LAW AND THE AMERICAN HEALTH CARE SYSTEM

SECOND EDITION

by

SARA ROSENBAUM
Harold and Jane Hirsh Professor, Health Law and Policy
George Washington University
School of Public Health and Health Services

&

DAVID M. FRANKFORD
Professor of Law
Rutgers University School of Law—Camden

SYLVIA A. LAW
Elizabeth K. Dollard Professor of Law, Medicine, & Psychiatry
New York University School of Law

RAND E. ROSENBLATT
Professor of Law
Rutgers University School of Law—Camden

FOUNDATION PRESS
2012

THOMSON REUTERS™

© 1997 FOUNDATION PRESS

© 2012 By THOMSON REUTERS/FOUNDATION PRESS

    1 New York Plaza, 34th Floor

    New York, NY 10004

    Phone Toll Free 1–877–888–1330

    Fax 646–424–5201

    foundation–press.com

Printed in the United States of America

ISBN 978–1–60930–088–3

Mat #41208224

AUTHORS' ACKNOWLEDGEMENTS

We all have many people to thank for this book.

Sara Rosenbaum thanks the many students who have worked with her over the years, Johanna Inglis, her partner in all endeavors for nearly two decades, and the George Washington University School of Public Health and Health Services and its Department of Health Policy, which have provided a wonderful home for the study of health law and policy. She thanks her coauthors, especially David Frankford, for the privilege of collaboration. Above all, she thanks her mother, Selma Rosenbaum, her sister, Ellen Rosenbaum, her daughter, Rachel Chavkin, her son-in-law, Jake Heinrichs, and especially her husband, Dan Hawkins, who have lovingly supported this effort for so many years.

David Frankford too thanks many research assistants over the years who have worked on this project and students in his classes who both have endured manuscripts in need of improvement and have helped make those improvements possible through their astute questions and observations. Martha Swartz, with whom he has taught for many years, deserves special mention, for she has taught him so much. Friends and family have contributed more support than can ever be repaid, particularly, of course, Judy, Rachel, Melissa and now Rena. Finally, Sara Rosenbaum has kept this whole vessel going and with her boundless energy and good spirit has pushed us all along, defining the meaning of colleague.

Sylvia A. Law acknowledges the legacy of the late Edward V. Sparer who inspired her and many others to become health law teachers, activists and scholars and grounded us in the profound human importance and complexity of the enterprise. She is grateful to generations of students and colleagues at NYU School of Law and Hawaii's Richardson School of Law who made invaluable contributions to the book.

Rand Rosenblatt also thanks the students in many health law classes who have used, and whose questions have improved, the manuscript, and Rutgers University School of Law—Camden for its long-term support of this project. Particular thanks go to Debbie Carr, his assistant for many years, and to Debbi Leak, his current assistant, for help with the manuscript, and to Reference Law Librarian David Batista for research assistance. He too wishes to thank his coauthors, especially Sara Rosenbaum, the community of health law legal academics, his wife and colleague Ann Freedman, and his sons David and Adam Rosenblatt, all of whom have been models of generosity and support.

PREFACE

LAW AND THE AMERICAN HEALTH CARE SYSTEM was first published in 1997. The three original authors, Rand Rosenblatt, Sylvia Law, and Sara Rosenbaum, were joined in 2001 by David Frankford with the publication of a formal supplement. In the intervening years the book was informally updated several times. This second edition builds on the original textbook. It continues the tradition of a textbook that offers a combination of law and policy. It is not possible to understand the interaction between the law and the health care system without an empirical and policy context and framework that helps students understand the complex workings of the health care system and the relationships from which legal principles emanate.

This textbook is organized into four parts focusing on four major dimensions of health care law: access to care; health insurance and health care financing; health care quality; and regulation of health care transactions.

Part One: Access to Health Care. As in the original textbook, the second edition opens with a focus on access to health care. It explores the extent to which Americans lack access to health care services, and the impact that has on lives and health. It asks whether there is a legal right to health care and thus, a corresponding legal duty to provide care. It examines the ways in which both the courts and legislatures have grappled with these questions, through both common law doctrine and statutory interventions. When, if ever, do individuals possess a right to health care, how is this right conditioned, and what types of institutions and professionals operate under a duty of care? If there is a duty to provide health care, how can that obligation be enforced? How much legal discretion do health care institutions and professionals retain to select their patients in a fashion that discriminates against those in genuine need? To what extent do civil rights laws limit that discretion? Finally Part One examines public safety-net health providers.

Part Two: Health Care Financing. Part Two examines the extraordinary body of law governing public and private health insurance coverage and employer-sponsored health plans. Part Two also introduces the complex and sweeping reforms in health insurance coverage contained in the Patient Protection and Affordable Care Act (PPACA), which became law on March 23, 2010. Part Two's principal job is to explore the diverse pathways by which Americans gain health insurance (mostly through the workplace) and how each of these pathways is regulated. This Part examines the Employee Retirement Income Security Act (ERISA), enacted in 1974, and the heart of the federal regulatory system for employer-sponsored health plans. It also presents the relationship between ERISA and state law, one that has grown more complex in the wake of passage of PPACA. In addition, Part Two examines Medicare and Medicaid, which together insure more than one-third of all Americans. Part Two concludes with a discussion of health care cost containment techniques and health care payment, two of the driving dimensions of all forms of health insurance.

In exploring health insurance, Part Two addresses several basic questions. Who qualifies for coverage? What health care services are included? What are the legal rights of patients and providers who disagree with determinations of insurers and insurance programs? How does insurance allocate the risk of health care cost among individuals, providers, insurers and employer-sponsored health plans? What is the role of health care payment, and how do modern payment structures operate? What is the relationship between health care cost containment and the accessibility and quality of health care itself? What are the respective roles of state and federal law in answering these questions? How is regulatory oversight spread among legislative bodies, administrative agencies, and the courts?

Part Three: Health Care Quality. Until the mid-twentieth century, the law of health care quality was limited to state licensure statutes and the body of common law principles and state statutes focusing on medical liability of individual doctors for negligence. Today the legal aspects of health care quality are far more complex, with questions of quality pervading not only the physical act of health care practice but also the structures used to pay health care provider and incentivize health care quality performance and improvement. The intersection of health care quality and law raises issues of eternal interest and passion. Should hospitals, physicians and other health care providers face legal liability to individual patients when their conduct falls below reasonable professional norms? How should those reasonable norms be determined? Is the professional norm always the right measure of legal reasonableness, or should health professionals be held to standards of reasonableness not limited by their own professional customs? What are the roles of licensure and accreditation and how do those roles comport with other forms of legal regulation? Are questions of liability to individual patients answered differently if it turns out that licensure and accreditation agencies, charged with system oversight, do not do their job? And should payers themselves face liability if their incentives induce inappropriate conduct or their coverage and payment denials result in injury to patients?

Part Four: Regulation of Health Care Transactions. Part Four examines the manner in which law regulates the health care sector as a modern, commercialized and industrialized enterprise. It involves, most fundamentally, the ambivalence that characterizes our society's and our law's approach to health care. Health care is now organized fully around market transactions but simultaneously we try to limit the extent to which health care should be organized under market principles, an inherent contradiction. Many of the major organizations of the sector are nonprofit. What does that mean when the larger social and legal environment encourages the sector to compete and compete hard? Nonprofits are entitled to various exemptions from taxation. Why should they be, and is something expected in return? If so, what is it?

Fraud and abuse laws are applied to health care transactions, but what is the definition of fraud and abuse? We'll see that the fraud and abuse laws purport to ban remuneration for referrals. What can that mean in a system in which referrals of patients are the life blood of the sector? Given that basic fact, where and how does one draw appropriate lines? Indeed, can any lines be drawn on a principled basis? Another important anti-fraud law proscribes physicians and their families from having financial interests in entities to which they refer, such as imaging centers. Financial interest is defined to include contractual relationships. What can this proscription mean, given that such transactions are the essential means by which the system is integrated—and integration is essential to the delivery of coordinated care? Again, is it possible to draw principled lines and if so, what are they? Enforcement of fraud is shared among a number of governmental agencies and private actors, who are given causes of action to sue. How can this joint authority be rationalized given differing incentives and institutional capacities?

Finally, Part Four examines the application of antitrust law to the health care sector in an effort to assure competition. It is this application, which began in earnest in the mid–1970s, that has been the most important factor in infusing the sector with the ethics of the market and grounding the transactional basis of contemporary relationships. How should antitrust be applied, given the numerous ways in which health care markets do not conform to ordinary expectations of markets? What doctrinal ramifications flow from the fact that health care is enormously complex, as far from the widget we use as our primary illustrative tool for much of legal reasoning? Can antitrust account for the fact that health care providers possess enormous power that is not simply a reflection of economics but of the importance of life itself? What about the unequal distribution of access to health care? Finally, given that delivery of care requires coordination among numerous actors, including ones that compete against each other, can antitrust law be coherently applied since its primary premise is that competitor collaboration is inherently suspicious?

* * *

This book reflects the view that American health law and policy— including the PPACA—have been strongly influenced by three principal models or perspectives: professionalism; social contract; and market competition. Rand E. Rosenblatt, *The Four Ages of Health Law*, 14 HEALTH MATRIX 155 (2004). Each offers a vision of by whom and by what criteria questions about access, financing, quality, and transactions should be answered. The first model, which dominated judicial decisions and legislation from around 1880 to around 1960, is centered around the *professional authority and professionalism* of physicians. Under this paradigm, legal authority over virtually all aspects of health care delivery, including access, financing, and quality, was delegated to the medical profession—indeed to individual physicians in private practice—and justified by what was seen as doctors' scientific expertise and the trust appropriately accorded their "professionalism."

A second model, which became dominant in health law from about 1960 to about 1980 and continues to the present, is that of the *modestly egalitarian social contract*. This paradigm holds that patients and society as a whole, as well as physicians and other providers, have legitimate rights and interests in the health care system. The role of law in this model is to achieve a fair resolution of conflicting interests, especially in the light of highly unequal information and power that often exists between patients and other actors. Given this model's egalitarian values, fairness has typically been articulated as access to care largely on the basis of health care needs (rather than ability to pay), high quality of care, and respect for patient autonomy, privacy, and dignity. In practice, this model allowed physicians to retain considerable influence over the access, financing, and quality questions, but located the ultimate authority to decide them in legislation and judge-made law. By the standards of the rest of the developed world, notably western Europe and Canada, the American social contract has been limited and uneven—hence the phrase "modestly egalitarian."

A third perspective holds that however modest by international standards, the American social contract is far too regulatory and redistributive, and should be replaced by legal principles appropriate to full-fledged *market competition*. The function of law in this model is to ensure that choices about health insurance and health services are made by individual patients or consumers based as much as possible on their own immediate preferences and financial resources, with a modest nod toward helping the very poorest. Some versions of the model seek to eliminate as much as possible hidden "cross-subsidies" of the type that invariably arise when the focus of health insurance is a group of individuals with varying age, gender, and health characteristics. Market advocates believe that advancing individual coverage and individual choice coupled with strong financial constraints will maximize efficiency, since people should pay only for coverage or services that really benefit them directly. Insurers and providers will, under this theory, respond by economizing to optimize costs and benefits. Individual choice under economic constraint is to also said to maximize, or perhaps constitute, freedom, properly understood.

Each of these three models continues to exercise influence in political and legal contexts, and all three perspectives have been contending actively for influence over numerous issues of health policy and law. The vocabulary or rhetoric of this struggle among the three models is often presented primarily as a matter of practical, empirical utilitarianism: which model will in fact achieve our agreed-upon goals of access to health care and of at least adequate quality at a cost we believe we can afford? This framing is of course a valid way of thinking about the models and an important area of empirical or health services research. But the struggle among the three models is not only an empirical disagreement about how to achieve agreed-upon goals most effectively or efficiently. It is also a disagreement at least in part among different perceptual frames and normative values: the varying "realities" that we see and the conflicting values or "identities" we embody as a nation.

Underlying these models is the basic question of what kind of nation we want to be. This epic struggle between social contract and individual freedom has always defined this nation. DEBORAH STONE, THE SAMARITAN'S DILEMMA: SHOULD GOVERNMENT HELP YOUR NEIGHBOR? (2008). Nowhere do we see this struggle play out more clearly or painfully than in health care. For example, from the perspective of the egalitarian social contract, broadly inclusive public or private health insurance is seen as a way of guaranteeing that people will get the care they need for conditions caused by factors that are mostly out of their control. This approach advances the value and experience of solidarity and mutual support, and assures that health care delivery will be financed in a stable and widely-shared way. But from the market competition perspective, such insurance is seen as forcing relatively healthy people to pay for the health care of relatively unhealthy people, thereby diminishing the liberty of the healthy to associate only with each other ("**us**") in insurance pools and exclude the unhealthy ("**them**"). The value or experience (from one perspective) of solidarity and mutual support is experienced from another perspective as constraint and coercion, and of course evaluated very differently.

The legal doctrines and vocabulary of judicial decisions always have been closely related to underlying models, perspectives, and values, although most judges and lawyers rarely openly acknowledge it. In the late nineteenth and early twentieth centuries, legal discourse often proclaimed that it was independent of conflicting values and perspectives and simply reflected "natural law," "reality,"—or the "logic"—of distinctive "legal reasoning" or "legal science." The greatest and most candid judges and lawyers knew that this was not so. As Oliver Wendell Holmes memorably put it in 1881, "The life of the law has not been logic: it has been experience. The felt necessities of the time, the prevalent moral and political theories, and intuitions of public policy, avowed or unconscious, have had a good deal more to do than the syllogism in determining the rules by which men should be governed." OLIVER WENDELL HOLMES, THE COMMON LAW 5 (1881, Mark DeWolfe Howe ed., 1963); What Holmes terms "the felt necessities of the time, the prevalent moral and political theories, [and] intuitions of public policy, avowed or unconscious" is another way of describing the models, perspectives, and paradigms that we seek to make more visible and available for discussion and choice.

Our final introductory observation—one that has permeated our collective writings in the field of health law—is the question of social fairness. As with the first edition, the second edition of LAW AND THE AMERICAN HEALTH CARE SYSTEM will ask readers in many different ways, and in many different contexts, to consider the role of law in advancing a fair society and a more equitable distribution of health and health care resources. These questions will remain front and center in health law, notably in the implementation of the PPACA, for many reasons that will become clear in the materials that follow.

We do not believe that we are being naïve in this regard. We are cognizant that in any society, the most affluent inevitably will receive proportionately greater benefits; indeed, countries with national health insurance typically permit those at the top to supplement the "norm." What makes the U.S. health care system such a sobering subject however, has been the absence of any floor of decency, any unified theory for ensuring that people simply are not excluded from the health care system because they are too poor, too sick, in poor health, speak the wrong language, look the wrong way, or some other consideration unrelated to their basic dignity as human beings and the beneficial nature of health care. The law plays a foundational role in advancing social fairness. These materials have been designed to make readers think about the role of law in a fair and just health care system.

ACKNOWLEDGEMENTS

Abraham, Kenneth S., and Paul C. Weiler, Enterprise Medical Liability and the Evolution of the American Health Care System, 108 Harvard Law Review, pp. 381–419 (1994). Copyright © 1994 by the Harvard Law Review Association. Reprinted by permission of the Harvard Law Review and Kenneth S. Abraham and Paul C. Weiler.

Abramson, Bradley, [Colorado Rule of Evidence] 803(18): The Learned Treatise Exception to the Hearsay Rule, 38 Colorado Law Review, pp. 39, 40 (March 2009). Copyright © 2009 by the University of Colorado Law Review. Reprinted by permission.

Baker, Tom, Health Insurance, Risk, and Responsibility After the Patient Protection and Affordable Care Act, 159 University of Pennsylvania Law Review, pp. 1579–1580 (2011). Copyright © 2011 by the University of Pennsylvania Law Review. Reprinted by permission, the University of Pennsylvania Law Review and Fred B. Rothman & Co.

Biles, Brian, Geraldine Dallek, and Lauren Hersch Nicholas, Medicare Advantage, Déjà vu All Over Again? Health Affairs (Web Exclusive) (December 15, 2004). Copyright © 2004 by Project HOPE—The People-to-People Health Foundation, Inc. Reprinted by permission.

Blumstein, James F., The Fraud and Abuse Statute in an Evolving Health Care Marketplace: Life in the Health Care Speakeasy, 22 American Journal of Law and Medicine, p. 218 (1996). Copyright © 1996 by the American Society of Law, Medicine and Ethics. Reprinted by permission.

Chassin, Mark R. and Jerod M. Loeb, The Ongoing Quality Improvement Journey, 30(4) Health Affairs, pp. 562–63 (April 2011). Copyright © 2011 by Project HOPE–The People-to-People Health Foundation, Inc. Reprinted by permission.

Frankford, David M., The Complexity of Medicare's Hospital Reimbursement System, 78 Iowa Law Review, pp. 635–636 (1993). Copyright © by the University of Iowa (Iowa Law Review). Reprinted by permission.

Frankford, David M., Creating and Dividing the Fruits of Collective Economic Activity: Referrals Among Providers, 89 Columbia Law Review, pp. 1910–1911 (1989). Copyright © 1989 by David M. Frankford. Reprinted by Permission.

Frankford, David M., Measuring Health Care: Political Fate and Technocratic Reform, 19 J. Health Policy Politics and Law, p. 660 (1994). Copyright © 1994 by Duke University Press. Reprinted by permission.

Frankford, David M., Privatizing Health Care: Economic Magic to Cure Legal Medicine, 66 Southern California Law Review, pp. 22–23 (1992). Copyright © 1992 by David Frankford. Reprinted by permission.

Furrow, Barry R., Regulating Patient Safety: The Patient Protection and Affordable Care Act, 159 University of Pennsylvania Law Review, pp. 1731–33, 1752. Copyright © 2011 by the University of Pennsylvania Law Review. Reprinted by permission, the University of Pennsylvania Law Review and Fred B. Rothman & Co.

Jacobson, Peter D. and Stephanie A. Doebler, We Were All Sold a Bill of Goods: Litigating the Science of Breast Cancer Treatment, 52 Wayne Law Review, pp. 46–47, 60–62 (2006). Copyright © 2006 by Wayne State Law Review. Reprinted by permission.

Langbein, John H., The Supreme Court Flunks Trusts, 1990 Supreme Court Review, pp. 207–227 (1991) (Gerhard Cooper, Dennis J. Hutchinson, and David A Strauss, eds.). Copyright © 1991 by the University of Chicago. Reprinted by permission.

Law, Sylvia A., and Steven Polan, Pain and Profit: The Politics of Malpractice. Copyright © 1978 by Sylvia A. Law and Steven Polan. Reprinted by permission of Harper Collins Publishers and the authors.

MacEachern, Malcolm T., Hospital Organization and Management, p. 35 (3d. ed., 1957). Copyright © 1957 by Physicians Record Company. Reprinted by permission.

Mello, Michelle M., Of Swords and Shields: The Role of Clinical Practice Guidelines in Medical Malpractice Litigation, 149 University of Pennsylvania Law Review, pp. 647–649 (2001). Copyright © 2001 by the University of Pennsylvania Law Review. Reprinted by permission, the University of Pennsylvania Law Review and Fred B. Rothman & Co.

Mitchell, Allison, Clinton Regrets "Clearly Racist" U.S. Study, N. Y. Times, May 17, 1997, p. 10. Copyright © 1997 by The New York Times Co. Reprinted by permission.

Moon, Marilyn, Medicare: A Policy Primer, pp. 1–2. Copyright © 2006 by The Urban Institute. Reprinted by permission, Urban Institute Press.

Newhouse, Joseph P., Consumer–Directed Health Plans and the RAND Health Insurance Experiment, 23(6) Health Affairs, p. 107 (2004). Copyright © 2004 by Project Hope—The People-to-People Health Foundation, Inc. Reprinted by permission.

Reinhardt, Uwe, How Much Money Do Insurance Companies Make? A Primer. Copyright © 2009 by the New York Times Co. Reprinted by permission.

Reinhardt, Uwe, The Pricing of U.S. Hospital Services: Chaos Behind a Veil of Secrecy, 25(1) Health Affairs, p. 59 (2006). Copyright © 2006 by Project HOPE—The People-to-People Health Foundation, Inc. Reprinted by permission.

Sanford, Sallie Thieme, Candor After Kadlec: Why, Despite the Fifth Circuit's Decision, Hospitals Should Anticipate an Expanded Obligation To Disclose Risky Physician Behavior, 1 Drexel Law Review, pp. 402–403 (2009). Copyright © 2009 by Drexel Law Review. Reprinted by permission.

Schlesinger, Mark and Bradford Gray, Nonprofit Organizations and Health Care: Paradoxes of Persistent Scrutiny, in The Nonprofit Sector (Walter W. Powell and Richard Steinberg, eds.), p. 399 (2006). Copyright © 2006 by Yale University Press. Reprinted by permission.

Siliciano, John, Wealth, Equity and the Unitary Medical Malpractice Standard, 77 Virginia Law Review, pp. 465–66, 475–481 (1991). Copyright © 1991 by the University of Virginia Law Review. Reprinted by permission of the Virginia Law Review and Fred B. Rothman & Co.

Vladeck, Bruce C., Medicare's Prospective Payment System at Age Eight: Mature Success or Midlife Crisis?, 14 University of Puget Sound Law Review, pp. 479–80 (1991). Copyright © 1991 by University of Puget Sound. Reprinted by permission.

Winn, Peter, Confidentiality in Cyberspace: The HIPAA Privacy Rules and the Common Law, 33 Rutgers Law Journal, p. 619 (2002). Copyright © 2002 by University of Rutgers Law Journal. Reprinted by permission.

SUMMARY OF CONTENTS

TABLE OF CONTENTS

CHAPTER 25. The Application of Antitrust to Health Care -- 1195

TABLE OF CASES

Principal cases are in bold type. Non-principal cases are in roman type. References are to Pages.

TABLE OF STATUTES AND REGULATIONS

LAW AND THE AMERICAN HEALTH CARE SYSTEM

PART ONE

ACCESS TO HEALTH CARE: RIGHTS, DUTIES, AND ENFORCEMENT

CHAPTER 1

BARRIERS TO ACCESS AND THE RIGHT TO HEALTH CARE

How health care is structured, organized and paid for, along with the rules of conduct that society and law apply to health care providers, are fundamental to the question of whether health care is available and affordable, whether people have reasonably equitable access to it, and whether care is of appropriate quality. Most health care in wealthy nations, including the United States, is furnished by private physicians and hospitals. Powerful private industries such as pharmaceutical manufacturers and medical device and equipment companies are dominant players throughout the world.

When faced with the need to balance fundamental societal needs against market expectations, other industrial democracies have opted to use the law to temper health care and health care financing markets in order protect the social good. For the most part, until very recently, the United States has not taken this step. TIMOTHY STOLTZFUS JOST, DISENTITLEMENT? THE THREAT FACING OUR PUBLIC HEALTH-CARE PROGRAMS AND A RIGHTS-BASED RESPONSE (2003). Until passage of the Patient Protection and Affordable Care Act in March 2010, we relied on a combination of voluntary public and private coverage for non-elderly adults and children. As a result, for the non-elderly, access to health care has been a matter of having a lot of money, being fortunate enough to qualify for either public or private insurance, or some combination thereof. (As you will learn in Part Two, the Affordable Care Act became law at a time when an already-weakened employer-sponsored health insurance system has been in further decline).

Beyond the question of health insurance coverage, access to health care is influenced by other factors considered "non-economic" such as race, culture, language, citizenship, or disability. The legal aspects of health care access considered in Part One focus on when and how the law establishes and recognizes obligations on the part of health care providers—in particular, physicians and hospitals—to provide treatment regardless of the ability to pay at the point at which treatment is needed. Part One also examines how the law deals with provider refusals to treat on the basis of race or national origin, disability, and gender. The separate problem of insurers refusing to extend any, or reasonable, coverage to certain individuals and groups is examined in Part Two.

Money matters. Chapter 1 opens with a brief overview of health insurance coverage. These issues are explored more fully in Part Two.

Chapter 2 explores the common law "no duty" norm, developed in the 19th and first half of the 20th centuries, under which neither doctors nor hospitals had any legal duty to serve people. This principle remains alive today, albeit with modifications, and coexists uneasily with non-legal social beliefs and professional norms and expectations. Beginning in the 1960s, state courts and legislatures began to challenge the "no duty" principle. The state efforts were mostly weak and ineffectual in practice, but provided important legal concepts and a model for federal reform.

Chapter 3 explores federal efforts to amend the common law "no duty" principle in the context of people seeking necessary medical care in hospital emergency departments. Defining and enforcing the duty of hospitals to provide screening and some treatment for emergency conditions regardless of ability to pay has proved to be a complex and contentious undertaking, revealing the challenges of defining a non-market access principle in a predominantly market-driven system.

Chapter 4 returns to the theme that access to health care is not only a matter of an individual's insurance or ability to pay, nor should the question of access focus solely on access to health care in true medical emergencies. Primary and preventive health care are essential throughout childhood and adulthood, as is ongoing treatment to manage serious health conditions such as diabetes or high blood pressure or depression. Therefore, it is important to think about barriers such as those associated with race and national origin, gender, disability, and citizenship, that might exist at all points along the health care continuum. Access also can be affected by community conditions.

Poor communities with high numbers of uninsured residents lack the overall economic wherewithal to maintain health care facilities, just as they lack the economic means to anchor grocery stores, banks, and shopping centers. Not only is access to health care profoundly affected in these communities, so is community health. Chapter 5 describes the safety-net health care providers—public hospitals and community health centers— that supply care to people who are medically underserved and that have been established in law to help overcome the systematic, physical shortages of health care that confront economically disadvantaged and geographically isolated communities.

1.   HEALTH INSURANCE AND THE UNINSURED

In the United States, health insurance—public or private—is associated with significantly greater levels of access to virtually all types of health care, from routine and preventive services to advanced care for serious and chronic health conditions. INSTITUTE OF MEDICINE, INSURING AMERICA'S HEALTH (2004). Health insurance coverage does not guarantee access to necessary care, but it makes a huge difference.

The Patient Protection and Affordable Care Act (PPACA) (which we will refer to frequently as the Affordable Care Act) is reviewed at length in

Part Two. The Act essentially resets the legal framework for health insurance coverage among persons under age 65 and introduces the concept of accessible and affordable health insurance as both a right and an obligation on the part of most Americans. Historically, however, the nation has relied on a voluntary system of employer-sponsored group coverage for workers and their families, supplemented by a weak-to-non-existent individual market, and a public program for certain low income people known as Medicaid. People age 65 and older and certain workers with severe disabilities are entitled to Medicare, compulsory and universal government-sponsored health insurance for persons covered by the Social Security system. As of 2009, almost 50 million persons, 16 percent of the nonelderly population, lacked health insurance coverage. Kaiser Family Foundation, *Health Insurance Coverage in the United States* (2009), http://facts.kff.org/chart.aspx?ch=477.

Employer-sponsored health insurance coverage reached its height in the 1970s, but even at its zenith, the system excluded millions of (predominantly) lower wage workers and their families. Over the past quarter century or so, employer coverage has begun to crumble under the weight of multiple factors: a labor market that has decisively moved away from higher paying manufacturing jobs that carry good benefits and toward a labor market characterized by lower paying jobs with fewer benefits; an increase in the proportion of families headed by single parents, which in turn reduces the likelihood that a household will contain a wage earner with access to coverage; and exponentially increasing health care costs that have caused employers (particularly smaller, low wage employers) to eliminate coverage. For most of this period, the proportion of non-elderly persons without coverage remained relatively constant at between 15 and 18 percent. Wilhelmine Miller et al., *Covering the Uninsured: What Is It Worth?*, HEALTH AFFAIRS w4–157 (March 31, 2004), http://content.health affairs.org/content/early/2004/03/31/hlthaff.w4.157.full.pdf+html. But between 2000 and 2006, even as the economy boomed, the number of uninsured Americans increased by 6 million persons as a result of eroding employer coverage, particularly among small firms. John Holahan & Allison Cook, *The U.S. Economy and Changes in Health Insurance Coverage, 2000–2006*, 27(2) HEALTH AFFAIRS w135 (2008).

Employers are not required to offer and subsidize group health coverage as a part of their employees' wages and compensation, and as we discuss more fully below, the ACA only minimally modifies this situation. In 2005, 50.1 percent of U.S. were employed by a firm that did not offer health benefits to any worker. Paul Fronstin, *Employment–Based Health Benefits: Access and Coverage, 1988–2005*, EBRI, ISSUE BRIEF 303 1 (March 2007). The actual number of workers with employer-sponsored coverage actually stood at about 61 percent that year, since some proportion of workers without plans of their own are able to secure coverage through a spouse's plan. Jane Norman, *Employer Health Coverage Draws Yet More Scrutiny from Researchers*, CQ HealthBeat News, June 21, 2011. What is shocking though is that the "mainstream" system for insuring workers and their families actually covers barely half of all employment and that only about three-fifths of people who work have employer coverage. So much for "mainstream."

For children matters are even worse. Fewer than 60 percent of children have employer-sponsored coverage, in part because children tend to be poorer than adults and live in families that lack good jobs with good benefits. Family benefit plans are costly (over $13,000 for a family plan offered by an employer in 2011). Children are particularly reliant on public insurance, especially Medicaid and its small companion program for low income, Medicaid-ineligible children known as the Children's Health Insurance Program (CHIP). Kaiser Family Foundation, *Holding Steady, Looking Ahead: Annual Findings Of a 50–State Survey of Eligibility Rules, Enrollment and Renewal Procedures, and Cost Sharing Practices in Medicaid and CHIP*, 2010–2011 (2011), http://www.kff.org/medicaid/upload/8130.pdf.

[handwritten: child]

Individuals and families without access to employer-sponsored group coverage and ineligible for public insurance (discussed at length in Part Two) essentially are up a creek. Prior to passage of the Affordable Care Act, neither federal law nor states other than Massachusetts (which enacted comprehensive health reform in 2006) guaranteed access to affordable and reasonable coverage in the individual market. With a collapsing employer-insurance system and inadequate public programs, the proportion of people (particularly adults) without any insurance coverage has risen commensurately. As of 2010, 49.9 million people, 16.3 percent of the total population, were uninsured, a 25 percent increase from 1987. UNITED STATES CENSUS BUREAU, INCOME POVERTY AND HEALTH INSURANCE COVERAGE IN THE UNITED STATES: 2010, CURRENT POPULATION REPORTS (P60–239), http://www.census.gov/prod/2011pubs/p60–239.pdf.

The number of persons without health coverage for the entire year tells only a portion of the story. The Congressional Budget Office, which advises Congress on long-term economic trends, as well as the cost and economic impact of federal legislation, reports that if the definition of being uninsured includes people who are uninsured for a portion of the year, the number of uninsured is actually much higher. A CBO study, conducted when the number of full-year uninsured persons stood at 40 million, showed that the number rose to more than 60 million when persons uninsured for part of the year also were counted. CONGRESSIONAL BUDGET OFFICE, HOW MANY PEOPLE LACK HEALTH INSURANCE AND FOR HOW LONG? (2003), http://www.cbo.gov/showdoc.cfm?index=4211 & sequence=0.

Underinsurance is also a significant and growing part of the uninsurance problem. Underinsurance measures being financially exposed to high out-of-pocket health care costs even when insured; its two main causes are low income in relation to the value of coverage or exceptionally high medical bills that exhaust the coverage limits found in a typical insurance policy. Underinsurance is defined by experts as financial exposure exceeding 10 percent of annual income in the case of non-low income persons and 5 percent in the case of persons with incomes below twice the federal poverty level. Underinsurance also means having an insurance policy whose deductible (the amount a covered individual must pay out of pocket before

[handwritten: definition of underinsured]

insurance coverage begins) equals 5 percent or more of family income. Cathy Schoen et al., *How Many are Underinsured: Trends Among U.S. Adults, 2003 and 2007*, 27(4) HEALTH AFFAIRS w298 (2008). Based on this formula, study authors found that in 2007 an estimated 25 million adults ages 19–64 were underinsured, a 60 percent increase in the number of underinsured adults since 2003. Using a slightly different timeframe, Figure 1 graphically displays the extent of the problem.

Rapidly rising health care costs have caused employers to trim coverage by increasing premiums, deductibles, coinsurance and copayments (out-of-pocket payments collected at the point of care), and by tightening benefits and adding strict annual and lifetime limits to the total value of coverage (e.g., no more than $1 million in coverage over a lifetime, an amount that one critically ill infant can cost a family in the first year of life alone). These changes left many of the 158 million Americans with employer-sponsored coverage struggling to meet basic expenses. Reed Abelson & Milt Freudenheim, *Even the Insured Feel the Strain of Health Costs*, NY TIMES (May 4, 2008), at A–1. Between 2004 and 2007, the percentage of low income insured Americans (persons with family incomes twice the federal poverty level or below) spending more than 10 percent of their income out-of-pocket for premiums and uncovered services rose from 13 percent to 18 percent. Jon Gabel et al., *Trends in Underinsurance and the Affordability of Employer Coverage, 2004–2007*, 28(4) HEALTH AFFAIRS w595 (2009).

Figure 1. An Estimated 116 Million Adults Were Uninsured, Underinsured, Reported a Medical Bill Problem, and/or Did Not Access Needed Health Care Because of Cost, 2007

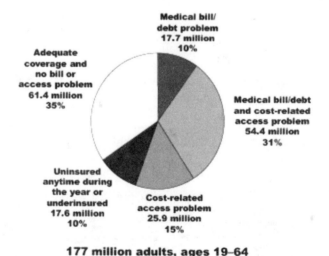

177 million adults, ages 19–64

Source: The Commonwealth Fund Biennial Health Insurance Survey (2007).

Other wealthy nations with political and economic landscapes similar to our own make only limited use of a voluntary commercial insurance market. Instead these nations finance universal coverage as a form of social welfare investment with contributions in the form of taxes and private payments by individuals. Their systems are administered directly by the government, government-chartered entities, or nonprofit insurers that act as national or regional plan administrators. TIMOTHY STOLTZFUS JOST, DISEN-TITLEMENT? THE THREAT FACING OUR PUBLIC HEALTH-CARE PROGRAMS AND A RIGHTS-BASED RESPONSE (2003); T. R. REID, THE HEALING OF AMERICA (2009).

Employment-based health insurance. The heart of the U.S. health insurance system for working-age Americans and their families—both before and after PPACA—is voluntary, employer-sponsored coverage (although under PPACA, large employers that elect not to insure their employees will be required to contribute to the cost of coverage through state health insurance Exchanges; more to follow in Part Two). This voluntary system first made its appearance in the 1920s, as other nations were moving toward universal and compulsory systems; the turn of events in the U.S. is credited by and large to a libertarian culture coupled with fierce resistance to compulsory coverage by physicians and hospitals seeking to ward off direct government involvement in health care financing. In order to compensate for the absence of a government-directed approach to assuring universal access to coverage, health care providers in the U.S., began to offer prepaid health plans to employers and employees.

This strategy of evasion and appeasement slowly took hold; voluntary coverage grew steadily but slowly during the 1930s. As the Depression left people without the means to pay for increasingly costly but necessary medical care out of pocket, states sanctioned the formal creation of nonprofit, community-based Blue Cross plans offering hospital coverage and Blue Shield plans covering physician services. Both were controlled by—you guessed it—hospitals and doctors. David Blumenthal, *Employer Sponsored Health Insurance in the United States: Origins and Implications*, 355 NEW ENG. J. MED. 82 (2006); PAUL STARR, THE SOCIAL TRANSFORMATION OF AMERICAN MEDICINE (1982); SYLVIA LAW, BLUE CROSS: WHAT WENT WRONG? (1976); Randall Bovjberg et al., *U.S. Health Care Coverage and Costs*, 21. J. L. MED. & ETHICS 102 (1993).

Employer-sponsored coverage arrangements continued to grow throughout the 1940s, when the federal War Labor Board, established to control wages and prices during World War II, exempted fringe benefits from wage freezes, and an IRS ruling classified such compensation arrangements as tax exempt while recognizing the employer's contribution as a deductible business expense. An amendment to the Internal Revenue Code in 1952 permanently codified this policy and led to another surge in coverage, while simultaneously incentivizing creation of a vast commercial insurance market for employer-sponsored plans.

At its apex employer-sponsored health insurance reached only about three quarters of all non-elderly Americans, even though over 90 percent of the working-age population lived in families with at least one member employed. Between 1977 and 1998, the percentage of Americans covered by job-based health insurance fell from 71 percent to 64 percent. Jon R. Gabel, *Job Based Health Insurance, 1977–1998: The Accidental System Under*

Scrutiny, 18(6) HEALTH AFFAIRS 62 (1999). By 2010, 69 percent of all U.S. firms offered health insurance. Kaiser Family Foundation, *Employer Health Benefits 2010 Annual Survey*, 4 (2010), http://ehbs.kff.org/pdf/2010/8085. pdf. As noted, since employment positions are unevenly distributed, only about half of all employees actually work at a firm that offers a plan.

As noted, even in the wake of the Affordable Care Act employers remain free not to establish and operate health plans, although larger employers that do not (more than 50 full-time employees) will be expected to contribute toward the cost of worker coverage. How well the Act stems the tide—or whether its new system of state health insurance Exchanges opens up a rush to the door by all but the largest employers, eager to get out from under the burden of having to run a health plan in addition to doing whatever it is they were formed to do—will not be known for years. There is no question that the employment-based system has steadily eroded in the face of changing demographics, worldwide economic competition, labor trends and the high cost of care. With per capita health care expenditures double those of other industrialized nations, discussed in Part Two, employers increasingly find themselves unable to offer subsidized coverage, whose costs rise far faster than payrolls; this trend is particularly true for smaller firms with relatively low-wage payrolls.

Individual "freedom" to remain uninsured. Historically, just as health insurance coverage was voluntary for employers, the same was true for individuals. But the notion of being free to eschew coverage is misplaced: people without it generally cannot afford it. Among individuals who have the option not to purchase coverage when it is available, those who do not purchase coverage overwhelmingly cite cost as the most important factor, leaving millions at risk for being unable to pay for health care when they need it. In 2010, the average premium for individual coverage surpassed $5,000 and stood at $13,770 for family coverage. Kaiser Family Foundation, *Employer Health Benefits 2010 Annual Survey, 1 (2010)*, http://ehbs.kff.org/ pdf/2010/8085.pdf. That year, only 5 percent of all firms paid the entire cost of their workers' family coverage, and average worker contributions amounted to several thousand dollars per year. *Id*.

People without access to an employer group plan might look to the individual insurance market. But traditionally insurers have medically underwritten in the individual market, meaning that they medically profile applicants to determine if they are good "stand-alone" risks. Few states have intervened to curb such practices. Even where a state attempts to limit underwriting practices, the cost of coverage can be so stratospheric (especially for anyone over age 30) that products simply are out of reach. Even when they are available, individual policies may be riddled with exclusions, limitations and vast coverage gaps (discussed more in Part Two). A federal law enacted in 1996, The Health Insurance Portability and Accountability Act (HIPAA) (discussed at length in Part Two) placed limits on medical underwriting in the employer-sponsored group market, but with a very narrow exception for people who previously and continuously had been covered under a group plan, HIPAA failed to curb underwriting in the individual market. Unfortunately, the lack of regulation made sense, since without any requirement to purchase coverage or a structured market designed to assure a strong and healthy coverage pool over whom financial risks could be spread, insurers forced to sell to anyone regardless of health status would have collapsed.

The bottom line is that even if someone is brave enough to venture into the pre-health reform individual market (the vast changes enacted under the Affordable Care Act do not go into effect until January 1, 2014), chances are that he or she either will be denied a policy entirely or else may be offered coverage only if larded with exclusions, and limitations. For example a young woman with a history of hay fever might be told that she qualifies for coverage but only if she agrees to a policy containing an exclusion covering all upper respiratory conditions (hay fever can exacerbate conditions such as influenza or pneumonia). Karen Pollitz et al., *How Accessible is Individual Health Insurance for Consumers in Less–Than–Perfect Health?*, KAISER FAMILY FOUNDATION (2001), http://www.kff.org/insurance/20010620a-index.cfm. Imagine getting pneumonia and discovering that your "pre-existing condition" means absolutely no treatment.

A weak public system fails to compensate for the failures of voluntary employer-sponsored benefits and unaffordable individual coverage. Medicaid is the behemoth of public insurance programs, covering nearly 70 million people in 2010 and accounting for about 17 percent of all U.S. health care expenditures. MEDICAID AND CHIP PAYMENT AND ACCESS COMMISSION (MACPAC), REPORT TO CONGRESS (June 2011). Yet despite its vast size (estimated expenditures surpassed $400 billion in 2010, Centers for Medicare and Medicaid Services, 2010 Actuarial Report on the Financial Outlook for Medicaid, 18 (Dec. 21, 2010), http://www.cms.gov/ActuarialStudies/downloads/MedicaidReport2010.pdf), Medicaid historically has covered less than half of all low-income persons. Prior to the Affordable Care Act, whose Medicaid expansions (discussed in Part Two) are set to commence January 1, 2014, Medicaid has for all practical purposes excluded poor non-elderly adults unless they happen to be pregnant, severely disabled, or extraordinarily impoverished parents of minor children. (By "extraordinarily" impoverished, we don't mean simply having income at the federal poverty level (about $15,000 annually for a family of 3 in 2011); we mean having income that in some states is as low as *20 percent* of the federal poverty level, or about $3000 annually. Sara Rosenbaum, *Medicaid and National Health Reform*, 361 NEW ENG. J. MED. 2009 (2009)).

Over the past two decades, Congress has enacted modest but important expansions in public insurance programs such as Medicaid, particularly for low-income pregnant women and children. Until enactment of the Affordable Care Act, which as you will learn, extends Medicaid coverage to virtually all poor nonelderly adults, Medicaid's fundamental failure to cover low-income adults who are neither pregnant, parents, nor disabled went unaddressed. This failure in part can be attributed to ideological opposition to expanding what traditionally has been considered a welfare program (and one that, as you will learn, pays low rates to providers, to boot, a source of constant upset). In part, the failure to extend Medicaid to poor adults* also could be attributed to assertions by some economists that Medicaid expansion for the poor would "crowd out" the (declining and already weak for poor workers) employer market and the (nonexistent) individual market. (Other analysts have been skeptical of this theory, pointing to the serious structural deficiencies built into the individual and group health insurance markets and evident to all who cared to look. Judy Feder, *Reflections from the Experts: Crowd–Out and the Politics of Health Reform*, 32 J. L. MED. & ETH. 461, 477–92 (2004).) The Medicaid expansions in the Affordable Care Act effectively declare that coverage of the poorest Americans is the responsibility of federal and state governments.

Prior to passage of the PPACA, Medicare, the federal health insurance program for Social Security beneficiaries ages 65 and older and recipients of Social Security disability benefits, was the only U.S. program similar to the national health insurance systems in place in other industrial democracies. However, Medicare coverage is limited and cost sharing is significant. Persons found eligible for Social Security disability benefits also must wait 24 months until coverage begins. As a result, many people who qualify for Medicare also depend upon Medicaid (if they are sufficiently low income) or buy private supplemental "Medigap" plans as they are known, which are special supplemental insurance plans jointly regulated by the federal and state governments. Kaiser Family Foundation, *Examining Sources of Coverage Among Medicare Beneficiaries: Supplemental Insurance, Medicare Advantage, and Prescription Drug Coverage* (2008), http://www.kff.org/medicare/upload/7801.pdf. Slightly more than 20 percent of Medicare beneficiaries are poor enough to also qualify for Medicaid. Kaiser Family Foundation, *Duals as a Percent of Medicare Enrollees*, http://www.state healthfacts.org/comparemaptable.jsp?ind=304&cat=6. Only about one-third of all employees have retiree coverage through work, a figure that has fallen by half since the mid–1980s and is projected to disappear virtually entirely because of its high cost.

2.   THE CONSEQUENCES OF BEING UNINSURED

The uninsured are poorer and sicker than the general population. Almost half of poor adults are uninsured, and poor non-elderly adults

---

* A small number of states have received permission from the United States Department of Health and Human Services to operate their Medicaid programs on a demonstration basis under § 1115 of the Social Security Act (42 U.S.C. § 1315), which permits research and demonstrations that further the objectives of the program. In these states, greater numbers of low income adults may qualify for Medicaid coverage. Section § 1115 demonstrations must be "budget neutral," meaning that total aggregate expenditures cannot cost more under a state's demonstration than the federal contribution to a state's Medicaid program would cost on a non-demonstration basis. Kaiser Commission on Medicaid and the Uninsured, *Five Key Questions and Answers About Medicaid Section 1115 Demonstration Waivers* (2011), http://www.kff.org/medicaid/upload/8196.pdf. Philosophical opposition to Medicaid expansion, as well as provider opposition to the Medicaid payment rate cuts needed to free up money to invest in expanded eligibility on a budget neutral basis, has meant that few states have taken advantage of this demonstration authority over the years.

report far higher rates of physical and mental illness. Kaiser Commission on Medicaid and the Uninsured, *Low Income Adults Under Age 65—Many Are Poor, Sick, and Uninsured* (Washington D.C. 2009). Being uninsured has a dramatic impact, not only on individuals, but on families, communities, and the nation. Between 2000 and 2003, the Institute of Medicine (IOM) of the National Academy of Sciences undertook a sustained study of the consequences of being uninsured. The studies produced in this series span six volumes: COVERAGE MATTERS: INSURANCE AND HEALTH CARE (2001); HEALTH INSURANCE IS A FAMILY MATTER (2002); CARE WITHOUT COVERAGE: TOO LITTLE, TOO LATE (2003); HIDDEN COSTS, VALUE LOST: UNINSURANCE IN AMERICA (2003); A SHARED DESTINY: COMMUNITY EFFECTS OF UNINSURANCE (2004); INSURING AMERICA'S HEALTH: PRINCIPLES AND RECOMMENDATIONS (2004). The IOM series definitively rejects any notion that the health insurance crisis is either transient or lacks the types of "externalities" that justify a national response.

The IOM found that the consequences of the nation's insurance problem extend to entire communities, as well as the nation's overall economy. A widespread lack of coverage takes a broad toll on community health systems, which in turn lack the revenues they need to operate properly. High uninsured rates in urban areas—in Los Angeles, for example, more than one in four persons have no health insurance coverage— affect more than persons without coverage. These communities also have fewer hospital beds, offer fewer specialized services for vulnerable populations, and are less likely to have advanced emergency services, and burn and shock/trauma systems. Rural hospitals serving disproportionately uninsured communities have fewer intensive care and inpatient psychiatric services and lower operating margins; depressed operating margins, in turn, make systems more vulnerable to economic downturns.

Public health systems located in communities with high proportions of uninsured persons can face serious budgetary shortfalls, with essential functions such as public health disease surveillance and emergency preparedness adversely affected. See, e.g., *A City Where Hospitals Are as Ill as the Patients*, NY TIMES (June 5, 2008), which describes the health care access consequences for South Los Angeles residents following the collapse of Martin Luther King Jr.–Harbor Health Care Hospital in 2007.

The IOM studies also document other national consequences that flow from the shortage of insurance, including diminished health and premature mortality, financial stress for families, reduced workforce productivity, and greater financial stresses on government programs. Most important perhaps, is the IOM's estimate of the lost "health capital" that results from poor health status over a lifetime. The IOM found that the annual, aggregated cost of not adequately financing health care for the population as a whole ranged between $65 and $130 billion.

These studies show that the insurance problem inflicts serious financial consequences, as well. The IOM estimated that in 2001, the nation spent some $99 billion on health care for uninsured persons. Of this amount, the uninsured bore about 25 percent of this cost on their own, insurers another 40 percent as a result of their part-year coverage of otherwise uninsured persons, and the government, more than one third— spending an estimated $35 billion on direct public subsidies to health care providers. Although critics of significant health insurance reform frequently argue that universal coverage is unaffordable, the IOM study demonstrates precisely the opposite of course, namely the high cost of leaving so many Americans without coverage, a bill that we all pay through cost-shifting onto our insurance premiums and as taxpayers.

The absence of health insurance coverage and its impact on access to health care have real and measurable health consequences, particularly where premature death and disability from chronic and preventable causes are concerned. The U.S. lags well behind other industrialized nations. Peter A. Muennig & Sherry A. Glied, *What Changes in Survival Rates Tell Us About US Health Care*, 29(11) HEALTH AFFAIRS 2103 (2010), http://content. healthaffairs.org/content/29/11/2105.full.pdf+html?sid=ca0291b3–33e5– 4213–a89f-e9f1a935e39e; Stephen C. Schoenbaum, *Reducing Preventable Deaths Through Improved Health System Performance* (Oct. 8, 2008), http://www.commonwealthfund.org/Content/From-the-President/2008/ Re- ducing–Preventable–Deaths–Through–Improved–Health–System–Perform- ance.aspx. The U.S. compares poorly against international measures of population health such as life expectancy, infant mortality, and chronic illness, and ranks highly in the degree of economic inequity in health care. Eddy Van Doorslaer, *Income Related Inequality in the Use of Medical Care in 21 OECD Countries* (2004), http://www.oecd.org/dataoecd/14/0/31743034. pdf.

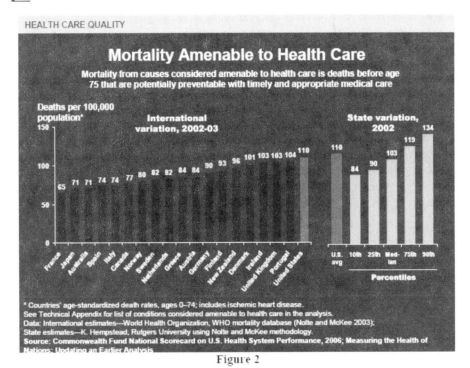

Figure 2

Figure 2. Mortality Amenable to Health Care

Decisions to allow the health care industry relatively unfettered freedom to choose its markets and engage in practices designed to increase sales have far-reaching ramifications for society. Other nations have concluded that health care is different from ordinary private markets because of its relative imperviousness to the normal operation of markets. These countries have chosen not only to finance health care across the population but also to simultaneously intervene to control spending on care through various forms of cost controls. Timothy Stoltzfus Jost, *Why Can't We Do What They Do? National Health Reform and America's Uninsured*, 32 J.L. MED. & ETHICS 410 (S. Rosenbaum, ed. 2004).

Studies of health care among patients in eight OECD nations are perhaps the most interesting. These studies show that health care abroad is more accessible and of better quality, particularly for sick patients. One study found that the U.S. leads other nations in the proportion of patients who experienced access problems because of cost, care coordination problems, and medical errors. The report found that U.S. adults were "by far" the most likely to report foregoing necessary medical care because of high cost. Cathy Schoen et al., *In Chronic Condition: Experiences of Patients with Chronic Health Conditions in Eight Countries*, 28(1) HEALTH AFFAIRS WEB EXCLUSIVE w1 (2009), http://content.healthaffairs.org/cgi/reprint/28/1/w 1. Figure 3 shows how the U.S. fares in terms of access for persons with chronic illness.

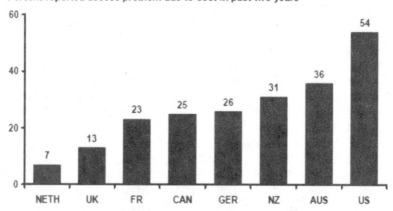

Figure 3. Cost-Related Access Problems Among the
Chronically Ill, in Eight Countries, 2008

Base: Adults with any chronic condition

Percent reported access problem due to cost in past two years*

* Due to cost, respondent did NOT: fill Rx or skipped doses, visit a doctor when had a medical problem, and/or get recommended test, treatment, or follow-up.
Data: The Commonwealth Fund International Health Policy Survey of Sicker Adults (2008).
Source: C. Schoen et al., "In Chronic Condition: Experiences of Patients with Complex Healthcare Needs in Eight Countries. 2008." *Health Affairs* Web Exclusive, Nov. 13, 2008.

3. A RIGHT TO HEALTH CARE?

Paradoxically, the common law "no duty" of care principle—and hence no legal "right" to care—has always coexisted with social norms and professional and political rhetoric favoring or suggesting in some sense a "right" to or at least legitimate expectation of care. Writing in 1982, sociologist Paul Starr stated that in prior decades, the assertion that health care is a matter of right, not privilege, was "so widely acknowledged as almost to be uncontroversial." PAUL STARR, THE SOCIAL TRANSFORMATION OF AMERICAN MEDICINE 389 (1982). *See also* Steven D. Jamar, *The International Human Right to Health*, 22 S.U. L. REV. 1 (1994); Jennifer Prah Ruger, *Health, Health Care, and Incompletely Theorized Agreements: A Normative Theory of Health Policy Decision Making*, 32 J. HEALTH POL. POL'Y & L. 51 (2007). Opinion polls consistently show that Americans generally believe that people who need health care should be able to obtain it on reasonable, non-onerous terms. See sources cited in Rand Rosenblatt, *The Four Ages of Health Law*, 14 HEALTH MATRIX 155, 156–158 (2004).

Ringing proclamations of health care as a basic human right have been found, not only in the speeches of reformers, but in the assertions of American presidents and presidential commissions. John Arras, *Retreat from the Right to Health Care: The President's Commission and Access to Health Care*, 6 CARDOZO L. REV. 321, 321 (1984). In his 1944 State of the Union Address, President Franklin Roosevelt stated "we have accepted, so to speak, a second Bill of Rights under which a new basis of security and prosperity can be established for all—regardless of station, race, or creed." CASS R. SUNSTEIN, THE SECOND BILL OF RIGHTS: FDR'S UNFINISHED REVOLUTION AND WHY WE NEED IT MORE THAN EVER 242–245 (2004). Among these rights were "the right to adequate medical care and the opportunity to achieve and enjoy good health." *Id*. at 243. In 1952, a commission established by President Truman proclaimed that "access to the means for attainment and preservation of health is a basic human right." PRESIDENT'S COMMISSION ON THE HEALTH NEEDS OF THE NATION, 3 (1953). In recent years, prestigious committees have called for reforms that enable reasonable access for all persons. See, e.g., INSTITUTE OF MEDICINE, INSURING AMERICA'S HEALTH (2003). Nonetheless, the message still seems lost on some leaders. For example, President George W. Bush, while opposing expansion of the SCHIP program for poor children, commented, "People have access to health care in America. After all, you just go to an emergency room." The White House, President Bush Visits Cleveland, Ohio, http://georgewbush-whitehouse. archives.gov/news/releases/2007/07/20070710–6.html.

Access to health care is also seen as a matter of international human rights. The Constitution of the World Health Organization provides, "The enjoyment of the highest attainable standard of health is one of the fundamental rights of every human being without distinction of race, religion, political belief, economic or social condition." Article 25(1) of the Universal Declaration of Human Rights of 1948 recognizes the right to medical care as an international human right. Article 25(1) states: "Everyone has the right to a standard of living adequate for the health and well-being of himself and his family, including food, clothing, housing, and medical care and necessary social services, and the right to security in the event of unemployment, sickness, disability, widowhood, old age or other lack of livelihood in circumstances beyond his control." http://www.un.org/ Overview/rights.html. For a discussion of this Article and the movement for international human rights as it relates to health care, see PAUL FARMER, PATHOLOGIES OF POWER: HEALTH, HUMAN RIGHTS, AND THE NEW WAR ON THE POOR 213–246 (2003). For a discussion of the background of the Universal Declaration of Human Rights and the role of Eleanor Roosevelt in its drafting and adoption, see MARY ANN GLENDON, A WORLD MADE NEW: ELEANOR ROOSEVELT AND THE UNIVERSAL DECLARATION OF HUMAN RIGHTS (2002). More than two-thirds of the nations of the world have Constitutions addressing health or health care. In most Constitutions the provision of health care is expressed in universal terms rather than being limited to certain populations. Eleanor D. Kinney & Brian Alexander Clark, *Provisions for Health and Health Care in the Constitutions of the Countries of the World*, 37 CORNELL INT'L L.J. 285 (2004).

The view that an individual has a right to help in time of need—and that appropriate medical care should not be contingent upon anything except need—clashes with other important strains of American political and legal philosophy, particularly the notion of individual freedom. Because the existence of a legal right necessitates a corresponding legal duty, some assert that the "right" to health care necessarily interferes with the individual liberty of both patients and doctors. Dr. Robert Sade, *Medical Care as a Right: A Refutation*, 285 NEW ENG. J. MED. 1288, 1289 (1971), asserts "[t]he concept of medical care as the patient's right is immoral because it denies the most fundamental of all rights, that of a man to his own life and the freedom of action to support it. Medical care is neither a right nor a privilege; it is a service that is provided by doctors and others to people who wish to purchase it."

In addition to the moral argument against a right to health care, many reject the claim of right as unworkable and futile. For example law Professor Richard J. Epstein asserts that the reforms necessary to enforce a right to health care "poses [sic] a mortal peril to the very ends they are supposed to advance: the health and prosperity of society." RICHARD A. EPSTEIN, MORTAL PERIL: OUR INALIENABLE RIGHT TO HEALTH CARE? (1997). Government intervention into markets or professional arrangements "quickly leads to an endless tangle of hidden subsidies, perverse incentives and administrative nightmares." *Id.* at 2–3. More specifically, he argues that Medicare establishes "a single-payer monopoly for large parts of the health care market—a perfect microcosm of a command and control economy." *Id.* at 152. Epstein disapproves of EMTALA, the 1986 federal law requiring hospitals to examine and stabilize patients with "emergency medical conditions" (reviewed later in this Part), arguing that it imposes unreasonable hidden costs on hospitals, *Id.* at 96–98, and that common law principles do "a far better job of providing health care than the endless set of legislative and judicial innovations of our day." *Id.* at 23.

As you study the materials presented in this text, consider what, concretely, the "right to health care" means. What are the roles of health care providers, localities, states and the federal government in making rights meaningful? What are the roles of courts in enforcing these rights? Are conservatives and libertarians correct in saying that the "right to health care" has been tried and found wanting? Are there alternative means, other than the definition and enforcement of rights, for assuring that all members of a society have reasonable access to essential medical care?

CHAPTER 2

THE COMMON LAW: FROM "NO DUTY OF CARE" TO LIMITED SOCIAL RESPONSIBILITY

Before the 1970s, the main source of law in the United States regarding a possible duty of care (or, from the patient's perspective, a right to health care) was the common law, i.e., judge-made law of tort and contract. This Chapter traces the evolution and modification of the "no duty" principle, examining the ways in which the law has acted to alter this most basic of all health care doctrines.

1. A BRIEF OVERVIEW OF AMERICAN COMMON LAW

For most of western history, most healers were unsung local people, many of them women, not formally trained or organized as a profession and belonging to relatively low-status groups such as apothecaries or barber-surgeons. University or hospital-trained physicians were few in number and unavailable to most people. *See, e.g.,* PAUL STARR, THE SOCIAL TRANSFORMATION OF AMERICAN MEDICINE (1982). Informal, low-status healers began to be displaced and legally prohibited in the late 19th century with the rise of scientific medicine, the organization of the medical profession, and the enactment of state medical licensure laws.

The American common or judge-made law of contracts and torts applicable to medical care began taking its modern shape in the same period. In considering the interaction between common law doctrines and medical care, four aspects of the common law should be kept in mind. The first was the pervasiveness of the charitable tradition, which vested the broadest discretion in the donor and was inconsistent with concept of legal obligation.

Both non-professionals and professionals might acknowledge a moral duty to help some of those who could not pay, but this was regarded as a matter of charity, not legal obligation. Before the late 19th century there were very few hospitals, and these were designed for those who could not be cared for in their homes. In the cities, the destitute were sent to public (government-owned) hospitals and almshouses, the first being the Philadelphia General Hospital in 1734. These were places of misery and despair, whose purpose was more to control, isolate, and reform than to cure. To serve the "respectable poor," such as workers in urban seaports, and occasional well-to-do people in special circumstances (such as travelers), and to provide patients for medical education, "voluntary" or private charitable hospitals were developed, the first being Philadelphia's Pennsylvania Hospital in 1752. Both governmental and voluntary hospitals were firmly in the charitable tradition. No one had a "right" to their services, and hospital staff could—and did—refuse care, discharging patients on numerous grounds, including misbehavior. CHARLES E. ROSENBERG, THE CARE OF STRANGERS: THE RISE OF THE AMERICAN HOSPITAL SYSTEM (1995).

A second important aspect of the common law was that the society in which American legal principles were being shaped was one dominated during the late 19th and early 20th centuries by an exceptionally strong commitment to unregulated markets and individual liberty. This cultural orientation effectively suppressed some of the countervailing traditions of fairness and interdependence that had been earlier recognized in the common law.

A third consideration that helps put the cases and the legal doctrine of "no duty" into perspective is the meteoric rise of the medical profession itself during the late 19th and early 20th centuries. This period saw an impressive rise in the status and social authority of the medical profession, linked to expanding scientific knowledge and efficacy, astute political organization and sensibility by the profession, and other cultural factors. STARR, *supra*. Of particular importance, the nature of the hospital changed dramatically, from a small number of charitable institutions for the poor or the transient to a large number of "modern" institutions seemingly based on the fast-developing science of medicine. Hospitals now displaced the home as the preferred site of surgery, and doctors could and did bring their paying patients into the hospital, where they paid fees both to the doctor and the hospital.

As will be explored at greater length in Part Three, doctors were typically not employees of hospitals and were not paid by them. Rather, doctors had "staff privileges" at hospitals, which entitled them to treat their (paying) patients in the hospital. In return, the doctors would donate their time to some hospital functions, such as serving on hospital committees, providing care to charitable patients, and serving as the "on-call" doctor for the emergency room. In large U.S. cities, established voluntary charitable hospitals expanded and transformed themselves into "temples of science," while in the more sparsely populated communities one hospital might be built on government land and formally owned by the local government. However, these seemingly "public" hospitals served doctors' paying patients and often claimed the right to exclude patients just as private charitable hospitals did. The new authority of doctors further reinforced the reluctance of the common law doctrines that held sway during this time to impose legal duties on physicians and hospitals.

Fourth, the common law developed in the context of a pervasive and powerful tradition of racial and other forms of discrimination. The late 19th and early 20th centuries were a time of virulent racism in the United States, expressed in violent suppression of African Americans' constitutional right to vote, lynching, use of the criminal and civil law to re-institute in effect forms of slavery, and pervasive segregation and denial of services on the grounds of race. *See, e.g.,* DOUGLAS A. BLACKMON, SLAVERY BY ANOTHER NAME (2008). Some of the most shocking refusals of emergency care involve people of color and these continue well into the last half of the 20th century. See, e.g., New Biloxi Hosp. v. Frazier, 146 So.2d 882 (Miss. 1962) ("a 42 year old Negro man," disabled World War II veteran, admitted to hospital emergency room with gunshot wounds and, in the words of the Mississippi Supreme Court, "permitted to bleed to death" without treatment by the nurses and doctors; in this case, since the hospital had formally accepted the patient, a jury verdict imposing liability was affirmed); Childs v. Weis, 440 S.W.2d 104 (Tex. Civ. App. 1969) ("negro girl" in the process of childbirth refused care by hospital emergency room and on-call emergency doctor; infant dies after birth in automobile; no violation of duty found); Campbell v. Mincey, below. It is not surprising that a society committed to racial exclusion and oppression would be reluctant to recognize a "duty of care." W. MICHAEL BYRD & LINDA A. CLAYTON, AN AMERICAN HEALTH DILEMMA: RACE, MEDICINE AND HEALTH CARE IN THE UNITED STATES (1900–2000) 48 (2002) conclude an epic study examining the social conditions of southern Black residents saying: "medical and public health facilities provided no assistance for rural blacks. In many areas no doctors or nurses were willing to treat black patients, and blacks who needed hospitalization had to find an urban medical facility that had a Jim Crow ward."

The story of American common law from the early 1900s to the 1960s and beyond involves a struggle between the legal models or perspectives premised on professional (physician) authority and market liberty on the one hand and an emerging worldview of egalitarian social contract on the other, one that recognized but sought to balance physician authority and market liberty with fairness to individuals, communities, and society at large.

2.   THE BASIS OF THE "NO DUTY" PRINCIPLE

Hurley v. Eddingfield

59 N.E. 1058 (Ind. 1901)

■ BAKER, JUSTICE:

The appellant sued appellee for $10,000 damages for wrongfully causing the death of his intestate. The court sustained appellee's demurrer to the complaint and this ruling is assigned as error.

The material facts alleged may be summarized thus: At and for years before decedent's death appellee was a practicing physician at Mace, in Montgomery County, duly licensed under the laws of the state. He held himself out to the public as a general practitioner of medicine. He had been decedent's family physician. Decedent became dangerously ill, and sent for appellee. The messenger informed appellee of decedent's violent sickness, tendered him his fee for his services, and stated to him that no other physician was procurable in time, and that decedent relied on him for attention. No other physician was procurable in time to be of any use, and decedent did rely on appellee for medical assistance. Without any reason whatever, appellee refused to render aid to decedent. No other patients were requiring appellee's immediate service, and he could have gone to the relief of decedent if he had been willing to do so. Death ensued, without decedent's fault, and wholly from appellee's wrongful act.

The alleged wrongful act was appellee's refusal to enter into a contract of employment. Counsel does not contend that, before the enactment of the law regulating the practice of medicine, physicians were bound to render professional service to everyone who applied. The [licensing] act provides for standards of qualification and penalties for practicing without license. The act is a preventive, not a compulsive, measure. In obtaining the state's license (permission) to practice medicine, the state does not require, and the licensee does not engage, that he will practice at all or on other terms than he may choose to accept. Counsel's analogies, drawn from the obligations to the public on the part of innkeepers, common carriers, and the like, are beside the mark. Judgment affirmed.

Notes

1. The lost facts of Hurley v. Eddingfield. The Indiana Supreme Court's opinion in *Hurley*, summarizing the plaintiff's complaint, does not identify the "decedent" in any way, nor anything about why or how the decedent was "dangerously ill." The plaintiff's complaint and brief provided more information. George Hurley, the named plaintiff, was the administrator of the estate of the deceased patient, Charlotte M. Burk. The complaint alleged that early on July 6, 1899, Mrs. Burk was "seized with child birth pains and labor" and that she sent for Dr. Eddingfield and requested him to attend her. When he refused, Mrs. Burk's husband Thomas sent for him two additional times, saying no other doctor was available, and tendered a fee. Dr. Eddingfield refused to respond "without reason or excuse" and by reason of this refusal Mrs. Burk "was caused to suffer great pain of body and anguish of mind, thereby causing [her] and her unborn child both to die."

2. The court's reasoning: individual liberty versus public duty. The Indiana Supreme Court's decision rests on the core principle that at common law, private parties have no obligation to enter into a contract, and that nothing in Indiana's licensure law alters this basic tenet by changing the basic relationship between physicians and society. The reasoning of the Indiana Supreme Court shows how the professional authority and market competition models can be mutually reinforcing. The court's main narrative presents the defendant as an abstract seller of services in the market. Dr. Eddingfield's position as a doctor (with a prior relationship to the patient, no less) virtually disappears, and the "logical" legal question then becomes a function of market liberty: does he have a duty to accept a contract of employment, the general answer being in the negative. The professional authority model hovers over the later stages of the argument: the medical licensure law does not impose a duty to render care, or even to practice at all, and the analogies to innkeepers, common carriers, "and the like" are "beside the mark," implicitly distinguishing the work of professionals from that of innkeepers and blacksmiths.

While the Indiana Supreme Court presents its opinion as a set of logical propositions abstracted from any substantive values or concrete facts about the patient and the doctor, the opinion actually reflects, as Oliver Wendell Holmes said judicial opinions inevitably do, "[t]he felt necessities of the time, the prevalent moral and political theories, [and] intuitions of public policy, avowed or unconscious." *The Common Law* 1 (1881). By the late 19th century, contract and tort doctrines had been largely re-cast in the individualistic, market-oriented "no duty" mode, reflecting the dominant laissez-faire and Social Darwinist substantive values of the era. *See, e.g.,* Lochner v. New York, 198 U.S. 45, 74 (1905) (Holmes, J., dissenting); RICHARD HOFSTADTER, SOCIAL DARWINISM IN AMERICAN THOUGHT (1944). These market-oriented social beliefs and attitudes that dominated this period in American history were reflected in the judicial "framing" of the precise relationship between physicians and individuals seeking medical care.

But earlier English cases reveal another tradition in the common law that recognized and enforced social interdependence and mutual obligations in ways that limited the no duty principle. As a result of numerous social and political factors in the 20th century, including the Depression, the New Deal, World War II, and the civil rights movement, the "social contract" theme in the common law became prominent again, contributing to egalitarian social contract models of law generally, including in health law. With respect to health law, *see, e.g.,* Rosenblatt, "The Four Ages of Health Law" at 166–175; Doe v. Bridgeton Hosp. Ass'n, Inc., 366 A.2d 641 (N.J. 1976); and Tunkl v. Regents of the University of California, 383 P.2d 441 (Cal. 1963).

---

3.   TERMINATION AND FORMATION OF THE DOCTOR-PATIENT RELATIONSHIP: "UNDERTAKING" AND "ABANDONMENT"

Ricks v. Budge

64 P.2d 208 (Utah 1937)

■ EPHRAIM HANSON, JUSTICE:

This is an action for malpractice against the defendants who are physicians and surgeons at Logan, Utah. [The plaintiff's (Rick's) infected right hand had been treated by Dr. S.M. Budge at the Budge Hospital from March 11 to March15, when Ricks left the hospital against Dr. Budge's advice. Rick's sought Dr. Budge's care again for the hand on March 17. The trial court granted a directed verdict for the defendants.]

[T]he evidence shows that when plaintiff left the hospital on March 15th, Dr. Budge advised him to continue the same treatment that had been given him at the hospital, and that if the finger showed any signs of getting worse at any time, plaintiff was to return at once to Dr. Budge for further treatment; that on the morning of March 17th, plaintiff telephoned Dr. Budge, and explained the condition of his hand; that he was told by the doctor to come to his office, and in pursuance of the doctor's request, plaintiff reported at the doctor's office at 2 p.m. of that day. Dr. Budge again examined the hand and told plaintiff the hand was worse; he called in Dr. D. C. Budge, another of the defendants, who examined the hand, scraped it some, and indicated thereon where the hand should be opened. Dr. S. M. Budge said to plaintiff: "You have got to go back to the hospital." Upon arriving [at the hospital, plaintiff] testified: "He [meaning Dr. S. M. Budge] came into my room and said, 'You are owing us. I am not going to touch you until that account is taken care of.'" (The account referred to was, according to plaintiff, of some years' standing and did not relate to any charge for services being then rendered.) Plaintiff testified that he did not know what to say to the doctor, but that he finally asked the doctor if he was going to take care of him, and the doctor replied: "No, I am not going to take care of you. I would not take you to the operating table and operate on you and keep you here thirty days, and then there is another $30.00 at the office, until your account is taken care of." Plaintiff replied: "If that is the idea, if you will furnish me a little help, I will try to move."

Plaintiff testified that this help was furnished, and that after being dressed, he left the Budge Memorial Hospital to seek other treatment. He walked to the Cache Valley Hospital, a few blocks away, and there met Dr. Randall, who testified that the hand was swollen with considerable fluid oozing from it; that the lower two thirds of the forearm was red and swollen from the infection which extended up in the arm, and that there was some fluid also oozing from the back of the hand, and that plaintiff required immediate surgical attention. About two weeks after the plaintiff entered the Cache Valley Hospital, it became necessary to amputate the middle finger and remove about an inch of the metacarpal bone.

Dr. S. M. Budge testified that at the time he sent the plaintiff to the Budge Memorial Hospital on March 17th, plaintiff was in a dangerous condition and needed immediate surgical and medical attention; that the reason for sending him to that hospital was in order to give him the necessary immediate surgical and medical attention. There can be no question from the evidence that it was the intention of Dr. S. M. Budge to operate at once on plaintiff's hand.

Defendants contend: (1) That there was no contract of employment between plaintiff and defendants and that defendants in the absence of a valid contract were not obligated to proceed with any treatment; and (2) that if there was such a contract, there was no evidence that the refusal of

Dr. S. M. Budge to operate or take care of plaintiff resulted in any damage to plaintiff.

We cannot agree with either of these propositions. The evidence shows that plaintiff had been under the care and treatment of the defendants at the Budge Memorial Hospital from March 11th to March 15th; that when he left that hospital on March 15th, Dr. S. M. Budge said to him: "If you are going home, you had better follow out the treatment at home just as near as you can the same as you were doing here. Here is another thing I want to tell you, if you see any signs of that finger getting worse at any time, you come in and see me immediately." On March 17th, plaintiff, realizing that his condition was getting worse, telephoned Dr. S. M. Budge and was told by that doctor to come to the doctor's office, which plaintiff did; that there both Dr. S. M. Budge and Dr. D. C. Budge examined the hand; that Dr. D. C. Budge indicated on it where it should be opened; and that under the instructions of these doctors plaintiff was returned to the hospital for no other purpose than having his hand operated upon at once.

Under this evidence, it cannot be said that the relation of physician and patient did not exist on March 17th. It had not been terminated after its commencement on March 11th. When the plaintiff left the hospital on March 15th, he understood that he was to report to Dr. S. M. Budge if the occasion required and was so requested by the doctor. Plaintiff's return to the doctor's office was on the advice of the doctor. While at the doctor's office, both Dr. S. M. Budge and Dr. D. C. Budge examined plaintiff's hand and they ordered that he go at once to the hospital for further medical attention. That plaintiff was told by the doctor to come to the doctor's office and was there examined by him and directed to go to the hospital for further treatment would create the relationship of physician and patient. That the relationship existed at the time the plaintiff was sent to the hospital on March 17th cannot be seriously questioned.

We believe the law is well settled that a physician or surgeon, upon undertaking an operation or other case, is under the duty, in the absence of an agreement limiting the service, of continuing his attention, after the first operation or first treatment, so long as the case requires attention. The obligation of continuing attention can be terminated only by the cessation of the necessity which gave rise to the relationship, or by the discharge of the physician by the patient, or by the withdrawal from the case by the physician after giving the patient reasonable notice so as to enable the patient to secure other medical attention. A physician has the right to withdraw from a case, but if the case is such as to still require further medical or surgical attention, he must, before withdrawing from the case, give the patient sufficient notice so the patient can procure other medical attention if he desires. [numerous citations omitted].

We cannot say as a matter of law that plaintiff suffered no damages by reason of the refusal of Dr. S. M. Budge to further treat him. The evidence shows that from the time plaintiff left the office of the defendants up until the time that he arrived at the Cache Valley Hospital his hand continued to swell; that it was very painful; that when he left the Budge Memorial

Hospital he was in such condition that he did not know whether he was going to live or die. That both his mental and physical suffering must have been most acute cannot be questioned. While the law cannot measure with exactness such suffering and cannot determine with absolute certainty what damages, if any, plaintiff may be entitled to; still those are questions which a jury under proper instructions from the court must determine.

■ FOLLAND, JUSTICE (concurring in part, dissenting in part):

As I view the case the contract of employment between Dr. Budge and Mr. Ricks was terminated by Ricks at the time he paid his bill and left the hospital on March 15th. There is no dispute whatsoever in the testimony with respect to the fact that he did this without the consent and against the advice of Dr. Budge. The testimony of Dr. D. C. Budge and Dr. S. M. Budge shows their protest was much more emphatic than indicated by plaintiff's testimony. A physician ought not to be censured or held liable for any bad results following the voluntary action of a patient in leaving the hospital where he could receive proper treatment.

The theory of plaintiff as evidenced in his complaint is that there was no continued relationship from the first employment but that a new relationship was entered into. He visited the clinic on March 17th; the Doctors Budge examined his hand and told him an immediate operation was necessary and for him to go to the hospital. I do not think a new contract was entered into at that time. There was no consideration for any implied promise that Dr. Budge or the Budge Clinic would assume the responsibility of another operation and the costs and expenses incident thereto. As soon as Dr. Budge reached the hospital he opened negotiations with the plaintiff which might have resulted in a contract, but before any contract arrangement was made the plaintiff decided to leave the hospital and seek attention elsewhere. As soon as he could dress himself he walked away. There is conflict in the evidence as to the conversation. Plaintiff testified in effect that Dr. Budge asked for something to be done about an old account. The doctor's testimony in effect was that he asked that some arrangement be made to take care of the doctor's bill and expenses for the ensuing operation and treatment at the hospital. The result, however, was negative. No arrangement was made. The plaintiff made no attempt whatsoever to suggest to the doctor any way by which either the old account might be taken care of or the expenses of the ensuing operation provided for.

Of course, for the purpose of deciding the rightfulness of the trial court's action in directing a verdict, we must take plaintiff's version as true. The jury might well have found that the doctor's version was far more reasonable and the true version of what actually happened. Under either view Dr. Budge had a right to refuse to incur the obligation and responsibility incident to one or more operations and the treatment and attention which would be necessary. If it be assumed that the contract relationship of physician and patient existed prior to this conversation, either as resulting from the first employment or that there was an implied contract entered into at the clinic, yet Dr. Budge had the right with proper notice to discontinue the relationship. While plaintiff's condition was acute and needed immediate attention, he received such immediate attention at the Cache Valley Hospital. There was only a delay of an hour or two, I am satisfied from my reading of the record that no injury or damage resulted from the delay occasioned by plaintiff leaving the Budge Hospital and going to the Cache Valley Hospital. He was not in such desperate condition but that he was able to walk the three or four blocks between the two hospitals. Dr. Randall testified he gave the same treatment and performed the same operation as would have been given and performed two or three hours earlier.

4.   MEDICAL ETHICS AS THE BASIS OF A DUTY OF CARE

The American Medical Association provides Principles of Medical Ethics for physicians. See *Principles of Medical Ethics*, American Medical Association (June 17, 2001), http://www.ama-assn.org/ama/pub/category/2512.html. The Principles state in pertinent part as follows:

Preamble

The medical profession has long subscribed to a body of ethical statements developed primarily for the benefit of the patient. The following Principles adopted by the American Medical Association (AMA) are not laws, but standards of conduct which define the essentials of honorable behavior for the physician.

Principles of medical ethics

VI.   A physician shall, in the provision of appropriate patient care, except in emergencies, be free to choose whom to serve, with whom to associate, and the environment in which to provide medical care.

VII.   A physician shall recognize a responsibility to participate in activities contributing to the improvement of the community and the betterment of public health.

VIII.   A physician shall, while caring for a patient, regard responsibility to the patient as paramount.

IX.   A physician shall support access to medical care for all people.

How do you reconcile ethical principle VI with ethical principles VII and IX? Would the defendant's behavior in *Hurley* be consistent with these medical ethics principles? How do you think the concept of "emergency" would be understood in the context of the AMA's ethical standards, and who would get to define the term? Are these ethical principles internally consistent? How does a physician work to improve the community and the public health and support access to medical care for all people, while simultaneously retaining total freedom to choose whom to serve and under what circumstances except in "emergencies?"

Prior to 1957, the AMA Principles contained an ethical duty to render charitable care. *Principles of Medical Ethics*, American Medical Association (1955). Some physicians continue to regard care for those unable to pay as an ethical duty, while others reject such ethical concepts on economic or political grounds. See discussion in Rand E. Rosenblatt, *Medicaid Primary Care Case Management, the Doctor–Patient Relationship, and the Politics of Privatization*, 36 CASE W. RES. L. REV. 915, 925 n.37 (1986).

---

5.   THE EVOLUTION OF THE "NO DUTY OF CARE" PRINCIPLE UNDER THE COMMON LAW

There is no "duty to rescue" at common law. Tort law historically draws a sharp distinction between action and inaction. It holds people liable when careless actions cause injury to others, but does not require affirmative action to help others in distress, even when essential help could be provided without inconvenience or danger.

Campbell v. Mincey

413 F. Supp. 16 (N.D. Miss. 1975), *aff'd without opinion*, 542 F.2d 573 (5th Cir. 1976)

■ ORMA R. SMITH, DISTRICT JUDGE:

On the morning of March 21, 1974, Hattie Mae Campbell gave birth to her third child, a son whom she named Frederick, under circumstances which counsel for plaintiffs in this case maintains would "disgrace a nation of savages." On August 19, 1974, Ms. Campbell and her son filed suit against the chairman and members of the Board of Trustees of the Marshall County Hospital in Holly Springs, Mississippi, and the Administrator, Chief of Staff, and Director of Nursing at the hospital. [P]laintiffs alleged that on the occasion of the birth of her son, Ms. Campbell was refused admittance to the Marshall County Hospital and its emergency room because of her race (she is black) and financial condition (she is indigent). Because Ms. Campbell and her son sought to prosecute the action on behalf of a plaintiff class, an evidentiary hearing to determine whether the suit could be maintained as a class action. Counsel for the parties subsequently agreed that the case be deemed submitted for decision on the merits on the basis of the testimony introduced at the class hearing. [The motion for class certification was denied subsequent to the hearing].

The course of events giving rise to this litigation began in the early morning hours of March 21, 1974, when Ms. Campbell was awakened by labor contractions. The child was not expected before April; however, Ms. Campbell, accompanied by her sister, secured the services of a neighbor to drive her from their home some eight miles north of Holly Springs, Mississippi, to Oxford, Mississippi, where Ms. Campbell received prenatal care from a local physician. Upon reaching Holly Springs, the occupants of the automobile concluded that it would not be possible for them to arrive at the Oxford–Lafayette County Hospital, located some thirty miles south of

Holly Springs, prior to the birth of Ms. Campbell's child. Ms. Campbell had not previously visited the Marshall County Hospital during the course of the pregnancy here in issue.

Upon arrival at the Marshall County Hospital, Ms. Campbell and her sister entered the emergency room where they encountered a staff nurse. Upon learning that Ms. Campbell was of the opinion that she was about to deliver, the nurse informed Ms. Campbell and her sister that they should go to the hospital in Oxford where Ms. Campbell had received prenatal care and have the baby delivered there. The nurse did call the emergency room doctor, the only physician on duty in the hospital at that time, and informed him that Ms. Campbell's labor contractions were occurring at the rate of one every five minutes, that her water was intact, and that she had been seeing a doctor in Oxford. The emergency room doctor then affirmed the nurse's directive to Ms. Campbell that she should go to Oxford for the delivery of her child.

Following the hospital staff's refusal to admit her, Ms. Campbell and her sister returned to the parking lot where she gave birth on the front seat of the neighbor's automobile. After Frederick's birth, Ms. Campbell's sister again went into the hospital and requested the nurse to admit Ms. Campbell and her newly-born son. Once again the nurse refused to admit plaintiffs but did go out into the parking lot to look over the mother and child. The only assistance which the nurse provided was in the form of a sheet in which the baby could be wrapped. The nurse did not notify the emergency doctor of the birth of the child and no other post-natal care was afforded mother or child by the staff of the Marshall County Hospital. The staff did, however, summon a Holly Springs ambulance which delivered the mother and child to the Oxford–Lafayette County Hospital where the plaintiffs were promptly admitted and treated. The evidence shows that the mother and son suffered no physical injury due to their inability to gain admittance to and treatment at the Marshall County Hospital. The report of the attending physician at the Oxford hospital indicates Ms. Campbell's delivery was normal in all respects other than the location and the absence of a doctor at the immediate time of the birth.

In addition to their allegation that the defendants' conduct violated their constitutional rights, plaintiffs also maintain that the defendants have violated [a provision of Mississippi's hospital licensure code which] requires hospitals operating within the state to comply with certain "rules, regulations and standards" promulgated by the Mississippi Commission on Hospital Care, failing which their licenses may be revoked. It is readily apparent that [the provision in question] imposes no duties upon the defendants which are owed to plaintiffs and/or other patients of the Marshall County Hospital, but merely establishes an enforcement system which may be utilized to compel compliance with state regulations governing the operation of hospitals. [The court further ruled that any statutory duties imposed only on the hospital as a corporate entity were not relevant because the hospital was not a named defendant and that state regulations that might impose duties were beyond judicial notice.]

Turning now to plaintiffs' claim that defendants' conduct on the night of March 20–21, 1974 constitutes a breach of a common law duty owed plaintiffs, it is plaintiffs' position that both public and private hospitals in this state operating an emergency room must accept, treat, and admit every individual who comes to them seeking assistance. The court can find no cases in this jurisdiction discussing the duty of a hospital to undertake to render emergency treatment to anyone seeking such aid, nor have the parties cited any decisions relative to that duty to the court.[3] However, the court has noted the existence of what may be described as a "trend" in the common law of this country toward imposing liability upon a hospital which refuses to admit and treat, on an emergency basis, a seriously injured person. Without discussing each of the more recent cases on the point, the court would observe that, in most instances, liability was predicated upon the defendant's arbitrary refusal to treat the plaintiff in question, which refusal was a marked departure from previous hospital custom and procedure. The refusal of the staff of the Marshall County Hospital to admit or treat the plaintiffs here was in compliance with, rather than a departure from, hospital policy not to admit patients who are not referred by local physicians.

The following excerpts from the bylaws of the Marshall County Hospital furnished the motivation underlying the defendants' refusal to treat or admit plaintiffs:

> All inpatients shall be admitted and attended only by members of the medical staff. If during an emergency the attending physician is unavailable then the on call or staff physician may be asked to serve in the emergency. All emergency outpatients shall be attended by members of the medical staff, according to the posted call system or by the staff physician on duty in the hospital. In the case of an emergency the physician attending the patient shall be expected to do all in his power to save the life of the patient, including the calling of such consultation as may be available. For the purpose of this section an emergency is defined as a condition in which the life of the patient is in imminent danger and in which any delay in administering treatment would increase the danger.

Both the administrator and chief of staff of the hospital testified as to the manner in which the above-quoted bylaws function to govern the day-to-day operation of the hospital. There are no staff physicians on duty at the hospital between 6:30 PM and 7:00 AM. During those hours, the only physician on duty is the emergency room doctor. The Marshall County Hospital has an agreement with the University of Tennessee Medical School at Memphis under the terms of which the University supplies the hospital with doctors who have completed their general medicine degrees and are pursuing a specialty residence, either in surgery or radiology, at the

---

3. The only Mississippi case concerning emergency room treatment which the court has been able to locate involved a factual situation wherein the defendant hospital clearly undertook to render emergency treatment to the plaintiff but failed to render such aid in a competent manner. New Biloxi Hospital, Inc. v. Frazier, 146 So.2d 882 (1962).

medical school. The emergency room doctors are not considered to be members of the medical staff of the Marshall County Hospital in the contemplation of the aforequoted bylaws. Because the emergency room doctors are not available to afford follow-up or continuing treatment for in-patients, patients may be admitted to the hospital only upon the authorization of a local physician who is a member of the medical staff.

According to hospital policy, when an individual appears at the emergency room seeking treatment between the hours of 6:30 PM and 7:00 AM, and such individual has not been referred for treatment and/or admission by a local physician, the emergency room doctor will see the individual but only for the limited purpose of determining whether the patient should be treated at the Marshall County Hospital or carried to another facility. That is, the emergency room doctor exercises his medical judgment as to whether the individual in question can best be treated at the Marshall County Hospital or should be referred to a hospital with better accommodations, expertise, or equipment.

Plaintiffs were twice examined by a staff nurse who determined that no "emergency," as that term is defined by the regulations of the hospital, existed. The nurse's determination that no emergency existed prior to Frederick's birth was confirmed by the emergency room doctor. The nurse's conclusion that no emergency existed after Frederick's birth was confirmed by the report of treating physician in Oxford who recorded his observation that Ms. Campbell's delivery and post-partum recovery was "uneventful" except for a loss of blood during the ambulance trip.

While the court is disturbed by the seemingly cursory examinations performed on Ms. Campbell by the staff nurse and by the fact that Ms. Campbell was never examined by the emergency room physician, the court must conclude that plaintiffs suffered no tortious injury at the hands of the defendants on the date in question. This conclusion is primarily compelled by the evidence indicating that the nurse's determination that Ms. Campbell's delivery did not amount to an "emergency" situation, as that term is customarily used in the furnishing of hospital and medical services, was proved substantially correct by subsequent events. Further, neither the emergency room doctor nor the staff nurse was joined as a defendant in the case and the plaintiffs did not allege that their injuries resulted from the failure of this doctor and this nurse to adhere to established hospital procedure. Rather, the basic tenor of plaintiffs' complaint, as the court understands it, is that the hospital regulations concerning operation of the emergency room function in an unconstitutional manner.

Another fact worthy of consideration in determining the propriety of the actions taken by the hospital personnel on the night here in question is that the ambulance which carried Ms. Campbell and her child to the Oxford–Lafayette County Hospital had already arrived at the Marshall County Hospital by the time the nurse became aware that the child had been born. The court feels that the nurse's actions in allowing the plaintiff to proceed to Oxford at that time were reasonable in view of her knowledge that there was no doctor in Holly Springs who accepted obstetric cases and that Ms. Campbell had a regular physician in Oxford, some thirty minutes away by ambulance.

[The court also notes that had liability been imposed on the hospital, it would have been entitled to sovereign immunity to monetary damages under state law unless plaintiffs could establish that the hospital had secured medical liability insurance coverage.]

Turning finally to the constitutional issues raised in the complaint, the plaintiffs claim that they were refused admittance to the hospital and treatment in the emergency room because of their race and indigency. The overwhelming weight of the evidence in the record is to the effect that plaintiffs' race and financial condition had nothing at all to do with the defendants' refusal to admit or treat plaintiffs. The court, as the finder of fact, has concluded that defendants' refusal was based solely on the hospital policy not to admit patients who are not referred by local physicians. In fact, Ms. Campbell herself was a patient of the Marshall County Hospital on the occasion of a previous pregnancy. The evidence shows that the hospital and its emergency room are used more frequently by blacks than by whites. Plaintiff's claim that she was the victim of racial discrimination is simply untenable.

The argument that Ms. Campbell was refused treatment because of her financial condition is likewise unpersuasive. Ms. Campbell had in her possession a Medicaid card which guaranteed payment of her hospital bills. She was never questioned by any member of the hospital staff as to her ability to pay. The proof shows that a large portion of the patients treated in the Marshall County Hospital are Medicaid patients. Plaintiffs offered no proof or even explanation as to why defendants would single out these particular individuals for unfavorable treatment because of their indigency. The court is convinced that there can be no explanation because the claimed discrimination never in fact occurred.

In support of their contention that a constitutional right has been denied them at the hands of the defendants, plaintiffs argue that, even in the absence of racial or financial motivation, the defendants denied plaintiffs the use of a governmental facility in an arbitrary and capricious manner so extreme as to amount to the deprivation of a constitutional right. Plaintiffs maintain that the Equal Protection Clause of the Fourteenth Amendment entitles them to use of the Marshall County Hospital on the same basis as all other individuals and that by refusing them admission and treatment, the defendants infringed this right.

In considering plaintiffs' equal protection claim, the court must first identify the classification which has been established and which results in disparate treatment of certain individuals by the Marshall County Hospital. The classes here may be defined as those persons who are referred to the hospital for admission and treatment by a local physician and those persons who seek admission and treatment at the hospital but have not been referred by a local doctor. It is the policy of the hospital to accept the former and reject the latter.[4] This policy clearly results in different treatment of certain individuals according to the classification into which they fall; however, the fact that a classification has been made, or that different treatment is afforded certain individuals on the basis of that classification, does not of itself establish a violation of the Equal Protection Clause. To establish an equal protection violation, plaintiffs must show that the classification and consequent dissimilar treatment fail to advance any legitimate state interest.

In the final analysis, disposition of this case reduces to a determination of whether the hospital regulations requiring reference of incoming patients by local physicians except in true "emergency" situations operates in a reasonable manner to further a legitimate state objective. On the basis of this record, the court cannot but conclude that the regulation does so function. The operation of the rule in this case resulted in no injury to plaintiffs according to the report of the attending physician at the transferee hospital. There was no evidence introduced which tended to show that true "emergency" cases were refused treatment at the Marshall County Hospital and suffered actual injury thereby. In the absence of some proof that this regulation has or can operate in some manner to inflict an injury upon some individual, the court must accept the considered judgment of the medical specialists who are charged with the responsibility of administering the hospital. Without some concrete evidence to the contrary, the court cannot say that the justification of the regulation offered by the hospital (which was to the effect that a local physician must authorize admission of a patient in order to insure a doctor will be available for follow-up treatment of that patient) is not a reasonable restriction upon the use of this public facility by plaintiffs and other similarly-situated individuals.

Notes

1. Physicians and hospitals and hospital admission. As explored more fully in Part Three, the relationships described by the bylaws of the Marshall County Hospital were common in the 1970s. Most of the doctors treating patients at the hospital were members of the "medical staff." Members of the medical staff have the privilege to admit and treat their patients at the hospital, but are not employed by the hospital. The only doctor available at night was a recent medical school graduate who had no authority to admit patients to the hospital. The bylaws recite that members of the medical staff might be expected to be available "according to the

---

4. It could be argued that the classes created by the policies of the Marshall County Hospital are composed of those persons who seek admission to the hospital and are adjudged to be true "emergency" cases by the emergency room doctor and those persons seeking admission who are not considered "emergency" cases pursuant to the hospital by-laws discussed, infra. However, no evidence was introduced by the parties as to the medical standards upon which emergency situations may be distinguished from non-emergency situations. A determination of this sort is therefore beyond the competency of the court on the basis of this record and is better left to medical judgment of trained physicians.

posted call system," but no member of the medical staff was at the hospital that night.

What is the logic of this organizational structure? The court suggests that the arrangement is motivated by the desire to assure that each patient is sponsored by a local physician "available to afford follow-up or continuing treatment." Today, most hospitals have emergency rooms staffed by doctors who are authorized to admit patients to the hospital. But, as you will see in Part Three, there are often significant differences in hospital treatment depending on whether a patient has a pre-existing relationship with a doctor with admitting privileges, or rather is admitted from the emergency room, without a relationship with a doctor with medical staff privileges. The doctors of Marshall County Hospital might say, "We just want to provide the best care possible. We want all of our patients to have a personal professional relationship with an individual doctor selected for our staff. We want the doctors to control the mission of the hospital and do not want the shape of our service to be driven by the unpredictable demands of ER patients with whom we have no prior relationship." What is wrong with that vision?

2. *Legal services and civil rights.* In 1964, as part of the War on Poverty, President Lyndon Johnson established the Office of Economic Opportunity to administer a neighborhood-based Community Action Program ("CAP"). During 1966, three hundred federally-funded neighborhood legal services programs were created throughout the country. MARTHA DAVIS, BRUTAL NEED: LAWYERS AND THE WELFARE RIGHTS MOVEMENT, 1960–1973 (1993). Mrs. Campbell was represented by two lawyers from North Mississippi Legal Services.

By 1974, lawyers representing low-income and minority patients were mounting legal challenges to hospital exclusionary practices, using a variety of legal theories to challenge policies that denied essential medical care on the basis of race or poverty.

Title VI of the Civil Rights Act of 1964, 42 U.S.C. § 2000d, prohibits discrimination based on race by recipients of federal financial assistance. Regulations interpreting the law reach both intentional discrimination and practices, such as facially neutral hospital admitting privilege rules that have the effect of discriminating. In *Campbell* the court rejected plaintiff's assertion of intentional racial discrimination. In many situations, rules providing that patients can be admitted to a hospital only by a doctor with staff privileges have a racially discriminatory impact, but proving that impact is difficult and it seems that the plaintiff's lawyers did not present evidence to support this claim. *See* below, Part One, Chap. 4(1).

The Hill–Burton Act of 1946 required that hospitals receiving federal construction funds ensure that services "will be made available to all persons residing in the territorial area." 42 U.S.C. § 291c(e). In 1979, the statute was interpreted to prohibit Hill Burton facilities from using admissions policies that limit admission to patients referred by physicians with medical staff privileges and to prohibit discrimination on the basis of public insurance status. 42 C.F.R. § 24.603(d)(1).

3. Women in labor. The failure of the court to view a woman in the final stages of labor as a medical emergency is remarkable given the clinical realities of, and normal human reaction to, labor and delivery. Pregnancy and childbirth are, of course, an integral part of the cycle of life. At the same time, 40 percent of pregnant women will develop some form of a pregnancy-related complication, and 15 percent will develop a life-threatening complication. Joy Lawn et al., *The Healthy Newborn: A Reference Manual for Program Managers, Part 1—The Unheard Cry for Newborn Health* 1.6 (Centers for Disease Control, CARE, Care/CDC Health Initiative, 2001), http://www.care.org/careswork/whatwedo/health/downloads/healthy_newborn_manual/part1.pdf. Between one and two percent of women will die giving birth. Evidence has shown that it is nearly impossible to predict which women will have a complication, so both comprehensive pregnancy care throughout the pregnancy, as well as safe and appropriate hospital care, is essential. Complications of labor can lead to, among other matters, strokes, lethal infections, uncontrolled bleeding, and loss of life. The American College of Obstetricians and Gynecologists reiterates long-standing opposition to home birth, even when the woman is at low risk and attended by a trained and certified nurse-midwife. ACOG Statement on Home Births, Feb. 6, 2008, http://www.acog.org/from_home/publications/press_releases/nr02–06–08–2.cfm.

4. Can New Biloxi Hospital *truly be distinguished?* What a difference evidence of even a nominal health care undertaking can make to the outcome of a case. In New Biloxi Hospital, Inc. v. Frazier, 146 So.2d 882 (Miss. 1962), cited in *Campbell v. Mincey*, a hospital was found liable for negligent conduct following the admission of a Black man who was allowed to slowly bleed to death while nurses and doctors literally stood around and watched. In the case, a family sought care for a "42 year old Negro man, who had lost his left eye and his left arm, just below the elbow, during World War II" and who had been shot. Id.

> He bled considerably at the scene, and on the ambulance cot during the five minute trip to the New Biloxi Hospital. Ambulance attendants carried him into the emergency room, where one of the Hospital's nurses just looked at him and walked away. He was bleeding profusely at that time. There was blood all over the ambulance cot, and while waiting in the hospital, blood was streaming from his arm to the floor, forming a puddle with a diameter of 24–30 inches. After about twenty minutes, another Hospital nurse came, looked at Frazier and walked away.
>
> Shortly after that, upon insistence by the ambulance attendants, he was placed on the table of the emergency room by the nurses and strapped down. During all of this time Frazier had been trashing about and cursing in a nasty manner. The registered nurse in charge, Mrs. Perrein, an employee of the Hospital, looked Sam over, took his blood pressure and his pulse, and attempted to call the doctor who was on first emergency call for the staff of the Hospital. There was no doctor in the Hospital on emergency call at

all times. The first doctor on the list could not be reached; Dr. Smith was contacted, and arrived about thirty minutes after being called, apparently around 11:30 p.m. or shortly thereafter.

In the meantime Frazier's wife and several of his friends arrived. They noticed that he was still bleeding and struggling; his wound was unbandaged, and there was blood on him and the table. Before Smith's arrival, the nurse placed a towel around the wound, but made no attempt to stop any bleeding, although she knew that this was an important factor. Mrs. Perrein denied Frazier was bleeding, but the jury manifestly found otherwise. She had no other particular duties to perform. She did not advise Dr. Smith of the extent of Frazier's bleeding. Smith, after looking at the wound, and learning Frazier was a veteran, recommended that he be transferred to the Veterans' Administration Hospital for surgical procedures. Frazier and his wife, both of whom were most distraught, acquiesced in the transfer. Smith left the room to see about obtaining an ambulance, but there was considerable delay in getting one.

After Smith examined the patient, Mrs. Perrein wrapped another towel around the wound. Neither she nor the doctor made any effort to stop the bleeding in any way. She continued to come in and out of the emergency room on occasions, but simply looked at Frazier. He asked to see his little boy, and for water. His bleeding continued. Mrs. Perrein was aware of the symptoms of shock: low blood pressure, high pulse rate, sweating and cold, clammy skin. Dr. Smith said he was relying on her to observe the patient and advise him of any changes. However, she did nothing for him other than to observe him, except to take his blood pressure upon his first being placed on the table in the treatment room.

He continued sweating; his skin was cold, but his thrashing about began to diminish, and he asked again for water. Mrs. Perrein did not report any of these facts to Dr. Smith, who said that Frazier probably had started into shock before he left the Hospital. A blood pressure reading would have revealed that. Smith was relying on the nurses to advise him about the patient's condition. If the condition had changed, he would have held the patient and given him additional treatment.

At about 1 a.m., Frazier was placed in another ambulance for a ten minute ride to the VA Hospital. When he arrived, he was practically moribund and, although every type of emergency measure was taken, he was pronounced dead at 1:25 a.m. An autopsy revealed that the sole cause of death was hemorrhage with resultant shock.

The administrator of the Hospital stated that nurses on duty in the emergency room have instructions to administer such treatment and render such first aid as they can, until a doctor arrives. Frazier was admitted to the emergency room as a patient, and a record was made of his admission.

Id. at 194–196

Does it strike you as odd the common law recognized that blatant disregard of a patient with a life and death medical emergency lying inside the emergency department was actionable, while a similarly blatant disregard of someone just outside the hospital doors did not amount to a legal violation? If, in *New Biloxi*, a nurse and medical resident had "eyeballed" the man and had refused to admit him because he had no sponsoring physician with staff privileges (as in *Campbell*), would the hospital have escaped liability entirely? Could the staff claim that they saw no life-threatening injury but just some blood? Does this case offer evidence of the very fine practical line which can separate a legal undertaking from its absence? Pay close attention when you read the cases and materials on EMTALA later in this Part, particularly the extent to which the statute and regulations prevent hospitals from refusing to commence a health care undertaking when presented with a patient with a medical emergency, but also which allow emergency room staff to fail to "perceive" emergency conditions, and therefore terminate their undertaking of care.

5. *Evolving concepts of duty: detrimental reliance, undertaking, and public accommodations.* The "no duty to rescue" principle, which reflects a strong vision of an individual's legal right to disregard the interests of others except under narrowly defined circumstances, has long been challenged as blind to moral and social values of interdependence and community; *see* Francis H. Bohlen, *The Moral Duty to Aid Others as a Basis of Tort Liability*, 56 U. PA. L. REV. 217 (1908), and as masking the realities of governmental and corporate power to create and permit harmful risks. Kenneth M. Casebeer, *The Empty State and Nobody's Market: The Political Economy of Non–Responsibility and the Judicial Disappearing of the Civil Rights Movement*, 54 U. MIAMI L. REV. 247 (2000). For a defense of individualism protected by the no duty principle, as applied to a woman's right to choose an abortion, see Donald H. Regan, *Rewriting Roe v. Wade*, 77 MICH. L. REV. 1569 (1979).

Beginning in the early 1960s, state courts, working with common law principles, began to modify the "no duty" principle in the context of hospital emergency care. Several basic theories emerged: detrimental reliance, undertaking, public function, and emergency.

a. *Detrimental reliance.* An influential 1961 decision of the Delaware Supreme Court rested on a theory of detrimental reliance to deny a hospital's motion to dismiss the claim of a child who died after being denied care.

A private hospital owes the public no duty to accept any patient not desired by it, and it is not necessary to assign any reason for its refusal to accept a patient for hospital service. Does that rule apply to the fullest extent to patients applying for treatment at an emergency ward? It may be conceded that a private hospital is under no legal obligation to the public to maintain an emergency ward. But the maintenance of such a ward to render first-aid to injured persons has become a well-established adjunct to the main business of a hospital. If a person, seriously hurt, applies for such aid at an emergency ward, relying on the established custom to render it, is it still the right of the hospital to turn him away without any reason? [S]uch a refusal might well result in worsening the condition of the injured person, because of the time lost in a useless attempt to obtain medical aid. Such a set of circumstances is analogous to the case of the negligent termination of gratuitous services, which creates a tort liability.

Wilmington Gen. Hosp. v. Manlove, 174 A.2d 135, 138–139 (Del. 1961); see also Stanturf v. Sipes, 447 S.W.2d 558 (Mo. 1969) (holding that where the hospital had a long established custom of accepting all persons for emergency treatment upon payment of $25, and plaintiff relied on the custom, the hospital had a duty to provide care). A duty premised on detrimental reliance raises many questions: How can the plaintiff establish that he or she relied on a hospital's custom of providing emergency care? How can the plaintiff show that the defendant's refusal of care put her in a worse position? The duty recognized in these cases is limited to "emergencies." How are emergencies to be identified?

b.   Undertaking. General tort principles require that, even if an individual has no duty to help, anyone who undertakes to provide aid must continue to act with reasonable care. Courts often find that a hospital has undertaken to provide care. In O'Neill v. Montefiore Hosp., 202 N.Y.S.2d 436 (App. Div. 1960), the emergency room nurse called the personal physician of a patient suffering a heart attack. The court held that the jury could determine whether the hospital had thereby undertaken to provide reasonable care when an intern examined a patient, took a throat culture and a blood test, and discharged the patient, who died shortly thereafter. Le Juene Rd. Hosp. v. Watson, 171 So.2d 202 (Fla. Dist. Ct. App. 1965), found that the patient's continued presence in the hospital rendered the hospital liable for failure to treat.

The "undertaking" issue is particularly important in cases in which a physician, rather than a hospital, has failed to provide care. Courts scrutinize the complexity of doctor-patient interactions to determine whether the jury should be allowed to conclude that the physician has undertaken to care for the patient. Clanton v. Von Haam, 340 S.E.2d 627 (Ga. Ct. App. 1986), held that a doctor returning a patient's calls and counseling her over the phone did not create a relationship of duty. In Lyons v. Grether, 239 S.E.2d 103 (Va. 1977), a blind woman called a doctor's office and made an appointment to be seen for a vaginal infection. When she arrived, accompanied by her guide dog, the physician evicted her from his office. Virginia state law prohibited discrimination against blind people accompanied by guide dogs. The court, while recognizing that merely having an appointment did not establish a doctor-patient relationship, found that such a relationship did exist in this instance. "The unmistakable implication is that plaintiff had sought and defendant had granted an appointment at a designated time and place for the performance of a specific medical service, one within the defendant's professional competence." *Id.* at 105.

Courts are divided on whether a physician who is contractually obligated to be on call at a hospital emergency room owes a duty of care to individuals who seek treatment there. In Childs v. Weis, 440 S.W.2d 104 (Tex. Civ. App. 1969), the physician on call refused to come to the hospital to see a woman from another town who was in labor. She gave birth on the highway an hour later, and the baby died shortly thereafter. The court held, as a matter of law, that the physician owed the patient no duty. By contrast, Hiser v. Randolph, 617 P.2d 774 (Ariz. Ct. App. 1980), held that a doctor who agrees to be on call owes a duty to patients who seek emergency aid. The patient in Hiser v. Randolph died when treatment for an acute diabetic episode was delayed. Her husband alleged that the doctor refused care because the husband was a lawyer. In Dillon v. Silver, 520 N.Y.S.2d 751 (App. Div. 1987), hospital bylaws required attending physicians to be on call for certain periods and to accept all patients referred to them. Plaintiff received care in the hospital emergency room and was referred to the defendant physician, who had been assigned to provide follow-up care at that time. When plaintiff's condition worsened, she contacted the defendant and he refused to see her because he had never met her. She returned to the emergency room, and the emergency room doctors called the defendant to perform emergency surgery. He refused. The emergency room doctors performed the surgery, but the plaintiff died as a result of the delay. The court held that the hospital bylaws imposed a duty on the defendant, providing a basis for the plaintiff's claim.

In Mead v. Legacy Health System, 220 P.3d 118 (Or. App. 2009), the Oregon Court of Appeals found that telephone calls between an on-call physician and the emergency room physician created an indirect but real physician-patient relationship between the patient and the on-call physician. The on-call consultation between the defendant, a neurologist, and the emergency room medical resident physician involved a patient who arrived at the hospital in great pain and unable to walk. After recommending her release, the defendant eventually agreed that she should be admitted because of her condition. Ultimately, after a delay of several days, surgery was performed but by then the patient was left permanently injured. In defending against a medical liability claim, the defendant neurologist claimed that no physician-patient relationship existed at the time he rendered his opinion, and the jury agreed. Noting the element of mutual consent that defines the physician-patient relationship, the Court of Appeals found that the facts presented—his on call status, his consultation to the resident on duty, his opinion regarding the patient's admission for observation rather than ordering her immediate surgery—all supported a finding that a physician-patient relationship existed, even if indirect. The Court concluded that the conduct demonstrated the type of affirmative behavior toward a patient that, even in the absence of an express agreement to treat, can form the basis for a finding of undertaking. The defendant was, in the court's view, making medical decisions regarding the patient's care, which in turn gave rise to a physician-patient relationship from the time the consultation began. The duties of on-call physicians and specialists under EMTALA, the federal emergency treatment act, are discussed Chapter 3 below.

What does it take to end a relationship once begun? In Payton v. Weaver, 182 Cal. Rptr. 225 (Ct. App. 1982), Dr. Weaver provided Ms. Payton hemodialysis for three years. The patient's life depended upon having her blood cleaned through a machine three times a week. Her condition also made it extraordinarily dangerous for her to use drugs or alcohol or to eat certain foods. Nonetheless, she persisted in these self-destructive behaviors. Dr. Weaver attempted to work with and to support her. She held him in great respect. She said: "Dr. Weaver is and was and still is the man between me and death other than God, I don't think of nobody higher than I do Dr. Weaver." *Id.* at 227. Finally, the doctor notified Ms. Payton that unless she changed her habits and entered therapy, he would no longer treat her. He advised her of other sources of dialysis treatment. Ms. Payton sued both the physician and the hospital at which the physician practiced and sought an order compelling her continued treatment. The court rejected her claim, albeit with possible qualifications discussed below.

Patient economic abandonment cases such as *Budge*, above, are not a thing of the past. Muse v. Charter Hosp. of Winston Salem, 452 S.E.2d 589 (N.C. App. 1995), discussed in Part Three, involved corporate liability on the part of a hospital whose administration ordered a treating physician to discharge a severely mentally ill teenager when his insurance ran out. Following this inappropriate discharge, the teenager committed suicide. The court found that the hospital's active interference with the patient's treatment constituted an abandonment of the boy and amounted to part of the chain of causation that ultimately led to his suicide.

Courts have ruled that provider network agreements create a legal undertaking on the part of the participating provider and health plan. In Hand v. Tavera, 864 S.W.2d 678, 679 (Tex. Ct. App. 1993), a member of the Humana Health Care Plan went to the emergency room complaining of a persistent headache, the severity of which increased and decreased in accordance with his blood pressure. The emergency room doctor contacted defendant, Dr. Tavera, the person responsible for authorizing admissions to the hospital that evening. Tavera determined that Hand, the plaintiff, could be treated on an outpatient basis. Plaintiff went home and suffered a stroke. In the ensuing litigation, Dr. Tavera moved for summary judgment on the ground that "he and Hand never established a physician-patient relationship and therefore he owed Hand no duty." The court held that "when a patient who has enrolled in a prepaid medical plan goes to a hospital emergency room and the plan's designated doctor is consulted, the physician-patient relationship exists and the doctor owes the patient a duty of care." Id. at 680. Part Two examines health insurance and discusses modern insurance products that rely on coverage through a provider network of physicians, hospitals, and other providers who have agreed to accept the insurer's payment rates and abide by the plan's terms of participation.

  c. Public function and public accommodations. General tort law has long prohibited certain actors, such as common carriers, innkeepers and public utilities, from denying services on an arbitrary basis unrelated to the purpose of the enterprise. Doe v. Bridgeton Hosp. Ass'n, Inc., 366 A.2d 641 (N.J. 1976), *cert. den.*, 433 U.S. 914 (1977), applied this concept to invalidate policies of three private nonprofit hospitals that prohibited physicians from providing most abortions in the hospitals. The New Jersey Supreme Court reasoned as follows:

> The hospitals are non-profit corporations organized to serve the public by operating medical facilities. Each receives substantial financial support from federal and local governments and the public. Each is the beneficiary of tax exemptions. Each is an institution whose medical facilities are available to the public, particularly those who live in their primary service areas. The properties of these hospitals are devoted to a use in which the public has an interest and are subject to control for the common good. See also De Portibus Maris, 1 Hargrave Law Tracts 77–78 (1787). As quasi-public institutions, their actions must not contravene the public interest. They must serve the public without discrimination. Their boards of directors or trustees are managing quasi-public trusts and each has a fiduciary relationship with the public.

Doe v. Bridgeton, 366 A.2d at 645. For commentary on the common law regarding innkeepers, *see, e.g.* A. K. Sandoval–Strausz, *Travelers, Strangers, and Jim Crow: Law, Public Accommodations, and Civil Rights in America*, 23 LAW & HIST. REV. 53 (2005).

  The lower court in *Manlove*, above, predicated liability for refusal of emergency care on a finding that the hospital was a "quasi-public" institution, although the Delaware Supreme Court rejected that reasoning and found liability on the detrimental reliance theory, as noted above. Generally, courts considering whether a hospital has a common law obligation to provide emergency care have not drawn distinctions on the basis of hospital ownership. But Williams v. Hospital Authority of Hall County, 168 S.E.2d 336 (Ga. Ct. App. 1969), held that public hospitals have an obligation to provide emergency service.

  Mercy Medical Center of Oshkosh v. Winnebago County, 206 N.W.2d 198, 201 (Wis. 1973), recognized a hospital's duty to provide essential care:

> It would shock the public conscience if a person in need of medical emergency aid would be turned down at the door of a hospital having emergency service because that person could not at that moment assure payment for the service. The public expects such service; the public support of a hospital and the government grants in aid to hospitals to increase their facilities all substantiate the

fact that hospitals with emergency service cannot refuse it to the needy.

Many of the justifications for considering even private, nonprofit hospitals "quasi-public" entities or "public accommodations" (public funding through grants, tax exemption, extensive regulation, and in some cases protection from competition through health planning), do not apply to doctors' private practices. Moreover, the burden on individual physicians of a duty to serve the public could be significant. For these and no doubt other reasons, doctors' private practices are not considered public accommodations, except in the context of the Americans with Disabilities Act, discussed later in this Part.

The *Payton* court rejected the self-destructive dialysis patient's claim that the hospital had violated the state statute requiring provision of emergency care. Nonetheless, the court found,

> It does not necessarily follow that a hospital, or other health care facility, is without obligation to patients in need of continuing medical services for their survival. [I]t is questionable whether a hospital which receives public funding can reasonably be said to be "private." Rather, where such a hospital contains a unique, or scarce, medical resource needed to preserve life, it is arguably in the nature of a "public service enterprise," and should not be permitted to withhold its services arbitrarily, or without reasonable cause. And, while disruptive conduct on the part of a patient may constitute good cause for an individual hospital to refuse continued treatment, since it would be unfair to impose serious inconvenience upon a hospital simply because such a patient selected it, it may be that there exists a *collective* responsibility on the part of the provider of scarce health resources in a community, enforceable through equity, to *share* the burden of difficult patients over time, through an appropriately devised contingency plan. Whatever the merits of such an approach, it cannot serve as a basis for imposition of responsibility upon these respondents under the circumstances present here. Whatever collective responsibility may exist, it is clearly not absolute, or independent of the patient's own responsibility.

Payton v. Weaver, 182 Cal. Rptr. at 230.

The decision underscores courts' willingness to separate the duties of a hospital from those of any particular physician, a theme that emerges throughout the evolution of hospital emergency services in both statute and at common law. But even assuming that hospitals can be held to legal duties that do not apply to individual physicians, how could a court, even in "equity," enforce "collective" responsibilities on hospitals? Are certain treatments and services more amenable to "collective" responsibilities? What may have sparked this change from viewing hospitals as private institutions to quasi-public organizations?

d. *Physicians as a public accommodation and the Patient Protection and Affordable Care Act.* The Affordable Care Act does not alter the basic legal relationship between health care providers and individuals. As you will see throughout this book, the Act makes sweeping reforms in federal laws related to public and private insurance coverage, laws aimed at improving the accessibility, quality, and efficiency of health care, laws curbing fraud and abuse, and laws aimed at assuring greater community involvement by nonprofit hospitals. But the Act leaves untouched the fundamental underlying proposition that physicians and hospitals (other than in cases of hospital emergency departments) owe no duty of care to individuals.

Many commentators have noted the serious health care access problems that arise as a result of the shortage of physicians generally and primary care physicians in particular (e.g., family medicine specialists and pediatricians). Furthermore, many practicing primary care physicians are unwilling to treat lower income people who depend on Medicaid because of low rates, what they perceive as greater administrative hassles, and the greater social and clinical challenges involved in caring for poorer patients. (Physician payment will be discussed at greater length in Part Two). The national shortage of primary care physicians has been projected at 150,000. Suzanne Sataline & Shirley Wang, *Medical Schools Can't Keep Up*, WALL ST. J. (April 12, 2010), http://online.wsj.com/article/SB100014240 52702304506904575180331528424238.html. Furthermore, fewer than 20% of all primary care physicians (who by and large practice in clinical and institutional settings such as public hospitals and community health centers) report being willing to treat a high share of Medicaid patients, with the concept of "high share" defined as 26 percent of all patients served or greater. Most physicians report treating only moderate or low numbers of Medicaid patients; 80 percent of low-share physicians report treating no new Medicaid patients. Anna Sommers et al., *Physician Willingness and Resources to Serve More Medicaid Patients: Perspectives from Primary Care Physicians* (Kaiser Family Foundation 2011).

---

6.   STATE EFFORTS TO IMPOSE DUTIES TO PROVIDE EMERGENCY MEDICAL CARE

In the 1970s and 1980s, many state legislatures enacted laws requiring that hospitals provide care to people seeking essential services. Most required provision of emergency care, regardless of ability to pay. New York provided that "no general hospital shall transfer any patient to another hospital or health care facility on the grounds that the patient is unable to pay or guarantee payment for services rendered." N.Y. Pub. Health Law, § 2805(b)(1) (McKinney 1988). The Texas law is discussed infra.

Thompson v. Sun City Community Hospital, Inc.

688 P.2d 605 (Ariz. 1984)

■ FELDMAN, JUSTICE:

Michael Jessee, plaintiff's son, was injured on the evening of September 4, 1976. Jessee was 13 years old. He was rushed by ambulance to the

Boswell Memorial Hospital operated by Sun City Community Hospital, Inc. Among Jessee's injuries was a transected or partially transected femoral artery. The injury was high in the left thigh and interrupted the flow of blood to the distal portion of the leg. Upon arrival at the emergency room at 8:22 p.m., Jessee was examined and initially treated by Dr. Steven Lipsky, the emergency room physician. Fluids were administered and blood was ordered. The leg injury prompted Dr. Lipsky to summon Dr. Alivina Sabanas, an orthopedic surgeon. She examined Jessee's leg and determined that he needed surgery. Dr. Jon Hillegas, a vascular surgeon, was consulted by phone.

At some time after 9:30 p.m., Jessee's condition "stabilized" and the decision was made to transfer him to County Hospital. There is no clear indication in the record of who ordered the transfer. Dr. Lipsky determined that Jessee was "medically transferable," but stated that "Michael Jessee was transferred for economic reasons after we found him to be medically transferable." Dr. Lipsky had no authority to admit patients to Boswell. Dr. Sabanas, who did have such authority and who knew that Jessee needed vascular surgery, claimed that Jessee was transferable from an orthopedic standpoint. Dr. Hillegas told Dr. Lipsky that Jessee could be transferred when "stabilized." A witness for the plaintiff testified that "The doctor at Boswell [apparently Dr. Lipsky] said [to Ada Thompson], I have the shitty detail of telling you that Mike will be transferred to County...." A Boswell administrator testified that emergency "charity" patients are transferred from Boswell to County whenever a physician, in his professional judgment, determines that "a transfer could occur."

Thus, at 10:13 p.m. Jessee was discharged from the Boswell emergency room, placed in an ambulance, and taken to County. The doctors who attended to him at County began administering fluids and ordered blood. They testified that Jessee's condition worsened but that he was eventually "stabilized" and taken to surgery at about 1:00 a.m. Jessee underwent abdominal surgery and, immediately thereafter, surgery to repair his torn femoral artery. He survived but has residual impairment of his left leg. His mother brought a malpractice action against Boswell and the physicians.

The trial record reveals a confusion of the issues of duty of care and causation. In any case such as this there are two types of causation questions. The first, relating to the question of breach of duty, pertains to the cause for the transfer to another hospital. Was the patient transferred for medical or other reasons? The second question relates to the cause of injury and is concerned with whether the transfer, with its attendant movement and delay, caused a new or additional injury or aggravated any injury which already existed. The first question was answered by defense counsel. "We admit and stipulate that the plaintiff in this case was transferred from Boswell to County Hospital for financial reasons. There is no question about it." This stipulation was prompted by a record which clearly indicates that the transfer was made because the type of insurance available for the patient did not satisfy the hospital's financial requirements for admission.

The [trial] court gave the following jury instructions:

Now, Defendant Boswell Hospital is a private hospital and as such may establish its own eligibility requirements regarding ability to pay. It does have a duty to provide immediate and necessary emergency care to all persons regardless of ability to pay. The hospital may properly determine a patient's eligibility according to its own rules before admitting a patient as an in-patient for further definitive treatment, and may transfer a patient to another appropriate hospital if the patient is medically transferable. A patient is medically transferable when in the judgment of the staff or emergency physician the patient may be transferred without subjecting the patient to an unreasonable risk of harm to his life or health.

[The intermediate appeals court affirmed the trial court's statement of the law. The appeals court distinguished the most applicable precedent, Guerrero v. Copper Queen Hospital, 537 P.2d 1329 (1975), as being about the total denial of care in an unmistakably emergency situation, rather than about "medical transferability" of a patient unable to pay. The appeals court further reasoned that prohibiting transfers of patients unable to pay would destroy the distinction between private hospitals, for whom the right to exclude patients was at the core of their private status, and public hospitals, whose mission was primarily to treat the poor. This distinction was supported by explicit Arizona statutes authorizing counties to pay private hospitals for indigent care only when the county hospital was unable to do so, and by long-standing custom of the medical profession. Thompson v. Sun City Community Hosp., 688 P.2d at 654–55 (Ariz. Ct. App.1983). Finally, the appeals court found the JCAH emergency care and patients rights standards, and the state licensing regulations too vague to require a contrary result, and in any event deferential to what was "medically indicated," which, according to the court of appeals, overlapped with the concept of "medical transferability." Id.]

[W]e address the following issues: (1) Did the instruction set forth the proper standard of care for emergency services? (2) If not, did the trial court err in refusing to affirmatively instruct the jury that the defendant hospital had breached its duty of care? Put differently: Should the trial court have ruled, as a matter of law, that the transfer was a breach of duty which the hospital owed its patient? (3) Did the trial court err in failing to instruct the jury properly on the issue of causation?

[The Standard of Care: The Hospital]

In this state, the duty which a hospital owes a patient in need of emergency care is determined by the statutes and regulations interpreted by this court in Guerrero v. Copper Queen Hospital, 112 Ariz. 104, 537 P.2d 1329 (1975). Construing the statutory and regulatory scheme governing health care and the licensing of hospitals as of 1972, we held that it was the "public policy of this state" that a general "hospital may not deny emergency care to any patient without cause." *Id.* at 106, 537 P.2d at 1331.

In *Guerrero*, we referred primarily to the statutes governing the licensing of hospitals. [I]n 1973, the Director of Health Services was required to adopt regulations for the licensure of health care facilities. As guidelines for minimum requirements, the director was mandated to use the standards of the Joint Commission for Accreditation of Hospitals (JCAH). The emergency services section of the JCAH states that "[n]o patient should arbitrarily be transferred if the hospital where he was initially seen has means for adequate care of his problem." JCAH, Accreditation Manual for Hospitals 69 (1976). The "Patient's Rights" section of the JCAH manual [states that] "no person should be denied impartial access to treatment or accommodations that are available and medically indicated, on the basis of such considerations as . . . the nature of the source of payment for his care." Id. at 23.

Principles governing the functioning of hospitals were not left in the abstract. Specific regulations adopted in 1976, concerning "emergency departments," provided that "general hospitals shall provide facilities for emergency care." In addition, such hospitals were required "to have on call one or more physicians licensed to practice medicine and surgery in Arizona or resident physician or intern physician."[2] Our holding in Guerrero is reinforced by [an Arizona statute providing]:

> A. When an indigent emergency medical patient is received by an emergency receiving facility from a [licensed] ambulance . . ., the county shall be liable . . . to the ambulance service for the cost of transporting the patient and to the facility for the reasonable costs of all medical services rendered to such indigent by the facility until such patient is transferred by the county to the county hospital, or some other facility designated by the county.

The quoted statute provides the answer to a serious problem. Charging hospitals with a legal duty to render emergency care to indigent patients does not ignore the distinctions between private and public hospitals. Imposition of a duty to render emergency care to indigents simply charges private hospitals with the same duty as public hospitals under a statutory plan which permits reimbursement from public funds for the emergency care charges incurred at the private hospital.

[A]s a matter of public policy, licensed hospitals in this state are required to accept and render emergency care to all patients who present themselves in need of such care. The patient may not be transferred until all medically indicated emergency care has been completed. This standard of care has, in effect, been set by statute and regulation embodying a public

---

2. The current regulation, which replaced R9–10–248, is R9–10–218. Although not in effect in 1976, it is useful in understanding the past intent of providing health care to emergency patients. It specifically requires all general hospitals to render "necessary emergency medical services . . . to any person in need of them." We do not view this as a change in the law, but simply as administrative adoption of the law as we construed it in *Guerrero*.

policy which requires private hospitals to provide emergency care that is "medically indicated" without consideration of the economic circumstances of the patient in need of such care. Interpreting the standard of care in accordance with the public policy defined in *Guerrero*, we hold that reasonable "cause" for transfer before completion of emergency care refers to medical considerations relevant to the welfare of the patient and not economic considerations relevant to the welfare of the hospital. A transfer based on the forbidden criterion of economic considerations may be for the convenience of the hospital, but it is hardly "medically indicated."

Given the duty imposed in Arizona—that a general hospital may not deny emergency care to any person without valid cause—there are three possible defenses a hospital may raise in an appropriate fact situation: (1) that the hospital is not obligated (or capable) under its state license to provide the necessary emergency care, (2) there is a valid medical cause to refuse emergency care, or (3) there is no true emergency requiring care and thus no emergency care which is medically indicated.

Neither of the first two defenses is at issue under the facts of this case. The third is more troublesome. Many people who enter the doors of an emergency room do not truly require "emergency care." The statutes and regulations do not apply to those who go to an "emergency room;" they apply to those in need of "emergency care." What constitutes an emergency is a matter of some disagreement. There are various definitions; the need for immediate attention seems to be the common thread. Ordinarily it is for the jury to determine the factual question of the duration of an emergency and the treatment modalities that are a necessary component of emergency care.

Given the stipulation that Boswell ordered the transfer of Jessee to County Hospital because of financial reasons, the relevant inquiries in the case at bench did not relate to "stabilization" and "transferability," but rather to the nature and duration of the emergency. The question was whether, before transfer, the hospital had rendered the emergency care medically indicated for this patient. The facts of this case indicate that emergency surgery was indicated for Jessee. Dr. Hillegas testified that "once the diagnosis is made, you should move on with definitive treatment," and that "you want to repair the arterial injury just as soon as you can." Dr. Lipsky [and] Dr. Sabanas believed Jessee needed emergency surgery. [The trial judge noted that Jessee was transferred to County Hospital by an ambulance with emergency lights flashing]. The undisputed evidence established that the patient was transferred for financial reasons while emergency care was medically indicated. As a matter of law this was a breach of the hospital's duty. Thus, the only question before the jury on the issue of the hospital's liability was whether its breach of duty was a cause of some compensable damage.

[The Standard of Care: The Physicians]

The duty of care owed by a physician to a patient is different from the hospital's duty. No statute requires the physician to provide services separate and apart from those which the hospital is required to provide. Thus, the duty of care owed by a physician is determined by common law principles which require reference to that which is usually done by members of the profession. Dr. Lipsky was not a specialist in either orthopedic or vascular surgery. He was an emergency room physician. Even if qualified, he could not have performed the needed surgery unless Jessee had been admitted. Lipsky had no power to admit and could not have admitted Jessee if he had wanted to do so. Nothing in the record indicates that any act or omission of Dr. Lipsky was a cause of the refusal to admit Jessee.

Plaintiff argues that the vascular surgeon [Dr. Hillegas] breached his duty in failing to come to the hospital to attend Jessee. [P]hysicians were on duty and present at Boswell to care for emergency patients; specialists were "on call," prepared to come to the hospital and treat patients who needed specialized attention. Boswell did not request this physician to come. To the contrary, Boswell's refusal to admit Jessee would have made Dr. Hillegas' arrival at the hospital an empty gesture.

[Causation]

Boswell's theory of the case was that the breach of duty, if any, in transferring the patient had caused no damage, since Jessee's serious injuries might have led to precisely the residual injury which he did sustain. At defendant's request, the court instructed the jury that plaintiff could not recover absent proof of a probability that the acts or omissions of the defendant had aggravated the original injury. Plaintiff sought an additional instruction that such cause was established if plaintiff had proved that defendant's acts or omissions had "increased the risk of harm" to plaintiff.

We acknowledge the difficulty in resolving the question of causation in cases where defendant has negligently breached an undertaking to prevent a certain harm. Historically, courts have been liberal with the causation issue in such cases and have allowed the jury to decide whether defendant's breach of duty was a cause or substantial factor in the final result. Generally, two different rules have evolved. The first holds that the plaintiff must introduce evidence from which the jury may find a probability that because of the defendant's negligence the ultimate result was different from or greater than that attributable to the original injury or condition. Under this rule, plaintiff fails in his burden of proof and a verdict is directed if the evidence does not warrant a finding that the chance of recovery or survival absent defendant's negligence, was over 50 percent.

Under the second rule, even if the evidence permits only a finding that the defendant's negligence increased the risk of harm or deprived plaintiff of some significant chance of survival or better recovery, it is left for the jury to decide whether there is a probability that defendant's negligence was a cause in fact of the injury.

There is much to be said against the [first] rule. It puts a premium on each party's search for the willing witness. [F]or every expert witness who evaluates the lost chance at 49 percent there is another who estimates it at closer to 51 percent. Also, the rule tends to defeat one of the primary functions of the tort system—deterrence of negligent conduct.

The unsatisfactory result from application of the [first] rule is well illustrated by the facts of the case at bench. Defense experts testified that even if the failure to admit caused a delay in vascular surgery, the chances were only five to 10 percent that plaintiff would have achieved complete recovery with prompt surgery. Though unwilling or unable to quantify the chance of complete recovery with prompt surgery, plaintiff's experts testified that there would have been a "substantially better chance" of full recovery had surgery been performed at once. They testified that the longer the delay, the greater the risk of residual injury. We believe the [increased risk of harm] rule to be better than the [first] rule. We acknowledge that it permits the case to go to the jury on the issue of causation with less definite evidence of probability than the ordinary tort case. To this extent, no doubt, it permits the jury to engage in some speculation with regard to cause and effect. However, the jury is still instructed that they must find for the defendant unless they find a *probability* that defendant's negligence was a cause of plaintiff's injury. We must remember further, that we are dealing with the limited class of cases in which defendant undertook to protect plaintiff from a particular harm and negligently interrupted the chain of events, thus increasing the risk of that harm. Defendant's negligent act or omission made it impossible to find with certainty what would have happened and thus forced the court to look at the proverbial crystal ball in order to decide what might have been. Such determinations, of course, have traditionally been the province of the jury rather than the judge.

We caution that this [second] rule fits only in those situations where the courts traditionally have allowed juries to deal more loosely with causation—the cases where the duty breached was one imposed to prevent the type of harm which plaintiff ultimately sustained. [W]here the law governing duty encompassed "the chance interest within [its] range of protection" (and the harm from which defendant was to have protected the plaintiff occurred), greater latitude is given to the trier of fact to find causation under any plausible theory. "Hence the interest which the law is protecting is the chance itself, and the chief problem is the evaluation of the chance, which is a function peculiarly within the province of the jury." This formulation, of course, merely recognizes that juries often discount damages according to the statistical evidence in order to accurately evaluate the true loss.

We hold, therefore, that because the protection of the chance interest was within the range of the duty breached by defendant and the harm which followed was the type from which the defendant was to have protected the plaintiff, the jury may be allowed to consider the increase in the chance of harm on the issue of causation. If the jury finds that defendant's failure to exercise reasonable care increased the risk of the harm he undertook to prevent, it may from this fact find a "probability" that defendant's negligence was the cause of the damage.

Notes

1. *Loss of chance doctrine.* American jurisdictions have divided sharply over the "increased risk of harm" or "loss of a chance" approach to causation. *See, e.g.*, Matsuyama v. Birnbaum, 890 N.E.2d 819 (Mass. 2008). In this decision, the court surveys cases and finds that a "substantial and growing majority of the States that have considered the question have endorsed the loss of chance doctrine, in one form or another, in medical malpractice actions." The usual reason for adhering to the traditional "all or nothing rule" (i.e., the plaintiff gets nothing if she cannot prove by a preponderance of the evidence (i.e., more than 50 percent) that the negligence caused the harm at issue) is that without such a limitation the liability and cost effects on health care and many other professions could be significant. An influential article, Joseph King, *Causation, Valuation, and Chance in Personal Injury Torts Involving Preexisting Injuries and Future Consequences* 90 Yale L.J. 1353 (1981), argues that the loss of a chance doctrine should be adopted, but its cost effects should be mitigated by calculating damages according to the percentage that the chance of cure was reduced. For example, if the patient originally had a 40 percent chance of cure, and negligence reduced that chance to 25 percent, then the patient should receive 15 percent (40 percent minus 25 percent) of the total damages.

2. *Duty of care and hospital collection actions.* In recent years, much attention has focused on the fact that hospitals charge the highest amounts to the uninsured. Overall, insurers pay hospitals about 40 percent of the listed charges billed to the uninsured. Gerard Anderson, *From Soak the Rich to Soak the Poor: Recent Trends in Hospital Pricing*, 26(3) Health Affairs 780 (2007); Uwe E. Reinhardt, *The Price of U.S. Hospital Services: Chaos Behind a Veil of Secrecy*, 25(1) Health Affairs 58 (2006). When the uninsured are unable to pay, hospitals aggressively seek to collect unpaid bills through practices that include seizures of homes and attachment of modest earnings. Melissa B. Jacoby & Elizabeth Warren, *Beyond Hospital Misbehavior: An Alternative Account of Medical–Related Financial Distress*, *100* Nw. U. L. Rev. 535 (2006) (documenting that "hospitals overcharged the uninsured, improperly applied charity care policies, and engaged in inappropriate debt collection," but arguing for a "broader structural inquiry" into "the entanglement between the health care system and the debtor-creditor system").

Insurers, including Medicare, Medicaid and all private insurers negotiate with hospitals to set the terms and amounts they will pay for the people they insure. No one negotiates for the uninsured. Mark A. Hall & Carl E. Schneider, *Patients as Consumers: Courts, Contracts, and the New Medical Marketplace*, 106 Mich. L. Rev. 643, 663–666 (2008). Hospital executives concede that "the vast majority of [charges] have no relation to anything, and certainly not to cost" and see "no method to this madness." *Id.* at 665.

Since 2000 law students, legal services program and clinics, and personal injury lawyers in dozens of cities, including New Haven, New York, Chicago, and Oxford, Mississippi have documented and publicized these practices. Joel S. Weissman, *The Trouble with Uncompensated Hospital Care*, 352 NEW ENG. J. MED. 1171 (2005); Jonathan Cohn, *Uncharitable?* N.Y. TIMES MAG. (Dec. 19, 2004); HOSPITALS CHARGE UNINSURED AND "SELF-PAY" PATIENTS MORE THAN DOUBLE WHAT INSURED PATIENTS PAY, JOHNS HOPKINS BLOOMBERG SCHOOL OF PUBLIC HEALTH PUBLIC HEALTH NEWS CENTER (May 8, 2007), http://www.jhsph.edu/publichealthnews/press_releases/2007/anderson_hospital_charges.html.

Many lawsuits challenged the practices as violating state laws against deceptive and unfair trade practices, and the obligations of "charitable" organizations that enjoy exemptions under state and local tax laws. The lawsuits have not been successful. *See e.g.*, Kizzire v. Baptist Health Systems, Inc., 343 F. Supp.2d 1074 (N.D. Ala. 2004) (holding that economic injuries are not compensable under the Emergency Medical Treatment and Labor Act (EMTALA), discussed below); Galvan v. Northwestern Memorial Hosp., 888 N.E.2d 529 (Ill. App. 1 Dist. 2008) (rejecting claims under state Consumer Fraud and Deceptive Business Practices Act); Colomar v. Mercy Hosp. Inc., 461 F. Supp.2d 1265 (S.D. Fla. 2006) (summary judgment for hospital that charged uninsured patient four times as much as patients with insurance).

In 2006, the New York legislature adopted "Manny's Law," named for a man who died when he avoided the hospital because he had been subject to aggressive collection efforts after previous hospitalizations. Francis J. Serbaroli, *New Law Curbs Hospital Charges, Collection Actions*, N.Y. L.J., May 30, 2006, at 1. The New York Law requires hospitals to offer free or reduced fee care to low income people, not limited to emergency care. It demands that hospitals assess patients' income and resources to determine whether they are eligible for such free or reduced cost care. It prohibits hospitals from charging low-income people more than twenty percent more than the amount paid by the highest of Medicaid, Medicare or its highest volume insurer. While some New York hospitals complied with the law, many have not. *Many New York Hospitals Fail to Follow New Law Protecting Hospital Patients from High Bills and Aggressive Collection*, CITIZEN ACTION OF NEW YORK (March 21, 2008), http://citizenactionny.org/2008/03/many-new-york-hospitals-fail-to-follow-new-law-protecting-hospital-patients-from-high-bills-and-aggressive-collection/550. Nonprofit hospitals' obligation to reform their billing practices as part of their federal tax-exempt status is discussed in Part Four.

CHAPTER 3

FEDERAL LEGISLATIVE REFORM OF THE "NO DUTY" PRINCIPLE: THE EMERGENCY MEDICAL TREATMENT AND LABOR ACT (EMTALA)

1. INTRODUCTION

Setting the stage for EMTALA. Campbell v. Mincey and *Thompson v. Sun City* reflect the types of crises faced by individuals in need of emergency care and the range of philosophical and legal viewpoints which were brought to bear on the question of hospitals' emergency care obligations in a changing health care system. By 1980, the hospital industry had emerged as the behemoth of American medical spending, consuming over 41 percent of all personal health expenditures. Centers for Disease Control and Prevention, United States Department of Health and Human Services, Pub. No. 2004–1232, Health, United States, 2004 Table 118 (2004). By the 1980s, state hospital licensure law and industry accreditation standards identified emergency care capacity as a basic feature of general community hospitals.

The Hill–Burton Act of 1946 provided grants and loans to state governments to build hospitals; acceptance of funding triggered two basic obligations. First, hospitals receiving Hill–Burton funds were required to make "available ... a reasonable volume of services to persons unable to pay therefore" [the so-called free care obligation]. Second, hospitals were required to ensure that services "will be made available to all persons residing in the territorial area" [the so-called community service obligation]. 42 U.S.C. § 291c(e). Between 1946 and 1976, the Hill–Burton program subsidized the construction of 40 percent of all hospital beds built in the United States. *See generally* Rand E. Rosenblatt, *Health Care Reform and Administrative Law: A Structural Approach*, 88 Yale L.J. 243, 264–86 (1978) (discussing the Hill–Burton Act and subsequent litigation).

During the 1970s, legal services lawyers mounted significant efforts to enforce the free care obligation through private legal actions. Hospitals defended, asserting that the Hill–Burton obligations could be enforced only through federal or state administrative action and created no judicially enforceable rights in beneficiaries. Courts rejected these defenses. *See e.g.,* Cook v. Ochsner Foundation Hospital, 319 F. Supp. 603 (E.D. La. 1970), *aff'd*, 559 F.2d 968 (5th Cir. 1977). The community service obligation received less attention because the community service obligation lacked a similar measurable dollar value and thus yielded less obvious financial worth to poor clients.

In 1979, the United States Department of Health and Human Services reissued earlier Hill–Burton regulations as part of a broader public enforcement initiative. The new regulations significantly strengthened the earlier rules, clarifying the meaning of both free care and community service. In response to a renewed and broadened interest in the intersection of health care and civil rights policy, the 1979 regulations clarified, among other matters, that that Hill–Burton facilities were prohibited from discriminating against persons based on their insurance status. 42 C.F.R § 124.603(c)(ii). The rules also were modified to require the provision of emergency care to the entire community without regard to ability to pay for care at the time that emergency services were actually rendered. The emergency care regulation, *id.* § 124.603(b)(1), does not define the term "emergency;" it provides that "[a] facility may not deny emergency services to any person who resides . . . in the facility's service area on the ground that the person is unable to pay for those services."

Hospitals' response to the rules was (an unsuccessful) challenge to their legality. American Hospital Association v. Schweiker, 721 F.2d 170 (7th Cir. 1983), *cert. den.,* AHA v. Heckler, 466 U.S. 958 (1984). In the 1980s, academic studies and news reports documented stories of denial of emergency care, and states adopted laws to address the problem. The most notable of these state efforts was the 1984 passage of emergency care legislation by the Texas legislature, a state known for its hard-charging hospital industry and conservative attitudes about aid to the poor. The Texas legislation, commonly referred to by state lawmakers as the "anti-dumping" act, was passed in response to a series of spectacular incidents reported in the press, including the outright refusal of care (as in the case of Hattie May Campbell) or the transfer (i.e., dumping) of an unstable patient to a public hospital. The gravity of the examples, coupled with unusually strong leadership from public health advocates (most notably Dr. Ronald Anderson of Parkland Hospital in Dallas, the county's public facility) led to enactment of the 1984 law. Robert Reinhold, *Treating an Outbreak of Patient Dumping in Texas*, NY TIMES (May 25, 1984).

In the wake of the Texas legislation, Democratic leaders in the U.S. House of Representatives introduced legislation to replicate the law at the federal level. A Democratic House and a Republican Senate passed—and President Ronald Reagan signed into law—legislation adding to the Medicare program federal legislative standards related to the provision of hospital emergency care. The Consolidated Omnibus Budget Reconciliation Act of 1985 (COBRA), Section 9121(b), Pub. L. No. 99–272. The new law arrived on the scene during a decade in which hospital revenues were rising at an average annual rate of around 13 percent. Centers for Disease Control and Prevention, United States Department of Health and Human Services, Pub. No. 2004–1232, Health, United States, 2004 Table 118 (2004). The legislation built on and strengthened the 1984 Texas statute and similar state laws, while amending the Medicare statute to establish a national and uniform duty on the part of all Medicare-participating hospitals with emergency departments to treat patients with medical emergencies.

EMTALA. The Emergency Medical Treatment and Labor Act (EMTALA)* imposes certain basic obligations on all Medicare participating hospitals with emergency departments. First, the hospital must "provide for an appropriate medical screening examination . . . to determine whether or not an emergency medical condition . . . exists." 42 U.S.C. § 1395dd(a). Second, "if an individual at a hospital has an emergency medical condition which has not been stabilized . . . the hospital must stabilize the patient." If, however, a transfer prior to stabilization is medically indicated and certain requirements are satisfied, the hospital may effectuate a transfer. *Id.* § 1395dd(c)(1). In addition to enforcement by the federal government, EMTALA creates express private enforcement rights.

EMTALA's principal aim was to stop the denial or termination of care to medically indigent persons. But the law applies to all persons. Furthermore, its provisions extend beyond the physical limits of a hospital's emergency department and into inpatient service units as well, although the extent of EMTALA's reach has been a source of considerable legal controversy, as you will see below. EMTALA also requires hospitals to ensure their staff specialists—not merely medical residents staffing the emergency department—are available to help with assessment and stabilization; again, however, the extent of hospitals' duty where on-call specialists are concerned has been the stuff of controversy.

EMTALA's obligations have triggered considerable debate among hospitals and their lawyers. *After 25 Years, EMTALA Compliance Issues Remain Varied, Complex, Practitioners Say*, 20 HEALTH LAW REPORTER (BNA) 1726 (2011). Unhappiness focuses on conflicts between hospitals emergency department physicians and their on-call specialists, inter-hospital conflicts over patient transfers, the threat of federal surveyors looking for violations that could lead to Medicare termination or civil penalties, the challenge of caring for patients who are mentally ill, ambiguity over EMTALA's reach into hospitals' inpatient facilities (discussed below), and EMTALA's overall economic and operational impact at a time of intense competition.

EMTALA duties hit hospitals at a time of unprecedented use of their emergency care facilities. Between 1993 and 2003, the U.S. population grew by 12 percent, hospital admissions grew by 13 percent, and emergency department visits grew by 26 percent. Institute of Medicine, *Hospital Based Emergency Care: At the Breaking Point*, (Washington D.C., 2007), http://

---

* The law is sometimes referred to as the Emergency Medical Treatment and *Active* Labor Act (emphasis added). In fact, this was the law's original name. Evidence of hospitals' refusal to treat pregnant women with emergency medical conditions short of active labor led Congress subsequently to eliminate the word "Active" in order to assure that labor, by itself, would be considered sufficient to trigger an emergency response, regardless of the stage of labor. *See* Pub. L. No. 101–239 § 6211(h)(2) (101st Cong., 1st Sess. 1989).

books.nap.edu/openbook.php?record_id=11621&page=2;   Arthur   Keller-
man, *Crisis in the Emergency Department*, 355 N. ENG. J. MED. 1300, 1303
(2006). Over this time period the nation experienced a net loss of more
than 700 hospitals and over 400 emergency departments. The report notes
the varied factors that account for this enormous growth, including the
need to compensate for the shortage of primary health care services, the
demand for high technology interventions for emergent and urgent health
needs, and hospitals' obligations in mass public health emergencies, whether intentional or the result of natural disease outbreaks. Heavy use among
insured patients is notable. Nicholas Bakalar, *E.R.'s Are Busy, But Fewer
Patients Are Uninsured*, NY TIMES (May 6, 2008), at A–1.

Overcrowding has exacerbated wait times for the sickest patients. For
example, between 1997 and 2004, one study found that wait times for
patients with acute myocardial infarctions increased by more than 11
percent annually. Andrew Wilper, *Waits to See an Emergency Department
Physician: U.S. Trends and Predictors, 1997–2004*, 27(2) HEALTH AFFAIRS
w84 (2008). One study suggests that uninsured patients and people insured
by Medicaid have more serious conditions and waited longer to be seen.
Peter J. Cunningham and Jessica H. May, *Insured Americans Drive Surge
in Emergency Department Visits*, CENTER FOR STUDYING HEALTH SYSTEMS
CHANGE, ISSUE BRIEF NO.70, http://hschange.org/CONTENT/613. "A growing
number of specialists are either refusing to take after-hours call or demanding payments for doing so. After-hours and weekend gaps in coverage have
real consequences; mortality rates associated with acute myocardial infarction and other time-critical conditions are significantly higher on weekends
than on weekdays." John Maa, *The Waits That Matter*, 364 N. ENG. J. MED.
2279 (2011). A 2009 Government Accountability Office report on emergency department conditions found that "the main factor" underlying overcrowding was the lack of available inpatient beds as a result of "scheduled
admissions" of patients. That is, hospitals are admitting so many patients
for scheduled inpatient care that they lack the capacity to manage the flow
of patients who arrive at the emergency department and need unscheduled
admission. GAO, Crowding Continues to Occur and Some Patients Continue to Wait Longer than Recommended Time Frames (GAO–09–347, April,
2009). Bear this finding in mind as you read the materials below regarding
whether hospitals' EMTALA stabilization obligations extend into inpatient
settings.

Consistent with the high dependence on emergency departments by all
patients—insured or otherwise—as well as the sizable anticipated remaining uninsured population even after full implementation of health reform
(discussed in Part Two), the Affordable Care Act does not alter hospitals'
EMTALA obligations. The Act provides, "Nothing in this Act shall be
construed to relieve any health care provider from providing emergency
services as required by State or Federal law, including section 1867 of the
Social Security Act (popularly known as EMTALA)." 42 U.S.C. § 1303(c).
In addition the Act provides that, effective in fiscal year 2014, Medicaid
Disproportionate Share Hospital (DSH) payments (which are made to
hospitals with a high volume of low income patients, discussed in Part

Two) will be reduced by 75 percent and that payments will subsequently be increased based on the percent of the population uninsured and the amount of uncompensated care provided. 42 U.S.C. § 1396r–4.

2. THE EMTALA STATUTE AND IMPLEMENTING REGULATIONS

The Text of EMTALA (Social Security Act § 1867; 42 U.S.C. § 1395dd)

§ 1395dd. Examination and treatment for emergency medical conditions and women in labor

(a) Medical screening requirement. In the case of a hospital that has a hospital emergency department, if any individual (whether or not eligible for benefits under this title) comes to the emergency department and a request is made on the individual's behalf for examination or treatment for a medical condition, the hospital must provide for an appropriate medical screening examination within the capability of the hospital's emergency department, including ancillary services routinely available to the emergency department, to determine whether or not an emergency medical condition (within the meaning of subsection (e)(1) of this section) exists.

(b) Necessary stabilizing treatment for emergency medical conditions and labor.

> (1) In general. If any individual (whether or not eligible for benefits under this title) comes to a hospital and the hospital determines that the individual has an emergency medical condition, the hospital must provide either—
>
> > (A) within the staff and facilities available at the hospital, for such further medical examination and such treatment as may be required to stabilize the medical condition, or (B) for transfer of the individual to another medical facility in accordance with subsection (c).
>
> (2) Refusal to consent to treatment. A hospital is deemed to meet the requirement of paragraph (1)(A) with respect to an individual if the hospital offers the individual the further medical examination and treatment described in that paragraph and informs the individual (or a person acting on the individual's behalf) of the risks and benefits to the individual of such examination and treatment, but the individual (or a person acting on the individual's behalf) refuses to consent to the examination and treatment. The hospital shall take all reasonable steps to secure the individual's (or person's) written informed consent to refuse such examination and treatment.

(3) Refusal to consent to transfer. A hospital is deemed to meet the requirement of paragraph (1) with respect to an individual if the hospital offers to transfer the individual to another medical facility in accordance with subsection (c) of this section and informs the individual (or a person acting on the individual's behalf) of the risks and benefits to the individual of such transfer, but the individual (or a person acting on the individual's behalf) refuses to consent to the transfer. The hospital shall take all reasonable steps to secure the individual's (or person's) written informed consent to refuse such transfer.

(c) Restricting transfers until individual stabilized.

(1) Rule. If an individual at a hospital has an emergency medical condition which has not been stabilized (within the meaning of subsection (e)(3)(B) of this section), the hospital may not transfer the individual unless—

(A)(i) the individual (or a legally responsible person acting on the individual's behalf) after being informed of the hospital's obligations under this section and of the risk of transfer, in writing requests transfer to another medical facility, (ii) a physician (within the meaning of section 1395x(r)(1) of this title) has signed a certification that based upon the information available at the time of transfer, the medical benefits reasonably expected from the provision of appropriate medical treatment at another medical facility outweigh the increased risks to the individual and, in the case of labor, to the unborn child from effecting the transfer, or (iii) if a physician is not physically present in the emergency department at the time an individual is transferred, a qualified medical person (as defined by the Secretary in regulations) has signed a certification described in clause (ii) after a physician (as defined in section 1395x(r)(1) of this title), in consultation with the person, has made the determination described in such clause, and subsequently countersigns the certification; and (B) the transfer is an appropriate transfer (within the meaning of paragraph (2)) to that facility.

A certification described in clause (ii) or (iii) of subparagraph (A) shall include a summary of the risks and benefits upon which the certification is based.

(2) Appropriate transfer. An appropriate transfer to a medical facility is a transfer—

(A) in which the transferring hospital provides the medical treatment within its capacity which minimizes the risks to the individual's health and, in the case of a woman in labor, the health of the unborn child; (B) in which the receiving facili-ty—(i) has available space and qualified personnel for the treatment of the individual, and (ii) has agreed to accept transfer of the individual and to provide appropriate medical treatment; (C) in which the transferring hospital sends to the receiving facility all medical records (or copies thereof), related to the emergency condition for which the individual has presented, available at the time of the transfer, including records related to the individual's emergency medical condition, observations of signs or symptoms, preliminary diagnosis, treatment provided, results of any tests and the informed written consent or certification (or copy thereof) provided under paragraph (1)(A), and the name and address of any on-call physician (described in subsection (d)(1)(C) of this section) who has refused or failed to appear within a reasonable time to provide necessary stabilizing treatment; (D) in which the transfer is effected through qualified personnel and transportation equipment, as required including the use of necessary and medically appropriate life support measures during the transfer; and (E) which meets such other requirements as the Secretary may find necessary in the interest of the health and safety of individuals transferred.

(d) Enforcement.

(1) Civil money penalties.

(A) A participating hospital that negligently violates a requirement of this section is subject to a civil money penalty of not more than $50,000 (or not more than $25,000 in the case of a hospital with less than 100 beds) for each such violation. The provisions of section 1320a–7a of this title (other than subsections (a) and (b)) shall apply to a civil money penalty under this subparagraph in the same manner as such provisions apply with respect to a penalty or proceeding under section 1320a–7a(a) of this title.

(B) Subject to subparagraph (C), any physician who is responsible for the examination, treatment, or transfer of an individual in a participating hospital, including a physician on-call for the care of such an individual, and who negligently violates a requirement of this section, including a physician who—(i) signs a certification under subsection (c)(1)(A) of this section that the medical benefits reasonably to be expected from a transfer to another facility outweigh the risks associated with the transfer, if the physician knew or should have known that the benefits did not outweigh the risks, or (ii) misrepresents an individual's condition or other information, including a hospital's obligations under this section, is subject to a civil money penalty of not more than $50,000 for each such violation and, if the violation is gross and flagrant or is repeated, to exclusion from participation in this title and State health care programs. The provisions of section 1128 [42 U.S.C. § 1320a–7a, relating to the mandatory exclusion of certain individuals from participating in Medicare, Medicaid and other federal programs] (other than subsection (a) and subsection (b)) shall apply to a civil money penalty and exclusion under this subparagraph in the same manner as such provisions apply with respect to a penalty, exclusion, or proceeding under section 1128A(a).

(C) If, after an initial examination, a physician determines that the individual requires the services of a physician listed by the hospital on its list of on-call physicians (required to be maintained under section 1866(a)(1)(I)) and notifies the on-call physician and the on-call physician fails or refuses to appear within a reasonable period of time, and the physician orders the transfer of the individual because the physician determines that without the services of the on-call physician the benefits of transfer outweigh the risks of transfer, the physician authorizing the transfer shall not be subject to a penalty under subparagraph (B). However, the previous sentence shall not apply to the hospital or to the on-call physician who failed or refused to appear.

(2) Civil enforcement.

(A) Personal harm. Any individual who suffers personal harm as a direct result of a participating hospital's violation of a requirement of this section may, in a civil action against the participating hospital, obtain those damages available for personal injury under the law of the State in which the hospital is located, and such equitable relief as is appropriate.

(B) Financial loss to other medical facility. Any medical facility that suffers a financial loss as a direct result of a participating hospital's violation of a requirement of this section may, in a civil action against the participating hospital, obtain those damages available for financial loss, under the law of the State in which the hospital is located, and such equitable relief as is appropriate.

(C) Limitations on actions. No action may be brought under this paragraph more than two years after the date of the violation with respect to which the action is brought.

(3) Consultation with peer review organizations. [Omitted.]

(4) Notice upon closing an investigation. The Secretary shall establish a procedure to notify hospitals and physicians when an investigation under this section is closed.

(e) Definitions. In this section:

(1) The term "emergency medical condition" means—

(A) a medical condition manifesting itself by acute symptoms of sufficient severity (including severe pain) such that the absence of immediate medical attention could reasonably be expected to result in—

(i) placing the health of the individual (or, with respect to a pregnant woman, the health of the woman or her unborn child) in serious jeopardy,

(ii) serious impairment to bodily functions, or

(iii) serious dysfunction of any bodily organ or part; or

(B) with respect to a pregnant women who is having contractions—

(i) that there is inadequate time to effect a safe transfer to another hospital before delivery or,

(ii) that transfer may pose a threat to the health or safety of the woman or the unborn child.

(2) The term "participating hospital" means hospital that has entered into a provider agreement under section 1395cc of this title.

(3)(A) The term "to stabilize" means, with respect to an emergency medical condition described in paragraph (1)(A), to provide such medical treatment of the condition as may be necessary to assure, within reasonable medical probability, that no material deterioration of the condition is likely to result from or occur during the transfer of the individual from a facility, or, with respect to an emergency medical condition described in paragraph (1)(B), to deliver (including the placenta).

(B) The term "stabilized" means, with respect to an emergency medical condition described in paragraph (1)(A), that no material deterioration of the condition is likely, within reasonable medical probability, to result from or occur during the transfer of the individual from a facility, or, with respect to an emergency medical condition described in paragraph (1)(B), that the woman has delivered (including the placenta).

(4) The term "transfer" means the movement (including the discharge) of an individual outside a hospital's facilities at the direction of any person employed by (or affiliated or associated, directly or indirectly, with) the hospital, but does not include such a movement of an individual who (A) has been declared dead, or (B) leaves the facility without the permission of any such person.

(5) The term "hospital" includes a critical access hospital (as defined in section 1395x(mm)(1) of this title).

(f) Preemption. The provisions of this section do not preempt any State or local law requirement, except to the extent that the requirement directly conflicts with a requirement of this section.

(g) Nondiscrimination. A participating hospital that has specialized capabilities or facilities (such as burn units, shock-trauma units, neonatal intensive care units, or (with respect to rural areas) regional referral centers as identified by the Secretary in regulation) shall not refuse to accept an appropriate transfer of an individual who requires such specialized capabilities or facilities if the hospital has the capacity to treat the individual.

(h) No delay in examination or treatment. A participating hospital may not delay provision of an appropriate medical screening examination required under subsection (a) of this section or further medical examination and treatment required under subsection (b) of this section in order to inquire about the individual's method of payment or insurance status.

(i) Whistleblower protections. A participating hospital may not penalize or take adverse action against a qualified medical person described in subsection (c)(1)(A)(iii) or a physician because the person or physician refuses to authorize the transfer of an individual with an emergency medical condition that has not been stabilized or against any hospital employee because the employee reports a violation of a requirement of this section.

Notes

1. *2003 Federal EMTALA regulations.* Federal regulations implementing EMTALA are found at 42 C.F.R. § 489.24. The Centers for Medicare and Medicaid Services has primary enforcement oversight, while the DHHS Inspector General is responsible for investigations and application of sanctions. Regulations were initially promulgated in 1994 (59 Fed. Reg. 32,086). Substantial revisions were issued in 2003 (68 Fed. Reg. 53,222). As detailed as it might at first appear, the EMTALA statute (like most laws) contains numerous and critical ambiguities. The 2003 regulatory revisions resolve these ambiguities in an effort to narrow hospitals' EMTALA obligations in several fundamental respects: the point at which EMTALA's screening and stabilization or transfer duties commence; the relationship between the screening and stabilization obligations; the locations to which EMTALA duties apply; the point at which EMTALA duties cease; and the extent of the duty owed by "on-call" specialists during both screening and stabilization. This narrowing of EMTALA appears to be consistent with the views expressed by the hospital industry, professional medical specialty associations, and a number of legal scholars. This regulatory limitation on EMTALA's reach also adopts as national policy certain judicial rulings in recent years, which have taken a more narrow interpretation of EMTALA, while rejecting other decisions which appear to broaden EMTALA's reach. At the same time, as you will see in the materials that follow, the regulations themselves have created controversy, and at least one federal court has rejected a portion of the regulations aimed limiting hospitals' duties as an arbitrary and capricious reading of the statute.

2. *EMTALA and public health emergencies.* As noted, hospital emergency departments provide an extraordinary amount of health care. In the case of public health emergencies, two competing considerations are at

work. The first is the need for an organized response to a public health emergency, which may argue for a first response by entities that are explicitly trained to manage a mass casualty, thereby permitting hospitals effectively to triage individuals to other sources of care without performing initial screening and stabilization duties. In contrast, an argument can be made that all hospitals with emergency capabilities should be expected to have the competencies needed in such a situation and that EMTALA obligations should remain firmly in effect; without such a policy and competencies, a first response system, no matter how robust, could become quickly overwhelmed.

Section 1135 of the Social Security Act, 42 U.S.C. § 1320b–5, added by the Project Bioshield Act of 2004, Pub. L. No. 108–276, tends to come down (somewhat mushily) in the middle. The Act authorizes the Secretary of Health and Human Services to waive, "in any emergency area and during an emergency period" laws and regulations pertaining to, among other matters,

> actions under section 1867 (relating to examination and treatment for emergency medical conditions and women in labor) for—(A) a transfer of an individual who has not been stabilized in violation of subsection (c) of such section if the transfer arises out of the circumstances of the emergency; (B) the direction or relocation of an individual to receive medical screening in an alternative location—(i) pursuant to an appropriate State emergency preparedness plan; or (ii) in the case of a public health emergency described in subsection (g)(1)(B) that involves a pandemic infectious disease, pursuant to a State pandemic preparedness plan or a plan referred to in clause (i), whichever is applicable in the State;

The provision is designed to waive enforcement of EMTALA's screening, stabilization and transfer obligations rather than the obligations themselves, and it authorizes the Secretary of DHHS to describe the extent of these obligations during an emergency. On August 14, 2009, the Centers for Medicare and Medicaid services issued a memorandum (Ref. S & C–09–52) describing the obligations of hospitals during an influenza pandemic as part of planning for a surge in emergency department need. The memorandum details the Section 1135 EMTALA waiver procedure, the circumstances under which waivers will be granted, and the obligations of hospitals notwithstanding a waiver if granted, to establish alternative screening sites that must be in place to address the demands created by a surge. President Obama signed such an emergency declaration waiver on October 24, 2009. *See* http://www.flu.gov/professional/federal/h1n1emergency 10242009.html. Under President Obama's administration, waivers have also been issued for the storms in North Dakota during 2009. HHS Acting Secretary Declares Public Health Emergency for North Dakota Storms, http://www.hhs.gov/news/press/2009pres/03/20090325a.html.   Previously, the Bush Administration issued waivers during Hurricane Katrina. HHS Declares Public Health Emergency for Hurricane Katrina, http://www.hhs. gov/katrina/ssawaiver.html. *See generally* HHS, Waiver or Modification of

Requirements under Section 1135 of the Social Security Act, http://www.
cms.hhs.gov/H1N1/Downloads/1135WaiverSigned_H1N1.pdf. For a description of the Act and the process for considering and granting waivers, see
Centers for Medicare and Medicaid Services, http://www.liebertonline.com/
doi/abs/10.1089/bsp.2008.0825.

No evaluation of these waivers have been undertaken in order to
determine the extent to which they were exercised by hospitals, whether
individuals seeking emergency care were appropriately diverted to specially
designated "alternative" locations, whether the care received at alternative
locations was timely and appropriate, or whether population health was
affected by diversion.

3.   THE DUTY TO PROVIDE AN "APPROPRIATE" SCREENING

Power v. Arlington Hospital Association

42 F.3d 851 (4th Cir. 1994)

■ WILLIAMS, CIRCUIT JUDGE:

[Susan] Power brought this suit against Arlington Hospital alleging
that it violated the Emergency Medical Treatment and Active Labor Act of
1986 (EMTALA), 42 U.S.C.A. § 1395dd (West 1992), by failing to provide
her an "appropriate medical screening" when she initially presented to the
emergency room.

[T]he jury returned a verdict in favor of Power on the appropriate
medical screening claim, and awarded actual damages of $5 million.

Power, a citizen of Great Britain, was brought by her fiancé to the
emergency room at Arlington Hospital on February 24, 1990, at approximately 5:45 a.m. At the time, she was 33 years old, unemployed, and had
no health insurance. Power complained of pain in her left hip, lower left
abdomen, pain in her back running down her leg, and that she was unable
to walk. She was shaking and had severe chills. Power also had a sizeable
boil visible on her cheek, though the emergency room nurses and physicians testified they did not see the boil and there is no mention of it in the
medical records for that day.

Power was initially taken to a treatment room and seen by a nurse,
Barbara Goldy, R.N., who took a brief medical history from her, did a
nursing assessment, and performed a "dip stick" urinalysis. The medical
information which was recorded on Power's chart indicated that she was
unemployed and uninsured. Power was next seen by an emergency room
physician, Dr. Heiman, who spoke with her, examined her hip, did a motor
examination and leg extension test, all of which were within normal limits,
and ordered x-rays. Shifts changed at 7:00 a.m., and Dr. Semmes, another
emergency room physician, examined Power. Based on his examination, Dr.
Semmes believed that Power's pain was localized and musculoskeletal in
nature, and that she did not have an infection and was not ill. The hip x-
ray was negative in all respects. Before the results of the urinalysis came

back from the lab, Dr. Semmes discharged Power. He gave her a prescription for anti-inflammatory and pain medications and instructed her to avoid bearing weight on her left leg. Dr. Semmes also told Power that if her pain persisted or became worse, she should return to the emergency room or call the orthopedic surgeon whose name, address, and phone number he had given to her.

When her pain worsened, Power returned to the Arlington Hospital emergency room at approximately 10:15 p.m. on the following day, February 25, 1990. She presented with the same symptoms as the day before except that by this time she was in an unstable condition with virtually no blood pressure. Her vital signs signified that she was in severe shock, which the doctors believed was probably septic in nature, and she was admitted to the intensive care unit at Arlington Hospital at approximately 1:00 a.m. An orthopedic surgeon concluded that the hip pain was not the source of Power's problems, and an internist, in consultation with an infectious disease specialist, decided to treat her with antibiotics pending the results of her blood work. The ultimate etiology of Power's illness was that she had "seeded" an infection in her blood approximately 10 days earlier when she had attempted to lance the boil on her face.

Power was in critical condition for the first several months of her hospitalization. Because of her level of shock, the medications required to control her infection and maintain her blood pressure, and the circulatory problems caused by these medications, Power had to have both legs amputated below the knee. She also lost sight in one eye and developed severe and permanent lung damage. By mid-April, Power's status was no longer critical. On July 1, 1990, Power was transferred on a gurney by commercial airliner to Central Middlesex Hospital in London, England.

Dr. Heiman and Dr. Semmes testified that Arlington Hospital had no written protocols or procedures describing how doctors should conduct an appropriate medical screening for patients presenting to the emergency room. Dr. Semmes did describe the typical procedure as the following: "take a history, perform a physical exam, have a differential diagnosis in your mind, order appropriate diagnostic tests, develop a treatment plan, determine a need whether to admit or discharge the patient, and implement the treatment plan." Dr. Semmes testified unequivocally that he would not have treated any other patient with the same complaints and vital signs any differently than he treated Power. There was also testimony, however, that Dr. Semmes did not follow the usual procedure at Arlington Hospital when he (1) did not record Power's medical history on her chart; (2) failed to record the results of Power's x-ray on her chart; and (3) discharged Power before the results of her urinalysis were returned.

Power presented testimony from Dr. George Colson, a qualified medical expert in emergency medicine, that a blood test was a necessary component of an appropriate medical screening examination for a patient who presented at the emergency room with Power's symptoms. She also offered testimony from Dr. Margo Smith, a qualified medical expert in infectious diseases, that if Power had received an appropriate medical screening, including a blood test, when she first came to the emergency room, it was more probable than not that her infection would have been detected and properly treated.

We turn now to several legal questions involving EMTALA. We begin with Arlington Hospital's argument that we adopt a standard that requires proof of a non-medical reason or an improper motive for a hospital's treatment or discharge decision before a plaintiff can recover for a breach of EMTALA.

Congress enacted EMTALA to address a growing concern with preventing "patient dumping," the practice of refusing to provide emergency medical treatment to patients unable to pay, or transferring them before emergency conditions were stabilized. EMTALA is not a substitute for state law malpractice actions, and was not intended to guarantee proper diagnosis or to provide a federal remedy for misdiagnosis or medical negligence. Count I of Power's complaint alleged that Arlington Hospital failed to provide "an appropriate medical screening examination," a requirement found in § 1395dd(a). EMTALA does not define the phrase "appropriate medical screening examination" other than to state that its purpose is to identify an "emergency medical condition." [In prior cases] we held that "[t]he plain language of [EMTALA] requires a hospital to develop a screening procedure designed to identify such critical conditions that exist in symptomatic patients and to apply that screening procedure uniformly to all patients with similar complaints." The key requirement is that a hospital "apply its standard of screening uniformly to all emergency room patients, regardless of whether they are insured or can pay. The Act does not impose any duty on a hospital requiring that the screening result in a correct diagnosis."

[T]his is not a case in which the EMTALA claim is based solely on allegations that emergency room personnel failed to make a proper diagnosis. Here, Power has clearly presented evidence from which a jury could conclude that she was treated differently from other patients presenting to the Arlington Hospital emergency room, and that the Hospital did not apply its standard screening procedure, such that it was, uniformly. Although the facts might also give rise to a claim under state law for misdiagnosis or malpractice, that is not what Power has alleged or argued here. Her evidence is sufficient to meet the threshold requirement of an EMTALA claim, namely that the screening she was provided by Arlington Hospital deviated from that given to other patients. Nevertheless, the Hospital contends that evidence of disparate treatment alone is not enough to recover under EMTALA.

Arlington Hospital argues that in order for Power to establish a violation of the screening requirement of EMTALA she must prove that any disparate treatment was given or withheld for a non-medical reason or improper motive. According to the Hospital, Power has failed to demonstrate such an improper motive on its part, therefore the judgment in her favor should be reversed. The Hospital contends that under the Sixth Circuit's holding in Cleland v. Bronson Health Care Group, Inc., 917 F.2d

266, 272 (6th Cir. 1990), disparate treatment provided or withheld based upon legitimate medical considerations is still an appropriate medical screening examination. The Cleland court stated:

> We believe that the terms of the statute, specifically referring to a medical screening exam by a hospital "within its capabilities" precludes resort to a malpractice or objective standard of care as the meaning of the term "appropriate." Instead, "appropriate" must more correctly be interpreted to refer to the motives with which the hospital acts. If it acts in the same manner as it would have for the usual paying patient, then the screening provided is "appropriate" within the meaning of the statute. Id. at 272.

The court also suggested that race, sex, ethnic group, politics, occupation, education, personal prejudice, drunkenness, and spite were all possible improper motives resulting in liability under EMTALA.

Power urges us to disregard the dicta in *Cleland* and follow the reasoning of the D.C. Circuit in Gatewood v. Washington Healthcare Corp., 933 F.2d 1037, 1041 (D.C. Cir. 1991), in which it stated:

> The motive for such departure [from standard screening procedures] is not important to this analysis, which applies whenever and for whatever reason a patient is denied the same level of care provided others and guaranteed him or her by subsection 1395dd(a).

We are persuaded that the D.C. Circuit's rejection of an improper motive requirement is indeed the correct approach. First, there is nothing in the statute itself that requires proof of indigence, inability to pay, or any other improper motive on the part of a hospital as a prerequisite to recovery. The language of subsection 1395dd(a) simply refers to "any individual" who presents to the emergency room. Second, it seems to us that the expanse of motives suggested by the Sixth Circuit in *Cleland* is so broad as to be no limit at all, and as a practical matter amounts to not having a motive requirement. Anyone who alleges that she did not receive an appropriate medical screening examination can simply find an improper motive that fits, whether it is sex, nationality, income, or occupation, and simply allege it. Which leads, thirdly, to the most fundamental problem with the motive requirement: the proof predicament. We agree with Power's position that having to prove the existence of an improper motive on the part of a hospital, its employees or its physicians, would make a civil EMTALA claim virtually impossible. We do not believe that proving the inner thoughts and prejudices of attending hospital personnel is required in order to recover under EMTALA.

[W]e are sympathetic to the Hospital's concern that "mere statistical comparison of patients with similar complaints on presentation to the emergency department should not be used as the basis to require uniformity of diagnostic studies ordered unless the physician caring for the patient believes that such tests are medically necessary for the particular patient." [A]pplication of the screening procedure "necessarily requires the exercise of medical training and judgment. Hospital personnel must assess a patient's signs and symptoms and use their informed judgment to determine whether a critical condition exists."

The question still remains as to how best to formulate the legal standard of recovery in an EMTALA case in order to address these legitimate concerns regarding medical judgment and flexibility. We believe the best approach, and the standard we now adopt, is to allow a hospital, after a plaintiff makes a threshold showing of differential treatment, to offer evidence rebutting that showing either by demonstrating that the patient was accorded the same level of treatment that all other patients receive, or that a test or procedure was not given because the physician did not believe that the test was reasonable or necessary under the particular circumstances of that patient.

If a hospital offers such rebuttal evidence, fairness dictates that the plaintiff should be allowed to challenge the medical judgment of the physicians involved through her own expert medical testimony. This is especially true in a case such as this where a hospital has denied that it has any standard emergency room protocols or procedures. As other courts have observed, Arlington Hospital cannot "simply hide behind this lack of standard emergency room procedures." We agree with the district court's conclusion below that, "absent such standard protocols," an EMTALA claim may be established through "proof of a failure to meet the standard of care to which the Hospital adheres." Although allowance of such proof potentially blurs the line somewhat between a malpractice claim and an EMTALA claim, they are still distinct causes of action as the following illustration given by district court elucidates:

> Consider a situation in which a hospital adheres to a standard requiring tests A, B, and C as part of an appropriate emergency room medical screening. In many instances, this standard will also be the malpractice standard of care. Thus, failure to perform test C, for example, would violate both EMTALA and the standard of care applicable in a malpractice claim. But if tests A, B, and C are performed and the doctor evaluating the results draws an incorrect conclusion, a violation of EMTALA may not be established, but medical negligence may be. In short, the issue is not whether the Hospital's treatment was adequate as measured against a malpractice standard of care, . . . but rather whether the claimant received the same screening examination regularly provided to other patients in similar circumstances.

To summarize, Power's claim is not inherently deficient because she did not offer proof of an improper motive on the part of Arlington Hospital personnel. She met her threshold burden of proof by presenting evidence of differential treatment. Arlington Hospital properly had the opportunity to submit evidence that she was not treated differently, or that any disparate treatment was based on the judgment of the treating physicians as to what was medically necessary. Power then offered evidence from qualified medical experts who testified that, among other things, a blood test was a necessary component of an appropriate medical screening examination at

Arlington Hospital, for a patient who presented at the emergency room with her symptoms. The jury found in favor of Power on the factual question of whether she received an appropriate medical screening, and we affirm its verdict.

Summers v. Baptist Medical Center Arkadelphia

91 F.3d 1132 (8th Cir. 1996) (en banc)

■ RICHARD S. ARNOLD, CHIEF JUDGE:

Harold Summers brought this case against Baptist Medical Center Arkadelphia (Baptist), a hospital in Arkadelphia, Arkansas. The case arises under [EMTALA], 42 U.S.C. § 1395dd. Summers claims that he was not appropriately screened for treatment when he was brought in to Baptist's emergency room after a deer-hunting accident. The District Court granted Baptist's motion for summary judgment and dismissed the complaint. Summers appealed, and a panel of this Court reversed and remanded for trial, one judge dissenting. Summers v. Baptist Medical Center Arkadelphia, 69 F.3d 902 (8th Cir. 1995). We granted Baptist's suggestion for rehearing en banc, thus vacating the opinion and judgment of the panel. Having heard oral argument before the Court en banc, we now affirm the judgment of the District Court. We hold that something more than, or different from, ordinary negligence in the emergency-room screening process must be shown to make out a federal claim under EMTALA.

We state the facts in the light most favorable to the plaintiff, the party opposing summary judgment. On October 25, 1992, Summers fell out of a tree stand while deer hunting near Arkadelphia. An ambulance brought him to Baptist's emergency room. A nurse took the medical history, and a physician saw Summers immediately. Summers testified that the doctor pressed "on my stomach and stuff." Summers said he "was hurting in my chest real bad and I was hearing this popping noise every time I breathed.... I [told the doctor] I was hurting [in my chest].... I heard this snapping, and he told me I was having muscle spasms." Summers also complained of pain in his back.

The emergency room physician ordered four x-rays of the patient's spine. (Other routine tests were done, but they are not material for present purposes.) Both the thoracic and the lumbar spine were covered. The physician recalls the patient's complaining of pain in his back, and Baptist conceded in the District Court that Summers complained of chest pain, but the doctor testified that Summers did not complain of pain in the front part of his chest. The doctor pressed on the front and back of the chest, noticed no difficulty in breathing, and heard no popping or crackling-type sounds on listening to the chest[.] The doctor did not remember the patient's saying he could hear popping-type sounds, and felt or heard nothing to indicate a broken sternum. "If he had complained of pain in the sternum or pain in the ribs, we would have x-rayed those."

No x-rays of the chest were taken. The spinal x-rays showed, in the opinion of the physician at Baptist, only an old break at the eighth thoracic vertebra. Summers was told that he was suffering from muscle spasms. He said he was in pain and asked to be admitted to the hospital. He was told no. Summers then said he had insurance and $1,200 in cash, in case the hospital felt his admission would cause some sort of financial problems, but he was still refused admission. The doctor thought he did not need to be admitted to the hospital. Summers was given pain injections and discharged with instructions to see a doctor at home (Jonesboro, Arkansas) the next day. He was loaded into a pick-up truck and had to endure the five-hour drive home in pain.

The next day Summers felt too sore to get out of bed, and did not go to his family doctor. The day after that, though, October 27, he was in such pain that he went by ambulance to St. Bernard's Regional Medical Center. He was given, among other tests, a chest x-ray. This x-ray was difficult to read, so a CT (computerized tomography) scan was done. The scan revealed a fresh break of the seventh thoracic vertebra. In addition, the x-ray showed a broken sternum and a broken seventh rib. According to Rebecca Barrett–Tuck, M.D., a Jonesboro neurosurgeon, the chest injury "certainly does constitute a life threatening injury," Summers was kept in the hospital at Jonesboro for 14 days, some of that time in intensive care. It is fair to conclude that if a chest x-ray had been taken at Arkadelphia, the broken breast-bone and rib would have been discovered, Summers would have been hospitalized at once, and the patient would have been spared at least two unnecessary days of anxiety and pain.

The plaintiff's main claim is that, on the basis of this record, a jury could properly find Baptist had failed to "provide for an appropriate medical screening examination within the capability of [its] . . . emergency department. . . ." 42 U.S.C. § 1395dd(a). Baptist agrees that patients complaining of pain in the front of their chest, or of snapping or popping noises when breathing, would normally be given a chest x-ray. The jury could find that Summers did so complain, but he was not given a chest x-ray. His screening examination was therefore not "appropriate."

What is meant by the word "appropriate?" One possible meaning, perhaps the most natural one, would be that medical screening examinations must be correct, properly done, if not perfect, at least not negligent. It would be easy to say, for example, simply as a matter of the English language, that a negligently performed screening examination is not an appropriate one. So far as we can determine, however, no court has interpreted the statute in such an expansive fashion, and it is easy to understand why.

[T]he purpose of the statute was to address a distinct and rather narrow problem—the "dumping" of uninsured, underinsured, or indigent patients by hospitals who did not want to treat them. [O]n the other hand, that it is the statute, and not a committee report, that is signed by the President and has therefore become law. [T]he fact that Baptist's motivation in this particular case was obviously not to dump an uninsured or indigent patient does not defeat the plaintiff's action.

[E]very court that has considered EMTALA has disclaimed any notion that it creates a general federal cause of action for medical malpractice in emergency rooms. The law of this Circuit is to the same effect. Williams v. Birkeness, 34 F.3d 695, 697 (8th Cir. 1994) (appropriate medical screening does not mean correct diagnosis).

[I]f improper motive is not required, and if the statute does not create a federal remedy for medical malpractice in emergency rooms, what does the statute do? Something more than or different from negligence must be shown, but what is that "something?" We have previously taken the position that the "something" required is lack of uniform treatment. Williams v. Birkeness, supra 34 F.3d at 697. An inappropriate screening examination is one that has a disparate impact on the plaintiff. Patients are entitled under EMTALA, not to correct or non-negligent treatment in all circumstances, but to be treated as other similarly situated patients are treated, within the hospital's capabilities. It is up to the hospital itself to determine what its screening procedures will be. Having done so, it must apply them alike to all patients.

As we understand the positions taken by both parties to this case they would accept, at least in general, all of the principles so far laid out in this opinion. Plaintiff, for example, concedes that he has to show non-uniform or disparate treatment in order to succeed. He takes the position, however, that he has met this requirement. According to the hospital's own admission, a patient complaining of snapping and popping noises in his chest would have been given a chest x-ray. Plaintiff, as we must assume for purposes of this motion for summary judgment, did make just such a complaint, but was not given the chest x-ray. He was therefore treated differently from other patients, and differently from the treatment prescribed by the hospital's normal screening process. Therefore he is entitled to recover under EMTALA.

The argument has a surface appeal. On reflection, we are not convinced.

The important point for us is that the very respect in which the plaintiff's screening is said to be non-uniform—failure to order a chest x-ray for a patient complaining of popping noises in his chest—is nothing more than an accusation of negligence. It would almost always be possible to characterize negligence in the screening process as non-uniform treatment, because any hospital's screening process will presumably include a non-negligent response to symptoms or complaints presented by a patient. To construe EMTALA this expansively would be inconsistent with the principles and cases set out earlier in this opinion.

The emergency-room physician is required by EMTALA to screen and treat the patient for those conditions the physician perceives the patient to have. So here, the physician, we must assume through inadvertence or inattention, did not perceive Summers to have cracking or popping noises in his chest, or pain in the front of his chest. This is why no chest x-rays were taken. In the medical judgment of the physician, Summers did not need a chest x-ray. Summers did receive substantial medical treatment. It was not perfect, perhaps negligent, but he was treated no differently from any other patient perceived to have the same condition.

[I]nstances of "dumping," or improper screening of patients for a discriminatory reason, or failure to screen at all, or screening a patient differently from other patients perceived to have the same condition, all are actionable under EMTALA. But instances of negligence in the screening or diagnostic process, or of mere faulty screening, are not. The District Court was therefore correct to dismiss Summers's claim that the failure to give him a chest x-ray violated EMTALA.[1]

■ HEANEY, CIRCUIT JUDGE, with whom McMILLIAN, CIRCUIT JUDGE, joins, dissenting:

In affirming the dismissal of Summers' claim, the majority assumes facts against Summers' position and significantly limits the scope of the statute. I believe that Summers' claim presents a genuine issue of material fact that the district court should have permitted to go to the jury. Thus, I respectfully dissent.

EMTALA [does not establish] a vast range of claims for medical negligence. EMTALA has a much more limited application than state malpractice law: it applies only to emergency rooms of hospitals that have provider agreements under the Medicare program. EMTALA also does not establish a national standard of care. Rather, it requires hospitals to develop screening procedures to detect emergency medical conditions. The more a hospital's established procedures are unwritten and loosely-defined—or essentially equivalent to "due care"—the more an EMTALA cause of action may overlap with a state medical malpractice claim.

Baptist agrees that patients complaining of pain in the front of their chest, or of snapping or popping noises when breathing, would normally be given a chest x-ray. The majority, considering the facts in a light most favorable to the non-moving party, accepts as true that Summers complained to the doctor about his chest pains and throbbing chest. Baptist even concedes this point. The majority assumes, however, that the physician:

> through inadvertence or inattention, did not perceive Summers to have cracking or popping noises in his chest, or pain in the front of his chest. This is why no chest x-rays were taken. In the medical judgment of the physician, Summers did not need a chest x-ray. Summers did receive substantial medical treatment.

[T]he majority effectively usurps the role of the jury and makes the factual findings necessary to dismiss Summers' claim as one of mere negligence. It was for the jury, not the district court or this court, to

---

1. In fairness to the plaintiff, we observe that Power v. Arlington Hospital Ass'n, 42 F.3d 851 (4th Cir. 1994), comes close, on its facts, to supporting his position.

determine the relative credibility of the parties and what occurred in the emergency room that day. We should not assume that the doctor did not hear Summers or forget about his complaints. Nor should we assume that it was the physician's medical judgment that prompted his failure to give Summers a chest x-ray. It is possible that the doctor heard Summers' complaints and, for no legitimate reason, failed to do anything about them. That alternative would establish the essentials of an EMTALA cause of action.

The majority's inappropriate resolution of this appeal from a grant of summary judgment is driven by its fear of giving EMTALA too "expansive" an interpretation such that it would apply in situations traditionally covered only by state malpractice law. Not only is this fear unwarranted, it cannot justify significantly altering the plain language of the statute.

The majority gives lip service to following the literal language of the statute by not requiring proof of bias on the part of the hospital. Yet its strained definition of "appropriate," (i.e., "uniform" or that which would be given to a similarly situated patient) effectively limits the statute's application to only those cases that involve bias or discrimination. I see no way for a plaintiff to prove non-uniform or disparate treatment without evidence of the hospital's bias against a particular group to which he belongs. While the Sixth Circuit is the only circuit that admits to requiring bias evidence for an EMTALA violation, see Cleland v. Bronson Health Care Group, Inc., 917 F.2d 266, 272 (6th Cir. 1990), the only circuit court decisions that permit an EMTALA claim to go forward involve evidence of bias.

In light of Congress' intent to address patient "dumping" in enacting EMTALA, the majority is understandably frustrated by the plain language of the statute. Its limitation of the statute's application perhaps even meets Congress' objective better than the law enacted by Congress. It is not our role, however, to re-draft the statute and to alter its plain language.

Under the statute as written, credible allegations that a hospital has failed to follow its own established screening procedures in the treatment of a particular patient constitute a threshold showing of an EMTALA violation.

Notes

1. *Defining what constitutes an "appropriate" screening.* Other cases confirm the difficulty of prevailing on EMTALA screening claims. In Fisher v. New York Health and Hospitals Corporation, 989 F. Supp. 444 (E.D.N.Y. 1998), a six year old boy, hit by a snowball over the left eye, complained of headaches for two days, as well as fever, loss of appetite, and generalized body pain. He was given a pediatric examination in a hospital emergency room, which did not reveal any abnormal findings with regard to the boy's heart, lungs, skin, head, eyes, ears, nose, or throat. He was diagnosed as having a viral infection, given Tylenol, and discharged. He returned to the emergency room three days later with similar but worse symptoms, was

diagnosed as having appendicitis and was operated on, revealing a normal appendix. Five days later, a CT scan was performed, revealing a severe brain abscess. The boy was then rushed to Kings County Hospital, where he was diagnosed with a severe festering brain abscess, subdural bilateral empyemas, and epidural hematoma.

In opposition to the hospital's motion for summary judgment on the EMTALA screening claim, the boy's attorney submitted an affidavit from a physician stating that the emergency room treatment of the boy fell below acceptable medical practice and emergency medical care. For purposes of the motion, the court accepted the allegation that the emergency room physician had been negligent in his failure to order blood tests, x-rays, and other diagnostic tests, but the court ruled that this evidence did not sustain a claim under EMTALA. *Id.* at 449. The court held that EMTALA decisions stood for the proposition that "[t]he appropriateness of the screening examination is determined by reference to how the hospital treats other patients who are perceived to have the same medical condition. If patients who are perceived to have viral illnesses are screened similarly by the hospital, EMTALA has not been violated. That is true even if the hospital's perception of a particular patient is based on a misdiagnosis; EMTALA is implicated only when individuals who are perceived to have the same medical condition receive disparate treatment." *Id.*

For a vivid example of the kind of facts needed to overcome a provider's motion for summary judgment based on "non-perception" of the patient's condition, consider Lewellen v. Schneck Medical Center, 2007 WL 2363384 (S.D. Ind. 2007). Lewellen, a registered nurse anesthetist, was involved a serious one-vehicle automobile accident in which his car rolled over and ended in a ditch well off the highway. His blood alcohol level was four times the legal limit. He was brought to the county-owned Schneck Memorial Hospital complaining of severe lower back pain, but was discharged without treatment into police custody after less than an hour at the hospital, before the X-rays of his back had been printed and reviewed. Lewellen refused to sign the discharge papers, complained of great pain, could not stand or walk, and was discharged in a wheelchair. The arresting officers refused to sign the discharge papers and questioned whether more care was needed, to which a nurse responded that "Lewellen was fine, he was just drunk." Two hours later a radiologist reviewing the X-rays "could not completely exclude" a spinal fracture, but failed to take effective action to notify the emergency room physician who had discharged Lewellen, or the jail authorities holding him. When the jail authorities themselves called the hospital to report Lewellen's continuing pain and incontinence, the nurse informed the officer that an "abnormality" had been found in the X-ray, but instructed the officer not to tell Lewellen and not to bring him back to the hospital. The officers were so upset with this response that they arranged to discharge Lewellen from custody and for an ambulance to take him back to the hospital. When the officer went to Lewellen's cell to inform him of these plans, he "noticed blood on the wall of the cell and [saw] a deep laceration on [Lewellen's] arm that had not been treated in any way. The cut still had grass and dirt in it." 2007 WL 2363384 at 3–5.

Lewellen sued the hospital, and two doctors and two nurses involved in his treatment under 42 U.S.C. § 1983 for violating his 14th Amendment right as a pretrial detainee to adequate medical care, and for violating EMTALA's duty to screen for emergency medical conditions. The 14th Amendment due process right to medical care "is violated when a state official [which can and in this case did include health care providers under contract to the state] 'acts with deliberate indifference toward the detainee's serious medical needs.'"

Meeting this standard requires both an objective and a subjective element. Objectively, a condition must be serious, meaning "the failure to treat [the] condition could result in further significant injury or the unnecessary and wanton infliction of pain." Subjectively, the defendants must have acted with deliberate indifference, in other words, they "[knew] of and disregard[ed] an excessive risk to [detainee's] health or safety; the official must both be aware of facts from which the inference could be drawn that a substantial risk of serious harm exists, and [they] must also draw the inference."

A showing of negligence on the part of the official will not be enough to show deliberate indifference. On the other hand, plaintiffs do not have to show that the officials intended for the inmate to suffer harm. "It is enough to show that the defendants actually knew of a substantial risk of harm to the inmate and acted or failed to act in disregard of that risk." This may be established by showing that "the danger was objectively so great that actual knowledge of the danger could be inferred."

That Lewellen satisfied the objective part of the test is beyond question. He arrived at Schneck with an unstable burst fracture in his lower spine. Failure to treat the condition not only could lead to further significant injury, it did.

[The defendants] do argue that they were not deliberately indifferent to this serious medical need. Defendant nurses argue that Lewellen failed to produce any evidence that they knew about his condition. Without a showing that they actually knew he had a serious medical need, the failure to treat him is merely negligent, which does not rise to the level of a Constitutional violation. But knowledge may be inferred "when the medical professional's decision is such a substantial departure from accepted professional judgment, practice, or standards as to demonstrate that the person responsible did not base the decision on such a judgment."

Plaintiff has demonstrated that there is a genuine issue of material fact on whether Dr. Reisert [the emergency room physician] was deliberately indifferent to Lewellen's serious medical needs. According to evidence presented by Plaintiff, Dr. Reisert knew that Plaintiff had been in an automobile accident and was complaining of back pain. However, the x-rays that Dr. Reisert ordered were being printed off almost contemporaneously to Lewellen's discharge. Two doctors, Drs. Schwartz and Fulbright, testified that a burst fracture is clearly visible on the x-rays that were being printed off as Lewellen was discharged. As explained above, a trier of fact could use this evidence to determine that Dr. Reisert ordered Lewellen discharged before even looking at these x-rays. Given that Plaintiff was in an automobile accident and was in such visible agony that a State Trooper questioned the decision to discharge Lewellen, discharging Lewellen without looking at an x-ray was such a deviation from accepted professional judgment that a trier of fact could easily determine that Dr. Reisert did not base his decision to discharge Plaintiff on it. The § 1983 claim against Dr. Reisert survives summary judgment. [analysis of additional evidence in support of Lewellen's § 1983 claim omitted].

Id. at 11–12.

Consider the similarity and differences between the § 1983 "deliberate indifference" standard and what a patient must show to survive a hospital's EMTALA summary judgment motion that it did not perceive a patient's condition, and hence cannot be held liable for failing to conduct an appropriate screening examination. Recall that under *Summers*, a hospital physician's *negligent* failure to perceive symptoms does not constitute a violation of EMTALA's screening duty, just as a physician's negligence does not constitute "deliberate indifference" for constitutional purposes. As federal District Judge John Daniel Tinder put it in *Lewellen*, "EMTALA's screening requirement means something more than an inadvertent failure to follow the regular screening process in a particular case." What is that "something more?" Judge Tinder cited a Ninth Circuit opinion stating that a screening examination comparable to that offered to patients with similar symptoms is sufficient, "unless the examination is so cursory that it is not 'designed to identify acute and severe symptoms that alert the physician of the need for immediate medical attention to prevent serious bodily injury.'" Judge Tinder held that a reasonable trier of fact could find the emergency room doctor's failure to read Lewellen's X-rays before discharge "so cursory" as not to be designed to identify acute and severe symptoms. More generally, "Lewellen's stay at the hospital was alarmingly brief considering he was in a motor vehicle accident and complaining of severe back pain so bad he could not stand or sit in a chair correctly. Lewellen still had a bleeding gash in his arm with grass and dirt in it when he arrived at prison." In short, Lewellen's injuries, or risk of serious injury, were obvious from the symptoms and the circumstances, and the health providers must have been, or are deemed to be, aware of them. The claim of "non-perception" is not credible, and the deviation from professional standards is worse than negligent. Negligence implies an effort to meet the professional standard, but falling short. These facts suggest an abandonment of the professional standard, and the substitution of other motivations (in this case, hostility to a drunk driver) that inspired EMTALA's enactment, while not being formally required to prove an EMTALA violation.

The sometimes elusive distinction between a negligent failure to adhere to the professional standard (implying a good faith effort to do so)—which is not an EMTALA violation—and a deeper failure even to try to adhere to it—which is an EMTALA violation with respect to screening—is further illustrated by Trivette v. North Carolina Baptist Hospital, 507 S.E.2d 48 (N.C. Ct. App. 1998), *aff'd without opinion*, 512 S.E.2d 425 (N.C. 1999). The plaintiff, a severely disabled adult, was taken to the hospital in an ambulance because he was unconscious, choking, vomiting, and limp. He was given a variety of tests that showed that his white blood count was elevated, his iron levels were low, and his eyes were fully dilated. Randy Trivette's survivors argued that his symptoms and initial test results were the classic signs of "gastrointestinal bleeding, which itself requires immediate medical intervention to prevent serious damage to patient's health." Moreover, they also argued that his symptoms were clear signs that an EEG and a neurological consult were needed, which were in fact ordered by the emergency room physician but not performed. Instead, Trivette was perceived by hospital personnel as having had a seizure, admitted to the hospital, and discharged the next morning, although the complaint alleged that he was still experiencing all of the other presenting symptoms, including unconsciousness. Within twelve hours he was admitted to another hospital where he was diagnosed with gastrointestinal bleeding and a cerebral hemorrhage. He remained there for 21 days and died four months later.

Just as Lewellen argued that his inability to stand or walk, and the bleeding gash in his arm, were so obvious that hospital personnel were required to perform an adequate screen for those conditions, Trivette's survivors argued that his symptoms were so clear as to make additional tests for gastrointestinal bleeding and cerebral hemorrhage required as part an "appropriate screening examination" for patients with those perceived symptoms. But the courts (over a dissent in the court of appeals) did not see it that way. Rather, the trial and appeals court majority perceived the hospital as having made a good faith effort to diagnose Trivette's condition, and, perhaps through negligence, failed to perceive two serious medical problems. The *Trivette* majority mistakenly considered the ordered but not given tests as part of "treatment," when they clearly were part of a process to determine what Trivette's condition was, i.e., screening (the point made by the dissenting judge). EMTALA explicitly provides that an appropriate medical screening examination must "includ[e] ancillary services routinely available to the emergency department, to determine whether or not an emergency medical condition ... exists." § 1395dd(a). The appeals court majority acknowledged that

> a hospital's screening standard can be so low as to constitute a "failure to treat," and hence constitute an EMTALA violation. Although plaintiffs have raised the "failure to treat" issue, we need not address it because we believe that the defendant hospital, by giving Randy a battery of tests and admitting him to the hospital, had an adequate screening procedure which certainly could not equate to a "failure to treat."

Trivette, 507 S.E.2d at 51 n.1. In short, the majority simply assumed that because the defendant hospital did "something" that looked from a "common sense" view like a good faith effort to determine the patient's condition, any shortcomings in that process were "negligence" rather than an EMTALA violation. This perspective also ignores the fact that Trivette was a "severely disabled adult" whose superficial diagnosis and hasty discharge might well have been discrimination against "a difficult patient"—the sort of refusal EMTALA was designed to prohibit—as well as a possible violation (not pled) of the American with Disabilities Act (ADA) discussed in Chapter 4.

If the duty to screen is satisfied and no emergency condition is found, then there is no duty to stabilize. The reasoning goes as follows: since the stabilization duty is triggered only when an emergency medical condition is found, if the hospital has not "found" an emergency, then it has no duty to stabilize. In *Trivette* this reasoning extended to the apparently extreme facts alleged in the complaint, that the patient was discharged while still unconscious. According to the court, since "[t]here is no evidence that the defendant hospital perceived or actually knew of Randy's cerebral hemorrhage, it did not have a duty under EMTALA to stabilize it." *Trivette*, 507 S.E.2d at 53.

2.   Summary judgment standards. The procedural context for answering these questions is typically a summary judgment motion by the hospital. A hospital defending against an EMTALA claim of failure to provide an appropriate screening ordinarily supplies affidavits from the treating emergency room physician and other personnel that an appropriate screening, consistent with the hospital's usual procedures, was provided. The hospital then moves for summary judgment.

Since the 1960s there has been a steady and substantial increase in the rate of case termination by summary judgment in federal civil cases. Stephen B. Burbank, *Vanishing Trials and Summary Judgment in Federal Civil Cases: Drifting Toward Bethlehem or Gomorrah?*, 1 J. EMPIRICAL LEGAL STUD. 591 (2004). Although summary judgment can be granted in favor of either a plaintiff or a defendant, it is granted far more often in favor of the defendant. *Id.* at 616. Some praise this development as promoting efficiency. Randy J. Kozel & David Rosenberg, *Solving the Nuisance–Value Settlement Problem: Mandatory Summary Judgment*, 90 VA. L. REV. 1849 (2004). Others question whether increased reliance on summary judgment promotes efficiency. *See, e.g.* Arthur R. Miller, *The Pretrial Rush to Judgment: Are the "Litigation Explosion," "Liability Crises," and Efficiency Cliches Eroding out Day in Court and Jury Trial Commitments?*, 78 N.Y.U. L. REV. 982 (2003); John Bronsteen, *Against Summary Judgment*, 75 GEO. WASH. L. REV. 522 (2007). Yet others argue that the increased reliance on summary judgment is unfair to plaintiffs, e.g. Patricia M. Wald, *Summary Judgment at Sixty*, 76 TEX. L. REV. 1897 (1998); Elizabeth Schneider, *The Dangers of Summary Judgment: Gender and Federal Civil Litigation*, 59 RUTGERS L. REV. 705 (2007). Suja Thomas contends that summary judgment violates the Seventh Amendment to the U.S. Constitution, which guarantees the right to a jury trial in civil cases. Suja A. Thomas, *Why Summary Judgment is Unconstitutional*, 93 Va. L. Rev. 139 (2007). Nathan S. Richards, *Note, Judicial Resolution of EMTALA Screening Claims at Summary Judgment*, 87 N.Y.U. L. Rev. (forthcoming 2012), criticizes the excessive use of summary judgment in EMTALA cases and argues for a new approach to EMTALA liability that would encourage reliance on protocols or "check-lists" that would both promote quality of care and protect emergency rooms that adopt them.

4. What Does It Mean to "Come to" the Hospital's Emergency Department?

Hospitals' duty under EMTALA to screen is triggered by three factors: (1) an individual "comes to" an "emergency department" and (2) a "request is made" for (3) "examination or treatment for a medical condition." 42 U.S.C. § 1395dd(a). Regulations promulgated in 2003 clarify the meaning of both "comes to" and "emergency department." The regulations, 42 C.F.R. § 489.24(b), create an elaborate classification scheme that attempts to address a variety of means of arrival at various locations as falling within—or outside of—the triggering event for EMTALA. The result is that the concept of "comes to" (and thus, the condition precedent for a "request" that triggers the EMTALA duties) has been narrowed to certain specific circumstances. The regulations divide "comes to" into three categories. An individual might present (1) at "a hospital's dedicated emergency department"; (2) "on hospital property other than the dedicated emergency department"; or (3) "in a ground or air ambulance."

Presentation at a hospital's dedicated emergency department was the paradigm around which the statute was drafted and has, therefore, posed fewer problems of interpretation. The 2003 regulations define dedicated emergency department as follows:

> *Dedicated emergency department* means any department or facility of the hospital, regardless of whether it is located on or off the main hospital campus, which meets at least one of the following requirements:
>
> (1) It is licensed by the State in which it is located as an emergency room or emergency department;
>
> (2) It is held out to the public (by name, posted signs, advertising, or other means) as a place that provides care for emergency medical conditions on an urgent basis without requiring a previously scheduled appointment; or
>
> (3) During the calendar year immediately preceding the calendar year in which a determination under this section is being made, based on a representative example of patient visits that occurred during that calendar year, it provides at least one-third of all outpatient visits for the treatment of emergency medical condi-

tions on an urgent basis without requiring a previously scheduled appointment.

42 C.F.R. § 489.24(b) (emphasis added).

Hospital departments other than the emergency department might fall within this definition. In the preamble to the final rule, the agency elaborated that what counts is the function of the department:

> In response to the comment concerning labor and delivery departments, we would like to clarify that CMS believes that EMTALA requires that a hospital's dedicated emergency department would not only encompass what is generally thought of as a hospital's "emergency room," but would also include other departments of hospitals, such as labor and delivery departments and psychiatric units of hospitals, that provide emergency or labor and delivery services, or both, to individuals who may present as unscheduled ambulatory patients but are routinely admitted to be evaluated and treated. Because labor is a condition defined by statute as one in which EMTALA protections are afforded, any area of the hospital that offers such medical services to treat individuals in labor to at least one-third of the ambulatory individuals who present to the area for care, even if the hospital's practice is to admit such individuals as inpatients rather than treating them on an outpatient basis, *would* be considered a dedicated emergency department under our revised definition in this final rule. In such cases, whether the department of the hospital chooses to directly admit the emergency patient upon presentment is irrelevant to the determination of whether the department is a dedicated emergency department.

68 Fed. Reg. 53,229 (Sept. 9, 2003).

The 2003 regulations also clarified what happens in situations like that presented in *Campbell* above in which an individual is somewhere on hospital property such as the parking lot, alley ways and the like. The regulations provide that an individual has "come to" the hospital emergency department, within the meaning of 42 U.S.C. § 1395dd(a), when the individual "has presented on hospital property" defined as:

> *Hospital property* means the entire main hospital campus including the parking lot, sidewalk, and driveway but excluding other areas or structures of the hospital's main building that are not part of the hospital such as physician offices, rural health centers, skilled nursing facilities, or other entities that participate separately under Medicare, or restaurants, shops, or other nonmedical facilities.

42 C.F.R. § 489.24(b) (emphasis added).

The third and most complicated situations in which an individual might be deemed to have "come to" the hospital emergency department involve individuals who are being transported by ground or air ambulance. The 2003 regulations provide that an individual has "come to" the hospital emergency department if the individual:

> (3) Is in a ground or air ambulance owned and operated by the hospital for purposes of examination and treatment for a medical condition at a hospital's dedicated emergency department, even if

the ambulance is not on hospital grounds. However, an individual in an ambulance owned and operated by the hospital is not considered to have "come to the hospital's emergency department" if

> (i) the ambulance is operated under communitywide emergency medical services (EMS) protocols that direct it to transport the individual to a hospital other than the hospital that owns the ambulance: for example to the closest facility;

> (ii) the ambulance is operated at the direction of a physician who is not employed or otherwise affiliated with the hospital that owns the ambulance; or

(4) Is in a ground or air nonhospital-owned ambulance on hospital property for presentation for examination and treatment for a medical condition at a hospital's dedicated emergency department. However, an individual in a nonhospital-owned ambulance is not considered to have come to the hospital's emergency department, even if a member of the ambulance staff contacts the hospital by telephone or telemetry communications and informs the hospital that they want to transport the individual to the hospital for examination and treatment. The hospital may direct the ambulance to another facility if it is in "diversionary status," that is, it does not have the staff or facilities to accept any additional emergency patients. If, however, the ambulance staff disregards the hospital's diversion instructions and transports the individual onto hospital property, the individual is considered to have come to the emergency department.

Id.

Notice the priorities established by the rule. To begin, an individual has come to a hospital if it owns the ambulance whether or not the ambulance has actually arrived. However, this conclusion does not obtain if the ambulance is operating under communitywide EMS protocols or if emergent care during transport has already begun at the direction of a physician on staff at another hospital. Highest priority, therefore, is given to communitywide protocols or emergent care begun during transport. Otherwise, if a hospital owns and operates the ambulance, it owns the patient too (so to speak).

By contrast, if an individual is in an ambulance owned by a third-party, the individual has come to a hospital contacted by the ambulance unless that hospital is on formal "diversionary status." In this respect the rules adopt the holding in Arrington v Wong, 237 F.3d 1066 (9th Cir. 2001). Before *Arrington*, the courts generally followed a simple pattern: "coming to" the emergency department was determined by the ownership of the ambulance. Thus, if a patient was transported in a hospital-owned vehicle, the "comes to" requirement was automatically satisfied. However, if the patient was transported in a non-hospital-owned ambulance, the "comes to" requirement was not satisfied unless or until the ambulance actually arrived on hospital property. *Id.* at 1046.

In *Arrington*, a non-hospital-owned ambulance picked up a man in severe respiratory distress. The ambulance crew contacted the nearest hospital before reaching the hospital property to inform them that they were bringing in a patient with severe respiratory distress. Before the ambulance reached hospital grounds, however, it was instructed to go to another hospital farther away at which the patient had previously received care. The majority held that the plain language of the CMS regulation in effect at the time demonstrated that the "comes to" requirement is satisfied once the hospital receives a radio call from any ambulance, unless the emergency department is in formal diversionary status. *See* Tricia J. Middendorf, *Ambulances: Hospital Property or Not? Interpreting the Expanding Boundaries of EMTALA Through* Arrington v. Wong, 46 St. Louis U. L.J. 1035 (2002). The CMS regulations adopt *Arrington* to the extent to which it applies to third-party owned ambulances that have contacted a hospital not on diversionary status.

In Morales v. Sociedad Espanola de Auxilio Mutuo y Beneficencia, 524 F.3d 54 (1st Cir. 2008), *cert. den.*, 555 U.S. 1097 (2009), the first "comes to" court of appeals decision following the promulgation of the new regulations, the United States Court of Appeals for the First Circuit followed *Arrington* in ruling that the new regulations prohibited a hospital from denying access to a non-hospital-owned ambulance unless it was on formal diversionary status. The case involved a woman being transported with an ectopic pregnancy-related emergency. The evidence suggested that, the hospital was not on formal diversionary status, but also that the emergency department physician inquired both as to whether the woman was in reality experiencing the effects of a self-induced abortion and also whether she had insurance before "abruptly terminat[ing]" the call from the ambulance driver. The lower court dismissed plaintiff's claim and refused to recognize the applicability of the 2003 regulations. The First Circuit held that it was reasonable for the Secretary to require hospitals to respond to non-hospital-owned ambulances unless they were on formal diversionary status.

> This sensible construction also preserves the practice of ambulances contacting hospitals prior to arrival when perceived emergencies exist. That practice is salutary because it enables emergency rooms to undertake suitable preparatory measures. Yet, if the crew of an ambulance fears refusal because of, say, the absence of medical insurance, the crew may well decide to approach under cover of silence. Upon arrival, the emergency room would be required to examine and/or treat the individual, but precious time would have been lost.

524 F.3d at 61.

In its 2007 study, Emergency Medicine at the Crossroads (NAS Press, Washington D.C.), the Institute of Medicine of the National Academy of Sciences stressed the evidentiary importance, from a safety and quality perspective, of ensuring that complex emergency care be furnished at hospitals with specialized emergency capabilities, such as critical newborn care, shock/trauma, and other emergency sub-specialties. The IOM recommended that this evidence be used to guide EMS personnel in the selection of the appropriate hospital. Does 42 C.F.R. § 489.24(b)(4), authorizing hospitals to use diversionary status, square with an evidence-based approach? Do you see any alternative to permitting a specialized hospital emergency care system to implement diversionary status? How likely do you think it is that an EMS transport, having been told that the hospital is on diversion, nonetheless would come to the facility as the rule contemplates?

Even though the concept of "diversion" is central to defining hospital obligations under EMTALA, federal law does not define the circumstances in which a hospital may declare that it is on full or partial diversion. In the absence of state law, these decisions are left to the discretion of individual hospitals. In addition, as emergency room use has increased, diversion, previously a stopgap measure used by a hospital in the rare event that its emergency department became extremely crowded, has become endemic. One study estimated that, in 2003, about 500,000 ambulances were diverted from their initial hospital destination. Finally, reliable information about diversion is not routinely collected. *See* Justin Gundlach, *Note: The Problem of Ambulance Diversion, and Some Potential Solutions*, 13 N.Y.U. J. LEGIS. & PUB. POL'Y 175 (2010).

---

5. THE DUTY TO STABILIZE PERSONS WITH EMERGENCY MEDICAL CONDITIONS

In the Matter of Baby "K"

16 F.3d 590 (4th Cir. 1994)

■ WILKINS, CIRCUIT JUDGE:

The Hospital instituted this action against Ms. H, Mr. K, and Baby K, seeking a declaratory judgment that it is not required under the Emergency Medical Treatment and Active Labor Act (EMTALA), 42 U.S.C.A. § 1395dd to provide treatment other than warmth, nutrition, and hydration to Baby K, an anencephalic infant. Because we agree with the district court that EMTALA gives rise to a duty on the part of the Hospital to provide respiratory support to Baby K when she is presented at the Hospital in respiratory distress and treatment is requested for her, we affirm.

I.

Baby K was born at the Hospital in October of 1992 with anencephaly, a congenital malformation in which a major portion of the brain, skull, and scalp are missing. While the presence of a brain stem does support her autonomic functions and reflex actions, because Baby K lacks a cerebrum, she is permanently unconscious. Thus, she has no cognitive abilities or awareness. She cannot see, hear, or otherwise interact with her environment.

When Baby K had difficulty breathing on her own at birth, Hospital physicians placed her on a mechanical ventilator. This respiratory support allowed the doctors to confirm the diagnosis and gave Ms. H, the mother, an opportunity to fully understand the diagnosis and prognosis of Baby K's condition. The physicians explained to Ms. H that most anencephalic infants die within a few days of birth due to breathing difficulties and other complications. Because aggressive treatment would serve no therapeutic or palliative purpose, they recommended that Baby K only be provided with supportive care in the form of nutrition, hydration, and warmth. Physicians at the Hospital also discussed with Ms. H the possibility of a "Do Not Resuscitate Order" that would provide for the withholding of lifesaving measures in the future.

The treating physicians and Ms. H failed to reach an agreement as to the appropriate care. Ms. H insisted that Baby K be provided with mechanical breathing assistance whenever the infant developed difficulty breathing on her own, while the physicians maintained that such care was inappropriate. As a result of this impasse, the Hospital sought to transfer Baby K to another hospital. This attempt failed when all of the hospitals in the area with pediatric intensive care units declined to accept the infant. In November of 1992, when Baby K no longer needed the services of an acute-care hospital, she was transferred to a nearby nursing home.

Since being transferred to the nursing home, Baby K has been readmitted to the Hospital three times due to breathing difficulties. Each time she has been provided with breathing assistance and, after stabilization, has been discharged to the nursing home. Following Baby K's second admission, the Hospital filed this action to resolve the issue of whether it is obligated to provide emergency medical treatment to Baby K that it deems medically and ethically inappropriate. Baby K's guardian *ad litem* and her father, Mr. K, joined in the Hospital's request for a declaration that the Hospital is not required to provide respiratory support or other aggressive treatments. Ms. H contested the Hospital's request for declaratory relief. After the district court issued its findings of fact and conclusions of law denying the requested relief, the Hospital, Mr. K, and Baby K's guardian *ad litem* noticed this appeal.

II.

Congress enacted EMTALA in response to its "concern that hospitals were "dumping" patients [who were] unable to pay, by either refusing to provide emergency medical treatment or transferring patients before their emergency conditions were stabilized." Through EMTALA, Congress sought "to provide an 'adequate first response to a medical crisis' for all patients." First, those hospitals with an emergency medical department must provide an appropriate medical screening to determine whether an emergency medical condition exists for any individual who comes to the emergency medical department requesting treatment. A hospital fulfills this duty if it utilizes identical screening procedures for all patients complaining of the same condition or exhibiting the same symptoms.

An additional duty arises if an emergency medical condition is discovered during the screening process. When an individual is diagnosed as presenting an emergency medical condition the hospital must provide either "—(A) within the staff and facilities available at the hospital, for such further medical examination and such treatment as may be required to stabilize the medical condition, or (B) for the transfer of the individual to another medical facility in accordance with subsection (c) of this section." 42 U.S.C.A. § 1395dd(b)(1).

The treatment required "to stabilize" an individual is that treatment "necessary to assure, within reasonable medical probability, that no material deterioration of the condition is likely to result from or occur during the transfer of the individual from a facility." 42 U.S.C.A. § 1395dd(e)(3)(A). Therefore, once an individual has been diagnosed as presenting an emergency medical condition, the hospital must provide that treatment necessary to prevent the material deterioration of the individual's condition or provide for an appropriate transfer to another facility.

In the application of these provisions to Baby K, the Hospital concedes that when Baby K is presented in respiratory distress a failure to provide "immediate medical attention" would reasonably be expected to cause serious impairment of her bodily functions. Thus, her breathing difficulty qualifies as an emergency medical condition, and the diagnosis of this emergency medical condition triggers the duty of the hospital to provide Baby K with stabilizing treatment or to transfer her in accordance with the provisions of EMTALA. Since transfer is not an option available to the Hospital at this juncture, the Hospital must stabilize Baby K's condition.

The Hospital acknowledged in its complaint that aggressive treatment, including mechanical ventilation, is necessary to "assure within a reasonable medical probability, that no material deterioration of Baby K's condition is likely to occur." Thus, stabilization of her condition requires the Hospital to provide respiratory support through the use of a respirator or other means necessary to ensure adequate ventilation. In sum, a straightforward application of the statute obligates the Hospital to provide respiratory support to Baby K when she arrives at the emergency department of the Hospital in respiratory distress and treatment is requested on her behalf.

III.

In an effort to avoid the result that follows from the plain language of EMTALA, the Hospital offers four arguments. The Hospital claims: (1) that this court has previously interpreted EMTALA as only requiring uniform treatment of all patients exhibiting the same condition; (2) that in prohibiting disparate emergency medical treatment Congress did not intend to require physicians to provide treatment outside the prevailing standard of medical care; (3) that an interpretation of EMTALA that requires a hospital or physician to provide respiratory support to an anencephalic infant fails to recognize a physician's ability, under Virginia law, to refuse to provide medical treatment that the physician considers medically or ethically inappropriate; and (4) that EMTALA only applies to patients who are transferred from a hospital in an unstable condition. We find these arguments unavailing.

A.

Relying on the decisions of this court in Baber v. Hospital Corp. of America, 977 F.2d 872 (4th Cir. 1992), and Brooks v. Maryland Gen. Hosp. Inc., 996 F.2d 708 (4th Cir. 1993), the Hospital contends that it is only required to provide Baby K with the same treatment that it would provide other anencephalic infants—supportive care in the form of warmth, nutrition, and hydration. The Hospital quotes language from *Baber* and *Brooks* as supporting the proposition that EMTALA only requires participating hospitals to provide uniform treatment to all patients exhibiting the same emergency medical condition. Advancing the proposition that anencephaly, as opposed to respiratory distress, is the emergency medical condition at issue, the Hospital concludes that it is only required to provide uniform treatment to all anencephalic infants. We disagree.

In *Baber* and *Brooks*, this court addressed the "appropriate medical screening" requirement of EMTALA. In the absence of a statutory definition for this term, we concluded that it should be defined as requiring participating hospitals to apply uniform screening procedures to all individuals coming to the emergency room of the hospital requesting treatment. These cases dealt with screening procedures; neither addressed a hospital's duty to provide stabilizing treatment for an emergency medical condition.

With this issue now before us, we conclude that the duty of the Hospital to provide stabilizing treatment for an emergency medical condition is not coextensive with the duty of the Hospital to provide an "appropriate medical screening." Congress has statutorily defined the duty of a hospital to provide stabilizing treatment as requiring that treatment necessary to prevent the material deterioration of a patient's condition. If, as the Hospital suggests, it were only required to provide uniform treatment, it could provide any level of treatment to Baby K, including a level of treatment that would allow her condition to materially deteriorate, so long as the care she was provided was consistent with the care provided to other individuals. The definition of stabilizing treatment advocated by the Hospital directly conflicts with the plain language of EMTALA.

Even if this court were to interpret EMTALA as requiring hospitals to provide uniform treatment for emergency medical conditions, we could not find that the Hospital is only required to provide Baby K with warmth, nutrition, and hydration. As the Hospital acknowledged during oral argument, Baby K resides at the nursing home for months at a time without requiring emergency medical attention. Only when she has experienced episodes of bradypnea or apnea[1] has Baby K required respiratory support to prevent serious impairment of her bodily functions. It is bradypnea or

---

1. Bradypnea is an "abnormal slowness of breathing." Dorland's Illustrated Medical Dictionary 230 (27th ed. 1988). In an infant who has established and sustained spontaneous breathing, apnea describes the cessation of respiration for more than 60 seconds.

apnea, not anencephaly, that is the emergency medical condition that brings Baby K to the Hospital for treatment. Uniform treatment of emergency medical conditions would require the Hospital to provide Baby K with the same treatment that the Hospital provides all other patients experiencing bradypnea or apnea. The Hospital does not allege that it would refuse to provide respiratory support to infants experiencing bradypnea or apnea who do not have anencephaly. Indeed, a refusal to provide such treatment would likely be considered as providing *no* emergency medical treatment.

B.

The second argument of the Hospital is that, in redressing the problem of disparate emergency medical treatment, Congress did not intend to require physicians to provide medical treatment outside the prevailing standard of medical care. The Hospital asserts that, because of their extremely limited life expectancy and because any treatment of their condition is futile, the prevailing standard of medical care for infants with anencephaly is to provide only warmth, nutrition, and hydration. Thus, it maintains that a requirement to provide respiratory assistance would exceed the prevailing standard of medical care. However, the plain language of EMTALA requires stabilizing treatment for any individual who comes to a participating hospital, is diagnosed as having an emergency medical condition, and cannot be transferred. The Hospital has been unable to identify, nor has our research revealed, any statutory language or legislative history evincing a Congressional intent to create an exception to the duty to provide stabilizing treatment when the required treatment would exceed the prevailing standard of medical care. We recognize the dilemma facing physicians who are requested to provide treatment they consider morally and ethically inappropriate, but we cannot ignore the plain language of the statute. The appropriate branch to redress the policy concerns of the Hospital is Congress.

C.

The Hospital further argues that EMTALA cannot be construed to require it to provide respiratory support to anencephalics when its physicians deem such care inappropriate, because Virginia law permits physicians to refuse to provide such care. Section 54.1–2990 of the Health Care Decisions Act (HCDA) of Virginia provides that "[n]othing in this article shall be construed to require a physician to prescribe or render medical treatment to a patient that the physician determines to be medically or ethically inappropriate." Va. Code Ann. § 54.1–2990 (Michie Supp. 1993). The Hospital maintains that EMTALA only obligates a hospital to provide stabilizing treatment "within the staff and facilities available at the hospital," 42 U.S.C.A. § 1395dd(b)(1)(A). It reasons that because its physicians object to providing respiratory support to anencephalics, it has no physicians available to provide respiratory treatment for Baby K and, therefore, is not required by EMTALA to provide such treatment. We disagree.

The duty to provide stabilizing treatment set forth in EMTALA applies not only to participating hospitals but also to treating physicians in participating hospitals. 42 U.S.C.A. § 1395dd(d)(1)(B). EMTALA does not provide an exception for stabilizing treatment physicians may deem medically or ethically inappropriate. Consequently, to the extent § 54.1–2990 exempts physicians from providing care they consider medically or ethically inappropriate, it directly conflicts with the provisions of EMTALA that require stabilizing treatment to be provided.

It is well settled that state action must give way to federal legislation where a valid "act of Congress, fairly interpreted, is in actual conflict with the law of the state," Savage v. Jones, 225 U.S. 501, 533 (1912), and EMTALA provides that state and local laws that directly conflict with the requirements of EMTALA are preempted. 42 U.S.C.A. § 1395dd(f).

D.

The final contention advanced by the Hospital is that EMTALA only applies to patients who are transferred from a hospital in an unstable condition. As previously stated, § 1395dd(b) requires a hospital to provide stabilizing treatment to any individual who comes to a participating hospital, is diagnosed as presenting an emergency medical condition, and cannot be transferred in accordance with the provisions of subsection (c). The use of the word "transfer" to describe the duty of a hospital to provide stabilizing treatment evinces a Congressional intent to require stabilization prior to discharge or that treatment necessary to prevent material deterioration of the patient's condition during transfer. It was not intended to allow hospitals and physicians to avoid liability under EMTALA by accepting and screening a patient and then refusing to treat the patient because the patient cannot or will not be transferred.

IV.

It is beyond the limits of our judicial function to address the moral or ethical propriety of providing emergency stabilizing medical treatment to anencephalic infants. We are bound to interpret federal statutes in accordance with their plain language and any expressed congressional intent. Congress rejected a case-by-case approach to determining what emergency medical treatment hospitals and physicians must provide and to whom they must provide it; instead, it required hospitals and physicians to provide stabilizing care to any individual presenting an emergency medical condition. EMTALA does not carve out an exception for anencephalic infants in respiratory distress any more than it carves out an exception for comatose patients, those with lung cancer, or those with muscular dystrophy—all of whom may repeatedly seek emergency stabilizing treatment for respiratory distress and also possess an underlying medical condition that severely affects their quality of life and ultimately may result in their death. Because EMTALA does not provide for such an exception, the judgment of the district court is affirmed.

■ SPROUSE, SENIOR CIRCUIT JUDGE, dissenting:

I have no quarrel with the majority's conclusion that the duty imposed on hospitals by EMTALA to provide stabilizing treatment for an emergency condition is different from its duty to provide "appropriate medical screening." There is no question that once a medical condition is characterized as an "emergency medical condition" contemplated by EMTALA, the patient must be stabilized to prevent material deterioration of the condition.

I simply do not believe, however, that Congress, in enacting EMTALA, meant for the judiciary to superintend the sensitive decision-making process between family and physicians at the bedside of a helpless and terminally ill patient under the circumstances of this case. Tragic end-of-life hospital dramas such as this one do not represent phenomena susceptible of uniform legal control. In my view, Congress, even in its weakest moments, would not have attempted to impose federal control in this sensitive, private area. Rather, the statute was designed narrowly to correct a specific abuse: hospital "dumping" of indigent or uninsured emergency patients. There is no indication in the legislative history of EMTALA that Congress meant to extend the statute's reach to hospital-patient relationships that do not involve "dumping." In light of the purposes of the statute and this child's unique circumstances, I would find this case to be outside the scope of EMTALA's anti-dumping provisions.

I also submit that EMTALA's language concerning the type and extent of emergency treatment to be extended to all patients was not intended to cover the continued emergencies that typically attend patients like Baby K. The law was crafted to effect the purpose of preventing disparate treatment between emergency patients. In my view, Baby K is not that kind of emergency patient contemplated by the statute, although by the very nature of her terminal illness, she will suffer repeated medical emergencies during her day-to-day maintenance care. The hospital argues that anencephaly, not the subsidiary respiratory failure, is the condition that should be reviewed in order to judge the applicability *vel non* of EMTALA. I agree. I would consider anencephaly as the relevant condition and the respiratory difficulty as one of many subsidiary conditions found in a patient with the disease.

The tragic phenomenon Baby K represents exemplifies the need to take a case-by-case approach to determine if an emergency episode is governed by EMTALA. Baby K's condition presents her parents and doctors with decision-making choices that are different even from the difficult choices presented by other terminal diseases. Specifically, as an anencephalic infant, Baby K is permanently unconscious. She cannot hear, cannot see, and has no cognitive abilities. She has no awareness of and cannot interact with her environment in any way. Since there is no medical treatment that can improve her condition, she will be in this state for as long as she lives. Given this unique medical condition, whatever treatment appropriate for her unspeakably tragic illness should be regarded as a continuum, not as a series of discrete emergency medical conditions to be considered in isolation. Humanitarian concerns dictate appropriate care.

However, if resort must be had to our courts to test the appropriateness of the care, the legal vehicle should be state malpractice law.

Notes

1. *Reaction to* Baby K. The Court of Appeals' EMTALA decision, as well as the lower court's ruling that withholding emergency medical treatment for apnea from an infant with anencephaly would violate federal disability law, provoked substantial commentary. *See, e.g.*, Scott B. Smith, *The Critical Condition of the Emergency Medical Treatment and Active Labor Act: A Proposed Amendment to the Act After In the Matter of Baby K*, 48 VAND. L. REV. 1491 (1995); Giles R. Scofield, *Medical Futility Judgments: Discriminating or Discriminatory?*, 25 SETON HALL L. REV. 927 (1995). For a description of one state's effort to provide a process for resolving disputes about futility between professionals and families see Robert D. Truog, *Tracking Medical Futility in Texas*, 357 N. ENG. J. MED. 1 (2007).

2. *The professional standard of care versus EMTALA stabilization duties.* In Part Three you will read about the professional standard of care and its relationship to medical liability. Note the court's refusal to rely on the professional standard of care for the management of futile cases in the context of an EMTALA stabilization claim. Essentially the court concludes that what otherwise might be an appropriate standard of care in a non-emergency setting does not alter the duty of the hospital emergency department staff to stabilize the patient, which in this particularly tragic example, means helping the infant resume her breathing function, no matter how futile her long-term prognosis is. Does it make sense to you that EMTALA should be read to require hospitals to furnish even futile treatments in order to achieve what might at best be temporary stabilization of hopeless cases? In your view, what policy arguments might best justify such an approach?

---

6. THE DUTY TO STABILIZE AND FURNISH A MEDICALLY APPROPRIATE TRANSFER

Cherukuri v. Shalala

175 F.3d 446 (6th Cir. 1999)

■ MERRITT, CIRCUIT JUDGE:

This appeal by Dr. Cherukuri, a surgeon, arises from the decision of the Secretary of Health and Human Services that the transfer of two patients violates EMTALA.

In this case, five auto accident patients, two with severe head injuries and internal abdominal injuries and bleeding, who were later transferred to another hospital, were brought by ambulance in the early morning hours to the emergency room of a small rural hospital in south Williamson, Kentucky, in the Appalachian Mountains on the border between Kentucky and

West Virginia, 85 miles South of Huntington, West Virginia. The Williamson Hospital had no trauma center, had no equipment for monitoring the effect of anesthesia on the brain during surgery, and had a longstanding policy of not performing neurosurgery on injuries to the brain. Rather, as on the evening of the events in question, it always transferred such patients to other larger hospitals, often to St. Mary's Hospital in Huntington, a teaching hospital with a trauma center and the medical expertise and equipment to perform brain surgery.

There is no question of improper motive, "patient dumping" based on uninsured status, or other discriminatory treatment by Dr. Cherukuri in this case. It is also undisputed that the condition of the two patients did not in fact deteriorate during transfer to St. Mary's in Huntington.

The issue before us is more technical in nature. The question is whether Dr. Cherukuri, the emergency room surgeon on call that night at Williamson Hospital, should be found guilty of violating the "stabilization" language of § (b) of EMTALA because he transferred the two patients with head injuries to the trauma center at St. Mary's Hospital in Huntington (1) before operating on their stomach injuries to stop internal bleeding and (2) before receiving express consent to transfer from the physicians at the Huntington hospital. The Inspector General commenced an enforcement action to suspend the surgeon's license and assess the maximum "civil penalty" of $100,000. An administrative law judge employed by the Secretary wrote a 35,000–word opinion finding the surgeon guilty and imposing a fine of $100,000. The "Departmental Appeals Board" in the Office of the Secretary declined to review or comment on the decision and made it final and binding, subject to review in the Court of Appeals.

The ALJ concluded that the surgeon failed to "stabilize" the two patients before transfer in violation of the statute. She held in cases where there is internal bleeding that "stabilization" necessarily requires an abdominal operation by the surgeon on the two patients before transfer. This legal conclusion was based in turn on a finding of fact that an anesthesiologist willing to "put the patients to sleep" was available so that surgery could proceed. After oral argument, a careful reading of the transcribed testimony of each witness and a review of the extensive record, we decline to enforce the order. We set the administrative decision aside and dismiss the charges. We conclude that Dr. Cherukuri sufficiently "stabilized" the two patients to permit transfer and, alternatively, that he did not have anesthesiology available so that he could operate.

I. The Statute

Sections (b), (c), (d) and (e), the critical sections in this case, regulate treatment and restrict transfer of emergency patients. Subsection (b) provides:

(b) ... the hospital must provide either—

(A) within the staff and facilities available at the hospital, for such further medical examination and such treatment as may be required *to stabilize* the medical condition, or

(B) for *transfer* of the individual to another medical facility in accordance with subsection (c) of this section.

Id. § 1395dd(b) (emphases added). Under subsection (c), a patient who "has *not* been stabilized" may be transferred (1) only upon "a certification that based upon the information available at the time of transfer, the medical benefits reasonably expected from the provision of appropriate medical treatment at another medical facility outweigh the increased risk to the individual . . . from effecting the transfer" and (2) only if "the receiving facility . . . has agreed to accept transfer of the individual and to provide appropriate medical treatment. . . ." *Id.* § 1395dd(c) (emphasis added). Only *unstable* patients require a certification and consent of the receiving hospital. A patient who has been "stabilized" in the emergency room of the transferring hospital may be transferred to a receiving hospital without a certification, as described above, and without obtaining the express agreement of the receiving hospital. "Stabilized" patients may be transferred without limitation under the language of the statute.

In subsection (e), EMTALA's definition subsection, the word "stabilized" is defined, but the definition is not given a fixed or intrinsic meaning. Its meaning is purely contextual or situational. The definition depends on the risks associated with the transfer and requires the transferring physician, faced with an emergency, to make a fast on-the-spot risk analysis. The definition says that "stabilized" means "that no material deterioration of the condition is likely, within reasonable medical probability, to result from or occur during the transfer of the individual." *Id.* § 1395dd(d). The bottom line is that under the language of subsections (b) and (c), including the definition of "stabilized" in subsection (e), a physician may transfer any emergency room patient to another hospital without any certifications and without the express consent of the receiving hospital if he reasonably believes that the transfer is not likely to cause a "material deterioration of the patient's condition." *Id.* Obviously a surgeon in Dr. Cherukuri's position must weigh what he can do for the patient at his hospital versus the services available at the receiving hospital, as well as the present condition of the patient and the risk that he will get worse during the transfer.

Section (d) defines the burden of proof for the government when prosecuting a physician in a civil penalty enforcement action. Subsection (d)(1)(B) provides for a "civil money penalty" against "any physician who is responsible for the . . . transfer of an individual . . . and who negligently violates a requirement of this section, including a physician who . . . signs a certification . . . that the medical benefits reasonably to be expected from a transfer to another facility outweigh the risks associated with the transfer, *if the physician knew or should have known that the benefits did not outweigh the risks.*" *Id.* § 1395dd(d)(1)(B) (emphasis added). In order to prove a transfer violation under sections (b), (c) and (e), the government must show in a civil penalty case not only that the transferred patient was not "stabilized" and not accepted by the receiving hospital. It must show that the doctor was "negligent" in transferring the patient in the sense that, under the circumstances, "the physician knew or should have known that the benefits [of transfer] did not outweigh the risks."

II.   The Emergency Room Situation, the Transfer, and the Application of the Law to the Facts

At about 3:30 on Sunday morning, September 15, 1991, five injured auto accident victims were brought to the Williamson Hospital. Dr. Hani, the emergency room doctor, and registered nurse Judy Hatfield were then on duty in the emergency room. They immediately called Dr. Cherukuri, the general surgeon on-call that night, a man in his mid–50s with many years experience and with a good reputation in his profession prior to this prosecution. Dr. Cherukuri and nurses White and Hatfield were at the hospital for the next six hours dealing with the five patients. The two nurses both testified that the small emergency room was "almost over-whelmed" by the situation. Two of the accident victims, Crum and Mills, were critically injured, another very seriously injured and two more were hurt in the accident and needed treatment.

As soon as Dr. Cherukuri arrived, he spent about 30 minutes diagnos-ing the injuries. He found Crum to be nonresponsive with massive cranial injuries, very low blood pressure and fixed dilated pupils indicating that the brain may be near death. He made a small incision in Crum's stomach and found internal bleeding. He tentatively concluded that Crum might not survive but would need immediate blood and other liquid transfusions to stabilize his blood pressure. He set that treatment in motion. He also concluded at that time he would have to operate on Crum's abdomen to find and stop the bleeding before transferring him to Huntington for brain surgery.

He found Mills to be responsive but unconscious with a serious head injury and low blood pressure. A similar stomach incision showed internal bleeding. After taking similar steps to administer blood and liquids, he examined the other three patients. He tried unsuccessfully to find another surgeon to come in to help with the five patients.

After four hours of treatment, Crum and Mills, the two patients with cranial injuries, were transferred by ambulance to Huntington. Time was lost trying without success to get a helicopter in to transfer the two patients to Huntington. Due to heavy fog in the river valley where the Williamson Hospital is located, the helicopter pilots finally advised that they were afraid to land in this mountainous country. Transfer was also delayed because of difficulties in finding an anesthesiologist.

A.   Anesthesiology

It is undisputed that Dr. Cherukuri determined by 4:00 A.M. that it would be best to operate on both Crum and Mills to stop the internal bleeding so that he could raise their blood pressure to assure a sufficient blood supply to the brain and other organs. But he was unable to do so for the next three hours because Dr. Thambi, the anesthesiologist on call, advised strongly against operating and did not come to the hospital. He testified that he advised Dr. Cherukuri and Nurse White that the patients should be immediately transferred to St. Mary's Hospital in Huntington. He testified that he advised repeatedly and adamantly that administering anesthesia for the abdominal surgery was too risky because they had no equipment to monitor its effect on the pressure in the brain. Dr. Thambi himself testified that he would only have provided anesthesia "under protest" if ordered to do so.

Dr. Cherukuri and Pat White testified that over the next two hours each requested Dr. Thambi by phone several times to come to the hospital but he maintained that anesthesia was out of the question and did not come. They tried to locate other anesthesiologists during this period but were unsuccessful. Finally, when Dr. Thambi came two and a half hours later, he testified that he told the parents of the patients that they must be transferred to Huntington for surgery because it could not be performed at Williamson. He continued to advise the staff that anesthesiology on the brain injured patients was out of the question. All witnesses who heard and observed Dr. Thambi so testified. No one testified to the contrary.

While recognizing that Dr. Thambi had made his position very clear that he did not intend to provide anesthesiology because it might kill the brain injured patients, the ALJ concluded that EMTALA required the surgeon to force Dr. Thambi to perform by expressly ordering him to administer anesthesia. The ALJ states repeatedly throughout her long opinion that the law "necessarily required" Dr. Cherukuri to stop the bleeding for the patients to be considered "stabilized" under the statute and that this required Dr. Cherukuri to force Dr. Thambi against his will to administer anesthesia. Nothing in EMTALA demands such a confrontation, and for good reasons.

Special care must be exercised in sedating parties who have sustained head injuries, as the level of consciousness is an important diagnostic and prognostic sign. It is difficult to distinguish between a desirable drug effect and the progression of intracranial pathology. Even mild drug-induced respiratory depression with its associated hypercania can result in significant elevations of the intracranial pressure. Lewis A Coveler, *Anesthesia*, in TRAUMA 219 (Ernest E Moore et al., eds., 2d ed. 1991). We thus regard the ALJ's conclusions as erroneous. Dr. Thambi testified that he probably would have administered anesthesia, if ordered, but strongly opposed it, delayed coming to the hospital for 2–1/2 hours so that the patients could be transferred and personally advised the parents not to allow surgery at Williamson but to transfer to Huntington.

B.   "Stabilization"

All witnesses in the case, as well as the ALJ, agreed that by the time the two patients were transferred by ambulance four hours after they arrived, the emergency room staff had normalized their blood pressure so that a sufficient blood supply was flowing to the organs of the body. But two witnesses, an emergency room doctor (Dr. Harrigan) and a general surgeon (Dr. Browning) testified for the government as experts that "stabilization" for transfer to another hospital could not occur, as a matter of definition, unless abdominal surgery was performed to stop the internal bleeding. They testified that the word "stabilize" in the statute has an intrinsic, *a priori* meaning requiring that patients not be transferred while internal bleeding remains. The ALJ accepted their testimony and adopted the inflexible meaning they gave to the word "stabilize" in the statute.

The two government experts, and the ALJ, viewed transfer with internal bleeding as improper because it was possible that the patients could start hemorrhaging during the 1-1/2 hour ambulance trip to Huntington. Even though attendants giving blood transfusions accompanied the patients, the two government witnesses believed that the risk of "deterioration" during travel was too great. All witnesses, as well as the ALJ, agreed that in this case the two patients in fact arrived at the Huntington Hospital without further injury or deterioration, that their blood pressure and breathing remained stable and did not deteriorate, and that the travel did not further exacerbate the patients' conditions. Although Crum died later of his injuries, the evidence was that there was nothing Dr. Cherukuri, or the staff in Huntington, could have done to save him. Mills survived, recovered from his injuries and was released.

Eight expert witnesses, including Dr. Cherukuri, testified either expressly, or in effect, that "stabilize" must be given a more flexible meaning and that the on-the-spot risk analysis of Dr. Cherukuri leading to transfer was appropriate under the circumstances. Among the witnesses, who so testified in addition to Dr. Cherukuri, were Dr. Sircus Arya, the receiving surgeon at Huntington who operated on Mills and Crum when they arrived; Dr. Thambi, the anesthesiologist, who testified that from the beginning he believed that Dr. Cherukuri had no choice but to transfer; and Dr. Hossein Sakhai, a Huntington-based, Vanderbilt-trained neurosurgeon with 31 years experience, who testified that he had carefully reviewed the hospital records at Williamson and Huntington and that the transfer "should have been done" when it was done and that there was "good cause and good reason" to transfer without an abdominal operation. After going over the blood pressures of the patients in detail, he testified repeatedly on direct and cross-examination that he could find no fault with the way Dr. Cherukuri handled the problem.

In addition, Dr. William Aaron, a board certified "quality assurance" and peer review physician, Dr. Paul Fowler, specializing in legal medicine, R.N. Judy Hatfield, the emergency room nurse at Williamson, and Pat White, the nurse who attended Dr. Cherukuri, also testified as experts that the two patients were sufficiently stabilized to transfer and, like Drs. Arya, Sakhai, and Thambi, testified that Dr. Cherukuri had no other viable choice under the circumstances but to transfer.

The ALJ treatment of the testimony of Drs. Sakhai, Aaron and Fowler is clearly erroneous and must be rejected. She rules out their testimony as irrelevant because "they did not have the opportunity to observe the patients' condition," deriving "their opinions solely from a review of the medical records." JA 24–25. Yet the ALJ appears to accept fully the testimony of government witnesses Harrigan and Browning—who also "did not have the opportunity to observe the patient's condition"—that the patients remained "unstable" so long as no abdominal operation was performed. No explanation is given for the inconsistent treatment of the two government experts and the three defense experts.

Nor does the ALJ give any credence to any of the five experts on the scene who observed the patients—Drs. Cherukuri, Thambi, Arya and Nurses White and Hatfield—and who all testified, either expressly or in effect, that after blood pressure was restored the patients were sufficiently stable and that transfer was the only reasonable choice.

We agree with the eight witnesses—Drs. Cherukuri, Thambi, Arya, Sakhai, Aaron, Fowler, and Nurses White and Hatfield. The statutory definition of "stabilize" requires a flexible standard of reasonableness that depends on the circumstances. The two government witnesses and the ALJ erred in giving the concept a fixed meaning which necessarily, and in all events, requires an abdominal operation before transfer. Nothing in the statute so requires, and the rigidity of the representatives of the Office of the Secretary on this subject is misplaced.

In our view Dr. Cherukuri acted properly under very trying and difficult circumstances and should be exonerated of any wrongdoing. Certainly any possible fault does not rise to the level prescribed by § (d) of EMTALA, which states that a civil penalty can only be imposed on a doctor who "knew or should have known that the benefits [of transfer] did not outweigh the risks." 42 U.S.C. § 1395dd(d).

C. The Transfer

At about 4:00 A.M., after Dr. Thambi advised Dr. Cherukuri that anesthesia should not be given to Crum and Mills, Dr. Cherukuri talked to the chief surgeon at Huntington, Dr. Arya, briefly describing the situation and his problem in finding an anesthesiologist. Dr. Arya advised him to try to find an anesthesiologist somehow and to perform an abdominal operation on each to stop the bleeding. Dr. Arya testified that he was irate when he learned later that morning that the patients were on their way by ambulance. He called Williamson and told Nurse White to recall the patients and perform the abdominal operations. He testified he was angry, suspected patient dumping and reported the incident as an improper transfer. The Administrator at the hospital in Huntington, Dr. Arya, and others who initially heard about what had happened thought that Dr. Cherukuri had violated EMTALA by transferring unstable patients without consent of the receiving hospital. On the basis of these initial complaints, the government undertook the investigation that led to this prosecution.

The Huntington Administrator and Dr. Arya both changed their minds completely once they learned the circumstances facing Dr. Cherukuri. They both had the courage to admit their error in sworn testimony and testified that their initial view was mistaken. Dr. Arya was a government witness, and the government does not seek to attack his credibility or expertise. The government argues, and the ALJ found, that Dr. Cherukuri lied when he told Nurse White that he had received permission from Dr. Arya to transfer the patients to St. John's in Huntington. Although it is true that Dr. Cherukuri did not have express permission to transfer, the record does not quite bear out a conclusion that he acted in bad faith and intentionally misrepresented the situation. In answer to a question by government counsel on direct examination, "after having this conversation [about 4:00 A.M. with Dr. Cherukuri] what was your expectation of what should occur before transfer," Dr. Arya gave this answer:

> Difficult for me to say what was going on in the other side. I thought that he would probably find a way to take care of the patient [by operating]. At the same time it is conceivable he was so desperate to do something, he sent the patient over. That is quite conceivable to me.

This answer states, contrary to the finding of the ALJ, that Dr. Arya's "expectation" was that "it is quite conceivable to me" that Dr. Cherukuri might be so "desperate" as to send "the patient over." This testimony from the government's own witness does not support the finding that Dr. Cherukuri lied.

The ALJ does not mention this exculpatory testimony in her long opinion repeatedly condemning Dr. Cherukuri, nor does she mention that Dr. Arya said he believes that Dr. Cherukuri saved Mills' life by keeping him alive and transferring him under extremely difficult circumstances.

Therefore, we conclude that the ALJ did not apply the proper meaning of "stabilization" and hence the proper standard for transfer and seriously erred in concluding that anesthesiology was available. It is unfortunate that the errors we have uncovered were not caught earlier in the administrative process. When the administrative "Review Board" established to administer EMTALA cases chooses without explanation to make an ALJ decision in an important case binding without review, the burden on the Court of Appeals to comb the record is substantially increased. We respectfully suggest that the Board should review cases like this one closely and should not simply pass them on to a federal appellate court without providing a reasoned disposition of the objections raised by the parties. Our own close review of the record clearly shows that the decision is not supported by substantial evidence on the record as a whole, does not justify the legal conclusion made by the ALJ that Dr. Cherukuri "knew or should have known that the benefits [of transfer] did not outweigh the risks" (§ 1395dd(d)(1)(B)), and accordingly must be set aside.

Note

The agency versus the court. The differences between the ALJ and the court are striking, as is the court's harsh scolding of the agency for its handling of the case. The ALJ found on the facts that the transfer was medically inappropriate because internal bleeding is conclusive evidence of instability and further found that Dr. Cherukuri lied about the status of the patients. The court rejected so simplistic an approach to the question of what constitutes "stabilization," given the fact-driven nature of the definition itself. It also found baseless the government's assertion that the trial testimony showed that Dr. Cherukuri had intentionally tried to send unstable patients to Huntington.

What seems to have moved the court beyond the facts is its view regarding the need for flexibility, particularly in desperate and complex injury cases such as this one. The incident that gave rise to the prosecution occurred in south Williamson, Kentucky, an unincorporated small coal-mining town near the Kentucky–Virginia border. This case also illustrates the tension around the proper role in the health care system for small rural hospitals. On one hand these hospitals may provide access for minor incidents while helping anchor medical practices within a community. On the other, in responding to major accidents such as this one they are incapable of providing even initial stabilization, much less full treatment. When trauma care is concerned, experts recommend that a superior strategy is a regional approach that relies on sophisticated ground and air transport directly to a highly advanced trauma center rather than one in which patients first languish at small facilities incapable of furnishing extreme lifesaving care. In this case the government seems to have been intent on throwing the book at the hospital for even attempting to deal with this type of case at all, while the court seems to have taken a far more charitable view based on the facts in the record.

7. THE DUTIES OF TRANSFEREE HOSPITALS

EMTALA provides, 42 U.S.C. § 1395dd(g), that:

> (g) Nondiscrimination. A participating hospital that has specialized capabilities or facilities (such as burn units, shock-trauma units, neonatal intensive care units, or (with respect to rural areas) regional referral centers as identified by the Secretary in regulation) shall not refuse to accept an appropriate transfer of an individual who requires such specialized capabilities or facilities if the hospital has the capacity to treat the individual.

In St. Anthony Hosp. v. U.S. Department of Health & Human Servs., 309 F.3d 680 (10th Cir. 2002), the Tenth Circuit affirmed an ALJ decision finding a hospital liable for refusing to accept transfer of an unstable patient. The emergency room physician of a small hospital attempted to transfer an unstable patient to St. Anthony, "a large modern hospital in Oklahoma City with state of the art surgical facilities." St. Anthony's on-call thoracic and vascular surgeon declined the transfer, saying he was not interested in taking the case and that it was another hospital's problem. St. Anthony had the equipment on hand to do the necessary surgery, available specialists on-call, and available space to perform the procedure. The court upheld the imposition of a civil monetary penalty, finding that the hospital violated the EMTALA reverse-dumping provisions in refusing to accept the transfer. Federal law has always required hospitals to maintain on-call specialists as part of Medicare's conditions of participation. § 1866(a)(1)(I)(iii) of the Social Security Act. However, *St. Anthony* was the first decision in which a hospital's medical specialists were treated as a "specialized capability" of a hospital. Robert Wanerman, *The EMTALA Paradox*, 40 ANN. OF EMERG. MED. 464 (2002).

---

8.   ON-CALL SPECIALISTS

The EMTALA statute, 42 U.S.C. § 1395dd(d)(1)(C), provides:

(C) If, after an initial examination, a physician determines that the individual requires the services of a physician listed by the hospital on its list of on-call physicians (required to be maintained under section 1866(a)(1)(I)) and notifies the on-call physician and the on-call physician fails or refuses to appear within a reasonable period of time, and the physician orders the transfer of the individual because the physician determines that without the services of the on-call physician the benefits of transfer outweigh the risks of transfer, the physician authorizing the transfer shall not be subject to a penalty under subparagraph (B). However, the previous sentence shall not apply to the hospital or to the on-call physician who failed or refused to appear.

Federal law has always required hospitals to maintain on-call specialists as part of Medicare's conditions of participation. § 1866(a)(1)(I)(iii) of the Social Security Act. EMTALA requires that hospitals "maintain a list of physicians who are on call for duty after the initial examination to provide treatment necessary to stabilize an individual with an emergency medical condition." 42 U.S.C. § 1395cc(a)(1)(I)(iii). If a physician on the list is called by a hospital to provide emergency screening or treatment and either fails to appear or refuses to appear within a reasonable period of time, the hospital may be in violation of EMTALA. *Id.* § 1395dd(d)(1)(C). *St. Anthony* was the first decision in which a hospital's medical specialists were treated as a "specialized capability" of a hospital. Wanerman, *The EMTALA Paradox* at 467.

In addition, physicians are directly liable if they are on call and do not respond. In Burditt v. United States Department of Health and Human Services, 934 F.2d 1362 (5th Cir. 1991), an on-call physician was found liable when he refused to come in and treat an unstable pregnant woman because he "didn't want to." The physician did not want to treat the woman because she was uninsured and had received no prenatal care. In this case, the physician was fined $20,000.

In a 2001 report on EMTALA enforcement, the U.S. Government Accountability Office (GAO) found hospitals to be greatly concerned about federal enforcement of the on-call specialist requirements because administrators lack leverage over their physicians. *Emergency Care: EMTALA Implementation and Enforcement Issues*, United States Government Accountability Office (GAO 02–28). Many U.S. hospitals confront a shortage of physicians, particularly specialists, willing to serve on-call. Physicians typically are not employees of hospitals, but rather are independent contractors. Private physicians contract with hospitals for staff privileges, including the right of physicians to admit their private patients and use the hospital's facilities. On-call physicians are generally not paid by hospitals, but serve on-call as a condition of receiving staff privileges. Erin M. McHugh, *The New EMTALA Regulations and the On–Call Physician Shortage: In Defense of the Regulations*, 37 J. HEALTH L. 61 (2004). Traditionally, the obligation to serve on-call provided doctors the opportunity to meet new patients and build a practice. With the growth of managed care, however, physicians can no longer use the emergency room to recruit patients to a fee-for-service practice. The practices among managed care organizations (MCOs) vary, but most do not pay non-participating on-call doctors for emergency care, or pay doctors for being on-call.

The shortage of on-call specialists is also worsened by the emergence of specialty care centers, including specialty hospitals, ambulatory surgical centers, imaging and diagnostic centers, and other "niche providers." MaryAnn Lando, *The Specialty Care Debate: Is There an Answer?*, 18 HEALTHCARE EXECUTIVE 1 (Jan. 1, 2003), available at 2003 WL 10898939. These specialty care centers do not operate emergency departments and, therefore, are not subject to EMTALA.

Some hospitals provide stipends for on-call physicians. *See On–Call Coverage: Hospitals Offer Carrots and Sticks to Specialists Reluctant to Answer ER's Call*, 8 HEALTH L. REPORTER (BNA) 1823 (1999). Some states require MCOs to pay for emergency care services performed by non-network physicians, regardless of whether the physician has a relationship with the MCO. Many states set maximum response times for on-call physicians. *See* Loren A. Johnson et al., *The Emergency Department On–Call Backup Crisis: Finding Remedies for a Serious Public Health Problem*, 37 ANN. EMER. MED. 495, 497 (2001).

EMTALA does not impose a direct obligation on physicians to undertake on-call duty. Physicians' EMTALA obligations arise only after they have agreed to serve on call and fail to respond to calls in an adequate manner. EMTALA thus imposes an obligation on hospitals to provide emergency care but does not impose a corresponding obligation on physicians to serve on call. "Thus, the duty to maintain on-call backup has been described as a legal responsibility for hospitals and, at best, a shared ethical responsibility for the medical staff, where individual physician participation can be assured only through clearly defined medical staff bylaws and hospital policies." Johnson, *The Emergency Department On–Call Backup Crisis* at 496.

In 2003, CMS issued regulations providing that a hospital's on-call list must be maintained in a manner that "best meets the needs of the hospital's patients who are receiving services required under EMTALA in accordance with the capability of the hospital, including the availability of on-call physicians." *See* Medicare Program; Clarifying Policies Related to Responsibilities of Medicare–Participating Hospitals in Treating Individuals with Emergency Medical Conditions, 68 Fed. Reg. 53,222, 53,252 (Sept. 9, 2003).

The revised standard requires hospitals simply to maintain

An on-call list of physicians who are on the hospital's medical staff, or who have privileges at the hospital, or who are on staff or have privileges at another hospital participating in a formal community call plan . . . available to provide treatment necessary after the initial examination to stabilize individuals with emergency medical conditions . . .

42 C.F.R. § 489.20(r)(2).

In its Preamble to the final rule, HHS explained that the rule changes are intended to give hospitals flexibility.

CMS allows hospitals flexibility to comply with EMTALA obligations by maintaining a level of on-call coverage that is within their capability. We understand that some hospitals exempt senior medical staff physicians from being on call. This exemption is typically written into the hospital's medical staff bylaws or the hospital's rules and regulations, and recognizes a physician's active years of service (for example, 20 or more years) or age (for example, 60 years of age or older), or a combination of both. We wish to clarify that providing such exemptions to members of hospitals' medical staff does not necessarily violate EMTALA. On the contrary, we believe that a hospital is responsible for maintaining an on-call list in a manner that best meets the needs of its patients as long as the exemption does not affect patient care adversely. Thus, CMS allows hospitals flexibility in the utilization of their emergency personnel. We also note that there is no predetermined "ratio" that CMS uses to identify how many days a hospital must provide medical staff on-call coverage based on the number of physicians on staff for that particular specialty.

68 Fed. Reg. 53,222, 53,250 (Sept. 9, 2003).

Consider Dabney v. H.C.A. Fort Walton Beach Medical Center, 2007 WL 3072448 (N.D. Fla. 2007). The court presented the facts as follows:

On August 12, 2005, Plaintiff was transported by Emergency Medical Services to Defendant FWBMC after being found on the floor in his home. After examination and tests, it was determined Plaintiff required a neurosurgical consult. Defendant FWBMC had a neurosurgeon scheduled to be on call, but when called for the neurosurgical consult, the neurosurgeon advised he was unable to come in due to illness. Defendant FWBMC had no backup neurosurgeon to cover for the unavailable on-call neurosurgeon. When Defendant FWBMC attempted to obtain consent for an impromptu transfer to three nearby hospitals that had the capacity to stabilize Plaintiff's emergency medical condition, all refused to accept the transfer of the Plaintiff. Defendant FWBMC had no pre-arranged inter-hospital transfer agreement with any nearby hospital.

The court dismissed the complaint in a few sentences:

> The availability of an on-call physician may be taken into account in determining whether treatment is within a hospital's capacity.

> Here, it was not within Defendant FWBMC's capacity to stabilize the Plaintiff because the on-call neurosurgeon was unavailable due to illness. The statute does not require on a hospital to have a back-up plan when an on-call physician is unavailable. The Defendant FWBMC attempted to transfer Plaintiff to three nearby hospitals, but all refused. The statute does not require that a hospital have a procedure in place guaranteeing transfer of a patient. To be successful under EMTALA, Plaintiff must allege that Defendant FWBMC could have successfully transferred Plaintiff to a reasonably available hospital but did not to take that course of action. Plaintiff does not make such an allegation.

Should it be this easy to avoid EMTALA liability? The court did not even appear to consider the "best meets the need" standard of the 2003 regulation. Consider how regulations addressing hospital obligations might better be crafted to assure that EMTALA is effective in assuring that essential care is available, while at the same time recognizing the diverse practical constraints confronting a variety of hospitals? Why doesn't EMTALA require that doctors participating in Medicare be available to serve on-call? What would an amendment imposing such an obligation say?

9. HOW DOES THE EMTALA STABILIZATION DUTY APPLY TO INPATIENTS?

These issues arise in several contexts. First, what are the EMTALA obligations of hospitals to individuals who arrive at the hospital with a medical emergency and subsequently are admitted? Second, what are hospitals' EMTALA obligations to individuals who have been admitted for medically necessary—but not emergency—care (e.g., a scheduled Caesarean section delivery, scheduled surgery), and who subsequently develop an emergency while inpatients? Third, under either scenario (the emergency admission or the scheduled admission) what are the obligations of hospitals with specialized capabilities to accept inpatient transfers when an emergency has developed?

Whether patients first enter a hospital as an emergency admission or a scheduled admission, inpatients are patients of the hospital, and as you will learn in Part Three, the hospital and its staff owe their patients a duty of reasonable care. Thus, a hospital that fails to adequately stabilize a patient in distress and take reasonable steps to provide or arrange for medically necessary care (including a transfer if medically indicated to a more specialized facility) may be liable in negligence if its failure results in death or injury. However, EMTALA raises the ante, not only for the treating hospital, but also for the transferee facility.

Under EMTALA, hospitals with specialized capabilities must respond to transferring hospitals that are attempting to make an appropriate medical transfer. 42 U.S.C. § 1395dd(g). (Think of a routine delivery of a newborn that goes wrong in a community hospital with limited capabilities, thereby compelling the newborn's transfer to a hospital with specialized neonatal intensive care capabilities). In the absence of EMTALA protections, a hospital with specialized capabilities to which a transfer is sought simply can refuse to accept a medical transfer on the "no duty" principle. For this reason, EMTALA's application to inpatients is a matter of great medical importance.

The law appears to impose an unconditional stabilization duty that protects anyone who comes to a hospital and that extends to all of the "staff and facilities available at the hospital" without regard to whether those staff and facilities are located in an inpatient or outpatient setting. Furthermore, the stabilization duty continues until the patient is stabilized or transferred in accordance with legal standards that permit the transfer of certain unstable patients.

Nonetheless, several courts have determined that the stabilization obligation is legally linked to the screening obligation. Under this interpretation, a hospital's stabilization duties would apply only to patients screened in the emergency department, and furthermore, would apply only in the event of a transfer from the emergency department. Under this interpretation of the law, a hospital's EMTALA duties would end once a patient who arrives at the emergency department is admitted as an inpatient. Furthermore, EMTALA never would apply to individuals admitted as inpatients in the first place without admission through the emergency department. Other courts explicitly have rejected this interpretation, finding that the screening and stabilization duties are separate.

In the Supreme Court's only decision interpreting EMTALA, Roberts v. Galen of Virginia, 525 U.S. 249 (1999), the Court implicitly applied the stabilization requirement to inpatients, determining that plaintiffs in EMTALA stabilization cases need not prove financial motive. The case involved the transfer of a woman, admitted through the emergency room, after a long inpatient stay for serious injuries. The Court noted that, unlike the screening provision that requires an "appropriate medical screening," the stabilization provision requires "such further medical examination and such treatment as may be required to stabilize the medical condition." 42 U.S.C. § 1395dd(b). The Court said, it "does not require an 'appropriate' stabilization, nor can it reasonably be read to require an improper motive." On remand, a jury ultimately returned a verdict in favor of the hospital. *Federal Jury Exonerates Kentucky Hospital of EMTALA Violation in Patient Transfer Case*, BNA HEALTH CARE POLICY REPORT 339–40 (March 5, 2001).

In 2003, however, the Department of Health and Human Services adopted regulations, 42 C.F.R. § 489.24, providing that EMTALA's stabilization duties apply only to persons who are screened in the emergency department and only while they are in the emergency department. The text of the regulation reads as follows:

(d) Necessary stabilization treatment for emergency medical conditions.—

> (2) *Exception: Application to inpatients.* (i) If a hospital has screened an individual and found the individual to have an emergency medical condition and admits the individual as an inpatient in good faith in order to stabilize the emergency medical condition, the hospital has satisfied its [EMTALA] responsibilities. (ii) This section is not applicable to an inpatient who was admitted for elective (nonemergency) diagnosis or treatment.

42 C.F.R. § 489.24(d)(2)(i).

In creating this EMTALA "stopping point" at the moment of inpatient admission and in tying the stabilization obligation to the screening of persons who enter the hospital through the emergency department, the 2003 regulations thus impose a significant constraint on the reach of the law. The Preamble to the final rule noted that hospitals that provide substandard care to hospital inpatients, including premature discharge, face potential malpractice liability under state law.

The circuit courts have split over whether EMTALA's stabilization duty applies to inpatients, and the Supreme Court declined in 2008 and 2010 to hear cases raising the issue. *See* Morgan v. North Mississippi Medical Center, Inc., 552 U.S. 1098 (2008) (denying certiorari) (district court opinion discussed below); Providence Hospital v. Moses, 130 S. Ct. 3499 (2010) (denying certiorari) (discussed below). As summarized by federal district judge William H. Steele in *Morgan*, three distinct approaches had emerged in the circuit courts prior to the 2003 regulation:

> The Fourth Circuit has imputed a fuzzy, ill-defined temporal limitation on all § 1395dd(b) claims, such that the stabilization requirement is confined to "the hospital's care of the patient only in the immediate aftermath of the act of admitting her for emergency treatment and while it considered whether it would undertake longer-term full treatment or instead transfer the patient." Bryan v. Rectors and Visitors of University of Virginia, 95 F.3d 349, 352 (4th Cir. 1996) (holding that EMTALA was not violated where patient had been admitted to hospital for 12 days, during which time she received stabilizing treatment).
>
> On the other end of the spectrum, the Sixth Circuit has endorsed a position that EMTALA's stabilization requirements can apply well after the patient is admitted to a hospital. In Thornton v. Southwest Detroit Hosp., 895 F.2d 1131 (6th Cir. 1990), the panel interpreted § 1395dd(b) as meaning that "once a patient is found to suffer from an emergency medical condition in the emergency room, she cannot be discharged until the condition is stabilized, regardless of whether the patient stays in the emergen-

cy room." *Id.* at 1134. The *Thornton* court expressed concern that if the law were otherwise, hospitals might circumvent EMTALA by admitting emergency room patients then immediately discharging them.

If the Fourth Circuit's construction of the temporal limits of § 1395dd(b) is too draconian, and if the Sixth Circuit's is too permissive, then, much like Goldilocks in the famed fairy tale, the Ninth Circuit's approach may be just right. In Bryant v. Adventist Health System/West, 289 F.3d 1162 (9th Cir. 2002), the court weighed both the Fourth and Sixth Circuit alternatives before holding "that EMTALA's stabilization requirement ends when an individual is admitted for inpatient care." *Id.* at 1168. [T]he Ninth Circuit added an important caveat to its inpatient rule, stating that "[i]f a patient demonstrates in a particular case that inpatient admission was a ruse to avoid EMTALA's requirements, then liability under EMTALA may attach," notwithstanding such admission. *Id.* at 1169.

Morgan v. North Mississippi Medical Center, 403 F. Supp.2d 1115, 1128–29 (S.D. Ala. 2005). Judge Steele applied the Ninth Circuit's "subterfuge" or "good faith admission" standard to a hospital's motion to dismiss the complaint containing the following allegations:

[O]n August 22, 2003, decedent Morgan sustained serious injuries (including fractured ribs and vertebrae, a dislocated shoulder, and a pulmonary contusion) in a fall from a tree stand at a hunting camp near Calhoun City, Mississippi. Mr. Morgan, who did not have medical insurance, was rushed to NMMC's hospital in Tupelo, Mississippi where he received emergency trauma care and was admitted as a patient. Immediately following Morgan's arrival at the Hospital, Hospital personnel notified [Mrs. Morgan] that she would need to make financial arrangements right away for her husband's treatment. After several stalled attempts commencing within a day after his admission, the Hospital discharged Mr. Morgan on August 31, 2003 (nine days after he was admitted), without conducting an MRI scan of his badly injured back, and despite his serious ongoing medical difficulties. An ambulance owned and/or controlled by the Hospital transported Mr. Morgan to his home in Foley, Alabama, where ambulance attendants physically carried him inside the house to his bed on a stretcher. Approximately 12 hours later, Mr. Morgan died from untreated injuries relating to his fall on August 22.

Id. at 1117–18. Judge Steele dismissed the plaintiff's disparate screening claim regarding the hospital's failure to perform an MRI, but denied the hospital's motion to dismiss the stabilization claim on the grounds that the complaint's allegations stated a "colorable claim" that the patient's admission had been in bad faith or a subterfuge. However, the hospital ultimately prevailed on its summary judgment motion on the merits of the bad faith admission claim. Morgan v. North Mississippi Medical Center, Inc., 458 F.

Supp.2d 1341 (S.D. Ala. 2006), *aff'd*, 225 F. App'x. 828 (11th Cir. 2007). Judge Steele found that while the Hospital business office had inquired about payment and various discharge planning steps had taken place, all of these could be explained on legitimate grounds and the facts did not support a bad faith admission claim, particularly when the hospital had provided nine days of inpatient care. The fact that the treating doctor focused on one set of Mr. Morgan's symptoms and missed another set of (ultimately fatal) symptoms may have been negligence but did not violate EMTALA's duty to stabilize *perceived* emergency conditions.

Torretti v. Main Line Hospitals, Inc., 580 F.3d 168 (3d Cir. 2009), deferred to the 2003 regulation and held that EMTALA's stabilization obligations did not apply to a pregnant woman whose emergency arose after her inpatient admission and who did not initially present at a hospital emergency department. By contrast the Sixth Circuit remains firmly committed to its reading of the law, explicitly rejecting more restrictive interpretations including the 2003 regulation. Moses v. Providence Hospital, 561 F.3d 573 (6th Cir.), *reh. denied en banc,* 573 F.3d 397 (6th Cir. 2009), *cert. den.,* 130 S. Ct. 3499 (2010), set aside a summary judgment ruling for the defendant hospital in a case involving a murder of a woman following the discharge of her severely mentally ill husband, who had been hospitalized only days before with psychotic symptoms. The court rejected the hospital's defense that, as a matter of law, it could not be held liable under EMTALA because the husband had been admitted as an inpatient prior to his discharge. The hospital rested its defense on the 2003 regulation extinguishing EMTALA duties following inpatient admission. The Court was having none of it:

> Contrary to Defendants' interpretation, EMTALA imposes an obligation on a hospital beyond simply admitting a patient with an emergency medical condition to an inpatient care unit. The statute requires "such treatment as may be required to stabilize the medical condition," § 1395dd(b), and forbids the patient's release unless his condition has "been stabilized," § 1395dd(c)(1). A patient with an emergency medical condition is "stabilized" when "no material deterioration of the condition is likely, within reasonable medical probability, to result from or occur during" the patient's release from the hospital. § 1395dd(e)(3)(B). Thus, EMTALA requires a hospital to treat a patient with an emergency condition in such a way that, upon the patient's release, no further deterioration of the condition is likely. In the case of most emergency conditions, it is unreasonable to believe that such treatment could be provided by admitting the patient and then discharging him.

> "Congress sought to insure that patients with medical emergencies would receive emergency care. Although emergency care often occurs, and almost invariably begins, in an emergency room, emergency care does not always stop when a patient is wheeled from the emergency room into the main hospital. Hospitals may

not circumvent the requirements of the Act merely by admitting an emergency room patient to the hospital, then immediately discharging that patient. *Emergency care must be given until the patient's emergency medical condition is stabilized. Id.* at 1135 (emphasis added). Thus, the statute requires more than the admission and further testing of a patient; it requires that actual care, or treatment, be provided as well." [quoting *Thornton* above].

To support their narrower reading of EMTALA's requirements, Defendants point to a rule promulgated by the Centers for Medicare and Medicaid Services ("CMS"), the agency responsible for implementing EMTALA, that effectively ends a hospital's EMTALA obligations upon admitting an individual as an inpatient. 42 C.F.R. § 489.24(d)(2)(i).

Although "[a]n agency's construction of a statutory scheme that it is entrusted to administer is entitled to a degree of deference ... we must ... 'reject administrative constructions which are contrary to clear congressional intent.' " The CMS rule appears contrary to EMTALA's plain language, which requires a hospital to "provide ... for such further medical examination *and such treatment* as may be required to stabilize the medical condition[.]" § 1395dd(b)(1)(A) (emphasis added). Although "treatment" is undefined in the statute, it is nevertheless unambiguous, because it is unreasonable to believe that "treatment as may be required to stabilize" could mean simply admitting the patient and nothing further. Moreover, the statute requires the patient to be "stabilized" upon release; "[i]f an individual at a hospital has an emergency medical condition which has not been stabilized ... the hospital may not transfer the individual unless" the patient requests a transfer in writing or a physician or qualified medical person certifies that the risks of further treatment outweigh the benefits. § 1395dd(c)(1)(A). Therefore, a hospital may not release a patient with an emergency medical condition *without first determining that the patient has actually stabilized,* even if the hospital properly admitted the patient. Such a requirement would be unnecessary if a hospital only needed to admit the patient in order to satisfy EMTALA. Because the CMS rule is contrary to the plain language of the statute, this Court does not afford it *Chevron* deference. *See Gallagher,* 89 F.3d at 278.

In 2010, Providence Hospital asked the Supreme Court to review the Sixth Circuit's ruling. The Court asked the Solicitor General to advise whether certiorari should be granted. 130 S. Ct. 1318 (2010). The Solicitor General opined that the question whether EMTALA's screening obligations continue after a patient is admitted to the hospital is not unambiguously answered by the statute, and that the circuit courts are in conflict. Nonetheless, the SG urged that the Court deny review. According to the SG, the circuit conflict is "shallow" and "further percolation is warranted." In addition, the SG noted that HHS "is committed to promulgating a request for comment in 2010, and a notice of proposed rulemaking in 2011. In these circumstances, the Court should not grant review to address the same question." Brief for the United States as Amicus Curiae, Providence Hospital v. Moses (May 2010), http://www.justice.gov/osg/briefs/2009/2pet/6 invit/2009–0438.pet.ami.inv.pdf. The Supreme Court declined to hear the case. 130 S. Ct. 3499 (2010). *See* W. Adam Malizio, *Moses v. Providence Hospital: The Sixth Circuit Dumps the Federal Regulations of the Patient Anti-dumping Statute*, 27 J. CONTEMP. HEALTH L. & POL'Y 213 (2010).

In 2010 (75 Fed. Reg. 80,762) and *again* in 2012 (76 Fed. Reg. 5213–17) the Centers for Medicare and Medicaid Services issued Requests for Comments regarding the applicability of EMTALA toward inpatients, as well as the related question as to whether transferee hospitals with specialized capabilities have duties toward inpatients with medical emergencies. In its 2012 Request, which offered the public a second chance to comment on CMS's decision to stand by its 2003 regulation, the agency reviewed the 2003 regulation, the subsequent litigation, and its ongoing effort to discern whether its policies had created "real world" problems for inpatients with emergency medical needs. Concluding that commenters offered no evidence of problems, and that other commenters (hospitals naturally) had offered overwhelming support for the 2003 limiting standards, CMS decided to stand pat:

Applicability of EMTALA to Hospital Inpatients

In the 2003 EMTALA final rule, we took the position that a hospital's obligation under EMTALA ends when that hospital, in good faith, admits an individual with an unstable emergency medical condition as an inpatient to that hospital. In that rule, we noted that other patient safeguards including the [Medicare hospital conditions of participation] as well as State malpractice law protect inpatients. In response to our request for comments as to whether we should revisit the policies that were established in the 2003 EMTALA final rule, very few commenters took the position that the admitting hospital should continue to have an EMTALA obligation after the individual is admitted as an inpatient. Most commenters expressed support for the current policy that EMTALA does not apply to any inpatient of a hospital, even a patient who was admitted through that hospital's dedicated emergency department and continues to be unstable. [C]ommenters appreciated the clarity and predictability of a bright line policy. Commenters also noted that our current policy regarding inpatients is achieving Congress' intent by ensuring that every individual, regardless of their ability to pay for emergency services, should have access to hospital services provided in hospitals with emergency departments. Therefore, in light of the comments we received regarding the extension of the EMTALA obligations for hospitals admitting an individual through their dedicated emergency departments, we are not proposing to change the current EMTALA requirements for these hospitals. That is, we are maintaining our current policy that, if an individual "comes to the [hospital's] emergency department," as we have defined that term in regulation, and the hospital provides an appropriate medical screening examination and determines that an [emergency medical condition] exists, and then admits the individual in good faith in order to stabilize the EMC, that hospital has satisfied its EMTALA obligation towards that patient.

Applicability of EMTALA to Hospitals With Specialized Capabilities

Under current regulations, if an individual comes to the hospital's dedicated emergency department, is determined to have an EMC, is admitted as an inpatient, and continues to have an unstabilized EMC which requires the specialized capabilities of another hospital, the EMTALA obligation for the admitting hospital has ended and a hospital with specialized capabilities also does not have an EMTALA obligation towards that individual. [M]ost comments supported making no change to the current policies regarding the applicability of EMTALA to hospitals with specialized capabilities. Therefore, at this time, we are making no proposals with respect to our policies regarding the applicability of EMTALA to hospitals with specialized capabilities. However, we will continue to monitor whether it may be appropriate in the future to reconsider this issue.

How do you think the agency might go about monitoring these two problems? By requesting information from transferee hospitals on the details of rejected transfers? By examining data related to the status of inpatients at the time of discharge? Is it an acceptable justification in your view that no commenter could come up with "real world" examples of actual transfer denials or unstable discharges, and therefore, that there was no need for CMS to revisit its earlier position? Are the cases described above in this note not "real world" enough?

CMS essentially took what some might call an "evidenced-based" approach to the problem, but particularly in this instance, such an approach has obvious shortcomings. First, the agency lacks any system for gathering "evidence." Second, since the 2003 rule effectively closed the book on EMTALA protections for inpatients, why would any hospitals have been keeping any "evidence" of the impact of the restrictions on inpatient health care or outcome?

Based on the language of the statute, who do you think has the better of the argument? Go back and look at the statute's structure. Does it read: "If any individual comes to the emergency department, then the hospital must (a) screen appropriately; (b) stabilize; or (c) transfer appropriately?" What do you make of the fact that each of subsections (a), (b), and (c) states *separate* condition precedents to the duty mandated by that subsection? Subsection (a) states that "if any individual comes to the emergency department," there is a duty to screen appropriately. Subsection (b) states that "if any individual comes to a hospital and the hospital determines that the individual has an emergency medical condition, the hospital must either" stabilize or transfer appropriately. Subsection (c) states that "if an individual at a hospital has an emergency medical condition which has not been stabilized, the hospital may not transfer the individual unless" specified conditions are satisfied. Does this structure suggest to you that the duties stated in subsections (b) and (c) are dependent on the condition precedent stated in subsection (a)? Are federal courts and agencies entitled to ignore statutory language because regulated entities believe they need bright clear rules?

10. PATIENTS' OBLIGATIONS TO PAY FOR SERVICES

As noted in Chapter 2, hospitals commonly charge the highest prices to uninsured people and make aggressive effort to collect bills. EMTALA, 42 U.S.C. § 1395dd(h), provides that a "participating hospital may not delay provision of an appropriate medical screening examination ... or ... medical examination and treatment ... in order to inquire about the individual's method of payment or insurance status." Unlike the Hill–Burton Act, EMTALA establishes no obligation to provide uncompensated emergency care.

In Grant v. Trinity Health–Michigan, 390 F. Supp.2d 643, 653–55 (E.D. Mich. 2005), the court ruled that a nonprofit hospital did not breach EMTALA in charging uninsured patients substantially higher rates for emergency care than the rates applicable to insured patients. Plaintiffs did not allege that "Trinity Health delayed providing them a medical screening or treatment. Rather, they merely allege that before Trinity provided them with treatment, it first analyzed their ability to pay and required them to sign forms agreeing to pay Trinity in full for their medical care. These allegations are insufficient to state a claim under EMTALA." As provided in the EMTALA regulations,

> Hospitals may follow reasonable registration processes for individuals for whom examination or treatment is required by this section, including asking whether an individual is insured and, if so, what that insurance is, so long as that inquiry does not delay screening or treatment.

42 C.F.R. § 489.24(d)(4)(iv).

11. THE INTERACTION OF EMTALA WITH MEDICAL MALPRACTICE AND STATE CAPS ON DAMAGES

EMTALA specifies that "[a]ny individual who suffers personal harm as a direct result of a participating hospital's violation of a requirement of this section may, in a civil action against the participating hospital, obtain those damages available for personal injury under the law of the State in which the hospital is located, and such equitable relief as is appropriate." 42 U.S.C. § 1395dd(d)(2)(A). It further provides that the "provisions of this section do not preempt any State or local law requirement, except to the extent that the requirement directly conflicts with a requirement of this section." Id. § 1395dd(f).

In *Barris v. County of Los Angeles*, 972 P.2d 966 (Cal. 1999), *cert. den.*, 528 U.S. 868 (1999), the California Supreme Court concluded that California's caps on damages for malpractice cases apply to EMTALA cases. *Barris* involved the Martin Luther King/Drew Medical Center, one of Los Angeles County's hospitals, which was found liable for failure to stabilize a perilously sick baby who died shortly after the transfer.

Mychelle Williams, an 18–month–old baby who was a member of the Kaiser Foundation Health Plan, was taken to King/Drew because it was the closest facility. At the time of her arrival "she had suffered episodes of vomiting and diarrhea, was lethargic, and was having difficulty breathing. Her temperature was 106.6 degrees, her pulse and respiratory rate were abnormally fast, she had abnormally low pulse oxygenation, and she had infections in the middle ear in both ears." The pediatric emergency physician on call "noted signs and symptoms" of sepsis, a "life threatening bacterial infection that he knew requires prompt treatment with antibiotics." The physician failed to obtain the complete blood culture that would have confirmed sepsis because "he believed that he had to obtain authorization from Kaiser." Kaiser's Emergency Prospective Review Program (EPR) deals with situations where a Kaiser member is brought to a non-Kaiser facility for emergency medical care to facilitate the transfer of such patients to a Kaiser facility. When the emergency room physician, Dr. Dang, called Kaiser, he was instructed by the physician in charge of the EPR program not to conduct any blood tests or begin treatment. The baby suffered a seizure and her condition worsened. Three and a half hours after arriving at King/Drew, the baby was transferred to a Kaiser facility, where she died of cardiac arrest 15 minutes after her arrival.

At trial, Dr. Dang testified that he knew sepsis was possible, but he did not believe that she had sepsis at the time of her transfer (even though he also knew that blood work was necessary). He further testified that he thought that her condition was stable at the time of the transfer. Experts in the case testified that Dr. Dang had violated standard of care by failing to begin antibiotic treatment for suspected sepsis based on clinical symptoms, even before confirmatory laboratory tests were done. The jury found that the hospital violated EMTALA stabilization requirements and concluded that the defendants were liable for professional negligence. It awarded $3,000 for funeral expenses and $1.35 million in punitive damages. The trial court then reduced the non-economic damages to $250,000 in accordance with Civil Code Section 3333.2, which limits non-economic damages in professional medical liability cases.

Justice Mosk, writing for the California Supreme Court, affirmed the lower court's decision to apply the cap:

> In stabilizing a patient, a hospital must, within the staff and facilities available to it, meet requirements that relate to the prevailing standard of professional care: it must give the treatment medically necessary to stabilize a patient and it may not discharge or transfer the patient unless it provides [treatment that professional experts agree would prevent severe and threatening conse-

quences during a transfer]. A claim under EMTALA for failure to stabilize is thus necessarily "based on professional negligence" within the meaning of MICRA [the acronym for California's professional liability statute]—it involves "a negligent-omission to act by a health care provider in the rendering of professional services"—although it requires more. Proof of professional negligence does not suffice as proof of a violation of EMTALA. EMTALA differs from a traditional state medical malpractice claim principally because it also requires *actual knowledge* by the hospital that the patient is suffering from an emergency medical condition and because it mandates only stabilizing treatment, and only such treatment as can be provided *within the staff and facilities available at the hospital*. EMTALA thus imposes liability for failure to stabilize a patient only if an emergency medical condition is actually discovered, rather than for negligent failure to discover and treat such a condition. In addition, EMTALA imposes only a limited duty of medical treatment: a hospital need provide only sufficient care, within its capability, to stabilize the patient, not necessarily to improve or cure his or her condition. Once the medical condition is stabilized, the hospital may discharge or transfer the patient without limitation.

Congress expressly provided that state law provisions limiting the recovery of damages are applicable to EMTALA claims: "Any individual who suffers personal harm as a direct result of a participating hospital's violation of a requirement [under EMTALA] may, in a civil action against the participating hospital, obtain *those damages available for personal injury under the law of the State in which the hospital is located*, and such equitable relief as is appropriate." (42 U.S.C. § 1395dd(d)(2)(A).)

As discussed, EMTALA expressly incorporates state substantive limits on "damages available for personal injury." [W]e are persuaded that Congress's choice of the term "personal injury" was intended to be inclusive, i.e., to incorporate not only any *general* provisions for personal injury damages, but also any *specific* provisions, such as limits applicable to malpractice damages. Congress was not required to refer specifically to malpractice damages caps or limitations on noneconomic damages, or to use other explicitly limiting language in order to incorporate such limits.

We discern no conflict between the purposes of providing for a private right to damages for violations of EMTALA and state law limits on malpractice damages. "[T]he ends of both the federal and state statutes are to keep medical care accessible." Indeed, the apparent intent of Congress was to balance the deterrence and compensatory goals of EMTALA with deference to the ability of states to determine what limits are appropriate in personal injury actions against health care providers. Thus, the legislative history suggests that in drafting EMTALA to incorporate state law limits on personal injury damages, Congress was specifically responding to concern "regarding 'the potential impact of these enforcement provisions on the current medical malpractice crisis.' " H.R. Rep. No. 99–241, at 6 (1986), *reprinted* in 1986 U.S.C.C.A.N. 42, 728.

Most federal courts that have addressed the point have applied particular state caps on malpractice damages to EMTALA claims. In determining whether a particular state's damages cap applies to an EMTALA violation, federal courts have looked at the underlying conduct challenged and its legal basis to determine whether, *if brought under state law,* it would constitute a cause of action subject to the cap. Thus, in Power v. Arlington Hospital Association, 42 F.3d 851 (4th Cir. 1994), the Fourth Circuit determined that although the plaintiff alleged disparate treatment, not a breach of the standard of care associated with a traditional medical malpractice claim, damages for the EMTALA violation would nonetheless be subject to Virginia's $1 million cap on malpractice damages because the cap applies broadly to "any tort based on health care or professional services rendered, or which should have been rendered, by a health care provider, to a patient."

We find the analytical approach of the Fourth Circuit on this point persuasive. Accordingly, the issue here is whether a claim under EMTALA based on failure to stabilize, *if brought under state law,* would constitute an action subject to [MICRA]. We conclude that it would.

The cap on damages under Civil Code section 3333.2 applies to injuries "based on professional negligence," i.e., medical treatment falling below the professional standard of care. As discussed, although it is not identical to a state malpractice claim because it includes additional requirements, an EMTALA claim for failure to stabilize is based on professional negligence. A plaintiff must prove that the hospital did not, within its available staff and facilities provide a patient known to be suffering from an emergency medical condition with medical treatment necessary to assure, within reasonable medical probability, that no deterioration of the condition would likely occur. The standard of "reasonable medical probability" is an objective one, inextricably interwoven with the professional standard for rendering medical treatment.

To be sure, every claim for professional negligence does not also constitute an EMTALA claim for failure to stabilize. A claim under EMTALA also requires proof that the hospital actually determined that the patient was suffering from an emergency medical condition, and a hospital must provide required treatment only to stabilize a patient, i.e., to assure, within its capability, "no material deterioration of the condition" upon transfer or discharge. But an EMTALA claim based on failure to provide medically reasonable treatment to stabilize a patient would, if brought under state law, constitute a claim of "professional negligence" as defined by Civil Code section 3333.2. The EMTALA claim for failure to stabilize has additional, but no inconsistent, elements. Thus, the medical causation proof required to establish an EMTALA claim that a hospital failed to provide medical treatment to assure, within reasonable medical probability, that the patient's condition would not materially deteriorate is the same as that which would be required to prove "a negligent act or omission to act by a health care provider ... which ... is the proximate cause of personal injury or wrongful death." (Civ.Code, § 3333.2, subd. (c)(2).) The trier of fact must, under EMTALA as in a medical negligence claim, consider the prevailing medical standards and relevant expert medical testimony to determine whether material deterioration of the patient's condition was reasonably likely to occur.

* * *

It is not just the actual amount of damages that will be subject to state law; it is the right to any damages recovery in light of underlying procedural requirements that apply to claims for damages under state law. In Hardy v. New York City Health & Hospitals Corp., 164 F.3d 789 (2d Cir. 1999), the patient was brought by ambulance to the Queens Hospital Center with a gravely elevated blood pressure of 195/143, nausea, vomiting, dizziness, and diarrhea. Seven hours later she was discharged, with instructions to have her blood pressure checked every day. Twenty-four hours later emergency medical personnel brought her back to the hospital, where she was soon diagnosed as suffering a cerebral hemorrhage and admitted. She remained in the hospital for eleven months. When she was discharged, she was partially paralyzed and permanently disabled. Just under two years after her discharge, she filed suit asserting that the hospital failed to provide an appropriate medical screening exam on her first visit, and had discharged her without having stabilized her medical condition.

Under New York law, plaintiffs who seek to sue the City must file a notice of claim within ninety days of the incident that gives rise to the claim. They can, however, apply for a waiver of this requirement, if they do so within two years of the incident. In dismissing plaintiff's EMTALA claim for failure to comply with the New York notice of claim requirement, the federal district court relied on EMTALA § 1395dd(d)(2)(A). In affirming the district court, the Second Circuit recognized that:

> A respectable argument can be made that Congress intended us to read § 1395dd(d)(2)(A) narrowly, as referring only to the specific type and amount of damages available under New York law. See generally *Power*, 42 F.3d at 866 (We do not read § 1395dd(d)(2)(A) as expressly or impliedly incorporating state-mandated procedural requirements for EMTALA claims).

Nonetheless, the Second Circuit relied, as best as can be ascertained, on the following chain of reasoning: (1) Congress did not mean EMTALA to supplant state medical malpractice law; (2) rather, Congress meant to "supplement" and "defer" to state medical malpractice law or "fill its gaps" with respect to a duty of emergency care; (3) since EMTALA is "filling the gaps" of state medical malpractice law, it should be interpreted as incorporating and not displacing any part of state medical malpractice law, unless the state law directly conflicts with EMTALA; (4) moreover, EMTALA's legislative history demonstrates that Congress was concerned about "the potential impact" of EMTALA on "the current medical malpractice crisis"; Congress also expressed concern that an unbridled EMTALA could unduly burden hospitals and thereby "result in a decrease in available emergency care" rather than the intended increase in such care (citing H.R. Rep. No. 99–241 at 27 (1986), *reprinted in* 1986 U.S.C.C.A.N. 42, 728); (5) New York's notice of claim law, "by promoting timely settlement of claims and protecting municipal hospitals from unnecessary or excessive litigation expenses, helps to alleviate these concerns." *Hardy*, 164 F.3d at 794.

Ms. Hardy protested that it was physically impossible for her to file the notice of claim because she remained in the hospital and gravely ill for the entire ninety days. The court rejected her argument, noting that, if she had acted more quickly after discharge, she could have filed a petition for a waiver within the two years allowed by state law.

Most courts have rejected hospitals' assertions that EMTALA plaintiffs must meet the procedural restrictions applicable to state malpractice claims. See, e.g., Brooks v. Maryland Gen. Hosp. 996 F.2d 708 (4th Cir. 1993) (holding that state law mandating arbitration for medical malpractice claims does not reach EMTALA disparate screening claims); Hewett v. Inland, 39 F. Supp.2d 84 (D. Me. 1999); Merce v. Greenwood, 348 F. Supp.2d 1271 (D. Utah 2004); *but see* Draper v. Chiapuzio, 9 F.3d 1391 (9th Cir. 1993) (holding that a one-year notice of claim provision is not preempted by EMTALA's two-year statute of limitation because it is not physically impossible to comply with both).

Both *Hardy* and *Barris* involved public hospitals. The financial situation confronting public hospitals and the communities they serve can be very dire. In Los Angeles County, for example, more than 25 percent of the population has no health insurance; similar problems plague New York City. Are there legitimate reasons not to permit unlimited non-economic damages in such situations? And in *Barris*, wasn't the real issue the legitimacy of the Kaiser Health Plan practice of requiring prior authorization before emergency screening and stabilization of a member at a non-Kaiser hospital could commence? Health insurance and cost containment are discussed in Parts Two and Three.

---

12. FEDERAL ENFORCEMENT OF EMTALA OBLIGATIONS

As noted earlier, the experience under the Hill–Burton Act was that neither federal nor state agencies took action to enforce the free care and community service requirements of the Act until legal services lawyers, representing individuals, persuaded federal courts to begin the process of enforcing the requirements of the Act. At that point, federal regulators became more involved, issuing regulations defining the general terms of the statute. Learning from that experience, Congress explicitly provided that individuals injured by violations of EMTALA could sue in federal court. Congress also provided for administrative enforcement of EMTALA.

EMTALA enforcement is assigned to both the Centers for Medicare and Medicaid Services (CMS, the DHHS agency that administers the Medicare and Medicaid programs) and the Office of the Inspector General (OIG). CMS has the authority to exclude from Medicare hospitals and facilities found in violation of the law, while the OIG has the authority to impose lesser "civil money penalties." The OIG's role is particularly important. Exclusion from Medicare, the "death penalty," is unlikely to be invoked, while civil monetary penalties, as "intermediate sanctions," are a more plausible deterrent against possible violations. Sara Rosenbaum & Brian Kamoie, *Finding a Way Through the Hospital Door: The Role of EMTALA in Public Health Emergencies*, 31 J. L. MED. & ETHICS 590, 593 (2003). Hospitals report that an EMTALA investigation, the potential loss of Medicare provider participation status, and the presence of federal investigators lead hospital administrators to take EMTALA complaints seriously.

DHHS initially assumed that EMTALA would be enforced by private civil actions. In recent years, however, DHHS has taken a more active oversight role. Robert Wanerman, *The EMTALA Paradox*, 40 ANN. EMERGENCY MED. 464 (2002). Wanerman notes that during the statute's first 10 years, the federal government collected about $1.8 million in penalties, while in 1998 alone this amount was obtained in 54 separate cases including four against physicians. Id. A 2001 GAO study reported that hospital officials found EMTALA burdensome because of the stresses which it placed on their emergency departments. *Emergency Care: EMTALA Implementation and Enforcement Issues (2001)*, General Accounting Office, GAO 01–747, http://www.gao.gov/new.items/d01747.pdf. An entire EMTALA legal industry has sprung up, a testament to the reach and perceived impact that a major EMTALA action can have on a hospital's operations. Both CMS and the Inspector General have issued numerous guidelines related to the interpretation, application, and enforcement of the statute, as well as extensive corporate compliance manuals for hospitals and their legal counsel. These materials can be found in electronic version at the websites of the two agencies (www.hcfa.gov and www.hhs.oig.gov).

CHAPTER 4

CIVIL RIGHTS LAW AND ACCESS TO HEALTH CARE

While the lack of health insurance itself is highly correlated with race, class, and ethnic origin, Chapter 1 explains that disparities in access to care and treatment exist regardless of insurance status. This Chapter explores disparities in access to health insurance based on factors other than health insurance coverage. It explores special access problems that confront members of racial and ethnic minority groups as well as problems related to access to insurance and access to care that confront women, people with disabilities and immigrants.

The Patient Protection and Affordable Care Act of 2010 prohibits discrimination on the basis of race, color, national origin, sex, age, or disability in health programs or activities that receive federal financial assistance. Sec. 1557(a) provides, "an individual shall not, on the ground prohibited under title VI of the Civil Rights Act of 1964, title IX of the Education Amendments of 1972, the Age Discrimination Act of 1975, or section 504 of the Rehabilitation Act of 1973, be excluded from participation in, be denied the benefits of, or be subjected to discrimination under, any health program or activity, any part of which is receiving Federal financial assistance, including credits, subsidies, or contracts of insurance, or under any program or activity that is administered by an Executive Agency or any entity established under this title."

Each of the prior Acts cited is quite different, in terms of the people protected and the allegedly discriminatory actions prohibited. As you read the materials in this section, consider whether and how the ACA modifies the ground rules of discrimination.

---

1. PROHIBITING DISCRIMINATION ON THE BASIS OF RACE AND NATIONAL ORIGIN BY RECIPIENTS OF FEDERAL FINANCIAL ASSISTANCE UNDER TITLE VI OF THE 1964 CIVIL RIGHTS ACT

   a. Evidence of disparities. Life expectancy and infant mortality are widely used measures of the general health of a population. While the life expectancy of the U.S. population increased substantially in the 20th century, African American life expectancy at birth remained persistently five to seven years lower than that of European Americans. CDC, Natl. Center for Health Statistics, Fast Stats, Table 22, (2010), http.www.cdc.gov

/nchs/faststats/lifeexpec.htm. In 2005, there was a more than threefold difference in infant mortality rates by race and ethnicity, from a high of 13.63 infant deaths for 1,000 live births for non-Hispanic black women to a low of 4.42 for Cuban women. Puerto Rican and American Indian and Alaska Native women also experienced infant mortality rates above the high U.S. average. After a century in which U.S. infant mortality rates declined, the U.S. infant mortality rate did not change significantly for any race/ethnicity group from 2000 to 2005. Marian F. MacDorman & T.J. Mathews, *Recent Trends in Infant Mortality in the United States*, CDC, NCHS, (2008), http.www.cdc.gov/nchs/data/databriefs/db09.htm.

At the request of Congress, the Institute of Medicine organized a large national study to assess the extent of racial and ethnic disparities in health care, the sources of disparities and intervention strategies. UNEQUAL TREATMENT: CONFRONTING RACIAL AND ETHNIC DISPARITIES IN HEALTH CARE, INSTITUTE OF MEDICINE (2003) found that African Americans and Hispanics tend to receive low quality health care across a range of diseases including cancer, cardiovascular disease, HIV/AIDS, diabetes, mental health, and other chronic and infectious diseases. Disparities are found even when clinical factors, such as stage of disease presentation, co-morbidities, age, and severity of disease are taken into account. Racial disparities persist even when insurance status and ability to pay for care are the same. Disparities are found in a range of clinical settings, including public and private hospitals, teaching and non-teaching hospitals. Disparities in care are associated with higher mortality among minorities.

People of color are more likely than whites to live in neighborhoods that lack adequate health care resources. 28% of Latinos and 22% of African Americans report having little or no choice in where to seek care, while only 15% of whites report this difficulty. Even among the insured, African Americans and Latinos are twice as likely as whites to rely upon a hospital clinic or outpatient department as their regular source of care, rather than on a private physician or other office-based provider. Marsha Lillie–Blanton & Caya B. Lewis, *Policy Challenges and Opportunities in Closing the Racial/Ethnic Divide in Health Care*, Kaiser Family Fund, Issue Brief (March 2005).

Racial differentiation also extends to individual treatment decisions. A study, published in the New England Journal of Medicine in 1999, described a structured a demonstration in which a group of physicians were shown a series of randomly assigned videos. Each video was of an actor depicting a patient who discussed symptoms suggesting the potential presence of cardiovascular disease. All patients were dressed identically. All had identical health insurance. All described their symptoms in identical terms and presented identical diagnostic tests. Their only distinguishing features were race and sex. Researchers found that diagnosis and treatment recommendations varied according to both, and that black women were less likely to be referred for diagnostic testing and treatment. Kevin Schulman et al., *The Effect of Race and Sex on Physicians' Recommendations for Cardiac Catheterization*, 340 NEW ENG. J. MED. 618 (1999).

The 1999 publication unleashed a storm of responses, reactions, and criticisms, questioning its methods, findings, and conclusions. Lisa Schwartz et al., *Misunderstandings About the Effects of Race and Sex on Physicians' Referrals for Cardiac Catheterization*, 341 NEW ENG. J. MED. 279 (1999). The study also inspired more extensive research on "health disparities," i.e., differences in health care treatment among populations that cannot be explained by factors related to health care need or economics. The overwhelming majority of dozens of studies confirm racial disparities in the treatment of patients with comparable insurance and the same illness. Lillie–Blanton & Lewis, *Policy Challenges and Opportunities*.

Researchers from Yale University's School of Public Health and the Urban Institute looked at discharge data for 133,821 patients in the greater New York City area between 2002 and 2004 to determine whether there were racial differences in the care provided. As you will see in Part Three, many studies have shown that surgeons and hospitals who perform more procedures are likely to produce better outcomes. The researchers examined ten procedures for breast cancer, colorectal cancer, gastric cancer, lung cancer, pancreatic cancer, coronary artery bypass grant, angioplasty, abdominal aortic aneurysm repair, carotid endarterectomy and total hip replacement. The study found, that for all 10 procedures, white patients were more frequently treated by both high-volume hospitals and surgeons than were blacks, Asians or Hispanics. Averaging all procedures together, white patients benefited from both high-volume hospitals and high-volume surgeons in 37.6% of cases, compared to 20.6% of cases for black patients, 24.4% of cases for Asian patients, and 25.5% of cases for Latino patients. Andrew J. Epstein et al., *Racial and Ethnic Difference in the Use of High– Volume Hospitals and Surgeons*, 145 ARCHIVES OF SURGERY 179 (2010).

Despite the now overwhelming evidence of racial disparities in medical treatment, most of the public and medical professionals deny the phenomena. Over two-thirds (67%) of whites believe African Americans get the same quality of care as they do, and over half (59%) of whites believe Latinos get the same quality of care. The misperceptions of the public are shared by medical professionals. Less than a third (29%) of physicians say the health care system "very or somewhat often" treats people unfairly based on their racial/ethnic background. Among those who believe disparities exist, the most common perception is that they are largely a result of differences in patient characteristics—especially insurance, education, and personal preferences. "This perception persists despite an abundance of studies that control for these patient level characteristics." Lillie–Blanton & Lewis, *Policy Challenges and Opportunities*.

   b. History. In the forward to W. Michael Byrd and Linda A. Clayton's monumental, two volume, chronicle of race and health care, Jack Geiger observes, "Slavery is America's original sin and racism is its chronic disease." AN AMERICAN HEALTH DILEMMA: VOL. 1, A MEDICAL HISTORY OF AFRICAN AMERICANS AND THE PROBLEM OF RACE: BEGINNINGS TO 1900 (2000); VOL. 2, RACE, MEDICINE, AND HEALTH CARE IN THE UNITED STATES, 1900–2000 (2002). Bryd and Clayton depict a threefold dilemma: a social expectation that minority

Americans will experience substandard health status; a highly privatized health system that accords broad discretion to entrepreneurs and marginalizes poor and minority members; and a widespread refusal to acknowledge the problem of racial segregation and exclusion in health care.

It has only been slightly more than a half century since racial segregation was official policy in federal health care programs, such as the Hill–Burton Act, which initially authorized the construction of segregated hospitals and nursing homes. Even after de jure segregation in health care was declared unconstitutional, and the passage of Title VI of the 1964 Civil Rights Act began a process that led to the desegregation of private hospitals, de facto segregation persisted through the use of numerous strategies by hospitals, including the denial of privileges to physicians who agreed to treat Medicaid patients. DAVID BARTON SMITH, HEALTH CARE DIVIDED (1999).

Following the United States Supreme Court's decision in Brown v. Board of Education, 349 U.S. 294 (1955), and the rise of the Civil Rights Movement, civil rights activists challenged racial discrimination in many spheres, including health care, and federal courts extended Brown's prohibition on segregation and discrimination. In 1963, Simkins v. Moses H. Cone Memorial Hospital, 323 F.2d 959 (4th Cir. 1963), *cert. den.*, 376 U.S. 398 (1964), declared unconstitutional hospital policies refusing to consider African American physicians seeking staff privileges. There was nothing subtle about the policies struck down in *Simkins*; the hospital flatly refused to consider black doctors for staff privileges. Rather, the difficult legal question was whether the actions of the ostensibly "private" hospital constituted "state action" subject to the Fourteenth Amendment. The *Simkins* court found that extensive state regulation, federal Hill–Burton construction funds, and the public importance of hospital services made the private hospital a state actor. In more recent years, the state action aspect of *Simkins* has been largely rejected. The hospital also defended its actions arguing that separate, but equal hospitals were available to Black doctors and patients and that Hill–Burton authorized segregation. The courts rejected that defense, based on *Brown*. SMITH, HEALTH CARE DIVIDED at 78–95. As of 1963, when the case was decided, out of more than 3000 Hill–Burton construction projects, 104 segregated facilities had been built, 84 for Whites only, and 20 for Black patients. BYRD AND CLAYTON, AN AMERICAN HEALTH DILEMMA: RACE, MEDICINE, AND HEALTH CARE IN THE UNITED STATES 1900–2000 at 267.

The Civil Rights Act of 1964 is broadly remedial, reaching public accommodations, federally funded programs, and employment. Coming in the midst of the 1964 Civil Rights Act debate, the decision in *Simkins* had a major impact on the fashioning of Title VI, which prohibits race discrimination in federally assisted programs. SMITH, HEALTH CARE DIVIDED at 105–21. The legislative history of the 1964 Civil Rights Act is replete with evidence that federal lawmakers had health care in mind when they enacted Title VI; indeed, the Title VI regulations, which were promulgated within months of passage, contain numerous explicit references to health care services.

The link between federal assistance and prohibited discrimination, established by Title VI, figured prominently in the Medicare debate, which took place only one year later. Organized medicine opposed any notion that the receipt of Medicare payments would expose physicians to anti-discrimination laws and would thereby prohibit them from selecting their patients as they chose. SMITH, HEALTH CARE DIVIDED at 96–142. The Southern Senators who championed their cause were so strong in their demand for a statutory exemption for physicians under Title VI that, in order not to jeopardize Medicare's passage, the Johnson Administration orally pledged not to enforce Title VI against physicians in private practice. *Id.*

The Administration based its pledge on an interpretation of the legal implications, for purposes of enforcing Title VI, flowing from the legal structure of Medicare's physician payment provisions. In its original form, Medicare Part B (pertaining to coverage for physician services) operated very differently from Medicare Part A (pertaining to the hospital insurance component). Part A provided for direct payment to hospitals, while Part B was structured to replicate the indemnity insurance arrangements of the time; as a result, it indemnified patients who had paid their physicians directly. Since, technically speaking, no money changed hands between the Medicare program and physicians in private practice, Administration officials promised that for purposes of enforcing Title VI, Medicare Part B would not be treated as the type of federal assistance that triggers application of the law's bar against discrimination in federally assisted programs. Thus, even though Title VI contains no statutory exemption for Medicare Part B payments and Medicare's original indemnification structure has long since been replaced by direct payments to physicians, the federal government continues to treat Part B physician payments as exempt. 45 C.F.R. 80.1 et seq. (Appendix).

Despite the sidestepping of Title VI enforcement in the case of Medicare Part B-funded physician services, one of the most important historical exercises of governmental authority under Title VI occurred in a health care context. In the months following the enactment of Medicare and Medicaid in 1965, the Johnson Administration, in an extraordinary exercise of its implementation powers, required every hospital to sign a Title VI assurance of non-discrimination as a condition of being allowed to participate in the Medicare program. This historic use of the Secretary's Title VI powers to bring the nation's hospital industry into compliance with the Act (at least on paper), demonstrated the potential power of Title VI to achieve fundamental change in the operation of health services. SMITH, HEALTH CARE DIVIDED at 146–96.

Following the election of Richard Nixon in 1968 (who's famed Southern Strategy capitalized on the divisiveness within the Democratic Party of civil rights legislation), civil rights enforcement was itself segregated from general federal healthcare program administration. The Nixon Administration isolated federal civil rights officials in a separate unit of the Department of Health Education and Welfare (subsequently renamed Health and Human Services) with the result that they were stripped of all direct authority over federal spending programs, such as Medicare and Medicaid. In other words, a federal remedial law, which depended on its application to federal spending laws for its power, was separated operationally from the federal spending programs themselves, leaving the remedial statute essentially afloat and disconnected from federal program expenditures. Indeed, given the legislative text below, the extent to which this separation adheres to Congressional intent would appear open to question. Federal civil rights officials were effectively stripped of the power to meaningfully enforce Title VI, except to the extent that they could persuade administrators of federal spending programs to jointly adopt their standards as their own. By the mid–1990s, active government enforcement of Title VI had all but ceased. SMITH, HEALTH CARE DIVIDED.

   c.   Title VI. The Title VI statute and regulations define discrimination in sweeping terms. 42 U.S.C. § 2000d provides that "No person in the United States shall, on the ground of race, color, or national origin, be excluded from participation in, be denied the benefits of, or be subjected to discrimination under any program or activity receiving Federal financial assistance."

Title VI regulations were developed concomitantly with enactment of the law through a unified regulatory process. The rules applicable to health, educational, and welfare services contain considerable references to health care services and set forth a more detailed enforcement scheme, including the provision of non-discrimination assurances, data reporting, and compliance monitoring. Relevant provisions are set forth below.

45 C.F.R. § 80.3 Discrimination prohibited.

   (a) General. No person in the United States shall, on the ground of race, color, or national origin be excluded from participation in, be denied the benefits of, or be otherwise subjected to discrimination under any program to which this part applies.

   (b) Specific discriminatory actions prohibited. (1) A recipient under any program to which this part applies may not, directly or through contractual or other arrangements, on ground of race, color, or national origin: (i) Deny an individual any service, financial aid, or other benefit provided in a different manner, from that provided under the program; (ii) Provide any service, financial aid, or other benefit to an individual which is different, or is provided in a different manner, from that provided to others under the program; (iii) Subject an individual to segregation or separate treatment in any matter related to his receipt of any service, financial aid, or other benefit under the program; (iv) Restrict an individual in any way in the enjoyment of any advantage or privilege enjoyed by others receiving any service, financial aid, or other benefit under the program; (v) Treat an individual differently from others in determining whether he satisfies any admission, enrollment, quota, eligibility, membership or other requirement or condition which individuals must meet in order to be provided any service, financial aid, or other benefit provided under the program; (vi) Deny an individual an opportunity to participate in the program through the provision of services or otherwise or afford him an opportunity to do so which is different from that afforded others under the program.

(2) A recipient, in determining the types of services, financial aid, or other benefits, or facilities which will be provided under any such program, or the class of individuals to whom, or the situations in which, such services, financial aid, other benefits, or facilities will be provided under any such program, or the class of individuals to be afforded an opportunity to participate in any such program, may not, directly or through contractual or other arrangements, utilize criteria or methods of administration which have the effect of subjecting individuals to discrimination because of their race, color, or national origin, or have the effect of defeating or substantially impairing accomplishment of the objectives of the program as respect individuals of a particular race, color, or national origin.

(3) In determining the site or location of a facility, an applicant or recipient may not make selections with the effect of excluding individuals from, denying them the benefits of, or subjecting them to discrimination under any programs to which this regulation applies, on the ground of race, color, or national origin, or with the purpose or effect of defeating or substantially impairing the accomplishment of the objectives of the Act or this regulation.

African American people have relied on Title VI to challenge hospital decisions to relocate from center city locations to the suburbs. In NAACP v. Wilmington Medical Center, Inc., 491 F. Supp. 290 (D. Del. 1980), *aff'd*, 657 F.2d 1322 (3d Cir. 1981), the Office of Civil Rights of the U.S. Department of Health Education and Welfare found the defendants' initial relocation plan in violation of Title VI and entered into a compliance agreement approving a modified plan. Plaintiffs' challenge to the modified plan was rejected. Bryan v. Koch, 627 F.2d 612 (2d Cir. 1980), considered a challenge to New York City's decision to close a public hospital which served a population which consisted of 98% minority group members. The majority held that there was no evidence of discriminatory intent and that, despite the racially discriminatory impact, the City had demonstrated a rational basis for its action. Judge Kearse dissented from the determination on discriminatory impact, finding that once the impact has been shown, the defendant had an obligation to demonstrate a rational basis for its decision, including consideration of the alternatives. By contrast, courts have been more willing to find a Title VI violation where a health care provider segregates patients on the basis of whether they were insured by Medicaid or private insurance, creating de facto racial segregation, with lower quality care to the Medicaid patients who were disproportionately racial minorities. *See, e.g.*, Linton v. Carney, 779 F. Supp. 925 (M.D. Tenn. 1990), *motion to dismiss den.*, 30 F.3d 55 (6th Cir. 1994), *aff'd*, Linton v. Commissioner, 65 F.3d 508 (6th Cir. 1995).

For several reasons, the application of Title VI to health care organizations has proven to be difficult. The organization of health care services is complex and responsibility is diffused. The legal standards are demanding. *See* Sydney Watson, *Reinvigorating Title VI: Defending Health Care Discrimination—It Shouldn't Be So Easy*, 58 FORDHAM L. REV. 939 (1990); Vernilia R. Randall, *Slavery, Segregation and Racism: Trusting the Healthcare System Ain't Always Easy! An African–American Perspective on Bioethics*, 15 ST. LOUIS U. PUB. L. REV. 191–242 (1996).

Racial disparities are particularly sharp in relation to the quality of long-term care. As you will see in Part Two, a significant portion of Medicaid funding—16%—supports long term care in nursing homes. As you will see in Part Three, in response to scandals in the 1970s about the quality of care provided in nursing homes, Congress has required a more systemic, state-based quality monitoring program than is applicable to other health care services. This review documents, but does not correct, persistent race-based segregation in long-term care, with African Americans relegated to substandard services. Ruqaiijah Yearby, *African Americans Can't Win, Break Even, or Get Out of the System: the Persistence of "Unequal Treatment" in Nursing Home Care*, 82 TEMP. L. REV. 1177 (2010).

d. *The importance of data.* Most Title VI discrimination cases in a health care context have involved practices that have discriminatory effects, rather than cases of intentional discrimination. These disparate impact cases, turn on access to large amounts of relevant statistical data. Neither Title VI nor the Medicaid and Medicare standards require that racial data be gathered on the services supported with federal funds. Thus proof of racial disparity is extremely difficult. Madison–Hughes v. Shalala, 80 F.3d 1121 (6th Cir. 1996), rejected plaintiffs' claim seeking to compel the federal government to include queries as to the race and ethnic identity of patients on a standard billing form used by health care institutions seeking reimbursement from federally sponsored health programs. While neither Medicare nor Medicaid requires that these data be gathered, several major health insurers, including United Health Group and Aetna, have undertaken efforts systematically to examine racial patterns in health care access among members. A 2004 survey of 137 health plans representing nearly 90 million members found that 51 percent either ask beneficiaries to furnish racial data voluntarily (e.g., on enrollment forms) or use other methods to obtain the type of racial data that would permit aggregate comparisons of health care access and receipt of services. Ron Winslow, *To Close Gaps in Care, More Health Plans Ask About Race*, WALL ST. J. (June 1, 2004). Some states, including New York, have required collection of racially identified data about health care. *See* Andrew J. Epstein et al., *Racial and Ethnic Difference in the Use of High–Volume Hospitals and Surgeons*, 145 ARCHIVES OF SURGERY 179 (2010), discussed above. Collection of data about race and care is essential to research that can form the basis of evidence-based medicine, as well as to litigation under a disparate impact standard.

Section 4302 of the Affordable Health Care Act provides that the Secretary of DHHS "shall ensure that, by not later than 2 years after enactment of this title, any federally conducted or supported health care or public health program, activity or survey ... collects and reports, to the extent practicable (A) data on race, ethnicity, sex, primary language, and disability status for applicants, recipients and participants." On its face, this requirement represents a stunning change in federal data collection policy. The Secretary is not simply authorized to demand collection of data, which has probably always been allowed, but is required to do so. The data collection mandate applies to any federally supported health care program or activity. At a minimum it seems to require collection of this data on all billing forms for federally financed programs. In addition, it demands collection of data about "applicants," as well as "recipients and participants."

The Affordable Care Act, § 4302, also requires that the Secretary collect and present this data in a form accessible to researchers and to the public. It insists on reliance on self-reported data. In relation to people with disabilities, it mandates detailed surveys to determine the services available to people with disabilities, and to assess whether providers of those services are sensitive to the needs those people.

Section 4302 could have a dramatic impact on the collection and reporting of data on race, ethnicity, sex, primary language, and disability status. The Secretary of HHS issued a request for comment on data collection standards. 76 Fed. Reg. 38,396 (June 30, 2011). The Secretary went beyond the mandate of the statute in noting that HHS was "in the process of developing and validating standard approaches for collecting data about sexual orientation and gender identity."

Issues of data collection standards raise important questions that have been extensively addressed for decades. For example, in relation to race, there is a trade-off between collecting data that paint a big picture, and seeking data that are more granular and recognize the important differences between dozens of different kinds of people of Asian, Hispanic, Pacific Island, African–American, Middle Eastern, European or mixed ethnicity. The category of people with disabilities raises similar, perhaps greater, complexities. Even gender, seemingly a simple binary category, is not simple for transsexual people.

While standards for data collection are important, the more consequential issues may be whether and how the data collection requirements will be applied to health care providers and insurers. How do these questions get integrated into standard billing forms? Should the data collection requirements apply to individual practitioners? (Recall doctors' success is resisting the application of Title VI to physicians receiving Medicare payments.) Is the push for more detailed, granular data collection in conflict with a desire to gather data about broad-based patterns? The Leadership Conference on Civil and Human Rights, Recommendations Related to Data Collection Requirements in Section 4302, Aug. 1, 2011, http://www.healthlaw.org/images/stories/issues/healthdisparities/2011_4_28_LCCR_Data_Collection.pdf.

e. Sandoval. In 2001, a deeply divided Supreme Court held in Alexander v. Sandoval, 532 U.S. 275 (2001), that there is no private right of action to enforce the Title VI disparate impact regulations. Justice Stevens' dissent argued that Justice Scalia's majority opinion was inconsistent with a long line of cases, including numerous health care cases, in which private litigants, relying on Title VI regulations, challenged state administrative practices that were discriminatory in effect. *Sandoval* arose as a challenge to the policy of the Alabama Department of Public Safety (DPS), a recipient of federal financial assistance, of administering its driving test only in English. Martha Sandoval brought suit on behalf of a class of similarly situated non-English speaking persons alleging that Alabama's practices violated Title VI, citing Lau v. Nichols, 414 U.S. 563 (1974). The *Sandoval* decision has been widely criticized as inconsistent with the Civil Rights Act and Congressional intent. *See e.g.*, John Arthur Laufer, Alexander v. Sandoval *and Its Implications for Disparate Impact Regimes*, 102 COLUM. L. REV. 1613 (2002). The majority's opinion is consistent with many years of dissenting and eventually majority opinions by Justice (later Chief Justice) Rehnquist and Justice Scalia attacking the concept of inferred or implied rights in many doctrinal contexts, discussed further in Part Two regarding entitlement to Medicaid. *See also* Rand E. Rosenblatt, *The Courts, Health Care Reform, and the Reconstruction of American Social Legislation*, 18 J. HEALTH POL. POL'Y & L. 439 (1993).

f. Administrative enforcement. In the wake of *Sandoval*, commentators explore ways in which federal and state administrative agencies might do more to monitor racial discrimination in health care and seek corrective action. Sara Rosenbaum & Joel Teitelbaum, *Civil Rights Enforcement in the Modern Healthcare System: Reinvigorating the Role of the Federal Government in the Aftermath of Alexander v. Sandoval*, 3 YALE J. HEALTH POL'Y L. & ETHICS 215 (2003); June Elchner & Bruce C. Vladeck, *Medicare As A Catalyst For Reducing Health Disparities*, 24(2) HEALTH AFFAIRS 365 (2005).

Ruqaiijah Yearby, *Litigation, Integration, and Transformation: Using Medicaid to Address Racial Inequities in Health Care*, 13 J. HEALTH CARE L. & POL'Y 325 (2010) argues that civil rights enforcement should be integrated into the existing processes for monitoring the quality of care provided in nursing homes funded by Medicaid. Yearby explores whether nursing home patients, whose care is financed by Medicaid, have a judicially enforceable claim to force the Secretary of HHS to implement such a change. These issues are considered in Part Two. Apart from the complex question whether federal courts could order the Secretary to implement such a change, consider why federal administrators would decline, as a matter of administrative discretion, to gather data on race and integrate them into the quality care enforcement process.

g. Title VI and language access. Despite *Sandoval*, Title VI's Limited English Proficiency (LEP) Guidelines Applicable to Health and Human Services Providers have continued to have significant impact. In Lau v. Nichols, the Supreme Court held that discrimination on the basis of limited

English proficiency constituted discrimination on the basis of national origin and thus gave rise to Title VI protections. In 2000, the United States Department of Health and Human Services, Office for Civil Rights (OCR), issued Guidance to Federal Financial Assistance Recipients Regarding Title VI Prohibition Against National Origin Affecting Limited English Proficient Persons. 65 Fed. Reg. 52,762 (August 30, 2000). The Guidance, which details federal expectations regarding Title VI compliance by covered entities, was reissued in a revised form in August 2003, pursuant to Executive Order 13,166 and following the Supreme Court's decision in *Sandoval.* 68 Fed. Reg. 47,311 (August 8, 2003).

The LEP Guidance is one of the few examples of comprehensive Title VI standards governing the conduct of federally assisted programs and services. Citing a Department of Justice Memorandum written in 2002, the Preamble clarifies that despite the doubts cast on the validity of the disparate impact rule by the Court in *Sandoval,* the Administration has the authority under Title VI to regulate conduct that is non-intentional but discriminatory in effect. 68 Fed. Reg. 47,312 (August 8, 2003). The growing need for language access services, federal enforcement efforts, and community activism have led many health care providers to develop creative approaches to providing language access. Jennifer B. Lee, *What is the Two–Headed Phone,* N.Y. Times, (May 12, 2009), http://cityroom.blogs.nytimes. com/2009/05/13/what-is-that-two-headed-phone/?pagemode=print.

The Guidance creates a "meaningful access" standard. It notes that the Office of Civil Rights (OCR) will apply a "flexible and fact-dependent standard," using a four-factor test in determining if meaningful access has been achieved: "(1) The number or proportion of LEP persons eligible to be served or likely to be encountered by the program or grantee; (2) the frequency with which LEP individuals come in contact with the program; (3) the nature and importance of the program, activity, or service provided by the program to people's lives; and (4) the resources available to the grantee/recipient and costs." 68 Fed. Reg. 47,314 (August 8, 2003). *See generally* Alvaro Decola, *Making Language Access to Health Care Meaningful: The Need for a Federal Health Care Interpreters' Statute,* 24 J.L. & HEALTH 151 (2011).

The Guidance sets forth situations in which the use of a professional interpreter (as opposed to a family member) would be expected:

> Again, while the use of a family member or friend may be appropriate, if that is the choice of the LEP person, the following are examples of where the recipient should provide an interpreter for the LEP individual:

> A woman or child is brought to an emergency room and is seen by an emergency room doctor. The doctor notices the patient's injuries and determines that they are consistent with those seen with victims of abuse or neglect. In such a case, use of the spouse or a parent to interpret for the patient may raise serious issues of conflict of interest and may, thus, be inappropriate.

A man, accompanied by his wife, visits an eye doctor for an eye examination. The eye doctor offers him an interpreter, but he requests that his wife interpret for him. The eye doctor talks to the wife and determines that she is competent to interpret for her husband during the examination. The wife interprets for her spouse as the examination proceeds, but the doctor discovers that the husband has cataracts that must be removed through surgery. The eye doctor determines that the wife does not understand the terms he is using to explain the diagnosis and, thus, that she is not competent to continue to interpret for her husband. The eye doctor stops the examination and calls an interpreter for the husband. A family member may be appropriate to serve as an interpreter if preferred by the LEP person in situations where the service provided is of a routine nature such as a simple eye examination. However, in a case where the nature of the service becomes more complex, depending on the circumstances, the family member or friend may not be competent to interpret.

48 Fed. Reg. 47,318 (Aug. 8, 2003).

Imagine that you are Counsel and Corporate Compliance Officer for a large private urban teaching hospital whose service area includes more than 1,000,000 individuals speaking some 25 different languages. Your hospital offers not only advanced inpatient care and full trauma services, but sponsors a network of eight clinics throughout the service area. What information would you want in order to assess your facility's interpretations obligations and fashion your implementation plan? With whom would you consult? What if the hospital CEO refused to approve your request for resources to conduct this work, stating, "but you told me that because of the *Sandoval* decision, no one can sue the hospital any more anyway?" What arguments might you make regarding the importance of complying with the Guidance?

The concept of culturally competent care is much broader than simply language access. ANNE FADIMAN, THE SPIRIT CATCHES YOU AND YOU FALL DOWN (1998). Hospitals, medical education programs and state and federal regulators have developed programs to encourage more culturally sensitive care. *See generally* Darci L. Graves et al., *Legislation as Intervention: A Survey of Cultural Competence Policy in Health Care*, 10 J. HEALTH CARE L. & POL'Y 339 (2008).

2. GENDER DISCRIMINATION AND ACCESS TO HEALTH SERVICES

Given the deep history of patriarchy and gender hierarchy in the United States, it is not surprising to find that women have been subject to discrimination in access to health services and health insurance. Many of the most serious forms of discrimination involve women's reproductive capacity. So, for example, in the 19th Century when allopathic physicians enlisted state authority to protect their hegemony over healing, abortions were commonly performed by "abortionists," a medical subspecialty dominated by women. The allopaths neither wanted to provide these services nor to allow the existence of alternative providers of medical services. Hence, they persuaded state legislatures to make abortion a crime. LINDA GORDON, THE MORAL PROPERTY OF WOMEN: THE HISTORY OF THE BIRTH CONTROL MOVEMENT IN THE UNITED STATES, 59–60 (1976); JAMES C. MOHR, ABORTION IN AMERICA: THE ORIGINS & EVOLUTION OF NATIONAL POLICY, 1800–1900, at 147–70 (1978). As another example, in the 20th Century, as doctors sought to move childbirth from the home to the hospital, the law and medical culture effectively restricted, and in many areas eliminated, the practice of nurse midwives. Many women preferred childbirth in a hospital. But hospital based, physician controlled childbirth often involves mandatory, sometimes arbitrary, constraints. BOSTON WOMEN'S HEALTH COLLECTIVE, OUR BODIES, OURSELVES: PREGNANCY AND CHILDBIRTH (2011). Until the 1970s, professional medical standards and official state policies denied women access to surgical sterilization unless she was middle-aged and had given birth to several children; at the same time, professional practice conditioned the availability of childbirth or other medical services on the "agreement" of young, low-income women of color to be sterilized. Lisa C. Ikemoto, *Infertile by Force and Federal Complicity: The Story of* Relf v. Weinberger, *in* LAW STORIES: WOMEN (ELIZABETH SCHNEIDER & STEPHANIE WILDMAN, eds., 2010). In short, discrimination against women has long been common in health care, particularly in relation to reproductive health.

Nonetheless, the landmark Civil Rights Act of 1964, prohibiting discrimination on the basis of race on the part of entities receiving federal funds, did not prohibit discrimination on the basis of gender. Again this is not surprising because the women's movement of the 1970s, transforming public consciousness about gender discrimination and the legal status of women, had not yet begun. It was not until the Affordable Care Act of 2010 that any federal law explicitly prohibited discrimination on the basis of gender in the provision of health care. The legislative history suggests that the provisions are intended to prohibit gender rating in individual insurance policies. Congress heard testimony that insurance companies in the individual market charged higher rates to all women, without actuarial justification, and denied coverage to women who had given birth by C-section or who were victims of domestic violence. Denise Grady, *Law Will Lower The Costs of Being a Woman*, N.Y. TIMES, March 29, 2010.

Many of the most common forms of discrimination against women involve reproductive health services and health insurance coverage. Since the early 1970s, the Supreme Court's interpretation of the Fourteenth Amendment's equal protection clause has generally required strong justification for laws that discriminate against women, but that constitutional protection has often been denied to women who are pregnant.

   a. Pregnancy and Childbirth. Historically, private insurance policies excluded coverage for maternity care and some still do. ALAN GUTTMACHER INSTITUTE, BLESSED EVENTS AND THE BOTTOM LINE: FINANCING MATERNITY CARE IN

THE U.S. 20 (1987). In 1974 the Supreme Court held that, under the 14th Amendment, discrimination against pregnant women is not based on gender. Geduldig v. Aiello, 417 U.S. 484 (1974). The challenged law involved a state sponsored disability policy that provided coverage for all disabilities except those related to pregnancy. The Court said, "the policy does not exclude anyone from benefit eligibility because of gender but merely removes one physical condition—pregnancy—from the list of compensable disabilities. While it is true that only women can become pregnant, it does not follow that every legislative classification concerning pregnancy is a sex-based classification. The program divides potential recipients into two groups—pregnant women and nonpregnant persons. While the first group is exclusively female, the second includes members of both sexes. There is no risk from which men are protected and women are not [and] no risk from which women are protected and men are not." 417 U.S. at 496–97.

Even though Title VI of the Civil Rights Act did not cover discrimination based on gender, Title VII of the Civil Rights Act of 1964, prohibiting discrimination in employment, included gender discrimination. In 1976, the Court extended the logic of *Geduldig* to Title VII. General Electric Co. v. Gilbert, 429 U.S. 125, held that an otherwise-comprehensive insurance program that excluded pregnancy-related disabilities from coverage did not constitute sex discrimination prohibited by Title VII of the Civil Rights Act of 1964. Congress quickly rejected *Gilbert's* assertion that discrimination against pregnant women was not discrimination based on sex by adopting the Pregnancy Discrimination Act of 1978 (PDA). The PDA prohibits covered employers from discriminating "on the basis of pregnancy, childbirth, or related medical conditions" and requires that "women affected by pregnancy, childbirth, or related medical conditions shall be treated the same for all employment-related purposes, including receipt of benefits under fringe benefit programs, as other persons not so affected but similar in their ability or inability to work."

The scope of the Pregnancy Discrimination Act is limited. It only applies to discrimination in employment and does not extend to discrimination in other spheres, such as medical care. Even in the employment context, it explicitly does not prohibit discrimination against abortion. Many states have protected women against discrimination in access to health care and health insurance. For example, many states adopted anti-discrimination laws prohibiting insurance discrimination against childbirth services. But, as you will see in Part Two, a state's power to protect women from discriminatory employment benefit policies is limited by the federal ERISA law that broadly preempts state regulation of employment-based benefit plans.

b. Contraception. Almost half (49%) of the pregnancies in the U.S. are unintended, more than 3 million unintended pregnancies a year. James Trussell et al., *Cost Effectiveness of Contraceptives in the United States*, 79 CONTRACEPTION 5 (2009). The U.S. rate of unintended pregnancy is higher than the world average, and much higher than that in other industrialized nations. Unintended pregnancy costs over $11 million a year in direct public medical costs for births, abortions, miscarriages and infant medical care. Adam Sonfield et al., *The Public Costs of Births resulting from Unintended Pregnancies: National and State–Level Estimates,* GUTTMACHER INSTITUTE (2011); Adam Monea and Adam Thomas, *Unintended Pregnancy and Taxpayer Spending,* BROOKINGS INSTITUTION (2011). The human and health costs to the 3 million women who experience unintended pregnancies each year are more difficult to quantify.

In the U.S., the most commonly used forms of contraception are the pill (28% of users) and female surgical sterilization (27%). *Facts on Contraceptive Use in the United States,* GUTTMACHER INSTITUTE (June 2010), http:// www.guttmacher.org/pubs/fb_contr_use.pdf. U.S. women have access to a narrower range of contraceptive choices than their European counterparts, largely because the IUD, inexpensive, effective and popular in Europe, is generally not available in the U.S. Sylvia A. Law, *Tort Liability and The Availability of Contraceptive Drugs and Devices in the United States,* 23 NYU REV. L. & SOC. CHANGE 339 (1997–1998). No other developed country has a rate of surgical sterilization as high as the U.S.

The dispute over access to emergency contraception (Plan B) is one graphic example of how contested politics over contraception is in the United States. Plan B is an emergency contraceptive that can be used within 72 hours after unprotected sex to reduce the risk of pregnancy. When used as directed, it reduces the risk of pregnancy by 89 percent. It does not have any known serious or long-term side effects, though it may cause nausea or abdominal pain. *See* Tummino v. Torti, 603 F. Supp.2d 519, 522 (E.D.N.Y. 2009). The FDA approved Plan B for prescription-only use in 1999. It is available without a prescription or age restriction in much of the world, including virtually all major industrialized nations. *Id.*

In 2001, a coalition of women's organizations, supported by the drug companies marketing Plan B, filed a Citizens' Petition asking the FDA to make Plan B available, without a prescription, to women of all ages. *Id.* at 523. The FDA scientific review staff agreed that women of all ages could use Plan B without a prescription safely and effectively, but the FDA did not act on these recommendations. In 2006, the FDA acted on the Citizen Petition, announcing that it would approve the distribution of emergency contraception without a prescription, but only behind the counter at pharmacies and only for women 18 or older who could produce government-issued identification as proof of age. No other over-the-counter drug is subject to these requirements. *Id.* at 526–28.

In 2009, a federal district court found that the FDA "acted in bad faith and in response to political pressure," "departed in significant ways from the agency's normal procedures," "engaged in repeated and unreasonable delays" and that the asserted justification for denying over-the-counter access to 17 year olds "lacks all credibility." The court required the FDA to approve Plan B, without prescription, for women 17 years and older, but remanded to the FDA to reconsider the restrictions requiring that: women younger than 17 obtain a prescription; Plan B be kept behind the counter at pharmacies; and that women present government-issued identification to obtain it. In December, 2011, despite the fact that the FDA recommended over-the-counter access to Plan B for minors, DHHS Secretary Kathleen Sebelius rejected the FDA recommendation, http://www.hhs.gov/news/press/ 2011pres/12/20111207a.html. In her rejection Secretary Sebelius stated that "[a]fter careful consideration of the FDA Summary Review, I have concluded that the data, submitted by [the drug manufacturer], do not conclusively establish that Plan B One–Step should be made available over the counter for all girls of reproductive age." *Id*. The decision has been widely criticized for its rejection of the scientific evidence. Gardiner Harris, *Plan to Widen Availability of Morning–After Pill is Rejected*, N.Y. TIMES (Dec. 7, 2011), at A–1. Experts such as Dr. Susan Wood have noted that drugs with greater risks, such as Acetaminophen (the main ingredient in Tylenol) are made accessible to minors on an over-the-counter basis; political observers have posited that the decision reflects the politics of sexual activity among minors rather than a careful consideration of the evidence.

Some pharmacists, corporations and hospitals have claimed a right to refuse to dispense Plan B, even in situations involving victims of rape. GUTTMACHER INSTITUTE, STATE POLICIES IN BRIEF, EMERGENCY CONTRACEPTION (MAY 1, 2011), http://www.guttmacher.org/statecenter/spibs/spib_EC.pdf. Some states require pharmacies to dispense FDA approved drugs regardless of claimed conscientious objection, and courts have divided over whether such requirements are constitutional. *See e.g.*, Stormans, Inc. v. Selecky, 586 F.3d 1109 (9th Cir. 2009) (rejecting pharmacy and pharmacists' free exercise claims against Washington State regulation requiring pharmacies to deliver lawfully prescribed FDA-approved medications); Morr–Fitz, Inc. v. Blagojevich, 2011 WL 1338081 (Ill. Cir. 2011), http://www.aclj.org/media/ pdf/JudgeRienziRuling_20110405.pdf (granting declaratory and injunctive relief for pharmacists and corporations objecting to selling emergency contraceptives as required by Illinois law because it violated the state conscience clause, the Free Exercise clause, and Illinois' Religious Freedom Restoration Act). Other states explicitly allow pharmacists to refuse to dispense contraceptives, including emergency contraception. Wal–Mart initially refused to stock emergency contraception, and then reversed itself in response to pro-choice advocacy, noting that in some parts of the country, Wal–Mart is the only pharmacy. Michael Barbaro, *In Reversal, Wal–Mart Will Sell Contraceptive*, N.Y. TIMES, March 4, 2006.

In 2008, 36 million U.S. women were sexually active, able to get pregnant and not trying to get pregnant. Between 2004 and 2008, the average annual cost of contraceptive services rose from $203 to $257. Slightly more than half of these women were able to pay for contraception services from private physicians or health plans. 17.4 million women sought publicly funded services and supplies. 29% of the women seeking services in public clinics were younger than 20. 71% were adult women with family incomes below 250% of the poverty line. Jennifer J. Frost et al., *Contraceptive Needs and Services: National and State Data, 2008 Update*, GUTTMACHER INSTITUTE (2010), http://www.guttmacher.org/pubs/win/contraceptive-needs-2008.pdf.

While almost all insurance policies cover prescription drugs, as recently as 1995, only fifteen percent of traditional private insurance plans covered all of the most commonly used reversible prescription contraceptives, and

49% cover none

forty-nine percent of plans cover none of these methods. Guttmacher Institute, *Uneven and Unequal: Insurance Coverage for Reproductive Health* Services (1995). Some women insured under employment-based plans challenged this pattern, arguing that excluding contraception from otherwise comprehensive coverage for prescription drugs violated the Pregnancy Discrimination Act. Sylvia A. Law, *Sex Discrimination and Insurance for Contraception*, 73 WASH. L. REV. 363 (1998). Courts have divided as to whether the PDA allows employers who provide comprehensive coverage for prescription drugs to exclude coverage for contraception. Erickson v. Bartell Drug Co., 141 F. Supp.2d 1266 (W.D. Wash. 2001) (exclusion violates the PDA); In re Union Pac. R.R. Co., 479 F.3d 936 (8th Cir. 2007) (PDA does not apply to contraception because users are not pregnant). By 2011, 28 states prohibited private insurance plans that offer coverage for prescription drugs from excluding coverage for the full range of contraceptive drugs and devices approved by the FDA. Alan Guttmmacher Institute, Insurance Coverage of Contraceptives, Aug. 1, 2011, http://www.guttmacher.org/statecenter/spibs/spib_ICC.pdf. Ninety percent of employer-based plans now cover a full range of prescription contraceptives, three times the proportion that did so just a decade before. *Facts on Contraceptive Use in the United States, 2010.*

The Affordable Care Act requires insurers to cover preventative health services, without deductibles or co-insurance payments. The Obama Administration asked the Institute of Medicine to recommend the preventive services that should be included. In July 2011, the IOM recommended that contraception be included as a preventive health services and the administration accepted that recommendation. Robert Pear, *Insurance Coverage for Contraception Is Required*, N.Y. TIMES, Aug. 1, 2011. Other preventive services include mammograms, colonoscopies, blood pressure checks, childhood immunizations, and many other services. Insurers remain free to use "reasonable medical management techniques" to control costs and promote the efficient delivery of care. For example, an insurer can charge co-payments for brand-name drugs if a lower-cost generic version is available and equally safe and effective. Secretary Kathleen Sebelius, the Secretary of Health and Human Services, said, "These historic guidelines are based on science and existing literature and will help ensure women the preventive health benefits they need."

An amended Interim Final Rule, issued in 2011, contained a narrowly drawn exemption for health plans offered by a "religious employer," defined for purposes of the ACA's preventive services coverage policy, as "one that: (1) has the inculcation of religious values as its purpose; (2) primarily employs persons who share its religious tenets; (3) primarily serves persons who share its religious tenets; and (4) is a non-profit organization under [certain sections of the Code]." 76 Fed Reg. 46,621, 46,625 (August 3, 2011). According to the federal agencies, the federal definition reflects definitions used by states that exempt religious employers from compliance with state mandates to cover contraceptive services. The definition shields churches and other religious houses of worship but not religiously-affiliated non-profit institutions such as hospitals, universities, and social service agencies.

allows them to escape having to comply

Following more than 200,000 comments, on January 20, 2012, Secretary Sebelius announced, without further amending the 2011 Interim Final Rule, that religiously-affiliated employers not covered by the narrow exemption for religious employers would have an additional year (August 1, 2013 rather than the interim rule's August 2012 effective date) to comply, http://www.hhs.gov/news/press/2012pres/01/20120120a.html. An absolute deluge of opposition from across the political spectrum then followed, framing the narrow regulatory exemption as violating religious freedom rather than protecting women's health. *See, e.g.,* David Gibson, Five Reasons Why Obama Is Losing the Contraception Fight, WASHINGTON POST, February 8, 2012, http://www.washingtonpost.com/national/on-faith/five-reasons-why-obama-is-losing-the-contraception-fight/2012/02/08/gIQACC0 kzQ_story.html; U.S. Bishops Vow to Fight HHS Edit, http://www.usccb.org/news/2012/12–012.cfm (Jan. 20, 2012).

[handwritten margin note: complained of violating]

The Administration issued a final rule on February 10, 2012, http://www.whitehouse.gov/the-press-office/2012/02/10/fact-sheet-women-s-preventive-services-and-religious-institutions, that, while retaining the narrow religious exemption, specifies that insurers that sell insured group health plan products to religiously-affiliated nonprofit sponsors must provide contraceptive coverage at levels defined in federal guidelines at no charge. This policy aimed both to guarantee women the right to full coverage while at the same time exempting religiously-affiliated sponsors from having to pay a premium for the coverage. According to the White House, research shows that the contraceptive coverage component of a group health plan carries no cost, since contraceptive coverage actually reduces insurer outlays.

[handwritten margin note: group Health must provide coverage]

This final policy turn answered the question (sort of) for religiously-affiliated employers that purchase insurance products by effectively sparing religiously-affiliated plan sponsors from having to pay premiums for contraception. However, you will learn in Part Two that this fig-leaf solution (assuming one needs a solution at all given the constitutionality of public health regulations against claimed religious freedom rights when such regulations are impartially and universally applied) leaves two big issues unanswered. First, even if the benefit is free, it remains part of the employer's benefit plan under ERISA. Second, the solution does nothing for employers that self-insure and that use insurers merely as third-party administrators of their own self-insured plans. Many large, religiously-affiliated employers such as hospitals or universities are self-insured. The final rule does not explain how self-insured plans will be accommodated. The White House has said that this "detail" will be worked out during the period of the moratorium.

[handwritten margin note: Issues @ BAY]

Because so many women lack insurance, and/or a regular source of medical care, in 1970, Congress acted to encourage the development of family planning clinics. Title X is the popular name for the Family Planning Services and Population Research Act of 1970, 42 U.S.C. §§ 300–300a–8. It provides grants to qualified providers of family planning services which meet a variety of standards, including a requirement that federal funds be matched with resources from other sources. Title X provides that: "None of the funds appropriated under this subchapter shall be used in programs where abortion is a method of family planning." 42 U.S.C. § 300a–6 (1982).

In 2006, more than 7 million women received contraceptive services from more than 8,000 subsidized family planning clinics. Guttmacher Institute, Contraceptive Needs and Services, 2006, (2009), http://www. guttmacher.org/pubs/win/allstates2006.pdf. Thirty-three percent were health department clinics, twenty-seven percent were community or migrant health centers, twenty percent were other clinics, eleven percent were Planned Parenthood centers and nine percent were hospital clinics. *Id.* The Planned Parenthood Clinics tend to serve more people than those sponsored by local health departments. In addition to Title X, under Medicaid, family planning services is a mandatory basic service which must be covered for eligible people; under Medicaid, family planning services are supported by a 90% federal match. *See* Part Two, below. Efforts to deny funding to family planning organizations that also provide abortions are discussed in the next section.

c. Abortion: shifting Constitutional principles. In Roe v. Wade, 410 U.S. 113 (1973), the Supreme Court held that the Fourteenth Amendment protects a doctor's right to practice medicine in accordance with his or her professional judgment and a woman's right to choose whether to have a child, including the right to abortion. Because the health risks of child birth are so much greater than the risks of abortion in the first trimester, states may not regulate in that period; in the second trimester states may regulate to promote maternal health. Only in the third trimester may states act to protect the fetus, and then a woman's abortion choice is protected if continued pregnancy poses a threat to her life or health. From 1973 until 1992, applying these standards, the Court struck down many state laws designed to restrict access to abortion. *See e.g.* Akron v. Akron Center for Reproductive Health, Inc., 462 U.S. 416 (1983) (striking down biased and burdensome requirements of hospitalization, "informed consent" and parental consent). The major exceptions were cases in which the Court approved complex rules for parental consent, Bellotti v. Baird, 443 U.S. 622 (1979), and approved the exclusion of abortion from Medicaid funding, discussed below. During these two decades, changes in the composition of the Court reduced the majority supporting *Roe v. Wade,* and almost all cases were decided by a 5–4 vote.

In Planned Parenthood of Southeastern Pennsylvania v. Casey, 505 U.S. 833 (1992), the Court, 5–4, technically affirmed *Roe,* but changed the constitutional standard used to evaluate the constitutionality of state laws restricting access to abortion. Under *Casey*, prior to viability, states may regulate abortions in ways that make it more costly or difficult to obtain, unless the law "imposes an undue burden on a woman's ability to make this decision. A finding of an undue burden is shorthand for the conclusion that a state regulation has the purpose or effect of placing a substantial obstacle in the path of a woman seeking an abortion of a nonviable fetus." 505 U.S. at 874, 877. In *Casey*, the Court found that Pennsylvania's requirement that women seeking abortions inform their husbands constituted an "undue burden." The *Casey* court approved many of the provisions of the Pennsylvania law that lower courts had found burdensome and irrational, including biased informed consent requirements and a mandatory 24-hour waiting period between consent and the abortion procedure. Since then, states have adopted hundreds of laws imposing serious burdens on pre-viability abortions, but none has been held unconstitutional. Kathryn Kolbert et al., *Preserving the Core of Roe: Reflections on Planned Parenthood v. Casey*, 18 YALE J. L. & FEMINISM 317 (2006).

Beginning in the 1990s, states began criminalizing a procedure commonly referred to as "partial birth" abortion. Nebraska adopted a law, typical of laws enacted in 30 other states, prohibiting "an abortion procedure in which the person performing the abortion partially delivers vaginally a living unborn child before killing the unborn child and completing the delivery." The law also defined a fetus as an "unborn child" from the moment of conception. Read literally, the law prohibited most common abortions because the phrase "partially delivers" could apply to a single limb delivered in the common dilation-and-evacuation abortion procedure. In Stenberg v. Carhart (*"Carhart I"*), 530 U.S. 914 (2000), the Supreme Court, 5–4, held that the Nebraska law was unconstitutional because it lacked an exception for preserving the health of the woman and created a serious risk of prohibiting most second-trimester, pre-viability abortions.

Congress responded by adopting a federal ban on "partial birth" abortions that was substantially identical to the Nebraska law, although it tightened the definition of the prohibited procedure. The composition of the Court had changed since *Casey*, with Justice Alito substituting for Justice O'Connor. In Gonzales v. Carhart (*"Carhart II"*), 550 U.S. 124 (2007), the Court upheld the federal law. Justice Ginsburg, dissenting for four justices, noted the absence of an exception safeguarding a woman's health, the failure to distinguish between abortions pre- and post-viability, and the failure to demand the close scrutiny previously required, at least as a formal matter, by *Casey*. The majority opinion deferred to the judgment of Congress that the prohibited procedure was never medically necessary, despite the disagreement of most of the organized medical profession and many individual physicians. Justice Kennedy also speculated that "some women come to regret their choice to abort the infant life they once created and sustained. Severe depression and loss of esteem can follow." *Id.* at 159.

d.   Abortion: availability of services. Abortion rates are much higher in the United States than in any other developed country. Megan L. Kavanaugh & Eleanor Bimla Schwarz, *Counseling About and Use of Emergency Contraception in the United States*, Perspectives on Sexual and Reproduc-

tive Health, June 1, 2008, http://www.articlearchives.com/medicine-health/
sexual-reproductive-health-contraception/962684–1.html. In recent years
U.S. policy has denied young people access to fact-based sexual education.
The medical profession and drug industry offer a narrower range of
contraception than is available in other developed countries. Most women
seeking abortions are in their twenties and have children. The most
commonly reported reasons for seeking abortion are the responsibilities of
parenthood and family life and the inability to meet the demands that
another child would present.

Abortion remains the most common surgical procedure in the United
States. Nearly half of pregnancies among American women are unintended,
and four in ten of these are terminated by abortion. In 2006, 22% of all
pregnancies (excluding miscarriages) end in abortion. In 2006, 1.21 million
abortions were performed, down from 1.31 million in 2000. Guttmacher
Institute, *Facts on Induced Abortion in the United States* (2008).

In 2005 eighty-seven percent of all U.S. counties lacked an abortion
provider. Thirty-five percent of women of reproductive age live in those
counties. Between 2000 and 2005, the number of U.S. abortion providers
declined by 2 percent. Rachel K. Jones & Kathryn Kooistra, *Abortion
Incidence and Access to Services in the United States, 2008*, 43 PERSP. ON
SEXUAL & REPRODUCTIVE HEALTH 41 (2011) [hereinafter *Abortion Access*,
2008.]

Most abortions, 95%, are performed in specialized abortion clinics.
Abortion Access, 2008, at 42. Some 82% of abortion clinics experienced
some form of harassment in 2000. Most commonly, harassment took for
form of picketing and physical contact with or blocking of patients, but 15%
of large providers received a bomb threat. *Id*. In addition, in most states,
abortion providers must comply with a wide range of restrictive laws that
have been adopted to discourage abortion and approved as constitutional
under *Casey's* "undue burden" standard.

Safe, legal abortion is inaccessible for many women. For example, in
New York City, Medicaid pays for abortions for poor women, and there are
more abortion providers than other areas of country, but women still seek
illegal abortions because they do not know that legal services are available
or they fear that their privacy will be sacrificed. Jennifer Lee & Cara
Buckley, *For Privacy's Sake, Taking Risks to End Pregnancy*, N.Y. TIMES,
Jan. 5, 2009, http://www.nytimes.com/2009/01/05/nyregion/05abortion.html.
The Medical Director of a clinic in northern Manhattan reports that she
sees at least one patient every week who has tried to end a pregnancy on
her own, often with tragic results. Anne Davis, Letter to the Editor, N.Y.
TIMES, Jan. 12, 2009, at A22.

The problem of access to safe abortion services has been intensified by
efforts on the part of numerous states to go beyond the "demand side"
strategy of placing regulatory constraints on women's ability to choose
abortion. Many states are now trying "supply side" efforts to impose strict
regulations on facilities that perform abortions, even in the early stages.
These state laws impose operating requirements and conditions that signifi-

cantly exceed levels considered reasonable for a relatively minor procedure. For example, regulations adopted by Virginia's public health authority in 2011 provide that any abortion facility performing five or more abortions per month will be considered a hospital and will be required to meet hospital-level licensure conditions. As of 2004, 12 states had fewer than five non-hospital-based abortion providers. Ninety-four percent of all U.S. abortions are performed in large clinics that perform more than 400 abortions annually. Theodore Joyce, *the Supply–Side Economics of Abortion,* 365 NEW ENG. J. MED. 1466 (2011).

Only a small portion of medical students and residents are trained to perform abortions. This paucity is understandable since doctors who perform abortions are subject to harassment and sometimes violence. In recent years, the medical profession, led by the student organization Medical Students for Choice, has encouraged training in abortion. Emily Bazelon, *The New Abortion Providers*, N.Y. TIMES, July 12, 2010, http://www.ny times.com/ 2010/07/18/magazine/18abortion-t.html?_r1. The American College of Obstetrics and Gynecology ("ACOG") has recognized the essential role of all physicians in assuring access to services that patients need and seek. An ethics opinion on these issues provides, in part:

> Where conscience implores physicians to deviate from standard practices, including abortion, sterilization and provision of contraceptives, they must provide potential patients with accurate and prior notice of their personal moral commitments. Physicians and other health care professionals have the duty to refer patients in a timely manner to other providers if they do not feel that they can in conscience provide the standard reproductive services that their patients request. In resource poor areas, access to safe and legal reproductive services should be maintained.

American College of Obstetrics and Gynecology Committee on Ethics, *The Limits of Conscientious Refusal in Reproductive Medicine,* 110 OBSTETRICS GYNECOLOGY 1203 (2007). Are these principles wise? Should a doctor who opposes abortion be ethically required to provide a referral to a patient who seeks one? Wise or not, the ACOG principles are often not followed in practice. Sylvia A. Law, *Silent No More: Physicians' Legal & Ethical Obligations to Patients Seeking Abortions*, 21 NYU REV. L. SOC. CHANGE 279 (1994–1995).

   e.   Abortion: funding. When the Supreme Court transformed abortion from a crime to a right in *Roe* in 1973, state Medicaid programs, as well as private health insurance policies, covered abortions. Abortion is a surgical procedure performed by physicians and typically covered by insurance, private and public. The vast majority of private insurance plans still cover abortions. Adam Sonfield, *Toward Universal Insurance Coverage: A Primer for Sexual and Reproductive Health Advocates*, 11 GUTTMACHER POL'Y REV. 11, 15 (2008). Soon after *Roe* several states restricted Medicaid payment for abortion by requiring doctors to document the reasons that abortions were "medically necessary."

Between 1973 and 1977, numerous federal courts held that such restrictive and discriminatory definitions of medical necessity violated the Medicaid statute, the federal constitution, or both. Medicaid funded 250,-000 to 300,000 abortions each year from 1973 to August 4, 1977. McRae v. Califano, 491 F. Supp. 630, 639 (E.D.N.Y. 1980). In Beal v. Doe, 432 U.S. 438 (1977), the Supreme Court, 5–4, upheld state restrictions on abortion. The Court rejected plaintiffs' statutory claim that the Medicaid statute prohibits limits based on diagnosis or condition. See Part Two, below. The Court noted that "serious statutory questions might be presented if a state Medicaid plan excluded necessary medical treatment from its coverage." 432 U.S. at 445. A companion case, Maher v. Roe, 432 U.S. 464 (1977), rejected the claim that the burdensome and unique Medicaid limits on abortion funding violated equal protection.

The "serious statutory questions" that the Court noted in *Beal*, disappeared in 1976 when Congress passed a rider to an appropriations bill (popularly known as the Hyde Amendment) prohibiting federal funding for the performance of abortions "except where the life of the mother would be endangered if the fetus were carried to term." When the Hyde Amendment was challenged, extensive medical evidence showed that that it is virtually never possible for doctors to predict when pregnancy will endanger the life of a woman. McRae v. Califano, 491 F. Supp. at 639. Pregnancy and delivery always pose greater risks to women than abortion. Many factors increase risk, including whether the woman wants to bear a child. Dozens of federal courts held that the Hyde Amendment violated the Equal Protection Clause by making Medicaid funding contingent upon a woman's sacrifice of her constitutionally protected right to reproductive choice, undermining the health of women, and serving no public purpose in terms of cost savings or population growth.

The Supreme Court reversed, 5–4, in Harris v. McRae, 448 U.S. 297 (1980), holding that the "principle recognized in *Wade* and later cases—protecting a woman's freedom of choice—did not translate into a constitutional obligation" to subsidize abortions. Ignoring the medically necessary nature of many of the excluded abortions, the majority ruled: "[I]t simply does not follow that a woman's freedom of choice carries with it a constitutional entitlement to the financial resources to avail herself of the full range of protected choices." *Id.* at 316. The Court continued, "It cannot be that because government may not prohibit the use of contraceptives, or prevent parents from sending their child to a private school, government, therefore, has an affirmative constitutional obligation to ensure that all persons have the financial resources to obtain contraceptives or send their children to private schools." *Id.* at 318.

Addressing the question presented by the plaintiffs, i.e. whether there was a rational basis for excluding medically necessary abortions from the otherwise comprehensive Medicaid program, the Court held: "[T]he Hyde Amendment bears a rational relationship to its legitimate [state] interest in protecting the potential life of the fetus. Abortion is inherently different from other medical procedures, because no other procedure involves the purposeful termination of potential life." *Id.* at 324–25.

The anti-abortion movement sees the Hyde Amendment and the Supreme Court's decision in *McRae* as one of its greatest successes. Douglas Johnson of the National Right to Life Committee says, "At the very minimum, there are over 1 million Americans walking around today alive because of the Hyde amendment." http://www.npr.org/templates/story/story.php?storyId=104184421.

In seventeen states, pro-choice advocates persuaded states to include abortion in Medicaid. (Four do so by legislative choice and the rest do so under court orders holding that the exclusion of abortion from Medicaid violates state constitutions, most often state constitutional prohibitions against gender discrimination). About 13 percent of all abortions in the United States are paid for with public funds, virtually all provided by state governments. Five states prohibit private insurance from covering abortion, except when a woman's life is in danger. Guttmacher Institute, *Restricting Insurance Coverage of Abortion* (2009). In other countries abortion services are covered by insurance to the extent that they are allowed by the law. Guttmacher Institute, *Sharing Responsibility: Women, Society and Abortion Worldwide*, at 12–16, 1999, http://www.Guttmacher.org/pubs/sharing.pdf.

Congress has extended the ban on federal funding for abortion to other groups including military personnel and their dependents, federal employees and their dependents, teenagers participating in the State Children's Health Insurance Program, low-income residents of the District of Columbia, members of the Peace Corps, disabled recipients of Medicare, federal prison inmates and Native Americans, among others. *Discriminatory Restrictions on Abortion Funding Threaten Women's Health, NARAL Pro–Choice America Foundation* 2, http://www.prochoiceamerica.org/assets/files/Abortion–Access-to-Abortion–Women–Government–Discriminatory–Restrictions.pdf. Some of the restrictions are even more stringent than those applicable to poor women eligible for Medicaid. For example, women serving in the military cannot obtain a federally funded abortion even when the pregnancy results from rape or incest; military doctors and health care facilities cannot provide abortion even if the woman is stationed in a remote area and is willing to pay. National Abortion Federation, *Service Women Overseas Deserve Better Access to Safe and Legal Health Care* (2006), http://www.prochoice.org/policy/congress/women_military.html.

The restrictions have been challenged by women with life threatening pregnancies and by women carrying fetuses that are unlikely to survive after birth. Following *McRae,* federal courts have upheld the denial of insurance coverage even in these extreme circumstances. Doe v. United States, 372 F.3d 1308 (Fed. Cir. 2004) (unanimous decision denying payment to a Navy wife with anencephalic fetus); Britell v. United States, 372 F.3d 1370 (Fed. Cir. 2004) (denying payment to a federal employee with an anencephalic fetus; state's interest in promoting potential life controls even though no possibility exists that the fetus will survive).

underdeveloped brain & incomplete skull

The denial of funding discourages abortion. Between 20 percent and 27 percent of the women denied Medicaid coverage for abortion carry the pregnancy to term. When a woman is forced to carry a pregnancy to term against her own best judgment, she may suffer, as may the future child and her other children. Some women, denied access to legal abortion, obtain illegal abortions and a small number die. Most, however, raise the money to have a legal abortion, often by foregoing essential food and shelter for themselves and their children. When Medicaid is denied, poor women wait on average 2–3 weeks longer than other women to have an abortion because of difficulties in obtaining the necessary funds. When abortion is delayed, health risks to the woman increase. A second trimester abortion costs about twice as much as a first trimester procedure. Heather Boonstra & Adam Sonfield, *Rights Without Access: Revisiting Public Funding of Abortion for Poor Women,* 3 Guttmacher Rep. on Pub. Pol'y 8, 10 (2000). Unintended pregnancy costs over $11 million a year in direct public medical costs for births, abortions, miscarriages and infant medical care. Adam Sonfield et al., *The Public Costs of Births resulting from Unintended Pregnancies: National and State–Level Estimates,* Guttmacher Institute, (2011); Adam Monea & Adam Thomas, *Unintended Pregnancy and Taxpayer Spending,* Brookings Institution (2011).

The Patient Protection and Affordable Care Act contains provisions whose purpose is to reduce financing for abortion by limiting the extent to which qualified health plans sold in state health insurance Exchanges (discussed in Part Two) may sell products that cover abortions other than abortion procedures linked to rape, incest, or life endangerment. The Act retains prior restrictions on federal funding while also banning privately purchased qualified health plans from covering additional abortions unless the additional coverage is set up and sold as a separate plan with separate administration. Premiums must be collected in a separate check and be deposited into a second separate account, and the abortion coverage must be separately administered. Insurers must determine the actuarial value of the separate coverage for abortion. Patient Protection and Affordable Care Act § 1303(b)(2)(C), as replaced by § 10104(c). In making that actuarial estimate the health plan insurer "may not take into account any cost reduction estimated to result from such services, including prenatal care, delivery, or postnatal care." Affordable Care Act, § 1303(b)(2)(D). As a practical matter, no insurer is likely to offer this separate, highly regulated, administratively cumbersome product for abortion coverage. Sara Rosenbaum et al., *An Analysis of the Impact of the Stupak/Pitts Amendment on Coverage for Abortion,* http://www.gwumc.edu/sphhs/departments/health policy/dhp_publications/pub_uploads/dhpPublication_FED314C4–5056–9D 20–3DBE77EF6ABF0FED.pdf.

In 2011, empowered by Republican gains in the mid-term elections and the Supreme Court's 2007 indication in *Gonzales v. Carhart* that abortion restrictions that were previously unconstitutional might now pass muster, anti-choice legislators in Congress and the states pushed for broader restrictions. In April, the House passed a bill that would have denied Title X funds for family planning services to Planned Parenthood, but the Senate rejected the bill. In May, the House passed a bill that would have denied tax credits to small businesses that offer private health plans that cover abortion services, as some 87 percent of private plans do. It also would eliminate the medical-expense deduction for abortion and prohibits reimbursement from individual medical savings accounts. Editorial, *New Attacks on Women's Rights,* N.Y. TIMES, May 9, 2011.

In 2011, legislatures in many states passed laws restricting access to abortion. Over this time period, at least 64 new pieces of anti-abortion legislation have been enacted based on what one writer characterizes as a "campaign" that is the "largest in history." Emily Bazelon, *The Reincarnation of Pro–Life,* N.Y. TIMES, May 27, 2011; The Guttmacher Institute, *States Enact Record Number of Abortion Restrictions in First Half of 2011* (July 13, 2011), http://www.guttmacher.org/media/inthenews/2011/07/13/index.html. Newly introduced legislation both places constraints on the ability to gain access to services in a timely fashion as well as restrictions on the ability to establish and operate facilities where abortions can be safely carried out. States also have introduced limitations on insurers' ability to offer products that cover medically indicated abortion procedures just as they would cover any other medically necessary hospital and medical procedure. *Id.* Federal courts issued preliminary injunctions against state laws requiring that women meet with anti-abortion counselors and wait for 72 hours before obtaining an abortion. David Bailey, *Federal Judge Blocks South Dakota Abortion Law,* Reuters.com, (June 30, 2011), http://www.reuters.com/article/2011/07/01/us-abortion-southdakota-idUSTRE76009M20110701; John Hanna, *Kansas Abortion Law Blocked by Federal Judge,* HuffPost Politics, HuffingtongPost.com (July 1, 2011), http://www.huffingtonpost.com/2011/07/01/kansas-abortion-law-judged-blocked-planned-parenthood_n_889021.html; Alicia Gallegos, *More States Face Legal Battles Over Abortion Laws,* amednews.com, (July 18, 2011), http://www.ama-assn.org/amednews/2011/07/18/gvsc0718.htm.

Following the example of the U.S. House, Indiana and six other states, targeted Planned Parenthood by prohibiting state agencies from entering contracts with or making grants to "any entity that performs abortions or maintains or operates a facility where abortions are performed." The law effectively denied Planned Parenthood payment for family planning services, cancer and STD screening and other services provided to people eligible for Medicaid. (Federal payment for abortion has long been denied under the Hyde Amendment.) As you will see in Part Two, states have wide latitude in determining who is a qualified Medicaid provider. But, an Indiana federal district court held that Planned Parenthood and the patients they serve had a right to sue under 42 U.S.C. § 1983 and that the state's exclusion of Planned Parenthood violated Medicaid's requirement that beneficiaries have free choice in selecting qualified providers. Planned Parenthood of Indiana, Inc. v. Commissioner of the Indiana State Department of Health, 794 F. Supp.2d 892 (S.D. Ind. 2011). Robert Pear, *Indiana Law to Cut Planned Parenthood Funding is Blocked,* N.Y. TIMES, June 24, 2011.

3. PROHIBITING DISCRIMINATION ON THE BASIS OF DISABILITY: THE AMERICANS WITH DISABILITIES ACT AND THE REALIZATION OF HEALTH CARE AS A PUBLIC ACCOMMODATION

The Americans with Disabilities Act of 1990 (ADA), 42 U.S.C. § 12101 et seq., is designed to overcome the long tradition of stereotyping and discrimination against persons with disabilities. Building on the earlier and still-applicable Section 504 of the Rehabilitation Act of 1973, 29 U.S.C. § 794, and drawing on the Civil Rights Act of 1964, the ADA prohibits discrimination against persons with disabilities (or regarded as such) in employment (Title I), governmental services (Title II), and predominantly privately-owned "public accommodations" (Title III), including the "professional office of a healthcare provider" and an "insurance office." 42 U.S.C. § 12181(7)(f). Title V includes "safe harbor" provisions with respect to insurance, and all the Titles contain qualifications on, or defenses to, the antidiscrimination principle, notably that in many contexts the disabled are entitled to reasonable accommodations.

The ADA is examined in several places in this textbook. This Chapter examines the Title III public accommodations provisions in the context of health care access. Part Two explores the application of Titles I and III in the context of health insurance products, as well as the powerful intersection of Title II and Medicaid.

a. The Statutory Text of the ADA

The ADA is a complex and lengthy statute, cobbled together from a series of measures passed by multiple Congressional committees, each of which had jurisdiction over various components of the Act. The ADA's complexity results from the fact that the legislation addresses both publicly funded practices and purely private conduct, including the conduct of health professionals and health care institutions regardless of their participation in federally assisted programs. The following statutory provisions are excerpts from the Act's Preamble.

Americans With Disabilities Act: Selected Text

42 U.S.C § 12101

§ 12101.   Findings and purpose

(a) Findings

The Congress finds that—

(1) some 43,000,000 Americans have one or more physical or mental disabilities, and this number is increasing as the population as a whole is growing older;

(2) historically, society has tended to isolate and segregate individuals with disabilities, and, despite some improvements, such forms of discrimination against individuals with disabilities continue to be a serious and pervasive social problem;

(3) discrimination against individuals with disabilities persists in such critical areas as employment, housing, public accommodations, education, transportation, communication, recreation, institutionalization, health services, voting, and access to public services;

(4) unlike individuals who have experienced discrimination on the basis of race, color, sex, national origin, religion, or age, individuals who have experienced discrimination on the basis of disability have often had no legal recourse to redress such discrimination;

(5) individuals with disabilities continually encounter various forms of discrimination, including outright intentional exclusion, the discriminatory effects of architectural, transportation, and communication barriers, overprotective rules and policies, failure to make modifications to existing facilities and practices, exclusionary qualification standards and criteria, segregation, and relegation to lesser services, programs, activities, benefits, jobs, or other opportunities;

(6) census data, national polls, and other studies have documented that people with disabilities, as a group, occupy an inferior status in our society, and are severely disadvantaged socially, vocationally, economically, and educationally;

(7) individuals with disabilities are a discrete and insular minority who have been faced with restrictions and limitations, subjected to a history of purposeful unequal treatment, and relegated to a position of political powerlessness in our society, based on characteristics that are beyond the control of such individuals and resulting from stereotypic assumptions not truly indicative of the individual ability of such individuals to participate in, and contribute to, society;

(8) the Nation's proper goals regarding individuals with disabilities are to assure equality of opportunity, full participation, independent living, and economic self-sufficiency for such individuals; and

(9) the continuing existence of unfair and unnecessary discrimination and prejudice denies people with disabilities the opportunity to compete on an equal basis and to pursue those opportunities for which our free society is justifiably famous, and costs the United States billions of dollars in unnecessary expenses resulting from dependency and nonproductivity.

(b) Purpose

It is the purpose of this Part—

(1) to provide a clear and comprehensive national mandate for the elimination of discrimination against individuals with disabilities;

(2) to provide clear, strong, consistent, enforceable standards addressing discrimination against individuals with disabilities;

(3) to ensure that the Federal Government plays a central role in enforcing the standards established in this Part on behalf of individuals with disabilities; and

(4) to invoke the sweep of congressional authority, including the power to enforce the fourteenth amendment and to regulate commerce, in order to address the major areas of discrimination faced day-to-day by people with disabilities.

Notes

The Preamble of the ADA was prompted by Supreme Court rulings since 1994 significantly limiting Congress' Constitutional powers. Some of the most important cases that have considered the reach of Congress' powers have arisen under the ADA. Tennessee v. Lane, 541 U.S. 509 (2004); Board of Trustees of Univ. of Ala. v. Garrett, 531 U.S. 356 (2001). *See* JOHN T. NOONAN, JR., NARROWING THE NATION'S POWER: THE SUPREME COURT SIDES WITH THE STATES (2002). In addition to chronicling the ways in which public and private interests systematically segregated, excluded, and discriminated against persons with disabilities, the Preamble provides a clear statement for the courts regarding Congress' underlying theory of its powers to protect persons with disabilities from discrimination in numerous settings.

Compare the extensive language of the ADA with Title VI of the 1964 Civil Rights Act. Unlike the earlier Act, in which the statutory language is modest and the rules are relatively detailed, the ADA embeds detailed standards directly into the statute. Why would Congress draft such extensive legislation as opposed to enacting a broad outline and permitting federal agencies to "fill in the blanks?" The ADA was adopted by a Democratic Congress in the middle of a Republican Presidential Administration. The legislation was bipartisan, passed the House of Representatives by a vote of 377 to 38, and in the Senate by a vote of 91 to 6. *Righting the ADA*, National Council on Disability (Dec. 2004), http://www.ncd.gov/news room/publications/2004/righting_ada.htm. President George H.W. Bush called the ADA the most important achievement of his Presidency. Nonetheless a Democratic Congress was not willing to leave the details to a Republican Administrative Branch. *See* Chai R. Feldblum, *Medical Examinations and Inquiries under the Americans with Disabilities Act: A View from the Inside*, 64 TEMP. L. REV. 521 (1991).

b.   Health Care as a Public Accommodation: The Obligation of Health Professionals to Treat Qualified Persons With Disabilities

Bragdon v. Abbott

524 U.S. 624 (1998)

■ KENNEDY, J., delivered the opinion of the Court, in which STEVENS, SOUTER, GINSBURG, and BREYER, JJ., joined. STEVENS, J., filed a concurring opinion, in which BREYER, J., joined. GINSBURG, J., filed a concurring opinion. REHNQUIST, C. J., filed an opinion concurring in the judgment in part and dissenting in part, in which SCALIA AND THOMAS, JJ., joined, and in Part Two of which O'CONNOR, J., joined. O'CONNOR, J., filed an opinion concurring in the judgment in part and dissenting in part.

■ JUSTICE KENNEDY delivered the opinion of the Court.

We address in this case the application of the Americans with Disabilities Act (ADA) to persons infected with the human immunodeficiency virus (HIV). We granted certiorari to review, first, whether HIV infection is a disability under the ADA when the infection has not yet progressed to the so-called symptomatic phase; and, second, whether the Court of Appeals, in affirming a grant of summary judgment, cited sufficient material in the record to determine, as a matter of law, that respondent's infection with HIV posed no direct threat to the health and safety of her treating dentist.

Respondent Sidney Abbott has been infected with HIV since 1986. When the incidents we recite occurred, her infection had not manifested its most serious symptoms. On September 16, 1994, she went to the office of petitioner Randon Bragdon in Bangor, Maine, for a dental appointment. She disclosed her HIV infection on the patient registration form. Petitioner completed a dental examination, discovered a cavity, and informed respondent of his policy against filling cavities of HIV-infected patients. He offered to perform the work at a hospital with no added fee for his services, though respondent would be responsible for the cost of using the hospital's facilities. Respondent declined.

Respondent sued petitioner under § 302 of the ADA, 42 U.S.C. § 12182, alleging discrimination on the basis of her disability. Section 302 of the ADA provides:

"No individual shall be discriminated against on the basis of disability in the full and equal enjoyment of the goods, services, facilities, privileges, advantages, or accommodations of any place of public accommodation by any person who operates a place of public accommodation." § 12182(a).

The term "public accommodation" is defined to include the "professional office of a health care provider." § 12181(7)(F).

A later subsection qualifies the mandate not to discriminate. It provides:

"Nothing in this subchapter shall require an entity to permit an individual to participate in or benefit from the goods, services, facilities, privileges, advantages and accommodations of such entity where such individual poses a direct threat to the health or safety of others." § 12182(b)(3).

The District Court ruled in favor of the plaintiffs, holding that respondent's HIV infection satisfied the ADA's definition of disability. The court held further that petitioner raised no genuine issue of material fact as to whether respondent's HIV infection would have posed a direct threat to the health or safety of others during the course of a dental treatment. The court relied on affidavits submitted by Dr. Donald Wayne Marianos, Director of the Division of Oral Health of the Centers for Disease Control and Prevention (CDC). The Marianos' affidavits asserted it is safe for dentists to treat patients infected with HIV in dental offices if the dentist follows the so-called universal precautions described in the Recommended Infection-control Practices for Dentistry issued by CDC in 1993 (1993 CDC Dentistry Guidelines).

The Court of Appeals affirmed. It held respondent's HIV infection was a disability under the ADA, even though her infection had not yet progressed to the symptomatic stage. The Court of Appeals also agreed that treating the respondent in petitioner's office would not have posed a direct threat to the health and safety of others. Unlike the District Court, however, the Court of Appeals declined to rely on the Marianos' affidavits. Instead the court relied on the 1993 CDC Dentistry Guidelines, as well as the Policy on AIDS, HIV Infection and the Practice of Dentistry, promulgated by the American Dental Association in 1991 (1991 American Dental Association Policy on HIV).

We first review the ruling that respondent's HIV infection constituted a disability under the ADA. The statute defines disability as: "(A) a physical or mental impairment that substantially limits one or more of the major life activities of such individual; (B) a record of such an impairment; or (C) being regarded as having such impairment." § 12102(2).

We hold respondent's HIV infection was a disability under subsection (A) of the definitional section of the statute. In light of this conclusion, we need not consider the applicability of subsections (B) or (C).

Our consideration of subsection (A) of the definition proceeds in three steps. First, we consider whether respondent's HIV infection was a physical impairment. Second, we identify the life activity upon which respondent relies (reproduction and child bearing) and determine whether it constitutes a major life activity under the ADA. Third, tying the two statutory phrases together, we ask whether the impairment substantially limited the major life activity. In construing the statute, we are informed by interpretations of parallel definitions in previous statutes and the views of various administrative agencies which have faced this interpretive question.

The first step in the inquiry under subsection (A) requires us to determine whether respondent's condition constituted a physical impairment. The HEW regulations, which appear without change in the current regulations issued by the Department of Health and Human Services, define "physical or mental impairment" to mean:

> (A) any physiological disorder or condition, cosmetic disfigurement, or anatomical loss affecting one or more of the following body systems: neurological; musculoskeletal; special sense organs; respiratory, including speech organs; cardiovascular; reproductive, digestive, genitourinary; hemic and lymphatic; skin; and endocrine; or

(B) any mental or psychological disorder, such as mental retardation, organic brain syndrome, emotional or mental illness, and specific learning disabilities. 45 CFR § 84.3(j)(2)(i) (1997).

In issuing these regulations, HEW decided against including a list of disorders constituting physical or mental impairments, out of concern that any specific enumeration might not be comprehensive. The commentary accompanying the regulations, however, contains a representative list of disorders and conditions constituting physical impairments, including "such diseases and conditions as orthopedic, visual, speech, and hearing impairments, cerebral palsy, epilepsy, muscular dystrophy, multiple sclerosis, cancer, heart disease, diabetes, mental retardation, emotional illness, and drug addiction and alcoholism."

HIV infection is not included in the list of specific disorders constituting physical impairments, in part because HIV was not identified as the cause of AIDS until 1983. HIV infection does fall well within the general definition set forth by the regulations, however.

The disease follows a predictable and, as of today, an unalterable course. Once a person is infected with HIV, the virus invades different cells in the blood and in body tissues. Certain white blood cells, known as helper Tlymphocytes or CD4+ cells, are particularly vulnerable to HIV. The virus eventually kills the infected host cell. CD4+ cells play a critical role in coordinating the body's immune response system, and the decline in their number causes corresponding deterioration of the body's ability to fight infections from many sources. Tracking the infected individual's CD4+ cell count is one of the most accurate measures of the course of the disease.

The initial stage of HIV infection is known as acute or primary HIV infection. In a typical case, this stage lasts three months. The virus concentrates in the blood. The assault on the immune system is immediate. The victim suffers from a sudden and serious decline in the number of white blood cells. There is no latency period. Mononucleosis-like symptoms often emerge between six days and six weeks after infection, at times accompanied by fever, headache, enlargement of the lymph nodes (lymphadenopathy), muscle pain (myalgia), rash, lethargy, gastrointestinal disorders, and neurological disorders. Usually these symptoms abate within 14 to 21 days. HIV antibodies appear in the bloodstream within three weeks; circulating HIV can be detected within 10 weeks.

After the symptoms associated with the initial stage subside, the disease enters what is referred to sometimes as its asymptomatic phase. The term is a misnomer, in some respects, for clinical features persist throughout, including lymphadenopathy, dermatological disorders, oral lesions, and bacterial infections. Although it varies with each individual, in most instances this stage lasts from seven to 11 years.

In light of the immediacy with which the virus begins to damage the infected person's white blood cells and the severity of the disease, we hold it is an impairment from the moment of infection. As noted earlier, infection with HIV causes immediate abnormalities in a person's blood, and the infected person's white cell count continues to drop throughout the course of the disease, even when the attack is concentrated in the lymph nodes. In light of these facts, HIV infection must be regarded as a physiological disorder with a constant and detrimental effect on the infected person's hemic and lymphatic systems from the moment of infection. HIV infection satisfies the statutory and regulatory definition of a physical impairment during every stage of the disease.

The statute is not operative, and the definition not satisfied, unless the impairment affects a major life activity. Respondent's claim throughout this case has been that the HIV infection placed a substantial limitation on her ability to reproduce and to bear children. Given the pervasive, and invariably fatal, course of the disease, its effect on major life activities of many sorts might have been relevant to our inquiry. Respondent and a number of amici make arguments about HIV's profound impact on almost every phase of the infected person's life. In light of these submissions, it may seem legalistic to circumscribe our discussion to the activity of reproduction. We have little doubt that had different parties brought the suit they would have maintained that an HIV infection imposes substantial limitations on other major life activities.

From the outset, however, the case has been treated as one in which reproduction was the major life activity limited by the impairment. It is our practice to decide cases on the grounds raised and considered in the Court of Appeals and included in the question on which we granted certiorari. We ask, then, whether reproduction is a major life activity.

We have little difficulty concluding that it is. As the Court of Appeals held, "the plain meaning of the word 'major' denotes comparative importance" and "suggests that the touchstone for determining an activity's inclusion under the statutory rubric is its significance." Reproduction falls well within the phrase "major life activity." Reproduction and the sexual dynamics surrounding it are central to the life process itself.

While petitioner concedes the importance of reproduction, he claims that Congress intended the ADA only to cover those aspects of a person's life which have a public, economic, or daily character. The argument founders on the statutory language. Nothing in the definition suggests that activities without a public, economic, or daily dimension may somehow be regarded as so unimportant or insignificant as to fall outside the meaning of the word "major." The breadth of the term confounds the attempt to limit its construction in this manner.

As we have noted, the ADA must be construed to be consistent with regulations issued to implement the Rehabilitation Act. See 42 U.S.C. § 12201(a). Rather than enunciating a general principle for determining what is and is not a major life activity, the Rehabilitation Act regulations instead provide a representative list, defining term to include "functions such as caring for one's self, performing manual tasks, walking, seeing, hearing, speaking, breathing, learning, and working." As the use of the term "such as" confirms, the list is illustrative, not exhaustive.

These regulations are contrary to petitioner's attempt to limit the meaning of the term "major" to public activities. The inclusion of activities such as caring for one's self and performing manual tasks belies the suggestion that a task must have a public or economic character in order to be a major life activity for purposes of the ADA. Petitioner advances no credible basis for confining major life activities to those with a public, economic, or daily aspect.

The final element of the disability definition in subsection (A) is whether respondent's physical impairment was a substantial limit on the major life activity she asserts. The Rehabilitation Act regulations provide no additional guidance.

Our evaluation of the medical evidence leads us to conclude that respondent's infection substantially limited her ability to reproduce in two independent ways. First, a woman infected with HIV who tries to conceive a child imposes on the man a significant risk of becoming infected. Second, an infected woman risks infecting her child during gestation and childbirth, i.e., perinatal transmission. Petitioner concedes that women infected with HIV face about a 25 percent risk of transmitting the virus to their children. [Even if] antiretroviral therapy can lower the risk of perinatal transmission to about 8 percent [i]t cannot be said as a matter of law that an 8 percent risk of transmitting a dread and fatal disease to one's child does not represent a substantial limitation on reproduction.

The Act addresses substantial limitations on major life activities, not utter inabilities. Conception and childbirth are not impossible for an HIV victim but, without doubt, are dangerous to the public health. This meets the definition of a substantial limitation. The decision to reproduce carries economic and legal consequences as well. There are added costs for antiretroviral therapy, supplemental insurance, and long-term health care for the child who must be examined and, tragic to think, treated for the infection. The laws of some States, moreover, forbid persons infected with HIV from having sex with others, regardless of consent.

In the end, the disability definition does not turn on personal choice. When significant limitations result from the impairment, the definition is met even if the difficulties are not insurmountable. For the statistical and other reasons we have cited, of course, the limitations on reproduction may be insurmountable here. Testimony from the respondent that her HIV infection controlled her decision not to have a child is unchallenged. In the context of reviewing summary judgment, we must take it to be true. We agree with the District Court and the Court of Appeals that no triable issue of fact impedes a ruling on the question of statutory coverage. Respondent's HIV infection is a physical impairment which substantially limits a major life activity, as the ADA defines it. In view of our holding, we need not address the second question presented, i.e., whether HIV infection is a per se disability under the ADA.

Our holding is confirmed by a consistent course of agency interpretation before and after enactment of the ADA. Every agency to consider the issue under the Rehabilitation Act found statutory coverage for persons with asymptomatic HIV. One comprehensive and significant administrative precedent is a 1988 opinion issued by the Office of Legal Counsel of the Department of Justice (OLC) concluding that the Rehabilitation Act "protects symptomatic and asymptomatic HIV–infected individuals against discrimination in any covered program." OLC determined further that asymptomatic HIV imposed a substantial limit on the major life activity of reproduction. The Opinion said: "Based on the medical knowledge available to us, we believe that it is reasonable to conclude that the life activity of procreation is substantially limited for an asymptomatic HIV–infected individual. In light of the significant risk that the AIDS virus may be transmitted to a baby during pregnancy, HIV–infected individuals cannot, whether they are male or female, engage in the act of procreation with the normal expectation of bringing forth a healthy child."

Every court which addressed the issue before the ADA was enacted in July 1990, moreover, concluded that asymptomatic HIV infection satisfied the Rehabilitation Act's definition of a handicap. The uniform body of administrative and judicial precedent confirms the conclusion we reach today as the most faithful way to effect the congressional design.

[We granted certiorari on the following additional question]:

When deciding under Title III of the ADA whether a private healthcare provider must perform invasive procedures on an infectious patient in his office, should courts defer to the health care provider's professional judgment, as long as it is reasonable in light of then-current medical knowledge?

The question is phrased in an awkward way, for it conflates two separate inquiries. In asking whether it is appropriate to defer to petitioner's judgment, it assumes that petitioner's assessment of the objective facts was reasonable. The central premise of the question and the assumption on which it is based merit separate consideration.

Again, we begin with the statute. Notwithstanding the protection given respondent by the ADA's definition of disability, petitioner could have refused to treat her if her infectious condition "posed a direct threat to the health or safety of others." 42 U.S.C. § 12182(b)(3). The ADA defines a direct threat to be "a significant risk to the health or safety of others that cannot be eliminated by a modification of policies, practices, or procedures or by the provision of auxiliary aids or services."

The ADA's direct threat provision stems from the recognition in School Bd. of Nassau Cty. v. Arline, 480 U.S. 273, 287 (1987), of the importance of prohibiting discrimination against individuals with disabilities while protecting others from significant health and safety risks, resulting, for instance, from a contagious disease. In *Arline*, the Court reconciled these objectives by construing the Rehabilitation Act not to require the hiring of a person who posed "a significant risk of communicating an infectious disease to others." Congress amended the Rehabilitation Act and the Fair Housing Act to incorporate the language. It later relied on the same language in enacting the ADA. Because few, if any, activities in life are risk free, *Arline* and the ADA do not ask whether a risk exists, but whether it is significant.

The existence, or nonexistence, of a significant risk must be determined from the standpoint of the person who refuses the treatment or accommodation, and the risk assessment must be based on medical or other objective evidence. *Arline, supra.* As a health care professional, petitioner had the duty to assess the risk of infection based on the objective, scientific information available to him and others in his profession. His belief that a significant risk existed, even if maintained in good faith, would not relieve him from liability. To use the words of the question presented, petitioner receives no special deference simply because he is a health care professional. It is true that *Arline* reserved "the question whether courts should also defer to the reasonable medical judgments of private physicians on which an employer has relied." At most, this statement reserved the possibility that employers could consult with individual physicians as objective third-party experts. It did not suggest that an individual physician's state of mind could excuse discrimination without regard to the objective reasonableness of his actions.

Our conclusion that courts should assess the objective reasonableness of the views of health care professionals without deferring to their individual judgments does not answer the implicit assumption in the question presented, whether petitioner's actions were reasonable in light of the available medical evidence. In assessing the reasonableness of petitioner's actions, the views of public health authorities, such as the U.S. Public Health Service, CDC, and the National Institutes of Health, are of special weight and authority. *Arline.* The views of these organizations are not conclusive, however. A health care professional who disagrees with the prevailing medical consensus may refute it by citing a credible scientific basis for deviating from the accepted norm.

We have reviewed so much of the record as necessary to illustrate the application of the rule to the facts of this case. For the most part, the Court of Appeals followed the proper standard in evaluating the petitioner's position and conducted a thorough review of the evidence. Its rejection of the District Court's reliance on the Marianos' affidavits was a correct application of the principle that petitioner's actions must be evaluated in light of the available, objective evidence. The record did not show that CDC had published the conclusion set out in the affidavits at the time petitioner refused to treat respondent.

A further illustration of a correct application of the objective standard is the Court of Appeals' refusal to give weight to the petitioner's offer to treat respondent in a hospital. Petitioner testified that he believed hospitals had safety measures, such as air filtration, ultraviolet lights, and respirators, which would reduce the risk of HIV transmission. Petitioner made no showing, however, that any area hospital had these safeguards or even that he had hospital privileges. His expert also admitted the lack of any scientific basis for the conclusion that these measures would lower the risk of transmission. Petitioner failed to present any objective, medical evidence showing that treating respondent in a hospital would be safer or more efficient in preventing HIV transmission than treatment in a well-equipped dental office.

We are concerned, however, that the Court of Appeals might have placed mistaken reliance upon two other sources. In ruling no triable issue of fact existed on this point, the Court of Appeals relied on the 1993 CDC Dentistry Guidelines and the 1991 American Dental Association Policy on HIV. This evidence is not definitive. As noted earlier, the CDC Guidelines recommended certain universal precautions which, in CDC's view, "should reduce the risk of disease transmission in the dental environment." The Court of Appeals determined that, "while the guidelines do not state explicitly that no further risk-reduction measures are desirable or that routine dental care for HIV-positive individuals is safe, those two conclusions seem to be implicit in the guidelines' detailed delineation of procedures for office treatment of HIV–positive patients." In our view, the Guidelines do not necessarily contain implicit assumptions conclusive of the point to be decided. The Guidelines set out CDC's recommendation that the universal precautions are the best way to combat the risk of HIV transmission. They do not assess the level of risk.

Nor can we be certain, on this record, whether the 1991 American Dental Association Policy on HIV carries the weight the Court of Appeals attributed to it. The Policy does provide some evidence of the medical community's objective assessment of the risks posed by treating people infected with HIV in dental offices. It indicates:

> Current scientific and epidemiologic evidence indicates that there is little risk of transmission of infectious diseases through dental treatment if recommended infection control procedures are routinely followed. Patients with HIV infection may be safely treated in private dental offices when appropriate infection control procedures are employed. Such infection control procedures provide protection both for patients and dental personnel.

We note, however, that the Association is a professional organization, which, although a respected source of information on the dental profession, is not a public health authority. It is not clear the extent to which the Policy was based on the Association's assessment of dentists' ethical and professional duties in addition to its scientific assessment of the risk to which the ADA refers. Efforts to clarify dentists' ethical obligations and to encourage dentists to treat patients with HIV infection with compassion may be commendable, but the question under the statute is one of statistical likelihood, not professional responsibility. Without more information on the manner in which the American Dental Association formulated this Policy, we are unable to determine the Policy's value in evaluating whether petitioner's assessment of the risks was reasonable as a matter of law.

The court considered materials submitted by both parties on the cross motions for summary judgment. The petitioner was required to establish that there existed a genuine issue of material fact. Evidence which was merely colorable or not significantly probative would not have been sufficient.

We acknowledge the presence of other evidence in the record before the Court of Appeals which, subject to further arguments and examination, might support affirmance of the trial court's ruling. For instance, the record contains substantial testimony from numerous health experts indicating that it is safe to treat patients infected with HIV in dental offices. We are unable to determine the import of this evidence, however. The record does not disclose whether the expert testimony submitted by respondent turned on evidence available in September 1994.

There are reasons to doubt whether petitioner advanced evidence sufficient to raise a triable issue of fact on the significance of the risk. Petitioner argues that, as of September 1994, CDC had identified seven dental workers with possible occupational transmission of HIV. These dental workers were exposed to HIV in the course of their employment, but CDC could not determine whether HIV infection had resulted. It is now known that CDC could not ascertain whether the seven dental workers contracted the disease because they did not present themselves for HIV testing at an appropriate time after their initial exposure. It is not clear on this record, however, whether this information was available to petitioner in September 1994. If not, the seven cases might have provided some, albeit not necessarily sufficient, support for petitioner's position. Standing alone, we doubt it would meet the objective, scientific basis for finding a significant risk to the petitioner.

[Because we declined to grant certiorari on whether petitioner raised a genuine issue of fact for trial, the briefs and arguments presented to us did not concentrate on the question of sufficiency in light all of the submissions in the summary judgment proceeding.] We conclude the proper course is to give the Court of Appeals the opportunity to determine whether our analysis of some of the studies cited by the parties would change its conclusion that petitioner presented neither objective evidence nor a triable issue of fact on the question of risk. In remanding the case, we do not foreclose the possibility that the Court of Appeals may reach the same conclusion it did earlier. A remand will permit a full exploration of the issue through the adversary process.

■ Justice Stevens, with whom Justice Breyer joins, concurring.

The Court's opinion demonstrates that respondent's HIV infection easily falls within the statute's definition of "disability." Moreover, the Court's discussion in Part III of the relevant evidence has persuaded me that the judgment of the Court of Appeals should be affirmed. I do not believe petitioner has sustained his burden of adducing evidence sufficient to raise a triable issue of fact on the significance of the risk posed by treating respondent in his office.

There are not, however, five Justices who agree that the judgment should be affirmed. Nor does it appear that there are five Justices who favor a remand for further proceedings consistent with the views expressed in either Justice Kennedy's opinion for the Court or the opinion of The Chief Justice. Because I am in agreement with the legal analysis in Justice Kennedy's opinion, in order to provide a judgment supported by a majority, I join that opinion even though I would prefer an outright affirmance.

■ JUSTICE GINSBURG, concurring.

HIV infection, as the description set out in the Court's opinion documents, has been regarded as a disease limiting life itself. The disease inevitably pervades life's choices: education, employment, family and financial undertakings. It affects the need for and, as this case shows, the ability to obtain health care because of the reaction of others to the impairment. No rational legislator, it seems to me apparent, would require nondiscrimination once symptoms become visible but permit discrimination when the disease, though present, is not yet visible. I am therefore satisfied that the statutory and regulatory definitions are well met. HIV infection is "a physical impairment that substantially limits major life activities," or is so perceived, including the afflicted individual's family relations, employment potential, and ability to care for herself.

I further agree, in view of the "importance [of the issue] to health care workers," that it is wise to remand, erring, if at all, on the side of caution. By taking this course, the Court ensures a fully informed determination whether respondent Abbott's disease posed "a significant risk to the health or safety of [petitioner Bragdon] that [could not] be eliminated by a modification of policies, practices, or procedures. . . ."

■ CHIEF JUSTICE REHNQUIST, with whom JUSTICE SCALIA and JUSTICE THOMAS join, and with whom JUSTICE O'CONNOR joins as to Part, concurring in the judgment in part and dissenting in part.

[T]he ADA's definition of a "disability" requires that the major life activity at issue be one "of such individual." The Court truncates the question, perhaps because there is not a shred of record evidence indicating that, prior to becoming infected with HIV, respondent's major life activities included reproduction (assuming for the moment that reproduction is a major life activity at all). At most, the record indicates that after learning of her HIV status, respondent, whatever her previous inclination, conclusively decided that she would not have children. There is absolutely no evidence that, absent the HIV, respondent would have had or was even considering having children. Indeed, when asked during her deposition whether her HIV infection had in any way impaired her ability to carry out any of her life functions, respondent answered "No." It is further telling that in the course of her entire brief to this Court, respondent studiously avoids asserting even once that reproduction is a major life activity to her. To the contrary, she argues that the "major life activity" inquiry should not turn on a particularized assessment of the circumstances of this or any other case.

But even aside from the facts of this particular case, the Court is simply wrong in concluding as a general matter that reproduction is a "major life activity." Unfortunately, the ADA does not define the phrase "major life activities." But the Act does incorporate by reference a list of such activities contained in regulations issued under the Rehabilitation Act. The Court correctly recognizes that this list of major life activities "is illustrative, not exhaustive," but then makes no attempt to demonstrate that reproduction is a major life activity in the same sense that "caring for one's self, performing manual tasks, walking, seeing, hearing, speaking, breathing, learning, and working" are.

Instead, the Court argues that reproduction is a "major" life activity in that it is "central to the life process itself." In support of this reading, the Court focuses on the fact that "major" indicates "comparative importance," ignoring the alternative definition of "major" as "greater in quantity, number, or extent." It is the latter definition that is most consistent with the ADA's illustrative list of major life activities.

No one can deny that reproductive decisions are important in a person's life. But so are decisions as to who to marry, where to live, and how to earn one's living. Fundamental importance of this sort is not the common thread linking the statute's listed activities. The common thread is rather that the activities are repetitively performed and essential in the day-to-day existence of a normally functioning individual. They are thus quite different from the series of activities leading to the birth of a child.

Both respondent and the United States as amicus curiae argue that reproduction must be a major life activity because regulations issued under the ADA define the term "physical impairment" to include physiological disorders affecting the reproductive system. If reproduction were not a major life activity, they argue, then it would have made little sense to include the reproductive disorders in the roster of physical impairments. This argument is simply wrong. There are numerous disorders of the reproductive system, such as dysmenorrhea and endometriosis, which are so painful that they limit a woman's ability to engage in major life activities such as walking and working. And, obviously, cancer of the various reproductive organs limits one's ability to engage in numerous activities other than reproduction.

But even if I were to assume that reproduction is a major life activity of respondent, I do not agree that an asymptomatic HIV infection "substantially limits" that activity. The record before us leaves no doubt that those so infected are still entirely able to engage in sexual intercourse, give birth to a child if they become pregnant, and perform the manual tasks necessary to rear a child to maturity. While individuals infected with HIV may choose not to engage in these activities, there is no support in language, logic, or our case law for the proposition that such voluntary choices constitute a "limit" on one's own life activities.

The Court responds that the ADA "addresses substantial limitations on major life activities, not utter inabilities." I agree, but fail to see how this assists the Court's cause. Apart from being unable to demonstrate that she is utterly unable to engage in the various activities that comprise the reproductive process, respondent has not even explained how she is less able to engage in those activities.

Respondent contends that her ability to reproduce is limited because "the fatal nature of HIV infection means that a parent is unlikely to live long enough to raise and nurture the child to adulthood." But the ADA's definition of a disability is met only if the alleged impairment substantially "limits" (present tense) a major life activity. Asymptomatic HIV does not presently limit respondent's ability to perform any of the tasks necessary to bear or raise a child. Respondent's argument, taken to its logical extreme, would render every individual with a genetic marker for some debilitating disease "disabled" here and now because of some possible future effects.

In my view, therefore, respondent has failed to demonstrate that any of her major life activities were substantially limited by her HIV infection.

While the Court concludes to the contrary as to the "disability" issue, it then quite correctly recognizes that petitioner could nonetheless have refused to treat respondent if her condition posed a "direct threat." I agree that the [Court of Appeals' judgment on this issue] should be vacated, although I am not sure I understand the Court's cryptic direction to the lower court.

I agree with the Court that "the existence, or nonexistence, of a significant risk must be determined from the standpoint of the person who refuses the treatment or accommodation," as of the time that the decision refusing treatment is made. I disagree with the Court, however, that "in assessing the reasonableness of petitioner's actions, the views of public health authorities are of special weight and authority." Those views are, of course, entitled to a presumption of validity when the actions of those authorities themselves are challenged in court, and even in disputes between private parties where Congress has committed that dispute to adjudication by a public health authority. But in litigation between private parties originating in the federal courts, I am aware of no provision of law or judicial practice that would require or permit courts to give some scientific views more credence than others simply because they have been endorsed by a politically appointed public health authority (such as the Surgeon General). In litigation of this latter sort, which is what we face here, the credentials of the scientists employed by the public health authority, and the soundness of their studies, must stand on their own. The Court cites no authority for its limitation upon the courts' truthfinding function, except the statement in *Arline* that in making findings regarding the risk of contagion under the Rehabilitation Act, "courts normally should defer to the reasonable medical judgments of public health officials." But there is appended to that dictum the following footnote, which makes it very clear that the Court was urging respect for medical judgment, and not necessarily respect for "official" medical judgment over "private" medical judgment: "This case does not present, and we do not address, the question whether courts should also defer to the reasonable medical judgments of private physicians on which an employer has relied."

Applying these principles here, it is clear to me that petitioner has presented more than enough evidence to avoid summary judgment on the "direct threat" question. In June 1994, the Centers for Disease Control and

Prevention published a study identifying seven instances of possible transmission of HIV from patients to dental workers. While it is not entirely certain whether these dental workers contracted HIV during the course of providing dental treatment, the potential that the disease was transmitted during the course of dental treatment is relevant evidence. One need only demonstrate "risk," not certainty of infection. See Arline, supra, at 288 (" 'the probabilities the disease will be transmitted' " is a factor in assessing risk). Given the "severity of the risk" involved here, i.e., near certain death, and the fact that no public health authority had outlined a protocol for eliminating this risk in the context of routine dental treatment, it seems likely that petitioner can establish that it was objectively reasonable for him to conclude that treating respondent in his office posed a "direct threat" to his safety.

In addition, petitioner offered evidence of 42 documented incidents of occupational transmission of HIV to healthcare workers other than dental professionals. The Court of Appeals dismissed this evidence as irrelevant because these health professionals were not dentists. But the fact that the health care workers were not dentists is no more valid a basis for distinguishing these transmissions of HIV than the fact that the health care workers did not practice in Maine. At a minimum, petitioner's evidence was sufficient to create a triable issue on this question, and summary judgment was accordingly not appropriate.

■ JUSTICE O'CONNOR, concurring in the judgment in part and dissenting in part.

I agree with The Chief Justice that respondent's claim of disability should be evaluated on an individualized basis and that she has not proven that her asymptomatic HIV status substantially limited one or more of her major life activities. In my view, the act of giving birth to a child, while a very important part of the lives of many women, is not generally the same as the representative major life activities of all persons—"caring for one's self, performing manual tasks, walking, seeing, hearing, speaking, breathing, learning, and working"—listed in regulations relevant to the Americans with Disabilities Act of 1990. Based on that conclusion, there is no need to address whether other aspects of intimate or family relationships not raised in this case could constitute major life activities; nor is there reason to consider whether HIV status would impose a substantial limitation on one's ability to reproduce if reproduction were a major life activity.

Notes

1. Health care as a public accommodation. From a broad health policy perspective, the most notable aspect of the ADA may be the Title III public accommodation provisions, which classify health care providers as "public accommodations." No other civil rights law has made such an advance. Rather than making a deliberate decision to reject previous, narrower doctrines regarding the duty of care, the ADA expanded to reach health care out of a common sense view that in the modern world, health professionals ought not to be able to pick and choose their patients based on their personal attributes. Indeed, the American Medical Association was an active sponsor of the legislation. There appears to be no legislative history on the decision to include health care services as a public accommodation. Joel Teitelbaum & Sara Rosenbaum, *Medical Care as a Public Accommodation: Moving the Discussion to Race*, 29 AM. J. L. & MED. 381 (2003). For a discussion of the extent to which the ADA departed from other civil rights laws in its use of the term, see Joseph William Singer, *No Right to Exclude: Public Accommodations and Private Property*, 90 Nw. U. L. REV. 1283, 1411 (1996).

In Howe v. Hull, 874 F. Supp. 779 (N.D. Ohio 1994), the plaintiff sued a hospital and the on-call physician for violation of the ADA. as well as other claims for failure to admit and stabilize him when he arrived at the hospital suffering from what appeared to the examining physician to be a possible case of Toxic Epidermal Necrolysis (TEN), a severe allergic reaction to certain drugs. Examining the plaintiff and learning of his underlying HIV status, the emergency room physician determined that admission and stabilization was appropriate. He telephoned Dr. Hull, the on-call member of the medical staff, whose authorization was required for admission. Dr. Hull refused to admit the patient and never attempted to meet with or examine him. Instead he ordered his transfer to the Medical College of Ohio, stating, "if you get an AIDS patient in the hospital, you will never get him out." The patient ultimately was transferred and treated at the Medical College of Ohio. After disposing of the EMTALA claim by allowing the claim to proceed against the hospital but dismissing the individual claim against defendant Hull, the court considered the liability of the hospital and physician under Title III of the ADA, which prohibits discrimination by "any person who owns, leases (or leases to), or operates a place of public accommodation." 42 U.S.C. § 12182(a).

> [Dr. Hull's motion for summary judgment turns] on whether Dr. Hull can be personally liable as an operator of a public accommodation within the meaning of the ADA.
>
> In common usage "operate" implies the performance of some sort of function, in conjunction with a degree of sanctioned authority. This seems consistent with the ADA, which contemplates that an owner or an operator of a public accommodation may be held liable for violations of its provisions.
>
> The Court is aware that there is a line of authority that has been loathe to allow individual liability for violations of Title VII [prohibiting discrimination in employment on grounds of race, color, gender, national origin, and religion] and the [Age Discrimination in Employment Act (ADEA)]. See, e.g., Miller v. Maxwell's International, 991 F.2d 583, 587 (9th Cir. 1993) (holding that Congress did not intend for individual employees to be liable as an "employer" for violations of Title VII and the ADEA).
>
> Cases not allowing individual liability for Title VII and ADEA violations in the employment context are not, however, applicable

to the law and facts in the case at bar. The Title VII employment cases precluding personal liability had their genesis at the time when Title VII only allowed for back pay as damages; it thus seems logical to construe the earlier version of that statute not to apply to individuals. Given the broad language and remedial purposes of the ADA, however, allowing individual liability in some circumstances under 42 U.S.C. § 12182(a) is consistent with both the plain language of the statute and congressional intent. To hold differently would allow individuals with both the authority and the discretion to make decisions based on a discriminatory agenda to violate the ADA with a degree of impunity not envisioned by Congress.

This Court holds that, under 42 U.S.C. § 12182(a), an individual may be liable as an operator of a public accommodation where (a) he or she is in a position of authority; (b) within the ambit of this authority he or she has both the power and discretion to perform potentially discriminatory acts; and (c) the discriminatory acts are the result of the exercise of the individual's own discretion, as opposed to the implementation of institutional policy or the mandates of superiors.

On these facts, the Court is unable to say as a matter of law that defendant Hull did not operate Memorial Hospital. It appears that defendant Hull was in a position of some authority within Memorial Hospital: he was a Vice Chief of Staff, the Medical Director of Special Services, and as the on-call admitting physician he had the authority and discretion to admit Charon to the hospital for treatment. The "business" of a hospital is the treatment of sick patients, and based on this evidence a jury could find that defendant Hull used his authority and discretion to deny plaintiff treatment for his non-HIV-related drug reaction solely on the basis of his HIV status. Defendant Hull's motion for summary judgment on plaintiff's ADA claim is not well taken.

874 F. Supp. at 787–90.

The Court also considered the defendants' motion for summary judgment on the grounds that the evidence did not show that the plaintiff was denied treatment solely because of his HIV status and furthermore, that he was not an otherwise qualified person with a disability because his preliminary diagnosis of TEN placed him beyond the hospital's alleged sphere of competence.

Before examining the merits of defendants' contentions, the Court must look at and compare the applicable parameters of the ADA and FRA [Federal Rehabilitation Act]. There are three basic criteria plaintiff must meet in order to establish a prima facie case of discrimination under the ADA: a) the plaintiff has a disability; b) the defendants discriminated against the plaintiff; and c) the discrimination was based on the disability. The discrimination can take the form of the denial of the opportunity to receive medical treatment, segregation unnecessary for the provision of effective medical treatment, unnecessary screening or eligibility requirements for treatment, or provision of unequal medical benefits based upon the disability. A defendant can avoid liability by establishing that it was unable to provide the medical care that a patient required.

As this Court has already stated, a reasonable jury could conclude that the TEN diagnosis was a pretext and that Charon was denied treatment solely because of his disability. Further, there is no evidence to support the conclusion that Memorial Hospital was unable to treat a severe allergic drug reaction. In fact, the evidence indicates that Dr. Reardon initially planned to admit Charon for treatment. Therefore, Charon was "otherwise qualified" for treatment within the meaning of the FRA. Defendants' arguments in this regard are not persuasive.

The Court notes that defendant Memorial hospital argues that the "solely on the basis of" standard that appears in the FRA should be imported into the ADA as well. This argument is without merit.

The ADA reads "No individual shall be discriminated against on the basis of disability." It is abundantly clear that the exclusion of the "solely by reason of disability" language was a purposeful act by Congress and not a drafting error or oversight. The inquiry under the ADA, then, is whether the defendant, despite the articulated reasons for the transfer, improperly considered Charon's HIV status. More explicitly, was Charon transferred for the treatment of a non-AIDS related drug reaction because defendant unjustifiably did not wish to care for an HIV–positive patient? Viewing the evidence in the light most favorable to the plaintiff, the Court finds plaintiff has presented sufficient evidence to preclude a grant of summary judgment on these claims. Defendant Memorial Hospital's motion for summary judgment on the plaintiff's ADA and FRA claims will be denied.

874 F. Supp. at 788–89.

Finally, the court considered whether Dr. Hull could be found liable under the Federal Rehabilitation Act ("FRA"), which, like Title VI, applies to recipients of federal financial assistance:

Defendant Hull further argues that the FRA does not apply to him in this instance because, even though Memorial Hospital receives federal funding, Hull did not with respect to plaintiff's care. [But] the FRA was amended and the scope of its application broadened by Congress in The Civil Rights Restoration Act of 1987.

For the purposes of the FRA, a program or activity that receives federal funds is defined as:

> all of the operations of [a] corporation, partnership, or other
> private organization, or an entire sole proprietorship which is
> principally engaged in the business of providing healthcare
> any part of which is extended Federal financial assistance.

Defendant Hull in his various capacities at Memorial Hospital is a
part of the "operations of" the hospital. Defendant also receives
Medicare and Medicaid funding in his own practice. Defendant
cannot receive federal funds on the one hand, and on the other
deny he is covered by the FRA simply because he received no
federal funds for his involvement with Charon. Defendant's motion for summary judgment on plaintiff's FRA claim is not well
taken.

874 F. Supp. at 789–90.

2. *When does a disability exist?* A core question in *Bragdon* was
whether asymptomatic HIV is a disability within the terms of the ADA. In
order to invoke the protections of the ADA, an individual must be considered to have a "disability" within the meaning of the law. The Supreme
Court has issued a series of decisions that considerably narrowed the
definition of disability in an employment context. Sutton v. United Air
Lines, 527 U.S. 471 (1999), and Toyota Motor Mfg., Kentucky, Inc. v.
Williams, 534 U.S. 184 (2002), held that correctable impairments cannot be
considered disabling. The cases were criticized as contrary to the intent of
the ADA (e.g., could Congress have really intended that a person who can
ambulate with a wheelchair is not "disabled"?). *Righting the ADA,* Nation-
al Council on Disability (NCD); Chai R. Feldblum, *Definition of Disability
Under Federal Anti–Discrimination Law: What Happened? Why? And What
Can We Do About It?*, 21 BERKELEY J. EMP. & LAB. L. 91 (2000); *but see*
Michael J. Puma, *Respecting the Plain Language of the ADA: A Textualist
Argument Rejecting the EEOC's Analysis of Controlled Disabilities*, 67 GEO.
WASH. L. REV. 123, 124 (1998).

The ADA Amendments Act of 2008 explicitly reversed *Sutton* and
reinstated a definition of disability that includes many impairments that
can be corrected or ameliorated through mitigating measures. 42 U.S.C.
§ 12102(3), amended by Pub. L. No. 110–325, § 3. Specifically the Act
amends the definition of disability in part as follows:

> (E)(i) The determination of whether an impairment substantially
> limits a major life activity shall be made without regard to the
> ameliorative effects of mitigating measures such as—(I) medi-
> cation, medical supplies, equipment, or appliances, low-vision de-
> vices (which do not include ordinary eyeglasses or contact lenses),
> prosthetics including limbs and devices, hearing aids and cochlear
> implants or other implantable hearing devices, mobility devices, or
> oxygen therapy equipment and supplies; (II) use of assistive tech-
> nology; (III) reasonable accommodations or auxiliary aids or ser-
> vices; or (IV) learned behavioral or adaptive neurological modifica-
> tions.

(ii) The ameliorative effects of the mitigating measures of ordinary eyeglasses or contact lenses shall be considered in determining whether an impairment substantially limits a major life activity.

(iii) As used in this subparagraph—(I) the term "ordinary eyeglasses or contact lenses" means lenses that are intended to fully correct visual acuity or eliminate refractive error; and (II) the term "low-vision devices" means devices that magnify, enhance, or otherwise augment a visual image.

3. *Asymptomatic HIV as an impairment, and reproduction as a major life activity.* Despite the growing restriction on the meaning of disability, *Bragdon* is notable for its classification of reproduction as a "major life activity," for its holding that asymptomatic HIV infection "substantially limits" reproduction, and for what an individual must show to establish that HIV infection substantially limits her or him personally with respect to reproduction. Consider the implications of Chief Justice Rehnquist's position that, even if reproduction is considered a "major life activity" as a general matter under the ADA (a point with which Chief Justice Rehnquist disagreed), an ADA claimant must also show that reproduction is a "major life activity" for her or himself. Presumably, a person who is married and has had a child, and who had made plans to have a second child, but then was deterred from doing so by HIV infection, would be the ideal ADA plaintiff, with the right not to be discriminated against in a wide range of contexts, such as access to health providers, employment, insurance, and public accommodations. Conversely, an asymptomatic, HIV-positive person who could not demonstrate a pre-infection commitment to childbearing would have, according to Chief Justice Rehnquist, no rights at all under the ADA, at least under this theory of disability. Do you think it is likely that Congress intended to make access to dental (and other health) care turn on patients' differential histories and plans with respect to childbearing?

Does Justice Kennedy's opinion make clear whether, under the majority's approach, an ADA defendant can question whether reproduction is a "major life activity" for a particular plaintiff? Additionally, what effect would adoption of Justice Rehnquist's view have on the administration of the ADA and the need for entities subject to its requirements to know when they have obligations? *See* Elizabeth C. Chambers, *Asymptomatic HIV as a Disability Under the Americans with Disabilities Act*, 73 Wash. L. Rev. 403, 423 (1998) (arguing that asymptomatic HIV is a disability, but that courts have erred in analyzing the question under the "actual disability" prong because this analysis excludes those with HIV, such as children, post-menopausal women, and celibate monks, who do not, or cannot, engage in reproduction); Mary Crossley, *The Disability Kaleidoscope*, 74 Notre Dame L. Rev. 621 (1999) (integrating theories of disability with the issues arising in the cases).

Granting *Bragdon's* holding that reproduction is a major life activity, what constitutes an "impairment" that "substantially limits" it? While a literal reading of the regulatory definition of "impairment" would appear to include pregnancy itself as a "condition affecting [the] reproductive [system]," EEOC guidelines provide that pregnancy plain-and-simple is not an impairment, although complications resulting from pregnancy may be. Eq. Empl. Compl Man. (CBC) § 902.2(c)(3) (1995). Following this reasoning, courts have sought to distinguish between an uncomplicated pregnancy and a pregnancy manifesting problems that medical science regards as unusual. *See, e.g.*, Cerrato v. Durham, 941 F. Supp. 388 (S.D.N.Y. 1996) (summarizing cases). For a critique see Crossley, *The Disability Kaleidoscope* at 669–74.

4. *Direct threat to the health and safety of others.* The second major issue addressed in Bragdon was whether the plaintiff's HIV positive condition posed a "direct threat" to the health or safety of the defendant dentist. Because these terms constitute an exception to the duty of non-discrimination, presumably the defendant-provider has the burden of proving that treating the patient would pose "a significant risk to the health or safety of others that cannot be eliminated by a modification of policies, practices, or procedures or by the provision of auxiliary aids or services." 42 U.S.C. § 12182(b)(3).

All of the Justices agreed that "the existence, or nonexistence, of a significant risk must be determined from the standpoint of the person who refuses the treatment or accommodation," as of the time that the decision refusing treatment is made. *Bragdon*, 524 U.S. at 564, 661. The Justices also agreed that the determination of whether a condition poses a "direct threat" must be made on the basis of "objective scientific evidence." In reaching this conclusion, the Court rejected the claim of Dr. Bragdon and other doctors that, because they are medical professionals, their personal assessment of risk is entitled to deference.

Beyond these core principles, the Court's decision left open many questions in relation to the "direct threat" defense to a claim of discrimination under the ADA. The First Circuit Court of Appeals had granted the plaintiff summary judgment on the "direct threat" issue, relying on the findings of the Centers for Disease Control, the Surgeon General, and the American Dental Association that patients with HIV and AIDS do not pose a significant threat to dentists when recommended precautions are used. The First Circuit rejected a rule of "absolute capitulation" to the views of public health authorities, and instead adopted a principle assigning their views "prima facie force," but providing for their rebuttal "by persuasive evidence adduced from other recognized experts in a given field." The defendant, Dr. Bragdon, offered no scientific evidence to rebut these expert assessments.

Nonetheless, the Supreme Court remanded the direct threat issue for further fact finding. Justice Kennedy held that the views of public health officials possess "special weight and authority," but can be rebutted by "citing a credible scientific basis for deviating from the accepted norm." Chief Justice Rehnquist, writing for the four-person dissent on this issue, disagreed.

On remand, the First Circuit took supplemental briefings and a new round of oral arguments. The Circuit Court affirmed the objective and scientific basis of the CDC guideline, noted that the American Dental Association guidelines were promulgated by its Council for Scientific Affairs, not its Council on Ethics, and were supported by objective scientific evidence, and observed that Ms. Abbott had offered "the opinions of several prominent experts to the effect that, in 1994, the cavity-filling procedure could have been performed safely in a private dental office." The court re-examined Dr. Bragdon's evidence and found it "too speculative or too tangential (or in some instances, both) to create a genuine issue of material fact." 163 F.3d at 90.

The *Bragdon* opinions reflect some interesting complexities in what might be called "the politics of deference" to "established" medical, scientific, or public health authority. In *Bragdon* the dentist asserted his subjective belief regarding the dangers he faced in treating HIV-infected patients. Given Chief Justice Rehnquist's skepticism about the weight to be given to professional society consensus and public health agency guidelines, what evidence would be sufficient to overcome his beliefs? The *Bragdon* opinions reflect a difficult choice between objective and subjective opinions in the context of discrimination litigation. Should Dr. Bragdon's beliefs absolve him of liability? What about the fact that, as the First Circuit decided on remand, all the weight of expert authority at the time pulled in the opposite direction? Shouldn't the defendant be charged with such knowledge? What would be the effect of the contrary result, that people get to engage in discrimination based on their ungrounded prejudices? Should the standard differ depending on whether or not a defendant has, or is supposed to have, expertise, such as professional knowledge? If Justice Rehnquist places little value in the deliberations of the CDC and professional societies, what might he value? A randomized controlled trial to test HIV exposure among dentists who work with patients with HIV with and without universal precautions? Is this remotely feasible or ethical? At what point does public health consensus necessarily become essential to the development of evidence? These issues will be explored in Part Three.

Outside the health context, several post-*Bragdon* cases have found that HIV positive people pose a "direct threat" to others, on the basis of thin evidence, findings that have absolved differential and often quite harsh treatment. *See, e.g.*, Onishea v. Hopper, 171 F.3d 1289 (11th Cir. 1999), *cert. den. sub nom.*, Davis. v. Hopper, 528 U.S. 1114 (2000) (segregation of HIV positive inmates for prison activities was not a violation of the ADA because those with HIV-positive status pose a "significant risk" to the safety and health of other prisoners; one judge dissented arguing that the risk was not significant); Montalvo v. Radcliffe, 167 F.3d 873 (4th Cir. 1999), *cert. den.*, 528 U.S. 813 (1999) (an HIV-positive child was denied admission to a martial arts school. The court held that his condition would pose significant risk to the health and safety of others because of the possibility of blood to blood contact, and that altering teaching style was not a reasonable accommodation).

5. *HIV and direct threat in a health care context. Abbott* and *Howe* both involve patients denied medical care because they were HIV positive.

Early in the HIV epidemic, denial of medical care to patients who were perceived to be HIV positive, or even perceived to be gay, was tragically common. Dr. Joel Neugarten, *Note, The Americans with Disabilities Act: Magic Bullet or Band–Aid for Patients and Health Care Workers Infected with the Human Immunodeficiency Virus?* 57 BROOK. L. REV. 1277 (1992).

In these early years, some lawmakers urged screening all patients for HIV. These recommendations were rejected by the CDC and the medical profession. Jean Hagen, *Routine Preoperative Screening for HIV*, 259 JAMA 1357 (1988) (screening a low-risk population would require testing 1,3000,-000 individuals to prevent one case of HIV infection). Rather, the CDC and the medical profession have promoted universal precautions to protect health care workers from the risk of infection from HIV, hepatitis B, and other infectious diseases. Generations of health care professional have now been trained in settings that implement universal precautions to prevent injuries from needle sticks and cuts. While prevention is the most important strategy for reducing the risk of exposure, the CDC and the profession have developed standards for post exposure prophylaxis. Through December 2001, there were 57 documented cases of occupational HIV transmission to health care workers in the United States. Between 2001 and 2011, only one reported case has been confirmed. CDC, Division of HIV/AIDS Prevention, *Occupational HIV Transmission and Prevention among Health Care Workers*, (Feb. 2011), http://www.cdc.gov/hiv/resources/factsheets/hcw prev.htm.

Health care workers with HIV have not fared well under the ADA. In 1991, the CDC suggested that most health care workers do not need to know their HIV status, or inform patients that they are HIV positive, if they practice recommended universal precautions. 40 MMWR RR–8 (1991). However, the CDC also recommends that health care workers who perform "exposure prone invasive procedures" should know whether they are infected with HIV or hepatitis and "should not perform exposure-prone procedures unless they have sought counsel from an expert review panel and been advised under what circumstances, if any, they may continue to perform these procedures. Such circumstances would include notifying prospective patients of the [health care workers'] seropositivity before they undergo exposure-prone invasive procedures." In several cases, courts have rejected the ADA claims of HIV-positive health care workers, even though they did not perform exposure-prone procedures and the risks of transmission were acknowledged to be very small. *See* Estate of Mauro ex rel. Mauro v. Borgess Med. Ctr., 137 F.3d 398, 407 (6th Cir.) (affirming summary judgment against HIV-positive surgical technician who was removed from his position, and collecting cases), *cert. den.*, 525 U.S. 815 (1998).

Is the disparity between HIV positive patients and HIV positive health care workers, in the application of the "direct threat" defense of the ADA, justifiable? Neugarten, *supra*, argues that it is not, as does *The Supreme Court 1997 Term*, 112 HARV. L. REV. 283, 292 (1998).

Apart from the six patients, apparently infected by a single dentist in Florida, noted by Chief Justice Rehnquist, there have been very few documented cases of HIV transmission from a health care worker to a patient. Though CDC has yet to determine how the transmission occurred in those instances, no additional CDC studies have found HIV transmission from a health care worker to a patient. Most of the other documented cases occurred early in the HIV epidemic and were from infected donor tissue that was used due to failures to follow properly the universal precautions and infection control guidelines. CDC, Division of HIV/AIDS Prevention, *HIV Transmission: Are patients in a health care setting at risk of getting HIV?* (Last Modified Mar. 25, 2010) (www.cdc.gov/hiv/pubs/faq/faq29.htm).

For a review of the state of cases and enforcement actions as of 2006 that involve health care services as places of public accommodation, see SARA ROSENBAUM, THE AMERICANS WITH DISABILITIES ACT IN A HEALTH CARE CONTEXT, THE FUTURE OF DISABILITY IN AMERICA (National Academy Press, 2007).

---

4.   IMMIGRANTS AND ACCESS TO HEALTH CARE

Approximately thirty million non-citizens live in the United States and, of these, 11.6 million are estimated to be undocumented immigrants, that is, individuals who are not legally present in the U.S (a category that technically includes persons falling into both immigration and non-immigration status, such as temporary visitors who overstay a visa). KAISER FAMILY FOUNDATION, THE KAISER COMMISSION ON MEDICAID AND THE UNINSURED, *Immigrants and Health Care Coverage: A Primer* 1 (2004), http://www.kff.org/uninsured/upload/7451–03.pdf. Immigrants are workers. They represent twelve percent of the population and fifteen percent of the workforce. KAISER FAMILY FOUNDATION, THE KAISER COMMISSION ON MEDICAID AND THE UNINSURED, *The Role of Employer–Sponsored Health Insurance Coverage for Immigrants: A Primer* (2006), http://www.kff.org/uninsured/upload/7524.pdf. But immigrants are likely to be uninsured because they work in low-wage jobs, in small firms, and in service, agriculture or other occupations that are less likely to offer health benefits.

Undocumented immigrants use less ambulatory care than citizens, and are less likely to be hospitalized, except for childbirth. Mark L. Berk et al., *Health Care Use Among Undocumented Latino Immigrants*, 19(4) HEALTH AFFAIRS, 51, 56 (2000); Mary Engel, *Latinos' Use of Health Services Studied*, L.A. TIMES, Nov. 27, 2007, at B–1 (illegal immigrants were 50 percent less likely to use emergency rooms than native born citizens).

Before 1996, immigrants who were in the United States legally, or whose status was ambiguous or under consideration, qualified for Medicaid. Julia Field Costich, *Legislating a Public Health Nightmare: The Anti–Immigrant Provisions of the "Contract With America" Congress*, 90 KY. L. J. 1043, 1047 (2002). The Personal Responsibility and Work Opportunity Reconciliation Act ("PRWORA") of 1996 denied Medicaid to immigrants whose status was ambiguous or under consideration, and it required that legal permanent and temporary residents wait five years to qualify for Medicaid. 8 U.S.C. §§ 1601–46 (2001). In 2009, Congress gave states the option to eliminate the five-year prohibition on services to legal immigrants for pregnant women and children. Children's Health Insurance Program Reauthorization Act of 2009, Pub. L. No. 111–3, 123 Stat. 8; Robert Pear, *House Votes to Expand Children's Health Care*, N.Y. TIMES, Jan. 14, 2009, http://www.nytimes.com/2009/01/15/washington/15healthcare.html?scp=2 & sq=schip & st=cse.

Denial of federal Medicaid to people who are neither citizens nor legally present in the U.S. has a serious impact on states and hospitals, as well as the non-citizens and their families. Some states have responded by imposing even harsher restrictions on immigrant health care, but other states provide health care to immigrants with state funds, particularly for prenatal care and child health. THE KAISER COMMISSION ON MEDICAID AND THE UNINSURED, *Covering New Americans: A Review of Federal and State Policies Related to Immigrants' Eligibility and Access to Publically Funded Health Insurance* ii (2004), http://www.kff.org/medicaid/7214.cfm (reporting the 22 states, including California, New York, Florida, Massachusetts, Maryland and Virginia provide state-funded coverage to immigrants); Sarah Kershaw, *New York, Faulting U.S., Says It Will Pay for Cancer Care for Illegal Immigrants,* N.Y. TIMES (Sept. 26, 2007); Kevin Sack & Catrin Einhorn, *Deal Would Provide Dialysis to Illegal Immigrants in Atlanta,* N.Y. TIMES, August 31, 2010. Some courts have held that state constitutions prevent application of the restrictions on health benefits for immigrants authorized by federal law. In Ehrlich v. Perez, 908 A.2d 1220 (Md. 2006) the Maryland Court of Special Appeals held that denial of Medicaid to pregnant women and children violated the state Declaration of Human Rights. In Aliessa ex rel. Fayad v. Novello, 754 N.E.2d 1085 (N.Y. 2001), the New York Court of Appeals held that excluding lawful resident aliens from Medicaid violated the equal protection clause of the state constitution.

EMTALA applies to all persons regardless of legal U.S. status. An obvious tension exists between EMTALA and the PRWORA: hospitals receiving federal funds must treat all individuals in an emergency under EMTALA, but federal law prohibits funding for services to immigrants. Federal law allows Medicaid payment "for treatment of an emergency medical condition, not related to an organ transplant procedure, of an alien who would qualify but for his or her immigration status." 42 U.S.C. § 1396b(v)(2) (2009). The statute defines an "emergency medical condition" as: "a medical condition (including emergency labor and delivery) manifesting itself by acute symptoms of sufficient severity (including severe pain) such that the absence of immediate medical attention could reasonably be expected to result in: (A) placing the patient's health in serious jeopardy, (B) serious impairment to bodily functions, or (C) serious dysfunction of any bodily organ or part." *Id.* § 1396b(v)(3). Hospitals and states struggle to draw the line between emergency and non-emergency care. Kaiser Family Fund, *Health Care for Undocumented Immigrants Cost $1.1B in 2000, Study Finds*, http://dailyreports.kff.org/Daily–Reports/2006/

November/21/dr00041208.aspx. The statutory definition leaves ample room for debate as to which diagnoses should be defined as emergency conditions. Courts and states have divided over whether chemotherapy, dialysis, paralysis requiring ventilation, and other serious conditions constitute "emergencies."

Hospitals providing services to the uninsured are also entitled to disproportionate share payments under Medicare. Additional federal funds are provided to states and hospitals providing a disproportionate volume of emergency services to uninsured immigrants. Robert Pear, *Payments to Help Hospitals Care for Illegal Immigrants*, N.Y. Times, May 10, 2005, at A11.

Without federal oversight or regulation some hospitals transport immigrant patients who cannot pay their hospital bills back to their native countries. Deborah Sontag, *Immigrants Facing Deportation by U.S. Hospitals*, N.Y. Times, Aug. 3, 2008, A1, http://www.nytimes.com/2008/08/03/us/03deport.html?ref=us. Private companies offer hospitals a commercial service to transport uninsured patients to Mexico. Lisa Richardson, *Patients Without Borders: Amid Rising Health Costs, Illegal Immigrants in San Diego–Area Hospitals are Being Transferred Back to Mexico for Treatment*, L.A. Times, Nov. 5, 2003, at A1.

In 1996, Congress heightened citizenship proof requirements for demonstrating Medicaid eligibility. Deficit Reduction Act ("DRA"), 42 U.S.C. §§ 1396a(a)(46)(B). While targeted at non-citizens, these requirements have a serious impact on anyone who lacks ready access to official documentation of citizenship, particularly the frail elderly, the disabled, and the homeless. *See* Donna Cohen Ross, *Medicaid Documentation Requirement Disproportionately Harms Non–Hispanics, New State Data Show: Rule Mostly Hurts U.S. Citizen Children, Not Undocumented Immigrants*, Ctrs. on Budget & Policy Priorities, July 10, 2007, http://www.cbpp.org/7–10–07 health.pdf (data from Alabama, Kansas, and Virginia show that white and African–American children are much more likely than Hispanic children to have Medicaid coverage delayed, denied, or terminated as a result of this new requirement); Mike Mitka, *Proving Citizenship Difficult*, 298 JAMA 1153 (2007) (citing conclusions from the Government Accountability Office ("GAO") and a House committee's majority staff that "22 [out of 44] states reported declines in Medicaid enrollment due to the documentation requirement, with the majority of these states attributing the decreases to delays or losses of Medicaid coverage for those who appeared to be eligible citizens"); Robert Pear, *Medicaid Hurdles for Immigrants May Hurt Others*, N.Y. Times, Apr. 16, 2006, at A1; Kaiser Family Fund, Citizenship Documentation in Medicaid (2007), http://www.kff.org/medicaid/upload/7533_03.pdf.

The Patient Protection and Affordable Health Care Act of 2010 made few changes in the situation of non-citizens and persons not legally present in the U.S. Most notably, the Act bars persons not lawfully present in the U.S. from receiving premium subsidies or cost-sharing reduction assistance (discussed in Part Two) through state insurance Exchanges but also from buying coverage at any price through the state Exchange market. Under the Act, a person is not considered a "qualified individual" entitled to purchase insurance through a state Exchange if he or she is not a U.S. citizen or an alien lawfully present in the United States. Affordable Care Act, § 1312(f)(3) and § 1402(e); Kaiser Family Fund, *Immigrants' Health Coverage and Health Reform: Key Questions and Answers*, Dec. 2009, http://www.kff.org/healthreform/upload/7982.pdf. In general see Brietta R. Clark, *The Immigrant Health Care Narrative and What it Tells Us About the U.S. Health Care System*, 17 Ann. Health L. 229 (2008).

CHAPTER 5

DIRECT PUBLIC PROVISION OF MEDICAL CARE: SAFETY–NET HOSPITALS AND COMMUNITY HEALTH CENTERS

As Chapter 1 demonstrates, access to health care is strongly influenced by having health insurance or money. Chapter 4 explores forms of discrimination that limit access to care. But even if neither discrimination nor ability to pay is an issue, necessary health care may be unavailable. Ordinarily, people obtain health care close to home. For obvious reasons, when a child has a high fever, an adult experiences a sharp pain in the chest, or when anyone seeks a routine check-up or vaccination, they seek care locally. For health care, the rubber hits the road locally, not in Washington or at the state capitol. This section explores two major components of the effort to assure that necessary care is actually available: safety-net hospitals and Community Health Centers.

1. SAFETY–NET HOSPITALS

Until the late nineteenth century, most medical care, even surgery, was delivered in the patient's own home. The home was correctly regarded as safer than hospitals, and the best way to receive nursing care was from the patient's own relatives. The first hospitals—Philadelphia General Hospital (PGH), 1734, and Bellevue Hospital in New York City, 1736—were the infirmary wards of almshouses used to incarcerate destitute people who did not have family to care for them. In the 19th Century, the few American hospitals—only 178 in the entire country in 1873, of which about a third were mental hospitals—were designed to serve those who could not be cared for in their homes and to provide a location for medical education, for which students paid fees. PAUL STARR, SOCIAL TRANSFORMATION OF AMERICAN MEDICINE 177–79 (1982); CHARLES ROSENBERG, THE CARE OF STRANGERS: THE RISE OF AMERICA'S HOSPITAL SYSTEM (1987). From the 1873 to 1910 hospitals and medical education underwent a remarkable transformation in which hospitals moved from the periphery to the center of medical practice and education. By 1910 there were over 4,300 hospitals in the United States.

In 2003 there were about 3,900 nonfederal, short-term, acute-care general hospitals in the United States. Most, about 62 percent, were private nonprofits. The rest included local public hospitals (20 percent) and for-profit hospitals (18 percent). In terms of service to the needy, the large urban public hospitals have a long tradition of extensive involvement in medical education and charitable care. But other "public" hospitals strictly limited their services. (Recall that the Holly Springs hospital in *Campbell v. Mincy*, above in Chapter 2, was a public hospital.) Similarly, some nonprofit hospitals provided substantial care to people unable to pay, either because of the hospitals' ethical traditions or because of state and federal efforts to enforce charitable care requirements. Profit-making hospitals provide little charitable care. Gloria J. Bazzoli et al., *An Update on Safety–Net Hospitals: Coping with the Late 1990s and Early 2000s,* 24(4) HEALTH AFFAIRS 1047 (2005).

In 2000, the Institute of Medicine coined the term "safety net hospitals" for those that provide significant amounts of charitable care. INSTITUTE OF MEDICINE, AMERICA'S SAFETY NET: INTACT BUT ENDANGERED (2000). Safety net hospitals deliver a significant level of health care to uninsured, Medicaid eligible and other vulnerable patients and, either by legal mandate or adopted mission, offer care to patients regardless of ability to pay. Urban general hospitals comprise a large portion of the safety net hospitals. Nat'l Assn. of Public Hospitals and Health Systems (NAPH), *2009 Annual Survey: Safety New Hospitals and Health Systems Fulfill Mission in Uncertain Times* (Feb. 2011), http://www.naph.org/Main–Menu–Category/Publications/Characteristics–Brief–Feb–2010.aspx?FT=.pdf.

In 2009 public safety net hospitals were only 2 percent of the hospitals in the nation, but were responsible for 20 percent of the costs of uncompensated care. Public safety net hospitals are frequently the only providers of services that are particularly difficult and costly to deliver. For example, in 2009, public safety net providers offered the only trauma center in many cities, including Albuquerque, Los Vegas, Memphis, Richmond, and San Francisco. In the ten largest U.S. cities, public safety net hospitals represent only 12 percent of local acute care hospitals, but provide a disproportionate share of critical services, including 63 percent of burn care beds, 33 percent of outpatient visits, and 23 percent of emergency department visits. *2009 NAPH Annual Survey.* In many areas, public safety net providers are sole providers of emergency inpatient psychiatric care, services to prisoners, and other costly, but important care.

Part Two and the chapter on tax exemption in Part Four describe how these services are financed. As demand has increased and financing has declined or not kept pace, many safety net hospitals have closed. Between 1996 and 2002, while the number of hospitals nationwide declined slightly, large numbers of public hospitals closed. More public hospitals closed (16 percent in cities and 27 percent in suburbs) than for-profit hospitals (11 percent in cities and 11 percent in suburbs) or non-profit hospitals (11 percent in cities and 2 percent in the suburbs). Dennis Andrulis, *Hospital Care in the 100 Largest Cities and Their Suburbs, 1996–2002: Implications for the Future of the Hospital Safety Net in Metropolitan America* (SUNY Downstate Medical Center, 2005), http://www.rwjf.org/pr/product.jsp?id=

21808. Further, this study shows that the high-poverty suburbs were relatively underserved by hospitals, compared to low-poverty suburbs. The lead author comments, "Public hospitals may become an endangered species. Not only are public hospitals disappearing from the inner cities across the country, they are disappearing from the suburbs as well."

As the number of people without insurance increases, so too does the demand for the services of safety net hospitals, including emergency care. Between 1993 and 2003, emergency department visits grew by 26 percent. Over that period, the number of emergency departments declined by 425. Institute of Medicine, Hospital-Based Emergency Care: At the Breaking Point (2006). Between 1990 and 2009, the number of hospital emergency departments in non-rural areas dropped from 2,446 to 1,779, even as the total number of emergency room visits nationwide increased by roughly 35 percent. Emergency rooms were more likely to close if they served large numbers of poor people, were at commercially operated hospitals, were in hospitals with skimpy profit margins, or were operated in highly competitive markets. Renee Y. Hsia, *Factors Associated with Closures of Emergency Departments in the United States*, 305 JAMA 620 (2011).

Beyond the phenomenon of emergency department closure is the problem of emergency department overcrowding. Emergency departments in many communities are so overcrowded that an ambulance a minute is diverted away to another source of care. IOM, Hospital-Based Emergency Care (2006). Patients who actually make it through the door are backed up, often because inpatient beds are full; in effect, these patients become "boarded" in the emergency department, sometimes for 48 hours or more. *Id.*

---

2. Community Health Centers

Community health centers were established as a federal pilot program in 1965 under the auspices of the Office of Economic Opportunity. Their mission was to provide comprehensive primary care services to populations and communities designated as "medically underserved" because of elevated health risks and a significant lack of access to primary health care. Juniper Lesnik, Community Health Centers: Health Care as it Could Be, 19 J. L. & Health 1 (2005). In 1975 the program was established as a legislative authority of the Public Health Service Act (PHSA § 330, 42 U.S.C. § 254b). Following a 35–year legislative cycle of periodic reauthorizations, the program was made a permanent legislative authority of the Public Health Service Act as part of the Patient Protection and Affordable Care Act, PPACA § 5601. In addition, $11 billion in mandatory funding was earmarked for the expansion of health centers under the ACA, in advance of full implementation, when demand for health care is expected to increase exponentially and the shortage of primary health care providers is expected to become critical. Sara Rosenbaum et al., *Community Health Centers: Opportunities and Challenges of Health Reform* (Kaiser Family Foundation, 2010), http://www.kff.org/uninsured/upload/8098.pdf.

Community health centers (known as "federally qualified health centers" for purposes of Medicare and Medicaid coverage and payment) are private non-profit health care clinics that must meet four essential conditions in order to qualify for federal grants. First, they must be located in or serve communities or populations designated as medically underserved. Second, they must furnish comprehensive primary health care services, which are defined under federal law. Third, health centers must prospectively adjust their charges on the basis of patients' ability to pay (an obligation that, as you will see in Part Four, has led to the creation of special exemptions from federal laws aimed at curbing the use of bribes and kickbacks to lure paying customers). Fourth, health centers must be governed by community boards, the majority of whose members are patients of the health center, a characteristic that distinguishes health centers from public clinics as well as from free clinics that typically are organized and governed by health care professionals who donate their time. Sara Rosenbaum et al., Assessing and Addressing Legal Barriers to the Clinical Integration of Community Health Centers and Other Community Providers (Commonwealth Fund, 2011), http://www.commonwealthfund. org/Publications/Fund-Reports/2011/Jul/Clinical-Integration.aspx. Because health centers represent a central source of primary health care in medically underserved communities, as well as a powerful economic development mechanism, community legal services programs frequently have been involved in their development. Brian Glick, *Neighborhood Legal Services as House Counsel to Community-Based Efforts to Achieve Economic Justice: The East Brooklyn Experience*, 23 NYU REV. OF L. & SOC. CHANGE 105 (1997).

Health centers represent a disproportionate source of primary health care to low-income publicly insured and uninsured patients. In 2008 nearly 1100 health centers operating in over 7500 locations provided care to more than 17 million patients, over 90 percent of whom had family incomes under twice the federal poverty level, and more than one-third of whom were insured through Medicaid. Although grants under the Public Health Service Act form the core of health centers' finances, Medicaid is their chief source of health care financing, comprising more than one-third of all operating revenues. Kaiser Family Foundation, *Community Health Centers, Opportunities and Challenges*, at 2–4. Observers have noted that health centers present an approach to health care that is "an anomaly in the U.S. system," Juniper Lesnik, *Community Health Centers*, because of their unique combination of primary clinical services and an approach to health care grounded in principles of broader community and public health.

Health centers have been widely credited for the quality of their primary health care, their cost-efficiency, their ability significantly to improve access to health care, their impact on community economic development, and their cost-effectiveness. Eli Adashi et al., *Health Care Reform and Primary Care: The Growing Importance of the Community Health Center*, 362 NEW ENG. J. MED. 2047 (2010). At the same time, health centers face important challenges, beginning with access to specialty care. While CHCs provide a broad range of high quality primary care, they cannot provide everything. Some CHC patients have difficulty obtaining services that are not provided directly by the CHC, such as specialty care, pharmaceuticals, and sophisticated diagnostic testing. Suzanne Felt–Lisk et al., *Monitoring Local Safety–Net Providers: Do They Have Adequate Capacity*, 21(5) HEALTH AFFAIRS 277 (2002). Referral problems are particularly acute for patients who lack insurance or who are insured by Medicaid. Nakela L. Cook et al., *Access of Specialty Care and Medical Services in Community Health Centers*, 26(5) HEALTH AFFAIRS 1469 (2007). Uninsured patients and patients eligible for Medicaid confront similar problems obtaining access to specialty referrals when they are seen in the clinics of academic medical centers. Joel S. Weissman et al., *Limits to the Safety Net: Teaching Hospital Faculty Report on Their Patients' Access to Care*, 22(6) HEALTH AFFAIRS 156 (2003).

Health centers also face challenges recruiting sufficient numbers of primary health care personnel (a problem that plagues the entire health care system, as you see throughout the book). A 2004 national survey of 890 CHCs found serious shortages of physicians, especially family physicians, who make up the primary physician workforce of the CHCs. Since then, the CHCs expanded their services from 8 million patients per year at 3,300 delivery sites to 18 million patients + 6,600 delivery sites. Carl G. Morris & Frederick M. Chen, *Training Residents in Community Health Centers: Facilitators and Barriers*, 7 ANN. OF FAMILY MED. 1488, 1488 (2009). At the same time, there has been a sharp decline in the number of family medicine residents and family medicine residency programs generally. Morris and Chen examine the small number of CHC family medicine residency programs that have trained doctors for the past twenty years and explore the administrative and financial challenges confronting these programs. They urge expansion of CHC family medicine residencies, quoting a health center administrator with years of CHC–FMR experience as saying, ''I still believe this is a match made in heaven. It's a little rocky path to heaven sometimes.'' *Id.* at 493. With the adoption of health reform in Massachusetts and at the federal level, there is increased interested in creating CHC-based programs to expand training care opportunities for primary care physicians. *See* Carl G. Morris et al., *Family Medical Residency Training in Community Health Centers: A National Survey*, 85 ACADEMIC MED. 1640 (2010); Thomas Bodenheimer & Hoagmai H. Pham, *Primary Care: Current Problems and Proposed Solutions*, 29(5) HEALTH AFFAIRS 799 (2010).

CHCs rely more heavily on non-physician providers than do other forms of health care. Between 2006 and 2008, physicians provided care for 69 percent of CHC patient visits, nurse practitioners provided care for 21 percent of visits, physician assistants 9 percent of visits, and certified nurse midwives one percent. Esther Hing & Roderick S. Hooker, *Community Health Centers: Providers, Patients, and Content of Care*, HHS, CDC, Nat'l Center for Health Statistics (July 2011), http://www.cdc.gov/nchs/data/data briefs/db65.pdf. The pressure to grow, along with long-term economic sustainability, represent additional challenges. Funding made available through the Patient Protection and Affordable Care Act is expected to generate an expansion of health centers to 50 million patients by 2019.

Kaiser Family Foundation, *Community Health Centers, Opportunities and Challenges of Health Reform*, at 12. Growth of this magnitude will require recruitment of thousands of health professionals and the additional investment of billions of dollars in capital expansion funding. Ronda Kotelchuck et al., *Community Health Centers and Community Development Financial Institutions: Joining Forces to Address Determinants of Health,* 30(11) HEALTH AFFAIRS 2090 (2011).

Health centers' ability to grow to meet expanding need depends on full state implementation of the PPACA Medicaid eligibility expansions (discussed in Part Two), given Medicaid's role as the central financier of health center services. Health centers are expected to be active participants in provider networks to be offered by qualified health plans marketed through state insurance Exchanges and discussed in Part Two. But the deep poverty of their patients makes health centers particularly sensitive to evolving state Medicaid coverage and payment policy and the Medicaid coverage expansions (also discussed in Part Two). One estimate projects that by 2019, the year of full implementation of the Affordable Care Act, the proportion of health center patients covered by Medicaid can be expected to rise to 44 percent. Kaiser Family Foundation, *Community Health Centers, Opportunities and Challenges of Health Reform* at 7.

The extent to which states fully implement the Medicaid provisions of health reform and enable Medicaid-eligible individuals actually to enroll and obtain coverage will be an important factor in health centers' ability to achieve major growth. Although insurance enrollment is required of all taxpayers (discussed in Part Two), this mandate does not apply to the poorest Americans whose incomes fall below federal income tax liability thresholds. PPACA § 1401. The Affordable Care Act requires states to take considerable steps to ease Medicaid enrollment, a reform discussed in Part Two. In a clear example of how legal reforms to one part of the health care system in the end influence the power and effectiveness of other parts of the system, how actively states embrace their heightened Medicaid eligibility and enrollment responsibilities in turn will play a significant role in determining health centers' ultimate reach, because of the intimate relationship between the sustainability of health centers and national Medicaid policy.

PART TWO

HEALTH CARE FINANCING

HEALTH CARE COSTS AND THE RISE AND EVOLUTION OF HEALTH INSURANCE: FROM "CASH AND CARRY" TO THE PATIENT PROTECTION AND AFFORDABLE CARE ACT

1. HEALTH CARE COSTS AND THE SEARCH FOR SOLUTIONS

Cost is the starting point for the study of health insurance, because health insurance just costs so much. As you read in Part One, without substantial subsidies, most American families would be uninsured because the cost of health insurance eats up such a significant portion of family income. This introductory material explores some of the underlying cost drivers and compares the U.S. experience to that of other wealthy democracies.

International comparisons of health care costs are startling. Over a 40–year time period, U.S. health care spending increased six-fold, a rate that surpassed nearly all other nations, with expenditures growing (in 2005 dollars) from $187 billion to $1.9 trillion. CONGRESSIONAL BUDGET OFFICE, TECHNOLOGICAL CHANGE AND THE GROWTH OF HEALTH CARE SPENDING (2008). Between 1960 and 2006, health care spending grew on average by 9.9 percent per year. Health economists calculate that this rate of increase exceeded the annual growth of GDP by 2.5 percentage points, with the result that the proportion of GDP devoted to health care increased from 5.2 percent in 1960 to 16 percent in 2006. Adjusted for inflation, the rate of inflation for health care spending in the United States is more than twice as large as the growth of GDP. Paul Ginsburg, *High and Rising Health Care Costs: Demystifying U.S. Health Care Spending*, ROBERT WOOD JOHNSON FOUNDATION, Research Synthesis Project, Report #16, 2008, http://www.rwjf.org/files/research/101508.policysynthesis.costdrivers.rpt.pdf (May 27, 2011).

As expenditures grow inexorably, the cost of health insurance crowds out spending by families, businesses, and governments alike for other life essentials. It reduces take-home pay, diminishes profits, and erodes critical public services. The dramatic rise in health insurance costs has been particularly striking when compared to wages: between 1999 and 2008, inflation-adjusted median household income declined by more than 4.3 percent, while the cost of an average employer-sponsored plan rose by 69 percent. Escalating insurance costs are literally crowding out take-home pay. WHITE HOUSE COUNCIL OF ECONOMIC ADVISORS, ECONOMIC REPORT TO THE PRESIDENT, CHAPTER 7 REFORMING HEALTH CARE (2009), http://www.white house.gov/sites/default/files/microsites/economic-report-president-chapter–7 r2.pdf. Similarly, retiree health benefits, once a common feature of most employer-sponsored plans, are disappearing entirely, leaving millions of older workers without any realistic means of securing coverage, because they are not yet eligible for Medicare and because they have been forced out of their jobs. Remarkably, even in the face of this dissolution of the private retiree coverage system, legislation was introduced in Congress in 2011 to roll back the age of Medicare eligibility to 67, which would add even more persons to the ranks of the uninsured. *Dems Reject Plan to Raise Medicare Eligibility Age*, KAISER HEALTH NEWS (Accessed June 29, 2011), http://www.kaiserhealthnews.org/daily-reports/2011/june/29/coburn-leiberman-medicare-plan.aspx?referrer=search.

In the public sector, the problem of rising costs takes a terrible toll. In 2011, according to the Congressional Business Office ("CBO"), which advises Congress on federal spending matters and provides cost estimates of pending legislation, Medicare and Medicaid comprised 35 percent of all spending on health care. *See* MEDICAID AND CHIP PAYMENT AND ACCESS COMMISSION, REPORT TO CONGRESS, 18 Figure 1–1 (March, 2011). The two programs alone are projected to account for 40 percent of the two trillion dollars in federal "mandatory" spending (i.e., spending required by law for things such as health care, civilian and military retirement programs, and nutrition assistance). CONGRESSIONAL BUDGET OFFICE, REDUCING THE DEFICIT: SPENDING AND REVENUE OPTIONS (March, 2011) Table 2–1. Fifteen of 32 options put forth by CBO to reduce the deficit focus on health care, and most of these focus on Medicare and Medicaid. *Id.* at 18–64. Reacting to this cost explosion and further propelled by a more general opposition to federal entitlement programs, the House of Representatives on April 15, 2011 passed a Fiscal 2012 federal budget resolution that, among other things, would restructure Medicare and Medicaid to place flat limits on federal spending regardless of the cost of care. *See generally* HOUSE BUDGET COMMITTEE, THE PATH TO PROSPERITY, (April 5, 2011). These changes would profoundly harm both beneficiaries and state governments by shifting costs away from the federal government and directly onto them. Meredith Rosenthal, *Alternatives for Reining In Medicare and Medicaid Spending*, 364 NEW ENG. J. MED. 1887 (2011).

State economies, heavily damaged by the economic collapse that began in 2008, are struggling under the weight of Medicaid, whose costs they bear in significant part. Despite the impoverishment of Medicaid beneficiaries, most states in 2011 planned some combination of program reductions, including elimination of benefits and deep reductions in provider payments, thereby increasing the already high proportion of physicians who refuse to treat Medicaid patients. Anna Sommers et al., *Physician Willingness and*

Resources to Serve More Medicaid Patients: Perspectives from Primary Care Physicians, KAISER FAMILY FOUNDATION (2011), http://www.kff.org/medicaid/upload/8178.pdf. Even these reductions were insufficient in some states' view, and some states sought Congress's permission to eliminate coverage completely for certain populations. *Legislation Advanced to Repeal Medicaid Maintenance of Effort Provisions*, KAISER HEALTH NEWS (May 4, 2011), http://www.kaiserhealthnews.org/daily-reports/2011/may/04/medicaid-moe.aspx. Opposition to the Medicaid provisions of the Patient Protection and Affordable Care Act, which not only expanded coverage for the poorest Americans but also required states to maintain eligibility standards (even for optional groups) that were in place at the time of the law's 2010 enactment, has figured prominently in litigation challenging the Act's constitutionality, discussed at the end of Part Two.

How we have arrived at this astounding state of affairs is a complicated story that carries enormous consequences for us all. Much of the story has to do with the underlying cost of health care, while a good part has to do with the additional financial burdens created by our approach to health insurance coverage. Despite evidence that a great deal of our health care is vastly overpriced and that some is of questionable value, our apparent tolerance of this situation heavily reflects the political might of health care professionals and the health care industry, with their strength drawn from the health care sector's relative size in the economy (claiming a quarter of the GDP by 2025 if nothing changes, according to CBO), and from the unique relationship that exists between health care providers and patients. Efforts to curb runaway costs inevitably are met with protests of rationing and damage to the physician/patient relationship. Lawmakers freeze in their tracks.

As a result, over many decades, reforms that might have controlled costs and improved access have been defeated because of the combined power of professionals and the health care sector's growing industrial might. Numerous industry players have helped kill proposals that would scrutinize costly new technologies (as you will see, a major cost driver), reduce the high fees paid for specialty care while simultaneously increasing those paid for primary care, slow the rate of growth in high cost procedures, or move the nation toward cost containment across the population as a whole instead of affecting only discrete populations, particularly Medicare and Medicaid. The health care industry writ large—not just physicians but insurers, hospitals, other health care providers, pharmaceutical companies, companies that manufacture medical devices and equipment, and in recent years, the health information technology industry—is now a political powerhouse virtually unrivaled in Washington, D.C. For example, by October 2009, sixth months prior to passage of the Patient Protection and Affordable Care Act of 2010, industry lobbyists had spent nearly $400 million in an effort to preserve the status quo; an estimated six lobbyists walked the halls for every Member of Congress. Charles McGreal, *Revealed: Millions Spent by Lobbyists Fighting Obama's Health Reform*, THE GUARDIAN, Oct. 1, 2009, http://www.guardian.co.uk/world/2009/oct/01/lobbyists-millions-obama-healthcare-reform.

Our spending greatly eclipses that of other nations, whether measured relative to overall GDP or per capita. Furthermore, despite what we spend, preventable mortality in the U.S. remains high, and access to health care remains compromised, as discussed in Part One. The United States does poorly compared to other nations on measures of mortality as well as conditions that health care can favorably affect such as diabetes and high blood pressure. Even so, U.S. health care spending dwarfs that of other countries (**Figure 1**), outstripping some nations by better than two to one.

Figure 1. International Comparison of Spending on Health, 1980–2007

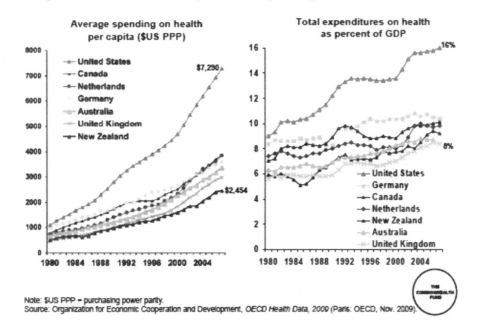

Note: $US PPP = purchasing power parity.
Source: Organization for Economic Cooperation and Development, *OECD Health Data, 2009* (Paris: OECD, Nov. 2009).

This story of dramatically elevated aggregate spending is likewise reflected in the cost of individual goods and services. For example, lengths of hospital stay in the United States are shorter than those in other nations, but spending per discharge is far higher. (**Figures 2 and 3**). As another example, the most popular, prescribed drugs, available in all wealthy nations, are far costlier here.

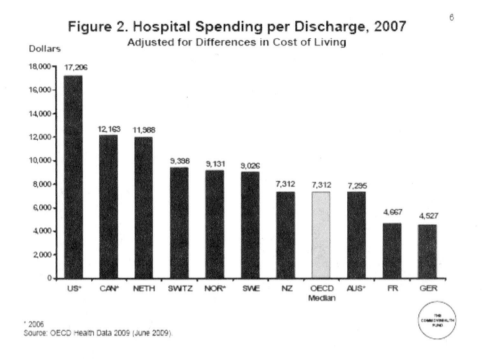

Figure 2. Hospital Spending per Discharge, 2007
Adjusted for Differences in Cost of Living

* 2006
Source: OECD Health Data 2009 (June 2009).

Figure 3. Average Length of Hospital Stay for Acute Myocardial Infarction,[8] 2007

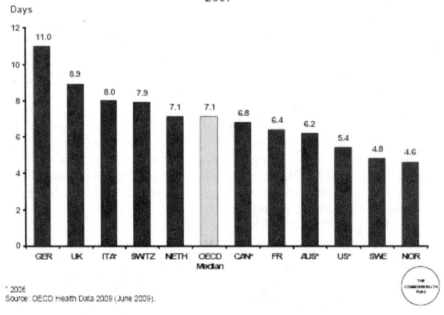

* 2006
Source: OECD Health Data 2009 (June 2009).

Many factors account for our high health care costs. One factor is the absence of any meaningful ability to control either the price of health care or the introduction and diffusion of costly yet unproven technologies. David Cutler & Mark McClellan, *Is Technological Change in Medicine Worth It?* 20(5) HEALTH AFFAIRS 11 (2001); HOWARD GREENWALD, HEALTH CARE IN THE UNITED STATES: ORGANIZATION, MANAGEMENT, AND POLICY (2010); PAUL STARR, THE SOCIAL TRANSFORMATION OF AMERICAN MEDICINE (1982); Gerard Anderson et al., *It's the Prices Stupid: Why the United States is So Different from Other Countries*, 22(3) HEALTH AFFAIRS 89 (2003). Another factor is a fragmented delivery system that often furnishes care in the most costly and least appropriate setting. We seem incapable of bringing an organized clinical response to serious community-wide medical problems, and the cost consequence is very high. Overall, we have a health insurance system that creates a large financial burden without effectively controlling costs. William Sage, *Brand New Law! The Need to Market Health Care Reform*, 159 U. PA. L. REV. 2121, 2133–34 (2011).

Not only are health care costs high but for reasons that are not well understood, they vary from place to place. For decades researchers have documented in the Dartmouth Atlas of Health Care (http://www.dartmouth atlas.org/) how health care spending varies among different regions in the nation. For example, they report that in 2007, total annual per capita Medicare spending for Parts A and B (which you will learn about later in Part Two) amounted to $5763 in Bismarck, North Dakota, compared to $17,274 in Miami, Florida. What could possibly account for this difference? Speculation runs from rampant fraud, to variation in practice style (particularly in the use of high cost technology), to the possibility that in some localities there exists a general approach to the practice of medicine that employs every possible strategy to maximize patient revenue regardless of quality or the value of care.

Dr. Atul Gawande, a surgeon and a gifted chronicler of medicine and culture, has illustrated the point by comparing McAllen, Texas, the site of the nation's most costly Medicare spending, with El Paso, Texas, where Medicare expenditures are literally half those of McAllen. See *The Cost Conundrum: What a Texas Town Can Teach Us About the Cost of Health Care*, THE NEW YORKER, June 1, 2009, at 52–61. Dr. Gawande probes the question of how these expenditures can be so different between two locations that are quite similar demographically. His conclusion is troubling: McAllen physicians use far higher levels of health care technology and cutting edge services and are far more likely to jump to the costliest procedures compared with physicians in El Paso. At the same time, McAllen patients are no healthier and its hospitals perform worse on standard measures of clinical quality.

Policy makers are consumed by attempts to deal with these regional spending variations, and some proposals are draconian. For example, in *Reducing the Deficit: Spending and Revenue Options* (March, 2011), at 34, CBO recommends that Medicare simply adopt uniform payment rates, which would effectively paper over the huge variations. As CBO itself pointed out, such an approach might curb spending in high-cost areas, but at the same time might actually increase spending in low-cost areas, even for care of questionable quality.

Public programs like Medicare receive the most attention because data are readily available, while comparable figures for private plans are not. Ironically, however, spending by the federal government in the United States accounts for a much lower proportion of the nation's total health care spending than comparable figures in other nations. Gerard Anderson & Patricia Markovich, *Multinational Comparisons of Health Systems Data (2009)*, COMMONWEALTH FUND, http://www.commonwealthfund.org/Content/Publications/Chartbooks/2009/Multinational–Comparisons-of-Health–Systems–Data–2009.aspx. The evidence shows that the high level of U.S. spending is the result of far higher out-of-pocket payments by individuals and employers' contributions to workers' health insurance coverage. *Id.* at 5.

Health care spending is a function of quantity—how much health care is used (on an individual or aggregate basis)—and the price paid for that care. Ginsburg, *High and Rising Health Care Costs* at 5. Quantity is increased by poor health, and Americans are in poorer health than citizens of other nations on some key measures such as infant mortality and premature, preventable mortality due to chronic illnesses such as cardiovascular disease, diabetes and obesity. *Multinational Comparisons,* at 17–26; *World Health Report*, WORLD HEALTH ORGANIZATION (2008), http://www.who.int/whr/2008/en/index.html. Obesity, for example, raises individual spending by an estimated 50 percent. *See* CBO, TECHNOLOGY AND THE GROWTH OF HEALTH CARE SPENDING 10 (2008) (By contrast, U.S. adult smoking rates are significantly lower than those in other nations with better overall health indicators, *Multinational Comparisons* at 22). However, evidence also shows that Americans are less likely than citizens of other nations to have access to health care that can improve outcomes for people with conditions like obesity. Ellen Nolte & C. Martin McKee, *Measuring the Health Care of Nations: Updating an Earlier Analysis*, 27(1) HEALTH AFFAIRS 58 (2008). Lack of access to the right care in the right place at the right time thus becomes a significant factor in higher costs.

International comparisons show that overall Americans actually receive less—and in some cases much less—health care than residents of other nations, as measured by utilization of hospital inpatient and physician care. (By contrast, however, on a *per capita* basis, we consume significantly higher levels of pharmaceutical products. *Multinational Comparisons* at 7–12). Nor does the U.S. have a vastly greater supply of physicians, which in turn might be expected to drive utilization since it is physicians (and other health care providers) who make the actual purchasing decisions in the course of prescribing and treating patients. Ginsburg, *High and Rising Health Care Costs* at 8. Indeed, the U.S. has fewer physicians than other nations, although the number is skewed toward specialty care. For example, while the U.S. has 2.4 practicing physicians per 1000 population, the comparable average among OECD countries is 3.2. *Multinational Comparisons* at 10. Indeed, an estimated 100 million Americans live in communities designated by the federal government as medically underserved because of poor health indicators and lack of access to primary health care. Leighton Ku et al., *Estimating the Effects of Health Reform on Health Centers' Capacity to Expand to New Medically Underserved Communities and Populations*, GEORGE WASHINGTON UNIVERSITY (July 2009), http://www.gwumc.edu/sphhs/departments/healthpolicy/dhp_publications/index.cfm?mdl=pubSearch & evt=view & PublicationID=9889E996–5056–9D20–3D1F89027D3F9406.

Others might point to an aging society as the cause of our high spending. But societies are aging all over the world, particularly in wealthy nations with economies similar to our own, and yet, as the evidence shows, other nations are able to keep costs in check. Furthermore, as noted health economist Uwe Reinhardt has written, while spending inevitably rises as people age, aging is happening too slowly to account for the vast differences between the U.S. and other nations. Uwe Reinhardt, *Does the Aging of the Population Really Drive the Demand for Health Care?*, 22(6) HEALTH AFFAIRS 27 (2003). According to the Center for Studying Health System Change, the aging of the population accounts for less than 10 percent of rising health care costs. Bradley Strunck & Paul Ginsburg, *Aging Plays Limited Role in Health Care Cost Trends*, Data Bulletin #23 (2002), http://www.hschange.com/CONTENT/473/?words=aging%20as%20a%20health%20care%20cost%20factor.

Experts from across the political spectrum tend to agree on the root cause of the high cost of U.S. health care: a rapid diffusion of health care technologies (e.g., drugs, equipment, costly medical procedures), and the prices paid for these technologies, as well as the high price of physician, particularly specialist, care. TECHNOLOGICAL CHANGE AND THE GROWTH OF HEALTH CARE SPENDING at 10; Miriam Laugesen & Sherry A. Glied, *Higher Fees Paid to U.S. Physicians Drive Higher Spending For Physician Services Compared to Other Countries*, 30(9) HEALTH AFFAIRS 1646 (2011). Because of how the nation has chosen to structure and operate its systems of health care and health care financing, we consistently favor what is termed the "increased capability of medicine," that is, the steady and rapid introduction into the health care economy of high priced technologies, whose effectiveness and value are not well-analyzed before they become available. *Id.*; Ginsburg, *High and Rising Health Care Costs* at 13; Gerard Anderson et al., *It's the Prices Stupid*. The same structural attributes—fragmentation of purchasing and the resulting ability to command high prices in disorganized local markets by an enterprise that makes its money from high-volume, high-cost procedures—also prevent the more rapid diffusion of innovations in health care efficiencies that lower costs through reduced use of technology. Victor R. Fuchs & Arnold Milstein, *The $640 Billion Question: Why Does Cost–Effective Care Diffuse So Slowly?*, NEW ENG. J. MED. (2011).

There is considerable disagreement among economists as to whether our massive investment in health care produces value to patients and society in terms of patient care, population health, and jobs created.

Ginsburg, *High and Rising Health Care Costs* at 8. The American health care marketplace is both dynamic and more likely to provide access to cutting edge technology more quickly than in other nations (at least for those who can afford it). At the same time, we lack other nations' mechanisms for balancing rapid introduction of costly technologies against their added value not only to society as a whole but also to individual patients. Treatments lacking in value are nonetheless paid for by insurers.

Even procedures of highly proven value that are widely available among wealthy nations are far more costly in the U.S., simply because we lack the means of controlling price. **Figure 4** shows how much costlier it is to repair a fractured hip or replace a knee in the U.S. (Two-to-one differences in the case of knees, and an astounding four-to-one difference in the case of hip prostheses).

Figure 4. Cost of Knee and Hip Prostheses to Providers, 2004[19]
GDP Adjusted, US $

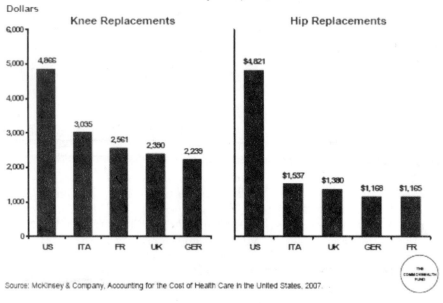

Source: McKinsey & Company, Accounting for the Cost of Health Care in the United States, 2007.

* * *

Beyond the problem of price is the problem of how the health care system is organized and care delivered. Other nations that show greater efficiency and effectiveness emphasize the training and deployment of large numbers of primary care physicians, whose costs are far lower and who are trained to manage routine care as well as ongoing care and treatment for serious and chronic health conditions. These health professionals (pediatricians, obstetricians and gynecologists, family practice physicians, and general internal medicine physicians), as well as nurse practitioners, physicians assistants, and other primary care professionals, should be the locus of most of the care we receive. Instead, in the U.S. a remarkable 58 percent of all acute care (defined as treatment for newly arising health care problems) is furnished by emergency departments, specialists and hospital outpatient departments, all of which are far more costly. Stephen R. Pitts et al., *Where Americans Get Acute Care: Increasingly It's Not at Their Doctor's Office*, 29(9) HEALTH AFFAIRS 1620 (2010). Notably, the percentage of Americans who visit hospital emergency departments for problems that could have been treated in a primary care setting is three times greater than the proportion using such locations in either the Netherlands or Germany. *Id.* Through Medicare payments for graduate medical education, the federal government invests nearly $10 billion annually in the training of physicians, and yet we have a critical shortage (some estimate as many as 90,000) of primary care physicians.

Commentators note that not only is care delivered in inappropriate settings, but it is also fragmented and irrational. The health care system may respond at the point of immediate treatment while missing the larger picture entirely. In *The Hot Spotters,* THE NEW YORKER, Jan. 24, 2011, at 41–56, Dr. Gawande describes the work of several remarkable researchers who have worked to identify and address the causes of high health care spending. He focuses on a physician named Jeffrey Brenner in Camden, New Jersey, one of the state's poorest cities. Among other astonishing revelations, Dr. Brenner's work documented that a single building in central Camden "sent more people to the hospitals with serious falls—fifty-seven elderly in two years—than any other in the city, resulting in almost three million dollars in health-care bills." Gawande, *Hot Spotters* at 42. Not only was the safety of the building overlooked as a basic factor in controlling expenditures, but no one at the city's hospital emergency departments put two and two together until Dr. Brenner's research unveiled the root cause.

Only in rare communities have more comprehensive delivery systems been created in which hospitals and physician practices are combined into a single enterprise that provides more complete and integrated care to patients. These rare examples include the Geisinger Clinic in Pennsylvania; Kaiser Permanente, which operates mainly in the West, where prepaid group health practices first flourished on a more widespread basis; and the Cleveland Clinic. These health care systems may offer insurance plans or may instead contract with public and private health insurers and employer-sponsored group health plans. However, most Americans still receive their care from individual providers and hospitals that do not work together in a coordinated fashion to improve the quality and efficiency of care; indeed, they have no incentive to do so, since profitability is based on the high-volume sale of high-cost procedures. Responding to this incentive, medicine has become hyper-specialized and increasingly fragmented, triggering greater disintegration in quality and higher costs related to inefficiency and error. *See* Einer Elhauge, *Why We Should Care About Health Care Fragmentation and How to Fix It, in* THE FRAGMENTATION OF U.S. HEALTH CARE 1 (Einer Elhauge, ed., 2010). The resistance to integration and accountability for cost, quality, and outcome has grown, particularly to innovations that would reduce volume and profitability. Fuchs & Milstein, *The $640 Billion*

Question. Some of this resistance is the result of concern over the loss of income; but physicians also fear being labeled unethical or of not acting in the best interests of their patients if they do not push the latest technology and procedures. Fuchs & Milstein, *The $640 Billion Question*; Gawande, *The Cost Conundrum.*

Some states have attempted to break this cycle by enacting, in the name of public health, laws designed to curb health care costs and inefficiencies. In Sorrell v. IMS Health Inc., 131 S. Ct. 2653 (2011), the United States Supreme Court struck down on First Amendment grounds Vermont's Prescription Drug Confidentiality Law, which barred the use of prescriber-identifying information purchased from pharmacies and used by the pharmaceutical industry to target physicians for door-to-door sales (known as detailing). The purpose of detailing is to persuade physicians to prescribe higher-cost brand-name drugs. Vermont's law allowed use of the information if physicians expressly authorized such contacts. Detailers claimed that the law (a similar law was enacted in Maine and upheld by the First Circuit Court of Appeals) violated their right to free speech, since the state did not ban the use of prescribing data entirely but instead allowed its use for other purposes, such as educating physicians on cost-effective prescribing practices. The case offers an important lesson in the tension between economic and public health regulation (which is permissible) and the regulation of speech, which is not. In the end, as has historically been the case, interests in favor of commercialization and the utilization that accompanies it won out, this time on constitutional grounds.

Commercialation v. Utilization

* * *

Our spending problem is further exacerbated by the high cost of health insurance. Rather than pooling risks across the entire population and minimizing administrative costs as other nations tend to do, the U.S. relies on large national and regional companies to sell insurance and plan administration products to employer-sponsored groups and, to a much smaller extent, to individuals. The result is a multitude of competing insurers and countless purchasers. Each company looks for the best risks while keeping out the bad ones to the greatest degree possible. Furthermore, each company attempts to shield itself by creating multiple risk pools in multiple markets and setting customized price points that reflect variable risk. The results are the perverse effects that flow from risk selection, market instability, higher administrative costs, insurance tied to employment—which can be lost when a job is lost—the inability to control costs, and an unpredictable and uncontrollable flow of financing compared with nations that have created more unified insurance and financing mechanisms.

In recent years, considerable consolidation has occurred within the insurance industry, but premium rates have not fallen in response; it is difficult to be a small insurer, of course, because of the need to spread risk across large groups of covered lives. In many states insurers face little competition. The Center for American Progress, a liberal think tank in Washington D.C., offers a map that allows readers to see for themselves

how concentrated the insurance market is in various states. *See* http://
www.americanprogress.org/issues/2009/06/health_competition_map.html. A
2009 GAO review of the literature on insurer market concentration found
growing concentration in certain markets, which in turn raised potential
antitrust concerns, addressed in Part Four, because of the potential to lead
to higher premium rates (although evidence was limited). Findings also
varied on whether a growing concentration led to an increase or decrease in
utilization and pricing. U.S. Gov'T ACCOUNTABILITY OFFICE, GAO–10–632R,
Letter to the Honorable Herbert Kohl (July 31, 2009), http://www.gao.gov/
new.items/d09864r.pdf.

Large insurance companies show handsome rates of return to investors
on the sale of products sold in both the individual and group markets, as
well as on the sale of third-party administered products for larger corporations that self-insure (more about this later in this Part). These large firms
also profit from the sale of information technology services, worksite
wellness services, health plans to public purchasers such as Medicare and
Medicaid, and (increasingly) direct medical care through insurer-owned and
operated clinics. Anahad O'Connor, *WellPoint Joins Other Insurers in
Strong Earnings*, NEW YORK TIMES, April 27, 2011, http://prescriptions.blogs.
nytimes.com/2011/04/27/wellpoint-joins-other-insurers-in-strong-
earnings/?ref=humanainc. As Americans increasingly put off care because
of its cost, insurers are generating enormous returns, since premiums
remain high but utilization has fallen off. Reed Abelson, *Health Insurers
Making Record Profits as Many Postpone Care*, NEW YORK TIMES, May 13,
2011, http://www.nytimes.com/2011/05/14/business/14health.html?_r=1 &
scp=1 & sq=healthïnsuranceprofits & st=Search.

Acclaimed health economist, Professor Uwe Reinhardt of Princeton,
offers the following primer on where insurers make their money. *How
Much Money Do Insurance Companies Make? A Primer,* NEW YORK TIMES,
Sept. 25, 2009, http://economix.blogs.nytimes.com/2009/09/25/how-much-
money-do-insurance-companies-make-a-primer/?scp=4 & sq=healthïnsur-
anceprofits & st=Search. His primer is based on a WellPoint income
statement, because it is "fairly typical" of statements generated by large
insurers selling mostly group policies to larger employers:

> WellPoint Inc. was formed from the merger of two companies that
> were once known as Blue Cross and Blue Shield of Indiana and
> Blue Cross of California, both originally not-for-profit plans. It is
> now one of the nation's largest commercial health insurers. In-
> come statements are part of the annual reports called a 10–K that
> every publicly traded company must submit to the Securities and
> Exchange Commission. A firm's 10–K reveals much of the bowels
> of a company, including the business risks it faces and executive
> compensation.
>
> **Revenues**: According to WellPoint's income statement for 2008,
> the company's *total revenue* that year was $61,579.2 million. Of
> that, 93.2 percent came from *premium revenues*, and 6.3 percent
> came from fees for merely administering the claims of employers

who self-insure (that is, these firms set aside their own funds for their employees' health benefits and bear full risk for them).

Revenue From the "Float": About 1 percent of WellPoint's *total revenue* came from a category simply called "other revenue." For the most part this probably comes from interest earned on the "float." An insurer's "float" is the money temporarily on hand when premium payments come in earlier than the outlays for insurance claims covered by these premiums. In times when interest rates are high, an insurer's float can be a major source of revenue, which is why sometimes health insurers stand accused of deliberately dragging out claims processing, strictly to increase the size of the float at any point in time. As the Federal Reserve has lowered short-term interest rates to close to zero, however, the interest earned on an insurer's float is now trivial—as it is in WellPoint's case—meaning that more costs must be recovered through premiums.

The Health Benefit Ratio (alias Medical Loss Ratio): WellPoint's payments for health benefits in 2008 equal the sum of what it calls "health benefits" ($47,742.4 million) and the "cost of drugs" ($468.5 million). Together these health benefits came to $48,210.9 million. As a fraction of total *premium revenue* of $57,101.0 million in 2008, total health benefits amounted to 84.4 percent of *premium revenue*. Traditionally, actuaries had called this fraction the *medical loss ratio* (M.L.R.), because it represents what insurers "lose," so to speak, to doctors, hospitals and other providers of health care. Because that terminology comes across as indelicate, however, the preferred term now is the mellower *health benefit ratio* (H.B.R.).

Marketing and Administrative Expenses, or S.G. & A.: The firm's total marketing (selling) expenses for 2008 were $1,778.4 million. General administrative expenses were $7,242.1 million. The sum of these two items goes by the acronym "S.G. & A." One should relate these S.G. & A. expenses not just to *premium revenue*, but also to *total revenue*. In this case, S.G. & A. expenses amounted to 14.7 percent of total revenue in 2008.

The Profit Margin: WellPoint's *net income* (profits) after all expenses and the provision for income taxes in 2008 was 4.07 percent of *total revenue*. In accounting jargon, it is called the "profit margin." In 2007, that margin had been 5.47 percent. In 2006 it was 5.42 percent. Were WellPoint's profits in 2008 high? It depends how we look at it. Profits were not that big a deal as a fraction of *premium revenue*. S.G. & A. expenses typically are a far bigger enchilada worthy of attention. It is here that the health insurance industry is being challenged to search for economies. As a percentage of *total assets* of $48,403.2 million deployed by the company (measured at the reported book value on the firm's balance sheet), WellPoint's profits in 2008 amounted to 5.14

percent in 2008 and 6.42 percent in 2007. As a percentage of the equity shareholders had in WellPoint (also measured at the book values reported by accountants), WellPoint's profits in were 11.62 percent in 2008 and 14.55 percent in 2007. Relative to other industries, these are not particularly high numbers, nor are they particularly low.

A key point is that no entity—not at the federal or state level—regulates these costs.

Professor Reinhardt takes a different view of the individual insurance market, in which policies are sold, not to employer-sponsored groups, but instead, directly to individuals:

[A]dd-ons for marketing, administration and profits on top of expected outlays for health care to set the insurance premiums can be astonishingly high for individually sold policies. Up to half the premium can go for these non-medical items. It is the reason why that market urgently needs to reformed.

* * *

Across the political spectrum, health experts agree that the nation faces an enormous, structural problem as a result of health care costs. But a philosophical gulf exists when it comes to how to remedy it. The Patient Protection and Affordable Care Act, Pub. L. No. 111–148, 124 Stat. 119 (2010), commonly referred to as the Affordable Care Act and discussed at length later in this chapter, represents an attempt to bridge this gulf. The political fallout has been strong, and as of February 2012, the Act's bitter politics had spilled over into one of the most important Constitutional cases to reach the United States Supreme Court in decades. These developments underscore the difficulty of finding a middle ground between the two principal opposing views that define the modern debate. To be sure, middle ground exists, but it is worth understanding the extremes views in their purest form. Because CBO has projected that health care will consume 25 percent of the GDP by 2025 if nothing is done to change the current trajectory, the stakes for the nation as a whole, for politicians, the government, and the health care industry could not be greater. CBO, THE LONG TERM OUTLOOK FOR HEALTH CARE SPENDING, http://www.cbo.gov/ftpdocs/87xx/doc8758/MainText.3.1.shtml.

View #1: Health care is a complex social good that should be subject to collective control. The first view reflects a fundamental belief that health care is a social good whose importance to the population is such that substantial governmental intervention—even into private health care markets—is essential to keep a nation's health care system from collapsing under the weight of uncontrollable costs. Experts holding this basic viewpoint see health care as a resource to be managed for the good of the nation, much like one might manage any national resource. This social good view is shared by all wealthy industrial nations, other than the U.S.; these other nations most often have private health care systems and vibrant private economies. Although the details differ from country to country, the basic outline of their approach remains the same.

These social-good theorists argue that unlike most market goods and services, the demand for health care is not simply a matter of choice, like buying a television set; instead, health care is a matter of necessity and largely outside of individual control. We never know when we will get terribly sick or be badly injured, and it is impossible to pay for such care at the point of treatment in the absence of great wealth or insurance. Even the preventive services people need to stay healthy are costly and must be part of organized financing. (In Washington D.C. in 2011, simple prophylactic dental care consisting of an exam, x-rays, and a cleaning costs upwards of $200. A full round of immunizations for infants and preschool-age children costs in excess of $2000).

These facts, according to social good theorists, warrant direct governmental involvement in the health care market to control costs and preserve access. In other wealthy nations, either government or coordinated, highly regulated nonprofit entities (typically termed sickness funds) collect the revenues needed to operate and maintain the country's health care system; they expend these revenues to pay for health care on behalf of covered individuals. The government might make these disbursements directly or it might utilize the sickness funds that, much like insurers, enroll individuals as members, negotiate with providers, and purchase health care on their behalf. (Switzerland and the Netherlands use more competitive models that have been criticized as less effective in controlling health care costs, but nonetheless, both nations maintain a central interventionist role in regulating the market to assure universal access. *See* G.H. Kieke et al., *Managed Competition for Medicare? Sobering Lessons from the Netherlands*, NEW. ENG. J. MED. [online first] (June 15, 2011), http://www.nejm.org/doi/full/10. 1056/NEJMp1106090.

The social good model extends beyond the basic fact of coverage. Interventionist governments also negotiate with the health care industry over price, volume, and the introduction of costly new technologies such as the latest surgical robotics or advanced cancer treatment drugs. A government that regards health care as a social good also may sponsor research to discover more efficient ways to organize and deliver health care in order to hold down costs while improving quality. England's National Institute of Health and Clinical Effectiveness (NICE) is an example of such a government-sponsored effort. *See, e.g.*, Kalipso Chalkidou et al., *Evidence–Based Decision Making: When Should We Wait for More Information?*, 27(6) HEALTH AFFAIRS 1642 (2008). (For a fascinating article comparing the dynamics of U.S. and British health policy and exploring the underlying factors that led Great Britain toward its strong social good approach to health care and health care financing, see Howard Glennerster & Robert C. Lieberman, *Hidden Convergence: Toward a Historical Comparison of U.S. and U.K. Health Policy*, 36 J. HEALTH POL. POL'Y & L. 5 (2011)).

In sum, wealthy nations built on private economies and dependent on private healthcare providers nonetheless take an interventionist approach to the problem. These governments sometimes also allow wealthier people to supplement their government insurance with privately purchased coverage that gives them a wider choice of physicians and hospitals and potentially more rapid access to treatment. But each government maintains responsibility for assuring affordable coverage for the vast majority of the population. Of course, the details for each nation differ, but the basic contours described here apply to France, Canada, Switzerland, Germany, Israel, the Netherlands, Australia, and other nations with advanced economies similar to our own and with a highly privatized health care sector. (Great Britain, by contrast, relies extensively on a National Health Service that combines government-administered health care with contracted relationships between the NHS and private physicians).

View #2: Health care should be allocated through individual choice in a competitive market. The second viewpoint, held by other experts, reflects a fundamental belief that health care is a market commodity like any other. Health care, according to this view, is no different from any other product that consumers buy; what has led to runaway health spending is the extent to which consumers are insulated from its true cost and thus are allowed to make wasteful and inefficient decisions. This tendency to overspend when cost is not an issue is known in health economics as "moral hazard," and it is compounded, according to this philosophical outlook, by the fact that those most likely to overspend are people who consume a lot of health care because of the presence of higher health risks (a phenomenon known in insurance practice as "adverse selection"). According to this perspective, the way to fix this problem is to expose consumers to the true cost of their choices while providing them the information they need to make smarter decisions about staying healthy and using health care. Likewise, according to this viewpoint, insurers, as consumers' fiscal agents, must be freed from the alleged restrictions that preclude them from getting tough on providers. If enough consumers act smartly and their agents are freed up, the market will begin to behave differently.

The remedy as viewed through a market-solution lens is well described by Professor Timothy Stoltzfus Jost. TIMOTHY STOLTZFUS JOST, HEALTH CARE AT RISK (2007). Advocates of this approach believe that the root cause of our cost inflation is the lack of competition. They believe that even though insured Americans already face high premiums and cost-sharing, the population is still excessively insured and prone to careless spending and excess, results of moral hazard. Deborah Stone, *Moral Hazard*, 36 J. HEALTH POL. POL'Y & L. 887 (2011); Malcolm Gladwell, *The Moral Hazard Myth: The Bad Idea Behind our Failed Health–Care System*, THE NEW YORKER, August 29, 2005. Those who believe in moral hazard in health insurance would argue that the cost of health insurance and health care is too high because benefits and coverage are too rich. These higher costs mean that younger and healthier people choose not to buy coverage, leading to an insurance death spiral in which the risk pool is filled with high-cost users, which causes premiums to rise, which causes healthier people to drop coverage, which causes premiums to rise further, in endless spiral.

From this market-oriented perspective, the solution lies in significantly reducing coverage still further, thereby exposing individuals to an even greater level of direct economic consequences for their health and health care decisions. Many of these experts recognize that all Americans need help with the cost of a plan, and they propose to give individual subsidies to everyone to help pay for an individual insurance policy in lieu of group coverage through an employer. They also propose to require insurers to sell products to all people and to bar the denial of coverage based on health status.

In this model, the level of subsidy would be adjusted for income, but the subsidy could be used only to buy a "consumer-driven" health insurance product (as they are known) that offers limited coverage and exposes the insured to a far greater proportion of the direct cost of care. Subsidized products supported through tax rebates (insurers would remain free to sell more generous coverage products to wealthy people, as in other nations) would offer only limited coverage and would tie coverage to very high deductibles (i.e., the amount that must be paid before coverage begins) on the order of $5000 for an individual and $10,000 for a family in 2011 dollars. Benefits would be narrow, and point-of-service cost-sharing (copayments and coinsurance payable at the time services are furnished) would be high, with the potential exception of certain preventive services. People could buy more coverage, but insurers could "experience rate" these richer policies (i.e., take buyers' health status into account), meaning that the sickest people would pay the highest premiums. Their (inevitable) alternative would be to buy only a very basic plan which covers only catastrophic loss and thereby leaves the insured with the risk of very heavy out-of-pocket expenses.

In recent years, market advocates, observing that Americans reject the notion of limited coverage coupled with the risk of high out-of-pocket expense, have tailored their proposals to accommodate these concerns. Certain "wellness" benefits would be shielded from a policy's deductible so that coverage for preventive services would be available on a first-dollar basis to encourage their use. Examples of such procedures would be well-baby and well-child exams, childhood immunizations, mammograms and Pap smears to detect cervical cancer. Products would also use "value-based insurance design" techniques, as they are known, in order to encourage people to manage chronic conditions. For example, in value-based insurance design, copayments for high blood pressure medication would be eliminated to incentivize adherence. Mark Fendrick et al., *Applying Value–Based Insurance Design to Low–Value Health Services*, 29(11) HEALTH AFFAIRS 2017 (2010); Neetesh Choudry et al., *Assessing the Evidence for Value–Based Insurance Design*, 29(11) HEALTH AFFAIRS 1998 (2010). Apart from these exceptions, coverage would be limited, and point-of-service costs would remain high. (In fact, the sheer cost of health insurance is driving employers in this direction anyway, as premiums, deductibles, and cost-sharing inexorably rise in the face of skyrocketing costs.)

Market advocates assert that in a market-oriented approach to the health care cost problem, insurers and providers would act more like sellers of goods and services that commonly are purchased through comparative shopping (think about price-quality comparison shopping for a television set). Insurers would provide their members with information about the quality and cost of physicians in their network, the performance of hospitals and their medical and surgical outcomes, and information about effective treatments versus treatments that don't work. (The Geisinger Clinic, noted earlier as one of the nation's most respected regional health systems, now offers "warranties" for certain procedures. Reed Abelson, *In Bid for Better Care, Surgery with a Warranty*, N.Y. TIMES, May 17, 2007, http://www.nytimes.com/2007/05/17/business/17quality.html).   Advocates also assert that insurers also would offer wellness programs (such as gym memberships) to incentivize people to stay healthy by reducing premiums for members who lose weight, keep their blood pressure under control, or hold their diabetes in check. In short, market advocates would combine techniques that incentivize healthy behaviors with design features that create economic barriers to high-cost care. In their view, consumer behavior would change over time, people would stop using excessively costly care, and prices would drop.

Both the social good and market approaches raise challenges. In a social good model, the danger exists that important innovations and advances in health care will lag because of government-imposed economic constraints. In such a situation, the level of care made available to the population could prove inadequate. For example, a serious concern in many countries with national health systems is that government experts will exert such tight controls on health care spending that promising interventions will not be allowed to become broadly available to the population, thereby limiting access only to the wealthiest people with supplemental coverage.

But think about the market-driven model. Doesn't it raise a similar risk of inadequacy? Isn't the key difference that, rather than affecting a broader population (and thereby allowing the democratic process to limit the risk), the risk of inadequacy instead, in a market-driven world, would fall on individuals who at any point in time are sick or injured (even despite their best efforts to remain healthy)? Think of the people you know who may have been born with a disability, or who have developed cancer or multiple sclerosis or schizophrenia, or whose healthy pregnancy suddenly has become high risk, or whose baby was born too soon and too small, or who have been seriously injured in an accident. Illness and disability happen to people, even to people who have many advantages and who take excellent care of themselves.

Should we as individuals be responsible for bringing down the cost of health care through our daily consumption choices? And if we fail because illness stands outside of our control, should the penalty be that we each bear the financial burden of being ill without having adequate access to coverage and care? Is this a challenge that turns on individual behavior or that requires collective action? To be sure, individual autonomy and patient engagement are paramount values in the health care system, as you will read in Part Three. But can individuals—particularly when they are sick or injured and dependent on the treatment choices made by their physicians in many instances—be the ones who will bear the primary responsibility for bargaining over value and choice? And will individual bargaining add up to the kinds of controls that can move the entire system? Indeed, research suggests that where the responsibility for controlling health care costs lies with individuals and individual choice, the results can be serious under-utilization of both high-cost and preventive benefits. Melinda Beeuwkes Buntin et al., *Healthcare Spending and Preventive Care in High–Deductible and Consumer–Driven Health Plans*, 17(3) AM. J. MANAG. CARE 222 (March 2011). Furthermore, consumer-driven plans seem to have had little effect on the financial burdens faced by the sickest people. Allison Galbraith et al., *Nearly Half of Families in High–Deductible Health Plans Whose Members Have Chronic Conditions Face Substantial Financial Burden*, 30(2) HEALTH AFFAIRS 322 (2011) (finding that high-deductible plans with deductibles of $1000 per individual and $2000 per family left nearly half of all families with chronic conditions exposed to health care-related financial burdens, compared to 21 percent of similar families enrolled in traditional plans. Researchers found a particularly severe impact on lower income families.).

Even the models of consumer-driven health care that rely on the use of agents to act for consumers—whether those agents be plan sponsors or insurance companies—underestimate the vulnerability experienced by healthy people, much less those who are already ill. Indeed, even sophisticated purchasers have had trouble peering into the "black-box" of managed care in order to get a better handle on price and quality.

Those who see health care as a social good argue that only government, with its enhanced buying power and regulatory authority, can keep costs in balance for the population as a whole. Market advocates argue that if people just have the right information and are forced to confront the full cost of care they receive, they will make the types of choices that will drive prices down, presumably by refusing to buy a hip replacement (recall the price figures above) unless a physician, the hospital, and the medical device company that manufactures the prosthesis all agree to cut their prices. How realistic is this approach when applied to real patients? Does it depend on virtually all patients in need of hip replacements becoming savvy shoppers at the same time, so that in the aggregate, enough refusals to buy a hip replacement begin to catch the attention of the industry? Do you think that people in need of a hip replacement (the pain and disability from a degenerating hip are extraordinary) would want to sit around and wait for a sale? Even if those consumers are represented by their fiscal agents, what does the evidence presented above regarding spending tell you about how effective those agents have been?

Certainly there are cases in which consumer response to high health care prices has been effective. Proponents of the consumer incentive approach might point to areas of health care that tend to be less well-insured. In the case of eyeglasses, for example, advances in mass production technology coupled with consumer sensitivity to price, better information and less complexity, have resulted in enormous reductions in price, putting at least single lens correction lenses and frames within reach of even those with modest incomes.

Those who favor direct government intervention argue that in fact, much of health care does not lend itself to the analytic framework that applies to eyeglasses, which are mass produced and for which information concerning price and quality is readily available. Buyers can look through a lens and tell right away if the prescription improves vision. They can select among frames ranging from simple and functional to high-end designer, with the latter desirable only for reasons of vanity. Buying eyeglasses thus rests on the power of choice. So routine is the prescribing of corrective-vision care that eyeglass manufacturers tend to employ their own in-house discount optometrists who can rapidly and efficiently diagnose the necessary correction and prescribe the right, low-cost treatment.

But what about a more complex case? Imagine being the parent of a child born with Type 1 diabetes. Type 1 diabetes is a condition in which the body's own immune cells destroy the pancreas' ability to generate insulin, which is essential to breaking down sugar. The inability to break down sugar in turn leads to terrible consequences including the collapse of kidney function, the loss of vision, and damage to the heart resulting in heart attack and stroke. Children born with Type 1 diabetes certainly may need single-lens correction eyeglasses, but their vision needs obviously are much more extensive. In addition to superb overall pediatric care, they need constant monitoring by experts for signs and symptoms of diabetes' *sequelae*. This type of health care need is—to state the obvious—no longer a matter of parental choice. Parents obviously do not choose to have children who are born with conditions such as diabetes. Most parents would never "choose" to forgo the best pediatric care as early as possible in order to maximize their child's chances of living a healthy, productive life. In a situation in which recommended care is beyond a parent's financial means, the concept of "choice" loses any real meaning.

Advocates of imposing greater direct cost on consumers at the point of care would argue that even in a situation in which health care is necessary, people should be much better shoppers, whether they are directly choosing health care services or they are choosing among health insurance plans. This of course implies that it is possible to shop for pediatric care for a child with diabetes, or to anticipate in advance what insurance one needs and to understand, in advance, the consequences—at the point of treatment—of the multitude of different plans with different coverage and cost-sharing rules. Leaving aside families who live in one of the nation's thousands of medically underserved urban or rural communities and therefore have no choice where they go for their care, it is an interesting exercise to actually try to find information.

If the task is buying a flat screen television for the family's living room, the shopping experience would be a relative pleasure. A quick scan of the Internet reveals that in Spring, 2012 a 46″ high definition resolution flat screen television made by RCA can be found at Wal–Mart for $539.00. (In 1997, when these televisions were first mass produced on a scale large enough to be within the reach of ordinary consumers, the going price was $15,000, a testament to the impact of technological advances, coupled with mass production and consumer price sensitivity, in creating economic and social value).

Now repeat this experiment, but this time use the Web to search for pediatricians in your community who specialize in the care of children with diabetes—or to check into which insurance plans even offer pediatricians in their networks who are known for the quality of their care for children with diabetes.* Screen insurers' provider panels of such specialists in order to get the "specs" on them for purposes of comparison. Look for their pricing policies, their proximity to your home, their office hours, the number of such children they care for (higher quality care in the case of specialty services is associated with volume), and their success rate in protecting vision-loss among children with diabetes. Just such a search (finding a pediatrician in my community who cares for children with diabetes) turns up practically nothing. One site, About.com, offers only bromides about finding a pediatrician ("When choosing a pediatrician, you should likely avoid these extremes, make sure you 'like' your new doctor, and see if you agree on important parenting topics, such as breastfeeding, discipline, not overusing antibiotics, etc.") *See* http://pediatrics.about.com/od/choosingapediatrician/Choosing_a_Pediatrician.htm. The site also runs endless ads on everything from diapers to life insurance. For health care providers that have elected to display their services on the site (a few from around the country can be found), parents might be able to type in their name and their child's needs and get a list of doctors, with no information about the physicians.

To be sure, once a parent is connected with a doctor, it is possible—and indeed highly appropriate—to use economic incentivizes to encourage effective health care services (e.g., making patient adherence easier through lower cost-sharing for regularly scheduled appointments and necessary drugs and supplies). But imagine being a parent who is simply attempting to enter the health care system on her child's behalf. Word of mouth might help pick a practice, but there is no doubt about the need for care; nor is it clear what measures would apply in selecting the right pediatrician, assuming for the moment that as with televisions, there *are* competing pediatri-

---

* Of course, in the spirit of risk avoidance, it is not clear that most insurers would want to advertise such specialists out of fear of attracting tons of parents of children with diabetes. How the goal of empowered consumers aligns with the business interests of insurers is one of the more complicated questions. In a perfect world insurers would receive a "risk adjusted" premium reflecting the higher anticipated costs of families with children who have elevated health risks. But the science of risk adjustment is only slowly evolving, and to a considerable degree, the aggregation of information needed to make a risk adjustment system work time is only beginning to emerge.

cians with the requisite skills. (This turns out to be a big assumption; in many communities, pediatric specialists are non-existent). Laura Landro, *For Severely Ill Children, A Dearth of Doctors*, WALL ST. J., Jan. 20, 2010, http://online.wsj.com/article/SB1000142405274870365210457465232 11818328216.html.

In short, the assertions of economists who favor maximizing economic incentives at the individual level as the central answer to our problem seem to unravel pretty quickly once the traps are run on an actual case. It turns out that the information needed to make informed decisions is absent and furthermore that the entire notion that there is a choice—the choice whether to seek the care, as well as the choice among competing health care professionals—rests on shaky grounds. Even when the issue is the choice among agents, consumers need massive amounts of information and remarkable sophistication to make sense of that information.

Of course, this is not to say that sensitivity to price in health care, combined with much better information about quality, and the use of financing mechanisms that stimulate sound patient decision-making are not important. However, existing evidence regarding actual behavior is sobering. Medicare, discussed in this Part, has attempted to introduce greater consumer choice into its structure and operations. For example, Nursing Home Compare, administered by the federal Centers for Medicare and Medicaid Services (CMS), offers information about nursing home quality at a community level. *See* http://www.medicare.gov/NHCompare/ Include/DataSection/Questions/HomeSelect.asp. But the cost of implementing such a measurement system is vast, particularly in the absence of a national, interoperable electronic health information system that, like the electronic banking system, ties together the nation's nursing homes with federal and state regulators. This means that information must be submitted manually to CMS, which must in turn compile results for each nursing home and post the results. Furthermore, because the type of health services research needed to measure quality is so costly and painstakingly slow, the measures that exist tend to be very broad and not particularly helpful when considering which home to use for a particular patient with a particular condition. (Again, all of this assumes that there even is a choice of nursing homes with open capacity in one's community). The Nursing Home Compare website offers a few measures, limited to overall rating, health inspections, staffing, and quality. But the site offers no definitions for "quality rating," "health inspections," "staffing" and "overall rating." In HEALTH CARE AT RISK, Professor Jost relates a story told by economist Uwe Reinhardt, who compares buying health care to buying a shirt with absolutely no information on size, quality, or price, only to be presented with an incomprehensible bill at some point down the road that bears no evident relationship to the product purchased.

2.   THE EVOLUTION OF HEALTH INSURANCE AND HEALTH INSURANCE LAW

a.   The Evolution of Private Health Insurance

Until the twentieth century, people consumed very little health care and modern health insurance did not exist. Health insurance became necessary only because modern medicine increased the cost of care such that individuals alone could not bear the risk of illness. By early in the 20th century, Germany had established the first national compulsory "sickness insurance" for its workforce, and other nations, including Norway, Serbia, Great Britain, Russia, the Netherlands, and to a lesser extent, France and Italy followed suit. Sweden, Switzerland, and Denmark all were heavily subsidizing sickness funds for the population. Starr, The Social Transformation of American Medicine at 237–40. Professor Starr, a leading chronicler of the history of medicine, writes that "social insurance [in Europe] represented a new stage in the management of destitution in capitalist societies.... The advent of social insurance at the end of the nineteenth century signified a return to social protection by providing a right to benefits instead of charity [and] represented an extension of [governmental] obligation as well as freedom." Starr, The Social Transformation of American Medicine at 237–38.

An American reform movement did in fact emerge, with calls for change issued during the first two decades of the 20th century. Perhaps the most important was the 1927 formation of the Committee on the Cost of Medical Care ("CCMC"), funded with private foundation support, whose charge was "to study the economic aspects of the care and prevention of illness." Milton Roemer & I.S. Falk, *The Committee on the Cost of Medical Care, and the Drive for National Health Insurance*, 75(8) Am. J. Pub. Health 841 (1985). The CCMC made five recommendations in 1933: (1) the organization of medical and hospital care into integrated group practices that could promote quality, efficiency and continuity of care; (2) universal access to basic preventive health services through public health departments; (3) universal coverage for medical care needs (termed prepayment), although not compulsory; (4) greater study, coordination, and evaluation of medical care needs, particularly in underserved areas of the nation; and (5) major revisions in professional education to create health professionals with far greater knowledge of the social conditions of health and the social aspects of medicine.

The recommendations went essentially nowhere under President Franklin Roosevelt. Intense opposition from organized medicine prevented inclusion of national health insurance in the original Social Security Act, which instead focused on old-age pensions, welfare subsistence aid to indigent widows and their children (whose meager allowances were structured to at least theoretically include an allotment for health care costs), and modest grants to states for provision of public health services to destitute mothers and their children, as well as "crippled" children. Starr, The Social Transformation of American Medicine at 265–69. Subsequent efforts to bring comprehensive health reform, capable of addressing the needs of the entire population, would fall victim to intense political opposition both inside and outside government under successive presidential administrations. DAVID BLUMENTHAL & JAMES MORONE, THE HEART OF POWER: HEALTH AND POLITICS IN THE OVAL OFFICE (2009).

However, in what Professor Starr has brilliantly termed "the Triumph of Accommodation," THE SOCIAL TRANSFORMATION OF MEDICINE, at 290–330, physicians and hospitals recognized the need for some response, both because of mounting need for subsidization of patients' health care costs, and because of hospitals' need for a steady flow of income (during the 1930s half of all U.S. hospitals went bankrupt). Health insurance ultimately emerged, but under the close control of providers themselves. Specifically, hospitals and then physicians succeeded in persuading state legislatures to allow them to establish corporations that would sell health service plans to the population. Hospital insurance came first, with the advent of Blue Cross plans; physicians subsequently created Blue Shield. Together the Blues fostered the growth of voluntary, community-wide health insurance. Blue Cross and Blue Shield were organized as state-based, not-for-profit corporations, and products were priced and sold on a community-rated basis, with open enrollment so that the young and healthy cross-subsidized older and sicker members of the community. Corporate boards dominated by providers set coverage standards, premiums, payment rules (which reflected physicians' charges and hospitals' costs) and the terms of payment. STARR, THE SOCIAL TRANSFORMATION OF AMERICAN MEDICINE at 307–10; SYLVIA LAW, BLUE CROSS: WHAT WENT WRONG? (1974).

Under these service benefit plans, provider payments were open-ended, with separate fees for separate services and procedures, a payment structure that Atul Gawande terms "piecework." Atul Gawande, *Piecework*, NEW YORKER, April 1, 2005, http://www.newyorker.com/archive/2005/04/04/050404fa_fact; Sage, *Brand New Law! The Need to Market Health Care Reform* at 2133. Each medical procedure would be compensated at a price set by the physician (the usual and customary charge, as it was called) and without regard to any overall, annual, aggregated level of spending per person. Hospitals similarly were paid the reasonable cost of care (as defined by them) for each day spent in a facility. The Blues' model provided financing without any oversight of health care delivery. Rising costs were passed along in rising premiums. This profession-centric world is at times referred to as the fee-for-service era, because hospitals and physicians were paid the fees they commanded, without regulatory or market constraints.

Concurrent with the creation of the Blues, a very different model also emerged, known as prepaid group practice, in very limited areas of the country. This model reflected the aims advocated by the CCMC, including use of an integrated group health practice care arrangement consisting of a hospital and an affiliated physician practice group, as well as a financing mechanism designed to permit the prepayment of care over a defined time period. In some cases, the prepaid practice arrangement involved corporate ownership of physician practices and a hospital. In others, joint ventures were undertaken between physician groups on the one hand and a fiscal intermediary on the other, and included hospital and other provider services as well. Kaiser Permanente, which still dominates the health insurance market in the West, is perhaps the best-known example of this model.

In some communities, prepaid practice arrangements sprang from local medical and hospital organizations themselves, which sold their services to workers and families; a well-known model of this type was the Baylor Hospital Health Plan in Texas. In other cases, industrialists built prepaid practice arrangements for their employees; the best known example of this was the medical plan instituted by industrialist Henry Kaiser, who recognized the need for health care for his employees during the construction of the Grand Coulee Dam. STARR, THE SOCIAL TRANSFORMATION OF AMERICAN MEDICINE at 320–22. LAWRENCE BROWN, POLITICS AND HEALTH CARE ORGANIZATION: HMOS AS FEDERAL POLICY (1983). From the time of their emergence until the mid–1980s, prepaid group practice arrangements grew slowly, in part because of anticompetitive conduct aimed against them from organized medicine, something we discuss in the antitrust chapter in Part Four.

Federal labor and tax law spurred the growth of voluntary, employment-based health insurance in the U.S. during the Second World War. The federal government imposed wage and price controls and then exempted health benefits from those controls. Employers could recruit workers in a tight labor market by offering health benefits. Jon Gabel, *Job Based Health Insurance, 1977–1998: The Accidental System under Scrutiny*, 18(6) HEALTH AFFAIRS 62, 63 (1999). A ruling by World War II's War Labor Board exempted health benefits from federal wage controls and set the stage for a special 1943 ruling by the Internal Revenue Service recognizing such benefits as exempt income to employees and a tax-deductible expense for employers. The IRS ruling ultimately was codified into the Internal Revenue Code in 1952, IRC §§ 104, 105, 106, 3121(a)(2) and 3306(a)(2), thereby making this tax-favored arrangement permanent and creating a strong financial incentive for employers to raise employees' compensation by offering health benefit plans. Employers and employees were thereby encouraged to make coverage more comprehensive. Plans began to offer not only protection against major medical events but also more routine health services such as dental care, well-child exams, and prescription drugs. Providers in turn, felt free to raise prices still further given the availability of comprehensive insurance coverage. JOST, HEALTH CARE AT RISK ch. 2.

As tax policy shifted and the experience of the Blues plans demonstrated that it was possible to create and market health insurance, commercial—i.e., for-profit—insurers entered the employment-based health insurance market. Unlike the Blues, the commercial insurers had no commitment to open-enrollment or community rating. Indeed the commercial insurers sought to market to employers with relatively young and healthy workforces, "cherry-picking" or "cream-skimming" the good risks. This competition was a crucial factor in causing the Blue Cross/Blue Shield plans to abandon their commitment to community service and community-rating. Gabel, *The Accidental System Under Scrutiny*; LAW, BLUE CROSS: WHAT WENT WRONG? Commercial insurers also began to offer health coverage on an individual basis, but accompanied by extensive exclusions designed to deny and limit coverage to people who most needed medical care. Gary Claxton, *How Private Health Coverage Works: A Primer*, KAISER FAMILY FOUNDATION (2008) http://www.kff.org/insurance/7766.cfm.

What ultimately evolved was a private health insurance system comprised of employer-sponsored plans covering most of the insured working population and their families, with limited experience-rated individual policies for others. Congress and the states did little to regulate either the group or individual markets. Although medical underwriting was overwhelming in the individual market, it played a decided role in group health insurance as well, particularly in the case of smaller employer groups, a fact that ultimately helped lead to federal reforms in group-market insurance practices in the mid–1990s.

Voluntary employment-based health insurance reached its apex in the early 1970s and ultimately accounted for 93 percent of all privately insured Americans. Gabel, *The Accidental System* at 66, Figure 2. But this model simply could not be sustained given the absence of any cost controls and rampant price inflation. As noted above, the much greater expenditures in the United States, compared with those of other advanced countries, cannot be explained by different levels or intensity of service. Rather, other wealthy nations simply did not permit financing to grow without a cost-containment strategy, whereas here, in both public and private insurance, growth in expenditures remained unchecked. By the late 1970s, price explosions coupled with a major recession began to take its toll. In 1977 more than 82% of all workers were offered coverage by their employers; by 1987, that figure had declined to 72%. Gabel, *The Accidental System* at 66, Exhibit 2. By 2009, the figure had dropped by another 10 percent.

Many changes over the past two decades in the types of insurance products offered and the share of premiums borne by employees reflect the absence of a broader strategy. As noted, employees have borne an increasing proportion of the cost for workplace coverage. Insurance coverage itself has eroded, with increasing deductibles and a growing presence of "high-deductible health plans" (deductibles of at least $1000 for individuals and $2000 for families). In 2010, five percent of all workers in large firms and 9 percent of workers in small firms were enrolled in such plans, the higher penetration in smaller firms consistent with their more limited bargaining power. *Kaiser/HRET Employer Health Benefits Survey*, KAISER FAMILY FOUNDATION/HRET (§ 8), http://ehbs.kff.org/?page=charts & id=1 & sn=14 & p=1. The use of selective contracting of provider networks also has grown over the past two decades, with significant out-of-network penalties, including both higher cost-sharing and full exposure to balance billing (i.e., the difference between what an insurer pays and a physician charges). So-called "consumer-driven" plans that increasingly use the prospect of high cost-sharing to drive patients toward less consumption of health care can perhaps be best understood as a desperate effort to keep employer-sponsored coverage alive. David Blumenthal, *Employer Sponsored Insurance— Riding the Health Care Tiger*, 355 NEW ENG. J. MED. 195 (2006). Despite all of this, the proportion of persons with employer-sponsored coverage continues to decline.

b. Medicare and Medicaid

Even as comprehensive reform eluded the nation, the enactment of Medicare and Medicaid in 1965 represented both a political triumph and government response to market failure; Medicare and Medicaid are a watershed in U.S. social welfare policy. Joined at the legislative hip, the programs together fill critical needs whose roots could be traced to the nation's decision to rely on private employer-sponsored coverage arrangements.

Both programs are creatures of an era when the concept of a strong role for government in assuring the population's well-being was ascendant. RASHI FEIN, MEDICAL CARE MEDICAL COSTS (1987); STARR, THE SOCIAL TRANSFORMATION OF AMERICAN MEDICINE at 350–60. A classic example of social contract, Medicare, like health insurance systems in other nations, is a compulsory and universal entitlement that vests in workers covered through the Social Security system and that rests on a financing base comprised of employer/employee payroll taxes, individual premium payments, and general governmental financing. While Medicare's financing was modeled on private pensions, its health care delivery was modeled after private health insurance. Therefore, Medicare covers primary services, including some specified preventive procedures, and medical care for conditions requiring costly and advanced curative care. However, Medicare does not cover long-term care furnished at home, in institutions or in community settings. Medicare's structure and administration are explored in depth later in this Part.

Medicare's contribution to the health care system is enormous. An insurer of 47 million people in 2010 (39 million beneficiaries ages 65 and older and 8 million persons with serious disabilities), the program provides coverage for both medical and institutional care, as well as outpatient prescription drugs, added through amendments to the law in 2003. In 2008 Medicare accounted for 23 percent of total health care spending, including 29 percent of all hospital expenditures, 21 percent of total expenditures for physician services and 22 percent of spending for prescription drugs. *Medicare: A Primer*, KAISER FAMILY FOUNDATION at 16 (2010), http://www.kff. org/medicare/upload/7615-03.pdf. Medicare participation by hospitals and other institutional providers is conditioned on compliance with federal civil rights laws including Title VI of the 1964 Civil Rights Act, and historians have credited the program with desegregating hospitals, which, as a condition of participation, agreed to halt the segregated treatment and exclusion of minority patients. DAVID BARTON SMITH, HEALTH CARE DIVIDED (1999). Medicare acts like a vast pumping machine, propelling an explosion in hospital growth, technological innovation, advances in surgical and medical techniques, and in later years tremendous diffusion of care to the outpatient sector. Indeed, the advent of Medicare and Medicaid has been associated with significant improvements in population health (including a major decline in infant mortality) and the reduction of disparities in health and health care. KAREN DAVIS & CATHY SCHOEN, HEALTH AND THE WAR ON POVERTY (1977).

Medicare provides relatively modest benefits compared to large employer-group plans. Medicare offers less in the way of coverage (for example, dental and vision care and hearing aids are not Medicare benefits). Medicare also leaves beneficiaries exposed to greater levels of cost-sharing, even for covered services. One actuarial study shows that in 2007, Medicare covered only 74 percent of health care costs compared to 85 percent in the large private-employer sector and 83 percent under the Federal Employee Health Benefit Plan ("FEHBP") (which provides insurance for federal workers). With regard to outpatient prescription drug coverage, the differentials in value are even more striking: in 2007 Medicare covered 51 percent of outpatient prescription drug costs compared to 80 percent under the FEHBP. As patients' health worsens, Medicare remains limited in value compared to employer plans, leaving the sickest patients exposed to out-of-pocket costs between 50 and 100 percent greater than those incurred by the sickest members of large employer-group plans. Patricia Neuman & Michelle Kitchman Strollo, *How Does the Benefit Value of Medicare Compare to the Benefit Value of Typical Large Employer Plans?* KAISER FAMILY FOUNDATION 3–7 (September 2008), http://www.kff.org/medicare/upload/7768.pdf.

The political developments that led to Medicare's enactment have been extensively chronicled. *See, e.g.*, FEIN, MEDICAL CARE MEDICAL COSTS; STARR, THE SOCIAL TRANSFORMATION OF AMERICAN MEDICINE at 360–65; THEODORE MARMOR, THE POLITICS OF MEDICARE (2d ed., 2000). Two aspects of the political compromises that led to Medicare's enactment were critical. First, although Part A (hospital and after-care in certain institutions) is compulsory and financed through payroll taxes, Part B (physician and medical-supplier services including home health care) is voluntary and financed through premiums and general revenues. The voluntary structure of Part B was a concession to attract the support of organized medicine, which violently opposed enactment. Second, the original law allowed physicians and hospitals to control the terms of payment and lacked any cost control mechanisms to address price, coverage design, or utilization of benefits. FEIN, MEDICAL CARE MEDICAL COSTS at 60–70. Physician payment was based on their "usual and customary" fees (meaning that payment essentially tracked what physicians charged, amounts that were greatly increased just before Medicare became effective), while hospital payments were tied to their "reasonable" costs as determined in accordance, with cost principles developed by Blue Cross and the American Hospital Association. The original Medicare legislation also assured doctors and hospitals that the "medical necessity" of care could only be reviewed by professional peer processes. Throughout the 1970s, Medicare costs exploded, leading to the introduction of major payment reforms in physician and hospital care in the 1980s, discussed later in this Part. These reforms have slowed the program's rate of growth but have not addressed the underlying dynamic causing price and volume to increase.

Medicare's legislative companion, Medicaid, plays a central role in the health care system. In 2010 Medicaid covered 68 million persons. *See* MEDICAID AND CHIP PAYMENT AND ACCESS COMMISSION (MACPAC), REPORT TO CONGRESS at 2 (March 2011). Medicaid operates like health insurance, covering individuals entitled to assistance and acting as a third-party payer of covered health care services. This structure represents a fundamental aim of Medicaid, to move the nation away from direct financing of public health care systems in public hospitals and clinics as the central, segregated means by which the poor receive their care. ROBERT AND ROSEMARY STEVENS, WELFARE MEDICINE IN AMERICA: A CASE STUDY OF MEDICAID (1974). At the same time, Medicaid is the single most important source of health care financing for health care safety net providers such as public hospitals and community health centers, described in Part One.

In 2010, Medicaid covered one in three children and one in three births, a testament to the low incomes of women of childbearing age and children in the U.S., as well as a reflection of somewhat more generous eligibility for these two populations. That year, Medicaid also covered some 8 million poor children and adults with disabilities as well as 9 million low-income Medicare beneficiaries. Kaiser Commission on Medicaid and the Uninsured, *Medicaid Matters: Understanding Medicaid's Role in Our Health Care System* (March, 2011), http://www.kff.org/medicaid/upload/8165.pdf. But the program's historical connection to cash-welfare programs has meant that coverage of poor non-elderly adults who are neither disabled nor pregnant, nor the deeply impoverished caretakers of minor children, historically has been exceptionally low; indeed, coverage of parents in some states hovers around 20 percent of the federal poverty level (meaning an annual income for a family of 3 of about $3800 in 2012). Sara Rosenbaum, *Can the States Pick Up the Health Reform Torch?*, 362 NEW ENG. J. MED. 1 (2010). At the same time, Medicaid has played a vital role not only for families with children but also as a supplement for Medicare coverage in the case of low-income Medicare beneficiaries, known as "dual eligibles." *See generally* STEVENS AND STEVENS, WELFARE MEDICINE IN AMERICA.

Not only is Medicaid the nation's single largest source of insurance, but it carries responsibilities borne by no other payer, particularly in the areas of long-term institutional and community care for children and adults with disabilities; expenditures for these populations account for two-thirds of all program spending. MACPAC, REPORT TO CONGRESS (March 2010). Medicaid contains no pre-existing condition exclusion clauses and no waiting periods (persons with disabilities who qualify for Social Security must wait 24 months before Medicare coverage begins). In the case of Medicaid, enrollment at the point of health care need is not only possible, but under federal law, coverage can be extended on a retroactive basis, beginning up to 3 months prior to the date of application and thereby allowing for retrospective coverage of high-cost procedures. Sara Rosenbaum, *Health Policy Report: Medicaid*, 346 NEW ENG. J. MED. 635 (2002).

As with Medicare, Medicaid did not have spending constraints built directly into the law, but by far its biggest constraint is that the program has a structure of "cooperative federalism," meaning that it is administered and partially funded by the states and that federal spending is tied to the level of state expenditures. As a result, there is much variation in Medicaid, and many states have elected over the decades to cover relatively fewer people, to place stricter limitations on benefits and to keep provider payments low. MACPAC REPORT TO CONGRESS 38–42 (March 2010). Medicaid comprises a significant portion of state budgets; in FY 2010, state Medicaid expenditures exceeded $130 billion. *Id.* The federal/state tensions inherent in this structure are legion, reflecting state concerns over the extent of federal requirements related to coverage and expenditures. At the same time, Medicaid is the single largest source of federal grant funding to the states, making the program a central feature of state economies. Alan Weil, *There's Something About Medicaid*, 22(1) HEALTH AFFAIRS 13 (2003).

Although Medicaid eligibility standards prior to enactment of the Affordable Care Act were limited, its coverage rules historically have been far broader than those that define private insurance and Medicare. Rosenbaum, *Health Policy Report: Medicaid.* These broader coverage rules reflect both the deep impoverishment and poorer health of program beneficiaries. Coverage thus spans not only treatments and services linked to preventive and primary health care and treatments of acute problems, but also long-term institutional and home and community services for individuals with severe activity limitations who require ongoing health care to maintain their health, gain or preserve functional capabilities, or avert serious diminution in health status. Cases on private health insurance coverage explored later in this Part reveal how commercial insurance typically excludes coverage for treatments and services linked to the long-term health support of individuals with disabilities. Rosenbaum, *Health Policy Report: Medicaid.*

c. An Evolving State Regulatory Framework

As the private health insurance industry grew, so did the attention of state regulators. Insurance regulation has been the purview of the states, with some twists and turns. In 1868 the Supreme Court held that states have the power to regulate contracts of insurance (the issue was the whether a state could require out-of-state insurance agents doing business in the state to post security bonds), and that insurers do not enjoy exemption from state regulation either because they engage in interstate commerce or are protected by the Article IV Privileges and Immunities Clause. Paul v. Virginia, 75 U.S. 168, 181–83 (1868). *Paul v. Virginia* was then overruled in United States v. South–Eastern Underwriters Ass'n, 322 U.S. 533 (1944), with the result that the Sherman Antitrust Act then applied to the insurance industry. Congress quickly responded to this potential evisceration of state authority by enacting the McCarran–Ferguson Act, which declared that the "business of insurance" should continue to be "subject to the laws of the several States which relate to the regulation or taxation of such business." 15 U.S.C. § 1012. McCarran–Ferguson also provided that federal regulation "would be applicable to the business of insurance to the extent that such business is not regulated by state law." *Id.* Thus, the Act essentially preserved the primacy of state law except to the extent that state law was silent on a particular issue. Only some time later, as you will see in the ERISA preemption cases that are explored later in this Part, did Congress sharply limited state power to regulate employer-sponsored group health plans.

State insurance law serves several purposes. First, states attempt to ensure solvency of insurers through requirements regarding licensure, capitalization, operations and management (including control of experience rating and medical underwriting practices) and by means of other stipulations to ensure financial stability. Companies must maintain adequate reserves to pay claims and are generally subject to agency oversight. State agencies also have the power to order the rehabilitation or liquidation of companies that have insufficient reserves. David J. Brummond, *Federal Preemption of State Insurance Regulation under ERISA*, 62 IOWA L. REV. 57, 81–82 (1976); ROBERT KEETON & ALAN WIDISS, INSURANCE LAW 938–40 (1988).

Second, states regulate insurer conduct in the market, prohibiting overreaching, unfairness, fraud, and deceptive practices. Laws require the registration and licensure of insurance sales agents, they prohibit deceptive trade practices and high-pressure sales tactics, and they mandate fairness in claims processing. States typically require approval of the form of sales contracts and often provide appeals processes to ensure appropriate enforcement of insurance contracts. Insurance departments may have investigatory powers as well as the power to impose penalties or issue cease and desist orders. Brummond, *Federal Preemption of State Insurance Regulation under ERISA* at 82.

Third, states regulate both access to insurance and the content of coverage itself. These state laws define who must be allowed access to individual and group policies, when coverage may be restricted through the use of pre-existing condition exclusions and waiting periods (subject to federal restrictions we discuss immediately below), and what benefits must be covered in the individual and group markets, such as coverage of treatments and procedures related to mental illness or substance abuse, maternity care, prescribed drugs, and other services. Some states limit insurers' ability to vary premiums in relation to the characteristics of certain individual or small-group policyholders, such as age, gender, health status or prior claims experience. Claxton, *How Private Health Coverage Works* at 9–11; GENERAL ACCOUNTING OFFICE, FEDERAL PREEMPTION OF STATE INSURANCE REGULATION AND HEALTH INSURANCE REGULATION: WIDE VARIATION IN STATES' AUTHORITY OVERSIGHT AND RESOURCES, GAO–HRD–94–26 (1993).

While states thus have the power to set strong standards for content, marketing, and business practices, as a practical matter these powers often tend to get exercised modestly. Many insurance companies operate in national markets or are subsidiaries of multi-national corporations, which gives them political power at the state level because they aren't so dependent on the business of many states. Further, state insurance commissions in individual states often do not have the resources to regulate wisely or to engage in enforcement. Insurance commissioners have attempted to remedy this mismatch through creation of the National Association of Insurance Commissioners ("NAIC") (http://www.naic.org/), which allows state authorities to pool data and ideas and share model regulation. The health insurance industry, as is true of other parts of the insurance industry, is powerful.

Sometimes state regulators fear that national companies will leave the state if regulation is too demanding. For example, many states historically have set insurers' "medical-loss ratios" (i.e., the proportion of a premium that must be spent on payment of medical claims and permissible administration costs) very low so that insurers are able to reap large profits in relation to the amount of premiums paid out in claims. The Patient Protection and Affordable Care Act established a federal floor of 80 percent for medical-loss ratios in the individual market, a requirement that takes effect in 2011, before the Act's universal coverage provisions commence in January, 2014. Because this ratio is considerably more stringent than most states' previous standards, implementation of the new standard in 2011 led to requests from numerous states that DHHS either wholly or partially waive the federal standard out of fear that insurers would cease to sell individual policies in their states. Dave Hogberg, *Louisiana is Ninth State to Seek Waiver from ObamaCare's Medical Loss Rules*, INVESTOR BUSINESS DAILY, March 29, 2011, http://blogs.investors.com/capitalhill/index.php/home /35–politicsinvesting/2544–louisiana-is-ninth-state-to-seek-waiver-from-obamacares-medical-loss-rules; *Iowa, Kentucky Get Extra Time to Comply with MLR Rule*, KAISER HEALTH NEWS, July 25, 2011, http://www.kaiser healthnews.org/daily-reports/2011/july/25/mlr.aspx.

State insurance codes are long and dense, but careful examination of state "standards" often reveals that laws are weak and leave enormous discretion to the industry. The following example indicates the limited nature of state regulatory standards governing health insurance. As part of their regulation of the group health insurance market, more than 35 states require health insurers to cover childhood immunizations to some degree. Yet one review of state insurance laws governing immunizations found that no state required insurers to cover the full complement of childhood vaccines recommended by the Centers for Disease Control and Prevention ("CDC") for children under age 18; indeed, only one state required coverage up to the CDC-established scientific standard for young children, when immunizations arguably are most important. Sara Rosenbaum et al., *The Epidemiology of U.S. Immunization Law: Mandated Coverage of Immunizations under State Health Insurance Law* (George Washington University 2003) http://www.gwumc.edu/sphhs/healthpolicy/immunization/reports. html.

The Health Insurance Portability and Accountability Act of 1996 (HIPAA) was the first significant effort by Congress to address directly the techniques used by insurers to select against poor risk—i.e., to engage in risk selection. The law did so by setting minimum federal standards barring discrimination based on health status at the point of sale, enrollment, and renewal. HIPAA provided that exclusion of coverage under employer plans for pre-existing conditions could not "look back" more than six months. Because in some existential sense virtually all conditions except trauma and infections may have pre-existed, many insurers denied coverage in a broad range of cases. HIPAA did not mandate any other minimum insurance coverage or design. Title XXVII of the Public Health Service Act, 42 U.S.C. § 300gg–1.

Nonetheless HIPAA represented a breakthrough by prohibiting insurers from rejecting small employer groups or singling out certain employees for exclusion from a group or refusing to renew coverage policies on the basis of costs and claims experience. HIPAA also established portability protections for individuals continuously covered by a group plan or other form of "creditable coverage," allowing individuals to move from one employee group to another, or from group coverage (or other form of insurance) into the individual market, without being subject to a pre-existing condition exclusion or lengthy waiting period. Unfortunately, the law was to some extent a paper tiger because persons lost their protection if they had a "gap in coverage" of 63 days (essentially two months), which often occurred when persons lost their jobs and could not afford to maintain continuation coverage under their employers' plans. Consequently, when they (and their dependents) found new employment with new insurance, they were subject to pre-existing illness exclusions and waiting periods. Also, while HIPAA offered coverage continuation, it did not regulate premiums, with the result that many individuals, faced with higher premiums, could no longer afford them. Renewability was therefore guaranteed only in a formal sense.

Beyond laws that directly regulate "the business of insurance," numerous types of state laws of general applicability, as well as broadly applicable common law principles, also apply to insurers. Examples include civil rights laws prohibiting discrimination, labor laws relating to wages, benefits and the conditions of work, general consumer protection laws aimed at curbing bad faith practices, and laws creating remedies for injuries sustained as a result of negligence. For example, a state law prohibiting discrimination against certain persons in the sale of an insurance contract may be part of state insurance law but could just as conceivably be codified as part of the state's civil rights or labor laws.

Over the years, the courts have developed rules for the interpretation of disputes between individuals and insurers; these principles build on longstanding common law principles, whose purpose is to address the unequal bargaining power between insurers and insured persons. Chief among these principles is the doctrine of *contra proferentem,* under which ambiguities in an insurance contract are construed against the drafter. This doctrine brings some degree of balance to the highly unequal bargaining arrangement that is inherent in insurance contracts generally and particularly in group-coverage arrangements. KEETON AND WIDISS, INSURANCE LAW at 628. State courts also have applied the common law principle of "bad faith breach of contract" to the insurance industry in cases of injury, thereby allowing recovery of not merely liquidated contractual damages (typically the value of health care withheld) but also compensatory and punitive damages for tortious conduct in cases in which the claimant can show that the insurer engaged in "failure to deal fairly and in good faith with [the] insured by refusing, without proper cause, to compensate [the] insured for a loss covered by the policy". Gruenberg v. Aetna Insurance Co., 510 P.2d 1032 (Cal. 1973). These principles are explored later in this Part.

d. The Employee Retirement Income Security Act (ERISA)

Even as federal law relegated regulation of the insurance market to the states, an important legal developments has worked to shape the health insurance marketplace and figures prominently in the structure of the Affordable Care Act. Enacted in 1974 to address a crisis in private pensions, The Employee Retirement and Income Security Act (ERISA), Pub. L. No. 93–406, codified at 29 U.S.C. § 1001 et seq., discussed extensively later in this Part and in Part Three, established a limited regulatory framework for group health benefit plans sponsored by private employers. ERISA set standards for disclosure, plan administration, and the review of claims for benefits. Over the years, ERISA was amended to add coverage requirements related to very small groups of people or discreet problems: mothers and newborns threatened with premature discharge from hospitals following birth; women with breast cancer; genetic non-discrimination; continuation coverage (popularly known as COBRA coverage after the public law containing the amendments) for certain qualified individuals; non-discrimination and portability requirements; and mental health parity.

ERISA has had an enormous impact on both insurance law and the evolution of the market for employer-sponsored health benefits itself because of the law's preemptive effect, in the case of self-insured plans, on state laws that regulate health insurance. ERISA preempts a great deal of state insurance law, as well as other state laws that create legal remedies for people who are injured as a result of the negligence or bad faith of an insurer or health plan administrator. Preemption is not limited to ERISA of course. HIPAA establishes minimum standards for non-discrimination and portability in coverage for insurance otherwise subject to state regulation. Medicare similarly precludes application of state insurance laws to insurers participating in the Medicare program. Medicaid sets conditions of participation that states must meet. In sum, despite the McCarran Ferguson Act's preservation of state regulatory power over insurance, the history of federal health insurance legislation over the past 45 years or so has been much about taking this authority back in the face of great need and uneven and dysfunctional state regulation.

However, this renewed assertion of federal authority has been somewhat limited and has been drawn around arbitrary lines. In its interpretation of ERISA in Metropolitan Life Ins. Co. v. Massachusetts, 471 U.S. 724 (1985), reviewed later in this Part, the United States Supreme Court effectively created two basic classes of employer-sponsored group health plans: those that purchase state-regulated group health insurance (known as "insured" plans), and those that self-insure and typically use an insurance company only as a "third-party administrator." Plans that self-insure are exempt from state laws that regulate insurance, because their plans do not involve the purchase of a state-regulated insurance product (or so the Court ruled). Furthermore, even in the case of insured plans, ERISA's exclusive remedies, as you will learn, completely preempt state law remedies that otherwise would be available to individuals harmed by the negligent or bad-faith conduct of insurers. *See* Pilot Life v. Dedeaux, 481 U.S. 41 (1987), discussed later in this Part.

3. ESCALATING COSTS AND NEW MODELS OF HEALTH INSURANCE

As public and private insurance costs escalated and as uniform mechanisms for controlling costs remained absent, the situation devolved into every payer for itself, including public payers. Congress stepped in to halt the growth of Medicaid by eliminating requirements for universal state implementation of full coverage up to federal limits. STEVENS & STEVENS, WELFARE MEDICINE IN AMERICA. Congress also introduced utilization review into Medicare and pressed states to follow suit in Medicaid.

Moreover, as Medicare costs escalated, Congress searched for ways to change how hospitals and physicians were paid. Relatively modest preliminary reforms enacted in the 1970s gave way to relatively sweeping changes by the 1980s. Beginning in 1972 Congress adopted a series of provisions to assure that Medicare payment was provided only for care that was actually medically necessary. These largely unsuccessful efforts to curb unnecessary utilization are discussed later in this Part. In 1982 Congress enacted legislation that replaced Medicare's retrospective cost-based payment system for hospitals, which essentially paid hospitals for the costs they incurred in furnishing care without regard to any efficiencies such as decreased length of stay, reduced volume or intensity of procedures, or prices. Congress replaced this "blank check" with a prospective payment system (PPS) that paid hospitals flat rates for inpatient services tied to treatments for particular conditions. Congress similarly revised Medicare's physician payment formula to replace the "usual and customary rate" structure used by public and private insurers alike and tied to physicians charges. This system was replaced by one known as a "resource based relative value scale" (RBRVS), which sets fees for both primary and specialty care. Provider payment mechanisms are reviewed later in this Part.

In the 1970s, the Carter administration (which tried and failed to obtain national health reform) moved against the rapidly rising cost of hospital care by creating hospital rate-setting experiments to enable states to set hospital rates not only for Medicare but also for private insurers ("all-payer" rate setting). New York State Conference of Blue Cross and Blue Shield Plans v. Travelers Ins. Co., 514 U.S. 645 (1995), reviewed in this Part, describes a New York program that served as one model for this experimentation. The purpose of all-payer rate-setting experiments was to curb the fastest-growing portion of the health care sector at the time, while halting cross-payer cost-shifting, through the use of tools that effectively treated hospitals as public utilities and established the rates that they could charge all payers. By 2011, only one state (Maryland) continued to operate an all-payer rate-setting system.

In this era, the federal government took a weak stab at a more holistic, regulatory approach to cost containment. Building on earlier legislation beginning with the Hospital Survey and Construction Act of 1946 (Hill Burton), Congress enacted the National Health Planning and Resource Development Act of 1974 (Pub. L. No. 93–641), whose purpose (further strengthened by amendments in 1979) was to introduce formal planning procedures into the development and growth of new health care resources. The law established state and local health planning agencies operating under federal oversight and (in theory at least) with the power to control capital investment and expansion, and with a particular focus on hospitals and major capital equipment purchases. Intense industry opposition, as well as parochialism, lack of resources, and professional capture stunted implementation, and the legislation was repealed in 1986 in the midst of the Reagan Administration's deregulatory fever.

Additionally, in 1973, Congress enacted legislation to spur the growth of what had been termed prepaid practice plans, renamed as health maintenance organizations. Pub. L. No. 93–222. The purpose of HMOs, championed by President Nixon and Dr. Paul Ellwood, his chief health advisor, was to integrate financing and health care into hybrid entities that, through greater clinical and financial integration, could both insure the population while managing care through greater emphasis on prevention and efficiencies. The HMO model was simply a newer moniker for the same type of integration championed by the Committee on the Cost of Medical Care, with ties to both insurance and health care. To spur development of HMOs, the law required employers of 25 or more to offer federally qualified HMOs as an option where they existed. By 1981 less than 10 percent of the employed population was enrolled in an HMO or other prepaid group practice arrangement. For many reasons, particularly physician opposition to intermediary control, and the fact that organizations like Kaiser–Permanente don't just spring into existence out of thin air, creation of HMOs that met the federal qualifications proved difficult. BROWN, HMOS AS FEDERAL POLICY.

In a fragmented payment system with multiple competing insurers and payers looking to protect only their own turf, these approaches were doomed to fail. Health care providers, faced with a cutback by one payer, as well as with millions of uninsured patients, simply raised prices in other less regulated markets.

Insurers began to respond to the demand for cost controls by introducing new models of coverage. Utilization review became a feature of private insurance. Utilization review was initially retrospective; that is, it was structured to review and deny payment after treatment had been given.

Judicial decisions sometimes struck down this approach as a form of bad faith breach of the implied covenant of good faith and fair dealing in insurance contracts. *See, e.g.,* Sarchett v. Blue Shield of California, 729 P.2d 267 (Cal. 1987).

In 1978, five years after enactment of the HMO Act, Professor Alain Enthoven, an industrial economist who had only recently turned his attention to health care—devoting tools he had applied to weapons procurement (a curious precedent perhaps)—wrote a seminal series of articles that appeared in the New England Journal of Medicine and enunciated a series of principles known as "managed competition." Alain Enthoven, *Consumer Choice Health Plan (I),* 298 NEW. ENG. J. MED. 650 (1978); Alain Enthoven, *Consumer Choice Health Plan (II),* 298 NEW ENG. J. MED. 709 (1978). Even as he acknowledged that health care was an unusual market, Enthoven essentially argued that in certain respects, buying health care required the same types of industrial organization techniques that companies brought to the purchase of an important manufacturing "input" such as rubber or steel. Thus, he claimed, the path to cost control was to organize health care into defined, vertically integrated products that could be sold to companies that in turn manufactured downstream products such as cars, refrigerators, retail services, or any other good or service sold in the economy and dependent on human input.

Enthoven's espoused techniques encompassed the use of competitive bidding from large integrated delivery and financing systems that in turn would use competitive purchasing of their own to select physicians and hospitals for their provider networks. Through selective purchasing, strict controls over coverage through the use of treatment guidelines, efforts to develop quality performance measures, and prospective controls designed to tame price and resource consumption, the American health care system would evolve into clinically and financially integrated health care products that operated on a prepaid basis. Essentially, Professor Enthoven described a competitive health care system dominated by large prepaid group practices and infused with vast amounts of transparent information about price and quality. Enthoven appreciated that public restrictions were required to prevent managed care organizations from competing by risk selection, i.e. marketing to the healthy. His model has never been fully adopted, although President Clinton's unsuccessful health reform plan of the 1990s followed it in many respects.

The managed care revolution of the 1990s was a response to the twin problems of cost and quality. In managed care (which can have many variations in form) large intermediaries offering insurance and/or plan administration services to self-insuring employers contract with provider networks, whose selection and practice they oversee, in exchange for the promise of patients and revenues. Jonathan Weiner & Gregory de Lissovoy, *Razing a Tower of Babel: A Taxonomy for Managed Care and Health Insurance Plans,* 18 J. OF HEALTH POL. POL'Y & L. 75, 83 (1993). The dominant feature of managed care is to combine financing and care within a single enterprise in which coverage is conditioned in whole or in part on use of a network, while providers' access to insured patients depends on their participation and acceptance of the insurer's control over access to coverage. Sara Rosenbaum et al., *Who Should Determine When Health Care Is Medically Necessary?* 340 NEW ENG. J. MED. 229 (1999). In this sense, managed care comes close—at least in concept—to the ideals espoused by Enthoven, although resistance by patients and providers has precluded the exclusivity that would enable full integration.

In its early years, managed care seemed to control costs, as the model spread across both employer plans and Medicaid, and as plan administrators were able to wring price concessions from hospitals, physicians and other providers as a *quid pro quo* for network membership and volume. Indeed, in the mid–1990s, health insurance premiums actually declined slightly. However, for a number of reasons this so-called "managed-care shock" was a temporary, one-time phenomenon. For one thing, both Congress and state governments enacted "patient protection reforms" that included laws aimed at preventing the arbitrary exclusion of providers from networks (known as any willing provider laws), laws establishing external review of insurers' treatment decisions, and laws requiring the disclosure of information about coverage and care. *See* Stephanie Lewis & Karen Pollitz, *Consumer Protection in Private Health Insurance: State Implementation and Enforcement Experience,* HHS Contract No. 100–97–0005 (Institute for Health Care Research and Policy, Georgetown University, 2000), http://aspe.hhs.gov/health/reports/consumer/stateimp/private.htm. A number of the cases presented in Parts Two and Three deal with state efforts to constrain insurers' conduct in managed care arrangements.

However, factors other than these legal reforms played a larger part in the "managed care backlash." *See, e.g.,* Mark A. Hall, *The Death of Managed Care: A Regulatory Autopsy,* 30 J. HEALTH POL. POL'Y & L. 427 (2005). To some extent, managed care coincided with and enhanced the normal up and down cycle of insurance premiums, which rise and fall according the cyclical rhythms of health insurance underwriting and competition among insurers. Prediction of expenditures is not an exact science and so at times premiums are set too high relative to the losses that then occur, as expected losses exceed the actual losses that follow. In the next wave of the cycle, premiums are set too low relative to actual losses, as actual losses turn out to be higher than predicted. Moreover—particularly when profits are high—firms at times will set premiums low relative to expected losses in order to gain market share, effectively a form of "loss leading." The "managed-care shock" coincided with the downward part of the cycle in which premiums fall or don't increase as fast, but the initial price discounting by providers outran actuarial predictions. This development accentuated the downward cycle, and the unexpectedly high profits led to aggressive lowering of premiums to gain market share. These combined effects did not eliminate the cycle but elongated it, making the low part lower and longer in duration. The upward rebound in premiums, accounting for the unexpected and abnormally large losses that followed the nadir, was even higher than normal. The downward swing in premiums that occurred when managed care took hold, therefore, did not prove that managed care could hold down price or utilization over the longer term, but was instead evidence of the cumulative effects of the ordinary cycle and the initial price shock that the introduction of managed care caused. *See* Joy M. Grossman & Paul B. Ginsburg, *As the Health Insurance Underwriting Cycle Turns: What Next?*, 23(6) HEALTH AFFAIRS 91 (2004).

Even when control of providers' prices works in the short term, eventually the underlying drivers of higher costs begin to rebound, particularly as providers learn how to maximize income within a new set of rules. This dynamic was particularly evident in the early years of managed care as physicians and hospitals initially panicked, fearful of their exclusion from access to pools of patients; and they willingly offered deep discounts in order not to be swept away by the tide. Then reality set in, and resistance to the model by physicians and patients proved too great for really tightly managed, exclusionary networks, to be socially and politically sustainable. *See, e.g.,* Alain Enthoven & Sara Singer, *The Managed Care Backlash and the Task Force in California*, 17(4) HEALTH AFFAIRS 95 (1998). Ultimately managed care's tight utilization controls and closed networks gave way to looser structures that partially shield payers from cost by shifting it directly onto patients through the use of discounting provider networks, coupled with tight coverage rules, high cost-sharing, and exposure to balance billing for going out of network. As cost-sharing has climbed ever higher, things might be swinging back somewhat in the other direction, as insurers have once again begun to emphasize a more managed approach that promises better coverage in exchange for acceptance of more utilization controls and more direct control over provider practice. *See, e.g.,* Reed Abelson, *Insurers Push Plans That Limit Choice of Doctors*, N.Y. TIMES, July 18, 2010. Managed care, in sum, has not held down costs—for reasons we explore in much greater deal in this Part—but the structural changes it wrought—competitive networks selected and managed by intermediaries and tighter prospective utilization controls—reflect a fundamental shift in the structure of U.S. health insurance. These two basic structural reforms—now amped up by rapidly rising point-of-service cost-sharing—are here to stay.

Insurers that developed managed care products for large employers eventually introduced them into the small-employer and individual markets. In the employer sector, health plans that do not use participating provider networks and that indemnify members for costs they incur when using the provider of their choice (a model known as indemnity insurance) has virtually disappeared. *Kaiser/HRET Employer Health Benefits Survey* (2010). In 1988, by contrast, coverage through insurer-controlled provider networks accounted for only 27 percent of all workers covered under an employer-sponsored plan. *Id.* at Ex. 6.1. Plan administrators and insurers typically have replaced the complete exclusion of coverage for out-of-network care with the use of "preferred provider networks" that typically contract with multiple plans. Insurers and plan administrators in turn use higher cost sharing for covered services, along with exposure to balance billing for out-of-network care, as the financial lures to encourage members to remain in-network. The financial consequences of out-of-network coverage will be explored in cases later in Part Two.

Managed care also grew in the public programs. Between 1976 and 2005, Medicare and Medicaid were amended through a series of reforms to explicitly give the insurance industry access to both programs. In the case of Medicare, the Medicare Advantage (MA) program was established in 2003, an outgrowth of earlier shifts toward participation by private, risk-bearing plans. MARILYN MOON, MEDICARE: A POLICY PRIMER ch. 5 (2006). As of 2009, MA plans enrolled 22 percent of the Medicare population. Spending on the enrolled population was projected to be 114 percent of comparable expenditures in the traditional Medicare program, as a result of the industry's selection of relatively younger and healthier beneficiaries and provision of additional benefits not ordinarily offered through Medicare, such as vision and dental care. Enhanced benefits cost Medicare $3.00 for every dollar in enhancements spent. MEDICARE PAYMENT AND ACCESS COMMIS-SION (MedPAC), REPORT TO CONGRESS ch. 5 (2009).

In the case of Medicaid, managed care proliferated, with more than 70 percent of all Medicaid beneficiaries enrolled in some sort of "managed care entity" (the term used in the Medicaid statute) following federal legislative amendments enacted in 1997 that established managed care as a state option for most beneficiaries, without the need for special federal permission. MACPAC, REPORT TO CONGRESS 7–16 (2011).

The evolution of managed care from insurers' efforts to manage price and utilization to plans that couple high cost-sharing with limited benefits and discounted provider networks has led some experts to declare managed care "dead." James C. Robinson, *The End of Managed Care*, 285 JAMA 2622 (2001). Others have pointed out that even if altered, the modern insurance product includes the same network and cost-management techniques associated with managed care. Glen P. Mays et al., *Managed Care Rebound: Recent Changes in Health Plans' Cost Containment Strategies*, HEALTH AFFAIRS (Web Exclusive) w427 (Aug. 6, 2004), http://content.health affairs.org/content/early/2004/08/11/hlthaff.w4.427.full.pdf + html?sid= d4897b14-414b-488b-974e-b753bfce0cde. In any event, managed care has failed miserably at controlling costs.

The modern insurance market is increasingly populated by products that go under the monikers of "consumer driven" (which emphasizes high deductibles) and "value-based purchasing" (which emphasizes higher cost-sharing for treatments deemed ineffective by insurers and experts). In the context of health insurance the term "consumerism" essentially has become a name for insurance plans that expose members to a higher share of the cost of covered treatments and services—effectively "de-insurance"—even as plans tighten the terms of what is actually covered at all. Paul Fronstin & Sara Collins, *Early Experience with High–Deductible and Consumer Driven Health Plans: Findings from the EBRI/Commonwealth Consumerism in Health Care Survey*, COMMONWEALTH FUND (2005); JOST, HEALTH CARE AT RISK; Gladwell, *The Moral Hazard Myth*. Some people who favor consumer-driven plans assert that previous efforts to rein in costs simply did not go far enough and that only even harsher withdrawal of coverage will achieve the necessary impact. Alan Hubbard, *A Tax Cure for Health Care*, WALL ST. J., July 24, 2007, at A15; FEDERAL TRADE COMMISSION, A DOSE OF COMPETITION (2003).

John Goodman, director of the National Center for Policy Analysis, is a leading proponent of consumerism who calls himself "The Father of Health Savings Accounts." He writes at his blog (http://www.john-goodman-blog.com/):

HSAs Explained

Suppose we passed a law tomorrow prohibiting all insurance companies (including Medicare and Medicaid) from paying any medical bills less than $5,000. What would happen? The medical marketplace would transform almost overnight. Within a couple of months, there would be no such thing as a primary care physician (PCP) who did not post prices—at least for routine procedures. PCPs would offer telephone and email consultations. They would keep patient records electronically (just like lawyers and accountants). Overall, there would develop a teeming, bustling, entrepreneurial marketplace for primary care, diagnostic tests and most prescription drugs.

Specialty markets would develop for the chronically ill, as doctors competed for their business instead of trying to avoid them. Patient education would become an emerging field, with providers offering to teach diabetics, asthmatics, etc. how to manage their own care. Internet drug sales would double, triple and quadruple, as brand drugs faced increasing competition from generic, therapeutic and over-the-counter substitutes. At the same time, overall health care spending would plummet. (Just thinking about it makes you wonder why we haven't done this already.)

Now, can the widespread use of HSAs create this same transformation? Certainly HSAs along with an even greater number of uninsured and a still larger number of employees facing higher deductibles and co-payments, are already having an impact on the market. How else can you explain the exploding number of walk-in clinics, the growth of internet drug sales, and $4–a-month-for-generics at Wal–Mart and other big box retailers?

Even as health care costs continue to climb at rates exceeding the general rate of inflation and growth in GDP, increasing numbers of employers have moved to offer such plans as either an option or sole choice. As of 2010, consumer-driven plans were offered by 15 percent of all employers. *Kaiser/ HRET Employer Health Benefits Annual Survey* ch. 8 (2010). These plans are a marriage of health insurance and savings accounts. That is, under such a plan, traditional coverage by the insurer or plan is linked to one of two types of tax-favored savings accounts whose exclusion from income is allowed under the Internal Revenue Code (a health reimbursement account (HRA) or a health savings account (HSA)) to a high deductible health plan (deductible at least $1000 for an individual and $2000 for a family). Employers can contribute to these accounts, and as is the case with employer insurance generally, individuals with employer contributions to their accounts tend to be higher income. HRA and HSA funds can be applied toward health care costs recognized by the IRS but excluded from coverage. The insurance portion of this type of coverage arrangement is typically a PPO or an HMO with a "point of service" option, that is, an HMO that maintains a tight network but allows individuals to go out-of-network for an additional fee. *Id.*

In addition to having no measurable impact on the rising cost of health care, early research suggests that the consumer-driven plan model raises new types of problems. First, high deductible plans appear to be incapable of distinguishing between the unnecessary use of high cost services and the use of large amounts of care to address significant health care needs. As a result, evidence suggests a greater likelihood that individuals in consumer-driven plans will forego necessary care, including preventive care, and are more likely to have unpaid bills.

Second, people who buy these products tend to be younger, leaving older workers increasingly concentrated in more traditional plans and thereby raising the cost of those plans. Third, lower income workers appear not to receive employer contributions to their health savings accounts. Unless they can contribute out of their own earnings, they are effectively left uninsured up to a (much higher) deductible level, thereby threatening access to care. Fronstin & Collins, *Findings from the 2007 EBRI/Commonwealth Fund Consumerism in Health Survey*; U.S. GOV'T ACCOUNTABILITY OFFICE, GAO–06–798, CONSUMER DIRECTED HEALTH PLANS: EARLY ENROLLEE EXPERIENCES WITH HEALTH SAVINGS ACCOUNTS AND ELIGIBLE HEALTH PLANS (August 2006).

Renowned health economist Karen Davis has written that the consumer driven model appears to have its greatest success among persons who do not use health care; 85% of all consumer-directed plan enrollees reported in one study that they spent less than $1000 annually on health care. Karen Davis, *Will Consumer Directed Health Care Improve System Performance?*, COMMONWEALTH FUND (August 2004). Economist Joseph Newhouse of Harvard, who in the 1970s led what is still considered the seminal study aimed a measuring the impact of cost sharing on the use of health care—the "RAND experiment"—is similarly skeptical about the ability of consumer-driven plans to tame costs:

> Just as managed care did not ultimately hold back the wave of increased health care costs, there is little reason to think that today's increased initial cost sharing and more sophisticated tools such as disease management will hold it back, either. Although these tools should leave health care costs lower at each point in time than they otherwise would be, it is less clear that they will greatly affect the steady-state growth rate of costs. This conclusion assumes that the steady-state growth rate of costs is mainly influence by the ongoing increase in the capabilities of medicine,

capabilities that for the most part we and others around the world want to pay for.

Joseph P. Newhouse, *Consumer–Directed Health Plans and the RAND Health Insurance Experiment*, 23(6) HEALTH AFFAIRS 107 (2004).

---

4.   THE PATIENT PROTECTION AND AFFORDABLE CARE ACT (ACA)

a.   The Prelude to Reform

As the preceding materials have made clear, federal law has played a central role in the design and regulation of health insurance, despite the authority reserved to the states under the McCarran Ferguson Act. ERISA, whose preemptive impact on state insurance laws will be explored later in this Part, governs health plans covering nearly 150 million people and sponsored by private employers. Hinda Ripps Chaikin, *ERISA Regulation of Health Plans* (CRS, 2003), http://www.allhealth.org/briefingmaterials/erisaregulationofhealthplans–114.pdf. Other federal laws define coverage for the federal military and civilian workforces, with special federal laws for such disparate workgroups as the U.S. Postal Service. Together Medicare and Medicaid cover more than 100 million people and represent about 35 percent of all U.S. health care expenditures. To be sure, states maintain the power to regulate health insurance products, but because of ERISA preemption, they cannot regulate third-party-administered products sold to self-insuring employers. Furthermore, ERISA has been held to preempt state efforts to regulate the scope and quality of self-insured plans indirectly by setting coverage and performance standards for the reinsurance sold to self-insuring employers under so-called "stop loss" arrangements. American Medical Security v. Bartlett, 111 F.3d 358 (4th Cir. 1997). In the period leading up to enactment of the Patient Protection and Affordable Care Act, about 8 percent of the population was covered by an individual private insurance plans purchased directly from an issuer and subject to both state and federal regulation. United States Census Bureau, *Income Poverty and Health Insurance: Coverage in the United States (2009)* 24–26 (2010), http://www.census.gov/prod/2010pubs/p60–238.pdf. Individual coverage thus was the weak sibling among insurance pathways.

Whatever the legal framework has been, the market itself also has been voluntary for individuals and employers. Thus, in the period preceding the ACA, insurers and health plan administrators for self-insuring employer-sponsored plans deployed risk-shielding behaviors that built on the concept of fair actuarial risk, which holds that individuals or pools with higher risks should pay more for the same coverage. The result of this approach was that sicker people inevitably faced greater barriers to health care.

To this end, prior to the ACA insurers used three types of risk-shielding techniques: (1) keeping bad risks out of the pool to begin with both through outright exclusion (either entirely or for "pre-existing conditions") and through rescissions (cancellations) as part of their practice of medically underwriting individuals and groups (HIPAA put limits on but did not bar these tactics in the group market); (2) exorbitant pricing; and (3) limiting coverage coupled with a lot of treatment exclusions and high cost-sharing in order to hold down unanticipated coverage costs. Thus, for example, a health plan would reserve the right not to pay for costs associated with any health problem that "relates to a condition (whether physical or mental), regardless of the cause of the condition, for which medical advice, diagnosis, care, or treatment was recommended or received within the [x]-month period ending on the enrollment date." (This is a typical pre-existing condition exclusion clause; the "look-back" period embedded in the clause might be six months, 24 months, 36 months, or any number of months). Similarly, the plan might impose an annual coverage limit of $500,000, or it might exclude treatments that could not be expected to "cure" an "illness or injury," thereby excluding from coverage treatments that might prevent a degenerative chronic condition from worsening.

As we discussed above, in a limited fashion HIPAA dealt with certain pre-enrollment risk-shielding practices in certain markets. At the same time, HIPAA essentially left post-enrollment techniques unaddressed. In addition to imposing annual and lifetime limits on the value of a policy, as well as high deductibles and cost-sharing, plan administrators could require that members and providers comply with extensive prior authorization requirements before treatment was covered. Plan administrators could likewise deny coverage for emergency care furnished by an out-of-network provider, maintain limited provider networks in order to make getting an appointment difficult, select physicians who adhered to the plan's practice guidelines, and incentivize practice styles that emphasized the limited use of resources. You will see cases arising from these types of practices in Part Three. *See generally* Mary Crossley, *Discrimination Against the Unhealthy in Health Insurance*, 54 KANSAS L. REV. 73 (2005); Sara Rosenbaum, *Insurance Discrimination Based on Health Status*, O'NEILL INSTITUTE FOR NATIONAL AND GLOBAL HEALTH LAW, GEORGETOWN UNIVERSITY (2009), http:// www.law.georgetown.edu/oneillinstitute/national-health-law/legal-solutions-in-health-reform/Discrimination.html; Deborah Stone, *Protect the Sick: Health Insurance Reform in One Easy Lesson*, 36(4) J. LAW, MED. ETHICS, 652 (2008); Karen Bleier, *Managed Care Enters the Exam Room as Insurers Buy Doctors Groups*, WASHINGTON POST, July 3, 2011 (reporting on the trend and on significant savings yielded by the practice), http://www.washington post.com/insurers-quietly-gaining-control-of-doctors-covered-by-companies-plans/2011/06/29/AG5DNftH_story.html.

These risk-shielding techniques have not been limited to groups purchasing insurance. Even large employers that self-insure utilize risk-avoidance practices in order to keep their plans solvent and to qualify for reinsurance. Furthermore, since self-insuring employers in fact tend to use insurers as their third-party administrators, their plan structure and operations are typically not much different from the plans that insurers sell to group purchasers on an insured basis.

At one time, and in keeping with the underlying classic theory of insurance, health insurance products might have focused on protection against catastrophic health care expenses such as those incurred in accidents or grave illnesses. Over time, as health care costs have climbed, employer-sponsored plans and public insurance programs increasingly have been expanded to offer at least some protections for the routine costs of health care that arise in daily life, a feature of coverage in other countries. Cathy Schoen et al., *Primary Care and Health System Performance: Adults' Experience in Five Countries*, COMMONWEALTH FUND (2004), http://www. commonwealthfund.org/Content/Publications/In-the-Literature/2004/Oct/ Primary–Care-and-Health–System–Performance—Adults–Experiences-in-Five–Countries.aspx. *See also* Wendy Mariner, *Health Reform: What's Insurance Got to Do With It? Recognizing Health Insurance as a Separate Species of Insurance*, 36 AM. J.L. & MED. 436 (2010) (arguing that in fact, U.S. health insurers have abandoned the classic insurance model and that health insurance is now a separate species of insurance that has moved far beyond the coverage of "fortuitous losses." Insurance in the U.S. now finances "a service component to pay for regular care" and should be understood and regulated as such). In the period prior to the Affordable Care Act, coverage of at least certain preventive and wellness services such as well-child exams, immunizations, and cancer screening for breast, colon, and certain other cancers also have been a feature of large employer-sponsored plans. Medicare offered only limited preventive screening and treatment services, Medicaid preventive services were pretty much confined to children under age 21, and family planning services and supplies for beneficiaries of childbearing age.

b.   Why Did Reform Happen?

The political process that led to enactment of the Affordable Care Act was dramatic. The Act itself is a complex piece of engineering, in good part because its builds on the complicated federal/state legal structure already in place, evolving out of an existing multi-payer, multi-tiered regulatory framework rather than displacing it. The legislation alters multiple bodies of federal law, overlaying on a market-oriented system a layer of social contract in order to achieve near-universal coverage. Because the Act weaves a new coverage regime out of the multiple and disparate skeins already in place, its fabric is dense and its implementation will be challenging.

Fundamentally the Affordable Care Act rejects the notion that the way in which to keep health care costs down is to exclude the sick. Instead, a requirement to purchase affordable coverage is established, the *quid pro quo* being regulation of previous risk-shielding practices, coupled with financial supports to make coverage more affordable. In this sense, the Act represents market-facilitating legislation that rests on concepts of socially shared risks. *See* Nan D. Hunter, *Health Insurance Reform and the Intimation of Citizenship*, 154 U. PA. L. REV. 1955, 1956 (2011) (The Affordable Care Act "creates the potential for broad public conversation—as has never before occurred in the United States—regarding the question of what the relationship should be between membership in the American community and meaningful access to health care.'').

Answering the question of why health reform happened in 2010 is complicated. Political scientist Mark Peterson writes that "[as] Barack Obama's administration and the members of the 111th Congress took office, by conventional accounting we were at the seventh significant episode of health care reform debate in a century. Each time before, reform not only failed, it crashed spectacularly." Mark Peterson, *It Was a Different Time: Obama and the Unique Opportunity for Health Care Reform*, 36 J. HEALTH POL. POL'Y & L. 429 (2011). Peterson's assessment of why this attempt succeeded focuses on two basic dimensions of the law's enactment. The first was a belief that "problems amenable to public-sector intervention actually exist." *Id.* at 430. What Peterson identifies as the related problems of "costs, coverage, and consequences" (which he defines as inefficiencies, inequities, and their health impact on the nation) were understood as having reached such an acute state as to have made political action possible. The President's predecessors were unfortunate enough to have attempted reform when change simply appeared less urgent. Health insurance was little more than a blip on the screen politically under President Franklin Roosevelt, and employer-sponsored coverage was just taking off when President Truman made his attempt at reform. Professor Peterson argues that it was not until President Bill Clinton's failed attempt in 1993–94 that policymakers came to appreciate the problem as having reached a critical stage.

The second dimension that receives Peterson's attention was the process of enactment itself, a focus shared by other scholars. *See, e.g.,* Jacob Hacker, *Why Reform Happened*, 36 J. HEALTH POL. POL'Y & L. 437 (2011); Judith Feder, *Too Big to Fail: The Enactment of Health Care Reform*, 36 J. HEALTH POL. POL'Y & L. 412 (2011); Lawrence Brown, *The Elements of Surprise: How Health Reform Happened*, 36 J. HEALTH POL. POL'Y & L. 420 (2011). Together these scholars hone in on several aspects of passage, the first of which was relatively strong and unified support among the major political interest groups, a crucial missing element in 1993–94. In response to President Clinton's agonizingly detailed health reform plan, most important groups, particularly private insurers, came out swinging against the Clinton plan. In 2009, by contrast, insurers, hospitals, the pharmaceutical industry and physicians (who ironically failed to get the very item at the top of their wish list, a more permanent fix to Medicare's physician payment problems discussed later in this Part) were fairly united behind the measure, sensing the magnitude of the underlying problems that threatened their individual economic positions. They also were united in realizing that the legislation also would potentially bring them a major new financing stream with the movement of millions of people from uninsured to the ranks of the insured. The support of these interest groups also hinged on the fact that the legislation effectively contained no serious attempt to alter the underlying costs of health care, a fact hidden by what Professor James Morone terms the law's "technical fixes" for health care costs, including a raft of pilots, demonstrations, new research, and health information technology, together weakly masking the fact that costs will not be controlled. James Morone, *Big Ideas, Broken Institutions, and the Wrath at the Grass Roots*, 36 J. HEALTH POL. POL'Y & L. 375, 380 (2011). In deploying these devices, the ACA gives the aura of much commotion without any real movement.

This point is perhaps best illustrated by the demise of the so-called "Medicare option," which would have allowed persons under age 65—i.e., not eligible for Medicare yet—to buy into Medicare. The insurance industry fought this proposal tooth and nail, for they understood it to be what it was, a Trojan horse. Medicare's administrative costs are far lower than private plans' administrative expenses, and, at least as initially proposed, this option could have used Medicare's payment methods—which we will examine later in this Part—that have allowed Medicare to achieve prices far lower than those obtained by the private sector—largely because of its huge bargaining power. Consequently, Medicare option would have been able to set premiums much lower than private plans could afford. One doesn't have to be Ross Perot to hear the sucking sound, of individuals being pulled out of private insurance. With the demise of this proposal, cost control was no longer seriously on the table, except for the bells and whistles we just described.

All of the political scientists cited above understand the critical nature of the manner in which the political story played out. In contrast to the Clinton strategy, which was to send a fully cooked (ultimately viewed as half-baked) piece of legislation to Capitol Hill, President Obama allowed the legislation to develop in Congress itself. The process that ensued was unbelievably messy, made all the more so by the eruption of vitriolic Town Hall meetings that confronted Members of Congress as they returned home for their summer 2009 recess and ultimately helped fuel the widespread political backlash that erupted in the 2010 midterm elections following passage.

And yet at the same time, as Judy Feder and James Morone point out, the very messiness of the process caused the House and Senate leadership to make sure that their Members—from the most liberal to the most conservative—were invested as never before in getting the job done. The pivotal moment came with the January 2010 special election to fill the seat of Senator Edward Kennedy (D–MA), who had died five months earlier. Once the seat was filled by Republican Scott Brown, the Senate Democrats lost their filibuster-proof majority, thereby forcing them to jettison the normal process of conferencing House and Senate-passed measures. In its place the House and Senate Leadership, with full White House support, launched what can only be described as a Hail Mary pass in which the much more politically-under-control House simply took up the Senate version of the legislation (hated by the House both for its structure and approach to coverage, as well as for its slightly less exclusionary treatment of abortion coverage), accepted and passed it, and sent it to the President.*

---

* The normal legislative disdain that each side feels for the other was magnified here. The House measure was dramatically different from the Senate bill, taking a far more federally-

This legislation, along with a companion bill, the Health Care and Education Reconciliation Act of 2010 (Pub. L. No. 111–152, 111th Cong., 2d Sess.), which contains a short list of important changes in, and extensions of, the main text of the Affordable Care Act itself, form the basis of the most far-reaching reform of American health care since the passage of Medicare in 1965.

c. Structure and Elements

Professor Tom Baker, a leading expert in insurance law writes:

The Affordable Care Act embodies a social contract of health care solidarity through private ownership, markets, choice, and individual responsibility. While some might regard this contract as the unnatural union of opposites—solidarity on the one hand and markets, choice, and individual responsibility on the other—those familiar with insurance history will recognize in the Act an effort to realize the dream of America's insurance evangelists: a "society united on the basis of mutual insurance." Public ownership and pure, tax-based financing are technically easier and almost certainly cheaper routes to health care solidarity, but they come at a cost to the status quo that Congress was not prepared to pay.

Tom Baker, *Health Insurance, Risk, and Responsibility After the Patient Protection and Affordable Care Act*, 159 U. PA. L. REV. 1577, 1579–80 (2011).

The Act is vast in scope, but despite its size, its elements present a relatively unified roadmap for moving ahead. The legislation is the ultimate meshing of many themes in U.S. health policy: the quest for near-universal coverage that had eluded lawmakers for three-quarters of a century; the preservation and strengthening of the employment-based insurance market; the preservation of a strong role for state regulation of insurance; the

structured approach to reform, while the Senate measure was built on a fundamental belief in a continuation of federal/state power-sharing over public and private health insurance. The House also resented the Senate because in an effort to accommodate Republicans (when there still was hope for bipartisanship) Senate leadership allowed months of negotiations to drag consideration through the fall and into Christmas, 2009, thereby allowing Democrats in both Houses to twist in the wind under a massive political onslaught that set in for good after the 2009 summer Town Hall meetings. Furthermore, while the Senate measure allowed health plans to continue to offer coverage for abortions under certain circumstances, the House measure would have barred from Exchange participation any health plan covering abortions other than those necessary to address rape or incest or save the life of the mother. Abortion politics are, of course, unlike any other, since some of the most passionate opponents of abortion (as was the case in the House) are also liberal Members of Congress. The Democratic majority was able to prevail in the House only after anti-abortion liberal Members agreed to accept the less restrictive Senate approach and the White House intervened to pledge energetic enforcement as well as aggressive enforcement of already existing prohibitions under the so-called Hyde Amendment on the provision of abortion services at community health centers, whose $11 billion Trust Fund providing for expansion had been (inadvertently) drafted to lie outside of the restrictions on abortion services that normally apply to federal expenditures. For his concession, Congressman Stupak, a leading supporter of health reform and also a leading Democratic opponent of abortion, was forced out of office, and his family was tormented for months.

establishment of a viable individual market for people without access to coverage through a group plan or public insurance; the additional strengthening of social contract through reforms to Medicare and Medicaid; an emphasis on market-based tools for containing costs, including competitive bidding by insurers and value-based purchasing strategies aimed at incentivizing physicians and patients to make the right choices; and an emphasis on individual responsibility in health and health care. In keeping with American culture and politics, the legislation fails to introduce any central means by which costs can be controlled; at the same time, it strives to make use of every politically acceptable tool in the market reform toolbox to begin to make a dent in costs. Peter Orzag, *How Health Care Can Save or Sink America*, 90 FOREIGN AFFAIRS 42 (July/August 2011).

Upon enactment, the legislation immediately was met with a series of legal challenges to the constitutionality of its centerpiece, the individual mandate to purchase affordable insurance, as well as its Medicaid expansion. See O'Neill Institute for National and Global Health Law, Health Law and Litigation, http://www.healthlawandlitigation.com/, which provides an ongoing chronicle and update on all pending litigation. As of February 2012, the United States Supreme Court had granted certiorari to resolve multiple issues: the requirement that taxpayers who can afford to do so buy health insurance; whether the coverage requirement, if struck down as unconstitutional, can be severed from the insurance market reforms so that they may be preserved; whether the Medicaid expansion to cover all low-income nonelderly Americans amounts to unconstitutional coercion; and whether the Anti–Injunction Act bars consideration of the challenge to the coverage requirement. The issues pending before the Court will be explored at the end of this Part.

In addition to this litigation, a more conservative 112th Congress has threatened to roll back major elements of the law, if not the legislation in its entirety. These efforts have not been successful, although some important pieces of legislation did gain enactment, most notably—in a tit-for-tat—a law that repeals a tax loophole that had been closed to help pay for the cost of subsidizing coverage for lower income people, while simultaneously increasing penalties charged against low- and moderate-income people who receive advance subsidies that exceed allowable amounts in light of their final adjusted annual income. Comprehensive 1099 Taxpayer Protection and Repayment of Exchange Subsidy Overpayments Act of 2011, Pub. L. No. 112–9 (111th Cong., 1st Sess.). Because the correct amount of advance subsidy payment cannot be known until a year-end reconciliation of the subsidies against actual income earned, Congress initially had limited the recoupment exposure for low- and moderate-income families in order not to deter enrollment. As the penalties mount, of course, the number of individuals who will take advantage of the refundable tax credits used to make insurance affordable can be expected to precipitously decline given fears of non-repayable financial exposure at the end of any year because of a modest rise in income.

Hostile lawmakers have not been the only problem. Strikingly, the Obama Administration itself concluded that a major element of the law, the Community Living Assistance Services and Supports Program (CLASS Act), which would have established the nation's first national long-term care policy outside of Medicaid, could not be launched as designed because it lacked actuarially sound underpinnings. Robert Pear, Health Law to Be Revised by Ending a Program, N. Y. TIMES (October 14, 2011), http://www. nytimes.com/2011/10/15/health/policy/15health.html?_r=1. The 48–page report issued by the United States Department of Health and Human Services. THE ACTUARIAL, MARKETING AND LEGAL ANALYSES OF THE CLASS ACT PROGRAM (2011), http://aspe.hhs.gov/daltcp/reports/2011/class/index.pdf, presented information showing that as written the law could not be implemented on a sound basis and that the Secretary lacked the legal authority under the Act to make crucial adjustments in plan and premium design to modify the law in order to assure that it could operate in an actuarially sound and self-sustaining fashion. *See generally* David M. Frankford, *At Least We're Still Free to Choose to Die at Home: A CLASS Act*, 36 J. HEALTH POL. POL'Y & L. 533 (2011).

Despite these setbacks, implementation has been underway since the law's March 23, 2010 enactment, with power shared among three Cabinet-level Departments: Labor; Treasury; and Health and Human Services. As a result, more detailed versions of the Act's scores of provisions are continuously unfolding.

The heart of the law is a requirement that individuals who can afford to do so purchase health insurance for themselves and their families. Failure to comply results in payment of a tax penalty, with the poorest individuals exempmted. PPACA § 5001. The *quid pro quo* for this requirement is a fundamentally restructured health insurance market to eliminate discrimination against the sick, along with important changes in access and coverage in both the group and individual markets. To accomplish these goals, the Act builds on the federal regulatory framework added to the Public Health Service Act by HIPAA while extending most of these reforms to ERISA-governed employer-sponsored health plans (both fully insured and self-insured) as well. The Act also requires large employers (over 50 full-time employees) to contribute toward the cost of coverage for their employees, giving them a choice to offer their own plans (with at least a 60 percent employer contribution toward the cost of employees' premiums) or contribute toward the cost of covering employees and their families through newly created state health insurance Exchanges.

The Act makes major changes in public insurance as well. The law significantly revises Medicare to improve coverage of preventive care and prescription drugs. The legislation also imposes higher premiums on wealthier beneficiaries for prescription drug coverage and scales back the rate of Medicare payment increases for providers and suppliers, including Medicare Advantage plans. The Act also expands Medicaid to extend coverage to all low-income nonelderly adults with family incomes below 133 percent of the federal poverty level. Low-income legal residents barred from

Medicaid during their first five years of U.S. residency will be eligible to enroll in subsidized health plans offered through state health insurance Exchanges.

The Act's reforms reach beyond health insurance. The law makes new investments in health care access for medically underserved populations through expansion of the community health centers program, described in Part One, along with investment in the National Health Service Corps, which provides scholarships and loan repayment assistance to health professions students and health professionals who agree to furnish primary health care in urban and rural communities designated as having a shortage of primary health care professionals. In addition, the law contains a wide array of provisions that seek to promote health care quality and efficiency, discussed in Part Three. The legislation provides for creation and adoption of a National Quality Strategy, investments in comparative effectiveness research (whose aim is to test competing treatments against one another to determine which one works best), investments in pilots and demonstrations whose aim is to improve the quality and efficiency of care, and the establishment of new service delivery models known as "medical homes" and "Accountable Care Organizations," discussed in Part Three.

In an effort to improve population health, the Act creates an ongoing investment in a Public Health Trust Fund whose purpose is to stimulate the growth of community initiatives aimed at improving population health. Finally, the Act expands the community benefit obligations of nonprofit hospitals that seek federal tax exempt status and makes various other types of payment reforms and enhancements to the fight against health care fraud (all discussed in Part Four).

The Act contains several large limitations. First, as has been much noted, the law lacks a meaningful cost-containment strategy that applies to all payers and that gives government the power and means to control high health care spending and unsustainable cost increases. Second, by retaining a state-based approach to health insurance markets and market regulation, along with employment-based coverage, the Act fails to create a national risk pool (or at least large regional pools) capable of spreading risk across the entire population. Instead the law leaves in place multiple insurance pools that remain subject to local fragmentation and market selectivity and manipulation, since insurers can continue to pick the states in which they do business, the parts of states in which they wish to compete, and the employers to whom they sell insured and third-party-administered products.

Third, Medicaid beneficiaries remain segregated in a coverage arrangement that, while comprehensive, often pays providers such low rates that they refuse to accept Medicaid patients. Medicaid agencies are expected under the law to align enrollment and retention of coverage in order to minimize the potential for gaps in coverage as low-wage workers and their families are forced continually to switch between the Exchange and Medicaid markets because of minor fluctuations in income that put them over or under the Medicaid eligibility cutoff. The potential for churning lower income workers and their families among markets and plans is very great, estimated in one study to be as high as a 50 percent turnover in any 12–month period. Benjamin Sommers & Sara Rosenbaum, *Issues in Health Reform: How Changes in Eligibility May Move Millions Back and Forth Between Medicaid and Health Insurance Exchanges,* 30(2) HEALTH AFFAIRS, 228 (2011).

Fourth, the Act contains provisions aimed at protecting newly established state insurance Exchanges from adverse risk selection but leaves states with leeway to encourage Exchanges to act as high-risk pools for the sickest and poorest patients, while retaining non-Exchange markets for healthier and wealthier populations. Timothy Stoltzfus Jost, *Health Insurance Exchanges and the Affordable Care Act: Eight Difficult Issues*, COMMONWEALTH FUND (2010), http://www.commonwealthfund.org/Content/Publications/Fund–Reports/2010/Sep/Health–Insurance–Exchanges-and-the-Affordable–Care–Act.aspx; Allison Hoffman, *Oil and Water: Mixing Individual Mandates, Fragmented Markets, and Health Reform*, 36 AM. J.L. & MED. 7 (2010).

Fifth, with the exception of a modest new program to train primary care physicians at "teaching health centers," the Act fails to redirect even a portion of the billions of dollars in federal Medicare funding spent annually on graduate medical education into building the primary care specialties such as family practice, general internal medicine, pediatrics, obstetrics and gynecology, dental practice, nursing practice, the training of physician assistants or the public health workforce. (The community health center and National Health Service Corps investments stand as major exceptions to this fundamental shortcoming in the law).

Sixth, the Act excludes coverage of persons not legally present in the U.S., who are barred from participating in state Exchanges, as well as from Medicaid. As noted in Part One, this exclusion affects over 11 million persons.

The materials that follow summarize the Act's major coverage-related provisions.

Private insurance and employer-sponsored health plans

The individual requirement to purchase affordable coverage. The Act establishes a qualified requirement to purchase insurance coverage. Effective January 1, 2014 and for every month thereafter, most people in the U.S. (known as "applicable individuals") will be required to "ensure" that they have "minimum essential coverage." 26 U.S.C. § 5000A (PPACA § 1501) Individuals who fail to meet their obligations are subject to a monetary "penalty," although the penalty does not apply to people with family incomes below the federal tax threshold (approximately $19,000 for a family in 2012).

The term "applicable individual" means all individuals but excludes certain groups: individuals who qualify for a religious exemption as defined under the Act; individuals "not lawfully present" in the U.S.; and individuals who are incarcerated in any given month. The law also exempts from any penalty any applicable individual for any month in which the individual's "required contribution" exceeds 8 percent of the individual's household income. The law also recognizes a "hardship" exemption (which is to be determined in accordance with standards set by the Secretary of Health and Human Services). *Id.* Individuals with incomes below the federal tax filing threshold are exempt from the penalty, thereby effectively exempting Medicaid-eligible individuals from the mandate; for this population, enrollment remains an essentially voluntary activity. In addition the law exempts from the mandate members of federally recognized Indian tribes. *Id.*

The term "minimum essential coverage" means coverage under any government program (i.e., Medicare or Medicaid) or coverage under an "eligible" employer plan, defined as any plan offered by a public or private employer. *Id.* Minimum essential coverage also encompasses "grandfathered plans" that were in effect on March 23, 2010 and that remain exempt from many of the Act's requirements until they make what are identified under interim final federal regulations as significant changes in premiums, cost-sharing, or coverage. 75 Fed. Reg. 34538 (June 17, 2010).

The role of employers. The Act similarly imposes obligations on employers. The law does not mandate that employers offer coverage. Instead, certain employers are subject to a "shared responsibility" obligation. Any "applicable large employer" (defined as an employer with 50 full-time employees or more on average) that does not offer "full-time" employees and their "dependents" the "opportunity to enroll" in minimum essential coverage must instead pay an "assessable payment" to the federal government. A similar financial assessment is imposed on large employers that offer coverage but do not provide a sufficient contribution to the cost of the monthly premium, such that their low- and moderate-income employees qualify for premium tax credits for coverage available through state Exchanges. I.R.C. § 4980H (PPACA § 1513).

Subsidies to make insurance affordable. Low- and moderate-income individuals subject to the mandate and ineligible for any other form of minimum essential coverage (including Medicaid) are eligible for premium tax credits to obtain for health insurance purchased through their state health insurance Exchanges. PPACA § 1311(d) and § 1312(f). The law targets premium tax credits on individuals and their families with household incomes between the Medicaid eligibility ceiling and 400 percent of the federal poverty level although subsidies also are available to Medicaid-ineligible legal U.S. residents with below-poverty income. Additionally, the law provides additional cost-sharing assistance to defray the cost of high deductibles and coinsurance for low-income persons. PPACA § 1402. Thus, while the Act does not make it unlawful for insurers to sell individual policies outside a state Exchange (where such policies will be less regulated), subsidies are limited to policies bought through the Exchange.

Premium tax credit eligibility is figured for a taxable year based on an individual's prior year's tax filing. Because eligibility is based on retrospective income, individuals who experience an increase in family income (either actual or as a result of a change in living arrangements) during a year in which the credits are received are subject to "recoupment" of their "excess advance payment." 26 U.S.C. § 36B (PPACA § 1401). The law directs the Secretary to develop an eligibility determination process for determining whether coverage is affordable, whether an individual is eligible for premium tax credits and reduced cost-sharing (and if so, their size), whether individuals meet the citizenship and legal status tests, and whether individuals qualify for an "individual responsibility exemption." (PPACA § 1411).

In order to make coverage affordable, premium tax credits are designed to be paid in advance, based on a family's income in the most recent tax year. Of course, if income rises, the size of the advance tax credit would fall. Under the Act as passed, families' exposure to the potential for recoupment of an inappropriate high advance premium tax credit was kept relatively low in order to incentivize low- and moderate-income people to seek coverage rather than seek hardship exemptions or pay a penalty. The Comprehensive 1099 Taxpayer Protection and Repayment of Exchange Overpayments Act of 2011, Pub. L. No. 112–9, passed by Congress early in 2011 and signed by the President, considerably increased the size of the potential recoupment in order to offset the cost of restoring a business tax loophole that in fact had been closed by the Act to help pay for the premium subsidies. Under the Affordable Care Act as passed, the maximum IRS recoupment amount against families could not exceed $400 in the first year, rising by a set amount in ensuing years. The 2011 law raises the first-year cap on recoupment for the poorest families to $600. Families with larger incomes are subject to caps on recoupment that increase with income up to $2500 for families with incomes of 300 percent of poverty or more.

Individual and group market reforms. The Act contains numerous reforms in the individual and group markets, revising and expanding the earlier reforms contained in HIPAA, whose minimum standards apply to insured plans, regulated by state insurance law, and self-insured ERISA plans, not regulated by state insurance law due to ERISA preemption (covered later in this Part). The Act also creates three forms of risk mitigation for insurers in order to avert destabilizing the insurance market as millions of people with potentially higher health risks obtain coverage: a transitional state reinsurance program covering individuals with high health costs; a federal temporary stop-loss program to protect against unanticipated losses; and a permanent risk-adjustment program for policies sold in state Exchanges in order to smooth risks associated with variable enrollment patterns. Mark A. Hall, *The Three Types of Reinsurance Created by Federal Health Reform*, 29(6) HEALTH AFFAIRS 1168 (2010); Mark A. Hall, *Risk Adjustment Under the Affordable Care Act: A Guide for Federal and State Regulators*, COMMONWEALTH FUND (2010).

With certain exceptions, the reforms that are codified into Title XXVII of the Public Health Service Act ("PHSA") (42 U.S.C. § 300gg et seq.), and thus made applicable to plans regulated by state law, also are codified in ERISA and thus made applicable to self-insured plans regulated only by

ERISA. ERISA § 715; 29 U.S.C. § 1185d. The Act's insurance reforms effectively eliminate insurers' ability to shield themselves against risks in either the individual or group markets, and at either initial sale and enrollment or renewal. In addition, the reforms strengthen the depth and quality of coverage, particularly in the individual and small group markets.

The Act bars the use of pre-existing condition exclusions in either the group or individual markets (PHSA § 2704), requires insurers to accept all employers and individuals applying for coverage (PHSA § 2702), guarantees the renewability of coverage (PHSA § 2703), and bars rescissions (PHSA § 2712) and "excessive" waiting periods of more than 90 days before coverage begins (PHSA § 2708).

The Act also requires insurers to comply with a modified community-rating system for insurance premiums in order to limit the extent to which insurers can vary the rates they charge to customers. Rates may vary by age (no more than a 3–to–1 variation), family status, and state-approved geographic rating areas. Rates also may be raised for people who use tobacco. Thus, by extending HIPAA's group-plan reforms, the Act prohibits insurers from using premium pricing to discriminate and the Act applies this prohibition to the individual market. At the same time and under certain circumstances, the law allows employers to establish "employee wellness programs" that condition financial incentives (in the form of reduced premiums) not simply on participating in the wellness program but also on achieving actual health outcomes such as lower blood pressure, smoking cessation, or weight loss. PHSA § 2705.

The Act bars the imposition of annual and lifetime dollar limits on "essential coverage," meaning coverage that falls within one or more "essential health benefit" coverage categories (PHSA § 2011). Note however, that a ban on annual or lifetime dollar limits is not the same as banning annual or lifetime *treatment* limits such as 10 visits to the doctor in a year. This type of limitation is not prohibited, although, as will be discussed later in this Part, any such treatment limitations would have to comply with separate mental health "parity" requirements when applicable. The Department of Health and Human Services has the power to waive compliance with the ban on dollar limits.

As of April 2011, HHS had received more than 1,400 applications from insurers and employer-sponsored health plans asking that HHS waive the annual limits requirements for 2011 because of the alleged cost impact of such a requirement on policies and plans. The Department approved virtually all applications. (Many employers such as national fast food chains offer their employees only what are known as "mini-med" plans that offer extremely limited coverage of a few thousand dollars annually for their premiums; one of the ACA's purposes was to eliminate such products in the employer market.) U.S. Gov't Accountability Office, GAO–11–725R, Private Health Insurance: Waivers of Restrictions on Annual Health Benefits (June 14, 2011), http://democrats.energycommerce.house.gov/sites/default/files/documents/GAOReport_06.14.11.pdf.

The Act requires an extension of dependent coverage to age 26 (PPACA § 1001) (typically insurers and health plans have ended dependent coverage at 18 or upon completion of higher education), the development and use of uniform explanation of coverage documents and standardized definitions (PHSA § 2715), and mandatory reporting on health care quality measures identified by the Secretary of HHS (PHSA § 2717).

A notable feature of the ACA is that it fails to create an express federal right of action to enforce the federal guaranty of individual coverage created under the Act. Certain insurance arrangements such as ERISA and Medicare contain express enforcement rights, as you will learn. But how about protections for the people who become newly entitled to individual coverage through state health insurance Exchanges? What if a state Exchange turns away an applicant because she fails to satisfy state residency tests or because her income is too low? What if her policy excludes family planning coverage even though federal law says that all individual policies sold in state Exchanges must cover family planning? What if her coverage is terminated for erroneous reasons? What are her remedies? While the ACA creates a new appeals process for plan denials involving the medical necessity of care (more about this later), these types of situations transcend a ''simple'' medical necessity case and instead involve the wholesale denial of coverage, ostensibly on legal grounds.

You will learn that under ERISA, participants and beneficiaries have an express federal right of action to enforce benefits that are due to them under the terms of their plan. Similarly, Medicare beneficiaries have an express right of action under the Social Security Act to enforce their right to coverage. But the ACA creates no parallel express set of federal enforcement rights for people whose benefits are secured through the individual Exchange market. The absence of federal enforcement rights for people covered through the individual market previously has arisen in the context of the protections added to the Public Health Service Act under HIPAA. In these situations, federal courts have refused to infer a federal right of action under the Public Health Service Act, ruling instead that people have only those remedies granted under state law. *See* O'Donnell v. Blue Cross Blue Shield of Wyoming, 173 F. Supp.2d 1176 (D. Wyo. 2001); Means v. Independent Life and Accident Ins. Co., 963 F.Supp. 1131 (M.D. Ala. 1997); Brock v. Provident America Ins. Co., 144 F. Supp.2d 652 (N.D. Tex. 2001); Acara v. Banks, 470 F.3d 569 (5th Cir. 2006).

As you will read later in Part Two, once upon a time, the courts might have recognized an implied cause of action arising under the Supremacy Clause to enforce federal protections against states whose laws fail to comply with federal requirements (e.g., the state refuses to follow the ACA's federal family planning coverage requirements under its own insurance code governing the individual and small group markets). The earlier HIPAA cases, coupled with recent developments in Medicaid (which raises similar issues), suggest that the days of inferring individual federal enforcement rights are over, particularly in laws such as Medicaid and the Public Health Service Act's insurance reform provisions, which give federal enforcement rights to the Secretary of HHS. We address this issue much more in Chapter 11 below. So could a state effectively nullify a provision of the ACA (such as coverage of comprehensive contraceptive services) simply by excluding coverage from its Exchange policies and then barring private state law enforcement actions to challenge policy limits that fail to meet federal or state standards?

Coverage for preventive services and essential health benefits. The Act requires all health plans sold or offered in the individual and group markets to cover certain preventive health services recommended by the U. S. Preventive Services Task Force, the Advisory Committee on Immunization Practice, and (in the case of women's and children's health), the Health Resources and Services Administration of the United States Department of Health and Human Services (PHSA § 2713). Interim final rules published in 2010, 75 Fed. Reg. 41,726 (July 19) and supplemented in 2011, 76 Fed. Reg. 46,621 (Aug. 3, 2011), define contraceptive benefits as one of the preventive services that must be covered without cost-sharing. As noted in Part One, this coverage definition has generated significant controversy.

In addition, the law requires that health plans sold in state-regulated individual- and small-group markets (100 full time employees) cover an "essential health benefits package" consisting of 10 classes of benefits and valued at one of four actuarially set premium tiers, known as the "metals" tiers (bronze, silver, gold, and platinum) with cost-sharing dropping as the premium tier rises. Individuals who receive premium subsidies also would be entitled to cost-sharing reduction assistance if their family incomes are below 250 percent of the federal poverty level. PPACA §§ 1401 and 1402. The value of this assistance will, at the silver tier level, give health plans an actuarial value of about 70 percent of the cost of covered services, a value well below many employer-sponsored plans.

In December 2011, following an Institute of Medicine report recommending a broadly preemptive approach to the state-regulated insurance market, the United States Department of Health and Human Services, in its initial policy steps toward implementation of the essential health benefits statute, chose essentially the opposite approach. In so doing, the Secretary essentially relinquished her own arguably broad discretion under PPACA § 1302 to define the parameters of an essential health benefit package in detail and instead ceded regulatory primacy to the states.

The IOM had argued for a broadly preemptive approach that would have displaced state insurance law benefit mandates (even when falling within an essential benefit class) in favor of federal guidelines vesting broad power in insurers themselves to define the extent and limitations of coverage in relation to a tightly managed premium price increase model. INSTITUTE OF MEDICINE, ESSENTIAL HEALTH BENEFITS: BALANCING COVERAGE AND COSTS (2011), http://www.iom.edu/Reports/2011/Essential–Health–Benefits–Balancing–Coverage-and-Cost.aspx. In other words, the IOM essentially recommended giving insurers selling products in the state-regulated individual and small group insurance markets the type of power to override state law that is now held only by third-party administrators for self-insured ERISA health plans, which you will learn about in Chapter 8.

Taking the opposite approach, and one that arguably is more consistent with the state-based nature of insurance regulation that characterizes the individual- and small-group markets under both current law and the ACA, the HHS policy issued in December 2011 vests broad discretion in states to both define and limit the range and scope of essential health benefits. The policy proposes to allow states to define the scope of the 10 classes of required benefits in relation to a state-selected benchmark (the most popular plans sold in the small-group market, the state-employee-group market, the federal employee health benefit plan market, or the most popular HMO product). In the case of required essential health benefit classes not typically covered in group products (such as habilitation services for children and adults with developmental disabilities, which, as you will learn in Chapter 8, frequently are excluded from group plans, even good ones), states are expected to develop coverage standards for any excluded essential health benefit coverage class by referencing other group insurance plans that do offer such coverage. United States Department of Health and Human Services, CCIIO, Essential Health Benefits Bulletin (Dec. 16, 2011), http://cciio.cms.gov/resources/files/Files2/12162011/essential_health_benefits_bulletin.pdf. The HHS policy thus assigns lead responsibility over insurance benefit design in the individual- and small-group markets to the states, under broad federal direction, thereby leaving these markets without a nationally uniform approach to what constitutes coverage. This is probably a not-too-surprising result given the fundamentally state-oriented nature of the Affordable Care Act itself, but a disappointment to some policy analysts and the health insurance industry, which long has sought national uniformity and state law preemption.

Was the Secretary's decision to cede the power to define coverage itself to the states a wise one? *See, e.g.*, Jennifer Prah Ruger, *Fair Enough? Inviting Inequities in State Health Benefits*, NEW ENG. J. MED. [Online First, Feb. 8, 2012], http://www.nejm.org/doi/full/10.1056/NEJMp1200751 (arguing that by giving states the flexibility to define what is an essential health benefit by referencing models already approved for sale or in use in the state, the HHS Secretary has allowed the perpetuation of inequities across the states and encouraged states to engage in discrimination against people with costly and rare diseases and conditions by permitting products that limit coverage of high-cost treatments and procedures). By contrast, state health policy expert Alan Weil argues in *The Value of Federalism in Defining Essential Health Benefits*, NEW ENG. J. MED. [Online First, February 8, 2012], http://www.nejm.org/doi/full/10.1056/NEJMp1200693, that an approach which offers states flexibility in coverage options not only makes political sense given the complexity of the implementation process but also allows states to act as laboratories, testing the capacity of the new Exchange insurance market through variable approaches to coverage. Weil argues for deference to states even in the case of a benefit such as "habilitative" services, where insurers and state regulatory insurance agencies lack a tradition of understanding and defining such a benefit (payment for which is pretty much limited to Medicaid as a result of its unusually broad coverage parameters). In its December 16 Bulletin, HHS notes that it plans to monitor state approaches to defining essential health benefits. Put yourself in the Secretary's shoes. Under what circumstances might you decide—and after how many years of monitoring—that it is time to create at least minimal federal definitions of what it means to be insured ?

The decision by HHS to allow states to define essential health benefits also met with objections from some Members of Congress. On February 6, 2012, seven House Members wrote to Secretary Sebelius that in enacting the law, it was their intent that the decision as to the meaning of coverage be a federal one, in order to protect consumers and patients from discriminatory insurer practices and to assure that coverage would be transparent and understandable. The members pointed out that by allowing states to turn to their own state-regulated small-group markets for a definition of essential health benefits, the HHS policy invited "very lean" coverage, with "restrictive amount, duration, and scope limitations":

> For example, small group plans are not required to meet state benefit mandates in many states and have not had to meet mental health parity or other insurance requirements. A recent GAO report found that 34% of employers surveyed exclude at least one broad mental health condition or substance use disorder from their covered benefits. Furthermore, many state laws require parity only for coverage of treatment for certain mental health conditions (serious or biologically based conditions). [I]f a state selects one of these small group plans as the EHB benchmark, individuals could have less than adequate coverage for mental illness and substance abuse disorders, or other illnesses that affect them.

Letter from Members of Congress to the Honorable Kathleen Sebelius, Feb. 6, 2012.

Later in Part Two, you will learn that mental health parity represents one of the few examples of Congressional action to stop insurers' use of terms of coverage to discriminate against persons with mental illness. The 2008 federal mental health parity amendments, which broadly extended the meaning of parity, also exempted employers of fewer than 50 employees. While the Affordable Care Act applies the mental health parity statute to the new Exchange market (PPACA § 1311), it specifies that parity would apply "in the same manner and to the same extent" as the law already applied to insurers and group health plans. If Congress was so concerned about equal treatment for persons with mental illness and addiction disorders, why did it include such a major exemption for employers of fewer than 50 employees to the federal parity act, and why did it allow the exemption apparently to continue in Exchanges? Does protection of small businesses require allowing them to discrimination against persons with mental illness and addiction disorders?

Regarding abortion, federal law as revised by the Affordable Care Act is anything but deferential to state policy. For health insurance products (known as qualified health plans) sold in state Exchanges, special abortion coverage restrictions will apply, barring the use of federal premium subsidies to defray the cost of nearly all abortion coverage other than abortions related to rape, incest, or physical conditions that threaten the life of the mother. PPACA § 1303. Health plans may offer coverage that includes all abortion procedures but, as noted in Part One, only if they comply with complex requirements to segregate individual premiums paid for this additional level of coverage from the federally subsidized premiums; as noted, states may bar the sale of products covering abortion altogether.

The Act establishes a new federal standard related to insurance coverage and participation in clinical trials. Under the law, all individual and group plans would be barred from denying payment for routine health care and otherwise covered health care treatments and services that otherwise would be covered for patients not participating in a clinical trial. PHSA § 2709. This new standard parallels earlier Medicare reforms introduced through administrative policy in 2006, whose purpose was to incentivize participation in clinical trials by beneficiaries.

The Act requires plans to report to the HHS Secretary on their "medical loss ratios" (that is, the ratio of medical claims paid to total insurer costs) so that the Secretary may identify plans that do not return a statutorily set minimum value to individual and group policyholders (85 percent in the large-group market and 80 percent in the individual- and small-group markets). PHSA § 2718. The Act also strengthens existing internal and external appeals processes available to all ERISA plan participants and beneficiaries (reviewed later in this Part) and requires states to maintain appeals processes meeting minimum federal requirements for state-regulated plans. (PHSA § 2719). As of the summer of 2011, two rounds of interim final rules implementing the appeals reforms had been issued. 76 Fed. Reg. 37,208 (June 24, 2011). In addition, the Act establishes certain patient protections applicable to all health plans: coverage of emergency hospital services; and direct access, without prior authorization, to obstetrical providers participating in plan networks. PHSA § 2719A.

State health insurance Exchanges: The Act establishes state health insurance Exchanges, whose purpose is to act as purchasing markets for individuals who are lawfully present in the U.S. and not incarcerated, as well as in small-employer groups, defined as employers with 100 or fewer full-time employees. (Beginning in 2017, states may open their Exchanges to larger employer groups). States can elect to establish an Exchange or can opt to have HHS establish and operate a federal Exchange for individuals and small businesses (known as SHOP Exchanges). PPACA § 1311. States that elect to establish an Exchange can do so either as public agencies or as private non-profit corporations subject to state oversight. Exchanges operating under state law are subject to federal standards, but funding to operate Exchanges after their initial creation period must be generated by the Exchanges themselves. *Id.*

Under the law, the central role of Exchanges is to create an active and stable market for the sale of individual and small group products by "qualified health plans" (PPACA § 1301) (QHPs) that meet federal standards for coverage, quality, accessible provider networks that include "essential community providers," and other matters. (PPACA § 1311). In carrying out this role, Exchanges are required to certify "qualified health plans" (either all such plans or selectively based on price and quality) that meet federal and state standards (including, at state option, coverage of additional state-mandated benefits beyond those falling within federal essential health benefit requirements). Exchanges are also required to rate health plans on quality and performance, provide accessible information through special websites and facilitate plan enrollment for both individuals and employer groups. Exchanges also must facilitate eligibility determinations for premium tax credits and cost-sharing assistance and coordinate enrollment procedures with state Medicaid agencies, since tax credits and cost sharing assistance are available only to individuals who are ineligible for Medicaid. PPACA §§ 1311 and 1401.

Without eliminating anything that has come before, health insurance Exchanges effectively superimpose a new, subsidized health insurance market on states' pre-existing markets for public and private health insurance. The purpose of Exchanges, combined with the individual and group market reforms, is essentially to stabilize employer benefits in the small-group market while creating a stable fourth stool leg as it were, so that people without employer benefits, Medicare, and Medicaid can secure affordable coverage of relatively decent scope and quality. In creating a brand new insurance market, a number of different issues can arise.

One potential issue is risk selection—aka cream-skimming—against Exchanges. A principal concern is that insurers will seek to manipulate their highest individual- and small-group risk populations into the subsidized Exchange market while selling cut-rate products to lower-cost populations outside the Exchange. The Act contains certain protections to minimize this risk, which would leave Exchanges burdened by the worst health risks and subject to failure as stable insurance markets for affordable coverage for millions of people. As noted, all insurers selling in the individual- and small-group markets must offer plans that not only cover certain essential health benefits but also have an actuarial value satisfying minimum standards specified under the law (ranging from a high of 90 percent of the full actuarial value for covered benefits in the case of the most expensive "platinum" plans down to 60 percent in the case of the least costly bronze plans). Furthermore, the ability to engage in discriminatory pricing is limited, pre-existing condition exclusions are barred, and other protections designed to avert risk avoidance are included. Similarly, federal medical loss ratio standards apply to all plans, not just those sold in Exchanges. Jost, *Health Insurance Exchanges and the Affordable Care Act: Eight Difficult Issues.* An additional protection under the law is the fact that premium tax credits and cost sharing assistance (as well as special assistance for small employers with 25 or fewer employees) can be secured only for products purchased through Exchanges. While individuals who use Exchanges are expected to be disproportionately lower income with higher health risks, the Exchange population is also expected to include millions of young healthy workers with relatively low wages. Benjamin Sommers & Sara Rosenbaum, *Issues in Health Reform: How Changes in Eligibility May Move Millions Back and Forth Between Medicaid and Insurance Exchanges*, 30(2) HEALTH AFFAIRS 228 (2011); *A Profile of Health Insurance Exchange Enrollees*, KAISER FAMILY FOUNDATION (2011), http://www.kff.org/health reform/upload/8147.pdf.

A second concern is whether employers will drop group coverage in favor of sending employees into their state Exchanges to purchase coverage on a subsidized individual basis. Professor Amy Monahan argues that the Act creates incentives for larger employers, not subject to essential benefit requirements, to design their plans not to appeal to older sicker workers, thereby encouraging those workers to purchase coverage through exchanges. Amy Monahan & Daniel Schwarz, *Will Employers Undermine Health Care Reform by Dumping Sick Employees?*, 97 VA. L. REV. 125 (2011). However the law was amended in 2011 to eliminate a special and narrow "employee free choice" voucher program, which would have permitted certain employees to obtain vouchers from their employers to purchase an alternative product through their state Exchange. Pub. L. No. 112–10 § 1858, 125 Stat. 38, 168–70 (2011). With these vouchers repealed, the crossover of employees would be difficult, since tax credits would be unavailable to them if their employers contribute to the cost of coverage. Thus, while older sicker workers could elect to purchase their minimum essential coverage through an Exchange, they would have to do so on an unsubsidized basis, an unlikely outcome.

There is, however, nothing in the law (or in prior law) that requires an employer to continue to offer a group health plan, and there is much speculation as to whether the establishment of Exchanges will hasten employers' exit from the health insurance business. An Exchange, after all, makes reasonable products available, with tax subsidies for low- and moderate-income workers. One check against this result is that ending employer-sponsored plans featuring employer contributions would end the generous funding for health insurance enjoyed by highly compensated workers, for whom the Internal Revenue Code's tax exclusion is particularly beneficial. Of course, this would not be a check in the case of employers whose workforce is comprised of low-wage workers and who might establish different compensation schemes for highly skilled and highly compensated employees. The elimination of employer-sponsored benefits does not appear to have happened in Massachusetts, which enacted universal coverage in 2006. Sharon Long & Karen Stockley, *Massachusetts Health Reform: Employer Coverage from Employees' Perspective*, 28(6) HEALTH AFFAIRS (Web Exclusive) w1079 (2009). But it is unclear whether the behavior of Massachusetts employers mirrors that of employers elsewhere, or whether, over the long term, Massachusetts employers will elect to pull out of the health plan business. Much may depend on the strength and attraction of state Exchanges. If viewed as attractive places to buy good quality coverage from a lot of participating plans familiar to employees, the Exchanges may offer real competition to what clearly is a problematic employer-sponsored system. By contrast, if seen as mainly catering to lower income, higher risk people without any form of coverage, Exchanges may lapse into something akin to a high risk pool for people unable to secure coverage through work or in the individual non-subsidized market. (In its cost estimates accompanying the final legislation, CBO estimated virtually no movement away from the employer market over the ten-year window used to calculate costs).

A third issue arising from state Exchanges is their relationship with Medicaid programs. Because the two coverage arrangements are divided literally by pennies (family income is either over or under the Medicaid eligibility cutoff) there exists considerable potential for frequent movement between the two coverage systems as a result of even slight fluctuations in family income. Exchanges are obligated to determine eligibility and enroll individuals in the form of assistance for which they qualify, whether Medicaid or premium tax credits. PPACA § 1311. At the same time, individuals, once determined eligible for Medicaid, are barred from enrolling in an Exchange-participating qualified health plan unless the plan also participates in the Medicaid program. If their incomes rise, the same individuals would be disqualified from Medicaid and would be obligated to re-enroll through the Exchange for a tax subsidy and membership in a qualified health plan. A high proportion of low-income individuals and families are subject to this risk of "churning," that is, moving from one system to the other; as noted, over the course of a year, 50 percent of all adults with family incomes under twice the federal poverty level can be expected to experience this change according to one study. Sommers & Rosenbaum, *Issues in Health Reform*. Similar patterns of enrolling, disenrolling and re-enrolling have occurred under the State Childrens Health Insurance Program ("SCHIP"), a joint federal-state health insurance program for low-income children. Stabilizing coverage for low income families is particularly important because of the link, as a result of managed care, between one's source of coverage and access to health care itself.

Public Insurance

Medicaid reforms. The centerpiece of the Medicaid reforms contained in the ACA is the extension of coverage on a mandatory basis, effective January 1, 2014, to all citizens and legally present persons with family incomes under 133 percent of the federal poverty level. PPACA § 2001. However, in the case of persons who are not citizens but are legally present in the country, federal Medicaid law imposes a five-year waiting period before Medicaid coverage can begin. During this waiting period, individuals are entitled to receive premium tax credits and thus subsidized coverage through a state Exchange. As the *quid pro quo* for this mandatory extension of coverage, the federal government, which on average funds about 58 percent of all state Medicaid expenditures, will pay 100 percent of the costs associated with the expansion population over the first two years of implementation, gradually declining to 90 percent in later years.

Medicare reforms. The Act does not fundamentally alter Medicare, retaining its structure and benefit design. The scope of preventive services is expanded (PPACA § 4003), Part D outpatient prescription drug premiums are newly tied to an income-based test as is now the case for Part B (PPACA § 3308), the payroll tax that supports Part A is increased for high-wage earners (PPACA § 9015), and the Part D prescription drug cost-sharing formula is adjusted downward, thereby reducing point-of-sale co-payments. (Health Care and Education Reconciliation Act of 2010 (HCERA), Pub. L. No. 111–152 § 1101). In addition, the Act reduces payments to Medicare Advantage plans and imposed an 85 percent medical loss ratio on them. HCERA § 1103.

* * *

Professor Baker observes that the Affordable Care Act transforms the distribution of health care costs, away from individuals and toward a broader population-based design. Medicare will continue to bear the risk of health care costs associated with aging and disability, other than long-term care, which is the purview of Medicaid. For the poorest Americans, Medicaid will continue to bear the primary responsibility for health care costs, given the poor's limited access to employer-sponsored benefits. Health care risks among workers and their families will be borne by employers and employees in the case of employers offering health plans. State health insurance Exchanges will be the locus of risk for populations (predominantly lower income working age individuals) unaffiliated with any of the first three risk pools.

In Professor Baker's view, the expansion of Medicaid, the reforms of the insurance market coupled with the establishment of a stable population-wide risk pool as a result of the mandate, and the creation of a stable, subsidized market for insurance for persons without access to membership in one of the other major coverage groups, collectively establish the Act as a significant (although not complete) rejection of the concept of actuarial fairness and individual risk in favor of a greater level of risk solidarity reflecting the experiences of other wealthy nations. Tom Baker, *Health Insurance, Risk and Responsibility* at 1600–07.

Actuarial fairness principles—adjusting the cost of health insurance to reflect the risks of the insured—do remain to some degree, and they take a number of forms. Baker, *Health Insurance Risk and Responsibility*. For example, the law allows modified community-rating practices that permit age adjustment, as well as the charging of higher rates for tobacco use (1.5:1). Actuarial fairness principles also can be seen in the law's wellness incentives, which allow employers that sponsor approved wellness programs to sanction employees, through higher premiums, for poor performance or outcomes. PHSA § 2705. Actuarial fairness can be seen in the design of "qualified health plans" (QHPs) sold in state Exchanges, whose relatively low actuarial value at the "silver" level (for which premium tax credits are available) will leave members with significant deductibles and coinsurance obligations that will be only partially offset through cost-sharing assistance. The emphasis on expanded coverage of preventive services also can be read as a strong encouragement for individuals to adopt better health practices, a continuing philosophy that individuals control their health. Furthermore, the preservation and expansion of Medicaid represents a decisive (and controversial) decision to maintain the poorest Americans in a separate pool whose benefits are rich but exists in isolation from other payers, and contributes to the health care segregation of the poor through low provider payment rates.

The biggest challenges to implementation and continuing political and economic stability may be overcoming the Act's failure to address costs in a comprehensive way, and its counterpart, the fact that insurance will remain practically, if not legally, unaffordable for many. Financial assistance for low- and moderate-income Americans is relatively modest; limited subsidies (constrained by limits on how much Congress and the President were willing to spend) mean that the price reductions offered through health insurance Exchanges may not be generous enough to make coverage affordable. As a result, many may elect simply to pay the relatively weak tax penalty that will be due if "affordable" coverage (a figure that under the law amounts to 8 percent of family income) is not secured.

Regarding cost controls, the law is bereft of teeth other than some provider rate cuts in the case of Medicare, aspirational efforts to achieve quality and efficiency without a true enforcement mechanism, and federal and state insurance rate-review activities that depend on states to stop unwarranted rate increases, a power that only some state legislatures give their insurance commissioners. In the beginning of the legislative process, Dr. Peter Orzag, former CBO Director and head of President Obama's Office of Management and Budget, was virtually everywhere, in every major political forum and on every talk show that would have him, exhorting the importance of legislation that would contain costs. The final law contains no comprehensive and decisive approach to cost containment, adopting instead an approach consisting of a blizzard of payment and organizational efficiency pilots and demonstrations, references to "value-based" purchasing and the ever-popular quest for "quality and efficiency," solemn pledges by researchers to find out "what works," and expanded scrutiny of insurers' premium rate increases. Recounting all of the ways in which the rhetoric of cost control culminated in legislation with no real cost control capabilities, political scientist Jonathan Oberlander argues that despite the law's mushiness, the Affordable Care Act may mark a watershed—ironically by its very deluge of seemingly disconnected provisions—in the politics of cost control, easing the way for future and more meaningful efforts in both the public and private sectors. Jonathan Oberlander, *Throwing Darts: Americans' Elusive Search for Health Care Cost Control*, 36 J. HEALTH POL. POL'Y & L. 477 (2011). Alternatively, the whole thing could, at some future date, crash and burn as it generates increased demand for health services, without concomitant controls, thereby fueling a greater expenditure crisis than we already have. We shall see.

CHAPTER 7

DEFINING INSURER OBLIGATIONS AND REMEDIES UNDER STATE LAW

---

1. REMEDIES FOR BAD FAITH BREACH OF CONTRACT IN DENYING COVERAGE

Albert H. Wohlers & Co. v. Bartgis

969 P.2d 949 (Nev. 1998)

■ PER CURIAM:

This is a case involving fraud, bad faith, and violations of the Nevada Unfair Claims Practices Act by a medical insurance company and its policy administrator. Bartgis is a court reporter who has been a member of the National Shorthand Reporters Association (NSRA) since 1973 [through whom she obtained insurance]. The medical insurance policies offered by NSRA to its members were underwritten by Mutual of New York (MONY), and were administered by Wohlers.

On September 24, 1990, MONY informed Wohlers by letter that it planned to increase the cost of premiums by fifty-five percent effective November 15, 1990. Wohlers contacted several other major medical insurance underwriters [including Allianz Life Insurance Company of North America (Allianz)] in an attempt to secure a medical insurance policy for NSRA before MONY's premium hike went into effect.

During their November 1990 negotiations, Wohlers and Allianz agreed to insert a new cost limitation on ancillary charges into the NSRA policy. Significantly, this "ancillary charges" cost limitation provision had not been included as a provision in NSRA's prior policy with MONY. Allianz's policy with NSRA defined the term "ancillary charges" as "a service or supply that is furnished by a Hospital or Extended Care Facility when a Member or Insured Dependent is Confined."

The maximum benefit for ancillary charges under the Allianz policy applied to a patient's confinement in a hospital and was computed as "the Daily Room Rate [multiplied by] the number of days of confinement [multiplied by] 2." Hospital confinement, for purposes of the Allianz policy, was defined as "confinement as a Registered Bed–Patient in a Hospital upon the advice of a Physician for a period of twenty-four (24) hours or longer and such confinement is for purposes other than convalescence or rehabilitation."

In November 1990, Wohlers informed Bartgis by letter that Allianz would now serve as her medical insurance policy underwriter because MONY had planned to raise its premiums by an unacceptable fifty-five percent. In its letter, Wohlers stated that Allianz had agreed to "continue this coverage offering comparable benefits without an increase in premiums," effective November 15, 1990. The letter specified that premiums were guaranteed until February 15, 1991, and assured plan participants that the "new NSRA plan [had] been carefully designed to [provide] the needed health care insurance protection at an affordable price."

Wohlers concluded its letter by encouraging all plan participants to compare the prior MONY policy benefits and coverage with those of the new Allianz policy. The policy outlines included information about deductibles and maximum coverage under the old MONY policy and the new Allianz policy. Under the new policy, Allianz would pay eighty percent of Bartgis' allowable hospital expenses up to $5,000.00. After expenses reached that amount, Allianz would pay one hundred percent. Significantly, the policy outlines did not notify plan participants of the new "ancillary charges" cost limitation provision that had been inserted into the Allianz policy, nor did the comparison outlines mention the provision or explain its intended effect.

Bartgis read both the letter and policy outlines in order to determine what changes had been made to her coverage. After comparing the details on the outlines, she concluded that the Allianz policy provided better coverage than her previous MONY policy. Bartgis did not read anything indicating limitations on ancillary charges.

On December 11, 1990, Allianz and Wohlers reviewed and accepted a final draft of the policy that contained the ancillary charges limitation provision. In January 1991, Wohlers sent a second letter to all NSRA members explaining the change of underwriters and providing policyholders with an insurance certificate. Bartgis read the letter, which again made no mention of the new ancillary charges limitation provision. Although the new ancillary charges limitation provision was noted in the policy certificate, there was no accompanying explanation that this provision represented a significant deviation in benefits when compared to NSRA's previous policy with MONY.

In 1991, Bartgis was diagnosed with pre-cancerous cells in her reproductive organs [and filed claims under the Allianz policy for a biopsy and an emergency room visit which, because they did not involve hospital stays beyond 24 hours, were reimbursed at the usual percentages]. Bartgis decided, per the recommendation of her physician, to undergo a total hysterectomy. She then perused the Allianz policy in order to determine the applicable coverage rate for the procedure. Her policy listed the procedure as an "elective" procedure, which meant that she would have to pay an additional $200.00 toward her deductible. Bartgis followed the pre-certification procedures required under the policy and obtained certification for a twenty-four hour stay. Based on her understanding of the policy,

Bartgis believed that she would only incur an additional $500.00 charge in the event that her hospitalization exceeded twenty-four hours.

The surgery was performed on December 29, 1992. As before, Bartgis assumed that Allianz would pay eighty percent of her medical expenses up to $5,000.00, and one hundred percent thereafter. Although Bartgis had only obtained certification for a twenty-four hour stay, she was hospitalized for approximately twenty-seven hours, including check-in and check-out time.

On Saturday, January 23, 1993, Bartgis received an explanation of covered expenses from Wohlers. Several of the itemized charges were covered by Allianz at the percentages and rates outlined in the November 1990 letter from Wohlers. However, the majority of the bill—$9328.75— was listed under a lump-sum charge of which Allianz covered only $930.00. The corresponding explanation code on the document identified the $9,328.75 as "ancillary charges." The detailed listing of charges from the hospital also revealed that Allianz had deemed all medical expenses beyond basic room and board as "ancillary charges."

Thus, Allianz categorized the expenses for Bartgis' operating room ($2,708.98), recovery room ($390.60), sutures and staples ($2,286.63), heart monitor ($103.80), anesthesia and anesthesia system ($401.70), and numerous other charges, as "ancillary" for coverage purposes. Accordingly, Allianz agreed to cover only ten percent of these "ancillary" medical expenses.

Upon receipt of the letter, Bartgis became extremely upset and frustrated. On Monday, January 25, 1993, Bartgis contacted Wohlers for an explanation as to why Allianz would only cover ten percent of the major medical expenses listed on her hospital bill. Delores Pricener, a Wohlers representative, explained that because Bartgis' hospitalization had exceeded twenty-four hours, Bartgis was classified as an in-patient and that such classification triggered the ancillary charges limitation provision in her policy. Pricener explained that when the ancillary charges limitation was in effect, essentially all charges from the hospital except for basic room and board were subject to the ancillary charges limitation provision contained in Bartgis' policy.

Bartgis then sought the assistance of her friend and attorney, Margaret Maines.

Distraught, Bartgis attempted to obtain a major medical insurance plan through another carrier but was unsuccessful because of her preexisting medical condition. Throughout this period, Bartgis became further upset, losing sleep and her appetite. During the following three months, she developed two bladder infections and an upper-respiratory infection, suffered dramatic weight loss, and felt "generally terrible."

On July 15, 1993, Bartgis filed a civil complaint against Allianz and Wohlers alleging breach of contract, fraud, bad faith, and violations of the Nevada Unfair Claims Practices Act. Bartgis sought both compensatory and punitive damages. At trial, the jury returned a verdict in favor of Bartgis and against Allianz and Wohlers on all claims: (1) $8,757.75 in contract damages; (2) $275,000.00 in non-economic compensatory damages for emotional distress; and (3) that both Allianz and Wohlers were subject to punitive damages. Following the punitive damage phase of the trial, the jury assessed exemplary damages in the amounts of $500,000.00 and $7,500,000.00 against Wohlers and Allianz respectively.

Allianz first contends that there is insufficient evidence to support the jury's finding of bad faith because it had reasonable grounds upon which to deny making full payment on Bartgis' claim. Specifically, Allianz asserts that based on the language of the ancillary charges limitation provision, a genuine issue existed as to its obligation under Bartgis' policy which, in turn, obviates its bad faith liability for failure to pay Bartgis' claim.[1] We disagree.

It is well settled in Nevada that "every contract imposes upon the contracting parties the duty of good faith and fair dealing." In Sparks v. Republic National Life Insurance Co., 647 P.2d 1127, 1137 (Ariz. 1982), the Arizona Supreme Court held:

> We disagree with the [insurance company's] contention that an insurer's belief that a portion of its insurance contract precludes coverage raises an absolute defense to a claim of bad faith. If the insurer's interpretation of its own contract as excluding coverage could render an insured's claim "fairly debatable," then insurers would be encouraged to write ambiguous insurance contracts, secure in the knowledge that an obscure portion of the policy would provide an absolute defense to a claim of bad faith.

In similar fashion, we reject Allianz's assertion that its interpretation of the ancillary charges limitation provision in Bartgis' policy provided reasonable grounds upon which to deny Bartgis' claim, thereby sheltering it from bad faith liability. Specifically, the jury heard evidence of the November 1990 letter from Wohlers to Bartgis, which had been pre-approved by Allianz, that made no mention of the harsh ancillary charges limitation provision. Further, the evidence adduced at trial established that in the same letter, Allianz and Wohlers made the significant misrepresentation that the new Allianz policy contained comparable benefits with Bartgis' previous MONY policy, a policy which did not contain the ancillary charges limitation provision. Additionally, the jury heard evidence that the defendants continued to conceal the ancillary charges limitation provision in subsequent communications to Bartgis. Finally, the evidence presented at

---

1. Allianz and Wohlers make two other challenges to Bartgis' favorable bad faith verdict. First, they contend that the jury's bad faith and fraud verdicts are "fatally inconsistent" because if they had fraudulently misrepresented the amount of coverage under the policy by informing Bartgis that the policy afforded more coverage than in fact it did, then they could not be held liable for bad faith failure to pay a claim. We reject this argument. It is preposterous to suggest that an insurer's fraudulent acts could, in turn, insulate it from bad faith liability and vice versa. Rather, from the evidence adduced at trial, the jury could have found that appellants'/ cross-respondents' fraudulent actions constituted a breach of the duty of good faith and fair dealing, thereby exposing them to bad faith liability.

trial established that by way of Allianz's and Wohlers's tortured interpretation of the arcane ancillary charges limitation provision, Bartgis' policy—which Allianz and Wohlers had ostensibly represented as a comprehensive major medical insurance policy—covered only hospital room and board. By interpreting the policy in a manner that denied coverage for all medically necessary procedures and expenses such as the operating and recovery room expenses, anesthesia, all medications, sutures, and roughly ninety percent of Bartgis' hospital bill, Allianz and Wohlers deprived Bartgis of the peace of mind and security for which she had bargained.

Based on these facts, we conclude that Allianz's failure to inform Bartgis of the significant reduction in coverage, its representation that coverage under the two policies was comparable, its absurd interpretation of the ancillary charges limitation provision, and its denial of Bartgis' claim pursuant to that provision, were unreasonable. Accordingly, we conclude that the jury's finding of bad faith is supported by substantial evidence.

Notes

1. *The significance of a cause of action for bad faith.* Under ordinary contractual principles, doesn't Bartgis have a duty of due diligence to protect herself? Why did the court not apply that rule to the facts of this case? The more usual fact pattern in which an insurer is liable for bad faith breach of contract involves its unreasonable interpretation of its insurance contract. An insurer might insist that the contract excludes coverage while it clearly includes coverage. Did Allianz or Wohlers misinterpret the contract they executed? The *Wohlers* court reasoned that the situation before it was analogous to an earlier decision that good faith interpretation of ambiguity in a contract is not an absolute defense to a bad faith claim because insurers will then have incentives to write ambiguous language to forestall potential bad faith liability. What was it that Wholers and Allianz did in order to be liable for bad faith? What do your answers to these questions tell you about the manner in which state law applies ordinary contractual principles to the relationship between an insurer and the insured covered under their contract? What are the reasons for such holdings that effectively have a sentinel effect?

2. *Should state law allow such deficient contracts to begin with?* The insurance contract sold to Ms. Bartgis and other stenographers was lawful under state law. What made the conduct unlawful here was the concealment techniques used by Allianz and Wohlers to shield the shift in the policy. Should the state ever have permitted insurers to sell a product that appears to cover inpatient care but in fact does not? Thinking back to the Introduction to Part Two, and imagining a debate within the state's Department of Insurance about allowing such policies, what defense of this sort of practice might be offered by a commissioner with a strong market orientation? What position might be taken by a commissioner with a strong orientation toward the social benefit role of insurance?

3. *When is a coverage limitation "disclosed?"* Let's think about disclosure. Assume for a moment that you are Ms. Bartgis and imagine that you received the following letter from Wohlers regarding a change in your coverage under Allianz:

> Under this policy, the term "ancillary charges" means "a service or supply that is furnished by a Hospital or Extended Care Facility when a Member or Insured Dependent is Confined." Beginning in the new coverage year, the maximum benefit for ancillary charges that will be applied to your confinement in a hospital will be computed as "the Daily Room Rate [multiplied by] the number of days of confinement [multiplied by] 2." Hospital confinement, for purposes of this policy is defined as "confinement as a Registered Bed–Patient in a Hospital upon the advice of a Physician for a period of twenty-four (24) hours or longer and such confinement is for purposes other than convalescence or rehabilitation."

Would you have any idea what this means?

4. *Disclosure and the Affordable Care Act.* Note that the coverage limitations were inserted into the "policy," while plan participants were given a "policy outline" that failed to describe the limitations. There is a big difference between getting a summary of what is in a policy (you will see in the ERISA materials that follow that participants and beneficiaries similarly are entitled to a "summary plan description") and understanding how the policy really operates.

Section 2715 of the Public Health Service Act, added by § 1001 of the Affordable Care Act, requires the Secretary to develop standards for use by insurers "in compiling and providing to applicants, enrollees, and policy-holders or certificate holders a summary of benefits and coverage explanation that accurately describes the benefits and coverage under the applicable plan or coverage." Summaries and explanations must include "a description of the coverage, including cost-sharing for each of the categories of essential health benefits and other benefits identified by the Secretary; . . . the exceptions, reductions and limitations on coverage; [and] a statement that the outline is a summary of the policy or certificate and that the coverage document itself should be consulted to determine the governing contractual provisions." PHSA § 2715(b)(3)(A)–(C), and (H). Section 2715 also directs the Secretary to develop standard definitions for "insurance-related" terms and certain medical terms specified in the statute along with other terms that she may identify. Among the statutory terms to be defined are "hospitalization" and "physician services." *Id.* § 2715(g). The term "ancillary services" is not listed.

Imagine that you are on the staff of the Centers for Medicare and Medicaid Services, the agency within HHS with the authority to implement § 2715 and other PHSA provisions related to insurance market reforms. What legal and policy decisions are needed in developing implementing regulations? Should the rules require plain-meaning terminology only in relation to services falling within an essential health benefit class, or should the Secretary use her discretion to require the use of such terminology in connection with any item or service in a coverage policy regardless of its status as an essential health benefit? (Note that the essential health benefit statute, PPACA § 1302, does not list inpatient surgery or medical care as a class of benefit, although it does list "hospitalization.")

The statute further instructs the Secretary to develop "standard definitions." Given the vast sea of coverage documents and insurance policies, how might you go about developing the evidence needed to arrive at a proposed "standard definition"? And since the potential range of insurance and medical terms is almost limitless, what might the federal government propose in the way of more generalized rules of conduct in order to address situations in which no specific standard or definition is contained in the federal rule? How would such a federal rule be enforced? What would be the duties of plan issuers (i.e., insurers) and state Departments of Insurance, who are obligated to carry out state insurance laws in a manner consistent with federal law?

Regulations published on February 14, 2012 (76 Fed. Reg. 8,668–8,706; 76 Fed. Reg. 8,706–8,709) outline final federal standards for the summary of benefits and coverage (SBC) and a uniform glossary for both insurers operating in the individual and group-plan markets as well as self-insured group plans. The regulations specify timing and content standards for provision of the SBC to plans and enrollees. The regulations also specify the minimum content of the SBC, including "uniform definitions of standards insurance terms and medical terms so that consumers may compare health coverage and understand the terms of (or exception to) their coverage, in accordance with guidance specified by the Secretary." 45 C.F.R. § 147.200(a)(2). The explanation must include a "description of the coverage, including cost sharing, for each category of benefits identified by the Secretary in guidance"; the "exceptions, reductions, and limitations of the coverage"; "the cost-sharing provisions of the coverage, including deducible, coinsurance, and copayment obligations; the renewability and continuation of coverage provisions"; and other matters. *Id.* Most interestingly perhaps, the rule requires insurers to include in the SBC certain coverage examples, including pregnancy and serious and chronic medical conditions, as specified by the Secretary, as well as actual benefit scenarios so that an insured person can have a realistic expectation of what will and will not be covered. *Id.*

Of course, there are several obvious limitations here. First, even plain-language documents are difficult to grasp. As noted previously in *Wohlers v Bartgis,* putting into plain language the fact that staying in the hospital more than a minute beyond the contractual maximum leads to a forfeiture of coverage is next to impossible, in part because it is so irrational. Second, it is not possible—even if one had an encyclopedic-length SBC (which sort of defeats the purpose of a "summary")—to offer enough scenarios to do justice to the infinite variety of conditions that patients can experience. Third, of course, disclosing limits and deciding whether limits should be enforced are two very different things. How knowing that cost-sharing can be in the thousands of dollars for a complicated pregnancy helps young couples to plan for a complicated pregnancy is pretty much beyond comprehension, given all of the other things that young couples need to plan for, financially speaking, in anticipation of the birth of their first child. And since families don't go into pregnancy thinking that it's going to be complicated, the orientation toward planning may not be too great to begin with. Disclosure of lousy coverage is important, of course, but will all the disclosure in the world help achieve a system that gives better coverage, uses better cost controls and has means to obtain efficient delivery of health care? Think about all the assumptions that are necessary to suppose that the disclosure will lead to such a system.

5. *Damages relief for insurers that engage in unfair claims practices.* Ordinarily, the remedy for breach of contract is limited to compensatory damages. Many states have adopted laws providing for exemplary damages and attorneys fees for bad faith breach of some contracts, including insurance contracts. *See* Tom Baker, *Constructing the Insurance Relationship: Sales Stories, Claims Stories, and Insurance Contract Damages*, 72 TEX. L. REV. 1395 (1994). Nevada law, in this case the Nevada Unfair Claims Practices Act, allows persons injured by such insurer conduct to sue for economic and noneconomic damages. In other states, as you will read in *Pilot Life*, 481 U.S. 41 (1987), later in this Part, such a remedy may exist at common law.

Consider two very different possible reactions to *Wohlers*. As you are no doubt aware, there is a thriving genre of popular writing and political commentary portraying the creative forces of American society, particularly American business, as being unfairly shackled by wasteful plaintiffs' litigation and grossly inflated jury awards. See, e.g., The American Tort Reform Association, which names Nevada as one of the nation's worst "judicial hell-holes" for defendants. *See* http://www.atra.org/. A proponent of this viewpoint might argue that this was a simple misunderstanding about how a perfectly lawful contract should deal with a $9,000 bill. Once the problem was brought to its attention, the insurer agreed to pay in full. Should the legal system allow a jury to exploit the "deep pockets" of the insurer and insurance administrator on behalf of an emotionally sympathetic plaintiff and award $275,000 in compensatory damages for "emotional distress" and $8 million in punitive damages? (The State Supreme Court later reduced the punitive award to $3.9 million).

The opposing side might argue first, that the state of Nevada could, of course, have stopped this problem from ever happening to begin with by disallowing contracts that permit such outrageous limitations on coverage but chose not to do so (state insurance departments, like regulatory agencies everywhere, tend to be captive of the industry they regulate, and they often lack sufficient resources). For most Americans a $9000 bill is a serious matter, predictably causing serious distress that in turn triggers future medical expenses. If the legal regime only requires that insurance companies pay compensatory damages when claims are unjustly denied, insurers have strong incentives to deny claims, knowing that they can simply pay if challenged. If only compensatory damages are available, most

Americans in this situation will not be able to find a lawyer to represent them in this situation. Many won't even complain in the first place. Exemplary damages provide appropriate incentives to enable insured people, and the contingent-fee lawyers who represent them, to serve as "private attorney generals" to discourage insurers from engaging in deceptive and abusive practices.

2.   RESCISSIONS OF HEALTH INSURANCE COVERAGE

Hailey v. California Physicians Services

69 Cal. Rptr.3d 789 (App. 2007)

■ ARONSON, J.:

Plaintiffs Cindy and Steve Hailey challenge a judgment entered after the trial court granted summary judgment in favor of defendants California Physicians' Service, doing business as Blue Shield of California (Blue Shield) on the Haileys' claims for breach of contract and breach of the covenant of good faith and fair dealing, and awarded $104,194.12 in damages to Blue Shield on its cross-complaint for rescission of the health services contract it had previously agreed to provide the Haileys.

The Haileys contend, inter alia, Health and Safety Code section 1389.3 precludes Blue Shield from rescinding unless it can prove the Haileys willfully misrepresented the condition of Steve's health at the time they applied for coverage. Because evidence of whether the Haileys' misrepresentations were willful presents a triable issue of fact, they contend the trial court erred in granting summary judgment. We conclude section 1389.3 precludes a health services plan from rescinding a contract for a material misrepresentation or omission unless the plan can demonstrate (1) the misrepresentation or omission was willful, or (2) it had made reasonable efforts to ensure the subscriber's application was accurate and complete as part of the precontract underwriting process. Because both of these issues turn on disputed facts, the trial court's summary judgment ruling cannot stand.

Blue Shield is a health care service plan licensed and regulated by the Department of Managed Health Care. To obtain coverage under a Blue Shield individual health contract, applicants must qualify based on their medical and health history. Accordingly, applicants must complete an application requesting specific information regarding their medical history. In signing the application, the applicant attests to the accuracy and completeness of the responses, and acknowledges the plan may revoke coverage if the applicant furnishes false or incomplete information.

Blue Shield underwrites all applicants for individual coverage by reviewing and analyzing the information contained in the applications submitted. An applicant's medical history and current medical conditions are assigned a point value. Some conditions are sufficient by themselves to warrant denial of coverage, while others may prompt a postponement in the process to allow Blue Shield to obtain additional information. Based on the point values, Blue Shield grants coverage, grants coverage at an increased rate, or denies coverage.

When Cindy started a new job in late 2000, she carried health insurance covering her family from a previous employer through COBRA.[3] Although she believed she could have obtained health insurance from her new employer, the new insurance did not cover the family's doctor. Learning Blue Shield would cover her family's physician, she contacted Timothy Patrick, an insurance agent, who sent her an application. According to Cindy, she believed she provided all of the information requested on the application. Nonetheless, she mistakenly believed the form sought information relating only to her health, and not that of her husband, Steve, or their son. Although she noted on the application matters concerning her own health, she omitted any health information regarding her husband or son. She also incorrectly listed Steve's weight as 240 pounds instead of his actual weight of 285 pounds.

Cindy sent the completed application to Patrick, who, after receiving it, asked Cindy some questions regarding her health history, but did not go over any of the application's questions and did not inform her of the application's health questions also applied to Steve and their son. Although Steve signed the application, he did not read it. Based on the information provided in the application, Blue Shield extended coverage to Cindy and her family at its "premier" or best rate beginning December 15, 2000.

In February 2001, Steve was admitted to the hospital for stomach problems. Because of this development, on February 8, 2001, Blue Shield's medical management department referred the Haileys' contract to its "Underwriting Investigation Unit" which "investigates potential fraud by Blue Shield subscribers." In its probe, Blue Shield obtained Steve's medical records, which revealed a history of undisclosed health issues, including obesity, hypertension, difficulty swallowing, and gastroesophageal reflux disease. Based on the information obtained from Steve's medical providers and Blue Shield's underwriting guidelines, Crary [the fraud investigator] determined the Haileys intentionally misrepresented and concealed Steve's medical information.

On March 19, 2001, an automobile accident left Steve completely disabled. He remained hospitalized until May 31, 2001, when he was released and sent home with instructions for additional home nursing care and physical therapy. Before his discharge, Blue Shield authorized healthcare providers to provide surgery, treatment, care, and physical therapy in an amount exceeding $457,000.

On June 1, 2001, Blue Shield sent the Haileys a letter informing them their health insurance coverage had been cancelled retroactively to Decem-

---

3. The Consolidated Omnibus Budget Reconciliation Act of 1985 (COBRA) mandates that certain employees and their dependents be offered the option of paying premiums to continue medical coverage for a limited time period after the termination of coverage under a group health plan. (29 U.S.C. §§ 1161–1167; 42 U.S.C. §§ 300bb–1 through 300bb–8.)

ber 15, 2000, the date Blue Shield issued the policy. Blue Shield based its cancellation on the Haileys' failure to disclose medical information Blue Shield had received from Los Alamitos Medical Center, which disclosed that in October 2000, Steve had been seen "for dysphagia, stricture/stenosis of the esophagus, essential hypertension, and a reported weight of 285 lbs." The letter noted the total amount of claims submitted during the period of February 6, 2001 to May 14, 2001 was $457,163.30. The letter demanded the Haileys pay Blue Shield $60,777.10, the difference between the amount Blue Shield had paid for Steve's medical care, and the premiums the Haileys had paid for their health insurance.

After Blue Shield cancelled the policy, the Haileys could no longer afford nursing care or physical therapy for Steve. In addition, third party medical providers demanded the Haileys pay for medical care previously provided. Blue Shield's rescission of the health care plan contract caused Steve delays in obtaining necessary medical care. Steve subsequently lost the use of his bladder, which he contends is permanently nonfunctional. Steve also asserts the lack of physical therapy has impaired his ability to walk, increased his pain, and resulted in further surgery and medication.

The Haileys sued Blue Shield, alleging in their second amended complaint causes of action for breach of contract, breach of the implied covenant of good faith and fair dealing, and intentional infliction of emotional distress. Blue Shield filed a cross-complaint seeking a declaration it legally rescinded its health care contract with the Haileys and was entitled to recover the money it spent on Steve's medical care before the rescission.

A. *A Triable Issue of Fact Exists Whether the Haileys Willfully Misrepresented Steve's Medical History*

Blue Shield is a health care service plan operating under the Knox–Keene Health Care Service Plan Act (Knox–Keene Act). To prevent providers from shifting the financial risk of health care back to the subscribers, the Legislature in 1993 enacted section 1389.3 as part of the Health Insurance Access and Equity Act. Section 1389.3 provides: "No health care service plan shall engage in the practice of postclaims underwriting. For purposes of this section, 'postclaims underwriting' means the rescinding, canceling, or limiting of a plan contract due to the plan's failure to complete medical underwriting and resolve all reasonable questions arising from written information submitted on or with an application before issuing the plan contract. This section shall not limit a plan's remedies upon a showing of willful misrepresentation."

Although the parties interpret section 1389.3 differently, the import of section 1389.3's last sentence is unmistakable: the provision does not affect a health care service plan's ability to rescind coverage if the subscriber willfully misrepresented his or her health condition in applying for plan coverage. Blue Shield contends the evidence conclusively demonstrates the Haileys willfully misrepresented Steve's medical history, thus providing a basis for upholding the judgment without further analysis. We disagree.

Although Cindy admittedly knew most of Steve's medical history when she filled out the application, she stated in her declaration that she believed the form sought only her health information, and not that of Steve or their son. Cindy's explanation for omission of Steve's information is not patently unbelievable.

For example, Part Two of the application form instructs: "List applicant and all family members you wish to cover." Implicit in this instruction is that Blue Shield did not consider family members as coapplicants for insurance. Part Three of the application, however, requests medical information for "you or any applying family member...." Moreover, the medical information checklist in Part Three did not provide separate questions for each family member, but required the applicant to answer each question as to herself and each family member. The form, although understandable upon close examination and reflection, is no model of clarity, and lends credence to Cindy's explanation of her omission of Steve's health information. [T]he Haileys have demonstrated a triable issue of fact whether they willfully misrepresented Steve's medical history.

Blue Shield asserts this triable issue is immaterial because even if Cindy negligently omitted the information it still had the right to rescind as a matter of law. In testing this assertion in our analysis below, we presume the Haileys' omissions were inadvertent and not willful.

B.   *A Triable Issue of Fact Exists Whether Blue Shield Engaged in Postclaims Underwriting*

1.   The Problem of Postclaims Underwriting

" 'Underwriting' is a label commonly applied to the process, fundamental to the concept of insurance, of deciding which risks to insure and which to reject in order to spread losses over risks in an economically feasible way." (Smith v. State Farm Mutual Automobile Ins. Co., 113 Cal. Rptr.2d 399 (2001). In essence, postclaims underwriting occurs when an insurer " 'wait[s] until a claim has been filed to obtain information and make underwriting decisions which should have been made when the application [for insurance] was made, not after the policy was issued." Thomas Cady and Georgia Gates, *Post Claims Underwriting*, 102 W.Va. L. Rev. 809, 813 (2000).

The harm from postclaims underwriting is manifest. An insurer has an obligation to its insureds to do its underwriting at the time a policy application is made, not after a claim is filed. It is patently unfair for a claimant to obtain a policy, pay his premiums and operate under the assumption that he is insured against a specified risk, only to learn *after* he submits a claim that he is *not* insured, and, therefore, cannot obtain any other policy to cover the loss. The insurer controls when the underwriting occurs. If the insured is not an acceptable risk, the application should [be] denied up front, not after a policy is issued.

In the present case, the record demonstrates Blue Shield conducted an extensive investigation into Steve Hailey's medical history after learning of

Steve's hospitalization for intestinal ailments. In contrast, Blue Shield apparently did little or no investigation into whether the medical information Cindy provided on the application was accurate.

Blue Shield argues that section 1389.3's prohibition on postclaims *underwriting* does not affect its right to perform a postclaims *investigation*. [P]ostclaims investigation and postclaims underwriting involve a common activity: Research into a subscriber's precontract health after a claim is made to determine whether to rescind the plan due to misrepresentations or omissions in the original application. The distinction between postclaims investigation and postclaims underwriting thus lies primarily in the quality of the underwriting process undertaken before the policy is issued.

2. The Plan's Duty Under Section 1389.3 to Make Reasonable Efforts to Ensure the Subscriber's Application Is Accurate and Complete as Part of the Precontract Underwriting Process.

Blue Shield argues section 1389.3 imposes no obligation to investigate the accuracy of a potential subscriber's application, unless questions arise from the answers given. We agree nothing on the Haileys' application raised any questions relating to Steve's health. But can a plan "complete medical underwriting" within the meaning of section 1389.3 by blindly accepting the responses on a subscriber's application without performing any inquiry into whether the responses were the result of mistake or inadvertence? Most people are capable of forgetting facts at the time they apply for insurance, especially if those facts relate to a condition or event in the past which is no longer (and perhaps never was) deemed a problem by the applicant. Given the likelihood of inadvertent error, accurate risk assessment requires a reasonable check on the information the insurer uses to evaluate the risk.

Blue Shield contends health care service plans may complete the "medical underwriting" required under section 1389.3 by simply taking the submitted application and assigning values to the risks disclosed. We are not persuaded the Legislature intended such a narrow construction. The unmistakable purpose of section 1389.3's prohibition on "postclaims underwriting" is to prevent the unexpected cancellation of health care coverage at a time coverage is needed most. Assuming the truth of the Haileys' evidence, the tragic situation in which they now find themselves could have been averted had a Blue Shield agent or underwriter simply asked Cindy if she had included information for her husband and son.

Blue Shield asserts that under the common law and the Civil Code, it is entitled to rescind upon a negligently made misrepresentation. Rescission, however, is an equitable remedy, with certain qualifications that limit its application. The cancellation of a health services contract presents unique challenges to returning the parties to the status quo, or achieving substantial justice. Here, the trial court granted Blue Shield rescission and a monetary award representing the money it expended for health care costs incurred before rescission. Rescission returned Blue Shield to the status quo, but rescission seeks to restore the status quo to *both parties*. The

Haileys assert they could have received coverage under the health plan offered by Cindy's new employer had they been denied coverage under the Blue Shield plan. Under that scenario, the medical costs of Steve's automobile accident would have been covered. The trial court's rescission order, however, failed to return the Haileys to the status quo—not only are the Haileys left with unpaid medical bills, but Steve is left with a new preexisting condition that may limit his ability to receive necessary health care. It is impossible to return the Haileys to the "status quo" under any definition of the term.

The decision regarding the extent of preissuance underwriting is primarily a marketing decision for the insurer. Insurers must decide whether to investigate their applicants at the beginning, in which case they will accept fewer applications but also insure better risks, or increase sales by simplifying their underwriting requirements at the time of purchase and risk adverse selection. Although the Legislature did not define "medical underwriting," we do not believe it intended to equate the term with whatever steps a plan took to evaluate the applicant based on its own marketing decisions or other considerations. Thus, in order to effectuate section 1389.3's purpose, and in light of the equitable nature of rescission, we interpret "medical underwriting" to require a plan to make reasonable efforts to ensure a potential subscriber's application is accurate and complete. Because the circumstances of each case vary, we do not precisely spell out what steps constitute a reasonable investigation. This will usually present a question of fact.

3. The Supreme Court's Remedy for Postclaims Underwriting

[P]ublic policy favors requiring a health care services plan to demonstrate reasonable care in ensuring the accuracy of a potential subscriber's application as part of the precontract underwriting process. The Knox–Keene Act's express purpose in transferring the *risk* of health care from patients to plans requires nothing less. The sudden loss of health insurance after the onset of an acute illness or serious injury presents not only a financial disaster to the former subscriber, but places an additional strain on health providers and government resources already overburdened by the vast number of those without health insurance. An applicant for a health services plan has a responsibility to exercise care in completing an application. In light of the potentially catastrophic consequences of an applicant's error in filling out an application, however, we believe the Legislature has placed a concurrent duty on the plan to make reasonable efforts to ensure it has all the necessary information to accurately assess the risk before issuing the contract, if the plan wishes to preserve the right to later rescind where it cannot show willful misrepresentation.

[The portion of the decision related to the Haileys' claim of intentional infliction of emotional distress is omitted]

Notes

1. *The outcome upon remand.* In 2009, a trial court found that the Haileys had indeed failed to appropriately disclose the facts about Steve

Hailey's health status and entered a directed verdict in favor of Blue Shield. Hailey v. California Physician Services (Case No. 03 CC 01789, Superior Court, Orange County). The judgment determined that Blue Shield acted reasonably, made a reasonable effort to find out the facts of Steve Hailey's health status, and that the Haileys willfully concealed the truth of Steve's health.

2. *Underwriting in the individual market.* To get a sense of the impact of the Affordable Care Act in prohibiting insurers from selecting which individuals they will insure and in imposing standards on how rates get set, consider the following information, available at California's Department of Insurance website:

Individual Market Underwriting

In California, medical underwriting is allowed without restriction. Each insurance company has its own underwriting guidelines, which are usually not made public. However, insurance companies marketing and selling individual health insurance policies in California must file information with the Department of Insurance pertaining to their policies, procedures, and underwriting guidelines for offering such insurance (Insurance Code Section 10113.95). We have summarized the information that companies have filed in the questions and answers and chart below.

What health conditions will cause a health insurance company to automatically refuse or deny my application for insurance?

There are many medical conditions that may cause an insurance company to automatically deny or not approve your application. These may include the following: Health problems for which you have not seen a doctor; Health problems that a doctor cannot explain; Health problems for which you have not completed treatment.

An insurance company may also automatically deny your application for the health conditions below. There may be other conditions that are not on this list: AIDS; Pregnancy, pregnancy of your spouse or significant other, planned surrogacy or adoption in progress; Cancer, under treatment; Sleep Apnea; Severe mental disorders, such as major depression, bipolar disorder, schizophrenia, or psychopathic personalities; Heart disease; Renal failure or Kidney Dialysis; Diabetes with complications; Cirrhosis; Multiple Sclerosis; Muscular Dystrophy; Systemic Lupus Erythematous; History of transplant Lymphedema; Current infertility treatment; Hepatitis; Hemochromatosis.

What will cause an insurance company to offer me insurance at a higher premium rate or limit the products or benefits I can get?

Insurance companies may offer you insurance at a higher premium and/or limit the products or benefits you can purchase if you had a health problem in the past but you have recovered or you have been without symptoms for some time. Insurance companies will also do this for minor health problem that you had in the past or may currently have. Insurance companies argue that these conditions pose a risk and that it will cost more for your health claims than if you were completely healthy. Each application and insurance company is different. An insurance company may charge a higher premium or limit the products offered for the health conditions below. There may be other health conditions and time frames that are not on this list: Stroke, after 10 years with no reoccurring [sic] problems; Allergies, while testing is in process; Ear infections, controlled with medications; Lyme's disease, without symptoms after one year; Breast implants (non-silicone); Ringworm; Joint sprain or strain, recovered and no restrictions; Migraine headache, mild and infrequent, with no emergency room visit; Mild depression.

Will a health insurance company look at my height and weight when I apply for insurance?

Yes. Insurance companies usually look at your height and weight when they decide to offer insurance. They may offer you insurance at a higher premium rate or refuse to insure you if you are overweight or obese.

3. *Bad faith*. The Haileys were permitted to proceed with a claim that the insurer's conduct amounted to bad faith breach of contract, which inflicted severe and emotional distress. What type of facts, exactly, must be present before a bad faith claim can proceed? It clearly is not enough that an insurer's practices caused injury to a plaintiff, even if those practices harm the insured's interests and may violate the terms of the contract. The types of practices identified by the court include the insurer's "wait and see" attitude: failing to conduct a reasonable assessment in advance, based in part on a business decision that marketing is more important than accuracy in underwriting; referring a case for investigation only after the claims began to come in and apparently being willing to continue to collect premiums so long as no claims were filed; continuing to collect premiums from the Haileys for months after it suspected something was up; leaving the Haileys with hundreds of thousands of dollars' worth of bills; and threatening the Haileys with litigation.

4. *Rescissions and the Affordable Care Act*. While the Act's broader insurance reforms do not take effect until January 1, 2014 (concurrent with the effective date of the mandate), the prohibition against rescissions took effect immediately. The statute amends the Public Health Service Act as follows:

§ 2712   Prohibition on Rescissions

A group health plan and a health insurance issuer offering group or individual health insurance coverage shall not rescind such plan or coverage with respect to an enrollee once the enrollee is covered under such plan or coverage involved, except that this section shall not apply to a covered individual who has performed an act or practice that constitutes fraud or makes an intentional misrepresentation of material fact as prohibited by the terms of the plan or coverage. Such plan or coverage may not be cancelled except with prior notice to the enrollee.

The Affordable Care Act applies the rescission policy to ERISA-governed health plans. PPACA § 1563.

Joint regulations issued June 28, 2010, by the United States Departments of Health and Human Services, Labor, and Treasury, 75 Fed. Reg. 37,188, 37,192–37,193 (June 28, 2010), provide the following explanation:

> This standard sets a Federal floor and is more protective of individuals with respect to the standard for rescission than the standard that might have previously existed under State insurance law or Federal common law. That is, under prior law, rescission may have been permissible if an individual made a misrepresentation of material fact, even if the misrepresentation was not intentional or made knowingly. Under the new standard for rescissions set forth in PHS Act section 2712 and these interim final regulations, plans and issuers cannot rescind coverage unless an individual was involved in fraud or made an intentional misrepresentation of material fact.

> For purposes of these interim final regulations, a rescission is a cancellation or discontinuance of coverage that has retroactive effect. A cancellation or discontinuance of coverage with only a prospective effect is not a rescission, and neither is a cancellation or discontinuance of coverage that is effective retroactively to the extent it is attributable to a failure to timely pay required premiums or contributions towards the cost of coverage.

> Moreover, PHS Act section 2719, as added by the Affordable Care Act and incorporated in ERISA section 715 and Code section 9815, addresses appeals of coverage determinations and includes provisions for keeping coverage in effect pending an appeal.

5. *Preemption of stricter state laws?* Note that unlike California law, the Affordable Care Act does not place a duty on insurers to reasonably ascertain the facts before issuing a policy; it simply bars cancellations except in the event of fraud or deliberate misrepresentations. The Public Health Service Act contains the following preemption statute applicable to federal market reforms:

> (a) CONTINUED APPLICABILITY OF STATE LAW WITH RESPECT TO HEALTH INSURANCE ISSUERS.—(1) IN GENERAL.—Subject to paragraph (2) and except as provided in subsection (b), this part and part C insofar as it relates to this part shall not be construed to supersede any provision of State law which establishes, implements, or continues in effect any standard or requirement solely relating to health insurance issuers in connection with

individual *or* group health insurance coverage except to the extent that such standard or requirement prevents the application of a requirement of this part.

PHSA § 2724, 42 U.S.C. § 300gg–23.

Were California to retain its pre-contract ascertainment requirement, would such a provision "prevent the application of a requirement of this part"? Could an insurer argue that federal law intends to lower the standard that insurers must meet before cancelling a contract and that such a law in fact prevents this lower standard from taking effect? In *O'Donnell*, 173 F. Supp.2d at 184, which concerned the predecessor HIPAA statute, amended by the Affordable Care Act, a federal court held that 42 U.S.C. § 300gg–23 does not preempt a state law that offers individual remedies for violation of HIPAA's restrictions against enforcement of pre-existing condition exclusions. By contrast, ERISA § 502(a), 42 U.S.C. § 1132(a) has been held to establish an exclusive federal remedy in claims for benefits brought by ERISA plan participants and beneficiaries. However, whereas ERISA creates an express private right of action to enforce claims against an ERISA plan, Title XVII of the Public Health Service Act containing the market reforms, contains none, as noted in Chapter 6. The Public Health Service Act applies to state-regulated plans generally, whether or not offered to ERISA-governed employers.

Suppose that California's imposition of a duty to investigate during underwriting applied to all forms of insurance, not just health insurance. What would be the effect, then, of the ACA's prohibition of rescission? Would the preemption clause save the more rigorous state law? When Congress amended ERISA to set forth standards for rescission do you think that it intended for ERISA's exclusive remedial scheme to preempt application of all state law pertaining to rescission, even state laws that are stricter than the "federal floor" created by the ACA? Do you think Congress intended to override cases like *O'Donnell* to the extent they apply to ERISA-governed plans? If not, how does one decide a federal preemption issue when one applicable statutory scheme points toward complete preemption while the other points toward only conflict preemption? If the answer is to apply complete preemption, then non-ERISA plans would be governed by stricter state law, whereas ERISA plans would be governed only by the ACA's federal floor. Do you think that Congress, in applying the federal floor to both the Public Health Service Act and ERISA, intended to preserve a legal status quo in which insurers' duties regarding rescission vary by whether or not their products happen to be sold to ERISA plans?

CHAPTER 8

THE EMPLOYEE RETIREMENT INCOME SECURITY ACT (ERISA)

1. INTRODUCTION

Although its main purpose was to protect pensions, The Employee Retirement Income Security Act (ERISA) is central to the study of health insurance and employer-sponsored health plans. Some 175 million workers and their families are covered through an ERISA-governed health plan. As discussed in Chapter 6, the Affordable Care Act amends ERISA in various ways while preserving its essential structure, its remedial provisions, and its extraordinary preemptive powers as they affect both state efforts to regulate insurance and the availability of individual remedies to address injuries caused by negligent or bad faith plan administration.

ERISA governs both insured coverage arrangements in which an ERISA health benefit plan buys a group health insurance product, as well as self-insured health benefit plans in which the employer retains the financial risk of loss (usually mitigated through the purchase of reinsurance coverage) while typically hiring a large insurer to provide third-party-administration services. You will see examples of self-insured plans with third-party administrators in both this chapter and in Part Three.

In amending ERISA, the Affordable Care Act retains this distinction between insured and self-insured plans. Furthermore, the Act creates an additional distinction between insured ERISA plans that involve small groups (under 100 employees) and those that involve large groups. Small-group plans are required to comply with the law's essential health benefit coverage requirements (discussed in Chapter 6), while larger insured groups are exempt from essential health benefits coverage standards. PPACA § 2707, applied to ERISA under PPACA § 1563.

In the context of health benefit plans, the study of ERISA can be divided into two segments. The first segment examines ERISA's standards and obligations as they apply to group health plans. The second explores ERISA's powerful preemptive effect on state laws that relate to health insurance, as well as on state law remedies for injuries caused by health plan administrators. The Affordable Care Act modifies ERISA requirements, while leaving its preemption doctrine untouched. At the same time, because the Affordable Care Act may alter the underlying picture where employer-sponsored health plans are concerned—potentially prompting employers, over time, to cease providing health plans and instead elect simply to contribute to a state health insurance Exchange—the future is a bit uncertain. In any event, ERISA's legal architecture remains central to the study of health insurance coverage for the vast majority of insured working-age Americans and their families.

Chapter 8 opens with a review of ERISA's key provisions related to the creation and administration of health plans, the fiduciary duties that attach to plan administrators, and the remedies available to employees (known as participants) and their family members (known as beneficiaries) in the event that a fiduciary duty is breached or a dispute arises over a claim for benefits. A typical dispute involves the denial of coverage on the ground that the treatment is medically unnecessary or excluded from the terms of coverage altogether.

The chapter then turns to ERISA preemption doctrine and examines the leading cases that together articulate this doctrinal framework. Two types of cases are presented here. In the first, the question is whether a state's laws regulating some aspect of insurance is superseded by ERISA's preemption provisions under ERISA § 514. In the second, the question is whether ERISA's remedial scheme has a *completely* preemptive effect on remedies available under state law in cases in which a participant or beneficiary alleges an injury caused by the plan administrator. Complete preemption arises, as you will see, from the United States Supreme Court's interpretation of the exclusivity of the federal remedial scheme set forth at ERISA § 502. This complete preemption has a sweeping impact on claims against ERISA plan administrators and fiduciaries and carries implications for state law remedies where substandard medical conduct is concerned, as you will read in Part Three.

2.   HISTORY AND STATUTORY STRUCTURE

The Employee Retirement Income Security Act (ERISA) of 1974 was primarily designed to assure the security of employer-sponsored pensions. Pensions faced two principal risks. The first was chronic under-funding by employers and unions, both of which sometimes refused to set aside sufficient reserves and relied on current profits and revenues to pay claims. These practices inevitably led to the second principal risk: pension failures during periods of economic disruption or decline. JOHN H. LANGBEIN & BRUCE WOLK, PENSION AND EMPLOYEE BENEFIT LAW 5–14 (2d ed., 1995).

ERISA's second purpose was to establish regulatory standards and remedial provisions to ensure that the law of trusts, with its fiduciary obligations, would apply to the administration of pension and benefit plans. Scandals involving the breach of fiduciary duties by pension and benefit plan administrators were abundant, and these scandals affected assets held not only for pensions but also health benefits, legal services, and other employee benefits. *Id.* at 509.

ERISA governs all "employee welfare benefit plans," defined as "(1) any plan, fund, or program which was heretofore or is hereafter established or maintained by an employer or by an employee organization, or by both, to the extent that such plan, fund, or program was established or is maintained for the purpose of providing for its participants or their beneficiaries, through the purchase of insurance or otherwise." 29 U.S.C. § 1002(1). Welfare plans include plans offering medical, surgical or hospital care or benefits in the event of sickness, accident, disability or death. *Id.* Exempted plans include public employee plans, plans for church employees, and plans maintained solely to comply with state laws regarding workers compensation, unemployment compensation, or disability insurance. ERISA § 4(b), 29 U.S.C. § 1003(b).

ERISA does *not* require employers to establish either a pension or health and welfare plan, the term used to describe the additional benefits that are part of employee compensation and governed by ERISA. Rather, *if* an employer chooses to establish a pension or health and welfare plan, then the plan is governed by ERISA. In the case of pension plans, ERISA imposes requirements related to "eligibility, participation, funding, vesting, and management as well as a mechanism to insure employees against pension plan insolvency." The content and design of health benefit plans is also addressed in the statute, although much discretion is left to employers and the health benefit corporations that sell insured or third-party administered products.

The original text of ERISA contained no regulation of the content of health benefit plans; nor did it offer any protection regarding renewal, termination or portability. As discussed in Chapter 6, HIPPA added some protection regarding the latter set of issues, as well as against some types of discrimination, just as COBRA before it had offered continuation coverage, commonly known as "COBRA" benefits, for health benefit plans covering 20 or more full-time employees. 29 U.S.C. § 1161. Also as noted above, the ACA added requirements regarding coverage of young adults. Numerous amendments, including those contained in the ACA, have added some content requirements. As noted earlier, the ACA added coverage of preventive services, services provided in clinical trials and, in the case of small-employer group health benefit plans, coverage of essential health benefits. PPACA § 1201 [adding PHSA § 2707] and PPACA § 1563. Earlier amendments stipulated that health benefit plans covering 50 or more employees must comply with standards relating to parity in coverage of mental health and substance abuse disorder benefits. 29 U.S.C. § 1185a. Additional requirements apply to coverage of benefits for mothers and newborns, prohibiting compelled discharge from the hospital within 24 hours after birth (29 U.S.C. § 1185), coverage of reconstructive surgery following mastectomies (29 U.S.C. § 1185b), and coverage of dependents on medically necessary leaves of absence from college (29 U.S.C. § 1189c).

ERISA's general provisions impose requirements for disclosure of information about eligibility and coverage (29 U.S.C. § 1021), and plan administrators must provide participants and beneficiaries with a "summary plan description" containing information about coverage, claims procedures, and the right of redress. 29 U.S.C. §§ 1022 and 1024. Plan administrators also must provide, upon written request, copies of any "instruments on which the plan is established or operated." 29 U.S.C. § 1024(b)(4). ERISA also provides beneficiaries with a right to "full and fair review" of claims for benefits (29 U.S.C. § 1133).

ERISA imposes fiduciary obligations on health plan administrators, who may be either the employer, the employer's insurer, or a third-party administrator, all of whom might be held to function as a "plan fiduciary," defined as an individual who "exercises any discretionary authority or discretionary control respecting management of such plan or exercises any authority or control respecting management or disposition of its assets." 29 U.S.C. § 1002(21). The law provides that a "fiduciary shall discharge his duties with respect to a plan solely in the interest of the participants and beneficiaries and for the exclusive purpose of: (i) providing benefits to participants and their beneficiaries." 29 U.S.C. § 1104(a)(1)(A). Plan administrators that breach this duty face liability "to make good to such plan any losses to the plan resulting from each such breach and shall be subject to such other equitable or remedial relief as the court may deem appropriate, including removal of such fiduciary." 29 U.S.C. § 1109.

The Secretary of Labor is empowered to enforce ERISA's terms. In addition, ERISA § 502, 29 U.S.C. § 1132, confers an express private right of action, in contrast to the Public Health Service Act:

ERISA § 502, 29 U.S.C. § 1132. Civil enforcement

(a) Persons empowered to bring a civil action. A civil action may be brought—(1) by a participant or beneficiary—(A) for the relief provided for in subsection (c) of this section, or (B) to recover benefits due to him under the terms of his plan, to enforce his rights under the terms of the plan, or to clarify his rights to future benefits under the terms of the plan; (2) by the Secretary, or by a participant, beneficiary or fiduciary for appropriate relief under section 1109 of this title [pertaining to breach of fiduciary duty]; (3) by a participant, beneficiary, or fiduciary (A) to enjoin any act or practice which violates any provision of this subchapter or the terms of the plan, or (B) to obtain other appropriate equitable relief (i) to redress such violations or (ii) to enforce any provisions of this subchapter or the terms of the plan.

c) Administrator's refusal to supply requested information; penalty for failure to provide annual report in complete form. (1) Any administrator * * * (B) who fails or refuses to comply with a request for any information which such administrator is required by this subchapter to furnish to a participant or beneficiary (unless such failure or refusal results from matters reasonably beyond the control of the administrator) * * * may in the court's discretion be personally liable to such participant or beneficiary in the amount of up to $100 a day from the date of such failure or refusal, and the court may in its discretion order such other relief as it deems proper.

In defining its relationship to state laws, ERISA § 514, 29 U.S.C. § 1144, provides as follows:

ERISA § 514, 29 U.S.C. § 1144. Other laws

(a) Supersedure; effective date

Except as provided in subsection (b) of this section, the provisions of this subchapter and subchapter III of this chapter shall supersede any and all State laws insofar as they may now or hereafter relate to any employee benefit plan described in section 1003 (a) of this title and not exempt under section 1003 (b) of this title.

(b) Construction and application * * * (2) (A) Except as provided in subparagraph (B), nothing in this subchapter shall be construed to exempt or relieve any person from any law of any State which regulates insurance, banking, or securities. (B) Neither an employee benefit plan described in section 1003 (a) of this title, which is not exempt under section 1003 (b) of this title * * * nor any trust established under such a plan, shall be deemed to be an insurance company or * * * to be engaged in the business of insurance * * * for purposes of any law of any State purporting to regulate insurance companies [or] insurance contracts.

 ### Note: Health Benefit Plan Administration and the Cast of Characters

Health benefit plan administration is a complex undertaking. A health benefit plan administrator would be an insurer in the case of an ERISA health plan that buys insurance. In the case of a self-insured plan, the administrator might be the employer itself that in turn subcontracts with a range of specialty companies. The plan administrator also might be a single corporation that carries out all functions associated with plan administration. For example, an employer that chooses to insure or administer its plan through a health benefit services corporation that operates a "staff model" HMO employing physicians and other health care professionals might be doing business with a company that does it all within a single corporate umbrella: benefit design and utilization management; a full range of primary and specialty service delivery including medical care, hospital care, prescribed drug coverage and other services; claims payment; quality oversight; actuarial services; information technology and management; and so forth.

Even comprehensive health benefit corporations often bring in partners, as do employers that administer their plans directly. These partners specialize in one or more aspects of plan administration. Thus a large insurer acting as the plan administrator might partner with a separate corporation (or a subsidiary) that specializes in the payment of claims (the claims administrator). The plan administrator also might contract with a corporation that sells medical services and operates under various names depending on structure and state law (e.g., a physician-hospital corporation, a physician practice network, an independent practice association, or an "Accountable Care Organization" (discussed at greater length in Part Three)). Numerous corporations sell a full range of plan administration products, such as actuarial services, information technology services, utilization management services, pharmacy benefit services, behavioral health services, pharmacy benefit management services (i.e., prescribed drug coverage and utilization management), internal claims appeals, and so forth. The proliferation of companies specializing in various phases of health benefit plan administration means that in cases involving challenges to plan administration, one might encounter many actors besides the plan administrator itself.

---

3. THE FIDUCIARY DUTY OF INFORMATION AND DISCLOSURE

Mondry v. American Family Mutual Insurance Company

557 F.3d 781 (7th Cir.), *cert. den.*, 130 S. Ct. 200 (2009)

■ ROVNER, CIRCUIT JUDGE:

When Sharon Mondry sought reimbursement from her workplace insurance plan for the speech therapy her son was receiving, she was advised that the therapy was not covered by the plan because it was "educational or training" and "not restorative." For the next sixteen months, Mondry repeatedly asked both the plan and claims administrators to supply her with the plan documents containing the language on which the claims administrator had relied in denying her claim. When the relevant documents were finally produced, it became patently clear that the provisions of these documents were inconsistent with the governing language of the insurance plan and that the claims administrator had inappropriately denied Mondry's claim for reimbursement. Once the error was exposed, Mondry prevailed. Mondry then filed suit against both the plan and claims administrators contending as relevant here that they had violated a statutory obligation to produce plan documents to her and misrepresented the terms of the plan to her in violation of their fiduciary duties. The district court dismissed these claims as against the claims administrator and entered summary judgment in favor of the plan administrator. We affirm in part and reverse in part.

Mondry worked for defendant American Family Mutual Insurance Company ("American Family") until September 2003. Mondry participated in the AmeriPreferred PPO Plan (the "Plan"), a self-funded group health insurance plan that American Family offered to its employees. Mondry also enrolled her son Zev, who was born in 1999, as a beneficiary of the Plan. The governance and terms of the plan were set forth in a Summary Plan Description ("SPD"). The SPD identified American Family as the Plan administrator but indicated that American Family had contracted with defendant Connecticut General Life Insurance Company [(CIGNA)] to handle the administration of claims for services pursuant to the Plan.

On the recommendation of his pediatrician, Zev began to receive speech therapy in July 2001. Initially, that therapy was provided to Zev through Wisconsin's Birth to Three program, a partially government-funded, early-intervention program for infants and toddlers with developmental delays and disabilities. As Zev approached his third birthday (at which time he would no longer be eligible to participate in the Birth to Three program), Mondry arranged for his therapy to continue at the Communication Development Center ("CDC"). When Mondry contacted American Family's Human Resources Department to ascertain the extent to which Zev's therapy would be covered by the Plan, she was directed to the company's internal website, where a copy of the SPD was posted. After reviewing the SPD, Mondry took Zev to his first speech therapy session at CDC on January 21, 2003 and to regular sessions thereafter. CDC submitted invoices to CIGNA seeking payment for the therapy.

On June 13, 2003, CIGNA's representative, Dr. Marsh Silberstein, wrote a letter to CDC, with a copy to Mondry, denying coverage for the speech therapy that Zev was receiving. In relevant part, the letter stated:

> Your plan provides coverage for specified Covered Services which are medically necessary. After a review of the information submitted, we have determined that the requested services are not covered under the terms of your plan. This coverage decision was made based on the following: The information provided does not meet plan language for speech therapy per CIGNA guidelines. Patient has expressive language skills delay and auditory comprehension skills impairment. Speech therapy to address this delay is *educational or training*. Speech therapy is *not restorative*.

Based on CIGNA's Benefit Resource Tools Guidelines–Speech Therapy. (Emphasis supplied).

Notably, one of the terms CIGNA used in its letter to characterize Zev's speech therapy—"not restorative"—is not found in the provisions of the Plan's SPD, and the terms "educational" and "training" are not used in the portion of the SPD dealing specifically with speech therapy. The SPD indicates that speech therapy will be covered so long as it is performed by a licensed or certified therapist and is referred by a doctor, subject to a maximum of thirty-five visits per injury or illness unless more are deemed necessary by physician. Moreover, as CIGNA's letter acknowledges, all claims against the Plan are subject to a general requirement, found in the SPD, that the treatment or services provided to a Plan participant be "medically necessary." By the terms of the SPD, treatment qualifies as "medically necessary" when:

> services and supplies are provided by a hospital, doctor, or other licensed medical provider to treat a covered illness or injury. The treatment must be appropriate for the symptoms or diagnosis, within the standards of acceptable medical practice, the most appropriate supply or level safe for the patient, and not solely for the convenience of the patient, doctor, hospital, or other licensed professional.

CIGNA's Benefit Interpretation Resource Tool for Speech Therapy ("BIRT"), which was cited in its letter to CDC and Mondry as the basis for CIGNA's conclusion that Zev's speech therapy was not covered by the Plan, is not part of the SPD and was not posted on American Family's internal website as a Plan document.

In response to CIGNA's letter, Mondry on June 30, 2003, wrote to both CIGNA and to American Family's benefits coordinator, Ken Dvorak, expressing her wish to appeal the adverse determination. She also requested a complete copy of the governing Plan documents, explaining, "The document I was told to pull off the American Family Intranet site is a Summary Plan Description, and is incomplete."

Mondry's first request for additional documentation of the Plan terms went unanswered. CIGNA treated her letter solely as a notice of appeal, and a CIGNA appeals processor wrote to Mondry on July 11, 2003, acknowledging her letter as such. The letter said nothing about Mondry's request for a complete copy of the Plan documents. American Family did not respond to the letter.

Dr. Patricia J. Loudis reviewed the case on CIGNA's behalf and upheld the denial of coverage for Zev's speech in a letter to Mondry dated July 23, 2003. Dr. Loudis set forth the following reasons for CIGNA's conclusion that Zev's speech therapy was not medically necessary: "The information provided does not justify the necessity of speech therapy. The patient has Expressive Language delays. Notes show that the goals of therapy are to improve speech skills not fully developed. Speech therapy is *not restorative.* Speech therapy, which is *not restorative,* is not a covered expense per the patient's *specific plan provisions. Reference CIGNA Clinical Resource Tool for Speech Therapy.*" (Emphasis supplied).

Notwithstanding Dr. Loudis's reference to "specific plan provisions" excluding speech therapy from expenses covered by American Family's Plan, the SPD in fact reflects that speech therapy generally *is* covered, and it contains no provision specifically conditioning coverage for speech therapy on the treatment being "restorative." And as with the BIRT mentioned in the June 13 letter denying Mondry's claim, the CIGNA Clinical Resource Tool for Speech Therapy ("CRT") mentioned by Loudis is not part of the SPD and was not posted on American Family's website as a Plan document.

On July 28, 2003, Mondry sent both CIGNA and American Family a second letter requesting "the total and complete copy of my Plan Documents." She noted that her first request for such documents had met with no response. By this time, Mondry had engaged a public interest law firm, Advocacy and Benefits Counseling for Health, Inc. ("ABC"), to represent her. She indicated in her July 28 letter that CIGNA and American Family should copy that firm on subsequent correspondence.

Mondry subsequently accepted a voluntary lay-off from American Family pursuant to a severance agreement effective September 19, 2003. Mondry elected not to exercise her right under the Consolidated Omnibus Budget Reconciliation Act of 1985 ("COBRA") to purchase continued coverage under the Plan. Mondry's counsel has represented that she instead obtained insurance coverage for herself and her son Zev through Wisconsin's Badger Care, a state-sponsored program offering insurance to families with children. However, Mondry and her counsel continued their efforts to obtain reimbursement from the Plan for the speech therapy Zev had received prior to her departure from American Family and the cessation of her coverage under the AmeriPreferred Plan.

ABC attorney Jonathan Cope wrote to both CIGNA and American Family on Mondry's behalf on September 23, 2003. Cope noted that Mondry had yet to receive a complete set of the Plan documents underlying CIGNA's adverse determination in response to her previous requests, but instead had been referred to a website. American Family responded to Cope's request in a letter dated October 16, 2003. Benefits Specialist Stacy McDaniel enclosed a copy of the SPD, and her letter stated that "This Summary Plan Description is the Plan document; we do not have a separate plan document."

Based on American Family's response, ABC attorney Bobby Peterson wrote to CIGNA's National Appeal Unit on October 30, 2003. Peterson noted that the only Plan document made available to Mondry was the SPD and that American Family had stated in its October 16 letter that there was no additional Plan document. Peterson asked CIGNA to confirm that the SPD was the legally binding Plan document. He also pointed out that Loudis's letter of July 23 referred to the CRT, which was not part of the SPD. "We are also requesting this Clinical Resource Tool, as well as any other information used to make your decision to deny these services, be sent to the undersigned."

CIGNA responded to Peterson's inquiry with a letter it faxed to Mondry's counsel on December 10, 2003. "In regards to the request for the Summary Plan Description (SPD)[,] you have to request this from your [previous] employer[;] per HIPAA guidelines and company policy we can[not] supply this item." The letter was silent as to Mondry's demand for a copy of the CRT.

On January 7, 2004, ABC attorney Peterson wrote another letter, this time to both CIGNA's National Appeals Unit and American Family. Peterson noted that Mondry's claim had been denied because it did not " 'meet the plan language for speech therapy per CIGNA guidelines.' " Yet, neither CIGNA nor the Plan Administrator had provided to Mondry any Plan document with the language CIGNA had relied on to deny her claim; the sole document provided to Mondry, the SPD, contained no such language. Peterson reiterated Mondry's demand for "a copy of the legally binding plan document in effect at the time the coverage was denied for this claim, a copy of the above-mentioned Clinical Resource Tool, as well as any other information used to make the decision to deny these services."

When CIGNA thereafter provided a packet of materials to ABC, it did not include either the CRT or any other document containing the specific Plan language that CIGNA had relied upon in denying Mondry's claim, which prompted ABC's Peterson to direct another letter to CIGNA on

January 28, 2004. Peterson noted that without a copy of the specific provisions on which CIGNA's decision was based, Mondry could not prepare for a second-level appeal of that decision. Peterson argued that CIGNA's refusal to supply the specific Plan language underlying its decision was contrary to ERISA regulations, which entitle a plan participant to a copy of any internal rule, guideline, protocol, or other criterion relied upon in making an adverse benefit determination. 29 C.F.R. 2560.503. He argued further that it was contrary to the SPD, which indicated that a Plan participant whose claim was denied had a right to know why it was denied and to obtain copies of any documents relating to that decision. "For the fourth time," the letter stated, "we are requesting the plan language and documents used as the premise for the denial of coverage for Zev Mondry's speech therapy." Peterson concluded:

> To remind you of the specific information requested, we are enclosing our prior three requests for this language. These documents refer to a CIGNA Clinical resource tool for Speech Therapy and to CIGNA's specific plan provisions. The words "Expressive Language Delays" are not found in the Summary Plan Document, and so they must exist somewhere in plan documents that have been withheld from Sharon Mondry and from ABC for Health, Inc., Sharon Mondry's authorized representative. We expect your prompt response.

A copy of the letter was sent to American Family.

CIGNA sent ABC a fax on February 20, 2004, denying Mondry's request for a copy of the CRT. "[T]he CIGNA tool used is only available to internal CIGNA agencies," wrote Appeals Processor Kimberly Schmitz. Schmitz suggested that Mondry's counsel contact CIGNA's Intracorp Medical Review unit by telephone to discuss the matter. But subsequent efforts by ABC staff to resolve the matter by phone proved fruitless.

ABC turned to American Family for help in securing a copy of the CRT from CIGNA, but American Family fared no better. After ABC's Kathryn Kehoe contacted her, Rosalie Detmer, American Family's Assistant General Counsel, agreed to contact CIGNA and see if it would release a copy of the CRT. Detmer spoke with Carl Peterson at CIGNA on April 23, 2004. Peterson informed her that CIGNA considered the CRT "propriety," that it was "too big to send anyway," and that CIGNA therefore would not produce the document to either Mondry or American Family. Peterson also advised Detmer that a "summary" had already been sent to Mondry and "that is all that is legally required." So far as the record reveals, Detmer and American Family accepted Peterson's response and made no further efforts to obtain the CRT or to clarify what CIGNA had relied upon in denying Mondry's claim. Nor did Detmer contact Kehoe at ABC to report the result of her inquiry.

ABC itself finally obtained a copy of the CRT in July 2004. CIGNA produced the CRT after John Pendergast, who was employed with CIGNA's National Appeals Unit, spoke by telephone with ABC legal intern Anne Berglund. According to Berglund, Pendergast told her that the CRT's provisions would be applied to Mondry's forthcoming Level Two appeal, and he agreed that disclosure of the CRT was required under ERISA. A copy of the CRT for Speech Therapy was faxed to ABC on July 2.

A review of the CRT revealed that it did not contain any of the key language that CIGNA had cited in denying Mondry's claim and sustaining the denial in her Level One appeal. The CRT did list the types of conditions for which CIGNA considered outpatient speech therapy to be "medically necessary," and it also identified the kinds of medical documentation that it would consider sufficient to support a finding of medical necessity. But the CRT did not employ any of the terminology that CIGNA had used in denying compensation to Mondry for Zev's speech therapy, including "expressive language delays," "educational or training," or "not restorative."

ABC's Berglund contacted CIGNA's Pendergast by letter on July 9, 2004, noting that the CRT lacked the language on which CIGNA had premised its denial of compensation to Mondry. ABC renewed its demand for any and all documents containing that language.

Pendergast declined ABC's request for additional documentation. On July 21, 2004, he left a voicemail for Berglund informing her that he had filed a Level Two on Mondry's behalf but that CIGNA would not be turning over any additional materials. Pendergast indicated that the Level Two review would be based "on the SPD, the plan contract, general service agreement, and [CIGNA's] criteria."

In the ensuing weeks, ABC continued to press CIGNA to produce additional information. ABC also demanded copies of the plan contract and the general service agreement. Initially, CIGNA produced to ABC a document entitled "CIGNA Healthcare Coverage Position" which related to speech therapy. But the effective date of that document was September 15, 2004—more than a year after Mondry's claim had been denied.

At last, ABC received by fax on October 5, 2004, a copy of the elusive BIRT—specifically, the "CIGNA Healthcare Benefit Interpretation Resource Tool for GSA 2001, Requested Service: Speech Therapy"—to which CIGNA had alluded in its June 13, 2003 letter to Mondry denying her claim for Zev's speech therapy. The BIRT was revelatory in several respects. First, the BIRT contained a definition of "medically necessary" that was significantly different from that found in the SPD.[3] Second, the BIRT cited as the governing Plan document not the AmeriPreferred SPD, but rather the CIGNA Healthcare Group Service Agreement 2001. Third, the BIRT

---

3.   Whereas the SPD defines treatment and services as "medically necessary" when they are appropriate for the symptom or diagnosis, within the standards of acceptable medical practice, the most appropriate supply or level safe for the patient, and not solely for the convenience of the patient or provider, the BIRT required that the provided services be "[n]o more than required to meet your basic health needs; and [c]onsistent with the diagnosis of the condition for which they are required; and [c]onsistent in type, frequency and duration of treatment with scientifically based guidelines as determined by medical research; and [r]equired for purposes other than [the] comfort and convenience of the patient or his Physicians; and [r]endered in the least intensive setting that is appropriate for the delivery of health care; and [o]f demonstrated medical value."

listed fourteen types of outpatient speech therapy that would not be covered, including the following: (1) "[s]peech therapy that is *not restorative* in nature"; (2)"[s]peech therapy that is considered custodial or *educational;*" (3) "[s]peech therapy that is intended to maintain speech communication"; (4) "[s]peech therapy that is being used to improve speech skills that have not fully developed"; and (5) "[s]ervices, *training,* or *educational* therapy for learning disabilities, developmental delays, autism or mental retardation." (Emphasis ours).

After further correspondence and telephone communication between ABC and CIGNA, ABC concluded that CIGNA had relied upon the wrong criteria in denying Mondry's claim. ABC law clerk Molly Bushman set forth that view in a lengthy letter to Pendergast dated December 21, 2004. After summarizing much of the back and forth between ABC and CIGNA over the relevant Plan documents, Bushman noted that the BIRT's definition of medical necessity departed from the standard articulated in the SPD:

> The provisions of the BIRT are much more detailed and potentially restrictive than the provisions of the contract [i.e., the SPD]. There is absolutely no basis in the contract for the exclusion of "Expressive Language Delays" or for the requirement that the treatment be "restorative." According to your statement above [that the SPD is the controlling Plan document] and to the law, the definition of "medically necessary" in the Plan should apply to this claim, not the extraneous provisions of the BIRT. In addition, as Sharon Mondry has maintained, there is strong evidence in the medical documentation that the claim at issue was for services that were, in fact, restorative.

Looking forward to Mondry's Level Two appeal, Bushman registered ABC's frustration with CIGNA's insistence that Mondry should frame her arguments based solely on the SPD rather than the BIRT or any of the additional documents that Mondry had sought from CIGNA, with or without success.

> While we agree that the BIRT is not contractually binding, it seems obvious that it was used to deny our client's claim.... [O]ur problem is that we do not know which standards will be applied to the medical facts. A voice mail you addressed to my colleague on July 21, 2004 stated that we should argue our case based on the SPD, plan contract, general service agreement, and [CIGNA's] criteria. You recently stated to me that the SPD is the plan contract, we do not need the general service agreement, and that CIGNA's criteria (which I take to mean the [CRT] and the BIRT) are not contractually binding. CIGNA has refused to send us the relevant documents, neglected to answer our phone calls and letters in a timely fashion, and basically protracted this process.

Apparently, there was no further document production from CIGNA following this correspondence.

When CIGNA's appeals committee heard Mondry's Level Two Appeal several months later, it agreed that her claim had been denied improperly. The hearing took place by telephone conference call on April 13, 2005; Peterson and Bushman of ABC represented Mondry at that hearing. Two days later, CIGNA sent Mondry a letter informing her that she had prevailed in her appeal. The letter provided no further explanation for CIGNA's change in position.[5]

Ten months after the decision in Mondry's favor at the Level Two Appeal hearing, CIGNA reimbursed her for most but, according to Mondry, not all of the expenses she had incurred for Zev's speech therapy in 2003, before she left American Family's employ and opted not to accept continued COBRA coverage under American Family's Plan. Mondry asserts that she has yet to be reimbursed for $303.89 of the money she is out-of-pocket for the speech therapy Zev received in 2003.

Mondry subsequently filed suit against both American Family and CIGNA pursuant to ERISA's civil enforcement provision, 29 U.S.C. § 1132. In Count One of her complaint, Mondry alleged that in failing to timely respond to her multiple written requests for plan documents, American Family and CIGNA had violated the obligation set forth in 29 U.S.C. § 1024(b)(4) to produce such documents and were liable for fines pursuant to 29 U.S.C. § 1132(c)(1)(B). In Count Two, Mondry alleged that American Family and CIGNA breached the fiduciary obligations they both owed to her under 29 U.S.C. § 1104(a)(1) to administer the AmeriPreferred Plan solely in the interest of Plan participants and beneficiaries, by misrepresenting the terms of the Plan and withholding from her information that she needed to pursue her Level Two appeal.

The district court dismissed Counts One and Two as to CIGNA and later entered summary judgment in favor of American Family as to both claims. With respect to Count One, the court held that only American Family, as the plan administrator, bore the statutory obligation to produce plan documents under § 1024(b)(4), and so CIGNA could not be held liable for any violation of that statutory provision. The court did agree with American Family that one of the documents that Mondry had demanded, the claims administration agreement between American Family and CIGNA, did not constitute a governing plan document that American Family was statutorily obligated to produce. But as to the other two documents Mondry had sought, the BIRT and CRT, the court concluded that those documents qualified as plan documents whose production was required under § 1024(b)(4). The court did not consider it to be a defense to liability that these documents were not in American Family's possession. However,

---

5. Although the record contains a copy of CIGNA's internal notes regarding Mondry's appeal, those notes shed no light on CIGNA's rationale for deciding the appeal in Mondry's favor. The appeal notes reflect Mondry's argument that previous denials of her claim had indicated that speech therapy must be restorative in nature, which is a condition not found in the Plan language. The notes reflect Mondry's additional contention that the previous denials relied on the BIRT, a set of guidelines intended for managed care plans, which the AmeriPreferred Plan was not.

the court later reversed itself on reconsideration, relying on the letter that ABC had written to CIGNA on Mondry's behalf on December 21, 2004, in which ABC acknowledged that the BIRT was not contractually binding on CIGNA in its handling of Plan claims. The Court viewed that letter as an admission by Mondry that both the BIRT and CRT were merely advisory, internal guidelines that CIGNA was not obligated to use in evaluating benefit claims and consequently were not documents that established or governed the Plan. Consequently, American Family had no obligation to produce those documents to Mondry under § 1024(b)(4).

As for the breach of fiduciary duty claim, the court dismissed that claim against CIGNA. The court saw no proof that American Family had breached its fiduciary duty by withholding material information from Mondry: rather, American Family had done what it could to help Mondry obtain the documents she sought from CIGNA. As for material misrepresentations, assuming that American Family had incorrectly represented to Mondry that the SPD was the only document that controlled the evaluation of her claim for benefits, there was no evidence that Mondry had relied on this representation to her detriment, because she continued to pursue her document requests.

A.   Count One: Failure to Produce Plan Documents

Pursuant to 29 U.S.C. § 1024(b)(4), the administrator of a plan has an obligation to produce to a plan participant certain documents upon her request:

> The administrator shall, upon written request of any participant or beneficiary, furnish a copy of the latest updated summary[ ] plan description, and the latest annual report, any terminal report, the bargaining agreement, trust agreement, contract, or other instruments under which the plan is established or operated.

The purpose of this disclosure provision is to "ensure [ ] that 'the individual participant knows exactly where he stands with respect to the plan [.]' " Firestone Tire & Rubber Co. v. Bruch, 489 U.S. 101 (1989). Knowing where one stands with respect to a plan includes having the information necessary to determine one's eligibility for benefits under the plan, to understand one's rights under the plan, to identify the persons to whom management of plan funds has been entrusted. Teeth are given to this obligation by 29 U.S.C. § 1132(c)(1)(B), which renders a non-compliant administrator liable for fines in the event he fails to timely produce requested plan documents.

Both the duty to produce and liability for the failure or refusal to produce plan documents are placed on the "administrator," and as that term is defined, it includes only American Family, not CIGNA. It is undisputed in this case that the SPD expressly designated American Family as the Plan administrator, thus rendering American Family the one and only "administrator," pursuant to § 1002(16)(A)(i). So it is American Family and American Family alone that bore the responsibility to honor Mondry's requests.

The next question is whether the documents that Mondry requested are the types of documents that § 1024(b)(4) required American Family to produce. We conclude that they are. We begin with the most straightforward of the documents that Mondry requested, the 1996 claims administration agreement between American Family and CIGNA.

Section 1024(b)(4) requires the plan administrator to produce (on request) copies of "the latest updated summary[ ] plan description, and the latest annual report, any terminal report, the bargaining agreement, trust agreement, contract, or other instruments under which the plan is established or operated." Needless to say, the claims administration agreement is a contract, but the relevant question is whether it is a contract "under which the plan is established or operated," such that it falls within the scope of § 1024(b)(4).

The claims administration agreement qualifies as such an agreement. That contract both established CIGNA as the claims administrator and identified the respective authority and obligations of American Family and CIGNA with respect to the plan: American Family bore responsibility for determining the eligibility of its employees to participate in the plan, enrolling eligible individuals in the plan, and communicating that information to CIGNA; whereas CIGNA bore responsibility for receiving benefit claims, determining whether claimants were eligible for benefits and the amount of money they were owed, disbursing payments, and providing appellate review of any adverse claims determinations. The district court believed that the agreement did not qualify for production under § 1024(b)(4) because it did not "define what rights or benefits [were] available to the Plan's participants and beneficiaries." But the agreement nonetheless governs the operation of the Plan in the sense that it defines the respective roles of American Family and CIGNA as the plan and claims administrators, respectively. Where the administration of a plan is divided, as is often the case, the extent of each administrator's authority is basic information that a plan participant needs to know. In that respect, we believe it qualifies as a contract under which the plan was operated, and Mondry was entitled to its production under § 1024(b)(4).[7]

The other documents that Mondry requested, the BIRT and CRT, present a closer question. The obligation, if any, to produce these documents arises from § 1024(b)(4)'s catch-all reference to "other instruments under which the plan is established or operated." In Ames v. Am. Nat'l Can Co., 170 F.3d 751, 758–59 (7th Cir. 1999), we rejected a broad construction of the catch-all language that would sweep within its reach all documents relevant to a plan and instead agreed with those courts which have construed the catch-all language narrowly to reach only those documents that formally govern the establishment or operation of a plan.

---

7. American Family points out that "a contract of insurance sold *to* a plan is not itself 'the plan. (citing Pegram v. Herdrich, 530 U.S. 211 (2000)). But that is not the type of contract that is at issue here. Connecticut General did not agree to provide insurance to American Family, but rather agreed to administer claims against the Plan on American Family's behalf.

Consistent with this limited construction of § 1024(b)(4), a number of courts have concluded that internal guidelines or memoranda that a claims administrator uses in deciding whether or not a claim for benefits falls within the coverage of a plan do not constitute "other instruments under which the plan is established or operated." *See also* Dep't of Labor Adv. Op. Letter 96–14a (July 31, 1996) ("it is the view of the Department of Labor that for purposes of section 104(b)(2) and 104(b)(4), any document or instrument that specifies procedures, formulas, methodologies, or schedules to be applied in determining or calculating a participant's or beneficiary's benefit entitlement under an employee benefit plan would constitute an instrument under which the plan is established or operated, regardless of whether such information is contained in a document designated as the 'plan document' "). The courts holding that internal guidelines and memoranda do not constitute plan documents within the scope of § 1024(b)(4) have reasoned that however relevant such guidelines and memoranda may be to a plan beneficiary's entitlement to benefits, as internal interpretative tools they are not binding on the claims administrator and therefore do not formally govern the operation of the plan. It is, instead, the language of the plan itself that remains dispositive of a beneficiary's rights, and of course § 1024(b)(4) expressly identifies both a plan and a summary plan description as documents to which the beneficiary is entitled.

There is also a separate statutory provision that may, in conjunction with regulations that the Secretary of Labor has promulgated, entitle a plan beneficiary to copies of the internal guidelines and other documents on which a claims administrator has relied in denying her claim for benefits. 29 U.S.C. § 1133 provides that "[i]n accordance with regulations of the Secretary, every employee benefit plan shall—. . . (2) afford a reasonable opportunity to any participant whose claim for benefits has been denied for a full and fair review by the appropriate named fiduciary of the decision denying the claim."

The Secretary's regulations in turn state that a plan will not be deemed to have afforded a claimant "full and fair review" unless, among other things, the claimant was provided "reasonable access to, and copies of, all documents, records, and other information *relevant to the claimant's claim for benefits*." 29 C.F.R. § 2560.503–1(h)(2)(iii) (emphasis ours). A document is deemed "relevant" if it "[w]as relied upon in making the benefit determination" or, in the case of a group health plan, the document "constitutes a statement of policy or guidance with respect to the plan concerning the denied treatment option or benefit for the claimant's diagnosis, without regard to whether such advice or statement was relied upon in making the benefit determination." § 2560.503–1(m)(8)(i) and (iv). Many items that do not qualify as documents that govern the establishment or operation of a plan for purposes of § 1024(b)(4) may qualify as documents that are relevant to a plan participant's claim for benefits for purposes of § 1133(2) and the Secretary's regulations.

Mondry did not seek relief under § 1133(2), but it is no mystery why she did not. Mondry ultimately obtained copies of the BIRT and CRT, and it was in large part the production of those documents that enabled her to show that CIGNA had improperly denied her claim for the speech therapy Zev had received. Mondry, in fact, prevailed at her Level Two appeal, convincing CIGNA to reverse its position and grant her claim. Having succeeded in her appeal, Mondry was in no position to argue that CIGNA denied her the full and fair review to which she was entitled under § 1133(2). The harm that she suffered was not the denial of full and fair review, but rather the lengthy delay in the production of documents that were key to her success in that review. That is why she contends that she was entitled to the timely production of the BIRT and CRT pursuant to § 1024(b)(4) and is now entitled to penalties pursuant to § 1132(c)(1)(B) for the defendants' failure to produce these documents within thirty days of her written demand for these documents.

We may assume, without deciding, that had CIGNA privately relied on the CRT and BIRT as reference materials to guide its interpretation and application of the plan language, these documents would not have come within the scope of § 1024(b)(4). In that circumstance, it would not be possible to characterize the CRT and BIRT as documents that formally established or governed the operation of the plan. The language of the plan itself would have remained dispositive of one's entitlement to benefits, and that language would be all that a plan participant would require in order to know her rights and to effectively appeal any adverse benefits determination. Had Mondry been denied copies of the BIRT and CRT and had she lost her Level Two appeal, she might have had an argument that her inability to see the interpretative tools that CIGNA had relied on in applying the plan language denied her the right to full and fair review accorded to her by § 1133(2). *See* 29 C.F.R. § 2560.503–1(h)(2)(iii)[cases omitted][.] She might also be entitled to the production of the BIRT and CRT in discovery in a lawsuit.

But CIGNA did not treat the BIRT and CRT as private guidelines that merely illuminated plan language—anything but. CIGNA expressly cited both documents as the basis for its decision to deny Mondry's claim for benefits and invited Mondry's reference to them. In short, CIGNA had been relying on the BIRT and CRT as the equivalent of plan language, treating the former documents as if they were dispositive and citing them to Mondry as such. Having expressly relied on the BIRT and CRT as the bases for its decision to deny Mondry's claim for benefits, CIGNA gave those guidelines the status of documents that govern the operation of a plan, and their production to Mondry thus became mandatory under § 1024(b)(4).

The fact that neither document was actually binding on CIGNA—indeed, that CIGNA had relied upon them improperly—is beside the point. What is relevant is that CIGNA expressly relied on them, and language from one of them, as dispositive in denying her claim. That is what entitled Mondry to the production of these documents as plan documents.

When a claims administrator expressly cites an internal document and treats that document as the equivalent of plan language in ruling on a participant's entitlement to benefits, the administrator renders that document one that in effect governs the operation of the plan for purposes of § 1024(b)(4), and production of that document is required. To hold otherwise would, in our view, allow a claims administrator to "hide the ball" from the participant, depriving her of access to the very documents that the claims administrator is saying are dispositive of her claim.

A final wrinkle here is that CIGNA rather than American Family had possession of the BIRT and CRT, and yet CIGNA was not the plan administrator with the statutory obligation to produce plan documents. American Family argues that this is a reason to relieve it of liability. Section 1132(c)(1)(B) itself indicates that a plan administrator will not be liable for penalties where its failure or refusal to produce plan documents "results from matters reasonably beyond the control of the administrator."

In the normal course of events, the plan administrator will possess all of the documents whose production is required by § 1024(b)(4) even where responsibility for administration of the plan is divided, as it was here. The universe of documents that qualify as ones "under which the plan is established or operated" for purposes of this statutory provision is small and is limited to those documents that formally, i.e., legally, govern the establishment or operation of the plan. The plan administrator will necessarily have those documents even when responsibility for handling claims for benefits has been assigned to a different party.

A problem will arise, as it has here, when the claims administrator mistakenly treats its own internal guidelines and checklists as binding, placing them on par with (or even displacing) the plan itself. When the claims administrator cites such internal documents as controlling, those documents will become subject to production pursuant to § 1024(b)(4), for the reasons we have discussed. And the duty to produce these documents will still belong to the plan administrator, just as it does with respect to other plan documents.

Any dilemma this may have posed for American Family did not excuse its statutory obligation to Mondry, however. It was American Family, of course, that decided to engage someone else as claims administrator, that chose CIGNA, and that gave CIGNA the authority to handle claims on its behalf. Once American Family was placed on notice that CIGNA was expressly relying on language not found in the plan itself to deny Mondry's claim and that Mondry was demanding copies of the documents containing that language, American Family had an obligation to obtain those documents from CIGNA and to produce them to Mondry. If the contract between American Family and CIGNA did not give American Family the right to insist on the production of internal documents such as the BIRT and CRT, this was certainly a right that American Family could have bargained for. Access to such documents thus was not a matter "reasonably beyond the control" of American Family as the plan administrator.

Mondry was entitled to copies of the service agreement between American Family and CIGNA, the BIRT, and the CRT, and American Family as the plan administrator is liable for its failure to produce these documents to Mondry within thirty days of her written requests for them.

We have no doubt that had these documents (in particular, the BIRT and CRT) been produced to her in a timely fashion, CIGNA's apparent negligence in denying Mondry's claim for reimbursement for her son's speech therapy would have been rectified much sooner than it was. Mondry is entitled to statutory penalties for the late production.

In Count Two of her complaint, Mondry alleges that both CIGNA and American Family violated the duties they owed to her as fiduciaries under 29 U.S.C. § 1104(a)(1). Neither defendant disputes that it qualifies as a fiduciary under ERISA. *See* 29 U.S.C. § 1002(21)(A)(i) & (iii). Mondry asserts that CIGNA breached its fiduciary obligations by misrepresenting the terms of the plan and failing to timely disclose material information necessary for her to pursue her Level Two appeal for benefits. Pursuant to 29 U.S.C. § 1132(a)(3), she seeks to hold CIGNA liable for $303.89 in medical expenses for which she alleges CIGNA has yet to reimburse her, additional medical expenses that she incurred because she declined COBRA coverage based on CIGNA's alleged misrepresentations, and the lost time value of funds that she spent on Zev's speech therapy before she was finally reimbursed following her successful Level Two appeal. As to American Family, Mondry alleges that her former employer failed to produce the information that she needed to prosecute her appeal of the original decision to deny her claim for benefits (again, the BIRT and CRT), misrepresented to her that the one and only Plan document was the SPD, and subjugated her interests to its own by taking a hands-off role in clarifying which documents governed her claim for benefits and in helping her to obtain those documents from CIGNA. Mondry contends that, like CIGNA, American Family is liable for the lost time value of the funds she used to pay for Zev's speech therapy until she prevailed in her Level Two appeal as well as the expenses Mondry incurred as a result of her decision to decline COBRA coverage.

The statutory provision pursuant to which Mondry seeks relief authorizes only a limited range of remedies, raising a threshold question as to whether the relief she demands is authorized. Section 1132(a)(3) provides:

> A civil action may be brought . . . by a participant, beneficiary or fiduciary (A) to enjoin any act or practice which violates any provision of this subchapter or the terms of the plan, (B) to obtain other appropriate equitable relief (i) to redress such violations, or (ii) to enforce any provisions of this subchapter or the terms of this plan.

The Supreme Court's decision in Varity Corp. v. Howe, 516 U.S. 489, 507–15 (1996), confirms that section 1132(a)(3) is an appropriate vehicle for remedying a breach of the fiduciary obligations owed to plan participants. But Mondry is seeking monetary rather than injunctive relief, and the former can be justified only if it falls within the scope of the "other appropriate equitable relief" authorized by the statute. The Court in Mertens v. Hewitt Assocs., 508 U.S. 248 (1993), rejected an expansive construction of "equitable relief" that might have included legal remedies, and instead construed the term to include only "those categories of relief that were *typically* available in equity...." The Court's subsequent decision in Great–West Life & Annuity Ins. Co. v. Knudson, 534 U.S. 204 (2002), reaffirmed that the "equitable relief" authorized by § 1132(a)(3) will normally not include monetary relief, even when the plaintiff asserts that an ERISA plan entitles him to the money he seeks:

> Here, petitioners seek, in essence, to impose personal liability on respondents for a contractual obligation to pay money-relief that was not typically available in equity. A claim for money due and owing under a contract is 'quintessentially an action at law. Almost invariably ... suits seeking (whether by judgment, injunction or declaration) to compel the defendant to pay a sum of money to the plaintiff are suits for 'money damages,' as that phrase has traditionally been applied, since they seek no more than compensation for loss resulting from the defendant's breach of legal duty.

As *Knudson* makes clear, Mondry's claim for the $303.89 that she claims CIGNA has yet to pay her as reimbursement for Zev's speech therapy is a form of legal relief that § 1132(a)(3) does not authorize. It is a demand for money to which Mondry believes the terms of the Plan entitle her. As such it is relief that Mondry could have sought under § 1132(a)(1)(B), which expressly authorizes a suit by a plan participant "to recover benefits due to him under the terms of the plan[.]" But Mondry has never invoked that provision as support for her claim. *Varity* observes that § 1132(a)(3) authorizes only "appropriate" equitable relief, and adds that where relief is available to a plan participant under other provisions of the statute, relief may not be warranted under § 1132(a)(3).

Consistent with *Varity*'s admonition, a majority of the circuits are of the view that if relief is available to a plan participant under subsection (a)(1)(B), then that relief is *un*available under subsection (a)(3).

Nor has Mondry shown that she is entitled to compensation for the additional medical expenses she was forced to pay as a result of her decision not to continue participating in the Plan under COBRA when she terminated her employment with American Family. Mondry's contention is that when CIGNA initially denied her claim for Zev's speech therapy, it represented to her, falsely, that the therapy was outside the scope of her coverage; thus, when the time came for her to decide whether to elect COBRA coverage, she concluded in reliance on that misrepresentation that there was no point in remaining with the Plan. She maintains that American Family itself played a supporting role in the misrepresentation by not taking meaningful steps to help her obtain from CIGNA the documents that she needed to expose the error in CIGNA's denial of her claim.

But what Mondry relied upon in electing to forgo continued participation in the Plan under COBRA was CIGNA's initial, erroneous decision to deny her claim. Yet, Mondry herself realized that CIGNA's decision was not final: she had appeal rights, she exercised those rights, and she ultimately prevailed. It takes more than a mistaken decision by the claims administrator to establish a breach of fiduciary duty. Nothing that CIGNA or American Family allegedly did or said coerced or deceived Mondry into waiving her COBRA rights and opting out of the AmeriPreferred Plan during the period of time when she was appealing CIGNA's adverse benefit determination.

However, we do think that Mondry has a viable claim against American Family for the lost time value of the money she was forced to expend on Zev's speech therapy until at last she obtained copies of the BIRT and CRT and was able to prevail in her Level Two appeal. Mondry could not have sought this form of relief under § 1132(a)(1)(B), for absent a provision in the plan that grants her the right to interest on past-due benefits (and the AmeriPreferred Plan contains no such provision), restitution of this sort is considered an extra-contractual remedy that is beyond the scope of that section. Of course, Mondry has already established American Family's liability for statutory penalties under § 1132(c)(1) for its failure to produce Plan documents to her under § 1024(b)(4), but the purpose of those penalties is to induce the plan administrator to comply with the statutory mandate rather than to compensate the plan participant for any injury she suffered as a result of non-compliance. This is not to say that the harm Mondry suffered due to the lengthy delay in obtaining the documents she sought is irrelevant to the assessment of statutory penalties; on the contrary, it is a material consideration, although not a prerequisite. But it is to say that the penalties imposed will not necessarily compensate her for her loss. Consequently, the door remains open to Mondry's request for relief under § 1132(a)(3), so long as what she seeks may be considered equitable relief.

Restitution amounts to a legal remedy in some circumstances and an equitable remedy in others. "[I]t is a legal remedy when sought in a case at law (for example, a suit for breach of contract) and an equitable remedy when sought in an equity case.... [H]owever, restitution is equitable when it is sought by a person complaining of a breach of trust...." Mondry is complaining of a breach of trust. American Family was a fiduciary, and Mondry charges that it breached its fiduciary obligation to her by failing to help her timely obtain the documents to which she was entitled under ERISA and that she needed to establish her right to Plan benefits. Because the AmeriPreferred Plan was self-funded, American Family arguably benefitted from the delay that Mondry experienced in obtaining those documents and reversing CIGNA's erroneous denial of her claim for benefits: it had the interest-free use of money that should have been paid to Mondry much sooner than it was. Restitution would thus force American Family to disgorge the gain it enjoyed from the delay that its breach of trust helped to bring about.

This assumes that American Family in some way breached its fiduciary obligations to Mondry. ERISA requires a fiduciary to discharge his duties with respect to

a plan solely in the interest of participants and beneficiaries and—
(A) for the exclusive purpose of: (i) providing benefits to partici-

pants and their beneficiaries; and (ii) defraying reasonable expenses of administering the plan; (B) with the care, skill, prudence, and diligence then prevailing that a prudent man acting in a like capacity and familiar with such matters would use in the conduct of an enterprise of a like character and with like aims....

29 U.S.C. § 1104(a)(1). Subsection (A) of this provision imposes a duty of loyalty upon plan administrators, and subsection (B) creates a duty of care in executing that duty.[8]

At common law, a trustee is obliged to provide beneficiaries, at their request, complete and accurate information as to the nature and amount of the trust property, and also "such information as is reasonably necessary to enable [them] to enforce [their] rights under the trust or to prevent or redress a breach of trust." (Restatement (Second) of Trusts § 173 & cmt. c. (1959)). In the ERISA context, our cases have recognized the fiduciary's duty not to mislead plan participants or misrepresent the terms or administration of a plan, although we have also cautioned that not all mistakes or omissions in conveying information about a plan amount to a breach of fiduciary duty, Frahm v. Equitable Life Assur. Soc., 137 F.3d 955, 960 (7th Cir. 1998); cf. Varity, 516 U.S. at 506 (reserving question as to whether ERISA fiduciaries have duty to provide truthful information to plan participants, whether on own initiative or in response to participants' inquiries, but agreeing that fiduciaries may not deliberately deceive plan participants and beneficiaries).

Against this legal backdrop, Mondry has presented evidence from which a factfinder could determine that American Family breached its fiduciary duty to her. Under the express terms of § 1024(b)(4), Mondry was entitled to copies of plan documents, and as we have held, those documents included the BIRT and CRT that the Plan's claims administrator had cited to Mondry as dispositive of her claim for benefits. Mondry could not effectively challenge CIGNA's decision to deny her claim based on these documents without knowing their contents. American Family had notice of the documents Mondry was seeking, her reasons for seeking these documents, and the apparent centrality of those documents to CIGNA's decisionmaking based on the correspondence that was directed to American Family, the telephonic contacts between American Family and Mondry's representatives, and the correspondence directed to CIGNA on which American Family was copied. A factfinder might conclude that American Family's heart was not in the effort, for its attorney not only accepted CIGNA's refusal without question, but did not even bother picking up the telephone to advise Mondry's counsel of CIGNA's refusal. Only weeks later, when Mondry's representative followed up with her, did American Family's counsel report the outcome of her inquiry. The factfinder might conclude that by not taking additional steps on Mondry's behalf to obtain these documents from CIGNA, its agent, American Family contributed to the

---

8. A fiduciary who breaches his obligations to a plan participant or beneficiary is "subject to such ... equitable or remedial relief as the court may deem appropriate...." 29 U.S.C. § 1109(a).

delay and failed to discharge its fiduciary duty as the plan administrator to provide her with the plan documents to which she was entitled by § 1024(b)(4) and which she needed in order to enforce her rights under the AmeriPreferred Plan.

Notes

1. *The scope of a plan administrator's duty to disclose documents upon written request under 29 U.S.C. § 1024.* As the court notes, ERISA's disclosure provision requires plan administrators, upon written request, to supply documents (including proprietary practice guidelines) that the administrator or its agents relies on when making a coverage decision. What converts a document from shielded to one that must be disclosed is whether it is used to operate the plan, which was the case here, since the guideline was instrumental to the claims administrator's (erroneous) interpretation of the plan's terms of coverage. As the court also points out, plan administrators must produce such documents when a participant or beneficiary appeals a coverage denial, if the document was used in the coverage decision.

You might wonder why was CIGNA so unwilling to supply the guidelines, particularly since in the event of an appeal under 28 U.S.C. § 1133, federal regulations require disclosure of any documents relied on by the plan administrator in adjudicating a claim. Plan guidelines are proprietary; furthermore, the guidelines, once released, allow claimants to do precisely what Ms. Mondry's lawyers did, namely, compare the guidelines relied on by the claims administrator against what the coverage documents actually say. In this case, CIGNA's guidelines grafted an "education" exclusion into the plan that was not part of the plan documents themselves; they also applied a more restrictive medical necessity standard than the plan documents actually stipulated. The lesson: in a coverage dispute, always ask for all written documents on which the administrator relied in making its decision, and do so at the earliest possible point.

Because of the determined efforts of Wisconsin's protection and advocacy agency, which provides individual representation for persons with developmental disabilities, the gulf between what the SPD said and how the plan was being administered came to light. The guidelines provide important insight into the level of prejudice against people with disabilities that are built into commercial insurance design and decision-making instruments. In this case, the little boy was denied speech therapy not because his condition did not require it and not because it was not clinically effective, but because the guideline arbitrarily classified the therapy in his case as "educational," presumably because CIGNA has concluded that such children should be cared for by school systems. Ironically, the Individuals with Disabilities Education Act (IDEA), 20 U.S.C. § 1400 et seq., the federal law mandating the appropriate education of children with disabilities, excludes payment for medical clinical treatment. The denial of therapy because it was "not restorative" likewise represents cruel discrimination. It evidences an attitude that the child was defective to begin with and will remain defective even with the therapy. Therefore, the little boy's speech could not be "restored" in the manner in which speech might be "restored" following a stroke. The fact that he might develop speech was irrelevant.

2. *Distinguishing between breach of fiduciary duty and a claim for benefits.* This case involves the breach of ERISA's fiduciary duty of disclosure, which arose as the plaintiff was preparing her appeal. It raises the question of what remedies are available in situations such as this. Note the care with which the court distinguishes between an ERISA § 502(a)(1)(A) claim (29 U.S.C. § 1132(a)(1)(A)) to "recover benefits due * * * under the terms of the plan," and a § 502(a)(3) claim (§ 1132(a)(3)) to "obtain any other appropriate equitable relief." Because the plaintiff prevailed at her full and fair review she recovered her benefits; even if she had not, she could not sue for benefits under § 502(a)(3), which authorizes the awarding of "appropriate equitable relief" separate and apart from the recovery of benefits. For this reason the court focused on the issue of what is recoverable under principles of restitution, which in her case involved valuation of the lost time she spent pursuing her son's therapy through other channels.

The classic situation in which this type of problem—the lack of a § 502(a)(1)(A) remedy—arises is one in which an individual relies on an oral assertion by a representative of the plan administrator that a particular procedure is covered only to discover later that in fact the treatment is expressly excluded under the terms of the plan, leaving the individual with nothing to appeal. This is precisely the situation faced in Kenseth v. Dean Health Plan, Inc., 610 F.3d 452 (7th Cir. 2010). The plaintiff, Deborah Kenseth, who had received gastric bypass surgery years before joining the Dean Health Plan, experienced subsequent complications and sought additional corrective surgery to treat her severe acid reflux. The list of exclusions and limitations contained in her plan Certificate and Summary (i.e., the summary plan description required of ERISA health plans) included "[s]ervices and/or supplies related to a non-covered benefit or service, denied referral or prior authorization, or denied admission." *Kenseth,* 610 F.3d at 456. The following year, this exclusion was amended to also cover "complications" from excluded treatments. The Certificate also encouraged:

> plan participants with questions about its provisions to call Dean's customer service department. On the third page of the 2005 Certificate, under the heading "Important Information," the reader is advised to make such a call "[f]or detailed information about the Dean Health Plan." Eight pages later, at the outset of the Certificate's summary of "Specific Benefit Provisions," a text box in bold lettering states, **"If you are unsure if a service will be covered, please call the Customer Service Department at 1–608–828–1301 or 1–800–279–1301 prior to having the service performed."**

Kenseth, 610 F.3d at 458.

Kenseth called her claims representative but neglected to indicate that the condition was related to much earlier gastric bypass surgery, which was excluded under the Dean plan. The claims representative indicated that Kenseth would be covered but "was not trained to tell, and does not tell, participants . . . that they cannot rely on her interpretation of benefits." *Kenseth,* 610 F.3d at 460. Kenseth did not ask for written confirmation and went ahead with the surgery, which according to the claims representative would be covered with only a relatively small deductible. The HMO then denied the claim.

Did she have a remedy? Ms. Kenseth could not pursue a § 502(a)(1)(B) remedy, since she was effectively seeking coverage for an excluded treatment, i.e., corrections of complications arising from gastric bypass surgery, itself an excluded treatment. (Note that the ambiguity that was further corrected by inserting the words "or complications" the following year might have given her an opening to appeal the denial on § 502(a)(1)(A) grounds but she did not).

Instead Ms. Kenseth filed a breach of fiduciary claim, charging a breach given both the ambiguity of the Certificate and the lack of any reliable process for clarifying the ambiguity. She also claimed separately that the denial amounted to an exclusion of a pre-existing condition in violation of Wisconsin's law (enacted in the wake of HIPAA) limiting pre-existing condition exclusions to 12 months. She sought recovery of the cost of her treatment and other relief. Dean took the position that it breached no duty and that Kenseth was attempting to recover through a suit for equitable relief the very remedy that she could not get through the claims appeal process. Following a loss on all counts, Kenseth appealed.

The court disposed of her pre-existing condition exclusion argument on the ground that what Kenseth experienced was a treatment exclusion, not an exclusion for a pre-existing condition. In so doing, the court noted that a *pre-existing condition exclusion* (which excludes otherwise-covered treatments for individuals with a particular condition) differs from a *treatment exclusion* which more narrowly excludes certain types of services and procedures for *all* participants, not just those with certain conditions.

With respect to her right to equitable relief for the cost of the acid reflux surgery, the court first determined that Dean was a plan fiduciary within the meaning of ERISA. The court then concluded that the fiduciary duty of disclosure under ERISA is more than simply not giving wrong information but creates an obligation to take affirmative steps to assure that participants and beneficiaries have the correct information, particularly where the plan takes steps to encourage reliance on its information ("call our information line"). This duty exists even in cases in which a participant may provide less than all material information to the plan. Here, not only were the documents unclear, but the plan encouraged the use of its claims line and then failed to train its own representatives to disclose the need for additional steps because their advice was unreliable. While the duty of disclosure is not "a guarantee of accuracy in all communications with the insured," *Kenseth,* 610 F.3d at 470, the fiduciary duty in this context compels "accurate and complete written explanations of the benefits available to plan participants and beneficiaries." *Id.* at 471. Expressly without determining whether a plan has a fiduciary duty to give "binding advice" in advance of any procedure for which coverage will be claimed, the court concluded that:

> [W]hen the plan documents are clear and the fiduciary has exercised appropriate oversight over what its agents advise plan participants and beneficiaries as to their rights under those documents, the fiduciary will not be held liable simply because a ministerial, non-fiduciary agent has given incomplete or mistaken advice to an insured. In that situation, the fiduciary has done what it can reasonably be expected to do to ensure that the insured receives accurate and complete information; that mistakes may nonetheless occur is an unfortunate fact of life that does not bespeak actionable negligence on the part of the fiduciary. But by supplying participants and beneficiaries with plan documents that are silent or ambiguous on a recurring topic, the fiduciary exposes itself to liability for the mistakes that plan representatives might make in answering questions on that subject. This is especially true when the fiduciary has not taken appropriate steps to make sure that ministerial employees will provide an insured with the complete and accurate information that is missing from the plan documents themselves.

Id. at 472

So did Ms. Kenseth have a remedy for breach of fiduciary duty? The court concluded that she was able to show real harm, since she relied on the advice from the claims representative to proceed with surgery that might otherwise have been put off. And yet, the court went on to note, "[i]t is not clear whether Kenseth seeks a remedy that ERISA authorizes for the asserted breach of fiduciary duty." *Id.* at 481. Noting that equitable remedies can include injunction, mandamus and restitution, the court went on to state that under principles of equity, restitution is available in equity only when used to secure the disgorgement of ill-gotten gains. Here, by contrast, the plan's conduct amounted to an arguably improper claim denial given the ambiguity of its own plan documents. Thus, the proper remedy according to the court was a § 502(a)(1)(B) action to recover benefits due, not a breach of fiduciary duty claim.

Unwilling to do in the plaintiff entirely, the court remanded the case for further development of the remedies question. On remand, the trial court determined that the case involved a claims denial, that her remedy lay in § 502(a)(1)(B), and that an injunction to prevent denial of the payment of the claim under § 502(a)(3) was a "thinly disguised" claim for money damages, not permitted under ERISA's equitable remedies provisions. *Kenseth v. Dean Health Plan, Inc.*, 784 F. Supp.2d 1081 (W.D. Wis. 2011).

Isn't there something wrong here? Aren't employers ordinarily held liable for the acts of their employees when the employees act within the scope of their duties? As between Kenseth and Dean Health Plan, who could have avoided the misunderstanding that occurred?

3. *How far do equitable remedies stretch under ERISA?* In CIGNA Corp. v. Amara, 131 S. Ct. 1866 (2011), decided after the *Kenseth* remand, CIGNA changed the terms of its pension plan and provided the plaintiff class with "incomplete and misleading" notice of the change (indeed, the change was billed as an improvement), thereby causing participants to lose thousands of dollars in pension value for each class member. Worse the trial court concluded that the errors were intentional. The court fashioned a remedy that would restore the previous value of the plan and ordered CIGNA to pay pensions under the reformulated remedy as if a claim for benefits was involved. The court based its order on § 502(a)(1)(B) because, in its view, prior Supreme Court decisions had seriously curtailed its ability to award relief under § 502(a)(3).

The Supreme Court concluded that § 502(a)(1)(B) did not apply in this instance, because the trial court had actually changed the terms of the plan rather than awarding benefits for a claim under the plan, a remedy that § 502(a)(1)(B) does not allow. (The Court also rejected the Solicitor General's argument that the misleading summary plan description was part of the plan's terms and thus could be enforced under § 502(a)(1)(B)). The question thus became whether, in the face of a breach of fiduciary duty, as in this case, the courts can fashion a remedy that alters plan terms to restore the status quo:

> If § 502(a)(1)(B) does not authorize entry of the relief here at issue, what about nearby § 502(a)(3)? That provision allows a participant, beneficiary, or fiduciary "to obtain other *appropriate equitable relief*" to redress violations of (here relevant) parts of ERISA "or the terms of the plan." 29 U.S.C. § 1132(a)(3) (emphasis added). The District Court strongly implied, but did not directly hold, that it would base its relief upon this subsection were it not for (1) the fact that the preceding "plan benefits due" provision, § 502(a)(1)(B), provided sufficient authority; and (2) certain cases from this Court that narrowed the application of the term "appropriate equitable relief."

> We have interpreted the term "appropriate equitable relief" in § 502(a)(3) as referring to " 'those categories of relief' " that, traditionally speaking (*i.e.,* prior to the merger of law and equity) " 'were *typically* available in equity.' " In *Mertens* we applied this principle to a claim seeking money damages brought by a beneficiary against a private firm that provided a trustee with actuarial services. We found that the plaintiff sought "nothing other than compensatory damages" against a nonfiduciary. And we held that such a claim, traditionally speaking, was legal, not equitable, in nature.

> In *Great–West*, we considered a claim brought by a fiduciary against a tort-award-winning beneficiary seeking monetary reimbursement for medical outlays that the plan had previously made

on the beneficiary's behalf. We noted that the fiduciary sought to obtain a lien attaching to (or a constructive trust imposed upon) money that the beneficiary had received from the tort-case defendant. [T]raditionally speaking, relief that sought a lien or a constructive trust was legal relief, not equitable relief, unless the funds in question were *"particular* funds or property in the defendant's possession."

The case before us concerns a suit by a beneficiary against a plan fiduciary (whom ERISA typically treats as a trustee) about the terms of a plan (which ERISA typically treats as a trust). *Varity Corp. v. Howe,* 516 U.S. 489, 496–497 (1996). It is the kind of lawsuit that, before the merger of law and equity, respondents could have brought only in a court of equity, not a court of law. 4 Austin Scott, William Fratcher, & Mark Ascher, Trusts § 24.1, at 1654 (5th ed. 2007) (hereinafter Scott & Ascher).

With the exception of the relief now provided by § 502(a)(1)(B), Restatement (Second) of Trusts §§ 198(1)–(2) (1957) (hereinafter Second Restatement); 4 Scott & Ascher § 24.2.1, the remedies available to those courts of equity were traditionally considered equitable remedies, see Second Restatement § 199; John Adams, Doctrine of Equity: A Commentary on the Law as Administered by the Court of Chancery 61 (7th Am. ed. 1881) (hereinafter Adams); 4 Scott & Ascher § 24.2.

The District Court's affirmative and negative injunctions obviously fall within this category. *Mertens, supra* (identifying injunctions, mandamus, and restitution as equitable relief). And other relief ordered by the District Court resembles forms of traditional equitable relief. That is because equity chancellors developed a host of other "distinctively equitable" remedies—remedies that were "fitted to the nature of the primary right" they were intended to protect. And the relief entered here, insofar as it does not consist of injunctive relief, closely resembles three other traditional equitable remedies.

First, what the District Court did here may be regarded as the reformation of the terms of the plan, in order to remedy the false or misleading information CIGNA provided. The power to reform contracts (as contrasted with the power to enforce contracts as written) is a traditional power of an equity court, not a court of law, and was used to prevent fraud.

Second, the District Court's remedy essentially held CIGNA to what it had promised, namely, that the new plan would not take from its employees benefits they had already accrued. This aspect of the remedy resembles estoppel, a traditional equitable remedy. Equitable estoppel "operates to place the person entitled to its benefit in the same position he would have been in had the representations been true." [E]quitable estoppel "forms a very essential element in ... fair dealing, and rebuke of all fraudulent misrepresentation, which it is the boast of courts of equity constantly to promote." 2 Story § 1533, at 776.

Third, the District Court injunctions require the plan administrator to pay to already retired beneficiaries money owed them under the plan as reformed. But the fact that this relief takes the form of a money payment does not remove it from the category of traditionally equitable relief. Equity courts possessed the power to provide relief in the form of monetary "compensation" for a loss resulting from a trustee's breach of duty, or to prevent the trustee's unjust enrichment. Restatement (Third) of Trusts § 95. Indeed, prior to the merger of law and equity this kind of monetary remedy against a trustee, sometimes called a "surcharge," was "exclusively equitable."

The surcharge remedy extended to a breach of trust committed by a fiduciary encompassing any violation of a duty imposed upon that fiduciary. Thus, insofar as an award of make-whole relief is concerned, the fact that the defendant in this case, unlike the defendant in *Mertens,* is analogous to a trustee makes a critical difference. In sum, contrary to the District Court's fears, the types of remedies the court entered here fall within the scope of the term "appropriate equitable relief" in § 502(a)(3).

Section 502(a)(3) invokes the equitable powers of the District Court. We cannot know with certainty which remedy the District Court understood itself to be imposing, nor whether the District Court will find it appropriate to exercise its discretion under § 502(a)(3) to impose that remedy on remand. We need not decide which remedies are appropriate on the facts of this case in order to resolve the parties' dispute as to the appropriate legal standard in determining whether members of the relevant employee class were injured.

The relevant substantive provisions of ERISA do not set forth any particular standard for determining harm. They simply require the plan administrator to write and to distribute written notices that are "sufficiently accurate and comprehensive to reasonably apprise" plan participants and beneficiaries of "their rights and obligations under the plan." § 102(a); see also §§ 104(b), 204(h). Nor can we find a definite standard in the ERISA provision, § 502(a)(3) (which authorizes the court to enter "appropriate equitable relief" to redress ERISA "violations"). Hence any requirement of harm must come from the law of equity.

Looking to the law of equity, there is no general principle that "detrimental reliance" must be proved before a remedy is decreed. To the extent any such requirement arises, it is because the specific remedy being contemplated imposes such a requirement. Thus, as CIGNA points out, when equity courts used the remedy of *estoppel,* they insisted upon a showing akin to detrimental reliance, *i.e.,* that the defendant's statement "in truth, influenced the conduct of" the plaintiff, causing "prejudic[e]." Accordingly, when a court exercises its authority under § 502(a)(3) to impose a remedy equivalent to estoppel, a showing of detrimental reliance must be made.

But this showing is not always necessary for other equitable remedies. Equity courts, for example, would reform contracts to reflect the mutual understanding of the contracting parties where "fraudulent suppression[s], omission[s], or insertion[s]," "materi-al[ly] ... affect[ed]" the "substance" of the contract, even if the "complaining part[y]" was negligent in not realizing its mistake, as long as its negligence did not fall below a standard of "reason-able prudence" and violate a legal duty. Nor did equity courts insist upon a showing of detrimental reliance in cases where they ordered "surcharge." Rather, they simply ordered a trust or bene-ficiary made whole following a trustee's breach of trust. In such instances equity courts would "mold the relief to protect the rights of the beneficiary according to the situation involved." Bogert § 861, at 4. This flexible approach belies a strict requirement of "detrimental reliance."

To be sure, just as a court of equity would not surcharge a trustee for a nonexistent harm, a fiduciary can be surcharged under § 502(a)(3) only upon a showing of actual harm—proved (under the default rule for civil cases) by a preponderance of the evidence. That actual harm may sometimes consist of detrimental reliance, but it might also come from the loss of a right protected by ERISA or its trust-law antecedents. In the present case, it is not difficult to imagine how the failure to provide proper summary information, in violation of the statute, injured employees even if they did not themselves act in reliance on summary documents— which they might not themselves have seen—for they may have thought fellow employees, or informal workplace discussion, would have let them know if, say, plan changes would likely prove harmful. We doubt that Congress would have wanted to bar those employees from relief.

The upshot is that we can agree with CIGNA only to a limited extent. We believe that, to obtain relief by surcharge for violations, a plan participant or beneficiary must show that the violation injured him or her. But to do so, he or she need only show harm and causation. Although it is not always necessary to meet the more rigorous standard implicit in the words "detrimental reli-ance," actual harm must be shown.

[W]e conclude that the standard of prejudice must be bor-rowed from equitable principles, as modified by the obligations and injuries identified by ERISA itself. Information-related circum-stances, violations, and injuries are potentially too various in nature to insist that harm must always meet that more vigorous "detrimental harm" standard when equity imposed no such strict requirement.

131 S. Ct. 1878–82.

4. *Revisiting* Kenseth *and* Mondry *after* CIGNA v. Amara. Given the Court's holding that where harm is shown, equitable principles allow the payment of money for a breach of fiduciary duty, how might this affect a case such as *Kenseth*, in which a breach of fiduciary is shown and harm is demonstrated? Could a court now fashion a remedy that involves modification of the plan document to cover the treatment that under normal circumstances unquestionably would have been excluded? Had Dean trained its claims representatives to do a better job of probing callers for more clarity around the circumstances of their coverage and to be clear about the need for a more definitive decision (particularly in a case such as this where there was no emergency and Ms. Kenseth could have waited), she would have discovered the exclusion problem. Does it make sense that in this type of situation, a court should be able to award coverage as if the plan terms had in fact allowed it?

Mondry of course is different. In fact, BadgerCare, the state's Medicaid program, ended up paying for the child's treatment. But according to the facts of the case, Ms. Mondry switched to BadgerCare because she had been misled into thinking that coverage for her child's condition was not available. Had *Amara* already been decided, might the Wisconsin state Medicaid agency have pursued the plan and argued for an equitable remedy consisting of repayment by the plan up to the level of coverage that should have been available to the child?

Because Medicaid offers more comprehensive coverage than other forms of insurance, federal law allows individuals to secure Medicaid as a form of secondary coverage to supplement other private or public insurance such as Medicare or an employer-sponsored plan. Thus, Medicaid beneficiaries can be "dually" insured, a common situation for low income Medicare beneficiaries, as noted in Chapter 6. (Dual insurance involving employer sponsored plans is less common because few low-income workers have access to employer-sponsored coverage). Because dual coverage is possible, federal law authorizes state Medicaid agencies to pursue "third party liability recovery" claims against private insurance and employer sponsored health plans in which its beneficiaries are enrolled. 42 U.S.C. § 1396a(a)(25). Would this have worked in this case? Remember that Ms. Mondry was no longer a plan participant, having elected to enroll in BadgerCare rather than pay for COBRA benefits. Can you fashion an argument that the state Medicaid agency might make to recover at least a portion of its costs?

5. *Coverage discrimination against children with developmental disabilities: commercial insurance versus Medicaid and the "essential health benefits" provisions of the Affordable Care Act.* Nowhere does the sharp distinction between commercial insurance and Medicaid show up more clearly than in services and treatments for children with developmental

disabilities. Here the clash between the concept of risk solidarity on one hand and risk avoidance on the other is in full view.

Mondry arose because despite the fact that speech therapy was a covered benefit class, the plan administrator, through its claims administrator, refused to cover the treatment for Zev because in the administrator's view the need was not "medical" but merely "educational." That is, even though the speech therapy was clinically appropriate for his condition and he needed the therapy to develop his speech, the administrator claimed an exclusion on the basis of his condition. The fact was that his developmental disability meant that he needed therapy to develop speech rather than restore previous speech (as might be the situation in a case involving a patient who has experienced a stroke).

The exclusion of otherwise covered treatments in the case of children and adults with disabilities is a theme that you will see again and again. *Cf. Bedrick v. Travelers Ins. Co.*, 93 F.3d 149 (4th Cir. 1996), later discussed in this Chapter. Commercial insurance typically excludes otherwise covered treatments that are considered "habilitative" in nature, that is they are needed to help develop function rather than regain normal function that was lost. A "habilitation" exclusion obviously works a serious hardship on families with children with conditions such as autism spectrum disorder, cerebral palsy, retardation, or other conditions that are present at birth and whose effects can be ameliorated through early clinical interventions.

In contrast, Medicaid, through its special "early and periodic screening diagnosis and treatment" benefit (EPSDT) covers a full range of clinical diagnostic and treatment services for children with developmental disabilities as well as other conditions. Sara Rosenbaum & Paul Wise, *Crossing the Medicaid/Private Insurance Divide: The Case of EPSDT*, 26(2) HEALTH AFFAIRS 382 (2007). One sees the differences between Medicaid (called BadgerCare in Wisconsin) and commercial insurance in another respect, as well: Ms. Mondry elected not to take "COBRA continuation" benefits, which are very costly (employers can charge up to 102 percent of the full group premium for coverage as a former employee), and to instead enroll in BadgerCare, which in Wisconsin is structured to allow moderate-income families to buy subsidized Medicaid coverage. Historically very few states have structured Medicaid to reach such families, a remarkably important social benefit particularly for families with sick or disabled children, because of the special EPSDT benefit.

This case reveals a core distinction between commercial insurance and Medicaid. Commercial insurers, as noted, are structured to cover costs associated with populations who have no long-term care needs. As a general matter, private plans cover selected clinical preventive services (a requirement of all health plans in the individual and group markets under the Affordable Care Act, PPACA § 1001), primary care, and more advanced treatment for acute illnesses and injuries, and a moderate level of rehabilitation services (e.g., 100 days in a skilled rehabilitation facility, 30 home health visits). Children and adults with serious and long-term conditions either from birth or that develop later in life often find that crucial treatments and services are excluded on "social," "educational," or other grounds unrelated to the need for treatment and the clinical appropriateness of the intervention. Rosenbaum, *Insurance Discrimination Based on Health Status.* Medicaid covers these treatments as an EPSDT benefit in the case of children under the age of 21. The program also covers services for individuals who on a long-term basis may need treatments to continue to maintain functioning or avert the loss of functioning.

One of the more important aspects of the Affordable Care Act's essential health benefits provisions (above, Chapter 6) is their inclusion of habilitation services as a required coverage class. PPACA § 1302(b). Furthermore, in interpreting and enforcing the essential health benefit statute, the Secretary of Health and Human Services is barred from making "coverage decisions, determin[ing] reimbursement rates, establish[ing] incentive programs, or design[ing] benefits in ways that discriminate against individuals because of their age, disability, or expected length of life." PPACA § 1302(d). Because the essential benefits statute binds only products sold in the individual and small-group markets, a large self-insured health benefit plan like the one in which Ms. Mondry was enrolled would not be legally obligated to offer such coverage. Rosenbaum et al., *The Essential Health Benefit Provisions of the Affordable Care Act.*

6. *What's in "the plan"?* Notice that everything turned in *Mondry* on what was deemed to be "inside" the plan and what was deemed to be "outside." The court read the SPD as being clearly inside the plan, and this view was grounded in ERISA's disclosure provision because the SPD is explicitly enumerated: "The administrator shall * * * furnish * * * a copy of the latest updated summary plan description * * *." 29 U.S.C. § 1024(b)(4). However, the ERISA provision goes on to specify that mandatory disclosure includes also "any * * * contract, or other instruments under which the plan is established or operated." Why weren't CIGNA's BIRT and CRT instruments under which the plan was operated? Because the plan administrator, American Family, had never seen them and probably did not even know about them? How many such documents do you think exist somewhere in the bowels of an entity like CIGNA that either insures or provides administrative services to its self-insured customers like American Family? Given the vast number of such documents written and used by firms like CIGNA, regardless of what the agreements stipulate—whether or not they state that entities like CIGNA exercise discretion—in actuality who *does* exercise discretion, American Family, CIGNA, or both?

This reality points to one of the Alice-in-Wonderland features of ERISA's application to health insurance. ERISA was drafted to regulate trusts, and with regard to a trust it's pretty easy to determine what the trust consists of: the articles of trust or other organic documents which create it. Moreover, such documents give relatively clear guidance regarding what the trust's benefits consist of, and compared with health insurance, benefits will be relatively few in number and certainly will not involve the payment of a vast multitude of claims involving an even larger universe of preventive, diagnostic and treatment modalities to patients who present in an infinite variety of ways. One can say with complete confidence that a health benefit plan does not consist in a document or a number of documents like an article of trust—much less the SPD—that enumerate extremely broad categories of coverage. Instead, the plan consists of the benefits as administered because only at that level of detail can one really know exactly what the enumerated benefits mean. Given that claims administration in health care necessarily involves the exercise of judgment, how can we possibly say that all the discretion is vested in a plan administrator like American Family and none in the claims administrator like CIGNA?

We will see this indeterminacy plague the law regarding ERISA and indeed, most of health law involving disputes regarding authority to design or administer benefits. Indeed, the court in *Mondry* played on the boundary between the inside and outside of "the plan" in two ways in achieving the result it did. On the one hand, because CIGNA made reference to, and apparently relied on, the BIRT and CRT, American Family was obligated to disclose them. Although as "internal documents" they weren't binding on American Family, according to the court, they were still subject to ERISA's disclosure rule as instruments under which the plan was operated. For purposes of disclosure, therefore, they were "inside." However, if they weren't binding on American Family, which supposedly had a monopoly on discretion in determining benefits, then they could not have been documents under which the plan was operated? Outside. Of the thousands of documents that are used in claims administration, which ones are part of "the plan"—inside—and which ones are not part of "the plan"—outside? If discretion in operating a benefit plan is scattered among the blockbuster-movie-like cast of characters we enumerated in the note preceding *Mondry*, whose documents and actions constitute "the plan"—inside—and which ones do not—outside?

It gets worse. You'll see in material that immediately follows, the plan settlor has discretion to design the benefit plan and can, by inclusion of certain language, make the exercise of that discretion virtually unreviewable. Where is the stopping point for this? Just what the SPD says? What about the documents under which entities like CIGNA exercise the discretion that necessarily exists in claims administration? What about CIGNA's choices in constituting the network it creates for plan sponsors like American Family? We'll see that issue drive the courts (and everyone else) nuts in the materials on ERISA preemption later in this Chapter.

And it doesn't stop at ERISA. What about internal instructions issued by the Secretary of DHHS to the contractors who administer Medicare benefits? Are the instructions akin to the quasi-legislative decision making typically granted to an administrative agency, analogous to "plan design," and committed to agency discretion—but one might suppose they would be subject to the Administrative Procedure Act or some sort of other public scrutiny—or are they part of administrative quasi-judicial decision making, such that claimants must exhaust administrative remedies before obtaining judicial review? In the material on Medicare in Chapter 10, we'll see that

one wreaking havoc in the courts. What about the numerous tasks performed by a registered nurse when she makes a home visit to a Medicaid beneficiary? She takes his vital signs, checks his skin, his weight, looks around the home for obstacles, assesses how much support he has in the home, monitors safety, etc., almost infinitum. The Medicaid "plan" submitted to the Secretary of DHHS for approval may list a category such as "home health care provided by a registered nurse" but it certainly does not drill down to anywhere near this level of specificity. Are these tasks part of the "state plan"? If not, when a Medicaid beneficiary with severe mental deficits and protected under the Americans with Disabilities Act proves that he will be forced to leave the community and enter a nursing home unless he can obtain safety monitoring, is he demanding a service that is not part of the "state plan"? We'll see these issues arise in Chapter 11. Finally—and we'll not test your patience anymore by going on, although we could ad nauseam—when a doctor, credentialed by an entity like CIGNA for inclusion in the network it sells to plan sponsors like American Family, harms a patient through negligence, are his actions part of "the plan"? We'll see numerous issues like this in Part Three.

The point, writ large, is this: Responsibility for health care—its delivery and its finance—is spread across numerous, fragmented actors in the United States. Law, however, assigns rights and duties only to specific actors for specific purposes. Ask yourselves—as you did with regard to the court's allocation of responsibilities among Mondry, American Family and CIGNA in this case—whether in a doctrinal area the lines drawn are arbitrary, whether they are drawn consistently across seemingly diverse doctrinal areas, and overall do they make sense?

4. FULL AND FAIR REVIEW OF CLAIMS

a. Statutory and Regulatory Structure

ERISA entitles plan participants and beneficiaries to "full and fair review" of claims when coverage is denied. The law provides as follows:

> In accordance with regulations of the Secretary, every employee benefit plan shall—(1) provide adequate notice in writing to any participant or beneficiary whose claim for benefits under the plan has been denied, setting forth the specific reasons for such denial, written in a manner calculated to be understood by the participant, and (2) afford a reasonable opportunity to any participant whose claim for benefits has been denied for a full and fair review by the appropriate named fiduciary of the decision denying the claim.

ERISA § 503, 29 U.S.C. § 1133.

Federal regulations governing coverage appeals involving health benefits, 29 C.F.R. § 2560.503–1 et seq., set forth appeals procedures for health benefit claims that provide for both fair process and for standard and expedited timeframes based on the urgency of the medical facts of the case. 29 C.F.R. § 2560.503–1(h). The "persistent core requirements" of full and fair review relate to knowing "what evidence the decision-maker relied upon, having an opportunity to address the accuracy and reliability of that evidence, and having the decision-maker consider the evidence presented by both parties prior to reaching and rendering his decision." Grossmuller v. International Union, United Auto. Aerospace & Agric. Implement Workers of Am., U.A.W., Local 813, 715 F.2d 853, 857 (3d Cir. 1983).

As prospective coverage reviews (i.e., reviews prior to the provision of care for which coverage will be sought) have become common, the potential for denial in advance of treatment raises important implications for access to health care access, an issue that you will see in *Corcoran v. United Health Care,* reviewed in Part Three. In 2000 the United States Department of Labor revised its full and fair hearing regulations to provide for expedited appeals in situations in which the health of the participant or beneficiary will be jeopardized by delay.

In addition, courts will waive ERISA's otherwise applicable exhaustion requirements through the full and fair review process in order to permit participants and beneficiaries to proceed directly to court under § 502(a)(1)(B); in these situations, a court may award coverage if the plaintiff is likely to succeed on the merits and the court finds a risk of irreparable injury, which in a health care case would be the denial of care itself. The potential availability of direct judicial intervention to halt a prospective denial with its attendant adverse effects on health care access figures strongly in the Court's decision in *Aetna Health Inc. v. Davila,* also reviewed in Part Three, which addresses the availability of remedies for injuries caused by the medical negligence of health benefit plan administrators.

In order to further protect participants and claimants facing the denial of a claim, the Affordable Care Act amended the Public Health Service Act both to strengthen the internal review procedures to be followed by health insurers and to provide for binding, independent external administrative review of adverse health benefit determinations by plan administrators. PHSA § 2719(b). These reforms were extended to all ERISA plans, whether fully insured or self-insured, PPACA § 1563(e), amending ERISA § 715.

Final regulations implementing ERISA, the Public Health Service Act, and the Internal Revenue Code,* were issued in 2011. 76 Fed. Reg. 37,208 (June 24, 2011). The final rules strengthen the notice requirements governing insurers and plan administrators, require insurers and plan administrators to defer to a treating health care provider's judgment regarding the urgency of a case for expedited appeals purposes, and deem the internal review process to have been exhausted if the plan or insurer provides

---

* ERISA is codified in both labor law and the Internal Revenue Code, an outgrowth of Congressional jurisdictional battles (separate Committees have authority over the nation's labor laws as opposed to its tax laws). This fact leads to much repetition in ERISA statutory terms. Add to this the fact that many ERISA provisions are crosswalked from the Public Health Service Act, and the complexity of understanding insurance law grows even more mind-boggling.

inadequate notice or fails to adhere to federal review requirements. 29 C.F.R. § 2590.715–2719(b).

Despite the fact that the Affordable Care Act itself draws no distinctions among the types of claims for which external independent review is available, the final rules limit access to binding, independent external reviews to certain situations.

§ 2590.715–2719 Internal claims and appeals and external review processes

(d)(1) *Scope*—(i) *In general.* Subject to the suspension provision in paragraph (d)(1)(ii) of this section and except to the extent provided otherwise by the Secretary in guidance, the Federal external review process established pursuant to this paragraph (d) applies to any adverse benefit determination or final internal adverse benefit determination (as defined in paragraphs (a)(2)(i) and (a)(2)(v) of this section), except that a denial, reduction, termination, or a failure to provide payment for a benefit based on a determination that a participant or beneficiary fails to meet the requirements for eligibility under the terms of a group health plan is not eligible for the Federal external review process under this paragraph (d).

(ii) *Suspension of general rule.* [T]he Federal external review process established pursuant to this paragraph (d) applies only to: (A) An adverse benefit determination (including a final internal adverse benefit determination) by a plan or issuer that involves medical judgment (including, but not limited to, those based on the plan's or issuer's requirements for medical necessity, appropriateness, health care setting, level of care, or effectiveness of a covered benefit; or its determination that a treatment is experimental or investigational), as determined by the external reviewer; and (B) A rescission of coverage (whether or not the rescission has any effect on any particular benefit at that time).

(iii) *Examples.* This rules of paragraph (d)(1)(ii) of this section are illustrated by the following examples:

Example 1. (i) *Facts.* A group health plan provides coverage for 30 physical therapy visits generally. After the 30th visit, coverage is provided only if the service is preauthorized pursuant to an approved treatment plan that takes into account medical necessity using the plan's definition of the term. Individual *A* seeks coverage for a 31st physical therapy visit. *A*'s health care provider submits a treatment plan for approval, but it is not approved by the plan, so coverage for the 31st visit is not preauthorized. With respect to the 31st visit, *A* receives a notice of final internal adverse benefit determination stating that the maximum visit limit is exceeded. (ii) *Conclusion.* In this *Example 1,* the plan's denial of benefits is based on medical necessity and involves medical judgment. Accordingly, the claim is eligible for external review during the suspension period under paragraph (d)(1)(ii) of this section. Moreover, the plan's notification of final internal adverse benefit determination is inadequate under [subsection (b)] because it fails to make clear that the plan will pay for more than 30 visits if the service is preauthorized pursuant to an approved treatment plan that takes into account medical necessity using the plan's definition of the term. Accordingly, the notice of final internal adverse benefit determination should refer to the plan provision governing the 31st visit and should describe the plan's standard for medical necessity, as well as how the treatment fails to meet the plan's standard.

Example 2. (i) *Facts.* A group health plan does not provide coverage for services provided out of network, unless the service cannot effectively be provided in network. Individual *B* seeks coverage for a specialized medical procedure from an out-of-network provider because *B* believes that the procedure cannot be effectively provided in network. *B* receives a notice of final internal adverse benefit determination stating that the claim is denied because the provider is out-of-network. (ii) *Conclusion.* In this *Example 2,* the plan's denial of benefits is based on whether a service can effectively be provided in network and, therefore, involves medical judgment. Accordingly, the claim is eligible for external review during the suspension period under paragraph (d)(1)(ii) of this section. Moreover, the plan's notice of final internal adverse benefit determination is inadequate under [subsection (b)] because the plan does provide benefits for services on an out-of-network basis if the services cannot effectively be provided in network. Accordingly, the notice of final internal adverse benefit determination is required to refer to the exception to the out-of-network exclusion and should describe the plan's standards for determining effectiveness of services, as well as how services available to the claimant within the plan's network meet the plan's standard for effectiveness of services.

Thus, the final rule distinguishes between the appeal of an "eligibility" claim, for which no external independent review is permissible and judicial recourse is the only option, and appeals involving "medical judgment" and rescissions of coverage, for which an external independent review in a non-judicial forum of plan administrators' decisions is permissible. In explaining their decision to distinguish between claims involving medical judgment and those that are "legal and contractual," the Departments of Labor, Health and Human Services, and Treasury (which issued the rules jointly in recognition of the fact that the rules implement three different statutes: the Public Health Service Act; ERISA; and the Internal Revenue Code) acknowledged that external review organizations currently consider contractual language as well as the fact that their decision leaves participants and beneficiaries restricted to recourse to the courts when the basis of the dispute is the interpretation of plan documents rather than medical judgment. At the same time, the agencies based their decision on their assertion that the fiduciary obligations of plan administrators mean that judicial review, rather than independent external review, is appropriate in cases in which plan documents must be considered. 76 Fed. Reg. 37,215–37,216. As you will see in the coverage cases that follow however, the denial of a claim for benefits often can involve both medical judgment and interpretation of plan documents in order to measure eligibility for coverage (e.g., the meaning of a plan coverage term). The regulations do not address what happens in this type of situation.

b. When Has a Plan Administrator Discharged Its Full and Fair Review Obligations?

Shelby County Health Care Corporation v. The Majestic Star Casino LLC Group Health Benefit Plan

581 F.3d 355 (6th Cir. 2009)

■ CLAY, CIRCUIT JUDGE:

Plaintiff, Shelby County Health Care Corporation ("the Med"), filed this action challenging the decision of Majestic Star Casino, LLC ("Majestic"), the plan administrator of The Majestic Star Casino, LLC Group Health Benefit Plan (the "Plan"), to deny the Med's claim for benefits. The Med filed the claim pursuant to an assignment of benefits by one of Majestic's employees insured under the Plan. The district court determined that Majestic erroneously denied benefits, and awarded benefits to the Med. Majestic appeals from that decision.

BACKGROUND

Damon Weatherspoon, an employee of Fitzgerald's Casino, a subsidiary of Majestic, sustained injuries as a result of a one-car accident on March 13, 2005. According to the Uniform Crash Report (the "Crash Report") completed by the responding Mississippi police officer, Weatherspoon was driving straight on a two-lane state highway when his car left the road, entered a ditch, and collided with a tree. The Crash Report indicated that, at the time of the accident, the road was dry, the weather was clear, and the road was not under construction. Additionally, the police officer reported that Weatherspoon was not wearing a seatbelt and did not have a driver's license or proof of insurance. The police officer also checked a box indicating that "driving under the influence" was a "contributing circumstance" to the accident, and noted that a blood test to determine Weatherspoon's blood-alcohol level was pending.

Following the accident, Weatherspoon received treatment for his multiple injuries at the Regional Medical Center, one of the Med's medical facilities, accumulating medical bills totaling over $400,000. On March 14, 2005, Weatherspoon assigned his insurance benefits to the Med, authorizing the Med to seek and recover all health insurance and hospitalization benefits available to Weatherspoon under the Plan. On June 10, 2005,

Weatherspoon submitted a claim for medical benefits, again authorizing the Plan to pay the benefits directly to the Med.

Weatherspoon filed his claim with Benefit Administrative Systems, Ltd. ("BAS"), the third-party administrator for the Plan. Under the terms of the Plan, BAS was "hired as the third party Contract Administrator by the Plan Administrator to perform claims processing and other specified administrative services in relation to the Plan." Importantly, the Plan Summary stated that BAS "is not a fiduciary of the Plan and does not exercise any of the discretionary authority and responsibility granted to the Plan Administrator." The Plan documents define Majestic as "the sole fiduciary of the Plan," and provide that Majestic "shall have the sole discretionary authority to determine eligibility for Plan benefits or to construe the terms of the Plan."

After receiving Weatherspoon's claim for medical benefits, BAS began its investigation of the claim. BAS sent a letter to the Mississippi Department of Public Safety ("DPS"). However, the DPS informed BAS that, because Weatherspoon did not have a driver's license, it could not determine whether he was convicted of driving under the influence. Despite being unable to ascertain whether Weatherspoon was driving under the influence at the time of the accident, BAS informed the Med that Weatherspoon's medical expenses were "ineligible" for coverage because the Plan excludes from coverage charges related to an illegal act. BAS based its conclusion on an exclusionary provision of the Plan:

> This Plan does not cover and no benefits shall be paid for any loss caused by, incurred for or resulting from.... [c]harges for or in connection with an injury or illness arising out of the participation in, or in consequence of having participated in, * * * an illegal or criminal act.

In a letter dated September 16, 2005, BAS sent counsel for the Med copies of the Plan Summary, the Crash Report, and the explanation of benefits denying coverage. On September 23, 2005, counsel for the Med sent a letter to BAS requesting an appeal of the denial of its claim for benefits, stating that "an accident report is not conclusive evidence of the commission of an illegal act."

To apprise Majestic of the status of Weatherspoon's claim, BAS sent an email to Sally Ramirez, Majestic's Corporate Director of Compensation and Benefits. The email from BAS informed Ramirez that "[w]e denied the claims based on 'an illegal act' " and that BAS "will be reviewing this case ... and ... will be contacting you to discuss further." On October 4, 2005, as part of its review of the Med's appeal, BAS requested information from the county clerk regarding the status of Weatherspoon's blood-alcohol test. BAS did not obtain the results of the blood test prior to completing its review of the Med's appeal and issuing the final decision to deny the benefits claim. On October 24, 2005, BAS sent a letter to counsel for the Med noting receipt of the Med's appeal. On November 18, 2005, BAS sent an email to Ramirez requesting that she "review and approve" the attached denial letter "before [BAS] send[s] it out." By letter dated November 21, 2005, BAS informed counsel for the Med that it was denying the benefits claim, stating that "[w]e have conducted a final review of the Plan's denial of benefits." The letter cited the illegal-act provision of the Plan, and noted that BAS's "final determination" was based on the Crash Report and BAS's independent investigation of whether Weatherspoon had a driver's license or automobile insurance.

Thus, although the denial letter identified three illegal acts potentially warranting application of the exclusionary provision—driving under the influence, driving without insurance, and driving without a license—BAS based the denial decision solely on driving without a license and driving without insurance. Because of the lack of evidence, BAS expressly disclaimed reliance on the citation for driving under the influence as a reason for denying benefits.

After receiving the final denial letter from BAS, on August 24, 2006, the Med filed an action for benefits pursuant to 29 U.S.C. § 1132(a)(1)(B). On the parties' cross-motions for summary judgment on the administrative record, the district court found in favor of the Med, concluding that Majestic improperly denied benefits. In reviewing the benefits decision, the district court recognized that the Plan documents conferred discretionary authority on Majestic, which generally would require the court to review Majestic's decision under an arbitrary and capricious standard of review. Nonetheless, the district court found that *de novo* review was appropriate because Majestic "was almost totally uninvolved in the decision to deny benefits to Weatherspoon."

Reviewing the denial of benefits *de novo*, the district court determined that the illegal-act provision did not provide a valid basis for denying Weatherspoon's claim for benefits. The district court concluded that there was insufficient evidence to prove that Weatherspoon was driving under the influence and that the two illegal acts BAS relied upon to deny the claim—driving without a license and driving without insurance—had an insufficient "causal link" to Weatherspoon's injuries. In addition to finding that Weatherspoon's claim was wrongly denied, the district court awarded benefits to the Med.

I. STANDARD OF REVIEW APPLICABLE TO THE DECISION TO DENY BENEFITS

[T]he parties dispute the standard of review applicable to the decision to deny Weatherspoon's benefits claim. Although ERISA creates a cause of action for plan participants to challenge a plan administrator's benefits determination, it does not specify the judicial standard of review applicable to such actions. The Supreme Court, however, has established that a denial of benefits "is to be reviewed under a *de novo* standard unless the benefit plan gives the administrator or fiduciary discretionary authority to determine eligibility for benefits or to construe the terms of the plan." *Firestone Tire & Rubber Co.,* 489 U.S. 101.

Nonetheless, even when the plan documents confer discretionary authority on the plan administrator, when the benefits decision "is made by a body other than the one authorized by the procedures set forth in a benefits plan," federal courts review the benefits decision *de novo*. Where a plan administrator does not make the benefits decision, the plan administrator has not exercised its discretionary authority, and therefore a deferential standard of review is not justified.

It is undisputed that the Plan documents give Majestic the discretionary authority to interpret the Plan and make the final determination regarding whether a plan participant is entitled to benefits. The parties also agree that the Plan explicitly denies BAS such authority. Therefore, to determine the appropriate standard of review applicable to the decision to deny benefits, the district court was required to resolve the factual issue of "who actually made the benefit determination."

Examining the administrative record, the district court determined that "Majestic was almost totally uninvolved in the decision to deny benefits to Weatherspoon.... Because BAS was *explicitly not* granted discretionary authority to determine eligibility for benefits and Majestic simply adopted its decision without engaging in any independent fact-finding, the Court will apply a *de novo* standard of review." The record supports the district court's finding. First, the record shows that BAS alone investigated Weatherspoon's claim. All requests for documents appeared on BAS letterhead and were sent by BAS representatives. The documents in the record also indicate that BAS was the entity that made the ultimate decision to deny the Med's claim.

Communications with counsel for the Med further demonstrate that Majestic did not make the benefits decision. The letters to counsel were on BAS letterhead and indicated that BAS was responsible for reviewing both the claim and the Med's appeal of the denial of benefits. Most significantly, BAS issued the final denial letter to the Med on BAS letterhead.

Although Ramirez submitted an affidavit stating that she was "in a continuing dialogue with BAS regarding whether [the] claim for benefits was payable pursuant to the terms of the Plan" and that she "approved the form and contents" of the denial letter before BAS sent the letter to the Med, the documents in the record suggest otherwise. For example, although the investigation into and initial denial of the Med's claim occurred in September 2005, Ramirez was unaware of the claim until at least October 3, 2005. In addition, although BAS asked Ramirez to "review and approve" the final denial letter, BAS never requested that Majestic approve its decision to deny benefits. Further, there is no evidence that Majestic even reviewed the letter, as Majestic did not make any changes to the denial letter or otherwise respond to BAS.[2]

2. Also suggesting a lack of review by Majestic is the fact that BAS sent the "review and approve" email in the afternoon on Friday, November 18, 2005, and sent the denial letter on Monday, November 21, 2005. While that may be sufficient time to proofread a letter, it seems unlikely that Majestic could review and approve the actual decision to deny coverage during that time.

Despite the extensive evidence indicating that Majestic did not make the decision to deny benefits, Majestic argues that it is entitled to deferential review because it retained the "sole discretionary authority to determine eligibility for Plan benefits or to construe the terms of the Plan." However, whether Majestic reserved for itself the discretion to determine eligibility under the Plan does not answer whether, in this particular case, Majestic exercised that discretionary authority.

II. DENIAL OF BENEFITS

[I]n denying Weatherspoon's claim for benefits, BAS relied on the following exclusionary provision:

> This Plan does not cover and no benefits shall be paid for any loss caused by, incurred for or resulting from.... [c]harges for or in connection with an injury or illness arising out of the participation in an illegal or criminal act.

Majestic argues that Weatherspoon's medical expenses are excluded from coverage under this provision because Weatherspoon was engaged in three illegal acts at the time of his accident: driving under the influence, driving without a license, and driving without insurance.

With respect to the DUI charge, Majestic relies on the Crash Report's indication that Weatherspoon was driving under the influence at the time of the accident to support the denial of benefits. Regardless of whether Majestic could have denied Weatherspoon's claim solely based on the Crash Report, BAS and Majestic expressly disclaimed reliance on the DUI allegation as the basis for denying the claim for benefits in the denial letter. Majestic relied solely on the illegal acts of driving without a license and driving without insurance to deny Weatherspoon's claim. Consequently, for Majestic's decision to deny benefits to be upheld, either driving without insurance or driving without a license must constitute an illegal act and also have a sufficient causal connection to Weatherspoon's injuries.

Weatherspoon was denied coverage pursuant to the illegal-act provision of the Plan which excludes coverage for injuries resulting from "being engaged in ... the commission or attempted commission of an illegal or criminal act." However, the Plan does not define the term "illegal." In denying Weatherspoon's claim for benefits, BAS concluded that driving without insurance and driving without a license constituted illegal acts because they were prohibited by Mississippi law. Therefore, BAS interpreted an illegal act as encompassing any action that is contrary to law, even if such action is not criminal. Because we review the decision to deny benefits *de novo*, this interpretation is entitled to no deference.

Majestic argues that the phrase "illegal act" is unambiguous because it plainly includes any act that is contrary to law. To support this interpretation, Majestic focuses on the fact that "illegal" appears in a disjunctive clause with "criminal." Majestic also relies on the dictionary definition of the word "illegal" as "contrary to or violating a law or rule or regulation or something else ... having the force of law."

However, the Med argues that the term "illegal act" is ambiguous because an illegal act could be limited to violations that result in a citation or rise to a certain level of wrongdoing or could encompass all acts contrary to law. We agree. Particularly in the context of the entire provision a reasonable interpretation of "illegal act" might not include driving without insurance or driving without a license. Thus, we conclude that the language of the Plan is ambiguous as to what level of wrongdoing is required to constitute an "illegal act" for purposes of the exclusionary provision.[5]

The district court concluded that the Plan's illegal-act provision did not exclude coverage for Weatherspoon's injuries because driving without a license and driving without insurance did not "cause" Weatherspoon's accident and resulting injuries. As noted above, the Plan excludes coverage for losses "caused by, incurred for or resulting from.... an illegal or criminal act." On appeal, Majestic argues that the district court "failed to acknowledge the strong causal connection ... between the illegal act of driving without a license and a motor vehicle crash." However, the administrative record provides no support for the assertion that driving without a license or driving without insurance "caused" Weatherspoon's accident and resulting injuries.

[The court ordered a direct payment of benefits to the Med rather than a remand for further proceedings, as sought by Majestic. In doing so, the court concluded that in contrast to cases in which the "plan administrator's decision suffers from a procedural defect or the administrative record is factually incomplete" and remand to allow for "full and fair review" is appropriate, in this case, the issue was not a procedural defect but a case in which the administrator reached the "wrong conclusion" that is "simply contrary to the facts."]

Notes

1. *The consequences of failing to conduct a full and fair review.* This case illustrates the consequences for plan fiduciaries of abdicating their responsibilities to review all of the evidence against the plan documents. Because Majestic rubber-stamped its contractor's work, it lost the "deferential" standard of review that is the hallmark of the judicial standard of review in ERISA cases, first articulated by the United States Supreme Court in *Firestone Tire & Rubber Co.*, 489 U.S. 101 (1989). This standard of review will be discussed in the materials that follow.

---

5. [T]he "other illegal act" phrase arguably would exclude coverage for injuries to beneficiaries who: (1) trip on a sidewalk while jaywalking; (2) have their cars hit by a semi-truck while driving one mile per hour over the posted speed limit or not wearing a seatbelt; (3) are hit by another vehicle while executing a turn without displaying a turn signal; (4) fall off a ladder while remodeling a house without all relevant governmental permits; (5) are bitten by their dog when they have not yet obtained a dog license; or (6) fall into a fire while burning yard debris with no burn permit. A reasonably intelligent person objectively examining the "other illegal act" phrase in the context of the entire exclusion would not expect a denial of coverage for these types of activities.

2. *Illegal-acts clauses.* An illegal-acts clause is a standard provision in many insurance contracts and employer-sponsored health benefit plans. See, e.g. Va. Code § 38.2–3504, which specifically authorizes insurers in the individual market to exclude coverage if the insured is "committing or attempting to commit a felony or engaging in an illegal occupation" and further allows exclusions for losses "resulting from the Insured's being drunk, or under the influence of any narcotic unless taken on the advice of a physician." This type of sanctioned exclusion is consistent with Professor Baker's "actuarial fairness" observation about the Affordable Care Act, discussed previously. At the same time, such an exclusionary clause can wreak havoc on health care providers like the Med, one of the nation's largest public hospitals (see Part One for a discussion of public hospitals). Public hospitals have a duty to serve their communities regardless of patients' insurance status; when a patient does have public or private health insurance, a hospital will bill the insurer. Furthermore, EMTALA requires that all hospitals with "dedicated emergency departments" screen persons who come to the hospital and for whom a request is made and to provide stabilization treatment if an emergency medical condition is found. (See discussion of EMTALA, Part One).

In your view, is this type of exclusionary clause wise public policy? What happens to these uncovered expenses do you think? A hospital receives a major trauma case and provides hundreds of thousands of dollars in care, only to discover that the patient, even if insured, is essentially dis-insured because of an illegal-acts exclusion. Should insurers be permitted to embed morals clauses into contracts if the effect is to shift the cost of illegal acts onto society at large? In recent years, the National Association of Insurance Commissioners has taken a formal position against such clauses. Joel Teitelbaum et al., *State Laws Permitting Intoxication Exclusions in Insurance Contracts: Implications for Public Health Policy and Practice*, 119 Pub. Health Reports 585–87 (Nov. 2004). The Affordable Care Act does not bar the use of such clauses.

For an interesting critique of the court's interpretation of the exclusion see John Utz, *Illegal Act Exclusions: Causality as the Sixth Circuit's Sword of Justice*, 17(6) ERISA Litig. Rep. 4. Writing that "Commonly, the plan exclusion, read literally, is so broad that a court will conclude that it just can't mean what it says. The court then has to try to make sense of the plan language, a task which seems to tempt judges to bring to bear their own personal sense of fairness." The author argues that the court's sympathy for the Med's plight led it to resolve the case as it did.

3. *Judicial deference.* The court's decision also underscores the consequences for a lazy plan administrator who fails to exercise its fiduciary duty and thus exposes itself to *de novo* review. As we mentioned earlier in this Part, in interpreting insurance contract clauses, courts traditionally applied the doctrine of *"contra proferentem."* Under this doctrine, the inherently unequal bargaining power represented by an insurance contract results in the construction of ambiguities against the drafter. *See, e.g.*, Farmers Auto Ins. Assn. v. Saint Paul Mercury Ins. Co., 482 F.3d 976 (7th Cir. 2007). For

a review of the doctrine and an argument favoring the elimination of the doctrine of *contra proferentem*, see Michael Rappaport, *The Ambiguity Rule and Insurance Law: Why Insurance Contracts Should Not Be Construed Against the Drafter*, 30 GA. L. REV. 171 (1995). Noting that courts have adopted the rule "with vigor" and arguing that the rule be replaced with one that resolves contracts consistent with the intent of the parties, Professor Rappaport categorizes the doctrine as the most important in all insurance law. The doctrine arises out of the concern that insurance contracts are subject to market failure because they are take-it-or-leave-it contracts of adhesion. Indeed, so strong is adherence to the doctrine that some state laws codifying the doctrine go so far as to apply it to all insurance contracts, even cases such as *Farmers Auto Insurance*, 482 F.3d 976, which involved two sophisticated purchasers.

4. *The obligation of employer-sponsored health benefit plans to pay for out-of-network emergency care in the wake of the Affordable Care Act.* The Affordable Care Act extends certain "patient protections" to privately insured people. One such protection is coverage of emergency services under what is known as a "prudent layperson" standard. (PHSA § 2719A, 42 U.S.C. § 300gg–19a, extended to ERISA under PPACA § 1563 amending ERISA § 715). Specifically, the emergency coverage statute provides as follows:

"(b) COVERAGE OF EMERGENCY SERVICES.—

"(1) IN GENERAL.—If a group health plan, or a health insurance issuer offering group or individual health insurance issuer, provides or covers any benefits with respect to services in an emergency department of a hospital, the plan or issuer shall cover emergency services (as defined in paragraph (2)(B))—(A) without the need for any prior authorization determination; (B) whether the health care provider furnishing such services is a participating provider with respect to such services; (C) in a manner so that, if such services are provided to a participant, beneficiary, or enrollee—(i) by a nonparticipating health care provider with or without prior authorization; or (ii)(I) such services will be provided without imposing any requirement under the plan for prior authorization of services or any limitation on coverage where the provider of services does not have a contractual relationship with the plan for the providing of services that is more restrictive than the requirements or limitations that apply to emergency department services received from providers who do have such a contractual relationship with the plan; and (II) if such services are provided out-of-network, the cost-sharing requirement (expressed as a copayment amount or coinsurance rate) is the same requirement that would apply if such services were provided in-network; (D) without regard to any other term or condition of such coverage (other than exclusion or coordination of benefits, or an affiliation or waiting period, permitted under section 2701 of this Act, section 701 of the Employee Retirement Income Security Act of 1974, or section 9801 of the Internal Revenue Code of 1986, and other than applicable cost-sharing).

(2) DEFINITIONS.—In this subsection: (A) EMERGENCY MEDI-CAL CONDITION.—The term 'emergency medical condition' means a medical condition manifesting itself by acute symptoms of sufficient severity (including severe pain) such that a prudent layperson, who possesses an average knowledge of health and medicine, could reasonably expect the absence of immediate medical attention to result in a condition described in clause (i), (ii), or (iii) of section 1867(e)(1)(A) of the Social Security Act. (B) EMER-GENCY SERVICES.—The term 'emergency services' means, with respect to an emergency medical condition—(i) a medical screening examination (as required under section 1867 of the Social Security Act) that is within the capability of the emergency department of a hospital, including ancillary services routinely available to the emergency department to evaluate such emergency medical condition, and (ii) within the capabilities of the staff and facilities available at the hospital, such further medical examination and treatment as are required under section 1867 of such Act to stabilize the patient. (C) STABILIZE.—The term 'to stabilize', with respect to an emergency medical condition (as defined in subparagraph (A)), has the meaning give in section 1867(e)(3) of the Social Security Act (42 U.S.C. 1395dd(e)(3)).

Imagine that you are counsel to the Med and that this statute now applies (the patient protection provisions of the law generally went into effect in 2010). What services could you bill for? What patient cost-sharing rules would apply to your claim? What if your claim is for hundreds of thousands of dollars? Will the plan have to pay? See 29 C.F.R. § 2590.715–2719A(b) (interim final rule), 75 Fed. Reg. 37,188 (June 28, 2010), which follows the statute in requiring payment of out-of-network services if the plan "provides any benefit with respect to services in an emergency department of a hospital." The rule also sets minimum payment standards equal to the greatest of what the plan pays its in-network providers, what the plan typically pays for out-of-network care (typically a percent of the provider's "usual and customary" rate) or the Medicare payment rate. *Id.* Furthermore, can the hospital, if out-of-network, balance bill the patient for the difference between what the plan or insurer pays (minus the required patient cost-sharing) and the full amount charged? The answer is yes according to the Departments of Labor, Health and Human Services, and Treasury, because the Affordable Care Act does not bar balance billing; indeed, the agencies base their minimum payment standard regulation on the fact that in the absence of such a standard or protection from balance billing, the provisions of the Act would effectively provide no protection at all, since plan administrators could pay next to nothing, leaving patients exposed to the entire charge. 75 Fed. Reg. at 37,194.

5. HEALTH BENEFIT PLAN DESIGN AND THE ERISA SETTLOR FUNCTION

McGann v. H & H Music Co.

946 F.2d 401 (5th Cir. 1991), *cert. den.,* 506 U.S. 981 (1992)

■ GARWOOD, CIRCUIT JUDGE:

Plaintiff-appellant John McGann (McGann) filed this suit under section 510 of the Employee Retirement Income Security Act of 1974, Pub.L. No. 93–406 (29 U.S.C. §§ 1001–1461) (ERISA), against defendants-appellees H & H Music Company (H & H Music), Brook Mays Music Company (Brook Mays) and General American Life Insurance Company (General American) (collectively defendants) claiming that they discriminated against McGann, an employee of H & H Music, by reducing benefits available to H & H Music's group medical plan beneficiaries for treatment for acquired immune deficiency syndrome (AIDS) and related illnesses. The district court granted defendants' motion for summary judgment on the ground that an employer has an absolute right to alter the terms of medical coverage available to plan beneficiaries. We affirm.

FACTS AND PROCEEDINGS BELOW

McGann, an employee of H & H Music, discovered that he was afflicted with AIDS in December 1987. Soon thereafter, McGann submitted his first claims for reimbursement under H & H Music's group medical plan, provided through Brook Mays, the plan administrator, and issued by General American, the plan insurer, and informed his employer that he had AIDS. McGann met with officials of H & H Music in March 1988, at which time they discussed McGann's illness. Before the change in the terms of the plan, it provided for lifetime medical benefits of up to $1,000,000 to all employees.

In July 1988, H & H Music informed its employees that, effective August 1, 1988, changes would be made in their medical coverage. These changes included, but were not limited to, limitation of benefits payable for AIDS-related claims to a lifetime maximum of $5,000.[1] No limitation was placed on any other catastrophic illness. H & H Music became self-insured under the new plan and General American became the plan's administrator. By January 1990, McGann had exhausted the $5,000 limit on coverage for his illness.

In August 1989, McGann sued H & H Music, Brook Mays and General American under section 510 of ERISA, which provides, in part, as follows:

"It shall be unlawful for any person to discharge, fine, suspend, expel, discipline, or discriminate against a participant or beneficiary for exercising any right to which he is entitled under the provisions of an employee benefit plan, ... or for the purpose of

---

1. Other changes included increased individual and family deductibles, elimination of coverage for chemical dependency treatment, adoption of a preferred provider plan and increased contribution requirements.

interfering with the attainment of any right to which such participant may become entitled under the plan ...'' 29 U.S.C. § 1140.

McGann claimed that defendants discriminated against him in violation of both prohibitions of section 510. He claimed that the provision limiting coverage for AIDS-related expenses was directed specifically at him in retaliation for exercising his rights under the medical plan and for the purpose of interfering with his attainment of a right to which he may become entitled under the plan.

Defendants, conceding the factual allegations of McGann's complaint, moved for summary judgment. These factual allegations include no assertion that the reduction of AIDS benefits was intended to deny benefits to McGann for any reason which would not be applicable to other beneficiaries who might then or thereafter have AIDS, but rather that the reduction was prompted by the knowledge of McGann's illness, and that McGann was the only beneficiary then known to have AIDS.[4] On June 26, 1990, the district court granted defendants' motion on the ground that they had an absolute right to alter the terms of the plan, regardless of their intent in making the alterations. The district court also held that even if the issue of discriminatory motive were relevant, summary judgment would still be proper because the defendants' motive was to ensure the future existence of the plan and not specifically to retaliate against McGann or to interfere with his exercise of future rights under the plan.

DISCUSSION

McGann contends that defendants violated both clauses of section 510 by discriminating against him for two purposes: (1) "for exercising any right to which [the beneficiary] is entitled," and (2) "for the purpose of interfering with the attainment of any right to which such participant may become entitled." At trial, McGann would bear the burden of proving the existence of defendants' specific discriminatory intent as an essential element of either of his claims. Kimbro v. Atlantic Richfield Co., 889 F.2d 869, 881 (9th Cir. 1989) (employee must prove employer's specific intent to retaliate for employee's exercise of rights under plan), cert. den., 498 U.S. 814 (1990). Thus, in order to survive summary judgment McGann must make a showing sufficient to establish that a genuine issue exists as to defendants' specific intent to retaliate against McGann for filing claims for AIDS-related treatment or to interfere with McGann's attainment of any right to which he may have become entitled.

Although we assume there was a connection between the benefits reduction and either McGann's filing of claims or his revelations about his illness, there is nothing in the record to suggest that defendants' motivation was other than as they asserted, namely to avoid the expense of paying for AIDS treatment (if not, indeed, also for other treatment), no more for McGann than for any other present or future plan beneficiary who might suffer from AIDS. McGann concedes that the reduction in AIDS benefits

4. We assume, for purposes of this appeal that the defendants' knowledge of McGann's illness was a motivating factor in their decision to reduce coverage for AIDS-related expenses, that this knowledge was obtained either through McGann's filing of claims or his meetings with defendants, and that McGann was the only plan beneficiary then known to have AIDS.

will apply equally to all employees filing AIDS-related claims and that the effect of the reduction will not necessarily be felt only by him. He fails to allege that the coverage reduction was otherwise specifically intended to deny him particularly medical coverage except "in effect." He does not challenge defendants' assertion that their purpose in reducing AIDS benefits was to reduce costs.

Furthermore, McGann has failed to adduce evidence of the existence of "any right to which [he] may become entitled under the plan." The right referred to in the second clause of section 510 is not simply any right to which an employee may conceivably become entitled, but rather any right to which an employee may become entitled pursuant to an existing, enforceable obligation assumed by the employer. "Congress viewed [section 510] as a crucial part of ERISA because, without it, employers would be able to circumvent the provision of *promised* benefits." Ingersoll–Rand Co. v. McClendon, 498 U.S. 133 (1990).

McGann's allegations show no *promised* benefit, for there is nothing to indicate that defendants ever promised that the $1,000,000 coverage limit was permanent. The H & H Music plan expressly provides: "Termination or Amendment of Plan: The Plan Sponsor may terminate or amend the Plan at any time or terminate any benefit under the Plan at any time." There is no allegation or evidence that any oral or written representations were made to McGann that the $1,000,000 coverage limit would never be lowered. Defendants broke no promise to McGann. The continued availability of the $1,000,000 limit was not a right to which McGann may have become entitled for the purposes of section 510.[5] To adopt McGann's contrary construction of this portion of section 510 would mean that an employer could not effectively reserve the right to amend a medical plan to reduce benefits respecting subsequently incurred medical expenses, as H & H Music did here, because such an amendment would obviously have as a purpose preventing participants from attaining the right to such future benefits as they otherwise might do under the existing plan absent the amendment. But this is plainly not the law, and ERISA does not require such "vesting" of the right to a continued level of the same medical benefits once those are ever included in a welfare plan. *See* Moore v. Metropolitan Life Insurance Co., 856 F.2d 488, 492 (2d Cir. 1988).

McGann appears to contend that the reduction in AIDS benefits alone supports an inference of specific intent to retaliate against him or to interfere with his future exercise of rights under the plan. McGann characterizes as evidence of an individualized intent to discriminate the fact that AIDS was the only catastrophic illness to which the $5,000 limit was applied and the fact that McGann was the only employee known to have AIDS. He contends that if defendants reduced AIDS coverage because they learned of McGann's illness through his exercising of his rights under

---

5. McGann does not claim that he was not fully reimbursed for all claimed medical expenses incurred on or prior to August 1, 1988; or that the full $5,000 has not been made available to him in respect to AIDS related medical expenses incurred by him on or after July 1, 1988.

the plan by filing claims, the coverage reduction therefore could be "retaliation" for McGann's filing of the claims.[6] Under McGann's theory, any reduction in employee benefits would be impermissibly discriminatory if motivated by a desire to avoid the anticipated costs of continuing to provide coverage for a particular beneficiary. McGann would find an implied promise not to discriminate for this purpose; it is the breaking of this promise that McGann appears to contend constitutes interference with a future entitlement.

McGann cites only one case in which a court has ruled that a change in the terms and conditions of an employee-benefits plan could constitute illegal discrimination under section 510.[7] *Vogel v. Independence Federal Sav. Bank,* 728 F.Supp. 1210 (D. Md. 1990). In *Vogel,* however, the plan change at issue resulted in the plaintiff and only the plaintiff being excluded from coverage. McGann asserts that the *Vogel* court rejected the defendant's contention that mere termination of benefits could not constitute unlawful discrimination under section 510, but in fact the court rejected this claim not because it found that mere termination of coverage could constitute discrimination under section 510, but rather because the termination at issue affected only the beneficiary. Nothing in *Vogel* suggests that the change there had the potential to then or thereafter exclude any present or possible future plan beneficiary other than the plaintiff. *Vogel* therefore provides no support for the proposition that the alteration or termination of a medical plan could alone sustain a section 510 claim. Without necessarily approving of the holding in *Vogel,* we note that it is inapplicable to the instant case. The post-August 1, 1988 $5,000 AIDS coverage limit applies to any and all employees.[8]

McGann effectively contends that section 510 was intended to prohibit any discrimination in the alteration of an employee benefits plan that results in an identifiable employee or group of employees being treated

---

6. We assume that discovery of McGann's condition—and realization of the attendant, long-term costs of caring for McGann—did in fact prompt defendants to reconsider the $1,000,000 limit with respect to AIDS-related expenses and to reduce the limit for future such expenses to $5,000.

7. Additionally, McGann relies on three cases involving wrongful termination claims brought under section 510. Fitzgerald v. Codex Corp., 882 F.2d 586 (1st Cir.1989); Kross v. Western Electric Co., 701 F.2d 1238 (7th Cir.1983); Folz v. Marriott Corp., 594 F. Supp. 1007 (W.D.Mo.1984). In none of these cases, however, did the employer alter the terms or conditions of the plan at issue. Nor did any one of the three suggest that the changing of the terms of the plan might constitute a violation of section 510.

8. As noted, the district court stated as one ground for its decision that an employer has an absolute right to alter the terms of an employee benefits plan, barring contractual provisions to the contrary. *See* Deeming v. American Standard, Inc., 905 F.2d 1124, 1127 (7th Cir.1990) ("allegation that the employer-employee relationship, and not merely the pension plan, was changed in some discriminatory or wrongful way" is "a fundamental prerequisite to a § 510 action"); Owens v. Storehouse, Inc., 773 F. Supp. 416, 418 (N.D.Ga.1991) (relying on *Deeming* in rejecting claim that employer violated section 510 by reducing AIDS benefits from $1,000,000 to $25,000 under employee health plan on ground that "§ 510 was designed to protect the 'employment relationship,' not the integrity of specific plans."). We do not find it necessary to decide this question.

differently from other employees. The First Circuit rejected a somewhat similar contention in Aronson v. Servus Rubber, Div. of Chromalloy, 730 F.2d 12 (1st Cir.), *cert. den.,* 469 U.S. 1017 (1984). In *Aronson,* an employer eliminated a profit sharing plan with respect to employees at only one of two plants. The disenfranchised employees sued their employer under section 510, claiming that partial termination of the plan with respect to employees at one plant and not at the other constituted illegal discrimination. The court rejected the employees' discrimination claim, stating in part:

> "[Section 510] relates to discriminatory conduct directed against individuals, not to actions involving the plan in general. The problem is with the word 'discriminate.' An overly literal interpretation of this section would make illegal any partial termination, since such terminations obviously interfere with the attainment of benefits by the terminated group, and, indeed, are expressly intended so to interfere.... This is not to say that a plan could not be discriminatorily modified, intentionally benefiting, or injuring, certain identified employees or a certain group of employees, but a partial termination cannot constitute discrimination per se. A termination that cuts along independently established lines—here separate divisions—and that has a readily apparent business justification, demonstrates no invidious intent." *Id.* at 16 (citation omitted).

The Supreme Court has observed in dictum: "ERISA does not mandate that employers provide any particular benefits, and does not itself proscribe discrimination in the provision of employee benefits." Shaw v. Delta Air Lines, Inc., 463 U.S. 85, [90] (1983). To interpret "discrimination" broadly to include defendants' conduct would clearly conflict with Congress's intent that employers remain free to create, modify and terminate the terms and conditions of employee benefits plans without governmental interference.

The Sixth Circuit, in rejecting a challenge to an employer's freedom to choose the terms of its employee pension plan, stated that

> "[i]n enacting ERISA, Congress continued its reliance on *voluntary* action by employers by granting substantial tax advantages for the creation of qualified retirement programs. Neither Congress nor the courts are involved in either the decision to establish a plan or in the decision concerning which benefits a plan should provide. In particular, courts have no authority to decide which benefits employers must confer upon their employees; these are decisions which are more appropriately influenced by forces in the marketplace and, when appropriate, by federal legislation. Absent a violation of federal or state law, a federal court may not modify a substantive provision of a pension plan." *Id.* (citation omitted) (emphasis in original).

The Sixth Circuit has subsequently declared that "the principle articulated in [*Reynolds Metals*] applies with at least as much force to welfare plans ...'' Musto v. American General Corp., 861 F.2d 897, 912 (6th Cir. 1988), *cert. den.,* 490 U.S. 1020 (1989).[9]

As persuasively explained by the Second Circuit, the policy of allowing employers freedom to amend or eliminate employee benefits is particularly compelling with respect to medical plans:

> "With regard to an employer's right to change medical plans, Congress evidenced its recognition of the need for flexibility in rejecting the automatic vesting of welfare plans. Automatic vesting was rejected because the costs of such plans are subject to fluctuating and unpredictable variables. Actuarial decisions concerning fixed annuities are based on fairly stable data, and vesting is appropriate. In contrast, medical insurance must take account of inflation, changes in medical practice and technology, and increases in the costs of treatment independent of inflation. These unstable variables prevent accurate predictions of future needs and costs." *Moore,* 856 F.2d at 492.

In *Metropolitan Life,* the court rejected an ERISA claim by retirees that their employer could not change the level of their medical benefits without their consent. The court stated that limiting an employer's right to change medical plans increased the risk of "decreas[ing] protection for future employees and retirees." *Id.* at 492; *see also Reynolds Metals,* 740 F.2d at 457 ("judicial interference into the establishment of pension plan provisions ... would serve only to discourage employers from creating voluntarily pension plans") (footnote omitted).

McGann's claim cannot be reconciled with the well-settled principle that Congress did not intend that ERISA circumscribe employers' control over the content of benefits plans they offered to their employees. McGann interprets section 510 to prevent an employer from reducing or eliminating coverage for a particular illness in response to the escalating costs of covering an employee suffering from that illness. Such an interpretation would, in effect, change the terms of H & H Music's plan. Instead of making the $1,000,000 limit available for medical expenses on an as-incurred basis only as long as the limit remained in effect, the policy would make the limit *permanently* available for all medical expenses as they might thereafter be incurred because of a single event, such as the contracting of AIDS. Under McGann's theory, defendants would be effectively proscribed from reducing coverage for AIDS once McGann had contracted that illness and filed claims for AIDS-related expenses. If a federal court could prevent an employer from reducing an employee's coverage limits for AIDS treatment once that employee contracted AIDS, the boundaries of judicial

---

9. *Musto* involved an ERISA claim by retirees that their former employer violated contractual and fiduciary duties by changing the terms of their medical coverage. The court rejected plaintiffs' claim that they had a vested interest in the terms of their medical coverage. *Musto,* like *Reynolds Metals,* noted that "[t]here is a world of difference between administering a welfare plan in accordance with its terms and deciding what those terms are to be. A company acts as a fiduciary in performing the first task, but not the second." *Id.* at 911.

involvement in the creation, alteration or termination of ERISA plans would be sorely tested.

As noted, McGann has failed to adduce any evidence of defendants' specific intent to engage in conduct proscribed by section 510. Proof of defendants' specific intent to discriminate among plan beneficiaries on grounds not proscribed by section 510 does not enable McGann to avoid summary judgment. ERISA does not broadly prevent an employer from "discriminating" in the creation, alteration or termination of employee benefits plans; thus, evidence of such intentional discrimination cannot alone sustain a claim under section 510. That section does not prohibit welfare plan discrimination between or among categories of diseases. Section 510 does not mandate that if some, or most, or virtually all catastrophic illnesses are covered, AIDS (or any other particular catastrophic illness) must be among them. It does not prohibit an employer from electing not to cover or continue to cover AIDS, while covering or continuing to cover other catastrophic illnesses, even though the employer's decision in this respect may stem from some "prejudice" against AIDS or its victims generally. The same, of course, is true of any other disease and its victims. That sort of "discrimination" is simply not addressed by section 510. Under section 510, the asserted discrimination is illegal only if it is motivated by a desire to retaliate against an employee or to deprive an employee of an existing right to which he may become entitled. The district court's decision to grant summary judgment to defendants therefore was proper. Its judgment is accordingly

AFFIRMED.

Notes

1.   *Reaction to* McGann. *McGann* provoked passionate criticism. The AARP, the AMA, the AHA, the National Governor's Association the U.S. Conference of Mayors and many others urged the first Bush Administration to ask the Supreme Court to reverse. Kathlynn L. Butler, *Securing Employee Benefits through ERISA and the ADA*, 42 EMORY L.J. 1197, 1230 (1993). The Administration filed an amicus brief supporting the *McGann* decision as a correct interpretation of ERISA, and noting that the Americans with Disabilities Act, which was enacted after the events in *McCann*, obviated the need for Supreme Court action. The application of the ADA to these facts is considered later in this Part. *McGann* led a wave of employers to also reduce HIV/AIDS coverage. Milt Freudenheim, *Patients Cite Bias in AIDS Coverage by Health Plans*, N.Y. TIMES, June 1, 1993, at A1.

2.   *Does the Affordable Care Act change the outcome in* McGann? As discussed in Chapter 6, ERISA contains certain substantive coverage provisions, most notably parity in the treatment of covered services for mental illness and substance abuse. (Mental health parity is discussed below following *Jones v. Kodak Medical Assistance Plan*, 169 F.3d 1287 (10th Cir. 1999)). *See.* ERISA § 712, PHSA § 2705. *See* 74 Fed. Reg. 5,409–5,451 (Feb. 2, 2010) (Interim Final Regulations).

Kenseth makes the point that coverage-based distinctions need to be distinguished from pre-existing condition exclusions, which were first limited in the group market under HIPAA, with the prohibition strengthened and extended to the individual insurance market under the Affordable Care Act. A pre-existing condition exclusion bars or limits coverage in the case of persons with certain conditions at the time of enrollment. By contrast, coverage exclusions of the sort seen in *McGann* apply to plan members, no matter when their health problems arose.

As noted in Chapter 6, the Affordable Care Act requires insurance products sold in the individual and small group markets to cover "essential health benefits" that encompass certain benefit classes (ambulatory patient services, emergency services, hospitalization, maternity and newborn care, mental health and substance use disorder services, including behavioral health treatment, prescription drugs, rehabilitative and habilitative services and devices, laboratory services, preventive and wellness services and chronic disease management, and pediatric services including oral and vision care). PPACA § 1302. In implementing this provision, in December 2011 the Secretary of HHS issued policy guidance that vests states with broad discretion to interpret the scope and range of essential health benefits. The notice does not address how the Secretary intends to interpret, apply and enforce against the states a crucial provision of the Act related to discrimination against persons with disabilities, despite the fact that the Act clearly instructs the Secretary ["shall" is a drafting term not used lightly] to set standards:

> In defining the essential health benefits, the Secretary shall—(B) not make coverage decisions, determine reimbursement rates, establish incentive programs, or design benefits in ways that discriminate against individuals because of their age, disability, or expected length of life.

PPACA § 1302(b)(4)(B).

Is it possible to square this statutory language with the agency's approach to implementation that tells states that they have the power to define coverage based on existing markets? The December 16, 2011 Bulletin on Essential Health Benefits, http://cciio.cms.gov/resources/files/Files2/12162011/essential_health_benefits_bulletin.pdf, provides that states may choose among several different market products in defining essential health benefits (e.g., the largest small-group product sold in the state, the largest HMO product sold in the state, the federal employee health benefit plan if the state so chooses) because other than cost-sharing (which is lower in more large plans and plans with higher premiums) product design is consistent across product markets:

> [Products sold] in the small group market, State employee plans, and the Federal Employees Health Benefits Program (FEHBP) Blue Cross Blue Shield (BCBS) Standard Option and Government Employees Health Association (GEHA) plans do not differ significantly in the range of services they cover. They differ mainly in cost-sharing provisions, but cost-sharing is not taken into account

in determining EHB. Similarly, these plans and products and the small group issuers surveyed by the IOM appear to generally cover health care services in virtually all of the 10 statutory categories.

Id. at 3.

Is this any sort of answer? What if all plans discriminate against persons with HIV by severely limiting and excluding coverage? Recall that under Bragdon v. Abbott, 524 U.S. 624 (1998) (Part One), HIV is a recognized disability under the Americans with Disabilities Act. Given the Act's language, which for the first time appears to reach the content of coverage itself, could a state select a product that limits or excludes coverage of treatment for HIV/AIDS? Is the Secretary at liberty to approve such a state selection? As you will learn in Doe v. Mutual of Omaha, 179 F.3d 557 (7th Cir. 1999), *cert. den.*, 528 U.S. 1106 (2000), discussed in Chapter 9, this type of across-the-board treatment limitation does not violate the Americans with Disabilities Act. For an argument that the disability discrimination "considerations" to be addressed by the Secretary would not necessarily bar across-the-board limitations and exclusions as long as such limitations and exclusions are applied to all conditions, *see* Sara Rosenbaum et al., *Crossing the Rubicon: The Impact of the Affordable Care Act on the Content of Coverage for Persons with Disabilities*, 25 NOTRE DAME J. OF L., ETHICS, & PUB. POL. 527 (2011).

Jones v. The Kodak Medical Assistance Plan

169 F.3d 1287 (10th Cir.1999)

■ KELLY, CIRCUIT JUDGE:

Russell Jones and Susan Jones appeal from entry of summary judgment for Kodak Medical Assistance Plan ("KMED" or "Plan") on claims to recover health benefits. The Joneses contend that the district court (1) should have reviewed KMED's decision to deny benefits for substance abuse treatment with less deference because of the Plan Administrator's alleged conflict of interest; (2) erred in concluding that the criteria upon which the Plan Administrator based his decision were part of the Plan and thus could not be reviewed; (3) should have held that the Plan Administrator acted arbitrarily and capriciously. [W]e affirm.

Background

Russell Jones worked for Eastman Kodak and was a participant in the KMED Plan. His wife, Susan Jones—at all relevant times a beneficiary of the Plan—had an alcohol abuse problem for which she sought treatment. Under the Plan, treatment for mental health and substance abuse problems are subject to pre-certification requirements, and the Plan Summary explicitly states that failure to obtain pre-certification may result in the reduction or denial of benefits. According to the Plan Summary, American PsychManagement ("APM") administers the managed care review process under which the medical appropriateness of substance abuse treatment is assessed. KMED informs Plan participants that it "does not cover expenses for services and items that are considered medically unnecessary, experimental, or investigational."

The Plan Administrator has "full discretionary authority in all matters related to the discharge of his responsibilities including, without limitation, his construction of the terms of the Plan and his determination of eligibility for Coverage and Benefits." The Plan Administrator is an Eastman Kodak employee, and the Plan is entirely self-funded, which means that Eastman Kodak employees do not contribute toward the premiums. Rather, payment for covered medical care comes out of company revenues.

On March 30, 1993, Sierra Tucson Hospital in Arizona contacted APM to obtain pre-certification for inpatient alcohol treatment of Mrs. Jones. APM denied pre-certification the same day on the grounds that (1) inpatient care was not medically necessary and (2) it would be too difficult for Mrs. Jones' family to participate in an out-of-state-program. APM determines the medical appropriateness of inpatient substance abuse treatment according to six criteria, three of which the patient must meet. Of the three criteria, one must be a history of either "structured outpatient rehab with less than one year sobriety/abstinence following completion of the outpatient program" or "two hospitalizations for detox with failure to follow up with structured outpatient rehab." Mrs. Jones did not meet these requirements.

After APM denied pre-certification for the Sierra Tucson program, Mrs. Jones suffered an alcoholic episode in which she contemplated suicide and, consequently, was admitted for a short stay at Charter Canyon Hospital in Utah, the state in which the Joneses resided. APM pre-certified this course of action. Dissatisfied with Charter Canyon, however, Mr. Jones notified APM on April 1, 1993, that he planned to take Mrs. Jones to Sierra Tucson. Mrs. Jones received inpatient treatment at Sierra Tucson from April 1 to May 1, 1993. Based on APM's refusal to pre-certify the Sierra Tucson program, the Plan declined to cover these services.

The Joneses pursued their claim through all levels of appeal available under the Plan. During this process, the Plan Administrator sent relevant medical information about Mrs. Jones to an independent reviewer, Dr. Richard B. Freeman, who concluded: "The patient did not meet APM's admission criteria. Therefore the case manager acted appropriately according to APM's guidelines." However, Dr. Freeman also opined that "the APM criteria are too rigid and do not allow for individualization of case management." The Plan Administrator nevertheless denied the Joneses' claim, and they filed suit in federal district court.

On June 10, 1996, the district court granted KMED's motion for summary judgment on the grounds that (1) the Plan Administrator's decision was neither arbitrary nor capricious and (2) KMED's failure to include the APM criteria in its Plan documents did not violate the disclosure requirements of ERISA. The Joneses were allowed to amend their complaint to allege that the APM criteria themselves were arbitrary and capricious. But the court subsequently granted KMED's second motion for summary judgment because it found that the APM criteria constituted part of the Plan and thus lay outside the scope of judicial review.

B. Reviewability of APM Criteria

In granting KMED's second motion for summary judgment, the district court found that the unpublished APM criteria were part of the Plan's terms and, hence, that it could not review them. We agree.

A plan participant has right to know where she stands with respect to her benefits. See *Firestone Tire & Rubber Co.*, 489 U.S. 101. However, ERISA's disclosure provisions do not require that the plan summary contain particularized criteria for determining the medical necessity of treatment for individual illnesses. Indeed, such a requirement would frustrate the purpose of a summary—to offer a layperson concise information that she can read and digest. In the instant case, the Plan Summary expressly authorized APM to determine eligibility for substance abuse treatment according to its own criteria. The APM criteria did not need to be listed in Plan documents to constitute part of the Plan.

Because we consider the APM criteria a matter of Plan design and structure, rather than implementation, we agree that a court cannot review them. Indeed, an employer may draft a benefits plan any way it wishes; it does not act as a fiduciary when it sets the terms of the plan. We hold that the district court properly granted summary judgment for KMED on the issue of whether the APM criteria were arbitrary and capricious.

C. Plan Administrator's Decision

The Joneses challenge the district court's determination that the Plan Administrator did not act arbitrarily and capriciously. Under the relevant standard of review, a court may not overturn a plan administrator's decision if it was reasonable, given the terms of the plan, and made in good faith. Even considering the alleged conflict of interest, ruling that inpatient care at Sierra Tucson was medically unnecessary and geographically inappropriate does not appear unreasonable. An impartial reviewer, Dr. Freeman, agreed with the Plan Administrator that Mrs. Jones "clearly [did] not meet the established American PsychManagement criteria for admission to an inpatient rehabilitation service." Because the APM criteria were part of the language of the Plan shielded from judicial review, and because Mrs. Jones presented no evidence that the criteria were applied in a discriminatory manner in her case, the Plan Administrator's reliance on them was neither arbitrary nor capricious.

The judgment of the district court is AFFIRMED.

Notes

1. *Treatment guidelines as part of benefit and coverage design. Jones* demonstrates that incorporating fixed treatment guidelines directly into plan documents can serve to effectively narrow coverage to the conditions and treatments enumerated in the guidelines. Once embedded in plan

documents, the guidelines become a limiting factor in coverage design and cannot be challenged, just as the clear exclusion of a treatment from the scope of coverage cannot be contested. In such a situation, it does not matter that the claimant would benefit from the excluded treatment or that the treatments authorized by the guidelines are not medically appropriate. Rather than expressing coverage in the form of broad benefit classes and leaving to the discretion of the plan administrator the decision as to whether the treatment is appropriate in a particular case, the guidelines act as an across-the-board limitation on coverage, binding the administrator and excluding other treatments from coverage.

In *Mondry* the documents on which CIGNA relied ultimately had to be disclosed, and the case was about how it is possible to win a disclosure battle. Here, as you can see in *Jones*, there is no way to win the larger coverage war. Sponsors can exclude anything, no matter how medically necessary. The administrator ultimately may have to come clean and disclose the documents, but in the end, coverage limits can be completely arbitrary and unfair and the plan will win on settler function grounds.

Why not disclose right away and just not even lead the beneficiaries and participants on? Why write vague documents that lead patients to believe they are going to get coverage when they won't? The answer may be three-fold: First, the materials used by administrators to determine whether *individual treatments* within any broad benefit class will be covered are so voluminous that disclosure is virtually impossible. Second, the material governing covered treatments is "proprietary" (everyone's favorite excuse). Third, sponsors of both insured and self-insured plans realize that given the horrible cost of health care, their premiums are too low to get coverage that truly encompasses all medically necessary health care, but they are too overwhelmed to be fully informed, nor can any mere mortal grasp it. Hence, they enter into vague agreements that give their plan administrators a vast amount of running room to impose exclusions under the vague terms in order to keep costs in line.

As the court points out, when coverage is expressed as a preset treatment menu, there is no denial from which a claimant may appeal within the claims process. This is why the distinction between plan interpretation and medical judgment in the full and fair hearing review regulations promulgated by the Treasury, Labor, and Health and Human Services Departments and discussed above becomes so important. Where the denial of coverage is based on medical judgment that a particular covered benefit is not necessary, the claimant can obtain an external and binding review. Where, however, the denial is based on the interpretation of plan documents and a finding by the administrator that the coverage sought is in fact excluded as a matter of plan interpretation, the claimant's only recourse is to challenge the administrator's decision in federal court, at which point, as you will see, the court's normal approach to the decision will be highly deferential to the plan. The practice of embedding limiting treatment guidelines into plan documents raises important questions regarding the quality of the guidelines, an issue explored more fully in Part Three.

2.   *The Affordable Care Act and the use of treatment guidelines to limit coverage.* While the Affordable Care Act requires products sold in the individual and small group markets to cover certain "essential health benefits," the law also appears to recognize the use of treatment guidelines as an explicit and permissible mechanism for limiting coverage:

> Notwithstanding any other provision of the Patient Protection and Affordable Care Act, nothing in such Act (or an amendment made by such Act) shall be construed to (1) prohibit (or authorize the Secretary of Health and Human Services to promulgate regulations that prohibit) a group health plan or health insurance issuer from carrying out utilization management techniques that are commonly used as of the date of enactment of this Act.

PPACA § 1563(d).

The question of course is whether embedded treatment guidelines are a "commonly used" "utilization management technique." This question has not yet been answered by the Secretary of Health and Human Services.

3.   *Mental health parity.* Since 1996, health insurers operating in the group health insurance market and ERISA-sponsored health benefit plans have been required to comply with certain requirements related to parity in coverage of treatment and services for mental illness. 42 U.S.C. § 300gg–26; 29 U.S.C. § 1185a. In 2008, the parity law, which applies to groups of 50 full-time employees or greater, was broadened to reach more types of limits and to extend parity requirements to substance use disorders. Paul Wellstone & Pete Domenici, Mental Health Parity and Addiction Equity Act, Pub. L. No. 110–343, 110th Cong., 2d Sess. (2008).* The Affordable Care Act extended the 2008 parity requirements to qualified health plans sold to individuals and small groups in state health insurance Exchanges "in the same manner and to the same extent as such section applies to health insurance issuers and group health plans." PPACA § 1311(j).

But where parity is concerned, what the ACA gives with one hand, it seemingly takes away with the other. Despite the fact that the ACA extends parity to qualified health plans sold through state health insurance Exchanges, the Act also appears to retain the 2008 parity law's small employer exemption. Furthermore, the ACA redefines the small employer group exemption to reach employers with *100 or fewer* fulltime employees, a literal doubling of the 2008 Act's small-employer exemption. As a result, although qualified health plans will be required to satisfy parity require-

---

* The parity provisions can be found at Title VIII of the 2008 Act, which created the Troubled Assets Relief Program (TARP). Needless to say, parity had nothing to do with troubled assets, but such are the ways of Congress, which sought to honor both Senator Wellstone, who had recently died in a tragic plane crash, and Senator Pete Domenici, who was retiring from the Senate. Both Senators, one the most liberal and the other quite conservative, had long careers advocating for the rights of persons with mental illness. This type of bipartisan advocacy to improve individual rights, once a relatively common occurrence, has become almost non-existent in 2011.

ments in the individual Exchange market, virtually all small-employer groups, whether or not they buy coverage through state Exchanges, will be exempt from parity requirements. *See* Amanda K. Sarata, *Mental Health Parity and the Patient Protection and Affordable Care Act of 2010*, at 6–8 (CONG. RES. SERV., Dec. 28, 2011), www.ncsl.org/documents/**health/** MH**parity** & mandates.pdf.

The parity statute does not require that employer plans to which it applies cover mental illness or provide benefits for substance abuse disorders (recall however, that under the Affordable Care Act, products subject to the essential health benefit requirements, which go into effect on January 1, 2014, will be required to cover both classes of benefits). Instead, the law's purpose is to assure parity with respect to whatever coverage is offered.

The 1996 amendments only established limited parity, barring just differential "aggregate lifetime limits." 29 U.S.C. § 1185a(a). The 2008 amendments broadened the concept of parity considerably to also reach plan coverage practices related to treatment limitations, patient cost-sharing and provider network rules. 29 U.S.C. § 1185a(a)(1)–(3). The concept of a treatment limitation was defined to include "limits on the frequency of treatment, number of visits, days of coverage, or other similar limits on the scope or duration of treatment." 29 U.S.C. § 1185a(a)(3)(B).

The parity statute, which applies to employers with more than 50 fulltime employees, also contains a Rule of Construction creating exceptions to the parity requirements. Prior to 2008, this Rule of Construction read in pertinent part as follows:

> b) Construction. Nothing in this section shall be construed—(2) as affecting the terms and conditions *(including requirements relating to medical necessity)* relating to the amount, duration, or scope of mental health benefits under the plan or coverage, except as specifically provided. (Emphasis added).

As revised by the 2008 amendments, 29 U.S.C. § 1185a(b)(2) now reads as follows:

> (b) Construction. Nothing in this section shall be construed—(2) as affecting the terms and conditions of the plan or coverage relating to such benefits under the plan or coverage, except as provided in subsection (a) [set forth above].

Thus, the 2008 amendments eliminated the parenthetical clause "(including requirements relating to medical necessity)" while leaving intact the general thrust of the Rule, which is designed to leave employers free to entirely exclude coverage of mental illness and substance use disorder treatments.

The question for the implementing agencies became the meaning of the striking of the medical necessity parenthetical provision, for which there was no legislative history. The Departments of Labor, Treasury, and Health and Human Services answered this question in 2010 with an interim final rule (79 Fed. Reg. 5,410–51, Feb. 10, 2010) that defines impermissible treatment limits to encompass both "quantitative" and "non-quantitative" limitations, thus barring not only quantitative limits (e.g., 30 visits) but also differential approaches to medical necessity, including the use of fixed treatment limits unless treatments for physical conditions similarly are curbed by fixed treatment rules.

> Treatment limitations include limits on benefits based on the frequency of treatment, number of visits, days of coverage, days in a waiting period, or other similar limits on the scope or duration of treatment. Treatment limitations include both quantitative treatment limitations, which are expressed numerically (such as 50 outpatient visits per year) and non-quantitative treatment limitations which otherwise limit the scope or duration of benefits for treatment under a plan.

29 C.F.R. § 2590.712(a)

The regulation then provides illustrative examples of prohibited treatment limits:

> Illustrative list of non-quantitative treatment limitations. Non-quantitative treatment limitations include—(A) medical management standards limiting or excluding benefits based on medical necessity or medical appropriateness, or based on whether the treatment is experimental or investigative; (B) formulary design for prescription drugs; (E) refusal to pay for higher-cost therapies until it can be shown that a lower cost therapy is not effective (also known as fail first policies or step therapy protocols); and (F) exclusions based on failure to complete a course of treatment.

29 C.F.R. § 2590.712(c)(4)(ii).

The regulations thus appear to address a common practice in health benefit plan administration in the case of mental illness and substance use disorders, that is, the use of fixed treatment guidelines that cannot be challenged, of the sort seen in *Jones*. Such practices presumably would be barred unless a plan administrator also can show that it uses a comparable approach to limiting coverage for physical health treatments. It is not possible to know whether embedded treatment guidelines that restrict coverage to certain pre-ordained treatments are more common in the case of mental illness and substance use disorders than they are in the case of coverage for physical conditions such as diabetes and cancer. In fact, as you will learn in Part Three, "evidence-based" treatment guidelines are a growing feature of coverage design and plan administration.

At the same time, the strong reaction from the health benefits industry, which filed suit to block the interim final rule on grounds that it violated the Administrative Procedure Act (APA), suggests that these types of fixed and irrefutable treatment limits may still be commonly used to limit coverage of mental illness and substance use disorders. *Behavioral Health Plans Sue HHS, Other Agencies to Block Parity Regulation*, 19 HEALTH LAW REP. 501, April 2, 2010; Robert Pear, *Fight Erupts Over Rules Issued for Mental Health Parity Insurance Law*, N.Y. TIMES, May 10, 2010, at A15. In June, 2010, a federal district court held that the government's interim final rule complied with the requirements of the APA. Coalition for Parity Inc. v. Sebelius, 709 F. Supp.2d 10 (D.D.C. 2010).

One final point: what is the effect of PPACA § 1563(d) on all of this? Recall that this provision, enacted in March 23, 2010, one month after the interim final parity rules were issued, bars the Secretary from prohibiting the use of "commonly used" techniques for "utilization management" that are in use as of the date of enactment. Assume that you are counsel for the Department of Labor. In your view, what impact might this provision have on the interim final rules? Do the parity regulations governing "non-quantitative" treatment limits involve restrictions on "commonly used" "utilization management" techniques? If so, will the final parity rules need to be revised if ERISA plans cannot be subject to restrictions on commonly used utilization management techniques in effect at the time of passage?

4. *Access to treatment guidelines.* ERISA requires disclosure of treatment guidelines if part of the plan documents or if relied upon as part of a claim review that is appealed. The Wellstone/Domenici Act, 29 U.S.C. § 1185a(a)(4), requires plans to make available information regarding their medical necessity criteria upon request. Why must people ask for these guidelines? Why aren't they automatically provided with the Summary Plan Description? For a discussion of the importance of disclosure as the *quid pro quo* for treatment and coverage limits, see Clark C. Havighurst, *Consumers Versus Managed Care: The New Class Actions*, 20(4) HEALTH AFFAIRS 8 (2001).

---

6. JUDICIAL REVIEW OF FIDUCIARY DECISIONS

a. Introduction

The preceding materials touch upon the issue of judicial review of fiduciary decisions. The standard of review is not addressed in ERISA itself; as a result, the United States Supreme Court and the lower courts have struggled to articulate an appropriate judicial approach. The principles that have evolved are grounded in the law of trusts, but as Chief Justice Roberts noted in Conkright v. Frommert, 130 S. Ct. 1640, 1648 (2010), "trust law does not tell you the entire story" but is merely a "starting point, after which courts must go on to ask whether, or to what extent, the language of the statute, its structure, or its purpose, require departing from common law trust requirements."

Judicial review of a fiduciary decision frequently arises in the context of a decision to deny a claim for coverage brought under ERISA § 502(a)(1)(B). An estimated 1.9 million ERISA plan beneficiaries experience a claims denial by a plan annually. C. Gresenz et al., *A Flood of Litigation?* 8 (1999), http:// www. rand. org/ pubs/ issue_ papers/ 2006/ IP 184.pdf. The number of claims that result in a judicial appeal is, of course, infinitesimal compared with the number of denials that go unchallenged, but each case offers important insight into the operations of health benefit plans and the relationship between plan administrators and the courts.

The preceding materials addressed the question of coverage design: that is, what benefits will be included in the health benefit plan for *any* participant or beneficiary? The types of decisions reviewed here focus instead on the question of whether a participant or beneficiary is entitled to receive a covered benefit. Here, the question frequently is whether the treatment for which coverage is requested is medically necessary. The answer to that question will depend on the plan's scope and extent of coverage, how the terms of coverage are defined, the plan's definition of medical necessity, and ultimately, on how the plan administrator applies the terms of the plan to the facts of the particular case. Resolving individual claims for benefits, whether under ERISA, Medicare, Medicaid, or any other form of insurance, thus involves the application of complex legal terms to individual facts. In the case of ERISA, judicial review of these determinations typically begins with a preliminary determination of how much deference to give the plan administrator.

Traditionally, challenges to the denial of a claim for benefits have been based on principles of contract law, and secondarily, on tort or quasi-tort principles. State courts normally do not see themselves as "reviewing" plan administration but instead as interpreting a contract; in this regard, two state contract law doctrines traditionally have been applied to insurance contracts. First, because these contracts are usually not negotiated by policyholders (whether individual or groups), they are treated as contracts of adhesion, with any ambiguity being construed against the contract drafter under the doctrine of *contra proferentum*. Second, because of the imbalance in knowledge and power between insurance companies and their policyholders, many (but not all) state courts, particularly since the early 1970s, have treated insurance companies as fiduciaries vis-à-vis their policyholders, liable for tort or expanded contractual damages for "bad faith breach of contract." See *Sarchett*, 729 P.2d 267. (The question of whether ERISA plan administrators (whether a self-insuring employer or a private insurer) can be held liable for negligence or bad faith breach of contract (as was the case in *Wohlers*, 969 P.2d 949, above) will be examined in the ERISA preemption materials as well as in Part Three).

By contrast, ERISA litigation has taken a different path. ERISA's fiduciary duty provisions were drafted in a manner similar to the fiduciary provisions in the earlier Labor Management Relations Act (LMRA); as a result, federal courts applying ERISA to claims appeals imported the "arbitrary and capricious" or "abuse of discretion" standard from the LMRA cases. *See, e.g.,* Bayles v. Central States, Southeast and Southwest Areas Pension Fund, 602 F.2d 97, 99–100 & n.3 (5th Cir. 1979). Under this standard, claimants challenging a denial of benefits bear a much heavier burden than under state contract or tort law, because "the actions of the trustees in the administration of the pension plan must be sustained as a matter of law unless plaintiff can prove such activities have been arbitrary or capricious." *Id.* at 99. In *Firestone Tire & Rubber Co.,* below, the United

States Supreme Court fashioned a new standard of review that on the one hand seems to move away from LMRA principles while on the other hand permits plan fiduciaries to cement their control over the use of plan resources, particularly when plan documents must be construed.

Firestone Tire & Rubber Co. v. Bruch

489 U.S. 101 (1989)

■ JUSTICE O'CONNOR delivered the opinion of the Court.

[Employees brought an action under ERISA § 502(a)(1)(B), 29 U.S.C. § 1132(a)(1)(B), for benefits due under Firestone's termination pay plan.]

ERISA does not set out the appropriate standard of review for actions under § 1132(a)(1)(B) challenging benefit eligibility determinations. To fill this gap, federal courts have adopted the arbitrary and capricious standard developed under the Labor Management Relations Act, 1947 (LMRA). [Because of differences between the LMRA and ERISA, LMRA principles offer no support for the adoption of the arbitrary and capricious standard insofar as § 1132(a)(1)(B) is concerned.]

ERISA abounds with the language and terminology of trust law. ERISA's legislative history confirms that the Act's fiduciary responsibility provisions, 29 U.S.C. §§ 1101–1114, "codif[y] and mak[e] applicable to [ERISA] fiduciaries certain principles developed in the evolution of the law of trusts." H. R. Rep. No. 93–533, at 11 (1973). Given this language and history, we have held that courts are to develop a "federal common law of rights and obligations under ERISA-regulated plans." See also Franchise Tax Board v. Construction Laborers Vacation Trust, 463 U.S. 1, 24, n. 26 (1983) (" '[A] body of Federal substantive law will be developed by the courts to deal with issues involving rights and obligations under private welfare and pension plans' ") (quoting 129 Cong. Rec. 29942 (1974) (remarks of Sen. Javits)). In determining the appropriate standard of review for actions under § 1132(a)(1)(B), we are guided by principles of trust law.

Trust principles make a deferential standard of review appropriate when a trustee exercises discretionary powers. See Restatement (Second) of Trusts § 187 (1959) ("Where discretion is conferred upon the trustee with respect to the exercise of a power, its exercise is not subject to control by the court except to prevent an abuse by the trustee of his discretion"). See also G. BOGERT & G. BOGERT, LAW OF TRUSTS AND TRUSTEES § 560, 193–208 (2d rev. ed. 1980). A trustee may be given power to construe disputed or doubtful terms, and in such circumstances the trustee's interpretation will not be disturbed if reasonable. *Id.*, § 559, at 169–171. Firestone can seek no shelter in these principles of trust law, however, for there is no evidence that under Firestone's termination pay plan the administrator has the power to construe uncertain terms or that eligibility determinations are to be given deference.

Finding no support in the language of its termination pay plan for the arbitrary and capricious standard, Firestone argues that as a matter of trust law the interpretation of the terms of a plan is an inherently discretionary function. But other settled principles of trust law, which point to *de novo* review of benefit eligibility determinations based on plan interpretations, belie this contention. As they do with contractual provisions, courts construe terms in trust agreements without deferring to either party's interpretation. The terms of trusts created by written instruments are "determined by the provisions of the instrument as interpreted in light of all the circumstances and such other evidence of the intention of the settlor with respect to the trust as is not inadmissible." Restatement (Second) of Trusts § 4, Comment d (1959).

The trust law *de novo* standard of review is consistent with the judicial interpretation of employee benefit plans prior to the enactment of ERISA. Actions challenging an employer's denial of benefits before the enactment of ERISA were governed by principles of contract law. If the plan did not give the employer or administrator discretionary or final authority to construe uncertain terms, the court reviewed the employee's claim as it would have any other contract claim by looking to the terms of the plan and other manifestations of the parties' intent.

ERISA was enacted "to promote the interests of employees and their beneficiaries in employee benefit plans," *Shaw*, 463 U.S. 85, 90, and "to protect contractually defined benefits," Massachusetts Mutual Life Ins. Co. v. Russell, 473 U.S., at 148. See generally 29 U.S.C. § 1001 (setting forth congressional findings and declarations of policy regarding ERISA). Adopting Firestone's reading of ERISA would require us to impose a standard of review that would afford less protection to employees and their beneficiaries than they enjoyed before ERISA was enacted.

Firestone and its amici also assert that a *de novo* standard would contravene the spirit of ERISA because it would impose much higher administrative and litigation costs and therefore discourage employers from creating benefit plans. Because even under the arbitrary and capricious standard an employer's denial of benefits could be subject to judicial review, the assumption seems to be that a *de novo* standard would encourage more litigation by employees, participants, and beneficiaries who wish to assert their right to benefits. Neither general principles of trust law nor a concern for impartial decision making, however, forecloses parties from agreeing upon a narrower standard of review. Moreover, as to both funded and unfunded plans,* the threat of increased litigation is not sufficient to outweigh the reasons for a *de novo* standard that we have already explained.

As this case aptly demonstrates, the validity of a claim to benefits under an ERISA plan is likely to turn on the interpretation of terms in the

---

* An unfunded plan is one in which "any benefits provided by the plan are paid directly by the employer out of its general corporate funds." Bruch v. Firestone Tire and Rubber Co., 828 F.2d 134, 138 (3rd Cir. 1987), *aff'd in part and rev'd in part*, 489 U.S. 101 (1989). A funded plan is one in which the employer has set aside money to pay claims in a special fund. Depending on how the funding mechanism is structured, an employer's annual contributions to the fund may not be dependent, or immediately dependent, on decisions to award benefits.

plan at issue. Consistent with established principles of trust law, we hold that a denial of benefits challenged under § 1132(a)(1)(B) is to be reviewed under a *de novo* standard unless the benefit plan gives the administrator or fiduciary discretionary authority to determine eligibility for benefits or to construe the terms of the plan. Because we do not rest our decision on the concern for impartiality that guided the Court of Appeals, we need not distinguish between types of plans or focus on the motivations of plan administrators and fiduciaries. Thus, for purposes of actions under § 1132(a)(1)(B), the *de novo* standard of review applies regardless of whether the plan at issue is funded or unfunded and regardless of whether the administrator or fiduciary is operating under a possible or actual conflict of interest. Of course, if a benefit plan gives discretion to an administrator or fiduciary who is operating under a conflict of interest, that conflict must be weighed as a "facto[r] in determining whether there is an abuse of discretion." Restatement (Second) of Trusts § 187, Comment d (1959).

Notes

1. *Empowering plan administrators.* Note that as far as Justice O'Connor was concerned the crucial defect in Firestone's decision making was the fact that the terms of the plan failed expressly to empower the plan administrator (in this case, Firestone itself) to construe the terms of the plan, nor did the plan indicate that the administrator's decision should be given deference. In the wake of *Firestone* all plan documents obviously contain the language of empowerment and deference in order to ensure that either the insurer (in the case of an insured health benefit plan) or the employer (in the case of a self-insured plan that uses a third-party administrator) is in possession of the powers that in turn create judicial deference in the form of review under an arbitrary and capricious standard.

It is this powerful and deferential relationship that the 2011 ERISA external appeals regulations, discussed previously, seek to sustain. As noted, the regulations allow external, independent, and binding reviews only in cases involving the exercise of medical judgment, while closing the door to external review in cases in which the plan documents themselves are the subject of interpretation. This curtailment of the Affordable Care Act's independent external review provisions to exclude cases in which the meaning of a plan document itself is on the line effectively preserves the courts' deferential treatment of plan administrators in construing their plan documents, without the threat of intervention by an independent reviewer.

2. Firestone's *ambivalence.* If you find *Firestone v. Bruch* puzzling, you are not alone. According to Professor John H. Langbein, the Supreme Court "flunk[ed] trusts"—and contracts and ERISA too. *See* John H. Langbein, *The Supreme Court Flunks Trusts*, 1990 SUPREME COURT REV. 207 (1991). First, "[a]lthough the Court says that it is instituting 'the trust law *de novo* standard of review,' that standard is not in fact particularly

characteristic of trust law. Would it have been better for the court to have said that it was preferring the contract standard of review to the trust standard?" LANGBEIN & WOLK, PENSION AND EMPLOYEE BENEFIT LAW at 810. Second, and more fundamentally,

> [The] puzzle about the Supreme Court's handling of the *Bruch* case is now easy to state but impossible to solve. If the Court was right to think that the arbitrary-and-capricious standard worsened the situation of plan participants and beneficiaries unacceptably, why did the Court permit plan drafters to reinstitute the arbitrary-and-capricious standard by means of boilerplate grants of discretion? Indeed, a quite plausible argument can be made that [ERISA] should be treated as preventing plan drafters from ousting the ordinarily applicable standard of review. If the purpose of ERISA fiduciary law is to protect plan participants from abusive management by the plan fiduciary, it seems transparently counterproductive to allow the employer to bootstrap around the safeguards of the statute by inserting boilerplate in the plan ordering the courts not to pay much attention to the misbehavior of an employer-dominated fiduciary.

> Thus, the deep issue that lurks in the standard-of-review dispute is not whether the particular plan actually claims discretion for the employer, but rather whether the protective policy of ERISA should allow such a plan to enforce its claim. ERISA is silent on the precise question. The Supreme Court in *Bruch* [waffled] on the question, inviting plan drafters to try it, while holding out the possibility that the resulting conflict of interest might be offensive enough to qualify "as a 'factor[ ] [to be weighed] in determining whether there is an abuse of discretion.' "

Langbein, *The Supreme Court Flunks Trusts* at 221–222, 226, 227.

3. *To protect employees or employers?* Nothing illustrates the Alice-in-Wonderland quality of ERISA better than Justice O'Connor's opinion in *Firestone*, which on the one hand describes ERISA's statutory purpose as being "to promote the interests of employees and their beneficiaries in employee benefit plans," and on the other hand defers deeply to what in most cases is the employer's unilateral drafting of the plan. (In most cases the plan is created by the employer without any bargaining with employees because only about 10 percent of private employees in the United States are represented by labor unions.) Justice O'Connor describes ERISA's statutory purpose, and the rationale of her holding that *de novo* review is the default standard, as follows:

> ERISA was enacted "to promote the interests of employees and their beneficiaries in employee benefit plans," *Shaw*, 463 U.S. 85 at 90, and *"to protect contractually defined benefits,"* *Massachusetts Mutual Life Ins. Co. v. Russell*, 473 U.S. at 148. See generally 29 U.S.C. § 1001 (setting forth congressional findings and declarations of policy regarding ERISA). Adopting Firestone's reading of ERISA [that arbitrary and capricious is the correct default stan-

dard of review] would require us to impose a standard of review that would afford less protection to employees and their beneficiaries than they enjoyed before ERISA was enacted.

Firestone Tire & Rubber Co., 489 U.S. 113–14 (emphasis added).

At the core of this passage is the emphasized phrase, *"to protect contractually defined benefits."* Once the genie of "freedom of contract" (or, given the usual lack of employer-employee bargaining, "freedom of unilateral employer drafting") is let out of the bottle, are there any limits as to how it can exercise its magic powers? Judge Richard Posner, never shy about following the logic of contractual freedom to places often considered outside the mainstream, seriously pondered whether an employer could, by artful plan drafting, exempt its decisions about claims for benefits from judicial review normally available under ERISA § 502. The case, Cutting v. Jerome Foods, Inc., 993 F.2d 1293 (7th Cir.), *cert. den.*, 510 U.S. 916 (1993), involved Mrs. Cutting, who had allegedly suffered $1 million damages in a serious automobile accident, but who had received only $126,000 from her uninsured motorist policy and $500,000 from a products liability claim. Yet when she submitted her $90,000 medical expenses to her husband's unfunded (i.e. no health insurance policy or special employer fund) employment-based health plan, she was told that her medical expenses would be covered only if she agreed to allow the plan, pursuant to its subrogation clause, to subrogate against other claims, i.e., that she reimburse the health benefits plan from any amounts she had received from other sources. Given the facts, this represented no coverage at all.

Mrs. Cutting argued that the federal court should adopt, as a matter of ERISA common law, the widely-applicable insurance law principle known as the "make-whole doctrine," under which an insurer's "rights of subrogation are enforceable only after the plan beneficiary has been made whole for the loss giving rise to the claim for benefits." *Cutting,* 993 F.2d at 1296. (Put another way, under this doctrine the insurer is allowed to reduce its own coverage exposure only if the injured insured has recovered benefits in excess of her actual damages.) The make-whole doctrine is generally treated as a "default rule," i.e., it applies unless the contract or plan "explicitly preclude[s] operation of the doctrine." Cagle v. Bruner, 112 F.3d 1510, 1521 (11th Cir. 1997). Since the Jerome Foods Plan did not explicitly preclude the doctrine, Mrs. Cutting argued that it should apply to her benefit.

Jerome Food countered that because its Plan provision stated that "all decisions concerning the interpretation or application of this Plan shall be vested in the sole discretion of the Plan Administrator," *Cutting,* 993 F.2d at 1295, that is, Jerome Foods itself, it must be allowed to interpret the plan's general subrogation provision as precluding the operation of the make-whole doctrine. The initial question explored by Judge Posner was whether Jerome Foods' interpretation of its subrogation provision was subject to any judicial review at all.

> The plan provides that "all decisions concerning the interpretation or application of this Plan shall be vested in the sole

discretion of the Plan Administrator,'' that is, Jerome Foods. Read literally, this terminology would extinguish all judicial review of refusals by Jerome Foods to pay benefits. The company concedes, however, that it should not be read literally—that it is not a license to make arbitrary or capricious decisions on applications for benefits. Were it otherwise, the coverage provided by the plan would be, not illusory exactly but noncontractual, because the company could turn down an application for benefits on whim. It might sometimes be tempted to do so. The plan is unfunded, with the result that every penny paid out in plan benefits comes out of the company's coffers; and even with funded or insured welfare plans, the employer has a financial stake in limiting the payment of benefits.

Of course, a company that is capricious in its bestowal of benefits may have to pay higher wages to compensate its workers for the anticipated reduction in the certainty and value of their benefits, or it may incur the potentially costly ill will of the workers. Some workers might prefer to rely on their employer's long-term self-interest in playing fair with benefits than to insist on a costly regime of legal rights for which they pay indirectly in lower wages or more limited benefits, just as many workers appear to prefer jobs in which they are employees at will to tenured positions as civil servants. We are not certain that there is any legal impediment to a plan's forbidding judicial review of the plan administrator's decisions. ERISA provides that "a civil action may be brought by a participant or beneficiary to recover benefits due," 29 U.S.C. § 1132(a)(1)(B), but if the plan entrusts the determination of what is due to the unreviewable discretion of the plan administrator, it can be argued that no benefits will be due unless the administrator awards them. And although the Supreme Court held in Firestone Tire & Rubber Co. v. Bruch, 489 U.S. 101, 115 (1989), that the default standard of judicial review of a plan administrator's decision is *de novo* review, it also held that if the plan gives the administrator discretion to construe its provisions the court will defer. *Id.* at 111, 115[.] Not defer completely, however—defer in the sense conveyed by such familiar and possibly synonymous terms as "abuse of discretion" and "arbitrary and capricious" (between which the Court found it unnecessary to choose), for which clear error may be a further synonym. It is one thing to interpret a provision that vests discretion in a plan administrator as commanding judicial deference within reason, another thing to interpret it as commanding complete deference. The indications that the latter was intended would have to be pretty conclusive to persuade us, and we agree with the parties that the reference to "sole discretion" is not (quite) conclusive evidence of such an intention and therefore should not be interpreted to strip the plan's beneficiaries of all legal remedies, especially given the conflict of interest inherent in an unfunded employer-administered plan. (Compare the hostility of trust law to efforts by a trustee to place himself beyond liability for profiting from a breach of trust. Restatement (Second) of Trusts § 222(2) (1959).) Otherwise the employees would have no contractual protection.

It is true, as we have pointed out, that employees often bargain away contractual protection. That is of the essence of the regime of employment at will, which is still the dominant regime for employment in this country. But this is only to say that employees normally will not pay for job insurance beyond what arrangements for unemployment compensation and severance pay provide them. They will pay for medical insurance and they usually want more assurance of insurance than an unenforceable promise from their employer would give them. Although an employer's concern for employee relations and good will inhibit him from indulging in wholly irrational self-serving interpretations, it is not a complete guarantee. A rational employer will trade off the cost of such an interpretation against the gain in reduced expense, which might be critical, especially for employers in a financially parlous state. A good business reputation is not a very valuable asset to a firm that has little confidence of being able to remain in business long enough to profit from that reputation. Long-run self-interest is a weak constraint on firms that have poor long-run prospects. So the Cuttings are entitled to judicial review of the company's ruling.

Cutting, 993 F.2d at 1295–96.

One of the most remarkable aspects of Judge Posner's analysis is how it renders virtually invisible or non-existent any public policy choices toward protecting employees that, according to Justice O'Connor, *were at the heart of the ERISA statute*. Instead, Judge Posner focuses on interpreting the "intention" of the Plan drafter, and concludes that an "intention" to "comman[d] complete [judicial] deference"

> would have to be pretty conclusive to persuade us, and we agree with the parties that the reference to "sole discretion" is not (quite) conclusive evidence of such an intention and therefore should not be interpreted to strip the plan's beneficiaries of all legal remedies, especially given the conflict of interest inherent in an unfunded employer-administered plan.

Cutting, 993 F.2d at 1296. While general trust law serves as a background to this reasoning, the central point seems to be that given sufficiently astute drafting, an ERISA plan could express its "intention" clearly enough to exempt itself from ERISA's own fiduciary duties and remedies for their violation.

Is it possible to reconcile Justice O'Connor's statement in *Firestone* of ERISA's statutory purposes with the breadth of employer liberty-of-drafting apparently envisaged by Judge Posner in *Cutting*? Judge Posner appears to concede that state law, and presumably pre-ERISA state law, embodied in the Restatement of Trusts, would have been hostile to such attempted immunity. Yet he takes seriously, and may even agree with, the remarkable proposition that the ERISA statute, enacted, according to Justice O'Connor, "to promote the interests of employees and their beneficiaries in employee benefit plans," and presumably not to "afford less protection to employees and their beneficiaries than they enjoyed before ERISA was enacted," should nonetheless be interpreted as allowing employers to exempt their benefit decisions from ERISA's own judicial review mechanism, while also enjoying preemption of state law. If Jerome Food had not itself disclaimed immunity from judicial review, can you ascertain just how and why Judge Posner would have ruled on the issue? Recall how *Jones* offers an alternative pathway that permits plans to insulate themselves from federal judicial review and/or state law by drafting generalized exclusions from coverage directly into plan documents.

On the merits, Judge Posner held that even though the Plan had not explicitly opted out of the make-whole doctrine, the Plan's—i.e., Jerome Food's—delegation of interpretive discretion to itself allowed it so to interpret the subrogation provision. Judge Posner noted that while many state courts might have ruled in favor of the Cuttings, in federal ERISA cases "the standard of judicial review [in this case, arbitrary and capricious] becomes critical and decides the case in favor of Jerome Foods. For we cannot say that the company was unreasonable in interpreting this plan as disclaiming the make-whole principle." *Cutting*, 993 F.2d at 1299. For an opinion reaching the opposite result on the same issue, with less intellectual brilliance but more fidelity to ERISA's statutory purpose of protecting beneficiaries, see *Cagle*, 112 F.3d at 1510, 1522 ("Under the *Cutting* approach, the Fund could avoid a default rule of insurance law applicable in the ERISA context merely by giving itself discretion to interpret the plan. We do not believe that ERISA gives the Fund that kind of authority, which is denied to insurance companies not governed by ERISA.").

b. Fiduciary Conflict of Interest

Metropolitan Life Insurance Company v. Glenn
554 U.S. 105 (2008)

■ JUSTICE BREYER delivered the opinion of the Court.

The Employee Retirement Income Security Act of 1974 (ERISA) permits a person denied benefits under an employee benefit plan to challenge that denial in federal court. 29 U.S.C. § 1132(a)(1)(B). Often the entity that administers the plan, such as an employer or an insurance company, both determines whether an employee is eligible for benefits and pays benefits out of its own pocket. We here decide that this dual role creates a conflict of interest; that a reviewing court should consider that conflict as a factor in determining whether the plan administrator has abused its discretion in denying benefits; and that the significance of the factor will depend upon the circumstances of the particular case. See *Firestone Tire & Rubber Co.,* 489 U.S. 101.

I

Petitioner Metropolitan Life Insurance Company (MetLife) serves as both an administrator and the insurer of Sears, Roebuck & Company's long-term disability insurance plan, an ERISA-governed employee benefit plan. The plan grants MetLife (as administrator) discretionary authority to determine whether an employee's claim for benefits is valid; it simultaneously provides that MetLife (as insurer) will itself pay valid benefit claims.

Respondent Wanda Glenn, a Sears employee, was diagnosed with severe dilated cardiomyopathy, a heart condition whose symptoms include fatigue and shortness of breath. She applied for plan disability benefits in June 2000, and MetLife concluded that she met the plan's standard for an initial 24 months of benefits, namely, that she could not "perform the material duties of [her] own job." MetLife also directed Glenn to a law firm that would assist her in applying for federal Social Security disability benefits (some of which MetLife itself would be entitled to receive as an offset to the more generous plan benefits). In April 2002, an Administrative Law Judge found that Glenn's illness prevented her not only from performing her own job but also "from performing any jobs [for which she could qualify] existing in significant numbers in the national economy." 20 CFR § 404.1520(g) (2007). The Social Security Administration consequently granted Glenn permanent disability payments retroactive to April 2000. Glenn herself kept none of the backdated benefits: three-quarters went to MetLife, and the rest (plus some additional money) went to the lawyers.

To continue receiving Sears plan disability benefits after 24 months, Glenn had to meet a stricter, Social–Security-type standard, namely, that her medical condition rendered her incapable of performing not only her own job but of performing "the material duties of any gainful occupation for which" she was "reasonably qualified." MetLife denied Glenn this extended benefit because it found that she was "capable of performing full time sedentary work."

After exhausting her administrative remedies, Glenn brought this federal lawsuit. The District Court denied relief. Glenn appealed to the Court of Appeals for the Sixth Circuit. Because the plan granted MetLife "discretionary authority to . . . determine benefits," the Court of Appeals reviewed the administrative record under a deferential standard. In doing so, it treated "as a relevant factor" a "conflict of interest" arising out of the fact that MetLife was "authorized both to decide whether an employee is eligible for benefits and to pay those benefits."

The Court of Appeals ultimately set aside MetLife's denial of benefits in light of a combination of several circumstances [including] conflict of interest. MetLife sought certiorari, asking us to determine whether a plan administrator that both evaluates and pays claims operates under a conflict of interest in making discretionary benefit determinations. The Solicitor

General suggested that we also consider " 'how' " any such conflict should " 'be taken into account on judicial review of a discretionary benefit determination.' " We agreed to consider both questions.

II

In *Firestone Tire & Rubber Co.,* 489 U.S. 101 this Court set forth four principles of review relevant here. (1) In "determining the appropriate standard of review," a court should be "guided by principles of trust law; it should analogize a plan administrator to the trustee of a common-law trust and consider a benefit determination to be a fiduciary act. (2) Principles of trust law require courts to review a denial of plan benefits "under a *de novo* standard" unless the plan provides to the contrary. (3) Where the plan provides to the contrary by granting the administrator or fiduciary *discretionary authority* to determine eligibility for benefits, trust principles make a deferential standard of review appropriate. (4) If a benefit plan gives discretion to an administrator or fiduciary who *is operating under a conflict of interest,* that conflict must be *weighed as a factor* in determining whether there is an abuse of discretion.

The questions before us, while implicating the first three principles, directly focus upon the application and the meaning of the fourth.

III

The first question asks whether the fact that a plan administrator both evaluates claims for benefits and pays benefits claims creates the kind of "conflict of interest" to which *Firestone's* fourth principle refers. In our view, it does. That answer is clear where it is the employer that both funds the plan and evaluates the claims. The employer's fiduciary interest may counsel in favor of granting a borderline claim while its immediate financial interest counsels to the contrary. Thus, the employer has an interest conflicting with that of the beneficiaries, the type of conflict that judges must take into account when they review the discretionary acts of a trustee of a common-law trust.

MetLife points out that an employer who creates a plan that it will both fund and administer foresees, and implicitly approves, the resulting conflict. But that fact cannot change our conclusion. At trust law, the fact that a settlor (the person establishing the trust) approves a trustee's conflict does not change the legal need for a judge later to take account of that conflict in reviewing the trustee's discretionary decisionmaking.

MetLife also points out that we need not follow trust law principles where trust law is "inconsistent with the language of the statute, its structure, or its purposes." MetLife adds that to find a conflict here is inconsistent (1) with ERISA's efforts to avoid complex review proceedings; (2) with Congress' efforts not to deter employers from setting up benefit plans, *ibid.*, and (3) with an ERISA provision specifically allowing employers to administer their own plans.

But we cannot find in these considerations any significant inconsistency. As to the first, we note that trust law functions well with a similar standard. As to the second, we have no reason, empirical or otherwise, to believe that our decision will seriously discourage the creation of benefit plans. As to the third, we have just explained why approval of a conflicted trustee differs from review of that trustee's conflicted decision-making.

The answer to the conflict question is less clear where (as here) the plan administrator is not the employer itself but rather a professional insurance company. Such a company, MetLife would argue, likely has a much greater incentive than a self-insuring employer to provide accurate claims processing. That is because the insurance company typically charges a fee that attempts to account for the cost of claims payouts, with the result that paying an individual claim does not come to the same extent from the company's own pocket. It is also because the marketplace (and regulators) may well punish an insurance company when its products, or ingredients of its products, fall below par.

We nonetheless continue to believe that for ERISA purposes a conflict exists. For one thing, the employer's own conflict may extend to its selection of an insurance company to administer its plan. An employer choosing an administrator in effect buys insurance for others and consequently (when compared to the marketplace customer who buys for himself) may be more interested in an insurance company with low rates than in one with accurate claims processing.

For another, ERISA imposes higher-than-marketplace quality standards on insurers. It sets forth a special standard of care upon a plan administrator, namely, that the administrator "discharge [its] duties" in respect to discretionary claims processing "solely in the interests of the participants and beneficiaries" of the plan, § 1104(a)(1); it simultaneously underscores the particular importance of accurate claims processing by insisting that administrators "provide a 'full and fair review' of claim denials," and it supplements marketplace and regulatory controls with judicial review of individual claim denials, see § 1132(a)(1)(B).

Finally, a legal rule that treats insurance company administrators and employers alike in respect to the *existence* of a conflict can nonetheless take account of the circumstances to which MetLife points so far as it treats those, or similar, circumstances as diminishing the *significance* or *severity* of the conflict in individual cases.

IV

We turn to the question of "how" the conflict we have just identified should "be taken into account on judicial review of a discretionary benefit determination." In doing so, we elucidate what this Court set forth in *Firestone*, namely, that a conflict should "be weighed as a 'factor in determining whether there is an abuse of discretion.'"

We do not believe that *Firestone*'s statement implies a change in the *standard* of review, say, from deferential to *de novo* review. Nor would we overturn *Firestone* by adopting a rule that in practice could bring about near universal review by judges *de novo—i.e.,* without deference—of the lion's share of ERISA plan claims denials. Neither do we believe it necessary or desirable for courts to create special burden-of-proof rules, or other special procedural or evidentiary rules, focused narrowly upon the evaluator/payor conflict. In principle, as we have said, conflicts are but one factor among many that a reviewing judge must take into account. Benefits decisions arise in too many contexts, concern too many circumstances, and can relate in too many different ways to conflicts—which themselves vary in kind and in degree of seriousness—for us to come up with a one-size-fits-all procedural system that is likely to promote fair and accurate review. Indeed, special procedural rules would create further complexity, adding time and expense to a process that may already be too costly for many of those who seek redress.

We believe that *Firestone* means what the word "factor" implies, namely, that when judges review the lawfulness of benefit denials, they will often take account of several different considerations of which a conflict of interest is one. This kind of review is no stranger to the judicial system. Not only trust law, but also administrative law, can ask judges to determine lawfulness by taking account of several different, often case-specific, factors, reaching a result by weighing all together.

In such instances, any one factor will act as a tiebreaker when the other factors are closely balanced, the degree of closeness necessary depending upon the tiebreaking factor's inherent or case-specific importance. The conflict of interest at issue here, for example, should prove more important (perhaps of great importance) where circumstances suggest a higher likelihood that it affected the benefits decision, including, but not limited to, cases where an insurance company administrator has a history of biased claims administration. It should prove less important (perhaps to the vanishing point) where the administrator has taken active steps to reduce potential bias and to promote accuracy, for example, by walling off claims administrators from those interested in firm finances, or by imposing management checks that penalize inaccurate decisionmaking irrespective of whom the inaccuracy benefits.

The Court of Appeals' opinion in the present case illustrates the combination-of-factors method of review. The record says little about MetLife's efforts to assure accurate claims assessment. The Court of Appeals gave the conflict weight to some degree; its opinion suggests that, in context, the court would not have found the conflict alone determinative. The court instead focused more heavily on other factors. In particular, the court found questionable the fact that MetLife had encouraged Glenn to argue to the Social Security Administration that she could do no work, received the bulk of the benefits of her success in doing so (the remainder going to the lawyers it recommended), and then ignored the agency's finding in concluding that Glenn could in fact do sedentary work. MetLife emphasized a certain medical report that favored a denial of benefits, had deemphasized certain other reports that suggested a contrary conclusion, and had failed to provide its independent vocational and medical experts with all of the relevant evidence. All these serious concerns, taken together with some degree of conflicting interests on MetLife's part, led the court to set aside MetLife's discretionary decision. We can find nothing improper in the way in which the court conducted its review.

■ CHIEF JUSTICE ROBERTS, concurring in part and concurring in the judgment.

I join all but Part IV of the Court's opinion. I agree that a third-party insurer's dual role as a claims administrator and plan funder gives rise to a conflict of interest that is pertinent in reviewing claims decisions. I part ways with the majority, however, when it comes to *how* such a conflict should matter. The majority would accord weight, of varying and indeterminate amount, to the existence of such a conflict in every case where it is present. The majority's approach would allow the bare existence of a conflict to enhance the significance of other factors already considered by reviewing courts, even if the conflict is not shown to have played any role in the denial of benefits. The end result is to increase the level of scrutiny in every case in which there is a conflict—that is, in many if not most ERISA cases—thereby undermining the deference owed to plan administrators when the plan vests discretion in them.

I would instead consider the conflict of interest on review only where there is evidence that the benefits denial was motivated or affected by the administrator's conflict. No such evidence was presented in this case. I would nonetheless affirm the judgment of the Sixth Circuit, because that court was justified in finding an abuse of discretion on the facts of this case—conflict or not.

■ JUSTICE KENNEDY, concurring in part and dissenting in part.

The Court sets forth an important framework for the standard of review in ERISA cases, one consistent with our holding in *Firestone Tire & Rubber Co. v. Bruch,* and I concur in those parts of the Court's opinion that discuss this framework. In my submission, however, the case should be remanded so that the Court of Appeals can apply the standards the Court now explains to these facts.

The Court has set forth a workable framework for taking potential conflicts of interest in ERISA benefits disputes into account. It is consistent with our opinion in *Firestone,* and it protects the interests of plan beneficiaries without undermining the ability of insurance companies to act simultaneously as plan administrators and plan funders. The linchpin of this framework is the Court's recognition that a structural conflict "should prove less important (perhaps to the vanishing point) where the administrator has taken active steps to reduce potential bias and to promote accuracy, for example, by walling off claims administrators from those interested in firm finances, or by imposing management checks that penalize inaccurate decisionmaking irrespective of whom the inaccuracy benefits." The Court acknowledges that the structural conflict of interest played some role in the Court of Appeals' determination that MetLife had abused its discretion. But as far as one can tell, the Court of Appeals made no effort to assess whether MetLife employed structural safeguards to avoid conflicts of interest, safeguards the Court says can cause the importance of a conflict to vanish. The Court nonetheless affirms the judgment, without giving MetLife a chance to defend its decision under the standards the Court articulates today.

■ JUSTICE SCALIA, with whom JUSTICE THOMAS joins, dissenting.

I agree with the Court that petitioner Metropolitan Life Insurance Company (hereinafter petitioner) has a conflict of interest. A third-party insurance company that administers an ERISA-governed disability plan and that pays for benefits out of its own coffers profits with each benefits claim it rejects. I see no reason why the Court must volunteer, however, that *an employer* who administers its own ERISA-governed plan "clear[ly]" has a conflict of interest.

The more important question is how the existence of a conflict should bear upon judicial review of the administrator's decision, and on that score I am in fundamental disagreement with the Court. Even if the choice were mine as a policy matter, I would not adopt the Court's totality-of-the-circumstances (so-called) "test," in which the existence of a conflict is to be put into the mix and given some (unspecified) "weight." This makes each case unique, and hence the outcome of each case unpredictable—not a reasonable position in which to place the administrator that has been explicitly given discretion by the creator of the plan, despite the existence of a conflict. More importantly, however, this is not a question to be solved by this Court's policy views; our cases make clear that it is to be governed by the law of trusts. Under that law, a fiduciary with a conflict does not abuse its discretion unless the conflict *actually* and *improperly motivates* the decision. There is no evidence of that here.

Notes

1. *How to weigh conflicts.* All the Justices appear to agree on the notion that trust law requires recognition of conflicts. Where they differ is on what to do when a conflict exists. Justice Breyer is careful to reaffirm the central elements of *Firestone:* (1) that trust law applies to ERISA appeals; (2) that the appropriate legal standard is *de novo* review; (3) that deference should be given where the plan documents vest discretion in the fiduciary; and (4) that a conflict of interest becomes a factor to be weighed in judicial review.

At the same time, *Glenn* appears to represent an important extension of *Firestone* in its unequivocal view regarding the inherent conflicts that exist in the fiduciary relationship (regardless whether the plan fiduciary is a self-insuring employer or an insurance company) and the need for evidence that the fiduciary has made an effort to manage the conflict. In Justice Breyer's view, a court must consider not only whether the decision is sufficiently supported by the evidence to meet an arbitrary and capricious standard, but also whether the decision maker has taken steps to manage the conflict of interest, particularly in "cases where an insurance company administrator has a history of biased claims administration."

Where an administrator can show that it has "taken active steps to reduce potential bias and to promote accuracy, for example, by walling off claims administrators from those interested in firm finances, or by imposing management checks that penalize inaccurate decision making irrespective of whom the inaccuracy benefits," then, as Justice Breyer notes, the fact of the conflict would be managed to the point of vanishing. In such a case, deference is applied so long as the settlor has so indicated that it wished the standard of deference to apply. By contrast, in the absence of proof that the conflict of interest has been managed, the standard of review becomes less deferential and reviewers should take into account the particulars of the conflict and the totality of the circumstances.

By contrast, Justice Roberts, while acknowledging the inherent conflicts in having one entity be responsible for both deciding claims and paying benefits, would seek actual evidence in the record that the conflict motivated or affected a claims denial before agreeing that a court can probe the decision in a less deferential fashion. Justice Scalia, on the other hand, argues that an inherent conflict of interest is of no import and argues that the courts should intervene only when a plaintiff actually proves that the particular decision resulted from an improper motive. Put differently, Justice Roberts places on the plaintiff a burden of coming forward with evidence that the conflict played a role in decision making before the standard of review is affected, while Justice Scalia would use the arbitrary and capricious test in all circumstances and therefore he would condition plaintiff's recovering on its proving that the fiduciary acted in self-interest.

2. *Can it be left to the market to determine the best way to manage conflict of interest?* One of MetLife's more interesting arguments was its claim that the market itself offers the best defense against the problem of conflicts of interest, since employers will reject contracts with insurers that act out of self-interest. The supporting links in this argument weren't spelled out, but they probably run along the lines that (1) employers must compete for workers; (2) in weighing offers from employers in this competitive process, workers will take into account how an ERISA plan is structured and administered, including the incentives given to its fiduciaries and how conflicts of interest are managed; (3) workers will prefer plans in which the conflict of interest is managed and resolved in a neutral fashion or even in their favor; and (4) employers will therefore contract with administrators who will act in such a fashion. To Justice Breyer's credit, he did not bite on the breath-taking quantity of empirical assumptions in these links but instead noted that some employers will be most swayed by price when they buy insurance or administrative services and that ERISA therefore "imposes higher-than-marketplace quality standards" for such purchases. To some extent, then, *Glenn* removes the structuring of plan administration from the marketplace. If a plan sponsor chooses to establish a benefit plan, it will not get the benefit of judicial deference in its or its agent's interpretation of the plan unless it builds in safeguards to account for its or its agent's conflict of interest as both payer and administrator of benefits.

In thinking about the practical significance of this doctrinal change, imagine you are counsel to an insurer that also sells third-party plan administration services to self-insuring employers. How would you advise clients in the wake of the decision? It appears that the consensus among experts is to attempt to keep the review process efficient while providing detailed denial letters, building in certain structures and avoiding contracts that clearly incentivize administrators to favor denials. Speaking at a post-*Glenn* conference, experts noted key steps for adhering to the principles of the case while maximizing the potential to be upheld on review: "wall off" claims decisions from financial departments; create a separate committee that acts as a fiduciary for claims decisions; document and follow procedures and practices for claims administration; produce thorough, carefully reasoned claims decisions; do not weigh the economic consequences of decisions to the plan sponsor; do not inquire into the amount of benefits that will be paid if they approve a claim "so that they can later argue that they did not consider the amount of benefits in approving or denying the claim"; give careful attention to the selection of outside claims administrators; "consider how claims decisions made by that administrator have been treated by courts in other decisions [and] in addition ask the administrator for their ratio of benefit approvals and benefit denials"; and minimize incentives for claim denials "by ensuring that claims examiners do not get paid more for denying claims than approving them." Jo-el J. Meyer, *Standard of Review: Practitioners Detail Steps Administrators Should Take to Ensure Deferential Review*, 68 BNA PENSION AND BENEFITS DAILY 130 (July 8, 2008).

3. *A "single honest mistake."* Before jumping to the conclusion that these structural safeguards will have a practical impact on claims administration, consider the more recent holding by the Supreme Court that even conflicted fiduciaries can be forgiven their mistakes, it seems, when there is no showing of bad faith. In *Conkright v. Frommert*, 130 S. Ct. 1640 (2010), the Xerox Corporation's pension plan was determined to have used an improper formula (one that naturally favored Xerox) to calculate pension value. The trial court upheld the company's formula, using a deferential standard of review. The United States Court of Appeals, however, overturned the use of the pension calculation formula, finding the administrator's actions to be unreasonable and an abuse of discretion, Frommert v. Conkright, 433 F.3d 254 (2d Cir. 2006). The case then was remanded to the trial court for further proceedings to determine the proper pension calculation. The fiduciary offered another self-favoring methodology, which was again challenged by the plan participants. This time, however, the trial court refused to treat the plan's decision with deference given the prior history, and the Court of Appeals affirmed, finding the plan language ambiguous and determining that in accordance with *Firestone,* a court "need not apply a deferential standards 'where the administrator ha[s] previously construed the same [plan] terms, and we found such construction to have violated ERISA.' " *Frommert,* 130 S. Ct. 1640, 1646.

Writing for the majority, Chief Justice Roberts concluded that loss of the deferential standard following the initial improper conduct was not appropriate under trust law in the absence of a showing that the trustee already has acted in bad faith rather than merely having previously erred. Furthermore, he noted, even if trust law did compel such a result, larger ERISA principles are also at play:

> Here trust law does not resolve the specific issue before us, but the guiding principles we have identified underlying ERISA do. Congress enacted ERISA to assure that employees would receive the benefits they had earned, but Congress did not require employers to establish benefit plans in the first place. Congress sought to create a system that is not so complex that administrative costs, or litigation expenses, unduly discourage employers from offering ERISA plans in the first place. ERISA induces employers to offer benefits by asserting a predictable set of liabilities, under uniform standards of primary conduct and a uniform regime of ultimate remedial orders and awards when a violation has occurred. *Firestone* deference protects these interests, and by permitting an employer to grant primary interpretive authority over an ERISA plan to the plan administrator, preserves the careful balancing on which ERISA is based.

Id. at 1648.

In his dissent, Justice Breyer found no support in either ERISA or principles of trust law for the notion that once an abuse of discretion is found, courts are obligated to defer to the fiduciary a second time around unless bad faith is shown.

> Trust law treatise writers say that [where abuse of discretion has been shown] a court *may* but need not exercise its own discretion rather than defer to a trustee's interpretation of trust language. Of course the fact that trust law grants courts discretion does not mean that they will exercise that discretion in all instances. [T]he majority reads [trust treatises] as establishing an absolute requirement that courts defer to a trustee's fallback position absent "reason to believe that [the trustee] will not exercise [his] discretion fairly—for example, upon a showing that the trustee has already acted in bad faith." I do not find trust law "unclear" on this matter. When a trustee abuses its discretion, trust law grants courts the authority either to defer anew to the trustee's discretion or to craft a remedy.
>
> In any event, it is far from clear that the Court's legal rule reflects an appropriate analysis of ERISA-based policy. To the contrary, the majority's "one free honest mistake rule" is impractical, for it requires courts to determine what is "honest," encourages appeals on the point, and threatens to delay further proceedings that already take too long. It also ignores what we previously have pointed out [in *Glenn*]—namely, that abuses of discretion arise in too many contexts and concern too many circumstances for this Court to come up with a one-size-fits all procedural [approach] that is likely to promote fair and accurate benefits

determinations. And finally, the majority's approach creates incentives for administrators to take "one free shot" at an employer-favorable plan interpretations and to draft ambiguous pension plans in the first instance with the expectation that they will have repeated opportunities to interpret (and possibly reinterpret) the ambiguous terms.

Id. at 1659–60.

How might a claimant go about showing that a denial based on the interpretation of plan documents was in fact made in bad faith? Does the Court in *Frommert* make too much of a line purportedly separating stupidity from bad faith? What good will all the structural safeguards in the world accomplish if fiduciaries are allowed to make repeated "mistakes" in favor of their own self-interest?

4. *Insured and self-insured plans. Glenn's* holding reaches both insured and self-insured plans. Defendant argued that since the money it managed wasn't coming out of its pocket, its conflict was attenuated compared with a self-insured plan-sponsor. It also argued that it would have financial and regulatory incentives to be "accurate" in claims administration. Justice Breyer was clearly unimpressed by the empirical assumptions in this argument too, responding simply that "the employer's own conflict may extend to its selection of an insurance company to administer its plan." Given ERISA's decision to remove management of the conflict of interest from the marketplace, the mere *possibility* that incentives in favor of self-interest *may* be transferred from the plan sponsor to the administrator or insurer it hires was sufficient to impose structural safeguards as a requirement for deference in reviewing denials by the plan administrator.

5. *Concerns about administrability.* How much does the workload of the courts weigh on the Justices' minds? Professor Timothy Stoltzfus Jost notes that one of the factors preserving the majority's avoidance of turning every ERISA appeal into a *de novo* review might be the extent to which a more active inquiry into the conduct of the fiduciary in ERISA cases might affect the considerable burden on the lower courts. In this sense, the Court's effort to preserve the limited review standard while still ascertaining the presence of conflicts management appears to be an effort to strike a middle ground. Timothy Stoltzfus Jost, *'MetLife v. Glenn': The Court Addresses a Conflict over Conflicts in ERISA Benefit Administration*, 27(5) HEALTH AFFAIRS (Web Exclusive) w430 (2008), http://content.healthaffairs.org/content/27/5/w430.full.pdf+html. The Court was also clearly concerned that complicating an administrative process could engender delays in plan beneficiaries' receipt of their benefits.

6. *State efforts to curb deference clauses.* The ERISA preemption materials below discuss efforts under state law to curb deference clauses in the context of insured health benefit plans. As you will learn, while these state laws have survived an ERISA preemption challenge, they do not apply to self-insured plans, which represent half the population of workers covered under ERISA plans (and growing).

c. Claims Denials Involving the Medical Necessity of Care

Bedrick v. Travelers Insurance Company

93 F.3d 149 (4th Cir. 1996)

■ K.K. Hall, Circuit Judge:

Ethan Bedrick and his parents appeal an order of the district court granting summary judgment for the defendant insurer in this dispute over medical insurance benefits provided under an ERISA welfare benefit plan. We affirm in part, reverse in part, and remand.

Ethan Bedrick was born January 28, 1992. His delivery went very badly, and he was asphyxiated. As a result, he suffers from severe cerebral palsy and spastic quadriplegia. "Spastic quadriplegia" means that Ethan's motor function is impaired in all four limbs because of hypertonia. Hypertonia is an abnormal resistance to passive stretching of the muscles. Ethan also has exaggerated reflexes and asymmetries of posture. The diabolical thing about hypertonia is that, unless properly treated, it can get much worse. Unless each hypertonic muscle is regularly stretched (and its abnormal resistance thereby overcome), the muscle itself changes. Long, flexible tissue is replaced by shorter, inflexible, fibrotic tissue. The resulting curled-up appendage is called a contracture.

Preventing contractures is especially difficult for a hypertonic infant. The path of least resistance is not to stretch, and a helpless baby follows that path. An adult must actively exercise the child's limbs. For this reason, Ethan was put on an intense regimen of physical, occupational, and speech therapy. [Physical therapy was prescribed on a twice weekly basis, with occupational and speech therapy at twice per month.] Travelers Insurance Company provides medical insurance to Ethan through an ERISA plan at his father's work. For a fixed premium from the employer, Travelers both funds and administers the plan, so it bears the financial consequences—and reaps the financial rewards—of its own coverage decisions.

When Ethan was fourteen months old, Travelers cut off coverage for speech therapy and limited his physical and occupational therapy to just fifteen sessions per year. This abrupt change was occasioned by a review of Ethan's case by Dr. Isabel Pollack, an employee of Travelers' ConservCo subsidiary. ConservCo performs "utilization review," i.e., it looks for places to cut off or reduce unnecessary services and thereby reduce the cost to Travelers.

Dr. Pollack called Ethan's pediatrician, Dr. R. L. Swetenburg, who told her that there was a "50/50 chance that the child will be able to walk by age 5." Ethan had a "poor prognosis[,] but [he] has shown some improvement [and] has some evidences of socialization[.]" She then called Dr. Philip Lesser, Ethan's pediatric neurologist, who stated that Ethan's "potential for progress is mild and that he would support whatever the physical therapist feels is necessary as far as home therapy by parents." Dr.

Pollack thereupon determined, without contacting the physical therapist whose opinion Dr. Lesser supported, that "I feel that further therapy is of minimal benefit[,] and ... I cannot in good conscience suggest that we continue." Ethan's therapies were cut back sharply. Travelers also denied his claims for certain prescribed durable medical equipment, including a bath chair and an upright stander. Dr. Swetenburg, Dr. Lesser, and the physical therapist, Donna Stout Wells, later sent letters to Travelers to protest the precipitous drop in coverage. Dr. Pollack did not see any of these letters until her deposition.

The denial was finally reviewed in Travelers' home office in October 1993, and only after Mr. Bedrick threatened to sue. This review was conducted by Dr. Kenneth Robbins. Though many months had passed, he did not update the file or contact any of Ethan's physicians. Instead, based on his general experience and a single New England Journal of Medicine article from 1988, Dr. Robbins concluded that intensive physical therapy does not speed the development of children with severe cerebral palsy. Dr. Robbins also concluded that the prescribed bath chair was a "convenience item" not covered by the plan.

Ethan and his parents filed suit in state court on February 4, 1994, alleging breach of contract, bad faith, and unfair and deceptive trade practices. Travelers removed the suit to district court. The bad faith and trade practices claims were dismissed as preempted by ERISA, and the breach of contract claim was recharacterized as one for benefits under an ERISA plan.

Decisions by administrators of ERISA plans are generally subject to *de novo* review, *Firestone Tire & Rubber Co.*, 489 U.S. 101, though, if the plan gives discretionary authority to the administrator, review is for abuse of discretion. Here, there is no plan-wide grant of discretion to Travelers; however, the "medically necessary" restriction on benefits does involve an exercise of discretion:

> The Travelers determines, in its discretion, if a service or supply is medically necessary for the diagnosis and treatment of an accidental injury or sickness. This determination is based on and consistent with standards approved by Travelers medical personnel. These standards are developed, in part, with consideration to whether the service or supply meets the following: It is appropriate and required for the diagnosis or treatment of the accidental injury or sickness. It is safe and effective according to accepted clinical evidence reported by generally recognized medical professionals and publications. There is not a less intensive or more appropriate diagnostic or treatment alternative that could have been used in lieu of the service or supply given. A determination that a service or supply is not medically necessary may apply to the entire service or supply or to any part of the service or supply.

This language clearly purports to give Travelers the discretion to determine the "medical necessity" of treatment. The problem, though, is that every exercise of this discretion has a direct financial effect upon

Travelers. Inasmuch as the law is highly suspect of "fiduciaries" having a personal interest in the subject of their trust, the "abuse of discretion" standard is not applied in as deferential a manner to such plans. *Firestone*, 489 U.S. at 115 (fiduciary's conflict of interest "must be weighed as a 'factor in determining whether there is an abuse of discretion.' "

Travelers concedes that it has a conflict of interest, but the parties debate what the conflict means. Travelers says its conflict is merely a "factor," citing the passage from *Firestone*, while the plaintiffs say that it changes the standard of review. [W]e apply *Firestone's* "factor" in this manner: When a fiduciary exercises discretion in interpreting a disputed term of the contract where one interpretation will further the financial interests of the fiduciary, we will not act as deferentially as would other-wise be appropriate. Rather, we will review the merits of the interpretation to determine whether it is consistent with an exercise of discretion by a fiduciary acting free of the interests that conflict with those of the benefi-ciaries. In short, the fiduciary decision will be entitled to some deference, but this deference will be lessened to the degree necessary to neutralize any untoward influence resulting from the conflict.

Another background legal point that bears on all issues here is ERISA's requirement of a "full and fair review" of all denied claims by an "appropriate named fiduciary." 29 U.S.C. § 1133(2); 29 C.F.R. § 2560.503-1(g)[.] Despite the Bedricks' protests, the denial of their claims was not referred to Dr. Robbins for Home Office Review until October 14, 1993, six full months after Dr. Pollack decided to sharply limit Ethan's therapy. The referral form is telling. It notes that the "[employee] says he is intending to sue," and that the field office "needs another opinion and support of Home Office." Dr. Robbins conducted his "review" without supplementing or updating the file. Finally, there is evidence that his exercise of judgment is not disinterested. At his deposition, Dr. Robbins acknowledged that his job involved "support for the legal department" and "support work for medical directors in the field who have problem cases[.]" In sum, we are very skeptical that the Bedricks received a "full and fair review."

According to its answer to an interrogatory, Travelers' decision that Ethan's intensive program of physical therapy was not medically necessary "was based upon a finding that the specified treatments did not reach a level of potential for significant progress which would allow the therapies to be provided on a medically necessary basis."

There are several deficiencies in this rationale. First and most funda-mentally, the "significant progress" requirement is not in the plan or Travelers' internal guidelines. Second, such a requirement makes no sense. If, as his doctors and therapists believe, intensive therapy is necessary to prevent harm (e.g., contractures), then it is medically necessary "treat-ment" for his cerebral palsy. It is as important not to get worse as to get better. Third, there is no medical evidence in the record from which Travelers could make such a "finding." Both Dr. Swetenburg and Dr. Lesser reported "progress," and Dr. Pollack did not even call Ms. Wells.

Fourth, the implication that walking by age five would not be "significant progress" for this unfortunate child is simply revolting.

Finally, the precipitous decision to give up on Ethan was made by Dr. Pollack, who could provide scant support for it at deposition. Travelers boldly states that she has "a wealth of experience in pediatrics and knowledge of cerebral palsy in children." We see nothing to support this statement in her deposition. In fact, she was asked whether, in her twenty years of practice (before she went to work for Travelers), she ever "prescribed either speech therapy, occupational therapy, or physical therapy for [her] cerebral palsy patients." Her answer:

> No. Because in the area where I practiced, the routine was to, and it was set up this way, say it is a closed panel, the routine was to send children with cerebral palsy to the Kennedy Center and the Albert Einstein College of Medicine. And they were cared for there. We took care of only their routine physical care.

So much for Dr. Pollack's "wealth of experience."

It gets worse. Dr. Pollack was asked whether physical therapy would prevent contractures. She said, "No." Why not? "Because it is my belief that it is not an effective way to prevent contractures." Where did this belief come from? "I cannot tell you exactly how I developed it because I haven't thought about it for a long time." The nadir of this testimony was reached soon thereafter, as the baselessness of Dr. Pollack's decision became apparent:

Q ... If Dr. Lesser and Dr. Swetenburg were of the opinion that physical therapy at that rate and occupational therapy at that rate was medically necessary for Ethan Bedrick, would you have any reason to oppose their opinion?

A I am not sure I understand the question. Using what definition of medical necessity?

Q Well, using the evaluation of medical necessity as what is in the best interests of the child, the patient?

A I think we are talking about two different things.

Q All right. Expand, explain to me what two different things we are talking about?

A I'm speaking about what is to be covered by our contract.

Q Is what is covered by your contract something that's different than the best interests of the child as far as medical treatment is concerned? [objection omitted]

A I find that's a little like "have you stopped beating your wife?"

Q That's why I ask it. [objection, question is rephrased]: If Dr. Swetenburg and if Dr. Lesser recommend physical therapy and occupational therapy at the rates prescribed, do you have any medical basis for why that is an inappropriate treatment that has been prescribed [for Ethan]? [objection omitted]

A I have no idea. I have not examined the patient whether it is appropriate or inappropriate. But that isn't a decision I was asked to make.

The fiduciary of an ERISA plan must act "solely in the interest of the participants and beneficiaries and for the exclusive purpose of providing benefits and defraying reasonable expenses." 29 U.S.C. § 1104(a)(1)(A). This duty of loyalty to plan participants presents the insurer-employee of an insurer-funded plan with a most difficult task.

To put it most charitably, we think it abundantly clear that Dr. Pollack at least "unconsciously" put the financial interest of Travelers above her fiduciary duty to Ethan. Indeed, this employee of Travelers' "ConservCo" was not even "asked to make" a judgment about the appropriateness of the prescribed care for Ethan, in whose interests ERISA demands that she solely act.

Moreover, Dr. Robbins' much-delayed review cannot cure the breach of duty. He views himself as a "supporter" of Travelers' "legal department" and "field office." He has not seen patients in seven years, and he admitted that he is not familiar with textbooks or treatises on cerebral palsy. His opinion was based on a single medical journal article, which is uncited here.

A fiduciary with a conflict of interest must act as if he is "free" of such a conflict. "Free" is an absolute. There is no balancing of interests; ERISA commands undivided loyalty to the plan participants. Travelers did not evaluate Ethan's physical and occupational therapy claims in a manner consistent with this duty. We reverse the denial of benefits.

The plan provides coverage for speech therapy, but there is a significant limitation: "These services must be given to restore speech." Ethan has never been able to talk, so the therapy he receives cannot be said to "restore speech." Medically necessary or not, there is just no coverage here. Because our review is *de novo* and disinterested, Travelers' conflict of interest is not relevant.

The policy provides coverage for durable medical equipment that is medically necessary and "which replaces a lost body organ or part or helps an impaired one to work."

Travelers denied the claim for an upright stander as "not medically necessary." The Bedricks challenged this finding, but neither Dr. Pollack nor Dr. Robbins ever reviewed the medical necessity of the stander. At his deposition, Dr. Robbins stated that the bath chair was a "convenience item." The district court cited the same deposition for the proposition that Dr. Robbins had deemed the bather and the stander as items of convenience. In its brief, Travelers twice repeats the district court's misreading of the record.

In short, it appears that Travelers never reviewed the medical necessity of the stander, and there is nothing in the record to rebut the opinion of Ethan's physical therapist:

> The upright stander and modifications provide support that allows
> a child with motor delays—such as Ethan—the opportunity to

stand with correct alignment of the hips, knees and ankles. This standing position is important to bone development as well as development of the hip joint. Reports in the professional literature indicate that there is a decrease in contractures and fractures in those disabled children who participate in a standing program. In addition, the upright stander will work to facilitate sustained neck and trunk extension for Ethan. The standing will also provide a symmetrical position for him, as well as the opportunity to develop movements of the shoulders and arms.

On this record,[4] a decision that the stander was not medically necessary would clearly be an abuse of discretion. We must therefore reverse. We reverse the judgment of the district court as to physical and occupational therapy and the upright stander, and we remand with instructions to grant summary judgment for the plaintiffs.

Notes

1. *Medical necessity and persons with disabilities; the impact of the Affordable Care Act.* As indicated in the notes following *Mondry*, above, cases such as those involving Zev Mondry and Ethan Bedrick illustrate the problems faced by children and adults with conditions that affect growth and development or that are severe, chronic and long-lasting. Patients such as these may need clinical interventions to develop their functional capabilities or to maintain them once developed, or to avert their deterioration and loss over time. The question of whether treatment will allow them to "recover" or will "restore" their prior level of functioning simply is misplaced or irrelevant. Instead, an appropriate medical necessity evaluation would turn on the health benefits to be derived given the facts of their cases.

One way in which insurers and health benefit plans shield themselves against having to pay these types of claims these types of cases is by limiting coverage either through plan discriminatory plan design (as in the speech therapy definition used by Travelers) or through the application of treatment guidelines that are biased against persons with disabilities by recognizing medical necessity only if restoration or recovery potential is present. Insurers and plans also may throw in irrelevant considerations such as whether the treatment would have spillover effects in other settings (such as Zev Mondry's situation, where the therapy also is key to his ability to gain educational achievement). Rosenbaum et al., *Crossing the Rubicon.*

---

4. In this regard, we must point out a rather egregious misstatement of the record Travelers makes in support of its denial of coverage for the stander: "Ethan Bedrick's condition is such that there is only a fifty percent chance he will ever walk. Therefore, Ethan will remain in a seated position for most of his life [and a stander is therefore unnecessary]." The joint appendix page cited actually reveals that Ethan's pediatrician told Dr. Pollack that Ethan had a 50/50 chance of walking by age 5. If Ethan is not going to "remain in a seated position for most of his life," the stander becomes even more necessary, in order to properly develop his hip joints.

As noted in Chapter 6, the essential health benefit provisions of the Affordable Care Act will apply to all health plans sold in the individual and small-group markets beginning in January 2014. The essential benefit statute contains several provisions that are fundamentally contradictory. On the one hand, the Act provides that in interpreting the essential benefit provisions, the Secretary of Health and Human Services must "ensure that the scope of the essential health benefits" is "equal to the scope of benefits provided under a typical employer plan." PPACA § 1302(b)(2). As you can see, the "typical" employer plan tends to offer limited benefits where children and adults with disabilities are concerned.

On the other hand, "habilitation" services (i.e., clinical treatments and therapies aimed at helping children and adults with disabilities develop function) are a required essential health benefit class. PPACA § 1302(b)(1). Furthermore, as noted earlier, the Secretary, in implementing the provisions, must "not make coverage decisions, determine reimbursement rates, establish incentive programs, or design benefits in ways that discriminate against individuals because of their age, disability, or expected length of life." PPACA § 1302(b)(4)(B). The task of course becomes how to reconcile the notion of a "typical" employer plan with habilitation coverage and non-discrimination. One step might be to bar the use of limitations such as "restore" or "recover" from medical necessity definitions, treatment guidelines, and other decision-making tools, regardless of whether these tools are actually part of plan documents or used informally to guide decision making. Another step might be to bar insurers and plan administrators from applying "educational" exclusions to deny otherwise covered treatments simply because a covered clinical treatment would have the added benefit of enabling greater learning and achievement. Rosenbaum et al., *Crossing the Rubicon*.

You will see later in Part Two that Medicaid is guided by principles that embrace treatments for children and adults with disabilities and as such, plays a singular role in health care financing.

2. *The impact of restrictive medical necessity standards on adults with disabilities.* The impact of (an often unwritten) bias against persons with disabilities in coverage determinations is equally evident in the case of adults. In McGraw v. The Prudential Insurance Company of America, 137 F.3d 1253 (10th Cir. 1998), Linda McGraw, a patient with multiple sclerosis (for which there is no known prevention or cure) appealed the denial of treatments that would provide a lessening of her symptoms and allow her to maintain functioning and independence. Her insurer denied coverage, citing an exclusion, set forth in the plan as follows:

> To be considered "needed," a service or supply must be determined by Prudential to meet all of these tests: (a) It is ordered by a Doctor. (b) It is recognized throughout the Doctor's profession as safe and effective, is required for the diagnosis or treatment of the particular Sickness or Injury, and is employed appropriately in a manner and setting consistent with generally accepted United

States medical standards. (c) It is neither Educational nor Experimental or Investigational in nature.

Denial was based on the ground that the in-home physical therapy McGraw requested "does not affect the course of MS" and was therefore not medically necessary even though her treating neurologist indicated that "physical therapy is recognized in the treatment of MS to provide essential physical support which improves the individual's strength and endurance as well as her ability to perform the activities of daily living (ADL)."

The testimony at trial showed that the insurer's denial was based on the assertion that the therapy cannot affect the course of MS. The insurer gave no weight to her medical records, the opinion of her physician, patient interviews, or the literature on treatment of MS. The medical claims reviewer stated that "his decision was based on the nature of MS. To warrant physical therapy, he explained, Prudential's internal protocols required a showing the condition would improve; and because there was no evidence any intervention would even have anything to do with maintenance, physical therapy, in his opinion, was not medically necessary." At the same time, the plan paid for 16 of approximately 40 outpatient visits on the basis of a nonbinding "confidential, internal Group Claim Division Memorandum (GCLM 90–42)" authorizing therapy for "short term, intensive and goal oriented treatment of a condition which has the potential for significant improvement, as compared to when the therapy began."

The court concluded:

> Prudential has modified its definition of "medically necessary" with the additional requirement the treatment provide a measurable and substantial increase in functional ability for "a condition having potential for significant improvement." This guideline is not binding but imposes on the "condition" of MS the requirement it has a "potential for significant improvement." However, under the terms of the Plan, the medical director and subsequent Prudential fiduciaries reviewing the claim were charged with assuring only that the treatment is ordered by a doctor; is generally accepted under United States medical standards; and is neither educational, experimental, or investigational in nature. Prudential's interpretation of the Plan with this criterion alters its scope and is unreasonable. Moreover, had Prudential's representatives read the hospital notes, medical records, and neurologists' letters, they might have discovered that each treating physician ordered physical therapy to enhance Ms. McGraw's strength, endurance, and motor functions. Ultimately, however, improving Ms. McGraw's functionality would permit her to live more comfortably. And that's the rub. Using GCLM 90–42, Prudential then characterized the means to that end as "medically beneficial" but not "medically necessary" because the treatment in its view would not alter the course of the disease.[14]

---

14. Arguably, were this criterion carried to its logical conclusion, no MS patient could qualify for reimbursement of certain medical services, and the contract of insurance would be illusory.

We apply the same analysis and reasoning to Prudential's [denial] of Ms. McGraw's claim for inpatient physical therapy at Baptist Medical Center. Dr. Lewis [Prudential's reviewer] explained in her affidavit the denial was based in part on [the fact that] a nurses' notes reflect that Mrs. McGraw left the hospital on a pass, accompanied by her husband, and had a good time. I believe the medical necessity of inpatient confinement is suspect where a patient is either able or allowed to leave the hospital on a pass." We find this statement shocking. There is nothing in the record suggesting proper inpatient physical therapy mandates a twenty-four hour confinement, or that periods away from the hospital when therapy is not being administered are incompatible with proper treatment.

Most egregiously, there is no indication in this record that the decision was ever based on a review of Ms. McGraw's medical records [or conversations with her treating physicians]. At each level of review, Prudential's fiduciaries did not evaluate the claims for Ms. McGraw's physical therapy "solely in the interest of the participants" as required under 29 U.S.C. § 1104(a)(1)(A), but more to reflect "defraying reasonable expenses." 29 U.S.C. § 1104(a)(1)(A). Because the fiduciary unreasonably interpreted the Plan, we therefore hold the denial of benefits for the two claims reviewed was arbitrary and capricious and reverse the contrary conclusion of the district court.

In *McGraw,* as in *Bedrick*, the restoration expectation was superimposed on the plan's medical necessity decision. The key question in the wake of the Affordable Care Act is whether given the language of § 1302(b)(4)(B), such a superimposition, even if an explicit written condition of coverage, would be lawful in the case of a qualified health plan.

Note: When Is Health Care Medically Necessary?

The definition of medical necessity can be critical to determining whether to cover a particular claim. Until the 1980s, most insurers and plan administrators took a much broader approach to the drafting of contracts and plan documents, covering broad classes of benefits, leaving key terms undefined or ambiguous, and using their general discretion to approve or deny claims. Insurers routinely paid all medical claims submitted to them and deferred to the judgment of treating clinicians as to whether covered treatments were medically necessary.

As health care costs escalated, insurers and plan administrators became more aggressive in three respects. First, they became more specific about the terms of coverage themselves, defining actual benefit classes to include or exclude certain conditions, treatments, or patients. You can see this in Traveler's definition of "speech therapy" in *Bedrick,* in which a restorative requirement is embedded into the definition of speech therapy itself.

Second, insurers and administrators became more specific about coverage exclusions, not only identifying treatments and services that fell outside the contract but also providing definitions that narrowed the scope of coverage while also, as predictable following *Firestone*, reserving to themselves the discretion to apply contract terms to a specific set of facts. Again, you can see this practice in *Bedrick,* in which Travelers argued for a deferential standard in its determination of whether physical therapy was medically necessary for Ethan.

Third, as you saw in *Jones,* drafters incorporated practice guidelines directly into the terms of coverage themselves, paradoxically in such situations in order to *limit* the discretion of their claims reviewers. A practice guideline that is part of the terms of coverage has the effect of limiting the utilization reviewers' power to approve any treatment other than the treatment specified in the guideline, since the guideline is part of the plan design. This can lead to disturbing results; as the behavioral health consultant in *Jones* noted, in his opinion the plan's permissible covered treatment for the plaintiff was inappropriate given her condition, and yet he lacked the authority of course to substitute his own medical judgment for the plan documents themselves. As we have seen, the purpose of something so at odds with medical rationality was to preclude review of discretion by drawing protocols into the plan itself and thereby eliminating the relevant of medical necessity.

Plan drafters also can also affect the outcome of coverage through the use of various types of definitions for the concept of "medically necessary" and its closely related companions, "experimental or investigational." Drafters can use very strict definitions of what will be considered "medically necessary" and therefore covered, or what will be excluded as "experimental."

The early medical necessity cases underscore the challenges faced in developing precise standards for when treatments will be denied because they are considered unnecessary or experimental. For example typical of the 1980s, in Dallis v. Aetna Life Ins. Co., 574 F. Supp. 547 (N.D. Ga. 1983), *aff'd*, 768 F.2d 1303 (11th Cir. 1985), the defendant insurance company, denying coverage for an unorthodox cancer treatment, relied on a provision in the policy that stated: "No insurance is afforded as to charges for care, treatment, services or supplies which are not necessary for the treatment of the injury or disease concerned." *Dallis*, 574 F. Supp. at 550. (The contract's failure to define "necessary" was typical of health insurance policies until quite recently.) The company argued that the term "necessary" meant "recognized as potentially efficacious and safe by the medical community, including all significant branches and agencies therein which are concerned with treatment of cancer." *Id.* at 550–51. In contrast, the plaintiff argued that the contract term " 'necessary for the treatment' implies that the care is, in some degree, beneficial to the patient." *Id.* at 551. The court surveyed other cases on the issue and found "no consensus among the courts as to the definition." Some courts had upheld insurer denials if the company had shown that the treatment was "worthless."

Other courts had interpreted the term to mean "appropriate" and "wise in the light of facts known at the time rendered." *Id.* at 551. The *Dallis* court concluded that the term "medically necessary" was ambiguous as a matter of law, and therefore, when considered in the light of all the rules of construction applicable to insurance contracts, was a matter of fact for a jury to decide. Like the term "medically necessary," the terms "experimental" or "investigational" have been frequently held by courts to be ambiguous. See Johnson v. District 2 Marine Eng'rs Beneficial Association—Associated Maritime Officers Medical Plan, 857 F.2d 514, 516 (9th Cir. 1988) ("in the context of modern medicine, the term experimental seems clearly ambiguous on its face"); Pirozzi v. Blue Cross–Blue Shield of Virginia, 741 F. Supp. 586, 589 (E.D. Va. 1990); Wolf v. Prudential Ins. Co., 50 F.3d 793, 799 (10th Cir. 1995) (applying Oklahoma law) (holding that the general exclusionary term "experimental" is ambiguous, but that a contract specifically excluding "all phases of clinical trials [and] all treatment protocols based upon or similar to those used in clinical trials" is not ambiguous).

Moreover, state law cases regarding health benefits denials rarely addressed whether the health insurance contract, contract law, or some other source of law required the insurance company or other payer to engage in a process of decision making that met any coherent criteria. Early cases, such as *Sarchett*, 729 P.2d 267, illustrate that insurers may decide cases involving questions of medical necessity or experimental/investigational without definitions, coherent written procedures, or adherence to their own procedures and guidelines, thereby violating their own policies through arbitrary and capricious conduct. Adverse judicial decisions increasingly have led insurers and plan administrators to become much more explicit and sophisticated in drafting their policies, with respect to both the definition of key terms and the articulation of criteria for decision.

One of the best known and most passionate battles over the separation of what is medically necessary from what is experimental occurred in the context of patients with metastatic breast cancer, whose physicians sought high-dose chemotherapy with autologous bone marrow transplant (HDC–ABMT) treatment for them. Such patients were routinely denied access to such treatment on the ground that they were experimental or some similar basis. In their article, *We Were All Sold a Bill of Goods: Litigating the Science of Breast Cancer Treatment*, 52 WAYNE L. REV. (2006), Peter D. Jacobson and Stephanie A. Doebler examined the scores of cases that were litigated during the 1990s across all forms of health insurance (ERISA-governed plans and otherwise):

> In the late 1980s and 1990s, thousands of women elected to undergo high-dose chemotherapy with autologous bone marrow transplant (HDC–ABMT) as a last-chance treatment for breast cancer, despite the fact that the procedure cost upwards of $100,000 and was also expensive in terms of risks and side effects. When their health insurers refused to cover the treatment, many women sought payment through the judicial system. The result

was a series of nearly a hundred courtroom battles, not to mention thousands of settlement negotiations, in which judges and juries were forced to determine whether women would have access to a new procedure that offered their only hope for survival. By the time studies were published conclusively showing that the procedure was ineffective, more than 30,000 women had already received the treatment, which often shortened their lives and added to their suffering, at a total cost of approximately $3 billion.

What went wrong? How could so much money have been spent and such suffering imposed for no apparent benefit? The natural reaction to these devastating accounts is to assign blame. Depending on one's political and philosophical views, blame might be apportioned in the following ways. First, in their quest to slash costs and raise the bottom-line, health insurers and managed care organizations ignored the needs of their policyholders. Second, physicians pressured their patients into undergoing a procedure with essentially unknown risks and benefits, in a desperate attempt to give them at least a few more years of life. Third, plaintiffs' attorneys saw the opportunity to make the insurers pay—both literally and figuratively—for their cold-heartedness and pursued these cases aggressively. Finally, courts, moved by the plight of the dying women who came before them, let sympathy trump the law.

Id. at 46–47.

In fact, the authors conclude, none of these "conventional wisdom" answers really explained the reality of the cases. Through extensive research, including interviews with many of the litigants, the authors conclude that no one was to blame, that the legal system worked as it should have both in terms of factual development and in applying the terms of coverage to the facts before the court. The authors concluded that the true culprit is an underlying health care system that permits the diffusion of medical and clinical technologies before they are ready. (Here, physicians clamored for the treatment on their patients' behalf even though Phase III randomized controlled trials had not yet been completed):

At its heart, the litigation reflected dramatically different moral, legal, and scientific views of the world. For metastatic and high-risk breast cancer patients, HDC–ABMT represented a promising therapy. Clinicians were divided, with breast cancer oncologists and bone marrow transplanters supporting the procedure and academic physicians wanting to wait for the results of randomized clinical trials (RCTs). For insurers, the procedure represented an unproven treatment whose use could actually adversely affect the patient's quality of life and lifespan. Given these disparate world views, it is not surprising that the plaintiffs' and defendants' narratives are very different, with little overlap between how the two frame the issue and their litigation strategies. An important consequence of the differing world views is that the plaintiffs' narrative can easily be framed in sound-bite terms, while the defense's narrative is inherently more complex. Not surprisingly, it seems much easier to "sell" the plaintiffs' narrative, especially to a jury than the defense's more complex story.

Id. at 47.

The authors summarized the positions of the litigants—the dying women and their families on one side, and the insurance industry on the other. Plaintiffs relied on three major themes to frame their cases—dying women, the sanctity of the physician/patient relationship, and the [just emerging] managed care industry, which could be portrayed as the villain. The defense, by contrast, relied on two theories of its own: first, the unproven nature of the treatment; and second, the treatment's potential actually to cause greater harm because of its extreme, potentially lethal nature. *Id.* at 61. The key to the cases in the authors' view was the factual development surrounding the standard of care* that in turn created the framework for judging the reasonableness of insurers' decisions:

At the core of the litigation was whether HDC–ABMT was the appropriate standard of care for metastatic breast cancer patients. To the insurance companies, there was no dispute about the standard of care for HDC–ABMT since it was and remains experimental. Hence, the standard of care for metastatic breast cancer patients did not include HDC–ABMT, at least outside of clinical trials. The plaintiff's job, therefore, was to demonstrate that the procedure's use was widespread among community oncologists. Defendants wanted the case tried on the lack of proven effectiveness. Plaintiffs wanted to try the case based on its widespread use regardless of what the research results indicated.

In many of the cases, plaintiffs' attorneys were able to show widespread use. For example, despite the absence of evidence from Phase III trials, many community oncologists and transplanters were avid supporters of the procedure. Their testimony carried great weight with the jury and counteracted that of the defense experts. From a judge's perspective, it was difficult to rule that the procedure was experimental when there was strong evidence from community physicians that they were actively using it.

Excerpts from the following trial transcript in 1994 clearly show the dilemma facing the judge and jury in determining the standard of care. The witness, a medical director of a CHAMPUS plan,** began by stating that HDC–ABMT "does not meet the generally accepted standards of usual medical practice in the general medical community" as defined in the plan's benefit contract. This colloquy followed:

---

* The issue of the professional standard of care will be reviewed extensively in Part Three.

** CHAMPUS was the acronym for employment based coverage for members of the military and their dependents. The system is now known as TRICARE.

Q: "Ms. X" was a little more straightforward in her affidavit. She stated in paragraph 10 that, "ABMT and PSCR [peripheral stem cell recovery] for breast cancer has gained acceptance among many oncologists." Would you agree with that statement?

A: Yes, sir.

Q: You would also agree that in 1991 the *Journal of Clinical Oncology* conducted a survey wherein 80% of oncologists polled felt that high-dose chemotherapy for the treatment of breast cancer was an alternative that should be offered to women. You would agree with that; wouldn't you?

A: I am not sure, sir.

Q: Are you familiar with the *Journal of Clinical Oncology* study?

A: Yes.

Q: You would agree with me 80% of oncologists felt that it was an alternative that should be offered; is that correct?

A: That is what was reported there, yes, sir.

Q: Do you know some piece of information why that is not accurate?

A: Yes, sir, I do.... It would be the consensus conference from Lyon, France published in last month's *Journal of Clinical Oncology* which states the international consensus of not only the Oncologists of America but also the oncologists of the world feel that [HDC/PSCR for] breast cancer should be confined solely to clinical trials.

Q: Now, when we talk about American oncologists, you would agree with me that the *Journal of Clinical Oncology* study ... polled 465 American oncologists; isn't that right?

A: Yes.

Q: It is 80% of those 465 American oncologists who say that it should be offered as an alternative; isn't that right?

A: Yes.

Q: It is safe to say if 80% of the oncologists polled in America say it should be offered as an alternative, then it is pretty safe to say that it is accepted by American oncologists; isn't that correct?

A: I wouldn't make that assumption.

Q: 80%, that figure speaks for itself; doesn't it?

A: Not in my opinion. [The witness then noted that six of the seven oncologists listed at the end of the article argued that HDC–ABMT was experimental.]

Q: Is it your testimony today that the participation of those seven American oncologists at that conference more weight should be placed upon that than the *Journal of Clinical Oncologists Survey*, is that what you are telling the court?

A: Yes, sir.

Q: Isn't it also true that some form of high-dose chemotherapy is available in most every major city and state in the United States, isn't that true?

A: I don't know that to be true.

Q: If you had to take a guess, you would agree it would be a good many?

A: It would be many major cities, yes, sir.

Q: It is available both at many academic institutions and hospitals?

A: That's correct.

Q: It is available from private providers also, isn't that correct?

A: That's true.

Q: It is available inpatient?

A: That's true.

Q: Outpatient?

A: True.

Q: Academicians administer the treatment, isn't that correct?

A: Yes, sir.

Q: Private oncologists administer the treatment. Isn't that right?

A: Yes.

Q: Community based oncologists administer the treatment, isn't that correct?

A: Yes.

Q: Pretty widespread, isn't it?

A: Yes.

From this exchange, the strategies of both sides can be seen, as can the conundrum facing the court. Plaintiffs' attorneys argued that if the procedure is widely used, it cannot be considered experimental or investigational. The defense countered that the mere fact of general use does not define the standard of care when the procedure's scientific effectiveness remains unproven. In similar exchanges in other cases, the defense made a strong case that the science does not support widespread use. Defense counsel attempted to show that the transplanting [physicians'] recommend[ed] actions were unique to the patient, without any agreed-upon standards in the community. By contrast, plaintiffs' counsel repeatedly focused on the final set of questions listed above to show that the procedure had spread to every corner of clinical practice.

Id. at 60–62.

* * *

Consider the following definition from the TennCare program, which is Tennessee's name for Medicaid. In Tennessee, virtually all services with limited exceptions are purchased from private insurers. Because the Medicaid statute contains no definition of medical necessity concerning coverage for individuals ages 21 and older (a comprehensive statutory definition applies in the case of children and adolescents), Tennessee insurers fashioned a definition, which in turn was enacted into law by the state legislature. It is an uncommonly comprehensive and tightly drafted statute that, read literally, places most forms of medical treatment into an "experimental" category, leaving insurers in a position to deny nearly all standard care on the ground that the care is not medically necessary. The definition is as follows:

> (a) Enrollees under the TennCare program are eligible to receive, and TennCare shall provide payment for, only those medical items and services that are: (1) within the scope of defined benefits for which the enrollee is eligible under the TennCare program; and (2) determined by the TennCare program to be medically necessary.

> (b) To be determined to be medically necessary, a medical item or service must be recommended by a physician who is treating the enrollee or other licensed healthcare provider practicing within the scope of his or her license who is treating the enrollee and must satisfy each of the following criteria: (1) It must be required in order to diagnose or treat an enrollee's medical condition. The convenience of an enrollee, the enrollee's family, or a provider, shall not be a factor or justification in determining that a medical item or service is medically necessary; (2) It must be safe and effective. To qualify as safe and effective, the type and level of medical item or service must be consistent with the symptoms or diagnosis and treatment of the particular medical condition, and the *reasonably anticipated medical benefits of the item or service must outweigh the reasonably anticipated medical risks based on the enrollee's condition and scientifically supported evidence;* (3) It must be the least costly alternative course of diagnosis or treatment that is adequate for the medical condition of the enrollee. When applied to medical items or services delivered in an inpatient setting, it further means that the medical item or service cannot be safely provided for the same or lesser cost to the person in an outpatient setting. Where there are less costly alternative courses of diagnosis or treatment, including less costly alternative settings that are adequate for the medical condition of the enrollee, more costly alternative courses of diagnosis or treatment are not medically necessary. An alternative course of diagnosis or treatment

may include observation, lifestyle or behavioral changes or, where appropriate, no treatment at all; and *(4)* It must not be experimental or investigational. *A medical item or service is experimental or investigational if there is inadequate empirically-based objective clinical scientific evidence of its safety and effectiveness for the particular use in question. This standard is not satisfied by a provider's subjective clinical judgment on the safety and effectiveness of a medical item or service or by a reasonable medical or clinical hypothesis based on an extrapolation from use in another setting or from use in diagnosing or treating another condition.*

Tenn. Ann. Code § 71–5–144 *(*emphasis added*)*.

The critical elements of the statute appear in the italicized language, which empowers claims reviewers to deny—either as not medically necessary or as experimental and investigational—any requested treatment for which there is no "scientifically supported evidence" or for which there is "inadequate empirically-based objective clinical scientific evidence of its safety and effectiveness." The "subjective clinical" judgment of treating clinicians, or even "reasonable medical hypotheses" based on use in another setting are insufficient to justify treatment.

Implementing regulations issued by Tennessee's Department of Finance and Administration, which oversees TennCare, further clarify the types of evidence considered sufficient to justify treatment:

> (22) HIERARCHY OF EVIDENCE shall mean a ranking of the weight given to medical evidence depending on objective indicators of its validity and reliability including the nature and source of the medical evidence, the empirical characteristics of the studies or trials upon which the medical evidence is based, and the consistency of the outcome with comparable studies. The hierarchy in descending order, with Type I given the greatest weight is: (a) Type I: Meta-analysis done with multiple, well-designed controlled clinical trials; (b) Type II: One or more well-designed experimental studies; (c) Type III: Well-designed, quasi-experimental studies; (d) Type IV: Well-designed, non-experimental studies; and (e) Type V: Other medical evidence defined as evidence-based: 1. Clinical guidelines, standards or recommendations from respected medical organizations or governmental health agencies; 2. Analyses from independent health technology assessment organizations; or 3. Policies of other health plans.

Department of Finance and Administration § 1200–13–16.01(22).

The definition of evidence, coupled with the discretion granted to the TennCare program and its contractors, means that any services and treatments whose need is based solely on the judgment of treating clinicians and consulting experts is subject to exclusion either as medically unnecessary or experimental. The hierarchy of evidence adopted by the TennCare program is one that is used by researchers when evaluating the efficacy of procedures undertaken as part of a clinical trial, where the goal is to test the effectiveness of a procedure, in a controlled clinical trial setting, that is not the standard medical response to a particular problem (e.g., a new drug, a new device, a new type of surgical procedure). See, e.g., David Evans, *Hierarchy of Evidence: A Framework for Ranking Evidence Evaluating Health Care Interventions*, 12 J. CLINICAL NURSING 77 (2003). Increasing the extent to which empirical research exists to support medical practice is considered one of the highest public policy priorities in health care quality research, but the state of this research is exceedingly limited. The net effect of importing this narrow definition of relevant evidence into an insurance definition of medical necessity is that it acts as a potential exclusionary rule for all otherwise covered treatments that lack an empirical base. Further, the basic goal of such pure research is to control for any confounding factors, with the result that extrapolation of research findings, derived from the purest of conditions, is simply a leap of faith into the "messy" world of actual clinical practice with real people.

The TennCare medical necessity definition received considerable attention when first enacted into law. Andy Schneider, *Tennessee's New Medical Necessity Standard: Uncovering the Insured?* KAISER COMMISSION ON MEDICAID AND THE UNINSURED (2004), http://www.kff.org/medicaid/upload/Tennessee-s-New-Medically-Necessary-Standard-Uncovering-the-Insured-Policy-Brief.pdf. It is not clear whether other insurers or plans have adopted the definition given its highly exclusionary qualities. The TennCare program has conducted no analyses to determine how this definition has been employed by contractors or the extent to which standard treatments for common conditions have been denied because they lack a scientific basis in evidence. Regardless, the basic message is that with appropriate drafting, much of clinical experience can be written out of an insurance plan and medical necessity rendered irrelevant.

d.   Claims Denials Involving Uncovered and Out-of-Network Care

Krauss v. Oxford Health Plans, Inc.

517 F.3d 614 (2d Cir. 2008)

■ SACK, CIRCUIT JUDGE:

The plaintiffs, Geri S. Krauss and Daniel J. Krauss, wife and husband, are members of an employer-provided health care plan that is governed by ERISA. The defendant Oxford administer[s] claims for benefits under the plan. In April 2003, Geri Krauss was diagnosed with breast cancer. Shortly thereafter, she underwent a double mastectomy and bilateral breast reconstruction surgery. The surgical procedures were performed in a single operative session by two different, unaffiliated doctors, neither of whom was a member of the plan's provider network. Following the operation, Mrs. Krauss received care from private-duty nurses. The Krausses paid for both the surgery and post-operative care themselves and sought reimbursement for those expenses from Oxford. Oxford refused payment for one-fourth of the cost of the breast reconstruction surgery and all expenses incurred for private-duty nursing.

After exhausting available administrative appeals, the Krausses filed this lawsuit in the United States District Court for the Southern District of New York. They allege that Oxford's denial of full reimbursement for the bilateral surgery and private-duty nursing care violated the Women's Health and Cancer Rights Act, 29 U.S.C. § 1185b ("WHCRA"), as well as various ERISA provisions. They further allege that Oxford violated ERISA by failing to make certain required disclosures and failing to respond to various grievances in the manner and time periods set forth by their plan. The district court ruled in favor of Oxford on all claims. [W]e affirm.

In April 2003, Mrs. Krauss was diagnosed with breast cancer. Her doctors, who were not members of Oxford's provider network, recommended that she undergo a double mastectomy and bilateral breast reconstruction,[1] to be performed in a single surgical session. On May 5, 2003, Oxford "pre-certified" (i.e., approved in advance) the breast-reconstruction portion of the surgery,[2] stating that "[p]ayment for approved services [would] be consistent with the terms, conditions, and limitations of [Mrs. Krauss's] Certificate of Coverage, the provider's contract, as well as with Oxford's administrative and payment policies." On May 13, 2003, Mrs. Krauss underwent bilateral mastectomy and reconstruction surgery. Following the surgery, upon the doctors' suggestion and the plaintiffs' request, private-duty nurses oversaw Mrs. Krauss's recovery.

The Krausses were at all relevant times participants in an ERISA-covered employee health insurance plan called the "Freedom Plan–Very High UCR" (the "Plan"). The Plan was established and sponsored by Mr. Krauss's employer, and claims for benefits under the Plan were administered by Oxford. The Plan's terms are set forth in three documents—the Summary of Benefits, the Certificate of Coverage (for payment of physicians and other providers who were part of the Oxford network), and the Supplemental Certificate of Coverage ("Supplemental Certificate") (for out-of-network care). Because the Supplemental Certificate concerns the use of out-of-network providers including the surgeons who operated on Mrs. Krauss, it is the document of primary relevance for purposes of this appeal. A Plan member utilizing an out-of-network provider must herself pay a higher portion of her medical expenses from her own pocket than must a member receiving care from in-network providers.

Oxford limits its plans' costs for medical services by, *inter alia,* (1) restricting the services that the insurance plan covers; (2) imposing deductibles and coinsurance payments; and (3) paying medical expenses in accordance with a schedule of "usual, customary, and reasonable" ("UCR") fees for various medical services. Charges in excess of the UCR rate or excluded from coverage by a plan, as well as the deductibles and coinsurance charges, are paid by the insured.

---

1. Bilateral Surgery is defined by the Centers for Medicare and Medicaid Services as procedures performed on both sides of the body during the same operative session or on the same day.

2. There is no dispute with respect to Oxford's reimbursement to the Krausses for doctors' charges for the double mastectomy.

The Plan expressly excludes "[p]rivate or special duty nursing" from Plan coverage. The Krausses had reached the Plan's annual limit on coinsurance and deductible charges at the time of Mrs. Krauss's surgery, so these charges did not reduce the amount of payments they received. They remained subject to the Plan's UCR schedule, however. The Supplemental Certificate makes several references to the UCR schedule. The subsection entitled "Your Financial Obligations," for example, states:

> A UCR schedule is a compilation of maximum allowable charges for various medical services. They vary according to the type of provider and geographic location. Fee schedules are calculated using data compiled by the Health Insurance Association of America (HIAA)[4] and other recognized sources. What We [sic] Cover/reimburse is based on the UCR.

Section XII, "Definitions," provides further that the UCR charge is "[t]he amount charged or the amount We [sic] determine to be the reasonable charge, whichever is less, for a particular Covered Service in the geographical area it is performed." According to the Supplemental Certificate, after Plan members receive care from an out-of-network provider, they must pay for services themselves and file a claim for reimbursement with Oxford.

Dr. Mark Sultan charged the Krausses $40,000 for Mrs. Krauss's breast reconstruction procedure and $200 for a pre-operation consultation. The private-duty nurses charged a total of $8,300 for her post-operative care.

The Krausses timely filed for reimbursement for both sets of services from Oxford. In response, on June 13, 2003, they received a check from Oxford in the amount of $30,200—$30,000 for the double-breast reconstruction and the $200 consultation fee. The accompanying Explanation of Benefits ("EOB") did not explain why the procedure was not fully reimbursed. It stated only that the maximum allowable benefit was $30,200 and that "[t]his claim reflects industry standards for payment of services which include two surgical procedures." Oxford did not explain the absence of reimbursement for the private-duty nursing.

On November 10, 2003, the Krausses filed a grievance with Oxford for the $10,000 of Dr. Sultan's fee and for the $8,300 cost for private-duty nursing that had not been reimbursed. By letter dated December 1, 2003, Oxford denied the Krausses' grievance as to the bilateral reconstruction surgery fee, "as the cpt code 19364–50x1[5] was paid at the usual and customary rate, because we have participating providers performing the

---

4. The HIAA now does business under the name Ingenix.

5. CPT is the commonly used abbreviation for "Current Procedural Terminology," a "system of terminology [that] is the most widely accepted medical nomenclature used to report medical procedures and services under public and private health insurance programs." American Medical Assn., CPT Process—How a Code Becomes a Code, http:// www. ama-assn. org/ ama/ pub/ category/ 3882. html (updated Oct. 30, 2007; last visited Feb. 25, 2008). CPT code 19364 is the code for "breast reconstruction with free flap."

procedure effectively, and there is no medical reason as to why to grant [sic] an exception outside the UCR. . . . ''

By letter dated December 3, 2003, Oxford notified the Krausses that it had referred the claim for the private-duty nursing care to its claims department. Oxford contends that it thereafter denied the Krausses' claim for private-duty nursing charges on the ground that private-duty nursing is not covered by the Plan, but the Krausses submit that they never received a report of Oxford's benefits determination in this regard.

On December 9, 2003, the Krausses, in two letters, requested additional information in aid of filing their "Second–Level" appeal regarding the unpaid portion of Dr. Sultan's operating fee. Oxford responded with three additional cursory denial letters dated December 11, 2003, January 21, 2004, and January 22, 2004. These letters stated, respectively, that in-network providers could have performed the surgery and that "there is no medical reason . . . to grant an exception outside the UCR."

On January 26, 2004, the Krausses filed a Second–Level appeal with Oxford's Grievance Review Board, asserting, among other things, that Oxford had not complied with ERISA disclosure requirements. Some three weeks later, by letter dated February 19, 2004, Oxford acknowledged its receipt of the Krausses' December letters and enclosed various Oxford documents that previously had not been disclosed to them, including its Bilateral Surgery Policy. This policy requires providers to identify bilateral procedures with the "modifier–50" attached to the standard billing code for the procedure at issue and indicates that procedures so identified would "be reimbursed at one and a half times the rate of the single procedure."

One week later, on February 26, 2004, the Krausses responded by letter contending that the Bilateral Surgery Policy was not set forth in their Plan's terms, had not been disclosed in Oxford's previous denial letters, violated state and federal laws requiring full compensation for post-mastectomy breast reconstruction, and had not been applied in other bilateral surgeries Mrs. Krauss had undergone.

By letter dated March 11, 2004, Oxford denied the Krausses' Second–Level appeal. Oxford asserted, for the first time, that the appropriate UCR under the Plan is "the level that 90% of all doctors (not 100% of all doctors) in the location would accept as full payment for the service," and that the UCR for CPT code 19364–50 was $20,000. The $30,000 reimbursement the Krausses received for the reconstruction surgery represented 150% of the UCR for a single reconstruction. The denial letter further stated that Oxford's Bilateral Surgery Policy was "consistent with well-established industry standards and in accordance with New York state insurance regulations," and was "not conceal[ed] . . . , but rather, [had been] publicize[d] . . . in its payment policies and on its explanations of benefits." Oxford further stated that its disclosures "far exceed[ed]" what ERISA requires, and that references in earlier letters to the availability of in-network providers referred to its understanding that the Krausses were requesting an "in-network exception," i.e., an exception to regular UCR rates that applies only if, unlike the procedure undergone by Mrs. Krauss, no in-network provider is available to perform it.

The Krausses responded to the denial of their administrative appeals by instituting this action. Their complaint asserts claims for: (1) recovery of unpaid benefits under ERISA § 502(a)(1)(B), on the grounds that Oxford's denial of benefits violated the WHCRA [Women's Health and Cancer Rights Act of 1988, 29 U.S.C. § 1185b] and the terms of the Plan; (2) breach of fiduciary duty in violation of ERISA § 502(a)(3), on the grounds that Oxford failed to provide benefits owed to the Krausses and improperly handled their claims for reimbursement and their appeals; (3) statutory damages under ERISA §§ 502(a)(3)(B)(1), (c)(1), in light of Oxford's alleged failure to make timely disclosures and to provide accurate reasons for the denials of their claims; (4) a declaratory judgment barring the application of Oxford's Bilateral Surgery Policy to post-mastectomy breast reconstruction surgeries; and (5) costs and attorney's fees.

The parties filed cross-motions for summary judgment. [The district court ruled against the Krausses on all counts].

II.   Claims for Unpaid Benefits

ERISA section 502(a)(1)(B) permits a participant or beneficiary of an ERISA-covered benefits plan to bring a civil action "to recover benefits due to him under the terms of his plan." The Krausses seek recovery of the unpaid portion of Dr. Sultan's breast reconstruction surgery fee and the costs of private-duty nursing care, benefits they say were owed to them either under the WHCRA or the terms of the Plan.

As a threshold matter, the Krausses argue that the district court erred in reviewing Oxford's benefits determination and their arguments with respect thereto under the arbitrary and capricious standard. Because Oxford's UCR benefit determination was not discretionary, they say, the court's review should have been *de novo*. On the merits, the Krausses contend (1) that Oxford's application of its Bilateral Surgery Policy to Mrs. Krauss's breast reconstruction surgery and its refusal to reimburse them for the costs of post-operative private-duty nursing care violate the terms of the WHCRA; (2) that even if the Bilateral Surgery Policy complies with the WHCRA, its application to the Krausses violates the terms of the Plan: it is not a UCR determination; was not properly disclosed; and was based upon an underlying HIAA-based UCR figure derived from a sample size too small to be meaningful; and (3) that the refusal to reimburse the costs incurred for private-duty nursing was contrary to the Plan's terms because the service was medically necessary and within the Plan's description of what it covers under the WHCRA.

A.   Standard of Review of Oxford's Actions

We agree with the district court that the Plan conferred discretionary authority on Oxford to make benefits determinations. Two clauses within the Plan's Supplemental Certificate governing care provided by out-of-network providers are relevant. The first appears under the heading

"General Provisions" and states that Oxford "may adopt reasonable policies, procedures, rules, and interpretations to promote the orderly and efficient administration of this Certificate...." The second is within the definition of UCR charges itself. It states that the UCR charge is either "[t]he amount charged or the amount We [sic] determine to be the reasonable charge, whichever is less...."

Despite a lack of clarity in our precedents as to what language conveys sufficient discretion to an administrator to require courts' "arbitrary and capricious" rather than *de novo* review of its actions, we conclude that the quoted language of the Oxford Plan does so. Oxford's UCR definition, which provides that the UCR charge is the lesser of the amount charged or the amount Oxford "determine[s] to be the reasonable charge," confers upon Oxford discretionary authority regarding one of the Plan terms here at issue. Accordingly, we will decide whether doing so was arbitrary or capricious, that is, if it was "without reason, unsupported by substantial evidence or erroneous as a matter of law."[7]

Separately, the Krausses' challenge under the WHCRA, see section II.B., below, raises questions of law which we review *de novo*. With respect to the Krausses' claim for reimbursement for private-duty nursing care, however, we assume, viewing the facts in the light most favorable to them as we must, that Oxford failed to inform them regarding the benefits determination made with respect to the nurses. For the reasons stated below, even assuming a *de novo* standard of review applies, we would deny the Krausses' claim for compensation for the private-duty nursing care under ERISA section 502(a)(1)(B).

B. The WHCRA

1. Dr. Sultan's Fees. The Krausses contend that under the WHCRA, the Plan was obligated to provide full reimbursement to them for Dr. Sultan's fee for Mrs. Krauss's bilateral reconstructive surgery. They also argue that the WHCRA requires reimbursement of the costs associated with the private-duty nursing care provided to her because it was pursuant to a medical decision made by her physician regarding the "manner" in which her breast reconstruction surgery would be carried out.

The WHCRA provides, in relevant part, that a group health plan that provides insurance coverage for mastectomies must also provide coverage for a subsequent breast reconstruction surgery:

> (a) In general. A group health plan ... shall provide, in a case of a participant or beneficiary who is receiving benefits in connection with a mastectomy and who elects breast reconstruction in connection with such mastectomy, coverage for—(1) all stages of reconstruction of the breast on which the mastectomy has been per-

---

7. The Krausses' additional arguments for *de novo* review are without merit. To contend that Oxford's application of the Bilateral Surgery Policy was not a discretionary decision because it simply "mechanically applied a formula," ignores the fact that the decision to enact the Bilateral Surgery Policy was itself a discretionary decision in the first instance.

formed . . . in a manner determined in consultation with the attending physician and the patient. *Such coverage may be subject to annual deductibles and coinsurance provisions* as may be deemed appropriate and as are consistent with those established for other benefits under the plan or coverage * * *(d) Rule of construction. Nothing in this section shall be construed to prevent a group health plan or a health insurance issuer offering group health insurance coverage from negotiating the level and type of reimbursement with a provider for care provided in accordance with this section.

29 U.S.C. § 1185b (emphasis added).

As to their claim for reimbursement of Dr. Sultan's fee, the gist of the Krausses' arguments is that the statutory language providing that insurers may limit their coverage by requiring "annual deductibles and coinsurance" precludes insurers from applying any other "cost-sharing" mechanisms that would render plan participants responsible for a portion of the procedure's costs. We agree with Oxford, however, that the WHCRA requires only that insurers "cover[ ]" such surgeries in a manner "consistent" with the policies "established for other benefits under the plan." 29 U.S.C. § 1185b(a).

The statutory provisions—which create a substantive floor for three different types of coverage—should not be construed to create specific rules regarding the means by which the statutorily mandated categories of services are provided. Congress was plainly focused on the question of coverage *vel non;* it was not concerned with the precise details of the coverage to be provided. In sum, the WHCRA includes an express statement of permission as to deductibles and coinsurance and is silent as to other cost-sharing possibilities; [the law ensures] that insurers apply the same devices to control costs of mandated benefits that they employ for benefits unrelated to the statutory provisions; and the legislative history of the WHCRA is silent regarding the entire concept of insurer-instituted cost control mechanisms.

   2. Private–Duty Nursing. Parallel reasoning applies to the Krausses' claim under the WHCRA for reimbursement for private-duty nursing care. We see nothing in the statute to support a reading that requires an insurer to pay for private-duty nurses where such services are not otherwise covered and where post-operative care in a different form could have satisfied the patient's medical needs as identified by her doctor. That the WHCRA requires coverage for "all stages of reconstruction of the breast on which the mastectomy has been performed . . . in a manner determined in consultation with the attending physician and the patient," 29 U.S.C. § 1285b(a)(1), does not, we think, categorically override every plan's specific exclusion of private-duty nursing care in these circumstances.

C.   The Plan's Terms

   The Krausses next argue that application of the Bilateral Surgery Policy to their claim for reimbursement for the reconstruction surgery and the denial of any reimbursement for the private-duty nursing care violated the terms of the Plan. They contend that the Bilateral Surgery Policy is not a UCR determination, was not properly disclosed, and was derived from an underlying HIAA-based UCR figure that was unreliable. They further assert that the private-duty nursing care was a service "related" to the reconstruction surgery that came within Oxford's pre-certification of the procedure. We conclude, however, that Oxford's decision to apply the Bilateral Surgery Policy is supported by substantial evidence, and that even under *de novo* review, the explicit exclusion of private-duty nursing care by the Plan governs the Krausses' claims.

1. Bilateral Surgery Policy. We find the Krausses' assertion that the Bilateral Surgery Policy violates the Plan's terms to be meritless, largely because it fails to give effect to the breadth of Oxford's UCR definition and description contained in the Supplemental Certificate. [T]he Supplemental Certificate states that UCR fee schedules are calculated by "using data compiled by the [HIAA] and *other recognized sources*." Its "definition" of "UCR" accords Oxford the discretion to employ an amount it deems "reasonable . . . for a particular Covered Service in the geographical area it is performed." Nothing in the Plan's terms forbids Oxford from adopting a UCR based not only on HIAA data, but on some other "recognized" source.

The Bilateral Surgery Policy, while arguably less than generous, comports with, and is based upon, Medicare's policy. The reimbursement rate of 150% of UCR was based, therefore, on both HIAA data and a "recognized source" (Medicare). [B]ecause the terms of the Supplemental Certificate indicate that Oxford did not intend the UCR charge necessarily to be equivalent to the HIAA amount, and because we, like the district court, are unprepared to conclude that Medicare's policy is arbitrary and capricious, we cannot conclude that Oxford's decision to apply the Bilateral Surgery Policy to determine the "reasonable" charge for Mrs. Krauss's surgery was an arbitrary or capricious application of the Plan.

There is also an insufficient basis for questioning Oxford's determination of what specific reimbursement rate applied to the Krausses' claim under the Bilateral Surgery Policy. Although the underlying HIAA-derived reimbursement rate of $20,000 for a single breast reconstruction was based on only ten comparable procedures, the Krausses do not challenge the ten-procedure sample or that Oxford derived the $20,000 amount from a standard industry source. *See, e.g.,* N.J. Admin. Code § 11:21–7.13(a) (defining "reasonable and customary" charges for small business health plans as "a standard based on the Prevailing Healthcare Charges System profile for New Jersey or other state when services or supplies are provided in such state, incorporated herein by reference published and available from . . . Ingenix, Inc. . . . .").

2. Private–Duty Nursing. Oxford's decision not to reimburse the Krausses for the costs of private-duty nursing care following the reconstruction surgery also did not violate the Plan. Reviewing *de novo* the Krausses' claim under the contract for compensation, we agree with the district court that the Plan's explicit and unambiguous exclusion of "[p]ri-vate or special duty nursing" from coverage.

We do not mean to imply that Mrs. Krauss should not have opted for the type of post-operative care that she and her doctor thought would be the most effective. But the Krausses' health care plan was amply clear that the nursing care she chose was not covered.

III.   Claims for Breach of Fiduciary Duty

The Krausses also bring a claim for breach of fiduciary duty pursuant to ERISA § 502(a)(3). Specifically, the Krausses assert that Oxford breach-ed that duty by failing to disclose certain information, by making false and affirmative misrepresentations regarding the true reason for denying their claims for reimbursement, and by failing to act on the Krausses' claims and appeals in a timely manner. First, the Krausses cannot recover money damages through their claim for breach of fiduciary duty. In order to state a claim under ERISA section 502(a)(3), the type of relief a plaintiff requests must be equitable. Second, in arguing that Oxford mishandled their claim through nondisclosure, misleading statements, and untimely responses, the Krausses are in essence claiming that Oxford denied them the full and fair review to which they were entitled under ERISA § 503(2). Here, however, now that the relevant information has been finally disclosed, we are confident that administrative remand would be futile. Oxford's benefits determination, even if not properly explained at the time of denial and during administrative review, was, as a substantive matter, an appropriate implementation of the Bilateral Surgery Policy under the Plan. We there-fore conclude that the Krausses are not entitled to relief for breach of fiduciary duty.

Note on Payment for "Out-of-Network" Coverage: The UCR Problem and the *Ingenex* Case

1.   *Krauss* sheds light on insurer payment practices for out-of-network care. Health plans with tightly managed provider networks strictly limit non-emergency coverage to providers that are members of their networks (recall that plans must now cover out-of-network emergency care in accor-dance with a "prudent layperson" standard as a result of the Affordable Care Act, PPACA § 1001). These plans tend to cost less both because plan administrators are able to negotiate deeper price discounts in exchange for volume and exclusivity and in part because if there are not enough network providers, health care access and utilization may be slowed (you will see this issue again in *Kentucky Association of Health Plans,* 538 U.S. 329 (2003), below, a leading ERISA preemption case).

More affluent people like the Krausses, however, if given the option to do so through their employers, will buy a product that does not entirely exclude out-of-network coverage for non-emergency care but instead allows them to continue to enjoy a pretty good level of coverage when they use out-of-network providers. These products, as explained in the decision, allow payment at a somewhat lower percentage than is the case for in-network care (e.g., 70 percent versus 90 percent), but this lower percentage is *paid based on* the "usual and customary rate" (UCR) rather than the provider's actual charges. The UCR, as you can see from this case, is a completely fictitious amount calculated by the insurer and based on a formula in which the insurer (or its affiliated company as in this case) aggregates and then averages charges for a geographic region. If Manhattan, say, is included in the same region as, say, Albany, the UCR average will reflect both the higher charges in Manhattan and the lower charges up the Hudson River Valley into Albany. If the insurer further throws out from the calculation all of the high end charges (the outliers), the average drops even further.

None of these arbitrary calculations of course are explained to plan participants, who have no idea that 70 percent of the UCR is not 70 percent of what *their particular physician* might charge them for a service. A plan offering out-of-network coverage can be considerably more costly than one with only in-network benefits. And yet, if the company offering the plan manipulates the UCR enough, it may end up paying no more for out-of-network coverage than in-network care (utilization may go up, however, since access is better). The participant, by contrast, is left not only with the expressly stated higher cost-sharing amount (30 percent versus 10 percent) but with a whopping balance bill for the difference between the UCR rate and the actual charge, since the out-of-network provider of course has not agreed to accept as full payment the deep discounts offered by in-network providers.

The arbitrary setting of the UCR sounds a lot like fraud, indeed, so much so that in 2008 then-New York Attorney General Andrew Cuomo announced an industry-wide investigation of insurer practices—specifically Ingenix—involving the manipulation of out-of-network payment rates and its concealment from plan participants and employers that bought these products. Characterizing the Ingenix system as a "scheme" to commit "fraud" on the public, General Cuomo's office summarized the case as follows:

> At the center of the scheme is Ingenix, Inc., the nation's largest provider of healthcare billing information, which serves as a conduit for rigged data to the largest insurers in the country. 16 subpoenas [have been issued] to the nation's largest health insurance companies including Aetna (NYSE: AET), CIGNA (NYSE: CI), and Empire BlueCross BlueShield (NYSE: WLP), and that [Cuomo] intends to file suit against Ingenix, Inc., its parent UnitedHealth Group (NYSE: UNH), and three additional subsidiaries.

> The six-month investigation found that Ingenix operates a defective and manipulated database that most major health insurance companies use to set reimbursement rates for out-of-network medical expenses. Further, the investigation found that two sub-

sidiaries of United (the "United insurers") dramatically under-reimbursed their members for out-of-network medical expenses by using data provided by Ingenix.

Under the United insurers' health plans, members pay a higher premium for the right to use out-of-network doctors. In exchange, the insurers promise to cover up to 80% of either the doctor's full bill or of the "reasonable and customary" rate depending upon which is cheaper. The Attorney General's investigation found that by distorting the "reasonable and customary" rate, the United insurers were able to keep their reimbursements artificially low and force patients to absorb a higher share of the costs.

Cuomo's investigation also found a clear example of the scheme: United insurers knew most simple doctor visits cost $200, but claimed to their members the typical rate was only $77. The insurers then applied the contractual reimbursement rate of 80%, covering only $62 for a $200 bill, and leaving the patient to cover the $138 balance.

The United insurers and many other health insurance companies relied on the Ingenix database to determine their "reasonable and customary" rates. The Ingenix database used the insurers' billing information to calculate a "reasonable and customary" rate for individual claims by assessing how much a similar type of medical service would typically cost, generally taking into account the type of service, physician, and geographical location. However, the investigation showed that the "reasonable and customary" rates produced by Ingenix were remarkably lower than the actual cost of typical medical expenses.

The United insurers and Ingenix are owned by the same parent corporation, United HealthGroup. When members complained their medical costs were unfairly high, the United insurers hid their connection to Ingenix by claiming the rate was the product of "independent research." The Attorney General's notice to United expressed concern that the company's ownership of Ingenix created a clear conflict of interest because their relationship gave Ingenix an incentive to set rates that benefited United and its subsidiaries.

http://www.oag.state.ny.us/press/2008/feb/feb13a_08.html.

In January 2009 the Attorney General and United entered into an *Assurance of Discontinuance Under Executive Law § 63(15),* http://www.oag.state.ny.us/bureaus/health_care/HIT2/pdfs/United%20Health.pdf. Specifically, the Attorney General found that "UnitedHealth has a conflict of interest in owning and operating the Ingenix Database in connection with determining reimbursement rates." Moreover, the Attorney General concluded that, "other health insurers have a financial incentive to manipulate the data they provide to the Ingenix database so that the pooled data will skew reimbursement rates downwards." The investigation found the rate of underpayment by insurers ranged from 10 percent to 28 percent for various medical services across NY State. *Health Care Report, The Consumer Reimbursement System is Code Blue*, State of New York, Office of Attorney General (January 13, 2009). In the settlement, United Healthcare agreed to close the Ingenix database and to pay a nearly $100 million fine to finance the establishment of an independent nonprofit corporation (now known as FairHealth) whose mission is to develop an impartial system for calculating the UCR information that insurers need in order to pay out-of-network claims. UnitedHealth also separately agreed to pay $350 million to the American Medical Association to resolve a class action lawsuit filed by providers challenging the insurer's reimbursement practices. The agreement between the AMA and UnitedHealth marked the largest class action lawsuit against a single U.S. health insurer in history.

The New York litigation was not an isolated incident. The findings of the Attorney General regarding the Ingenix Databases closely mirror those allegations asserted by class members in a New Jersey subscriber class action suit, McCoy v. Health Net, Inc. 569 F. Supp.2d 448 (2008). (Recall that the New Jersey statute discussed in Kraus specifically references Ingenix). Alleging violations of both ERISA and the Racketeer Influenced Corrupt Organizations Act ("RICO") (reviewed in the chapter on fraud in Part Four), plaintiffs claimed that the insurer was engaged in a conspiracy to manipulate UCR pricing data in order to underpay out-of-network providers and require members to pay more than their fair share of those services when the providers "balance billed" them. In assessing the reasonableness of the deep discounts generated by Ingenix, the court wrote:

> There are two serious flaws in Ingenix's data collection methods: one relates to Ingenix's data sources; the other relates to the number of data points collected for each medical procedure. The database is compiled from data submitted by several insurers pursuant to a purely voluntary data contribution program. Under this program, "some, but not all, of only those health insurers that are Ingenix clients submit information, on a purely voluntary basis, about the amounts they happen to have been billed by an undisclosed number of unidentified health care providers for specific CPT code services." At best, the Ingenix database includes the bills of an unspecified number of medical providers who, within a specific period of time, happened to have billed only those health insurers that were not only Ingenix clients, but also Ingenix clients that elected to participate in [Ingenix's] voluntary data contribution program.
>
> This method of data collection is considered by statisticians to be a "convenience sample." A convenience sample is the easiest way to collect the data, but it is haphazard. Convenience samples are chosen on the basis of expediency, cost, efficiency or other reasons not directly concerned with scientific sampling parameters. As a result, convenience samples are considered the most suspect type of sample. A convenience sample is not necessarily

invalid, but it must be subject to further testing to determine whether the data collected is in fact representative of what an insurer is trying to estimate.

Ingenix does not test the voluntarily submitted data to see if the data constitutes an accurate representative sample of charges for a particular procedure in a particular geographical area. Moreover, the data collection methodology provides no reassurance that the raw data collected is representative of the actual charges billed for any given procedure. This arrangement can encourage insurers to remove high charges before submitting their data, in order to ensure that a lot of it's not going to be knocked out during the data scrubbing process. Because other insurance companies who themselves use the database are permitted to choose what data to submit, there is a built in incentive to submit low cost data that will produce a lower UCR database that the submitting insurance company will itself use to calculate a lower UCR for its own reimbursements to its insureds.

Second, the database relies upon too few data points for each procedure. The database relies upon just four pieces of data for each submitted charge: date of service; 5–digit Current Procedural Terminology code ("CPT code"); the address where the procedure was performed; and the amount of the provider's billed charge. Ingenix relies upon these four data points to facilitate comparison among similar procedures and geographical zones. In other words, these data points represent the sum total of the information that purportedly allows an insurer to compare similarly situated procedures.

These four data points exclude several factors that are critical to the "core concepts" of UCR. These four data points do not identify: (1) the provider's licensure or qualifications; (2) the patient's age or health status; (3) the type of facility where the procedure was performed. The database does not take into account whether a particular procedure was performed by a highly-skilled Board Certified specialist or a general practitioner or a paraprofessional or a nurse. It is a matter of common sense that these factors may be fundamental to a comparison of charges. A procedure performed by a highly skilled physician is likely to be more expensive than one performed by a physician's assistant or nurse practitioner, but the physician's higher charge may nevertheless be the most valid comparator if an insured was treated by a physician of comparable skill and experience. Yet, by including every possible type of provider in the CPT Code Service, even a totally average bill from a skilled physician will be higher than the UCR yielded by the database.

These excluded data points may be the most important factors in determining "reasonable" and "customary" costs. One might expect that it would cost significantly more to have a highly skilled, Board Certified heart specialist interpret an echocardio-gram than it would to have a general practitioner do the same task. The database improperly assumes that these factors are all irrelevant for determining the usual and customary rate charged for particular procedures. Any accurate database would control for these additional factors. Ingenix's failure to control for these factors means that the database is not actually comparing similar-ly situated procedures when it purportedly yields a "usual" and "customary" rate for that procedure.

McCoy, 569 F. Supp.2d at 464–66.

---

7. ERISA AND PREEMPTION OF STATE LAW

The preceding materials have laid out ERISA's basic contours with respect to the design and administration of health and welfare benefit plans. A statute of unusually strong preemptive powers, ERISA has pro-foundly displaced much state law. ERISA's preemption clause, 29 U.S.C. § 1144 (commonly referred to as ERISA § 514 in the cases) displaces state laws that *relate to* an employee health or welfare benefit plan. However, section 514 also contains a "saving clause" which provides that state laws that *regulate insurance* are saved from preemption even if they "relate to" ERISA plans. Because the potential preemptive effects of section 514 are so vast, the United States Supreme Court has developed a complex approach to these two elements of section 514 preemption.

ERISA can preempt state laws by a route different from the preemp-tion provisions of § 514. Above we have read cases in which plaintiffs have brought suits to obtain benefits and other forms of relief under ERISA's § 502, 29 U.S.C. § 1132, which provides a private right of action for allowable claims arising under ERISA. As you will see, courts have held that § 502 remedies are exclusive for claims that arise under ERISA, thereby focusing a laser beam on what, exactly, is a "claim arising under ERISA" and whose remedies thereby are exclusive to ERISA, displacing all state law remedies. Part Three addresses at length the distinction between claims that arise under ERISA in a health care context and those that do not.

The Affordable Care Act does not change these ERISA preemption principles, at least not intentionally. Indeed, the preemption clause con-tained in the Public Health Service Act provisions setting minimum federal standards for the non-ERISA group and individual insurance markets states explicitly that "[n]othing in this part shall be construed to affect or modify the provisions of section 514 of the Employee Retirement Income Security Act of 1974 with respect to group health plans." PHSA § 2724, 42 U.S.C. § 300gg–23. An important question that will arise following imple-mentation of state health insurance Exchanges is whether employers which elect to purchase coverage by making a direct payment to an Exchange on behalf of individual employees rather than by purchasing group health coverage nonetheless will be considered to have established an employee health benefit plan within the meaning of 29 U.S.C. § 1001. The Department of Labor has not yet answered this question; its resolution will determine whether insurers that sell products in the Exchange's small employer group market (known as the SHOP Exchange) will continue to enjoy the benefits of the preemption "shield" whose contours can be seen in the cases that follow.

a.   The Meaning of "Relate to"

Shaw v. Delta Air Lines, Inc., 463 U.S. 85 (1983), focused on two New York statutes, one of which was the state's Human Rights Law, a law of general applicability which forbade discrimination on the basis of pregnancy. Several airline carriers offering ERISA welfare plans sued for declaratory relief that their welfare plans were not obligated to comply with this law. The United States Supreme Court previously had ruled that the practice of limiting or excluding benefits and services on the basis of pregnancy did not amount to unconstitutional discrimination, nor did it violate civil rights statutes. (Title VII of the 1964 Civil Rights Act would later be amended by the Pregnancy Discrimination Act to bar discriminatory employment practices). (See Part One, Chap. 4).

Taking a highly textualist, "plain language" approach to the question of preemption, Justice Blackmun, writing for a unanimous Court, held that the law was preempted because it "related to" the airlines' welfare benefit plans:

> We have no difficulty in concluding that the Human Rights Law and Disability Benefits Law "relate to" employee benefit plans. The breadth of § 514(a)'s preemptive reach is apparent from that section's language. A law "relates to" an employee benefit plan, in the normal sense of the phrase, if it has a connection with or reference to such a plan.[16] Employing this definition, the Human Rights Law, which prohibits employers from structuring their employee benefit plans in a manner that discriminates on the basis of pregnancy [is preempted]. We must give effect to this plain language unless there is good reason to believe Congress intended the language to have some more restrictive meaning. In fact, however, Congress used the words "relate to" in § 514(a) in their broad sense. To interpret § 514(a) to preempt only state laws specifically designed to affect employee benefit plans would be to ignore the remainder of § 514.
>
> Nor, given the legislative history, can § 514(a) be interpreted to preempt only state laws dealing with the subject matters covered by ERISA—reporting, disclosure, fiduciary responsibility, and the like. The bill that became ERISA originally contained a limited

---

16. *See* Black's Law Dictionary 1158 (5th ed.1979) ("Relate. To stand in some relation; to have bearing or concern; to pertain; refer; to bring into association with or connection with").

preemption clause, applicable only to state laws relating to the specific subjects covered by ERISA.[18] The Conference Committee rejected these provisions in favor of the present language, and indicated that the section's preemptive scope was as broad as its language. *See* H.R.Conf.Rep. No. 93–1280, p. 383 (1974); S.Conf. Rep. No. 93–1090, at 383 (1974). Statements by the bill's sponsors during the subsequent debates stressed the breadth of federal preemption. Representative Dent, for example, stated:

"Finally, I wish to make note of what is, to many, the crowning achievement of this legislation, the reservation to Federal authority the sole power to regulate the field of employee benefit plans. With the preemption of the field, we round out the protection afforded participants by eliminating the threat of conflicting and inconsistent State and local regulation." 120 Cong.Rec. 29197 (1974).

Senator Williams echoed these sentiments:

"It should be stressed that, with the narrow exceptions specified in the bill, the substantive and enforcement provisions of the conference substitute are intended to preempt the field for Federal regulations, thus eliminating the threat of conflicting or inconsistent State and local regulation of employee benefit plans. This principle is intended to apply in its broadest sense to all actions of State or local governments, or any instrumentality thereof, which have the force or effect of law."

Given the plain language of § 514(a), the structure of the Act, and its legislative history, we hold that the Human Rights Law and the Disability Benefits Law "relate to any employee benefit plan" within the meaning of ERISA's § 514(a).[21]

463 U.S. at 95–102.

This textualist interpretation of the statute lasted for more than a decade, engendering much controversy because of its fundamental clash with federalism principles. In 1995 this highly textualist approach began to give way to a more contextual and nuanced approach to ERISA preemption.

---

18. The bill that passed the House, H.R. 2, 93d Cong., 2d Sess., § 514(a) (1974), provided that ERISA would supersede state laws "relat[ing] to the reporting and disclosure responsibilities, and fiduciary responsibilities, of persons acting on behalf of any employee benefit plan to which Part One applies." The bill that passed the Senate, H.R. 2, 93d Cong, 2d Sess., § 699(a) (1974), provided for preemption of state laws "relat[ing] to the subject matters regulated by this Act or the Welfare and Pension Plans Disclosure Act."

21. Some state actions may affect employee benefit plans in too tenuous, remote, or peripheral a manner to warrant a finding that the law "relates to" the plan. *Cf.* American Telephone and Telegraph Co. v. Merry, 592 F.2d 118, 121 (CA2 1979) (state garnishment of a spouse's pension income to enforce alimony and support orders is not preempted). The present litigation plainly does not present a borderline question, and we express no views about where it would be appropriate to draw the line.

New York State Conference of Blue Cross & Blue Shield Plans v. Travelers Insurance Company

514 U.S. 645 (1995)

■ JUSTICE SOUTER delivered the opinion of the Court.

A New York statute requires hospitals to collect surcharges from patients covered by a commercial insurer but not from patients insured by a Blue Cross/Blue Shield plan, and it subjects certain health maintenance organizations (HMOs) to surcharges that vary with the number of Medicaid recipients each enrolls. This case calls for us to decide whether [ERISA] pre-empts the state provisions for surcharges on bills of patients whose commercial insurance coverage is purchased by employee health-care plans governed by ERISA and for surcharges on HMOs insofar as their membership fees are paid by an ERISA plan. We hold that the provisions for surcharges do not "relate to" employee benefit plans within the meaning of ERISA's pre-emption provision, § 514(a), 29 U.S.C. § 1144(a), and accordingly suffer no pre-emption.

New York's Prospective Hospital Reimbursement Methodology (NYPHRM) regulates hospital rates for all in-patient care, except for services provided to Medicare beneficiaries. The scheme calls for patients to be charged not for the cost of their individual treatment, but for the average cost of treating the patient's medical problem, as classified under one or another of 794 Diagnostic Related Groups (DRGs). The charges allowable in accordance with DRG classifications are adjusted for a specific hospital to reflect its particular operating costs, capital investments, bad debts, costs of charity care and the like.

Patients with Blue Cross/Blue Shield coverage, Medicaid patients, and HMO participants are billed at a hospital's DRG rate. Others, however, are not. Patients served by commercial insurers providing in-patient hospital coverage on an expense-incurred basis, by self-insured funds directly reimbursing hospitals, and by [certain other] funds, must be billed at the DRG rate plus a 13% surcharge to be retained by the hospital. For the year ending March 31, 1993, moreover, hospitals were required to bill commercially insured patients for a further 11% surcharge to be turned over to the State, with the result that these patients were charged 24% more than the DRG rate.

New York law also imposes a surcharge on HMOs, which varies depending on the number of eligible Medicaid recipients an HMO has enrolled, but which may run as high as 9% of the aggregate monthly charges paid by an HMO for its members' in-patient hospital care. This assessment is not an increase in the rates to be paid by an HMO to hospitals, but a direct payment by the HMO to the State's general fund.

ERISA's comprehensive regulation of employee welfare and pension benefit plans extends to those that provide "medical, surgical, or hospital care or benefits" for plan participants or their beneficiaries "through the purchase of insurance or otherwise." § 3(1), 29 U.S.C. § 1002(1). The federal statute does not go about protecting plan participants and their beneficiaries by requiring employers to provide any given set of minimum benefits, but instead controls the administration of benefit plans, see § 2, 29 U.S.C. § 1001(b), as by imposing reporting and disclosure mandates, § 101–111, 29 U.S.C. §§ 1021–1031, participation and vesting requirements, §§ 201–211, 29 U.S.C. §§ 1051–1061, funding standards, §§ 301–308, 29 U.S.C. §§ 1081–1086, and fiduciary responsibilities for plan administrators, §§ 401–414, 29 U.S.C. §§ 1101–1114. It envisions administrative oversight, imposes criminal sanctions, and establishes a comprehensive civil enforcement scheme. §§ 501–515, 29 U.S.C. §§ 1131–1145. It also pre-empts some state law. § 514, 29 U.S.C. § 1144.

On the claimed authority of ERISA's general pre-emption provision, several commercial insurers, acting as fiduciaries of ERISA plans they administer, joined with their trade associations to bring actions against state officials seeking to invalidate the 13%, 11%, and 9% surcharge statutes. The New York State Conference of Blue Cross and Blue Shield plans, Empire Blue Cross and Blue Shield (collectively the Blues), and the Hospital Association of New York State intervened as defendants, and the New York State Health Maintenance Organization Conference and several HMOs intervened as plaintiffs. The [district] court found that although the surcharges "do not directly increase a plan's costs or affect the level of benefits to be offered," there could be "little doubt that the surcharges at issue will have a significant effect on the commercial insurers and HMOs which do or could provide coverage for ERISA plans and thus lead, at least indirectly, to an increase in plan costs." It found that the "entire justification for the surcharges is premised on that exact result—that the surcharges will increase the cost of obtaining medical insurance through any source other than the Blues to a sufficient extent that customers will switch their coverage to and ensure the economic viability of the Blues." The District Court concluded that this effect on choices by ERISA plans was enough to trigger pre-emption under § 514(a) and that the surcharges were not saved by § 514(b) as regulating insurance. The District Court accordingly enjoined enforcement of "those surcharges against any commercial insurers or HMOs in connection with their coverage of ERISA plans."[4]

The Court of Appeals for the Second Circuit affirmed, relying on our decisions in Shaw v. Delta Air Lines, Inc., 463 U.S. 85 (1983) and District of Columbia v. Greater Washington Bd. of Trade, 506 U.S. 125 (1992), holding that ERISA's pre-emption clause must be read broadly to reach any state law having a connection with, or reference to, covered employee benefit plans. [T]he Court of Appeals relied on our statement in *Ingersoll–Rand Co.*, 498 U.S. [at 139] (1990) that under the applicable " 'broad common-sense meaning,' a state law may 'relate to' a benefit plan, and

---

4. [W]e [do not] address the surcharge statute insofar as it applies to self-insured funds. The trial court's ERISA analysis originally led it to enjoin defendants "from enforcing those surcharges against any commercial insurers or HMOs in connection with their coverage of ERISA plans," without any further mention of self-insured funds. The Court of Appeals, in turn, did not expressly address this application of the surcharge and, accordingly, we leave it for consideration on remand.

thereby be pre-empted, even if the law is not specifically designed to affect such plans, or the effect is only indirect."

The Court of Appeals agreed with the trial court that the surcharges were meant to increase the costs of certain insurance and health care by HMO's, and held that this "purposeful interference with the choices that ERISA plans make for health care coverage is sufficient to constitute [a] 'connection with' ERISA plans" triggering pre-emption. The court's conclusion, in sum, was that "the three surcharges 'relate to' ERISA because they impose a significant economic burden on commercial insurers and HMOs" and therefore "have an impermissible impact on ERISA plan structure and administration." In the light of its conclusion that the surcharge statutes were not otherwise saved by any applicable exception, the court held them pre-empted.

Our past cases have recognized that the Supremacy Clause, U.S. Const., Art. VI, may entail pre-emption of state law either by express provision, by implication, or by a conflict between federal and state law. And yet, despite the variety of these opportunities for federal preeminence, we have never assumed lightly that Congress has derogated state regulation, but instead have addressed claims of pre-emption with the starting presumption that Congress does not intend to supplant state law. Indeed, in cases like this one, where federal law is said to bar state action in fields of traditional state regulation, we have worked on the "assumption that the historic police powers of the States were not to be superseded by the Federal Act unless that was the clear and manifest purpose of Congress."

Since pre-emption claims turn on Congress's intent, we begin as we do in any exercise of statutory construction with the text of the provision in question, and move on, as need be, to the structure and purpose of the Act in which it occurs. The governing text of ERISA is clearly expansive. Section 514(a) marks for pre-emption "all state laws insofar as they relate to any employee benefit plan" covered by ERISA, and one might be excused for wondering, at first blush, whether the words of limitation ("insofar as they relate") do much limiting. If "relate to" were taken to extend to the furthest stretch of its indeterminacy, then for all practical purposes pre-emption would never run its course, for "really, universally, relations stop nowhere," H. JAMES, RODERICK HUDSON xli (New York ed., World's Classics 1980). But that, of course, would be to read Congress's words of limitation as mere sham, and to read the presumption against pre-emption out of the law whenever Congress speaks to the matter with generality. That said, we have to recognize that our prior attempt to construe the phrase "relate to" does not give us much help drawing the line here.

In *Shaw*, we explained that "[a] law 'relates to' an employee benefit plan, in the normal sense of the phrase, if it has a connection with or reference to such a plan." The latter alternative, at least, can be ruled out. The surcharges are imposed upon patients and HMOs, regardless of whether the commercial coverage or membership, respectively, is ultimately secured by an ERISA plan, private purchase, or otherwise, with the consequence that the surcharge statutes cannot be said to make "reference to" ERISA plans in any manner. Cf. *[District of Columbia v.] Greater Wash. Bd. of Trade, 506 U.S. [1992]* (slip op., at 4) (striking down District of Columbia law that "specifically refers to welfare benefit plans regulated by ERISA and on that basis alone is pre-empted"). But this still leaves us to question whether the surcharge laws have a "connection with" the ERISA plans, and here an uncritical literalism is no more help than in trying to construe "relate to." For the same reasons that infinite relations cannot be the measure of pre-emption, neither can infinite connections. We simply must go beyond the unhelpful text and the frustrating difficulty of defining its key term, and look instead to the objectives of the ERISA statute as a guide to the scope of the state law that Congress understood would survive.

As we have said before, § 514 indicates Congress's intent to establish the regulation of employee welfare benefit plans "as exclusively a federal concern." We have found that in passing § 514(a), Congress intended

> to ensure that plans and plan sponsors would be subject to a uniform body of benefits law; the goal was to minimize the administrative and financial burden of complying with conflicting directives among States or between States and the Federal Government, [and to prevent] the potential for conflict in substantive law requiring the tailoring of plans and employer conduct to the peculiarities of the law of each jurisdiction.

Ingersoll–Rand, 498 U.S. at 142. The basic thrust of the pre-emption clause was to avoid a multiplicity of regulation in order to permit the nationally uniform administration of employee benefit plans.

Accordingly in *Shaw*, for example, we had no trouble finding that New York's "Human Rights Law, which prohibited employers from structuring their employee benefit plans in a manner that discriminated on the basis of pregnancy, and [New York's] Disability Benefits Law, which required employers to pay employees specific benefits, clearly 'related to' benefit plans." These mandates affecting coverage could have been honored only by varying the subjects of a plan's benefits whenever New York law might have applied, or by requiring every plan to provide all beneficiaries with a benefit demanded by New York law if New York law could have been said to require it for any one beneficiary.

Similarly, Pennsylvania's law that prohibited "plans from requiring reimbursement [from the beneficiary] in the event of recovery from a third party" related to employee benefit plans within the meaning of § 514(a). FMC Corp. v. Holliday, 498 U.S. 52, 60 (1990). The law required plan providers to calculate benefit levels in Pennsylvania based on expected liability conditions that differ from those in States that have not enacted similar antisubrogation legislation, thereby frustrating plan administrators' continuing obligation to calculate uniform benefit levels nationwide. Elsewhere, we have held that state laws providing alternate enforcement mechanisms also relate to ERISA plans, triggering pre-emption. See *Ingersoll–Rand*, 498 U.S. 133, above.

Both the purpose and the effects of the New York surcharge statutes distinguish them from the examples just given. The charge differentials have been justified on the ground that the Blues pay the hospitals promptly and efficiently and, more importantly, provide coverage for many subscribers whom the commercial insurers would reject as unacceptable risks. The Blues' practice, called open enrollment, has consistently been cited as the principal reason for charge differentials. See, e.g., Kenneth Thorpe, *Does All–Payer Rate Setting Work? The Case of the New York Prospective Hospital Reimbursement Methodology*, 12 J. HEALTH POLITICS, POLICY, & LAW 391, 402 (1987). Since the surcharges are presumably passed on at least in part to those who purchase commercial insurance or HMO membership, their effects follow from their purpose. Although there is no evidence that the surcharges will drive every health insurance consumer to the Blues, they do make the Blues more attractive (or less unattractive) as insurance alternatives and thus have an indirect economic effect on choices made by insurance buyers, including ERISA plans.

An indirect economic influence, however, does not bind plan administrators to any particular choice and thus function as a regulation of an ERISA plan itself; commercial insurers and HMOs may still offer more attractive packages than the Blues. Nor does the indirect influence of the surcharges preclude uniform administrative practice or the provision of a uniform interstate benefit package if a plan wishes to provide one. It simply bears on the costs of benefits and the relative costs of competing insurance to provide them. It is an influence that can affect a plan's shopping decisions, but it does not affect the fact that any plan will shop for the best deal it can get, surcharges or no surcharges.

There is, indeed, nothing remarkable about surcharges on hospital bills, or their effects on overall cost to the plans and the relative attractiveness of certain insurers. Rate variations among hospital providers are accepted examples of cost variation, since hospitals have traditionally attempted to compensate for their financial shortfalls by adjusting their price schedules for patients with commercial health insurance. Charge differentials for commercial insurers, even prior to state regulation, "varied dramatically across regions, ranging from 13 to 36 percent," presumably reflecting the geographically disparate burdens of providing for the uninsured. [See, e.g.,] Mary Anne Bobinski, *Unhealthy Federalism: Barriers to Increasing Health Care Access for the Uninsured*, 24 U.C. DAVIS L. REV. 255, 267, and n. 44 (1990).

If the common character of rate differentials even in the absence of state action renders it unlikely that ERISA pre-emption was meant to bar such indirect economic influences under state law, the existence of other common state action with indirect economic effects on a plan's costs leaves the intent to pre-empt even less likely. Quality standards, for example, set by the State in one subject area of hospital services but not another would affect the relative cost of providing those services over others and, so, of providing different packages of health insurance benefits. Even basic regulation of employment conditions will invariably affect the cost and price of services.

Indeed, to read the pre-emption provision as displacing all state laws affecting costs and charges on the theory that they indirectly relate to ERISA plans that purchase insurance policies or HMO memberships that would cover such services, would effectively read the limiting language in § 514(a) out of the statute, a conclusion that would violate basic principles of statutory interpretation and could not be squared with our prior pronouncement that preemption does not occur if the state law has only a tenuous, remote, or peripheral connection with covered plans, as is the case with many laws of general applicability. While Congress's extension of pre-emption to all state laws relating to benefit plans was meant to sweep more broadly than state laws dealing with the subject matters covered by ERISA [such as] reporting, disclosure, fiduciary responsibility, and the like, nothing in the language of the Act or the context of its passage indicates that Congress chose to displace general health care regulation, which historically has been a matter of local concern.

In sum, cost-uniformity was almost certainly not an object of pre-emption, just as laws with only an indirect economic effect on the relative costs of various health insurance packages in a given State are a far cry from those "conflicting directives" from which Congress meant to insulate ERISA plans. Such state laws leave plan administrators right where they would be in any case, with the responsibility to choose the best overall coverage for the money. We therefore conclude that such state laws do not bear the requisite "connection with" ERISA plans to trigger pre-emption.

This conclusion is confirmed by our decision in Mackey v. Lanier Collection Agency & Service, Inc., 486 U.S. 825 (1988), which held that ERISA pre-emption falls short of barring application of a general state garnishment statute to participants' benefits in the hands of an ERISA welfare benefit plan. We took no issue with the argument of the Mackey plan's trustees that garnishment would impose administrative costs and burdens upon benefit plans, but concluded from the text and structure of ERISA's pre-emption and enforcement provisions that Congress did not intend to forbid the use of state-law mechanisms of executing judgments against ERISA welfare benefit plans, even when those mechanisms prevent plan participants from receiving their benefits. If a law authorizing an indirect source of administrative cost is not pre-empted, it should follow that a law operating as an indirect source of merely economic influence on administrative decisions, as here, should not suffice to trigger pre-emption either.

The commercial challengers counter by invoking the earlier case of *Metropolitan Life Insurance Co. v. Massachusetts*, 471 U.S. 724, which considered whether a State could mandate coverage of specified minimum mental-health-care benefits by policies insuring against hospital and surgical expenses. Because the regulated policies included those bought by employee welfare benefit plans, we recognized that the law directly affected such plans. Although we went on to hold that the law was ultimately saved from pre-emption by the insurance savings clause, respondents proffer the first steps in our decision as support for their argument that all laws affecting ERISA plans through their impact on insurance policies "relate to" such plans and are pre-empted unless expressly saved by the statute. The challengers take *Metropolitan Life* too far, however.

The Massachusetts statute applied not only to any blanket or general policy of insurance or any policy of accident and sickness insurance but also to any employees' health and welfare fund which provided hospital expense and surgical expense benefits. In fact, the State did not even try to defend its law as unrelated to employee benefit plans for the purpose of § 514(a). As a result, there was no reason to distinguish with any precision between the effects on insurers that are sufficiently connected with employee benefit plans to "relate to" the plans and those effects that are not. Even this basic distinction recognizes that not all regulations that would influence the cost of insurance would relate to employee benefit plans within the meaning of § 514(a). If, for example, a State were to regulate sales of insurance by commercial insurers more stringently than sales by insurers not for profit, the relative cost of commercial insurance would rise; we would nonetheless say, following *Metropolitan Life*, that such laws "do not 'relate to' benefit plans in the first instance." And on the same authority we would say the same about the basic tax exemption enjoyed by nonprofit insurers like the Blues since the days long before ERISA, and yet on respondents' theory the exemption would necessarily be pre-empted as affecting insurance prices and plan costs.

The New York surcharges do not impose the kind of substantive coverage requirement binding plan administrators that was at issue in *Metropolitan Life*. Although even in the absence of mandated coverage there might be a point at which an exorbitant tax leaving consumers with a Hobson's choice would be treated as imposing a substantive mandate, no showing has been made here that the surcharges are so prohibitive as to force all health insurance consumers to contract with the Blues. As they currently stand, the surcharges do not require plans to deal with only one insurer, or to insure against an entire category of illnesses they might otherwise choose to leave without coverage.

It remains only to speak further on a point already raised, that any conclusion other than the one we draw would bar any state regulation of hospital costs. The basic DRG system (even without any surcharge), like any other interference with the hospital services market, would fall on a theory that all laws with indirect economic effects on ERISA plans are pre-empted under § 514(a). This would be an unsettling result and all the more startling because several States, including New York, regulated hospital charges to one degree or another at the time ERISA was passed.

That said, we do not hold today that ERISA pre-empts only direct regulation of ERISA plans, nor could we do that with fidelity to the views expressed in our prior opinions on the matter. See, e.g., *Ingersoll–Rand*, 498 U.S. at 139; Pilot Life Ins. Co. v. Dedeaux, 481 U.S. 41, 47–48 (1987); *Shaw*, 463 U.S. 85 at 98. We acknowledge that a state law might produce such acute, albeit indirect, economic effects, by intent or otherwise, as to force an ERISA plan to adopt a certain scheme of substantive coverage or effectively restrict its choice of insurers, and that such a state law might indeed be pre-empted under § 514. But as we have shown, New York's surcharges do not fall into either category; they affect only indirectly the relative prices of insurance policies, a result no different from myriad state laws in areas traditionally subject to local regulation, which Congress could not possibly have intended to eliminate.

The judgment of the Court of Appeals is therefore reversed, and the cases are remanded for further proceedings consistent with this opinion.

Notes

1. *The public purpose of New York's law.* The New York legislation served an important public purpose, aiding the state in attempting to control costs through rate setting while simultaneously raising the funds needed to assure financing for its state Medicaid program, health professions education (a big industry in New York), and support for hospitals serving a disproportionate share of indigent patients. Professor Sylvia Law notes that more than 90 percent of the hospital surcharges collected under this law involved payments by ERISA health benefit plans.

2. Travelers' *impact on ERISA preemption doctrine.* The *Travelers* case represents an important change in the Supreme Court's method of interpreting ERISA's § 514(a), stressing context, structure and purpose, and opening the door for a balancing of federalism principles against indirect economic effects that burden plan administration and national uniformity. The *Travelers* opinion does not provide clear rules or guidelines on how to interpret § 514(a); rather, it establishes a framework of analysis, informed by certain principles and presumptions which it illustrates through examples; it effectively sets up an inquiry akin to conflict preemption. It left further development of the principles and presumptions for later cases. For additional discussion of the shift from textual to purposive styles of statutory interpretation in the context of preemption doctrine generally and ERISA preemption in particular, *see* Karen Jordan, *The Shifting Preemption Paradigm: Conceptual and Interpretive Issues*, 51 VAND. L. REV. 1149 (1998); *see also* Catherine L. Fisk, *The Last Article About the Language of ERISA Preemption? A Case Study of the Failure of Textualism*, 33 HARV. J. ON LEGIS. 35 (1996).

In California Division of Labor Standards Enforcement v. Dillingham Construction, N.A., Inc., 519 U.S. 316 (1997), the Court more sharply framed its emerging conflict-preemption, analytic approach. The question presented was whether California's labor laws regulating apprenticeship wages were preempted. (ERISA defines employee welfare benefit plans to include both plans that provide health benefits as well as those offering apprenticeship and training programs). In concluding that the state laws were not preempted, a unanimous Court held that California's laws did not "relate to" apprenticeship programs within the meaning of the statute.

Writing for the majority, Justice Thomas characterized the Court's prior ERISA preemption jurisprudence as follows:

> Our efforts at applying the provision have yielded a two-part inquiry: A "law 'relates to' a covered employee benefit plan for purposes of § 514(a) if it [1] has a connection with or [2] reference to such a plan.'" Under the latter inquiry, we have held pre-empted a law that imposed requirements by reference to [ERISA] covered programs; a law that specifically exempted ERISA plans from an otherwise generally applicable garnishment provision; and a common-law cause of action premised on the existence of an ERISA plan. Where a State's law acts immediately and exclusively upon ERISA plans, or where the existence of ERISA plans is essential to the law's operation, that "reference" will result in pre-emption.
>
> A law that does not refer to ERISA plans may yet be pre-empted if it has a "connection with" ERISA plans. [T]o determine whether a state law has the forbidden connection, we look both to the objectives of the ERISA statute as a guide to the scope of the state law that Congress understood would survive, as well as to the nature of the effect of the state law on ERISA plans.

Dillingham Construction, 519 U.S. at 336–37. The Court also invoked the "assumption," articulated in *Travelers,* that the "historic police powers of the States" are not to be preempted "unless that was the clear and manifest purpose of Congress." *Id.* at 338.

3. *The impact of* Travelers *on self-insured plans and the power of the "relate to" test in displacing preemption.* Although in footnote 4 the *Travelers* opinion remanded to the Second Circuit the question of whether New York could impose the surcharges on services delivered to members of self-insured plans, the logic of the opinion permitted only one answer: if the surcharges do not "relate to" ERISA plans that purchase health insurance, they equally do not "relate to" ERISA plans that do not purchase health insurance, and the Second Circuit so held on remand in Travelers Insurance Co. v. Pataki, 63 F.3d 89, 93–94 (2d Cir. 1995).

In a subsequent decision, the Supreme Court extended *Traveler's* framework to a tax that operated directly on the plan itself, thereby putting to rest any distinction between direct and indirect effects. In De Buono v. NYSA–ILA Medical and Clinical Services Fund, 520 U.S. 806 (1997), the plan not only provided coverage but actually operated two clinics offering care to active and retired longshoremen and their families and dependents; the clinics were subject to New York's Health Facility Assessment (HFA), a 0.6 percent gross receipts tax. The Court of Appeals for the Second Circuit, ruling before the *Travelers* decision, held that the HFA relates to ERISA plans, deciding that it "operates as an immediate tax on payments and contributions which were intended to pay for participants' medical benefits," and that it directly affects "the very operations and functions that make the Fund what it is, a provider of medical, surgical, and hospital care to its participants and their beneficiaries." The tax, concluded the court, thus "related to" the Fund because it reduced the amount of Fund assets that would otherwise be available to provide plan members with benefits, and could cause the plan to limit its benefits, or to charge plan members higher fees.

Reversing the lower court ruling, Justice Stevens stated:

[T]he historic police powers of the State include the regulation of matters of health and safety. While the HFA is a revenue raising measure, rather than a regulation of hospitals, it clearly operates in a field that " 'has been traditionally occupied by the States.' " Respondents therefore bear the considerable burden of overcoming "the starting presumption that Congress does not intend to supplant state law." [T]he HFA is one of "myriad state laws" of general applicability that impose some burdens on the administration of ERISA plans but nevertheless do not "relate to" them within the meaning of the governing statute. The HFA is a tax on hospitals. Most hospitals are not owned or operated by ERISA funds. This particular ERISA fund has arranged to provide medical benefits for its plan beneficiaries by running hospitals directly, rather than by purchasing the same services at independently run hospitals. If the Fund had made the other choice, and had purchased health care services from a hospital, that facility would have passed the expense of the HFA onto the Fund and its plan beneficiaries through the rates it set for the services provided. The Fund would then have had to decide whether to cover a more limited range of services for its beneficiaries, or perhaps to charge plan members higher rates. Although the tax in such a circumstance would be "indirect," its impact on the Fund's decisions would be in all relevant respects identical to the "direct" impact felt here. Thus, the supposed difference between direct and indirect impact—upon which the Court of Appeals relied in distinguishing this case from *Travelers*—cannot withstand scrutiny. Any state tax, or other law, that increases the cost of providing benefits to covered employees will have some effect on the administration of ERISA plans, but that simply cannot mean that every state law with such an effect is pre-empted by the federal statute.

520 U.S. at 816. Thus, a decision that a state law does not "relate to" ERISA plans is a far more powerful displacement of ERISA preemption than a decision that a state law is saved from preemption by the insurance saving clause. The latter decision permits a state law to apply only to insurance policies purchased by ERISA plans, and leaves self-insured ERISA plans free from the state law in question. By contrast, a holding that the statute simply fails to "relate to" ERISA plans altogether allows a state law to apply to all types of ERISA plans and their insurers or third-party administrators.

Note: ERISA Preemption and State Health Reform Efforts

In the run-up to passage of the Affordable Care Act, and indeed, for decades preceding, some states have wrestled with health reform. Inevitably, state efforts touched up against employer coverage, because employer coverage is so intrinsic to Americans' thinking about health care or because of the cost of attempting to entirely replace the model using public financing. This means, of course, that states seeking to regulate health insurance must consider ERISA preemption issues.

The first state to feel ERISA's preemptive force was Hawaii. In 1974, prior to ERISA's enactment, Hawaii lawmakers adopted its Prepaid Health Care Act requiring employers to provide full-time employees health insurance comparable to that negotiated by unionized employees for full-time workers. Sylvia A. Law, *Health Care in Hawaii: An Agenda for Research and Reform*, 26 AM J.L. & MED. 205 (2000). When Congress enacted ERISA, Standard Oil challenged the state's power to mandate insurance coverage. In 1980, the United States Court of Appeals for the Ninth Circuit held that the Hawaii statute "directly and expressly regulate[d] employers and the type of benefits they provide employees" and that it therefore "related to" ERISA plans under § 514 and was preempted by ERISA. The United States Supreme Court affirmed, Standard Oil Co. v. Agsalud, 633 F.2d 760 (9th Cir. 1980), *aff'd*, 454 U.S. 801 (1981). From 1974 to 1980, while the case was litigated in the federal courts, the Prepaid Health Care Act was broadly accepted by Hawaii employers and workers.

When the law was overturned in 1981, very few employers dropped coverage. In addition, as a small state with representatives with long tenure, Hawaii was able to persuade Congress to give it an exemption from ERISA, 29 U.S.C. § 1144(b)(5)(A). Organized labor strongly opposed the exemption. The Act specifically provides that the protection for the Hawaii program "shall not be considered a precedent with respect to extending such an amendment to any other state law," and limits the exemption to the Hawaii statute as it existed in 1974.

In 2007 the United States Court of Appeals for the Fourth Circuit struck down Maryland's Fair Share Health Care Fund Act (known popularly as the "Wal–Mart Law"), which required large employers (with 10,000 or more Maryland employees) to spend 8% of their total payrolls on health insurance or pay the difference to the state. The law was widely reported at the time as affecting only Wal–Mart, which was in a major, public, national dispute with unions over labor conditions. In Retail Industry Leaders Association v. Fielder, 475 F.3d 180 (4th Cir. 2007), the Court of Appeals for the Fourth Circuit held that the Maryland law was preempted, on the basis that the law was simply an attempt to force the store to provide health benefits at a level considered acceptable by the state and thus a direct demand that it change its employee health benefit plan:

> [T]he Secretary [of Maryland's Department of Health and Mental Hygiene] describes the Act as "part of the State's comprehensive scheme for planning, providing, and financing health care for its citizens." In his view, the Act imposes a payroll tax on covered employers and offers them a credit against that tax for their healthcare spending. The revenue from this tax funds a Fair

Share Health Care Fund, which is used to offset the costs of Maryland's Medical Assistance Program.

While an employer's one-time grant of some benefit that requires no administrative scheme does not constitute an ERISA "plan," a grant of a benefit that occurs periodically and requires the employer to maintain some ongoing administrative support generally constitutes a "plan." *See Fort Halifax Packing Co. v. Coyne,* 482 U.S. 1 (1987). Because the definition of an ERISA "plan" is so expansive, nearly any systematic provision of health-care benefits to employees constitutes a plan.

A state law that directly regulates the structuring or administration of an ERISA plan is not saved by inclusion of a means for opting out of its requirements. *See Egelhoff v. Egelhoff,* 532 U.S. 141, 150–51(2001). [A] state law has an impermissible "connection with" an ERISA plan if it directly regulates or effectively mandates some element of the structure or administration of employers' ERISA plans. On the other hand, a state law that creates only indirect economic incentives that affect but do not bind the choices of employers or their ERISA plans is generally not preempted. *See Travelers,* 514 U.S. at 658. In deciding which of these principles is applicable, we assess the effect of a state law on the ability of ERISA plans to be administered uniformly nationwide. Even if a state law provides a route by which ERISA plans can avoid the state law's requirements, taking that route might still be too disruptive of uniform plan administration to avoid preemption.

At its heart, the Fair Share Act requires every employer of 10,000 or more Maryland employees to pay to the State an amount that equals the difference between what the employer spends on "health insurance costs" (which includes any costs "to provide health benefits") and 8% of its payroll. As Wal–Mart noted by way of affidavit, it would not pay the State a sum of money that it could instead spend on its employees' healthcare. This would be the decision of any reasonable employer. Healthcare benefits are a part of the total package of employee compensation an employer gives in consideration for an employee's services. An employer would gain from increasing the compensation it offers employees through improved retention and performance of present employees and the ability to attract more and better new employees. In contrast, an employer would gain nothing in consideration of paying a greater sum of money to the State. Indeed, it might suffer from lower employee morale and increased public condemnation.

In effect, the only rational choice employers have under the Fair Share Act is to structure their ERISA healthcare benefit plans so as to meet the minimum spending threshold. The Act thus falls squarely under *Shaw's* prohibition of state mandates on how employers structure their ERISA plans. Because the Fair Share Act effectively mandates that employers structure their employee healthcare plans to provide a certain level of benefits, the Act has an obvious "connection with" employee benefit plans and so is preempted by ERISA.

[T]he choices given in the Fair Share Act [including both payment of a fee or establishing on-site clinics], on which the Secretary relies to argue that the Act is not a mandate on employers, are not meaningful alternatives by which an employer can increase its healthcare spending to comply with the Fair Share Act without affecting its ERISA plans. [E]ven if on-site medical clinics and contributions to Health Savings Accounts were a meaningful avenue by which Wal–Mart could incur non-ERISA healthcare spending, we would still conclude that the Fair Share Act had an impermissible "connection with" ERISA plans.

In short, the Fair Share Act leaves employers no reasonable choices except to change how they structure their employee benefit plans. Because the Act directly regulates employers' provision of healthcare benefits, it has a "connection with" covered employers' ERISA plans and accordingly is preempted by ERISA.

By contrast, in Golden Gate Restaurant v. City and County of San Francisco, 546 F.3d 639 (9th Cir. 2008); reh. en banc den. by Golden Gate Restaurant Assn. v. City and County of San Francisco, 558 F.3d 1000 (2009), *cert. den.,* 130 S. Ct. 3497 (2010), the Court of Appeals for the Ninth Circuit reached the opposite conclusion in a case that differed in certain important respects from *Fielder,* particularly its sweep and context and particularly in its establishment of a public insurance plan for city residents. The San Francisco city ordinance at issue established a Health Access Plan (HAP) to provide services for low and moderate income residents. Utilizing a payroll tax assessment measurement, the ordinance further required covered employers to spend a minimum amount on health care for covered employees in the form of contributions to a health savings account, reimbursement for health care expenditures, payments to a third party health services provider, or payments to the City to support HAP. The ordinance also required employers to maintain records, while exempting self-insured employers from the reporting requirements. The law applied to all employers, regardless of whether they offered any health benefits and required that payments be made directly to the City, which administered all aspects of HAP.

The Association and the amicus, the Secretary of Labor,* make two central arguments. First, they argue that the City-payment option under the Ordinance creates an ERISA plan. This argument takes two forms. The Association argues in its brief that the Ordinance's administrative obligations on employers create an

---

* Subsequent to this decision in the ninth circuit, the Obama Administration argued against the certiorari petition, claiming that the ordinance drew no impermissible connection with any ERISA plan, and further, that unlike the situation in *Fielder,* it left employers with realistic choices other than establishing ERISA plans. Brief for the United States as Amicus Curiae.

ERISA plan. The Secretary of Labor argues as amicus that the HAP itself is an ERISA plan. If either argument is correct, the Ordinance almost certainly makes an impermissible "reference to" an ERISA plan. Second, they argue that even if the City-payment option does not establish an ERISA plan, an employer's obligation to make payments at a certain level—whether or not the payments are made to the City—"relates to" the ERISA plans of covered employers and is thus preempted.

The first element of an employee welfare benefit plan is the existence of a "plan, fund or program." In the context of ERISA, the phrase "plan, fund or program" is a term of art. As relevant to this case, an ERISA "plan" is an "employee welfare benefit plan," defined as

> [a]ny plan, fund, or program which ... is ... established or maintained by an employer or by an employee organization, or by both, to the extent that such plan, fund, or program was established or is maintained for the purpose of providing for its participants ..., through the purchase of insurance or otherwise, ... medical, surgical, or hospital care or benefits, or benefits in the event of sickness, accident, disability, death or unemployment....

29 U.S.C. § 1002(1); *see also* § 1002(3).

The Supreme Court has emphasized that ERISA is concerned with "benefit plans," rather than simply "benefits," because "[o]nly 'plans' involve administrative activity potentially subject to employer abuse." *Fort Halifax Packing Co. v. Coyne,* 482 U.S. 1, 16 (1987). This focus on "benefit plans" is consistent with the first underlying purpose of ERISA—protecting employees against the abuse and mismanagement of funds.

Two Supreme Court cases tell us that an employer's obligation to make monetary payments based on the amount of time worked by an employee, over and above ordinary wages, does not necessarily create an ERISA plan. This is so even if the payments are made by the employer directly to the employees who are the beneficiaries of the putative "plan." First, in *Fort Halifax,* a Maine statute required an employer to pay employees one week's pay for every year worked if the employees were terminated because of a plant closing. The Court held that the statute did not create a "plan" within the meaning of ERISA: "The Maine statute neither establishes, nor requires an employer to maintain, an employee benefit *plan.* The requirement of a one-time, lump-sum payment triggered by a single event requires no administrative scheme whatsoever to meet the employer's obligation."

Second, in Massachusetts v. Morash, 490 U.S. 107, 109 (1989), a Massachusetts statute required employers to pay discharged employees their "full wages, including holiday or vacation payments, on the date of discharge." The Court held that the statute was not preempted by ERISA. The Court in *Morash* emphasized the importance of the fact that the employer made the payments out of its general assets.

The employer payments at issue under the San Francisco Ordinance, which the Association contends create an ERISA plan, are not made directly to employees. Rather, they are made to the City. But even if the employers made the payments directly to the employees, *Fort Halifax* and *Morash* indicate that those payments would not be enough to create an ERISA plan. Under the Ordinance, employers make the payments on a regular periodic basis and calculate those payments based on the number of hours worked by the employee. Further, as in *Morash*, employers make the payments "on a regular basis from [their] general assets."

The fact that an employer makes its payments to the City rather than to the employees confirms that the employer's administrative obligations under the City-payment option do not create an ERISA plan. Under the Ordinance, an employer has no responsibility other than to make the required payments for covered employees, and to retain records to show that it has done so. The payments are made for a specific purpose, but the employer has no responsibility for ensuring that the payments are actually used for that purpose. [A]n employer's administrative duties must involve the application of more than a modicum of discretion in order for those administrative duties to amount to an ERISA plan. It is within the exercise of that discretion that an employer has the opportunity to engage in the mismanagement of funds and other abuses with which Congress was concerned when it enacted ERISA.

The Secretary of Labor, as amicus curiae, argues that the HAP itself is an ERISA plan. If the Secretary is right, ERISA preempts not merely the employer spending requirements, but the HAP itself.

The first element of an employee welfare benefit plan is the existence of a "plan, fund or program." The HAP, administered by the City, is not an ERISA plan. Rather, the HAP is a government entitlement program available to low-and moderate-income residents of San Francisco, regardless of employment status.[4] It is

---

4. The Secretary also argues that the HAP operates as "a government-run program for private employers," and therefore it is not entitled to the exemption under 29 U.S.C. § 1003(b)(1) from ERISA regulations. The ERISA exemption to which the Secretary refers applies when a government establishes and maintains an employee welfare benefit plan for its own employees. *Id.; see also* 29 U.S.C. § 1002(32). As the Secretary correctly notes, a government plan of that type loses its exemption when it opens up its plan to employees of private employers. The Secretary's argument is that the City has opened its exempt plan for its own employees to private employees and has thus forfeited its exemption. The Secretary's argument is without foundation. The City does maintain an exempt employee welfare benefit

funded primarily by taxpayer dollars. Employer payments under the Ordinance provide only a small portion of the HAP's funding, and, although we do not know the precise numbers, employees covered under the Ordinance comprise substantially less than half of all HAP enrollees. The fact that a minority of HAP enrollees pay a discounted enrollment fee because their employers participate in the City-payment option is not enough to make the HAP a "plan, fund or program" within the meaning of ERISA.

The second element of an employee welfare benefit plan requires that the plan be "established or maintained by an employer through the purchase of insurance or otherwise." An employer electing the City-payment option does not "establish[ ] or maintain [ ]" the HAP through its payments. The HAP exists, and will continue to exist, whether or not any covered employer makes a payment to the City under the Ordinance. Further, the employer has no control over whether its employees are eligible for the HAP.

The Association's and the Secretary of Labor's second argument is that, even if the City-payment option does not create an ERISA plan, the Ordinance is preempted because it "relates to" *employers'* ERISA plans. The Ordinance in this case stands in stark contrast to the laws struck down in *Egelhoff*, *Shaw* and *Agsalud*. The Ordinance does not require any employer to adopt an ERISA plan or other health plan. Nor does it require any employer to provide specific benefits through an existing ERISA plan or other health plan. Any employer covered by the Ordinance may fully discharge its expenditure obligations by making the required level of employee health care expenditures, whether those expenditures are made in whole or in part to an ERISA plan, or in whole or in part to the City. The Ordinance thus preserves ERISA's "uniform regulatory regime." The Ordinance also has no effect on "the administrative practices of a benefit plan," *Fort Halifax*, 482 U.S. at 11, unless an employer voluntarily elects to change those practices.

In this case, the influence exerted by the Ordinance is even less direct than the influence in *Travelers*. In *Travelers,* the required surcharge on benefits provided under ERISA plans administered by commercial insurers inescapably changed the cost structure for those plans' health care benefits and thereby exerted economic pressure on the manner in which the plans would be administered. Here, by contrast, the Ordinance does not regulate benefits or charges for benefits provided by ERISA plans. Its only influence is on the employer who, because of the Ordinance, may choose to make its required health care expenditures to an ERISA plan rather than to the City.

---

plan for its own employees. The HAP, however, is not that plan. The City has never argued that the HAP is exempt from ERISA as a government-run plan for the City's own employees.

Further, the Ordinance does not "bind[ ] ERISA plan administrators to a particular choice of rules" for determining plan eligibility or entitlement to particular benefits. *See Egelhoff,* 532 U.S. at 147. Employers may "structur[e] their employee benefit plans" in a variety of ways and need not "pay employees specific benefits." *See Shaw,* 463 U.S. at 97. The Ordinance affects employers, but it "leave[s] plan administrators right where they would be in any case." *Travelers Ins. Co.,* 514 U.S. at 662.

Finally, the Ordinance does not impose on plan administrators any "administrative [or] financial burden of complying with conflicting directives" relating to benefits law. *Ingersoll–Rand Co.,* 498 U.S. at 142. The Ordinance does impose an administrative burden on covered employers, for they must keep track of their obligations to make expenditures on behalf of covered employees and must maintain records to show that they have complied with the Ordinance. But these burdens exist whether or not a covered employer has an ERISA plan. Thus, they are burdens on the employer rather than on an ERISA plan.

To determine whether a law has a forbidden "reference to" ERISA plans, we ask whether (1) the law "acts immediately and exclusively upon ERISA plans," or (2) "the existence of ERISA plans is essential to the law's operation." *Dillingham,* 519 U.S. at 325. Under the Ordinance in our case, by contrast, an employer's obligations to the City are measured by reference to the *payments* provided by the employer to an ERISA plan or to another entity specified in the Ordinance, including the City. The employer calculates its required payments based on the hours worked by its employees, rather than on the value or nature of the benefits available to ERISA plan participants. Thus the Ordinance in this case is not determined, in the words of § 514(a), by "reference to" an ERISA plan.

Here employers need not have any ERISA plan at all; and if they do have such a plan, they need not make any changes to it. Where a law is fully functional even in the absence of a single ERISA plan, it does not make an impermissible reference to ERISA plans.

Finally, the Association contends that the Ordinance is preempted under the analysis set forth in *Retail Industry Leaders Association v. Fielder,* Wal–Mart was the only employer in Maryland affected by the law's minimum spending requirements. On the face of the law, Wal–Mart appeared to have two options. To reach the required spending level of 8%, it could either increase contributions to its own ERISA plan, or it could pay money to the State of Maryland. But the Fourth Circuit concluded that, in practical fact, Wal–Mart had no choice.

In stark contrast to the Maryland law in *Fielder,* the City-payment option under the San Francisco Ordinance offers employers a meaningful alternative that allows them to preserve the existing structure of their ERISA plans.

In 2006, St. 2006 c.58, Massachusetts legislators enacted universal health insurance coverage legislation that became the prototype for the Affordable Care Act. For reasons related to the extraordinary political consensus that emerged around its reform law, Massachusetts did not experience an ERISA preemption challenge. Like the Affordable Care Act, the Massachusetts law mandates individual health insurance coverage and requires employers to contribute toward their employees' coverage. Sharon K. Long & Paul B. Masi, *Access and Affordability: An Update on Health Reform in Massachusetts, Fall 2008*, 28(4) HEALTH AFFAIRS (Web Exclusive) w578–87 (2009). *See also* Elizabeth A. Weeks, *Failure to Connect: The Massachusetts Plan for Individual Health Insurance Coverage*, 55 U. KAN. L. REV. 1283 (2007); John E. McDonough et al., *Massachusetts Health Reform Implementation: Major Progress and Future Challenges* 27(4) HEALTH AFFAIRS (Web Exclusive) w285–97 (2008).

* * *

A number of cases have addressed the issue of when a law can be said to fall on ERISA plans sufficiently to be preempted. In some of these cases, the law affects the entities that insure or administer plan services or that are part of a plan's offerings, such as the insurers in *Travelers* or the plan-owned clinics in *De Buono*. As you will see below, when a law is found to "relate to" a plan, the next step is to determine whether it can be saved. But if no relationship within the meaning of ERISA is found, ERISA's preemption principles are halted at the first stage. The two analyses ("relate to" and the "saving clause") are related: if a state law affects the conduct or practices of the seller of a product to an ERISA plan (i.e., an insurer) and can be said to only indirectly affect the price paid for the product by the ERISA plan, shouldn't the law not be preempted in the first place? Isn't that the message of *Travelers*?

In Foster v. Blue Cross and Blue Shield of Michigan, 969 F. Supp. 1020 (E.D. Mich. 1997), the court held that Michigan's enabling legislation for Blue Cross, although requiring Blue Cross to cover certain treatments for breast cancer, did not "relate to" the ERISA plans that purchased Blue Cross policies, but merely imposed

> an indirect economic influence on those plans choosing to use Blue Cross for their coverage[. T]he law itself does not regulate [ERISA] plans or impose a different administrative regimen upon them. It regulates Blue Cross, a company that some plans choose to hire to assist in the operation of their plans. The plans are still free to select another insurer for their coverage, in which case the requirements of those provisions would not apply.

Id. at 1027. The *Foster* court held, in the alternative, that "[e]ven if these sections did relate to an ERISA plan, they would be saved from preemption because they are state laws regulating insurance." *Id. Accord,* Sluiter v.

Blue Cross and Blue Shield of Michigan, 979 F. Supp. 1131 (E.D. Mich. 1997).

See also Washington Physicians Service Assoc. v. Gregoire, 147 F.3d 1039 (9th Cir. 1998), *cert. den.*, 525 U.S. 1141 (1999), holding that Washington State's requirement that HMOs and other health insurers reimburse "alternative health care providers" regulated insurers but did not "relate to" ERISA plans, or, alternatively, was saved from preemption by the insurance saving clause; American Drug Stores, Inc. v. Harvard Pilgrim Health Care, Inc., 973 F. Supp. 60 (D. Mass. 1997) (same alternative holdings with respect to Massachusetts' "any willing pharmacy law" imposing requirements on health insurers with limited provider networks).

b.   ERISA's Insurance Saving Clause

Metropolitan Life Insurance Company v. Massachusetts

471 U.S. 724 (1985)

■ JUSTICE BLACKMUN delivered the opinion of the Court.

A Massachusetts statute [section 47B] requires that specified minimum mental-health-care benefits be provided a Massachusetts resident who is insured under a general insurance policy, an accident or sickness insurance policy, or an employee health-care plan that covers hospital and surgical expenses. The first question before us in these cases is whether the state statute, as applied to insurance policies purchased by employee health-care plans regulated by the federal Employee Retirement Income Security Act of 1974, is pre-empted by that Act.

General health insurance typically is sold as group insurance to an employer or other group. Group insurance presently is subject to extensive state regulation, including regulation of the carrier, regulation of the sale and advertising of the insurance, and regulation of the content of the contracts. Mandated-benefit laws, that require an insurer to provide a certain kind of benefit to cover a specified illness or procedure whenever someone purchases a certain kind of insurance, are a subclass of such content regulation.

While mandated-benefit statutes are a relatively recent phenomenon, statutes regulating the substantive terms of insurance contracts have become commonplace in all 50 States over the last 30 years.

The substantive terms of group-health insurance contracts, in particular, also have been extensively regulated by the States. For example, the majority of States currently require that coverage for dependents continue beyond any contractually imposed age limitation when the dependent is incapable of self-sustaining employment because of mental or physical handicap; such statutes date back to the early 1960's. And over the last 15 years all 50 States have required that coverage of infants begin at birth, rather than at some time shortly after birth, as had been the prior practice in the unregulated market. Others require insurers either to offer or mandate that insurance policies include coverage for services rendered by a particular type of health-care provider.

Mandated-benefit statutes, then, are only one variety of a matrix of state laws that regulate the substantive content of health-insurance policies to further state health policy. [Section 47B] is typical of mandated-benefit laws currently in place in the majority of States. [I]t requires any general health-insurance policy that provides hospital and surgical coverage, or any benefit plan that has such coverage, to provide as well a certain minimum of mental-health protection. In particular, § 47B requires that a health insurance policy provide 60 days of coverage for confinement in a mental hospital, coverage for confinement in a general hospital equal to that provided by the policy for non-mental illness, and certain minimum outpatient benefits.

Section 47B was designed to address problems encountered in treating mental illness in Massachusetts. The Commonwealth determined that its working people needed to be protected against the high cost of treatment for such illness. It also believed that, without insurance, mentally ill workers were often institutionalized in large state mental hospitals, and that mandatory insurance would lead to a higher incidence of more effective treatment in private community mental-health centers.

In addition, the Commonwealth concluded that the voluntary insurance market was not adequately providing mental-health coverage, because of "adverse selection" in mental-health insurance: good insurance risks were not purchasing coverage, and this drove up the price of coverage for those who otherwise might purchase mental-health insurance. The legislature believed that the public interest required that it correct the insurance market in the Commonwealth by mandating minimum-coverage levels, effectively forcing the good-risk individuals to become part of the risk pool, and enabling insurers to price the insurance at an average market rather than a market retracted due to adverse selection. Section 47B, then, was intended to help safeguard the public against the high costs of comprehensive inpatient and outpatient mental-health care, reduce non-psychiatric medical-care expenditures for mentally related illness, shift the delivery of treatment from inpatient to outpatient services, and relieve the Commonwealth of some of the financial burden it otherwise would encounter with respect to mental-health problems.

It is our task in these cases to decide whether such insurance regulation violates or is inconsistent with federal law.

ERISA comprehensively regulates employee pension and welfare plans. Plans may self-insure or they may purchase insurance for their participants. Plans that purchase insurance—so-called "insured plans"—are directly affected by state laws that regulate the insurance industry.

ERISA imposes upon pension plans a variety of substantive requirements relating to participation, funding and vesting. It does not regulate the substantive content of welfare-benefit plans.

ERISA thus contains almost no federal regulation of the terms of benefit plans. It does, however, contain a broad pre-emption provision declaring that the statute shall "supersede any and all State laws insofar as they may now or hereafter relate to any employee benefit plan." § 514(a), 29 U.S.C. § 1144(a). Metropolitan argues that ERISA pre-empts Massachusetts' mandated-benefit law insofar as 47B restricts the kinds of insurance policies that benefit plans may purchase.

While § 514(a) of ERISA broadly pre-empts state laws that relate to an employee-benefit plan, that pre-emption is substantially qualified by an "insurance saving clause," § 514(b)(2)(A), 29 U.S.C. § 1144(b)(2)(A), which broadly states that, with one exception, nothing in ERISA "shall be construed to exempt or relieve any person from any law of any State which regulates insurance, banking, or securities." The specified exception to the saving clause is found in § 514(b)(2)(B), 29 U.S.C. § 1144(b)(2)(B), the so-called "deemer clause," which states that no employee-benefit plan, with certain exceptions not relevant here, "shall be deemed to be an insurance company or other insurer, bank, trust company, or investment company or to be engaged in the business of insurance or banking for purposes of any law of any State purporting to regulate insurance companies, insurance contracts, banks, trust companies, or investment companies." Massachusetts argues that its mandated-benefit law, as applied to insurance companies that sell insurance to benefit plans, is a "law which regulates insurance," and therefore is saved from the effect of the general pre-emption clause of ERISA.

In 1979, the Attorney General of Massachusetts brought suit in Massachusetts Superior Court for declaratory and injunctive relief to enforce § 47B. The Commonwealth asserted that since January 1, 1976, the effective date of § 47B, the insurers had issued policies to group policyholders that failed to provide Massachusetts-resident beneficiaries the mental-health coverage mandated by § 47B, and that the insurers intended to issue more such policies, believing themselves not bound by § 47B for policies issued outside the Commonwealth. In their answer, the insurers admitted these allegations.

The Superior Court issued a preliminary injunction requiring the insurers to provide the coverage mandated by § 47B. Addressing first the ERISA pre-emption question, the court recognized that § 47B is a law that " 'relate[s] to' benefit plans," and so would be pre-empted unless it fell within one of the exceptions to the pre-emption clause of ERISA. The court went on to hold, however, that § 47B is a law "which regulates insurance," as understood by the ERISA saving clause, § 514(b)(2)(A), and therefore is not pre-empted by ERISA.

Section 47B clearly "relate[s] to" welfare plans governed by ERISA so as to fall within the reach of ERISA's preemption provision, § 514(a). The broad scope of the preemption clause was noted recently in *Shaw*, where we held that the New York Human Rights Law and that State's Disability Benefits Law "relate[d] to" welfare plans governed by ERISA. The phrase "relate to" was given its broad common-sense meaning, such that a state law "relate[s] to" a benefit plan "in the normal sense of the phrase, if it has a connection with or reference to such a plan." The pre-emption provision was intended to displace all state laws that fall within its sphere, even including state laws that are consistent with ERISA's substantive requirements.

Though § 47B is not denominated a benefit-plan law, it bears indirectly but substantially on all insured benefit plans, for it requires them to purchase the mental-health benefits specified in the statute when they purchase a certain kind of common insurance policy. The Commonwealth does not argue that § 47B as applied to policies purchased by benefit plans does not relate to those plans, and we agree with the Supreme Judicial Court that the mandated-benefit law as applied relates to ERISA plans and thus is covered by ERISA's broad pre-emption provision set forth in § 514(a).

Nonetheless, the sphere in which § 514(a) operates was explicitly limited by § 514(b)(2). The insurance saving clause preserves any state law "which regulates insurance, banking, or securities." The two pre-emption sections, while clear enough on their faces, perhaps are not a model of legislative drafting, for while the general pre-emption clause broadly pre-empts state law, the saving clause appears broadly to preserve the States' lawmaking power over much of the same regulation. While Congress occasionally decides to return to the States what it has previously taken away, it does not normally do both at the same time.

Fully aware of this statutory complexity, we still have no choice but to "begin with the language employed by Congress and the assumption that the ordinary meaning of that language accurately expresses the legislative purpose." We also must presume that Congress did not intend to pre-empt areas of traditional state regulation.

To state the obvious, § 47B regulates the terms of certain insurance contracts, and so seems to be saved from preemption by the saving clause as a law "which regulates insurance." This common-sense view of the matter, moreover, is reinforced by the language of the subsequent subsection of ERISA, the "deemer clause," which states that an employee-benefit plan shall not be deemed to be an insurance company "for purposes of any law of any State purporting to regulate insurance companies, insurance contracts, banks, trust companies, [*Metropolitan Life Insurance Co.,* 471 U.S. 724, 741] or investment companies." § 514(b)(2)(B), 29 U.S.C. § 1144(b) (2)(B). By exempting from the saving clause laws regulating insurance contracts that apply directly to benefit plans, the deemer clause makes explicit Congress' intention to include laws that regulate insurance contracts within the scope of the insurance laws preserved by the saving clause. Unless Congress intended to include laws regulating insurance contracts within the scope of the insurance saving clause, it would have been unnecessary for the deemer clause explicitly to exempt such laws from the saving clause when they are applied directly to benefit plans.

The insurers nonetheless argue that § 47B is in reality a health law that merely operates on insurance contracts to accomplish its end, and that it is not the kind of traditional insurance law intended to be saved by § 514(b)(2)(A). We find this argument unpersuasive.

Initially, nothing in § 514(b)(2)(A), or in the "deemer clause" which modifies it, purports to distinguish between traditional and innovative insurance laws. The presumption is against pre-emption, and we are not inclined to read limitations into federal statutes in order to enlarge their preemptive scope. Further, there is no indication in the legislative history that Congress had such a distinction in mind.

Appellants assert that state laws that directly regulate the insurer, and laws that regulate such matters as the way in which insurance may be sold, are traditional laws subject to the clause, while laws that regulate the substantive terms of insurance contracts are recent innovations more properly seen as health laws rather than as insurance laws, which § 514(b)(2)(A) does not save. This distinction reads the saving clause out of ERISA entirely, because laws that regulate only the insurer, or the way in which it may sell insurance, do not "relate to" benefit plans in the first instance. Because they would not be pre-empted by § 514(a), they do not need to be "saved" by § 514(b)(2)(A). There is no indication that Congress could have intended the saving clause to operate only to guard against too expansive readings of the general pre-emption clause that might have included laws wholly unrelated to plans.

Moreover, it is both historically and conceptually inaccurate to assert that mandated-benefit laws are not traditional insurance laws. As we have indicated, state laws regulating the substantive terms of insurance contracts were commonplace well before the mid-70's, when Congress considered ERISA. The case law concerning the meaning of the phrase "business of insurance" in the McCarran-Ferguson Act also strongly supports the conclusion that regulation regarding the substantive terms of insurance contracts falls squarely within the saving clause as laws "which regulate insurance."

Cases interpreting the scope of the McCarran-Ferguson Act have identified three criteria relevant to determining whether a particular practice falls within that Act's reference to the "business of insurance": "first, whether the practice has the effect of transferring or spreading a policyholder's risk; second, whether the practice is an integral part of the policy relationship between the insurer and the insured; and third, whether the practice is limited to entities within the insurance industry." Union Labor Life Ins. Co. v. Pireno, 458 U.S. 119, 129 (1982) (emphasis in original). See also Group Life & Health Ins. Co. v. Royal Drug Co., 440 U.S. 205 (1979). Application of these principles suggests that mandated-benefit laws are state regulation of the "business of insurance."

Section 47B obviously regulates the spreading of risk: as we have indicated, it was intended to effectuate the legislative judgment that the risk of mental-health care should be shared. It is also evident that mandated-benefit laws directly regulate an integral part of the relationship between the insurer and the policyholder by limiting the type of insurance that an insurer may sell to the policyholder. Finally, the third criterion is present here, for mandated-benefit statutes impose requirements only on insurers, with the intent of affecting the relationship between the insurer and the policyholder.

Nothing in the legislative history of ERISA suggests a different result. There is no discussion in that history of the relationship between the general pre-emption clause and the saving clause, and indeed very little discussion of the saving clause at all. In the early versions of ERISA, the general pre-emption clause pre-empted only those state laws dealing with subjects regulated by ERISA. The clause was significantly broadened at the last minute, well after the saving clause was in its present form, to include all state laws that relate to benefit plans. The change was made with little explanation by the Conference Committee, and there is no indication in the legislative history that Congress was aware of the new prominence given the saving clause in light of the rewritten pre-emption clause, or was aware that the saving clause was in conflict with the general pre-emption provision. There is a complete absence of evidence that Congress intended the narrow reading of the saving clause suggested by appellants here.

We therefore decline to impose any limitation on the saving clause beyond those Congress imposed in the clause itself and in the "deemer clause" which modifies it. If a state law "regulates insurance," as mandated-benefit laws do, it is not preempted.

We are aware that our decision results in a distinction between insured and uninsured plans, leaving the former open to indirect regulation while the latter are not. By so doing we merely give life to a distinction created by Congress in the "deemer clause," a distinction Congress is aware of and one it has chosen not to alter. We also are aware that appellants' construction of the statute would eliminate some of the disuniformities currently facing national plans that enter into local markets to purchase insurance. Such disuniformities, however, are the inevitable result of the congressional decision to "save" local insurance regulation. Arguments as to the wisdom of these policy choices must be directed at Congress.

Notes

1. *The practical effect of the "deemer" clause.* As the court notes, the "deemer" clause, ERISA § 514(b)(2)(B), 29 U.S.C. § 1144(b)(2)(B), provides that employee benefit plans themselves cannot be considered insurance companies for purposes of state regulations. This division between insured health benefit plans (i.e., plans that purchase health insurance) and self-insured plans, means that people enrolled in self-insured health benefit plans (something that mere mortals never could be expected to know) may lack protections afforded members of insured plans that are subject to regulation under state law. Prior to the Affordable Care Act, for example, in more than 40 states participants and beneficiaries in insured plans had the right, under state law, to at least some level of independent external review, while participants in self-insured plans did not, because of the deemer clause. Similarly, people enrolled in insured plans would have

the right to coverage for benefits mandated under state law, while those enrolled in self-insured plans would not. Imagine two spouses, both enrolled in a Blue Cross/Blue Shield PPO plan. One works for a small trade association that buys the Blue Cross insurance product. The other works for a large university that self-insures and contracts with Blue Cross as a third-party administrator only. The two spouses have the same card (the University plan does not say "University Plan" but instead says "Blue Cross/Blue Shield of [pick your state]"). Yet despite the fact that the two spouses *think* they have the same coverage, in fact their coverage, along with their coverage protections, can differ markedly with respect to benefits, consumer protections, and other matters regulated by the state.

2. *Are HMOs insurers for purposes of the saving clause?* Health maintenance organizations are hybrid creatures that both insure or administer coverage while also providing or arranging for care through a participating provider network. Do laws regulating HMOs constitute laws regulating insurance for purposes of the saving clause? The United States Supreme Court answered this question in the affirmative in Rush Prudential HMO v. Moran, 536 U.S. 355 (2002). *Rush Prudential* concerned Illinois' external review statute, which provided insured individuals with a right to external review of an insurer's denial of benefits based on medical necessity. (External review rights, as noted above, are now a guarantee under certain circumstances under the Affordable Care Act).

Finding that the statute did not impermissibly add remedies to ERISA but instead operated as a law regulating insurance contracts, the Court concluded that the application of such laws to HMOs constituted the regulation of insurance and thus would be saved.

3. *Extending the reach of a "saved" law, modifying the saving clause test, and reconciling ERISA with the "business of insurance" provisions of the McCarran–Ferguson Act.* In Kentucky Association of Health Plans, Inc. v. Miller, 538 U.S. 329 (2003), the state of Kentucky had enacted a law (known as an "any willing provider" statute (AWP)) providing that "[a] health insurer shall not discriminate against any provider who is located within the geographic coverage area of the health benefit plan and who is willing to meet the terms and conditions for participation established by the health insurer." Moreover, any "health benefit plan that includes chiropractic benefits shall ... [p]ermit any licensed chiropractor who agrees to abide by the terms, conditions, reimbursement rates, and standards of quality of the health benefit plan to serve as a participating primary chiropractic provider to any person covered by the plan."

Kentucky's HMO association sued, arguing that the law could not be saved because it was directed at more than just insurers in that it also applied to physicians who formed provider networks to negotiate with HMOs and other insurers. Moreover, according to the plaintiff, the law failed the three-pronged test articulated in *Metropolitan Life Insurance v. Massachusetts,* in that the law regulated the relationship between insurers and providers, rather than the relationship between an insurer and the insured. The impact of the law, according to the Association, was its impairment of HMOs' ability to "limit the number of providers with access to their networks, and thus their ability to use the assurance of high patient volume as the *quid pro quo* for the discounted rates that network membership entails."

On behalf of a unanimous Court, Justice Scalia wrote:

It is well established in our case law that a state law must be "specifically directed toward" the insurance industry in order to fall under ERISA's savings clause; laws of general application that have some bearing on insurers do not qualify. At the same time, not all state laws "specifically directed toward" the insurance industry will be covered by [the savings clause], which saves laws that regulate *insurance,* not insurers. Petitioners contend that Kentucky's AWP laws fall outside the scope of [the savings clause] for two reasons. First, because Kentucky has failed to "specifically direc[t]" its AWP laws towards the insurance industry; and second, because the AWP laws do not regulate an insurance practice. We find neither contention persuasive.

Petitioners claim that Kentucky's statutes are not "specifically directed toward" insurers because they regulate not only the insurance industry but also doctors who seek to form and maintain limited provider networks with HMOs. That is to say, the AWP laws equally prevent *providers* from entering into limited network contracts with *insurers,* just as they prevent insurers from creating exclusive networks in the first place. We do not think it follows that Kentucky has failed to specifically direct its AWP laws at the insurance industry.

It is of course true that as a *consequence* of Kentucky's AWP laws, entities outside the insurance industry (such as health-care providers) will be unable to enter into certain agreements with Kentucky insurers. [T]he effects of these laws on noninsurers, significant though they may have been, [are not] inconsistent with the requirement that laws saved from pre-emption by [the savings clause] be "specifically directed toward" the insurance industry. Regulations "directed toward" certain entities will almost always disable other entities from doing, with the regulated entities, what the regulations forbid; this does not suffice to place such regulation outside the scope of ERISA's savings clause.[1]

---

1. Petitioners also contend that [Kentucky's AWP law] is not "specifically directed toward" insurers because it applies to "self-insurer or multiple employer welfare arrangement[s] not exempt from state regulation by ERISA." We do not think [the statute's] application to self-insured non-ERISA plans forfeits its status as a "law ... which regulates insurance" under [§ 514(b)(2)(A)]. ERISA's savings clause does not require that a state law regulate "insurance *companies*" or even "*the business of insurance*" to be saved from pre-emption; it need only be a "law ... which regulates *insurance,*" and self-insured plans engage in the same sort of risk pooling arrangements as separate entities that provide insurance to an employee benefit plan. Any contrary view would render superfluous ERISA's "deemer clause," which has effect only on state laws saved from pre-emption that would, in the absence of [the

Petitioners claim that the AWP laws do not regulate insurers with respect to an insurance practice because they do not control the actual terms of insurance policies. Rather, they focus upon the relationship between an insurer and *third-party providers*—which in petitioners' view does not constitute an "insurance practice."

In support of their contention, petitioners rely on *Group Life & Health Ins. Co. v. Royal Drug Co.*, which held that third-party provider arrangements between insurers and pharmacies were not "the 'business of insurance'" under § 2(b) of the McCarran–Ferguson Act. ERISA's savings clause, however, is not concerned (as is the McCarran–Ferguson Act provision) with how to characterize *conduct* undertaken by private actors, but with how to characterize *state laws* in regard to what they "regulate." It does not follow from *Royal Drug* that a law mandating certain insurer-provider relationships fails to "regulate insurance." Those who wish to provide health insurance in Kentucky (any "health insurer") may not discriminate against any willing provider. This "regulates" insurance by imposing conditions on the right to engage in the business of insurance; whether or not an HMO's contracts with providers constitute "the business of insurance" under *Royal Drug* is beside the point.

We emphasize that conditions on the right to engage in the business of insurance must also substantially affect the risk pooling arrangement between the insurer and the insured to be covered by ERISA's savings clause. Otherwise, any state law aimed at insurance companies could be deemed a law that "regulates insurance." A state law requiring all insurance companies to pay their janitors twice the minimum wage would not "regulate insurance," even though it would be a prerequisite to engaging in the business of insurance, because it does not substantially affect the risk pooling arrangement undertaken by insurer and insured. Petitioners contend that Kentucky's AWP statutes fail this test as well, since they do not alter or affect the terms of insurance policies, but concern only the relationship between insureds and third-party providers. We disagree. We have never held that state laws must alter or control the actual terms of insurance policies to be deemed "laws ... which regulat[e] insurance" under [the saving clause]; it suffices that they substantially affect the risk pooling arrangement between insurer and insured.[3] By expanding the number of providers from whom an insured may receive health

---

deemer clause] be allowed to regulate self-insured employee benefit plans. Under petitioners' view, such laws would never be saved from pre-emption in the first place.

3. [O]ur test requires only that the state law substantially *affect* the risk pooling arrangement between the insurer and insured; it does not require that the state law actually spread risk. The notice-prejudice rule [at issue in *Unum*] governs whether or not an insurance company must cover claims submitted late, which dictates to the insurance company the conditions under which it must pay for the risk that it has assumed. This certainly qualifies as a substantial effect on the risk pooling arrangement between the insurer and the insured.

services, AWP laws alter the scope of permissible bargains between insurers and insureds. No longer may Kentucky insureds seek insurance from a closed network of health-care providers in exchange for a lower premium. The AWP prohibition substantially affects the type of risk pooling arrangements that insurers may offer.

Our prior decisions construing [the savings clause] have relied, to varying degrees, on our cases interpreting §§ 2(a) and 2(b) of the McCarran–Ferguson Act. In determining whether certain practices constitute "the *business of* insurance" under the McCarran–Ferguson Act (emphasis added), our cases have looked to three factors: "*first,* whether the practice has the effect of transferring or spreading a policyholder's risk; *second,* whether the practice is an integral part of the policy relationship between the insurer and the insured; and *third,* whether the practice is limited to entities within the insurance industry."

We believe that our use of the McCarran–Ferguson case law in the ERISA context has misdirected attention, failed to provide clear guidance to lower federal courts, and, as this case demonstrates, added little to the relevant analysis. That is unsurprising, since the statutory language of [the savings clause] differs substantially from that of the McCarran–Ferguson Act. Rather than concerning itself with whether certain practices constitute "[t]he business of insurance," or whether a state law was "enacted . . . *for the purpose of* regulating the business of insurance," [the savings clause] asks merely whether a state law is a "law . . . which regulates insurance, banking, or securities." What is more, the McCarran–Ferguson factors were developed in cases that characterized *conduct* by private actors, not state laws.

We have never held that the McCarran–Ferguson factors are an essential component of the [savings clause] inquiry. *Metropolitan Life* initially used these factors only to buttress its previously reached conclusion that Massachusetts' mandated-benefit statute was a "law . . . which regulates insurance." Today we make a clean break from the McCarran–Ferguson factors and hold that for a state law to be deemed a "law . . . which regulates insurance" under [the savings clause], it must satisfy two requirements. First, the state law must be specifically directed toward entities engaged in insurance. Second, as explained above, the state law must substantially affect the risk pooling arrangement between the insurer and the insured. Kentucky's law satisfies each of these requirements.

Miller is an important signpost in the movement of section 514 toward a test that focuses on the functions of potentially conflicting state and federal law rather than some formalistic test, like the three-part test used under the McCarran–Ferguson Act. Justice Scalia is quite pointed about this change. He says correctly that the Court "has never held that the

McCarran–Ferguson factors are an essential component of the [saving clause] inquiry." You can look back at the Court's opinion in *Met Life* to verify this assertion, for the Court there used the McCarran–Ferguson factors to case light on interpretation of ERISA's saving clause and did not state that ERISA incorporated the analysis of McCarran–Ferguson. *See also UNUM Life Insurance Co. of America v. Ward*, 526 U.S. 358, 373–74 (1999). Justice Scalia in *Miller* candidly admits that the McCarran–Ferguson factors have generated more heat than light in ERISA jurisprudence: "We believe that our use of the McCarran–Ferguson case law in the ERISA context has misdirected attention, failed to provide clear guidance to lower federal courts, and, as this case demonstrates, added little to the relevant analysis." He points out that McCarran–Ferguson was passed to overrule an antitrust decision that subjected "*conduct* by private actors"—entities engaged in the business of insurance—to the federal antitrust laws, not to allocate state and federal powers more generally (though we will see this attempt to broaden the impact of McCarran–Ferguson in a number of other doctrinal areas). These passages, freeing ERISA from McCarran–Ferguson, truly spell the end of the era.

So, what has the new dawn brought? First, the focus of the saving clause is redirected to laws that regulate *insurance* as a function—the allocation and bearing of risk. Look back at footnote one, in which the Court responds to the argument that Kentucky's any-willing-provider law is over-inclusive—and therefore falls shy of the McCarran–Ferguson requirement that a law be specifically directed toward insurers—because it applies also to self-insured plans and multiple employer welfare arrangements. The Court points out, as did the Court in *Met Life*, that such over-inclusiveness is not a problem when the "non-insurance-company" entities are self-insured plans. "Any contrary argument would render superfluous ERISA's 'deemer clause.' " Yet the other justification is more telling. Justice Scalia wrote, "ERISA's savings clause does not require that a state law regulate 'insurance *companies*' or even '*the business of insurance*' to be saved from pre-emption: it need only be a 'law ... which regulates *insurance*,' and self-insured plans engage in the same sort of risk pooling arrangements as separate entities that provide insurance to an employee benefit plan" (emphasis in original). The focus of the saving clause, therefore, is on *insurance* not particular *companies* or *businesses*.

Yet what one hand giveth, the other taketh away because the Court then states the other part of its new test. Not only must the state law to be saved "substantially affect the risk pooling arrangement between the insurer and the insured" but it must also "be specifically directed toward entities engaged in insurance."

At this point, the opinion collapses into a muddle, since the renewed focus on entities is totally inconsistent with the focus on risk pooling, the function of insurance. Earlier in the opinion Justice Scalia had correctly shredded the Association's claim that Kentucky's law was over-inclusive because it "regulate[s] not only the insurance industry but also doctors who seek to form and maintain limited provider networks with HMOs."

The Court's answer was structurally the same as the one against the over-inclusiveness argument that the law likewise affected self-insured plans (although here the Court did not have the deemer clause as a backstop). It wrote, "Regulations 'directed toward' certain entities will almost always disable other entities from doing, with the regulated entities, what the regulations forbid; this does not suffice to place such regulations outside the scope of ERISA's savings clause." Then, in response to the argument that Kentucky's law likewise was not specifically aimed at insurance because it "focus[es] upon the relationship between an insurer and *third-party providers*—which in petitioners' view does not constitute an 'insurance practice[,]' " the Court responded:

> By expanding the number of providers from whom an insured may receive health services, AWP laws alter the scope of permissible bargains between insurers and insureds. No longer may Kentucky insureds seek insurance from a closed network of health-care providers in exchange for a lower premium. The AWP prohibition substantially affects the type of risk pooling arrangements that insurers may offer.

123 S. Ct. at 1477–78. Here we are back to the question whether the state law substantially affects the allocation and spreading of risk in insurance. Health insurance is the relationship between the plan, the patient and the pool of providers that constitute the plan's network. That relationship consists in the contracts between the plan, the patient and the pool of providers. Notice the word "contracts." The contracts are between entities, and it is the contracts that are being regulated, not the entities. For that reason, it is sheer nonsense to recognize this fact, by holding that Kentucky's any-willing-provider law regulates risk pooling, i.e., the contractual relationships, and simultaneously to hold that the state law regulates a particular entity.

Leave aside for the moment that the opinion is self-contradictory and consider whether or not this new two-part test is workable. First, how are we to know if a law is "specifically directed toward entities engaged in insurance"? The Court says that it is irrelevant that Kentucky's any-willing-provider law also affects providers because it is "specifically directed toward entities in the insurance industry." Q.E.D. Suppose that Kentucky's law read: "No licensed provider in this state shall execute a participation agreement with any insurer if the insurer refuses to offer identical terms to all providers who hold identical licenses." Is that law aimed at providers or insurers? It takes two to contract as well as tango. States often regulate insurance by passing laws that regulate the contracts that are executed between insurers and their contracting parties. The laws are aimed at the relationship, not one side of the contract or the other, and there is no rationale for saying that the law is "specifically directed" to one side or the other. So is the true meaning of the decision that relationships between insurers and their contracting providers are so intertwined that laws regulating the relationship, regardless of how they are drafted, should be considered saved?

Second, the boundaries of the other part of the test—that the state law "substantially affect the risk pooling arrangement between the insurer and the insured"—likewise is not so clear, particularly in light of the Court's holding, in *Pilot Life*, to which we turn next, that section 502 preempts state law remedies against insurers even though those remedies substantially affect risk pooling. To illustrate for now, recall that *Firestone Tire & Rubber Co.*, 489 U.S. 101, above, allows insurers to insert "deference clauses" into their contracts to assure that their decisions regarding eligibility and coverage receive deference from the courts in the event of a legal challenge. What happens when a state law bars the use of deference clauses in insurance contracts, thereby preserving classic principles of contract interpretation and *de novo* review of claims disputes? This was the question posed and answered in Standard Ins. Co. v. Morrison, 584 F.3d 837 (9th Cir. 2009), *cert. den. sub nom*, Standard Ins. Co. v. Lindeen, 130 S. Ct. 3275 (2010). Montana Code Ann. § 33-1-502 requires the commissioner of insurance to "disapprove any [insurance] form . . . if the form . . . contains . . . any inconsistent, ambiguous, or misleading clauses or exceptions and conditions which deceptively affect the risk purported to be assumed in the general coverage of the contract." The Insurance Commissioner determined that this state statute barred the incorporation of deference clauses in insurance contracts. The Court of Appeals concluded that this statutory interpretation was saved from preemption:

> Discretionary clauses are controversial. The National Association of Insurance Commissioners ("NAIC") opposes their use, arguing that a ban on such clauses would mitigate the conflict of interest present when the claims adjudicator also pays the benefit. According to NAIC, as of 2008, a dozen states had limited or barred the use of discretionary clauses in at least some form of insurance.

> Insurers and other supporters of discretionary clauses argue they keep insurance costs manageable. They assert that more cases will be filed in the absence of a discretionary clause and that the wide ranging nature of *de novo* review will lead to increased per-case costs as well. Failure to control litigation costs, they suggest, will discourage employers from offering employee benefit programs in the first place.

> Here, no one disputes that Commissioner Morrison's practice relate[s] to any [covered] employee benefit plan. It is thus preempted unless preserved by the savings clause. To fall under the savings clause, a regulation must satisfy a two-part test laid out in *Kentucky Ass'n of Health Plans, Inc. v. Miller*. "First, the state law must be specifically directed toward entities engaged in insurance." Also, it "must substantially affect the risk pooling arrangement between the insurer and the insured."

> Standard asserts initially that Morrison's practice of disapproving discretionary clauses is not specifically directed at insur-

ance companies because it is instead directed at ERISA plans and procedures. Unfortunately for Standard, ERISA plans are a form of insurance, and the practice regulates insurance companies by limiting what they can and cannot include in their insurance policies.[1] It is well-established that a law which regulates what terms insurance companies can place in their policies regulates insurance companies. That an insurance rule has an effect on third parties does not disqualify it from being a regulation of insurance.

Standard next argues that the practice is not specifically directed at insurers because it merely applies "laws of general application that have some bearing on insurers." To Standard, the practice is nothing more than an attempt to apply the common-law rule that contracts are interpreted against their drafter.

The cases Standard offers in support involve basic common-law rules which were applied to a wide variety of contracts. For instance, in *Pilot Life Insurance Co. v. Dedeaux*,, the Supreme Court found suits for "tortious breach of contract" or "the Mississippi law of bad faith" preempted under ERISA. The Court looked to "common-sense" to determine whether the state law was merely general in application, noting that the law applied to any insurance contract in the state and allowed for punitive damages. The court observed that the law of bad faith was "no more 'integral' to the insurer-insured relationship than any State's general contract law is integral to a contract made in that State." Finally, the law "developed from general principles of tort and contract law available in any Mississippi contract case."

However, the practice here—the disapproval of insurance forms which contain discretionary clauses—is specific to the insurance industry. The practice admittedly achieves some of the same ends as the common-law *contra proferentem* rule. It is, however, unexceptional that most state policies would further somewhat similar conceptions of the public interest. In any event, the state does not require approval of most contracts; its requirement that insurance forms be approved by the Commissioner is an expression of its special solicitude for insurance consumers. Thus, the state's bar on discretionary clauses addresses an insurance-specific problem, because discretionary clauses generally do not exist outside of insurance plans.

This view finds support in *Unum Life v. Ward,* 526 U.S. 358 (1999), which upheld California's notice-prejudice rule as falling

---

1. Furthermore, there is no evidence in the record to suggest that Morrison would allow any insurance company to issue forms containing "misleading . . . conditions which deceptively affect the risk purported to be assumed in the general coverage of the contract." Mont. Code Ann. § 33–1–502. Although the impact of the Commissioner's refusal to approve discretionary clauses is felt by the ERISA subsegment of the insurance market, his powers are part of a larger regulation of allegedly unfair and misleading practices in the insurance industry as a whole.

under the savings clause. The rule required that an insurer show substantial prejudice before denying a claim based on untimely filing. The court first looked to common sense. The Court rejected the insurer's view "that the notice-prejudice rule [was] merely an industry-specific application of the general principle that disproportionate forfeiture should be avoided in the enforcement of contracts."

Here, the Commissioner's practice forces all insurers to omit discretionary clauses. If it is an application of the general rule that contracts are interpreted against their drafters, it is clearly "an application of a special order." Furthermore, [in *Unum Life*] the Supreme Court found the "grounding" of the notice-prejudice rule "in policy concerns specific to the insurance industry" to be "key" to its decision. Likewise, Morrison's practice is grounded in policy concerns specific to the insurance industry, such as ensuring fair treatment of claims by insurers with potential conflicts of interest. It is indeed directed at insurance companies.

Turning now to the second *Kentucky Ass'n* prong, Standard asserts that the disapproval of discretionary clauses does not substantially affect the risk pooling arrangement. The requirement that insurance regulations substantially affect risk pooling ensures that the regulations are targeted at insurance practices, not merely at insurance companies. Standard argues for a definition of risk pooling that it claims is used in the insurance industry. According to such definition, risk is pooled at the time the insurance contract is made, not at the time a claim is made. "Administrative factors" such as "claim investigations, the appeals process, and litigation" can "affect amounts paid to insureds under [a] policy," but are outside of the risk pooling arrangement. We cannot accept such narrow conception, as a review of the Supreme Court's case law demonstrates that risk pooling extends to a much wider variety of circumstances than Standard's definition would suggest.

For instance, in *Kentucky Ass'n,* the state passed an "Any Willing Provider" ("AWP") statute, which forbade insurance companies from discriminating against any doctor who is willing to meet the terms and conditions of the health plan. This was enough to affect risk pooling substantially: "[b]y expanding the number of providers from whom an insured may receive health services, AWP laws alter the scope of permissible bargains between insurers and insureds.... No longer may Kentucky insureds seek insurance from a closed network of health-care providers in exchange for a lower premium."

Montana insureds may no longer agree to a discretionary clause in exchange for a more affordable premium. The scope of permissible bargains between insurers and insureds has thus narrowed. The Supreme Court has repeatedly upheld similar scope-narrowing regulations. *See, e.g., Rush Prudential* (scope of permissible bargains narrowed in that consumers could not agree to waive independent review of a medical decision); *UNUM Life* (scope narrowed in that insureds cannot reject notice-prejudice rule); *Metropolitan Life v. Massachusetts* (denying insureds the ability to accept plans without minimum mental-health coverage).

Consumers can be reasonably sure of claim acceptance only when an improperly balking insurer can be called to answer for its decision in court. By removing the benefit of a deferential standard of review from insurers, it is likely that the Commissioner's practice will lead to a greater number of claims being paid. More losses will thus be covered, increasing the benefit of risk pooling for consumers.

Standard next asserts that "[r]isk does not concern 'legal risks' borne by the insured or insurer, such as the availability of extra-contractual remedies." It may well be true that risk pooling does not contemplate damages for a bad faith breach of contract, *see Pilot Life*, or factor in the burden of contract misrepresentations. However the only risk at issue here is the risk of the insured's becoming disabled—the risk that the insurance company has contracted for, not a 'legal risk' created by state tort law or contract law. The Commissioner's practice merely alters the terms by which the presence or absence of the insured contingency is determined. It indeed affects the risk pooling arrangement.

ERISA provides an exclusive remedial scheme for insureds who have been denied benefits. 29 U.S.C. § 1132(a). An insured may sue "to recover benefits due to him under the terms of his plan, to enforce his rights under the terms of the plan, or to clarify his rights to future benefits under the terms of the plan." He may also seek an injunction or other appropriate equitable relief to enforce the provisions of ERISA or of the plan.

Standard asserts that the Commissioner's practice conflicts with this exclusive scheme. ERISA already provides several remedies for disgruntled litigants, including preliminary injunctions and restitution under 29 U.S.C. § 1132(a)(1)(B). However, only the value of the lost claim is recoverable under the statutory remedies. Here, however, there is no additional remedy. Insureds may only recover the value of the denied claim from their insurers. While it is true that the Commissioner's practice will lead to *de novo* review in federal courts, this is hardly foreign to the ERISA statute. Indeed, *de novo* review is the default standard of review in an ERISA case. *Firestone Tire*. Because the practice merely forces ERISA suits to proceed with their default standard of review, it cannot be said to "duplicate[ ]," "supplement[ ]," or "supplant[ ]" the ERISA remedy.

Finally, Standard argues that a state's forbidding discretionary clauses is inconsistent with the purpose and policy of the ERISA remedial system, which emphasizes a balance between protecting employees' right to benefits and incentivizing employers to offer benefit plans. It relies on the Supreme Court's decision in *Metropolitan Life Insurance Co. v. Glenn*, 554 U.S. 105. There, the Court rejected a call to repudiate *Firestone Tire* and instead retained the abuse-of-discretion standard (albeit tempered by consideration of the conflict), saying that it "would [not] overturn *Firestone* by adopting a rule that in practice could bring about near universal review by judges *de novo—i.e.,* without deference— of the lion's share of ERISA plan claims denials."

The Court's refusal to create a system of universal *de novo* review does not necessarily mean that states are categorically forbidden from issuing insurance regulations with such effect. The effect of disapproving discretionary clauses on ERISA plans is unclear. The *Firestone Tire* Court noted concerns "that a *de novo* standard would contravene the spirit of ERISA because it would impose much higher administrative and litigation costs and therefore discourage employers from creating benefit plans," but found them insufficient to justify a departure from a *de novo* standard where there was no discretionary clause. *Firestone Tire* and *Glenn* read together may suggest that Congress would prefer a system in which many if not most cases were reviewed for an abuse of discretion. Yet, *Firestone Tire*'s explicit acceptance of the *de novo* standard, coupled with *Glenn*'s acknowledgment that the conflict of interest could prove "of great importance" in some cases indicates that highly deferential review is not a cornerstone of the ERISA system.

Indeed, the Supreme Court has said as much. In *Rush Prudential,* the insurer argued that deferential review was a "substantive rule intended to be preserved by the system of uniform enforcement." Instead, the Court stated that it was perfectly appropriate for the state to "eliminate[ ] whatever may have remained of a plan sponsor's option to minimize scrutiny of benefit denials." In *Rush Prudential,* the state had "eliminat[ed] an insurer's autonomy to guarantee terms congenial to its own interests" by requiring an independent medical review when the patient's doctor and the HMO disagreed about medical necessity. That, however, was merely "the stuff of garden variety insurance regulation through the imposition of standard policy terms." And ensuring a level playing field for claims is at the heart of the state's power to regulate insurance: "[i]t is ... hard to imagine," said the Court, "a reservation of state power to regulate insurance that would not be meant to cover restrictions of the insurer's advantage in this kind of way."

We decline to create an additional exception from the savings clause here. Like the regulatory scheme in *Rush Prudential,* the Commissioner's practice "provides no new cause of action under state law and authorizes no new form of ultimate relief." The

Rush Prudential court emphasized that the scheme in that case "does not enlarge the claim beyond the benefits available" and does not grant relief other than "what ERISA authorizes in a suit for benefits under § 1132(a)." Neither does the Commissioner's practice.

The Commissioner's practice is directed at the elimination of insurer advantage, a goal which the Supreme Court has identified as central to any reasonable understanding of the savings clause. It creates no new substantive right, offers no additional remedy not contemplated by ERISA's remedial scheme, and institutes no decision makers or procedures foreign to ERISA. Although we acknowledge the tension between the Commissioner's practice and federal common law concerning the standard of review, we see nothing that would justify taking the extraordinary step of creating a new exclusion under the savings clause.

* * *

Consider whether the court's opinion hangs together. To do so, imagine that you are offered two health insurance plans. Written by the plan sponsor or the insurer it hires, one plan says: "We reserve the right to interpret the terms of this health insurance plan. You may bring suit under section 502 for remedies provided by ERISA but you agree that the court in which you bring suit may overrule our interpretation only if it is arbitrary and capricious." The alternative plan says: "We reserve the right to interpret the terms of this health insurance plan. You may bring suit under section 502 for remedies provided by ERISA and we agree that the court in which you bring suit will subject our interpretation to de novo review."

Are these two contracts the same? Of course not. In what respect do they differ? Isn't it one thing to execute a contract in which the insured takes on the risk that the insurer will interpret the contract in an arbitrary fashion and another thing entirely for the insurer to bear the risk of that error? Wasn't the court in *Morrison* correct that the Montana law, by prohibiting deference clauses, substantially affects the allocation and bearing of risk between the insurer and the insured? Was it likewise correct in holding that state law did not create a different remedy than that afforded by ERISA's section 502 (as interpreted by *Firestone, Glenn, Frommert* et al.)? Don't the two contracts above provide different remedies; and isn't the first one an illustration of the default under ERISA (so long as the necessary boilerplate reservation clause is included in the plan), while the second one illustrates the manner in which Montana law has rewritten the first?

We will suspend this line of questioning for now because it brings us first to *Pilot Life v. Dedeaux*, the final chapter—subject perhaps to further development by the Supreme Court—of our ERISA preemption story (at least until Part Three).

c. The Extraordinary Problem of ERISA's Complete Preemption of State Law Remedies

Pilot Life Insurance Co. v. Dedeaux

481 U.S. 41 (1987)

■ JUSTICE O'CONNOR delivered the opinion of the Court.

This case presents the question whether [ERISA] pre-empts state common law tort and contract actions asserting improper processing of a claim for benefits under an insured employee benefit plan.

In March 1975, in Gulfport, Mississippi, respondent Everate W. Dedeaux injured his back in an accident related to his employment for [Entex]. Entex had at this time a long term disability employee benefit plan established by purchasing a group insurance policy from petitioner, Pilot Life Insurance Co. (Pilot Life). Entex collected and matched its employees' contributions to the plan and forwarded those funds to Pilot Life; the employer also provided forms to its employees for processing disability claims, and forwarded completed forms to Pilot Life. Pilot Life bore the responsibility of determining who would receive disability benefits. Although Dedeaux sought permanent disability benefits following the 1975 accident, Pilot Life terminated his benefits after two years. During the following three years Dedeaux's benefits were reinstated and terminated by Pilot Life several times.

In 1980, Dedeaux instituted a diversity action against Pilot Life in the United States District Court for the Southern District of Mississippi. Dedeaux's complaint contained three counts: "Tortious Breach of Contract"; "Breach of Fiduciary Duties"; and "Fraud in the Inducement." Dedeaux sought "damages for failure to provide benefits under the insurance policy in a sum to be determined at the time of trial," "general damages for mental and emotional distress and other incidental damages in the sum of $250,000.00," and "punitive and exemplary damages in the sum of $500,000.00." Dedeaux did not assert any of the several causes of action available to him under ERISA.

At the close of discovery, Pilot Life moved for summary judgment, arguing that ERISA pre-empted Dedeaux's common law claim for failure to pay benefits on the group insurance policy. The District Court granted Pilot Life summary judgment, finding all Dedeaux's claims pre-empted. The Court of Appeals for the Fifth Circuit reversed, primarily on the basis of this Court's decision in Metropolitan Life Ins. Co. v. Massachusetts. We granted certiorari, and now reverse.

In ERISA, Congress set out to

protect participants in employee benefit plans and their beneficiaries, by requiring the disclosure and reporting to participants and beneficiaries of financial and other information with respect thereto, by establishing standards of conduct, responsibility, and obligation for fiduciaries of employee benefit plans, and by providing for appropriate remedies, sanctions, and ready access to the Federal courts.

§ 2, 29 U.S.C. § 1001(b).

ERISA comprehensively regulates, among other things, employee welfare benefit plans that, "through the purchase of insurance or otherwise," provide medical, surgical, or hospital care, or benefits in the event of sickness, accident, disability, or death. § 3(1), 29 U.S.C. § 1002(1).

Congress capped off the massive undertaking of ERISA with three provisions relating to the pre-emptive effect of the federal legislation:

> Except as provided in subsection (b) of this section [the saving clause], the provisions of this subchapter and subchapter III of this chapter shall supersede any and all State laws insofar as they may now or hereafter relate to any employee benefit plan.

§ 514(a), as set forth in 29 U.S.C. § 1144(a) (pre-emption clause).

> Except as provided in subparagraph (B) [the deemer clause], nothing in this subchapter shall be construed to exempt or relieve any person from any law of any State which regulates insurance, banking, or securities.

§ 514(b)(2)(A), as set forth in 29 U.S.C. § 1144(b)(2)(A) (saving clause).

> Neither an employee benefit plan nor any trust established under such a plan, shall be deemed to be an insurance company or other insurer, bank, trust company, or investment company or to be engaged in the business of insurance or banking for purposes of any law of any State purporting to regulate insurance companies, insurance contracts, banks, trust companies, or investment companies.

§ 514(b)(2)(B), 29 U.S.C. § 1144(b)(2)(B) (deemer clause).

To summarize the pure mechanics of the provisions quoted above: If a state law "relate[s] to employee benefit plan[s]," it is pre-empted. § 514(a). The saving clause excepts from the pre-emption clause laws that "regulat[e] insurance." § 514(b)(2)(A). The deemer clause makes clear that a state law that "purport[s] to regulate insurance" cannot deem an employee benefit plan to be an insurance company. § 514(b)(2)(B). We have observed in the past that the express pre-emption provisions of ERISA are deliberately expansive, and designed to "establish pension plan regulation as exclusively a federal concern." As we explained in *Shaw*, 463 U.S. 85 at 98:

> The bill that became ERISA originally contained a limited pre-emption clause, applicable only to state laws relating to the specific subjects covered by ERISA. The Conference Committee rejected those provisions in favor of the present language, and indicated that section's pre-emptive scope was as broad as its language." The House and Senate sponsors emphasized both the breadth and importance of the pre-emption provisions. Representative Dent described the "reservation to Federal authority [of] the sole power to regulate the field of employee benefit plans" as ERISA's

"crowning achievement." Senator Williams said: "It should be stressed that with the narrow exceptions specified in the bill, the substantive and enforcement provisions of the conference substitute are intended to preempt the field for Federal regulations, thus eliminating the threat of conflicting or inconsistent State and local regulation of employee benefit plans. This principle is intended to apply in its broadest sense to all actions of State or local governments, or any instrumentality thereof, which have the force or effect of law."

There is no dispute that the common law causes of action asserted in Dedeaux's complaint "relate to" an employee benefit plan and therefore fall under ERISA's express pre-emption clause, ERISA § 514(a). In both *Metropolitan Life* and *Shaw* we noted the expansive sweep of the pre-emption clause. In both cases "the phrase 'relate to' was given its broad common-sense meaning, such that a state law 'relate[s] to' a benefit plan 'in the normal sense of the phrase, if it has a connection with or reference to such a plan.' " [W]e have emphasized that the pre-emption clause is not limited to "state laws specifically designed to affect employee benefit plans." The common law causes of action raised in Dedeaux's complaint, each based on alleged improper processing of a claim for benefits under an employee benefit plan, undoubtedly meet the criteria for pre-emption under ERISA § 514(a). Unless these common law causes of action fall under an exception to ERISA § 514(a), therefore, they are expressly pre-empted. Dedeau[x] has described one of the counts [in his complaint]–called "tortious breach of contract" in the complaint, and "the Mississippi law of bad faith" in respondent's brief—as protected from the pre-emptive effect of ERISA § 514(a). The Mississippi law of bad faith, Dedeaux argues, is a law "which regulates insurance," and thus is saved from preemption by ERISA § 514(b)(2)(A).[1]

In *Metropolitan Life*, we were guided by several considerations in determining whether a state law falls under the saving clause. First, we took what guidance was available from a "common-sense view" of the language of the saving clause itself. Second, we made use of the case law interpreting the phrase "business of insurance" under the McCarran–Ferguson Act, 15 U.S.C. § 1011 et seq., in interpreting the saving clause. Three criteria have been used to determine whether a practice falls under the "business of insurance" for purposes of the McCarran–Ferguson Act:

> First, whether the practice has the effect of transferring or spreading a policyholder's risk; second, whether the practice is an integral part of the policy relationship between the insurer and the insured; and third, whether the practice is limited to entities within the insurance industry.

---

1. Decisional law that "regulates insurance" may fall under the saving clause. The saving clause, ERISA § 514(b)(2)(A), covers "any law of any State." For purposes of ERISA § 514, "the term 'State law' includes all laws, decisions, rules, regulations, or other State action having the effect of law, of any State." 29 U.S.C. § 1144(c)(1),(2).

Union Labor Life Ins. Co. v. Pireno, 458 U.S. 119. In the present case, the considerations weighed in *Metropolitan Life* argue against the assertion that the Mississippi law of bad faith is a state law that "regulates insurance."

As early as 1915 the Mississippi Supreme Court had recognized that punitive damages were available in a contract case when "the act or omission constituting the breach of the contract amounts also to the commission of a tort." See Hood v. Moffett (1915) (involving a physician's breach of a contract to attend to a woman at her approaching "accouchement"). In American Railway Express Co. v. Bailey, a case involving a failure of a finance company to deliver to the plaintiff the correct amount of money cabled to the plaintiff through the finance company's offices, the Mississippi Supreme Court explained that punitive damages could be available when the breach of contract was "attended by some intentional wrong, insult, abuse, or gross negligence, which amounts to an independent tort." In Standard Life Insurance Co. of Indiana v. Veal, 354 So.2d 239 (1977), the Mississippi Supreme Court upheld an award of punitive damages against a defendant insurance company for failure to pay on a credit life policy. Since *Veal*, the Mississippi Supreme Court has considered a large number of cases in which plaintiffs have sought punitive damages from insurance companies for failure to pay a claim under an insurance contract, and in a great many of these cases the court has used the identical formulation, first stated in *Bailey*, of what must "attend" the breach of contract in order for punitive damages to be recoverable. Recently the Mississippi Supreme Court stated that "we have come to term an insurance carrier which refuses to pay a claim when there is no reasonably arguable basis to deny it as acting in 'bad faith,' and a lawsuit based upon such an arbitrary refusal as a 'bad faith' cause of action." Blue Cross & Blue Shield of Mississippi, Inc. v. Campbell, 466 So.2d 833, 842 (1984).

Certainly a common-sense understanding of the phrase "regulates insurance" does not support the argument that the Mississippi law of bad faith falls under the saving clause. A common-sense view of the word "regulates" would lead to the conclusion that in order to regulate insurance, a law must not just have an impact on the insurance industry, but must be specifically directed toward that industry. Even though the Mississippi Supreme Court has identified its law of bad faith with the insurance industry, the roots of this law are firmly planted in the general principles of Mississippi tort and contract law. Any breach of contract, and not merely breach of an insurance contract, may lead to liability for punitive damages under Mississippi law.

Neither do the McCarran–Ferguson Act factors support the assertion that the Mississippi law of bad faith "regulates insurance." Unlike the mandated-benefits law at issue in *Metropolitan Life*, the Mississippi common law of bad faith does not effect a spreading of policyholder risk. The state common law of bad faith may be said to concern "the policy relationship between the insurer and the insured." The connection to the insurer-insured relationship is attenuated at best, however. In contrast to the mandated benefits law in *Metropolitan Life*, the common law of bad faith does not define the terms of the relationship between the insurer and the insured; it declares only that, whatever terms have been agreed upon in the insurance contract, a breach of that contract may in certain circumstances allow the policyholder to obtain punitive damages. The state common law of bad faith is therefore no more "integral" to the insurer-insured relationship than any State's general contract law is integral to a contract made in that State.

Finally, Mississippi's law of bad faith, even if associated with the insurance industry, has developed from general principles of tort and contract law available in any Mississippi breach of contract case. Cf. Hart v. Orion Ins. Co., 453 F.2d 1358 (CA10 1971) (general state arbitration statutes do not regulate the business of insurance under the McCarran–Ferguson Act). Accordingly, the Mississippi common law of bad faith at most meets one of the three criteria used to identify the "business of insurance" under the McCarran–Ferguson Act, and used in *Metropolitan Life* to identify laws that "regulat[e] insurance" under the saving clause.

In the present case, moreover, we are obliged in interpreting the saving clause to consider not only the factors by which we were guided in *Metropolitan Life*, but also the role of the saving clause in ERISA as a whole. On numerous occasions we have noted that "in expounding a statute, we must not be guided by a single sentence or member of a sentence, but look to the provisions of the whole law, and to its object and policy." Because in this case, the state cause of action seeks remedies for the improper processing of a claim for benefits under an ERISA-regulated plan, our understanding of the saving clause must be informed by the legislative intent concerning the civil enforcement provisions provided by ERISA § 502(a), 29 U.S.C. § 1132(a).

The Solicitor General, for the United States as amicus curiae, argues that Congress clearly expressed an intent that the civil enforcement provisions of ERISA § 502(a) be the exclusive vehicle for actions by ERISA-plan participants and beneficiaries asserting improper processing of a claim for benefits, and that varying state causes of action for claims within the scope of ERISA § 502(a) would pose an obstacle to the purposes and objectives of Congress. We agree. The conclusion that ERISA § 502(a) was intended to be exclusive is supported, first, by the language and structure of the civil enforcement provisions, and second, by legislative history in which Congress declared that the preemptive force of ERISA § 502(a) was modeled on the exclusive remedy provided by the Labor Management Relations Act of 1947 § 301 (LMRA), 29 U.S.C. § 185.

The civil enforcement scheme of ERISA § 502(a) is one of the essential tools for accomplishing the stated purposes of ERISA. Under the civil enforcement provisions of ERISA § 502(a), a plan participant or beneficiary may sue to recover benefits due under the plan, to enforce the participant's rights under the plan, or to clarify rights to future benefits. Relief may take the form of accrued benefits due, a declaratory judgment on entitlement to benefits, or an injunction against a plan administrator's improper refusal to pay benefits. A participant or beneficiary may also bring a cause of action for breach of fiduciary duty, and under this cause of action may seek removal of the fiduciary. ERISA § 502(a)(2), 409. In an action under these civil enforcement provisions, the court in its discretion may allow an award of attorney's fees to either party. Section 502(g). See *Massachusetts Mutual Life Ins. Co. v. Russell*, 473 U.S. 134 at 147. In *Russell*, we concluded that ERISA's breach of fiduciary duty provision, ERISA § 409(a), 29 U.S.C. § 1109(a), provided no express authority for an award of punitive damages to a beneficiary. Moreover, we declined to find an implied cause of action for punitive damages in that section, noting that " 'the presumption that a remedy was deliberately omitted from a statute is strongest when Congress has enacted a comprehensive legislative scheme including an integrated system of procedures for enforcement.' "

In sum, the detailed provisions of ERISA § 502(a) set forth a comprehensive civil enforcement scheme that represents a careful balancing of the need for prompt and fair claims settlement procedures against the public interest in encouraging the formation of employee benefit plans. The policy choices reflected in the inclusion of certain remedies and the exclusion of others under the federal scheme would be completely undermined if ERISA-plan participants and beneficiaries were free to obtain remedies under state law that Congress rejected in ERISA. "The six carefully integrated civil enforcement provisions found in § 502(a) of the statute as finally enacted provide strong evidence that Congress did not intend to authorize other remedies that it simply forgot to incorporate expressly."

The deliberate care with which ERISA's civil enforcement remedies were drafted and the balancing of policies embodied in its choice of remedies argue strongly for the conclusion that ERISA's civil enforcement remedies were intended to be exclusive. This conclusion is fully confirmed by the legislative history of the civil enforcement provision. The legislative history demonstrates that the pre-emptive force of § 502(a) was modeled after § 301 of the LMRA [Labor–Management Relations Act of 1947].

The Conference Report on ERISA describing the civil enforcement provisions of § 502(a) says:

> Under the conference agreement, civil actions may be brought by a participant or beneficiary to recover benefits due under the plan, to clarify rights to receive future benefits under the plan, and for relief from breach of fiduciary responsibility. With respect to suits to enforce benefit rights under the plan or to recover benefits under the plan which do not involve application of the title I provisions, they may be brought not only in U.S. district courts but also in State courts of competent jurisdiction. All such actions in Federal or State courts are to be regarded as arising under the laws of the United States in similar fashion to those brought under section 301 of the Labor–Management Relations Act of 1947.

H. R. Conf. Rep. No. 93–1280, at 327 (1974).

Congress was well aware that the powerful pre-emptive force of § 301 of the LMRA displaced all state actions for violation of contracts between an employer and a labor organization, even when the state action purported to authorize a remedy unavailable under the federal provision. Section 301 pre-empts any "state-law claim [whose resolution] is substantially dependent upon the analysis of the terms of an agreement made between the parties in a labor contract." Allis–Chalmers Corp. v. Lueck, 471 U.S. 202 at 220 (1985). Indeed, for purposes of determining federal jurisdiction, this Court has singled out § 301 of the LMRA as having "pre-emptive force so powerful as to displace entirely any state cause of action 'for violation of contracts between an employer and a labor organization.' Any such suit is purely a creature of federal law." Franchise Tax Board of Cal. v. Construction Laborers Vacation Trust for Southern Cal., 463 U.S. 1, 23 (1983).

Congress' specific reference to § 301 of the LMRA to describe the civil enforcement scheme of ERISA makes clear its intention that all suits brought by beneficiaries or participants asserting improper processing of claims under ERISA-regulated plans be treated as federal questions governed by § 502(a). The expectations that a federal common law of rights and obligations under ERISA-regulated plans would develop, indeed, the entire comparison of ERISA's § 502(a) to § 301 of the LMRA, would make little sense if the remedies available to ERISA participants and beneficiaries under § 502(a) could be supplemented or supplanted by varying state laws.

In *Metropolitan Life Ins. Co. v. Massachusetts*, 471 U.S. 724, this Court rejected an interpretation of the saving clause of ERISA's express preemption provisions, § 514(b)(2)(A), 29 U.S.C. § 1144(b)(2)(A), that saved from pre-emption "only state regulations unrelated to the substantive provisions of ERISA," finding that "nothing in the language, structure, or legislative history of the Act" supported this reading of the saving clause. *Metropolitan Life*, however, did not involve a state law that conflicted with a substantive provision of ERISA. Therefore the Court's general observation—that state laws related to ERISA may also fall under the saving clause—was not focused on any particular relationship or conflict between a substantive provision of ERISA and a state law. In particular, the Court had no occasion to consider in Metropolitan Life the question raised in the present case: whether Congress might clearly express, through the structure and legislative history of a particular substantive provision of ERISA, an intention that the federal remedy provided by that provision displaces state causes of action. Our resolution of this different question does not conflict with the Court's earlier general observations in *Metropolitan Life*. Considering the common-sense understanding of the saving clause, the McCarran–Ferguson Act factors defining the business of insurance, and, most importantly, the clear expression of congressional intent that ERISA's civil enforcement scheme be exclusive, we conclude that Dedeaux's state law suit asserting improper processing of a claim for benefits under an ERISA-regulated plan is not saved by § 514(b)(2)(A), and therefore is preempted by § 514(a). Accordingly, the judgment of the Court of Appeals is reversed.

Notes

1. Pilot Life's *impact.* The matter-of-fact tone that characterizes Justice O'Connor's decision certainly seems at odds with its reach. Its impact is to set aside state laws that provide remedies for injuries when the injury can be traced to the negligence or willful misconduct of an ERISA plan administrator, whether an insurer or a company acting as a third-party administrator of a self-insured plan. Because the decision ultimately turns on the exclusivity of ERISA § 502 remedies rather than on a § 514 preemption analysis, the distinction between insured and self-insured plans falls away. State remedies cannot be saved; instead, they are completely preempted by the power of ERISA § 502. Lower court decisions leading up to the Court's ruling, including that of the Fifth Circuit, held for the plaintiffs. In these cases the courts analyzed the problem as one arising under § 514. While Justice O'Connor dutifully sets out a § 514 preemption and saving clause analysis to demonstrate why the law relates to ERISA plans and cannot be saved, the real power of the court's holding is in her final, almost offhand conclusion that whatever one thinks of her § 514 handiwork, it is the power of § 502 that closes the deal for the Court. You will see this same analysis play out again in *Aetna v. Davila,* reviewed in Part Three. Perhaps all or most of her statements concerning the scope of both the "relate-to" clause, see *Travelers* above, and the saving clause, see *Kentucky Association of Health Plans, Inc. v. Miller,* above, have not stood the test of time, it is the grounding of preemption in the allegedly exclusive remedies of section 502 that packs a wallop.

2. *Limiting the scope of § 502.* And what a punch it is! When a claim under state law is brought against a plan administrator (whether an insurer or a company acting as a third-party administrator), defendant tries to set up the preclusive effect of § 502 by arguing that the claim *arises under* ERISA. Often the attempt is a one-two punch: removal of a case from state to federal court, and if defendant gets a knockout, a holding that ERISA provides the sole remedy and therefore preempts state law causes of action. As you will see in Part Three, there are cases in which the federal court will reject a removal attempt on the grounds that preemption, if it exists at all, is simply a defense to a legitimate claim arising under state law (e.g., medical or institutional negligence), in which event, the court tosses the case back to state court for further proceedings. ERISA preemption of the state law claim still may be a viable although potentially losing, defense. *See e.g.,* Pappas v. Asbel, 724 A.2d 889 (Pa. 1998), vacated and remanded, 530 U.S. 1241 (2000), *aff'd on remand,* 768 A.2d 1089 (Pa. 2001) (discussed in Part Three). You will see that over time the law has pulled its punches on ERISA § 514 field preemption claims, but as you will learn in Part Three, complete preemption of state law remedies when claims are determined to arise under ERISA itself is still the firmly entrenched doctrine. But as you will learn in *Dukes v. U.S. Healthcare* in Part Three and accompanying materials, certain types of claims based on the quality of care are considered not to arise under ERISA § 502.

Claims by health care providers seeking damages for breach of contract have been found not to arise under § 502. In Franciscan Skemp Healthcare, Inc. v. Central States Joint Bd. Health and Welfare Trust Fund, 538 F.3d 594 (7th Cir. 2008), a hospital sued an employee benefit plan in state court alleging negligence and estoppel in connection with a claim submitted for the care of a patient. The plan had confirmed the patient's participant status over the telephone at the time of admission, only later to deny the claim once submitted, on the ground that the patient had failed to pay her COBRA benefit continuation premiums and thus had lost her coverage. Reversing a dismissal by the lower court on § 502 grounds, the Court of Appeals for the Seventh Circuit concluded that the exclusivity of the ERISA remedy and the doctrine of complete preemption does not reach cases such as this one:

> Complete preemption, really a jurisdictional rather than a preemption doctrine, confers exclusive federal jurisdiction in certain instances where Congress intended the scope of a federal law to be so broad as to entirely replace any state-law claim. Of course the difficulty arises in drawing the line between what is completely preempted and what escapes the cast of the federal net. The Supreme Court in [Aetna Health Inc. v. Davila, 542 U.S. 200 (2004)] used a two-part analysis for determining when a claim has been completely preempted by ERISA:

> [I]f an individual brings suit complaining of a denial of coverage for medical care, where the individual is entitled to such coverage only because of the terms of an ERISA-regulated employee benefit plan, and where no legal duty (state or federal) independent of ERISA or the plan terms is violated, then the suit falls "within the scope of" ERISA § 502(a)(1)(B). . . . In other words, if an individual, at some point in time, could have brought his claim under ERISA § 502(a)(1)(B), and where there is no other independent legal duty that is implicated by a defendant's actions, then the individual's cause of action is completely pre-empted by ERISA § 502(a)(1)(B).

> Under the district court's and Central States's reasoning, Franciscan Skemp could have brought its state-law claims of negligent misrepresentation and estoppel under ERISA § 502(a)(1)(B). Franciscan Skemp took an assignment of benefits from Romine and filed a claim form with Central States. Franciscan Skemp requested that Central States be estopped from denying coverage benefits for the Romine medical services and that a judgment [be entered] against defendant for the services provided by Franciscan Skemp as would otherwise be covered by defendant's plan. The district court found that "[t]hese requests establish that the gravamen of plaintiff's cause of action is a desire to recover benefits it believes are due to it under the terms of the Plan."

What the district court and Central States too easily overlook, however, is that Franciscan Skemp is not bringing these claims as Romine's assignee. Franciscan Skemp is bringing these claims of negligent misrepresentation and estoppel, not as Romine's assignee, but entirely in its own right. These claims arise not from the plan or its terms, but from the alleged oral representations made by Central States to Franciscan Skemp. Franciscan Skemp *could* bring ERISA claims in Romine's shoes as a beneficiary for the denial of benefits under the plan; but it has not. In fact, Franciscan Skemp does not at all dispute Central States' decision to deny Romine coverage. Franciscan Skemp acknowledges that Romine is not entitled to benefits, because she failed to make her COBRA premium payments. Franciscan Skemp is bringing its own independent claims, and these claims are simply not claims to "enforce the rights under the terms of the plan." ERISA § 502(a)(1)(B).

See also Marin General Hospital v. Modesto and Empire Traction, 581 F.3d 941 (9th Cir. 2009) (hospital's claims for breach of contract, negligent misrepresentation, *quantum meruit*, and estoppel against a health plan that negligently failed to pay according to its agreement with the hospital not completely preempted by ERISA § 502, even though the claim for payment itself arose under ERISA § 502 on an assignment of the claim from the patient).

Cases like *Skemp* should not be confused with the Med's claim in the *Majestic* case earlier. In the *Majestic*, the hospital was standing in the participant's shoes, having taken an assignment of the claim and suing for benefits. In *Skemp* on the other hand, the claim, while triggered by the provision of a covered benefit to a participant, was not a claim for benefits within the meaning of ERISA § 502. Instead it was a state law claim challenging the breach of the underlying deal between the plan and the provider regarding the provider's participation in the plan's network.

3. *The continued viability of separate, two-track preemption under ERISA sections 502 and 514.* Return to the discussion in the notes following *Morrison*. The court was right that Montana's law prohibiting the enforcement of discretionary clauses affects the manner in which an insurance contract allocates risk. It was therefore correct in following *Miller* because the Montana law substantially affects the risk pooling arrangement between the insured and insurer; and in *Morrison*, since the regulatory scheme was administered by the Montana Commissioner of Insurance, the law was specifically directed toward entities engaged in insurance. That means the law was properly saved under ERISA's saving clause, as reinterpreted by *Miller*.

However, what about *Pilot Life*? The court in *Morrison* earnestly tried to find that the Montana law didn't change, alter, deviate from, supplement ERISA's remedial scheme, but the simple fact of the matter is that it did, at least if one concedes that altering the judicial standard of review goes to the heart of any remedy. As you've seen from the cases under ERISA, for the most part, determination of the standard of review is outcome-determinative. Thus, a cause of action under a reservation clause is very different than a cause of action in which the court will exercise de novo review—like, plaintiff has a chance! In the end, the *Morrison* court understood the dilemma but opined, "Although we acknowledge the tension between the Commissioner's practice and federal common law concerning the standard of review, we see nothing that would justify taking the extraordinary step of creating a new exclusion under the savings clause."

Yet, as we have seen, that is precisely what *Pilot Life* and its progeny have wrought: they "[took] the extraordinary step of creating a new exclusion under the savings clause." A state law, like Montana's aimed at discretionary clauses, might satisfy the criteria needed for inclusion in section 514's saving clause but nonetheless are completely preempted by section 502. That is simply the meaning of "complete preemption."

What has changed from *Pilot Life*, however, is that section 514 has gone in a new direction. With *Shaw* the Court started with a literalness standard that admitted of practically no boundary, and with *Met Life*, as the Court there noted, potentially what was taken away from the states in one subsection was seemingly given back to them with the following subsection. The Court deadpanned, "While Congress occasionally decides to return to the States what it has previously taken away, it does not normally do both at the same time."

As we've seen, first in *Travelers* and then in *Miller*, the Court understood that section 514 jurisprudence had gotten off on the wrong foot and it began to make the necessary adjustments. While the Court in *Travelers* refused to cut back the scope of the "relates to" clause to the core ERISA functions of regulating eligibility, funding, solvency, administration, disclosure, vesting and reporting—given the legislative history, related in the cases, it could not—at the same time it recognized that the literalness test set forth in *Shaw* had to be abandoned, and so it returned section 514 to a balance between state and federal power.

Miller likewise understood that a different kind of literalness test, embodied in the ERISA version of the three McCarran–Ferguson factors, was not workable. This literalness test focused on "the policy" and the entities "engaged in the business of insurance." It presupposed that in health care we could literally know what "the policy" consist of and who engages in "health insurance," and then we could construe the saving clause to preserve state power over anything that targets "the policy" and who engages in "health insurance."

However, as we began to develop in the notes following *Mondry* (and we warned that the issue would plague ERISA preemption), with regard to health insurance, identifying "the plan" is a messy endeavor given that health insurance consists of countless claims involving a vast array of services for patients who vary in number as do the stars in the sky. "The plan" consists of some rights and obligations reflected in some documents executed between or among some cast of characters. In modern health care, "the plan" consists of a multitude of documents executed among a horde of different entities involved in the finance and delivery of health care. Thus, use of the McCarran–Ferguson factors was as indeterminate as *Shaw's* literalness standard, with the result, puzzled over by the Court in *Met Life*, that under these twin interpretations, Congress had seemingly given back what it had taken away at the same time, and the only clause of significance in section 514 would be the deemer clause, a result that is absurd because if Congress wished only to preempt the application of state law to self-insured ERISA plans, it could have used language much more direct than the convoluted text of section 514.

For that reason, the Court in *Miller*, with regard to the saving clause, took action similar to what the Court had done in *Travelers* with regard to the "relate-to" clause, it went functional. The functions of insurance—as opposed to the specialized meaning of the "business of insurance" for the McCarran–Ferguson Act—consist of designing the plan's benefit scheme, calculating the premium, assembling and credentialing the network, negotiating a series of "downstreaming" risk agreements through "provider incentive" arrangements, handling disputes and appeals, running the claims payment system, overseeing internal quality controls, and so forth. These are all insurance functions because they all affect the basis of insurance—the pooling of defined risks for the payment of a set premium.

However, if that is our understanding of the power left to the states—absent a strong showing that, in accordance with *Travelers*, the application of state law will wreak havoc on national uniformity (which doesn't exist, by the way, whether or not state law is applied)—or will mandate plan structure or administration, such as with Maryland's Wal–Mart law, then how can *Pilot Life* survive? Viewed purely as an ERISA preemption question under section 514, as now interpreted by *Travelers* and *Miller*, it cannot. An insurance contract that allows for punitive damages for bad faith breach is certainly a different animal than one that does not; and if states force the rewriting of "the plan" to allow for such a remedy, then the insurer certainly bears a different risk—risk of error exists in interpretation and application of all legal documents—if it is subject to exposure to penal damages than if it is not.

The question then becomes whether complete preemption under section 502 can stand on its own while section 514 is interpreted in such a functional manner. You will see in *Aetna v Davila*, Part Three, that the Court's definite direction is to treat state laws that create damage remedies as completely preempted by section 502. The Court goes to great lengths to separate section 514 preemption from section 502's complete preemption of state remedies when the state remedy involves damages from injuries, regardless of the clash that this separation sets up with ERISA section 514 preemption cases that save state laws that directly affect the judicial process itself by altering the standard of review or, as in Rush Prudential HMO v. Moran, 536 U.S. 355 (2002), by giving claimants access to independent external reviews of insurers' medical necessity decisions (now, as previously noted, required under federal law as a result of the Affordable Care Act).

One might speculate that the Court in *Miller* understood that a holding which cut the saving clause adrift from its anchor to "entities engaged in insurance" would have forced the Court to overrule *Pilot Life* and its progeny (and we will see many more in Part Three). Moreover, such a holding would require abandoning the distinction, embedded in much precedent including *Pilot Life*, between laws of general applicability and laws "specifically directed toward entities in the insurance industry." If the Court was not ready to overrule these two lines of cases, then it tied the ship back to that anchor, which, as we've seen, is completely unworkable and totally inconsistent with the other part of the two-part test the Court in *Miller* created.

So, we must return to the question: as a matter of the structural integrity of the entire ERISA statute, can *Pilot Life* stand alone, even with all of the bolstering that the Court has attempted to provide through subsequent decisions? (As a blatant political decision, of course it can stand alone). If section 514 now stands for the proposition that Congress meant to respect state authority in areas states have traditionally regulated absent a strong countervailing need to preserve national uniformity or to protect ERISA settlors' fundamental right to design the benefit plans they offer to their employees, then can complete preemption of remedies be consistent with that understanding of congressional intent? In *UNUM*, discussed in many of the cases we've read here, the Solicitor General invited the Court to consider whether section 502 preempts remedies created by state laws that are saved under section 514. *See* 526 U.S. at 376–77. The Court in *UNUM* found that it could decide the case before it without resolving that issue. *See id.* at 377. Do you think that this question deserves a look when it is properly presented, particularly in light of the evolution of cases under section 514? In *Davila,* Part Three, you will see that the Court decided not to take the Solicitor General up on his invitation. At the same time, the *Amara* decision discussed earlier in this Part suggests that perhaps the Court has decided to slowly begin to move in a different direction, recognizing monetary relief directly under ERISA itself, at least in certain circumstances, as yet to be enunciated.

Note: Enforcing Federal Insurance Protections in the Non–ERISA Group and Individual Health Insurance Markets

As noted at the beginning of this chapter, ERISA exempts public employee health benefit plans and does not apply to the individual health insurance market. Instead, a separate body of federal law, codified in the Public Health Service Act, regulates state and local governmental group health plans as well as individual insurers. (Separate federal laws govern health plans covering federal civilian and military employees and their dependents).

The Health Insurance Portability and Accountability Act, discussed in Chapter 6, amended ERISA while also establishing new standards as part of the Public Health Service Act, thereby reaching insurers operating in the non-ERISA group market (e.g., public employer-sponsored plans) as well as, in some cases, the individual market. HIPAA represented Congress' initial legislative foray into the state-regulated insurance market, a notable limitation on Congress' earlier ceding of power to regulate insurers to the states under the McCarran–Ferguson Act. The Affordable Care Act essentially builds on this breakthrough HIPAA legal architecture, strengthening standards for group health plans in both the ERISA and non-ERISA public employee markets and establishing a far tougher regulatory framework for the state-regulated individual insurance market. The most far-reaching reforms—i.e., those pertaining to non-discrimination against people based on their pre-existing conditions or high health care costs—become effective on January 1, 2014, when the individual mandate takes effect.

In the meantime, however, important protections are already in place, including the ban on rescissions, coverage of young adults up to age 26, external appeals and patient protections such as coverage for out-of-network emergency care. (See discussion in Chapter 6). The ACA provisions essentially extend the HIPAA legal architecture, while strengthening it.

How do individuals enforce these protections? As you have seen in the case of ERISA, the law creates an express (albeit narrow) federal right of action to enforce a claim for benefits in court. This existence of an express right of action, an issue that will be revisited in the context of Medicaid, has grown increasingly important because of the Supreme Court's unwillingness to imply a federal right of action when none is expressly conferred by Congress. Alexander v. Sandoval, 532 U.S. 275 (2000); *see* Sara Rosenbaum & Joel Teitelbaum, *Civil Rights Enforcement in the Modern Healthcare System: Reinvigorating the Role of the Federal Government in the Aftermath of* Alexander v. Sandoval, 3 YALE J. OF HEALTH L. & POL'Y 215 (2003).

Courts that have considered cases brought against insurers to enforce Public Health Service Act protections uniformly have rejected arguments for the existence of either an express or implied federal right of action under the Public Health Service Act. In these decisions, courts have emphasized that unlike ERISA, the Public Health Service Act contains no preemption statute that supersedes state remedial laws of general applicability (including general remedies for tortuous breach of contract), nor does the Public Health Service Act confer *any* federal private right of action, much less one, like ERISA § 502, that might operate to the exclusion of state law remedies.

The Public Health Service Act's preemption statute, PHSA § 2724, 42 U.S.C. § 300gg–23(a), provides in pertinent part as follows:

> CONTINUED APPLICABILITY OF STATE LAW WITH RESPECT TO HEALTH INSURANCE ISSUERS (1) In general Subject to paragraph (2) [relating to ERISA plans] and except as provided in subsection (b) of this section [establishing special rules for state portability statutes], this part . . . shall not be construed to supersede any provision of State law which establishes, implements, or continues in effect any standard or requirement solely relating to health insurance issuers

in connection with group health insurance coverage except to the extent that such standard or requirement prevents the application of a requirement of this part.

Under this statute, the question in the context of state remedies becomes when does a state law "prevent the application of a requirement" of the Public Health Service Act? In O'Donnell v. Blue Cross Blue Shield of Wyoming, 173 F. Supp.2d 1176 (D. Wyo. 2001), a federal court dismissed for lack of subject matter jurisdiction plaintiff's claim against his Blue Cross plan for failing to honor a claim of coverage, the basis of which was the insurer's alleged violation of HIPAA's limited bar against the use of pre-existing condition clauses. In dismissing the federal claim the court found that the Public Health Service Act, as amended by HIPAA, created no federal right of action, nor could one be implied. At the same time, the court observed that nothing in the Act precluded any private right of action that a plaintiff might have under state law for bad faith breach of contract, since a state law remedy would not prevent the application of PHSA standards. A similar conclusion was reached in Brock v. Provident America Insurance Co., 144 F. Supp.2d 652 (N.D. Tex. 2001), in which an insurer similarly attempted to remove to federal court and dismiss a state law claim for bad faith breach of contract, in connection with the non-renewal of a coverage policy.

Under the Public Health Service Act the only entities empowered to enforce federal standards are the states and the federal government. PHSA § 2722, 42 U.S.C. § 300gg–22 underscores the primacy of state enforcement, while at the same time granting the Secretary of HHS unique powers in the event of state inaction:

> STATE ENFORCEMENT. (1) State authority. Subject to section 300gg–23 of this title, each State may require that health insurance issuers that issue, sell, renew, or offer health insurance coverage in the State in the small or large group markets meet the requirements of this part with respect to such issuers. (2) Failure to implement provisions. In the case of a determination by the Secretary that a State has failed to substantially enforce a provision (or provisions) in this part with respect to health insurance issuers in the State, the Secretary shall enforce such provision (or provisions) under subsection (b) of this section insofar as they relate to the issuance, sale, renewal, and offering of health insurance coverage in connection with group health plans in such State.

This power on the part of the Secretary to step into the breach where state inaction is determined (such a determination never has been made) formed the basis of the Affordable Care Act's state health insurance Exchange provisions, which in a similar manner, direct the Secretary to establish a federal exchange in the event that a state elects not to proceed or is unable to meet the Exchange establishment deadlines. 42 U.S.C. § 18041, added by PPACA § 1321. As of July, 2011, 13 states had enacted legislation authorizing the establishment of an Exchange, while about the same number had taken at least initial steps toward authorizing Exchange establishment. Kaiser Family Foundation, *Establishing Health Insurance Exchanges: An Update on State Efforts* (2011), http://www.kff.org/health reform/upload/8213.pdf. The litigation over the constitutionality of the Affordable Care Act, reviewed at the end of this Part, no doubt has cast a pall on the speed at which states are willing to crank up their considerable responsibilities in the ACA implementation machinery process. Unless states speed up the rate at which Exchange authorities are enacted and come online, the federal government could find itself administering Exchanges in the majority of states in 2014, including oversight of insurers' adherence to federal health insurance market reforms, compliance with which is a condition of participation in an Exchange. *See, e.g.*, Robert Pear, *Many States Take a Wait-and-See Approach on New Insurance Exchanges*, N.Y. TIMES, Feb. 27, 2012, at A11.

CHAPTER 9

PRIVATE HEALTH INSURANCE AND COVERAGE DISCRIMINATION

1. INTRODUCTION

Federal civil rights laws prohibit discrimination on the basis of numerous factors, including race, national origin, disability, gender, and age. 42 U.S.C. § 2000e et seq. (race, national origin, and sex); 29 U.S.C. § 794 (handicap in federally assisted programs); 42 U.S.C. § 12101 et seq. (disability); and 29 U.S.C. § 621 et seq. (age). Discrimination in employment is understood to encompass not only hiring, promotions, wages, and the like, but other "conditions of employment," which includes health benefits. See, e.g., 42 U.S.C. § 2000e–2(a) (prohibiting discrimination on the basis of race, sex or national origin). Many states have enacted laws that parallel these federal prohibitions.

A number of states have addressed discrimination based on sexual orientation through laws aimed at conferring spousal rights on members of same-sex couples. These laws have implications for access to employer-sponsored benefits for spouses. As of July, 2011, six states (New York, Connecticut, Iowa, Massachusetts, New Hampshire, and Vermont) and the District of Columbia extend marriage licenses to same sex couples. In addition, eight states (Delaware, California, Hawaii, Illinois, Nevada, New Jersey, Oregon and Washington State) have enacted civil union or domestic partnership laws that provide spousal rights to same sex couples. The question of whether ERISA would preempt a state law recognizing spousal rights in same sex couples for purposes of health and welfare benefit eligibility has not been addressed. Society for Human Resource Management, *Equal Benefits Gain Ground*, 56(6) HR MAGAZINE (Summer 2011), http://www.shrm.org/Publications/hrmagazine/EditorialContent/2011/0611/Pages/0611heylman.aspx. The Bureau of Labor Statistics reports that approximately one third of all workers have access to health care benefits for same-sex partners. Sabrina Tavernise, *Access to Health Care Benefits for Gay Partners is Gauged*, N.Y. TIMES (July 27, 2011), at A12.

2.   THE AMERICANS WITH DISABILITIES ACT

Equal Employment Opportunity Commission Interim Enforcement Guidance on the Application of the Americans With Disabilities Act of 1990 to Disability–Based Distinctions in Employer Provided Health Insurance

No. 915.002, June 28, 1993, (http://www.eeoc.gov/policy/docs/health.html)

This interim enforcement guidance sets forth the Commission's position on the application of the Americans with Disabilities Act to disability-based distinctions in employer provided health insurance.

I.   INTRODUCTION

The interplay between the nondiscrimination principles of the ADA and employer provided health insurance, which is predicated on the ability to make health-related distinctions, is both unique and complex. This interplay is, undoubtedly, most complex when a health insurance plan contains distinctions that are based on disability. The purpose of this interim guidance is to assist Commission investigators in analyzing ADA charges which allege that a disability-based distinction in the terms or provisions of an employer provided health insurance plan violates the ADA.

II.   BACKGROUND AND LEGAL FRAMEWORK

The ADA provides that it is unlawful for an employer to discriminate on the basis of disability against a qualified individual with a disability in regard to "job application procedures, the hiring, advancement, or discharge of employees, employee compensation, job training, and other terms, conditions, and privileges of employment." 42 U.S.C. § 12112(a). Section 1630.4 of the Commission's regulations implementing the employment provisions of the ADA further provides, in pertinent part, that it is unlawful for an employer to discriminate on the basis of disability against a qualified individual with a disability in regard to "[f]ringe benefits available by virtue of employment, whether or not administered by the [employer]." 29 C.F.R. § 1630.4(f). Employee benefit plans, including health insurance plans provided by an employer to its employees, are a fringe benefit available by virtue of employment. Generally speaking, therefore, the ADA prohibits employers from discriminating on the basis of disability in the provision of health insurance to their employees.

The ADA also prohibits employers from indirectly discriminating on the basis of disability in the provision of health insurance. Employers may not enter into, or participate in, a contractual or other arrangement or relationship that has the effect of discriminating against their own qualified applicants or employees with disabilities. 42 U.S.C. § 12112(b)(2); 29 C.F.R. § 1630.6(a). Contractual or other relationships with organizations that provide fringe benefits to employees are expressly included in this prohibition. 42 U.S.C. § 12112(b)(2); 29 C.F.R. § 1630.6(b). This means that an employer will be liable for any discrimination resulting from a contract or agreement with an insurance company, health maintenance organization (HMO), third party administrator (TPA), stop-loss carrier, or other organization to provide or administer a health insurance plan on behalf of its employees.

Another provision of the ADA makes it unlawful for an employer to limit, segregate, or classify an applicant or employee in a way that adversely affects his or her employment opportunities or status on the basis of disability. 42 U.S.C. § 12112(b)(1); 29 C.F.R. § 1630.5. Both the legislative history and the interpretive Appendix to the regulations indicate that this prohibition applies to employer provided health insurance. Appendix to 29 C.F.R. § 1630.5.

[E]mployees with disabilities must be accorded "equal access" to whatever health insurance the employer provides to employees without disabilities. See Appendix to 29 C.F.R. § 1630.16(f).

III. DISABILITY–BASED DISTINCTIONS

A. Framework of Analysis

Whenever it is alleged that a health-related term or provision of an employer provided health insurance plan violates the ADA, the first issue is whether the challenged term or provision is, in fact, a disability-based distinction. If the Commission determines that a challenged health insurance plan term or provision is a disability-based distinction, the respondent will be required to prove that that disability-based distinction is within the protective ambit of § 501(c) of the ADA.

In pertinent part, § 501(c) permits employers, insurers, and plan administrators to establish and/or observe the terms of an insured health insurance plan that is "bona fide," based on "underwriting risks, classifying risks, or administering such risks that are based on or not inconsistent with State law," and that is not being used as a "subterfuge" to evade the purposes of the ADA. Section 501(c) likewise permits employers, insurers, and plan administrators to establish and/or observe the terms of a "bona fide" self-insured health insurance plan that is not used as a "subterfuge." 42 U.S.C. § 12201(c). The text of § 501(c) is incorporated into § 1630.16(f) of the Commission's regulations.

Consequently, if the Commission determines that the challenged term or provision is a disability-based distinction, the respondent will be required to prove that: 1) the health insurance plan is either a bona fide insured health insurance plan that is not inconsistent with state law, or a bona fide self-insured health insurance plan; and 2) the challenged disability-based distinction is not being used as a subterfuge. If the respondent so demonstrates, the Commission will conclude that the challenged disability-based distinction is within the protective ambit of § 501(c) and does not violate the ADA. If, on the other hand, the respondent is unable to make this two-pronged demonstration, the Commission will conclude that the respondent has violated the ADA.

B.   What Is a Disability–Based Distinction?

It is important to note that not all health-related plan distinctions discriminate on the basis of disability. Insurance distinctions that are not based on disability, and that are applied equally to all insured employees, do not discriminate on the basis of disability and so do not violate the ADA.

For example, a feature of some employer provided health insurance plans is a distinction between the benefits provided for the treatment of physical conditions on the one hand, and the benefits provided for the treatment of "mental/nervous" conditions on the other. Typically, a lower level of benefits is provided for the treatment of mental/nervous conditions than is provided for the treatment of physical conditions. Similarly, some health insurance plans provide fewer benefits for "eye care" than for other physical conditions. Such broad distinctions, which apply to the treatment of a multitude of dissimilar conditions and which constrain individuals both with and without disabilities, are not distinctions based on disability. Consequently, although such distinctions may have a greater impact on certain individuals with disabilities, they do not intentionally discriminate on the basis of disability and do not violate the ADA.

Blanket pre-existing condition clauses that exclude from the coverage of a health insurance plan the treatment of conditions that pre-date an individual's eligibility for benefits under that plan also are not distinctions based on disability, and do not violate the ADA. Universal limits or exclusions from coverage of all experimental drugs and/or treatments, or of all "elective surgery," are likewise not insurance distinctions based on disability. Similarly, coverage limits on medical procedures that are not exclusively, or nearly exclusively, utilized for the treatment of a particular disability are not distinctions based on disability. Thus, for example, it would not violate the ADA for an employer to limit the number of blood transfusions or X-rays that it will pay for, even though this may have an adverse effect on individuals with certain disabilities.

Example 1.   The R Company health insurance plan limits the benefits provided for the treatment of any physical conditions to a maximum of $25,000 per year. CP, an employee of R, files a charge of discrimination alleging that the $25,000 cap violates the ADA because it is insufficient to cover the cost of treatment for her cancer. The $25,000 cap does not single out a specific disability, discrete group of disabilities, or disability in general. It is therefore not a disability-based distinction. If it is applied equally to all insured employees, it does not violate the ADA.

In contrast, however, health-related insurance distinctions that are based on disability may violate the ADA. A term or provision is "disability-based" if it singles out a particular disability (e.g., deafness, AIDS, schizophrenia), a discrete group of disabilities (e.g., cancers, muscular dystrophies, kidney diseases), or disability in general (e.g., non-coverage of all conditions that substantially limit a major life activity).

As previously noted, employers may establish and/or observe the terms and provisions of a bona fide benefit plan, including terms or provisions based on disability, that are not a "subterfuge to evade the purposes" of the ADA. Such terms and provisions do not violate the ADA. However, disability-based insurance distinctions that are a "subterfuge" do intentionally discriminate on the basis of disability and so violate the ADA.

Example 2.   R Company's new self-insured health insurance plan caps benefits for the treatment of all physical conditions, except AIDS, at $100,000 per year. The treatment of AIDS is capped at $5,000 per year. CP, an employee with AIDS enrolled in the health insurance plan, files a charge alleging that the lower AIDS cap violates the ADA. The lower AIDS cap is a disability-based distinction. Accordingly, if R is unable to demonstrate that its health insurance plan is bona fide and that the AIDS cap is not a subterfuge, a violation of the ADA will be found.

Example 3.   R Company has a health insurance plan that excludes from coverage treatment for any pre-existing blood disorders for a period of 18 months, but does not exclude the treatment of any other pre-existing conditions. R's pre-existing condition clause only excludes treatment for a discrete group of related disabilities, e.g., hemophilia, leukemia, and is thus a disability-based distinction. CP, an individual with acute leukemia who recently joined R Company and enrolled in its health insurance plan, files a charge of discrimination alleging that the disability-based pre-existing condition clause violates the ADA. If R is unable to demonstrate that its health insurance plan is bona fide and that the disability-specific pre-existing condition clause is not a subterfuge, a violation of the ADA will be found.

C.   The Respondent's Burden of Proof

Once the Commission has determined that a challenged health insurance term or provision constitutes a disability-based distinction, the respondent must prove that the health insurance plan is either a bona fide insured plan that is not inconsistent with state law, or a bona fide self-insured plan. The respondent must also prove that the challenged disability-based distinction is not being used as a subterfuge. Requiring the respondent to bear this burden of proving entitlement to the protection of § 501(c) is consistent with the well-established principle that the burden of proof should rest with the party who has the greatest access to the relevant facts. In the health insurance context, it is the respondent employer (and/or the employer's insurer, if any) who has control of the risk assessment, actuarial, and/or claims data relied upon in adopting the challenged disability-based distinction. Charging party employees have no access to such data, and, generally speaking, have no information about the employer provided health insurance plan beyond that contained in the employer provided health insurance plan description. Consequently, it is the employer who should bear the burden of proving that the challenged disability-based insurance distinction is within the protective ambit of § 501(c).

1.   The Health Insurance Plan Is "Bona Fide" and Consistent with Applicable Law

In order to gain the protection of section 501(c) for a challenged disability-based insurance distinction, the respondent must first prove that the health insurance plan in which the challenged distinction is contained is either a bona fide insured health insurance plan that is not inconsistent with state law, or a bona fide self-insured health insurance plan. If the health insurance plan is an insured plan, the respondent will be able to satisfy this requirement by proving that: 1) the health insurance plan is bona fide in that it exists and pays benefits, and its terms have been accurately communicated to eligible employees; and 2) the health insurance plan's terms are not inconsistent with applicable state law as interpreted by the appropriate state authorities. If the health insurance plan is a self-insured plan, the respondent will only be required to prove that the health insurance plan is bona fide in that it exists and pays benefits, and that its terms have been accurately communicated to covered employees.

2. The Disability–Based Distinction Is Not a Subterfuge

The second demonstration that the respondent must make in order to gain the protection of section 501(c) is that the challenged disability-based distinction is not a subterfuge to evade the purposes of the ADA. "Subterfuge" refers to disability-based disparate treatment that is not justified by the risks or costs associated with the disability. Whether a particular challenged disability-based insurance distinction is being used as a subterfuge will be determined on a case by case basis, considering the totality of the circumstances.

The respondent can prove that a challenged disability-based insurance distinction is not a subterfuge in several ways. A non-exclusive list of potential business/insurance justifications follows.

a. The respondent may prove that it has not engaged in the disability-based disparate treatment alleged. For example, where a charging party has alleged that a benefit cap of a particular catastrophic disability is discriminatory, the respondent may prove that its health insurance plan actually treats all similarly catastrophic conditions in the same way.

b. The respondent may prove that the disparate treatment is justified by legitimate actuarial data, or by actual or reasonably anticipated experience, and that conditions with comparable actuarial data and/or experience are treated in the same fashion. In other words, the respondent may prove that the disability-based disparate treatment is attributable to the application of legitimate risk classification and underwriting procedures to the increased risks (and thus increased cost to the health insurance plan) of the disability, and not to the disability per se.

c. The respondent may prove that the disparate treatment is necessary (i.e., that there is no nondisability-based health insurance plan change that could be made) to ensure that the challenged health insurance plan satisfies the commonly accepted or legally required standards for the fiscal soundness of such an insurance plan. The respondent, for example, may prove that it limited coverage for the treatment of a discrete group of disabilities because continued unlimited coverage would have been so expensive as to cause the health insurance plan to become financially insolvent, and there was no nondisability-based health insurance plan alteration that would have avoided insolvency.

d.   The respondent may prove that the challenged insurance practice or activity is necessary (i.e., that there is no nondisability-based change that could be made) to prevent the occurrence of an unacceptable change either in the coverage of the health insurance plan, or in the premiums charged for the health insurance plan. An "unacceptable" change is a drastic increase in premium payments (or in co-payments or deductibles), or a drastic alteration to the scope of coverage or level of benefits provided, that would: 1) make the health insurance plan effectively unavailable to a significant number of other employees, 2) make the health insurance plan so unattractive as to result in significant adverse selection, or 3) make the health insurance plan so unattractive that the employer cannot compete in recruiting and maintaining qualified workers due to the superiority of health insurance plans offered by other employers in the community.

e.   Where the charging party is challenging the respondent's denial of coverage for a disability-specific treatment, the respondent may prove that this treatment does not provide any benefit (i.e., has no medical value). The respondent, in other words, may prove by reliable scientific evidence that the disability-specific treatment does not cure the condition, slow the degeneration/deterioration or harm attributable to the condition, alleviate the symptoms of the condition, or maintain the current health status of individuals with the disability who receive the treatment.

* * *

In *McGann v. H & H Music*, discussed earlier in this Part, the Bush Administration argued that ERISA should not preclude employers from inserting disability-based distinctions against people with HIV in their plans because the then newly enacted ADA would address the issues. Both HIV and insurance coverage were central issues in the ADA debate. Nonetheless, after adoption of the ADA many employers and insurers were reluctant to abandon policies that denied or sharply limited health insurance coverage for people with HIV. They tried to enlist the aid of the courts in employing many tactics to limit the reach of the ADA. For example, Gonzales v. Garner Food Services, Inc., 89 F.3d 1523 (11th Cir. 1996), held that a former employee, disabled as a result of HIV, could not challenge his former employer's policy denying long-term disability coverage for HIV because he was no longer an employee protected under Title I of the ADA. (By contrast, Ford v. Schering–Plough Corp., 145 F.3d 601 (3d Cir. 1998), *cert. den.*, 525 U.S. 1093 (1999), held that the ADA applies to ex-employees seeking employment related benefits. The circuits remain divided on the issue.).

As another example, many entities, including union hiring halls and trade associations providing health insurance benefits for their members argued that they were free to deny coverage for people with HIV because they were not "employers," under the terms of Title I of the ADA. Carparts Distribution Center, Inc. v. Automotive Wholesaler's Assn., of New England, 37 F.3d 12 (1st Cir. 1994), rejected this claim and held that a trade association was an employer, subject to the terms of the ADA. As a third example of efforts to deny the applicability of the ADA, many insurance companies argued that the prohibition against discrimination by public accommodations in ADA, Title III, only required that the offices of insurance companies be accessible to people with disabilities and did not apply to the content of insurance coverage. The circuits were sharply divided on this question. See Pallozzi v. Allstate Life Insurance, Co., 198 F.3d 28 (2d Cir. 1999), as amended by Pallozzi v. Allstate Life Ins. Co., 204 F.3d 392 (2d Cir. 2000) (holding that Title III of the ADA covers the content of insurance and summarizing cases). In all these cases, if employers or insurers lost their claims that the ADA does not apply to them, they settled. There are no actuarial data to support the claim that HIV costs more than other catastrophic illnesses such as cancer or stroke, or other chronic conditions. Apart from HIV and mental health there is no tradition in health insurance in the U.S. of granting or denying coverage for particular conditions. See Carparts Distribution Center, Inc. v. Automotive Wholesaler's Assn. of New England, Inc., 987 F. Supp. 77 (D.N.H. 1997).

The following decision is widely influential in its holding that the ADA fails to regulate the content of health insurance. Although some courts still may scrutinize policies' disability-based distinctions, Judge Posner, as you will see, holds that the ADA is not violated so long as a disability-based coverage limitation applies across-the-board to all persons, regardless of its impact on persons with a disability and regardless of whether the insurer can justify the limit on actuarial grounds—or even if actuarial grounds actually do not exist.

Doe v. Mutual of Omaha Insurance Company

179 F.3d 557 (7th Cir. 1999), *cert. den.*, 528 U.S. 1106 (2000)

■ POSNER, CHIEF JUDGE:

Mutual of Omaha appeals from a judgment that the AIDS caps in two of its health insurance policies violate the public accommodations provision of the Americans with Disabilities Act. One policy limits lifetime benefits for AIDS or AIDS-related conditions (ARC) to $25,000, the other limits them to $100,000, while for other conditions the limit in both policies is $1 million. Mutual of Omaha has stipulated that it "has not shown and cannot show that its AIDS Caps are or ever have been consistent with sound actuarial principles, actual or reasonably anticipated experience, bona fide risk classification, or state law." It also concedes that AIDS is a disabling condition [from onset] within the meaning of the Americans with Disabilities Act. See Bragdon, v. Abbott, 524 U.S. 624. Mutual of Omaha argues that the Americans with Disabilities Act does not regulate the content of insurance policies.

Title III of the Act, in § 302(a), provides that "no individual shall be discriminated against on the basis of disability in the full and equal enjoyment of the goods, services, facilities, privileges, advantages, or accommodations of any place of public accommodation" by the owner, lessee, or operator of such a place. 42 U.S.C. § 12182(a). The core meaning of this provision, plainly enough, is that the owner or operator of a store, hotel, restaurant, dentist's office, travel agency, theater, Web site, or other facility (whether in physical space or in electronic space, Carparts Distribution Center, Inc. v. Automotive Wholesaler's Ass'n of New England, Inc., 37 F.3d 12), that is open to the public cannot exclude disabled persons from entering the facility and, once in, from using the facility in the same way that the nondisabled do. The owner or operator of, say, a camera store can neither bar the door to the disabled nor let them in but then refuse to sell its cameras to them on the same terms as to other customers. Department of Justice, Civil Rights Division, The Americans with Disabilities Act: Title III Technical Assistance Manual § III3.2000 (Nov. 1993); 28 C.F.R. § 36.202. To come closer to home, a dentist cannot refuse to fill a cavity of a person with AIDS unless he demonstrates a direct threat to safety or health, and an insurance company cannot (at least without pleading a special defense, discussed below) refuse to sell an insurance policy to a person with AIDS. 28 C.F.R. § 36.104 Place of Public Accommodation (6).

Mutual of Omaha does not refuse to sell insurance policies to such persons—it was happy to sell health insurance policies to the two plaintiffs. But because of the AIDS caps, the policies have less value to persons with AIDS than they would have to persons with other, equally expensive diseases or disabilities. This does not make the offer to sell illusory, for people with AIDS have medical needs unrelated to AIDS, and the policies give such people as much coverage for those needs as the policies give people who don't have AIDS. If all the medical needs of people with AIDS were AIDS-related and thus excluded by the policies, this might support an inference that Mutual of Omaha was trying to exclude such people, and such exclusion, as we shall see, might violate the Act. But that is not argued.

Since most health-insurance policies contain caps, the position urged by the plaintiffs would discriminate among diseases. Diseases that happened to be classified as disabilities could not be capped, but equally or more serious diseases that are generally not disabling, such as heart disease, could be. Moreover, the plaintiffs acknowledge the right of an insurance company to exclude coverage for an applicant's pre-existing medical conditions. If the applicant is already HIV-positive when he applies for a health-insurance policy, the insurer can in effect cap his AIDS-related coverage at $0. This "discrimination" is not limited to AIDS or for that matter to disabilities, which is why the plaintiffs do not challenge it; but it suggests that the rule for which they contend is at once arbitrary and unlikely to do much for people with AIDS.

The insurance company asks us to compare this case to one in which a person with one leg complains of a shoe store's refusal to sell shoes other than by the pair, or in which a blind person complains of a bookstore's refusal to stock books printed in Braille. We do not understand the plaintiffs to be contending that such complaints are actionable under

§ 302(a), even though there is a sense in which the disabled individual would be denied the full and equal enjoyment of the services that the store offers. In fact, it is apparent that a store is not required to alter its inventory in order to stock goods such as Braille books that are especially designed for disabled people. But it is apparent as a matter of interpretation rather than compelled by a simple reading which would place the present case on the other side of the line; and so the case cannot be resolved by reference simply to the language of § 302(a).

The common sense of the statute is that the content of the goods or services offered by a place of public accommodation is not regulated. A camera store may not refuse to sell cameras to a disabled person, but it is not required to stock cameras specially designed for such persons. Had Congress purposed to impose so enormous a burden on the retail sector of the economy and so vast a supervisory responsibility on the federal courts, we think it would have made its intention clearer and would at least have imposed some standards. There are defenses to a prima facie case of public-accommodation discrimination, but they would do little to alleviate the judicial burden of making standardless decisions about the composition of retail inventories. The only defense that might apply is that the modification of a seller's existing practices that is necessary to provide equal access to the disabled "would fundamentally alter the nature of . . . [the seller's] services," 42 U.S.C. § 12182(b)(2)(A)(ii), and it probably would not apply to either case and certainly not to the Braille one.

That the plaintiffs are asking that a limitation be removed rather than that a physical product be added or altered cannot distinguish these cases. [S]ince § 302(a) is not limited to physical products, but includes contracts and other intangibles, such as an insurance policy, a limitation upon the duty to serve cannot be confined to physical changes. An insurance policy is a product, and a policy with a $25,000 limit is a different product from one with a $1 million limit, just as a wheelchair is a different product from an armchair. A furniture store that does not stock wheelchairs knows that it is making its services less valuable to disabled than to nondisabled people, but the Americans with Disabilities Act has not been understood to require furniture stores to stock wheelchairs.

It might seem that the AIDS caps could be distinguished from the "refusal to stock" cases because the caps include complications of AIDS. If being infected by HIV leads one to contract pneumonia, the cost of treating the pneumonia is subject to the AIDS cap; if a person not infected by HIV contracts pneumonia, the costs of treating his pneumonia are fully covered. It looks, therefore, like a difference in treatment referable solely to the fact that one person is disabled and the other not.

But this is not correct. The essential point to understand is that HIV doesn't cause illness directly. What it does is weaken and eventually destroy the body's immune system. As the immune system falters, the body becomes prey to diseases that the system protects us against. These "opportunistic" diseases that HIV allows, as it were, to ravage the body are exotic cancers and rare forms of pneumonia and other infectious diseases.

Anthony S. Fauci & H. Clifford Lane, *Human Immunodeficiency Virus (HIV) Disease: AIDS and Related Disorders, in* 2 HARRISON'S PRINCIPLES OF INTERNAL MEDICINE 1791, 1824–45 (Anthony S. Fauci et al. eds., 14th ed. 1998). To refer to them as "complications" of HIV or AIDS is not incorrect, but it is misleading, because they are the chief worry of anyone who has the misfortune to be afflicted with AIDS. An AIDS cap would be meaningless if it excluded the opportunistic diseases that are the most harmful consequences of being infected by the AIDS virus.

What the AIDS caps in the challenged insurance policies cover, therefore, is the cost of fighting the AIDS virus itself and trying to keep the immune system intact plus the cost of treating the opportunistic diseases to which the body becomes prey when the immune system has eroded to the point at which one is classified as having AIDS. The principal opportunistic diseases of AIDS, such as Kaposi's sarcoma, Pneumocystis carinii pneumonia, AIDS wasting, and esophageal candidiasis, are rarely encountered among people who are not infected by HIV—so rarely as to be described frequently as "AIDS-defining opportunistic infections." It is these distinctive diseases that are the target (along with the costs of directly treating infection by HIV) of the AIDS caps. This is not a case of refusing, for example, to provide the same coverage for a broken leg, or other afflictions not peculiar to people with AIDS, to such people, which would be a good example of discrimination by reason of disability.

It is true that as the immune system collapses because of infection by HIV, the patient becomes subject to opportunistic infection not only by the distinctive AIDS-defining diseases but also by a host of diseases to which people not infected with HIV are subject. Even when they are the same disease, however, they are far more lethal when they hit a person who does not have an immune system to fight back with, which means they are not really the same disease. This is not a point that is peculiar to AIDS. The end stage of many diseases is an illness different from the one that brought the patient to that stage; nowadays when a person dies of pneumonia, it is usually because his body has been gravely weakened by some other ailment. If a health insurance policy that excluded coverage for cancer was interpreted not to cover the pneumonia that killed a patient terminally ill with cancer, this would not be "discrimination" against cancer.

To summarize the discussion to this point, we cannot find anything in the Americans with Disabilities Act or its background, or the nature of AIDS and AIDS caps, to justify so radically expansive an interpretation as would be required to bring these cases under § 302(a) without making an unprincipled distinction between AIDS caps and other product alterations—unless it is § 501(c)(1) of the Act. That section provides that Title I (employment discrimination against the disabled) and Title III (public accommodations, the title involved in this case) "shall not be construed to prohibit or restrict an insurer from underwriting risks, classifying risks, or administering such risks that are based on or not inconsistent with State law," 42 U.S.C. § 12201(c)(1), unless the prohibition or restriction is "a subterfuge to evade the purposes" of either title. § 12201(c).

Even with the "subterfuge" qualification, § 501(c) is obviously intended for the benefit of insurance companies rather than plaintiffs and it may seem odd therefore to find the plaintiffs placing such heavy weight on what is in effect a defense to liability. But a defense can cast light on what is to be defended against, that is, what the prima facie case of a violation is. Suppose, for example, that a statute regulated the sale of "animals" but it was unclear whether the legislature had meant to include fish. Were there a statutory exclusion for goldfish, it would be pretty clear that "animals" included fish, since otherwise there would be no occasion for such an exclusion. And, with that clarified, the advocate of regulating the sale of a particular goldfish would have to show only that the exclusion was somehow inapplicable to him. That is the plaintiffs' strategy here. They use the insurance provision to show that § 302(a) regulates content, then argue that the excluding provision is narrow enough to allow them to challenge the coverage limits in Mutual of Omaha's policies. There is even some legislative history, which the plaintiffs hopefully call "definitive," to § 501(c) that suggests that an insurance company can limit coverage on the basis of a disability only if the limitation is based either on claims experience or on sound actuarial methods for classifying risks. H.R. Rep. No. 485, 101st Cong., 2d Sess. 136–37 (1990); S. Rep. No. 116, 101st Cong., 1st Sess. 84–86 (1989). And Mutual of Omaha conceded itself out of relying on § 501(c)'s safe harbor by stipulating that it cannot show that its AIDS caps are based on sound actuarial principles or claims experience or are consistent with state law.

The plaintiffs argue, consistent with our goldfish example, that the insurance exemption has no function if § 302(a) does not regulate the content of insurance policies, and so we should infer that the section does not [sic] regulate that content. But this reasoning is not correct. If it were, it would imply that § 302(a) regulates the content not only of insurance policies but also of all other products and services, since the section is not limited to insurance. The insurance industry may have worried that the section would be given just the expansive interpretation that the district court gave it in this case, and so the industry may have obtained the rule of construction in § 501(c) just to backstop its argument that § 302(a) regulates only access and not content. Or it may have worried about being sued under § 302(a) for refusing to sell an insurance policy to a disabled person. Remember that the right of full and equal enjoyment as we interpret it includes the right to buy on equal terms and not just the right to enter the store. For Mutual of Omaha to take the position that people with AIDS are so unhealthy that it won't sell them health insurance would be a prima facie violation of § 302(a). But the insurance company just might be able to steer into the safe harbor provided by § 501(c), provided it didn't run afoul of the "subterfuge" limitation, as it would do if, for example, it had adopted the AIDS caps to deter people who know they are HIV positive from buying the policies at all.

The legislative history is consistent with this interpretation. Both committee reports on which the plaintiffs rely give the example of refusing to sell an insurance policy to a blind person, as does the gloss placed on

§ 501(c) by the Department of Justice. 28 C.F.R. Pt. 36, App. B § 36.212, at 601 (1998). A refusal to sell insurance to a blind person is not the same thing as a provision in the policy that if the insured becomes blind, the insurer will not pay the expense of his learning Braille. We find nothing in the language or history of the statute to suggest that the latter refusal would be unlawful. The Department's Technical Assistance Manual, above, § III–3.11000, contains somewhat broader language than either the statute or the regulation or the committee reports, language about insurers' being forbidden to discriminate on the basis of disability in the sale, terms, or conditions of insurance contracts; but basically this just parrots the statute and the regulation and does not indicate a focused attention to coverage limits. There is, as we have pointed out, a difference between refusing to sell a health-insurance policy at all to a person with AIDS, or charging him a higher price for such a policy, or attaching a condition obviously designed to deter people with AIDS from buying the policy (such as refusing to cover such a person for a broken leg), on the one hand, and, on the other, offering insurance policies that contain caps for various diseases some of which may also be disabilities within the meaning of the Americans with Disabilities Act.

The Department has filed an amicus curiae brief that effaces this distinction and embraces the plaintiffs' interpretation of the Act. The Department's regulations interpreting the Americans with Disabilities Act are entitled to *Chevron* deference, but, as we have just seen, do not compel the interpretation for which these plaintiffs contend. We noted recently, that it is unsettled how much *Chevron* deference is to be given to an agency's informal policy pronouncements. This category includes the Technical Assistance Manual as well as the amicus curiae brief; and though we know from Auer v. Robbins, 519 U.S. 452, 462 (1997), that, in some circumstances at least, an agency's amicus brief is entitled to some deference, it cannot be very great when it is the brief of an agency that has, and has exercised, rulemaking powers yet has unaccountably failed to address a fundamental issue on which the brief takes a radical stance. Displacing the regulation of the insurance industry into the federal courts is a sufficiently far-reaching interpretive stride to justify us in requiring the Department to invite deference by a more deliberative, public, and systematic procedure than the filing of an amicus curiae brief.

We conclude that § 302(a) does not require a seller to alter his product to make it equally valuable to the disabled and to the nondisabled, even if the product is insurance. This conclusion is consistent with all the appellate cases to consider this or cognate issues. And if it is wrong, the suit must fail anyway, because it is barred by the McCarran–Ferguson Act.

That Act, so far as bears on this case, forbids construing a federal statute to "impair any law enacted by any State for the purpose of regulating the business of insurance unless such Act specifically relates to the business of insurance." 15 U.S.C. § 1012(b). Direct conflict with state law is not required to trigger this prohibition; it is enough if the interpretation would "interfere with a State's administrative regime." Humana Inc.

v. Forsyth, 119 S. Ct. 710, 717 (1999). The interpretation of section 302(a) of the Americans with Disabilities Act for which the plaintiffs contend would do this. State regulation of insurance is comprehensive and includes rate and coverage issues, see Couch on Insurance §§ 2:7, 2:20, 2:26, 2:35 (3d ed. 1997), so if federal courts are now to determine whether caps on disabling conditions (by no means limited to AIDS) are actuarially sound and consistent with principles of state law they will be stepping on the toes of state insurance commissioners.

It is one thing to say that an insurance company may not refuse to deal with disabled persons; the prohibition of such refusals can probably be administered with relatively little interference with state insurance regulation, and anyway this may be a prohibition expressly imposed by federal law because encompassed within the blanket prohibition of § 302(a) of the Americans with Disabilities Act, and so outside the scope of the McCarran–Ferguson Act. It is another thing to require federal courts to determine whether limitations on coverage are actuarially sound and consistent with state law. Even if the formal criteria are the same under federal and state law, displacing their administration into federal court—requiring a federal court to decide whether an insurance policy is consistent with state law—obviously would interfere with the administration of the state law.

It is true that we are not being asked in this case to decide whether the AIDS caps were actuarially sound and in accordance with state law. But if the McCarran–Ferguson Act does not apply, then we are certain to be called upon to decide such issues in the next case, when the insurer does not stipulate to them. Mutual of Omaha didn't want to get into these messy issues if it could show that the Americans with Disabilities Act did not apply. If the ADA is fully applicable, insurers will have to defend their AIDS caps by reference to § 501(c), and the federal courts will then find themselves regulating the health-insurance industry, which McCarran–Ferguson tells them not to do.

Section 501(c) itself specifically relates to insurance and thus is not within the scope of McCarran–Ferguson. But the interpretation that the McCarran–Ferguson Act bars is not an interpretation of § 501(c); it is an interpretation of § 302(a) that injects the federal courts into the heart of the regulation of the insurance business by the states.

Of course, we can infer from § 501(c)—we have done so earlier in this opinion—and Mutual of Omaha does not deny, that section 302(a) has some application to insurance: it forbids an insurer to turn down an applicant merely because he is disabled. To that extent, as we have already suggested, we can accept (certainly for purposes of argument) that § 302(a) relates specifically to the business of insurance. But thus limited to a simple prohibition of discrimination, § 302(a) does not impair state regulation of insurance; no state wants insurance companies to refuse to insure disabled people.

Both because § 302(a) of the Americans with Disabilities Act does not regulate the content of the products or services sold in places of public accommodation and because an interpretation of the section as regulating the content of insurance policies is barred by the McCarran–Ferguson Act, the judgment in favor of the plaintiffs must be reversed with directions to enter judgment for the defendant. This does not, however, leave the plaintiffs remediless. If in fact the AIDS caps in the defendant's policies are not consistent with state law and sound actuarial practices (and whether they are or not, the defendant may be bound by its stipulation, though this we needn't decide), the plaintiffs can obtain all the relief to which they are entitled from the state commissioners who regulate the insurance business. Federal law is not the only source of valuable rights. Reversed.

■ EVANS, CIRCUIT JUDGE, dissenting.

The Americans with Disabilities Act is a broad, sweeping, protective statute requiring the elimination of discrimination against individuals with disabilities. Because I believe the insurance policies challenged in this case discriminate against people with AIDS in violation of the ADA, I dissent.

The majority believes we are being asked to regulate the content of insurance policies—something we should not do under the ADA. But as I see it we are not being asked to regulate content; we are being asked to decide whether an insurer can discriminate against people with AIDS, refusing to pay for them the same expenses it would pay if they did not have AIDS. The ADA assigns to courts the task of passing judgment on such conduct. And to me, the Mutual of Omaha policies at issue violate the Act.

Chief Judge Posner's opinion likens the insurance company here to a camera store forced to stock cameras specially designed for disabled persons. While I agree that the ADA would not require a store owner to alter its inventory, I think the analogy misses the mark. The better analogy would be that of a store which lets disabled customers in the door, but then refuses to sell them anything but inferior cameras. To pick up on another analogy raised at oral argument, we are not being asked to force a restaurant to alter its menu to accommodate disabled diners; we are being asked to stop a restaurant that is offering to its nondisabled diners a menu containing a variety of entrees while offering a menu with only limited selections to its disabled patrons. Section 501(c)'s "safe harbor" would allow Mutual of Omaha to treat insureds with AIDS differently than those without AIDS if the discrimination were consistent with Illinois law or could be justified by actuarial principles or claims experience. But Mutual of Omaha conceded that its AIDS and ARC caps do not fall under the ADA's safe harbor protection.

The parties stipulated that the very same affliction (e.g., pneumonia) may be both AIDS-related and not AIDS-related and that, in such cases, coverage depends solely on whether the patient has AIDS. In my view that is more than enough to trigger an ADA violation. Chief Judge Posner reasons that, although the policies appear to discriminate solely based on an insured's HIV status, they really don't, when you consider the nature of AIDS. He suggests that the phrase "AIDS related conditions" embodies a unique set of symptoms and afflictions that would make it easy for the insurance company to determine with certainty whether an expense incurred for a particular illness is "AIDS-related" and therefore subject to the cap. His analysis—charitable to Mutual of Omaha to be sure—may very well be medically sound. But it doesn't come from the insurance policies. The policies don't even hint at what illnesses or afflictions might fall within the ARC exclusion. Nor has the medical community embraced an accepted definition for what "conditions" are "AIDS-related." The practical effect of all this, as Mutual of Omaha concedes, is that coverage for certain expenses would be approved or denied based solely on whether the insured had AIDS. Given that the ADA is supposed to signal a "clear and comprehensive national mandate for the elimination of discrimination against individuals with disabilities," see 42 U.S.C. § 12101(b)(1), I would use the statute to right the wrong committed by Mutual of Omaha.

I also part company with the majority on the McCarran–Ferguson Act analysis, and I think the faultiness of its conclusion is evident in the way the issue is framed. The Chief Judge writes: "It is one thing to say that an insurance company may not refuse to deal with disabled persons; the prohibition of such refusals can probably be administered with relatively little interference with state insurance regulation. It is another thing to require federal courts to determine whether limitations on coverage are actuarially sound and consistent with state law." This is somewhat misleading because, as the majority acknowledges, the question of whether these caps are actuarially sound or consistent with state law has been taken out of the equation by Mutual of Omaha's concession in the parties' stipulation. Consistent with McCarran–Ferguson we can—and we should—decide exactly what the majority seemed to think is permissible: whether an insurer may refuse to deal with disabled persons on the same terms as nondisabled persons. Because any conceivable justification for the caps (under § 501(c)) is not at issue, and because an insurer cannot legally decide to pay or not pay expenses based solely on whether an insured has AIDS and is therefore disabled under the ADA, I dissent from the opinion of the court.

Notes

1. *Customization or reasonable modification? Does Judge Posner make sense here?* With his strong orientation toward framing disputes in market terms, Judge Posner essentially argues that the plaintiffs are demanding customized products, that is, that they want a product that offers better coverage of HIV/AIDS treatments, not just the "standard off the shelf" insurance product with its limited coverage. But isn't this precisely the point? Didn't the insurer in fact customize its product—without any actuarial basis for doing so—wholly to make it nearly worthless for patients with HIV/AIDS? And isn't the issue whether such avoidance tactics, singled out against one particular group of patients as opposed to an entire class of conditions considered disabling, run afoul of the ADA? Furthermore, given the fact that there are no actuarial data to support the distinction, how can it be anything other than discrimination within the meaning of the ADA's legal framework, to impose special restrictions based

solely on a particular disability, i.e. HIV? Once Mutual of Omaha conceded that it had no actuarial basis for its classification targeting people disabled by HIV, how could it be seen as other than discriminatory?

2. *The ADA safe harbor.* One of the more peculiar aspects of Judge Posner's decision is his emphatic rejection of the language of the ADA insurance "safe harbor," which provides that the Act "shall not be construed to prohibit or restrict an insurer from underwriting risks, classifying risks, or administering such risks that are based on or not inconsistent with State law," 42 U.S.C. § 12201(c)(1), unless the prohibition or restriction is "a subterfuge to evade the purposes" of either title. § 12201(c). Despite the fact that the EEOC, which has expertise in matters of employment benefits, laid out a framework for analyzing insurer conduct in relation to the safe harbor provisions, Judge Posner simply rejected this framework out of hand as not worth his deference and announced that it is not the place of the federal courts to "step on the toes" of state insurance commissioners. Isn't it precisely the job of the courts to decide when a state law runs afoul of federal standards?

3. *Disability protections and the content of health insurance.* Is the real problem for the court in this case the fact that the ADA seems to be all about physical places (e.g., health care facilities such as the dental office as in *Bragdon,* 524 U.S. 624, segregated facilities, as you will see later in this Part in Olmstead v. L.C., 527 U.S. 581 (1999)), and not about the content of coverage? And yet, the discrimination in *Doe* is so utterly blatant, and the court so dismissive of the EEOC's efforts to control such blatant discrimination that more is at work here than just physical place versus the more abstract concept of coverage. The type of conduct presented in *Doe* also can be distinguished from facially neutral, across-the-board limits that impact people with disabilities more seriously, the situation presented in Alexander v. Choate, 469 U.S. 287 (1985). In *Choate,* which involved Medicaid, Justice Thurgood Marshall, writing for a unanimous court, upheld a 14–day annual limit on inpatient hospital care imposed under Tennessee's Medicaid program, despite strong evidence that the limit had a disproportionately severe impact on persons with handicaps. The Court concluded that uniformly applied across-the-board treatment limits that do not single out any specific condition and thus do not run afoul of Section 504 of the Rehabilitation Act. Justice Marshall reasoned that across-the-board limits apply to all beneficiaries and

> will not deny respondents meaningful access to Tennessee Medicaid services or exclude them from those services. The new limitation does not invoke criteria that have a particular exclusionary effect on the handicapped; the reduction, neutral on its face, does not distinguish between those whose coverage will be reduced and those whose coverage will not on the basis of any test, judgment, or trait that the handicapped as a class are less capable of meeting or less likely of having. Moreover, it cannot be argued that "meaningful access" to state Medicaid services will be denied by the 14–day limitation on inpatient coverage; nothing in the record

suggests that the handicapped in Tennessee will be unable to benefit meaningfully from the coverage they will receive under the 14–day rule. The reduction in inpatient coverage will leave both handicapped and non-handicapped Medicaid users with identical and effective hospital services fully available for their use, with both classes of users subject to the same durational limitation. The 14–day limitation, therefore, does not exclude the handicapped from or deny them the benefits of the 14 days of care the State has chosen to provide.

To the extent respondents further suggest that their greater need for prolonged inpatient care means that, to provide meaningful access to Medicaid services, Tennessee must single out the handicapped for *more* than 14 days of coverage, the suggestion is simply unsound. At base, such a suggestion must rest on the notion that the benefit provided through state Medicaid programs is the amorphous objective of "adequate health care." But Medicaid programs do not guarantee that each recipient will receive that level of health care precisely tailored to his or her particular needs. Instead, the benefit provided through Medicaid is a particular package of health care services, such as 14 days of inpatient coverage. That package of services has the general aim of assuring that individuals will receive necessary medical care, but the benefit provided remains the individual services offered-not "adequate health care."

The federal Medicaid Act makes this point clear. The Act gives the States substantial discretion to choose the proper mix of amount, scope, and duration limitations on coverage, as long as care and services are provided in "the best interests of the recipients." The District Court found that the 14–day limitation would fully serve 95% of even handicapped individuals eligible for Tennessee Medicaid, and both lower courts concluded that Tennessee's proposed Medicaid plan would meet the "best interests" standard. That unchallenged conclusion indicates that Tennessee is free, as a matter of the Medicaid Act, to choose to define the benefit it will be providing as 14 days of inpatient coverage.

Section 504 does not require the State to alter this definition of the benefit being offered simply to meet the reality that the handicapped have greater medical needs. To conclude otherwise would be to find that the Rehabilitation Act requires States to view certain illnesses, *i.e.,* those particularly affecting the handicapped, as more important than others and more worthy of cure through government subsidization. Nothing in the legislative history of the Act supports such a conclusion. Section 504 seeks to assure evenhanded treatment and the opportunity for handicapped individuals to participate in and benefit from programs receiving federal assistance. The Act does not, however, guarantee the handicapped equal results from the provision of state Medicaid, even assuming some measure of equality of health could be constructed.

427 U.S. at 302–04.

Does Judge Posner's opinion tell us that far from uniformly and impartially applying limits on coverage, the business of the private insurance industry is to arbitrarily and prejudicially exclude and discriminate in the name of "actuarial fairness," even when no actuarial evidence can be mustered on behalf of such conduct? Does he say that stopping this type of practice is one that lies in the political realm and that it is not the courts' problem if states are too politically weak to stop such conduct? Then why was the ADA passed in the first place?

4. *Implications of disability law rulings for interpretation of the Affordable Care Act's essential health benefit non-discrimination provision.* As noted earlier in Chapter 8, the Affordable Care Act's essential health benefit provisions require the Secretary to take certain "considerations" into account in interpreting the scope of the requirement. Specifically she must "not make coverage decisions, determine reimbursement rates, establish incentive programs, or design benefits in ways that discriminate against individuals because of their age, disability, or expected length of life." PPACA § 1302(b)(4)(B).

Were you advising the Secretary on the meaning of this provision in a disability context given prior interpretations of both the ADA and § 504, what would your advice be? Would you differentiate between across-the-board limits (note, of course that with passage of an expanded mental health parity statute, one of the most common disability-based distinctions is now prohibited) and what the EEOC calls "disability-based" distinctions, i.e., the singling out of specific conditions for differential treatments? How then do you deal with practice guidelines, which are all about distinguishing among conditions for purposes of covered treatments? Do you allow condition-specific treatment guidelines as long as they are prevalent in plan management rather than used only to limit treatment options for certain conditions? What would you do about restrictions on certain covered benefits that make them available only when prior functioning can be restored or when recovery is possible, thereby eliminating coverage for persons with disabilities whose developmental or chronic conditions require treatment to develop or maintain functioning or avert the loss of functioning? Would this in your view amount to a disability-based distinction or a valid, across-the-board limit that applies to everyone?

3.   Age Discrimination and Health Benefits for Retired Workers

One of the most compelling arguments for the enactment of the Affordable Care Act was the plight of older workers facing early retirement and left without access to health insurance. As health care costs have skyrocketed and as employee compensation has stagnated, the proportion of employers offering health insurance coverage for early retirees has plummeted. In 1988, 66 percent of all large employers offered retiree health benefit plans; by 2006, this figure had dropped to 35 percent, with significant increases in the percent of premiums borne by retirees who still have access to retiree benefits. *Kaiser/Hewitt 2006 Survey on Retiree Health Benefits* 1, http://www.kff.org/medicare/upload/7587.pdf. In 2006 74 percent of employers increased retiree premiums, and 11 percent eliminated subsidies altogether for new workers. Phyllis C. Borzi, *Retiree Health VEBAs: A New Twist on an Old Paradigm: Implications for Retirees, Unions, and Employers*, KAISER FAMILY FOUNDATION 1 (March 2009).

The crisis created by the escalation of costs and termination of employer-sponsored retiree health plans means that retirees under age 65 who have not yet reached Medicare age may find themselves completely without coverage or faced with untenable costs and heavy medical underwriting in the individual insurance market. The Affordable Care Act addresses this issue by curbing health-related discrimination in the individual insurance market, providing modified community rating that controls the cost of premiums, establishing health insurance Exchanges through which early retirees can purchase coverage, and offering premium tax credits and cost-sharing assistance.

Proposals under consideration in the 112th Congress to raise Medicare eligibility to age 67 increases the importance of establishing an alternative subsidized and accessible individual insurance market. Raising the Medicare retirement age would save money to the Medicare program while simultaneously increasing costs for employers. Among the 7 million affected persons ages 65 to 66, one study estimates that 42 percent would turn to their employer plans for coverage as either active workers or retirees, 38 percent would enroll in qualified health plans offered through health insurance Exchanges once available, and 20 percent would enroll in Medicaid. The shift of older adults away from Medicare and into qualified health plans sold in Exchanges also could be expected to raise premiums by an estimated $141 annually for all individuals covered through Exchange plans as a result of the Affordable Care Act's modified community rating provisions. Tricia Neuman & Juliette Cubianski, *Raising the Age of Medicare Eligibility: A Fresh Look Following Implementation of Health Reform*, KAISER FAMILY FOUNDATION (July 2011), http://www.kff.org/medicare/upload/8169.pdf.

American Association of Retired Persons v. Equal Employment Opportunity Commission, 489 F.3d 558 (3d Cir. 2007), *cert. den.*, 552 U.S. 1279 (2008), addressed the question of whether under the Age Discrimination in Employment Act (ADEA), employers can distinguish in their retiree plans between younger and older, Medicare-eligible retirees. They can. In 2003, the Equal Employment Opportunity Commission (EEOC) issued a proposed rule exempting from the ADEA an employer's decision to terminate eligibility for retiree benefits at the point of Medicare eligibility. 68 Fed. Reg. 41,542 (July 14, 2003). Previously the EEOC had taken the opposite position. The AARP filed suit to enjoin the rule on both ADEA and

Administrative Procedure Act grounds. Initially the trial court granted summary judgment for AARP. However, the United States Supreme Court then decided National Cable and Telecommunications Assn. v. Brand X Internet Services, 545 U.S. 967 (2005), which held that prior judicial interpretation of a statute bars subsequent agency interpretations only where the precedent "unambiguously forecloses the agency's interpretation, and therefore contains no gap for the agency to fill." On this basis, the district court reversed its earlier ruling and found that the EEOC had the power to revise its earlier policy.

The Court of Appeals for the Third Circuit affirmed, finding that the EEOC's revised policy violated neither the ADEA nor the APA:

> There is a well-trodden two-step approach to judicial review of an agency regulation. Chevron, U.S.A., Inc. v. Natural Res. Def. Council, 467 U.S. 837 (1984). Step one asks whether Congress has directly spoken to the precise question at issue. "If the intent of Congress is clearly expressed in the statute, "that is the end of the matter; for the court, as well as the agency," and such intent must be given effect." "[I]f the statute is silent or ambiguous with respect to the specific issue," then the court proceeds to a step-two determination of whether the agency interpretation is based on a "permissible construction" of the statute.

> The precise question in this case is whether the EEOC has the power to issue a regulation exempting from the prohibitions of the ADEA employer-sponsored benefits plans that coordinate retiree health benefits with eligibility for Medicare or state-sponsored health benefits programs. Section 9 of the ADEA authorizes the EEOC to "establish such reasonable exemptions to and from any or all provisions of [the Act] as it may find necessary and proper in the public interest." 29 U.S.C. § 628. The EEOC acknowledges this source of authority in its notice of the proposed rulemaking, stating that "[a]fter an in-depth study, the Commission believes that the practice of [coordinating retiree health benefits with Medicare eligibility] presents a circumstance that warrants Commission exercise of its ADEA exemption authority."

> Section 9 clearly and unambiguously grants to the EEOC the authority to provide, at least, narrow exemptions from the prohibitions of the ADEA. By stating that *"any or all* provisions" may be subject to exemptions, Congress made plain its intent to allow limited practices not otherwise permitted under the statute, so long as they are "reasonable" and "necessary and proper in the public interest." 29 U.S.C. § 628 (emphasis added). Because the language of § 9 expressly grants to the EEOC the power to implement such exceptions, there is no question that a limited exemption shown by the agency to be reasonable, necessary, and proper falls within the agency's authority under the statute.

> AARP argues that the proposed exemption exceeds the EEOC's authority under section 9 because it would allow certain

employer practices otherwise prohibited by the ADEA. AARP points to section 4 of the ADEA, which states that "[i]t shall be unlawful for an employer . . . [to] discriminate against any individual with respect to his compensation, terms, conditions, or privileges of employment, because of such individual's age." 29 U.S.C. § 623(a)(1). As discussed previously, however, it is clear that Congress intended to permit limited exemptions from the ADEA.

[S]ection 9 limits permissible exemptions to those that are shown to be "reasonable" and "necessary and proper in the public interest." 29 U.S.C. § 628. Here, the EEOC issued the proposed regulation in response to its finding that employer-sponsored retiree health benefits were decreasing. 68 Fed. Reg. at 41,543–44. Rather than maintaining retiree benefits at pre-Medicare eligibility levels for all retirees in order to avoid discrimination under the ADEA, some employers chose to reduce all retiree health benefits to a lower level. Further, in addition to rising health care costs and increased demand for retiree benefits, the EEOC correctly noted that employers are not required to provide any retiree health benefits, or to maintain such plans once they have been established. Retiree benefits often face elimination under these constraints, and the EEOC issued the proposed exemption to "permit[ ] employers to offer [retiree] benefits to the greatest extent possible." We recognize with some dismay that the proposed exemption may allow employers to reduce health benefits to retirees over the age of sixty-five while maintaining greater benefits for younger retirees. Under the circumstances, however, the EEOC has shown that this narrow exemption from the ADEA is a reasonable, necessary and proper exercise of its § 9 authority, as over time it will likely benefit all retirees.

Because we have found that the proposed regulation, being narrowly drawn to meet the goals of the ADEA and being in the public interest, is expressly authorized by the ADEA, this argument is unavailing. The EEOC has shown the regulation to be reasonable, necessary, and proper according to the terms and purposes of the statute. In the notice of proposed rulemaking, the EEOC set forth its reasons for adopting the new exemption, and indicated that the regulation is intended to respond to the unintended negative effects of its prior approach: namely, that employers have chosen to terminate retiree benefits rather than adhere to a standard that has proven too costly to sustain. 68 Fed. Reg. at 41,542–43. The EEOC's review of available material and careful explanation of its reasoning on this point demonstrates that its change in policy is neither arbitrary nor capricious.

AARP claims that the EEOC did not fully consider that a number of employers offer full health benefits to all retirees. In the notice of proposed regulation, however, the EEOC indicated a number of relevant studies and applicable statistics to support its reasoning on this point. Relying substantially on these reports, the EEOC concluded that the proposed exemption is necessary to counteract the effects of rising health care costs and to encourage employers to provide retiree health benefits to the greatest possible extent. Similarly, AARP's assertion that the EEOC failed to consider the potential effect on all workers, particularly retirees over the age of sixty-five, is contradicted by the EEOC's explanations accompanying the proposed regulation. The EEOC recognized that "many retirees in this age group rely on employer-sponsored benefits," and that such programs are "valuable benefit[s] for older persons [and] should be protected and preserved." The EEOC determined that the proposed exemption would be in the interests of all retirees, "permit[ting] employers to provide a valuable benefit to early retirees who otherwise might not be able to afford health insurance coverage and allow[ing] employers to provide valuable supplemental health benefits to retirees who are eligible for Medicare."

4. NON-DISCRIMINATION AND THE AFFORDABLE CARE ACT

The Affordable Care Act contains the following provision:

SEC. 1557. NONDISCRIMINATION.

(a) IN GENERAL.—Except as otherwise provided for in this title (or an amendment made by this title), an individual shall not, on the ground prohibited under title VI of the Civil Rights Act of 1964 (42 U.S.C. 2000d et seq.), title IX of the Education Amendments of 1972 (20 U.S.C. 1681 et seq.), the Age Discrimination Act of 1975 (42 U.S.C. 6101 et seq.), or section 504 of the Rehabilitation Act of 1973 (29 U.S.C. 794), be excluded from participation in, be denied the benefits of, or be subjected to discrimination under, any health program or activity, any part of which is receiving Federal financial assistance, including credits, subsidies, or contracts of insurance, or under any program or activity that is administered by an Executive Agency or any entity established under this title (or amendments). The enforcement mechanisms provided for and available under such title VI, title IX, section 504, or such Age Discrimination Act shall apply for purposes of violations of this subsection.

(b) CONTINUED APPLICATION OF LAWS.—Nothing in this title (or an amendment made by this title) shall be construed to invalidate or limit the rights, remedies, procedures, or legal standards available to individuals aggrieved under title VI of the Civil Rights Act of 1964 (42 U.S.C. 2000d et seq.), title VII of the Civil Rights Act of 1964 (42 U.S.C. 2000e et seq.), title IX of the Education Amendments of 1972 (20 U.S.C. 1681 et seq.), section 504 of the Rehabilitation Act of 1973 (29 U.S.C. 794), or the Age

Discrimination Act of 1975 (42 U.S.C. 611 et seq.), or to supersede State laws that provide additional protections against discrimination on any basis described in subsection (a).

(c) REGULATIONS.—The Secretary may promulgate regulations to implement this section.

The nondiscrimination provision reaches all programs and activities under Title I of the Act, which establishes the insurance reforms, the subsidy arrangements, and the state health insurance Exchanges. The provision extends the reach of, among other laws, Title VI and VII of the 1964 Civil Rights Act (recall that Part One addresses Title VII and sex discrimination in health care and coverage), and Section 504 of the Rehabilitation Act to any entity receiving federal funding, including "contracts of insurance," thereby appearing to clarify the reach of the laws to qualified health plans sold in state health insurance Exchanges, for which the government provides premium subsidies and cost-sharing reduction assistance. As of December, 2011, this provision has not been interpreted by the Secretary of Health and Human Services. Given the decision in *Choate,* as well as the analogous decision in *Mutual of Omaha,* it would probably be safe to say that across-the-board exclusions that fall particularly heavily on patients with disabilities nonetheless would not be considered discriminatory. But what if, as in *Bedrick,* (discussed in Chapter 8), a health plan were to deny otherwise covered physical therapy to a child with cerebral palsy on the ground that, as in *Bedrick,* children with such a condition cannot "recover" and thus, care is never medically necessary? Would such a limitation potentially violate not only the Exchange statute's non-discrimination clause but arguably also § 504?

Regarding discrimination based on race or national origin, recall the LEP requirements for federally assisted entities discussed in Part One. As general counsel to a qualified health plan what advice would you give with respect to the plan's obligation to comply with the LEP requirements that apply to other federally assisted health care entities?

CHAPTER 10

MEDICARE

1. INTRODUCTION

Dr. Marilyn Moon, one of the nation's leading Medicare analysts, writes of Medicare:

> Medicare has contributed substantially to the well-being of America's oldest and most disabled citizens. For some Medicare represents a model of what national health insurance could be in the United States. With low administrative costs, the program is popular with both beneficiaries and the general population. At the same time, Medicare is one of the fastest growing programs in the federal budget, gobbling up new resources at the rate of 12 percent each year during its first 37 years

Medicare: A Policy Primer, URBAN INSTITUTE 1–2 (2006).

Medicare's successes have been enormous. In the wake of its controversial enactment, Medicare "almost immediately doubled the share of people age 65 and over with insurance," with 97 percent of the elderly enrolled by 1970. Medicare not only created access to health care among the elderly but also led to a nearly 50 percent decline in the financial burden on older Americans and their families. Its vast financing capabilities have transformed the health care system, pumping trillions of dollars into the health economy over nearly a half century. Through the introduction of financial incentives at a seminal time in American history, Medicare played a central role in the desegregation of hospitals and the medical care system more generally. The health care that it has financed has contributed to a significant rise in life expectancy among persons who reach age 65. *Id.* at 2–3.

In 2010, Medicare covered 47 million persons, 39 million persons ages 65 and older and 8 million persons with disabilities. Moon, *Medicare: A Policy Primer*. Although, as noted in Chapter 6, the extent of Medicare coverage leaves beneficiaries subject to significant out-of-pocket costs, its financial impact on the standard of living has been enormous. In 2004, Medicare on a per capita basis contributed $6,670 to each program beneficiary, almost 46 percent of the median income of beneficiaries ages 65 and older that year. Moon, *Medicare: A Policy Primer* at 3.

The politics of Medicare have been extensively chronicled. MARMOR, THE POLITICS OF MEDICARE; FEIN, MEDICAL CARE MEDICAL COSTS; STARR, THE SOCIAL TRANSFORMATION OF AMERICAN MEDICINE. Because of its size as well as its emblematic stature as one of the nation's two most important programs of social contract (Social Security being the other), Medicare rests in the crosshairs of a political environment far more conservative than the one in which it was forged in 1965. Opponents of direct government insurance advocate replacing Medicare's defined benefit structure with one that would provide a "defined contribution" pegged to a rate of growth well below the rate of medical inflation. Beneficiaries of this contribution would then use their defined contribution to seek health insurance from a participating private health plan, much in the way that state health insurance Exchanges are anticipated to operate for working-age Americans and their families. Medicare Part D, enacted in 2003, provides outpatient prescription drug coverage to beneficiaries and offers a limited precedent for this approach.

Opponents of switching Medicare to a defined-contribution program point to two central facts. First, unlike health insurance Exchanges, whose stability is linked to the enrollment of millions of younger healthier people, it is not clear how a market comprised of elderly and often sick beneficiaries could survive without such massive infusion of financing that all cost savings associated with a defined contribution would be lost. Indeed, the experience of the Medicare Advantage program, Medicare's private health insurance component, has been annual costs between 12 percent and 19 percent higher than those of the traditional program. Second, over the past several decades, Medicare has been more successful than private health insurance in holding down *per capita* cost growth. Moon, *Medicare: A Policy Primer* at 112–113; Karen Davis et al., *Medicare versus Private Insurance, Rhetoric and Reality*, HEALTH AFFAIRS (Web Exclusive) w2–311 (Oct. 9, 2002). Indeed, the politics of Medicare in relation to private insurers is no less complicated than its interaction with hospitals, physicians, and medical technology suppliers: e.g., Part D bars the federal government from engaging in aggressive price negotiations in selecting participating prescription drug plans.

Medicare is one of the most complex of all federal laws, spelling out in extensive—some would say excruciating—detail all program elements. This detail arises in part from Medicare's entitlement structure, but it is also the result of the almost immeasurable political stakes that physicians, hospitals and the health care industry have in the program. Medicare represented 12 percent of the total $3.6 trillion federal outlay in 2010. One third of these outlays went for hospital care and another 18 percent, for physician services. Surprisingly, perhaps, given the level of advocacy for privatization of the program, 35 percent of all Medicare outlays in 2010 went to the purchase of private health insurance coverage for beneficiaries enrolled in private prescription drug plans (11 percent) and in Medicare Advantage Plans (24 percent), which are private insurers that sell products to Medicare; in 2010 Medicare Advantage plans enrolled nearly one quarter (11.4 million) of all beneficiaries. Moon, *Medicare: A Policy Primer* at 9–17.

2. DEFINING THE SIZE, SCOPE, AND LIMITS OF THE SOCIAL CONTRACT

In approaching the study of a subject as complex as Medicare law, it is useful to break the subject into several basic components. First, how is the program structured? Second, who is entitled to coverage? Third, what benefits are covered, how is the extent and scope of coverage (including cost-sharing) defined, and how are individual claims decisions made? Fourth, how do beneficiaries actually receive their coverage and how are participating providers and suppliers paid? (How Medicare pays providers is examined later in this Part). Fifth, how is Medicare administered and what are the rights of beneficiaries and participating providers in disputes over claims for benefits?

a.   Program Structure

Medicare consists of 4 distinct components. The 1965 legislation established Part A (known as Hospital Insurance), which covers institutional care, and Part B (known as Supplementary Medical Insurance), which covers all other health care goods and services. This structure reflects the compromise that mollified the opposition of organized medicine to compulsory government insurance. While Part A is compulsory, Part B is voluntary, a concession to organized medicine.

This compromise has drastically affected the financing, and related politics, of each part. Part A is funded through a 2.9 percent payroll tax shared by employers and workers covered under the Social Security system. Beginning in 2013, the Affordable Care Act increases the tax on high income taxpayers (over $200,000/individual and $250,000/couple) by 0.9 percentage points. Moon, *Medicare: A Policy Primer* at 1. This revenue is deposited in a trust fund, and over the years projected shortfalls have given rise to claimed "crises," which have sparked significant payment reforms we discuss later in this Part in the chapter on payment. See generally JONATHAN OBERLANDER, THE POLITICAL LIFE OF MEDICARE (2003).

By contrast, Part B, because it is voluntary, is financed through a combination of monthly individual premiums (with higher income beneficiaries charged higher premiums) and general federal revenues. Unlike Part A, Part B relies on general revenue for survival. In 2010, Part B premiums were $110.00 per month; these premium payments account for only about 25 percent of total Part B expenditures. *Moon, Medicare: A Policy Primer* at 1.

Part C was passed in response to growing pressure from an increasingly market-oriented Congress intent on reducing the role of government and expanding the role of private, risk-bearing health plans in both Medicare and Medicaid. Part C established The Medicare+Choice program ("Medicare+C") in 1997 as part of the Balanced Budget Act, Pub. L. No. 105–33 (105th Cong., 1st Sess.). Medicare+C was succeeded in 2003 by Medicare Advantage (MA), enacted as part of the Medicare Prescription Drug, Improvement, and Modernization Act, Pub. L. No. 108–173 (108th Cong., 1st Sess.). Building on the 1997 legislation, MA created large financial incentives to attract private health insurers into Medicare while offering an array of new private health insurance options for Medicare beneficiaries. Because of this generous funding, MA plans frequently offer coverage for items and services not covered by traditional Medicare, such as eyeglasses and dental care.

By 2010, enrollment in the array of entities allowed to market under the MA mantle surpassed 11 million, a quarter of all beneficiaries. *Medicare Advantage 2010 Data Spotlight*, KAISER FAMILY FOUNDATION, http://www. kff.org/medicare/upload/8080.pdf. This surge in enrollment (owing to more attractive coverage) exacerbated the fact that MA plan compensation levels averaged between 112% and 119% of the amount that the traditional Medicare program would have paid for the same services offered to the same beneficiaries. The most significant overpayment problems appear to have affected the MA "fee for service" market, which operates in heavily rural areas, whose health care costs are lower to begin with, thereby making the business even more profitable. MEDPAC, REPORT TO CONGRESS (2006); Moon, *Medicare: A Policy Primer*; Marsha Gold, *Medicare Advantage 2006–2007: What Congress Intended?*, 26(4) HEALTH AFFAIRS (Web Exclusive) w445 (2007); Robert Berenson, *Medicare Disadvantaged and the Search for the Elusive Level Playing Field*, HEALTH AFFAIRS (Web Exclusive) w4–572 (December 15, 2004), http://content.healthaffairs.org/cgi/reprint/hlthaff.w4.572v1.

Because their benefits are more generous, MA plans have attracted significant enrollment among beneficiaries with modest incomes who cannot afford to purchase private supplemental insurance coverage (known as Medigap policies, discussed below), which offers additional coverage to offset Medicare cost-sharing and certain coverage limits and exclusions. *Medicare Advantage 2010 Data Spotlight,* KAISER FAMILY FOUNDATION, http://www.kff.org/medicare/upload/8080.pdf. MA plans also disproportionately enroll lower income Medicare beneficiaries, including so-called dual enrollees or eligibles, who are entitled to both Medicare and Medicaid coverage (also discussed more fully below). MA plans thus serve higher numbers of patients with limited discretionary funds available to them and limited levels of education and health literacy. Sarah Lueck, *Insurers Fight to Defend Lucrative Medicare Business* WSJ, April 30 2007, at A1. (For a contrary view see Edwin Park & Robert Greenstein, *Low Income and Minority Beneficiaries Do Not Rely Disproportionately on Medicare Advantage Plans*, CENTER ON BUDGET AND POLICY PRIORITIES (Washington D.C. 2007), claiming that industry figures are misleading).

Ironically, then, the subjects of Medicare's experimentation with competing, risk-bearing plans are the portion of Medicare beneficiaries least capable of exercising the "choice" supposedly allowed by the availability of MA plans. Because the MA population is elderly, disproportionately low-income, and has lower levels of education and health literacy, they are the least prepared among Medicare beneficiaries to navigate the world of private health insurance. (Many Medicare beneficiaries of advanced age may well have experienced their first insurance coverage with Medicare, and "traditional" Medicare as it is sometimes known, is relatively straightforward compared to private insurance). In their 2004 review of Medicare Advantage, as well as the Part D prescription drug program, Brian Biles and colleagues identified several major "challenges" that would arise, given the history of Medicare managed care:

First, the complexity of enrollment and the potential for confusing and misleading information and practices, owing to the relative inexperience of beneficiaries in choosing, combined with the fact that the "actuarial equivalence" standard governing both MA and the Part D benefit (meaning the absence of a standardized benefit package) allows plans to offer "a seemingly limitless" variety of plan packages with little variation but enough to create enormous confusion. The authors note that many of the consumer aid tools created by the government depend on use of the internet, a reality for only 19 percent of beneficiaries. They also note evidence of the confusion that sets in when elderly or cognitively impaired beneficiaries are asked to make choices.

Second, since only 5 percent of Medicare beneficiaries incur nearly 50 percent of all program costs, the authors predicted efforts by plans to avoid high cost enrollees through location, marketing, and deceptive sales practices and techniques. The actuarial leeway given to coverage design under the law means that marketing abuses can be coupled with product designs that attract low cost members (health club memberships, low cost eyeglasses) and high cost sharing for benefits and services used by more costly enrollees.

The third challenge involves instability in benefit design and provider networks, as plans enter and exit the market, change networks, and tinker with benefit design. The authors note that "from 1997 to 2003 the number of private M+C plans decreased by more than half, from 346 plans in 1998 to 155 plans in November 2003. Private plan enrollment dropped from 6.2 million beneficiaries in 1998 to 4.6 million in November 2003, a reduction of 26 percent."

Fourth, plan enrollment is structured to lock in beneficiaries for a minimum period (annually) much as enrollment periods work in private group coverage. The lock in feature means that beneficiaries who are sick and underserved cannot leave.

Fifth is the problem of geographic inequity, meaning serious underservice in certain parts of the country and a glut in others. High plan location variation means that in different parts of the country, not only is access different, but so is Medicare plan design itself, losing the consistency and dependability that has been the program's hallmark.

Sixth is the risk of plan over-payment, which, as noted, has had a long history in Medicare because of the crudeness of premium risk adjustments.

Brian Biles et al., *Medicare Advantage, Déjà vu All Over Again?* HEALTH AFFAIRS (Web Exclusive) w4–586 (December 15, 2004), http://content. healthaffairs.org/cgi/reprint/hlthaff.w4.586v1.

Over the years there has been evidence of MA marketing abuses, particularly in communities in which the gap between the MA payment rate and prevailing traditional Medicare payments is the widest. Extensive Congressional testimony has described harsh sales tactics coupled with evidence that once enrolled, beneficiaries, particularly those living in rural areas and enrolled in "fee-for-service" plans, have been unable to locate any participating providers. Paradoxically, although the fee for service plans operate without networks, their interaction with private physicians has been so poor that doctors reportedly have been unwilling to accept patients with fee-for-service plan coverage. Robert Pear, *For Recipient of Medicare, the Hard Sell*, N.Y. TIMES, Dec. 17, 2007. The problems were so great that in July 2007, CMS issued a memorandum to all MA and Part D organizations establishing a Special Election Period to allow disenrollment by MA enrollees who had been tricked into enrollment by fraudulent marketing. Memorandum to All Medicare Advantage and Part D Organizations, July 18 2007 from Anthony Culotta, reported in BNA Daily Health Care Policy Reporter (July 20, 2007).

Evidence of abuse, coupled with overpayments to MA plans, combined to underscore the fact that this "privatization," rather than disentangling Congress from the headaches of Medicare policy and politics, was sucking it in deeper. *See, e.g.*, U.S. GOV'T ACCOUNTABILITY OFFICE, GAO–08–827R, MEDICARE ADVANTAGE ORGANIZATIONS: ACTUAL EXPENSES AND PROFITS COMPARED TO PROJECTIONS FOR 2005 (June 24, 2008); Robert Berenson & Melissa M. Goldstein, *Will Medicare Wither on the Vine? How Congress Has Advantaged Medicare Advantage—and What's a Level Playing Field Anyway?* 1 ST. LOUIS U. J. HEALTH L. & POL'Y. 5 (2007). (Noting $160 billion in excess MA payments between FY 2008 and 2018).

In 2008 and then as part of the Affordable Care Act, Congress took certain steps to address the twin problems of excess payments and marketing abuses. The Medicare Improvement for Patients and Providers Act of 2008, Pub. L. No. 110–275, § 103, prohibits certain sales and marketing activities under both Medicare Advantage and by Medicare Part D plans. The 2008 amendments also established stricter provider participation requirements for fee-for-service MA plans and trimmed payment. The Affordable Care Act replaced the 2003 payment methodology to bring costs into line with the original program, a reform that might be expected to result in the withdrawal of MA plans from less profitable markets, as well as to reduction in the additional coverage they offer.

Part D, enacted in 2003, provides coverage of outpatient prescription drugs. As with Part C, Part D effectuates coverage not through a direct government program but instead through contracts with private entities that offer "prescription drug plans" (all Medicare Advantage plans also must offer a Part D outpatient prescription drug plan as a condition of participation). As with Part B, Part D financing involves both premium payments and general revenues. In addition, states contribute to Part D, which, by extending coverage for outpatient drugs to individuals dually enrolled in Medicare and Medicaid, obviates the need for state Medicaid expenditures on prescription drug coverage (Medicaid is a secondary payer to Medicare). As will be the case with the state health insurance Exchanges, Part D offers both premium support and cost-sharing assistance to low-income beneficiaries. As of April, 2010, 27.6 million beneficiaries were enrolled in a Part D plan.

In 2010, the standard Part D plan had a $310 deductible and a $25 percent coinsurance up to the initial part D coverage limit of $2,830 in total drug costs. This exposure is then followed by a coverage gap, in which enrollees in 2010 with at least $2,830 in total costs paid 100 percent of their drug costs until they spent $4,550 out of pocket (excluding premiums). At that point, known as a catastrophic threshold, Part D coverage kicks in again, limiting individual payments to 5 percent of the drug cost (or a minimum copayment) for the remainder of the year. Of course, all of this would start again in the following year. The Affordable Care Act slowly phases in gap coverage between 2011 and 2020. Moon, *Medicare: A Policy Primer* at 11–12.

Since 2006, monthly Part D premiums have risen significantly. A special Low Income Subsidy exists to help individuals who are ineligible for Medicaid but have low income and assets. In 2009, more than 36 percent of all Part D recipients received low income subsidies, but only about 65 percent of those eligible for them actually received the help. *Low Income Assistance Under the Medicare Drug Benefit,* KAISER FAMILY FOUNDATION (2009), http://www.kff.org/medicare/upload/7327–05.pdf.

b. Eligibility

Medicare entitles nearly all persons age 65 and older to Medicare Part A, if either they or their spouse are eligible for Social Security payments and have contributed to the Social Security payroll system for at least 10 years (40 quarters). Medicare eligibility is also conditioned on U.S. citizenship or permanent legal residence. Because Medicare is a universal entitlement, individuals become eligible without regard to their medical history or preexisting conditions and do not need to meet an income or asset test. Moon, *Medicare: A Policy Primer* at 2.

Medicare also entitles adults under age 65 to coverage if they are entitled to Social Security Disability Income (SSDI) and have received payments for 24 months. The minimum 40–quarter rule applicable to coverage at age 65 does not apply to persons with disabilities. In the case of individuals with end-stage renal disease (ESRD) (who qualify for Medicare regardless of age) or Lou Gehrig's Disease, the 24–month waiting period does not apply.

Part A is available on a monthly premium basis to individuals who attain age 65 but who did not pay enough into the Social Security system to qualify for automatic coverage. Additionally, individuals entitled to Part A and others age 65 and older may elect to enroll in Part B. Approximately 95 percent of persons with Part A are also enrolled in Part B. For most individuals who become entitled to Part A, enrollment in Part B is automatic unless an individual opts out. People who work past age 65 and their spouses may delay enrollment until retirement without having to pay a late enrollment penalty.

Part A entitlement coupled with Part B enrollment allows individuals to select enrollment in a Part C MA plan in lieu of traditional Medicare if they wish. As with private health insurance, MA is subject to annual open enrollment rules to reduce the risk of adverse selection, with late enrollment fees and certain exceptions to the late enrollment penalty applicable. A similar approach is taken in the case of Part D, with eligibility conditioned on Part A entitlement and Part B enrollment. Enrollment is into either a "stand alone" prescription drug plan in the case of beneficiaries covered through the traditional Medicare program or through a MA plan. As with MA, Part D has established open enrollment periods, with penalties for late enrollment unless an exception applies.

c. Benefits and Coverage

The Medicare statute and regulations operate like the plan documents that govern private insurance, and they are detailed and dense with respect to coverage. The Secretary of Health and Human Services is empowered to interpret and apply the terms of the statute and furthermore is authorized to make "National Coverage Determinations (NCD)" regarding coverage of a very limited number of new procedures and technologies. 42 U.S.C. § 1395ff. Even in the case of Parts C and D, both of which allow plan administrators considerable discretion over benefit design and claims decisions, the Medicare statute and regulations impose extensive requirements.

Medicare initially was structured to resemble a commercial insurance plan of its time. Although benefits have been considerably broadened since 1965, the program still has as its central focus coverage and payment for acute episodes of illness followed by relatively brief convalescent periods. Thus, for example, it offers no long-term custodial care, and services for individuals who live in communities and need assistance with the normal activities of daily living are quite limited. Medicare has been expanded to include greater coverage of preventive services and outpatient prescription drugs (an addition that did not come until the program was nearly 40 years old); coverage is still lacking for routine vision and dental and oral care.

Part A is centered on inpatient hospital stays. As such, it covers inpatient care and any following "after-care," which may include short-term stays in skilled nursing facilities and home health care. It also covers hospice care and home blood infusion therapy. While there is no premium for Part A for most beneficiaries—as stated earlier, it is financed largely out of payroll taxes—patients must pay a deductible before coverage begins. In 2010, the Part A deductible for each "spell of illness" stood at $1,100 for an inpatient hospital stay. Part A also requires the payment of coinsurance for both inpatient hospital care ($275 per day for days 61–90 in 2010) and services of skilled nursing facilities ($137.50 per day for days 21–100 in

2010). Although home health care is furnished without cost-sharing, it should be readily apparent that out-of-pocket costs can be significant.

Part B covers outpatient services, such as outpatient hospital care, physician visits, and other medical services, including preventive services such as mammography, colorectal screening and certain vaccines. Part B also covers ambulance services, clinical laboratory services, durable medical equipment (such as wheelchairs and oxygen), kidney supplies and services, outpatient mental health care, and diagnostic tests such as x-rays and magnetic resonance imaging. The Affordable Care Act expanded the range of preventive services available under Part B, adding a free annual comprehensive wellness visit and a personalized prevention plan. The Act also empowers the Secretary of DHHS to modify coverage of Medicare-covered preventive services to conform to the recommendations of the U.S. Preventive Services Task Force (USPSTF), whose recommendations also guide coverage of preventive services offered in the individual and group health plan markets.

Part B, as noted, imposes a monthly premium, which rises in connection with Social Security cost of living increases ("COLA"). In years in which there is no increase, the premium remains constant for most beneficiaries, but new enrollees, higher income beneficiaries, and low-income beneficiaries (whose premium is paid through either Medicaid or a separate subsidy) are subject to annual Part B premium increases regardless of COLA.

Beneficiaries enrolled in Medicare Advantage plans remain entitled to all benefits covered under Parts A, B and D. MA enrollees pay their Part B premiums to their MA plans and may be required to pay an additional premium for more extended coverage. Similarly, Part D enrollees pay premiums as well as cost-sharing.

Unlike Parts A and B, Part D lacks a statutory definition of coverage. Instead, Part D plans must meet "standard coverage" rules linked to broad prescription drug benefit classes and cost-sharing levels; administrators are given considerable discretion to design actuarial equivalency tests for coverage as long as the dollar value of coverage meets the law's tests of value. Part D is significantly different from the "traditional" Medicare program as a result of the politics surrounding its enactment. A major achievement of the Bush Administration and a Republican Congress, Part D was designed by highly market-oriented experts and relies on the philosophy of market competition, discussed in Chapter 6. At the same time, the competition is not exactly full-bore: Medicare remains at risk for the highest-cost beneficiaries.

Part D plans (either "stand alone" prescription drug plans (PDPs) and Medicare Advantage plans offering Part D coverage) compete for business, marketing products that meet the minimum federal coverage design rules. Within these broad benefit classes (which consist of classes and categories of prescribed drugs and biologicals including vaccines not covered under Part B), plans have a good deal of leeway to design their products. For example, within any class, a plan may cover certain brands and not others.

The plan may charge higher cost-sharing for certain brands (known as tiered cost-sharing) or may require beneficiaries to fail first in relation to a lower cost drug before a higher cost drug will be dispensed. In this sense, the structure of the Part D model clearly emerges as a federal prototype for qualified health plans operating in state health insurance Exchanges and offering "essential health benefits."*

Certain consumer protections apply to both MA and Part D plans. For example, a Part D plan member may request an "exception" to his or her plan formulary in order to get a non-covered drug or to seek a reduction in higher cost-sharing requirements; in these cases plans are given the discretion to approve the exception based on the strength of the evidence presented. Part D beneficiaries, as well as Medicare Advantage beneficiaries, have appeal rights for disputes over claims. Both MA and Part D plans are held to certain network adequacy standards. Part D formularies must be based on scientific standards and must be overseen by a formulary committee that adheres to the therapeutic classes and categories required of all Part D plans.

In order to stimulate the creation of the Part D plan market, Congress created significantly favorable conditions. As a result, as is the case with Medicare Advantage plans, even when a Part D plan operates at "full risk," it in fact is provided with a "risk corridor" that under law guarantees that Medicare will effectively hold the plan harmless by picking up the costs of coverage once certain cost thresholds are met. Thus, once the costs incurred by a prescription drug plan (PDP) for a particular beneficiary reach 102.5 percent of a target set by law, Medicare will cover 75 percent of the plan's costs in order to stem its losses; if the costs rise to more than 105 percent of the target, Medicare stop-loss payments will rise to 80 percent. Medicare therefore still bears the risk of catastrophic prescription coverage, even though it enrolls beneficiaries in private at-risk plans.

In sum, while Medicare offers broad coverage, it also leaves significant gaps particularly in relation to custodial long-term care services offered either at home or in an institution. Nor does the program pay for routine dental care and dentures, routine vision care or eyeglasses, or hearing exams and hearing aids. Further, as we have discussed, Part D was enacted with significant limitations in coverage, including a so-called "donut hole" aimed at reducing moral hazard. This coverage hole leaves beneficiaries completely exposed to out-of-pocket costs once an initial annual coverage threshold is reached. Coverage then resumes once the catastrophic threshold is met. The Affordable Care Act gradually phases out the donut hole and offers beneficiaries access to discounted brand name drugs during this phase-down period.

---

* In fact, the State Children's Health Insurance Program (SCHIP, renamed CHIP in 2009), offered the real prototype of this approach in which the federal government moved away from a defined benefit for coverage and toward one in which benefits are sketched out in law and private companies are given leeway to vary the benefit design as long as they meet federally defined actuarial value standards in relation to patient cost-sharing for covered services.

Because Medicare coverage is relatively narrow and cost-sharing is high, beneficiaries carry significant financial exposure to health care costs. Between 1997 and 2006, median out-of-pocket spending as a share of beneficiary income rose from 11.9 percent to 16.2 percent. Moon, *Medicare: A Policy Primer* at 6. As a result, nearly 90 percent of beneficiaries have supplemental insurance. In addition, Medicare lacks a stop-loss benefit that shields beneficiaries from excessive out-of-pocket spending (ironically, perhaps, even as it creates stop-loss coverage for MA plans and prescription drug plans). Individuals may buy supplemental coverage, but of course this costs extra, leaving millions of beneficiaries with exposure to high out-of-pocket costs.

If they are sufficiently poor, Medicare beneficiaries qualify for Medicaid as a form of supplemental coverage. In 2010, 34 percent of beneficiaries had employer-sponsored coverage, 22 percent were enrolled in Medicare Advantage plans offering supplemental coverage, and 17 percent purchased "Medigap" policies, special supplemental insurance coverage that became subject to federal regulation in the 1980s in response to extensive evidence of fraudulent marketing practices and excessively low medical-loss ratios. Medigap policies can range from limited to extensive under federal coverage standards, but the 2003 prescription drug coverage legislation bars the sale of plans offering additional prescription drug coverage, thereby guaranteeing financial exposure by beneficiaries with high prescription drug costs unless they are poor enough to qualify for "low income assistance." See generally, CCH, MEDICARE EXPLAINED ¶ 740 (2011).

Note: Making Part D Work for Low-Income Beneficiaries

Because of the enormous interest in Medicare Part D, there already exists a considerable literature on early experiences with most phases of the program, from market response to its effects on beneficiary access and use of prescription drugs. Early evidence suggests that beneficiaries are generally satisfied with their Part D plans, including their current costs and access to medications under the program. ERICH ANDREAS DROTLEFF, THE MEDICARE PART D PRESCRIPTION DRUG BENEFIT: WHO WINS AND WHO LOSES? 148 (Marquette Elder's Advisor Fall 2006). At the same time, interviewees indicated substantial dissatisfaction with program design (particularly the deductibles and coverage gaps) and program administration. They are conflicted about the process of choosing and indicate that they would have preferred a program more like traditional Part A/B Medicare Coverage. Florian Heiss et al., *Who Failed to Enroll In Medicare Part D, And Why? Early Results*, 25(5) HEALTH AFFAIRS (Web Exclusive) w352 (August 1, 2006).

Of particular concern has been the experience of low-income beneficiaries, as well as the poorest Medicare beneficiaries, i.e., the dual eligibles. Some 27 percent of all Medicare beneficiaries, and a higher proportion of dual enrollees, have a cognitive impairment. (The number of dual eligibles with dementia or psychiatric illness is estimated at 2.4 million persons). The transition of dual eligibles into Part D was chaotic, with many states unable to ensure their connection with a plan and forced to pay millions of dollars in costs in order to keep coverage going during the transition. Part D enrollment is compulsory for dual eligibles, and this group is automatically assigned to plans without a guarantee that their drugs will be covered under the formulary (many duals may be on multiple drugs because of severe and co-occurring physical and mental conditions). Because Medicaid drug coverage is broader than Part D, the movement of dual eligibles from Medicaid to Medicare Part D means a decline in coverage, a problem that adversely affects dual eligibles in need of unusual drugs. Finally, because the government subsidy for duals permits enrollment only in basic benefit plans, some states are experiencing the loss of Part D participating plans that will accept duals, even as the number of plans offering costly supplemental coverage burgeons. As a result, dual enrollees may experience frequent disruptions in coverage and plan switching. *See generally Dual Eligibles and Medicare Part D*, KAISER COMMISSION ON MEDICAID AND THE UNINSURED (May, 2006); U.S. GOV'T ACCOUNTABILITY OFFICE, GAO–07–272, CHALLENGES IN ENROLLING NEW DUAL-ELIGIBLE BENEFICIARIES (2007).

Part D offers subsidies (known as low-income subsidies, LIS) to low-income Medicare beneficiaries who are ineligible for Medicaid, a precursor of the premium tax credits available to low-income individuals through state health insurance Exchanges. As with premium tax credits, even a slight fluctuation in income can result in the loss of the subsidy and the need to begin enrollment again. In 2007 an estimated 600,000 low-income beneficiaries with LIS are expected to lose their subsidy and will join the nearly 3 million who never made it into the subsidy system at all. JENNIFER O'SULLIVAN, MEDICARE: ENROLLMENT IN MEDICARE DRUG PLANS (Cong. Res. Serv., Library of Congress, Washington D.C. Updated Nov. 29, 2006).

In any major insurance program, a basic problem is how to make enrollment work properly. Enrollment in Parts A and B are relatively straightforward; that is, the Part A premium is pre-funded through payroll taxes, while the Part B premium is uniform and updated annually.

Part D is a different matter. Beneficiaries choose from dozens of plans with different premiums. Changes in plan offerings or operations can cause mid-year changes, and annual shifts in enrollment can affect the premium owed on a beneficiary-by-beneficiary basis.

In order to ease matters for beneficiaries, the law provides for a deduction of premiums from monthly Social Security checks, as is the case with Part B. But the complexity of Part D means that the deduction process is highly prone to error because the enormous number of choices by beneficiaries must be transmitted from CMS, which administers Part D, to the Social Security Administration, which administers the Social Security payment system.

Within months of program implementation, it was clear that the system was seriously flawed. The failure to operationalize the enrollment and deduction system properly led to erroneous deductions from the monthly Social Security checks received by thousands of lower income beneficiaries, whose checks in some cases were so significantly reduced as a result of government errors that beneficiaries' ability to subsist was seriously impaired. Machado v. Leavitt, 542 F. Supp.2d 185 (D. Mass. 2008), concerned the harms that befell beneficiaries as implementation began, with significant over-withholding of Social Security payments because of unreliable information about variable plan premiums (recall that unlike Part B, which is uniform, Part D plan premiums can vary widely). The court's opinion allowing the case to proceed on Constitutional grounds began with this notable introduction:

> Phrased generally, this lawsuit raises the following question: how egregious does an agency's failure to make timely corrections of its own mistakes have to be, and how much suffering do these uncorrected errors have to inflict, before a violation of due process may be found? Specifically, these low-income Plaintiffs contend they have suffered erroneous and excessive deductions from their monthly Social Security checks as a result of blunders by Defendants in the calculation of their prescription drug plan premiums under Medicare Part D. These mistakes, which at this point are undisputed, have deprived Plaintiffs of hundreds of dollars for periods lasting from five to seventeen months.

Id. at 187–88. A settlement in *Machado* was announced in June, 2008 as the two federal agencies were able to establish systems for the more rapid correction of erroneous Social Security payment withholding.

d. Provider and Supplier Participation and Payment

Much of the Medicare statute is devoted to defining the program's conditions of participation and payment rules for Part A providers, Part B suppliers, Medicare Advantage plans (authorized under Part C), and Medicare Part D prescription drug plans. Since 1980, methods for paying providers under Parts A and B have been transformed in certain fundamental ways. Since Medicare represents nearly 40% of hospital revenues and 25% of physician revenues, one can begin to appreciate the extent to which Medicare not only is integral to the modern health care system but has payment rules that are so heavily a creature of political action.

Medicare payment principles are described in a later chapter in this Part. Medicare's broader social benefit role is evident in these principles. For example, Medicare's inpatient hospital payment formula includes additional payments to hospitals that serve a "disproportionate share" of low-income Medicare and Medicaid beneficiaries. 42 U.S.C. § 1395ww(d). Medicare hospital financing also explicitly includes payments for the direct and indirect costs of "graduate medical education," 42 U.S.C. § 1395ww(d), as well as payments for the cost of training nurses and allied health professionals. 42 U.S.C. § 1395x(v). Medicare also explicitly recognizes capital related costs. 42 U.S.C. § 1395ww(g). Finally, Medicare pays for routine costs associated with clinical trials as well as investigational devices. *See* http://www.cms.hhs.gov/manuals/downloads/Pub06_PART_35.pdf; Mark Barnes & Jerald Korn, *Medicare Clinical Trials*, 38 J. HEALTH L. 609 (2005) (discussing the relationship between the coverage determination process discussed below and coverage of clinical trials). Indeed, Medicare payment policies for routine costs associated with clinical trials served as the basis for the clinical trials provision of the Affordable Care Act, PHSA § 2709, added by PPACA § 1201.

e. Coverage Limitations and Exclusions; National Coverage Determinations and Local Coverage Decisions

Medicare contains important limitations and exclusions on coverage. The core principle that guides Medicare, as is the case with every form of health insurance, is that the program excludes items and services that are "not reasonable and necessary for the diagnosis or treatment of illness or injury, or to improve the functioning of a malformed body part." 42 U.S.C. § 1395y(a)(1)(A)–(E). Over the decades of Medicare administration, the federal government has developed regulations and more detailed guidance specifying when items and services are considered reasonable and necessary; coverage can vary depending on the nature of the condition. In the case of new and emerging treatments and services, the Secretary is empowered to make national coverage determinations (NCDs), discussed at greater length, below. The federal government, in making NCDs, maintains a manual detailing excluded procedures. *National Coverage Determinations Manual,* Pub. 100–03. When no national coverage determination exists, Medicare contractors that process claims (i.e., insurers acting as third-party administrators) are authorized to make local coverage decisions based on the reasonable and necessity of coverage.

Coverage decisions made during claims processing rest on the evidence in the record, including the patient's medical record and the conclusions and recommendations of the patient's physician, but in Medicare as in private insurance, the physician's decision of medical necessity is not binding, nor does it receive presumptive weight. *HCFA Ruling 93–1,* May 18, 1993.

f. Medicare Administration and Appeals

In administering Medicare Parts A and B, the federal government assumes a role not dissimilar to that of a self-insuring employer. That is, the government brings in contractors (known as Medicare administrative contractors (MACs)), previously known as intermediaries and carriers but renamed as contractors by the Medicare Modernization Act of 2003, Pub. L. No. 108–173 § 911. These contractors are typically large private insurance companies which act as third-party administrators for CMS. Indeed, reliance on private insurers to administer Medicare was a key element in securing the support of the American Hospital Association in the program's enactment in 1965.

In the case of Parts C and D, Medicare's role is more that of a purchaser of products than a self-insuring employer who uses third-party administrators for its own plan. MA and PDP plans have more leeway to design their products, risk is shared with the federal government, and the entities operate in the manner of regulated private entities rather than as direct agents of the government.

Beyond claims administrators and Medicare Advantage and Prescription Drug plans, Medicare contracts with a dizzying array of entities involved in program administration: Quality Improvement Organizations that carry out peer-review activities (discussed at greater length in Part Three), Recovery Audit Contractors (RACs), who perform audit functions), qualified independent contractors (QICs), which perform independent external review, and other entities.

Medicare provides a lengthy process of administrative review of claims (which may be expedited under certain conditions), including appeals involving entitlement and enrollment, as well as a uniform appeals process for reviewing claims under Parts A and B. The uniform system establishes a four-level review process beginning with a redetermination by the Medicare contractor and is followed by a "reconsideration" conducted by a "qualified independent contractor." The third level of review is conducted by an administrative law judge, with final review by the Medicare Appeals Council. SSA § 1869(b)–(d). Patients enrolled in Part C MA plans and Part D PDPs are entitled to independent external review as well as internal plan appeals. Separate appeals processes apply to national coverage determinations and local coverage decisions.

Quality Improvement Organizations (QIOs) make initial determinations regarding patients' continued eligibility for inpatient care. 42 C.F.R. § 405.924 (c). Patients who receive notices of non-coverage while hospitalized may request an expedited review and benefits are continued pending the review. 42 C.F.R. §§ 405.1206, 405.1208, 312.42(c)(3). The advance notice and expedited appeals process also applies to beneficiaries who are informed that skilled nursing facility, hospice, home health, and comprehensive outpatient treatment facility services are about to end. 42 C.F.R. § 405.1200.

Medicare providers and suppliers are entitled to their own process of administrative appeal for adverse determinations, as well as judicial review. As in the case of private insurance and employer-sponsored plans, providers and suppliers can accept assignment of claims, thereby allowing them to appeal coverage denials. Providers and supplier appeal rights also include appeals of recovery audit contractor (RAC) determinations, provider status determinations, the impositions of fines and civil money penalties, and suspensions and exclusions from Medicare participation. 42 C.F.R. Part 498. The appeals system for providers and suppliers also permits challenges to cost reports for those providers to which cost-reporting requirements apply. 42 C.F.R. § 405.1801. In each case, multi-phased review procedures are used, and judicial review is available. Provider status reviews, which address continued participation in the program or suspensions and fines, are heard before the Departmental Appeals Board (DAB), while appeals of provider audits and cost report findings are heard by the Provider Reimbursement Review Board.

Federal law places important limits on the power of courts to consider Medicare appeals from adverse decisions in claims administration. The Medicare statute, 42 U.S.C. § 1395ii, incorporates the Social Security Act's limitations on judicial review, 42 U.S.C. § 405(h), which requires exhaustion of administrative remedies before a claimant may seek judicial review. Parts A and B involve a five-level process, which begins with an initial determination, followed by a redetermination of the initial denial by the administrative contractor. This "internal" redetermination is followed by a review conducted by a qualified independent contractor. This phase then leads to a full evidentiary review before an administrative law judge and a final appeal to the Medicare Appeals Council. The Medicare Modernization Act also revised the rules for amount in controversy, requiring that the minimum threshold increase by the annual percentage increase in the medical component of the consumer price index. 42 U.S.C. § 1395ff(b)(1)(e).

---

3.   DEFINING THE SCOPE AND LIMITS OF THE MEDICARE ENTITLEMENT

Heckler v. Ringer

466 U.S. 602 (1984)

■ JUSTICE REHNQUIST delivered the opinion of the Court.

Respondents are individual Medicare claimants who raise various challenges to the policy of the Secretary of Health and Human Services (Secretary) as to the payment of Medicare benefits for a surgical procedure known as bilateral carotid body resection (BCBR). The United States District Court for the Central District of California dismissed the action for lack of jurisdiction, finding that in essence respondents are claiming entitlement to benefits for the BCBR procedure and therefore must exhaust their administrative remedies pursuant to 42 U.S.C. § 405(g), before pursuing their action in federal court. The Court of Appeals for the Ninth Circuit reversed and remanded for consideration on the merits. Ringer v. Schweiker, 697 F.2d 1291 (1982). We granted certiorari to sort out the thorny jurisdictional problems which respondents' claims present, and we now reverse as to all respondents.

Title XVIII of the Social Security Act, 42 U.S.C. § 1395 et seq., commonly known as Medicare, establishes a federally subsidized health insurance program to be administered by the Secretary. Part A of the Act, 42 U.S.C. § 1395c et seq., provides insurance for the cost of hospital and related post-hospital services, but the Act precludes reimbursement for any "items or services ... which are not reasonable and necessary for the diagnosis or treatment of illness or injury." § 1395y(a)(1). The Medicare Act authorizes the Secretary to determine what claims are covered by the Act "in accordance with the regulations prescribed by him." § 1395ff(a). Judicial review of claims arising under Medicare is available only after the Secretary renders a "final decision" on the claim, in the same manner as is provided in 42 U.S.C. § 405(g)[2] for old age and disability claims arising under Title II of the Social Security Act. 42 U.S.C. § 1395ff(b)(1)(C).

---

2. Title 42 U.S.C. § 405(g) provides in part as follows: "Any individual, after any final decision of the Secretary made after a hearing to which he was a party, irrespective of the

Pursuant to her rulemaking authority, see 42 U.S.C. §§ 1395hh, 1395ii (incorporating 42 U.S.C. § 405(a)), the Secretary has provided that a "final decision" is rendered on a Medicare claim only after the individual claimant has pressed his claim through all designated levels of administrative review.[3] First, the Medicare Act authorizes the Secretary to enter into contracts with fiscal intermediaries providing that the latter will determine whether a particular medical service is covered by Part A, and if so, the amount of the reimbursable expense for that service. 42 U.S.C. § 1395h, 42 CFR § 405.702 (1983). If the intermediary determines that a particular service is not covered under Part A, the claimant can seek reconsideration by the Health Care Financing Administration (HCFA) [renamed the Centers for Medicare and Medicaid Services by the Bush Administration in 2001] in the Department of Health and Human Services. 42 CFR §§ 405.710–405.716 (1983). If denial of the claim is affirmed after reconsideration and if the claim exceeds $100 the claimant is entitled to a hearing before an administrative law judge (ALJ) in the same manner as is provided for claimants under Title II of the Act. If the claim is again denied, the claimant may seek review in the Appeals Council. If the Appeals Council also denies the claim and if the claim exceeds $1,000 only then may the claimant seek judicial review in federal district court of the "Secretary's final decision." 42 U.S.C. §§ 1395ff(b)(1)(C), (b)(2).

In January 1979, the Secretary through the HCFA issued an administrative instruction to all fiscal intermediaries, instructing them that no payment is to be made for Medicare claims arising out of the BCBR surgical procedure when performed to relieve respiratory distress. See 45 Fed. Reg. 71431–71432 (1980) (reproducing the instruction).[4] Relying on information from the Public Health Service and a special Task Force of the National Heart, Lung and Blood Institute of the National Institutes of Health, the HCFA explained that BCBR has been "shown to lack [the] general acceptance of the professional medical community" and that "controlled clinical

---

amount in controversy, may obtain a review of such decision by a civil action. The court shall have power to enter, upon the pleadings and transcript of the record, a judgment affirming, modifying, or reversing the decision of the Secretary, with or without remanding the cause for a rehearing. The findings of the Secretary as to any fact, if supported by substantial evidence, shall be conclusive. The judgment of the court shall be final except that it shall be subject to review in the same manner as a judgment in other civil actions."

3. The Secretary has recognized one exception which is not applicable here. She has provided by regulation that when the facts and her interpretation of the law are not in dispute and when the only factor precluding an award of benefits is a statutory provision which the claimant challenges as unconstitutional, the claimant need not exhaust his administrative remedies beyond the reconsideration stage. 42 CFR §§ 405.718–405.718e (1983); 20 CFR §§ 404.923–404.928 (1983).

4. BCBR, first performed in this country in the 1960's, involves the surgical removal of the carotid bodies, structures the size of a rice grain which are located in the neck and which control the diameter of the bronchial tubes. Proponents of the procedure claim that it reduces the symptoms of pulmonary diseases such as asthma, bronchitis, and emphysema. Although the Secretary concluded that BCBR for that purpose is not "reasonable and necessary" within the meaning of the Medicare Act, she did note that the medical community had accepted the procedure as effective for another purpose, the removal of a carotid body tumor in the neck. 45 Fed. Reg. 71431 (1980).

studies establishing the safety and effectiveness of this procedure are needed." It concluded that the procedure "must be considered investigational" and not "reasonable and necessary" within the meaning of the Medicare Act.

Many claimants whose BCBR claims were denied by the intermediaries as a result of the instruction sought review of the denial before ALJs, who were not bound by the Secretary's instructions to the intermediaries. Until October 1980, ALJs were consistently ruling in favor of individual BCBR claimants. The Appeals Council also authorized payment for BCBR Part A expenses in a consolidated [1980] case involving numerous claimants.

In response to the rulings of the ALJs and the Appeals Council, on October 28, 1980, the Secretary through the HCFA issued a formal administrative ruling, intended to have binding effect on the ALJs and the Appeals Council, prohibiting them in all individual cases from ordering Medicare payments for BCBR operations occurring after that date. In the ruling the Secretary noted that she had consulted with the Public Health Service, and again had concluded that the BCBR procedure was not "reasonable and necessary" within the meaning of the Medicare Act.

On September 18, 1980, respondents in this case filed a complaint in the District Court for the Central District of California, raising numerous challenges focused on the Secretary's January 1979 instructions to her intermediaries precluding payment for BCBR surgery.* On November 7, 1980, after the Secretary issued the formal ruling binding on the ALJs and the Appeals Council as well as the intermediaries, respondents amended their complaint to challenge that ruling as well.

The individuals named in the amended complaint, who are respondents before this Court, are four individual Medicare claimants. Their physician, who has developed a special technique for performing BCBR surgery and who has performed the surgery over 1,000 times, prescribed BCBR surgery for all four respondents to relieve their pulmonary problems. Respondents Sanford Holmes, Norman Webster–Zieber, and Jean Vescio had the surgery before October 28, 1980, and all three filed a claim for reimbursement with their fiscal intermediary. At the time that the amended complaint was filed, none of the three had exhausted their administrative remedies, and thus none had received a "final decision" on their claims for benefits from the Secretary. The fourth respondent, Freeman Ringer, informally inquired of the Secretary and learned that BCBR surgery is not covered under the Medicare Act. Thus he has never had the surgery, claiming that he is unable to afford it.

---

* The plaintiffs challenged HCFA's reimbursement denials under both Parts A and B. At this point in the history of the Medicare program, no judicial review of Part B claims was permitted. Several cases already had unsuccessfully challenged the constitutionality of this denial of judicial review for Part B claims (see e.g., Schweiker v. McClure, 456 U.S. 188 (1982); United States v. Erika, Inc., 456 U.S. 201 (1982)). The Court dismissed this portion of the challenge without reaching the merits, once again finding a lack of subject matter jurisdiction. Congress subsequently amended Medicare to permit judicial review of Part B appeals. See 42 C.F.R. § 405.857 (2003).

The essence of their amended complaint is that the Secretary has a constitutional and statutory obligation to provide payment for BCBR surgery because overwhelmingly her ALJs have ordered payment when they have considered individual BCBR claims. According to the complaint, the Secretary's instructions to the contrary to her intermediaries violate constitutional due process and numerous statutory provisions in that they force eligible Medicare claimants who have had BCBR surgery to pursue individual administrative appeals in order to get payment, even though ALJs overwhelmingly have determined that payment is appropriate. The complaint seeks a declaration that the Secretary's refusal to find that BCBR surgery is "reasonable and necessary" under the Act is unlawful, an injunction compelling the Secretary to instruct her intermediaries to provide payment for BCBR claims, and an injunction barring the Secretary from forcing claimants to pursue individual administrative appeals in order to obtain payment.

The District Court dismissed the complaint in its entirety for lack of jurisdiction. It concluded that "[t]he essence of [respondents' claim] . . . is a claim of entitlement [to] benefits for the BCBR procedure," and that any challenges respondents raise to the Secretary's procedures are "inextricably intertwined" with their claim for benefits. Thus the court concluded that 42 U.S.C. § 405(g) with its administrative exhaustion prerequisite provides the sole avenue for judicial review. Relying on our decision in Mathews v. Eldridge, 424 U.S. 319 (1976), the court concluded that none of respondents' claims are so "collateral" to their overall claim for benefits that the exhaustion requirement should be waived as to those claims.

On appeal the Court of Appeals for the Ninth Circuit reversed. It concluded that the thrust of respondents' claim is that "the Secretary's presumptive rule that the BCBR operation is not reasonable and necessary was an unlawful administrative mechanism for determining awards of benefits." The Court of Appeals concluded that to the extent that respondents are seeking to invalidate the Secretary's procedure for determining entitlement to benefits, those claims are cognizable without the requirement of administrative exhaustion.

The Court of Appeals agreed with the District Court that respondents also had raised substantive claims for benefits, in that they had sought an injunction requiring the Secretary to declare that BCBR is reasonable and necessary under the Act. Acknowledging that § 405(g) with its exhaustion prerequisite provides the only jurisdictional basis for seeking judicial review of claims for benefits, the court nonetheless concluded that the District Court had erred in requiring respondents to exhaust their administrative remedies in this case. Relying on our opinions in Weinberger v. Salfi, 422 U.S. 749 (1975), and Mathews v. Eldridge, supra, the Court of Appeals concluded that exhaustion would be futile for respondents and that it may not fully compensate them for the injuries they assert because they seek payment without the prejudice—and the necessity of appeal—resulting from the existence of the instructions and the rule. Because we disagree with the Court of Appeals' characterization of the claims at issue in this case and its reading of our precedents, we now reverse.

Preliminarily, we must point out that, although the Court of Appeals seemed not to have distinguished them, there are in fact two groups of respondents in this case. [The first group] had BCBR surgery before October 28, 1980, and have requested reimbursement at some, but not all, levels of the administrative process. [T]here is no dispute that the Secretary's formal administrative ruling simply does not apply to those three respondents' claims for reimbursement for their BCBR surgery. Their claims only make sense then if they are understood as challenges to the Secretary's instructions to her intermediaries, instructions which resulted in those respondents' having to pursue administrative remedies in order to get payment. They have standing to challenge the formal ruling as well only because, construing their complaint liberally, they argue that the existence of the formal rule creates a presumption against payment of their claims in the administrative process, even though the rule does not directly apply to bar their claims.

It seems to us that it makes no sense to construe the claims of [these] respondents as anything more than, at bottom, a claim that they should be paid for their BCBR surgery. Arguably respondents do assert objections to the Secretary's "procedure" for reaching her decision—for example, they challenge her decision to issue a generally applicable rule rather than to allow individual adjudication, and they challenge her alleged failure to comply with the rulemaking requirements of the APA in issuing the instructions and the rule. We agree with the District Court, however, that those claims are "inextricably intertwined" with respondents' claims for benefits. Indeed the relief that respondents seek to redress their supposed "procedural" objections is the invalidation of the Secretary's current policy and a "substantive" declaration from her that the expenses of BCBR surgery are reimbursable under the Medicare Act. We conclude that all aspects of respondents' claim for benefits should be channeled first into the administrative process which Congress has provided for the determination of claims for benefits. We, therefore, disagree with the Court of Appeals' separation of the particular claims here into "substantive" and "procedural" elements. We disagree in particular with its apparent conclusion that simply because a claim somehow can be construed as "procedural," it is cognizable in federal district court by way of federal-question jurisdiction.

The third sentence of 42 U.S.C. § 405(h),[10] made applicable to the Medicare Act by 42 U.S.C. § 1395ii, provides that § 405(g), to the exclusion of 28 U.S.C. § 1331, is the sole avenue for judicial review for all "claim[s] arising under" the Medicare Act. See Weinberger v. Salfi, supra, 422 U.S.,

---

10. That provision reads as follows: "The findings and decisions of the Secretary after a hearing shall be binding upon all individuals who were parties to the hearing. No findings of fact or decision of the Secretary shall be reviewed by any person, tribunal, or governmental agency except as herein provided. No action against the United States, the Secretary, or any officer or employee thereof shall be brought under section 1331 or 1346 of title 28 to recover on any claim arising under this subchapter." 42 U.S.C. § 405(h).

at 760–761. Thus, to be true to the language of the statute, the inquiry in determining whether § 405(h) bars federal-question jurisdiction must be whether the claim "arises under" the Act, not whether it lends itself to a "substantive" rather than a "procedural" label. See *Weinberger*, 424 U.S. 319 (recognizing that federal-question jurisdiction is barred by 42 U.S.C. § 405(h) even in a case where claimant is challenging the administrative procedures used to terminate welfare benefits).

In *Weinberger*, 422 U.S. 749, we construed the "claim arising under" language quite broadly to include any claims in which "both the standing and the substantive basis for the presentation" of the claims is the Social Security Act. In that case we held that a constitutional challenge to the duration-of-relationship eligibility statute pursuant to which the claimant had been denied benefits, was a "claim arising under" Title II of the Social Security Act within the meaning of 42 U.S.C. § 405(h), even though we recognized that it was in one sense also a claim arising under the Constitution.

Under that broad test, we have no trouble concluding that all aspects of [the cases brought by respondents with claims pending in the administrative appeals process] "aris[e] under" the Medicare Act. It is of no importance that respondents here, unlike the claimants in *Weinberger*, 422 U.S. 749, sought only declaratory and injunctive relief and not an actual award of benefits as well. Following the declaration which respondents seek from the Secretary—that BCBR surgery is a covered service—only essentially ministerial details will remain before respondents would receive reimbursement.

The Court of Appeals also relied on the mandamus statute as a basis for finding jurisdiction over a portion of those three respondents' claims. We have on numerous occasions declined to decide whether the third sentence of § 405(h) bars mandamus jurisdiction over claims arising under the Social Security Act, either because we have determined that jurisdiction was otherwise available under § 405(g)

Assuming without deciding that the third sentence of § 405(h) does not foreclose mandamus jurisdiction in all Social Security cases it is clear that no writ of mandamus could properly issue in this case. The common-law writ of mandamus, as codified in 28 U.S.C. § 1361, is intended to provide a remedy for a plaintiff only if he has exhausted all other avenues of relief and only if the defendant owes him a clear nondiscretionary duty.

Here respondents clearly have an adequate remedy in § 405(g) [and] [t]he Secretary's decision as to whether a particular medical service is "reasonable and necessary" and the means by which she implements her decision, whether by promulgating a generally applicable rule or by allowing individual adjudication, are clearly discretionary decisions.

Respondents urge us to hold them excused from further exhaustion and to hold that the District Court could have properly exercised jurisdiction over their claims under § 405(g). We have held that the Secretary herself may waive the exhaustion requirement when she deems further exhaustion futile. We held that *Mathews,* 424 U.S. 319 was such a case, where the plaintiff asserted a procedural challenge to the Secretary's denial of a pretermination hearing, a claim that was wholly "collateral" to his claim for benefits, and where he made a colorable showing that his injury could not be remedied by the retroactive payment of benefits after exhaustion of his administrative remedies.

The latter exception to exhaustion is inapplicable here where respondents do not raise a claim that is wholly "collateral" to their claim for benefits under the Act, and where they have no colorable claim that an erroneous denial of BCBR benefits in the early stages of the administrative process will injure them in a way that cannot be remedied by the later payment of benefits. [Furthermore] as we have pointed out above, the administrative ruling is not even applicable to respondents' claims because they had their surgery before October 28, 1980. We therefore agree with the Secretary that exhaustion is in no sense futile for these three respondents and that the Court of Appeals erred in second-guessing the Secretary's judgment.

Respondents also argue that there would be a presumption against them as they pursue their administrative appeals because of the very existence of the Secretary's instructions and her formal ruling and thus that exhaustion would not fully vindicate their claims. The history of this litigation as recited to us by respondents belies that conclusion. Indeed, according to respondents themselves, in every one of 170 claims filed with ALJs between the time of the Secretary's instructions to her intermediaries and the filing of this lawsuit, before the formal ruling became effective, ALJs allowed recovery for BCBR claims. In promulgating the formal ruling, the Secretary took pains to exempt from the scope of the ruling individuals in respondents' position who may have had the surgery relying on the favorable ALJ rulings. Although respondents would clearly prefer an immediate appeal to the District Court rather than the often lengthy administrative review process, exhaustion of administrative remedies is in no sense futile for these respondents, and they, therefore, must adhere to the administrative procedure which Congress has established for adjudicating their Medicare claims.[12]

Respondent Ringer is in a separate group from the other three respondents in this case. He raises the same challenges to the instructions and to the formal ruling as are raised by the other respondents. His position is different from theirs, however, because he wishes to have the operation and

---

12. We noted in *Weinberger v. Salfi,* 422 U.S. 749 (1975), that the purpose of the exhaustion requirement is to prevent "premature interference with agency processes" and to give the agency a chance "to compile a record which is adequate for judicial review." This case aptly demonstrates the wisdom of Congress' exhaustion scheme. Several respondents in this case pursued their administrative remedies during the pendency of this litigation and the claims of respondents Holmes and Webster–Zieber were denied on grounds not even related to the instructions and rule which they now seek to challenge in federal court. Further, the ALJ determined that the formal rule was not even applicable to respondent Vescio's claim because of the date of her surgery, and he thus concluded that additional evidence was necessary to determine whether she was entitled to payment.

claims that the Secretary's refusal to allow payment for it precludes him from doing so. Because Ringer's surgery, if he ultimately chooses to have it, would occur after the effective date of the formal ruling, Ringer's claim for reimbursement, unlike that of the others, would be covered by the formal ruling. Ringer insists that, just as in the case of the other three respondents, the only relief that will vindicate his claim is a declaration that the formal ruling, and presumably the instructions as well, are invalid and an injunction compelling the Secretary to conclude that BCBR surgery is "reasonable and necessary" within the meaning of the Medicare Act.

Again, regardless of any arguably procedural components, we see Ringer's claim as essentially one requesting the payment of benefits for BCBR surgery, a claim cognizable only under § 405(g). Our discussion of the unavailability of mandamus jurisdiction over the claims of the other three respondents is equally applicable to Ringer. As to § 1331 jurisdiction, as with the other three respondents, all aspects of Ringer's claim "aris[e] under" the Medicare Act in that the Medicare Act provides both the substance and the standing for Ringer's claim.

Ringer's situation does differ from that of the other three respondents in one arguably significant way. Because he has not yet had the operation and thus has no reimbursable expenses, it can be argued that Ringer does not yet have a "claim" to present to the Secretary and thus that he does not have a "claim arising under" the Medicare Act so as to be subject to § 405(h)'s bar to federal-question jurisdiction. The argument is not that Ringer's claim does not "arise under" the Medicare Act as we interpreted that term in *Weinberger*, 422 U.S. 749; it is rather that it has not yet blossomed into a "claim" cognizable under § 405(g). We find that argument superficially appealing but ultimately unavailing.

Although it is true that Ringer is not seeking the immediate payment of benefits, he is clearly seeking to establish a right to future payments should he ultimately decide to proceed with BCBR surgery. The claim for future benefits must be construed as a "claim arising under" the Medicare Act because any other construction would allow claimants substantially to undercut Congress' carefully crafted scheme for administering the Medicare Act.

If we allow claimants in Ringer's position to challenge in federal court the Secretary's determination, embodied in her rule, that BCBR surgery is not a covered service, we would be inviting them to bypass the exhaustion requirements of the Medicare Act by simply bringing declaratory judgment actions in federal court before they undergo the medical procedure in question. Congress clearly foreclosed the possibility of obtaining such advisory opinions[.] Under the guise of interpreting the language of § 405(h), we refuse to undercut that choice by allowing federal judges to issue such advisory opinions. Thus it is not the case that Ringer has no "claim" cognizable under § 405(g); it is that he must pursue his claim under that section in the manner which Congress has provided. Because Ringer has not given the Secretary an opportunity to rule on a concrete claim for reimbursement, he has not satisfied the non-waivable exhaustion requirement of § 405(g).

With respect to our holding that there is no jurisdiction pursuant to § 1331, the dissent argues that § 405(h) is not a bar to § 1331 jurisdiction because Ringer's challenge to the Secretary's rule is "arising under" the Administrative Procedure Act, not the Medicare Act. But the dissent merely resurrects an old argument that has already been raised and rejected before by this Court in *Weinberger*, 422 U.S. 749. Ringer's claim may well "aris[e] under" the APA in the same sense that Salfi's claim arose under the Constitution, but we held in Salfi that the constitutional claim was nonetheless barred by § 405(h).

The dissent suggests that Salfi is distinguishable on two grounds. First, it seems to suggest that Salfi is distinguishable because, after rejecting the claim that there was jurisdiction under § 1331, the Court in Salfi went on to conclude that there was jurisdiction under § 405(g). We fail to see how the Court's conclusion that the claimants in Salfi had satisfied all of the prerequisites to jurisdiction under § 405(g) has anything at all to do with the proper construction of § 405(h). If the dissent is suggesting that the meaning of § 405(h) somehow shifts depending on whether a court finds that the waivable and non-waivable requirements of § 405(g) are met in any given case, that suggestion is simply untenable.

Second, the dissent seems to suggest that Salfi is distinguishable because the claimants there appended a claim for benefits to their claim for declaratory and injunctive relief as to the unconstitutionality of the statute. Again, as we have already pointed out, there is no indication in Salfi that our holding in any way depended on the fact that the claimants there sought an award of benefits. Furthermore, today we explicitly hold that our conclusion that the claims of [respondents who appealed] are barred by § 405(h) is in no way affected by the fact that those respondents did not seek an award of benefits.

The crux of the dissent's position as to § 1331 jurisdiction then seems to be that Ringer's claims do not "arise under" the Medicare Act so as to be barred by § 405(h) because Ringer and his surgeon have not yet filed, and indeed cannot yet file, a concrete claim for reimbursement because Ringer has not yet had BCBR surgery. But that argument amounts to no more than an assertion that the substance of Ringer's claim somehow changes and "arises under" another statute simply because he has not satisfied the procedural prerequisites for jurisdiction which Congress has prescribed in § 405(g).

With respect to our holding that Ringer has not satisfied the nonwaivable requirement of § 405(g), the dissent adopts the remarkable view that the Secretary's promulgation of a rule regarding BCBR surgery satisfies that nonwaivable requirement. The dissent would thus open the doors of the federal courts in the first instance to everyone—those who can and those who cannot afford to pay their surgeons without reliance on Medicare—who thinks that he might be eligible to participate in the Medicare program, who thinks that someday he might wish to have some kind of surgery, and who thinks that this surgery might somehow be affected by a rule that the Secretary has promulgated. [I]t is of no great moment to the dissent that Congress, who surely could have provided a scheme whereby claimants could obtain declaratory judgments about their entitlement to benefits, has instead expressly set up a scheme that requires the presentation of a concrete claim to the Secretary.

The dissent's concern is with those perhaps millions of people, like Ringer, who desire some kind of controversial operation but who are unable to have it because their surgeons will not perform the surgery without knowing in advance whether they will be victorious in challenging the Secretary's rule in the administrative or later in the judicial process. But that concern exists to the same degree with any claimant, even in the absence of a generally applicable ruling by the Secretary. For example, a surgeon called upon to perform any kind of surgery for a prospective claimant would, in the best of all possible worlds, wish to know in advance whether the surgery is "reasonable and necessary" within the meaning of the Medicare Act. And indeed some such surgeons may well decline to perform the requested surgery because of fear that the Secretary will not find the surgery "reasonable and necessary" and thus will refuse to reimburse them. The logic of the dissent's position leads to the conclusion that those individuals, as well as Ringer, are entitled to an advance declaration so as to ensure them the opportunity to have the surgery that they desire.

Furthermore, the solution that the dissent provides for Ringer—allowing him to challenge the Secretary's rule in federal court—hardly solves the problem that the dissent identifies. It is mere speculation to assume, as the dissent does, that a surgeon who is unwilling to perform surgery because of the existence of a rule will all of a sudden be willing to perform the surgery if the rule is struck down.

We hold that the District Court was correct in dismissing the complaint as to all respondents. [The respondents who already have appealed] are not subject to the Secretary's formal ruling and stood the chance of prevailing in administrative appeals. Respondent Ringer has not undergone the procedure and could prevail only if federal courts were free to give declaratory judgments to anyone covered by Medicare as to whether he would be entitled to reimbursement for a procedure if he decided later to undergo it.

In the best of all worlds, immediate judicial access for all of these parties might be desirable. But Congress, in § 405(g) and § 405(h), struck a different balance, refusing declaratory relief and requiring that administrative remedies be exhausted before judicial review of the Secretary's decisions takes place. Congress must have felt that cases of individual hardship resulting from delays in the administrative process had to be balanced against the potential for overly casual or premature judicial intervention in an administrative system that processes literally millions of claims every year. If the balance is to be struck anew, the decision must come from Congress and not from this Court.

■ JUSTICE STEVENS, with whom JUSTICE BRENNAN and JUSTICE MARSHALL join, concurring in the judgment in part and dissenting in part.

The Medicare Act is designed to insure the elderly against the often crushing costs of medical care. To that end, § 1862(a)(1) of the Act guarantees payment of all expenses "reasonable and necessary for the diagnosis or treatment of illness or injury."[2] The Secretary has issued a formal ruling stating that she will not pay the costs of bilateral carotid body resection (BCBR) surgery performed after October 28, 1980, in order to treat pulmonary distress because for that purpose BCBR is neither medically reasonable nor necessary. Respondents contend that the rule was not adopted in accord with the relevant limitations on the Secretary's authority.

The three respondents who have undergone the BCBR procedure all did so prior to October 28, 1980. The Secretary's ruling as of that date does not prevent them from obtaining payment for BCBR, and in fact states that they may prevail if they demonstrate that they underwent the procedure in reliance on previous rulings indicating that BCBR is reimbursable. I agree with the Court that the Secretary's ruling does not foreclose relief for them and that it is therefore appropriate to require them to exhaust their administrative remedies.

The claim of respondent Ringer, however, stands on a different footing. The complaint indicates that Ringer cannot afford it unless the Secretary agrees to pay for it. The Secretary, however, has formally ruled that she will not pay for it, and has taken the position that Ringer cannot challenge her ruling, except in a proceeding seeking reimbursement for the cost of the surgery. Yet precisely because Ringer cannot afford the surgery, the Secretary will not permit him to file a claim for reimbursement, since he has incurred no expense that can be reimbursed.

Today, the majority holds that Ringer must have the operation that he cannot afford and cannot obtain because of the Secretary's ruling before he can challenge that ruling. [T]he Court concludes that there is no federal-question jurisdiction over this case under 28 U.S.C. § 1331 because Ringer has a "claim arising under the Medicare Act," which cannot be asserted under § 1331 by virtue of § 205(h) of the Social Security Act. Therefore, the Court continues, jurisdiction over this case can be exercised if at all under § 205(g). Yet the Court also holds that there is no jurisdiction under § 205(g) because Ringer has not submitted a claim for reimbursement.

The Court's mistaken analysis of Ringer's claim stems from its failure to recognize that the jurisdictional limitation in § 205(h) refers only to actions "to recover on any claim arising under this subchapter"—claims that are within the jurisdictional grant in § 205(g). Section 205(h) is simply inapplicable to a claim that cannot be asserted in an action under § 205(g),

---

2. "Notwithstanding any other provision of this subchapter, no payment may be made under part A or part B for any expenses incurred for items or services—(1) which are not reasonable and necessary for the diagnosis or treatment of illness or injury or to improve the functioning of a malformed body member," 42 U.S.C. § 1395y(a)(1).

and hence does not preclude the assertion of jurisdiction over such a claim under § 1331.

A careful reading of the plain language of the relevant statutes indicates that the statutory scheme does not preclude jurisdiction over Ringer's challenge to the Secretary's ruling under 28 U.S.C. § 1331. That is because the preclusive provision on which the Court relies, § 205(h), simply does not apply to Ringer's claim.[9]

Section 1869(a) of the Medicare Act provides that the determination whether an individual is entitled to Medicare benefits shall be made by the Secretary pursuant to prescribed regulations. Since the Secretary and the Court agree that Ringer has submitted no "claim" on which the Secretary could have acted, it is perfectly clear that the Secretary has made no determination pertaining to Ringer that is covered by § 1869(a). Section 1869(b)(1)(C) states that an individual "dissatisfied with any determination made under subsection (a)" is entitled to the kind of hearing authorized by § 205(b) of Title II of the Social Security Act, and to judicial review as prescribed in § 205(g) of that Title. Since there has been no "determination" in this case, this provision does not apply to Ringer either.

We come then to § 1872, which in relevant part provides that § 205(h) shall "apply with respect to this subchapter to the same extent as [it is] applicable with respect to subchapter II of this chapter." Nowhere in this reticulated statutory scheme is there any requirement that every "question" arising under the Medicare Act must be litigated in an action brought under § 205(g). Quite the contrary § 1872 applies § 205(h) to "this subchapter," i.e., to the provisions concerning reimbursement determinations contained in § 1869. Yet not one of the provisions in that section is relevant to Ringer. Ringer's claim is not the type of claim covered by "this subchapter," since the subchapter applies only to the type of hearing provided for in § 205(b). What Ringer seeks is not the type of hearing provided for in § 205(b), which would arise under "this subchapter," but instead an action under the right-of-review provisions of the Administrative Procedure Act (APA), 5 U.S.C. §§ 701–706.[16] Hence 28 U.S.C. § 1331 provides jurisdiction to entertain such a claim.

This analysis is confirmed by Weinberger v. Salfi, 422 U.S. 749 (1975). In that case, on which the majority relies so heavily, the Court held that when a claimant seeks payment of benefits under the Social Security Act, his claim "arises under" that Act within the meaning of § 205(h) and

---

9. The Court's analysis is confined to the question whether Ringer's action is one "arising under" the Medicare Act; it never attempts to construe the immediately preceding words in § 205(h): "any claim to recover." The majority thereby is able to attack a straw man, since by focusing only on the words "arising under" it avoids the question of how Ringer can have "any claim to recover arising under" that Act when he cannot submit any claim for Medicare benefits because he cannot afford the operation.

16. In particular, the APA provides: "A person suffering legal wrong because of agency action, or adversely affected or aggrieved by agency action within the meaning of a relevant statute, is entitled to judicial review thereof...." 5 U.S.C. § 702. "Agency action made reviewable by statute and final agency action for which there is no other adequate remedy in a court are subject to judicial review...." § 704.

hence may not be brought pursuant to 28 U.S.C. § 1331. The obvious difference between this case and Salfi is that Salfi had a claim which could be raised under §§ 205(b) and (g); indeed the Court upheld the exercise of jurisdiction over that case under § 205(g).

Thus, what Salfi holds is that § 205(h) "precludes federal-question jurisdiction in an action challenging denial of claimed benefits." Mathews v. Eldridge, 424 U.S. 319 (1976). In contrast to Salfi, Ringer has no "claim" within the meaning of the Social Security Act—because he is unable to have the operation, he cannot file an application for reimbursement and no "decision of the Secretary" has been made denying such a claim which could fall under § 205(h). Because Ringer cannot afford the operation and obtain judicial review under the relevant provisions of the Medicare Act, he has no "claim" that "arises under" that Act and is unable to generate one.[19]

There is yet another fundamental reason why § 205(h) does not preclude Ringer's claim. Section 205(h) precludes only actions "to recover" on a claim arising under the Social Security Act. That language plainly refers to an action in which the claimant seeks payment of benefits. Today's majority finds § 205(h) applicable because Ringer "is clearly seeking to establish a right to future payments should he ultimately decide to proceed with BCBR surgery." If Ringer were seeking payment of benefits, this might well be a different case, but that is plainly not what he seeks. Ringer seeks a declaration that the Secretary's BCBR rule is invalid and an injunction against its operation. He alleges that it is the "irrefutable presumption" contained in the rule—which denies administrative law judges discretion to decide in a hearing under § 205(b) whether BCBR is reimbursable—that prevents him from having the operation. Ringer disavows any desire to obtain a judicial determination that benefits must be paid to him. Thus, Ringer is not seeking "to recover." Instead he seeks an injunction against this "irrefutable presumption."

Ringer is not seeking to "bypass the exhaustion requirements of the Medicare Act," but rather to be able to exhaust—something he can only do if the rule is enjoined so that he and his surgeon can seek reimbursement through the administrative process. Ringer's challenge to the operation of a rule that prevents him from having a "claim" he can pursue under § 205 is therefore not a claim covered by § 205(h)—it is a challenge to a procedural rule that could prove meritorious even if Ringer is ultimately not entitled to reimbursement. Hence it can be asserted under § 1331.

Unfortunately the majority's errors in this case are not limited to its construction of § 205(h). For even if we assume that § 205(h) is applicable to Ringer's case, and that he can obtain judicial review only through § 205(g), the majority's disposition would still be incorrect.

---

19. There is a wealth of authority in the lower courts for the proposition that when the Social Security Act provides no avenue for review, there is no claim arising under that Act within the meaning of § 205(h) and hence no bar to jurisdiction under 28 U.S.C. § 1331.

Section 205(g) contains three jurisdictional prerequisites to judicial review: a "[1] final [2] decision of the Secretary [3] made after a hearing...." In Salfi, the Court decided that the first and third elements are "waivable" upon an appropriate showing, whereas the second element is nonwaivable and must be satisfied in all cases before judicial review may be obtained.

Ringer has plainly satisfied the nonwaivable element. [T]he Secretary has made a decision here. By issuing the challenged BCBR regulation, she decided that BCBR can in no event be reimbursable. If that is not a "decision of the Secretary," I do not know what is. The regulation was issued to prevent claimants from litigating the reimbursability of BCBR in an adjudicatory context. Thus, the relevant decision of the Secretary here could not be any decision made in the administrative process; rather it is the decision to issue the BCBR regulation. That "decision of the Secretary" satisfies the nonwaivable portion of § 205(g).

The waivable elements are satisfied as well. In Salfi, the Court held that waiver was appropriate when there is no chance that the claimant could prevail in the administrative process. In such circumstances, "further exhaustion would not merely be futile for the applicant, but would also be a commitment of administrative resources unsupported by any administrative or judicial interest." Here, just as in Salfi, a hearing [would] be futile and wasteful. Indeed, in light of the dispositive rule, there is no reason to believe that the Secretary would waste her resources by holding a hearing to see if Ringer's claim could be denied on some other ground, and the Secretary has not represented that such a hearing in fact would be held.

Moreover, even if a claim such as Ringer's should ordinarily be exhausted, the waivable element is satisfied when there is a "colorable claim" that the claimant will be injured if forced to exhaust in a way that cannot be remedied by later payment of benefits. Ringer clearly has such a claim. He suffers from serious pulmonary distress, and represents that if he does not get BCBR he faces a risk of continued deterioration in his health, and even death.[31] Surely, the injury Ringer faces while awaiting judicial review—which on the majority's view he in any event can never obtain because of his inability to afford the operation—constitutes a collateral injury not remedied even if Ringer somehow could exhaust his administrative "remedy."

"To allow a serious illness to go untreated until it requires emergency hospitalization is to subject the sufferer to the danger of a substantial and irrevocable deterioration in his health. Cancer, heart disease, or respiratory illness, if untreated for a year, may become all but irreversible paths to pain, disability, and even loss of life. The denial of medical care is all the more cruel in this context, falling as it does on indigents who are often

---

31. One of the original plaintiffs in the District Court, Ernie M. Haley, was, like Ringer, unable to afford the operation and died while awaiting BCBR. Brief for Respondents 9. Thus, the risk Ringer faces because of his inability to obtain judicial review at this juncture is far from speculative.

without the means to obtain alternative treatment." Memorial Hospital v. Maricopa County, 415 U.S. 250, 261(1974).

Thus, Ringer "has raised at least a colorable claim that because of his physical condition and dependency on [Medicare] benefits, an erroneous termination would damage him in a way not recompensable through retroactive payments." Ringer should be permitted to challenge the BCBR rule which causes this injury without satisfying the waivable requirements of § 205(g).

Thus, jurisdiction over this case is appropriate under § 205(g). The Secretary has surely made a "decision" on BCBR within the meaning of that statute, and to require further pursuit of adjudicatory remedies when the purpose of the challenged rule is to preclude adjudication is a potentially tragic exercise in futility.

The Court's inability to find a jurisdictional basis for Ringer's challenge to the Secretary's formal ruling stems in part from a concern that the Secretary and the federal courts would otherwise be flooded by requests for advisory opinions by individuals contemplating various forms of medical treatment. There is no need to evaluate this purely hypothetical concern because this case presents no question concerning Ringer's "right" to an advisory opinion or the Secretary's "duty" to provide one. [T]he Secretary has already issued an advisory opinion on BCBR. That is exactly what her BCBR regulation is. The regulation was specifically designed to prevent this issue from arising in a concrete adjudicatory context. Indeed, her ruling is far more significant than mere advice; it is a formal pronouncement directing the bureaucracy under her command to reject all claims for reimbursement for BCBR surgery, despite the uniform course of decision by a variety of Administrative Law Judges, as well as the Secretary's Appeals Council, that such claims qualify for reimbursement. Thus, this is not a case concerning a "right" to an advisory opinion. Rather, this case poses the question whether, once the Secretary issues a rule which has the effect of denying a Medicare beneficiary surgery, that beneficiary may obtain judicial review as to the validity of the rule.[33]

The majority has decided that it is proper to prevent a citizen from ever challenging a rule which denies him surgery he desperately needs. Ringer cannot afford the operation and therefore his "claim" can never be "pursued" in a reimbursement proceeding. In making this decision, the Court ignores a basic proposition of administrative law. Abbott Laboratories v. Gardner, 387 U.S. 136 (1967), is but one in a long line of cases

---

33. The majority argues that the logic of my position applies to any person who wishes to obtain an advisory opinion from the Secretary. It does not. If a surgeon thinks that a given procedure is medically necessary and reasonable, he should be confident of his ability to convince an administrative law judge of exactly that, and therefore will provide the operation with the expectation of receiving reimbursement after the fact through the administrative process. Indeed that is the way that most surgery is in fact provided under Medicare; the surgeon does not require prepayment precisely because he is confident he will be reimbursed. That is certainly true here—Ringer's surgeon would provide the surgery if he were given an opportunity to obtain a hearing after the fact.

holding that nothing less than clear and convincing evidence of legislative intent to preclude judicial review is required before a statute will be construed to preclude the citizen's right to seek judicial redress for violations of his rights.

In this case Ringer, whose only sin is that he is unable to afford BCBR surgery, is denied access to any judicial review of what we must take to be a rule that violates the Secretary's statutory duty to assure reimbursement of necessary and reasonable medical expenses under a health insurance program. Because he cannot afford the surgery, he will never be able to seek administrative or judicial review.

When the issue is properly phrased in terms of whether there is clear and convincing evidence that Congress intended to preclude judicial review of such a case, it is essential to remember that the entire statutory scheme was enacted for the benefit of the aged, the infirm, and the impoverished. It was the medically needy that Congress sought to aid through the provision of health insurance under the Medicare program. Yet those most in need of comprehensive medical insurance are those with the least ability to assert their statutory right to such insurance under the majority's approach. In telling Ringer that "he must pursue his claim" under § 205(g), the Court indicates that he will have the "right" to judicial review only if he can pay for it—and he cannot.

On the majority's view it would appear the rich and the poor alike also have the right to front the money for major surgery. I cannot believe that is what Congress intended, or what our precedents require.

Of course, the integrity of the administrative exhaustion mechanism created by Congress is vital, and the Act should not be construed in a way that would undermine that system. But all Ringer seeks to do is challenge a rule that prevents him from having the operation and then seeking reimbursement through the statutory review system. It is not Ringer who is bypassing the administrative review system, but the Secretary, whose BCBR rule prevents persons such as Ringer from seeking administrative review of a concrete claim for benefits. I can find no evidence, much less clear and convincing evidence, that Congress intended to prohibit judicial review in these circumstances.

Notes

1. *How the dissent and majority opinions view coverage exclusions in relation to legal rights.* The Secretary's BCBR ruling had the effect of totally excluding the surgery for persons whose conditions were like those of Mr. Ringer. Clearly, if Justice Stevens had carried the day, the courts would have decided the question of whether the Medicare statute permits the Secretary to promulgate across-the-board exclusionary policies on medical necessity grounds, and if so, whether her actions were constitutional. But the question as to whether Medicare would have paid for *Mr. Ringer's* surgery still would have been up in the air, no? In fact, as you have seen in the previous cases involving private insurance, even where there is no

across-the-board coverage exclusion, the question still remains as to whether a covered benefit is medically necessary for a particular patient. This was the point made by Justice Stevens—that is, that litigation by Ringer over the legality of an exclusionary rule would not, in fact, have settled the question as to whether the treatment was medically necessary as to him, and therefore, Ringer was not litigating a claim for benefits.

The majority would have none of this, arguing instead that Ringer was attempting to get a declaratory ruling on his actual coverage. In Justice Rehnquist's view, Ringer's case was nothing more than an attempt to evade the claims process set out in the statute. The fact that Congress created no avenue for challenging the legality of coverage exclusions was an issue to be resolved by Congress. In fact, Congress subsequently (some 16 years subsequently) took such action.

2. *The Medicare national coverage determination process.* The Medicare, Medicaid, and SCHIP Benefits Improvement and Protection Act of 2000 (BIPA), Pub. L. No. 106–554, §§ 521 and 522, formalized the process for making coverage determinations. Prior to the legislation coverage determinations were made at both the national and local levels. The 2000 amendments formalized procedures for national coverage determinations (NCDs), made at the national level, and local coverage determinations (LCDs), made by the Medicare contractors at the local level. The amendments also added a provision allowing direct access to judicial review in cases in which there are no material facts in dispute and the only question is the constitutionality or legality of a rule. 42 U.S.C. § 1395ff(f)(3).

The amendments create review procedures for both national and local coverage determinations. See 68 Fed. Reg. 63,692–731 (Nov. 7, 2003). Implementing regulations clarify that challenges to LCDs or NCDs are separate from individual claims appeals, 42 C.F.R. § 426.310, and they establish a multi-level process for challenging a determination, which places the burden of proof on the challenger to bring forth new evidence of a sufficient strength and quality such that it has the "potential to significantly affect the ALJ's or the Board's evaluation of the LCD/NCD provision(s) in question under the reasonableness standard." 42 C.F.R. § 426.340. In light of the extensive evidentiary record that goes into making a NCD, this burden of proof is high indeed.

Under separate policies describing the process used to make determinations, 68 Fed. Reg. 55,634–42 (Sept. 26, 2003), the Centers for Medicare and Medicaid Services provided this explanation of a NCD:

> Medicare payment is contingent upon a determination that a service meets a benefit category, is not specifically excluded from coverage, and the item or service is "reasonable and necessary." Section 1862(a)(1)(A) of the Act states that, subject to certain limited exceptions, no payment may be made for any expenses incurred for items or services that are not "reasonable and necessary" for the diagnosis and treatment of illness or injury or to improve the functioning of a malformed body member. For over 30 years, we have exercised these authorities to make a coverage

determination regarding whether a specific item or service meets one of the broadly defined benefit categories and can be covered under the Medicare program.

As revised by section 522 of BIPA, an NCD is now defined to be a determination by the Secretary with respect to whether or not a particular item or service is covered nationally under title XVIII of the Act, but does not include a determination with respect to the amount of payment for a particular covered item or service. In general, an NCD is a national policy statement granting, limiting, or excluding Medicare coverage for a specific medical item or service. Often, an NCD is written in terms of a particular patient population that may receive (or not receive) Medicare reimbursement for a particular item or service. An NCD is binding on all [contractors and Medicare providers].

68 Fed. Reg. at 55,635.

BIPA sets forth standards that CMS must consider in making a NCD: (1) consideration of applicable information including clinical experience as well as medical, technical and scientific evidence with respect to the subject matter of the determination; (2) a clear statement of the basis for the determination including responses to public comments; (3) a statement of the assumptions underlying the NCD; and (4) making the evidence publicly available. Certain requests travel in parallel with the FDA review process, since the task of determining the safety and effectiveness of a drug or device is closely linked to the question of whether it should be a candidate for financing (drugs and devices that are determined to fall outside of Medicare obviously stand next to no chance of making it in the market). The request process is designed also to disclose information submitted to the FDA.

The NCD also includes a comprehensive health technology assessment (HTA) that consists of an independent review of the available clinical and scientific evidence on a technology. CMS has the authority to request an HTA when the evidence is scientifically complex or conflicting, since the HTA will assist in determining if the item at hand is "reasonable and necessary" and thereby covered. CMS is guided by a Medicare Coverage Advisory Committee, which makes recommendations to the Secretary based on interpretations of the Act and relevant evidence.

The 2000 legislative reforms also articulate the relationship between NCDs and LCDs. These determinations may vary from region to region, since they involve regional contractors rather than CMS itself. In the absence of a NCD, local contractors have the discretion to make a coverage determination in the context of reviewing an individual claim. That is, the local contractor, in the context of a single claims review, may make a decision to adopt a more broadly exclusionary standard as well as to clarify payment limitations and exclusions. 42 U.S.C. § 1395ff(f)(1) and (2). In making an LCD the contractor must consider medical literature, the advice of local medical societies and medical consultants, public comments, and comments from the provider community.

In Erringer v. Thompson, 371 F.3d 625 (9th Cir. 2004), the court held that the Secretary's unpublished manual of guidelines to local contractor for their making of LCDs does not violate the APA's requirement that agency regulations be promulgated under notice-and-comment rulemaking. The court held that the guidelines are not substantive regulations but instead are internal interpretive rules or policies. The particular guideline in question set forth the principle of "Least Costly Alternative," which effectively requires contractors to limit payment for durable medical equipment to the cost of "an existing and available medically appropriate alternative." *Id.* at 629.

In her review of the coverage decision-making process and the overhaul of NCDs, Professor Eleanor Kinney notes that despite the changes, the new process can be expected to be as controversial as the less formalized process that DHHS started to use in 1989, the date when it first began to use an evidence-based review process for new services and technologies. The new process, like the old, focuses on the ultimate and fundamental question: whether beneficiaries should have access to all new clinical innovations and technologies, regardless of cost, that might potentially be effective. Eleanor Kinney, *Medicare Coverage Decision Making and Appeal Procedures: Can Process Meet the Challenge of New Technology?*, 60 WASH. & LEE L. REV. 1461 (2003). The relevant provisions of the Affordable Care Act illustrate how politically touchy the issue is because it provides that in using the evidence gained from comparative clinical effectiveness research, the Secretary shall not "deny coverage of items or services" under Medicare "solely on the basis of comparative clinical effectiveness research." SSA § 1182, added by PPACA § 6301. In your view, given the Secretary's already existing power to adopt exclusions and limitations via LCDs and NCDs, what is gained by barring her from making coverage determinations based on what Congress considers to be such high-quality evidence that lawmakers have committed to invest billions of dollars over 2010–2019 to produce it?

3. *Applying* Ringer *to provider appeals.* In 2000, the Supreme Court extended its reasoning in *Ringer* to challenges by Medicare providers to administrative actions other than coverage denials. In Shalala v. Illinois Council on Long Term Care, 529 U.S. 1 (2000), the Court denied nursing homes the right to bring a constitutional challenge to nursing home quality enforcement rules that provide for the immediate termination of an institution's provider agreement, or for the use of receivership, in the event that a safety inspection reveals certain types of violations that "immediately jeopardize the health or safety of residents." The regulations also provide for less severe, but nonetheless substantial, sanctions in the event of less serious violations. Nursing homes found to be in "substantial compliance" would not face more than minimal sanctions for violations.

A group of Illinois nursing homes sued to enjoin implementation of the regulation on both substantive and procedural Constitutional grounds. The Medicare statute's nursing home quality provisions specifically extend the § 405 appeals mechanism to nursing facilities dissatisfied with the results of inspections. 42 U.S. C. § 1395cc(h)(1) The District Court dismissed the suit for lack of subject matter jurisdiction but the appeals court reversed, citing the Court's post-*Ringer* decision in Bowen v. Michigan Academy of Family Physicians, 476 U.S. 667 (1986), as having modified the *Ringer* rule of "virtually exclusive" jurisdiction under § 405(g).

As in *Ringer,* a critical issue was the meaning of § 405(h), which precludes alternative bases for jurisdiction to "recover on any claim arising under" the Medicare program. While noting the statute's clear application to claims for benefits, Justice Breyer, writing for a 5–4 majority, identified the inherent difficulty in applying § 405's administrative procedures for the adjudication of *claims for care already provided* to cases involving *potential future claims* such as the ones raised by the Illinois Council. Nursing homes barred from the program were caught in the paradoxical situation—analogous to Ringer's dilemma—that they could challenge their exclusion only first by providing care and then filing a claim for that care. Nonetheless, finding that "the bar of § 405(h) reaches beyond ordinary administrative law principles," Justice Breyer concluded that even hardships to providers such as total program exclusion could not defeat the reach of the limitations on federal jurisdiction imposed by the Medicare statute:

> Insofar as § 405(h) prevents application of the "ripeness" and "exhaustion" exceptions, *i.e.,* insofar as it demands the "channeling" of virtually all legal attacks through the agency, it assures the agency greater opportunity to apply, interpret, or revise policies, regulations, or statutes without possibly premature interference by different individual courts applying "ripeness" and "exhaustion" exceptions case by case. But this assurance comes at a price, namely, occasional individual, delay-related hardship. In the context of a massive, complex health and safety program such as Medicare, embodied in hundreds of pages of statutes and thousands of pages of often interrelated regulations, any of which may become the subject of a legal challenge in any of several different courts, paying this price may seem justified. In any event, such was the judgment of Congress as understood in *Salfi* and *Ringer*.

529 U.S. at 13. The majority turned aside all attempts to distinguish cases like *Ringer*:

> Claims for money, claims for other benefits, claims of program eligibility, and claims that contest a sanction or remedy may all similarly rest upon individual fact-related circumstances, may all similarly dispute agency policy determinations, or may all similarly involve the application, interpretation, or constitutionality of interrelated regulations or statutory provisions. There is no reason to distinguish among them in terms of the language or in terms of the purposes of § 405(h).

Id. at 13–14.

Justice Thomas (joined by Justices Stevens, Kennedy and (partially) Scalia) dissented on the grounds that the *Ringer* bar to the exercise of general federal question jurisdiction in a Medicare case is inapplicable to cases in which the legal action is first, general and prospective and second, aimed at preventing future harm. In essence, the dissenters argued, there are certain types of cases in which, despite the fact that no "claim" exists and thus, no § 405 jurisdiction is appropriate, the special Medicare bar to general jurisdiction should give way to permit "preenforcement judicial review" of the legitimacy of severe sanctions.

What policy considerations might justify denying individuals like Ringer pre-claims challenges to coverage denials under Medicare while allowing entities like the nursing homes in *Illinois Council* review of pre-enforcement claims? Do you agree with Justice Breyer in *Illinois Council* and Justice Rehnquist in *Ringer* that the normal presumption of federal jurisdiction (particularly where the harm arising from a lack of judicial intervention could be irreversible) should give way in the case of Medicare because of the program's enormous complexity? Do you consider this presumption to be more or less sensible in light of the overhaul by Congress of the NCD process?

Hays v. Sebelius

589 F.3d 1279 (D.C. Cir. 2009)

■ TATEL, CIRCUIT JUDGE:

Appellee, a Medicare Part B beneficiary, challenges a decision by a regional Medicare contractor to reimburse for a particular drug only up to the price of its least costly alternative. The district court held that the Medicare Act unambiguously forecloses that determination and requires instead that Medicare pay for covered items or services at a statutorily prescribed rate. Agreeing with the district court, we affirm.

Medicare Part B provides the disabled and elderly with outpatient items and services, including durable medical equipment and certain prescription medications. The threshold for Medicare Part B coverage appears in 42 U.S.C. § 1395y(a)(1)(A), which states that "no payment may be made ... for any expenses incurred for items or services which ... are not reasonable and necessary for the diagnosis or treatment of illness or injury or to improve the functioning of a malformed body member[.]"

The Secretary of Health and Human Services administers the Medicare Act and may delegate certain functions to contractors, including the development of local coverage determinations. 42 U.S.C. § 1395kk–1(a)(4). The Medicare Act defines local coverage determinations as decisions "whether or not a particular item or service is covered" in the contractor's geographic area "in accordance with section 1395y(a)(1)(A)." 42 U.S.C. § 1395ff(f)(2)(B). The Secretary has instructed contractors that when determining whether a treatment is "reasonable and necessary" under section 1395y(a)(1)(A), they may apply the so-called least costly alternative policy. Ctrs. for Medicare and Medicaid Servs., Medicare Program Integrity Manual § 13.4.A (Rev.71, Apr. 9, 2004). Under that policy, Medicare provides reimbursement for treatments only up to the price of their "reasonably feasible and medically appropriate" least costly alternatives. Ctrs. for Medicare and Medicaid Servs., Medicare Benefit Policy Manual § 110.1.C.3 (Rev.93, July 25, 2008). Application of the policy is discretionary with regard to prescription drugs—the subject of this case—but mandatory with regard to durable medical equipment. *See* Medicare Program Integrity Manual § 13.4.A.

This case arose when Medicare contractors applied the least costly alternative policy to DuoNeb, an inhalation drug used to treat Chronic Obstructive Pulmonary Disease. DuoNeb provides a combination of albuterol sulfate and ipratropium bromide in one dose and can be slightly more expensive than separate doses of the two component drugs. Appellee Ilene Hays is a Medicare Part B beneficiary suffering from Chronic Obstructive Pulmonary Disease who has used DuoNeb for approximately four years. During that time, Medicare, pursuant to a statutory formula, provided reimbursement for DuoNeb at 106% of the drug's average sales price. 42 U.S.C. §§ 1395w–3a(b)(1), 1395u(*o*)(1)(G)(ii).

In 2008, four Medicare contractors announced that the medical necessity of administering the two drugs in a combined dose, as compared to separate doses, had not been established. *See* NHIC (Region A), LCD for Nebulizers, L11499 (Apr. 10, 2008). Thus, pursuant to the least costly alternative policy, payment for the combination drug "[would] be based on the allowance for the least costly medically appropriate alternative," the two component drugs as administered separately. *Id.* Hays challenged this decision in the United States District Court for the District of Columbia pursuant to a provision of the statute that allows beneficiaries to proceed without exhausting administrative remedies where "there are no material issues of fact in dispute, and the only issue of law is . . . that a regulation, determination, or ruling by the Secretary is invalid." 42 U.S.C. § 1395ff(f)(3). Hays argued that section 1395y(a)'s "reasonable and necessary" standard modifies "items and services." Accordingly, she contended, the Secretary may determine only whether DuoNeb is reasonable and necessary; if it is, Medicare must reimburse based on the 106% statutory formula. *See* 42 U.S.C. § 1395w–3a. The district court agreed with Hays and granted her motion for summary judgment. The Secretary appeals, and our review is *de novo*.

The Secretary argues that section 1395y(a) is ambiguous and that we should defer to her reasonable interpretation of the statute. *See Chevron U.S.A. Inc. v. Natural Res. Def. Council, Inc.*, 467 U.S. 837 (1984). Several features of the Medicare statute, however, convince us that it unambiguously forecloses the Secretary's interpretation.

In relevant part, section 1395y provides: "(a) Items or services specifically excluded. Notwithstanding any other provision of this subchapter, no payment may be made . . . for any expenses incurred for items or services— (1)(A) which . . . are not reasonable and necessary for the diagnosis or treatment of illness or injury or to improve the functioning of a malformed body member[.]"

The dispute in this case centers on whether "reasonable and necessary" modifies "expenses" (as the Secretary argues), or "items and services" (as Hays contends). If the Secretary is correct, then Medicare may, as it has here, partially cover an item or service, declining to reimburse expenses associated with the marginal difference in price between a prescribed item or service and its least costly and medically appropriate alternative. If Hays and the district court are correct, then the Secretary may make only a binary coverage decision, namely to reimburse at the full statutory rate or not at all.

We agree with Hays and the district court. As they point out, only a dependent clause separates "reasonable and necessary" from the phrase "items or services." *See* § 1395y(a)(1) ("for any expenses incurred for items or services-which, ..., are not reasonable and necessary ..."). "Expenses," by contrast, appears earlier in the sentence. "Ordinarily, qualifying phrases are to be applied to the words or phrase immediately preceding and are not to be construed as extending to others more remote." *United States v. Pritchett,* 470 F.2d 455, 459 (D.C. Cir. 1972). To be sure, this "Rule of the Last Antecedent" is not an absolute and can assuredly be overcome by other indicia of meaning. Here, however, section 1395y contains no indication that the rule is inapplicable. Quite to the contrary, not only is the phrase "items or services" much nearer to the phrase "reasonable and necessary," but subsection (1)(A), which introduces the "reasonable and necessary" standard, is set off from the introductory language and nowhere mentions "expenses."

Several other characteristics of section 1395y(a) reinforce this conclusion. First, subsection (1)(A) prohibits payment for expenses incurred for items or services "which, except for items and services described in a succeeding subparagraph ..., are not reasonable and necessary...." 42 U.S.C. § 1395y(a)(1)(A). By defining the scope of the word "which," this language provides powerful evidence that "reasonable and necessary" applies to "items and services." Moreover, the "succeeding subparagraph[s]" to which subsection (1)(A) refers discuss coverage of specific items and services including "hospice care," § 1395y(a)(1)(C), "screening mammography," § 1395y(a)(1)(F), "home health services," § 1395y(a)(1)(I), and "ultrasound screening," § 1395y(a)(1)(N).

Second, to be covered something—either expenses or items and services—must be "reasonable and necessary for the diagnosis or treatment of illness or injury or to improve the functioning of a malformed body member." 42 U.S.C. § 1395y(a)(1)(A). Items and services diagnose, treat, and improve; expenses do not.

Finally, section 1395y(a) is entitled "Items or services specifically excluded." 42 U.S.C. § 1395y(a). Although "the title of a statute and the heading of a section cannot limit the plain meaning of the text," they remain "tools available for the resolution of a doubt" about statutory meaning. *Bhd. of R.R. Trainmen v. Baltimore & Ohio R.R. Co.,* 331 U.S.

519, 528–29 (1947). Here, the title, which says nothing about expenses, confirms the obvious: that items or services, not expenses, must be reasonable and necessary to qualify for Medicare coverage.

Our conclusion finds support elsewhere in the Medicare Act, specifically its mandatory reimbursement formulas. Section 1395w–3a provides that for multiple source drugs like DuoNeb, "the amount of payment . . . *is*" 106% of the average sales price, as determined under the statutory formula. 42 U.S.C. § 1395w–3a(b)(1) (emphasis added). The statutory formula is in turn based on the volume-weighted average of the average sales prices of drugs within the same Healthcare Common Procedure Coding System (HCPCS) billing and payment code. 42 U.S.C. § 1395w–3a(b)(6). DuoNeb's HCPCS code includes neither component drug.

The Secretary insists that the least costly alternative policy comports with the Medicare Act's mandatory reimbursement formulas because payment under that policy is based on the statutory rate as applied to an item or service's least costly alternative. But this argument would permit an end-run around the statute. The statutory formula requires the Secretary to reimburse a particular drug at 106% of the average sales price for drugs within its billing and payment code. 42 U.S.C. § 1395w–3a(b)(1). By reimbursing DuoNeb at 106% of the average sales price of its two component drugs—which have different billing and payment codes—the Secretary would fundamentally alter the reimbursement scheme. Like the district court, we think it quite unlikely that "Congress, having minutely detailed the reimbursement rates for covered items and services, intended that the Secretary could ignore these formulas whenever she determined that the *expense* of an item or service was not reasonable or necessary."

To be sure, Congress could have written the Medicare Act to authorize the least costly alternative policy. For example, if the statute read, "no payment may be made . . . for any expenses which are incurred for items and services *and* which are not reasonable and necessary for the diagnosis or treatment of illness or injury," then the phrase "reasonable and necessary" would indeed modify "expenses." And if the reimbursement formulas were either discretionary or based on the cost of an item or service's therapeutic equivalents, the Secretary would have authority to refuse payment for the difference in cost between a prescribed item or service and its least costly alternative. But this is not the statute Congress wrote. As written, the statute unambiguously authorizes the Secretary to make only a binary choice: either an item or service is reasonable and necessary, in which case it may be covered at the statutory rate, or it is unreasonable or unnecessary, in which case it may not be covered at all. Nothing in the statute authorizes the least costly alternative policy.

■ RANDOLPH, SENIOR CIRCUIT JUDGE, concurring:

Invoking *Chevron, U.S.A., Inc. v. NRDC,* 467 U.S. 837 (1984), the Secretary asked us to defer to the interpretation of the statute embodied in the local coverage determination of a private contractor. The court rightly declines on the ground that the statute—42 U.S.C. § 1395y(a)(1)(A)—clearly forecloses application of the least costly alternative policy to Duo-

Neb. If the statute had not been so clear, one may wonder whether deference of the *Chevron* variety would have been due. No decision of the Secretary applied the least costly alternative policy to this product. That was the doing of four private contractors the Secretary hired to administer the program. [T]here is a substantial question whether, in requesting deference, the Secretary was actually asking us to defer to a private contractor's determination of the meaning of the statute as applied to DuoNeb. It is not apparent why the rationale of *Chevron* would support the Secretary's request. Still less is it clear that Congress authorized the Secretary to delegate lawmaking functions to private contractors or could do so consistently with the Constitution.

Notes

1. *Consideration of costs.* The question of whether cost can be considered in a medical necessity determination is a contentious one. The court's decision underscores that nothing in the Medicare Act's provisions related to the medical necessity of care expressly allows the Secretary to take cost into account in reaching her decision. Indeed, the debate over the Affordable Care Act was punctuated throughout by accusations that the Act would lead to the elimination of more costly care for beneficiaries and the rationing of whatever care was covered. Should cost in fact be taken into account if the price for equally effective treatments is different? Can "coverage" and "cost" be so neatly cleaved apart?

2. *The concurrence and the application of* Chevron. Judge Randolph's skepticism about *Chevron* deference in the case of contractor decisions is an important one. Here it was not the Secretary's decision that led to the appeal but instead, the local coverage determination of regional subcontractors. For sake of argument suppose Congress grants the Secretary discretion to take cost in account in making decisions regarding medical necessity. May the Secretary delegate that decision to private contractors, and if so, would their decision in any particular case be treated as final decisions of the Secretary? These questions loom large for Medicare because of the extensive use of private contractors to administer a public program.

4. APPEALS OF INDIVIDUAL MEDICARE CLAIMS DENIALS

Ringer concerns the broad question whether outside of a concrete dispute over a claim, a challenge can be mounted against the Secretary's power to place design limits on Medicare coverage through the imposition of across-the-board exclusionary limits on the amount and scope of benefits based on broad evidence regarding the medical necessity of treatments. Far more common are appeals from individualized determinations of medically necessity. Indeed, the cases are as countless as the stars in the sky. Appeals under Medicare parallel those that arise in an ERISA § 502 action, and focus both on whether the denial is consistent with the legal provisions governing coverage and second, whether the denial is supported by the evidence. In Medicare, however, principles of administrative law define the conceptual framework for judicial review of agency action, while in the case of ERISA, the framework is found in the federal common law of trusts developed under ERISA. Both types of reviews are deferential, and in either case, the question is whether the decision maker acted in a manner consistent with governing law and the facts of the case.

The following case is illustrative of the types of facts that can give rise to an appeal under Medicare concerning the appropriate level of care. The case also raises important questions about the validity of the Secretary's approach to defining medical necessity.

Papciak v. Sebelius

742 F. Supp.2d 765 (W.D. Pa. 2010)

■ CATHY BISSOON, UNITED STATES MAGISTRATE JUDGE:

This is an appeal from the final decision of the Secretary of the Department of Health and Human Services ("Secretary") denying Medicare coverage under Part C of the Medicare Program for care provided to Wanda Papciak ("Plaintiff"), between July 10 through July 19, 2008. The administrative law judge (the "ALJ") found that Plaintiff did not require Medicare-covered skilled nursing services. The Medicare Appeal Counsel ("MAC") affirmed. Plaintiff contends that the decision denying coverage is not supported by substantial evidence in the record. Conversely, the Secretary asserts that the decision is supported by substantial evidence. For the reasons that follow, the Court will deny the Secretary's motion for summary judgment and will grant Plaintiff's motion for summary judgment and will remand the case for instruction to award Plaintiff benefits.

At the time of the Secretary's decision, Plaintiff was 81 years old and had undergone a hip replacement surgery on April 28, 2008. Plaintiff received twenty days of therapy and was discharged to her home for home health care on May 22, 2008. Subsequently, Plaintiff developed a urinary tract infection and she was readmitted to the hospital. On June 3, 2008, Plaintiff was discharged by Dr. Tuchinda to ManorCare to receive skilled nursing care, physical therapy and occupational therapy. Upon Plaintiff's admission to ManorCare, Plaintiff was unable to ambulate and could not use her walker due to numbness of her hands due to what was later diagnosed as carpal tunnel syndrome. Plaintiff also had a history of cellulitis, anemia, cholecystectomy, chronic atrial fibrillation, hypertension, anxiety and depression.

Plaintiff received therapy five days a week; however, she made slow progress during her stay. Plaintiff's therapy included physical and occupational therapy, treatment, self-care, therapeutic exercises and therapeutic activities. Her initial treatment was primarily for ambulation. Medicare paid for the skilled care Plaintiff received from June 3 through July 9, 2008. It was determined, however, that effective July 10, 2008, Plaintiff no longer needed skilled care because Plaintiff had made only minimal progress in some areas, had regressed in other areas, and had been determined to have met her maximum potential for her physical and occupational therapy. As a result, Medicare denied payment from July 10 through July 19 because Plaintiff was only receiving "custodial care," not the skilled nursing services required for Medicare coverage.

Subsequent to Plaintiff's treatment at ManorCare, Plaintiff was admitted to the UPMC South Side Emergency Room as an inpatient for a possible infection and generalized weakness. After three days in the hospital, she was transferred to a different facility, Baldwin Health Center. At the new location, she was given physical therapy treatment. The treating physician determined that she would benefit from continued occupational therapy treatment. This assessment proved to be accurate and she met three of her goals prior to discharge on August 21, 2008. Her physical therapist also expressed that she had good recovery potential.

Plaintiff appealed the decision denying coverage and the appeal was subsequently denied by Quality Insights of PA on July 9, 2008. On November 13, 2008, the ALJ held a telephonic hearing, and on November 20, 2008, the ALJ issued a decision denying Plaintiff Medicare coverage. Plaintiff appealed that decision to the MAC. The MAC upheld the ALJ's decision. The MAC decision is the final decision of the Secretary. 42 C.F.R. § 405.730. Therefore, Plaintiff has exhausted her administrative remedies and now seeks relief from this court.

Judicial review of the Secretary's denial of Medicare coverage is proper pursuant to 42 U.S.C. § 405(g). The role of this Court on judicial review is to determine whether there is substantial evidence in the administrative record to support the Secretary's final decision. Any findings of fact made by the ALJ must be accepted as conclusive, provided that they are supported by substantial evidence. 42 U.S.C. § 405(g).

Substantial evidence has been defined as such relevant evidence as a reasonable mind might accept as adequate to support a conclusion. The district court's function is to determine whether the record, as a whole, contains substantial evidence to support the Secretary's findings. Furthermore, the Court also must determine whether the Secretary applied the proper legal standard in denying Medicare benefits.

During the time period in question, Plaintiff was insured by Keystone Health Plan West/Highmark Security Blue, a Medicare Advantage plan. Medicare Advantage plans are required to cover the same medical services that Medicare would cover. 42 C.F.R. § 422.101. One of the exclusions of coverage from Medicare is for expenses considered to be "custodial care." 42 U.S.C. § 1395y(a)(9). The regulations state that "custodial care is any care that does not meet the requirements for coverage as [skilled nursing facility ("SNF")] care as set forth in §§ 409.31 through 409.35 of this chapter." 42 C.F.R. § 411.15(g).

Under the Medicare program, Skilled Nursing Care ("SNC") that is provided at an SNF is defined as services that: (1) Are ordered by a physician; (2) Require the skills of technical or professional personnel such as registered nurses, licensed practical (vocational) nurses, physical thera-pists, occupational therapists, and speech pathologists or audiologists; and (3) Are furnished directly by, or under the supervision of, such personnel. 42 C.F.R. § 409.31(a). Furthermore, the level of care requirements for SNC is that "the beneficiary must require skilled nursing or skilled rehabilita-tion services, or both, on a daily basis" and "the daily skilled services must be ones that, as a practical matter, can only be provided in a SNF, on an inpatient basis." 42 C.F.R. § 409.31(b). Personal care services, such as general supervision and maintenance, which do not require the skills of qualified technical or professional personnel are not skilled services; howev-er, special medical complications can render personal care services to be considered SNC. 42 C.F.R. §§ 409.32(b), 409.33(d).

Courts, in trying to distinguish "custodial care" from SNC, have been guided by two general principles. "First, the decision should be based upon a common sense, non-technical consideration of the patient's condition as a whole. Second, the Social Security Act is to be liberally construed in favor of beneficiaries." Friedman v. Secretary of HHS, 819 F.2d 42, 45 (2d Cir. 1987). In Ridgely v. Secretary, 345 F.Supp. 983 (D. Md. 1972), Chief Judge Northrop stated:

> [T]he purpose of the custodial care disqualification in § 1395y(a)(9) was not to disentitle old, chronically ill and basically helpless, bewildered and confused people like [plaintiff] from the broad remedy which Congress intended to provide for our senior citizens. Rather, the provision was intended to stop cold-blooded and thoughtless relatives from relegating an oldster who could care for him or herself to the care of an [extended care facility] merely so that that oldster would have a place to eat, sleep, or watch television. But when a person is sick, especially a helpless old person, and when those who love that person are not skilled enough to take care of that person, Congress has provided a remedy in the Medicare Act, and that remedy should not be eclipsed by an application of the law and findings of fact which are blinded by bureaucratic economics to the purpose of the Congress.

Ridgely, 345 F.Supp. at 993, *aff'd,* 475 F.2d 1222 (4th Cir. 1973). As a result, [t]he courts have interpreted custodial care to be care that can be provided by a lay person without special skills and not requiring or entailing the continued attention of trained or skilled personnel.

Plaintiff presents two arguments as to why the decision of the Secre-tary lacks the support of substantial evidence in the record. First, Plaintiff argues that the Secretary failed in only considering whether Plaintiff's condition would no longer materially improve with additional SNC. Plain-tiff asserts that the Secretary is required to also consider whether SNC would be required to maintain Plaintiff's level of functioning. Second, Plaintiff argues that the Secretary failed to consider Plaintiff's condition as a whole, and ignored evidence in the record, in coming to the conclusion that Plaintiff required only custodial care. Each argument will be addressed in turn.

A. *The Secretary Failed to Apply the Correct Legal Standard*

Plaintiff argues that the Secretary failed to properly consider *Medicare Skilled Nursing Facility Manual* Chapter 2 § 214.3 in that no consideration was given to Plaintiff's need for SNC to maintain her level of functioning. The relevant portion reads: "The services must be provided with the expectation, based on the assessment made by the physician of the patient's restoration potential, that the condition of the patient will improve materially in a reasonable and generally predictable period of time, *or* the services must be necessary for the establishment of a safe and effective maintenance program." *Skilled Nursing Facility Manual* Chapter 2 § 214.3(A)(1), 2002 WL 34445032 (emphasis added). Plaintiff argues that the question of whether services were necessary for a maintenance program was not considered by the Secretary, and thus the Secretary failed to apply the proper legal standard.[2]

In the decisions by the MAC and the ALJ, no discussion was provided as to Plaintiff's potential need for a rehabilitative maintenance program. In the ALJ's decision, he concluded that "[i]t became apparent that no matter how much more therapy the Beneficiary received, she was not going to achieve a higher level of function." Similarly, the MAC stated that "[d]espite the appellant's arguments to the contrary, the enrollee made little or no progress in therapy from the time of her admission to ManorCare through her discharge from skilled care on or around July 10, 2008." Nothing else in either discussion addresses whether plaintiff required SNC to maintain her level of functioning following her hip replacement.

The Secretary's regulations state that "[t]he restoration potential of a patient is not the deciding factor in determining whether skilled services are needed. Even if full recovery or medical improvement is not possible, a patient may need skilled services to prevent further deterioration or preserve current capabilities." 42 C.F.R § 409.32(c). Despite this, the Secretary concluded that Plaintiff lacked any future restoration potential and therefore no longer required SNC and only required "custodial care." Furthermore, the Secretary's decision lacks a sufficient discussion of the alternative reason for rehabilitative SNC. As a result, the decision denying Plaintiff Medicare coverage cannot be affirmed.

B. *The Secretary Failed to Consider Plaintiff's Condition as a Whole*

Plaintiff argues that the Secretary ignored evidence that Plaintiff was improving in her functional capacity. In particular, Plaintiff points out that she had improvement in the ability to use her hands and that she could stand with moderate assistance thus enabling her to begin to use a walker. Furthermore, subsequent to Plaintiff's treatment at ManorCare, Plaintiff's condition improved such that she was meeting her occupational therapy goals and had a positive outlook and engaged in group activities.

---

2. Interpretative guidelines of an agency's regulations do not rise to the level of a regulation and do not have the effect of law. However, such guidelines are persuasive interpretation of the agency's regulations, which are binding and carry the force and effect of law.

[T]he MAC's decision stated that "[t]he record clearly and unequivocally reflects a patient who was unmotivated and resistant to participation in therapy throughout her entire stay." In making this finding, however, no consideration was given to Plaintiff's other impairments that were limiting her ability to progress in her functional capacity. In particular, Plaintiff was diagnosed as having anxiety and situational depression that affected her motivation to ambulate. Plaintiff's depression also included symptoms of suicidal ideation and crying spells. In making the finding that Plaintiff had reached her maximum functional capacity, no consideration was given as to the treatment of Plaintiff's depression and anxiety and whether her physical capacity was being limited by her mental impairments. Indeed, in the progress notes subsequent to Plaintiff's treatment at ManorCare, it was noted that she had become more cooperative, was willing and able to participate in group activities with other residents and stated that she felt like she was doing better.

Furthermore, Plaintiff points to treatment notes by Plaintiff's physicians indicating that she would benefit from continued rehabilitative care, as well as treatment notes that showed Plaintiff's improvement during and subsequent to Plaintiff's stay at ManorCare. Also, Plaintiff's subsequent treatment notes show that she had made progress with her occupational therapy and some limited progress with her physical therapy. Finally, in a note by Plaintiff's physical therapist dated October 20, 2008, it is stated that "she has made tremendous progress in transfers and ambulation. She is able to walk five feet, twice with walker and minimal assist. She is able to do transfer and walker and minimal assist."

[T]his evidence was not discussed by the Secretary in the decision denying plaintiff Medicare coverage. As a result, the decision by the Secretary is not supported by substantial evidence. Because the Secretary's conclusion that Plaintiff "could not reasonably have been expected to reach a higher level of function from further skilled therapy," is in direct conflict with the evidence that Plaintiff's physical capacity did improve subsequent to her stay at ManorCare, it is appropriate for this case to be reversed and remanded with instructions to award Plaintiff benefits. In considering the entire record as a whole, in light of the Secretary's regulations, the *only* possible conclusion that can be reached is that Plaintiff would have benefited from continued SNC during the relevant time because she had not yet reached her peak functional capacity. Indeed (and ironically), the facts of this case quite nearly mirror the example given in the *Medicare Skilled Nursing Facility Manual*.

> EXAMPLE 1: An 80–year–old, previously ambulatory, post-surgical patient has been bedbound for one week and, as a result, has developed muscle atrophy, orthostatic hypotension, joint stiffness and lower extremity edema. To the extent that the patient requires a brief period of daily skilled physical therapy services to restore lost functions, those services are reasonable and necessary.

Skilled Nursing Facility Manual Chapter 2 § 214.3, 2002 WL 34445032. While Plaintiff's progress was slow during the period in question, the

Secretary failed to consider the cause of Plaintiff's slow progress and whether it was, in fact, a permanent limitation. Because the record, when considered as a whole, indicates that Plaintiff would have benefited from SNC during the period in question, this case will be reversed and remanded to the Secretary with instruction to award Plaintiff benefits.

Note

The chasm between the regulations, the facts, and the administrative decision. This case illustrates the gulf that often can lie between an administrative decision and the actual law and the facts of the case and underscores the importance of judicial review. It seems pretty clear that both the administrative law judge and the Medicare Appeals Council ignored the regulations that apply to nursing facility treatment, not to mention the facts surrounding her case. In key respects, Mrs. Papciak's condition harkens back to that of Ethan Bedrick, earlier in this Part, in that a decision maker essentially has elected to graft onto the legal terms of coverage additional tests not found anywhere in the controlling law. In both situations, the decisionmakers demanded evidence that was not and could not be there: in Ethan's case, proof that somehow treatment could completely correct the effects of cerebral palsy, with the conclusion then following that treatment was really not useful for children like Ethan); in Mrs. Papciak's case, the reviewers wanted major improvements (although ironically she did subsequently make them), rather than evidence that the treatment was medically appropriate to maintain her functional capabilities and avert further deterioration. In both cases, the medical necessity determination substantially diminished the value of insurance coverage for persons with severe disabilities.

CHAPTER 11

MEDICAID

1. INTRODUCTION

It is difficult to overstate Medicaid's importance to the U.S. health care system, because in many ways Medicaid is built to compensate for all of the limitations on coverage described throughout Part Two. Medicaid makes coverage possible for individuals whose poverty and health status put them beyond the reach of the market. Although the January 2014 implementation of state health insurance Exchanges offering subsidized insurance products will provide enormous benefits for lower income people, these expansions will rest on an expanded Medicaid base. Furthermore, Medicaid continues to play a vital role for low-income disabled children and adults, for whom the limited design of private insurance is inadequate, as well as for low-income Medicare beneficiaries for whom Medicaid is the central source of supplemental coverage. Despite enactment of the Affordable Care Act, in other words, Medicaid remains a fundamental building block of the American health care system. Sara Rosenbaum, *A Customary and Necessary Program*, 362 NEW ENG. J. MED. 1955 (2010).

Medicaid is complex, in ways that even Medicare cannot rival. To be sure, there is variation in Medicare coverage owing to the differences among regional contractors' coverage decisions and practices, and additional variation has been introduced as a result of the Medicare Advantage and the Prescription Drug plans. But Medicare is governed by uniform federal standards that ensure commonality in eligibility, entitlement, and the important contours of coverage.

This uniformity is not the case with Medicaid, which in reality consists of 51 separate state programs (as well as programs in the Commonwealth and Trust Territories) that are designed and operate under broad federal standards, the enforcement of which is limited to recoupment of disallowed state claims for payment. Indeed, national headlines reflected the surprise generated by CMS's disapproval of a state plan amendment submitted by Indiana in the spring of 2011 that would have debarred Planned Parenthood clinics from its program because it provides legal abortions. (Planned Parenthood also is the state's single largest providers of family planning services, preventive cancer screenings, and treatment of sexually transmitted diseases). Robert Pear, *U.S. Objects to New Law on Clinics in Indiana*, N.Y. TIMES, May 22, 2011. CMS has no injunctive powers, nor does it have the legal authority to step in and take over administration of a state's program when the state fails to comply with federal requirements, as is the case with federal enforcement of insurance market reforms under the Public Health Service Act (see Chapter 6, above). As a result, until June,

2011, when a federal injunction was issued against Indiana's policy as a violation of Medicaid's "free choice of provider" requirement, discussed below, thousands of Medicaid recipients simply were cut off from care as clinics lost their major source of funding. Indeed, the role of the United States was reduced to filing a Statement of Interest at trial, underscoring its own lack of enforcement authority. Planned Parenthood of Indiana v. Commissioner of the State Department of Health, 794 F. Supp.2d 892 (S.D. Ind. 2011)

The literature on Medicaid is enormous. At once foundational to health care and reviled as "welfare medicine," Medicaid represents the nation's attempt to overcome the failure of a market-driven system to take care of people too poor to participate in the market. Termed by one judge decades ago (when the program was far simpler) "an aggravated assault on the English language,"* Medicaid is considered particularly impervious to straightforward interpretation and understanding.

In 1965, Congress created a three-layer cake: Medicare Part A, guaranteeing hospital coverage to all seniors; Medicare Part B, a voluntary program providing seniors insurance for physician and other medical services; and Medicaid, a welfare program for the poor. Medicaid was an outgrowth of the nation's welfare tradition rather than the blossoming social insurance vision reflected in Medicare. At once enormous and limited, Medicaid has withstood the test of time, precisely because its contributions are so elemental and powerful and because it is impossible to craft any single successor program. Indeed, it is Medicaid's unmatched ability to compensate for other limitations in the U.S. health care system that led to its enormous expansion under the Affordable Care Act; Medicaid will account for half the newly insured population when the law is fully implemented in 2014.

2. FINANCING HEALTH CARE FOR MEDICALLY INDIGENT PERSONS, PRE–MEDICAID

The structure and policies of Medicaid are rooted in a tradition of market-supporting charity, combined in complex ways with the egalitarian social contract and professional autonomy models, and, more recently, with market competition in the delivery of care. Market-supporting charity embodies a charitable response to human suffering, but is also structured to ensure that charitable benefits do not undermine the economic or market incentive to work. Thus the English and American Poor Laws of the 19th century and before required local units of government to "relieve" the poor, but to do so in such a limited, discretionary, and often humiliating fashion as to make the condition of the recipient less desirable than that of the lowest paid worker. Moreover, the Poor Laws distinguished the "worthy" from the "unworthy" poor, i.e., those who had a socially legiti-

---

* Friedman v. Berger, 409 F. Supp. 1225, 1225 (S.D.N.Y.), aff'd, 547 F.2d 724 (2d Cir. 1976).

mate reason for poverty and not working (such as advanced age, illness and physical disability), versus those who did not.

The Social Security Act of 1935 reflected this tradition in its provisions for cash assistance. Under this law, the federal government promised to match state cash assistance (or "welfare") expenditures for certain "categories" of low-income people: the aged, the blind and totally disabled, and children with a single parent (statutorily termed "dependent children", and until 1996 known as the "Aid to Families with Dependent Children" (AFDC) program). The states had discretion to set the eligibility lines and amounts of actual payment.* *See generally* Edward V. Sparer, *The Right to Welfare, in* THE RIGHTS OF AMERICANS (Norman Dorsen ed., 1971); FRANCES FOX PIVEN & RICHARD A. CLOWARD, REGULATING THE POOR (1971); Rand E. Rosenblatt, *Social Duties and the Problem of Rights in the American Welfare State, in* THE POLITICS OF LAW 90 (David Kairys ed., rev. ed., 1990). After remaining in place for over 60 years, this structure—welfare as we know it—was repealed and replaced by a "workfare" program, the Personal Responsibility and Work Opportunity Act of 1996, Pub. L. No. 104–193 (generally known as "welfare reform"). However, as discussed below, the welfare categories comprised the foundation of Medicaid's eligibility, underscoring the enormity of the policy departure embodied in the Affordable Care Act's provisions extending Medicaid to all low-income people.

Prior to 1965, governmental health care programs for the poor were largely local and discretionary. State statutes typically authorized, but did not require, counties and municipalities to spend a portion of their tax revenues on health care for the poor, either by constructing and operating public hospitals and clinics, or by purchasing care in the private sector, usually at well below market rates. Decisions about eligibility, coverage, and reimbursement were generally discretionary with each locality, and policy was determined not by the medical needs of the poor, but by budget limitations and concepts of what kind of care was "appropriate" for low-income patients.

The result of these governmental policies and private charitable practices was a "dual track" health care system explicitly stratified along the lines of economic class and its frequent correlates, race and national origin/ethnicity. Larger cities often had (and some continue to have) two separate sets of health care institutions: public hospitals and clinics for the poor; and private nonprofit hospitals with associated private physician practices for those with private insurance or personal financial resources. Even when a private hospital admitted poor patients, as many did, these patients were placed in multi-bed hospital "wards" and treated primarily

---

* The Social Security Act Amendments of 1972 consolidated the non-AFDC categories of cash assistance (i.e. the aged, blind, and permanently and totally disabled) into a new program titled Supplemental Security Income (SSI). This new program established federal eligibility and benefit standards, and permitted the states both to augment cash benefits above the federal levels and to "freeze" Medicaid eligibility standards for SSI recipients at levels below the updated federal SSI standards. Subject to several qualifications, the states retained discretion to set AFDC eligibility and benefit levels.

by doctors-in-training (under varying degrees of supervision by more senior physicians), while middle-income patients occupied semi-private rooms (usually two beds) and upper income patients had private accommodations. *See generally* RAYMOND S. DUFF & AUGUST B. HOLLINGSHEAD, SICKNESS AND SOCIETY (1968) (analyzing in detail the impact of socioeconomic class on treatment decisions and provider-patient relationships in a large teaching hospital).

Whether the tracking took place among or within institutions, the consequences were similar: underfunded, fragmented, crisis-oriented care for the poor, often organized around the educational needs of the medical profession, compared with, at least in theory, comprehensive, patient-centered care for the middle and upper classes. *See, e.g.*, Greater Washington D.C. Area Council of Senior Citizens v. District of Columbia Government, 406 F. Supp. 768 (D.D.C. 1975) (public hospital serving indigents "fell far short of recognized and acceptable standards in this community"); Meyer v. Massachusetts Eye and Ear Infirmary, 330 F. Supp. 1328, 1330 (D. Mass. 1971) (plaintiff-physician alleges that "[i]n contrast to the quality personalized attention afforded private patients," "clinic" patients receive inferior treatment and are exposed to greater risks for experimental and educational purposes without their informed consent).

3. MEDICAID'S IMPORTANCE TO THE HEALTH CARE SYSTEM

The largest of all means-tested entitlements, Medicaid covered 68 million persons in 2010, including 33 million children, 11 million persons with disabilities, 17 million non-disabled adults, and 6 million elderly people. MEDICAID AND CHIP PAYMENT AND ACCESS COMMISSION (MACPAC), REPORT TO CONGRESS 10 (March 2011). Medicaid's role in extending meaningful Medicare coverage to low-income beneficiaries is enormous; in 2010 the program covered 9 million disabled and elderly persons with low family incomes. *Medicaid Matters: Understanding Medicaid's Role in Our Health Care System*, KAISER FAMILY FOUNDATION (2011), http://www.kff.org/medicaid/upload/8165.pdf. Medicaid enables states to provide extended coverage to Medicare beneficiaries with disabilities so that they can work. Its far smaller companion, the State Children's Health Insurance Program (SCHIP), covered 8 million "targeted low income children" that year, who have low family incomes (generally below 300 percent of the federal poverty level) but were ineligible for Medicaid. *Id.*

In 2010, total federal and state Medicaid outlays surpassed $400 billion. Medicaid accounted for slightly more than 8 percent of U.S. outlays and represented 33 percent of all nursing home expenditures, 36 percent of all home health expenditures, and 25 percent of total spending on mental health and substance disorder treatment services. *Id.* Along with CHIP, Medicaid accounted for 18 percent of total hospital expenditures. *Id.* Medicaid is the single largest source of funding for community health centers and public hospitals, discussed in Part One.

4.   MEDICAID'S HISTORY

a.   Enactment

Medicaid was enacted in 1965 as part of the same legislation that established Medicare. Although their names are similar and the two programs often are confused, Medicaid and Medicare have very different financing, methods of administration, and social missions. At the same time the programs share joint coverage of low-income Medicare beneficiaries, known as "dual eligibles."

The vision of Medicaid as an egalitarian social contract for the poor was stated most expansively by the program's original administering federal agency, the Department of Health, Education, and Welfare (HEW).

> The passage of Title XIX marks the beginning of a new era in medical care for low-income families. The potential of this new title can hardly be overestimated, as its ultimate goal is the assurance of complete, continuous, family-centered medical care of high quality to persons who are unable to pay for it themselves. The law aims much higher than the mere paying of medical bills, and States, in order to achieve its high purpose, will need to assume responsibility for planning and establishing systems of high quality medical care, comprehensive in scope and wide in coverage.

HEW Supplement D, § D–5140.

This vision would have been challenging to implement in the best of circumstances, because it would cost a great deal of money, challenge the professional autonomy, income, and power of health care providers, and shock the fiscal and provider-dominated policies of state governments. Overcoming such obstacles would have required a large, well-organized, and long-lasting social movement. While the elements of such a movement did exist among the elderly, the civil rights movement, the labor movement, and the nascent anti-poverty movement, the political and administrative officials who crafted Medicaid (and Medicare) resolutely refused to help build such a movement or to conceive of the legislation in those terms.

> Far from being presented as the triumph of a long movement for compulsory health insurance or as a needed social service provided under government guarantee, Medicare appeared in the guise of an insurance company, and Medicaid as an extension of welfare programs in the states. The absence of any clear commitment, on the part of either Medicare or Medicaid, to the goal [of] ensuring a basic right to health services meant that both programs were open to future cutbacks in entitlements, funding, and eligibility.

STEVENS & STEVENS, WELFARE MEDICINE IN AMERICA: A CASE STUDY OF MEDICAID 53 (1974). This lack of commitment was evident in Medicaid's own financing and other structural and political features. Most decisively, the program's substantial reliance on state funding and its linkage of eligibility to cash welfare categories has sharply limited the number of beneficiaries and its political appeal. In 1965, many states did not even have income taxes; revenues were raised by sales and property taxes, which fall more heavily on those with lower incomes. In effect, states were being asked to raise money from hard-pressed employed average-income families to pay for broadly defined benefits for some of the nonworking population, when many working families themselves did not have adequate or any health benefits. *See* Edward V. Sparer, *Gordian Knots: The Situation of Health Care Advocacy for the Poor Today*, 15 CLEARINGHOUSE REV. 1 (1981), discussed in Rand E. Rosenblatt, *Equality, Entitlement, and National Health Care Reform: The Challenge of Managed Competition and Managed Care*, 60 BROOK. L. REV. 105, 114–116 (1994). Needless to say, this was not politically popular, although eventually the states were pressed by the federal government (including the courts) to establish relatively comprehensive benefits and access for eligible low-income children.

b. Structure, Achievements, and Challenges

In enacting Medicaid, Congress set a goal of doing nothing less than eliminating traditionally segregated and inferior health care for the poor, and integrating them into "mainstream" or middle-class patterns of hospital and medical care. The program's general strategy was to provide eligible poor persons with the equivalent of health insurance coverage, which in turn would enable them to leave the charity wards and clinics in order to purchase services in the private sector. The precise terms of these health care benefits were to be set by the states operating under federal standards establishing substantive provisions governing eligibility, enrollment, receipt of medical assistance, coverage, provider participation and (to a limited degree) provider payment, cost-sharing, and general methods of administration. From the beginning, Medicaid was freed of the types of careful ground rules on coverage and payment that governed Medicare. STEVENS AND STEVENS, WELFARE MEDICINE IN AMERICA at 73–90.

The administrative centerpiece of this complex reform effort was (and remains) the statutory requirement that each participating state establish a uniform, state-wide medical assistance program embodied in a federally-approved "state plan." (Uniformity rules have been considerably relaxed over the years to permit coverage variations by sub-class of recipient, class of services and items, and geographic region). *See* Rand E. Rosenblatt, *Health Care Reform and Administrative Law: A Structural Approach*, 88 YALE L.J. 243, 289 (1978) (citing relevant statutory and regulatory provisions); Andy Schneider et al., *Medicaid Source Book*, KAISER FAMILY FOUNDATION (2003); State Medicaid Directors Letter (Aug 15, 2006), http://www.cms.hhs.gov/SMDL/SMD/itemdetail.asp?filterType=dual,%20date & filterValue=2/yyyy & filterByDID=1 & sortByDID=1 & sortOrder=ascending & itemID=CMS1202222 & intNumPerPage=10.

Under Medicaid, the federal government contributes toward the cost of state expenditures for "medical assistance" furnished to eligible low-income persons by participating providers. Because the 1965 federal legislation allowed each state considerable discretion in designing its own Medicaid program, there have always been 50 Medicaid programs (54 actually, counting the District of Columbia, which is treated like a state for purposes of Medicaid payments and administration, as well as the U.S. territories, which have modified Medicaid programs). These programs operate under federal standards of varying clarity and legal force.

The statutory federal payment formula for determining amounts owed to state programs for the "medical assistance" furnished to eligible persons varies in accordance with a state's per capita income; by contrast, federal contributions toward states' administrative costs are set in accordance with a nationally uniform formula. Thus, a poor state, such as Mississippi, may receive four federal dollars for every one state dollar spent on medical assistance, while an affluent state, such as New Jersey, receives a dollar in medical assistance contributions for every state dollar spent. Family planning services and supplies are covered by a special payment rate equaling 90 percent, while states also receive federal contributions ranging from 50 percent to 90 percent for costs associated with state plan administration. 42 U.S.C. § 1396b. In 2009, legislation to incentivize the adoption and "meaningful use" of electronic health records (EHRs) established a 100 percent contribution rate for state incentive payments. American Reinvestment and Recovery Act of 2009, Pub. L. No. 111–5 (Division B, Title IV) (111th Cong., 1st Sess.) The federal government will finance nearly all medical assistance costs associated with coverage of individuals made newly eligible for coverage under the Affordable Care Act as of January 1, 2014. PPACA § 2001 (federal financial participation of 100 percent in calendar years 2014–2016, declining to 90 percent in 2020 and for years thereafter). PPACA § 2001, adding 42 U.S.C. § 1396d(y).

Whether entitled to a high federal medical assistance contribution or a lower one, states have an enormous incentive to use Medicaid to finance health care services to the poor, because of the availability of open-ended federal contributions to the cost of paying for covered services. Medicaid represents the single largest federal grant transfer to states. Once a state plan for medical assistance is approved (subsequent changes in eligibility, scope of coverage, payment rates, conditions of participation, and other matters are also subject to a state plan approval process), the federal government contributes to state expenditures in accordance with each state's plan. Federal contributions are treated as a legal entitlement in each state, and federal law establishes appeals and judicial review protections governing the Secretary of DHHS' determinations as to state entitlement to payments. Thus, for example, DHHS' decision to disapprove Indiana's state plan amendments is subject to an appeals process with a right of judicial review in the state. 42 U.S.C. § 1316. *See* 76 Fed. Reg. 44,591 (July 26, 2011) (announcing reconsideration of the Indiana state plan amendment disapproval).

Federal law imposes numerous obligations on state programs. Among the most important are the following: first, state medical assistance programs must meet requirements related to comparability of services and uniformity across the state, 42 U.S.C. § 1396a(a)(1) and (a)(10), although important exceptions apply in order to allow variations in services to meet the needs of special populations. Second, states must assure that medical assistance (defined under the Affordable Care Act as not only payment for services but access to the services themselves) is furnished "with reasonable promptness." 42 U.S.C. § 1396a(a)(8). Third, state eligibility standards and coverage rules must be reasonable and must comply with certain federal requirements related to the methods and standards for evaluating income and assets. 42 U.S.C. § 1396a(a)(17). Fourth, states must provide beneficiaries with the right to seek services from the qualified provider of their choice. 42 U.S.C. § 1396a(a)(23) (although states can condition coverage (other than family planning and emergency care) for most populations on enrollment in managed care entities). 42 U.S.C. § 1396u–2. Fifth, states must provide "fair hearings" for individuals whose claims for medical assistance have been denied or are not acted upon with reasonable promptness. 42 U.S.C. § 1396a(a)(4). Sixth, states must assure that payments are sufficient to enlist enough providers to make care accessible. 42 U.S.C. § 1396a(a)(30)(A). Within this framework, states retain substantial discretion to determine income eligibility levels and the shape of the benefit package, beyond a basic, federal minimum.

The heart of the statute, from the perspective of individuals, is 42 U.S.C. § 1396a(a)(10), which defines the individuals who are entitled to medical assistance, as well as the scope of assistance required. Tracking classic concepts of welfare law, the original groups of individuals entitled to medical assistance on a mandatory basis consisted of "dependent" children and their caretaker relatives who received Aid to Families with Dependent Children (AFDC),* elderly and disabled persons receiving welfare under cash assistance programs (which were replaced in 1974 by the Supplemental Security Income Program covering both disabled children and adults as well as the indigent elderly). Mandatory coverage subsequently was added for all "poverty level" children and pregnant women as well as for certain additional groups of low-income Medicare beneficiaries. MACPAC, REPORT TO CONGRESS (March 2011) at 11–16.

In addition, federal law establishes approximately four dozen "optional" coverage groups, including many categories defined by their illness, their place of residence, or other descriptors designed to parse the "deserving" from the "non-deserving" poor. Historically the statute also gave states enormous leeway to define who is poor, thereby leading to state Medicaid eligibility standards for adults as low as 20% of the federal poverty level. Sara Rosenbaum, *Medicaid and National Health Care Reform*, 361 NEW ENG. J. MED. 2009 (2009).

---

* AFDC was replaced in 1996 with the Temporary Assistance to Needy Families (TANF) program. The repeal statute retained the original requirement that state Medicaid programs cover "AFDC-related" individuals, defined as persons who would have been entitled to AFDC under the state's 1996 rules. Because cash welfare payments in 1996 were already low and have of course eroded further, as a practical matter, no child or adult would be eligible for coverage under this standard today. States uniformly provide Medicaid to children and adults who receive TANF.

Addressing this enormous gap in federal Medicaid coverage policy—a legacy of the program's welfare roots—was a centerpiece of the Affordable Care Act, which as of January 1, 2014, establishes an obligation in all participating states to cover all individuals (with a 5–year waiting period imposed on individuals who are legally present in the U.S.) with family incomes below 133% of the federal poverty level. Furthermore, the Act bars the use of asset tests and requires use of a new "modified adjusted gross income" methodology for calculating financial eligibility, in order to smooth coverage transitions between Medicaid and state health insurance Exchanges. PPACA § 2001. This change is anticipated to result in more uniform eligibility rules for nonelderly, non-disabled, non-pregnant adults, and an assurance that all adults and children living below a uniform concept of poverty will be eligible for program benefits. The Act provides enhanced federal payments for newly eligible adults, while imposing aggressive outreach and enrollment obligations on the states to assure that newly eligible adults and children are enrolled.

The term "medical assistance" is defined in the statute. 42 U.S.C. § 1396d(a). Medicaid provides for certain "required benefits," as well as a broad array of optional benefits. MACPAC, REPORT TO CONGRESS (March 2010). What is "required" versus what is "optional" is an artifact of history and unrelated to medical need. For example, prescription drugs are an "optional" Medicaid service, while the services of rural health clinics are required. In 2004, 30 percent of all state Medicaid spending could be attributed to "optional" items and services, which include many of the program's most important items and services (e.g., prescription drugs, institutional care for persons with mental retardation, home and community care). *An Overview of Spending on Mandatory vs. Optional Populations and Services*, KAISER COMMISSION ON MEDICAID AND THE UNINSURED, Fig. 5 (2005), http://www.kff.org/medicaid/upload/Medicaid–An–Overview-of. Spending-on.pdf

Medicaid's enormous power as a funder of health care services is evident not only in the eligibility categories it recognizes but also in the rules of coverage it imposes. Unlike Medicare and commercial insurance, Medicaid prohibits arbitrary, condition-specific limits on required services. 42 C.F.R. § 440.230. The statute requires that state medical necessity definitions be reasonable and that coverage requirements be non-discriminatory. 42 U.S.C. §§ 1396a(a)(17)(A) and (a)(30)(B); 42 C.F.R. § 440.230(b)–(d). Furthermore, coverage requirements for children under the age of 21 are unprecedented in U.S. pediatric health care policy. The Medicaid Early Periodic Screening Diagnostic and Treatment (EPSDT) benefit requires that all categories of benefits and services falling within the federal definition of "medical assistance" be furnished to persons under age 21, even if not covered for adults. In addition, EPSDT requires broad coverage of preventive services such as checkups, immunizations, vision, dental and hearing care, and it eliminates state discretion to impose fixed limits on coverage unrelated to the medical necessity of care for individual children. Rosenbaum & Wise, *Crossing The Medicaid/Private Insurance Divide* at 382–93.

Medicaid gives states broad discretion to develop provider participation and compensation standards, while setting minimum standards for disproportionate share hospitals, federally qualified health centers, and rural health clinics. As noted, federal law gives recipients the right to select from among "qualified providers" while at the same time permitting states to condition coverage on enrollment in a managed care entity that restricts beneficiaries to care received through the entity. Certain free choice of provider exceptions apply in the case of emergency care and family planning services and supplies. 42 U.S.C. § 1396a(a)(23). As of 2010, approximately 70 percent of all beneficiaries were enrolled in some form of managed care. MACPAC, REPORT TO CONGRESS (June 2011).

In sum, federal law imposes broad limits to assure that state discretion is exercised in a manner consistent with program goals. Indeed, as discussed in the materials that follow, the courts have interpreted Medicaid as creating not one but three separate sets of legal entitlements and enforceable federal obligations: that of participating states to federal financial assistance; that of eligible individuals to coverage; and certain enforceable federal obligations in the case of certain participating providers.

Medicaid's achievements have been enormous. The program has been amended numerous times to respond to major social and population health needs. MACPAC, REPORT TO CONGRESS 14–15 (March 2011). When the limits of employer-sponsored coverage for the poor became evident, Congress, with considerable state support, expanded Medicaid to cover all "poverty level" pregnant women, infants and children (income eligibility up to 133 percent of the federal poverty level for pregnant women and infants, and 100 percent of the federal poverty level for children ages 1–18). As the need for stable financing for the health care safety net became clearer, Medicaid was amended to provide "disproportionate share" payments to public hospitals and enhanced payments to community health centers (known as federally qualified health centers in Medicaid parlance). Enhanced payments to community health centers, discussed in Part One, coupled with expanded coverage for the low-income patients served by health centers, led to a doubling of community health center capacity over the years 1985–2005. Sara Rosenbaum & Peter Shin, *Health Center Reauthorization: An Overview of Achievements and Challenges*, KAISER COMMISSION ON MEDICAID AND THE UNINSURED (2006).

Medicare's failure to account adequately for the special needs of the poor were addressed by expanding Medicaid rather than by amending Medicare. The demand for non-institutional long-term care for children, adults, and the elderly with serious disabilities but capable of living in community settings—propelled forward by civil rights laws for persons with disabilities—led to a series of broad reforms to enable greater Medicaid financing for home and community-based care. Through its coverage of community-based long-term care, Medicaid has been a powerful force for the integration into society of children and adults with severe disabilities. John Iglehart, *Medicaid Revisited: Skirmishes over a Vast Public Enter-*

prise, 356 NEW ENG. J. MED. 734 (2007); Rosenbaum, *Health Policy Report: Medicaid* at 635–40; Weil, *There's Something About Medicaid.*

Concerns about population health, such as high infant mortality, resulted in program restructuring to extend Medicaid to all low-income pregnant women. Today Medicaid pays for health care for more than one-third of all births and one in three children. *Understanding Medicaid's Role in Our Health Care System*, KAISER FAMILY FOUNDATION, http://www.kff.org/medicaid/upload/8165.pdf. Indeed, Medicaid has been credited with the dramatic decline in infant mortality that followed its enactment. DAVIS & SCHOEN, HEALTH AND THE WAR ON POVERTY.

Medicaid, in combination with Medicare, led to a dramatic increase in the use of health care among low-income Americans; by 1973 Medicaid had nearly ended the nominal disparities in health care utilization (prior to adjusting for health status) between the non-poor and the poor; health care utilization rates for low-income children became virtually identical to those for privately insured children. DAVIS & SCHOEN, HEALTH AND THE WAR ON POVERTY at 65. Medicaid eliminated out-of-hospital births among low-income African American women in the South, and is credited with much of the 50 percent decline in infant mortality which occurred in the United States between the late 1960s and 1980. Sara Rosenbaum, *Medicaid Expansions and Access to Health Care, in* THE MEDICAID FINANCING CRISIS: BALANCING RESPONSIBILITIES, PRIORITIES AND DOLLARS 45, 61 (Diane Rowland et al., eds.,1993).

A review of Medicaid's impact on more than 30 separate health care markets identified 8 distinct types of health care goods and services in which the proportion of total market revenue represented by Medicaid equaled or exceeded 40 percent. Kevin Quinn & Martin Kitchener, *Medicaid's Role in the Many Markets for Health Care*, HEALTH CARE FIN. REV. 28, 69–82 (Summer 2007). Medicaid accounts for nearly half of all nursing home revenues, and it is not uncommon for Medicaid patients to constitute half or more of a hospital's maternity and newborn patient census. A groundbreaking study examining Medicaid's role in improving access to health centers found that following the random assignment of low-income people to the Medicaid program under a special Oregon lottery system, people enrolled in Medicaid received significantly greater amounts of health care. Amy Finkelstein et al., *The Oregon Health Insurance Experiment: Evidence from the First Year*, NBER WORKING PAPER SERIES #17190 (2011), www.nber.org/papers/w17190.

Despite its achievements, Medicaid faces serious challenges. Despite evidence of its beneficial impact on opening health care doors for the poor, Medicaid has had a particularly difficult time achieving equal health care access because of low provider participation, the isolation of poor communities, and inadequate numbers of community health centers, public hospitals and health systems. MACPAC, REPORT TO CONGRESS ch. 4 (March 2011). MACPAC attributes this failure to a combination of factors: the unique characteristics of beneficiaries, which creates greater clinical challenges; frequent fluctuations in coverage because of its strict eligibility limitations;

the availability of providers; the rate of provider participation in the program; and factors affecting utilization, including geographic and cultural isolation. Because of the uneasy financial base on which Medicaid rests, provider payment rates frequently are far below those paid by private insurance and even Medicare. Stephen Zuckerman et al., *Trends in Medicaid Physician Fees, 2003–2008*, 28(3) HEALTH AFFAIRS (Web Exclusive) w510 (April 28, 2009) (showing Medicaid-to-Medicare fee ratios as low as 47% in some states). As a result, already inadequate health care access, due to poverty and medical underservice in poor communities, has been exacerbated by low fees, even as—paradoxically—"mainstreaming" care of the poor was a major aim of the original legislation. STEVENS & STEVENS, WELFARE MEDICINE IN AMERICA. *See also* Vanessa Fuhrmanns, *Note to Medicaid Patients: the Doctor Won't See You*, Wall St. J., July 19, 2007, at A1.

One major approach to reforming Medicaid has been the use of special federal demonstration authority under § 1115 of the Social Security Act, 42 U.S.C. § 1315, to test new approaches to shaping the program. This authority has been used to expand coverage, institute compulsory managed care, and expand home- and community-based services. These demonstrations have helped propel broader statutory reforms in eligibility, coverage, and service delivery. John Holahan et al., *Insuring the Poor Through Section 1115 Medicaid Waivers*, 14(1) HEALTH AFFAIRS 199 (1995). At the same time, concerns have been raised regarding the lack of transparency in demonstration design and implementation, as well as the use of demonstration powers to reduce the scope of coverage. U.S. GOV'T ACCOUNTABILITY OFFICE, GAO–07–694R, MEDICAID DEMONSTRATION WAIVERS: LACK OF OPPORTUNITY FOR PUBLIC INPUT DURING FEDERAL APPROVAL PROCESS STILL A CONCERN (July 24, 2007).

The problem is larger, however, than anything that can be solved through demonstrations: Medicaid's gains have come with a big political and financial price tag. As with the individual coverage requirement, political resistance to the Affordable Care Act's Medicaid expansion had, by December, 2011, been translated into an epic constitutional battle that had journeyed all the way to the United States Supreme Court, despite the fact that the Court of Appeals for the Eleventh Circuit, whose decision striking down the individual coverage requirement is on appeal, had, along with every other federal court to consider the issue, determined that Medicaid's status as a voluntary program places it beyond states' claims of unconstitutional "coercion." 648 F.3d 1235, 1260–67 (11th Cir.,), *cert. granted*, 2011 WL 5155564.

The fact that Medicaid's requirements may be a constitutional *quid pro quo* for the trillions of dollars that the federal government has given the states since Medicaid's enactment* (not to mention no serious enforcement of federal requirements *ever*, to wit, never having found a state out of compliance to the point of a major withholding federal funds), does not stop states from absolutely despising the program, even as they depend com-

---

* Of course, the minimum eligibility requirements may not be constitutional, depending on what the Supreme Court does.

pletely on it. Even before the ACA expansion, Medicaid was the subject of enormous federal/state tension resulting from the program's shared federal-state participation rates; and the large number of federal requirements, even when unenforced by the federal government, have led to countless private enforcement actions by program beneficiaries and providers. Where the federal government has been active has been in audits and recoveries aimed at reclaiming funds that the government considers to have wrongfully paid for uncovered services, ineligible populations or for services rendered by non-qualified providers. These recovery actions, while minor compared to the vast sums that states receive, are a major irritant to states and usually find the states at the short end of the legal stick. *See, e.g.,* Minnesota v. CMS, 495 F.3d 991 (8th Cir. 2007) (upholding a final ruling denying the state the right to amend its state plan to provide increased payments for nursing home care on the ground that the state's proposed payment scheme for county operated nursing homes violated applicable requirements).

The federal/state financial relationship lies at the heart of the tension. Medicaid consumes a major portion of state spending, and the rate of growth far exceeds state revenue growth, particularly in bad economic times. Congress simply has been unwilling to shoulder a higher proportion of overall costs; indeed, if anything, Congress historically has expanded both mandates and options even as it has sought to contain costs. At the same time, states have enormous policy and economic incentives to expand their Medicaid program. If the state, or doctors and hospitals in the state, are likely to provide a service to a particular population, the cost is borne at the state and local level unless that state chooses to include the care in its Medicaid program, in which case the cost is shared by the federal government. State desire for federal matching funds drives increases in Medicaid costs.

Congress' favorite approach to containing federal Medicaid spending is to limit how much money states can receive, not merely by reducing its federal contribution levels (Congress did this in 1981 on a temporary basis), but by making it harder for states to come up with their share of the program costs. Because Medicaid is structured as a federal contribution to state programs, the more limited the level of state spending, the more constrained the federal contribution.

Congress and succeeding Administrations have focused particularly on two state practices. The first involves the use by states of special "provider-based" taxes that in turn generate funds that states can use to expand their programs and increase provider payments—often to the very providers that were taxed to begin with. Indeed, the New York State taxing scheme that lay at the heart of the *Travelers* decision earlier in this Part involved the generation of revenues that were used in part to finance the state's Medicaid program. Congress has sought to curb what it considers to be phantom state financing arrangements through amendments that limit states' ability to generate state funding through provider taxes and donations. U.S. GOV'T ACCOUNTABILITY OFFICE, GAO–08–255T, MEDICAID FINANCING:

LONG-STANDING CONCERNS ABOUT INAPPROPRIATE STATE ARRANGEMENTS SUPPORT NEED FOR IMPROVED FEDERAL OVERSIGHT (2007), http://www.gao.gov/new.items/d08255t.pdf.

A second Congressional and agency focus has been to halt state efforts effectively to bootstrap federal Medicaid funding by building public institutional facilities such as public nursing homes, which then are paid at rates that far exceed payments made to private institutions. Rather than leaving these funds in the facilities to strengthen their performance, states and participating localities then collect funding back from them and return the money to their general treasuries, thereby using these institutions—and the people in them—to launder federal Medicaid funding. Perhaps the worst example of this occurred in San Francisco, where the Laguna Honda nursing facility warehoused more than 1400 disabled adults in violation of federal civil rights laws even as it received hundreds of millions of dollars of federal Medicaid contributions, much of which was taken out of the facility by the city to run its general services. Sara Rosenbaum, *The Case of Laguna Honda*, 120(4) PUBLIC HEALTH REPORTS 970 (2005). Federal reforms aimed at limiting how much state agencies can pay public providers are designed to stop what is viewed as money-laundering by states. States in turn grow furious, given what they see as the unsustainable position into which they are put. The fighting goes on, and Medicaid remains a perpetual subject of state and federal frustration over size, cost, and which form of government bears a disproportionate burden. *See, e.g.,* CONGRESSIONAL BUDGET OFFICE, TESTIMONY OF PETER ORZAG, DIRECTOR before the United States House of Representatives (July 8, 2008), http://www.cbo.gov/ftpdocs/95xx/doc9563/07–16–HealthReform.1.2.shtml; Statement of the Honorable Haley Barbour, Governor of Mississippi, before the United States House of Representatives, Committee on Energy and Commerce, The Consequences of ObamaCare: Impact on Medicaid and State Health Reform (March 1, 2011) ("The Medicaid Program is broken from both a budget and health outcomes perspective. The growth in federal Medicaid medical service spending is unsustainable, increasing almost 8 percent annually during the past 10 years.")

5. MEDICAID AND THE LEGAL BASIS OF STATUTORY ENTITLEMENT

Health insurance coverage takes the form of a contractual or a statutorily protected right. Both ERISA and Medicare create express private rights of action to enforce claims of entitlement and coverage. Medicaid is different. The statute creates explicit rights in states to enforce their entitlement to federal payments. The question of whether the statute creates a privately enforceable legal right to coverage or a federal legal right to payment among providers is less clear. Equally uncertain is whether providers and beneficiaries have the ability to enforce federal Medicaid obligations because the statute creates no express private right of action. Private parties, therefore, can sue only if they can find a source of an implied cause of action. To do so, they must ground a right in the statutory text or mount a claim under the U.S. Constitution. Even if many provisions are not rights-creating, they nonetheless establish crucial duties imposed on the states to guarantee results like access to services and prompt assistance. Sara Rosenbaum, *Medicaid and Access to the Courts*, 364 NEW ENG. J. MED. 1489 (2011). The question remains, however, exactly how those duties can be enforced.

The Medicaid statute does not explicitly provide that beneficiaries have a "right" to services or that providers have a "right" to reimbursement, and it does not explicitly create a federal cause of action parallel to ERISA § 502 or the Medicare appeals statute, 42 U.S.C. § 405(g). The federal Medicaid statute does require state Medicaid agencies to provide "fair hearings" for applicants and recipients "whose claim for assistance is denied or not acted upon promptly" or if the Medicaid agency "takes action to suspend, terminate or reduce services." 42 C.F.R. § 431.200. Applications must be considered within specific time frames, and coverage may not be reduced or terminated without prior notice. 42 C.F.R. §§ 435.911, 435.912 and 435.916. Prior to final agency action, states must conduct fair hearings if the action adversely affects current recipients, and agencies must afford certain procedural due process requirements. 42 C.F.R. §§ 435. 230, 435.232–.246. Individuals who wish to enroll in the program must be given the opportunity to do so, and medical assistance must be furnished with "reasonable promptness." 42 U.S.C. § 1396a(a)(8).

At the same time, however, state fair hearing procedures typically afford only limited relief. Under state administrative procedures acts, a fair hearing officer typically does not have jurisdiction to declare a state official's action to be in violation of federal law. It is possible that a fair hearing officer might not even have the authority to declare a state procedures manual to be in violation of state regulations or enabling legislation. Furthermore, the fair hearing process is time-consuming and provides no immediate relief to individuals who challenge the denial of aid rather than its termination. Additionally, both rights of action to proceed in state court, as well as remedies, may be limited under state law in the case of denials of welfare assistance. Finally, the fair hearing process gives states the option, but does not require, a group process in the event that a grievance is shared by a class.

The Administrative Procedure Act (APA), 5 U.S.C. §§ 701–706, creates a right to judicial review of many actions by federal agencies, including those of DHHS with respect to Medicaid, but the APA also exempts from judicial review decisions committed by law to the agency's "discretion," 5 U.S.C. § 701(a)(2), such as whether or not a state Medicaid program is out of compliance with federal law. Furthermore, the federal agency itself has only limited powers. It cannot step in to administer an unlawful program, nor can it issue an injunction to stop unlawful state action. DHHS can threaten a state with disallowance of what it considers to be erroneous expenditures, but it is unclear how this stick works in the common situation in which the state is *refusing* to spend money in a legally required way (as in the Indiana family planning example), rather than spending in ways of which the federal government disapproves. Further, DHHS may totally end federal contribution to a state Medicaid program that refuses to comply with federal conditions. This is an elephant-gun remedy that would cause incalculable damage to vulnerable people, providers and states, and not surprisingly the death penalty has never been invoked or credibly threatened. Perhaps DHHS could go to federal court to seek an injunction enforcing state compliance with Medicaid requirements so long as the state continues to participate in the program; this enforcement remedy has not been tested.

The establishment of modern legal services programs and the rise of an organized welfare rights movement in the 1960s led to the filing of federal lawsuits against state Medicaid (and welfare) agencies that required courts to address the question of recipient entitlement under federal law. The courts responded in basically one of two ways. Some judges adhered to the traditional "right/privilege distinction," under which rights are created primarily by market transactions or by very explicit statutory provisions. Charitable or "gratuitous" payments, such as cash welfare assistance and Medicaid, are not rights but "privileges," and since such programs can be totally abolished (there being no constitutional duty on government to establish them), they can also be conditioned or administered with total government discretion. *See* Smith v. Board of Commissioners, 259 F. Supp. 423 (D.D.C. 1966), *aff'd on other grounds*, 380 F.2d 632 (D.C. Cir. 1967).

By the middle and late 1960s, however, the right/privilege distinction was on the defensive. The civil rights movement was dramatizing the injustice and the social danger of placing large numbers of citizens outside the effective protection of the law. A small but remarkable group of legal scholars and scholar-advocates were articulating a more inclusive concept of law and citizenship. In a famous article titled *The New Property*, 73 YALE L.J. 733 (1964), Professor Charles Reich of the Yale Law School argued that government benefits of all sorts, including welfare benefits, were as important to individual liberty as traditional property, and should be accorded the same kind of procedural and substantive legal protection. In a series of influential articles, speeches, and legal briefs, Professor Edward V. Sparer of the University of Pennsylvania Law School (and founder of several innovative legal service and advocacy programs) documented how his low-income clients were routinely denied their statutory rights to desperately needed food and shelter, and how an expanded recognition of legal rights could avoid these unnecessary tragedies and enhance human dignity and social welfare. *See* SPARER, *The Right to Welfare*; Goldberg v. Kelly, 397 U.S. 254 (1970) (requiring hearing prior to termination of welfare benefits consistent with constitutional standards of procedural due process); Rosenblatt, *Equality, Entitlement, and National Health Care Reform* at 112–16 (discussing and citing Sparer's work).

In four landmark cases decided between 1968 and 1970, the United States Supreme Court rejected the right/privilege distinction and adopted a "statutory entitlement" approach to welfare benefits provided under federal law. One of these cases, a cash assistance case titled *Rosado v. Wyman*, 397 U.S. 397 (1970), focused on the issues of statutory interpretation and judicial remedies at the heart of the question of entitlement to welfare or Medicaid benefits. Rand E. Rosenblatt, *The Courts, Health Care Reform, and the Reconstruction of American Social Legislation*, 18 J. HEALTH POL. POL'Y & L. 439, 444–49 (1993); Rosenblatt, *Social Duties and the Problem of Rights in the American Welfare State* at 92–96.

The six-justice majority opinion was authored by Justice John Marshall Harlan (then considered a conservative Republican), and joined by justices across the political spectrum: his fellow Republican Stewart, liberal Democrats Douglas, Brennan, and Marshall, and conservative Democrat White. Justice Harlan rejected the argument made in Justice Black's dissent that Congress had meant to give HEW "primary jurisdiction" to enforce federal funding requirements and thereby preclude judicial review, at least until after HEW (the predecessor name for the United States Department of Health and Human Services) had acted. See *Rosado,* 397 U.S. at 431 (Black, J., dissenting). Rather, held Justice Harlan, the fact that Congress has delegated to a federal agency authority to define and enforce the statutory conditions does not preclude judicial action to enforce them against state agencies on behalf of recipients, unless Congress has clearly indicated such preclusion. This is particularly so where neither Congress nor the agency has given beneficiaries access to the administrative process or effective administrative remedies. "We are most reluctant," wrote Justice Harlan, "to assume that Congress has closed the avenue of effective judicial review to those individuals most directly affected by the administration of the program." *Rosado,* 397 U.S. at 420.*

Rosado also articulated important principles of statutory interpretation. Even obscure statutory provisions, dealing with complex issues of social policy (in *Rosado*, about cost-of-living adjustments to welfare eligibility standards), should be interpreted if at all possible as sources of meaningful law. Thus courts should not shrink from a full inquiry into complex statutes and legislative history. "Congress," wrote Justice Harlan, "as it frequently does, has voiced its wishes in muted strains and left it to the courts to discern the theme in the cacophony of political understanding." *Id.* at 412. Congressional compromise may result in a statute that contemplates not a clear rule or benefit, but a process of structured discretion, in which a federal or state agency may make a policy choice, but also is supposed to take certain information and values into account. Even though such a provision confers discretion, it also creates an obligation to take certain factors into account in exercising it, and a corollary "right" on behalf of the ultimate beneficiaries to have that consideration take place. In particular, courts (and agencies) should avoid reading statutes in ways that make them "a futile, hollow, even deceptive gesture," *Id.* at 415—laws that

---

* One year after *Rosado*, two federal district courts applied its reasoning to the Medicaid program and enjoined the state of New York from reducing its medical benefits in violation of federal statutory standards. See Bass v. Rockefeller, 331 F. Supp. 945 (S.D.N.Y. 1971); Bass v. Richardson, 338 F. Supp. 478 (S.D.N.Y. 1971).

seem to promise something for the poor, but really mean nothing more than formal assurances and empty bureaucratic labels.

These principles of statutory entitlement are analogous to state law doctrines about health insurance contracts discussed earlier in this Part: that ambiguities should be construed against the drafter, that the contract should be interpreted in the light of the insured's reasonable expectations, and that the insurance company should deal with its policyholders in good faith. Imagine the judicial and popular reaction if an employer attempted to create a system in which a group health insurance contract was regarded as simply an agreement between the employer and the insurer, with no rights for the employee beneficiaries. The contract would "promise" various benefits, but the beneficiaries would have no means of enforcement, other than to hope that the employer might disregard his possibly conflicting economic interests and take some action on the employee's behalf.

Between 1970 and 1990, the *Rosado* principles achieved remarkable acceptance by Congress, the lower federal courts, and the Supreme Court. The lower federal courts decided hundreds, perhaps thousands of cases brought by beneficiaries and providers involving federal funding requirements in the Medicaid (and other benefit) programs, some of which are set forth below. The Supreme Court decided many of these cases on the merits, and further clarified the statutory basis of the *Rosado* principles. In Maine v. Thiboutot, 448 U.S. 1 (1980), a cash assistance case, the Court held that any federal statute, including those imposing conditions on federal funding, could create a right enforceable in federal court under the general federal cause of action statute, 42 U.S.C. § 1983.*

Over the past 20 years, the conditions under which a § 1983 right of action is available to enforce the terms of federal welfare laws, including Medicaid, have been increasingly narrowed. For this reason, the right of private parties to enforce federal requirements directly through the Constitution's Supremacy Clause has grown in importance. In February 2012, the United States Supreme Court left this right untouched—at least for the time being—in Douglas v. Independent Living Center for Southern California, 132 S. Ct. 1204 (1202). The question of when Medicaid gives rise to private enforcement actions under modern jurisprudential principles, including the decision in *Douglas*, as discussed later in this chapter.

---

* This statute, first enacted in 1871, provides a federal cause of action (that is, a right to seek federal judicial relief) to any person who has been deprived under color of state law of "any rights, privileges, or immunities, secured by the Constitution and laws. . . ." 42 U.S.C. § 1983. Although originally enacted in the context of assuring equal legal rights for the newly-emancipated slaves, the law has long referred to rights secured "by the Constitution and laws," without specific reference to the issue of racial discrimination. The Court's opinion in *Thiboutot* confirmed the implicit position of many precedents that the Social Security Act and other federal laws could be judicially enforced on the basis of this general statute.

6.   JUDICIAL INTERPRETATION OF STATE MEDICAID COVERAGE OBLIGATIONS

Curtis v. Taylor

625 F.2d 645 (5th Cir. 1980)

■ RUBIN, CIRCUIT JUDGE:

In October, 1977, Florida [instituted] several reductions in its Medicaid program because of a deficit in its Medicaid budget. [The reductions were contained in a notice that read in part as follows]:

> Effective November 1, 1977 because of the projected Medicaid budgetary deficit (lack of money) it will be necessary to make the following changes in the Medicaid Program:
>
> 1.Physicians Services Outside the Hospital.
>
> a.   Three (3) Doctor Visits Per Month (except for emergencies).

[P]laintiffs alleged that Florida's plan to reduce Medicaid expenses by paying for a maximum of three physicians' visits per month, except for emergencies, violated federal regulations [regarding amount, duration, and scope of service and non-discrimination on the basis of diagnosis or condition].

Whether Florida may limit the number of paid physicians' visits to three per calendar month depends on whether three visits are sufficient "to reasonably achieve" the purpose of going to the doctor's office. The data submitted to the trial court indicates that most Medicaid recipients do not require more than three visits in any calendar month.[10] However, a few, including some of the plaintiff-representatives, do. The answer to the question posed turns on whether the state may place limits on the amount of physicians' services available to a recipient, even though those limits may result in a denial of some medically necessary treatment, if most recipients do not need treatment beyond that provided.[11] The plaintiffs contend that the sufficiency of the service provided must be determined with regard to each individual who receives medical services, and that, if only a handful out of thousands needs to see a doctor more than three times a month, the limitation defeats the regulatory requirement. The logic

---

10.   In 1976, persons eligible for Medicaid required, on the average, 5.6 physicians' visits a year. In Florida, only 3.9% of the second quarter 1977 Medicaid population required more than three physicians' visits in any month of that quarter. Only .5% required in excess of three visits in more than one month. On the basis of these statistics, meager as they are, Florida contends that three physicians' visits per month is sufficient "to reasonably achieve" the purpose of the program.

11.   The state may place appropriate limits on a service based on medical necessity. The state does not, however, contend that the three-visit limit is based on the lack of medical necessity of treatment for any individual. Indeed it could not. The plaintiffs include several persons with a documented need for more than three visits per month. For example, one of the plaintiffs suffers from several ailments, including cirrhosis of the liver, tuberculosis, and chronic anemia. His physician concluded that proper treatment would not be possible within the three-visit-per-month limitation. Several doctors testified that a variety of illnesses could not be adequately treated with such a limit. These illnesses included asthma, urinary tract infections, pneumonia, and acute tonsillitis.

of this argument would preclude any limitation on any medically necessary service. It would require the state to pay for thirty visits per month if any Medicaid recipient needed such services or hospital stays of indefinite duration.

Florida's limitation is not unprecedented: at least seventeen states limit physicians' services in a similar fashion, and HEW has apparently approved the practice. Several courts of appeal have considered the validity of state plans that provide certain services only for certain illnesses. These decisions do not resolve our problem. Considering medical treatment generally provided through a Medicaid program, they prohibit its denial to individuals solely on the basis of the "diagnosis, type of illness, or condition" those individuals suffered from if the denial is unrelated to medical necessity. The limitation proposed by Florida is not based "solely" upon the "diagnosis, type of illness, or condition" of the recipient. Medicaid funding for physicians' visits is limited to three per month for all persons who need a physician's services except in emergencies. The district judge concluded that the exception for emergencies discriminates based on condition. However, Florida's decision to pay for no more than three physicians' visits per month does not discriminate on the basis of "condition" between persons who need three or fewer visits and those who need four or more. Neither does its decision to pay for emergency visits beyond the three-visit limitation discriminate against those with less severe "conditions." It simply reflects a judgment by the state that those persons who need emergency care have a higher degree of medical necessity than those who do not. That conclusion is compassionate as well as rational. The provision of emergency services beyond the three-visit-per-month limit is patently based on a medical necessity standard, the existence of an exigent need.

The limitation here is completely unlike state limitations on treatment [that single out specific conditions for treatment limits]. Here, no particular medical condition is singled out for unique treatment or given care only in restricted situations. All medical conditions are treated equally. Those conditions that result in emergency medical situations, where care is most crucial, may receive exceptional treatment, but the conditions entitled to such treatment are described only in terms of medical necessity, not in terms of the "diagnosis, type of illness or condition."

The consistent pattern of [HEW] approval of similar limitations satisfies us that HEW views a limitation on the "amount, scope or duration" of a required service as "reasonable" if the coverage provided is adequate to serve the medical needs of most of the individuals eligible for Medicaid assistance. In our opinion, the district court erred in ignoring the interpretation given to the regulation by HEW and was mistaken in its application of precedent. We reverse its judgment that the regulations are violated by the three-physician-visit-per-month limitation.

Notes

1. *Across-the-board limits on Medicaid-covered services. Curtis* illustrates the ability of a state to impose across-the-board limits on a required service without running afoul of the reasonableness test. Essentially a non-

discriminatory normative coverage standard passes muster with the courts, as noted in *Alexander v. Choate*, discussed in Chapter 9 and holding that across-the-board limits that satisfy the normative needs of more than 90% of the Medicaid population do not violate § 504 of the Rehabilitation Act of 1973, even though such limits disproportionately disadvantage Medicaid beneficiaries with handicaps.

2. *Limits targeted at particular diagnosis and conditions.* The original regulations promulgated by HEW provided that "the State may not arbitrarily deny or reduce the amount, duration, or scope of, such services to an otherwise eligible individual solely because of the diagnosis, type of illness or condition. Appropriate limits may be placed on services based on such criteria as medical necessity or those contained in utilization or medical review procedures." 42 C.F.R. § 440.230(b) (earlier codifed at 45 C.F.R. § 249.10(a)(5)(i)). The provision reflected a commitment to equality, recognizing the need to limit coverage based on medical need, but, appreciating the danger of limited coverage based on "diagnosis, type of illness or condition."

In 1976, Pennsylvania offered eye glasses, an optional service, but only to people who needed glasses for eye pathology, rather than refractive error. Poor people who needed glasses for refractive error challenged the policy. Ophthalmologists testified that some persons with refractive error, but without eye pathology, were more visually handicapped than those with eye pathology and that while eyeglasses will correct a refractive error, they are not helpful in many cases of eye disease. White v. Beal, 555 F.2d 1146 (3d Cir. 1977), held that Pennsylvania's rule, distinguishing between eye glasses needed for pathology and those needed refractive error violated Medicaid's prohibition against discrimination on the basis of diagnosis or condition.

In Pinneke v. Preiser, 623 F.2d 546 (8th Cir. 1980), the Iowa state Medicaid agency denied coverage for sex-reassignment surgery on the grounds that the State of Iowa's Medicaid plan specifically excluded coverage for sex reassignment surgery. The state defended its rule as an exercise of its "discretion to formulate an irrefutable presumption that treatment of transsexualism by alteration of healthy tissue cannot be considered 'medically necessary.'" *Id.* at 548. Given that physician and hospital care are required services under the statute, and that such surgery is "the only successful treatment known to medical science," *id.* at 549, the Eighth Circuit held that Iowa's rule was an "arbitrary denial of benefits based solely on the 'diagnosis, type of illness, or condition.'" The Eighth Circuit further held that Iowa's exclusion "is not consistent with the objectives of the Medicaid statute," because the statute and legislative history indicate that "[t]he decision of whether or not certain treatment or a particular type of surgery is 'medically necessary' rests with the individual recipient's physician and not with clerical personnel or government officials." *Id.* at 550. By contrast, the Fifth Circuit reversed a district court's grant of summary judgment in favor of a Medicaid patient seeking coverage for sex-reassignment surgery, where the exclusion was based on the assertion that the treatment was experimental, discussed below. Rush v. Parham, 625 F.2d 1150 (5th Cir. 1980). Smith v. Rasmussen, 249 F.3d 755 (8th Cir. 2001) upheld Iowa's categorical exclusion of transsexual surgery, based on growing "disagreement regarding the efficacy of sex reassignment surgery."

McGann v. H. & H. Music Company (Chapter 8) and *Doe v. Mutual of Omaha Insurance Co.,* discussed in Chapter 9, involved private insurance rules that single out a specific condition for exclusionary treatment in the provision of otherwise covered benefits. This type of diagnosis-based exclusion, while permissible under ERISA and the ADA, would violate the Medicaid principle prohibiting discrimination against a diagnosis or condition (in contrast to *Alexander v. Choate,* Chapter 9, which involved a non-diagnosis-based limitation on a covered benefit (i.e., all hospital services for any condition) that hurt people with disabilities more than those without disabilities because of their greater need for health care generally). Does the principle of non-discrimination on the basis of "diagnosis, type of illness or condition" make sense? The underlying purpose is to protect certain people who are not only sick but social vulnerable (e.g., people with mental illness, people with HIV). On the other hand, are some diagnoses or types of illness or conditions—apart from the traditional exclusions for cosmetic and experimental care—that are likely to be less worthy of financial support, or less likely to be helped by medical intervention and hence appropriate for categorical exclusion from insurance funding?

3. *EPSDT and state Medicaid benefit limits.* States' discretion to deny coverage of medically necessary services is sharply reduced with respect to persons under the age of 21, even if treatment is experimental. *See, e.g.,* Miller v. Whitburn, 10 F.3d 1315 (7th Cir. 1993) (rejecting state refusal to pay for a liver transplant for a child unless its definition of "experimental" could be shown to be reasonable). Individuals under age 21 are entitled to Medicaid coverage at a far greater level than individuals 21 and older as a result of the EPSDT benefit, added to the Medicaid statute in 1967. The requirement was added because studies showed extensive health problems among young children participating in early Head Start demonstrations. Additionally, a special, never-repeated 1963 study of the health status of young military draftees produced disturbing results. Sara Rosenbaum et al., *National Security and U.S. Child Health Policy: The Origins and Continuing Role of Medicaid and EPSDT*, GWU SPHHS (2005), http://www. gwumc.edu/sphhs/departments/healthpolicy/dhp_publications/index.cfm? mdl=pubSearch & evt=view & PublicationID=35A8D671–5056–9D20– 3DEFF238AEFA7071.

EPSDT benefits consist of comprehensive periodic health exams to assess physical and mental health and potential developmental delays. Also included are immunizations, comprehensive vision, dental and hearing services, and any "medically necessary" treatment recognized as medical assistance. 42 U.S.C. § 1396d(r). Limitations permissible for adults are barred in the case of children. Rosie D v. Romney, 474 F. Supp.2d 238 (D.

Mass. 2007); Sara Rosenbaum & Paul Wise, *Crossing the Medicaid/Health Insurance Divide.*

EPSDT has generated intense litigation because of the breadth of the statutory entitlement and the range of covered services. For example, dental services, while an optional benefit for adults, are a required service for children under EPSDT. When in 1979, the Texas Legislature cut the amount of funds for the EPSDT program by forty-five percent, the Texas Department of Human Resources (TDHR) replaced annual dental checkups with one checkup every three years. During the three-year period, the EPSDT child could receive dental services only if the particular dental condition fell within one of three limited exceptions: (1) the "emergency" exception; (2) the "obvious need" exception; or (3) the "medical necessity" exception. TDHR also eliminated eight previously available dental services, including topical fluoride, posterior root canals, and antibiotic injections. These limitations were reviewed in Mitchell v. Johnston, 701 F.2d 337 (5th Cir. 1983), the most sweeping dental case handed down under the program.

Defining the "purpose" of EPSDT dental services as "aimed at reducing future Medicaid expense by detecting and remedying incipient dental problems with children who could reasonably be anticipated to become adult Medicaid recipients," the court then asked whether the reduced Texas dental plan was "sufficient in 'amount, duration, and scope to reasonably achieve these purposes.' " *Id.* at 347–48. When "several expert witnesses, including TDHR's own expert, testified that triennial access to preventive dental services [even with the three exceptions, and elimination of the eight services] is wholly inadequate to meet the reasonable dental needs of the children," *id.* at 348, the court had little difficulty concluding that "the resulting package of available services denies preventive, restorative and maintenance care to a child solely because of the child's diagnosis, type of illness, or condition." *Id.* at 349.

4. *Defining what is medically necessary.* The Medicaid statute, unlike Medicare, contains no definition of medical necessity other than a requirement that state coverage limits be "reasonable." 42 U.S.C. § 1396a(a)(17) In Cowan v. Myers, 232 Cal. Rptr. 299 (App. 1986), *cert. den.*, 484 U.S. 846 (1987), a California court considered an amount, duration, and scope challenge to a California law limiting Medicaid benefits to services necessary to "protect life, to prevent significant disability or illness, or to alleviate severe pain." The court upheld the standard embodied in California's law.

> [T]he fundamental question presented [is]: Who decides what Medi–Cal services qualify as "medically necessary," the physician or the State? [Although] *Rush* and *Pinnecke* appear completely at odds [t]he two cases can be reconciled[.] A state may place a generic limit on Medicaid services based upon a judgment as to the degree of medical necessity of those services, so long as it does not discriminate on the basis of specific medical condition which occasions the need. [See Curtis v. Taylor].

232 Cal. Rptr. at 306. Rejecting the "horrendous picture" painted by amici welfare rights organizations "in which Medi–Cal recipients are routinely denied benefits for painful and contagious disorders because they are not life-threatening [or, presumably, involving sufficiently 'significant' disability or illness or sufficiently 'severe' pain]," *id.* at 306–07, the California appellate court upheld the coverage limitation as "reasonable."

The court offered three reasons for its decision. First, the court dismissed the importance of the California statute's operative adjectives, "significant" disability or illness and "severe" pain, as not prohibiting any truly needed care. *Id.* at 307. If this were the case, one wonders why the coverage limitation was enacted at all. Moreover, imagine the reaction of consumers (or reviewing courts) in the private insurance market to a company's attempt to add such adjectives overtly to a health insurance policy. Second, the court held that the amount, duration, and scope regulation, 42 C.F.R. § 440.230(b), requires only that program resources be adequate to achieve the program's purposes as defined by the state. If the state chooses to define the purpose of its Medicaid program as only providing service to save life and prevent significant disability, illness and severe pain, then the federal regulation requires only resources sufficient to meet this level of service. *Id.* Finally, "and most important," the federal agency's approval of the California state Medicaid plan containing this provision is entitled to deference, and "should be followed unless there are compelling indications that it is wrong." *Id.* at 308. (Recall Justice Harlan's opinion in *Rosado*, section 5 above, holding that the federal agency's oversight function did not displace the role of the courts in interpreting and enforcing the statute.) In *Cowen*, one judge dissented, arguing that the court's proper role was to interpret the federal statute.

The *Cowen* opinion represents a marked departure from the precedents it purports to follow. What if evidence had been presented at trial in *Cowen* showing that 70 percent of all treatments for covered services were for conditions other than those needed "protect life, to prevent significant disability or illness, or to alleviate severe pain"? Would such evidence be relevant to a challenge on grounds of "reasonableness," consistency with the statute's objectives, or the amount, duration and scope regulation as interpreted in *Curtis*? Should the state be able to define the meaning of "purpose" in the way suggested by the *Cowen* court? Could the California standard be applied to children in light of *Mitchell*?

Earlier, in Chapter 8, TennCare's definition of medical necessity, as used in its Medicaid managed care program, was discussed. Managed care contracts are complex documents that are analogous to a third-party administration agreement that a self-insuring employer might write with a company hired to act as the third-party administrator. As such, federal regulations related to Medicaid managed care arrangements specify that in establishing such agreements with their contractors, state Medicaid agencies must use the same medical necessity standards that govern their Medicaid programs generally. 42 C.F.R. § 438.210(a). The purpose of this regulation is to assure that Medicaid contractors do not use more restrictive definitions of medical necessity than those used in the underlying state Medicaid program (i.e., the sponsor of the managed care arrangement). At the same time, the Centers for Medicare and Medicaid Services (CMS), which administers Medicaid, lacks a systematic means to measure whether contractors' actual medical necessity determinations adhere to a state's medical necessity definition. Instead, CMS relies on states to exercise oversight over this and a myriad of other issues concerning whether managed-care entities comply with their contractual obligations.

What incentive might a state have to monitor contractors' decisions regarding medical necessity? In Rosie D. v. Romney, 474 F. Supp.2d 238 (D. Mass. 2007), the incentive was the state's continuing responsibility to provide all medically necessary EPSDT treatment services, regardless of the fact that the state permitted its managed care contractors to impose more restrictive coverage standards on treatments for the state's severely mentally ill children enrolled in managed care. The court held that regardless of their enrollment in managed care plans, the children retained their enforceable rights to all EPSDT treatments require by federal law, meaning that if the contractor did not administer the plan in conformance with federal requirements, the state, as the accountable entity, was still on the hook. Given the its rule that coverage standards used in managed care be as broad as those used in the underlying state plan, should CMS disallow Massachusetts' claim for extra federal funding as reimbursement for the additional services it was ordered to cover? After all, the state negotiated a contract with its plans that was supposed to be equal in scope to its fee-for-service program. Should the state be instructed instead to inform its plans to eat the loss? In fact, states typically include a clause in their managed care agreements to cover just such a situation, in which the state is required to pay for treatments that fall within the scope of benefits outlined in their contracts.

5. *What is "experimental" treatment?* Like Medicare and private insurance contracts, Medicaid excludes coverage of "experimental" treatments. But what is "experimental"? In Weaver v. Reagen, 886 F.2d 194 (8th Cir. 1989), Missouri's Medicaid program refused to pay for the drug AZT except for patients whose diagnoses and conditions matched the conditions specified on the labeling for the drug as approved by the federal Food and Drug Administration (FDA). The state defended its coverage limitation on two grounds. The first basis was that it was "a reasonable exercise of [its] discretion to place limitations on covered services based on medical necessity and utilization controls," see 42 C.F.R. § 440.230(d) ("Appropriate limits [may be placed] on a service based on such criteria as medical necessity or utilization control procedures."). *Weaver*, 886 F.2d at 198. The second reason was:

> that prescribing AZT outside the FDA approved indications is per se "experimental" in the sense that there is [sic] no scientific data derived from clinical trials documenting the efficacy and safety of AZT use outside the FDA guidelines. According to defendants,

because such AZT use is experimental, it can never be deemed medically necessary treatment.

Id. The Eighth Circuit rejected both arguments. As to the first, the court noted that:

> Contrary to defendants' assertions, FDA approved indications were not intended to limit or interfere with the practice of medicine nor to preclude physicians from using their best judgment in the interest of the patient. According to a drug bulletin issued by the FDA, "[t]he [Food, Drug and Cosmetic] Act does not, limit the manner in which a physician may use an approved drug. Once a product has been approved for marketing, a physician may prescribe it for uses or in treatment regimens or patient populations that are not included in approved labeling. Such "unapproved" or, more precisely, "unlabeled" uses may be appropriate and rational in certain circumstances, and may, in fact, reflect approaches to drug therapy that have been extensively reported in medical literature.

Id. at 198.

The court then concluded that "[i]t would be improper for the State of Missouri to interfere with a physician's judgment of medical necessity by limiting coverage of AZT based on criteria that admittedly do not reflect current medical knowledge or practice." *Id.* With respect to the argument about experimental status, the court adopted the definition of "experimental" used in *Rush,* 625 F.2d 1150: a treatment not "generally accepted by the professional medical community as an effective and proven treatment for the condition" or "rarely used, novel or relatively unknown." *Id.* at 1156 n. 11, quoted at *Weaver,* 886 F.2d at 198–99. Since the plaintiffs' experts testified that "AZT is generally accepted by the medical community as an effective and proven treatment for AIDS patients who do not meet the criteria in the FDA indications," under the *Rush* standard "the prescription of AZT beyond its labeled indications is not experimental." *Weaver,* 886 F.2d at 199.

In *Miller,* 10 F.3d 1315, the issue was a liver transplant for a child. In addition to holding that the EPSDT coverage standard bars a state from prohibiting medically necessary care, the court also stipulated that a beneficiary could challenge in court an administrative finding that a procedure is experimental:

> When Tiffany applied for Medicaid coverage for her proposed liver-bowel transplant, the Department denied her request for one reason and one reason only: the Department considered the procedure "experimental." [T]he Department took the position that a liver-bowel transplant was not a "necessary treatment" because its effectiveness is unproven.
>
> As a result, the issue in this litigation has been from the outset the judicial reviewability and propriety of the Department's determination that liver-bowel transplants are experimental. [A]

Medicaid recipient may "challenge the reasonableness of a state's decision regarding the medical necessity of a lifesaving procedure." Specifically, Tiffany contends that the Department's characterization of liver-bowel transplantation as experimental is "arbitrary and capricious" and asks for judicial review of that determination. Tiffany does not contend that the Department must pay for her liver-bowel transplant simply because her physician has determined that it is a medically necessary treatment. Rather, Tiffany argues that the transplant procedure is a "necessary treatment" for which the Department is obligated to pay pursuant to § 1396d(r)(5) [the EPSDT medical necessity coverage standard]. The Department has rested exclusively on the established doctrine that a Medicaid-participating state is under no obligation to pay for experimental procedures, *Rush*, 625 F.2d at 1154–55. Thus, the Department has effectively conceded that it must pay for the transplant if its characterization of liver-bowel transplants as experimental falls outside of its admittedly substantial discretion.

Various courts have addressed the meaning of "experimental," as that word is used to refer to medical procedures. The former Fifth Circuit adopted what we believe to be a workable definition of that term, which we quote in its entirety:

> "The clearest articulation of the considerations that go into determining whether a particular service is experimental is found in a letter Medicare uses to explain to its clients and providers why a service is ineligible for reimbursement: 'In making such a decision [whether to provide payment for a particular service], a basic consideration is whether the service has come to be generally accepted by the professional medical community as an effective and proven treatment for the condition for which it is being used. If it is, Medicare may make payment. On the other hand, if the service is rarely used, novel or relatively unknown, then authoritative evidence must be obtained that it is safe and effective before Medicaid [sic] may make payment.' "

Rush, 625 F.2d at 1156. Clearly, the best indicator that a procedure is experimental is its rejection by the professional medical community as an unproven treatment. The quoted passage suggests, however, that different definitions of "experimental" may be necessary depending upon the notoriety of the treatment under review. Indeed, certain procedures may be so new and, as a result, relatively unknown, that the medical community may not yet have formed an opinion as to their efficacy. We agree with the court in *Rush* that such procedures are not per se experimental. If "authoritative evidence" exists that attests to a procedure's safety and effectiveness, it is not "experimental."

7.   MEDICAID AND ACCESS TO HEALTH CARE: THE LIMITS OF PRIVATE ENFORCEMENT OF FEDERAL OBLIGATIONS

a. Introduction

Health care access has been an enduring problem in Medicaid. Data suggest that compared to the uninsured, Medicaid insured adults are more likely to have a usual source of health care and to have received preventive care in the preceding two years. *Medicaid: A Primer*, KAISER COMMISSION ON MEDICAID AND THE UNINSURED, 19 (2010), http://www.kff.org/medicaid/upload/7334–04.pdf. But compared to privately insured people, Medicaid beneficiaries encounter serious problems in securing access to specialty care. There are a number of reasons for this, including residential segregation (Medicaid beneficiaries are more likely to live in medically underserved communities with high poverty concentration and serious shortages of health personnel, particularly specialists), and an unwillingness of specialists to accept as many referrals from safety net providers serving the poor, such as community health centers. Michael Gusmano et al., *Exploring the Limits of the Safety Net: Community Health Centers and Care for the Uninsured*, 21(6) HEALTH AFFAIRS 188 (2002).

The federal Medicaid statute contains two provisions of particular importance to issues of access. The first is known as the reasonable promptness statute, while the second is commonly called the equal access statute.

The reasonable promptness statute provides that state plans for medical assistance must "provide that all individuals wishing to make application for medical assistance under the plan shall have opportunity to do so, and that such assistance shall be furnished with reasonable promptness to all eligible individuals." 42 U.S.C. § 1396a(a)(8). In Doe v. Chiles, 136 F.3d 709 (11th Cir. 1998), this obligation was interpreted to mean not merely prompt access to payment for care but access to the care itself, thus overturning limits imposed by Florida on inpatient residential facility beds that in turn resulted in years-long waiting lists for care. However, in Bruggeman v. Blagojevich, 324 F.3d 906 (7th Cir. 2003), *Doe* was rejected in favor of an interpretation that limited the definition of medical assistance under 42 U.S.C. § 1396d(a) to "payment" for the cost of care and services. *See also* Oklahoma Chapter of the American Academy of Pediatrics v. Fogarty, 472 F.3d 1208 (10th Cir. 2007); Mandy v. Owens, 464 F.3d 1139 (10th Cir. 2006). In yet another case, Sabree v. Richman, 367 F.3d 180 (3d Cir. 2004), the Third Circuit Court of Appeals followed the lead in *Doe*. Authority is therefore divided.

The Affordable Care Act clarified the "prompt access" requirement by revising the definition of medical assistance, 42 U.S.C. § 1396d(a), to define medical assistance as "payment of part or all of the cost of the following care and services or the care and services themselves, or both." 42 U.S.C.

§ 1396d(a), as amended by PPACA § 2304. As of December, 2011, the revised reach of 42 U.S.C. § 1396a(a)(8) had not been tested judicially.

The Medicaid equal access statute is more complex. This provision of law provides in pertinent part as follows:

> A state plan for medical assistance must ... provide such methods and procedures related to the utilization of, and payment for, care and services under the plan ... as may be necessary ... to assure that payments are consistent with efficiency, economy, and quality of care and are sufficient to enlist enough providers so that care and services are available under the plan at least to the extent that such care and services are available to the general population in the geographic area.

42 U.S.C. § 1396a(a)(30)(A).

Because access has been so problematic, and payments for Medicaid services have been so low, over the years beneficiaries and providers have used this statute to challenge state Medicaid payment policies. In particular, providers and beneficiaries have used the equal access rule to challenge state rate reductions in court in order to enjoin their implementation. Medicaid provider payment rate reductions are particularly likely during major economic downturns, when states are desperate to save money and cutting provider payments (particularly to large institutional providers of high cost care) offers a fast way to save money. See, e.g., Clark v. Kizer, 758 F. Supp. 572 (E.D. Cal. 1990), *aff'd in part, rev'd in part,* Clark v. Coye, 967 F.2d 585 (9th Cir. 1992); Arkansas Med. Society v. Reynolds, 6 F.3d 519 (8th Cir. 1993); Orthopaedic Hospital v. Belshe, 103 F.3d 1491 (9th Cir. 1997), *cert. den.,* Belshe v. Orthopaedic Hospital, 522 U.S. 1044 (1998); Independent Living Center of So. Calif. v. Shewry, 543 F.3d 1050 (9th Cir. 2008). For a full listing of cases through 2009 see, Sara Rosenbaum, *Medicaid Payment Rate Lawsuits: Evolving Court Views Mean Uncertain Future for MediCal,* CALIFORNIA HEALTH CARE FOUNDATION (2009), http://www.chcf.org/% EB/media/MEDIA% 20LIBRARY% 20Files/PDF/M/PDF% 20MediCalProviderRateLitigation.pdf.

The equal access cases have been grounded in two distinct jurisprudential theories. Under the first theory, the Medicaid equal access statute creates a right enforceable under 42 U.S.C. § 1983. Under the second theory, the equal access statute is a federal law that preempts contrary state law, with an implied right of action in beneficiaries and providers to pursue such a claim arising under the Supremacy Clause of the U.S. Constitution. Both theoretical bases of private enforcement have been tested in the courts.

b. Does Medicaid Create Private Rights Legally Enforceable Under § 1983?

As noted earlier, Medicaid itself contains no express provision creating private causes of action but *Maine,* 448 U.S. 1, established the right on the part of welfare beneficiaries to proceed under 42 U.S.C. § 1983 to enforce rights created by federal laws including federal welfare programs. This approach to granting a private right of action to enforce federal law reached its apex in Wilder v. Virginia Hospital Association, 496 U.S. 498 (1990). A closely divided majority held that the (later repealed) Boren Amendment, governing hospital payment, gave rise to an enforceable right which could be enforced using 42 U.S.C. § 1983. In so doing, the majority distinguished the federal Medicaid hospital payment statute from other federal laws that created general federal policies rather than individually enforceable rights:

> We must therefore determine whether the Boren Amendment creates a "federal right" that is enforceable under Section 1983. Such an inquiry turns on whether "the provision in question was intend[ed] to benefit the putative plaintiff." If so, the provision creates an enforceable right unless it reflects merely a "congressional preference" for a certain kind of conduct rather than a binding obligation on the governmental unit, Pennhurst State School and Hospital v. Halderman, 451 U.S. 1, 19 (1981), or unless the interest the plaintiff asserts is " 'too vague and amorphous' " such that [it] is " 'beyond the competence of the judiciary to enforce.' " Under this test, we conclude that the [Boren Amendment] creates a right enforceable by health care providers under § 1983 to the adoption of reimbursement rates that are reasonable and adequate to meet the costs of an efficiently and economically operated facility that provides care to Medicaid patients. The right is not merely a procedural one that rates be accompanied by findings and assurances (however perfunctory) of reasonableness and adequacy; rather the Act provides a substantive right to reasonable and adequate rates as well.

> [W]e conclude that the Boren Amendment imposes a binding obligation on States participating in the Medicaid program to adopt reasonable and adequate rates and that this obligation is enforceable under § 1983 by health care providers. The Boren Amendment is cast in mandatory rather than precatory terms[.] Moreover, provision of federal funds is expressly conditioned on compliance with the Amendment and the Secretary is authorized to withhold funds for noncompliance with this provision.

> [T]he statute and regulation set out factors which a State must consider in adopting its rates.[17] In addition, the statute requires the State, in making its findings, to judge the reasonableness of its rates against the objective benchmark of an "efficiently and economically operated facility" providing care in compliance with federal and state standards while at the same time ensuring "reasonable access" to eligible participants. That the Amendment

17. For example, when determining methods of calculating rates that are reasonably related to the costs of an efficient hospital, a State must consider: (1) the unique situation (financial and otherwise) of a hospital that serves a disproportionate number of law income patients, (2) the statutory requirements for adequate care in a nursing home, and (3) the special situation of hospitals providing inpatient care when long term care at a nursing home would be sufficient but is unavailable. 42 U.S.C. § 1396a(a)(13)(A) (1982 ed., Supp. V).

gives the States substantial discretion in choosing among reasonable methods of calculating rates may affect the standard under which a court reviews whether the rates comply with the Amendment, but it does not render the Amendment unenforceable by a court. While there may be a range of reasonable rates, there certainly are some rates outside that range that no State could ever find to be reasonable and adequate under the Act. Although some knowledge of the hospital industry might be required to evaluate a State's findings with respect to the reasonableness of its rates, such an inquiry is well within the competence of the judiciary.

Wilder, 496 U.S. at 510–15.

A differently constituted Court (with the retirement of Justices Brennan and Marshall in 1990 and 1991, respectively) revisited the question of when laws create statutory entitlements that private parties can enforce under § 1983. In Suter v. Artist M., 503 U.S. 347 (1992), a case involving the Adoption Assistance and Child Welfare Act of 1980, the Court modified the *Wilder* test to tighten considerably the standard for measuring the existence of an enforceable right for purposes of § 1983 litigation. The Adoption Assistance and Child Welfare Act provides federal financial support for qualified state foster care and adoption services. To participate in the program, a state must have a plan which "provides that in each case, reasonable efforts will be made (A) to prevent or eliminate the need for removal of the child from his home, and (B) to make it possible for the child to return to his home." 42 U.S.C. § 671(a)(15)(A) & (B). Children in foster care challenged the reasonableness of the state program. Relying on *Wilder,* the lower courts held that plaintiffs could enforce the reasonableness requirement under § 1983 and required the state to set up a program to assign each child a case worker within three days after he or she was placed in foster care.

The Supreme Court reversed. Chief Justice Rehnquist reasoned:

the Act is mandatory in its terms. However, we must examine exactly what is required of States by the Act. Here, the terms of § 671(a) are clear; "In order for a State to be eligible for payments under this part, it shall have a plan approved by the Secretary." Therefore the Act does place a requirement on the States, but that requirement only goes so far as to ensure that the State have a plan approved by the Secretary which contains the 16 features [listed in the statute.]"

Suter, 503 U.S. at 358.

Chief Justice Rehnquist's opinion went on to provide that there must be evidence of rights-creating statutory language before § 1983 enforcement would be proper. In re-stating the *Wilder* test, the majority opinion nonetheless attempted to distinguish *Wilder* on its facts:

[In *Wilder*] we held that the Boren Amendment actually required the States to adopt reasonable and adequate rates, and that this obligation was enforceable by the providers. We relied in part on the fact that the statute and regulations set forth in some detail the factors to be considered in determining the methods for calculating rates.

Id. at 359. By contrast, the majority asserted, the Child Welfare Act does not define the term "reasonable efforts." "How the State was to comply with this directive, and with the other provisions of the Act, was, within broad limits, left up to the State." *Id.* at 360. In short, the Court held that this federal law does not place "any requirement for state receipt of federal funds other than the requirement that the State submit a plan to be approved by the Secretary." *Id.* at 361. "[T]he 'reasonable efforts' language does not unambiguously confer an enforceable right upon the Act's beneficiaries [and can] at least as plausibly [be] read to impose only a rather generalized duty on the State, to be enforced not by private individuals, but by the Secretary." *Id.* at 363. (Chief Justice Rehnquist had characterized the Boren Amendment in precisely these terms in his *Wilder* dissent).

Justice Blackmun dissented on three grounds. First, he concluded, the plaintiff children were the intended beneficiaries of the requirement that the State make "reasonable efforts" to prevent unnecessary removal and to reunify children with their families. "Second, the 'reasonable efforts' clause impos[ed] a binding obligation on the State because it [was] 'cast in mandatory rather than precatory terms.' " Third, the "reasonable efforts" standard [was] as precise and judicially enforceable as that which the Court enforced in *Wilder*. *Id.* at 368–69 (Blackmun, J., dissenting).

In 1994, Congress responded to the *Suter* decision by adding a new section to the Social Security Act:

> In an action brought to enforce a provision of this chapter [i.e. the Social Security Act], such provision is not to be deemed unenforceable because of its inclusion in a section of the Act requiring a State plan or specifying the required contents of a State plan. This section is not intended to limit or expand the grounds for determining the availability of private actions to enforce State plan requirements other than by overturning any such grounds applied in Suter v. Artist M., 112 S. Ct. 1360 (1992), but not applied in prior Supreme Court decisions respecting such enforceability; provided, however, that this section is not intended to alter the holding in Suter v. Artist M. that section 671(a)(15) of the Act is not enforceable in a private right of action.

Pub. L. No. 103–382, 108 Stat. 4057 (codified at 42 U.S.C. § 1320a–2 (1995)). Courts have divided somewhat on the meaning of § 1320a–2. In one case in which plaintiffs sought to enforce provisions of the Adoption Assistance Act that require prompt delivery of services to children in foster care, the court held that while *Suter's* holding regarding 42 U.S.C.§ 671(a)(15) remained good law, courts

> must "rewind the clock" and look to cases prior to *Suter* to determine the enforceability of other provisions under the Adop-

tion Assistance Act. More broadly, the amendment overrules the general theory in *Suter* that the only private right of action available under a statute requiring a state plan is an action against the state for not having that plan. Instead, the previous tests of *Wilder* and *Pennhurst* apply to the question of whether or not the particulars of a state plan can be enforced by its intended beneficiaries.

Jeanine B. by Blondis v. Thompson, 877 F. Supp. 1268, 1283 (E.D. Wis. 1995).

Then, in Blessing v. Freestone, 520 U.S. 329 (1997), the Supreme Court tightened the test of when a law creates enforceable rights still further, in the context of Title IV–D of the Social Security Act, which established a federal child support enforcement program. As in *Suter,* Justice O'Connor, writing for the Court, found that the law did not create individually enforceable rights insofar as it obligated the states to make general efforts on behalf of children and families to whom child support payments are owed. Reiterating that § 1983 is available to enforce federal rights, not merely to litigate "violations of federal law," *id.* at. 339, the Court held that beneficiaries could not sue generally to enforce its requirements against the state under § 1983—despite the state of Arizona's dismal performance, to wit, in 1992, nearly three-quarters of Arizona's 275,000 child support cases were still in the earliest stages of the enforcement process; in 42% of all cases, paternity had yet to be established; and in nearly 30% the absent parent had been identified but his or her whereabouts were unknown. Justice O'Connor characterized the women's action as one to force the state to comply generally with the law rather than an action to require the state to carry out specific duties they were owed under the law:

> In their complaint, respondents sought a broad injunction requiring the director of Arizona's child support agency to achieve "substantial compliance ... throughout all programmatic operations." Without distinguishing among the numerous rights that might have been created by this federally funded welfare program, the Court of Appeals agreed in sweeping terms that "Title IV–D creates enforceable rights in families in need of Title IV–D services." The Court of Appeals did not specify exactly which "rights" it was purporting to recognize, but it apparently believed that federal law gave respondents the right to have the State substantially comply with Title IV–D in all respects. It was incumbent upon respondents to identify with particularity the rights they claimed, since it is impossible to determine whether Title IV–D, as an undifferentiated whole, gives rise to undefined "rights."

> [I]n *Wilder*, we held that health care providers had an enforceable right to reimbursement at "reasonable and adequate rates" as required by a particular provision in the Medicaid statute. And in *Suter*, where we held that Title IV–E of the Social Security Act did not give the plaintiffs the right that they asserted, we again

analyzed the claim in very specific terms: whether children had a right to have state authorities undertake "reasonable efforts to prevent removal of children from their homes and to facilitate reunification of families where removal had occurred."

The Court of Appeals did not engage in such a methodical inquiry. As best we can tell, the Court of Appeals seemed to think that respondents had a right to require the director of Arizona's child support agency to bring the State's program into substantial compliance with Title IV–D. But the requirement that a State operate its child support program in "substantial compliance" with Title IV–D was not intended to benefit individual children and custodial parents, and therefore it does not constitute a federal right. Far from creating an individual entitlement to services, the standard is simply a yardstick for the Secretary to measure the system wide performance of a State's Title IV–D program.

Blessing, 520 U.S. at 341–45.

Justice O'Connor therefore remanded the case with instructions that to bring a case under § 1983, plaintiff must identify specific rights that are left to private enforcement, and that a state could defeat such a showing only by showing that a statutory scheme is so comprehensive that it leaves no room for private rights enforceable under § 1983:

We do not foreclose the possibility that some provisions of Title IV–D give rise to individual rights. For example, respondent Madrid alleged that the state agency managed to collect some support payments from her ex-husband but failed to pass through the first $50 of each payment, to which she was purportedly entitled under the pre–1996 version of [the child support enforcement act.] Although [the pass through provision] may give her a federal right to receive a specified portion of the money collected on her behalf by Arizona, she did not explicitly request such relief in the complaint.

Because we leave open the possibility that Title IV–D may give rise to some individually enforceable rights, we pause to consider [the State's] final argument that no remand is warranted because the statute contains "a remedial scheme that is 'sufficiently comprehensive ... to demonstrate congressional intent to preclude the remedy of suits under § 1983.'" *Wilder.* Because [the Secretary] does not claim that any provision of Title IV–D expressly curtails § 1983 actions, she must make the difficult showing that allowing § 1983 actions to go forward in these circumstances "would be inconsistent with Congress' carefully tailored scheme."

Only twice have we found a remedial scheme sufficiently comprehensive to supplant § 1983. [Discussion of the "unusually elaborate enforcement provisions" of the Federal Water Pollution Control Act and the Education of the Handicapped Act omitted.]

We have also stressed that a plaintiff's ability to invoke § 1983 cannot be defeated simply by "[t]he availability of administrative mechanisms to protect the plaintiff's interests." [In *Wilder*, even though significant federal] oversight powers were accompanied by limited state grievance procedures for individuals, we found that § 1983 was still available.

The enforcement scheme that Congress created in Title IV–D contains no private remedy—either judicial or administrative— through which aggrieved persons can seek redress. The only way that Title IV–D assures that States live up to their child support plans is through the Secretary's oversight. The Secretary can audit only for "substantial compliance" on a programmatic basis. Furthermore, up to 25 percent of eligible children and custodial parents can go without most of the services enumerated in Title IV–D before the Secretary can trim a State's AFDC grant. These limited powers to audit and cut federal funding closely resemble those powers at issue in *Wilder*. Although counsel for the Secretary suggested at oral argument that the Secretary "has the same right under a contract as any other party to seek specific performance," this possibility was not developed in the briefs. Even assuming the Secretary's authority to sue for specific performance, no private actor would have standing to force the Secretary to bring suit for specific performance. To the extent that Title IV–D may give rise to individual rights, therefore, we agree with the Court of Appeals that the Secretary's oversight powers are not comprehensive enough to close the door on § 1983 liability.

Id. at 345–47.

In 2002, the Supreme Court further tightened its restrictions on the use of § 1983, this time in the context of the Family Educational Rights and Privacy Act (FERPA). In Gonzaga University v. Doe, 536 U.S. 273 (2002), a suit to recover damages for an unauthorized disclosure of student records, Chief Justice Rehnquist reviewed the Court's past decisions regarding the availability of 42 U.S.C. § 1983 to enforce provisions of Spending Clause statutes. The opinion stated in even stronger terms than previously the need for unequivocal proof of Congressional intent to create an enforceable private right before § 1983 is available and further clarified the parallel nature of the burden of proof imposed on plaintiffs in private enforcement suits, regardless of whether the suit is brought under § 1983 or is based on an implied right of action. The Chief Justice wrote:

Some language in our opinions might be read to suggest that something less than an unambiguously conferred right is enforceable by § 1983. We now reject the notion that our cases permit anything short of an unambiguously conferred right to support a cause of action brought under § 1983. Section 1983 provides a remedy only for the deprivation of "rights, privileges, or immunities secured by the Constitution and laws" of the United States. Accordingly, it is *rights,* not the broader or vaguer "benefits" or "interests," that may be enforced under the authority of that section. This being so, we further reject the notion that our implied right of action cases are separate and distinct from our § 1983 cases. To the contrary, our implied right of action cases should guide the determination of whether a statute confers rights enforceable under § 1983.

We have recognized that whether a statutory violation may be enforced through § 1983 "is a different inquiry than that involved in determining whether a private right of action can be implied from a particular statute." But the inquiries overlap in one meaningful respect—in either case we must first determine whether Congress *intended to create a federal right.* Thus we have held that "[t]he question whether Congress . . . intended to create a private right of action [is] definitively answered in the negative" where "a statute by its terms grants no private rights to any identifiable class." But even where a statute is phrased in such explicit rights-creating terms, a plaintiff suing under an implied right of action still must show that the statute manifests an intent "to create not just a private *right* but also a private *remedy.*" *Alexander v. Sandoval,* 532 U.S. 275 (2001).

Plaintiffs suing under § 1983 do not have the burden of showing an intent to create a private remedy because § 1983 generally supplies a remedy for the vindication of rights secured by federal statutes. Once a plaintiff demonstrates that a statute confers an individual right, the right is presumptively enforceable by § 1983. But the initial inquiry—determining whether a statute confers any right at all—is no different from the initial inquiry in an implied right of action case.

A court's role in discerning whether personal rights exist in the § 1983 context should therefore not differ from its role in discerning whether personal rights exist in the implied right of action context. Both inquiries simply require a determination as to whether or not Congress intended to confer individual rights upon a class of beneficiaries. Accordingly, where the text and structure of a statute provide no indication that Congress intends to create new individual rights, there is no basis for a private suit, whether under § 1983 or under an implied right of action.

536 U.S. at 282–86.

In his concurrence, Justice Breyer, writing for himself and Justice Souter, noted that while he agreed with the outcome in this case (i.e., that FERPA created no enforceable rights),

[T]he statute books are too many, the laws too diverse, and their purposes too complex, for any single legal formula to offer more than general guidance. I would not, in effect, pre-determine an outcome through the use of a presumption—such as the majority's

presumption that a right is conferred only if set forth "unambiguously" in the statute's "text and structure."

Id. at 291.

In the wake of this ever-tightening (and confusing) vise, courts have
varied enormously in deciding which provisions of the Medicaid statute are
considered as creating enforceable private rights and which are not. In
2006 the United States Supreme Court refused to review a decision by the
United States Court of Appeals, Watson v. Weeks, 436 F.3d 1152 (9th Cir.
2006), in which the court concluded (as have five other circuits in the wake
of *Gonzaga)* that § 1902(a)(10) (which defines who is entitled to medical
assistance) met the *Gonzaga* test for the creation of a clear and legally
enforceable right.

At the same time, some of the most crucial aspects of Medicaid state
plan administration—e.g., the obligation to permit individuals to apply and
to have their eligibility determined with reasonable promptness; the obligation to furnish fair hearings; the obligation to use reasonable standards
to determine eligibility and the amount of medical assistance; and the
"equal access" obligation—are state obligations that may or may not be
considered rights-creating by the courts. In these cases, the courts have
been far more scattered in their views, with some finding certain sections
enforceable and others not. Favorable findings on reasonable promptness:
Sabree, 367 F.3d 180 and Bryson v. Shumway, 308 F.3d 79 (1st Cir. 2002);
no enforceable rights in relation to standards of reasonable promptness:
Watson, 436 F.3d 1152; no enforceable rights with respect to reasonable
access: Westside Mothers v. Olszewski, 454 F.3d 532 (6th Cir. 2006); no
enforceable rights in the equal access statute: Sanchez v. Johnson, 416 F.3d
1051 (9th Cir. 2005) (which contains a particularly good review of the
history of the private enforceability cases); no enforceable rights in the
equal access statute: Long Term Pharmacy Alliance v. Ferguson, 362 F.3d
50 (1st Cir. 2004); Oklahoma Chapter of America Academy of Pediatrics v.
Fogarty, 472 F.3d 1208 (10th Cir. 2007); *but see* Pediatric Specialty Care v.
Arkansas Dept. of Human Services, 443 F.3d 1005 (8th Cir. 2006), finding
an enforceable right to equal access. In sum, the current state of judicial
affairs over what is or is not a privately enforceable Medicaid right is a
mess.

c. Can Private Parties Use the Supremacy Clause to Enforce States' Federal Medicaid Obligations? Medicaid's "Equal Access" Statute and *Douglas v. Independent Living Center of Southern California*

(1) *Introduction*

Medicaid creates an enforceable right in eligible individuals to "medical assistance" as defined under federal law. 42 U.S.C. §§ 1396a(a)(10) and
1396d. But as discussed in the previous section, the scope of Medicaid
"rights" enforceable under § 1983 is narrow, particularly in relation to the
vast array of provisions in the Medicaid statute that impose obligations on
states as a condition of federal funding, which ranges between 50 percent
and more than 80 percent of total program expenditures.

Among the many duties that states must agree to perform are numerous requirements that obligate states to take steps to ensure that health care is accessible. Medicaid's access provisions are important because of the vulnerabilities of Medicaid beneficiaries; and they are provisions have no counterpart in private health insurance For example, states must act "promptly" not only to determine eligibility for benefits but also to actually furnish covered health care services. 42 U.S.C. § 1396a(a)(8). States also must use reasonable standards in determining eligibility and the extent of medical assistance, 42 U.S.C. § 1396a(a)(17)(A), and must permit beneficiaries to choose among "qualified providers" of covered services, 42 U.S.C. § 1396a(a)(23). Significantly, states must maintain payment standards that are sufficient to enlist enough providers so that care is accessible.

These federal obligations may or may not constitute federally enforceable "rights" under 42 U.S.C. § 1983. (The courts have varied in the answer to this question as enforcement cases have arisen). *See* National Health Law Program, THE ADVOCATE'S GUIDE TO THE MEDICAID PROGRAM (2011); Rochelle Bobroff, *Section 1983 and Preemption: Alternative Means of Court Access for Safety Net Statutes*, 10 LOYOLA J. PUB. INTEREST L. 28 (2008). But together, the access requirements go to the heart of Medicaid's original and enduring purpose, namely, to help promote beneficiaries' access to "mainstream" health care. ROBERT & ROSEMARY STEVENS, WELFARE MEDICINE IN AMERICA: A CASE STUDY OF MEDICAID (1974); Sara Rosenbaum, *Medicaid and Access to Health Care: A Proposal for Continued Inaction?* 365 NEW ENG. J. MED. 102 (2011). Nonetheless, federal enforcement of these obligations is seriously limited. In briefs filed with the United States Supreme Court in Douglas v. Independent Living Center of Southern California, 132 S. Ct. 1204 (2012), set forth below, both Members of Congress and former HHS officials acknowledged that Congress never has appropriated the funding necessary to put in place the personnel and technology to assure effective federal oversight, and therefore private enforcement of state obligations is essential. Brief of Former HHS Officials as Amici Curiae in Support of Respondents (Aug. 5, 2011); Brief of Members of Congress as Amici Curiae in Favor of Respondents (Aug. 5, 2011).

The question thus becomes whether the intended beneficiaries of these obligations—the providers that furnish covered treatment and especially the beneficiaries for whom Medicaid represents a lifeline to care—can seek the aid of the federal courts when a state fails to abide by federal requirements. The Medicaid statute provides no mechanism by which individuals can seek redress through agency channels; instead, federal agency action is limited to direct Secretarial oversight of the states, which, if not actively and continually carried out, effectively leaves the law unenforced. For providers or beneficiaries, therefore, it is either access to the courts in the event that a state fails to live up to its obligations, or no remedy at all.

For years, the presumed answer to the question of whether the courts will entertain private enforcement action by a program's intended beneficiaries was yes. This changed with Alexander v. Sandoval, 532 U.S. 275 (2001), discussed in Part One, in which the United States Supreme Court effectively declared implied right of action theory dead. The Court has held that beneficiaries have no cause of action unless Congress clearly and unambiguously grants one, with regard to specific provisions in a specified class of beneficiaries.

Unlike Medicare or ERISA, as we have pointed out, the Medicaid statute contains no right of action. In the case of Medicaid "rights" secured by law, as previously noted, this right of action may be enforced through the remedy provided by 42 U.S.C. § 1983. The problem is that numerous courts (including the Ninth Circuit Court of Appeals whose decision led to the *Douglas* case, below) have concluded that the federal requirement governing Medicaid payment rates (known as the "equal access" requirement) is a broad mandate and not an enforceable "right" that attaches to any discrete class of individuals.

With regard to these types of broad federal mandates, the courts, including the United States Supreme Court, have allowed a separate remedy—grounded directly under the Constitution's Supremacy Clause—when a state's conduct or law conflicts with this type of broad mandate. In 2003, for example, the Supreme Court decided Pharmaceutical Research and Manufacturers of America v. Walsh, 538 U.S. 644 (2003). *Walsh* involved a Maine law whose aim was to lower the cost of prescription drugs for low-income residents *in*eligible for Medicaid. Under the law, drug manufacturers who sold drugs to Maine's Medicaid program also were required to make their drugs available at a reduced price to Medicaid-ineligible low-income residents. The law further provided if manufacturers refused to discount the price of their drugs for the non-Medicaid poor, they would face additional prior authorization requirements before their products would be covered by Medicaid, a hurdle that no manufacturer wants to face, given the additional administrative burdens such requirements place on health care professionals who wish to prescribe the manufacturer's products. Essentially, the state used its considerable leverage over the Medicaid prescription drug market to try to lower the cost of drugs for all low-income people, not just Medicaid beneficiaries. *See generally* Kimberley Fox et al., *State Pharmacy Discount Programs: A Viable Mechanism for Addressing Prescription Drug Affordability*, 60 N.Y.U. Ann. Survey Am. L. 187 (2004). By 2004, Medicaid was spending about $30 billion on prescription drugs, a figure that will drop considerably given the fact that state Medicaid agencies now contribute to the cost of the Medicare Part D drug program for their dually eligible Medicare beneficiaries rather than covering the cost directly. Statement of Douglas Holtz Eakin, Director, Congressional Budget Office, before the United States Senate Special Committee on Aging (July 20, 2005), http://www.cbo.gov/sites/default/files/cbofiles/ftpdocs/65xx/doc6564/07–20–medicaidrx.pdf. Even with this drop, however, states continue to spend enormous sums on prescription drugs, and thus can have considerable impact on the drug industry.

In *Walsh*, the Pharmaceutical Research and Manufacturers of America ("PhRMA"), the drug manufacturers' trade association, sought to block implementation of Maine's law (known as the Rx Program). PhRMA alleged that the Rx Program violated both the Commerce Clause and federal Medicaid law, which regulates state agency practices related to prescription drug coverage and utilization management techniques such as prior authorization. A federal district court preliminarily enjoined implementation of the law, determining that PhRMA was likely to succeed on the merits. On appeal however, the injunction was dissolved. Although the Supreme Court rarely takes cases in such a preliminary stage, it agreed to hear the manufacturers' claim.

The Court upheld Maine's law, dismissing the Commerce Clause claim and finding that the statute did not abridge federal Medicaid requirements. But our interest here is not with the merits of the case but instead, with the fact that no Justice, other than Justice Thomas, questioned the manufacturers' right to be in court, even though the Medicaid statute appeared to grant them no "rights" enforceable under § 1983. In his concurrence, Justice Thomas wrote that:

> I make one final observation with respect to petitioner's preemption claim. The Court has stated that Spending Clause legislation "is much in the nature of a contract." *Pennhurst State School and Hospital*, 451 U.S. at 17. This contract analogy raises serious questions as to whether third parties may sue to enforce Spending Clause legislation—through pre-emption or otherwise. In contract law, a third party to the contract (as petitioner is here) may only sue for breach if he is the "intended beneficiary" of the contract. When Congress wishes to allow private parties to sue to enforce federal law, it must clearly express this intent. Under this Court's precedents, private parties may employ 42 U.S.C. § 1983 or an implied private right of action only if they demonstrate an "unambiguously conferred right." *Gonzaga Univ.*, 536 U.S. at 283. Petitioner quite obviously cannot satisfy this requirement and therefore arguably is not entitled to bring a pre-emption lawsuit as a third-party beneficiary to the Medicaid contract. Respondents have not advanced this argument in this case. However, were the issue to be raised, I would give careful consideration to whether Spending Clause legislation can be enforced by third parties in the absence of a private right of action.

538 U.S. at 682–83.

Justice Thomas made no mention of Ex parte Young, 209 U.S. 123 (1908), the landmark decision by the United States Supreme Court establishing the right of private parties to seek injunctive relief under the Supremacy Clause from state laws and conduct that violate federal law. ERWIN CHEMERINSKY, CONSTITUTIONAL LAW: PRINCIPLES AND POLICIES 201–04 (2006).

(2) *Medicaid's "Equal Access" Statute, Private Enforcement and the* Douglas *Decision*

Federal Medicaid law provides in pertinent part that "A state plan for medical assistance must":

> provide such methods and procedures relating to . . . the payment for care and services . . . as may be necessary . . . to assure that payments are consistent with efficiency, economy, and quality of care and are sufficient to enlist enough providers so that care and services are available under the plan at least to the extent that such care and services are available to the general population in the geographic area[.]

42 U.S.C. § 1396a(a)(30)(A).

Beginning in 2008, however, the state of California, facing epic budget deficits, began slashing Medicaid provider payment rates. In fact, even in better times the state had a history of deep provider payment cuts, and so by the arrival of the financial crisis that began in 2008, the United States Court of Appeals for the Ninth Circuit already had ruled, in a widely cited decision in the wake of *Gonzaga,* that 42 U.S.C. § 1396a(a)(30)(A) did not create rights enforceable under § 1983. Sanchez v. Johnson, 416 F.3d 1051 (9th Cir. 2005). In the face of a new round of cuts, providers and beneficiaries, taking a page out of the *Walsh* playbook, sued to enjoin the enacted payment reductions, this time claiming that they had an implied cause of action directly under the Supremacy Clause. Reversing the district court, the United States Court of Appeals for the Ninth Circuit held that despite the absence of rights creating language, § 1396a(a)(30)(A) lent itself to private enforcement under the Supremacy Clause. Independent Living Center of Southern California v. Shewry, 543 F.3d 1050 (9th Cir. 2008). On remand, the trial court issued a preliminary injunction against the payment reductions, and the state once again appealed. The Ninth Circuit, reiterating the existence of a Supremacy Clause right of action, affirmed the lower court's preliminary injunction in 2009. Independent Living Center of Southern California v. Maxwell–Jolly, 572 F.3d 644 (9th Cir. 2009). The Supreme Court granted certiorari on the question whether the Supremacy Clause provides a right of action for prospective injunctive relief when a private party seeks to halt implementation of a state Medicaid rate cutback under 42 U.S.C. § 1396a(a)(30)(A) in advance of federal agency review. Maxwell Jolly v. Independent Living Center of Southern California, 131 S. Ct. 992 (2012).

After having initially opposed grant of certiorari, the Solicitor General of the United States, in a move that shocked many, filed a brief on behalf of California. Brief for the United States as Amicus Curiae Supporting Petitioner. In his brief, the Solicitor General argued that by its terms and in the case of provisions such as (a)(30)(A), which create duties but not enforceable rights, federal Medicaid law assigns exclusive enforcement power to the federal agency, here HHS. As a result, according to the Solicitor General, the principle of *Ex parte Young* does not apply. The provider and beneficiary respondents argued that the foundational legal principles embodied in *Ex Parte Young* apply to all private efforts to seek an injunction against state officials who refuse to comply with any federal law, including laws based on Congress's Spending Clause Powers. In their view, as was evident in *Walsh,* private parties have the right to seek injunctive relief when they face the threat of injury as a result of unlawful action by a state Medicaid agency. Furthermore, argued plaintiffs, unlike *Walsh,* the injury they alleged was not merely the loss of profits but in fact amounted to the life-threatening diminution or withdrawal of care.

The Supreme Court's 2011–2012 term opened with the oral argument in *Douglas* (October 3, 2011). But then things got really complicated. Only a few weeks after oral argument the Centers for Medicare and Medicaid Services, which had initially rejected California's request to reduce provider payment rates, reversed course and approved some of the rate reductions and disapproved others. As a result, the Court sought the views of the parties as to whether this latest shoe to drop changed anything. The answer was a resounding "no" since the question before the Court was the right of parties to seek injunctive relief *in advance of,* rather than following, federal agency action. Against this backdrop, the Court issued its decision in February, 2012.

Douglas v. Independent Living Center of Southern California, Inc.

132 S. Ct. 1204 (2012)

■ JUSTICE BREYER delivered the opinion of the Court.

We granted certiorari in these cases to decide whether Medicaid providers and recipients may maintain a cause of action under the Supremacy Clause to enforce a federal Medicaid law—a federal law that, in their view, conflicts with (and pre-empts) state Medicaid statutes that reduce payments to providers. Since we granted certiorari, however, the relevant circumstances have changed. The federal agency in charge of administering Medicaid, the Centers for Medicare & Medicaid Services (CMS), has now approved the state statutes as consistent with the federal law. In light of the changed circumstances, we believe that the question before us now is whether, once the agency has approved the state statutes, groups of Medicaid providers and beneficiaries may still maintain a Supremacy Clause action asserting that the state statutes are inconsistent with the federal Medicaid law. For the reasons set forth below, we vacate the Ninth Circuit's judgments and remand these cases for proceedings consistent with this opinion.

I

A

Medicaid is a cooperative federal-state program that provides medical care to needy individuals. To qualify for federal funds, States must submit to a federal agency (CMS, a division of the Department of Health and Human Services) a state Medicaid plan that details the nature and scope of the State's Medicaid program. It must also submit any amendments to the plan that it may make from time to time. And it must receive the agency's approval of the plan and any amendments. Before granting approval, the agency reviews the State's plan and amendments to determine whether they comply with the statutory and regulatory requirements governing the Medicaid program. See 42 U.S.C. §§ 1316(a)(1), (b), 1396a(a), (b); 42 CFR § 430.10 *et seq.* (2010); *Wilder* v. *Virginia Hospital Assn.*, 496 U.S. 498, 502 (1990). And the agency's director has specified that the agency will not provide federal funds for any state plan amendment until the agency approves the amendment. See Letter from Timothy M. Westmoreland, Director, Center for Medicaid & State Operations, Health Care Financing Admin., U.S. Dept. of Health and Human Servs., to State Medicaid Director (Jan. 2, 2001).

The federal statutory provision relevant here says that a State's Medicaid plan and amendments must:

"provide such methods and procedures relating to the utilization of, and the payment for, care and services available under the plan ... as may be necessary to safeguard against unnecessary utilization of such care and services and *to assure that payments are consistent with efficiency, economy, and quality of care and are sufficient to enlist enough providers so that care and services are available under the plan at least to the extent that such care and services are available to the general population in the geographic area.*" 42 U.S.C. § 1396a(a)(30)(A) (emphasis added).

B

In 2008 and 2009, the California Legislature passed three statutes changing that State's Medicaid plan. The first statute, enacted in February 2008, reduced by 10% payments that the State makes to various Medicaid providers, such as physicians, pharmacies, and clinics. See 2007–2008 Cal. Sess. Laws, 3d Extraordinary Sess. ch. 3, §§ 14, 15. The second statute, enacted in September 2008, replaced the 10% rate reductions with a more modest set of cuts. See 2008 Cal. Sess. Laws ch. 758, §§ 45, 57. And the last statute, enacted in February 2009, placed a cap on the State's maximum contribution to wages and benefits paid by counties to providers of in-home supportive services. See 2009–2010 Cal. Sess. Laws, 3d Extraordinary Sess. ch. 13, § 9.

In September and December 2008, the State submitted to the federal agency a series of plan amendments designed to implement most of the reductions contained in these bills. Before the agency finished reviewing the amendments, however, groups of Medicaid providers and beneficiaries filed a series of lawsuits seeking to enjoin the rate reductions on the ground that they conflicted with, and therefore were pre-empted by, federal Medicaid law, in particular the statutory provision that we have just set forth. They argued that California's Medicaid plan amendments were inconsistent with the federal provision because the State had failed to study whether the rate reductions would be consistent with the statutory factors of efficiency, economy, quality, and access to care. In effect, they argued that California had not shown that its Medicaid plan, as amended, would "enlist enough providers" to make Medicaid "care and services" sufficiently available. 42 U.S.C. § 1396a(a)(30)(A).

The consolidated cases before us encompass five lawsuits brought by Medicaid providers and beneficiaries against state officials. Those cases produced seven decisions of the Court of Appeals for the Ninth Circuit. See 572 F.3d 644 (2009); 342 Fed. Appx. 306 (2009); 596 F.3d 1098 (2010); 563 F.3d 847 (2009); 374 Fed. Appx. 690 (2010); 596 F.3d 1087 (2010); and 380 Fed. Appx. 656 (2010). The decisions ultimately affirmed or ordered preliminary injunctions that prevented the State from implementing its statutes. They (1) held that the Medicaid providers and beneficiaries could directly bring an action based on the Supremacy Clause; (2) essentially accepted the claim that the State had not demonstrated that its Medicaid plan, as amended, would provide sufficient services; (3) held that the amendments consequently conflicted with the statutory provision we have quoted; and (4) held that, given the Constitution's Supremacy Clause, the federal statute must prevail. That is to say, the federal statute preempted the State's new laws.

In the meantime, the federal agency was also reviewing the same state statutes to determine whether they satisfied the same federal statutory conditions. In November 2010, agency officials concluded that they did not satisfy those conditions, and the officials disapproved the amendments. California then exercised its right to further administrative review within the agency. The cases were in this posture when we granted certiorari to decide whether respondents could mount a Supremacy Clause challenge to the state statutes and obtain a court injunction preventing California from implementing its statutes.

About a month after we heard oral argument, the federal agency reversed course and approved several of California's statutory amendments to its plan. In doing so, the agency also approved a limited retroactive implementation of some of the amendments' rate reductions. The State, in turn, withdrew its requests for approval of the remaining amendments, in effect agreeing that it would not seek to implement any unapproved reduction.

II

All parties agree that the agency's approval of the enjoined rate reductions does not make these cases moot. For one thing, the providers and beneficiaries continue to believe that the reductions violate the federal provision, the agency's view to the contrary notwithstanding. For another, federal-court injunctions remain in place, forbidding California to implement the agency-approved rate reductions. And, in light of the agency's action, California may well ask the lower courts to set those injunctions aside.

While the cases are not moot, they are now in a different posture. The federal agency charged with administering the Medicaid program has determined that the challenged rate reductions comply with federal law.

That agency decision does not change the underlying substantive question, namely whether California's statutes are consistent with a specific federal statutory provision (requiring that reimbursement rates be "sufficient to enlist enough providers"). But it may change the answer. And it may require respondents now to proceed by seeking review of the agency determination under the Administrative Procedure Act (APA), 5 U.S.C. § 701 *et seq.*, rather than in an action against California under the Supremacy Clause.

For one thing, the APA would likely permit respondents to obtain an authoritative judicial determination of the merits of their legal claim. The Act provides for judicial review of final agency action. § 704. It permits any person adversely affected or aggrieved by agency action to obtain judicial review of the lawfulness of that action. § 702. And it requires a reviewing court to set aside agency action found to be "arbitrary, capricious, an abuse of discretion, or otherwise not in accordance with law." § 706(2)(A).

For another thing, respondents' basic challenge now presents the kind of legal question that ordinarily calls for APA review. The Medicaid Act commits to the federal agency the power to administer a federal program. And here the agency has acted under this grant of authority. That decision carries weight. After all, the agency is comparatively expert in the statute's subject matter. And the language of the particular provision at issue here is broad and general, suggesting that the agency's expertise is relevant in determining its application.

Finally, to allow a Supremacy Clause action to proceed once the agency has reached a decision threatens potential inconsistency or confusion. In these cases, for example, the Ninth Circuit, in sustaining respondents' challenges, declined to give weight to the Federal Government's interpretation of the federal statutory language. (That view was expressed in an *amicus curiae* brief that the United States submitted in prior litigation.) See *Independent Living Center of Southern Cal., Inc.* v. *Maxwell-Jolly*, 572 F.3d 644, 654 (CA9 2009) (referring to the United States' certiorari-stage invitation brief in *Belshe* v. *Orthopaedic Hospital*, 522 U.S. 1044 (1998) (denying writ of certiorari)). And the District Court decisions that underlie injunctions that now forbid California to implement its laws may rest upon similar analysis.

But ordinarily review of agency action requires courts to apply certain standards of deference to agency decisionmaking. See *National Cable & Telecommunications Assn.* v. *Brand X Internet Services*, 545 U.S. 967 (2005) (describing deference reviewing courts must show); *Chevron U.S.A. Inc.* v. *Natural Resources Defense Council, Inc.*, 467 U.S. 837 (1984). And the parties have not suggested reasons why courts should not now (in the changed posture of these cases) apply those ordinary standards of deference.

Nor have the parties suggested reasons why, once the agency has taken final action, a court should reach a different result in a case like this one, depending upon whether the case proceeds in a Supremacy Clause action rather than under the APA for review of an agency decision. Indeed, to permit a difference in result here would subject the States to conflicting interpretations of federal law by several different courts (and the agency), thereby threatening to defeat the uniformity that Congress intended by centralizing administration of the federal program in the agency and to make superfluous or to undermine traditional APA review. Cf. *Astra USA, Inc.* v. *Santa Clara County*, 563 U.S. ___, ___ (2011) (slip op., at 2) (noting that the treatment of lawsuits that are "in substance one and the same" "must be the same, '[n]o matter the clothing in which [plaintiffs] dress their claims'" (quoting *Tenet* v. *Doe*, 544 U.S. 1, 8 (2005)). If the two kinds of actions should reach the same result, the Supremacy Clause challenge is at best redundant. And to permit the continuation of the action in that form would seem to be inefficient, for the agency is not a participant in the pending litigation below, litigation that will decide whether the agency-approved state rates violate the federal statute.

III

In the present posture of these cases, we do not address whether the Ninth Circuit properly recognized a Supremacy Clause action to enforce this federal statute before the agency took final action. To decide whether these cases may proceed directly under the Supremacy Clause now that the agency has acted, it will be necessary to take account, in light of the proceedings that have already taken place, of at least the matters we have set forth above. It must be recognized, furthermore, that the parties have not fully argued this question. Thus, it may be that not all of the considerations that may bear upon the proper resolution of the issue have been presented in the briefs to this Court or in the arguments addressed to and considered by the Court of Appeals. Given the complexity of these cases, rather than ordering reargument, we vacate the Ninth Circuit's judgments and remand the cases, thereby permitting the parties to argue the matter before that Circuit in the first instance.

It is so ordered.

■ CHIEF JUSTICE ROBERTS, with whom JUSTICE SCALIA, JUSTICE THOMAS, and JUSTICE ALITO join, dissenting.

The Medicaid Act established a collaborative federal-state program to assist the poor, elderly, and disabled in obtaining medical care. The Act is Spending Clause legislation; in exchange for federal funds a State agrees to abide by specified rules in implementing the program. One of those rules is set forth in § 30(A) of the Act, which requires States to meet particular criteria in establishing Medicaid reimbursement rates for those providing services under the Act. 42 U.S.C. § 1396a(a)(30)(A). In 2008 and 2009, California enacted legislation reducing the rates at which it would compensate some providers. Certain providers and individuals receiving Medicaid benefits thought the new reimbursement rates did not comply with the criteria set forth in § 30(A). They sued the State to prevent the new rates from going into effect.

But those plaintiffs faced a significant problem: Nothing in the Medicaid Act allows providers or beneficiaries (or anyone else, for that matter) to sue to enforce § 30(A). The Act instead vests responsibility for enforcement with a federal agency, the Centers for Medicare & Medicaid Services (CMS). See, *e.g.,* 42 U.S.C. § 1316(a)(1). That is settled law in the Ninth Circuit. See *Sanchez* v. *Johnson,* 416 F.3d 1051, 1058–1062 (2005) ("[T]he flexible, administrative standards embodied in [§ 30(A)] do not reflect a Congressional intent to provide a private remedy for their violation"). And it is the law in virtually every other circuit as well. See, *e.g., Long Term Care Pharmacy Alliance* v. *Ferguson,* 362 F.3d 50, 57–59 (CA1 2004) (holding that it would be inconsistent with this Court's precedent to find that § 30(A) creates rights enforceable by private parties). The respondents have never argued the contrary. Thus, as this case comes to us, the federal rule is that Medicaid reimbursement rates must meet certain criteria, but private parties have no statutory right to sue to enforce those requirements in court.

The providers and beneficiaries sought to overcome that difficulty by arguing that they could proceed against the State directly under the Supremacy Clause of the Constitution, even if they could not do so under the Act. They contended that the new state reimbursement rates were inconsistent with the requirements of § 30(A). The Supremacy Clause provides that a federal statute such as § 30(A) preempts contrary state law. Therefore, the providers and beneficiaries claimed, they could sue to enforce the Supremacy Clause, which requires striking down the state law and giving effect to § 30(A). The Ninth Circuit agreed with this argument and blocked the new state reimbursement rates.

During briefing and argument in this case, the parties have debated broad questions, such as whether and when constitutional provisions as a general matter are directly enforceable. It is not necessary to consider these larger issues. It is not even necessary to decide whether the Supremacy Clause can ever provide a private cause of action. The question presented in the certiorari petitions is narrow: "Whether Medicaid recipients and providers may maintain a cause of action under the Supremacy Clause to enforce [§ 30(A)] by asserting that the provision preempts a state law reducing reimbursement rates." To decide this case, it is enough to conclude that the Supremacy Clause does not provide a cause of action to enforce the requirements of § 30(A) when Congress, in establishing those requirements, elected not to provide such a cause of action in the statute itself.

The Supremacy Clause operates differently than other constitutional provisions. For example, if Congress says in a law that certain provisions do not give rise to a taking without just compensation, that obviously does not resolve a claim under the Takings Clause that they do. The Supremacy Clause, on the other hand, is "not a source of any federal rights." *Chapman* v. *Houston Welfare Rights Organization,* 441 U.S. 600, 613 (1979); accord, *Dennis* v. *Higgins,* 498 U.S. 439, 450 (1991) (contrasting, in this regard, the Supremacy Clause and the Commerce Clause). The purpose of the Supremacy Clause is instead to ensure that, in a conflict with state law, whatever Congress says goes.

Thus, if Congress does not intend for a statute to supply a cause of action for its enforcement, it makes no sense to claim that the Supremacy Clause itself must provide one. Saying that there is a private right of action under the Supremacy Clause would substantively change the federal rule established by Congress in the Medicaid Act. That is not a proper role for the Supremacy Clause, which simply ensures that the rule established by Congress controls.

Indeed, to say that there is a federal statutory right enforceable under the Supremacy Clause, when there is no such right under the pertinent statute itself, would effect a complete end-run around this Court's implied right of action and 42 U.S.C. § 1983 jurisprudence. We have emphasized that "where the text and structure of a statute provide no indication that Congress intends to create new individual rights, there is no basis for a private suit, whether under § 1983 or under an implied right of action." *Gonzaga Univ.* v. *Doe*, 536 U.S. 273, 286 (2002). This body of law would serve no purpose if a plaintiff could overcome the absence of a statutory right of action simply by invoking a right of action under the Supremacy Clause to the exact same effect. Cf. *Astra USA, Inc.* v. *Santa Clara County*, 563 U.S. ___, ___ (2011) (slip op., at 7) (rejecting contention that contract incorporating statutory terms could be enforced in private action when statute itself could not be; "[t]he absence of a private right to enforce the statutory ceiling price obligations would be rendered meaningless if [contracting] entities could overcome that obstacle by suing to enforce the contract's ceiling price obligations instead").

The providers and beneficiaries argue, however, that the traditional exercise of equity jurisdiction supports finding a direct cause of action in the Supremacy Clause. This contention fails for the same reason. It is a longstanding maxim that "[e]quity follows the law." 1 J. Pomeroy, Treatise on Equity Jurisprudence § 425 (3d ed. 1905). A court of equity may not "create a remedy in violation of law, or even without the authority of law." *Rees* v. *Watertown*, 19 Wall. 107, 122 (1874). Here the law established by Congress is that there is no remedy available to private parties to enforce the federal rules against the State. For a court to reach a contrary conclusion under its general equitable powers would raise the most serious concerns regarding both the separation of powers (Congress, not the Judiciary, decides whether there is a private right of action to enforce a federal statute) and federalism (the States under the Spending Clause agree only to conditions clearly specified by Congress, not any implied on an ad hoc basis by the courts).

This is not to say that federal courts lack equitable powers to enforce the supremacy of federal law when such action gives effect to the federal rule, rather than contravening it. The providers and beneficiaries rely heavily on cases of this kind, most prominently *Ex parte Young*, 209 U.S. 123 (1908). Those cases, however, present quite different questions involving "the pre-emptive assertion in equity of a defense that would otherwise have been available in the State's enforcement proceedings at law." *Virginia Office for Protection and Advocacy* v. *Stewart*, 563 U.S. ___, ___ (2011)

(KENNEDY, J., concurring) (slip op., at 1). Nothing of that sort is at issue here; the respondents are not subject to or threatened with any enforcement proceeding like the one in *Ex parte Young*. They simply seek a private cause of action Congress chose not to provide.

The Court decides not to decide the question on which we granted certiorari but instead to send the cases back to the Court of Appeals, because of the recent action by CMS approving California's new reimbursement rates. But the CMS approvals have no impact on the question before this Court. If, as I believe, there is no private right of action under the Supremacy Clause to enforce § 30(A), that is the end of the matter. If, on the other hand, the Court believes that there is such a cause of action, but that CMS's recent rate approvals may have an effect on that action going forward, then the Court should say just that and *then* remand to the Ninth Circuit for consideration of the effect of the agency approvals.

I am not sure what a remand without answering the preliminary question is meant to accomplish. The majority claims that the agency's recent action "may change the [lower courts'] answer" to the question whether the particular state rates violate § 30(A). But that fact-specific question is not the one before us; we chose not to grant certiorari on the question whether California's rates complied with § 30(A), limiting our grant to the cause of action question.

The majority also asserts that the lower courts must "decide whether these cases may proceed directly under the Supremacy Clause now that the agency has acted." The majority contends that the parties have not "fully argued this question." But the agency proceedings that ultimately led to the CMS approvals were well underway when this Court granted certiorari. The parties debated the import of the parallel administrative proceedings in their initial briefs and at oral argument. See, *e.g.*, Brief for Petitioner 28–29 ("Private lawsuits ... interfere with ... CMS's own enforcement procedures," as is "vividly demonstrated in the present cases"); Brief for Respondents Santa Rosa Memorial Hospital et al. in No.10–283, p. 46 ("This case vividly illustrates why the [administrative] enforcement scheme ... cannot substitute for a constitutional preemption claim"). No party— nor the United States as *amicus curiae*—argued that any action by CMS would affect the answer to the question we granted certiorari to review. See, *e.g.*, Tr. of Oral Arg. 53–54 (counsel for respondents) (arguing that, "to be sure," there would be a cause of action under the Supremacy Clause even after the agency took action on the challenged rates).

Once the CMS approvals were issued, this Court directed the parties to file supplemental briefs to address "the effect, if any, of the [CMS approvals] on the proper disposition of this case." Again, no one argued on supplemental briefing that the CMS approvals affected the answer to the question before this Court. See, *e.g.*, Supp. Letter Brief for Certain Respondents 6 ("The CMS findings do not directly resolve whether the Constitution supports a right of action"); Supp. Letter Brief for Petitioner 6 (agreeing that "*if* a preemption cause of action may be stated here against the State, [CMS] approval may affect its merits but not its existence"). It seems odd, then, to claim that the parties have not had the opportunity to fully address the impact of the agency action on the question that we granted certiorari to review: whether the Ninth Circuit correctly recognized a private cause of action under the Supremacy Clause to enforce § 30(A).

So what is the Court of Appeals to do on remand? It could change its view and decide that there is no cause of action directly under the Supremacy Clause to enforce § 30(A). The majority itself provides a compelling list of reasons for such a result: "The Medicaid Act commits to the federal agency the power to administer a federal program"; "the agency is comparatively expert in the statute's subject matter"; "the language of the particular provision at issue here is broad and general, suggesting that the agency's expertise is relevant"; and APA review would provide "an authoritative judicial determination." Allowing for both Supremacy Clause actions and agency enforcement "threatens potential inconsistency or confusion," and imperils "the uniformity that Congress intended by centralizing administration of the federal program in the agency."

Still, according to the majority, the Court of Appeals on remand could determine that the Supremacy Clause action may be brought but then must abate "now that the agency has acted," *ibid.*—as everyone knew the agency would. A Court concerned with "inefficien[cy]" should not find that result very palatable, and the majority cites no precedent for a cause of action that fades away once a federal agency has acted. Such a scenario would also create a bizarre rush to the courthouse, as litigants seek to file and have their Supremacy Clause causes of action decided before the agency has time to arrive at final agency action reviewable in court.

Or perhaps the suits should continue in a different "form," by which I understand the Court to suggest that they should morph into APA actions. The APA judicial review provisions, however, seem to stand in the way of such a transformation. To convert the litigation into an APA suit, the current defendant (the State) would need to be dismissed and the agency (which is not currently a party at all) would have to be sued in its stead. 5 U.S.C. §§ 701–706. Given that APA actions also feature—among other things—different standards of review, different records, and different potential remedies, it is difficult to see what would be left of the original Supremacy Clause suit. Or, again, why one should have been permitted in the first place, when agency review was provided by statute, and the parties were able to and did participate fully in that process.

I would dispel all these difficulties by simply holding what the logic of the majority's own opinion suggests: When Congress did not intend to provide a private right of action to enforce a statute enacted under the Spending Clause, the Supremacy Clause does not supply one of its own force. The Ninth Circuit's decisions to the contrary should be reversed.

Notes

1. *Wait a minute: what just happened?* In a seeming judicial sleight of hand and without dismissing the claim as moot, the majority ruled that

circumstances had changed and that it would no longer decide the very issue that formed the basis of its decision to hear the case to begin with, namely, "whether the Ninth Circuit properly recognized a Supremacy Clause action to enforce this federal statute before the agency took final action." In essence, the majority left open the question of whether the Supremacy Clause can provide a cause of action even in situations in which Congress, in enacting a Spending Clause statute, has created no right of action within the statute itself.

Writing for the dissent, Justice Roberts not unsurprisingly called the majority out for evading the question in the case, namely, whether the Supremacy Clause can fill in when Congress, in enacting a social welfare program, does not create private enforcement remedies of its own. Indeed, as he noted, the parties and the Solicitor General explicitly had agreed that nothing about the agency's decision after the grant of certiorari had altered the very question the Court had agreed to decide, namely whether the Supremacy Clause provides a private party with a right of action to secure injunctive relief to enforce Medicaid (a)(30)(A), a provision of law that recognizes no private enforcement rights. The majority, apparently not willing to decide this question, simply vacated the Ninth Circuit injunction, leaving the matter for another day and suggesting that the next logical step was a new action filed by the plaintiffs against the Secretary under the APA.

With this nifty sidestep of the central issue, the Court's liberal wing apparently succeeded in picking up Justice Kennedy's vote. Perhaps Justice Kennedy was not yet ready (as was the dissent) to institute the nuclear option by limiting the reach of *Ex parte Young* to situations in which a plaintiff preemptively seeks a federal injunction in the face of threatened state action to which he can assert, as a defense, that the state action violates federal law. In fact, had the dissent prevailed, this limitation on the *Ex parte Young* doctrine could have had far-reaching implications for a host of federal Spending Clause statutes in the areas of health, education, and social welfare. Without the threat of meaningful federal enforcement and absent private rights of action under the Supremacy Clause, states could flagrantly flout Congressional requirements to the detriment of the very people who are supposed to be assisted by the federal program.

Medicaid, of course, presents the most compelling example of this effect because states' failure to comply with the statutory mandates to assure access would threaten the basic health and safety of millions of people, especially beneficiaries like those in *Douglas,* who were extremely fragile institutionalized children and adults. Particularly striking would have been a rollback of *Ex Parte Young* even in the face of evidence that federal enforcement depends on a grossly underfunded federal agency lacking meaningful enforcement tools and furthermore, that the enforcement system affords affected providers and beneficiaries no means to seek swift protection from an agency charged with their protection. Thus, the liberal majority maneuvered matters to make the case simply go away, even while not declaring it moot.

What exactly is the Ninth Circuit supposed to do now? It still has jurisdiction over the case, of course, but its injunction has been dissolved. Should it, like Justice Breyer, hope that the plaintiffs move to dismiss the case and instead file a claim under the APA that the HHS Secretary's approval of the rate cut was arbitrary and capricious? Since the case is not moot, should the parties perhaps move for a declaratory ruling on the original issue, namely, whether they have a right of action under the Supremacy Clause to proceed in the event that the state institutes future cuts? Rather than filing a new action under the APA, should the plaintiffs amend and seek to enjoin the state from proceeding with the federally approved cuts on the ground that the Secretary's approval of the reductions is arbitrary and capricious?

In fact, this last option—relying on the Supremacy Clause to halt the state from proceeding with a Secretarially-blessed reduction—is exactly what *another* group of plaintiffs did in the wake of HHS approval of state rate cuts, in California Medical Association v. Douglas, 2012 WL 273768 (C.D. Cal. 2012). In a 30–page decision, Judge Christina Snyder threw the book at HHS for its baseless and deeply flawed approval of yet *another* California law (enacted in early 2011 whose purpose was to once again reduce a broad array of MediCal provider fees). The plaintiffs' argument was that in approving the cuts, the Secretary had failed to do the type of careful cost impact analysis previously identified by the Ninth Circuit as essential to proper review.

This time, HHS moved (relatively) quickly, approving the state's June 2011 rate reduction request by October. (The approval process, as noted, does not provide for a formal hearing in which affected interests can present evidence in opposition to the reduction). Plaintiffs filed suit in December, 2011. The state, with HHS at its side, filed briefs in opposition by the middle of January 2012, slightly more than four weeks before the Supreme Court handed down its *Douglas* decision.

Judge Snyder began by finding that the agency deference standard articulated in *Chevron* (and discussed by Justice Breyer) in fact did *not* apply to the approval by CMS. In her view, *Chevron* was inapplicable because the process involved no formal adjudication whatsoever, afforded affected interests no opportunity to present evidence and be heard, and was completely conclusory with no supporting evidence to show why the state's proposed fee reductions would not place the state in violation of Medicaid's access requirement under (a)(30)(A). Second, as Judge Snyder noted, the Secretary essentially admitted in her brief to the court that her agency lacked reasonable standards or procedures for determining when a state's payment reductions raise access issues:

> [The CMS approval letter] does not provide any reasons on its face as to why provider costs [argued by the plaintiffs as essential to measuring the impact of a rate reduction] should not be considered in determining whether the SPA's rate reduction will result in lower quality of care or decreased access to services. Given the logical and empirical relationship between reimbursement rates

and the willingness of providers to make services available [under Ninth Circuit precedent], the absence of a reasoned decision to not require cost studies to justify the SPA makes the decision to approve the SPA less appropriate for *Chevron* deference. Further, the record reflects that CMS states even though it "does not currently interpret [Section 30(A)] of the Act to require cost studies in order to demonstrate compliance," CMS is "currently reviewing and refining, in a rulemaking proceeding, guidance on how states can adequately document access to services," suggesting that a formal notice and comment rulemaking process, accompanied by the procedural safeguards of such a proceeding, is contemplated by CMS. Besides the fact that no explanation is given for not requiring cost studies other than the statement that CMS "believe[s] the appropriate focus in [sic] on access," this statement by CMS suggests that its position regarding cost studies is not necessarily settled.

CMA v. Douglas, 2012 WL 273768 at 7.

Indeed, Judge Snyder concluded, the CMS decision here was not even entitled to a level of "respect" under the standard set by the United States Supreme Court in Skidmore v. Swift & Co., 323 U.S. 134 (1944), because the Secretary's analysis of California's rate reduction was not even consistent with the Secretary's *own* prior positions on the relevance of provider cost data in decisions over whether rate reductions were reasonable. *Id.* The Secretary was not even considering factors that she herself had found relevant in previous situations involving the reasonableness of Medicaid provider payment rates.

As for the merits of plaintiffs' claims, Judge Snyder found a likelihood of success on the merits, given CMS' utter failure to establish a general methodology that would yield reliable findings:

The Court finds that plaintiffs have shown a substantial likelihood of success on the merits of their claim that CMS' acceptance of DCHS' [the state agency's] access analyses and monitoring plan was arbitrary and capricious. In this regard, the Court finds significant that DHCS' access analyses failed to include projections of what impact the rate reduction would have on beneficiary access or comparisons of Medi–Cal payment rates to Medicare payment rates, average commercial payment rates or provider costs. Furthermore, DHCS' analyses lack any meaningful geographic comparisons. This is so because DHCS reviewed access by "geographic peer groups," which apparently have nothing to do with geographic proximity and include providers from disparate regions of the State. Next, the Court finds it likely that the Secretary's acceptance of the monitoring plan as adequately ensuring access to quality services will also be found to be arbitrary and capricious. This is so because the monitoring plan merely creates a potential response after an access problem has been identified. To the extent reduced rates cause providers to close their doors, increased rates will not necessarily result in the reopening of those facilities. More fundamentally, during the period between the detection of an access problem and its potential remedy through increased reimbursements, Medi–Cal beneficiaries will necessarily suffer from reduced access to services. Finally, the Ninth Circuit has found it unreasonable to rely on independent provisions of federal and state law to ensure quality of care, precisely what the monitoring plan purports to do here.

Id. at 8.

For these reasons, the court issued yet another preliminary injunction. Now, of course, the question is whether California will move to dissolve the injunction based on the Supreme Court's decision in *Douglas*. But what exactly did the Court say? It did *not* hold that private parties have no right to seek injunctive relief. It *did* suggest that the Administrative Procedure Act was the appropriate vehicle to review the agency's action once the agency has acted, but at the same time, as Chief Justice Robert's dissenting opinion pointed out, the majority's holding is silent on the crucial question whether plaintiffs have any rights at all which they can enforce by any vehicle, whether that remedy be directly under the Supremacy Clause, § 1983 or the APA. If there is no right, then there is no remedy— anywhere. The dissenters simply followed out the logic of *Gonzaga*, which the majority did not discuss at all much less overrule.

In the meantime, of course, beneficiaries face ongoing threats to health and safety.

2. *Chief Justice Roberts' effort to distinguish between situations in which* Ex parte Young *can be invoked and those in which it cannot.* Chief Justice Roberts, along with Justices Thomas, Scalia, and Alito, appear to be ready to limit *Ex parte Young* to situations in which a plaintiff, threatened with enforcement of state law against him to which federal law provides a defense, seeks a federal injunction preemptively to stop the a state official from enforcing an unconstitutional law. Why such a limitation? His opinion offers no basis for drawing this distinction but instead merely asserts that *Ex Parte Young* should be so construed, as close as possible, to its facts:

> This is not to say that federal courts lack equitable powers to enforce the supremacy of federal law when such action gives effect to the federal rule, rather than contravening it. The providers and beneficiaries rely heavily on cases of this kind, most prominently *Ex parte Young*, 209 U.S. 123 (1908). Those cases, however, present quite different questions involving "the pre-emptive assertion in equity of a defense that would otherwise have been available in the State's enforcement proceedings at law." *Virginia Office for Protection and Advocacy v. Stewart*, 563 U.S. __ __, __, 131 S.Ct. 1632, 1642 (2011) (KENNEDY, J., concurring). Nothing of that sort is at issue here; the respondents are not subject to or threatened with any enforcement proceeding like the one in *Ex parte Young*. They simply seek a private cause of action Congress chose not to provide.

But why limit *Ex Parte Young* in such a fashion? Wasn't the point of *Ex Parte Young* that federal courts have equitable powers to force a state official to conform his actions to federal law *before* harm occurs because after the fact either plaintiff has suffered irreparable harm or because a federal court's ordering of *retrospective* relief involves far greater intrusion on the states? Isn't this precisely the point of plaintiffs' action in *Douglas*, to seek a federal injunction to force California's compliance with Medicaid's requirements *prospectively*?

Is some distinction being drawn about the nature of the harm? Carry the logic through. Sure, the logic goes, if Delta Airlines is threatened with the imposition of a fine by the state of New York for failing to cover pregnancy-related services under its disability plan (the situation that led to its suit against the state of New York in *Shaw v. Delta Airlines,* Chapter 8), then of course the Supremacy Clause affords a right of action to halt the unlawful state prosecution. But according to the Chief Justice, *Ex Parte Young* provides no such protection based on federal law when the issue instead involves a cut in Medicaid payment rates that threatens the health if not the lives of millions of low-income Medicaid beneficiaries. Delta Airlines receives protection against fines, while low-income Medicaid beneficiaries receive no analogous protection. Is the point that harm to Delta Airline's pocketbook is of higher priority than the health and welfare of millions of low-income Medicaid beneficiaries?

And if the point is the prevention of imminent harm that is caused by unconstitutional state action, of what significance is it that this harm is wrought, not through formal legal proceedings, like that threatened against Delta Airlines, but instead through action that will cause an irreparable impact on health and safety? Should a plaintiff be able to call on federal courts to force state officials to defend the constitutionality of their actions only when the threat to the plaintiff is formal legal action like a fine or imprisonment? What is this, some distinction between *de jure* and *de facto* harm? If so, why should federal courts be available only against the former, rather than the latter? *Isn't the whole point the prospective assertion of the Supremacy of federal law against threatened state action that is unconstitutional?* For an argument why *Ex Parte Young* provides a mechanism to enforce civil rights statutes and safety-net protections, see Rochelle Bobroff, Ex Parte Young *as a Tool to Enforce Safety Net and Civil Rights Statutes,* 40 U. Tol. L. Rev. 819 (2009). For a lengthy disposition on why the *Young* doctrine has no place in American jurisprudence, including Spending Clause cases, see James Leonard, *Ubi Remedium Ibi Jus, Or Where There's a Remedy There is a Right: A Skeptic's Critique of* Ex parte Young, 54 Syracuse L. Rev. 215 (2004).

Finally, reflect carefully on the premise embedded in this proposition: "This is not to say that federal courts lack equitable powers to enforce the supremacy of federal law when such action gives effect to the federal rule, rather than contravening it." The assertion that the injunctive relief sought by the plaintiffs in *Douglas* would "contravene" federal law rests on the proposition that because Congress failed explicitly to grant beneficiaries and providers a cause of action, the courts' doing so would "contravene" federal law:

> Thus, if Congress does not intend for a statute to supply a cause of action for its enforcement, it makes no sense to claim that the Supremacy Clause itself must provide one. Saying that there is a private right of action under the Supremacy Clause would substantively change the federal rule established by Congress in the Medicaid Act. That is not a proper role for the Supremacy Clause, which simply ensures that the rule established by Congress controls.

Seriously? How long ago was *Ex Parte Young* decided? Imagine you are staff counsel in Congress responsible for drafting legislation. Given the interpretation of *Ex Parte Young* that has prevailed for decades, wouldn't you think that it is unnecessary to include a provision giving plaintiffs like those in *Douglas* an express cause of action under the Supremacy Clause? What exactly is the contravention of the rule of law here? Doesn't the federal law that is Supreme include interpretations by the judiciary and the exercise of administrative discretion in the Executive Branch? Do the dissenters seriously believe that lawmaking stops at one end of Constitution Avenue? We return to this issue—the significance of settled law, in which beneficiaries and providers have had rights in Medicaid's three-legged entitlement—at the very end of this Part in the context of a potential holding that when Congress spends, it coerces the states.

3. *Douglas's implications for private enforcement of the Public Health Service Act's federal insurance standards.* Earlier in this Part you learned that the Affordable Care Act creates no private enforcement rights for individuals covered through qualified health plans offered through state health insurance Exchanges, which are subject to a raft of federal requirements. Among these requirements are coverage of comprehensive family planning services, coverage of other preventive services without patient cost-sharing, coverage of essential health benefits, and coverage of routine medical care costs incurred as a participant in a clinical trial. Were a state to fail to modify its insurance laws to mandate that qualified health plans sold in its Exchanges comply with these federal coverage mandates, could a group of plaintiffs file an action to enjoin operation of the state's Exchange coverage until the state-approved products were brought into compliance with federal requirements? How about a simple contract enforcement action against a plan for coverage of federal benefits that the issuer plan is required to include in its policy? What if the state law barred policyholders covered through Exchange plans from bringing actions against the plans?

4. *The impact of low provider payment rates.* In February 2007, a 12-year-old Maryland child, Deamonte Driver, died as the result of an untreated tooth infection. Despite his being insured through Medicaid, the boy's mother was unable to find a dentist to treat her son. *Dental Clinic Opens in Charles County: Initiative Is First Aimed at Southern Maryland Children.* WASHINGTON POST, June 16, 2008, http://www.washingtonpost.com/wp-dyn/content/article/2008/06/15/AR2008061501865.html. Before he died, Deam-

onte Driver cost the Maryland Medicaid program a quarter million dollars in catastrophic inpatient care to treat the brain infection that killed him. Is this an "efficient" and "economic" use of Medicaid resources within the meaning of § 1902(a)(30)(A)? A quarter million dollars would pay for complete dental care for about 5000 Medicaid-enrolled children.

As you consider the ramifications of *Douglas* for access under Medicaid, think about the nearly overwhelming problem of having to mount private litigation every time beneficiaries face barriers to access. How many lawsuits possibly can be brought, even if there is continued viability to *Ex parte Young* to preclude states from flouting Medicaid's requirements? Doesn't a better answer lie in a well-funded federal agency with the power to rapidly review and adjust state Medicaid rates when they are set deeply below prevailing market rates? More funding to develop health care services where they are needed? Better cost controls so that Medicaid payments are not such grievous outliers? Stronger state regulation of health care providers to prohibit them from simply turning their backs on the poor if they want to hold a license to practice? Better training of health professions students and practitioners in their ethical duties? What is the answer here?

8. MEDICAID'S INTERACTION WITH THE AMERICANS WITH DISABILITIES ACT

As public programs, state Medicaid agencies are governed by Title II of the Americans with Disabilities Act, as well as by the predecessor statute, Section 504 of the Rehabilitation Act. The outcome is very different, however, depending on whether the issue at hand is discrimination in the *administration* of a public program or discrimination in the design of benefits, as the cases below illustrate.

Olmstead v. L. C.

527 U.S. 581 (1999)

■ JUSTICE GINSBURG announced the judgment of the Court and delivered the opinion of the Court with respect to Parts I, II, and III–A, and an opinion with respect to Part III–B, in which O'CONNOR, SOUTER, and BREYER, JJ., joined.

I

This case concerns the proper construction of the anti-discrimination provision contained in the public services portion (Title II) of the Americans with Disabilities Act of 1990 [ADA]. Specifically, we confront the question whether the proscription of discrimination may require placement of persons with mental disabilities in community settings rather than in institutions. The answer, we hold, is a qualified yes. Such action is in order when the State's treatment professionals have determined that community placement is appropriate, the transfer from institutional care to a less restrictive setting is not opposed by the affected individual, and the placement can be reasonably accommodated, taking into account the resources available to the State and the needs of others with mental disabilities. We remand the case for further consideration of the appropriate relief, given the range of facilities the State maintains for the care and treatment of persons with diverse mental disabilities, and its obligation to administer services with an even hand.

In the opening provisions of the ADA, Congress stated findings applicable to the statute in all its parts. Most relevant to this case, Congress determined that

> (2) historically, society has tended to isolate and segregate individuals with disabilities, and, despite some improvements, such forms of discrimination against individuals with disabilities continue to be a serious and pervasive social problem; (3) discrimination against individuals with disabilities persists in such critical areas as ... institutionalization ...; (5) individuals with disabilities continually encounter various forms of discrimination, including outright intentional exclusion, ... failure to make modifications to existing facilities and practices, ... [and] segregation...." 42 U.S.C. § 12101(a)(2), (3), (5).[1]

Congress then set forth prohibitions against discrimination in employment (Title I, § 12111–12117), public services furnished by governmental entities (Title II, § 12131–12165), and public accommodations provided by private entities (Title III, §§ 12181–12189). The statute as a whole is intended "to provide a clear and comprehensive national mandate for the elimination of discrimination against individuals with disabilities." § 12101(b)(1).

There is no dispute that L.C. and E.W. are disabled within the meaning of the ADA. This case concerns Title II, the public services portion of the ADA. The provision of Title II centrally at issue reads:

> "Subject to the provisions of this subchapter, no qualified individual with a disability shall, by reason of such disability, be excluded from participation in or be denied the benefits of the services, programs, or activities of a public entity, or be subjected to discrimination by any such entity."

§ 12132.

Title II's definition section states that "public entity" includes "any State or local government," and "any department, agency, [or] special

---

1. The ADA, enacted in 1990, is the Federal Government's most recent and extensive endeavor to address discrimination against persons with disabilities. Earlier legislative efforts included the Rehabilitation Act of 1973, 29 U.S.C. § 701 et seq., and the Developmentally Disabled Assistance and Bill of Rights Act, 42 U.S.C. § 6001 et seq., enacted in 1975. In the ADA, Congress for the first time referred expressly to "segregation" of persons with disabilities as a "for[m] of discrimination," and to discrimination that persists in the area of "institutionalization." §§ 12101(a)(2), (3), (5).

purpose district." § 12131(1)(A), (B). The same section defines "qualified individual with a disability" as

> an individual with a disability who, with or without reasonable modifications to rules, policies, or practices, the removal of architectural, communication, or transportation barriers, or the provision of auxiliary aids and services, meets the essential eligibility requirements for the receipt of services or the participation in programs or activities provided by a public entity.

§ 12131(2).

On redress for violations of § 12132's discrimination prohibition, Congress referred to remedies available under § 505 of the Rehabilitation Act of 1973. See 42 U.S.C. § 12133.[4]

Congress instructed the Attorney General to issue regulations implementing provisions of Title II, including § 12132's discrimination proscription. See § 12134(a) [statutory excerpts omitted]. The Attorney General's regulations, Congress further directed, "shall be consistent with this chapter and with the coordination regulations ... applicable to recipients of Federal financial assistance under [§ 504 of the Rehabilitation Act]." 42 U.S.C. § 12134(b). One of the § 504 regulations requires recipients of federal funds to "administer programs and activities in the most integrated setting appropriate to the needs of qualified handicapped persons." 28 CFR § 41.51(d) (1998).

As Congress instructed, the Attorney General issued Title II regulations, see 28 CFR Part Three 5 (1998), including one modeled on the § 504 regulation just quoted; called the "integration regulation," it reads:

> A public entity shall administer services, programs, and activities in the most integrated setting appropriate to the needs of qualified individuals with disabilities. 28 CFR § 35.130(d) (1998).

The preamble to the Attorney General's Title II regulations defines "the most integrated setting appropriate to the needs of qualified individuals with disabilities" to mean "a setting that enables individuals with disabilities to interact with non-disabled persons to the fullest extent possible." 28 CFR pt. 35, App. A, 450 (1998). Another regulation requires public entities to "make reasonable modifications" to avoid "discrimination on the basis of disability," unless those modifications would entail a "fundamenta[l] alter[ation]"; called here the "reasonable-modifications regulation," it provides:

---

4. Section 505 of the Rehabilitation Act incorporates the remedies, rights, and procedures set forth in Title VI of the Civil Rights Act of 1964 for violations of § 504 of the Rehabilitation Act. See 29 U.S.C. § 794a(a)(2). Title VI, in turn, directs each federal department authorized to extend financial assistance to any department or agency of a State to issue rules and regulations consistent with achievement of the objectives of the statute authorizing financial assistance. 42 U.S.C. § 2000d–1. Compliance with such requirements may be effected by the termination or denial of federal funds, or "by any other means authorized by law." Ibid. Remedies both at law and in equity are available for violations of the statute. See § 2000d–7(a)(2).

A public entity shall make reasonable modifications in policies, practices, or procedures when the modifications are necessary to avoid discrimination on the basis of disability, unless the public entity can demonstrate that making the modifications would fundamentally alter the nature of the service, program, or activity. 28 CFR § 35.130(b)(7) (1998).

II

With the key legislative provisions in full view, we summarize the facts underlying this dispute. Respondents L.C. and E.W. are mentally retarded women; L.C. has also been diagnosed with schizophrenia, and E. W., with a personality disorder. Both women have a history of treatment in institutional settings. In May 1992, L.C. was voluntarily admitted to Georgia Regional Hospital at Atlanta (GRH), where she was confined for treatment in a psychiatric unit. By May 1993, her psychiatric condition had stabilized, and L.C.'s treatment team at GRH agreed that her needs could be met appropriately in one of the community-based programs the State supported. Despite this evaluation, L.C. remained institutionalized until February 1996, when the State placed her in a community-based treatment program.

E.W. was voluntarily admitted to GRH in February 1995; like L.C., E.W. was confined for treatment in a psychiatric unit. In March 1995, GRH sought to discharge E.W. to a homeless shelter, but abandoned that plan after her attorney filed an administrative complaint. By 1996, E.W.'s treating psychiatrist concluded that she could be treated appropriately in a community-based setting. She nonetheless remained institutionalized until a few months after the District Court issued its judgment in this case in 1997.

In May 1995, when she was still institutionalized at GRH, L.C. filed suit in the United States District Court for the Northern District of Georgia, challenging her continued confinement in a segregated environment. Her complaint invoked 42 U.S.C. § 1983 and provisions of the ADA, §§ 12131–12134. L.C. alleged that the State's failure to place her in a community-based program, once her treating professionals determined that such placement was appropriate, violated, inter alia, Title II of the ADA. L.C.'s pleading requested, among other things, that the State place her in a community care residential program, and that she receive treatment with the ultimate goal of integrating her into the mainstream of society. E.W. intervened in the action, stating an identical claim.[6]

The District Court granted partial summary judgment in favor of L.C. and E.W. The court held that the State's failure to place L.C. and E.W. in an appropriate community-based treatment program violated Title II of the ADA. In so ruling, the court rejected the State's argument that inadequate funding, not discrimination against L.C. and E.W. "by reason of" their

---

6. L.C. and E.W. are currently receiving treatment in community-based programs. Nevertheless, the case is not moot. [I]n view of the multiple institutional placements L.C. and E.W. have experienced, the controversy they brought to court is "capable of repetition, yet evading review."

disabilities, accounted for their retention at GRH. Under Title II, the court concluded, "unnecessary institutional segregation of the disabled constitutes discrimination per se, which cannot be justified by a lack of funding."

In addition to contending that L.C. and E.W. had not shown discrimination "by reason of [their] disabilit[ies]," the State resisted court intervention on the ground that requiring immediate transfers in cases of this order would "fundamentally alter" the State's activity. The State reasserted that it was already using all available funds to provide services to other persons with disabilities. Rejecting the State's "fundamental alteration" defense, the court observed that existing state programs provided community-based treatment of the kind for which L.C. and E.W. qualified, and that the State could "provide services to plaintiffs in the community at considerably less cost than is required to maintain them in an institution."

The Court of Appeals for the Eleventh Circuit affirmed the judgment of the District Court, but remanded for reassessment of the State's cost-based defense. As the appeals court read the statute and regulations: When "a disabled individual's treating professionals find that a community-based placement is appropriate for that individual, the ADA imposes a duty to provide treatment in a community setting—the most integrated setting appropriate to that patient's needs"; "[w]here there is no such finding [by the treating professionals], nothing in the ADA requires the deinstitutionalization of th[e] patient."

The Court of Appeals recognized that the State's duty to provide integrated services "is not absolute"; under the Attorney General's Title II regulation, "reasonable modifications" were required of the State, but fundamental alterations were not demanded. The appeals court thought it clear, however, that "Congress wanted to permit a cost defense only in the most limited of circumstances." In conclusion, the court stated that a cost justification would fail "[u]nless the State can prove that requiring it to [expend additional funds in order to provide L.C. and E.W. with integrated services] would be so unreasonable given the demands of the State's mental health budget that it would fundamentally alter the service [the State] provides." Because it appeared that the District Court had entirely ruled out a "lack of funding" justification, the appeals court remanded, repeating that the District Court should consider, among other things, "whether the additional expenditures necessary to treat L.C. and E.W. in community-based care would be unreasonable given the demands of the State's mental health budget." *Id.* at 905.[7]

---

7. After this Court granted certiorari, the District Court issued a decision on remand rejecting the State's fundamental-alteration defense. See 1:95–cv–1210–MHS (ND Ga., Jan. 29, 1999), at 1. The court concluded that the annual cost to the State of providing community-based treatment to L.C. and E.W. was not unreasonable in relation to the State's overall mental health budget. *Id.*, at 5. In reaching that judgment, the District Court first declared "irrelevant" the potential impact of its decision beyond L.C. and E.W. 1:95–cv–1210–MHS (ND Ga., Oct. 20, 1998), at 3. The District Court's decision on remand is now pending appeal before the Eleventh Circuit.

III

Endeavoring to carry out Congress' instruction to issue regulations implementing Title II, the Attorney General, in the integration and reasonable-modifications regulations made two key determinations. The first concerned the scope of the ADA's discrimination proscription, 42 U.S.C. § 12132; the second concerned the obligation of the States to counter discrimination. As to the first, the Attorney General concluded that unjustified placement or retention of persons in institutions, severely limiting their exposure to the outside community, constitutes a form of discrimination based on disability prohibited by Title II. See 28 CFR § 35.130(d) (1998) ("A public entity shall administer services ... in the most integrated setting appropriate to the needs of qualified individuals with disabilities.") Regarding the States' obligation to avoid unjustified isolation of individuals with disabilities, the Attorney General provided that States could resist modifications that "would fundamentally alter the nature of the service, program, or activity." 28 CFR § 35.130(b)(7) (1998).

The Court of Appeals essentially upheld the Attorney General's construction of the ADA. [T]he court then remanded with instructions to measure the cost of caring for L.C. and E.W. in a community-based facility against the State's mental health budget.

We affirm the Court of Appeals' decision in substantial part. Unjustified isolation, we hold, is properly regarded as discrimination based on disability. But we recognize, as well, the States' need to maintain a range of facilities for the care and treatment of persons with diverse mental disabilities, and the States' obligation to administer services with an even hand. Accordingly, we further hold that the Court of Appeals' remand instruction was unduly restrictive. In evaluating a State's fundamental-alteration defense, the District Court must consider, in view of the resources available to the State, not only the cost of providing community-based care to the litigants, but also the range of services the State provides others with mental disabilities, and the State's obligation to mete out those services equitably.

A.

We examine first whether, as the Eleventh Circuit held, undue institutionalization qualifies as discrimination "by reason of ... disability." The Department of Justice has consistently advocated that it does. Because the Department is the agency directed by Congress to issue regulations implementing Title II, its views warrant respect. We need not inquire whether the degree of deference described in *Chevron* is in order; "[i]t is enough to observe that the well-reasoned views of the agencies implementing a statute 'constitute a body of experience and informed judgment to which courts and litigants may properly resort for guidance.'" [Additional cases omitted]

The State argues that L.C. and E.W. encountered no discrimination "by reason of" their disabilities because they were not denied community placement on account of those disabilities. Nor were they subjected to "discrimination," the State contends, because " 'discrimination' necessarily requires uneven treatment of similarly situated individuals," and L.C. and E.W. had identified no comparison class, i.e., no similarly situated individuals given preferential treatment. We are satisfied that Congress had a more comprehensive view of the concept of discrimination advanced in the ADA.[10]

The ADA stepped up earlier measures to secure opportunities for people with developmental disabilities to enjoy the benefits of community living. The Developmentally Disabled Assistance and Bill of Rights Act (DDABRA), a 1975 measure, stated in aspirational terms that "[t]he treatment, services, and habilitation for a person with developmental disabilities . . . should be provided in the setting that is least restrictive of the person's personal liberty." 42 U.S.C. § 6010(2) (1976 ed.); see also *Pennhurst State School and Hospital*, 451 U.S. at 24. In a related legislative endeavor, the Rehabilitation Act of 1973, Congress used mandatory language to proscribe discrimination against persons with disabilities. Ultimately, in the ADA, enacted in 1990, Congress not only required all public entities to refrain from discrimination, see 42 U.S.C. § 12132; additionally, in findings applicable to the entire statute, Congress explicitly identified unjustified "segregation" of persons with disabilities as a "for[m] of discrimination." See § 12101(a)(2) (historically, society has tended to isolate and segregate individuals with disabilities, and, despite some improvements, such forms of discrimination against individuals with disabilities continue to be a serious and pervasive social problem"); § 12101(a)(5) ("individuals with disabilities continually encounter various forms of discrimination, including . . . segregation").[11]

Recognition that unjustified institutional isolation of persons with disabilities is a form of discrimination reflects two evident judgments. First,

---

10. The dissent is driven by the notion that "this Court has never endorsed an interpretation of the term 'discrimination' that encompassed disparate treatment among members of the same protected class," that "[o]ur decisions construing various statutory prohibitions against 'discrimination' have not wavered from this path,"and that "a plaintiff cannot prove 'discrimination' by demonstrating that one member of a particular protected group has been favored over another member of that same group[.]" The dissent is incorrect as a matter of precedent and logic. See O'Connor v. Consolidated Coin Caterers Corp., 517 U.S. 308, 312 (1996) (The Age Discrimination in Employment Act of 1967 "does not ban discrimination against employees because they are aged 40 or older; it bans discrimination against employees because of their age, but limits the protected class to those who are 40 or older. The fact that one person in the protected class has lost out to another person in the protected class is thus irrelevant, so long as he has lost out because of his age."); cf. Oncale v. Sundowner Offshore Services, Inc., 523 U.S. 75, 76 (1998) ("[W]orkplace harassment can violate Title VII's prohibition against 'discriminat[ion] . . . because of . . . sex,' 42 U.S.C. § 2000e–2(a)(1), when the harasser and the harassed employee are of the same sex."); Jefferies v. Harris County Community Action Assn., 615 F.2d 1025, 1032 (C.A.5 1980) ("[D]iscrimination against black females can exist even in the absence of discrimination against black men or white women.").

11. Unlike the ADA, § 504 of the Rehabilitation Act contains no express recognition that isolation or segregation of persons with disabilities is a form of discrimination. Section 504's discrimination proscription, a single sentence attached to vocational rehabilitation legislation, has yielded divergent court interpretations.

institutional placement of persons who can handle and benefit from community settings perpetuates unwarranted assumptions that persons so isolated are incapable or unworthy of participating in community life. [The Court's discussion of relevant cases is omitted]. Second, confinement in an institution severely diminishes the everyday life activities of individuals including family relations, social contacts, work options, economic independence, educational advancement, and cultural enrichment. In order to receive needed medical services, persons with mental disabilities must, because of those disabilities, relinquish participation in community life they could enjoy given reasonable accommodations, while persons without mental disabilities can receive the medical services they need without similar sacrifice.

The State urges that, whatever Congress may have stated as its findings in the ADA, the Medicaid statute "reflected a congressional policy preference for treatment in the institution over treatment in the community." The State correctly used the past tense. Since 1981, Medicaid has provided funding for state-run home and community-based care through a waiver program. Indeed, the United States points out that the Department of Health and Human Services (HHS) "has a policy of encouraging States to take advantage of the waiver program, and often approves more waiver slots than a State ultimately uses." (Further observing that, by 1996, "HHS approved up to 2109 waiver slots for Georgia, but Georgia used only 700").

We emphasize that nothing in the ADA or its implementing regulations condones termination of institutional settings for persons unable to handle or benefit from community settings. Title II provides only that "qualified individual[s] with a disability" may not "be subjected to discrimination." 42 U.S.C. § 12132. "Qualified individuals," the ADA further explains, are persons with disabilities who, "with or without reasonable modifications to rules, policies, or practices, . . . mee[t] the essential eligibility requirements for the receipt of services or the participation in programs or activities provided by a public entity." § 12131(2).

Consistent with these provisions, the State generally may rely on the reasonable assessments of its own professionals in determining whether an individual "meets the essential eligibility requirements" for habilitation in a community-based program. Absent such qualification, it would be inappropriate to remove a patient from the more restrictive setting. See 28 CFR § 35.130(d) (1998) (public entity shall administer services and programs in "the most integrated setting appropriate to the needs of qualified individuals with disabilities"; cf. School Bd. of Nassau Cty. v. Arline, 480 U.S. 273, 288 (1987) ("[C]ourts normally should defer to the reasonable medical judgments of public health officials.").[13] Nor is there any federal require-

---

13. Georgia law also expresses a preference for treatment in the most integrated setting appropriate. See Ga. Code Ann. 37–4–121 (1995) ("It is the policy of the state that the least restrictive alternative placement be secured for every client at every stage of his habilitation. It shall be the duty of the facility to assist the client in securing placement in noninstitutional community facilities and programs.").

ment that community-based treatment be imposed on patients who do not desire it. See 28 CFR § 35.130(e)(1) (1998) ("Nothing in this part shall be construed to require an individual with a disability to accept an accommodation ... which such individual chooses not to accept."); 28 CFR pt. 35, App. A, 450 (1998) ("[P]ersons with disabilities must be provided the option of declining to accept a particular accommodation."). In this case, however, there is no genuine dispute concerning the status of L.C. and E.W. as individuals "qualified" for noninstitutional care: The State's own professionals determined that community-based treatment would be appropriate for L.C. and E. W., and neither woman opposed such treatment.[14]

B.

The State's responsibility, once it provides community-based treatment to qualified persons with disabilities, is not boundless. The reasonable-modifications regulation speaks of "reasonable modifications" to avoid discrimination, and allows States to resist modifications that entail a "fundamenta[l] alter[ation]" of the States' services and programs. 28 CFR § 35.130(b)(7) (1998). The Court of Appeals construed this regulation to permit a cost-based defense "only in the most limited of circumstances," and remanded to the District Court to consider, among other things, "whether the additional expenditures necessary to treat L.C. and E.W. in community-based care would be unreasonable given the demands of the State's mental health budget."

The Court of Appeals' construction of the reasonable-modifications regulation is unacceptable for it would leave the State virtually defenseless once it is shown that the plaintiff is qualified for the service or program she seeks. If the expense entailed in placing one or two people in a community-based treatment program is properly measured for reasonableness against the State's entire mental health budget, it is unlikely that a State, relying on the fundamental-alteration defense, could ever prevail. Sensibly construed, the fundamental-alteration component of the reasonable-modifications regulation would allow the State to show that, in the allocation of available resources, immediate relief for the plaintiffs would be inequitable, given the responsibility the State has undertaken for the care and treatment of a large and diverse population of persons with mental disabilities.

When it granted summary judgment for plaintiffs in this case, the District Court compared the cost of caring for the plaintiffs in a community-based setting with the cost of caring for them in an institution. That simple comparison showed that community placements cost less than institutional confinements. As the United States recognizes, however, a comparison so simple overlooks costs the State cannot avoid; most notably, a "State ... may experience increased overall expenses by funding commu-

---

14. We do not in this opinion hold that the ADA imposes on the States a "standard of care" for whatever medical services they render, or that the ADA requires States to "provide a certain level of benefits to individuals with disabilities." We do hold, however, that States must adhere to the ADA's nondiscrimination requirement with regard to the services they in fact provide.

nity placements without being able to take advantage of the savings associated with the closure of institutions."[15]

As already observed the ADA is not reasonably read to impel States to phase out institutions, placing patients in need of close care at risk. Nor is it the ADA's mission to drive States to move institutionalized patients into an inappropriate setting, such as a homeless shelter, a placement the State proposed, then retracted, for E.W. Some individuals, like L.C. and E.W. in prior years, may need institutional care from time to time "to stabilize acute psychiatric symptoms." For other individuals, no placement outside the institution may ever be appropriate.

To maintain a range of facilities and to administer services with an even hand, the State must have more leeway than the courts below understood the fundamental-alteration defense to allow. If, for example, the State were to demonstrate that it had a comprehensive, effectively working plan for placing qualified persons with mental disabilities in less restrictive settings, and a waiting list that moved at a reasonable pace not controlled by the State's endeavors to keep its institutions fully populated, the reasonable-modifications standard would be met. In such circumstances, a court would have no warrant effectively to order displacement of persons at the top of the community-based treatment waiting list by individuals lower down who commenced civil actions.[16]

For the reasons stated, we conclude that, under Title II of the ADA, States are required to provide community-based treatment for persons with mental disabilities when the State's treatment professionals determine that such placement is appropriate, the affected persons do not oppose such treatment, and the placement can be reasonably accommodated, taking into account the resources available to the State and the needs of others with mental disabilities.

---

15. Even if States eventually were able to close some institutions in response to an increase in the number of community placements, the States would still incur the cost of running partially full institutions in the interim.

16. We reject the Court of Appeals' construction of the reasonable-modifications regulation for another reason. The § 504 regulation upon which the reasonable-modifications regulation is based provides now, as it did at the time the ADA was enacted: "A recipient shall make reasonable accommodation to the known physical or mental limitations of an otherwise qualified handicapped applicant or employee unless the recipient can demonstrate that the accommodation would impose an undue hardship on the operation of its program." 28 CFR § 41.53

While the Part Four regulations do not define "undue hardship," other § 504 regulations make clear that the "undue hardship" inquiry requires not simply an assessment of the cost of the accommodation in relation to the recipient's overall budget, but a "case-by-case analysis weighing factors that include: (1) [t]he overall size of the recipient's program with respect to number of employees, number and type of facilities, and size of budget; (2) [t]he type of the recipient's operation, including the composition and structure of the recipient's workforce; and (3)[t]he nature and cost of the accommodation needed." 28 CFR § 42.511(c) (1998); see 45 CFR § 84.12(c) (1998) (same). Under the Court of Appeals' restrictive reading, the reasonable-modifications regulation would impose a standard substantially more difficult for the State to meet than the "undue burden" standard imposed by the corresponding § 504 regulation.

■ JUSTICE STEVENS, concurring in part and concurring in the judgment.

Unjustified disparate treatment, in this case, "unjustified institutional isolation," constitutes discrimination under the Americans with Disabilities Act of 1990. If a plaintiff requests relief that requires modification of a State's services or programs, the State may assert, as an affirmative defense, that the requested modification would cause a fundamental alteration of a State's services and programs. In this case, the Court of Appeals appropriately remanded for consideration of the State's affirmative defense. On remand, the District Court rejected the State's "fundamental-alteration defense." If the District Court was wrong in concluding that costs unrelated to the treatment of L.C. and E.W. do not support such a defense in this case, that arguable error should be corrected either by the Court of Appeals or by this Court in review of that decision. In my opinion, therefore, we should simply affirm the judgment of the Court of Appeals. But because there are not five votes for that disposition, I join JUSTICE GINSBURG's judgment and Parts I, II, and III–A of her opinion.

■ JUSTICE KENNEDY, with whom JUSTICE BREYER joins as to Part I, concurring in the judgment.

[T]he States have acknowledged that the care of the mentally disabled is their special obligation. They operate and support facilities and programs, sometimes elaborate ones, to provide care. It is a continuing challenge, though, to provide the care in an effective and humane way, particularly because societal attitudes and the responses of public authorities have changed from time to time.

Beginning in the 1950's, many victims of severe mental illness were moved out of state-run hospitals, often with benign objectives. The so-called "deinstitutionalization" has permitted a substantial number of mentally disabled persons to receive needed treatment with greater freedom and dignity. It may be, moreover, that those who remain institutionalized are indeed the most severe cases. Nevertheless, the depopulation of state mental hospitals has its dark side. [discussion of the effects of deinstitutionalization omitted].

It would be unreasonable, it would be a tragic event, then, were the Americans with Disabilities Act of 1990(ADA) to be interpreted so that States had some incentive, for fear of litigation, to drive those in need of medical care and treatment out of appropriate care and into settings with too little assistance and supervision. The opinion of a responsible treating physician in determining the appropriate conditions for treatment ought to be given the greatest of deference.

In light of these concerns, if the principle of liability announced by the Court is not applied with caution and circumspection, States may be pressured into attempting compliance on the cheap, placing marginal patients into integrated settings devoid of the services and attention necessary for their condition. This danger is in addition to the federalism costs inherent in referring state decisions regarding the administration of treatment programs and the allocation of resources to the reviewing authority of the federal courts. It is of central importance, then, that courts apply today's decision with great deference to the medical decisions of the responsible, treating physicians and, as the Court makes clear, with appropriate deference to the program funding decisions of state policymakers.

With these reservations made explicit, in my view we must remand the case for a determination of the questions the Court poses and for a determination whether respondents can show a violation of 42 U.S.C. § 12132's ban on discrimination.

[T]here is no allegation that Georgia officials acted on the basis of animus or unfair stereotypes regarding the disabled. Discrimination under this statute might in principle be shown in the case before us, though further proceedings should be required.

Putting aside issues of animus or unfair stereotype, I agree with JUSTICE THOMAS that on the ordinary interpretation and meaning of the term, one who alleges discrimination must show that she "received differential treatment vis-a-vis members of a different group on the basis of a statutorily described characteristic." In my view, however, discrimination so defined might be shown here. Although the Court seems to reject JUSTICE THOMAS' definition of discrimination, it asserts that unnecessary institutional care does lead to "[d]issimilar treatment." According to the Court, "[i]n order to receive needed medical services, persons with mental disabilities must, because of those disabilities, relinquish participation in community life they could enjoy given reasonable accommodations, while persons without mental disabilities can receive the medical services they need without similar sacrifice."

Although this point is not discussed at length by the Court, it does serve to suggest the theory under which respondents might be subject to discrimination in violation of § 12132. If they could show that persons needing psychiatric or other medical services to treat a mental disability are subject to a more onerous condition than are persons eligible for other existing state medical services, and if removal of the condition would not be a fundamental alteration of a program or require the creation of a new one, then the beginnings of a discrimination case would be established.

Of course, it is a quite different matter to say that a State without a program in place is required to create one. No State has unlimited resources and each must make hard decisions on how much to allocate to treatment of diseases and disabilities. If, for example, funds for care and treatment of the mentally ill, including the severely mentally ill, are reduced in order to support programs directed to the treatment and care of other disabilities, the decision may be unfortunate. The judgment, however, is a political one and not within the reach of the statute. Grave constitutional concerns are raised when a federal court is given the authority to review the State's choices in basic matters such as establishing or declining to establish new programs. It is not reasonable to read the ADA to permit court intervention in these decisions. In addition, as the Court notes, by regulation a public entity is required only to make "reasonable modifications in policies, practices, or procedures" when necessary to avoid discrimination and is not even required to make those if "the modifications would fundamentally alter the nature of the service, program, or activity." 28

CFR § 35.130(b)(7). It follows that a State may not be forced to create a community-treatment program where none exists.

To establish discrimination in the context of this case, and absent a showing of policies motivated by improper animus or stereotypes, it would be necessary to show that a comparable or similarly situated group received differential treatment.

Unlike JUSTICE THOMAS, I deem it relevant and instructive that Congress in express terms identified the "isolat[ion] and segregat[ion]" of disabled persons by society as a "for[m] of discrimination," § 12101(a)(2), (5), and noted that discrimination against the disabled "persists in such critical areas as ... institutionalization," § 12101(a)(3). These findings do not show that segregation and institutionalization are always discriminatory or that segregation or institutionalization are, by their nature, forms of prohibited discrimination. Nor do they necessitate a regime in which individual treatment plans are required, as distinguished from broad and reasonable classifications for the provision of health care services. Instead, they underscore Congress' concern that discrimination has been a frequent and pervasive problem in institutional settings and policies and its concern that segregating disabled persons from others can be discriminatory. Both of those concerns are consistent with the normal definition of discrimination—differential treatment of similarly situated groups. The issue whether respondents have been discriminated against under § 12132 by institutionalized treatment cannot be decided in the abstract, divorced from the facts surrounding treatment programs in their State.

The possibility therefore remains that, on the facts of this case, respondents would be able to support a claim under § 12132 by showing that they have been subject to discrimination by Georgia officials on the basis of their disability. This inquiry would not be simple. Comparisons of different medical conditions and the corresponding treatment regimens might be difficult, as would be assessments of the degree of integration of various settings in which medical treatment is offered. However, as petitioners observe, "[i]n this case, no class of similarly situated individuals was even identified, let alone shown to be given preferential treatment." As a consequence, the judgment of the courts below, granting partial summary judgment to respondents, ought not to be sustained. In addition, as JUSTICE GINSBURG's opinion is careful to note, it was error in the earlier proceedings to restrict the relevance and force of the State's evidence regarding the comparative costs of treatment. The State is entitled to wide discretion in adopting its own systems of cost analysis, and, if it chooses, to allocate health care resources based on fixed and overhead costs for whole institutions and programs.

I would remand the case to the Court of Appeals or the District Court for it to determine in the first instance whether a statutory violation is sufficiently alleged and supported in respondents' summary judgment materials and, if not, whether they should be given leave to replead and to introduce evidence and argument along the lines suggested above.

■ JUSTICE THOMAS, with whom the CHIEF JUSTICE and JUSTICE SCALIA join, dissenting.

The majority concludes that petitioners "discriminated" against respondents—as a matter of law—by continuing to treat them in an institutional setting after they became eligible for community placement. I disagree. Temporary exclusion from community placement does not amount to "discrimination" in the traditional sense of the word, nor have respondents shown that petitioners "discriminated" against them "by reason of" their disabilities.

Until today, this Court has never endorsed an interpretation of the term "discrimination" that encompassed disparate treatment among members of the same protected class.

Our decisions construing various statutory prohibitions against "discrimination" have not wavered from this path. [the discussion of discrimination in the context of Title VII of the Civil Rights Act and Section 504 of the Rehabilitation Act are omitted].

Despite this traditional understanding, the majority derives a more "capacious" definition of "discrimination," as that term is used in Title II of the ADA, one that includes "institutional isolation of persons with disabilities." It chiefly relies on certain congressional findings contained within the ADA. To be sure, those findings appear to equate institutional isolation with segregation, and thereby discrimination. The congressional findings, however, are written in general, hortatory terms and provide little guidance to the interpretation of the specific language of § 12132. In my view, the vague congressional findings upon which the majority relies simply do not suffice to show that Congress sought to overturn a well-established understanding of a statutory term (here, "discrimination"). Moreover, the majority fails to explain why terms in the findings should be given a medical content, pertaining to the place where a mentally retarded person is treated. When read in context, the findings instead suggest that terms such as "segregation" were used in a more general sense, pertaining to matters such as access to employment, facilities, and transportation.

Elsewhere in the ADA, Congress chose to alter the traditional definition of discrimination. Title I of the ADA, § 12112(b)(1), defines discrimination to include "limiting, segregating, or classifying a job applicant or employee in a way that adversely affects the opportunities or status of such applicant or employee." Notably, however, Congress did not provide that this definition of discrimination, unlike other aspects of the ADA, applies to Title II. The majority's definition of discrimination—although not specifically delineated—substantially imports the definition of Title I into Title II by necessarily assuming that it is sufficient to focus exclusively on members of one particular group. Under this view, discrimination occurs when some members of a protected group are treated differently from other members of that same group. As the preceding discussion emphasizes, absent a special definition supplied by Congress, this conclusion is a remarkable and novel proposition that finds no support in our decisions in analogous areas. For example, the majority's conclusion that petitioners "discriminated" against respondents is the equivalent to finding discrimination under Title VII where a black employee with deficient management skills is denied in-house training by his employer (allegedly because of lack of funding) because other similarly situated black employees are given the in-house training. Such a claim would fly in the face of our prior case law, which requires more than the assertion that a person belongs to a protected group and did not receive some benefit.

At bottom, the type of claim approved of by the majority does not concern a prohibition against certain conduct (the traditional understanding of discrimination), but rather imposition of a standard of care.[6] As such, the majority can offer no principle limiting this new species of "discrimination" claim apart from an affirmative defense because it looks merely to an individual in isolation, without comparing him to otherwise similarly situated persons, and determines that discrimination occurs merely because that individual does not receive the treatment he wishes to receive. By adopting such a broad view of discrimination, the majority drains the term of any meaning other than as a proxy for decisions disapproved of by this Court.

Further, I fear that the majority's approach imposes significant federalism costs, directing States how to make decisions about their delivery of public services. We previously have recognized that constitutional principles of federalism erect limits on the Federal Government's ability to direct state officers or to interfere with the functions of state governments. We have suggested that these principles specifically apply to whether States are required to provide a certain level of benefits to individuals with disabilities.

The majority may remark that it actually does properly compare members of different groups. Indeed, the majority mentions in passing the "[d]issimilar treatment" of persons with and without disabilities. It does so in the context of supporting its conclusion that institutional isolation is a form of discrimination. It cites two cases as standing for the unremarkable proposition that discrimination leads to deleterious stereotyping. The majority then observes that persons without disabilities "can receive the services they need without" institutionalization and thereby avoid these twin deleterious effects. I do not quarrel with the two general propositions, but I fail to see how they assist in resolving the issue before the Court. Further, the majority neither specifies what services persons with disabilities might need, nor contends that persons without disabilities need the

---

6. In mandating that government agencies minimize the institutional isolation of disabled individuals, the majority appears to appropriate the concept of "mainstreaming" from the Individuals with Disabilities Education Act (IDEA), 20 U.S.C. § 1400 et seq. But IDEA is not an antidiscrimination law. It is a grant program that affirmatively requires States accepting federal funds to provide disabled children with a "free appropriate public education" and to establish "procedures to assure that, to the maximum extent appropriate, children with disabilities ... are educated with children who are not disabled." §§ 1412(1), (5). Ironically, even under this broad affirmative mandate, we previously rejected a claim that IDEA required the "standard of care" analysis adopted by the majority today. See Board of Ed. of Hendrick Hudson Central School Dist., Westchester Cty. v. Rowley, 458 U.S. 176, 198 (1982).

same services as those with disabilities, leading to the inference that the dissimilar treatment the majority observes results merely from the fact that different classes of persons receive different services—not from "discrimination" as traditionally defined.

Finally, it is also clear petitioners did not "discriminate" against respondents "by reason of [their] disabili[ties]," as § 12132 requires. We have previously interpreted the phrase "by reason of" as requiring proximate causation. This statute should be read as requiring proximate causation as well. Respondents do not contend that their disabilities constituted the proximate cause for their exclusion. Nor could they—community placement simply is not available to those without disabilities. Continued institutional treatment of persons who, though now deemed treatable in a community placement, must wait their turn for placement, does not establish that the denial of community placement occurred "by reason of" their disability. Rather, it establishes no more than the fact that petitioners have limited resources.

For the foregoing reasons, I respectfully dissent.

Notes

1. Olmstead *on remand*. On remand, the state of Georgia and the plaintiffs ultimately reached a settlement that required the state to expand community services for institutionalized persons. Olmstead v. L.C., No. 1:95 CV 1210 (July 11, 2000).

2. *Meaning of discrimination in* Olmstead. Perhaps the greatest significance of the majority's decision was its adoption of "undue institutionalization" as discrimination under Title II of the ADA. Its reference to Congress' findings regarding the deleterious effects of segregating the disabled in institutions is pregnant with the implication that separate is almost inherently unequal. Moreover, reflect on the manner in which this holding affects a plaintiff's burden in bringing such a claim. The dissent would have required that a plaintiff show differential treatment relative to an unprotected class, and accused the majority of ignoring precedent—and logic—in allowing claims of discrimination to rest on disparate treatment within the protected class.

We have seen already how in many different contexts persons with mental disabilities are accorded diminished insurance benefits in relation to their need for health care than compared with persons who are challenged by physical disabilities. Although the mental health parity protections discussed earlier in this Part offer modest mitigations, employers remain free to exclude entire mental health conditions from treatment or even to offer no treatment for mental illness. And the parity law applies only to private health insurance and employer-sponsored plans, not to Medicaid fee-for-service coverage, the typical form of coverage for persons with severe mental illness and other mental disabilities.

The question thus becomes whether what Georgia—and many other states did—i.e., refusing to pay for approved community services for mentally ill persons that already were covered under its Medicaid plan—was discriminatory. The dissent would hold that qualified individuals with a mental disability could not prove discrimination under Title II by showing that qualified individuals with a physical disability were accorded a greater level of services as a matter of plan design and administration. The only relevant comparison, according to the dissent, would be between mentally disabled persons, for whom community-based services were medically appropriate, and non-disabled persons similarly situated, i.e., for whom community-based services were medically appropriate. Who could possibly be a member of the latter class? Do you know of any non-disabled persons for whom community-based services are medically necessary in order to treat their [??????]? Is it any wonder, then, that plaintiffs failed to identify such a class?

The decision in *Olmstead*, therefore, enabled institutionalized, mentally disabled persons to show that discrimination exists when the only choice of care given to persons with disabilities is medically unwarranted institutionalization, coupled with a paucity of community-based services. This holding sparked significant rethinking at all levels of government about how "*Olmstead* obligations" could be satisfied and how Medicaid should be reconfigured to move away from policies that essentially favored institutional placements while encouraging the under-funding of community-based care. Although there was no majority opinion on the issue of exactly what those obligations consisted of, at the very least, after the decision it was clear that some sort of obligation did exist. In *Olmstead's* wake, numerous states expanded their community-based services and Congress amended the federal Medicaid statute to create more state options for further community integration of persons with disabilities. For a summary of the Clinton and Bush Administrations' and Congressional responses, as well as the state reforms, *see, e.g.*, Sara Rosenbaum & Joel Teitelbaum, *Olmstead at Five: Assessing the Impact*, KAISER COMMISSION ON MEDICAID AND THE UNINSURED (2004), http://www.kff.org/medicaid/upload/Olmstead-at-Five–Assessing-the-Impact.pdf.

3. *Post-Olmstead litigation.* The history of litigation in the wake of *Olmstead* is spotty at best, with both winners and losers. Generally, when the claim has been understood as the failure properly to administer available resources (i.e., underuse of community resources approved for financing in the state plan, as was the case with Georgia), courts have found for plaintiffs on a reasonable modification theory. But once a case is perceived as involving a request for the addition of resources to cover more Medicaid services in the community or make more community residential placements available, the cases lose on a fundamental alteration theory. The cases are erratic, because much depends on how a court understands the gist of the argument. For example, in a situation in which a state Medicaid agency (lawfully) cuts off eligibility for home and community based benefits at a specific monthly dollar income amount, persons with incomes above that amount are entitled only to nursing home care. Sounds

like a design case, no? Wrong, this fact pattern has given rise to a holding of discriminatory administration/reasonable modification. Sara Rosenbaum, *The ADA in a Health Care Context, IOM, Disability in America,* NATIONAL ACADEMY PRESS (Washington D.C. 2007).

4. *Coverage design and the ADA.* As in private health insurance, the remedial protections of disability rights law have not been understood as reaching otherwise lawful Medicaid benefit design choices. In *Alexander v. Choate,* 469 U.S. 287, discussed earlier in this Part, the United States Supreme Court held that Tennessee's 14–day inpatient hospital limit as permissible under federal Medicaid law because it met the *Curtis,* 625 F.2d 645, normative test, did not become unlawful because it fell with disproportionate force on persons with disabilities. Nothing changed with the enactment of the ADA.

Rodriguez v. City of New York, 197 F.3d 611 (2d Cir. 1999), *cert. den.,* 531 U.S. 864 (2000), concerned the City of New York's practice of denying coverage for safety monitoring as part of in-home personal care services furnished to seriously disabled persons with mental illness. In New York State (as in about half of all states), county governments administer Medicaid and thus have authority over Medicaid eligibility determinations and coverage decision-making. The *Rodriguez* case arose when the City refused, as part of its personal care program for persons with disabilities, to cover and pay for safety monitoring (i.e., the presence of an aid in the home to assure that an individual with serious disabilities is performing tasks associated with the activities of daily living) as an independent service. The City did cover and pay for safety monitoring when furnished as an incidental service to other personal care services for persons with physical disabilities.

Personal care services are one of the optional services that state Medicaid programs can elect to cover under their state plans. 42 U.S.C. § 1396d(a)(22). Neither the statute nor the federal regulations (42 C.F.R. § 440.167) define the term "personal care" other than to specify that the service must be (a) furnished to an individual who is not a resident of a Medicaid institution, (b) provided by a qualified individual who is not a member of the beneficiary's family, and (c) furnished in the beneficiary's home or another location specified by the state.

New York City provides extensive coverage of personal health services. Under the City's rules, safety monitoring qualified for coverage when furnished as "incidental" to another personal care service including "bathing, toileting, taking medication, assisting with personal hygiene, dressing, feeding, light housekeeping or shopping," but the City would neither recognize nor pay for safety monitoring as an independent personal care service. This decision meant that safety monitoring was unavailable to persons whose only disabilities were mental in nature and who, under observation, could dress, bathe, shop, eat, etc. Without access to safety monitoring, the ability of beneficiaries with mental illness to exist safely outside of an institution could be jeopardized (the very issue that was litigated in *Olmstead*).

The plaintiffs in *Rodriguez* sued the city under both federal Medicaid law and Title II of the ADA (the same Title at issue in *Olmstead*). The trial court found for the plaintiffs on both counts, determining that the City's limits on coverage violated Medicaid's reasonableness and anti-discrimination standards as well as the non-discrimination provisions of the ADA. The Court of Appeals reversed.

With respect to the respondents' claims that the City's coverage limits were unreasonable, the Court began by dismissing arguments that the City's refusal to cover safety monitoring as a direct benefit and only as an incidental benefit violated Medicaid's "comparability of services" requirement, 42 U.S.C. § 1396a(a)(10)(B):

> When Congress passed the Medicaid Act in 1965, it sought to ensure that "the primary concern of the states in providing financial assistance should be those persons who lack sufficient income to meet their basic needs—termed the categorically needy." Camacho v. Perales, 786 F.2d 32, 38 (2d Cir. 1986). This group—*i.e.*, those listed in subparagraph (A)—were contrasted with the medically needy, those who have resources to meet most of their basic needs but not their medical ones. Section 1396a(a)(10)(B) guarantees that if a state elects to provide Medicaid to the medically needy, it must also provide it to the categorically needy and that it may not provide more assistance to the former group than to the latter. *Id.* at 39. Moreover, states may not provide benefits to some categorically needy individuals but not to others. [additional citations omitted]. Section 1396a(a)(10)(B) thus precludes states from discriminating against or among the categorically needy.

> Appellees' discrimination claim is entirely different from the types of discrimination described above. They do not contend that the medically needy receive coverage in New York not afforded to the categorically needy or that some distinction is drawn among the categorically needy. Instead, they claim that, because safety monitoring is "comparable" to the personal care services already provided by New York, the failure to provide such monitoring violates Section 1396a(a)(10)(B). Appellees attempt to graft a new requirement on this Section: If two different benefits are "comparable" and one is provided, the other must be as well. Thus, they conclude, once a state provides assistance for any personal-service activity comparable to safety monitoring, it must also provide safety monitoring.

> *However, Section 1396a(a)(10)(B) does not require a state to fund a benefit that it currently provides to no one.* Its only proper application is in situations where the same benefit is funded for some recipients but not others. [case citations omitted]. A holding to the contrary would both substantially narrow the "broad discretion" the Medicaid Act confers "on the States to adopt standards for determining the extent of medical assistance," and create a

disincentive for states to provide services optional under federal law lest a court deem other services "comparable" to those provided—an elastic concept—thereby increasing the costs of the optional services. Beal v. Doe, 432 U.S. 438, 444 (1977). The Act therefore "requir[es] only that such standards be 'reasonable' and 'consistent with the objectives' of the Act." Appellants' decision to distinguish between safety monitoring and other tasks thus does not implicate Section 1396a(a)(10)(B).

We reject appellees' further contention that because incidental safety monitoring is provided to those receiving other personal care services, it must be provided to appellees as well. Caregivers of course monitor safety while providing other personal-care services to patients. *See Rodriguez,* 44 F. Supp.2d at 619. If a caregiver failed to monitor a patient's safety while he/she was providing another service, he/she would obviously not be providing reasonable care. A clear and legitimate distinction exists, therefore, between providing safety monitoring as an incidental benefit when the care-giver is assisting with another task and providing it as an independent task, when the caregiver is present only to monitor the patient's safety.

Because New York's program does not impermissibly discriminate under Section 1396a(a)(10)(B), New York may prevail simply by showing that the decision not to include safety monitoring as an optional benefit was reasonable. *Beal,* 432 U.S. at 446 n. 11 (finding Pennsylvania's lack of funding for nontherapeutic abortions to be "entirely consistent" with Section 1396a(a)(10)(B) and noting that the state had "reasonable justification" for making this decision).

Rodriguez, 197 F.3d at 615–16 (emphasis added).

With respect to respondents' claim that the City's coverage limits were unreasonable and a violation of federal Medicaid non-discrimination standards (see *Pinneke,* 623 F.2d 546, above) the court concluded as follows:

[B]ecause the cost of personal-care services would be significantly greater if safety monitoring were provided, New York had legitimate fiscal reasons for its decision. Moreover, the federal Health Care Financing Agency [sic]—which is responsible for administering the Medicaid program—informed New York that its decision was not only reasonable but proper. (" '[W]e believe that the supervising/monitoring of an individual, by itself, without the provision of recognized personal care services, would not be considered personal care services for Medicaid purposes.' ")

Appellees next contend that appellants' plan violated two regulations promulgated pursuant to the Medicaid Act, 42 C.F.R. § 440.230(b) & (c). Title 42 C.F.R. § 440.230 reads in relevant part as follows: (b) Each service must be sufficient in amount, duration, and scope to reasonably achieve its purpose. (c) The

Medicaid agency may not arbitrarily deny or reduce the amount, duration, or scope of a required service under §§ 440.210 and 440.220 to an otherwise eligible recipient solely because of the diagnosis, type of illness, or condition.

[W]e see no conflict with these regulations.

Title 42 C.F.R. § 440.230(b) looks to the purpose of the particular service provided. Appellees argue that the purpose of the personal care services is to enable recipients to reside in their homes and, their argument goes, because safety monitoring enables appellees to remain at home, it must be provided. *This analysis is, however, at the incorrect level of generality. Instead of examining the particular need addressed by a particular service, it focuses on the presumed purpose of an entire package of personal care services. This approach is contrary to the text of the regulation and to the purpose of the Medicaid Act.*

The regulation looks to the purpose of "[e]ach service" provided, *see* 42 C.F.R. § 440.230(b), and where a state like New York provides numerous different services, each is to be examined independently.[4] Moreover, interpreting the regulation to require examination of the overall purpose of a broad category of optional services provided instead of the purpose of a particular benefit would undermine the discretion that the Medicaid Act affords states. *See Beal*, 432 U.S. at 444. Under appellees' reading of the regulation, for example, a state that provided one benefit that allowed some patients to remain at home would be required to provide virtually all benefits needed to enable all Medicaid recipients to remain at home. Thus, even if safety monitoring is essential to enable appellees to reside safely in their homes, 42 C.F.R. § 440.230(b) is not violated by New York's failure to provide it.

Appellees' claim under subsection (c) also suffers from a fatal problem. The regulation states that "[t]he Medicaid agency may not arbitrarily deny or reduce the amount, duration, or scope of a *required* service under §§ 440.210 and 440.220 to an otherwise eligible recipient solely because of the diagnosis, type of illness, or condition." 42 C.F.R. § 440.230(c) (emphasis added). Personal care services are not a required service under Section 440.210 or Section 440.220.[5] Thus, this provision gives no support to appellees' claim.

---

4. We note that courts construing this regulation have viewed as the relevant question the propriety of the manner in which a particular benefit was provided, not whether a new benefit was mandated. For example, in Charleston Memorial Hospital v. Conrad, 693 F.2d 324, 330 (4th Cir. 1982), the Fourth Circuit found no violation of the Medicaid Act or 42 C.F.R. § 440.230(b) when South Carolina reduced the number of annual hospital visits it would reimburse. *See also Curtis*, 625 F.2d at 650–53 (finding limitation on physician visits to three per month did not violate regulation), *modified by* 648 F.2d 946 (5th Cir. 1980).

5. Section 440.210 does require states to provide the home health services described in Section 440.70, but those required services do not include the type of personal care services at issue here.

Rodriguez, 197 F.3d at 616–18 (emphasis added).

The court then dismissed the respondents' ADA claims as well:

> Under the ADA, "no qualified individual with a disability shall, by reason of such disability, be ... denied the benefits of the services or programs of a public entity, or be subjected to discrimination by any such entity." 42 U.S.C. § 12132. A "qualified individual with a disability" is defined as "an individual with a disability who ... meets the essential eligibility requirements for the receipt of services or the participation in programs or activities provided by a public entity." 42 U.S.C. § 12131(2). There is no dispute that the appellees are disabled under the statute.
>
> Appellees contend that they satisfy the eligibility requirements for personal care services but are effectively denied the services because of their disability. We disagree. We begin by noting that New York *provides identical services to mentally and physically disabled Medicaid recipients.* Although the district court did state that "it is not clear that [certain] services are consistently provided to the mentally disabled, while *comparable* services are provided to the physically impaired," this observation turns on the district court's incorrect view of the role of comparability. See above. The district court did not, for example, find that the enumerated services New York provides as part of its personal-care services package were denied to the mentally disabled. Instead, appellees' claim is that New York's decision not to provide safety monitoring renders the providing of personal-care services ineffective for many who are mentally disabled. At its crux, the claim is that the provision of Medicaid-funded services to one group of disabled persons discriminated against other disabled persons who need different services.
>
> Appellees again fail to focus on the particular services provided by appellants. *See Alexander v. Choate,* 469 U.S. 287, 303 (holding that Medicaid "benefits" under the Rehabilitation Act [and hence ADA] are "the individual services offered" not the "amorphous objective of 'adequate health care' "). The ADA requires only that a particular service provided to some not be denied to disabled people. As discussed above, the services that New York provides to the mentally disabled are no different from those provided to the physically disabled. *Neither group is provided with independently tasked safety monitoring.* Hence, what appellees are challenging "is not illegal discrimination against the disabled, but the substance of the services provided." *Id.* at 84. Thus, New York cannot have unlawfully discriminated against appellees by denying a benefit that it provides to no one. *See* 42 U.S.C. § 12132. Nor do appellees "meet[ ] the essential eligibility requirements for the receipt" of separately tasked safety monitoring services because New York does not even have any such requirements. *Id.* § 12131(2).

Appellees place much reliance on the Supreme Court's recent decision in *Olmstead,* 527 U.S. 581 (1999). In *Olmstead,* the Court examined whether Georgia's refusal to provide services to mentally disabled persons in "community settings," instead of institutions, violated the ADA. The Court held that such action would violate the ADA only "when the State's treatment professionals have determined that community placement is appropriate, the transfer from institutional care to a less restrictive setting is not opposed by the affected individual, and the placement can be reasonably accommodated, taking into account the resources available to the State and the needs of others with mental disabilities." 119 S. Ct. at 2181. This decision is inapposite.

In *Olmstead,* the parties disputed only—and the Court addressed only—*where* Georgia should provide treatment, not *whether* it must provide it. *Id.* at 2183–84 (detailing state's provision of treatment to mentally disabled patients in institutions). Georgia already had numerous state programs that provided community-based treatment that the *Olmstead* respondents were qualified to receive. *Id.* at 2183–84, 2188. The state contended that even though these services existed, it had a cost justification to keep certain mentally disabled individuals institutionalized.

The portion of the opinion most relevant to the instant dispute was the Court's statement that it was explicitly not holding that "the ADA imposes on the States a standard of care for whatever medical services they render, or that the ADA requires States to provide a certain level of benefits to individuals with disabilities." *Id.* at 2188 n. 14 (internal quotation marks omitted). *Olmstead* does not, therefore, stand for the proposition that states must provide disabled individuals with the opportunity to remain out of institutions. Instead, it holds only that "States must adhere to the ADA's nondiscrimination requirement with regard to the services *they in fact provide.*" *Id.* (emphasis added).

Appellees want New York to provide a new benefit, while Olmstead reaffirms that the ADA does not mandate the provision of new benefits. Under the ADA, it is not our role to determine what Medicaid benefits New York must provide. *See Cercpac,* 147 F.3d at 168 ("[T]he disabilities statutes do not guarantee any particular level of medical care for disabled persons, nor assure maintenance of service previously provided."). Rather, we must determine whether New York discriminates on the basis of a mental disability with regard to the benefits it does provide. Because New York does not "task" safety monitoring as a separate benefit for anyone, it does not violate the ADA by failing to provide this benefit to appellees.[6]

---

6. Because New York did not discriminate against appellees in violation of the ADA, we need not reach whether separately tasking safety monitoring is a "reasonable modification[ ]" required under the ADA by 28 C.F.R. § 35.130(b)(7).

Rodriguez, 197 F.3d at 618–19 (emphasis added).

The *Rodriguez* case underscores just how crucial factual development can be in Medicaid coverage litigation. Reading the decision, one can see that there is a world of difference between how the beneficiaries and the City each characterized the facts and the "theory of the case." In a nutshell, the City's theory of the case was that beneficiaries were attempting to force New York to expand Medicaid coverage in order to better tailor the program to the needs of mentally ill persons (in this regard, recall Judge Posner's characterization of the patient's claim in *Doe v. Mutual of Omaha,* earlier in this Part). To build its case, the City argued the facts as follows: Safety monitoring is not a covered personal care service, and beneficiaries' attempt to characterize it as one is wrong. At best, safety monitoring is recognized simply an incidental part of an otherwise covered personal care service, such as assistance with bathing. Indeed, it would be impossible to furnish a covered personal care service to a beneficiary *without* engaging in at least some level of safety monitoring as an intrinsic dimension of personal care. The City makes no provision for direct and independent billing of safety monitoring in our provider claims manuals. Furthermore, the City offers the same personal care services to all persons. Thus, the beneficiaries' arguments amount to nothing more than a blatant attempt to force the city at great cost to "customize" its personal care program to meet the needs of persons with mental illness. Since neither Medicaid nor the ADA requires a state agency to alter the coverage design of its Medicaid plan, we win.

(The City was helped in this argument by the seemingly tautological letter from the Health Care Financing Administration, which stated that if no personal care services are furnished, then safety monitoring cannot be covered. Of course, if safety monitoring *is* a personal care service (and nothing in the statute or rule states otherwise), then HCFA's letter is completely without meaning).

For the beneficiaries, the theory of the case was that the City does in fact cover safety monitoring and is engaging in discrimination against mentally ill beneficiaries in the administration of its personal care program by denying beneficiaries with mental illness access to the service. Beneficiaries' arguments thus would go something like this: The state Medicaid plan covers safety monitoring as a personal care service but limits coverage only to those situations in which the service is furnished along with another personal care service for persons with physical disabilities. Furthermore, in the context of persons with mental illness, safety monitoring *is* assistance with bathing, toileting, eating, etc. Just because mentally ill people can physically execute certain functions does not render safety monitoring any less "personal care" assistance. The City's interpretation of coverage limits through its provider claims manuals thus constitutes unlawful administration. The City's administration is no less than an attempt to limit access to safety monitoring only to people who have a physical disability, thereby depriving persons with mental disabilities from getting a service that is fundamental to remaining in their homes. As a result, the City's program violates both Medicaid and the ADA.

The court obviously accepted the City's factual presentation and its theory of the case. Its legal analysis then became relatively easy. Viewed as a lawsuit to force a state to *expand the coverage limits of its Medicaid plan,* the beneficiaries' challenge failed under every legal theory. As *Curtis,* 625 F.2d 645, above illustrates, Medicaid coverage rules require comparable coverage and prohibit unreasonable limits on coverage, but they do not force a state to add coverage, no matter how desirable the coverage might be. In this respect the case presents an analogy to ERISA benefit design cases such as *Jones* and *McGann* in Chapter 8. Courts are loathe to dictate plan design to sponsors (in this case, a Medicaid agency; in the ERISA cases, employers), although in Medicaid, a state may be found liable for failing to adjust its benefit design to federal content requirements. Furthermore, while the ADA (and its predecessor statute the Rehabilitation Act of 1973) prohibit differential treatment based on disability *within the scope of coverage,* courts are unwilling to read the ADA to require the modification of *insurance design* to suit the needs of a subset of subscribers or beneficiaries. If the court had accepted the beneficiaries' view of the case, the legal result would have been different. Had the court understood the New York program as covering safety monitoring but only for persons who receive the service in combination with another personal care service, then the comparability arguments might have succeeded. The reasonableness of the City's limits would have been thrown into doubt under the *Curtis* test, because the limitation on coverage would have excluded a very large portion of the beneficiary population (i.e., persons with mental but not physical illnesses) from the reach of the service. Finally, the ADA claim would have been a claim regarding the *discriminatory administration of a covered benefit,* rather than a claim for a benefit that was not covered. In this regard, the City's actions arguably would have fit directly within the prohibitions of the ADA's anti-discrimination rules.

Thus—and as in all litigation—facts are everything. How a court understands the facts in the case it adjudicates effectively determines the outcome. One might superficially characterize the case as one involving a court that empathizes with a public defendant and is determined not to force it to spend millions of additional dollars on services for persons with mental illness (although it might be tempting to view the decision in this fashion, given the fact that the opinion is filled with platitudes regarding the need to give states discretion to place limits on their Medicaid programs). However, the dynamic of this decision runs more deeply and concerns the fundamental question of how judges take in and understand facts. The lower court in *Rodriguez* saw the case as involving the arbitrary denial of a covered benefit from persons with mental illness. The court of appeals on the other hand saw the case as a demand to modify New York's Medicaid program.

Are you surprised that the crucial fact in the case—is the care covered or not—could be so elusive? As a condition of receiving federal funds, state

Medicaid programs must file "state plans" with the federal government that describe eligibility, benefits and coverage, provider qualification standards, compensation formulas, and other matters. The summaries of state Medicaid plans can be viewed in the CCH Medicare/Medicaid Guide. Wouldn't you suppose that the trial court could have ascertained the answer simply by asking for the state plan? In fact many services covered in state Medicaid plans "fly below the radar" in the sense that they are covered procedures within general classes of services. The only way to ascertain coverage is by careful examination of the minute details of provider claims manuals. Since states need only list in their plans the broad classes of benefits they cover and any express limits on amount, duration and scope (e.g., three physician visits per month)—and states do not identify all of the covered procedures within a class—it is possible that only detailed analysis of actual claims analysis can reveal the limits of state Medicaid programs.

In this regard, the most far-reaching aspect of the court's analysis of federal Medicaid standards related to the legality of coverage limits is its assertion that in setting limits on coverage of optional Medicaid services, a state may permissibly "unbundle" a broad optional service category and carve out specific procedural limits as a matter of coverage design. Furthermore, the court tacitly approves state strategies of expressing limits through provider claims payment procedures rather than through publicly disclosed limits on coverage under the official state plan. What does all this tell you about the ability of DHHS to monitor states' compliance with the statute? Further, what does this tell you about the importance of their being private rights of enforcement, by beneficiaries and providers who are the ones issuing claims that are denied?

One final point is worth noting: The court correctly notes that the federal Medicaid anti-discrimination rule, 42 C.F.R. § 440.230(c), applies only to "required" services and that personal care services are optional, and that nothing appears to prohibit a state, in the court's view, from selecting out certain procedures used by certain types of individuals and restricting or eliminating their coverage altogether. However, in the case of children under 21, federal law requires the provision of all medically necessary services enumerated in 42 U.S.C. § 1396c(a) of the Social Security Act. 42 U.S.C. § 1396d(r). Sara Rosenbaum & David Rousseau, *Medicaid at Thirty–Five*, 45 St. Louis U.L.J. 7, 22 (2001). As a result, the anti-discrimination rule would apply to personal care services when furnished to children.

Note: The Pathologies of Fragmented Financing, Risk–Bearing and Payment

We have now canvassed the major streams of revenue that together comprise the financing of health care in the United States. Take an inventory of what you have read thus far: Medicare; Medicaid—actually 51 different programs; the approximately one million ERISA plans; and individual health insurance coverage. We have barely touched on other significant revenue streams: the Children's Health Insurance Program; TRI-CARE, covering our armed forces and their families; and the Federal Employees Health Benefit Program, covering the federal civilian workforce. Then add the state health insurance Exchanges stipulated by the ACA, potentially numbering up to at least 51, depending on how many states create their own Exchanges and how many states decide to create subsidiary Exchanges rather than one large pool. This situation is fragmentation, with a capital "F."

In the next chapter we draw some comparisons with other nations' systems. Some depend on forms of taxation to finance their systems. Others rely on premiums collected by private organizations. *None* has anything close to the fragmentation in raising revenue that exists in the United States. Moreover, *none* relies primarily on private entities to engage in the function most fundamental to modern health care, to-wit, the underwriting of risk, aka risk pooling or social solidarity. Finally, *none* fails to coordinate the means by which they pay providers—the subject of our next chapter—into a single ("single-payer") or collective ("all-payer") system. By contrast, the United States fragments all three functions—raising revenue, bearing risk and paying providers—across a horde of competing, private and public entities.

To be sure, the Affordable Care Act sets a number of reforms in motion that, over time, may bring greater national cohesion to health care finance and delivery. The Act introduces some level of standardization of coverage into the individual and small-group markets, while moving toward a more unified vision of clinical preventive coverage across all markets. The Act makes investments in primary health care and the training of primary health care professionals in order to limit the tilt toward specialty care. The Act seeks to introduce more tightly controlled payment models, known as payment bundling (which will be discussed in the next chapter) in order to decrease volume associated with constant hospital readmission of patients whose conditions are allowed to deteriorate in the community. The Act also attempts to stimulate investment in more efficient health care delivery models such as "medical homes" and "Accountable Care Organizations" that are more clinically and financially integrated. These entities (which will be discussed in Part Three) are designed to emphasize a team approach to health care in order to substitute lower cost professionals where possible. They are also structured to better coordinate care to avoid unnecessary procedures while improving its quality (for example, by providing better follow-up care following a serious spell of illness to avoid relapse and hospital readmission). Providers that practice in this fashion are likely to be paid using a single global rate rather than separate payments for each procedure, in order to incentivize lowering the volume of costly individual procedures and negotiating for better prices.

However, as we have noted throughout this Part, the ACA builds on top of and preserves this fiercely fragmented system. As a result, for the most part it's business as usual, continuing all the pathologies we have examined so far in this book. In the culture and organization of U.S. health care—to borrow a phrase—it's every man for himself. Each payer is confronted with the enormity of controlling volume and pricing. Insurers and plan administrators want to show a profit for their efforts, and public sponsors such as Medicare and Medicaid want to bring down the cost curve. What do they do? Each payer attempts to use the arsenal of weapons at its disposal at any given time, given the state of legal regulation, to keep its costs under control. These strategies and tactics can be grouped into four major camps, whose parameters the cases presented throughout this Part have brought into view.

1. *Avoid the most costly cases.* The history of health insurance in the individual and group health insurance markets shows the efforts to which insurers have gone, in the name of actuarial fairness, to avoid individuals and groups considered bad health risks and to force bad risks to pay excessively high prices for coverage. These practices of course come to an end with full implementation of the Affordable Care Act, whose central achievement is to stop punishing the sick. To be sure, the Act retains some principles of actuarial fairness, such as the use of wellness incentives to charge higher rates to individuals who fail to maintain their health, the use of modified community rating that raises the price of insurance for older people, and the permissibility of higher rates for tobacco users, but it comes as close as we have, at least since the demise of community rating, to eliminating health status as a factor in one's insurability.

Whether wellness incentives will lead to a new form of discrimination against less healthy employees, who disproportionately will be lower income, is a matter of concern. Harald Schmidt et al., *Carrots, Sticks and Health Care Reform—Problems with Wellness Incentives*, 364 NEW ENG. J. MED. E3 (Jan. 14, 2010). At the same time, a signature achievement of the Act may be the mitigation of nearly unchecked power to avoid bad risks by prohibiting discrimination in enrollment and pricing based on health status. With this tool effectively gone, insurers must look elsewhere. (And of course, Medicaid and Medicare do not possess these tools because of their essential purpose and structure, with the exception of risk-bearing plans and providers who participate in the program).

Although the Act takes away the most blatant weapons—the pre-existing condition exclusion and discriminatory pricing—there still are arrows left in the quiver. For example, insurers might lobby state legislatures hard to set up subsidiary Exchanges rather than a single state health insurance Exchange with uniform rating and pricing. They then might avoid the costliest subsidiary markets (in their view). In states with single Exchanges they could bid only for certain geographic areas on the basis that their networks are confined to certain communities. Insurers acting as plan administrators could selectively pitch their third-party administered products in the non-Exchange group health market, avoiding employers whose employees are associated with elevated health risks.*

---

* One of the more interesting questions is whether elevated health risks equate with elevated financial risk. In fact, if a product is designed to shield the payer from too much coverage risk and the network is weak enough, it may be that the sickest patients end up using far less care.

2. *Buy as little health care as possible.* Another technique—and one that grows in importance as the outright risk avoidance techniques described in #1 are curbed—is to buy less care. The cases throughout Part Two illustrate this approach. An insurer, plan sponsor or public insurer can define the scope of coverage narrowly. This tactic might mean excluding higher cost treatments for patients with long-term health needs, as in *Mondry* or *Bedrick*. It might mean, in Medicaid, covering long-term care in institutions or community settings as little as possible, eliminating "optional" services such as adult dental and vision care, or not offering personal attendant services for people with serious disabilities.

Beyond coverage design are the techniques of utilization management, prior authorization, and claims denials. A payer can arbitrarily deny coverage as in *Majestic Casino* or *Papciak* and hope that the beneficiary or provider simply does not appeal. The payer might make the appeals process particularly onerous to cut down on claims. (The Affordable Care Act limits these practices to some degree, but recall that the easier-to-use external independent review process is available only for certain types of "medical judgment" claims, and is closed to challenges to wrongful interpretation of plan documents).

An insurer might design networks to deter use. The provider network might lack enough specialists or have too few pharmacies. There might not be enough dentists. Waits for a new patient appointment might take months. You will see the worst consequences of network limits in *Jones v. Chicago HMO* in Part Three, below. Not only might this cut down on use but it might also encourage people to go out of network, thereby exposing them to higher cost-sharing and balance-billing, as in *Krauss.*

3. *Pay as little as possible for the health care that is purchased.* An insurer or plan can pay deeply discounted rates for the services it covers, as in *ILC*, 543 F.3d 1050, in the hope that either providers will somehow survive on less money or cut back on care. For FY 2012, 49 states plan additional cuts in Medicaid provider payment rates. Edward Williams et al., *State Budget Cuts in the New Fiscal Year Are Unnecessarily Harmful*, CENTER ON BUDGET AND POLICY PRIORITIES (2011), http://www.cbpp.org/cms/index.cfm?fa=view & id=3550. If the insurer or plan pays low enough rates, serious access problems could develop of course, and the results could be higher costs, as in the example of Diomonte Driver, above, the Maryland child who died for lack of a dentist, but not before the Medicaid program paid a quarter of a million dollars in hospital costs. What often happens, however, particularly in the case of low-income people, is that patients simply go without the care. Further, often the payer won't bear the long-term consequences of such skimping because the individual who has been short-changed is no longer in the payer's insurance pool. As we discuss immediately below, even with the reforms in the ACA, incentives and multiple means to cost shift still exist.

An insurer or plan might also pay its claims slowly in order to stem the flow of funds. It also might deny a large proportion of claims and make providers fight with it over payment. *Majestic Casino* offers a variation of this strategy. The formal name for payment delays is "pended claims."

4. *Push the risk onto someone else.* There are multiple options here. For starters, insurers might design health insurance plans that rely on very high deductibles and coinsurance. This technique has two benefits. First, it means that a large portion of the cost of care is borne by the insured. Second, it also depresses utilization because people cannot afford to pay their out-of-pocket share and simply go without treatment. (This technique of course may ultimately result in higher expenditures if people get really sick, but if the payer is thinking only about the next quarter or off-loading costs into the next fiscal year, this strategy buys time).

Another technique, seen in Medicare Advantage, the Medicare Part D prescription drug program, and in Medicaid managed care, is to agree to provide coverage only with attractive stop-loss arrangements that push responsibility for excess costs back onto the sponsor. Defining coverage narrowly also pushes the risk back onto individuals by making them directly responsible for all of the excluded treatments or forcing them to go without. The TennCare medical necessity statute, described in Chapter 8, offers an example of this type of financial risk-avoidance technique. Really low provider payment rates also push risk back onto providers by exposing them to payments that are less than even the cost of efficiently furnished care.

Yet another technique is to pay network providers low fees or develop contracts that call for them to share in part of the losses if the money turns out not to be enough to cover all claims. Managed care arrangements often use risk-sharing contracts with participating providers. Some of these arrangements work; others, explored in the next chapter and in Part Three, may lead to major disruption in care because of provider inexperience in managing financial risks.

The problem with all of these techniques is that it is every insurer, employer plan, provider, federal or state governmental unit aiming for its own book of business, its own population, its own budget. In this situation, an entire regional health care system might be upended as every payer seeks to cut costs without regard to its spillover effects. In affluent communities with good levels of health insurance, providers may succeed in shifting costs to some other payer by hiking rates. In communities with many uninsured residents, there may be no viable economic model for maintaining services at a reasonable level without an infusion of funding—such as funding to run a public hospital or a grant to build a community health center—to keep services adequate.

Most importantly perhaps, in this "every-man-for-himself" approach to cost containment, the nation loses not only the ability to rationally control costs but also the potential to use its resource investment capacity to improve quality and population health. In this dog-eat-dog world, the only real questions are which providers and populations will come out on top, and who gets stuck holding the bag in the end.

CHAPTER 12

PAYING FOR HEALTH CARE: CONCEPTUAL AND STRUCTURAL CONSIDERATIONS

1. INTRODUCTION

Our explication of payment to providers must begin with a return to basics, the nature of illness and the nature of health insurance. Illness is a probabilistic event, meaning that the probability of occurrence for a given person—the risk that a given individual will become ill—cannot confidently be predicted in advance. Health insurance works because as a result of the "law of large numbers," actuarial predictions can be made for a class of persons who are insured. It's like tossing a coin. If the coin is tossed just twice, one has little confidence that one toss will be heads and one will be tails, but if the coin is tossed one million times, one can be much more confident that half the tosses will be heads and half will be tails. Thus, while one cannot predict the illness that might befall an individual, one can predict the illnesses that will befall a large insurance pool.

Similar uncertainty characterizes not only the probability of loss but also its magnitude. In advance one cannot confidently predict how much a given illness will cost for any particular individual. Suppose that two individuals suffer heart attacks. One might be so lucky as to have the attack right at a hospital emergency department and the condition might be treated much more quickly and easily than one that occurs fifteen minutes away (by ambulance). Moreover, individuals differ in their general state of health, and so a heart attack in one person might be quite different from a heart attack in another. Further, potentially the heart attack might be treated in a small community hospital or a massive academic medical center; the doctor could be an emergency specialist, a cardiac surgeon, or a general practitioner, and the actual services provided might vary by the technologies that are necessary or available. These examples can be multiplied almost to infinity, but if one has data concerning the cost of illness across a multitude of individuals, then one can derive a statistical norm of the magnitude of loss for the "average" heart attack.

As we discussed earlier in this part, before the advent of modern health care, payment was essentially cash and carry. Some people, like the dying woman's servant in *Hurley v. Eddingfield* (Part One), tendered cash. Others were expected to work for the privilege of what went for hospital "health care" back then, essentially "bed and board," a place off the streets. As we describe in a bit more detail below, insurance became necessary only when doctors and hospitals began to experience trouble collecting payment. The original form of health insurance in the United States (including Medicare when it was first enacted) was indemnity insurance, meaning that patients paid providers and then submitted bills for reimbursement by the health insurer. Hence the term "reimbursement," which has dominated the lexicon as opposed to the more appropriate term "payment."

An indemnity insurance arrangement not only enabled the pooling of risk, the essential element of insurance, but also allowed a patient—aka the "insured"—unfettered choice among providers. Likewise, reimbursement as a form of payment not only was a feature of early social insurance systems (sickness programs in Prussia, for example, reimbursed families for their lost wages) but also was consistent with commercial insurance norms. Reimbursement also was simpatico with the individualism that is the hallmark of American society and culture, since it left providers without any duty of care, as discussed in Part One and free to bargain with their patients over the terms of care. Indemnity insurance thus was one means—not the only possible means, but one means—to spread risk over an insurance pool. It also was a way of dealing with the fact that in advance of illness one cannot identify which particular patient in the pool of patients will fall ill and what services he or she will need—i.e., the types of providers who will furnish services. Indemnity insurance effectively covered all insured persons for any illness and any type of service because once ill, the patients could seek treatment from any provider.

However, as we also described earlier in this Part, a characteristic of indemnity insurance in the United States was that, aside from participation agreements executed between hospitals and insurance companies, no prior contractual relationship existed between providers and insurers. Hospitals simply were reimbursed for their costs in providing services. They were reimbursed either directly by patients or, if they had executed a participation agreement, by the patient's insurer. Doctors were paid by patients for whatever they could charge patients, who then submitted the doctors' charges to their insurers—and most often patients got stuck with whatever balance they owed above what insurers deemed to be the "reasonable" charge, the limit above which they refused to reimburse patients.

This form of "retrospective reimbursement" furnished no means by which payers could control costs. Insurers or patients reimbursed hospitals' costs, and patients paid doctors whatever charges the market would bear. As a result, as costs have increased, retrospective reimbursement has been replaced by "prospective payment," in which providers are supposed to be paid at prices set in advance of treatment, a means that theoretically allows payers to control costs. To the degree to which payment is set in advance, prospective payment succeeds in shifting risk back to providers, because in the modern system they are organized into networks through which patients must receive care if they want to receive the full value of their insurance. Providers in turn must accept a discounted payment rate in order to remain in the networks. This system is prospective if payers refuse to make retroactive adjustments—we'll see below that prospective payment has not controlled costs because payers have failed to make it stick—and if it is made to stick, it binds participating providers to the insurer's fee schedule (minus deductibles, coinsurance and copayments).

With the introduction of prospective payment, indemnity insurance in the United States could no longer work because contracting must occur before the time services are furnished. Conceivably an insurer could execute contracts with all providers from whom a patient might seek care. This situation effectively obtains in other countries' national health insurance systems. If health insurance is directly provided by government—e.g., the Canadian provinces—the government sets payment in advance, and citizens are still free to seek the services of any provider.* Likewise, if national health insurance exists through nation-wide coordination of sickness funds—e.g., the social security countries of France and Germany—the coordinated funds and providers negotiate price in advance, and citizens choose among providers. However, as we have previously described, in the United States, health insurance is generally private and fragmented, with the result that payment, to be prospective, must be determined in advance through contracts executed between an insurer and providers it selects. Prospective payment thus requires that a pool of potential providers—aka, the network—be identified in advance of treatment and further, that a budget constraint be imposed on them. What makes prospective payment so difficult is the fact that this obligation to pay is set in advance of delivery of services before it can be known exactly what services will be provided, to whom they will be provided, and from whom they will be provided.

As discussed above, actuarial predictions over a pool of potential patients—and a pool of potential providers—can be made, but the examples we used simplify too much because both the occurrence and magnitude of loss are somewhat affected by events that occur after insurance is initiated, a phenomenon known as "moral hazard." In the ideal, insurance involves the pooling of the risk of loss in which a sum certain, the premium, is fixed at the time of contracting and paid to shift the risk of loss to the insurance pool. In this ideal both the risk of occurrence—illness—and the magnitude of loss—the cost of treatment—are known and fixed at the time of contract formation. Health insurance, however, deviates from this ideal in that actions of persons insured and providers from whom they seek health care affect both the risk and magnitude of loss. Individuals can quite literally eat and smoke themselves to death, thereby triggering a long bout of health care expenditures. Some types of providers, particularly physicians, likewise can affect both the risk and magnitude of loss by varying the volume or intensity of the services they provide in treating illness—they too can treat

---

* Some national health services, like the UK, have used selective contracting in internal markets. The insurance function is collective but selection of providers occurs within that bubble. *See, e.g.,* Joseph White, *Targets and Systems of Health Care Cost Control*, 24 J. HEALTH POL. POL'Y & L. 653, 661–62 (1999) [hereinafter White, *Targets and Systems of Health Care Cost Control*]. *See generally* HEALTH CARE REFORM THROUGH INTERNAL MARKETS: EXPERIENCE AND PROPOSALS (Monique Jerôme–Forget et al., eds., 1995).

a patient to death or, more optimistically, back to life. As we discuss more fully in Part Three, substantial variation exists in the manner in which providers treat many conditions, evidence of the fact that providers exercise discretion over the loss insured against.*

At the extreme, then, some providers—again, particularly physicians—can decide how much income they will receive. Economists have fought long and hard over the extent to which providers "induce" demand for their services. Most health economists now take the position that "supplier-induced demand" exists at least to some extent in the health care sector, *see, e.g.,* Roger Feldman & Michael A. Morrisey, *Health Economics: A Report on the Field,* 15 J. HEALTH POL. POL'Y & L. 627, 640–41 (1990); and some take the position that a major constraint on provider incomes, particularly physicians, is how many hours they wish to work in order to meet a "target income," a "profit-satisficing" model, in which doctors don't try to maximize profit but just make do, so to speak, by supporting the lifestyle they wish. *See* Joseph P. Newhouse, *A Model of Physician Pricing,* 37 S. ECON. J. 174, 181 n.30 (1970); *see also, e.g.,* Robert G. Evans, *Supplier–Induced Demand: Some Empirical Evidence and Implications, in* THE ECONOMICS OF HEALTH AND MEDICAL CARE 162 (Mark Perlman, ed., (1974)). In short, to some extent providers often can respond to reductions in prices by increasing volume or substituting pricier procedures for less pricey ones. Prediction and control of spending, therefore, are difficult.

Obviously, then, the unique nature of health insurance creates great challenge for any payment system. Although the ideal is unattainable—probability and magnitude of loss perfectly calculable in advance—a system is more predictable if its mechanisms ensure a relatively high degree of predictability, a goal that is easily stated but not easily achieved. Expenditures for any given accounting period are the product of the prices of goods and services provided and the intensity and volume of services. Prices are determined in negotiations between providers and insurers, whether those negotiations occur in political or economic markets. Hence they are predictable in that they are "set" in advance as a product of negotiation or as a system of administered pricing (i.e., the setting of the price by the payer). However, the mix or "intensity" of services—e.g., are constant severe headaches diagnosed with a CT scan or an MRI?—and volume may fall more within the discretion of health care providers and the preferences of patients. Attaining predictability of expenditures, therefore, is a very complicated process with numerous moving, interacting parts. In the end,

---

* The welfare effects of moral hazard are debatable. Health economics and policy in the United States has been dominated by the argument, deriving initially from Mark V. Pauly, *The Economics of Moral Hazard: Comment,* 58 AM. ECON. REV. 531 (1968), that moral hazard reduces welfare because at the point of purchase, consumers over-consume because they face lower costs than they would absent insurance. This claim, which has delegitimized comprehensive insurance, *see, e.g.,* Deborah Stone, *Moral Hazard,* 36 J. HEALTH POL. POL'Y & L. 887 (2011), has recently come under attack within economics, largely on the ground that it ignores the income effects of health insurance—that what consumers gain in welfare from the purchase of insurance is income protection when they are ill. *See, e.g.,* John A. Nyman, *American Health Policy: Cracks in the Foundation,* 32 J. HEALTH POL. POL'Y & L. 760 (2007).

expenditures must match up with revenues, whether obtained in the form of premiums or taxation, or else the system becomes politically and economically unstable to the point of insolvency.

Below we discuss in more detail some mechanisms to attain predictability and long-term financial and political stability, and we contrast the historical development of payment in the United States with systems in other industrialized nations. By and large we use Medicare as the domestic example because it is the largest payer in the United States, because private insurers tend to adopt its methods, and because its methods are in the public domain, in contrast to those of private payers, who consider their methods, to the extent they differ from Medicare's, to be proprietary. We also focus on physician and hospital payment. Entire treatises can be written on health payment systems, which vary by the type of good or service considered. Thus for example, prescription drug payment is a world unto itself. Payment for durable medical equipment (such as wheel chairs and walkers) is a long and technical journey through the intricacies of how the industry operates and the relationships it has developed with third-party payers. Similarly complex is payment for medical devices and new technologies. Suffice it to say that much of the field of health law practice, particularly when representing the health care industry, is learning—and ultimately mastering—the payment systems that drive the industry and that (inevitably) the industry has had a big hand in creating. This is the structural and political reality of Medicare, where relatively speaking, passing attention is paid to who is eligible and what benefits and services are covered, and thousands of pages of statutory and regulatory text are devoted to paying the medical-industrial complex.

Similarly, as partially described earlier in the Part, a complex administrative and appellate procedure exists for contesting methods of payment and application of the method to particular providers. For example, below we discuss a wage index that has been used to adjust Medicare payments to hospitals. A complicated administrative procedure exists by which hospitals can obtain reclassification, and a special board—one of many in the administration of Medicare payment—exists for making such decisions.

Our purpose, then, is not to teach you details of payment but instead to teach you basic history and concepts. We believe that armed with this history and conceptual knowledge, you will then be able to master the details of any particular payment system.

Before proceeding to a more detailed discussion of Medicare's methods of paying hospitals and doctors, we briefly summarize some basic requirements of any type of payment system.

* * *

Attaining long-term financial and political stability and predictability requires that a compensation system be administratively simple and foster relatively cooperative relationships among patients, providers and payers, with institutionalized mechanisms for dispute resolution when cooperation ends. Constant strife without institutionalized means to resolve conflict only produces instability. Providers, particularly physicians, have remarkable power to cause massive disruptions of health care institutions like hospitals when they are extremely dissatisfied. They can even spark system-wide turmoil, whether in the form of actual strikes, such as occurred in some Canadian provinces, or the "backlash" that occurred against managed care in the United States, when providers and patients found common cause in the name of "freedom of choice," "quality" and what was framed as preservation of the provider/patient relationship.

The ideal compensation system is also part of long-term relationships between large pools of stably insured patients and large pools of providers. As we indicated, in advance no one can identify which patients will be sick, what those illnesses will be, who will treat them, and what goods and services will be necessary. One can make confident predictions across a pool of patients—and conversely across a pool of providers—and therefore the task of modern health care insurance is to link pools of potential patients, aka insured individuals (in an insurance system) or citizens (in a national health insurance system), with panels of a multitude of types of providers. If compensation is short-term as part of constantly changing relationships—like the ideal widget of simple microeconomic models in which all resources are instantaneously mobile so that they can flow without friction to highest valued use—then no one has any long-term incentives, much less long-term bonds that we describe with terms like "solidarity," "loyalty," and "commitment." Health care works best, then, when its provision is far away from the fragmented ideal of economic models—when payers, patients and providers are joined together for the long-haul in integrated pools such that there is continuity of care, incentives to invest in prevention, stability in revenue generation—one side of the "revenues = expenditures" equation—and stability in payment—the other side of the equation.

Notice that we use "best" in two senses: appropriate costs and quality. In an ideal system costs are controlled and set in some manner that accords with social value, whether that value be determined through markets or through democratic processes, a distinction about which for the moment we can be agnostic. Analogously, quality is appropriate both in the aggregate and at the level of each case, an enormous subject we explore in Part Three. For now, all we need to observe is that payment can affect both aspects of health care, but it is also crucial to separate the two analytically in discussing the merits of various payment methods. *See generally* White, *Targets and Systems of Health Care Cost Control.*

The ideal system also uses a pricing structure that reflects some degree of relative value among types of goods and services and the achievement of commonly held social values and goals. As one example, highly specialized care undoubtedly has great benefit and usually costs more to provide. Highly skilled orthopedists who specialize only in treatment of wrists can provide superior care for some types of wrist conditions than can orthopedists who do not so specialize, much less general surgeons. The training for such subspecialization is longer, and the expense is higher, as is the concomitant debt students most often accumulate. Specialized equipment is also necessary, and it is often more expensive. At the same time, a solid base of readily available primary care is essential for any health care system to provide cost-effective, high quality care; and for decades the United States has been a laggard in this regard. A key factor in this problem has been that relative to payment for specialty care; payment for primary care has been too low to attract medical students into this form of practice.

A payment system also needs mechanisms to bring norms to bear in the policing of outliers. Some variation in the goods and services provided for illness is to be expected given that illnesses "present" in whole persons who may share a common diagnosis but differ in other respects. We use the terms "comorbidities" and "complications" to encompass the whole of this variation; but those terms fail to capture the variation in life circumstances and the goals of the whole people in whom illnesses exist. Further, variations exist because technical capacity can differ from area to area; consensus regarding modality of treatment does not always exist; our tools to detect "variation" in care may be imprecise and so we incorrectly conclude that variation exists when it does not; and so on. While we examine these issues more fully below in Part Three, here we only note that sometimes gross variation from a professional norm indicates either poor quality, the need for remediation of the provider, or perhaps simple, rapacious behavior (we examine fraud in Part Four). Reimbursement systems must balance the need to make adequate comparisons—something we examine below as the necessity for "inter-institutional comparability"—the recognition that some variation is necessary to provide quality care, and the need to reign in providers who are simply operating beyond the pale.

Finally, with the exception of the United States, most systems also rely on some degree of control over human and capital resources, meaning the numbers and types of health professionals, health care institutions, and technologies deployed in society. Control over capacity is not "the answer" any more than control over price or utilization is "the answer." The task of controlling cost and policing quality is too multifaceted to be boiled down to "the answer." However, control over capacity remains a useful lever; in terms of the tools deployed internationally, the United States remains the outlier. We have relied much more on control at the "micro-level" of care, through such means as utilization review and selective contracting, but exercising control at the micro-level means that, in terms of controlling costs and preventing harm to patients, the horses have long left the barn (which by then is also burning, to mix metaphors).

Health care is relatively unique in that human and capital resources, once in existence, often find a way to be used—or to use themselves. As Professor Joseph White colorfully wrote, "to paraphrase the movie *Field of Dreams*, if you do not build it they cannot come." White, *Targets and Systems of Health Care Cost Control* at 659. This observation is an update of Roemer's Law, famously coined by pioneering physician and health services researcher Milton Roemer in 1961 when he wrote that a "built bed is a filled bed." Milton I. Roemer, *Bed Supply and Hospital Utilization: A*

Natural Experiment, 35 Hospitals 36 (Nov. 1, 1961). Most other countries have learned a lesson we have not, which is that it is often administratively easier and more feasible politically to regulate supply than it is to constrain its utilization after the fact. After all, in the end, controlling utilization means reducing someone's income, *see, e.g.,* Morris L. Barer et al., *It Ain't Necessarily So: The Cost Implications of Health Care Reform*, 13(4) Health Affairs 88, 95 (1994), and that means compelling either loss of investment or diminishing expected returns. Control over capacity, therefore, is one tool among many, and payment systems have a role to play in this regard too.

While some payment systems "work" better than others—again in the dual sense of setting resource expenditure and providing high quality of care—the unfortunate, simple truth of the matter is that all payment systems are flawed in some respect. We'll see, for example, that different systems use various "units of payment" as the basis of compensation. A hospital stay, for example, might be reimbursed based on the number of days the patient was in the hospital. Such a mechanism creates incentives to increase length of stay. That result may waste money and be harmful—iatrogenic—to patients. The hospital stay might be paid based on the primary diagnosis for which the patient was admitted. Such a mechanism creates incentives to game the diagnosis system or to discharge medically unstable patients or to discharge and readmit patients, thereby causing financial harm and poor quality care. A hospital also might be paid based on a projected annual budget, but such a scheme lacks a means to monitor activity on a smaller scale. This approach to payment could induce providers to furnish care that is too low in volume or intensity, with the result that patients may be harmed, as may society also in that too much money is expended for the care actually provided. The basic point is that because providers exercise discretion, they are able to use that discretion to increase their compensation through greater volume or intensity or to diminish the services for which a prospective payment has been made. Different systems provide different incentives but no system is airtight. That is the nature of the beast.

Further, payment systems, like all social practices, are not the result of rational planning. Rather, they are the products of what is handed down through historical accretion, boosted by the politics of the moment, particularly in the case of public insurance programs. Sometimes a rational intervention might be applied to change the contours of that flow, with expected and unexpected consequences. It is useful to think of the "design" of payment like flood control of a large river like the Mississippi. In many places and in many times we might prefer that the Mississippi flow elsewhere, be wider, be narrower, or flow more swiftly or more slowly, but at any moment, the river is what it is. We can build levees, dams, flow-ways and the like in various places, which will affect the flow in various ways—again, with some expected and some unexpected consequences—but we can never plot the course of the river from scratch in some grand design that gets exactly what we want (were it possible ever to know exactly what that is!). Like the mighty Mississippi, payment systems are epochal, with histories—and seemingly—wills of their own.

Finally, and probably most important, payment involves one inexorable law: one person's "cost" is another person's "payment," i.e., their income. This point is axiomatic: "One person's expenditure *is*, by definition, another's income; and many of the basic conflicts over health care policy flow from that ineluctable fact." Robert G. Evans, *Coarse Correction—And Way Off Target*, 22 J. HEALTH POL. POL'Y & L. 503, 504 (1997). It follows that, as Professor Uwe Reinhardt wrote in the 1980's, resource allocation to health care involves—on the one side—the transfer of services to patients, and—on the other—social and political processes that allocate lifestyles to providers. Uwe E. Reinhardt, *Resource Allocation in Health Care: The Allocation of Lifestyles to Providers*, 65 MILBANK Q. 153 (1987). Study after study has shown that the vast disparity between the dollars devoted to health care in the United States and the rest of the industrialized world is not accounted for so much in first part of that equation—the quantum and quality of services devoted to patients—but instead much more in the second—the prices paid to providers. *See, e.g.,* Victor R. Fuchs & James S. Hahn, *How Does Canada Do It? A Comparison of Expenditures for Physicians' Services in the United States and Canada*, 323 NEW ENG. J. MED. 884 (1990); Mark V. Pauly, *U.S. Health Care Costs: The Untold True Story*, 12(3) HEALTH AFFAIRS 152 (1993); Gerard F. Anderson et al., *It's the Prices, Stupid: Why the United States Is So Different from Other Countries*, 22(3) HEALTH AFFAIRS 89 (2003); Carlos Angrisono et al., *Accounting for the Cost of Health Care in the United States*, MCKINSEY GLOBAL INSTITUTE (2007), http://www. mckinsey.com/mgi/rp/healthcare/accounting_cost_healthcare.asp; Paul B. Ginsburg, *Reforming Provider Payment—The Price Side of the Equation*, 365 NEW ENG. J. MED. 1268 (2011); Miriam J. Laugesen & Sherry A. Glied, *Higher Fees Paid to US Physicians Drive Higher Spending for Physician Services Compared to Other Countries*, 30(9) HEALTH AFFAIRS 1647 (2011).

Thus, at its heart, payment is as much, if not more, about the allocation of power—both political and economic—as it is about technique. The United States has failed to assert countervailing power against providers because we have failed to consolidate payment into a "single-payer" or "all-payer" system. That simple fact is reflected in the history and contemporaneous condition of our payment system, which is completely fragmented. *See, e.g.,* Bruce C. Vladeck & Thomas Rice, *Market Failure and the Failure of Discourse: Facing Up to the Power of Sellers*, 28(5) HEALTH AFFAIRS 1305 (2009); Jonathan Oberlander & Joseph White, *Public Attitudes Toward Health Care Spending Aren't the Problem; Prices Are*, 28(5) HEALTH AFFAIRS 1285 (2009).

2. A BRIEF HISTORY OF (PROBLEMATIC) PAYMENT IN THE UNITED STATES

a. Retrospective Cost–Based Hospital Reimbursement

Hospital reimbursement began in the United States as hospitals took their modern form as centers of intensive technological care, for which third-party payment was necessary. Their growth as complex medical institutions moved them away from their religious and charitable roots, and their need for a payment model that was not dependent on cash at the point of care became increasingly evident. In Western Europe the sickness funds, fraternal societies organized largely around crafts and grounded in social solidarity and mutual aid, began to reimburse hospitals for care provided to their members. By contrast, in the United States the economic catastrophe of the Great Depression gave rise to the first Blue Cross nonprofit organizations, whose purpose was to ensure that the hospitals were paid. *See generally* SYLVIA A. LAW, BLUE CROSS: WHAT WENT WRONG? ch. 1 (2d ed. 1976). As private insurance spread, the flow of revenues grew, ultimately to be boosted mightily by the advent of public insurance.

The modern hospital is a fairly odd creature in modern capitalism. Its revenues derive almost entirely from payment by pools or collectives— government receipts and private insurers. Its product, if we can talk about a product at all, is extremely difficult to define and at best consists of a multitude of diverse goods and services which are extremely heterogeneous, a phenomenon we address in much greater deal in the antitrust chapter in Part Four. Moreover, the structure of a hospital in no way resembles the ideal-type of rational capitalist organization—that hierarchically organized firm in which authority flows down from the top through rational-legal bureaucracy. Rather, as will be discussed in Part Three, the organized medical staff, officers, trustees and others are independent power bases that sometimes cooperate and sometimes do not.

In the social security systems of Western Europe, none of these characteristics presented insuperable reimbursement problems. Hospitals had always been thought of as a unit, and they were reimbursed as a unit. A standard charge was calculated to be used for the increasingly fewer self-paying patients and for the increasingly more numerous third-party payers. There were always shortfalls after these payments—hospitals were not self-supporting organizations—and these shortfalls were made up by payments from charity and from government support in various forms. Since in these countries the basic unit to be reimbursed was the hospital, the task of hospital reimbursement was simply to divide up the pie and to give slices to the different payers.*

---

* This section draws on many comparative works. Particularly notable studies, although somewhat dated, of practices in numerous countries are JOSEPH WHITE, COMPETING SOLUTIONS: AMERICAN HEALTH CARE PROPOSALS AND INTERNATIONAL EXPERIENCE (1995), and the copious writings of William A. Glaser, including HEALTH INSURANCE IN PRACTICE: INTERNATIONAL VARIATIONS IN FINANCING, BENEFITS, AND PROBLEMS (1991); PAYING THE HOSPITAL: THE ORGANIZATION, DYNAMICS, AND EFFECTS OF DIFFERING FINANCIAL ARRANGEMENTS (1987); HEALTH INSURANCE BARGAINING: FOREIGN LESSONS FOR AMERICANS (1978) [hereinafter "GLASER, HEALTH INSURANCE BARGAINING"]; and PAYING THE DOCTOR: SYSTEMS OF REMUNERATION AND THEIR EFFECTS (1970).

Various units of payment for reimbursement may be chosen. Hospitals may be paid as a unit by use of a budget, on the basis of a day's worth of care, on the basis of numbers or types of cases, or based on the number of patients served. The crucial point here is that the unit of payment does not matter for attaining cost control nearly as much as whether payers and political authority are relatively united or fragmented, which is connected to the type of financing system, because the more fragmented the finance system, the harder the task of coordination among payers (which raises antitrust issues, a subject of Part Four). In fact, the unit of payment chosen itself reflects whether payment is relatively fragmented or united. Compared with the United States, the western European social security systems usually make relatively few entities responsible for paying a slice of hospital cost pie and, compared with payers in the United States, coordination among payers is grounded in an ethic of mutual support. Given the strong bonds of traditionalism that tied the sickness fund system together, the funds have been relatively stable, as has been the relationship among them. As a result, it was relatively uncontroversial simply to take a rough cut average across all patients in a hospital or group of hospitals, with every sickness fund paying on the basis of this average.

Thus, in many social security systems the basic unit of payment traditionally was a daily rate (known as a *per diem* rate). One takes the total operating costs of the hospital, divides it by the total number of patient-days of care the hospital provides, and gets an average charge for an average day in a hospital or in groups of hospitals. Alternatively, the mutual aid societies banded together, with or without government participation or sponsorship, and negotiated with a hospital or a group of hospitals over a budget for a hospital or group of hospitals for an upcoming year. That budget was the basis for what the hospital was paid as a whole. This approach has been stable and predictable, easy to administer, and relies on continuous relationships between groups and extant institutional mechanisms for resolving disputes.

Compared with the United States, this approach also has allowed a greater degree of cost control. Organizations of the sickness funds, and governments, have bargained with hospitals or hospital groups, and have been able to exert some pressure in holding down costs. In this context, use of a simple standard unit of payment that is fairly comparable across hospitals achieves cost control, stability and predictability. In this respect, the fact that a unit of payment like the per diem provides less than a perfect degree of comparability among hospitals has not been very important because there has been a relatively high degree of cooperation among hospitals and payers, who are relatively unified in their exertion of fiscal power.

The situation in the United States has been as different as night is to day. As we have discussed earlier in this Part, the payment "system" has been fragmented into a vast sea of public insurers and employer-sponsored health plans, with insurers operating in the individual coverage market thrown in for good measure. In contrast with the rest of the industrialized world, payers are neither unified into an all-payer or single-payer system, nor linked in long-term relationships with providers, with the rare exception of entities like Kaiser–Permanente, Group Health of Puget Sound, the Geisinger System, and a few others. Particularly with the entry of the commercial insurance sector as competitors against the Blue Cross organizations starting in the 1930's, in the United States the name of the game has been for payers to compete against each other in a fragmented payment and political system.

Regulation of hospital payment—or more precisely the lack thereof—has both been a cause of this fragmentation and has been driven by it. From the inception of hospital reimbursement in the United States in the 1930s, the name of the game for each insurer has been to pay less than everyone else. If an insurer pays less than its competitors, it can offer lower premiums and get more subscribers. Because unlike the social security systems, insurers failed to cooperate and political power was fragmented, no single insurer had the incentive or the power to force down costs. Instead, paying less meant that each insurer made sure that its allocation of the total costs of the hospital was as low as possible. Cost shifting, whether at the level of government, among organizations, or within an organization, is often a path of least resistance, *see, e.g.,* Robert G. Evans, *Tension, Compression, and Shear: Direction, Stresses, and Outcomes of Health Care Cost Control*, 15 J. HEALTH POL. POL'Y & L. 101 (1990). It's often easier to shift costs than to face down powerful interests, overcome problems of collective action, or challenge an organization's technical core.* Thus, very ironically, competition took the form of attempting to palm off costs onto one's competitors—cost shifting. As Professor Ted Marmor recently wrote, "The *fragmentation* of finance has meant that, once payers are aroused, the problem they separately address is that of their own costs, not of American medicine." Theodore R. Marmor, *American Health Care Policy and Politics: Is Fragmentation a Helpful Category for Understanding Health Reform Experience and Prospects?, in* THE FRAGMENTATION OF U.S. HEALTH CARE: CAUSES AND SOLUTIONS 343, 352 (Einer R. Elhauge, ed., 2010). For a relatively recent description of the cost-shifting game, *see, e.g.,* Uwe E. Reinhardt, *The Pricing of U.S. Hospital Services: Chaos Behind a Veil of Secrecy*, 25(1) HEALTH AFFAIRS 57 (2006).

An effective way to engage in cost-shifting was to splinter the hospital into a zillion different so-called "cost centers" and "revenue centers." Cost centers are just conventions used to allocate costs; one takes the joint costs of the hospital, which predominate, and allocates them to these centers. In the western European systems, cost centers have by and large been organized around the clinical departments: pediatrics, orthopedics, etc. Thus there was relatively more rationality in the cost accounting. Because

---

* Further, the effects run in the other direction too in that, as we discuss below, fragmentation in finance, payment and delivery are mutually reinforcing. Cost shifting is corrosive of social solidarity needed to create consolidated insurance, *see, e.g.,* Elizabeth Kilbreth, *Paying by the Rules: How Eliminating the Cost Shift Could Improve the Chances for Successful Health Care Reform*, 35 J. HEALTH POL. POL'Y & L. 177 (2010), a corrosive effect that is probably a barrier to consolidated payment and integrated delivery too.

the doctors organized care, and since different types of care were organized around the clinical departments, it is rational to allocate costs around the departments.

In the United States, however, the function of the cost accounting is to allocate costs among the relatively large number of payers, all of whom are pressuring the hospital to get a lower allocation than its competitors. The best way to engage in fancy, undetectable allocation is to use a large number of cost centers, and to use inconsistent methods of allocating costs to those centers. Thus a typical hospital might have had the following cost centers in the 1960s (the list would be much larger today): operating room; recovery room; delivery room & labor room; anesthesiology; radiology-diagnostic; radiology-therapeutic; radioisotope; laboratory; whole blood and packed red blood cells; blood storing, processing and transfusion; intravenous therapy; oxygen (inhalation) therapy; physical therapy; occupational therapy; speech pathology; electrocardiography; electroencephalography; medical supplies charged to patients; drugs charged to patients; renal dialysis; kidney acquisition. The end result is that there is a very fractionated, cumbersome system of accounting, with no standardization within a single hospital, much less among types of hospitals. *See, e.g.,* DONALD F. BECK, PRINCIPLES OF REIMBURSEMENT IN HEALTH CARE (1984).

Medicare stepped into this situation in the mid–1960s. Two very important points are worth noting. First, Medicare is not a universal insurance system; it provides benefits to a limited group in our society. Second, Medicare saw its role as paying just for its beneficiaries and making sure that it paid just for its beneficiaries—its "fair share." In other words, Medicare was going to play the same cost-accounting, cost-shifting game as everyone else had been playing so that as much cost as possible was paid by someone else. However, with the entry of Medicare, the game became far more intense. Although Medicare acted like just any other payer clamoring to pay only its fair share and no more, it obviously wasn't just some other payer. It was the federal government, and it had the largest pool of patients in tow—something like 20–40% depending on how one counted—and everyone knew that there was a strong possibility that Medicare would exercise its clout to get a good deal, thereby shifting substantial costs to private payers. The stakes of the game thus got much higher and more visible, since unlike the private sector, federal agencies and lawmakers were watching, cost increases were being published, and alarm bells thus were ostentatiously public.

Nonetheless, until roughly the 1980s, Medicare did relatively little to stop the total of its costs from growing. It was a claims-paying agency, in which decisions of doctors and hospitals just passed-through. *See, e.g.,* JUDITH M. FEDER, MEDICARE: THE POLITICS OF FEDERAL HOSPITAL INSURANCE (1977). Medicare did little to constrain that activity; it just played the shove-cost-to-someone-else game. *See, e.g.,* David M. Frankford, *The Complexity of Medicare's Hospital Reimbursement System: Paradoxes of Averaging*, 78 IOWA L. REV. 517 (1993) [hereinafter Frankford, *The Complexity of Medicare's Hospital Reimbursement System*].

However, in the late 70s and the early 80s the cost bubble burst. You will recall that we were then living an era of double-digit inflation to begin with, and hospital expenditures managed even to exceed that high rate of inflation. In that economic climate, one of a series of "crises" in the Medicare Part A Trust Fund occurred, see JONATHAN OBERLANDER, THE POLITICAL LIFE OF MEDICARE (2003), and Medicare finally moved to control its costs. Now we must stress that those words "control its costs" have a double meaning. Medicare continued to play the shove-off-costs-to-others-game, but, for the first time, it became serious about holding down its aggregate level of spending. Prospective payment in the United States was born.*

b.   Prospective DRG–Based Payment for Inpatient Hospital Services

Cost-based reimbursement was just that—cost-based. To be entitled to reimbursement, hospitals had to account for the costs they incurred, and once those costs were documented, they were paid retrospectively. The entire exercise was in essence simply a cost-accounting enterprise. As long as costs could be documented, they were paid. The reimbursement system was, in short, a blank check.

Prospective payment, by contrast, puts providers on a diet. Payment for an accounting period is set in advance and the prospective payment is made to stick. As we discuss below, the distinction between "retrospective reimbursement" and "prospective payment" is less than meets the eye because adjustments are often made in arrears, but there is still some beef to the distinction, for the question is one of degree: to what extent will payment be fixed in advance and to what extent will providers be forced to live within prospectively set means?

As might be expected, the United States has been exceptional in its method of setting payment prospectively. Any unit of payment could be used—although we'll see there are differences among them—for the key point is not the unit of payment, but the fact that payment is set and thereby limited in advance of the provision of services. Hence, as European systems shifted from cost-based reimbursement to prospective payment, they continued to use units of payment like the hospital budget or per diem allocations—we'll discuss more recent modifications below. As before, with fewer payers squabbling over their "fair share" of total payment and with greater cooperation among them—backed by the unified political power of the state—averaging was relatively noncontroversial.

In the United States, by contrast, the stakes were higher because of the fragmented payment system. Competing insurers, including Medicare as one competing payer among many, want to pay only for their patients—and no more. Further, they all want discounts to boot. To accomplish that,

---

* For an excellent discussion of the political and administrative shift from administering benefits and paying claims to controlling program costs, *see* JONATHAN OBERLANDER, THE POLITICAL LIFE OF MEDICARE ch. 5 (2003); *see also* Frankford, *The Complexity of Medicare's Hospital Reimbursement System*.

the dominant payer in the United States, Medicare, peers all the way down to the "case"—per-case reimbursement. Cost-shifting thereby got much more scientific—and much more intense. *See, e.g.,* RICK MAYES & ROBERT A. BERENSON, MEDICARE PROSPECTIVE PAYMENT AND THE SHAPING OF U.S. HEALTH CARE (2006) [hereinafter MAYES & BERENSON, MEDICARE PROSPECTIVE PAYMENT].

After some experimentation at the state level—experiments which were still incompletely evaluated at the time—in 1983 Congress enacted Medicare's inpatient prospective payment system ("IPPS").* Case-based payment is accomplished by categorizing patients into what were initially, when first implemented by Medicare in 1984, "diagnosis-related groups" ("DRGs"), and are now "Medicare severity-adjusted diagnosis-related groups" ("MS–DRGs"). The reason for the use of categories of patients is simple. If a payer were to pay what each patient actually costs, then the payment system would be retrospective, not prospective, and the payment system would again give a blank check to providers. To fix payment in advance, some standardized unit of payment must be calculated, and payment must be made on the basis of that standardized unit. That's how hospitals are made to stick with their diet—they are given a certain number of calories in advance and they must tailor care accordingly.

Prospective payment, American-style, is therefore grounded in averaging, just like all prospective payment must be grounded in averaging, but the averages used are set at the level of the case, rather than for an average day of care or for the annual budget of a type of hospital.** Upon discharge, each patients is categorized or "coded" into one of 335 "base DRGs"—e.g., "concussion"—most of which are divided into two or three subcategories that, for the most part, account for comorbidities or complications—e.g., "concussion without comorbidities or complications"; "concussion with comorbidities or complications"; "concussion with multiple comorbidities or complications." This categorization of illnesses yields a total of 751 MS–DRGs. Each of these categories is assigned a relative weight—.7297; .9809; and 1.6177, respectively for the concussion MS–DRGs—and thus effectively the entire array of DRGs constitutes a relative-value scale whereby different illnesses are ranked relative to each other, i.e., the relative value scale is supposed to be an index of severity of illness. Then, each year a

---

* The IPPS was the first and, for a number of years, the only prospective payment system, and therefore it was known simply as "PPS." It is now one of a large number prospective payment systems for a number of different providers—SNFs, home health agencies, ASCs, etc.—and so it is now known as the "IPPS."

** The current DRG-based prospective payment system for acute inpatient care is described in numerous sources, including the latest regulations, which at this writing were those for fiscal year 2012. *See* Dep't Health & Human Services, Centers for Medicare & Medicaid Services, Medicare Program; Proposed Changes to the Hospital Inpatient Prospective Payment System for Acute Care Hospitals and the Long–Term Care Hospital Prospective Payment System and Fiscal Year 2012 Rates, 76 Fed. Reg. 25,788 (May 5, 2011) [hereinafter *Proposed IPPS Rules for FY 2012*]; Dep't Health & Human Services, Centers for Medicare & Medicaid Services, Medicare Program; Hospital Inpatient Prospective Payment System for Acute Care Hospitals and the Long–Term Care Hospital Prospective Payment System and FY 2012 Rates; Hospitals' FTE Resident Caps for Graduate Medical Education Payment; Final Rules, 76 Fed. Reg. 51,476 (Aug. 18, 2011).

"conversion factor" is applied to the weight such that the amount to be paid for each illness is set in advance. Hospitals are supposed to stay within these fixed means. If they spend less than the norm for a particular patient, then they keep the surplus they are paid; if they spend more than the norm, they eat the shortfall. In the ideal, given a sufficient number of patients the overage and underage for particular patients wash out, and each hospital is paid an amount stipulated in advance adjusted for its mix of particular patients, as represented by the sum total of DRGs serviced—its "case mix."

To function in this manner as a means of measuring each hospital's case-mix, each DRG must represent a homogeneous group of patients, and concomitantly, a homogeneous use of resources for that type of patient both within a hospital and among diverse hospitals. In other words, each DRG, in the economist's way of thinking, represents a product of a hospital which is a multi-product firm. Costs are collected around each type of DRG, with the result that the DRGs (supposedly) provide uniform, standard, predictable, and clinically coherent units of comparison across all hospitals. The DRGs are then ranked into a hierarchy, which reflects the resources allocated to each type of case, or the hospital products. That's the manner by which the DRGs form a relative value scale. Then the payment for any discharge is derived from multiplying the weight against the average operating costs of the average case in the average hospital in the United States—the so-called "standardized payment amount" or "operating base payment rate."* The DRG multiplied by the operating base payment rate yields the average costs of the average case of that type in the average hospital. The sum total of DRGs for a given hospital represents its case mix compared with the case mixes of other hospitals. Hence, the sum total of its DRGs times the standardized payment amount equals precisely the amount of resources that should be expended as an average across all hospitals. Voila: perfect inter-institutional comparability (particularly compared with those crude averages like the per diem or budget used in less technically "advanced" systems):

> Payment on the basis of a per-case rate for each DRG is intended to create specific financial incentives that encourage hospital management to adopt desirable methods of controlling the cost of care. It was hoped that hospital management, facing a separate payment rate per discharge for each DRG, would have strong incentives to: (1) improve productivity; (2) use less expensive inputs where possible; (3) influence physicians to reduce the length of stay, limit the volume of inpatient services, and use a less expensive mix of services to treat each patient; (4) specialize in treating types of cases the hospital can produce efficiently; and (5)

---

* Actually, there are two base payment rates, one for operating costs and one for capital. For simplicity we ignore the latter although this separation has caused problems as hospitals try to shift money from "operating expenses" to "capital expenditures" in their accounting systems.

adopt cost-reducing technologies, while avoiding cost-increasing technologies.

PROSPECTIVE PAYMENT ASSESSMENT COMMISSION ("PROPAC"), REPORT AND REC-OMMENDATIONS TO THE DEPARTMENT OF HEALTH AND HUMAN SERVICES 16 (Mar. 1, 1990). *See generally* David M. Frankford, *The Medicare DRGs: Efficiency and Organizational Rationality*, 10 YALE J. REG. 273 (1993) [hereinafter Frankford, T*he Medicare DRGs*].*

If only the health care payment and health care could be made scientifically simple through use of Ockham's Razor.**

(1). The annual complexity of payment. The first layer of complexity stems from the fact that the classification system yields national averages, which are then applied to the delivery of health care, which is largely local and occurs within a diversity of hospitals across the United States, a large, heterogeneous geographic area. As a consequence, numerous adjustments for types of hospitals, local variation, differences among types of cases, and so on are made. It is the use of national averages as the basis of payment that spawns a complex system to take into account enormous variation, in a form of "rough justice" in reimbursement. SEE MAYES & BERENSON, MEDICARE PROSPECTIVE PAYMENT at 60–63; *see also* Frankford, *The Complexity of Medicare's Hospital Reimbursement System.*

The concept of the prospective payment system was simple. The DRGs "explain" in statistical terms a fairly large percentage of cost variation in treating different kinds of cases, meaning that each DRG represents severity of illness, something supposedly beyond the control of hospitals.*** Some portion of the variation "unexplained" by the DRGs could be accounted for statistically in different ways: some was the result of labor costs, some the result of the fact that patients in teaching hospitals are sicker than average, some attributable to the fact that poor patients are sicker than average, and so on. These factors also are supposedly beyond

---

* You can see, then, that the DRG-based reimbursement system was instituted, not just to cap expenditures, but also to spur hospitals to act as rational profit-maximizers. For a critique of the heroic assumptions regarding organizational behavior, *see* Frankford, *The Medicare DRGs.*

** All things being equal, simpler is better than more complicated.

*** In 1982, two analysts at HCFA, Julian Pettengill and Jules Vertrees studied a sample comprised of 1.93 million Medicare inpatient hospital discharges in 1979 from 5,947 short-stay hospitals. The sample in turn comprised 20% of all such discharges in that year. Their study combined diagnosis, categorized by DRG, with several hospital characteristics into a causal model that would "explain" the variations observed in the treatment of all Medicare patients. They reported that this model could account for far more cost variation than had ever been achieved before. Based on this sample and the differentiation of the discharges through use of the 467 DRGs, Pettengill and Vertrees concluded that their model accounted for 72% of the variation in the Medicare cost per case. *See* Julian Pettengill & James Vertrees, *Reliability and Validity in Hospital Case–Mix Measurement*, 4 HEALTH CARE FINANCING REV. 101, 113 (Dec. 1982). The role of the Pettengill–Vertrees study in the adoption of the DRGs as a case-mix measure is discussed in DAVID G. SMITH, PAYING FOR MEDICARE: THE POLITICS OF REFORM 34–35 (1992) [hereinafter SMITH, PAYING FOR MEDICARE].

the control of hospitals, but any other sources of unexplained variation are within their control (and therefore can be excised as "fat").

The system, therefore, requires three basic calculations. First, as described above, types of cases have to be arrayed in terms of their severity. The DRGs serve that purpose. Second, costs must be stripped down to an average cost for an average case in an average hospital. That's the role of the base payment rate, which, when Medicare was implemented in 1983, was constructed from the actual historical cost experience of individual hospitals during a "base-year period." These individual costs were "standardized" to eliminate the recognized factors—local labor wages, the higher per-case costs correlated with teaching, the costs of caring for the poor, etc.—which would cause a hospital's actual historical cost experience to vary from the average case. These factors were quantified and subtracted from each individual hospital's costs, which then were aggregated to yield an average cost—the standardized payment amount—representing the average cost of the average case in the average hospital. Third, these factors of "uncontrollable variation" are then given back, where appropriate, as payment "add-ons."

In very simplified form, then, the sequence of calculations goes like this (illustrated graphically in the figure below). In order to account for wage variations among different localities, the base payment rate, the standardized payment amount, is separated into two portions, a labor-related part and a non-labor-related part. The labor-related portion is then adjusted by a wage index applicable to the area in which a hospital is located (yielding the "base rate adjusted for geographic factors"). The sum of the non-labor portion of the base rate and the portion adjusted for geographic factors—the labor-related portion adjusted by the wage index—is then multiplied by the MS–DRG weight for the case's relevant DRG. The result, the "adjusted base payment rate"—see the top half of the figure below—is then the payment for the type of case, unless an add-on applies—the add-ons are illustrated by the bottom half of the figure.

The most important add-ons are the following:

Disproportionate Share Hospitals ("DSH"). If the hospital serves a certain percentage of defined low-income persons, Medicare pays a percentage add-on for serving those patients. Hospitals that receive this add-on payment qualify by virtue of one of two statutorily provided formulae and are known as "disproportionate share hospitals" ("DSH"). State Medicaid programs also make DSH payments, but add-on payments for treating high levels of low income patients are, of course, unheard of in the private insurance market.

Indirect medical education adjustment ("IME"). If the hospital meets the definition of a teaching hospital, Medicare pays an add-on for its "indirect medical expenses"—the "IME adjustment"—which are the higher per-case expenses associated with the patient population of teaching facilities. State Medicaid programs also may pay IME costs. Again, this is unheard of in the private insurance market.

New technology adjustment. If the case involves a new technology or new service that is a substantial improvement over technologies or services otherwise available that, absent an add-on, would be inadequately compensated under the DRG-based payment, then Medicare allows an add-on for technology. Again, this type of policy is unique to Medicare.

Outlier payment. If a case is unusually expensive and meets the definition of an "outlier case," then Medicare applies another add-on. By contrast, other costs, like the direct costs of graduate medical education (e.g., time spent in instruction) (GME), are taken out of the system completely and paid separately. The GME payments are derived from hospital-specific costs per resident in a base year, although currently they are capped at hospitals with amounts above 140 percent of the national average.

Finally—and we're still explicating a very simplified version of the basic calculation—the system takes into account the fact that hospitals sometimes transfer patients after a short stay. When a patient's length of stay is at least one day less than the geographic mean length of stay for the MS–DRG and the patient is transferred to another acute care hospital or, for a limited number of MS–DRGs, to a post-acute-care facility—e.g., a skilled nursing facility ("SNF"), then the hospital is reimbursed based on a per diem rate, not the full DRG-based payment.

In sum, the calculation of payment looked like the following for fiscal year 2011, as shown by a figure from the website of the Medicare Payment Advisory Committee ("MedPAC"), which advises Congress on Medicare payment (MEDPAC, HOSPITAL ACUTE INPATIENT SERVICES PAYMENT SYSTEM at 2 (Oct. 2011)) (http://www.medpac.gov/documents/MedPAC_Payment_Basics_11_hospital.pdf):

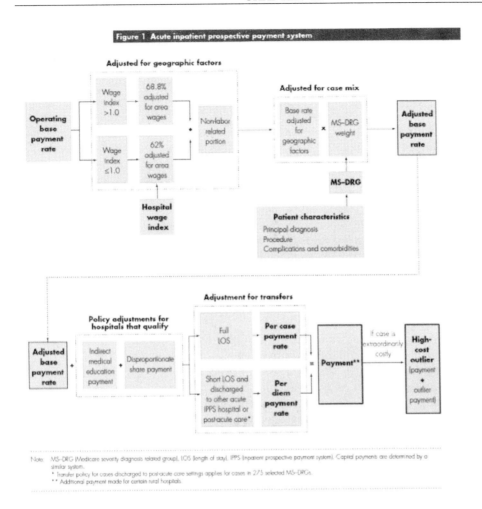

Figure 1 Acute inpatient prospective payment system

Note: MS-DRG (Medicare severity diagnosis related group), LOS (length of stay), IPPS (Inpatient prospective payment system). Capital payments are determined by a similar system.
   * Transfer policy for cases discharged to post-acute care settings applies for cases in 275 selected MS-DRGs.
   ** Additional payment made for certain rural hospitals.

Each step in this complex calculation can itself be extremely complicated and controversial and has given rise to a vast amount of litigation. We illustrate this point by discussing the wage index—just one example of the multitude of illustrations we could use to demonstrate complexity and controversy. As we noted, the adjustment of the labor-related portion of the standardized payment amount accounts for variations in local labor conditions by means of the wage index. The wage index is supposed to indicate how the price of labor in a wage labor area compares to the average price of labor nationwide. The index uses 1.0 as the mean, i.e., there is effectively no adjustment up or down to the average payment. Wage labor areas with wages above the national average, e.g., New York City, are assigned an index figure greater than 1.0, i.e., an adjustment, to varying degrees, upward. Wage labor areas with wages below the national average, e.g., Wyoming, are assigned an index figure less than 1.0, i.e., an adjustment, again in varying degrees, downward. For fiscal year 2011, as reflected in the figure above, CMS had calculated that 68.8% of the base payment rate was comprised of labor-related expenses for hospitals with a wage index above 1.0; and Congress had set the labor-related portion of the standard-ized payment amount at 62% for hospitals with a wage index below 1.0. *See* 42 U.S.C. § 1395ww(d)(3)(E)(ii).* That adjustment supposedly measures, accurately, the labor-wage price variation among hospitals, a factor over which they have no control—it's the higher cost of housing in New York, for example—and for which they should be compensated.

To understate, the "accuracy" of the wage-labor adjustment has been particularly controversial and well litigated because substantial amounts of money can ride on the index applied to a particular hospital. Four aspects have proved particularly nettlesome. First, hospitals located near the border of a labor area—particularly hospitals in rural areas adjacent to metropolitan ones—have often claimed that the price of their labor is more represented by the labor wage areas to which they are adjacent, not the ones in which they are located. The somewhat arbitrary lines drawn at the boundaries separating areas have been characterized as "wage cliffs." As a consequence, over time administratively cumbersome reclassifications and exceptions have developed that have either reclassified hospitals or allowed hospitals to challenge their classifications. *See, e.g.,* 42 U.S.C. § 1395ww(d)(8)(B), (d)(10).

Second, labor costs in an area might differ from the national average because of the mix of labor inputs used, e.g., a higher ratio of RNs to LPNs, not because wages in the area are different. It has been claimed that the wage index does not account adequately for the mix of labor inputs because it does not adjust adequately for skill level or sufficiently cover relevant occupational groups, and controversy exists over what mix of labor inputs should constitute the norm. Third, it has been claimed that the wage index has not adequately accounted for non-cash forms of remuneration, particu-larly benefits like pensions. Fourth, it has been claimed that the method used to calculate the wage index has a perverse effect, particularly if a hospital is dominant in a geographic area. If such a hospital were to put downward pressures on its wages, then the index applied to it could fall and it would be penalized; conversely, if its wages increased, then the index applied to it would increase and it would be rewarded. The wage index, it is said, has no means to account for such circularity. *See* PPACA, Pub. L. No. 111–148 § 3137(b) (2010) (mandating submission of plan for new wage index to solve these problems). *See generally* MEDPAC, REPORT TO THE CONGRESS: PROMOTING GREATER EFFICIENCY IN MEDICARE 127–31 (June 2007), http://www.medpac.gov/documents/jun07_entirereport.pdf; Thomas MaCur-dy et al., *Revision of Medicare Wage Index,* ACUMENT, LLC (Apr. 2009), https://www.cms.gov/AcuteInpatientPPS/downloads/Acumen_Study_on_Wage_Index.zip; Margaret Edmunds & Frank A. Sloan, eds., *Geographic Adjustment in Medicare Payment Phase I: Improving Accuracy*, INSTITUTE OF MEDICINE (2d ed., Sept. 28, 2011), http://www.iom.edu/Reports/2011/Geographic–Adjustment-in-Medicare–Payment–Phase–I–Improving–Accuracy.aspx.

---

* The proportions for fiscal year 2012 will be the same. *See* Proposed IPPS Rules for FY 2012 at 25,889–90.

Similar complication and controversy attend each element of the figure above: the DSH payments; the IME adjustment; the add-on for new technologies; the policies regarding transfers; the manner in which outliers are defined and paid; etc. We could fill a book describing these issues.

(2). The complexity over time. Thus far, we have explicated the complexity of the payment calculation for just one year. The second level of complexity stems from the fact that each year the entire system must be updated. The two major tasks are updating the standardized payment amount and "recalibrating" the DRG weights.

As we described above, when the IPPS was implemented in 1984, the standardized payment amount was constructed from the actual historical cost experience of individual hospitals during a "base-year period." It was expected that the historicity of the base payment amount would fade with time. In theory it could be updated annually in a scientific manner devoid of politics (or anything else) such that the payment system would reflect only the efficient payment of cases calibrated by their severity, i.e., the DRGs. This expectation is a perfect example of the American faith in technocratic fixes as a means to avoid tough political and economic choices.* *See, e.g.,* David M. Frankford, *Measuring Health Care: Political Fate and Technocratic Reform*, 19 J. HEALTH POL. POL'Y & L. 647 (1994) [hereinafter Frankford, *Measuring Health Care*]. *See generally* James A. Morone, *American Political Culture and the Search for Lessons from Abroad*, 15 J. HEALTH POL. POL'Y & L. 129 (1990); Gary A. Belkin, *The Technocratic Wish: Making Sense and Finding Power in the "Managed" Medical Marketplace*, 22 J. HEALTH POL. POL'Y & L. 509 (1997). The reality has not matched the theory.

The basic idea has been to update the standardized payment amount by "forecasting" the legitimate rate of "inflation" for the upcoming year. The basic means to predict inflation has been to use forecasted changes in the "market basket index," a proxy for the costs of hospital inputs, coupled with an additional number, which has been called the "discretionary adjustment factor," that supposedly accounts for changes in technology, productivity and case mix. Neither part of the update has been "automatic," devoid of distributional choices.

The hospital market basket:

is constructed by (a) specifying the inputs that hospitals purchase, (b) determining a weight for each component that represents its share of hospital expenses, (c) identifying proxy measures of price change for each input, and (d) forecasting price changes. The overall change in the price of the market basket is computed by

---

* "Diderot, the French Encyclopedist and philosopher, is credited with the slogan, 'Despotism and statistics cannot coexist.' This slogan rested on the kind of optimistic belief shared by many who helped design and implement [PPS]: that a fair and technically sound system of hospital payments could be designed, would win assent and be enacted into law, and could be administered without being destroyed by 'politics.' " SMITH, PAYING FOR MEDICARE at 71–72; *see id.* at 4, 11, 84, 86, 100, 106, 232–33, 246–47.

multiplying each component's price change by its weight, and summing across all components.

PROPAC, TECHNICAL APPENDIXES TO THE REPORT AND RECOMMENDATIONS TO THE SECRETARY, DEPARTMENT OF HEALTH AND HUMAN SERVICES 27 (April 1985). The market basket is a "fixed-weight price index," which means that it relies on weights calculated from the mix of goods and services used in a base year, and it is then updated periodically for inflation in those goods and services as originally weighted. The index is therefore not sensitive to changes either in the mix or quality of goods and services used, and periodically it must be rebased and reweighted to account for such changes.

The key point here is to focus on part "(c)," which is "identifying proxy measures of price change for each input." If the update relied just on actual price changes for hospital inputs, the prospective payment system would be prospective no more. Hospitals would determine the inputs they use and the prices at which those inputs would be purchased, and these decisions would just pass through the index—retrospective cost-based reimbursement once again.

As a result, the index is a "normative price index" in that "the PPS index is an approximation of *what hospital care price changes would be if demand and supply were determined in efficient markets*. In principle, basing Medicare payments on these normative indices means that CMS is subsidizing only that part of health care cost increases that actually reflects increases in consumer welfare." Global Insights, Inc., *Hospital Compensation Costs: An Analysis of Escalation in ECI Wage and Benefit Costs Indices Relative to PPS Proxies*, PREPARED FOR CMS OFFICE OF THE ACTUARY 4 (Sept. 2002), https://www.cms.gov/MedicareProgramRatesStats/downloads/wage studyfinal.pdf. In other words, the market basket index represents, quite simply, a political decision by CMS and Congress regarding how much Medicare will pay, in an upcoming period, for hospital inputs. *See* 42 U.S.C. § 1395(b)(3)(B). *See also* PPACA § 3401(a) (mandating a partial reduction to the standardized payment amount based on a 10–year economy-wide index of private, non-farm factor costs).

The other component of the update to the standardized payment amount, the "discretionary adjustment factor," is similar. In the annual MedPAC reports and CMS analyses, one finds consideration of whether payments are adequate. The factors canvassed have included at various times: beneficiaries' access to care (e.g., number of hospitals and beds, growth of specialized services, volume of services, hospitals' access to capital); quality of care (e.g., safety indicators; satisfaction measures; readmission rates); new technologies; changes in site of care; coding behavior; changes in productivity; provider costs; Medicare margins; total margins; projected costs and margins; prior under or overpayments; "one-time factors"; and the general health care environment. These considerations are stirred in a pot—a report—and out pops a recommendation, e.g.:

> In considering its update recommendation, the Commission has struck a balance between a number of competing factors. On the one hand, average total Medicare margins are negative (–5

percent in 2009 and projected to reach –7 percent in 2011). On the other hand, our update framework indicators (access to care, including supply and service volume; quality of care; and access to capital) are positive. Furthermore, the negative Medicare margins are due at least in part to the lack of private financial pressure for cost containment, and the set of hospitals identified as efficient have a median Medicare margin of about 3 percent. On the basis of these circumstances, the Commission contemplated an update of 2.5 percent.

However, two additional considerations led the Commission to its recommended update of 1 percent. For inpatient services, the Commission and others have documented past and ongoing over-payments resulting from changes in documentation and coding after implementation of MS–DRGs in 2008. Current law does not allow full recovery of past overpayments and no action has been taken to stop the ongoing overpayments. The Commission believes that all overpayments should be recovered and that the most urgent step is to stop the ongoing overpayments. To accomplish this objective, the Commission would reduce the ongoing overpay-ment by 1.5 percentage points—that is, the difference between its contemplated update of 2.5 percent and its recommended update of 1 percent. This adjustment would account for 1.5 percentage points of the 3.9 percent adjustment needed to fully prevent accumulation of further overpayments.

MEDPAC, REPORT TO THE CONGRESS: MEDICARE PAYMENT POLICY 60 (March 2011), http://www.medpac.gov/documents/mar11_entirereport.pdf [hereinaf-ter MEDPAC MARCH 2011 REPORT]. *See generally* Frankford, *The Complexity of Medicare's Hospital Reimbursement System* at 618–35.

This is simply a very, very global budget. It is a political judgment how much money should be devoted to Medicare hospitals nationwide for acute inpatient care. This extremely macro-judgment is then drilled down to the individual hospital and to the individual case through the complex mecha-nisms of the IPPS.

(3).   Categories of special hospitals. The third complication is that a diversity of types of hospitals, predominantly rural, are carved out and accorded special, preferential but varying treatment: rural referral centers; critical access hospitals; sole community hospitals; Medicare-dependent hospitals; and low-volume hospitals. Rural referral centers are high-volume rural hospitals to which other hospitals and non-staff physicians refer patients for relatively sophisticated treatment. *See* 42 U.S.C. § 1395ww(d)(5)(C). Such hospitals receive preferable treatment for DSH payments and for geographic classification. *See* Proposed IPPS Rules for FY 2012 at 25,937–38. Critical access hospitals, which are reimbursed for 101% of their reasonable costs, *see* 42 U.S.C. § 1395f(*l*)(1), are small, usually geographically remote facilities that have no more than twenty-five beds. They must provide 24–hour emergency services, have an average length of stay of 96 hours or less, be more than 35 miles (or 15 miles in mountainous

terrain) from the nearest hospital, or be designated by its state as a "necessary provider." *See id.* § 1395i–4(c)(2)(B).

Sole community hospitals receive the higher of the regular IPPS payment or a hospital-specific rate based on their costs in a base year (the highest of fiscal years 1982, 1987, 1996 or 2006). *See id.* § 1395(d)(5)(D)(i). To be defined as a sole community hospital, the facility must be located more than 35 road miles from another hospital or, by reason of factors such as isolated location, or weather or travel conditions, the hospital is the sole source of hospital inpatient services reasonably available to Medicare beneficiaries. *See id.* § 1395ww(d)(5)(D)(iii). A Medicare-dependent hospital is a hospital located in a rural area that has no more than 100 beds and is not a sole community hospital, and has a high percentage of Medicare discharges (not less than 60 percent of its inpatient days or discharges). *See id.* § 1395ww(d)(5)(G)(iv). Such a hospital is paid the higher of the regular IPPS payment or the regular payment plus 75 percent of the amount by which the regular payment is exceeded by the highest of its fiscal year 1982, 1987 or 2002 hospital-specific cost-based rate. *See id.* § 1395ww(d)(5)(G)(i)–(ii). Finally, a low-volume hospital is located more than 15 road miles from another facility and has fewer than 1600 Medicare discharges in a year. Low-volume hospitals are entitled to an add-on payment. *See id.* § 1395ww(d)(12).

(4). Measuring case mix initially and over time. The final—at least as space allows—and probably most important complication has been the capacity of the classifications themselves, the DRGs. One of us has previously characterized the task at hand as follows:

> The DRG weights and hospital case-mix indices were designed to measure the resources actually used for different types of patients in different kinds of hospitals. As such, they were also supposed to account for the severity of illness. The inferential chain connecting these two goals—linking measurement with actual resource use and then with severity of illness—is long and attenuated: (1) the data "reflect" the use of resources; (2) the use of resources is rationally organized around types of cases; and (3) the types of cases are expressions of underlying types and degrees of illnesses. More fully, four conditions would have to be satisfied. First, HCFA's [now CMS's] assignment of costs to each DRG, leading to the original DRG weights, must have "accurately reflected" actual patterns of resource use. Second, this "accuracy in reflection" must be maintained over time through changes in the classification system and the associated weights and indices. Third, the classification scheme itself—the DRGs—in combination with the various factors used in standardization must "accurately reflect" the underlying patterns of resource use. Stated differently, either the DRGs are completely "homogeneous" in that all patients in each DRG evoke exactly the same use of resources, or the variations that remain are completely explained by the other variables used—the adjustments for variations due to different

wages, the indirect costs of teaching activities, the special costs associated with indigent patients, and the removal of outlier cases. Fourth and finally, the practice patterns commanding the flow of resources must "reflect" an underlying type and severity of illness.

Frankford, *The Complexity of the Medicare DRGs* at 635–36.

For a number of reasons these conditions have been in doubt for decades. First, until very recently the weights were derived from hospitals' billed charges, rather than costs. Given variations in accounting among hospitals, the relationship between charges and costs varies. Some weights, therefore, have been too high and some too low. Second, the prevalence of high-cost outliers in some DRGs has distorted the weights for those DRGs. Third, research showed that the DRGs just were not homogeneous; significant variation existed among patients coded within the same DRG—so-called "within-DRG severity"—because of factors like age, comorbidities and complications. As a result, in 1991, Dr. Bruce C. Vladeck, a former Medicare administrator, could observe:

> The tighter that payment rates get relative to costs and the more that is learned about the system, the more it appears that hospitals suffer or prosper under [prospective payment] for reasons at least partially outside their control. The root problem lies in the system of uniform national rates tied to measures of case-mix. These measures are far superior than any other available tool to measure hospital outputs, but they are still far from adequate as the basis for the kind of system [prospective payment] has created. As reasonably homogeneous measures of what hospitals produce, DRGs are getting better all the time, but they simply are not that good. At least, DRGs are not good enough to support a system of flat rates.

Bruce C. Vladeck, *Medicare's Prospective Payment System at Age Eight: Mature Success or Midlife Crisis?*, 14 U. Puget Sound L. Rev. 453, 479–80 (1991).*

As early as 1992, ProPAC, the predecessor Congressional agency to MedPAC's advisory role with regard to the IPPS, signaled that perhaps major refinements to the DRGs were needed, *see* ProPAC, Report and Recommendations to the Congress 46–47 (March 1992); and in 1995 it recommended that significant changes be made. *See* ProPAC, Report and Recommendations to the Congress 44–47 (March 1995). However, after

---

* This view was shared by Judith Lave, who was the Director of HCFA's Office of Research from 1980 to 1982. *See* Judith R. Lave et al., *A Proposal for Incentive Reimbursement for Hospitals*, 11 Med. Care 79, 85–89 (1973) (proposing the use of a case-adjusted per-case reimbursement system with cost sharing between the government and a hospital for deviations from the per-case rate, and with periodic readjustment to account for technological change); Judith R. Lave, *Hospital Reimbursement Under Medicare*, 62 Milbank Memorial Fund Q. 251, 254–56 (1984) (recommending the immediate abandonment of the use of national rates); Judith R. Lave, *The Impact of the Medicare Prospective Payment System and Recommendations for Change*, 7 Yale J. on Reg. 499, 521–27 (1990) (recommending various changes to reduce the reliance upon national rates).

internal experimentation with severity-adjusted DRGs, HCFA declined to adopt any changes, stating that it could not accurately predict the effects that would be caused by switching to the new classification system. *See* Dep't Health & Human Services, Health Care Financing Administration, Medicare Program; Changes to the Hospital Inpatient Prospective Payment Systems and Fiscal Year 1995 Rates, 59 Fed. Reg. 27,708, 27,715–16 (May 27, 1994); Dep't Health & Human Services, Health Care Financing Administration, Medicare Program; Changes to the Hospital Inpatient Prospective Payment Systems and Fiscal Year 1996 Rates; Proposed Rule, 60 Fed. Reg. 29,202, 29,209, 29,246–47 (June 2, 1995). MedPAC renewed its recommendation in its March and June 2000 reports, largely in the context of its assessment of payment to teaching hospitals. *See* MedPAC, REPORT TO THE CONGRESS: MEDICARE PAYMENT POLICY 71–80 (March 2000); MedPAC, REPORT TO THE CONGRESS: SELECTED MEDICARE ISSUES ch. 3 (June 2000). Again no change occurred, perhaps because of the perception that teaching hospitals were faring rather well under the IPPS, and because the uneven distributional effects of any changes divided the hospital industry.

It was not until the middle portion of this past decade (2000–2010) that change finally came. When it did arrive, the issue was no longer some technocratic fight over the number of standard deviations within a single DRG. Instead the debate got fired with jet fuel, because it became entangled with the growth of physician-owned specialty hospitals. According to general community hospitals, these newcomers were cherry-picking lucrative areas like heart surgery and types of orthopedic surgery—and they were enriching their surgeon-owners who were, it was claimed, churning volume at the facilities to increase the revenue from their ownership interests. At this point the hospital industry could unite around the need for refinement of the DRGs to stave off the (despicable) competition of doctor-owned specialty hospitals.

Congress first acted in 2003 by imposing an 18–month moratorium during which physician-investors in new specialty hospitals could not refer Medicare or Medicaid patients to those hospitals. This moratorium effectively halted development of new ones. Further, Congress ordered both MedPAC and the Secretary of HHS to study the issues raised. *See* Medicare Prescription Drug, Improvement, and Modernization Act of 2003, Pub. L. No. 108–173, § 507.

MedPAC's report, issued in 2005 to satisfy the Congressional mandate, could hardly have been more categorical regarding the effect of the relevant DRGs. MedPAC found that cardiac specialty hospitals were specializing in cardiac surgical DRGs that were relatively more profitable than the average DRG and ones in which payment exceeded cost. Moreover, both the cardiac and orthopedic surgical hospitals were taking advantage of the fact the DRGs in which they were specializing failed to account for within-DRG severity of illness. Because for these types of illness severity is observable and predictable, the specialty hospitals were selecting the less severely ill patients—the ones in which the margins were highest because for those cases the payment to cost ratios were the greatest. The conclusions regarding the problems with the DRGs were starkly presented:

> ● *The DRG definitions.* The DRG definitions fail to adequately isolate differences in severity of illness associated with substantial differences in the cost of hospital inpatient care.

> ● *The DRG relative weights.* The relative weights appear to over- or understate the expected relative costliness of treatment for typical cases in the DRGs due to differences in charge-setting practices across and within hospitals and differences in the level of costs across hospitals.

> ● *The outlier policy.* The extraordinary charges associated with outlier cases appear to inflate the relative weights for DRGs with a disproportionate share of outliers.

MEDPAC, REPORT TO THE CONGRESS: PHYSICIAN-OWNED SPECIALTY HOSPITALS 36 (MARCH 2005).

Recall that one of the reasons for adopting per-case reimbursement—rather than using a larger unit of payment such as a per diem or a hospital budget—was to create incentives for specialization. The growth of the specialty hospitals in part represented specialization with a vengeance.* Although MedPAC recommended that the DRGs be improved by adding severity-of-illness indicators, that the weights be improved by rebasing them on estimated costs, not charges, and that outliers be removed from the calculation of some DRG weights, it also indicated that adverse selection against Medicare will remain endemic to per-case payment:

> [O]pportunities for selection never fully disappear for two reasons. First, our profitability measure is an average for each severity-adjusted DRG category, based on Medicare cost report data that may differ from a hospital's own cost accounting data. Second, physicians always know more than CMS about individual patients' expected costs.

Id. at 38.

CMS has responded by phasing in the recommended changes over a number of years. It rebased the weights based on costs and added severity levels. The result was, as noted above, the differentiation of the original DRGs into the current 751 MS–DRGs. *See, e.g.,* Proposed IPPS Rules for FY 2012 at 25,797–81, 25,808–10; Dep't of Health & Human Services, Centers for Medicare & Medicaid Services, Medicare Program; Changes to

---

* The reason for the caveat "in part" is that another possible reason for the growth of these hospitals was that physician-owners could profit by "self-referring" their own patients there for procedures. This issue is one of those covered in the fraud chapter in Part Four below. MedPAC found that specialty hospitals did not lower costs. *See also* MEDPAC, REPORT TO THE CONGRESS: PHYSICIAN-OWNED SPECIALTY HOSPITALS REVISITED (Aug. 2006). In the PPACA Congress banned physician-owned hospitals created after December 31, 2010, from Medicare participation and proscribed the expansion of existing ones except in narrowly prescribed circumstances. *See* PPACA, Pub. L. No. 111–148 § 6001 (2010).

the Hospital Inpatient Prospective Payment Systems and Fiscal Year 2008 Rates, Final Rule, 47,130, 47,138–200 (Aug. 27, 2007).

However, the result of these changes was easily predictable—in fact it had been predicted. As hospitals became better acquainted with the new MS–DRGs, they changed their procedures for documentation and coding, with the result that there was an upward "creep" in the DRGs into which patients were classified. The resultant "overpayment" has spurred both regulatory and Congressional responses to reduce the standardized payment amount to "recoup" the overpayments. The basic task is to figure how much of the upward creep reflects "real" changes in severity of illness and how much is an artifact of changes to the coding system. *See, e.g.,* Proposed IPPS Rules for FY 2012 at 25,801–05. Needless to say, substantial money has probably been redistributed among hospitals.

These recent issues bring forth a strong feeling of déjà vu. Writing in 1992, one of us canvassed identical issues that occurred in the early years of the DRG-based per-case payment system and noted the conceptual muddle that still pertains. The system is based on a notion of "accuracy" in that it attempts to track "real" changes, as noted above. Yet if it tracks "real" changes in hospital behavior, then it becomes, again, a system of cost-based, retrospective reimbursement, albeit an enormously complex one. To preclude that result, a complicated, technical process is invoked to identify in reported data the "real" or "efficient" or "true" costs, which itself is hypothecation: how a hypothetical hospital would perform in a hypothetical market free of the "distortions" that characterize the actual markets that exist in health care. Given this process, it is not clear what "accuracy" could possibly mean other than that federal officials are ultimately deciding how much resources to inject into the health care sector for Medicare patients: "The word 'real' thus has an unintended double meaning: (1) 'real' in the sense that a phenomenon occurs independently of measurement; (2) 'real' in the sense that the phenomenon will be recognized as 'happening' by the system and built into rates." Frankford, *The Complexity of Medicare's Hospital Reimbursement System* at 659.

In 1992 one of us critically reviewed the question whether the prospective payment system is "working." The answer then, as now, is yes, in that compared with other payers in the United States, Medicare is holding down its costs, principally by setting a price lower than that paid by other payers. However, that answer should come as no surprise because Medicare does not have to bargain with anybody for anything at all. It is THE STATE. It has the power to impose an overall budgetary cap on Medicare's inpatient expenditures, and hospitals cannot afford to refuse its "offer" by turning away Medicare patients.

However, the conclusion that IPPS is "working" because it is holding down Medicare costs is like admiring a new arrangement of deck chairs on the Titanic while it is sinking. Expenditures for hospital services continue to rise. Some observers place the blame on Medicare: Medicare is effectively imposing a tax on private payers because as its rates are ratcheted down, costs are shifted to private payers. If Medicare had to internalize this tax, then its record on controlling costs would not look as successful. *See, e.g.,* Allen Dobson, *The Cost–Shift Payment "Hydraulic": Foundation, History, and Implications*, 25(1) HEALTH AFFAIRS 22 (2006). Other observers point the finger of blame at private payers: they have failed to hold down costs, particularly in markets in which hospitals possess bargaining power, with the result that costs for everyone, including Medicare, continue to rise.

Proponents of this argument claim that the causality of cost shifting is reversed, in that the high payments of private payers induce high costs, which then make Medicare margins appear to be low because Medicare pays less than private payers. *See, e.g.,* Austin B. Frakt, *How Much Do Hospitals Cost Shift?*, 89 MILBANK Q. 90 (2011); Jeffrey Stensland, *Private–Payer Profits Can Induce Negative Medicare Margins*, 29(5) HEALTH AFFAIRS 1045 (2010).* Others, like your authors, conclude that this chicken-and-egg argument is irrelevant because regardless of which side is correct, the continuing cost escalation is a joint product of Medicare and private payers—they're both in it together because the problem is fragmented payment. *See, e.g.,* Uwe E. Reinhardt, *The Many Different Prices Paid to Providers and the Flawed Theory of Cost Shifting: Is It Time for a More Rational All–Payer System?*, 30(5) HEALTH AFFAIRS 2125 (2011); Uwe E. Reinhardt, *The Pricing of U.S. Hospital Services: Chaos Behind a Veil of Secrecy*, 25(1) HEALTH AFFAIRS 57 (2006) [hereinafter Reinhardt, *The Pricing of U.S. Hospital Services*]. As a result, in 1992 as now, the answer to the issue whether the IPPS is working is that such a formulation begs the questions that must be asked: (1) what is the effect of the IPPS on total acute inpatient expenditures in the United States, not just on Medicare expenditures; and (2) are the *DRGs* working—could Medicare hold down its costs and achieve appropriate distributional results without this massively complicated nationwide per-case payment system?

Numerous other countries, *in the context of their single or all-payer systems*, are using DRG-like patient classification systems in a multitude of ways—to monitor activity within a budgeting system; as a means to allocate funds in internal markets; as a portion of overall compensation; as payment for select services; as payment for select types of hospitals; as part of distributing aggregate spending among regions in a regionalized system; as payment for patients who cross regional boundaries; as a method in one region of a larger system; for internal management, benchmarking quality, research, epidemiology or planning; and so on. With a few notable excep-

---

* Some economists dispute that cost shifting occurs or is widespread because it implies that when hospitals are not feeling the pinch from Medicare, they do not fully exercise market power against private payers, effectively leaving money on the table, to be taken up only when Medicare puts greater pressure on hospital rates. This implication is at odds with the assumption that hospitals maximize profits. By contrast Professors Richard Steinberg and Burton Weisbrod have developed a model in which nonprofit hospitals "bonofice," in that they use price discrimination and other strategies to achieve mission rather than profit maximization. *See* Richard Steinberg & Burton A. Weisbrod, *Nonprofits with Distributional Objectives: Price Discrimination and Corner Solutions*, 89 J. PUB. ECON. 89 (2004); Richard Steinberg & Burton A. Weisbrod, *Pricing and Rationing by Nonprofit Organizations with Distributional Objectives*, in TO PROFIT OR NOT TO PROFIT: THE COMMERCIAL TRANSFORMATION OF THE NONPROFIT SECTOR 65 (Burton A. Weisbrod ed., 1998).

tions like France—which has moved to a per-case payment system that is top-down like the United States but also highly regionalized—the trend internationally is to use a mixture of methods, particularly to combine a relatively "global" payment, like a budget, with a means to monitor activity, or to use both global and activity-based payments. Such mixtures enable consolidated payers and hospitals to share the inevitable risk of "inaccuracy" in the patient classification systems, and this risk sharing dilutes the incentives for providers to select against "underpaid" categories or against patients who are more severely ill than the norm built into the categories. Using mixed systems also dilutes incentives of providers to shift patients to different sites of care, e.g., discharge patients earlier to skilled nursing facilities.

Furthermore, even where per-case payment is being used exclusively, as in France and, to a lesser extent, in Germany, the insurance function has been fully or largely nationalized, and because all payers use the same mechanism of payment—"all-payer"—the social and political context is vastly different from that in the United States, in which a multitude of insurers compete to pay as little of hospital expenses as they can. Cost-shifting among payers, in such a context, is either irrelevant or far diminished compared with the United States (although, as just mentioned, providers might still engage in risk selection among patients, or alter site of care to game the system).*

By contrast, in the United States, *outside the context of a single or all-payer system*, we are using national averages in an extremely comprehensive fashion, across a vast and diverse landscape, and our expenditures continue to rise at frightening rates while those of our peer nations remain stable. Use of DRGs or similar patient classification systems in other

---

* Internationally, huge variation exists in the types of patient classification systems used and in the purposes for which they are deployed. We have therefore generalized among them. The most comprehensive recent study is THE GLOBALIZATION OF MANAGERIAL INNOVATION IN HEALTH CARE (John R. Kimberly et al., eds., 2008) [hereinafter Kimberly et al., eds., THE GLOBALIZATION OF MANAGERIAL INNOVATION IN HEALTH CARE], which updates and expands the editors' earlier work, THE MIGRATION OF MANAGERIAL INNOVATION (John R. Kimberley et al., eds., 1993). Other recent, cross-national studies include Aoife Brick et al., *Resource Allocation, Financing and Sustainability in Health Care, vol I*, AN RIONN SLAINTE DEPARTMENT OF HEALTH (2010), http://www.dohc.ie/publications/resource_allocation_financing_health_sector.html; Stephanie Ettelt & Ellen Nolte, *Funding Intensive Care—Approaches in Systems Using Diagnosis–Related Groups*, RAND CORPORATION (2010), http://www.rand.org/pubs/technical_reports/TR792.html; Sheila O'Dougherty et al., *Case-Based Hospital Payment Systems*, in DESIGNING AND IMPLEMENTING HEALTH CARE PROVIDER PAYMENT SYSTEMS ch. 3 (John C. Langenbrunner et al., eds., 2009), (http://www.rbfhealth.org/rbfhealth/library/doc/248/designing-and-implementing-health-care-provider-payment-systems-how-manuals); Jacques Cremer et al., *Protecting Equity While Improving Efficiency: Some Possibilities for Expanding the Role of Competition and Choice in Health Care Delivery, in Financing Sustainable Healthcare in Europe: New Approaches for New Outcomes* (2007), http://www.euractiv.sk/fileadmin/images/The_Cox_Report.pdf#page= 13; Jonas Schreyögg et al., *Methods To Determine Reimbursement Rates for Diagnosis Related Groups (DRG): A Comparison of Nine European Countries*, 9 HEALTH CARE MGMT. SCI. 215 (2006) (entire issue devoted to per-case payment in Europe); Dana A. Forgione et al., *The Impact of DRG–Based Payment on Quality of Care in OECD Countries*, 31(1) J. HEALTH CARE FINANCE 41 (2004); Francis H. Roger France, *Case Mix Use in 25 Countries: A Migration Success But International Comparisons Failure*, 70 INT'L J. MED. INFORMATICS 215 (2003).

countries perhaps enable better monitoring of activity as a means of attaining distributional goals. In the United States, however, the Medicare DRGs enable the federal government either to win the game of shifting costs to other payers or to stand idly by as weaker payers allow everyone's costs to rise. Either way, everyone is losing.

Additionally, in the United States, the use of averaging on such a large scale appears also, unfortunately, to be precluding appropriate distributional decisions. Below we describe how other nations are doing a better job of holding down aggregate costs with better distributional results than ours, and so the answer in the United States remains that the DRGs are not necessary and may even be hindering the process. National averages are national averages, and because the United States is a *big* and *diverse* place, the adjustments downward from such a great height cannot replicate decisions that could be made in much more particularized ways—such as through budgets—with appropriate inter-institutional comparisons and monitoring of activity, as many other nations accomplish. *See* generally Frankford, *The Medicare DRGs.**

c.   Retrospective Charge–Based Physician Reimbursement

Insurance payment for physician services developed on a very different basis from payment to hospitals and other organized institutions. While hospitals were paid on the basis of some estimate of costs, physicians traditionally have been paid their charges on a fee-for-service basis. No one would argue, especially considering the preceding material in this section, either that hospital costs were carefully monitored and controlled or that hospitals were precluded from building a lot of "fat" into their reimbursement. Still, there was a fundamental difference between the reimbursement of hospitals and physicians: hospitals had to justify their rates, but physicians did not.

The differences between hospitals and physicians are more than formal: they are also reflected in different institutional relationships between insurers and providers. In the 1930s and 1940s, Blue Cross and Blue Shield were formed as separate, though closely related, insurance programs. Hospitals controlled their insurance program, Blue Cross, while doctors governed Blue Shield. The distinction between the two was based on the fact that it is more feasible to determine the "costs" of an organization like a hospital with a budget and salaried employees than those of an individual provider, who is compensated for human services and time. In 1965, Congress incorporated these distinctions in creating Medicare. Part A, which pays hospitals, originally provided reimbursement on a cost basis, administered for the federal government by Blue Cross. Part B, which pays for the services of physicians and other suppliers of medical services, is administered for the government by Blue Shield and other insurers, which pay on a fee-for-service basis.

---

* For a crisp discussion how actual budgeting functions, *see* Joseph White, *Markets, Budgets, and Cost Control*, 12(3) HEALTH AFFAIRS 44 (1993).

Fee-for-service insurance typically paid physicians in one of three ways: actual charges, fee schedules, or charge-based reimbursement. Insurance that pays actual charges is simple but expensive and has always been rare. Under a fee schedule, the insurance program (which traditionally was controlled by providers) sets the fees that it will pay. Such schedules can be set high or low and adjusted to account for a number of variables including: the diagnosis, the service provided, the training, experience, and specialty status of the provider, and the setting in which care is given. Historically both commercial insurers and Blue Shield, as well as Medicaid and other state insurance programs for the poor, paid doctors on the basis of a fee schedule. A major risk with fee schedules is that if they are not updated on a timely basis, payment rates can fall to levels that physicians view as unacceptable; in these instances physicians will limit services to patients insured by programs that pay too little, unless the patient is able to pay the balance of the bill.

In the 1950s, Blue Shield developed a new method of paying physicians called charge-based reimbursement. Fee-for-service payments were set on the basis of the historic charges of individual physicians and their medical colleagues at some period in the recent past. These were "customary" fees. The insurer would pay the lesser of: the individual physician's actual billed charge; the amount that he or she customarily charges for that service; or the prevailing charge in the community. The payment system became known as the "Usual, Customary and Reasonable" ("UCR") system. Since the payment a doctor receives is determined by the stated charge at some time in the recent past, doctors have strong economic incentives to keep stated charges high. Moreover, since the prevailing charge in the community set one of the parameters of the system, physicians had an obvious reason to join together in determining the rates they would charge. As a result, insurance programs using charged-based reimbursement most often set their rates to reflect the prevailing charge in the community (although actual payments would take into account applicable deductibles and copayments).

When Congress enacted Medicare in 1965, the AMA was strongly opposed, and many feared that physicians would boycott the program. To encourage physicians' participation, Congress gave the doctor-sponsored Blue Shield programs responsibility for paying doctors and required that Medicare follow Blue Shield's practice of paying doctors based on physicians' customary, prevailing, and reasonable charges.

Theoretically, a charge-based reimbursement system can constrain or prevent unjustifiable increases in physician fees. In theory, the doctor will set "charges" in transactions with patients who negotiate prices for services paid out of pocket, and the insurance program can piggy-back onto the charges reached in free market transactions. But when most patients are insured, and those who are not have no money, the concept of "charges" loses meaning. The uninsured cannot realistically pay any significant price for their care, while insured patients do not need to bargain because they are insured. As a result, the concept of prevailing charges became an instrument in physicians' hands to maximize insurance payments. This result was particularly true for surgical procedures and other services that are widely insured and thereby insulated from market forces. Charge-based reimbursement also legitimated a pattern under which the most technologically sophisticated physicians (e.g., heart surgeons) are paid at vastly higher rates than physicians trained in less technical primary care specialties such as family practice, even when both types of doctors performed exactly the same services.

One further important point is relevant before proceeding to prospective payment. Some physicians executed participation agreements with insurers, whereby, like hospitals, they agreed to accept the insurer's payment in full for the services provided. However, many if not most physicians did not execute such agreements, with the result that, as previously noted in this Part, they billed patients the balance not covered by insurance payments and patient cost-sharing.

d. Prospective RBRVS–Based Physician Payment

Because physicians were given a blank check, between the enactment of Medicare in 1965 and the mid–1980s, spending for physicians' services increased at an average annual rate of more than 13% and averaged 16% a year during the first half of the 1980s. Increases in both Medicare and private insurance expenditures for physicians' services consistently outpaced growth in both the gross domestic product and total health care expenditures. Physician Payment Review Commission, Annual Report to Congress (Sept. 11, 1995).

Beginning in 1984, Congress took steps to control the cost of physician services. As part of the Deficit Reduction Act of 1984 (P.L. 98–369) Congress froze physician fees and instituted conditions and procedures for updating payment rates. Then, in 1989, Congress adopted a fundamentally new approach to physician reimbursement in the Physician Payment Reform Act, enacted as part of the Omnibus Budget Reconciliation Act of 1989. 42 U.S.C. § 1395w–4(a)–(j). The cornerstone of the new approach, implemented in 1992, was the creation of a Medicare fee schedule based on a "resource-based relative-value scale" ("RBRVS"). The RBRVS system was developed by economists and colleagues at Harvard and tested and refined by the federal Health Care Financing Administration (HCFA), the Physician Payment Review Commission, the expert body then for physicians fees (now one of MedPAC's responsibilities), and various professional organizations.

The Physician Payment Reform Act (which was incorporated into OBRA '89) sought to accomplish four objectives: make the system of physician payment more rational and equitable; control the costs of professional services provided under Medicare, Part B; ensure access to physicians for Medicare beneficiaries; and protect and improve quality of care. In particular, one aim in developing the RBRVS was to increase payments to generalists relative to specialists as a means to induce more medical graduates to enter primary care. *See, e.g.,* William C. Hsiao et al., *Results and Policy Implications of the Resource–Based Relative–Value Study*, 319

NEW ENG. J. MED. 881 (1988); William C. Hsiao et al., *Results, Potential Effects, and Implementation Issues of the Resource–Based Relative Value Scale*, 260 JAMA 2429 (1988); PHYSICIAN PAYMENT REVIEW COMMISSION, MEDICARE PHYSICIAN PAYMENT: AN AGENDA FOR REFORM 4–5, 20–21, 35 (March 1987). Hence, the new fee schedule was designed to increase payment for "cognitive" services and reduce payment to practitioners of procedurally oriented disciplines, such as ophthalmology, surgery and anesthesia.

The RBRVS departed dramatically from the previous system of basing payment on charges. The resource basis of the Medicare fee schedule is embodied in the relative value scale ("RVS") specified in the federal legislation. The RVS has three components, each of which is called a "relative value unit" ("RVU"): a "physician work" RVU that reflects the time, mental effort and judgment, technical skill and physical effort, and stress arising from potential risk for the patient, of the physician's providing a service; a "practice expense" ("PE") RVU that includes costs such as office rent, staff salaries, equipment, and supplies; and a "physician liability" ("PL") RVU that reflects professional liability premium expenses. Each RVU is adjusted for local variation by a "geographical practice cost index" ("GPCI") specifically designed for each one.

The unit of payment for physicians services, therefore, is the individual service, such as an office visit or a diagnostic procedure, which are sometimes bundled together, such as a surgical procedure which is bundled together with pre and post-operative care. The payment for a service is the conversion factor—which is analogous to the standardized amount for the IPPS—multiplied by the sum of the three relevant RVUs, each of which has been adjusted by the GPCI pertaining to it. Analogous to the standardized amount for the IPPS, the conversion factor is updated every year to account for change and to control aggregate payments. This update is somewhat different than that applied to the standardized amount for the IPPS in that the principal concern is that physicians will increase the volume and intensity of their services in response to decreased revenue, i.e., take advantage of supplier-induced demand. The current mechanism to prevent greater volume from increasing aggregate payments is a complex formula known as the "sustainable growth rate" ("SGR"), a calculation that is supposed to take back any increase in aggregate expenditure resulting from increased volume—an "expenditure target." However, given the large increases in volume that have occurred in recent years, as we discuss below, the SGR formula would have led to large decreases in payment—"negative updates"—and under pressure from organized medicine and beneficiary groups, Congress has enacted "overrides," effectively abandoning use of the SGR formula. *See* 42 U.S.C. § 1395w–4(d). *See generally* MEDPAC, MARCH 2011 REPORT at 70, 73.

The sum of the three geographically adjusted RVUs, multiplied by the conversion factor, yields the "adjusted fee schedule payment rate," which is then potentially adjusted for a number of so-called policy factors, three of which we discuss here: (1) physicians who fail to participate in Medicare—effectively preserving their right to balance bill beneficiaries up to a cap of

15%, see 42 U.S.C. § 1395w–4(g)—are penalized for their failure to participate in Medicare by receiving only 95% of the full RBRVS payment; (2) a
bonus is awarded to physicians who practice in health professional shortage
areas ("HPSAs"), payments intended to attract physicians to practice in
those areas; and (3) the PPACA created a 10% increase for primary care
services and major surgical procedures. *See* PPACA, Pub. L. No. 111–148
§ 5501 (2010).

In sum, as illustrated in the following figure from MedPAC, (MEDPAC,
PHYSICIANS AND OTHER HEALTH PROFESSIONALS PAYMENT SYSTEM 2 (Oct. 2011),
http://www.medpac.gov/documents/MedPAC_Payment_Basics_11_
Physician.pdf), the entire calculation looks like the following:

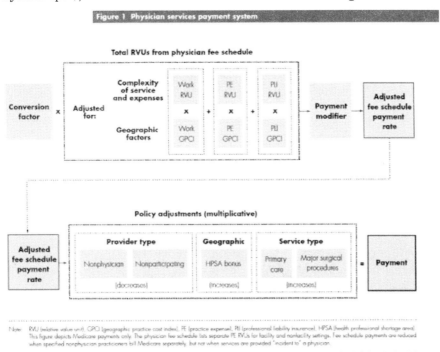

The issues regarding the Medicare RBRVS are somewhat analogous to
those we examined with regard to Medicare's IPPS. Therefore, our explication can be briefer, and we focus on only two examples of many. Problems
have arisen with regard to the relative value scale itself and the SGR
formula, which, to iterate, imposes an expenditure target if physicians
increase the volume of services in response to reduced payments.

(1).   Updates to the Work RVU

Analogous to the DRG values that form the basic of the case-mix
measure for the IPPS, the physician-fee RVUs can change over time,
reflecting such factors as enhanced efficiency, technology diffusion or
substitution, allied health personnel substitution, modifications, or changes
in patient severity. As a result, Congress mandated that CMS update the

RVUs every five years. *See* 42 U.S.C. § 1395w–4(c)(2)(B)(i). Because among the three RVUs, the work RVU accounts for, on average, 48% of the total payment, *see, e.g.,* MedPAC, Report to the Congress: Medicare and the Health Care Delivery System 13 (June 2011) [hereinafter MedPAC June 2011 Report], in the interest of time we limit our discussion to just that one.

Aside from the issue, discussed above with regard to the IPPS, of what "accuracy" means in these updates, there is a special issue pertaining to the RBRVS-based fee schedule, which concerns the process for updating. As we indicated above, the original RVS was developed by researchers at Harvard in cooperation with HCFA. By contrast, in conducting the five-year reviews, CMS relies heavily on the American Medical Association's Relative Value Scale Update Committee ("RUC"). Writing in 2006, Med-PAC found that contrary to one of the purposes in implementing the scale, the dominance of the RUC in the update process was skewing the scale in favor of specialists, particularly those who performed procedures or used imaging. Contributing to this result were a number of factors, including: (1) the RUC is dominated by specialists; (2) most requests for revaluing an RVU come from specialty societies; (3) the great majority of weights reviewed have been ones that were allegedly undervalued, with the result that review has most often led to an increase in value; (4) any increase in one weight diminishes the value of others because adjustments are "budget neutral"; and (5) CMS generally accepts the RUC's recommendations. *See* MedPAC, Report to the Congress: Medicare Payment Policy ch. 3 (March 2006) [hereinafter MedPAC March 2006 Report]; *see also* MedPAC June 2011 Report at 12–17.

Additionally, numerous studies have shown that the work estimates that form the basis of the RVUs for specialty services, estimates derived from data garnered by specialty society surveys, substantially inflate the values of the specialty work RVUs; and that many of these RVUs should be reduced—but have not been—to reflect productivity gains that have occurred (To some extent, the PE RVUs for specialists are similarly inflated). *See, e.g., id.;* MedPAC, Report to the Congress: Medicare Payment Policy 87 (March 2010); Jerry Cromwell et al., *Missing Productivity Gains in the Medicare Physician Fee Schedule: Where Are They?*, 67 Med. Care Res. & Rev. 676 (2010); Thomas Bodenheimer et al., *The Primary Care–Specialty Income Gap: Why It Matters*, 146 Ann. Internal Med. 301 (2007); Nancy McCall et al., *Validation of Physician Survey Estimates of Surgical Time Using Operating Room Logs*, 63 Med. Care Res. & Rev. 764 (2006); Jerry Cromwell et al., *Validating CPT Typical Times for Medicare Office Evaluation and Management (E/M) Services*, 63 Med. Care Res. & Rev. 236 (2006).

The consequence of these effects, coupled with other factors—including most importantly, as discussed more fully below, a great increase in volume of procedures compared with cognitive services—is that primary care physicians over the lifetime of the RBRVS-based fee system have lost ground relative to specialists. Moreover, this significant disparity in compensation is one factor, although not the only one, in the career choices of undergraduate medical students. In recent years, the number of graduates who have chosen primary care has fallen dramatically. While in absolute terms the RBRVS system has increased the compensation of primary care somewhat, the relative disparity between compensation of generalists and specialists remains too great to attract a sufficient number of students away from specialization and subspecialization toward primary care. *See, e.g.,* MEDPAC MARCH 2011 REPORT at 88–94; Robert Berenson et al., *What If All Physician Services Were Paid under the Medicare Fee Schedule? An Analysis Using Medical Group Management Association Data*, MEDPAC (March 2010), http://medpac.gov/documents/Mar10_Physician_Fee Schedule_CONTRACTOR_v2.pdf.

To redress the manner in which the updates to the weights have contributed to this trend, in 2006 MedPAC issued some fairly strong recommendations, all designed to reduce CMS's reliance, in performing the update, on the medical specialty societies. Most importantly, MedPAC recommended that CMS form an expert panel of its own to advise it in its review of the RVUs. Under the recommendation, the panel, composed of experts in health economics and physician payment, would not "supplant" the RUC but would "augment" it by providing an independent source of expertise. MedPAC also recommended that, separately from the Congressionally required five-year reviews, CMS should, based on a number of factors MedPAC specified, identify values that might be ripe for reduction. *See* MEDPAC MARCH 2006 REPORT at 142–48.

CMS has adopted some of the recommendations, some of which were also codified in PPACA § 3134, Pub. L. No. 111–148 (2010). Over the past several years, it began identifying misvalued services along the lines of criteria MedPAC recommended; it has obtained input from nonphysicians; and it has announced that it will conduct annual reviews instead of five-year ones. *See, e.g.,* Dep't Health & Human Services, Center for Medicare & Medicaid Services, Medicare Program; Payment Policies Under the Physician Fee Schedule and Other Revisions to Part B for CY 2012, 76 Fed. Reg. 42,772, 42,788–93 (July 19, 2011). However, CMS has failed to adopt MedPAC's most important recommendation, the establishment of a review panel independent of specialty society control. As a result, it is not clear whether the RVUs' drift toward widening the disparity between primary and specialty compensation will end. *See, e.g., Letter from Glenn M. Hackbarth, Chairman, MedPAC to Donald Berwick, Administrator*, CMS (July 22, 2011), http://www.medpac.gov/documents/07222011_Physician_COMMENT_KH.pdf.

(2). Controlling aggregate expenditures

In two respects the Sustained Growth Rate formula has been the most problematic feature of the RBRVS-based physician fee schedule. First, its use to control aggregate expenditures is an utter failure. Second, its use has enhanced the disparity between primary and specialty care.

As we discussed above, health care providers, particularly physicians, often have some capacity to offset lost income as a result of diminished prices by increasing the volume or intensity of services they provide. The

SGR formula and its predecessor, the Volume Performance Standard ("VPS"), were supposed to be used to counteract increased volume as a means to control aggregate expenditures—i.e., to keep the prospective system prospective.

As noted above, the SGR formula and the VPS both provide what are called expenditure targets, mechanisms that are also used in other nations. The concept is that if the target is exceeded in one year, in the next year aggregate payments are reduced to some extent. According to some, the targets provide a mechanism to deter physicians from increasing volume in response to diminished fees—they are behavioral controls. According to others, the targets are simply means to maintain fiscal control. If the target is $1,000,000 per annum, and if in one year expenditures exceed that amount, the excess is taken back in the next year so that the target is met. The point is not to affect behavior but to keep aggregate expenditures at the stipulated level.

The story of what has happened in the United States is a very troubling one, and speaks volumes (sorry!) about how fragmentation in financing leads to a loss of control over expenditures. The SGR expenditure target allows for Medicare rates to grow but only if that growth is justified by an increase in (1) the nation's per capita gross domestic product; (2) the number of beneficiaries enrolled in fee-for-service—"traditional"—Medicare; (3) the practice costs of physicians and other health professionals; or (4) services covered by Medicare. *See* 42 U.S.C. § 1395w–4(f). As MedPAC describes it:

> With respect to the first factor—per capita GDP—the SGR formula essentially allows the volume of fee schedule services to grow at the same rate as per capita GDP. Additionally, the SGR expenditure target is adjusted to account for three other factors: changes in the number of Medicare beneficiaries, changes in physician practice costs, and changes in covered services due to law and regulation. When these rates increase, so does the expenditure target, essentially allowing higher aggregate spending.

MEDPAC, JUNE 2011 REPORT at 7. Put simply, "Growth in GDP—the measure of goods and services produced in the United States—is used as a benchmark of how much additional growth in expenditure society can afford." MEDPAC, REPORT TO THE CONGRESS: ASSESSING ALTERNATIVES TO THE SUSTAINABLE GROWTH RATE SYSTEM 11 (March 2007) [hereinafter MEDPAC, ASSESSING ALTERNATIVES TO THE SUSTAINABLE GROWTH RATE SYSTEM].

In the first few years of its use, the SGR formula did not result in take-backs in a successive year. However, from 2001 forward, in each year actual expenditures have exceeded the target, and the projected take-backs have grown very large because Congress has intervened each year to reduce the take-back for that year. Because the formula then compounds the shortfall in successive years—just like an interest rate compounds each year by adding to the base over which it is taken—and because updates in any given year are based on what fees would have been had the full reductions occurred, the effects are very substantial:

• The cumulated overage between actual and target spending compounds every year that the fee reductions are postponed—retrospectively and prospectively. Also, the spending attributable to the 2003–2006 overrides was added to the total amount of dollars that must be recouped in accordance with the SGR formula. Thus, these overrides resulted in increasing the deficit between actual cumulative spending and the SGR cumulative target.

• Under current law, the reduced future fees would become the base for payment levels in all subsequent years. So, while cumulative spending would equal the SGR target after the 30 percent cut, the updates would be based on much lower fees. In other words, a fee that is $100 today is scheduled to drop to $70 in 2012, and subsequent updates would start from the $70 level.

Id. at 8.

Given the number of "overrides" enacted by Congress to decrease or eliminate the formula's effect, fees for calendar year 2012 would have to be cut a whopping 29.5%; and any updates in future years would start at that reduced level. That sort of shock to providers is unreasonable. For that reason, in 2012 Congress has again suspended application of the SGR, thereby continuing a payment freeze. See Pub. L. No. 112–96 § 3003, 112th Cong., 2d Sess. (2012).

How did we end up in such a fix? We return to a point made very early in this chapter. Other nations control costs either because governments set prices for some relevant geographic unit—nation, state, or province—in a "single-payer" system, or because payers are organized together, with or without state sponsorship, into an "all-payer" system. As Professor Joe White has summarized (and some of these points we elaborate in the next section):

Such *coordinated payment* rules have a series of major advantages:

1) Because payers have more power in the rate-setting, prices are systematically lower in all-payer systems than in the United States [citation omitted]. This directly lowers total costs.

2) Standardization leads to two kinds of administrative savings. Compared to the United States, insurers save from not having to negotiate and then keep track of many different prices from many different plans negotiated with different providers; caregivers do not need to maintain elaborate billing operations to deal with inconsistent insurer payment rules.

3) All-payer systems are much more transparent for both caregivers and consumers. If there is cost-sharing, the prices paid by the insurers are not trade secrets, so consumers know if the insurers are charging the correct amounts (an unfortunate concern in the U.S., as discussed below).

4) The standard payments can also substantially standardize medical record-keeping. It becomes possible, for example, to combine

files to review practice patterns—or even to coordinate billing through a central clearinghouse, and analyze patterns through that database.

5) In an all-payer system, the different payers see themselves as having a shared interest in cost control. This is very different from in the United States, where fears of cost-shifting mean that employers, for example, are not a lobby in support of better cost control for Medicare.

Joseph White, *Implementing Health Care Reform with All–Payer Regulation, Private Insurers, and a Voluntary Public Insurance Plan* 5 (May 3, 2009), http://www.ourfuture.org/files/JWhiteAllPayerCostControl.pdf.

By contrast, the way Medicare is run is analogous to spitting into the wind: "The adequacy of Medicare payments is assessed relative to the costs of treating Medicare beneficiaries, and the Commission's recommendations address a sector's Medicare payments, not total payments." MedPAC March 2011 Report at 30. In other words, Medicare sets its rates with indifference to the effect on other payers or the health care system more generally. As we have noted, this "Medicare-only" policy has allowed Medicare to control its costs relative to other payers, but as costs are shifted to other payers as a result, more revenues are poured into the health care system, which adds fuel to the expenditure fire, further driving the system, including Medicare, which alone cannot tamp down the fire, as big as it is. The whole massive, technically beautiful apparatus is self-defeating because Medicare's attempts to drive down its costs alone are just self-defeating. It isn't working.*

This dynamic not only increases aggregate expenditures but also has pernicious distributional effects because it also is a major factor in the continued and growing disparity between the incomes of primary care physicians and specialists. As MedPAC and others have noted over and over again, generalists, who perform more cognitive services and fewer procedures, have much less "opportunity" to increase the volume of their services than do specialists, e.g., a specialist can order many more tests and images, while a primary doctor can only do so much to increase the number of office visits, given limited hours in a day. As a consequence, volume has

---

* In the PPACA Congress added a spending cap designed to apply, not just to physician fees, but to Medicare as a whole, administered by an independent board composed of experts, the Independent Payment Advisory Board, which is supposed to propose cuts to aggregate Medicare spending if specified targets are not met. The Board's proposal becomes law without a Congressional override, which requires a three-fifth vote in the Senate. *See* PPACA, P.L. 111–148 § 3403 (2010). *See generally* Timothy Stoltzfus Jost, *The Independent Payment Advisory Board,* 363 New Eng. J. Med. 103 (2010). One wonders if this mechanism will suffer the same fate as the SGR formula—if it survives at all: Strong Congressional support for killing it abounds—particularly since the targets would have been met in only four of the last 25 years, and the targets are similar to those under the SGR formula, which Congress has overridden now for almost a decade. *See* Richard S. Foster, *Estimated Financial Effects of the "Patient Protection and Affordable Care Act,"* as Amended 10 (Washington D.C.: Centers for Medicare and Medicaid Services, April 22, 2010), http://www.cms.gov/ActuarialStudies/Downloads/PPACA_2010-04-22.pdf.

increased much more for procedures, tests and imaging, compared with service codes that require "face-to-face" time with patients. When this disparity in volume increase is coupled with budget neutrality, the increase in services provided by specialists comes at a substantial reduction in the compensation of primary care physicians. *See, e.g.,* MEDPAC MARCH 2011 REPORT at 83–84, 89; Stephanie Maxwell et al., *Use of Physicians' Services Under Medicare's Resource–Based Payments*, 356 NEW ENG. J. MED. 1853 (2007); Stephanie Maxwell & Stephen Zuckerman, *Impact of Resource–Based Practice Expenses on the Medicare Physician Volume*, 29(2) HEALTH CARE FIN. REV. 65 (Winter 2007–2008). It is a zero-sum game. In this regard too, Medicare's "Medicare-only" stance is self-defeating for it defeats its own policy of increasing the supply of primary-care doctors.

Unfortunately, there is just no other way to put the point: we have a mess. Reams of paper are filled with numerous, complicated, sometimes ingenuous, means to fix the SGR formula (some of which we would present if space allowed).* Given the underlying dynamic—fragmentation—our view is that Rome burns while Nero fiddles.

3.   THE INEXORABLE TRADEOFFS OF PAYMENT METHODS

As we stated above, all methods of payment have advantages and disadvantages. Following a format inspired by Professor Joe White's typography of targets and systems of payments, *see* White, *Targets and Systems of Health Care Cost Control*, we analyze systems and methods along three dimensions: (1) the level of aggregation or disaggregation of units of payment; (2) the aggregation or disaggregation of providers; and (3) the degree of coordination or fragmentation among payers.

a.   Aggregation–Disaggregation of Units of Payment

As we have seen, the unit for payment of different entities may vary. A physician might be reimbursed for each service performed, for each patient the physician takes care of—per head or capita—or for some unit of time like an annual salary. A hospital might be paid for each day a patient stays, for each service it provides, based on the diagnosis by which each patient is admitted, or for an annual budget. Units of payment are relatively "aggregated" or "global"—e.g., per capita payment to physicians or a hospital's annual budget—when they "bundle" together goods and services that could be "unbundled" and billed separately—e.g., the per capita payment to the physician encompasses office visits and procedures performed for the patient over the relevant accounting period. By contrast, units of payment are relatively "disaggregated" when units of service are broken down into

---

* *See, e.g.,* MEDPAC 2011 JUNE REPORT ch. 1; MedPAC 2011 March Report at 73–75; MEDPAC, ASSESSING ALTERNATIVES TO THE SUSTAINABLE GROWTH RATE SYSTEM. MedPAC has recently recommended to Congress that it repeal the SGR formula and replace it with a 10–year schedule of updates coupled with plans to accelerate increasing the accuracy of the RVS and other reforms to alter the organizations for delivery of services. *See Letter from Glenn M. Hackbarth, Chairman, MedPAC to The Honorable Max Baucus et al.*, MedPac (Oct. 14, 2011), http://www.medpac.gov/documents/10142011_MEDPAC_SGR_letter.pdf.

smaller and smaller units, e.g., surgery for hip replacement is billed as each equipment used, the time spent by each type of professional, and so forth.

Let's start with disaggregated units since they have dominated prospective payment in the United States and are therefore more familiar to you at this point. What are the advantages of paying hospitals on a per-case basis, physicians per service, and so on across various providers?

To begin, we can generalize that smaller units of payment potentially allow payers to monitor and control exactly what is being performed. For example, as we have seen, the MS–DRGs and the RVUs are assigned weights based on what the statistical norm implies for treatment of each case. Because the level of aggregation of these payments is relatively small, in theory payers have more control over services than if the unit of payment is set at a much more aggregated level, such as per diem and capitated payments, respectively for hospitals and physicians.

The caveat "in theory," however, is crucial. As we have seen, the theory is that providers will respond to the incentives built into the relative values and concomitant weights, and those responses will allow payers to achieve their aims. For a number of reasons, that may not be true. First, as we have seen individual providers may respond, e.g., cardiac surgeons may create and invest in cardiac specialty hospitals, while organizations may have much more difficulty in responding, e.g., hospitals have harder time rationalizing care involving multiple actors, departments, etc.

Second, a payer might not have the technical capacity to attain its desired end, e.g., mistakes in setting the time element in the work RVU—by far the most important element—may "overvalue" specialty care and shift income from primary care to specialty care. The law of unintended consequences should be taken as a norm; and in the United States, with the American penchant to use technological fixes to avoid the use of political power, compensation systems are technically refined, and refined, and refined again, with seemingly little critical perspective about the limits of techné, particularly in the face of a very messy social and political world.

Third, when units of payment are not global—e.g., not capitation—providers are able to differentiate care into smaller units and seek payment for each one. This unbundling must then be countered by a re-bundling by the payer. Medicare, for example, maintains a "3–day payment window" during which pre-admission services provided on an outpatient basis prior to an inpatient stay are deemed to be part of the inpatient stay and are only paid by the DRG-based payment. *See* 42 U.S.C. § 1395ww(a)(4). Congress recently amended this provision to clarify that the 3–day window applies to all nondiagnostic services unless the hospital certifies that the services were unrelated to the inpatient stay that followed. *See* Preservation of Access to Care for Medicare Beneficiaries and Pension Relief Act of 2010, Pub. L. No. 111–192 § 101; *see also* Proposed IPPS Rules for FY 2012 at 25,960–61. This amendment was necessary to stop the unbundling of outpatient procedures from the inpatient stay, which effectively allowed double payment, once as an outpatient service and once under the relevant DRG. Similarly, a significant concern now is that imaging services are being unbundled and billed as smaller and smaller units. Hence, in light of the fact that physicians' utilization of imaging has soared in recent years, particularly to facilities they own, *see, e.g.,* Laurence C. Baker, *Acquisition of MRI Equipment by Doctors Drive Up Imaging Use and Spending*, 29(12) HEALTH AFFAIRS 2252 (2010); Bruce J. Hillman & Jeff Goldsmith, *Imaging: The Self–Referral Boom and the Ongoing Search for Effective Policies to Contain It*, 29(12) HEALTH AFFAIRS 2231 (2010), there is discussion of reforms to re-bundle such services into larger units of payment. *See* MedPAC June 2011 Report ch. 2. Congress more generally in the PPACA authorized the creation of the Center for Medicare and Medicaid Innovation, with the broad mandate to explore more global forms of payment, and the National Pilot Program on Payment Bundling, as one specific experiment for bundling hospital stays with other after-care components of the "episode." *See* PPACA §§ 3021, 3023, Pub. L. No. 111–148 (2010). *See generally, e.g.,* Paul B. Ginsburg, *Rapidly Evolving Physician–Payment Policy—More Than the SGR*, 364 NEW ENG. J. MED. 172 (2011). Providers can also game the system through up-coding, something that can be defeated through policing coding, as described in the chapter on fraud in Part Four below, or through re-bundling.

Fourth, to the extent that the relevant type of provider can churn volume, smaller units of payment enhance that capacity. For example, Medicare is about to begin a program of penalizing "excess" hospital readmissions. *See* PPACA, Pub. L. No. 111–148 § 3025 (2010); Proposed IPPS Rules for FY 2012 at 25,928–37. This complicated new program is necessary in part because hospitals have incentives to discharge patients early, and if anything, they gain financially from readmission. *See* MEDPAC, REPORT TO THE CONGRESS: PROMOTING GREAT EFFICIENCY IN MEDICARE ch. 5 (June 2007); MEDPAC, REPORT TO THE CONGRESS: REFORMING THE DELIVERY SYSTEM ch. 4 (June 2008). More generally, as we discussed, the United States (and other nations) have used expenditure targets as a means to mitigate the effects of increased volume in response to diminished payment (or to reduce the incentives to engage in such behavior).

Relatively aggregated units of payments present in almost the opposite manner. As just stated, units of payment set at relatively global levels eliminate incentives to unbundle. At the extreme, organizations may be combined together into entities like ACOs, discussed below in Part Three. *See generally* Neeraj Sood et al., *Medicare's Bundled Payment Pilot for Acute and Postacute Care: Analysis and Recommendations on Where to Begin*, 30(9) HEALTH AFFAIRS 1708 (2011); Michael Chernow, *Bundled Payment Systems: Can They Be More Successful This Time*, 45 HEALTH SERVS. RES. 1141 (2010); Robert E. Mechanic & Stuart H. Altman, *Payment Reform Options: Episode Payment Is a Good Place To Start*, 28(2) HEALTH AFFAIRS w262 (2009); Glenn Hackbarth et al., *Collective Accountability for Medical Care—Toward Bundled Medicare Payments*, 359 NEW ENG. J. MED. 3 (2008). Such "bundling" reduces the opportunity of providers to game the system through unbundling, upcoding or transferring patients to other sites of care earlier, like discharging a patient from the hospital early into nursing or home care. Bundling providers into one unit also promises to enhance coordination of care, something we address below in Part Three.

More global units of payment also involve less need for "accuracy" in the way that DRG- or RBRVS-based payment does. For example, where hospital budgets are used, the payer or groups of coordinating payers can take the budget for the prior year, make some adjustments based on how much additional (or diminished) resources can be afforded, and base payment largely on that basis. Of course we are exaggerating to a degree, because more sophisticated and technical adjustors are used, but the degree of fine-tuning present in the contrasting U.S. systems doesn't exist. Also, to have an aggregate effect, larger units of payment also require that either a single payer exist or that there be a relatively high degree of cooperation among payers. Hospital budgeting is not possible unless all payers together set the organization's entire income or if there is a single payer. That's the definition of budgeting. Similarly, as we have seen, without such coordination or consolidation other units of payment cannot achieve desired aggregate effects. An insurance plan with a small percentage of a doctor's, medical group's, or hospital's overall practice cannot greatly affect the behavior of the capitated entity, particularly if from year to year providers and patients are changing plans. As we started with early in the chapter, fragmented insurers, providers and payment systems tend to go together—actors tend just to shift costs and otherwise seek to gain advantage of one another, and the game of cost shifting is enhanced with fragmented methods of payment. Stable systems with larger units of payment tend to stick together. As we will discuss below, joint negotiations can work wonders.

More global units of payment may diminish unbundling and upcoding and be easier to administer but they also make care less visible and controllable because less information is conveyed about what services are actually provided. As we have observed, some nations give hospitals budgets set in advance, a payment mechanism that reflects the unity of the entity being paid and is less dependent on "accuracy" at the micro-level. Analogously, doctors might be put on salary. However, payment set at such a macro-level gives providers incentives to slack off and reduce levels of service. Hence, many countries that use budgets for hospitals are using a DRG-like patient classification system as a basis to monitor level of care.* This effort is an attempt to account for providers' incentive and ability to reduce volume of services, the mirror image of methods used to counter providers' attempts to increase volume.

Analogously, more aggregated payment doesn't allow incentives to attain ends related to specialization. Regulators in the United States were able to shift select services from higher-cost inpatient settings to lower-cost outpatient settings because they were able to vary rates for certain targeted procedures, i.e., payment increased some capacity and created incentive to

---

* Notice that it's one thing to suppose that the DRGs are accurate enough to monitor activity, and quite another to suppose that they are so accurate as to enable per-case payment, particularly on the scale of all acute-care hospitals in the United States.

reduce the use of substitute, but more costly, capacity. Global payments do not allow that type of fine-tuning. On the other hand, diffusing technology and procedures into the less "aggregated" outpatient sector may not have been such a good idea after all, because as a unified site of care, the hospital is a much easier entity to regulate than the diffuse outpatient sector, and because use of marginal cost pricing can rationalize payment for the expensive inpatient setting. *See* Uwe E. Reinhardt, *Spending More Through "Cost Controls:" Our Obsessive Quest To Gut the Hospital*, 15(2) HEALTH AFFAIRS 145 (1996). These considerations illustrate our point: nothing is perfect.

b.   Aggregation–Disaggregation of Providers

Providers can be paid in aggregated or disaggregated provider units. Physicians may be paid individually or in groups into which they have been aggregated. Likewise, hospitals can be subject to budgets that apply, with some individual variation, across regions.* The extent to which providers are aggregated affects the viability of different units of payment; and payment systems often combine elements of aggregation and disaggregation. Aggregation has its advantages and disadvantages, as does disaggregation.

Take Medicare's RBRVS-based fee schedule as an example. Physicians are paid on a completely disaggregated basis, fee for service to the individual physician. The payment of one physician affects no other physicians. However, as we have seen, the level of payment *for all* is affected by whether or not an expenditure target is met. Hence, if the expenditure target is given effect—and as we have discussed it largely has not been enforced—then over- or underutilization by individual physicians affects the compensation of all.

This externality, so to speak, has given rise to two complaints against the SGR and its predecessor, the VPS. First, some say that an aggregate expenditure target is inequitable in that the compensation of physicians who do not increase volume is diminished by those who do. As we have seen, primary care doctors can certainly complain that specialists have diminished the payment of primary care. Second, some say that expenditure targets are ineffective in reducing aggregate expenditures because they are not targeted sufficiently to penalize physicians who overuse and reward those who do not. Technically that is not correct because if a single payer or a coordinated group of payers decides to hold providers to the target, then the target does control aggregate expenditures. However, the distributional effects may be too hard to bear politically, with the result that the target remains unenforced, which is what we have seen for about a decade with regard to the SGR as Congress repeatedly "overrides" it because the distributional impact is undesirable.

---

* Reforms in Germany in 1992 spread one hospital's overrun of its budget limit across other hospitals' funds. *See* WHITE, COMPETING SOLUTIONS at 85. At one time, France used regional global budgets spread across a region's hospitals. *See* William A. Glaser, *How Expenditure Caps and Expenditure Targets Really Work*, 71 MILBANK Q. 97, 106 (1993) [hereinafter Glaser, *How Expenditure Caps and Expenditure Targets Really Work*].

The incentive for overutilization can be eliminated by use of a more global payment, such as capitation, but then other problems arise. Capitation amounts can be set with some degree of accuracy only if, as we discussed at the very beginning of the chapter, one can predict the risk of loss with some degree of confidence over a sufficiently large pool of patients. As a result, individual physicians (and low-volume hospitals) do not have sufficient scale to be capitated and bear risk; an outlier patient or two can be financially devastating. Such small scale also necessarily enhances incentives for physicians to avoid patients who are more severely ill and to select patients who are less so. Physicians collected into large enough groups (or hospitals with sufficient scale) might be able to bear risk sufficiently. However, when they are so aggregated, we return to the problem that one physician's utilization affects others' compensation; and it's difficult to link individual and group incentives. That's why cost control and maintenance of high quality in a large group practice depends also—or much more on—institutional culture and process, and on coordination along the continuum of care within a vertically integrated organization that owns or contracts exclusively with diverse types of providers. *See, e.g.,* JOHN G. SMILLIE, CAN PHYSICIANS MANAGE THE QUALITY AND COSTS OF HEALTH CARE? THE STORY OF THE PERMANENTE MEDICAL GROUP (1991); *see also* Joseph White, *Markets and Medical Care: The United States*, 1993–2005, 85 MILBANK Q. 395 (2007). We discuss below how payment works best within a much larger institutional context than as the sole lever to control overall expenditures and achieve distributional goals.

Hybrid methods are also possible. *See, e.g.,* James C. Robinson & Francis Megerlin, *Physician Payment Innovations in the United States and France, in* FINANCE AND INCENTIVES OF THE HEALTH CARE SYSTEM 49 (Antti Suvanto & Hannu Vartiainen, eds., 2007). For example, physicians have been paid on a fee-for-service basis subject to all sorts of incentives, in the form of withholds or bonuses, tied to volume as a means to counter volume effects. Analogously, portions of compensation—say 50% of total pay—can be capitated, while the rest is paid on a fee-for-service basis; and mixtures of methods can be matched with types of physicians. Specialists whose practices consist largely of tests and procedures can, as we have seen, increase volume much more easily than can primary care physicians who mostly provide cognitive services. Therefore, specialists can be subject to capitation to prevent their churning of services, while primary-care physicians, who are less able to churn volume, can be paid fee for service. All methods have advantages and disadvantages.

c. Coordination–Fragmentation of Payers

However, as we stated early in the chapter, by far the most important part of payment is the extent to which payers are consolidated—single-payer at the extreme—or coordinated in an all-payer system. A canard in the debate in the United States concerning health care reform, that one hears tirelessly repeated, is that the problem here is "fee-for-service medicine." International comparison proves this claim to be completely false. Other nations have long paid physicians on a fee-for-service basis, using other mechanisms to counteract volume effects, and their expenditures are almost half of those in the United States. Some countries have also used per diems for hospitals, without nearly the cost inflation here, but again the key is coordination among payers. Budgets clearly work better than per diems, and budgets by definition imply consolidated or coordinated payers.

We present only a few examples to round out discussion. We use the control of physician expenditures because it is much harder than controlling hospital expenditures because of the number of physicians, compared with hospitals; because doctors typically fight control more than hospitals, which in addition are subject to substantial regulation; and because physicians have greater ability to induce demand, and thereby defeat cost control, than any other actor in the health care sector. We draw principally on Germany and Canada because they share some aspects of our sector. Canada, our immediate neighbor to the north, shares some cultural features of our medical practice, particularly a practice style that is relatively aggressive compared with doctors working in our trading partners in Europe. However, Canada's provinces do use a single-payer payment method, something unlikely to obtain in the United States, with our multitude of insurers. For that reason, on this dimension the better comparison might be Germany because for most years Germany has had numerous sickness funds, far more than France for example, although with free choice among funds the number has shrunk from about 1200 in 1992 to 260 in 2006 as a wave of consolidation continues. *See, e.g.,* Günter Neubauer & Florian Pfister, *DRGs in Germany: Introduction of a Comprehensive, Prospective DRG Payment System by 2009, in* Kimberly et al., eds., THE GLOBALIZATION OF MANAGERIAL INNOVATION IN HEALTH CARE at 153, 154. This comparison too should not be overdrawn because competition among funds in social security countries is extremely regulated such that incentives to risk select are absent or heavily diluted. Moreover, the funds coordinate in all-payer systems with governmental oversight. Still, despite the differences, with appropriate caution about transferability of methods into different social, political and historical contexts, comparisons can illuminate.

In Germany local physicians are organized into associations, as are the sickness funds.* In this "corporatist" society, such "peak associations" negotiate to represent the interests of their members. Periodically they create a relative-value scale, and prior to 1986, they negotiated a conversion factor. However, this system failed to control costs, and therefore it was replaced with a point system. A physician would submit bills to the regional physician association, and each service was worth a number of points. On a quarterly basis the total points and resultant payments would be tallied, and if the total exceeded the cap that had been negotiated, each point would be worth less, with the result that payments to physicians were reduced immediately if volume and intensity had increased. This system stands in marked contrast to our RBRVS-based system in which overpayments from exceeding the expenditure target in one year is supposed to,

---

* Most of this discussion derives from WHITE, COMPETING SOLUTIONS ch. 4, and Glaser, *How Expenditure Caps and Expenditure Targets Really Work* at 108–111.

but hasn't, resulted in a diminution of aggregate expenditure in the next. The German system adjusts fees immediately and is the product of negotiation between peak associations, thereby lending it legitimacy and cooperation among its members.

However, payment is not the only means to control expenditures. A joint committee of the funds and physicians retrospectively oversees utilization. Using centralized data, the committee builds practice profiles that compare comparable practices. The committee is thereby able to flag significant deviations from the norm, and the committee consults with the physician who is an outlier. The process is more consultative and educational than punitive, although the committee does have authority to deduct excesses from future payments. All this occurs in the context of regulation of medical education to control physician supply (which went awry and produced too many physicians for a while), and, more importantly, regulating the diffusion of capital.

One ironic fact of the RBRVS-based system in the United States is that when it was implemented, in their use of the VPS, creators thought they were modeling methods used in British Columbia in the 1980s. *See* Paul B. Ginsburg & Philip R. Lee, *Defending U.S. Physician Payment Reform*, 8(4) HEALTH AFFAIRS 67 (1989); *see also* SMITH, PAYING FOR MEDICARE at 198. However, the designers failed to understand the difference between imposing an aggregate target or cap and negotiating one, and moreover, they missed the fact that to succeed, a target has to be used in conjunction with other methods. The overall institutional structure just discussed in Germany illustrates those points, as do many features of the situation in British Columbia that designers of our VPS ignored. In more detail, much more could have been learned from British Columbia:

> First, for example, the "informal" negotiating structure represented by the PPRC, whether it results in a national or state-wide volume performance standard,[5] simply does not resemble bilateral negotiations between parties who are locked together for the long haul,[6] as any labor lawyer in the United States could readily tell us. Second, by the mid–1980s there was growing concern in British Columbia (and in other provinces) that volume controls would prove ineffective and politically unstable.[7] Third, British Columbia in those years was, in draconian fashion, eliminating ***current*** physician stock by refusing to grant, or severely restricting geographically, billing numbers for some physicians.[8] Fourth, the

---

5. SMITH, PAYING FOR MEDICARE at 15–16.

6. GLASER, HEALTH INSURANCE BARGAINING.

7. Morris L. Barer & Robert G. Evans, *Riding North on a South–Bound Horse? Expenditures, Prices, Utilization and Incomes in the Canadian Health Care System, in* MEDICARE AT MATURITY: ACHIEVEMENTS, LESSONS AND CHALLENGES 53, 144–49 (Robert G. Evans & Greg L. Stoddart, eds., 1986); Jonathan Lomas & Morris L. Barer, *And Who Shall Represent the Public Interest? The Legacy of Canadian Manpower Policy, in* MEDICARE AT MATURITY: ACHIEVEMENTS, LESSONS AND CHALLENGES 221 (Robert G. Evans & Greg L. Stoddart, eds., 1986).

8. Morris L. Barer, *Regulating Physician Supply: The Evolution of British Columbia's Bill 41*, 13 J. HEALTH POL'Y & L. 1 (1988).

Canadian provinces were actively preventing the diffusion of capital into and within the ambulatory care sector, instead of reimbursing it, as we do, and (worse still) instead of spreading its recovery, as does the RBRVS system, across a relative value scale.[9]

Frankford, *Measuring Health Care* at 660 (footnote with references added).

Writing in 1989, Bill Glaser put his finger on the point about American policy regarding payment and cost control. As we have seen above, in the United States "policy analysis in health care finance has specialized in technical economics rather than in the construction of politically feasible structures." William A. Glaser, *The Politics of Paying American Physicians*, 8(3) HEALTH AFFAIRS 129, 131 (1989); *see also* William A. Glaser, *Designing Fee Schedules by Formulae, Politics, and Negotiations*, 80 AM. J. PUB. HEALTH 804 (1990). Rather than uniting payers and providers into institutionalized mechanisms through which they can face off and try to resolve disputes, instead in the United States we have been creating technically beautiful apparatuses that purportedly work their technocratic magic in an institutional vacuum in an attempt to mimic a hypothetical market's magic hand. It may be true that Glaser tended to paint too rosy a picture of consensus rather than the assertion of power, *compare, e.g.*, William A. Glaser, *Doctors and Public Authorities: The Trend Toward Collaboration*, 19 J. HEALTH POL. POL'Y & L. 795 (1994), *with, e.g.*, Victor G. Rodwin, *Physician Payment Reform: Lessons from Abroad*, 8(4) HEALTH AFFAIRS 76 (1989), it is nonetheless true that the United States remains weak in institutions that connect payers and providers together and forces them to resolve disputes, or at least allows the assertion of power, whether through arbitration or other institutionalized mechanisms. As Joe White remarked concerning negotiations and arbitration in Canadian provinces, "Kicking and screaming in many cases, both sides have been dragged into recognizing that they have to live together, that rules are necessary, and neither side should be able to impose its will." WHITE, COMPETING SOLUTIONS at 69. By contrast, our institutional vacuum isn't working.

The fragmentation we get instead produces three results: higher expenditures, increased administrative cost, and dysfunctional delivery of care. The first point we have explicated throughout the chapter. The second point has been shown in numerous studies, the most recent of which includes Lawrence P. Casalino et al., *What Does It Cost Physician Practices to Interact with Health Insurance Plans?*, 28(4) HEALTH AFFAIRS w533 (2009), in which the authors found the cost to physician practices of dealing with the multitude of insurers to be $31 billion, which is 6.9% of all U.S. expenditures for physician and clinical services. *Id.* A more recent study from the same research team found that this figure amounted to nearly four times what is spend in Canada. Dante Morra et al., *US Physician Practices Versus Canadians: Spending Nearly Four Times as Much Money Interacting with Payers*, 30(8) HEALTH AFFAIRS 1 (2011). Professor Reinhardt

---

9. Morris L. Barer et al., *Fee Controls as Cost Control: Tales from the Frozen North*, 66 MILBANK Q. 1, 10 (1988).

made the same point in his description of hospitals' practices for dealing with the insurance horde:

> An individual hospital might be paid by a dozen or more distinct third-party payers, each with its own distinct set of rules for and levels of payment, which are negotiated separately with each private insurer once a year. Medicare and Medicaid have their own extensive rules for paying hospitals. Relative to hospitals paid under the much simpler national health insurance schemes in other countries, the contracting and billing departments of U.S. hospitals therefore are huge enterprises, often requiring large cadres of highly skilled workers backed up by sophisticated computer systems that can simulate the revenue implications of the individual contract negotiations. Furthermore, because violations of contracts with the government programs can trigger severe civil or criminal penalties, hospital billing departments are strictly monitored and supervised by sizable internal control operations.

Reinhardt, The Pricing of U.S. Hospital Services at 59.

The third point—fragmentation in delivery—should not be overlooked as less important than cost control. We are about to turn to quality more generally in the next Part of this book, but the point here is simply that fragmentation in payment can kill.

Early in this chapter we noted that health care works best when payers, patients and providers are joined together for the long-haul in integrated pools such that there is continuity of care, incentives to invest in prevention, stability in revenue generation—one side of the revenue and expenditure equation—and stability in payment—the other side of the equation. In this chapter we have discussed how a very fragmented payment system feeds on itself and becomes entrenched in culture and institutions in that the fragmentation enables cost shifting, volume generation, shifting of sites of care, risk selection, upcoding and the like. This behavior is then countered by payers' moves to rebundle services, even to rebundle providers into entities like ACOs (and numerous other examples). However, these efforts are likely to be successful only in a marginal way because they are swimming upstream against so much fragmentation elsewhere. Despite efforts to bundle up the provider side we will still have both a multitude of different public and private entities contributing the "system's" revenues—e.g., Medicare, the 51 Medicaid plans, a million private ERISA plans, individual plans, (the soon to be added 51 state Exchange plans)—all operating with varying rules, and a multitude of different entities engaged in payment, who likewise operate with varying rules. In principle under highly regulated circumstances the finance side can remain somewhat disaggregated—like in Germany or moreover, in Switzerland and the Netherlands—while the payment side is coordinated.* However, in the

---

* For a truly illuminating discussion of how carefully calibrated such a system must be, *see* Tsung–Mei Cheng, *Understanding the "Swiss Watch" Function of Switzerland's Health System*, 29(8) HEALTH AFFAIRS 1442 (2010).

United States, at least right now, that appears unlikely to occur with so much fragmentation in all parts of the system.*

This fragmentation has consequences for quality of care, to which we turn in Part Three. We offer just one piece of empirical information for now. A recent study, Steven D. Pizer & Johan A. Gardner, *Is Fragmented Financing Bad for Your Health?*, 48 INQUIRY 109 (2011), examined the correlation between fragmented financing and the probability of hospitalization (and re-hospitalization) for certain chronic conditions that, if well controlled through ambulatory care, would lead to fewer hospitalizations—asthma, diabetes, congestive heart failure, etc. As the authors explain, continuity of care has been associated with better outcomes in a number of ways: higher quality primary care; lower probability of hospitalization; fewer visits to the emergency room; better immunization and other prevention; etc. The authors further described how our system promotes numerous disruptions in continuity of care because patients are separated from providers with whom they have established relationships when they switch—or are switched from—insurance plans and when providers are deselected from their patients' plan. What this study did was to connect these two parts to examine how fragmented financing affects outcomes. The authors found, first, that persons who have these types of chronic illnesses need a multitude of providers, and given these diverse needs, changes in insurance or in the provider pool are more likely to result in fragmentation of financing. The authors found, second, that higher fragmentation was highly correlated with higher rates of hospitalization.

Fragmentation does indeed kill. The fragmentation in payment discussed in this chapter has defeated our attempts to control expenditures; it appears to be part of a dynamic which skews our system away from primary care and the prevention that goes along with it; and in the United States at least, fragmentation in payment is institutionally linked with fragmentation in finance and delivery, which in turn is linked with adverse quality, our next subject.

---

4. REIMBURSEMENT AS SOCIAL POLICY: PUBLIC GOODS (E.G., EDUCATION); STAND-BY CAPACITY (E.G., TRAUMA UNITS); AND DISTRIBUTIVE JUSTICE (E.G., A SAFETY NET)

Before turning to quality, however, we wish to focus a bit on financing of public goods like education, stand-by capacity—like trauma centers, that we don't ordinarily use but sure need them to be there when we need

---

* We've been here before anyway: "Yesterday's conviction that capitation and integrated delivery systems held the key to stemming medical costs has been resurrected in the current fad for accountable care organizations and bundling, with scant acknowledgement that we have been down this road before." Jonathan Oberlander, *Throwing Darts: Americans' Elusive Search for Health Care Cost Control*, 36 J. HEALTH POL. POL'Y & L. 477, 481 (2011). "Americans are . . . determined to try all available cost control options—except those that actually succeed elsewhere." *Id.* at 482.

them—and distributive goals, like maintaining a safety net for those who cannot afford to pay for their care. As we indicated above, these purposes are not incorporated into the DRG-based system. As we noted, the direct costs of graduate medical education ("GME") are excluded from the DRG-based system altogether and paid separately.* Other goals, like the DSH payments, are all add-ons—directly targeted payments for particular activities like serving a disproportionate share of poor patients.

To say the least, the methods of paying for these items and the amount to be paid have been very controversial. In the interest of space, we just want to give you a flavor of the debates, and so we only briefly describe some of MedPAC's current proposals to reform medical education through Medicare funding.

There are three related underlying motivations behind the proposals we describe. The first concerns overall supply. As we have seen, an increase in the number of physicians has historically been correlated with an increase in the volume of services. Hence, the first motivation behind the proposals is that funding for education be related to the need to control aggregate expenditures through controlling the supply of physicians.

The second motivation arises from the fact that, as we have seen, specialists can expand the volume of services much more easily than can primary-care physicians. Coupled with an overall lack of generalists relative to specialists—historically in the United States we have overfunded the education of specialists—and coupled with payment skewed toward specialists, as we have seen—control over aggregate expenditures and addressing the imbalance in the mix of physicians are linked.**

The third motivation relates to the fact that, as we've also discussed, in the United States we pay for care in a fragmented fashion although the care should be continuous; and the fragmentation of payment and the fragmentation of care are related as chickens are to eggs. Bundling payments together, whether into "episodes of care" or into aggregations of providers, e.g., ACO's, should in theory, as we've also discussed, reduce aggregate expenditures and also improve quality. As a result, graduates of our medical education programs should be trained, not only to be technically proficient in what they do as individuals, but also be proficient in coordinating across the continuum of care, acting within teams of different types of professionals, and acting effectively within organizations that integrate what are now disaggregated sites and stages of care that need to be more integrated.

---

* The Indirect Medical Education ("IME") adjustment is not designed to pay for education but for the fact that the patients in teaching hospitals are more severely ill, or complex, than the norm reflected in the DRGs. This adjustment too has been very controversial. There is almost universal agreement that it has been set too high since the inception of the IPPS as a way to buy off teaching hospitals (and their elected supporters). *See, e.g.,* MAYES & BERENSON, MEDICARE PROSPECTIVE PAYMENT at 44–45.

** The locus classicus for the historical overemphasis on specialization is ROSEMARY STEVENS, AMERICAN MEDICINE AND THE PUBLIC INTEREST: A HISTORY OF SPECIALIZATION (updated ed., 1998).

Given these interlocking motivations, a portion of a 2010 MedPAC report focused on Medicare's funding of education begins, "Our nation's system of medical education and graduate training produces superbly skilled clinicians while contributing to stunning advances in medical science. Yet, it is not aligned with the delivery system reforms essential for increasing the value of health care in the United States." MedPAC, Report to the Congress: Aligning Incentives in Medicare 103 (June 2010). This statement concerns all of the facts that too many residents are being training for specialty care, that too many specialists drive up volume and expenditures, and that coordination across a continuum of care is sorely lacking. MedPAC continues, "Medicare is the single largest payer of graduate medical education (GME)—$9.5 billion in 2009—but requires minimal accountability from its recipients for achieving education and training goals." *Id.* The reform task, therefore, is to obtain accountability.

MedPAC proposes to accomplish this task through attention both to the mix of physicians trained and the content and outcomes of that training. It proposes, first, starting in October 2013, the implementation of a new incentive program, funded out of further reduction to the IME, in which payments will be awarded based on satisfaction of specified educational standards and outcomes: "The standards established by the Secretary should specify ambitious goals for practice-based learning and improvement (including quality measurement), interpersonal and communication skills (including cultural sensitivity), professionalism (including patient-centered care), and systems-based practice (including integration of care across community- and hospital-based settings)." *Id.* at 113. Notably, this program will not draw current funds out of direct GME spending, although the Commission stated that "[f]uture assessment of the GME payment system might consider making even larger portions contingent on performance." *Id.* at 114.

MedPAC's second and third proposals are related to each other. Payments for graduate medical education go, not to medical schools, but directly to teaching hospitals. Educators have complained that they have little idea how hospitals are using resources. The aim of these two proposals, therefore, is increased transparency. One proposal is that teaching hospitals be required to report information concerning their direct GME and IME payments, the number of residents reported for those calculations, and Medicare's share of their GME costs. *See id.* at 115. The other proposal is that CMS report similar information annually for each teaching hospital that receives GME funding. *See id.* at 116–17.

The fourth and final proposal we discuss is that CMS should conduct a workforce study to determine the total number of residency slots needed and the mix of specialties. MedPAC recommends that the workforce study not just count numbers but also consider "what education and training the workforce will require." *Id.* at 118. Moreover, the calculation should be tied to specific workplace settings: "The Commission strongly recommends that an analysis of our 21st century health care workforce needs be driven by the requirements of a high-value, affordable health care delivery system. In calculating benchmarks for physicians and specialty mix, this study should take into account successful examples of high-performing, integrated delivery systems." *Id.* (reference omitted). The purpose is clearly to link, as we described above, aggregate expenditures and the distribution of those expenditures—fiscal goals—with creation of an educational system that can meet the needs of a delivery system reorganized to achieve those ends: "A study is needed to assess how major improvements in the delivery system would affect the demand for physicians. If Medicare is unsustainable without delivery system reform, as the Commission maintains, a health care workforce that is consonant with a reformed delivery system is essential." *Id.*

These are laudable goals, but they should be put in historical perspective. Similar proposals have been raised for decades, probably close to half a century now. Some of them have been internal to medicine, produced by various associations like the Association of American Medical Colleges, and some have been external to medicine, produced by various foundations and commissions, like the Pew Charitable Trusts. However, many observers would conclude that these efforts have produced change only at the margins, because specialization is so strongly entrenched within medical schools, within hospitals, within the profession as represented by various specialty societies, and as we have stressed in this chapter, within the payment system. What MedPAC proposes is clearly very different in that its proposal would be backed by the power of the purse. Nonetheless, whether these proposals can get through Congress and be implemented successfully is not clear. We can be hopeful but history teaches how difficult it is to change the system in the United States oriented toward specialization and high-technology care.

THE PATIENT PROTECTION AND AFFORDABLE CARE ACT IN THE UNITED STATES SUPREME COURT

On November 14, 2011 the United States Supreme Court agreed to hear arguments on four issues that have arisen as a result of more than two dozen legal challenges to the Affordable Care Act that were filed upon or immediately following enactment. Eventually, four appeals courts ruled on multiple aspects of the challenges: whether the parties had standing and their claims were ripe; whether the federal courts have jurisdiction to hear claims regarding the constitutionality of the individual coverage requirement under the Anti–Injunction Act; whether the coverage requirement is constitutional, and if not, whether its provisions are severable from the rest of the Act; whether the obligations of employers are constitutional; and whether the Medicaid expansions violate the Tenth Amendment and are unconstitutionally coercive. Ultimately one appellate court overturned the individual coverage requirement as unconstitutional in Florida v. United States Department of Health and Human Services, 648 F.3d 1235 (11th Cir. 2011), while upholding the Medicaid expansions. Two other circuits found the individual coverage requirement constitutional. Thomas More Law Center v. Obama, 651 F.3d 529 (6th Cir. 2011) and Susan Seven–Sky v. Holder, 661 F.3d 1 (D.C. Cir. 2011). A fourth appellate court decision dismissed the individual coverage requirement claim on grounds that it was precluded by the Anti–Injunction Act. Liberty University v. Geithner, 2011 WL 3962915 (4th Cir. 2011).

Underscoring the seminal nature of the case, the Supreme Court itself has created a special website for briefs and related materials. http://www.supremecourt.gov/docket/PPAACA.aspx.

From this mass of litigation the Supreme Court will consider four issues: (1) Whether Congress has the power under Article I of the Constitution to enact the minimum coverage provision; (2) If the individual mandate is found unconstitutional, whether it is severable from the remainder of the Act; (3) Whether the ACA's requirement that states expand Medicaid eligibility or risk losing federal funds is unduly coercive in violation of the Tenth Amendment; and (4) Whether the individual coverage requirement is a tax for purposes of the Anti–Injunction Act, meaning that it precludes plaintiffs from challenging the requirement until it takes effect in 2014.

The constitutionality of the individual coverage requirement

The constitutionality of the individual coverage requirement raises questions regarding the scope and limits of Congressional powers under both the General Welfare Clause and the Commerce Clause. Recall that the ACA effectuates the coverage requirement through amendments to the Internal Revenue Code, by imposing a "penalty" on applicable taxpayers who do not present evidence of "minimum essential coverage" (i.e., employer coverage, coverage purchased individually, Medicare, Medicaid, TRI-CARE, veterans health care programs certified by the Secretaries of Health and Human Services and Veterans Affairs, and certain other forms of coverage). 26 U.S.C. § 5000A(f). The penalty for failure to maintain such coverage is relatively low; after a phase-in period, the penalty will be capped at $695.00, adjusted after 2016 for inflation, or 2.5 percent of taxable income above the filing limit. *Id.* § 5000A(c)(3)(D).

Although the Justice Department consistently argued that Congress' taxing and spending powers offered a basis for the coverage requirement, the Eleventh Circuit rejected this argument, concluding that the law was structured as a penalty rather than a revenue-raising tax, that Congress did not intend the law to operate as a tax, and that the minimum essential coverage requirement thus failed to meet the minimum essential elements of a tax under Supreme Court precedent. ("The government would have us ignore all of this and instead hold that any provision found in the Internal Revenue Code that will produce revenue may be characterized as a tax. This we are unwilling to do."). *Florida,* 648 F.3d at 1315–19. The Court of Appeals for the Sixth Circuit reached a similar conclusion in *Thomas More,* 651 F.3d 529, holding that the coverage requirement was a regulatory penalty, not an "enforced contribution to provide for the support of government." *Thomas More,* 651 F.3d at 544 (Sutton, J., concurring).

Where the lower courts disagreed was over whether the requirement could be upheld as a valid exercise of Congress' Commerce Clause powers. The disagreement essentially boiled down to two matters: first, whether the individual conduct regulated is reachable under the Commerce Clause; and second, whether the solution (i.e., a requirement to purchase private insurance) amounts to a constitutional exercise of Congressional powers under the Commerce and the Necessary and Proper Clauses. On these two matters, the appellate decisions diverge sharply, with the *Thomas More* and *Seven Sky* majorities (along with a particularly strong concurring opinion by Judge Jeffrey Sutton in *Thomas More*) finding the requirement constitutional, and the *Florida* majority reaching the opposite conclusion.

In reaching opposite conclusions, the appellate courts nonetheless agreed on the basic parameters of the Commerce Clause as well as on the defining Supreme Court precedents that ultimately will help shape the outcome.* However, consensus broke down over what the various courts

---

* Certain cases are cited repeatedly in the appellate decisions, regardless of whether the decision is to uphold or strike down the individual coverage requirement. These are Wickard v. Filburn, 317 U.S. 111 (1942) (prohibition against the growing of wheat for personal consump-

found to be the key regulatory purpose of the coverage requirement and the validity of the requirement itself. In essence, the lower courts disagreed over the essential purpose of the law as well as the validity of a law that effectively requires individuals to establish a relationship to a private insurance market.

Underlying this disagreement was accord on Congress' power under the Commerce Clause to regulate individual behavior that by itself has no impact on interstate commerce and is wholly intrastate in nature, as long as such behavior is considered to "substantially affect" interstate commerce. The two sides also agree that under longstanding precedent, Wickard v. Filburn, 317 U.S. 111 (1942), Congress can "aggregate" individual conduct in measuring substantial impact. The lower courts also agree that the Necessary and Proper Clause affords Congress additional authority to establish requirements that might not otherwise survive, when they are a broader part of a comprehensive regulatory scheme. Gonzalez v. Raich, 545 U.S. 1 (2005). (As Professor Mark Hall has pointed out, to the extent that opponents of the minimum coverage requirement argue that the requirement is unseverable from the Act's insurance market reforms (United States Supreme Court, Brief of the NFIB, NFIB v. Sebelius et al., 11–393 and 11–400), they seem to concede that establishment of a minimum insurance pool to support the market reforms is a necessary and proper exercise of Congress's authority to establish a broad regulatory scheme governing the health insurance market. Mark Hall, New York University, Annual Symposium on American Health Law, Feb. 17, 2012). Where the agreement ends—as with so many legal disputes—is not over the fundamental legal principles but over their application to specific facts. The two sides disagree over precisely what Congress is trying to regulate and over whether its solution is kosher.

The appellate court opinions favoring the constitutionality of the individual coverage requirement (the majority and concurring opinions in *Thomas More Law Center v. Obama* and *Susan Seven Sky v. Holder*) concluded that the ACA's fundamental focus is on stabilizing the health care system economy as a whole, and that this frame of reference is essential because all Americans need and use health care, and their need is essentially unpredictable. The majorities upholding the coverage requirement focus on Congress' lengthy findings (PPACA § 1501) regarding the impact of uninsured people on the health care economy (over $40 billion in bad debt that is passed along to everyone through higher insurance premiums), the problems created by having so many Americans attempting to self-insure, the need for a stable and accessible insurance system, and the resulting need for a healthy insurance pool. These related findings, for the majorities favoring constitutionality, form a solid basis for Congress'

---

tion held constitutional), United States v. Morrison, 529 U.S. 598 (2000) (the Violence Against Women Act held unconstitutional); United States v. Lopez, 514 U.S. 549 (1995) (the Gun Free School Zones Act held unconstitutional); Gonzalez v. Raich, 545 U.S. 1 (the Controlled Substances Act's prohibition applied to the growing of marijuana for personal use held constitutional); and Heart of Atlanta Motel v. United States, 379 U.S. 241 (1964) (the Civil Rights Act of 1964 applied to individual motel owner held constitutional).

decision to regulate individual conduct where the "when and how" of paying for health care is concerned.

The favorable rulings expressed no concern with the allegedly unprecedented nature of the mandate. Furthermore, from their perspective, the modern Supreme Court has given Congress a wide berth to test innovative solutions to complex problems of national policy (Judge Sutton goes back further, pointing to the creation of the first national bank as an example of Congressional innovation). In so doing, the majorities reject the notion that Congress is forcing Americans into a market and thereby punishing inactivity rather than economic activity, a point repeatedly made by the challengers. Indeed, in his *Thomas More* concurrence Judge Sutton, noted for his conservative judicial philosophy, dismisses the assertion that not buying a product could be characterized as "inactivity" at all: "No one is inactive when deciding how to pay for health care, as self-insurance and private insurance are two forms of action for addressing the same risk. Each requires affirmative choices; one is no less active than the other; and both affect commerce." 651 F.3d at 561.

Furthermore, the *Seven–Sky* and *Thomas More* majorities found no problem with an individual requirement to buy private insurance as a resolution of the problem. In their view, Congress devised a quintessentially American solution to an intractable problem in the market, one that reshapes the market and individuals' relationship to it, no different from reshaping individual farmers' relationship to the market for wheat. In his *Thomas More* concurrence, Judge Sutton was clear in pointing out that such a solution is not unconstitutional because it had never previously been attempted, noting that any solution that hinged on a Medicare-like approach of extending public insurance to all residents through use of the taxing power, while clearly constitutional, had proved to be politically impossible, leaving Congress with no choice but to forge a new path.

In striking down the individual coverage requirement, the Eleventh Circuit majority held that rather than reshaping the market for health care, the purpose of the law was to force Americans into a private insurance market that they had chosen to remain outside of. In this respect, the majority asserted, the Act could be distinguished from other cases such as *Wickard* and *Raich,* which reordered pre-existing relationships between individuals and markets; this was an instance of forcing relationships that do not exist. What appeared to move the Eleventh Circuit into the "no" column was not the inactivity argument, which it dismissed as unhelpful. Instead, the appeals court suggested that the mandate crossed a line from a constitutional perspective, since it was "a mandate that Americans purchase and maintain health insurance from a private company for the entirety of their lives." 648 F.3d at 1288. Even more important, perhaps, the *Florida* majority wrote that "even assuming that decisions *not* to buy insurance substantially affect interstate commerce," 648 F.3d at 1293, no connection could be found between the coverage requirement and commerce, because the requirement was not linked to an actual act of commerce itself, namely the use of health care:

[W]hat matters is the regulated subject matter's connection to interstate commerce. That nexus is lacking here. It is immaterial whether we perceive Congress to be regulating inactivity or a financial decision to forego insurance. Under any framing the regulated conduct is defined by the *absence of* both commerce or even "the production, distribution, and consumption of commerce."

Id.

As such, the *Florida* majority lumped the minimum coverage requirement into the same camp as laws regulating the mere possession of guns on school grounds, United States v. Lopez, 514 U.S. 549 (1995), and the commission of a local crime, United States v. Morrison, 529 U.S. 598 (2000). In so doing, the majority refused to defer to Congress' own findings regarding the link between not being insured and the health care economy. In its view, even extensive findings could not save a law whose purpose and structure simply are too attenuated to commerce to be considered connected to it, a position taken by the Supreme Court in declaring unconstitutional the Violence Against Women's Act in *United States v. Morrison.*

The Eleventh Circuit majority also dismissed the argument that the cumulative uncompensated care burden across the health care system—an express finding by Congress—provided evidence of the nexus between the decision to forego insurance coverage and commerce. Relying on *Lopez,* the majority concluded that it is not enough to assert a connection between conduct and commerce; Congress simply was unable to show the type of link that the Commerce Clause requires:

Here the decision to forego insurance similarly lacks an established interstate tie or any "case-by-case inquiry." Aside from the categories of exempted individuals, the individual mandate is applied across-the-board without regard to whether the regulated individuals receive, or have ever received, uncompensated care—or indeed, seek any care at all either now or in the future. Thus the Act contains no language "which might limit its reach to a discrete set of [activities] that additionally have an explicit connection with or effect on interstate commerce."

648 F.3d at 1294 (quoting *Lopez*).

In response to the assertion that all people will need health care at some point, the majority responded that such an assertion made the mandate's constitutionality even shakier because it underscored the absence of any *current* connection between the requirement and individual conduct. The majority further pointed out that Congress would, of course, be well within its powers in enacting a law banning the use of health care by uninsured people ("[w]hen the uninsured actually enter the stream of commerce and consume health care, Congress may regulate their activity at the point of consumption.") 648 F.3d at 1295. In the majority's view, however, the law's fatal flaw is its failure to regulate insurance coverage at the point of consumption.*

In keeping with political arguments made both during and following enactment, the *Florida* majority was troubled by the lack of "limiting principles" for such a law and expressed its dissatisfaction with the federal government's suggestion that the political process itself would place limits on Congress' use of its power to regulate individuals' relationship with markets ("If Congress may compel individuals to purchase health insurance from a private company, it may similarly compel the purchase of other products from private industry, regardless of the 'unique conditions' the government cites as warrant for Congress's regulation here." 648 F.3d at 1298). Finally, the majority rejected the notion that the individual coverage requirement was a necessary component of a broader regulatory scheme, holding that Congress could regulate the insurance industry without question but that an individual purchase requirement is not necessary to that task. Acknowledging the insurance crisis that might arise from regulating the market without connecting the regulation to a stable purchasing pool, the majority concluded that this was not its problem.

Severability

The Eleventh Circuit majority ruled that the mandate could be severed from the remainder of the Act and that numerous options remained available to Congress to address the Act's constitutional deficiencies. (In so doing, the court was perhaps mindful of Professor Hall's excellent observation.) Essential to its decision were several considerations: the weak penalties that attach to those who refuse to buy coverage; the fact that no severability clause was included in the Act; and the fact that the market reforms make no reference to the mandate. From the majority's perspective, the better part of valor would be to send the law back to Congress intact but missing the mandate, with Congress free to grapple with alternatives.**

Whether the Medicaid expansion is unconstitutionally coercive

Recall that the ACA's Medicaid expansion creates a new mandatory Medicaid eligibility category consisting of nonelderly adults who are neither pregnant, persons with the level of disability required to achieve Medicaid coverage, nor eligible caretakers of minor children. PPACA § 2001. Coverage of the new eligibility group thus becomes a condition of state entitle-

---

* Of course you learned at the beginning of this Part that such an approach basically would blow up the insurance system, not to mention being utterly inhumane. Are people supposed to tell the ambulance to stop at the insurance company on the way to the hospital?

** One alternative might be to substitute a voluntary enrollment provision that provides for fixed open enrollment periods and penalties for late enrollment, in order to reduce the potential for adverse selection. Jonathan Oberlander, *Under Seige—The Individual Mandate for Health Insurance and its Alternatives*, 364 NEW ENG. J. MED. 1085 (2011). Such an alternative, notes Professor Oberlander, might allow preservation of the insurance reforms but would significantly reduce the number of insured people, and the penalties for late enrollment would need to be very stiff for a voluntary system to work.

ment to federal Medicaid payments; for coverage of the newly eligible group, however, the legislation rewards states with heavily enhanced federal funding that begins at 100 percent for most states and declines to 90 percent in 2020. *Id.*

The Eleventh Circuit, the only court to reach the Medicaid coercion claim, rejected the challenge. The Supreme Court's granting certiorari on this issue has been perhaps the biggest surprise of all, because the latest Medicaid expansion follows the pattern of numerous mandatory expansions that preceded it (e.g., mandated coverage of all recipients of Supplemental Security Income in 1972; mandatory coverage of all federally defined "poverty level" pregnant women and children). Furthermore, the original Medicaid statute, as you have learned, mandated that certain populations (e.g., recipients of cash welfare) be covered by states. In this respect, the Medicaid coercion issue potentially becomes at least as, if not more, consequential than the mandate. Striking down the individual coverage requirement would leave Congress and the President with possible alternatives. Striking down the Medicaid expansion as coercive calls into question all Spending Clause statutes that impose minimum state operational requirements as a quid pro quo for federal funding.

The states' argument is based on the "coercion doctrine," a theory characterized as "amorphous" by the Eleventh Circuit. *Florida*, 648 F.3d at 1251. Set forth by the United States Supreme Court in the New Deal era, the doctrine relates to Congress' Spending Clause powers and was most recently addressed by the Court in South Dakota v. Dole, 483 U.S. 203 (1987). In *Dole,* the Court upheld as non-coercive a federal law that conditioned five percent of federal highway funds on states' agreeing to raise the minimum drinking age to 21. Chief Justice Rehnquist, writing for the majority, stated, "Our decisions have recognized that, in some circumstances, the financial inducement offered by Congress might be so coercive as to pass the point at which 'pressure turns into compulsion.'" 483 U.S. at 221.

Based on this doctrine, the states argued in *Florida* that the Medicaid expansion amounts to unconstitutional coercion because failure to comply potentially could result in loss of federal funding and even more specifically, because the only source of health care financing for the poor under the Affordable Care Act comes from Medicaid (Recall that premium tax credits are available only to individuals with incomes that exceed Medicaid eligibility standards, with the exception of impoverished legal residents who have not yet satisfied Medicaid's waiting period. PPACA § 1401). Since it is Medicaid or nothing for the poorest residents, argue the states, what has historically been an optional program has been effectively converted into a coercive law.

In rejecting this argument, the Eleventh Circuit concluded that under coercion doctrine theory, states had not met the bar. First, nothing in the statute forces the Secretary to withhold all funds. Indeed, the law gives her flexibility to engage in only partial withholding; thus, the states' claim of all or nothing was wrong. Second, the Eleventh Circuit pointed out that while the expansion may create a difficult choice for states, a hard choice is not the same as unconstitutional coercion. Medicaid remains voluntary. Third, the court noted that in keeping with the doctrine, Congress gave the states plenty of notice (the Medicaid expansions do not become effective until 45 months following the ACA's enactment). Should a state wish to pull out of Medicaid and go it alone for its poorest residents, it can do so. In addition, as the Department of Justice pointed out in its response to the states' petition for certiorari on the coercion question, the coercion doctrine comes into play only when an insubstantial obligation is tied to a substantial loss of funding. A Medicaid expansion covering some 16 million people is hardly an insubstantial requirement; nor is nearly full federal funding a substantial loss for the states.

The Anti–Injunction Act

The argument under the Anti–Injunction Act is that if the legislation is deemed to have a constitutional basis in Congress' taxing and spending powers, then the federal courts have no jurisdiction to hear a challenge before the effective date of the coverage requirement and the imposition of a penalty. The United States Court of Appeals for the Fourth Circuit, in *Liberty University v Geithner*, 2011 WL 3962915, concluded that the individual coverage requirement in fact is a tax despite the term "penalty" that appears in the legislation, and on this basis dismissed the challenge. Because the Obama Administration has taken the position that the case should be decided on its merits as soon as possible, special counsel will argue the Anti–Injunction Act claim.

What Does All of This Mean?

Whatever the final result (a June 2012 decision is likely), the consequences emerge at a couple of levels.

From a constitutional perspective, the decision of course has profound implications for the scope of Congressional powers. A decision holding that Congress cannot reach individual interactions with broad markets as part of an effort to stabilize such markets within the national economy—and furthermore, that Congress cannot utilize market-based solutions to broad social problems if the solutions go beyond the merely voluntary—raises questions about other Congressional interventions to complex questions of social welfare. For example, one proposed solution to Medicare's uncontrolled growth is to scrap the "traditional" government insurance program in favor of a premium support system that would parallel that used in the Affordable Care Act's approach to coverage in the individual market. Would such a solution—typically advanced by conservative free-market thinkers—immediately be off the table since it would replace public insurance with compulsory participation in a decidedly market-based system?

The Medicaid coercion aspect of the case arguably is even more far-reaching. Not only would a decision in the states' favor call into question Medicaid's basic structure, but such a decision would place a bull's-eye on a host of federal laws—ranging form health care to transportation to civil rights laws—in which Congress ties large amounts of federal funding to states' agreement to abide by minimum national standards. Perhaps the most eloquent statement on the consequences of such an outcome for Congressional lawmaking was offered by Senator Charles Grassly (R–IA) who, in an extraordinary Senate speech delivered on December 15, 2011, warned his colleagues of the meaning of a coercion ruling that adopts the states' position:

> Mr. President, if the Supreme Court rules the individual mandate unconstitutional, it will have the effect of striking down a new law that hasn't been fully implemented. If the Supreme Court rules the Medicaid expansion in the Affordable Care Act unconstitutional, it has the potential to cause significant changes in a program that has been in operation for the last 46 years. [I]t is difficult to overstate the potential implications of this particular aspect of the Affordable Care Act case. A ruling for the states could affect future Medicaid policy, current Medicaid policy and broader federal-state partnerships. Mr. President, if the federal government cannot require expansion of the Medicaid program and pick up 92% of the tab, what can the federal government require? Would a mandatory expansion be constitutional if the federal government permanently paid for 100% of the cost? [I]f the current mandatory expansion of Medicaid is unconstitutional, what does that imply for previous expansions and policies? In 1989 and 1990, when Congress required states to expand eligibility for women and children, Congress did so without providing ANY additional funding for the states beyond the normal federal share. Mr. President, if the Supreme Court rules in favor of the states, will previous mandatory expansions of Medicaid be subject to challenge?

> [A] Supreme Court ruling on a coercion test necessarily has broader implications for all federal-state partnerships. A Supreme Court ruling in favor of the states will necessarily bring into question every agreement between the federal government and the states where the federal government conditions 100% of the federal funds on states meeting requirements determined by the federal government. It is certainly possible that such a Supreme Court ruling could require future Congresses to carefully consider a "coercion test" in designing legislation. It could threaten the fundamental structure of the Medicaid program by bringing into question all the requirements in the program today. It could require future Congresses to reconsider the structure of every federal-state partnership. If the Supreme Court accepts the states' argument, a host of constitutional questions will surround the operation of many federal funding streams to the states. It would be difficult to overstate the significance of such a ruling.

Statement of Senator Charles Grassley, 157 Cong. Rec. (S. 8619–20, Dec. 15, 2011).

From a health policy perspective, the meaning of the decision is much murkier. A new Congress and (potentially) a new President who meet up in

2013 could—regardless of the outcome of the case—decide to revisit the Act's basic tenets including its coverage mandate, its Medicaid expansion, its insurance reforms, and more. Remember, aside from some important but relatively modest changes, the major restructuring of the insurance market under the Act does not take effect until January 1, 2014. As a result, the 111th Congress and President Obama left themselves vulnerable to the most crucial form of attack, namely a political attack in which the major advances achieved under the law are so delayed in having an impact that a subsequent President and Congress can quash them without having to actually deprive anyone of anything.

The one signal that so complete a reversal of fortune may be unlikely can be found in the budget deficit wars that have raged throughout 2011. Even with all of the talk of deficits and deficit reduction, *no* serious effort was made to roll back the Medicaid expansion and the premium tax credits (although to be sure, Congress, as noted, has increased repayment penalties that will be imposed on people who receive more advance credits than they ultimately qualify for). The absence of a major attack on the investment in health insurance expansion for over 30 million people may signal that while mandates may become options, and expansion timetables may slow, future Congresses will see the Act as having crossed a fundamental threshold in U.S. health policy. The ACA ultimately stands for two propositions: the belief that insurance ought to be accessible; and the belief that it ought to be affordable. Even if implementation is agonizingly slow, these two basic beliefs are, in fact, shared by both political parties, and one only can hope that they will not abandon them entirely, no matter what transpires politically.

HEALTH CARE QUALITY AND LAW: DEFINING STANDARDS AND STRUCTURING ENFORCEMENT AND ACCOUNTABILITY

CHAPTER 13

OVERVIEW

Part Three addresses the law of health care quality. Quality in American health care is now, and historically has been, characterized by astonishing paradoxes and contradictions. Once quality was all about the individual doctor and his or her relationship to an individual patient, and that relationship was grounded in and shaped by medical custom. Today the quality concept is embedded in bigger picture thinking as well: how practices in individual patient care and the use of resources for specific cases square with broader goals of population health and more global sensitivities about the quality and value of population investments that are made. Indeed one of the great paradoxes in U.S. health law and policy is that even as health care financing has remained a fractured mess, the debate over health care quality increasingly has come to reflect more global thinking about how best to invest available resources to achieve good outcomes—not only to achieve good outcomes at the individual clinical level, but across populations as well. Over time, this emphasis on accountability for matters of broader health and quality, beginning at the point of individual practice, can only help spur complementary coverage and payment reforms. You will see this the impact of this link between practice, quality, health, and resources in the discussion of Accountable Care Organizations, later in this Part.

Historically quality has focused on individual patient outcomes, and rightly so, since concerns about quality grew initially out of the unique relationship between doctors and their patients. For example, the pioneers of scientific hospital medicine in early 20th century, and professional leaders ever since, emphasized rigorous attention by physicians to the patient's condition and intense commitment to the patient's well being (as conceived by physicians). Thus in a surgical residency training program in a large urban hospital in the 1970s, young physicians were expected to be very thorough in their efforts to detect patients' possible postoperative problems. "Fatigue [of the doctor], pressing family problems, a long queue of patients waiting to be seen, a touch of the flu—all the excuses that individuals routinely use in everyday life, are inadmissible [for resident doctors] on a surgery service." CHARLES BOSK, FORGIVE AND REMEMBER: MANAGING MEDICAL FAILURE 55 (1979).

But in actual practice, physician behavior could be quite different, a reflection of geography, technology, resources, and institutional and local "medical culture." Thus in 1978 a rural Mississippi surgeon performed gastrointestinal surgery on a patient, monitored her postoperative condition for an hour and a half, and then left the hospital, with apparently no clear understanding of who was responsible for keeping track of his patient's condition and under what circumstances he should be contacted. The nurses on duty discounted the patient's pain, difficulty breathing, and problematic vital signs, resulting in the patient's death without any medical attention. The doctor's defense—successful at the trial level and consistent with existing legal doctrine until reversed by the state supreme court—was that his actions were consistent with the actual practices of his local medical peers, and that the plaintiff's out-of-state eminent surgical expert was not qualified to testify as to the applicable local standard of care. The lack of communication and teamwork among the surgeon and the nurses was apparently not unusual, nor was the hospital's apparent lack of oversight and patient-protective systems. As explored in Chapter 14, legal doctrine on these issues was split, with some legal norms reinforcing the apparent national consensus and others impeding its effective implementation. *See* Hall v. Hilbun, 466 So.2d 856 (Miss. 1985), discussed later in this Part.

In the ensuing thirty years, much has changed and much has remained the same. The relatively simple concept of "medical error"—an individual doctor's failure to implement competently a clear medical (and hence legal) standard of care with respect to an individual patient—remains important, but is now seen in a much wider, systemic context. Two related insights and areas of research have had enormous impact, at least at the level of policy debates. First, as discussed in Part Two, "geographic variations research" pioneered by Dr. John Wennberg and others in the 1970s and thereafter found very large differences in rates of hospitalization and surgery for the same medical conditions in effectively identical localities, especially for the many conditions and procedures about which "clinical science is weak, [and] medical opinion [about outcomes] is only loosely constrained by medical evidence [and where physicians assume patient preferences for intervention rather than engage in informed shared decision making]." JOHN E. WENNBERG, TRACKING MEDICINE: A RESEARCHER'S QUEST TO UNDERSTAND HEALTH CARE 258–59 (2010). "For example, I have observed that in Maine, by the time women reach 70 years of age in one hospital market the likelihood they have undergone a hysterectomy is 20 percent while in another market it is 70 percent." John Wennberg, *Dealing With Medical Practice Variations: A Proposal for Action*, 3(2) HEALTH AFFAIRS 6, 9–10 (1984) (reporting similar variations for prostatectomies in Iowa and tonsillectomies in Vermont). Wennberg could not explain these differences on the basis of population characteristics, age, illness rates, insurance coverage, or access to service, and concluded that the best explanation was varying "practice styles" among doctors. Geographic variations and the relatively high rate of inappropriate or unnecessary procedures, strongly suggest that the problem of quality of care is not simply a matter of error or deviance by individual doctors. When thousands of physicians are making similar "errors," or even more seriously, when no one can explain why the rate of "appropriate" surgery varies by several hundred percent among seemingly similar populations, there are likely to be more general problems than individual deviations from established norms.

Some of the sources of these problems—a medical "entrepreneurial culture" and pervasive financial incentives that reward quantity and use of technology rather than careful risk/benefit assessment and informed patient decision-making—are explored in Dr. Atul Gawande's famous 2009 article about McAllen, Texas, discussed in Part Two. To Gawande's surprise, in the midst of McAllen's low-income population he found "sleek and modern" health care facilities filled with the latest technology. The mystery he sought to understand was why Medicare expenditures per person in McAllen had "exploded" from 1992 (when they had been at the national average) to $15,000 per person in 2006, almost twice the national average. El Paso County, 800 miles to the north, had the same lifestyle and socioeconomic demographics, the same state medical malpractice law, and the same modern facilities, and managed to spend half as much on its population with no measurable differences in health outcomes. The McAllen doctors and hospital CEOs with whom Gawande talked did not know this information, and, for the most part, did not want to know. One practicing surgeon, once his standard denials had been demolished by Gawande's data, admitted that " '[t]here is overutilization here, pure and simple.' Doctors, he said, were racking up charges with extra tests, services, and procedures." Since his arrival in McAllen in the mid–1990s, "the way to practice medicine has changed completely. Before, it was about how to do a good job. Now it is about 'How much will you [the doctor] benefit?' " Atul Gawande, *The Cost Conundrum: What a Texas Town Can Teach Us About Health Care*, THE NEW YORKER MAGAZINE, June 1, 2009, at 52.

Part Two explored the impact of these "out of control costs" on health insurance and on efforts at national health reform. Part Three focuses on the quality dimension. McAllen is not only a story about the likely vast waste of resources; it also illustrates the counterintuitive paradox that "more" high technology health care may, in an excessively profit-driven culture, also constitute low quality care. This is so for at least three reasons. First, excessive invasive tests, surgery, and other procedures are themselves risky as well as expensive. They cause harm and kill people, without adequate therapeutic justification. This surely constitutes low quality, as well as wasteful care. *See* AVEDIS DONABEDIAN, THE DEFINITION OF QUALITY AND APPROACHES TO ITS ASSESSMENT 6 (1980) ("[T]he quality of technical care consists in the application of medical science and technology in a manner that maximizes its benefits to health without correspondingly increasing its risks. The degree of quality is, therefore, the extent to which the care provided is expected to achieve the more favorable balance of risks and benefits.")

Second, population-based data show that high-cost regions also tend to have less effective and/or less accessible primary care, leading to less lower-cost (and often more effective) preventive care. This was confirmed by Gawande's conversations with McAllen's doctors, who admitted that patients with uncomplicated gallstone or chest pain would likely receive expensive diagnostic testing and even surgery, on the assumption that the patients were incapable of adhering to much lower cost (and less profitable) wellness programs. Again, this is a quality as well as a cost concern.

Third and most fundamental is the culture of what might be called "profitable ignorance," which Gawande found in McAllen and which is built into the heart of American health care nationwide, including the law that is supposed to assure quality of care. McAllen's doctors and hospital leaders did not know about their region's high expenditures and very high use of expensive tests and procedures. Furthermore, they did not want to know, because, in their view and (they would argue) in the view of the system itself, *it wasn't their job*. The doctors saw their job as deploying the best technology, presumably "appropriately," to care for individual patients. The hospital leaders saw their job as having a well-equipped hospital that would deliver "appropriate" care in a way that maximized the hospital's revenues or "business model." But who defines "appropriateness," and on the basis of what standards? Should the standard of care be limited (as it traditionally has been in medical malpractice law) to the *actual practices* of similarly-situated doctors providing services to individual patients, traditionally under fee-for-service, open-ended insurance payments? What if those actual practices have no scientific validation, and/or vary enormously among similar geographic localities (e.g., McAllen vs. El Paso)? What role should population-based studies (i.e., beyond the context of providing care to individuals), "evidence-based medicine," "clinical-practice guidelines," safety protocols, and comparative effectiveness and cost-effectiveness analysis play, if any? Within the new world of more population-based or collective standards and trade-offs, what are the major operative values, especially as between scarcity-constrained market liberty and a revised, professionally-informed social contract? This is the terrain on which is being fought what Dr. Gawande calls "a battle for the soul of American medicine," Gawande, *The Cost Conundrum*, and is the subject of Part Three.

The second and related major insight has been that medical errors—e.g., wrong-site surgery, mistaken drugs and dosages, failure to control infections through hand-washing and other measures—involve not only individual deviations from a quality norm, but systemic failures to support actions and behaviors essential to patient safety. The Institute of Medicine's (IOM) famous report, *To Err is Human* (2000), projected "44,000 to 98,000 deaths per year due to hospital errors, and hundreds of thousands of avoidable injuries and extra days of hospitalization," and fueled a "patient-safety movement in the United States." Barry R. Furrow, *Regulating Patient Safety: The Patient Protection and Affordable Care Act*, 159 U. PA. L. REV. 1727, 1728 (2011). The quality assurance focus of hospital industry and medical profession leaders has shifted from assigning individual blame and rooting out "bad apples" to uncovering the systemic flaws (such as lack of standardized anesthesia machines, dispensing drugs in multiple dose units, or lack of checklists) that fail to prevent, and even exacerbate, inevitable human error.

At the level of national professional ideals, we appear to be light years away from the classic professional authority model of health care quality, which glorified and protected the "clinical judgment" (i.e., practice experience rather than peer-reviewed science) of the individual practitioner through the locality rule and other legal doctrines. Yet, as we shall see in Chapter 14, medical malpractice law remains in flux about whether, and how, to accommodate new concepts into the legal standard of medical care: what role should be played by evidence-based medicine, population studies, informed patient preferences, and of huge importance, cost-effectiveness and cost-containment research? Moreover, despite considerable efforts at systemic improvement by many sectors of the health professions and industries, "[t]en years after the IOM Report, the level of adverse events in hospitals has not improved in any major way." Furrow, *Regulating Patient Safety* at 1728. While some "health care systems" (e.g., Veterans Administration hospitals and the Mayo Clinic) have been shown to perform well in coordinating care and improving outcomes, much medical and hospital care remains poorly coordinated and managed. Thus Dr. Peter J. Pronovost, one of the leaders of the patient-safety movement, can report with pride on new protocols and methods to measure performance and "improve culture and teamwork among physicians, nurses, and administrators," When implemented in more than 100 intensive care units in Michigan, these advances led to a median infection rate of zero for more than three years for central line-associated bloodstream infection (CLABSI), compared with the death of 31,000 patients annually from CLABSI in the United States. Peter J. Pronovost, *Learning Accountability for Patient Outcomes*, 304 JAMA 204 (2010). On the other hand, Dr. Pronovost notes that "[h]ospital enrollment in the [CLABSI prevention] program has been surprisingly slow. In many states, less than 20% of hospitals have volunteered to participate." *Id.*

Writing in the major health policy journal HEALTH AFFAIRS in April 2011, the president and vice president of the Joint Commission—the leading private health quality assurance organization—state that

> Health care quality and safety today are best characterized as showing pockets of excellence on specific measures or in particular services at individual health care facilities. Excellence across the board is [also] emerging on some important quality measures [such as use of beta-blockers for heart attack patients]. The pockets of excellence mentioned above coexist with enormously variable performance across the delivery system. Along with some progress, we are experiencing an epidemic of serious and preventable adverse events. Moreover, the available evidence suggests that the risk of harmful error in health care may be increasing. As new devices, equipment, procedures, and drugs are added to our therapeutic arsenal, the complexity of delivering effective care increases. Complexity greatly increases the likelihood of error, especially in systems that perform at low levels of reliability.

> The need for major improvements in safety and quality has never been greater. Yet current approaches are not producing the

pace, breadth, or magnitude of improvement that all stakeholders desire. Along with a number of other observers, we believe that it is essential to look outside health care for solutions. Specifically, we should first get a clear picture of how complex organizations establish and maintain extremely high levels of safety. [Examples of reliable management of major risks include the nuclear power industry, commercial air travel, and the flight decks of aircraft carriers.] Then we must apply the lessons we learn from them to health care.

Mark R. Chassin & Jerod M. Loeb, *The Ongoing Quality Improvement Journey*, 30(4) HEALTH AFFAIRS 559, 562–63 (2011).

Drawing on the relevant literature, Chassin and Loeb summarize the characteristics of "high reliability" organizations as "collective mindfulness" (acute awareness by all in the organization of the need to perceive, report, and remedy "even small failures in safety protocols or processes"). *Id.* at 563. It is hard to imagine a more dramatic contrast to the noncommunicative surgeon and nurses and passive hospital in the Mississippi case, *Hall v. Hilbun*, summarized above and set forth below. Chassin and Loeb concede that the literature does not provide much "practical insight into how organizations [such as many hospitals] can move from low to high reliability." The difficulty is intensified by the importance of the spirit or values with which "collective mindfulness" is conceived and implemented. An overly punitive, "top down" approach will add additional burdens to already stressed personnel and likely backfire; the great challenge is how to respond to both simple and complex problems in a way that is both regulatory and punitive when needed, and also cooperative and supportive. *See, e.g.*, ATUL GAWANDE, THE CHECKLIST MANIFESTO: HOW TO GET THINGS RIGHT 72–85 (2009) (noting the need to distinguish simple, routine quality issues from complex, non-routine problems requiring "judgment aided—and even enhanced—by procedure," at 79; observing that high reliability systems dealing with complex quality problems must use centralized power and decision-making carefully, in an "unexpectedly democratic" way to "giv[e] people power" "to adapt [and take responsibility] based on their experience and expertise," at 72–73); Pauline W. Chen, *Sharing the Stresses of Being a Doctor*, N.Y. TIMES WELL BLOG, Sept. 15, 2011, http://well.blogs.nytimes.com/2011/09/15/sharing-the-stresses-of-being-a-doctor/?scp=3 & sq=dr% 20pauline% 20chen & st=cse (describing the additional stress on doctors of "new mandates, how-to tips, scorecards" and reimbursement policies linked to the new standards [regarding, ironically, "compassionate care"], and the value of foundation-funded "Schwartz Rounds" in which doctors and other providers can confidentially share the deep dilemmas and stresses of their work in a supportive context).

The insights of geographic variations research and systemic analysis of patient safety have generated five broad strategies relevant to the law of health care quality; *see* Furrow, *Regulating Patient Safety* at 1731:

    1. Standardizing and Implementing Good Medical Practices. This approach attempts to reduce medical practice variation by promot-

ing evidence based medicine, clinical practice guidelines, and cost-effectiveness research;

2. Tracking and Disclosing Provider Performance: collection of adverse event and "near-miss" data; reporting it to hospital quality assurance programs, state and federal regulators and quasi-regulators such as the Joint Commission; publication of performance data designed for use by payers and consumers; disclosure of adverse events to patients injured by them; disclosure of "material" physician-specific information about credentials, experience, and risks when requested by patients, as part of informed consent;

3. Expansion of Provider Responsibility: in addition to expanded duties of data collection and disclosure in (2) above, expanded fiduciary and corporate (e.g., hospital or managed care organization) responsibility and liability for quality of care problems;

4. Reforming Payment Systems: using financial incentives to reward and penalize quality-related actions;

5. Coordinating and Integrating Care: the most ambitious of these strategies, encouraging the formation of more integrated "health care delivery systems" that arguably have superior capacity and incentives to improve quality and manage costs.

The Patient Protection and Affordable Care Act does not directly address health care quality improvement in the clinical or professional sense. For example, the Act does not establish national standards for the licensure of health care professionals or institutions, nor does the Act establish national compulsory public reporting standards for serious adverse events. The Act does not condition Medicare and Medicaid participation on reforms in health care practice aimed at improving clinical performance and efficiency such as requiring physicians and hospitals to practice in the types of large, integrated care arrangements that are structured to develop the type of continuous improvement approach to health care quality noted by Chassin and Loeb.

At the same time, the Act tries to nudge the health care system toward better performance. As Barry Furrow notes in *Regulating Patient Safety: The Patient Protection and Affordable Care Act*, the Act has an "astonishing" number of provisions whose purpose is to improve safety and quality. How many of these provisions will produce tangible results is unclear, although the Act's emphasis on insurance expansion, incentivizing greater clinical integration across physicians and hospitals, and linking payment to quality is evident.

The Act contains a series of reforms aimed at achieving a more unified quality improvement strategy across the multiple public and private health insurers and health plans that finance care. The Act also links participation in federal health care financing programs, including Medicare, Medicaid, and qualified health plans sold through state health insurance Exchanges and subsidized with premium tax credits, to expanded reporting about health care quality and patient outcomes of care. The Act also ups the ante for improving health care quality by barring payment under federal programs for certain "never" events and adverse outcomes of care that are discussed later in this Part.

In order to foster greater cross-payer alignment, the Act establishes a National Quality Strategy under which the Secretary of Health and Human Services is required to identify national priorities for improving "the delivery of health care services, patient health outcomes, and population health." These "national priorities" must be ones that "have the greatest potential for improving the health outcomes, efficiency, and patient centeredness of health care for all populations, identify areas in the delivery of health care services that have the greatest potential for rapid improvement, address gaps in quality, efficiency, comparative effectiveness information, and health outcomes measures, improve federal payment policy to emphasize quality and efficiency, enhance the use of health care data, address the health care provided to patients with high-cost chronic diseases, [and] reduce health disparities." 42 U.S.C. § 241 et seq., amended by PPACA § 3011.

In March 2011 the federal government issued the first National Quality Strategy. *See* http://www.healthcare.gov/law/resources/reports/national qualitystrategy032011.pdf. The Report, which is aspirational rather than legally binding, sets out three major aims: better quality care, affordable care, and healthier people and communities. To reach these aims, the Report essentially acts as a bully pulpit, calling on all participants within the health care system to do a better job, within six principal areas: (1) making care safer by reducing harm caused in the delivery of care; (2) ensuring that each person and family are engaged as partners in their care; (3) promoting effective communication and coordination of care; (4) promoting the most effective prevention and treatment practices for the leading causes of mortality, starting with cardiovascular disease; (5) working with communities to promote wide use of best practices to enable healthy living; and (6) making quality care more affordable for individuals, families, employers, and governments by developing and spreading new health care delivery models.

The extent to which these aims are advanced through federal financing programs, specifically Medicare, Medicaid, and the new premium subsidy system to support the purchase of health insurance through state health insurance Exchanges, is explored later in this Part.

This Part presents several contexts in which the law has attempted, often together with the medical profession, the health care industry, and, more recently, health care payers, to define and enforce quality of care standards, while simultaneously serving other (often conflicting) values such as professional autonomy, managerial flexibility, and cost containment, cost-benefit and profitability decisions made by a variety of actors.

Following this overview, Chapter 14 turns to the core of medical malpractice law—the standard of care applicable to doctors—and traces the debate between the professionally-deferential "actual or customary practices" and "locality" rules and the more patient-protective "national standard," itself in transition from "professional custom" to a more "evidence-based" standard. This section also examines permitted variations from the prevailing standard and how the law should respond to professional disagreement or multiple standards of care.

Chapter 15 presents the doctrine of informed consent, and the related matter of physician conflicts of interest. Chapter 16 focuses on electronic health information, health information privacy and the evolution of the professional standard of care. Chapter 17 considers medical malpractice reform. Chapter 18 focuses on the rise of vicarious and corporate liability on the part of hospitals and the shift away from the view of hospitals as passive workplaces for private physicians to one in which hospitals possess an independent, institutional responsibility for quality of care.

Chapter 18 also covers the hospital quality assurance process, paying particular attention to hospitals' efforts to regulate quality through the use of physician staff privileges. Chapter 18 also describes the burgeoning movement toward health care quality improvement and patient safety, with its emphasis on avoidable error reduction. This section considers the law of professional privilege and other laws that shield shortfalls in health system quality from efforts to make such information more widely available.

Chapter 19 considers the relationship of state licensing agencies and industry accreditation to quality assurance. Chapters 20 and 21 explore the issues that arise when health care payers—Medicare, Medicaid, and the large health benefit services companies that insure or administer group health benefit plans—become centrally involved in questions of health care quality. This involvement takes the form of incentivization (an issue also explored in the previous materials on payment), "pay for performance," "quality tiering," and other "value purchasing" methods, that is, using the power of health care purchasing to get the best care for the money, not necessarily the cheapest care. It also takes the form of decisions to cover—or deny coverage and payment for—the diagnosis or treatment of medical conditions, not infrequently (in the case of denials, especially) over the protests of treating physicians. These final two sections also address the troubling legal issues that arise when patients attempt to hold payers accountable for medical injury or death arising from decisions to deny or reduce coverage for necessary treatment.

Although it is often uncomfortable to acknowledge, cost considerations must be viewed as a central factor in health policy and law, because of the impact of cost on the extension of adequate coverage to all without crowding out other essential social needs such as education and environmental protection. How cost management may legitimately affect health care quality and increased risk is a challenging and hot-button issue, as the extraordinary uproar over health reform and "death panels" demonstrated. *See, e.g.*, Jim Rutenberg & Jackie Calmes, *False 'Death Panel' Rumor Has Some Familiar Roots*, N.Y. TIMES, Aug. 14, 2009. The most sophisticated practitioners of this quest to find a balance between costs and quality, such as Dr. David Eddy or Dr. Troyen Brennan (each of whom has had a career grounded in both financing and health care), would say that any responsible health care system must consider both quality and cost, as well as patients' own values, when making treatment decisions at all levels—for individual patients, on behalf of health care institutions, and in relation to society at large. *See, e.g., Interview: Reflections on Science, Judgment, and Value in Evidence Based Decision Making: A Conversation with David Eddy*, 26(4) HEALTH AFFAIRS (Web Exclusive) w500 (June 19, 2007); Christine K. Cassel & Troyen E. Brennan, *Managing Medical Resources: Return to the Commons?*, 297 JAMA 2518 (2007). But how to get to this Valhalla-like state—in which health care providers balance money and medicine without regard to economic self-interest and patients appreciate and accept this balance after open and transparent discourse—remains a daunting challenge.

One final note: any chapter on the law of quality of care inevitably focuses on the lack of quality—on system deficiencies, on story after story of incompetence, insensitivity, and venality, broken occasionally by a good doctor candidly confessing error, or a physician struggling to convince a managed care organization that a patient needs more care than the guidelines call for. It is therefore worth considering for a moment on medicine's enormous capacity for good: physicians and health professionals who have dedicated their lives to providing the best possible care for patients, community health clinics practicing in medically underserved areas, and furnishing the best patient care they can working with limited resources; leaders in clinical education and scientific endeavor, who have dedicated their lives to training young professionals, advancing scientific and clinical knowledge and population health; and the many thousands of physicians whose daily choices for their patients are grounded in a strong ethical base.

CHAPTER 14

MEDICAL MALPRACTICE AND HEALTH CARE QUALITY

1. WHAT DOES MEDICAL MALPRACTICE TELL US ABOUT HEALTH CARE QUALITY?

When considering the concept of "quality of care," most lawyers and law students probably turn immediately, and perhaps exclusively, to the law of medical malpractice. This law consists of the principles used by judges and juries to decide whether doctors, hospitals, and other providers (and their insurance companies) must pay for the costs of particular medical errors and adverse outcomes with respect to individual patients. In theory, these decisions about liability should serve as a quality assurance system, with damage awards signaling that certain errors should be avoided, certain procedures revised, or individual practitioners monitored and disciplined. Indeed, economist Patricia M. Danzon argues that "the primary economic rationale for tort liability is deterrence [of injury-producing behavior]. In principle, the law of negligence can create an incentive structure designed to induce physicians to invest optimally in injury prevention." PATRICIA DANZON, MEDICAL MALPRACTICE 9 (1985). *See also* Randall Bovbjerg, *Medical Malpractice on Trial: Quality of Care Is the Important Standard*, 49 LAW & CONTEMP. PROBS. 321 (Spring 1986).

In fact, at least until recently, medical malpractice law has made relatively little contribution to assuring quality of care or deterring doctor-caused injuries. First, malpractice litigation is expensive, and is largely financed on the plaintiffs' side by contingent attorney's fees. Thus, most lawyers in private practice will not provide representation (or will drop the case without obtaining compensation) unless the case has a substantial dollar value. Consequently, the vast majority of quality of care issues are never even touched by the malpractice system.

Second, while malpractice insurance premiums charged to individual doctors vary greatly with practice specialty and geographic region, they are not "experience rated," i.e., based on the claims experience of the individual doctor. As Kenneth Abraham and Paul Weiler explain,

> the individual Miami obstetrician or New York surgeon typically pays the same premium as his colleagues even if he has never been the target of a malpractice suit, let alone a successful one.
>
> The implicit premise underlying the absence of experience rating is that prior claims experience is generally a poor index of comparative physician quality and of the physician's likely future claims

experience. From the perspective of the health care system as a whole, many malpractice claims within different regions and specialties are brought. In contrast, from the individual physician's perspective, being named as a malpractice defendant is a comparatively rare event. It occurs only a handful of times in the entire careers of even physicians who practice in the high-risk specialties. Even the actual commission of malpractice produces a tort claim only if the error in question happened to cause an injury serious enough to make litigation worthwhile. And the chance that a patient will make a claim turns at least as much on the tone of her personal relations with the physician as on the quality of treatment actually rendered. Thus, with the exception of a tiny number of malpractice recidivists, past claims experience tends not to be a reliable index of future liability risk.

Kenneth Abraham & Paul Weiler, *Enterprise Medical Liability and the Evolution of the American Health Care System*, 108 HARV. L. REV. 381, 410 (1994). *See also* Lori L. Darling, *The Applicability of Experience Rating to Medical Malpractice Insurance*, 38 CASE W. RES. L. REV. 255 (1987) (discussing pros and cons of experience rating and experience rating legislation in New York and Massachusetts).

Third, medical malpractice litigation is widely perceived, particularly by doctors, as not sending reliable signals about quality of care. Anecdotal evidence and some studies suggest that many physicians regard malpractice judgments against their colleagues as artifacts of the legal system—of skillful plaintiffs' lawyers and emotional juries—rather than as reliable signals regarding quality of care. *See, e.g.*, PAUL C. WEILER, MEDICAL MALPRACTICE ON TRIAL 6 (1991). For an analysis of studies and powerful critique of this belief as a "myth," see TOM C. BAKER, THE MEDICAL MALPRACTICE MYTH (2005).

Fourth, even if physicians with special quality of care responsibilities— hospitals chiefs of staff, or members of state licensing boards—wish to use malpractice awards as part of a quality feedback system, they often lack (or lacked until recently) the institutional support, information, resources, and (in the case of licensing boards) legal authority to undertake effective action. *See* SYLVIA LAW & STEVE POLAN, PAIN AND PROFIT: THE POLITICS OF MALPRACTICE 39–50 (1978); Sylvia Law, *A Consumer Perspective on Medical Malpractice*, 49 LAW & CONTEMP. PROBS. 305, 310–15 (Spring 1986).

Reviewing Professor Paul Weiler's MEDICAL MALPRACTICE ON TRIAL, and drawing on data from the Harvard Medical Practice Study Group (whose study, by Troy Brennan et al., entitled INCIDENCE OF ADVERSE EVENTS AND NEGLIGENCE IN HOSPITALIZED PATIENTS: RESULTS OF THE HARVARD MEDICAL PRACTICE STUDY, http://www.oshmanlaw.com/Harvard–Medical–Practice–Study.pdf, is considered a classic in the field), Professor Stephen Sugarman summarizes the relationship of the medical malpractice system to patient injuries as follows:

> Based on the Harvard Study, Weiler explains that of every 100,000 patients discharged from hospitals, nearly 4,000 suffered

an "adverse event" from their medical treatment. [In the Harvard Study, a hospital occurrence counted as an adverse event if it prolonged the patient's stay in the hospital by at least one day or caused the patient's death.] About one-fourth of these are the result of medical malpractice. In short, hospital patients on average run about a four percent risk of an adverse event and about a one percent risk of medical malpractice.

These 100,000 patient discharges and 1,000 malpractice-caused injuries generate about 125 legal claims. About sixty of the 125 claimants actually receive compensation. The rest of the claims lose at trial or are dropped. Of those sixty successful claimants, about twenty receive payment before they have filed a lawsuit, about thirty-five after a suit is filed but before (or during) trial, and only about five win at trial.

According to neutral physicians reviewing the records, however, of every 125 claims that plaintiffs make, no malpractice occurred in about eighty-five cases.... [Thus] about thirty to thirty-five of every 1,000 malpractice victims use the legal system to obtain compensation for their losses, although only perhaps four out of every 1,000 obtain an award of individualized justice through a jury of their peers. At the same time, twenty-five to thirty people who were probably not victims of malpractice nevertheless receive payment from the system....

[The above figures are based on occurrences per 100,000 hospital discharges.] In fact, we are talking about some forty million annual hospitalizations across America. These numbers translate into about a million and a half adverse events and 400,000 torts (one percent of 40 million) every year. Yet, the system's compensation shortfall is enormous: only 25,000 medical malpractice claimants, out of 50,000 who claim and 400,000 who are injured, are likely to receive some compensation, of whom only 12,500 to 15,000 were actually malpractice victims....

Projecting the findings nationally, the Harvard Study suggests that every year the approximately 1.5 million adverse events from medical treatment in hospitals seriously and permanently disable approximately 150,000 people and kill more than 150,000 people (many of whom, admittedly, are elderly and perhaps frail at the outset). Medical negligence accounts for greater than a quarter of those more than 300,000 substantial harms, only a small portion of which are actually compensated through the current tort system....

[After analyzing litigation and other administrative costs, high malpractice insurance premiums for some specialties, defensive medicine and many other factors, Sugarman concludes] [i]n sum, from the viewpoint of compensating victims, whether we focus only on victims of malpractice or on all victims of adverse events from medical treatment, Weiler's analysis demonstrates that the current system is a disaster and a disgrace. The few are lucky lottery winners, so to speak, only about half of whom should even have been given lottery tickets. The many are ignored. Although it may not be fair to say that "only the lawyers win," it can hardly be said that, from the compensation perspective, patients as a class win.

Stephen D. Sugarman, *Doctor No, Review of Medical Malpractice on Trial by Paul C. Weiler*, 58 U. CHI. L. REV. 1499, 1500–1502, 1504 (1991). *See also* Randall Bovbjerg, *Review of A Measure of Malpractice*, 79 VA. L. REV. 2155, 2177–78, 2163–65 (1992) (noting that New York statistics may not be nationally representative, and that the Harvard Study's "neutral doctors" may have underestimated actual negligence because of professional bias, and because their case reviews were based on hospital records only, and hence did not include additional information developed during discovery or evidence from patients).

Given these limitations, we put medical malpractice law near the beginning of Part Three not because it is the most important or best means of assuring quality, but rather because historically it was one of the earliest, and for many years largely the only, system of reviewing physician actions against some standard of quality of care.

2.   FROM PHYSICIAN AUTHORITY TO EGALITARIAN SOCIAL CONTRACT AND MARKET COMPETITION: MEDICAL MALPRACTICE LAW AND THE TRANSFORMATION OF THE PROFESSIONAL STANDARD OF CARE

In the period between roughly 1870 and 1960, the dominant concepts of American health law were dedicated to protecting the authority and autonomy of the physician in solo private practice, and of the nonprofit or charitable hospital vis-à-vis its charitable patients. This was accomplished in considerable part by tort doctrines that made it very difficult or impossible to establish liability against doctors and hospitals, and simultaneously deprived hospitals of authority over the quality of care provided by doctors to hospital patients. The central premise of these doctrines was that a doctor's legal duty of competence to his patients should be largely defined by doctors' *actual practices*—what was known as the "professional" and "established custom" standard of care. Beginning in the 1940s and gaining ground from roughly 1960 to 1980, a vision of a modestly egalitarian social contract that influenced many areas of law challenged this enormous delegation of authority to physicians, and expanded both physician and hospital liability and hospital responsibility and authority for physicians' quality of care. The market competition model of health law and policy that arose in the 1970s added its own powerful perspectives and energies to this trend. The concept of a "professional standard of care" has remained, but is in the process of being transformed—with much variation, complication, and unevenness—into a "reasonably prudent physician" model, which does not accept doctors' actual practices as conclusive evidence of reasonable care, and—as in tort law generally—opens the door to evaluating those practices in the light of scientific knowledge and standards of reasonableness defined from a broader perspective by professional societies and analogous institutions (such as hospitals and accreditation programs), peer-reviewed research, government-sponsored standard-setting, and courts, juries, legislatures, and administrative agencies. The details of these developments with respect to physicians, and varying explanations and justifications for them, are explored in this chapter as well as Chapter 15, addressing informed consent. The story with respect to hospitals is covered in Chapter 18, and with respect to managed care organizations (MCOs), in Chapter 21.

a. The Role of Law in the Age of Expanding Medical Authority: c.1870 to c.1960

The social authority and internal organization of the medical profession increased dramatically in the period between 1870 and 1960. *See* PAUL STARR, THE SOCIAL TRANSFORMATION OF AMERICAN MEDICINE (1982). Law—statutes as well as judicial decisions—provided indispensable support for these developments by granting doctors virtually unreviewable power over training, operating, and financing their profession. Entry into the profession was controlled by state licensing boards, whose functions and composition were defined by the state medical societies. Medical education was controlled through an accreditation process operated by the medical profession and hospital industry. Appointments to hospital medical staffs, discussed later in this Part, were in practice controlled by existing staff physicians without significant external review. As we have seen in Part Two, how insurers paid for care was, until the 1980s, also dominated by the interests of organized doctors and hospitals. Finally, if a patient wanted to sue a doctor for damages, she or he would encounter two doctrines of medical malpractice law that effectively delegated the liability decision to the local medical profession itself.

b. The Professional Standard as "Established" or "Customary" Practice

As a general matter, a person whose activity imposes risks of (and actual) harm on others is held to a socially-defined "duty of reasonable care" (also known as "ordinary care" or "reasonable prudence"). A homeowner whose steep outside steps with no railing and no light cause harm cannot successfully require a jury to rule in his favor by showing that such conditions are customary in the neighborhood. Evidence of customary practice is certainly admissible and often persuasive as to what constitutes "ordinary care" or "reasonable prudence," but the jury may give customary practice the weight it feels it deserves, and may conclude that "reasonable care" requires different or additional precautions than those customarily taken. *See* Kenneth S. Abraham, *Custom, Noncustomary Practice, and Negligence*, 109 COLUM. L. REV. 1784, 1788–92 (2009). This now-dominant approach to custom emerged in the 1930s, most famously in Judge Learned Hand's opinion in *The T.J. Hooper*, 60 F.2d 737 (2d Cir. 1932) (set forth below), and supplanted a doctrine prominent in the late 19th and early 20th century, under which a defendant's proof of compliance with custom "provided a safe harbor and resulted in a holding that the defendant was free from negligence as a matter of law." Abraham, *Custom, Noncustomary Practice* at 1792.

Where the proper performance of risky activities involves technical and specialized knowledge not accessible to a lay jury (or, for that matter, judge) without expert testimony, the law has traditionally allowed the relevant specialists, and especially physicians, to define, or at least heavily influence, the definition of "reasonable care," and hence has been more deferential to the customary practices of the relevant professionals. As early as 1767, an English court indicated that in order to recover damages against a surgeon, a patient had to show that the doctor had violated "the usage and law of surgeons ... the rule of the profession ..." as testified to by other surgeons themselves. Slater v. Baker and Stapleton, 95 Eng. Rpts. 860, 862 (King's Bench 1767). Although English and American law before the mid-nineteenth century was unclear about whether professional custom preempted general principles of ordinary care, by the later nineteenth century American judicial doctrine accorded the customary practices of doctors virtually conclusive weight as to what constituted "reasonable care." *See* Theodore Silver, *One Hundred Years of Harmful Error: The Historical Jurisprudence of Medical Malpractice*, 1992 WIS. L. REV. 1193 (1992).

This "safe harbor" deference to customary medical practice continues to be applied by some courts in the current era, despite its inconsistency with reasonable care doctrine dominant in most areas of tort law. *See, e.g.*, Doe v. American Red Cross Blood Serv., 377 S.E.2d 323, 326 (S.C. 1989) (blood bank failure to screen for HIV/AIDS at a time when such screening was not customary practice cannot constitute negligence as a matter of law; plaintiff must prove defendant "failed to conform to the generally recognized and accepted practices in his profession.") This doctrine not only looks to doctors to define what the risks and feasible means of avoiding them are, but also delegates to doctors the critical cost-benefit decisions of which precautions are "reasonable" and therefore required, and which risks are "worth taking" given the benefits of treatment and the costs of precautions. *See* Randall Bovbjerg, *The Medical Malpractice Standard of Care: HMO's and Customary Practice*, 1975 DUKE L.J. 1375, 1390–97 [hereinafter cited as "Bovbjerg, *HMO Standard*"] (arguing that reliance on medical custom is a practical necessity, but flawed by doctors' lack of competence to assess the social costs of medical custom, lack of informed bargaining between doctors and patients over the costs and benefits of medical and treatment risks and by the anti-bargaining effects of open-ended insurance reimbursement); *see also* Philip G. Peters, *The Quiet Demise of Deference to Custom: Malpractice Law at the Millennium*, 57 WASH. & LEE L. REV. 163, 164–169, 192–202 (2000) (documenting the "conventional wisdom" of judicial deference to medical custom, arguing that it is in fact eroding, and suggesting that the causes of the deference and its erosion are much more complex than "technical expertise" and involve multiple reasons for the rise and decline of the social authority of physicians).

One of the most important consequences of defining the legal standard of care in terms of professional custom is to require the plaintiff, in most instances, to find an expert medical witness willing to testify as to the content of the professional standard, and that the defendant doctor violated it. *See, e.g.,* Bovbjerg, *HMO Standard* at 1392–97. Without such a witness, the plaintiff cannot prove the first two elements of his case: the content of the defendant doctor's duty ("the standard of care") and breach of the duty in this case. *See, e.g., Hall,* 466 So.2d 856, 860, 864 (trial court granted directed verdict for defendant after excluding the testimony of plaintiff's two expert witnesses because they were not familiar with the "standard of professional skill, including surgical skills and post-operative care, practiced by general surgeons in Pascagoula, Mississippi.") The most prominent exceptions to the requirement of an expert witness is when the issue of negligence is accessible to "common knowledge," *see, e.g.,* Gannon v. Elliot, 23 Cal. Rptr.2d 86 (1993) (plastic cap of surgical instrument left in patient's hip socket after surgery), and when the doctrine of "res ipsa loquitur" applies: (1) the accident must be of a kind that ordinarily does not occur without someone's negligence; (2) the accident must be caused by an agency or instrumentality within the exclusive control of the defendant; and (3) the accident must not have been due to any voluntary action or contribution on the part of the plaintiff. See Ybarra v. Spangard, 154 P.2d 687 (Cal. 1944) (patient injured while unconscious during surgery; medical expert testimony for plaintiff on likely cause of injury shifts burden of explanation to the defendants). As *Ybarra* indicates, medical expert testimony may still be needed to establish the elements of "ordinarily does not occur without negligence" and causation. In some states, the res ipsa doctrine contains a fourth component: that "evidence of the true explanation of the event must be more readily accessible to the defendant than to the plaintiff." Locke v. Pachtman, 521 N.W.2d 786, 793 (Mich. 1994).

Early American courts, like the English courts, defined the doctor's legal duty in terms of the "reasonable skill and diligence as are ordinarily exercised in his profession...." McCandless v. McWha, 22 Pa. (10 Harris) 261, 267–68 (1853). Although one early court defined the applicable standard as that which "thoroughly educated surgeons ordinarily employ," most American courts rejected this standard as too high and required only the standard set by the actual practices of the "average" or "ordinary" practitioner. *See, e.g.,* Smothers v. Hanks, 34 Iowa 286 (1872).

c. The Locality Rule

Equal in importance to the professional standard was the geographic scope by which that standard was to be determined. By the 1870s and 1880s, a number of courts had ruled that a doctor practicing in a rural area or small town was

> bound to possess that skill only which physicians and surgeons of
> ordinary ability and skill, practicing in similar localities, with
> opportunities for no larger experience, ordinarily possess; and he

was not bound to possess that high degree of art and skill possessed by eminent surgeons practicing in larger cities, and making a specialty of the practice of surgery.

Small v. Howard, 128 Mass. 131, 132, 35 Am. Rep. 363, 365 (1880) (trial court charge approved by state supreme court).

Some courts required the plaintiff to prove a violation of the customary professional standard in the *particular* locality where the defendant practiced; thus, only doctors who practiced in that same community were qualified to be expert witnesses. Needless to say, finding one doctor to testify against another in a small community was often impossible. Many courts relaxed the standard enough to allow experts from the "same or similar locality," which gave rise to much uncertainty and litigation over what a "similar" locality was. *See* Jon Waltz, *The Rise and Gradual Fall of the Locality Rule in Medical Malpractice Litigation*, 18 DePaul L. Rev. 408, 410–12 (1969). Moreover, proof of a doctor's deviation from local medical custom did not necessarily establish a breach of duty; courts permitted (and most still permit) the defendant doctor to justify his actions as consistent with those of a "respectable" or "reputable" minority of medical practitioners (discussed below), or as a "medical judgment" about which reasonable doctors might disagree.

3.   FROM LOCAL MEDICAL CUSTOMARY PRACTICES TO A "NATIONAL STANDARD" OF "ACCEPTABLE CARE"

a.   Introduction

The trend in medical malpractice law from roughly the 1960s to the present has been the gradual abandonment of the local customary standard of care, generally with the effect of raising the applicable standard. There have been two ways of thinking and talking about this change. The first, and by far the dominant, is that the medical profession itself has adopted national standards, through medical school, hospital, and specialty accreditation and certification programs, and a complex nation-wide process of disseminating the results of research and clinical experience. Under this view, the expanded tort liability characteristic of the social contract approach is actually a revised professional standard, in which the courts enforce a purported national consensus of what constitutes reasonable or acceptable care. *See, e.g.*, Blair v. Eblen, 461 S.W.2d 370, 373 (Ky. 1970). As applied to small towns and rural areas, this view normally leads to raising the local standard of care by allowing medical experts from larger cities or out of state to testify that local practices have lagged behind medical developments in more sophisticated settings. *See, e.g.*, *Hall*, 466 So.2d 856, discussed below. *But see* Mark F. Grady, *Why Are People Negligent: Technology, Nondurable Precautions, and the Medical Malpractice Explosion*, 82 Nw. U. L. Rev. 293 (1988) (arguing that the expansion of medical malpractice liability has not been caused primarily by "technology lag" of this sort, but rather by difficulties in using new technology in the larger urban centers).

The second account of this change articulates the abandonment of the "safe harbor" doctrine for medical custom, and the assimilation of medical malpractice law into the modern tort law approach to custom. In this view, medical customary practices, like customary practices generally, are "evidence" of what ought to be done, but not conclusive evidence; in the final analysis, as Justice Holmes put it (in a non-medical case), "what ought to be done is fixed by a standard of reasonable prudence, whether it is usually complied with or not." Texas & P. Rwy. v. Behymer, 189 U.S. 468, 470 (1903). *See* Phillip G. Peters, Jr., *The Role of the Jury in Modern Malpractice Law*, 87 IOWA L. REV. 909, 913–18 (2002) (reporting that in eleven states and the District of Columbia, "the jury decides whether the physician behaved reasonably, not whether she complied with custom[ary practices]," *id.* at 915–16; "another nine states, although not explicitly addressing the role of custom, have also endorsed the 'reasonable physician' test," *id.* at 914; and several additional states, while purporting to apply the medical custom approach, in fact allow juries latitude to decide the reasonableness of the physician's action, as informed by competing expert testimony. *Id.* at 915.)

In theory, the "reasonable care" approach could allow a court to overrule directly a professional cost-benefit consensus, but in fact such action has been extremely rare and controversial, (*see* Helling v. Carey, 519 P.2d 981 (Wash. 1974), discussed below). More typical and fruitful have been a variety of doctrines acknowledging the contested and dynamic nature of medical knowledge and standards, and focusing on the processes by which individual providers and, where applicable, standard-setting committees or institutions reach their decisions.

Although many judges and legal commentators have celebrated the trend toward rising standards, few have been willing to address the law's de facto (and at times de jure) lowering of the standard of care with respect to the poor. The trend of lowering the standard of care, or of creating multiple standards of care based on ability to pay, is now assuming unprecedented importance because it is beginning to affect middle-income patients through a variety of cost-containment programs and the phenomenon of managed care in the context of market competition. This topic was discussed in the context of insurance coverage in Part Two, and is further addressed in Chapter 21 below.

In addition, in response to a perceived crisis in the cost and availability of medical malpractice insurance, many state legislatures have imposed procedural and substantive restrictions on medical malpractice procedures, testimony, and remedies, discussed in Chapter 17, and at least one state (Georgia) has lowered the standard of care to "gross negligence" for all patients receiving emergency services in a hospital emergency department or obstetrical unit, and in surgery after admission through the emergency department. *See* Gliemmo v. Cousineau, 694 S.E.2d 75 (Ga. 2010). Almost all states have also enacted "Good Samaritan statutes" that apply either a gross negligence or "good faith" standard to health care providers (and others) rendering emergency care outside a hospital at the scene of emergency need. *See, e.g.*, Thomas Lateano et al., *Does the Law Encourage or Hinder Bystander Intervention? An Analysis of Good Samaritan Laws*, 44(5) CRIM. L. BULL. ART. 4 (2008).

b.   The Assault on the Locality Rule and the Concept of a National Standard

Critics of the locality rule repeatedly pointed out its two major defects: it permitted perhaps dubiously competent practitioners to set an authoritative local "standard," and it often made it impossible for injured patients to find a medical expert willing to testify even against gross negligence. *See, e.g.*, Waltz, *Medical Malpractice Litigation* at 420; Pederson v. Dumouchel, 431 P.2d 973, 977 (Wash. 1967). Moreover, the stated justifications for the locality rule—the isolation and rudimentary conditions of small-town or rural medical practice—seemed increasingly untenable as medical education and hospital procedures became, or were at least claimed to be, standardized under national accreditation programs. *See, e.g.*, Shilkret v. Annapolis Emergency Hospital, 349 A.2d 245, 249–50 (Md. 1975); Brune v. Belinkoff, 235 N.E.2d 793 (Mass. 1968) (reversing a trial judge's instruction that an anesthesiologist in New Bedford, Mass., a city of 100,00 about 50 miles from Boston, need only comply with the local standard of care, even if that were "fifty percent inferior to that which existed in Boston," and overruling the locality rule announced in 1880 in *Small v. Howard*, above). By the mid–1970's, many state courts had abandoned the traditional locality rule, and now held physicians to

> that degree of care and skill which is expected of a reasonably competent practitioner in the same class to which he belongs, acting in the same or similar circumstances. Under this standard, advances in the profession, availability of facilities, specialization or general practice, proximity of specialists and special facilities, together with all other relevant considerations, are to be taken into account.

Shilkret, 349 A.2d at 253. In announcing this doctrine, the *Shilkret* court explicitly rejected the "strict locality" and "similar locality" rules, and characterized its formulation as a national standard applicable both to specialists and general practitioners. This version of the standard, which is fairly typical, seems to point in both "national" and "local" directions. The phrases "same or similar circumstances," "availability of facilities," and "all other relevant considerations" appear to open the door for consideration of at least some "local" factors, which might fall below or exceed some national norm. Despite this textual tension, the clear intent and consequence of *Shilkret* and similar decisions is to allow plaintiffs to use expert witnesses from outside the locality and even outside the state to testify as to the content of the applicable standard of care and whether the defendant complied with it in the particular case. The simultaneous effort to define and enforce "national standards" and to allow consideration of "legitimate" local factors and practices is vividly displayed in the following case.

Hall v. Hilbun

466 So.2d 856 (Miss. 1985)

■ ROBERTSON [JUSTICE]:

[Plaintiff Glenn Hall was the husband of a deceased patient, 37 year-old Terry O. Hall, who complained of "abdominal discomfort" and underwent an exploratory laparotomy by general surgeon Dr. Glyn R. Hilbun. Following surgery Mrs. Hall was moved to a recovery room at 1:35 pm, where Dr. Hilbun attended her until about 2:50 pm. At that time her vital signs "were stable." Terry's husband Glen remained with her continuously thereafter. At 9:00 pm Mrs. Hall complained of pain and was given morphine for relief, after which she fell asleep. Thereafter Glen Hall reported to the nurses several times his concerns with his wife's difficulty breathing (including "making noise"), restlessness, pain and color and was assured that these symptoms were normal and routine. At various times during the evening and early morning there were "fluctuations" in Mrs. Hall's vital signs; at 4:00 am her pulse rate was recorded at 140. At no time in response to any of these symptoms did the nurses contact Dr. Hilbun or any other physician, nor had Dr. Hilbun left any instructions that they do so, nor did Dr. Hilbun see Mrs. Hall after he left the recovery room at 2:50 pm. Around 5:00 am Mr. Hall noticed that his wife "had stopped making that noise," determined that "she was having a real hard problem breathing and ... was turning ... a bluish color. And I went to screaming." Apparently Mr. Hall himself telephoned Dr. Hilbun, who rushed to the hospital only to find his patient already dead from adult respiratory distress syndrome (cardio-respiratory failure).

Glenn Hall called as his medical expert witnesses Dr. Hoerr, a distinguished retired surgeon from Cleveland, Ohio, and Dr. David Sachs, a specialist in pulmonary diseases also from Cleveland. Dr. Hoerr's proffered testimony was heard by the trial judge out of the presence of the jury. Dr. Hoerr stated that serious pulmonary complications were a well-known postoperative risk of this type of surgery, and that general surgeons had a duty to closely monitor their patients "particularly in the first few hours" after surgery. This could be accomplished by briefly examining the patient and checking the vital signs, or by delegating this task to another physician or an experienced nurse. If the doctor has doubts about the quality of the nursing staff, he should leave very explicit instructions that he should be contacted if the vital signs exceed or fall below certain levels. Because Dr. Hilbun had done none of these things, and made no effort to ascertain Terry Hall's condition after 2:50 pm, Dr. Hoerr concluded that Dr. Hilbun "was negligent in not following his patient."

Dr. Hoerr conceded that he was not familiar with the "standard of professional skill, including surgical skills and post-operative care, practiced by general surgeons in Pascagoula, Mississippi,"—that is, the actual local customary practices—but "he did know what the standard should have been." Dr. Sachs was also unfamiliar with local standard of care. On the basis of what appeared to be existing Mississippi Supreme Court precedent, the trial judge excluded their testimony as not consistent with "the locality rule."

The defendant Dr. Hilbun was called by the plaintiff as an adverse witness. Dr. Hilbun agreed that he remained "one of [Terry Hall's] physicians" after her surgery, and that his custom was to "follow" such a patient "until she leaves the hospital," "as long as my services are needed." In addition, Dr. Donald Dohn testified for the defendant. Also from Cleveland, Dr. Dohn had practiced at the world-famous Cleveland Clinic and had moved to Pascagoula about a month before the trial. Although having practiced in Pascagoula for only three weeks, and "still in the process of acquainting himself with the local conditions," he testified that "there was a great difference in the standard of care [between Cleveland and Pascagoula]." At the Cleveland Clinic there was a large and well-organized staff of resident doctors and experienced nurses, while "here we have no staff. So it is up to us [the doctors] to do the things that our residents would have done there."

At the close of the plaintiff's case, defendant moved for a directed verdict on the grounds that since the plaintiff's medical experts had been excluded, he had failed to present evidence of the standard of care and its breach, and the trial judge granted the motion.]

III.

A. General Considerations

Medical malpractice is legal fault by a physician or surgeon. It arises from the failure of a physician to provide the quality of care required by law. When a physician undertakes to treat a patient, he takes on an obligation enforceable at law to use minimally sound medical judgment and render minimally competent care in the course of the services he provides. A physician does not guarantee recovery. A competent physician is not liable *per se* for a mere error of judgment, mistaken diagnosis or the occurrence of an undesirable result.

C. The Physician's Duty of Care: A primary rule of substantive law

2. *The Inevitable Ascendency of National Standards*

We would have to put our heads in the sand to ignore the "nationalization" of medical education and training. Medical school admission standards are similar across the country. Curricula are substantially the same. Internship and residency programs for those entering medical specialties have substantially common components. Nationally uniform standards are enforced in the case of certification of specialists. Regarding the basic matter of the learning, skill and competence a physician may bring to bear in the treatment of a given patient, state lines are largely irrelevant. A patient's physiological response to an exploratory laparotomy and needs regarding post-operative care following such surgery do not vary from Ohio to Mississippi. A pulse rate of 140 per minute provides a danger signal in Pascagoula, Mississippi, the same as it does in Cleveland, Ohio. Bacteria, physiology and the life process itself know little of geography and nothing of political boundaries.

3. *The Competence–Based National Standard of Care: Herein Of the Limited Role of Local Custom*

All of the above informs our understanding and articulation of the competence-based duty of care. Each physician may with reason and fairness be expected to possess or have reasonable access to such medical knowledge as is commonly possessed or reasonably available to minimally competent physicians in the same specialty or general field of practice throughout the United States, to have a realistic understanding of the limitations on his or her knowledge or competence, and, in general, to exercise minimally adequate medical judgment. Beyond that, each physician has a duty to have a practical working knowledge of the facilities, equipment, resources (including personnel in health related fields and their general level of knowledge and competence), and options (including what specialized services or facilities may be available in larger communities, e.g., Memphis, Birmingham, Jackson, New Orleans, etc.) reasonably available to him or her as well as the practical limitations on same.

In the care and treatment of each patient, each physician has a non-delegable duty to render professional services consistent with that objectively ascertained minimally acceptable level of competence he may be expected to apply given the qualifications and level of expertise he holds himself out as possessing and given the circumstances of the particular case. The professional services contemplated within this duty concern the entire caring process, including but not limited to examination, history, testing, diagnosis, course of treatment, medication, surgery, follow-up, after-care and the like.

Mention should be made in this context of the role of good medical judgment which, because medicine is not an exact science, must be brought to bear in diagnostic and treatment decisions daily. Some physicians are more reluctant to recommend radical surgery than are other equally competent physicians. There exist legitimate differences of opinion regarding medications to be employed in particular contexts. "Waiting periods" and their duration are the subject of bona fide medical controversy. What diagnostic tests should be performed is a matter of particularly heated debate in this era of ever-escalating health care costs. We must be vigilant that liability never be imposed upon a physician for the mere exercise of a bona fide medical judgment which turns out, with the benefit of 20–20 hindsight, (a) to have been mistaken, and (b) to be contrary to what a qualified medical expert witness *in the exercise of his good medical judgment* would have done. We repeat: a physician may incur civil liability only when the quality of care he renders (including his judgment calls) falls below minimally acceptable levels.

Different medical judgments are made by physicians whose offices are across the street from one another. Comparable differences in medical judgment or opinion exist among physicians geographically separated by much greater distances, and in this sense local custom does and must continue to play a role within our law, albeit a limited one.

We recognize that customs vary within given medical communities and from one medical community to another. Conformity with established medical custom practiced by minimally competent physicians in a given area, while evidence of performance of the duty of care, may never be conclusive of such compliance. *Cf. Helling v. Carey.* The content of the duty of care must be objectively determined by reference to the availability of medical and practical knowledge which would be brought to bear in the treatment of like or similar patients under like or similar circumstances by minimally competent physicians in the same field, given the facilities, resources and options available. The content of the duty of care may be informed by local medical custom but never subsumed by it.

4. *The Resources–Based Caveat to the National Standard of Care*

The duty of care, as it thus emerges from considerations of reason and fairness, when applied to the facts of the world of medical science and practice, takes two forms: (a) a duty to render a quality of care consonant with the level of medical and practical knowledge the physician may reasonably be expected to possess and the medical judgment he may be expected to exercise, and (b) a duty based upon the adept use of such medical facilities, services, equipment and options as are reasonably available. With respect to this second form of the duty, we regard that there remains a core of validity to the premises of the old locality rule.

A physician practicing in Noxubee County, for example, may hardly be faulted for failure to perform a CAT scan when the necessary facilities and equipment are not reasonably available. In contradistinction, objectively reasonable expectations regarding the physician's knowledge, skill, capacity for sound medical judgment and general competence are, consistent with his field of practice and the facts and circumstances in which the patient may be found, *the same everywhere.*

As a result of its resources-based component, the physician's non-delegable duty of care is this: given the circumstances of each patient, each physician has a duty to use his or her knowledge and therewith treat through maximum reasonable medical recovery, each patient, with such reasonable diligence, skill, competence, and prudence as are practiced by minimally competent physicians in the same specialty or general field of practice throughout the United States, who have available to them the same general facilities, services, equipment and options.

As we deal with general principles, gray areas necessarily exist. One involves the case where needed specialized facilities and equipment are not available locally but are reasonably accessible in major medical centers— New Orleans, Jackson, Memphis. Here as elsewhere the local physician is held to minimally acceptable standards. In determining whether the physician's actions comport with his duty of care, consideration must always be given to the time factor—is the physician confronted with what reasonably appears to be a medical emergency, or does it appear likely that the patient may be transferred to an appropriate medical center without substantial risk to the health or life of the patient? Consideration must also be given to the economic factors—are the proposed transferee facilities sufficiently superior to justify the trouble and expense of transfer? Further discussion of these factors should await proper cases.

D.   Who May Qualify As Expert Medical Witness In Malpractice Case: A Rule of Evidence

Medical malpractice cases generally require expert witnesses to assist the trier of fact to understand the evidence. Generally, where the expert lives or where he or she practices his or her profession has no relevance per se with respect to whether a person may be qualified and accepted by the court as an expert witness.

In view of the refinements in the physician's duty of care, we hold that a qualified medical expert witness may without more express an opinion regarding the meaning and import of the duty of care, given the peculiar circumstances of the case. Based on the information reasonably available to the physician, i.e., symptoms, history, test results, results of the doctor's own physical examination, x-rays, vital signs, etc., a qualified medical expert may express an opinion regarding the conclusions (possible diagnoses or areas for further examination and testing) minimally knowledgeable and competent physicians in the same specialty or general field of practice would draw, or actions (not tied to the availability of specialized facilities or equipment not generally available) they would take.

Before the witness may go further, he must be familiarized with the facilities, resources, services and options available. This may be done in any number of ways. The witness may prior to trial have visited the facilities, etc. He may have sat in the courtroom and listened as other witnesses described the facilities. He may have known and over the years interacted with physicians in the area. There are no doubt many other ways in which this could be done, but, significantly, we should allow the witness to be made familiar with the facilities (and customs) of the medical community in question via a properly predicated and phrased hypothetical question.

Once he has become informed of the facilities, etc. available to the defendant physician, the qualified medical expert witness may express an opinion what the care duty of the defendant physician was[10] and whether the acts or omissions of the defendant physician were in compliance with, or fell substantially short of compliance with, that duty.

V.   Disposition of the Case At Bar

[W]e are confident that the first 24 hours post-surgery for any patient present matters within the common knowledge of any surgeon. Subject to variation with the patient's age, history and general state of health prior to surgery, there are surely a number of commonly known and reasonably to

---

10.   The duty "was" what it "reasonably should have been"—see the point regarding the non-controlling effect of local medical custom or practice stated above in subsection III(c)(3).

be anticipated complications and danger signals common to all post-operative patients.[14] These are matters with respect to which surgeons such as Dr. Hilbun have a duty of care to their patients.

Dr. Hilbun held himself out to the public in general and to Terry O. Hall in particular as being competent to perform the surgery in question. He thereby acquired an obligation to Mrs. Hall to perform all facets of the surgery with that level of competence and diligence as might be expected of minimally competent surgeons under the circumstances. The relevant circumstances include those of the particular patient, any objectively sound local medical custom, and the facilities, resources and options available as discussed in Section III(C)(4) above. He particularly became obligated to direct the post-operative care of Mrs. Hall and to ensure that, with respect to all post-operative dangers or complications reasonably to be anticipated under the circumstances, adequate provision was made for prompt diagnosis and treatment.

In view of what we have said in Section III(D) above, it was error to exclude the testimony of [Doctors Hoerr and Sachs] in its entirety. Each was clearly competent to testify regarding matters related to the level of knowledge, skill, medical judgment and general competence a surgeon should have brought to bear in prescribing and administering the post-operative regimen for a patient such as Mrs. Hall.

Insofar as the record reflects [including Dr. Dohn's testimony], the only possible basis for Dr. Hilbun's contention that there are relevant differences between Cleveland, Ohio, and Pascagoula, Mississippi, regards the general quality and competence of nursing personnel. By establishing the inadequacy of the nursing and personnel resources available to him in Pascagoula, Mississippi, Dr. Hilbun only increases his own responsibility. Where a physician is working with medical personnel of known modest competence, his duty of instruction and control is increased. That Dr. Hilbun may have had doubts about the quality of nursing care at the Singing River Hospital lends considerable credibility to the expert testimony of Dr. Hoerr to the effect that far more specific post-operative orders or instructions should have been provided in the case of Mrs. Hall.

[The Court held that the trial court's exclusion of the plaintiff's experts' testimony was error, and remanded the case for a new trial, in which those experts would be permitted to testify "without limitation" as to "such medical knowledge as is commonly possessed or is reasonably available to minimally competent surgeons throughout the country. Each may be permitted to express an opinion as to whether the quality of post-operative care rendered Mrs. Hall by Dr. Hilbun conformed to objectively ascertained minimally acceptable levels. In expressing such an opinion, each should consider such legitimate differences of opinion as may exist within the medical profession regarding the regimen of post-operative care

---

14. On retrial it should be developed more fully whether and to what extent a 140 pulse rate and adult respiratory distress syndrome are "commonly known and reasonably to be anticipated complications."

that ought to have been provided a patient such as Mrs. Hall. Further, to the extent that, in order to express such an opinion, consideration need be given to the facilities, equipment, personnel and general medical resources available, Drs. Hoerr and Sachs must be fully apprised of and required to assume these prior to answering."]

Notes

1. *The conspiracy of silence.* The facts and litigation process in *Hall* reveal several remarkable features of the previously dominant locality rule. First, Dr. Hilbun did not dispute that he remained Mrs. Hall's doctor for post-operative care, and that it was his (and presumably local) customary practice to "follow" such patients until they left the hospital. Then what was his theory of the case? That with less hospital resources, individual doctors were "stretched thin" and therefore could not monitor post-operative patients as closely as could doctors in larger hospitals? That it was his (and local medical) practice to rely on the hospital nurses to inform him of any emerging difficulties, and not to give the nurses any instructions about when to do so? As the *Hall* opinion points out, Dr. Hilbun's and his witness Dr. Dohn's testimony about the unevenness of the nurses logically supports a greater duty of physician supervision and pro-active patient management. In fact, the locality rule functioned to suppress this kind of dialogue about or interrogation of local practices. If the plaintiff could not find an expert knowledgeable about local practices, he could not put on his case at all, and the defendant doctor had no need to explain anything, except if called by the plaintiff as an adverse witness, when he would be expected to testify that his actions did not violate the standard of care. It is remarkable that on these facts apparently not a single local physician was willing to testify for the plaintiff, and indeed that a physician newly arrived in the locality from a major medical center apparently thought it to be in his interest to testify for the defendant. It is also worth noting the financial investment in out-of-state expert testimony that the plaintiff's attorney likely made in this case, knowing that he would likely lose at the trial level in the hope of persuading the state supreme court to overrule long-standing precedent.

2. *Challenging the local customary standard.* Under *Hall*, a jury is no longer *required* to find that compliance with local customary medical practices is not negligence. But the jury is still *permitted* to find that local customary practices are not negligent. Under *Hall*, under what circumstances—in response to what kinds of evidence—is the jury permitted to reach that conclusion? Under *Hall*, through what mechanisms is it now easier for a plaintiff's out-of-state expert to express a (presumably critical) opinion about local customary practices?

3. *Applying the* Hall *doctrine.* In his book HEALING THE WOUNDS (1985), Dr. David Hilfiker describes a particularly harrowing childbirth. A woman whose pregnancy has been "wonderfully normal," and who has traveled over 50 miles to be attended by Dr. Hilfiker because he believes in natural

childbirth, is in the hospital and about to give birth when the nurse listening to the fetus' heart rate suddenly notices that it has increased sharply. When the baby is born a minute or so later, it is blue, with a pulse of only 40 (instead of the normal 140), and not trying to breathe. Dr. Hilfiker and a nurse resuscitate the baby, and through a blood sample Hilfiker identifies the immediate problem as low blood sugar. Unsure of the proper concentration or how to administer it, Hilfiker calls a specialist, Dr. Mary Donaldson, at the Newborn Intensive Care Unit in Duluth. After Hilfiker describes the situation as succinctly as he can, their conversation is as follows:

"Did you have a fetal monitor [an electronic device for measuring fetal heart rate] on during labor?" she [Dr. Donaldson] asks. "What was the heart rate then?"

"We don't have the monitor yet, Mary." How can I explain to her that our little hospital can't afford the $10,000 piece of equipment since it would be used only a few times a year? "The nurses listened, of course, but the heart rate seemed normal to them. We must have missed the decelerations in heartbeat."

"Yes, I think so. You said the baby's small? Did you get an ultrasound picture during pregnancy?"

"No, I didn't. The baby seemed normal size to me on examination, so I didn't get an ultrasound. I suppose I should have."

"Well, it might have tipped you off that something was wrong. But then, we don't always get them down here either, and these surprises can happen.... I think you should get some glucose in as soon as possible to prevent brain damage."

"OK," I say. "What route should we use for administration, and what dosages?"

"I think an intraumbilical catheter [a plastic tube through a vein in the belly button] would be best. Just give five percent glu—"

I interrupt her. "I've never put in an intraumbilical line." I feel so ignorant—one more skill, one more bit of information I should have.... "I'm not even sure we have the correct supplies up here."

"Oh ... well, then put an IV into a scalp vein and give a simple five percent glucose solution. If you can't get an IV going, you can put a gavage tube down into the baby's stomach and instill ten percent glucose; that would be better than nothing.... I'd suggest we come up in the ambulance and bring the baby down here for intensive care...."

[Jean Appleton, the head nurse] and I work unsuccessfully for fifteen minutes trying to pass an IV catheter into one of the fragile veins of the baby's scalp. I haven't had to do this since my internship five years ago and my skills have noticeably deteriorated. The small veins keep breaking. Finally we give up on the IV and put a tube in the baby's stomach. Fortunately, one of the newly recruited nurses used to work in a newborn intensive care unit. We get her out of bed ... and she hurries to help me manage the gavage tube, since I've never done that either....

During the next two hours while we are waiting for the specialized neonatal transport ambulance from Duluth, the baby seems to do pretty well. I, however, am a nervous wreck! I remember vaguely that abnormal levels in blood minerals, trouble getting enough oxygen to the brain, and numerous other problems can plague [small] babies ... but I don't have the knowledge or skills, nor does our hospital have the equipment, to do the required testing or treatment.

[After a few months of complications, concern, and treatment in Duluth, the baby is pronounced fine.]

DAVID HILFIKER, HEALING THE WOUNDS 45–47 (1985).

Assume, however, that the baby was permanently and seriously brain damaged because of inadequate blood sugar at and after childbirth. Assume further that you are representing Dr. Hilfiker in the subsequent malpractice suit, and that the *Hall v. Hilbun* opinion is the governing law. (1) Is Dr. Hilfiker likely to be liable for (a) never having put in an intraumbilical line, and not knowing whether he had the supplies to do so?; (b) not being able to pass an IV catheter into the baby's scalp?; and (c) not having an electronic fetal monitor? What kinds of testimony and witnesses would each side call on these issues? (2) Does the fact that Dr. Hilfiker consulted the Duluth specialist constitute compliance with the *Hall* doctrine regarding a rural doctor's relationship with sources of more advanced care? As his attorney, what would you want to ask Dr. Hilfiker about his conversations with the pregnant woman when she was deciding to become his patient?

4. *Applying the* Hall *Doctrine: a second example.* Assume that the following case arises under the *Hall* doctrine. A women in her thirty-third week of pregnancy experienced significant bleeding and sought care at a small rural hospital, where she was treated by the doctor on call, a family physician. The doctor correctly diagnosed a dangerous emergency condition and began arranging for neonatal transport to be dispatched from a tertiary care hospital. The doctor was also aware that if the emergency condition became less stable than it was at the moment and progressed to the point where the baby was not receiving adequate oxygen, he would have roughly fifteen minutes to deliver the baby by cesarean section to avoid permanent injury to the child. Because the family physician did not himself perform cesarean sections, he began making phone calls to line up the personnel (a nurse anesthetist, a scrub nurse, a circulating nurse, a labor and delivery nurse, a surgeon, a physician to assist the surgeon, and a pediatrician for the baby) who could deliver the baby and assist in the infant's resuscitation if that became necessary. The family physician did not, however, actually mobilize a surgical team to come to the hospital at this time.

Before the medical transport arrived, the baby's heart rate dropped precipitously, and the surgical team was assembled at the hospital. The baby was delivered thirty minutes later and was then transferred to the tertiary care hospital by the neonatal transport team that had been dispatched when the emergency arose. The child died the next evening.

The trial, a classic battle of the experts, centered on the conflicting testimony of the plaintiffs' experts and the defendant's experts. The plaintiffs' experts were critical of several aspects of the family physician's care, but most significantly of his failure to assemble a surgical team to stand by at the hospital for an emergency cesarean section should the baby's oxygenation become compromised. They believed that had a surgical team been ready, the baby could have been delivered within ten to fifteen minutes instead of over thirty minutes, and the baby's chances of survival would have been good.

The family physician testified that at a community hospital such as his, physicians do not call in a surgical team until surgery is actually needed. He said human resources are limited in rural areas, and in some cases a physician is on call fifty percent of the time. Consequently, on-call personnel are summoned only when it is certain that their services will be required. The defense experts echoed this testimony and conclusions. They confirmed that in rural areas surgical teams are not assembled on a standby basis; when personnel are limited, having them on standby may disrupt the on-call providers' attention to other matters. As one physician simply summarized, "We don't have that many personnel."

Plaintiff's experts and attorney argued that *Hall's* "resources-based" locality rule did not apply, because the personnel needed to perform an immediate cesarean section were actually available, and therefore, there was no resource-based limitation on the family doctor's ability to comply with the standard of care requiring immediate delivery if needed. In essence, they argued that because a surgical team *could* have been called to the hospital on a standby basis, reasonable care *required* that the surgical personnel be summoned even before surgery was determined to be necessary. If you were representing the defendant, how would you cross examine plaintiff's experts on this issue? Under *Hall*, should the trial judge allow the jury to consider the defendant's resource-based limitations argument? What result under the *Shilkret* version of the medical standard of care?

5. *Application of a national standard of care.* National standards have been and are typically applied to specialists, even in states that retain a version of the local standard for general practitioners. *See, e.g.*, Robbins v. Footer, 553 F.2d 123, 126–30 (D.C. Cir. 1977), in which a Washington, D.C. obstetrician was sued for negligent administration of pitocin during childbirth. One of the defendant's experts testified that "actual common practice" among obstetricians in Washington, D.C. was "more lax" than the national specialty standard; on this basis, the trial judge excluded testimony about the national standard and instructed the jury to apply the standards actually used among specialists in the locality. The District of Columbia Circuit Court of Appeals reversed, holding that nationally certified specialists must meet a national standard, i.e. "that degree of care and skill expected of a reasonably competent practitioner in his specialty acting in the same or similar circumstances." The fact that specialists in one

locality may have followed a lower standard was no defense, unless that deviation was justified by "[t]he availability of medical facilities, accessibility of professional consultation and the communication and transportation systems of the area...."

6. *Application of a national standard of care to hospitals.* Traditionally, hospitals, like physicians, were only held to the standard of care practiced by similar hospitals in their own locality. However, the existence of national hospital accreditation, state-wide licensure, and increasingly comprehensive state regulatory systems has convinced most state courts to reject a locality standard for hospitals, and to apply a roughly uniform national standard. Thus, "a hospital is required to use that degree of care and skill which is expected of a reasonably competent hospital in the same or similar circumstances. As in cases brought against physicians, advances in the profession, availability of special facilities and specialists, together with all other relevant considerations, are to be taken into account." *Shilkret*, 349 A.2d at 254. For further discussion of hospitals' duties of care, see Chapter 18 below. Like doctors and hospitals, nurses are also now generally held to a national standard of care expected of a "reasonably prudent and competent registered nurse." George Annas et al., The Rights of Doctors, Nurses, and Allied Health Professionals 28 (1981).

7. *The ambiguity of national versus local standards.* Although many state supreme courts have abandoned the locality rule in favor of a national standard, the exact status of the rule, or of local factors, is not clear in several jurisdictions, and in others the courts and/or legislatures have retained or reinstated the locality rule. *See, e.g.,* Annot., 99 A.L.R.3d 1133 (originally published in 1980; cases updated weekly) (stating that the status of the locality rule is unclear in thirteen jurisdictions, including New York, California, Pennsylvania, and Texas); McCullough v. University of Rochester Strong Memorial Hosp., 794 N.Y.S.2d 236 (App. Div. 2005) ("the standard of care in a medical malpractice action is measured against local, statewide, or nationwide standards and the 'superior knowledge and skill' that a provider actually possesses," *id.* at 237); Gubler v. Boe, 815 P.2d 1034 (Idaho 1991) (on the basis of Idaho Code section 6–1012, plaintiffs' out-of-state expert witness excluded because although expert had consulted with an Idaho physician about the local standard of care, plaintiff could not prove that the local physician so consulted had been practicing in the particular town in the particular year in which the alleged negligence took place).

8. *Is there really a "national" standard of care?* The common law courts' interest in and at least partial endorsement of "national standards of care" exists in a very curious context: the medical profession's traditional resistance to formal, systematic, or evidence-based standards, a vigorous contemporary movement by many actors in health care delivery (including physicians) to develop such standards and practices, and the continuing sense that such efforts have not taken hold on a large scale. For most of American history, including the present, there has been no national, institutionalized system of establishing "standards of care" or the efficacy

of new surgical and diagnostic procedures (in contrast to new drugs, whose use is regulated—albeit controversially—by the Food and Drug Administration). "Most clinical policies derive from a flow of reports in the literature, at meetings, and in peer discussions. Over a period of time, hundreds of separate comments come together to form a clinical policy. If this becomes generally accepted, it becomes 'standard practice.'" BARRY R. FURROW ET AL., HEALTH LAW at 266–67 (2d ed., 2000); *see also* David M. Eddy, *Clinical Policies and the Quality of Clinical Practice*, 307 NEW ENG. J. MED. 343 (1982).

For the past twenty and more years, there has been an immense amount of research, advocacy, and organizational experimentation attempting to make the traditional fragmented process of diffusing medical knowledge more systematic and evidence-based. *See, e.g.*, Atul Gawande et al., *10 Steps to Better Health Care*, N.Y. TIMES, August 13, 2009; ATUL GAWANDE, THE CHECKLIST MANIFESTO; Lars Noah, *Medicine's Epistemology: Mapping the Haphazard Diffusion of Knowledge in the Biomedical Community*, 44 ARIZ. L. REV. 373 (2002); Mark A. Hall, *The Defensive Effect of Medical Practice Policies in Malpractice Litigation*, 54 LAW & CONTEMP. PROBS. 119 (Spring 1991) [hereafter cited as Hall, *Defensive Effect*]. As early as 1991, Professor Mark Hall could refer to a 1988 review issue of American Medical News, the official newspaper of the American Medical Association "detail[ing] the coordinated efforts of the AMA, medical specialty societies, private research groups, and the government to bring greater standardization to medical treatment" [including "over 1,100 existing practice policies, and reporting that fifteen of the twenty-four specialty societies are actively developing practice policies, with the rest likely to follow suit."] "These developments stand in stark contrast to organized medicine's traditional opposition to any sort of formal standard-setting." Hall, *Defensive Effect* at 121–22. In the same article, Hall wrote that the "present state of medical science thoroughly fails to conform to the legal ideal of an established standard of care. In most instances, no such definitive standard exists. Instead, there are vast differences in the frequency with which different groups of doctors employ many medical procedures. Practice patterns vary so greatly because 'uncertainty pervades medical diagnosis and treatment.' 'Medical knowledge is engulfed and infiltrated by uncertainty.' It 'creeps into medical practice through every pore.'" *Id.* at 127–28. Writing in 2008, Professor James Gibson echoed this assessment: "most medical practices have little or no support in the scientific literature. Instead, physicians do what they see other physicians do, or what they were taught in medical school. Even more disillusioning is that when scientific evidence becomes available—e.g., randomized clinical trials of a common procedure—those in the field often remain ignorant of or misapply the results." James Gibson, *Doctrinal Feedback and (Un)Reasonable Care*, 94 VA. L. REV. 1641, 1663–64 (2008). The issue of how to apply findings from studies like randomized trials in practice is difficult because conditions in the field differ in many ways from the idealized conditions of the studies, which require relatively "sterile" conditions in order to avoid confounding the results and to attain statistical significance. The patients included in a randomized trial also may bear little resemblance to patients actually under treatment, since in order to test the impact of an intervention on certain conditions (for example, a new medical procedure for managing a cardiology condition) the trial may screen out people with co-morbidities such as diabetes and depression.

Parts of the movement toward more formal standards and evidence-based medicine were explored in Part Two in the context of health insurance coverage exclusions and "pay for performance" initiatives. The Affordable Care Act seeks to stimulate these developments even further. Before considering these recent and ongoing developments, it is important to examine how medical liability law has evolved in dealing with diversity and change in medical and scientific knowledge and practices.

4. THE PROBLEM OF COMPETING STANDARDS: THE "TWO SCHOOLS OF THOUGHT" OR "RESPECTABLE (OR REPUTABLE) MINORITY" DOCTRINE

Jones v. Chidester

610 A.2d 964 (Pa. 1992)

■ PAPADAKOS [JUSTICE]:

A medical practitioner has an absolute defense to a claim of negligence when it is determined that the prescribed treatment or procedure has been approved by one group of medical experts even though an alternate school of thought recommends another approach, or it is agreed among experts that alternative treatments and practices are acceptable. The doctrine is applicable only where there is more than one method of accepted treatment or procedure. [W]e are called upon in this case to decide once again whether a school of thought qualifies as such when it is advocated by a "considerable number" of medical experts or when it commands acceptance by "respective, reputable and reasonable" practitioners. The former test calls for a quantitative analysis, while the latter is premised on qualitative grounds.

The facts indicate that in November, 1979, Appellant, Billy Jones, underwent orthopedic surgery on his leg performed by Dr. John H. Chidester. In order to create a bloodless field for the surgery, the surgeon employed a tourniquet which was elevated and released at various intervals. Because of subsequent problems with the leg, the patient was referred to a neurosurgeon who determined that Jones had suffered nerve injury to the leg.

At trial Jones complained, inter alia, that his nerve injury was the result of Dr. Chidester's use of the tourniquet. Both sides presented testimony by medical experts supporting their positions. Unsurprisingly, Dr. Chidester's experts told the court and jury that his technique was acceptable medically in this particular case, and the plaintiffs' experts insisted that it constituted unacceptable practice.

[At the close of the evidence, the court instructed the jury:]

Ladies and gentlemen, I instruct you upon this additional principle of law known as the two schools of thought doctrine. This principle provides that it is improper for a jury to be required to decide which of two schools of thought as to proper procedure should have been followed in this case, when both schools have their respective and respected advocates and followers in the medical profession.

In essence, then, a jury of lay persons is not to be put in a position of choosing one respected body of medical opinion over another when each has a reasonable following among the members of the medical community.

Thus, under the two schools of thought doctrine, a physician in the position of Dr. Chidester will not be held liable to a plaintiff merely for exercising his judgment in applying the course of treatment supported by a reputable and respected body of medical experts, even if another body of medical experts' opinion would favor a different course of treatment.

The jury returned a verdict in favor of Dr. Chidester. At trial and on appeal, Jones argues that [the trial court's instruction to the jury on the two schools of thought doctrine was reversible error because] under Pennsylvania law, the test for the doctrine is "considerable number" rather than "reputable and respected" as the court had charged the jury.

The "two schools of thought doctrine" provides a complete defense to malpractice. It is therefore insufficient to show that there exists a "small minority" of physicians who agree with the defendant's questioned practice. Rather, there must be a considerable number of physicians, recognized and respected in their field, sufficient to create another "school of thought." We, therefore, provide the following as a correct statement of the law: Where competent medical authority is divided, a physician will not be held responsible if in the exercise of his judgment he followed a course of treatment advocated by a considerable number of recognized and respected professionals in his given area of expertise.

In recognizing this doctrine, we do not attempt to place a numerical certainty on what constitutes a "considerable number." The burden of proving that there are two schools of thought falls to the defendant. The burden, however, should not prove burdensome. The proper use of expert witnesses should supply the answers. Once the expert states the factual reasons to support his claim that there is a considerable number of professionals who agree with the treatment employed by the defendant, there is sufficient evidence to warrant an instruction to the jury on the two "schools of thought." It then becomes a question for the jury to determine whether they believe that there are two legitimate schools of thought such that the defendant should be insulated from liability.

Reversed and remanded for a new trial consistent with this opinion.

■ McDERMOTT, JUSTICE, concurring:

When a physician is charged with employing a course of treatment and it fails of its purpose though properly and carefully administered, the issue becomes whether that treatment was an acceptable medical procedure which the physician was justified in believing would work a cure. The question involved is not was it done negligently, but should it have been done at all. That question is beyond the ability of laymen to answer: whether it were best to chill or heat, use medicines, intervene with scalpel or await nature, or approach from back, front, top or bottom to reach the site of ill, are questions over which doctors disagree. One group of doctors, of skill and competence may withhold the scalpel, another group of equal competence may believe in quick response. When each group has its advocates, and each has its arguable reasons, a doctor of either, cannot be faulted if he properly administers the one to his knowledge and experience seems the better, so long as that group is comprised of a sufficient number of reputable and respected members.

■ ZAPPALA, JUSTICE, concurring:

While I join in the opinion, I vehemently disagree with the majority that the existence of two schools of medical thought may ever be a question of fact to be submitted to a jury. The majority states that, "It then becomes a question for the jury to determine whether they believe that there are two legitimate schools of thought such that the defendant should be insulated from liability." It is the responsibility of the trial judge to determine in the first instance whether there are two schools of medical thought so that competent medical authority as to a course of treatment is divided. It is a question of law for the trial judge. It is not a question of fact. In all other respects, I agree with the majority's analysis.

Notes

1. *The evolution and continuing relevance of the "two schools of thought" doctrine.* Courts have long recognized that medicine is a variable craft, and protected doctors not only from standards outside their locality, but also from varying approaches within their locality or among their local, regional, or national professional peers. This was particularly important in the late nineteenth and early twentieth centuries, when competing "schools" of medicine (e.g. medicine emphasizing surgery or pharmaceuticals, versus medicine emphasizing skeletal alignment) had sharply different views regarding appropriate treatment. *See* PAUL STARR, THE SOCIAL TRANS-FORMATION OF AMERICAN MEDICINE 93–112; Ennis v. Banks, 164 P. 58 (Wash. 1917) (homeopathic doctor cannot testify as to the standard of care applicable to an allopathic doctor). More generally, most jurisdictions recognized, and continue to recognize, that "[w]here doctors differ as to what procedure is appropriate, physicians may depart from the majority's customary practice to follow that of a 'reputable' or 'respectable' minority of practitioners." Bovbjerg, *HMO Standard* at 1385; *see, e.g.*, Dahl v. Wagner, 151 P. 1079 (Wash. 1915).

While the concept of "two schools of thought" or a "respectable minority" is easy to articulate, applying it in a particular case raises challenging questions about the degree to which the authority to set and to question "standards of care" (and hence legal duty) is delegated to individual doctors, or to more or less small groups of doctors, or, conversely, is held by judges and juries presumably informed by expert testimony and by the values of the society and the traditions of the law. Who (the judge? the jury?) is to determine whether a minority medical view has sufficiently widespread support (the "quantity" issue) or is sufficiently (scientifically? clinically? reputationally?) plausible (the "quality" issue) to be "respectable" or "legitimate"? What kind of expert witnesses, and what kind of evidence, should be allowed to inform these decisions?

How the law should handle competing standards of care is likely to become an increasingly important issue. Geographic variations research has highlighted the degree to which medical "practice styles" differ between even nearby geographic areas. The proliferation of new technology, on the one hand, and resource-constrained practice guidelines, managed care plans, and competitive market pressures on the other, are likely to generate even greater diversity in both standards and practice.

2. *Safe harbors against ambiguous standards.* Often there are not two competing standards of equal reputability, but rather less clear plausibility and/or influence of one or more standards. In these circumstances, the two schools of thought doctrine has great difficulty providing a "safe harbor" or "shield" for the defendant, or removing the substantive merits from the jury. (To be sure, where the validity and influence of the purported standard is not clear, many would argue that it should not provide a safe harbor, and the jury should evaluate the merits of the standard.) There is a substantial academic literature, and some legislation, calling for "certification" or other official or quasi-official approval of clinical practice guidelines, which, if adopted, would effectively revive the safe harbor quality of the two schools of thought doctrine. Under this approach, if, for example, a government agency designated by statute approved or certified a clinical practice guideline, it would at the very least be considered a reasonable and reputable standard, and hence a physician who appropriately followed such a guideline in an individual case would be shielded by the two schools of thought doctrine, even if there were other standards or guidelines more favorable to the plaintiff. *See* Arnold J. Rosoff, *Evidence–Based Medicine and the Law: The Courts Confront Clinical Practice Guidelines*, 26 J. HEALTH POL. POL'Y & L. 327, 362 (2001), discussed further in the section on clinical practice guidelines below.

5.   OVERRIDING THE PROFESSIONAL OR INDUSTRY STANDARD OF CARE

The T.J. Hooper

60 F.2d 737 (2d Cir.) *cert. den.*, 287 U.S. 662 (1932)

■ LEARNED HAND, CIRCUIT JUDGE:

[The relevant issue in *The T.J. Hooper* was whether tugboats pulling coal-laden barges along the east coast of the United States in March 1928 were negligent for not having functioning radios on board through which they could have heard weather reports that would have probably caused them to seek shelter and avoid a damaging storm.]

[The tugs did not receive the weather reports] because their private radio receiving sets, which were on board, were not in working order. These belonged to [the crew] personally, and were partly a toy, partly a part of the equipment, but neither furnished by the owner, nor supervised by it. It is not fair to say that there was a general custom among coastwise carriers so as to equip their tugs. One line alone did it; as for the rest, they relied upon their crews, so far as they can be said to have relied at all. An adequate receiving set suitable for a coastwise tug can now be got at small cost and is reasonably reliable if kept up; obviously it is a source of great protection to their tows. Twice every day they can receive these predictions based upon the widest possible information. Whatever may be said as to other vessels, tugs towing heavy coal laden barges, strung out for half a mile, have little power to maneuver, and do not, as this case proves, expose themselves to weather which would not turn back stauncher craft. They can have at hand protection against dangers of which they can learn in no other way.

Is it then a final answer that the business had not yet generally adopted receiving sets? There are yet, no doubt, cases where courts seem to make the general practice of the calling the standard of proper diligence. Indeed in most cases reasonable prudence is in fact common prudence; but strictly it is never its measure; a whole calling may have unduly lagged in the adoption of new and available devices. It may never set its own tests, however persuasive be its usages. Courts must in the end say what is required; there are precautions so imperative that even their universal disregard will not excuse their omission. But here there was no custom at all as to receiving sets; some had them, some did not; the most that can be urged is that they had not yet become general. Certainly in such a case we need not pause; when some have thought a device necessary, at least we may say that they were right, and the others too slack.

Notes

1. *Overriding the professional standard or industry custom.* Courts have occasionally overridden (or allowed juries to override) professional standards or industry custom on the basis of general criteria of "reasonable prudence." The details of *The T.J. Hooper* are revealing about what is involved in trumping an industry or professional practice, and about the relationship between liability and new technology. The case usually is cited for the proposition that when the cost of a precaution is greatly outweighed by the benefit gained by the precaution, a professional standard that neglects the precaution can be overridden by the general principle of reasonable care or reasonable prudence. While Judge Hand certainly articu-

lated this principle, the facts of the case show that there was no strong industry consensus. Rather, the case could be characterized as involving "two schools of thought," with some tugboat companies taking systematic responsibility for having working radios, and others relying in what Judge Hand suggests was a haphazard manner on the crew's private radios. With an effective precaution costing so little, and the value of the cargoes at risk so great, Judge Hand found it easy to decide that one "school" was "too slack."

How could this decision be re-framed in terms of the two schools of thought doctrine explored above? The defendants apparently easily satisfied the "quantity" requirement; nothing in Judge Hand's opinion suggests that most tugboat companies supplied working radios, and that the defendants in *The T.J. Hooper* were a small minority or "outliers." So the decision must rest on the "quality" requirement, i.e., that the cost-benefit decision of not having the radios so egregiously disregarded the interests of the cargo owners that the non-radio approach could no longer be regarded (by a court applying the general standard of reasonable prudence) as "respectable" or "reputable," notwithstanding the contrary view of many in the industry. Of course, the plaintiff had to persuade the court that having radios was either the only reasonable "emerging standard" or was required by the general principle of reasonable care.

2. *The impact of new technology.* The facts of *The T.J. Hooper* exquisitely straddle the distinction made by Professor Mark Grady between two ways that new technology increases the risk of liability: "technology lag" and "failure to use nondurable precautions." *See* Grady, *Why Are People Negligent.* The invention of the kidney dialysis machine, a new incubator for premature infants, the carbon dioxide monitor at issue in the *Washington v. Washington Hospital Center* case below, or the radios at issue in *The T.J. Hooper* transform "natural" risk into potential legal liability: what was once unavoidable death or injury is now avoidable, given appropriate use of the new technology. Liability can come from an individual defendant's (e.g. *Washington v. Washington Hospital Center)* or entire industry's (e.g., *T.J. Hooper*) failure to adopt the technology at all; in this version, the function of tort liability is to assure fast diffusion of new technology, and to override the mistaken cost-benefit calculations of individual defendants or (occasionally) entire professions or industries.

Professor Grady argues that the actual pattern of increased malpractice liability reveals that most of the new liability is imposed in urban centers, where the new technology is most quickly adopted. The predominant reason for the new liability, Grady contends, is not failure to adopt new technology, but failure to implement the "nondurable precautions" (i.e., repetitive maintenance and operations) that the new technology requires, e.g., properly connecting the dialysis machine to the patient, carefully testing the hemodialytic solution, regularly checking the patient's shunts, and so forth. Indeed, although Professor Grady, like most commentators, describes *The T.J. Hooper* as a technology lag case, it actually can also be thought of as "nondurable precautions" case. As Judge Hand made clear, there were radios on the defendant tugboats; the problem was that they were not working, i.e., that "nondurable precautions" had not been taken. Similarly, the *Washington v. Washington Hospital Center* case, below, can be seen not so much as a "technology lag" case (because the hospital was "attempting" to adopt the technology), but rather as a "failure to use nondurable precautions," i.e., failing to get the procurement process to work effectively.

3. *Overriding industry custom in a health care context.* The most famous (and largely unique) health law case purporting to overrule a professional standard is *Helling v. Carey*, in which several ophthalmologists defended their failure to give their 32–year old patient a low-risk, inexpensive pressure test for glaucoma on the grounds that the professional standard required such tests on a "routine" basis only for patients over 40. Bypassing possible evidence that the patient had presented sufficient symptoms to have required the test for her on an individualized rather than "routine" basis, the Washington Supreme Court assumed that the professional standard had been correctly applied, and challenged the professional standard itself. Citing *The T.J. Hooper*, the court concluded that "[t]he precaution of giving this test to detect the incidence of glaucoma to patients under 40 years of age is so imperative that irrespective of its disregard by the standards of the ophthalmology profession, it is the duty of the courts to say what is required." In fact, "even though the [*Helling*] court does not seem to have known it, physicians in almost every other state were routinely testing for glaucoma in the early 1970s." GEORGE J. ANNAS ET AL., AMERICAN HEALTH LAW 329 (1990). *Helling* thus could have been decided as a "national vs. local standard" or "two schools of thought" case, in which the local or minority standard was no longer deemed consistent with the national standard or with reasonable care. *See also* Harris v. Robert C. Groth, M.D., Inc., 663 P.2d 113 (Wash. 1983) (discussing legislative and litigation developments in the state of Washington after *Helling*).

6. WHEN HAS A NEW STANDARD EMERGED? THE "BEST JUDGMENT RULE" AND THE PROBLEM OF NEW KNOWLEDGE AND TECHNOLOGIES

As discussed above, the locality rule was successfully criticized for failing to penalize doctors whose local customs of practice did not keep pace with advancing medical knowledge. The shift to a "national standard" could be characterized as both a more scientifically accurate version of a "professional standard," and as society's insistence (through the courts) that local medical custom remain consistent with a social or general standard of reasonable care (i.e., a social contract model) informed by advances in medical knowledge. Both sources of legal duty were articulated in cases involving the "best judgment doctrine," under which reliance on local or customary practice is not adequate where the physician knows, or has reason to know, that customary practice is problematic. In other words, the doctor has a duty to exercise his "best judgment," even if that judgment differs from the customary standard.

A number of cases involving this principle arose out of the fact that in the early 1950's there was extensive debate among doctors about whether administration of high doses of oxygen (six liters per minute) to premature infants actually benefited them at all, and whether it caused blindness. Shortly before a study conclusively showed that any oxygen treatment was pointless and harmful, and hence while such treatment still remained the standard, albeit subject to debate, a pediatrician who knew about the controversy attempted to mitigate the risk of the treatment by ordering four liters of oxygen per minute be administered to two premature infants, rather than the customary six. The nurses failed to follow the four liter per minute order, and administered the usual six, causing the infants' blindness. In a subsequent lawsuit the doctor was found not liable for having ordered the oxygen—since it was still considered the standard—but the question arose whether he might be liable for failing to ascertain that the hospital staff had mistakenly increased the dosage. The doctor argued that since the "mistaken" dosage was still the customary standard, he should not be held liable for the mistake. The New York Court of Appeals disagreed, reasoning as follows:

> [E]vidence that a physician conformed to accepted community standards of practice usually insulates him from tort liability. There is, however, a second principle involved in medical malpractice cases. Having its genesis in the reasonable man rule, this principle demands that a physician should use his best judgment and whatever superior knowledge, skill and intelligence he has. Thus, a specialist may be held liable where a general practitioner may not.
>
> The necessary implication of this latter principle is that evidence that the defendant followed customary practice is not the sole test of professional malpractice. If a physician fails to employ his expertise or best judgment, and that omission causes injury, he should not automatically be freed from liability because in fact he adhered to acceptable practice. There is no policy reason why a physician, who knows or believes there are unnecessary dangers in the community practice, should not be required to take whatever precautionary measures he deems appropriate.

Toth v. Community Hospital at Glen Cove, 239 N.E.2d 368, 373 (N.Y. 1968). The court noted that requiring doctors to use their "best judgment" and thereby perhaps deviate from customary practice increased their risk of legal liability if harm was caused, and suggested that this risk could be mitigated by the "two schools of thought" doctrine discussed above.

As customary practices come under the increasing scrutiny of geographic variations research and other quality assessment programs discussed in this Part, at what point should a doctor be required to use his or her "best judgment" in questioning conventional tests and treatments? One desirable and perhaps legally required way to deal with this issue is for the doctor to inform the patient of the competing perspectives, so as to enable the patient to exercise truly informed choice. *See* Burton v. Brooklyn Doctors Hosp., 452 N.Y.S.2d 875, 880–81 (App. Div. 1982) (doctor who raised premature infant's oxygen to high levels for experimental rather than therapeutic purposes liable both for violating her duty to use her best judgment, and her duty to explain to infant's parents the risks and options so as to obtain informed consent). See further discussion of informed consent later in this Part.

Washington v. Washington Hospital Center

579 A.2d 177 (D.C. App. 1990)

■ FARRELL, ASSOCIATE JUDGE:

On the morning of November 7, 1987, LaVerne Alice Thompson, a healthy 36–year–old woman, underwent elective surgery at the Washington Hospital Center [WHC] for an abortion and tubal ligation, procedures requiring general anesthesia. At about 10:45 a.m., nurse-anesthetist Elizabeth Adland, under the supervision of Dr. Sheryl Walker, the physician anesthesiologist, inserted an endotracheal tube into Ms. Thompson's throat for the purpose of conveying oxygen to, and removing carbon dioxide from, the anesthetized patient. The tube, properly inserted, goes into the patient's trachea just above the lungs. Plaintiffs alleged that instead Nurse Adland inserted the tube into Thompson's esophagus, above the stomach. After inserting the tube, Nurse Adland "ventilated" or pumped air into the patient while Dr. Walker, by observing physical reactions—including watching the rise and fall of the patient's chest and listening for breath sounds equally on the patient's right and left sides—sought to determine if the tube had been properly inserted.

At about 10:50 a.m., while the surgery was underway, surgeon Nathan Bobrow noticed that Thompson's blood was abnormally dark, which indicated that her tissues were not receiving sufficient oxygen, and reported the condition to Nurse Adland, who checked Thompson's vital signs and found them stable. As Dr. Bobrow began the tubal ligation part of the operation, Thompson's heart rate dropped. She suffered a cardiac arrest and was resuscitated, but eventually the lack of oxygen caused catastrophic brain injuries. Plaintiffs' expert testified that Ms. Thompson remains in a persistent vegetative state and is totally incapacitated; her cardiac, respiratory and digestive functions are normal and she is not "brain dead," but, according to the expert, she is "essentially awake but unaware" of her surroundings. Her condition is unlikely to improve, though she is expected to live from ten to twenty years.

[After various claims against various defendants were settled or dismissed, the case went to the jury primarily on Ms. Thompson's personal injury claim against WHC [the hospital] for "failing to provide the anesthesiologists with a device known variously as a capnograph or end-tidal carbon dioxide monitor which allows early detection of insufficient oxygen in time to prevent brain injury." The jury awarded Ms. Thompson $4.586 million.]

In a negligence action predicated on medical malpractice, the plaintiff must carry a tripartite burden, and establish: (1) the applicable standard of care; (2) a deviation from that standard by the defendant; and (3) a causal relationship between that deviation and the plaintiff's injury. [E]xpert testimony is usually required to establish each of the elements, except where the proof is so obvious as to lie within the ken of the average lay juror.

Generally, the "standard of care" is "the course of action that a reasonably prudent [professional] with the defendant's specialty would have taken under the same or similar circumstances." With respect to institutions such as hospitals, this court has rejected the "locality" rule, which refers to the standard of conduct expected of other similarly situated members of the profession in the same locality or community, in favor of a national standard. Thus, the question for decision is whether the evidence as a whole, and reasonable inferences therefrom, would allow a reasonable juror to find that a reasonably prudent tertiary care hospital, at the time of Ms. Thompson's injury in November 1987, and according to national standards, would have supplied a carbon dioxide monitor to a patient undergoing general anesthesia for elective surgery.

WHC argues that the plaintiffs' expert, Dr. Stephen Steen, failed to demonstrate an adequate factual basis for his opinion that WHC should have made available a carbon dioxide monitor. WHC contends that [Dr.] Steen gave no testimony on the number of hospitals having end-tidal carbon dioxide monitors in place in 1987, and that he never referred to any written standards or authorities as the basis of his opinion. We conclude that Steen's opinion rested upon a broader foundation than [that argued by the defense] and that combined with the other evidence concerning standard of care, it was sufficient to create an issue for the jury.

Dr. Steen testified that by 1985, the carbon dioxide monitors were available in his hospital (Los Angeles County–University of Southern California Medical Center (USC)), and "in many other hospitals." In response to a question whether, by 1986, "standards of care" required carbon dioxide monitors in operating rooms, he replied, "I would think that by that time, they would be [required]." As plaintiffs concede, this opinion was based in part on his own personal experience at USC, which cannot itself provide an adequate foundation for an expert opinion on a national standard of care. But Steen also drew support from "what I've read where [the monitors were] available in other hospitals." He referred to two such publications: The American Association of Anesthesiology (AAA) Standards for Basic Intra–Operative Monitoring, approved by the AAA House of Delegates on October 21, 1986, which "encouraged" the use of monitors, and an article entitled *Standards for Patient Monitoring During Anesthesia at Harvard Medical School*, published in August 1986 in the JOURNAL OF AMERICAN MEDICAL ASSOCIATION, which stated that as of July 1985 the monitors were in use at Harvard, and that "monitoring end-tidal carbon dioxide is an emerging standard and is strongly preferred."

WHC makes much of Steen's concession on cross-examination that the AAA Standards were recommendations, strongly encouraged but not mandatory, and that the Harvard publication spoke of an "emerging" standard. In its brief WHC asserts, without citation, that "[p]alpable indicia of widespread *mandated* practices are necessary to establish a standard of care" (emphasis added), and that at most the evidence spoke of "recommended" or "encouraged" practices, and "emerging" or "developing" standards as of 1986–87. A standard of due care, however, necessarily embodies what a reasonably prudent hospital would do, and hence care and foresight exceeding the minimum required by law or mandatory professional regulation may be necessary to meet that standard. It certainly cannot be said that the 1986 recommendations of a professional association (which had no power to issue or enforce mandatory requirements), or an article speaking of an "emerging" standard in 1986, have no bearing on an expert opinion as to what the standard of patient monitoring equipment was fully one year later when Ms. Thompson's surgery took place.

Nevertheless, we need not decide whether Dr. Steen's testimony was sufficiently grounded in fact or adequate data to establish the standard of care. The record contains other evidence from which, in combination with Dr. Steen's testimony, a reasonable juror could fairly conclude that monitors were required of prudent hospitals similar to WHC in late 1987. [This evidence showed that at least eight university teaching hospitals had adopted carbon dioxide monitors by the time of Ms. Thompson's surgery. In response to WHC's argument in its reply brief that teaching hospitals had significantly enhanced financial resources to accelerate their testing and implementation of new and improved technologies that "inherently, were not yet required for the general populace of hospitals [such as WHC]," the court noted that Dr. Steen had reviewed the WHC's President's Report for 1986–87 and concluded that WHC was a teaching hospital. "Counsel for the hospital could have identified and probed fully before the jury any differences between WHC and the hospitals relied on to establish the standard of care. To the extent the record was not so developed, the jury could credit Steen's testimony that WHC was required to adhere to the standard applicable to teaching hospitals."]

Perhaps most probative was the testimony of WHC's own Chairman of the Department of Anesthesiology, Dr. Dermot A. Murray, and documentary evidence associated with his procurement request for carbon dioxide monitors. In December 1986 or January 1987, Dr. Murray submitted a requisition form to the hospital for end-tidal carbon dioxide units to monitor the administration of anesthesia in each of the hospital's operating rooms, stating that if the monitors were not provided, the hospital would "fail to meet the national standard of care." The monitors were [supposed] to be "fully operational" in July of 1987 [but were not].

Note

Technology diffusion and the professional standard of care. Does a doctor's or hospital's knowledge that new, safer equipment or procedures are available create a duty on that particular doctor or hospital to adopt the new equipment or procedure, even though there is often no formal and authoritative process through which medical organizations declare that a new technology is "the standard"? At what point does the diffusion of technology begin to alter the standard of care? Is even limited evidence of incorporation of technology into health care practice enough to alter the standard? The *Washington Hospital Center* case suggests that it may not take much depending on the complexity of the technology, the commonality of its use, and its cost. The technology at issue here was not a multi-million dollar piece of diagnostic or treating equipment, but instead consisted of a relatively simple (and inexpensive) monitor whose use in all operating rooms might dramatically reduce the risk of death or permanent disability.

Note: Medical Expert Testimony

As the *WHC* opinion states, "[g]enerally, the 'standard of care' is 'the course of action that a reasonably prudent [professional] *with the defendant's specialty* [sic] would have taken under the same or similar circumstances.' " (Emphasis supplied). The plaintiff has the burden of proving, almost always through expert testimony, what that standard of care is. Not surprisingly, both the common law and numerous state statutes generally require that the plaintiff's expert be within the same specialty as the defendant physician.

There are also, however, numerous exceptions to this principle, with many variations among the states. In jurisdictions with a flexible approach based on the expert's actual knowledge, the touchstone is not limited to the expert's formal credentials (although these are certainly relevant), but rather whether the expert is knowledgeable about the standard of care involved in the particular facts of the case. Thus a more specialized physician can testify with respect to the actions of a less specialized defendant physician, as long as the specialist can satisfy the trial court that he/she is knowledgeable and testifying about the standard of care relevant to the defendant non-specialist. *See, e.g.*, Fiedler v. Spoelhof, 483 N.W.2d 486, 489 (Minn. App. 1992) (cardiologist can testify about a family physician's care for a prison inmate; "record indicates that [cardiologist] has experience with and knowledge of the standard of care exercised by family practitioners[;] [a]lthough [the cardiologist] was never a prison physician, this factor does not render him incompetent to testify but instead goes to the weight of his testimony.")

Conversely, a less specialized physician can testify with respect to the action of a specialist, as long as the non-specialist can satisfy the trial court that he/she is knowledgeable and testifying about a non-specialist standard of care relevant to the defendant specialist's actions. *See, e.g.*, Hauser v. Bhatnager, 537 A.2d 599, 601 (Me. 1988) ("although [plaintiff's general surgeon expert witness] might not been qualified to give testimony regarding the specific surgical technique involved in the eyebrow lift performed in the instant case, he was competent to testify whether [the defendant plastic surgeon] followed proper general surgical procedures.'') As part of ''medical malpractice reform'' discussed later in this Part, many states have enacted statutes extensively defining medical experts' qualifications, including whether they are now in active clinical practice or recently retired. Some of these statutes delegate discretion to the courts to waive particular requirements if the witness can demonstrate relevant knowledge; other statutes are more restrictive, including re-instating some aspects of the locality rule. *See, e.g.*, Justin H. Werner, *Double Checking the Doctor's Credentials: The New Medical Expert Qualification Statute of MCARE*, 67 U. PITT. L. REV. 661 (2006) (analyzing Pennsylvania's Medical Care Availability and Reduction of Error Act (''MCARE'') of 2002); *Harris*, 663 P.2d at 118 n.4 (statute establishes ''reasonably prudent practitioner'' standard but limits ''those who set the standard of care to health care providers within the state of Washington.'').

In the context of a defendant hospital, as in *WHC*, the concept of the appropriate comparison group may be analogous to a medical ''specialty,'' as in the case of a medically specialized hospital or unit within a hospital, such as a children's hospital or a specialized trauma unit. Most hospitals are not medically specialized in this way, and the comparison group is typically defined as it was in *WHC* by the broad categories of ''secondary'' or ''community'' hospital versus ''tertiary'' or ''teaching'' hospital. *WHC*'s attorneys apparently failed to dispute whether WHC was a teaching hospital, thereby sacrificing an opportunity to challenge Dr. Steen's qualifications (was he knowledgeable about the standard of care applicable to non-teaching hospitals, if WHC was a non-teaching hospital?) and/or the relevance of his testimony about the applicable standard of care.

The basis of expert testimony about the standard of care

Note the court's careful attention in *WHC* to the exact basis of Dr. Steen's testimony about the standard of care applicable to the defendant hospital. The court notes that Dr. Steen's ''own personal experience at USC [with carbon dioxide monitors] cannot itself provide an adequate foundation for an expert opinion on a national standard of care.'' This is because the fact (standing alone) that one particular hospital was using the monitors at the relevant time does not permit an inference that such monitors were ''the standard of care.'' Appropriate evidence of ''a standard of care'' has been summarized as follows:

> The personal opinion of the testifying expert as to what he or she would do in a particular case, without reference to a standard of care, is insufficient to prove the applicable standard of care. ''[I]t is insufficient for an expert's standard of care testimony to merely recite the words 'national standard of care.' '' The testifying expert must establish that a particular course of treatment is followed nationally either through ''reference to a published standard,'' ''[discussion] of the described course of treatment with practition-

ers outside the [locality] ... at seminars or conventions," or through presentation of relevant data. [Other sources of evidence of a standard include] [a] certification process, current literature, conference or discussion with other knowledgeable professionals.

Strickland v. Pinder, 899 A.2d 770, 773–74 (D.C. Ct. App. 2006). The emphasis in *Hall v. Hilbun* on the national standard of care as an "*objectively ascertained* minimally acceptable leve[l]," 466 So.2d at 871 (emphasis added), points to the same concern: to differentiate "the standard of care" from a particular expert's "subjective" or personal practices. *See* Estate of Northrop v. Hutto, 9 So.3d 381, 384–87 (Miss. 2009).

One the other hand, the law's long recognition of medical care as a variable craft or "art" rather than an "exact science," with inevitable differences in "medical judgment," has led courts to emphasize that the standard of care applicable to medical *practice* is grounded significantly in practice rather than solely in "theory" or even scientific knowledge. For example, a patient sued her family physician for damages caused by the allegedly negligent prescription of, and failure to monitor the effects of, the drug Thorazine. She offered as her expert witness a Ph.D. psychologist, Dr. Rucker, who, in the court's opinion,

> has admirable qualifications as a psychologist, with extensive training and experience in the areas of psychology and pharmacology, including a doctorate in biopsychology. Dr. Rucker has also done consultant work for drug companies and has engaged in research and laboratory studies on the psychopharmacologic aspects of drug dependence. He has read books and journals, attended lectures, and trained graduate students, and he may well have the requisite scientific knowledge to testify about the nature of Thorazine, its dangers and uses. What the witness lacks, however, is practical experience or knowledge of what physicians do. He himself has never prescribed Thorazine for a patient. It is one thing to study Thorazine in the laboratory and to discuss it in the classroom, but it is quite another thing to prescribe the drug for a patient under the circumstances of a family medical practice. Dr. Rucker does not know how physicians themselves customarily use Thorazine in treatment of their patients.

Lundgren v. Eustermann, 370 N.W.2d 877, 880–81 (Minn. 1985).

The Minnesota Supreme Court upheld the trial court's ruling that Dr. Rucker was not qualified to give an opinion on the standard of medical care involved. *But see* Thompson v. Carter, 518 So.2d 609, 615 (Miss. 1987), in which plaintiff's expert, with master's degrees in pharmacology and toxicology and serving as state-wide poison control coordinator, permitted to testify both as to causation and as to the medical standard of care in a case involving alleged physician negligence in prescribing and monitoring use of drug: "[The plaintiff's expert,] who taught medical students and advised and counseled physicians as to drug use and administration, through his skill, knowledge, training, and education, knew the standard of care to which physicians adhered when prescribing [the drug]. Therefore, this

Court holds that he was qualified to deliver expert testimony, notwithstanding his lack of a medical degree, on the issue of a physician's standard of care in the use and administration of this drug." *Id.*

The ambivalence of the law's conception of the "standard of care" is further reflected in doctrines that permit attorneys to cross examine adverse medical expert witnesses on whether their own personal practice varies from what they assert to be the standard of care, and some courts have allowed juries to weigh an expert's personal practice more heavily than the asserted and documented "standard." *See* Wallbank v. Rothenberg, 74 P.3d 413, 417 (Colo. App. 2003), in which the court found that "testimony regarding an expert's personal practices may either bolster or impeach the credibility of that expert's testimony concerning the standard of care," a point on which it elaborated (quoting C. Frederick Overby, *Trial Practice and Procedure*, 51 Mercer L. Rev. 487, 501–02 (1999)):

> The relevance and importance of a medical expert's personal choice of a course of treatment is highly probative of the credibility of the expert's opinion concerning the standard of care. A jury is free to disregard the expert's opinion entirely and find that the standard of care is reflected by the course of treatment the expert would have chosen, a highly probable scenario if other evidence admitted in the case supports this proposition.

The Role of Learned Treatises: pharmaceutical package inserts, the Physicians Desk Reference (PDR), and other publications regarding the standard of care

The common law's emphasis on the medical standard of care as based on practicing physicians' actual clinical or customary practices, and its suspicion of admitting out-of-court statements as evidence (the hearsay problem), led many jurisdictions to develop highly restrictive rules about the circumstances under which published standards or knowledge could be admitted as evidence in medical malpractice cases. *See, e.g.,* Jacober by Jacober v. St. Peter's Medical Center 608 A.2d 304 (N.J. 1992) (explicating, but refusing to follow, highly restrictive state law doctrines that allowed medical experts to deny the authoritativeness of learned medical treatises and thereby prevent their use in cross-examination). By contrast, Federal Rule of Evidence 803(18) established the following exception to the hearsay rule:

> (18) Learned treatises. To the extent called to the attention of an expert witness upon cross-examination or relied upon by the expert witness in direct examination, statements contained in published treatises, periodicals, or pamphlets on a subject of history, medicine, or other science or art, established as a reliable authority by the testimony or admission of the witness or by other expert testimony or by judicial notice. If admitted, the statements may be read into evidence but may not be received as exhibits.

The majority of the states have adopted similar rules of evidence. As explained by the New Jersey Supreme Court, "the federal rule allows texts to be established as reliable authority by experts other than the cross-examined expert, as well as by judicial notice. Secondly, expert witnesses may refer to statements from learned treatises on direct examination, to the extent that they relied on those statements in forming their own opinion. Finally, the contents of learned treatises may be introduced as substantive evidence on both direct and cross-examination." *Jacober*, 608 A.2d at 312.

As with so many aspects of the medical standard of care, there is much variation among (and even within) states regarding the admissibility of published sources of standards. Labels supplied by pharmaceutical manufacturers and inserted into drug packaging, which under regulation by the federal Food and Drug Administration (FDA) set forth proper dosages and warnings of complications and contraindications, and which are compiled in the Physicians Desk Reference (PDR), are generally admissible under the common law hearsay exception "for published compilations generally used and relied upon by the public or by persons in particular occupations" or its modern equivalent under federal and state evidence rules, as long as a live medical expert witness testifies that the label or PDR "is accepted by him as one source of information and by the medical profession in the [local] area as a standard of care in the administration of drugs." *Thompson v. Carter*, 518 So.2d 609, 612. The Mississippi Supreme Court described the relationship of the pharmaceutical package insert to the standard of care as follows:

> The package insert can be given weight as authoritative published compilation by a pharmaceutical manufacturer. It is some evidence of the standard of care, but it is not conclusive evidence. The prescribing physician can be permitted to rebut this implication and explain its [sic] deviation from the manufacturer's recommended use on dosage. The holding will shift the burden of persuasion to the physician to provide a sound reason for his deviating from the directions for its use, and will require corroborative evidence to determine whether the physician met or violated the appropriate standard.

Id. at 613.

Expert opinion and scientific reliability

As we have seen, testimony by medical experts has traditionally been based on the diffuse methods through which doctors have traditionally learned from each other what they consider the proper approach or "standard of care": personal clinical experience and knowledge of customary professional practice gathered through professional conferences, "grand rounds" (case discussion within hospitals), the professional literature, and numerous formal and informal communications. *See, e.g.*, Sandra Tanenbaum, *Knowing and Acting in Medical Practice: The Epistemological Politics of Outcomes Research*, 19 J. HEALTH POL. POL'Y & LAW 27 (1994), discussed in Rosoff, *Evidence–Based Medicine and the Law* at 346–47.

Medical malpractice law never required medical expert witnesses to "validate" these clinical norms (such as the plaintiff's expert testimony in *Hall v. Hilbun* that a surgeon must effectively monitor the vital signs of a post-operative patient) with formal scientific methods and evidence. But when litigants' experts (first in non-medical cases) began relying on purportedly scientific methods and theories—particularly "novel" ones—courts had to devise criteria for their admissibility. For many the years the governing doctrine, derived from Frye v. United States, 293 Fed. 1013 (D.C. Ct. App. 1923), was that "expert opinion based on a scientific technique is inadmissible unless the technique is 'generally accepted' as reliable in the relevant scientific community." Daubert v. Merrell Dow Pharmaceuticals, Inc., 509 U.S. 579 (1993) (holding that the *Frye* test had been superseded by Congressional enactment of the Federal Rules of Evidence, and setting forth a new doctrine). As discussed in Part Two in connection with the contested meaning of "medically necessary" and "experimental" limitations on health insurance coverage, in *Daubert*, 509 U.S. 579, the Supreme Court abandoned the exclusive reliance on "general acceptance" and adopted a more flexible or nuanced "gatekeeping" role for the trial judge. Summarizing its analysis of the components of Federal Rule of Evidence 702, the Supreme Court stated:

> Faced with a proffer of expert scientific testimony, then, the trial judge must determine at the outset, whether the expert is proposing to testify to (1) scientific knowledge that (2) will assist the trier of fact to understand or determine a fact in issue. This entails a preliminary assessment of whether the reasoning or methodology underlying the testimony is scientifically valid and of whether that reasoning or methodology properly can be applied to the facts in issue. Many factors will bear on the inquiry, and we do not presume to set out a definitive checklist or test. But some general observations are appropriate.

> Ordinarily, a key question to be answered in determining whether a theory or technique is scientific knowledge that will assist the trier of fact will be whether it can be (and has been) tested. Another pertinent consideration is whether the theory or technique has been subjected to peer review and publication. Publication (which is but one element of peer review) is not a sine qua non of admissibility. But submission to the scrutiny of the scientific community is a component of "good science." Additionally, in the case of a particular scientific technique, the court ordinarily should consider the known or potential rate of error, and the existence and maintenance of standards controlling the technique's operation.

> Finally, "general acceptance" can yet have a bearing on the inquiry. A "reliability assessment does not require, although it does permit, explicit identification of a relevant scientific community and an express determination of a particular degree of acceptance within that community." Widespread acceptance can be an

important factor in ruling particular evidence admissible, and "a known technique that has been able to attract only minimal support within the community," may properly be viewed with skepticism.

Daubert, 509 U.S. at 592–95.

The fascinating (and perhaps somewhat surprising) question for medical malpractice cases is the extent to which medical expert testimony is intended to be, and/or offered as, "expert *scientific* testimony." (emphasis supplied). To be sure, much testimony in medical malpractice cases is presented as "scientific," especially regarding causation, where the testimony asserts that "action or omission X caused result/damage Y." But what about testimony about the content of "the standard of care"? Two factors are of critical importance. First, if the "standard of care" is conceived, as it has traditionally been, as doctors' actual customary practices, then this is a descriptive inquiry rather than one based on scientific methodology. (For a discussion of the difficulties surrounding proposals to use scientific, statistical methods to ascertain doctors' actual customary practices, see Michelle Mello, *Using Statistical Evidence To Prove The Medical Malpractice Standard of Care: Bridging Legal, Clinical, and Statistical Thinking*, 37 WAKE FOREST L. REV. 821 (2002) (exploring the deep differences among law, clinical practice, and scientific research)). Second, the methods doctors themselves actually use to learn about their colleagues' actual practices, and that the law traditionally regarded as the basis of medical expertise, are largely unscientific in a rigorous sense. *See, e.g.* Palandjian v. Foster, 842 N.E.2d 916, 921–22 (Mass. 2006) ("factors relevant in assessing expert testimony on standard of care include expert's training, board certification, specialized medical experience, attendance at seminars and meetings, familiarity with medical literature, and discussions with other physicians."); *see also* articles by Professors Mark Hall and James Gibson, quoted in the notes following *Hall v. Hilbun*, above, that are sharply critical of the non-scientific basis of much medical practice.

To be sure, some medical knowledge is developed from studies using rigorously scientific methods and disseminated through peer-reviewed journals, and when an expert testifies about the standard of care on the basis of this kind of knowledge, a *Daubert* inquiry seems clearly applicable. But as the cases discussed above indicate, testimony about the standard of care often does not have this kind of scientific basis, and indeed, some courts have held that Ph.D. level scientists with undoubted scientific expertise in (for example) the proper usage and risks of pharmaceuticals, are not permitted to testify as *medical* experts because, in effect, the practice of medicine is not "science" in this sense, but rather a scientifically-informed "art" or "craft" in which clinical experience treating individual patients and immersion in medical culture is the necessary basis of "expertise." *See, e.g.*, *Lundgren*, 370 N.W.2d 877, 880–81, excerpted above. (There is sharp disagreement among judges on this issue.) *See also* Mello, *Bridging Legal, Clinical, and Statistical Thinking*; Tanenbaum, *Knowing and Acting in Medical Practice*; Rosoff, *Evidence–Based Medicine and the Law*.

In Palandjian, 842 N.E.2d at 922–23 (Mass. 2006), the Massachusetts Supreme Court made the following interesting effort to reconcile the tension between medical tradition and scientific method by defining medical tradition as a special kind of "science" that can be handled by a flexible use of *Daubert* (and its federal progeny) and its Massachusetts state-law analogues.

In *Daubert v. Merrell Dow Pharms., Inc.* the United States Supreme Court addressed the admissibility of scientific expert testimony under the Federal Rules of Evidence. The Court, emphasizing the need for a flexible inquiry, provided a nonexhaustive list of factors to consider in evaluating the reliability of the expert's testimony, including testing, peer review and publication, error rates, and general acceptance in the relevant scientific community. This court adopted the basic reasoning of *Daubert* in *Commonwealth v. Lanigan,* 419 Mass. 15, 641 N.E.2d 1342 (1994), although we suggested that general acceptance in the relevant scientific community likely would remain the most important factor in determining reliability.

In *Canavan's Case,* we extended the holding of *Lanigan* to apply to expert opinions based on personal observations and clinical experience, and concluded that medical expert testimony concerning diagnosis and causation should be subject to a *Lanigan* analysis. "Observation informed by experience is but one scientific technique that is no less susceptible to *Lanigan* analysis than other types of scientific methodology." We based this conclusion in part on the reasoning of the United States Supreme Court in *Kumho Tire Co. v. Carmichael,* 526 U.S. 137 (1999), in which the Court held that *Daubert*'s gatekeeping obligation applies to all expert testimony, whether based on scientific, technical, or other specialized knowledge. *Id.* at 149. In *Canavan's Case,* we again emphasized that the test of reliability is flexible, and that a trial judge has broad discretion in determining which factors to apply to assess the reliability of proffered expert testimony.

Relying on the reasoning of *Canavan's Case,* Foster argues that *Daubert–Lanigan* should apply to medical expert testimony concerning the standard of care, just as it applies to medical opinions relating to diagnosis and treatment, to ensure that the judge admits only reliable expert opinions.

The plaintiffs argue that the judge improperly used *Lanigan.* They maintain that the purpose of *Daubert–Lanigan* is to screen new or untested scientific evidence to prevent the admission of "junk science," and note that courts in at least two other jurisdictions have held that *Daubert* does not apply to testimony about the standard of care because it does not involve novel scientific evidence.

We agree with the plaintiffs that expert testimony concerning the standard of care generally need not be subject to a *Daubert–*

Lanigan analysis. Such testimony is based on the expert's knowledge of the care provided by other qualified physicians, not on scientific theory or research: "How physicians practice medicine is a fact, not an opinion derived from data or other scientific inquiry by employing a recognized methodology."[12] However, when the proponent of expert testimony incorporates scientific fact into a statement concerning the standard of care, that science may be the subject of a *Daubert–Lanigan* inquiry. Because expert opinion about increased risk, like diagnosis and causation, involves the application of science to patient care, *Daubert–Lanigan* would be applied to that portion of an expert's testimony, requiring the proponent of such evidence, if challenged, to demonstrate its relevance and reliability.

Palandjian, 842 N.E.2d at 922–23.

Of course, the *Palandjian* opinion asserts (and/or assumes) that "actual medical custom" is and should remain the legal standard of care for medical malpractice. That position is the subject of great debate and contest, particularly in contexts where various kinds of science suggest that actual medical custom causes more harm than benefit.

7. CLINICAL PRACTICE GUIDELINES AND THE STANDARD OF CARE

The practice of embedding practice guidelines into health benefit plan documents was identified in Part Two in cases such as *Mondry* and *Jones v. Kodak* as a highly effective means of narrowing and limiting otherwise-broad terms of coverage. For example, rather than specifying that speech therapy is a covered item or service when medically necessary, thereby requiring the plan administrator to make individualized, discretionary (and thus challengeable) determinations of medical necessity in specific cases, a plan might instead list the types of speech therapy treatments that will be covered and the conditions that will merit treatment, with treatment limits spelled out with precision. To be sure there still may be factual issues (e.g., whether a patient's condition falls into the scope of a guideline, whether the plan was correct in selecting among enumerated treatment guidelines given the facts of the case). At the same time, however, the use of treatment guidelines can eliminate the need for broadly conceived, fact-driven reviews of medical necessity; if a patient's condition does not meet the guideline definition for coverage, or if the treatment sought does not

---

12. Indeed, it is difficult to imagine how Daubert–Lanigan, with its emphasis on methodology, would apply to testimony concerning the standard of care. Because the standard of care is determined by the care that the average qualified physician would provide, it is "generally accepted" almost by definition. Moreover, the "methodology" employed by an expert testifying to the applicable standard of care will almost always be the same: the testimony will be based on the expert's experience and education. The focus, then, is not truly on the "methodology" underlying the expert's opinion, but on whether the expert's qualifications create a foundation adequate to support the expert's statement of the standard of care.

satisfy guideline requirements, the "default" is no coverage at all. This is what happened to the claimant in *Jones v. Kodak,* discussed in Part Two, who sought long-term treatment but whose condition and history of prior treatment meant that she did not qualify for additional coverage under the plan's guidelines, which in turn were read as elements of plan design and thus beyond legal challenge.

The contractual (and in the case of ERISA, trust) doctrines that underlie the question of coverage mean that whether guidelines make any sense at all is irrelevant from a legal perspective. No matter how irrational, the terms of a plan can limit extended residential treatment for severe mental illness to cases in which multiple less costly treatments had been attempted and failed, and courts will not challenge such limits on quality grounds unless the law giving rise to the plan itself proscribes arbitrary and unreasonable limits. Thus, in the absence of higher controlling law, a plan administrator could refuse to pay for perfectly appropriate medical care simply on the ground that the patient had not first tried multiple types of interventions even though experts might agree that those interventions are inappropriate care, given the severity of the patient's condition. (Recall in *Metropolitan Life Insurance Company v. Glenn* (Part Two), which presented a particularly egregious case of abuse of discretion tied to a conflict of interest, Metropolitan Insurance argued that the market was the best check on such bad conduct, since employers would not buy such defective plans. The Supreme Court gave this argument short shrift).

In the case of ERISA-sponsored plans, as we have seen in cases in Part Two such as *McGann v. H & H Music Company* and *Jones v. Kodak Medical Assistance Plan*, plan sponsors are not subject to any review at all of the medical reasonableness of their plan designs. As a legal matter, plan sponsors can create wholly inappropriate terms of coverage and modify them to their hearts' content without risking liability for arbitrariness, or even any liability at all. There are certain checks on such arbitrariness to be sure, such as the Mental Health Parity Act, but these checks are few and far between. By contrast, federal Medicaid law does place constraints on how state programs can design their coverage, because it specifies certain minimum benefit classes and requires that state agencies use reasonable limits in establishing the amount, duration, and scope of medical assistance. 42 U.S.C. § 1396a(a)(17). Federal regulations implementing this reasonableness standard also bar discrimination in coverage for required benefits on the basis of a patient's medical condition. This prohibition against condition-based treatment limits might conceivably limit the use of guidelines that bar medically beneficial treatments or require medically unjustifiable care (such as prior failure rules) for certain conditions. Similarly, Medicare's coverage standards, as we have seen in *Papciack,* Part Two, places reasonableness constraints on the level of coverage to which beneficiaries may be entitled in certain settings.

Ultimately however, with the possible exception of Medicaid's reasonableness standard, no law requires that the treatment guidelines relied on by insurers (whether to impose fixed limits on plan coverage or to aid decision-making) be proven clinically reasonable by any criteria of evidence, much less scientific evidence. But while insurers might be able to limit coverage by relying on guidelines of questionable quality, at least so far guidelines will not likewise serve as a shield for malpractice litigation against health professionals. As you will see in Wickline v. State of California, 239 Cal. Rptr. 810 (App. 1986), discussed later in this Part, it is no defense to a liability action that a physician was guided in his or her treatment decisions by plan administrators' questionable coverage determinations.

Where the quality of care itself is concerned, there has been and remains intense controversy over the desirability of purportedly "scientific," "evidence-based," or "objective" standards of care, as distinct from the traditional standard of doctors' actual practices. This controversy often appears in the legal and health policy literature, and many would predict that it will appear with increasing frequency in legislation and litigation focused on the use of "clinical practice guidelines."

A preliminary discussion of terminology is needed. "[E]vidence-based medicine (EBM) [is] defined as the conscientious, explicit, and judicious use of current best evidence in making decisions about the care of individual patients." Rosoff, *Evidence–Based Medicine and the Law* (citing DAVID SACKETT ET AL., EVIDENCE–BASED MEDICINE: HOW TO PRACTICE AND TEACH EBM (1997)).

A major way that EBM has impacted medical practice has been through the development, dissemination, and use of clinical practice guidelines (CPGs). The Institute of Medicine's widely cited 1990 report [MARILYN FIELD & KATHLEEN LOHR, CLINICAL PRACTICE GUIDELINES: DIRECTIONS FOR A NEW PROGRAM] defines CPGs as "systematically developed statements to assist practitioner and patient decisions about appropriate health care for specific clinical circumstances." CPGs can be used to guide practitioners in undertaking treatment of various kinds of conditions and to help third-party payers, regulatory bodies, and courts determine whether care given in a particular instance was adequate and appropriate. Thus CPGs have relevance both for the practice of medicine by physicians and for the regulation of that practice by others.

Because CPGs are the most common practical embodiment of EBM, the terms "clinical practice guidelines" and "evidence-based medicine" and their acronyms have often been used interchangeably, or nearly so. It should be understood, however, that they are distinct terms and can be used in contexts where they are not interchangeable. EBM can show up in forms other than CPGs—for example, in journal articles, unpublished studies, and expert testimony. Conversely, CPGs are not necessarily based upon EBM— although the vast majority of the CPGs being generated nowadays are, or at least purport to be. [G]uidelines generated primarily through a professional consensus process—the traditional approach—may differ from those based more directly on hard, empirical evidence—the EBM approach. This last point is especially important, because courts, in deciding what weight to accord to CPGs, may find it useful, even necessary, to distinguish between those that are based on EBM and those that are not.

Rosoff, *Evidence–Based Medicine and the Law* at 328–29.

Michelle Mello, Professor of Health Policy and Law in the Department of Health Policy and Management of the Harvard School of Public Health, and a leading opponent of the use of CPGs in medical liability litigation, describes their promise and problems.

Efforts to reduce costs in the medical malpractice system should be aimed at three targets: discouraging defensive medicine, lowering the costs of producing accurate outcomes, and decreasing the incidence of incorrect outcomes. In the last ten years, there has been increasing attention paid to the possibility of using clinical practice guidelines ("CPGs") to accomplish these goals.

At first blush, this proposal is attractive. The reformers point out that at present, the medical malpractice system is pervaded by uncertainty: uncertainty as to what constitutes the legal standard of care, uncertainty as to what evidence will be sufficient to prove a breach of that standard, and uncertainty as to the magnitude of the damages a jury will award if it is convinced by that evidence. This uncertainty is manifested in physicians' pursuit of defensive medicine. Unsure about exactly what is required of them, and averse to the risk of being sued, physicians protect themselves by ordering tests and other services that may be medically unnecessary but that will create a "paper trail" that they can later invoke in defense of the care rendered. If physicians knew ex ante that the standard of care to which they had a legal duty to conform was inscribed in black and white in a compendium of CPGs, it is argued, two benefits would be reaped. Physicians would operate under less uncertainty, and consequently would practice medicine less defensively. Additionally, physicians would have an incentive to comply with CPGs, which represent our best estimate of what constitutes good quality care.

[W]hile there may be certain efficiencies associated with the use of CPGs as the legal standard of care, their use is deeply problematic. While empirical evidence indicates that CPGs currently are being used both as exculpatory evidence (by physician defendants) and as inculpatory evidence (by plaintiffs), statutory reforms enacted to date provide for the one-way, "shield-only" use of CPGs. Indeed, there are good reasons to disallow their inculpatory use. Chief among these is that CPGs do not, in fact, appear to represent prevailing medical practice in most instances. But permitting physicians to use CPGs as an affirmative defense in malpractice litigation while denying plaintiffs the right to use this evidence to prove their own case would also be problematic. Restricting one party's access to relevant, probative, and otherwise admissible evidence on a key element of a legal claim is an anomaly in the law and requires strong justification. There is no such justification for restricting the use of CPGs. Thus, CPGs should either be available to all parties or to none. Because of the problems associated with the inculpatory use of CPGs, the best course of action is to restrict their use by both plaintiffs and defendants.

Michelle M. Mello, *Of Swords and Shields: The Role of Clinical Practice Guidelines in Medical Malpractice Litigation*, 149 U. PA. L. REV. 645, 647–49 (2001).

Professor Mello also argues that the multiplicity of CPGs, their frequent departure from established custom, their frequent generality and disclaimer of establishing a "rule," and controversy about their methodology and validity, will increase uncertainty among physicians about what is required, and therefore lead to more rather than less defensive medicine.

The most straightforward way for CPGs to be admitted into evidence in medical malpractice litigation would be though the "learned treatise" exception to the hearsay rule embodied in Federal Rule of Evidence (FRE) 803(18) and its state law analogues, and, where appropriate for novel scientific theories, through a *Daubert* inquiry (and its state law analogues). (A significant number of states have not adopted either the FRE approach to learned treatises or *Daubert*.). Attorneys seeking to introduce CPGs as substantive evidence (as distinguished from "the inadmissible basis of expert opinion" and "demonstrative evidence" discussed below) must formally offer them for admission, including "authentication" of their reliability through expert opinion or (rarely) judicial notice. (Recall Chief Justice Rehnquist's questioning of the reliability of even the CDC's universal precaution guidelines in *Bragdon v. Abbott* in Part One).

It is not enough, at least in many courts, for a witness to state that the publication is authoritative. An attorney must formally offer it as substantive evidence in order to give opposing counsel a fair opportunity to object and to alert the court that the evidence is not being used only for impeachment purposes, which was its traditional function.

> [F]or a learned treatise to be introduced as substantive evidence under Rule 803(18), the treatise must be offered into evidence like any other exhibit, including: 1) having the treatise marked by the reporter for identification; 2) authenticating the treatise by the testimony of a witness (in the case of a learned treatise, authentication means expert testimony that the treatise is reliably authoritative); 3) offering the treatise into evidence; 4) permitting adverse counsel to examine the treatise; 5) allowing adverse counsel to object to the treatise, if he or she so chooses; 6) submitting the treatise to the court for examination, if the court so desires; 7) the court's ruling on admission of the learned treatise; and 8) if the learned treatise is admitted into evidence, presenting it to the jury by reading it to the jury (the only option under the federal Rule), passing it among the jurors, or other means. In other words, the attorney seeking admission of a learned treatise as substantive

evidence must proceed through the formalities applicable to the admission of any document as evidence, paying particular attention to the authentication of the learned treatise as being reliably authoritative.

Bradley S. Abramson, *[Colorado Rule of Evidence] 803(18): The Learned Treatise Exception to the Hearsay Rule*, 38 COLO. LAW. 39, 40 (March 2009), citing Maggipinto v. Reichman, 481 F.Supp. 547 (E.D. Pa. 1979).

As we have seen with expert testimony about an emerging standard of care (see *Washington Hospital Center* above), it is not sufficient for an expert witness to state in a conclusory fashion that a guideline issued by a professional organization "is the standard of care," as revealed in the following case.

Diaz v. New York Downtown Hospital

784 N.E.2d 68 (N.Y. 2002)

MEMORANDUM:

Plaintiff was sexually assaulted by a male technician while undergoing a transvaginal sonogram at defendant New York Downtown Hospital. At the time of the incident, plaintiff and the technician were alone in the examination room. Plaintiff commenced this action against the hospital alleging that it negligently hired, trained, supervised and retained the sonography technician. The hospital moved for summary judgment dismissing the complaint, asserting that it had no prior knowledge of any propensity of the technician to commit such acts. In opposition to the motion, plaintiff submitted the affirmation of Dr. Jessica Fuchs Berkowitz, a board-certified radiologist. Dr. Berkowitz opined that the hospital deviated from the standard of care for performing transvaginal ultrasounds on female patients by not instituting a policy requiring the presence of a female staff member during such procedures. In support of her opinion, Dr. Berkowitz cited guidelines promulgated by two national radiological organizations (the American College of Radiology and the American Institute of Ultrasound in Medicine) which recommend that a woman be present as an examiner or chaperone for vaginal sonograms. Dr. Berkowitz asserted that one purpose of the recommended policy was to "ensure the personal safety of the female patient."

[The trial court] granted the hospital's motion and dismissed plaintiff's causes of action, except with respect to the negligent supervision claim, holding that the expert affirmation created a question of fact as to whether the hospital deviated from the applicable standard of care by failing to implement the recommended protocol. On the hospital's appeal, the Appellate Division reversed and dismissed plaintiff's complaint in its entirety as against the hospital. The majority of the Court concluded that the guidelines relied on by plaintiff's expert failed to establish an industry standard and that the physician proffered no evidence to support the existence of an actual practice or custom in the radiological community requiring the presence of a chaperone during vaginal ultrasounds. The dissent determined that the guidelines recommended by two national organizations, paired with the expert's assertion that the protocol constituted an industry standard, created an issue of fact with respect to the hospital's negligence. Upon a two-Justice dissent, plaintiff appeals as of right.

In other contexts, this Court has recognized that "[o]rdinarily, the opinion of a qualified expert that a plaintiff's injuries were caused by a deviation from relevant industry standards would preclude a grant of summary judgment in favor of the defendants." Where the expert's ultimate assertions are speculative or unsupported by any evidentiary foundation, however, the opinion should be given no probative force and is insufficient to withstand summary judgment.

Here, the Appellate Division correctly determined that plaintiff's expert affirmation, offered as the sole evidence to defeat the hospital's summary judgment motion, did not create a triable issue with respect to the existence of an accepted industry practice or standard. The guidelines of both professional organizations merely recommend the presence of female staff members for vaginal sonogram procedures; in fact, the materials from the American College of Radiology clearly state that its guidelines "are not rules."

Moreover, plaintiff's expert failed to provide any factual basis for her conclusion that the guidelines establish or are reflective of a generally-accepted standard or practice in hospital settings. Dr. Berkowitz made no reference either to her own personal knowledge acquired through professional experience or to evidence that any hospitals have implemented such a standard. Thus, the expert's affirmation lacked probative force and was insufficient as a matter of law to overcome the hospital's motion for summary judgment on plaintiff's negligent supervision claim.

* * *

The admissibility of CPGs is made more complex by the fact that attorneys and judges may use (or attempt to use) other evidentiary routes to get testimony about the CPG before the jury, particularly in states with more restrictive doctrines about learned treatises as substantive evidence. For example, Hinlicky v. Dreyfuss, 848 N.E.2d 1285 (N.Y. 2006), involved a 71-year-old patient who died 25 days after an apparently successful endarterectomy (surgery to remove plaque buildup in the carotid artery). The central question in the subsequent lawsuit was whether the defendant physicians were negligent in not obtaining a preoperative cardiac evaluation to insure that Mrs. Hinlicky's heart could tolerate the surgery. One of her non-defendant physicians testified he had followed a flow chart, or algorithm, in deciding to allow the surgery without the cardiac evaluation. An important question on appeal was whether the trial court properly exercised its discretion in admitting the algorithm into evidence. The trial court admitted the algorithm not as substantive evidence of the applicable standard of care, but rather as "demonstrative evidence" (similar to a model, map, or chart) introduced to help the jury understand the witness's testimony about his actual decision-making process. Despite the obvious difference between a model or map, that the jury could not confuse with direct evidence, and an algorithm or guideline that a doctor actually used in making decisions about the patient, the New York Court of Appeals declined to reverse the trial court because the plaintiff had not asked for a limiting instruction, and further declined to address when a CPG might be admitted under the "professional reliability" exception to the hearsay rule, "which enables an expert witness to provide opinion evidence based on otherwise inadmissible hearsay, provided it is demonstrated to be the type of material commonly relied on in the profession."

---

8. CHALLENGING PROFESSIONAL AND INDUSTRY STANDARDS: THE "EQUALLY WELL–INFORMED EXPERT" AND "AVAILABLE AND PROVEN SCIENTIFIC SAFEGUARDS" DOCTRINES

United Blood Services v. Quintana

827 P.2d 509 (Colo. 1992)

■ QUINN [JUSTICE]:

[A patient who contracted AIDS from a May 1983 blood transfusion sued the blood bank [UBS], which had received the blood from a donor in April 1983. The focus of the appeal from a jury verdict in favor of the blood bank was on the trial court's ruling that Colorado's blood bank liability statute "impos[ed] a professional standard of care on a blood bank in acquiring, preparing, and transferring human blood or its components for transfusion into a human being and that the trial court, in its evidentiary rulings and jury instructions, also erred by applying the professional standard of care in a manner that rendered UBS's compliance with the professional standard the equivalent of conclusive proof of reasonable care. In place of the professional standard of care applied by the trial court, the [intermediate] court of appeals reasoned that UBS's conduct 'should be measured against what a reasonable and prudent blood bank would or should have done under the same or similar circumstances' and that, under that standard of ordinary care, compliance with governmental regulations and industrial customs and practices would merely constitute evidence of reasonable care and would not be conclusive proof on that issue."

The trial court had granted the defendant's motion to block testimony by plaintiff's witnesses (who did not work in the blood bank industry, but who were said to be as knowledgeable about the relevant issues as the witnesses offered by the industry) regarding the standard of care, which would have shown that by the date of the injury in question, blood banks were well aware of the dangers posed by the HIV virus, were equally aware of screening procedures and governmental guidelines, and were also aware of additional steps to screen blood donors that should have been taken as a result of ongoing discussions within the industry itself. In remanding the case for a new trial, the Colorado Supreme Court determined that under the Colorado blood bank statute, the applicable standard of care was a "professional standard," and that the jury was entitled to evaluate existing industry custom in the light of evidence "that the blood banking community had adopted unreasonably deficient practices and procedures in place of substantially more protective and readily available safeguards."]

[I]n ordinary negligence cases, an actor is required to conform his or her conduct to a standard of objective behavior measured by what a reasonable person of ordinary prudence would or would not do under the same or similar circumstances. For those practicing a profession involving specialized knowledge or skill, reasonable care requires the actor to possess "a standard minimum of special knowledge and ability," and to exercise reasonable care in a manner consistent with the knowledge and ability possessed by members of the profession in good standing.

While a defendant practicing a profession is entitled to be judged by the standard of care applicable to the professional school to which the defendant belongs, that standard is not always conclusive proof of due care. Judge Learned Hand, in addressing this problem of insulating a particular calling's standard of care from any challenge whatever, put the matter this way:

> There are, no doubt, cases where courts seem to make the general practice of the calling the standard of proper diligence; we have indeed given some currency to the notion ourselves.... Indeed in most cases reasonable prudence is in fact common prudence; but strictly it is never its measure; a whole calling may have unduly lagged in the adoption of new and available devices. It never may set its own tests, however persuasive be its usages. Courts must in the end say what is required; there are precautions so imperative that even their universal disregard will not excuse their omission.

The T.J. Hooper. If the standard adopted by a practicing profession were to be deemed conclusive proof of due care, the profession itself would be permitted to set the measure of its own legal liability, even though that measure might be far below a level of care readily attainable through the adoption of practices and procedures substantially more effective in protecting others against harm than the self-decreed standard of the profession.

To be sure, there is a presumption that adherence to the applicable standard of care adopted by a profession constitutes due care for those practicing that profession. The presumption, however, is a rebuttable one, and the burden is on the one challenging the standard of care to rebut the presumption by competent evidence. In a professional negligence case, therefore, a plaintiff should be permitted to present expert opinion testimony that the standard of care adopted by the school of practice to which the defendant adheres is unreasonably deficient by not incorporating readily available practices and procedures substantially more protective against the harm caused to the plaintiff than the standard of care adopted by the defendant's school of practice. A plaintiff may establish that proposition by the opinion testimony of a qualified expert practicing in the same school or by the opinion testimony of an expert practicing in another school if the expert is sufficiently familiar with the standard of care applicable to the school in question as to render the witness's testimony as well-informed on the applicable standard of care as would be the opinion of an expert witness practicing the same profession as the defendant, or if the standard of care at issue is substantially identical to both schools of practice.

If the plaintiff offers competent and credible evidence [of unreasonable deficiency of the professional standard] the issue of whether the standard of care adopted by the defendant's school constitutes due care is a question for the jury to resolve under appropriate instructions. If the jury is convinced by a preponderance of the evidence that the standard of care adopted by the defendant's school of practice is unreasonably deficient, it must resolve the issue of the defendant's negligence on the basis of all the evidence concerning the practices and procedures available to the defendant's profession under the circumstances existing at the time of the events in question. If, on the other hand, the jury is not convinced by a preponderance of the evidence that the standard of care adopted by the defendant's school is unreasonably deficient, the jury must accept the standard of the defendant's school of practice as conclusive evidence of reasonable care and must determine the issue of negligence on the basis of the defendant's compliance or noncompliance with that standard.

[The Colorado Supreme Court concluded that, consistent with the conclusion reached in other jurisdictions, and the national regulatory characteristics of the blood banking industry, Colorado's blood bank statute imposed a professional standard of care rather than a general negligence standard of ordinary reasonable care. Blood banks were subject to guidelines of both the Centers for Disease Control and Prevention and the Food and Drug Administration. Furthermore the Colorado statute specified that the banking of blood for transfusion purposes involved "scientific knowledge, skills, and materials" and that the banking of blood was part of the provision of health care requiring "the use of available and proven scientific safeguards" and the "exercise of sound medical judgment." As such, the statute limited liability to "instances of negligence and willful misconduct." § 13–22–104, 6A C.R.S. (1987)]

At the time of the events underlying the instant litigation, scientific information on the etiology and epidemiology of AIDS was in the developmental stages. There did not exist at that time what might be characterized as "state of the art" screening and testing procedures, but articles published in 1982 by the Centers for Disease Control clearly suggested that AIDS well might be transmitted through blood and blood products. Source plasma centers [related to, but different than the whole blood industry], acting on the above information, began to implement aggressive screening procedures by asking donors if they were homosexual, intravenous drug users, recent arrivals from Haiti, or hemophiliacs, and also began to employ surrogate testing of donated blood.

It is also noteworthy that in March 1983, the Food and Drug Administration issued recommendations calculated to decrease the risk of transmitting AIDS through donated blood and source plasma. [Details of March 1983 FDA recommendations omitted. These recommendations, and the fact that they did not incorporate the more extensive precautions undertaken by the source plasma centers (see preceding paragraph) had been the subject of intense controversy in meetings among the regulators, scientists, and blood bank industry.].

In the instant case, UBS's compliance with the Food and Drug Administration's recommendations and with the guidelines developed by the national blood banking community was some evidence of due care, but was not conclusive proof that additional precautions were not required. The record shows that the three expert witnesses from whom the Quintanas unsuccessfully sought to elicit opinion evidence were sufficiently familiar with the standard of care applicable to the national blood banking community as to render their opinions on the need for additional precautions as well-informed as the opinion of an expert engaged in procuring and processing human blood for use in medical treatment. The Quintanas' expert opinion evidence was calculated to show that the national blood banking community's screening and testing procedures on which UBS relied were unreasonably deficient in guarding against the transmission of the AIDS virus through blood and blood components and that those procedures, in that respect, were not in accordance with the then "available and proven safeguards" designed to be substantially more protective against the risk of transmitting AIDS through contaminated blood. Indeed, given the growing suspicion in the early months of 1983 that the AIDS virus might be transmitted through blood or blood components, and in light of the extreme caution recommended by the Food and Drug Administration and other groups within the blood banking community in dealing with donated blood, as well as the implementation by some blood and plasma centers of substantially stricter screening and testing procedures than those used by the national blood banking community, the significance of the excluded evidence to a fair and informed resolution of this case is compelling.

The trial court's ruling prohibiting the Quintanas from offering expert opinion evidence on the unreasonably deficient character of the blood banking community's screening and testing procedures was tantamount to permitting the blood banking community to establish its own standard of legal liability despite the existence of expert opinion evidence tending to show unreasonabl[e] deficien[cy].

If the Quintanas had been permitted to present their expert opinion evidence, the jury then would have been required to consider whether the blood banking community's standard of care was indeed adequate. If the jury had determined that the national blood banking community's standard was itself unreasonably deficient, it would have been required to resolve the issue of UBS's negligence on the basis of all the evidence bearing on UBS's conduct in procuring and processing the blood donation in question, including the data generated by the Centers for Disease Control, the Food and Drug Administration's recommendations for whole blood centers and source plasma centers, the data and recommendations generated by various groups within the national blood banking community, and the practices employed by particular entities in attempting to minimize the risk of transmitting AIDS through blood and plasma transfusion.

Note

Blood transfusions and the standard of care. By June 1995, 7,128 people diagnosed with AIDS (two percent of the total cases) had acquired it through transfusion of contaminated blood and blood products. Additionally, at least 6,000 to 8,000 persons with hemophilia became infected with HIV through use of contaminated factor concentrate products. *4 Drug Companies Ordered to Pay Hemophiliacs*, N.Y. TIMES, May 8, 1997, at D12. (For a higher estimate of about 12,000 infected people with homophilia, see Linda M. Dorney, *Comment: Culpable Conduct with Impunity: The Blood Industry and the FDA's Responsibility for the Spread of AIDS Through Blood Products*, 3 J. PHARMACY & LAW 129, 130 (1994)). In 1994, there were between three and five hundred pending lawsuits, but very few had resulted in awards for the plaintiffs. Joseph Kelly, *The Liability of Blood Banks and Manufacturers of Clotting Products to Recipients of HIV–Infected Blood: A Comparison of the Law and Reaction in the United States, Canada, Great Britain, and Australia*, 27 J. MARSHALL L. REV. 465 (1994).

Osborn v. Irwin Mem. Blood Bank, 7 Cal. Rptr.2d 101 (Ct. App. 1992), squarely disagreed with the reasoning in *Quintana*. The patient contracted HIV from a transfusion in February 1983. Relying on a version of the "accepted practice," *Osborn* held that

> professional prudence is defined by actual or accepted practice within a profession, rather than theories about what "should" have been done. It follows that Irwin cannot be found negligent for failing to perform tests that no other blood bank in the nation was using.

Id. at 128. The *Osborn* opinion noted that *Quintana* had held to the contrary that prevailing practice with respect to surrogate testing for AIDS may have been deficient, but the *Osborn* court did not attempt to engage in a dialogue with *Quintana* or any other differing opinion.

However, in Advincula v. United Blood Services, 678 N.E.2d 1009 (Ill. 1996), involving the same defendant as in *Quintana* and blood collected in February 1984, ten months after the blood collection in *Quintana*, the Illinois Supreme Court essentially agreed with the reasoning of the Colorado Supreme Court in *Quintana*, although it reversed the judgment for the patient's estate and remanded for a new trial under the proper standard of care. Interpreting the relevant Illinois statute to mean that the blood bank's actions should be evaluated by a "professional standard of care," the meandering majority opinion also held that under the statute "the [blood] bank is bound to exercise care which is due." *Id.* at 1021.

Quintana, *Osborn*, and *Advincula* dramatically illustrate the interplay of the three models of health law discussed throughout this book. The once-dominant professional authority perspective, reflected in statutes about blood bank liability and still considered authoritative in *Osborn*, holds that a defendant's compliance with professional customary or accepted practice is a complete defense. Note that the professional authority model does not easily fit the donor screening policies of blood banks, because these policies are not developed by physicians in the context of doctor-patient relationships (or perhaps not even by physicians at all), but rather are managerial cost-benefit decisions made with great concern for the costs of the precautions. In this instance, what is called "the professional standard of care" may be more realistically considered as the market competition model, insulating managerial cost-benefit decisions from the general standard of care championed by *The T.J. Hooper* and its progeny.

The courts in *Quintana* and *Advincula*, while considering themselves bound by statute to apply a professional standard, interpret the concept of a "professional standard" in a more socially protective way. Aware that a profession can be split on the proper cost-benefit analysis regarding precautions, and that the dominant view can be influenced by the self-interest of the profession's members and/or of institutions such as hospitals and blood banks, these courts are willing to open a modest door to expanding or re-conceiving the professional standard: where, as *Quintana* puts it, the plaintiffs can put on testimony by an expert "as well-informed as" someone engaged in the industry, to the effect that the dominant view is "unreasonably deficient in not incorporating available safeguards," then the jury can, on the basis of that expert's testimony, decide the case on the basis of what is in effect a revised, more risk-averse professional standard. This test functions as a detector of excessive professional or industry self-interest because it asks, if there was an "available safeguard" that could have prevented much harm at relatively little cost (to be sure, a debatable matter), then why wasn't it adopted? The likelihood of some "illegitimate" factor (professional or institutional self-interest) is relatively high, and the need for insisting on appropriate weighing of patients' interests through a modestly egalitarian social contract between providers on the one hand and patients on the other is apparent.

9.   SHOULD THE PROFESSIONAL STANDARD OF CARE BE ADJUSTED TO ACCOUNT FOR PATIENTS' ECONOMIC CIRCUMSTANCES?

Murray v. UNMC Physicians

806 N.W.2d 118 (Neb. 2011)

■ GERRARD, J.:

This case involves a failure to provide medical treatment. The treatment at issue is a very expensive drug that must be administered indefinitely. But it also may cause serious and even deadly symptoms if its administration is interrupted. In this case, the patient's treating physicians, wary of those health risks, decided not to administer the drug until the patient's insurer approved it or another source of payment could be found. But, regrettably, the patient died before either happened. The question presented in this appeal is whether under such circumstances, an expert medical witness is permitted to opine that under the customary standard of care, a physician should consider the health risks to a patient who may be unable to pay for continued treatment. We conclude that such testimony is admissible and, therefore, reverse the district court's order granting a new trial.

BACKGROUND

This is a medical malpractice case in which Robert Murray, individually and as special administrator of the estate of his wife, Mary K. Murray, alleges that the defendants caused the death of Mary by negligently failing to administer Flolan therapy to treat her pulmonary arterial hypertension. The defendants were the Nebraska Medical Center, the Board of Regents of the University of Nebraska, UNMC Physicians (UNMC), and several associated individual employees, although UNMC was the only defendant remaining by the time of trial.

Pulmonary arterial hypertension is a chronic medical condition in which the blood vessels in the lungs constrict, and the resulting pressure on the heart leads to heart failure. Flolan is a vasodilator that relaxes blood vessels and prevents blood clotting. It is administered by a pump, connected to a port and catheter usually inserted above the collarbone. Flolan is very expensive and short acting, so patients on Flolan treatment need a constant supply of the drug, because if its administration stops, pulmonary blood pressure rebounds and can be life threatening. And because Flolan is a chronic treatment, patients who begin Flolan need to remain on it, essentially, for the rest of their lives—it must be administered 24 hours a day and costs approximately $100,000 a year. The parties do not seem to disagree that generally, Flolan therapy is the appropriate course of treatment for chronic pulmonary arterial hypertension. Nor do the parties seem to dispute that there are significant and potentially deadly risks associated with interrupting Flolan treatment.[1]

The course of treatment relevant to this case began in late June 2006, as Mary's treating physician, Austin Thompson, M.D., was preparing to treat Mary's pulmonary arterial hypertension with Flolan. On June 29, Mary underwent a heart catheterization to confirm her diagnosis and eligibility for Flolan; in fact, Thompson had already written the Flolan order before the catheterization, pending the results of the catheterization and insurance approval.

On July 4, 2006, Mary reported to the medical center with swollen legs and fluid around her heart. She was given diuretics and hospitalized until July 8. She was discharged and was supposed to begin Flolan after port

---

1. See Physicians' Desk Reference 1181–82 (54th ed. 2000).

placement the following week. But on July 10, she reported to the emergency room with a rapid heartbeat and shortness of breath. She began to seize, then her heartbeat stopped, and medical efforts failed to resuscitate her.

At trial, the parties disputed both the cause of Mary's death and whether UNMC had breached the standard of care. Robert presented expert medical testimony that the proximate cause of Mary's death was pulmonary arterial hypertension. UNMC, on the other hand, presented expert medical testimony that myocarditis, an inflammation of the heart usually caused by viral or bacterial infection, was a contributing factor to Mary's death—a conclusion with which Robert's experts disagreed. And Robert presented expert medical testimony that immediate Flolan administration, even a day or two before Mary's death, would have prevented her death; UNMC, on the other hand, presented expert medical testimony that Flolan would have made no difference.

Specifically, Robert's experts testified that Mary's pulmonary arterial hypertension was acute by June 29, 2006, based on the results of her heart catheterization, and that Flolan can be administered as an emergent treatment for acute pulmonary arterial hypertension. Robert adduced expert medical testimony that UNMC's treatment of Mary fell below the relevant standard of care after June 29, because the medical center should have paid for and provided Flolan by July 4 or 5—in other words, that the standard of care for a patient as sick as Mary was to start Flolan and obtain insurance approval afterward.

UNMC's witnesses, on the other hand, testified that Flolan was not effective as an emergent treatment, because it did not work immediately. And they testified that their practice was to wait for insurance approval before beginning Flolan, because most patients are not able to pay for the drug without insurance and it can be more dangerous if treatment is started and then stopped. The UNMC attending physician during Mary's July 2006 hospitalization, James Murphy, M.D., explained that because Flolan treatment can last for years and require hundreds of thousands of dollars, it was important to make sure the treatment was sustainable before commencing. And another of UNMC's experts, William Johnson, M.D., explained that the standard of care required finding some source of payment for a patient, but that if insurance was unavailable, it was still usually possible to find some other payment on a "compassionate need basis" within the 12–week timeframe that Johnson opined was appropriate for treatment of chronic pulmonary arterial hypertension.

Robert moved for a directed verdict on the standard of care, arguing that as a matter of law, insurance coverage cannot dictate what doctors do. UNMC replied that according to its experts, a continuing source for treatment is something that doctors should consider in determining how treatment is to be administered. Robert's motion was overruled. Robert also asked that the jury be instructed that if the standard of care requires prescription of a drug, it is not a defense to a claim the standard of care has been violated that the drug would not be provided until approved by an insurance carrier. That instruction was refused.

The jury returned a general verdict for UNMC. But Robert filed a motion for new trial that the district court granted. The court explained:

> The evidence offered by [Robert's] expert on the issue of standard of care indicated that after the confirmation of [pulmonary arterial hypertension] by a right heart catheterization, the standard of care required the commencement of FLOLAN therapy. The evidence offered by [UNMC's] expert was basically the same with one major difference. [UNMC's] expert opined that the standard of care required the commencement of FLOLAN therapy after payment approval by the patient's insurance carrier. On cross-examination, [UNMC's] expert conceded that if no outside funds were available to subsidize the treatment to a patient who needed it, then treatment would be provided on a "humanitarian" basis. The substance of this concession was that the treatment was required by the standard of care regardless of how it was to be paid for. This Court is of the opinion that, as a matter of law, a medical standard of care cannot be tied to or controlled by an insurance company or the need for payment. This Court cannot determine the basis upon which the jury found in favor of [UNMC]. It could have been on the standard of care issue and it could have been on the causation issue. This Court erred in not directing the jury that the standard of care had not been met by [UNMC]. This error taints the entire verdict of the jury and requires a new trial.

UNMC appeals from the order granting Robert's motion for new trial. But the discretion of a trial court in ruling on a motion for new trial is only the power to apply the statutes and legal principles to all facts of the case; a new trial may be granted only where legal cause exists.

ANALYSIS

It is important, from the outset, to carefully note what issues this appeal does *not* present. This appeal arises against a backdrop of increasing concern about the costs of health care, among health care providers, insurers, government officials, and consumers. That concern has prompted a great deal of discussion, among commentators and in the public arena, about what should be done to control health care costs or to allocate potentially limited resources. As we will explain below, the question presented in this appeal is narrow and does not require us to address the more sweeping issues that are the subject of greater public policy debate. But some discussion of the broader picture will help us clarify what this case is about—or, more precisely, what it is not about.

In Nebraska, in cases arising (like this one) under the Nebraska Hospital–Medical Liability Act, the standard of reasonable and ordinary care is defined as "that which health care providers, in the same community or in similar communities and engaged in the same or similar lines of work, would ordinarily exercise and devote to the benefit of their patients under like circumstances."[6] That standard is consistent with the general common-law rule and is a so-called unitary, or wealthblind, standard of care.[7] In other words, the standard of care is found in the customary practices prevailing among reasonable and prudent physicians and must not be compromised simply because the patient cannot afford to pay.[8] That standard of care, however, developed in a world of fee-for-service medicine and persisted while health insurance still primarily provided first-dollar unlimited coverage.[9] Today,

> [h]ealth plans and self-insured corporations are placing increasing-ly stringent controls on health care resources, thereby limiting physicians' freedom to practice medicine as they see fit. Clinical guidelines have proliferated from a wide variety of sources: man-aged care organizations, medical subspecialty societies, malpractice insurers, entrepreneurial guideline-writing firms, and others. Each guideline purports to tell physicians the best way to practice. Yet often they conflict with each other, with traditional practice pat-terns, and with patients' expectations.[10]

But "[b]ecause tort law expects physicians to provide the same stan-dard of care regardless of patients' ability to pay, and because this standard sometimes encompasses costly technologies no longer readily available for the poorest citizens," physicians are "caught in a bind between legal expectations and economic realities."[11] Courts have been accused of being "oblivious to the costs of care, essentially requiring physicians to comman-deer resources that may belong to other parties, regardless of whether those other parties owe the patient these resources."[12]

It has been suggested that at a fundamental level, a unitary, wealth-blind standard of care cannot be reconciled with the growth of technology and the stratification of available health care. Custom is increasingly difficult to identify in today's medical marketplace, as resource distinctions produce fragmentation and disintegration.[13] It has also been suggested that maintaining a unitary standard of care disadvantages those who may not be able to pay for health care. Physicians remain free, for the most part, to decline to treat those who cannot pay, and "an outright refusal to treat an

---

6. See Neb. Rev. Stat. §§ 44–2810.

7. See E. Haavi Morreim, Cost Containment and the Standard of Medical Cure, 75 Cal. L. Rev. 1719 (1987).

8. See id. See, also, John A. Siliciano, Wealth, Equity, and the Unitary Medical Malprac-tice Standard, 77 Va. L. Rev. 439 (1991).

9. See E. Haavi Morreim, Stratified Scarcity: Redefining the Standard of Care, 17 L. Med. & Health Care 356 (1989).

10. E. Haavi Morreim, Medicine Meets Resource Limits: Restructuring the Legal Stan-dard of Care, 59 U. Pitt. L. Rev. 1, 5 (1997).

11. Id. at 4–5.

12. Id. at 4.

13. See James A. Henderson, Jr. & John A. Siliciano, Universal Health Care and the Continued Reliance on Custom in Determining Medical Malpractice, 79 Cornell L. Rev. 1382 (1994).

indigent patient, in contrast to a decision to treat in a manner inconsistent with the unitary malpractice standard, rarely creates the threat of liability."[14] So, it has been argued that rather than assume the burden of paying for a patient's treatment, or the potential liability of providing some but not all possible care, the unitary standard makes it more likely that "providers will now sidestep the entire problem simply by refusing to accept some, or all, of such patients for treatment."[15]

On the other hand, it has been argued that permitting physicians to make medical decisions based on resource scarcity would compromise the fiduciary relationship between patient and physician, creating a conflict of interest because the patient's well-being would no longer be the physician's focus.[16] The question is how the value judgments inherent in the development of the standard of care might evolve in response to a societal interest in controlling health care costs.[17] It has been explained that a physician's initial value judgment, in treating a patient,

> is made in light of conclusions reached about the likely benefits that services would have had for the plaintiff patient. It involves an evaluation as to whether the services should have been provided given their likely benefits, the risk of iatrogenic harm, and the gravity of the problem experienced by the patient. Normally the value judgment does not involve an explicit consideration of the costs of caring for a patient, although economics are implicitly considered. Physicians do not do everything conceivably possible in caring for a patient—they draw what they consider to be reasonable boundary lines. For example, physicians do not order every diagnostic test available for a patient that requests a physical examination, even though doing so might reveal interesting information. Instead, they order tests which are indicated given the age and physical characteristics of the patient.[18]

A physician's initial value judgment, in other words, is constrained by reason but does not include a societal interest in conserving costs or resources, and certainly does not include weighing the physician's own economic interests.

In short, the traditional ethical norms of the medical profession and the legal demands of the customary standard of care impose significant restrictions on a physician's ability to consider the costs of treatment, despite significant and increasing pressure to contain those costs. Whether the legal standard of care should change to alleviate that conflict, and how

---

14. Siliciano, supra note 8 at 457.

15. Id.

16. See, Maxwell J. Mehlman, The Patient–Physician Relationship in an Era of Scarce Resources: Is There a Duty to Treat?, 25 Conn. L. Rev. 349 (1993); Edward B. Hirshfeld, Should Ethical and Legal Standards for Physicians Be Changed to Accommodate New Models for Rationing Health Care?, 140 U. Pa. L. Rev. 1809 (1992).

17. Hirshfeld, supra note 16.

18. Id. at 1835.

it might change, has been the subject of considerable discussion. It has been suggested that the customary standard of care could evolve to permit the denial of marginally beneficial treatment—in other words, when high costs would not be justified by minor expected benefits.[20] Others have suggested that the standard of care should evolve to consider two separate components: (1) a skill component, addressing the skill with which diagnoses are made and treatment is rendered, that would not vary by a patient's financial circumstances and (2) a resource component, addressing deliberate decisions about how much treatment to give a patient, that would vary so as to not demand more of physicians than is reasonable.[21] It has been suggested that physicians should be permitted to rebut the presumption of a unitary standard of care when diminution of care arises by economic necessity instead of negligence.[22] And many have suggested that custom should no longer be the benchmark for the standard of care;[23] instead, practice standards or guidelines could be promulgated that would settle issues of resource allocation.[24]

All of the concerns discussed above are serious, and they present difficult questions that courts will be required to confront in the future. But we do not confront them here, because under the unique facts of this case, they are not presented. Contrary to the district court's belief, this is not a case in which insurance company "bean counters" overrode the medical judgment of a patient's physicians[25] or in which those physicians allowed their medical judgment to be subordinated to a patient's ability to pay for treatment.[26] Nor is this a case in which the parties disputed the cost-effectiveness of the treatment at issue.[27] Rather, UNMC's evidence was that its decision to wait to begin Flolan treatment was not economic—it was a medical decision, based on the health consequences to the patient if the treatment is interrupted.

Whether a medical standard of care can appropriately be premised on such a consideration is a matter of first impression in Nebraska, and the parties have not directed us to (nor are we aware of) any other authority speaking directly to that issue. But as a general matter, we have said that while the identification of the applicable standard of care is a question of

---

20. See Mark A. Hall, Rationing Health Care at the Bedside, 69 N.Y.U. L. Rev. 693 (1994).

21. See, Mark A. Hall, Paying for What You Get and Getting What You Pay For: Legal Responses to Consumer–Driven Health Care, 69 Law & Contemp. Probs. 159 (2006); Morreim, supra note 10; Morreim, supra note 9.

22. Morreim, supra note 9.

23. See Morreim, supra note 10.

24. See, Daniel W. Shuman, The Standard of Care in Medical Malpractice Claims, Clinical Practice Guidelines, and Managed Care: Towards a Therapeutic Harmony?, 34 Cal. W. L. Rev. 99 (1997); Hirshfeld, supra note 16; Peter H. Schuck, Malpractice Liability and the Rationing of Care, 59 Tex. L. Rev. 1421 (1981). But see Siliciano, supra note 8.

25. Compare Long v. Great West Life & Annuity Ins., 957 P.2d 823 (Wyo. 1998).

26. Compare Wickline v. State, 239 Cal. Rptr. 810 (1986).

27. Compare Helling v. Carey, 519 P.2d 981 (1974).

law, the ultimate determination of whether a party deviated from the standard of care and was therefore negligent is a question of fact. And it is for the finder of fact to resolve that issue by determining what conduct the standard of care would require under the particular circumstances presented by the evidence and whether the conduct of the alleged tort-feasor conformed with that standard.

Malpractice, as alluded to above, is defined as a health care provider's failure to use the ordinary and reasonable care, skill, and knowledge ordinarily possessed and used under like circumstances by members of his or her profession engaged in a similar practice in his or her or in similar localities. The district court granted a new trial based on its conclusion that UNMC's expert testimony was inconsistent with the standard of care. So the question is whether, as a matter of law, UNMC's expert opinion testimony was inconsistent with the standard of care as defined above.

The district court determined that it was. But the district court's reasoning was erroneous in three respects. First, the district court understood Johnson's testimony to concede that "if no outside funds were available to subsidize the treatment to a patient who needed it, then treatment would be provided on a 'humanitarian' basis." The "substance of this concession," the court reasoned, "was that the treatment was required by the standard of care regardless of how it was to be paid for."

But that is not exactly what Johnson said. The import of Johnson's testimony, as revealed by the record, was that if a patient was unable to obtain insurance coverage for Flolan, it was Johnson's practice to try to work with the patient to find another way for the patient to get the drug on a "compassionate need" basis. Johnson's testimony in that regard was about his practice, not the general standard of care. Nor did Johnson testify that the drug would be started regardless—he simply said that if insurance was unavailable, he would try to find another way for the patient to obtain the medication. Nothing in Johnson's testimony is contrary to his basic opinion that the standard of care requires a doctor to make sure that a payment source is in place before beginning Flolan treatment, because of the risks associated with interruption of treatment.

Second, the customary standard of care in this case is defined by statute, and it is not a court's place to contradict the Legislature on a matter of public policy. UNMC's witnesses testified that UNMC's treatment of Mary was consistent with the statutory standard of care—in other words, that health care providers in the same community or in similar communities and engaged in the same or similar lines of work would ordinarily defer Flolan treatment until payment for a continuous supply had been secured. We cannot depart from the customary standard of care on policy grounds, even if it is subject to criticism, because the standard of care is defined by statute and public policy is declared by the Legislature. Robert was, of course, free to argue and present evidence that UNMC's experts were wrong when they opined about customary practice. But that was a jury question.

Finally, and more fundamentally, the district court's concerns about health care policy, while understandable, are misplaced in a situation in which the patient's ability to continue to pay for treatment is still a *medical* consideration. In other words, even when the standard of care is limited to medical considerations relevant to the welfare of the patient, and not economic considerations relevant to the welfare of the health care provider,[33] the standard of care articulated by UNMC's witnesses in this case was still consistent with a medical standard of care.

This case does not involve a conflict of interest between the physician and patient—there was no evidence, for instance, of a financial incentive for UNMC's physicians to control costs.[34] As explained by UNMC's witnesses, the decision to defer Flolan treatment was not based on its financial effect on UNMC, or subordinating Mary's well-being to the interests of other patients, or even considering Mary's own financial interest. Instead, when making its initial value judgment regarding Mary's treatment, UNMC's physicians were not weighing the risk to Mary's health against the risk to her pocketbook, or UNMC's budget, or even a general social interest in controlling health care costs. UNMC's physicians were weighing the *risk to Mary's health* of delaying treatment against the *risk to Mary's health* of potentially interrupted treatment. Stated another way, this was not a case in which a physician refused to provide beneficial care—it was a case in which the physicians determined that the care *would not be beneficial* if it was later interrupted. In fact, it could be deadly.

As explained by Murphy, Thompson, and Johnson, the reason for waiting to begin Flolan until after insurance approval had been obtained was out of concern for the health of the patient. That was not meaningfully different from any number of other circumstances in which a health care provider might have to base a treatment decision upon the individual circumstances of a patient. For instance, a physician with concerns about a particular patient's ability to follow instructions, or report for appropriate follow-up care, might treat the patient's condition differently in the first instance. And a health care provider who is told that a patient cannot afford a particular treatment may recommend a less expensive but still effective treatment, reasoning that a treatment that is actually used is better than one that is not. These are difficult decisions, and there may be room to disagree, but it is hard to say they are unreasonable as a matter of law, or that an expert cannot testify that such considerations are consistent with the customary standard of care.

And as noted above, Robert's witnesses were free to disagree with UNMC's witnesses; Robert could (and did) argue that the standard of care required more than UNMC's witnesses said it did. And the evidence might have supported the conclusion that given Mary's deteriorating condition, there was little risk in beginning Flolan even without a payment source in

33. See, e.g., Thompson v. Sun City Community Hosp., Inc., 688 P.2d 605 (1984); Wilmington Gen. Hospital v. Manlove, 174 A.2d 135 (1961). Cf. Creighton–Omaha Regional Health Care Corp. v. Douglas County, 277 N.W.2d 64 (1979).

34. Compare Shea v. Esensten, 622 N.W.2d 130 (Minn. App. 2001).

place. (Although we note, for the sake of completeness, that Johnson also testified that Mary's weakening condition militated against beginning Flolan on an emergent basis, because its side effects could have been deadly.)

In other words, the jury *could* have found that in this case, given the facts and testimony, the standard of care required Flolan to be administered immediately. But it was a question for the jury, and there was also competent evidence supporting a conclusion that the standard of care had not been breached. The court erred in concluding that it should have directed a verdict on the standard of care. And for that reason, the court abused its discretion in granting Robert's motion for new trial. UNMC's assignment of error has merit.

UNMC's evidence and opinion testimony reflect difficult medical decisions—but still *medical* decisions. Therefore, the scope of our holding is limited. We need not and do not decide whether the standard of care can or should incorporate considerations such as cost control or allocation of limited resources. Although the decision (or lack thereof) of a third-party payor contributed to the circumstances of this case, UNMC's decisions were still (according to its evidence) premised entirely upon the medical well-being of its patient. In a perfect world, difficult medical decisions like the one at issue in this case would be unnecessary. But we do not live in a perfect world, and we cannot say as a matter of law that UNMC's decisions in this case violated the standard of care.

CONCLUSION

For the foregoing reasons, the district court's order granting Robert's motion for new trial is reversed.

Reversed.

Notes

1. *A careful parsing of the issues.* The court took great care to separate the problem of paying for Flolan from the precise decision that the physicians made: "This case does not involve a conflict of interest between the physician and patient. UNMC's physicians were not weighing the risk to Mary's health against the risk to her pocketbook, or UNMC's budget, or even a general societal interest in controlling health care costs. UNMC's physicians were weighing the *risk to Mary's health* of delaying treatment against the *risk to Mary's health* of potentially interrupted treatment." Had Mary's insurer rapidly approved Flolan, would the physicians have gone through this assessment? There may be other reasons why Flolan would need to be halted; we don't know anything about the risks of Flolan from this case, but it is conceivable that in any situation, physicians must weigh the risks of starting and stopping treatment. What makes this case unusual is its degree of clarity regarding how financial considerations may influence clinical thinking.

How much do or should physicians need to think about the financial risks that any course of treatment might create for their patients? Imagine that Mary Murray had been employed and that her insurer had rapidly approved Flolan. Six months later, with her health too fragile to continue, Mary had taken early retirement and lost her employer benefits (she might have eked out an additional 18 months through payment of COBRA extension premiums, but the cost was too high). Should her physicians have anticipated that she might not be insured forever and avoided putting her on a treatment whose interruption could kill her? Where does this end for physicians? Should physicians in fact routinely think about whether the treatments they are prescribing are sustainable for patients?

Or is the court going too far in its effort to shield the hospital and physicians here? According to the evidence, Flolan was not an appropriate emergency stabilization response, so the potential violation of EMTALA's stabilization requirements does not appear to be an issue here. But once she was stabilized, should the hospital and her physicians have contacted the manufacturer of Flolan to explain the situation and determine the availability of compassionate use that would supply her with Flolan at much reduced costs? Is this a case in which Mary Murray's health care providers failed her from an ethical perspective if not a legal one, by not advocating on her behalf to the best of their ability? Flolan is manufactured by GlaxoSmithKline. At its corporate website, Glaxosmithkline, the maker of Flolan, offers a compassionate use program for people who cannot afford their drugs. Should the hospital and physicians have taken action on her behalf?

2. *Social class and patient communication.* Physician-patient communications in stratified social class settings were the subject of a remarkable study. In 1968, Dr. Raymond S. Duff, Chair of Pediatrics at Yale University, and Dr. August B. Hollingshead, Chair of the Sociology Department, published SICKNESS AND SOCIETY, a study of the organization of work, provision of care, and interpersonal relations at one of the nation's most prestigious university teaching hospitals. The study excels in its systematic and detailed description of work and personal relationships in a hospital.

The central observation of SICKNESS AND SOCIETY is that the care people receive in the hospital and the relationships patients have with everyone who works there are stratified along the lines of socioeconomic class. Although in 1968 hospital accommodations were also organized along class lines (private, semi-private and ward, i.e., large rooms with many patients), the primary mechanism of class stratification was the patient/physician relationship.

Duff and Hollingshead distinguished four types of patient/physician relations. "Committed sponsorship," the relation between the highest class patients and their doctors, involved an assumption of responsibility for the patient by the specialist physician that extended beyond the doctor's interest in the patient's disease, and protected the patient from much contact with "house staff" (i.e., resident doctors and medical students). The next highest class of patients had a relationship of "casual sponsorship" with their physicians, characterized by a focus on "the symptoms of the disease and the diagnostic and treatment procedures," with more involvement by house staff but still significant control of the case by the private physician. Moving down the class ladder, "semicommittee sponsorship" involved a private physician who was nominally responsible for the patient's diagnosis and treatment, but in fact house staff assumed actual responsibility for diagnosis and treatment, as well as communication with the patient. Finally, the lowest class of patients, "committee sponsored" or ward (charitable) patients, had no private physicians. Responsibility for patient care rested with a committee of house staff and students, whose membership shifted as people rotated through their educational process. These patients were admitted to the hospital by a staff physician from an outpatient clinic or emergency room. They were significantly more ill than other patients, and communication between patients and physicians was very poor. RAYMOND S. DUFF & AUGUST B. HOLLINGSHEAD, SICKNESS AND SOCIETY 127–45 (1968).

Duff and Hollingshead found that no one on the hospital staff, either doctors or nurses, knew much about the patients as people, their personal situations, mental status, or feelings about their illness. By contrast, both nurses and doctors had consistent and accurate knowledge of the patient's social status. The failure to know the patients as people led to high levels of misdiagnosis, particularly failure to recognize alcoholism, mental illness and pain, in all classes of patients. Few dying patients were informed of their prognosis, and all who were told were white men of high status.

Lack of communication had adverse consequences upon the hospital's workers, as well as upon the patients. Registered nurses (RN's) felt conflicts most acutely. They felt they should do more bedside care and know their patients better, but administrative requirements of the bureaucratic structure within which they worked placed heavy demands upon their time. Although the aides and licensed practical nurses (LPNs) spent most time in direct patient care, and the LPNs had greatest knowledge of the patients' emotional and personal circumstances, that knowledge was not used or valued. Communication among various groups of hospital workers flowed in only one direction, from the top down.

How much has changed since Duff and Hollingshead made their observations in the mid–1960s? "Ward" accommodations have largely disappeared from American hospitals, and the implementation of Medicare and Medicaid has allowed many elderly and low-income patients to have their own private physicians. Moreover, the hospital industry and medical profession at least have made gestures, and at times and places more than that, toward more respect for patients through patients' "bills of rights," informed consent practices, and more emphasis on adequate communications with patients. The women's movement and varying labor and health care market conditions may have increased nurses' influence vis-à-vis physicians, at least to a modest extent, as have recurring efforts at conceiving of health care as provided by a "team." On the other hand, the pressure from public and private insurers to hold down costs, the extensive involvement of payers in treatment decisions, and a perpetual workforce shortage, particularly in nursing, have further complicated matters. These factors threaten quality of care for virtually all patients, and particularly for lower-income groups for whom resources are the most limited.

The question of physician/patient communication and in particular the impact of socioeconomic status on the extent and quality of that communication continues to be a topic central to efforts to improve the quality of health care and the related question of informed consent to treatment, discussed in Chapter 15. What makes the Hollingshead and Duff study so brilliant is that it puts its finger on physician attitudes and beliefs. An equally powerful ethical, historic, and systemic examinations of the question of poverty and medicine is Rebecca Skloot's best-selling and award-winning book, THE IMMORTAL LIFE OF HENRIETTA LACKS (2010). In the book, Skloot tells the story of Henrietta Lacks. Lacks, a vibrant young woman who resided with her family in Baltimore and her poverty, like that of so many of the city's African American residents in the 1950s, resulted in a dependence on what charitable care might be available through Johns Hopkins Hospital. Lacks died in agony of cervical cancer, which was found and (minimally) treated when it was too late. Yet she is known for all time to scientists throughout the world, not as a person but because it was her cells—taken without her knowledge or permission as she lay dying in a segregated hospital ward—that became the HeLa cell line, which has been used as an irreplaceable tool in modern medicine for more than a half century. Lacks' cells were unique, capable of growing and dividing ad infinitum in a Petri dish, making possible ground-breaking research in countless fields of medicine, technology, and science. Her family was told virtually nothing about her treatment or the capture of her cell line, and it was never given the opportunity to consent to the use of her cell line or to share in the immense profits made by universities and companies that sold the lines and patented the products. Lacks' impoverished family survivors lacked the health insurance needed to buy the drugs that Henrietta's cells had helped produce.

Numerous studies have considered the issue of socio-economic status ("SES") and its impact on the relationship between providers and patients. Researchers have noted the impact of SES on communication and informed consent, given the complexity of the process. *See, e.g.*, Jaime S. King et al., *The Potential of Shared–Decision Making to Reduce Health Disparities*, 39 J. LAW. MED. & ETHICS 30 (2011). Others, testing approaches to informed consent and finding significant evidence of patient uncertainty and confusion, have noted the important additional factors created by low literacy and limited language proficiency. Andrea Akkad et al., *Patients' Perception of Written Consent: A Questionnaire Study*, 333 BRIT. MED. J. 528 (2006). In their analysis of the impact of race and ethnicity on provider/patient communication, Lisa Cooper and Deborah Roter note the association between low socioeconomic status, which disproportionately affects minority patients, and their ability to achieve meaningful interaction with health care providers as a result of low literacy. Lisa Cooper & Deborah Roter, *The Effect of Race and Ethnicity on Process and Outcomes of Healthcare, in* UNEQUAL TREATMENT: CONFRONTING RACIAL AND ETHNIC DISPARITIES IN HEALTH CARE (Institute of Medicine, 2003). *See also* Rachel L. Johnson Thornton et al., *Patient–Physician Social Concordance, Medical Visit Communication, and Patients' perception of quality*, 85 PATIENT EDUC. COUNS. e201.

Yet low literacy is hardly the only problem. Part One, Chapter 4, which deals with race and access to health care, described what is considered one of the most important studies ever conducted on the issue of race and health disparities. In the study, physicians were shown identically dressed and equally well-spoken patients reporting symptoms and were then asked to formulate a diagnosis and treatment plan. Significant racial and gender differences were measured in physicians' responses, with greater resources recommended for the treatment of white male patients. The study generated enormous controversy but was rapidly followed by a landmark study by the Institute of Medicine, UNEQUAL TREATMENT: CONFRONTING RACIAL AND ETHNIC DISPARITIES IN HEALTH CARE (2003). Examining the evidence, the IOM found measurable differences that could not be explained by patient characteristics and that appeared to be associated with the health care system itself and the institutional structures and customs that underlie physician/patient interactions, including bias, stereotyping, and uncertainty. From its exhaustive findings the IOM recommended numerous interventions, including improvements in training and structures for provider/patient communications, greater enforcement of civil rights protections, greater parity in public and private insurance programs to reduce discrimination against the poor, and the development of clinical practice guidelines sensitive to matters of racial and socioeconomic disparities.

3. *A wealth-based standard of care?* The court conducts an extensive review of the legal literature on the relationship between resources, the quality of care, and a legal system that holds physicians to a unitary standard of care regardless of the economic circumstances of patients. Many commentators have grappled with this problem, none more so than Professor John Siliciano, who argues forcefully for a professional standard of care that departs from what he views as the too-simplistic approach of unified medical custom and for one that that is relative to patient wealth. In Professor Siliciano's view, a unified standard of care has done harm to patients by disincentivizing physicians to care for the under-resourced poor, thereby further impairing their access to appropriate treatments. As a result, he argues, physicians should be allowed to recognize explicitly the economic standard of their patients in determining the level of treatment to furnish and should be held to a liability standard only in relation to the level of care chosen. John A. Siliciano, *Wealth, Equity, and the Unitary Medical Malpractice Standard*, 77 VA. L. REV. 439 (1991). He writes:

> This is not a nation where all can afford the best that medicine has to offer. Instead, the medical profession must serve at least two very different populations, one reasonably well-insured and able to afford a relatively high standard of care and the other, poor and uninsured, wholly dependent on direct and indirect forms of charity for the care that it receives. In addition, because the unitary standard's insistence on complete equality of treatment effectively discourages many providers from offering

any treatment at all, the poor are forced to utilize the health care system in an inefficient manner.

Because of the wealth-blind nature of that unitary standard, the legal significance of patient indigence has never been addressed by tort law. Analytically, however, it seems that the provision of care to the poor has three separate quality-related components, each potentially affecting the configuration of a modified malpractice rule. First, there is an allocation decision, a determination by a health care provider to expend resources to treat a specific indigent. It is important to note that, at least in theory, this decision involves not only the initial question of whether to treat a given patient, but also the ancillary question of what amount of resources should be committed to a patient accepted for treatment. Once this two-part allocation decision is made, a determination as to the method of treatment—what particular array of diagnostic and remedial techniques will be employed—is necessary. Finally, the competence with which the selected techniques are implemented provides the third component bearing on the quality of care.

Under the existing unitary standard, the first component—the allocation decision—is simply not addressed. The law allows physicians the contractual freedom to refuse care to indigents altogether, but, if care is undertaken, the unitary standard disables providers from allocating less than full resources to treatment. This flat proscription against differentiating between accepted patients based on resource concerns also applies under the unitary standard to the choice of method and competence components of the treatment process: the same treatments are to be used, with the same degree of care, regardless of the patient's economic status.

Obviously, moving away from the unitary standard requires rethinking the legal significance of these three quality-related factors. The ultimate substantive goal of the law is to articulate a legal standard that allows physicians greater latitude in determining the amount and nature of the care provided the indigent, thus encouraging the voluntary treatment of greater numbers of such poor while still providing adequate assurance that the care provided will be competent and reasonable under the circumstances. Even so, consistent with process concerns, any modified standard must be one that, in the context of a malpractice action, can be applied in a reasonably predictable and consistent fashion by the trier of fact.

1. Competence in the Rendering of Services

Clearly, the simple issue of technical competence—whether the chosen diagnosis or treatment was conducted with reasonable care—should continue to be an issue under a resource-sensitive malpractice standard just as it is an issue under the unitary standard. Since the primary substantive justification for abrogating the unitary malpractice standard is to increase the overall adequacy of health care delivery to the poor, any modified standard must, at the very least, continue to protect the poor against the incompetent, that is, the harmful or wholly ineffective delivery of care.

2.   Allocations of Care and Resources

[Since society is plainly unwilling to fund full care for all of the poor, some denial of access is inevitable. If this is so, there are no standards by which tort law could judge an individual provider's refusal of treatment (except in cases of emergency, where the need for care is clearly determinable).] For similar process-based reasons, the second component of the allocation decision, the amount of resources to be spent on an indigent patient accepted for treatment, should remain a medical, rather than legal, judgment. As noted earlier, many medical conditions are susceptible, with varying degrees of success and varying attendant costs, to different types of treatment. Locating an optimal point along this spectrum is problematic under the best of circumstances, but it becomes exceedingly difficult to promulgate legally governing decisional criteria when other patients, with other conditions and their own array of treatment options, are vying for the limited funds allocated to treatment of the indigent. Any such standard would implicitly have to resolve exceedingly complex and essentially political questions that society has, thus far, shown little success in negotiating. These questions include whether we as a society prefer to treat large numbers of the poor with minimum levels of care, or limited numbers of the poor with full care, or something in between; whether we wish to focus resources on certain diseases and conditions over others; and whether we want to allow such criteria as age, family status, or potential social contribution to affect the decision to offer treatment.

To be sure, leaving this multifaceted resource allocation decision to health care professionals might yield inconsistent outcomes, with poor patients suffering similar conditions receiving different amounts of care. Yet there is little hope that the tort system, functioning through numerous, independent lay juries acting in unrelated lawsuits, would produce any better results. Indeed, the tort system is almost certain to do worse, for juries in individual actions, when confronted with an injured and sympathetic plaintiff, are easily distracted from the broad social implications of individual allocation decisions. The jury's answer in such cases will almost always be that more should have been done; that, however, is an answer that society has steadfastly refused to finance.

[U]nder the revised standard proposed here choices [of methods of diagnosis and treatment] are no longer assessed against a unitary assumption of full resources, but instead must be judged against whatever level of resources were actually allocated to treatment of a particular patient. This task, of course, poses some process problems, for once the traditional assumption of full care is jettisoned, the "customary" practice of the medical profession with respect to a given condition no longer serves as an automatic benchmark for reasonable care. Instead, for any given condition, the appropriate response will now depend not only on what is medically indicated, but also on what is financially feasible. The interjection of this resource question into the equation undoubtedly increases the complexity of the malpractice determination, but there are reasons to believe that the tort process can handle the added burden.

First, in many other areas where tort law concerns itself with the safety of a good or the carefulness of a service, it already adjusts its inquiry to account for the amount that the plaintiff paid for the good or service. [Thus,] tort law does not insist that Volkswagens be as safe as Volvos, nor does it require that a Legal Aid attorney handle a client's matrimonial problems in the same manner as would Donald Trump's team of lawyers. Indeed, the unitary medical malpractice standard is distinctive in large part because of departure from tort law's general recognition of the inevitable interplay between quality and cost. Thus, although a resource-sensitive malpractice standard is doubtless more difficult to administer than a unitary one, it presents no special challenge that tort law has not already met and mastered in other, similar areas of concern.

Moreover, it is unlikely that the single, customary treatment now prescribed under the unitary standard will give way to an infinitely variable number of treatments, the reasonableness of each depending on the precise dollar amount allocated to the care of each specific indigent. Instead, methods of diagnosis and treatment tend to be limited in number, and allocations of resources to patient care tend to come in discrete increments.

Siliciano, *Wealth, Equity, and the Unitary Medical Malpractice Standard.*

What do you make of this argument? Does Professor Siliciano accurately divide the world? As the incomes of Americans have stagnated or declined, and as the cost of health insurance has exploded, more people are not only uninsured but underinsured, a concept, as you learned in Part Two, that signifies both the presence of insurance and the simultaneous exposure to health care costs as a result of deductibles, coinsurance, and coverage limits that are considered economically unreasonable. Can the Siliciano approach be modified to consider gradients of underinsurance?

And how are physicians supposed to know the economic status of their patients? Increasingly physicians practice in large groups. By the time a patient is sitting in a robe on an examining table, the physician rushing from exam room to exam room trying to do her level best only knows that the patient needs her attention. Is she supposed to first ask the patient about his wealth, his insurance status, and whether he is adequately insured, under-insured, or uninsured? Should the patient have been given the choice to begin with as to whether to seek the Cadillac care, the Toyota care, or the used car level of care?

Is Professor Siliciano realistic in suggesting the feasibility of adjusting for wealth at the bedside or even desirable? Might an alternative approach, perhaps, be to take a page out of *Hall v. Hilbun,* in which the unified standard of practice essentially is modified to fit the realities facing any particular physician and patient? Can we ask more of physicians than that they do professionally with what they have to work with? As Professor Siliciano points out, no one realistically expects that an uninsured patient cared for at a community health center has all the treatment options that are available to a corporate CEO cared for in a posh practice in McLean, Virginia. But shouldn't both patients know the range of possible treatments and their pros and cons? And should it perhaps be part of the unitary standard of care in the case of under-resourced patients for physicians not only to do the best with what they have but also to attempt to secure the necessary additional resources in the event that a costlier approach is in fact the better and more desired approach?

* * *

While the ACA will bring coverage to an estimated 94 percent of the population, this fact alone will not assure across-the-board quality for all insured people. You read in Part One about the inequities in health care access that transcend issues of coverage alone. Residential segregation, racial and cultural distinctions in the population, and residual bias within the health care system keep the quality of care uneven. The very structure of the health care system militates against this result. Even when they participate in multiple payment systems, insurers may maintain subsidiaries that specialize in only public insurance programs such as Medicaid, maintaining segregated and lesser networks of participating physicians and hospitals. You will see the results of this type of segregated access to treatment in *Jones v. Chicago HMO* in the materials that follow. As noted in Parts One and Two, physicians may refuse to accept certain types of payment, eschewing participation in health practice networks that are dominated by public payers because payments are lower and patients, more clinically and socially complex. Differences in coverage and personal wealth may mean that some patients receive the most advanced treatment (although more treatment definitely is not always the best treatment), and some of the most accomplished specialists in a community may refuse to treat the insured poor. Health centers, high quality sources of primary health care, nonetheless face serious problems finding sources of specialty care even for their insured populations. As noted in Part One, public hospitals, with their disproportionate dependence on public payers who often pay less, may lack the resources to offer the most sophisticated treatments and adopt the newest technologies.

In UNEQUAL TREATMENT: CONFRONTING RACIAL AND ETHNIC DISPARITIES IN HEALTH CARE, the IOM reviewed massive evidence regarding the factors that contribute to the ongoing problem of disparities in access and quality. UNEQUAL TREATMENT at 125–79. Central to the challenge is the personal discretion over the use of health care resources that physicians exercise. Although the standard of care is thought of as unified, in fact, part of this unified standard of care may be very different decision-making approaches to the same problems encountered in different patients. Clinical judgment may encourage a physician to prescribe costly and aggressive treatment for certain patients, while seeking out less ambitious treatment regimens for patients whose prognosis, in his or her judgment, may be poorer as a result of greater resource constraints. Added to the underlying problem of uncertainty in clinical decision-making generally, this built-in bias may result in notable differences in how patients of different classes are treated.

This is what Hollingshead and Duff showed so brilliantly nearly 50 years ago. Not only are treatment choices different based on physicians' perceptions of their patients, but even the threshold question of whether to test for certain conditions or complications may vary from patient to patient. The IOM found evidence that race pervades even the most basic aspects of clinical care, reporting on one study showing that the length of office visits varied by the race of both physicians and patients, with visits between white physicians and African–American patients being of the shortest duration. *Id.* at 133 The researchers attributed this discrepancy in part to the lack of cultural ease between physicians and patients of different races and ethnic backgrounds. *Id.* Past history and experience with a discriminatory health care system, a dominant life experience for so many minority families, may shape their ability to meaningfully engage with health care providers, a problem reinforced by providers' disdain for health and health care practices that may be based in poverty and disadvantage rather than personal preferences *per se*. The very fact that disadvantaged Americans have far fewer opportunities to effectively choose health by where they live, what they eat, how much they exercise, and the daily habits they adopt, may result not only in poorer health but also in impatience and avoidance within the health care system itself.

CHAPTER 15

INFORMED CONSENT TO TREATMENT

1. INTRODUCTION

Until relatively recently, the dominant view among physicians was that patients should be told as little as possible about their condition and treatment. An essay attributed to Hippocrates advised physicians to adopt a manner of self-confident reserve, "concealing most things from the patient while you are attending to him," and "revealing nothing of the patient's future or present condition, [f]or many patients through this cause [i.e. disclosure] have taken a turn for the worse." MELVIN KONNER, MEDICINE AT THE CROSSROADS 4–5 (1993). While much has changed between Hippocrates' ancient Greece and the present, Dr. Jay Katz, a modern champion of informed consent, wrote in 1984 that "disclosure and consent, except in the most rudimentary fashion, are obligations alien to medical thinking and practice." THE SILENT WORLD OF DOCTOR AND PATIENT 1 (1984).

Three major developments have helped modify the medical profession's traditional resistance to sharing information with patients and seeking their informed consent. The first has been the concept of basic human rights of self-determination and dignity, often denied to vulnerable populations such as African Americans, immigrant populations, prisoners, and in most extreme form, inmates of the Nazi concentration camps. At the Nuremberg trials of German physicians who carried out murderous "experiments" in the camps, the German doctors argued, accurately but unsuccessfully, that American and British medical researchers of that era often did not obtain consent from their human subjects. Ten principles of research ethics articulated at the trial, commonly known as the Nuremberg Code, require, inter alia, voluntary consent of the subject and avoidance of all unnecessary physical and mental suffering and injury. These principles have been adopted, expanded, and specified in extensive federal legislation and regulations governing federally-funded biomedical and behavioral research. *See* 45 C.F.R. Part 46, often referred to as Common Rule. Nevertheless, the effectiveness of these regulations has repeatedly come under criticism. *See, e.g.,* Kurt Eichenwold & Gina Kolata, *Drug Trials Hide Conflicts for Doctors,* N.Y. TIMES, May 16, 1999, at A1; Editorial: *Patients for Hire, Doctors For Sale,* N.Y. TIMES, May 22, 1999, at A–12; Sheryl Gay Stolberg, *"Unchecked" Experiments on People Raise Concern,* N. Y. TIMES, May 14, 1997, at A1.

In July, 2011, the Obama Administration published an "Advance Notice of Proposed Rulemaking" (ANPRM) whose purpose is to update the Common Rule. 76 Fed. Reg. 44,512 (July 26, 2011). The ANPRM reviews the history of the Common Rule and its evolution from the Nuremburg Code, the subsequent Declaration of Helsinki issued by the World Medical Association, and the Belmont Report developed under an Act of Congress in response to widespread evidence of gross violations of research ethics, most notably, the Tuskegee Study described below. The ANPRM pays particular attention to research protocols used for social and behavioral research, a vast and rapidly growing field that measures the relationship of behavior and society to health and health care. A special focus of the proposal is the use of informed consent in order to assure patient and subject understanding of research participation and its impact, while balancing the need to advance large-scale studies that involve minimal invasion of personhood and privacy while collecting important information about population health.

But modern thinking about how to better enable population-based research does not obviate the need for rigorous attention to research that carries risks to health. Much of our modern thinking about informed consent in research comes from Nuremburg as well as from the notorious "Tuskegee Study," in which for forty years (from the early 1930s to 1972) doctors working for the federal government's Public Health Service, together with local physicians, deceptively withheld treatment for syphilis from 400 unknowing African American men, who were told they were receiving treatment for "bad blood." Despite the Tuskegee study's serious ethical and scientific failings, a Public Health Service review of the project in 1969 "decided to continue to withhold treatment from the survivors," without informing the subjects or evaluating whether individuals would be helped by treatment. The study was not terminated until 1972, and then only after a courageous junior Public Health Service employee and journalists exposed it. *See generally* JAMES H. JONES, BAD BLOOD: THE TUSKEGEE SYPHILIS EXPERIMENT (rev. ed., 1992).

On May 16, 1997, President Bill Clinton formally apologized at the White House to the few remaining survivors of the Tuskegee Study. "The Government," he said, "did something that was wrong—deeply, profoundly, morally wrong. It was an outrage to our commitment to integrity and equality for all our citizens." Alison Mitchell, *Clinton Regrets "Clearly Racist" U.S. Study*, N. Y. TIMES, May 17, 1997, at A10. The article went on to note that while the government had paid $10 million in compensation to the Tuskeegee victims since 1973, there had never been a formal apology for a seminal event that left "a legacy of Government distrust among black Americans" that in turn hindered efforts to combat HIV/AIDS within the African American community.

At least as a matter of theory, American common law also viewed the patient as an autonomous person with the "right to determine what shall be done with his own body; and a surgeon who performs an operation without his patient's consent, commits an assault, for which he is liable in damages." Schloendorff v. Society of New York Hospital, 105 N.E. 92, 93 (N.Y. 1914) (Cardozo, J.). The problem was that what constituted "consent" under the law of assault or battery was usually primitive: that the patient did not object when the doctor said that surgery was needed. The patient's explicit or implicit consent under these circumstances effectively eliminated most real opportunities for patient choice, and delegated decision-making power to physicians.

While assault or battery remains the legal theory applicable to situations where no patient consent at all has been given, most states now treat the issue of the adequacy of the consent—and of the disclosures preceding it—as an issue of negligence. The legal issues surrounding the negligence theory of informed consent are explored in the following materials and cases.

Before turning to informed consent doctrine, it is worth noting two other major factors that have challenged medical resistance to patient information and consent. The first is "consumerism," which builds on both the tradition of patient rights and also on the ascendant market model of health care delivery. Patient-rights liberals and pro-market conservatives can often find common ground on measures requiring disclosure of "adverse events" and consumer-oriented "report cards" and other metrics that encourage informed consumer "shopping" among providers and health plans. The second force is led by safety and quality-oriented leaders of the health care professions explored in Chapter 13. They often agree with these measures and support an even more ambitious model of "shared decision-making" between providers and patients that would improve quality and patient compliance and well-being, while counteracting doctors' all too easy (and profitable) assumption that the patient always wants the most interventionist (and expensive) procedures.

2.   THE RISE OF A PATIENT-ORIENTED STANDARD OF INFORMED CONSENT

Canterbury v. Spence

464 F.2d 772 (D.C. Cir. 1972)

■ SPOTTSWOOD W. ROBINSON, III, CIRCUIT JUDGE:

[Plaintiff Canterbury sought damages for personal injuries allegedly sustained as a result of an [spinal] operation negligently performed by Dr. Spence, a negligent failure by Dr. Spence to disclose a risk of serious disability inherent in the operation, and negligent post-operative care by Washington Hospital Center. On close examination of the record, we find evidence which required submission of these issues to the jury. We accordingly reverse the judgments for the defendants and remand the case to the District Court for a new trial.]

I

The record we review tells a depressing tale. A youth troubled only by back pain submitted to an operation without being informed of a risk of paralysis incidental thereto. A day after the operation he fell from his hospital bed after having been left without assistance while voiding. A few hours after the fall, the lower half of his body was paralyzed, and he had to be operated on again. Despite extensive medical care, [he is now] a victim of paralysis of the bowels and urinary incontinence. In a very real sense this lawsuit is an understandable search for reasons.

At the time of the events which gave rise to this litigation, appellant was nineteen years of age, a clerk-typist employed by the Federal Bureau of Investigation. In December, 1958, he began to experience severe pain between his shoulder blades. He consulted two general practitioners, but the medications they prescribed failed to eliminate the pain. Thereafter, appellant secured an appointment with Dr. Spence, who is a neurosurgeon.

[After several examinations and tests, including a myelogram] Dr. Spence told appellant that he would have to undergo a laminectomy—the excision of the posterior arch of the vertebra—to correct what he suspected was a ruptured disc. Appellant did not raise any objection to the proposed operation nor did he probe into its exact nature.

Appellant explained to Dr. Spence that his mother was a widow of slender financial means living in Cyclone, West Virginia, and that she could be reached through a neighbor's telephone. Appellant called his mother the day after the myelogram was performed and, failing to contact her, left Dr. Spence's telephone number with the neighbor. When Mrs. Canterbury returned the call, Dr. Spence told her that the surgery was occasioned by a suspected ruptured disc. Mrs. Canterbury then asked if the recommended operation was serious and Dr. Spence replied "not any more than any other operation." He added that he knew Mrs. Canterbury was not well off and that her presence in Washington would not be necessary. The testimony is contradictory as to whether during the course of the conversation Mrs. Canterbury expressed her consent to the operation. Appellant himself apparently did not converse again with Dr. Spence prior to the operation.

Dr. Spence performed the laminectomy on February 11 at the Washington Hospital Center. Mrs. Canterbury traveled to Washington, arriving on that date but after the operation was over, and signed a consent form at the hospital. The laminectomy revealed several anomalies: a spinal cord that was swollen and unable to pulsate, an accumulation of large tortuous and dilated veins, and a complete absence of epidural fat which normally surrounds the spine.

For approximately the first day after the operation appellant recuperated normally, but then suffered a fall and an almost immediate setback.[4] Several hours later, paralysis seems to have been virtually total from the waist down. At the time of the trial in April, 1968, appellant required

---

4. The one fact clearly emerging from the otherwise murky portrayal by the record, however, is that appellant did fall while attempting to void and while completely unattended.

crutches to walk, still suffered from urinal incontinence and paralysis of the bowels, and wore a penile clamp.

II

Against Dr. Spence it alleged, among other things, negligence in the performance of the laminectomy and failure to inform him beforehand of the risk involved. Against the hospital the complaint charged negligent post-operative care in permitting appellant to remain unattended after the laminectomy, in failing to provide a nurse or orderly to assist him at the time of his fall, and in failing to maintain a side rail on his bed.

Appellant introduced no evidence to show medical and hospital practices, if any, customarily pursued in regard to the critical aspects of the case, and only Dr. Spence, called as an adverse witness, testified on the issue of causality. Dr. Spence admitted that trauma [e.g. from the fall] can be a cause of paralysis. Dr. Spence further testified that even without trauma paralysis can be anticipated "somewhere in the nature of one percent" of the laminectomies performed, a risk he termed "a very slight possibility." He felt that communication of that risk to the patient is not good medical practice because it might deter patients from undergoing needed surgery and might produce adverse psychological reactions which could preclude the success of the operation.

At the close of appellant's case in chief, each defendant moved for a directed verdict and the trial judge granted both motions. The judge did not allude specifically to the alleged breach of duty by Dr. Spence to divulge the possible consequences of the laminectomy.

We reverse. The testimony of appellant and his mother that Dr. Spence did not reveal the risk of paralysis from the laminectomy made out a prima facie case of violation of the physician's duty to disclose which Dr. Spence's explanation did not negate as a matter of law.

III

True consent to what happens to one's self is the informed exercise of a choice, and that entails an opportunity to evaluate knowledgeably the options available and the risks attendant upon each. The average patient has little or no understanding of the medical arts, and ordinarily has only his physician to whom he can look for enlightenment with which to reach an intelligent decision. From these almost axiomatic considerations springs the need, and in turn the requirement, of a reasonable divulgence by physician to patient to make such a decision possible.[15]

---

15. The doctrine that a consent effective as authority to form therapy can arise only from the patient's understanding of alternatives to and risks of the therapy is commonly denominated "informed consent." See, e.g., Waltz and Scheuneman, Informed Consent to Therapy, 64 Nw. U. L. Rev. 628, 629 (1970). The same appellation is frequently assigned to the doctrine requiring physicians, as a matter of duty to patients, to communicate information as to such alternatives and risks. See, e.g., Comment, Informed Consent in Medical Malpractice, 55 Calif. L. Rev. 1396 (1967). While we recognize the general utility of shorthand phrases in literary expositions, we caution that uncritical use of the "informed consent" label can be

The context in which the duty of risk-disclosure arises is invariably the occasion for decision as to whether a particular treatment procedure is to be undertaken. To the physician, whose training enables a self-satisfying evaluation, the answer may seem clear, but it is the prerogative of the patient, not the physician, to determine for himself the direction in which his interests seem to lie. To enable the patient to chart his course understandably, some familiarity with the therapeutic alternatives and their hazards becomes essential.

A reasonable revelation in these respects is not only a necessity but, as we see it, is as much a matter of the physician's duty. It is a duty to warn of the dangers lurking in the proposed treatment, and that is surely a facet of due care. It is, too, a duty to impart information which the patient has every right to expect. The patient's reliance upon the physician is a trust of the kind which traditionally has exacted obligations beyond those associated with arm's length transactions. His dependence upon the physician for information affecting his well-being, in terms of contemplated treatment, is well-nigh abject. We now find, as a part of the physician's overall obligation to the patient, a similar duty of reasonable disclosure of the choices with respect to proposed therapy and the dangers inherently and potentially involved. [This represents a logical and modest extension of the physician's traditional duty] on pain of liability for unauthorized treatment, to make adequate disclosure to the patient.[36]

---

misleading. See, e.g., Plante, An Analysis of "Informed Consent," 36 Ford. L. Rev. 639, 671–72 (1968).

In duty-to-disclose cases, the focus of attention is more properly upon the nature and content of the physician's divulgence than the patient's understanding or consent. Adequate disclosure and informed consent are, of course, two sides of the same coin—the former a sine qua non of the latter. But the vital inquiry on duty to disclose relates to the physician's performance of an obligation, while one of the difficulties with analysis in terms of "informed consent" is its tendency to imply that what is decisive is the degree of the patient's comprehension. As we later emphasize, the physician discharges the duty when he makes a reasonable effort to convey sufficient information although the patient, without fault of the physician, may not fully grasp it. Even though the fact-finder may have occasion to draw an inference on the state of the patient's enlightenment, the fact-finding process on performance of the duty ultimately reaches back to what the physician actually said or failed to say. And while the factual conclusion on adequacy of the revelation will vary as between patients—as, for example, between a lay patient and a physician-patient—the fluctuations are attributable to the kind of divulgence which may be reasonable under the circumstances.

36. We discard the thought that the patient should ask for information before the physician is required to disclose. Caveat emptor is not the norm for the consumer of medical services. Duty to disclose is more than a call to speak merely on the patient's request, or merely to answer the patient's questions; it is a duty to volunteer, if necessary, the information the patient needs for intelligent decision. The patient may be ignorant, confused, overawed by the physician or frightened by the hospital, or even ashamed to inquire. See generally Note, Restructuring Informed Consent: Legal Therapy for the Doctor–Patient Relationship, 79 Yale L.J. 1533, 1545–51 (1970). Perhaps relatively few patients could in any event identify the relevant questions in the absence of prior explanation by the physician. Physicians and hospitals have patients of widely divergent socio-economic backgrounds, and a rule which presumes a degree of sophistication which many members of society lack is likely to breed gross inequities. See Note, Informed Consent as a Theory of Medical Liability, 1970 Wis. L. Rev. 879, 891–97.

IV

Duty to disclose has gained recognition in a large number of American jurisdictions, but more largely on a different rationale. The majority of courts dealing with the problem have made the duty depend on whether it was the custom of physicians practicing in the community to make the particular disclosure to the patient. If so, the physician may be held liable for an unreasonable and injurious failure to divulge, but there can be no recovery unless the omission forsakes a practice prevalent in the profession. We agree that the physician's noncompliance with a professional custom to reveal, like any other departure from prevailing medical practice, may give rise to liability to the patient. We do not agree that the patient's cause of action is dependent upon the existence and nonperformance of a relevant professional tradition.

There are, in our view, formidable obstacles to acceptance of the notion that the physician's obligation to disclose is either germinated or limited by medical practice. To begin with, the reality of any discernible custom reflecting a professional consensus on communication of option and risk information to patients is open to serious doubt. We sense the danger that what in fact is no custom at all may be taken as an affirmative custom to maintain silence, and that physician-witnesses to the so-called custom may state merely their personal opinions as to what they or others would do under given conditions. We cannot gloss over the inconsistency between reliance on a general practice respecting divulgence and, on the other hand, realization that the myriad of variables among patients makes each case so different that its omission can rationally be justified only by the effect of its individual circumstances. Nor can we ignore the fact that to bind the disclosure obligation to medical usage is to arrogate the decision on revelation to the physician alone. Respect for the patient's right of self-determination on particular therapy demands a standard set by law for physicians rather than one which physicians may or may not impose upon themselves.

We have admonished that "the special medical standards are but adoptions of the general standard to a group who are required to act as reasonable men possessing their medical talents presumably would." There is, by the same token, no basis for operation of the special medical standard where the physician's activity does not bring his medical knowledge and skills peculiarly into play. And where the challenge to the physician's conduct is not to be gauged by the special standard, it follows that medical custom cannot furnish the test of its propriety, whatever its relevance under the proper test may be. The decision to unveil the patient's condition and the chances as to remediation, as we shall see, is oft times a non-medical judgment and, if so, is a decision outside the ambit of the special standard. Where that is the situation, professional custom hardly furnishes the legal criterion for measuring the physician's responsibility to reasonably inform his patient of the options and the hazards as to treatment.

In sum, the physician's duty to disclose is governed by the same legal principles applicable to others in comparable situations, with modifications only to the extent that medical judgment enters the picture. We hold that the standard measuring performance of that duty by physicians, as by others, is conduct which is reasonable under the circumstances.

V

Once the circumstances give rise to a duty on the physician's part to inform his patient, the next inquiry is the scope of the disclosure the physician is legally obliged to make. In our view, the patient's right of self-decision shapes the boundaries of the duty to reveal. That right can be effectively exercised only if the patient possesses enough information to enable an intelligent choice. The scope of the physician's communications to the patient, then, must be measured by the patient's need, and that need is the information material to the decision.

From these considerations we derive the breadth of the disclosure of risks legally to be required. The scope of the standard is not subjective as to either the physician or the patient; it remains objective with due regard for the patient's informational needs and with suitable leeway for the physician's situation. In broad outline, we agree that "[a] risk is thus material when a reasonable person, in what the physician knows or should know to be the patient's position, would be likely to attach significance to the risk or cluster of risks in deciding whether or not to forego the proposed therapy."

The topics importantly demanding a communication of information are the inherent and potential hazards of the proposed treatment, the alternatives to that treatment, if any, and the results likely if the patient remains untreated. The factors contributing significance to the dangerousness of a medical technique are, of course, the incidence of injury and the degree of the harm threatened. A very small chance of death or serious disablement may well be significant; a potential disability which dramatically outweighs the potential benefit of the therapy or the detriments of the existing malady may summon discussion with the patient.

VI

Two exceptions to the general rule of disclosure have been noted by the courts. The first comes into play when the patient is unconscious or otherwise incapable of consenting, and harm from a failure to treat is imminent and outweighs any harm threatened by the proposed treatment. When a genuine emergency of that sort arises, it is settled that the impracticality of conferring with the patient dispenses with need for it. Even in situations of that character the physician should, as current law requires, attempt to secure a relative's consent if possible. But if time is too short to accommodate discussion, obviously the physician should proceed with the treatment.

The second exception obtains when risk-disclosure poses such a threat of detriment to the patient as to become unfeasible or contraindicated from a medical point of view. It is recognized that patients occasionally become so ill or emotionally distraught on disclosure as to foreclose a rational decision, or complicate or hinder the treatment, or perhaps even pose psychological damage to the patient. Where that is so, the cases have generally held that the physician is armed with a privilege to keep the information from the patient, and we think it clear that portents of that type may justify the physician in action he deems medically warranted. The critical inquiry is whether the physician responded to a sound medical judgment that communication of the risk information would present a threat to the patient's well-being.

The physician's privilege to withhold information for therapeutic reasons must be carefully circumscribed, however, for otherwise it might devour the disclosure rule itself. The privilege does not accept the paternalistic notion that the physician may remain silent simply because divulgence might prompt the patient to forego therapy the physician feels the patient really needs. That attitude presumes instability or perversity for even the normal patient, and runs counter to the foundation principle that the patient should and ordinarily can make the choice for himself. Nor does the privilege contemplate operation save where the patient's reaction to risk information, as reasonably foreseen by the physician, is menacing. And even in a situation of that kind, disclosure to a close relative with a view to securing consent to the proposed treatment may be the only alternative open to the physician.

VII

No more than breach of any other legal duty does nonfulfillment of the physician's obligation to disclose alone establish liability to the patient. An unrevealed risk that should have been made known must materialize, for otherwise the omission, however unpardonable, is legally without consequence. Occurrence of the risk must be harmful to the patient, for negligence unrelated to injury is nonactionable. And, as in malpractice actions generally, there must be a causal relationship between the physician's failure to adequately divulge and damage to the patient.

A causal connection exists when, but only when, disclosure of significant risks incidental to treatment would have resulted in a decision against it. The patient obviously has no complaint if he would have submitted to the therapy notwithstanding awareness that the risk was one of its perils. On the other hand, the very purpose of the disclosure rule is to protect the patient against consequences which, if known, he would have avoided by foregoing the treatment. The more difficult question is whether the factual issue on causality calls for an objective or a subjective determination.

It has been assumed that the issue is to be resolved according to whether the fact-finder believes the patient's testimony that he would not have agreed to the treatment if he had known of the danger which later ripened into injury. We think a technique which ties the factual conclusion on causation simply to the assessment of the patient's credibility is unsatisfactory. It places the physician in jeopardy of the patient's hindsight and bitterness. It places the fact-finder in the position of deciding whether a speculative answer to a hypothetical question is to be credited.

Better it is, we believe, to resolve the causality issue on an objective basis: in terms of what a prudent person in the patient's position would have decided if suitably informed of all perils bearing significance. If adequate disclosure could reasonably be expected to have caused that person to decline the treatment because of the revelation of the kind of risk or danger that resulted in harm, causation is shown, but otherwise not. The patient's testimony is relevant on that score of course but it would not threaten to dominate the findings. And since that testimony would probably be appraised congruently with the fact-finder's belief in its reasonableness, the case for a wholly objective standard for passing on causation is strengthened.

Notes

1. *The President's Commission: a survey and a doctor-patient dialogue.* According to the President's Commission for the Study of Ethical Problems in Medicine and Biomedical and Behavioral Research, "Although the informed consent doctrine has substantial foundations in law, it is essentially an ethical imperative." MAKING HEALTH CARE DECISIONS 2 (1982). The Commission surveyed both the public and physicians on their attitudes toward informed consent. Among its findings, "Regardless of race, income, education, age, or gender, the vast majority of people surveyed by the Commission felt that patients have a right to information and ought to participate in decisions regarding their health care." *Id.* at 17. More than 80 percent of patients and 90 percent of physicians believe physicians should initiate the informed consent discussion. *Id.* at 79. And more than three-quarters of physicians and the public think physicians should initiate discussion about uncertainty in medical treatment and outcomes. *Id.* at 88. On the other hand, most physicians report that they sometimes withhold information from patients for the following reasons: the family asks doctor not to tell; the patient tells doctor not to tell; the information might lead patient not to accept treatment recommendation. *Id.* at 97–99. Finally, 76 percent of physicians and 88 percent of the public think informed consent should be protected by law. *Id.* at 105.

As a practical matter, it is sometimes difficult to know what is being communicated and what the patient wants to have communicated. The following is a transcript of an informed consent discussion concerning cardiac catheterization. What do you think about it? Does it seem consistent with *Canterbury's* principles? If the doctor asked you to comment on his remarks, what would you tell him about how to act toward the next similar patient?

Having explained why the procedure should be done and what information it would provide, the physician went on to describe how it was done and what it would feel like, including that the patient would feel very hot for about 20 seconds.

Patient: Oh, seconds only, that's all right. But I do want this explanation because I knew I would get this for 25 years. I guess I've heard a lot of things about it. Friends of mine have had it and so forth.

Doctor: Yes, some people like it and some people say it's the worst thing that happened to them in their lives. I think I ought to tell you that there's some possibility that we may have to do a transeptum catheterization [and he explained what this consisted of]. There's some potential risks. I think you will find they are terrifying, but I want you to remember we weigh the risks both of doing it and not doing it before we recommend it to you.

Patient: Maybe you shouldn't tell me until tomorrow.

Doctor: Well, I could wait until tomorrow, but I do have to tell you this. I want you to know the risk is low. We are talking about a one in a thousand chance of a major risk. There's some minor ones, too. But they can all be dealt with. Some of the major ones can, too, but they're not very likely. Here are some of them. First of all we have to go into the vessel, and we can injure the vessel, and that can sometimes require surgery, which can be difficult in its own right. The second one is that you might have hardening of the arteries already, and some sort of blockage could result from pushing through them. This can require surgery also to make it better, and even so there's a low risk of a heart attack or of stroke from it. Then another thing is that some people are allergic to the dye, and this can put somebody into shock, and usually we can treat that with medicine, but it's quite serious. Another thing it can do is it can cause an irregular heartbeat, and you can even need an electric shock because it can cause your heart to stop. But of course you would be asleep then, and you wouldn't feel it. Another thing is that if we need to do the transeptal catheterization, that can cause a puncture of the heart and bleeding. The blood can get between the heart and the sac around it, and then we would have to drain that. One of the minor risks is that you can have a hematoma around where we put in the catheter. That's not much of a real problem, but you can get black and blue, and that happens because of the Heparin we put in to prevent the clotting I talked about earlier.

Patient: You know, I can't remember any of that stuff.

Doctor: Well, I know it's scary, but I want you to understand that it's my feeling that it is a higher risk not to have it done. But of course ultimately it's your decision, not mine.

Patient: Do you do this often?

Doctor: Yeah, this is a big center for that sort of thing, for valve replacements, and we see a lot of these.

Patient: You see it's all new to me.

Doctor: And one other thing is that you're going to have to sign a consent form. The nurse'll bring that in later tonight.

Patient: Well, you have to do it because it's the best procedure. [*Id.* at 81–82.]

2. *Varying state informed consent standards.* Either by judicial decision or by statute, about one half the states have retained the professionally-based standard of informed consent, and measure the duty to disclose by the standard of the similarly situated reasonable physician. *See* Jaime Staples King & Benjamin Moulton, *Rethinking Informed Consent: The Case for Shared Medical Decisionmaking*, 32 AM. J.L. & MED. 429, 493–501 (2006). Expert testimony is required to establish the standard and its breach. *See, e.g.*, Culbertson v. Mernitz, 602 N.E.2d 98, 102–04 (Ind. 1992) (expert testimony of professional standard of disclosure required except where deviation from the standard of care is a matter commonly known to lay persons). The *Canterbury* patient-based approach was followed quickly in Cobbs v. Grant, 502 P.2d 1 (Cal. 1972), and over the years in other states, e.g. Sard v. Hardy, 379 A.2d 1014 (Md. 1977), Largey v. Rothman, 540 A.2d 504 (N.J. 1988), and Korman v. Mallin, 858 P.2d 1145 (Alaska, 1993).

3. *The doctrinal and normative underpinning of informed consent.* Some commentators have suggested that Judge Robinson was mistaken in section IV of his *Canterbury* opinion in asserting that the patient-oriented informed consent standard was simply the uniform application of negligence principles to an area of medical practice (informing the patient of material risks) "where the physician's activity does not bring his medical knowledge and skills peculiarly into play." According to this view, "the negligence principle normally evaluates the conduct of the reasonable actor—not the expectations of a reasonable victim. The values served by the [*Canterbury*] doctrine—patient autonomy and dignity—are unrelated to the values served by the doctrine of negligence. Informed consent really serves the values we otherwise identify with the doctrine of battery. It is ironic that a doctrine developed to foster and recognize individual choice should be measured by an objective standard." BARRY R. FURROW ET AL., HEALTH LAW: CASES, MATERIALS AND PROBLEMS 241 (6th ed., 2008). Are you persuaded by this view? It appears to rest on a strong opposition between a doctor's (sole) duty to comply with technical professional norms, and a totally separate realm ("battery") concerned with patient autonomy and dignity.

4. *Is a bodily invasion a condition precedent to breach?* Is an affirmative physical act required before a physician can be liable for failing to secure an informed consent? In McQuitty v. Spangler, 976 A.2d 1020 (Md. App. 2009), the Maryland Court of Appeals considered the liability of a physician for his failure to inform a pregnant patient at high risk of premature labor of changes in her condition and that an early Caesarean delivery, as an alternative treatment, might have spared her child permanent disability. A trial resulted in a finding of non-negligence on Dr. Spangler's part for the actual management of Mrs. McQuitty's care. A second trial resulted in a verdict for Mrs. McQuitty on the issue of informed consent. Dr. Spangler appealed, arguing that as a matter of law, he could not be found liable for negligence in connection with a failure of

informed consent, because there had been no affirmative violation of the patient's physical integrity; instead, his only allegedly wrongful conduct was not to inform her of alternate options to the treatment she already was undergoing to stave off preterm labor.

The McQuittys argue that it is well established that an informed consent claim is separate from that for medical malpractice, and that "artificial restriction[s] borrowed from the law of battery," such as the requirement of an "affirmative invasion of the physical integrity of the patient," have no place in the doctrine of informed consent. To this end, the McQuittys argue that Mrs. McQuitty and Dylan were receiving ongoing treatment from Dr. Spangler during the period in which Mrs. McQuitty was admitted to the hospital and placed on bed rest, and that Dr. Spangler had a "continuing duty to inform Mrs. McQuitty of material changes in her condition or that of her baby," as well as risks and alternative treatments associated therewith, material to Mrs. McQuitty's decision-making regarding whether to continue a pre-established course of treatment.

[T]he gravamen [of an informed consent claim] is the health-care provider's duty to provide information, rather than battery or the provider's physical act. [R]equiring a physical invasion to sustain an informed consent claim contravenes the very foundation of the informed consent doctrine—to promote a patient's choice. "[T]he paramount purpose of the doctrine of informed consent [is] to vindicate the patient's right to determine what shall be done with [her] body and when," and that a healthcare provider's duty to obtain a patient's informed consent is "to enable . . . the choice about whether or not to undergo . . . *treatment.*" (emphasis added). When describing the scope of that duty, we held that a healthcare provider has a duty to inform of those risks "which are material to the intelligent decision of a reasonably prudent patient." An affirmative physical invasion requirement countermands a patient's choice by permitting the healthcare provider to make treatment decisions [that do not involve physical invasion], in lieu of patient involvement in the healthcare choice.

"Conventional medical judgments during the course of treatment remain for the physician to make, subject to ordinary malpractice controls. But determinations bearing upon which course of treatment to adopt are the capable patient's prerogative, assisted by as much information and advice as the physician may reasonably be able to furnish. To the extent the physician has a view as to which of the reasonably available alternative courses of treatment is the best in the circumstances as a matter of medical judgment, the physician must also give the patient the benefit of a recommendation. There is no reasonable basis for the apprehension, as expressed by defendant in argument before the trial judge, that the physician will ever be required to perform surgery or administer any other course of treatment that he or she believes to be contraindicated. If the patient selects a course, even from among reasonable alternatives, which the physician regards as inappropriate or disagreeable, the physician is free to refuse to participate and to withdraw from the case upon providing reasonable assurances that basic treatment and care will continue. In such circumstances, there can be no liability for the refusal." [quoting Matthies v. Mastromonaco, 709 A.2d 238 (N.J. Super. Ct. App. Div. 1998).]

For a similar holding, see Truman v. Thomas, 611 P.2d 902 (Cal. 1980) (doctor has duty to warn patient of the risks of her refusal to follow his advice to have a pap smear).

5. *The role of expert witnesses.* Under the patient-oriented standard, the question of whether the doctor disclosed the risks that a reasonable patient would find material is for the trier of fact, and expert testimony is not required on the issue of materiality. But expert testimony may still be needed to establish what are the risks of a particular treatment, alternative treatments and their risks, and the risks if the patient declines treatment altogether. *See, e.g., Sard,* 379 A.2d 1014. Information to be disclosed includes the risks and benefits of diagnostic tests, the diagnosis, the risks of the treatment, the probability of success, and treatment alternatives and their risks and consequences.

6. *Does the doctor's duty to disclose include information relevant to non-medical decision making?* Does a physician have a duty to inform his patient with pancreatic cancer of the relevant mortality statistics, either as an element of informed consent to the proposed treatment, or to enable the patient to put his affairs in order in contemplation of death? In Arato v. Avedon, 858 P.2d 598 (Cal. 1993), the California Supreme Court declined to mandate such disclosure, leaving it to the jury to decide what information "the physician knows or should know would be regarded as significant by a reasonable person in the patient's position when deciding to accept or reject a recommended medical procedure." Moreover, the court defined the disclosure duty as related solely to the patient's decision about medical treatment, and rejected any argument that physicians have a fiduciary duty to disclose information important to their patients' financial affairs.

7. *Patient decision aids, shared medical decision-making, and the Affordable Care Act.* In recent years, researchers have developed increasingly sophisticated methods for aiding patients in complex medical decisions, known as decision-aid programs, in which patients are systematically armed with extensive information as well as patient support staff who help guide them through difficult decisions related to treatments for advanced illnesses. The Affordable Care Act defines "Patient Decision Aid" at §§ 3506 and 936(b)(1), as an "educational tool that helps patients, caregivers, or authorized representatives understand and communicate their beliefs and preferences related to their treatment options, and to decide with their caregiver what treatments are best for them based on their treatment options, scientific evidence, circumstances, beliefs, and preferences." In-

creasingly there may be multiple options—some aggressive and some less so—for treating conditions such as advanced cancer or heart disease. Health care providers are using these more sophisticated decision support techniques more often. A principal finding is that when given a full array of options, patients may be more likely to choose less invasive and lower-cost care than that perhaps preferred by their physicians, or assumed by physicians to be preferred by their patients, thereby improving quality of care and patient well-being, and lowering costs associated with high-use geographic variations highlighted by Atul Gawande in McAllen, Texas and by John Wennberg in New England and elsewhere. *See, e.g.,* John E. Wennberg & Philip G. Peters, *Unwanted Variations in the Quality of Health Care: Can the Law Help Medicine Provide a Remedy/Remedies?*, 37 WAKE FOREST L. REV. 925, 925–941 (2002); Atul Gawande, *The Cost Conundrum*; King & Moulton, *Rethinking Informed Consent*; Laura Landro, *Weighty Choices, in Patients' Hands*, WALL ST. J., Aug. 5, 2009, at D2. Think about the *Washington Hospital Center* case, as well as the provisions of the ACA immediately below. What is the possibility that the move toward more sophisticated decision-making aids could result in liability on the part of providers for patient injury as a result of an aggressive intervention, if the provider has relied on less supportive techniques that fail fully to inform a patient of all choices and that fail to provide extensive decision support?

The Affordable Care Act supports the use of decision aids for what it terms "preference-sensitive care," i.e., "medical care for which the clinical evidence does not clearly support one treatment option such that the appropriate course of treatment depends on the values of the patient or the preferences of the patient, caregivers, or authorized representatives regarding the benefits, harms, and scientific evidence for each treatment option." ACA §§ 3506 and 936(b)(2). "[T]he use of such care should depend on the informed patient choice among clinically appropriate treatment options." *Id.*

The ACA requires the Secretary of HHS to develop standards and certification for such aids (through contract with an independent entity) "for use in federal health programs and by other interested parties." *Id.* § 936(c)(1). The ACA emphasizes development of standards for decision aids, certification of particular aids that meet the standards, educating providers on their use, including through academic conferences, and making the decision aids available to the public. *Id.* § 936(d). Left unsaid is whether use of such decision aids will become (to the extent they exist) a new legal standard of informed consent, either in federally-funded programs (such as Medicare and Medicaid) or for health care more generally. *Cf.* Furrow, *Regulating Patient Safety* at 1767 (arguing that such aids "must replace the normal process of informed consent disclosure, first in Medicare health plans, but realistically in most settings as providers strive for consistency in their informed consent approaches"). The state of Washington has already amended its informed consent statute to provide for developing and certifying decision aids, and requiring that such certified aids be used. Rev. Code Wash. § 7.70.060 creates a presumption of informed consent if a provider uses a decision aid, which can only be rebutted by clear and convincing evidence that the aid failed to convey sufficient information.

3.   INFORMED CONSENT AND DISCLOSURE OF PHYSICIAN-SPECIFIC QUALIFICATIONS AND RISKS

While the general *Canterbury* standard requires disclosure of "material risks," the more detailed *Canterbury* disclosure doctrine focuses solely on the risks of the proposed procedure and alternatives to it, without any reference to risks that might vary among physicians or other providers with different credentials or levels of experience. As medical procedures and specialization have become ever more complex, and patients' knowledge and "consumer orientation" have increased, the law of informed consent has had to consider disclosure of physician-specific information.

One of the leading cases on this topic is Johnson v. Kokemoor, 545 N.W.2d 495 (Wis. 1996). The plaintiff Donna Johnson underwent a CT scan to determine the cause of her headaches, and was referred to Dr. Kokemoor, who is described in the court's opinion as a "neurosurgeon" but who was not board-certified in neurosurgery—a fact he did not disclose to the patient. Dr. Kokemoor diagnosed an enlarging aneurysm at the rear of the plaintiff's brain and recommended surgery to clip the aneurysm. He later acknowledged at trial that the aneurysm was not the cause of the plaintiff's headaches—an error that apparently was so common that it was not the basis for a viable claim of negligence (The plaintiff voluntarily dismissed before trial her claim that Dr. Kokemoor had been negligent in performing the surgery.). Dr. Kokemoor performed the operation and clipped the aneurysm, thereby "rendering the surgery a technical success. But as a consequence of the surgery, the plaintiff, who had no neurological impairments prior to surgery, was rendered an incomplete quadriplegic. She remains unable to walk or to control her bowel and bladder movements. Furthermore, her vision, speech and upper body coordination are partially impaired."

The issue at trial was whether Dr. Kokemoor had failed to obtain the patient's informed consent. Specifically, Dr. Kokemoor appealed the trial court's decision to admit evidence that he had failed (1) to divulge the extent of his experience in performing this type of operation; (2) to compare the morbidity and mortality rates for this type of surgery among experienced surgeons and inexperienced surgeons like himself; and (3) to refer the plaintiff to a tertiary care center staffed by physicians more experienced in performing the same surgery. The Wisconsin Supreme Court noted that the "admissibility of such physician-specific evidence in a case involving the doctrine of informed consent raises an issue of first impression in this court and is an issue with which appellate courts have had little experience."

The facts revealed egregious behavior on the part of Dr. Kokemoor. "According to testimony introduced during the plaintiff's case in chief, when the plaintiff questioned the defendant regarding his experience, he replied that he had performed the surgery she required "several" times; asked what he meant by "several," the defendant said "dozens" and "lots of times." In fact, however, following residency, the defendant had performed aneurysm surgery on six patients with a total of nine aneurysms. He had operated on basilar bifurcation aneurysms only twice and had never operated on a large basilar bifurcation aneurysm such as the plaintiff's aneurysm." Dr. Kokemoor also grossly understated the risks of this complex surgery when performed by a doctor of his own level of experience, i.e., lack of experience.

> According to the plaintiff's witnesses, the defendant had told the plaintiff that her surgery carried a two percent risk of death or serious impairment and that it was less risky than the angiogram procedure she would have to undergo in preparation for surgery.

> The plaintiff's neurosurgical experts testified that even the physician considered to be one of the world's best aneurysm surgeons, who had performed hundreds of posterior circulation aneurysm surgeries, had reported a morbidity and mortality rate of ten-and-seven-tenths percent when operating upon basilar bifurcation aneurysms comparable in size to the plaintiff's aneurysm. Furthermore, information in treatises and articles which the defendant reviewed in preparation for the plaintiff's surgery set the morbidity and mortality rate at approximately fifteen percent for a basilar bifurcation aneurysm. The plaintiff also introduced expert testimony that the morbidity and mortality rate for basilar bifurcation aneurysm operations performed by one with the defendant's relatively limited experience would be between twenty and thirty percent, and "closer to the thirty percent range."[13]

> Finally, the plaintiff introduced into evidence testimony and exhibits stating that a reasonable physician in the defendant's position would have advised the plaintiff of the availability of more experienced surgeons and would have referred her to them. The plaintiff also introduced evidence stating that patients with basilar aneurysms should be referred to tertiary care centers—such as the Mayo Clinic, only 90 miles away—which contain the proper neurological intensive care unit and microsurgical facilities and which are staffed by neurosurgeons with the requisite training and experience to perform basilar bifurcation aneurysm surgeries.

Johnson, 545 N.W.2d at 499–500.

Dr. Kokemoor argued on appeal that "the doctrine of informed consent should be viewed as creating a 'bright line' rule requiring physicians to

---

13. The plaintiff introduced into evidence as exhibits articles from the medical literature stating that there are few areas in neurosurgery where the difference in results between surgeons is as evident as it is with aneurysms. One of the plaintiff's neurosurgical experts testified that experience and skill with the operator is more important when performing basilar tip aneurysm surgery than with any other neurosurgical procedure.

disclose only significant complications intrinsic to the contemplated procedure," i.e., of "risks associated with particular 'treatments' rather than the
risks associated with particular physicians." The Wisconsin Supreme Court
rejected such a "bright line rule." "The question of whether certain
information is material to a patient's decision and therefore requires
disclosure is rooted in the facts and circumstances of the particular case in
which it arises. The state's informed consent statute, Wisconsin Stat.
§ 448.30, explicitly requires disclosure of more than just treatment complications associated with a particular procedure. Physicians must, the statute
declares, disclose 'the availability of all alternate, viable medical modes of
treatment' in addition to 'the benefits and risks of these treatments.' " In
effect and at times explicitly, the court interpreted "all alternate, viable
modes of medical treatment" and their "benefits and risks" to include well-
documented differential risks and benefits depending on the surgeon's
experience and qualifications, especially where, as here, the patient explicitly inquired about such factors, and the defendant-physician undertook to
discuss (misleadingly) the risks in statistical terms.

The *Johnson* court explicitly approved the trial court's admission of
"comparative risk statistics purporting to estimate and compare the morbidity and mortality rates when the surgery at issue is performed, respectively, by a physician of limited experience such as the defendant and by
the acknowledged masters in the field."

> The defendant concedes that the duty to procure a patient's
> informed consent requires a physician to reveal the general risks
> associated with a particular surgery. The defendant does not
> explain why the duty to inform about this general risk data should
> be interpreted to categorically exclude evidence relating to provid-
> er-specific risk information, even when that provider-specific data
> is geared to a clearly delineated surgical procedure and identifies a
> particular provider as an independent risk factor. When different
> physicians have substantially different success rates, whether sur-
> gery is performed by one rather than another represents a choice
> between "alternate, viable medical modes of treatment" under
> § 448.30.

Johnson, 545 N.W.2d at 507.

In short, when medical experts testify that the data known in the
profession show that physician-specific characteristics are significant risk
factors regarding a particular surgery, such risks are "material" to a
reasonable patient's decision and must be disclosed. Similarly, when there
is a well-established professional consensus that less experienced surgeons
should refer very complex or risky cases of a particular type to more
qualified surgeons at larger medical centers, that professional standard
defines an "alternate, viable mode of medical treatment [at the other
institution]" that must be disclosed. In this case, the patient should have
been told by Dr. Kokemoor that far more qualified surgeons were available
"in the immediate geographical vicinity" (e.g., the Mayo Clinic, 90 miles
away) where she could obtain at least a second opinion.

Finally, the defendant argues that if his duty to procure the plaintiff's informed consent includes an obligation to disclose that she consider seeking treatment elsewhere, then there will be no logical stopping point to what the doctrine of informed consent might encompass. We disagree with the defendant. As the plaintiff noted in her brief to this court, "[i]t is a rare exception when the vast body of medical literature and expert opinion agree that the difference in experience of the surgeon performing the operation will impact the risk of morbidity/mortality as was the case here," thereby requiring referral. At oral argument before this court, counsel for the plaintiff stated that under "many circumstances" and indeed "probably most circumstances," whether or not a physician referred a patient elsewhere would be "utterly irrelevant" in an informed consent case. In the vast majority of significantly less complicated cases, such a referral would be irrelevant and unnecessary.

Johnson, 545 N.W.2d at 510.

The *Johnson* court also addressed the overlap between informed consent and misrepresentation.

The defendant also argues that the plaintiff is trying to disguise what is actually a negligent misrepresentation claim as an informed consent claim so that she might bring before the jury otherwise inadmissible evidence regarding the defendant's experience and relative competence. The tort of negligent misrepresentation occurs when one person negligently gives false information to another who acts in reasonable reliance on the information and suffers physical harm as a consequence of the reliance. *Restatement (Second) of Torts,* § 311(1) (1965). An overlap exists between a claim pleading this tort and one alleging a failure to provide informed consent. As the commentary to § 311 of the *Restatement* points out:

The rule stated in this Section finds particular application where it is a part of the actor's business or profession to give information upon which the safety of the recipient or a third person depends. Thus it is as much a part of the professional duty of a physician to give correct information as to the character of the disease from which his plaintiff is suffering, where such knowledge is necessary to the safety of the patient or others, as it is to make a correct diagnosis or to prescribe the appropriate medicine.

Restatement (Second) of Torts, § 311(1) cmt. b (1965). Because of this overlap between negligent misrepresentation and informed consent, it is not surprising that allegations made and evidence introduced by the plaintiff might have fit comfortably under either theory. But this overlap does not preclude the plaintiff from making allegations and introducing evidence in an informed consent case which might also have been pled in a negligent misrepresentation case. This case was pled and proved under the tort of failure to procure informed consent.

Johnson, 545 N.W.2d at 503 n.29

Notes

1. *When is a physician's failure to respond accurately to a patient's question about credentials relevant to an informed consent claim?* In Howard v. University of Medicine and Dentistry of New Jersey, 800 A.2d 73 (N.J. 2002), the patient's wife claimed that she asked the defendant professor of neurosurgery whether he was "Board Certified," and he replied that he was. (The defendant physician disputed this allegation.). In fact, the physician was "board eligible" and did not become board certified until over two years after he performed the surgery on the patient. The plaintiffs also claimed that the defendant told them he had performed "approximately sixty" surgeries of the type he was recommending for the patient, when in fact he had performed "a couple dozen" such surgeries. The New Jersey Supreme Court ruled that plaintiffs' cause of action for fraud had to be considered as an informed consent claim. The court further held that in general physicians had no affirmative duty to disclose their credentials and experience as part of obtaining informed consent. However, if a patient or other party requests such information, "a serious misrepresentation concerning the quality or extent of a physician's professional experience, viewed from the perspective of the reasonably prudent patient assessing the risks attendant to a medical procedure, can be material to the grant of intelligent and informed consent to the procedure."

> If defendant's true level of experience had the capacity to enhance substantially the risk of paralysis from undergoing a corpectomy, a jury could find that a reasonably prudent patient would not have consented to that procedure had the misrepresentation been revealed. That presumes that plaintiff can prove that the actual level of experience possessed by defendant had a direct and demonstrable relationship to the harm of paralysis, a substantial risk of the procedure that was disclosed to plaintiff. Put differently, plaintiff must prove that the additional undisclosed risk posed by defendant's true level of qualifications and experience increased plaintiff's risk of paralysis from the corpectomy procedure.

> The standard for causation that we envision in such an action will impose a significant gatekeeper function on the trial court to prevent insubstantial claims concerning alleged misrepresentations about a physician's experience from proceeding to a jury. We contemplate that misrepresented or exaggerated physician experience would have to significantly increase a risk of a procedure in order for it to affect the judgment of a reasonably prudent patient in an informed consent case. As this case demonstrates, the proximate cause analysis will involve a two-step inquiry.

The first inquiry should be, assuming a misrepresentation about experience, whether the more limited experience or credentials possessed by defendant could have substantially increased plaintiff's risk of paralysis from undergoing the corpectomy procedure. We envision that expert testimony would be required for such a showing. The second inquiry would be whether that substantially increased risk would cause a reasonably prudent person not to consent to undergo the procedure. If the true extent of defendant's experience could not affect materially the risk of paralysis from a corpectomy procedure, then the alleged misrepresentation could not cause a reasonably prudent patient in plaintiff's position to decline consent to the procedure. The court's gatekeeper function in respect of the first question will require a determination that a genuine issue of material fact exists requiring resolution by the factfinder in order to proceed to the second question involving an assessment by the reasonably prudent patient. Further, the trial court must conclude that there is a genuine issue of material fact concerning both questions in order to allow the claim to proceed to trial.

Howard, 800 A.2d at 84–85. Thus the burden is on the plaintiff to show not only actual misrepresentation, but also that the misrepresentation was "material" in the sense that the defendant's undisclosed lesser credentials or experience "could have substantially increased plaintiff's risk"—a standard easily satisfied in *Johnson v. Kokemoor* but perhaps not so easily in *Howard*.

2. *Non-disclosure of prior outcomes and informed consent.* In Duffy v. Flagg, 905 A.2d 15 (Conn. 2006), a pregnant patient was interested in attempting a vaginal birth after previously having had a cesarean section.

[T]he defendants [physicians] informed the plaintiff of the risks of the procedure known as "vaginal birth after cesarean section," including the risk of uterine rupture and the possibility of a resulting risk of death to the plaintiff and her infant. On one occasion, while discussing the procedure with Flagg, the plaintiff asked Flagg whether she had encountered any difficulty in her prior vaginal birth after cesarean section deliveries. Flagg responded that there had been "a bad outcome" because of a uterine rupture. The plaintiff did not inquire further about the result of the uterine rupture, and Flagg did not tell the plaintiff that the infant had died as a result of that uterine rupture. The plaintiff thereafter decided to attempt a vaginal birth after cesarean delivery and executed written consent forms therefor, which specifically detailed the nature, risks, alternatives and benefits of the procedure.

Id. at 16–17. The patient's baby died after uterine rupture, and she sued Dr. Flagg for both medical malpractice and lack of informed consent. The trial court granted the defendant doctor's motion to exclude any mention of the previous death and the fact that it was not disclosed to the plaintiff, and the Connecticut Supreme Court affirmed. The court distinguished *Johnson v. Kokemoor* and *Howard* as cases in which the plaintiff either had evidence, or might have had evidence, that the non-disclosed information significantly increased the risk of the proposed procedure, while in this case, "[i]n response to the trial court's inquiry, the plaintiff's counsel acknowledged that there would be no evidence that Flagg's prior experience with vaginal birth after cesarean section increased the risk of harm to the plaintiff from such a procedure." The court rejected the plaintiff's argument that knowing the prior outcome of death would have led her to forego the vaginal attempt, characterizing her claim as her subjective preference, not protected by the informed consent doctrine's concern with the objective decisions of a reasonable patient responding to accurate information about significant risks. Was the court necessarily correct in assuming that the doctor's prior adverse outcome was not related to the risk faced by the plaintiff?

4. CONFLICTS OF INTEREST AND THE PHYSICIAN'S FIDUCIARY DUTY

Moore v. The Regents of the University of California

793 P.2d 479 (Cal. 1990)

■ PANELLI [JUSTICE]:

[The opinion quotes extensively from Moore's 50–page complaint]. Moore first visited UCLA Medical Center on October 5, 1976, shortly after he learned that he had hairy-cell leukemia. After hospitalizing Moore and "withdr[awing] extensive amounts of blood, bone marrow aspirate, and other bodily substances," [Dr. David] Golde [the attending physician] confirmed that diagnosis. At this time all defendants, including Golde, were aware that "certain blood products and blood components were of great value in a number of commercial and scientific efforts" and that access to a patient whose blood contained these substances would provide "competitive, commercial, and scientific advantages."

On October 8, 1976, Golde recommended that Moore's spleen be removed. Golde informed Moore "that he had reason to fear for his life, and that the proposed splenectomy operation was necessary to slow down the progress of his disease." Based upon Golde's representations, Moore signed a written consent form authorizing the splenectomy. Before the operation, Golde and [Shirley] Quan [a researcher at the University] "formed the intent and made arrangements to obtain portions of [Moore's] spleen following its removal" and to take them to a separate research unit. These research activities "were not intended to have any relation to [Moore's] medical care." However, neither Golde nor Quan informed Moore of their plans to conduct this research or requested his permission. Surgeons at UCLA Medical Center, whom the complaint does not name as defendants, removed Moore's spleen on October 20, 1976.

Moore returned to the UCLA Medical Center several times between November 1976 and September 1983. He did so at Golde's direction and based upon representations "that such visits were necessary and required for his health and well-being, and based upon the trust inherent in and by virtue of the physician-patient relationship." On each of these visits, Golde withdrew additional samples of "blood, blood serum, skin, bone marrow aspirate, and sperm." On each occasion Moore traveled to the UCLA Medical Center from his home in Seattle because he had been told that the procedures were to be performed only there and only under Golde's direction. "In fact, [however,] throughout the period of time that [Moore] was under [Golde's] care and treatment, the defendants were actively involved in a number of activities which they concealed from [Moore]." Specifically, defendants were conducting research on Moore's cells and planned to "benefit financially and competitively [by exploiting the cells] and [their] exclusive access to [the cells] by virtue of [Golde's] ongoing physician-patient relationship." Sometime before August 1979, Golde established a cell line from Moore's T-lymphocytes. On January 30, 1981, the Regents applied for a patent on the cell line, listing Golde and Quan as inventors. "[B]y virtue of an established policy, [the] Regents, Golde, and Quan would share in any royalties or profits arising out of [the] patent." The patent issued on March 20, 1984, naming Golde and Quan as the inventors of the cell line and the Regents as the assignee of the patent. (U.S. Patent No. 4,438,032 (Mar. 20, 1984)).

With the Regents' assistance, Golde negotiated agreements for commercial development of the cell line and products to be derived from it. Under an agreement with Genetics Institute, Golde "became a paid consultant" and "acquired the rights to 75,000 shares of common stock." Genetics Institute also agreed to pay Golde and the Regents "at least $330,000 over three years, including a pro-rata share of [Golde's] salary and fringe benefits, in exchange for exclusive access to the materials and research performed" on the cell line and products derived from it. On June 4, 1982, Sandoz "was added to the agreement," and compensation payable to Golde and the Regents was increased by $110,000. "[T]hroughout this period, Quan spent as much as 70 [percent] of her time working for [the] Regents on research" related to the cell line.

III. Discussion

A. *Breach of Fiduciary Duty and Lack of Informed Consent*

Moore repeatedly alleges that Golde failed to disclose the extent of his research and economic interests in Moore's cells before obtaining consent to the medical procedures by which the cells were extracted. These allegations, in our view, state a cause of action against Golde for invading a legally protected interest of his patient. This cause of action can properly be characterized either as the breach of a fiduciary duty to disclose facts material to the patient's consent or, alternatively, as the performance of medical procedures without first having obtained the patient's informed consent.

Our analysis begins with three well-established principles. First, [a competent adult person has the right to determine whether or not to submit to lawful medical treatment]. Second, "the patient's consent to treatment, to be effective, must be an informed consent." Third, in soliciting the patient's consent, a physician has a fiduciary duty to disclose all information material to the patient's decision.

These principles lead to the following conclusions: (1) a physician must disclose personal interests unrelated to the patient's health, whether research or economic, that may affect the physician's professional judgment; and (2) a physician's failure to disclose such interests may give rise to a cause of action for performing medical procedures without informed consent or breach of fiduciary duty.

Indeed, the law already recognizes that a reasonable patient would want to know whether a physician has an economic interest that might affect the physician's professional judgment. As the Court of Appeal has said, "[c]ertainly a sick patient deserves to be free of any reasonable suspicion that his doctor's judgment is influenced by a profit motive." Magan Medical Clinic v. Cal. State Bd. of Medical Examiners, 57 Cal. Rptr. 256 (Cal. App. 1967) [upholding a state regulation prohibiting physicians from having an ownership interest in pharmacies]. The desire to protect patients from possible conflicts of interest has also motivated legislative enactments. Under [Business and Professions Code section 654.2(a)], a physician may not charge a patient on behalf of, or refer a patient to, any organization in which the physician has a "significant beneficial interest, unless [the physician] first discloses in writing to the patient, that there is such an interest and advises the patient that the patient may choose any organization for the purposes of obtaining the services ordered or requested by [the physician]." See also Bus. & Prof. Code, § 654.1 [referrals to clinical laboratories].

[A] physician who treats a patient in whom he also has a research interest has potentially conflicting loyalties. This is because medical treatment decisions are made on the basis of proportionality—weighing the benefits to the patient against the risks to the patient. A physician who adds his own research interests to this balance may be tempted to order a scientifically useful procedure or test that offers marginal, or no, benefits to the patient.[8] The possibility that an interest extraneous to the patient's health has affected the physician's judgment is something that a reasonable patient would want to know in deciding whether to consent to a proposed course of treatment. It is material to the patient's decision and, thus, a prerequisite to informed consent.

Golde argues that the scientific use of cells that have already been removed cannot possibly affect the patient's medical interests. The argument is correct in one instance but not in another. If a physician has no plans to conduct research on a patient's cells at the time he recommends

---

8. This is, in fact, precisely what Moore has alleged with respect to the postoperative withdrawals of blood and other substances.

the medical procedure by which they are taken, then the patient's medical interests have not been impaired. In that instance the argument is correct. On the other hand, a physician who does have a preexisting research interest might, consciously or unconsciously, take that into consideration in recommending the procedure. In that instance the argument is incorrect: the physician's extraneous motivation may affect his judgment and is, thus, material to the patient's consent. We acknowledge that there is a competing consideration. To require disclosure of research and economic interests may corrupt the patient's own judgment by distracting him from the requirements of his health. But California law does not grant physicians unlimited discretion to decide what to disclose.

Accordingly, we hold that a physician who is seeking a patient's consent for a medical procedure must, in order to satisfy his fiduciary duty[10] and to obtain the patient's informed consent, disclose personal interests unrelated to the patient's health, whether research or economic, that may affect his medical judgment.

Notes

1. Physicians have always had economic interests that were in tension with the patient's health. Under fee-for-service reimbursement, doctors have economic incentives, and practice within a professional culture, that encourages them to perform procedures. Acknowledging this tension, Opinion 8.03 of the American Medical Association's Code of Medical Ethics (1994 ed.) states that:

> Under no circumstances may physicians place their own financial interests above the welfare of their patients. The primary objective of the medical profession is to render service to humanity; reward or financial gain is a subordinate consideration. For a physician unnecessarily to hospitalize a patient, prescribe a drug, or conduct diagnostic tests for the physician's financial benefit is unethical. If a conflict develops between the physician's financial interest and the physician's responsibilities to the patient, the conflict must be resolved to the patient's benefit.

However, it was easy for physicians to believe that the procedures on which their income depended were also "medically necessary," resulting in many thousands of dubiously justified tonsillectomies, hysterectomies, coronary bypass operations, and numerous other procedures. In mitigation of this, one could argue that "everybody knew" that doctors were being paid for doing procedures, and that patients at least had a theoretical opportunity to question the doctor's proposal before consenting. In the contemporary

---

10. In some respects the term "fiduciary" is too broad. In this context the term "fiduciary" signifies only that a physician must disclose all facts material to the patient's decision. A physician is not the patient's financial adviser. As we have already discussed, the reason why a physician must disclose possible conflicts is not because he has a duty to protect his patient's financial interests, but because certain personal interests may affect professional judgment.

world of market competition and managed care, by contrast, patients do not know that their doctor may be financially rewarded for not doing tests or referring them to a specialist. *See generally* BRADFORD H. GRAY, THE PROFIT MOTIVE AND PATIENT CARE: THE CHANGING ACCOUNTABILITY OF DOCTORS AND HOSPITALS (1991); MARC A. RODWIN, MEDICINE, MONEY, AND MORALS: PHYSICIANS' CONFLICTS OF INTEREST (1993); Susan M. Wolf, *Health Care Reform and the Future of Physician Ethics*, 24 HASTINGS CTR. REP. 28 (Mar.– April 1994); Mary Anne Bobinski, *Autonomy and Privacy: Protecting Patients From Their Physicians*, 55 U. PITT. L. REV. 291 (1994); Deven C. McGraw, *Financial Incentives to Limit Services: Should Physicians Be Required to Disclose These To Patients?* 83 GEO. L.J. 1821 (1995). To a substantial extent, the area of health care fraud and abuse, covered in Part Four, concerns these conflicts of interest.

2. In *Checklist*, discussed earlier, Dr. Atul Gawande, describes the efforts by a Johns Hopkins physician to introduce a checklist approach to intensive-care management to reduce the problem of line infection. Following this pioneering effort, a group of 67 hospitals in Michigan decided to pursue the approach and, being responsible systems, sought to collect information on performance and patient outcomes before and after instituting the checklist. Although this research involved observation of changes in the provision of routine health care (rather than an experimental treatment), the HHS Office of Human Research Protections (OHRP) investigated the proposed plan and ordered it halted on the ground that the informed consent of patients had not been secured. The Johns Hopkins institutional review board had judged the research exempt, but OHRP ruled that the investigation did indeed constitute human subject research and ordered the Michigan program halted in the absence of informed consent.

Writing about the episode Franklin Miller and Ezekiel Emanuel concluded that the observation did constitute research because it "prospectively implemented a protocol of infection control interventions and tested hypotheses regarding its effectiveness." Nonetheless, they concluded, the research could have been classified as one posing minimal risks, because the research was undertaken as part of routine clinical practice and involved no invasive collection of information. Franklin Miller & Ezekiel Emanuel, *Quality Improvement Research and Informed Consent*, 358 NEW ENG. J. MED. 765 (2008). The question however is whether the introduction of safe, evidence-based standards in hospitals should be considered research at all or should be classified as exempt. The authors conclude that this type of research poses "no meaningful infringement" of patients' autonomy and thus should be exempt. *Id.* at 767.

What if researchers had divided patients in the ICU into two groups, one of which would receive the safety intervention, while the other would not? At what point does observational research on clinical practice reforms in fact reach a level at which informed consent is needed?

CHAPTER 16

THE CONFIDENTIALITY OF HEALTH INFORMATION AND HEALTH INFORMATION PRIVACY

1. INTRODUCTION

Maintaining the confidentiality of patient information is a foundational duty on the part of health care providers. A related issue is the privacy of health information. Although the two subjects raise the issue of control over information, they are also different, since not all information given in confidence involves a private or personal matter. A breach of confidentiality happens when an individual who holds information in confidence breaches the confidence, whereas a breach of privacy can involve any third party, clinical or otherwise, not merely one who holds the information on a confidential basis. Thus, for example, in a major privacy breach reported in 2011, the personal information of thousands of emergency department patients was inadvertently published and remained on a public website for a year, when a contractor for Stanford University Hospital posted online a bar graph depicting patient emergency room data and left the underlying data identifying in detail particular patients attached to the bar graph. The Office for Civil Rights of the United States Department of Health and Human Services, which oversees enforcement of the Health Information Portability and Accountability Act's Privacy Rule, has investigated numerous such incidents of inadvertent disclosure of private patient information by third parties including both clinicians and business contractors who have access to patient data as part of their business agreements with health care providers. Kevin Sack, *Patient Data Posted Online in Major Breach of Privacy*, N.Y. TIMES, Sept. 8, 2011.

Several possible theories govern actions against health care providers for the disclosure of confidential information. Under one theory, it is a breach of the professional standard of care to disclose confidential information. Under the second, the cause of action would be for invasion of privacy by the health care professional. State law would determine which type or types of cause of action apply. Thus, for example, the unauthorized disclosure of patient information may be considered a breach of privacy. Anderson v. Glissmann, 577 F. Supp. 1506 (D. Colo. 1984). In some jurisdictions, however, unauthorized disclosures also can give rise to a cause of action based in the inherent nature of the relationship between physicians and patients.

MacDonald v. Clinger

84 A.D.2d 482 (N.Y. 1982)

■ DENMAN, J:

We here consider whether a psychiatrist must respond in damages to his former patient for disclosure of personal information learned during the course of treatment and, if he must, on what theory of recovery the action may be maintained. We hold that such wrongful disclosure is a breach of the fiduciary duty of confidentiality and gives rise to a cause of action sounding in tort.

The complaint alleges that during two extended courses of treatment with defendant, a psychiatrist, plaintiff revealed intimate details about himself which defendant later divulged to plaintiff's wife without justification and without consent. As a consequence of such disclosure, plaintiff alleges that his marriage deteriorated, that he lost his job, that he suffered financial difficulty and that he was caused such severe emotional distress that he required further psychiatric treatment. The complaint set forth three causes of action: breach of an implied contract; breach of confidence in violation of public policy; and breach of the right of privacy guaranteed by article 5 of the Civil Rights Law. Defendant moved to dismiss for failure to state a cause of action, asserting that there was in reality only one theory of recovery, that of breach of confidence, and that such action could not be maintained against him because his disclosure to plaintiff's wife was justified. The court dismissed the third cause of action but denied the motion with respect to the first two causes of action and this appeal ensued.

Research reveals few cases in American jurisprudence which treat the doctor-patient privilege in this context. That is undoubtedly due to the fact that the confidentiality of the relationship is a cardinal rule of the medical profession, faithfully adhered to in most instances, and thus has come to be justifiably relied upon by patients seeking advice and treatment. This physician-patient relationship is contractual in nature, whereby the physician, in agreeing to administer to the patient, impliedly covenants that the disclosures necessary to diagnosis and treatment of the patient's mental or physical condition will be kept in confidence.

Examination of cases which have addressed this problem makes it apparent that courts have immediately recognized a legally compensable injury in such wrongful disclosure based on a variety of grounds for recovery: public policy; right to privacy; breach of contract; breach of fiduciary duty. (See, generally, Ann., 20 ALR 3d 1109; 61 Am Jur 2d, Physicians, Surgeons and Other Healers, § 169). As the Supreme Court of Washington stated in *Smith v Driscoll* (94 Wash 441, 442): "Neither is it necessary to pursue at length the inquiry of whether a cause of action lies in favor of a patient against a physician for wrongfully divulging confidential communications. For the purposes of what we shall say, it will be assumed that, for so palpable a wrong, the law provides a remedy."

An excellent and carefully researched opinion exploring the legal ramifications of this confidentiality is *Doe v Roe* (93 Misc 2d 201), a decision after a nonjury trial in which plaintiff sought injunctive relief and damages because of the verbatim publication by her former psychiatrist of extremely personal details of her life revealed during years of psychoanalysis. The court considered several proposed theories of recovery, including violation of public policy and breach of privacy rights. We agree with the court's observation that the several statutes and regulations requiring physicians to protect the confidentiality of information gained during treatment are clear evidence of the public policy of New York (see, e.g., CPLR 4504, subd [a]; 4507; Education Law, § 6509, subd [9]; 8 NYCRR 29.1 [b] [8]; Mental Hygiene Law, § 33.13, subds [c], [d]; Public Health Law, § 2803–c, subd 3, par f; § 2805–g, subd 3), but that there is a more appropriate theory of recovery than one rooted in public policy.

Neither do we believe that an action for breach of the right of privacy may be maintained despite some current predictions to the contrary.

Another instructive discussion of the legal consequences emanating from the physician-patient relationship is found in *Hammonds v Aetna Cas. & Sur. Co.* (243 F Supp 793), in which plaintiff sought damages from an insurance carrier for procuring his medical records from his physician by falsely representing that plaintiff was suing the physician for malpractice. Looking to Ohio law, the court found that such disclosure was contrary to the public policy of the State, evidence of which could be found in the medical code of ethics; the Ohio statute on privileged communications; and the Ohio licensing statute which prohibited betrayal of confidential information.

Attempting to fashion a remedy based on a traditional legal theory, the court discussed the contractual nature of the relationship: "Any time a doctor undertakes the treatment of a patient, and the consensual relationship of physician and patient is established, two jural obligations ... are simultaneously assumed by the doctor. Doctor and patient enter into a simple contract, the patient hoping that he will be cured and the doctor optimistically assuming that he will be compensated. As an implied condition of that contract, this Court is of the opinion that the doctor warrants that any confidential information gained through the relationship will not be released without the patient's permission. Almost every member of the public is aware of the promise of discretion contained in the Hippocratic Oath, and every patient has a right to rely upon this warranty of silence. The promise of secrecy is as much an express warranty as the advertisement of a commercial entrepreneur. Consequently, when a doctor breaches his duty of secrecy, he is in violation of part of his obligations under the contract." (*Hammonds v Aetna Cas. & Sur. Co., supra,* p 801.) The court then determined that from that contractual relationship arose a fiduciary obligation that confidences communicated by a patient should be held as a trust (*Hammonds v Aetna Cas. & Sur. Co., supra,* p 803).

That position was generally adopted by the court in *Doe v Roe* (93 Misc 2d 201, 210–211, *supra*), thus: "I too find that a physician, who enters into an agreement with a patient to provide medical attention, impliedly covenants to keep in confidence all disclosures made by the patient concerning the patient's physical or mental condition as well as all matters discovered by the physician in the course of examination or treatment. This is particularly and necessarily true of the psychiatric relationship, for in the dynamics of psychotherapy '[t]he patient is called upon to discuss in a candid and frank manner personal material of the most intimate and disturbing nature.' "There can be little doubt that under the law of the State of New York and in a proper case, the contract of private parties to retain in confidence matter which should be kept in confidence will be enforced by injunction and compensated in damages."

It is obvious then that this relationship gives rise to an implied covenant which, when breached, is actionable. If plaintiff's recovery were limited to an action for breach of contract, however, he would generally be limited to economic loss flowing directly from the breach (5 Corbin, Contracts, § 1019, at pp 113–115) and would thus be precluded from recovering for mental distress, loss of his employment and the deterioration of his marriage. We believe that the relationship contemplates an additional duty springing from but extraneous to the contract and that the breach of such duty is actionable as a tort. Indeed, an action in tort for a breach of a duty of confidentiality and trust has long been acknowledged in the courts of this State. In *Rich v New York Cent. & Hudson Riv. R. R. Co.* (87 NY 382) the court recognized that there was no clear line of demarcation between torts and breaches of contract: "Ordinarily, the essence of a tort consists in the violation of some duty due to an individual, which duty is a thing different from the mere contract obligation. When such duty grows out of relations of trust and confidence, as that of the agent to his principal or the lawyer to his client, the ground of the duty is apparent, and the tort is, in general, easily separable from the mere breach of contract."

The relationship of the parties here was one of trust and confidence out of which sprang a duty not to disclose. Defendant's breach was not merely a broken contractual promise but a violation of a fiduciary responsibility to plaintiff implicit in and essential to the doctor-patient relation.

Such duty, however, is not absolute, and its breach is actionable only if it is wrongful, that is to say, without justification or excuse. Although public policy favors the confidentiality described herein, there is a countervailing public interest to which it must yield in appropriate circumstances. Thus where a patient may be a danger to himself or others (see, e.g., *Tarasoff v Regents of Univ. of Cal.*, 17 Cal 3d 425; *Berry v Moench*, 8 Utah 2d 191; *Simonsen v Swenson*, 104 Neb 224), a physician is required to disclose to the extent necessary to protect a threatened interest. "The protective privilege ends where the public peril begins" (*Tarasoff v Regents of Univ. of Cal., supra*, at p 442).

Contending that disclosure here was justified because it was made only to plaintiff's wife, defendant relies on *Curry v Corn* (52 Misc 2d 1035) in support of that position. In that case the court found justifiable the disclosure of information to a husband by his wife's doctor who knew the information would be used by the husband in a pending matrimonial action. Even overlooking the shortcomings of that determination, it was based at least in part upon the husband's status as head of the marital household and responsible for his wife's debts. It is thus inapplicable here where it is the wife who sought disclosure and is outmoded in any event.

Although the disclosure of medical information to a spouse may be justified under some circumstances, a more stringent standard should apply with respect to psychiatric information. One spouse often seeks counseling concerning personal problems that may affect the marital relationship. To permit disclosure to the other spouse in the absence of an overriding concern would deter the one in need from obtaining the help required. Disclosure of confidential information by a psychiatrist to a spouse will be justified whenever there is a danger to the patient, the spouse or another person; otherwise information should not be disclosed without authorization. Justification or excuse will depend upon a showing of circumstances and competing interests which support the need to disclose (cf. *Berry v Moench*, 8 Utah 2d 191, *supra*). Because such showing is a matter of affirmative defense, defendant is not entitled to dismissal of the action.

■ SIMONS, J. P. (Concurring):

Plaintiff seeks in this action to recover from defendant, his psychiatrist, for defendant's allegedly unjustified and damaging disclosure of confidential information about plaintiff's condition to plaintiff's wife. The members of the court are agreed that he may do so and that the action sounds in tort. We are divided about the nature of the cause of action, however, the majority believing it to be a "breach of fiduciary duty to confidentiality," while I believe the cause of action to be for malpractice. The difference is one of substance, for the majority hold plaintiff may recover if he submits evidence of the professional relationship, the disclosure of confidential information and damages. Once plaintiff does so, it is for the doctor to offer evidence of justification and for the jury to weigh it. Plaintiff's right to recover, as they see it, rests on proof of an unauthorized disclosure, the breach of an implied promise to hold confidential information received during treatment. In my view, plaintiff's right to recover must rest upon his proof that the disclosure was wrongful or unjustified.

When a physician undertakes treatment of a patient, he impliedly represents that he possesses, and the law places upon him the duty of possessing, the reasonable degree of learning and skill possessed by physicians in the community generally. Culpable fault exists if the physician fails to live up to this standard. Confidentiality, particularly in the case of a psychiatrist, is a significant and important aspect of medical treatment and a promise of nondisclosure may readily be implied from the physician-patient relationship. Thus, the relationship has elements of a contract, as plaintiff's first cause of action suggests, but commonly malpractice is a tort action predicated upon the physician's violation of his duty to supply the quality of care promised when he undertook to treat the patient. The physician's duty to honor this implied promise of confidentiality is merely another aspect of the treatment rendered and should be judged similarly.

The majority, by taking the cause of action out of the malpractice area, hold that all unauthorized disclosures, prima facie, violate reasonable medical care. The disclosure may be excused only if defendant proves that it was precipitated by danger to the patient, spouse or another. No other disclosure is permissible, apparently, even if mandated by statute.

But further than that, the established rules of professional malpractice base liability upon an objective standard measured by the general quality of care of the professional community (see *Toth v Community Hosp. at Glen Cove*, 22 NY2d 255, 262). The rule advanced by the majority permits the standard of care in unauthorized disclosure cases to be set by the jury. Thus, in every case of disclosure, the physician is exposed to the danger of a damage verdict resting upon the jury's subjective view of his explanation of his conduct even if it was in accordance with accepted medical practice. Thus, a jury disbelieving a physician's evaluation that a patient is assaultive or suicidal may hold the physician liable for the most limited but necessary disclosure relating to such commonplace matters as advice to ensure that the patient takes prescribed medication or avoids stressful situations.

In short, to avoid a nonsuit, a plaintiff should submit evidence of more than an unauthorized disclosure by the physician. There should be evidence that the physician has engaged in the unskilled practice of medicine. The relationship between the parties, after all, is medical, not fiduciary. The doctor is hired to treat the patient and his liability, if any, should be predicated upon his failure to do so properly.

Notes

1. *The nature of the action: the full force of professional custom.* The *MacDonald* majority finds that an action for the unauthorized disclosure of confidential information is grounded in the very nature of the relationship between health care professionals and their patients and that a breach of such a relationship gives rise not simply to a breach of contract claim but to a tort claim because of the special fiduciary relationship that exists between patient and professional. It is this relationship that in turn creates a duty of confidentiality, particularly in sensitive relationships such as those between psychiatrists and their patients. The dissent, on the other hand, would base the action in malpractice, arguing that confidentiality goes to the standard of care. What is the effect of this position? In the concurrence's view, this would permit a defendant to introduce evidence of professional custom rather than being limited to a narrower range of disclosures recognized in law. It is this position that also was rejected in *Canterbury v. Spence* on the ground that in an informed consent case, professional custom holds no place where the custom of the profession is to withhold information from a patient. Here, too, the issue becomes the broader interests of society in protecting communications between patients and their treating health care professionals, even in cases in which, a

professional claims the right to exercise his or her own professional judgment over disclosures.

2. *Unauthorized disclosures.* Laws governing disclosures of confidential information also authorize certain types of disclosures. Thus, for example, a health care professional may (and in certain cases must) disclose confidential information when the safety of the patient or others may be in jeopardy. Disclosures may also be required as a matter of public policy, such as the disclosure of evidence of child abuse to law enforcement authorities following the examination of a child.

The question of whether physicians have a duty not to disclose information given to them in confidence can arise in numerous contexts. For example, in cases in which a physician supplies evidence against a patient by disclosing confidential information, the question is whether such disclosures violate the confidentiality of the physician-patient relationship. Where the answer to this question is in the affirmative, it is probably not long before jurisdictions will recognize the legal right of individuals harmed by such disclosures to sue for damages arising from a disclosure to which there has been no consent. See Joseph White, *Physicians' Liability for Breach of Confidentiality: Beyond the Limitations of the Privacy Tort,* 49 S.C. L. REV. 1271 (1998) (reviewing the evolution of South Carolina's tort and evidentiary laws to recognize a duty of confidentiality).

2. HEALTH INFORMATION PRIVACY: THE HIPAA PRIVACY RULE

In 2000 the United States Department of Health and Human Services published a Privacy Rule, 65 Fed. Reg. 82,462, 82,471 (Dec. 28, 2000), later modified in relatively minor respects in 2002, 67 Fed. Reg. 53,182 (Aug. 14, 2002). The Rule establishes a federal privacy regulatory policy and is an outgrowth of the Health Insurance Portability and Accountability Act of 1996 (HIPAA) (Pub. L. No. 104–191), whose insurance-related reforms were reviewed in Part Two. The Rule establishes no federal private right of action against unauthorized disclosures of "personal health information" ("PHI"). Peter Winn, *Confidentiality in Cyberspace: The HIPAA Privacy Rules and the Common Law,* 33 RUTGERS L.J. 617 (2002). At the same time, Professor Winn argues, the Privacy Rule in effect sets the stage for individual enforcement actions at common law:

> The failure of the HIPAA Privacy Rules to create a private federal remedy does not imply that the Rules will exist in a parallel federal universe with no influence on state common law doctrines. The HIPPA Privacy Rules, although federal, are likely to be adopted by state common law courts to establish a national minimum standard for liability for breach of confidentiality under state law. Like the HIPAA Privacy Rules, most early state statutes and ethical rules establishing a duty of confidentiality did not create a private right of action for their violation. However, these

apparently toothless statutes and ethical rules constituted the basis of the early cases establishing the common law tort of breach of confidentiality. While it does not appear likely that courts will use HIPAA to imply a federal private cause of action for breach of the Rules, it does appear that the minimum federal standard established by the HIPAA Privacy Rules are likely to be adopted in private state actions for breach of confidentiality as establishing the duty whose breach is the predicate for the underlying tort claim.

Id. at 619.

Official guidance on the Privacy Rule can be found at the website of the Office for Civil Rights within the United States Department of Health and Human Services, which is the federal agency charged with enforcement. The following materials provide an overview of the Rule:

The Health Insurance Portability and Accountability Act of 1996 directed the Secretary of Health and Human Services to promulgate regulations governing the privacy of health information if Congress failed to enact such legislation within 3 years. HIPAA also provided that, should such regulations become necessary, they should not supersede "more stringent" state law. Health Insurance Portability and Accountability Act of 1996, P.L. 104–191, Sec. 264(c)(2) (Aug. 21, 1996). "More stringent" was not defined in the Act. But in the implementing regulations a "more stringent" state law is defined as "in the context of a comparison of a provision of State law and a standard [under the HIPAA regulations], a State law that meets one or more of the following criteria: (1) with respect to a use or disclosure, the law prohibits or restricts a use or disclosure in circumstances under which such use or disclosure otherwise would be permitted [under the HIPAA regulations], except if the disclosure is [required by the Secretary of HHS to determine compliance with the HIPAA regulations] or to the individual who is the subject of the individually identifiable health information; . . . (4) With respect to the form, substance, or the need for express legal permission from an individual, who is the subject of the individually identifiable health information, for use or disclosure of individually identifiable health information, provides requirements that narrow the scope or duration, increase the privacy protections afforded . . ., or reduce the coercive effect of the circumstances surrounding the express legal permission, as applicable." 45 C.F.R. § 160.202.

When Congress failed to enact legislation, HHS promulgated the HIPAA Privacy Rule in accordance with the Act, creating a federal "floor" of privacy protections. Standards for Privacy of Individually Identifiable Health Information, Final Rule, 65 Fed. Reg. 82,462, 82,464 (Dec. 28, 2000). The Privacy Rule is in essence a grand balancing effort consisting of two independent balancing acts: balancing individuals' interest in health information privacy against the need for a free flow of information in a number of key contexts; and balancing the need for uniformity in privacy standards against the custom and practice [and] state law, on whose foundations the Privacy Rule rests. In this regard, HIPAA represents a market departure from ERISA preemption, which simply swept away state regulatory law in its path without laying down any content of its own.

The Privacy Rule applies to "covered health care entities," which consist of health plans, health care clearinghouses, or health care providers who transmit any health information in electronic form for certain administrative purposes. 45 C.F.R. §§ 160.102(a), 164.500 [In 2009 the Rule was extended to entities known as Business Associates as well]. The Privacy Rule affords protection to individually identifiable health information (called "protected health information") held by these entities. With very limited exceptions, the Privacy Rule does not distinguish between types of data. The Rule does, however, recognize that existing federal and state privacy and confidentiality laws accord great protection for certain types of health information and leaves these laws undisturbed.

In general, the Privacy Rule permits a covered entity to use and disclose protected health information for certain core purposes, including for treatment, payment and health care operations, without an individual's written permission (called "consent").* However, the Rule also recognizes professional traditions and ethical obligations by permitting covered entities to obtain consent to use and disclose health information for these core purposes as part of their privacy policies. The Rule establishes no format or content requirements for consent.

For most purposes, including payment and health care operations, the Rule limits covered entities' uses, disclosures, and requests from other covered entities of protected health information to the minimum amount necessary to accomplish the intended purpose of the use or disclosure. 45 C.F.R. §§ 164.502(b), 164.508. However, the minimum necessary rule does not apply to requests for or disclosures of protected health information for treatment purposes. The Privacy Rule does however impose the minimum necessary requirement on internal uses of protected health information, generally requiring a covered entity to identify the individuals within the organization who need access to such information to perform their duties and to limit their access to the type and amount of information needed. See 45 C.F.R. § 164.514(d)(2). This

* The Privacy Rule distinguishes between written permission to use and disclose protected health information for treatment, payment and health care operations (called "consent") and written permission to use and disclose protected health information for other purposes. In the latter case, the written permission is called an "authorization" and must meet specific format and content requirements. See 45 C.F.R. §§ 164.506(b) and 164.508.

means that for treatment purposes, providers can share any information they determine necessary, while internal management activities are governed by more rigorous "need to know" provisions.

Covered entities may also use and disclose protected health information without an individual's written permission for other purposes closely related to the provision of care and, subject to conditions, for other national priority purposes. There are over a dozen fairly broad categories for which health information can be used and disclosed without written permission. Among the most important are the following: First, covered entities are free to disclose protected health information to the individual who is the subject of the information without authorization. 45 C.F.R. § 164.502(a)(2)(i). Second, when the individual has been given an opportunity to agree or object, for example regarding disclosures to family members or others involved in the care of the individual, no authorization is needed. 45 C.F.R. § 164.510. This also includes facility directories, for notification purposes, in limited situations when the individual is not present, and for disaster relief purposes. Third, no authorization is needed when the use or disclosure is "incident to" an otherwise permitted use and disclosure, meaning that a secondary use or disclosure stems from an otherwise permitted one. 45 C.F.R. § 164.502(a)(1)(iii). Fourth, covered entities are permitted to use and disclose protected health information without an individual's authorization for a variety of national priority purposes including for health care oversight, public health, research, law enforcement and when required by other law. 45 C.F.R. § 164.512.

With respect to using and disclosing protected health information for purposes other than treatment, payment, and health care operations, or the exceptions noted above, the Rule requires that entities obtain written permission (called "authorizations") from patients. These permissions must meet specific content and format requirements.

[P]sychotherapy notes are covered by this special authorization rule. "Psychotherapy notes" are "notes recorded (in any medium) by a health care provider who is a mental health professional documenting or analyzing the contents of conversation during a private counseling session or a group, joint, or family counseling session and that are separated from the rest of the individual's medical record. Psychotherapy notes exclude medication prescription and monitoring, counseling session start and stop times, the modalities and frequencies of treatment furnished, results of clinical tests, and any summary of the following items: diagnosis, functional status, the treatment plan, symptoms, prognosis, and progress to date." 45 C.F.R. § 164.501. This special rule applies to Psychotherapy notes even though such notes arguably relate to treatment, payment, and health care operations, and should therefore be covered by the general disclosure rule. HIPAA accords these notes greater protection in deference to longstanding legal and policy concerns and professional custom.

The Rule also sets forth the essential elements of an authorization. 45 C.F.R § 164.508(c). Authorizations must be written in plain language and contain: a specific and meaningful description of the information to be disclosed or used; the name or specific identification of the person(s) authorized to disclose the information; the name or specific identification of the person(s) to whom the information can be disclosed; a description of each purpose of the requested use or disclosure; an expiration date or event; the signature of the individual and date; and required statements to place the individual on notice of his/her rights, including the right to revoke consent.

For routine disclosures of protected health information to a third party who performs business functions for a covered entity, the covered entity must enter into an agreement with the "business associate." A business associate is a person or organization who, on behalf of the covered entity, but "other than in the capacity of a member of the workforce of such covered entity or arrangement" performs "a function or activity involving the use or disclosure of individually identifiable health information, including claims processing or administration, data analysis, processing or administration, utilization review, quality assurance, billing, benefit management, practice management and repricing ..." or "legal, actuarial, accounting, consulting, data aggregation, management, administrative, accreditation, or financial services to or for such covered entity." 45 C.F.R. § 160.103. Such agreements must include assurances that the business associate will appropriately safeguard protected health information. 45 C.F.R.§ 164.502(e).

HIPAA regulates provider conduct but creates no new and independent federal individual legal right to privacy. The regulations have been upheld as constitutional, Association of American Physicians & Surgeons, Inc. v. U.S. Dept. Of Health and Human Services, 224 F. Supp.2d 1115, 194 A.L.R. Fed. 711 (S.D. Tex. 2002); aff'd, 67 Fed. Appx. 252 (5th Cir. 2003), and its routine disclosure provisions have also been upheld as constitutional. Citizens for Health v. Leavitt, 428 F.3d 167 (3d Cir. 2005).

* * *

HIPAA's Relationship to State Law

HIPAA does not operate in a vacuum. Instead, it is a part of a complex fabric of federal and state laws that govern privacy and the confidentiality of patient information. The framework of the HIPAA Rule essentially establishes a "roadmap" for reconciling this legal diversity. Sara Rosenbaum et al., *Does HIPAA Preemption Pose a Legal Barrier to Health Information Transparency and Interoperability?* 15(11) BNA HEALTH CARE

Pol'y Report, ER (Mar. 19, 2007). This "roadmap" can be summarized as follows:

First, HIPAA generally preempts state laws that are "contrary to" it. A state law is contrary to the HIPAA Privacy Rule when it would be impossible to comply with both the state and federal requirements or when the provisions of the state law would be an obstacle to the accomplishment and execution of the HIPAA Privacy Rule. *See* 45 C.F.R. § 160.202. HIPAA permits covered entities to comply with state disclosure laws and disclose information without patient consent under a permissive disclosure standard. 45 C.F.R. 164.512(a).

Second, HIPAA also specifies that its standards do not supersede a contrary provision of state law, if the provision of state law imposes requirements, standards, or implementation specifications that are "more stringent than" HIPAA's own standards. Pub. L. No. 104–191 § 264(c)(2). In essence, HIPAA sets a conduct "floor" where privacy is concerned. State laws that accord greater privacy protections—those that either provide individuals greater access to their own records or contain more restrictive use and disclosure requirements—are considered "more stringent than" HIPAA.

Third, HIPAA does not preempt mandatory state reporting laws that require reporting of various types of information, including but not limited to, disease, injury, child abuse, public health surveillance, and health plan requirements such as management or financial audits. 45 C.F.R. § 160.203(d).

A 2006 review of nearly 500 judicial opinions interpreting the HIPAA privacy rule shows the great range of questions that can arise under this roadmap outlining the relationship between HIPAA and state laws. Rosenbaum et al., *Does HIPAA Preemption Pose a Legal Barrier to Health Information Transparency and Interoperability?* These cases do not deal with provider-to-provider exchange of health information for treatment reasons. Instead they focus on the disgorgement of patient information as part of the legal process, such as a state law governing malpractice litigation (where one side is attempting to discover treatment records concerning a party to the suit), or a federal or state criminal subpoena. In these cases, providers may raise HIPAA as a defense as a means of shielding information that could hurt their position or their patients. The question in these cases becomes whether HIPAA or state law controls; where state law is "more stringent" it will apply, but in the absence of state law, the HIPAA rule—i.e., that the health care entity generally has discretion over whether or not to produce evidence—will apply. Furthermore, although state laws do not apply to federal legal proceedings, HIPAA itself may create a shield against disclosure unless it is the provider's custom to disclose.

For a review of the special privacy laws that come into play when substance abuse is present, see J. Zoe Beckerman et al., *Health Information Privacy, Patient Safety, and Health Care Quality: Issues and Challenges in the Context of Treatment for Mental Illness and Substance Abuse*, 16(2) BNA HEALTH CARE POL'Y REPORT (Jan. 14, 2008).

Notes

1.   Legal standards to assure health information privacy represent an important dimension of implementing a national framework that is expected to spur increased use of health information technology and electronic health records and transactions. *See generally* Deven McGraw, *Privacy and Health Information Technology*, O'NEILL INSTITUTE FOR NATIONAL AND GLOBAL HEALTH LAW (2009). National health reform has intensified the pressure to move the U.S. health care system, by means of health information technology (HIT), to one that is built on the use of electronic health records (EHRs). The use of EHRs represents a strategy to improve quality and efficiency, goals sought by virtually all wealthy nations with national health insurance systems. Commonwealth Fund, *Health Care Spending and Use of Information Technology, in OECD Countries* (2006). The diffusion of HIT in the U.S. was potentially aided by 2009 amendments to the Social Security Act financially to incentivize HIT adoption by certain Medicare and Medicaid providers. American Reinvestment and Recovery Act 0f 2009, Pub. L. No. 111–5 §§ 4101–4201 (111th Cong. 1st Sess.). These legislative incentives were enacted in the face of substantial evidence of low HIT adoption rates in the U.S. Ashish Jha et al., *The Use of Electronic Health Records in U.S. Hospitals*, 360 NEW ENG. J. MED. 1628 (2009); Catherine Des Roches, *Electronic Records in Ambulatory Care*, 359 NEW ENG. J. MED. 50 (2008).

At the same time, EHRs make information previously buried in health care provider-owned paper medical records vastly more accessible, thereby elevating the potential for privacy breaches, not to mention greater scrutiny of medical practice generally. *See* Sara Rosenbaum & Michael Painter, *When New is Old: Professional Liability in the Information Age, in* MEDICAL PROFESSIONALISM IN THE NEW INFORMATION AGE (David J. Rothman & David Blumenthal, eds., 2010). As a result, pressure has grown to assure heightened privacy and security safeguards for an electronic information age. At the core of HIPAA is the power of covered entities to use information without consent (in most instances) for "treatment, payment, and business operations." Government agencies also are given broad authority under law to gain access to personal information held in electronic format. These exceptions under the rule allow widespread access to health information by employer-sponsored health plans and public insurers and create an inevitable tension between the potential gains from widespread adoption of HIT and individual rights. McGraw, *Privacy and Health Information Technology. See also* Sharona Hoffman & Andy Podgurski, *Finding a Cure: The Case for Regulation and Oversight of Electronic Health Record Systems*, 22 HARV. J.L. & TECH. 104 (2008) (arguing for a broad EHR federal regulatory framework because of EHRs' potential to not merely record information but actually affect clinical practice through decision-support functions).

Thus, in addition to incentivizng HIT adoption, the American Recovery and Reinvestment Act of 2009 (ARRA), Pub. L. No. 111–5, also makes various changes to the HIPAA Privacy Rule as a means of strengthening the rule in advance of a major national investment in health information technology (HIT). Chief among the reforms are stronger enforcement requirements, extension of the Privacy Rule to business associates with access to data but not themselves covered entities, and clarification of the right of individuals who pay for treatment in cash to withhold consent to the disclosure of information for purposes of payment or health care operations. Pub. L. No. 111–5, §§ 13401–13405.

2. *Health care corporate compliance.* The tension between access to data and individual privacy also raises corporate compliance concerns for health care entities. *See* Linda A. Malek & Jay D. Meisel, *Electronic and Personal Health Records: The Risks and Benefits for Providers* 17(16) HEALTH LAW REPORTER (BNA) 555 (April 17, 2008). Malek and Singer note that during a single hospital stay, as many as 150 people have access to a patient's medical records and an estimated 600,000 separate payers. Additionally, health information data warehouses have access to individual health information. All of these people are authorized to view records. Corporate concerns are intense even though the United States Department of Health and Human Services exercises what might be charitably termed anemic oversight of HIPAA Privacy Rule compliance; despite lax federal oversight, state laws pose a major source of potential liability, particularly in the case of highly sensitive information such as information on mental illness, substance abuse, and conditions that are perceived as carrying stigma, such as HIV or other sexually transmitted diseases.

3. *Private enforcement rights.* The HIPAA Privacy Rule creates no independent enforceable rights according to virtually every court that has considered the matter. *See* Acara v. Banks, 470 F.3d 569, 571–72 (5th Cir. 2006); Doe v. Board of Trustees of University of Illinois, 429 F. Supp.2d 930, 944 (N.D. Ill. 2006); Dominic J. v. Wyoming Valley West High School, 362 F. Supp.2d 560, 573 (M.D. Pa. 2005); Logan v. Department of Veterans Affairs, 357 F. Supp.2d 149, 155 (D.D.C. 2004); University of Colorado Hosp. v. Denver Pub. Co., 340 F. Supp.2d 1142, 1145 (D. Colo. 2004); Spencer v. Roche, 755 F. Supp.2d 250 (D. Mass. 2010).

Federal HIPAA enforcement is very limited because of significant resource constraints. In this light, the HIPAA Privacy Rule can best be thought of as a series of rules meant to move medical custom and practice toward greater vigilance over patient privacy in the face of technology that enables far greater access to sensitive information.

CHAPTER 17

MEDICAL LIABILITY AND THE POLITICS OF LEGAL CHANGE

1. INTRODUCTION

Over the past century, health care liability law has shifted from the protection of physicians to greater protection of patients. In response, physicians, other health care providers, and the malpractice insurance industry have sought to shield themselves through the enactment of state laws that accomplish two basic goals: first, the creation of legal, financial, and practical barriers to instituting liability actions; and second, disincentivizing such actions by significantly reducing recoverable amounts. Some of these shielding efforts appear to have been effective in curbing claims, particularly the establishment of caps on the size of noneconomic damages that juries can award. At the same time, it is not evident whether the claims that have been curbed are those that, as suggested by the Harvard study discussed earlier in this Part, might be considered non-meritorious because evidence of negligence is lacking. Furthermore, of course, simply shielding physicians, hospitals, and other providers from exposure to costly litigation does nothing to address the basic problem of assuring adequate care and support for individuals who have experienced preventable and serious injuries as a result of the conduct of health care providers. Nor does reducing liability exposure do anything to assure that preventable errors are swiftly addressed through corrective actions or that health care professionals and institutions whose performance is substandard are quickly dealt with in order to reduce the risk of future death or injury. Indeed, as you will read in the materials on licensure and accreditation below, while the health care industry has become far more engaged in patient safety and health care quality, effective and swift interventions are lacking, whether through governmental action or industry sanction.

In considering medical liability reform, several questions arise. First, what is the magnitude of the medical liability problem? Second, how might the liability system be reformed to reduce the likelihood of frivolous cases while nonetheless permitting significant actions to proceed? Third, should the liability system be replaced? Rather than relying on tort principles that employ private enforcement and the concepts of fault and damages, should injury compensation be carried out through another type of system, such as a no-fault arrangement coupled with rapid interventions to address preventable injuries?

2.   WHAT IS THE NATURE AND EXTENT OF THE MEDICAL LIABILITY PROBLEM?

There have been periodic assertions of a medical liability "crisis" particularly in the latter part of the 20th century. The first wave of "crisis" claims appeared in the 1970s, as courts took a more expansive view of liability through modifications of the basic common law principles that underlay professional and (as you will see later in this Part) institutional negligence. As the professional standard of care was broadened to move beyond mere local custom, the testimony of national experts became permissible, and long-standing legal barriers to claims against hospitals began to come down, the health care industry—physicians, hospitals, and malpractice insurers—inevitably faced more frequent claims and claims of greater size and scope (i.e., a rise in incidence and severity). Ken Thorpe, *The Medical Malpractice 'Crisis': Recent Trends and the Impact of State Tort Reforms*, HEALTH AFFAIRS (Web Exclusive) W4 (Jan. 21, 2004). This trend, coupled with falling rates of return on insurers' premium investments, caused a number of insurers to exit the market while simultaneously leading to a rise in self-insuring entities and physician-owned companies. The second "crisis" wave of the 1980s led to a rise in state laws to reform and limit medical liability cases. The third wave, which occurred early in the 21st century, has created greater momentum for state reform while also triggering new rounds of federal reform proposals.

Professor Frank Sloan, a leading economic expert in the field of medical liability who advocates retention of a fault system but one that is more fairly balanced, writes of "five myths" associated with medical malpractice:

Myth 1:	There are too many medical malpractice claims.
Myth 2:	Only "good" doctors are sued.
Myth 3:	Dispute resolution in medical malpractice is a lottery.
Myth 4:	Medical malpractice claimants are overcompensated for their losses.
Myth 5:	Medical care is costly because of medical malpractice.

FRANK A. SLOAN & LINDSEY M. CHEPKE, MEDICAL MALPRACTICE (2008).

Professor Sloan's description of these myths is based on in considerable empirical research that has led him to conclude that claims of crisis are significantly inaccurate, while the remedies simply shield health care providers without fundamentally assuring that economic incentives are deployed to promote patient safety and quality.

As for the first myth, Professor Sloan notes that two major studies (the Harvard study carried out in New York State in the 1980s and a similar study conducted in California) found a vast gap between the incidence of negligence-caused injury and medical liability claims (only 2 percent of negligence-caused injuries in the New York study led to any malpractice claim). Thus, while both studies showed significant numbers of "invalid" claims (i.e., claims where records showed no evidence of negligence), the proportion of such claims was exceeded by the large number of valid claims that went unfiled. SLOAN & CHEPKE, MEDICAL MALPRACTICE at 17–19.

Myth 2, according to Professor Sloan, is belied by the fact that the evidence drawn from litigation shows that the physicians who are sued are neither better nor worse than other physicians and furthermore that, contrary to assertions from the medical profession, being a cutting-edge and technological innovator does not expose physicians to greater liability. *Id.* at 81–83. Indeed, while past adverse claims are the best predictor of future claims, the evidence suggests that the quality of care from physicians who have been the subject of more frequent adverse claims is not distinguishable from that of other physicians.

With regard to myths 3 and 4, the evidence shows that the outcomes of legal disputes do in fact show a relationship, although imperfect, to independent assessments of liability and injury cost. Furthermore, the evidence shows that malpractice claimants tend to be under- rather than overcompensated. Finally, Professor Sloan notes, the medical liability system adds to the overall cost of health care, but the additional costs are modest.

Professor Sloan's fifth myth, regarding the modest nature of liability costs, was reinforced by 2011 cost estimates prepared by the Congressional Budget Office for the Help Efficient, Accessible, Low-cost, Timely Healthcare (HEALTH) Act of 2011, a bill that would have imposed preemptive federal legal curbs on medical liability litigation including a $250,000 cap on noneconomic damages. CBO estimated that total savings to the federal health care budget, including Medicare, Medicaid, and tax expenditures linked to the exclusion from income of employer-sponsored health insurance premium payments would amount to about $50 billion over 10 years. CBO COST ESTIMATE (May 4, 2011). This figure pales in comparison with total projected federal spending for Medicare, Medicaid, and employer-sponsored coverage of more than $10 trillion over the same time period.

The description of the medical liability "crisis" as myth has been reinforced by the earliest studies to address the problem. In response to the first round of "crisis" claims, including assertions that medical liability exposure led to "defensive medicine" (i.e., tests and services not actually needed by patients but provided by doctors in the belief that such services would help avoid malpractice liability), the Secretary of Health, Education & Welfare established a Commission on Medical Malpractice in 1970 to investigate the entire system. The Commission's findings, issued in 1972, infuriated the American Medical Association by refuting the doctors' claims of a "crisis."

The Commission found that a large number of physician-caused injuries for which claims were never made; that 75 percent of jury verdicts were for the defendant; that malpractice insurance was available, albeit at rising premiums; that most hospitals had experienced little litigation; that defensive medicine was widely believed to exist but impossible to measure, because of difficulties in identifying services provided solely or primarily to avoid legal liability; and that state licensing agencies had little authority, staff, or inclination to discipline incompetent or "impaired" (alcoholic, drug-addicted, or mentally-ill) physicians. Indeed, the Commission's report revealed an actual or incipient "crisis" very different from the one asserted by doctors: that of a medical malpractice system that fails to compensate enough patients or effectively penalize the relatively small number of doctors responsible for a disproportionate share of injuries and claims.

Despite the HEW Commission's findings, by 1975 the American Medical Association was able to persuade state legislatures that a "crisis" existed and that statutory change was necessary. The basis for its success was an alarming rise in malpractice insurance premiums, coupled with threatened or actual withdrawal of companies from the malpractice insurance market. (A similar spike in malpractice insurance premiums has tended to precede subsequent federal and state legislative efforts to curtail liability litigation). *See* LAW & POLAN, PAIN AND PROFIT 166 (describing premium rises of 82 and 93 percent in North Carolina and New York in 1974); *see also* Glen Robinson, *The Medical Malpractice Crisis of the 1970s: A Retrospective*, 49 LAW & CONTEMP. PROBS. 5, 7–9 (Spring 1986) (noting that malpractice insurance premiums increased from 1960 to 1972 from an average of 600 to 900 percent in different risk categories).

Although the reality of the crisis was not in dispute, a sharp debate arose regarding its nature and causes. The American Medical Association, and the insurance industry, argued that plaintiffs' lawyers, hungry for contingent fees, brought unjustified suits, and that allegedly liberalized malpractice law (e.g., easier qualification of expert witnesses following abandonment of the locality rule, expanded use of *res ipsa loquitur*, and patient-oriented informed consent) made it all too easy for lay juries to render unjustified and excessive verdicts for plaintiffs. This analysis led predictably to calls for legislative restrictions of plaintiffs' rights and remedies, including limitations on plaintiffs' attorneys' contingent fees. The American Trial Lawyers Association (ATLA), representing the plaintiffs' bar, responded that doctors had failed totally to discipline their own ranks, either through state licensing boards or through in-hospital peer review, and that existing malpractice law was one of the few protections against widespread substandard care. Predictably, the ATLA also attacked the costs generated by defense lawyers. Some independent analysts agreed that doctors had done little to deter malpractice, and also pointed to the unregulated and cyclical nature of the malpractice insurance industry, in which companies set unrealistically low premiums to collect capital for investment, and then radically raise premiums or abandoned the market when investment strategies falter. *See* LAW & POLAN, PAIN AND PROFIT at 161–95.

In their examination of medical liability, Michelle Mello and David Studdert note that although many types of health professionals may be liable for malpractice, physicians are the "primary targets" of malpractice claims. Michelle M. Mello & David M. Studdert, *The Medical Malpractice System: Structure and Performance, in* MEDICAL MALPRACTICE AND THE U.S.

HEALTH CARE SYSTEM 12 (William M. Sage & Rogan Kersh, eds., 2006). The authors report that the as of 2003, the average payout among paid claims ranged between $160,000 and $200,000. *Id.* at 13 (much research into the field of malpractice is based on legal claims for recovery that have been filed or that have been resolved in some manner and closed). A United States Department of Justice report examining medical malpractice claims between 2000 and 2004 and using data collected from seven states that require malpractice insurers to report claims information, also confirms the limited nature of recoveries. Researchers found that "most medical malpractice claims were closed without any compensation" provided to injury claimants (between 12 percent and one third of all claims resulted in any payout in the reporting states), and that a small proportion of claims with any payouts had payouts of $1 million or higher. Thomas Cohen & Kristen Hughes, Medical Malpractice Insurance Claims in Seven States, 2000–2004, at 1 (U.S. Department of Justice, March 2007, NCJ 216339).

Claims payouts are not the only means of measuring the impact of liability law, however. First, although very difficult to measure accurately and susceptible to exaggeration, the risk of liability does appear to elevate clinician concern and lead to "defensive medicine". Mello & Studdert, *The Medical Malpractice System* at 23–25; Frank M. Studdert et al., *Medical Malpractice*, 350 NEW ENG. J. MED. (2004). Second, liability risk may have effects on physician behavior, leading to what Mello and Studdert term "bristling" and "cloaking" behaviors (i.e., suspicion and distrust or a refusal to share information that would permit a full discussion of error and improvements in patient safety). Mello & Studdert, *The Medical Malpractice System* at 25–27. *See* U.S. GOV'T ACCOUNTABILITY OFFICE, GAO–03–836, MEDICAL MALPRACTICE: IMPLICATIONS OF RISING PREMIUMS ON ACCESS TO HEALTH CARE (August 2003) (finding little evidence of widespread avoidance behavior but spot problems by geographic region and sub-specialty).

Having medical liability insurance is a condition of health care practice. Health professionals who practice in federal institutions or federally funded entities such as the Veterans Administration, the Indian Health Service and its physician contractors, and community health centers are insured under the Federal Tort Claims Act (FTCA), 28 U.S.C. § 1346(b), which waives sovereign immunity to allow liability recoveries for economic damages as well as limited liability for noneconomic damages. State and local health departments and community public hospitals similarly are covered under comparable state sovereign immunity waivers. Savings to the health centers program from self-funded coverage offered by the U.S., rather than commercial insurance, are estimated to run about $100 million annually, which translates into comprehensive primary health care for nearly 1 million low-income uninsured patients.

Private liability insurance can be costly, and evidence suggests that insurers raise their rates in response to various events, including losses on premiums, changes in investment income, and rising reinsurance rates. U.S. GOV'T ACCOUNTABILITY OFFICE, GAO 03–702, MEDICAL MALPRACTICE INSURANCE: MULTIPLE FACTORS HAVE CONTRIBUTED TO INCREASED PREMIUM RATES (June

2003). At the same time, an analysis of malpractice insurance premiums in Massachusetts, using data from the National Practitioner Data Bank, established by the Health Care Quality Improvement Act, found that even in a high risk state for malpractice claims, when adjusted for inflation, premiums paid by most physicians in 2005 were lower than the levels paid in 1990. Mark Rodwin et. al., *Malpractice Premiums in Massachusetts, a High Risk State: 1975 to 2005*, 27(3) HEALTH AFFAIRS 835 (2008). The authors note that previous studies conducted by the AMA between 1970 and 2000 show stable premiums, with costs averaging about 7% of practice costs for most physicians and 12.7% for OB/GYN physicians. Because the incomes of obstetricians are considerably higher however, this higher proportional payment did not threaten the viability of their practices. *Id.* at 835–36.

Recoveries involve several different types of compensation: recovery for economic losses (e.g., medical care, long-term treatment and services, lost wages); and non-economic damages for pain and suffering or to impose punishment in cases involving particularly egregious conduct. But despite the types of compensation that *might* be available, whether injured persons ever recover anything is a different question entirely. Evidence from three major studies of compensation show that the proportion of injured patients who actually recover is extremely small in relation to the prevalence of actual injury. Mello & Studdert, *The Medical Malpractice System* at 15–17. Collectively the studies, which focused on hospital inpatient injury, found that only a small proportion of patients suffered the types of injuries for which a negligence recovery might have been warranted (about 1 percent of cases). However, the studies also found that only 2 percent of persons whose injuries appeared connected to negligence ever filed a negligence action and moreover, that only about one sixth of these claimants ever recovered anything. In addition, the studies found that while claims may be filed in cases with no evidence of negligence, those whose injuries are found to be related to negligent conduct are more likely to file claims than individuals whose records show no evidence of negligence. *Id.*

In sum, the result is a system that may cost money (a figure estimated at 2.4 percent of total health care spending in 2008 dollars, Michelle Mello et. al., *National Costs of the Medical Liability System*, 29(9) HEALTH AFFAIRS 1569 (2010)), but not ruinous costs. The system appears to trigger various forms of undesirable conduct (in particular, shielding and secretive behavior) on the part of health professionals and health care institutions. It also deters broader system reforms aimed at quickly identifying, publicly reporting, and correcting errors, as well as compensating patients for injuries that are the result of medical errors (preventable or otherwise). Of every dollar spent on medical liability insurance, only 40% ever reaches injured patients. The rest is consumed by attorneys' fees and insurance overhead. Mello & Studdert, *The Medical Malpractice System* at 22. By contrast, the amount of funding allocated to claimants in non-judicial compensation systems is on the order of 70–90%. *Id.*

In her review of major malpractice liability studies Professor Michelle Mello, a leading medical liability researcher, finds that several show a significant relationship between the malpractice litigation climate (as measured by insurance premiums, claims frequency and state claims payment) and physician supply, while others do not. Robert Wood Johnson Foundation, *Medical Malpractice: Impact of the Crisis and Effect of State Tort Reforms* (2008). The studies vary in the extent to which they are able to control for other market changes that also may affect physician supply, such as certain types of insurer conduct, hospital closures, and the like. Her findings also suggest that the evidence on whether malpractice affects the supply of certain specialists is unclear, but also that defensive medicine, while difficult to measure, may become more common as physicians sense themselves to be in a heightened malpractice environment.

Reporting on state malpractice reforms, Professor Mello finds that as of 2008, 26 states had placed caps on damages, particularly in the case of noneconomic damages. Other than damages caps, whose efficacy is mixed, as shown in research, other reforms such as limits on attorney's fees, shortened statutes of limitations, and structured claims payouts, appear to have had little effect. According to Professor Mello, the research on damages caps suggest that they reduce the size of the awards but not their frequency and may have a small positive effect on physician supply. For an empirical study which found that such "caps" reduced malpractice awards by 19 percent within two years of enactment, see PATRICIA DANZON, THE FREQUENCY AND SEVERITY OF MEDICAL MALPRACTICE CLAIMS, Rand R–2870–ICJ/HCFA (1982) (cited in U.S. GENERAL ACCOUNTING OFFICE, MEDICAL MALPRACTICE: NO AGREEMENT ON PROBLEMS OR SOLUTIONS 19 (1986)).

Aside from their effects on malpractice premiums, Sylvia Law and Steve Polan argue that

> as a matter of principle, laws restricting the amounts recoverable by seriously injured patients are outrageous. The actions of many people contribute to the malpractice crisis: doctors, hospitals, lawyers, insurance companies, and perhaps patients who press frivolous claims. No one suggests that the crisis is caused by patients who suffer very serious injuries. Although we all ultimately pay for soaring malpractice premiums through rising health care costs, it seems grossly unjust to impose a disproportionate share of these costs on people who are unfortunate enough to be seriously injured as a result of negligent medical treatment.

LAW & POLAN, PAIN AND PROFIT. *See also* Abraham & Weiler, *Enterprise Medical Liability* at 405 (opposing fixed-dollar caps on total tort recoveries or on pain and suffering awards "because of their disparate impact on patients who have suffered the most severe injuries from negligent treatment," while proposing "pain and suffering damages guidelines" that would constrain jury discretion).

The AMA and others argue that jury assessments of damages, particularly for noneconomic injuries, are inherently untrustworthy and must be limited by strict rules. Aside from its debatable premises and conclusions,* the problem with this argument is that while some legislatures applied it to medical malpractice cases, many state courts, with apparent legislative acquiescence, simultaneously expanded the power of juries to award damages for emotional and other non-physical and noneconomic injuries in other types of torts cases, such as accidents and products liability. *See* David Smith, *Battling a Receding Tort Frontier: Constitutional Attacks on Medical Malpractice Laws*, 38 OKLA. L. REV. 797 (1985). Reflecting these tensions, at least six state courts found medical malpractice damages limitations to be in violation of state constitutions. See, *e.g.*, Lucas v. United States, 757 S.W.2d 687 (Tex. 1988); Carson v. Maurer, 424 A.2d 825 (N.H. 1980); Smith v. Department of Insurance, 507 So.2d 1080 (Fla. 1987).

One method of reducing medical liability litigation is to curb the willingness of physicians to act as expert witnesses for plaintiffs. As you have learned from the cases presented in this Part, expert testimony regarding the professional standard of care and its breach is a basic dimension of a professional liability case. In response to the willingness of physicians to act as experts against other physicians, at least 18 separate medical societies had, as of 2009, instituted boards of conduct to investigate members who agree to serve as witnesses, while others were considering it. These boards take complaints only from members; hence, as a practical matter it is not possible for an injured plaintiff to file a complaint with a board over the conduct of a defense expert who mischaracterized the professional standard of care or its breach. Aaron S. Kesselheim & David Studdert, *Professional Oversight of Physician Witnesses: An Analysis of Complaints to the Professional Conduct Committee of the American Association of Neurological Surgeons, 1992–2006*, 249 ANNALS OF SURGERY 1168 (2009). The authors of this study found, probably not surprisingly, that the most common complaint (about two-thirds of the total) received by the neurosurgery board was a misrepresentation of the standard of care, characterized by the authors as "presentation of testimony contrary to the broad spectrum of neurosurgical practice." *Id.* at 170. Approximately one third of all complaints filed were dismissed in preliminary review, while 68% led to some action by the board, in some cases, expulsion. Overwhelmingly, the primary defendant in a case was the source of the complaint that led to the investigation. The society's oversight system has itself been the subject of litigation, and while the courts have expressed concerns about the inherent unfairness of a system that sanctions only plaintiffs' experts, the sanctions have been upheld. *Id. See, e.g.*, Austin v. American Association of Neurological Surgeons, 253 F.3d 967 (7th Cir. 2001).

---

* See NEIL VIDMAR, MEDICAL MALPRACTICE AND THE AMERICAN JURY: CONFRONTING THE MYTHS ABOUT JURY INCOMPETENCE, DEEP POCKETS, AND OUTRAGEOUS DAMAGE AWARDS (1995); Neil Vidmar, *Are Juries Competent To Decide Liability in Tort Cases Involving Scientific/Medical Issues? Some Data from Medical Malpractice*, 43 Emory L.J. 885 (1994); Neil Vidmar, The Unfair Criticism of Medical Malpractice Juries, 76 JUDICATURE 118 (1992); Michael Rustad & Thomas Koenig, *Reconceptualizing Punitive Damages in Medical Malpractice: Targeting Amoral Corporations, Not "Moral Monsters,"* 47 RUTGERS L. REV. 975 (1995).

3.   FIXING THE MEDICAL LIABILITY "CRISIS"

Several strategies might be pursued to address the problem of medical liability.

No-fault systems

One approach might be to move to a no-fault compensation model that would provide controlled payments for the economic (medical, lost earnings) consequences of injury, coupled with effective and swift actions to reduce the risk of future injury through investigation and corrective action. In the case of injuries caused by vaccines, Congress enacted a no-fault compensation system in 1986 in order to avert market exit by vaccine manufacturers. National Vaccine Injury Act of 1986, 42 U.S.C. § 300aa–10 et. seq. The Act provides compensation in accordance with a Vaccine Injury Schedule of recognized adverse reactions, while leaving persons alleging injuries with the ability to reject a compensation order and pursue private liability claims. Claimants who demonstrate a listed injury within an appropriate window of time in relation to receipt of a vaccination may recover without proof of causation. Compensation includes medical costs, special education and social costs, vocational training, and diminished earnings. Deaths are compensated at $250,000. Claimants need not show defects in the design or manufacturing of vaccines, because the law displaces design and manufacturing defects as the basis of recovery. The Act has been upheld against legal challenges attempting to limit its preemptive effects. Bruesewitz v. Wyeth LLC, 131 S. Ct. 1068 (2011).

Improving on a fault-based system

A second approach might be to reform the existing fault-based liability system to create incentives for more rapidly separating claims that are meritorious from those that lack real merit, while encouraging prompt resolution and settlement. Litigants could be required to present their claims to special administrative bodies empowered to halt further action if the evidence is deemed insufficient to at least make out a prima facie claim for a jury. U.S. GOV'T ACCOUNTABILITY OFFICE, GAO–08–836, MEDICAL MALPRACTICE: IMPLICATIONS OF RISING PREMIUMS ON ACCESS TO HEALTH CARE (2003), State disclosure and apology laws might be used to encourage defendants to quickly reveal errors and engage in dispute resolution.

Experts have noted the importance of disclosure of errors to patients. Disclosure of harmful errors is perceived to be an important step in reform, because transparency in communication between professionals and patients has been shown to be a significant step in reducing liability exposure. Thomas Gallagher et al., *Disclosing Harmful Medical Errors to Patients*, 356 NEW. ENG. J. MED. 2713 (2007). In 2001, the Joint Commission, which accredits hospitals and other health care organizations, developed nationwide disclosure standards, which is understood to have been an important step in adopting disclosure as a national standard of practice. The Joint

Commission standard calls for disclosing all outcomes of care including "unanticipated outcomes." *Id.* In recent years, this early effort has been amplified through further efforts to develop working disclosure standards and to make disclosure a formal part of "safe" health care practice.

A separate but related issue is whether errors must be reported to public health agencies, licensing authorities, or accreditation bodies. Malpractice reform proposals often couple disclosure to patients with broader disclosures in order to better achieve both better information to patients while also a greater level of knowledge about the nature and extent of errors across the population. Thus, the clinical aspects of error disclosure are joined to population-level reforms whose purpose is to allow a far more robust understanding of the presence of error on a system-wide basis.

A study of state adverse-event reporting systems found that as of 2007, 25 states plus the District of Columbia maintained mandatory adverse-event reporting systems. Almost half of all states with any reporting system, mandatory or voluntary, had adopted a core list of reportable adverse events developed by the National Committee on Quality Assurance. Only one state had the capacity to receive information electronically. The study's authors note that the "current trend is toward strong, comprehensive data protection in state reporting system legislation." Eleven states required health care facilities to report adverse events to patients and families who have experienced such events, while 16 states release data in the aggregate that prevents the identification of individual facilities. Jill Rosenthal & Mary Takach, *2007 Guide to State Adverse Event Reporting Systems*, NATIONAL ACADEMY FOR STATE HEALTH POLICY 1:1, at 1–2 (Portland, ME).

An analysis of the extent to which physicians are willing to report medical errors publicly surveyed more than 1000 physicians in two states and found that more than 83% had reported an error but did so by word of mouth rather than through formalized institutional reporting systems such as a risk management system or a patient safety program. Physicians reported that they would use a reporting system if it was confidential, non-discoverable, and rapid. Jane Garbutt et. al., *Lost Opportunities: How Physicians Communicate About Medical Errors*, 27(1) HEALTH AFFAIRS 246 (2008). For an argument in favor of compelling disclosure of errors to patients, see Richard Bourne, *Medical Malpractice: Should Courts Force Doctors to Confess Their Own Negligence to Their Patients?* 61 ARK. L. REV. 620 (2009). Professor Bourne notes that numerous courts have treated as fraudulent concealment, justifying both equitable estoppel and damages, health care providers' failure to disclose errors in sufficient time to avoid the running of statutes of limitations. *Id.* at 635. Professor Bourne also reports on decisions in which courts have sanctioned physicians for failure to disclose financial conflicts of interest. *Id.* at 641 (citing Shea v. Esensten 208 F.3d 712 (8th Cir. 2000), and *Moore*, 793 P.2d 479 (Cal. 1990), discussed earlier in this Part). In Professor Bourne's view, the duty of disclosure springs from the special fiduciary relationship between physicians and patients and should not depend on a demonstration of injury, and in this vein, fraudulent concealment of error should be a tort in its own right.

As noted, some commentators have recommended that physicians be able to establish a complete defense to a claim of liability by demonstrating that they adhered to established standards of care. The quality of such standards may be open to question. Moreover, since a crucial aspect of health care quality is the reasonable professional exercise of individual clinical judgment on behalf of a specific patient, who is to say that any particular standard was appropriate for a particular patient? Conversely, should failure to live up to standards be conclusive evidence of negligence, or are practice standards more aspirational and thus intended to guide the allocation of resources rather than establishing the standard of care in specific situations? Michelle Mello et. al., *The Leapfrog Standards: Ready to Jump from Marketplace to Courtroom?*, 22(2) HEALTH AFFAIRS 46 (2003).

Shielding health care providers from the risk of medical liability

The most common response to the crisis, as noted, has been to enact laws that shield defendants from liability claims and limit recoveries. Without question, the legal landmark in this area is MICRA, a California law, enacted in 1975, which placed limits on noneconomic damages while also limiting insurance rate increases. Experts have noted that MICRA's actual impact on insurance costs and malpractice litigation has been difficult to measure. For example, a comprehensive study released in 2004 by the Rand Corporation found that the law limited defendant expenditures but that their results could not show whether MICRA had in fact "translated into reduced premiums, greater availability of coverage, and a more stable delivery system." Rogan Kersh, *Medical Malpractice and the New Politics of Health Care, in* MEDICAL MALPRACTICE AND THE U.S. HEALTH CARE SYSTEM 57 (William M. Sage & Rogan Kersh, eds., 2006). The Rand researchers found that the claims most affected by the cap on noneconomic damages were those with the severest injuries (brain damage, paralysis, or various catastrophic injuries) and plaintiffs less than a year old. *Id.*

Despite the absence of evidence that MICRA made health care less expensive or improved the quality of care, medical liability reforms at the state level tend to follow the MICRA example. Common elements of such laws encompass numerous strategies. One is to elevate the burden of proof for claimants (e.g., substituting a gross negligence standard for certain types of errors such as negligence associated with emergency care or treatment of Medicaid beneficiaries). Another is to shorten the statute of limitations for filing lawsuits. Still another would be to cap economic and noneconomic damages in order to reduce the perceived value of lawsuits. Other reforms include capping attorneys' contingency fees, the establishment of collateral source rules to limit the liability of any single alleged tortfeasor when multiple defendants are involved, and reform of the malpractice insurance market in order to lower premiums. Thorpe, *The Medical Malpractice Crisis* at w-4, w22–w23; SLOAN & CHEPKE, MEDICAL MALPRACTICE ch. 4.

Studies of various strategies show mixed results. Capping noneconomic damages has been found to have a significant impact on the cost of malpractice premiums. Thorpe, *The Medical Malpractice Crisis* at w–4–w26. One study of a Texas statute aimed at capping noneconomic damages found that the legislation affected 47% of jury verdicts and reduced the mean allowed noneconomic damages, mean allowed verdicts, and mean allowed total payouts by 73%, 38% and 27%, respectively. David Hyman et al., *Estimating the Effect of Damages Caps in Medical Malpractice Cases*, 1(1) J. of Legal Analysis 355 (Winter 2009). The total dollar value of the cap on verdicts was $150 million on cases closed between 1988 and 2004, but the effect on payouts was only $60 million. The authors found that the small actual impact of the cap on actual payouts could be attributable to the fact that above-cap damages were not actually being paid to begin with. The authors also examined the damages cap laws in effect (30 states as of 2009) and found that the states in which the largest impact could be felt were those that capped all damages, both economic and noneconomic. Discussing the fact that noneconomic damages caps had a relatively limited impact on actual payouts, the authors concluded that the "de facto" effects of malpractice insurance policy limits worked to defeat actual payouts, quite apart from legislative efforts. The authors also found that noneconomic damages laws had a greater effect on deceased persons and unemployed plaintiffs, and that this discriminatory impact could be found at the point of jury verdict rather than at the point of actual payout. Noting the rarity of malpractice trials and the tendency of such cases to settle, the authors found that the impact of a damages cap was to lower the level of settlement. The authors also concluded that noneconomic damages caps could reduce the willingness of counsel to accept malpractice cases to begin with, while raising the incentive to prove economic damages.

Federal incursions into medical liability reform

The federal government has made some incursions into medical liability reform. The HEALTH Act, (H.R. 5, 112th Cong., 1st Sess.) noted above, is an attempt to establish preemptive federal standards mirroring the noneconomic damages caps in MICRA (without any updating from the $250,000 cap established in 1975), as well as other reforms intended to shield defendants from liability. The Patient Protection and Affordable Care Act makes little change in the fabric of U.S. liability laws. Its reforms focus on modest funding for state liability reform demonstrations and the required use of "decision aids."

The PPACA state liability reform demonstrations are "limited in scope" and focus on the development by states of alternative dispute resolution systems. Furrow, *Regulating Patient Safety*. With discretionary grants from the Secretary of DHHS, a participating state must undertake a demonstration that: (A) makes the medical liability system more reliable by increasing the availability of prompt and fair resolution of disputes; (B) encourages the efficient resolution of disputes; (C) encourages the disclosure of health care errors; (D) enhances patient safety by detecting, analyzing, and helping to reduce medical errors and adverse events; (E) improves access to liability insurance; (F) fully informs patients about the differences in the alternative and current tort litigation; (G) gives patients the ability to opt out of or voluntarily withdraw from participating in the alternative dispute system at any time and to pursue other options, including litigation; (H) would not conflict with State law at the time of the application in a way that would prohibit the adoption of an alternative to current tort litigation; and (I) would not limit or curtail a patient's existing legal rights, ability to file a claim in or access a State's legal system, or otherwise abrogate a patient's ability to file a medical malpractice claim. 42 U.S.C. § 280g–15.

Decision aids, which as discussed earlier have received increased focus in recent years, are designed to assist providers in their interactions with patients around "preference-sensitive care," that is, care in which there is no definitive evidence favoring a single approach and in which careful interactions between patients and providers are key to understanding benefits and tradeoffs. In these types of situations, incorporating patient preferences into treatment plans is highly important. Decision aids are practice support tools that offer patients specific and in-depth information about treatment options, outcomes, and tradeoffs and help them think through what they value and what is important to them from care. Some states already have incorporated decision aids into their informed consent statute. Professor Barry Furrow writes that the PPACA requirement to use decision aids amounts to a "federal requirement that overlays the common law of informed consent," which will affect only Medicare health plans in the short-term, but will over time be extended "realistically [to] most settings as providers strive for consistency in" their approach to informed consent. In this way, the PPACA effectively "sets the standard of care for the disclosure of risks and benefits," establishing the decision aid as the standard of care for conveying information. Furrow, *Regulating Patient Safety* at 1762.

4. DOES HEALTH CARE QUALITY IMPROVEMENT AFFECT MEDICAL LIABILITY RISK?

The past three decades have witnessed an important evolution in the degree to which health care providers are involved in efforts to systematically improve the quality of care. Some of these efforts have come at the initiative of health care providers, while others, as you will learn later in this Part, have come at the insistence of payers. These efforts are not without controversy in relation to medical liability exposure. This potential linkage exists because in systemic improvement efforts, performance standards are identified, and health care providers (typically hospitals but increasingly physicians in community practice) are then expected to provide ongoing reports regarding their adherence to such standards or their progress toward meeting them. Examples span both intermediate measures (proportion of children under two who are fully immunized) and "outcome" standards, some of which are "zero tolerance" measures for especially preventable outcomes, considered "never events" (e.g., amputation of the wrong limb, dosage errors, bedsores, infected lines).

Health care defense lawyers see these metrics, in particular the so-called "never events," as having "inadvertently handed the plaintiffs' bar a strong new weapon against health care facilities," effectively creating "a healthcare version of strict liability" as a result of the "mere designation" of never events. Charles Brown et al., *Litigation Impact of Never Events*, AM. HEALTH LAWYERS ASS'N. (Feb. 2, 2008). The authors note that the National Quality Forum, a nonprofit organization specializing in health care quality reform and to which many health care system leaders belong, has designated 27 "never events" for hospitals. Examples include the unintended retention of a foreign object in a patient after surgery or other procedure; patient death or serious disability associated with medication error (wrong drug, wrong dose, wrong patient, wrong time, wrong rate, wrong preparation, wrong routine administration); surgery performed on the wrong part of the body; falls; or patient death or serious disability associated with an intravascular embolism while being cared for in a health care facility. *Id.* at 1–2. As discussed later in this Part, Medicare and other payers now tie payment to hospitals to the absence of such never events unless they are present on admission. See 42 U.S.C. § 1395ww(d)(4)(D)(i) (describing the Medicare "never event" payment requirement). The authors point out that at least in the case of falls, many situations can give rise to a fall, such as a patient who decides against medical advice to get out of bed without a nurse present.

The authors point out that under traditional liability concepts, a defendant sued over a "never event" could call experts to testify as to the professional standard (such as not restraining patients, normal staffing ratios that require patients to wait a period of time for a nurse to arrive, and the frequency of patient falls that are initiated by patients who move against medical advice). But under a strict liability standard, such a defense would not be available. The authors conclude that the "best and only solution to a strict liability problem is to keep CMS' responsibility determination from the jury" and that doing so will require arguing the irrelevance of CMS standards in determining the standard of care. In this regard, the authors point to the fact that a number of state courts have held that hospital policies and procedures, as well as the policies and procedures of the Joint Commission on Health Care Organizations discussed later in this Part, are *not* admissible as evidence of the professional standard of care. *Id.* at 4–5, citing O'Mara v. Wake Forest University Health Sciences Center, 646 S.E.2d 400, 406 (N.C. App. 2007); Moyer v. Reynolds, 780 So.2d 205 (Fla. Dist. App. Ct. 2001); Pogge v. Hale, 625 N.E.2d 792 (Ill. App. Ct. 1993); and other cases.

Think about what it takes to get a provider organization to concede that certain events can be considered "never events." Do you agree that these events are so cutting edge as to create new and insurmountable performance standards for hospitals? Or are they really simply an industry consensus that certain events simply should not happen in a reasonably well-functioning hospital? Do you think that in 2008 a plaintiff would have a difficult time, in the absence of the CMS standards, in calling experts to testify that cutting off the wrong limb is evidence of substandard practice? To be sure, some of the never events, such as falls, present more ambiguous problems, but are the authors here at least somewhat engaged in setting up a "straw man" as a tactical means for argue against giving weight in a liability context to payer-established performance standards?

5.   ENTERPRISE LIABILITY

An idea that gained prominence in the 1990s is the concept of enterprise medical liability, one that is reflected in the notion that health systems as a whole should bear liability for the consequences of negligence.

Kenneth S. Abraham & Paul C. Weiler, Enterprise Medical Liability and the Evolution of the American Health Care System

108 HARV. L. REV. 381, 382–84, 407–13, 415–19 (1994)

The concept of enterprise medical liability [EML] had been quietly analyzed in scholarly publications for a number of years, but the idea gained public prominence in the spring of 1993 as the Clinton Administration made ready its proposed health care reforms. Reports circulated that the legislation would completely abolish the liability of individual physicians for medical malpractice. Common law physician liability was to be replaced by "enterprise liability," under which the statutorily defined health plans that were to provide care under the new system* would bear all liability for medical malpractice. Enterprise liability had the potential simultaneously to garner individual physicians' support for the Administration's broader health care reforms and to place legal responsibility for health care decision making on a business enterprise whose role was to be central in the Administration's vision of the reformed health system.

What happened next should be recorded as one of the great ironies in the history of political lobbying. Primarily through two of its major organizations, the American Medical Association (AMA) and the Physician Insurer Association of America (PIAA),** the medical profession descended on

---

* The health plans proposed by the Administration essentially were what would be considered HMOs, that is, clinically and financially integrated corporate entities that combined health care financing with service delivery. The aspiration to merge financial and clinical activities into large integrated arrangements that can deliver health care efficiently (much like the replacement of small mom and pop shops with large grocery stores) is a constantly recurring theme in the U.S., which is accustomed to large, competitive enterprises across many fields. We never seem to get there. The chapter on antitrust in Part Four is one illustration of how our legal system pushes in the other direction.

** The PIAA is the association of malpractice liability insurers started by members of the industry, like physician groups, hospitals, and dentists (www.piaa.us).

Washington, and began to work strenuously to persuade the Administration to reconsider its plan to immunize physicians from personal liability for their negligence. Having bemoaned for decades the baneful effects of malpractice liability, doctors now pleaded, in effect, "Please don't take our liability away from us!"

A number of institutional and ideological concerns produced this surprising reaction to the Administration's trial balloons. The PIAA was evidently concerned that if physicians no longer were liable for malpractice, they would no longer need liability insurance. In that brave new world, physician-owned mutual malpractice insurers would have lost their raison d'etre. The AMA, which had seen national health care reform as a possible vehicle for securing its favored malpractice reform—the highly regressive California model of a fixed ($250,000) ceiling on pain and suffering awards—was unwilling to settle for a second-best option such as enterprise liability. And many physicians, especially those represented by the AMA, were wary of a proposal that, while promising to get lawyers off their backs, might simply put insurance company bureaucrats or hospital administrators in the lawyers' place. [W]hen physicians' organizations made it publicly clear that they did not find enterprise liability particularly attractive, the Administration retreated.

[W]hen the Administration's reform package finally saw the light of day in the fall of 1993, it revived enterprise liability in the form of a proposal for federal funding of demonstration projects that would test the value of this alternative assignment of medical malpractice liability.

C. *EML as a More Effective Injury–Prevention System*

[Under current doctrines that impose liability on individual physicians], [t]he individualistic quality of malpractice litigation is more of an obstacle to, than a vehicle for, effective injury prevention. Malpractice insurance is a near-universal feature of physician practice. Malpractice liability insurers, not physicians, actually pay the awards to malpractice claimants—thus diluting the direct incentives that physicians might otherwise have to enhance their quality of care in order to avoid paying jury verdicts to injured patients. Moreover, the premiums physicians pay for their malpractice coverage are eventually accounted for in fee schedules established in the nation's health insurance plans (paid by or for patients) that routinely cover this item in physician practice overhead.

[I]njury-prevention incentives could be preserved even for insured physicians if premiums paid by individual physicians were adjusted to take account of their claims experience. However, a noteworthy feature of malpractice insurance is the almost total absence of experience rating of individual physicians' premiums. The implicit premise underlying the absence of experience rating is that prior claims experience is generally a poor index of comparative physician quality and of the physician's likely future claims experience. [F]rom the individual physician's perspective, being named as a malpractice defendant is a comparatively rare event. Thus, with the exception of a tiny number of malpractice recidivists, past claims experience tends not to be a reliable index of future liability risk.

In contrast, the premiums that insurers charge health care enterprises for malpractice coverage can reliably reflect the prior claims experience of the particular institution. Indeed, larger systems such as the Harvard Medical School teaching hospitals are self-insured, and thus their liability costs reflect only their own claims experience. Such enterprises generate sufficient claims experience within usable time frames to make this experience an actuarially credible index of the probability that future claims will be brought. It follows that shifting the focus of liability from the individual physician to the hospital, or to some other health care enterprise, could vastly increase injury-prevention incentives.

Even more importantly, such a shift to EML would target the component of the health care system that possesses the greatest capacity for continuously improving the quality of care. No better illustration of this assertion can be found than the transformation of anesthesia safety that was initiated in the Harvard teaching hospitals during the 1980s. In the mid–1980s, anesthesiologists' premiums at Harvard, as elsewhere, were among the highest for any specialty, due in large part to the severity of anesthesia-related mishaps. Anesthesia procedures generated only three percent of claims but eleven percent of payments. Close scrutiny by an arm of Harvard's own insurance company of the cases that had generated suits and payments over the prior decade disclosed that the bulk of the claims were valid and that the patient injuries in question could and should have been avoided. But rather than focus on the different physicians involved in these tragic incidents, the study group recommended that the hospitals prescribe new procedures and technologies designed to avoid similar results in the future.

The desire of the Harvard hospitals' administrators to endorse and establish these new standards of practice evoked considerable controversy among their physician staffs about the dangers of "cookbook" styles of medical practice. The hospitals eventually decided, however, to mandate compliance with the new standards. When experience under those standards was reviewed several years later, it became clear that anesthesia-related mishaps and claims had dropped sharply and that malpractice premium ratings for Harvard anesthesiologists had been cut in half. The new practice standards are now spreading throughout the rest of the country.

[T]he inevitable human frailty of individual physicians and the undeniable effectiveness of "team" approaches to reducing patient injury point to the health care enterprise as the most effective mechanism for addressing medical malpractice. The truth is that the individual physician is now typically a member—admittedly a crucial member—of a larger team of medical personnel, all of whom have their own special training and responsibilities for the course of treatment of the same patient.

A.   *The Responsible Enterprise*

Viewed along the three dimensions of compensation, administration, and prevention, the hospital is a far better candidate for malpractice liability than are individual physicians. Hospitals do not so clearly emerge as the better candidate, however, when compared to other health care enterprises—insurance companies financing health insurance, network HMOs, or the newly developing integrated health plans that the Clinton Administration sought to make the centerpiece of its health care reform. The central question concerns whether the subjects of malpractice liability should be institutions such as hospitals or HMOs that actually deliver health care to patients, or institutions such as health plans or other health insurers that finance the provision of health care.

On the face of it, the preferable option is the enterprise that actually delivers, rather than merely finances, health care. The vast majority of the injuries that result from malpractice stem from treatment delivered under the auspices of hospitals—if only by physicians with the right to admit their patients to the hospital. Hospitals are typically responsible for selecting and providing the supplies, facilities, and equipment used in treatment, as well as for hiring and firing the employees who play an important role on the patient care team. Hospitals also grant admitting privileges to physicians, and can restrict, suspend, or terminate the privileges of doctors whose poor quality of treatment has come to the hospital's attention. In each of these respects, hospitals are in the best position to make judgments about whether any such steps will reduce the risk of injuries to their patients. And some hospitals—particularly the more prominent teaching hospitals—are most likely to conduct serious research and development about ways of enhancing the quality of care in the overall health care system. To the extent, then, that imposing malpractice liability may influence these cost-benefit judgments about patient safety, hospitals would seem to be the prime candidates for that legal role.

At present, utilization decisions are increasingly influenced by financing enterprises. However, health care providers bear liability for malpractice. This bifurcation of responsibility creates conflicting incentives. Financing enterprises have the incentive to press providers to achieve lower utilization rates (in effect to require lower utilization through managed care), whereas providers have the incentive to protect themselves against liability for malpractice by increasing utilization through the practice of defensive medicine. In contrast, under financing-based enterprise liability, the same enterprise would bear the consequences of both under-utilization and over-utilization. Utilization might thus be more nearly optimized.

Similar optimization, however, is beginning to occur under delivery-based EML. Financing enterprises are finding it in their interest to contract with hospitals and even individual physicians on a capitation (or DRG-like) basis. Thus, if a hospital contracts with a financing enterprise to treat coronary patients for a specified dollar amount per patient, the hospital bears the same incentive as the financing enterprise to optimize the mix of treatment quality and cost. It is easy to envision such incentives under either delivery—or financing-based EML, because they currently exist in the DRG reimbursement model under Medicare and in much managed care provided under private health insurance contracts.

In the future, of course, the distinction between financing-based and delivery-based enterprises may become increasingly cloudy as insurers, hospitals, and physicians become linked in integrated health care networks. Under tighter forms of managed competition these networks might be held to higher standards of accountability and therefore behave more like health care deliverers and less like pure financiers. In such a world, liability might optimally be imposed on these networks, which could not easily be classified in our binary analysis.

Notes

1. *The enduring nature of claims against individual physicians.* Even though doctrinal developments expanding corporate and vicarious liability have moved the law toward enterprise liability, most malpractice claims continue to involve allegations of negligence against individual doctors. Michelle M. Mello & David M. Studdert, *Deconstructing Negligence: The Role of Individual and Systemic Factors in Causing Medical Injuries*, 96 GEO. L. REV. 599, 601–602 (2008).

2. *Downstream consequences of enterprise liability.* As Abraham and Weiler suggest, with respect to hospitals their proposed EML system seems most appropriate for large, sophisticated teaching hospitals. As you read the following materials, consider whether most community hospitals would have the capacity to control risks and absorb the extensive liability that Abraham and Weiler propose. Ask yourselves what assumptions do the authors make about hospital organization and governance and if those assumptions are realistic? Consider also what changes in internal organization might be spurred by EML and whether those changes are desirable? Think also about the different types of occurrences that might give rise to malpractice claims. Should they all be lumped together into a one-size-fits-all system? Additionally, if Abraham and Weiler's EML proposal ever were implemented, would it likely accelerate the already strong trend toward consolidation of hospitals into larger networks and delivery systems that would have the requisite institutional capacities? Further, what assumptions do they make about the nature of all the different entities that now fly under the broad banner of "HMO"? Aside from a very small number of the traditional HMOs that truly integrate financing and delivery across the continuum of care, most of what goes by the name of "HMO" these days relies largely on contractual arrangements as "integration." You will see the full impact of this pale shadow of meaningful integration later in this Part when we discuss the potential avenues of holding these purported "entities" liable for negligent care within their "networks," a term that is more suggestive of a social club rather than a fully integrated enterprise that can manage the upside and downside risks in the way Abraham and Weiler propose. A term that was fashionable a few decades ago—"clinics without walls"—is all too descriptive of most of these arrangements. Further, if, as the authors suggest, EML were applied to health plans, would this hasten the end of loosely configured networks and push the health care system toward more fully integrated models in which members receive their care from highly structured closed panels, with very limited access to "out-of-network" treatments, and only then, with the approval of the plan administrator?

CHAPTER 18

HOSPITALS AND HEALTH CARE QUALITY

1. INTRODUCTION

Hospital liability for injuries to patients, including those caused by physicians' malpractice, has been a major arena in which the shift from physician autonomy to egalitarian social contract has taken place. As in the area of physician liability, expanded hospital liability can be seen as judicial enforcement of the hospital industry's and medical profession's own "best" vision of quality assurance and accountability. Alternatively, or perhaps simultaneously, this expanded liability can be seen as part of the general trend in tort and regulatory law toward more conscious protection of those injured by risk-creating activity. From yet another perspective, there is evidence that the effort to improve quality through institutional oversight has had only variable success and a number of spectacular failures, reflecting serious structural weaknesses in hospitals and in the institutions designed to monitor them.

Expanded liability converged with other important trends. Just at the moment when hospitals were being given greater institutional authority over and responsibility for quality of care, they were also affected—beginning in the late 1970s—by increasingly powerful efforts by the state and federal governments to limit payments to hospitals. These cost containment efforts were greatly magnified by the sharp turn toward a more market-oriented approach to health care financing that began in the 1980s, as employers, Medicaid programs, and health insurers and plan administrators began aggressive bargaining for price discounts and instituted utilization controls such as advance approval and prior authorization. This pressure on cost controls in turn rippled through the hospital industry in a number of ways, changing business practices, workforce staffing and other aspects of hospital administration, as you will see in the cases below that focus on efforts by hospitals to rid themselves of non-profitable patients, and potentially, physicians.

2. THE ROLE OF LAW IN THE AGE OF EXPANDING HOSPITAL AUTHORITY

In the same time period—roughly 1870 to 1960—that physicians were largely insulated from malpractice liability by the locality and reputable minority rules, hospitals were also insulated by the doctrines of charitable immunity, the locality rule, and the characterization of doctors as independent contractors and nurses as doctors' borrowed servants. All of these doctrines have been substantially eroded or entirely overruled with respect to hospitals. Nevertheless, it is difficult to understand current debates about hospitals' (and ultimately, managed care organizations') legal duties without some knowledge of these doctrines—especially the doctrine of the doctor as independent contractor—and of the forces that led to their change.

For most of the nineteenth century American hospitals were charitable institutions whose primary patients were the poor. Not surprisingly, the charitable immunity doctrine dates from this period. In 1876, the Massachusetts Supreme Court held that the Massachusetts General Hospital was a "public charity," conducted for "the great public purpose" of serving the sick without compensation, and that therefore its limited funds, held in trust for its beneficiaries, should be immune from depletion by tort judgments. The corporation's only legal responsibility was to use due care in selecting its agents; apart from that, it could not be subjected to liability for any negligence by its doctors or other staff toward its beneficiaries. *See* McDonald v. Massachusetts General Hospital, 120 Mass. 432 (1876). The remarkable thing about the charitable immunity doctrine was not that it existed in 1876, but that it continued to exist into the 1950s and 1960s, long after hospitals had transformed themselves into large economic entities serving paying as well as lower income patients.

The independent contractor and borrowed servant doctrines must be understood against the broader background of vicarious liability in tort. There are generally two ways that a hospital or any other corporate organization can be held liable for negligence: (1) directly, for its own corporate or organizational failure, and (2) vicariously, for the negligence of its employees or agents, despite the organization's own lack of direct involvement in the act or omission causing harm. An example of direct or "corporate negligence" would be the failure of the hospital's board of trustees, administration, and medical staff to review the credentials of doctors applying for permission to practice at the hospital. An example of vicarious liability would be holding the hospital liable for the negligence of an employee such as a technician, despite all proper precautions having been taken regarding credentials, training, and supervision.

Vicarious liability has been traditionally justified by the employer's right, at least in theory, to "control" the actions of the employee. Where the employer is thought not to have a right of control—as in the case of an "independent contractor," or where the employer's own employee becomes actually subject to the control of a second employer or principal, and hence a "borrowed servant"—vicarious liability is said not to apply. Both of these principles were used by Judge Cardozo to defeat a claim for damages for unauthorized surgery (hence battery) against a hospital in the famous case of *Schloendorff*, 105 N.E. 92 (1914). Judge Cardozo's opinion in *Schloendorff* continues to be widely cited for its ringing statement of the principle of patient self-determination: "Every human being of adult years and sound mind has a right to determine what shall be done with his own body; and a surgeon who performs an operation without his patient's consent, commits an assault, for which he is liable in damages." *Id.* at 93. However, while Mrs. Schloendorff may have had a claim against the surgeon, her suit against the *hospital* still failed, because even though she did not choose or pay the doctors, and even though they were chosen by the hospital, "[t]he wrong was not that of the hospital; it was that of physicians, who were not the defendant's servants, but were pursuing an independent calling, a profession sanctioned by a solemn oath, and safeguarded by stringent penalties. If, in serving their patient, they violated her commands, the responsibility is not the defendant [hospital's]; it is theirs." *Id.* at 94. Similarly, Judge Cardozo ruled that nurses, even though paid by the hospital, when treating a patient, "are not acting as the servants of the hospital. The superintendent is a servant of the hospital; the assistant superintendents, the orderlies, and the other members of the administrative staff are servants of the hospital. But nurses are employed to carry out the orders of the physicians, to whose authority they are subject. The hospital undertakes to procure for the patient the services of a nurse. It does not undertake through the agency of nurses to render those services itself." *Id.*

3. HOSPITALS' INSTITUTIONAL STRUCTURE AND IDEALIZED SELF-IMAGE: THE RIVAL VISIONS OF PRIVATE WORKSHOP AND COMMUNITY RESPONSIBILITY

Understanding the assumptions underlying the independent contractor and borrowed servant doctrines, and the reasons for their demise, requires knowledge of the system of staff privileges through which physicians receive permission to practice in particular hospitals, and the accreditation process designed and administered by the Joint Commission on Accreditation of Healthcare Organizations, formerly the Joint Commission on Accreditation of Hospitals.

Written in 1914, Judge Cardozo's *Schloendorff* opinion presents a powerful image of the charitable hospital as a workshop that simply makes its facilities and equipment available to independent, individual medical and nursing practitioners. (For a collection of judicial expressions of this image, see B. Abbott Goldberg, *The Duty of Hospitals and Medical Staffs to Regulate the Quality of Patient Care: A Legal Perspective*, 14 PAC. L.J. 55, 66 n.64 (1982)). In some respects this image was accurate, at least with respect to paying patients. "While certain physicians were designated to treat the poor in charity wards, the private rooms were open to the patients of almost any private physician. Thus, the typical American voluntary hospital in the late nineteenth and early twentieth centuries came to be known as having an 'open staff.' There was no systematic policy in voluntary hospitals toward exercise of controls over the work of private physicians." MILTON ROEMER & JAY FRIEDMAN, DOCTORS IN HOSPITALS 34 (1971).

In other words, to say that a doctor was "on the hospital's staff" did *not* mean that he was an employee of the hospital; on the contrary, what it meant was that he had permission—"staff privileges"—to use the hospital's facilities for his own private, fee-generating practice of medicine. Of course, a strong contrary argument could have been made in Mrs. Schloendorff's case, because she had not selected and paid her own physician, and was relying on the hospital's designation of particular doctors to serve charitable patients. More fundamentally, what Cardozo did not mention (and perhaps did not know) was that the system of unsupervised, unaccountable individual practice in hospitals was being contested within the medical profession at the time.

The great expansion in the number of hospitals, along with the numbers of doctors wanting to work in them, raised the question of who should be permitted to practice medicine in a hospital, and in particular to practice surgery. On the one hand, the American laissez-faire and entrepreneurial tradition precluded the European solution, which was to limit hospital practice to a small number of highly qualified doctors and relegate all other doctors to general office practice. On the other hand, truly wide-open hospital practice threatened the economic interests and professional status of the new specialty of surgeons. Moreover, any restrictions on and organization of hospital practice had to be justified, at least at a rhetorical level, in terms of patient welfare. Finally, with the decline of hospitals' traditional missions of hierarchical charity and social control, a new legitimizing image was needed to link the lucrative private practice of medicine in hospitals with broader community interests that would justify philanthropic and later governmental support.

The response to these conflicting pressures that gradually emerged in the first half of the twentieth century was, from the perspective of physicians, brilliantly successful. At the level of national ideology, the hospital standardization principles of the American College of Surgeons (ACS), formulated in 1919, were adopted by many hospitals. These standards set such goals as adequately staffed laboratories and X-ray departments, and a formal commitment that the "hospital" and its "medical staff" would be institutionally responsible for the quality of patient care, at least through the staffs' careful granting of privileges and its retrospective review of its members' work. Thus Dr. Malcolm MacEachern, a leading authority on hospital administration, advocate of hospital standards, and Director of Professional Relations of the American Hospital Association, wrote in 1935 that

> twentieth century developments have made [the distinction between public and private ownership] inaccurate, and those terms should be abandoned. With the exception of a limited number of hospitals owned by private individuals or corporations, operated for profit and admitting only pay patients, all hospitals are public in that they are directly or indirectly owned by the community and may admit free and part-pay patients as well as those who are able to pay the full cost of their care. Further than this, all hospitals

have a definite relationship to the community. They must give adequate service if they are to continue to exist. [These hospitals] draw their support from the community, and, if they are to continue to receive that support, they must earn it by giving equally good service.

MALCOLM MACEACHERN, HOSPITAL ORGANIZATION AND MANAGEMENT 35 (1935, 3d ed., 1957).

Although the rhetoric promised institutional responsibility and oversight of the private practice of medicine, there were no publicly-accountable mechanisms of enforcement. Adherence to the standards was voluntary with each hospital, and compliance was widely resisted, not only by the less elite general practitioners, but also by most physicians who wanted to avoid bitter intra-professional disputes.

Passage of the federal Hill–Burton Act in 1946, discussed in Part One, required states to enact hospital licensure laws as a condition of receiving federal funds for hospital construction; not surprisingly, the states relied heavily on the ACS standards in drafting their statutes, thereby applying them to all hospitals and backing them, at least in theory, with state regulatory enforcement. Again, however, the reality was that the states had no staff or other resources for enforcement, and more fundamentally, they had no desire to regulate medical practice in or out of hospitals. In 1951 the ACS standards program was succeeded by a more powerful but still resolutely private organization, the Joint Commission on Accreditation of Hospitals (JCAH), whose governing board was (and still is to some extent) composed of representatives from the two major interest groups—the American Medical Association (AMA) and the American Hospital Association (AHA), as well as from a number of more specialized professional organizations. For a detailed discussion of the origins and development of the JCAH, see Timothy Stoltzfus Jost, *The Joint Commission on Accreditation of Hospitals: Private Regulation of Health Care and the Public Interest*, 24 B.C. L. Rev. 835 (1983).

From physicians' perspective, the brilliant characteristic of this private regulatory apparatus was its voluntary, wholly professional, and often illusory quality. Under the JCAH standards, permission to practice in a hospital could be granted to virtually any doctor with a degree from an approved medical school. The hospital was then supposed to create various categories of staff privileges and control mechanisms to attempt to regulate the dangers of wide-open, unsupervised hospital practice. As Roemer and Friedman perceptively point out, the entire American structure of accreditation standards, control committees, and legal requirements derive (paradoxically) from our primary commitment to unsupervised and—in a telling phrase—"private" practice in hospitals. (Such structures are largely absent in Europe, where hospital practice is professionalized.) *See* ROEMER & FRIEDMAN, DOCTORS IN HOSPITALS at 59.

The highest level of staff privileges, termed "active" privileges, is given to experienced doctors who have made a commitment to focus their practice at the particular hospital. Such doctors are considered full members of the medical staff, with voting privileges and committee responsibilities. "Relatively firm standards could be applied to attainment [of this level], and to these physicians would be entrusted duties for which the hospital was legally responsible, such as service to indigent patients or various functions in administration and teaching." *Id.* at 43. In return, these doctors are given preferential access to scarce hospital resources, e.g., beds for their patients. A second category, termed "associate," is for more junior doctors who are in a probationary status. These doctors may have some committee responsibilities, but do not have a vote or participate in policymaking.

A third category, termed "courtesy," simply allows doctors to treat their private patients in the hospital. This category of doctor comes closest to the model of the independent practitioner simply using the hospital as a workshop. Nevertheless, it is important to note that no source of hospital law—statutes, regulations, accreditation standards, or the common law—has ever suggested that hospitals have less responsibility for quality of care depending on the doctor's category of privileges. Indeed, following the Roemer and Friedman analysis above, an argument could be made that hospitals should have *more* responsibility to monitor the care of the less affiliated courtesy staff, whose credentials may be weaker than those of the active staff, and who in any case are less involved in day-to-day professional interactions.

Most doctors—whether active, associate, or courtesy staff members—derived (and still derive) the majority of their income from the private practice of medicine. Three types of doctors represent at least partial exceptions to this rule. Anesthesiologists, radiologists, and pathologists are often termed "hospital-based physicians" because they are normally selected by the hospital, rather than by patients, and because their practices are primarily hospital-based. At the same time, these doctors are sometimes still not "employees" of the hospital, have complex contracts with the hospital regarding compensation, insurance liability, time commitment to the hospital, and other matters, and may sometimes bill patients directly for their services.

4. THE COLLAPSE OF CHARITABLE IMMUNITY AND THE RISE OF RESPONDEAT SUPERIOR

Paradoxically, many of the hospitals' greatest successes in the 1930s and 1940s undermined the doctrines that insulated hospitals from legal responsibility for quality of care. The establishment and expansion of Blue Cross as the financing arm of American hospitals, discussed in Part Two, helped transform large numbers of formerly charity or near-charity patients into paying patients, and hospitals themselves into the "hospital industry." Moreover, individual hospitals, the AHA, and the JCAH repeatedly articulated the vision of the nonprofit, voluntary hospital as a community institution that "provided" high quality care. All of these developments were inconsistent with Judge Cardozo's image of the hospital as a passive charity removed from operational responsibility.

This shift in hospitals' self-image and public expectations led many state supreme courts to abandon the doctrines insulating hospitals from liability. Thus in 1957, New York's Chief Judge Fuld overruled his predecessor Chief Judge Cardozo's 1914 *Schloendorff* opinion, as well as the doctrine of charitable immunity. "Present-day hospitals, as their manner of operation plainly demonstrates, do far more than furnish facilities for treatment. Certainly, the person who avails himself of 'hospital facilities' expects that the hospital will attempt to cure him, not that its nurses or other employees will act on their own responsibility." Henceforth "the test should be, for [hospitals], whether charitable or profit-making, as it is for every other employer, was the person who committed the negligent injury-producing act one of its employees and, if he was, was he acting within the scope of his employment." Bing v. Thunig, 143 N.E.2d 3 (N.Y. 1957).

Nurses and non-professional employees fit easily into the traditional respondeat superior doctrine: they are formally employees of the hospital, and for the most part are subject to hospital managerial control. The obvious exception to this generalization is where the nurse or technician is functioning under the orders or supervision of a physician who is not himself a hospital employee. The modern trend is to recognize that *both* the hospital and the non-employee physician may be supervising the hospital employee, and hence both may be liable for the employee's negligence. For example, Truhitte v. French Hospital, 180 Cal. Rptr. 152 (App. 1982), involved a suit for damages caused by a sponge left inside the patient's abdomen. Responsibility for insuring that all sponges were removed was shared by the surgeon and by the operating room nurses who prepared the sponges and counted them before and after the operation. Under the "captain of the ship" doctrine (which held surgeons responsible for all negligence in the operating room), the nurses would have been considered the borrowed servants of the surgeon, and the hospital would have been absolved of liability for the negligence of its employees. *See* Annot., 29 A.L.R. 3d 1065, 1075 (1970). But the *Truhitte* court rejected that reasoning.

> We question whether the "captain of the ship" doctrine has any remaining independent existence: the vicarious liability of a surgeon for the independent negligence of nurses and other assistants is determined in the cases under the general rules of agency. The "captain of the ship" doctrine arose from the need to assure plaintiffs a source of recovery for malpractice at a time when many hospitals enjoyed charitable immunity; other jurisdictions are moving away from a strict application of the doctrine. A theory that the surgeon directly controls all activities of whatever nature in the operating room certainly is not realistic in present day medical care. Today's hospitals hire, fire, train and provide day-to-day supervision of their nurse-employees. Fortunately, hospitals can and do implement standards and regulations governing good surgery practices and techniques and are in the best position to enforce compliance; hospitals also are in a position to insure against the risk and pass the cost to consumers.

The argument of the hospital in the trial court and on appeal confuses two distinct concepts: the nondelegable nature of the surgeon's duty to remove sponges, and the basis for imposing vicarious liability on the surgeon under the borrowed-servant doctrine for the independent negligence of the nurses. It is the law of California that the surgeon's duty to remove all sponges and other foreign objects from the patient's body is nondelegable. However, it does not follow that the hospital may escape liability for its independent negligence in failing to devise adequate sponge-accounting procedures or in negligently carrying out such procedures through its employee-nurses.

Truhitte, 180 Cal. Rptr. at 160–61. *See also* Brickner v. Normandy Osteopathic Hosp., Inc., 746 S.W.2d 108 (Mo. App. 1988) (hospital can be held vicariously liable for the negligence of a second-year resident doctor, employed by the hospital, when performing surgery under the supervision of an attending physician, i.e., a more senior doctor who was not an employee of the hospital).

---

5. Non-Employee Physicians and the Expanding Concepts of Agency and Nondelegable Duty

As discussed above, much medical care and surgery delivered in hospitals is performed by physicians who are not employees of the hospital. Nevertheless, as discussed above and below, the work of these non-employee physicians takes place in a complex context of hospital oversight and responsibility for quality of care. Does this context mean that hospitals should be vicariously liable for physician negligence, even if the hospital has exercised due care in granting privileges and other corporate responsibilities? The doctrines of "apparent agency" and "nondelegable duty" have been applied particularly to the "hospital-based physicians"—anesthesiologists, radiologists, and pathologists—who are usually chosen by the hospital rather than by individual patients, and hence who can be characterized as the apparent agents of the hospital.

Section 267 of the *Restatement (Second) of Agency* states that:

One who represents that another is his servant or other agent and thereby causes a third person justifiably to rely upon the care or skill of such apparent agent is subject to liability to the third person for harm caused by the lack of care or skill of the one appearing to be a servant or other agent as if he were such.

The comment to this section states that "[t]he mere fact that acts are done by one whom the injured party believes to be the defendant's servant is not sufficient to cause the apparent master to be liable. There must be such reliance upon the manifestation as exposes the plaintiff to the negligent conduct. The rule normally applies where the plaintiff has submitted himself to the care or protection of an apparent servant *in response to an invitation from the defendant to enter into such relations with such serv-ant."* (emphasis supplied).

A somewhat broader version of apparent agency liability can also be found in Section 429 of the *Restatement (Second) of Torts* (1965), which provides:

> One who employs an independent contractor to perform services for another which are accepted in the reasonable belief that the services are being rendered by the employer or by his servants, is subject to liability for physical harm caused by the negligence of the contractor in supplying such services, to the same extent as though the employer were supplying them himself or by his servants.

As the Alaska Supreme Court commented on the Torts version: "[t]wo factors are relevant to a finding of ostensible agency: (1) whether the patient looks to the institution, rather than the individual physician, for care; and (2) whether the hospital "holds out" the physician as its employee." Jackson v. Power, 743 P.2d 1376, 1380 (Alaska 1987). Thus in the Torts version of the doctrine, the plaintiff need only prove a "reasonable belief" in the apparent agency relationship, which can be based on a hospital "holding out" the physician as its employee, rather than having to prove reliance on "an invitation" by the hospital to "enter into relations" with the doctor.

Most appellate opinions in the last few decades concerning the apparent agency of hospital-based physicians have upheld denials of hospital motions for summary judgment and permitted the cases to go to juries to find liability if the facts warrant. However, in theory, and at times in practice, an apparent agency claim can be thrown into question or even defeated by proof that the patient did not rely on an express or implied representation by the hospital. The following case suggests some of the difficulties in applying the law of agency to relationships among patients, doctors, and hospitals, and the virtues of the alternative doctrine of nondelegable duty.

Jackson v. Power

743 P.2d 1376 (Alaska 1987)

■ BURKE, J.:

[In May 1981, sixteen year old Brett Jackson was seriously injured when he fell from a cliff, and was airlifted to Fairbanks Memorial Hospital (FMH), the only general hospital emergency room north of Anchorage. Jackson was examined by John Power, M.D., an emergency room physician on duty at the time. Dr. Power's examination revealed extensive injuries, including gastric distension, suggesting possible internal injuries. Dr. Power ordered several tests, but did not order certain procedures that could have been used to ascertain whether there had been damage to the patient's kidneys. Jackson had, in fact, suffered damage to the renal arteries and veins which supply blood to and remove blood from the kidneys. This damage, undetected for approximately 9 to 10 hours after Jackson's arrival at FMH, ultimately caused Jackson to lose both of his kidneys.

Jackson and his mother filed suit. In their complaint they alleged negligence in the diagnosis, care and treatment Jackson received at FMH. Jackson moved for partial summary judgment seeking to hold FMH vicariously liable as a matter of law for the care rendered by Dr. Power. In support of his motion, Jackson advanced three separate theories: (1) enterprise liability; (2) apparent authority; and (3) non-delegable duty.

The trial court rejected the enterprise liability theory, and ruled that genuine issues of material fact precluded summary judgment on the two remaining theories. The Alaska Supreme Court granted Jackson's petition for review of the trial court's ruling.]

Initially, it is important to clarify the exact issue that we have been asked to resolve. Jackson has conceded, for purposes of this appeal, that Dr. Power was not an employee of FMH, but an independent contractor employed by respondent Emergency Room, Inc. (ERI), and that ERI and FMH are separate legal entities. Jackson also makes no claim that FMH was itself negligent in its selection, retention, or supervision of Dr. Power. Consequently, we have no occasion to consider the doctrine of corporate negligence. Jackson asks us to resolve only whether a hospital should be vicariously liable, as a matter of public policy, for the negligence or malpractice of an independent contractor/physician, committed while treating a patient in the hospital's emergency room [under the three theories stated above].

[Enterprise Liability]

Jackson contends [that] if the enterprise impacts society and the negligent act occurred during an activity performed for the benefit or in the interest of the enterprise, the enterprise is liable. [Although the court notes that two courts in other states have indicated some willingness to accept this theory, and that it has been advocated by some commentators, it declines to adopt it where the negligence has been committed by a person who was not an employee of the enterprise.]

[Apparent Authority]

[On this point the Alaska Supreme Court reviewed cases from other states, noted the "strong trend [in other states] toward liability against hospitals that permit or encourage patients to believe that independent contractor/physicians are, in fact, authorized agents of the hospitals," as well as the Restatements of Torts and Agency, and nonetheless affirmed the trial court's ruling that genuine issues of material fact precluded summary judgment for the plaintiff on this theory. Among the facts noted by the court as relevant for trial were the lack of a contract between FMH and ERI, and the absence of any role by FMH employees in scheduling or monitoring the emergency room physicians. In addition, the court considered it relevant that there was a sign adjacent to the desk of the admissions clerk in the emergency room "indicat[ing] that physicians from ERI were working in the emergency room," (this being the court's description of the sign's wording, apparently not a direct quotation of the sign) and that Jackson was not unconscious when he arrived at the hospital.]

[Non-delegable duty]

Physicians, not hospitals, FMH asserts, have a duty to practice medicine non-negligently. Thus, according to FMH, a hospital cannot be held to have delegated away a duty it never had.

FMH is licensed as a "general acute care hospital." As such, it is required to comply with state regulations designed to promote "safe and adequate treatment of individuals in hospitals in the interest of public health, safety and welfare." These regulations provided, at the time of Jackson's accident, that an acute care hospital shall "insure that a physician is available to respond to an emergency at all times." Thus, at a minimum, the law imposed a duty on FMH to provide emergency care physicians on a 24–hour basis.

FMH, however, voluntarily assumed a much broader duty. At the time of Jackson's accident, FMH was accredited by the Joint Committee on the Accreditation of Hospitals (JCAH). In order to receive and maintain accreditation, FMH had to comply with the JCAH's standards promulgated in the Accreditations Manual For Hospitals, Emergency Services. Standard I mandates that all accredited hospitals implement a well defined plan for emergency care based on community need and the capability of the hospital. The JCAH standards also mandate, among other things, that: (1) FMH's emergency room be directed by a physician member of the active medical staff (Standard II); (2) FMH's emergency room be integrated with other units and departments of the hospital (Standard III); (3) that emergency care be guided by written policies and procedures; and (4) that the quality of care be continually reviewed, evaluated and assured through establishment of quality control mechanisms (Standard V).

Additionally, FMH's own bylaws provided for the establishment and maintenance of an emergency room [and] for the creation of an emergency room committee which is required among other things to: (a) formulate rules and regulations for the continuous coverage of the emergency room; and (b) supervise the clinical work in that department.

Based upon the above, it cannot seriously be questioned that FMH had a duty to provide emergency room services and that part of that duty was to provide physician care in its emergency room. Having so determined, we must next ascertain whether FMH's duty to provide physician care in the emergency room is non-delegable.

A non-delegable duty is an established exception to the rule that an employer is not liable for the negligence of an independent contractor. [S]uch a duty "may be imposed by statute, by contract, by franchise or by charter, or by the common law." [After reviewing many particular non-delegable duties, such as those of common carriers to passengers, landlords to tenants, etc., the court quoted Prosser and Keeton that] "[i]t is difficult to suggest any criterion by which the non-delegable character of such duties may be determined, *other than the conclusion of the courts that the responsibility is so important to the community that the employer should not be permitted to transfer it to another.* (emphasis added)" [Prosser & Keeton on THE LAW OF TORTS 511–12 (5th ed., 1984)].

[After discussing a recent Alaska case holding that a scheduled airline could not delegate its duty to provide safe passage to a sub-contracting carrier, the court stated that] the importance to the community of a hospital's duty to provide emergency room physicians rivals the importance of the common-carriers' duty for the safety of its passengers. We also find a close parallel between the regulatory scheme of airlines and hospitals. Undoubtedly, the operation of a hospital is one of the most regulated activities in this state. Besides the license, and certificate of need a hospital must comply with state regulations promulgated to control its activities, adopt a state approved risk management program "to minimize the risk of injury to patients," and undergo "annual inspections and investigations" of its facilities. Failure to comply with these statutory requirements can lead to suspension or revocation of the hospital's license.

The hospital regulatory scheme and the purpose underlying it manifests the legislature's recognition that it is the hospital as an institution which bears ultimate responsibility for complying with the mandates of the law. It is the hospital that is required to ensure compliance with the regulations and thus, relevant to the instant case, it is the hospital that bears final accountability for the provision of physicians for emergency room care. We, therefore, hold that a general acute care hospital's duty to provide physicians for emergency room care is non-delegable. Thus, a hospital such as FMH may not shield itself from liability by claiming that it is not responsible for the results of negligently performed health care when the law imposes a duty on the hospital to provide that health care.

We are persuaded that the circumstances under which emergency room care is provided in a modern hospital mandates the rule we adopt today. Not only is this rule consonant with the public perception of the hospital as a multifaceted health care facility responsible for the quality of medical care and treatment rendered, it also treats tort liability in the medical arena in a manner that is consistent with the commercialization of American medicine. Finally, we simply cannot fathom why liability should depend upon the technical employment status of the emergency room physician who treats the patient. It is the hospital's duty to provide the physician, which it may do through any means at its disposal. The means employed, however, will not change the fact that the hospital will be responsible for the care rendered by physicians it has a duty to provide.

This holding is necessarily limited. We do not change the standard of care with which a physician must comply, nor do we extend the duty which we find non-delegable beyond its natural scope. Our holding does not extend to situations where the patient is treated by his or her own doctor in an emergency room provided for the convenience of the doctor. Such situations are beyond the scope of the duty assumed by an acute care hospital. Rather our holding is limited to those situations where a patient comes to the hospital, as an institution, seeking emergency room services and is treated by a physician provided by the hospital. In such situations, the hospital shall be vicariously liable for damages proximately caused by a physician's negligence or malpractice. Jackson is [thus] entitled to partial summary judgment on the issue of FMH's vicarious liability.

Notes

1.   The *Jackson* opinion analyzes the doctrines of non-delegable duty and apparent agency with markedly different perspectives. Regarding non-delegable duty, the court looks to general statutory policy, regulations, accreditation standards, and public perception, and finds that hospitals cannot escape liability through sub-contracting for the critical institutional function of emergency care. But regarding apparent agency, the court surprisingly suggests that it might be appropriate for a jury to relieve a hospital of vicarious liability because it did *not* have a contract with its emergency room sub-contractor, in apparent gross violation of the JCAH standards and the hospital's own by-laws, or because the severely-injured Jackson may have been dimly aware of an ambiguous sign at the admissions desk. Perhaps the court's approach to apparent agency was the result of the fact that this was an appeal from the trial court's denial of the *plaintiff's* motion for summary judgment, i.e., the court was "over-explaining" why this issue could not be taken from the jury. For a more patient-protective version of apparent agency, which requires the hospital to rebut the appearance of agency with a "meaningful written notice to the patient, acknowledged at the time of admission," see Burless v. West Virginia University Hospitals, Inc., 601 S.E.2d 85 (W. Va. 2004) (reversing trial court's granting *defendant's* motion for summary judgment and expanding apparent agency from the emergency room to the hospital's "High Risk [obstetrical] Clinic").

2.   Many state appellate courts have ruled that hospitals may be held vicariously liable for the negligence of hospital-based physicians not chosen by the patients themselves. *See, e.g.*, Mehlman v. Powell, 378 A.2d 1121 (Md. 1977) (emergency room physician under contract to hospital found to be hospital's apparent agent; court contrasts public's expectations about gas stations, where franchising under national brand names is well known, with public's reliance on hospital as source of care and impracticality of patient inquiries about precise status of numerous members of the hospital staff); Hannola v. City of Lakewood, 426 N.E.2d 1187 (Ohio App. 1980) (court distinguishes agency and reliance doctrines in commercial context, where customer has time to read and act on disclaimers of liability, from hospital emergency-room context, where patient often has no realistic opportunity to absorb or react to information about ownership and control); Beeck v. Tucson General Hospital, 500 P.2d 1153 (Ariz. App. 1972) (court finds hospital vicariously liable for negligence of radiological technician; opinion focuses not only on the fact that the hospital furnished all the equipment for the radiology department, had entered into an exclusive

contract with a particular group of radiologists, and exercised extensive control over the employment of the technicians, but also that radiology "was an inherent function of the hospital, a function without which the hospital could not properly achieve its purpose.").

Some courts in other jurisdictions have refused to join this trend. *See, e.g.,* Gunn v. St. Elizabeth Medical Center, 1993 WL 503239 (Ohio Ct. App. 1993) (plaintiff failed to provide evidence showing that the hospital made representations causing the decedent to believe that the doctor was operating as an apparent agent under the hospital's authority or that he was induced to rely upon the agency relationship; the court noted that the contract between the hospital and the group that provided emergency room services specifically provided that the doctors were independent contractors and that the hospital had no control over the manner or mode in which the emergency room doctor practiced medicine with the exception that all services would be performed within generally accepted and approved medical standards); Holmes v. University Health Service, Inc., 423 S.E.2d 281 (Ga. App. 1992) (finding no apparent agency where hospital consent form and signs in patient registration area assert that physicians providing services in the hospital are not employees or agents of the hospital).

Other courts sharply disagree with these rulings and will allow juries to find apparent agency not only with respect to emergency room doctors and anesthesiologists, but also with respect to other specialists "supplied" by the hospital (rather than chosen by the patient). According to Coleman v. McCurtain Memorial Medical Management, Inc., 771 F. Supp. 343 (E.D. Okla. 1991),

> The relevant inquiry for the application of this doctrine is "whether the plaintiff, at the time of his admission to the hospital, was looking to the hospital for treatment of his physical ailments or merely viewed the hospital as the situs where his physician would treat him for his problems." The physician's status as an independent contractor, whether it be by virtue of a contract with the hospital or by an assessment of the control exercised by the hospital over the physician, is of little significance with regard to the resolution of the ostensible agency question. [T]he critical factor in the evaluation of an ostensible agency proposal is the existence of a preexisting physician-patient relationship.

Id. at 348–49. In Kashishian v. Port, 481 N.W.2d 277 (Wis. 1992), the Wisconsin Supreme Court held that, in part because of advertising by the defendant hospital and hospitals in general, it was a jury question whether a patient who was admitted to a hospital by her family physician could establish that the cardiologist who treated her was the hospital's apparent agent. *See also* Cuker v. Hillsborough County Hospital Authority, 605 So.2d 998 (Fla. App. 1992) (obstetricians who contracted to staff hospital department may be hospital's apparent agents vis-à-vis patient transferred to tertiary care hospital because of childbirth complications); Fulton v. Quinn, 1993 WL 19674 (Del. Super. 1993) (hospital's "on call" orthopedic surgeon may be hospital's apparent agent vis-à-vis a patient admitted through the emergency room).

Who should have the burden of proof regarding "holding out" or "reliance" in establishing or refuting claims of apparent agency? And what are the appropriate elements of this burden? Should a plaintiff be able to rely on generalized public expectations? If so, should a hospital then be allowed to rebut that proof by a showing that it affirmatively disavowed any employer-employee relationship between it and the physician accused of negligence? If that rebuttal is allowed, what evidence is necessary? A small sign? A big sign with flashing neon lights? Tiny print buried in a long form giving consent for treatment? Big bold print? Instead, should a plaintiff have to show that his or her particular expectations were established by affirmative acts of the hospital? If that is the burden of proof, again, what would constitute sufficient evidence to allow a plaintiff to take the question to a jury? How likely will it be that such evidence exists? How do these answers regarding burden and elements of proof for apparent agency differ from the evidence on which the court in *Jackson* relied in establishing a nondelegable duty? In thinking about this last question, remember that the court granted Jackson partial summary judgment on the issue of nondelegable duty. To what extent, if any, were issues regarding "holding out" or "reliance" relevant to this grant of partial summary judgment? Finally, consider carefully whether your answers to these questions should pertain to all of a hospital's operations or just to some discrete portions and, concomitantly, to certain types of physicians, as well as to other types of health care professionals or employees who work within a hospital. Particularly with regard to nondelegable duties, think about the various factors on which the court relied, in establishing nondelegable duties, and consider whether those factors are pertinent to the multitude of types of services offered in hospitals? Do these rationales apply to the whole operation, to parts and if the latter, to which parts?

6.   THE RISE OF HOSPITAL CORPORATE LIABILITY

a.   The Scope of Corporate Liability and the Structure of Hospital Governance

Thus far the focus has been on the hospital's liability for the actions of its employees or agents engaged in patient treatment. The question is whether a hospital can be liable for its "own" acts and omissions. Such acts can be performed not only by the board of directors and senior administrative and medical officials, but also by any employee or medical staff member whose organizational role involves carrying out a duty or function of the hospital as an institution. Four areas in particular have given rise to litigation about hospitals' direct duties to patients regarding quality of care. The first involves the hospital's duty to screen out incompetent physicians and other providers at the time of initial appointment or reappointment to the medical staff, a duty recognized even by the *McDonald* court in 1876. For a modern example, see Johnson v. Misericordia Community Hospital,

301 N.W.2d 156 (Wis. 1981) (hospital breached duty of reasonable care by failing to check with previous hospitals where physician's privileges had been revoked). Second, hospitals have been held liable for failing to respond to apparent serious errors by physicians as they occur. *See* Darling v. Charleston Community Memorial Hospital, 211 N.E.2d 253 (Ill. 1965), set out below.

Third, and related, hospitals have been held liable for failing to monitor the performance of particular physicians, and of failing to restrict or terminate doctors with a track record of significant mistakes. *See, e.g.,* Elam v. College Park Hospital, 183 Cal. Rptr. 156 (App. 1982); Corleto v. Shore Memorial Hospital, 350 A.2d 534 (N.J. Super. 1975). Fourth, hospitals have a duty to provide adequate equipment, policies, training and supervision to their employees, a point made in the *Truhitte* case regarding systems for counting surgical sponges. For a similar description of the scope of hospital corporate liability, see Thompson v. Nason Hospital, 591 A.2d 703 (Pa. 1991). Cutting across these particular duties are questions about the relative powers, duties, and rights of the major actors in the hospital: the doctors, nurses, administration, organized medical staff, and governing board.

The typical structure of the private nonprofit hospital has been described as a "triad" composed of the governing body, the administration or management, and the "self-governing" medical staff. According to standards promulgated by the Joint Commission (formerly the Joint Commission on the Accreditation of Hospitals), the governing body is responsible for establishing policy, maintaining quality patient care, and providing for institutional management and planning. The medical staff is described as having overall responsibility for the quality of the professional services as well as the responsibility of accounting therefore to the governing body. Accountability is said to be consistent with a framework of self-governance of the medical staff; neither the governing body nor the medical staff may unilaterally amend the medical staff bylaws. The administrator or chief executive officer is appointed by and responsible to the governing body, but has no direct authority over the medical staff, which has the right of direct access to the governing body.

Despite these tensions and ambiguities, the clear message of the Joint Commission standards is that according to the hospital industry and medical profession themselves, hospitals have important and specific responsibilities as institutions for the quality of care delivered under their auspices. However, as articulated by the Joint Commission and as expressed in actual hospital practice, these responsibilities are allocated among, and often shared by, the governing body, the medical staff, and hospital administration, and numerous committees and joint committees. As K. J. Williams, a doctor and hospital consultant puts it, "[w]hat frequently happens is that responsibility and authority are diffused and diluted throughout committees of the medical staff rather than being pinpointed in certain officials. Accordingly, that which is everyone's business becomes no one's business." K. J. Williams, *The Quandary of the*

Hospital Administrator in Dealing with the Medical Malpractice Problem, 55 NEB. L. REV. 401, 407 (1976). The question for the courts has been the extent to which the accreditation standards, their analogues in state licensure laws and hospital bylaws, and more broadly the social expectations of the hospital's mission that they both define and reflect, should function not only as voluntary industry guidelines with often minimal effects, but also as legal standards for assessing hospitals' responsibility for quality of care.

b.   The Hospital's Duty to Monitor Ongoing Treatment Provided by Independent Physicians With Staff Privileges

Darling v. Charleston Community Memorial Hospital

211 N.E.2d 253 (Ill. 1965)

■ SCHAEFER, JUSTICE:

On November 5, 1960, the plaintiff [Dorrence Darling II], who was 18 years old, broke his leg while playing in a college football game. He was taken to the emergency room at the defendant [Charleston Community Memorial Hospital] where Dr. Alexander, who was on emergency call that day, treated him. Dr. Alexander, with the assistance of hospital personnel, applied traction and placed the leg in a plaster cast. A heat cradle was applied to dry the cast. Not long after the application of the cast plaintiff was in great pain and his toes, which protruded from the cast, became swollen and dark in color. They eventually became cold and insensitive. On the evening of November 6, Dr. Alexander 'notched' the cast around the toes, and on the afternoon of the next day he cut the cast approximately three inches up from the foot. On November 8 he split the sides of the cast with a Stryker saw; in the course of cutting the cast the plaintiff's leg was cut on both sides. Blood and other seepage were observed by the nurses and others, and there was a stench in the room, which one witness said was the worst he had smelled since World War II. The plaintiff remained in Charleston Hospital until November 19, when he was transferred to Barnes Hospital in St. Louis and placed under the care of Dr. Fred Reynolds, head of orthopedic surgery at Washington University School of Medicine and Barnes Hospital. Dr. Reynolds found that the fractured leg contained a considerable amount of dead tissue which in his opinion resulted from interference with the circulation of blood in the limb caused by swelling or hemorrhaging of the leg against the construction of the cast. Dr. Reynolds performed several operations in a futile attempt to save the leg but ultimately it had to be amputated eight inches below the knee.

[In the subsequent lawsuit against Dr. Alexander and the hospital, Dr. Alexander paid $40,000 in settlement. The jury returned a verdict against the hospital for $150,000, which amount was reduced by the $40,000 paid by Dr. Alexander. The judgment against the hospital was affirmed by the intermediate appellate court, which summarized the evidence in a lengthy opinion, 200 N.E.2d 149 (Ill. App. 1964).]

The plaintiff contends that it established that the defendant [hospital] was negligent in permitting Dr. Alexander to do orthopedic work of the kind required in this case, and not requiring him to review his operative procedures to bring them up to date; in failing, through its medical staff, to exercise adequate supervision over the case, especially since Dr. Alexander had been placed on emergency duty by the hospital, and in not requiring consultation, particularly after complications had developed. Plaintiff contends also that in a case which developed as this one did, it was the duty of the nurses to watch the protruding toes constantly for changes of color, temperature and movement, and to check circulation every ten to twenty minutes, whereas the proof showed that these things were done only a few times a day. Plaintiff argues that it was the duty of the hospital staff to see that these procedures were followed, and that either the nurses were derelict in failing to report developments in the case to the hospital administrator, he was derelict in bringing them to the attention of the medical staff, or the staff was negligent in failing to take action. Defendant is a licensed and accredited hospital, and the plaintiff contends that the licensing regulations, accreditation standards, and its own bylaws define the hospital's duty, and that an infraction of them imposes liability for the resulting injury.

The defendant's position is stated in the following excerpts from its brief: "It is a fundamental rule of law that only an individual properly educated and licensed, and not a corporation, may practice medicine. Accordingly, a hospital is powerless under the law to forbid or command any act by a physician or surgeon in the practice of his profession. A hospital is not an insurer of the patient's recovery, but only owes the patient the duty to exercise such reasonable care as his known condition requires and that degree of care, skill and diligence used by hospitals generally in that community. Where the evidence shows that the hospital care was in accordance with standard practice obtaining in similar hospitals, and Plaintiff produces no evidence to the contrary, the jury cannot conclude that the opposite is true even if they disbelieve the hospital witnesses. A hospital is not liable for the torts of its nurse committed while the nurse was but executing the orders of the patient's physician, unless such order is so obviously negligent as to lead any reasonable person to anticipate that substantial injury would result to the patient from the execution of such order. The extent of the duty of a hospital with respect to actual medical care of a professional nature such as is furnished by a physician is to use reasonable care in selecting medical doctors. When such care in the selection of the staff is accomplished, and nothing indicates that a physician so selected is incompetent or that such incompetence should have been discovered, more cannot be expected from the hospital administration."

The basic dispute, as posed by the parties, centers upon the duty that rested upon the defendant hospital.

Custom is relevant in determining the standard of care because it illustrates what is feasible, it suggests a body of knowledge of which the defendant should be aware, and it warns of the possibility of far-reaching consequences if a higher standard is required. But custom should never be conclusive.

In the present case the regulations, standards, and bylaws which the plaintiff introduced into evidence, performed much the same function as did evidence of custom. This evidence aided the jury in deciding what was feasible and what the defendant knew or should have known. It did not conclusively determine the standard of care and the jury was not instructed that it did.

The Standards for Hospital Accreditation, the state licensing regulations and the defendant's bylaws demonstrate that the medical profession and other responsible authorities regard it as both desirable and feasible that a hospital assume certain responsibilities for the care of the patient.

We now turn to an application of these considerations to this case. [A]n entire verdict is not to be set aside if one or more of the grounds is sufficient. Therefore we need not analyze all of the issues submitted to the jury. Two of them were that the defendant had negligently: "5. Failed to have a sufficient number of trained nurses for bedside care of all patients at all times capable of recognizing the progressive gangrenous condition of the plaintiff's right leg, and of bringing the same to the attention of the hospital administration and to the medical staff so that adequate consultation could have been secured and such conditions rectified; ... 7. Failed to require consultation with or examination by members of the hospital surgical staff skilled in such treatment; or to review the treatment rendered to the plaintiff and to require consultants to be called in as needed."

We believe that the jury verdict is supportable on either of these grounds. On the basis of the evidence before it the jury could reasonably have concluded that the nurses did not test for circulation in the leg as frequently as necessary, that skilled nurses would have promptly recognized the conditions that signaled a dangerous impairment of circulation in the plaintiff's leg, and would have known that the condition would become irreversible in a matter of hours. At that point it became the nurses' duty to inform the attending physician, and if he failed to act, to advise the hospital authorities so that appropriate action might be taken. As to consultation, there is no dispute that the hospital failed to review Dr. Alexander's work or require a consultation; the only issue is whether its failure to do so was negligence. On the evidence before it the jury could reasonably have found that it was.

Notes

1. *A landmark case. Darling* is widely viewed as the landmark opinion that inaugurated the doctrine of corporate liability for hospitals. *See* I. Trotter Hardy, *When Doctrines Collide: Corporate Negligence and Respondeat Superior When Hospital Employees Fail to Speak Up*, 61 TUL. L. REV. 85, 92 n.25 (1986).

2. *Measuring the hospital standard of care.* As the Illinois Supreme Court recognized in its *Darling* opinion, the crucial doctrinal breakthrough was its rejection of the hospital's argument that hospital duties should be defined solely by the local customary practices of similarly situated hospitals, and rather could be defined by state licensing regulations and national accreditation standards. Indeed, in an ironic moment at trial, a hospital administrator called by the defense to testify that the hospital was in compliance with customary practice, conceded on cross-examination that he agreed with the famous Dr. MacEachern that a hospital is more than just bricks and mortar, and that the governing board of the hospital is responsible for the proper care of the patient, and has the power to choose the standard of medicine practiced in the hospital. *Darling*, 200 N.E.2d at 173. Thus did MacEachern's vision of the hospital as a community corporation move from often ignored rhetoric to judicially-enforceable law.

3. *Further elaboration of the corporate liability doctrine.* Applying Thompson v. Nason Hospital, 591 A.2d 703 (Pa. 1991), the Pennsylvania Supreme Court case adopting hospital corporate liability, an intermediate appeals court explained the doctrine as follows:

> The Thompson theory of corporate liability will not be triggered every time something goes wrong in a hospital which harms a patient. Acts of malpractice occur at the finest hospitals, and these hospitals are subject to liability under theories of respondeat superior or ostensible agency. To establish corporate negligence, a plaintiff must show more than an act of negligence by an individual for whom the hospital is responsible. Rather, Thompson requires a plaintiff to show that the hospital itself is breaching a duty and is somehow substandard. This requires evidence that the hospital knew or should have known about the breach of duty that is harming its patients. Thus, a hospital is not directly liable under Thompson just because one of its employees or agents makes a mistake which constitutes malpractice. Just as regular negligence is measured by a reasonable person standard, a hospital's corporate negligence will be measured against what a reasonable hospital under similar circumstances should have done. Thompson contemplates a kind of systemic negligence, such as where a hospital knows that one of its staff physicians is incompetent but lets that physician practice medicine anyway; or where a hospital should realize that its patients are routinely getting infected because the nursing staff is leaving catheters in the same spot for too long, yet the hospital fails to formulate, adopt or enforce any rule about moving catheters.

Edwards v. Brandywine Hospital, 652 A.2d 1382, 1386 (Pa. Super. 1995).

Negligent credentialing of medical staff is a particularly fertile ground for claims against hospitals in cases involving negligence by physicians with staff privileges who nonetheless work as independent contractors.

4. Think back to the discussion of nondelegable duties in *Jackson* and the following notes. Are the factors to which the court pointed in *Jackson*

the same or different from the factors discussed to establish corporate liability? How about the duties imposed under each category? Are they the same or do they differ? Until very recently the conditions to be licensed by the state or to obtain private accreditation from the Joint Commission pertained to the structure of the hospital—e.g., the ratio of registered nurses to patients—or to processes by which care was delivered—e.g., the points to be covered at the time of an admission, aka an "in-take." Only very recently has private accreditation moved to some attempt to measure actual outcomes of care—e.g., what is the survival rate following a particular surgical procedure? If a hospital has a duty to monitor ongoing care, is that duty satisfied by its attention to the structure in which care is provided, the process of its delivery, or all the way "out" to the outcomes of care (or some combination of these three ways to assure quality)? Should distinctions be drawn around the particular corporate responsibility? For example, what burdens should be imposed with regard to initial credentialing, in contrast to re-credentialing, curtailing or eliminating privileges, dealing with reported errors, patterns of errors, and so on? The search costs with regard to initial credentialing have been eased somewhat by the creation of the National Practitioner Data Bank, discussed more fully below in Chapter 19, which is a repository of some types of "reportable events," such as termination of privileges at a hospital.

Think also back to the questions raised in the notes following *Jackson* regarding the areas of the hospital and the types of physicians, other professionals, employees and services to which nondelegable duties may apply. Both *Jackson* and *Darling* involved negligent care provided in the emergency room. One could say that in no part of a hospital might the corporate responsibilities be higher, because in the great majority of cases, no established relationship exists between a patient presenting at the emergency department and the professionals who staff it. This of course helps explain why the *Jackson* court was so inclined to read state law as barring delegation of responsibility at that point. What about the labor and delivery department? The operating theaters? And so on? Can distinctions be drawn based either on the nature of relationships between staff and patients in these different contexts or on the burden imposed on the hospital, as a corporate entity, to monitor ongoing care in these different domains?

Finally, can and should distinctions be drawn around types of errors? The negligence in *Darling* was so "gross," literally and figuratively as it could be smelled like the stench of war, that one might say that bad facts make bad law that is not and should not be easily and readily generalized. In Chapter 20 we will discuss errors that are characterized as "never events"—e.g., removing a patient's healthy kidney instead of the diseased one, with the result that the patient is left to kidney dialysis for the rest of his or her life or to a transplant should he or she qualify for one and make it to the top of the queue. Never events just should never occur. Should corporate liability, particularly its duty to monitor ongoing care, be limited to never events or some other subset of errors? At some point, does the imposition of nondelegable duties or corporate liability swallow the rule that doctors are independent contractors? Should it? Consider all these questions in the context of the next note, describing the reality of the "political economy" of the hospital, and then return to these questions following your reading of *Muse*, the next reprinted case. Is the corporatization of the hospital an unmitigated good and if not, what kinds of lines can and should be drawn?

5. *An accurate depiction of the realities of hospital administration?* Although the *Darling* opinion is consistent with the rhetoric of the Joint Commission and the hospital industry that the hospital medical staff, and the hospital itself, are responsible in some sense for quality of care in the hospital, how consistent is this expectation with the realities of power and influence in hospitals? Is it realistic to expect non-physician administrators and lay governing board members to overrule or even seriously question well-known senior physicians?

In a 1976 article, Dr. K. J. Williams, a doctor and hospital consultant, detailed the hospital administrator's and governing board's lack of real power over the medical staff. *See* Williams, *The Quandary of the Hospital Administrator in Dealing with the Medical Malpractice Problem.* Although in theory the medical staff is supposed to be an "integral" part of the hospital that functions as an "organizational extension" of the governing board in assuring quality of care, in practice, Dr. Williams wrote, medical staff strongly resist any direction or oversight from the administrator and governing board. Indeed, even as a formal matter, Joint Commission standards and AHA Model Bylaws, incorporated into most hospital bylaws, restrict governing board authority by requiring any change in the medical staff (as distinct from the hospital) bylaws to be approved by both the governing board and the medical staff. *See* St. John's Hospital Medical Staff v. St. John Regional Medical Center, Inc., 245 N.W.2d 472 (S.D. 1976).

Williams reported that hospital administrators, not to mention governing boards, are often not told of patterns of substandard physician care well known to the medical and nursing staff. Even when hospital management does find out about such problems, it must rely on the medical staff to do something about them. The medical staff leaders in turn are often effectively disabled from acting by vague bylaws, lack of clear standards and institutional traditions, and rotating leadership and overlapping committees that diffuse responsibility. Williams closes his analysis of the hospital administrator's "quandary" by focusing on a case of a repeatedly incompetent physician who severely injured a teenage patient by negligently "treating" him for the wrong condition. If the hospital's mission is truly to safeguard patients' interests, Williams asks, should not the patient be told of the nature and cause of his injury? (Recall the duty of disclosure arguments discussed in the informed consent materials, above). This suggestion was regarded by the hospital's governing board "as akin to asking them to commit suicide," thereby further dramatizing the tensions in the hospital's responsibility for quality of care.

To point out these difficulties and realities is not to suggest that the doctrine of corporate liability be abandoned. The point is rather that seriously pursuing the goals of the corporate liability doctrine and the industry's own standards is a long-term and complex process in which malpractice law has played, and will continue to play, an important role, both in its own right, and as a stimulus to other regulatory efforts.

For an article exploring the management and regulation of physician/hospital relationships in a far more market-driven environment, see James F. Blumstein, *Of Doctors and Hospitals: Setting the Analytical Framework for Managing and Regulating the Relationship*, 4 IND. HEALTH L. REV. 209 (2007). Professor Blumstein argues that the increasingly entrepreneurial environment in which hospitals and physicians function argues for a liberalization of laws that constrain certain types of market conduct so that entities can "adapt to entrepreneurial opportunities":

> The objective of regulatory policy should be to develop a regulatory regime that is neutral to organizational form and that allows institutions and physicians to cooperate or compete according to market conditions, provided that market conditions are maintained and that quality outcomes are properly encouraged.

Id. at 213.

What do you think Professor Blumstein has in mind when he states that quality outcomes should be encouraged? Keep this approach to encouraging quality in mind as you read the materials below that focus on pay for performance and performance incentivization.

c. Corporate Interference With Appropriate Medical Care

Muse v. Charter Health Care

452 S.E.2d 589 (N.C. App. 1995)

■ LEWIS, JUDGE:

This appeal arises from a judgment in favor of plaintiffs in an action for the wrongful death of Delbert Joseph Muse, III (hereinafter "Joe"). Joe was the son of Delbert Joseph Muse, Jr. (hereinafter "Mr. Muse") and Jane K. Muse (hereinafter "Mrs. Muse"), plaintiffs. The jury found that defendant Charter Hospital of Winston–Salem, Inc. (hereinafter "Charter Hospital" or "the hospital") was negligent in that, *inter alia,* it had a policy or practice which required physicians to discharge patients when their insurance expired and that this policy interfered with the exercise of the medical judgment of Joe's treating physician, Dr. L. Jarrett Barnhill, Jr. The jury awarded plaintiffs compensatory damages of approximately $1,000,000. The jury found that Mr. and Mrs. Muse were contributorily negligent, but that Charter Hospital's conduct was willful or wanton, and awarded punitive damages of $2,000,000 against Charter Hospital. Further, the jury found that Charter Hospital was an instrumentality of defendant Charter Medical Corporation (hereinafter "Charter Medical") and awarded punitive damages of $4,000,000 against Charter Medical.

On 12 June 1986, Joe, who was sixteen years old at the time, was admitted to Charter Hospital for treatment related to his depression and suicidal thoughts. Joe's treatment team consisted of Dr. Barnhill, as treating physician, Fernando Garzon, as nursing therapist, and Betsey Willard, as social worker. During his hospitalization, Joe experienced auditory hallucinations, suicidal and homicidal thoughts, and major depression. Joe's insurance coverage was set to expire on 12 July 1986. As that date neared, Dr. Barnhill decided that a blood test was needed to determine the proper dosage of a drug he was administering to Joe. The blood test was scheduled for 13 July, the day after Joe's insurance was to expire. Dr. Barnhill requested that the hospital administrator allow Joe to stay at Charter Hospital two more days, until 14 July, with Mr. and Mrs. Muse signing a promissory note to pay for the two extra days. The test results did not come back from the lab until 15 July. Nevertheless, Joe was discharged on 14 July and was referred by Dr. Barnhill to the Guilford County Area Mental Health, Mental Retardation and Substance Abuse Authority (hereinafter "Mental Health Authority") for outpatient treatment. Plaintiffs' evidence tended to show that Joe's condition upon discharge was worse than when he entered the hospital. Defendants' evidence, however, tended to show that while his prognosis remained guarded, Joe's condition at discharge was improved. Upon his discharge, Joe went on a one-week family vacation. On 22 July he began outpatient treatment at the Mental Health Authority, where he was seen by Dr. David Slonaker, a clinical psychologist. Two days later, Joe again met with Dr. Slonaker. Joe failed to show up at his 30 July appointment, and the next day he took a fatal overdose of Desipramine, one of his prescribed drugs.

On appeal, defendants present numerous assignments of error. We find merit in one of defendants' arguments.

I.

[The Court first holds that Chartered Hospital was an instrumentality of Chartered Health Care Corporation and each could incur joint and several liability in its own right. The failure to so instruct resulted in reversible error, leading to remand on the issue of punitive damages alone.]

II.

Defendants next argue that the trial court submitted the case to the jury on an erroneous theory of hospital liability that does not exist under the law of North Carolina. As to the theory in question, the trial court instructed: "[A] hospital is under a duty not to have policies or practices which operate in a way that interferes with the ability of a physician to exercise his medical judgment. A violation of this duty would be negligence." The jury found that there existed "a policy or practice which required physicians to discharge patients when their insurance benefits expire and which interfered with the exercise of Dr. Barnhill's medical judgment." Defendants contend that this theory of liability does not fall within any theories previously accepted by our courts.

In *Blanton v. Moses H. Cone Memorial Hospital, Inc.*, 354 S.E.2d 455 (1987), our Supreme Court held that the appropriate standard for determining whether a valid claim exists against a hospital is the standard of the ordinary, reasonable, and prudent person. *Id.* at 375, 354 S.E.2d at 457. The Court further stated: "Actionable negligence is the failure of one owing a duty to another to do what a reasonable and prudent man would ordinarily have done, or doing what such a person would not have done, which omission or commission is the proximate cause of injury to another." *Id.*

[H]ospitals in this state owe a duty of care to their patients. *Id.* In *Burns v. Forsyth County Hospital Authority, Inc.*, 344 S.E.2d 839, 845 (1986), this Court held that a hospital has a duty to the patient to obey the instructions of a doctor, absent the instructions being obviously negligent or dangerous. Another recognized duty is the duty to make a reasonable effort to monitor and oversee the treatment prescribed and administered by doctors practicing at the hospital. In light of these holdings, it seems axiomatic that the hospital has the duty not to institute policies or practices which interfere with the doctor's medical judgment. We hold that pursuant to the reasonable person standard, Charter Hospital had a duty not to institute a policy or practice which required that patients be discharged when their insurance expired and which interfered with the medical judgment of Dr. Barnhill.

III.

Defendants next argue that even if the theory of negligence submitted to the jury was proper, the jury's finding that Charter Hospital had such a practice was not supported by sufficient evidence. The issue before us is whether the trial court erred in denying defendants' motion for judgment notwithstanding the verdict. In reviewing the denial of a defendant's motion for judgment notwithstanding the verdict, the question is whether the evidence, when viewed in the light most favorable to the plaintiff, giving the plaintiff the benefit of every reasonable inference, was sufficient to go to the jury. We conclude that in the case at hand, the evidence was sufficient to go to the jury.

Plaintiffs' evidence included the testimony of Charter Hospital employees and outside experts. Fernando Garzon, Joe's nursing therapist at Charter Hospital, testified that the hospital had a policy of discharging patients when their insurance expired. Specifically, when the issue of insurance came up in treatment team meetings, plans were made to discharge the patient. When Dr. Barnhill and the other psychiatrists and therapists spoke of insurance, they seemed to lack autonomy. For example, Garzon testified, they would state, "So and so is to be discharged. We must do this." Finally, Garzon testified that when he returned from a vacation, and Joe was no longer at the hospital, he asked several employees why Joe had been discharged and they all responded that he was discharged because his insurance had expired. Jane Sims, a former staff member at the hospital, testified that several employees expressed alarm about Joe's impending discharge, and that a therapist explained that Joe could no longer stay at the hospital because his insurance had expired. Sims also testified that Dr. Barnhill had misgivings about discharging Joe, and that Dr. Barnhill's frustration was apparent to everyone. One of plaintiffs' experts testified that based on a study regarding the length of patient stays at Charter Hospital, it was his opinion that patients were discharged based on insurance, regardless of their medical condition. Other experts testified that based on Joe's serious condition on the date of discharge, the expiration of insurance coverage must have caused Dr. Barnhill to discharge Joe. The experts further testified as to the relevant standard of care, and concluded that Charter Hospital's practices were below the standard of care and caused Joe's death. We hold that this evidence was sufficient to go to the jury.

Defendants further argue that the evidence was insufficient to support the jury's finding that Charter Hospital engaged in conduct that was willful or wanton. An act is willful when it is done purposely and deliberately in violation of the law, or when it is done knowingly and of set purpose, or when the mere will has free play, without yielding to reason ... It is wanton when it is done of wicked purpose, or when it is done needlessly, with reckless indifference to the rights of others. We conclude that the jury could have reasonably found from the above-stated evidence that Charter Hospital acted knowingly and of set purpose, and with reckless indifference to the rights of others. Therefore, we hold that the finding of willful or wanton conduct on the part of Charter Hospital was supported by sufficient evidence.

IV.

Defendants' next argument is that the trial court erred in not granting their motion for judgment notwithstanding the verdict, on the ground that the negligent acts of the Muses and Dr. Barnhill were superseding causes of Joe's death. Defendants' contention is that the superseding negligence of the Muses and Dr. Barnhill insulated the negligence of Charter Hospital as a matter of law, and that, therefore, the hospital's negligence was not a proximate cause of the suicide.

The doctrine of superseding, or intervening, negligence is well established in our law. In order for an intervening cause to relieve the original wrongdoer of liability, the intervening cause must be a new cause, which intervenes between the original negligent act and the injury ultimately suffered, and which breaks the chain of causation set in motion by the original wrongdoer and becomes itself solely responsible for the injury. The intervening cause must be an independent force which turns aside the natural sequence of events set in motion by the original wrongdoer and produces a result which would not otherwise have followed, and which could not have been reasonably anticipated. The rule in this jurisdiction is that except in cases so clear that there can be no two opinions among fair-minded people, the question should be left for the jury to determine whether the intervening act and the resultant injury were such that the original wrongdoer could reasonably have expected them to occur as a result of his own negligence.

The evidence, when viewed in the light most favorable to plaintiffs, with all reasonable inferences being afforded to plaintiffs, tended to show that the hospital had a policy of requiring the discharge of patients when their insurance expired and that this policy interfered with Dr. Barnhill's medical judgment regarding Joe's discharge. Dr. Barnhill was thereby put in a position such that he could not disclose the severity of Joe's condition to the Muses. He then discharged Joe, transferring him to outpatient treatment at the public facility. Any negligence of Dr. Barnhill in discharging Joe and in not warning the Muses, or of the Muses, in not properly supervising Joe after discharge, did not turn aside the natural sequence of events set in motion by the hospital's misconduct. Rather, the alleged intervening acts, in the natural and ordinary course of things, could have been anticipated by defendants as not entirely improbable. Thus, the hospital's negligence was not superseded, and thereby insulated, as a matter of law. Accordingly, the trial court properly denied defendants' motion for judgment notwithstanding the verdict.

Defendants also contend that the trial court erred in directing a verdict for plaintiffs on the issue of whether Dr. Slonaker's alleged negligence was a superseding cause of Joe's death. In reviewing the granting of a directed verdict, the question is whether the evidence, when viewed in the light most favorable to the non-movant, and giving the non-movant the benefit of every reasonable inference, was sufficient to go to the jury. When viewed in this light, the evidence tended to show that Joe saw Dr. Slonaker at the Mental Health Authority on two occasions after his discharge from Charter Hospital, that Dr. Slonaker had reviewed Joe's discharge summary, and that Joe reported to Dr. Slonaker that he was still having hallucinations. Further, one of plaintiffs' experts testified that Dr. Slonaker's treatment was "[s]o totally inadequate that he could possibly not have had [the documents in Joe's Charter Hospital file] to review, or if he did review them, he paid no damned attention to them." However, defendants have pointed to no evidence in the record which tends to show that Dr. Slonaker's treatment of Joe was a cause of Joe's suicide. Thus, there was not sufficient evidence to submit to the jury the issue of whether Dr. Slonaker's alleged negligence was a superseding cause of Joe's death, and the trial court did not err in directing a verdict for plaintiffs on this issue.

Defendants next contend that Joe's suicide was a superseding cause of his death and that the trial court erred in granting summary judgment for plaintiffs on the issue. This question is apparently one of first impression in this state. However, we cannot agree with defendants' contention. The rule must be that where a psychiatric hospital has assumed the care of a suicidal patient, and as a result of its negligence, the patient commits suicide, the hospital cannot claim that the suicide was a superseding cause, insulating the hospital from liability. Were the rule otherwise, the wrongdoer "could become indifferent to the performance of his duty [to care for the suicidal patient] knowing that the very eventuality that he was under a duty to prevent would, upon its occurrence, relieve him from responsibility.'' Accordingly, we conclude that the trial court properly granted summary judgment in favor of plaintiffs on this issue.

V.

Defendants' next argument is that the contributory negligence of the Muses bars their recovery as beneficiaries of Joe's estate. This argument is without merit, however, as contributory negligence does not bar recovery in a wrongful death action where, as here, the defendants' conduct was found to be wanton or willful.

VI.

Defendants next contend that the trial court erred in admitting certain testimony by plaintiffs' experts. However, in each instance, the first time such testimony was offered, defendants failed to object. Thus, the subsequent admission of similar testimony over objection was not prejudicial error. Accordingly, defendants' contention is without merit.

VII.

[the Court concluded that punitive damages did not violate defendants' due process rights as unreasonably in excess of the harm and compensatory damages and that no error was committed in connection with the punitive award]

VIII.

[the Court rejects defendants' other objections to the verdict and award]

■ ORR, J., dissents:

After a careful review of the record and applicable law, I must respectfully dissent from the majority on the submission of the issue on willful or wanton conduct. While recognizing the severe emotional impact of the facts surrounding the case, my research concludes that there was insufficient evidence to warrant the submission of willful and wanton conduct by defendant to the jury. Therefore, in my opinion, the damage awards that were predicated on the jury's positive answer to the willful or wanton conduct issue must fail.

Plaintiffs contend that acts of the defendant hospital constituted negligence in that (1) there was a policy or practice of requiring physicians to discharge patients from the hospital when their insurance benefits expired, and (2) defendant allowed this policy or practice to operate in a way that interfered with Dr. Barnhill's medical judgment, thereby causing Dr. Barnhill to discharge Joseph Muse, III in a medically-inappropriate manner.

For purposes of this analysis, we can assume that there was such a policy and that there was some evidence from which a jury could find that this policy influenced or interfered with Dr. Barnhill's medical judgment and his decision to discharge Joseph Muse, III. That being the case, plaintiff arguably has made out a case of negligence and the jury so determined. However, the crux of the case rests squarely on the issue of whether the evidence, taken in a light most favorable to the plaintiff, is sufficient to submit the further issue of willful or wanton conduct to the jury.

Our Supreme Court in *Akzona, Inc. v. Southern Railway Co.,* 334 S.E.2d 759, 763 (1985), defined willful and wanton conduct as follows:

> An act is done willfully when it is done purposely and deliberately in violation of law, or when it is done knowingly and of set purpose, or when the mere will has free play, without yielding to reason. "The true conceptions of willful negligence involves a deliberate purpose not to discharge some duty necessary to the safety of the person or property of another, which duty the person owing it has assumed by contract, or which is imposed on the person by operation of law." An act is wanton when it is done of wicked purpose, or when done needlessly, manifesting a reckless indifference to the rights of others. Further, while "[o]rdinary negligence has as its basis that a person charged with negligent conduct should have known the probable consequences of his act," we have said "[w]anton and willful negligence rests on the assumption that he knew the probable consequences, but was recklessly, wantonly or intentionally indifferent to the results."

Turning now to the facts of this case, there is, as previously noted, evidence that defendant hospital had a policy or practice of discharging patients when their insurance ran out. This practice was obviously done for a business purpose; however, the evidence reveals that the policy was subject to being overridden on occasion by request of the treating physician or other financial consideration. Although there also was some evidence that this policy may have affected Dr. Barnhill's decision to discharge the plaintiffs' son, such evidence, while perhaps supporting a negligence theory, does not go beyond that.

Dr. Barnhill testified that the policy did not influence his decision, and more importantly, that a range of treatment options including a state psychiatric hospital were available for the patient. No evidence was presented that could lead a jury to conclude that the policy in question involved a deliberate purpose not to discharge some duty necessary to the safety of the person in question. While it can be said that the policy to discharge was deliberate, there is no evidence that the hospital expected, anticipated or intended for the patient to be released in circumstances that put the person's safety in jeopardy. In fact, Joseph Muse, III was discharged into the custody and care of another physician and a community based mental health facility as well as the care of his parents with specific instructions for his care.

The trial court instructed the jury that "... a hospital is under a duty not to have policies or practices which operate in a way that interferes with the ability of a physician to exercise his medical ... judgment. A violation of this duty would be negligence."

While the jury found that defendant was negligent, I find insufficient evidence to raise the defendant's conduct to the level required to submit the issue of willful and wanton conduct to the jury. A policy to terminate a patient's hospitalization based upon insurance benefits ending in and of itself is not willful or wanton conduct. To sustain plaintiff's contention there must be, according to our law, a deliberate purpose not to discharge a duty necessary for a person's safety. If the hospital had simply discharged the patient with no referral to another physician or medical facility, then a cognizable claim for willful or wanton conduct would have been established. Such was not the case here, as I read the record, and although Dr. Barnhill's care in discharging the patient may well have been negligent, there is nothing to suggest that the hospital's policy or its implementation by Dr. Barnhill was done with reckless or deliberate disregard for the patient's safety. Therefore, I conclude that the trial court erred in submitting the issue of willful and wanton conduct to the jury and would accordingly vote to reverse.

Notes

1. *Is this how it really works?* What do you make of Judge Orr's dissent, that it was the normal course of business to discharge patients when the insurance ran out, and all the doctor had to do in order to get more time for the patient was to ask?

2. The court found sufficient evidence that the hospital engaged in a policy or practice of almost always discharging patients when their insurance ran out regardless of patients' medical conditions and needs. Suppose that instead the hospital had a policy that when insurance was nearly exhausted there would be a meeting of the health care team during which both the financial situation and the patient's medical conditions and needs were discussed. Suppose that the evidence showed that as a result of these meetings, patients were sometimes discharged, and sometimes not, when their insurance was exhausted. Same result on the negligence question? On the question of willful and wanton conduct? In thinking about these questions, reflect back on *Murray v. UNMC Physicians*, in Chapter 14 above, in which a medical center decided not to begin treatment with a drug, Flucan, until payment had been secured because stopping the drug after it had been started might have been fatal to the patient.

Look also how the lower and appellate courts framed the issue in very traditional terms: Did the hospital's policy interfere with the individual physician's medical judgment? Are there other ways to frame the issue so that it is not about protecting individual professional autonomy and yet still brings in consideration of the patient's medical condition and needs?

3. *Health care corporations versus payers and financial interference with care.* The materials later in this Part dealing with payers and health care quality make clear that insurers and health plans routinely "interfere" with medical practice by delineating what they do or do not cover, refusing to approve recommended treatments, rewarding or deterring conduct in ways that may cloud medical judgment, and steering patients away toward network providers considered to provide better "value." You also will learn that even where payers' restrictions are involved in death and injury, thereby creating the potential for liability under state law, ERISA

(whose preemption principles were introduced in Part Two) shields plan administrators and fiduciaries from the consequences of their conduct.

Not so with health care corporate providers. A hospital is a health care entity and thus has the duties attributed to health care providers under the law. It can face liability if resource constraints pressure it to push or direct medical staff toward patient care practices that kill or injure. As you will learn, there are times when entities that are treated as plan administrators in certain contexts nonetheless may be considered health care providers in other contexts. This is particularly true with entities licensed as health maintenance organizations, which by definition are hybrids—both paying for care and furnishing it.

4. *Institutional neglect.* Neglect of patients in health care institutions has been a basis of extensive institutional negligence actions. The classic study in the field is BRUCE C. VLADECK, UNLOVING CARE: THE NURSING HOME TRAGEDY (1982). *See also,* e.g., John Bellflower, *Respecting Our Elders: Can Tennessee Do More to Protect its Elders from Institutional Abuse and Neglect?* 66 TENN. L. REV. 819 (1999) (reporting that 5% of the state's nursing home population has experienced abuse and that 40% of the state's nursing homes have experienced at least 1 reported violation). Problems are particularly serious in poor communities with high minority populations and a high Medicaid dependence. David Barton Smith et. al., *Separate and Unequal: Racial Segregation and Disparities In Quality Across U.S. Nursing Homes,* 26(5) HEALTH AFFAIRS 1448 (2007). A range of legal theories, including fraud and abuse (discussed in Part Four) under the Federal False Claims Act, 31 U.S.C. §§ 3729–3733, and state false claims acts have been applied in cases involving nursing home abuse, as well as other types of pervasive neglect and abuse situations. *See* John Munich & Elizabeth Lane, *When Neglect Becomes Fraud: Quality of Care and False Claims Act,* 43 ST. LOUIS U. L.J. 27 (1999). The false claim (which you will learn more about in Part Four) constitutes payment for care that either was never rendered or else rendered in such a substandard manner as to be worthless.

7.   THE CHARITABLE IMMUNITY DOCTRINE AND CONTRACTUAL "RELEASES"

As noted above, the charitable immunity doctrine has fallen away as the provision of health care increasingly has been understood as a major business. May a hospital effectively re-instate charitable immunity through contract, i.e., by requiring patients to sign agreements releasing the hospital from liability as a condition of admission?

Tunkl v. Regents of University of Cal.

383 P.2d 441 (Cal. 1963)

■ TOBRINER, JUSTICE:

This case concerns the validity of a release from liability for future negligence imposed as a condition for admission to a charitable research hospital. For the reasons we hereinafter specify, we have concluded that an agreement between a hospital and an entering patient affects the public interest and that, in consequence, the exculpatory provision included within it must be invalid under Civil Code section 1668.

The University of California at Los Angeles Medical Center admitted Tunkl as a patient on June 11, 1956. The Regents maintain the hospital for the primary purpose of aiding and developing a program of research and education in the field of medicine; patients are selected and admitted if the study and treatment of their condition would tend to achieve these purposes. Upon his entry to the hospital, Tunkl signed a document setting forth certain 'Conditions of Admission.' The crucial condition number six reads as follows:

> RELEASE: The hospital is a nonprofit, charitable institution. In consideration of the hospital and allied services to be rendered and the rates charged therefor, the patient or his legal representative agrees to and hereby releases The Regents of the University of California, and the hospital from any and all liability for the negligent or wrongful acts or omissions of its employees, if the hospital has used due care in selecting its employees.

We begin with the dictate of the relevant Civil Code section 1668. The section states: 'All contracts which have for their object, directly or indirectly, to exempt anyone from responsibility for his own fraud, or willful injury to the person or property of another, or violation of law, whether willful or negligent, are against the policy of the law.'

[Judicial decisions have disagreed on whether the statute prohibits exculpation of any negligence, or only negligent disregard of statutory duties, or only gross negligence. Despite this diversity, there has been agreement on one doctrine.] The cases have consistently held that the exculpatory provision may stand only if it does not involve 'the public interest.'[6]

If, then, the exculpatory clause which affects the public interest cannot stand, we must ascertain those factors or characteristics which constitute the public interest. The social forces that have led to such characterization are volatile and dynamic. No definition of the concept of public interest can be contained within the four corners of a formula. The concept, always the subject of great debate, has ranged over the whole course of the common law; rather than attempt to prescribe its nature, we can only designate the situations in which it has been applied. We can determine whether the instant contract does or does not manifest the characteristics which have been held to stamp a contract as one affected with a public interest.

In placing particular contracts within or without the category of those affected with a public interest, the courts have revealed a rough outline of

---

6. The view that the exculpatory contract is valid only if the public interest is not involved represents the majority holding in the United States.

that type of transaction in which exculpatory provisions will be held invalid. Thus the attempted but invalid exemption involves a transaction which exhibits some or all of the following characteristics. It concerns a business of a type generally thought suitable for public regulation. The party seeking exculpation is engaged in performing a service of great importance to the public, which is often a matter of practical necessity for some members of the public. The party holds himself out as willing to perform this service for any member of the public who seeks it, or at least for any member coming within certain established standards. As a result of the essential nature of the service, in the economic setting of the transaction, the party invoking exculpation possesses a decisive advantage of bargaining strength against any member of the public who seeks his services. In exercising a superior bargaining power the party confronts the public with a standardized adhesion contract of exculpation, and makes no provision whereby a purchaser may pay additional reasonable fees and obtain protection against negligence. Finally, as a result of the transaction, the person or property of the purchaser is placed under the control of the seller, subject to the risk of carelessness by the seller or his agents.

While obviously no public policy opposes private, voluntary transactions in which one party, for a consideration, agrees to shoulder a risk which the law would otherwise have placed upon the other party, the above circumstances pose a different situation. In this situation the releasing party does not really acquiesce voluntarily in the contractual shifting of the risk, nor can we be reasonably certain that he receives an adequate consideration for the transfer. Since the service is one which each member of the public, presently or potentially, may find essential to him, he faces, despite his economic inability to do so, the prospect of a compulsory assumption of the risk of another's negligence.

[W]e think that the hospital-patient contract clearly falls within the category of agreements affecting the public interest. To meet that test, the agreement need only fulfill some of the characteristics above outlined; here, the relationship fulfills all of them. Thus the contract of exculpation involves an institution suitable for, and a subject of, public regulation. That the services of the hospital to those members of the public who are in special need of the particular skill of its staff and facilities constitute a practical and crucial necessity is hardly open to question.

The hospital, likewise, holds itself out as willing to perform its services for those members of the public who qualify for its research and training facilities. While it is true that the hospital is selective as to the patients it will accept, such selectivity does not negate its public aspect or the public interest in it. The hospital is selective only in the sense that it accepts from the public at large certain types of cases which qualify for the research and training in which it specializes.

In insisting that the patient accept the provision of waiver in the contract, the hospital certainly exercises a decisive advantage in bargaining. The would-be patient is in no position to reject the proffered agreement, to bargain with the hospital, or in lieu of agreement to find another hospital.

The admission room of a hospital contains no bargaining table where, as in a private business transaction, the parties can debate the terms of their contract. As a result, we cannot but conclude that the instant agreement manifested the characteristics of the so-called adhesion contract. Finally, when the patient signed the contract, he completely placed himself in the control of the hospital; he subjected himself to the risk of its carelessness.

We turn to a consideration of the two arguments urged by defendant to save the exemptive clause. Defendant first contends that while the public interest may possibly invalidate the exculpatory provision as to the paying patient, it certainly cannot do so as to the charitable one. Defendant secondly argues that even if the hospital cannot obtain exemption as to its 'own' negligence it should be in a position to do so as to that of its employees. We have found neither proposition persuasive.

As to the first, we see no distinction in the hospital's duty of due care between the paying and nonpaying patient. The duty, emanating not merely from contract but also tort, imports no discrimination based upon economic status. To immunize the hospital from negligence as to the charitable patient because he does not pay would be as abhorrent to medical ethics as it is to legal principle.

Defendant's second attempted distinction, the differentiation between its own and vicarious liability, strikes a similar discordant note. In form defendant is a corporation. In everything it does, including the selection of its employees, it necessarily acts through agents. A legion of decisions involving contracts between common carriers and their customers, public utilities and their customers, bailees and bailors, and the like, have drawn no distinction between the corporation's 'own' liability and vicarious liability resulting from negligence of agents. We see no reason to initiate so far-reaching a distinction now. If, as defendant argues, a right of action against the negligent agent is in fact a sufficient remedy, then defendant by paying a judgment against it may be subrogated to the right of the patient against the negligent agent, and thus may exercise that remedy.

[D]efendant urges that otherwise the funds of the research hospital may be deflected from the real objective of the extension of medical knowledge to the payment of claims for alleged negligence. Since a research hospital necessarily entails surgery and treatment in which fixed standards of care may not yet be evolved, defendant says the hospital should in this situation be excused from such care. But the answer lies in the fact that possible plaintiffs must prove negligence; the standards of care will themselves reflect the research nature of the treatment; the hospital will not become an insurer or guarantor of the patient's recovery. To exempt the hospital completely from any standard of due care is to grant it immunity by the side-door method of a contractual clause exacted of the patient.

We must note, finally, that the integrated and specialized society of today, structured upon mutual dependency, cannot rigidly narrow the concept of the public interest. From the observance of simple standards of due care in the driving of a car to the performance of the high standards of hospital practice, the individual citizen must be completely dependent upon the responsibility of others. The fabric of this pattern is so closely woven that the snarling of a single thread affects the whole. We cannot lightly accept a sought immunity from careless failure to provide the hospital service upon which many must depend. Even if the hospital's doors are open only to those in a specialized category, the hospital cannot claim isolated immunity in the interdependent community of our time. It, too, is part of the social fabric, and prearranged exculpation from its negligence must partly rend the pattern and necessarily affect the public interest.

Notes

1. *The reasoning underlying the decision.* Justice Tobriner's opinion in *Tunkl* stands as one of the most clear and eloquent legal expressions of what we have termed the "modestly egalitarian social contract." Bound by the jury's verdict that the patient "either knew or should have known the significance of the release," the California Supreme Court held that the law itself would not permit such contracts that altered the otherwise applicable standard of care. There were essentially two reasons for this holding. First, the court regarded the contract as coercive as a matter of law; the parties' inequality of bargaining power, the patient's desperate circumstances, and the large degree of risk that the contract shifted to the (by definition) low-income patient, meant that a jury should not be permitted to find the bargain voluntary. Second, the court viewed the hospital's contract as too inconsistent with a background legal model of social contract, reflected in the "practical and crucial necessity" to the public of hospital services, public regulation of those services, the protective doctrines of the common law, and the court's understanding of legitimate social expectations in "the interdependent community of our time."

2. *What conduct might cost charitable institutions their immunity from liability?* In University of Virginia Health Services Foundation v. Morris, 657 S.E.2d 512 (Va. 2008), the question was whether the Health Services Foundation, a nonprofit medical group practice arrangement serving the University's medical school faculty, was entitled to charitable immunity in a liability action. Established as a nonprofit corporation under § 501(c)(3) of the Internal Revenue Code (which we'll explore in Part Four), the Foundation's Articles of Incorporation stated, in part, "No part of the Foundation's net earnings shall inure to the benefit of a director or officer of the Foundation or to any private individual." The Articles also declared that one of its purposes was the provision of medical care to "benefit patients who might not otherwise receive or be able to afford medical attention" and it purported to provide treatment to all persons regardless of their ability to pay. The Foundation also participated in all public and private insurance programs and used an elaborate salary structure to pay its member physicians.

In defending against a series of liability actions, the Foundation asserted its exemption from liability as a charitable institution under the doctrine of charitable immunity, an assertion that was denied by the trial courts. Citing Virginia precedent on the Commonwealth's charitable immunity doctrine, the court concluded that no charitable immunity was appropriate given HSF's actual financial conduct:

> "To establish charitable immunity as a bar to tort liability, an entity must prove at least two distinct elements. The absence of either element makes the bar of charitable immunity inapplicable. First, the entity must show it is organized with a recognized charitable purpose and that it operates in fact in accord with that purpose. In conducting this inquiry, Virginia courts apply a two-part test, examining (1) whether the organization's articles of incorporation have a charitable or eleemosynary purpose and (2) whether the organization is in fact operated consistent with that purpose. Second, assuming the entity has met the foregoing test, it must then establish that the tort claimant was a beneficiary of the charitable institution at the time of the alleged injury."

Evidence that actual operations were not in accordance with charitable purposes, even if such purposes existed, thus could eliminate the charitable immunity defense.

> We articulated ten factors that are indicative of whether a charitable organization operates in fact with a charitable purpose: (1) Does the entity's charter limit the entity to a charitable or eleemosynary purpose? (2) Does the entity's charter contain a not-for-profit limitation? (3) Is the entity's financial purpose to break even or earn a profit? (4) Does the entity in fact earn a profit, and if so, how often does that occur? (5) If the entity earns a profit (a surplus beyond expenses) must that be used for a charitable purpose? (6) Does the entity depend on contributions and donations for a substantial portion of its existence? (7) Is the entity exempt from federal income tax and/or local real estate tax? (8) Does the entity's provision of services take into consideration a person's ability to pay for such services? (9) Does the entity have stockholders or others with an equity stake in its capital? (10) Are the directors and officers of the entity compensated and if so, on what basis? The factors are not exclusive, and no one factor is determinative.

> Reviewing the record in the case, the court concluded that the real purpose of HSF was to make money, that its charitable activities were modest at best, and that its true activities involved aggressive billing and collections efforts:

> > The founding Chief Executive Officer of HSF, William Edgar Carter, Jr., testified that a primary reason for the creation of HSF was to improve the billing system that was used to collect fees for the clinical services of the physicians employed by the Medical School. The billing system used at the time was inadequate, such that not enough money was being collected and not enough revenue was returned to the Medical School. HSF's primary goal at

inception was to find, set up, and operate a new billing system to collect more of the receivables generated by providing patient care.

The record reflects that the HSF Billings and Collections Department employs 115 people. Of those people, five full-time employees (four collectors and one clerical employee) are involved in the legal collection unit. In addition, HSF contracts with an attorney that represents HSF if it goes to trial for collections purposes.

Once a week, a representative from the legal collection unit goes to the Charlottesville General District Court to file warrants in debt. From 2001 to 2005, HSF filed 16,158 warrants in debt and obtained 5,885 judgments. In those years, HSF sought $124,108,445 and collected $7,009,718 through these efforts. HSF expended an estimated 45,760 employment hours in "efforts to obtain legal collection of payment[s] on behalf of HSF" between 2001 and 2005.

HSF was created to increase the amount of revenue received by the Medical Center and aggressively pursues legal collections. The magnitude of these practices suggests that HSF operates more like a for-profit business with a financial purpose of earning a profit than a charitable organization.

In 2005, HSF's total revenue from billing for patient services, reimbursements from the University for services provided to the Medical Center, and "other miscellaneous revenue" was $216,780,000, with additional income from investments and gains from sales of capital assets of $9,118,000. HSF's financial statements show foregone collections of approximately $22.5 million in 2005 as a result of providing medical care to indigent patients. Haws testified that this figure reflects the amount that would have been billed if collection efforts had not been waived for indigency. However, [an HSF employee] testified that HSF usually collects only about thirty-five to thirty-eight percent of the amount billed from insurance companies and paying patients. Therefore, by treating medically indigent patients in 2005, HSF actually failed to receive approximately $7–8 million in collections.

Moreover, the Commonwealth reimburses the University up to the level of the costs of treating indigent patients. In 2005, the Commonwealth reimbursed the University $5.5 million, which was transferred to the faculty (the physicians employed by HSF) as compensation. Taking into account the Commonwealth's reimbursement, HSF's actual shortfall in 2005 was only about $1.5 million as a result of providing medical care to indigent patients. The ratio of this shortfall to HSF's total revenue and other income of $225,898,000 in 2005 is only about 0.66%. The minimal cost of HSF's charity work as compared to its income illustrates how small a portion of HSF's work is charitable.

(c) Physician Incentive Payments

The trial court was concerned with the manner in which HSF's surplus is distributed. The trial court found that the incentive payment system, by which a large part of HSF's revenue is distributed to its physician employees, was "diametrically opposed" to the model of how a charitable institution uses its profit or surplus. HSF's method of revenue distribution, not the amount, was the subject of the trial court's analysis. This analysis is clearly relevant to whether an institution operates in accordance with its stated charitable purpose.

After HSF pays its operating expenses and the Dean's Tax, the balance of HSF's revenue is transferred to the various departments of the Medical School, depending on which departments generate the revenue. The departments group this revenue with money from the Medical School and use it to pay physician salaries and benefits. A department may then pay out incentive payments to the physicians who work for the department.

HSF spends an average of $12 to 17 million a year in incentive payments. When the incentive payments are added to the fixed compensation paid to the physicians, the physicians are compensated on average at about the forty-fifth to fifty-fifth percentile of the AAMC survey of salaries for physicians employed in academic medical centers. We recognize that this level of payment is necessary to recruit and retain talented physicians. The Medical Center is a world-class medical facility, in large part because of the high quality of the physicians employed by HSF. However, what is important to this analysis is not the reason the physicians are paid at a certain level or whether it is necessary to recruit and retain physicians, but how HSF uses its substantial revenue, including its surplus.

HSF's incentive payment structure includes a distribution of surplus revenue in a manner more consistent with a successful commercial business than a charitable organization. The revenue is distributed by HSF to the Medical Center departments in accordance with how much revenue those departments generated, rather than how much indigent care is provided, how much research is performed, or how many hours their physicians spent teaching. The departments then distribute the incentive payments as determined by the chair of the department and the Dean of the Medical School. Surgical departments (plastic surgery, cardiovascular surgery, general surgery, and neurological surgery) tend to generate more revenue than other departments, such as pediatrics or psychiatry, because they perform procedures that are highly compensated. The surgical departments receive more revenue from HSF, and the physicians who work for those departments tend to receive the biggest incentive payments. For example, the Chair of the Department of Surgery, who also served on the HSF Board of

Directors, received incentive payments, in addition to a base salary provided by the Medical School, between $430,000 and $600,000 a year from 2002 to 2005. In comparison, the Chair of the Department of Internal Medicine, who also served on the HSF Board of Directors, received incentive payments between $10,000 and $15,000 a year from 2003 to 2005.

The HSF incentive payment structure is functionally a profit-based bonus system. The departments that generate the most revenue receive the most money from HSF, and those physicians who are the most financially productive in their departments generally receive the biggest incentive payments. In this respect, HSF follows the model of a profitable commercial business, not a charitable institution.

(d) No Charitable Gifts

HSF receives no charitable contributions or donations. In fact, under its affiliation agreement with the Medical School, HSF is precluded from receiving contributions or donations. Because charitable immunity in Virginia is based on public policy, this factor is not without importance. We have justified granting charitable immunity to a charitable hospital in the past, saying:

> It cannot be debated that the care of the sick and injured is a public purpose, a matter of public concern. When a portion of the responsibility therefor is borne by the gifts of the philanthropic-minded, so much of the burden is removed from the public. If a portion of those gifts is diverted to the payment of tort claims, without restriction, the spirit and intent of the gifts are, at once, nullified and that much of the burden is again cast upon the public.

If HSF is required to pay tort awards to the various plaintiffs in the present cases, no philanthropic-minded intentions will be nullified, because no gifts are received.

3. *Teaching institutions.* Hospitals that are part of academic teaching programs for medical students and residents (i.e., physicians who have completed their undergraduate medical training and are in their period of formal apprenticeship) face complex liability issues. It is essential during the training process to permit students and residents to be actively part of the process of care, and yet their inexperience obviously elevates patient risk. As a result, teaching hospitals work in care teams, with the senior teaching physicians and other senior clinical staff leading the team and with sufficient team safeguards to reduce the potential for error. Nonetheless, teamwork failure and lapses in supervision are well documented. A study of 1452 closed claims from 5 malpractice insurers and involving a significantly elevated error rate involving trainees and concluded that the most prevalent factors were those associated with team breakdown: failures of communication, errors in judgment, and lack of supervision were the most prevalent types of teamwork-associated problems. Also in evidence

was excessive workload and technical problems, the most significant of which involved substandard diagnostic decision making and failure to monitor the patient. Trainee errors were more complex than those committed by non-trainees. Hardeep Singh et al., *Medical Errors Involving Trainees: A Study of Closed Malpractice Claims from Five Insurers* 167(19) ARCH. INT. MED. 2030 (2007).

---

8. STRUCTURING THE HOSPITAL PEER REVIEW PROCESS: STATE-LAW IMMUNITY, PRIVILEGE, AND REGULATION

At common law, false statements that tend to injure a person's reputation or business relationships—which might well occur in the course of hospital peer review—would be considered defamatory per se, with both malice and injury presumed. But peer review participants would probably be protected by a common law privilege granted to

> communication[s] made in good faith on any subject matter in which the person communicating has an interest, or in reference to which he has a right or duty, if made to a person having a corresponding interest or duty on a privileged occasion and in a manner fairly warranted by the duty, right or interest. The privilege arises from the necessity of full and unrestrained communication concerning [the] matter.

Mayfield v. Gleichert, 484 S.W.2d 619, 625 (Tex. Ct. Civ. App. 1972) (applying qualified privilege to written report of physician misconduct from department head to hospital medical staff). The effect of the privilege is to eliminate the presumption of malice and require the plaintiff to prove actual malice, meaning knowledge of falsity or reckless disregard of the truth. The privilege is typically termed "conditional" or "qualified," because it can be defeated by a showing of "bad faith." In some circumstances, e.g., when the hospital proceedings are considered quasi-judicial or when the physician has requested the disclosure, the privilege can be deemed "absolute." See Arthur Southwick & Debora Slee, *Quality Assurance in Health Care*, 5 J. LEG. MED. 343, 382–86 (1984).

By the mid-1970s, at least thirty-five states had enacted statutes granting immunity from damages for good faith hospital-based peer review. See David Jorstad, *The Legal Liability of Medical Peer Review Participants for Revocation of Hospital Staff Privileges*, 28 DRAKE L. REV. 692, 694 n.11 (1978–79) (citing statutes). These statutes varied greatly in how they defined the activity or entity that qualifies for the immunity, with some referring to hospital-based medical review committees, others including any "review organization," and still others encompassing all proceedings that "resemble" judicial proceedings. The degree of protection also varied, with most granting qualified immunity based on "good faith," while some were interpreted in more absolute terms. The concept of immunity is of course broader than that of privilege; while the latter only provides some protection for communications against defamation claims, the former provides wider protection against all types of civil actions.

Congress passed more comprehensive legislation in an attempt to strengthen hospital-based quality assurance. The event that precipitated Congressional action in this area was a federal jury award in 1985 of $2.2 million in antitrust damages in favor of an Oregon physician who claimed—with much justification—that peer review sanctions against him were part of a conspiracy to monopolize medical practice. *See* Patrick v. Burget, 486 U.S. 94 (1988). Although the facts in *Patrick* may have justified relief, several national medical and hospital organizations argued that federal antitrust and state-law liability threatened good faith peer review, and Congress responded to their concerns by enacting the Health Care Quality Improvement Act of 1986, Pub. L. No. 99–660, 42 U.S.C. § 11101 et seq.

Bryan v. James E. Holmes Regional Medical Center

33 F.3d 1318 (11th Cir. 1994)

■ TJOFLAT, CHIEF JUDGE:

In this case, a Florida hospital, after completing a lengthy internal disciplinary process, terminated the clinical staff privileges of a staff physician. The physician sued the hospital, alleging various state and federal causes of action and seeking money damages. After an eleven-day trial, a federal jury concluded that the hospital had revoked the physician's staff privileges in violation of its bylaws and awarded the physician nearly $4.2 million in damages for breach of contract. The hospital appeals that judgment as well as the district court's denial of its post-trial motion for judgment as a matter of law, which contended that the hospital was immune from liability in money damages under the Health Care Quality Improvement Act of 1986 ("HCQIA"), 42 U.S.C. §§ 11101–11152 (1988 & Supp. IV 1992), and under Florida law, Fla.Stat.Ann. § 395.0193(5) (West 1993). Because we conclude that the hospital was entitled to protection from monetary liability under HCQIA, we reverse.

I.

Peer review, the process by which physicians and hospitals evaluate and discipline staff doctors, has become an integral component of the health care system in the United States. Congress enacted the Health Care Quality Improvement Act [HCQIA] to encourage such peer review activities, "to improve the quality of medical care by encouraging physicians to identify and discipline other physicians who are incompetent or who engage in unprofessional behavior." 1986 U.S.C.C.A.N. 6287, 6384, 6384. In furtherance of this goal, HCQIA grants limited immunity, in suits brought by disciplined physicians, from liability for money damages to those who participate in professional peer review activities. *Id.* § 11111(a).

HCQIA is designed to facilitate the frank exchange of information among professionals conducting peer review inquiries without the fear of reprisals in civil lawsuits.[2] The provision of HCQIA that limits the availability of damages for professional review actions provides as follows:

> If a professional review action (as defined in . . . this title) of a professional review body meets all the standards specified in section 11112(a) of this title, (A) the professional review body, (B) any person acting as a member or staff to the body, (C) any person under a contract or other formal agreement with the body, and (D) any person who participates with or assists the body with respect to the action, shall not be liable in damages under any law of the United States or of any State (or political subdivision thereof) with respect to the action.

42 U.S.C. § 11111(a)(1).[4] The standards that professional review actions must satisfy to entitle the participants to such protection are enumerated in § 11112(a) as follows:

> For purposes of the protection set forth in § 11111(a) of this title, a professional review action must be taken—(1) in the reasonable belief that the action was in the furtherance of quality health care, (2) after a reasonable effort to obtain the facts of the matter, (3) after adequate notice and hearing procedures are afforded to the physician involved or after such other procedures as are fair to the physician under the circumstances, and (4) in the reasonable belief that the action was warranted by the facts known after such reasonable effort to obtain facts and after meeting the requirement of paragraph (3).

Id. § 11112(a). Importantly, HCQIA also creates a rebuttable presumption of immunity: "A professional review action shall be presumed to have met the preceding standards necessary for the protection set out in section

---

2. In another set of provisions, HCQIA requires health care entities to report certain specific disciplinary actions taken against a staff physician (or the acceptance of a resignation or suspension in return for not conducting investigations or disciplinary proceedings) to a national clearinghouse established to collect and disseminate information on health care providers. 42 U.S.C. § 11133–34. Then, prior to admitting a physician to its staff, a hospital must obtain that physician's records from the clearinghouse. Id. § 11135. These reporting requirements were designed to "restrict the ability of incompetent physicians to move from State to State without disclosure or discovery of the physician's previous damaging or incompetent performance." Id. § 11101(2) (reciting congressional findings).

The Secretary of Health and Human Services may, following an investigation, publish in the Federal Register the name of a health care entity that has failed to comply with these reporting requirements; a hospital so identified then loses the protection of HCQIA immunity provisions for three years. 42 U.S.C. § 11111(b).

4. Section 11111(a)(1) expressly excludes from its coverage suits brought under 42 U.S.C. § 1983 or Title VII of the Civil Rights Act of 1964, but it clearly does apply to antitrust claims. See Patrick v. Burget, 486 U.S. 94, 105 n. 8 (1988). The section states, however, that "nothing in this paragraph shall prevent the United States or any Attorney General of a State from bringing an action, including an action under [section 4C of the Clayton Act, 15 U.S.C. 15C], where such an action is otherwise authorized." 42 U.S.C. § 11111(a)(1). And HCQIA "does not restrict the rights of physicians who are disciplined to bring private causes of action for injunctive or declaratory relief." 1986 U.S.C.C.A.N. at 6391.

11111(a) of this title unless the presumption is rebutted by a preponderance of the evidence." *Id.*

Section 11112(b) of HCQIA then enumerates the minimum, or "safe harbor" procedures that will, in every case, satisfy the adequate notice and hearing requirement of section 11112(a)(3). *Id.* § 11112(b). Organized in the form of a detailed checklist, the provision defines what hospitals conducting peer review disciplinary procedures must do to obtain the Act's protections for itself and the members of its peer review bodies. We discuss this checklist in more detail infra in part III. Congress was careful to explain, however, that "[a] professional review body's failure to meet the conditions described in this subsection shall not, in itself, constitute failure to meet the standards of subsection (a)(3) of this section." *Id.*

The legislative history of § 11112(a) indicates that the statute's reasonableness requirements were intended to create an objective standard of performance, rather than a subjective good faith standard. As the House Committee on Energy and Commerce explained:

> Initially, the Committee considered a "good faith" standard for professional review actions. In response to concerns that "good faith" might be misinterpreted as requiring only a test of the subjective state of mind of the physicians conducting the professional review action, the Committee changed to a more objective "reasonable belief" standard. The Committee intends that this test will be satisfied if the reviewers, with the information available to them at the time of the professional review action, would reasonably have concluded that their action would restrict incompetent behavior or would protect patients.

H.R. Rep. No. 903, at 10, reprinted in 1986 U.S.C.C.A.N. at 6392–93.

II.

The appellant, Holmes Regional Medical Center ("Holmes" or "the Hospital"), is a nonprofit corporation operating a private hospital in Melbourne, Florida. The appellee, Dr. Floyd T. Bryan, is a board-certified physician who specializes in general and vascular surgery. Bryan became a member of the Holmes medical staff in 1976; he is generally acknowledged to be an excellent surgeon, often undertaking long, detailed vascular procedures that other physicians in the field avoid. Bryan also has a reputation for being a volcanic-tempered perfectionist, a difficult man with whom to work, and a person who regularly viewed it as his obligation to criticize staff members at Holmes for perceived incompetence or inefficiency. Hospital employees, however, often viewed Bryan's "constructive criticism" as verbal—or even physical—abuse. Because the Holmes board of directors found Bryan's behavior inappropriate and unprofessional, it terminated his medical staff privileges in November 1990. The means by which Holmes accomplished this termination is the subject of the dispute in this case.

A.

The organizational structure at Holmes, as is the case at most hospitals, is bifurcated, reflecting the distinct roles of the Hospital administration and of the medical staff. Holmes is governed by a board of directors, comprised mostly of non-physicians, that retains the ultimate responsibility for the operation of the facility. The board employs a staff, led by a president and chief executive officer ("CEO"), to manage the hospital on a day-to-day basis. The medical staff organization, which consists of all doctors with privileges to practice at Holmes, represents the physicians in the Hospital's government. The medical staff is led by an elected chief of staff who presides over the medical executive committee, which comprises the chairpersons of the various clinical departments as well as several officers elected by the staff at large.

The Holmes board of directors promulgates bylaws for the medical staff, by which all physicians receiving staff privileges at the Hospital agree to be bound. The bylaws provide a detailed series of procedures for handling physician disciplinary actions. Under those bylaws, the medical staff, through its executive committee, may recommend that the board of directors suspend or revoke the privileges of a physician. Although the board retains the ultimate authority over staff privileges, the recommendations of the medical staff are given considerable weight. This system, which is known as peer review, is designed to raise the quality of medical care by encouraging physicians to police themselves. Florida law mandates that hospitals provide for peer review of their staff doctors.

Under the Holmes bylaws, certain hospital officials may request an executive committee investigation into a physician's conduct if the medical staff member fails to comply with the ethics of the medical profession or with the Hospital's bylaws, or if "the Staff appointee is unable to work harmoniously with others to the extent that it affects the orderly operation of the hospital or Medical Staff organization." Grounds for investigation also include questions regarding a physician's clinical competence or his care and treatment of patients.

Once an investigation is initiated, the executive committee is charged with making a recommendation to the board of directors concerning the level of discipline that should be imposed. The executive committee's recommendation may range from a written warning to revocation of clinical privileges, but a recommendation involving the reduction, suspension, or revocation of clinical privileges entitles the physician to the extensive procedural hearing rights outlined in the bylaws. The executive committee's recommendation is forwarded to the CEO of the hospital, who notifies the physician under scrutiny. The physician has twenty days from receipt of the notice to make a written request for a hearing. If the physician waives his or her right to a hearing, the CEO forwards the recommendation (along with the supporting documentation) to the board of directors for a final disposition of the matter.

When a physician requests a formal hearing, the executive committee appoints a hearing panel consisting of seven members of the medical staff who have not taken active part in consideration of the matter contested; mere knowledge of the matter does not preclude a staff member from serving on a hearing panel. According to the bylaws, "the purpose of the hearing shall be to recommend a course of action to those acting for the hospital.... The duties of the Hearing Panel shall be so defined and so carried out."

The medical staff bylaws contain detailed procedures governing the hearing process, including provisions for written notice of the time and place for the hearing, prompt scheduling, and lists of witnesses. The physician requesting the hearing is entitled to representation, and has full rights of cross-examination and confrontation of witnesses. The executive committee designates someone, who may be an attorney, to present the disciplinary recommendation that led to the hearing and to examine witnesses. In addition, the CEO appoints a hearing officer, who must be an attorney, to preside over the hearing and to rule on the admissibility of evidence; the hearing officer must not act as a prosecuting officer or as an advocate for the hospital.

The decision of the hearing panel is to be based on the evidence produced at the hearing, whether in the form of oral testimony of witnesses or documentary evidence. The "burden of proof" is established as follows: "The Hearing Panel shall recommend against the [physician] who requested the hearing unless it finds that said [physician] has proved that the recommendation which prompted the hearing was unreasonable, not sustained by the evidence, or otherwise unfounded."

After reaching a decision, the hearing panel is to "render a recommendation, accompanied by a report, which shall contain a concise statement of the reasons justifying the recommendation made...." The report is then forwarded to the executive committee for whatever modification, if any, it may wish to make in its original recommendation. The executive committee's decision on modification is purely discretionary.

Within fifteen days after the affected physician is notified of final adverse action by the executive committee, the doctor may make a written request for appellate review by the board of directors. If appellate review is not requested within the fifteen-day period, the affected individual is deemed to have accepted the recommendation involved "and it shall thereupon become final and immediately effective." The terms of the bylaws limit the grounds upon which an adverse disciplinary recommendation may be appealed to the following:

> [1] there was substantial failure on the part of the Executive Committee or Hearing Panel to comply with the hospital or Medical Staff Bylaws in the conduct of hearings and recommendations based upon hearings so as to deny due process or a fair hearing; or [2] the recommendation was made arbitrarily, capriciously, or with prejudice; or [3] the recommendation of the Executive Committee or Hearing Panel was not supported by the evidence.

Under time constraints imposed by the bylaws, the chairman of the board appoints a board review panel (consisting of three or more persons, including board members or "reputable persons outside the hospital") to consider the record upon which the disciplinary recommendation was made. The review panel may accept additional evidence, subject to the same procedural guarantees that apply to hearing panels, and both sides have an opportunity to present arguments. The review panel then recommends action to the full board.

The board of directors may affirm, modify, or reverse the recommendations of either the appellate review panel or the executive committee, or, in its discretion, refer the matter for further review and recommendation. When made, the board's ultimate decision is final, immediately effective, and is not subject to further review under the bylaws.

B.

Bryan's disciplinary problems began shortly after he arrived at Holmes in 1976, and they continued throughout his tenure at the Hospital. Indeed, prior to his termination, Bryan was the subject of more than fifty written incident reports involving unprofessional or disruptive behavior, usually complaints regarding Bryan's abusive treatment of nurses, technicians, and even fellow physicians. By December 1987, nurses in the intensive care unit at Holmes were refusing to care for Bryan's patients on anything but a rotating basis for fear of becoming the object of his volcanic temper. For their part, surgical nurses complained that Bryan's verbal abuse compounded an already stressful environment, precluding them from operating at peak performance.

In October 1988, for example, Bryan falsely reported to a nurse supervisor that one of her patients had just hanged himself in his room; in fact, the patient was fine. At trial, Bryan explained that he had intended the episode as a "joke" to teach the nurse "responsibility." After additional incidents during the fall of 1988, the executive committee met to consider disciplinary action.

Despite the board's warning, Bryan was involved in four additional incidents in the first five months of 1990; these four incidents led directly to the termination of Bryan's medical staff privileges. First, surgical technologist Tina Stark filed an incident report stating that, on March 7, Bryan slapped her hands—apparently as a reprimand for a perceived mistake in handling a catheter—while she was assisting him in an operation. On May 16, 1990, while nurse Michael Greene assisted Bryan on an operation, Bryan struck Greene's hands with a surgical instrument; Greene claimed that his hand hurt for several minutes afterwards.

During the same period, Bryan twice ordered the wrong patient prepared for surgery, first in March of 1990 and then in May. On both occasions, the mistake was caught by another physician after the patient had been transferred to the surgical intensive care unit in advance of the operation.

On May 29, 1990, the executive committee convened to interview the witnesses to the four recent incidents. Bryan presented his version of events to the committee: He attributed what were perceived as slaps to the hands of the nurses as a form of "nonverbal communication" (the use of hand motions by a physician to give directions during surgery) to correct the nurses' mistakes; similarly, although he admitted the misdirections of the patients for surgery, he minimized these mistakes because they were detected in time and no harm had come to the individuals involved. After considering these latest incidents in light of Bryan's history of disruptive behavior and the hospital's varied attempts to correct such behavior—as well as the board's explicit warning a few months before that further unprofessional conduct would result in Bryan's dismissal—the executive committee recommended that Bryan's staff privileges be permanently revoked.

Throughout the disciplinary process, neither Bryan nor the expert witnesses who testified on his behalf contended that the various incident reports that formed the basis for the disciplinary action were fraudulent fabrications. Indeed, Bryan himself admitted that, in each instance, some sort of interaction occurred between himself and the author of the incident report. Bryan merely disagreed both with the Hospital's judgment concerning the propriety of his conduct and the severity of the sanction imposed.

C.

On December 5, 1990, in the United States District Court for the Middle District of Florida, Bryan filed a complaint on behalf of himself and his professional association against the Hospital, the individual members of its board of directors, members of the medical staff executive committee, and two nurses. The complaint included federal and state antitrust claims as well as state law claims for defamation, negligent supervision of the peer review process (against only the individual members of the board of directors), and breach of contract for failing to follow the medical staff bylaws during the disciplinary process (against the Hospital). The complaint demanded damages and, only with respect to the count of negligent supervision, injunctive relief. The central allegation in the complaint was that the defendants, "individually and in concert, acted in bad faith and with intentional fraud, resulting in the destruction of Dr. Bryan's medical practice."

Beginning with their answer denying liability on all counts, the Hospital and the other defendants consistently claimed immunity from monetary liability for their actions in terminating Bryan's clinical privileges because they were functioning in this matter, individually and collectively, as a professional review body in a peer review process. Later, the defendants filed motions for summary judgment, contending, inter alia, that they were immune from Bryan's suit for damages under HCQIA, 42 U.S.C. § 11111(a), and under Florida law, Fla.Stat.Ann. § 395.0193(5).

III.

A.

HCQIA immunity is a question of law for the court to decide and may be resolved whenever the record in a particular case becomes sufficiently developed.

As the Ninth Circuit has explained, the rebuttable presumption of HCQIA section 11112(a) creates an unusual summary judgment standard that can best be expressed as follows: "Might a reasonable jury, viewing the facts in the best light for [the plaintiff], conclude that he has shown, by a preponderance of the evidence, that the defendants' actions are outside the scope of § 11112(a)?" *Austin*, 979 F.2d at 734. If not, the court should grant the defendant's motion. In a sense, the presumption language in HCQIA means that the plaintiff bears the burden of proving that the peer review process was not reasonable.

B.

Before determining whether the procedural standards for proper peer review proceedings were satisfied in this case, we first note that the events and entities at issue here fall squarely within the definitions of HCQIA's operative terms. The disciplinary action at issue here is the November 1990 decision by the Holmes board of directors to revoke Bryan's staff privileges. The term "professional review action" is defined in HCQIA as follows:

> An action or recommendation of a professional review body which is taken or made in the conduct of professional review activity, which is based on the competence or professional conduct of an individual physician (which conduct affects or could affect adversely the health or welfare of a patient or patients), and which affects (or may affect) adversely the clinical privileges ... of the physician.

42 U.S.C. § 11151(9).[29] The revocation of Bryan's staff privileges therefore qualifies as such a professional review action.

A "professional review body" is defined as "a health care entity and the governing body or any committee of a health care entity which conducts professional review activity, and includes any committee of the medical staff of such an entity when assisting the governing body in a professional review activity." *Id.* § 11151(11). Furthermore, the term "health care entity" includes "a hospital that is licensed to provide health care services by the State in which it is located." *Id.* § 11151(4)(A)(i). The Holmes decision makers in Bryan's case fall within those categories. As a result, the Hospital is entitled to immunity from monetary liability under section 11111(a) of HCQIA if the peer review process met the standards set forth in section 11112(a).

C.

As stated above, a professional review action must satisfy the four standards of section 11112(a) in order to qualify for the immunity protec-

---

29. While its meaning is generally apparent, the statute does provide the following definition of "professional review activity": An activity of a health care entity with respect to an individual physician—

(A) to determine whether the physician may have clinical privileges with respect to, or membership in, the entity, (B) to determine the scope or conditions of such privileges or membership, or (C) to change or modify such privileges or membership.

42 U.S.C. § 11151(10). Again, the termination of Bryan's medical staff privileges clearly falls within HCQIA definition.

tions of section 11111(a). We discuss each in turn and conclude that the Hospital's termination of Bryan's clinical privileges met HCQIA requirements.

First, a review of the record makes clear that the decision to terminate Bryan's clinical privileges at Holmes was taken "in the reasonable belief that the action was in the furtherance of quality health care." *Id.* § 11112(a)(1). This prong of the HCQIA immunity test is met if "the reviewers, with the information available to them at the time of the professional review action, would reasonably have concluded that their action would restrict incompetent behavior or would protect patients." 1986 U.S.C.C.A.N. at 6393. The record in this case reveals that the revocation of Bryan's privileges was prompted by the reasonable belief that doing so would promote quality health care. Bryan had exhibited a pattern of unprofessional conduct over a period of many years, and he was given a series of opportunities to remedy his difficulties in interacting with other staff members. Eventually, the Hospital concluded that, because of his behavior, Bryan's presence in the operating room and in patient rooms was disruptive and interfered with the important work of other employees. Moreover, the board was properly concerned about the circumstances surrounding the misdirection of the two patients to surgery. Accordingly, the Hospital dealt appropriately with the perceived situation in terminating Bryan's privileges.

At trial, Bryan asserted that the members of the board of directors and the executive committee were primarily motivated by personal animosity and not by concern for patient care. He introduced no evidence, however, that such hostility determined the outcome of the peer review process. Moreover, Bryan's "assertions of hostility do not support his position [that the Hospital is not entitled to the HCQIA's protections] because they are irrelevant to the reasonableness standards of § 11112(a). The test is an objective one, so bad faith is immaterial. The real issue is the sufficiency of the basis for the [Hospital's] actions." *Austin*, 979 F.2d at 734. We therefore conclude that Bryan failed to provide sufficient evidence to permit a jury to find that he had overcome, by a preponderance of the evidence, the presumption that the Hospital's disciplinary action was taken in the reasonable belief that it would further quality patient care.

Second, a review of the record reveals that the Holmes board of directors took its action "after a reasonable effort to obtain the facts of the matter." 42 U.S.C. § 11112(a)(2). The board terminated Bryan's medical staff privileges only after Bryan's conduct had been evaluated by the executive committee, the Chanda peer review panel, and an appellate review panel of board members. Each of those groups submitted reports to the board, which made its decision based upon the documentary record developed during the various peer review proceedings and after Bryan had the opportunity to make a presentation. Bryan introduced no competent evidence at trial to suggest that the Hospital's efforts to obtain the facts before terminating his staff privileges were not reasonable.

Third, Bryan's staff privileges were revoked only "after adequate notice and hearing procedures [were] afforded to the physician involved or after such other procedures as [were] fair to the physician under the circumstances." *Id.* § 11112(a)(3). As noted above, § 11112(b) sets forth the "safe harbor" conditions that a health care entity must meet regarding adequate notice and hearing. Section 11112(b) provides as follows:

A health care entity is deemed to have met the adequate notice and hearing requirement of subsection (a)(3) of this section with respect to a physician if the following conditions are met (or are waived voluntarily by the physician):

(1) Notice of proposed action—The physician has been given notice stating (A)(i) that a professional review action has been proposed to be taken against the physician, (ii) reasons for the proposed action, (B)(i) that the physician has the right to request a hearing on the proposed action, (ii) any time limit (of not less than 30 days) within which to request such a hearing, and (C) a summary of the rights in the hearing under paragraph (3).

(2) Notice of hearing—If a hearing is requested on a timely basis under paragraph (1)(B), the physician involved must be given notice stating—(A) the place, time, and date, of the hearing, which date shall not be less than 30 days after the date of the notice, and (B) a list of the witnesses (if any) expected to testify at the hearing on behalf of the professional review body.

(3) Conduct of hearing and notice—If a hearing is requested on a timely basis under paragraph (1)(B)—(A) subject to subparagraph (B), the hearing shall be held (as determined by the health care entity)—(i) before an arbitrator mutually acceptable to the physician and the health care entity, (ii) before a hearing officer who is appointed by the entity and who is not in direct economic competition with the physician involved, or (iii) before a panel of individuals who are appointed by the entity and are not in direct competition with the physician involved; (B) the right to the hearing may be forfeited if the physician fails, without good cause, to appear; (C) in the hearing the physician has the right—(i) to representation by an attorney or other person of the physician's choice, (ii) to have a record made of the proceedings, copies of which may be obtained by the physician upon payment of any reasonable charges associated with the preparation thereof, (iii) to call, examine, and cross-examine witnesses, (iv) to present evidence determined to be relevant by the hearing officer, regardless of its admissibility in a court of law, and (v) to submit a written statement at the close of the hearing; and (D) upon completion of the hearing, the physician involved has the right—(i) to receive the written recommendation of the arbitrator, officer, or panel, including a statement of the basis for the recommendations, and (ii) to receive a written decision of the health care entity, including a statement of the basis for the decision.

Id. § 11112(b).

As the summary of the facts of the case in part II of this opinion reflects, each of these procedural requirements of § 11112(b) was satisfied. Documents introduced at trial indicate that the Hospital complied with the notice requirements and that the hearings were held in a timely fashion and in accordance with the Hospital's bylaws. Bryan was afforded full rights of representation, cross-examination, and confrontation.

It should be noted that § 11112(b) specifically provides that the failure of a review body to meet the enumerated conditions does not, per se, constitute a failure to meet the standards of § 11112(a)(3). Indeed, "if other procedures are followed, but are not precisely of the character spelled out in [section 11112(b)], the test of 'adequacy' may still be met under other prevailing law." 1986 U.S.C.C.A.N. at 6393. Moreover, Bryan made no contemporaneous objections to the manner in which the hearing procedures were conducted; § 11112(b) explicitly provides that compliance with its terms is not required if the physician voluntarily waives them. On the record of this case, we conclude that no reasonable jury could conclude that the Hospital had not afforded Bryan the adequate procedures.

Finally, there is no question that the board decided to terminate Bryan "in the reasonable belief that the action was warranted by the facts known." 42 U.S.C. § 11112(a)(4). Again, the record reveals that the board certainly had a factual basis for its action. Bryan concedes that the incidents that led to his termination actually occurred; his only argument is that they did not justify the severe sanction he received. HCQIA clearly grants broad discretion to hospital boards with regard to staff privileges decisions. Accordingly, as in all procedural due process cases, the role of federal courts "on review of such actions is not to substitute our judgment for that of the hospital's governing board or to reweigh the evidence regarding the renewal or termination of medical staff privileges." No reasonable jury could conclude that Bryan had demonstrated, by a preponderance of the evidence, that the Hospital board did not act in the "reasonable belief that the [termination] was warranted by the facts known after reasonable effort to obtain facts" as required by § 11112(a)(4). 42 U.S.C. § 11112(a)(4).

Given that all of the section 11112(a) standards were satisfied, we conclude that the Hospital was entitled to the immunity from damages liability granted by HCQIA in § 11111(a).[30]

Notes

1. *Bad faith allegations.* Do you agree with the Eleventh Circuit's opinion in *Bryan* that evidence of "bad faith" on the part of peer review decision makers is irrelevant to immunity under the HCQIA? Although the

---

30. Because our holding on this point disposes of all of the claims in the case, we need not reach the question of whether the Hospital was protected from monetary liability under the Florida peer review statute, Fla. Stat. Ann. § 395.0115(5).

facts of the case seem amply to support revocation of privileges, one can imagine other facts that would raise more troubling questions. For example, what if a doctor had performed below standard on some occasions, and hence there was a reasonable basis for discipline, but what if other doctors also typically fell short in this way, and this doctor was being "selectively prosecuted" in order to drive him out of the market? Would facts of this sort be relevant to overcoming the HCQIA presumption?

2.   *Ongoing liability exposure despite statutory protections.* Because of the trial judge's erroneous rulings in *Bryan,* the HCQIA failed to achieve its major goal, i.e., to protect peer review participants from massive litigation costs. Section 11113 of the HCQIA requires courts to award attorney's fees in cases in which the defendant "substantially prevails," and in which the plaintiff's claim was "frivolous, unreasonable, without foundation, or in bad faith." Does the fact that Dr. Bryan won favorable rulings from the trial judge and a jury verdict mean by definition that his claim was not frivolous? The Eleventh Circuit's refusal to rule on the Florida state law claims (see footnote 30) may have had considerable monetary significance, because the Florida law awards attorney's fees to peer review defendants prevailing against physician plaintiffs without regard to the reasonableness of the plaintiff's claim. See 1988 Fla. Sess. Law Serv. Ch. 88–1, sec. 3, amending Fla. Stat. sec. 395.0115(8)(a).

3.   *What constitutes a professional review action?* Several courts have ruled that only the ultimate decision to restrict or revoke privileges is a "professional review action" that must meet the four standards set out in HCQIA § 11112(a). Preliminary investigations and reviews of case files that lead up to the final decision are "professional review activity" that do not require notice and opportunity to comment, although they are often provided. *See, e.g.,* Mathews v. Lancaster Gen. Hosp., 883 F. Supp. 1016 (E.D. Pa. 1995). In Wahl v. Charleston Area Medical Center, 562 F.3d 599 (4th Cir. 2009), the Court of Appeals affirmed a suspension under the HCQIA even though no hearing occurred after finding that the physician was repeatedly warned of his rights and suggested hearing dates but the physician never responded, suggesting that he was stalling. The court concluded that a suspension can be upheld even though the HCQIA hearing procedure never transpires if the process is fair to the physician under the totality of the circumstances. In *Wahl,* the record showed a history of problems, repeated warnings, a suspension and months of communication regarding the hearing procedure.

4.   *What level of proof is needed to uphold peer reviewer conclusions?* In Poliner v. Texas Health Systems, 537 F.3d 368 (5th Cir. 2008), *cert. den.,* 555 U.S. 1149 (2009), the Court of Appeals overturned a $33 million judgment in favor of a cardiologist whose privileges were temporarily revoked, holding that the hospital and its peer review system were immune from damages under the HCQIA. The Court of Appeals ruled that the HCQIA's reasonable belief standard is satisfied if the reviewers, with the information available to them at the time of the professional review action, would reasonably have concluded that their action would restrict incompe-

tent behavior or would protect patients. The court held that the HCQIA does not require that professional review result in an actual improvement of the quality of health care, nor does it require that reviewers' conclusions be factually correct.

In *Poliner* the hospital temporarily restricted the plaintiff's catheter lab privileges as the result of a peer-review investigation. The court found that the restriction was objectively reasonable, as required for immunity under the HCQIA, because there was evidence that the cardiologist missed a complete blockage of a patient's left anterior descending artery, which was a critical diagnostic error. This failure of diagnosis was made all the more troubling by the fact that two other physicians saw the blockage, the cardiologist himself described the blockage as obvious and clear in an addendum, and the concerns that flowed from the missed blockage were amplified by the problems with the cardiologist's other patients that had been brought to the peer-review leader's attention. Nearly half of all 44 reviewed cases showed evidence of negligence. The early investigation led to a suspension of privileges while further investigation was underway, and continuation of the restriction fell within the HCQIA's emergency provisions. The failure to comply with hospital bylaws was held not to defeat immunity.

5. *Peer pressure not to review.* Kadlec Medical Center v. Lakeview Anesthesia Associates, 527 F.3d 412 (5th Cir. 2008), reveals the pressures on hospitals to avoid formal action against impaired physicians, thereby arguably avoiding reporting duties under the HCQIA, and (controversially) avoiding liability although contributing to serious harm. Dr. Robert Berry, a Louisiana anesthesiologist, was a shareholder in Louisiana Anesthesia Associates (LAA) (an anesthesiology practice group) and (through LAA's exclusive anesthesiology contract), on the active staff of Lakeview Regional Medical Center (Lakeview Medical), a hospital. Lakeview Medical nurses "expressed concern" at Dr. Berry's "undocumented and suspicious withdrawals of Demerol," and "a small management team" of the hospital found excessive and undocumented withdrawals. When Dr. Berry did not comply with his remedial plan, and was found groggy and impaired at the hospital, his partners at LAA sent him a "for cause" termination letter noting that his impaired condition "puts our patients at significant risk." Although the hospital CEO was fully aware of this action, and indeed had been involved informally in Dr. Berry's termination, the hospital

> did not initiate a formal peer review, did not revoke or suspend Dr. Berry's privileges, and did not make a report to the NPDB [HCQIA's National Practitioner Data Bank], the Louisiana State Board of Medical Examiners (which licenses physicians), or the Physicians Health Foundation of Louisiana (which works with impaired physicians). However, since LAA had an exclusive contract to provide anesthesia services at the hospital and Dr. Berry was no longer with LAA, he never again worked at the facility. Additionally, as the Fifth Circuit relates, "Lauderdale [the hospital CEO] took the unusual step of locking away in his office all files,

audits, plans, and notes concerning Dr. Berry and the investigation," and "ordered the Chief Nursing Officer to notify the administration if Dr. Berry returned."

Sallie Thieme Sanford, *Candor After Kadlec: Why, Despite The Fifth Circuit's Decision, Hospitals Should Anticipate An Expanded Obligation To Disclose Risky Physician Behavior*, 1 DREXEL L. REV. 383, 402–403 (2009).

When Dr. Berry sought a new position in the state of Washington, Kadlec Medical Center requested referral letters from LAA and Lakeview Medical. Physicians at LAA sent actively misleading letters praising Dr. Berry as an "excellent clinician," while staff at Lakeview Medical claimed that they were too busy to provide details, and simply noted the dates of Dr. Berry's membership on the hospital staff, without any mention of his impaired condition. Dr. Berry was allowed to practice at Kadlec, with devastating consequences to a patient. After Kadlec (the Washington hospital) paid a $7 million malpractice judgment because of Dr. Berry's malfeasance as its apparent agent, Kadlec sued LAA and Lakeview Medical for failure to disclose the truth about Dr. Berry. While LAA was found liable under Louisiana law for active misrepresentation, Lakeview Medical was found by the Fifth Circuit (sitting in diversity jurisdiction) to have had no state law affirmative duty of disclosure. The HCQIA was never discussed by the Fifth Circuit, and while the HCQIA does deprive non-complying hospitals of federal immunity, imposition of actual liability often depends on varying state law.

9.   SUBSTANTIVE GROUNDS FOR ADVERSE HOSPITAL ACTION

a.   Negative Categorical Exclusions: Race and Non–M.D. Providers

With respect to negative categories, courts on their own have played a relatively limited role. To be sure, one major traditional negative category—exclusion of black and other minority practitioners—has been ruled illegal, first by the federal courts on equal protection grounds (with the help of greatly expanded "state action" doctrine in the case of private nonprofit hospitals), and then by Titles VI and VII of the 1964 Civil Rights Act, which respectively prohibit discrimination on grounds of race, color, or national origin in federally-funded activities, and discrimination on grounds of (among others) race in employment. *See* Simkins v. Moses H. Cone Memorial Hospital, 323 F.2d 959 (4th Cir. 1963) (granting injunction prohibiting racial discrimination in staff privilege decisions by private nonprofit hospitals and holding "separate but equal" provision of the federal Hill–Burton Act, 42 U.S.C. § 291e(f) (1963) unconstitutional); Titles VI and VII of the 1964 Civil Rights Act, 42 U.S.C. §§ 2000d, 2000e (1982); *but see* Diggs v. Harris Hosp.–Methodist Inc., 847 F.2d 270 (5th Cir. 1988) (neither staff privileges nor doctor-patient relationship is "employment" under Title VII, hence challenge to staff privilege termination on racial discrimination grounds dismissed). In addition, as noted above, the New Jersey Supreme Court's landmark 1963 *Greisman* opinion ruled invalid on state common law grounds the widespread hospital categorical exclusion of doctors of osteopathy.

For the most part, however, hospital categorical exclusions have been ruled illegal not by the courts, but by state legislation prohibiting particular categorical exclusions. *See, e.g.,* Shaw v. Hospital Authority of Cobb County, 614 F.2d 946 (5th Cir. 1980) (upholding a public hospital bylaw categorically excluding podiatrists against federal constitutional challenges); Calif. Health & Safety Code § 1316 (1979) (prohibiting categorical exclusion of osteopaths and podiatrists); New York Public Health Law § 2801–b (McKinney 1985 & 1987 Supp.) (prohibiting categorical exclusion of physicians, podiatrists, optometrists and dentists); D.C. Code Ann. § 32–1307(c) (1986) (prohibiting categorical exclusion of certified nurse midwives, nurse anesthetists, nurse practitioners, and psychologists). Antitrust law, further discussed in Chapter 25, has played some role in these developments, particularly in persuading the Joint Commission to drop its requirement that only individuals "fully licensed to practice medicine" were eligible for staff privileges. *See* Jane Davis, *Health Professionals' Access to Hospitals: A Retrospective and Prospective Analysis*, 34 VAND. L. REV. 1161, 1190 (1981).

At least three federal circuits have ruled that state peer review privileges do not apply in cases involving federal civil rights claims. Adkins v. Christie, 488 F.3d 1324 (11th Cir. 2007); Memorial Hospital v. Shadur, 664 F.2d 1058 (7th Cir. 1981); and Viramani v. Novant Health Inc. 259 F.3d 284 (4th Cir. 2001). As part of a claim of a racially motivated firing, Dr. Adkins sought all peer review documents for all physicians during the seven years he had been on the medical staff. The trial court granted a limited production order; upon reviewing the evidence the court dismissed the claim. On appeal Adkins argued that the trial court had improperly limited the scope of his discovery request. In holding for the appellant the Appeals Court noted the general presumption against privileges and the public interest in transparency in the absence of "a public good transcending the normally predominant principle of utilizing all rational means for ascertaining truth." *Adkins*, 488 F.3d at 1339. The court concluded that the plaintiff needed the full body of evidence to prove his disparate treatment case, as well as that the trial court had other means to limit harms, such as issuance of protective orders, confidentiality agreements, and *in camera* review.

b.   Functional Categorical Exclusions

A functional categorical exclusion occurs where a hospital purports not to make any judgment about an individual practitioner's capabilities, but rather denies privileges on assertedly neutral, functional grounds. The two most typical reasons are: (1) that the hospital staff is "full"—i.e., that the facilities and staff cannot support more services of the type that the applicant wishes to provide; and (2) that the hospital wishes to grant a particular group of doctors a monopoly over certain functions, typically the hospital-based practices of anesthesiology, pathology, and radiology.

In defending these hospital policies against legal attack, hospitals must show that they are rationally related to legitimate institutional goals. In contrast to hospital actions based on individual performance, which, at least in some states must rest on "sufficient reliable evidence, including hearsay," actions based on broad policies (such as staff closure) need only be "reached in the normal and regular course of conducting affairs and [be] based on adequate information, regardless of form, origin, or authorship, that is generally considered reasonable and reliable by professional persons responsibly involved in the health care field." Desai v. St. Barnabas Medical Center, 510 A.2d 662, 669 (N.J. 1986). Thus a New Jersey hospital convinced the state supreme court that the primary function of its new satellite facility was to treat urgent and emergency cases, thereby providing a "rational basis" for closure of surgical appointments until the pattern of usage became clear. Guerrero v. Burlington County Mem. Hosp., 360 A.2d 334, 341 (N.J. 1976). Similarly, expert testimony persuaded New Jersey courts that because surgeons control patient usage of anesthesia services, an exclusive contract between a hospital and a particular group of anesthesiologists was a reasonable way to avoid undue accumulation of power by surgeons and resulting tensions and disruption of service. Belmar v. Cipolla, 475 A.2d 533, 539–40 (N.J. 1984).

In both *Guerrero* and *Belmar*, the courts emphasized that they would intervene if exclusions were "motivated by a desire to exclude newcomers in order to maintain the status quo of the staff." *Guerrero*, 360 A.2d at 341. Thus a hospital policy closing its staff except to newcomers joining one of the hospital's existing medical practices was found to "arbitrarily discriminat[e] against qualified applicants." The hospital's arguments that this exception improved public health by increasing coverage among the partnership, without increasing the patient load in the crowded facility, were dismissed as "pure supposition." *Desai*, 510 A.2d at 671, 670. *See also* Berman v. Valley Hospital, 510 A.2d 673 (N.J. 1986) (rejecting exclusion of non-affiliated doctors who had practiced in area for more than two years; asserted health rationales lack any empirical or academic support, therefore do not mitigate discriminatory and exclusionary impact).

c. Individual Performance: Medical Incompetence, Inability to Work With Others, and Other Risk–Creating Grounds

(1). Medical Incompetence

Protecting patients from medical incompetence is clearly the central justification for hospital-based peer review, and therefore hospitals do and should have the authority to deny, restrict, suspend, and revoke staff privileges on that ground. Serious risks to patient well-being can justify summary suspension, as long as a post-suspension hearing is held within a reasonable time. *See* Woodbury v. McKinnon, 447 F.2d 839 (5th Cir. 1971). Revocations are normally based on a pattern of substandard care, and a doctor's periodic reappointment to the medical staff does not preclude the hospital from relying on incidents preceding the reappointment. Miller v. Indiana Hospital, 419 A.2d 1191, 1194 (Pa. Super. 1980) (proper for hospital to rely on prior misconduct "which may not have been so egregious in any one year as to warrant denial of reappointment, but the cumulative effect of which called for [the doctor's] dismissal from the staff"). However, a single incident of substandard care, if sufficiently serious, can also justify termination of privileges. Storrs v. Lutheran Hospitals and Homes Soc. of America, 661 P.2d 632 (Alaska 1983). Finally, "impairment"—disabilities caused by drugs, alcohol, and age—is a permissible basis for revocation. Theissen v. Watonga Mun. Hosp. Bd., 550 P.2d 938 (Okla. 1976). *See generally* Edward E. Hollowell, *Medical Staff Credentialing*, 15 LEGAL ASPECTS OF MED. PRAC. 1 (Sept. 1987).

(2). Inability to Work With Others and Other Risk-related Grounds

Revocation of privileges because of "inability to work with others" or similar grounds is troublesome and controversial. Decisions typically require the hospital to show specific physician behaviors that create the kind of disharmony that presents a "realistic and specific threat to the quality of medical care." Miller v. Eisenhower Med. Ctr., 614 P.2d 258, 269 (Cal. 1980).

Physicians' staff privileges are occasionally revoked not because of specific instances of substandard care, but because of other behavior that creates a reasonable concern for patient well-being or hospital liability. *See* Miller v. National Medical Hosp. of Monterey Park, 177 Cal. Rptr. 119 (App. 1981) (doctor's conviction of conspiracy to murder his wife); Holmes v. Hoemako Hosp., 573 P.2d 477 (Ariz. 1977) (refusal to carry malpractice insurance).

(3). "Economic Performance" and Staff Privileges

Economic competition and performance-based payment tying hospital compensation and status as "preferred providers" to their performance, means that hospitals may be quite aggressive in efforts to lower costs, increase efficiency, maximize revenue, and defend and expand their "market share." To what extent may hospitals encourage and even require doctors to promote these institutional objectives in the doctors' patterns of practice and patient care, and penalize them if they do not? These questions have barely been touched on by courts or legislatures, but they represent the potential cutting edge of staff privilege law in the age of cost containment and entrepreneurial hospital management, and will be discussed with respect to managed care organizations in the final section.

Issues regarding a doctor's economic performance can be seen as arising in three different contexts. The first, not necessarily linked to cost containment, is where public policy requires the hospital to take certain actions with economic consequences, which actions can only be performed by doctors who themselves are not under a similar duty. The clearest example is the federal regulatory requirement that hospitals that have accepted federal construction funds under the Hill–Burton Act (discussed in Part One) assure that their facilities are actually available to Medicaid recipients and, at least with respect to emergencies, all low-income people. Aside from hospital bylaws, individual doctors are not themselves required to accept Medicaid patients, or to treat any particular patient, even in an emergency. But in order to fulfill its own regulatory duties, a hospital may condition its staff privileges on doctors' accepting low-income patients or rendering other services, and may revoke privileges for refusal to satisfy that condition. *See* Clair v. Centre Community Hosp., 463 A.2d 1065 (Pa. Super. 1983).

A second dimension of economic performance, often combined with non-economic considerations, arises when a hospital seeks institutional objectives through means that deny staff privileges to competent physicians, or attempts to regulate where or through whom certain procedures are performed. The most familiar example of this problem is exclusive contracting for hospital-based physicians, under which a hospital will require all anesthesiology services to be performed by a particular group of doctors, and will deny privileges to other anesthesiologists regardless of competence. Despite numerous legal challenges to this practice on state and federal grounds, the courts have uniformly upheld it because it contributes to important institutional objectives such as availability of services, efficiency of scheduling, familiarity with equipment, maintenance of quality, and performance of administrative and educational functions. *See, e.g.*, Adler v. Montefiore Hosp. Assn. of W. Pa., 311 A.2d 634 (Pa. 1973), *cert. den.*, 414 U.S. 1131 (1974); *Belmar*, 475 A.2d 533; *see also* Jefferson Parish Hosp. Dist. No.2 v. Hyde, 466 U.S. 2 (1984) (upholding exclusive anesthesiology contract against federal antitrust challenge; discussed in Chapter 25). Similarly, a hospital policy prohibiting neurologists on its medical staff from transporting hospital patients to their own privately-owned CAT scanner, and requiring them to use the hospital's scanner, was upheld as a reasonable effort "to deal with the complex task of providing comprehensive medical services to the citizens of our state." Cobb County–Kennestone Hosp. Authority v. Prince, 249 S.E.2d 581 (Ga. 1978).

Another, more complex version of this issue arises when a hospital has adopted an institutional strategy to develop itself along certain lines, emphasizing certain kinds and styles of practice. May a hospital then deny privileges to a competent doctor whose style or pattern does not fit the desired economic-institutional mold? A fascinating case addressing this issue is Robinson v. Magovern, 521 F. Supp. 842 (W.D. Pa. 1981), *aff'd*, 688 F.2d 824 (3d Cir.), *cert. den.*, 459 U.S. 971 (1982). This case arose when Dr. Robinson, a thoracic (open-heart) surgeon with good academic credentials (but debatable practical experience) was denied staff privileges at Allegheny General Hospital in Pittsburgh on three major grounds. First, Dr. Robinson's pattern of practicing at several hospitals, and refusing to make a major commitment to Allegheny General, was said to "prevent him from adequately covering his heart patients at Allegheny General." *Id.* at 915. Second, Dr. Robinson was said not to have the ability or the interest to contribute to the hospital's research and educational programs, e.g., by doing research or joining the medical school faculty. Third, the medical staff had serious doubts about Dr. Robinson's ability to function harmoniously with his fellow doctors, residents, and support personnel. *Id.* These reasons were important to Allegheny General not only on general grounds of high-quality patient care, but also because of the hospital's specific institutional objectives and competitive strategy. Dr. Robinson challenged the legitimacy of those objectives and of the specific criteria applied to his application by suing the hospital and Dr. Magovern, the head of the surgical department and chief thoracic surgeon, on federal antitrust and analogous state-law grounds.

To determine whether the hospital's objectives and criteria imposed an unreasonable restraint on competition or trade, the trial judge undertook exhaustive analyses of the hospital industry, the specialized market in open-heart surgery, and the institutional development of Allegheny General. He determined that Allegheny General was a "regional referral" or "secondary teaching" hospital, midway between community hospitals offering basic health services and major teaching hospitals. Hospitals such as Allegheny General provide both basic health care to their immediate areas and advanced care units in some subspecialties for patients from larger, regional areas. *Id.* at 857–58. In the late 1960's, Allegheny General sought to reverse an era of financial decline and low morale by developing its educational and research programs in particular specialties, notably cancer and heart disease. *Id.* at 859–60. Under Dr. Magovern's leadership, the open-heart surgery department "greatly expanded its research activities, and developed a reputation for providing secondary and tertiary level patients with high quality, innovative care. [These] achievements have attracted a large volume of patients to Allegheny General." *Id.* at 862–63.

Against this background, the court concluded that the hospital's highly selective criteria for granting staff privileges—such as the insistence that physicians have an active interest in research, be eligible for appointment to a medical school faculty, and be willing to concentrate their practices at Allegheny General—were related to legitimate hospital objectives. Moreover, while these criteria did have some anticompetitive effects—e.g., by excluding competent doctors who did not wish to do research or make a primary commitment to Allegheny General—these effects were outweighed in the court's view by the procompetitive effects of enhancing Allegheny General's ability to compete and by raising the prevailing level of patient care. *Id.* at 919. Finally, the hospital's policies and market share did not preclude Dr. Robinson from practicing at other hospitals in the area, or even from receiving referrals from doctors at Allegheny General. For these reasons, and others, the judge found against Dr. Robinson on all of his federal and state claims.

Robinson reflects unusually strong facts in the hospital's favor. The hospital had hired a consulting firm in the late 1960's, had formally adopted explicit institutional objectives and a competitive strategy, and had implemented that strategy by hiring strong administrators and department chairs. In other words, the hospital could credibly claim that its selective, exclusionary staff privilege criteria were not simply serving to protect the power and income of established doctors, but were rather designed to heighten the research and educational reputation of the hospital and hence its competitive position. Moreover, Dr. Robinson had a history of personality conflict and rigidity that might have justified denial even without special institutional objectives. The lesson of *Robinson* thus cuts two ways; hospitals may be able to justify exclusion on the basis of special institutional and competitive objectives, but (perhaps) not if all that is taking place is the dressing up of self-interest of existing practitioners in the rhetoric of high quality care.

CHAPTER 19

LICENSURE, ACCREDITATION AND CERTIFICATE OF NEED

1. LICENSURE AND ACCREDITATION

a. Introduction

As you learned in *Hurley v. Eddingfield* in Part One, licensure is a mechanism whose principal purpose is to protect patients and communities from unsafe or substandard health care. State licensure laws, which typically operate in connection with the privately administered health professional and institutional accreditation process, set the standards that determine qualification for entry into professional practice or operation of a health care institution. In recent years, the field of licensure has been expanded to require proof of ongoing compliance with measures of health care quality such as continuing professional education and institutional accreditation. Licensure also may be linked to compliance with certain types of reporting requirements such as adverse event reporting systems, a compulsory aspect of health care quality oversight in 25 states and the District of Columbia as of 2007. Rosenthal & Takach, *2007 Guide to State Adverse Event Reporting Systems*.

Licensure serves other purposes beyond health and safety. Licensure can advance social goals by setting value-based standards that define the legal provision of health care. Licensure also can create a protective cocoon around the professionals and institutions that hold any particular class of license, barring potential competitors from the licensed field of practice. For example, in recent years, nurses have sought to extend the reach of what is considered nursing practice to encompass diagnosis and treatment, two activities long associated with the practice of medicine. Numerous schools of nursing now offer a "doctor of nursing" degree, which is designed to train candidates to practice at a level of performance associated with medical care. State medical societies, in turn, have sought to squelch this movement, assuring that nursing remains defined as a field of practice more limited in scope than the practice of medicine—a "subordinate" profession—and restricting the use of the moniker "Doctor" to persons trained and licensed as physicians. Gardiner Harris, *Calling More Nurses 'Doctor' A Title Physicians Begrudge*, N.Y. TIMES, October 2, 2011, at A1. For this reason, discussions of licensure as well as its semi-companion, the certificate of need, often vacillate between issues of quality and concerns that licensure statutes are being used to stifle competition.

Viewed from these vantage points, it becomes evident that health professional and institutional licensure laws are part of the economic foundation of health care, since they determine not only which individuals and institutions can enter and maintain a field of practice but also the "scope of practice" powers that any particular licensed class will hold. For this reason a licensure discussion necessarily deals with the intersection of competition on the one hand and quality standard-setting through licensure and accreditation on the other. Holding a license is basic to participation in public and private health insurance programs. State licensing laws also define the scope of practice powers of license holders, at times allowing overlapping fields of practice and in other cases rigidly circumscribing the scope of powers of those who otherwise would be potential competitors.

The modern medical licensure era began in the late 19th century with an 1873 Texas medical licensure statute; over the next 30 years, licensure requirements reached all states, aided by a decision of the United States Supreme Court in Dent v. West Virginia, 129 U.S. 114 (1889), upholding a state's power to regulate medical practice. Timothy Stoltzfus Jost, *Oversight of the Quality of Medical Care: Regulation, Management, or the Market?*, 37 ARIZ. L. REV. 825, 828–829 (1995). As Professor Jost notes, the movement that emerged at this point was "merely the most 'legal' manifestation of a broader structure of self-regulation that physicians constructed beginning in the nineteenth century." *Id.* This movement consisted of medical education reform, the closure of substandard training colleges, and self-regulatory efforts to organize and improve specialty practice into subspecialties. *Id.*

In the case of hospitals, the widespread growth of state hospital licensure schemes in the mid–20th century followed passage of the Hospital Survey and Construction Act of 1946 (Hill Burton, discussed in Part One), which made hospital licensure and enforcement a condition of state participation. Cases such as *Thompson v. Sum City* (Part One) and *Jackson v. Power* (Part Three) illustrate the extent to which state legislatures have used hospital licensure schemes to advance other broad social purposes, such emergency care as a basic duty of all community hospitals and the duty to screen and stabilize emergency medical conditions.

From the beginning, the license to practice medicine was broadly conceived; that is, a physician would acquire a license as a condition of entry into the profession and could then engage in any form of medical practice, from primary care to specialized surgery. In response to the potential for incompetence to emerge among licensed physicians, the profession itself created private specialty boards whose purpose was to certify and oversee fitness to engage in medical practice within the primary care and sub-specialty fields. Today these boards, which are part of a federation of specialty boards known as the American Board of Medical Specialties, oversee practice competency on an ongoing basis through initial certification and periodic recertification exams. Hospital staff privileges may be conditioned on accreditation within that specialty. It is unusual for a state to confine medical licensure to certain sub-specialty practices; instead medical licensure permits physicians entry into the field of medicine generally, with private specialty accreditation requirements linked to hospital privileges and coverage under medical liability insurance policies.

A state's licensure enterprise consists of statutes that broadly delegate authority to various professional boards. Boards tend to be dominated by the health care professionals and institutions that are subject to licensure and may have little involvement by patients, consumers, or health care experts. INSTITUTE OF MEDICINE (IOM), THE FUTURE OF NURSING: LEADING CHANGE, ADVANCING HEALTH ch. 3 (2011); Jost, *Oversight of the Quality of Medical Care* at 835–36.

The move of licensure laws into matters of ongoing fitness and competence emerged in the 1970s, along with relatively modest efforts to broaden the composition of licensure boards. Jost, *Oversight of the Quality of Medical Care* at 833. In more recent years, the field of health professions licensing has faced broader pressures to act as an external locus of control over the quality of medical care itself. This greater interest in the role of licensing in policing ongoing competency has emerged simultaneously with the evolution of physician practice arrangements—away from solo and small physician-owned practices into larger and more accountable practice groups, as well as hospital and institutional employment—and with the entry of payers into the field of quality regulation, explored later in this Part. See Jost, *Oversight of the Quality of Medical Care* at 832–839.

At the same time, the number of individual disciplinary actions remain modest, with most instances focusing on gross violations of professional norms and laws, as well as substance abuse. *Id.* at 861–62. Even this may be a gross overstatement of just how much medical licensure boards actually engage in quality oversight. A 2011 study by Public Citizen found that despite the fact that the federal National Practitioner Data Bank, established by the Health Care Quality Improvement Act, contained the names of nearly 11 thousand physicians who faced either the revocation of restriction of clinical privileges, only 45 percent also had faced state licensing actions. Among the physicians for whom no licensing action was taken, 220 were disciplined as an "Immediate Threat to Health or Safety," more than 1100 had been disciplined because of incompetence, negligence or malpractice, and over 600 had been disciplined because of substandard care. One example offered by researchers involved a physician who had been disciplined for 26 separate medical malpractice violations but who nonetheless faced no state medical licensure action. The findings are particularly shocking because state licensure boards have ready access to both the hospital licensure actions that gave rise to most of the cases, as well as to the National Practitioner Data Bank. Alan Levine et al., *State Medical Boards Fail to Discipline Doctors with Hospital Actions Against Them* (PUBLIC CITIZEN, 2011) The resounding failure of the licensure system to be a tool for ongoing, effective oversight of clinical quality stems from numerous factors: the autonomy of the profession and its cultural if not outright controlling relationship over licensure authorities; the lack of a continuous system of information reporting about practice quality; the limited authority given to licensure agencies, (in some cases) the uncertainties of assessment, particularly of isolated practitioners—by far the group most likely to fall behind in competence; and the high expense of remediation.

Using licensing to protect the medical profession has been extensively chronicled by historians. *See, e.g.*, PAUL STARR, THE SOCIAL TRANSFORMATION OF AMERICAN MEDICINE. Starr notes that physicians sought to protect their financial interests against competitors like pharmacists, homeopaths, and herbalists, but that strong resistance to licensure grew within the profession itself, since stiff entry standards threatened the livelihoods of commercial medical schools of the time, who were busily churning out marginal graduates. Liberals and populists also opposed licensure as a tool for preventing the economic advancement by the lower classes; these writers were willing to trade what they saw as marginal improvements in safety (that could be accomplished through better education of providers) for a more open economic opportunity terrain.

As noted, the role of licensure as a basis of economic power is an important one. As Professor Starr observes, physicians themselves sought broad licensure status as a means of consolidating power and moved quickly to occupy the field through laws that defined the practice of medicine as broadly as possible and criminalized practice by anyone who was not a licensed physician. In its report on the future of nursing, the IOM offers insight into how defining medical practice can work not only to protect the public but also to empower regulated entities. In its report on the future of nursing, the IOM offered an early Washington State medical licensure statute defined the practice of medicine as any action "to diagnose, cure, advise, or prescribe for any human disease, ailment, injury, infirmity, deformity, pain or other condition, physical or mental, real or imaginary, by any means or instrumentality" or "to administer or prescribe drug or medicinal preparations to be used by any other person" or to "[sever or penetrate] the tissues of human beings." As a result of broad scope of practice powers and limited oversight, physicians as a regulated industry were able to capture the field and quash competition from other classes of health professionals. The use of licensure to advance anticompetitive behavior as been broadly criticized. FEDERAL TRADE COMMISSION & DEPARTMENT OF JUSTICE, IMPROVING HEALTH CARE: A DOSE OF COMPETITION (2003); Jost, *Oversight of the Quality of Medical Care* at 841.

An example of the ways in which scope of practice acts might restrain greater competition in health care can be seen in the field of immunization practice. When patients receive an immunization, they typically don't give a lot of thought to the health professional furnishing the vaccine. But in fact, immunizations represent a powerful illustration of how scope of practice laws can be used to constrain health care practice in ways that are not easily justified by evidence related to either patient quality or health care safety. Usually the person who administers the vaccine is a nurse, although some states also permit immunizations by specially trained immunization workers. In the case of nurses, however, the deeper "scope of practice" question is whether a nurse who immunizes is doing so under his or her *own nursing license* (i.e., whether immunizations fall into the nursing scope of practice under state law) or whether immunization is considered to fall exclusively within the scope of medical practice under state law. In the latter case, the nurse immunizes effectively under a *delegation of powers* from a physician (known as working under a physician's license), with supervision of the delegating physician required. In many states, the law is silent on a question such as this; faced with silence, a state medical licensure board typically will fall back on the basic concept of delegation of powers and will permit physicians to delegate to their medical practice powers to nurses who work under their supervision. The hazier the delegation, the less likely it is that professionals working under delegated powers will be able to compete effectively.

Scope of practice restrictions fall with particular severity on certain health professions, whose ability to practice in many states may be far more limited than the capability imparted by education and training. For example, although nurse practitioners have been found sufficiently skilled and trained to provide safely and effectively over 90 percent of all pediatric primary care and 75 percent of all general primary care, only 14 states plus the District of Columbia, according to one study, maintain nursing practice acts that allow nurse practitioners to treat primary care patients under their own licenses and without physician supervision. IOM, THE FUTURE OF NURSING at 3–11 to 3–12. Constraints on practice also mean that professionals excluded from certain types of practice are unable to bill insurers for their services when operating under their own licenses. An immunization in a state with restrictive nurse licensure laws could be billed only as an "ancillary" aspect of a physician office visit, thereby precluding independent practice by nurses. Even where state law explicitly recognizes immunization as both nursing *and* medical practice, thereby allowing nurses to assess and treat independently for vaccine-preventable diseases, insurers may refuse to cover and pay for an immunization up to the full scope of permissible practice under state law. That is, an insurer may elect to cover and pay for the procedure only when furnished by, or under the supervision of, a physician.

In order to guard against such results, some states with broader scope of practice laws have enacted laws barring insurers from discriminating against health professionals working within their state-law-defined scope of practice. In turn, these laws have been challenged by employer-sponsored health benefit plans and insurers that insure or administer such plans as preempted by ERISA. *See, e.g.*, Washington Physicians Service Ass'n v. Gregoire, 147 F.3d 1039 (9th Cir. 1998) *cert. den.*, 525 U.S. 1141 (1999). The Patient Protection and Affordable Care Act also addresses the issue of insurer discrimination against licensed health professionals in states that have adopted broad scope of practice laws by amending the Public Health Service Act to bar discrimination against health care providers (42 U.S.C. § 300gg–5, added by PPACA § 1201) as follows:

(a) PROVIDERS.—A group health plan and a health insurance issuer offering group or individual health insurance coverage shall not discriminate with respect to participation under the plan or coverage against any health care provider who is acting within the scope of that provider's license or certification under applicable State law. This section shall not require that a group health plan or health insurance issuer contract with any health care provider willing to abide by the terms and conditions for participation established by the plan or issuer. Nothing in this section shall be construed as preventing a group health plan, a health insurance issuer, or the Secretary from establishing varying reimbursement rates based on quality or performance measures.

This provision applies to all ERISA-governed health plans, whether fully or self-insured. PPACA § 1563.

Beyond establishing quality and safety standards and providing economic protections, state laws may advance broader social aims. Despite the fact that complications from a first trimester abortion are exceedingly rare (88 percent of women who have an abortion do so in the first trimester, and 99.5 percent of these women have either no complication or one simple enough to be handled in the office or clinic where the abortion is performed), the Commonwealth of Virginia promulgated regulations in 2011 that bar legal first-trimester abortions at clinics unless they can satisfy the types of standards applicable to outpatient clinics where complex ambulatory surgery occurs. *See, e.g.,* Sabrina Tavernise, *Virginia Health Board Tightens Rules on Abortion Clinics*, N.Y. TIMES, Sept. 15, 2011.

In a similar vein, state health care licensure laws aimed at protecting health and safety can evoke a strong social response. In Stormans Inc. v. Selecky, 586 F.3d 1109 (9th Cir. 2009), Washington State's pharmacy licensure board adopted a regulation requiring all licensed pharmacies to stock and dispense an FDA-approved emergency contraception drug known as Plan B. As described in Part One, the purpose of Plan B is to prevent the implantation of a fertilized egg in a womb following intercourse. In order to be effective, Plan B should be taken within 12 to 24 hours of intercourse and becomes ineffective if taken 72 hours after intercourse or later, losing all effectiveness after 120 hours. Plan B is approved for over-the-counter sale but must be held behind the pharmacist's desk, and persons 17 or younger must present a medical prescription. Reviewing the evidence, the state pharmacy licensure board concluded that there were no grounds on which a licensed pharmacy could legitimately refuse to fill the prescription. The rule allowed any individual pharmacist to refuse to dispense the prescription but in such cases also required a pharmacy either to have another pharmacist onsite to fill the prescription or to make one available by telephone.

A handful of Washington State pharmacies refused to stock or dispense the drug on moral and religious grounds; they and several individual pharmacists opposed Plan B on their belief that the drug causes abortions, and they sued to enjoin the application of the licensure board's requirement to them. The district court awarded an injunction, finding that the law burdened the free exercise of religion and as such was subject to strict scrutiny, a standard of review it failed to satisfy.

Reversing the trial court's decision, the court of appeals concluded that the law was facially neutral and not designed to discriminate against religious beliefs or conduct. As such, it needed to satisfy only a lower standard of proof, since a state acting under its licensing powers, can prescribe broad conduct for health professionals, even if such facially neutral standards have an incidental impact on free exercise of religion. Citing a long line of cases upholding the power of states to enact laws to protect the public even if such laws incidentally burden the free exercise of religion, the court wrote:

> [Washington State's] rules operate neutrally. They do not suppress, target, or single out the practice of any religion because of religious content. The evidentiary record—though thin given the procedural posture of this case—sufficiently reflects that the object of the rules was to ensure safe and timely patient access to lawful and lawfully prescribed medications. As such, the new rules eliminate all objections that do not ensure patient health, safety, and access to medication. They require delivery of all lawfully prescribed medications, save for when one of several narrow exemptions permits refusal. Thus, aside from the exemptions, any refusal to dispense a medication violates the rules, and this is so regardless of whether the refusal is motivated by religion, morals, conscience, ethics, discriminatory prejudices, or personal distaste for a patient.

> That the rules may affect pharmacists who object to Plan B for religious reasons does not undermine the neutrality of the rules. The Free Exercise Clause is not violated even though a group motivated by religious reasons may be more likely to engage in the proscribed conduct. The neutrality of the new rules is not destroyed by the possibility that pharmacists with religious objections to Plan B will disproportionately require accommodation under the rules.

Stormans Inc., 586 F.3d at 1131.

b. Licensure Standards and Enforcement

González–Droz v. González–Colon

660 F.3d 1 (1st Cir. 2011)

■ SELYA, CIRCUIT JUDGE:

For many years, all licensed physicians in Puerto Rico could perform cosmetic surgery. The landscape changed in 2005, when the Puerto Rico Board of Medical Examiners (the Board) promulgated a first-in-the-nation regulation that limited the practice of cosmetic medicine to particular classes of medical specialists. In due course, the Board enforced the regulation against a physician who, though generally licensed to practice medicine, did not possess the required specialty board certification. This litigation arises in consequence of that enforcement effort [and] challenges the constitutionality of both the regulation and the license suspension. [W]e affirm the entry of judgment for the defendants.

I. BACKGROUND

We start with the dramatis personae. The plaintiff (the appellant here) is Efraín González–Droz, a physician licensed to practice in Puerto Rico. The defendants are the members of the Board and its investigative officer. The Board, acting under the authority of the Puerto Rico Department of Health, is responsible for medical licensure in the Commonwealth. At the times relevant hereto, it was empowered to promulgate regulations relating to the practice of medicine.

After graduating from medical school, the plaintiff obtained board certification in obstetrics and gynecology. He began practicing that specialty in Puerto Rico in 1995. While practicing, he took a number of continuing medical education courses and gradually shifted the focus of his endeavors toward cosmetic medicine. As time went by, procedures such as liposuction and breast augmentation came to dominate his practice. The plaintiff's odyssey was not unique. In the same time frame, other doctors began to extend their practices to include cosmetic procedures. Concerned by this trend and by the lack of any recognized specialty accreditation in cosmetic medicine, the Board looked into the matter.

On October 19, 2005, it issued a public notice—in effect, a regulation—explaining that it had conducted research into and analysis of the field of aesthetic medicine and had determined that: 1. The majority of professionals that market their services as "aesthetic medicine" are, in reality, general physicians that have no formal training supervised at a duly accredited institution able to offer the same, in the skills that are purportedly offered to the public. 2. There is no medical field that goes by the name of "aesthetic medicine", according to the "American Board of Medical Specialties" and it is not, and never has been a recognized specialty. 3. The procedures commonly marketed as "aesthetic medicine" in reality are competencies of specialties recognized by the American Board of Medical Specialties and the [Board], to wit, dermatology and plastic surgery. 4. In reality, the so called "aesthetic medicine" is but a group of techniques and procedures belonging to dermatology and plastic surgery that is conducted by physicians lacking in the training required for such specialties that are required for the certification of professionals as qualified for the safe practice of said techniques for the benefit of the patient. 5. It will be deemed to be illegal practice of medicine [when] any person advertises, practices or purports to practice the procedures that only fall under the competence of dermatologists or plastic surgeons without possessing the certification in the corresponding specialty.

The plaintiff is not board-certified in either plastic surgery or dermatology. Thus, the new rule, which we shall call "the Regulation," barred him from the practice of cosmetic medicine. Despite this impediment and notwithstanding that the Regulation survived a constitutional challenge in the local courts, the plaintiff continued to advertise and perform cosmetic procedures. The Board did not take the plaintiff's actions lightly; on December 12, 2006, it voted to suspend his medical license provisionally pending a hearing. At around the same time, the plaintiff (apparently unaware of this vote) moved to California and opened an office there. He did not, however, lose sight of the Regulation: on December 18, 2006, he filed suit in the United States District Court for the District of Puerto Rico, challenging its constitutionality.

On May 2, 2007, while visiting Puerto Rico, the plaintiff received a copy of the Board's written resolution memorializing its decision [on public health and safety grounds including the possible death of a patient] provisionally to suspend his license [pending a hearing]. The suspension took effect upon the plaintiff's receipt of the resolution, with a hearing to be held within fifteen days thereafter. The plaintiff was invited to appear at the hearing (with or without counsel) and present evidence. If he was unable to attend on the date designated by the Board, he could request an extension; without such a request, the hearing would proceed in his absence.

Instead of responding to the resolution, on May 11, 2007, the plaintiff—who had by then returned to California—moved in the federal court to enjoin the hearing. Three days later (May 14), the plaintiff received a summons dated May 10, setting the hearing for the afternoon of May 15. He responded through counsel that he would not attend because the matter should be pursued through the courts, "not in a kangaroo 'administrative hearing.'" He did not request a continuance.

The district court refused to grant an injunction, and the hearing proceeded as scheduled. The Board reserved decision and, on April 4, 2008, issued a final decision, suspending the plaintiff's license for five years and fining him $5,000. The plaintiff asked the district court to enjoin enforcement of the suspension and fine, but the court demurred. On an interlocutory appeal, this court affirmed the denial of injunctive relief. The plaintiff on October 30, 2009 filed a second amended complaint. In it, he asserted that the Regulation transgressed both the Fourteenth Amendment and federal antitrust law, that the suspension of his medical license took place without due process, and that the suspension was prompted by a retaliatory animus.

Following the completion of pretrial discovery, the plaintiff moved for partial summary judgment. The defendants cross-moved for summary judgment on all of the claims. On June 15, 2010, the district court denied the plaintiff's motion and essentially granted the defendants' cross-motion. The court rejected the plaintiff's antitrust claim on predictable grounds. It rejected the remaining claims on immunity grounds. It stated, however, that it considered the Regulation to be a proper exercise of the Board's authority to promulgate restrictions anent the practice of medicine. This timely appeal ensued.

II. ANALYSIS

Here, the district court's single-minded emphasis on immunity issues put the cart before the horse. In the circumstances of this case, no combination of immunity doctrines can obviate the need to decide the question of the constitutionality of the Regulation. We take a different approach. Where, as here, the district court does not decide the dispositive issues presented in fully briefed motions for summary judgment, we may elect in our discretion either to remand or to decide the issues. In this instance, the issues are purely legal and the outcome is clear. We proceed, therefore, to the merits.

As we envision it, the proper decisional matrix in this case presents three sets of issues. First, we decide whether the Regulation withstands equal protection and due process challenges. We then decide whether the actions undertaken to suspend the plaintiff's medical license offended procedural due process. Finally, we determine whether the suspension itself is open to attack on either substantive due process or First Amendment (retaliation) grounds. We address these matters below.

A. *The Regulation.*

The plaintiff launches two constitutional challenges against the validity of the Regulation. We address them separately.

1. *Rational Basis.* With considerable assistance from the amicus, the plaintiff charges that limiting the practice of cosmetic medicine to board-certified plastic surgeons and dermatologists transgresses the Equal Protection and Due Process Clauses. U.S. Const. amend. XIV, § 1. In mounting this argument, the plaintiff does not allege either that he is a member of a suspect class or that the Regulation infringes a fundamental right. Consequently, we take the measure of the Regulation under rational basis review.

Rational basis review is a paradigm of judicial restraint. The general rule is that legislation is presumed to be valid and will be sustained if the classification drawn is rationally related to a legitimate state interest. The challenger has the devoir of persuasion and must negate any and all conceivable bases upon which the challenged regulation might appropriately rest. If any such ground exists to support the classification employed, the regulation must be upheld even if it is drawn from rational speculation unsupported by evidence or empirical data. [internal quotes omitted]

In this instance, the interests that the Regulation purposes [sic] to serve are unarguably legitimate. States have a profound interest in assuring the health of the public and, thus, in regulating the practice of medicine. As a corollary of this proposition, states may act to safeguard the integrity and ethics of the medical profession and to protect "vulnerable groups ... from abuse, neglect, and mistakes" at the hands of medical practitioners. The plaintiff strives to convince us that the Regulation is not rationally related to these salutary purposes but, instead, draws an arbitrary distinction that is useless in promoting safe and effective health care.

He begins this effort by pointing out that cosmetic medicine deals with the achievement of aesthetic ideals, whereas plastic surgery and dermatology deal with medically indicated needs for treatment and reconstruction. But this argument, which depends on oversimplification and unproven generalities, fails to demonstrate the absence of a rational basis.

Rational basis review requires only that the state could rationally have concluded that the challenged classification *might* advance its legitimate interests. The Board's decision to limit access to the practice of cosmetic medicine by reference to board certification in plastic surgery and dermatology satisfies this standard. In adopting the certification requirement, the Board repeatedly remarked upon the dangers attendant to cosmetic procedures and the need to guide patients to qualified practitioners.

The Board thought that a general license to practice medicine is not enough to ensure competence in this field and decided to use as a proxy for competence two closely related specialty boards. The plaintiff's arguments against that choice emphasize the lack of perfect symmetry between those specialties and cosmetic medicine. But perfect symmetry is not required: as long as the premises underlying the state's reasoning are at least "arguable," the state's judgment about a matter subject to rational basis review is protected from constitutional attack. In this case, there is no accredited specialty board for cosmetic medicine, and certification in the closely related fields of plastic surgery and dermatology arguably could be seen as a surrogate. To pass rational basis review, it is enough that the classification falls within the universe of reasonable alternatives that might serve to foster improved patient care and safety. The Regulation achieves this benchmark.

We reject the plaintiff's insistence that the selection of this alternative is wholly arbitrary. During their specialized residency training, both plastic surgeons and dermatologists are exposed to procedures that are indigenous to cosmetic medicine. They develop a skill set compatible with that practice area. Perhaps more important, both plastic surgeons and dermatologists are trained in general concepts that advance their abilities to understand and perform cosmetic procedures. It was not arbitrary for the Board to conclude that such training would, on the whole, contribute to improved patient care and safety in this rapidly evolving field.

The fact that the actual practice of any particular plastic surgeon or dermatologist may not include performance of cosmetic procedures does not undercut this conclusion. The training needed to obtain board certification in these specialties overlaps substantially with the knowledge needed to practice cosmetic medicine safely and effectively. That is enough, as a constitutional matter, to justify the Board's solution.

The plaintiff complains that a classification based on board certification in other specialties is an ineffective way to foster patient choice and safety. He notes that residency programs and other prerequisites for certification in plastic surgery and/or dermatology do not encompass all, or even most, cosmetic medicine procedures; yet under the Regulation, a board-certified plastic surgeon or dermatologist may practice cosmetic medicine without proof of any additional training. In contrast, other doctors (who may have undergone additional procedure-specific training) cannot.

This plaint is unavailing. In conducting rational basis review, courts are not tasked with deciding whether a better or more effective means of classification exists. While the Regulation may draw an imperfect line, that circumstance alone does not render it unconstitutional. The wisdom of the Board's choice is not within the judiciary's purview. The plaintiff seeks to derive sustenance from the fact that no other state has adopted a similar limitation with respect to the practice of cosmetic medicine. Differences in classifications among the several states, without more, do not betoken irrationality.

The plaintiff[ ] next [argues] that, by virtue of both training and experience, he is superbly qualified to practice cosmetic medicine. That may be so—and the Board could, if it so chose, conduct a case-by-case assessment of each physician's qualifications in cosmetic medicine as a prerequisite to permitted practice in that field. But the Constitution does not demand so specific a decisional matrix. The state may paint with a broader brush as long as the criteria that it chooses are rationally related to some legitimate governmental purpose. Board certification, as a practice criterion, satisfies this requirement.[6] *See* Am. Med. Ass'n, *State Medical Licensure Requirements and Statistics* 128 (2011). Although the point may be debatable, *see, e.g., id.* at 167 (discussing conflicting views among national professional organizations over precise value of board certification), the Board's decision to limit the practice of cosmetic medicine to physicians who have achieved board certification in closely related fields represents a permissible choice.

In sum, the Board, acting within the scope of its delegated authority, settled upon a regulatory classification that bears a rational relationship to the legitimate objective of promoting safe and effective medical care. Consequently, the Regulation does not contravene the Equal Protection or Due Process Clauses.

2. *Vagueness.* The plaintiff also claims that the Regulation is unconstitutionally vague because it does not clearly define its limitations. This claim need not detain us. It is a basic principle of due process that an enactment is void for vagueness if its prohibitions are not clearly defined. This does not mean, however, that a law or a regulation must be precise to the point of pedantry. Where a profession-specific regulation affords sufficient indicia of its meaning and application to those of ordinary intelligence in the profession, it is not subject to invalidation on vagueness grounds. In this instance, the Regulation identifies the covered procedures as those "commonly marketed" as "aesthetic medicine" and defines them with

---

6. The amicus contends that the Board's reliance on certification is inconsistent with a federal regulation prohibiting hospitals from awarding staff privileges on the basis of board certification alone. See 42 C.F.R. § 482.12(a)(7). This argument was not raised below, and we repeatedly have held that while amicus briefs are helpful in assessing litigants' positions, an amicus cannot introduce a new argument into a case.

reference to plastic surgery and dermatology. This is enough to avoid a general charge of vagueness. It may be that a particular procedure exists on the margin that would leave a physician of ordinary intelligence to wonder whether that procedure is covered by the Regulation. But no such uncertainty plagued the plaintiff in this case (or, if it did, he has not offered an example). For aught that appears, the plaintiff's practice consisted of liposuction, breast augmentation, and other procedures that fell squarely within the compass of the Regulation. There could be no doubt among medical professionals that the Regulation reaches those procedures.

B. *The Suspension.*

Taking aim at a different target, the plaintiff assails, on constitutional grounds, both the procedures used to suspend his license and the suspension itself. The Due Process Clause prohibits a state from depriving a person of "life, liberty, or property, without due process of law." U.S. Const. amend. XIV, § 1. This guarantee has both substantive and procedural components. The plaintiff's broadside, and our ensuing analysis, implicate both theories. We also address under this rubric the plaintiff's claim of retaliation.

1. *Procedural Due Process.* The plaintiff contends that the actions undertaken to effect the suspension of his license violated his procedural due process rights. We think not. To establish a procedural due process violation, the plaintiff must identify a protected liberty or property interest and allege that the defendants, acting under color of state law, deprived [him] of that interest without constitutionally adequate process. Because the Board stripped the plaintiff of his license (and, thus, took away a means of earning his livelihood), he has made the necessary showing of a deprivation of a constitutionally protected property interest. The question, then, is whether the process leading to that deprivation passes constitutional muster.

The basic guarantee of procedural due process is that before a significant deprivation of liberty or property takes place at the state's hands, the affected individual must be forewarned and afforded an opportunity to be heard " 'at a meaningful time and in a meaningful manner.' " No rigid taxonomy exists for evaluating the adequacy of state procedures in a given case; rather, due process is flexible and calls for such procedural protections as the particular situation demands. In this case, the plaintiff identifies the lack of a pre-deprivation hearing, the brevity of the notice afforded in advance of the hearing, and the nature of the hearing itself as hallmarks of a constitutional shortfall. We examine this asseverational array.

In order to determine both when a pre-deprivation hearing is compulsory and what process is due, an inquiring court must balance a myriad of factors, including the private and public interests involved, the risk of an erroneous deprivation inherent in the procedures employed by the state, and the likely benefit that might accrue from additional procedural protections. *Mathews v. Eldridge*, 424 U.S. 319 (1976). Whether the deprivation was, in fact, justified is not an element of the procedural due process inquiry.

The plaintiff first upbraids the defendants for their vote to suspend his license, albeit provisionally, without an antecedent hearing. To begin, it is difficult to imagine what value there would have been in a pre-deprivation hearing. The plaintiff does not challenge the Board's key finding that precipitated its action: their determination that the plaintiff was practicing cosmetic medicine in violation of the Regulation. The lack of any dispute over that key finding is telling. *Codd v. Velger,* 429 U.S. 624 (1977) (per curiam) (finding no pre-deprivation hearing necessary when there was no factual dispute). Although the plaintiff implies that he would have challenged the constitutionality of the Regulation at the hearing, that is a question for adjudication by the courts, not the Board.

The plaintiff's criticism overlooks that due process does not invariably require a hearing before the state can interfere with a protected property interest. A key datum is whether "some form of hearing is [provided] before an individual is *finally* deprived of [the] interest." *Mathews,* 424 U.S. at 333 (emphasis supplied). Considering that the license suspension was at that point provisional (not final), that the balance of the private and public interests involved favored immediate action, and that the risk of an erroneous deprivation was very small, we conclude that a prompt post-deprivation hearing was constitutionally adequate.

In working this calculus, we give great weight to the proposition that when the state reasonably determines that a license-holder poses a risk to patient safety, pre-deprivation process typically is not required. *Patel v. Midland Mem'l Hosp. & Med. Ctr.,* 298 F.3d 333, 339–40 (5th Cir. 2002). In these circumstances, moreover, the need for a pre-deprivation hearing is further diminished by the state's strong interest in upholding the integrity of [a] state-licensed profession[ ] ... The Board's concern that González–Droz "may harm patients" because he lacks the "training required by the [Regulation] to carry out such procedures" provided a sufficient basis for a founded conclusion that no pre-deprivation hearing was constitutionally compelled.

Neither the possible risk of an erroneous deprivation nor the possible benefit of additional safeguards shifts the balance. Especially in cases involving public health and safety and the integrity of professional licensure, the force of these factors is significantly diminished by the ready availability of prompt post-deprivation review. In this case, the provisional suspension did not take effect until May 2, 2007. The plaintiff was afforded a hearing roughly two weeks later (prior to the Board's decision to make the suspension final).

The plaintiff's assault on the adequacy of the notice provided in advance of the post-deprivation hearing is easily repulsed. The plaintiff focuses with tunnel vision on the summons that he received on May 14 to support an allegation that he had only a few hours' notice of the May 15 hearing. This is sheer persiflage. In reality, the notice afforded to the plaintiff and his opportunity to prepare were much greater. The plaintiff was aware more than five months earlier that his continued practice of cosmetic medicine flew in the teeth of the Regulation and placed his medical license in jeopardy. The suit that he filed in December of 2006 attests to this awareness. Moreover, the resolution that the Board delivered to the plaintiff in hand on May 2 advised him that a hearing would be held within fifteen days. Taken together, these facts demonstrate that the plaintiff had ample notice of the hearing, a fair indication of when it would occur, and a sufficient opportunity to prepare for it.[7] If more were needed— and we doubt that it is—the resolution explained that if the plaintiff was unable to attend the hearing or to proceed, he could request a continuance. He eschewed that opportunity, instead telling the defendants that the issues should be resolved through litigation. This steadfast insistence on boycotting the hearing further erodes the plaintiff's claim of inadequate notice.

What remains is to determine whether the hearing itself offered adequate safeguards. The plaintiff's contrary claim rests primarily on an assertion that defendant José Jiménez–Rivera (Jiménez), the Board's investigative officer and the de facto prosecutor at the May hearing, infected the proceeding with a risk of bias because the plaintiff had named him months earlier as a defendant in this suit. Certainly, a biased decision maker [is] constitutionally unacceptable. But Jiménez's duties as the Board's investigative officer do not involve decision making.

In a further attack on the conduct of the hearing, the plaintiff asserts that the Board failed to demand sufficient evidence in connection with the patient grievances to which it referred in its suspension decision. Here, however, the plaintiff had the opportunity to engage counsel and present rebuttal evidence at the hearing. He could have submitted his patient files for consideration but did not do so. Given this tactical decision, he hardly can complain about the Board's reference to the dissatisfied patients' unopposed testimony, and we do not, in any event, read the Board's decision as resolving the issue of the patient grievances.

2.   *Substantive Due Process.* The constitutional guarantee of substantive due process functions to protect individuals from particularly offensive actions on the part of government officials. In other words, a substantive due process claim implicates the essence of state action rather than its modalities. The plaintiff bears the burden of showing that the challenged actions were so egregious as to shock the conscience. To sink to this level, the challenged conduct must be truly outrageous, uncivilized, and intolerable. The plaintiff claims that the suspension of his license was so heavy-handed as to work a denial of substantive due process. We reject this claim out of hand. In this case, neither the Board's actions nor the result of those actions (the license suspension) remotely approach the level of a substantive due process violation. Consequently, summary judgment was inevitable on this claim.

---

7.   It is difficult to discern what additional safeguards might have benefitted the plaintiff. The resolution unambiguously stated that a hearing would occur within fifteen days, yet the plaintiff elected to return to California.

3. *Retaliation.* The plaintiff has one more shot in his sling. He argues that the suspension of his license cannot stand because the Board's decision was in retaliation for filing this suit and his testimony in favor of another physician in a separate 2005 license-suspension case. This claim is without merit. Citizens have a First Amendment right to engage in certain kinds of speech, including the filing of civil actions. A party seeking to establish a claim of retaliation under the First Amendment must show that the conduct in which he engaged was a substantial or motivating factor in the challenged decision. This showing necessitates proof of a causal connection between the allegedly protected speech and the allegedly retaliatory response.

In the case at hand, the plaintiff insists that the suspension decision followed two instances of protected speech and that this temporal proximity, without more, supports a conclusion that a causal connection exists between these events. Temporal proximity alone may, in certain circumstances, support an inference of retaliation. Here, however, neither of the described incidents forges the necessary causal link.

We start with the plaintiff's suit. The Board made its decision to suspend the plaintiff's license on December 12, 2006. This occurred *before* the plaintiff filed the original complaint on December 18 and, thus, cannot plausibly be viewed as an act of retaliation. This leaves the plaintiff's testimony in another physician's case. The testimony occurred in October of 2005 (more than a year before the Board voted provisionally to suspend the plaintiff's license). In order to raise an inference of causation, temporal proximity must be close. With no other evidence of causation, an interval of this magnitude cannot establish the necessary linkage between protected speech and some challenged action.

At any rate, a defendant may avoid liability in a retaliation case by showing that it would have reached the same decision absent the protected speech. The plaintiff does not dispute that his actions (continuing to advertise and perform cosmetic surgery) contravened the Regulation. The Board's decision was based on those actions (which under the Regulation constituted illegal practice). It is, therefore, clear beyond hope of contradiction that the Board would have reached the same conclusion regardless of the plaintiff's 2005 testimony.

Notes

1. *Using board certification as a measure of quality in state licensing laws.* Dr. González–Droz challenged Puerto Rico's regulation barring cosmetic surgery by physicians without a specialty in either dermatology or plastic surgery on the grounds that the link between quality and board certification in either specialty was factually unsupported. The plaintiff had pursued advanced training in the field of cosmetic surgery and took the position that in order to be legitimate, the rule had to provide for a case-by-case review of competency rather than setting across-the-board competency thresholds linked to certification status. The court rejected this argument,

taking the same deferential approach to matters of licensure standard that is evident in peer review cases and allowing the Board to rely on broad evidence of certification as the threshold measure of qualification.

There is evidence to suggest that specialty-certified physicians are more likely to pass the clinical knowledge component of the U.S. Medical Licensure examination survey. Donna B. Jeffe & Dorothy Andriole, *Factors Associated with American Board of Medical Specialties Member Board Certification Among U.S. Medical School Graduates*, 306 JAMA 901 (2011). Other studies have linked board certification with patient health outcome. *See, e.g.*, Jay Prystowksy et al., *Patient Outcomes for Segmental Colon Resection According to Surgeon's Training, Certification and Experience*, 132 SURGERY 663 (2002); Joyce V. Kelly & Fred Hellinger, *Physician and Hospital Factors Associated with Mortality of Surgical Patients*, 24 MED. CARE 785 (1986); J. J. Norcini et al., *Certification and Specialization: Do They Matter in the Outcome of Acute Myocardial Infarction*, 75 ACAD. MED. 1193 (2000). At the same time, studies linking certification to outcome have been found to be flawed. L. K. Sharp et al., *Specialty Board Certification and Clinical Outcomes: the Missing Link*, 77 ACAD. MED. 534 (2002).

Furthermore, evidence suggests that the volume of care performed in a particular sub-specialty field or type of institutional practice may be a strong predictor of quality. Benjamin Spencer et al., *Quality-of-Care Indicators for Early Prostate Cancer*, 21 J. CLINICAL ONCOLOGY 1928 (2003); Harold Luft et al., *Should Operations be Regionalized?* 301 NEW ENG. J. MED. 1364 (1979). The latter study, considered the landmark in the field of quality assessment in relation to volume, found very large differences in the quality of care across low-volume and high-volume hospitals in 14 separate surgical procedures. The study measured operative mortality in relation to volume, defining such mortality as death prior to hospital discharge or within 30 days of the operative procedure. John D. Birkemeyer et al., *Hospital Volume and Surgical Mortality in the United States*, 346 NEW ENG. J. MED. 1128 (2002). High-volume hospitals may, of course, be the most likely to attract physicians with more advanced training, certification, and experience in a field, which in turn boosts the volume of care furnished within that field.

The question thus becomes whether the key factor in quality is the level of training, the level of experience, or both. If the former, then it makes sense to link licensure, as Puerto Rico does, to board certification status, although it is unclear whether certification in dermatology or surgery gets at the core issue of qualification to provide a certain type of surgery, or whether added training and experience are better predictors, in fact. As the opinion notes, the American Academy of Cosmetic Surgery filed an amicus brief on behalf of the plaintiff; the brief underscores that experience and volume, as evidenced in Medicare's national hospital privileging standard, is the central issue rather than board certification alone:

> Defendants offer no evidence, or even a logical explanation that the Ruling will protect the public's health and welfare. Instead, Defendants [sic] argument is based on nothing but an

unsound, and false, assertion that board certified plastic surgeons and dermatologists are "better trained and better educated" than other cosmetic surgeons. By contrast, AACS provided this Court with the following undisputed information demonstrating there can be no rational relationship between the public's health and welfare, and the Ruling which reduces patient choice and jeopardizes public safety:

The criteria used to assess a physician's qualifications to perform any medical procedure include education, training, experience, and proven competence. The "national privileging standard" is endorsed by the American Medical Association ("AMA"), the Joint Commission, the American Osteopathic Association's Healthcare Facilities Accreditation Program, the American Board of Medical Specialties and the federal government. The Ruling which uses board certification to determine whether physicians are qualified to perform cosmetic procedures in Puerto Rico is inconsistent with the national privileging standard. No state in the U.S. utilizes board certification to determine a physician's competency or right to perform cosmetic procedures. Cosmetic surgery, plastic surgery, and dermatology are different areas of medicine, and education, training, and experience in one area does not render a physician qualified in another. AMA recognizes cosmetic surgery as a separate medical specialty. There is no Accreditation Council for Graduate Medical Education ("ACGME") recognized residency in cosmetic surgery. The residency programs physicians must complete to become board certified in dermatology, general surgery, obstetrics and gynecology, oral and maxillofacial surgery, ophthalmology, otolaryngology, plastic surgery and other ABMS member specialties do not typically include adequate training to render a graduate competent to perform the vast array of cosmetic surgery procedures. Physicians develop the majority of their cosmetic surgery skills through specialized post-residency education, training, and experience. Plastic surgery and dermatology residency programs encompass inadequate training, and in some cases no training with respect to many cosmetic procedures. Several studies found significantly higher rates of morbidity, mortality, and malpractice claims among board certified plastic surgeons over all other medical specialties performing certain cosmetic procedures.

AACS Amicus Brief, 2011 WL 1977753

Why do you believe that the Puerto Rico Medical Board may have acted as it did? Would a case-by-case review using criteria of advanced training and actual experience be fairer and more in accord with the research? What are the downsides of such an approach? Does the Puerto Rico licensure standard in fact guarantee a greater level of safety given the weak link between certification and cosmetic surgery outcomes? Given the squishiness of the evidence linking board certification to quality (and in this case, the total absence of a system of board certification in cosmetic surgery), does Puerto Rico's standard do much to advance quality, or is it more a strategy for keeping the competition in check?

2. *Due process.* As in the case of the suspension or revocation of hospital admitting privileges, courts uniformly rule that as long as an individual can challenge such a decision through a fair process that provides for impartial review, the right to present and review evidence and the right to representation, procedural due process does not require a pre-decisional hearing. As with the substantive standards that determine licensure, courts defer to boards over matters of process, as long as basic thresholds are met. However, numerous challenges from all states have successfully addressed defects in the notice and hearing procedures. *See generally* Randy Koenders, *Right as to Notice and Hearing in Proceeding to Revoke or Suspend License to Practice Medicine,* 10 A.L.R. 5th 1 (2011). Courts will uphold the constitutionality of broadly worded state licensure laws as long as substandard conduct is well documented. Thus, a requirement that health professionals maintain ''complete treatment records'' is not unconstitutionally vague in the context of facts showing extensive failure by a health professional to document the appropriateness of his diagnosis of a condition and administration of treatment. Faghih v. Washington State Department of Health, Dental Quality Assurance Commission, 202 P.3d 962 (Wash. 2009).

3. *Oversight of licensed health professionals and institutions; state investigations and the National Practitioner Data Bank.* As a general matter, ongoing oversight of the quality of health care is carried out by professional and institutional accrediting organizations, as well as, to a growing degree, health care payers, as discussed later in this Part. A 2009 report from the Federation of State Medical Boards describes advances in medical licensure including a multi-state application process, online evaluation, credentialing, information exchange to promote cross-state linkages, and a technology based credentials verification system. FEDERATION OF STATE MEDICAL BOARDS, STATE OF THE STATES: PHYSICIAN REGULATION (2009), http://www.fsmb.org/pdf/2009_state_of_states.pdf.

Federal law addresses the qualifications of physicians only to a limited degree, most notably in the context of the Health Care Quality Improvement Act of 1986, reviewed earlier in this Part, which, along with reforms to shield further the medical peer review process, also established the National Practitioner Data Bank (NPDB) that allows hospitals and health care institutions to examine the qualifications of physicians on a national basis. The NPDB is a repository of medical malpractice claims payments that encompasses payment by settlement, arbitration award or verdict. The NPDB also holds information on other ''adverse actions'' involving licensure revocation or sanctions or the suspension or revocation of hospital privileges. The NPDB was a response to concerns that under the state-based method of medical oversight, physicians sanctioned for poor quality care in one jurisdiction could escape notice simply by moving to another.

Under federal NPDB requirements, 45 C.F.R. § 60.1 et seq., malpractice insurers must, with certain limited exceptions, report medical liability claims payments made for physicians, dentists, and other health professionals. In addition, state licensing boards must report licensure disciplinary actions based on professional competence and misconduct. Reportable actions include revocation, suspension, restriction, or acceptance of surrender of a license, as well as censure, reprimand, or probation of a licensed physician or dentist based on professional competence or professional conduct. Reporting requirements under the law also extend to hospitals and other health care entities in cases in which physicians and dentists are the subject of any professional review action, related to professional competence or conduct, that affects clinical privileges for longer than 30 days; or voluntary surrender or restriction of clinical privileges while under, or to avoid, investigation. Similarly covered are professional societies, which must report, for physicians and dentists, any professional review action linked to professional competence or conduct. Finally, all information related to exclusion of health professionals from Medicare and Medicaid must be reported to the NPDB.

Federal regulations permit access to the NPDB by hospitals and health care entities, health professionals seeking information about themselves and state licensing boards. Only in narrow circumstances can plaintiffs in medical liability cases secure information from the NPDB, whose regulations limit plaintiffs' access to actions involving allegations of hospital as well as physician negligence in which information is not accessible from the hospital directly. A 2003 study examining the impact of the NPDB on the settlement of medical malpractice claims found that the introduction of the NPDB actually reduced the proportion of claims that were settled, particularly small claims. These results suggested to researchers that the impact of the NPDB has been to reduce the proportion of questionable claims that receive compensation. Teresa Waters et al., *Impact of the National Practitioner Data Bank on Resolution of Malpractice Claims*, 40 INQUIRY 283 (2003).

In explaining the role of state professional licensure investigators, the Federation of State Medical Boards provides as follows:

> Depending on the size of a state's physician population, medical boards typically will receive hundreds to thousands of complaints annually. The most common complaint received by medical boards is allegations a physician has deviated from the accepted standard of medical care in a state. According to board investigators, some of the most common standard-of-care complaints include: Overprescribing or prescribing the wrong medicine; Failure to diagnose a medical problem that is found later; Misreading X rays to identify a medical problem; Failure to get back to a patient with medical test results in a timely manner, which can lead to harm to that patient; Failure to provide appropriate post-operative care; Failure to respond to a call from hospital to help a patient in a traumatic situation. Other complaints allege sexual impropriety or substance abuse. Even complaints about rudeness could be indicative of a bigger issue.

Most complaints to medical boards are related to the standard of health care, but some involve allegations of criminal conduct, such as drug dealing, rape or homicide. In some states, the medical board acts as an independent, self-contained unit, and investigators work strictly on medical board cases. In other states, the medical board is part of a larger umbrella agency, and investigators work on cases for several boards.

Federation of State Medical Boards, State of the States: Physician Regulation 2009.

Despite the investigative machinery, news accounts provide many examples of major failures in health care quality with little action by licensing agencies. For example, the young playwright Jonathan Larsen who composed the opera *Rent,* died the day before the acclaimed work opened on Broadway in 1996, a victim of the failure of two hospitals to detect the massive aortic aneurism that took his life. Both times the hospitals instead sent him home, once with a diagnosis of the flu, and again, with food poisoning. The two hospitals paid small fines, a sanction that lawyers for Mr. Larson applauded because such action by a licensure agency was considered so rare. *Two Hospitals Fined in the Wake of Death of 'Rent' Creator*, N.Y. Times, Dec. 13, 1996.

The death of Libby Zion, daughter of reporter Sidney Zion, had wider ramifications. An 18–year–old college freshman brought to the New York Hospital by her father in 1984, she was running a high fever and exhibiting "mysterious jerking" movements. She also had a history of depression, was taking a strong antidepressant. Several hours after her treatment (hydration and the administration of an opiate to stop the shaking) began, Zion became increasingly agitated and the first-year resident who had done the initial evaluation ordered that she be placed in restraints. With "dozens" of other patients to cover, the resident never visually evaluated Zion again. The second-year resident on the case had left to get a few hours of sleep. Zion's fever skyrocketed to 107 degrees and she suffered cardiac arrest.

What emerged from Sidney Zion's subsequent efforts to investigate the cause of his daughter's death was a shocking story: overwhelmed and exhausted young physicians in training who were forced to work 36–hour shifts; the complete absence of supervising physicians; and an utter failure of care as evidenced by the lack of ongoing monitoring and evaluation, the use of restraints, and rampant fever. A subsequent 1994 malpractice trial "assigned equal blame" to the hospital and to Zion for concealing her past use of cocaine.

What emerged from grand jury proceedings convened by the Manhattan District Attorney was more significant however. Describing the case 25 years later, Dr. Barron Lerner, who had been a New York City medical resident at the time, recalled that the case came as no surprise to other residents, who understood the "insanity" of a system that forced young physicians to attempt to learn the practice of medicine while awake for 36 hours: "Deprived of sleep, we roamed the wards, dreaming of when we could finally leave, dozing off on rounds, screaming at patients and colleagues, and praying we would not make any grievous mistakes." Dr. Lerner notes that it was the highly critical findings of the Manhattan grand jury that ultimately influenced the adoption of reforms that limited medical residents practicing in New York State to no more than 80 hours per week and no more than 24 hours in a row, with "significantly more on-site supervision from senior physicians." In 2003, the Accreditation Council for Graduate Medical Education, which accredits all training and residency programs, adopted the reforms as a binding national standard. In 2010 the Institute of Medicine recommended even stricter controls and issued a stinging critique of medical residency training in a report entitled "Optimizing Graduate Medical Trainee (Residency) Hours and Work Schedules to Improve Patient Safety." Barron Lerner, *A Life–Changing Case for Doctors in Training*, N. Y. Times, August 14, 2011.

4. *Physicians who abuse their powers to prescribe controlled substances.* Licensure revocation and suspension may involve physicians who abuse their licenses by consistently and indiscriminately prescribing painkillers and other controlled substances. *See, e.g.*, Matter of Binenfield v. New York State Department of Health, 640 N.Y.S.2d 924 (1996) (revocation of medical practice license after years of evidence of prescribing abuses, including a long history of warnings and more limited sanctions). Particularly notable, perhaps, is the absence of action by state licensure boards against physicians who overprescribe painkillers or worse, who are receiving kickbacks for steering patients to certain drugs, even in the face of strong evidence including the indictment of drug companies and the naming of physicians as co-conspirators in indictments. Tracy Weber & Charles Ornstein, *Doctors Avoid Penalties in Lawsuits Against Medical Firms Alleging Kickbacks, Fraud*, Wash. Post, Sept. 16, 2011.

5. *Drug and alcohol-impaired physicians.* What do medical licensure boards do in the face of extensive and ongoing evidence of alcohol or drug impairment? Alcohol and drug abuse are among the leading causes of disciplinary actions by licensing boards in the U.S. One study of longitudinal patterns in disciplinary actions between 1990 and 2000 showed frequent restoration of licenses followed by subsequent disciplinary action. The study author speculated that such patterns could indicate both ongoing monitoring as well as repeated relapses. Matthew Holtman, *Disciplinary Careers of Drug–Impaired Physicians*, 64 Soc. Sci. & Med. 543 (2007).

A particularly spectacular example of precisely this syndrome involved Vice President Cheney's personal internist, Dr. Gary Malakoff, about whom there was extensive evidence of drug dependency. The evidence showed that not only did Dr. Malakoff have a long record of abuse, but that his own colleagues "may even have facilitated Malakoff's problem by their deferential treatment, raising questions about the suitability of having physicians in practice together overseeing the recovery of one of their own." Rick Weiss, *Internist's Relapse Into Drug Use Undetected*, Wash. Post, July 8, 2004, at A1. The story documented the extent to which, once the physician's impairment was discovered, the Washington D.C. medical licensure board not only permitted him to continue practicing medicine but allowed the D.C. Medical Society to oversee his rehabilitation treatment. The practice of assigning oversight to a private medical society is not uncommon; what was unusual about this case was that the Society in turn placed him under the management of the very medical group practice of which he was a member, specifically personal colleagues and younger physicians who literally practiced under his direction. The medical group, the George Washington University Medical Faculty Associates, agreed to such an arrangement and provided information claiming his recovery, when in fact he continued to extensively abuse drugs:

> The psychiatrist and neurologist overseeing care for Malakoff— then the director of the medical center's internal medicine division—repeatedly prescribed the drugs the internist was known to have been abusing, medical charts show. And when the neurologist, Perry Richardson, needed to document Malakoff's progress to the local medical society, he let Malakoff craft the letter, Richardson acknowledged in a deposition.
>
> "I have no concerns about his thought processes or judgment," Malakoff wrote about himself for Richardson's signature. "I truly believe that he is stable enough to see and take care of patients as well as teach our medical students and residents." The documents, along with interviews of doctors familiar with the case, paint a picture of an insular and ineffective system of oversight in which Malakoff's doctors accepted his assurances of well-being at face value while he continued to order thousands of dollars of drugs on the Internet, repeatedly crashed his car and managed to bamboozle scores of urine tests. By doing so, the records show, Malakoff's physicians effectively, if unwittingly, protected him from further disciplinary action by the District's medical licensing board.
>
> It is not clear, however, why earlier periods of ongoing drug use by Malakoff were not picked up by drug tests demanded by the medical society. One thing that became clear is that [Vice President] Cheney has known about Malakoff's problems for some time. Jonathan Reiner, director of GWU's cardiac catheterization laboratory, said in an interview that Cheney "has known for years" about Malakoff's drug dependence, although he would not be specific. "Dr. Malakoff had frank discussions with the vice president for quite a period of time about this," Reiner said. "This was not just recent news. He has kept him apprised." Reiner said he had "no concern" that Malakoff's problems affected Cheney's care, saying that Malakoff was "a member of a team of doctors" that made collective decisions.
>
> Several doctors and medical administrators said Malakoff's story is emblematic of a larger problem of the difficulties doctors face in applying the tough love their impaired colleagues need. Malakoff continued to treat patients from the fall of 1999—when he was first caught using other doctors' names to prescribe drugs

for himself—until May [2004] when the medical society determined he was failing to stay clear of drugs and insisted he stop practicing or face possible action by the District's medical licensing board.

Records, obtained by The Post indicate that in the first years of Malakoff's treatment, when his doctors documented his purported recovery, he spent about $50,000 on bulk orders of Stadol, an opiate; fiorinal, a barbiturate; codeine, a narcotic; Xanax, an anti-anxiety drug; Ambien, a sleeping aid; and other prescription drugs. Similarly, when Gerald Perman—the psychiatrist on Malakoff's treatment team—was told by a lawyer in January 2002 that Malakoff had secretly continued to order large quantities of drugs during treatment in 2001, Perman seemed unalarmed.

"There are many things in the world I don't know about, and there are many things my patients do, I'm sure, that they don't tell me about or that I don't know about," Perman is quoted as saying in legal documents related to Malakoff. He added, "It tells me that he may have felt embarrassed and ashamed about this problem." In the course of Malakoff's treatment, Richardson, the neurologist, prescribed fiorinal and codeine, two drugs that Malakoff had been abusing, with the stated aim of helping Malakoff deal with headaches and sinus pain. Malakoff's psychiatrist, Perman, added Xanax and Ambien to the mix—two drugs Malakoff had used heavily during his times of drug dependence.

Perman said yesterday that prescribing drugs that the patient has had trouble kicking can help a physician develop a "relationship" with the patient before gradually discontinuing the drug. But he conceded that others would strongly disagree. Those prescriptions gave Malakoff plausible deniability for his occasional positive drug tests. The real question, several doctors said, is how Malakoff managed to pass virtually all of those tests—more than 150 of them in one stretch, according to one doctor who was monitoring his progress.

In the early years of his treatment—the only period for which records were obtained—Malakoff had multiple automobile accidents. Repair shop records, citations and other documents indicate he had at least 20 crashes between April 1998 and October 2001. Many of them were on the George Washington Parkway, which he would drive daily from his home in Great Falls, and several involved rental cars he had while his car was in for repairs. The records indicate that Malakoff attributed many instances of car damage to parking garage incidents.

6. *Licensure and moral conduct.* State licensure laws focus not only on technical competence but also on moral character and conduct. Thus, courts have upheld disciplinary actions against physicians based on gun possession and the absence of good moral character even though there was no evidence that possession of firearms actually adversely affected quality

of practice. Raymond v. Board of Registration in Medicine, 443 N.E.2d 391 (Mass. 1982). More common are license-revocation cases in which the evidence shows egregious acts of mistreatment of patients. It is not uncommon for a medical professional to be well known to legal authorities, with a record showing repeated instances of medical misconduct.

7. *Ongoing quality reporting and hospital accreditation.* The Joint Commission, which accredits hospitals, measures hospital performance on an ongoing basis. As part of this measurement system the Commission has developed a performance measurement system that considers 12 million separate and specific treatment actions (such as giving a heart attack patient an aspirin upon admission). In this sense, the Commission's quality measurement system emphasizes the process of care rather than its outcome. JOINT COMMISSION, IMPROVING AMERICA'S HOSPITALS (2011).

The 2011 Joint Commission report showed that the highest performing hospitals on its quality measures were not the nation's best known hospitals. Kevin Sack, *Report Finds Improved Performance by Hospitals*, N.Y. TIMES, Sept. 15, 2011, at A–20. The Commission found that hospitals followed specified standards more than 97 percent of the time, up from 83 percent in 2002. Furthermore, over 90 percent of hospitals had composite scores of over 90 percent, a four-fold improvement, according to the Commission, from the beginning of the decade. The 405 hospitals noted as the best (14 percent of all hospitals whose performance was measured) received composite scores of over 95 percent. Most significantly perhaps, none of the hospitals listed by U.S. News and World Report on its *Best Hospitals Honor Roll*, one-third of whose score reflects the opinions of physicians, made the best hospital cutoff used by the Joint Commission based on more objective performance measures. *Id.* Hospitals on the U.S. News Honor Roll, but omitted from the Joint Commission's list, included the Mayo Clinic, the Johns Hopkins Hospital, the Cleveland Clinic, and others. No hospitals in New York City made the list. Because the Joint Commission measures tend to focus on process, experts could offer little in the way of explanation regarding the high failure rate among the hospitals with the best reputations, noting that unlike outcomes, case-mix differences (i.e., sicker patients being treated at larger medical centers) should not have affected the results.

8. *The impact of health information technology and telemedicine on state licensure.* Health information technology has enabled online medical practice, transforming what is possible in terms of extending even advanced diagnostic and treatment technologies into remote and medically underserved communities. Similarly, physician/patient communications via the Internet represent an increasingly important dimension of the provider/patient relationship. At the same time, technology raises important questions such as how to avert dangerous and fraudulent practices, particularly uncontrolled e-prescribing of controlled substances and the establishment of standards governing the use of Internet services in provider patient communications.

A 1997 Telemedicine Report to Congress identified a series of approaches to addressing this issue including the growth of multi-state licensing systems based on interstate compacts, reciprocity procedures, cross-state registration, special licensure categories in all states for health professionals engaged in telemedicine practice, and the replacement of a state-based system with a national licensure scheme. As of 2000, most states with telemedicine licensure laws had elected instead to require a full and unrestricted license to practice, as opposed to adopting one of the more streamlined alternatives. Nursing has been somewhat more successful in achieving cross-state licensure cooperation through the use of interstate compacts. Ross D. Silverman, *The Changing Face of law and Medicine in the New Millennium*, 26 Am. J. L. & Med. 255 (2000).

An analytic compilation by the Federation of State Medical Boards through 2008 shows widespread refusal by states to recognize as lawful e-prescribing in the absence of a physical examination. (Internet prescribing is of course separate from internet pharmacy services, which are a big business and which dispense in accordance with physician treatment orders once prescribed). FEDERATION OF STATE MEDICAL BOARDS, INTERNET PRESCRIBING BY STATE (2008).

In 2002 the Federation published Model Guidelines for the Appropriate Use of the Internet in Medical Practice. The Guidelines are intended for use by state medical boards in the oversight of licensed physician practice in their state. The Guidelines reinforce the importance of a formally established physician/patient relationship as a condition of internet practice, but also allow some wiggle room, noting that "the relationship is clearly established when the physician agrees to undertake diagnosis and treatment of the patient and the patient agrees, whether or not there has been a personal encounter between the physician (or other supervised health care practitioner) and patient." Recall the health care undertaking cases reviewed in Part One. It is evident that a physical examination may not be essential to establishing the existence of a physician/patient relationship, particularly in the case of consultation services. However, the Guidelines are predicated on the use of Internet technology as part of an ongoing, physically established physician patient relationship:

Guidelines for the Appropriate Use of the Internet in Medical Practice

Evaluation of the Patient

A documented patient evaluation, including history and physical evaluation adequate to establish diagnoses and identify underlying conditions and/or contra-indications to the treatment recommended/provided, must be obtained prior to providing treatment, including issuing prescriptions, electronically or otherwise.

Treatment

Treatment and consultation recommendations made in an online setting, including issuing a prescription via electronic means, will be held to the same standards of appropriate practice as those in traditional (face-to-face) settings. Treatment, including issuing a prescription, based solely on an online questionnaire or consultation does not constitute an acceptable standard of care.

Electronic Communications

Written policies and procedures should be maintained for the use of patient-physician electronic mail. Such policies and procedures should address (1) privacy, (2) health-care personnel (in addition to the physician addressee) who will process messages, (3) hours of operation, (4) types of transactions that will be permitted electronically, (5) required patient information to be included in the communication, such as patient name, identification number and type of transaction, (6) archival and retrieval, and quality oversight mechanisms. Transmissions, including patient e-mail, prescriptions and laboratory results must be secure within existing technology (i.e., password protected, encrypted electronic prescriptions, or other reliable authentication techniques). All patient-physician e-mail, as well as other patient-related electronic communications, should be stored and filed in the patient's medical record. Turnaround time should be established for patient-physician e-mail and medical practice sites should clearly indicate alternative form(s) of communication for urgent matters. E-mail systems should be configured to include an automatic reply to acknowledge message delivery and that messages have been read. Patients should be encouraged to confirm that they have received and read messages.

Informed Consent

A written agreement should be employed documenting patient informed consent for the use of patient/physician e-mail. The agreement should be discussed with and signed by the patient and included in the medical record. The agreement should include the following terms: Types of transmissions that will be permitted (prescription refills, appointment scheduling, patient education, etc.); Under what circumstances alternate forms of communication or office visits should be utilized; Security measures, such as encrypting data, password protected screen savers and data files, or utilizing other reliable authentication techniques, as well as potential risks to privacy; Hold harmless clause for information lost due to technical failures; Requirement for express patient consent to forward patient-identifiable information to a third party; Patient's failure to comply with the agreement may result in physician terminating the e-mail relationship.

Medical Records

The medical record should include copies of all patient-related electronic communications, including patient-physician e-mail, prescriptions, laboratory and test results, evaluations and consultations, records of past care and instructions. Informed consent agreements related to the use of e-mail should also be filed in the medical record.

Compliance with State and Federal Laws and Web Standards

Physicians should meet or exceed applicable federal and state legal requirements of medical/health information privacy. Physicians who treat or prescribe through Internet Web sites are practicing medicine and must possess appropriate licensure in all jurisdictions where patients reside.

Disclosure

Physician medical practice sites should clearly disclose: Owner of the site; Specific services provided; Office address and contact information; Licensure and qualifications of physician(s) and associated health care providers; Fees for online consultation and services and how payment is to be made; Financial interests in any information, products or services; Appropriate uses and limitations of the site, including providing health advice and emergency health situations; Uses and response times for e-mails, electronic messages and other communications transmitted via the site; To whom patient health information may be disclosed and for what purpose; Rights of patients with respect to patient health information; Information collected and any passive tracking mechanisms utilized.

Accountability

Medical practice sites should provide patients a clear mechanism to: access, supplement and amend patient-provided personal health information; provide feedback regarding the site and the quality of information and services; register complaints, including information regarding filing a complaint with the applicable state medical board(s).

9. *State adverse event reporting systems.* A highly influential 1999 report by the Institute of Medicine of the National Academy of Sciences titled TO ERR IS HUMAN: BUILDING A SAFER HEALTH SYSTEM, called for a nationwide state-based system of mandatory reporting of adverse events across multiple types of patient care settings, from hospitals and nursing homes to pharmacies, ambulatory surgery centers, hospices, laboratories and other settings. As of 2007, 25 states and the District of Columbia maintained compulsory adverse-event reporting systems administered by state government agencies. NATIONAL ACADEMY FOR STATE HEALTH POLICY (NASHP), GUIDE TO STATE ADVERSE EVENT REPORTING SYSTEMS (2007).

As noted earlier in this Part, adverse-event reporting is a technique used to measure the quality of health care on a population-wide basis. The National Quality Forum is a private body that develops national quality performance standards across a broad range of care settings, including performance measures under contract to the federal government and other public and private sponsors. In 2002, in a report entitled SERIOUS REPORTA-

BLE EVENTS IN HEALTHCARE: A CONSENSUS REPORT, the NQF identified a core group of "never events." As of 2011, this core list of "never events" stands at twenty-nine. Examples of "never events" are wrong site surgery, patient falls, medication errors, and certain types of post-operation complications.

Despite the existence of a standardized list of "never events" endorsed by experts, only about half of all state adverse-event reporting systems use the list, while the remainder use measures that they have developed separately. While hospitals have been the major NQF focus and thus dominate state adverse-event reporting systems, the United States Department of Health and Human Services has funded NQF to expand its work into other care settings such as ambulatory and office-based surgery centers, long-term care institutions, and physicians' offices.

Hospitals are the overwhelming setting identified in state adverse-event reporting systems, but some state systems reach other provider classes as well. State systems tend to focus on the most serious adverse events that result in serious harm or death. States may use their systems to impose sanctions for poor performance or for the provision of public information about patient safety and health care quality. Because states vary in the reporting measures they require and the standards applicable to the development of reports, the number and range of reported incidents can vary enormously. Some states report staggeringly high figures (200,000 separate reported events in Pennsylvania in 2007, 7000 of which were classified as serious). NASHP, GUIDE TO STATE ADVERSE EVENT REPORTING SYSTEMS at 8. Of the twenty-six mandatory systems in existence in 2007, all but three publicly released at least "some" of the information reported to the state, typically in the form of an annual report released on a website. *Id.* For a review of state mandatory adverse-event reporting systems and the problem of underreporting and vague and inaccurate reporting, see Maxine M. Harrington, *Revisiting Medical Error: Five Years After the IOM Report, Have Reporting Systems Made a Measurable Difference?*, 15 HEALTH MATRIX 329 (2005).

2. CERTIFICATE OF NEED

As with licensure, the certificate of need (CON) process is a double-edged sword, a tool for promoting quality in health care while at the same time a mechanism viewed by its opponents as a tool for giving certain powerful interests a franchise over particular types of health care practice to the exclusion of all others. Both the Federal Trade Commission and the Antitrust Division of the United States Justice Department have called for the abolition of state certificate of need laws, IMPROVING HEALTH CARE: A DOSE OF COMPETITION (2004). Despite the opposition of advocates for greater market competition, thirty-six states maintain certificate of need laws as of 2011. Tracey Yee et al., *Health Care Certificate-of-Need Laws: Policy or Politics?*, NATIONAL INSTITUTE FOR HEALTH CARE REFORM (2011).

The origin of the certificate of need program can be found in efforts to promote greater planning for the allocation of health care resources. The Hill Burton program, enacted in 1946, was an early health planning law that succeeded in not only developing thousands of hospitals but also transforming the landscape of hospital licensure. In 1966 Congress amended the Public Health Service Act to create state and local Comprehensive Health Planning Agencies. As health care costs escalated, Congress revisited the issue of comprehensive planning in 1972 with amendments to the Social Security Act that barred Medicare and Medicaid payments to unapproved facilities and projects. These amendments were followed by passage of the National Health Planning and Resources Development Act of 1974, which strengthened the certificate-of-need process. By the 1980s, the concept of government intervention to control capacity as a cost-containment strategy was all but dead and the Act was repealed in 1986. The CON literature varies, with some studies suggesting an impact on cost and volume and others finding that states with CON programs actually experience an increase in volume and cost. Yee, *Health Care Certificate of Need Laws* at 2. Regardless of the experience in the U.S., as we pointed out in Chapter 21 in Part Two, other nations have controlled cost in part by regulating the supply side of health care.

State certificate of need laws vary significantly by the types of services for which a CON may be required as a condition of expansion (e.g., a new dialysis facility), as well as in the dollar threshold to which the CON process applies (e.g., a CON required for capital construction projects of $1 million or greater). A state might require documentation of community need for all regulated services regardless of the cost, while another state may impose documentation requirements only in the case of high-cost projects. Some states may require a CON in order to close or move a facility in order to guard against the loss of access to care, particularly in underserved areas or with regard to safety net providers, and require a community assessment of the impact of closure on the population threatened with curtailment of services.

A six-state study of the CON process found that the approval process itself may be subjective and prone to politics. Yee, *Health Care Certificate of Need Laws* at 2–8. Because of intense competition and high political stakes, the CON process is lengthy, highly legally regulated, and subject to appeals and court challenges. A common form of procedural challenge is one brought by a competitor who lost out on a bid to the competition (we touch on this in Chapter 25, dealing with antitrust, in Part Four). Approval rates tend to be high (between 88 percent and 96 percent in the study states). CON agencies tend to be understaffed, making appropriate evaluation of applications difficult. Interviews with respondents in the states studied suggested that hospitals and other health care institutions, as well as other types of health care entrepreneurs, view the process "opportunistically" as a political challenge to be navigated. Other respondents reported that facilities sought legislative exemption from the process in order to circumvent CON requirements.

Study respondents reported that the CON process was a mechanism for setting quality standards beyond the threshold offset by licensure alone. The CON process in effect allows a state to develop and apply standards of quality as a condition of growth and expansion. Thus for example, researchers reported, Michigan limits certain types of cardiac catheterization procedures to hospitals that also can perform cardiothoracic surgery. Because, as noted earlier in this chapter, volume is often associated with quality, a CON statute may impose minimum volume levels to assure higher quality of complex care like transplants. Opponents of CON noted that a lengthy CON process can slow the introduction of new technologies and several respondents in the study noted that the quality measures, combined with high cost-thresholds, led some entrepreneurs to develop smaller mediocre facilities.

Yakima Valley Memorial Hospital v. Washington State Department of Health

654 F.3d 919 (9th Cir. 2011)

■ FISHER, CIRCUIT JUDGE:

The Washington State Department of Health (Department) will not license Yakima Valley Memorial Hospital (Memorial) to perform certain procedures known as elective percutaneous coronary interventions (PCI), which are used to treat diseased arteries of the heart. Examples of such procedures include stent implantation and laser angioplasty. Although Memorial already performs PCI in emergencies (no license required), it cannot perform "elective" procedures without a license that is required as part of the state's broader "certificate of need" regulatory regime. *See* Wash. Admin. Code § 246–310–700. According to the Department, the community Memorial serves does not need another PCI provider.

The concept of certificate of need regimes, which many states enforce, is to avoid private parties making socially inefficient investments in healthcare resources they might make if left unregulated. A certificate of need program corrects the market by requiring preapproval for certain investments and, in theory, thereby ensures that providers will make only necessary investments in health care. One type of investment the state of Washington regulates is the capacity to perform "tertiary health services," which are specialized health-care services including PCI. *See* Wash. Rev. Code § 70.38.105(4)(f). Congress made certificate of need regimes part of the federal government's national health planning policy in the National Health Planning and Resources Development Act of 1974 (NHPRDA). In response, Washington enacted its current certificate of need framework in 1979. *See* Wash. Rev.Code § 70.38.015. Although Congress repealed the NHPRDA in 1986, leaving states free to abandon their certificate of need programs, Washington has continued its program.

In 2007, the Washington legislature passed a law directing the Department to promulgate regulations requiring a certificate of need for elective

PCI. The Department responded in 2008 by promulgating the PCI regulations Memorial now challenges. *See* Wash. Admin. Code §§ 246–310–700–755. The PCI regulations, which are explained in detail below, (a) require that a licensed hospital perform at least 300 elective PCI procedures per year; and (b) provide that the Department shall issue a certificate of need only if projected demand in an applicant's geographic market exceeds the capacity of incumbent certificate holders by *at least* 300 procedures. Under this formula, Memorial has no hope of receiving a certificate of need in the near future. Memorial operates a single nonprofit hospital in Yakima, Washington. The surrounding market is already served by the for-profit Yakima Regional Medical and Cardiac Center, which holds an elective PCI certificate and is the only competing hospital in the city of Yakima. The Department does not contest Memorial's assertion that the market's "need" will not exceed 300 procedures until 2022.

Memorial sued the Department after it promulgated the PCI regulations, arguing that the certificate of need requirement violates the dormant Commerce Clause by unreasonably burdening interstate commerce. Memorial also claimed that the Department's methodology for defining "need" is anticompetitive and preempted by § 1 of the Sherman Act because it allows incumbent certificate holders to expand their capacity and preclude new certificates. The Department moved to dismiss the case for failure to state a claim and lack of standing to raise a dormant Commerce Clause challenge. Although the district court held that Memorial had standing, it dismissed the case on the pleadings pursuant to Federal Rule of Civil Procedure 12(c).

The district court held that Memorial failed to state a claim of antitrust preemption, holding that the PCI regulations were a unilateral restraint of trade not barred by the Sherman Act. With regard to the dormant Commerce Clause, the district court found Memorial had standing because it alleged it would participate in an interstate market for PCI patients, doctors and supplies. Nevertheless, the district court found that any burden on Memorial's interstate commercial activity was expressly authorized by Congress' approval of certificate of need regimes, making a dormant Commerce Clause violation impossible. Memorial appeals the judgment, and the Department cross-appeals the ruling on standing. We agree that Memorial failed to state a claim of antitrust preemption because the PCI regulations are a unilateral licensing requirement rather than an agreement in restraint of trade. We also agree that Memorial has standing under the dormant Commerce Clause, but we reverse the district court's judgment on that claim because the Department failed to prove congressional authorization for the PCI regulations.

A.   The Sherman Act
[Sherman Act discussion omitted]

B.   The Dormant Commerce Clause
Memorial's complaint alleges that the PCI regulations violate the dormant Commerce Clause by placing an undue burden on interstate

commerce.[16] If it were not for the licensing requirement, Memorial would offer elective PCI to out-of-state patients, as well as hire out-of-state doctors and import medical supplies from out-of-state to perform the procedures. There is no allegation of intentional discrimination against interstate commerce, but even laws that are applied even-handedly and impose only an incidental burden on interstate commerce can be unconstitutional. Where a law only incidentally burdens interstate commerce, it will be upheld unless the burden imposed on interstate commerce is clearly excessive in relation to the putative local benefits.

We must decide whether Memorial has standing to raise a dormant Commerce Clause challenge and if so, whether the PCI regulations are immunized by congressional authorization. The ultimate question of whether the PCI regulations survive scrutiny is not before us.

[The court determined that although Memorial Hospital operated only an in-state hospital it nonetheless had standing to raise a dormant commerce clause claim because it demonstrated an economic interest in being free of trade barriers that would permit it to develop a cross-state business in PCI procedures but was hampered from doing so because it could not secure a state CON. As such the hospital had standing to challenge what it alleged was an unjustified burden on commerce.]

Congress has not authorized the 2008 PCI regulations

"It is well established that Congress may authorize the States to engage in regulation that the Commerce Clause would otherwise forbid." *Maine v. Taylor*, 477 U.S. 131, 138 (1986). Congressional authorization must be " 'unmistakably clear' " and "unambiguous." *Taylor*, 477 U.S. at 139. Congress must clearly evince its intent "to alter the limits of state power otherwise imposed by the Commerce Clause." Congressional authorization is a defense that the state must prove.

The district court granted judgment on the pleadings to the Department because it concluded Congress had authorized certificate of need programs in the National Health Planning and Resources Development Act of 1974 (NHPRDA). See above n. 4. Although recognizing that the NHPRDA had been repealed in 1986 before the Department promulgated the challenged regulations in 2008, the district court accepted the repealed statute as a prima facie authorization and erroneously put the burden on Memorial to prove the significance of repeal. We reverse because the Department has failed to show that the NHPRDA, a statute repealed without a savings clause, provides the requisite clear statement of authorization for the 2008 PCI regulations. We do not decide whether the NHPRDA is sufficient authorization for certificate of need requirements established prior to repeal.

---

16. The Commerce Clause of the Constitution explicitly grants Congress authority to regulate interstate commerce. See U.S. Const. art. I, § 8, cl. 3. As a corollary, the Commerce Clause implicitly limits the regulatory authority of the states over interstate commerce. This inference is commonly referred to as the dormant Commerce Clause. See Nat'l Ass'n of Optometrists & Opticians LensCrafters, Inc. v. Brown, 567 F.3d 521, 523 (9th Cir. 2009).

The Department argues that the NHPRDA was a clear statement of authorization for certificate of need regimes because the statute made them a condition of federal funding. Memorial disputes whether this suffices as a sufficiently clear statement of authorization, but we need not decide the question. Whatever the NHPRDA authorized prior to 1986, after Congress repealed the statute there was no NHPRDA left to authorize a regulation promulgated in 2008. For more than a century, "the general rule ... [has been] that when an act of the legislature is repealed, it must be considered, except as to transactions past and closed, as if it never existed." *Ex Parte McCardle,* 74 U.S. 506, 514, (1868). Even in a pending action, "no judgment could be rendered ... after the repeal of the act under which it was brought and prosecuted." *Id.* A statute that Congress snuffed out of existence by repeal leaves no residual clear statement of authorization.

Had Congress meant to perpetuate its alleged authorization for certificate of need programs, it could have included a savings clause in the repeal.[19] The savings clause would then itself be an unmistakably clear statement of authorization. Savings clauses can be used to preserve state authority from implied preemption when Congress passes a statute. By the same token, Congress could enact a savings clause to avoid the natural implication of repealing an act. Instead, Congress repealed the NHPRDA with terse language that, at best, leaves it ambiguous whether Congress affirmatively contemplated the fate of state certificate of need programs.

To the extent there is ambiguity, the Department offers no legislative history to inform our interpretation of it. The district court relied on President Reagan's signing statement, but even if a presidential signing statement could establish an unmistakably clear *legislative* intent, President Reagan's opinion does not amount to an unmistakably clear statement of authorization for the Department's PCI regulations. *See* Statement of President Ronald Reagan upon Signing S. 1744, 22 Weekly Comp. Pres. Doc. 1565, 1566 (Nov. 14, 1986).[20] Ultimately, the Department is reduced to arguing that we can infer authorization from congressional silence—that Congress could not have meant to pull the rug out from under the states after inducing their transition to certificate of need programs, so Congress must have meant to leave undisturbed its authorization for certificates of need. As the district court's agreement demonstrates, that may be a

---

19. The repeal stated:

Sec. 701. Repeal of Title XV

(a) Repeal—Title XV of the Public Health Services Act is repealed effective January 1, 1987. (b) Funds—The repeal made by subsection (a) shall not affect any funds obligated for the purposes of title XV of the Public Health Service Act before January 1, 1987. Pub.L. No. 99–660, tit. VII, § 701, 100 Stat. 3743, 3799 (1986).

20. "It is also with great pleasure that I can finally lay to rest the Federal health planning authorities. I have sought their repeal since I assumed office. These authorities, while perhaps well-intentioned when they were enacted in the 1970's, have only served to insert the Federal Government into a process that is best reserved to the marketplace. Health planning has proved to be a process that was costly to the Federal Government, in the last analysis without benefit, and even detrimental to the rational allocation of economic resources for health care."

reasonable inference. Congressional silence is not a clear statement, however. Accordingly, we hold that the repealed NHPRDA does not provide congressional authorization for the 2008 PCI certificate of need regulation.

Notes

1. *The merits of the case.* The Court of Appeals' decision does not reach the ultimate merits of the case, namely whether the CON law can be upheld as a valid exercise of Washington State's licensing powers. As noted previously, the health services research literature suggests that the volume of some procedures is associated with better health outcomes in hospitals. Given the literature, should the results of a review of the merits of the PCI licensure regulation be any different from the results in *Gonzalez–Droz?* Is the basis of the 300–procedure rule, which does appear to be directly tied to a valid measure of volume, any less or more defensible than a requirement that a provider hold accreditation in specialties that appear even less connected to measures of health care quality? Is the CON statute any different from a licensure law that prevents an in-state physician from practicing a specialty that might draw customers from across state lines?

2. *The 300–procedure rule.* Where does the 300–procedure threshold specified in the Washington State regulation come from? There is no indication as to whether this number was based on studies linking PCI specifically to measures of volume. Should it matter whether there is empirical evidence to support this threshold or whether it is the result of professional consensus?

CHAPTER 20

PAYERS AND HEALTH CARE QUALITY: AWAKENING THE SLEEPING GIANT

1. INTRODUCTION: OLD CONCERNS, OLD TECHNIQUES, AND THE RISE OF "VALUE-BASED PURCHASING"

Part Two introduced basic concepts of payment. Over the past generation, no development in the evolution of health care has had more implications for the law than the collective—albeit disjointed—decision by payers to insert themselves aggressively into matters of quality by engaging in "value-based purchasing." A series of developments accounts for this fundamental shift on the part of public and private insurers, and this shift has now reached health care consumers who find themselves increasingly exposed to the cost of care as a result of shrinking insurance plans riddled with coverage limitations and exclusions and subject to high deductibles and cost-sharing at the point of service. Increasingly payers—insurance companies and people—want to know what they are getting for their money, what it will cost them, and how costs compare. They want value for their money.

The first major development of course is the high price of care coupled with exponential cost increases and widespread evidence of questionable quality and waste. With the failure of all prior attempts to control costs, including managed care, payers—including political actors—simply are scrambling to find some tool they think will work. In this search, they have latched onto research which suggests that at least in some communities much health care is wasted. Other studies suggest that even when the right type of health care for a particular condition is known, a lot of health professionals simply don't use such knowledge. See, e.g., Elizabeth A. McGlynn et. al., *The Quality of Health Care Delivered to Adults in the United States*, 348 NEW ENG. J. MED. 2635 (2003) (finding that adults receive recommended treatments only about half the time). Commentators like Atul Gawande, whose work is reviewed earlier in this Part, have vividly brought this research to real-life situations and in an easy-to-digest form for politicians, policy elites and the public. The pay-for-performance movement is more about the politics of cost containment than it is grounded in science. Perhaps the most ironic part of it is that very little evidence exists that it can either improve quality or constrain costs. *See, e.g.*, Sandra J. Tanenbaum, *Pay for Performance in Medicare: Evidentiary Irony and the*

Politics of Value, 34 J. HEALTH POL. POL'Y & L. 717 (2009); *see also* Joseph White, *Prices, Volume, and the Perverse Effects of the Variations Crusade*, 36 J. HEALTH POL. POL'Y & L. 776 (2011) (discussing how variations research is oversold by those who generate it and overconsumed by the policy and political worlds in a way that distracts the United States from focusing on solutions that work in other nations).

High and rapidly rising costs have led to reductions in coverage. They also have led insurers and patients alike to begin to demand greater price transparency and more information about quality in order to enable better decisions about health care spending. (Of course as you have learned, the vast majority of insured Americans are effectively limited in *where* they can shop for covered services by the networks that their insurers have assembled for them (Recall *Krauss v. Oxford Health Plans* in Part Two). At the same time, provider network restrictions do not apply to uncovered services, and even within networks there may be a choice of providers whose quality and prices differ.)

Many insurers now offer their members basic quality rating information, as does Medicare, as discussed in Part Two. But this information is pretty limited given the dearth of detailed information on the quality of care. As discussed in Part Two, health care purchasing remains a distinct field for many reasons. A patient who needs open heart surgery, assuming that she even has the time to shop for it, can't simply log onto *Consumer Reports* to find the 10 best cardiac surgeons in the region, do a price comparison, and pick one (assuming any of the best are in her network). Nor is it clear, given the complexities of health care quality measurement (performance measures are difficult to identify, data are difficult to collect, and performance data must be adjusted to take into account key differences in types of patients served) that *Consumer Reports*-style shopping ever would be the most sensible way to find a good doctor. Furthermore, much of the information about quality available through popular online shopping sites may be of questionable value. For example, *U.S. News* ranks the nation's top hospitals across 16 specialty areas using federal data provided to Medicare and by surveying physicians to produce a "reputation" score, http://health.usnews.com/health-news/best-hospitals/articles/2011/07/18/best-hospitals-2011-12-the-methodology (Nov. 1, 2011). But as noted, the official 2011 Joint Commission national accreditation survey of hospital performance across more than 12 million reportable measurements found that none of the *U.S. News* top performers in fact ranked tops on accreditation performance.

The drive toward better consumer information on quality also runs into practical problems regarding its usefulness. For example, many of the people who are most in need of this information in fact are the sickest people with the highest health care costs. Much of the information may be too general to help them make the very granular types of treatment decisions that their conditions may necessitate. Some economists who believe that direct exposure to the cost of care is an essential ingredient in making patients wiser users of health care also argue that information on quality has less utility for these patients from an efficiency perspective because they are likely to have met their annual or lifetime out-of-pocket cost-sharing obligations. James C. Robinson, *Consumer Directed Health Insurance: the Next Generation*, HEALTH AFFAIRS (Web Exclusive) w5–583 (Dec. 13, 2005).

Proponents of health information technology ("HIT") claim that ultimately HIT may help produce the evidence that is needed to more accurately measure performance and tie performance measurement to pricing data. Dr. David Blumenthal, who led the Obama Administration's initial efforts to implement the HITECH Act, whose purpose, as discussed below, is to incentivize financially the adoption and "meaningful" use of health information technology, has written that the advent of electronic health information will not only help clinicians improve the quality of their health care but also yield far greater information for patients about the quality of care they receive generally. David Blumenthal & Marilyn Tavenner, *The Meaningful Use Regulation for Electronic Health Records*, 363 NEW ENG. J. MED. 501 (2010). But health information technology is diffusing slowly across the medical care system; as of 2008 only 4 percent of physicians had a fully functioning EHR system, while only 13 percent had what could be considered a basic system. Catherine DesRoches et al., *Electronic Health Records in Ambulatory Care: A National Survey of Physicians*, 359 NEW ENG. J. MED. 60 (2008). Similarly dismal results are evident for hospitals. David Blumenthal & John Glaser, *Health Policy Report: Information Technology Comes to Medicine* 356 NEW ENG. J. MED. 2524 (2007).

Changes in the law also have helped spur greater involvement by payers. For example, Medicare changes enacted in the 1970s represented a national policy breakthrough on the role of payer involvement in clinical quality peer review with the creation of what were then-called Professional Standards Review Organizations ("PSROs"), discussed below. Similarly, as illustrated in *Heckler v. Ringer*, (Part Two), HHS has used its Medicare administrative authority to exclude from coverage treatments of no proven clinical or health value. The Patient Protection and Affordable Care Act broadly expands Medicare's involvement in payment innovations aimed at incentivizing greater health care quality and efficiency.

Regarding private insurance, two legal important developments likely spurred greater linkage between payment and quality. First, the enactment of ERISA (Part Two) effectively freed self-insured employer-sponsored health plans from state insurance laws, thereby allowing them to test models of coverage and payment that would have been blocked in a world in which provider preferences and customs dominated the structure of health insurance. By the 1990s, as the full scope of ERISA's preemptive impact on provider-friendly state insurance laws had become clear, self-insured employers became more aggressive in their efforts to manage care and costs. Large employers became well known for their implementation of new approaches to managing quality and cost through the expansion of "managed care" arrangements that utilized selective provider contracting, the formation of "preferred" provider networks, more aggressive prior authorization, and provider payment incentives designed to reward what plan administrators considered to be the more efficient use of resources. M. Gregg Bloche, *One Step Ahead of the Law: Market Pressures and the Evolution of Managed Care, in* THE PRIVATIZATION OF HEALTH CARE REFORM (M. Gregg. Bloche, ed., 2003). The companies that administered these products for self-insured plans carried these new approaches into the world of state-regulated insurance products. While providers were able to battle back these reforms in some cases (perhaps best illustrated by *Kentucky Association of Health Plans v. Miller* in Part Two, which concerned providers' efforts to blunt selective contracting through passage of state "any-willing-provider" laws), provider opposition could not halt the sweeping changes in the design of insurance.

A second legal development that inevitably influenced the movement of payers directly into matters of quality and efficiency was the decision in Arizona v. Maricopa County Medical Society, 457 U.S. 332 (1982), discussed more fully in Chapter 25, which ruled *per se* unlawful under Section 1 of the Sherman Act collective efforts by medical societies to control medical care pricing. With the prohibition of providers' engaging in their own collective efforts to control price, and the rejection of quality as a rule-of-reason defense to blatant evidence of price-fixing, the courts effectively opened the doors to the unilateral imposition of payer-driven health care pricing structures, including financing strategies that payers believed would produce better "value" in terms of better care at a more affordable price. As payers sought to get more bang for the buck by linking payment to quality and as part of this effort created "preferred" practice networks, physicians could not jointly band together to push back without fear of running afoul of antitrust law. (The relaxation of antitrust principles to encourage collective action in order to promote efficiency and quality through the formation of Accountable Care Organizations (ACOs) is discussed in Part Four).

While payers' efforts to stem the tide of rising prices has had little impact, it is clear that over the past 30 years, the relationship between payers and providers over matters of quality has fundamentally changed. While the fragmented nature of health care financing has left the nation without the ability to act collectively to control matters of quality and efficiency, there is no question that payers have become aggressive in using whatever financial tools are at their disposal to push health system performance. Today, a large number of health care professionals and institutions, particularly those practicing in larger groups in metropolitan regions, take it as a given that they will need to provide performance information and engage in quality improvement efforts as a condition of being paid. Indeed, it is this expectation on the part of hospitals and physicians that the quality of their care will be measured—they have simply accommodated themselves to this future just as they accommodated themselves to payment reforms like prospective payment (discussed in Part Two)—that may help quicken the pace of health information technology adoption because of its central role in the collection and aggregation of clinical performance information.

Payers have several basic strategies for enforcing the value-based payment standards they elect to use: (1) excluding providers from program participation altogether or disincentivizing patients from using uncooperative providers' services by making their care more costly; (2) rewarding providers for good performance, and conversely, denying payment for care that fails to meet quality standards; and (3) organizing payment in a manner that nudges (providers might say pushes) providers, in turn, to change their own organizational and operational structures in ways that are calculated to improve the quality and efficiency of health care. Payers can use positive incentives, such as higher prices or bonus payments for providers who satisfy specified practice arrangements. *See, e.g.*, Robert E. Mechanic & Stuart H. Altman, *Payment Reform Options: Episode Payment is a Good Place to Start*, 28(2) HEALTH AFFAIRS (Web Exclusive) w262 (Jan. 27, 2009); MEDPAC, IMPROVING INCENTIVES IN THE MEDICARE PROGRAM (2009). They also can impose penalties. Undergirding modern payer efforts to use financing to influence quality is the growing emphasis on a special type of health services research known as comparative effectiveness research, whose purpose is to build knowledge about what works in health care, particularly with respect to high cost treatments and conditions. INSTITUTE OF MEDICINE, INITIAL NATIONAL PRIORITIES FOR COMPARATIVE EFFECTIVENESS RESEARCH (National Academy Press, 2009).

The full flowering of this national effort—a bandwagon effect, if you will—to move toward value-based purchasing can be seen in Patient Protection and Affordable Care Act, which contains a raft of provisions that collectively are aimed at using the power of public insurance financing to drive changes in quality and efficiency in order to reduce what Professor Einer Elhauge terms "the fragmentation of U.S. health care." EINER ELHAUGE, THE FRAGMENTATION OF U.S. HEALTH CARE: CAUSES AND SOLUTIONS (2010). In his analysis of the numerous ways in which the Affordable Care Act addresses matters of patient safety and health care quality, Professor Barry Furrow discusses the extent to which the provisions speak to what he identifies as six major areas of regulatory reform in the area of patient safety: (1) standardizing good medical practices to promote best practices, practice guidelines, and research on what works and is cost effective; (2) tracking adverse events in hospitals in order to select those that are the most serious and in need of the greatest attention; (3) disclosure of provider performance including hospital adverse events and "near misses"; (4) the reform of payment systems through financial incentives that are intended to promote patient safety including payment bonuses and "docking" reimbursement for failure to meet minimum standards along with the use of insurance exchanges to promote the purchase of qualified health plans that offer good quality care; (5) new financing models to coordinate and integrate health care; and (6) expanding provider fiduciary responsibilities and accountability for poor outcome. Furrow, *Regulating Patient Safety* at 1731–33. In his optimistic summary of the Act, Professor Furrow writes:

> The passage of PPACA promises to take patient safety to the next level of regulatory intensity in American health care delivery, in part through the infusion of money into patient-safety research

and into payment reforms in particular. PPACA has an astonishing variety of provisions aimed at improving the quality of the U.S. health care system, reducing errors, and generally promoting patient safety. The Act sets out an ambitious research agenda and provides funding and other incentives to accomplish its goals. It launches demonstration projects through which the federal government funds particular forms of health care or health care delivery system with a requirement that their performance be studied, often with the intent of examining their potential for wider adoption. [P]ayment strategies will be expanded and tested to determine how the Medicare payment system can better promote best practices and outcomes.

In other words, the premise is that as knowledge is gained, health care financing—both coverage and payment—will become the major tools for infusing that knowledge into the health care system. Also embedded in the ACA is a major investment in such research through the establishment of the Patient Centered Outcomes Research Institute (PCORI), PPACA § 6301, whose job is to commission research that produces evidenced-based information about treatment outcomes.

The subject of using payment to try to steer the health system toward greater quality and efficiency is vast. Key examples are peer review and provider exclusion from insurance programs, "tiered" physician networks, efforts to reduce "never events," reducing excessive and wasteful use of resources by curbing unnecessary care such as frequent hospital readmission of the same patient, incentives to adopt and "meaningfully" use health information technology, and payment incentives to stimulate the formation of clinically and more financially integrated practice groups known as Accountable Care Organizations. All of these efforts can be grouped under a general heading known as "value-based purchasing," meaning strategies that are intended to create changes in provider and patient behavior in ways that improve the quality of care while holding down cost. *See* MEDPAC, REPORT TO CONGRESS ch. 1. (2005).

Value-based purchasing techniques can exist in relation to both patients and providers. An example of a patient-oriented value-based purchasing technique would be exempting prescription medications needed to manage chronic conditions (such as medications to control hypertension) from deductible and cost-sharing requirements in order to encourage patient adherence. Robinson, *Consumer Directed Health Insurance* at w5–590 (2005). A provider-oriented example would be the use of what are known as "pay for performance" (P4P) strategies (discussed below) in which compensation is at least partially tied to care processes associated with high quality care and positive patient outcomes. Evidence from the British National Health Service suggests that only relatively high incentives can meaningfully affect behavior (e.g., primary care physicians in the NHS derive as much as 25 percent of total practice income based on their performance); however in the U.S., the proportion of payment that is performance-based remains low, as suggested by the MedPAC recommendation and other experts. Whether this is a good or bad thing is debatable. See, e.g., John Rowe, *Pay-for-Performance and Accountability: Related Themes in Improving Health Care*, 145 ANN. INT. MED. 695 (2009) (finding widespread physician support for value-based purchasing initiatives that use P4P incentives, identifying the utility of both cash and non-cash incentives such as reduced administrative burdens or reputational enhancements, but concluding that most incentives are too simple to adequately deal with performance in relation to complex patients who generate most of the costs). See also Meredith Rosenthal et al., *Employers' Use of Value Based Purchasing Strategies*, 298 JAMA 2281 (2007), finding a relatively limited employer response to value-based purchasing as of 2006.

Part of the reason for slower implementation of such strategies than proponents would have liked has been the fragmented payment and insurance system we have described throughout the book. Development and implementation of such strategies create externalities given this fragmentation. Payers who make necessary investments confer benefits on their competitors to the extent they succeed. Their methods can then be copied, and any increases in health may not inure to them unless they are locked into those patients over the long-term, which is not possible in our fragmented system. By contrast, they might also incur a "negative externality" to the extent that their efforts incur the wrath of plan sponsors, providers or patients, who can then switch to competitors. As a result, part of the bandwagon effect stems from the ACA's achievement of near-universal coverage of Americans. With the Act's diminution of externalities it becomes more realistic to focus intently on strategies for improving efficiencies and quality that previously eluded reformers as a result of large gaps in coverage that may have deterred access to more appropriate health care, as well as provider cost-shifting aimed at offsetting financial exposure to uncompensated care, problems reviewed in Parts One and Two.

Nonetheless, commentators have identified what they see as numerous potential "legal barriers" to the aggressive diffusion and development of broader value-based purchasing techniques as a means of simultaneously controlling costs, improving quality, and maintaining access to care. These legal barriers involve "statutory, regulatory, and common law impediments to the widespread or efficient adoption of each promising effort." Anne B. Claiborne et al., *Legal Impediments to Implementing Value–Based Purchasing in Health Care*, 35 AM. J. L. & MED. 442 (2009).

In their analysis of "legal impediments" to value-based purchasing, the authors identify "Four Cornerstones defined by the federal government to recognize, reinforce, and facilitate the implementation of the core elements of health system reform developed by the health policy community over time." *Id.* at 443. The first of these is health information technology (HIT), which was launched as a formal national policy effort by Congress in 1996 with the passage of HIPAA and championed by successive Administrations—and extended still further through passage of the HITECH Act, as part of the 2009 American Recovery and Reinvestment Act (Pub. L. No. 111–5, 111th Cong., 1st Sess.), and the Affordable Care Act. Focused on the widespread adoption of interoperable HIT, this effort has, since the 1990s been seen as the means "to facilitate, among other things, reducing medical errors, enhancing the provision of evidence-based health care, and increasing administrative efficiency in health care delivery," through the sharing of clinical, administrative, and financial information "throughout the health care system in an accurate, effective, secure and consistent manner." *Id.* at 448.

The second "Cornerstone" according to the authors is measuring and publishing information about the quality of care. This effort, an outgrowth of a 2004 Executive Order issued by President George W. Bush, calls for measuring and publishing the results of provider performance, using quality metrics developed by federal health care agencies overseeing Medicare, Medicaid, federal employee health benefit programs and other federal health care programs and working in concert with private payers. *Id.* at 449. The effort has resulted in innovations such as Medicare's "Hospital Compare" website, which provides certain information to beneficiaries about hospital performance. Private payers similarly measure and publish information about quality. *See e.g.*, The Leapfrog Group hospital comparison information, which allows comparison of hospitals across the country on about a dozen measures ranging from management of heart attacks (where shopping and choice might be constrained by time and networks) to weight loss surgery (where more limited coverage for the procedure might make insurance networks essentially irrelevant and there may be more time to shop). The goal of being able to compare physicians based on quality and cost is also advanced under the ACA, which requires the federal government to establish a similar public website for physician services as the technology and knowledge to produce robust and accurate information becomes available. PPACA § 10331. Furrow, *Regulating Patient Safety* at 1750–52.

A third cornerstone, the authors continue, is greater pricing transparency, with some pricing information available through Hospital Compare and through private insurers. Claiborne et. al., *Legal Impediments to Implementing Value–Based Purchasing in Health Care* at 449. A final Cornerstone is the concept of "pay for performance (P4P)," which is the explicit tying of payment to specific performance measures. P4P traces its origins to efforts to collect and report information on important health care events (both positive and negative) such as comparative hospital mortality rates. David A. Hyman & Charles Silver, *You Get What You Pay For: Results–Based Compensation for Health Care*, 58 WASH. & LEE L. REV. 1427, 1437 (2001). For example, in the early 1990s, New York State and Pennsylvania began to issue report cards on how hospitals in the state performed in certain procedures, such as Coronary Artery Bypass Graft (CABG) surgery, because of the relatively high mortality risks associated with this common surgical procedure. As a result of this effort, interest grew in payment innovations that would draw overt links between provider payment and specific, measurable results (often referred to as quality "metrics"). For this reason, the "performance" that might be the focus of P4P efforts may be greater transparency in the form of simply reporting information (both good and bad) to a payer. Legislation enacted by Congress in 2005 directed the federal government to develop a P4P system for hospital inpatient care, later broadened to include physician services. Claiborne et al., *Legal Impediments to Implementing Value–Based Purchasing* at 450.

Modern P4P arrangements tie provider payments to explicit measures of quality developed by organizations such as the National Committee for Quality Assurance (NCQA) and the National Quality Forum (NQF). Examples might be the percentage of adults in care immunized against influenza, the proportion of women falling within age appropriate groups who receive mammography screens, or the proportion of adults ages 18 and older who have had their blood pressure measured within the preceding two years. Performance measurement entities receive major contracts from the federal government and from the private insurers and health plans to develop, test, and validate as reliable performance benchmarks that use information from health care practice (such as medical records or claims data). These measures are then used by payers to measure provider performance against the performance benchmarks, with testing and validation as the means by which to bring greater reliability to the process and shield payers against provider concerns that such measurement is unreliable or unfair.

Performance benchmarks typically are updated, so that as performance improves, the benchmark also becomes tougher. For example, if the national provider performance norm is 50 percent of all adults appropriately immunized against influenza, the benchmark might be raised to 60 percent in order to incentivize stronger performance. Many of the benchmarks are designed to measure relatively simple and discrete preventive events, such as a mammogram as opposed to completed and appropriate treatment for breast cancer within a medically appropriate number of weeks of initial detection. This is because the state of knowledge about health care—and the ability to measure a complete episode of treatment—is still very crude. At the same time, researchers are attempting to develop more sophisticated measures, a major aim, as Professor Furrow notes, of the Affordable Care Act's investment in quality measurement.

One of the greatest "barriers" to performance measurement is that frequently it is unclear what good practice is. Certain events, known as "never events," have gained prominence because of the clear evidence demarcating such incidents that things that never should happen in a health care system that functions appropriately. The concept of the "never event" was first advanced by the National Quality Forum (NQF) in the wake of the Institute of Medicine's landmark study, To ERR IS HUMAN. Since then, the NQF has identified a series of such events, including, for example, surgery performed on the wrong body part, surgery performed on the wrong patient, wrong surgical procedure performed on a patient, the "unintended retention of a foreign object in a patient after surgery or other procedure," mismatched blood transfusions, major medication errors, and others. National Quality Forum, *Serious Reportable Events in Health Care*, 2006 Update. Furrow, *Regulating Patient Safety* at 1745. Over 20 states had adopted reporting requirements for "never events" as of 2011. *Id.* The ACA mandates the greater disclosure of never events as a matter of more general public knowledge through a newly established Center for Quality Improvement and Patient Safety. *Id.* at 1749–1750.

Such events, however, are clearly just low-hanging fruit. No diagnosis of complex conditions is necessary, nor is a patient's history, a complicated treatment plan that must account for multiple complications, as well as the rest of the patient's life, coordination among a multitude of providers in many organizations, with differing incentives, expertise, and agendas; nor are data difficult to define and collect; endpoints difficult to define, much less endpoints infused with value choices, not just the "technical" aspects of care—just to name *a few* of the challenges. Compared with the vast range of complex conditions and treatments, ensuring that surgery occurs on the correct limb is remarkably easy and avoids all the problems listed above and many more—and preventing even wrong-site surgery alone has been difficult to achieve. Building a movement linking payment to "value" from such simplistic situations to the rest of health care is breathtakingly simple-minded.

Other measures of quality are harder to demarcate. For example, hospitals increasingly use "hospitalists," who are physicians employed by the hospital, in the belief that physicians who are full-time hospital employees will better manage inpatient care and thereby increase efficiency, reduce errors, and promote quality. But the use of hospitalists may, in fact, disrupt the continuity of care after discharge. See, e.g., Gudshan Sharma et al., *Continuity of Outpatient and Inpatient Care by Primary Care Physicians for Hospitalized Older Adults*, 301 JAMA 1671 (2009). (finding that more than half of hospitalized older adults had been seen by at least one physician in an outpatient setting in the preceding year, and that the use of hospitalists was associated with reduced continuity of care and an elevated risk of readmission). The body of comparative effectiveness research on which performance measures rest is still very crude, with very few measures capable of capturing the quality of performance for rare but costly procedures or complex conditions.

Despite the gaps that abound in measuring quality—not to mention any meaningful, scientifically valid link between titrating payment types and levels to accomplish a scientifically valid outcome—experts in performance measurement view P4P as a mechanism for aligning provider and payer interests. INSTITUTE OF MEDICINE, REWARDING PROVIDER PERFORMANCE: ALIGNING INCENTIVES IN MEDICARE (2006). Most P4P systems use a mix of measures across both clinical and non-clinical performance, patient experiences in care, and use of health information technology. Thus, for example, the thirty-six P4P measures that will be used to measure the performance of Accountable Care Organizations discussed below range from adoption and use of electronic health records to the proportion of patients receiving recommended mammograms and appropriate medication management for patients with chronic illness and the results of patient surveys to measure their experience in health care.

At the time of passage of the Affordable Care Act, P4P strategies had gained greatly in popularity and political attractiveness. One study that attempted to measure the growth of P4P activities estimated a four-fold growth in the number of reported formal programs in use, from 35 in 2003 to an estimated 160 such programs by 2008, accounting for health care to some 85 million patients. Michelle D. Apodaca, *Medicare and the Physicians' Pay-for-Performance Program; Will it Create More Problems Than it Can Solve?* 9(2) J. HEALTH CARE COMPLIANCE 37, 38 (2007). See also Katharina Janus et al., *Medicare as Incubator for Innovation in Payment Policy*, 32 J. HEALTH POL. POL'Y & L. 293 (2007).

While it is relatively easy to describe payment strategies such as value-based purchasing and P4P, it is much harder to implement them. Measures must be carefully developed in order to assure that the candidate measures are considered evidence-based, that is, proven to be tied to actual desired outcomes such as reducing mortality following a heart attack by quickly administering aspirin. Furthermore, the measures selected must be tested under real-world circumstances and evaluated in order to gain knowledge as to whether they produce reliable results in practice, whose output can be properly measured through available clinical and administrative data. As a result, the purported scientific basis of performance measurement is a slowly unfolding phenomenon. By contrast, the Congressional investment in sustained quality improvement research under the Affordable Care Act represents an effort to try to speed things up, Furrow, *Regulating Patient Safety* at 1737–1743, an effort that involves, not science, but the politics of cost containment, and it is moving forward regardless of the scientific pace. *See, e.g.*, Tanenbaum, *Pay for Performance in Medicare*.

One final point in this summary of a vast subject: Value-based purchasing operates at the "micro level"—i.e., at the point where health care treatment of individual patients occurs. It links payment to quality in an attempt to obtain value through financial incentives that operate either on the demand side—patients—or the supply side—providers. This effort is much different from trying to exert broader "macro level" controls over the supply and diffusion of technologies, the size of community-wide investment in capital equipment, and the training of health care professionals. As we have pointed out, the ACA contains numerous and significant efforts to shape the workforce and utilization of services. But for the most part, these controls are not direct regulation of physical and human capital, as other nations do *in addition* to more targeted initiatives aimed at improving the clinical quality of patient care. Instead, the U.S. strategy is constrained and indirect, with "value-based purchasing" a veritable pinpoint strategy in a sea of challenges. Rather than adopting a broad range of strategies, the U.S. seemingly is on an endless experiment to reach better system balance in the most cramped way possible.

2. LEGAL ISSUES IN VALUE–BASED PURCHASING

The steady march of payment and financing into the terrain of quality raises many legal questions. Some of these questions can be framed as legal impediments to progress. Claiborne et al., *Legal Impediments to Implementing Value–Based Purchasing in Health Care*. Others might be thought of as legal consequences arising from the entwinement of payment and quality, with some degree of skepticism toward this brave new world. Whether as an inhibitor of transformation or a consequence of it, the law's impact on the intersection of payment and health care quality is enormous.

a. Health Information Technology

The HITECH Act, part of the 2009 American Recovery and Reinvestment Act (Pub. L. No. 111–5, Division A, Title XIII (establishing the office of the National Coordinator) and Division B, Title IIV (related to Medicare and Medicaid incentives for adoption and meaningful use)), creates a complex national legislative policy and administrative machinery which was initially launched as an Executive Order in 2004. HITECH put into place the DHHS Office of the National Coordinator whose purpose is to oversee (along with other federal agencies) the development of nationwide interoperable HIT standards, refine the necessary health information privacy and security standards, provide technical support to physicians and hospitals to speed adoption, and incentivize adoption and use through Medicare and Medicaid payments to "meaningful users."

In dealing with HIT adoption and use, however, the federal government has had to address potential legal barriers. Examples of such barriers include federal fraud and abuse laws that potentially bar the donation of HIT hardware and software by hospitals or large group practices to physicians and clinics who cannot afford the capital expenditure to obtain it (federal fraud laws are discussed in Part Four). Such donations by nonprofit hospitals likewise could violate federal tax laws, also discussed in Part Four. In addition, HIT adoption and resulting information sharing has been viewed as creating potential antitrust problems, by permitting competitors to engage in collusive conduct in restraint of trade, concepts discussed in Part Four. Claiborne et al., *Legal Impediments to Implementing Value–Based Purchasing in Health Care* at 456–64. These authors also note other legal issues that arise in HIT adoption including state licensure questions related to "telemedicine" (i.e., the use of HIT to engage in the interstate practice of medicine, a problem of licensure we discussed above), and problems of medical liability for negligent use of technology. *See also* Rosenbaum & Painter, *When Old is New* (discussing the liability implications of failing to adopt and meaningfully use HIT as the technology diffuses).

b. Publishing Information About Price and Quality and Using Data to Tier Physician Networks and Sanction Hospitals for "Never Events," and "Excessive" Readmissions

The publication of information about health care quality raises additional legal and practical issues. Providers may fear that reporting creates liability and may actively resist efforts to uncloak information without strong liability shields such as immunity or privilege. Claiborne et al., *Legal*

Impediments to Implementing Value–Based Purchasing in Health Care at 465–472. The federal Patient Safety and Quality Improvement Act of 2005 (PSQIA) (Pub. L. No. 109–41, 109th Cong., 1st Sess.) was intended to create such a federal privilege for quality improvement information collected, aggregated, analyzed, and potentially reported by "Patient Safety Organizations" ("PSOs"). Under federal implementing regulations, information collected and analyzed by PSOs acting under federal standards is considered privileged and confidential. However, the privilege does not extend to information collected by payers, nor does it cover information held by individual providers. Furthermore, the patient safety evaluation systems required to qualify for the privilege generally do not yet exist. Clairborne et al., *Legal Impediment to Implementing Valve–Based Purchasing* at 470–71. Without such a shield, such information would likely be discoverable in litigation.

Provider reporting systems that deal with both quality and cost also raise questions and resistance from health care professionals and institutions, particularly when reporting may result in various types of financial penalties, such as being placed on a lower "tier" (which translates into higher copayments for patients) or potentially being excluded from a network entirely. Providers charge that quality measurement systems are biased, unfair, opaque, and immune from inquiry and challenge. For these reasons, providers have claimed that these systems violate common law or statutory fair process standards and are possibly even defamatory.

The stakes in the accuracy of this information are therefore very high. Recall from Part Two that physician networks are now the norm in health insurance benefit design. In 1980, networks were rare; as of 2006, only 7 percent of all employers offered a health benefit plan whose terms of coverage were not tied to a provider network; at 54 percent, preferred provider organizations (PPOs) represented the most common type of plan offering that year. Kaiser HRET, Employer Health Benefits, 2006, Table 4.3. (August 18, 2007). Similarly, both Medicare Advantage plans and Medicaid managed care arrangements rely on provider networks. Medicare Advantage Fact Sheet (KAISER FAMILY FOUNDATION, 2007); Deborah Draper et al., *High Performance Health Plan Networks: Early Experiences* (CENTER FOR STUDYING HEALTH SYSTEMS CHANGE 2007).

The use of information about quality to determine whether a physician or hospital can be a member of a network is hardly new. Yet value-based purchasing techniques aimed at tiering physicians based on their quality and efficiency (with the "best" performers on quality and price subject to the lowest cost-sharing) is relatively new. In these insurance arrangements, payers classify their networks and rank their members based on certain quality and efficiency measures selected and calculated by the plan. Deborah Draper et al., *High Performance Health Plan Networks: Early Experiences. See also* J. William Thomas, *What We Know and Do Not Know About Tiered Provider Networks*, 4 J. HEALTH CARE FIN. 53 (Summer 2007); Cara Lesser & Paul B. Ginsberg, *Strategies to Enhance Price and Quality Competition In Health Care: Lessons Learned from Tracking Local Markets,*

31 J. HEALTH POL. POL'Y & L. 557, 561 (2006). One study that examined the use of tiered networks in "high performing" employer-sponsored health plans suggests that these arrangements may be more common among plans offered by self-insuring employers. No comparable information exists on the growth of tiering arrangements in Medicare or Medicaid managed care plans, or in plans offered by other sponsors. Draper et al., *High Perform- ance Health Plan Networks*.

The use of tiering for physician services typically is targeted at special- ized, selected high cost procedures. Tiering techniques and methods may be tied to physician performance against evidence-based guidelines and con- sensus standards specified by the plan, with actual performance calculated via algorithms. Both the tiering measures and the tiering algorithms may be proprietary (and therefore opaque to the provider), with substantial variation from plan to plan. Draper et al., *High Performing Health Plan Networks*. Performance assessments may be limited to what can be ascer- tained through claims data at the individual provider level, and results may or may not be aggregated to the practice group level. Plans also can vary in the proportion of network physicians designated as high performers. *Id.* In addition, plans may show much variation in the techniques they employ to incentivize their plan members' selection of high performing physicians. Research suggests that incentives can range from simple disclosure of physician performance information to members and patients, to the use of tiered cost-sharing that effectively penalizes low performers, and to the outright exclusion of under-performing physicians. As you have learned in Part Two, self-insured ERISA-governed employer sponsored plans that use these approaches would be shielded from state regulations aimed at regu- lating such practices when performed by insurers, although as *Miller* (Part Two) intimates, states might effectively attain the same result with regard to self-insured plans by directly regulating the conduct of physician practice networks that sell their services to plans and insurers.

Even though health plans have credentialed and overseen networks for years now, new terms and monikers inevitably can create a new round of legal challenges. The potential for such challenges understandably increas- es when physicians—who previously beat back selective contracting through market pressures and legal interventions like "any-willing-provid- er" laws (e.g., *Kentucky Ass'n of Health Plans v. Miller*, Part Two)—face a new strategy that promises to affect their livelihood, this time through lower rankings. Thus, while federal and state laws regulating insurance and employer-sponsored health benefit plans currently leave the formation of networks largely unlimited, with the exception of any-willing-provider laws, the use of tiering is a new twist which may bring new litigation.

In *Washington State Medical Assoc. v. Regence BlueShield* (No. 06–2– 30665–1SEA, filed Nov. 29, 2006, Seattle WA Superior Court) (settlement announced August 2007), reported in 12 HEALTH LAW REPORTER (BNA) 153 (Aug. 9, 2007), multiple legal claims were used to halt tiering practices in one major insurance market. Sara Rosenbaum et al., *An Assessment of Legal Issues Raised in "High Performing" Health Plan Quality and*

Efficiency Tiering Arrangements: Can the Patient be Saved? 39 BNA
HEALTH CARE POL'Y REPORT 1325 (Oct. 8, 2007). Similarly, in 2007 then-New
York Attorney General Andrew Cuomo filed charges against United Health
Care for alleged violations of various New York State laws in its use of
network tiering arrangements. (Letter from New York State Attorney
General to United Health Care, July 13, 2007). In both cases, the claims
ran the gamut, from defamation to the absence of a fair process and to
fraud. See also Claiborne et al., *Legal Impediments to Implementing Value–
Based Purchasing* at 479–82; Sara Rosenbaum et al., *An Assessment of
Legal Issues Raised in High Performing Health Plan Quality and Efficiency
Tiering Arrangements*. While they covered a range of legal theories, the
claims had their origins in three specific aspects of tiering: the secrecy in
both the standards and algorithms used to create the rankings and to
assign providers within them; the absence of a transparent rational basis
for the methods chosen; and the absence of a process by which physicians
can examine the data on which their rankings rest and challenge errors in
data or methodology. The *Washington Medical Association* settlement
suggests the types of modifications considered important by physicians:

1.   Prior to implementing any new or revised performance measurement program, the plan will give physicians an opportunity of
meaningful input, including input on the data to be used, the
methods used to compare physician performance, and the methods
of communicating ratings and scores.

2.   The insurer will make efforts to offer actual, advance notice
(10 days) to physicians that new scores are forthcoming.

3.   Physician scores will be posted in an electronic format, along
with an explanation of the methodology, an explanation of the data
relied on to calculate the score, and a means to identify the types
of patients included in the calculation of the score.

4.   Physicians will have the opportunity to make a timely appeal
of their scores; where a score is challenged on a timely basis, it will
be withheld until the appeal is completed. Where a physician's
challenge is outside of the time limits permitted for an appeal, the
score will be posted but with a clear notation that a challenge is
underway.

5.   Determinations by the insurer regarding the accuracy of its
scoring will be appealable to an independent external reviewer
based on the same materials used in the internal review.

See also, discussion of the New York State settlement in Claiborne et al.,
Legal Impediments to Implementing Value–Based Purchasing at 482–83.

Of course, similar issues might be raised about other payment sanctions. For example, if a payer were to withhold payment from a hospital for
a "never event," e.g., wrong-site surgery, would a hospital have the
opportunity to review the information on which the penalty is based for its
reliability and accuracy? Might the reliability of the measure be challenged
to begin with? How about a penalty imposed on a hospital for excessive

readmissions resulting from the poor quality of care? Could the measure of what is a "poor quality" readmission measure be challenged as too vague or unreliable to be the basis of a payment sanction? Does it matter whether the sanction is imposed by a public or private insurer? Where Medicare is concerned, what types of procedures might the program be required to follow before a particular readmissions penalty measure is adopted? Once the readmissions measure is adopted and in use, should hospitals be permitted to appeal its imposition and the application of a sanction? Should judicial review be allowed? (See *Heckler v. Ringer*, Part Two, for a discussion of judicial review of administrative actions under Medicare).

In fact, these questions are far beyond speculative. In its 2007 Report to Congress, MedPAC identified many hospital readmissions as potentially preventable. MedPAC, Report to Congress 108 (2007). MedPAC suggested that rates would drop with better hospital discharge planning and more transparent public reporting on rates. Congress included the Hospital Readmissions Reduction Program in the Patient Protection and Affordable Care Act in response to these recommendations, PPACA § 3025(a), and in 2011 CMS issued a final rule (76 Fed. Reg. 51,660, August 18) implementing the law. The final rule specifies the readmissions for "applicable conditions" that will be the focus of the program, as well as the time periods in which an admission will in fact be considered a "readmission" for purposes of imposing sanctions. Furthermore, the rule establishes a readmissions frequency threshold. That is, an isolated readmission is not enough to trigger a sanction under the rule. Instead, a hospital essentially must display a pattern of readmissions. The MS–DRGs that are considered candidates for readmissions sanctions are those that are associated with high cost or prevalence and for which a public process has been used to develop applicable performance measures. 76 Fed. Reg. 51,660, 51,665. The readmissions "window" will be 30 days, and data on readmissions will be "risk-adjusted," a technique that is used to ensure that hospitals which care for the sickest and most socially at-risk patients will not be inappropriately accused of poor performance. Providers will have the right to appeal a sanction, but not the measurement. Importantly, a hospital that inappropriately causes a readmission can be sanctioned when the patient is readmitted to a hospital other than the facility that initially discharged the patient. 76 Fed. Reg. 51,666.

In a companion effort to further incentivize a reduction in inappropriate hospital readmissions, the Patient Protection and Affordable Care Act directed the Department of Health and Human Services to develop a pilot program of "payment bundling" techniques. PPACA § 3023. Furrow, *Regulating Patient Safety* at 1763. The concept of "payment bundling" is not unlike paying an inpatient episode according to DRGs, reviewed in Part Two. However, this program encompasses bundling procedures performed by multiple sources of health care rather than the care furnished by a single facility during a single admission. Thus, for example, a hospital that admits a patient for open heart surgery would be paid not only for the treatment of the heart attack but also for the post-discharge treatment for what experts would define as a full "episode of care." The episode might include the pre-operational procedures to prepare the patient for surgery, the surgery and hospital aftercare, care then furnished by a nursing facility and/or a home health care provider, and follow-up care of the patient's surgeon and primary care physician. See Glenn Hackbarth et al., *Collective Accountability for Health Care—Toward Bundled Medicare Payments*, 359 NEW ENG. J. MED. 3 (2008).

Such a payment arrangement is complex. First, it involves a fair degree of financial risk, since there is always the chance that some patients will fare poorly and require extensive readmission care, even if quality is good. Second, the payment structure involves some sort of affiliation or joint venture relationship across providers using an intermediary to collect the bundled payment and to administer and reconcile component payments, as well as coordinated care management and quality control. Where the bundled payment is made to a single highly integrated health care entity this level of integration is inherent in the provider system. But most providers are not integrated. Furthermore, as discussed in the materials that follow, getting independent providers actually to participate as members of a broader enterprise that coordinates clinical and financial activities on their behalf raises a host of additional legal matters that must be addressed.

It should be obvious that this is extremely technical stuff. To some extent, Medicare and Medicaid use processes that are open and, in certain circumstances, subject to challenge and review. However, what about similar practices in the private sector? Past experience suggests that the practices will be great in number and vary tremendously among payers, and that the method and data used will be considered proprietary. Absent intervention like that described above by the New York Attorney General or a challenge in court, will the methods and data used be accurate? What does the material earlier in the chapter concerning challenges to ERISA plan design suggest about the viability of obtaining judicial review through private challenges? Shouldn't we just leave it to the market? Recall the litigation described in Part Two concerning the manner in which private insurers calculated reasonable and necessary charges for physician services, calculations which were used to determine how much patients would be balance billed and how much providers would be paid. The methods and data used by Ingenix were so poor as to constitute a fraud. What does that suggest about leaving the data and methods discussed here—which are light-years more complicated than the relatively simple calculation of reasonable and necessary fees—to the market?

c. Incentivizing Provider Performance Through Medicare Shared Savings: Accountable Care Organizations

The fourth Cornerstone identified in *Legal Impediments to Implementing Value–Based Purchasing in Healthcare*, above, is incentivizing provider performance, specifically the performance of physicians toward greater quality and a more clinically integrated approach to health care practice. As noted, a more clinically integrated approach, physicians who otherwise might be competitors, affiliate with one another into practice management groups that oversee collaboration to achieve commonly adopted quality improvement aims, share in the tasks and responsibilities of performance oversight, and are willing to sanction members (to the point of exclusion) for poor performance. In these arrangements, physicians may remain legally independent of one another rather than merging into a single, vertically integrated practice group such as the Mayo Clinic (which in fact is comprised of a single large group practice along with hundreds of affiliated independent physicians). At the same time, the physicians work jointly through a single practice management enterprise to improve performance and keep costs low.

Beginning in 2002, the Centers for Medicare and Medicaid Services (CMS), which oversees Medicare, launched a "Physician Quality Reporting Initiative (PQRI)" whose purpose was to move physicians toward more integrated practice and performance improvement and reporting. This move on CMS' part was accompanied by similar efforts on the part of private payers to incentivize physicians to work together toward common and more transparent quality improvement. Claiborne, *Legal Impediments to Implementing Value–Based Purchasing in Healthcare* at 482–484.

These efforts—whether they take the form of physician collaborations or collaborations across independent entities participating in a bundled payment demonstration—raise numerous legal questions. Paradoxically, cross-provider collaboration has perched at the apex of the modern quality improvement effort for decades; indeed, the clinical integration of care has been recognized as a national policy ideal since the seminal report, issued nearly a century ago, by an early reform group known as the Committee on the Costs of Medical Care. PAUL STARR, THE SOCIAL TRANSFORMATION OF AMERICAN MEDICINE 261–267.

But the laws of market competition and fraud don't favor collaborations among independent competitors, as the materials in Part Four illustrate. Furthermore, federal tax laws applicable to not-for-profit health care entities that seek tax-exempt status similarly discourage financial arrangements that could result in profits from activities considered as unrelated to the charitable purpose of the undertaking, treating such profits as taxable income. The major problem of course is that such collaborations raise the specter of numerous potential violations of federal laws aimed at curbing fraud and abuse, anticompetitive conduct in the health care marketplace, and in the case of nonprofit providers, legal violations of tax laws aimed at barring financial gains unrelated to charitable purpose. Claiborne, *Legal Impediments to Implementing Value–Based Purchasing in Healthcare* at 485–490.

The Patient Protection and Affordable Care Act, § 3022, establishing § 1899 of the Social Security Act, seeks to break through this morass by formally sanctioning such collaborations—and the shared savings that at least in theory they may produce. This shift in policy to favor collaborations across independent health care actors is accomplished through the establishment of the Medicare Shared Savings Program (MSSP), which permits the Medicare program to share savings with entities known as Accountable

Care Organizations that are certified as satisfying the law's organizational and operational requirements and that are able to produce savings while providing care of measurable good quality.

The purpose of the MSSP is to create a program that "promotes accountability for a patient population and coordinates items and services under [Medicare] parts A and B, and encourages investment in infrastructure and redesigned care processes for high quality and efficient service delivery." Social Security Act § 1899(a)(1). The PPACA defines ACOs as "groups of providers of services and suppliers who work together to manage and coordinate care for Medicare fee-for-service beneficiaries," *id.* § 1899(a)(1)(A), meaning beneficiaries who are not enrolled in Medicare Advantage organizations but who continue to be treated by physicians, hospitals, and other Medicare health professionals and institutions that are not part of formal managed care networks. Beneficiaries who remain in the Medicare fee-for-service program can continue to receive care from the hospitals, physicians, and pharmacies of their choice. Although free choice of provider is the basic ideal on which Medicare is based, remaining in the fee-for-service system is considered to raise the potential for fragmented and uncoordinated care, the inefficient use of health care resources, and poor health care quality and patient health outcomes in the form of too little primary care, uncoordinated use of medications, too-frequent hospitalizations and readmissions, and poor management of chronic conditions. Studies of Medicare Advantage patients do not show health outcomes that are appreciably different; nonetheless, coordination remains an ideal, and this ideal, in turn, led Congress to seek strategies for overcoming the financial, legal, cultural, and practical barriers that inhibit closer collaboration.

As Robert Berenson and Rachel Burton have written:

> For many the holy grail of health care policy-making has been to find a model that aligns health care providers' and patients' interests. In the 1980s and '90s, some thought that health maintenance organizations (HMOs) might be such a model, but patients, encouraged by their physicians, eventually objected to HMOs' perceived intrusion into patient care decisions, causing HMOs to back off from some of their earlier approaches and now to fade from prominence. Two decades later, the next great hope has become accountable care organizations (ACOs).

Robert A. Berenson and Rachel A. Burton, *Accountable Care Organizations in Medicare and the Private Sector: A Status Update*, ROBERT WOOD JOHNSON FOUNDATION/URBAN INSTITUTE 1 (November 2011).

Berenson and Burton note that the ACO concept made the "leap" into formal national payment policy with the MSSP program but that private payers have been experimenting with the model for years. *Id.* at 2. They also note that "Medicare's ACO approach may influence many more health plans because it provides a model for an intermediary form of health care delivery: putting providers in a position somewhere between being paid solely through volume-increasing fee-for-service payments and operating within tightly managed, prospectively defined capitated budgets that place providers at full financial risk for all spending for their enrolled populations. *Id.* The authors report that in addition to being an outgrowth of—and simultaneously a veering away from—the payer-driven HMO model (which combines the functions of an insurance intermediary with integrated health care), ACOs have roots in an earlier "provider-sponsored organization" model of health care established in Medicare amendments under the Balanced Budget Act of 1997. Even more than HMOs, this model never took off because of their greater complexity and requirement of formal patient enrollment. *Id.*

The term "accountable care organization" was coined in 2006 by MedPAC based on findings from Dr. Elliott Fisher, who reported that in fact, even Medicare beneficiaries in the fee-for-service program receive most of their care "from relatively stable sets of local physicians and hospitals," *id.*, and therefore, that it should be possible to group providers together into "virtual organizations" accountable for the cost and quality of the full continuum of care delivered to these patients." *Id.* Based on these findings, MedPAC formally recommended the establishment of ACOs as part of its 2009 *Report to Congress*, which in turn helped shape the Affordable Care Act.

Final MSSP regulations released by the Obama Administration in 2011 (76 Fed. Reg. 67,802, Nov. 2, 2011) followed a preliminary set of regulatory requirements that garnered intense opposition as raising too many barriers to ACO formation and operation. The final rules establish what Berenson and Burton identify as "three major characteristics that differentiate ACOs from existing health plan and provider arrangements:" (1) shared savings that allow ACOs to layer bonus payments from Medicare savings on top of their regular fee-for-service payments "if their patients' health care costs are below a projected amount based on their own historic spending, regardless of whether the level of their historic spending is high or low;" (2) accountability for quality, which entails measuring ACO performance based on numerous "quality metrics" such as those discussed previously; and (3) free choice of providers that leaves patients assigned to ACOs for shared savings purposes based on their patterns of health care use still free to see other physicians and Medicare providers not participating in ACOs. *Id.* at 3–4.

The authors are skeptical, based on evaluations of precursor demonstrations conducted by the federal government, that ACOs will generate savings, although the evidence suggests that the quality of care will improve. *Id.* at 4–5. The absence of savings results in part from the anticipated investments in infrastructure and care process that ACOs will require, approximately $1.7 million, on average, in 2011 dollars. Thus, while mature ACOs may produce cost efficiencies, in the short term, financial gains may not be realized, because of both start-up and early performance costs and also because the model, which continues to recognize procedure-based payments, is not tough enough to bring about deeper cultural changes in the consumption of resources. At the same time, the model is a permanent alteration to the Medicare landscape and thus potentially positioned to show cost-savings over time.

A major concern about ACOs is that the desire to produce shared savings may cause participating providers ultimately to skimp on quality. In order to avoid this result, the final CMS regulations include clinical processes and patient experience-of-care measures [that] fall into four domains: patient/caregiver experience, care coordination/patient safety, preventive health, and at-risk population measures. But Berenson and Burton are somewhat skeptical about the safeguards created by the market basket of measures:

> It is unclear whether quality measures currently are up to one of the tasks assigned them, that is, to ensure that cost savings will not be achieved by stinting on care. Although the selected quality measures address some areas that have not been given sufficient attention in current volume-based payment systems, such as care coordination and care of at-risk populations, they do not cover the full range of areas that an organization responsible for the entire continuum of care for a population of Medicare beneficiaries should address, for example, appropriate referral to specialized centers outside the ACO, when specialized expertise is needed to treat particular forms of cancer.

Berenson & Burton, *Accountable Care Organizations in Medicare and the Private Sector* at 7–8.

CMS projects that between 50 and 270 ACOs will be formed, saving an estimated $940 million over the first four years of the program (during this time, Medicare will spend somewhere north of $2 trillion, making estimated savings from ACOs a drop in the bucket). In order to further incentivize ACO formation, CMS also announced an "advance payment" initiative that will permit certain small ACO startups to secure their savings in advance so that they can have access to the capital costs needed to get off the ground. 76 Fed. Reg. 68,012 (Nov. 2, 2011).

In order to put the health care system on the road to formation of ACOs, both CMS and federal regulatory agencies charged with oversight of a competitive marketplace driven to high profitability, made important changes in critical underlying laws. First, the United States Justice Department and the Federal Trade Commission released *Statement of Antitrust Enforcement Policy Regarding Accountable Care Organizations Participating in the Medicare Shared Savings Program* (the "Policy Statement"). The Policy Statement provides that ACO formation will be permitted without pre-formation antitrust oversight, thereby allowing the formation of large ACOs, even in marketplaces where such entities might be considered to have market power by their very existence. The concept of market power, and its implications in the context of horizontal arrangements that can unlawfully affect price, is discussed in Part Four.

The decision effectively to permit the formation of large entities that are able to meet CMS' ACO structural and operational requirements is important; it reflects a deliberate national policy decision to favor collaboration for purposes of efficiency and quality improvement through the use of a far gentler "rule of reason" test (reviewed in Part Four) to measure the legality of market conduct and a willingness to allow ACOs actually to form and operate, even if such entities grow very large (e.g., more than 50 percent of the market), with impact measured only after the fact. The question of whether ACOs, as dominant players in their communities, may eventually raise prices for private insurers is an important one, but one that will be answered in a "letting the horse out of the barn" manner, only after ACOs have begun operating and flexing their (potential) muscle. Even so, antitrust experts viewed the final Policy Statement with some skepticism, noting concerns over the potential for aggressive post-enforcement oversight, as well as an uncertain role played by State Attorneys General. Stephan Paul Mahinka, *FTC/DOJ Final Policy on Accountable care Organizations: Important Antitrust Issues Remain Unanswered*, 20 BNA HEALTH LAW REPORTER 1760 (Dec. 1, 2011).

Second, the Inspector General and the CMS jointly announced final policies related to the applicability of federal fraud and abuse laws to ACOs. Under these ACO specific policies, entities that are certified to participate in the MSSP will be given broader latitude to share in savings both among the ACO provider participants and between participants and other health care providers to whom patients are referred. 76 Fed. Reg. 67,992 (Nov. 2, 2011).

The relaxation of federal antitrust and fraud and abuse standards in the case of CMS-certified and actively participating ACOs was accompanied by an IRS document entitled *Fact Sheet: Tax–Exempt Organizations Participating in the Medicare Shared Savings Program through Accountable Care Organizations*, FS–2011–11 (Oct. 20, 2011). The Fact Sheet explains how the Agency will analyze the structure and activities of such organizations for purposes of establishing or maintaining tax-exempt status. Under the IRS statement of policy, an ACO may be structured as either a corporation or a partnership for federal tax purposes, and the organization may be either taxable or tax-exempt under federal regulations. The fact sheet also clarifies that participation in an ACO furthers a tax-exempt organization's charitable purpose "of lessening the burdens of government" within the meaning of § 501(c)(3), thereby opening the door to tax-exempt status by virtue of the organization's participation in the Shared Savings Program, if it meets all other requirements.

d. Should Payers Face Liability for Injuries or Deaths Linked to Value–Based Purchasing?

As payers become users of information about health care quality and increasingly insert themselves into the structure, process, and outcomes of health care, a logical question is whether they should face potential liability when they use compensation to steer health care in certain directions which are then alleged to be linked to death or injury. Many payment incentives may not comport with what turns out to be the reasonable standard of care for a patient. See Robert A. Berenson & Christine K.

Cassel, *Consumer–Driven Health Care May Note Be What Patients Need—Caveat Emptor*, 301 JAMA 321 (2009).

This question of the relationship between payers and liability for medical injury is explored in the next chapter. An additional question is whether payers and health care providers involved in P4P arrangements should disclose their economic interests to members and patients, particularly if the incentive involves reducing the use of specialized care. The issue of physician obligations to disclose a direct financial interest in the process or outcome of patient care was explored in *Moore v. Regents* earlier in Part Three. From one perspective, traditional fee-for-service payment creates a direct financial interest in maximizing procedures regardless of quality, an incentive that typically is never discussed with patients. This interest in maximizing physician revenue through overtreatment—potentially to the point of harming patients—was illuminated by Dr. Atul Gawande in his story of McAllen Texas, described earlier in this Part. Perhaps patients are inured to this conflict of interest because fee-for-service payment arrangements have been the norm; and perhaps only for this reason arrangements in which physicians are rewarded for reducing the use of health care resources are seen as somehow more suspect.

In Shea v. Esensten, 107 F.3d 625 (8th Cir.), *cert. den.*, 522 U.S. 914 (1997), the failure of an HMO to disclose to its plan members the fact that its network physicians were financially rewarded for holding down the use of specialty care was treated as a breach of ERISA fiduciary duty because of the materiality of such information. *Shea* (which years later resulted in a state Supreme Court decision absolving the physician of negligence, Shea v. Esensten 622 N.W.2d 130 (Minn. App. 2001)) involved the death of a patient from heart failure. Suffering chest pains and enrolled in an HMO that required prior authorization for specialty care, the patient sought a referral to a cardiologist from his primary care physician. The physician refused, indicating that specialty care was unnecessary but not disclosing the fact that the HMO paid a bonus (P4P) for reducing referrals. The patient subsequently died of a massive heart attack. His widow brought a wrongful death action against the HMO for fraudulent disclosure, which the defendant successfully removed to federal court. Concluding that removal was proper because the state law claim was completely preempted under ERISA's § 502 complete preemption* the federal district court then dismissed the case on the ground that physician compensation information was not material and therefore was not covered by ERISA's fiduciary disclosure requirements.

In reversing the lower court on the question of fiduciary duty, the appeals court concluded that

> from the patient's point of view, a financial incentive scheme put in place to influence a treating doctor's referral practices when the

---

* ERISA and complete preemption of state law remedies for medical injury will be discussed in the chapter that follows; the concept of completion preemption of state remedies for tortuous injury was introduced in Pilot Life v. Dedeaux, discussed in Part Two.

patient needs specialized care is certainly a material piece of information. This kind of patient necessarily relies on the doctor's advice about treatment options, and the patient must know whether the advice is influenced by self-serving financial considerations created by the health insurance provider.

Shea, 107 F.3d at 628.

Of course, as you learned in Part Two, the remedies available under ERISA in cases of breach of fiduciary duty may be modest indeed, although the Supreme Court has indicated a greater openness to allowing financial recovery under "make whole" theory. At the same time, *Shea* raises the broader question of whether insurers and plan administrators have a fiduciary obligation to provide information to participants and beneficiaries about the various compensation arrangements they use and how these compensation arrangements may influence provider conduct. The Affordable Care Act requires the Secretary of DHHS to develop regulations mandating that health plans and insurers disclose terms of coverage and cost-sharing. 42 U.S.C. § 300gg–15 (Public Health Service Act, applied to ERISA-governed plans by PPACA § 1563). However, these provisions do not address the disclosure of payment arrangements, although pre-existing federal ERISA regulations require the disclosure of material information about compensation arrangements when requested by participants.

Final CMS regulations implementing the MSSP program, discussed above, contain extensive disclosure provisions. While Medicare fee-for-service beneficiaries, as provided under the final rules, are free to receive care from the provider of their choice, research shows that most beneficiaries in fact receive most of their care from a regular physician and hospital. Therefore they would have no idea that their providers are suddenly part of an ACO. For this reason, the final MSSP regulations mandate the disclosure of substantial information:

> **42 C.F.R. § 425.312 Notification to beneficiaries of participation in shared savings program.** (a) ACO participants must do all of the following: (1) Notify beneficiaries at the point of care that their ACO providers/suppliers are participating in the Shared Savings Program. (2) Post signs in their facilities to notify beneficiaries that their ACO providers/suppliers are participating in the Shared Savings Program. (3) Make available standardized written notices regarding participation in an ACO . . . Such written notices must be provided by the ACO participants in settings in which beneficiaries receive primary care services.

Should Medicare also require providers to notify beneficiaries that they do not participate in an ACOs and explain the implications for quality of remaining outside a more organized health care setting?

e.   Excluding Substandard Health Care Professionals Through Peer Review

Even in the early years of the program, the explosive growth of Medicare spending caused Congress to begin to rethink its highly deferential approach to coverage and payment. By the late 1960s, Congress began to introduce oversight techniques into Medicare in the form of utilization review of medical necessity. The initial foray was pretty weak. Hospitals were expected, as a condition of participation, to establish physician-directed "utilization review" (UR) committees whose job was to review the medical necessity of hospitalization, length of stay, and professional services. However, for most cases the review was only retrospective and applied just to a sample of cases. Only if a stay was of "extended duration" was UR conducted on a concurrent basis (i.e., while services were still being delivered). *See* 42 U.S.C. § 1395x(k)(1), (3); SYLVIA A. LAW, BLUE CROSS: WHAT WENT WRONG? 118–20 (2d ed. 1976); JUDITH FEDER, MEDICARE: THE POLITICS OF FEDERAL HOSPITAL INSURANCE 33 (1977). Utilization review committees were required to consult with the treating physician regarding the necessity of extended stays. If the committee disagreed with the attending, they were required to notify the physician, hospital, and patient that continued hospitalization was no longer necessary. Medicare payments then could be made for only four days after such notice was given, to allow the patient time to make alternative arrangements for care. LAW, BLUE CROSS, WHAT WENT WRONG? 119–120.

While some aspects of the UR program related to quality of care, the main thrust of the effort was to save money by denying payment for unnecessary hospitalization. When, not surprisingly, in-hospital committees failed to perform this function, DHEW (the predecessor of DHHS) quietly authorized Blue Cross, which functioned as the fiscal intermediary for Medicare, to deny payment retrospectively for services it deemed "custodial" (rather than skilled nursing) care. See LAW, BLUE CROSS, WHAT WENT WRONG? 121–30 (analyzing in detail the role of Blue Cross in carrying out Medicare UR from 1968–1972). Thus the term "utilization review" became associated with cost containment and denial of payment by the payer's agent on the basis of (often undisclosed) criteria of "necessity," while "quality assurance" (QA) or "medical audit" (MA) remained a more ad hoc and educational function, itself often without clear standards or enforcement, and under physician and hospital control.

Clearly dissatisfied with the performance of the UR program, in 1972 Congress established the Professional Standards Review Organizations ("PSROs"). The explicit purpose of this new program was to transfer the UR function from Blue Cross to regional (i.e., multi-county) organizations controlled by state and local medical societies, which were supposed to establish standards to be used by revived in-hospital UR committees now operating under PSRO surveillance, and by the PSROs themselves. See FEDER, MEDICARE: THE POLITICS OF FEDERAL HOSPITAL INSURANCE at 43–45. Although PSROs were clearly supposed to perform UR functions, the program attempted to induce physician buy-in by emphasizing quality assurance and educational goals. *See id.*; Clark C. Havighurst & James F. Blumstein, *Coping with Quality/Cost Trade-offs: The Role of PSROs*, 70 NW. U.L. REV. 6, 38–45 (1975).

Given the PSROs' multiple and inconsistent functions, their local character, and their lack of a clear national mandate and quantifiable goals, it is not surprising that Havighurst and Blumstein's 1975 prediction was largely vindicated: the PSROs were generally unable to "achieve more than minor improvements over 'business as usual.'" *Id.* at 68.

Congress reacted in 1982 by transforming the PSROs into Peer Review Organizations ("PROs"), which were to be responsible for determining whether Medicare-covered care and services were reasonable and medically necessary, furnished in the most economic setting, and consistent with professionally accepted standards. *See* 42 U.S.C. § 1320c–3(a). PROs possessed some of the same programmatic functions as the PSROs and as with the PSROs, PROs were granted civil immunity for actions taken with due care. 42 U.S.C. § 1320c–6. Moreover, 43 of the 54 new PROs were former PSROs for all or part of the area served.

However, the new program differed from the old one in several major respects. First, the geographic areas for each PRO were much larger, now typically covering an entire state rather than several counties. Second, the degree of required physician sponsorship or support was much lower, thereby weakening the influence of the profession as a whole. Third, the contracts between DHHS and the nongovernmental PROs were written to contain specific and quantified objectives. Fourth, the PRO law was amended to require explicitly that health care practitioners and institutions were to provide care that met standards of necessity, quality, and efficiency, and the legislation gave both the PROs and the Secretary of DHHS important new powers to enforce these provisions. *See* Social Security Act § 1156, 42 U.S.C. § 1320c–5.

Finally, and most importantly, the mission of the PROs was heavily affected by the adoption of Medicare's prospective payment system (PPS), based on DRGs, in 1983. Congress added several new functions to the original 1982 PRO mandate, in the nature of what might be termed "DRG police." First, PROs were given the authority to validate the diagnostic and procedural information that is used to determine a patient's DRG, and hence the hospital's reimbursement; without such validation, hospitals could code patients into more lucrative categories, a process colloquially known as "DRG creep." Second, PROs were authorized to guard against "churning"—multiple discharges and admissions of the same patient—by reviewing *prospectively* the appropriateness of admissions and discharges. Third, PROs were empowered to review the appropriateness of care for which outlier payments were sought, to counteract hospitals' financial incentives to extend the length of difficult cases into the outlier category. Fourth, PROs were given an express mandate to review "the completeness, adequacy, and quality of care provided," to guard against the general financial incentive provided by DRGs to reduce the resources devoted to patient care. See 42 U.S.C. § 1395cc(a)(1)(F)(i).

In 2002, the Centers for Medicare and Medicaid Services changed the term "Peer Review Organization" to "Quality Improvement Organizations" ("QIOs"), signifying their expanded role in not only evaluating the quality of care but also prospectively and affirmatively carrying out a Health Care Quality Improvement Program, whose aim is to improve the quality of care across patient settings. 67 Fed. Reg. 36539 (May 24, 2002). QIOs continue to carry out peer review activities as part of their function. As private health care quality improvement organizations, QIOs contract with Medicare and agree to develop comprehensive quality improvement plans setting forth specific quality indicators for various types of treatments and services (e.g., management of stroke recovery care in skilled nursing facility settings); from these indicators, QIOs undertake specific quality improvement projects aimed at measuring and improving performance.

The structure and process of peer review reflects the accommodation between purchasers and health care providers in how quality is defined, measured, and enforced. Although QIOs, like PROs, function as contractors to CMS, they do so, as noted, through a process that heavily involves community physicians. In order to secure contracts with the federal government, a QIO either must be sponsored by a significant number of physicians in active practice in its designated service areas, or else it must have a sufficient number of physicians available to it to conduct peer review. 42 U.S.C. § 1320c–3.

QIOs also are responsible for reviewing quality of care at the level of individual beneficiaries, including non-coverage notices if inpatient care is no longer necessary. At the request of a beneficiary or a representative, a QIO will review a non-coverage decision, and during this review process, the termination of coverage is stayed. 42 U.S.C. § 1354(e). QIOs also investigate potential EMTALA violations, as well as the performance of ambulatory surgery centers and certain outpatient surgical procedures.

Federal law prohibits physicians from billing patients for services for which payment has been denied by the QIO on the basis of substandard quality of care. Social Security Act § 1842(b)(3)(B)(ii). In addition, beneficiaries must be indemnified for cost sharing associated with disallowed claims. *Id.* § 1879(b).

QIOs' power to sanction for poor quality care is statutory. In addition to reviewing the reasonableness and medical necessity of care and whether care was furnished at an appropriate level (e.g. hospital or nursing home), QIOs determine whether "the quality of such services meets professionally recognized standards of care." 42 U.S.C. § 1354(a)(1)(B). This power to sanction providers and suppliers for poor quality care was added to the legislation by § 9403 of the Consolidated Omnibus Budget Reconciliation Act of 1985, P.L. No. 99–272.

QIOs must have written criteria against which they assess the standard of care, and their reviewers for initial reviews must be clinically qualified personnel. 42 C.F.R.§ 476.98(a). Consistent with their statutory authority, QIOs engage in a broad scope of review: (1) whether the services are "reasonable and necessary for the diagnosis and treatment of illness or injury or to improve functioning of a malformed body member" or, with respect to vaccines, for prevention of illness or (in the case of hospice care (which is covered under Medicare)) for the palliation and management of terminal illness; (2) whether the quality of care meets professionally recognized standards; (3) whether services furnished or proposed to be furnished on an inpatient basis could be effectively furnished consistent with appropriateness and efficiency and economically on an outpatient basis or in an inpatient health care facility of a different type; (4) the validity of the diagnostic procedural code information supplied by the hospital in the case of hospital care; (5) the completeness and adequacy of hospital care; (6) the medical necessity and appropriateness of inpatient hospital admissions and discharges; (7) the medical necessity of inpatient care in situations in which hospitals claim additional payments because their patients are sufficiently ill to be considered "outliers" under the DRG coding system; and (8) the accuracy of a hospital's decision to admit or readmit a patient. 42 C.F.R. §§ 412.82–.84; 42 C.F.R. § 476.74.

If a QIO believes that a practitioner or provider has engaged in repeated violations of the obligation under Medicare to furnish care that is economical, medically necessary or of proper quality, and if it properly documents this pattern, it must submit a report and recommendation to the Secretary of DHHS regarding actions to be taken, including program exclusion from Medicare and Medicaid and the imposition of fines. If the Secretary imposes penalties, the law establishes a post-termination due process hearing for providers and practitioners that have been so sanctioned. Social Security Act § 1156(b)(4), 42 U.S.C. § 1320c–5. In addition, both beneficiaries and providers can appeal QIO non-coverage determinations, known as initial denials. 42 C.F.R. § 478.12–.16. Appeals from initial denials are governed by Medicare's appeals system, described in *Heckler v. Ringer*, Part Two.

Doyle v. Secretary of Health and Human Services

848 F.2d 296 (1st Cir. 1988)

■ BREYER, CIRCUIT JUDGE:

On December 31, 1986, the Inspector General of the Department of Health and Human Services ("HHS") entered an order forbidding Dr. Robert Doyle, the plaintiff in this case, from receiving reimbursement for treatment of Medicare patients for at least five years. In doing so, the Inspector General accepted a recommendation of a Maine peer review organization ("PRO") that he impose this serious sanction because Dr. Doyle "grossly and flagrantly violated" his obligation to provide medical care "of a quality which meets professionally recognized standards of health care," in particular by improperly treating three patients.

[Under the statute and regulations], [i]f a PRO "identifies" a "substantial violation" of professional health care standards in "a substantial number" of a doctor's "cases," or a "violation" that is "gross and flagrant," it is to notify the doctor in writing. The doctor must have a chance to submit information to the PRO or to meet with it to review its initial finding, or both. If the PRO still believes the doctor has violated Medicare standards, it will submit a report and a sanction recommendation to HHS's Inspector General. The PRO must send a copy of the report and recommendation to the doctor. The doctor may submit additional material to the Inspector General. The Inspector General will then decide whether to apply a sanction. He must notify the doctor of the sanction decision. If he imposes a sanction, it will take effect two weeks after notification. At that time, the Inspector General must also notify members of the medical community (hospitals, medical societies, etc.) and publish notice in the newspaper.

The statutes and the regulations provide further administrative remedies for a doctor whom the Inspector General sanctions. The doctor is entitled to a hearing before an Administrative Law Judge (ALJ). The doctor may appeal an adverse ALJ decision to the Secretary's Appeals Council. And, he can obtain judicial review of the final decision of the Secretary. See generally 42 U.S.C. §§ 1320c–1 through 13; 42 C.F.R. §§ 1004.30–130.

The relevant facts here are as follows:

1. A private company called Health Care Review, Inc., ("HCRI") is under contract with HHS to run the peer review system in Maine. It employs nurses who examine medical charts of 25 percent to 30 percent of Maine's Medicare patients. If he or she finds a possible problem, the reviewing nurse alerts a doctor, who may refer the matter to a Quality Review Committee (four doctors), which may refer the matter to the Maine Advisory Committee (six doctors), which may make recommendations to the Inspector General.

2. HCRI followed this process in respect to Dr. Doyle. The Quality Review Committee found seven instances in which Dr. Doyle may have committed a sanctionable offense. The Maine Advisory Committee, after hearing from Dr. Doyle, unanimously found there was a "gross and flagrant" violation in three instances, and recommended a five-year exclusion from the Medicare program. After reviewing Dr. Doyle's further submissions, the Inspector General adopted that recommendation.

3. At this point, during the two weeks before the sanction would take effect, Dr. Doyle brought his suit in district court. After hearing evidence about how the Maine Advisory Committee had conducted its deliberations, the court concluded that the committee had not properly applied the factors listed in a particular HHS regulation. That regulation says: The PRO's specific recommendation must be based on a consideration of: (a) The type of the offense involved; (b) The severity of the offense; (c) The deterrent value; (d) The practitioner's or other person's previous sanction record; (e) The availability of alternative sources of services in the community; and (f) Any other factors that the PRO considers relevant (for example, the duration of the problem). 42 C.F.R. § 1004.80 (1987). (At the time of Dr. Doyle's sanction, the fifth factor, availability of alternative sources of services in the community, was not part of the list. 42 C.F.R. § 474.6 (1985), amended 1986.) For this reason, the court enjoined "enforcement and publication" of plaintiff's five-year exclusion. The court ordered a new meeting of the Maine Advisory Committee to reconsider its sanction recommendation, this time on the basis of the factors in § 1004.80.

The Secretary argues that the district court could not legally issue an injunction because Dr. Doyle came to court before exhausting his administrative remedies. We believe the Secretary is right. In the Medicare area, Congress has elevated the ordinary administrative "common law" principle of exhaustion into a statutory requirement. The Medicare statute allows judicial review only after a "final decision by the Secretary."

In this instance, Dr. Doyle's claim has "been presented" to the Secretary; indeed one of the Secretary's administrators, the Inspector General, has imposed the very sanction about which Dr. Doyle complains. Dr. Doyle, however, has not "exhausted" the Department's administrative appeals; and, there is no "final" decision of the Secretary because the Secretary has not "waived" exhaustion.

Dr. Doyle argues that his claim fits within a narrow exception to the exhaustion rule, an exception where courts have found the agency must waive exhaustion. That exception applies to an "entirely collateral" matter where the agency has deprived an individual of something important and "full relief cannot be obtained" later from the agency. In our view, however, Dr. Doyle's case does not fall within this exception.

To understand why, one must first understand the policy basis of an exhaustion rule:

> [Exhaustion] allows the agency to develop a factual record, to apply its expertise to a problem, to exercise its discretion, and to correct its own mistakes, all before a court will intervene. Insofar as specialized administrative understanding is important, the doctrine thereby promotes accurate results, not only at the agency level, but also by allowing more informed judicial review. By limiting judicial interruption of agency proceedings, the doctrine can encourage expeditious decision making. Insofar as Congress has provided that an agency will decide a matter in the first instance, to apply the doctrine normally furthers specific Congressional intent. And, as a general matter, the doctrine promotes a sensible division of tasks between the agency and the court: litigants are discouraged from weakening the position of the agency by flouting its processes, while court resources are reserved for dealing primarily with those matters which could not be resolved administratively. Thus, the doctrine serves the interests of accuracy, efficiency, agency autonomy and judicial economy.

Given these policy principles, one can understand why, for example, when a plaintiff attacks the lawfulness of an important "systemwide" agency policy (say, a constitutional challenge to a policy disqualifying a large class of potential Social Security recipients), the Supreme Court has held that the agency must waive its exhaustion requirements. In that sort of case exhaustion serves little purpose; the agency's policy is well-established and unlikely to change; agency expertise is not particularly likely to help the court; and, at the same time, to insist upon exhaustion of agency procedures might well physically harm a plaintiff needing benefits. Where the plaintiff's claims, however, raise issues where the agency's expertise may be helpful, or attack policies to which the agency is less firmly attached, or seem more closely confined to the facts of a particular case, exhaustion is required.

The case before us is one that falls within the rule, not the exception. Dr. Doyle's case involves one plaintiff, not a class. In Dr. Doyle's case, agency expertise can help the court evaluate whether or not the Advisory Committee recommendation was "based on a consideration of" the relevant factors, because the agency (HHS) is likely better to understand (1) how a PRO does, or should, go about considering those factors, (2) how HHS, which wrote the regulation, interprets the word "consideration, and (3) whether, given the statute, rules, and regulations, any PRO deviation from the regulation's norm made a significant difference to Dr. Doyle. There is no reason here to think the agency has a closed mind on these matters. It is not wedded to a particular long-standing policy that is under attack. If the PRO has made a mistake in applying the agency's rules, the agency will likely correct it.

Dr. Doyle cross-appeals from the district court's rejection of his claims that the Inspector General's decision violated the Constitution. Since all parties wish us to hear the merits of these arguments, and the Secretary, at oral argument, expressly waived any exhaustion requirement, we shall do so.

1. Dr. Doyle argues that the relevant statute's terms, punishing those who "grossly and flagrantly violated" the "obligation" to "assure services . . . of a quality which meets professionally recognized standards of health care," are so vague that the Constitution's Due Process Clause prohibits Congress from using the statute to deprive him of part of his income.

Other courts, holding this provision constitutional, have done so in part because "(t)he definition of adequate medical care cannot be boiled down to a precise mathematical formula; it must be grounded in what, from time to time, other health professionals consider to be acceptable standards of medical care." To the medical profession, which will administer this standard, it has reasonably clear meaning.

2. Dr. Doyle argues that the procedure that HHS uses to decide whether, and how, to institute a sanction is constitutionally inadequate. In particular, he says that the Constitution entitles him to a full evidentiary hearing before the Inspector General imposes a sanction.

Even if we assume, however, for the sake of argument, that Dr. Doyle's injury amounts to a deprivation of "liberty" or "property," within the terms of the Fifth Amendment, we must still reject his argument, for HHS provides Dr. Doyle with all of the "process" that is constitutionally "due." While a full, formal, courtroom-type evidentiary hearing prior to the Inspector General's imposition of a sanction might offer still more protection against one kind of agency mistake (wrongly sanctioning a doctor), it would offer Medicare patients less protection against another equally important kind of mistake (failing to warn patients against a doctor whose services are seriously deficient). Under the Constitution, the agency should, and does, have leeway to balance these two risks. And, the procedural result of that balancing here is reasonable.

3. Dr. Doyle claims that the PRO's recommendation deprived him of "property" or "liberty" without due process of law because the PRO was "biased" against him. Insofar as this argument rests upon the PRO's dual role as prosecutor and judge, the Supreme Court has explicitly rejected it. Withrow v. Larkin, 421 U.S. 35 (1975). Insofar as it rests on his claim that the Committee decided against him because it was "under pressure" to find a "victim" and impose a sanction, the district court rejected it as a matter of fact. Similarly, the court found that the Committee's recommendation did not rest on any personal bias against Dr. Doyle growing out of his attacks on the Committee.

The part of the judgment of the district court upholding the constitutionality of the Secretary's sanction decision is affirmed. The part of the judgment of the district court declaring the Secretary's sanction decision an invalid violation of agency regulations and enjoining further agency action is reversed.

Notes

1. As Judge (now Justice) Breyer points out, one of Dr. Doyle's claims was that he had been deprived of liberty or property without due process of law because the Maine PRO (HCRI) was biased against him due to Doyle's prior criticism of HCRI. The district court summarized the evidence on this point as follows:

> Dr. Doyle is the first physician ever sanctioned by HCRI, and in fact is the first physician to be sanctioned by any peer review organization in all of New England. Although it falls far short of being substantive proof of any impropriety, the Court is nevertheless given some pause by the fact that the first physician to be sanctioned by HCRI is someone who is well known to that organization and who has been one of the most vocal critics of its operations in Maine. The Court is particularly troubled by the testimony of former HCRI Medical Director Michael Lacombe that when HCRI Vice President Edward Lynch was told that Doyle's opposition was making it difficult to recruit physician reviewers in Bridgton, Lynch suggested doing a review of every Medicare patient treated by Dr. Doyle so as to make him "feel the heat." Although this complete review never took place, it is clear that Lynch and perhaps other HCRI administrators considered Doyle to be a thorn in their sides.

Doyle v. Bowen, 660 F.Supp. 1484, 1488–89 (D. Me. 1987), *aff'd in pertinent part*, 848 F.2d 296 (1st Cir. 1988). The district court ultimately found that although HCRI had audited Dr. Doyle's practice at a higher-than-average rate, there was no proof that this was not based on neutral criteria, such as the types of diagnoses involved. The district court also stressed the apparent neutrality and unanimity of the multi-layer review process.

(a) In the light of Judge Breyer's opinion, should Dr. Doyle's claim of PRO bias against him for prior criticism be considered a "collateral issue" not subject to the normal requirement of exhaustion of administrative remedies?

(b) If your answer to question (a) is negative—i.e. if you insist that Dr. Doyle first present his claim of bias through the administrative process—does that affect your answer to the question of whether an ALJ hearing is constitutionally required before sanctions can be imposed?

(c) Whoever hears the bias claim, should the burden of proof be shifted if the accused doctor can make out a prima facie case? The district court apparently placed the burden on Dr. Doyle to prove by a preponderance of the evidence that the PRO had targeted him for an illegitimate reason, and ultimately ruled that Dr. Doyle had not carried that burden. But do the facts summarized by the district court above make out at least a prima facie case of bias, justifying shifting the burden to the PRO to explain the neutral criteria that led to the selection of Dr. Doyle as the first object of sanctions?

2.   In developing the Omnibus Budget Reconciliation Act of 1987, P.L. 100–203 (hereinafter OBRA 1987), the House of Representatives passed a provision that attempted to balance physicians' strong desire for a formal evidentiary hearing before sanctions were imposed with the strong opposition of DHHS and the PROs to such a provision as endangering patient care. The House bill provided that "before an exclusion took effect, the provider would be entitled to a decision by an administrative law judge as to whether patients would be at serious risk if the provider were to continue furnishing services during the review process." H.R. Rep. 100–391, at 427. In other words, a provider would be entitled to a limited pre-sanction hearing before an ALJ on whether sanctions could be postponed until after a full hearing on the merits without posing a "serious risk" to patients. The Senate had passed no comparable provision, and the conferees accepted the House version but limited it to providers located in rural health manpower shortage areas or in counties with fewer than 70,000 people. See *Joint Explanatory Statement of the Committee of Conference* at 664–65; Social Security Act § 1156(b)(5), 42 U.S.C. § 1320c–5(b)(5). Since the amendment grants retroactive relief to doctors who received their exclusion notices up to 365 days before the effective date of the Act (December 22, 1987), Dr. Doyle would apparently have been entitled to a limited ALJ hearing if he qualified as a rural practitioner.

CHAPTER 21

LIABILITY FOR MEDICAL NEGLIGENCE: SPECIAL ISSUES THAT ARISE IN SITUATIONS INVOLVING INSURERS AND HEALTH PLAN ADMINISTRATORS

1. INTRODUCTION

The preceding materials have explored concepts of professional and institutional medical liability as well as the rising importance of payers in matters of health care quality. This chapter explores the intersection of payment and care in a medical liability context; it focuses on the special liability questions that arise in the case of insurers and health plan administrators, who also control health care—either de-facto through medical management and prospective utilization controls or explicitly through practice networks selected and overseen by the insurer or plan administrator. In these situations, both types of liability principles presented thus far—those in connection with the provision of medical care as well as liability arising from negligence or bad faith in administering an insurance plan—come into play. To further complicate matters there is the question of what happens when the plan administrator involved is connected to an ERISA health benefit plan.

The defendants in these cases span the world of payers today. They are public insurers (*Wickline v. State of California*, below), HMOs selling their products to both private and public group sponsors (*Boyd v. Albert Einstein*, *Jones v. Chicago HMO*, and *Dukes v. U.S. Healthcare*, below), and health benefit services companies acting as claims administrators for self-insured ERISA plans (*Corcoran v. United Health Care*, below). What binds these cases together is that the defendant accused of negligence in connection with injury or death is a payer, although as you will learn, the negligent medical conduct that is alleged may be in the context of either payment or the provision of health care. Part of the reason that there are so many types of defendants is the proliferation of the types of hybrid entities in the wake of the HMO Act of 1973, as companies sought to replicate the hybrid nature of the HMO (offering both coverage and care) but without all of the obligations that accompanied federally-qualified HMO status under that Act. *See* Jonathan Weiner & Gregory de Lissovoy, *Razing a Tower of Babel:*

A Taxonomy for Managed Care and Health Insurance Plans, 18 J. HEALTH POL. POL'Y & L. 75, 76–78 (1993).

From these cases two basic questions emerge. First, what is the plaintiff's theory of liability? Is it connected to negligence in the actual provision of medical care, or alternatively, does it relate to the exercise of medical judgment in connection with a decision not to cover or pay for treatment in the context of plan administration? The theory of liability is critical not only because it may determine whether the plaintiff has a cause of action under state law but also because of the ERISA preemption implications that can arise when the liability theory ties back to what the courts consider to be plan administration.

The second basic question is whether the defendant is acting as part of an ERISA health benefit plan, and if so, whether its status as a plan administrator has any bearing on the claim. Recall from *Pilot Life v. Dedeaux* (Part Two), that ERISA § 502 completely preempts state law remedies in cases in which the claim itself can be said to "arise under" ERISA. Deciding when a claim challenging the quality of medical decision making in fact arises under ERISA turns out to be no small matter, as you will see, and the results can be quite anomalous.

Many judges and commentators have, as you will see in *Aetna v. Davila,* which completes this cycle of cases, called for Congressional intervention to address situations in which persons injured by the medical judgment of an ERISA plan administrator are left without a remedy because of ERISA's extraordinary preemptive powers. Congress has not so intervened. The Patient Protection and Affordable Care Act, while making significant changes to ERISA's coverage requirements, does not alter ERISA's remedial provisions. The closest Congress came to rectifying the complete absence of a remedy for medical injuries sustained as a result of negligence or bad faith on the part of an ERISA plan administrator came on the eve of the attacks on the Pentagon and the World Trade Center on September 11, 2001. At that time, Congress was wrestling with the question, as part of the Patient Protection Act, of whether ERISA-governed health plans should be shielded from liability for medical injury. In its bill, (S. 872, 107th Cong., 1st Sess.), the Senate called for the elimination of the ERISA liability shield in such situations, which would have allowed injured persons to pursue plan administrators under whatever state law claims might have been available. (*Aetna v. Davila,* decided in 2004, presents an example of such a state law). At the urging of President George W. Bush and his supporters, the House of Representatives, on the other hand, under H.R. 2563 (107th Cong., 1st Sess.), pressed for creation of a federal remedy that would have allowed monetary relief in ERISA medical negligence cases arising from plan administration. The attacks in New York and Washington D.C. caused both Chambers to abandon the effort even though conferencing had begun, and the matter of remedies for medical injuries arising from plan administration thus remains a major dimension of law and public policy in health care quality today.

This chapter begins with an overview of cases that explore the application of state law liability theories of medical negligence in connection with payment and care under health insurance arrangements. Following these cases, this chapter explores how these liability theories intersect with ERISA.

---

2. INSURER NEGLIGENCE IN CONNECTION WITH COVERAGE DETERMINATIONS

Wickline v. State of California

239 Cal. Rptr. 810 (App. 1986)

■ ROWEN, ASSOCIATE JUSTICE:

Principally, this matter concerns itself with the legal responsibility that a third party payer, in this case, the State of California, has for harm caused to a patient when a cost containment program is applied in a manner which is alleged to have affected the implementation of the treating physician's medical judgment. The plaintiff, respondent herein, Lois J. Wickline sued defendant, appellant herein, State of California (State or Medi–Cal). The essence of the plaintiff's claim is [that state employees negligently terminated Wickline's eligibility for medical assistance, causing her to be discharged prematurely from Van Nuys Community Hospital. As a result of this premature discharge, plaintiff suffered a complete occlusion of the right infra-renoaorta, necessitating an amputation of plaintiff's right leg.]

I

Responding to concerns about the escalating cost of health care, public and private payers have in recent years experimented with a variety of cost containment mechanisms. We deal here with one of those programs: The prospective utilization review process. At the outset, this court recognizes that this case appears to be the first attempt to tie a health care payer into the medical malpractice causation chain and that it, therefore, deals with issues of profound importance to the health care community and to the general public.

Traditionally, quality assurance activities, including utilization review programs, were performed primarily within the hospital setting under the general control of the medical staff. The principal focus of such quality assurance review schema was to prevent overutilization. Early cost containment programs utilized the retrospective utilization review process. In that system the third party payer reviewed the patient's chart after the fact to determine whether the treatment provided was medically necessary. If, in the judgment of the utilization reviewer, it was not, the health care provider's claim for payment was denied.

In the cost containment program in issue in this case, prospective utilization review, authority for the rendering of health care services must be obtained before medical care is rendered. Its purpose is to promote the well-recognized public interest in controlling health care costs by reducing unnecessary services while still intending to assure that appropriate medical and hospital services are provided to the patient in need. However, such a cost containment strategy creates new and added pressures on the quality assurance portion of the utilization review mechanism. The stakes, the risks at issue, are much higher when a prospective cost containment review process is utilized than when a retrospective review process is used. A mistaken conclusion about medical necessity following retrospective review will result in the wrongful withholding of payment. An erroneous decision in a prospective review process, on the other hand, in practical consequences, results in the withholding of necessary care, potentially leading to a patient's permanent disability or death.

II

[Wickline was diagnosed by Dr. Polonsky, a specialist in vascular surgery, as having [an] obstruction of the terminal aorta. Dr. Polonsky concluded that it was necessary to remove a part of the plaintiff's artery and insert a synthetic (Teflon) graft in its place. After receiving authorization from Medi–Cal for the operation and 10 days of hospitalization, Dr. Polonsky performed the surgery on January 7, 1977.]

Later that same day Dr. Polonsky was notified that Wickline was experiencing circulatory problems in her right leg. He concluded that a clot had formed in the graft. As a result, Wickline was taken back into surgery, the incision in her right groin was reopened, the clot removed and the graft was resewn. [After further pain and spasms in Wickline's lower leg vessels] Dr. Polonsky performed a lumbar sympathectomy. A lumbar sympathectomy is a major operation in which a section of the chain of nerves that lie on each side of the spinal column is removed. Dr. Polonsky was assisted in all three surgeries by Dr. Leonard Kovner a board certified specialist in the field of general surgery and the chief of surgery at Van Nuys. Dr. Daniels [Mrs. Wickline's primary care physician] was [also present for some of the surgery].

On or about January 16, 1977, Dr. Polonsky concluded that "it was medically necessary" that plaintiff remain in the hospital for an additional eight days beyond her then scheduled discharge date. Drs. Kovner and Daniels concurred in Dr. Polonsky's opinion. Dr. Polonsky cited many reasons for his feeling that it was medically necessary for plaintiff to remain in an acute care hospital for an additional eight days, such as the danger of infection and/or clotting. His principal reason, however, was that he felt that he was going to be able to save both of Wickline's legs and wanted her to remain in the hospital where he could observe her and be immediately available, along with the hospital staff, to treat her if an emergency should occur.

In order to secure an extension of Wickline's hospital stay, it was necessary to complete and present to Medi–Cal a form called "Request for Extension of Stay in Hospital," commonly referred to as an "MC–180" or "180." It is the hospital's responsibility to prepare the 180 form. The hospital must secure necessary information about the patient from the responsible physician. It then submits the 180 form to Medi–Cal's representative and obtains appropriate authorization for the hospital stay extension. The physician's responsibility in the preparation of the 180 form is to furnish (to the hospital's representative) the patient's diagnosis, significant history, clinical status and treatment plan in sufficient detail to permit a reasonable, professional evaluation by Medi–Cal's representative, either the "on-site nurse" or/and the Medi–Cal Consultant, a doctor employed by the State for just such purpose.

The Medi–Cal Consultant's responsibility is to review requests submitted by private physicians on behalf of their patients for hospital treatment they believe necessary and to review requests for extensions of hospital time submitted on behalf of hospitalized patients. The Medi–Cal Consultant is not permitted to approve the request unless the information furnished is timely, complete and indicates the medical necessity of the requested treatment. At Van Nuys, Patricia N. Spears (Spears), an employee of the hospital and a registered nurse, had the responsibility for completing 180 forms. In this case, as requested by Dr. Polonsky, Spears filled out Wickline's 180 form and then presented it to Dr. Daniels, as plaintiff's attending physician, to sign, which he did, in compliance with Dr. Polonsky's recommendation. All of the physicians who testified agreed that the 180 form prepared by Spears was complete, accurate and adequate for all purposes in issue in this matter.

Doris A. Futerman (Futerman), a registered nurse, was, at that time, employed by Medi–Cal as a Health Care Service Nurse, commonly referred to as an "on-site nurse." As such, her primary duties were to contact, daily, a group of hospitals assigned to her to review requests for extensions of hospital stays prepared on behalf of patients in those particular hospitals. Van Nuys was one of the hospitals to which she was assigned. Futerman had the authority, after reviewing a 180 form, to approve the requested extension of time without calling a Medi–Cal Consultant. She could not, however, either reject the request outright or authorize a lesser number of days then requested. If, for any reason, she felt she could not approve the extension of time in the hospital as requested, she was required to contact a Medi–Cal Consultant and that physician would make the ultimate decision on the request.

Futerman, after reviewing Wickline's 180 form, felt that she could not approve the requested eight-day extension of acute care hospitalization. While conceding that the information provided might justify some additional time beyond the scheduled discharge date, nothing in Wickline's case, in Futerman's opinion, would have warranted the entire eight additional days requested and, for those reasons, she telephoned the Medi–Cal Consultant. She reached Dr. William S. Glassman (Dr. Glassman), one of the Medi–Cal Consultants on duty at the time in Medi–Cal's Los Angeles office. The Medi–Cal Consultant selection occurred randomly. As was the practice, whichever Medi–Cal Consultant was available at the moment took the next call that came into the office.

Dr. Glassman was board certified in general surgery and had practiced in that field until 1975 when he became employed by the Department of Health of the State of California as a Medi–Cal Consultant I. At the time of trial Dr. Glassman was not employed by the State and attempts to personally serve him with a subpoena to appear as a witness in this case were without success. Without objection from the State, Dr. Glassman's testimony was taken at trial by the reading of his deposition in open court.

After speaking with Futerman on the telephone, Dr. Glassman rejected Wickline's treating physician's request for an eight-day hospital extension and, instead, authorized an additional four days of hospital stay beyond the originally scheduled discharge date. Dr. Glassman testified that since the initial request for extension of hospital stay is made to him by way of a telephone call from the on-site nurse, he does not actually see the 180 form itself until after he has acted on it, when it is forwarded to him for his signature. While there are appropriate places provided on the 180 form to indicate what the on-site nurse's recommendation is and the reason given for disapproval of the requested hospital stay extension by the Medi–Cal Consultant, both of those places were left blank on Wickline's 180 form. Dr. Glassman could not recall why he granted a four-day extension rather than the eight days requested by plaintiff's treating physician.

Neither Futerman nor Dr. Glassman had any specific recollection of the Wickline case. Each testified based upon their ordinary practice and procedure except where requested to state their opinion based on information provided to them at the time their respective testimony was taken as, for example, regarding information appearing on Wickline's 180 form. After review of Wickline's 180 form, Dr. Glassman testified that the factors that led him to authorize four days, rather than the requested eight days, was that there was no information about the patient's temperature which he, thereupon, assumed was normal; nothing was mentioned about the patient's diet, which he then presumed was not a problem; nor was there any information about Wickline's bowel function, which Dr. Glassman then presumed was functioning satisfactorily. Further, the fact that the 180 form noted that Wickline was able to ambulate with help and that whirlpool treatments were to begin that day caused Dr. Glassman to presume that the patient was progressing satisfactorily and was not seriously or critically ill.

Dr. Glassman testified that he had no recollection of reviewing any documentary information available to him before rejecting the requested eight-day extension and authorizing four days instead. Initial treatment authorization requests, form MC–161, which had to be completed by the plaintiff's physician in order to obtain prior authorization from Medi–Cal for her initial hospitalization was, according to the State's own witness, Dr. Harry Kaufman (Dr. Kaufman), the chief Medi–Cal Consultant at the Los Angeles field office (and Dr. Glassman's supervisor), always supported by documentation submitted by the physician before such authorization was granted. Therefore, such material was apparently available to Dr. Glassman for review before he acted.

Further, it is reasonable to conclude from the record that Dr. Glassman did not consult with a specialist in peripheral vascular surgery before making his decision. Such specialists were employed by Medi–Cal, according to Dr. Kaufman, and were made available to Medi–Cal Consultants to confer with for special information and guidance in areas beyond the Medi–Cal Consultants' own general knowledge, training and experience.

In essence, respondent argues, Dr. Glassman based his decision on signs and symptoms such as temperature, diet and bowel movements, which were basically irrelevant to the plaintiff's circulatory condition for which she was being treated and did not concern himself with those symptoms and signs which an ordinary prudent physician would consider to be pertinent with regard to the type of medical condition presented by Wickline.

Complying with the limited extension of time authorized by Medi–Cal, Wickline was discharged from Van Nuys on January 21, 1977. Drs. Polonsky and Daniels each wrote discharge orders. At the time of her discharge, each of plaintiff's three treating physicians were aware that the Medi–Cal Consultant had approved only four of the requested eight-day hospital stay extension. While all three doctors were aware that they could attempt to obtain a further extension of Wickline's hospital stay by telephoning the Medi–Cal Consultant to request such an extension, none of them did so.

Dr. Polonsky, the senior man on the Wickline matter, and the specialist brought in specifically to treat Wickline's condition, was acknowledged by his associates as the doctor with primary responsibility in making decisions regarding her case. It would appear that both Drs. Daniels and Kovner, observing nothing that looked threatening to the patient, deferred to Dr. Polonsky and allowed Wickline to be discharged at the expiration of the period authorized by Dr. Glassman, the Medi–Cal Consultant.

At trial, Dr. Polonsky testified that in the time that had passed since the first extension request had been communicated to Medi–Cal, on January 16th or 17th, and the time of her scheduled discharge on January 21, 1977, Wickline's condition had neither deteriorated nor become critical. In Dr. Polonsky's opinion no new symptom had presented itself and no additional factors had occurred since the original request was made to have formed the basis for a change in the Medi–Cal Consultant's attitude regarding Wickline's situation. In addition, he stated that at the time of Wickline's discharge it did not appear that her leg was in any danger.

Dr. Polonsky testified that at the time in issue he felt that Medi–Cal Consultants had the State's interest more in mind than the patient's welfare and that that belief influenced his decision not to request a second extension of Wickline's hospital stay. In addition, he felt that Medi–Cal had the power to tell him, as a treating doctor, when a patient must be discharged from the hospital. Therefore, while still of the subjective, non-communicated, opinion that Wickline was seriously ill and that the danger to her was not over, Dr. Polonsky discharged her from the hospital on January 21, 1977. He testified that had Wickline's condition, in his medical judgment, been critical or in a deteriorating condition on January 21, he would have made some effort to keep her in the hospital beyond that day even if denied authority by Medi–Cal and even if he had to pay her hospital bill himself.

Dr. Daniels testified that he believed it was medically proper to discharge Wickline from the hospital on January 21, 1977. Dr. Kovner testified that while he did not recall whether or not he saw Wickline on January 21, as he was given credit for doing in a nurse's note in the hospital record, he did see her on January 19, 1977, and from his knowledge of her case he had no objection to her discharge from the hospital. Dr. Kovner stated that if he had seen (on the day of her discharge) "a grossly infected wound, that in anyway looked threatening to the patient," he would have done whatever was necessary to take measures to continue her hospitalization. All of the medical witnesses who testified at trial agreed that Dr. Polonsky was acting within the standards of practice of the medical community in discharging Wickline on January 21, 1977.

Had the eight-day extension requested on Wickline's behalf been granted by Medi–Cal, she would have remained in the hospital through the morning hours of January 25, 1977. In Dr. Polonsky's medical opinion, based upon hypothetical questions derived from Wickline's recollection of her course subsequent to her discharge from the hospital, had she been at Van Nuys on January 22, 23 or 24, he would have observed her leg change color, would have formed the opinion that she had clotted and would have taken her back into surgery and reopened the graft to remove the clot again, not an uncommon procedure in this type of case. As previously stated, he had performed a similar procedure on the first day of surgery, January 7, 1977. In addition thereto, Dr. Polonsky testified that had Wickline developed an infection while she was in the hospital, it could have been controlled with the vigorous use of antibiotics.

In Dr. Polonsky's opinion, to a reasonable medical certainty, had Wickline remained in the hospital for the eight additional days, as originally requested by him and her other treating doctors, she would not have suffered the loss of her leg.

Dr. Polonsky testified that in his medical opinion, the Medi–Cal Consultant's rejection of the requested eight-day extension of acute care hospitalization and his authorization of a four-day extension in its place did not conform to the usual medical standards as they existed in 1977. He stated that, in accordance with those standards, a physician would not be permitted to make decisions regarding the care of a patient without either first seeing the patient, reviewing the patient's chart or discussing the patient's condition with her treating physician or physicians.

III

From the facts thus presented, appellant takes the position that it was not negligent as a matter of law. Appellant contends that the decision to discharge was made by each of the plaintiff's three doctors, was based upon the prevailing standards of practice, and was justified by her condition at the time of her discharge. It argues that Medi–Cal had no part in the plaintiff's hospital discharge and therefore was not liable even if the decision to do so was erroneously made by her doctors.

"All persons are required to use ordinary care to prevent others being injured as a result of their conduct." And, "in the absence of statutory provision declaring an exception to the fundamental principle enunciated by section 1714 of the Civil Code, no such exception should be made unless clearly supported by public policy." A departure from this fundamental principle involves the balancing of a number of considerations; the major ones are the foreseeability for harm to the plaintiff, the degree of certainty that the plaintiff suffered injury, the closeness of the connection between the defendant's conduct and the injury suffered, the moral blame attached to the defendant's conduct, the policy of preventing future harm, the extent of the burden to the defendant and consequences to the community of imposing a duty to exercise care with resulting liability for breach, and the availability, cost, and prevalence of insurance for the risk involved.

Applying those standards to the facts in issue in this matter causes this court to conclude that appellant's contentions are well taken and that it is absolved from liability in this case as a matter of law.

Dr. Kaufman, the chief Medi–Cal Consultant for the Los Angeles field office, was called to testify on behalf of the defendant. He testified that in January 1977, the criteria, or standard, which governed a Medi–Cal Consultant in acting on a request to consider an extension of time was founded on title 22 of the California Administrative Code. That standard was "the medical necessity" for the length and level of care requested. That, Dr. Kaufman contended, was determined by the Medi–Cal Consultant from the information provided him in the 180 form. The Medi–Cal Consultant's decision required the exercise of medical judgment and, in doing so, the Medi–Cal Consultant would utilize the skill, knowledge, training and experience he had acquired in the medical field.

Dr. Kaufman supported Dr. Glassman's decision. He testified, based upon his examination of the MC–180 form in issue in this matter, that Dr. Glassman's four-day hospital stay extension authorization was ample to meet the plaintiff's medically necessary needs at that point in time. Further, in Dr. Kaufman's opinion, there was no need for Dr. Glassman to seek information beyond that which was contained in Wickline's 180 form.

Dr. Kaufman testified that it was the practice in the Los Angeles Medi–Cal office for Medi–Cal Consultants not to review other information that might be available, such as the TAR 160 form (request for authorization for initial hospitalization), unless called by the patient's physician and requested to do so and, instead, to rely only on the information contained in the MC–180 form. Dr. Kaufman also stated that Medi–Cal Consultants did not initiate telephone calls to patient's treating doctors because of the volume of work they already had in meeting their prescribed responsibilities. Dr. Kaufman testified that any facts relating to the patient's care and treatment that was not shown on the 180 form was of no significance.

As to the principal issue before this court, i.e., who bears responsibility for allowing a patient to be discharged from the hospital, her treating physicians or the health care payer, each side's medical expert witnesses agreed that, in accordance with the standards of medical practice as it existed in January 1977, it was for the patient's treating physician to decide the course of treatment that was medically necessary to treat the ailment. It was also that physician's responsibility to determine whether or not acute care hospitalization was required and for how long. Finally, it was agreed that the patient's physician is in a better position than the Medi–Cal Consultant to determine the number of days medically necessary for any required hospital care. The decision to discharge is, therefore, the responsibility of the patient's own treating doctor.

Dr. Kaufman testified that if, on January 21, the date of the plaintiff's discharge from Van Nuys, any one of her three treating doctors had decided that in his medical judgment it was necessary to keep Wickline in the hospital for a longer period of time, they, or any of them, should have filed another request for extension of stay in the hospital, that Medi–Cal would expect those physicians to make such a request if they felt it was indicated, and upon receipt of such a request further consideration of an additional extension of hospital time would have been given.

Title 22 of the California Administrative Code section 51110, provided, in pertinent part, at the relevant time in issue here, that: "The determination of need for acute care shall be made in accordance with the usual standards of medical practice in the community."

The patient who requires treatment and who is harmed when care which should have been provided is not provided should recover for the injuries suffered from all those responsible for the deprivation of such care, including, when appropriate, health care payers. Third party payers of health care services can be held legally accountable when medically inappropriate decisions result from defects in the design or implementation of cost containment mechanisms as, for example, when appeals made on a patient's behalf for medical or hospital care are arbitrarily ignored or unreasonably disregarded or overridden. However, the physician who complies without protest with the limitations imposed by a third party payer, when his medical judgment dictates otherwise, cannot avoid his ultimate responsibility for his patient's care. He cannot point to the health care payer as the liability scapegoat when the consequences of his own determinative medical decisions go sour.

There is little doubt that Dr. Polonsky was intimidated by the Medi–Cal program but he was not paralyzed by Dr. Glassman's response nor rendered powerless to act appropriately if other action was required under the circumstances. If, in his medical judgment, it was in his patient's best interest that she remain in the acute care hospital setting for an additional four days beyond the extended time period originally authorized by Medi–Cal, Dr. Polansky should have made some effort to keep Wickline there. He himself acknowledged that responsibility to his patient. It was his medical judgment, however, that Wickline could be discharged when she was. All the plaintiff's treating physicians concurred and all the doctors who testified at trial, for either plaintiff or defendant, agreed that Dr. Polonsky's medical decision to discharge Wickline met the standard of care applicable at the time. Medi–Cal was not a party to that medical decision and therefore cannot be held to share in the harm resulting if such decision was negligently made.

In addition thereto, while Medi–Cal played a part in the scenario before us in that it was the resource for the funds to pay for the treatment sought, and its input regarding the nature and length of hospital care to be provided was of paramount importance, Medi–Cal did not override the medical judgment of Wickline's treating physicians at the time of her discharge. It was given no opportunity to do so. Therefore, there can be no viable cause of action against it for the consequences of that discharge decision.

The California Legislature's intent, in enacting the Medi–Cal Act, was to provide "mainstream" medical care to the indigent. The Legislature had expressly declared that Medi–Cal recipients should be able "whenever possible and feasible, to the extent practical, to secure health care in the same manner employed by the public generally, and without discrimination or segregation based purely on their economic disability." (Welf. & Inst. Code, § 14000.) [Hospitalization is covered by Medi–Cal subject to prior authorization of medical necessity.] In the case before us, the Medi–Cal Consultant's decision, vis-à-vis the request to extend Wickline's hospital stay, was in accord with then existing statutory law.

V

This court appreciates that what is at issue here is the effect of cost containment programs upon the professional judgment of physicians to prescribe hospital treatment for patients requiring the same. While we recognize, realistically, that cost consciousness has become a permanent feature of the health care system, it is essential that cost limitation programs not be permitted to corrupt medical judgment. We have concluded, from the facts in issue here, that in this case it did not.

The judgment is reversed.

Notes

1. In a crucial sentence, the *Wickline* opinion states that "[t]hird party payers of health care services can be held legally accountable when medically inappropriate decisions result from defects in the design or implementation of cost containment mechanisms as, for example, when appeals made on a patient's behalf for medical or hospital care are arbitrarily ignored or unreasonably disregarded or overridden." What are the elements of "design" or "implementation"? Individual determinations of the medical necessity of covered treatments that do not consider the facts of a particular case and that fail to take into account clinical and health measures that have a reasonable relationship to the patient's condition, as

in *Wickline*? Medical management design features that are actually part of the plan itself, such as medical necessity definitions that are irrationally restrictive and that allow treatments only to improve health while denying treatments necessary to avert a loss of health, as in *Bedrick v. Travelers Insurance* (Part Two)? Arbitrary and fixed treatment limits that leave patients undertreated for health conditions as in *Jones v. Kodak Health Plan* (Part Two)? Is the court really suggesting that insurers should be held accountable when plan design itself is implicated in substandard care that leads to injury or death? Do you think that a state legislature would ever create a cause of action against an insurer—public or private—for "defects" in "design"?

2. *A whodunnit.* In *Wickline* the court focused more on the decisions made by individual physicians, including those acting for Medi–Cal, than it did on the manner in which the prospective utilization process was structured. Clearly, the process failed because Dr. Glassman did not get the information he needed, and the court pointed out that defects in the design and administration of utilization management could lead to payer liability. Ultimately, however, the court seemed to lay sole blame for the breakdown in communication on the treating physicians' failure to raise objections to Wickline's discharge. Is that the end of the story? What about the fact that the relevant form, the MC–180, was unsigned, that crucial fields were left blank, and that Dr. Glassman made his decision before even seeing it? Didn't FAX machines exist back then? What about the contents of the form? Was it up to the task of conveying the information needed for a patient like Wickline? What about Dr. Glassman's credentials as a reviewer? Was he competent to review Wickline's case? Why didn't he consult with a specialist?

These characteristics all might have created a basis for liability in this case were it not for Wickline's physicians' own conduct. In the end, the court absolves Medi–Cal from liability because Wickline's physicians did not complain, noting that reviewers like Dr. Glassman don't have time to contact treating physicians. Do you think Wickline's doctors had nothing but time on their hands? The court effectively allocates the sole responsibility to them, because they had the chance and the responsibility as her physicians to witness Medi–Cal's really shoddy practices and, based on those practices, fight for extra days or refuse to discharge her. In the end, it was her physicians who pronounced her good to go, not Medi–Cal.

Does this allocation of responsibility back to the treating physician at least implicitly set up a presumption that the reviewing entity's decision is correct unless the physician, as the "committed sponsor" of the patient, intervenes to pull back the curtains on the defects and errors? Given that the attending physicians are closest to the particular facts and circumstances of the case, doesn't the court get it backwards, that the treating physicians' recommendations should be presumed to be correct unless the reviewers contact them? Even so, one must ask oneself whether, even if the treating doctors were indisputably correct, they ultimately should bear the liability here because they stood by and acquiesced to what they knew to be a flawed discharge.

3.   In Frank v. Kizer, 261 Cal. Rptr. 882 (App. 1989), a state appellate court ordered the state Medi–Cal agency to comply with federal regulations requiring: (1) 10–day written notice to recipients before termination, reduction, or suspension of services; (2) inclusion in the written notice of the intended action, the reasons for the action, the specific regulation or law that supports the action, and an explanation of the recipient's right to a hearing and the circumstances under which Medicaid coverage is continued if a hearing is requested. The court stated that these federal regulations were adopted "in part to prevent a hasty or imprudent medical decision to terminate or reduce services lest serious injury to the patient result," and cited *Wickline* as a case which, although the state agency was exonerated, "presents a graphic example of harm to the recipient when the fiscal 'bottom-line' takes precedence over the medical needs of the recipient."

McEvoy v. Group Health Cooperative of Eau Claire

570 N.W.2d 397 (Wis. 1997)

■ ANN WALSH BRADLEY, J.:

Group Health Cooperative of Eau Claire, Inc. ("GHC"), a health maintenance organization, seeks review of a decision of the court of appeals that reversed the circuit court's entry of summary judgment dismissing Angela and Susan McEvoy's complaint. The court of appeals determined that the tort of bad faith can be applied to health maintenance organizations. GHC asserts that the tort of bad faith pertains only to insurance companies. In addition, GHC argues that its patient-related decisions are subject to the medical malpractice statute, Wis. Stat. ch. 655 (1991–92), which precludes any bad faith tort claims. Because we determine that the common law tort of bad faith applies to all health maintenance organizations making out-of-network benefit decisions and that Wis. Stat. ch. 655 does not preclude the McEvoys' claims, we affirm the decision of the court of appeals.

In the fall of 1991, 13–year–old Angela McEvoy began to suffer from anorexia nervosa, a potentially fatal eating disorder characterized by an aversion to food. At the time of diagnosis, Dr. Lawrence McFarlane of GHC was Angela's primary care physician. GHC insured Angela as a dependent of her mother, Susan McEvoy, a government employee and health care benefits policyholder. A portion of that policy required GHC to cover up to 70 days of inpatient psychological care.

GHC is a staff model health maintenance organization ("HMO") organized as a cooperative under Wis. Stat. ch. 185. It offers health care services to network participants through staff physicians that operate within GHC's clinics in Eau Claire, Wisconsin. When GHC is unable to care adequately for a network subscriber's health care needs, GHC refers its patients to out-of-network providers. Pursuant to the contractual terms of its subscriber's policy, GHC will pay for that out-of-network care up to the policy's limits.

After confirming his diagnosis of anorexia, McFarlane approached GHC's administration about referring Angela to the inpatient eating disorder program at the University of Minnesota Hospital ("UMH"). Neither GHC nor its network affiliates had previously treated a patient for anorexia nervosa.

Dr. Stuart Lancer, GHC's Medical Director, was responsible for GHC's cost containment programs and medical management. His approval was necessary for any staff physician referrals to out-of-network providers. At McFarlane's request, Lancer agreed that GHC would cover the cost of a two-week period of inpatient treatment for Angela at UMH. Lancer subsequently approved continued coverage that totaled an additional four weeks of inpatient care. He never personally met or treated Angela.

After six weeks of treatment by UMH physicians, Lancer decided to discontinue coverage of Angela's care at UMH. This decision was based on phone calls Lancer or members of his administrative staff had with individuals treating Angela at UMH. As one notation in GHC's records indicated: "SRL [Lancer] OK'ed thru Wed. Jan. 1st 1992 will be Angela's last day. Appt with Lloyd Thurs. (sic) NO MORE EXTENSIONS. SRL doesn't want to talk to them anymore. No excuses. Discharge, or no payment."

Both Angela's treating physician and her psychiatrist at UMH opposed Lancer's decision because Angela had not achieved UMH's established eating disorder treatment goals as of the time of discharge. UMH staff also objected to GHC's alternative treatment choice, placement in a newly-formed, in-network, Eau Claire outpatient group therapy session for compulsive overeaters that met only once a week. At the time of Lancer's termination of coverage order, approximately four weeks of inpatient psychological care benefits remained under Angela's contract with GHC.

On December 31, 1991, Angela was discharged back into the care of GHC's network providers. Upon discharge she weighed 95 pounds. Lancer had no further involvement with Angela's care within the GHC network beyond occasionally receiving unsolicited copies of progress notes. Angela relapsed almost immediately. On February 27, 1992, GHC readmitted Angela to UMH's inpatient eating disorder program. At the time of readmission, she weighed 74 pounds.

GHC's coverage of Angela's inpatient psychological care at UMH terminated in late March, 1992. Upon termination of that financial coverage, Lancer's involvement in Angela's case ended. Angela remained at UMH and continued treatment at her own personal expense.[3]

Angela and her mother commenced an action against GHC in the circuit court of Eau Claire County, alleging that GHC "in breach of the

---

3. Angela and GHC later disputed whether the terms of her contract with GHC required that coverage terminate in late March of 1992. After beginning arbitration of this contract dispute, GHC offered Angela a settlement and agreed to pay for the remainder of her care during her second stay at UMH.

policy, and in bad faith, denied and threatened to deny Angela McEvoy coverage for her treatment and failed to authorize appropriate treatment.'' They demanded compensatory and punitive damages. GHC moved for summary judgment, arguing for dismissal of the suit on the grounds that the McEvoys' action was actually one for medical malpractice governed by Wis. Stat. ch. 655. The plaintiffs, in opposing the motion, pointed to the dual nature of GHC as both a health care provider and an insurer and argued for application of the tort of bad faith.

The question of whether HMOs can be sued by subscribers under the common law tort of bad faith traditionally applied to insurance companies is a question of first impression for this court and one that has not received significant discussion in other jurisdictions.[4] To properly resolve this issue, we must consider the rationale underlying our previous adoption of the common law tort of bad faith, the nature and purpose of HMOs, the legislature's pronouncements concerning the regulation and organization of HMOs, and the policy implications behind labeling HMOs as insurers under bad faith tort. These considerations convince us that for purposes of the application of the common law doctrine of bad faith, HMOs making out-of-network benefit decisions are insurers.

This court explicitly adopted the common law tort of bad faith as applied to first party claims under insurance contracts in Anderson v. Continental Ins. Co., 271 N.W.2d 368 (1978). Our adoption of this doctrine recognized that ''bad faith conduct by one party to a contract toward another is a tort separate and apart from a breach of contract per se'' and that separate damages may be recovered for this tort. The rationale underlying a bad faith cause of action is to encourage fair treatment of the insured and penalize unfair and corrupt insurance practices. By ensuring that the policyholder achieves the benefits of his or her bargain with the insurer, a bad faith cause of action helps to redress a bargaining power imbalance between parties to an insurance contract.

Next we consider the nature and purpose of HMOs. HMOs are modern health care entities that cover over 52.5 million Americans. Each HMO is a hybrid entity encompassing characteristics of both traditional health care providers and traditional insurers in such a way as to encourage a restrained use of available health care resources. HMOs currently exist in three forms. Under a staff model HMO, the HMO employs its own doctors as salaried employees and runs its own delivery facilities such as hospitals and clinics. In a group model HMO, alternatively known as a network HMO, the HMO owns its own facilities, but establishes network health care delivery contracts with individual physicians and physician practice groups that continue to provide fee-for-services care to non-plan participants. Finally, in an Independent Practice Association (''IPA'') HMO, the HMO contracts with an Independent Practice Association (a partnership or

4. See, e.g., Williams v. HealthAmerica, 535 N.E.2d 717, 719–21 (1987) (reversing circuit court's grant of summary judgment to HMO based on plaintiff's claims of bad faith since issues of material fact remained); Rederscheid v. Comprecare, Inc., 667 P.2d 766, 767 (Colo. Ct. App. 1983) (reinstating plaintiff's bad faith tort claim against an HMO as an insurer).

cooperative composed of physicians) which in turn has contracted with groups of individual physicians. The individual providers affiliated with an HMO are part of its health care network. Where such network physicians are not equipped to provide necessary medical care to a subscriber, the HMO, pursuant to its contract, may authorize coverage for payment for out-of-network treatment. HMOs, like insurance companies, may also place contractual limits on their liability for unapproved care.

In the course of the contractual relationship between the HMO and subscriber, a power imbalance similar to that between a classical insurer and policyholder exists. An HMO subscriber has little effective negotiating power since policy terms, like those in insurance contracts, are usually prepackaged and subject to a significant number of regulations and rules. When faced with a problem, HMO subscribers, like many insurance policy-holders, may encounter bureaucratic or procedural hurdles in asserting their contractual health care rights. As a practical matter, HMO subscribers are similarly situated vis-à-vis their HMOs as insurance policyholders are to their more traditional insurance companies.

A review of legislative declarations in the Wisconsin statutes specifically applicable to GHC supports our general characterization of HMOs as insurers for bad faith purposes. Like traditional insurance companies, HMOs are required to establish contracts with subscribers with set terms of coverage. See Wis. Stat. § 185.981(2). While staff model HMOs organized under Wis. Stat. ch. 185 may not be organized for the sole purpose of providing insurance, and may not enter indemnity contracts, those same HMOs may be authorized to engage in the insurance business. See Wis. Stat. § 185.981 & 601.04. Such HMOs are also subject to many of the same regulations as insurance companies. See Wis. Stat. § 185.983(1).[5] Moreover, Wis. Stat. § 600.03 defines "insurer" to include some HMOs. See Wis. Stat. § 600.03(23), (27). Wis. Stat. ch. 609 also gives the Office of the Commissioner of Insurance the power to regulate HMOs. Accordingly, based on the practical and legal similarities of HMOs and traditional insurance companies, we determine that the common law tort of bad faith applies to HMOs making out-of-network benefit decisions.

Public policy also supports our decision to equate HMOs and insurers for purposes of applying bad faith tort to HMOs. Research on the benefits of particular medical treatments to patient communities supports contentions by health care financing entities such as HMOs that some medical practices are wasteful. Through contractual arrangements with physicians and patients, HMOs are able to exert significant influence on, if not outright control over, the costs of treatment regimens administered to

5. While these HMOs are excused from compliance with many statutory insurance provisions, they are subject to significant regulation that parallels the insurance industry. They must comply with insurance statutory mandates concerning (but not limited to) certificates of authority, deposits and financial services, fees paid to and powers of the Commissioner of Insurance, required reports, and examination of affairs by the Commissioner of Insurance. For a list of provisions from which such HMOs are not exempt, consult Wis. Stat. § 185.983(1).

patients, thereby limiting waste. The fears attendant with such arrangements, however, revolve around the economic model of health care financiers focusing on reducing aggregate costs while failing to recognize and to protect adequately the medical needs of individual subscribers.

This fear is particularly acute in the present high-cost medical economy where an adverse benefits ruling means not just that the financier will not provide payment, but also that the medical care itself is effectively denied. The tort of bad faith was created to protect the insured from such harm. Because HMO subscribers are in an inferior position for enforcing their contractual health care rights, application of the tort of bad faith is an additional means of ensuring that HMOs do not give cost containment and utilization review such significant weight so as to disregard the legitimate medical needs of subscribers.

Based on the observations discussed above, and the fact situation as alleged in this case, we recognize that HMOs making out-of-network benefit decisions are insurers for purpose of application of the tort of bad faith. The question then becomes how to best distinguish between decisions made by an HMO employee that create liability for medical malpractice and those that place liability on HMOs for bad faith tort. Because HMOs by their nature are an amalgamation of characteristics from health care providers and insurers designed to reduce medical costs, this inquiry does not adhere well to bright line rules, particularly since cases will exist where a particular HMO action or omission may constitute both bad faith and malpractice. However, despite this difficulty, several boundaries can be applied to the inquiry.

First, we emphasize that it is not the case that all malpractice cases against HMO physicians may also be pursued under the guise of the tort of bad faith. The tort of bad faith is not designed to apply to classic malpractice cases arising from mistakes made by a health care provider in diagnosis or treatment. If a surgeon amputates the wrong leg, no claim for bad faith is established. If a primary care physician fails to order an effective diagnostic procedure through negligence or medical mistake, no claim for bad faith arises.

Second, the bad faith cause of action is not limited to decisions made by an HMO's medical director. The official capacity of the decision maker is not the touchstone of our bad faith inquiry. Rather, we are concerned with the underlying basis for any decision made by an HMO employee that effectively denies coverage for out-of-network care under a subscriber's contract where the weight of internal financial considerations overcomes concern for the subscriber's reasonably necessary medical care.

Third, the facts as alleged in this case present an excellent example of where a bad faith claim should survive a summary judgment motion. Where a staff model HMO refers a subscriber to an out-of-network provider pursuant to that subscriber's needs and contract with the HMO, and it is alleged that the HMO then denies reimbursement for that out-of-network care without an established reasonable basis (i.e., due to internal financial considerations), the HMO is acting purely as an insurer. Because the referral passes primary medical responsibility to the out-of-network provider, the HMO staff member reviewing coverage requests, absent a sufficient showing of participation in treatment, is making a nonmedical, coverage-related decision. Thus, the HMO should be held to the same level of responsibility for its actions as a traditional insurance company. The more closely a particular decision made by an HMO or HMO employee resembles coverage decisions made by traditional insurers, the more appropriate the tort of bad faith becomes.

Fourth, bad faith tort claims cannot arise in out-of-network provider situations unless an HMO unreasonably refuses to provide a service or cover payments to outside providers for which it is contractually obligated. Thus, an HMO insurer that denies payment for care because contractual coverage of such care is reasonably debatable cannot be held liable for bad faith tort.

Having acknowledged that reasonably debatable claims are not subject to bad faith, we find unconvincing GHC's contention that it was not required to pay for Angela's extended care since its contract required GHC's prior authorization for expenditures. Such unilateral authority would give GHC the sole power to determine when and to what extent it would be bound by its subscriber contracts. This unbridled discretion may subject such contracts to the argument that they are illusory. The HMO is under a contractual duty to provide or pay for reasonable services to remedy the subscriber's condition up to the subscriber's policy limits. Where an HMO authorizes a referral to an out-of-network provider, the HMO may not end that referral against the recommendation of the treating physicians solely on the basis of cost-containment concerns when the subscriber has not reached the contractual coverage limits. Thus, such an improper denial can constitute a bad faith denial under *Anderson* and the boundaries set out above.

Accordingly, in certain factual circumstances, bad faith claims may properly be maintained against HMOs. To prevail on a bad faith tort claim asserted against an HMO, a plaintiff must plead facts sufficient to show, upon objective review, i) the absence of a reasonable basis for the HMO to deny the plaintiff's claim for out-of-network coverage or care under his or her subscriber contract; and ii) that the HMO, in denying such a claim, either knew or recklessly failed to ascertain that the coverage or care should have been provided. A plaintiff must make this showing by evidence that is clear, satisfactory, and convincing.

An HMO, regardless of its organizational format, may be liable in bad faith when it has denied a request for out-of-network care or coverage without a reasonable basis. Such a bad faith cause of action may arise when an HMO refuses to consider a patient or physician request for care or coverage, if the HMO makes no reasonable investigation of a request for care or referral put to it, if the HMO conducts its evaluation of a care or coverage request in such a way as to prevent it from learning the true facts upon which the plaintiff's claims are based, or if, as the plaintiffs allege in this case, the HMO conducts its evaluation of a request and bases its decision primarily on internal cost-containment mechanisms, despite a demonstrated medical need and a contractual obligation. When a bad faith breach occurs, the HMO is liable for any damages which are the proximate result of that breach. Unlike in medical malpractice cases, punitive damages may be demanded for bad faith where the defendant is guilty not only of bad faith, but also of "oppression, fraud, or malice."

We do not apply the bad faith tort doctrine to HMOs so as to give HMO subscribers carte blanche authority to demand out-of-network treatments or diagnostic procedures beyond what a physician, in exercising his or her medical judgment, finds reasonably necessary. Rather, because bad faith actions are designed to give a weaker party to a contract the benefit of the bargain, we think bad faith actions may arise where the plaintiff is able to show by clear, satisfactory, and convincing evidence that an HMO acted improperly and that financial considerations were given unreasonable weight in the decision maker's cost-benefit analysis.[6]

Notes

1. *Split accountability. McEvoy* clarifies that under Wisconsin law, an HMO essentially wears two hats and thus can face two distinct types of liability. In its role as a provider of health care, a Wisconsin HMO is subject to state medical liability law through its physicians (and presumably through its hospitals and other network providers). As you will see below, both vicarious and corporate liability theories would be relevant, depending on the law of the state. On the other hand, when the HMO acts as an insurer, it can face liability as would any other insurer in the state for conduct judged to amount to bad faith claims administration.

HMOs have often argued that they are medical providers and thus insulated from laws regulating insurers. Following McEvoy, in Rush Prudential HMO Inc. v. Moran, 536 U.S. 355 (2002), the HMO industry made a losing argument to the Supreme Court that state laws regulating HMO practices (specifically their obligation to submit to an external review of certain coverage denials) could not be saved as laws regulating insurance under ERISA's preemption statute, ERISA § 514(b)(2)(A). Taking a "commonsense" view, Justice Souter, writing for the majority, noted that in

---

6. In rendering this decision, we are cognizant of the limitations placed upon the scope of our ruling by [ERISA]. ERISA specifically preempts all state court claims that "relate to" covered employee benefit plans (which include most private employer health care plans). See 29 U.S.C. § 1144. The Supreme Court, in Pilot Life Insurance Co. v. Dedeaux, 481 U.S. 41, 51 (1987), held that state common law causes of action, such as the insurance tort of bad faith, sufficiently "relate to" employee benefits plans to fall under ERISA preemption. Thus our conclusion that the tort of bad faith is applicable to HMOs reaches only a small portion of Wisconsin's populace—those HMO subscribers who either receive health care benefits as part of an ERISA-exempt plan or else purchase their subscription plans individually. The McEvoys' claims are not preempted in this case because Mrs. McEvoy receives her insurance plan as an employee benefit from a government employer. See 29 U.S.C. § 1003(b). Nevertheless, because we recognize the similarity between HMOs and insurance companies and the protective benefits of the bad faith doctrine, we apply the common law doctrine of bad faith tort to those HMO contracts that we can reach.

enacting the HMO Act of 1973, Congress expressly recognized that it was creating a new type of entity that would act both as a licensed insurer under state law, even as it also provided health care:

Rush contends that seeing an HMO as an insurer distorts the nature of an HMO, which is, after all, a health care provider, too. This, Rush argues, should determine its characterization, with the consequence that regulation of an HMO is not insurance regulation within the meaning of ERISA. The answer to Rush is, of course, that an HMO is both: it provides health care, and it does so as an insurer. Nothing in the saving clause requires an either-or choice between health care and insurance in deciding a preemption question, and as long as providing insurance fairly accounts for the application of state law, the saving clause may apply. There is no serious question about that here, for it would ignore the whole purpose of the HMO-style of organization to conceive of HMOs without their insurance element.

"The defining feature of an HMO is receipt of a fixed fee for each patient enrolled under the terms of a contract to provide specified health care if needed." *Pegram v. Herdrich,* 530 U.S. 211 (2000). "The HMO thus assumes the financial risk of providing the benefits promised: if a participant never gets sick, the HMO keeps the money regardless, and if a participant becomes expensively ill, the HMO is responsible for the treatment...." *Id.* at 218–219. The HMOs actually underwrite and spread risk among their participants, a feature distinctive to insurance.

So Congress has understood from the start, when the phrase "Health Maintenance Organization" was established and defined in the HMO Act of 1973. The Act was intended to encourage the development of HMOs as a new form of health care delivery system, see S. Rep. No. 93–129, pp. 7–9 (1973), and when Congress set the standards that the new health delivery organizations would have to meet to get certain federal benefits, the terms included requirements that the organizations bear and manage risk. See, *e.g.,* Health Maintenance Organization Act of 1973, § 1301(c), 87 Stat. 916, as amended, 42 U.S.C. § 300e(c); S. Rep. No. 93–129, at 14 (explaining that HMOs necessarily bear some of the risk of providing service, and requiring that a qualifying HMO "assum[e] direct financial responsibility, without benefit of reinsurance, for care . . . in excess of the first five thousand dollars per enrollee per year"). The Senate Committee Report explained that federally qualified HMOs would be required to provide "a basic package of benefits, consistent with existing health insurance patterns," *id.* at 10, and the very text of the Act assumed that state insurance laws would apply to HMOs; it provided that to the extent state insurance capitalization and reserve requirements were too stringent to permit the formation of HMOs, "qualified" HMOs would be exempt from such limiting regulation. See § 1311, 42 U.S.C. § 300e–

10. This congressional understanding that it was promoting a novel form of insurance was made explicit in the Senate Report's reference to the practices of "health insurers to charge premium rates based upon the actual claims experience of a particular group of subscribers," thus "raising costs and diminishing the availability of health insurance for those suffering from costly illnesses," S. Rep. No. 93–129, at 29–30. The federal Act responded to this insurance practice by requiring qualifying HMOs to adopt uniform capitation rates, see § 1301(b), 42 U.S.C. § 300e(b), and it was because of that mandate "pos[ing] substantial competitive problems to newly emerging HMOs," S. Rep. No. 93–129, at 30, that Congress authorized funding subsidies, see § 1304, 42 U.S.C. § 300e–4. In other words, one year before it passed ERISA, Congress itself defined HMOs in part by reference to risk, set minimum standards for managing the risk, showed awareness that States regulated HMOs as insurers, and compared HMOs to "indemnity or service benefits insurance plans."

This conception has not changed in the intervening years. Since passage of the federal Act, States have been adopting their own HMO enabling Acts, and today, at least 40 of them, including Illinois, regulate HMOs primarily through the States' insurance departments, although they may be treated differently from traditional insurers, owing to their additional role as health care providers. Finally, this view shared by Congress and the States has passed into common understanding. HMOs (broadly defined) have "grown explosively in the past decade and [are] now the dominant form of health plan coverage for privately insured individuals." Gold & Hurley, The Role of Managed Care "Products" in Managed Care "Plans," in Contemporary Managed Care 47 (M. Gold ed. 1998). While the original form of the HMO was a single corporation employing its own physicians, the 1980's saw a variety of other types of structures develop even as traditional insurers altered their own plans by adopting HMO-like cost-control measures. See Weiner & de Lissovoy, Razing a Tower of Babel: A Taxonomy for Managed Care and Health Insurance Plans, 18 J. of Health Politics, Policy and Law 75, 83 (Spring 1993). The dominant feature is the combination of insurer and provider. R. Rosenblatt, S. Law, & S. Rosenbaum, Law and the American Health Care System 552 (1997). Rush cannot checkmate common sense by trying to submerge HMOs' insurance features beneath an exclusive characterization of HMOs as providers of health care.

536 U.S. at 367–69:

2. *When does the bad faith breach of contract theory apply to HMOs?* In attempting to delineate the situations in which a plaintiff could pursue a bad faith breach of contract claim against an HMO, the court in *McEvoy* framed the issue as an in-versus-out-of-network one:

Where a staff model HMO refers a subscriber to an out-of-network provider pursuant to that subscriber's needs and contract with the

HMO, and it is alleged that the HMO then denies reimbursement for that out-of-network care without an established reasonable basis (i.e., due to internal financial considerations), the HMO is acting purely as an insurer. Because the referral passes primary medical responsibility to the out-of-network provider, the HMO staff member reviewing coverage requests, absent a sufficient showing of participation in treatment, is making a nonmedical, coverage-related decision. Thus, the HMO should be held to the same level of responsibility for its actions as a traditional insurance company. The more closely a particular decision made by an HMO or HMO employee resembles coverage decisions made by traditional insurers, the more appropriate the tort of bad faith becomes.

Does this delineation make sense to you? Should the court have assumed complete integration between the decisions of HMO in-network providers and those of the utilization management staff? What if a network provider wanted to furnish extra care to Angela McEvoy and the utilization management staff declared without reasoning that enough was enough and treatment was over? Isn't the issue more nuanced than simply in-versus-out of network in all but the most tightly integrated staff model HMOs, where the financing function is essentially conceptualized as an aspect of medical practice itself? Talk to most HMO physicians and they will tell you that even in tightly structured HMOs where maximum integration is sought between treatment and resources, there are tensions between the payment and practice functions of the HMO.

On the other hand, think of the earlier materials in this Part and Part Two, which reviewed the question of integrating financing and health care into more highly structured entities whose performance is continuously measured in order to promote quality, efficiency, and accountability. If this is a sensible aspiration in a health care system overwhelmed by both high cost and care of questionable quality, then should public policy promote the growth of tightly integrated HMOs by holding them to institutional quality standards while sparing them exposure to the full impact of a bad faith breach of contract claim when their decisions cause harm? Can one both integrate finance and delivery and then separate them as the court in *McEvoy* tried to do?

---

3. LIABILITY FOR MEDICAL INJURIES ARISING FROM HEALTH CARE NEGLIGENCE

a. Vicarious Liability and Agency

Boyd v. Albert Einstein Medical Center

547 A.2d 1229 (Pa. Super. 1988)

■ OLSZEWSKI, J.:

Appellant asserts that the trial court erred in granting the motion for summary judgment when there existed a question of material fact as to whether participating physicians are the ostensible agents of HMO.

Decedent's husband became eligible for participation in a group plan provided by HMO through his employer. Upon electing to participate in this plan, decedent and her husband were provided with a directory and benefits brochure which listed the participating physicians. Restricted to selecting a physician from this list, decedent chose Doctor David Rosenthal and Doctor Perry Dornstein as her primary care physicians.

In June of 1982, decedent contacted Doctor David Rosenthal regarding a lump in her breast. Doctor Rosenthal ordered a mammogram to be performed which revealed a suspicious area in the breast. Doctor Rosenthal recommended that decedent undergo a biopsy and referred decedent to Doctor Erwin Cohen for that purpose. Doctor Cohen, a surgeon, is also a participating HMO physician. The referral to a specialist in this case was made in accordance with the terms and conditions of HMO's subscription agreement.[2]

On July 6, 1982, Doctor Cohen performed a biopsy of decedent's breast tissue at Albert Einstein Medical Center. During the procedure, Doctor Cohen perforated decedent's chest wall with the biopsy needle, causing decedent to sustain a left hemothorax. Decedent was hospitalized for treatment of the hemothorax at Albert Einstein Hospital for two days.

In the weeks following this incident decedent complained to her primary care physicians, Doctor David Rosenthal and Doctor Perry Dornstein, of pain in her chest wall, belching, hiccoughs, and fatigue. On August 19, 1982, decedent awoke with pain in the middle of her chest. Decedent's husband contacted her primary care physicians, Doctors Rosenthal and Dornstein, and was advised to take decedent to Albert Einstein hospital where she would be examined by Doctor Rosenthal. Upon arrival at Albert Einstein emergency room, decedent related symptoms of chest wall pain, vomiting, stomach and back discomfort to Doctor Rosenthal. Doctor Rosenthal commenced an examination of decedent, diagnosed Tietz's syndrome [an inflammatory condition], and arranged for tests to be performed at his office where decedent underwent x-rays, EKG, and cardiac isoenzyme tests.[4] Decedent was then sent home and told to rest.

During the course of that afternoon, decedent continued to experience chest pain, vomiting and belching. Decedent related the persistence and worsening of these symptoms by telephone to Doctors Rosenthal and Dornstein, who prescribed, without further examination, Talwin, a pain medication. At 5:30 that afternoon decedent was discovered dead in her

---

2. Doctor Rosenthal admitted in his deposition that HMO limited specifically the doctors to whom decedent could have been referred.

4. HMO avers that decedent was returned to the doctor's office for testing because it was more comfortable and convenient for her. Appellant, however, asserts that the tests were performed in the doctor's office, rather than the hospital, in accordance with the requirements of HMO whose primary interest was in keeping the medical fees within the corporation.

bathroom by her husband, having expired as a result of a myocardial infarction.

The group master contract provides that HMO "operates a comprehensive prepaid program of health care which provides health care services and benefits to Members in order to protect and promote their health, and preserve and enhance patient dignity." HMO was incorporated in 1975 under the laws of Pennsylvania and converted from a non-profit to a for-profit corporation in 1981. HMO is based on the individual practice association model (hereinafter IPA), which means that HMO is comprised of participating primary physicians who are engaged in part in private practice in the HMO service area. Under the plan, IPA contracts with HMO to provide medical services to HMO members. IPA selects its primary and specialist physicians and enters into an agreement with them obligating the physician to perform health services for the subscribers of HMO.

When an interested physician calls the IPA, the Provider relations representative reviews the physician's credentials and the reasons for his interest in HMO. The physician then subsequently receives an application packet that requests the applicant's curriculum vitae, four letters of recommendation, copies of the state license, and evidence of malpractice insurance. Soon thereafter, the IPA coordinator visits the applicant's practice in order to: (1) observe how the office is run, how the office personnel treat patients, and the ability of the office to absorb a number of new patients; (2) inspect the actual physical plant to ensure that appropriate procedures, space, and necessary medical equipment are available; (3) explain the payment system, the incentive program, and the rights and responsibilities of an IPA physician; and (4) set up a medical director's interview.

After interviewing the applicant,[8] the medical director makes a recommendation that is forwarded to the membership committee, which thoroughly discusses and determines whether the applicant has met all the criteria for membership. The criteria include: Twenty-four-hour-a-day coverage provided with another IPA member for office and hospital patients, with any exclusions being approved by the executive committee; prior routine hospitalization of patients on his own service at a participating HMO hospital; specific routinely performed procedures including minor surgery and office gynecology; scheduling of appointments at a rate of no more than five patients per hour per doctor; and office records that are legible, reproducible, and pertinent.

The membership committee makes a recommendation to the executive committee, which makes the final decision regarding the applicant. Those accepted into the IPA are called by an IPA coordinator, who schedules an office orientation.

The primary physician's role is defined as the "gatekeeper into the health care delivery system." "An HMO member must consult with his

---

8. During the interview, the medical director reviews applicant's understanding of the HMO and IPA, the physician's referral pattern, how he would handle various medical problems, and his medical charts.

primary physician before going to a specialist and/or the hospital." If the primary physician deems it necessary, he arranges a consultation with an HMO participating specialist, which constitutes a second opinion. "Basically, with the primary physicians 'screening' the members' illnesses, excessive hospitalization and improper use of specialists can be reduced."

Primary physicians are paid through a mechanism termed "capitation." Capitation is an actuarially determined amount prepaid by HMO to the primary physician for each patient who has chosen his office. The dollar amount is based upon a pre-determined rate per age group. The primary physicians are paid 80% of the capitation amount and the remaining 20% is pooled by IPA and goes back into a pooled risk-sharing fund as a reserve against specialty referral costs and hospital stays. Each primary care office has its own specialist fund and hospital fund established by allocating a pre-determined amount each month for each member who has chosen that primary care office. The surplus from the specialist fund is returned to the primary care office. The hospital fund, however, is governed by a hospital risk/incentive-sharing scheme which anticipates a number of inpatient days per members per year. If the actual hospital utilization is less than anticipated, the HMO and IPA each receive 50% of the savings. IPA must place the savings in the Special IPA risk-sharing account and must use the funds to offset losses resulting from unanticipated physician costs. If utilization is greater than anticipated, IPA is responsible for 50% of the loss up to the amount of uncommitted funds in the Special IPA risk sharing account.

Appellant asserts that he has raised a question of material fact as to whether the treating physicians were the ostensible agents of HMO. Pennsylvania courts have determined that the two factors relevant to a finding of ostensible agency are: (1) whether the patient looks to the institution, rather than the individual physician for care, and (2) whether the HMO "holds out" the physician as its employee.

HMO asserts that because the theory of ostensible agency has been applied in Pennsylvania only to the relationship between hospitals and independent contractor physicians, the theory is not appropriate in the instant situation. [H]owever, when this Court introduced the concept of ostensible agency [with respect to hospitals] we based that decision in large part upon "the changing role of the hospital in society [which] creates a likelihood that patients will look to the institution" for care. Because the role of health care providers has changed in recent years, the rationale for applying the theory of ostensible agency to hospitals is certainly applicable in the instant situation.

We find that the facts indicate an issue of material fact as to whether the participating physicians were the ostensible agents of HMO. HMO covenanted that it would "[provide] health care services and benefits to Members in order to protect and promote their health." "HMO PA operates on a direct service rather than an indemnity basis." Appellant paid his doctor's fee to HMO, not to the physician of his choice. Then, appellant selected his primary care physicians from the list provided by HMO.

Regardless of who recommended appellant's decedent to choose her primary care physician, the fact remains that HMO provides a limited list from which a member must choose a primary physician. Moreover, those primary physicians are screened by HMO and must comply with a list of regulations in order to honor their contract with HMO.

Further, as mandated by HMO, appellant's decedent could not see a specialist without the primary physician's referral. As HMO declares, the primary physician is the "gatekeeper into the health care delivery system." [Thus] appellant's decedent had no choice as to which specialist to see. In our opinion, because appellant's decedent was required to follow the mandates of HMO and did not directly seek the attention of the specialist, there is an inference that appellant looked to the institution for care and not solely to the physicians; conversely, that appellant's decedent submitted herself to the care of the participating physicians in response to an invitation from HMO.

Notes

1. *The ambiguity of Boyd.* There appears to be a core ambiguity in the *Boyd* opinion. The court spends a great deal of time—much of it not included in this edited opinion—demonstrating that the HMO exercises significant supervision and control over the participating physicians. The main evidence comes from physician manuals and other documents internal to the HMO about which patients are presumably unaware. All of this is relevant to showing that the doctors are actual agents of the HMO, because the HMO exercises de facto supervision and control over them, regardless of how their relationship is formally characterized. But neither the plaintiff nor the court focuses on actual agency, but rather on ostensible agency. As the court points out, the key to ostensible agency is whether the patient is (reasonably) "looking to" the HMO rather than the individual doctor as the provider of care, and whether the HMO has "held out" the physician as its employee or agent. As to these factors, the record is much less clear. Here is some of the evidence discussed by the court but not included in the edited opinion above:

> The record reflects that, through his employer, appellant became eligible for and ultimately chose to participate in a group plan provided by the Health Maintenance Organization of Pennsylvania (hereinafter HMO).[6] As part of its services, HMO provided its members with a brochure explaining, in general outline form only, the main features of the program of benefits. The brochure

---

6. In a document entitled "Why offer HMO–PA?," HMO reasoned to employers that HMO "is a total care program which not only insures its subscribers, but provides medical care, guarantees the quality of the care and controls the costs of health care services." The document also claimed that "HMO–PA is more than just another health insurance plan. HMO–PA is an entire health care system. HMO–PA provides the physicians, hospitals and other health professionals needed to maintain good health. HMO–PA assures complete security, when illness or injury arises." Finally, the document provided that HMO–PA "[a]ssumes responsibility for quality and accessibility."

also provided a directory of participating primary physicians and declared that the complete terms and conditions of the plan were set forth in the group master contract.

The group master contract provides that HMO "operates a comprehensive prepaid program of health care which provides health care services and benefits to Members in order to protect and promote their health, and preserve and enhance patient dignity."[7]

547 A.2d at 1232.

It is apparent from the above that the HMO's "holding out" of its "total care program" was done in material directed to employers, and in the "group master contract." Did the patient or her husband ever see these documents, much less rely on them? Of course, it is possible that this employee may have asked to see the group master contract, but no such allegation was reported in the opinion. Alternatively, the court might have developed a "surrogate ostensible agency doctrine," where a principal may be held liable to an ultimate consumer if the principal holds out an agent to the consumer's own agent, i.e., the employer who chooses which health plan to offer.

Notwithstanding the HMO's statements quoted above, which are unlikely to have been seen by the patient, it is not clear how much "holding out" there is in an HMO of the IPA type. Unlike the staff-model HMO, the patient does not go to an HMO building or office, and may not encounter literature or other material associating the HMO with the direct care. Rather, after selecting the primary care doctor from the HMO list, doctor-patient encounters may appear similar to those in the traditional indemnity model: at the doctor's private office, with little or no visible presence of the HMO as an entity. How true this is may vary among HMOs, but at least one would expect this to be an issue of contention for a court following classic ostensible agency theory. Yet none of this appears in the *Boyd* opinion.

The *Boyd* court makes much of the fact that the HMO restricts the choice of primary care physicians to those from a list. But what if the list contains dozens or even a hundred choices? What if the patient actually chose the doctor on the basis of a friend's advice, just the way she might have done in an indemnity system? Could the HMO have shown that the patient actually regarded the HMO not as a provider of care, but rather as another type of insurance company? Since this was a reversal of a summary judgment ruling, presumably these issues might have been explored at the trial.

The point is not that *Boyd* was wrongly decided, but that the court's reliance on the doctrine of ostensible agency was factually questionable. This problem becomes clear when one compares cases like Chase v. Inde-

---

7. The introduction to the group master contract also provides that "HMOPA operates on a direct service rather than indemnity basis. The interpretation of the Contract shall be guided by the direct service nature of HMOPA's prepaid program."

pendent Practice Association, Inc., 583 N.E.2d 251 (Mass. App. 1991), described below, and McClellan v. Health Maintenance Organization of Pennsylvania, reprinted below. *See also* Dunn v. Praiss, 606 A.2d 862 (N.J. Super. A.D. 1992) (finding physician to be an actual, not merely apparent, agent of HMO when, inter alia, physician is paid on a capitation basis, is not free to reject HMO-referred patients, and examines patients at HMO's office).

2. *Justifiable reliance.* In Petrovich v. Share Health Plan of Illinois, Inc., 719 N.E.2d 756 (Ill. 1999), the Illinois Supreme Court held that an HMO could be held vicariously liable under the doctrine of "apparent authority" for the acts of its independent contractor physicians. Important to the court was the fact that the patient's employer had offered its employees only one health plan. The HMO therefore argued that the patient had not "relied" on any representation by the HMO, because the patient had only one choice within the employment-based plan. The court analyzed this issue as follows:

B.   Justifiable Reliance

A plaintiff must also prove the element of "justifiable reliance" to establish apparent authority against an HMO for physician malpractice. The element of justifiable reliance is met where the plaintiff relies upon the HMO to provide health care services, and does not rely upon a specific physician. This element is not met if the plaintiff selects his or her own personal physician and merely looks to the HMO as a conduit through which the plaintiff receives medical care.

Share maintains that plaintiff cannot establish the justifiable reliance element because she did not select Share. Share argues that, unless the plaintiff actually selects the HMO, there is no reliance upon the HMO and thus no nexus between the HMO's alleged wrongful conduct and the plaintiff's injury. Share takes the position that, if a person did not select the HMO, then that person can never claim apparent agency, regardless of what the HMO does, says or leads the person to believe.

We reject Share's argument. It is true that, where a person selects the HMO and does not rely upon a specific physician, then that person is relying upon the HMO to provide health care. Equally true, however, is that where a person has no choice but to enroll with a single HMO and does not rely upon a specific physician, then that person is likewise relying upon the HMO to provide health care.

In the present case, the record discloses that plaintiff did not select Share. Plaintiff's employer selected Share for her. Plaintiff had no choice of health plans whatsoever. Once Share became plaintiff's health plan, Share required plaintiff to obtain her primary medical care from one of its primary care physicians. If plaintiff did not do so, Share did not cover plaintiff's medical costs.

In accordance with Share's requirement, plaintiff selected Dr. Kowalski from a list of physicians that Share provided to her. Plaintiff had no prior relationship with Dr. Kowalski. As to Dr. Kowalski's selection of Dr. Friedman [the specialist] for plaintiff, Share required Dr. Kowalski to make referrals only to physicians approved by Share. Plaintiff had no prior relationship with Dr. Friedman. We hold that these facts are sufficient to raise the reasonable inference that plaintiff relied upon Share to provide her health care services.

Were we to conclude that plaintiff was not relying upon Share for health care, we would be denying the true nature of the relationship among plaintiff, her HMO and the physicians. Share, like many HMOs, contracted with plaintiff's employer to become plaintiff's sole provider of health care, to the exclusion of all other providers. Share then restricted plaintiff to its chosen physicians. Under these facts, plaintiff's reliance on Share as the provider of her health care is shown not only to be compelling, but literally compelled. Plaintiff's reliance upon Share was inherent in Share's method of operation.

719 N.E.2d at 768–69.

3. *The impact of corporate practice of medicine laws on agency theory.* In Williams v. Good Health Plus, Inc., 743 S.W.2d 373 (Tex. App. 1987), the court held that because of the corporate practice of medicine doctrine, an HMO could not as a matter of law hold itself out as providing medical care, and hence could not be held liable under apparent agency. Moreover, because of that doctrine and the actual agreement between the HMO and its physician group, the physicians were independent contractors in the provision of medical services for whom the HMO could not be liable on any theory of agency or respondeat superior.

4. *Agency theory in multi-layered contractual arrangements.* Hybrid entities that combine coverage and care frequently, as noted in *McEvoy*, build their systems through layers of contractual arrangements, by entering into agreements with Independent Practice Associations (IPAs) that in turn contract with medical groups. These layered arrangements can lead to a down-streaming of liability away from the parent and toward the individual physician or medical group. In *Chase*, 583 N.E.2d 251 (Mass. App. 1991) the facts involved injury to a patient who received her care from physicians practicing in an IPA, which in turn contracted with individual medical groups and sold its collection of physician and group practice services to the patient's HMO. In the case, the court found that the IPA could not be held vicariously liable for the negligence of one of its physicians, Dr. Kaufman, in failing to administer certain tests to plaintiff Rae Ann Chase, whose baby subsequently was born with cerebral palsy and retardation.

The plaintiff was a member of an HMO (Valley Health Plan, (VHP)) that contracted with the IPA. The contract provided that the IPA would "have the sole and exclusive right and obligation to select, negotiate with, and arrange for, each and every individual, group and organization who, or whose employees, may become and continue to be an IPA Health Professional." VHP paid the IPA a monthly capitation rate and retained the right to review the quality of the IPA's care. At the same time, the IPA was required to monitor its staff for over-and under-utilization and provide continuing education to its members. The obstetrical group practice of which the treating physician was a member was, in turn, a contractor to the IPA and likewise was paid on a monthly capitation basis. The contract clarified that the "relationship of the parties was to be that of purchaser (IPA) and provider" and that neither would be "the agent or representative of the other, nor shall either party have any express or implied right or authority to assume or create any obligation on behalf of or in the name of the other." Supervision of the physicians was carried out by the group practice, not the IPA. As a result, the court concluded that "the plaintiff would be unable to prove at trial that any negligence on the part of Dr. Kaufman or [the group practice] was attributable to IPA by virtue of its contractual arrangements with VHP or the [obstetrical group]."

Unlike the HMO in [Gugino v. Harvard Community Health Plan, 380 Mass. 464 (1980)], [the HMO] did not employ physicians directly. Instead, it contracted with IPA to arrange for medical services to its members. IPA in turn contracted with [the obstetrical group] who in turn employed Dr. Kaufman. IPA does not pay any physician employees and functions in effect as a third-party broker, arranging for services on behalf of VHP members.

IPA is also not liable under a theory of "ostensible" or "apparent" agency. Other courts which have considered this theory in a medical malpractice context have found that an HMO may be liable if the HMO creates an appearance that the physician is its employee, regardless of a physician's actual status. See, e.g., Boyd v. Albert Einstein Med. Center.

There is no factual basis in this record to support a theory of ostensible agency. Ms. Chase's membership agreement with VHP defines IPA as "a corporation formed to arrange for professional health services for members having contracts with [VHP] and other health professionals to provide such services." Standing alone, Ms. Chase's statement in her affidavit that she was not "made aware that doctors that were providing her prenatal care were not employees of [VHP]" is insufficient to raise a claim of ostensible agency. Moreover, Ms. Chase does not allege that she believed Dr. Kaufman or [the obstetrical group] were employees or agents of IPA, only that she was not aware they were not employees of VHP. In order to hold IPA liable under an ostensible agency theory, there would have to be a showing of reliance on representations by IPA, that Dr. Kaufman and HCGO were its agents or employees. The plaintiffs do not allege that such representations were made by IPA and they therefore cannot prevail on this claim.

Summary judgment was properly granted in favor of the defendant IPA.[9]

583 N.E.2d at 254–56.

Think about the consequences of this layer-cake arrangement, particularly for a patient battling medical negligence in a health care system that functions through a cascade of contracts knitting one layer of management to the next. The court finds that the obstetrical group is the only entity in control of Dr. Kaufman and the other physicians in the group. So, Chase can't sue up the managed-care food chain on a theory of actual control and is thrown back into ostensible agency. The court rejects that the IPA had apparent authority over the practice group because Chase could show only that she did not know that the physicians weren't employees of VHP, the HMO. The court says that there must be some affirmative representations that would set up a reliance interest. How likely is that in this sort of arrangement with multiple layers of brokering? Would you have any idea, when you see your doctor, who actually has an ownership or controlling interest in her practice? You might know that the doctor is part of a group, but you typically would have no way of knowing that the group is part of a multi-group network whose management, like farmworker labor jobbers, sells services to big insurers and self-insured plans. What normal patient would be aware that various entities exist in packaging the whole network together or that the medical care is or is not controlled by the HMO or the IPA? How does that affect her ability to establish that representations were made and reliance evoked, and against whom could those claims be asserted? Conceivably a court could rely on evidence such as the master agreement that was the subject of review in *Boyd*, but remember our discussion in the notes after *Boyd* that for the most part, the evidence relied on by the court in *Boyd* all went to actual, not ostensible, agency. The layer-cake in *Chase* is reminiscent of the "faceless bureaucracy" in which no one has any authority because authority is so defuse.

b.   Corporate Liability

McClellan v. Health Maintenance Organization of Pennsylvania

604 A.2d 1053 (Pa. Super. 1992)

■ McEwen, Judge:

Marilyn McClellan, appellants' decedent, a 39–year–old teacher employed by the School District of Philadelphia, was the wife of appellant Ronald M. McClellan and the mother of three young children. Sometime

---

9. The facts of this case, together with the continuing growth of HMOs and the increasing complexity of the health care industry, might suggest another case in which a health insurance entity attempts, by raising multiple layers of corporate and contractual relationships, to escape accountability for the negligence of physicians and other health care providers, to whom they direct their members or subscribers for care. This, however, is not that case.

prior to June of 1985 Marilyn McClellan contracted, through her employer, the School District of Philadelphia, with Health Maintenance Organization of Pennsylvania, an HMO operated by appellees, for health care coverage for herself and her family.

HMOs, authorized by the Health Maintenance Organization Act, 40 P.S. §§ 1551 *et seq.,* are defined as "an organized system which combines the delivery and financing of health care and which provides basic health services to voluntarily enrolled subscribers for a fixed prepaid fee." 40 P.S. § 1553. Appellees allege in their brief that HMO PA is a modified IPA model HMO[2] "in which the HMO contracts with the independent, private physicians as independent contractors." A primary care physician is assigned to each subscriber and is the "physician who supervises, coordinates, and provides initial and basic care to members; initiates their referral for specialist care; and maintains continuity of patient care." 28 Pa. Code § 9.2.

Marilyn McClellan selected Joseph A. Hempsey, D.O., as her family's primary care physician from the list of participating physicians provided by HMO of Pennsylvania. Appellants allege that Dr. Hempsey removed a mole from Mrs. McClellan's back on October 28, 1985, and, even though Mrs. McClellan had related to Dr. Hempsey that the mole had recently undergone a marked change in size and color, Dr. Hempsey discarded the mole without obtaining a biopsy or other histological exam. Appellants claim that as a result of Dr. Hempsey's failure to submit the tissue sample for testing, Mrs. McClellan's malignant melanoma was not timely diagnosed or treated, and Mrs. McClellan died on January 1, 1988.

Appellants commenced a medical malpractice action against Dr. Hempsey, and later instituted suit against appellees [HMO of PA], alleging that the negligence of appellees in selecting and retaining Dr. Hempsey as a primary care physician contributed to the condition which caused the death of Mrs. McClellan. Appellants also sought to hold appellees liable for breach of contract and misrepresentation based upon the express representations made by appellees concerning the competency of their primary care physicians and the availability to subscribers of consultation and treatment by medical specialists whenever warranted through primary care physician referrals. The trial court sustained the demurrer and this appeal timely followed.[6]

---

2. An individual practice association (IPA) HMO is defined as "an HMO that contracts for delivery of services with a partnership, corporation, or association whose major objective is to enter into contractual arrangements with health professionals for the delivery of such health services." 28 Pa. Code § 9.2

6. Appellants include in their complaint an allegation that the agreements between appellees and their "primary care physicians" are themselves tortious since it is "against the 'primary care physician's' personal or pecuniary interest to give proper medical advice and make appropriate referral." This allegation suggests as issues whether the essential elements of the HMO system violate public policy, and whether the HMO system itself contributed to the asserted malpractice in this case. It is settled beyond peradventure, however, that the judicial branch is precluded by constitutional mandate from addressing the ethical, moral, or social implications of a health care program which indirectly provides a diminished compensa-

I. CLAIMS BASED UPON NEGLIGENCE.

Appellants sought, in their complaint, to state a cause of action in negligence utilizing theories of ostensible agency and corporate negligence.

[The court concludes that the plaintiff raised sufficient facts regarding the presence of ostensible agency to survive a motion to dismiss. The plaintiff alleged that Dr. Hempsey was held out as an agent of the HMO and that the HMO represented that its "primary care physicians were carefully screened and fully qualified physicians who would render competent medical care to HMO members and who would obtain timely consultation and/or treatment for HMO members with medical specialists whenever such treatment was warranted."]

(b) *Corporate Negligence.*

Appellants' argument that their complaint also sets forth sufficient facts to state a valid cause of action in negligence based upon a theory of corporate negligence, as defined by our Supreme Court in *Thompson v. Nason Hospital* [591 A. 2d 703 (1991)] is not as easily resolved. The Court there reasoned:

> the corporate hospital of today has assumed the role of a comprehensive health center, with responsibility for arranging and coordinating the total health care of its patients.... Courts have recognized several bases on which hospitals may be subject to liability including respondeat superior, ostensible agency and corporate negligence.
>
> Corporate negligence is a doctrine under which the hospital is liable if it fails to uphold the proper standard of care owed the patient, which is to ensure the patient's safety and well-being while at the hospital. This theory of liability creates a non-delegable duty which the hospital owes directly to a patient
>
> The hospital's duties have been classified into four general areas: (1) a duty to use reasonable care in the maintenance of safe and adequate facilities and equipment; (2) a duty to select and retain only competent physicians; (3) a duty to oversee all persons who practice medicine within its walls as to patient care; and (4) a duty to formulate, adopt and enforce adequate rules and policies to ensure quality care for the patient

Thompson v. Nason, supra, 591 A. 2d 706.

While HMO PA could be viewed as having "assumed the role of a comprehensive health center", only two of the four duties defined by the Court in *Thompson v. Nason* could be imposed upon a modified IPA model HMO since such an HMO has no facilities or equipment and thus cannot "oversee.... patient care [within its walls]." It is reasonable, however, to require that an IPA model HMO "select and retain only competent physi-

---

tion for a provider who deems further medical attention necessary or desirable. The fundamental prerogative and duty of considering and establishing social policy, including, of course, the regulation of health care providers, is vested solely in the legislature.

cians" and "formulate, adopt and enforce adequate rules and policies to ensure quality care for [its subscribers]." *Id.*, 591 A.2d at 707.

It would appear unnecessary, however, to extend the theory of corporate negligence to IPA model HMOs in order to find that such HMOs have a non-delegable duty to select and retain only competent primary care physicians. [The court proceeded to find that HMO/PA had a duty of reasonable care under the existing common law, as reflected in Section 323 of the Restatement (Second) of Torts,* to exercise due care in "in the selection, retention, and/or evaluation of the primary care physician," without formally reaching a decision about whether the doctrine of corporate negligence applied to HMOs of the IPA variety.]

Notes

1. *The sources and nature of corporate or nondelegable duties.* Think back to *Jackson, Darling,* and other cases in Chapter 18 which relied on corporate liability or nondelegable duty to impose responsibility on hospitals for negligence committed within their facilities. In what ways do these theories change plaintiffs' burdens of proof? Consider then the nature of those burdens to fall within the holding in *McClellan* and compare the evidence necessary to establish apparent agency in cases like *Boyd* and *Chase*? Think also about the analogy drawn between hospitals and managed-care networks discussed carefully in *McClellan,* and notice that the court in dictum stated that it would extend the analogy only with regard to a corporate obligation to credential network providers. Do you think it would have been willing to extend corporate liability to a duty to monitor ongoing care, as did the court in *Darling*? Finally, notice that the court relied on general tort principles, reflected in section 323 of the Restatement (Second) of Torts, to impose a nondelegable duty to credential only competent physicians. Compare the discussion of the no-duty principle in Part One and the exceptions for established relationships and care undertaken. How far can this reliance interest take a plaintiff? Again, consider whether a court could impose a duty to monitor ongoing care under such a theory. We will return to these questions again after each of the next two cases, *Shannon* and *Jones.*

2. McClellan *on remand.* After winning reinstatement of the complaint from the Superior Court (Pennsylvania's intermediate appeals court) in the opinion above, (*McClellan I*) plaintiffs moved for discovery of documents related to Dr. Hempsey's application to join HMO PA and later investigations of his care of patients. HMO PA objected to several of McClellan's document requests, citing the confidentiality provisions of

---

* Section 323 of the Restatement (Second) of Torts provides: "One who undertakes, gratuitously or for consideration, to render services to another which he should recognize as necessary for the protection of the other's person or things, is subject to liability to the other for physical harm resulting from his failure to exercise reasonable care to perform his undertaking, if (a) his failure to exercise such care increased the risk of harm, or (b) the harm is suffered because of the other's reliance upon the undertaking."

Pennsylvania's Peer Review Protection Act (the Act). The Act's confidentiality provision, section 425.4, protects a "professional health care provider" from compelled disclosure during discovery in a civil action of proceedings and records of a peer review committee.

In a 1995 opinion, the Superior Court held that an IPA-model HMO such as HMO PA is not a "health care provider" within the meaning of the Act and is therefore not protected by its confidentiality provision. McClellan v. HMO PA, 660 A.2d 97 (Pa. Super. 1995) (*McClellan II*). The *McClellan II* court suggested that while staff-model HMOs (which own their own health care facilities and employ physicians and other providers) and group-model HMOs (which often own their own facilities and contract with physician groups to provide services) might qualify as health care providers under the Act, "IPA model HMOs, like HMO PA, that do not operate their own facilities, but merely act as insurers or quasi-insurers," should not be covered by the Act.

In McClellan v. Health Maintenance Organization of Pennsylvania, 686 A.2d 801 (Pa. 1996), an evenly divided court upheld the order, concluding that the peer review statute did not cover entities such as IPA HMOs, which lack the attributes of a facility and furthermore, that their operations do not involve the type of "candor" and "frank" discussions that must take place within a health care institution in order to promote care of appropriate quality. Because the policy underpinnings promoting peer review were not, in the view of some of the judges, present in the case of entities with a loose IPA structure, the statute did not apply, even though the Act specified application of its terms to "(11) A corporation or other organization operating a hospital, a nursing or convalescent home or other health care facility." 63 P.S. § 425.2. The opposing viewpoint, 686 A.2d at 809, which would have reversed the order of the lower court, offered insight into the complexities of modern health care enterprises:

> The majority holds that an IPA model HMO cannot be regarded as an administrator of a health care facility because it cannot oversee patient care within its walls. This conclusion ignores the reality of health care today. A corporation operating a health care facility—one of the examples of a professional health care provider in the statute—may not be in a place where it can oversee patient care "within its walls." More importantly, HMOs dictate the care provided in health care facilities. They prescribe the tests patients receive, the doctors patients see, and the time patients stay in health care facilities. HMOs administrate, directly or through contracts with physician groups, health care facilities.
>
> Because HMOs manage patient care, they have the same duty as other health care facilities to select and retain competent physicians. *McClellan v. Health Maintenance Organization of Pennsylvania*, 604 A.2d 1053, 1058–59 (1992). They may be held liable for the failure to do so. *Id.* To fulfill this responsibility, HMOs, like other health care facilities, evaluate and review doctors' qualifications and choose doctors to provide their subscribers'

care. HMOs conduct peer review to select competent doctors. If other health care facilities that conduct peer review for this purpose are protected from producing confidential peer review documents, HMOs also should be protected.

Think about this opposing viewpoint in the context of accountable care organizations, discussed in the preceding chapter. Would their activities qualify for peer review privilege even though their model, by definition, stipulates that groups of independent competitors must function together as a joint enterprise?

Shannon v. McNulty

718 A.2d 828 (Pa. Super. 1998)

■ ORIE MELVIN, JUDGE:

The theory of corporate liability as it relates to hospitals was first adopted in this Commonwealth in the case of *Thompson v. Nason*, 591 A.2d 703. Our supreme court upheld a direct theory of liability against the hospital, stating:

> Corporate negligence is a doctrine under which the hospital is liable if it fails to uphold the proper standard of care owed the patient, which is to ensure the patient's safety and well-being while at the hospital. This theory of liability creates a nondelegable duty which the hospital owes directly to a patient. Therefore, an injured party does not have to rely on and establish the negligence of a third party.

Id. at 707. The court then set forth four general areas of corporate liability: (1) A duty to use reasonable care in the maintenance of safe and adequate facilities and equipment; (2) A duty to select and retain only competent physicians; (3) A duty to oversee all persons who practice medicine within its walls as to patient care; (4) A duty to formulate, adopt and enforce adequate rules and policies to ensure quality care for patients.

The evidence introduced by the Shannons may be summarized as follows. Mrs. Shannon testified during the trial of this case that she was a subscriber of the HealthAmerica HMO when this child was conceived. It was Mrs. Shannon's first pregnancy. When she advised HealthAmerica she was pregnant in June 1992, they gave her a list of six doctors from which she could select an OB/GYN. She chose Dr. McNulty from the list. Her HealthAmerica membership card instructed her to contact either her physician or HealthAmerica in the event she had any medical questions or emergent medical conditions. The card contained the HealthAmerica emergency phone number, which was manned by registered nurses. She testified it was confusing trying to figure out when to call Dr. McNulty and when to call HealthAmerica because she was receiving treatment from both for various medical conditions related to her pregnancy, including asthma and reflux.

She saw Dr. McNulty monthly but also called the HealthAmerica phone line a number of times for advice and to schedule appointments with their in-house doctors. She called Dr. McNulty on October 2, 1992 with complaints of abdominal pain. The doctor saw her on October 5, 1992 and examined her for five minutes. He told Mrs. Shannon her abdominal pain was the result of a fibroid uterus, he prescribed rest and took her off of work for one week. He did no testing to confirm his diagnosis and did not advise her of the symptoms of pre-term labor.

She next called Dr. McNulty's office twice on October 7 and again on October 8 and October 9, 1992, because her abdominal pain was continuing, she had back pain, was constipated and she could not sleep. She asked Dr. McNulty during the October 8th call if she could be in pre-term labor because her symptoms were similar to those described in a reference book she had on labor. She told Dr. McNulty her pains were irregular and about ten minutes apart, but she had never been in labor so she did not know what it felt like. He told her he had just checked her on October 5th, and she was not in labor. The October 9th call was at least her fourth call to Dr. McNulty about her abdominal pain, and she testified that Dr. McNulty was becoming impatient with her. *Id*.

On October 10th, she called HealthAmerica's emergency phone line and told them about her severe irregular abdominal pain, back pain, that her pain was worse at night, that she thought she may be in pre-term labor, and about her prior calls to Dr. McNulty. The triage nurse advised her to call Dr. McNulty again. Mrs. Shannon did not immediately call Dr. McNulty because she did not feel there was anything new she could tell him to get him to pay attention to her condition. She called the HealthAmerica triage line again on October 11, 1992, said her symptoms were getting worse and Dr. McNulty was not responding. The triage nurse again advised her to call Dr. McNulty. Mrs. Shannon called Dr. McNulty and told him about her worsening symptoms, her legs beginning to go numb, and she thought that she was in pre-term labor. He was again short with her and angry and insisted that she was not in pre-term labor.

On October 12, 1992, she again called the HealthAmerica phone service and told the nurse about her symptoms, severe back pain and back spasms, legs going numb, more regular abdominal pain, and Dr. McNulty was not responding to her complaints. One of HealthAmerica's in-house orthopedic physicians spoke with her on the phone and directed her to go to West Penn Hospital to get her back examined. She followed the doctor's advice and drove an hour from her house to West Penn, passing three hospitals on the way. At West Penn she was processed as having a back complaint because those were HealthAmerica's instructions, but she was taken to the obstetrics wing as a formality because she was over five (5) months pregnant. She delivered a one and one-half pound baby that night. He survived only two days and then died due to his severe prematurity.

The Shannons' expert, Stanley M. Warner, M.D., testified he had experience in a setting where patients would call triage nurses. Dr. Warner opined that HealthAmerica, through its triage nurses, deviated from the standard of care following the phone calls to the triage line on October 10, 11 and 12, 1992, by not immediately referring Mrs. Shannon to a physician or hospital for a cervical exam and fetal stress test. As with Dr. McNulty, these precautions would have led to her labor being detected and increased the baby's chance of survival. Dr. Warner further testified on cross examination that Mrs. Shannon turned to HealthAmerica's triage nurses for medical advice on these three occasions when she communicated her symptoms. She did not receive appropriate advice, and further, if Health-America's triage nurses intended for the referrals back to Dr. McNulty to be their solution, they had a duty to follow up Mrs. Shannon's calls by calling Dr. McNulty to insure Mrs. Shannon was actually receiving the proper care from him.

CORPORATE LIABILITY

In granting the nonsuit the trial court concluded the Shannons failed to present sufficient evidence to establish negligence on the part of Health-America under either a corporate or vicarious liability theory. After first questioning the applicability of corporate liability to an HMO such as HealthAmerica, the trial court offered the following rationale with respect to the inadequacy of the evidence of corporate negligence:

> First, only two of the four duties set forth in *Thompson, supra,* could conceivably apply to a health maintenance organization such as HealthAmerica. There was no discussion, for example, of how HealthAmerica selected participating physicians or the criteria used in monitoring the physicians' performance. Similarly, Plaintiffs produced no evidence regarding the formulation, adoption or enforcement of rules or policies by HealthAmerica in carrying out its duty to provide adequate care to its subscribers. In the absence of such evidence, it is apparent that Plaintiffs failed to meet their burden of establishing the necessary elements to maintain a cause of action for corporate negligence, thereby justifying the granting of a compulsory nonsuit.

Without addressing the trial court's conclusion that a lack of evidence regarding the formulation, adoption or enforcement of rules or policies by HealthAmerica defeats the Shannons' claim of corporate negligence, we find the third duty is applicable. In assessing whether the Shannons evidence was sufficient to allow the case to go the jury on the theory of corporate liability pursuant to this third duty, we find Welsh v. Bulger, 698 A.2d 581 (Pa. 1997) to be instructive. [In *Welsh,* the Pennsylvania Supreme Court found evidence of hospital nurses' failure to perceive need for emergency caesarean section to be a sufficient basis for hospital corporate negligence under *Thompson v. Nason.*]

In adopting the doctrine of corporate liability the *Thompson v. Nason* court recognized "the corporate hospital's role in the total health care of its patients." Likewise, we recognize the central role played by HMOs in the total health care of its subscribers. A great deal of today's healthcare is channeled through HMOs with the subscribers being given little or no say so in the stewardship of their care. Specifically, while these providers do not practice medicine, they do involve themselves daily in decisions affecting their subscriber's medical care. These decisions may, among others, limit the length of hospital stays, restrict the use of specialists, prohibit or limit post hospital care, restrict access to therapy, or prevent rendering of emergency room care. While all of these efforts are for the laudatory purpose of containing health care costs, when decisions are made to limit a subscriber's access to treatment, that decision must pass the test of medical reasonableness. To hold otherwise would be to deny the true effect of the provider's actions, namely, dictating and directing the subscriber's medical care.

Where the HMO is providing health care services rather than merely providing money to pay for services their conduct should be subject to scrutiny. We see no reason why the duties applicable to hospitals should not be equally applied to an HMO when that HMO is performing the same or similar functions as a hospital. When a benefits provider, be it an insurer or a managed care organization, interjects itself into the rendering of medical decisions affecting a subscriber's care it must do so in a medically reasonable manner. Here, HealthAmerica provided a phone service for emergent care staffed by triage nurses. Hence, it was under a duty to oversee that the dispensing of advice by those nurses would be performed in a medically reasonable manner. Accordingly, we now make explicit that which was implicit in *McClellan* and find that HMOs may, under the right circumstances, be held corporately liable for a breach of any of the *Thompson* duties which causes harm to its subscribers.

Note

The nature and degree by which managed care inserts itself into treatment decision making. In *Wickline* and in *McEvoy* the insurer/managed care entity inserted itself directly into the decision-making that led to the adverse event. As we discussed in the notes following *Wickline* one could say that the negligence was a joint product of the manner in which utilization review was structured and conducted and the manner in which the treating physicians simply accepted that framework. In *McEvoy* the authority appeared to lie almost completely in the hand of the HMO's medical director. He just ordered that there be no more extensions. Think back to *Muse* also (Chapter 18), in which the young patient committed suicide after being discharged from the inpatient psychiatric facility at the medical staff's orders and as a result of the hospital's blatant policy of terminating when insurance has been exhausted. Perhaps the professionals involved in treating the patient could have gotten an exception—and in that sense responsibility was shared, as in *Wickline*—but the evidence seemed to show that exceptions were rarely if ever granted.

Boyd, Chase and *McClellan* were different, weren't they? One could say that responsibility for the error was joint in the manner in which they managed—core entities structured their networks, and perhaps in the way they set up their plan members' expectations that they would exercise due care over at least credentialing, but the linkage between the structure of their networks and the treating physicians' negligence was more attenuated than the connection in *Wickline* and *McEvoy*. The entwinement between institutional decision-making and the actual medical care was not on display in these three cases the way it was in *Wickline* and *McEvoy*.

What about *Shannon*? Where does it fit in these fact patterns? Perhaps the key sentence in the opinion is: "When a benefits provider, be it an insurer or a managed care organization, interjects itself into the rendering of medical decisions affecting a subscriber's care it must do so in a medically reasonable manner." How does this reasoning compare with the reasoning in *McClellan* that the HMO had at least undertaken a duty to credential its physicians with due care? Given the nature of the undertaking in *Shannon*, does the corporate duty extend only to credentialing, as in *McClellan*, or is it more like the duty to monitor ongoing care like in *Darling*? If you were counsel to an HMO like the one in *Shannon*, what modifications would you suggest they make in their hotline? What advice would you offer them about having any hotline at all?

Jones v. Chicago HMO Ltd. of Illinois

730 N.E.2d 1119 (Ill. 2000)

■ JUSTICE BILANDIC delivered the opinion of the court:

This appeal asks whether a health maintenance organization (HMO) may be held liable for institutional negligence. We answer in the affirmative.

FACTS

On January 18, 1991, Jones' three-month-old daughter Shawndale was ill. Jones called Dr. Jordan's office, as she had been instructed to do by Chicago HMO. Jones related Shawndale's symptoms, specifically that she was sick, was constipated, was crying a lot and felt very warm. An assistant advised Jones to give Shawndale some castor oil. When Jones insisted on speaking with Dr. Jordan, the assistant stated that Dr. Jordan was not available but would return her call. Dr. Jordan returned Jones' call late that evening. After Jones described the same symptoms to Dr. Jordan, he also advised Jones to give castor oil to Shawndale.

On January 19, 1991, Jones took Shawndale to a hospital emergency room because her condition had not improved. Chicago HMO authorized Shawndale's admission. Shawndale was diagnosed with bacterial meningitis, secondary to bilateral otitis media, an ear infection. As a result of the meningitis, Shawndale is permanently disabled.

The medical expert for the plaintiff, Dr. Richard Pawl, stated in his affidavit and deposition testimony that Dr. Jordan had deviated from the standard of care. In Dr. Pawl's opinion, upon being advised of a three-month-old infant who is warm, irritable and constipated, the standard of care requires a physician to schedule an immediate appointment to see the infant or, alternatively, to instruct the parent to obtain immediate medical care for the infant through another physician. Dr. Pawl gave no opinion regarding whether Chicago HMO was negligent.

Although Jones filed this action against Chicago HMO, Dr. Jordan and another party, this appeal concerns only counts I and III of Jones' second amended complaint, which are directed against Chicago HMO. Count I charges Chicago HMO with institutional negligence for, *inter alia,* (1) negligently assigning Dr. Jordan as Shawndale's primary care physician while he was serving an overloaded patient population, and (2) negligently adopting procedures that required Jones to call first for an appointment before visiting the doctor's office or obtaining emergency care. Count III charges Chicago HMO with breach of contract and is based solely on Chicago HMO's contract with the Department of Public Aid.

Chicago HMO is a for-profit corporation. During all pertinent times, Chicago HMO was organized as an independent practice association model HMO under the Illinois Health Maintenance Organization Act (Ill. Rev. Stat.1991, ch. 111 1/2, par. 1401 *et seq.*).

In her deposition testimony, Jones described how she first enrolled in Chicago HMO while living in Park Forest. A Chicago HMO representative visited her home. According to Jones, he "was telling me what it was all about, that HMO is better than a regular medical card and everything so I am just listening to him and signing my name and stuff on the papers. I asked him what kind of benefits you get out of it and stuff, and he was telling me that it is better than a regular card."

The "HMO ENROLLMENT UNDERSTANDING" form signed by Jones in 1987 stated: "I understand that all my medical care will be provided through the Health Plan once my application becomes effective." Jones remembered that, at the time she signed this form, the Chicago HMO representative told her "you have got to call your doctor and stuff before you see your doctor; and before you go to the hospital, you have got to call." [Ms. Jones was approached by a Chicago HMO solicitor a second time after she moved to Chicago Heights, and told that person she was already enrolled in Chicago HMO.]

When Jones moved to Chicago Heights, she did not select Dr. Jordan as Shawndale's primary care physician. Rather, Chicago HMO assigned Dr. Jordan to her. Jones explained: "They gave me Dr. Jordan. They didn't ask me if I wanted a doctor. They gave me him. They told me that he was a good doctor for the kids because I didn't know what doctor to take my kids to because I was staying in Chicago Heights so they gave me him so I started taking my kids there to him."

Dr. Mitchell J. Trubitt, Chicago HMO's medical director, testified at his deposition that Dr. Jordan was under contract with Chicago HMO for two sites, Homewood and Chicago Heights. [Dr. Trubitt stated that Chicago HMO patients in Chicago Heights had no practical choice of physician, because "Dr. Jordan was Chicago HMO's only physician who was willing to

serve the public aid membership in Chicago Heights. Dr. Trubitt characterized this lack of physicians as "a problem" for Chicago HMO."]

Dr. Jordan testified at his deposition that, in January of 1991, he was a
solo practitioner. He divided his time equally between his offices in Homewood and Chicago Heights. Dr. Jordan was under contract with Chicago
HMO for both sites. In addition, Dr. Jordan was under contract with 20
other HMOs, and he maintained his own private practice of non-HMO
patients. Dr. Jordan estimated that he was designated the primary care
physician of 3,000 Chicago HMO members and 1,500 members of other
HMOs. In contrast to Dr. Jordan's estimate, Chicago HMO's own "Provider Capitation Summary Reports" listed Dr. Jordan as being the primary
care provider of 4,527 Chicago HMO patients as of December 1, 1990.

I.   Institutional Negligence

Institutional negligence is also known as direct corporate negligence.
Since the landmark decision of *Darling v. Charleston Community Memorial
Hospital,* 211 N.E.2d 253 (1965), Illinois has recognized that *hospitals* may
be held liable for institutional negligence. *Darling* acknowledged an independent duty of hospitals to assume responsibility for the care of their
patients. Ordinarily, this duty is administrative or managerial in character.
To fulfill this duty, a hospital must act as would a "reasonably careful
hospital" under the circumstances. Liability is predicated on the hospital's
own negligence, not the negligence of the physician.

Underlying the tort of institutional negligence is a recognition of the
comprehensive nature of hospital operations today. The hospital's expanded
role in providing health care services to patients brings with it increased
corporate responsibilities.

In accordance with the preceding rationale, we now hold that the
doctrine of institutional negligence may be applied to HMOs. [See *Petrovich,* 719 N.E.2d 756; *Shannon,* 718 A.2d 828]. HMOs, like hospitals,
consist of an amalgam of many individuals who play various roles in order
to provide comprehensive health care services to their members. Moreover,
because HMOs undertake an expansive role in arranging for and providing
health care services to their members, they have corresponding corporate
responsibilities as well. *Shannon,* 718 A.2d at 835–36; see *Petrovich,* 719
N.E.2d 756 (recognizing that HMOs act as health care providers and
attempt to contain the costs of health care); 215 ILCS 125/1–2(9) (West
1998) (defining an HMO as "any organization formed to provide or arrange
for one or more health care plans under a system which causes any part of
the risk of health care delivery to be borne by the organization or its
providers"); Current Amicus Briefs of Labor Department on Medical Malpractice, 68 U.S.L.W. 2249–50 (November 2, 1999) (noting that, according
to the United States Department of Labor, HMOs wear "three different
hats," one of which is "medical provider"). Our nationwide research has
revealed no decision expressing a contrary view, and Chicago HMO makes
no argument against extending the doctrine of institutional negligence to
HMOs. Hence, we conclude that the law imposes a duty upon HMOs to

conform to the legal standard of reasonable conduct in light of the apparent risk. To fulfill this duty, an HMO must act as would a "reasonably careful" HMO under the circumstances.

■ JUSTICE RATHJE, concurring in part and dissenting in part:

I strongly disagree with the majority's holding that Chicago HMO can be liable under a theory of institutional liability. Generally, institutional liability attaches when an organization breaches a duty it owes as an organization. Under *Darling,* hospitals are vulnerable to institutional liability partly because, as organizations, they offer complete medical services, including nurses, doctors, orderlies, and administration.

In *Shannon v. McNulty*, 718 A.2d 828 (Pa. Super. 1998), the case upon which the majority relies, the defendant HMO was not serving simply as a vehicle through which a member's medical bills are paid. Instead, the HMO employed nurses to work its own triage service and to advise members on medical decisions such as whether to seek treatment at a hospital. [In contrast,] [u]nder Chicago HMO's contract with Dr. Jordan, Chicago HMO is responsible for enrolling members, providing the doctor's group with a current list of those members, paying capitation fees, providing a list of hospitals and health care providers, providing other funding, and obtaining the appropriate regulatory licensure for the doctor's group. The doctor's group is solely responsible for providing the health services. Moreover, Chicago HMO's member's handbook specifically explains that the individual doctors are responsible for nurses and all other medical attention. Unlike the HMO in *Shannon,* which "provid[ed] health care services," Chicago HMO "merely provid[ed] money to pay for services." Thus, institutional liability is inappropriate in this case.

The primary flaw in the majority's analysis is that it attempts to create a rule of general application that fails to take into account not only the differences that exist between a hospital and an HMO but also those that exist among HMOs. To determine whether an HMO should have the same duty to its members that a hospital has to its patients, a court must assess not only whether hospitals are similar to HMOs but also whether the patient's relationship to the hospital is similar to the member's relationship to the HMO.

Hospitals are "institutions holding themselves out as devoted to the care and saving of human life." Institutional liability makes sense in the hospital context because a person in need of treatment must be assured that the hospital will abide by a sufficient standard of care. That patient generally does not have the time or opportunity to compare hospital bylaws or look for the hospital with the best administrative policies and the highest standard of care. A person goes to the nearest hospital in an emergency or to a hospital where his doctor has privileges in a nonemergency. In many cases, including most emergent cases, the patient has no time to make an informed choice. In his relationship with a hospital, the patient is at a severe disadvantage, which the law acknowledges by subjecting hospitals to institutional liability.

By contrast, the goal of an HMO is to provide health care in a cost-sensitive manner. Barry Furrow, *Managed Care Organizations and Patient Injury: Rethinking Liability*, 31 GA. L. REV. 419, 457 (1997). HMOs offer medical services, but they do not do so in the same way that hospitals do. HMOs offer the funding and the contact with the medical professionals. In Chicago HMO, for instance, the way in which daily business is conducted, the duties of nurses and other staff, and other day-to-day decisions are made by the individual doctor or hospital with whom the HMO has contracted.[2] This type of HMO makes no decision as to what type of care is ultimately given; they only decide whether the HMO will pay for that care.

Moreover, when a person joins an HMO, he knows beforehand what that HMO will cover and, in most cases, chooses which HMO he will join based on his assessment of the costs and benefits. To become a member, that person usually has to contract with the HMO.[3] As a result, the HMO will be held accountable for any failure to comply with its own policies through a contract action.

In this case, the Chicago HMO representative arrived at plaintiff's door and asked her whether she would prefer to receive her public aid medical benefits through the HMO or continue receiving them directly through public aid. He reviewed the policies, and plaintiff made the decision to join, signing a statement that her participation in the HMO was voluntary and that she could disenroll at any time. Plaintiff was given the opportunity to make an informed choice and chose to receive her medical services through an HMO.

I wish to stress that I by no means believe that HMOs should not be held accountable for their actions. Ordinarily, an HMO will be accountable to its members through the contract that is signed by both parties. Unfortunately, in this case, plaintiff was receiving benefits from the HMO through public aid and, therefore, did not contract with the HMO. Consequently, as the majority correctly holds, her particular situation leaves her unable to enforce the policy provisions because she was not a party to the contract. While I sympathize with plaintiff's unenviable position, the fact remains that plaintiff's theory of [contract] liability is not one permissible under our laws. [The majority allowed the plaintiff's corporate negligence claim against Chicago HMO for allegedly assigning the doctor an excessive number of patients to survive a motion to dismiss.]

Notes

1. *How do different factors give rise to the nature and scope of institutional liability of managed-care organizations?* Let's continue the inquiry in the note following *Shannon*. How is *Jones* different from or similar to *Wickline, McEvoy, Boyd, Chase, McClellan* and *Shannon*? Was

2. Some HMOs do employ the staff and provide the facilities for care, but most do not.

3. This case is an exception to that rule because the HMO membership was given to plaintiff by the Department of Public Aid.

there any claim that Chicago HMO had directly inserted itself into the care provided by the treating physician as in *Wickline, McEvoy* or *Shannon* (or *Muse* in Chapter 18)? On the other hand, what do you think about the degree of connection between the treating doctor's error and the managed-care entity's construction of its network? Is the connection in *Jones* relatively stronger or more attenuated than in *Boyd* or *Chase*?

Compare the factors in the cases concerning whether corporate liability or nondelegable duties would or would not be imposed and the manner in which those factors shape the reach of liability. As we've seen, *McClellan* grounded a duty in the managed-care entity's undertaking of due care in construction of its network—after all, that's the most basic of what they all do, isn't it, they package networks?—but that rationale took us only so far as imposing duties with regard to credentialing the members in its network. By contrast, because the HMO in *Shannon* had directly "interject[ed] itself into the rendering of medical decisions affecting a subscriber's care it [was obligated] do so in a medically reasonable manner." That undertaking extended its duty to the responsibility to monitor ongoing care, as in *Darling*.

Consider though how fact-dependent imposition of these duties can be. Think back to *Jackson* in Chapter 18, a decision in which the court imposed nondelegable duties on a hospital to take responsibility over its emergency department because that's what it was supposed to do under licensure, private accreditation and its own bylaws. We raised in the notes following the case, and again in the notes following *Darling*, questions concerning how far nondelegable duties and corporate liability might extend—to different areas of the hospital, different types of professionals and employees, different types of treatment, and different types of errors.

Analogously, in many of the cases you now have read that involve liability of managed-care organizations, you have seen the courts question how tightly the managed care/hospital analogy might be drawn. You also have seen the courts draw distinctions among types of networks: staff-model, group-model, IPA-type, or modified-IPA types. For the most part, the imposition of duties at all, and the reach of those duties, rest on a complex assessment on the part of courts. Judges in essence are called upon to decide what exactly it is that these new managed-care entities do in relation to the patient, and they undertake these decisions against a legal landscape comprised of the legal principles applied to all of the complex health care system relationships that have come before them. In essence, the court has to decide what is really going on, and whether principles, established previously to deal with an increasingly complex health care system, in fact fit the new reality so as to establish duties and determine their scope.

With regard to *Jones*, in which the court had no problem extending the principles of *Darling* to managed care, consider three pieces of evidence. The first was that Ms. Jones did not select her physician—she was assigned to him by the HMO as the only physician available for her baby. The second came out in the trial during the cross-examination of the Chicago

HMO's medical director. Jones' counsel asked the medical director whether some consideration is given to the volume of patients assigned to physicians in the network, and the answer was "yes."

The next question concerned who sets the limit. The medical director's recollection was that the Health Care Finance Administration (the predecessor to CMS), which oversees Medicaid managed care, had promulgated a rule that the maximum ratio allowed was 3500 Medicaid beneficiaries per one primary care doctor.* The third piece of evidence was one of the contracts executed by the state Medicaid agency and Chicago HMO, which provided: "There shall be at least one full-time equivalent, board eligible physician to every 1,200 enrollees, including one full-time equivalent, board certified primary care physician for each 2,000 enrollees. There shall be one pediatrician for each 2,000 enrollees underage 17." (Note that to its credit, the state at least on paper, established a provider:patient ratio lower than the federal government permitted).

Are these facts—the assignment of patients to providers without any possibility of choice, federal standards regarding networks, and state network standards in its contracts—relevant to imposing a nondelegable duty on Chicago HMO with regard to the construction of its network? Are the obligations more or less specific than the sorts of factors relied on in other cases, such as licensure, private accreditation, bylaws, undertaking, the type of HMOs, and so on? Finally, does it matter that the potential source of any duties that might be imposed is not the private contracting by which a network is arranged, or private accreditation, or bylaws, or licensure, which, as you saw in Chapter 19, aims pretty broadly at the structure and processes through which care is delivered? The court had before it a grant of Chicago HMO's motion for summary judgment, which it reversed, finding that plaintiff had shown enough to establish the existence of a duty, but the court did not determine what the relevant standard of care would be. If you were representing Jones, would you introduce that regulation and those contracts in evidence, and what might be the result of doing so?

In thinking about these issues regarding the importance of the source of duties and the manner in which the sources can affect their scope, consider Pagarigan v. Aetna U.S. Healthcare of California, Inc., 2005 WL 2742807 (Cal. Ct. App. 2005), which arose under California's statutory scheme for regulating HMOs—and reflect back to the comparative lack of a regulatory scheme governing the HMO involved in *Chase*, in which the HMO was effectively allowed to contract away its duty to exercise reasonable care in selecting its providers. Like the HMO in *Chase*, Aetna U.S. Healthcare of California had contracted out its responsibilities to a diffuse

---

* This itself is astonishing since 1:3500 is the measure that the federal government uses to assign National Health Service Corps physicians to areas considered so deprived of health care personnel that they are treated as "health professions shortage areas." Why would any state with this degree of health care shortage (much more common in poor communities than you might think, as the community health center material in Chapter One pointed out) be permitted by the federal government *at all* to restrict people to a managed-care provider network that by definition was insufficient to serve members?

network of providers rather than taking the classic staff-model approach that was the hallmark of the original prepaid group practices but is seldom found today. In *Pagarigan,* the court concluded that an HMO "owes a duty to avoid contracting with deficient providers or negotiating contract terms which require or unduly encourage denials of service or below-standard performance by its providers."

The case involved an elderly woman, Johnnie Pagarigan, who died in a nursing home, a victim of both malpractice and abuse. A member of a Medicare Advantage plan (see Part Two for a discussion of Medicare managed care), her plan Administrator, Aetna, had entered into multi-layered contract agreements with its network. According to the court, "Aetna had contracted with a management organization, Greater Valley Management Services Organization, which contracted with medical groups Greater Valley Medical Group and Greater Valley Physician Association (collectively "Greater Valley"), which contracted with Magnolia Gardens nursing home (owned and operated by Libby Care Center, Inc. and Long-wood Management Corp.) and a physician, Dr. Buttleman, to care for decedent." Following their mother's death, the children sued every layer, all the way to the top. Aetna moved to dismiss the claim and the trial court concurred.

On appeal, the court considered the structure of the modern HMO and its implications for liability of a parent corporation under California's Civil Code:

> [T]he classic form of HMO, such as the original Kaiser Permanente plan, employs its own doctors and operates its own hospitals. Thus, these HMOs are liable both for any improper denials of coverage and for any malpractice their patients experience.
>
> Aetna calls its plan an HMO, but it is far from the classic model. Rather, in common with a classic fee-for-service health insurer, Aetna's plan employs no doctors and owns no hospitals. Consequently, it purports to avoid liability for any malpractice its insureds may suffer. But unlike many current fee-for-service insurance plans, it also makes no coverage decisions, and thus claims to avoid liability for denials of service, as well. Instead of making coverage decisions itself, Aetna shifts that decision-making responsibility, financial risk, and attendant liability for service denials and malpractice to the providers and intermediary management organizations with which it contracts.
>
> The shift in decision-making responsibility and financial risk is accomplished through what the industry calls a "capitation" arrangement. Aetna agrees to pay the management firm or provider a specified amount per year for each person its "HMO" has admitted into its "HMO" plan and then assigns to that firm or provider. The management firm or provider receives the same amount for a particular person whether that insured is so healthy he or she never incurs a single health-related expense the entire year as it receives for one who instead experiences a serious

disease requiring hospitalization and a series of operations entailing hundreds of thousands of dollars in medical expenses over the year. Furthermore, if some patient's only chance for recovery is some expensive but experimental or otherwise problematical treatment, in theory at least it is not Aetna but the management firm or provider who must decide whether to offer—and pay for—that treatment. It also is that management firm or provider Aetna expects to bear the consequences should an insured or the insured's survivors successfully sue because the denial of some extraordinary or even ordinary treatment caused the insured serious injury or death.

[T]he Pagarigans essentially allege Aetna's negligent conduct caused decedent's injuries and ultimate death. Aetna responded and the trial court ruled Aetna owed no duties to decedent which it breached. Whatever happened to decedent at Magnolia Gardens nursing home was the responsibility of the nursing home staff and the supervising physician (Dr. Buttleman). Vicarious liability may extend to the owners and operators of the nursing home, but not to Aetna which was just the insurance company that paid the nursing home and physician to take care of decedent.

As their primary theory of liability, the Pagarigans focus on Aetna's role as a health management organization. They urge as such Aetna has "non-delegable" duties toward its enrollees for the quality of the care they receive from the health care providers Aetna contracts to provide that care. The Pagarigans find these "non-delegable" duties in the language of certain statutes. While we conclude Aetna is not directly responsible for its contractees' breaches of duties they owe the plan's enrollees, we also conclude Aetna owes its own duties to those enrollees. These include a duty of due care when choosing the providers who will supply health services to enrollees. They also include a duty to avoid executing contracts with those providers containing terms, especially low levels of capitation payments, which foreseeably require or unduly encourage below-standard care.

[California Civil Code] Section 3428 appears to exempt health insurance plans, such as Aetna, from liability for acts of malpractice committed by health care providers it contracts to care for its enrollees. "This section does not create any new or additional liability on the part of a health care service plan or managed care entity for harm caused that is attributable to the medical negligence of a treating physician or other treating health care provider."

That same code section, however, also imposes a general duty on Aetna and like plans—a duty of due care when arranging health care services for its enrollees. "A health care service plan or managed care entity ... shall have a duty of ordinary care to arrange for the provision of medically necessary health care service to its subscribers and enrollees ... and shall be liable for any and all harm legally caused by its failure to exercise that ordinary care ..." [Cal. Civ. Code § 3428(a)]

Such a duty of due care is not satisfied by contracting with just any old providers or on any terms whatsoever. To select a provider or to allow the selection of a provider the plan knows or should know is deficient or prone to malpractice is to violate that duty. Moreover, this breach of the plan's own specific duty toward its enrollees also constitutes a contributing cause when an enrollee suffers injury or death due to malpractice attributable in part to the plan's careless selection of the deficient provider organization.

A plan likewise breaches this duty when "arranging" services for its enrollees if it negotiates contract terms with a provider—or allows the negotiation of contract terms with such provider—that foreseeably enhance the likelihood the provider will offer below-standard services that will injure or kill a substantial number of the plan's enrollees. Although other terms may have this result, the most critical term is the level of the "capitation" payment. The plan breaches its duty of ordinary care in arranging services for its enrollees if the plan negotiates a per capita payment so low the plan knows or should know it will require the provider to furnish substandard services and/or deny medically necessary services in order to survive. And, once again this breach of the plan's own duty to its enrollees qualifies as a contributing cause of any injury or death an enrollee suffers at the hands of a provider the plan is seriously underpaying for the services it is expected to supply.

2. What should the standard of liability be for HMOs and similar insurers? In a 1975 article widely cited in the academic literature, Randall Bovbjerg sharply contrasted the traditional perspective on quality of care with that of an HMO committed to serving a defined population for a fixed, prepaid sum. Unlike the solo physician, "[t]he comprehensiveness and integration of their services give HMOs numerous occasions to evaluate alternatives in seeking to achieve maximum health benefits for given expenditures." Health benefits may be considered not only, or even primarily, from the perspective of individual patients, but from the perspective of the enrolled population as a group. "Thus, there might be universal agreement that a certain test improves the accuracy of a diagnosis from ninety to ninety-five percent in some moderately serious and generally treatable condition; a fee-for-service doctor would almost certainly perform such a test if it were readily available and covered by insurance, since no obvious benefit for his patient or himself could be achieved by foregoing the potential insurance payment. On the other hand, an HMO might decide that its subscribers' resources were better spent, for example, on upgrading the staff of its emergency room than on the test." Traditional malpractice law standards, based on traditional medical practice, do not contemplate justifying an increased risk for a particular patient, or all patients, by a

reduced risk or improved quality in some other aspect of health care. Bovbjerg, *HMO Standard* at 1375, 1379, 1390, 1391–1407.

Bovbjerg defines the resulting dilemma as follows: on the one hand, it is important to subject HMOs to potential malpractice liability, in order to guard against economically motivated underservice and unreasonably low quality of care. On the other hand, malpractice law should not be permitted to interfere "inappropriately with HMOs' desirable ability to count costs in evaluating what care to provide." *Id.* at 1379 n.5. Bovbjerg's proposed solution to this dilemma is for the courts to recognize "HMO custom" as the appropriate standard for HMO care. Where the dispute concerns alternative procedures or approaches about whose medical efficacy doctors disagree, this would amount to a restatement of the "reputable minority" rule discussed above.

The harder case is where an HMO foregoes a test or procedure whose medical efficacy is clear in order to improve quality in some other aspect of health care delivery. Bovbjerg admits that the courts' case-by-case process is not well-suited to resolving these issues, nor does he begin to suggest the substantive standards by which they might be evaluated, other than "HMO custom" itself. Defining and implementing an "HMO custom" standard presents numerous difficulties, particularly in the modern era (as opposed to 1975 when Bovbjerg wrote), when the variety of HMOs and managed care organizations is far greater than before. In this context, it seems unlikely that the community of HMO's will have made sufficiently similar trade-offs to establish a customary standard. Other, perhaps surmountable problems include defining an "HMO" to insure that the financial incentives are "appropriate," defining appropriate comparison groups of similarly-situated HMOs, and defining the kind of notice that consumers must be given of the HMO's cost-benefit criteria.

Where state law tort liability theories survive preemption, some commentators argue for their displacement. Professors Richard Epstein and Clark Havighurst make a similar argument about contractual alteration of the standard of care for medical malpractice purposes. *See* Richard Epstein, *Medical Malpractice: The Case for Contract*, 1976 AM. B. FOUND. RES. J. 87; Clark C. Havighurst, *Altering the Applicable Standard of Care*, 49 LAW & CONTEMP. PROBS. 265 (Spring 1986); Clark C. Havighurst, *Prospective Self-Denial: Can Consumers Contract Today to Accept Health Care Rationing Tomorrow?* 140 U. PA. L. REV. 1755 (1992).

Professor Havighurst argues that "some health insurance policies are appropriately conceptualized as agreements by which members of the covered group mutually elected to be bound in order that the fund created by their contributions would be sufficient to cover their essential needs and would not be squandered on nonessential, inefficacious, or overly costly services demanded by any individual." *Id.* at 1771. "One untried set of feasible contractual innovations are voluntary agreements limiting the tort-law rights of plan subscribers." *Id.* at 1793. Havighurst believes that "well-crafted modifications of legal rights" would or at least might be more acceptable to the courts than a "pure exculpatory clause." *Id.* at 1793 n.91.

In a 1986 article, Havighurst presented a draft of the kind of contractual clause he had in mind, which would purportedly leave the substantive standard of professional custom formally unchanged, but "specif[y] that the plaintiff has not established a prima facie case just by showing a departure from customary practice." Havighurst, *Altering the Applicable Standard of Care* at 265, 271. Rather, to establish the applicable standard and its violation, the plaintiff would be limited "solely [to] the testimony of experts knowledgeable about scientific studies bearing on the appropriateness of the actions taken and about what, in the light of all the circumstances including the cost of alternative measures, constitutes appropriate medical care." *Id.*

3.   *The special problems posed by Medicaid managed care.* Note that in *Jones,* the plaintiff did not even get to select from among a network of physicians: she was assigned to the only physician available in the community in which she lived, despite the fact that he was overwhelmed with patients. Shortages of participating physicians—managed care, fee-for-service, or otherwise, are a critical problem for Medicaid—as discussed in Part Two. *See* MEDICAID AND CHIP PAYMENT AND ACCESS COMMISSION (MACPAC), REPORT TO CONGRESS (June, 2011). Many reasons have been cited for the shortage, including low payment levels, the administrative burdens of Medicaid participation (although whether the program is any more burdensome than other insurance programs is not clear), and the stigma of participating in a large welfare program. There was some hope that the assumption of Medicaid administration duties by private companies would cure some of these problems and "mainstream" patients into coverage arrangements that enrolled members regardless of which sponsor pays the enrollment fee. Anna Sommers et. al., *Physician Willingness and Resources to Serve More Medicaid Patients: Perspectives from Primary Care Physicians*, KAISER COMMISSION ON MEDICAID AND THE UNINSURED (Apr. 2011), http://www.kff.org/medicaid/upload/8178.pdf.

It hasn't worked out that way. The Medicaid managed care business tends to be a specialty industry, with either companies that focus exclusively on the population or all-Medicaid subsidiaries of commercial firms. The business is highly profitable, and the 10 largest companies in the nation responsible for more than 25 million enrollees. Phil Galewitz, *Medicaid Managed Care Programs Grow: So Do Issues*, U.S.A. TODAY, Nov. 12, 2010. In general, beneficiaries report access to care that is no worse under managed care than in the Medicaid fee-for-service programs, but of course broad population satisfaction surveys can mask terrible local situations such as the one in *Jones*.

The Patient Protection and Affordable Care Act is expected to intensify Medicaid managed care competition as millions of new people become eligible for benefits, with companies vying for business. *Id.* Although the Act's expansion of community health centers into more medically underserved communities (PPACA § 5602) may somewhat ease the primary health care shortage for these communities, experts estimate that as many as 22.4 million people may enroll in Medicaid as a result of health reform, including 16 million new eligible children and adults, along with millions more who were eligible under pre-reform standards but could not enroll because of administrative barriers that have been eased under the law's simplified enrollment procedures. These same experts estimate that an additional 4,500–12,000 primary care physicians alone will be needed. Benjamin Sommers et. al., *Policy Makers Should Prepare for Major Uncertainties in Medicaid Enrollment, Costs, and Needs for Physicians Under Health Reform*, 30(11) HEALTH AFFAIRS 2186 (2011).

In *Jones,* enrollment in Medicaid managed care was voluntary. Today Medicaid managed care is a mandatory condition of participation in most states, with 70 percent of all Medicaid beneficiaries enrolled in some form of managed care arrangement. *Id.* In your view should state Medicaid programs be permitted to mandate managed care enrollment in communities in which the health care shortages are as critical as that in which Ms. Jones lived? Does managed care, with its contractual structure of financing plus a network, actually force state Medicaid programs to confront provider access shortages as they build their systems (access to care for Medicaid beneficiaries generally is discussed in Part Two), or is it a strategy for pushing off the problem onto private companies? What does the structure of Medicaid managed care now suggest about the more generally applicability of the holding in *Jones*? If choice does not exist in any meaningful way, isn't there necessarily a condition precedent to holding that non-delegable duties apply?

And do companies have the right incentives to solve the problem? Think of the (at least) short-term profitability of enrolling far too many people in plans with insufficient capacity to serve them, as the rate of health care utilization plummets. Do managed care firms have an economic interest in addressing the issue through higher payment rates and better support for provider networks? (Just to add to the dilemma, Medicaid enrollment historically has tended to last about nine months on average, and so forget long-term incentives such as keeping children and adults healthy today in order to avert costly conditions down the road). If you were a Medicaid director faced with this challenge, how important would health care access performance standards be? How would you go about developing standards, and what enforcement tools would you want to be able to use with your contractors?

4.   WHEN DOES ERISA PREEMPT THE MEDICAL LIABILITY OF INSURERS AND PLAN ADMINISTRATORS?

a.   Medical Negligence in Connection With Medical Utilization Review by an ERISA Plan Administrator

Wickline, above, presents the problem of prospective utilization review and its implications for health care quality when negligently performed. In *Wickline,* the court concluded that it was the physician's decision to discharge rather than Medi–Cal's negligent performance of its utilization review functions that constituted the proximate cause of the plaintiff's injury. Nonetheless, the decision left open the door for a state law claim of medical negligence against an insurer related to coverage determinations. Such a case in fact materialized in Wilson v. Blue Cross of Southern California, 271 Cal. Rptr. 876 (App. 1990), in which a California intermediate appeals court held that ordinary tort and contract principles apply to utilization review programs in the context of private health insurance. The court further held that a utilization review company could be held liable for negligence or breach of contract, even if the treating physician had not sought review of the negative decision on coverage. In other words, the court held that a utilization review program owes a duty of reasonable care to the patient. Because the court was only reversing a lower court's granting of summary judgment for the defendants, it did not address the substantive standard of care.

The question is how ERISA would affect such a state law claim.

Corcoran v. United Healthcare, Inc.

965 F.2d 1321 (5th Cir.), *cert. den.*, 506 U.S. 1033 (1992)

■ KING, CIRCUIT JUDGE:

This appeal requires us to decide whether ERISA pre-empts a state-law malpractice action brought by the beneficiary of an ERISA plan against a company that provides "utilization review" services to the plan. We also address the availability under ERISA of extracontractual damages. The district court granted the defendants' motion for summary judgment, holding that ERISA both pre-empted the plaintiffs' medical malpractice claim and precluded them from recovering emotional distress damages. We affirm.

The basic facts are undisputed. Florence Corcoran, a long-time employee of South Central Bell Telephone Company (Bell), became pregnant in early 1989. In July, her obstetrician, Dr. Jason Collins, recommended that she have complete bed rest during the final months of her pregnancy. Mrs. Corcoran applied to Bell for temporary disability benefits for the remainder of her pregnancy, but the benefits were denied. This prompted Dr. Collins to write to Dr. Theodore J. Borgman, medical consultant for Bell, and explain that Mrs. Corcoran had several medical problems which placed her "in a category of high risk pregnancy." Bell again denied disability benefits. Unbeknownst to Mrs. Corcoran or Dr. Collins, Dr. Borgman solicited a second opinion on Mrs. Corcoran's condition from another obstetrician, Dr. Simon Ward. In a letter to Dr. Borgman, Dr. Ward indicated that he had reviewed Mrs. Corcoran's medical records and suggested that "the company would be at considerable risk denying her doctor's recommendation." As Mrs. Corcoran neared her delivery date, Dr. Collins ordered her hospitalized so that he could monitor the fetus around the clock.[1]

---

1. This was the same course of action Dr. Collins had ordered during Mrs. Corcoran's 1988 pregnancy. In that pregnancy, Dr. Collins intervened and performed a successful Caesarean section in the 36th week when the fetus went into distress.

Mrs. Corcoran was a member of Bell's Medical Assistance Plan (MAP or "the Plan"). MAP is a self-funded welfare benefit plan which provides medical benefits to eligible Bell employees. It is administered by defendant Blue Cross and Blue Shield of Alabama (Blue Cross) pursuant to an Administrative Services Agreement between Bell and Blue Cross. The parties agree that it is governed by ERISA. Under a portion of the Plan known as the "Quality Care Program" (QCP), participants must obtain advance approval for overnight hospital admissions and certain medical procedures ("pre-certification"), and must obtain approval on a continuing basis once they are admitted to a hospital ("concurrent review"), or plan benefits to which they otherwise would be entitled are reduced.

QCP is administered by defendant United Healthcare (United) pursuant to an agreement with Bell. United performs a form of cost-containment service that has commonly become known as "utilization review." See Blum, *An Analysis of Legal Liability in Health Care Utilization Review and Case Management*, 26 Hous. L. Rev. 191, 192–93 (1989) (Utilization review refers to "external evaluations that are based on established clinical criteria and are conducted by third-party payers, purchasers, or health care organizers to evaluate the appropriateness of an episode, or series of episodes, of medical care."). The Summary Plan Description (SPD) explains QCP as follows:

> The Quality Care Program (QCP), administered by United HealthCare, Inc. assists you and your covered dependents in securing quality medical care according to the provisions of the Plan while helping reduce risk and expense due to unnecessary hospitalization and surgery. They do this by providing you with information which will permit you (in consultation with your doctor) to evaluate alternatives to surgery and hospitalization when those alternatives are medically appropriate. In addition, QCP will monitor any certified hospital confinement to keep you informed as to whether or not the stay is covered by the Plan.

Two paragraphs below, the SPD contains this statement: "When reading this booklet, remember that all decisions regarding your medical care are up to you and your doctor." It goes on to explain that when a beneficiary does not contact United or follow its pre-certification decision, a "QCP Penalty" is applied. The penalty involves reduction of benefits by 20 percent for the remainder of the calendar year or until the annual out-of-pocket limit is reached. Moreover, the annual out-of-pocket limit is increased from $1,000 to $1,250 in covered expenses, not including any applicable deductible. According to the QCP Administrative Manual, the QCP penalty is automatically applied when a participant fails to contact United. However, if a participant complies with QCP by contacting United, but does not follow its decision, the penalty may be waived following an internal appeal if the medical facts show that the treatment chosen was appropriate.

A more complete description of QCP and the services provided by United is contained in a separate booklet. Under the heading "WHAT QCP DOES" the booklet explains:

> Whenever your doctor recommends surgery or hospitalization for you or for a covered dependent, QCP will provide an independent review of your condition (or your covered dependent's). The purpose of the review is to assess the need for surgery or hospitalization and to determine the appropriate length of stay for a hospitalization, based on nationally accepted medical guidelines. As a part of the review process, QCP will discuss with your doctor the appropriateness of the treatments recommended and the availability of alternative types of treatments—or locations for treatment—that are equally effective, involve less risk, and are more cost effective.

The next paragraph is headed, "INDEPENDENT, PROFESSIONAL REVIEW" and states:

> United Health Care, an independent professional medical review organization, has been engaged to provide services under QCP. United's staff includes doctors, nurses and other medical professionals knowledgeable about the health care delivery system. Together with your doctor, they work to assure that you and your covered family members receive the most appropriate medical care.

At several points in the booklet, the themes of "independent medical review" and "reduction of unnecessary risk and expense" are repeated. Under a section entitled "THE QUALITY CARE PROGRAM ... AT A GLANCE" the booklet states that QCP "Provides independent, professional review when surgery or hospitalization is recommended—to assist you in making an enlightened decision regarding your treatment." QCP "[p]rovides improved quality of care by eliminating medically unnecessary treatment," but beneficiaries who fail to use it "may be exposed to unnecessary health risks" Elsewhere, in the course of pointing out that studies show one-third of all surgery may be unnecessary, the booklet explains that programs such as QCP "help reduce the unnecessary and inappropriate care and eliminate their associated costs." Thus, "one important service of QCP will help you get a second opinion when your doctor recommends surgery."

The booklet goes on to describe the circumstances under which QCP must be utilized. When a Plan member's doctor recommends admission to the hospital, independent medical professionals will review, with the patient's doctor, the medical findings and the proposed course of treatment, including the medically necessary length of confinement. The Quality Care Program may require additional tests or information (including second opinions), when determined necessary during consultation between QCP professionals and the attending physician. When United certifies a hospital stay, it monitors the continuing necessity of the stay. It also determines, for certain medical procedures and surgeries, whether a second opinion is necessary, and authorizes, where appropriate, certain alternative forms of care. Beneficiaries are strongly encouraged to use QCP to avoid loss of benefits: "fully using QCP means following the course of treatment that's recommended by QCP's medical professionals."

In accordance with the QCP portion of the plan, Dr. Collins sought pre-certification from United for Mrs. Corcoran's hospital stay. Despite Dr. Collins's recommendation, United determined that hospitalization was not necessary, and instead authorized 10 hours per day of home nursing care. Mrs. Corcoran entered the hospital on October 3, 1989, but, because United had not pre-certified her stay, she returned home on October 12. On October 25, during a period of time when no nurse was on duty, the fetus went into distress and died.

Mrs. Corcoran and her husband, Wayne, filed a wrongful death action in Louisiana state court alleging that their unborn child died as a result of various acts of negligence committed by Blue Cross and United. Both sought damages for the lost love, society and affection of their unborn child. In addition, Mrs. Corcoran sought damages for the aggravation of a pre-existing depressive condition and the loss of consortium caused by such aggravation, and Mr. Corcoran sought damages for loss of consortium. The defendants removed the action to federal court on grounds that it was pre-empted by ERISA.

Shortly thereafter, the defendants moved for summary judgment. They argued that the Corcorans' cause of action, properly characterized, sought damages for improper handling of a claim from two entities whose responsibilities were simply to administer benefits under an ERISA governed plan. They contended that their relationship to Mrs. Corcoran came into existence solely as a result of an ERISA plan and was defined entirely by the plan. Thus, they urged the court to view the claims as "relating to" an ERISA plan, and therefore within the broad scope of state law claims pre-empted by the statute. In their opposition to the motion, the Corcorans argued that "this case essentially boils down to one for malpractice against United HealthCare." They contended that under this court's analysis in Sommers Drug Stores Co. Employee Profit Sharing Trust v. Corrigan Enterprises, Inc. 793 F.2d 1456 (5th Cir. 1986), cert. den., 479 U.S. 1034 (1987), their cause of action must be classified as a state law of general application which involves an exercise of traditional state authority and affects principal ERISA entities in their individual capacities. This classification, they argued, together with the fact that pre-emption would contravene the purpose of ERISA by leaving them without a remedy, leads to the conclusion that the action is permissible notwithstanding ERISA.

The district court, relying on broad ERISA pre-emption principles developed by the Supreme Court and the Fifth Circuit, granted the [defendants'] motion [for summary judgment]. The court noted that ERISA pre-emption extends to state law claims "of general application including tort claims where ERISA ordinarily plays no role in the state law at issue." (citing Pilot Life Ins. Co. v. Dedeaux). The court found that the state law claim advanced by the Corcorans "related to" the employee benefit plan and therefore was pre-empted, because, but for the ERISA plan, the defendants would have played no role in Mrs. Corcoran's pregnancy; the sole reason the defendants had anything to do with her pregnancy is because the terms of the ERISA plan directed Mrs. Corcoran to the defendants (or at least to United HealthCare) for approval of coverage of the medical care she initially sought. The court held that, because the ERISA plan was the source of the relationship between the Corcorans and the defendants, the Corcorans' attempt to distinguish United's role in paying claims from its role as a source of professional medical advice was unconvincing.

The Corcorans filed a motion for reconsideration under Rule 59 of the Federal Rules of Civil Procedure. They did not ask the district court to reconsider its pre-emption ruling, but instead contended that language in the district court's opinion had implicitly recognized that they had a separate cause of action under ERISA's civil enforcement mechanism, sec. 502(a)(3).[5] They argued that the Supreme Court's decision in Massachusetts Mutual Life Ins. Co. v. Russell, did not foreclose the possibility that other compensatory damages such as they sought constituted "other appropriate equitable relief" available under sec. 502(a)(3) for violations of ERISA or the terms of an ERISA plan. The district court denied the motion. Although the court recognized that there was authority to the contrary, it pointed out that "the vast majority of federal appellate courts have held that a beneficiary under an ERISA health plan may not recover under section 509(a)(3) [sic] of ERISA compensatory or consequential damages for emotional distress or other claims beyond medical expenses covered by the plan." Moreover, the court pointed out, a prerequisite to recovery under sec. 502(a)(3) is a violation of the terms of ERISA itself. ERISA does not place upon the defendants a substantive responsibility in connection with the provision of medical advice which, if breached, would support a claim under sec. 502(a)(3). The court entered final judgment in favor of Blue Cross and United and this appeal followed.

The law in [the area of utilization review] is only beginning to develop, and it does not appear to us that Louisiana law clearly forecloses the possibility of recovery against United. Thus, assuming that on these facts the Corcorans might be capable of stating a cause of action for malpractice, our task now is to determine whether such a cause of action is pre-empted by ERISA]

C. *Pre-emption of the Corcorans' Claims.*

Initially, we observe that the common law causes of action advanced by the Corcorans are not that species of law "specifically designed" to affect ERISA plans, for the liability rules they seek to invoke neither make

---

5. The district court had stated that "because the plaintiffs conceded that the defendants have fully paid any and all medical expenses that Mrs. Corcoran actually incurred that were covered by the plan, the plaintiffs have no remaining claims under ERISA." In a footnote, the court indicated that Mrs. Corcoran could have (1) sued under ERISA, before entering the hospital, for a declaratory judgment that she was entitled to hospitalization benefits; or (2) gone into the hospital, incurred out-of-pocket expenses, and sued under ERISA for these expenses.

explicit reference to nor are premised on the existence of an ERISA plan. Rather, applied in the case against a defendant that provides benefit-related services to an ERISA plan, the generally applicable negligence-based causes of action may have an effect on an ERISA-governed plan. In our view, the pre-emption question devolves into an assessment of the significance of these effects.

1. United's Position—it makes benefit determinations, not medical decisions

United's argument in favor of pre-emption is grounded in the notion that the decision it made concerning Mrs. Corcoran was not primarily a medical decision, but instead was a decision made in its capacity as a plan fiduciary about what benefits were authorized under the Plan. All it did, it argues, was determine whether Mrs. Corcoran qualified for the benefits provided by the plan by applying previously established eligibility criteria. The argument's coup de grace is that under well-established precedent, participants may not sue in tort to redress injuries flowing from decisions about what benefits are to be paid under a plan. One commentator has endorsed this view of lawsuits against providers of utilization review services, arguing that because medical services are the "benefits" provided by a utilization review company, complaints about the quality of medical services (i.e., lawsuits for negligence) "can therefore be characterized as claims founded upon a constructive denial of plan benefits." Chittenden, *Malpractice Liability and Managed Health Care: History and Prognosis*, 26 TORT & INS. LAW J. 451, 489 (1991).

In support of its argument, United points to its explanatory booklet and its language stating that the company advises the patient's doctor "what the medical plan will pay for, based on a review of [the patient's] clinical information and nationally accepted medical guidelines for the treatment of [the patient's] condition." It also relies on statements to the effect that the ultimate medical decisions are up to the beneficiary's doctor. It acknowledges at various points that its decision about what benefits would be paid was based on a consideration of medical information, but the thrust of the argument is that it was simply performing commonplace administrative duties akin to claims handling.

Because it was merely performing claims handling functions when it rejected Dr. Collins's request to approve Mrs. Corcoran's hospitalization, United contends, the principles of *Pilot Life* and its progeny squarely foreclose this lawsuit. In *Pilot Life,* a beneficiary sought damages under various state-law tort and contract theories from the insurance company that determined eligibility for the employer's long term disability benefit plan. The company had paid benefits for two years, but there followed a period during which the company terminated and reinstated the beneficiary several times. 481 U.S. at 43. The Court made clear, however, that ERISA pre-empts state-law tort and contract actions in which a beneficiary seeks to recover damages for improper processing of a claim for benefits. *Id.* at 48–49. United suggests that its actions here were analogous to those of the insurance company in *Pilot Life*, and therefore urges us to apply that decision.

2. The Corcorans' position–United makes medical decisions, not benefit determinations

The Corcorans assert that *Pilot Life* and its progeny are inapposite because they are not advancing a claim for improper processing of benefits. Rather, they say, they seek to recover solely for United's erroneous medical decision that Mrs. Corcoran did not require hospitalization during the last month of her pregnancy. This argument, of course, depends on viewing United's action in this case as a medical decision, and not merely an administrative determination about benefit entitlements. Accordingly, the Corcorans, pointing to the statements United makes in the QCP booklet concerning its medical expertise content that United exercised medical judgment which is outside the purview of ERISA pre-emption.

The Corcorans suggest that a medical negligence claim is permitted under the analytical framework we have developed for assessing pre-emption claims. Relying on Sommers Drug Stores Co. Employee Profit Sharing Trust v. Corrigan Enterprises, Inc. 793 F.2d 1456 (5th Cir. 1986), *cert. denied*, 479 U.S. 1034 (1987), they contend that we should not find the state law under which they proceed pre-empted because it (1) involves the exercise of traditional state authority and (2) is a law of general application which, although it affects relations between principle ERISA entities in this case, is not designed to affect the ERISA relationship.

3. Our View—United makes medical decisions incident to benefit determinations

We cannot fully agree with either United or the Corcorans. Ultimately, we conclude that United makes medical decisions—indeed, United gives medical advice—but it does so in the context of making a determination about the availability of benefits under the plan. Accordingly, we hold that the Louisiana tort action asserted by the Corcorans for the wrongful death of their child allegedly resulting from United's erroneous medical decision is pre-empted by ERISA.

Turning first to the question of the characteristics of United's actions, we note that the QCP booklet and the SPD lend substantial support to the Corcorans' argument that United makes medical decisions. United's own booklet tells beneficiaries that it "assesses the need for surgery or hospitalization and determines the appropriate length of stay for a hospitalization, based on nationally accepted medical guidelines." United "will discuss with your doctor the appropriateness of the treatments recommended and the availability of alternative types of treatments." Further, "United's staff includes doctors, nurses, and other medical professionals knowledgeable about the health care delivery system. Together with your doctor, they work to assure that you and your covered family members receive the most appropriate medical care." According to the APD United will "provide you with information which will permit you (in consultation with your doctor) to evaluate alternatives to surgery and hospitalization when those alternatives are medically appropriate."

United makes much of the disclaimer that decisions about medical care are up to the beneficiary and his or her doctor. While that may be so, and while the disclaimer may support the conclusion that the relationship between United and the beneficiary is not that of doctor-patient, it does not mean that United does not make medical decisions or dispense medical advice. See Wickline, 239 Cal. Rptr. at 819 (declining to hold Medi–Cal liable but recognizing that it made a medical judgment); [i]n response, United argues that any such medical determination or advice is made or given in the context of administrating the benefits available under the Bell plan. Supporting United's position is the contract between United and Bell, which provides that "[United] shall contact the Participant's physician and based upon the medical evidence and normative data determine whether the Participant should be eligible to receive full plan benefits for the recommended hospitalization and the duration of benefits."

United argues that the decision it makes in this, the prospective context, is no different than the decision an insurer makes in the traditional retrospective context. The question in each case is "what the medical plan will pay for, based on a review of [the beneficiary's] clinical information and nationally accepted medical guidelines for the treatment of [the beneficiary's] condition." See QCP Booklet at 4. A prospective decision is, however, different in its impact on the beneficiary than a retrospective decision. In both systems, the beneficiary theoretically knows in advance what treatments the plan will pay for because coverage is spelled out in the plan documents. But in the retrospective system, a beneficiary who embarks on the course of treatment recommended by his or her physician has only a potential risk of disallowance of all or a part of the cost of that treatment, and then only after treatment has been rendered. In contrast, in a prospective system a beneficiary may be squarely presented in advance of treatment with a statement that the insurer will not pay for the proposed course of treatment recommended by his or her doctor and the beneficiary has the potential of recovering the cost of that treatment only if her or she can prevail in a challenge to the insurer's decision. A beneficiary in the latter system would likely be far less inclined to undertake the course of treatment that the insurer has at least preliminarily rejected.

By its very nature, a system of prospective decisionmaking influences the beneficiary's choice among treatment options to a far greater degree than does the theoretical risk of disallowance of a claim facing a beneficiary in a retrospective system. Indeed, the perception among insurers that prospective determinations result in lower health care costs is premised on the likelihood that a beneficiary, faced with the knowledge of specifically what the plan will and will not pay for, will choose the treatment option recommended by the plan in order to avoid risking total or partial disallowance of benefits. When United makes a decision pursuant, QCP, it is making a medical recommendation which—because of the financial ramifications—is more likely to be followed.

Although we disagree with United's position that no part of its actions involves medical decisions, we cannot agree with the Corcorans that no part of United's actions involves benefit determinations. In our view, United makes medical decisions as part and parcel of its mandate to decide what benefits are available under the Bell plan. As the QCP Booklet concisely puts it, United decides "what the medical plan will pay for." When United's actions are viewed from this perspective, it becomes apparent that the Corcorans are attempting to recover for a tort allegedly committed in the course of handling a benefit determination. The nature of the benefit determination is different than the type of decisions that was at issue in *Pilot Life*, but it is a benefit determination nonetheless. The principle of *Pilot Life* that ERISA pre-empts state-law claims alleging improper handling of benefit claims is broad enough to cover the cause of action asserted here.

Moreover, allowing the Corcorans' suit to go forward would contravene Congress's goals of "ensuring that plans and plan sponsors would be subject to a uniform body of benefit law" and "minimizing the administrative and financial burdens of complying with conflicting directives among States or between States and the Federal Government."

[A]lthough imposing liability on United might have the salutary effect of deterring poor quality medical decisions, there is a significant risk that state liability rules would be applied differently to the conduct of utilization review companies in different states. The cost of complying with varying substantive standards would increase the cost of providing utilization review services, thereby increasing the cost to health benefit plans of including cost containment features such as the Quality Care Program (or causing them to eliminate this sort of cost containment program altogether) and ultimately decreasing the pool of the plan funds available to reimburse participants.

It may be true, as the Corcorans assert, that Louisiana tort law places duties on persons who make medical judgments within the state, and the Louisiana courts may one day recognize that this duty extends to the medical decisions made by utilization review companies. But it is equally true that Congress may pre-empt state-law causes of action which seek to enforce various duties when it determines that such actions would interfere with a carefully constructed scheme of federal regulation. See *Pilot Life*, 481 U.S. at 48. The acknowledged absence of a remedy under ERISA's civil enforcement scheme for medical malpractice committed in connection with a plan benefit determination does not alter our conclusion. While we are not unmindful of the fact that our interpretation of the pre-emption clause leaves a gap in remedies within a statute intended to protect participants in employee benefit plans, the lack of an ERISA remedy does not affect a pre-emption analysis. Congress perhaps could not have predicted the interjection into the ERISA "system" of the medical utilization review process, but it enacted a pre-emption clause so broad and a statute so comprehensive that it would be incompatible with the language, structure and purpose of the statute to allow tort suits against entities so integrally connected with a plan.

Note

Benefit determination, medical decision, or both, and the absence of either state or federal remedies for injury. As the *Corcoran* opinion points out, the shift from retrospective to prospective and concurrent "utilization review" significantly changes the impact of the enterprise. More fundamentally, the way that the United presents its "Quality Care Program" (QCP), casts serious doubt on whether "utilization review" is the appropriate term to describe it. The program material certainly does not give the patient/subscriber the impression that QCP is designed simply to determine whether a proposed treatment is covered, but rather promises that the professionally-qualified reviewers, "together with your doctor work to assure that you and your covered family members receive the most appropriate medical care." This blending of cost-containment and quality-assurance functions is now perhaps best captured in the phrase "managed care." The exact nature of this function is also the central legal issue in *Corcoran*.

The *Corcoran* case represents one of a nightmare scenario. A physician recommends an expensive course of treatment (hospitalization) for a patient with a genuine medical problem (high-risk pregnancy). A second physician concurs with the first. Yet an unnamed "person or persons" at United HealthCare (United), the sub-contractor administering the QCP, refuses to pre-certify the hospitalization and substitutes treatment consisting of ten hours per day of home nursing care. As a result, the patient is discharged from the hospital. Two weeks later, with no nurse on duty, the fetus goes into distress and dies.

According to the Fifth Circuit opinion, the central legal question is: Does United make "benefit determinations" or "medical decisions?" If the former, then what United does is part of administering an employee benefit plan, and ERISA both pre-empts all state-law remedies and denies any compensatory damages as a matter of federal law, in light of the bar against monetary awards even if a plaintiff prevails on a breach of fiduciary responsibility claim, which the Corcorans also brought. (Recall that in *Cigna v. Amara*, Part Two, the United States Supreme Court appears to have opened the door at least a crack to the possibility of monetary awards as a form of equitable relief, but how *Amara* may play out in the context of medical negligence claims related to coverage decisions cannot be known at this point).

The question is why the court did not view what United did as a form of medical practice and remand the case back to the state courts for a full trial, at which point the firm could raise a § 514 ERISA preemption claim—as opposed to the § 502 complete preemption claim recognized in *Pilot Life*—as a defense. In a separate portion of the *Corcoran* opinion, not reproduced above but included here, the Fifth Circuit responds to this argument:

We find Independence HMO, Inc. v. Smith, 733 F. Supp. 983 (E.D. Pa. 1990), cited by the Corcorans, distinguishable on its facts. In *Smith,* the district court did not find pre-empted a state court malpractice action brought against an HMO by one of its members. The plaintiff sought to hold the HMO liable, under a state-law agency theory, for the alleged negligence of a surgeon associated with the HMO. The case appears to support the Corcorans because the plaintiff was attempting to hold an ERISA entity liable for medical decisions. However, the medical decisions at issue do not appear to have been made in connection with a cost containment feature of the plan or any other aspect of the plan which implicated the management of plan assets, but were instead made by a doctor in the course of treatment.

Corcoran, 965 F.2d at 1333 n.16.

While it is true that *Smith* can be distinguished as a vicarious liability case, the question lingers as to whether what United did should be viewed as medical care, as the Corcorans argued (and as a Texas law enacted in 1997 and the subject of *Aetna v. Davila,* below, explicitly sought to accomplish). Of course, United would not have been liable on corporate or institutional grounds, since it was merely the claims administrator: note that Bell separately contracted with Blue Cross for its provider network, essentially constructing its own managed care system using a popular provider network for its participants and beneficiaries, while assuring that a more tenacious—and non-conflicted—entity would oversee the network's resource consumption.* Because United's fundamental role was to manage plan assets, the fact that it did so through medical decision-making was not controlling, even though its own materials suggested its direct involvement in treatment planning and management—and even though the company effectively made a treatment decision for Mrs. Corcoran by "prescribing" home nursing care in lieu of hospital care. The court wrote:

> Although we disagree with United's position that no part of its actions involves medical decisions, we cannot agree with the Corcorans that no part of United's actions involves benefit determinations. In our view, United makes medical decisions as part and parcel of its mandate to decide what benefits are available under the Bell plan. As the QCP Booklet concisely puts it, United decides "what the medical plan will pay for." When United's actions are viewed from this perspective, it becomes apparent that the Corcorans are attempting to recover for a tort allegedly committed in the course of handling a benefit determination. The nature of the benefit determination is different than the type of decision that

---

* This of course raises a separate interesting question of whether Bell itself should have faced corporate liability for negligence in the selection of its claims management company. If Bell decided to run a health care company (with some telephone services on the side) should it, as the ERISA sponsor and plan fiduciary, face liability when its medical management system causes death and injury? No case directly implicating a self-insuring employer ever appears to have been decided.

was at issue in *Pilot Life*, but it is a benefit determination nonetheless. The principle of *Pilot Life* that ERISA pre-empts state-law claims alleging improper handling of benefit claims is broad enough to cover the cause of action asserted here.

965 F.2d at 1332. Thus, United may have made treatment decisions, but its principal job, indeed, its only contractual job, was to manage plan assets. *Corcoran's* reasoning was widely embraced, creating a complete preemption shield of ERISA § 502, as established in *Pilot Life v. Dedeaux*, whenever a defendant plan administrator's conduct could be characterized as falling within the scope of "plan administration," even where the conduct involved medical decision-making and even where the decision-making was demonstrably negligent.

How workable is this distinction between a "medical decision" and a "benefit determination"? *Corcoran* was an easy case because United Health Care made an explicit decision to deny Corcoran's obstetrician's request for hospitalization and substitute a (limited) home nursing benefit (although one could argue that what United did went well beyond a simple benefit determination, since it did not merely deny one form of treatment but actually ordered up another instead). But suppose that United Health had influenced the course of care in less explicit, more subtle ways. Suppose it used a payment system that subjected Corcoran's obstetrician to a payment withhold with the year-end "bonus" (i.e., a return of the withhold) tied to a target level of prescribed hospitalizations over the course of the year? Suppose it sent him a binder with practice guidelines stating criteria under which hospitalization should occur? Suppose it used practice profiling in its contracting with physicians and chose Corcoran's doctor in part based on his lower level of hospitalizations? Suppose he decided on his own that it was unnecessary to hospitalize his patient? Which of these decisions would create an avenue for imposition of corporate or vicarious liability against United Health if the obstetrician decides against hospitalization? In turn, which of these situations involves a "benefit determination," giving rise to ERISA preemption, and which involves a "medical decision," for which there would be no preemption? What is the relationship between the strength of the plaintiff's case for imposing liability on United Health and the strength of that United Health's argument that plaintiff's claim is preempted?

b. The Pegram v. Herdrich "Interlude" and the Aetna v. Davila "Resolution"

Despite its widespread adoption, the *Corcoran* "rule" seemingly was stood on its head for a few years as a result of the United States Supreme Court's decision in Pegram v. Herdrich, 530 U.S. 211 (2000). *Pegram* concerned the question of whether HMO physician incentive arrangements, by inducing a lower use of resources, by their very nature amount to a breach of fiduciary responsibility under ERISA. In *Pegram* the decision maker over resource use in fact was the plaintiff's treating clinician, but that did not stop the decision from being applied broadly.

The facts in *Pegram* were as follows:

The events in question began when a Carle [HMO] physician, petitioner Lori Pegram [who in addition to being an HMO treating physician was also a co-owner of the for-profit HMO] examined [Cynthia] Herdrich, who was experiencing pain in the midline area of her groin. Six days later, Dr. Pegram discovered a six by eight centimeter inflamed mass in Herdrich's abdomen. Despite the noticeable inflammation, Dr. Pegram did not order an ultrasound diagnostic procedure at a local hospital, but decided that Herdrich would have to wait eight more days for an ultrasound, to be performed at a facility staffed by Carle more than 50 miles away. Before the eight days were over, Herdrich's appendix ruptured, causing peritonitis.

Pegram, 530 U.S. at 215.

Herdrich sued Dr. Pegram and the Carle HMO in state court for medical malpractice and state-law fraud. The defendants removed the case to federal court, where the trial judge ruled that ERISA preempted the state-law fraud claims, and gave Herdrich leave to amend her complaint to reframe the fraud claims under ERISA. Herdrich's amended complaint

alleg[ed] that provision of medical services under the terms of the Carle HMO organization, [financially] rewarding its physician owners for limiting medical care, entailed an inherent or anticipatory breach of an ERISA fiduciary duty, since these terms created an incentive to make decisions in the physicians' self-interest, rather than the exclusive interests of plan participants [as required by ERISA's fiduciary duty].

Id. at 216. Herdrich specifically alleged that the Carle HMO's year-end financial distributions in effect "contract[ed] with CARLE owner/physicians to provide the medical services contemplated in the Plan and then having those contracted owner/physicians: (1) minimize the use of diagnostic tests; (2) minimize the use of facilities not owned by CARLE; and (3) minimize the use of emergency and non-emergency consultation and/or referrals to non-contracted physicians." *Id.* at 216 n.3.

Herdrich's ERISA claim against the HMO (as distinct from the malpractice claim against the individual doctor and the HMO, for which she won a $35,000 jury verdict), challenged as a breach of ERISA's fiduciary duty *not* the treating doctor's particular decision to delay Herdrich's care until an in-network provider was available, but rather *the very existence* of a "year-end fund" from which doctors would be rewarded for medical cost savings. ("[A]t oral argument [Herdrich's] counsel confirmed that the ERISA count could have been brought, and would have been no different, if Herdrich had never had a sick day in her life." *Id.* at 226.) As summarized by Justice Souter,

[Herdrich's] claim is that Carle, acting through its physician owners, breached its duty to act solely in the interest of beneficiaries by making decisions affecting medical treatment while influenced by the terms of the Carle HMO scheme, under which the physician owners ultimately profit from their own choices to minimize the medical services provided.

Id.

Justice Souter began his analysis of this claim by making two points. First, the HMO was merely the product sold to the ERISA plan and not the plan itself; it adopted its year-end payout scheme independently of, and before entering into a contract to provide health care to, ERISA plan members. "The HMO is not the ERISA plan, and the incorporation of the HMO preceded its contract with the State Farm plan. See 29 U.S.C. § 1109(b) (no fiduciary liability for acts preceding fiduciary status)." *Id.* at 227.

Second, the decision of Herdrich's employer, State Farm, to purchase the Carle HMO product (including its year-end payout incentive), was part of the employer's "plan design," and hence not subject to ERISA's fiduciary duty. (The concept of plan design as a complete shield to any challenge to the impact of the design or a claim of rights arose in *McGann v. H. & H. Music* as well as in *Jones v. Kodak,* both in Part Two). So, properly understood according to Justice Souter, Herdrich's ERISA claim must be that when Carle HMO contracted to become a fiduciary under State Farm's ERISA plan, its year-end payout scheme amounted to an "anticipatory breach" of Carle's duty to exercise its fiduciary function "solely in the interest of beneficiaries." *Id.* at 227.

Writing for a unanimous Court, Justice Souter then rejected this broadside attack on all (or most) cost containment financial incentives.

> Since the provision for profit is what makes the HMO a proprietary organization, [Herdrich's] remedy in effect would be nothing less than elimination of the for-profit HMO [and possibly nonprofit HMO schemes as well]. It is enough to recognize that the Judiciary has no warrant to precipitate the upheaval that would follow a refusal to dismiss Herdrich's ERISA claim. The fact is that for over 27 years the Congress of the United States has promoted the formation of HMO practices. The Health Maintenance Organization Act of 1973, allowed the formation of HMOs that assume financial risks for the provision of health-care services, and Congress has amended the Act several times. If Congress wishes to restrict its approval of HMO practice to certain preferred forms, it may choose to do so. But the Federal Judiciary would be acting contrary to the congressional policy of allowing HMO organizations if it were to entertain an ERISA fiduciary claim portending wholesale attacks on existing HMOs solely because of their structure, untethered to claims of concrete harm.

Id. at 233–34.

Focusing more precisely on the facts in *Pegram,* Justice Souter distinguished two types of decisions made by managed care entities such as Carle. The first he termed a "pure eligibility decision." To understand this, imagine a health benefit plan that expressly excludes (i.e. will not pay for) a certain category of treatment, e.g., dental care, or high-dose chemotherapy for breast cancer. Treatment would be denied not based on medical judgment but instead because of a flat exclusion that involved no exercise of judgment about the patient's case. In contrast, assume that the policy does cover "medically necessary" high-dose chemotherapy for breast cancer. In that case, if a patient were to seek coverage for such care, the question would be whether a covered service was medically necessary, thereby triggering medical judgment for that particular patient, i.e., a question involving assessment of the particular patient's medical condition and the necessity of that treatment.

In *Pegram,* that judgment was in fact exercised by the treating physician on the plan's behalf, once she decided not to order rapid (and presumably more expensive) diagnostic tests for her patient. But in writing the opinion, Justice Souter appeared to sweep relatively broadly, reaching all such mixed decisions even when made by a plan's utilization management staff or medical director:

> In practical terms, these [mixed] eligibility decisions cannot be untangled from physicians' judgments about reasonable medical treatment, and in the case before us, Dr. Pegram's decision was one of that sort. She decided (wrongly, as it turned out) that Herdrich's condition did not warrant immediate action; the consequence of that medical determination was that Carle would not cover [pay for] immediate care, whereas it would have done so if Dr. Pegram had made the proper diagnosis and judgment to treat. The eligibility decision and the treatment decision were inextricably mixed, as they are *in countless medical administrative decisions every day.* [emphasis added]

Id. at 229. Thus, although the decision-maker in *Pegram* was the treating clinician acting under delegated powers from the plan, the decision was interpreted to reach further. This interpretation was reinforced by Justice Souter's discussion of ERISA's history. Concluding that in creating ERISA's fiduciary duty, Congress was focusing overwhelmingly on financial decisions (notably management and payout of pension funds), not medical care, *id.* at 231–32, Justice Souter reflected that to allow ERISA fiduciary actions about mixed eligibility/treatment decisions would open the federal courts to a flood of "fiduciary malpractice" litigation, a prospect that the Court regarded with barely-concealed horror and could not imagine Congress having intended. *Id.* at 235–37.

For all of these reasons, Justice Souter's opinion concluded that "mixed eligibility decisions by HMO physicians are not fiduciary decisions under ERISA." *Id.* at 237. In doing so, however, the opinion implied that a mixed eligibility decision could be understood as any decision involving the exercise of individual medical judgment, not merely those decisions in which the "mixed" decision-maker was the treating physician.

Taking a cue from the ambiguity of this final point, and perhaps out of exasperation with Congress' failure to create a proper remedy, many lower federal courts began to classify claims in which the medical judgment of the plan administrator was implicated as the type of "mixed eligibility" decisions to which the Court had alluded in *Pegram*. Numerous cases were remanded to state court for trial as a result.

Remember: even in a remanded case, ERISA preemption still can arise, this time as an ERISA § 514 defense raised by the plan administrator, in which case, the entire action might still be dismissed before state trial. Then again, of course the plaintiff's case might survive the motion to dismiss, thus raising the ante for the defendant.

A fascinating example of a case in which ERISA § 514 preemption arose as a defense in a state court action occurred in Pappas v. Asbel, 724 A.2d 889 (Pa. 1998). In *Pappas*, an ERISA participant sued his physician and hospital for negligence in treating a medical emergency. The hospital brought a third-party complaint against U.S. Healthcare, which administered the plaintiff's ERISA plan, for negligence in failing to approve the plaintiff's transfer to an out-of-network hospital with greater emergency management capabilities. U.S. Healthcare moved in state court to dismiss the claim against it on ERISA § 514 grounds. The trial court granted the motion but the appellate court and Pennsylvania Supreme Court reversed, ruling based on *Travelers* (Part Two) that the claim was one for medical negligence involving the quality of care, not a claim related to the ERISA plan.

U.S. Healthcare then appealed the case to the Supreme Court, which simultaneously with its decision in *Pegram,* vacated the Pennsylvania Supreme Court's ruling and remanded the case for further review. (The remand served to reinforce the interpretation of *Pegram* that its principles applied to all medical judgment, not just the judgment of treating clinicians). *See* U.S. Healthcare Systems of Pennsylvania, Inc. v. Pennsylvania Hosp. Ins. Co., 530 U.S. 1241 (2000).

On remand, the Pennsylvania Supreme Court reaffirmed its earlier decision, holding that the third-party claim was one for medical negligence in the quality of health care and thus not preempted under ERISA § 514 principles. Pappas v. Asbel, 768 A.2d 1089 (Pa. 2001). The United States Supreme Court denied certiorari in U.S. Healthcare Systems of Pennsylvania, Inc. v. Pennsylvania Hosp. Ins. Co., 536 U.S. 938 (2002).

Pappas underscores the extent to which medical conduct versus plan administration may be in the eye of the beholder. Despite the fact that the claim involved the refusal of U.S. Healthcare's utilization management staff to authorize a transfer to a higher level of care, the Pennsylvania Supreme court characterized the conduct as medical in nature, thereby bringing the claim within the ambit of state medical liability law. And of course once the challenged conduct fell on the medical care side of the ledger, the *Travelers* principle (Part Two) came into full play; the state law in question was considered too remote and tenuous to "relate to" the plaintiff's ERISA plan:

> Applying *Travelers* and its progeny to the case *sub judice,* we determined that the negligence claims in plaintiffs' complaint,

which Haverford incorporated by reference against U.S. Health-care in its third party complaint, are not preempted. *Pappas I,* 724 A.2d at 894. We found that they do not "relate to" an ERISA plan within the meaning of 29 U.S.C. § 1144(a), and that local negligence laws, like many laws of general applicability, are only remotely connected to ERISA plans. *Id.* at 893, 894. In view of the Supreme Court's determination that Congress did not intend to preempt state laws aimed at regulating health care, we held it would have been inappropriate to conclude that Haverford's claims, in which the issue of U.S. Healthcare's allegedly dilatory delivery of contractually-guaranteed medical benefits were intertwined with the question of safe medical care, are preempted by ERISA. *Id.* at 893.

Pappas v Asbel, 768 A.2d at 1093. In a footnote the court explained that Haverford's third party complaint was worded as follows: "The negligence consisted of the following: a. Failing to transfer the patient to a hospital capable and competent of administering to his acute medical condition in a prompt and timely fashion; b. Delaying inordinately in transferring the patient, keeping him at [Haverford] during which time his spinal cord compression continued, with resulting permanent damage to the patient's spinal cord." *Id.*

Think about the workability of *Pegram's* terminology. Essentially Justice Souter distinguishes among three types of decisions. The first consists of "pure eligibility" decisions made by ERISA plan fiduciaries that involve issues such as whether a patient is an eligible plan participant, or whether the patient has satisfied the deductible, or whether physical therapy is listed as a plan benefit. The second type of decision—which Souter takes out of the fiduciary realm—is what he calls "mixed eligibility" decisions, which involve the interaction between medical judgment and the allocation of plan resources (e.g., is the lab test *so* medically necessary that it should be done on an urgent basis through an out-of-network provider rather than through the backed-up HMO lab?). The third type of decision-making is, of course, the type that institutional and professional health care providers engage in all the time, to-wit treatment decisions. Should I order a stat test? Is this patient ready to be discharged? The law assigns these decisions to the realm of "treatment." But can one really tell the difference between treatment and a mixed eligibility decision? When Dr. Pegram decided not to buck the system and order a stat test, was she making a resource decision or a treatment decision? And if in fact she was making a resource allocation decision on the plan's behalf, then why would her decision not have been that of the plan fiduciary? Teasing apart treatment decisions and mixed eligibility decisions is clearly very hard and not particularly workable, while potentially leaving plan fiduciaries without the ERISA liability shield in cases in which medical judgment is part of the plan resource allocation decision. The result is of course precisely the opposite of that in *Corcoran,* which is why so many observers were so stunned by *Pegram* and the implications of Justice Souter's terminology. We see this potential impact in *Pappas,* a decision in which a plan was stripped of its ERISA preemption shield in what arguably was a resource allocation case.

We flagged the complexity of this all in the notes following *Corcoran*. In each case, consider a state malpractice action brought against the HMO, or the plan sponsor, or an intermediary with which State Farm might have contracted to select among providers like the Carle HMO. Suppose that Dr. Pegram made her decision based on practice guidelines developed by the Carle HMO for when out-of-network testing should occur? Suppose that State Farm or an intermediary between it and the HMO had developed those guidelines? Suppose Carle HMO had used practice profiling in selection and retention of its physicians? Would there be a difference if State Farm or an intermediary between it and the Carle HMO had used profiling in its selection process and had contracted with the Carle HMO based on its ability to keep care within network? Suppose that on her own Dr. Pegram had decided that it was unnecessary to send her patient out of network for the ultrasound? Which of these decisions would create an avenue for imposition of corporate or vicarious liability against the Carle HMO, State Farm or an intermediary between the two if Dr. Pegram decides to delay the ultrasound so it can be done within network? In turn, which of these situations involves a "pure eligibility" decision, giving rise to ERISA preemption, or a "mixed eligibility" decision or a "treatment decision," for which there would be no preemption? What is the relationship between the strength of the Herdrich's case for imposing liability on the Carle HMO or some other entity higher in the food chain and the strength of the argument that her claim is preempted?

The Court did not think through the logic of holding that "mixed eligibility" decisions stand outside of fiduciary responsibility. Think of the coverage cases in Part 2. Most saliently, *Firestone* held that the default standard imposed by ERISA for judicial review of fiduciaries' medical necessity determinations was de novo review; that plan administrators could reserve their rights to deferential review under an arbitrary and capricious standard; and that a fiduciary's conflict of interest in making medical necessity determinations could count as a factor in this review. *Glenn* then expanded on this holding, imposing an obligation to minimize the impact of the fiduciary's conflicts of interest by taking steps to ensure the accuracy of decision making. This line of cases, all involving "mixed eligibility" decisions, is rendered incoherent by the reasoning in *Pegram*, for the cases are all completely grounded in the fact that these decisions are rendered by fiduciaries. Indeed, interpreting *Pegram* as focused on the type of decision—which many courts then proceeded to do—rather than the identity of the decision maker, as implied by *Corcoran*, effectively eliminates the existence of any fiduciary function in medical necessity determinations. The Court in *Pegram* seemed intent on removing from ERISA's ambit cases involving the exercise of medical judgment by treating physicians but given that treatment decisions and benefit determinations are, as the Court put it, "often practically inextricable from one another," the Court was effectively at a loss how to disentangle the two so as to wall off decisions of treating physicians in managed care, so as not to sweep them all within ERISA, while leaving intact the discretion exercised by plan administrators in medical necessity determinations.

Rush Prudential HMO, Inc. v. Moran, 536 U.S. 355 (2002), discussed in the notes following *Boyd* in the previous chapter, came right on the heels of *Pegram* and seemingly contradicted *Pegram's* theory that mixed eligibility decisions somehow lie beyond the ERISA fiduciary pale. In *Rush* the plaintiff sought coverage for back surgery which the plan administrator denied on medical grounds. Based on Illinois law, she then took her case to an independent external reviewer and won, and the HMO argued that as an insurer of an ERISA plan, it was exempt from state-mandated external review under *Pilot Life,* because the external review process effectively created an additional remedy. Thus, *Rush* raised the question of whether ERISA preempts a state insurance law that regulates contract interpretation by guaranteeing insurance policyholders the right to an impartial external review of their health plan's medical necessity decisions. The answer, according to Justice Souter and the *Rush* majority, was no, that external review simply regulates how insurance contracts are to be interpreted and applied to particular cases and does not add a remedy in violation of ERISA § 502.

At the same time—and weirdly—the conduct that lay at the heart of *Rush* (i.e., the denial of care considered medically unnecessary) amounted to *exactly* the type of decision that the Court seemingly had told everyone just two years before in *Pegram* should not be regarded as an ERISA decision at all (i.e., it involved the "when and how" of health care). Yet Justice Souter made no mention of this seeming inconsistency; indeed, no Justice—not the majority, not the dissent—questioned the fact that, in deciding *Rush,* the Court was confronted with the conduct of an ERISA fiduciary. This fact alone should have been a signal to the world that to read *Pegram* as placing all medical judgment decisions outside the scope of ERISA fiduciary conduct was wrong. However, it took *Davila,* decided two years after *Rush,* to whack people over the head about the Court's true intentions, namely extending the principle of *Pilot Life* to give maximum liability protection to both insured and self-insured ERISA plans while stopping the ERISA Preemption Express at some magic point known as "treatment," at which point state law would become relevant again.

Given the confusion that reigned after *Pegram,* it was not surprising that four years later, in *Aetna v. Davila,* the Court revisited its *Pegram* holding as part of a case that directly tested the validity of a state law that broadly classified negligent medical judgment affecting health care treatment as an actionable tort.

Aetna Health, Inc. v. Davila

542 U.S. 200 (2004)

■ JUSTICE THOMAS delivered the opinion of the Court.

In these consolidated cases, two individuals sued their respective health maintenance organizations (HMOs) for alleged failures to exercise ordinary care in the handling of coverage decisions, in violation of a duty imposed by the Texas Health Care Liability Act (THCLA), Tex. Civ. Prac. & Rem. Code Ann. §§ 88.001–88.003. We granted certiorari to decide whether the individuals' causes of action are completely pre-empted by the "interlocking, interrelated, and interdependent remedial scheme," *Massachusetts Mut. Life Ins. Co. v. Russell*, 473 U.S. 134, 146 found at § 502(a) of the Employee Retirement Income Security Act of 1974 (ERISA), 29 U.S.C. § 1132(a). We hold that the causes of action are completely pre-empted and hence removable from state to federal court. The Court of Appeals, having reached a contrary conclusion, is reversed.

I

A

Respondent Juan Davila is a participant, and respondent Ruby Calad is a beneficiary, in ERISA-regulated employee benefit plans. Their respective plan sponsors had entered into agreements with petitioners, Aetna Health Inc. and CIGNA Healthcare of Texas, Inc., to administer the plans. Under Davila's plan, for instance, Aetna reviews requests for coverage and pays providers, such as doctors, hospitals, and nursing homes, which perform covered services for members; under Calad's plan sponsor's agreement, CIGNA is responsible for plan benefits and coverage decisions.

Respondents both suffered injuries allegedly arising from Aetna's and CIGNA's decisions not to provide coverage for certain treatment and services recommended by respondents' treating physicians. Davila's treating physician prescribed Vioxx to remedy Davila's arthritis pain, but Aetna refused to pay for it. Davila did not appeal or contest this decision, nor did he purchase Vioxx with his own resources and seek reimbursement. Instead, Davila began taking Naprosyn, from which he allegedly suffered a severe reaction that required extensive treatment and hospitalization. Calad underwent surgery, and although her treating physician recommended an extended hospital stay, a CIGNA discharge nurse determined that Calad did not meet the plan's criteria for a continued hospital stay. CIGNA consequently denied coverage for the extended hospital stay. Calad experienced post surgery complications forcing her to return to the hospital. She alleges that these complications would not have occurred had CIGNA approved coverage for a longer hospital stay.

Respondents brought separate suits in Texas state court against petitioners. Invoking THCLA § 88.002(a), respondents argued that petitioners' refusal to cover the requested services violated their "duty to exercise ordinary care when making health care treatment decisions," and that these refusals "proximately caused" their injuries. *Ibid.* Petitioners removed the cases to Federal District Courts, arguing that respondents' causes of action fit within the scope of, and were therefore completely pre-empted by, ERISA § 502(a). The respective District Courts agreed, and declined to remand the cases to state court. Because respondents refused to amend their complaints to bring explicit ERISA claims, the District Courts dismissed the complaints with prejudice.

B

Both Davila and Calad appealed the refusals to remand to state court. The United States Court of Appeals for the Fifth Circuit consolidated their cases with several others raising similar issues. The Court of Appeals recognized that state causes of action that "duplicat[e] or fal[l] within the scope of an ERISA § 502(a) remedy" are completely pre-empted and hence removable to federal court. *Roark v. Humana, Inc.,* 307 F.3d 298, 305 (2002). After examining the causes of action available under § 502(a), the Court of Appeals determined that respondents' claims could possibly fall under only two: § 502(a)(1)(B), which provides a cause of action for the recovery of wrongfully denied benefits, and § 502(a)(2), which allows suit against a plan fiduciary for breaches of fiduciary duty to the plan.

Analyzing § 502(a)(2) first, the Court of Appeals concluded that, under *Pegram v. Herdrich,* 530 U.S. 211 (2000), the decisions for which petitioners were being sued were "mixed eligibility and treatment decisions" and hence were not fiduciary in nature. The Court of Appeals next determined that respondents' claims did not fall within § 502(a)(1)(B)'s scope. It found significant that respondents "assert tort claims," while § 502(a)(1)(B) "creates a cause of action for breach of contract," and also that respondents "are not seeking reimbursement for benefits denied them," but rather request "tort damages" arising from "an external, statutorily imposed duty of 'ordinary care.' " From *Rush Prudential HMO, Inc. v. Moran,* 536 U.S. 355 (2002), the Court of Appeals derived the principle that complete pre-emption is limited to situations in which "States ... duplicate the causes of action listed in ERISA § 502(a)," and concluded that "[b]ecause the THCLA does not provide an action for collecting benefits," it fell outside the scope of § 502(a)(1)(B).

II

B

Congress enacted ERISA to "protect ... the interests of participants in employee benefit plans and their beneficiaries" by setting out substantive regulatory requirements for employee benefit plans and to "provid [e] for appropriate remedies, sanctions, and ready access to the Federal courts." 29 U.S.C. § 1001(b). The purpose of ERISA is to provide a uniform regulatory regime over employee benefit plans. To this end, ERISA includes expansive pre-emption provisions, which are intended to ensure that employee benefit plan regulation would be "exclusively a federal concern." *Alessi v. Raybestos–Manhattan, Inc.,* 451 U.S. 504, 523 (1981).

ERISA's "comprehensive legislative scheme" includes "an integrated system of procedures for enforcement." *Russell,* 473 U.S., at 147. This integrated enforcement mechanism, ERISA § 502(a), 29 U.S.C. § 1132(a), is a distinctive feature of ERISA, and essential to accomplish Congress' purpose of creating a comprehensive statute for the regulation of employee benefit plans. Therefore, any state-law cause of action that duplicates, supplements, or supplants the ERISA civil enforcement remedy conflicts with the clear congressional intent to make the ERISA remedy exclusive and is therefore pre-empted.

III

A

ERISA § 502(a)(1)(B) provides:

> "A civil action may be brought—(1) by a participant or beneficiary— . . . (B) to recover benefits due to him under the terms of his plan, to enforce his rights under the terms of the plan, or to clarify his rights to future benefits under the terms of the plan. 29 U.S.C. § 1132(a)(1)(B)."

This provision is relatively straightforward. If a participant or beneficiary believes that benefits promised to him under the terms of the plan are not provided, he can bring suit seeking provision of those benefits. A participant or beneficiary can also bring suit generically to "enforce his rights" under the plan, or to clarify any of his rights to future benefits.

It follows that if an individual brings suit complaining of a denial of coverage for medical care, where the individual is entitled to such coverage only because of the terms of an ERISA-regulated employee benefit plan, and where no legal duty (state or federal) independent of ERISA or the plan terms is violated, then the suit falls "within the scope of" ERISA § 502(a)(1)(B). In other words, if an individual, at some point in time, could have brought his claim under ERISA § 502(a)(1)(B), and where there is no other independent legal duty that is implicated by a defendant's actions, then the individual's cause of action is completely pre-empted by ERISA § 502(a)(1)(B).

To determine whether respondents' causes of action fall "within the scope" of ERISA § 502(a)(1)(B), we must examine respondents' complaints, the statute on which their claims are based (the THCLA), and the various plan documents. Davila alleges that Aetna provides health coverage under his employer's health benefits plan. Davila also alleges that after his primary care physician prescribed Vioxx, Aetna refused to pay for it. The only action complained of was Aetna's refusal to approve payment for Davila's Vioxx prescription. Further, the only relationship Aetna had with Davila was its partial administration of Davila's employer's benefit plan.

Similarly, Calad alleges that she receives, as her husband's beneficiary under an ERISA-regulated benefit plan, health coverage from CIGNA. She alleges that she was informed by CIGNA, upon admittance into a hospital for major surgery, that she would be authorized to stay for only one day. She also alleges that CIGNA, acting through a discharge nurse, refused to authorize more than a single day despite the advice and recommendation of her treating physician. Calad contests only CIGNA's decision to refuse coverage for her hospital stay. And, as in Davila's case, the only connection between Calad and CIGNA is CIGNA's administration of portions of Calad's ERISA-regulated benefit plan.

It is clear then, that respondents complain only about denials of coverage promised under the terms of ERISA-regulated employee benefit plans. Upon the denial of benefits, respondents could have paid for the treatment themselves and then sought reimbursement through a § 502(a)(1)(B) action, or sought a preliminary injunction, see *Pryzbowski v. U.S. Healthcare, Inc.,* 245 F.3d 266, 274 (C.A.3 2001) (giving examples where federal courts have issued such preliminary injunctions).[2]

Respondents contend, however, that the complained-of actions violate legal duties that arise independently of ERISA or the terms of the employee benefit plans at issue in these cases. Both respondents brought suit specifically under the THCLA, alleging that petitioners "controlled, influenced, participated in and made decisions which affected the quality of the diagnosis, care, and treatment provided" in a manner that violated "the duty of ordinary care set forth in §§ 88.001 and 88.002." Respondents contend that this duty of ordinary care is an independent legal duty. They analogize to this Court's decisions interpreting LMRA § 301, 29 U.S.C. § 1081, with particular focus on Caterpillar Inc. v. Williams, 482 U.S. 386 (1987) (suit for breach of individual employment contract, even if defendant's action also constituted a breach of an entirely separate collective bargaining agreement, not pre-empted by LMRA § 301). Because this duty of ordinary care arises independently of any duty imposed by ERISA or the plan terms, the argument goes, any civil action to enforce this duty is not within the scope of the ERISA civil enforcement mechanism.

The duties imposed by the THCLA in the context of these cases, however, do not arise independently of ERISA or the plan terms. The THCLA does impose a duty on managed care entities to "exercise ordinary care when making health care treatment decisions," and makes them liable for damages proximately caused by failures to abide by that duty. § 88.002(a). However, if a managed care entity correctly concluded that, under the terms of the relevant plan, a particular treatment was not covered, the managed care entity's denial of coverage would not be a proximate cause of any injuries arising from the denial. Rather, the failure of the plan itself to cover the requested treatment would be the proximate cause.[3] More significantly, the THCLA clearly states that "[t]he standards in Subsections (a) and (b) create no obligation on the part of the health insurance carrier, health maintenance organization, or other managed care entity to provide to an insured or enrollee treatment which is not covered by the health care plan of the entity." § 88.002(d). Hence, a managed care entity could not be subject to liability under the THCLA if it denied

---

2. Respondents also argue that the benefit due under their ERISA-regulated employee benefit plans is simply the membership in the respective HMOs, not coverage for the particular medical treatments that are delineated in the plan documents. Respondents did not identify this possible argument in their brief in opposition to the petitions for certiorari, and we deem it waived.

3. To take a clear example, if the terms of the health care plan specifically exclude from coverage the cost of an appendectomy, then any injuries caused by the refusal to cover the appendectomy are properly attributed to the terms of the plan itself, not the managed care entity that applied those terms.

coverage for any treatment not covered by the health care plan that it was administering.

Thus, interpretation of the terms of respondents' benefit plans forms an essential part of their THCLA claim, and THCLA liability would exist here only because of petitioners' administration of ERISA-regulated benefit plans. Petitioners' potential liability under the THCLA in these cases, then, derives entirely from the particular rights and obligations established by the benefit plans. So, unlike the state-law claims in *Caterpillar, supra,* respondents' THCLA causes of action are not entirely independent of the federally regulated contract itself. Cf. *Allis–Chalmers Corp. v. Lueck,* 471 U.S. 202, 217 (1985) (state-law tort of bad faith handling of insurance claim pre-empted by LMRA § 301, since the "duties imposed and rights established through the state tort . . . derive[d] from the rights and obligations established by the contract"); *Steelworkers v. Rawson,* 495 U.S. 362 (1990) (state-law tort action brought due to alleged negligence in the inspection of a mine was pre-empted, as the duty to inspect the mine arose solely out of the collective-bargaining agreement).

Hence, respondents bring suit only to rectify a wrongful denial of benefits promised under ERISA-regulated plans, and do not attempt to remedy any violation of a legal duty independent of ERISA. We hold that respondents' state causes of action fall "within the scope of" ERISA § 502(a)(1)(B), *Metropolitan Life,* 481 U.S., at 66, and are therefore completely pre-empted by ERISA § 502 and removable to federal district court.[4]

B

The Court of Appeals came to a contrary conclusion for several reasons, all of them erroneous. First, the Court of Appeals found significant that respondents "assert a tort claim for tort damages" rather than "a contract claim for contract damages," and that respondents "are not seeking reimbursement for benefits denied them." But, distinguishing between pre-empted and non-pre-empted claims based on the particular label affixed to them would "elevate form over substance and allow parties to evade" the pre-emptive scope of ERISA simply "by relabeling their contract claims as claims for tortious breach of contract." *Allis–Chalmers, supra,* at 211.

Second, the Court of Appeals believed that "the wording of [respondents'] plans is immaterial" to their claims, as "they invoke an external, statutorily imposed duty of 'ordinary care.' But as we have already dis-

---

4. Respondents also argue that ERISA § 502(a) completely pre-empts a state cause of action only if the cause of action would be pre-empted under ERISA § 514(a); respondents then argue that their causes of action do not fall under the terms of § 514(a). But a state cause of action that provides an alternative remedy to those provided by the ERISA civil enforcement mechanism conflicts with Congress' clear intent to make the ERISA mechanism exclusive. See Ingersoll–Rand Co. v. McClendon, 498 U.S. 133, 142 (1990) (holding that "[e]ven if there were no express pre-emption [under ERISA § 514(a)]" of the cause of action in that case, it "would be pre-empted because it conflict[ed] directly with an ERISA cause of action").

cussed, the wording of the plans is certainly material to their state causes of action, and the duty of "ordinary care" that the THCLA creates is not external to their rights under their respective plans.

Nor would it be consistent with our precedent to conclude that only strictly duplicative state causes of action are pre-empted. Frequently, in order to receive exemplary damages on a state claim, a plaintiff must prove facts beyond the bare minimum necessary to establish entitlement to an award. Cf. *Allis–Chalmers,* 471 U.S., at 217 (bad-faith refusal to honor a claim needed to be proved in order to recover exemplary damages). Congress' intent to make the ERISA civil enforcement mechanism exclusive would be undermined if state causes of action that supplement the ERISA § 502(a) remedies were permitted, even if the elements of the state cause of action did not precisely duplicate the elements of an ERISA claim.

C

Respondents also argue—for the first time in their brief to this Court—that the THCLA is a law that regulates insurance, and hence that ERISA § 514(b)(2)(A) saves their causes of action from pre-emption (and thereby from complete pre-emption). This argument is unavailing. The existence of a comprehensive remedial scheme can demonstrate an "overpowering federal policy" that determines the interpretation of a statutory provision designed to save state law from being pre-empted. *Rush Prudential,* 536 U.S., at 375. ERISA's civil enforcement provision is one such example. See *ibid.*

As this Court stated in *Pilot Life,* "our understanding of [§ 514(b)(2)(A)] must be informed by the legislative intent concerning the civil enforcement provisions provided by ERISA § 502(a), 29 U.S.C. § 1132(a)." 481 U.S., at 52. The Court concluded that "[t]he policy choices reflected in the inclusion of certain remedies and the exclusion of others under the federal scheme would be completely undermined if ERISA-plan participants and beneficiaries were free to obtain remedies under state law that Congress rejected in ERISA." *Id.* at 54. The Court then held, based on

> "the common-sense understanding of the saving clause, the McCarran–Ferguson Act factors defining the business of insurance, and, *most importantly,* the clear expression of congressional intent that ERISA's civil enforcement scheme be exclusive, ... that [the plaintiff's] state law suit asserting improper processing of a claim for benefits under an ERISA-regulated plan is not saved by § 514(b)(2)(A)."

Id., at 57 (emphasis added).

Pilot Life's reasoning applies here with full force. Allowing respondents to proceed with their state-law suits would "pose an obstacle to the purposes and objectives of Congress." *Id.* at 52. As this Court has recognized in both *Rush Prudential* and *Pilot Life,* ERISA § 514(b)(2)(A) must be interpreted in light of the congressional intent to create an exclusive federal remedy in ERISA § 502(a). Under ordinary principles of conflict pre-emption, then, even a state law that can arguably be characterized as "regulating insurance" will be pre-empted if it provides a separate vehicle to assert a claim for benefits outside of, or in addition to, ERISA's remedial scheme.

IV

Respondents, their *amici,* and some Courts of Appeals have relied heavily upon *Pegram v. Herdrich,* 530 U.S. 211 (2000), in arguing that ERISA does not pre-empt or completely pre-empt state suits such as respondents'. They contend that *Pegram* makes it clear that causes of action such as respondents' do not "relate to [an] employee benefit plan," ERISA § 514(a), 29 U.S.C. § 1144(a), and hence are not pre-empted.

Pegram cannot be read so broadly. In *Pegram,* the plaintiff sued her physician-owned-and-operated HMO (which provided medical coverage through plaintiff's employer pursuant to an ERISA-regulated benefit plan) and her treating physician, both for medical malpractice and for a breach of an ERISA fiduciary duty. The treating physician was also the person charged with administering plaintiff's benefits; it was she who decided whether certain treatments were covered. See *id.* at 228. We reasoned that the physician's "eligibility decision and the treatment decision were inextricably mixed." *Id.* at 229. We concluded that "Congress did not intend [the defendant HMO] or any other HMO to be treated as a fiduciary to the extent that it makes mixed eligibility decisions acting through its physicians." *Id.* at 231.

A benefit determination under ERISA, though, is generally a fiduciary act. See *Bruch,* 489 U.S., at 111–113. "At common law, fiduciary duties characteristically attach to decisions about managing assets and distributing property to beneficiaries." *Pegram, supra,* at 231; cf. 2A A. Scott & W. Fratcher, Law of Trusts §§ 182, 183 (4th ed.1987); G. Bogert & G. Bogert, Law of Trusts & Trustees § 541 (rev.2d ed.1993). Hence, a benefit determination is part and parcel of the ordinary fiduciary responsibilities connected to the administration of a plan. See *Varity Corp. v. Howe,* 516 U.S. 489 (1996) (relevant plan fiduciaries owe a "fiduciary duty with respect to the interpretation of plan documents and the payment of claims"). The fact that a benefits determination is infused with medical judgments does not alter this result.

Pegram itself recognized this principle. *Pegram,* in highlighting its conclusion that "mixed eligibility decisions" were not fiduciary in nature, contrasted the operation of "[t]raditional trustees administer[ing] a medical trust" and "physicians through whom HMOs act." 530 U.S., at 231–232. A traditional medical trust is administered by "paying out money to buy medical care, whereas physicians making mixed eligibility decisions consume the money as well." *Ibid.* And, significantly, the Court stated that "[p]rivate trustees do not make treatment judgments." *Id.* at 232. But a trustee managing a medical trust undoubtedly must make administrative decisions that require the exercise of medical judgment. Petitioners are not the employers of respondents' treating physicians and are therefore in a somewhat analogous position to that of a trustee for a traditional medical trust.[6]

ERISA itself and its implementing regulations confirm this interpretation. ERISA defines a fiduciary as any person "to the extent . . . he has any discretionary authority or discretionary responsibility in the administration of [an employee benefit] plan." § 3(21)(A)(iii), 29 U.S.C. § 1002(21)(A)(iii). When administering employee benefit plans, HMOs must make discretionary decisions regarding eligibility for plan benefits, and, in this regard, must be treated as plan fiduciaries. See *Varity Corp., supra,* at 511 (plan administrator "engages in a fiduciary act when making a discretionary determination about whether a claimant is entitled to benefits under the terms of the plan documents"). Also, ERISA § 503, which specifies minimum requirements for a plan's claim procedure, requires plans to "afford a reasonable opportunity to any participant whose claim for benefits has been denied for a full and fair review by the appropriate named fiduciary of the decision denying the claim." 29 U.S.C. § 1133(2). This strongly suggests that the ultimate decision maker in a plan regarding an award of benefits must be a fiduciary and must be acting as a fiduciary when determining a participant's or beneficiary's claim. The relevant regulations also establish extensive requirements to ensure full and fair review of benefit denials. See 29 CFR § 2560.503–1 (2004). These regulations, on their face, apply equally to health benefit plans and other plans, and do not draw distinctions between medical and nonmedical benefits determinations. Indeed, the regulations strongly imply that benefits determinations involving medical judgments are, just as much as any other benefits determinations, actions by plan fiduciaries. See, *e.g.,* § 2560.503–1(h)(3)(iii). Classifying any entity with discretionary authority over benefits determinations as anything but a plan fiduciary would thus conflict with ERISA's statutory and regulatory scheme.

Since administrators making benefits determinations, even determinations based extensively on medical judgments, are ordinarily acting as plan fiduciaries, it was essential to *Pegram*'s conclusion that the decisions challenged there were truly "mixed eligibility and treatment decisions," 530 U.S., at 229, *i.e.,* medical necessity decisions made by the plaintiff's treating physician *qua* treating physician and *qua* benefits administrator. Put another way, the reasoning of *Pegram* "only make[s] sense where the underlying negligence also plausibly constitutes medical maltreatment by a party who can be deemed to be a treating physician or such a physician's employer." *Cicio[v Does]* 321 F.3d, at 109 (Calabresi, J., dissenting in part).

---

6. Both Pilot Life and Metropolitan Life support this understanding. The plaintiffs in Pilot Life and Metropolitan Life challenged disability determinations made by the insurers of their ERISA-regulated employee benefit plans. See Pilot Life Ins. Co. v. Dedeaux, 481 U.S. 41, 43 (1987); Metropolitan Life Ins. Co. v. Taylor, 481 U.S. 58, 61 (1987). A disability determination often involves medical judgments. See, e.g., ibid. (plaintiff determined not to be disabled only after a medical examination undertaken by one of his employer's physicians). Yet, in both Pilot Life and Metropolitan Life, the Court held that the causes of action were pre-empted. Cf. Black & Decker Disability Plan v. Nord, 538 U.S. 822 (2003) (discussing "treating physician" rule in the context of disability determinations made by ERISA-regulated disability plans).

Here, however, petitioners are neither respondents' treating physicians nor the employers of respondents' treating physicians. Petitioners' coverage decisions, then, are pure eligibility decisions, and *Pegram* is not implicated.

■ JUSTICE GINSBURG, with whom JUSTICE BREYER joins, concurring.

The Court today holds that the claims respondents asserted under Texas law are totally preempted by § 502(a) of the Employee Retirement Income Security Act of 1974. That decision is consistent with our governing case law on ERISA's preemptive scope. I therefore join the Court's opinion. But, with greater enthusiasm, as indicated by my dissenting opinion in *Great–West Life & Annuity Ins. Co. v. Knudson,* 534 U.S. 204 (2002), I also join "the rising judicial chorus urging that Congress and [this] Court revisit what is an unjust and increasingly tangled ERISA regime." *DiFelice v. AETNA U.S. Healthcare,* 346 F.3d 442, 453 (C.A.3 2003) (Becker, J., concurring).

Because the Court has coupled an encompassing interpretation of ERISA's preemptive force with a cramped construction of the "equitable relief" allowable under § 502(a)(3), a "regulatory vacuum" exists: "[V]irtually all state law remedies are preempted but very few federal substitutes are provided." *Id.* at 456 (internal quotation marks omitted).

A series of the Court's decisions has yielded a host of situations in which persons adversely affected by ERISA-proscribed wrongdoing cannot gain make-whole relief. First, in *Massachusetts Mut. Life Ins. Co. v. Russell,* 473 U.S. 134 (1985), the Court stated, in dicta: "[T]here is a stark absence—in [ERISA] itself and in its legislative history—of any reference to an intention to authorize the recovery of extracontractual damages" for consequential injuries. *Id.* at 148. Then, in *Mertens v. Hewitt Associates,* 508 U.S. 248 (1993), the Court held that § 502(a)(3)'s term " 'equitable relief' . . . refer[s] to those categories of relief that were *typically* available in equity (such as injunction, mandamus, and restitution, but not compensatory damages)." *Id.* at 256 (emphasis in original). Most recently, in *Great–West,* the Court ruled that, as "§ 502(a)(3), by its terms, only allows for *equitable* relief," the provision excludes "the imposition of personal liability . . . for a contractual obligation to pay money." 534 U.S., at 221 (emphasis in original).

As the array of lower court cases and opinions documents, see, *e.g., DiFelice; Cicio v. Does,* 321 F.3d 83 (C.A.2 2003), *cert. pending sub nom. Vytra Healthcare v. Cicio,* fresh consideration of the availability of consequential damages under § 502(a)(3) is plainly in order. See 321 F.3d, at 106, 107 (Calabresi, J., dissenting in part) ("gaping wound" caused by the breadth of preemption and limited remedies under ERISA, as interpreted by this Court, will not be healed until the Court "start[s] over" or Congress "wipe[s] the slate clean"); *DiFelice,* 346 F.3d, at 467 ("The vital thing . . . is that either Congress or the Court act quickly, because the current situation is plainly untenable."); Langbein, What ERISA Means by "Equitable": The Supreme Court's Trail of Error in *Russell, Mertens,* and *Great–West,* 103 Colum. L. Rev. 1317, 1365 (2003) (hereinafter Langbein) ("The Supreme Court needs to . . . realign ERISA remedy law with the trust remedial tradition that Congress intended [when it provided in § 502(a)(3) for] 'appropriate equitable relief.' ").

The Government notes a potential amelioration. Recognizing that "this Court has construed § 502(a)(3) not to authorize an award of money damages against a *non-fiduciary,*" the Government suggests that the Act, as currently written and interpreted, may "allo[w] at least some forms of 'make-whole' relief against a breaching *fiduciary* in light of the general availability of such relief in equity at the time of the divided bench." As the Court points out, respondents here declined the opportunity to amend their complaints to state claims for relief under § 502(a); the District Court, therefore, properly dismissed their suits with prejudice. But the Government's suggestion may indicate an effective remedy others similarly circumstanced might fruitfully pursue.

"Congress . . . intended ERISA to replicate the core principles of trust remedy law, including the make-whole standard of relief." Langbein 1319. I anticipate that Congress, or this Court, will one day so confirm.

Notes

1. *The value of appeals rights and the ability to bring an emergency § 502 challenge in federal court.* As the Court notes, and as discussed in Part Two, federal ERISA regulations provide for expedited appeals in cases involving urgent care. The expedited review standard was carried over in regulations implementing the expanded appeals rights granted under the Patient Protection and Affordable Care Act (PPACA § 1001, adding Public Health Service Act § 2719). Furthermore, as Justice Thomas points out, it is possible to file a § 502 claim directly in court and seek waiver of appeals requirements under equitable principles.

In your view, do speedy appeals rights and direct access to the courts in extreme circumstances amount to a total replacement for the right to a remedy in the event of death or injury? Imagine you are Ruby Calad. You are lying in a hospital bed one day after major surgery and in a world of pain. At 7:00 a.m., a nurse comes around and tells you with a big smile that you are going home that day, will be discharged by noon, and that your family should come and get you. What do you do first? Call your doctor to find out why you are being sent home? Call your ERISA-knowledgeable lawyer and ask for an expedited appeal or an emergency claim to the closest federal court? What if your physician is willing to fight for you to stay and refuse to sign the discharge order? Do you risk losing and owing thousands of dollars to the hospital? Is this really what you are thinking about? Hopefully you might have a family member who can think about all of these options and realities, ideally one who went to law school and took health law.

For an analysis of the limited number of appeals pursued by privately insured enrollees see David M. Studdert & Carol Roan Gresenz, *Enrollee Appeals of Preservice Coverage Denials* 289 JAMA 889 (2003). Why do you think that appeals may be pursued so rarely? Since appeals are pursued so rarely, is it realistic to view the appeals process as a replacement for the ability of individuals to pursue recovery when determinations result in harm? Do an appeals system and laws permitting recovery for damages caused by negligent or bad faith conduct on the part of an insurer serve the same purpose, as the *Davila* decision seems to suggest?

2. *After* Davila. Following the decision, the hammer fell fast and hard, as courts began to dismiss pending "mixed eligibility" claims and reject new cases that they viewed as essentially raising coverage questions rather than health care quality matters. *See e.g.*, Lind v. Aetna Health, Inc., 466 F.3d 1195 (10th Cir. 2006); Barber v. Unum Life Ins. Co. of America, 383 F.3d 134 (3d Cir. 2004); Mayeaux v. Louisiana Health Service and Indem. Co., 376 F.3d 420 (5th Cir. 2004): Cicio v. Does, 385 F.3d 156 (2d Cir. 2004); and Land v. CIGNA Healthcare of Florida, 381 F.3d 1274 (11th Cir. 2004).

3. In thinking about the implications of *Davila*, don't forget what we covered in Chapter 8 in Part Two with regard to *Amara*. Conceivably *Amara* makes possible monetary make-whole equitable-relief remedies under ERISA § 502. Possibly those remedies would extend to harm flowing from denials of benefits. If that were to happen, then there would be a federal remedy and *Davila's* holding that state remedies are completely preempted would have less bite. The question, of course, would be what constitutes an *equitable* monetary remedy. Presumably compensatory damages, damages for pain and suffering, and punitive damages would not be feasible. But according to Justice Ginsburg, make-whole relief should be. So how about restitution for the losses suffered by a patient who relied on a health plan to carry out its fiduciary obligation to act in the patient's best interest in selecting and overseeing a health plan network? Later in this part you will read about a scandal in Las Vegas that involved an endoscopy center that exposed thousands of patients to hepatitis C through the use of infected drugs and substandard procedures. Health plans included the center into their networks, thereby effectively selecting the source of treatment for plan members and were sued on this basis under state law theories. Could this type of conduct be refashioned as a federal claim for breach of fiduciary duty, with attendant recoveries?

For a pre-Amara discussion of *Davila* and the possibility of make-whole relief in cases of medical injury, see Stacey Rogers Sharp, *ERISA Preemption and MCO Liability: The Court's Search in* Aetna Health Inc. v Davila *for Congress's Elusive Intent*, 84 TEX. L. REV. 1347 (2006).

c. The Final Step: ERISA Preemption in Cases in Which Claims Involve Negligent Treatment

Dukes v. U. S. Healthcare, Inc.

57 F.3d 350 (3d Cir.), *cert. den.*, 516 U.S. 1009 (1995)

■ STAPLETON, CIRCUIT JUDGE:

The plaintiffs in these two cases filed suit in state court against health maintenance organizations ("HMOs") organized by U.S. Healthcare, Inc., claiming damages, under various theories, for injuries arising from the medical malpractice of HMO-affiliated hospitals and medical personnel. The defendant HMOs removed both cases to federal court, arguing (1) that the injured person in each case had obtained medical care as a benefit from a welfare-benefit plan governed by the [ERISA], (2) that removal is proper under the Metropolitan Life Insurance Co. v. Taylor, 481 U.S. 58 (1987), "complete preemption" exception to the "well-pleaded complaint rule," and (3) that the plaintiffs' claims are preempted by § 514(a) of ERISA, 29 U.S.C. § 1144(a). The district courts agreed with these contentions and dismissed the plaintiffs' claims against the HMOs. The plaintiffs appeal those rulings and ask that their claims against the HMOs be remanded to state court.

We hold that on the record before us, the plaintiffs' claims are not claims "to recover [plan] benefits due under the terms of [the] plan, to enforce rights under the terms of the plan, or to clarify rights to future benefits under the terms of the plan" as those phrases are used in § 502(a)(1)(B) of ERISA, 29 U.S.C. § 1132(a)(1)(B). Accordingly, we hold that *Metropolitan Life's* "complete preemption" exception is inapplicable and that removal of these claims from state court was improper. We will reverse the judgments of the district courts and will remand each case to district court with instructions to remand the cases to the state courts from which they were removed.

Suffering from various ailments, Darryl Dukes visited his primary care physician, defendant Dr. William W. Banks, M.D., who identified a problem with Darryl's ears. A few days later, Banks performed surgery and prepared a prescription ordering that blood studies be performed. Darryl presented that prescription to the laboratory of Germantown Hospital and Medical Center but the hospital refused to perform the tests. The record does not reveal the reasons for the hospital's refusal.

The next day, Darryl sought treatment from defendant Dr. Edward B. Hosten, M.D. at the Charles R. Drew Mental Health Center, who also ordered a blood test. This time, the test was performed. Darryl's condition nevertheless continued to worsen and he died shortly thereafter. Darryl's blood sugar level was extremely high at the time of his death. That condition allegedly would have or could have been diagnosed through a timely blood test.

Darryl received his medical treatment through the United States Health Care Systems of Pennsylvania, Inc., a federally qualified health maintenance organization organized by U.S. Healthcare. As a qualified HMO under the federal Health Maintenance Organization Act of 1973, 42 U.S.C. §§ 300e–300e–17 (1988), this U.S. Healthcare HMO provides basic and supplemental health services to its members on a pre-paid basis. As is often the case, Darryl received his membership in the HMO through his participation in an ERISA-covered welfare plan sponsored by his employer.

Darryl's wife, Cecilia Dukes, brought suit in state court alleging medical malpractice and other negligence against numerous defendants, including Banks, Hosten, the Germantown Hospital, and the Drew Center. She also brought suit against the HMO, alleging that as the organization through which Darryl received his medical treatment, it was responsible, under a Pennsylvania state law ostensible agency theory (the "agency theory"), for the negligence of the various doctors and other medical-service providers. See Boyd v. Albert Einstein Medical Ctr., 547 A.2d 1229, 1234–35 (Pa. Super. Ct. 1988) (holding that an HMO may be held liable for malpractice under an ostensible agency theory where a patient looks to the HMO for care and the HMO's conduct leads the patient to reasonably believe that he or she is being treated by an employee of the HMO). She alleged further that the HMO failed to exercise reasonable care in selecting, retaining, screening, monitoring, and evaluating the personnel who actually provided the medical services (the "direct negligence theory").

The HMO removed the case to district court pursuant to the *Metropolitan Life* complete-preemption exception to the "well-pleaded complaint rule." In its notice of removal, it claimed that the HMO is part of—or at least plays a role in—the ERISA plan to provide health benefits and that Dukes' claims, properly construed, "are directed to the structure and operation of the employer benefit plan." In its view, Dukes' claims therefore "relate to" the welfare plan and accordingly are preempted under ERISA § 514(a).

Dukes moved for a remand and the HMO moved to dismiss. The district court denied Dukes' motion and granted the HMO's, explaining that Dukes' claims "related to" an ERISA plan—and thus were preempted—because (1) "any ostensible agency claim must be made on the basis of what the benefit plan provides and is therefore 'related' to it" and (2) "the treatment received must be measured against the benefit plan and is therefore also 'related' to it." Dukes v. United States Health Care Sys., Inc., 848 F. Supp. 39, 42 (E.D. Pa. 1994). It remanded to state court the remainder of Dukes' claims against the other defendants. *Id.* at 43.

Ronald and Linda Visconti are the biological parents of Serena Visconti, who was stillborn. During the third trimester of her pregnancy with Serena, Linda apparently developed symptoms typical of preeclampsia. The Viscontis claim that Linda's obstetrician, Dr. Wisniewski, negligently ignored these symptoms and that this negligence caused Serena's death. Like Darryl Dukes, Linda received her medical treatment through a federally qualified HMO organized by U.S. Healthcare. This HMO was called the Health Maintenance Organization of Pennsylvania/New Jersey. The Viscontis received their membership in the HMO through an ERISA-covered welfare plan.

Ronald Visconti, as administrator of Serena's estate, and Ronald and Linda, in their own right (collectively, "the Viscontis"), brought suit in the Philadelphia County Court of Common Pleas. They attempted to hold the HMO liable for Dr. Wisniewski's malpractice under ostensible and actual agency theories, alleging that when Linda became pregnant, the HMO held out Dr. Wisniewski as a competent and qualified participating obstetrician/gynecologist. They also sued the HMO under a direct negligence theory, claiming, among other things, that the HMO was negligent in its selection, employment, and oversight of the medical personnel who performed the actual medical treatment.

The HMO removed the case to federal court, asserting that the Viscontis' claims were completely preempted by ERISA. It then filed a motion to dismiss, and the Viscontis filed a motion to remand, contending that removal was improper and that ERISA did not preempt their state law claims. The district court denied the Viscontis' motion but granted the HMO's motion to dismiss. Visconti ex rel. Visconti v. U.S. Health Care, 857 F.Supp. 1097, 1105 (E.D. Pa. 1994).

The *Visconti* and *Dukes* cases have been consolidated on appeal.

The HMOs removed these cases to federal court pursuant to 28 U.S.C. § 1441, alleging that the district courts had original jurisdiction over the claims, because the claims "[arose] under the Constitution, treaties or laws of the United States." § 1441(b); 28 U.S.C. § 1331. To determine whether a claim "arises under" federal law—and thus is removable—we begin with the "well-pleaded complaint rule." See Metropolitan Life Ins. Co. v. Taylor, 481 U.S. 58, 63 (1987)

Under the well-pleaded complaint rule, a cause of action "arises under" federal law, and removal is proper, only if a federal question is presented on the face of the plaintiff's properly pleaded complaint. A federal defense to a plaintiff's state law cause of action ordinarily does not appear on the face of the well-pleaded complaint, and, therefore, usually is insufficient to warrant removal to federal court. Thus, it is well-established that the defense of preemption ordinarily is insufficient justification to permit removal to federal court.

The Supreme Court has recognized an exception to the well-pleaded complaint rule—the "complete preemption" exception—under which "Congress may so completely pre-empt a particular area that any civil complaint raising this select group of claims is necessarily federal in character." *Metropolitan Life*, 481 U.S. at 63–64. The complete preemption doctrine applies when

> the pre-emptive force of [the federal statutory provision] is so powerful as to displace entirely any state cause of action [addressed by the federal statute]. Any such suit is purely a creature of federal law, notwithstanding the fact that state law would provide a cause of action in the absence of [the federal provision].

Franchise Tax Bd., 463 U.S. at 23. Claims to enforce a collective-bargaining agreement under § 301 of the Labor Management Relations Act of 1947, 29 U.S.C. § 185, present a typical example of the complete-preemption doctrine at work The Supreme Court has determined that Congress intended the complete-preemption doctrine to apply to state law causes of action which fit within the scope of ERISA's civil-enforcement provisions. Metropolitan Life, 481 U.S. at 66. It explained:

The legislative history consistently sets out [Congress's] clear intention to make § 502(a)(1)(B) suits brought by participants or beneficiaries federal questions for the purposes of federal court jurisdiction in like manner as § 301 of [the Labor Management Relations Act of 1947, 29 U.S.C. § 185.] For example, Senator Williams, a sponsor of ERISA, emphasized that the civil enforcement section would enable participants and beneficiaries to bring suit to recover benefits denied contrary to the terms of the plan and that when they did so "it is intended that such actions will be regarded as arising under the laws of the United States, in a similar fashion to those brought under section 301 of the Labor Management Relations Act."

481 U.S. at 66. Thus, courts have found that the *Metropolitan Life* complete-preemption doctrine permits removal of state law causes of action in a host of different ERISA-related circumstances. See *id.* at 63–67 (holding that state common law causes of action asserting improper processing of a claim for benefits under an employee benefit plan are removable to federal court).

That the Supreme Court has recognized a limited exception to the well-pleaded complaint rule for state law claims which fit within the scope of § 502 by no means implies that all claims preempted by ERISA are subject to removal. Instead, as the U.S. Court of Appeals for the Sixth Circuit wrote recently, "removal and preemption are two distinct concepts." Warner v. Ford Motor Co., 46 F.3d 531, 535 (6th Cir. 1995). Section 514 of ERISA defines the scope of ERISA preemption, providing that ERISA "supersedes any and all State laws insofar as they may now or hereafter relate to any employee benefit plan described in [§ 4(a) of ERISA] and not exempt under [§ 4(b) of ERISA]." (Emphasis added.) The *Metropolitan Life* complete-preemption exception, on the other hand, is concerned with a more limited set of state laws, those which fall within the scope of ERISA's civil enforcement provision, § 502. State law claims which fall outside of the scope of § 502, even if preempted by § 514(a), are still governed by the well-pleaded complaint rule and, therefore, are not removable under the complete-preemption principles established in *Metropolitan Life*.

The difference between preemption and complete preemption is important. When the doctrine of complete preemption does not apply, but the plaintiff's state claim is arguably preempted under § 514(a), the district court, being without removal jurisdiction, cannot resolve the dispute regarding preemption. It lacks power to do anything other than remand to the state court where the preemption issue can be addressed and resolved.

The district courts in these cases found that the plaintiffs' state law claims against the U.S. Healthcare HMOs fall within the scope of § 502(a)(1)(B) and that the *Metropolitan Life* complete-preemption doctrine therefore permits removal. We disagree. To determine whether the state law claims fall within the scope of § 502(a)(1)(B), we must determine whether those claims, properly construed, are "to recover benefits due under the terms of [the] plan, to enforce rights under the terms of the plan, or to clarify rights to future benefits under the terms of the plan." In making that determination, it would be helpful to have a complete understanding in each case of the relationships among the HMO, the employer, and the other defendants, the nature of the plan benefits, and the rights of participants and beneficiaries under the plan. We are somewhat hampered here because these cases come to us on appeal from orders granting motions to dismiss. Because of this procedural status, the parties have had little chance to develop the records and, accordingly, we know very little about the nature of the plan benefits or about the role—if any—that U.S. Healthcare's HMOs play in the respective ERISA welfare plans.

We recognize that there are issues in dispute. The plaintiffs and the Department of Labor as amicus curie, for example, claim that the U.S. Healthcare HMOs are separate from the ERISA plans and that the sole benefit that participants and beneficiaries receive from each plan is the plaintiffs' membership in the HMOs. In their view, the plaintiffs' claims thus have nothing at all to do with § 502(a)(1)(B) because no one contests that the plaintiffs in fact have received their plan benefits (their membership in the HMO). Instead, under their view, the plaintiffs' claims merely attack the behavior of an entity completely external to the ERISA plan.

U.S. Healthcare, on the other hand, claims that the plan benefits are more than just the plan participants' or beneficiaries' memberships in the respective HMOs; it argues that the medical care received is itself the plan benefit. As a corollary to that position, it also disagrees with the plaintiffs' view that the HMOs are completely distinct from the respective ERISA plans, arguing that the HMOs in fact play a role in the delivery of plan benefits. It further maintains that ERISA is implicated because both the plaintiffs' agency claims and their direct negligence claims relate to the quality of the plan benefits and the HMOs' role as the entity that arranges for those benefits for the ERISA plans.

We need not here resolve these disputes about how to characterize the plan benefits or the HMOs' role in the respective ERISA plans. We will assume, without deciding, that the medical care provided (and not merely the plaintiffs' memberships in the respective HMOs) is the plan benefit for the purposes of ERISA. We will also assume that the HMOs, either as a part of or on behalf of the ERISA plans, arrange for the delivery of those plan benefits. We thus assume, for example, that removal jurisdiction would exist if the plaintiffs were alleging that the HMOs refused to provide the services to which membership entitled them.

Given those assumptions, we nevertheless conclude that removal was improper. We are compelled to this conclusion because the plaintiffs' claims, even when construed as U.S. Healthcare suggests, merely attack the quality of the benefits they received: The plaintiffs here simply do not claim that the plans erroneously withheld benefits due. Nor do they ask the state courts to enforce their rights under the terms of their respective plans or to clarify their rights to future benefits. As a result, the plaintiffs' claims fall outside of the scope of § 502(a)(1)(B) and these cases must be remanded to the state courts from which they were removed.

Nothing in the complaints indicates that the plaintiffs are complaining about their ERISA welfare plans' failure to provide benefits due under the plan. Dukes does not allege, for example, that the Germantown Hospital refused to perform blood studies on Darryl because the ERISA plan refused to pay for those studies. Similarly, the Viscontis do not contend that Serena's death was due to their welfare plan's refusal to pay for or otherwise provide for medical services. Instead of claiming that the welfare plans in any way withheld some quantum of plan benefits due, the plaintiffs in both cases complain about the low quality of the medical treatment that they actually received and argue that the U.S. Healthcare HMO should be held liable under agency and negligence principles.

We are confident that a claim about the quality of a benefit received is not a claim under § 502(a)(1)(B) to "recover benefits due under the terms of [the] plan."

The text [of the statute] lends no support to U.S. Healthcare's argument. On its face, a suit "to recover benefits due under the terms of [the] plan" is concerned exclusively with whether or not the benefits due under the plan were actually provided. The statute simply says nothing about the quality of benefits received.

Nor does anything in the legislative history, structure, or purpose of ERISA suggest that Congress viewed § 502(a)(1)(B) as creating a remedy for a participant injured by medical malpractice. When Congress enacted ERISA it was concerned in large part with the various mechanisms and institutions involved in the funding and payment of plan benefits. That is, Congress was concerned "that owing to the inadequacy of current minimum [financial and administrative] standards, the soundness and stability of plans with respect to adequate funds to pay promised benefits may be endangered." § 2, 29 U.S.C. § 1001(a). Thus, Congress sought to assure that promised benefits would be available when plan participants had need of them and § 502 was intended to provide each individual participant with a remedy in the event that promises made by the plan were not kept. We find nothing in the legislative history suggesting that § 502 was intended as a part of a federal scheme to control the quality of the benefits received by plan participants. Quality control of benefits, such as the health care benefits provided here, is a field traditionally occupied by state regulation and we interpret the silence of Congress as reflecting an intent that it remain such. See, e.g., Travelers Ins. Co., 115 S. Ct. 1671 (noting that while quality standards and work place regulations in the context of hospital services will indirectly affect the sorts of benefits an ERISA plan can afford, they have traditionally been left to the states, and there is no indication in ERISA that Congress chose to displace general health care regulation by the states).

We also reject the HMOs' attempts to characterize the plaintiffs' state court complaints as attempts to enforce their "rights under the terms of the [respective welfare] plans." That phrase is included, we believe, so as to provide a means of enforcing any contract rights other than the right to benefits, as for example the various plan-created rights of plan participants to benefit-claim and benefit-eligibility procedures. Just as § 502(a)(1)(B) provides the means by which a participant can insist on the promised benefits, so too does it provide the means for insisting on the plan-created rights other than plan benefits.

The HMOs point to no plan-created right implicated by the plaintiffs' state law medical malpractice claims. The best they can do is assert that the plaintiffs' medical malpractice claims "attempt to define a participant's rights under the plan." We cannot accept that characterization. The plaintiffs are not attempting to define new "rights under the terms of the plan"; instead, they are attempting to assert their already-existing rights under the generally-applicable state law of agency and tort. Inherent in the phrases "rights under the terms of the plan" and "benefits due under the terms of [the] plan" is the notion that the plan participants and beneficiaries will receive something to which they would not be otherwise entitled. But patients enjoy the right to be free from medical malpractice regardless of whether or not their medical care is provided through an ERISA plan.

Much of the above analysis also precludes us from concluding that the plaintiffs are asking the state courts to "clarify [their] rights to future benefits under the terms of the plan." As noted, there is no allegation here that the HMOs have withheld plan benefits due. Moreover, nothing in the complaints remotely resembles a request that the court clarify a right to a future benefit; instead, the plaintiffs' complaints center on past events.

We recognize that the distinction between the quantity of benefits due under a welfare plan and the quality of those benefits will not always be clear in situations like this where the benefit contracted for is health care services rather than money to pay for such services. There well may be cases in which the quality of a patient's medical care or the skills of the personnel provided to administer that care will be so low that the treatment received simply will not qualify as health care at all. In such a case, it well may be appropriate to conclude that the plan participant or beneficiary has been denied benefits due under the plan. This is not such a case, however. While the Dukes complaint alleges that the Germantown Hospital committed malpractice when it decided not to perform certain blood tests, no one would conclude from that malpractice that Germantown Hospital was not acting as a health care provider when it made those decisions. Similarly, while the Viscontis claim that Dr. Wisniewski was incompetent, there is no indication that he was not performing health care services at the time he allegedly committed the malpractice charged.

We also recognize the possibility that an ERISA plan may describe a benefit in terms that can accurately be described as related to the quality of the service. Thus, for example, a plan might promise that all X-rays would be analyzed by radiologists with a prescribed level of advanced training. A plan participant whose X-ray was analyzed by a physician with less than the prescribed training might well be entitled to enforce the plan's promise through a suit under § 502(a)(1)(B) to secure a denied benefit.

Much of the HMOs' argument in these cases is at root a contention that the employer and the HMO impliedly contracted that the health care services provided would be of acceptable quality and, accordingly, that these damage suits rest on a failure to provide services of acceptable quality. Since we do not have before us the documents reflecting the agreements between the employers and the HMOs, we are not in a position to determine whether such a commitment was implicit in their respective agreements. However, the burden of establishing removal jurisdiction rests with the defendant. Accordingly, the HMO is not in a position to press this argument.

Moreover, we hasten to add that while we have no doubt that all concerned expected the medical services arranged for by the HMOs to be of acceptable quality, this seems to us beside the point. The relevant inquiry is not whether there was an expectation of acceptably competent services, but rather whether there was an agreement to displace the quality standard found in the otherwise applicable law with a contract standard.

It may well be that an employer and an HMO could agree that a quality of health care standard articulated in their contract would replace the standards that would otherwise be supplied by the applicable state law of tort. We express no view on whether an ERISA plan sponsor may thus by contract opt out of state tort law and into a federal law of ERISA contract. We will reserve that issue until a case arises presenting it.[5] Nothing in this record suggests an agreement to displace the otherwise applicable state laws of agency and tort.

The HMOs take heart in a recent case, Corcoran v. United Healthcare, Inc., 965 F.2d 1321 (5th Cir.), *cert. den.*, 113 S. Ct. 812 (1992), in which the U.S. Court of Appeals for the Fifth Circuit held that ERISA preempts a medical malpractice claim against a medical consulting company for decisions it made as the third-party administrator of a welfare plan's "precertification" review program. We agree with the HMOs that under *Corcoran*, third-party private companies may, in some circumstances, play a role in an ERISA plan and that claims against such companies may fall within the scope of § 502(a). We nevertheless find *Corcoran* inapposite on the facts and claims alleged in this case.

The HMOs argue that we should read *Corcoran* broadly to hold that medical malpractice claims against an HMO should be removable under *Metropolitan Life* whenever an HMO provides the complained-about medical treatment as a benefit of an ERISA-covered health plan. The HMOs' reliance on *Corcoran* is misplaced. Although United's decisions in *Corcoran* were in part medical decisions, United, unlike the HMOs here, did not provide, arrange for, or supervise the doctors who provided the actual medical treatment for plan participants. (Blue Cross played that role in *Corcoran*.) Instead, United only performed an administrative function

---

5. It would seem to Judge Roth that, if a plan were to adopt its own standard of acceptable health care to be made available to beneficiaries, the plan should provide concurrently, through insurance or otherwise, an appropriate remedy to beneficiaries for any failure of the plan care providers to meet that standard or, in the alternative, should inform plan beneficiaries that tort law remedies for medical malpractice would not be available to them under the plan.

inherent in the "utilization review." The difference between the "utilization review" and the "arranging for medical treatment" roles is crucial for the purposes of § 502(a)(1)(B) because only in a utilization-review role is an entity in a position to deny benefits due under an ERISA welfare plan.[6]

In these cases, the defendant HMOs play two roles, not just one. In addition to the utilization-review role played by United in *Corcoran*, the HMOs also arrange for the actual medical treatment for plan participants. Only this second role is relevant for this appeal, however: on the faces of these complaints there is no allegation that the HMOs somehow should be held liable for any decisions they might have made while acting in their utilization-review roles. Stated another way, unlike *Corcoran*, there is no allegation here that the HMOs denied anyone any benefits that they were due under the plan. Instead, the plaintiffs here are attempting to hold the HMOs liable for their role as the arrangers of their decedents' medical treatment.

For the foregoing reasons, the district courts' judgments in these cases will be reversed and remanded with instructions to remand the cases to the state courts from which they came. Our holding that the districts courts lack removal jurisdiction, of course, leaves open for resolution by the state courts the issue of whether the plaintiffs' claims are preempted under § 514(a).

Notes

1. *Quality of care and ERISA preemption. Dukes* stands for the proposition, universally adhered to today, that quality of care claims will not be preempted by ERISA, either at the point of federal removal or via a defense raised in a state court action (see *Pappas v. Asbel,* following the discussion of *Pegram,* above.) The name of the game, then, for a plaintiff is to frame a claim as one that a court will understand as raising matters of the quality of care, either vicariously or through direct institutional negligence. Thinking about all of the cases reviewed in this chapter, do you consider them helpful? Do the theories advanced in non-ERISA cases allow plaintiffs a fair amount of latitude to attempt to maneuver a case into quality territory, or is it inevitable that most cases of medical injury involving ERISA plans will instead confront their characterization as treatment decisions made as part of resource allocation?

Attempting to draw a distinction between quality of care and plan administration can be difficult. Cases in which a plan substitutes what it considers to be a therapeutic equivalent for a prescribed drug have been treated as plan administration decisions, with predictable results, even where the impact is devastating to a patient. See Lind v. Aetna Health Care, 466 F.3d 1195 (10th Cir. 2006) (dismissing a liability action against a

---

6. As noted, we are assuming, without deciding, that the medical care provided (and not merely the plaintiffs' memberships in the respective HMOs) is the plan benefit for the purposes of ERISA. So viewed, when acting in their utilization-review role, the HMOs are making benefit determinations.

plan that substituted Ritalin for the patient's MS drug, over his physician's vocal objections). Why is this so different from the type of institutional interference evident in *Muse,* discussed in Chapter 18? Is the issue the plan's lack of direct control over treatment decisions?

But then there is the fascinating, post-*Davila case of* Insco v. Aetna Health and Life Insurance Co., 673 F. Supp.2d 1180 (D. Nev. 2009). The case arose out of a major scandal in Nevada, the infection of numerous patients with hepatitis C as a result of massive quality control problems at the Endoscopy Center of Southern Nevada. The patient, an employee of Ross Dress for Less, which insured its employees through Aetna, sued, claiming, among other matters, that Aetna had a "duty to evaluate, audit, monitor, and supervise" its network providers under Nevada laws applicable to the duty of health care entities. The District Court concluded that this case amounted to medical negligence (i.e., the negligent selection of treating providers) and thus did not fall into the *Davila* abyss of ERISA preemption. Citing Bui v. AT&T, 310 F.3d 1143 (9th Cir. 2002), Aetna moved to dismiss arguing that under *Bui,* such practices are considered plan administration decisions. No, said the *Insco* judge, the issue actually comes down to whether Aetna made its network decisions as part of administering an ERISA plan, *or instead,* as part of its ongoing internal operations related to building its products, which it *then sold* to ERISA plans. In other words, was the selection of the Endoscopy Center part of the plan administration or instead, part of the underlying managed care product design that ultimately led to the sale of products to ERISA plans and their subsequent administration? Thus was the key factual question raised.

> In *Bui,* the Court distinguished causes of action involving medical decisions made in the course of treatment, which are not preempted, from those that involve administrative decisions made in the course of administering an ERISA plan, which are preempted. Under *Bui,* a claim based on negligence in selection or retention of a provider, regardless of the source of the duty, "is a necessary part of the administration of an ERISA plan," not provision of services. [B]ut Aetna's decision to select providers to be in its Network was not an ERISA decision. This seemed to be Plaintiff's position at oral argument, although Plaintiff's brief does not draw this distinction clearly. To make this argument, Plaintiff must convince the Court that Aetna's decision to retain certain providers in its Network is not preempted, because Aetna's decisions in this regard were not made as part of administration of an ERISA plan, but simply as management of its internal affairs, which affected all of its clients, ERISA or not. A claim based on Aetna's alleged negligence under the statutory and common law duties existing in Nevada is not preempted by ERISA if Aetna's decisions in this regard do not concern administration of an ERISA plan. In other words, under *Bui,* the Court would have to find that any negligence claim against [the plan administrator] for selection and retention of Aetna is preempted, but that a similar claim

against Aetna for selection or retention of negligent providers is not similarly preempted unless it was done specifically in relation to an ERISA plan. If Aetna were purely the administrator of the plan, it could not under *Bui* be sued for negligent selection or retention of a provider. Both Defendants and Plaintiff refer to Aetna as the "administrator" of the plan throughout, which makes the distinction that Plaintiff attempts more difficult to see. Plaintiff's argument rests on the distinction that although Aetna may in fact be an administrator, it is not purely an administrator for the purposes of ERISA preemption, because even though this is its formal function under the contract, it is not only a delegate of Ross for administering the plan, but also a healthcare organization with its own duties under the Nevada Code. It is Aetna's actions in the latter capacity that are not preempted by ERISA § 514(a).

The Court therefore agrees with Plaintiff that a state law claim based on Aetna's allegedly negligent selection and retention of healthcare providers in its Preferred Provider Network is not preempted by ERISA § 514(a), because these choices are made not in conjunction with Aetna's contractual administration of an ERISA plan, but rather on Aetna's own accord, regardless of the existence of any ERISA plans. Aetna cannot wear its later grant of access to its pre-existing Preferred Provider Network as armor against Nevada's health and welfare regulations simply because it often grants access to the Network pursuant to an ERISA-administration contract with an employer. Aetna's choice of providers in the network is made independently from its contractual duties to administer any ERISA plan. Aetna's choice to grant access to its Network as it exists, or its direct selection of providers for Ross under the contract, are not subject to suit under state law, but Aetna's choice of providers within its own preexisting healthcare Network is.

Insco, 673 F. Supp. at 1188–89.

But then there is Cervantes v. Health Plan of Nevada, 263 P.3d 261 (Nev. 2011), another Endoscopy Center injury case in which the Supreme Court of Nevada refused to follow *Insco*. In *Cervantes,* the defendant was not an insurer but a self-funded union plan (recall that ERISA § 502 remedies do not distinguish between insured and self insured plans) that retained the defendant to help it build its plan network. Here, unlike *Insco,* in which Aetna sold a pre-packaged product to a plan sponsor, the insurer (Health Plan of Nevada) was brought in simply to help the sponsor design *its own plan.* Because the provider network selection was found to be part of plan administration as opposed to the sale of a prepackaged network to the plan, the plaintiff's claim was considered completely preempted under ERISA § 502.

Now isn't this ridiculous? Regardless of whether they are selling a prepackaged product or administering an ERISA plan, companies that put defective networks together—that participants must use if they want to be insured—get away with this conduct? Don't you assume that HPN was using the same network providers for its administered products sold to self-insured plan sponsors that it used in its prepackaged insured products? Should the availability of a deterrent remedy such an institutional liability really turn on which hat the insurance company happens to be wearing at any given moment? How is this remotely just?

Here is a postscript, a story from the Las Vegas Sun (http://www.las vegassun.com/blogs/news/2008/feb/27/hepatitis-outbreak-springs-endoscopy-center-nevada/) that gives you the full flavor of how this catastrophe was handled by state and federal officials.

Hepatitis C Outbreak Springs from Endoscopy Center of Nevada; 40,000 at risk (Feb. 27, 2008; updated June 2, 2009)

Steve Marcus

Southern Nevada Health District officials announced today they have identified six cases of hepatitis C, five of which stemmed from procedures occurring on the same day that involved anesthesia at the Endoscopy Center of Nevada. Following a joint investigation with the Nevada State Bureau of Licensure and Certification (BLC) and with consultation from the Centers for Disease Control and Prevention, the health district determined that unsafe injection practices related to the administration of anesthesia medication might have exposed patients to the blood of other patients. The health district is recommending 40,000 patients who had procedures requiring injected anesthesia at the clinic between March 2004 and January 11, 2008, contact their primary care physicians or health care providers to get tested for hepatitis C as well as hepatitis B and HIV.

Here is the company's response:

On behalf of the Endoscopy Center of Southern Nevada, we want to express our deep concern about this incident to the many patients who have put their trust in us over the years. As always, our patients remain our primary responsibility and we have already corrected the situation. The recent events related to the Southern Nevada Health District study mark the first time anything like this has ever happened at our facility. We have already taken steps to ensure that it will never happen again.

The health district began its investigation in January, and we have been fully cooperating with them. We were officially notified by the health district on February 6, 2008 and submitted our detailed Plan of Correction on February 15, 2008. All concerns noted by the health department were addressed immediately. We continue to work closely with the Southern Nevada Health District and other health agencies during this ongoing review. We want to be sure that every patient who may have been exposed is informed and tested. To help us with these issues, we have engaged the services of nationally renowned experts who have extensive epidemiological experience and that have worked closely with the Centers for Disease Control in the past. In addition to our corrective actions, we are on a mission to maintain the trust our patients have had in us during our years of service to southern Nevada.

We wish to emphasize that the actual risk of anyone being affected by this is extremely low, but as a precaution, anyone who has undergone procedures at the Endoscopy Center who required anesthesia should be tested. As I'm sure you understand this situation brings with it a number of complex elements including patient privacy and regulatory guidelines. At this time, our counsel has asked that we limit our comments to this statement, and we are unable to take questions.

CORRECTION: Earlier this blog said "Health officials say that practitioners were routinely using the same syringe on more than one patient, which is widely known to pass on infection." Actually, the same syringe was not being used on multiple patients. But single dose vials of medication, which had become infected through their initial use, were being used again. Health officials say this is widely known to pass infection.

2. *Pulling all the cases together: trying to unscramble the managed-care egg.* In the last note after *Mondry* in Part Two, we started developing the conceptual problem of what a "plan" consists of and what falls outside of the "plan." Throughout the ERISA materials, we have seen this theme recur. Clearly, if the plan administrator makes a decision to shape benefits under plan design, ERISA preempts a negligence action arising out of that decision and brought under state law. The key question is to decide whether a decision constitutes plan design. Similarly, if a decision is characterized as part of plan administration performed by one of the number of entities in the managed-care food chain, then a negligence action arising out of that decision is also preempted. However, as we have seen in these cases, the characterization question is by no means clear cut. *Dukes* leaves us with the distinction between decisions relating to the "quality" of treatment itself, which are not preempted, and decisions relating to plan design and administration, which are preempted, but, as should be clear by now, many decisions affect both quality and finance simultaneously.

This conceptual problem also intersects with the state-law doctrinal elements that a plaintiff must satisfy to bring a state-law negligence action against an entity other than the doctor who ultimately is responsible for treatment. You have probably realized by now that a plaintiff has a greater possibility of imposing vicarious liability against an actor in the managed-care food chain if that actor was more greatly involved in some manner in a decision directly connection with treatment. However, the dictates of state law, combined with the doctrine regarding ERISA preemption, puts the plaintiff between a rock and a hard place because the stronger the claim for assigning responsibility up the food chain, the greater the chance that the state law will be preempted.

Start with two extremes, one at the each end of a continuum. Suppose that the treating physician commits one of the "never-events" we discussed earlier in this Part. He or she operates on the wrong site or wrong patient. Suppose that there are no facts like those in *Jones v. Chicago HMO*, above, which might support a claim that the managed-care entity contracting with the provider has created a situation in which such an event becomes likely (a claim that would be very difficult to mount under almost any conceivable circumstances that could lead to a never-event). It would be almost inconceivable that the never-event was linked to financial incentives, provider selection, provider profiling, guidelines or any other activity that is a function somewhere within the managed-care food chain. This example is a close as we can get to a "quality" problem to which, under *Dukes*, one could escape preemption but likewise, fail to mount a claim for vicarious or corporate liability. Preemption doctrine, therefore, is irrelevant anyway because state law only creates liability against the individual providers, the surgeon and the hospital. The buck stops there.

At the other extreme are cases like *Corcoran*, *Davila* or *McEvoy*, should that case have involved an ERISA plan. At its fullest intensity is the *Wickline* situation in which a plan administrator refuses to authorize payment for any more treatment, and the physician bows to the decision without protest. In such cases, the plan administrator explicitly denies coverage. As we have written in the notes after these cases, it's easy to conclude that there has been a "pure eligibility decision" (*Pegram's* language) or a "benefit determination" (*Corcoran's* language). Or think back to *Jones v. Kodak* in Part Two, in which the practice guideline precluding the mental health benefit was explicitly incorporated into the plan. This too is an easy case to hold both that the plan has made the decision that caused harm and therefore to mount successfully a corporate liability claim under state law, but concomitantly an easy case to hold that ERISA preemption applies.

In between these two extremes, a vast middle ground exists. Network formation and administration are extremely complicated, and the question of the manner in which these aspects affect a particular decision in a particular case is always multifaceted. Isn't assembling an incompetent network directly parallel to a hospital failing to select its medical staff with reasonable care? Why is one type of misconduct classified as plan design or administration while the other is corporate medical negligence? Think about the layer upon layer of contracting parties that existed in *Chase*, discussed earlier in the notes following *Boyd*. At any layer, financial incentives may be involved, guidelines created and deployed, providers profiled, providers selected and deselected, ongoing care supervised to differing degrees and among various parties, pay-for-performance imposed, quality reporting used, and so on, and so on, and so on. Suppose a plaintiff can link an adverse event to some of these actions as influencing the treatment provided or not provided. We've seen that the imposition under state law of vicarious or corporate liability is totally fact dependent, sensitive to the degree to which there was actual control of the treating physician, whether apparent authority was conveyed to the patient, or whether corporate responsibility should be imposed for the situation created by some entity in the managed-care food chain. Indeed, because the structures of these layer cakes are so variable, the question whether there is "any there, there" up above in the food chain—any sort of institutionalization that we can say makes appropriate the analogy of imposing vicarious or corporate liability in hospitals—is enormously fact-sensitive. The same is true, then, whether a claim can be characterized as involving "quality" or "benefit determination."

A few more examples to close. As we have seen, *Wickline* involved a breakdown in communication—all so typical of malpractice. As we developed in the notes following the opinion, this breakdown was jointly created by the manner in which Medi–Cal organized its review process, the manner in which Dr. Glassman, his supervisor, and the on-site nurse, Nurse Futerman, conducted the process, and the action of Wickline's attending physicians in authorizing the discharge, the manner in which their decisions were made—which were a mixture of medical considerations in that her condition had not deteriorated during the four days prior to discharge—as well as their failure to press their view in the review system, an omission which in turn may have been induced by Medi–Cal's repeated denials, making argument futile. What caused the loss of Wickline's leg? *All of it*. If she had belonged to an ERISA plan and had sued the plan or any of the intermediaries in the managed-care layer cake for negligence, would her claim relate to quality of care? Definitely. Would it have involved administration of a benefit plan? Quite arguably too.

In *Shannon v. McNulty*, Shannon was on the phone constantly with HealthAmerica HMO as the sad sequence of events unfolded. She likewise saw and then was in constant phone contact with Dr. McNulty, who became increasingly irascible toward her, totaling discounting the possibility that she was experiencing preterm labor. She didn't understand when to call the staff of the HMO and when to call McNulty; and no one straightened this out for her. Moreover, no one at HealthAmerica decided to pull the plug on McNulty until it was too late for the baby. Who caused the death of this baby? *They all did*. Is her claim against them all one that involves "quality" or does it relate to the manner in which the benefit plan is organized and administered? Both.

We could raise example after example. The manner in which Dr. Jordan was assigned far more cases than any human being could ever cover in *Jones v. Chicago HMO*. A variation of these same financial incentives are in play in *Pegram*, *Boyd* and other cases. How does one distinguish between credentialing the treating doctors or the medical reviewer? Dr. Glassman in *Wickline* only wanted to know whether Wickline had fever, could ambulate, defecate, and eat properly. None of this was in the least relevant to the question regarding the risk of another clot forming at the site of the synthetic graft. Dr. Glassman was as qualified to make that decision as you or we.

The point is simply this: Managed care, whether to manage costs, quality or both, is supposed to infuse considerations of both cost and quality *into treatment* through the numerous means discussed in this note and illustrated throughout the cases and notes in this Part. In a few cases like *Corcoran* and *Davila*, we see that ERISA shields a plan from liability even when medical judgment and medical decisions led to death and injury. Yet in *McEvoy* and *Jones v. Chicago HMO*, we see how state law can be used to hold plans accountable when their conduct or decisions lead to harm. So what this all comes down to is whether a patient's coverage is through a plan that is shielded or not shielded. Does this make sense? In the end, from a broader policy perspective of assuring that actors in health care quality remain accountable for injuries caused by substandard care, ERISA § 502 not only fails to make sense whatsoever but is simply unjust. For those reasons, Justice Ginsburg in her concurring opinion in *Davila* was absolutely correct that it's time for Congress to fix this mess. We're still waiting, despite the passage of the ACA.

3. *What is a physician's duty of advocacy in the utilization management process?* Related to what might be termed a physician's "duty of advocacy" on behalf of the patient in the utilization review process, should a physician be expected to see a patient promptly regardless of HMO documentation problems and to submit prompt referral requests? A 1999 New York case involved a patient receiving cardiac care whose employer switched its insurance carrier from Blue Cross/Blue Shield to a choice of three HMOs. The patient promptly enrolled in one of the HMOs, selected a primary care physician, attempted to see that physician, and obtain a referral to his existing out-of-network specialist, whom he was still permitted to use under the plan. The patient experienced a more than six-week delay in arranging care through the new primary care physician, through a combination of delays in receiving an accurate HMO card, the primary care physician's refusal to see him with an incorrect card, the primary care physician's 10–day delay in submitting the specialist referral form, and the HMO's refusal to authorize out-of-network care. The patient died of a heart attack the day before his appointment with an in-network specialist.

In his wife's subsequent state law suit against the primary care physician, the HMO Director, the HMO and two of its subsidiaries, the claims against all defendants except the primary care physician were removed to federal court and dismissed as preempted by ERISA The primary care physician then argued in state court that the claims against him based on medical malpractice, breach of contract, and breach of (state law) fiduciary duty were preempted by ERISA, presumably because they related to the patient's status as an HMO enrollee and the procedures for processing referral requests. The New York Court of Appeals held that while the plaintiff's claims did make some reference to the HMO's administrative framework, that reference with respect to a primary care physician was "too tenuous, remote or peripheral" to constitute "relating to" an ERISA plan. Nealy v. US Healthcare HMO, 93 N.Y.2d 209, 711 N.E.2d 621 (1999).

PART FOUR

REGULATION OF HEALTH CARE TRANSACTIONS

CHAPTER 22

OVERVIEW

Health care has always been a business. Riding under the banner of professionalism, providers used to try to hide the fact that they made money, but that has always been the case. They have always made money.

Nonetheless, the question is one of degree. As has been documented throughout this book, the health care world of today does not resemble periods that existed prior to what might be thought of as the modern era, when: (1) private third-party health care financing began in the 1930s; (2) in the immediate post-Second World War period, specialization really took off and the modern hospital began to take its current form; (3) in 1965, Medicare and Medicaid were passed, and the amount of money pouring into the system increased tremendously, as did governmental involvement in the sector, and for-profit skilled nursing facilities were created in vast numbers; (4) in the mid–1970s, for-profit hospitals and for-profit insurance companies began seriously challenging the predominance of non-profits across much larger areas of the country than ever before; and focus began to get placed on the standardization of medical practice, just as ERISA effectively freed self-insuring employers from provider-dominated state insurance regulation; (5) in 1983, the Medicare inpatient prospective payment system began a revolutionary change in how providers are paid; (6) in roughly the mid–1990s, with the advent of managed care, investor capital flowed massively into for-profit managed care organizations, perhaps taking the cue from the adoption of managed competition by the Clinton health plan, even as it went down in flames; and (7) beginning shortly thereafter, following the lead of the insurance industry, physicians and hospitals began to organize themselves into ever-growing medical business ventures in order to increase their bargaining power.

Our health care system is now fully industrialized. It is the "industrial-medical complex," the arrival of which Dr. Arnold S. Relman, then-editor of the prestigious and influential *New England Journal of Medicine*, announced in 1980. *The New Medical–Industrial Complex*, 303 NEW ENG. J. MED. 963. The fact that health care in America is a fully commercialized enterprise is no longer a hidden, nasty, whispered secret. Making money—and mega-money at that—has become the coin of the realm.

And with a vengeance—but don't please tell anyone—emerged the contradiction which thematically dominates this Part. If we may be excused for creating yet one more "ism," the watch word is now "transactionism"; and they are everywhere. Transactions occur between patients and doctors, patients and hospitals, patients and nursing homes, patients and home health agencies, patients and their insurance plans, patients and.... And everyone is doing it with everyone else: doctors with doctors, doctors with plans, doctors with hospitals, hospitals with hospitals, hospitals with plans, hospitals with nursing homes, etc., etc., and so forth.

The institutional blessing for this massive degree of entanglement has all been brought to you by law, the subject of this Part. Yet, the law likewise sends a counter-revolutionary message: Don't do it too much. Be bound, not to your transactional partners but to your patients; not to your investors but to your patients; not to sharing the enormous wealth you are creating among yourselves but to your patients; not to the gigantic quantity of care you produce but to the high quality of care you owe to your patients.

This tension is the subject of this Part—and in fact, the entire book— the love our country has for full-scale, unfettered, brutish and nasty capitalistic war in health care, with all of its benefits of raw, unvarnished efficiency, weeding out the weak and the sick for special treatment under health care programs for the poor and medically vulnerable such as Medicaid—but also our great fear of all of capitalistic health care's effects, the collateral damage that is wrought on those who get left behind by markets, and the massive, resource-sucking effect that our capitalism has. It has become clear that the demand-generating capacity of advanced, modern capitalism's health care organizations is power unsurpassed, except for the power of the modern nation-state, which in the United States we fear even more.

Our description in this Part of this ambivalence, this love-hate affair, begins with the exemption from taxation for nonprofit health care providers, the subject of Chapter 23. The exemption is grounded in community, in solidarity. It is about supporting organizations that are supposed to stand against the gales of profit-maximization, that are supposed to create public good and public benefit, elevating altruism and mission over taking advantage of power over patients, over health plans, against the rest of society. It is supposed to be about freedom from reliance on the capital markets for resources, against the sole loyalty to investors that is the primary legal obligation that comes with that form of capitalization.

Yet there is the other side of the coin, for as we shall see, the tax exemption has been under attack for decades now, by academics who question its utility, who document how little is obtained in return, particularly as the amount of charity care provided has dropped, and by many states and federal actors, who likewise demand that they get something in exchange for the public dollars that are paid to the nonprofits from the value of the exemption, even though exchange is the antithesis of the notion that health care is to be founded in communal solidarity and obligation. As this debate has raged, other parts of law, particularly antitrust, examined in Chapter 25, and payment, examined in Chapter 13 of Part Two, have encouraged all actors in the sector, nonprofit and for-profit alike, to compete and compete hard. A vicious cycle, therefore, has been put in place by law, in which nonprofits are encouraged and forced by survival in the market to act like for-profits, but as they do so, there are fewer resources to spend on mission, with the result that their tax-exempt status is less legitimate, made less tenable, even though the squeezing out of cross-subsidization of unprofitable services makes profit-maximization appear to be the only viable alternative to keeping any money for mission alive. We trace this tension and debate in the doctrine of the tax exemption, as more is demanded of nonprofits in a world that allows them to do less and simultaneously counts less of what they do as nonprofit activity.

We then turn, in Chapter 24, to the subject of fraud in health care. This topic had its beginning in the common-sense meaning of fraud—inducing someone to give something for nothing or for something that is worthless, but we'll see that the subject has now turned into a monster to face down the monster that haunts us: that in our totally commercialized society oriented to joint venturing with as many partners as possible, in order to make as much money as possible, health care providers are doing too much joint venturing, and making too much money. We trace the doctrinal basis of the huge war that is being fought as health care fraud, defined indeterminately as too much transactionsim going on, too great profiteering, making too much money. Health care fraud is an illustration of our legal regime at war with itself. Numerous laws and policies encourage integration, generating as much efficiency and surplus as possible, and the creation of the transactional bonds that through integration enable that wealth to be generated. Yet the fraud laws simultaneously attempt to put at risk many of these transactions and the sharing of the enormous wealth being created. We'll see that the laws of fraud now potentially exact an extremely high price, with massive fines and the threat of jail time even for executives at the head of these enterprises.

And finally, we turn to antitrust, that great engine of capitalism. Antitrust blew apart that cozy world in which money-making was a secret. It destroyed the collective power of professionalism, an ideology that many would say kept the lid on the demand-generating capacity of health care professionals and largely prevented professionals' enlistment in organizations to which they could accommodate and become much more powerful in generating the holy dollar. Antitrust largely splintered this world and enabled it to be assembled anew in the transactionism of today. Antitrust destroyed the collective economic front of the medical profession and hospitals and opened up the world to new organizational fields, particularly for-profit health insurers, who now assemble the different professional players as inputs in networks to be purveyed to plan sponsors. In the doctrine we will trace how this happened, through at least initially treating collaboration among doctors as suspect, and thereby atomizing them in transactions, to be picked off by insurance companies in the assembly of their networks. However, antitrust also invited a counter-revolution to occur here as well, through exceptions and safe harbors that attempt to balance quality and the aspiration for coordinated delivery, on the one side, against the ban on collective and anti-competitive conduct, on the other. This equivocation allowed providers to consolidate into organizations that possess greater market power than ever before and that can better bear the risk imposed on them by prospective payment. Antitrust has not succeeded in breaking down these new forms of consolidation because much of it has occurred in a favored form, so-called vertical arrangements, to be explained below, and because our laws in other ways, examined in the chapter on payment and in the quality materials of Part Three, are pushing for the coordination and consolidation of providers in order to improve the delivery of care. There also has been, quite frankly, solicitude for doctors, who have engaged in illegal practices time and time again without feeling the full brunt of the law. The result, documented increasingly of late, has been consolidation on both sides of the marketplace and then cooperation between them, as margins and power on both sides increase.

The law examined in Part Four, therefore, has largely fought itself to a standstill, and we are stuck. Our costs continue to rise, and we continue to have the tremendous problems of fragmentation in delivery and payment that weaken the effort to improve the quality of care and reduce its costs. This stalemate has been the subject of the book, and so it should come as no surprise that it is the subject of this final Part.

CHAPTER 23

TAX EXEMPTION IN THE MODERN HEALTH CARE SYSTEM

The words creating the so-called "Section 501(c)(3)" exemption from federal income taxation are seemingly simple. Organizations are exempt from federal income taxation if they are "organized and operated exclusively for religious, charitable, scientific, or educational purposes," I.R.C. § 501(c)(3), known as "exempt purposes." To qualify for the exemption, an organization must satisfy both an "organizational test" and an "operational test." *See* Treas. Reg. § 1.501(c)(3)–1(a). The organizational test is purely formal in that it requires only that the entity be organized solely to achieve exempt purposes. Hence, the documents establishing the entity—its articles of incorporation, articles of trust, operating agreement, partnership agreement, etc.—must specify that the organization's powers are limited solely to exempt purposes. *See id.* § 1.501(c)(3)–1(b)(4). The operational test, by contrast, goes to actual operations, not just what is written in the organization's formative documents. Hence, the operational test requires that the organization actually be operated for exempt purposes.

However, the simplicity ends right there for one basic reason (among others we'll explore). Focus on the words "organized *and* operated *exclusively*" for exempt purposes. We, the authors of this textbook, are employed by tax-exempt universities. We assure you that our universities are "organized exclusively" for exempt purposes because their constitutional documents stipulate as such. We likewise assure you that our universities are *not* "operated exclusively" for exempt purposes. We are paid. Yet, despite paying us, our universities do satisfy the operational test because they cannot engage in education—at least not yet—without us (including pay). Put simply, in pursuing exempt purposes, an organization inexorably confers some degree of private benefit, as reflected in the fact that the Treasury Department's regulations conveniently substitute the word "primarily" for the word "exclusively" in the operational test: to be exempt, an organization must be operated *primarily* for exempt purposes, *see id.* § 1.501(c)(3)–1(c), which in the health care context is now taken to mean that the health care organization must operate primarily to confer *community*—not *private*—benefit. As we will explore in great detail, the word "primarily" tells you that there is no per se rule against private benefit; instead the exemption involves a process of balancing in which some degree of private benefit is allowed as necessary to attain the community benefit conferred by an organization claiming to be exempt.

This balancing pervades the doctrine although, as with any area of law in which there is balancing, some activities are beyond the pale. For example, the hallmark of an exempt organization—"EO" for short—is that it is legally barred from distributing its earnings to individuals. It is subject to the so-called "non-distribution constraint." *See* Henry B. Hansmann, *The Role of Nonprofit Enterprise*, 89 YALE L.J. 835 (1980) [hereinafter Hansmann, *The Role of Nonprofit Enterprise*]. Like any taxable organization, an EO must generate income that exceeds its costs because if costs exceed income to a great enough extent or over a long enough period of time, the organization would dissipate its assets and collapse. However, the paradigmatic instance of private—as opposed to community—benefit would be for the organization to distribute that surplus to individuals, e.g., dividends. Hence, to be exempt, the entity must be organized and operated as a nonprofit, an organizational form that is a necessary condition of exemption (but we will see in the notes following *Geisinger I* below that organization as a nonprofit and refraining from distributing earnings is not a sufficient condition to obtain an exemption). Tax-exempt organizations may earn surplus but that surplus must be retained, plowed back into operations that confer community benefit.

Particularly dangerous is the possibility that earnings would be distributed to or benefit conferred on "insiders"—essentially defined as persons in a position to exercise a significant degree of control over the EO. This danger has given rise to the so-called rule against "private inurement." *See* Treas. Reg. § 1.501(c)(3)–1(c)(2). This rule is a subspecies of the more general rule that an EO cannot primarily confer private benefit, but it is stricter than the more general rule because, given their position of control, insiders are seen as more dangerous than outside private actors upon whom benefit might be conferred. Hence, the rule against private inurement is essentially prophylactic in that there is no de minimus standard, no balancing, and it is said that any amount of private inurement will lead to loss of the tax exemption.

Yet, even in the face of such strong rules, the need to balance creeps in because community and private benefit inexorably are jointly produced in the delivery of services. Where does the retained and reinvested surplus go? Hospitals often have very plush offices, including lavishly furnished board rooms. We're sure that the board of trustees and executives greatly enjoy these amenities. Anesthesiologists, employed by hospitals, draw handsome salaries. Orthopedic surgeons operate with the latest, most fancy and expensive technology, thereby attracting lucrative reimbursement for the patients they serve. Do these facts violate the non-distribution constraint? Moreover, all of these individuals are considered insiders. What has happened to the per se rule against private inurement? On the other hand, doesn't the hospital have to attract trustees, executives, anesthesiologists, orthopedists, and, most importantly, patients?

To attract patients and to keep doctors on staff, these days hospitals operate cafeterias, they often provide lodging for patients' families, they even often have adjacent health clubs. Such is the stuff of modern health care. Despite these activities the nonprofit hospitals are still tax exempt. Again, there are limits. Suppose a hospital builds a large country club with a golf course and other amenities on its campus, and the revenue from the club dwarfs the revenue it gains from operation of the hospital. Under such circumstances, it would be quite a stretch to say the hospital is operated primarily for exempt purposes even if the revenue from the club is used to subsidize the hospital's activities. Nonetheless, the tax code does allow an EO to earn income that is "unrelated" to its exempt purposes, *see* I.R.C. § 501(b), although this income is taxed, *see id.* § 511, and it must be "insubstantial" for the entity to remain exempt. *See* Treas. Reg. § 1.501(c)(3)–1(b)(1)(III), (c)(1), (e) (though we'll see below that even this rule can be avoided by creating taxable subsidiaries). The words "unrelated" and "insubstantial" should indicate to you that these issues are not clear-cut but instead involve difficult, complex questions of degrees.

These questions have gotten even harder than they were in the past because the *business* dimension of health care—even for nonprofit institutions—is so much sharper than it was a few decades ago. Application of these rules was *relatively* uncomplicated in the health care world of the 1950s, 1960s, and 1970s, in which indemnity insurance predominated, reimbursement was cost-based, competition among health care organizations pertained largely to the acquisition of sophisticated technology, the major organizational forms in the health care sector were unaffiliated hospitals or relatively small, religious-based hospital chains, and for-profit organizations existed only in relatively small numbers confined to limited areas of the country. To be sure, as described below in *Geisinger I*, there were some twists and turns, such as the question whether a hospital had to maintain an open emergency room in order to support a conclusion that the hospital was operating for charitable purposes.

However, the difficulty posed by those questions of interpretation pale against those that arise now. The demise of indemnity insurance and the rise of competitive insurance provider networks, the growth of for-profit, particularly investor-owned, systems operating across the country, the proliferation of diverse types of service entities, and the use of provider payment systems that require health care organizations to compete over price have all meant that there is intense competition among exempt organizations and between for-profits and EOs, with the result that EOs must maintain a complex number of affiliations and engage in for-profit activities in order to survive. These developments have spawned a huge number of organizational forms and have greatly complicated the question whether an organization or its constituent parts should be tax exempt.

As you will see, the doctrine in this technical area of the law raises questions fundamental to the situation of American health care in the twenty-first century. The tax exemption subsidizes qualifying nonprofit organizations involved in delivering health care goods and services. Why should this be? Does the enactment of the Patient Protection and Affordable Care Act (which, even as it promises to insure 94 percent of all Americans also preserved but tightened the standards applicable to nonprofit hospitals seeking tax-exempt status, discussed below) eliminate the need to maintain tax-exempt health care entities? Would an exemption from federal income taxation still be either necessary or justifiable? Should all income from all health care activity be taxed, with proceeds applied toward the financing of health insurance coverage, the provision of health services to persons unable to pay for care, or both? To whom do tax-exempt assets belong and to what purposes should the proceeds of their sale be devoted?

This latter question dominated debates during the 1990s when there was a surge in the conversion of nonprofit health entities such as hospitals and Blue Cross/Blue Shield plans to for-profit status. *See, e.g.,* Gary Claxton et al., *Public Policy Issues in Nonprofit Conversions: An Overview; Does Ownership Status of Hospital and Health Plans Make A Difference?*, 16(2) HEALTH AFFAIRS 9 (1997); JUDITH BELL ET AL., THE PUBLIC INTEREST IN CONVERSIONS OF NONPROFIT HEALTH CHARITIES (Milbank Memorial Fund 1997); James Fishman, *Checkpoints on the Conversion Highway: Some Trouble Spots in the Conversion of Nonprofit Health Care Organizations to For–Profit Status*, 23 J. CORP. L. 701 (1998). This question likewise dominates contemporaneous debates because, as you will see below, one of the most pressing issues of the day concerns the relevance and meaning of "community benefit," which is the entire basis of the tax exemption in health care. In these debates, decision makers tend to focus on, among other matters, whether the entity claiming the right to an exemption is providing uncompensated care. In a nation in which at the end of 2011 more than 50 million Americans are uninsured, it is probably inevitable that the "legal eye" tends to travel immediately to evidence of charitable care, and it is easy for the provision of charity care to become the focus of the legal justification for the receipt of a public subsidy whether through a tax exemption or the receipt of a federal grant such as those formerly made under the Hill Burton program (discussed in Part One).

However, even if there were universal health coverage, it may still make sense to discriminate between charitable and non-charitable activities or enterprises and provide a subsidy to the former. Even when everyone has the ability to pay for care, the health care industry still has powerful incentives to segment the market for the very reasons explored in Chapter 1: poverty, minority status, and disability, all of which can result in discrimination and exclusion even of "paying customers." Given the instinct of a market-driven system to seek out the best customers, maldistribution of services and facilities might still be problems. Would health care entities try to avoid "undesirable" neighborhoods in favor of wealthy and desirable communities, particularly when one adds into the mix the need for a swanky location as a means of attracting health professionals to work at the facility? Would patients with HIV or mental illness be welcomed even if they all can pay for care? Was the ability to pay for care even an issue in *Abbott v. Bragdon* (presented in Part One)? Could we expect that out of the goodness of their hearts, health care entities would undertake activities that fall outside the limits of health insurance, such as health education classes or patient support programs for immigrants? Could the health system simply be expected to undertake health research or the education and training of medical and health professionals? Who would care for individuals like undocumented workers who might be excluded from national health insurance? Is there any reason to support the existence of nonprofits through a tax exemption other than their provision of goods and services which for-profits likewise furnish? Does the term "community hospital" still resonate for reasons other than the mere provision of health care?

Tax exemption is a means of transferring revenues to qualifying entities in order to achieve stated or unstated public policy goals. Even in a world of universal coverage, many worthy public goals might still justify public funding. It is certainly possible that federal and state lawmakers could elect to pay directly for such public good. However, for reasons related to the politics of government spending, it is often politically easier to transfer income by means of a tax benefit than through a direct transfer. Thus, as you work to master the remarkable doctrinal complexity of the application of tax law to the health care sector, bear in mind that many of these intricacies have at their roots the need to grapple with some of the most difficult policy problems confronting the American health system. For that reason, this area is not one of doctrinal simplicity.

1. THE NATURE OF COMMUNITY BENEFIT

Geisinger Health Plan v. Commissioner of Internal Revenue (*Geisinger I*)

985 F.2d 1210 (3d Cir. 1993)

■ LEWIS, CIRCUIT JUDGE:

The Commissioner of the Internal Revenue Service ("Commissioner" or "IRS") appeals from a Tax Court decision granting appellee Geisinger Health Plan ("GHP") tax-exempt status under 26 U.S.C. § 501(c)(3). This case requires us to decide whether a health maintenance organization (an "HMO") which serves a predominantly rural population, enrolls some Medicare subscribers, and which intends to subsidize some needy subscribers but, at present, serves only its paying subscribers, qualifies for exemption from federal income taxation under 26 U.S.C. § 501(c)(3). We hold that it does not. We will remand this case to the Tax Court on a subsidiary issue, however. On remand, the Tax Court is to determine whether GHP should be considered an integral part of the health care system to which it belongs so as to qualify for tax-exempt status based upon the status of entities related to it.

I.

GHP, which qualifies as an HMO under both Pennsylvania and federal law, operates as part of a system of health care organizations in northeastern and northcentral Pennsylvania (the "Geisinger System").

The Geisinger System consists of GHP and eight other nonprofit entities. All are involved in some way in promoting health care in 27 counties in northeastern and northcentral Pennsylvania. They include: the Geisinger Foundation (the "Foundation"); Geisinger Medical Center ("GMC"); the Geisinger Clinic (the "Clinic"); Geisinger Wyoming Valley Medical Center ("GWV"); Marworth; Geisinger System Services ("GSS") and two professional liability trusts. Each of these entities is exempt from federal income taxation under one or more sections of the Internal Revenue Code (the "Code").

In order to provide cost-effective delivery of health care to areas it had identified as medically underserved, GMC experimented with a pilot pre-paid health plan between 1972 and 1985. The results were sufficiently favorable that the Geisinger System formed GHP to provide its own prepaid health plan. GHP's service area encompasses 17 predominantly rural counties within the area served by the Geisinger System. As of November 30, 1987, according to a finding of a bureau of the federal Department of Health and Human Services, 23 percent of GHP's subscribers resided in medically underserved areas while 65 percent resided in counties containing medically underserved areas.

GHP's articles of incorporation provide that it was incorporated "for the purpose of conducting exclusively charitable, scientific and educational activities within the meaning of Section 501(c)(3) of the Internal Revenue Code," and list a number of specific purposes relating to the provision of health care through a prepaid fee arrangement. Its articles also prohibit GHP from lobbying, participating in political campaigns and engaging in activity that would invalidate its tax-exempt status. No earnings or profit may inure to the benefit of its members, directors, officers or other private persons; upon its dissolution, GHP's board of directors must pay any assets that remain to a tax-exempt charitable organization.

Any person, whether or not a resident of Pennsylvania, may serve on GHP's board of directors. GHP's president and the senior officers of the Geisinger Foundation, the Geisinger System's umbrella organization, automatically serve as directors. The remaining directors are elected by GHP's members, who can be directors themselves. Pennsylvania law requires that at least one-third of GHP's directors be GHP subscribers.

GHP has two types of subscribers. First, it is open to all adult individuals who reside in its service area and satisfactorily complete a routine questionnaire regarding their medical history. From its inception through June 30, 1987, GHP accepted all but 11 percent of its individual applicants. Second, it enrolls group subscribers. Any individual who resides in GHP's service area and belongs to a group of at least 100 eligible enrollees may enroll as a group subscriber without completing a health questionnaire. Individual applicants belonging to groups of less than 100 eligible enrollees must usually complete the questionnaire required of individual subscribers, however.

GHP describes itself as "providing health services." In reality, it contracts with other entities in the Geisinger System (at least one of which will contract with physicians from outside the Geisinger System) to provide services to GHP's subscribers. It also contracts with entities such as pharmacies to provide medical and hospital services to its subscribers in exchange for compensation. Under the terms of these contracts, GHP reimburses the hospitals and clinics by paying a negotiated per diem charge for inpatient services and a discounted percentage of billed charges for outpatient services. For the fiscal year ended June 30, 1987, the Clinic and GWV provided 80 percent of all hospital services to GHP subscribers. The remaining 20 percent were provided by other hospitals.

All physician services are provided to GHP subscribers pursuant to a contract between GHP and the Clinic. The contract requires the Clinic to open its emergency rooms to all GHP subscribers, regardless of ability to pay, just as the Clinic's emergency rooms are open to all members of the public, regardless of ability to pay. The Clinic will contract with unaffiliated physicians to provide required services, but for the year ended June 30, 1987, more than 84 percent of the physician services which the Clinic provided to GHP's subscribers were performed by physicians who were employees of the Clinic. GHP compensates the Clinic for the physicians' services by paying a fixed amount per subscriber.

GHP has adopted a subsidized dues program which has not yet been implemented. The program would establish a fund comprised of charitable donations and operating funds to subsidize GHP subscribers who are unable to pay their premiums. The fund would, in GHP's view, "add to the security of [subscribers], any of whom may at some time suffer financial misfortune due to loss of employment, physical or mental disability or other causes beyond their control and which impute no dishonor to the [subscriber]." Although the program makes reference to subsidizing people who are already subscribers, GHP's submissions indicate that it also intends to admit people who require subsidization at the time they apply.

Despite GHP's initial projection that it would fund the program by raising $125,000 in contributions over its first three years of operation, it has been unable to do so, it claims, because potential donors cannot be assured that contributions will be deductible on their federal income tax returns until GHP receives recognition of tax-exempt status under section 501(c)(3). GHP has likewise been unable to support the program with operating funds because it operated at a loss from its inception through the time the record in this case closed.

GHP enrolls some subscribers who are covered by Medicare and Medicaid. As of March 31, 1988, it had enrolled 1,064 Medicare recipients at a reduced rate on a wraparound basis, meaning that it will cover what Medicare does not. It also has enrolled a small number of Medicaid recipients in a few exceptional situations. Generally, however, GHP cannot offer coverage to Medicaid recipients until and unless it contracts with the Pennsylvania Department of Welfare, which administers Pennsylvania's Medicaid program. GHP has negotiated with the Department to obtain such a contract, but efforts to reach agreement have thus far been unsuccessful.

II.

Shortly after its incorporation, GHP applied to the IRS for recognition of exemption. The Commissioner ruled that GHP was not exempt because (1) it was not operated exclusively for exempt purposes under section 501(c)(3); and (2) it could not vicariously qualify for exemption as an "integral part" of the Geisinger System.

GHP filed suit in Tax Court, requesting a declaratory judgment that it was exempt. The parties submitted the case to the Tax Court on a stipulated administrative record. The Tax Court reversed the Commissioner's ruling in an opinion dated December 30, 1991, which was made final by an order dated February 20, 1992. On May 15, 1992, the Commissioner appealed.

III.

The first issue is whether GHP, standing alone, is entitled to tax-exempt status under section 501(c)(3).

Generally, "[c]haritable exemptions are justified on the basis that the exempt entity confers a public benefit—a benefit which the society or the community may not itself choose or be able to provide, or which supplements and advances the work of public institutions already supported by tax revenues." Thus, charitable exemptions from income taxation constitute a *quid pro quo:* the public is willing to relieve an organization from paying income taxes because the organization is providing a benefit to the public.

The parties' dispute flows directly from an application of the second prong of the test set forth in the IRS regulations, the so-called "operational test." This test mandates that, in addition to being organized exclusively for exempt purposes, GHP must be operated exclusively for exempt purposes to qualify for tax-exempt status under section 501(c)(3).

GHP argues that it qualifies for exemption because it serves the charitable purpose of promoting health in the communities it serves. There are no published revenue rulings and only one previously litigated case addressing whether an HMO may qualify for exemption under section 501(c)(3). The sole case on this issue is a Tax Court case, *Sound Health Association v. Commissioner,* 71 T.C. 158 (1978), *acq.* 1981–2 C.B. 1.

Thus, we face what is apparently a case of first impression among the United States Courts of Appeals. Under these circumstances, our task necessarily involves both outlining the proper test to be applied in determining whether an HMO may qualify for tax-exempt status and applying that test to the facts at hand.

A.   *The Appropriate Test*

In *Sound Health,* the Tax Court applied the law pertaining to nonprofit hospitals as charitable entities in measuring an HMO's claim for exemption. Although this case does not involve a hospital, neither the IRS nor GHP argue that this distinction rendered inappropriate the Tax Court's reliance upon *Sound Health* in examining GHP's request for exemption. To the contrary, in fact, the IRS concedes that GHP's stated purpose, like a hospital's stated purpose, is to promote health; it simply argues that *Sound Health* and the hospital precedents require more than mere promotion of health in order to qualify for tax exemption. The IRS argues that the relevant precedents require at least some "indicia of charity" in the form of serving the public and providing some services free of charge.

1. *Nonprofit Hospitals as Tax–Exempt Entities*

Initially, the IRS required that nonprofit hospitals provide some free care in order to qualify for tax exemption under section 501(c)(3). *See* Rev.Rul. 56–185, 1956 C.B. 202. This reflected an early view that hospitals and other health care institutions were only exempt as "charitable" if they both provided relief to the poor and promoted health.

In 1969, however, the IRS modified that requirement and established an alternative "community benefit" standard for hospitals seeking exempt status. Thus, in Rev.Rul. 69–545, the IRS modified Rev.Rul. 56–185 to remove "the requirements relating to caring for patients without charge or at rates below cost." Rev.Rul. 69–545, 1969–2 C.B. 117. It did so in the context of a hospital which provided emergency care to all, regardless of ability to pay.

In Rev.Rul. 69–545, the IRS stated that "the promotion of health is a charitable purpose." Indeed, the word "charitable" is used in its generally accepted legal sense in section 501(c)(3), 26 C.F.R. § 1.501(c)(3)–1(d)(2), and promotion of health has long been considered a charitable purpose under the traditional law of charitable trusts. *See Sound Health*, 71 T.C. at 178.

By issuing Rev.Rul. 69–545, however, the IRS did not abolish entirely the requirement that nonprofit hospitals provide free care. Shortly after it was issued, the United States Court of Appeals for the District of Columbia Circuit held that Rev.Rul. 69–545 did not overrule Rev.Rul. 56–185, but that it

> simply provide[d] an alternative method whereby a nonprofit hospital can qualify as a tax exempt charitable organization. That method entails the operation of an emergency room open to all regardless of their ability to pay and providing hospital services to those able to pay the cost either directly or through third party reimbursement. Thus, to qualify as a tax exempt charitable organization, a hospital must still provide services to indigents.

Eastern Kentucky Welfare Rights Organization v. Simon, 506 F.2d 1278, 1289 (D.C.Cir.1974), *vacated on other grounds,* 426 U.S. 26 (1976). *See also Sound Health,* 71 T.C. at 181 n. 9.

In 1983, the IRS went a step further, issuing Rev.Rul. 83–157, in which it ruled that a nonprofit hospital need not even maintain an emergency room open to all, regardless of ability to pay, if doing so would result in needless duplication of services in the area. This ruling made clear, however, that other "significant factors" demonstrating that the hospital operated "exclusively to benefit the community" must be present to dispense with the requirement that the hospital need not maintain an open emergency room. Rev.Rul. 83–157, 1983–2 C.B. 94. But the ruling did not provide complete illumination; it did not explain, for example, what was meant by the word "benefit" or, more importantly for purposes of this appeal, who or what would constitute the "community." There have been no further pronouncements in the form of revenue rulings or regulations.

In sum, no clear test has emerged to apply to nonprofit hospitals seeking tax exemptions. Instead, a nonprofit hospital will qualify for tax-exempt status if it primarily benefits the community. One way to qualify is to provide emergency room services without regard to patients' ability to pay; another is to provide free care to indigents. A hospital may also benefit the community by serving those who pay their bills through public programs such as Medicaid or Medicare. For the most part, however, hospitals must meet a flexible "community benefit" test based upon a variety of indicia.

2. *HMOs as Tax–Exempt Entities*

Overlaid against this background is *Sound Health*. In *Sound Health*, the Tax Court applied the hospital precedents in ruling that an HMO was exempt from taxation.

The *Sound Health* HMO resembled GHP in many ways. Its articles of incorporation listed a number of charitable purposes relating to the promotion of health. Like GHP's subscribers, its subscribers paid for services based upon a community rating system, and a subsidized dues program assisted those who could not afford subscribership. Subscribers also had to satisfy eligibility requirements similar to GHP's. *Sound Health*, 71 T.C. at 168–69, 172–73.

Unlike GHP, however, the *Sound Health* HMO provided health care services itself rather than simply arranging for others to provide them to its subscribers. It also employed doctors, health care providers and medical personnel who were not affiliated with the HMO to provide health care to its subscribers. Significantly, the *Sound Health* HMO provided services to both subscribers and members of the general public through an outpatient clinic which it operated and at which it treated all emergency patients, subscribers or not, and regardless of ability to pay. *Id.* at 172. It also adjusted rates for and provided some free care to patients who were not subscribers. It offered public educational programs regarding health.

The court described the IRS' approach to tax exemptions for health care providers, as embodied in the hospital precedents, as reflecting a

"community benefit" approach. A charity will benefit the community if the class served is not so small that its relief is not of benefit to the community. This concept has been stated as follows:

A trust is not a charitable trust if the persons who are to benefit are not of a sufficiently large or indefinite class so that the community is interested in the enforcement of the trust. This is true even though the purpose of the trust is to promote health....

> The requirement that the community must benefit from a chari-
> ty's activities has, as its natural corollary, that private interests
> must not so benefit in any substantial degree.

Sound Health, 71 T.C. at 181, *quoting* 4A Scott, *Scott on Trusts,* § 372.2 at
2897.

The *Sound Health* court went to great lengths to find a benefit to the
community rather than simply a benefit to the HMO's subscribers. It
rejected the argument that the HMO at issue benefited only its subscribers,
finding:

> The most important feature of the Association's [subscribership]
> form of organization is that the class of persons eligible for
> [subscribership], and hence eligible to benefit from the Associa-
> tion's activities, is practically unlimited. The class of possible
> [subscribers] of the Association is, for all practical purposes, the
> class of members of the community itself. The major barrier to
> [subscribership] is lack of money, but a subsidized dues program
> demonstrates that even this barrier is not intended to be abso-
> lute.... It is safe to say that the class of persons potentially
> benefitted [sic] by the Association is not so small that its relief is
> of no benefit to the community.

Id. at 185.

As we have observed, however, the court listed several factors in
addition to open subscribership as indications that the *Sound Health* HMO
was operated for charitable purposes. Chief among these were the HMO's
operation of an emergency room open to all persons, subscribers or not, and
regardless of ability to pay; rendering some free care to both subscribers
and those who did not subscribe; conducting research; and offering an
educational program. *Id.* at 184. GHP refers to these as "marketing
techniques," but, as the *Sound Health* court noted, the HMO benefited the
community by engaging in these activities.

Thus, the *Sound Health* court did not entirely dispense with the
requirement that an entity seeking tax exemption must benefit the community, either by providing services to those who cannot afford to pay or
otherwise. *Sound Health* was decided before Rev.Rul. 83–157 was issued,
but provision of emergency care was only one of the factors relied upon in
holding that the HMO was exempt from taxation under section 501(c)(3).
The HMO in *Sound Health* demonstrated that it benefited the community
in several ways beyond merely providing emergency services regardless of
ability to pay.

3.   *The Resulting Test*

In administrative proceedings in this case, the IRS contended that
GHP had to meet a strict, fourteen-factor test based upon the facts of
Sound Health in order to qualify for tax-exempt status. Upon review, we
cannot agree that any strict, multi-factor test is appropriate when determining whether an HMO qualifies for tax-exempt status under section
501(c)(3). Rather, the determination must be based upon the totality of the

circumstances, with an eye toward discerning whether the HMO in question benefits the community in addition to its subscribers.

B.   *GHP's Status as a Tax–Exempt Entity*

Viewed in this light, GHP standing alone does not merit tax-exempt status under section 501(c)(3). GHP cannot say that it provides any health care services itself. Nor does it ensure that people who are not GHP subscribers have access to health care or information about health care. According to the record, it neither conducts research nor offers educational programs, much less educational programs open to the public. It benefits no one but its subscribers.

GHP argues that the *Sound Health* requirement that an HMO seeking exemption must provide an emergency room open to all is rendered obsolete by Rev.Rul. 83–157. This may indeed be the case. Under the logic of Rev.Rul. 83–157, GHP need not provide an emergency room if doing so would unnecessarily duplicate services offered elsewhere in the area. Because the Clinic and other Geisinger System facilities provide emergency care to GHP's subscribers, requiring GHP to operate an emergency room may be unnecessarily duplicative and wasteful.

This conclusion would not, however, automatically bestow upon GHP an entitlement to tax-exempt status. The test remains one of community benefit, and GHP cannot demonstrate that it benefits anyone but its subscribers.

It is true that GHP is open to anyone who can afford to pay and that, like the HMO in *Sound Health,* GHP apparently intends to lower, or even to remove, this potential economic barrier to subscribing through its subsidized dues program. As we explain below, however, the mere presence of the subsidized dues program does not necessarily invite a conclusion that GHP benefits the community.

First, the *Sound Health* court ventured too far when it reasoned that the presence of a subsidized dues program meant that the HMO in question served a large enough class that it benefited the community. The court ruled that because there was no economic barrier to subscribership, "the class of persons potentially benefitted [sic] by the Association is not so small that its relief is of no benefit to the community." *Sound Health,* 71 T.C. at 185. In doing so, however, the court misconstrued the relevant inquiry by focusing on whether the HMO benefited the community at all rather than whether it primarily benefited the community, as an entity must in order to qualify for tax-exempt status.

The mere fact that a person need not pay to belong does not necessarily mean that GHP, which provides services only to those who do belong, serves a public purpose which primarily benefits the community. The community benefited is, in fact, limited to those who belong to GHP since the requirement of subscribership remains a condition precedent to any service. Absent any additional indicia of a charitable purpose, this self-imposed precondition suggests that GHP is primarily benefiting itself (and, perhaps, secondarily benefiting the community) by promoting subscribership throughout the areas it serves.

There may be circumstances in which an HMO will be able to demonstrate that the purpose of self-promotion is not so "substantial in nature" that it should not be accorded section 501(c)(3) status, even though access to service is premised upon membership. In this case, however, self-promotion appears to be the primary purpose for requiring membership. We are unaware of, and GHP has not identified, evidence which would lead to any other conclusion. Under these circumstances, we conclude that the presence of a subsidized dues program does not, in and of itself, primarily benefit the community sufficiently to enable GHP to qualify for tax-exempt status.

Second, the *Sound Health* court need not have gone as far as it did. The presence of a subsidized dues program was not the only factor it considered when deciding that the HMO in question qualified for tax-exempt status. For example, the HMO in *Sound Health* "in effect, [ran] a substantial outpatient clinic as an important ingredient of its medical care services." *Id.* It also provided free care even to persons who did not subscribe and offered educational programs to the public.

Finally, even considering the subsidized dues program, the amount of benefit GHP intends to confer on people other than paying subscribers is minuscule. GHP anticipates subsidizing approximately 35 people. We cannot say that GHP operates primarily to benefit the community at large rather than its subscribers by arranging for health care for only 35 people, who would not otherwise belong, as compared to more than 70,000 paying subscribers. GHP argues that the HMO in *Sound Health* had provided only $158.50 in subsidies when it was granted tax-exempt status. This is true, but, as previously noted, the HMO in that case also benefited the community in other ways, most notably by providing free or reduced-cost care to people who were not subscribers. An HMO must primarily benefit the community, not its subscribers plus a few people, in order to qualify for tax-exempt status under section 501(c)(3).

In sum, GHP does not qualify for tax-exempt status under section 501(c)(3) since it does no more than arrange for its subscribers, many of whom are medically underserved, to receive health care services from health care providers. This is so even though it has a program designed to subsidize the subscribership of those who might not be able to afford the fees required of all other subscribers. Arranging for the provision of medical services only to those who "belong" is not necessarily charitable, particularly where, as here, the HMO has arranged to subsidize only a small number of such persons. GHP, standing alone, is not entitled to tax-exempt status under section 501(c)(3).

IV.

Alternatively, GHP argues that it is entitled to tax-exempt status under section 501(c)(3) because it is an integral part of the Geisinger System.

We decline to address the merits of the integral part doctrine at this stage, and instead remand the question of its application to this case to the Tax Court for clarification.

Notes

1. *The contested "community benefit" standard.*

a. Geisinger's *application of the community benefit test. Geisinger I* was silly in ruling that GHP pursued private benefit in servicing only its own members, because that's what HMOs do. Suppose that an HMO is the only form of health care financing in an entire community and that everyone in the community is a member. Does that mean that the HMO fails to provide community benefit? Of course not. Unless an HMO's membership is so vanishingly small—e.g., one member, a "community of one"—that in no way can its membership be characterized as "community" in the meaning of "community benefit," the only relevant question regarding whether it operates for exempt purposes is the nature of its operations.

Perhaps the denial of an exemption was warranted because GHP had not done enough to subsidize membership or otherwise operate for community benefit, but the fact that it serviced its members alone is irrelevant and evidences muddled thinking. Moreover, as we shall see following the discussion of *Geisinger III* reprinted immediately below, when GHP is considered within the context of the activities of the overall system, the rest of which was exempt, then it is relatively clear that GHP too should have been exempt. As Professor John Colombo has argued, the Geisinger System provided services to underserved areas and populations that the market was unlikely to serve, and it is this point that should have driven the analysis but does not appear in the opinion. *See* John C. Colombo, *Health Care Reform and Federal Tax Exemption: Rethinking the Issues*, 29 WAKE FOREST L. REV. 215, 246–47 (1994) [hereinafter Colombo, *Rethinking the Issues*]; John C. Colombo, *The Role of Access in Charitable Tax Exemption*, 82 WASH. U. L. Q. 343, 357 (2004) [hereinafter Colombo, *The Role of Access*].

b. *The doctrinal history of the community benefit test.* The court's analysis, however, stems in part from the history and meaning of the community benefit standard itself. As indicated above, in relevant part section 501(c)(3) provides an exemption for entities organized and operated for "religious, charitable, scientific, or educational purposes." In 1923 the Service had imposed the requirement that for an entity to be engaged in "charitable" purposes, it had to provide "relief to the poor," i.e., charity. *See* I.T. 1800, II–2 Cum. Bull. 152 (1923). However, in 1956 the Service relaxed the standard somewhat such that hospitals need only provide charity care to the extent of their "financial ability." *See* Revenue Ruling 56–185, 1956–1 C.B. 202. Following, in 1969 in Revenue Ruling 69–545, 1969–2 C.B. 117, the Service ruled that hospitals could be exempt without providing charity care so long as they provided community benefit. The "community benefit" test was born. Apparently the IRS accepted the nonprofit hospital industry's view that nonprofit hospitals furnished community benefit by advancing medical science and taking care of the sick, and that Medicare and Medicaid had rendered the charity care obligation "anachronistic." *See* Daniel M. Fox & Daniel C. Schaffer, *Tax Administration as Health Policy: Hospitals, the Internal Revenue Service, and the Courts*, 16 J. HEALTH POL. POL'Y & L. 251 (1991). The Service ruled that "[t]he promotion of health, like the relief of poverty and the advancement of education and religion, is one of the purposes in the general law of charity that is deemed beneficial to the community as a whole even though the class of beneficiaries eligible to receive a direct benefit from its activities does not include all members of the community, such as indigent members of the community, provided that the class is not so small that its relief is not of benefit to the community." 1969–2 C.B. at 118.

At this point, a red flag should go off in your head. If the provision of health care is sufficient to establish exempt status, then every entity in the health care sector would be tax exempt. That cannot be the state of the law; and it never was in that at the very least, Revenue Ruling 69–545 required that to be exempt, a hospital must maintain an emergency room open to all; possibly, the ruling also required acceptance of Medicare and Medicaid patients. *See generally* Fox & Schaffer, *Tax Administration as Health Policy*. The Service also noted that the hospital used its surplus "to improve the quality of patient care, expand its facilities, and advance its medical training, education, and research programs"; that it maintained an open medical staff; and that its board of trustees was "composed of independent civic leaders." Thus, the Service articulated a community benefit standard in the context of particular facts—a "facts and circumstances" test—and a good lawyerly reading of the revenue ruling leads to the conclusion that "promotion of health" constitutes a section 501(c)(3) charitable purpose when it has some or all of the elements engaged in by the nonprofit organizations that were the subject of the revenue ruling. Nonetheless, there was sufficient ambiguity in the language that as the health care world changed, and through processes of competition the behavior of for-profits and nonprofits started to converge, critics of this convergence, from both the political right and left, could start to wonder why the promotion of health by nonprofits should be exempt while promotion of health by for-profits is not.

One solution to this purported dilemma would be simply to hew to the requirement that EOs be nonprofit and make this form of organization sufficient for tax exempt status. So long as the non-distribution principle is maintained—an entity claiming exempt status does not distribute earnings to shareholders or influential insiders—but instead retains surplus to support its operations, the entity would be exempt. *See, e.g.*, Rob Atkinson, *Altruism in Nonprofit Organizations*, 31 B.C.L. REV. 501 (1990) [hereinafter Atkinson, *Altruism in Nonprofit Organizations*]. Status as a nonprofit alone is what would matter. However, the law has not moved in this direction. Non-distribution of earnings is a necessary but not a sufficient condition to maintain an exemption.

The other solution is to attempt to adumbrate criteria by which "community benefit" is indicated, and as *Geisinger I* recounts, the law has gone in this direction. The Service has vacillated over time regarding exactly what is required but for the most part the requirements have been structural: an open emergency room, at least for an acute-care hospital; an independent board of directors drawn from the community; an open medical staff; the existence of policies prohibiting discrimination against Medicare or Medicaid patients and for the provision of charity care; and so on. *See generally, e.g.*, Douglas M. Mancino, *The Impact of Federal Tax Exemption Standards on Health Care Policy and Delivery*, 15 HEALTH MATRIX 5 (2005). A recent court of appeals decision characterized these requirements as a "plus" criterion: something in addition to the provision of health care. See IHC Health Plans, Inc. v. Commissioner, 325 F.3d 1188, 1197 (10th Cir. 2003). "Free or below-cost services" clearly count as a "plus," but so might "devoting surpluses to research, education and medical training." *See id.*

c. *The terms of the controversy over the community benefit test.* To understate, the meaning of "community benefit" has been vigorously contested over roughly the past half century, and the literature is vast and rich. Necessarily, the question of what constitutes community benefit is related to the question whether there should be a tax exemption at all, which in turn is linked to questions concerning the nature of nonprofit activity. As described immediately below, various theoretical explanations have been offered to "explain" the existence and behavior of nonprofits in health care. Although those explanations provide a useful starting point for analyzing the community benefit standard and the merits of a tax exemption altogether, we must keep in mind that the questions why nonprofits exist and whether they deserve a tax exemption should be kept separate. For example, nonprofits may spur innovation to a greater extent than for-profits, but arguably that marginal level of innovation does no public good and should not be subsidized. Nonprofits may, as another example, promote diversity but we as a society might determine that such a value is not worth protecting. The legal and policy question is what we value, not why nonprofits exist—although again, as we shall see, these questions are linked.

We begin our explication of the debate over the community benefit standard and the tax exemption altogether with the search for explanations regarding why nonprofits exist in the health care sector. This inquiry itself reflects American exceptionalism because it starts from the premise that nonprofits in health care are something to be "explained" as deviant forms of organization in a world dominated by for-profits. *See, e.g.*, Hansmann, *The Role of Nonprofit Enterprise*; Robert Charles Clark, *Does the Nonprofit Form Fit the Hospital Industry?*, 93 HARV. L. REV. 1416 (1980) [hereinafter Clark, *Does the Nonprofit Form Fit?*]. Many of these explanations—or are they normative too?—point to nonprofits as solving or ameliorating purported "market failures," situations in which the ordinary incentive to maximize and distribute profit is inadequate to maximize welfare (assuming for the moment that that is what markets do).* Mission, altruism, or nonpecuniary forms of reward such as prestige substitute for (monetary) greed, and even if nonprofits act to maximize surplus, a normatively or legally imposed non-distribution constraint directs by law or causes (by motivation, for example) nonprofit actors to do public good. All these activities provide "community benefit" in the sense that were everything "private," embodied in a system of private exchange in which any form of "commons" has been eradicated, the benefits would be lost because of "market failure."

Hence, out of a sense of mission or desire for prestige (or due to other posited causes or motivations) nonprofits are said to provide *public goods* like information, the classic public good, that would otherwise be underprovided by the market. For-profits, the theory goes, tend to under-invest in creating information to the extent that the information is not proprietary, with the result that others cannot be excluded from its use, an external benefit. Nonprofits, it is said, by contrast beat to a different drummer and ignore the public good nature of the information they generate. Since they do not aim to maximize profit, they are unconcerned with conferring external benefit. Examples of such information might include education and research, innovative forms of delivery and organization, including, for instance, practice standards, and information regarding the quality of providers or health plans.

Nonprofits are also said to exist because of *spillover effects*, positive or negative externalities. An example of the former might be investment in population health, e.g., vaccination programs, the benefits of which inure to other actors, while an example of negative spillover effects might be risk selection, which involves the dumping of health care risk onto others, the imposition of an external cost. Nonprofits, the theory goes, will ignore such externalities because their goal is neither to capture all the benefits of investment nor to impose costs on others. By contrast, for-profit firms will forego investments that generate positive externalities because they cannot garner the full benefit, while they will impose negative externalities because they do not bear the full cost.

---

* These explanations are discussed in various sources, albeit categorized differently and with various emphases, including Mark A. Hall & John D. Colombo, *The Charitable Status of Nonprofit Hospitals: Toward a Donative Theory of Tax Exemption*, 66 WASH. L. REV. 307 (1991) [hereinafter Hall & Colombo, *Toward a Donative Theory*]; M. Gregg Bloche, *Health Policy Below the Waterline: Medical Care and the Charitable Exemption*, 80 MINN. L. REV. 299 (1995) [hereinafter Bloche, *Health Policy Below the Waterline*]; Mark Schlesinger et al., *Charity and Community: The Role of Nonprofit Ownership in a Managed Health Care System*, 21 J. HEALTH POL. POL'Y & L. 697 (1996) [hereinafter Schlesinger et al., *Charity and Community*]; Mark Schlesinger et al., *Measuring Community Benefits Provided by Nonprofit and For–Profit HMOs*, 40 INQUIRY 114 (2003) [hereinafter Schlesinger et al., *Measuring Community Benefits*]; Colombo, *The Role of Access*; Jill R. Horwitz, *Why We Need the Independent Sector: The Behavior, Law, and Ethics of Not-for-Profit Hospitals*, 50 UCLA L. REV. 1345 (2003) [hereinafter Horwitz, *Why We Need the Independent Sector*]; Jill R. Horwitz, *Does Nonprofit Ownership Matter?*, 24 YALE J. ON REG. 139 (2007) [hereinafter Horwitz, *Does Nonprofit Ownership Matter?*].

Nonprofits in health care are also said to exist because of the nature of health care. Because of its complexity, contracts must be "open" or "incomplete," and *information is asymmetric*. Lacking the incentive to maximize and distribute surplus, or spurred by mission, nonprofits might not exploit this information asymmetry, just as they might not take advantage of negative externalities and might ignore, to the detriment of profit, positive spillover effects.

Finally, nonprofits are said to exist to provide *unprofitable services* that markets, political or economic, do not furnish. Charity care is the classic example but unprofitable activities also might include such services as emergency care, trauma centers and prenatal care.

Another set of explanations or normative accounts, by contrast, stems not from purported market structure, imperatives or failure but instead from visions of democracy and justice and affective attachments that characterized the *Gemeinschaft* ("community") of old rather than the *Gesellschaft* ("association") of modern capitalism.* These claims start with the fact that nonprofits are "voluntary" in the traditional senses of, first, maintaining independence from government; second, standing outside of profit-seeking incentives; and, third, relying on the intimacy of voluntariness in communities bound by the sense of mutual solidarity that derives from shared, lived, local space. Independent of government, voluntaries are not directed by the political economy of the modern polity, whether that be conceived of as interest-group competition or some other theoretical construct. Standing outside of the market, voluntaries are bound not by processes of exchange but by other forms of accountability. Because these ties that bind combine rationality and affection, they are relationships of trust and mutuality, rather than unilateral direction and rational-legal accountability. They are forms of representation and participation rather than artifacts of contract. They therefore enable, somewhat paradoxically, both the breadth of representativeness across diversity and responsiveness to heterogeneity—pluralism, in short—with particular attentiveness to the weak and vulnerable, to those who are economically and politically disen-

---

* For illustrative descriptions of these accounts, albeit again with varying categories and emphases, see J. David Seay & Bruce C. Vladeck, *Mission Matters* [hereinafter Seay & Vladeck, *Mission Matters*], *in* IN SICKNESS AND IN HEALTH: THE MISSION OF VOLUNTARY HEALTH CARE INSTITUTIONS 1 (J. David Seay & Bruce C. Vladeck, eds., 1988); J. David Seay & Robert Sigmond, *Community Benefit Standards for Hospitals: Perceptions and Performance*, 5 FRONTIERS OF HEALTH SERVS. MGMT. 3 (1989); J. David Seay, *Tax–Exemption for Hospitals: Towards an Understanding of Community Benefit*, 2 HEALTH MATRIX 35 (1992); Bloche, *Health Policy Below the Waterline* at 339–49; Schlesinger et al., *Charity and Community*; Mark Schlesinger et al., *A Broader Vision for Managed Care, Part 2: A Typology of Community Benefits*, 17(5) HEALTH AFFAIRS 26 (1998) [hereinafter Schlesinger et al., *A Typology of Community Benefits*]; Horwitz, *Why We Need the Independent Sector*; Schlesinger et al., *Measuring Community Benefits*; Jill R. Horwitz, *Nonprofit Ownership, Private Property, and Public Accountability*, 25(4) HEALTH AFFAIRS w308 (2006) [hereinafter Horwitz, *Nonprofit Ownership, Private Property, and Public Accountability*]; Horwitz, *Does Nonprofit Ownership Matter?. See also* Mark Schlesinger, *Paradigms Lost: The Persisting Search for Community in American Health Policy*, 22 J. HEALTH POL. POL'Y & L. 937 (1997); David M. Frankford & Thomas R. Konrad, *Responsive Medical Professionalism: Integrating Education, Practice, and Community in a Market-driven Era*, 73 ACADEMIC MED. 138 (1998).

franchised. Finally, they are the institutional specification of a normative aspiration that health care is not just another commodity but instead stems from social obligation.

d. The great empirical debate over the community benefit test. These arguments frame the debate whether there should be a tax exemption at all for nonprofits in health care, whether that exemption should rely on a community benefit standard or something else, and what activities should constitute community benefit. Almost universally, the debate is first joined empirically, as proponents and opponents of the exemption and the relevant standards attempt to establish the extent to which nonprofits conform to the predicted behavior, or normative aspirations, just detailed.*

Provision of public goods. Opponents of the tax exemption or the use of a community benefit standard typically point to evidence that there is little ownership-related difference in the adoption of innovation and that there is great variability in the extent to which nonprofits engage in such activities as research and education. In claiming that the type of ownership does not affect behavior, they often rely on the fact that a relatively small portion of the sector, mainly academic medical centers, account for most of the provision of public goods. Otherwise, they claim, there is little if any difference between the activities of for- and nonprofit entities. They argue, moreover, that the creation of public goods can be directly subsidized in research, grants and other forms of payment; at the very least, the need for

---

* Much scholarship summarizes the empirical literature and draws policy and normative implications from it. The most comprehensive and nuanced recent work is Mark Schlesinger & Bradford H. Gray, *Nonprofit Organizations and Health Care: Some Paradoxes of Persistent Scrutiny* [hereinafter Schlesinger & Gray, *Paradoxes of Persistent Scrutiny*], in THE NONPROFIT SECTOR: A RESEARCH HANDBOOK 378 (2nd ed., Walter W. Powell & Richard Steinberg eds., 2006); *see also* Mark Schlesinger & Bradford H. Gray, *How Nonprofits Matter in American Medicine, and What to Do About It*, 25(4) HEALTH AFFAIRS w287 (2006) [hereinafter Schlesinger & Gray, *How Nonprofits Matter*]. For examples from opponents of the tax exemption or the community benefit standard, see Hall & Colombo, *Toward a Donative Theory*; Bloche, *Health Policy Below the Waterline*; Colombo, *The Role of Access*; John D. Colombo, *The Push and Pull of Tax Exemption Law on the Organization and Delivery of Health Care Services: The Failure of Community Benefit*, 15 HEALTH MATRIX 29 (2005) [hereinafter Colombo, *Failure of Community Benefit*]; Thomas L. Greaney & Kathleen M. Boozang, *Mission, Margin, and Trust in the Nonprofit Health Care Enterprise*, 5 YALE J. HEALTH POL'Y L. & ETHICS 1 (2005); John D. Colombo, *Federal and State Tax Exemption Policy, Medical Debt and Healthcare for the Poor*, 51 ST. LOUIS U. L.J. 433 (2007). *See generally* David A. Hyman & William M. Sage, *Subsidizing Health Care Providers Through the Tax Code: Status or Conduct?*, 25(4) HEALTH AFFAIRS W312 (2006) [hereinafter Hyman & Sage, *Status or Conduct?*]; M. Gregg Bloche, *Tax Preference for Nonprofits: From Per Se Exemption to Pay-For-Performance*, 25(4) HEALTH AFFAIRS W304 (2006) [hereinafter Bloch, *From Per Se Exemption to Pay-For-Performance*]. For examples from supporters of the extant or modified exemption or community benefit standard, see Schlesinger & Gray, *Paradoxes of Persistent Scrutiny*; Schlesinger & Gray, *How Nonprofits Matter*; Horwitz, *Why We Need the Independent Sector*; Horwitz, *Does Nonprofit Ownership Matter?*; Jill R. Horwitz, *What Do Nonprofits Maximize? Nonprofit Hospital Service Provision and Market Ownership Mix*, NBER WORKING PAPER No. 13246 (July 2007); Jill R. Horwitz & Austin Nichols, *Hospital Ownership and Medical Services: Market Mix; Spillover Effects; and Nonprofit Objectives*, 28 J. HEALTH ECON. 924 (2009); Jill R. Horwitz & Austin Nichols, *Rural Hospital Ownership: Medical Service Provision, Market Mix, and Spillover Effects*, NBER WORKING PAPER No. 16926 (April 2011).

public goods does not justify that nonprofits be exempt as charitable organizations but that they can instead be exempt under the other clauses of section 501(c)(3) for education and scientific research. Proponents of the exemption or community benefit standard stress the opposite side of the coin. They point to literature showing that nonprofits are more likely to conduct community needs assessments, collaborate with local health departments and agencies to address local needs for services like immunization, prevention of obesity, diabetes and the like, and that nonprofits are more likely to offer such services to improve community health.

Information asymmetries. Opponents of the tax exemption or community benefit standard argue that nonprofit providers do take advantage of their agency, which exists because consumers or payers cannot judge or have difficulty judging the price or quality of care. They point to studies that purport to find that between nonprofits and for-profits there is little difference in cost, quality, or exercise of market power. They contend that any differences that do exist are due to locality rather than ownership type. Proponents of the tax exemption or the community benefit standard point to studies showing that nonprofits have lower markups, prices and administrative expenses; are less likely to upcode services in submitting claims for reimbursement; are more likely to provide higher quality care when quality is less visible, less easily measured, or provided to more vulnerable patients; and that nonprofits have committed fewer instances of large-scale, organizationally directed fraud.

Unprofitable services. Critics of the tax exemption or the community benefit standard claim that some empirical studies show that nonprofits provide charity care—defined variously as uncompensated care, including or excluding bad debt; unreimbursed cost of services for uninsured or Medicaid or Medicare patients; or services to some population otherwise defined as indigent—at the same rate as for-profit entities; that the amount of such care is exceeded by the value of nonprofits' favorable tax treatment; and that it cannot be shown that the tax exemption "causes" nonprofits to provide such care at a greater level than they would absent favorable treatment.* The other side of this argument is that although some studies reach different results, the literature nonetheless consistently shows that nonprofit hospitals provide charity care, again variously defined, at greater rates than for-profits; that variation is due not to nonprofit status but local conditions, depending particularly on the extent to which nonprofits have to compete against for-profits; that nonprofits are more likely to offer unprofitable services, treat more complex and therefore more expensive cases, and locate in areas in which they will draw indigents and uninsured patients; and that although the charity care provided by a single nonprofit

---

* For a recent discussion of the variation in defining charity care, and in fact community benefit as a whole, see U.S. GENERAL ACCOUNTABILITY OFFICE, GAO–08–880, NONPROFIT HOSPITALS: VARIATION IN STANDARDS AND GUIDANCE LIMITS COMPARISON OF HOW HOSPITALS MEET COMMUNITY BENEFIT REQUIREMENTS (Sept. 2008) (http://www.gao.gov/products/GAO–08–880) [hereinafter GAO 2008 COMMUNITY BENEFIT REPORT]; *see also* INTERNAL REVENUE SERVICE, EXEMPT ORGANIZATIONS HOSPITAL STUDY, FINAL REPORT (Feb. 2009) (http://www.irs.gov/charities/charitable/article/0,,id=203109,00.html).

may not exceed by a wide margin that provided by a single for-profit facility, in the aggregate the difference is substantial and nonprofits as whole, therefore, provide significant social benefit (similar arguments regarding aggregate, as opposed to single facility, effects are made with regard to other dimensions of care like quality).

Spillover effects. Firms in a market can influence one another, whether through market segmentation, local norms, isomorphism or competition. Opponents of the tax exemption or the community benefit standard stress how the presence of for-profits, particularly coupled with greater penetration of managed care, causes nonprofits to act like for-profits (i.e., the behavior of the two ownership forms converge). Hence, they point to studies showing that a larger presence of for-profits in a market induces nonprofits to add profitable services and reduce unprofitable ones, to avoid more costly complex cases, and to reduce treatment of the uninsured. By contrast, supporters of the tax exemption or the community benefit standard point to spillover effects in the other direction, i.e., the manner in which the presence of a nonprofit or nonprofits in a local market with for-profits influences the latter. For example, there is evidence that nonprofits attract vulnerable patients because they are deemed "trustworthy," i.e., patients know that nonprofits won't take advantage of the information asymmetries just discussed. The market then segments in that the unsophisticated patients gravitate toward the nonprofits while more sophisticated patients (or payers or plan sponsors) populate the for-profits, which, then, because of the sophistication of their market segment, cannot exploit their information advantage to the extent they would were the nonprofits not in the market. As another example, discussed more fully below, evidence suggests that in markets in which nonprofits dominate, for-profits, to gain legitimacy, are more likely to mimic nonprofits by offering higher quality care and unprofitable services. Form of ownership, it is argued, therefore does matter.

Community solidarity, representation, and participation; pluralism; and preservation of altruism. Opponents of the exemption or community benefit standard claim that the vision of volunteerism has no empirical bite in the world. Most critics here too rely on some version of the convergence theory and they deny that nonprofits are any more diverse, representative, or responsive to their communities than for-profit organizations. Some go so far as to claim that volunteerism is mere ideology and that the nonprofit form is a façade for ordinary rent-seeking behavior, as some group like physicians or hospital managers "capture" nonprofit organizations and use them to serve their own selfish ends. Other detractors go less far but they point to unattractive features of progressivism, such as paternalism, arrogance, a history of racial, ethnic and religious discrimination, and a regressive tax impact. By contrast, supporters of the tax exemption or community benefit standard point to studies showing that nonprofit health plans and providers are more involved with their communities. Nonprofit health plans, for example, are more supportive of safety-net infrastructure like community and mental health centers. They are also, as another example, more engaged in general philanthropy in their communities. They are also more likely to be influenced by their community-based board of directors and to adopt local norms of medical practice.

To say that this literature is complex is surely an understatement. Unfortunately, much of this empirical debate is also quite sterile. Health care is a remarkably complex endeavor, characterized by a complex division of labor and concomitant diverse organization types and forms. Although national and regional chains exist, it is still a largely local enterprise, and localities across the United States are necessarily diverse and varied. It should not be surprising, therefore, that great variation exists in motivations, practices, organizational culture, market structure and the like; and it is even less surprising that empirical studies of behavior reach different results. If one poses the empirical question to be: "Do nonprofits behave differently?," one is almost bound to reach conflicting empirical results. Additionally, the question itself presupposes that the only activity that counts is that which can be measured, i.e., behavior. Any other activity does not count because it is not on the radar screen; and, perversely, the effect of policy's focus on what can be counted results in nonprofits' withdraw of investment from activities that "do not count" but may nonetheless provide significant public good. Finally, if one then phrases the policy question to be, "Do nonprofits deserve favorable treatment?," and, moreover, if one demands a dichotomous, yes/no, answer, then the policy outcome is almost presupposed. Given that results are "inconsistent," one concludes that nonprofits do not consistently fulfill whatever responsibility is presupposed in the examined behavior.

The contemporaneous, dominant discourse has largely followed this logic. As Schlesinger and Gray note in one of their literature reviews, this interpretation of the empirical literature, although mistaken or misleading, is repeated so often in academic and policy contexts that it is taken to be true. Schlesinger & Gray, *How Nonprofits Matter* at W288.

Yet, one cannot possibly understand the behavior of nonprofits and draw appropriate legal and policy lessons by posing the question so broadly, by effectively having the empirical evidence turn on one variable, whether the organization is nonprofit or for-profit. As Schlesinger and Gray develop at great length and nuance in their *Paradoxes of Persistent Scrutiny*, the seeming inconsistency in the studies can be explained by a number of interacting considerations.* First, there is the sheer magnitude of different services and organizational forms in the health care sector. One simply cannot generalize across acute-care hospitals, long-term-care hospitals, rehabilitation hospitals, psychiatric hospitals, nursing homes, home health care agencies, outpatient dialysis facilities, HMOs, hospice facilities, and so on, and answer a unitary question: "Does the form of ownership affect behavior?" As one might expect, the answer depends on the type of service but in the literature that answer—"sometimes"—translates into "inconsistent results," and the conclusion follows that ownership type is not correlated with behavior, i.e., it doesn't matter.

---

* *See also* Bradford H. Gray & Mark Schlesinger, *Health*, in THE STATE OF NONPROFIT AMERICA 65 (Lester M. Salmon, ed., 2002).

Second, the history of development of the different services has affected behavior in various locations and different time periods. Most often for-profit entities initially entered service types and locations where nonprofits did not exist or were less entrenched. Nonprofit hospitals, for example, long dominated and filled most demand outside of later-developing areas of the country such as the Southwest. For that reason, for-profit hospitals entered those areas first and only very recently began to appear in areas like the Northeast. Hence, until the past three decades or so, local markets contained one type or the other; nonprofits competed largely only with other nonprofits and for-profits with for-profits. This cabinization, in turn, affected the mode of competition. Nonprofits competed against each other largely by providing technology and amenities to physicians and competing in other ways for prestige and community support. By contrast, for-profits competed against each other on other dimensions, including price. However, as for-profit hospitals began to enter against nonprofit ones, and as managed care penetration increased, nonprofits in some markets then began to compete on other bases, most notably price. While one can debate the normative implications of this change, the only point here is that it is fallacious to pose an abstract question, "how do nonprofits behave?," and expect to get a meaningful answer with such abstraction.

Third and related, the development of the different service sectors has been affected by the state of technology and technology diffusion, the availability of reimbursement, and governmental policy. During most of the twentieth century the major technology advancement occurred in inpatient acute care, fueled in good part by funding for hospital construction, post-graduate medical education, and NIH money for research. Already ensconced, nonprofits dominated this activity. However, as funding became available for other types of care, as pressure increased to move care out of the very expensive inpatient setting, and as technology to move the site of care developed—all in symbiotic relationship—for-profits moved in to fill the demand that nonprofits failed to satisfy.

For example, in the 1930s Social Security fueled the development of for-profit nursing homes because it created reimbursement for non-acute-care housing of the elderly. A second boom period of for-profit entry occurred with the passage of Medicaid and in particular the creation of the "middle-class entitlement" for nursing home care. As another example, for-profits came to dominate outpatient dialysis as Medicare funding became available in the early 1970s and 80s and as concomitant technologies developed to take such care outside of hospitals. Other examples of for-profit expansion spurred by changing technology, reimbursement and regulatory policy include home health agencies, rehabilitation hospitals and HMOs; more recent phenomena today include the development of a large for-profit presence in ambulatory surgical centers and specialty hospitals.

By contrast, at the opposite end of the boom-or-bust cycle, subsequent to such for-profit expansion sectors can become saturated and profits squeezed by payers. Participants then withdraw capacity and act in different ways than when demand is expanding. For-profits are subject to the demands of capital markets to maximize profits—particularly over the short-run—and they are therefore particularly sensitive to such market saturation and payer pressure. Just as increased demand attracts investor capital, decreased or stable demand causes it to flee. As one prominent example, the for-profit nursing home sector contracted significantly in the 1990s, spurred in good part by policies aimed at keeping patients in community settings. A boom in for-profit psychiatric hospital capacity in the 1970s and 80s was followed by a rapid decline in the 1990s as the emphases on managed care and drug therapy set in, along with a number of instances of high profile fraud committed by for-profit chains. Again, the point for now is not to draw normative conclusions but to observe that behavior varies along the dimension of such cycles and cannot be reduced to the general abstract question whether behavior is correlated with ownership type.

Fourth and for our purposes, finally, in health care, like in real estate, what matters is "location, location, location." Compare two markets. One is suburban in which only for-profit hospitals exist. They provide little indigent care. Why? Because they lack mission? Because there are few indigents in their service area? The other market is urban poor, and the only hospitals are nonprofit. They serve more indigents than the for-profits in the suburban area. Why? Because of their commitment to charitable care? Because there are indigents in their service area? Of course it makes no sense to compare behavior of nonprofits and for-profits by comparing these two markets because the contexts are so different. Therefore, studies to compare behavior of nonprofits and for-profits consider markets in which both ownership types are located and compete. In such circumstances a study might conclude that the behavior of the two types of actors converges. What about the fact that for-profits typically locate in areas in which they cannot face indigent care? Such a comparison does not capture that crucial difference.

Indeed, the behavior of nonprofit and for-profit actors varies greatly on the characteristics of local markets. A for-profit that enters a market dominated by nonprofits will tend to emulate their behavior. "When in Rome...." By contrast, a nonprofit in a sea of for-profits will emulate the latter's behavior. Further, to some extent markets vary not just along structural factors but also sometimes have unique histories and culture. Rochester, New York, for example was long dominated by Kodak, with the result that for many years one could say that health care was more "civic-minded" than in most areas of the country. For many years entities like Kaiser Permanente and Group Health of Puget Sound were different than other nonprofit health plans.

The bottom line, then, is that there is no inherent behavior of nonprofits and for-profits, for one must consider a vast multitude of factors and not simply average them out with conclusions that are so general as to approach banality. In too much of the literature straw men are being built up only then to be torn down. As Schlesinger and Gray summarize:

Most fundamentally, we believe that [the misperceptions that ownership form is irrelevant] reflect researchers' essentially asking the wrong questions. Those who see only inconsistency in the empirical literature are asking, sometimes implicitly, whether ownership form "matters" in some fashion that holds for all forms of health care under all local market conditions. From this perspective, if ownership seems to matter for some studies but not others, or appears to produce significant effects on performance for some organizations but not others, then the findings are "inconsistent" and the answer to the question is "no." We believe the quest for such a generalized prediction about the implications of ownership is fundamentally misguided, leading researchers to miss substantial effects of ownership that vary across services."

Schlesinger & Gray, *Paradoxes of Persistent Scrutiny* at 399 (footnote omitted).

e. Proposed reforms to the community benefit test. If one ignores such complexity, one can propose blanket policy conclusions: on the one side, award the tax exemption to nonprofits simply by virtue of their organizational form with few if any strictures, *see* Atkinson, *Altruism in Nonprofit Organizations*; or, on the other side, eliminate it altogether because nonprofits do nothing that for-profits don't already. *See, e.g.,* Clark, *Does the Nonprofit Form Fit?* at 1473–77; Bloche, *Health Policy Below the Waterline* at 404. Absent this dichotomy, many positions occupy a substantial middle ground.

"Status" as nonprofit should be insufficient or irrelevant: the turn to buying outcomes. Many observers now propose that the tax exemption be awarded based on performance or outcomes of targeted activities. Based on the argument that the empirical literature fails to prove—notice where the burden of proof is placed—either that the nonprofit form is associated with socially desired behavior or that the value of that behavior exceeds the cost of the tax exemption, these observers contend that the link between nonprofit status and the tax exemption should be broken entirely or attenuated greatly. Some of these critics remain hard-nosed about what matters as "charitable" activity: if it can't be counted—like the number of indigent patients served—then it is not relevant. Others are more willing to recognize that not all of social life can be reduced to quantitative measures; nonetheless, even they assert that as a matter of law and policy, these unquantifiable benefits alone are insufficient to justify the favorable treatment of nonprofits.

Tellingly, all of these claims are made in the language of exchange: *what the tax exemption is about is government's purchase of benefits.* Similarly, all of these scholars object to the "facts and circumstances" nature of the community benefit standard, which they characterize with terms like "nebulous," *see* David A. Hyman, *The Conundrum of Charitability: Reassessing Tax Exemption for Hospitals*, 16 AM. J.L. & MED. 327, 375 (1990), failing, in our view, to recognize the distinction between incoherence, on the one hand, and flexibility, on the other, and a recognition that phenomena aren't always quantifiable. This claim sets up their argument that current law is based solely on nonprofit status, requires no types of performance and is therefore in need of reform. Some go so far as to state that the new exemption should be "entity-neutral," rewarding specified behavior whether engaged in by for-profit or nonprofit entities. *See, e.g.,* Clark, *Does the Nonprofit Form Fit?*; Nina J. Crimm, *Evolutionary Forces: Changes in For–Profit and Not-for-Profit Health Care Delivery Structures; A Regeneration of Tax Exemption Standards*, 37 B.C.L. REV. 1 (1995) [hereinafter Crimm, *A Regeneration of Tax Exemption Standards*]; Bloch, *From Per Se Exemption to Pay–For–Performance*; Hyman & Sage, *Status or Conduct?*. Others are concerned that nonprofits do provide unmeasured or immeasurable benefits, and they are therefore open to retaining the requirement that the exempt entity be nonprofit. *See, e.g.,* Colombo, *Failure of Community Benefit*; Colombo, *The Role of Access.*

Proposals also differ as to what a tax exemption should "buy." Many critics of the current regime still point to the purchase of charity care as a key component of the tax exemption. *See, e.g.,* Bloche, *From Per Se Exemption to Pay–For–Performance*. *But see* John D. Colombo, *The Role of Tax Exemption in a Competitive Health Care Market*, 31 J. HEALTH POL. POL'Y & L. 623, 636–37 (2006) (questioning on a number of grounds whether mandating charity care is a wise policy choice). The exemption could also pay for various sorts of specific public goods like development of medical records, tools to assess outcomes and other means to enhance quality. *See, e.g.,* Bloche, *From Per Se Exemption to Pay–For–Performance*. Others expand the list more generally and flexibly to include community-regional services, underprovided by the market, that in their context are deserving of funding, e.g., a free shuttle in New York City that takes indigent patients from emergency rooms to neighborhood clinics for non-emergent care. *See, e.g.,* Crimm, *A Regeneration of Tax Exemption Standards* at 106. Professor Colombo similarly would generalize the exemption to include services that "enhance access" by either providing commercially available services to populations ignored by for-profit or government providers, or by creating services that are not commercially available, i.e., are not provided by markets. See Colombo, *Failure of Community Benefit*; Colombo, *The Role of Access*. Notice that all these proposals are based on the market-failure explanation of nonprofit existence and behavior.

Only some of these proposals flesh out the administrative mechanisms by which these purchases will be made. One exception, provided by Professor Nina Crimm, is quite ambitious. *See* Crimm, *A Regeneration of Tax Exemption Standards*. Professor Crimm imagines a complicated regulatory scheme in which a community or region-based certification panel would draw up plans for needed resources and would weight particular charitable activities in such areas as improving preventive services for vulnerable populations; quality enhancement; research; and other public goods or services not provided by the market. These plans would then provide a benchmark against which to evaluate an institution's particular charitable activities and programs, as well as a dissemination vehicle to spark investment. The certification panel would also issue report cards for each institution.*

Other observers shy away from such complexity, pointing out that prior planning efforts have been prone to expert capture and anticompetitive use, *see, e.g.*, Hyman & Sage, *Status or Conduct?* at W315, and that flexibility is likely to be lost in administrative implementation. *See, e.g.*, Colombo, *Failure of Community Benefit* at 61–62. Professor Colombo, for example, seeks to draw on both process and outcome-based requirements. *See* Colombo, *Failure of Community Benefit*; Colombo, *The Role of Access*. To satisfy the former, a nonprofit would have to create a mission-based plan adumbrating the means of enhancing access, including specific benchmarks and implementation plans; to satisfy the latter, the nonprofit would have to show that in the relevant domain it is outperforming for-profits, e.g., providing more uncompensated care or unprofitable services, and that the commitment of resources is substantial, meaning central to its mission and activities and not what Colombo terms a "sideshow." *Id.* at 374.

Regardless of these details of definition and implementation, all these proposals to change to a performance-based exemption require a turn to quantifiable outcomes. The value of the tax exemption, whether available only to nonprofits or also to for-profits, is determined by the quantified outcomes. A number of concerns can be and have been raised about this shift. We can only briefly canvass them here.

First, generating the necessary information is not costless. Hospitals are complex and often very decentralized organizations. As a result, the qualifying activities are likely to be spread across many departments. Information may not be readily available, and allocation of costs involves complicated accounting. Ambiguities will have to be resolved, and information systems created. *See, e.g.*, Bradford H. Gray & Mark Schlesinger, *The Accountability of Nonprofit Hospitals: Lessons from Maryland's Community Benefit Reporting Requirements*, 46 INQUIRY 122 (2009) [hereinafter Gray & Schlesinger, *Lessons from Maryland's Community Benefit Reporting Requirements*]. To be sure, a taxpayer bears the burden of justifying an exemption, but that does not answer the policy question. Critics of the community benefit standard demand that proponents prove that the standard is justified. Why shouldn't the proponents of these performance standards have to prove that the cost of generating and administering the necessary data regarding outcomes is worth the expenditure of resources?

Second, quantitative measures are necessarily limited to activities and outcomes that can be measured. When the stipulated outcomes are backed by dollars, incentives are created for nonprofits to devote resources to satisfying those measures and not to other activities. Indeed, that is the very idea. However, just as teachers who "teach to the test" might impoverish other aspects of pedagogy, nonprofits who gear their activities

---

* *See also* Jessica Berg, *Putting the Community Back Into the "Community Benefit" Standard*, 44. GA. L. REV. 375 (2010) [hereinafter Berg, *Putting the Community Back*] (proposing reorientation of community benefit standard toward population health and the use of a community benefit board as part of the administrative mechanism for implementation).

to the performance required to obtain a tax exemption might neglect other activities deemed socially beneficial. The latter will simply fall under radar screen, so to speak, and their loss is an "unintended consequence" of a performance-based scheme. To the extent that social benefit is created in ways that lie beyond such measurement, it cannot be captured; to the degree that the extant tax exemption underwrites such activities and outcomes, they might be lost. Moreover, this problem pertains particularly to the use of data on expenditures, *see, e.g.*, Bradford H. Gray & Mark Schlesinger, *Charitable Expectations of Nonprofit Hospitals: Lessons from Maryland*, 28(5) HEALTH AFFAIRS W809, W820 (2009), which necessarily will constitute the guts of an outcome-based exemption system. In the end, even in narrowly conceived terms—we return to the broader vision immediately below—the benefit conferred by nonprofits in health care consists of the reduction of morbidity and mortality. We simply do not have the means to link expenditures to the outcomes that really matter.

Third, in this context as in antitrust (and elsewhere), the standard argument is that it is necessarily a good thing in a democracy to replace an implicit system of cross-subsidies with an explicit system of public payment, here in the form of a tax subsidy for defined outcomes. It is commonly claimed that payers are effectively taxed to confer community benefit and that at least in the financing of our health care system, this taxation is regressive.* However, it must be asked why in a world in which "cross-subsidies" are a fact of life, these particular ones are seen to be problematic; and it must be questioned whether the political process will in fact replace them with direct funding. Were that not to occur, then quite arguable inequality will be increased by their elimination, the opposite of the intended result. While the ideal may be pure, the reality may be much messier.

Fourth and perhaps most pertinent to the competing explanations—visions—of the tax exemption, it is fallacious to suppose that the tax exemption can "buy" performance and that, simultaneously, the nonprofit health care sector can maintain its identity as "voluntary." Professor Colombo's self-described "middle ground" imagines this possibility in that, he supposes, there is an alleged overlap between the market-failure explanation of nonprofit existence and behavior and the one he terms "pluralism" or "sociological/political." Colombo, *The Role of Access* at 364. The gist of this claim is that in providing a service that is not available—enhancing access under his test—a nonprofit both addresses market failure

---

* For a description of how nonprofits engage in price discrimination and other strategies to achieve the distributional objectives of their mission, see Richard Steinberg & Burton A. Weisbrod, *Nonprofits with Distributional Objectives: Price Discrimination and Corner Solutions*, 89 J. PUB. ECON. 89 (2004); Richard Steinberg & Burton A. Weisbrod, *Pricing and Rationing by Nonprofit Organizations with Distributional Objectives*, in TO PROFIT OR NOT TO PROFIT: THE COMMERCIAL TRANSFORMATION OF THE NONPROFIT SECTOR 65 (Burton A. Weisbrod ed., 1998). Not surprisingly, the authors conclude that when nonprofits face competition from for-profits, loss of the tax subsidy will mean that they cannot fund their missions because they must act like for-profit price-maximizers in order to survive.

and enhances pluralism. See *id.* at 367.* With due respect, this assertion is wrong. The vision of voluntarism—and it is a vision—is that the voluntaries should stand outside of a system of exchange, whether that system be private or public. Within this vision, the basis of the tax exemption is that it creates an incentive for nonprofits to exist and by subsidizing their creation it thereby unleashes social capacity for nongovernmental organizations to create and actualize their own ideas of the good. Necessarily, an outcomes-based tax exemption system that purchases specific behavior stands against this vision because in choosing which outcomes to fund and at what level, government must adjudicate among competing visions of good. It is a contradiction in terms to suppose that we can buy our way to organizations that are constituted outside of modes of exchange.

This tension in fact is the nub of the problem, to which we alluded in the introduction to this chapter and to which we return below when we address joint ventures between nonprofit and for-profit entities. Nonprofits in the health care sector are now dependent on service delivery as their primary mode of financing, yet we simultaneously expect them to stand outside of that market in their activities. It is a difficult balancing act indeed.

Accountable community benefit. It is in good part to resolve this basic tension that scholars like Gray, Schlesinger and colleagues (and others), and associations like the Catholic Health Association ("CHA") and the Voluntary Hospitals of America ("VHA"), *see* Catholic Health Association, *A Guide for Planning & Reporting Community Benefit* (original, 2006; rev. ed., 2008) [hereinafter CHA–VHA Guide for Planning & Reporting Community Benefit], have tried to fashion an alternative in which nonprofit health care organizations remain outside a system of governmentally adjudicated exchange but are nonetheless more accountable than they have been under the prevailing legal regime of community benefit. These proposals are combinations of government's conditioning the exemption on nonprofit status, the nonprofit's use of certain structure and process internally and externally, and its reporting of that structure, process and community benefit activities.

---

* His full statement of this point is the following:

The most interesting aspect of a doctrinal test for exemption based upon "enhancing access" is that the access criterion appears to bridge these two broad theoretical categories. Take health care organizations, for example, and assume that exemption required these organizations to prove that they substantially enhanced access to medical services either by providing services to previously-underserved segments of a community or else by providing the general community with specific services that otherwise were unavailable. In either of these situations, the organization meets the pluralism explanation of exemption: the organization in question has brought to the table new services and ways of delivering services that did not exist before, the essence of the pluralistic view of exemption. At the same time, the access criterion meets the economic explanations of exemption. By tying exemption to expansion of services to groups that otherwise were underserved, or to providing services otherwise unavailable to the general public, the organization has stepped in to cover a twin failure since the services were not previously provided either by the government or by the private market. *Id.*

We have seen in Part Three of this book, which focuses on health care quality, that defining quality is extremely difficult and controversial. Traditionally, definitions of quality have fallen into three categories: (1) the *structure* of the provision of care, e.g., does an operating theater have the necessary equipment if a patient aspirates food while under anesthesia?; (2) the *process* of providing care, e.g., is there a list of questions to be asked a patient before anesthesia is used, including inquiring when the patient last ate?; and (3) the *outcome* of providing care, e.g., how many patients under anesthesia died because they aspirated food they had previously eaten.

We have seen something similar in this area in which we have examined the quality of community benefit provided by exempt organizations. As mentioned in the beginning of this note, in examining such issues as the composition of the organization's governing board, whether its emergency room is open to all, or whether the EO has in place explicit policies prohibiting discrimination against Medicaid and Medicare patients, the Internal Revenue Service has utilized structure and process criteria as a means to gauge the quality of community benefit the EO confers. Proponents of accountability proffer means of strengthening these indicia of community benefit as an alternative to mandating outcomes, which, as we have seen, are goals dictated by government, a system of mandates at odds with the voluntary nature of nonprofits in health care.

One major task in creating accountability is simply to increase the visibility of community benefit within the organization. This task need not involve centralization but certainly involves committing financial and human resources, planning, budgeting, and changing the discourse within the organization so that the mission of community benefit is constantly in focus and clarified, and that the need for the organization to "accentuate" its distinctiveness from a for-profit is embedded in organizational culture. *See, e.g.,* Seay & Vladeck, *Mission Matters* at 23–26. It is probable that reporting requirements strengthen the hand of those in organizational politics who are more attentive to community benefit than those who are more disinterested or hostile.

Another major task to be accomplished in creating accountability is to increase engagement between nonprofit health organizations and the communities they serve. Requiring exempt organizations to conduct community needs assessments is an obvious part of this project. However, that process is too unidirectional, and therefore observers like Schlesinger and Gray suggest that states finance an infrastructure to support a dialogue between organizations and communities. Part of this infrastructure would consist in the state's creation of guidelines that "identify the full range of plausible community benefit activities associated with different health services." Schlesinger & Gray, *How Nonprofits Matter* at W298. Another part would consist of states' furnishing "communities with resources to organize and deliberate about these community-benefit activities." *Id.* Likewise, a "community benefit reporting process that uses credible categories and instructions about what should and should not be counted can start important conversations, both internally within [health care organizations] and in the larger health and tax policy communities, about charitable expectations." Gray & Schlesinger, *Lessons from Maryland* at W817. The word "empowerment" is perhaps overly used these days but it applies here. Community capacity, cohesion and commitment are to be created such that health care organizations and communities engage as equals and they thereby contribute to each others' goals and norms.

Proponents of an outcomes-based system of course are dissatisfied with such a framework. Because they are fixated on achieving quantifiable outcomes, they point to the weak or uncertain link between structure and process, on the one side, and quantifiable outcomes, on other. Since they demand particular quantified performance, they find the use of structure and process wanting. Coming from entirely different perspectives—the one based on improving the market and the other on maintaining some degree of freedom from the market—these two ships do indeed pass in the night.

However, some allies of maintaining the voluntary nature of nonprofits, including Professor Horwitz, likewise express great concern about the State's imposition of further structure, process and reporting requirements aimed even just at facilitating the dialogue explicated above. They point out that no matter how one slices it, structure and process requirements, including reporting, impose some degree of the uniformity and standardization that is the hallmark of rational-legal bureaucracy and is therefore in tension with the vision of allowing voluntaries breathing room to define their own vision of the good. *See* Horwitz, *Nonprofit Ownership, Private Property, and Public Accountability.* Professor Horwitz argues that the issue of trusting health care providers will not go away insofar as complex services or services the value of which is controversial. *See also* David M. Frankford, *Privatizing Health Care: Economic Magic to Cure Legal Medicine,* 66 S. CAL. L. REV. 1 (1992) [hereinafter Frankford, *Privatizing Health Care*] (discussing how the market-based rhetoric cannot avoid the agency question but can only move it around). Professor Horwitz argues that her empirical work and others' at least demonstrate correlation between the goals of the community benefit standard and nonprofit incentives, namely that nonprofits put some vision of public good above profit maximization.

The stakes, therefore, are high, because what is at risk is not only the loss of community benefits that cannot be boiled down to quantifiable outcomes, including the loss of voluntary organizations from the perspective of communitarianism or some other non-market normative vision, but also the spillover effects that flow from nonprofits to affect, in a way deemed socially beneficial, for-profits. The tax exemption, Professor Horwitz points out, may be a very blunt instrument to attain some of these benefits, particularly the ones that might be subject to quantification like charity care, but it is the only such means that is consistent with the less tangible benefits and, moreover, the vision of the voluntaries as standing outside of private or public markets. Additionally, as Schlesinger, Gray and colleagues point out in a number of places, while at the organizational level the benefits might be fairly small, in the aggregate across organizations they are very substantial. To preserve these benefits, Professor Horwitz and others claim, it is necessary to avoid even the sort of structure and process requirements supported by scholars like Schlesinger and Gray. The safer course is to allow "private actors, within broad constraints, to create and implement their own ideas of what counts as the public good." Horwitz, *Nonprofit Ownership, Private Property, and Public Accountability* at W310.

You should recognize this debate is in essence an iteration of the more general controversy concerning the relationship between procedure and substance. Liberal theory is founded on the notion that the State should remain neutral regarding definition of the good, and market theory, as a species of the more general argument, presupposes that the facilitation of markets—by addressing market failure through a tax exemption—is neutral. However, as our discussion indicates, facilitating markets is by no means neutral because markets are one means among others of organizing social and political activity. Professor Horwitz's concern is that the State's use of the tax exemption to facilitate communal discussion of the ends of health care will itself structure the terms of that discourse and therefore cannot be neutral. This debate is a large, difficult one, which we cannot answer here, but the fact that it is central to the controversy over the tax exemption for nonprofits in health care indicates why that issue cannot be boiled down to things like counting the number of indigent patients whom nonprofits serve.

In the end this controversy over the community benefit standard and the tax exemption altogether, and over the existence and nature of nonprofits and their appropriate role, comes down in good part to what our society values most and is willing to put at risk. As we have discussed, opponents of the community benefit standard start with the premise that supporters of community benefit bear the burden of proof that the tax exemption, administered under that standard, is justified. Opponents define the needed proof as quantifiable outcomes that are proven to be caused by the tax exemption. However, this burden of proof could only be carried with a "natural experiment," i.e., change or end the exemption and see what happens; if community benefit disappears, then it is proved that the exemption caused community benefit. *See* Horwitz, *Why We Need the Independent Sector* at 1409. Moreover, as we have discussed, the terms of this demand are at odds with the vision of voluntarism on which proponents rely. Since the premises with which opponents start cannot be satisfied by proponents, the opponents' policy conclusion to eliminate the community benefit standard or define it in very narrow, quantifiable terms, necessarily follows.

Proponents of community benefit start with different premises, different burdens of proof and different definitions of the nature of proof. Their highest values are maintenance of the system of the nonprofit voluntaries and the intangibles that they claim stem from the existence and activities of those organizations. Their demand, therefore, is that opponents of the community benefit standard prove that the intangibles cannot exist. The intangibles, however, stem from normative aspirations, and normative aspirations are not subject to empirical falsification. As a result, proponents of an outcomes-based tax exemption cannot meet the standard laid down by proponents of the community benefit regime. In the end, therefore, the policy question is which values should be put at risk and to what degree.

2. *Where are we headed?* The trend in federal law, at least pertaining to exempt hospitals, is certainly toward greater accountability (we briefly discuss state law below). Following a number of decades of pressure, in Congress and elsewhere, two significant changes have occurred regarding nonprofit hospitals' community benefit obligation. First, for the first time, beginning with tax year 2009, the IRS began to require specific reporting of community benefit activities. Prior to that year nonprofit hospitals were required to include only general, fairly open-ended descriptions of their activities in Form 990, their tax reports. *See, e.g.,* GAO 2008 COMMUNITY BENEFIT REPORT. Indeed, the IRS had not changed the Form 990 since 1979. By contrast, the revised Form 990 includes a Schedule H, which requires reporting of seven categories of activities: (1) charity care; (2) "community health improvement services and community benefit operations"; (3) "health professions education"; (4) "subsidized health services"; (5) "research"; (6) "cash and in-kind contributions to community groups"; and (7) "community building operations."

A couple of points are notable about these categories, which in good part are derived from the CHA–VHA Guide for Planning & Reporting Community Benefit. "Charity care" does not include any portion of bad debt or shortfalls from either Medicare payments or reimbursement from means-tested programs like Medicaid or SCHIP, although data from these items are collected elsewhere on the Schedule H. A recent study demonstrates that conclusions about the adequacy of charity care are very different depending on whether or not these items are included in the definition of charity care. *See* Gloria J. Bazzoli at al., *Community Benefit Activities of Private, Nonprofit Hospitals,* 35 J. HEALTH POL. POL'Y & L. 999 (2010). Additionally, "community building operations" are limited to activities that protect or improve the community's health or safety. This definition is not as expansive as the one discussed above, in which part of the model of a voluntary organization is that it helps build infrastructure to empower a community to engage with the organization as an equal. *See generally* Schlesinger et al., *A Typology of Community Benefits* (contrasting a model of building "community health" with one aimed at creating a "healthy community").

The second major recent development is Congress's imposition of "additional requirements for charitable hospitals" in the PPACA. Section 9007 of the Act added a new section 501(r) to the Internal Revenue Code, which requires, among other things, that a section 501(c)(3) hospital (1) conduct a community health needs assessment at least once every three years, adopt and publicize an implementation strategy to address those needs, and report each year in its Form 990 how it is addressing those needs or why it is not; (2) adopt, implement and widely publicize a written policy to provide financial assistance to patients, including the manner by which eligibility for assistance is established, how the amounts billed to patients are calculated, how a patient applies for assistance, and how the hospital will attempt to collect patients' unpaid debts; (3) limit the amount billed to individuals qualifying for assistance to that generally billed to insured individuals; and (4) refrain from "engag[ing] in extraordinary collection actions before the organization has made reasonable efforts to determine whether the individual is eligible for assistance under the financial assistance policy" the hospital is required to maintain. These provisions were written in part in response to some hospitals' failure to determine whether an individual was eligible for assistance before engaging in debt-collection procedures—a complicated issue because determination of financial status can be difficult and expensive; because many hospitals bill individuals based on charges, as opposed to costs, a practice described previous in Part Two above; and because some hospitals use abusive debt-collection practices. *See generally* Nancy M. Kane, *Tax–Exempt Hospitals: What Is Their Charitable Responsibility and How Should It Be Defined and Reported?*, 51 St. Louis L.J. 459 (2007).

The requirements that hospitals engage in needs assessments and actually develop and report on strategies for implementation are an attempt to go beyond reporting, in that hospitals, hopefully, will not simply collect cost information about the community benefit they confer but will take on a broader "hospitals as public health actors" role, actively embracing and engaging in community benefit planning and activity. *See generally* Gray & Schlesinger, *Lessons from Maryland's Community Benefit Reporting Requirements* (contrasting between accounting and managerial models of providing community benefit). This legal vision of a broader role for hospitals in promoting the health of their communities, rather than just treating people when they are sick, has been nudged along by numerous research studies that explore the social conditions of poor health and that link the burden of poor health to where one lives (often referred to in the literature as "place-based research"). *See, e.g.*, David Williams & James Marks, *Community Development Efforts Offer a Major Opportunity to Advance Americans' Health*, 30(11) Health Affairs 2052 (2011); Sandeep Kulkarni et al., *Falling Behind: Life Expectancy in U.S. Counties from 2000–2007 in an International Context*, 9 Population Health Metr. 16 (2011); Paula Braveman et al., *Socioeconomic Disparities in Health in the United States: What the Patterns Tell Us*, 100 Am. J. Pub. Health (Suppl.) 5186 (2010).

Importantly, although the Act requires that the Service review the community benefit activities of each exempt hospital once every three years, Congress did not adopt a proposal from Senator Grassley, then the ranking member of the Finance Committee, to impose a quota on hospitals that they devote five percent of their patient revenues or operating expenses, whichever is greater, to charity care. See S. Committee on Finance, Minority Staff, Tax-Exempt Hospitals: Discussion Draft (July 19, 2007), grassley.senate.gov/releases/2007/07182007.pdf. Federal law, therefore, has clearly moved in the direction of accountability but has yet to go to an outcomes-based tax exemption standard.

3. *State law*. By contrast, state law is much more mixed. Writing in March 2008 and analyzing just community benefit statutes and regulations, the GAO reported that "[s]tate community benefit requirements that hospitals must meet in order to qualify for state tax-exempt or nonprofit status vary substantially in scope and detail." In more detail:

> 15 of the states have community benefit requirements in statutes or regulations and 36 do not. Of the 15 states with requirements, 5 states—Alabama, Mississippi, Pennsylvania, Texas, and West Virginia—specify a minimum amount of community benefits required in order for hospitals to be compliant with state requirements. Another 4 of the 15 states—Illinois, Indiana, Maryland, and Texas—have penalties for hospitals that fail to comply with their community benefit requirements.

GAO 2008 COMMUNITY BENEFIT REPORT at 16.

Some states have moved toward requiring a quantified amount of charity care but most have not. Again writing in March 2008 and analyzing only statutes and regulations, the GAO summarized:

> Most states do not specify a minimum quantity of community benefits that must be provided in order to satisfy requirements. Five states require that hospitals provide a specified amount of community benefit. Alabama requires that "[t]o be exempt from ad valorem taxation, the treatment of charity patients must constitute at least 15 percent of the business of the hospital," while Texas requires that its hospitals comply with one or more of three standards: a level reasonable in relation to community needs; at least 100 percent of its tax-exempt benefits, excluding federal income tax; or at least 5 percent of its net patient revenue (in which case charity care and government-sponsored indigent care must be at least 4 percent of net patient revenue). In other states, the required minimum quantity is not a specified dollar amount or percentage. For example, Mississippi requires that, to be exempt from property tax, hospitals must maintain at least one ward for charity patients. West Virginia requires that charitable hospitals provide free and below-cost necessary medical services in an amount determined by their boards of trustees consistent with their ability to do so.

Id. at 56.

A similar division appears in the case law, the most important of which pertains to exemptions from property taxes (because that exemption is worth much more than federal and state income exemptions or state sales tax exemptions). In recent decades, as state and local budgets have been stressed and controversy over the tax-exempt status of nonprofits has increased, states and localities have become much more assertive in attempting to enforce their property tax laws against health care providers. The initial leading case was Utah County v. Intermountain Health Care, 709 P.2d 265 (Utah 1985), in which the Supreme Court of Utah denied tax exempt status to two nonprofit hospitals that "made every effort to recover payment for services rendered and devoted less than one percent of their gross revenues to providing charity care." *Id.* at 274. The Pennsylvania Supreme Court followed suit almost immediately, holding that a charitable organization has to "donate[ ] or render[ ] gratuitously a substantial portion of its services" in order to qualify for the state property tax exemption. Hospital Utilization Project v. Commonwealth, 487 A.2d 1306, 1317 (Pa. 1985). Illinois too has been aggressive in imposing a charity-care obligation, and has provided the most recent leading case, Provena Covenant Medical Center v. Department of Revenue, 925 N.E.2d 1131 (Ill. 2010), in which the Illinois Supreme Court held that Provena Hospital was properly denied a property tax exemption because "both the number of uninsured patients receiving free or discounted care and the dollar value of the care they received were *de minimus.*" *Id.* at 1149.*

Other recent cases, however, point in the exact opposite direction. For example, in Dialysis Clinic Inc. v. Levin, 938 N.E.2d 329 (Ohio 2010), the Supreme Court of Ohio upheld the denial of a property tax exemption because the dialysis provider, DCI, reserved the right to refuse care to uninsured patients in contravention of Ohio law's conditioning the exemption on the requirement that care be provided to all patients on a nondiscriminatory basis. However, the court also found that the tax commissioner went too far in "requir[ing] DCI to show that it provided unreimbursed care—that is, care financed by DCI itself from funds derived either from charitable donations or operating surpluses." *Id.* at 337. The court stated that "[b]ecause of the existence of Medicare and Medicaid, which reimburse providers for the provision of dialysis services to the indigent, few patients actually receive free care that is wholly unreimbursed. A threshold amount of unreimbursed care is not required, and the commissioner's contrary assertion is unfounded." *Id.* Similarly, in Wexford Medical Group v. City of Cadillac, 713 N.W.2d 734 (Mich. 2006), the Michigan Supreme Court refused to set such a requirement in the absence of a specific legislative mandate. It reasoned:

> To set such a threshold, significant questions would have to be grappled with. For instance, a court would have to determine how to account for the indigent who do not identify themselves as such but who nonetheless fail to pay. A court would have to determine whether facilities that provide vital health care should be treated more leniently than some other type of charity because of the

---

* The ruling of the Illinois Supreme Court was followed by three denials of property tax exemption by state regulators,. *See Illinois Hospitals Denied Tax Exemption; Revenue Department Cites State Court Ruling*, 20 HEALTH LAW REPORTER (BNA) 1270 (Aug. 18, 2011). Responding to the resultant shock wave sent through the industry, the Governor imposed a moratorium on further action pending further review. *See Illinois To Review Rules for Property Tax Exemptions for Nonprofit Hospitals*, 20 HEALTH LAW REPORTER (BNA) 1461 (Sept. 29, 2011). However, after a breakdown in negotiations, reportedly the state's review of current property tax exemptions has resumed. *See* Michael Bologna, *Hospital Tax Exemption Debate Heats Up As Illinois Resumes Review of Pending Cases*, 21 HEALTH L. REPORTER (BNA) 335 (Mar. 8, 2012).

nature of its work, or even if a health care provider in an underserved area, such as petitioner, is more deserving of exemption than one serving an area of lesser need. A court would need to consider whether to premise the exemption on whether the institution had a surplus and whether providing below-cost care constitutes charity. Clearly, courts are unequipped to handle these and many other unanswered questions.

Id. at 745–46.

A clear trend, by contrast, seems to be a slow movement toward the states' imposing requirements that hospitals take a more managerial approach toward conferring community benefit, defined as "community health" (but not "healthy communities"). Again, summarizing the statutory and regulatory law as of March 2008, the GAO found that the ten states which maintained detailed community benefit requirements "typically include[d] some combination of the following factors: a definition of community benefit, requirements for a community benefit plan that sets forth how the hospital will provide community benefits, community benefit reporting requirements, and penalties for noncompliance." GAO 2008 COMMUNITY BENEFIT REPORT at 18. See generally Berg, *Putting the Community Back* at 421–29.

In sum, the picture under state law is more mixed than under federal law. Much depends, of course, on the particular language of particular statutes, and, admittedly, decisions construing similar language vary from state to state. Some states have clearly moved to an outcomes-based tax exemption, focused particularly on a quantified level of charity care, while others have refused to move in that direction. By contrast, some have moved to a broader, more process-oriented standard, similar to that embodied in the new section 501(r) of the Internal Revenue Code, which, we have seen, requires the use of community needs assessments. Generalizations are hazardous but it is fair to say that the meaning of "community benefit" will remain in play for some time to come.

2. THE INTEGRAL PART DOCTRINE

As illustrated by the *Geisinger III* case, reprinted immediately below, for reasons unrelated to tax law an EO will create one or more nonprofit subsidiaries that, as separate entities, will be somewhat organizationally and operationally distinctive from the parent corporation. As in the Geisinger litigation, a system might create an HMO, which must be organized differently from other units of the overall system because of the need to satisfy state laws that license health care organizations (described more fully in Part Three of this book). The same might be true of various inpatient and outpatient facilities. As another example, state law often bans or limits corporations from engaging in the practice of medicine, which means that control over a system's clinical units or clinical decision-making must be vested in its medical staff. Because the individual doctors who are staff members engage in for-profit activity and are insiders, giving them control raises the possibility that the assets and income of the organization may be diverted for private purposes and that the rule against private inurement is violated. These examples and numerous others show how the requirements of state or federal law, or private accreditation, mandate certain modes of organization that threaten loss of the tax exemption for the subsidiary or, more broadly still, in very limited circumstances discussed below, the parent.

The Geisinger tax litigation illustrates the former danger. *Geisinger I* shows that by virtue of its own organization or operation, a subsidiary like the Geisinger Health Plan may not be entitled to a tax exemption. However, *Geisinger I* left open the possibility that the Health Plan may nonetheless have been exempt because it is an "integral part" of the overall system. That is the subject of *Geisinger III*.*

Geisinger Health Plan v. Commissioner of Internal Revenue (*Geisinger III*)

30 F.3d 494 (3d Cir. 1994)

■ LEWIS, CIRCUIT JUDGE:

In *Geisinger Health Plan v. Commissioner of Internal Revenue,* 985 F.2d 1210 (3d Cir.1993) ("*Geisinger I*"), we held that the Geisinger Health Plan ("GHP"), a health maintenance organization ("HMO"), was not entitled to exemption from federal income taxation as a charitable organization under 26 U.S.C. § 501(c)(3). We remanded the case for determination of whether GHP was entitled to exemption from taxation by virtue of being an integral part of the Geisinger System (the "System"), a comprehensive health care system serving northeastern and northcentral Pennsylvania. We will affirm the Tax Court's decision that it is not exempt as an integral part of the System.

I.

GHP is a prepaid health care plan which contracts with health care providers to provide services to its subscribers. The facts relevant to GHP's function are detailed in our opinion in *Geisinger I,* and we need not repeat them here. Instead, far more relevant to this appeal is GHP's relationship with the Geisinger System and its other constituent entities, a relationship which we must examine in some detail to decide the issue before us.

The Geisinger System consists of GHP and eight other entities, all involved in some way in promoting health care in 27 counties in northeastern and northcentral Pennsylvania. They are: the Geisinger Foundation (the "Foundation"), Geisinger Medical Center (AGMC"), Geisinger Clinic

---

* We use the term *"Geisinger I"* to describe the Court of Appeal's first decision, *"Geisinger II"* for the Tax Court's decision on remand, and *"Geisinger III"* for Court of Appeal's second decision. Some writers count from the Tax Court decision before *Geisinger I,* with the result that our I is their II and so on, with a *Geisinger IV* at the end.

(the "Clinic"), Geisinger Wyoming Valley Medical Center ("GWV"), Marworth, Geisinger System Services ("GSS") and two professional liability trusts. All of these other entities are recognized as exempt from federal income taxation under one or more sections of the Internal Revenue Code.

The Foundation controls all these entities, as well as three for-profit corporations. It has the power to appoint the corporate members of GHP, GMC, GWV, GSS, the Clinic and Marworth, and those members elect the boards of directors of those entities. The Foundation also raises funds for the Geisinger System. Its board of directors is composed of civic and business leaders in the area.

GMC operates a 569–bed regional medical center. As of March 31, 1988, it had 3,512 employees, including 195 resident physicians and fellows in approved postgraduate training programs. It accepts patients without regard to ability to pay, including Medicare, Medicaid and charity patients. It operates a full-time emergency room open to all, regardless of ability to pay. It also serves as a teaching hospital.

GWV is a 230–bed hospital located in Wilkes–Barre, Pennsylvania. It accepts patients regardless of ability to pay, and it operates a full-time emergency room open to all, regardless of ability to pay.

The Clinic provides medical services to patients at 43 locations throughout the System's service area. It also conducts extensive medical research in conjunction with GMC and physicians who perform medical services for GMC, GWV and other entities in the Geisinger System. As of March 31, 1988, it employed 401 physicians. It accepts patients without regard to their ability to pay.

Marworth operates two alcohol detoxification and rehabilitation centers and offers educational programs to prevent alcohol and substance abuse.

GSS employs management and other personnel who provide services to entities in the Geisinger System.

As we noted in *Geisinger I,* the Geisinger System apparently decided to create GHP after GMC experimented with a pilot prepaid health plan between 1972 and 1985. The experience was positive, and the Geisinger System formed GHP to provide its own prepaid health plan.

It organized GHP as a separate entity within the System (as opposed to operating it from within the Clinic, GMC or GWV) for three reasons. First, HMOs in Pennsylvania are subject to extensive regulation by the Commonwealth's Departments of Health and Insurance. Operating GHP separately enables other entities in the System to avoid having to comply with the burdensome requirements associated with that regulation. Second, those administering the System believe it preferable for GHP's organization and management to remain separate from those of the System's other entities because it serves a wider geographic area than any of those other entities. Finally, under Pennsylvania law at least one-third of GHP's directors must be subscribers. Establishing GHP as a separate entity avoids disrupting the governance of the other Geisinger System entities to comply with this requirement. For example, establishing an HMO within GMC would have required GMC to canvass its board of directors to ensure that one-third of them subscribed to the HMO. If they did not, GMC would have had to amend its by-laws or other governing documents to add director-ships so that one-third of the directors were subscribers. Incorporating GHP separately eliminates the need for such reorganization.

For the year which ended June 30, 1987, GHP generated 8.8 percent of the aggregate gross receipts of the five health care providers in the Geisinger System. At the time this case was first submitted to the Tax Court, projections indicated that by June 30, 1991, GHP would generate 14.35 percent of the System's aggregate gross receipts.

GHP's interaction with other Geisinger System entities is varied. Its most significant contact is with the Clinic, from which it purchases the physician services its subscribers require by paying a fixed amount per member per month, as set forth in a Medical Services Agreement. Eighty-four percent of physician services are provided by doctors who are employees of the Clinic; the remaining 16 percent are provided by doctors who are not affiliated with the Clinic but who have contracted with the Clinic to provide services to GHP subscribers. GHP has similarly entered into contracts with GMC and GWV, as well as 20 non-related hospitals. When GHP's subscribers require hospital care, these hospitals provide it pursuant to the terms of their contracts, for either a negotiated per diem charge or a discounted percentage of billed charges. GHP has also contracted with GSS to purchase office space, supplies and administrative services.

Except in emergency situations, only physicians who either work for the Clinic or have contracted with the Clinic may order that a GHP subscriber be admitted to a hospital. When such admission is ordered, it generally must be to GMC, GWV or one of the 20 other hospitals with which GHP has contracted. The only exceptions to this requirement are in a medical emergency outside of GHP's service area or when approved in advance by GHP's medical director; in those instances, a subscriber may be admitted to a hospital with which GHP has no contractual relationship.

GHP has also entered into contracts with pharmacies, durable medical equipment suppliers, ambulance services and physical therapists. Those entities' services are available to subscribers only (1) in a medical emergency or (2) when prescribed by a doctor who is employed by the Clinic or who is under contract with the Clinic to provide care to GHP subscribers.

The Tax Court considered GHP's role in the Geisinger System when, on remand from Geisinger I, it decided that GHP did not qualify for exempt status under the integral part doctrine. *Geisinger Health Plan v. Commissioner of Internal Revenue,* 100 T.C. 394 (1993) (*"Geisinger II"*). The court first distinguished a series of "group practice cases," in which incorporated groups of doctors on hospital or faculty medical staffs were held to be exempt from taxation as integral parts of the tax-exempt hospitals or medical schools with which they were associated. The Tax Court found that those cases did not control its decision because "[f]or [them] to apply here, the population of [GHP's] subscribers would have to overlap substantially with the patients of the related exempt entities [and t]he facts indicated that it does not." *Geisinger II,* 100 T.C. at 404. Moreover, it held, GHP was not entitled to tax-exempt status as an integral part of the System because it would produce unrelated business income for the Clinic, GMC or GWV if one of those entities were to absorb its activities. *Id.* at 404–06. A timely appeal followed; as noted previously, we will affirm, although we will do so on grounds which differ from those on which the Tax Court rested. Specifically, because we deem it unnecessary to decide, we will not reach the issue whether GHP would produce unrelated business income if it were part of some entity created by merging its operations with one of the other Geisinger System entities.

II.

Generally, separately incorporated entities must qualify for tax exemption on their own merits. In *Geisinger I,* we decided that GHP cannot qualify for tax exemption on its own merits. The question before us now is whether it comes within the "integral part doctrine," which may best be described as an exception to the general rule that entitlement to exemption is derived solely from an entity's own characteristics. As it did with the issue of whether it was entitled to exemption standing alone, GHP bears the burden of proving entitlement to exemption under the integral part doctrine.

A.

In *Geisinger I,* we described the integral part doctrine as follows:

> The integral part doctrine provides a means by which organizations may qualify for exemption vicariously through related organizations, as long as they are engaged in activities which would be exempt if the related organizations engaged in them, and as long as those activities are furthering the exempt purposes of the related organizations.

Geisinger I, 985 F.2d at 1220. The Tax Court on remand stated:

> The parties agree that an organization is entitled to exemption as an integral part of a tax-exempt affiliate if its activities are carried out under the supervision or control of an exempt organization and could be carried out by the exempt organization without constituting an unrelated trade or business.

Geisinger II, 100 T.C. at 402; *see* 26 C.F.R. § 1.502–1(b).

GHP argues that these statements require us to examine whether the Clinic or GMC could retain tax-exempt status if it were to absorb GHP. It thus compares the attributes of a hypothetically merged Clinic/GHP or GMC/GHP entity to the attributes of the HMO held to be exempt in *Sound Health.* Concluding that the merged entity would display more indicia of entitlement to exemption than the *Sound Health* HMO, GHP urges that it is exempt because of the characteristics of the hypothetical merged entity. Despite its superficial appeal, we reject this argument and hold that the integral part doctrine does not mean that GHP would be exempt solely because either GMC or the Clinic could absorb it while retaining *its* tax-exempt status. While this is a necessary condition to applying the doctrine, it is not the only condition. GHP is separately incorporated for reasons it found administratively and politically advantageous. While it may certainly benefit from that separate incorporation, it must also cope with the consequences flowing from it.

We acknowledge that interpreting the integral part doctrine in the manner GHP urges might enable entities to choose their organizational structures based on efficiency concerns rather than perverting those concerns by making tax considerations relevant. In our view, however, there are countervailing policy concerns which justify determining each entity's tax status based upon its own organizational structure. It is less complex and more certain for courts and administrators to assess an entity's tax status in light of its unique organizational composition and its association with another entity, and only to have to take into account some hypothetical combination of organizations as a second step in those relatively rare instances when an organization meets the other precondition of integral part status we set forth below. *See* II.C. *infra.* We recognize that it may appear overly technical to tax GHP differently from a GMC/GHP or a Clinic/GHP combination, for instance, merely because it is incorporated separately. On the other hand, to tax GHP differently merely because it is related to those entities, without searching for indicia that its association with them enhances its own tax-exempt characteristics, would be inconsistent with the narrow construction generally accorded tax exemptions.

Accordingly, we will determine whether GHP is exempt from taxation when examined not only in the context of its relationship with the other entities in the System, but also based upon its own organizational structure. In doing so, we bear in mind that we are not bound by the description of the integral part doctrine set forth in *dicta* in *Geisinger I.*

B.

As the Tax Court recognized, 100 T.C. at 401, the integral part doctrine is not codified. Its genesis may be found in a phrase contained within a regulation which speaks of a subsidiary being exempt "on the ground that its activities are an integral part of the activities of the parent organization." This reference to the doctrine is only fully understood, however, when one considers it in the context of the regulation and the statute it implements. Section 502 of the Internal Revenue Code (the "feeder organization rule") provides that an organization engaged in a trade or business for profit will be taxed even if it pays all of its profits over to an exempt organization. 26 U.S.C. § 502(a). *See generally* 9 Merten's Law of Federal Income Taxation § 34.01 at 5. The regulation interpreting this section of the Code makes clear that

> [i]n the case of an organization operated for the primary purpose of carrying on a trade or business for profit, exemption is not

allowed ... on the ground that all the profits of such organization are payable to one or more [exempt] organizations. . . .

26 C.F.R. § 502–1(b).

The integral part doctrine arises from an exception to this "feeder organization" rule. Regulation 502–1(b) states that despite the general rule of taxation of "feeder organizations,"

> [i]f a subsidiary organization of a tax-exempt organization *would itself be exempt on the ground that its activities are an integral part of the exempt activities of the parent organization,* its exemption will not be lost because, as a matter of accounting between the two organizations, the subsidiary derives a profit from its dealings with the parent organization[.]

26 C.F.R. § 1.502–1(b) (emphasis added). To illustrate how this exemption might apply to an entity, the regulation describes "a subsidiary organization which is operated for the sole purpose of furnishing electric power used by its parent organization, a tax-exempt organization, in carrying out its educational activities." *Id.*[5] *See also* Rev.Rul. 78–41, 1978–1 C.B. 148 (trust existing solely as a repository of funds set aside by nonprofit hospital for the payment of malpractice claims against the hospital, and as the payor of those claims, was exempt as an integral part of the hospital); Rev.Rul. 63–235, 1963–2 C.B. 210 (incidental publication and sale of law journals did not prevent journal corporation from being exempt as "adjunct to" an exempt law school); Rev.Rul. 58–194, 1958–1 C.B. 240 (bookstore used almost exclusively by university faculty and students was exempt as an integral part of the university with which it was associated).

GHP contends that as long as it would not generate unrelated business income if it were merged into any one of the other Geisinger System entities, it is exempt as an integral part of the System. The Tax Court, in fact, utilized unrelated business income concepts in analyzing GHP's claim for exemption. *See Geisinger II,* 100 T.C. at 404–07. We agree that an entity seeking exemption as an integral part of another cannot primarily be engaged in activity which would generate more than insubstantial unrelated business income for the other entity. That much is demonstrated by the remainder of 26 C.F.R. § 1.502–1(b), which cautions that

> the subsidiary organization is not exempt from tax if it is operated for the primary purpose of carrying on a trade or business which would be an unrelated trade or business (that is, unrelated to exempt activities) if regularly carried on by the parent organization. For example, if a subsidiary organization is operated primarily for the purpose of furnishing electric power to consumers other than its parent organization (and the parent's tax-exempt subsidiary organizations), it is not exempt since such business would be an unrelated trade or business if regularly carried on by the parent

---

5. Although the regulation speaks in terms of parent and subsidiary entities, the IRS does not contend that we should consider only GHP's relationship with its parent, the Foundation, in deciding this appeal.

organization. Similarly, if the organization is owned by several unrelated exempt organizations, and is operated for the purpose of furnishing electric power to each of them, it is not exempt since such business would be an unrelated trade or business if regularly carried on by any one of the tax-exempt organizations.

Id.

Although 26 C.F.R. § 502–1(b) clearly makes the absence of activity constituting an unrelated trade or business a necessary qualification for the operation of the integral part doctrine, because this regulation speaks in terms of disqualification from exemption rather than qualifications for exemption, it does not indicate or explain whether there are any other necessary qualifications—the issue we face in this case.

Both the revenue rulings cited earlier and case law similarly fail to state a comprehensive rule to assist in determining when an entity is exempt as an integral part of another. In *Squire v. Students Book Corp.,* 191 F.2d 1018 (9th Cir. 1951), for example, the court ruled that a corporation operating a bookstore and restaurant which sold college texts, was wholly owned by a college, used college space free of charge, served mostly faculty and students, and devoted its earnings to educational purposes was exempt because it "obviously bears a close and intimate relationship to the functioning of the [c]ollege itself." *Squire,* 191 F.2d at 1020. It did not, however, provide further explication for its rationale.

C.

Distilling § 1.502–1(b) and [prior cases] into a general rule leads us to conclude that a subsidiary which is not entitled to exempt status on its own may only receive such status as an integral part of its § 501(c)(3) qualified parent[6] if (i) it is not carrying on a trade or business which would be an unrelated trade or business (that is, unrelated to exempt activities) if regularly carried on by the parent, and (ii) its relationship to its parent somehow enhances the subsidiary's own exempt character to the point that, when the boost provided by the parent is added to the contribution made by the subsidiary itself, the subsidiary would be entitled to § 501(c)(3) status.

In considering whether the boost received by GHP from its association with GMC or the Clinic might be sufficient, when added to its own contribution, to merit § 501(c)(3) treatment, we must first look at the nature of the boost which was sufficient in those instances where the integral part doctrine has been applied. The electric company discussed in 26 C.F.R. § 502–1(b), for example, would not be entitled to an exemption standing alone, because the provision of electric power to others is not a charitable purpose.

---

6. Although we refer to the entity seeking application of the integral part doctrine as the "subsidiary" and the current holder of the § 501(c)(3) exemption as the "parent," we recognize that the relationship, as in this case, may be that of entities controlled by a common parent or some other form of affiliation.

However, the fact that the electric company is a subsidiary of an exempt university eliminates the characteristic which prevented the company from being exempt on its own. As a subsidiary of the university, the electric company acquires the purpose of the university—it produces electricity solely for the purpose of allowing education to occur. The "boost" it receives from its association with the educational institution transforms it from a company without to a company with a charitable purpose and thus enables it to qualify for tax-exempt status as an integral part of that institution. Like the electric company, the bookstores in *Squire* and Rev. Rul. 58–194, and the law journal in Rev.Rul. 63–235 had insufficiently charitable purposes to qualify for exempt status when considered alone. Selling books or a journal to the general public is not educational enough to qualify for exempt status as a charitable institution. But because these particular bookstores and this particular law journal were subsidiaries of universities and aided the universities' exempt missions of educating their students, the purposes of the bookstores and journal became more charitable, and they were entitled to an exemption. Absent receipt of such a "boost," we do not think that an institution is entitled to a tax exemption as an integral part. To hold otherwise might enable an organization that is not entitled to an exemption on its own to become tax-exempt *merely* because it happens to be controlled by an organization that is itself exempt.

Here, we do not think that GHP receives any "boost" from its association with the Geisinger System. In *Geisinger I,* we determined that while GHP helps to promote health, it does not do so for a significant enough portion of the community to qualify for tax-exempt status on its own. And, unlike the electric company, university bookstores or law journal in the regulations and case law, the contribution that GHP makes to community health is not increased at all by the fact that GHP is a subsidiary of the System rather than being an independent organization which sends its subscribers to a variety of hospitals and clinics.

As our examination of the manner in which GHP interacts with other entities in the System makes clear, its association with those entities does nothing to increase the portion of the community for which GHP promotes health—it serves no more people as a part of the System than it would serve otherwise. It may contribute to the System by providing more patients than the System might otherwise have served, thus arguably allowing the System to promote health among a broader segment of the community than could be served without it, but its provision of patients to the System does not enhance its own promotion of health; the patients it provides—its subscribers—are the same patients it serves without its association with the System. To the extent it promotes health among non-GHP-subscriber patients of the System, it does so only because GHP subscribers' payments to the System help finance the provision of health care to others. An entity's mere financing of the exempt purposes of a related organization does not constitute furtherance of that organization's purpose so as to justify exemption. *Cf.* 26 U.S.C. § 502 ("[a]n organization ... shall not be exempt from taxation under section 501 on the ground that all of its profits are payable to one or more organizations exempt from taxation under section 501"). Thus, it is apparent that GHP merely seeks to "piggyback" off of the other entities in the System, taking on their charitable characteristics in an effort to gain exemption without demonstrating that it is rendered "more charitable" by virtue of its association with them.

D.

It has not escaped our attention, of course, that both our decision today and our decision in *Geisinger I* may either set the tone for, or be superseded by, legislative activity in the near future. The executive and the legislative branches are currently debating the appropriate parameters of future governmental involvement in the provision and financing of health care in this country. The legislation which may result could significantly transform the structure and financing of health care delivery systems in ways both anticipated and unanticipated. Academic commentary on our decision in *Geisinger I* reinforces our common-sense impression that questions regarding the tax-exempt status of integrated delivery systems under 26 U.S.C. § 501(c)(3) may be addressed during these debates.

Whatever changes are wrought by the legislature in the future, however, today we are constrained to apply the law in its current form and to construe tax exemptions narrowly. Our interpretation of the integral part route to exemption under section 501(c)(3) reflects those constraints. Obviously, we express no opinion as to whether HMOs, whether structured like GHP or like the *Sound Health* HMO, can or should be exempt from federal income taxation after whatever transformation of the health care industry may be forthcoming.

III.

In sum, GHP does not qualify for exemption as an integral part of the Geisinger System because its charitable character is not enhanced by virtue of its association with the System. We will affirm the decision of the Tax Court.

Notes

1. *Subsidiaries and the "integral part" test.* A subsidiary is an integral part of a whole when its functions are so intertwined with and necessary to achieving the exempt purposes of the whole that it makes no sense to treat the part as nonexempt and the whole as exempt. Put differently, the activities of the subpart are related to the exempt purposes of the whole such that the subsidiary's income is not taxable as unrelated business income. An EO may create a subsidiary to engage in taxable unrelated business activities, and for purposes relevant here, the Revenue Service and the courts will respect the formal separation—meaning that the two entities are separate for tax purposes—so long the subsidiary is bona fide—it actually pursues a trade or business as those terms are used in tax law—and is operationally distinct. See Gen. Couns. Mem. 39,598

(Jan. 23, 1987). Put conversely in the terms of the integral part doctrine, if the subsidiary is operationally distinct and if its activities are not related to the whole's exempt purposes, then it is not an integral part of the whole, and its income is taxable as unrelated business income.

Relevant to the consideration of whether income is derived from unrelated business activity is the degree to which an EO would obtain a competitive advantage against for-profit entities, which are not eligible for an exemption. Treas. Reg. § 1.513–1(b). The Revenue Service and the courts balance the extent to which an activity is necessary to achieve an EO's exempt purposes against the competitive disadvantage that might be imposed on nonexempt entities from the proposed exemption for that activity. For example, an exempt hospital's pharmacy deprives competing nonexempt pharmacies of business when it services a hospital's patients, but that activity is intertwined with and essential to running a modern hospital and is therefore not unrelated business activity. On the other hand, the pharmacy's sales to the general public would be taxable. We will return to these sorts of issues when we discuss joint ventures below.

The Tax Court had found it relevant that GHP's membership was broader than the class of patients it sent to the Geisinger System's clinical units. 100 T.C. at 404–07. Although the Tax Court did not adequately explain why this fact was relevant, one can analogize the situation to the pharmacy example above. The fact that some of GHP's members are sent to the System's clinical units indicates that GHP's activities are intertwined with the clinical units; and the fact that the clinical units must have patients indicates that GHP's activities are necessary to attaining the clinical units' exempt purposes. The GHP members sent to clinical units are analogous to the hospital patients the pharmacy serves. However, the fact that a substantial portion of GHP's members are not sent to the clinical units indicates—the implicit reasoning of the Tax Court (and the Service) must go—that a substantial part of GHP's activities are neither intertwined with nor necessary to the clinical units' exempt purposes. Similarly, the Tax Court found it relevant that GHP had arranged for the provision of services to its members at facilities outside of the Geisinger System's clinical units. The Tax Court took this to mean that GHP was servicing unrelated entities. As such, a substantial portion of its activities were unrelated to the System's exempt purposes. These activities were like the pharmacy's sales to persons other than hospital patients. Because GHP had not shown them to be insubstantial, it had not carried its burden of proof to establish its exemption.

For two reasons, the Tax Court (and the Revenue Service) flunked health law. First, it is always the case that only a portion of an HMO's subscribers will use clinical services. Accordingly, the fact that GHP's membership was broader than the class of patients it sent to the clinical units is irrelevant. Second, it is equally irrelevant that GHP contracted with, and sent its patients, to non-Geisinger facilities. This too is the standard course of affairs in the sector because unless all of the needs of all patients in an HMO can be serviced just through the HMO's network, then the HMO must contract with facilities outside of the network. If the Geisinger System operated an HMO without creating a separate subsidiary, it too would have to execute those agreements with non-Geisinger facilities. Without question, the System's execution of those contracts would not affect its exempt status. Likewise, GHP's execution of those agreements should have been irrelevant.

2. *The "boost" test.* The Court of Appeals decided the case on a different basis than the Tax Court and found that GHP did not receive a boost from the activities of the Health System because its primary role was to send the System's other units only HMO members, but not non-members from the general community. Again, since the integral part doctrine focuses on the extent to which the activities of the subsidiary are causally related and necessary to attainment of the exempt purposes of the whole, shouldn't the question have been whether the HMO's sending patients to the rest of the Geisinger System was integrated with and necessary to the System's provision of care and education? Doesn't the boost test seem to turn the integral part doctrine on its head in that it asks what the whole does for the part rather than what the part does for the whole?

Additionally, the integral part doctrine is supposed to be an independent ground by which a separate entity can obtain an exemption even though on its own it is not so entitled. Given the rationale for deciding *Geisinger I*— that GHP serves only its own members—did the application of the test in *Geisinger III* that GHP only sends its members to the rest of the System add anything?

3. *The relevance of the separate HMO.* Isn't the crux of the case the fact that GHP members received care from the Geisinger System's clinical units, a result that would have been no different if Pennsylvania law allowed the System itself to act as an HMO rather than requiring it to form an HMO as a separate subsidiary? If the System—more precisely all the other units of the System—are tax exempt by virtue of their provision of care and pursuit of educational and scientific goals, then why does the separate organization of the Health Plan matter? What is the sense, then, of deciding separately whether the Geisinger System's various units, organized individually to achieve various business purposes and to satisfy the strictures of state law, are tax exempt? Keep in mind that the diverse units' organizational and operational features might raise different questions for each concerning private inurement and unrelated business income.

The Court of Appeals in *Geisinger III* evidently believed that the only way it could determine whether the whole engaged in exempt activities would be to add up the activities of the parts, a task it deemed to be "hypothetical." For that reason, it decided that the integral part doctrine had to work analytically in the opposite direction in that the parts are examined on their own merits except that they might achieve some "boost" from their role in the larger exempt enterprise.

The Court of Appeals was wrong, however, that it would have to assess the activities of a hypothetical entity in order to decide whether the Health

System as whole and therefore all its parts would be entitled to an exemption. Writing after the Tax Court had decided *Geisinger II* but before *Geisinger III* had been decided in the Court of Appeals, Professor Colombo observed that tax authorities and the courts could determine whether diverse units are subject to common ownership or management, or whether together they carry on activities that would be exempt if housed in one organization. See Colombo, *Rethinking the Issues* at 248–53. If all the activities were in fact housed in one organizational unit, tax authorities and the courts would have to determine whether that single entity is exempt and which of its activities would be taxable as unrelated business income. The fact that these activities are spread across diverse units does not somehow change the task, which tax authorities and the courts perform in numerous cases. If it is not a hypothetical exercise when there exists one entity, it does not magically become hypothetical when multiple entities exist instead.

4. *Separating unrelated business income into separate organizational units.* Given that unrelated business income is taxable, are there administrative reasons to encourage organizations to segregate unrelated business income into separate organizational units? Would this goal of administrative convenience be more effectively implemented if one examines the role the part plays in achieving the purposes of the whole—the standard formulation of the integrated part doctrine—or the Court of Appeal's boost test? Is the conceptual muddle introduced by the boost test necessary to attain this administrative efficiency?

Even if there are administrative reasons to encourage the segregation of unrelated activities into taxable subsidiaries, does anything in the Geisinger litigation indicate that GHP was created for that reason? Could the Geisinger System have organized itself so that it both satisfied state law and separated related activities from unrelated ones in separate entities? Assuming that the tax exemption in 501(c)(3) furthers public purposes—and given that Congress has decided that question affirmatively—should EOs be penalized because they cannot achieve both purposes?

5. *Doesn't Geisinger as a whole provide community benefit?* Aside from these arguments concerning administrative convenience, Professor Colombo is clearly right in characterizing the holdings regarding community benefit and the integral part doctrine as "idiocy." Colombo, *Rethinking the Issues* at 248. He makes a compelling case that GHP is organized and operated for exempt purposes if one considers the operation of the Geisinger System as a whole and GHP's role in those operations:

> The Geisinger System formed GHP to enhance health care delivery to its service area, mostly rural northeastern and north central Pennsylvania. In fact, at the time of litigation, 23% of GHP's members lived in medically underserved areas and 65% of its members lived in counties that contained medically underserved areas. GHP contracted with other members of the Geisinger System (the clinic and two hospitals) as well as some outside physicians and hospitals to provide physician and hospital services

to its members. GHP also contracted to provide drugs, durable medical equipment, rehabilitation therapy, and other services to members.

The only requirements for membership in GHP were that an individual be at least 18 years of age, reside in GHP's service area, and complete a medical history questionnaire. GHP also enrolled groups without the questionnaire procedure. At the time of litigation, GHP had turned down 11% of its applicants and had enrolled about 1000 Medicare recipients. It did not enroll any Medicaid recipients because it had not yet negotiated the necessary Medicaid contract with the state Department of Public Welfare. GHP had also adopted a subsidized dues program for indigent families in its service area, but had not implemented that program as of the date of litigation because of financial constraints. It had projected that the program would permit 35 indigent enrollees during the first three years of operation.

Id. at 232 (footnotes omitted).

At bottom, if one puts all the Geisinger decisions together, the Revenue Service and the courts have deprived the Geisinger System of money that could be used to further its exempt purposes. Depriving the System of these funds means that it is less able to provide nonprofit services. Is this or should it be what Congress had in mind?

6. *Section 501(m) and risk retention.* Denying a requested exemption for the HMOs operated by Intermountain Health Care ("IHC"), a large West Coast system, the Service relied largely on *Geisinger II and III* and found that IHC's HMOs do not engage in charitable purposes because, among other things, they provides services exclusively to their enrollees and because like GHP, they are not an integral part of the larger system. These decisions were affirmed by the Tax Court and the 10th Circuit. *See* IHC Health Plans, Inc. v. Commissioner, 325 F.3d 1188, 1197 (10th Cir. 2003). However, the Service also ruled that the HMOs were included within section 501(m)(1) of the Internal Revenue Code, which states that an exemption may be granted "only if no substantial part of [the organization's] activities consists of providing commercial-type insurance." According to the Service, section 501(m)(1) leads to the result that entities which retain risk are engaged in "commercial-type insurance" and are therefore not tax-exempt; entities that do not retain risk are therefore tax exempt. This distinction, in turn, depends on whether the HMO contracts with physicians and pays them on a fee-for-service basis—therefore retaining risk—or contracts with them and shifts risk to them by paying either a capitated rate or under a system in which a portion of their compensation is tied to the amounts and types of services they order for their patients (withholds). See *Exempt Status: HMO Does Not Qualify for Tax Exemption, According to Unreleased Advice from IRS*, 7 HEALTH LAW REPORTER (BNA) 1983 (1998). See also Priv. Ltr. Rul. 2000–44039 (Nov. 3, 2000); Tech. Adv. Mem. 2000–330346 (Aug. 18, 2000). The tax exemption of HMOs, therefore,

would turn on its risk relationship with providers. This portion of the ruling has not been tested in the courts.

The Service's interpretation is an extremely contested application of section 501(m)(1), which was passed to remove the tax exemption provided to the Blue Cross and Blue Shield organizations on the ground that they were acting just like commercial insurers, i.e., providing "commercial-type insurance." While it is clear that the provision was not intended to revoke the tax exemption provided to staff-model HMOs, which employ physicians, its application to entities like IHC's HMOs is very controversial, because it is not clear that the tax status of an HMO should turn on whether or not it uses risk-based reimbursement. In Notice 2003–31, I.R.B. 2003–21 (May 27, 2003), Treasury and IRS announced that they intend to propose regulations providing guidance under section 501(m) on the meaning of "commercial-type insurance" and address how section 501(m) applies to HMOs. In light of this reexamination, they withdrew the extant application of section 501(m) from their Manual and issued a field memorandum that they would not revoke an HMO's exemption on the basis of this section. See *IRS Official Predicts Continued Delay in HMO Tax Rules, Says Suspension Possible*, 13 HEALTH LAW REPORTER (BNA) 1552 (Oct. 28, 2004). As of February, 2012, no regulations have been issued and it is not clear whether the Service will issue them or enforce section 501(m) again against a non-staff model HMO because it retains risk.

7. *Counseling nonprofit clients.* You are advising a client regarding an acquisition, reorganization, or other transaction in which, as in the *Geisinger* litigation, the demands of state law, business purposes, and the requirements of tax law point in different directions. What is your role and what tasks are necessary for you to fulfill that role? If the ultimate decision requires that the client exercise a business judgment regarding the trade-offs between conflicting requirements, how do you help your client make those decisions? Think about different options as creating sets of beneficial opportunities accompanied by certain risks of loss.

3.   JOINT VENTURES WITH NONEXEMPT ENTITIES

The decisions whether entities are organized and operated to confer community or private benefit are perhaps most difficult when EOs enter into joint ventures with for-profit entities, which in turn is perhaps the most significant evidence of the fact that the lines between nonprofit and for-profit activities have become blurred relative to the much sharper demarcation that existed for roughly thirty years following the Second World War. These joint ventures vary greatly in scope. An EO might, for example, enter into a joint venture whereby it and a for-profit entity become partners in an ancillary service facility, such as an imaging center. At the other extreme, the EO might transfer all of its assets into the joint venture, as is the case of a so-called "whole hospital" joint venture we'll see in Revenue Ruling 98–15 discussed below. Joint ventures also vary greatly in organizational structure, formal and informal control, and operation, in that the interests held by the EO and the for-profit entity in the joint venture can vary, as can composition of relevant boards, the powers of the boards, designation of and restrictions on organizational purposes, management contracts, appointment of directors, officers, and key employees, etc.

To understand the tax issues involved here, we must refine our discussion of the distinction between community and private benefit. To reiterate prior discussion, an EO may pursue a nonexempt purpose, i.e., engage in an activity that confers private not community benefit, so long as that benefit is "no more than insubstantial," or in another word, "incidental." There is a qualitative and quantitative element to the question whether private benefit is incidental, both of which we have seen before in the analogous formulation of the integral part doctrine. The qualitative element is that the private benefit must be "a necessary concomitant of the activity which benefits the public at large [in that] the benefit to the public cannot be achieved without necessarily benefitting certain private individuals." Gen. Couns. Mem. 37,789 (Dec. 18, 1978). This qualitative element is the analogue of the requirement for the integral part doctrine that the part's activity must be causally related to the ability of the whole to attain public purposes. The quantitative element is that the private benefit must be insubstantial compared with the community benefit conferred, analogous to the requirement that an integral part of an exempt whole may only engage in insubstantial nonexempt activities.

This concept—that community benefit must outweigh the private benefit that is inexorably jointly created in conferring community benefit—pervades the tax treatment of joint ventures. Applying this concept to joint ventures is what makes the area so difficult and, simultaneously, interesting.

For our purposes joint ventures between an EO and a for-profit entity raise two tax questions. First, is the income from the joint venture returned to the EO taxable? The joint venture is a legal entity, formed between the EO and the for-profit entity. Below we'll discuss how the type of legal entity—partnership, limited partnership, corporation, LLC, etc.—can matter, but for now ignore this issue. Just focus on the fact that the joint venture is itself a legal entity which may or may not engage in exempt activities. As a shorthand, we can ask, "Is the joint venture tax exempt?" However, posing the question this way is just a shorthand and hides something important (or the more precise formulation is just taken for granted by those who already know the law). Each of the joint venturers usually contributes something to the joint venture, takes some risk, and shares an upside, i.e., is expecting a return. The way to think about this first tax question is that it asks whether the stream of income flowing to the EO from the joint venture is taxable. The other stream of income, flowing to the for-profit joint venturer, will always be taxable because income to the for-profit is, of course, always taxable. By contrast, if the joint venture engages in activities that are exempt, then the income flowing to the EO is likewise exempt. On the other hand, if the activities of the joint venture are not exempt, they are "unrelated" to the exempt activities for which the EO is awarded *its* tax exemption. Under these circumstances the EO will have to pay taxes on its share of the joint venture's income (leaving aside any potential application of the integral part exception). Technically this tax is known as the Unrelated Business Income Tax, or UBIT, a complicated subject that we will not address fully in this chapter.

The second question is different. It arises once it has been decided that the activities of the joint venture do not qualify for a tax exemption. As we have just indicated, under these circumstances, the EO must pay UBIT on its share of the income from the joint venture. To repeat, an EO may engage in activity unrelated to its exemption, but it must pay taxes on that activity. However, as we also indicated, there are limitations on the amount of unrelated activity permitted to an EO. When the EO engages in such activity, it is engaged in activity that confers private benefit, or, put in different tax language, does not confer community benefit. As we discussed in the beginning of the chapter and refined here, for the EO to remain exempt this unrelated activity must be insubstantial relative to the whole of the EO's activities, in the quantitative and qualitative sense just described. If the unrelated activity exceeds this threshold, then the EO's participation in the joint venture threatens its tax exemption. However, as we will see, the question whether its exemption will be revoked is more complicated because, as we discuss in the notes following *Redlands* below, here the choice of entity to house the joint venture—is the joint venture a general partnership, a limited partnership, a corporation, an LLC, etc.—has outcome-determinative consequences. For now please keep these two questions separate as you read the materials below: (1) Must the EO joint venturer pay UBIT on its share of income from the joint venture?; and (2) does the joint venture threaten the EO's tax exempt status?

As of the end of 2011, *Redlands*, the following case, is the leading authority in the area. Because the organizational structure involved in *Redlands* is complex, when reading the case, you should refer to the following chart, which the Tax Court prepared as an appendix to its decision. The chart also provides an excellent example of diagrams you can create on your own to understand similar cases.

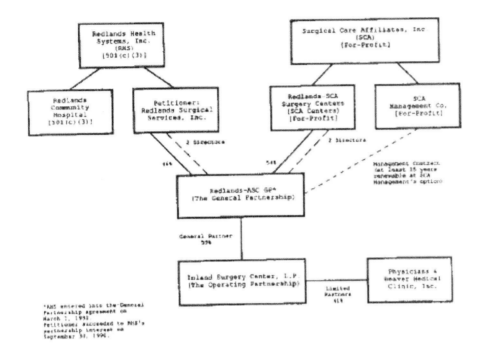

Redlands Surgical Services v. Commissioner of Internal Revenue

113 T.C. 47 (1999), *aff'd per curiam*, 242 F.3d 904 (9th Cir. 2001)

■ THORNTON, J.:

FINDINGS OF FACT

Petitioner is a California nonprofit public benefit corporation with its principal place of business in Redlands, California. It is a wholly owned subsidiary of Redlands Health Systems, Inc. (RHS), a California nonprofit public benefit corporation that has been recognized as exempt under section 501(c)(3) of the Code. RHS is the parent corporation of three subsidiaries in addition to petitioner, namely Redlands Community Hospital (Redlands Hospital) and Redlands Community Hospital Foundation (Redlands Foundation), both of which are California nonprofit public benefit corporations that have been recognized as exempt under section 501(c)(3); and Redlands Health Services, a for-profit corporation.

As described in more detail below, in 1990 RHS became co-general partner with a for-profit corporation, Redlands–SCA Surgery Centers, Inc. (SCA Centers), in a general partnership formed to acquire a 61–percent interest in an existing outpatient surgical center in Redlands, California, two blocks from the Redlands Hospital facility. This general partnership in turn became sole general partner in the California limited partnership that owns and operates the surgical center. Under a long-term management contract, SCA Management Co. (SCA Management)—a for-profit affiliate of SCA Centers—manages the day-to-day operations of the surgical center, in return for a percentage of gross revenues. Several months after forming the general partnership, RHS formed petitioner to succeed to its interest in it.

Petitioner has no activity other than its involvement with the partnerships. The question is whether petitioner is operated exclusively for exempt purposes within the meaning of section 501(c)(3). We hold that it is not.

Redlands Hospital

Since its founding in 1929, Redlands Hospital has been recognized by respondent as a charitable organization described in section 501(c)(3). Its mission includes providing necessary medical care free of charge, or at a discount, to individuals without insurance or other means of paying.

Redlands Hospital has its own outpatient surgery program within the hospital facility.

Inland Surgery Center, L.P.

Since its inception in 1983, the Inland Surgery Center Limited Partnership (the Operating Partnership) has operated a freestanding ambulatory surgery center (the Surgery Center) within two blocks of Redlands Hospital. During the 1980's, the Operating Partnership was a successful for-profit venture, serving only surgical patients who were able to pay, by insurance or otherwise. Prior to its affiliation with the General Partnership, the Operating Partnership comprised Beaver Medical Clinic, Inc., and some 30 physician partners, who were also physicians on the medical staff of Redlands Hospital.

The Affiliation of Redlands Hospital With the Surgery Center

Before 1990, Redlands Hospital desired to increase its outpatient surgery capacity but lacked the capital resources and experience to develop and operate its own freestanding outpatient facility. In addition, such a facility would have been in competition with the existing Surgery Center, and there was concern that the Redlands community could not sustain both.

On March 1, 1990, RHS and SCA Centers entered into a general partnership agreement to acquire jointly a 61–percent general partnership interest in the Surgery Center. The partnership is known as Redlands Ambulatory Surgery Center (the General Partnership).

SCA Centers is a for-profit, wholly owned subsidiary of Surgical Care Affiliates, Inc. (SCA), a publicly held corporation based in Nashville, Tennessee, and specializing in owning and managing ambulatory surgery centers.[3] Prior to formation of the General Partnership, neither SCA nor any of its affiliated entities had any relationship, contractual or otherwise, with RHS or any of its affiliated entities, or with the Surgery Center.

RHS contributed $1,131,289 to the General Partnership, borrowing $796,829 from SCA and the balance of $334,460 from Redlands Hospital.

---

3. As of 1995, SCA owned, in whole or part, and operated approximately 40 ambulatory surgery centers throughout the United States, some of which were owned in part by tax-exempt health care systems.

SCA Centers contributed $1,946,993 in cash and stock to the General Partnership. In return for its approximately 37–percent capital investment, RHS received a 46–percent interest in profits, losses, and cash-flows of the General Partnership. In return for its approximately 63–percent capital investment, SCA Centers received a 54–percent interest in profits, losses, and cash-flows of the General Partnership.

[The transaction was consummated in four steps. First, RHS and SCA executed the General Partnership Agreement that created the General Partnership, Redlands Ambulatory Surgery Center. Second, the General Partnership executed the Limited Partnership Agreement with the Operating Partner, Inland Surgery Center, and became the majority interest holder in and sole general partner of the Operating Partnership. Third, the Operating Partnership executed the Management Contract with SCA Management. Fourth, the Petitioner, Redlands Surgical Services (RSS), was incorporated as a wholly owned subsidiary to which RHS transferred its interest in the General Partnership.*

(1) The General Partnership Agreement. The General Partnership Agreement created four Managing Directors for the partnership, two of whom were chosen by RHS and two by SCA Centers. The Managing Directors were given power over all questions relating to the affairs of the partnership, except for questions relating to medical standards and policies. Decisions were to be made by majority vote, but in the case of a tie, either party could invoke arbitration by a panel consisting of one arbitrator appointed by each and a third appointed by the two other arbitrators. Questions regarding medical standards and policies were to be decided by a Medical Advisory Group, half of whom were appointed by the Managing Directors and half appointed by the Beaver Medical Clinic, one of the limited partners in the Operating Partnership. However, decisions regarding the creation of new ("non-listed") services at the ambulatory center were to be made solely by the Managing Directors. The General Partnership agreement contained no clauses regarding an obligation to operate for charitable purposes but merely stated that the "Partnership may engage in any and all other activities as may be necessary, incidental or convenient to carry out the business of the Partnership as contemplated by this Agreement."

The General Partnership agreement also specified that the Operating Partnership was to enter into the Management Contract with SCA Management, which would have plenary power for administering the day-to-day operation of the ambulatory center in accordance with the goals, policies and objectives of the Operating Partnership. It stipulated a term of 15 years with two 5–year extensions at SCA Management's sole discretion. It also provided that SCA Management was to be paid 6% of the Operating Partnership's gross revenues.

---

* RSS was created as a wholly owned subsidiary of RHS, and RHS's interest in the General Partnership was transferred to RSS, both to insulate Redlands Hospital and Redlands Foundation, also RHS subsidiaries, from the creditors of the Surgery Center, and to insulate RSS and the Surgery Center from the Hospital's debt.

Other clauses were relevant. SCA Management was to execute a Quality Assurance Agreement with RHS. Both parties agreed that for a period of two years they would not create competing facilities within a 20–mile radius of the center, and both parties agreed that neither would introduce new services at any existing facility within that geographic area.

(2) The Limited Partnership Agreement. Like the General Partnership Agreement, the Operating Partnership Agreement did not specify that the Operating Partnership must operate for charitable purposes.

(3) The Management Contract. The Management Contract gave SCA Management complete authority over the day-to-day operation of the center, including maintaining accreditation, employing all non-physician personnel, negotiating reimbursement, and creating non-medical operating procedures.

(4) RSS's Articles of Incorporation. The Articles of Incorporation creating the Petitioner, RSS, stipulated that the corporation was organized solely to carry out charitable purposes.]

OPINION

I.   *The Parties' Positions*

Respondent contends that petitioner is not operated exclusively for charitable purposes because it operates for the benefit of private parties and fails to benefit a broad cross-section of the community. In support of its position, respondent contends that the partnership agreements and related management contract are structured to give for-profit interests control over the Surgery Center. Respondent contends that both before and after the General Partnership acquired an ownership interest in it, the Surgery Center was a successful profit-making business that never held itself out as a charity and never operated as a charitable health-care provider.

Petitioner argues that it meets the operational test under section 501(c)(3) because its activities with regard to the Surgery Center further its purpose of promoting health for the benefit of the Redlands community, by providing access to an ambulatory surgery center for all members of the community based upon medical need rather than ability to pay, and by integrating the outpatient services of Redlands Hospital and the Surgery Center. Petitioner argues that its dealings with the for-profit partners have been at arm's length, and that its influence over the activities of the Surgery Center has been sufficient to further its charitable goals. Petitioner further contends that it qualifies for exemption because it is organized and operated to perform services that are integral to the exempt purposes of RHS, its tax-exempt parent, and Redlands Hospital, its tax-exempt affiliate.

II.   *Applicable Legal Principles*

A.   *Operational Test*

To qualify for exemption from Federal income tax, an organization must be "organized and operated exclusively for charitable purposes".

The operational test focuses on the actual purposes the organization advances by means of its activities, rather than on the organization's statement of purpose or the nature of its activities. To determine whether the operational test has been satisfied, we look beyond "the four corners of the organization's charter to discover 'the actual objects motivating the organization.'"

Although an organization might be engaged in only a single activity, that single activity might be directed toward multiple purposes, both exempt and nonexempt. If the nonexempt purpose is substantial in nature, the organization will not satisfy the operational test.

The fact that an organization engages in a trade or business is not conclusive of a substantial nonexempt purpose and does not, in and of itself, disqualify the organization from exemption under section 501(c)(3), provided the activity furthers or accomplishes an exempt purpose.

Whether an organization has a substantial nonexempt purpose is a question of fact to be resolved on the basis of all the evidence presented by the administrative record. "Factors such as the particular manner in which an organization's activities are conducted, the commercial hue of those activities, and the existence and amount of annual or accumulated profits are relevant evidence of a forbidden predominant purpose." *B.S.W. Group, Inc. v. Commissioner,* [70 T.C. 352, 358 (1978)].

The burden of proof is on petitioner to demonstrate, based on materials in the administrative record, that it is operated exclusively for exempt purposes and that it does not benefit private interests more than incidentally.

C. Proscription Against Benefiting Private Interests

An organization does not operate exclusively for exempt purposes if it operates for the benefit of private interests such as designated individuals, the creator or his family, shareholders of the organization, or persons controlled, directly or indirectly, by such private interests. The private benefit proscription inheres in the requirement that an organization operate exclusively for exempt purposes.

The mere fact that an organization seeking exemption enters into a partnership agreement with private parties that receive returns on their capital investments does not establish that the organization has impermissibly conferred private benefit. The question remains whether the organization has a substantial nonexempt purpose whereby it serves private interests. Compare *Plumstead Theatre Socy., Inc. v. Commissioner,* 675 F.2d 244 (9th Cir. 1982), affg. per curiam 74 T.C. 1324 (1980) (a nonprofit arts organization furthered its charitable purposes by participating as sole general partner in a partnership with private parties to produce a play), with *Housing Pioneers, Inc. v. Commissioner,* 49 F.3d 1395 (9th Cir. 1995), affg. T.C. Memo. 1993–120 (a nonprofit corporation's participation as co-general partner in low-income housing partnerships, structured to trade off its tax exemption to secure tax benefits for its for-profit partners, had a substantial nonexempt purpose and impermissibly served private interests).

The proscription against private benefit corresponds to a similar proscription in the law of charitable trusts. "A trust is not a charitable trust if the property or the income therefrom is to be devoted to a private use." 2 Restatement, Trusts 2d, sec. 376 (1959). An organization's property may be impermissibly devoted to a private use where private interests have control, directly or indirectly, over its assets, and thereby secure nonincidental private benefits.

For instance, in *est of Hawaii v. Commissioner,* 71 T.C. 1067 (1979), several for-profit 'est' organizations that had no formal structural control over the nonprofit entity in question nevertheless exerted "considerable control" over its activities. The for-profit organizations set fees that the nonprofit charged the public for training sessions, required the nonprofit to carry on certain types of educational activities, and provided management personnel paid for and responsible to one of the for-profits. Under a licensing agreement with the for-profits, the nonprofit was allowed to use certain intellectual property for 10 years, and at the end of the licensing agreement, all copyrighted material, including new material developed by the nonprofit, was required to be turned over to the for-profits. The nonprofit was required to use its excess funds for the development of 'est' or related research. The for-profits also required that trainers and local organizations sign an agreement not to compete with 'est' for 2 years after terminating their relationship with 'est' organizations.

In *est of Hawaii v. Commissioner, supra* at 1080, this Court agreed with respondent that the nonprofit was "part of a franchise system which is operated for private benefit and its affiliation with this system taints it with a substantial commercial purpose." We found that the "ultimate beneficiaries" of the nonprofit's activities were the for-profit corporations, and that the nonprofit "was simply the instrument to subsidize the for-profit corporations and not vice versa." *Id.* at 1082. This Court held that the nonprofit was not operated exclusively for exempt purposes. See also *Harding Hosp., Inc. v. United States,* 505 F.2d 1068 (6th Cir.1974) (impermissible private benefit resulted from a nonprofit hospital's contract with a physician group, giving them a virtual monopoly over care of the hospital's patients and the income stream they represented, and providing the physician group with fees for supervising the hospital's medical staff); *Sonora Community Hosp. v. Commissioner,* 46 T.C. 519 (1966) (impermissible private benefit resulted from an arrangement whereby a for-profit laboratory was permitted to occupy space in the nonprofit hospital rent-free, and paid the hospital's founding doctors a share of the laboratory's gross revenues in consideration of patient referrals and administrative services), affd. 397 F.2d 814 (9th Cir.1968).

III.   Petitioner's Claim to Exemption on a "Stand–Alone" Basis

A.   The Relevance of Control—The Parties' Positions

Respondent asserts that petitioner has ceded effective control over its sole activity—participating as a co-general partner with for-profit parties in the partnerships that own and operate the Surgery Center—to the for-profit partners and the for-profit management company that is an affiliate of petitioner's co-general partner. Respondent asserts that this arrangement is indicative of a substantial nonexempt purpose, whereby petitioner impermissibly benefits private interests.

Without conceding that private parties control its activities, petitioner challenges the premise that the ability to control its activities determines its purposes. Petitioner argues that under the operational test, "the critical issue in determining whether an organization's purposes are noncharitable is *not* whether a for profit or not for profit entity has control. Rather, the critical issue is the sort of conduct in which the organization is actually engaged." On brief, the parties agree that under an aggregate theory of partnership taxation, the partnerships' activities are considered petitioner's own activities. Petitioner's brief states: "The evidence in the administrative file demonstrates that [the Operating Partnership] has been operated in an exclusively charitable manner since 1990." Therefore, petitioner concludes, it should be deemed to operate exclusively for charitable purposes.

We disagree with petitioner's thesis. It is patently clear that the Operating Partnership, whatever charitable benefits it may produce, is not operated "in an exclusively charitable manner." As stated by Justice Cardozo (then Justice of the New York Court of Appeals), in describing one of the "ancient principles" of charitable trusts, "It is only when income may be applied to the profit of the founders that business has a beginning and charity an end." *Butterworth v. Keeler,* 219 N.Y. 446, 449–450, 114 N.E. 803, 804 (1916). The Operating Partnership's income is, of course, applied to the profit of petitioner's co-general partner and the numerous limited partners.[10] It is no answer to say that none of petitioner's income from this activity was applied to private interests, for the activity is indivisible, and no discrete part of the Operating Partnership's income-producing activities is severable from those activities that produce income to be applied to the other partners' profit.

Taken to its logical conclusion, petitioner's thesis would suggest that an organization whose main activity is passive participation in a for-profit health-service enterprise could thereby be deemed to be operating exclusively for charitable purposes. Such a conclusion, however, would be contrary to well-established principles of charitable trust law.

> Frequently, a business enterprise may have charitable effects. A private hospital relieves sickness and suffering. However, the primary object of these institutions is the pecuniary gain of the operators. Hence trusts to aid in the founding or maintenance of private hospitals or clinics, which are business enterprises operated for the purpose of making profits for stockholders or owners, are not charitable even though they involve incidentally some public benefits. "It is not charity to aid a business enterprise." [Bogert & Bogert, The Law of Trusts and Trustees, sec. 364

---

10. In making these observations, we are mindful that it is the status of petitioner, not of the General Partnership or the Operating Partnership, that is in issue. Indeed, it is not meaningful to speak of a partnership's exempt status, given that partnerships are nontaxable entities.

(Rev.2d ed. 1991) (quoting *Butterworth v. Keeler,* 219 N.Y. at 449, 114 N.E. at 804); fn. refs. omitted.]

Clearly, there is something in common between the structure of petitioner's sole activity and the nature of petitioner's purposes in engaging in it. An organization's purposes may be inferred from its manner of operations; its "activities provide a useful indicia of the organization's purpose or purposes." The binding commitments that petitioner has entered into and that govern its participation in the partnerships are indicative of petitioner's purposes. To the extent that petitioner cedes control over its sole activity to for-profit parties having an independent economic interest in the same activity and having no obligation to put charitable purposes ahead of profit-making objectives, petitioner cannot be assured that the partnerships will in fact be operated in furtherance of charitable purposes. In such a circumstance, we are led to the conclusion that petitioner is not operated exclusively for charitable purposes.

Based on the totality of factors described below, we conclude that petitioner has in fact ceded effective control of the partnerships' and the Surgery Center's activities to for-profit parties, conferring on them significant private benefits, and therefore is not operated exclusively for charitable purposes within the meaning of section 501(c)(3).

B.   Indicia of For–Profit Control Over the Partnerships' Activities

1.   No Charitable Obligation

Nothing in the General Partnership agreement, or in any of the other binding commitments relating to the operation of the Surgery Center, establishes any obligation that charitable purposes be put ahead of economic objectives in the Surgery Center's operations. The General Partnership agreement does not expressly state any mutually agreed-upon charitable purpose or objective of the partnership.

After the General Partnership acquired its 61–percent interest, the Operating Partnership—which had long operated as a successful for-profit enterprise and never held itself out as a charity—never changed its organizing documents to acknowledge a charitable purpose. Indeed, in at least one instance the Operating Partnership agreement explicitly acknowledges the partnership's noncharitable objectives. Section 16.5.2 of the Operating Partnership agreement in authorizing the General Partnership to amend the Operating Partnership as necessary to comply with legal requirements, specifies that this authority may be exercised only if "such amendments do not alter the economic objectives of the partnership or materially reduce the economic return to the limited partners."

2.   Petitioner's Lack of Formal Control

a.   Managing Directors

Under the General Partnership agreement, control over all matters other than medical standards and policies is nominally divided equally between petitioner and SCA Centers, each appointing two representatives to serve as managing directors. (As discussed *infra,* matters of medical standards and policies are determined by the Medical Advisory Group, half of whom are chosen by the General Partnership's managing directors.) Consequently, petitioner may exert influence by blocking actions proposed to be taken by the managing directors, but it cannot initiate action without the consent of at least one of SCA Center's appointees to the managing directors. For instance, petitioner lacks sufficient control unilaterally to cause the Surgery Center to respond to community needs for new health services, modify the delivery or cost structure of its present health services to serve the community better, or, as discussed in more detail *infra*, terminate SCA Management, if SCA Management were determined to be managing the Surgery Center in a manner inconsistent with charitable objectives.

The administrative record shows that petitioner has successfully blocked various proposals to expand the scope of activities performed at the Surgery Center. Petitioner's ability to veto expansion of the scope of the Surgery Center's activities, however, does not establish that petitioner has effective control over the manner in which the Surgery Center conducts activities within its predesignated sphere of operations. Nor does it tend to indicate that the Surgery Center is not operated to maximize profits with regard to those activities. Indeed, given that all the partners except petitioner are for-profit interests not shown to be motivated or constrained by charitable objectives, and given that all the limited partners except Beaver Medical Clinic were issued SCA common stock when the General Partnership acquired its interest in the Operating Partnership, and given that SCA Management derives a management fee computed as a percentage of gross revenues, we find, in the absence of evidence to the contrary, that a significant profit-making objective is present in the Surgery Center's operations. The high rates of return earned on the partners' investments (including petitioner's) in the Operating Partnership bolster this finding.

In sum, the composition of the managing directorship evidences a lack of majority control by petitioner whereby it might assure that the Surgery Center is operated for charitable purposes.[12] Consequently, we look to the binding commitments made between petitioner and the other parties to ascertain whether other specific powers or rights conferred upon petitioner might mitigate or compensate for its lack of majority control.

b. Arbitration Process

The General Partnership agreement provides for an arbitration process in the event that the managing directors of the General Partnership

---

12. The managing directors of the General Partnership are functionally equivalent to a hospital's board of directors, the importance of which has been described as follows:

> The board of directors, its composition, and its functions are relevant to tax exemption the composition of the board provides important evidence that the hospital serves public rather than private purposes. For example, it is fair to presume that a board of directors chosen from the community would place the interests of the community above those of either the management or the medical staff of the hospital. Thus, the relevance of the board is that its process should indicate whether the hospital is operated for the benefit of the community or to secure benefits for private interests. [Douglas M. Mancino, *Income Tax Exemption of the Contemporary Nonprofit Hospital*, 32 St. Louis U. L.J. 1015, 1051 (1988).]

deadlock over a matter other than medical standards and medical policies, such as approval of new surgical procedures. Under these provisions, in the event of a deadlock, each of the co-general partners selects one arbitrator, and these two arbitrators select a third. The arbitrators have final authority to decide matters referred to them. The ground rules for the arbitration process are minimal and provide petitioner no assurance that charitable objectives will govern the outcome. Under the General Partnership agreement, the arbitrators are not required to take into account any charitable or community benefit objective, but are simply required to "apply the substantive law of California."

Petitioner asserts that since 1990, neither co-general partner has invoked the arbitration clause. The administrative record is inconclusive on this point. Even assuming arguendo that petitioner's assertion is correct, it merely tends to show that petitioner and SCA Centers have avoided conflict with regard to those operating decisions that are subject to arbitration. Whether such conflicts have been avoided because petitioner's purposes and the purposes of its for-profit partner are so closely aligned, or for some other reason, the administrative record does not reveal. Clearly, however, the arbitration process does not significantly mitigate petitioner's lack of majority control to provide any assurance that the General Partnership will operate to put charitable objectives ahead of economic objectives.

c. The Management Contract

The management contract between the Operating Partnership and SCA Management confers broad powers on SCA Management to enter into contracts, to negotiate with third-party payers and State and Federal agencies, and to set patient charges for all services provided, with the exception of charges for physicians' services. In short, SCA Management is authorized to manage as it sees fit many of the day-to-day operations of the Surgery Center, reserving to the Medical Advisory Group of the Operating Partnership the authority to make all medical decisions.

Under the management contract, SCA Management is entitled to receive fees equaling 6 percent of the Operating Partnership's gross revenues each month, in addition to reimbursement of its direct expenses. This revenue-based compensation structure provides SCA Management an incentive to manage the Surgery Center so as to maximize profits.

As a practical matter, the Operating Partnership is locked into the management agreement with SCA Management for at least 15 years. At its sole discretion, SCA Management may renew the agreement for two additional 5–year periods on the same terms and conditions. The Operating Partnership has the right to terminate the management contract for breach, but only after the Operating Partnership has given written notice describing in detail the basis on which it believes termination is justified. Because the issuance of such a termination notice would require approval by a majority of the General Partner's managing directors, petitioner could not effect the issuance of such a notice without the consent of SCA Centers, which is an affiliate of SCA Management. Thus, even if petitioner determined that SCA Management were managing the Surgery Center in a manner inconsistent with charitable purposes, petitioner could not be assured of any remedy.

Moreover, neither the General Partnership agreement, the Operating Partnership agreement, nor the management contract itself requires that SCA Management be guided by any charitable or community benefit, goal, policy, or objective. Rather, the management contract simply requires SCA Management to render services as necessary and in the best interest of the Operating Partnership, "subject to the policies established by [the Operating Partnership], which policies shall be consistent with applicable state and Federal law."

Petitioner argues that the management contract "was negotiated at arm's length, between parties of equal bargaining strength." The administrative record does not support this contention. Although the General Partnership agreement was negotiated between RHS and SCA Centers, it contains only a sparse description of several key features to be included in the management contract. The actual management contract is between SCA Management and the Operating Partnership, and contains much more extensive and detailed provisions than are stipulated in the General Partnership agreement.

The administrative record does not reveal that petitioner or RHS had any role in negotiating the actual management contract. It is executed for both the Operating Partnership and SCA Management by the same individual—David E. Crockett—in his dual capacities as secretary of SCA Centers and vice president of SCA Management, raising the suggestion, if not the likelihood, of self-dealing between these two SCA affiliates.

Respondent asserts, and we agree, that this long-term management contract with an affiliate of SCA Centers is a salient indicator of petitioner's surrender of effective control over the Surgery Center's operations to SCA affiliates, whereby the affiliates were given the ability and incentive to operate the Surgery Center so as to maximize profits. This surrender of effective control reflects adversely on petitioner's own charitable purposes in contracting to have its sole activity managed in this fashion.

d. *Medical Advisory Group*

The Operating Partnership agreement delegates authority for making decisions about care and treatment of patients and other medical matters to the Operating Partnership's Medical Advisory Group. This group was inactive before the General Partnership became involved with the Operating Partnership, but there is no evidence to show that role, if any, petitioner played in reconstituting the Medical Advisory Group.

Only three of the six members of the Medical Advisory Group are selected by the General Partnership. The other three are selected by one of the limited partners, Beaver Medical Clinic. It is telling that the Medical Advisory Group is composed entirely of limited partners of the Operating Partnership, all of whom (except Beaver Medical Clinic) received common stock in SCA when the General Partnership acquired its Operating Partnership interest. Taking all these considerations into account, it is clear that petitioner lacks sufficient influence to determine the resolution of any matter brought before the Medical Advisory Group. Moreover, there is no evidence in the record that the decisions of the Medical Advisory Committee are subject to independent review by petitioner or Redlands Hospital.

e.   *Termination of Quality Assurance Activities*

As required by the General Partnership agreement, on April 30, 1990, SCA Management entered into a quality assurance agreement with RHS. The term of the quality assurance agreement was conditioned on maintenance of a specified level of surgery activity in the Surgery Center. Petitioner concedes that the quality assurance agreement terminated after the first year. Although the agreement required the parties to negotiate a new quality assurance agreement in the event of such a termination, there is no evidence in the record that such negotiations ever occurred.

The termination of the quality assurance agreement vividly evidences petitioner's lack of effective control over vital aspects of the Surgery Center's operations. Quality assurance agreements in the health-care industry serve the important dual functions of attempting to avoid inappropriate services (e.g., the wrong services for the patient's needs, or services that are improperly rendered), and seeking to assure that enough services are provided to meet the patient's needs. The record does not reflect that petitioner performed any quality assurance work. Likewise, the record is silent as to how petitioner, in the absence of any operable quality assurance agreement, purports to assure itself that these vital functions will be discharged consistently with charitable objectives.

3.   *Lack of Informal Control*

The administrative record provides no basis for concluding that, in the absence of formal control, petitioner possesses significant informal control by which it exercises its influence with regard to the Surgery Center's activities. Nothing in the administrative record suggests that petitioner commands allegiance or loyalty of the SCA affiliates or of the limited partners to cause them to put charitable objectives ahead of their own economic objectives. Indeed, until April 1992, petitioner was in a debtor relationship to SCA. The limited partners (except for Beaver Medical Clinic, Inc.) all became common stockholders of SCA when the General Partnership acquired its interest in the Operating Partnership.

The administrative record does not establish that petitioner has the resources or ability effectively to oversee or monitor the Surgery Center's operations. Petitioner has almost no resources apart from its assets invested in the General Partnership. The president of Redlands Hospital also serves as petitioner's president and as one of the four managing directors of the General Partnership.

On brief, petitioner argues that its influence in the partnerships is evidenced by various changes that it says occurred in the operation of the Surgery Center after April 1990, when the amended Operating Partnership agreement became effective. Petitioner suggests that these operational changes demonstrate that its influence is sufficient to allow it to achieve its charitable goals through the partnerships' activities and demonstrate that for-profit interests do not control the partnerships and the Surgery Center. As described in more detail below, the record does not support petitioner's contentions.

a. Change in Criteria for Procedures Performed at the Surgery Center

Petitioner asserts that after the General Partnership acquired its interest in the Operating Partnership, "the decision to perform a surgery at the Surgery Center was changed from an economic to exclusively a medical decision. Accordingly, RHS achieved its goal of providing complete access to freestanding ambulatory surgery center care for all members of the Redlands community irrespective of their ability to pay."

This proposed finding of fact is not supported by the record. Neither before nor after petitioner's involvement with it has the Surgery Center provided charity care. Moreover, the administrative record indicates that one aspect of ambulatory surgery centers that makes them attractive investment opportunities in the first instance is that they boast favorable "procedure and payer mixes."[18] Consequently, it is not apparent from the record to what extent the decision to perform a surgery at the Surgery Center has ever been an "economic" rather than a "medical" decision, or exactly how that situation might have changed after April 1990.

b. Provision for Indigent Patients

Petitioner concedes that as of December 31, 1993, Medi–Cal patients accounted for only 0.8 percent of total procedures performed at the Surgery Center. Petitioner argues that the type of services which the Service Center offers is not the type of services typically sought by low-income individuals. Petitioner notes that Redlands Hospital has negotiated certain provider agreements that designate the Surgery Center as a subcontractor to provide outpatient services for Medi–Cal patients, and that Redlands Hospital has caused the Surgery Center to increase its number of managed care contracts. Petitioner suggests that these efforts demonstrate petitioner's influence over the operations of the Surgery Center and evidence petitioner's charitable purposes.

We do not find petitioner's arguments convincing. The facts remain that the Surgery Center provides no free care to indigents and only negligible coverage for Medi–Cal patients. That low-income individuals may not typically seek the types of services the Surgery Center offers may partially explain the virtual absence of relief it provides for such individuals. But it provides no independent basis for establishing petitioner's

---

18. The administrative record includes an investment summary with respect to SCA and another national health-care provider, Medical Care International, published by Shearson Lehman Brothers, dated Aug. 7, 1991. The report states: "To a large extent the favorable payer mix is a function of the fact that many procedures safely performed on an outpatient basis happen to be those with a young patient population." Similarly, in its arguments to justify the Surgery Center's low rate of Medi–Cal patients, petitioner notes that the Surgery Center does not perform the types of procedures—emergency room treatments and obstetrics and gynecology—that typically account for a "substantial majority" of low-income surgical expenses for a community.

charitable purposes in its involvement with the Surgery Center. Moreover, the activities of Redlands Hospital in effecting some negligible degree of Medi–Cal coverage at the Surgery Center and in increasing the number of managed care contracts do not provide a basis for establishing petitioner's exemption.

Petitioner asserts that the Surgery Center has no requirement that patients demonstrate an ability to pay before receiving treatment. The record does not reflect whether any such policy has been communicated to its patients. Petitioner suggests that this policy is evidenced by the Surgery Center's "substantial Medicare" patronage. The record shows that Medicare accounted for 12 percent of invoices at the Surgery Center in the last half of 1993. The record does not reflect, however, whether the Surgery Center waives fees in excess of those covered by Medicare and accordingly does not establish that ability to pay is not a factor even for patients covered by Medicare. Moreover, the Surgery Center's treatment of Medicare patients cannot on this record be attributed to petitioner's influence over the Surgery Center's operations. According to the affidavit of Mr. James R. Holmes, who was president of petitioner and Redlands Hospital at the time of the affidavit, the Surgery Center "has regularly treated Medicare patients since before 1990."

c.   *Coordination of Activities of Redlands Hospital and the Surgery Center*

In arguing that it plays an active role in the conduct of the Surgery Center's activities, petitioner cites a number of ways in which Redlands Hospital has integrated its activities with those of the Surgery Center since the General Partnership acquired its interest in the Operating Partnership. These include Redlands Hospital's use of the Surgery Center as a site for training and surgeon proctoring, as well as various other cooperative training and educational activities between Redlands Hospital and the Surgery Center.

Although there may be cooperation between the Surgery Center and Redlands Hospital, nothing in the record suggests that these various cooperative activities are more than incidental to the for-profit orientation of the Surgery Center's activities.

C.   *Competitive Restrictions and Market Advantages*

By entering into the General Partnership agreement, RHS (petitioner's parent corporation and predecessor in interest in the General Partnership) not only acquired an interest in the Surgery Center, but also restricted its future ability to provide outpatient services at Redlands Hospital or elsewhere without the approval of its for-profit partner. Paragraph 16 of the General Partnership agreement prohibits the co-general partners and their affiliates from owning, managing, or developing another freestanding outpatient surgery center within 20 miles of the Surgery Center, without the other partner's consent. Moreover, Redlands Hospital may not "expand or promote its present outpatient surgery program within the Hospital." In fact, outpatient surgeries performed at Redlands Hospital decreased about

17 percent from 1990 to 1995, while those performed at the Surgery Center increased.

The General Partnership agreement also restricts the parties and their affiliates from providing outpatient surgery services and procedures that the agreement does not specifically authorize to be provided at the Surgery Center (hereinafter referred to as nonlisted services). Under this agreement, Redlands Hospital, but not the co-general partners or any of their other affiliates, is allowed to perform nonlisted outpatient services that were currently available to patients in California at the time the General Partnership agreement was executed. By contrast, neither Redlands Hospital nor the co-general partners or their affiliates are allowed to perform nonlisted outpatient services that first become available in California during the term of the General Partnership agreement (i.e., until March 31, 2020), unless the managing directors of the General Partnership approve.[20]

Consequently, RHS effectively restricted its own ability to assess and service community needs for outpatient services until the year 2020. It is difficult to conceive of a significant charitable purpose that would be furthered by such a restriction.

The administrative record contains a market research report on the ambulatory surgery center industry, prepared by Ernst & Young and transmitted to Redlands Hospital on October 20, 1994. This report describes the strong movement toward providing health care services in ambulatory settings, driven both by economic considerations and technological advances. The report notes that hospitals face "strong competition" in this market. It cites economic advantages that freestanding ambulatory surgery centers enjoy over hospitals. These advantages include, among other things, higher turn-over of operating rooms that increases the number of "fee-generating procedures" surgeons can do; lower nurse compensation that in turn leads to "higher margins"; and the "general tendency for private payers to account for a high percentage of a surgery center's mix, since most procedures performed in outpatient settings are elective (non-emergency) and are done on younger, non-Medicare patients." The report cites physician relations and capital as two major barriers to entering this market.

The Shearson Lehman Brothers investment summary, see *supra* note 18, contains similar facts and conclusions. The report indicates that SCA and Medical Care International are the two main surgical center chains, that they are highly profitable, and that their margins are likely to continue moving higher. The report notes that one reason for the high profitability of these chains is that "they typically shadow-price hospitals, which tend to charge very high rates for outpatient surgery so they can shift costs to the private sector and spread out their overhead." The report states that "one might expect hospitals to fight hard for this business by

---

20. As previously discussed, petitioner lacks sufficient control to dictate any such approval by the managing directors, and, in the event of deadlock, the matter would go to arbitration.

starting up their own FASCs [freestanding ambulatory surgery centers]," but that this had not happened to date because it is very hard for hospitals to do so, due partly to problems hospitals face in throwing off their own "culture" and creating an autonomous unit that is small, friendly, and efficient. The report states: "[SCA's] strategy of developing three-way joint ventures—consisting of a local hospital, surgeons, and the company—represents an attractive opportunity to address these cultural problems." The report notes:

> the FASC niche of the health care services industry has the further attraction of considerable consolidation opportunity. We believe that multispecialty, nonhospital FASCs currently number 600–700, with perhaps another 100 opening each year. Yet there are currently only two chains, Medical Care International and [SCA] affiliates, which have a total of 109 units.

> Once a surgical group decides to sell its center, there is generally only one bidder (Medical Care or [SCA]), with the price typically five to seven times pretax income. The key issue for MDs is not the modest amount of cash that comes from a sale but the operating environment for them once the center changes hands.

In the instant case, the Surgery Center had not one but two bidders, the General Partnership, offering four to five times earnings, and another unrelated, for-profit bidder, otherwise unidentified in the record, offering approximately six times earnings. A letter from Ernst & Young to respondent's representatives, dated July 14, 1992, indicates that the Surgery Center took the General Partnership's offer instead of the other, higher bid because of a desire to have an affiliation with Redlands Hospital for quality control and other reasons.

Viewed in its totality, the administrative record is clear that SCA and petitioner derive mutual economic benefits from the General Partnership agreement. By borrowing necessary up-front capital from SCA, RHS (petitioner's predecessor in interest in the General Partnership), overcame a capital barrier to gain entry into a profitable and growing market niche. By forming a partnership with RHS, SCA Centers was able to benefit from the established relationship between Redlands Hospital and the limited partner physicians to acquire its interest in the Surgery Center at a bargain price.

By virtue of this arrangement, petitioner and SCA Centers realized further mutual benefits by eliminating sources of potential competition for patients, as is evidenced by the restrictions on either party's providing future outpatient services outside the Surgery Center, and by Redlands Hospital's agreeing not to expand or promote its existing outpatient surgery facility at the hospital. In light of the statement in the record that it is typical for national chains such as SCA to "shadow-price" hospitals in charging for services at outpatient surgery centers, it seems most likely that one purpose and effect of the containment and contraction of Redlands Hospital's outpatient surgery activities is to eliminate a competitive constraint for setting Surgery Center fees (a matter delegated to SCA Management under the management contract, excluding charges for physicians' services). Moreover, market consolidation provided petitioner and SCA Centers mutual advantages by eliminating pressures to compete in spending for expensive equipment.

There is no per se proscription against a nonprofit organization's entering into contracts with private parties to further its charitable purposes on mutually beneficial terms, so long as the nonprofit organization does not thereby impermissibly serve private interests. In the instant case, however, RHS relied on the established relationship between Redlands Hospital and Redlands physicians to enable RHS and SCA affiliates jointly to gain foothold, on favorable terms, in the Redlands ambulatory surgery market. Then, by virtue of their effective control over the Surgery Center, the SCA affiliates have been enabled to operate it as a profit-making business, with significantly reduced competitive pressures from Redlands Hospital, and largely unfettered by charitable objectives that might conflict with purely commercial objectives. The net result to the SCA affiliates is a nonincidental "advantage; profit; fruit; privilege; gain; [or] interest" that constitutes a prohibited private benefit.

D.   *Conclusion*

Based on all the facts and circumstances, we hold that petitioner has not established that it operates exclusively for exempt purposes within the meaning of section 501(c)(3). In reaching this holding, we do not view any one factor as crucial, but we have considered these factors in their totality: The lack of any express or implied obligation of the for-profit interests involved in petitioner's sole activity to put charitable objectives ahead of noncharitable objectives; petitioner's lack of voting control over the General Partnership; petitioner's lack of other formal or informal control sufficient to ensure furtherance of charitable purposes; the long-term contract giving SCA Management control over day-to-day operations as well as a profit-maximizing incentive; and the market advantages and competitive benefits secured by the SCA affiliates as the result of this arrangement with petitioner. Taken in their totality, these factors compel the conclusion that by ceding effective control over its operations to for-profit parties, petitioner impermissibly serves private interests.

[The court went on to hold that petitioner could not prevail under the integral part doctrine].

Decision will be entered for respondent.

Notes

1. *The importance of being in control (and other issues).* Make a list of factors that the Tax Court found troubling indicators that the Surgery Center was organized and formally and informally operated for private benefit, and put yourself in the place of someone engaged in a transaction that involves a joint venture between a for-profit entity and an EO. Does the Tax Court tell you which factor to vary to obtain or maintain an exemption? In thinking about this, ask whether the court tells you which

factor or factors are necessary to an exemption, and which one or ones are sufficient? What do your answers indicate to you about the manner in which a "totality of the circumstances" test lends itself to predictability and certainty? Given that joint ventures are no longer per se a ground for loss or denial of an exemption—in other words, given that some degree of private benefit necessarily flows from the operation of the joint venture—are there doctrinal avenues that might allow some degree of predictability and certainty while simultaneously permitting flexibility and balancing? Can we have our cake and eat it too?

Organization and Formal Control. In thinking about these issues, consider the safe harbor delineated by the Revenue Service in its issuance of Revenue Ruling 98–15, 1998–1 C.B. 718 (Mar. 4, 1998). Prior to this ruling the Service had initially taken the position that an EO's participation as a general partner in a partnership with for-profit partners was per se incompatible with its maintaining its exempt status because the sharing of profits necessarily involved private inurement and because the general partnership's obligation to maximize partnership profits meant that the EO was acting for private benefit. Gen. Couns. Mem. 36,293 (May 30, 1975). The IRS gradually stepped back from this per se prohibition toward a more fact sensitive approach, *see* Gen. Couns. Mem. 39,005 (June 28, 1983); Gen. Couns. Mem. 39,444 (Nov. 13, 1985), in part due to adverse decisions against it in court. *See* Plumstead Theatre Society, Inc. v. Commissioner, 74 T.C. 1324 (1980), *aff'd*, 675 F.2d 244 (9th Cir.1982). While the fact-sensitive approach has introduced flexibility, something that was necessary given the changing health care sector, it has also created uncertainty.

Safe harbors are designed to reduce uncertainty by providing an example or examples of safe arrangements. Importantly, remember that a safe harbor just provides a safe place and therefore, the fact that an arrangement *falls outside* of the safe harbor does not indicate that it is legally infirm. It is just outside of the safety zone. Unfortunately, many lose sight of this important point, which applies equally to safe harbors provided against antitrust and fraud and abuse liability, discussed in this Part.

Revenue Ruling 98–15 contrasts two situations in which, common to both "whole hospital" joint ventures, an EO transferred all of its operating assets, including its hospital, to a limited liability company to which a for-profit entity also contributed, and ownership and control, and returns of capital and distributions of earnings, were divided proportionally to the contributions of each. In situation 1, in which the EO retained its exemption, the interests held by the EO and the for-profit joint venturer were 3–2, respectively, and the relevant governing documents limited the LLC (and its operation of the hospital) to charitable purposes, explicitly imposing the requirement that conflicts between the charitable obligation and the obligation to maximize profit were to be resolved in favor of the former. The governing board was given wide powers over capital and operating budgets, distribution of earnings, selection of key executives, acquisition and disposition of facilities, major contracts, changes in types of services offered, and execution of management agreements.

Additionally, the LLC had executed a management contract with a company unrelated to the joint venturers with a 5–year term and a renewal option that required the consent of both. Compensation was pegged to the LLC's gross revenues, and this term and others in the management contract were comparable to other such contracts in the industry. Finally, none of the directors, officers, or key employees of the EO possessed a conflict of interest such as promised employment by the LLC or the possession of an interest in the for-profit joint venturer. By contrast, in situation 2, in which the EO lost its exemption, the governing documents provided that there was no duty to place charitable purposes ahead of private ones, and control and interests, and returns of capital and distributions of earnings, were divided equally between the joint venturers. This board too was given substantial powers, along with a provision that the CEO and CFO were to come from the for-profit entity. In addition, the LLC executed a management agreement with a wholly owned subsidiary of the for-profit joint venturer with automatic renewal at the sole discretion of the for-profit entity and the LLC having the right to terminate only for cause.

A transaction that matches situation 1 is completely is safe, but one that does not falls outside of the safe harbor—remember, the fact that it is out of the safe harbor does not necessarily mean that it is illegal but only that it's no longer "safe." How does one predict how the Revenue Service will respond when a deal combines elements of the situations? Suppose, for example, that the governing documents in situation 2 or in *Redlands* gave the EO control of the joint venture's governing board irrespective of the joint venturers' ownership interests. Is that change in formal control necessary? Sufficient? Revenue Ruling 98–15 can be read to say it is necessary, *see* Douglas M. Mancino, *New Ruling Provides Guidance, Raises Questions for Joint Ventures Involving Exempt Organizations*, 88 J. TAX'N 294 (1998), although this interpretation is by no means compelled. It is clear, in any event, that the Revenue Ruling is silent on sufficiency.

How do you read *Redlands* on these points? As another example, suppose that the governing documents for the joint ventures in situation 2 and *Redlands* imposed the obligation, like that in situation 1, to pursue public purposes and that a conflict between for-profit incentives and public interest be resolved in favor of the latter? Is this change in organization necessary? Sufficient alone or in combination with changes in the composition of the governing board? Again, Revenue Ruling 98–15 has been read to require these organizational clauses, *see id.*, but again the Ruling is clearly silent on sufficiency. How do you read *Redlands* on these points? As the final example, suppose that the management contract in situation 2 and in *Redlands* were structured along the lines of the management contract in situation 1. In such an instance, the for-profit joint venturer could not act through its management company subsidiary to exercise day-to-day operational control. Arguably, then, this change in management would make it somewhat less likely that the joint venture's operations and use of assets would be devoted to private benefit. Is that change necessary? Sufficient alone or in combination with other factors? And so on.

To reiterate, Revenue Ruling 98–15 provides a safe harbor and transactions outside of its safety zone are not necessarily problematic. Because the hypotheticals of 98–15 involve whole-hospital joint ventures, it is possible that the Service and courts will apply less exacting standards to joint ventures for ancillary-care facilities like ambulatory surgical centers and imaging facilities. A potential signpost in this direction is Private Letter Ruling 2004–51 in which membership and control of the board of directors was equally divided between the tax-exempt university and the for-profit joint venturer, an entity that conducted interactive video training programs, in a venture offering seminars to school teachers to improve their skills. Some may take this approval to indicate that with regard to ancillary joint ventures the Service may not require that the EO be in control, *see, e.g.*, Nicholas A. Mirkay, *Relinquish Control! Why the IRS Should Change Its Stance on Exempt Organizations in Ancillary Joints Ventures*, 6 NEV. L.J. 21, 57–59 (2005).

However, one must be careful to note that the joint venture did not constitute a substantial part of the university's activities, ownership interests were proportional to contributions of capital and returns, the activities were substantially related to the university's exempt purposes—the seminars covered the same content as ones available on the university's campus and the joint venture therefore merely enabled the seminars to be made available to teachers who could not get to the campus—and the university "alone approve[d] the curriculum, training materials and instructors, and determine[d] the standards for successfully completing the seminars." 2004 WL 1038122 (IRS RRU) at 5. In short, the Service applied a totality of circumstances test in which under these circumstance, the income from the joint venture returned to the university was not taxable, i.e., not subject to UBIT. In different circumstances, the Service might require more than 50–50 formal control for an ancillary joint venture (and don't forget that the safe harbor, Revenue Ruling 98–15, involves a whole-hospital joint venture in which all of the EO's assets are at stake); and the Service might still deny *the safe harbor* of Revenue Ruling 98–15 to ancillary joint ventures in which there is 50–50 control even though it might approve *some of them* in particular facts and circumstances. We return to this balancing process in the notes following *St. David's* below.

Informal Control. How did the Tax Court in *Redlands* characterize the control and operation of the Surgery Center before and after it became part of the joint venture between Redlands and SCA? Do you think that its view of the amount of change, or lack thereof, influenced its decision? Would the conclusion of private benefit on similar facts be as compelling if the joint venture started the relevant facility or facilities from scratch? What if the evidence regarding operational control for exempt purposes had been stronger? How should the Revenue Service or a court decide cases in which the evidence of informal operational control shows, in degrees of strength that can vary across cases, that operational control is different than formal control? Remember that evidence of informal control for non-exempt purposes can defeat formal control pointing towards exempt purposes. What if the relationship is the opposite, in that formal control points toward non-exempt purposes but evidence regarding informal control points toward exempt purposes? Keep in mind that Revenue Ruling 98–15 concerns organization and formal control only. See *St. David's* below and the notes and questions that follow.

The Service's regulations stipulate that evidence of actual operation for exempt purposes will not override flaws in the entity's organization. Treas. Reg. § 501(c)(3)–1(b)(iv). However, as *Redlands* indicates, evidence regarding either or both of formal and informal control can be equivocal; and, as *Redlands* also indicates, courts are willing to entertain evidence of surrounding facts and circumstances, *see, e.g.*, Colorado State Chiropractic Society v. Commissioner, 93 T.C. 487 (1989), including organizational conduct. *See* Blake v. Commissioner, 29 T.C.M. (CCH) 513 (1970); Commissioner v. John Danz Charitable Trust, 284 F.2d 726 (9th Cir. 1960); Forest Press, Inc. v. Commissioner, 22 T.C. 265 (1954), *acq.*, 1954–2 C.B. 3.

   2.   *The importance of losing money?* Toward the end of the opinion the Tax Court makes much of the manner in which the Surgery Center was financially well positioned and projected to be of great mutual benefit. How is that relevant? Surely the profitability of the joint venture cannot lead to the conclusion that it is operated for private benefit. If that were the case, then the law would return to a per se prohibition (unless parties formed joint ventures with the purpose of losing money). How was the court's view of the profitability of the center affected by the existence of the non-compete clauses, the fact that Redlands could not raise the necessary capital alone, lacked the necessary expertise, was at a cost disadvantage in competing with ambulatory care facilities, and was indebted to SCA? What might this balance of power tell you about the balance of power between private and public purposes in both the structure and operation of the joint venture?

   3.   *The importance of organizational form (over substance).* Suppose that Redlands Surgical Service held assets other than its general partnership interest in the General Partnership. Would it still have lost its exemption due to its lack of formal and informal control over the General Partnership? It depends. As a result of the Tax Court's decision, activity of the General Partnership results in taxable income because it is business activity conducted for non-exempt purposes. Under the Code, the unrelated business activity of a partnership is attributed backward to the partners, see I.R.C. § 512(c), and therefore the unrelated activity of the General Partnership is attributed back to RSS. In turn, RSS could maintain its exemption only if its unrelated business activity is less than substantial. Since RSS held no assets other than its partnership interest and engaged in no other activities, the unrelated business activity attributed back from the General Partnership had to be substantial, with the result that RSS could not be exempt (the identical situation in Revenue Ruling 98–15).

Could the unrelated business activity of the General Partnership threaten the tax exempt status of RHS, the parent of RSS? If RHS held a partnership interest in RSS, the answer would be yes for the reasons just outlined. The activities of RSS would be attributed backward to RHS, the holder of a partnership interest in RSS. However, the relationship between RHS and RSS was not a partnership but that of a parent and subsidiary corporation, and the partnership attribution rules do not apply between a corporate parent and a corporate sub. Additionally, as we have seen, the separate corporate identities of a parent and subsidiary will be respected—they are separate taxable entities—unless it can be shown either that the subsidiary fails to pursue a trade or business or is operationally indistinct from the parent. Assuming that those criteria could be satisfied—and those issues were not before the Tax Court—yes, the buck does stop with RSS.

Is this distinction between a partnership and a corporation form over substance? Perhaps it is, an issue to which we return in the notes following *St. David's* below. For now, just note that avoidance of the partnership attribution rules is in part the reason that a health system like RHS will create a corporate subsidiary to house activity that might be deemed taxable. Of course, RHS was hoping that RSS would have been considered to be a nontaxable subsidiary, but the erection of RSS between RHS and the General Partnership also helped insulate the tax exempt status of RHS from an adverse determination. The use of a separate subsidiary also sheltered RHS from the reach of creditors of the Surgery Center.*

Suppose that RSS held a limited partnership interest in the Surgery Clinic, rather than that of a general partner. Would that make a difference? No, because the attribution rules apply to both limited and general partners. Of course, if RSS had been a limited partner, it would have been even harder to mount the argument that the joint venture was organized and operated for exempt purposes, because SCA would have been the sole general partner and RSS only a passive investor. The fact that in the actual case RSS was a co-general partner with SCA was the basis for the argument that the General Partnership was organized and operated for exempt purposes.

4. *The importance of community benefit redux.* EOs' joint ventures with physicians raise similar issues regarding the question whether the joint venture pursues public or private purposes. However, because the physician partners of the joint venture are often insiders of the EO, e.g., members of the EO's medical staff, special problems arise because of the rule against private inurement. *See* Gen. Couns. Mem. 39,862 (Dec. 2, 1991). The Revenue Service has made it clear that any joint ventures that violate the Medicare and Medicaid fraud and abuse laws, discussed in this Part, may not be exempt. *Id.* Because the so-called Stark II Law has prohibited physicians from holding ownership interests in many types of facilities to which they refer patients, prior favorable reviews by the IRS of

---

* Of course there is more to choice of entity than we can discuss here, e.g., limited liability and so-called double taxation of corporate earnings. We leave these issues to your course on business organizations.

physician-hospital joint ventures regarding these types of facilities have been rendered irrelevant.

St. David's Health Care System v. United States

349 F.3d 232 (5th Cir. 2003)

■ GARZA, CIRCUIT JUDGE:

St. David's Health Care System, Inc. ("St. David's") brought suit in federal court to recover taxes that it paid under protest. St. David's argued that it was a charitable hospital, and therefore tax-exempt under 26 U.S.C. § 501(c)(3). The Government responded that St. David's was not entitled to a tax exemption because it had formed a partnership with a for-profit company and ceded control over its operations to the for-profit entity. Both St. David's and the Government filed motions for summary judgment. The district court granted St. David's motion, and ordered the Government to refund the taxes paid by St. David's for the 1996 tax year. We conclude that this case raises genuine issues of material fact, and that the district court thus erred in granting St. David's motion for summary judgment. We therefore vacate the district court's decision, and remand for further proceedings.

I

For many years, St. David's owned and operated a hospital and other health care facilities in Austin, Texas. For most of its existence, St. David's was recognized as a charitable organization entitled to tax-exempt status under § 501(c)(3).

In the 1990s, due to financial difficulties in the health care industry, St. David's concluded that it should consolidate with another health care organization. Ultimately, in 1996, St. David's decided to form a partnership with Columbia/HCA Healthcare Corporation ("HCA"), a for-profit company that operates 180 hospitals nationwide. HCA already owned several facilities in the suburbs of Austin, and was interested in entering the central Austin market. A partnership with St. David's would allow HCA to expand into that urban market.

St. David's contributed all of its hospital facilities to the partnership. HCA, in turn, contributed its Austin-area facilities. The partnership hired Galen Health Care, Inc. ("Galen"), a subsidiary of HCA, to manage the day-to-day operations of the partnership medical facilities.

In 1998, the IRS audited St. David's and concluded that, due to its partnership with HCA, St. David's no longer qualified as a charitable (and, thus, tax-exempt) hospital. The IRS ordered St. David's to pay taxes. St. David's paid the requisite amount under protest, and subsequently filed the instant action, requesting a refund.

The parties filed cross-motions for summary judgment. The district court granted the motion filed by St. David's and ordered the Government to refund the taxes paid by the hospital for the 1996 tax year. The Government filed this appeal.

II

In order to qualify for tax-exempt status, St. David's was required to show that it was "organized and operated exclusively" for a charitable purpose. 26 C.F.R. § 1.501(c)(3)–1(a). The "organizational test" required St. David's to demonstrate that its founding documents: (1) limit its purpose to "one or more exempt purposes"; and (2) do not expressly empower St. David's to engage more than "an insubstantial part of its activities" in conduct that fails to further its charitable goals. *Id.* § 1.501(c)(3)–1(b). The parties agree that St. David's articles of incorporation satisfy the organizational test.

To pass the "operational test," St. David's was required to show: (1) that it "engage[s] primarily in activities which accomplish" its exempt purpose. The parties appear to agree that, because St. David's contributed all of its medical facilities to the partnership, we must look to the activities of the partnership to determine if St. David's satisfies the operational test.

The Government asserts that, because of its partnership with HCA, St. David's cannot show that it engages "primarily" in activities that accomplish its charitable purpose. The Government does not contend that a non-profit organization should automatically lose its tax-exempt status when it forms a partnership with a for-profit entity. Instead, the Government argues that a non-profit organization must sacrifice its tax exemption if it cedes control over the partnership to the for-profit entity. The Government asserts that, when a non-profit cedes control, it can no longer ensure that its activities via the partnership primarily further its charitable purpose. In this case, the Government contends that St. David's forfeited its exemption because it ceded control over its operations to HCA.

St. David's responds in part that the central issue in determining its tax-exempt status is not which entity *controls* the partnership. Instead, St. David's appears to assert, the pivotal question is one of *function*: whether the partnership engages in activities that further its exempt purpose. St. David's argues that it passes the "operational test" because its activities via the partnership further its charitable purpose of providing health care to all persons.

St. David's contends that its activities via the partnership more than satisfy the community benefit standard. St. David's notes that the partnership hospitals perform a number of charitable functions in the Austin community. According to St. David's, the partnership not only provides free emergency room care, but also has opened the rest of its facilities to all persons, regardless of their ability to pay. In addition, St. David's asserts, the partnership hospitals maintain open medical staffs. Finally, St. David's states that it uses the profits that it receives from the partnership revenues to fund research grants and other health-related initiatives.

We have no doubt that St. David's via the partnership provides important medical services to the Austin community. Indeed, if the issue in this case were whether the partnership performed any charitable functions, we would be inclined to affirm the district court's grant of summary judgment in favor of St. David's.

However, we cannot agree with St. David's suggestion that the central issue in this case is whether the partnership provides some (or even an extensive amount of) charitable services. It is important to keep in mind that § 501(c)(3) confers tax-exempt status only on those organizations that operate *exclusively* in furtherance of exempt purposes. 26 C.F.R. § 1.501(c)(3)–1(a). As a result, in determining whether an organization satisfies the operational test, we do not simply consider whether the organization's activities further its charitable purposes. We must also ensure that those activities do *not* substantially further other (non-charitable) purposes. If more than an "insubstantial" amount of the partnership's activities further non-charitable interests, then St. David's can no longer be deemed to operate *exclusively* for charitable purposes.

Therefore, even if St. David's performs important charitable functions, St. David's cannot qualify for tax-exempt status under § 501(c)(3) if its activities via the partnership substantially further the private, profit-seeking interests of HCA.

In order to ascertain whether an organization furthers non-charitable interests, we can examine the structure and management of the organization. In other words, we look to which individuals or entities *control* the organization. If private individuals or for-profit entities have either formal or effective control, we presume that the organization furthers the profit-seeking motivations of those private individuals or entities. That is true, even when the organization is a partnership between a non-profit and a for-profit entity. *See Redlands Surgical Servs. v. Commissioner,* 113 T.C. 47, 75, 1999 WL 513862 (1999) ("An organization's property may be impermissibly devoted to a private use where private interests have control, directly or indirectly, over its assets, and thereby secure nonincidental private benefits."). When the non-profit organization cedes control over the partnership to the for-profit entity, we assume that the partnership's activities substantially further the for-profit's interests. As a result, we conclude that the non-profit's activities via the partnership are not exclusively or primarily in furtherance of its charitable purposes. Thus, the non-profit is not entitled to a tax exemption. *See* Rev. Rul. 98–15, 1998–1 C.B. 718, 1998 WL 89783 (1998) ("[I]f a private party is allowed to control or use the non-profit organization's activities or assets for the benefit of the private party, and the benefit is not incidental to the accomplishment of exempt purposes, the organization will fail to be organized and operated exclusively for exempt purposes.").

Conversely, if the non-profit organization enters into a partnership agreement with a for-profit entity, and retains control, we presume that the non-profit's activities via the partnership primarily further exempt purposes. Therefore, we can conclude that the non-profit organization should retain its tax-exempt status.

The present case illustrates why, when a non-profit organization forms a partnership with a for-profit entity, courts should be concerned about the relinquishment of control. St. David's, by its own account, entered the partnership with HCA out of financial *necessity* (to obtain the revenues needed for it to stay afloat). HCA, by contrast, entered the partnership for reasons of financial *convenience* (to enter a new market). The starkly different financial positions of these two parties at the beginning of their partnership negotiations undoubtedly affected their relative bargaining strength. Because St. David's "needed" this partnership more than HCA, St. David's may have been willing to acquiesce to many (if not most) of HCA's demands for the final Partnership Agreement. In the process, of course, St. David's may not have been able to give a high priority to its charitable objectives. As a result, St. David's may not have been able to ensure that its partnership with HCA would continually provide a "public benefit" as opposed to a private benefit for HCA.

These precedents and policy concerns indicate that, when a non-profit organization forms a partnership with a for-profit entity, the non-profit should lose its tax-exempt status if it cedes control to the for-profit entity. *See Redlands,* 242 F.3d at 904 (holding that a non-profit organization is no longer entitled to tax-exempt status when it "has ceded effective control . . . to private parties") (internal quotation marks omitted). Therefore, in our review of the district court's summary judgment ruling, we examine whether St. David's has shown that there is no genuine issue of material fact regarding whether St. David's ceded control to HCA.

A recent IRS revenue ruling provides a starting point for our analysis. In Revenue Ruling 98–15, the IRS indicated how a non-profit organization that forms a partnership with a for-profit entity can establish that it has retained control over the partnership's activities. *See* Rev. Rul. 98–15, 1998–1 C.B. 718 (1998). The revenue ruling states that a non-profit can demonstrate control by showing some or all of the following: (1) that the founding documents of the partnership expressly state that it has a charitable purpose and that the charitable purpose will take priority over all other concerns; (2) that the partnership agreement gives the non-profit organization a majority vote in the partnership's board of directors; and (3) that the partnership is managed by an independent company (an organization that is not affiliated with the for-profit entity).

The partnership documents in the present case, examined in light of the above factors, leave us uncertain as to whether St. David's has ceded control to HCA. St. David's did manage to secure some protections for its charitable mission. First of all, Section 3.2 of the Partnership Agreement expressly states that the manager of the partnership "shall" operate the partnership facilities in a manner that complies with the community benefit standard.[10] This provision appears to comport with the first factor

---

10. Section 3.2 of the Partnership Agreement states:

in Revenue Ruling 98–15, which indicates that the partnership's founding documents should contain a statement of the partnership's charitable purpose. *See* Rev. Rul. 98–15, 1998–1 C.B. 718 (1998) (indicating that "[t]he governing documents" of the partnership should "commit [the partnership] to providing health care services for the benefit of the community as a whole and to give charitable purposes priority over maximizing profits"); *compare Redlands,* 113 T.C. at 78–79 (noting, as a factor suggesting that the non-profit organization lacked control, that the partnership documents did not expressly state that the partnership had a charitable mission).[11] St. David's asserts that if Galen, the manager of the partnership facilities, fails to adhere to this requirement, St. David's can sue in Texas state court for specific performance of the Partnership Agreement.

The Management Services Agreement between Galen and the Partnership further provides that, if Galen takes any action with a "material probability of adversely affecting" St. David's tax-exempt status, that action will be considered an "[e]vent of [d]efault." Management Services Agreement, section 7(d). The Management Services Agreement authorizes St. David's to unilaterally terminate the contract with Galen if it commits such a "default." *See* Management Services Agreement, section 7 ("If any Event of Default shall occur and be continuing, the non-defaulting party may terminate this Agreement.... Any action to be taken by the Partnership under this paragraph may be taken by the [St. David's] representatives on the Governing Board[.]").

In addition, St. David's can exercise a certain degree of control over the partnership via its membership on the partnership's Board of Governors. St. David's and HCA each appoint half of the Board. No measure can pass

---

In furtherance of the purposes of the Partnership described in Section 3.1, the Manager shall cause the Facilities to conduct the business and operations of the Partnership in such a manner as to satisfy the community benefits standard generally required of hospitals under Section 501(c)(3) of the Code of (i) accepting Medicare and Medicaid patients, (ii) accepting all patients in an emergency condition in their emergency rooms without regard to the ability of such emergency patients to pay, (iii) maintaining open medical staffs, (iv) providing public health programs of educational benefit to the community, and (v) generally promoting the health, wellness and welfare of the community by providing quality health care at a reasonable cost. The Partnership intends to operate its business in such a manner so as not to jeopardize the status of [St. David's] or the [St. David's] Affiliates, to the extent applicable, as organizations described in Section 501(c)(3) of the Code.

11. The Government contends that Section 3.2 of the Partnership Agreement does not meet the standard established by Revenue Ruling 98–15. The Government argues that it is not sufficient for a partnership agreement to state that a manager "shall" abide by the community benefit standard; the agreement must also *expressly* require the manager to place charitable concerns above other goals. We are not persuaded by the Government's narrow interpretation of Revenue Ruling 98–15. The term "shall" clearly indicates that the manager of this partnership is required to abide by the community benefit standard. As our discussion below indicates, Section 3.2 cannot, standing alone, ensure that St. David's has an adequate amount of control over partnership operations. Other provisions of the partnership documents must provide St. David's with an effective means of enforcing the manager's obligation to abide by the community benefit standard. *See infra.* Nevertheless, as a purely textual matter, the purpose statement in Section 3.2 appears to comply with the first factor listed in Revenue Ruling 98–15.

the Board without the support of a majority of the representatives of *both* St. David's and HCA. *See* Partnership Agreement, section 1.8 (noting that Board approval "means approval of not less than a majority of a quorum of [HCA] Governors and not less than a majority of a quorum of [St. David's] Governors"). Thus, through its voting power, St. David's can effectively veto any proposed action of the Board of Governors.

St. David's also contends that the Partnership Agreement gives it authority over the partnership's Chief Executive Officer ("CEO"). The agreement permitted St. David's to appoint the initial CEO, subject to the approval of the HCA members of the Board of Governors. *See* Partnership Agreement, section 8.2. The agreement further provides that either HCA or St. David's can unilaterally remove the CEO. See *id.* St. David's suggests that this termination power enables it to ensure that the CEO will promote charitable objectives.

Finally, St. David's argues that its power to dissolve the partnership provides it with a significant amount of control over partnership operations. The Partnership Agreement states that, if St. David's receives legal advice (from an attorney that has been deemed acceptable by both HCA and St. David's) that its participation in the partnership will hinder its tax-exempt status, St. David's can request dissolution. *See* Partnership Agreement, section 15.1(f). St. David's asserts that it can use the threat of dissolution to force the partnership to give priority to charitable concerns.

According to St. David's, the above protections in the partnership documents (the purpose statement in the Partnership Agreement; St. David's power to terminate the Management Services Agreement and the CEO; its ability to block proposed action of the Board of Governors; and its power of dissolution) provide it with a large measure of control over partnership operations.

However, as the Government argues, there are reasons to doubt that the partnership documents provide St. David's with sufficient control. First of all, St. David's authority within the Board of Governors is limited. St. David's does not control a majority of the Board. *See* Rev. Rul. 98–15, 1998–1 C.B. 718 (1998) (indicating that a non-profit can retain control over a partnership with a for-profit if it selects a majority of the partnership's board of directors, but will have difficulty controlling the partnership if it has only an equal share of the board). As a result, although St. David's can veto board actions, it does not appear that it can initiate action without the support of HCA. Thus, at best, St. David's can prevent the partnership from taking action that might undermine its charitable goals; St. David's cannot necessarily ensure that the partnership will take new action that furthers its charitable purposes. *See Redlands,* 113 T.C. at 79–80 (finding that the non-profit did not have sufficient control in part because the non-profit could only veto partnership action; the non-profit could not initiate action without the consent of the for-profit entity).[12]

---

12. St. David's appears to contend that its authority to appoint the chairman of the Board of Governors, *see* Partnership Agreement, section 8.4(b)(i), gives it a significant amount

Second, Galen, which manages the operations of the partnership on a day-to-day basis, is a for-profit subsidiary of HCA. As a result, it is not apparent that Galen would be inclined to serve charitable interests. It seems more likely that Galen would prioritize the (presumably non-charitable) interests of its parent organization, HCA. *See* Rev. Rul. 98–15, 1998–1 C.B. 718 (1998) (indicating that a charitable hospital is unlikely to be in control of a partnership with a for-profit entity when the partnership manager is a subsidiary of the for-profit entity); *see also Redlands,* 113 T.C. at 83–84 ("[T]his long-term management contract with an affiliate of [the for-profit entity] is a salient indicator of [the non-profit's] surrender of effective control over the [partnership's] operations").[13]

Galen's apparent conflict of interest is only partly mitigated by the fact that Section 3.2 of the Partnership Agreement requires the manager to abide by the community benefit standard. As the Government points out, that requirement is useful only to the extent that the governing documents of the partnership empower St. David's to enforce the provision. St. David's appears to assert that the primary means through which it can force Galen to comply with Section 3.2 is by taking legal action. Given the time and expense of judicial proceedings, we doubt that St. David's will resort to litigation every time Galen makes a single decision that appears to conflict with the community benefit standard.

St. David's also asserts that it can control the management of the partnership via its position on the Board of Governors. However, the power

---

of control over the Board. It is not clear, however, how this appointment power provides St. David's with any real authority. The Partnership Agreement does not appear to permit the chairman to make decisions or initiate action without the consent of the rest of the Board. *See* Partnership Agreement, section 8.4(c) ("[N]o member of the Governing Board, acting alone, shall have the authority to act on behalf of the Governing Board."). Thus, it does not seem that the chairman could initiate any action without the support of a majority of the HCA representatives on the Board.

13. Our concerns about Galen's affiliation with HCA are magnified by the fact that the partnership's contract with Galen appoints the manager for an extraordinarily long term. The Management Services Agreement states that Galen will remain the manager until 2050, as long as an HCA affiliate continues to be a general partner of the partnership. *See* Management Services Agreement, section 6. Such "job security" could make Galen less responsive to any allegations by St. David's that Galen was not managing the partnership in accordance with the community benefit standard. *See Redlands,* 113 T.C. at 82–83 (finding problematic the fact that the partnership was "locked into" a management contract with an affiliate of the for-profit partner, when the contract provided for a 15–year term and the possibility of renewing that term for two additional five-year periods). In addition, part of Galen's fee is computed as a percentage (1%) of the partnership's net revenues. *See* Management Services Agreement, section 5(a). Such a contingency could give Galen an incentive to maximize revenues, and to neglect charitable goals. This fact, standing alone, does not necessarily preclude tax-exempt status for the non-profit partner. *See* Rev. Rul. 98–15, 1998–1 C.B. 718 (1998) (noting that a partnership paid its manager a fee based on the partnership's gross revenues, and nonetheless concluding that the non-profit member of the partnership was entitled to tax-exempt status). However, this fact, particularly when considered in light of Galen's relationship with HCA, does suggest that Galen will not be inclined to prioritize charitable goals. *See Redlands,* 113 T.C. at 80 (citing the fact that the manager "derive[d] a management fee computed as a percentage of gross revenues" as a factor suggesting that the partnership had a "significant profit-making objective").

of the Board is limited in scope. The Board of Governors is empowered to deal with only major decisions, not the day-to-day operation of the partnership hospitals.[14] Thus, St. David's could not, via its position on the Board, overrule a management decision that fell outside the range of the Board's authority.

The Management Services Agreement does appear to provide St. David's with a certain degree of control over Galen. The agreement permits St. David's to unilaterally cancel the contract with Galen if the manager takes action that has a "material probability" of undermining St. David's tax-exempt status. It is not entirely clear whether St. David's would be willing to exercise this termination option without the consent of HCA. Nor is it clear whether St. David's could ensure that Galen was replaced by a manager that would prioritize charitable purposes. Nonetheless, the Management Services Agreement does appear to give St. David's some authority over Galen, and therefore seems to provide St. David's with a degree of control over partnership operations.

We are also uncertain about the amount of control that St. David's exercises over the partnership's CEO. St. David's appears to assert that its authority to appoint the initial CEO, and its power to terminate the officer, demonstrate its control within the partnership. The Government has created a general issue of material fact, however, regarding St. David's by pointing to instances in which the CEO failed to comply with the Partnership Agreement. Although the Partnership Agreement states that the CEO "shall" provide the Board of Governors with annual reports of the amount of charity care, *see* Partnership Agreement, section 8.4(f), it seems that no such report was prepared for 1996 (the first year of the partnership and the tax year at issue in this case). Indeed, it does not appear that any annual report on charity care was prepared until after the IRS began auditing the partnership. Despite St. David's assertions about its power over the CEO, the non-profit does not claim to have taken *any* punitive action against the CEO for failing to prepare these reports. If St. David's was in fact unable to enforce a provision of the Partnership Agreement dealing specifically with charity care, that raises serious doubts about St. David's capacity to ensure that the partnership's operations further charitable purposes.

Finally, we question the degree to which St. David's has the power to control the partnership by threatening dissolution. First of all, the Partnership Agreement appears to permit St. David's to request dissolution only when there is a change in the law, not simply when the partnership fails to perform a few charitable functions. *See* Partnership Agreement, section 15.1(f) (indicating that the partnership "shall" be dissolved upon "[t]he request of [St. David's] for dissolution . . . in the event [St. David's]

---

14. The Board can consider matters such as: (1) amendments to the Partnership Agreement, the Management Services Agreement, and other major partnership documents; (2) sales of substantially all partnership assets; (3) approval of annual operating and capital budgets; (4) the hiring the partnership's CEO; (5) any change in the mission of the partnership; and (6) authorization of debt in excess of 10% of the partnership's assets. *See* Partnership Agreement, section 8.4(c).

receives an opinion of counsel, from counsel reasonably acceptable to [St. David's] and the [HCA] Governors, that as a result of a rule, regulation, statute, Internal Revenue Service government pronouncement, or court decision ... enacted or issued subsequent to the date hereof which would cause the participation of [St. David's] or the [St. David's] Affiliates in the Partnership to be inconsistent with [their] Status ... as organizations described in Section 501(c)(3) of the Code"). Second, HCA may not take seriously any threat of dissolution made by St. David's. HCA must be aware that St. David's has a strong incentive not to exercise its power to dissolve the corporation. The partnership documents include a non-compete clause, which provides that, in the event of dissolution, neither partner can compete in the Austin area for two years. *See* Contribution Agreement, section 11.1. That result might be slightly unpleasant for HCA, but would not destroy the entity; HCA would still have its nationwide health care business. For St. David's, by contrast, dissolution would be disastrous. St. David's serves only the Austin community. If it were forbidden from competing in that area, St. David's would (in effect) cease to exist. In light of the realities of the situation, it seems unlikely that St. David's would exercise its option to dissolve the partnership even if the partnership strayed from St. David's charitable mission.

The evidence presented by the parties demonstrates that there remain genuine issues of material fact regarding whether St. David's ceded control to HCA. Therefore, we vacate the district court's grant of summary judgment in favor of St. David's.

Notes

1. *Formal control v. actual operations.* St. David's argued that what mattered was not who controlled the partnership but how it actually operated. Suppose that the relevant documents indicated that control was vested in HCA but what about the fact that St. David's provided a large amount of charitable care, did not discriminate against Medicare and Medicaid patients, operated an emergency room open to all regardless of ability to pay, provided educational and public health programs free of charge, and maintained open medical staffs? Aren't those activities the basis of community benefit and therefore an entitlement to tax exemption? What administrative burden would such a result place on the Internal Revenue Service?

2. *Exactly what did the government win?* On remand St. David's Health Care System won a jury *verdict*. *See* St. David's Health Care System v. United States, 2004 WL 555095 (2004). Given that result, exactly what did the Government win in the Court of Appeals? To answer the question, pay close attention to the procedural posture, burdens of proof and who got the benefit of inferences from the record.

a. *Formal control.* Make a list of the relevant factors. What did the relevant documents say about the mission of the partnership and the obligations of the Board, the officers and the management company? Who had the powers to appoint, dismiss and enforce? What was missing regarding the formal lines of the authority? Were there relevant issues of material fact regarding formal control?

b. Informal control. Make a list of the relevant factors. What did the court say about the overall context of the transaction and the possible set of incentives and power created out of this context? Were there relevant issues of material fact regarding actual control? Who got the benefit of any inferences in this regard? What does this analysis tell you regarding who bore the relevant burdens of proof? What does this tell you about the importance of formal or informal control in the court's decision to vacate and remand? Return to the point of the immediately preceding note and ask why the Service should get its cake and eat it too: it can stave off summary judgment by raising questions regarding informal control and operations while the taxpayer cannot prevail on proof regarding informal control and operations if it lacks formal control.

3. *Split board powers.* Citing *Redlands*, the court found fault with the fact that power on the Board of Directors was equally divided. The court concluded that such a split enabled St. David's to prevent action contrary to charitable purposes but also precluded St. David's from initiating new activities in furtherance of exempt purposes. Recall the operations of the surgical center in *Redlands* prior to the joint venture with a for-profit partner. Reflect on the operations of the hospital system in *St.* David's prior to the whole-hospital joint venture with HCA. Did the court in *St. David's* correctly cite *Redlands*? Were the cases analogous in terms of the effect of preserving the status quo ante?

4. *Saving public assets for some degree of public use.* Suppose that St. David's sold its hospital facilities to HCA. Could those operations have then been tax exempt? Exactly what did the hospital system sell to HCA? It has been clear for a long time that an EO cannot simply sell a portion of its revenue steam to a for-profit entity. *See, e.g.,* Gen. Couns. Mem. 39,862 (Dec. 2, 1991). What did St. David's obtain in return? If the health system needed an infusion of capital what alternatives could it pursue? Do you think that HCA would take an equity position in St. David's without obtaining control in return? What is the appropriate tax policy if the choice is between total loss of assets devoted to charitable purposes or transfer of public assets to private use to some extent? Where should this line be drawn and how is that reflected in the doctrine?

5. *Is form being elevated over substance?* Why is a partnership with a for-profit entity suspect? In this thinking about this question, keep in mind that with regard to for-profit activity we have seen different requirements imposed for different organizational forms. First, if a nonprofit engages in for-profit activity without creating a corporate subsidiary to house it, then the nonprofit's tax exemption is threatened if the unrelated business activity is more than insubstantial. Second, and by contrast, if the nonprofit creates a separate corporate subsidiary to pursue the unrelated activity, then no such requirement is imposed unless it can be shown either that the subsidiary fails to pursue a trade or business or is operationally indistinct

from the parent. EOs in the health sector have routinely taken advantage of this strong presumption against piercing the corporate veil to create numerous for-profit subsidiaries, and the fact that this unrelated business income is substantial does not threaten the parent's exempt status. Third, if the nonprofit forms a partnership with a for-profit entity, the unrelated business activities of the partnership are attributed to the partners, and the nonprofit's exemption is threatened unless, as in the first mode of organization, the activities are only insubstantial. The question is whether it makes sense to treat the use of the for-profit subsidiary differently than the joint venture partnership insofar as the amount of unrelated business activity allowed.

Remember that the basic premise of the tax exemption is that assets are to be devoted to creating community benefit, which leads to the requirements that an exempt entity be organized and operated to confer community benefit. One of the issues, then, in thinking about whether for-profit subsidiaries should be treated more deferentially than partnerships— or, stated conversely, whether partnerships with for-profit entities should be suspect—is whether the two forms vary in the extent to which the community benefits from allowing a nonprofit to earn for-profit income. The answer is by no means clear.

In the first form, where no corporate subsidiary is used, the nonprofit can gain little for-profit income because this option is legally barred for anything greater than insubstantial activity. To reiterate, the nonprofit cannot protect its exemption by pointing to the fact alone that it is using the income gained from the for-profit activity to fund nonprofit endeavors. In situation two, there is no similar requirement regarding the quality or quantity of incidental private benefit, and the parent's exemption is not threatened by the for-profit activity, but likewise there is no mandate requiring the nonprofit parent to use the fruits of the for-profit activity to subsidize nonprofit ones. Indeed, there is often a pyramiding scheme at work in the sector, where for-profit income gained by a nonprofit is used to sustain or create other for-profit activity.

As Professor Mark Hall put it in a useful metaphor in correspondence with one of us about this issue, to a great extent each boat floats on its own hull as for-profit assets fund for-profit activity and nonprofit assets support nonprofit endeavor. Thus, the extent to which for-profit revenue gained from a subsidiary is used to subsidize nonprofit activity may not differ much from the case when a partnership with a for-profit is used. This empirical question cannot simply be assumed away by pointing to the existence of different organizational forms and the fact that one but not the other involves a for-profit participant. Finally, where for-profit revenue is gained from the partnership, it may be true that private interests are to some extent siphoning off profits that might otherwise be available to the nonprofit if the nonprofit were to use a subsidiary. However, again because it is not clear how much for-profit revenue from a for-profit subsidiary funds a parent's nonprofit activity, it may be the cases that the use of the partnership changes the result very little.

Additionally, there is the assumption that the nonprofit has the option of using one form or the other, or, in other words it is assumed that the nonprofit's opportunity to generate for-profit revenue is equally available in the two situations. However, often this is not a valid assumption because sometimes it is the case, as in *Redlands*, that the nonprofit cannot pursue the venture without the for-profit partner, because it lacks necessary expertise or capital or because extant capacity in its service area makes that option unprofitable. Thus, it may be, as it seems to have been in *Redlands*, that the only way the for-profit money can be at all available to the nonprofit as a means to subsidize nonprofit activity is through a joint venture with a for-profit co-venturer. The St. David's Health System may have failed altogether without the infusion of income from HCA. Once again, an empirical question cannot be papered over simply by pointing to the existence of a for-profit partner. Last, if the concern is that the partnership will put at risk the nonprofit's other assets because other members of a partnership can reach the general partner's assets, then that problem is amply addressed by requiring that the nonprofit create a subsidiary to wall off its other assets, as was done in *Redlands*.

In short, is form being elevated over substance? Of course, an affirmative answer to this very complicated and difficult question does not resolve the larger question concerning the extent to which nonprofits should be allowed to earn for-profit income. It might be that more stringent requirements should be imposed on the use of for-profit corporate subsidiaries rather than allowing greater leniency for partnerships with for-profits. One can see it both ways. On the one hand, although the reasoning in *Redlands*, Revenue Ruling 98–15, and other Revenue Service releases, *see, e.g.*, Priv. Ltr. Rul. 2004–48048 (Aug. 31, 2004); Priv. Ltr. Rul. 2004–36022 (June 9, 2004); Priv. Ltr. Rul. 2001–18054 (Feb. 7, 2001); Priv. Ltr. Rul. 1999–13035 (Apr. 2, 1999); Priv. Ltr. Rul. 97–09014 (Feb. 28, 1997); Priv. Ltr. Rul. 97–05014 (Jan. 31, 1997); Priv. Ltr. Rul. 96–37050 (Sept. 13, 1996); Priv. Ltr. Rul. 96–16005 (Apr. 19, 1996); Priv. Ltr. Rul. 95–18014 (May 5, 1995); Priv. Ltr. Rul. 95–17029 (Apr. 28, 1995); Priv. Ltr. Rul. 93–23035 (June 11, 1993); Priv. Ltr. Rul. 93–23030 (June 11, 1993); Priv. Ltr. Rul. 90–24085 (June 15, 1990); Gen. Couns. Mem. 39,732 (May 27, 1988), can be best described as opaque, one can see a balancing process at work in which decision-makers weigh the amount of assets transferred by the nonprofit to the joint venture partnership, the degree to which the nonprofit's other assets are put at risk, the extent to which the nonprofit needs the participation of the for-profit partner, the amount of profit siphoned off to the for-profit entity as private inurement or private benefit, and the extent to which the joint venture will pursue public and private activity. It might be possible to develop analogous requirements regarding the transfer of assets to a for-profit subsidiary. On the other hand, it is possible that the requirements imposed on joint venture partnerships should be relaxed to allow nonprofits to engage in a larger number of joint ventures partnerships with for-profit entities, albeit with the erection of some barriers against a wholesale transfer of nonprofit assets to for-profit use and to police against egregious examples of private inurement and benefit.

In thinking about these possibilities, it should be clear why this area of the law is so controversial, because, as was said at the outset of the section on joint ventures, it presents in perhaps starkest relief the tensions regarding the mixing of public and private activity in the health care sector. Our society has now traveled relatively far down the road of allowing for-profit actors to engage in activity that was once largely the sole preserve of nonprofit ones; and we have made it increasingly difficult for nonprofits to use public and private reimbursement to subsidize activities like charitable care and education that the market does not currently and perhaps cannot support. Our law is thus part of a vicious circle in which we expect nonprofit organizations to act differently than for-profit ones but create an overall environment—particularly with respect to price competition—that makes it increasingly difficult for them to be different in fact. Then, as nonprofit organizations act more like for-profit ones, it becomes even harder for them to mount a legitimate claim that they deserve public subsidy, with the result that they are more likely to lose whatever forms of subsidization that are left to allow them to differ, and so they come to resemble for-profit actors all the more, and so on.* One can argue that nonprofits must have whatever income they can gain from for-profit activity to keep those non-market-supported activities afloat. On the other hand, as critics of the tax exemption point out, for various reasons, it is not clear that the tax exemption is the proper vehicle to achieve that end; and, as should be clear by now, there are substantial administrative costs involved. Still, continued elimination of opportunities for subsidization of nonprofit activities by for-profit ones is a risky social experiment because nonprofits may no longer provide those activities and, to the extent there are spillover effects, conceivably for-profits will provide them even less than they do now.

---

* As we developed at length in the notes following *Geisinger I*, the claim that the behavior of for-profit and nonprofit entities has "converged" is grossly oversimplified, *see generally* Schlesinger & Gray, *Paradoxes of Persistent Scrutiny*, and so we do not wish to overstate this point.

CHAPTER 24

HEALTH CARE FRAUD AND ABUSE

One could say without exaggeration that one of the most imperialistic areas of health law in our era is the category "fraud." Estimates of the amount of fraud vary, ranging from the $60 billion estimated by the United States Federal Bureau of Investigation, *see* http://www.fbi.gov/about-us/ investigate/white_collar/health-care-fraud, to $68 billion estimated by the National Health Care Anti–Fraud Association, *see* http://www.nhcaa.org/ eweb/DynamicPage.aspx?webcode=anti_fraud_resource_centr & wpscode =TheProblemOfHCFraud, or even more. Of course one must be wary of such estimates because they depend on the definition of fraud, which is necessarily contested and difficult to delineate, *see generally* Jerry L. Mashaw & Theodore R. Marmor, *Conceptualizing, Estimating, and Reforming Fraud, Waste, and Abuse in Healthcare Spending*, 11 YALE J. ON REG. 455 (1994); Joan H. Krause, *Following the Money in Health Care Fraud: Reflections on a Modern–Day Yellow Brick Road*, 36 AM. J. L. & MED. 343, 345–47 (2010) [hereinafter Krause, *Following the Money in Health Care Fraud*], but the problem is large and probably growing.

Equally large and growing are state and federal efforts to combat fraud. Numerous rounds of budget reconciliation bills and other legislation have poured more money and effort into the fight and created new programs. Among the recent endeavors, HIPAA directed more funds to federal agencies and created the Health Care Fraud and Abuse Control Account, a special account to fund antifraud activities to which some recoveries are deposited. *See* Pub. L. No. 104–191 § 201(b), 110 Stat. 1936, 1993–4 (1996) (codified as amended at 42 U.S.C. § 1395i). The Balanced Budget Act of 1997 added substantial new penalties and increased the budget still further. *See* Balanced Budget Act of 1997, Pub. L. No. 105–33 §§ 4304(b), 4314, 4331(c), 111 Stat. 251, 383–84, 389, 396 (codified as amended at 42 U.S.C. §§ 1320a–7a, 1395nn, 1320a–7).

The Deficit Reduction Act of 2005 funded a new Medicaid Integrity Program, which among other things, as discussed below, created incentives for states to enact their own false claims acts to prosecute Medicaid fraud. *See* Pub. L. No. 109–171, § 6031, 120 Stat. 4, 72–73 (codified as amended at 42 U.S.C. § 1396h). The Fraud Enforcement and Recovery Act of 2009 (FERA), also as discussed below, made enforcement easier in a number of ways and enhanced penalties. *See* Pub. L. No. 111–21, § 4, 123 Stat. 1617, 1621–25. The PPACA likewise increased the arsenal significantly by expanding the ability of private parties to act as attorney generals, as we will see below, and significantly adding to the funding available to state and federal authorities. *See* PPACA, Pub. L. No. 111–148 § 6402(i). As Professor Krause (under)states, the "typical legislative response to health care fraud is to throw both money and new enforcement authority at the problem." Krause, *Following the Money in Health Care Fraud* at 363. The resources are enormous and growing.

Typically one lists three animating purposes in the area: (1) protect programmatic fiscal integrity; (2) prevent or ameliorate financial incentives that might lead to overutilization; and (3) obviate incentives that might lead to poor quality care. Professors Pamela Bucy and Joan Krause, among others, have cogently explained why the United States health care system is particularly prone to fraud: it is decentralized and filled with paperwork. Those attributes make it easier to take the money and run and hide. *See* Krause, *Following the Money in Health Care Fraud* at 345–51. *See generally* Pamela H. Bucy, *Fraud by Fright: White Collar Crime by Health Care Providers*, 67 N.C. L. REV. 855 (1989).

For some the disadvantage of the rubric fighting health care fraud is that it potentially snares or deters efficient arrangements. *See, e.g.*, James F. Blumstein, *Rationalizing the Fraud and Abuse Statute*, 15(4) HEALTH AFFAIRS 118 (1996) [hereinafter Blumstein, *Rationalizing the Fraud and Abuse Statute*]. As you will see, fraud laws can also, if not modified, deal harshly with socially desirable investments, such as contributions of services by hospitals to community health centers or other health care safety net providers caring for large numbers of low income uninsured or underinsured patients.

For others, the advantage of introducing a strong anti-fraud gloss to health system oversight is that it is flexible enough to snare or deter fraudulent activity. *See, e.g.*, Timothy Stoltzfus Jost & Sharon Davies, *The Fraud and Abuse Statute: Rationalizing or Rationalization*, 15(4) HEALTH AFFAIRS 129 (1996) [hereinafter Jost & Davies, *The Fraud and Abuse Statute*]. Regardless of which view is correct—whether the glass is half empty or half full—both sides of the debate agree that the fraud and abuse regime can be applied quite broadly to a vast array of health care activity, as illustrated by the following situations:

1. On October 13, 2010 federal prosecutors brought charges against 44 individuals in what was then the largest ring ever prosecuted for fraudulent Medicare charges. According to the charges, the syndicate stole the identities of thousands of doctors and patients and used 118 phantom clinics across 25 states to bilk Medicare of over $100 million in bogus billings over four years. *See* William K. Rashbaum & Michael Wilson, *44 Charged in Huge Medicare Fraud Scheme*, N.Y. TIMES, Oct. 13, 2010 (http://cityroom.blogs.nytimes.com/2010/10/13/44–charged-in-huge-medicare-fraud-scheme/).

2. An Atlanta-based radiologist, Dr. Rajashakher P. Reddy, was convicted of numerous counts of fraud based on evidence that he signed 70,000 radiology reports in eight months although during that time he reviewed actual computer images only 5,900 times. Most of the reports, submitted to numerous hospitals, were prepared by non-physician assistants who were the only persons to review the images and who used an electronic signature

created for that purpose. *See, e.g., Atlanta Radiologist Guilty of Fraudulently Passing Off Diagnoses Prepared by Non–Physician Employees* (Press Release, United States Dep't of Justice, July 7, 2011) (http://www.justice. gov/usao/gan/press/2011/07–07–11.html); United States v. Reddy, 2010 WL 3210842 (N.D. Ga. 2010).

3. A psychiatrist in private practice largely treated Medicare and Medicaid patients in a mom-and-pop solo practice in which his wife and a single employee did all the billing. The government brought a case against him and his wife for, among other things, improper billing using CPT code 90844, which pertains to a 45–50 minute psychotherapy session, instead of CPT code 90843, used for a 20–30 minute session, or CPT code 90862, used for a "minimal psychotherapy" session. Since the alternative codes were reimbursed at lower rates than CPT code 90844, the government claimed actual damages of $245,392, although its prayer for relief, constructed out of the relevant statutes discussed below, also included both trebling those damages and civil penalties of $10,000 for each of the 8,002 allegedly false reimbursement claims submitted during the relevant time period, for total damages of $81 million. *See* United States v. Krizek, 111 F.3d 934 (D.C. Cir. 1997), reprinted below.

4. During the 1990s the Office of Inspector General (OIG) of the Department of Health and Human Services launched the Physicians at Teaching Hospitals (PATH) audits aimed potentially at all 125 teaching hospitals then associated with the nation's 125 medical schools. These audits involved the hospitals' part B billings to Medicare for services provided by teaching physicians. One part of the audits involved application of a requirement that a teaching physician could bill Medicare part B for care provided by residents only if the faculty member was physically present when the care was provided, a stricture that potentially conflicted with regulations that allowed for reimbursement of teaching physicians when residents acted under their supervision and direction. For example, a teaching hospital might bill for part B services when the attending physician reviewed a chart with a resident and provided instructions which the resident then carried out. *See generally* Pamela H. Bucy, *The Path from Regulator to Hunter: The Exercise of Prosecutorial Discretion in the Investigation of Physicians at Teaching Hospitals*, 44 Sᴛ. Lᴏᴜɪs U. L.J. 3 (2000) [hereinafter Bucy, *The Path from Regulator to Hunter*].

5. The psychiatrist discussed in situation #3 above treated many severely ill patients with psychiatric disorders like paranoid psychosis, organic brain dementia, chronic depression with delusions, acute schizophrenia, and hallucinations. These psychiatric illnesses were often coupled with somatic medical problems including colon cancer, diabetes, herpes infections, viral encephalitis, epilepsy, paralysis and substance abuse. In bringing the action for health care fraud, the government challenged not only defendants' coding practices but the psychiatrist's method of practice. Some patients, it argued, should have been discharged from the hospital sooner; others, it claimed, should not have been treated with psychotherapy; others, it claimed, needed less intensive therapy. *See* United States v.

Krizek, 859 F.Supp. 5 (D.D.C. 1994), *rev'd on other grounds*, 111 F.3d 934 (D.C. Cir. 1997), reprinted below and also discussed in the notes following *Mikes* reprinted below.

6. A spirometer is a device into which a patient blows air in order to test pulmonary function to detect lung diseases like asthma, emphysema and pulmonary fibrosis. According to a plaintiff's expert, spirometers are susceptible to inaccuracy through time and usage because they can become clogged, causing false readings. Erroneous readings can also occur through damage during cleaning and transportation or from variations in barometric pressure, temperature or humidity. According to plaintiff, guidelines published by the American Thoracic Society constituted the relevant standard of care for spirometry, and these guidelines recommended daily calibration of the spirometer by use of a three liter calibration syringe, the performance of three successive trials during administration of the testing to a patient, and appropriate training of technicians. Plaintiff claimed that defendants committed fraud by obtaining reimbursement for spirometry even though these guidelines were not followed. *See* United States ex rel. Mikes v. Straus, 274 F.3d 687 (2d Cir. 2001), reprinted below.

7. According to documents produced in discovery during litigation, a major pharmaceutical company used a medical communications firm to draft 26 papers that then appeared in 18 peer-reviewed medical journals between 1998 and 2005. The articles, which did not mention the pharmaceutical firm's role in producing the papers, supported the use of hormone replacement therapy for women, treatment which included the use of two of the company's products that generated $2 billion in revenue in 2001. The documents showed that after drafting the papers, the ghostwriting company solicited top physicians to sign their names to the articles although the physicians had contributed little or no writing. *See* Natasha Singer, *Medical Papers by Ghostwriters Pushed Therapy*, N.Y. TIMES, August 5, 2009, at A1.

8. A nonprofit health care system owned and operated the only hospital in a county and all outpatient procedures were performed there. Informed by its only gastroenterology group that the group was considering opening its own outpatient surgery center, and concerned that the specialists would perform their procedures solely at the competing facility because of their ownership interest, the hospital system, fearful of serious adverse financial consequences, entered into part-time employment contracts with the gastroenterologists and other local specialists. The agreements, executed between the specialists and two wholly-owned for-profit subsidiaries created for that purpose, obligated the physicians to provide professional and administrative services to the system and required the specialists, over a ten-year period, to perform all their outpatient procedures exclusively there. In executing these agreements the system obtained advice from various outside law firms and consultants, and obtained appraisals of the fair-market value and commercial reasonableness of the employment contracts. Various contractual options were considered and some were rejected as too risky. The one chosen compensated the specialists through a combi-

nation of a fixed base salary, a "productivity bonus" equal to 80% of the amounts collected by the system for the physicians' personally performed professional services, and an additional incentive bonus if certain perform- ance targets were met.

Quite a diversity of activity called "fraud," yes? In thinking about that point, we can start by considering a lay definition of fraud, which is that someone intentionally peddles something known to be of little or no value and receives remuneration in return. Situation #1 certainly meets that definition because it involved a massive, organized criminal scheme in which federal reimbursement was obtained for the provision of noth- ing: fictitious doctors provided fictitious patients with fictitious services. Situation #2 likewise seems to meet this definition although it is more complicated because radiological reports were submitted—something was provided—but because their value depended on a radiologist's viewing the relevant images and preparing the reports, we can reasonably conclude, as did the jury in that case, that nothing of worth was provided in return for payment, and the conduct was done with full knowledge and intent of providing nothing for something.

Situations #3 and #4, by contrast, are much more complicated because actual services were provided and there was no allegation that the services were worthless. Instead, the allegations were that the value conferred was less than the amount billed for and allowed under the relevant reimburse- ment scheme, i.e., there had been upcoding. You can see, then, that we've moved well beyond the lay definition of fraud and into the intricacies of reimbursement. On its face situation #3 seems simple enough, involving a couple of reimbursement codes, but as you will see in the case itself, nothing was quite that simple. Situation #4, involving the massively complicated reimbursement of academic medical centers for their provision of teaching in the context of providing patient care itself, is about as far away from lay-defined fraud as one can get.

Situations #5 and #6 get us more deeply into the standards by which health care is provided. Situation #5 involves a question of medical necessity, i.e., utilization. Some issues of this sort might be blatant, e.g., a surgeon removes a cataract that he or she knows is perfectly normal and then bills the surgery as reasonable and necessary care. However, in many other instances necessity is contested, as it was in the case presented in Situation #5. Somewhat related, situation #6 involves a question of quality of care. Again, blatant issues of fraud arise, such as situation #2, in which the care provided was so substandard as to be worthless, but again many more instances involve shades of grade. Therefore, as you read the materi- als, ask yourselves how the doctrine in this area can or should draw these lines.

Situation #7 starts attenuating the causal chain of fraud quite a bit. Something smells like fraud. The authors who were solicited to ghostwrite the articles published in the medical journals lent their names and authori- ty to the results, yet they did nothing. Perhaps that authority influenced their peers to write prescriptions. Maybe those prescriptions would have been written anyway, maybe not. Maybe those drugs helped patients, maybe they didn't, maybe the patients weren't even harmed. Federal dollars were spent, but maybe they would have been spent anyway. Maybe not. It's getting complicated, isn't it?

Situation #8 describes pending litigation in United States ex rel. Drakeford v. Tuomey, No. 10–254 (D.S.C.), in which, at this point, a new trial has been ordered for a portion of the allegations. See *Fourth Circuit Denies Petition by Hospital Seeking to Appeal Court's New Trial Order*, 19 HEALTH LAW REPORTER (BNA) 1516 (Nov. 4, 2010). The case involves the question whether the employment contracts fell into exceptions of the Stark law, on which we will spend substantial time below, and if the contracts did not, whether the violations were knowing, as defined technically by another statute we will spend much time explicating, the False Claims Act. You will see, as we go through this area, that some of it gets as technical as technical gets in a very specialized area of law. As you move through this dizzying landscape, keep in mind where we started in situations #1 and #2, how far away we are from those common-sense illustrations of fraud, whether through this technical haze we can even still "see" those common-sense meanings and what this says about the entire enterprise.

One way to think about the current regime is to compare the prosecution of members of organized crime—in fact, below we will take up the application to health care fraud of criminal laws against racketeering. Al Capone was put away for tax evasion, not the widespread mayhem and murder he and his criminal associates wrought. Other persons likewise involved in organized crime might be nailed on mail fraud, not the underlying crimes, which, for many reasons, remain beyond prosecution. Many would say that the current system of prosecuting health care fraud is similar in that the numerous causes of action lumped under the rubric of health care fraud are tools by which public and private enforcers are able to get at almost every type of activity involved in the health care sector by virtue of the fact that money is exchanged at some point. Under the name of fraud we are now regulating many diverse activities and pathologies of our health care sector with a very wide net that trawls through a vast, oceanic expanse. *Cf.* Krause, *Following the Money in Health Care Fraud* (incisively detailing how the entire health care fraud enterprise is lucrative to all sides—the fraudsters, prosecutors and policy makers).

What makes the area difficult to master, therefore, is its remarkable complexity. Some dimensions of health law, like tax and antitrust, are difficult to master conceptually. Fraud is different, however, in that the concepts are not difficult but are few in number or, as some would maintain, absent entirely. Given the vast landscape to which the label "fraud" now applies, the result is that detail is piled on detail which is piled on yet more detail. The old saw says that spaghetti thrown against the wall does not stick. The domain of health care fraud is more like ten varieties of pasta tossed at the wall.

1. FALSE CLAIMS

The law penalizing false claims is today one of the most important tools in the arsenal for fighting health care fraud and abuse. A number of statutes give rise to potential criminal or civil liability. Some of these are specifically tailored to health care, while some are of general applicability. The criminal statutes of general applicability include the mail and wire fraud statutes, 18 U.S.C. §§ 1341, 1343; laws prohibiting persons from knowingly making or presenting false or fraudulent claims to the United States, 18 U.S.C. § 287; statutes proscribing the making of false or fraudulent statements or representations, 18 U.S.C. § 1001; and the criminalization of money laundering, 18 U.S.C. §§ 1956–57. A separate statute, 42 U.S.C. § 1320a–7b(a), proscribes false claims with regard to the provision of Medicare and Medicaid services. It creates a felony punishable by either or both a fine of $25,000 and up to five-years imprisonment for knowingly and willfully making or causing to be made "any false statement or representation of a material fact in any application for any benefit or payment under a Federal health care program." Finally, we will see that the criminal portion of the general racketeering criminal statute, the Racketeer Influenced and Corrupt Organizations Act (RICO), 18 U.S.C. §§ 1961–68, may also be applied to false claims made by an "enterprise" engaged in interstate commerce.

Civil statutes of generally applicability include the Program Fraud and Civil Remedies Act, 31 U.S.C. §§ 3801–12, and the Federal False Claims Act (FCA), 31 U.S.C. §§ 3729–33, which subjects a person who "knowingly presents, or causes to be presented, a false or fraudulent claim for payment or approval" or "knowingly makes, uses, or causes to be made or used, a false record or statement material to a false or fraudulent claim," 31 U.S.C. § 3729(a)(1)(A)–(B), to liability for trebled actual damages and a civil penalty of $5,000 to $10,000 for each false claim.* The FCA allows the federal government to sue on its own behalf or, under specified circumstances, private individuals to bring "qui tam" actions on their own behalf as private attorney generals, colloquially known as "whistleblowers," litigation into which the United States has discretion to intervene. *See* 31 U.S.C. § 3730. RICO also provides civil remedies for racketeering.

A separate statute, 42 U.S.C. § 1320a–7a, creates civil monetary penalties for false claims committed in serving Medicare and Medicaid patients. Its core statutory language for civil false claims sweeps very broadly:

Civil Monetary Penalties for False Claims

42 U.S.C. § 1320a–7a.   Civil monetary penalties

(a) Improperly filed claims. Any person (including an organization, agency, or other entity, but excluding a beneficiary) that—

---

* By regulation, as a result of indexing for inflation, the current range is actually $5,500–$11,000 per claim. See 28 C.F.R. § 85.3(a)(9).

(1) knowingly presents or causes to be presented to an officer, employee, or agent of the United States, or of any department or agency thereof, or of any State agency (as defined in subsection (i)(1)), a claim (as defined in subsection (i)(2)) that the Secretary determines—

(A) is for a medical or other item or service that the person knows or should know was not provided as claimed, including any person who engages in a pattern or practice of presenting or causing to be presented a claim for an item or service that is based on a code that the person knows or should know will result in a greater payment to the person than the code the person knows or should know is applicable to the item or service actually provided,

(B) is for a medical or other item or service and the person knows or should know the claim is false or fraudulent,

(C) is presented for a physician's service (or an item or service incident to a physician's service) by a person who knows or should know that the individual who furnished (or supervised the furnishing of) the service—

(i) was not licensed as a physician,

(D) is for a medical or other item or service furnished during a period in which the person was excluded from the Federal health care program under which the claim was made pursuant to Federal law or

(E) is for a pattern of medical or other items or services that a person knows or should know are not medically necessary;

shall be subject, in addition to any other penalties that may be prescribed by law, to a civil money penalty of not more than $10,000 for each item or service. In addition, such a person shall be subject to an assessment of not more than 3 times the amount claimed for each such item or service in lieu of damages sustained by the United States or a State agency because of such claim. In addition the Secretary may make a determination in the same proceeding to exclude the person from participation in the Federal health care programs and to direct the appropriate State agency to exclude the person from participation in any State health care program.

(i) Definitions. For the purposes of this section:

(2) The term "claim" means an application for payments for items and services under a Federal health care program.

(3) The term "item or service" includes (A) any particular item, device, medical supply, or service claimed to have been provided to a patient and listed in an itemized claim for payment, and (B) in the case of a claim based on costs, any entry in the cost report, books of account or other documents supporting such claim.

(4) The term "agency of the United States" includes any contractor acting as a fiscal intermediary, carrier, or fiscal agent or any other

claims processing agent for a Federal health care program (as so defined).

* * *

Other portions of this statute imposing civil monetary penalties reach particularly specified conduct and in some instances impose different penalties. Some of these include: the provision of false or misleading information that could reasonably be expected to influence a hospital discharge decision regarding a Medicare beneficiary (42 U.S.C. § 1320a–7a(3)); the use of remuneration to induce beneficiaries to enroll or seek services (42 U.S.C. § 1320a–7a(5)); contracting for services with an individual that the contractor knows or should have known was excluded from participation in a federal health care program (42 U.S.C. § 1320a–7a(6)); making a false statement or misrepresentation with regard to a provider agreement (42 U.S.C. § 1320a–7a(11)); knowledge of and failure to report and return an overpayment for services (42 U.S.C. § 1320a–7a(12)); and payments by hospitals to physicians, as well as receipt of such payments by physicians, as remuneration to induce reduction of services (42 U.S.C. § 1320a–7a(b)). The statute (42 U.S.C. § 1320a–7a(7)) also imposes civil monetary penalties for violations of the Anti-kickback Statute, a subject we address in the next subsection.

There is much overlap among the different statutes and borrowing among them, although some important differences still exist. At this point the most important statute by far is the civil component of the FCA, and for that reason we focus on that part in our examination of false claims for health care services.

United States v. Krizek

111 F.3d 934 (D.C. Cir. 1997)

■ Sentelle, Circuit Judge:

This appeal arises from a civil suit brought by the government against a psychiatrist and his wife under the civil False Claims Act ("FCA"), 31 U.S.C. §§ 3729–3731, and under the common law. The District Court found defendants liable for knowingly submitting false claims and entered judgment against defendants for $168,105.39. The government appealed, and the defendants filed a cross-appeal. We hold that the District Court erred and remand for further proceedings.

I.

The government filed suit against George and Blanka Krizek for, *inter alia,* violations of the civil FCA, 31 U.S.C. §§ 3729–3731. Dr. George Krizek is a psychiatrist who practiced medicine in the District of Columbia. His wife, Blanka Krizek, worked in Dr. Krizek's practice and maintained his billing records. At issue are reimbursement forms submitted by the Krizeks to Pennsylvania Blue Shield ("PBS") in connection with Dr. Krizek's treatment of Medicare and Medicaid patients.

The government's complaint alleged that between January 1986 and March 1992 Dr. Krizek submitted 8,002 false or unlawful requests for reimbursement in an amount exceeding $245,392. The complaint alleged two different types of false claims: first, some of the services provided by Dr. Krizek were medically unnecessary; and second, the Krizeks "upcoded" the reimbursement requests, that is billed the government for more extensive treatments than were, in fact, rendered.

A doctor providing services to a Medicare or Medicaid recipient submits a claim for reimbursement to a Medicare carrier, in this case PBS, on a form known as the "HCFA 1500." The HCFA 1500 requires the doctor to provide his identification number, the patient's information, and a five-digit code identifying the services for which reimbursement is sought. A list of the five-digit codes is contained in the American Medical Association's Current Procedures Terminology Manual ("CPT"). For instance, the Manual notes that the CPT code "90844" is used to request reimbursement for an individual medical psychotherapy session lasting approximately 45 to 50 minutes. The CPT code "90843" indicates individual medical psychotherapy for 20 to 30 minutes. An HCFA 1500 lists those services provided to a single patient, and may include a number of CPT codes when the patient has been treated over several days or weeks.

Before the District Court, the government argued that the amount of time specified by the CPT for each reimbursement code indicates the amount of time spent "face-to-face" with the patient. The government focused on the Krizeks' extensive use of the 90844 code. According to the government, this code should be used only when the doctor spends 45 to 50 minutes with the patient, not including time spent on the phone in consultation with other doctors or time spent discussing the patient with a nurse. The government argued that the Krizeks had used the 90844 code when they should have been billing for shorter, less-involved treatments.

Based on its claims of unnecessary treatment and upcoding the government sought an extraordinary $81 million in damages. This amount included $245,392 in actual damages and civil penalties of $10,000 for each of 8,002 separate CPT codes. During a three-week bench trial, the District Court determined that the case would initially be tried on the basis of seven patients which the government described as representative of the Krizeks' improper coding and treatment practices. *United States v. Krizek,* 1994 U.S. Dist. LEXIS 21095, No. 93–0054 (D.D.C. March 9, 1994) (Protective Order). The determination of liability would then "be equally applicable to all other claims." *Id.* On July 19, 1994, the District Court issued a Memorandum Opinion, *United States v. Krizek,* 859 F. Supp. 5, 8 (D.D.C. 1994) [hereinafter *Krizek I*], holding that the government had not established that the Krizeks submitted claims for unnecessary services. The Court noted that the government's witness failed to interview the patients or any doctors or nurses. The District Court also rejected the government's theory that the Krizeks were liable for requesting reimbursement when some of the billed time was spent out of the presence of the patient. The Court found that it was common and proper practice among psychiatrists to bill for time spent reviewing files, speaking with consulting physicians, etc.

Despite having rejected the government's arguments on these claims, the Court determined that the Krizeks knowingly made false claims in violation of the FCA. The Court found that because of a "seriously deficient" system of recordkeeping the Krizeks "submitted bills for 45–50 minute psychotherapy sessions ... when Dr. Krizek could not have spent the requisite time providing services, face-to-face, or otherwise." *Id.* at 11, 12. For instance, on some occasions within the seven-patient sample, Dr. Krizek submitted claims for over 21 hours of patient treatment within a 24–hour period. The Court stated, "While Dr. Krizek may have been a tireless worker, it is difficult for the Court to comprehend how he could have spent more than even ten hours in a single day serving patients." *Id.* The Court stated that these false statements

> were not "mistakes" nor merely negligent conduct. Under the statutory definition of "knowing" conduct the Court is compelled to conclude that the defendants acted with reckless disregard as to the truth or falsity of the submissions. As such, they will be deemed to have violated the False Claims Act.

Id. at 13–14.

Having found the Krizeks liable within the seven-patient sample, the Court attempted to craft a device for applying the determination of liability to the entire universe of claims. Here, the District Court relied on the testimony of a defense witness that he could not recall submitting more than twelve 90844 codes—nine hours worth of patient treatment—for a single day. Based on this testimony, the District Court stated that nine hours per day was "a fair and reasonably accurate assessment of the time Dr. Krizek actually spent providing patient services." *Id.* The Court, accordingly, determined that the Krizeks would be liable under the FCA on every day in which

> claims were submitted in excess of the equivalent of twelve (12) 90844 claims (nine patient-treatment hours) in a single day and where the defendants cannot establish that Dr. Krizek legitimately devoted the claimed amount of time to patient care on the day in question.

Id. at 14.

On April 6, 1995, the District Court, with the consent of the parties, referred the matter to a Special Master with instructions to investigate the 8,002 challenged CPT codes and, applying the nine-hour presumption, to determine 1) the single damages owed by the Krizeks; 2) the amount of the single damages trebled; 3) the number of false claims submitted by defendants; and 4) the number of false claims multiplied by $5000. *United States v. Krizek,* 1995 U.S. Dist. LEXIS 21531, No. 93–0054 (D.D.C. April 6, 1995) (Order of Reference). After considering evidence submitted by the parties, the Special Master determined that the defendants requested reimbursement for more than nine hours per day of patient treatment on 264 days.

United States v. Krizek, No. 93–0054, at 15 (D.D.C. June 6, 1995) (Special Master Report). The Special Master found single damages of $47,105.39, which when trebled totaled $141,316.17. He then determined to treat each of the 1,149 false code entries as a separate claim, even where several codes were entered on the same HCFA 1500. Multiplied by $5000 per false claim, this approach produced civil penalties of $5,745,000.

After considering motions by the parties, the District Court issued a second opinion, *United States v. Krizek,* 909 F. Supp. 32 (D.D.C. 1995) [hereinafter *Krizek II*], which modified its earlier decision. The Court stated that it accepted the Special Master's factual findings, but was applying a different approach in calculating damages. First, the Court awarded damages of $47,105.38 to the government for unjust enrichment based on the nine-hour presumption. The Court then stated:

> While the Court set a nine hour benchmark to determine which claims were improper, the Court will now set an even higher benchmark for classifying claims that fall under the False Claims Act so that there can be no question as to the falsity of the claims. The Court has determined that the False Claims Act has been violated where claims have been made totaling in excess of twenty-four hours within a single twenty-four hour period and where defendants have provided no explanation for justifying claims made for services rendered virtually around the clock.

Id. at 34. Claims in excess of twenty-four hours of patient treatment per day had been made eleven times in the six-year period. The Court assessed fines of $10,000 for each of the eleven false claims, which, combined with single damages of $47,105.39, totaled $157,105.39. The Court also assessed Special Master's fees against the Krizeks in the amount of $11,000. The government appealed, and the Krizeks cross-appealed. We first turn to the government's appeal.

II.

The government argues that the District Court's use of a twenty-four hour presumption, having earlier announced its intent to use nine hours as the benchmark, prejudiced its prosecution of the claim. We agree and remand for further proceedings.

In *Krizek I,* the District Court found nine hours to be "a fair and reasonably accurate assessment of the time Dr. Krizek actually spent providing patient services" and held that defendants were presumptively liable for all claims in excess of nine hours per day. 859 F. Supp. at 12. Before the Special Master, the government relied on this finding by adopting conservative assumptions that favored the Krizeks. For instance, the government assumed that a 90843 code, indicating a 20 to 30 minute psychotherapy session, would be credited as a 20 minute treatment for determining whether the Krizeks had over-billed. Likewise, the government treated 90844 claims, which indicate 45 to 50 minute sessions, as 45 minutes of patient treatment. Considering the large number of claims submitted on any given day these assumptions may have had a material effect on the damages proved up by the government. However, because the damages were likely to be substantial already, the government chose not to proffer less generous approximations. The government also relied on *Krizek I* by declining to pursue discovery concerning Dr. Krizek's private pay patients. Presumably, if the government had introduced evidence on these additional patients it could have established that the Krizeks billed in excess of twenty-four hours on more days than indicated by Medicare and Medicaid records alone.

The District Court announced its intention to abandon the nine-hour presumption in favor of a stricter benchmark only after receiving the Special Master's Report. While this higher standard may have been permissible, the District Court erred in issuing judgment based on the new presumption without permitting the parties to introduce additional evidence. We do not hold, as urged by the government, that the District Court was prohibited from revisiting its earlier finding and replacing it with the twenty-four hour presumption. We hold instead that, even assuming the District Court was free to revisit this issue, it could not properly do so without allowing the parties to introduce additional evidence.

The government also asserts that the District Court impermissibly disregarded the factual findings of the Special Master in imposing liability for only eleven false claims as opposed to 1,149. We disagree. Under FED. R. CIV. PRO. 53(e)(2) "the court shall accept the master's findings of fact unless clearly erroneous." Findings of a special master are not to be disturbed unless the court "is left with the definite and firm conviction that a mistake has been committed." *Zenith Radio Corp. v. Hazeltine Research, Inc.*, 395 U.S. 100, 123 (1969) (internal quotations omitted); *see also* 9A WRIGHT & MILLER, CIVIL PRACTICE AND PROCEDURE: CIVIL § 2614, at 699 (2nd ed. 1995). However, the Special Master's Report did not determine, as a matter of fact, that 1,149 false claims had been made. His report stated only that, *applying the nine-hour presumption* established by the District Court, 1,149 claims had been made in excess of the benchmark. As the Special Master stated himself, "What I did was try to identify the number of claims in excess of nine hours a day, and pursuant to the Court's earlier ruling, I called those false claims and treated them as false claims." *United States v. Krizek*, 909 F. Supp. 32, 33 (D.D.C. 1995) (Transcript of Hearing). Therefore, the District Court did not reject the factual findings of the Special Master, but only afforded to those findings a different legal consequence.

III.

The Krizeks cross-appeal on the grounds that the District Court erroneously treated each CPT code as a separate "claim" for purposes of computing civil penalties. The Krizeks assert that the claim, in this context, is the HCFA 1500 even when the form contains a number of CPT codes.

The FCA defines "claim" to include

any request or demand, whether under a contract or otherwise, for money or property which is made to a contractor, grantee, or other recipient if the United States Government provides any portion of the money or property which is requested or demanded, or if the Government will reimburse such contractor, grantee, or other recipient for any portion of the money or property which is requested or demanded.

31 U.S.C. § 3729(c). Whether a defendant has made one false claim or many is a fact-bound inquiry that focuses on the specific conduct of the defendant. In *United States v. Bornstein,* 423 U.S. 303, 307 (1976), for instance, the Supreme Court considered the liability of a subcontractor who delivered 21 boxes of falsely labeled electron tubes to the prime contractor in three separate shipments. The prime contractor, in turn, delivered 397 of these tubes to the government and billed the government using 35 invoices. The trial court awarded 35 statutory forfeitures against the subcontractor, one for each invoice. The Court of Appeals reversed, holding that there was only one forfeiture because there had been only one contract. The Supreme Court disagreed with both positions and held that there had been three false claims by the subcontractor, one for each shipment of falsely labeled tubes. *Id.* at 313. The Court stated, "The focus in each case [must] be upon the specific conduct of the person from whom the Government seeks to collect the statutory forfeitures." *Id.* Because the subcontractor committed three separate causative acts—dispatching each shipment of the falsely marked tubes—it would be liable for three separate forfeitures. *Id.; see also United States ex rel. Marcus v. Hess,* 317 U.S. 537, 552 (1943) (holding that the government was entitled to a forfeiture for each project for which a collusive bid was entered even though the bids included additional false forms); *United States v. Grannis,* 172 F.2d 507, 515 (4th Cir.) (assessing ten forfeitures against defendant for each of ten fraudulent vouchers even though the vouchers listed 130 items), *cert. denied,* 337 U.S. 918 (1949).

Bornstein was applied by the United States Court of Claims in *Miller v. United States,* 550 F.2d 17, 24 (Ct.Cl. 1977), another case considering the FCA liability of a contractor. The contractor in *Miller* submitted five monthly billings to the government in which eleven invoices were enclosed. The Court found that there had been five false claims, one for each occasion on which the contractor made a request for payment. 550 F.2d at 23. Similarly, in *United States v. Woodbury,* 359 F.2d 370, 378 (9th Cir. 1966), the Ninth Circuit considered what civil penalties attached to ten false applications for payment when the applications included false invoices. Again, the Court imposed ten penalties, one for each separate submission, even though the false invoices were used to calculate the amount submitted. *Id.* at 377–78.

The gravamen of these cases is that the focus is on the conduct of the defendant. The Courts asks, "With what act did the defendant submit his demand or request and how many such acts were there?" In this case, the

Special Master adopted a position that is inconsistent with this approach. He stated,

> The CPT code, not the HCFA 1500 form, is the source used to permit federal authorities to verify and account for discrete units of medical service provided, billed and paid for. In sum, the government has demanded a specific accounting unit to identify and verify the services provided, payments requested and amounts paid under the Medicare/Medicaid program. The CPT code, not the HCFA 1500 form, is that basic accounting unit.

United States v. Krizek, No. 93–0054, at 21 (D.D.C. June 6, 1995) (Special Master Report). The Special Master concluded that because the government used the CPT code in processing the claims, the CPT code, and not the HCFA 1500 in its entirety, must be the claim. This conclusion, which was later adopted by the District Court, misses the point. The question turns, not on how the government chooses to process the claim, but on how many times the defendants made a "request or demand." 31 U.S.C. § 3729(c). In this case, the Krizeks made a request or demand every time they submitted an HCFA 1500.

Our conclusion that the claim in this context is the HCFA 1500 form is supported by the *structure* of the form itself. The medical provider is asked to supply, along with the CPT codes, the date and place of service, a description of the procedures, a diagnosis code, and the charges. The charges are then totaled to produce one request or demandline 27 asks for total charges, line 28 for amount paid, and line 29 for balance due. The CPT codes function in this context as a type of invoice used to explain how the defendant computed his request or demand.

The government contends that fairness or uniformity concerns support treating each CPT code as a separate claim, arguing that "to count woodenly the number of HCFA 1500 forms submitted by the Krizeks would cede to medical practitioners full authority to control exposure to [FCA] simply by structuring their billings in a particular manner." Precisely so. It is conduct of the medical practitioner, not the disposition of the claims by the *government,* that creates FCA liability. *See Alsco–Harvard Fraud Litigation,* 523 F. Supp. 790, 811 (D.D.C. 1981) (remanding for determination whether invoices were presented for payment at one time or individually submitted as separate demands for payment). Moreover, even if we considered fairness to be a relevant consideration in statutory construction, we would note that the government's definition of claim permitted it to seek an astronomical $81 million worth of damages for alleged actual damages of $245,392. We therefore remand for recalculation of the civil penalty.

The Krizeks also challenge the District Court's definition of claim on the ground that the penalties sought in the complaint would violate the Excessive Fines Clause. U.S. CONST. amend. VIII. Because we hold that the District Court incorrectly defined claim, we do not find it necessary to reach the Krizeks' Excessive Fines argument, in keeping with the principle that courts should avoid unnecessarily deciding constitutional questions. *See Ashwander v. TVA,* 297 U.S. 288 (1936) (Brandeis, J., concurring).

The Krizeks also challenge the District Court's use of a seven-patient sample to determine liability. As mentioned, the District Court did not consider specific evidence as to the truth or falsity of the vast majority of the challenged claims. Instead, the District Court determined to go to trial on the issue of liability using a sample comprised of cases selected by the government. As the Court explained,

> Given the large number of claims, and the acknowledged difficulty of determining the "medical necessity" of 8,002 reimbursement claims, it was decided that this case should initially be tried on the basis of seven patients and two hundred claims that the government believed to be representative of Dr. Krizek's improper coding and treatment practices. It was agreed by the parties that a determination of liability on Dr. Krizek's coding practices would be equally applicable to all 8,002 claims in the complaint.

Krizek I, 859 F. Supp. at 7 (citation omitted). The Krizeks assert that the District Court erred in freeing the government of its burden of proving the falsity of each and every claim. According to the Krizeks, they did not agree that the sample would form the basis of determining liability for the entire universe of claims; they agreed to the seven-patient sample only as a means of testing the government's theories.

We disagree with the Krizeks' interpretation of the scope of their agreement at trial. During a Status Hearing on October 19, 1993, counsel for the Krizeks not only agreed to, but proffered, the idea of going to trial based on a representative sample. At the hearing, the Court discussed with government counsel whether the Court might make an overall determination and then submit the case to a special master. Defense counsel stated,

> Judge, may I say that we did pick out this population or the government finally identified six people. They threw in a seventh for purposes of the summary judgment motion as their best cases. Why can't we try it on those? That is to get 8,336 separate billings for God knows how many patients over six years is—

The Court responded, "You want to try six of them, we'll try six of them." Defense counsel answered "Yes." Government counsel asked, "The seven that we've got, Your Honor?" The Court stated, "Yes, we'll try those seven." Understanding that the parties were agreeing to go to trial based on the seven representative patients, the District Court ordered,

> Having heard argument of the parties, the Court believes that it is unnecessary at this time for the Krizeks to search for and produce all of their records. The government has identified seven patients and two hundred claims for reimbursement that the government believes are representative of the Krizeks' improper coding and treatment practices. All document production for these patients and claims has already occurred. This case will go to trial on this issue of liability using these seven patients as a representative

sample. A determination of liability on the issue of improper coding would be equally applicable to all other claims. As to the allegations of performance of unnecessary services, it may be that further discovery will have to take place to establish liability for the other patients and claims alleged by the government.

United States v. Krizek, 1994 U.S. Dist. LEXIS 21095, No. 93–0054, at 2 (D.D.C. March 9, 1994) (Protective Order). This order met with no contemporaneous objection by the Krizeks. We conclude, therefore, that the Krizeks are bound by their agreement at trial that liability would be based on the seven-patient sample with damages to be extrapolated later.

Having determined that liability was properly determined by the seven-patient sample, we turn now to the question whether, in considering the sample, the District Court applied the appropriate level of scienter. The FCA imposes liability on an individual who "knowingly presents" a "false or fraudulent claim." 31 U.S.C. § 3729(a). A person acts "knowingly" if he:

(1) has actual knowledge of the information;

(2) acts in deliberate ignorance of the truth or falsity of the information; or

(3) acts in reckless disregard of the truth or falsity of the information, and no proof of specific intent to defraud is required

31 U.S.C. § 3729(b). The Krizeks assert that the District Court impermissibly applied the FCA by permitting an aggravated form of gross negligence, "gross negligence-plus," to satisfy the Act's scienter requirement.

In *Saba v. Compagnie Nationale Air France,* 78 F.3d 664 (D.C. Cir. 1996), we considered whether reckless disregard was the equivalent of willful misconduct for purposes of the Warsaw Convention. We noted that reckless disregard lies on a continuum between gross negligence and intentional harm. In some cases, recklessness serves as a proxy for forbidden intent. Id. (citing *SEC v. Steadman,* 967 F.2d 636, 641 (D.C. Cir. 1992)). Such cases require a showing that the defendant engaged in an act known to cause or likely to cause the injury. Use of reckless disregard as a substitute for the forbidden intent prevents the defendant from "deliberately blinding himself to the consequences of his tortious action." *Id.* at 668. In another category of cases, we noted, reckless disregard is "simply a linear extension of gross negligence, a palpable failure to meet the appropriate standard of care." *Id.* In *Saba,* we determined that in the context of the Warsaw Convention, a showing of willful misconduct might be made by establishing reckless disregard such that the subjective intent of the defendant could be inferred.

The question, therefore, is whether "reckless disregard" in this context is properly equated with willful misconduct or with aggravated gross negligence. In determining that gross negligence-plus was sufficient, the District Court cited legislative history equating reckless disregard with gross negligence. A sponsor of the 1986 amendments to the FCA stated,

> Subsection 3 of Section 3729(c) uses the term "reckless disregard of the truth or falsity of the information" which is no different than and has the same meaning as a gross negligence standard that has been applied in other cases. While the Act was not intended to apply to mere negligence, it is intended to apply in situations that could be considered gross negligence where the submitted claims to the Government are prepared in such a sloppy or unsupervised fashion that resulted in overcharges to the Government. The Act is also intended not to permit artful defense counsel to require some form of intent as an essential ingredient of proof. This section is intended to reach the "ostrich-with-his-head-in-the-sand" problem where government contractors hide behind the fact they were not personally aware that such overcharges may have occurred. This is not a new standard but clarifies what has always been the standard of knowledge required.

132 Cong. Rec. H9382–03 (daily ed. Oct. 7, 1986) (statement of Rep. Berman). While we are not inclined to view isolated statements in the legislative history as dispositive, we agree with the thrust of this statement that the best reading of the Act defines reckless disregard as an extension of gross negligence. Section 3729(b)(2) of the Act provides liability for false statements made with deliberate ignorance. If the reckless disregard standard of section 3729(b)(3) served merely as a substitute for willful misconduct—to prevent the defendant from "deliberately blinding himself to the consequences of his tortious action"—section (b)(3) would be redundant since section (b)(2) already covers such struthious conduct. *See Kungys v. United States,* 485 U.S. 759 (1988) (citing the "cardinal rule of statutory interpretation that no provision should be construed to be entirely redundant"). Moreover, as the statute explicitly states that specific intent is not required, it is logical to conclude that reckless disregard in this context is not a "lesser form of intent," *see Steadman,* 967 F.2d at 641–42, but an extreme version of ordinary negligence.

We are unpersuaded by the Krizeks' citation to the rule of lenity to support their reading of the Act. Even assuming that the FCA is penal, the rule of lenity is invoked only when the statutory language is ambiguous. *Deal v. United States,* 508 U.S. 129, 135 (1993). Because we find no ambiguity in the statute's scienter requirement, we hold that the rule of lenity is inapplicable.

We are also unpersuaded by the Krizeks' argument that their conduct did not rise to the level of reckless disregard. The District Court cited a number of factors supporting its conclusion: Mrs. Krizek completed the submissions with little or no factual basis; she made no effort to establish how much time Dr. Krizek spent with any particular patient; and Dr. Krizek "failed utterly" to review bills submitted on his behalf. *Krizek I,* 859 F. Supp. at 13. Most tellingly, there were a number of days within the seven-patient sample when even the shoddiest recordkeeping would have revealed that false submissions were being made—those days on which the Krizeks' billing approached twenty-four hours in a single day. On August

31, 1985, for instance, the Krizeks requested reimbursement for patient treatment using the 90844 code thirty times and the 90843 code once, indicating patient treatment of over 22 hours. Outside the seven-patient sample the Krizeks billed for *more* than twenty-four hours in a single day on three separate occasions. These factors amply support the District Court's determination that the Krizeks acted with reckless disregard.

Finally, we note that Dr. Krizek is no less liable than his wife for these false submissions. As noted, an FCA violation may be established without reference to the subjective intent of the defendant. Dr. Krizek delegated to his wife authority to submit claims on his behalf. In failing "utterly" to review the false submissions, he acted with reckless disregard.

IV.

We, therefore, conclude that the District Court erred in replacing the nine-hour presumption with a twenty-four hour benchmark without providing an opportunity for the litigants to present additional evidence. We also hold that the "claim" in this context is the HCFA 1500 form. We hold that cross-appellants are bound by their stipulation that liability would be determined by the seven-patient sample. In considering this sample the District Court properly interpreted "reckless disregard" to be a linear extension of gross negligence, or "gross negligence-plus." We remand to the District Court for further proceedings consistent with this opinion.

Notes

1. *Finding liability, i.e., the meaning of "false."* The government contended that the Krizeks had submitted 8,002 CPT codes that were false. Was each use of those codes contested? How would one prove that the submission of one such CPT code was false? Did the finding of any liability in the case rest on comparing the time billed for any one patient with Dr. Krizek's notes or some other documentation? What was the basis of liability, then, that the Krizeks had submitted claims that were false? Is the theory in these types of cases that each individual claim is false or that defendants have engaged in a pattern or practice of submitting false claims because they have consistently upcoded or consistently inadequately documented services for which they have billed? Refer back to 42 U.S.C. § 1320a–7a(a)(1)(A) above.

For purposes of finding liability the parties stipulated that a seven-patient sample was representative of the patients treated by Dr. Krizek. The court of appeals refused to allow defendants to escape the consequences of that stipulation. Why was liability in this case tried by using a representative sample? The government will often bring a civil action rather than a criminal case to avoid the protections afforded under criminal procedure and the constitution. *See, e.g.*, James G. Sheehan & Jesse A. Goldner, *Beyond the Anti-kickback Statute: New Entities, New Theories in Healthcare Fraud Enforcement*, 40 J. HEALTH L. 167, 178–79 (2007). If you were defending the Krizeks, would you be careful about entering into such a stipulation? Why? Unlike some contractors, e.g., military contractors building warplanes, health care providers submit a steady stream of small claims rather than one big one. *See, e.g.,* Joan H. Krause, *Health Care Providers and the Public Fisc: Paradigms of Government Harm under the Civil False Claims Act,* 36 GA. L. REV. 121 (2001) [hereinafter Krause, *Health Care Providers and the Public Fisc*]. The much greater risk of exposure from the number of potential claims is amplified by the need to try these cases using representative samples and benchmarks. *See, e.g.,* Timothy Stoltzfus Jost & Sharon L. Davies, *The Empire Strikes Back: A Critique of the Backlash Against Fraud and Abuse Enforcement,* 51 ALA. L. REV. 239, 259–60 (1999) [hereinafter Jost & Davies, *The Empire Strikes Back*].

2. *Scienter.* Citing legislative history that the term "reckless disregard" includes claims submitted in a "sloppy or unsupervised fashion," the court of appeals ruled that reckless disregard is "an extension of gross negligence." What exactly does this mean? How does one divine the nature of evidence required to meet this standard? Of what significance is the court's statement that "Mrs. Krizek completed the submissions with little or no factual basis; she made no effort to establish how much time Dr. Krizek spent with any particular patient; and Dr. Krizek 'failed utterly' to review bills submitted on his behalf. Most tellingly, there were a number of days within the seven-patient sample when even the shoddiest recordkeeping would have revealed that false submissions were being made—those days on which the Krizeks' billing approached twenty-four hours in a single day." Note that the court rejected application of a rule of leniency because it found the statutory language to be unambiguous. Note also that scienter in civil and criminal matters is one of the means by which we adjudicate responsibility.

3. *Damages, i.e., the number of "false claims."* Even though the finding of liability and scienter is grounded in a class of claims submitted, for purposes of deriving damages courts and other decision makers must determine (or estimate?) the number of false claims. Based on expert testimony the district court initially concluded that unless proven otherwise by the Krizeks, the Special Master should assume that any billing of more than twelve 45–50 minute face-to-face sessions in a single day—nine hours of treatment time—was false. The Special Master then came back with 264 days on which false claims were made—requested reimbursement of more than nine hours of patient treatment per day. This resulted in actual damages of $47,105.39, trebled to $141,316.17. The Special Master treated 1,149 CPT codes submitted on those days as false claims, to which a penalty of $5000 per false claim was applied, for a total civil penalty of $5,745,000. Subsequently, for purposes of calculating the civil penalty, the district changed the benchmark used such that claims were proven false only when more than twenty-four hours worth of services was billed for a twenty-four hour day. This yielded three days on which false claims were submitted, for a total of eleven CPT codes, to which a penalty of $10,000 per claim was applied, which coupled with the actual damages of $47,105.39, yielded a total penalty and damages of $157,105.39.

The court of appeals first held that the district court violated rules of procedural fairness in not affording the government the opportunity to introduce additional evidence in light of the changed benchmark. It then held that each HCFA 1500 form constituted a "claim," thereby overruling the district court's holding that each CPT code was a "claim." If the court of appeals had maintained that each CPT code constituted a claim, what potentially would have been the amount of penalties if the 9–hour benchmark was applied? If the 24–hour benchmark was applied? Given that the court of appeals remanded for reconsideration of the civil penalty under the 24–hour benchmark, and given that it held that the district court erred in treating each CPT code as a "claim," which side benefitted from the appellate court's ruling on calculation of the civil penalty?

The FCA defines a "claim" as a "request or demand for money." 31 U.S.C. § 3729(c). Does that definition help resolve the question? The court of appeals, purportedly following precedent, wrote that the number of claims "is a fact-bound inquiry that focuses on the specific conduct of the defendant" in which the appropriate question is, " 'With what act did the defendant submit his demand or request and how many such acts were there?' " Does that reasoning resolve the question? The Special Master stated that the HCFA 1500 form "is the source used to permit federal authorities to verify and account for discrete units of medical services provided, billed and paid for." Is the observation that the HCFA 1500 is a "source" a step in the reasoning process or a conclusion? If the latter, on what is it based? Responding to the government's contention that use of the HCFA 1500 form would allow health care providers to control their exposure to FCA by structuring their billings in a certain way, the court of appeals wrote, "even if we considered fairness to be a relevant consideration in statutory construction, we would note that the government's definition of claim permitted it to seek an astronomical $81 million worth of damages for alleged actual damages of $245,392." Although the court of appeals rejected a rule of leniency with regard to the scienter requirement—i.e., whether the Krizeks could be found liable at all for submitting any false claims—is its conclusion regarding the number of claims filed anything more than a means to monitor the penal aspect of the FCA?

Given that in these cases liability is grounded in a sample that establishes a pattern, and then damages and penalties are derived from inferences about how that sample can be universalized over a much larger number of claims, the nature of those inferences is crucial. The PATH audits, the subject of situation #4 above, illustrate these stakes in that results from a limited audit sample of one hundred randomly selected inpatient admissions were, through statistical methods, extrapolated to determine liability over an enormously larger number of claims. *See generally* U.S. GENERAL ACCOUNTING OFFICE, GAO/HEHS–98–174, CONCERNS WITH PHYSICIANS AT TEACHING HOSPITALS (PATH) AUDITS 98–174 (http://www.gao.gov/products/HEHS–98–174). Potentially each institution could have been liable for hundreds of millions of dollars for even a very small error rate such as two percent. See Bucy, *The Path from Regulator to Hunter.*

4. *Prosecutorial discretion.* To what extent was the program's fiscal integrity or the monitoring of utilization or quality of care furthered by the government's suing the Krizeks for $81 million? Does such litigation serve the ends of deterrence, recoupment of funds, or even retribution? Many scholars of criminal law believe that deterrence is more a function of the calculated likelihood of getting caught than the severity of punishment. Should resources be directed toward prosecuting the Krizeks—or making litigation against them of such high stakes—or toward ferreting out other activity, particularly the big-ticket items described in situations #1, 4, and 7. On the other hand, if repeated on a large scale, don't the losses represented by the other situations really add up? Regardless, it may be true that providers' complaints about increased fraud enforcement is indeed an instance of The Empire striking back, see Jost & Davies, *The Empire Strikes Back*, but do the Krizeks strike you as Darth Vader masquerading in Yoda's garb? For a vivid and disturbing description of this extremely sad litigation, see Thomas L. Greaney & Joan H. Krause, *United States v. Krizek*, *in* HEALTH LAW & BIOETHICS 187 (Sandra H. Johnson et al., eds., 2009).

United States ex rel. Mikes v. Straus

274 F.3d 687 (2d Cir. 2001)

■ CARDAMONE, CIRCUIT JUDGE:

On this appeal we review a complaint asserting violations of the False Claims Act (Act), 31 U.S.C. § 3729 *et seq.* (1994), brought by a plaintiff employee against her former employers, who are health care providers. The appeal raises issues of first impression in this Circuit concerning the applicability of medical standards of care to the Act.

Congress enacted the False Claims Act after disclosure of widespread fraud during the War–Between–The–States revealed that the union government had been billed for nonexistent or worthless goods, had been charged exorbitant prices, and had its treasury plundered by profiteering defense contractors. In 1986 the Act was substantially amended to combat fraud in the fields of defense and health care. As of February 2000 over half of the $3.5 billion recovered since that amendment derived from cases alleging fraud against the Department of Health and Human Services.

The Act contains a *qui tam* provision designed to encourage private individuals to file suit by offering them a percentage of any money recovered. Those persons bringing a *qui tam* suit are known colloquially as whistle-blowers. The plaintiff in this case purports to blow the whistle on those practices of her employers she believes violate the Medicare statute, payment for which would defraud the government. Regardless of whether such suit is successful or unsuccessful (and here it is unsuccessful), a tale-bearer stands out, and risks being thought as bad as those alleged to be the tale-makers.

BACKGROUND

A. *Facts*

In 1991 defendants Dr. Marc J. Straus, Dr. Jeffrey Ambinder and Dr. Eliot L. Friedman, physicians specializing in oncology and hematology, formed a partnership called Pulmonary and Critical Care Associates to extend their practice to include pulmonology, the branch of medicine covering the lungs and related breathing functions. In July of that year defendants hired plaintiff Dr. Patricia S. Mikes, a board-certified pulmonologist, to provide pulmonary and critical care services in defendants' offices in Westchester and Putnam Counties, New York. In September 1991 Mikes discussed with Dr. Straus her concerns relating to spirometry tests being performed in defendants' offices. Three months later, plaintiff was fired.

The parties dispute the reason for Mikes' termination. Plaintiff says she was fired because she questioned how defendants conducted their medical practice. Defendants declare that Mikes' employment agreement provided she was terminable-at-will, and that plaintiff had difficulty procuring privileges at area hospitals.

On April 16, 1992 Mikes commenced the instant litigation against defendants in the United States District Court for the Southern District of New York, asserting not only causes of action for retaliatory discharge and unlawfully withheld wages, but also a *qui tam* suit under the False Claims Act. She served the complaint on the United States Attorney who, on April 19, 1993, notified the district court that it declined its statutory right to substitute for Mikes in the prosecution of this litigation. *See* 31 U.S.C. § 3730 (b)(2), (b)(4)(B).

B. *Prior Proceedings*

Plaintiff's *qui tam* cause of action under the Act alleged that defendants had submitted false reimbursement requests to the federal government for spirometry services. Plaintiff contended that defendants' failure to calibrate the spirometers rendered the results so unreliable as to be "false" under the Act. In addition, Mikes averred that spirometry is an eligible service under the Medicare statute, and that defendants submitted Medicare claims for reimbursement during the period relevant to this dispute—now said to be 1034 claims from 1986 through 1993—for a total Medicare payout of $28,922.89.

Defendants moved for summary judgment. In granting defendants' motion, the district court ruled that submitting a claim for a service that was not provided in accordance with the relevant standard of care does not make that claim false or fraudulent for False Claims Act purposes. Defendants' submission of claims for reimbursement, the court continued, did not implicitly certify that their performance of spirometry conformed to any qualitative standard. And, it concluded, that even were the Medicare claims objectively false, plaintiff had not shown defendants submitted the claims with the requisite scienter.

C. *Spirometry*

Before turning to a discussion of the law, it will be helpful to define spirometry—a subject that lies at the heart of this case—and plaintiff's allegations regarding defendants' performance of this diagnostic test. Spirometry is an easy-to-perform pulmonary function test used by doctors to detect both obstructive (such as asthma and emphysema) and restrictive (such as pulmonary fibrosis) lung diseases. The type of spirometers used by defendants measures the pressure change when a patient blows into a mouthpiece, thereby providing the doctor with on-the-spot analysis of the volume and speed by which patients can exhale. The spirometry equipment consists of readily transportable lightweight machines, and defendants apparently used at least one in each of their several offices.

Plaintiff's expert stated that spirometers are susceptible to inaccuracy through time and usage because they become clogged, causing false readings. Erroneous measurements may also arise from damage to the instrument through cleaning or disturbance during transport, or from variations in barometric pressure, temperature or humidity. Mikes claims that guidelines first published in 1979 and later updated in 1987 and 1994 by the American Thoracic Society (ATS guidelines), a division of the American Lung Association, set out the generally accepted standards for spirometry. To ensure accuracy, these guidelines recommend daily calibration of spirometers by use of a three liter calibration syringe, the performance of three successive trials during test administration and the appropriate training of spirometer technicians. In support of her contention that the ATS guidelines are the medical standard for spirometry, Mikes notes they are incorporated by reference in the federal Longshore and Harbor Workers' Compensation Act, 33 U.S.C. § 902(10) (1994), and included in regulations promulgated pursuant to the Social Security Act, *see* 20 C.F.R. pt. 404, subpt. P, app. 1, pt. A, § 3.00(E) (2001), the Radiation Exposure Compensation Act, *see* 28 C.F.R. § 79.36(d)(1)(ii)(B)(1) (2001), and the Federal Mine Safety and Health Act, 52 Fed. Reg. 34,460, 34,551 (Sept. 11, 1987).

Mikes maintains further that defendants' performance of spirometry did not conform to the ATS guidelines and thus would yield inherently unreliable data. She argues that defendants allowed medical assistants to perform spirometry tests when they were not trained in its proper administration. Plaintiff states she personally observed the medical assistants fail to calibrate the spirometer daily and that she was informed the assistants could not recall the last time the machine had been calibrated. Moreover, defendants did not possess a three liter calibration syringe, nor did the assistants properly instruct the patients during the administration of the test or perform three successive tests.

Defendants insist that after plaintiff raised her concerns regarding the spirometer and its use in their practice, they told her to review exam results for inaccuracy, and to train the medical assistants in proper spirometric administration. Dr. Straus reports that plaintiff did not apprise the practice of any false readings in response to this directive, nor did she supervise the medical assistants. With this factual background, we turn to the law.

DISCUSSION

I Elements of Plaintiff's False Claims Act Causes of Action

Mikes challenges the district court's grant of summary judgment to defendants that resulted in the dismissal of her False Claims Act causes of action.

Liability under the False Claims Act occurs when a person

> (1) knowingly presents, or causes to be presented, to an officer or employee of the United States Government ... a false or fraudulent claim for payment or approval;

> (2) knowingly makes, uses, or causes to be made or used, a false record or statement to get a false or fraudulent claim paid or approved by the Government; [or]

> (3) conspires to defraud the Government by getting a false or fraudulent claim allowed or paid.

31 U.S.C. § 3729(a). Plaintiff brought suit under each of these subdivisions, but since our analysis applies equally to all three, we limit discussion primarily to the first. As the language of that subdivision makes clear, to impose liability under the Act Mikes must show that defendants (1) made a claim, (2) to the United States government, (3) that is false or fraudulent, (4) knowing of its falsity, and (5) seeking payment from the federal treasury.

The Act expansively defines the term "claim" to cover "any request or demand, whether under a contract or otherwise, for money or property ... if the United States Government provides any portion of the money or property which is requested or demanded." 31 U.S.C. § 3729(c). As required by the Medicare implementing regulations, *see* 42 C.F.R. § 424.32 (2000), defendants submitted Medicare reimbursement claims for spirometry on form "HCFA–1500" or an electronic equivalent. Each submission of the HCFA–1500 form meets the first two elements of a False Claims Act cause of action in that it qualifies as a claim made to the United States government. *See United States v. Krizek*, 111 F.3d 934, 940 (D.C. Cir. 1997) (holding that number of claims under Act based upon submission of HCFA–1500 forms).

Regarding the third element, the term "false or fraudulent" is not defined in the Act. A common definition of "fraud" is "an intentional misrepresentation, concealment, or nondisclosure for the purpose of inducing another in reliance upon it to part with some valuable thing belonging to him or to surrender a legal right." *Webster's Third New International Dictionary* 904 (1981). "False" can mean "not true," "deceitful," or "tending to mislead." *Id.* at 819. The juxtaposition of the word "false" with the word "fraudulent," plus the meanings of the words comprising the phrase "false claim," suggest an improper claim is aimed at extracting money the government otherwise would not have paid. *See* Clarence T.

Kipps, Jr. *et al.*, *Materiality as an Element of Liability Under the False Claims Act*, A.B.A. Center for Continuing Legal Educ. Nat'l Inst. (1998), WL N98CFCB ABA–LGLED B–37, B–46 ("[A] claim cannot be determined to be true or false without consideration of whether the decisionmaker should pay the claim—that is, a claim is 'false' only if the Government or other customer would not pay the claim if the facts about the misconduct alleged to have occurred were known.").

This notion also applies to subdivisions (2) & (3) of 31 U.S.C. § 3729(a). The former prohibits a party from knowingly using or making "a false record or statement *to get a false or* fraudulent *claim paid or approved* by the Government," *id.* § 3729(a)(2) (emphasis added), while the latter prohibits conspiring "to defraud the Government *by getting a false or fraudulent claim allowed or paid*," *id.* § 3729(a)(3) (emphasis added). The language of these provisions plainly links the wrongful activity to the government's decision to pay.

On this appeal, the parties' [sic] dispute whether defendants' Medicare claims rise to the level of being false or fraudulent. They disagree, in addition, as to the fourth element—*i.e.*, whether any false or fraudulent claims were "knowingly" made. The Act defines "knowingly" as either: (1) possessing actual knowledge; (2) acting in deliberate ignorance of falsity; or (3) acting in reckless disregard of falsity. *See id.* § 3729(b).

The fifth element of the Act further supports the conclusion that the statute reaches only those claims with the potential wrongfully to cause the government to disburse money. The Senate Report accompanying the 1986 amendments to the Act states that "the purpose of [the amendments] is to enhance the Government's ability to recover losses sustained as a result of fraud against the Government." S. Rep. No. 99–345, at 1, *reprinted in* 1986 U.S.C.C.A.N. 5266, 5266. The Supreme Court has further indicated that the Act's primary purpose is to indemnify the government—through its restitutionary penalty provisions—against losses caused by a defendant's fraud. *See United States ex rel. Marcus v. Hess*, 317 U.S. 537, 549, 551–52 (1943). With these understandings of the Act's language in mind, we turn to plaintiff's contentions.

II "Legally False" Certification Theory

The thrust of plaintiff's *qui tam* suit is that the submission of Medicare reimbursement claims for spirometry procedures not performed in accordance with the relevant standard of care, that is, the ATS Guidelines— violates the False Claims Act. Mikes relies principally on the "certification theory" of liability, which is predicated upon a false representation of compliance with a federal statute or regulation or a prescribed contractual term. *See* Lisa Michelle Phelps, Note, *Calling off the Bounty Hunters: Discrediting the Use of Alleged Anti–Kickback Violations to Support Civil False Claims Actions*, 51 Vand. L. Rev. 1003, 1014–15 (1998). This theory has also been called "legally false" certification. *See* Robert Fabrikant & Glenn E. Solomon, *Application of the Federal False Claims Act to Regulatory Compliance Issues in the Health Care Industry*, 51 Ala. L. Rev. 105, 111– 12 (1999). It differs from "factually false" certification, which involves an incorrect description of goods or services provided or a request for reimbursement for goods or services never provided. *Id.*

Although the False Claims Act is "not designed to reach every kind of fraud practiced on the Government," *United States v. McNinch*, 356 U.S. at 599, it was intended to embrace at least some claims that suffer from legal falsehood. Thus, "a false claim may take many forms, the most common being a claim for goods or services not provided, or *provided in violation of contract terms, specification, statute, or regulation.*" S. Rep. No. 99–345, at 9, *reprinted in* 1986 U.S.C.C.A.N. 5266, 5274 (emphasis added).

Just as clearly, a claim for reimbursement made to the government is not legally false simply because the particular service furnished failed to comply with the mandates of a statute, regulation or contractual term that is only tangential to the service for which reimbursement is sought. Since the Act is restitutionary and aimed at retrieving ill-begotten funds, it would be anomalous to find liability when the alleged noncompliance would not have influenced the government's decision to pay. Accordingly, while the Act is "intended to reach all types of fraud, without qualification, that might result in financial loss to the Government," *United States v. Neifert–White Co.*, 390 U.S. 228, 232 (1968), it does not encompass those instances of regulatory noncompliance that are irrelevant to the government's disbursement decisions.

We join the Fourth, Fifth, Ninth, and District of Columbia Circuits in ruling that a claim under the Act is legally false only where a party certifies compliance with a statute or regulation as a condition to governmental payment. *See United States ex rel. Siewick v. Jamieson Sci. & Eng'g, Inc.*, 214 F.3d 1372, 1376 (D.C. Cir. 2000) ("[A] false certification of compliance with a statute or regulation cannot serve as the basis for a *qui tam* action under the [False Claims Act] unless payment is conditioned on that certification."); *Harrison*, 176 F.3d at 786–87, 793; *United States ex rel. Thompson v. Columbia/HCA Healthcare Corp.*, 125 F.3d 899, 902 (5th Cir. 1997); *United States ex rel. Hopper v. Anton*, 91 F.3d 1261, 1266–67 (9th Cir. 1996).

We add that although materiality is a related concept, our holding is distinct from a requirement imposed by some courts that a false statement or claim must be material to the government's funding decision. *See, e.g., Harrison*, 176 F.3d at 785. A materiality requirement holds that only a subset of admittedly false claims is subject to False Claims Act liability. *Cf. United States ex rel. Cantekin v. Univ. of Pittsburgh*, 192 F.3d 402, 415 (3d Cir. 1999), *cert. denied*, 531 U.S. 880 (2000) (finding that *Hopper* held that not every regulatory violation is a "knowingly false statement" and distinguishing this holding from a materiality requirement). We rule simply that not all instances of regulatory noncompliance will cause a claim to become false. We need not and do not address whether the Act contains a separate materiality requirement.

A. *Express False Certification*

We analyze first plaintiff's argument that defendants' claims contained an express false certification. An expressly false claim is, as the term suggests, a claim that falsely certifies compliance with a particular statute, regulation or contractual term, where compliance is a prerequisite to payment.

Plaintiff contends that by submitting claims for Medicare reimbursement on HCFA–1500 forms or their electronic equivalent, defendants expressly certified that they would comply with the terms set out on the form. Form HCFA–1500 expressly says: "I certify that the services shown on this form were medically indicated and necessary for the health of the patient and were personally furnished by me or were furnished incident to my professional service by my employee under my immediate personal supervision." Both the form, which further provides "No Part B Medicare benefits may be paid unless this form is received as required by existing law and regulations," and the Medicare Regulations, *see* 42 C.F.R. § 424.32, state that certification is a precondition to Medicare reimbursement. We agree that defendants certified they would comply with the terms on the form and that such compliance was a precondition of governmental payment. *Cf. United States ex rel. Piacentile v. Wolk*, 1995 U.S. Dist. LEXIS 580, Civ.A.No.93–5773, 1995 WL 20833, at *2–3 (E.D. Pa. Jan. 17, 1995) (finding False Claims Act violation where defendant altered Medicare Certificates of Medical Necessity without doctor's authorization, because the forms contained a certification that the claims represented the physician's judgment).

Yet plaintiff's objections to defendants' spirometry tests do not implicate the standard set out in the HCFA–1500 form that the procedure was dictated by "medical necessity." The term "medical necessity" does not impart a qualitative element mandating a particular standard of medical care, and Mikes does not point to any legal authority requiring us to read such a mandate into the form. Medical necessity ordinarily indicates the level—not the quality—of the service. For example, the requisite level of medical necessity may not be met where a party contends that a particular procedure was deleterious or performed solely for profit, *see United States ex rel. Kneepkins v. Gambro Healthcare, Inc.*, 115 F. Supp.2d 35, 41–42 (D. Mass. 2000) (procedures chosen solely for defendants' economic gain are not "medically necessary" as required by claim submission form), or where a party seeks reimbursement for a procedure that is not traditionally covered, *see Rush v. Parham*, 625 F.2d 1150, 1156 (5th Cir. 1980) (upholding state's exclusion of experimental medical treatment from definition of "medically necessary" services under Medicaid).

This approach to the phrase "medically necessary"—as applying to *ex ante* coverage decisions but not *ex post* critiques of how providers executed a procedure—would also conform to our understanding of the phrase "reasonable and necessary" as used in the Medicare statute, 42 U.S.C. § 1395y(a)(1)(A) (1994) (disallowing payment for items or services not reasonable and necessary for diagnosis or treatment). *See New York ex rel. Bodnar v. Sec'y of Health & Human Servs.*, 903 F.2d 122, 125 (2d Cir. 1990) (acknowledging Secretary's authority, in determining whether procedure is "reasonable and necessary," to consider type of service provided and whether service was provided in appropriate, cost-effective setting); *Goodman v. Sullivan*, 891 F.2d 449, 450–51 (2d Cir. 1989) (per curiam) (affirming exclusion of experimental procedures from Medicare coverage pursuant to requirement that procedures be "reasonable and necessary"); *see also Friedrich v. Sec'y of Health & Human Servs.*, 894 F.2d 829, 831 (6th Cir. 1990) (noting that the Health Care Financing Administration, when determining whether a procedure is "reasonable and necessary," considers the procedure's safety, effectiveness, and acceptance by medical community).

Moreover, the section of the Medicare statute setting forth conditions of participation has separate provisions governing the medical necessity of a given procedure and its quality. *Compare* 42 U.S.C. § 1320c–5(a)(1) (1994) (practitioner shall assure that the service "will be provided economically and only when, and to the extent, medically necessary"), *with id.* § 1320c–5(a)(2) (1994) (practitioner shall assure that the service "will be of a quality which meets professionally recognized standards of health care"). This statutory design supports the conclusion that the medical necessity for a procedure and its quality are distinct considerations.

Inasmuch as Mikes challenges only the quality of defendants' spirometry tests and not the decisions to order this procedure for patients, she fails to support her contention that the tests were not medically necessary. Nor has she proffered evidence to support an allegation that the defendants did not "personally furnish" the spirometry tests as required by the HCFA–1500 form. The form allows for reimbursement when a procedure is "rendered under the physician's immediate personal supervision by his/her employee," which covers the medical assistants' performance of spirometry at defendants' direction. Thus, plaintiff's cause of action insofar as it is founded on express false certification is without merit.

B. *Implied False Certification*

1. *Viability of Implied Certification Theory*

Plaintiff insists that defendants' submissions to the government for payment were impliedly false certifications. An implied false certification claim is based on the notion that the act of submitting a claim for reimbursement itself implies compliance with governing federal rules that are a precondition to payment. *See* Phelps, *supra*, at 1015. Foundational support for the implied false certification theory may be found in Congress' expressly stated purpose that the Act include at least some kinds of legally false claims, *see* S. Rep. No. 99–345, at 9, *reprinted in* 1986 U.S.C.C.A.N. 5266, 5274, and in the Supreme Court's admonition that the Act intends to reach all forms of fraud that might cause financial loss to the government, *see Neifert–White Co.*, 390 U.S. at 232.

The implied certification theory was applied in *Ab–Tech Construction, Inc. v. United States*, 31 Fed. Cl. 429 (Fed. Cl. 1994), *aff'd*, 57 F.3d 1084 (Fed. Cir. 1995) (unpublished table decision). The Court of Federal Claims held that the defendants' submission of payment vouchers, although containing no express representation, implicitly certified their continued adherence to the eligibility requirements of a federal small business statutory program. *See id.* at 434. The failure by defendants to honor the terms of this certification rendered their claims for payment false, resulting in False Claims Act liability. *See id.* at 433–34.

But caution should be exercised not to read this theory expansively and out of context. The *Ab–Tech* rationale, for example, does not fit comfortably into the health care context because the False Claims Act was not designed for use as a blunt instrument to enforce compliance with all medical regulations—but rather only those regulations that are a precondition to payment—and to construe the impliedly false certification theory in an expansive fashion would improperly broaden the Act's reach. Moreover, a limited application of implied certification in the health care field reconciles, on the one hand, the need to enforce the Medicare statute with, on the other hand, the active role actors outside the federal government play in assuring that appropriate standards of medical care are met. Interests of federalism counsel that "the regulation of health and safety matters is primarily, and historically, a matter of local concern." *Hillsborough County v. Automated Med. Labs., Inc.*, 471 U.S. 707, 719 (1985); *accord Medtronic, Inc. v. Lohr*, 518 U.S. 470, 475 (1996).

Moreover, permitting *qui tam* plaintiffs to assert that defendants' quality of care failed to meet medical standards would promote federalization of medical malpractice, as the federal government or the *qui tam* relator would replace the aggrieved patient as plaintiff. *See* Patrick A. Scheiderer, Note, *Medical Malpractice as a Basis for a False Claims Action?*, 33 Ind. L. Rev. 1077, 1098–99 (2000). Beyond that, we observe that the courts are not the best forum to resolve medical issues concerning levels of care. State, local or private medical agencies, boards and societies are better suited to monitor quality of care issues. *See* Fabrikant & Solomon, *supra*, at 156–57.

For these reasons, we think a medical provider should be found to have implicitly certified compliance with a particular rule as a condition of reimbursement in limited circumstances. Specifically, implied false certification is appropriately applied only when the underlying statute or regulation upon which the plaintiff relies *expressly* states the provider must comply in order to be paid. *See Siewick*, 214 F.3d at 1376 (holding that court will "infer certification from silence" only when "certification was a prerequisite to the government action sought"). Liability under the Act may properly be found therefore when a defendant submits a claim for reimbursement while knowing—as that term is defined by the Act, *see* 31 U.S.C. § 3729(b)—that payment expressly is precluded because of some noncompliance by the defendant.

2. *Plaintiff's Allegations Under the Implied Theory*

Mikes asserts that compliance with §§ 1395y(a)(1)(A) and 1320c–5(a) of the Medicare statute is a precondition to a request for federal funds and that submission of a HCFA–1500 form attests by implication to the providers' compliance with both of those provisions.

a. *§ 1395y(a)(1)(A).* Section 1395y(a)(1)(A) of the Medicare statute states that "no payment may be made under [the Medicare statute] for any expenses incurred for items or services which … are not *reasonable and necessary* for the diagnosis or treatment of illness or injury or to improve the functioning of a malformed body member." 42 U.S.C. § 1395y(a)(1)(A) (emphasis added). Because this section contains an express condition of payment—that is, "no payment may be made"—it explicitly links each Medicare *payment* to the requirement that the particular item or service be "reasonable and necessary." The Supreme Court has noted that this section precludes the government from reimbursing a Medicare provider who fails to comply. *See Heckler v. Ringer*, 466 U.S. 602, 605 (1984); *see also United Seniors Ass'n v. Shalala*, 182 F.3d 965, 967 (D.C. Cir. 1999) ("If a service is deemed not to have been reasonable and necessary, Medicare will not make payment and the doctor generally is prohibited from charging the patient."); *Mount Sinai Hosp., Inc. v. Weinberger*, 517 F.2d 329, 334 (5th Cir. 1975) (explaining that § 1395y controls whether particular services are covered by Medicare). Since § 1395y(a)(1)(A) *expressly* prohibits payment if a provider fails to comply with its terms, defendants' submission of the claim forms implicitly certifies compliance with its provision.

Yet, Mikes' insistence that defendants' performance of spirometry was not reasonable and necessary is without support. As set forth in our discussion of express certification, the requirement that a service be reasonable and necessary generally pertains to the selection of the particular procedure and not to its performance. *See Goodman*, 891 F.2d at 450–51. While such factors as the effectiveness and medical acceptance of a given procedure might determine whether it is reasonable and necessary, the failure of the procedure to conform to a particular standard of care ordinarily will not. *See id.* at 450 (noting that under § 1395(y)(a)(1)(A) the Secretary of Health and Human Services prohibits "payment of benefits for any experimental, investigational, or unproven treatment or diagnostic method not yet generally accepted in the medical profession"). Since plaintiff contends only that defendants' performance of spirometry was *qualitatively* deficient, her allegations that defendants falsely certified compliance with § 1395y(a)(1)(A) may not succeed.

b. *§ 1320c–5(a).* Plaintiff's implied false certification claims rely more heavily upon § 1320c–5(a). That section does mandate a qualitative standard of care in that it provides

> It shall be the obligation of any health care practitioner … who provides health care services for which payment may be made … to assure, to the extent of his authority that services or items ordered or provided by such practitioner …
>
> (1) will be provided economically and only when, and to the extent, medically necessary;
>
> (2) *will be of a quality which meets professionally recognized standards of health care*; and

CHAPTER 24   HEALTH CARE FRAUD AND ABUSE

(3) will be supported by evidence of medical necessity and quality ... as may reasonably be required by a reviewing peer review organization in the exercise of its duties and responsibilities.

42 U.S.C. § 1320c–5(a) (emphasis added).

Mikes avers that the ATS guidelines comprise a "professionally recognized standard of health care" for spirometry, and that defendants' failure to conform to those guidelines violates the Medicare statute. She believes defendants, by submitting HCFA–1500 forms for spirometry tests that did not comply with the ATS guidelines, engaged in implied false certification. But plaintiff's allegations cannot establish liability under the False Claims Act because—unlike § 1395y(a)(1)(A)—the Medicare statute does not explicitly condition payment upon compliance with § 1320c–5(a).

Instead, § 1320c–5(a) simply states that "it shall be the obligation" of a practitioner who provides a medical service "for which payment may be made ... to assure" compliance with the section. Hence, it may be seen that § 1320c–5(a) acts prospectively, setting forth obligations for a provider to be eligible to participate in the Medicare program. *See Fischer v. United States*, 529 U.S. 667 (2000) (describing § 1320c–5(a) as a statutory obligation to qualify to participate in the Medicare program); *see also Corkill v. Shalala*, 109 F.3d 1348, 1350 (9th Cir. 1997) ("In order to qualify for reimbursement under the Medicare program, a physician must comply with three statutory requirements [including § 1320c–5(a)].").

The structure of the statute further informs us that § 1320c–5(a) establishes conditions of participation, rather than prerequisites to receiving reimbursement. The statute empowers peer review organizations to monitor providers' compliance with § 1320c–5(a). *See* 42 U.S.C. § 1320c–3(a) (1994). If a peer review organization determines that a provider has "failed in a substantial number of cases" to comply with the requirements of § 1320c–5(a) or that the provider has "grossly and flagrantly violated" the section, the organization may—after reasonable notice and an opportunity for corrective action—recommend sanctions. *See id.* § 1320c–5(b)(1) (1994 & Supp. V 1999). If the Secretary agrees that sanctions should be imposed, and further finds the provider unwilling or unable substantially to comply with its obligations, the Secretary may exclude the provider from the Medicare program. *See id.*; *see also Doyle v. Sec'y of Health & Human Servs.*, 848 F.2d 296, 298 (1st Cir. 1988) (explaining statutory and regulatory procedures).

The fact that § 1320c–5(b) permits sanctions for a failure to maintain an appropriate standard of care only where a dereliction occurred in "a substantial number of cases" or a violation was especially "gross[] and flagrant[]" makes it evident that the section is directed at the provider's continued eligibility in the Medicare program, rather than any individual incident of noncompliance. *See* Fabrikant & Solomon, *supra*, at 122–23 (arguing that quality of care standards are conditions of participation in the Medicare program and not conditions of payment). This conclusion is reinforced by the ultimate sanction provided by § 1320c–5(b)(1): exclusion of the provider from Medicare eligibility. Further, the section explicitly provides that the Secretary may authorize an alternate remedy—repayment of the cost of the noncompliant service to the United States—"as a condition to the continued eligibility" of the health care provider in the Medicare program. 42 U.S.C. § 1320c–5(b)(3). Accordingly, § 1320c–5(a) is quite plainly a condition of participation in the Medicare program.

Since § 1320c–5(a) does not expressly condition *payment* on compliance with its terms, defendants' certifications on the HCFA–1500 forms are not legally false. Consequently, defendants did not submit impliedly false claims by requesting reimbursement for spirometry tests that allegedly were not performed according to the recognized standards of health care.

Finally, our holding—that in submitting a Medicare reimbursement form, a defendant implicitly certifies compliance with § 1395y(a)(1)(A), but not § 1320c–5(a)—comports with Congress' purpose as discussed earlier in this opinion. Section 1395y(a)(1)(A) mandates that a provider's choice of procedures be "reasonable and necessary"; it does not obligate federal courts to step outside their primary area of competence and apply a qualitative standard measuring the efficacy of those procedures. The quality of care standard of § 1320c–5(a) is best enforced by those professionals most versed in the nuances of providing adequate health care.

III Worthless Services Claim

The government in its *amicus* brief and plaintiff at oral argument argue that the district court erred by not considering whether the defendants' submission of Medicare claims for substandard spirometry essentially constituted requests for the reimbursement of worthless services. An allegation that defendants violated the Act by submitting claims for worthless services is not predicated upon the false certification theory. Instead, a worthless services claim asserts that the knowing request of federal reimbursement for a procedure with no medical value violates the Act irrespective of any certification.

The Ninth Circuit's recent decision in *United States ex rel. Lee v. Smithkline Beecham, Inc.*, 245 F.3d 1048 (9th Cir. 2001), is the leading case on worthless services claims in the health care arena. In *Lee*, the relator alleged that defendant, an operator of regional clinical laboratories, falsified laboratory test data when test results fell outside the acceptable standard of error. The Ninth Circuit held that the false certification theory addressed in *Hopper*, 91 F.3d 1261, was only one form of action under the Act, and that the district court should have considered the distinct and separate worthless services claim. *Lee*, 245 F.3d at 1053. As the Ninth Circuit explained, "in an appropriate case, knowingly billing for worthless services or recklessly doing so with deliberate ignorance may be actionable under § 3729 [of the False Claims Act], regardless of any false certification conduct." *Id.*

We agree that a worthless services claim is a distinct claim under the Act. It is effectively derivative of an allegation that a claim is factually false because it seeks reimbursement for a service not provided. *See* Fabrikant &

Solomon, *supra*, at 111–12. In a worthless services claim, the performance of the service is so deficient that for all practical purposes it is the equivalent of no performance at all.

We nevertheless find no liability in the instant case because plaintiff makes no showing that defendants knowingly—as the Act defines that term—submitted a claim for the reimbursement of worthless services. We have adopted the Ninth Circuit's standard that the "requisite intent is the knowing presentation of what is known to be false" as opposed to negligence or innocent mistake. *Hagood v. Sonoma County Water Agency*, 81 F.3d 1465, 1478 (9th Cir. 1996) (quoted in *United States ex rel. Kreindler & Kreindler v. United Techs. Corp.*, 985 F.2d 1148, 1156 (2d Cir. 1993)).

Plaintiff fails to substantiate that defendants knew their Medicare claims for reimbursement were false. At best, plaintiff urges that defendants submitted Medicare claims knowing they did not conform to the ATS guidelines. This allegation alone fails to satisfy the standard for a worthless services claim. The notion of presenting a claim known to be false does not mean the claim is incorrect as a matter of proper accounting, but rather means it is a lie. *See id.* Defendants have presented such overwhelming evidence of their genuine belief that their use of spirometry had medical value, we conclude as a matter of law they did not submit their claims with the requisite scienter.

Initially, the defendants claim to have relied upon the spirometers' instruction manual which—contrary to the ATS guidelines—indicates that daily calibration is not required. Beside the heading "calibration," the manual provides that "the equipment is properly calibrated at the time of shipment so that no calibration is required except for periodical checks." Norman Levine, the defendants' former chief medical assistant and a non-party to this action, testified that he reviewed the spirometers' instruction manual at the time of purchase. A separate product information booklet states without qualification that the spirometer conforms to the ATS guidelines and controlling federal regulations. The booklet identifies a three liter calibration syringe as only an "optional item."

Moreover, Levine testified that the individual spirometers were sent out for periodic servicing, at which time the practice would use loaner machines. Defendant Friedman confirmed that on occasion he would direct Levine to send a spirometer out for recalibration. Levine also averred that he received practical training on the operation of the machine from the sales technicians who sold the spirometers. Finally, defendant Straus claims that, shortly after the confrontation with plaintiff, he requested that Levine pursue Mikes' complaints regarding the spirometers to see if anything could be done to rectify the alleged problem. Levine asserts that in response he thoroughly reviewed the practice's spirometry procedures and found no fault.

Defendants have thus proffered ample evidence—most of which derives from disinterested non-party witnesses—supporting their contention that they held a good faith belief that their spirometry tests were of medical value. In light of this evidence, plaintiff's unsupported allegations to the contrary do not raise a triable issue of fact sufficient to bar summary judgment. *See Lipton v. Nature Co.*, 71 F.3d 464, 472 (2d Cir. 1995) (summary judgment is appropriate even when mental state is at issue, so long as there are sufficient undisputed material facts); *see also Skouras v. United States*, 26 F.3d 13, 14 (2d Cir. 1994) (per curiam) (record justified district court's determination at summary judgment stage that defendants acted willfully).

Accordingly, the judgment of the district court is affirmed.

Notes

1. *The different aspects of utilization review.* *Mikes* illustrates cases in which there is an attempt to police utilization through use of the FCA. As we've seen, the Act uses a binary distinction in that a claim is labeled either as "false" or "not-false." The application of the Act to utilization is difficult, to say the least, because most often questions of medical necessity do easily fit within such a binary framework.

The court's analysis in *Mikes* relies on a distinction between the quantity and quality of services. It says that questions of medical necessity involve quantity, while the plaintiff's claims only go to quality. The court concludes that questions of quantity are within the compass of the FCA, while questions of the qualitative deficiency of services are not. You have to ask yourselves whether this quantity/quality distinction works.

In discussing utilization review, the court pushes together a number of different issues, about which we read in Part Three of this textbook, and it is helpful to separate them. The court also makes questionable distinctions.

a. *Exclusions from coverage.* As we have seen, certain categories of services, e.g., cosmetic services, are explicitly excluded from coverage. Attempts to bill for such services do not raise issues of utilization. The services may be medically indicated and they may be provided according to the relevant standard of care, but they are simply not part of Medicare or the relevant insurance plan. Hence, billing for such service is, in this context, the submission of a "false claim," and so long as the relevant scienter requirement is satisfied, there can be liability under the FCA. For example, suppose that a provider routinely bills for cosmetic surgery even though it knows that this is not a covered service. Such claims are "false." In pointing to cases involving, for example, experimental care that is excluded from coverage, the *Mikes* court got the conclusion right, *see, e.g.,* In re Cardiac Devices Qui Tam Litigation, 221 F.R.D. 318 (D. Conn. 2004) (court distinguished *Mikes* in case involving not breach of regulatory framework but billing violating terms of coverage that allegedly excluded cardiac devices that had yet to be approved by FDA and were provided in clinical trials), but its analysis needed to be more finely tuned.

b. *Services not medically indicated.* The court in *Mikes* drew a distinction between quantity and quality, finding that medical necessity involves determinations with regard to quantity but not quality. On the facts in

Mikes, the court's distinction worked because plaintiff made no claim that spirometry was not indicated for the patients to whom it was given, that it was not reasonable and necessary care for them. One could easily imagine instances of false claims based on this quantitative dimension. Suppose that plaintiff's claim was that every patient who walked in the door was given spirometry regardless of whether there were any signs or history of respiratory difficulty. Spirometry is clearly not reasonable and necessary care for a patient who presents with just a serious limp. However, that was not plaintiff's case. Rather, her theory was that the manner in which the spirometry was performed was qualitatively deficient.

However, most often there is less to this distinction than meets the eye. Suppose a man has just been diagnosed with prostate cancer. Suppose the treatment options are watchful waiting—doing nothing but watching to see if the cancer progresses—radiation, laser surgery, conventional surgery with a scalpel, etc. Which treatment is reasonable and necessary? Is this an issue of quantity or quality? Suppose that some medical centers have been performing laser surgery for a significant period of time, while others have just acquired the technology (because it is reimbursed in a lucrative manner, among other reasons). Is the decision that laser surgery at a particular center is "necessary" a quantitative or qualitative one? Suppose that this patient has laser surgery at a center that is just starting to offer the procedure; he is the first patient treated. A technician sets the device incorrectly so that the laser misses the malignancy entirely. Is this a quantitative or qualitative issue? Did the patient have "surgery" at all? Don't quantity and quality blend together?

Krizek amply illustrates the difficulty. As summarized in situation #5 above, Dr. Krizek treated many severely ill patients, and part of the government's FCA action was that he could have treated them differently than he did. Is the difference between an inpatient psychiatric stay and outpatient therapy sessions quantitative, qualitative or both? The district court dispatched the government's allegations easily:

> The government takes issue with Dr. Krizek's method of treatment of his patients, arguing that some patients should have been discharged from the hospital sooner, and that others suffered from conditions which could not be ameliorated through psychotherapy sessions, or that the length of the psychotherapy sessions should have been abbreviated. The government's expert witness's opinions on this subject came from a cold review of Dr. Krizek's notes for each patient. The government witness did not examine or interview any of the patients, or speak with any other doctors or nurses who had actually served these patients to learn whether the course of treatment prescribed by Dr. Krizek exceeded that which was medically necessary.

> Dr. Krizek testified credibly and persuasively as to the basis for the course of treatment for each of the representative patients. The medical necessity of treating Dr. Krizek's patients through psychotherapy and hospitalization was confirmed via the testimo-

ny of other defense witnesses. The Court credits Dr. Krizek's testimony on this question as well as his interpretation of his own notes regarding the seriousness of each patient's condition and the medical necessity for the procedures and length of hospital stay required. The Court finds that the government was unable to prove that Dr. Krizek rendered services that were medically unnecessary.

859 F.Supp. at 8. As you read the notes below, consider whether the court should have entertained these claims at all, based on differences in professional judgment regarding course of treatment rather than instances of blatantly terrible care such that it was worthless. Is this issue properly addressed by the purported distinction used in *Mikes* between quantitative and qualitative dimensions of care or in some other fashion? Additionally, as we observed with regard to the upcoding claims in *Krizek* and equally applicable to quality-of-care FCA claims, *see, e.g.,* Joan H. Krause, *Medical Error as False Claim*, 27 AM. J.L. & MED. 181, 191–92 (2001) [hereinafter Krause, *Medical Error as False Claim*], the issues addressed in the FCA cases are patterns or practices of conduct that might be categorized as submission of false claims; and we saw that complicated statistical analysis and benchmarks had to be applied to extrapolate a sample of cases across a much larger sample of allegedly false claims. How does one engage in such extrapolation when the issues involve courses of treatment represented by those claims?

2. *False certification.* As you can see from the *Mikes* decision, one way the courts try to disentangle when a claim is false and when it is not is through the doctrinal avenue of false certification. The discussion concerning "legal" falsity should be familiar to you. A contract contains a description of the goods or services to be provided and other expressly stated obligations. The contract is executed in the context of background practices and legal rules. Courts make some of these contextual rules and practices an implied part of the contract, and some are excluded. In actions brought under the FCA the argument concerning the regulatory context is exactly parallel. The parties argue over what part of that context is a condition of performance by the government, i.e., a precondition to payment, and what part of that context is a condition of performance by the health care provider, part of its "legal" certification. The *Mikes* court and others are surely correct that not every word in the Code of Federal Regulations is part of the bargain that leads to reimbursement. The fact that a hospital fails, for example, to have the exact number of florescent lights, as stipulated somewhere in the regulatory regime under which it functions, does not render all its submitted claims "false," but a claim submitted for an operation performed in the dark might render a bill for that surgery "false."

The *Mikes* court struggles with this issue of regulatory inclusion or exclusion through use of very broad pronouncements, such as the one that none of the conditions of eligibility for participation in the Medicare program are conditions for reimbursement and therefore cannot be the basis of a false certification claim. Many courts follow this distinction. *See, e.g.*, United States ex rel. Wilkins v. United Health Group, Inc., 659 F.3d 295 (3d Cir. 2011); United States ex rel. Conner v. Salina Regional Health Center, Inc., 543 F.3d 1211 (10th Cir. 2008). However, *some* conditions of eligibility are in fact preconditions to payment. As the case in situation #2 above shows, for example, services performed without the appropriate license can be the basis of a false claim. The radiological reports prepared under the radiologist's, Dr. Reddy's, signature were worthless because no radiologist had viewed the images and prepared the reports, and the expertise and participation of a radiologist was necessary for the services to have any value at all. *Compare, e.g.*, United States ex rel. Woodruff v. Hawaii Pacific Health, 560 F. Supp.2d 988 (D. Hawaii 2008), *aff'd*, 2010 WL 5072191 (9th Cir. 2010) (unpublished opinion) (billings for procedures performed by nurse practitioners (NPs) were not false because the procedures were within scope of the NPs' licensure although the procedures could have also been performed by physicians), *with* United States ex rel. Wright v. Cleo Wallace Centers, 132 F. Supp.2d 913 (D. Colo. 2000) (false claim properly pled because facility billed for swing-bed services without necessary state license to operate swing-beds). Appropriate licensure is a condition of participation *and* it is a condition of payment. Similarly strained was the court's ruling that 42 U.S.C. § 1320c–5(a)(2)'s requirement that services "will be of a quality which meets professionally recognized standards of health care" does not state a precondition of payment. Services are reimbursed when they are "reasonable and necessary," and part of the definition of "reasonable and necessary" is that they meet professionally defined standards of care. The court's conclusion in this regard is just flat wrong and stems from an overly broad, artificial separation of conditions of eligibility from conditions of reimbursement.

Indeed *Woodruff* shows how vacuous these distinctions between implied and express conditions—and between conditions of participation and conditions of payment—can be. In *Woodruff* plaintiffs claimed that defendant hospital failed to report on its cost reports that NPs performed certain procedures and that the NPs were allegedly acting outside their scope of license. In one decision the district court dismissed plaintiffs' allegations that the hospital had made *legally* false claims. Following *Mikes*, it broadly ruled that neither the cost reports, nor the hospital's participation agreement, nor state licensure law, conditioned payment on scope of licensure. *See* United States ex rel. Woodruff v. Hawaii Pacific Health, 2007 WL 1500275 (D. Hawaii 2007). In its subsequent decision the district court dismissed plaintiffs' charge that the hospital made *factually* false claims. The court found that the hospital had not represented that physicians actually performed the services; and it found that the hospital's billing was factually correct because the NPs acted within the scope of their licensure, i.e., reimbursement was properly paid given the scope of the NPs' licensure. *See Woodruff*, 560 F. Supp.2d 988.

If the scope of NP licensure was outcome determinative—if reimbursement was conditioned on whether the nurse practitioners acted within the scope of their licenses—what possible difference does it make whether we call that linkage—materiality—"legal" or "factual"? Express and implied requirements are both part of a contract, and at least in the civil context it is senseless to split hairs about what requirements stem from "inside" the contract and which ones derive from the "outside," i.e., what is "factually" required and what is "legally" required. In all this technical verbiage the courts and many scholars have lost the forest for the trees. *Accord* United States ex rel. Hutcheson v. Blackstone Medical, Inc., 647 F.3d 377 (1st Cir. 2011) (refusing to apply distinctions between factually false and legally false, and express certification and implicit certification, because these categories "do more to obscure than clarify"); New York v. Amgen Inc., 652 F.3d 103 (1st Cir. 2011) (same). In *Woodruff* the billing was not false because the NPs were legally authorized to perform the procedures and the hospital never represented that they were performed by anyone other than the NPs. That's it, plain and simple. *See also* United States ex rel. Riley v. St. Luke's Episcopal Hospital, 200 F. Supp.2d 673 (S.D. Tex. 2002) (false claims for service provided by foreign-licensed physician not licensed in Texas were dismissed because supervising physician signed for work and supervision arrangement was approved by Texas State Board of Medical Examiners), *rev'd*, 355 F.3d 370 (5th Cir. 2004) (claims improperly dismissed because fact of supervision was controverted).*

3. *Materiality or causation.* The courts have often implied a materiality or causation standard likewise to make the distinctions discussed above, sorting out regulatory requirements that are "technical" or "minor" from those that go to the "heart" or "core" of the provider's agreement with the government, the breach of which causes improper payment. *See, e.g.,* Luckey v. Baxter Healthcare Corp., 2 F. Supp.2d 1034, 1045 (N.D. Ill. 1998), *aff'd*, 183 F.3d 730 (7th Cir. 1999); *Mikes*, 84 F. Supp.2d at 435. *See generally* Krause, *Health Care Providers and the Public Fisc* at 189–201. In implying a materiality test, some courts had implied an "outcome materiality" requirement, a subjective standard by which plaintiff had to show an actual effect on government's decision to pay—that defendant acted with the purpose and effect of causing the government to pay out money it was not obligated to pay—while the majority of courts implying a materiality test had used a purportedly easier standard of "claim materiality," an objective standard which asks what the impact would be on a "reasonable" agency. *See generally* United States v. Southland Management Corp. 288 F.3d 665, 675–76 (5th Cir. 2002). Regardless of this history, the Fraud Enforcement and Recovery Act of 2009 ("FERA"), Pub. L. No. 111–21, § 4(a), 123 Stat. 1617, 1621, added an explicit materiality standard to the FCA, and adopted the purportedly more lenient approach of claim materiality, amending the FCA so that it now defines materiality as "having a natural tendency to influence, or be capable of influencing, the payment or receipt of money or property." 31 U.S.C. § 3729(b)(4). It is unclear, however, whether the amendment will alter any results. At least thus far in cases involving delivery of health care services, the choice of materiality

* Criminal prosecutions for false claims raise additional considerations and are not our focus in these materials.

test has for the most part not been outcome determinative, although predictions are perilous because the language is amorphous. *See* John T. Boese, *The Past, Present & Future of Materiality under the FCA*, 3 ST. LOUIS U. J. HEALTH L. & POL'Y 291 (2010); Krause, *Health Care Providers and the Public Fisc* at 189–201.*

4. *Worthless care.* In the end both the inquiries whether a legal requirement is part of a legal certification or whether it is material are incorrectly focused. The fact that a provider failed to comply with a regulation does not necessarily render its claim "false" within the meaning of the FCA. Nor is that issue decided by asking whether its failure to state something is material. The history of the FCA indicates its appropriate application to health care services. Passed during the Civil War, it was aimed at contractors who were paid for goods sold to the Union Army that either were not furnished, not furnished as described, or so defective as to be worthless, e.g., blind mules or sand substituted for gunpowder. That sort of fraud is what the FCA is aimed at, and in the end the court in *Mikes* gets it right in considering the claim of "worthless care" to be the only viable cause of action. *See, e.g.*, Krause, *Medical Error as False Claim* at 188; Joan H. Krause, *"Promises to Keep": Health Care Providers and the Civil False Claims Act*, 23 CARDOZO L. REV. 1363, 1402–05 (2002) [hereinafter Krause, *"Promises to Keep"*]. These sort of cases do not involve weighing the niceties of professional standards of care but instead present instances of care that is blatantly beyond the pale. *See, e.g.*, United States ex rel. Lee v. Smithkline Beecham, Inc., 245 F.3d 1048 (9th Cir. 2001) (motion to dismiss should have been denied given allegation that lab tests were worthless because results were falsified when control samples fell outside acceptable range instead of investigating or fixing source of error or retesting patients); United States v. NHC Healthcare Corp., 115 F. Supp.2d 1149 (W.D. Mo. 2000) (motion to dismiss denied given allegations that nursing home had such woefully inadequate staffing that it could not possibly have provided care billed for); United States ex rel. Aranda v. Community Psychiatric Centers, Inc., 945 F. Supp. 1485 (W.D. Okla. 1996) (defendant inpatient psychiatric facility's motion to dismiss denied given allegations of its knowledge that with sufficient frequency patients identified by treating physicians as dangerous physically or sexually assaulted

---

* There are retroactivity issues concerning the amendments that we discuss in this chapter from FERA and the PPACA. In the interest of space we do not discuss them. *See, e.g.,* United States ex rel. Carpenter v. Abbott Laboratories, Inc., 723 F. Supp.2d 395, 401–03 (D. Mass. 2010) (collecting and discussing cases interpreting meaning of "claims" in FERA's provision regarding retroactivity for FCA actions, FERA, § 4(f)(1), 123 Stat. at 1625); United States ex rel. Stone v. Omnicare, 2011 WL 2669659 (N.D. Ill. 2011) (discussing retroactivity issues with regard to changes made by FERA and PPACA for false claims due to overpayments). Nor do we discuss the constitutional issues attendant to retroactive application. *See, e.g., id.* (finding impermissible retroactivity); United States ex rel. Sanders v. Allison Engine Co., 667 F. Supp.2d 747 (S.D. Ohio 2009) (because FCA is punitive, retroactivity violates Ex Post Facto Clause); United States ex rel. Drake v. NSI, Inc., 736 F. Supp.2d 489 (D. Conn. 2010) (reaching opposite conclusion). *See generally* Matthew Titolo, *Retroactivity and the Fraud Enforcement and Recovery Act of 2009*, 86 IND. L.J. 257 (2011).

other patients due to inadequate separation of housing, staffing and monitoring equipment).

Cases like *Mikes* involving less serious deficiencies that do not render care worthless typically do not survive. *See, e.g.*, United States ex rel. Blundell v. Dialysis Clinic, Inc., 2011 WL 167246 (N.D.N.Y. 2011) (vague allegations of improper documentation, billing and staffing dismissed because no adequate allegation that dialysis provided was worthless); United States ex rel. Swan v. Covenant Care, Inc., 279 F. Supp.2d 1212 (E.D. Cal. 2002) (same); Luckey v. Baxter Healthcare Corp., 183 F.3d 730 (7th Cir. 1999) (summary judgment properly granted because dispute concerning effective testing of blood plasma not the same as not testing at all); United States ex rel. Landers v. Baptist Memorial Health Care Corp., 525 F. Supp.2d 972 (W.D. Tenn. 2007) (allegations of improper staffing and sterilization of equipment did not allege that care was rendered worthless).

5. *Institutional competence.* The question of institutional competence looms large in false claims actions that challenge conduct beyond billing for services not provided or worthless as provided. Sometimes the arguments are the standard ones that prosecutors, courts and juries do not have the adequate expertise to judge complicated issues like standards of care that are vague, subjective and best left to agencies or professionals—i.e., we should abandon malpractice too—*see, e.g.*, Robert Fabrikant & Glenn E. Solomon, *Application of the Federal False Claims Act to Regulatory Compliance Issues in the Health Care Industry*, 51 ALA. L. REV. 105, 156–60 (1999) [hereinafter Fabrikant & Solomon, *Application of the FCA to Regulatory Compliance*]. Other times the argument is the more substantial one that authority has indeed been vested elsewhere. *See, e.g., id.* at 131–32. After all, the theory of "legal falsity" rests on an alleged failure to conform to some requirement of the regulatory landscape, the enforcement of which ordinarily rests with the relevant agency. This argument is particularly strong when that agency is vested with its own prosecutorial discretion such that enforcement of a regulation under the FCA would deprive the agency of that discretion. *See, e.g.*, Krause, *Health Care Providers and the Public Fisc* at 198; Dayna Boyen Matthew, *Tainted Prosecution of Tainted Claims: The Law, Economics, and Ethics of Fighting Medical Fraud Under the Civil False Claims Act*, 76 IND. L.J. 525 (2001) [hereinafter Matthew, *Tainted Prosecution of Tainted Claims*]. However, you must ask yourselves whether the existence of that authority necessarily occupies the field or whether there is room for concurrent enforcement. You must also ask whether concurrent enforcement is necessarily redundant, overkill or, perhaps worse, inconsistent.

6. *Institutional competence again—qui tam.* The question of divided authority would be difficult enough if limited to division of authority between prosecutors and regulatory agencies. Prosecutors wield enormous authority to challenge fraud, and many observers claim that prosecutors have been overreaching in stretching the ambit of the FCA and in particular in applying it to enforce ambiguous, inconsistent or simply an overwhelming multitude of regulations. *See, e.g.*, Timothy P. Blanchard, *Medi-*

care Medical Necessity Determinations Revisited: Abuse of Discretion and Abuse of Process in the War Against Medicare Fraud and Abuse, 43 ST. LOUIS U. L.J. 91 (1999); Fabrikant & Solomon, *Application of the FCA to Regulatory Compliance. See generally* Krause, *"Promises to Keep"*; Matthew, *Tainted Prosecution of Taint Claims. But see generally* Jost & Davies, *The Empire Strikes Back*. In 1998 in response to such criticism, then-Deputy Attorney General Eric H. Holder, Jr., issued "Guidance on the Use of the False Claims Act in Civil Health Matters" (http://www.justice.gov/dag/readingroom/chcm.htm) as guidelines to attorneys.

Among other things these guidelines instruct federal prosecutors to consider whether the provider had appropriate notice of the rule or policy on which a case would be based; whether it is reasonable to conclude that the provider understood the rule or policy; and whether the provider reasonably relied on agency guidance. When a rule is technical or complex, prosecutors are instructed to communicate with knowledgeable staff within the relevant agency. In its final report on implementation of the guidelines, the GAO reported that the Department of Justice had successfully institutionalized compliance. *See* U.S. GENERAL ACCOUNTING OFFICE, GAO–02–546, MEDICARE FRAUD AND ABUSE: DOJ CONTINUES TO PROMOTE COMPLIANCE WITH FALSE CLAIMS ACT GUIDANCE (April 5, 2002) (http://www.gao.gov/htext/d02546.html).*

However, the question of divided authority is rendered enormously more complicated by the possibility of qui tam litigation. As indicated briefly in the introduction to this section, the FCA was passed during the Civil War with a qui tam provision to encourage individuals to sue to obtain a share of the amount bilked from the government. In 1943, Congress made it much more difficult for private relators to bring qui tam actions by stipulating that such actions could not be brought if the government had prior possession of the relevant information, by eliminating the relator's role in the litigation if the DOJ intervened, and by reducing the bounty available to private attorney generals. Then, in 1986 in the midst of one of the cycles of rising concern about health care fraud, Congress re-expanded the ability and incentive of private relators to come forward with the insider information they possess by again increasing the amounts they could recover, by allowing relators to sue based on public information so long as they were the "original source," 31 U.S.C. § 3730(e)(4), and, subject to caveats listed immediately below, by allowing the private relator "unrestricted participation" in the action even if the government intervened. *See id.* § 3730(c)(2)(C)–(D).

---

* The issue, however, has arisen again recently regarding complaints that at least one investigation, concerning the performance of kyphoplasty on an inpatient rather than outpatient basis—the "kyphoplasty initiative"—relied on data mining to find simple billing errors and therefore failed to comply with the Holder Memorandum. See *AHA Continues Discussions with DOJ over Alleged Misuse of Fraud Claims*, 19 HEALTH LAW REPORTER (BNA) 1742 (Dec. 16, 2010); *False Claims Act Investigations Targeting Billing Errors, Mistakes, AHA Letter Says*, 19 HEALTH LAW REPORTER (BNA) 1272 (Sept. 16, 2010); *Nine Hospitals Settle FCA Claims over Kyphoplasty*, 19 HEALTH LAW REPORTER (BNA) 712 (May 20, 2010).

Safeguards do exist to protect prosecutors' primary authority. The qui tam complaint is initially served on the government, along with "substantially all material evidence and information the person possesses." 31 U.S.C. § 3730(b)(2). The complaint is sealed for 60 days to allow the government to investigate and determine if it will intervene. *Id.* If the government does not intervene, it is entitled to copies of all pleadings during the case, *id.* § 3730(c)(3), and it may intervene later for "good cause." *Id.* If the government does intervene, it has "the primary responsibility for prosecuting the action, and shall not be bound by an act of the person bringing the action." *Id.* § 3730(c)(1). This responsibility includes the right to dismiss and settle although the relator has the right to a hearing and the court must determine that the settlement is fair, adequate and reasonable. See *id.* § 3730(c)(2)(A)–(B). The government also has the right under certain circumstances to seek limitations on the relator's participation in the litigation. See *id.* § 3730(c)(2)(C)–(D). (See also below regarding the public disclosure bar).

Yet, one can ask whether, particularly given the recent flood of qui tam litigation, these safeguards are sufficient. A somewhat persuasive argument can be mounted that qui tam litigation deprives prosecutors of the discretion that is needed to administer a statute that is potentially a club—and one that is very attractive to the plaintiffs' bar. *See, e.g.*, John T. Boese & Beth C. McClain, *Why Thompson Is Wrong: Misuse of the False Claims Act to Enforce the Anti–Kickback Act*, 51 ALA. L. REV. 1, 46–50 (1999) [hereinafter Boese & McClain, *Why Thompson Is Wrong*]. This argument is all the more compelling in that qui tam relators are pushing the boundaries of application of the FCA, like in *Mikes*, and seeking to enforce regulations for which there is no private cause of action; and although relators do serve as *crucial* sources of information and provide an important oversight function, prosecutors do not necessarily have the resources (or perhaps the proper incentives) needed to monitor the flood. *See, e.g.*, Krause, *Health Care Providers and the Public Fisc* at 203; Krause, *"Promises to Keep"* at 1413–14; Joan H. Krause, *A Conceptual Model of Health Care Fraud Enforcement*, 12 J.L. & POL'Y 55, 137–41 (2003) [hereinafter Krause, *A Conceptual Model*]; Dayna Bowen Matthew, *Moral Hazard Problem with Privatization of Public Enforcement: The Case of Pharmaceutical Fraud*, 40 U. MICH. J.L. REFORM, 281 (2007) [hereinafter Matthew, *Moral Hazard Problem*]. *See generally* Pamela H. Bucy, *Private Justice*, 76 CAL. L. REV. 1 (2002). In fact, over 80% of all false claims case, of which about 60% relate to health care, are brought, not by governmental prosecutors, but by private parties. *See* http://www.taf.org/statistics.htm (statistics maintained by Taxpayers Against Fraud, an advocacy group for qui tam actions). Prosecutors for the most part are concentrating on the cases discussed above in which breach of regulatory duty amounts to failure to provide services of any worth at all, but relators are pushing those boundaries rather hard. It is an open question whether qui tam litigation should be partially or fully reigned in.

7. *Public disclosure bar to qui tam suits.* If anything, recent amendments will increase the number and type of qui tam suits. As noted above, in 1943 Congress made it much more difficult for private relators to bring

qui tam actions by stipulating that such actions could not be brought if the government had prior possession of the relevant information, but in 1986 Congress relaxed this requirement by allowing relators to sue based on public information so long as they were the "original source." At that point the original source requirement was a jurisdictional bar and read as follows: "No court shall have jurisdiction over an action under this section based upon the public disclosure of allegations or transactions in a criminal, civil, or administrative hearing, in a congressional, administrative, or Government Accounting Office report, hearing, audit, or investigation, or from the news media, unless the action is brought by the Attorney General or the person bringing the action is an original source of the information." 31 U.S.C. § 3730(e)(4)(A) (2008). "Original source" was defined as "an individual who has direct and independent knowledge of the information on which the allegations are based and has voluntarily provided the information to the Government before filing an action under this section which is based on the information." *Id.* Further, the Supreme Court had extended the definition of public disclosure to state proceedings. See Graham County Soil & Water Conservation District v. United States ex rel. Wilson, 130 S. Ct. 1396 (2010) (decided after passage of the PPACA in 2010 but involving conduct to which the PPACA did not apply retroactively).

However, in 2010 the PPACA relaxed these barriers to qui tam suits even more. First, it reversed the Supreme Court's holding in *Graham County* such that now public disclosure is limited to federal actions and proceedings. PPACA, Pub. L. No. 111–148 § 10104(j)(2) (codified as 31 U.S.C. § 3730(e)(4)(A)). Second, the PPACA narrowed the definition of "original source" such that the individual need not have "direct and independent knowledge" but only "knowledge that is independent of and materially adds to the publicly disclosed allegations or transactions." *Id.* (codified as 31 U.S.C. § 3730(e)(4)(B)). Third, the public source requirement is no longer a jurisdictional bar but instead just an automatic ground for dismissal, which the government can prevent simply by opposing dismissal. See *id.* (codified as 31 U.S.C. § 3730(e)(4)(A)) ("The court shall dismiss an action or claim under this section, unless opposed by the Government."). Thus, effectively the DOJ is given responsibility for deciding when qui tam suits in which it has not intervened should go forward.

8.   *Failure to comply with the anti-kickback statute or Stark.* A special case of "legal falsity" or breach of implied certification that clearly raises the institutional competence issue is a provider's alleged failure to comply with the requirements of the anti-kickback statute (AKS) or Stark, statutory schemes we will discuss immediately below. The leading case is United States ex rel. Thompson v. Columbia/HCA Healthcare Corporation, 20 F. Supp.2d 1017 (1998), in which the court held that violations of the AKS and Stark automatically rendered certifications or cost reports false. In reaching this holding the court extended some more traditional FCA doctrine, namely that by violating the AKS and Stark, defendants were ineligible for reimbursement and therefore any billings were ipso facto "tainted" and false. The court also ruled that the government was injured, even though services were unaffected, in that the government suffered

losses in investigative and administrative costs. Finally, the court held that plaintiff had shown by affidavit, sufficient to stave off dismissal, that the government would not have paid defendants' claims had it known of the violations. See *id.* at 1047. Similar holdings have been United States ex rel. Pogue v. American Healthcorp, Inc., 914 F. Supp. 1507 (M.D. Tenn. 1996); United States ex rel. Roy v. Anthony, 914 F. Supp. 1504 (S.D. Ohio 1994); and United States ex rel. Bidani v. Lewis, 264 F. Supp.2d 612 (N.D. Ill. 2003). Many recent cases effectively hold the same thing as *Thomson* but with different language. *See, e.g.,* United States ex rel. Wilkins v. United Health Group, Inc., 659 F.3d 295 (3d Cir. 2011) (holding that satisfaction of the AKS is a condition of payment); McNutt ex rel. United States v. Haleyville Medical Supplies, Inc., 423 F.3d 1256 (11th Cir. 2005) (same); United States ex rel. Lisitza v. Johnson & Johnson, 765 F. Supp.2d 112 (D. Mass. 2011) (same). *But cf.* United States ex rel. Gonzalez v. Fresenius Medical Care North America, 761 F. Supp.2d 442 (W.D. Tex. 2010) (refusing to allow false claims action based on alleged violation of Civil Monetaries Penalty Law or Health Care Fraud Statute because enforcement of those statutes is left exclusively to government).

To say the least, *Thompson's* per se holding has been controversial. As we will see AKS and Stark are extremely complicated statutory schemes in which substantial discretion is vested in the regulating agencies when to pursue remedies available to them. Most important for our purposes, *Thompson* has been criticized as a usurpation of agency discretion, whether the FCA action is prosecuted by government prosecutors or by qui tam plaintiffs, while the displacement of agency authority is worse when actions are brought by relators. Some argue that the per se rule in *Thompson* presents total preclusion of agency discretion; others argue that imposition of an actual materiality or similar requirement would at least require government harm and a proven deleterious effect on utilization and patients; while others argue that any linkage between the FCA and the AKS or Stark is problematic. For a sample of these arguments, see Boese & McClain, *Why Thompson Is Wrong*; Krause, *"Promises to Keep"*; and Matthew, *Tainted Prosecution of Tainted Claims*. Despite this criticism the PPACA adopted *Thompson's* per se rule for AKS violations by adding a new subsection to the AKS so that as amended it now provides that "[i]n addition to the penalties provided for in this section or 42 U.S.C. § 1320a–7a, a claim that includes items or services resulting from a violation of this section constitutes a false or fraudulent claim for purposes of [the FCA]." 42 U.S.C. § 1320a–7b(g). *But see* United States ex rel. Hutcheson v. Blackstone Medical, Inc., 647 F.3d 377 (1st Cir. 2011) (reversing dismissal of false claim action founded on AKS violation and finding it unnecessary to construe PPACA amendment because materiality was plausibly alleged). A violation of Stark, by contrast, has been taken entirely out of the falsity/false certification framework because it creates an "overpayment," which, as discussed below, if not properly returned creates FCA liability.

9. *Cause-to-be-presented liability.* The FCA makes liable not only one who presents but also "causes to be presented" a false claim. 31 U.S.C. § 3729(a)(2). The traditional fact pattern giving rise to cause-to-be-present-

ed liability would be an employer-employee or principal-agent relationship in which a superior would direct someone to present a false claim. *Krizek* above resembles such a case in which Dr. or Ms. Krizek caused their employee to bill fraudulently.

However, some recent prosecutions have greatly expanded the range of such prosecutions to include various kinds of advisors who offer billing advice to health providers. Some of the firms subjected to these actions have offered software that upcoded claims for clients. One infamous qui tam action was brought against the giant accounting firm KPMG Peat Marwick for creating two sets of books for Medicare and Medicaid cost reports. *See generally* Krause, *"Promise to Keep"* at 1385–89. When we discuss AKS and Stark we will see there is the possibility of attorney liability. The "cause-to-be-presented" theory of liability has also recently been used against alleged fraud committed by pharmaceutical companies for allegedly engaging in off-label promotion for unapproved uses of pharmaceuticals, *see, e.g.,* United States ex rel. Franklin v. Parke–Davis, 147 F. Supp.2d 39 (D. Mass. 2001); United States ex rel. Westmoreland v. Amgen, Inc., 2011 WL 4342721 (D. Mass. 2011); United States ex rel. King v. Solvay S.A., 2011 WL 4834030 (S.D. Tex. 2011); *see generally* Allison D. Burroughs et al., *Off–Label Promotion: Government Theories of Prosecution and Facts That Drive Them*, 65 FOOD & DRUG L.J. 555 (2010), or kickbacks to physicians, *see, e.g., id.;* Krause, *"Promises to Keep"* at 1390–91, both of which thereby "caused" the physicians to present false claims.

Situation #7 presented in the beginning of the chapter, in which a pharmaceutical company has allegedly paid for ghostwriting scholarly articles to support the use of its product, poses the potential expansion of this theory because, quite arguably, the publication of those articles "causes" physicians to write prescriptions. *See* Strom ex rel. United States v. Scios, Inc., 676 F. Supp.2d 884 (N.D. Cal. 2009) (refusing to dismiss false claims prosecution based on allegations that included pharmaceutical company's hiring of ghostwriters for articles); *cf.* Simon Stern & Trudo Lemmens, *Legal Remedies for Medical Ghostwriting: Imposing Fraud Liability on Guest Authors of Ghostwritten Articles*, 8(8) PLoS MED e1001070 (Aug. 2, 2011) (http://www.plosmedicine.org/article/info% 3Adoi% 2F10.1371% 1Fjournal.pmed.1001070) (advocating RICO cause of action). For critical views along the lines adumbrated in these notes, *see generally* Matthew, *Moral Hazard Problem*; Vicki W. Girard, *Punishing Pharmaceutical Companies for Unlawful Promotion of Approved Drugs: Why the False Claims Act is the Wrong RX*, 12 J. HEALTH CARE L. & POL'Y 119 (2009). It is likely that the PPACA's adoption of *Thompson's* per se linkage of the AKS to the FCA will strengthen the arguments for such "downstream liability." *See, e.g.,* Katherine A. Blair, *In Search of the Right R[x]: Use of the Federal False Claims Act in Off–Label Drug Promotion Litigation*, 23 HEALTH LAWYER 44 (2011).

10. *Reverse false claims*. If the government overpays a provider, potentially there is a false claim. Following the amendments by FERA in 2009, the FCA now imposes liability for "knowingly conceal[ing] or know-

ingly and improperly avoid[ing] or decreas[ing] an obligation to pay or transmit money or property to the Government." 31 U.S.C. § 3729(a)(1)(G). This language replaces the prior subsection which made it unlawful to use a "false record or statement to conceal, avoid or decrease an obligation to pay money to the government." Hence, an affirmative act is no longer needed for liability. Instead, liability exists whenever a provider knowingly conceals or avoids an obligation to pay. Providers have to pay back overpayments within 60 days of the date on which the overpayments are "identified." *See* 42 U.S.C. § 1320a–7k(d). Unfortunately, the term "identified" is not defined. Recall also the civil monetary payments can be imposed for knowledge of and failure to report and return an overpayment for services. *See* 42 U.S.C. § 1320a–7a(a)(12). Finally, a violation of Stark, to be discussed below, creates an overpayment, *see* 42 U.S.C. § 1395nn(g)(2), which can now, given these amendments, trigger liability for civil monetary penalties and false claims if not returned within the stipulated time period.

11. *State false claims statutes.* States that did not have their own false claim statutes were given an incentive to pass them by the Deficit Reduction Act of 2005, which increased a state's share of Medicaid fraud recovery by ten percent if it has a statute modeled on the federal FCA, including equal civil penalties and equally effective qui tam provisions. *See* 42 U.S.C. § 1396h. The Office of Inspector General of the Department of Health and Human Services reviews the state statutes and maintains data concerning their status on its website (http://oig.hhs.gov/fraud/state-false-claims-act-reviews/index.asp). According to the Taxpayers Against Fraud, 28 states have false claims statutes, of which 18 have been successfully reviewed (some of those already approved are within the two-year waiting period for complying with recent amendments to the FCA). *See* http://www.taf.org/statefca.htm. For slightly different figures on the number of complying states, *see* http://www.statehealthfacts.org/comparetable.jsp?ind=260 & cat=4.

2. RICO

RICO has become an important part of the statutory arsenal deployed against health care fraud in good part because, unlike the FCA and the statutes we examine below, AKS and Stark, RICO's cause of action does not necessitate that payment be made by governmental money. Government prosecutors too have used RICO, but the fact that it also gives a cause of action when private money is involved means that numerous actions for health care fraud have been brought under RICO for the same type of conduct litigated under the other statutes we discuss. Hence, as principal examples, insurers have sued providers for improper billing and false representations; insurers have sued pharmaceutical companies for allegedly fraudulent marketing practices; pharmaceutical companies have been sued for their pricing practices; and insurance companies have been sued for allegedly fraudulent practices and representations in their payment of claims and marketing. It has truly been used as a catch-all statute to provide (substantial) federal relief for what would otherwise be state claims.

RICO creates three distinct categories of substantive offenses. First, under the statute, in relevant part, it is unlawful for any person

> who has received any income derived, directly or indirectly, from a pattern of racketeering activity or through collection of an unlawful debt in which such person has participated as a principal [within the meaning of the Title 18, § 2] to use or invest, directly or indirectly, any part of such income, or the proceeds of such income, in acquisition of any interest in, or the establishment or operation of, any enterprise which is engaged in, or the activities of which affect, interstate or foreign commerce.

18 U.S.C. § 1962(a). Second, the statute makes it unlawful for any person "through a pattern of racketeering activity or through collection of an unlawful debt to acquire or maintain, directly or indirectly, any interest in or control of any enterprise which is engaged in, or the activities of which affect, interstate or foreign commerce." *Id*. § 1962(b). Third, the Act makes it unlawful for any person "employed by or associated with any enterprise engaged in, or the activities of which affect, interstate or foreign commerce, to conduct or participate, directly or indirectly, in the conduct of such enterprise's affairs through a pattern of racketeering activity or collection of unlawful debt." *Id*. § 1962(c).

The terms "enterprise," "pattern" and "racketeering activity" are defined terms. The term "enterprise" means "any individual, partnership, corporation, association, or other legal entity, and any union or group of individuals associated in fact although not a legal entity." *Id*. § 1961(4). The term "pattern" refers to "at least two acts of racketeering activity, one of which occurred after the effective date of [the Act] and the last of which occurred within ten years after the commission of a prior act of racketeering activity." *Id*. § 1961(5). The term "racketeering activity" covers a very long series of federal and state offenses, called "predicate acts," among them mail and wire fraud, bribery, arson, extortion, murder, gambling, robbery, and drug dealing. *Id*. § 1961(1). Mail and wire fraud are broad enough to incorporate a vast range of fraudulent sales and marketing schemes.

Violations of the Act carry enhanced criminal penalties, criminal forfeiture, public and private injunctive relief, and treble damages in private actions. *Id*. §§ 1963–64. The sanctions authorized by RICO may be far tougher than those available under state law.

Many of the issues we examined under the FCA likewise arise under RICO, although sometimes the same concepts are examined under different "magic words" because the statutory language varies.

a. Falsity, materiality and causation. Similar to litigation under the FCA, the RICO plaintiff must prove that defendant did something that is false or fraudulent in a material way that caused the expenditure of money. This point may be illustrated by some of the rulings in the massive litigation over the marketing and sale of the drug Neurontin. Plaintiffs in the consolidated, multidistrict litigation alleged that defendants engaged in a fraudulent marketing campaign to convince doctors to prescribe Neurontin for numerous off-label uses that had not been approved by the FDA. *See* In re Neurontin Marketing and Sales Practices Litigation, 677 F. Supp.2d 479 (D. Mass. 2010); *see also* In re Neurontin Marketing and Sales Practices Litigation, 748 F. Supp.2d 34 (D. Mass. 2010). Defendants argued that the insurance plan plaintiffs were not injured by the alleged fraud, while the plans argued that had they known the truth about Neurontin's lack of efficacy for the off-label uses, they would have taken steps to limit the number of prescriptions written to plan members and paid for by the plans themselves. The plaintiff plans argued successfully that defendants made fraudulent representations by suppressing negative studies—offering "half-truths"—even in response to inquiries. *See In re Neurontin Marketing and Sales Practices Litigation,* 677 F. Supp.2d at 491–92.

One of the plaintiff insurance plans, Kaiser, was able to win its RICO claim because it showed, among other things, that it exercised strict control over its formulary, that it actively reviewed the uses of Neurontin, that it had made numerous requests for information from defendants, and that it had gotten false or misleading information in return. Kaiser was therefore able to show that defendants had made material misrepresentations on which it relied in constructing its formulary, causing it to make coverage decisions it would not have made had it not been misled. *See id.* at 495–97; *see also Pfizer Ordered to Pay $142 Million for Illegal Promotion of Neurontin,* 19 HEALTH LAW REPORTER (BNA) 450 (Mar. 25, 2010). By contrast, unlike Kaiser, the plaintiff plans Aetna and Guardian maintained no formulary controls around Neurontin, undertook no studies and failed to communicate with defendants. Therefore their RICO claims were dismissed. *See In re Neurontin Marketing and Sales Practices Litigation,* 677 F. Supp.2d at 497; *see also, e.g.,* American Dental Association v. Cigna Corp., 605 F.3d 1283, 1291–93 (11th Cir. 2010) (allegations of fraudulent claims processing dismissed for failure to show misrepresentations); Schoedinger v. United Healthcare, 557 F.3d 872, 879 (8th Cir. 2009) (unintentional billing errors although repeated will not support a RICO claim).

b. Standing. The civil remedies for RICO are available to "any person injured in his business or property by reason of a violation." 18 U.S.C. § 1964(c). In a number of cases, the leading one of which is Maio v. Aetna, Inc., 221 F.3d 472 (3d Cir. 2000), this requirement has created some difficulty.

Maio was a class action against Aetna's HMO plans in a number of states in which plaintiffs alleged that " 'Aetna's failure to disclose its restrictive and coercive internal policies and practices, which render its advertising, marketing and membership materials false and misleading in violation of RICO.' " *Id.* at 474. Plaintiffs claimed that " 'Aetna has engaged in a massive nationwide fraudulent advertising campaign designed to induce people to enroll in its HMO by representing that Aetna affirmatively manages its members' health care when in fact, Aetna designed undisclosed internal policies to improve defendants' profitability at the expense of quality of care.' " *Id.* Plaintiffs elaborated that Aetna represented that its "members would receive high quality health care from physicians who are solely responsible for providing all medical care and maintaining the physician-patient relationship, when in reality Aetna's internal policies restrict the physicians' ability to provide the high quality health care that appellants have been promised." *Id.* at 475. Plaintiffs alleged that "despite Aetna's representations that it compensated its physicians under a system that provides them with incentives based upon the quality of care provided, Aetna's provider contracts actually offer the physicians financial incentives to withhold medical services and reduce the quality of care to HMO members." *Id.*

The court of appeals affirmed the district court's dismissal of the complaint on grounds that plaintiffs failed to show they suffered injury. The court characterized plaintiffs' claims as allegations that they had been denied promised health care. It then repeatedly pointed to plaintiffs' failure to allege particularized instances in which their care had been diminished, and in its lengthy opinion the court repeatedly characterized plaintiffs' allegations of harm to the quality of care they were provided as speculative.

Maio raises many very interesting issues, only some of which we can discuss here. Ask yourselves first, what was it that plaintiffs bought, did they buy health care services or insurance for health care services? If the answer is the latter, was their complaint based on the denial of particular instances of care or on the structure of the plan itself? If the answer is the latter, can we not say, if we assume the truth of their allegations as we must on a 12(b)(6) motion, that they were injured because it was represented that they were sold one thing when in fact they were sold another? *See* In re Managed Care Litigation, 150 F. Supp.2d 1330, 1338–39 (S.D. Fla. 2001) (criticizing *Maio* for failing to distinguish between breach of contract and fraudulent inducement). Remember that the point of standing is to narrow the range of persons who can sue to those who are actually injured, as opposed to those who are affected only very remotely. If Aetna did engage in a complicated bait and switch scheme, as alleged by plaintiffs, weren't the plaintiffs, as the plan members, the ones harmed? We'll see in a minute that this question is not so easy to answer, but for now just ask yourselves, did the court's discussion go to whether or not plaintiffs had standing or the merits?

Let's think more, however, about who was harmed by asking, if the product at issue is insurance for health care services, who bought from Aetna? Aren't the plan sponsors the ones who were subjected to alleged fraud, not their employees, aka members, for whom the insurance was purchased? Or was it both? And if they were both harmed, how would a court go about measuring the harm to each one and allocating it among them? We've now moved into a very difficult area where for standing purposes, the law often draws a distinction between direct and indirect purchasers; and to avoid problems of speculative damages and potential double recovery, courts often deny standing to the indirect purchasers. *See, e.g.*, Hale v. Stryker Orthopaedics, 2009 WL 321579 (D.N.J. 2009) (patients who had joint replacements had no standing as indirect purchasers in RICO action against manufacturer which sold to hospitals or insurers). *Cf.* Longmont United Hospital v. Saint Barnabas Corp., 305 Fed. Appx. 892, 2009 WL 19343 (3d Cir. 2009) (class of hospitals could not maintain RICO action against hospital chain that inflated Medicare reimbursement because alleged injury of diminished reimbursement for outlier cases was too remote and the party directly harmed was government, which had settled qui tam action); Boca Raton Community Hospital, Inc. v. Tenet Healthcare Corp., 502 F. Supp.2d 1237 (S.D. Fla. 2007), *aff'd*, 582 F.3d 1227 (11th Cir. 2009) (same). This indirect purchaser doctrine can be much criticized on the ground, among others, that the direct purchasers in such cases are unlikely to sue, and that plaintiffs like those in *Maio* satisfy the standing rule articulated in a subsequent Supreme Court case, Bridge v. Phoenix Bond & Indemnity Co., 553 U.S. 639 (2008) (first-party reliance not necessary to establish RICO standing so long as some direct relation exists between plaintiff's alleged injury and defendant's fraudulent misrepresentation to third-party). However, we have to leave the issue at just providing food for thought.

As the last point before moving on, let's make sure we continue to think about the RICO cases as *fraud* cases. Plaintiffs in *Maio* could have tried to sue under a breach of contract or ERISA breach of fiduciary duty theory, although consider how that tactic would have affected their ability to certify a class action—much less a national one—and the remedies available to them—including the settlement value for class-action lawyers. By contrast, with a RICO case, we're talking about an entirely different animal. We saw above that in the context of the FCA the courts are reluctant to get involved in weighing claims of quality of care; and we've suggested that perhaps falsity, for purposes of the FCA, should be returned to its old meaning of services not provided entirely or of such low quality as to be worthless, i.e., not provided at all. Suppose that were the meaning of health care fraud too under RICO. Can we then say that the *Maio* plaintiffs were provided insurance that was worthless?; and if that is the meaning of "injury" for purposes of standing, were they injured?

    c. Preemption. When a civil RICO action is brought and private money is involved, preemption issues arise because RICO is a federal statute and because, as we have seen, the McCarran–Ferguson Act, stated generally, leaves regulation of the business of insurance to the states. The leading case here is Humana, Inc. v. Forsyth, 525 U.S. 299 (1999), which involved what was once a typical insurance practice, as we saw in the chapter on payment, in which beneficiaries' copayments are based on providers' charges—e.g., 20% of $10,000 = $20,000—rather than the lesser amount the insurer actually pays—e.g., 20% of $80,000 = $16,000. Claiming that such a scheme amounted to fraud, plaintiff beneficiaries in *Forsyth* brought suit under RICO, and Humana argued that this cause of action was barred by the McCarran–Ferguson Act.

Refusing to apply field preemption, the Supreme Court instead applied conflict preemption, and held that in the particular case before it, no conflict existed because application of RICO "would not frustrate any declared state policy or interfere with a State's administrative regime." *Id.* at 310. The Court found that in the case presented to it RICO was a "complement" (*id.* at 313) to Nevada's administrative and common-law remedies, the latter of which allowed punitive damages capped at much less than damages allowed under RICO but not capped in instances in which bad faith obtained. Additionally, Nevada had not asserted a contrary position.

Forsyth is important because it allows beneficiaries to mount a suit independent of both state law and ERISA, thereby providing what may be the only effective deterrent against conduct like Humana's. State insurance departments are often reluctant to impose substantial penalties against the insurance companies they regulate, and as the Supreme Court in *Forsyth* noted, see *id.* at 304 n.2, regulators effectively just slapped Humana on the wrist with a $50,000 fine for misconduct that probably caused beneficiaries losses in multiples of that amount. Under ERISA section 502(a)(1)(B) ERISA beneficiaries are limited to recovering just the benefits due under the plan, a remedy of no help to them here; and as discussed in Part Two, Pilot Life Ins. Co. v. Dedeaux, 481 U.S. 41 (1987), and Part Three, Aetna Health Inc. v. Davila, 542 U.S. 200 (2004), preempt beneficiaries' use of any available state remedies that could give them greater damages. Possibly Cigna Corp. v. Amara, 131 S. Ct. 1866 (2011), also discussed in Part Two, opens the door to equitable relief under section 502(a)(3), such as a rebate, but the scope of the equitable powers discussed in *Amara* have yet to be developed. Even if *Amara* allows beneficiaries a full accounting of the losses they suffer in a case like *Forsyth*—a proposition that remains speculative right now—RICO's remedies, if they satisfy *Forsyth* and are therefore not "reverse preempted," would still have much greater deterrent value.

Keep in mind that *Forsyth* requires a fact-specific inquiry regarding the extent to which a particular RICO claim impairs particular state laws. *See, e.g.*, Riverview Health Institute v. Medical Mutual of Ohio, 601 F.3d 505, 517–19 (6th Cir. 2010) (providers' RICO claims concerning defendant insurer's reimbursement practices preempted by Ohio's regulatory scheme for claims processing because of the absence of a private cause of action, the concomitant unavailability of bad faith penal damages, the existence of a comprehensive regulatory scheme and because Ohio asserted that application of RICO would chill insurers' willingness to cooperate with its regulators); Sandwich Chef of Texas, Inc. v. Reliance National Indemnity Insurance Co., 111 F. Supp.2d 867 (S.D. Tex. 2000) (RICO action based on premiums exceeding filed rates complements states' rate-filing laws by aiding enforcement); Campanelli v. Allstate Insurance Co., 97 F. Supp.2d 1211 (C.D. Cal. 2000), *rev'd on other grounds*, 322 F.3d 1086 (9th Cir. 2003) (California's enforcement of an insurance contract's one-year statute of limitation applies instead of RICO's four-year statute of limitation because application of RICO's statute of limitation would impair the policy behind California's enforcement of the shorter contractually stipulated period).

3. THE ANTI-KICKBACK STATUTE (AKS) AND STARK

We now move to direct consideration of the problem of kickbacks, bribes, rebates and the like exchanged for referrals. As we have seen, this conduct can be litigated under the FCA and RICO, effectively as "predicate acts." Up to this point, however, in analyzing whether causes of action could be mounted under the FCA and RICO, we have largely bracketed out direct examination of these predicates and effectively assumed their existence. Now we remove those brackets and give the "predicates" direct attention.

We reprint portions of the relevant federal statutes below but for now we can generalize by saying that the law on its face prohibits "remuneration for referral." The nub of the problem is this: the livelihood of every actor in the healthcare system depends on referrals. Without patients, there is no business; without referrals, there are no patients. Given that everyone needs referrals, transactions in the healthcare world are designed to create referrals. Yet remuneration for referral is facially banned. As one of us has put the matter,

> Economic production, like all other forms of social activity, requires collective action to generate wealth. The creation of almost every conceivable good and service requires, to some degree, the aggregation of capital and labor through a collective arrangement. This aggregation may fall into a variety of formal legal categories, ranging from full integration of ownership, management, plant and labor, to the combination of only one element necessary to production, such as the collection of capital in limited partnerships.
>
> In this respect, production of health care services is no different from the production of other goods and services in a modern economy. Wealth can be created from the production of health care only if hospitals, physicians, nurses, home health care agencies, nursing homes, laboratories and other members of the health care system are organized into formal and informal networks. Again, although the legal form of these organizations may vary, one fact alone is invariant—the need for collective activity among these multifarious participants.
>
> It is quite paradoxical, therefore, that numerous federal and state statutes, such as the Medicare and Medicaid antifraud and abuse provisions, as well as professional ethical standards, such as the Principles of Medical Ethics of the American Medical Association, purport either to regulate or to prohibit payments that are exchanged between different health care providers as compensation for the formation of collective activity. After all, since organizations do not simply spring into being, it is quite reasonable to ask: If collective action is necessary to produce health care, can

there be any principled content to legal and ethical requirements that it be organized without remuneration?

David M. Frankford, *Creating and Dividing the Fruits of Collective Economic Activity: Referrals Among Health Care Providers*, 89 COLUM. L. REV. 1861, 1862 (1989) [hereinafter Frankford, *Creating and Dividing the Fruits of Collective Economic Activity*].

Our laws are potentially at war with each other. For close to half a century now our society has taken the position that the health care sector ought to be largely or totally organized as any other sector in capitalist society. Simultaneously we maintain the position that there is something special about health care and that health care providers should not conduct themselves like other actors in a capitalist system. The polar ends of this extreme ambivalence intersect precisely at the laws regarding health care fraud. If our laws truly prohibit remuneration for referral, then our laws banish our health care sector.

The doctrine in this area, therefore, is a search for a middle ground, but it is a particular kind of search and type of middle ground because the basic principle—do not trade anything of value to obtain patients—is at odds with the basic principle around which the sector is organized—make money by obtaining patients. As a result, the law strives for compromises between these two protagonists by carving out certain categories of conduct or structures of activity as providing too much of a good thing—e.g., remuneration that is "unearned." *See* Mark A. Hall, *Making Sense of Referral Fee Statutes*, 13 J. HEALTH POL. POL'Y & L. 623 (1988). However, such adjectives merely move the question to another set of words, for we must ask, "When is remuneration earned? How much of a good thing is too much?" Because there is still no animating principle, the law devolves into a process of piling detail upon detail, exception upon exception, boring down, at the extreme, to regulating such things as the manner in which frequent flier miles can be allocated (We kid you not! See Health Care Financing Administration, Proposed Rule, Medicare and Medicaid Programs; Physicians' Referrals to Health Care Entities with Which They Have Financial Relationships, 63 Fed. Reg. 1659, 1699 (Jan. 9, 1998)). Typically we end up where we started: parties are entitled to enter into arrangements that reflect "fair market" profits, i.e., arrangements that make money but not too much. The resultant level of detail is truly mindboggling.

The Anti–Kickback Statute (AKS)

42 U.S.C. § 1320a–7b. Criminal penalties for acts involving Federal health care programs

(b) Illegal remunerations.

(1) Whoever knowingly and willfully solicits or receives any remuneration (including any kickback, bribe, or rebate) directly or indirectly, overtly or covertly, in cash or in kind—

(A) in return for referring an individual to a person for the furnishing or arranging for the furnishing of any item or service for which payment may be made in whole or in part under a Federal health care program, or

(B) in return for purchasing, leasing, ordering, or arranging for or recommending purchasing, leasing, or ordering any good, facility, service, or item for which payment may be made in whole or in part under a Federal health care program,

shall be guilty of a felony and upon conviction thereof, shall be fined not more than $25,000 or imprisoned for not more than five years, or both.

(2) Whoever knowingly and willfully offers or pays any remuneration (including any kickback, bribe, or rebate) directly or indirectly, overtly or covertly, in cash or in kind to any person to induce such person—

A) to refer an individual to a person for the furnishing or arranging for the furnishing of any item or service for which payment may be made in whole or in part under a Federal health care program, or

(B) to purchase, lease, order, or arrange for or recommend purchasing, leasing, or ordering any good, facility, service, or item for which payment may be made in whole or in part under a Federal health care program,

shall be guilty of a felony and upon conviction thereof, shall be fined not more than $25,000 or imprisoned for not more than five years, or both.

Civil Monetary Penalties for Kickbacks

42 U.S.C. § 1320a–7a. Civil monetary penalties

(a) Improperly filed claims. Any person (including an organization, agency, or other entity, but excluding a beneficiary) that—

(7) commits an act described in paragraph (1) or (2) of 42 U.S.C. § 1320a–7b(b);

shall be subject, in addition to any other penalties that may be prescribed by law, to a civil money penalty of not more than $50,000 for each such act. In addition, such a person shall be subject to damages of not more than 3 times the total amount of remuneration offered, paid, solicited, or received, without regard to whether a portion of such remuneration was offered, paid, solicited, or received for a lawful purpose. In addition the Secretary may make a determination in the same proceeding to exclude the person from participation in the Federal health care programs and to direct the appropriate State agency to exclude the person from participation in any State health care program.

United States v. Greber

760 F.2d 68 (3d Cir.), *cert. den.*, 474 U.S. 988 (1985)

■ WEIS, CIRCUIT JUDGE:

In this appeal, defendant argues that payments made to a physician for professional services in connection with tests performed by a laboratory cannot be the basis of Medicare fraud. We do not agree and hold that if one purpose of the payment was to induce future referrals, the Medicare statute has been violated. We find the district court's rulings consistent with our determinations and accordingly will affirm.

After a jury trial, defendant was convicted on 20 of 23 counts in an indictment charging violations of the mail fraud, Medicare fraud, and false statement statutes. Post-trial motions were denied, and defendant has appealed.

Defendant is an osteopathic physician who is board certified in cardiology. In addition to hospital staff and teaching positions, he was the president of Cardio–Med, Inc., an organization which he formed. The company provides physicians with diagnostic services, one of which uses a Holter-monitor. This device, worn for approximately 24 hours, records the patient's cardiac activity on a tape. A computer operated by a cardiac technician scans the tape, and the data is later correlated with an activity diary the patient maintains while wearing the monitor.

Cardio–Med billed Medicare for the monitor service and, when payment was received, forwarded a portion to the referring physician. The government charged that the referral fee was 40 percent of the Medicare payment, not to exceed $65 per patient.

Based on Cardio–Med's billing practices, counts 18–23 of the indictment charged defendant with having tendered remuneration or kickbacks to the referring physicians in violation of 42 U.S.C. § 1395nn(b)(2)(B) (1982).

The proof as to the Medicare fraud counts (18–23) was that defendant had paid a Dr. Avallone and other physicians "interpretation fees" for the doctors' initial consultation services, as well as for explaining the test results to the patients. There was evidence that physicians received "interpretation fees" even though defendant had actually evaluated the monitoring data.

The government also introduced testimony defendant had given in an earlier civil proceeding. In that case, he had testified that "... if the doctor didn't get his consulting fee, he wouldn't be using our service. So the doctor got a consulting fee." In addition, defendant told physicians at a hospital that the Board of Censors of the Philadelphia County Medical Society had said the referral fee was legitimate if the physician shared the responsibility for the report. Actually, the Society had stated that there should be separate bills because "for the monitor company to offer payment to the physicians ... is not considered to be the method of choice."

On appeal, defendant raises several alleged trial errors. He presses more strongly, however, his contentions that the evidence was insufficient to support the guilty verdict on the Medicare fraud counts, and that the charge to the jury on that issue was not correct.

I. MEDICARE FRAUD

The Medicare fraud statute was amended by P.L. 95–142, 91 Stat. 1183 (1977). Congress, concerned with the growing problem of fraud and abuse in the system, wished to strengthen the penalties to enhance the deterrent effect of the statute.

A particular concern was the practice of giving "kickbacks" to encourage the referral of work. Testimony before the Congressional committee was that "physicians often determine which laboratories would do the test work for their Medicaid patients by the amount of the kickbacks and rebates offered by the laboratory.... Kickbacks take a number of forms including cash, long-term credit arrangements, gifts, supplies and equipment, and the furnishing of business machines."

To remedy the deficiencies in the statute and achieve more certainty, the present version of 42 U.S.C. § 1395nn(b) (2) was enacted. It provides:

"whoever knowingly and willfully offers or pays any remuneration (including any kickback, bribe or rebate) directly or indirectly, overtly or covertly in cash or in kind to induce such person—

(B) to purchase, lease, order, or arrange for or recommend purchasing ... or ordering any ... service or item for which payment may be made ... under this title, shall be guilty of a felony."

The district judge instructed the jury that the government was required to prove that Cardio–Med paid to Dr. Avallone some part of the amount received from Medicare; that defendant caused Cardio–Med to make the payment; and did so knowingly and willfully as well as with the intent to induce Dr. Avallone to use Cardio–Med's services for patients covered by Medicare. The judge further charged that even if the physician interpreting the test did so as a consultant to Cardio–Med, that fact was immaterial if a purpose of the fee was to induce the ordering of services from Cardio–Med.

Defendant contends that the charge was erroneous. He insists that absent a showing that the only purpose behind the fee was to improperly induce future services, compensating a physician for services actually rendered could not be a violation of the statute.

The government argues that Congress intended to combat financial incentives to physicians for ordering particular services patients did not require.

The language and purpose of the statute support the government's view. Even if the physician performs some service for the money received, the potential for unnecessary drain on the Medicare system remains. The statute is aimed at the inducement factor.

The text refers to "any remuneration." That includes not only sums for which no actual service was performed but also those amounts for which some professional time was expended. "Remunerates" is defined as "to pay an equivalent for service." Webster Third New International Dictionary (1966). By including such items as kickbacks and bribes, the statute expands "remuneration" to cover situations where no service is performed. That a particular payment was a remuneration (which implies that a service was rendered) rather than a kickback, does not foreclose the possibility that a violation nevertheless could exist.

In *United States v. Hancock*, 604 F.2d 999 (7th Cir. 1979), the court applied the term "kickback" found in the predecessor statute to payments made to chiropractors by laboratories which performed blood tests. The chiropractors contended that the amounts they received were legitimate handling fees for their services in obtaining, packaging, and delivering the specimens to the laboratories and then interpreting the results. The court rejected that contention and noted, "The potential for increased costs to the Medicare–Medicaid system and misapplication of federal funds is plain, where payments for the exercise of such judgments are added to the legitimate cost of the transaction ... There [sic] are among the evils Congress sought to prevent by enacting the kickback statutes...." *Id.* at 1001.

Hancock strongly supports the government's position here, because the statute in that case did not contain the word "remuneration." The court nevertheless held that "kickback" sufficiently described the defendants' criminal activity. By adding "remuneration" to the statute in the 1977 amendment, Congress sought to make it clear that even if the transaction was not considered to be a "kickback" for which no service had been rendered, payment nevertheless violated the Act.

We conclude that the more expansive reading is consistent with the impetus for the 1977 amendments and therefore hold that the district court correctly instructed the jury. If the payments were intended to induce the physician to use Cardio–Med's services, the statute was violated, even if the payments were also intended to compensate for professional services.

A review of the record also convinces us that there was sufficient evidence to sustain the jury's verdict.

Having carefully reviewed all of the defendant's allegations, we find no reversible error. Accordingly, the judgment of the district court will be affirmed.

Notes

1. *The significance of intent to induce referral.* The AKS is an intent-based statute. The *Greber* court holds that the required intent is established if it is proven that "one purpose" of remuneration given to the referring provider is to induce a referral. Suppose the court had adopted the defendant's argument that the government must prove that the *only*

purpose of the remuneration was to induce the referral. What would have been the consequence of defendant's proof that referring physicians did perform some service? Under the court's test what is the consequence of that fact? Put differently, what is it that the government must prove to establish the requisite intent? Is it simply that money was exchanged between providers or something more? Does the statute as interpreted, then, literally ban "any remuneration" exchanged between providers or something else?

Suppose that the referring physicians had billed Medicare for the services they provided and suppose that Cardio–Med had likewise billed the program directly for the Holter-monitor, with the result that no cash passed between Cardio–Med and the referring physicians. Although there are referrals, is there remuneration for referral? What exactly, then, does the AKS regulate? Should prosecutors, judges and juries, through a criminal statute, be overseeing the value exchanged among providers when they engage in transactions? Should providers be placed at the risk of criminal penalties that prosecutors, judges and juries will decide after the fact that the value exchanged among the providers exceeded fair market value?

Some courts have formulated tests other than the "one-purpose test" of *Greber*—which the OIG has of course codified in its regs (42 C.F.R. § 1001.951(a)(2)(i))—in order to reduce the risk. *See, e.g.*, United States v. Bay State Ambulance and Hospital Rental Service, 874 F.2d 20, 30 (1st Cir. 1989) ("primary purpose") (dicta). Regardless, substantial risk remains because the evidence in these cases is almost always circumstantial. United States v. McClatchey, 217 F.3d 823 (10th Cir. 2000), a case that became infamous because attorneys were indicted too, is illustrative. One defendant, McClatchey, the chief operating officer of a hospital, had negotiated a new contract with two doctors, Robert and Ronald LaHue, who were the principals of a practice that provided care to nursing home patients whom they admitted to the hospital. McClatchey's conviction was sustained on review because the record showed that he knew that the LaHues had not provided some or all of the services specified by the prior contracts, had added services to the new contract that no one was interested in having performed, and because he understood how important the referrals were to the hospital's financial health. The evidence showed, therefore, that the fee paid to the LaHues for their service as "Co–Directors of Gerontology Services" was inflated relative to whatever duties, if any, they performed.

Given the high risk and high degree of uncertainty posed by alternative readings of such circumstantial evidence, you can understand why the statute is loaded with an increasing number of exceptions and why the regulatory regime has added on an ever-expanding number of safe harbors and advisory opinions, a subject we develop immediately below.

2. *Specific intent to violate the statute.* At least one circuit did in fact place substantial hurdles in the way of successful prosecution, barriers much higher than a formulation like the "primary-purpose test." In Hanlester Network v. Shalala, 51 F.3d 1390 (9th Cir. 1995), the ninth circuit held that not only did the AKS scienter requirement stipulate that

defendant had a purpose of inducing referrals but also that defendant must have acted with specific intent to violate the law, i.e., defendant knew that the specific conduct violates the AKS. The PPACA overrules this holding by amending the AKS to provide that "a person need not have actual knowledge of this section or specific intent to commit a violation of this section." PPACA, Pub. L. No. 111–148 § 6402(f) (codified as 42 U.S.C. § 1320a–7b(h)). Congress's purpose appears to have been to bring the ninth circuit in line with the rest of the country. *See* Scot T. Hasselman, *The Patient Protection and Affordable Care Act, As Amended by the Reconciliation Act: Analysis, Implications of Key Fraud Abuse and Program Integrity Provisions*, 19 HEALTH LAW REPORTER (BNA) 1115 (Aug. 5, 2010).

3. *State laws*. Many states have laws covering the subject area of the federal AKS (and also Stark, covered below). The variations are great. Some states mandate disclosure; some, particularly through regulation of medical licensure, prohibit fee-splitting; some are modeled more explicitly on AKS or Stark; and so on.

Exceptions to the AKS

42 U.S.C. § 1320a–7b. Criminal penalties for acts involving Federal health care programs

(b) Illegal remunerations.

(3) Paragraphs (1) and (2) shall not apply to—

(A) a discount or other reduction in price obtained by a provider of services or other entity under a Federal health care program if the reduction in price is properly disclosed and appropriately reflected in the costs claimed or charges made by the provider or entity under a Federal health care program;

(B) any amount paid by an employer to an employee (who has a bona fide employment relationship with such employer) for employment in the provision of covered items or services;

(C) any amount paid by a vendor of goods or services to a person authorized to act as a purchasing agent for a group of individuals or entities who are furnishing services reimbursed under a Federal health care program if—

(i) the person has a written contract, with each such individual or entity, which specifies the amount to be paid the person, which amount may be a fixed amount or a fixed percentage of the value of the purchases made by each such individual or entity under the contract, and

(ii) in the case of an entity that is a provider of services, the person discloses (in such form and manner as the Secretary requires) to the entity and, upon request, to the Secretary the amount received from each such vendor with respect to purchases made by or on behalf of the entity;

(D) a waiver of any coinsurance under part B by a Federally qualified health care center with respect to an individual who qualifies for subsidized services under a provision of the Public Health Service Act;

(E) any payment practice specified by the Secretary in regulations promulgated pursuant to [AKS safe harbors] or [or in a safe harbor for free goods and services to establish an electronic prescription system];

(F) any remuneration between an organization and an individual or entity providing items or services, or a combination thereof, pursuant to a written agreement between the organization and the individual or entity if the organization is [a Medicare MCO] or if the written agreement, through a risk-sharing arrangement, places the individual or entity at substantial financial risk for the cost or utilization of the items or services, or a combination thereof, which the individual or entity is obligated to provide;

(G) the waiver or reduction by pharmacies (including pharmacies of the Indian Health Service, Indian tribes, tribal organizations, and urban Indian organizations) of any cost-sharing imposed under part D, if the conditions [for specified types of financial need are satisfied];

(H) any remuneration between a federally qualified health center (or an entity controlled by such a health center) and a [Medicare Advantage organization];

(I) any remuneration between a [federally qualified health center] and any individual or entity providing goods, items, services, donations, loans, or a combination thereof, to such health center entity pursuant to a contract, lease, grant, loan, or other agreement, if such agreement contributes to the ability of the [federally qualified health center] to maintain or increase the availability, or enhance the quality, of services provided to a medically underserved population served by the [federally qualified health center]; and

(J) a discount in the price of an applicable drug of a manufacturer that is furnished to an applicable beneficiary under the Medicare coverage gap discount program.

Notes

1. *AKS exceptions.* Over the years the AKS exceptions have bred like rabbits as particular problem areas have been identified or as Congress has added new parts to Medicare and Medicaid. The point of listing them is not for you to learn the details but to understand the structure of AKS. Each exception has been added because remuneration passed between the specified types of health care providers in a specified way such that without the exception, the AKS ban on remuneration for referral would have been violated. Some of the exemptions immunize "ordinary" activity that would otherwise be at risk. As examples: (1) the first exception, in subsection (A),

is needed because ordinary discounts would have constituted remuneration for referral; (2) the second exception, in subsection (B), is needed because it is standard practice for employees, who are paid—i.e., they receive remuneration—to solicit business for their employers—i.e., they receive remuneration for referrals; (3) the third exception, in subsection (C), is needed because rebates are routinely given to group purchasing organizations; and (4) the "risk-sharing" exception, in subsection F, is needed because with the growth of managed care, risk-sharing methods of reimbursement—capitation, withholds, bonuses—result in money being shifted between providers and insurers who maintain referral relationships.

Other exceptions immunize payments for entities or beneficiaries favored by other social policies, and without the exception there would be remuneration for referrals. Two prominent examples of this interplay between social interests and the prohibition against health care fraud involve the two exceptions are found at 42 U.S.C. § 1320a–7b(b)(3)(D) and (I), which address specific situations in which federally qualified health centers (the Medicare and Medicaid names for community health centers, discussed in Part One) have found themselves in hot water with the federal government over allegations of fraud. Health centers operate with basic grant support under the Public Health Service Act but also are obligated under the Act to participate in all public and private insurance programs and bill third-party payers. The Public Health Service Act also obligates health centers to adjust charges prospectively in accordance with patients' ability to pay, with grant funds effectively subsidizing these lower charges. Health centers are comprehensive primary care practices located in medically underserved urban and rural communities that exhibit high levels of poverty and preventable health problems. Approximately 37 percent of all health center patients are uninsured, and over 90 percent are low-income.

In an exception (D) situation, health centers faced the prospect of AKS exposure because, in accordance with their own Public Health Service Act authorizing statute, 42 U.S.C. § 254b, they waived or reduced otherwise applicable cost-sharing charges owed by Medicare beneficiaries whose incomes were low enough to qualify for free or reduced-cost care under the terms of the health centers funding authority. Despite the fact that by law health centers are obligated to adjust charges in accordance with patients' ability to pay, the Office of the Inspector General—another branch of the same federal agency (i.e., the United States Department of Health and Human Services) that administered the health centers program—treated prospective adjustment of charges as an inducement to fraud. The Congressional response to this absurdity was to create an exception explicitly recognizing this legal requirement and exempt the waiver of cost sharing from the definition of fraud.

In an exception (I) situation, a health center might enter into an agreement with a hospital to send its insured patients to the hospital (e.g., use the hospital for all of its Medicaid-covered deliveries) in exchange for donated services such as laboratory tests, specialty consultations, or reduced cost inpatient hospital care. A hospital also might give a grant to a health center to help defray the cost of operation. Obviously in this situation, the health center and hospital could be viewed as trading something of value for Medicare and Medicaid business, a characterization that stopped cold numerous collaborations between health centers and other community providers and institutions, despite the fact that health centers are obligated under their own authorizing statute to collaborate with other community institutions and to maximize resources available to care for the poor. *See, e.g.,* Sara Rosenbaum et al., *Assessing and Addressing Legal Barriers to Clinical Integration of Community Health Centers and Other Community Providers,* COMMONWEALTH FUND (2011), http://www.commonwealthfund.org/?/media/Files/Publications/Fund20Report/2011/Jul/1525_Rosenbaum_assessing_barriers_clinical_integration_CHCs.pdf. The purpose of the (I) exception is to legitimize such arrangements, which were viewed by Congress as a public good rather than an invitation to fraud.

2. *Terms of AKS exceptions.* Notice the structure of many of the AKS exceptions. For example, the first exception in subsection (A) stipulates that the discount must be "properly disclosed and appropriately reflected in the costs claimed or charges made by the provider or entity under a Federal health care program." Similarly, the risk-sharing exception in subsection (F) requires that the risk-sharing arrangement be part of a written agreement. We will see analogous requirements in most of the safe harbors below. Always keep in mind the burden placed on regulators to police an enormous sector with diverse activities for violations of the fraud and abuse laws, and how certain stipulations, like requiring a writing, ease that burden, as well as possibly reduce incentives for overutilization.

The AKS Safe Harbors

Despite the exceptions provided by the statute itself many "ordinary activities" remained at risk. Therefore, in response to much pressure in 1987 Congress granted the Department of Health Human Services the authority to create safe harbors, codified as the exception in subsection (E) above, to immunize certain activities from the AKS. *See* Pub. L. No. 100–93 § 14(a), 101 Stat. 680, 697. It is important to remember the precise meaning of a safe harbor. Activity within the safe harbor is excepted from the reach of the statute (again, see 42 U.S.C. § 1320a–7b(b)(3)(E) reprinted above). Activity outside of the safe harbor falls outside of the statutory exception, i.e., the activity is still within the ambit of the statute. That fact doesn't mean that the activity necessarily violates AKS. It just means that the activity is outside of the exception provided for activities within the safe harbor.

As of December 2011, there are twenty-five safe harbors, codified at 42 C.F.R. § 1001.952. Among the more important ones are: large and small entity investment interests; contracts for equipment and space rentals; contracts for personal services and management services; sales of physician practices; physician recruitment; risk-sharing arrangements by MCOs; group practice arrangements; ambulatory surgical centers (ASCs); and electronic health records and electronic prescribing.

Sometimes the safe harbors reflect the fact that ordinary business arrangements can be used to generate referrals, and the safe harbors are designed to give parties an incentive to avoid such temptation, i.e., steer them from going too far (leaving aside how we define "too far"). For example, medical facilities need to contract with physicians to obtain their expertise, but those physicians are often in a position to refer to that facility. Therefore, overpayment of those physicians is a means to induce and reward referrals based, not on medical necessity and quality, but the fact that the physicians receive what are effectively kickbacks. As another example, it is convenient to patients, physicians and hospitals for hospitals to have medical office buildings on hospital medical campuses and to rent office space to members of their medical staffs. Undercharging rent is a means, again, to induce referrals for reasons unrelated to medical necessity and quality. Hence the safe harbors for personal service contracts and space rental are designed to preclude such overutilization by building in certain safeguards.

As you read the following safe harbor for rental space, think about the reason for each of its stated requirements. Remember that the purpose of your reading this safe harbor is not to master the details—and this is by far one of the simplest safe harbors out of all of them—but to understand how the safe harbors in general are structured to allow beneficial arrangements while precluding (too great) an inducement for referral.

Space Rental Safe Harbor

42 C.F.R. § 1001.952

(b) Space rental. As used in [42 U.S.C. § 1320a–7b], "remuneration" does not include any payment made by a lessee to a lessor for the use of premises, as long as all of the following six standards are met—

(1) The lease agreement is set out in writing and signed by the parties.

(2) The lease covers all of the premises leased between the parties for the term of the lease and specifies the premises covered by the lease.

(3) If the lease is intended to provide the lessee with access to the premises for periodic intervals of time, rather than on a full-time basis for the term of the lease, the lease specifies exactly the schedule of such intervals, their precise length, and the exact rent for such intervals.

(4) The term of the lease is for not less than one year.

(5) The aggregate rental charge is set in advance, is consistent with fair market value in arms-length transactions and is not determined in a manner that takes into account the volume or value of any referrals or business otherwise generated between the parties for which payment may be made in whole or in part under Medicare, Medicaid or other Federal health care programs.

(6) The aggregate space rented does not exceed that which is reasonably necessary to accomplish the commercially reasonable business purpose

of the rental. Note that for purposes of paragraph (b) of this section, the term fair market value means the value of the rental property for general commercial purposes, but shall not be adjusted to reflect the additional value that one party (either the prospective lessee or lessor) would attribute to the property as a result of its proximity or convenience to sources of referrals or business otherwise generated for which payment may be made in whole or in part under Medicare, Medicaid and all other Federal health care programs.

* * *

Sometimes safe harbors are based on recognition of the reality that in the sector remuneration is exchanged to induce referrals, while the arrangement also serves useful functions; and the safe harbor is designed to moderate the incentive to refer simply to increase that remuneration. Examples include the safe harbor for small entity investment interests and the safe harbor for ASCs. Both safe harbors reflect regulatory reconciliation to the fact that physicians invest in these endeavors to earn an investment return that will be enhanced by the referrals they make, but also that patients and the federal health programs can benefit from this financial interest. Physician-owners can contribute expertise to an entity and, in the case of ASCs, at least in some instances in rural areas, referring physicians—the physicians who would perform procedures at the ASC—were the only willing or the most appropriate investors. Again, the safe harbors contain safeguards to ameliorate incentives to churn volume simply to earn higher rates of return from these investment interests, e.g., return on investment cannot be directly tied to the volume or value of referrals. As we will see when we turn to Stark, by contrast, some similar investments were deemed to be so dangerous that they were simply banned as a prophylactic measure (or at least the idea was to create bright-clear lines).

Finally, another purpose animating some of the safe harbors is that they are designed to accomplish social ends. The safe harbor for ASCs, again, provides a good example. Program administrators were simply interested in seeing ASCs constructed in order to move site of care from expensive inpatient settings to less expensive outpatient ones. As a result, they turned a blind eye, in part, to the fact that physicians invest so that they can earn a higher rate of return for referrals to the ASCs in which they have an ownership stake. The safe harbor reduces the incentive from what it would otherwise be in an unfettered, unregulated marketplace.

The safe harbors for electronic prescribing and electronic health records provide a further example. The effort to promote the diffusion of health information technology (HIT) and electronic patient health records is viewed as vital to quality improvement and oversight of health care costs and patient conduct. *See* HHS Office of Health Information Technology, http://www.hhs.gov/healthit/; INSTITUTE OF MEDICINE, CROSSING THE QUALITY CHASM (2000). Yet, HIT capitalization is very costly because of the investment in both necessary hardware and software as well as technical support. Should hospitals, pharmaceutical companies, and medical suppliers be able to donate HIT to staff physicians? Regulators have answered with a qualified yes, for safe harbors were written for e-prescribing and electronic records transfer to promote such diffusion of technology by allowing donations under limited circumstances. See 42 C.F.R. §§ 1001.952(x)–(y).

The safe harbors permit donation of "non-monetary remuneration" (i.e., hardware, software, and training) related to e-prescribing and electronic health records. The safe harbors lay out specific donor/recipient relationships and spell out required conditions. While the selection of donees can take volume into account, there can be no direct financial *quid pro quo* (i.e., so many dollar's worth of prescriptions written per month). The technology that can be donated is specified (e.g., no general office suites). The technology must be interoperable with other technologies and cannot impose proprietary limits on the exchange of data. In other words, the technology must be compatible with the needs of multiple payers in order to permit cross-payer collection on provider practices across multiple groups of patients. While interoperable systems are desirable, the cost of adoption is prohibitive, and the real benefit to the donor therefore is that it is going to get a return on its investment. On the other hand, interoperability and prohibitions against exclusivity and dollar volume make this potentially beneficial investment more of a community benefit. As a consequence, this safe harbor and others are simply reflections of what we stated at the outset of this section, our ambivalence toward the unfettered incentives created by capitalist, for-profit ownership of health care. Life involves compromise.

AKS Advisory Opinions

In 1996 Congress responded to complaints that even with the addition of the safe harbors, too much uncertainty remained in interpreting the AKS, particularly given the "one-purpose" rule of *Greber*. Over the objection of the Clinton administration, Congress mandated that DHHS establish procedures whereby a party could seek an advisory opinion regarding whether an activity violates the statute. *See* Pub. L. No. 104–191 § 205, 110 Stat. 1936, 2000 (codified as 42 U.S.C. § 1320a–7d(b)). While the safe harbors adumbrate generalized requirements to fit within the exception for them in the AKS, advisory opinions analyze particular fact patterns by which the administering authority, the OIG, makes a determination, based on the facts the parties present to it—its conclusion is premised on the fact that what the parties say is true—whether the statute is violated. While the advisory opinion is binding only on the particular parties which sought it, and has no precedential effect, health care providers and their attorneys routinely rely on the advisory opinions for guidance. As of this writing, the OIG has issued 297 opinions, which are listed on their website, http://oig. hhs.gov/compliance/advisory-opinions/. CMS, which has regulatory authority over Stark, issues analogous opinions under that statute because of a mandate from Congress in 1997, *see* Pub. L. No. 105–33 § 4314, 111 Stat. 251, 389 (codified as 42 U.S.C. § 1395nn(g)(6)), although it has issued many, many fewer advisory opinions than has the OIG under AKS.

It is important to understand the relationship between advisory opinions and the safe harbors. The advisory opinion reprinted below concerns a joint venture between a hospital and orthopedists on its staff to create an ASC. The relevant portions of the pertinent safe harbor provides:

Safe Harbor for Ambulatory Surgical Centers

42 C.F.R. § 1001.952(r)

(r) Ambulatory surgical centers. As used in [the AKS], "remuneration" does not include any payment that is a return on an investment interest, such as a dividend or interest income, made to an investor, as long as the investment entity is a certified ambulatory surgical center (ASC), whose operating and recovery room space is dedicated exclusively to the ASC, patients referred to the investment entity by an investor are fully informed of the investor's investment interest, and all of the applicable standards are met within one of the following four categories [we reprint only two of the categories of ASCs]—

(1) Surgeon-owned ASCs—If all of the investors are general surgeons or surgeons engaged in the same surgical specialty, who are in a position to refer patients directly to the entity and perform surgery on such referred patients; surgical group practices (as defined in this paragraph) composed exclusively of such surgeons; or investors who are not employed by the entity or by any investor, are not in a position to provide items or services to the entity or any of its investors, and are not in a position to make or influence referrals directly or indirectly to the entity or any of its investors, all of the following six standards must be met [we include only three]—

(i) The terms on which an investment interest is offered to an investor must not be related to the previous or expected volume of referrals, services furnished, or the amount of business otherwise generated from that investor to the entity.

(ii) At least one-third of each surgeon investor's medical practice income from all sources for the previous fiscal year or previous 12–month period must be derived from the surgeon's performance of procedures (as defined in this paragraph).

(iv) The amount of payment to an investor in return for the investment must be directly proportional to the amount of the capital investment (including the fair market value of any pre-operational services rendered) of that investor.

(4) Hospital/Physician ASCs—If at least one investor is a hospital, and all of the remaining investors are physicians who meet the requirements of paragraphs (r)(1), (r)(2) or (r)(3) of this section; group practices (as defined in this paragraph) composed of such physicians; surgical group practices (as defined in this paragraph); or investors who are not employed by the entity or by any investor, are not in a position to provide items or services to the entity or any of its investors, and are not in a position to refer patients directly or

indirectly to the entity or any of its investors, all of the following eight standards must be met [we only include four]—

(i) The terms on which an investment interest is offered to an investor must not be related to the previous or expected volume of referrals, services furnished, or the amount of business otherwise generated from that investor to the entity.

(iii) The amount of payment to an investor in return for the investment must be directly proportional to the amount of the capital investment (including the fair market value of any pre-operational services rendered) of that investor.

(vi) All ancillary services for Federal health care program beneficiaries performed at the entity must be directly and integrally related to primary procedures performed at the entity, and none may be separately billed to Medicare or other Federal health care programs.

(viii) The hospital may not be in a position to make or influence referrals directly or indirectly to any investor or the entity.

(5) For purposes of paragraph (r) of this section, procedures means any procedure or procedures on the list of Medicare-covered procedures for ambulatory surgical centers in accordance with regulations issued by the Department and group practice means a group practice that meets all of the standards of paragraph (p) of this section. Surgical group practice means a group practice that meets all of the standards of paragraph (p) of this section and is composed exclusively of surgeons who meet the requirements of paragraph (r)(1) of this section.

OIG Advisory Opinion 08–08

We are writing in response to your request for an advisory opinion regarding an investment in an ambulatory surgery center by a group of surgeons and a health care corporation that owns hospitals (the "Arrangement").

You have certified that all of the information provided in your request, including all supplementary letters, is true and correct and constitutes a complete description of the relevant facts and agreements among the parties.

In issuing this opinion, we have relied solely on the facts and information presented to us. We have not undertaken an independent investigation of such information. This opinion is limited to the facts presented. If material facts have not been disclosed or have been misrepresented, this opinion is without force and effect.

Based on the facts certified in your request for an advisory opinion and supplemental submissions, we conclude that while the Arrangement could potentially generate prohibited remuneration under the anti-kickback statute, if the requisite intent to induce or reward referrals of Federal health care program business were present, the Office of Inspector General ("OIG") will not impose administrative sanctions. This opinion is limited to the Arrangement and, therefore, we express no opinion about any ancillary agreements or arrangements disclosed or referenced in your request letter or supplemental submissions, except as explicitly stated in this opinion.

I. FACTUAL BACKGROUND

[T]he "Hospital Corporation" is a not-for-profit corporation that owns three hospitals and other healthcare-related entities, including a large physician group practice consisting of primary-care and specialty-care physicians (the "Hospital–Owned Physician Practice").

[T]he "Surgeon Partnership" is limited liability company whose members (the "Surgeon Investors") are also members of two divisions of a large, multi-site physician group (the "Surgeon Group"). (The Surgeon Group is not the Hospital–Owned Physician Practice, nor do their memberships overlap.) All of the Surgeon Investors are orthopedic surgeons. Each Surgeon Investor made an initial capital contribution of $50,000 and a subsequent capital contribution of $11,000 to the Surgeon Partnership. Each of the Surgeon Investors owns an equal share of the Surgeon Partnership.

[T]he "Company" is an entity owned 70 percent by the Surgeon Partnership and 30 percent by the Hospital Corporation. Under the Arrangement, the Company owns and operates an ambulatory surgery center (the "ASC"). The Surgeon Partnership and the Hospital Corporation made financial contributions to the Company proportional to their ownership interests, in order to finance the development and operation of this ASC.

There are eighteen Surgeon Investors, of whom fourteen meet the following test: Each received at least one-third of his or her medical practice income for the previous fiscal year or previous 12–month period from the performance of procedures payable by Medicare when performed in an ambulatory surgery center ("ASC–Qualified Procedures"). The four remaining Surgeon Investors (the "Inpatient Surgeons") do not meet this test. Each of the Inpatient Surgeons derives at least one-third of his or her medical practice income from procedures requiring a hospital operating room setting, but receives little or no medical practice income from the performance of ASC–Qualified Procedures. The Requestors have certified that the Inpatient Surgeons rarely have the occasion to refer patients to other physicians for ASC–Qualified Procedures, except for pain management procedures. The Requestors also have certified that none of the Surgeon Investors will refer patients for pain management procedures to be performed at the ASC, unless the pain management procedure is to be performed personally by the referring Surgeon Investor.

The Hospital Corporation is in a position to make or influence referrals to the ASC. The Requestors have certified that, in order to limit such ability, the Hospital Corporation has refrained and will refrain from any actions to require or encourage physicians who are employees, independent contractors, and medical staff members ("Hospital–Affiliated Physicians") to refer patients to the ASC or to its Surgeon Investors, and has not and will not track referrals, if any, by Hospital–Affiliated Physicians to the ASC or to its Surgeon Investors. The Requestors have further certified that any compensation paid by the Hospital Corporation to Hospital–Affiliated Physicians has been and will be consistent with fair market value and has not been and will not be related, directly or indirectly, to the volume or value of any referrals Hospital–Affiliated Physicians may make to the ASC, its Surgeon Investors, or the Surgeon Group. The Hospital Corporation will inform Hospital–Affiliated Physicians annually of these measures.

The Company entered a written agreement (the "Anesthesia Agreement") with the Hospital–Owned Physician Practice to be the exclusive provider of anesthesiology (except for pain management services) at the ASC through its employed anesthesiologists and certified registered nurse anesthetists. The Hospital–Owned Physician Practice obtains payment for anesthesia services from third-party payers, including Federal health care programs, and from patients for uninsured amounts. Pursuant to the Anesthesia Agreement, one of the anesthesiologists employed by the Hospital–Owned Physician Practice serves, on a part-time basis, as Director of Anesthesiology and Medical Director of the ASC, for an annual fixed stipend paid by the Company to the Department of Anesthesiology of the Hospital–Owned Physician Practice. The duties of this individual, which are administrative and supervisory, are described in detail in the Anesthesia Agreement, and the Requestors have certified that the stipend is fair market value for these services and not determined in a manner that takes into account the volume or value of any referrals or business otherwise generated between the parties.

II. LEGAL ANALYSIS

A. Law

The anti-kickback statute makes it a criminal offense knowingly and willfully to offer, pay, solicit, or receive any remuneration to induce or reward referrals of items or services reimbursable by a Federal health care program. For purposes of the anti-kickback statute, "remuneration" includes the transfer of anything of value, directly or indirectly, overtly or covertly, in cash or in kind.

The statute has been interpreted to cover any arrangement where one purpose of the remuneration was to obtain money for the referral of services or to induce further referrals. United States v. Greber, 760 F.2d 68 (3d Cir.), cert. denied, 474 U.S. 988 (1985).

B. Analysis

Although joint ventures by physicians and hospitals are susceptible to fraud and abuse, the OIG recognizes that hospitals may be at a competitive disadvantage when they compete with ASCs owned by physicians, who principally control referrals. Thus, the OIG promulgated a safe harbor for investment income from ASCs jointly-owned by physicians and hospitals that meet certain conditions, 42 C.F.R. § 1001.952(r)(4). Among the ownership arrangements potentially protected by this safe harbor are ASCs jointly owned by hospitals and general surgeons or surgeons engaged in the same surgical specialty. Because all the Surgeon Investors in the ASC are engaged in the same surgical specialty (orthopedics), the safe harbor is potentially applicable to the Arrangement. The Arrangement does not qualify for protection by this safe harbor, however, for the reasons noted below. Because no safe harbor would protect the investment income from the ASC, we must determine whether, given all the relevant facts, the Arrangement poses a minimal risk under the anti-kickback statute.

First, the Arrangement does not qualify for the protection of the hospital/physician-owned ASC safe harbor, because the Surgeon Investors do not hold their investment interests in the ASC either directly or through a group practice composed of qualifying physicians. Rather, the Surgeon Investors hold their individual ownership interests in the Surgeon Partnership. The Surgeon Partnership, in turn, holds an interest in the Company that owns and operates the ASC. We have previously expressed concern that intermediate investment entities could be used to redirect revenues to reward referrals or otherwise vitiate the safeguards provided by direct investment, including distributions of profits in proportion to capital investment. However, in this case, the use of a "pass-through" entity does not substantially increase the risk of fraud or abuse. Each Surgeon Investor's ownership in the Surgeon Partnership is proportional to his or her capital investment.[2] The Surgeon Partnership's ownership interest in the Company is, in turn, proportional to its capital investment. Thus the individual Surgeon Investors receive a return on their ASC investments that is exactly the same as if they had invested directly.

Second, four of the eighteen Surgeon Investors (the Inpatient Surgeons) fail to meet the safe harbor requirement that at least one-third of a physician investor's income from medical practice for the previous fiscal year or previous 12-month period be derived from the performance of ASC-Qualified Procedures. This "one third" test helps ensure that the safe harbor applies only to investment income to physicians who are unlikely to use the investment as a vehicle for profiting from their referrals to other physicians using the ASC. Safe harbor protection is limited to physician-investors who, because they perform a substantial number of ASC-Qualified Procedures, are likely to use the ASC on a regular basis as part of their medical practices.

In the circumstances presented, notwithstanding that four Inpatient Surgeons will not regularly practice at the ASC, we conclude that the ASC is unlikely to be a vehicle for them to profit from referrals. The Requestors have certified that, as practitioners of sub-specialties of orthopedic surgery that require a hospital operating room setting, the Inpatient Surgeons rarely have occasion to refer patients for ASC-Qualified Procedures (other than pain management procedures, which are discussed below).[4] Moreover,

---

2. We express no opinion with regard to any future sales of membership interests in the Surgeon Partnership that may result in individual investors having ownership interests that are not proportional to their investment.

4. If this certification proves incorrect, this advisory opinion is without force and effect.

like the other Surgeon Investors, the Inpatient Surgeons are regularly engaged in a genuine surgical practice, deriving at least one-third of their medical practice income from procedures requiring a hospital operating room setting. The Inpatient Surgeons are qualified to perform surgeries at the ASC and may choose to do so (and earn the professional fees) in medically appropriate cases. Also, the Inpatient Surgeons comprise a small proportion of the Surgeon Investors, a majority of whom will use the ASC on a regular basis as part of their medical practice. This Arrangement is readily distinguishable from potentially riskier arrangements in which few investing physicians actually use the ASC on a regular basis or in which investing physicians are significant potential referral sources for other investors or the ASC, as when primary care physicians invest in a surgical ASC or cardiologists invest in a cardiac surgery ASC.

As noted above, the Inpatient Surgeons do have occasion to refer patients for pain management procedures that are ASC–Qualified Procedures. This raises the possibility that an Inpatient Surgeon or other Surgeon Investor might refer patients to other practitioners for pain management procedures performed at the ASC, for the purpose of generating a facility fee for the ASC. The Requestors have certified, however, that no Surgeon Investor will refer patients for pain management procedures to be performed at the ASC, unless the procedure is to be performed personally by the referring Surgeon Investor. This serves to mitigate the potential for abusive referrals, with regard to this type of procedure.

Third, the Arrangement does not qualify for the safe harbor for ASCs jointly owned by physicians and hospitals, because the Hospital Corporation is in a position to make or influence referrals to the ASC and to the Surgeon Investors. However, the Arrangement includes certain commitments limiting the ability of the Hospital Corporation to direct or influence such referrals. The Hospital Corporation refrains from any actions to require or encourage Hospital–Affiliated Physicians to refer patients to the ASC or to its Surgeon Investors; it does not track referrals, if any, by Hospital–Affiliated Physicians to the ASC or to its Surgeon Investors; any compensation paid to Hospital–Affiliated Physicians is at fair market value and does not take into account any referrals Hospital–Affiliated Physicians may make to the ASC or to its Surgeon Investors; and the Hospital Corporation informs Hospital–Affiliated Physicians annually of these measures. In light of these safeguards, the ability of the Hospital Corporation to direct or influence referrals to the ASC is significantly constrained.

Fourth, the Arrangement does not meet the requirement of the hospital/physician-owned ASC safe harbor that any services provided by the Hospital Corporation to the ASC must be pursuant to a contract that complies with the personal services and management contracts safe harbor set forth at 42 C.F.R. § 1001.952(d). Among the conditions of the personal services and management contracts safe harbor is that, if the agreement is intended to provide for services on a periodic, sporadic or part-time basis, rather than on a full-time basis for the term of the agreement, the agreement must specify exactly the schedule of such intervals, their precise length, and the exact charge for such intervals.

The Anesthesia Agreement does not meet this requirement. It provides for an employee of the Hospital–Owned Physician Practice to serve as Director of Anesthesiology and Medical Director of the ASC on less than a full-time basis, but does not specify a schedule for the services to be provided by this individual. However, all of the services to be provided are set out in the Anesthesia Agreement in detail, and the Requestors have certified that the services are reasonable and necessary for the ASC. They have further certified that the amount to be paid under the agreement—a fixed fee set in advance in the contract—is fair market value for the services described, as determined in an arms length transaction, and not determined in a manner that takes into account the volume or value of any referrals or business otherwise generated between the parties.[5] The parties will keep accurate and contemporaneous records, such as time cards, of the services provided by the Medical Director, and make them available to the Secretary and the OIG upon request. In these circumstances and given the nature of the contracted services, the lack of specificity of the schedule of services does not raise the risk of fraud and abuse under the Arrangement.

For all of the foregoing reasons, we conclude that, while the Arrangement poses some risk, the safeguards put in place by the Requestors make that risk sufficiently low that we would not subject the Arrangement to administrative sanctions in connection with the anti-kickback statute.

III. CONCLUSION

Based on the facts certified in your request for an advisory opinion and supplemental submissions, we conclude that while the Arrangement could potentially generate prohibited remuneration under the anti-kickback statute, if the requisite intent to induce or reward referrals of Federal health care program business were present, the OIG will not impose administrative sanctions [for violation of the AKS].

IV. LIMITATIONS

The limitations applicable to this opinion include the following:

This advisory opinion is applicable only to the statutory provisions specifically noted above. No opinion is expressed or implied herein with respect to the application of any other Federal, state, or local statute, rule, regulation, ordinance, or other law that may be applicable to the Arrangement, including, without limitation, the physician self-referral law, [Stark].

No opinion is expressed herein regarding the liability of any party under the False Claims Act or other legal authorities for any improper billing, claims submission, cost reporting, or related conduct.

---

5. We are precluded by statute from opining on whether fair market value shall be or was paid for goods, services, or property. See 42 U.S.C. § 1320a–7d(b)(3)(A). For purposes of this advisory opinion, we rely on the Requestors' certifications of fair market value. If the compensation is not fair market value, this opinion is without force and effect.

Notes

1. *Understand the entities.* It is always important to understand the entities to a transaction and then analyze the legal issues raised. In the deal reviewed under OIG Advisory Opinion 08–08 the surgeons did not invest directly in the legal entity holding ownership of the ASC, "the Company." Instead, they formed, and each individual surgeon invested in, the "Surgeon Partnership," organized as a limited liability company (LLC). The Surgeon Partnership, in turn, held the investment interest in the Company, i.e., the ASC. Undoubtedly, the reasons for this structure were to obtain limited liability, favorable tax treatment and the governance flexibility afforded by an LLC. We leave these issues to your courses on business organizations and transactions.

2. *The role of safe harbors and advisory opinions.* However, notice that this structure and other factors in the business deal made it impossible to fit within the safe harbor for ASCs.

   a. *Surgeons not individual investors.* The first problem, as the advisory opinion notes, is that the safe harbor requires that the individual surgeons be direct investors but, as just discussed, the partnership they formed was the direct investor in the ASC. As the OIG explicates, when an intermediate investor is used, the concern is that the intermediate can hide linkages between volume and value of referrals, ownership interests and returns on those interests, i.e., profits can be distributed such *that* they are tied to referrals not ownership interests. In the deal reviewed in Advisory Opinion 08–08, the OIG opined, no such problem exists because the LLC is only a pass-through: "Each Surgeon Investor's ownership in the Surgeon Partnership is proportional to his or her capital investment. The Surgeon Partnership's ownership interest in the Company is, in turn, proportional to its capital investment. Thus the individual Surgeon Investors receive a return on their ASC investments that is exactly the same as if they had invested directly." Why didn't the OIG, however, stick to its guns and enforce only the explicit terms of the safe harbor? Would that have elevated form over substance? What does that tell you about the nature of the safe harbors? What does that tell you about the relationship between the safe harbors and advisory opinions (and the job of giving legal advice to clients)? Be sure to compare your answers to these questions to the exceptions to Stark, discussed below. You'll see that the answers are very, very different.

   b. *One-third rule.* The safe harbor requires that one-third of the surgeon investor's income derive from his or her practice at the ASC. The purported rationale for this rule is that the ASC is really an extension of the physician's office practice. Investors who don't practice at the ASC have an incentive to refer *to* physicians who do, and thereby increase the return on their investments. Yet in this instance the OIG approved an arrangement in which four of the eighteen surgeon investors performed only inpatient surgery and therefore would not practice at the ASC. The OIG reasoned that there was little danger of remuneration from referral because the parties certified both that the inpatient surgeons rarely referred to the other surgeons and that the inpatient surgeons operated on their own patients in an inpatient setting. Again, why didn't the OIG strictly enforce the strict terms of the safe harbor (and all the other questions asked above)?

c. *The hospital investor in a position to refer.* The safe harbor explicitly states that the hospital investor must not be in a position to refer to the ASC in which it is investing (so as to be in a position to enhance its investment return). Won't any hospital investor in this type of transaction be in a position to refer? The OIG was satisfied that safeguards like not tracking referrals were sufficient to avoid AKS liability. Again, what does this tell you about the nature of the safe harbors and their relationship to advisory opinions? If the OIG wishes to see these sort of safeguards, why not write them directly into the safe harbor? What would be the result of doing so for any transaction that could not use those particular safeguards?

d. *The anesthesia agreement.* The agreement for anesthesia service deviated from the safe harbors for *personal* and management services in many ways. Ditto all the questions asked above.

3. *The FCA is the 100–pound gorilla in the room.* Keep in mind always—if you aren't already—that now lurking in the background must be the fact that a violation of AKS or Stark can form the basis of a false claim action that FERA and the PPACA have made easier for *qui tam* plaintiffs to bring. And keep in mind always—we know you are—the differences between AKS and Stark. Yes, we are asking you to keep in mind things you haven't read yet. See the discussion of Stark below. You'll see that while perhaps an FCA cause of action for an AKS violation isn't so bad—although many would say it is—potentially an FCA cause of action for a Stark violation is a horror because of the differences between the statutes. Please see below.

4. *Other forms of guidance.* The OIG also engages in a number of other activities to inform providers and attorneys about their obligations and the agency's intentions. Periodically the agency issues Special Fraud Alerts, which can pertain to AKS or Stark. Originally these documents were disseminated internally for purposes of enforcement but the agency decided to make them publicly available to provide external guidance. The alerts cover areas that the agency thinks are particularly prone to abuse, and the alerts identify "suspect practices." The alerts do not have the same force of law as regulations promulgated under the Administrative Procedure Act but constitute agency interpretation to which other authorities like courts often defer. Over the years the Special Fraud Alerts have covered such areas as sham joint ventures for durable medical equipment (DME) and other services; rental of office space; nursing home arrangements with hospice programs; and telemarketing by DME suppliers. Somewhat similar are special advisory bulletins that identify particular areas of problematic behavior. All of these sources are found on the OIG's website for compliance, http://oig.hhs.gov/compliance/. *See generally* Krause, *A Conceptual Model* at 90–110.

5. *Voluntary compliance.* Perhaps of greater importance in recent years have been the efforts to encourage voluntary compliance, activities

that grew out of corporate integrity agreements (CIAs), which were negotiated with the OIG or DOJ to settle investigations, administrative proceedings or litigation brought as enforcement actions. CIAs typically require that the provider hire a compliance officer or appoint a compliance committee; develop written standards and policies; implement a comprehensive employee training program; retain an independent review organization to conduct annual reviews; establish a confidential disclosure program; restrict employment of ineligible persons; report overpayments, other events and ongoing investigations and legal proceedings; and provide an implementation report and annual reports to the OIG. *See* http://oig.hhs.gov/compliance/corporate-integrity-agreements/index.asp. However, as Professor Krause describes, "emphasis has moved from compliance as a *remedy* to compliance as a *preventive* mechanism." Krause, *A Conceptual Model* at 96. Toward that end, the OIG has published "Compliance Program Guidances," which it describes on its website as "a series of voluntary compliance program guidance documents directed at various segments of the health care industry, such as hospitals, nursing homes, third-party billers, and durable medical equipment suppliers, to encourage the development and use of internal controls to monitor adherence to applicable statutes, regulations, and program requirements." http://oig.hhs.gov/compliance/compliance-guidance/index.asp. OIG has issued specific guidances to a wide range of the sector, including hospitals, clinical laboratories, home health agencies, third-party medical billing companies, DME suppliers, hospices, Medicare Advantage organizations, nursing facilities, physician practices, pharmaceutical manufacturers, and ambulance companies.

Stark

As we have seen, arrangements in which physicians have an ownership interest in entities to which they refer can, if the statutory requirements are satisfied, violate AKS. However, these types of remuneration-for-referral arrangements, known generally as "self-referrals," became particularly controversial after a series of state, federal and academic studies showed increased utilization by referring physicians with ownership interests, particularly in clinical laboratories but also in other types of ancillary facilities. *See, e.g.*, OFFICE OF INSPECTOR GENERAL, FINANCIAL ARRANGEMENTS BETWEEN PHYSICIANS AND HEALTH CARE BUSINESSES: REPORT TO CONGRESS (1989). As a result, in 1989 Congress passed legislation that had been introduced as The Ethics in Patient Referrals Act, *see* Pub. L. No. 101–239 § 6204, 103 Stat. 2106, 2236, the scope of which was expanded in 1993. *See* Pub. L. No. 103–66 § 13562, 107 Stat. 312, 2236. Both laws are known by the name of their principal sponsor, Representative Fortney "Pete" Stark, as "Stark I" and "Stark II," or collectively, "Stark."

The initial legislation pertained only to clinical laboratory services in which physicians had an ownership interest but Stark II expanded the scope to other "designated health services," as defined below. The proscribed financial arrangements are effectively given special treatment. They violate the AKS if the other requirements of AKS are satisfied, most saliently the scienter requirement. However, the idea of Stark is that certain arrangements present such great danger of overutilization that prophylactically they are prohibited (although, as we shall see, with the large number of exceptions and regulatory interpretations, bright-clear rules are no longer bright and clear). Hence, with the exception of some penalties mentioned below, Stark has no scienter requirement—unlike AKS it is not an intent-based law. If the banned form of financial arrangement exists, then Stark is violated.

The basic definition of the types of proscribed arrangements is as follows.

Stark's Proscribed Arrangements

§ 1395nn. Limitation on certain physician referrals

(a) Prohibition of certain referrals.

(1) In general. [I]f a physician (or an immediate family member of such physician) has a financial relationship with an entity specified in paragraph (2), then—

(A) the physician may not make a referral to the entity for the furnishing of designated health services for which payment otherwise may be made under this title, and

(B) the entity may not present or cause to be presented a claim under this title or bill to any individual, third party payor, or other entity for designated health services furnished pursuant to a referral prohibited under subparagraph (A).

(2) Financial relationship specified. For purposes of this section, a financial relationship of a physician (or an immediate family member of such physician) with an entity specified in this paragraph is—

(A) an ownership or investment interest in the entity, or

(B) a compensation arrangement (as defined in subsection (h)(1)) between the physician (or an immediate family member of such physician) and the entity.

An ownership or investment interest described in subparagraph (A) may be through equity, debt, or other means and includes an interest in an entity that holds an ownership or investment interest in any entity providing the designated health service.

(h) Definitions and special rules. For purposes of this section:

(1) Compensation arrangement; remuneration.

(A) The term "compensation arrangement" means any arrangement involving any remuneration between a physician (or an immediate family member of such physician) and an entity.

(B) The term "remuneration" includes any remuneration, directly or indirectly, overtly or covertly, in cash or in kind.

(5) Referral; referring physician.

(A) Physicians' services. Except as provided in subparagraph (C), in the case of an item or service for which payment may be made under part B, the request by a physician for the item or service, including the request by a physician for a consultation with another physician (and any test or procedure ordered by, or to be performed by (or under the supervision of) that other physician), constitutes a "referral" by a "referring physician."

(B) Other items. Except as provided in subparagraph (C), the request or establishment of a plan of care by a physician which includes the provision of the designated health service constitutes a "referral" by a "referring physician."

(C) Clarification respecting certain services integral to a consultation by certain specialists. A request by a pathologist for clinical diagnostic laboratory tests and pathological examination services, a request by a radiologist for diagnostic radiology services, and a request by a radiation oncologist for radiation therapy, if such services are furnished by (or under the supervision of) such pathologist, radiologist, or radiation oncologist pursuant to a consultation requested by another physician does not constitute a "referral" by a "referring physician."

(6) Designated health services. The term "designated health services" means any of the following items or services:

(A) Clinical laboratory services.

(B) Physical therapy services.

(C) Occupational therapy services.

(D) Radiology services, including magnetic resonance imaging, computerized axial tomography scans, and ultrasound services.

(E) Radiation therapy services and supplies.

(F) Durable medical equipment and supplies.

(G) Parenteral and enteral nutrients, equipment, and supplies.

(H) Prosthetics, orthotics, and prosthetic devices and supplies.

(I) Home health services.

(J) Outpatient prescription drugs.

(K) Inpatient and outpatient hospital services.

(L) Outpatient speech-language pathology services.

* * *

Violations of Stark can bring serious penalties. To begin with, no payment may be made for designated health services, known as "DHS," if the proscribed financial arrangement exists, *see* 42 U.S.C. § 1395nn(g)(1); and if any payment has been made, it has to be repaid as an overpayment. *Id.* § 1395nn(g)(2). Recall also our discussion of the FCA that an overpayment not returned within the specified time period can constitute a false claim, and all the severe sanctions that follow from that statutory scheme.

Stark also contains its own civil monetary penalties: "Any person that presents or causes to be presented a bill or a claim for a service that such person knows or should know is for a service for which payment may not be made under paragraph (1) or for which a refund has not been made under paragraph (2) shall be subject to a civil money penalty of not more than $15,000 for each such service." *Id.* § 1395nn(g)(3). These penalties are heightened for "circumvention schemes": "Any physician or other entity that enters into an arrangement or scheme (such as a cross-referral arrangement) which the physician or entity knows or should know has a principal purpose of assuring referrals by the physician to a particular entity which, if the physician directly made referrals to such entity, would be in violation of this section, shall be subject to a civil money penalty of not more than $100,000 for each such arrangement or scheme." *Id.* § 1395nn(g)(4). Exclusion likewise is an available sanction.

Notice that the prohibited transactions go beyond ownership interests but also include compensation arrangements, i.e., Stark bans "financial arrangements," defined as "ownership or investment interests" plus "compensation arrangements." As we said, the immediate spur for Stark I was, in particular, physician referrals to entities in which they held ownership interests. Why did the legislation extend, then, to "compensation arrangements"? Hint: Didn't some clever lawyers invent real property leases with 1,000–year terms, instead of using the fee simple absolute, in order to avoid the feudal obligations that went along with a fee simple interest? Can you think of ways to draft agreements that effectively grant investment returns without explicating creating an ownership interest?

Stark Exceptions

In contrast to AKS, Stark is an "exceptions-based" statute. Many of the exceptions cover arrangements likewise within the AKS exceptions and safe harbors. For example, there are exceptions for rental of office space or equipment, personal service arrangements, group practices, risk-sharing arrangements, large and small entity investments, in-office ancillary services, and physician recruitment. However, extreme caution must be exercised because the wording between an AKS safe harbor and a Stark exception is often different, which can lead to different results. For example, the AKS safe harbor for physician recruitment is designed to allow hospitals to recruit physicians to medically underserved areas and therefore one of its standards is that 75% of the new practice be from the underserved area or population, *see* 42 C.F.R. § 1001.952(n)(8), an illustration of a social purpose that can inform the creation of safe harbors. By contrast, the Stark statutory exception for physician recruitment contains no such stipulation. *See* 42 U.S.C. § 1395nn(e)(5). Under its authority to create additional exceptions that do not pose the risk of program abuse, *see id.* § 1395nn(b)(4), CMS created a separate exception for recruitment of physicians to underserved areas. *See* 42 C.F.R. § 411.357(t). In sum, one must read very carefully and not assume that the requirements under Stark and

AKS are the same (while always keeping in mind the basic difference that AKS is an intent-based statute but Stark is not; it is an exceptions-based statute).

Yet there is another point, which is that compared with the AKS safe harbors the amount of text and detail in the Stark regulations is encyclopedic. First there is simply the sheer scope of material, as CMS and its predecessor, HCFA, have published wave after wave of regulations, with accompanying lengthy but important preambles and with attendant numerous lengthy delays. *See, e.g.*, Krause, *A Conceptual Model* at 86–90 (describing only part of what at that time was the "ongoing saga" of producing Stark regulations). The first regulations implementing Stark I came in 1995, six years after the statute was passed. *See* 60 Fed. Reg. 41,914 (Aug. 14, 1995). What followed were Stark II, Phase I Regulations in 2001, 66 Fed. Reg. 856 (Jan. 4, 2001); Stark II, Phase II Regulations in 2004, 69 Fed. Reg. 16,054 (March 26, 2004); and then Stark II, Phase III Regulations in 2007, 72 Fed. Reg. 51,012 (Sept. 5, 2007). Additionally, CMS has implemented Stark in part through its annual updates to the hospital inpatient prospective reimbursement system and the physician fee schedule. For purposes of understanding the Stark exceptions the most important of these regulations were issued in the Calendar Year 2008 Physician Fee Schedule, 72 Fed. Reg. 66,222 (Nov. 27, 2007), and the Fiscal Year 2009 Hospital Inpatient Prospective Payment System Final Rule, 73 Fed. Reg. 48,434 (Aug. 19, 2008).

The second point is the level of detail in the Stark regulations, compared with the AKS safe harbors. To illustrate, let's return to physician recruitment. The AKS safe harbor states nine requirements for the recruitment arrangement: a writing; stipulations regarding revenues generated from new patients for the new practice; a maximum term for the agreement; a provision that referrals not be explicitly required; that the arrangement not be exclusive; that compensation not vary according to the volume or value of referrals; a nondiscrimination clause; the stipulation, mentioned above, regarding underserved populations or areas; and that no benefit be conferred on anyone in a position to refer other than the recruited physician. *See* 42 CFR § 1001.952(n). By contrast, the Stark regulations run on and on, canvassing such subjects as the zip codes which define the recruiting hospital's service area, how one defines practice revenue, including start-up costs if relevant, and how one allocates costs if a physician is to join a new practice. *See* 42 CFR § 411.350(e). Our example of regulation of frequent flier miles, used in the beginning of this section, was no exaggeration. The point regarding the remarkable level of detail could be illustrated by example after example. A financial arrangement might fall within an AKS safe harbor yet not within a more detailed Stark exception.

This piling of detail on detail stems from the structure of Stark. As we have seen its definition of a violation was meant to sweep very widely. Broadly defined financial relationships between physicians and the entities to which they can refer for DHS were to be banned as a prophylactic measure. However, the sweep of the prohibition captures and therefore bans relationships crucial to the health care sector. To deal with this reality, detailed exception upon detailed exception is necessary to regulate these relationships. Unlike AKS, no one can fudge under Stark by recourse to the claim that the requisite bad intent is absent, because intent is irrelevant. Conduct legal under AKS because the requisite intent is missing can still violate Stark. The type of arrangement is simply banned if it fits within the definition of proscribed financial arrangements. Thus exception after exception must be crafted to cover the vast number of possibilities—detail upon detail upon detail.

Further, when one gets down to it, many times the most important factor is the fair market value of the arrangement. The phrase "fair market value" or a similar one appears repeatedly in the regulations; and the issue whether remuneration is "fair" often depends on the quality of (massive) documentation and potentially competing, subjective appraisals, *see, e.g.,* David M. Deaton, *What Is "Safe" about the Government's Recent Interpretation of the Anti–Kickback Statute Safe Harbors? ... And Since When Was Stark an Intent–Based Statute?*, 36 J. HEALTH L. 549 (2003), something that is particularly problematic since most or all of the time the fair market value of an arrangement is inexorably tied to the value of referrals. *See generally* Frankford, *Creating and Dividing the Fruits of Economics Activity.* The Tuomey litigation that is behind situation #8 at the beginning of the chapter illustrates this point, as the parties' dueling experts joined battle over the fair market value and commercial reasonableness of the employment contracts that, the competing sides claim, do or do not fall inside the Stark exception for compensation arrangements. Given that the cases are replete with these battles of the experts, one must ask what happened to a statute that was supposed to proscribe certain transactions in a bright-clear manner that is now interpreted by hundreds of pages in the federal register; and, given how Stark has been implemented, is there any justification for its existence as a scheme independent from AKS?

Perhaps even more important is the fact that the importance of these questions has been magnified enormously by the recent linkage of violations of Stark to the FCA and the PPACA's empowerment of qui tam relators. The defendant in *Tuomey* (situation #8) publicly breathed a sigh of relief when a jury returned a verdict against it for "only" violating Stark, to the tune of $45 million in damages, relieving it of exposure to a $300 million award under the FCA—*see Federal Jury Finds Hospital Violated Stark, Not FCA; Possible Liability Cut to $45 Million*, 19 HEALTH LAW REPORTER (BNA) 530 (Apr. 15, 2010)—although the grant of the government's motion for a new trial on the FCA claims made that sigh of relief short lived; and consider this argument made to the Public Interest Committee of the American Health Lawyers Association:

> ***The Dangers of Disproportionality:*** The risk that a Stark violation might result in a level of exposure that could effectively bankrupt a hospital is a scenario that haunts [hospital] administrators. For example, assume that in 2001, a hospital enters into a medical director agreement with its most productive cardiac sur-

geon. The terms of the agreement are commercially reasonable and the compensation is set at fair market value. In 2002, the medical director agreement expires but the hospital mistakenly assumes that the agreement automatically renewed and continues to pay the surgeon. The surgeon also thinks the written agreement is still in place and continues to provide the services and submits weekly timesheets documenting the hours devoted to his medical director duties. In 2009, the hospital discovers that the medical director agreement expired in 2002. Under the Stark Law, the hospital has had a non-excepted financial relationship with the cardiac surgeon for the past seven years and *all* reimbursement that the hospital received during that period for services provided to Medicare patients pursuant to referrals from that cardiac surgeon are subject to recoupment by the government. The repayment liability in this instance could be millions of dollars. If the hospital made the same type of faulty assumption with respect to five agreements, the potential exposure grows accordingly. If this Stark violation is used as the basis for a False Claims Act case, civil penalties and treble damages could also be recovered. In short, the hospital's total exposure flowing from an expired medical director agreement could well be ruinous.

While the potential exposure for a Stark violation is enormous, historically the likelihood of enforcement has been low. CMS has not been actively seeking recoupment based on violations of the Stark Law. Enforcement of Stark through the False Claims Act is random and often not the sole or even primary focus of the government's case. The risk of a hospital facing disproportional penalties for an innocent Stark violation, however, is exacerbated to the extent that prosecutorial discretion has been effectively abdicated to whistleblowers under the *qui tam* provisions of the FCA. Given all these factors, the industry has viewed Stark enforcement as akin to lightning striking—unpredictable but deadly.

American Health Lawyers Association Public Interest Committee, A Public Policy Discussion: Taking the Measure of the Stark Law 10–11 (2009) (http://www.healthlawyers.org/Resources/PI/Policy/Pages/StarkConvener. aspx).

Remember that under AKS, liability in the example posed is questionable, if not unlikely, because the requisite intent could not be established, but liability under Stark for such a "mistake" depends on no such intent; and given how much greater detail typically is in the Stark exceptions and regulatory interpretations, compared with the AKS safe harbors, the linking of Stark overpayments to FCA liability is potentially much more dangerous for providers than the linking of AKS liability to false claims.

True, as we have seen, the FCA, as amended by FERA, has its own scienter requirements for overpayments—the overpayments must be "knowingly concealed or knowingly and improperly avoided or decreased," terms yet to be fleshed out—but given the potentially enormous exposure, the pressures to settle are great even for innocent defendants.* Among other scholars, Professor Krause in particular has written persuasively that such "regulation by settlement" is problematic. *See, e.g.*, Krause, *"Promises to Keep"* at 1410–17; Krause, *A Conceptual Model* at 113–47.

This brings us to our final point, which is the growing importance of voluntary compliance, something we addressed in our discussion of AKS, but which may be of even greater importance now under Stark, given the looming presence of FCA liability. Pursuant to a congressional mandate in the PPACA, *see* PPACA, Pub. L. No. 111–148 § 6409, CMS has developed, in cooperation with the OIG, and posted on its website a "Self–Referral Disclosure Protocol," which is designed to encourage providers to detect and report Stark violations. See CMS Voluntary Self–Referral Disclosure Protocol   (https://www.cms.gov/PhysicianSelfReferral/65_Self_Referral_ Disclosure_Protocol.asp#TopOfPage). This process is, under Congress's mandate, *see* PPACA, Pub. L. No. 111–148 § 6409(a)(3), separate from the procedure for obtaining an advisory opinion and is instead a procedure whereby a provider fesses up to a Stark violation in order to settle liability, including an accounting of overpayments owed. As a carrot to providers, Congress gave DHHS explicit authority to reduce he amount owed, including civil penalties. The agency may consider "(1) [t]he nature and extent of the improper or illegal practice[;] (2) [t]he timeliness of such self-disclosure[; and] (3) [t]he cooperation in providing additional information related to the disclosure." *Id.* § 6409(b)(1)–(3). CMS has stated that it will also consider "(4) the litigation risk associated with the matter disclosed; and (5) the financial position of the disclosing party." CMS Voluntary Self–Referral Disclosure Protocol at 6.** Importantly, this process suspends the running of the 60–day time period by which overpayments have to be reported to avoid violations and sanctions (and potential FCA exposure). Further, in requiring very detailed reporting in the protocol, the agency's intention is clearly to induce some providers to cop a plea so other participants can be identified:

> The disclosing party's diligent and good faith cooperation throughout the entire process is essential. Accordingly, CMS expects to receive documents and information from the disclosing party that relate to the disclosed matter without the need to resort

---

* Even if the pre-FERA FCA applies to an alleged false claim, there remains a scienter requirement, and the Stark violation has to be "willing" to establish false claim liability for it. *See, e.g.*, United States ex rel. Singh v. Bradford Regional Medical Center, 752 F. Supp.2d 602 (W.D. Pa. 2010) (plaintiffs granted summary judgment on Stark violation but trial required on FCA scienter requirement); United States ex rel. Kosenske v. Carlisle HMA Inc., 2010 WL 1390661 (M.D. Pa. 2010) (same).

** The OIG had established an earlier protocol under which it could reduce penalties for Stark violations, *see* Office of Inspector General, Dep't of Health and Human Services, An Open Letter to Providers (Apr. 24, 2006) (http://oig.hhs.gov/compliance/self-disclosure-info/ index.asp), but this protocol had been withdrawn for Stark violations, *see* OFFICE OF INSPECTOR GENERAL, DEP'T OF HEALTH AND HUMAN SERVICES, AN OPEN LETTER TO PROVIDERS (Mar. 24, 2009) (http://oig.hhs.gov/compliance/self-disclosure-info/index.asp), because the agency thought it lacked requisite authority, which Congress has clarified by the explicit grant in the PPACA.

to compulsory methods. If a disclosing party fails to work in good faith with CMS to resolve the disclosed matter, that lack of cooperation will be considered when CMS assesses the appropriate resolution of the matter. Similarly, the intentional submission of false or otherwise untruthful information, as well as the intentional omission of relevant information, will be referred to DOJ or other Federal agencies and could, in itself, result in criminal and/or civil sanctions, as well as exclusion from participation in the Federal health care programs. Furthermore, it is imperative for disclosing parties to disclose matters in a timely fashion once identified. As stated above, section 6402 of the ACA establishes a deadline for reporting and returning overpayments[.]

CMS Voluntary Self–Referral Disclosure Protocol at 6.

In proposed regulations, 77 Fed. Reg. 9,179 (Feb. 16, 2012), CMS gave some content to the crucial term "identified," which triggers the obligation to report the overpayment within sixty days. The agency stipulated that an overpayment is "identified" when a person "has actual knowledge of the existence of an overpayment, or acts in reckless disregard or deliberate ignorance of the overpayment." *Id.* at 9,182. This definition imposes a duty of reasonable diligence and gives incentives for providers to institute routine compliance efforts like self-audits, incentives strengthened by the fact that the proposed rules also stipulate that the obligation to report identified overpayments extends backwards for a whopping ten years, based on the FCA's statute of limitations.

As of February 2012, the effect of a provider's hewing to part of this protocol is murky. For a discussion of some of the risks, *see* Jason Christ et al., *CMS Opens Its Doors by Creating the Stark Voluntary Self–Referral Disclosure Protocol—But Enter at Your Own Risk*, 19 HEALTH LAW REPORTER (BNA) 1400 (Oct. 7, 2010). Clearly, if the provider discloses before the 60–day period has run, adheres to the protocol and successfully reaches a resolution with administrators, there is no "overpayment" and no "false claim," both as terms of art. However, if one of these three conditions is not satisfied, then there is potential exposure to the FCA, but much will depend on how a court interprets the language FERA added to define an overpayment, particularly the scienter requirement.

Additionally, the effect of the disclosure under the CMS protocol could affect the ability of a qui tam relator to bring suit. As discussed above, the PPACA loosened what had previously been a jurisdictional bar that the whistleblower have direct and independent knowledge of publicly disclosed information such that the qui tam plaintiff now can avoid dismissal if it "materially adds to the publicly disclosed allegations or transactions." PPACA, Pub. L. No. 111–148 § 10104(j)(2) (codified as 31 U.S.C. § 3730(e)(4)(B)). Moreover, also as discussed above, DOJ is given authority to prevent dismissal simply by opposing it. Exactly how these new provisions will interact with the new protocol is very unclear and has to be developed. Given the heft of the penalties under the FCA and the concomitant incentives of qui tam relators to bring false claim actions, these questions are very important.

4.   CLOSING REFLECTIONS AND QUESTIONS

We suspect that by now, after your having plowed through this astronomical level of technical detail and complexity, you are wasted. Therefore, let's relax, step out of the technical detail and reflect back to where we started. The law of health care fraud and abuse, quite simply, exists to deal with the fact that providers are in a position to take advantage of their expertise, of patients' cognitive and emotional dependence on them, and of the vulnerability of payers, including government, to behavior that ranges from outright theft to overutilization. Providers have a financial conflict of interest.

We have seen that in trying to regulate such a broad spectrum of what has been defined as fraud, the law has devolved into mind-boggling detail and complexity. We have also seen that thoughtful commentators, writing from a variety of perspectives, think that the legal regime has become extremely top-heavy, burdensome and even, heavy-handed.

However, different lessons have been drawn from this experience. For example, Professor James Blumstein has characterized the AKS as a "blunt tool," James F. Blumstein, *The Fraud and Abuse Statute in an Evolving Health Care Marketplace: Life in the Health Care Speakeasy*, 22 AM. J.L. & MED. 205, 209 (1996), that is completely out of sync with the health care sector. With characteristic flair, in 1996 he wrote:

> *Greber* makes illegal much restructuring in the health care marketplace that is appropriate in the rationalizing of the health care industry. In the current environment, it is a truism that the fraud and abuse law is being violated routinely but that those violations are acknowledged as not threatening the public interest. Indeed, they further the public interest and are needed to improve the functioning of the health care marketplace. Lack of prosecution leaves the industry living with economically and socially appropriate conduct. This poses a formidable civil liberties concern as prosecutors exercise enormous prosecutorial discretion, which is always subject to abuse. In sum, the modern American health care industry is akin to a speakeasy—conduct that is illegal is rampant and countenanced by law enforcement officials because the law is so out of sync with the conventional norms and realities of the marketplace and because respected leaders of the industry are performing tasks that, while illegal, are desirable in improving the functioning of the market.

Id. at 218.

There is an important point here but we agree with Professors Jost and Davies that it is not the one that Professor Blumstein thinks he has made. As Jost and Davies develop in response to Blumstein's argument,

Professor Blumstein is wrong that the laws governing health care fraud and abuse are a "blunt tool." *See* Jost & Davies, *The Fraud and Abuse Statute*. One cannot have read this chapter and come away with that conclusion. The laws are more and more finely tuned, becoming more so perhaps every day, as detail is piled on detail. The fraud and abuse laws are not out of step with the behavior in the sector so much as chasing it constantly in a wrestling match of move, counter-move, move, counter-move—a game that goes on endlessly, as countervailing power is matched against countervailing power. *See generally* David M. Frankford, *The Normative Constitution of Professional Power*, 22 J. HEALTH POL. POL'Y & LAW 185 (1997). The important point, then, is not that the instrument is blunt but, as we said at the outset of the chapter, that the laws promoting competition in the sector—of which Professor Blumstein and others have been important proponents—are at war with the laws trying to stop that competition. The market-based law and policies that would generally leave the health care sector unregulated are at odds with the heavy regulation that the health care fraud laws now represent.

However, to state that this conflict exists does not answer the question of which side of the conflict needs to go or be significantly modified. For example, above we have suggested that perhaps the FCA should be returned to its roots such that falsity is defined as care that is not provided or is worthless as provided. In other words, the heavy club of the FCA—and it is a club—should be applied only to outliers. Similarly, Professor Stephen Latham has proposed that financial incentives for physicians be regulated structurally such that they are allowed when they apply to broad classes of patients and providers but banned when they apply to very small classes. *See* Stephen R. Latham, *Regulation of Managed Care Incentive Payments to Physicians*, 22 AM. J.L. & MED. 399 (1996). Professor Saver's more recent proposal uses a similar animating principle. *See* Richard S. Saver, *Squandering the Gain: Gainsharing and the Continuing Dilemma of Physician Financial Incentives*, 98 NW. U. L. REV. 145, 227–28, 231–32 (2003). Both the AKS and Stark would have to be significantly modified to implement such proposals; and, in fact, as we stated in the chapter on payment in Part Two, our entire system needs to be moved toward creating long-lasting linkages between large pools of patients and large pools of providers, which is one of the key features providing relative stability in the social security systems of Europe.

By contrast, the lesson Professor Blumstein takes from the internecine warfare among our legal principles is to loosen significantly the antifraud regulation and to let the market dictate the arrangements that may be made. *See* Jost & Davies, *The Fraud and Abuse Statute* at 129 (Professor Blumstein "articulates the desire of many health care entrepreneurs to be free from the complex web of federal and state regulations that constrain their ability to structure their business relationships as they see fit."). Although his proposal seems anachronistic at this point, writing in 1996 he basically urged that the fraud and abuse laws be modified such that managed care organizations be free to "steer" patients around in whatever way the MCOs wished. Blumstein, *Rationalizing the Fraud and Abuse*

Statute at 125. We agree with him that regulation cannot eliminate providers' conflict of interest, but we need to ask in response to his and others' purported solution, does the market eliminate conflict of interest or does it merely shift it around from providers, to insurers, to plan sponsors, and so on? *See* Frankford, *Privatizing Health Care* at 59–60.

Put somewhat differently, Professor Blumstein and his ideological allies might be correct that the fraud and abuse laws should be returned to policing against run-of-the-mill fraud—services not provided and services clearly not medically necessary or provided in such a manner that they are qualitatively worthless. However, what follows from this? If we allow the market free play, creating and deploying the legal and social norm that providers should grab for all the gusto they can get, won't we just intensify the conflict of interest? Isn't the lesson instead that we need to change direction, that we need to get serious about using the methods that other nations deploy to control utilization—methods that are not market-based? Instead of regulating conflict of interest and "self-referral" indirectly through AKS and Stark, shouldn't we instead regulate diffusion of technology directly? More generally, do we not need to shift the cultural and legal landscape such that appetites all around are moderated?

CHAPTER 25

THE APPLICATION OF ANTITRUST TO HEALTH CARE

One could say with much justification that the application of antitrust law to the health care sector, starting in earnest in the mid–1970s, was the most important legal development in health law in the last century. Prior to that time, the health care sector was largely nonprofit and payment was cost-based in the case of hospitals, and charge-based in the case of physician services. As a result, price competition did not exist and providers, particularly hospitals, competed only over technological improvements.

Of course many explanations may be offered to explain the social organization of health care in the United States. For our purposes here, however, we can focus on just one, one that in fact became so well accepted in much of social and academic discourse that we can justifiably call it the "standard story."

According to the standard story, the fact that until recently health care was largely a nonprofit enterprise with little if any price competition stemmed from the medical profession's dominance of the (1) financing, (2) delivery, and (3) conceptualization of health care. Control over financing, the narrative runs, began with the creation of the Blue Cross and Blue Shield organizations by providers and continued largely through various anticompetitive practices. *See, e.g.*, Lawrence G. Goldberg & Warren Greenberg, *The Emergence of Physician–Sponsored Health Insurance: A Historical Perspective, in* COMPETITION IN THE HEALTH CARE SECTOR: PAST, PRESENT, AND FUTURE 231 (Warren Greenberg ed., 1978); Clark C. Havighurst, *Professional Restraints on Innovation in Health Care Financing*, 1978 DUKE L.J. 303; Lawrence G. Goldberg & Warren Greenberg, *The Effect of Physician–Controlled Health Insurance: U.S. v. Oregon State Medical Society*, 2 J. HEALTH POL. POLICY & L. 48 (1977).

Professional dominance over the delivery of health care stemmed from professional dominance of the licensure and accreditation of individual and institutional providers. *See, e.g.*, H.E. Frech III, *The Long–Lost Free Market in Health Care: Government and Professional Regulation of Medicine, in* A NEW APPROACH TO THE ECONOMICS OF HEALTH CARE 44 (Mancur Olson ed., 1981); Clark C. Havighurst & Nancy M.P. King, *Private Credentialing of Health Care Personnel: An Antitrust Perspective, Part One*, 9 AM. J.L. & MED. 131, *Part Two*, 9 AM. J.L. & MED. 263 (1983); Clark C. Havighurst, *Doctors and Hospitals: An Antitrust Perspective on Traditional Relationships*, 1985 DUKE L.J. 1071. Furthermore, the medical profession's control

1195

over the conceptualization of health care derived from its dominance of education and research, again a result of control over accreditation. As one of us has summarized this narrative:

> The profession has monopolized the education system, thus ensuring that a particular orthodoxy is adopted by all individual professionals. Further, it has dominated occupational licensure and institutional credentialing, thereby assuring that only the professionals it turns out, schooled in its orthodoxy, have a place in the market. Finally, it has dominated the insurance system, thereby preventing the rise of countervailing pressure for alternatives to its orthodoxy. It is as if some being from an alien planet landed on the earth and took over all institutions relating to the delivery of health care.

David M. Frankford, *Privatizing Health Care: Economic Magic to Cure Legal Medicine*, 66 S. Cal. L. Rev. 1, 22–23 (1992) (footnotes omitted) [hereinafter Frankford, *Privatizing Health Care*].

This situation persisted, the story went, because until Goldfarb v. Virginia State Bar, 421 U.S. 773 (1975), the medical professions' anticompetitive restraints were immune from application of antitrust law under the implied exception for the "learned professions." *Goldfarb*, which struck down a minimum fee schedule recommended by a local bar association, ended this exception. Rejecting the argument that the exception rested on state regulation, the Court stated:

> Whether state regulation is active or dormant, real or theoretical, lawyers would be able to adopt anticompetitive practices with impunity. We cannot find support for the proposition that Congress intended any such sweeping exclusion. The nature of an occupation, standing alone, does not provide sanctuary from the Sherman Act, nor is the public-service aspect of professional practice controlling in determining whether § 1 includes professions.

Id. at 787. Importantly, however, the Court noted that professions might deserve particular attention, something we'll see play a role in the doctrine we discuss below:

> The fact that a restraint operates upon a profession as distinguished from a business is, of course, relevant in determining whether that particular restraint violates the Sherman Act. It would be unrealistic to view the practice of professions as interchangeable with other business activities, and automatically to apply to the professions antitrust concepts which originated in other areas. The public service aspect, and other features of the professions, may require that a particular practice, which could properly be viewed as a violation of the Sherman Act in another context, be treated differently. We intimate no view on any other situation than the one with which we are confronted today.

Id. at 788 n.17. Regardless, the "gales of competition" were about to blow on the health care sector.

The historic changes wrought by application of the antitrust laws stems from the core of the antitrust doctrine we explore in this chapter. Stemming from the era of the great trusts, antitrust had its beginnings in the breaking up of the U.S. economy's great cartels—industry-wide combinations of sellers who fixed price. The motivating premise was that when competitors make agreements among themselves, their customers very often are victimized by those agreements because they are subject to higher prices, lower quality and discriminatory practices that favor the rich and harm the poor. This notion, we shall see, gave rise to the so-called "per se rule" against price fixing, a rule in which relatively few facts are relevant to judge the conduct illegal and in which, stated generally, defendants bear relatively heavy burdens of proof.

This simple doctrine in turn gave rise to a crucial distinction that we explore throughout the chapter: horizontal versus vertical conduct. Productive activity can be described as occurring over vertical stages of production. For example, gasoline sold at retail derives from prior stages: crude oil is found and pumped out of the ground or sea; it is then shipped to refineries, where it is refined; and then the final products like gasoline are distributed to retailers, which sell to the ultimate consumers at the pump. Similarly, health care providers like doctors provide health care, the final goods and services to patients, but the real product is insured health care, which, like the production of gasoline, necessitates vertical stages of production: providers like doctors are packaged together into networks by insurers, who likewise compete against each other to sell networks to plan sponsors. Figuratively, the stages of production looks like the following:

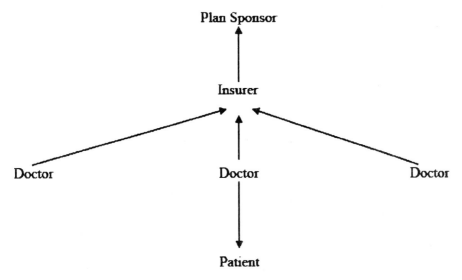

Notice the distinction between the horizontal and vertical dimensions. In this example, doctors compete at the same stage of production and so they are "horizontal competitors." By contrast, plan sponsors, insurers, and doctors stand in vertical relationships, particularly in modern insurance products in which insurers and plan administrators promise to deliver what they sell through their provider networks. Thus doctors can be thought of as inputs into the networks that insurers create by packaging the doctors and medical groups together. Insurers compete at their own horizontal level (not portrayed) to sell their health benefit services products, along with their networks, to plan sponsors.

The key point in antitrust doctrine is that collaboration among horizontal competitors is viewed with suspicion as possible means to coordinate over price and output—going back to the original cartels. Agreements among horizontal competitors are therefore potentially subject to the per se rule of illegality. By contrast, the vertical relationships are treated much more favorably because under ordinary circumstances they do not lead to cartelization. Rather than being subject to a per se rule of illegality, vertical relationships instead are assumed to benefit consumers because they represent complete and integrated products that are efficiently assembled. These arrangements receive examination under the more lenient so-called "rule of reason," about which we will have much to say below, but for now we can simply characterize as a very fact-sensitive inquiry in which generally plaintiffs bear heavier burdens of proof.

We will see that administering this distinction—between the rule of reason and the per se treatment—is extremely complex and that as with so many areas of law, how one categorizes the arrangements and conduct will effectively determine the legal outcome. For now, however, our point is mainly historical. Because providers, particularly doctors, are treated as horizontal competitors in an antitrust construct (as opposed to "collaborators," as you have learned, in a clinical-quality improvement construct, aye there's the rub), their coordination is treated with suspicion. Thus, as we shall see below, agreements among doctors—horizontal competitors—with regard to the terms and conditions of their deals with insurers, group health plan administrators, hospitals, standards of care, and other matters potentially are subject to per se condemnation. The historic change wrought by application of antitrust to the business of health care, which began in earnest with *Goldberg*, is that physicians can no longer assert collective economic power as they did in the past—in the form of boycotts, expulsions from medical societies, control over hospital privileges, and ethical codes—in defense of their economic interests. *See, e.g.*, Havighurst, *Doctors and Hospitals*; Havighurst, *Professional Restraints on Innovation in Health Care Financing*. The key case is *Maricopa* reprinted below. By contrast, as we shall see, full-bore economic power can be asserted against physicians when they contract "vertically" with insurance companies. The key case here is *Kartell*, also reprinted below.

Dissolving or greatly diluting horizontal power among physicians and subjecting them to economic power asserted vertically against them has had the effect of wresting control over the financing system away from them. The idea has been to transfer wealth and power away from medicine and medical institutions and toward consumers and the rest of society:

Because each individual health care professional is conceived of as a "producer," professionals are prohibited from asserting collective bargaining power against the institutions to which they are being encouraged to sell their labor. Those, institutions, however, are also aggregations—collections of buyers of the professional labor. Nonetheless, they are allowed to bargain collectively with individual health care professionals; they are allowed to assert collective economic power in the purchase of professional labor.

David M. Frankford, *Creating and Dividing the Fruits of Collective Economic Activity: Referrals Among Providers*, 89 Colum. L. Rev. 1861, 1910–11 (1989).

The institutional changes wrought by the full application of antitrust principles to health care have been enormous; the landscape of payment and practice is vastly different from what it was in the 1970s before this transformation. Writing in 1983, Professor Clark C. Havighurst, the most important early proponent of applying antitrust to health care, was able to declare, "With the end of the Supreme Court's 1981–1982 term, a term marked by five significant antitrust decisions involving professional services and health care, the legal revolution appears to be virtually complete." Clark C. Havighurst, *The Contributions of Antitrust Law to a Procompetitive Health Policy*, *in* MARKET REFORMS IN HEALTH CARE: CURRENT ISSUES, NEW DIRECTIONS, STRATEGIC DECISIONS 295, 317 (Jack A. Meyer, ed., 1983). The "antitrust explosion," *id*. at 300, has "decentralized" decision-making in health care, *see* Clark C. Havighurst, *The Changing Locus of Decision Making in the Health Care Sector*, 11 J. HEALTH POL. POL'Y & L. 697 (1986), fomenting and intensifying the pre-existing and extant fragmentation in payment and delivery that we've examined throughout this book. The application of antitrust to health care has also played a large part in "reeducating consumers, their agents, and providers to new realities and possibilities," *id*. at 714, as the spirit of capitalism has pervaded the culture of health care and fueled the rampant commercialization and industrialization of the sector. While empirically the goal of transferring wealth away from providers has not been achieved—the incomes of providers in the United States are much, much larger than in other comparable nations—we can certainly say that capitalism has triumphed as the sector has succeeded in the way that capitalism succeeds—by creating growth—and thereby gobbling up an exponentially increasing share of the GDP.

We return to this assessment at the end of the chapter. Before that, we dive into the heart of antitrust doctrine by examining market power, the core concern. We will see that the idea of market power is simply stated but that this intuitive appeal is misleading because in most instances finding that power exists is actually very complicated, difficult and expensive. In part for that reason, antitrust does not focus solely on the existence of power but relies also on, first, "barriers to entry" that preclude competition and, second, types of conduct which are "exclusionary," a term of art. These two elements of market structure and conduct are the subjects of the next two subparts. We then examine how the difficulties of determining power and the historical suspicion against horizontal collaboration combine to create the complex conceptual distinction between conduct subject to a per se rule and conduct subject only to the more lenient rule of reason. We finish our doctrinal exposition by exploring the often outcome-determinative distinction between horizontal and vertical conduct. We then assess the overall endeavor—the application of antitrust to health care—and indeed the primary reliance on markets to organize health care, something that is exceptional to the United States.

For our purposes, we focus only on sections 1 and 2 of the Sherman Act and sections 3 and 7 of the Clayton Act.

Section 1 of the Sherman Antitrust Act, 15 U.S.C. § 1, provides:

Every contract, combination in the form of trust or otherwise, or conspiracy, in restraint of trade or commerce among the several States, or with foreign nations, is hereby declared to be illegal. Every person who shall make any contract or engage in any combination or conspiracy hereby declared to be illegal shall be deemed guilty of a felony, and, on conviction thereof, shall be punished by fine not exceeding $100,000,000 if a corporation, or, if any other person, $1,000,000, or by imprisonment not exceeding 10 years, or by both said punishments, in the discretion of the court.

Section 2 of the Sherman Antitrust Act, 15 U.S.C. § 2, provides:

Every person who shall monopolize, or attempt to monopolize, or combine or conspire with any other person or persons, to monopolize any part of the trade or commerce among the several States, or with foreign nations, shall be deemed guilty of a felony, and, on conviction thereof, shall be punished by fine not exceeding $100,000,000 if a corporation, or, if any other person, $1,000,000, or by imprisonment not exceeding 10 years, or by both said punishments, in the discretion of the court.

Section 3 of the Clayton Act, 15 U.S.C. § 14, provides:

It shall be unlawful for any person engaged in commerce, in the course of such commerce, to lease or make a sale or contract for sale of goods, wares, merchandise, machinery, supplies or other commodities, whether patented or unpatented, for use, consumption or resale within the United States or any Territory thereof or the District of Columbia or any insular possession or other place under the jurisdiction of the United States, or fix a price charged therefor, or discount from, or rebate upon, such price, on the condition, agreement or understanding that the lessee or purchaser thereof shall not use or deal in the goods, wares, merchandise, machinery, supplies or other commodities of a competitor or competitors of the lessor or seller, where the effect of such lease, sale, or contract for sale or such condition, agreement or understanding may be to substantially lessen competition or tend to create a monopoly in any line of commerce.

Section 7 of the Clayton Act, 15 U.S.C. § 18, in relevant part provides:

No person engaged in commerce or in any activity affecting commerce shall acquire, directly or indirectly, the whole or any part of the stock or other share capital and no person subject to the jurisdiction of the Federal Trade Commission shall acquire the whole or any part of the assets of another person engaged also in commerce or in any activity affecting commerce, where in any line of commerce or in any activity affecting commerce in any section of the country, the effect of such acquisition may be substantially to lessen competition, or to tend to create a monopoly.

1. MARKET POWER

Section 1 of the Sherman Act proscribes collaboration among horizontal competitors in which the sole form of collaboration is an agreement to set price or divide markets. Section 2, by contrast, proscribes conduct by a fully integrated firm that consists of monopolization or attempted monopolization of a market. In a sense, then, sections 1 and 2 sit at two extremes of possible market organization. The ideal for section 1 is a fully atomized market in which each market participant acts independently of the rest. Section 2, in turn, condemns the conduct of a single entity that produces the output of an entire market if that entity's power has been gained, maintained or enhanced unlawfully, i.e., by means that are not, in antitrust terms, "honestly industrial." Indeed, it is assumed that a fully integrated firm that gains power by lawful means has done so precisely because it satisfied consumer demand. The classic example is an entrepreneurial firm that builds the proverbial better mouse trap, increases its capacity through internal expansion, and thereby puts all firms offering competing mouse traps out of business.

To understate the matter, these two visions of economic structure are anomalous in a modern, capitalist economy. Rarely does one find an extremely atomized market in which firms do not cooperate to some degree. As an example, there may be numerous firms supplying plumbing and electrical products but through a cooperative like a trade association the otherwise competing firms have standardized sizes so that parts produced by one firm fit onto the parts supplied by others. Moreover, much productive economic activity requires that there be greater degrees of cooperation, in which firms integrate with regard to some activities but do not fully integrate to such an extent that they have formed a single entity which is the subject of section 2 (but not section 1).

In either case, the core concern of antitrust, at least at present, is the illicit creation, use and maintenance of market power whether that power be possessed or exercised by a collective, raising a section 1 problem, or by a single entity, creating a problem under section 2. It is market power that gives a firm or firms the ability to raise price and reduce output; and, at least according to one school of thought, it is market power that enables a firm, perhaps paradoxically, to raise barriers of entry, explained below, which are means to perpetuate such power.

a. Market Share

In theory market power is easy to define because its definition tautologically stems from its untoward effects: market power is the ability to raise price or exclude competitors. This definition, in essence, stems from an ideal for markets, based on a vision of freedom, in which no seller or buyer has the power to affect price or quantity. Market power is thus the evil twin of the good twin of totally atomized power. If the latter pertains, buyers and sellers have unfettered freedom because no one can exercise power against them; if the former exists, buyers and sellers are subject to the will of the firm with power over price and quantity.

In theory a firm's power, its position, in a market is simple to express. A firm's power at any given moment consists of its share of the market at hand.* Market share, in turn, is simply expressed as the firm's production divided by the total market production:

$$\text{Defendant's Market Share} = \frac{\text{Defendant's Production}}{\text{Total Market Production}}$$

As the fraction illustrates, the most important task conceptually in antitrust is to define what that denominator, total market production, consists of, or, in other words, to define the relevant market. To use the classic widget as an example, suppose that a firm, ClassicWidget, manufactures widgets (of course). If we define the relevant market as "widgets made by ClassicWidget," then of course ClassicWidget has complete control over that market, as expressed by a market share of 100%, because "defendant's production" and "total market production" are one and the same. However, suppose that a zillion other firms manufacture widgets. Because a widget is, well, a widget, it would be absurd to define the total market production to consist of ClassicWidget's production alone. Instead, the denominator would have to include the production (or production capacity) of the zillion other firms. At the extreme ClassicWidget's production would be so infinitely small compared with total market production that its market share would approach zero. With these two examples we have the two extremes of market structure mentioned above: a 100% market share or total control over price, and a 0% market share or absolutely no control over price.

However, in most instances the real world is more complicated and a firm's actual share lies somewhere in between. Because, to reiterate, the illicit creation, use and maintenance of market power is at present the core concern of antitrust, determining market share can be outcome determinative and concomitantly, so is determination of the relevant market. Plaintiff's strategy is to make the defendant's share larger by increasing the

---

* We start here with the traditional, so-called "structural" approach to market power and introduce the many complications (and doubts) below. The classic statement of determining market power by Judge Hand in *Alcoa* is reprinted below.

numerator, decreasing the denominator, or both. Defendant's strategy is the opposite: decrease the numerator, increase the denominator, or both.

These two strategies are generally played out on two different battlefields. The first is geographic. Suppose that ClassicWidgets manufactures all the widgets in the United States. However, suppose also that there are a zillion other widget manufacturers spread throughout the world and that the cost of shipping a widget is, you guessed it, zero. Now put yourself in the position of a consumer in the United States. Do you care from whence you buy a widget? Absent patriotism or some other non-price motivation, the answer is clearly no because there is no shipping cost (and let's assume that the widgets can appear instantaneously anywhere because, after all, lost time is lost money). Because a widget from anywhere is, you guessed it again, identical to all other widgets, consumers would be more than happy to substitute widgets from other parts of the world for the ones made by ClassicWidgets in the United States. Hence, the "relevant geographic market" would be the entire world.

However, let's again return to the real world and relax the fiction that shipping costs, including time, are zero. In that case, assuming that shipping costs are reflected in prices, consumers would not be indifferent to the geographic provenance of a widget; and we must decide which locations should be "combined" to constitute the relevant geographic market and which locations should be "separated" from that market. The locations chucked into the relevant geographic market are said to be "good" or "close substitutes" in that consumers in the relevant locale would turn to all those locations to purchase their widgets. The locations separated from the relevant geographic market are said to be "poor substitutes" because consumers in that locale would find widgets made there to be too expensive relative to widgets manufactured in the locations included in the relevant market.

The second battlefield is conceptually similar but relates not to the place of manufacture and use but to the use and characteristics of a product. To understand this, relax the fiction that stands behind a widget, namely that the products of all manufacturers or sellers are identical, i.e., fungible, homogeneous, undifferentiated. Suppose the product at issue is chocolate ice cream. Is that the "relevant product market"? Well, there is also vanilla, strawberry, coffee, cherry and .... These days the list of flavors seems infinite. The question in defining our relevant product market is therefore the extent to which consumers will find these alternative flavors to be "close substitutes" for one another such that they will be combined to constitute the relevant product market; and the extent to which some flavors will be "poor substitutes" such that they should be separated from that market.

To put it all together, let's return to our two, ideal extremes. One side we've discussed already. ClassicWidgets makes all the widgets in the United States but widgets can be sent anywhere instantaneously at no cost. Additionally, a zillion other firms make a zillion other products—gidgets, didgets, bidgets, etc.—that are identical to the widget (yes, we know, they're all widgets, but please indulge us). In this instance the relevant geographic market includes everywhere and the relevant product market includes everything such that ClassicWidgets has a market share approaching zero.

The second extreme is a world in which every place and everything is completely unique. In this instance a buyer in a locale cannot buy the product, the "Unwidget," from anywhere else than its locale and from anybody else other than Unwidgets, the sole supplier. In this case the defendant's production and the total market production are one and the same and Unwidgets has a 100% market share.

If only the world were so simple.

United States v. Long Island Jewish Medical Center

983 F. Supp. 121 (E.D.N.Y. 1997)

■ SPATT, DISTRICT JUDGE:

In this case, the defendants Long Island Jewish Medical Center ("LIJ") and North Shore Health Systems, Inc. ("North Shore" or "NSHS") have agreed to merge. The United States of America (the "Government" or the "plaintiff") commenced this antitrust action to prevent this merger. The Government alleges that the proposed merger "may tend substantially to lessen competition in violation of Section 7 of the Clayton Act, as amended, 15 U.S.C. § 18."

I. THE TRIAL–FINDINGS OF FACT

A. The Hospitals

Long Island Jewish Medical Center is a not-for-profit voluntary hospital sponsored by the Federation of Jewish Philanthropies. This medical center consists of three institutions: LIJ, a 450 bed acute care adult facility; Schneider's Children Hospital, a 150 bed acute care facility; and Hillside Hospital, a psychiatric wing consisting of 220 beds. Dr. David Dantzker [is] its President and Chief Executive Officer. Dr. Dantzker and others at the hospital have described its network as an "anchor site" and as a "premier" hospital.

LIJ is also an academic teaching hospital primarily affiliated with the Albert Einstein School of Medicine, with missions of medical education and research.

Fifty percent of the LIJ patient population resides in Queens, thirty percent in Nassau, and the balance in Suffolk, Manhattan and Westchester. The primary competitors of LIJ in the psychiatric field are the Nassau County Medical Center and the Elmhurst Hospital in Queens. In pediatrics, LIJ competes "with almost every hospital on Long Island that has an in-patient pediatric service," which includes most of the hospitals, such as Winthrop University Hospital ("Winthrop") in Nassau, New York Hospital of Queens ("New York Hospital Queens"), Good Samaritan Hospital in Suffolk, and, in addition, the Manhattan hospitals.

North Shore Manhasset opened in 1953. John Gallagher is the President and CEO. He joined the hospital's administrative staff in 1962, when the hospital had 169 beds. Since then, the hospital's capacity has increased to 705 beds. According to Gallagher, NSM has four goals: (1) to render the highest quality of care, (2) to become a leading teaching center for Long Island; (3) to continue its commitment to research, and (4) to aid the poor through community service and outreach programs. NSM is an academic teaching hospital affiliated with New York University School of Medicine.

In terms of the services provided, an important consideration in this case, approximately 80 to 85 percent of the services provided by NSM and LIJ are primary/secondary services, which also are provided at all the community hospitals in Queens and Nassau. The remaining services are for tertiary care.

C. *Competition Among Local Hospitals*

Initially, the Court recognizes that North Shore Manhasset and Long Island Jewish are two of the premier hospitals on Long Island. As Robert Wheeler, CEO of northeast operations of United Health Care ("United"), the third largest health care insurer in the United States, covering 25 million persons and 1.1 million New Yorkers, testified, NSM and LIJ arc "must have" hospitals. NSM serves as the "premier hub of the North Shore System" and is "vital for [United's] customer base." Further, according to Wheeler, the only other Long Island hospital with the same "cachet" as NSM is LIJ.[4] Indeed, Wheeler went so far as to state that if United had to drop NSM and LIJ, it could not "build a marketable network on Long Island." Consistent with this testimony, Gerard Moran, the Acting Vice President of Labor Relations for the Long Island Rail Road, who is responsible for negotiating health care benefits, stated that accessibility to hospitals is an important consideration in bargaining with the union, which was interested in the "three major hospitals on Long Island ... North Shore, Long Island Jewish and Stony Brook." Connie Poirier, Vice President for Contracting and Network Development and Operations for Empire, testified that LIJ and NSM are the two top "anchor" hospitals in Long Island.

Richard Wildzunas is the Senior Vice President of MagnaCare, an MCO which operates as both a Preferred Provider Organization ("PPO") (a less restrictive form of managed care than an MCO) and an HMO, and procures 80 percent of its business from self-insured trust funds and 20 percent through insurance carriers. He negotiates the contracts with the hospitals. According to Wildzunas, LIJ and NSM are comparable premier tertiary care hospitals. At trial he testified that in order to operate in Long Island, "you have to have one of these facilities in [your] network." Wildzunas testified that although Winthrop offers the same services and quality of services as NSM and LIJ, it is not comparable to those hospitals

---

4. "Cachet" is roughly defined as prestige or high status.

because it does not have the same reputation as LIJ or NSM. However, he conceded that the reputation of Winthrop is "close" to LIJ and NSM. Roslyn Yasser is the administrator of the District Council 37 Health and Security Plan and Trust. She negotiates health care packages for approximately 300,000 active workers and 100,000 retirees over the age of 65 and their families. Yasser testified that NSM and LIJ have excellent reputations and are well-utilized. In Yasser's view, there are no other comparable hospitals in Nassau and Queens. She "could not conceive [an] . . . arrangement without those two hospitals."

Prior to the proposed merger, NSM and LIJ were fierce competitors. According to Wheeler, this competition "helped . . . Managed Care Organizations, sort of keep all parties on their toes." Poirier, Empire's chief negotiator, testified that LIJ is an MCO's only alternative to NSM and vice-versa. Similarly, Mario Vangeli, the hospital relations manager for Cigna Healthcare of New York ("Cigna"), which has a small share of the Queens–Nassau market, testified that if neither LIJ nor NSM were in his network. "Cigna would probably lose its current clients and not be able to market to a whole other population in the area." However, Vangeli testified that Winthrop is a large teaching hospital that he perceives "to have a certain respect in the community" and offers the same tertiary care services as LIJ and NSM. In addition, Vangeli conceded that the Cigna enrollees' admissions to Winthrop exceeded such admissions to both LIJ and NSM. In fact, in 1996, the hospital in Queens and Nassau with the most Cigna admissions was Winthrop. Further, he considers Winthrop to be a "center of excellence" along with LIJ, NSM and Stony Brook. Also, during negotiations with NSM as to cardiac rates, Cigna diverted patients from NSM to Lenox Hill and possibly Winthrop. After that move, NSM agreed to a discount for cardiothoracic surgery.

Dr. Dantzker, LIJ's President and CEO, stated in a February 1995 memorandum that an MCO "will contract with either us or with North Shore Hospital, but not with both." Indeed, in December 1995, LIJ sent a letter to the Federal Trade Commission and the Department of Justice complaining that the NSHS acquisitions on Long Island would lessen competition in the health care field. In the March 26, 1996 minutes of the LIJ Board of Trustees meeting, Dr. Dantzker predicted the development of two Queens–Long Island health care networks, one "coalescing around North Shore and the other around the Medical Center." Similarly, NSM's Strategic Plan for 1997–1998, prepared on October 11, 1996, prior to the merger discussions, states that NSM "competes primarily with other tertiary care centers, such as LIJ and Winthrop."

A major contested issue in this case is whether other hospitals are able to provide similar services to LIJ/NSM in the relevant markets. According to Wheeler, there are several other full service hospitals in the area, such as Winthrop in Nassau, which, although it provides excellent service (Winthrop was ranked as one of the "100 Best Hospitals" in the United States by U.S. News & World Report), lacks the reputation of NSM or LIJ necessary to build a network. Wheeler testified that attempting to form a network around Winthrop would "disrupt those preferences with our physicians and with our patients[,]" thereby causing United to "lose customers." Both Wheeler and Wildzunas testified that a network built around Manhattan hospitals would be untenable because people generally prefer to be hospitalized where they live. Poirier reached a similar conclusion, namely, that a Manhattan hospital would be an inappropriate anchor, recognizing that "[w]e [Empire] owe our members to receive acute care in their backyard, where their families can visit them, where they feel comfortable, where their physicians practice medicine." Wildzunas further stated that Stony Brook would not be a suitable alternative because of its distant location in Suffolk County.

Poirier testified that Winthrop is not a premier hospital because it is "not known as a teaching facilit[y] … which is clearly reflected in the graduate education medical dollars.… They [the other Long Island hospitals] do not have the history and prestige that the North Shore Manhasset and LIJ names carry." Wildzunas, senior negotiator for MagnaCare, similarly stated that although Winthrop offers the same services as NSM and LIJ, it lacks the same reputation, although he conceded that the reputations are "close." Both Wildzunas and Poirier testified that St. Francis Hospital is not comparable because it is a "specialty hospital, not a full service tertiary hospital with the full benefits of a teaching facility." In addition, both contract negotiators stated that New York Hospital Queens and Nassau County Medical Center also lack NSM's and LIJ's reputation, and as a result, could not be considered anchor hospitals.

When asked whether a developing affiliation between Winthrop and the local network of Catholic hospitals (comprised of St. Francis, Mercy, Good Samaritan, St. Charles and Mather hospitals, referred to as "CHNLI"), might be comparable to NSHS or LIJ, Poirier responded in a colorful fashion:

> First of all a patch work quilt of hospitals with different levels of clinical skills, you cannot treat or provide the full continuum of care to all patients, LIJ and North Shore on their campuses are full service facilities. So if a member with a brain trauma is at Manhasset, and they have a cardiac problem, there is the full breadth and depth of clinical services available to that patient under that roof. If you patch work quilted several acute care facilities with different clinical specialties, you would have to put that member in an ambulance and travel around the county to provide the full continuum of care. I consider that not only lack of quality, but irresponsible.

However, Dr. Stocker, who, as the President of Empire, is Poirier's superior, and is the spokesman authorized to address the public on the company's behalf, believes that Winthrop provides the same services as LIJ and NSM and therefore, is a viable alternative to those hospitals. Further, Dr. Stocker testified that Winthrop and LIJ share a similar reputation, although he concedes that NSM has the most "cachet." Consistent with this opinion, Anthony Watson, Chairman and Chief Executive Officer of the Health Insurance Plan of Greater New York ("HIP"), with 310,000 members in Queens, Nassau and Suffolk, testified that Montefiore Hospital "is the only hospital in a dominant position [as it] controls and dominates the Bronx and lower Westchester as no other hospital in this region does." However, as a member of the Board of Trustees of NSHS, Watson is an interested witness. Nevertheless, as the CEO of one of the major MCOs in the New York metropolitan area, it is Watson's opinion that by merging, LIJ and NSHS are "doing exactly what they should do . . . [to] enable them to deliver a better health care product . . . [and] a much more cost effective system."

In terms of vital statistics, NSM has 705 beds while LIJ and Winthrop have 591 beds each. In average daily population census, NSM is number one, LIJ number two and Winthrop number three. This ranking also holds true with respect to the number of attending physicians at each hospital. This latter statistic is particularly important because a hospital with a larger number of attending physicians is more likely to have a greater number of patients admitted. With regard to the number of residents, LIJ has the most, with NSM second and Winthrop a close third. In addition, in a statistical analysis of where admitted patients reside (categorized by zip code), NSM had the most patients from a diverse geographical area, with LIJ second and Winthrop third.

With respect to other sources of competition, Dr. Dantzker and Gallagher, the President and CEOs of LIJ and NSM respectively, and Katz, Chairman of the Board of Trustees for NSHS, gave undisputed testimony regarding the increased "colonization" of Long Island by Manhattan hospitals. As an example of this trend, Gallagher traced the extensive expansion of Mt. Sinai by affiliating with St. John's Smithtown in Suffolk, St. John's Hospital in Far Rockaway, Queens General, Elmhurst General, Long Beach Hospital and a number of nursing homes in Nassau and Suffolk. Further, Dr. Dantzker described this significant factor relating to market share and competition, namely, the rapid, growing infiltration of Manhattan hospitals into Queens, Nassau and Suffolk:

Q   Do Manhattan hospitals take affirmative steps to attract Queens, Nassau and Suffolk residents?

A   Absolutely. I would believe that it is already quite a hot market and it is heating up rapidly. *Manhattan hospitals are clearly looking at Queens, Long Island, as an area of what we call colonization.*

Q   And in what ways do they go about this?

A   There are a number of ways they have.

The most well recognized ways for them to develop affiliated relationships, or to purchase hospitals out on Long Island and Queens, this is the approach taken by New York Hospital in their purchase of both Flushing Hospital and New York Hospital of Queens, and by Mount Sinai. I am sure everybody has seen the Mount Sinai map of the world with its arrows and flags scattered throughout Queens and Long Island and its affiliated relationships with multiple hospitals in Queens and multiple hospitals in Nassau and Suffolk.

It is also done by the purchase or opening of medical groups. You already heard about Mount Sinai buying the North Shore Medical Group in—I am blocked on the Town.

Q Huntington?

A Huntington.

They also recently opened an ambulatory center in Hewlett, Long Island, which is in the southern parts of Nassau County. It is also done by courting and establishing relationships with physicians on Long Island, such as what was done, for example by Lenox Hill who established good and close relationships for the series of cardiologists out on the east end of Suffolk County, and now send all their cardiac surgical patients into Lenox Hill.

Speaking of them, they [Lenox Hill] already have opened up an ambulatory center essentially across the street from Long Island Jewish Medical Center to do orthopedics and sports medicine and a number of other areas.

There is an affiliation between Colombian [sic] Presbyterian Hospital and St. Francis.

There are a number of ways the Manhattan hospitals have used to colonize from a medical standpoint, Queens and Long Island.

Further, Sloan–Kettering recently announced a program with St. Francis and Mercy Hospital to bring its highly sophisticated and advanced cancer care program from Manhattan to Nassau County. This would diversify the health care furnished at St. Francis, which has been predominantly cardiac related. Mt. Sinai is opening a facility for primary care and specialist consultation services in Hewlett, which is in the southern portion of Long Island. Further, as stated above, Winthrop/South Nassau is actively pursuing an affiliation with the five Catholic hospitals on Long Island, which if consummated, would provide a clear competitive threat to a combined LIJ/NSHS entity.

Expanding on this point, Howard Gold, Senior Vice President in charge of NSHS's managed care negotiations, views North Shore's competitors on the primary and secondary care level to be every hospital in Queens, Nassau, Suffolk and Manhattan. On the tertiary care level, he views Winthrop, St. Francis, LIJ, Nassau County Medical Center, Stony Brook and the Manhattan hospitals as competitors. In addition, he places New York Hospital Queens in the latter category because it was purchased by New York Hospital, which is affiliated with Cornell University Medical School, and recently added a cardiac surgery department. In support of this contention that the Manhattan hospitals are colonizing Long Island and providing competition to Long Island hospitals, Dr. Dantzker testified that the Manhattan hospitals advertise "extensively":

Q Do the Manhattan hospitals advertise in media which reach Queens, Nassau and Suffolk residents?

A Endlessly. It is hard to turn on the radio without hearing an ad for one of the Manhattan hospitals. Even I know the number of MD [sic] Sinai. The ads are continuously in the Long Island edition of the New York Times, in Newsday, in all of the local newspapers, television ads. It is a veritable blitz of advertising in this area.

The Court further recognizes that large numbers of Queens, Nassau and Suffolk residents go to Manhattan hospitals for treatment. This is especially true for the speciality [sic] fields of cancer treatment, cardiac surgery and complex orthopedic surgery. For example, in 1996, almost 9,000 patients from Queens, Nassau, and Suffolk were admitted into Manhattan hospitals for cardiac surgery—3,000 from Queens, 3,000 from Nassau and 2,800 from Suffolk. In 1996, according to the testimony of the defendants' expert, Margaret Guerin–Calvert, approximately 50,000 patients from Queens, Nassau and Suffolk Counties sought primary, secondary and tertiary health care in Manhattan. Other statistics revealed that 15 percent of tertiary care patients from Queens, Nassau and Suffolk were treated at Manhattan hospitals.

D. *The Consumers*

At trial, the parties disagreed as to the identity of the consumers in the alleged relevant markets. The Government's expert, as to all phases of liability except "efficiencies," was Dr. Gregory S. Vistnes, Assistant Chief Economist at the Anti–Trust Division of the Department of Justice. Dr. Vistnes testified that the consumers are the managed care plans who "pick the appropriate hospitals for their hospital network ... assemble physicians and other attributes of the provider network ... which they then market or try to sell to their customer." Dr. Vistnes elaborated his view that the managed care plans are the "customers" or "consumers":

Q And what are the implications of focusing on the individual patient as the customer of the hospital rather than the managed care plan?

A I feel that by focusing on patients as the customer of the hospital, that that leads to a misleading or inappropriate analysis.

In particular while such a focus may have been appropriate in the past when indemnity plans were prevalent in the marketplace, and the principal means by which individuals were insured. That is no longer the case in today's health care marketplace. *Instead, it is the managed care plan which is driving the hospital's decisions.* It is clear that the managed care plans are the ones driving the hospital's decisions on whether or not, or why they should affiliate or merge. It is the managed care plans who are driving the hospital's decisions on what services they should or should not be offering. And it is managed care plans which are driving hospitals' decisions with regard to price.

Unless one focuses on managed care plans as a factor which is affecting today's marketplace in health care, one cannot come to a reliable conclusion as to the effect of this merger.

Dr. Vistnes further stated that the "customers are in general the employers and their employees." In sum, Dr. Vistnes testified that the "consumers" were (1) the managed care plans, (2) the employers, and (3) their employees.

On the other hand, Guerin–Calvert, the defendants' antitrust health care expert, testified that the "consumers" are the users of the hospitals' services, namely, the residents of Queens, Nassau and Suffolk. In her view, managed care plans account for less than 30 percent of the payers of hospital services. Other "consumers" include the Government through Medicare and Medicaid, indemnity insurers, self-insured employers, other employers, private individuals who pay for themselves, and increasingly, physician groups.

Given the evidence at the trial, the Court finds that there are five categories of "consumers" in this hospital merger case. First, there are the patients who are either self-payers or have indemnity insurance. Second, there are the physicians and the physician groups who control admissions. Third, there are the managed care plans as described by Dr. Vistnes. Fourth, there are the employers who exert control over the selection of the hospital network. Fifth, there are the Government payers.

II. *ADDITIONAL FINDINGS OF FACT–CONCLUSIONS OF LAW*

A. *Section 7 of the Clayton Act*

While the complaint includes a request for relief under Section 1 of the Sherman Act, 15 U.S.C. § 1, the Court will focus its attention on Section 7 of the Clayton Act, as that law applies equally to both statutes.

Section 7 of the Clayton Act, 15 U.S.C. § 18 ("Section 7"), provides in part that "no person engaged in commerce . . . shall acquire the whole or any part of the assets of another person . . . where . . . the effect of such acquisition may be substantially to lessen competition, or to tend to create a monopoly." To meet the requirements of Section 7, the Government must show a reasonable probability that the proposed merger would substantially lessen competition in the future. To determine whether there is a reasonable probability of a substantial lessening of competition, the courts have focused on whether the transaction has the "potential for creating, enhancing, or facilitating the exercise of market power-the ability of one or more firms to raise prices above competitive levels for a significant period of time." Generally, a plaintiff in a Section 7 Clayton Act antitrust matter may establish a *prima facie* case by demonstrating that the merged entity will have a large percentage of the "relevant market," so that it may raise prices above competitive levels. In order for a court to determine the effect of a merger on competition, the "relevant market" must first be defined. A "relevant market" consists of two components: a product market, and a geographic market. Further, the Government must prove that the defendants have "a dominant market share in a *well-defined* relevant market." The properly defined market excludes those potential suppliers whose product is sufficiently differentiated or too far away, and who are unlikely to offer a suitable alternative.

Applying these standards, the Government has the burden of proof and seeks to: (1) define the relevant product market; (2) define the relevant geographic market; and (3) prove that the merger will be anti-competitive and will result in an increase in prices above competitive levels for a significant period of time.

B. *The Relevant Product Market*

In defining the relevant product market, the Court must consider what products or services a consumer, confronting a price increase, would reasonably substitute for the products or services of the merging parties. If the consumer can reasonably substitute another product or service, then the substitute product or service can be considered part of the relevant product market.

The Government contends that the "relevant product market" consists of "the bundle of acute inpatient services provided by anchor hospitals to managed care plans." On the other hand, the defendants contend that, using the court's "traditional methodology," the relevant product market in this hospital merger case is "general acute care inpatient hospital services."

"Anchor hospitals," according to the plaintiff, are those having "prestigious reputations, broad ranging and highly sophisticated services, and high quality medical staffs." The plaintiff distinguishes between the "general acute care hospitals" and the major prestigious acute care "anchor" hospitals like NSM and LIJ, which are in "a [unique] market to serve as an anchor hospital for a managed care plan." The plaintiff asserts that "community hospitals are not reasonably interchangeable" with anchor hospitals.

The Government's version of the product market is limited to primary and secondary care and excludes tertiary care provided at the anchor hospitals. Thus, as will be discussed later, the Government is pursuing this Clayton Act Section 7 case based on a claimed anti-competitive price increase of 20 percent only for the primary/secondary services by the merged entity. In this regard, the following testimony by Dr. Vistnes is crucial:

> Q   Now, you hypothesized a 20 percent price increase by the merged entities after the merger; is that correct?
>
> A   Yes, I have.
>
> Q   That is not a 20 percent across the board for the whole bundle of services, is it, Dr. Vistnes?
>
> A   No, it is not.
>
> Q   It covers only non-tertiary services; is that correct?
>
> A   Yes, it does-or that is correct.
>
> Q   *And do you believe that after the merger of North Shore Manhasset and Long Island Jewish will be monopolist for tertiary care services?*
>
> A   *No, I do not.*

The Government's analysis of the relevant product market is flawed in several key respects. Preliminarily, the Court notes that the plaintiff's definition is unduly restricted to "anchor" hospitals. This definition does not comport with that applied in other hospital merger cases, namely, "general acute inpatient services." *Freeman Hospital,* 69 F.3d at 268 (government stipulated that the relevant product market was "acute care inpatient services"); *University Health,* 938 F.2d at 1210–11 (relevant market is "the provision of in-patient services by acute-care hospitals in the Augusta area"); *Rockford Memorial Corp.,* 898 F.2d at 1284 (relevant market is "the provision of inpatient services by acute-care hospitals"); *Butterworth Health Corp.,* 946 F. Supp. at 1290–91 (relevant product market is "general acute care inpatient hospital services" and "primary care inpatient services"); *Mercy Health Servs.,* 902 F. Supp. at 976 (government stipulated that the relevant product market was "acute care inpatient services"); *United States v. Carilion Health System,* 707 F. Supp. 840, 842 (W.D. Va.), (relevant product market is "acute inpatient hospital services and certain outpatient healthcare services provided by various clinics"), *aff'd without written opinion,* 892 F.2d 1042 (4th Cir. 1989).

However, even if the Court were to ignore the weight of authority in this particular urban-suburban locality, the Government has failed to establish that the acute inpatient services produced at these so called "anchor hospitals" are unique and would support its own relevant product market. As set forth above, approximately 85 percent of the services provided by LIJ and NSM involve primary and secondary care. The evidence is clear that these services are offered by numerous other hospitals in Nassau and Queens. The Court finds that with regard to primary and secondary care services, LIJ and NSM competes with the community hospitals in Nassau and Queens, such at Mercy, Mid–Island and South Nassau Community in Nassau and Elmhurst Hospital Center, Flushing Medical, Peninsula Hospital Center and St. John's Episcopal in Queens. Further, in the same area, Winthrop and New York Hospital Queens provides substantially all of the services offered by LIJ and NSM, including tertiary care. In addition, there is another major tertiary care hospital in the relevant product market, namely, the Nassau County Medical Center located in East Meadow.

The Government's position based on an "anchor hospital" monopoly did not materialize in Suffolk County, where it is conceded by all parties that the only anchor hospital's Stony Brook University Hospital. Under the Government's theory, Stony Brook would be in a position to raise prices in an anti-competitive manner. However, the evidence revealed that Stony Brook was and is charging competitive prices.

Indeed, in the Court's view, the Government essentially concedes this point. Rather than argue that these services are unavailable elsewhere, the plaintiff maintains that the "reputation" of LIJ and NSM is what separates them from the crowd. The main support for this proposition is the testimony of certain Government witnesses such as Poirier, Empire's Vice President who testified that LIJ and NSM are the only two hospitals in Nassau and Queens which share a prominent "reputation." The problem with this "reputation" evidence is that it is based on "perception" of where patients currently go, rather than where they could practically go for acute care inpatient services in the future. The more material question is not the present customer's perception of the available hospital care, but the future likelihoods.

The lack of weight of this evidence was driven home by the testimony of Dr. Stocker, who serves not only as Empire's President and CEO, but as Poirier's direct superior. According to Dr. Stocker, whose testimony the Court credits, NSM and LIJ compete with many other entities as to all acute inpatient care. With regard to primary/secondary care, which is the lion's share of their business, the defendant hospitals compete with all local health care institutions including teaching hospitals such as Winthrop, the community hospitals in Queens and Nassau, and the Nassau County Medical Center, a large municipal hospital. In this regard, the Court notes that, in Queens County, aside from LIJ and the Queens hospital in the NSHS, there are ten general acute care hospitals that supply all or most of the services provided by LIJ and NSM. Many of these hospitals provide some tertiary care. These hospitals include Elmhurst General with 516 beds; New York Hospital Queens with 487 beds; Flushing with 415 beds; and St. John's Episcopal with 314 beds. In Nassau County, other than the hospitals in the NSHS, there are eight general acute care hospitals that supply all or many of the services provided by LIJ and NSM, including some tertiary care services. These hospitals include Nassau County Medical Center with 1,384 beds; Winthrop with 518 beds; Hempstead General with 464 beds; South Nassau Communities with 429 beds; Long Beach Medical Center with 390 beds; and Mercy with 387 beds.

The defendant hospitals also compete with the recently "colonized" medical outposts of the Manhattan hospitals, such as the local oncology facilities opened by Sloan–Kettering and the physician practices purchased by Mt. Sinai. One of the most striking examples of competition resulting from this colonization is the recent purchase of Booth Memorial Hospital in Queens by New York Hospital, which is associated with the Cornell Medical Center. As stated above, this facility, now known as New York Hospital Queens, is on its way to being a major tertiary care teaching hospital, and, with reasonable certainty, will be a vigorous competitor with the merged hospitals, certainly in Queens County.

Furthermore, any attempts to distinguish LIJ and NSM based on their "reputations" as teaching facilities and providers of tertiary care must fail for two reasons. First, the Court finds that although several witnesses testified that both LIJ and NSM have a certain "cachet," there is another teaching facility in the area which performs similar services, namely, Winthrop, which has merged with South Nassau Communities Hospital and may also become affiliated with five major Catholic hospitals, two of those hospitals located in Nassau. Winthrop has become a formidable competitor, especially in cardiac services. The NSM strategic plan, drawn prior to the merger, acknowledged that Winthrop "is competing fiercely with NSUH–

M's market position" Every witness in this case who was questioned on the subject, testified that Winthrop is an excellent, premier, tertiary care teaching hospital.

Second, with respect to tertiary, services, the evidence is clear that people will travel to Manhattan to seek medical treatment. As set forth above, last year alone, approximately 9,000 Queens, Nassau and Suffolk patients sought cardiac treatment in Manhattan, and 50,000 traveled to Manhattan for all types of treatment. Accordingly, to the extent that there is a relevant product market to be considered, the Court finds that it would be for general acute care inpatient hospital services, rather than the provision of these services by anchor hospitals.

Also, the Court finds that the Government's characterization of an anchor hospital as a relevant product market is unnecessarily restrictive in that it fails to take into consideration the dynamics of the marketplace. This subject was discussed in *Belfiore v. New York Times Co.*, 826 F.2d 177, 180 (2d Cir. 1987), an antitrust case involving newspaper home delivery:

> In the district court, plaintiffs alleged that the Times monopolizes the "general interest daily newspapers directed primarily to upscale readers" market.... As the district court noted, this market definition is implausible as a theoretical matter. Plaintiffs' narrow definition is an awkward attempt to conform their theory to the facts they alleged; this market definition does not reflect any relevant market evidenced in the record.

Id. at 180. (Citing *U.S. v. Grinnell Corp.*, 384 U.S. 563, 590–91 [1966] [Fortas, J., with Stewart, J., dissenting] [criticizing narrow market definitions tailored only to those activities in which defendants engage; relevant market includes alternative sources of and substitutes for defendants' product reflecting "commercial realities.]). Accordingly, the Court finds that the relevant product market is the general acute care inpatient hospital services.

Even if the Government's definition of the relevant product market involving "anchor" hospitals was appropriate, it cannot prevail. The Court finds that Winthrop, which is a teaching facility providing primary, secondary and tertiary health care services, qualifies as an anchor hospital. In addition to the testimony of various witnesses supporting this conclusion, including Wheeler and Dr. Stocker, the Court notes again that U.S. News & World Report recently ranked Winthrop as one of the nation's top 100 hospitals. Moreover, the plaintiff's own expert witness, DOJ economist Dr. Vistnes, admitted that Winthrop provides essentially the same services as LIJ and NSM.

Thus, the Court finds that the Government failed to establish its definition of the relevant product market as an anchor hospital providing primary/secondary service. However, to complete the record, the Court will review and determine the remaining material issues in the case.

C. *The Relevant Geographic Market*

A geographic market is that area "to which consumers can practically turn for alternative sources of the product and in which the antitrust defendants face competition." The critical question is where can consumers of the product involved practically turn for alternative sources of the product should the merger be consummated and the merged hospitals prices increase. Determination of the relevant geographic market is highly fact sensitive.

Predictably, the parties have widely divergent views of the geographic market within which the merging hospitals compete. The Government's definition of the relevant geographic market vacillated throughout the proceeding. In its moving papers, the Government did not set forth a clearly defined relevant geographic market. It stated, in imprecise terms, that the geographic market is an area in Nassau and Queens surrounding the two merging anchor hospitals, but not extending to Suffolk or Manhattan. The Government's expert, Dr. Vistnes, testified that the relevant geographic market has no defined borders; it may be the entire counties of Queens and Nassau, but his best estimate is "that the geographic market would be a region of approximately five miles from the two merging hospitals," without a precise boundary. In its post-trial brief and at closing arguments, however, the Government firmly selected an outside boundary of Queens and Nassau Counties as the relevant geographic market.

The defendants maintain that the relevant geographic market includes Nassau, Queens, Western Suffolk and Manhattan. In support of their position, the hospitals rely on patient origin data (records of where people who receive medical care at certain hospitals reside), which demonstrates that LIJ and NSM draw patients from Queens, Nassau and Suffolk, and that patients residing in these areas also seek medical care in western Suffolk, Nassau, Queens and Manhattan.

As is often the case with such complex, fact sensitive issues, the reality lies somewhere in between the two versions. In the Court's view, the parties have oversimplified the relevant geographic market by attempting to impose a single market to their own advantage, where actually two such markets exist. *Accord Brown Shoe Co.,* 370 U.S. at 324 ("However, within this broad market, well-defined submarkets may exist which, in themselves, constitute product markets for antitrust purposes"); *Blue Cross & Blue Shield v. Marshfield Clinic,* 65 F.3d 1406, 1411 (7th Cir. 1995) (recognizing how multiple markets may complicate an antitrust proceeding and discussing "submarkets" and a "series of linked geographic markets") *cert. denied* 516 U.S. 1184 (1996); *U.S. Anchor Mfg., Inc. v. Rule Industries, Inc.,* 7 F.3d 986, 995 (11th Cir. 1993) ("defining a 'submarket' is the equivalent of defining a relevant product market for antitrust purposes") *cert. denied,* 512 U.S. 1221 (1994); *Butterworth Health Corp.,* 946 F. Supp. at 1293 (recognizing the possibility of two relevant geographic markets, one for general acute inpatient services, the other for primary care services).

On the one hand, there is evidence that in general, patients prefer to receive health care treatment relatively close to their homes. As Wheeler testified, when forming a hospital network it is important not to disrupt the preferences of physicians and patients. Further, several witnesses, including Wheeler and Wildzunas, testified that a network built around Manhattan hospitals would be untenable because people generally prefer to be hospitalized where they live. Poirier reached a similar conclusion, recognizing that Empire is obligated "to provide its members with acute care in their backyard, where their families can visit them, where they feel comfortable, where their physicians practice medicine."

Nevertheless, there was evidence adduced that large numbers of Queens, Nassau and Suffolk residents go to Manhattan hospitals for treatment. Vangeli of Cigna lauded the large, tertiary care hospitals in Manhattan and stated that Cigna enrollees "are willing to travel to Manhattan for certain services." This is especially true with regard to tertiary care in the speciality [sic] fields of cancer treatment, cardiac surgery and complex orthopedic surgery. As stated above, in 1996, approximately 50,000 patients from Queens, Nassau and Suffolk traveled to Manhattan for treatment. Other statistics revealed that 15 percent of tertiary care patients from Queens, Nassau and Suffolk went to Manhattan hospitals. The Court agrees with the description of the Manhattan "submarket" described by Dr. Stocker:

Q With respect to the Nassau–Queens market, Doctor, what impact do [sic] the Manhattan market have on competition and on pricing do you think?

A Substantial.

Q Would you please describe that?

A Well, unlike most marketplaces it is only what, 15 miles or so to get to the Manhattan tertiary care hospitals. They are very big, very famous and very attractive. And they attract a lot of business from Long Island to their hospitals. So New York Hospital, Columbia, Sloan–Kettering, Beth Israel, are all hospitals that almost in any other marketplace, you would be lucky if you have one of them, and we have ten academic centers in there.

Reviewing this evidence, the Court concludes that there are actually two relevant geographic markets in this case. The first geographic market is for primary and secondary care, which constitutes approximately 85 percent of the services provided by LIJ and NSM, and includes only Queens and Nassau. The Manhattan and Suffolk hospitals, including Stony Brook, are too far away from the consumers in the NSM/LIJ sphere of influence, to provide reasonably suitable alternative care. The second geographic market is for tertiary care, and includes Manhattan, Queens, Nassau and western Suffolk County. (*See* testimony regarding "carve-outs," or the "process by which a managed care company can contract with a hospital for just some services, but not all services"); (*see* testimony regarding "steering" patients away from certain institutions).

Having reached this determination, the Court notes a significant corollary which must be kept in mind when reviewing the alleged anticompetitive effects of the merger. Once the existence of two geographic markets is established, the relevant product market also must be revised. As the plaintiff conceded at trial, it would be virtually impossible for the Government to obtain injunctive relief if Manhattan were included in the relevant geographic area, given the numerous alternative anchor hospitals located in that area. Accordingly, assuming that a viable relevant product market had been demonstrated with respect to general acute inpatient care, as opposed to acute inpatient care provided by an anchor hospital, the inclusion of Manhattan as part of the relevant geographic market for tertiary services, effectively limits the overall relevant market to primary/secondary care at hospitals in Queens and Nassau.

Notes

1. *Defining the market as the defendant's production.* LIJ and NSM are both high-quality, sophisticated teaching hospitals in the New York metropolitan area, which has significant overcapacity and includes many premier teaching facilities and numerous general acute-care hospitals. Nonetheless, the government tried to exclude all or almost all of these competing facilities from the relevant market by characterizing LIJ and NSM as "anchor hospitals," defined as "those having 'prestigious reputations, broad ranging and highly sophisticated services, and high quality medical staffs' [and] which are in 'a [unique] market to serve as an anchor hospital for a managed care plan.'" 983 F. Supp. at 137. This argument, based in good part on some purchasers' testimony that they could not build adequate networks without LIJ and NSM, boiled down to the proposition that those two hospitals were unique in that area and therefore the relevant market largely consisted of just them, meaning that the defendants together had a market share close to 100%. The government lost because it was unable to convince the court that neighboring general acute-care hospitals and the teaching facilities in Manhattan were not good substitutes for LIJ and NSM. This holding increased the denominator of the hospitals' market share tremendously such that it was clear that together LIJ and NSM had a fairly small share. For careful criticism of the court's analysis of the geographic market, see Thomas L. Greaney, *Hospital Mergers, in* COMPETITION POLICY AND MERGER ANALYSIS IN DEREGULATED AND NEWLY COMPETITIVE INDUSTRIES 126, 141–42 (Peter Carstensen et al. eds., 2008); *Chicago's Procrustean Bed: Applying Antitrust Law in Health Care,* 71 ANTITRUST L.J. 857, 879–82 (2004) [hereinafter Greaney, *Chicago's Procrustean Bed*].

2. *Defining the product market—reasonable interchangeability.* The classic statement of the relevant question in defining a product market is to ask whether competing products are reasonably interchangeable for similar uses, considering their prices, characteristics, and quality. United States v. E.I. du Pont de Nemours & Co., 351 U.S. 377, 404 (1956) [*Cellophane*]. The fundamental question is whether to "combine" or "separate" products in defining the market. As with much of law presumptions can play an important role here. One could start with the assumption that similar

products should be "combined" unless proven otherwise. Erroneous judgments would result in understating a defendant's market power (because the denominator would incorrectly be increased). From the other direction, one could presume that fairly small differences between products indicate that they should be "separated." Errors would result in overstating a defendant's power (because the denominator would erroneously be diminished). The starting point for the opposite presumptions are beliefs concerning the extent to which market power can exist and be long lasting. If one is "Chicago–School" and believes that market power is rare and is quickly broken down by the gales of competition—the so-called "self-correcting" feature of markets—then one is more concerned about harm caused by erroneous legal intervention into a market. Given this view of the risk of error, it is preferable, the argument goes, to combine similar products. At the margin, this presumption will understate power but the self-correcting features of markets will minimize this harm. By contrast, if one has less faith in the "centripetal and centrifugal" forces of competition—if one believes that market power can exist and can be long-lasting—then one is more inclined to separate products. At the margin, this presumption will overstate power but this harm is outweighed by that caused by erroneously allowing continued, long-lasting exercise of market power. Use of this strategy sets the stage for greater legal intervention into the market, a proper consequence of the belief that law should err on the side of breaking up power. For the respective views, compare William M. Landes & Richard A. Posner, *Market Power in Antitrust Cases*, 94 HARV. L. REV. 937 (1981), with Louis Kaplow, *The Accuracy of Traditional Market Power Analysis and a Direct Adjustment Alternative*, 95 HARV. L. REV. 1817 (1982). *See generally* Robert Pitofsky, *New Definitions of Relevant Market and the Assault on Antitrust*, 90 COLUM. L. REV. 1805 (1990). For an interesting discussion about how these different "priors" affect antitrust policy in the United States and the European Union, see Ken Heyer, *A World of Uncertainty: Economics and the Globalization of Antitrust*, 72 ANTITRUST L.J. 375, 399–415 (2005).

Notice that the court in *Long Island Jewish Medical Center* decided that patients stayed close to home for relatively simple care but were willing to travel for more complex and serious conditions. There is an intuitive sense and substantial evidence to support such a distinction. For an arm that has been broken in the schoolyard, few patients (parents, here) would drive past local emergency rooms. However, to treat a rare form of advanced metastatic cancer, persons are much more willing to travel greater distances. What does this indicate regarding the homogeneity of the multiple services that hospitals offer? Nonetheless, for the most part in merger cases decision makers have been content to combine those services into fairly crude categories, "clusters," such as acute inpatient care or outpatient care. *But see* FTC v. ProMedica Health System, Inc., 2011 WL 1219281 (N.D. Ohio 2011) (in granting preliminary injunction to preclude final consummation of merger pending administrative enforcement action, court accepted submarket of inpatient obstetrical services because of separable demand and entry conditions). In non-merger cases where conduct is at issue decision makers have drawn narrower markets. For example, Jefferson Parish Hospital District No. 2 v. Hyde, 466 U.S. 2 (1984), involved a challenge to the defendant hospital's use of an exclusive contract for anesthesia, and the relevant product market was anesthesiology services. Using narrower markets, drawn with reference to the challenged conduct, makes sense because the remedy for illegal conduct would be merely to open up the contracting process. Likewise, when multi-product pharmaceutical companies merge, the remedy for undue power over one of the merging companies' products would be divestiture of that one product. At least so far, no one has suggested that merging hospitals divest themselves of a particular service, say orthopedics, if the merger creates power over that service.

Aside from administrative convenience, the rationale for using broad clusters is that on the demand side for the most part payers contract with hospitals for such broad clusters instead of narrower, more specialized segments, while on the supply side many services are produced from a common base—e.g., all surgery uses anesthesia and nursing. This complementarity in supply would enable one hospital to enter in response to another's attempted exercise of market power. *See* DEBORAH HAAS-WILSON, MANAGED CARE AND MONOPOLY POWER: THE ANTITRUST CHALLENGE 100–105 (2003) [hereinafter HAAS-WILSON, MANAGED CARE AND MONOPOLY POWER]; *see also* United States v. Philadelphia Nat'l Bank, 374 U.S. 321, 356–57 (1963). *See generally* Jonathan Baker, *The Antitrust Analysis of Hospital Mergers and the Transformation of the Hospital Industry*, 51 L. & CONTEMP. PROBS. 93, 123–140 (1988). Neither of these rationales is terribly satisfying but we leave fuller consideration to our discussion of *Evanston Northwestern Healthcare Corporation* immediately below.

Decision makers have been far more willing to define product markets for other products and services much more narrowly than broad categories like "acute-inpatient care." Product markets for physician services, for example, are usually drawn about the relevant CPT codes such as those for vascular surgeons or gastroenterologists, *see, e.g.*, Letter from Joel I. Klein, Assistant Attorney General, Antitrust Division, U.S. Department of Justice to Bob D. Tucker (Re: CVT Surgical Center and Vascular Surgery Associates) (Apr. 16, 1997) (http://www.usdoj.gov/atr/public/busreview/1099.htm); Letter from Joel I. Klein, Assistant Attorney General, Antitrust Division, U.S. Department of Justice to Donald L. Lipson (Gastroenterology Associates Limited et al.) (July 7, 1997) (http://www.usdoj.gov/atr/public/bus review/1099.htm), although substitution among types of physicians should be a consideration, as well as the fact that buyers sometimes group services together, raising the possibility of using clusters of services. *See generally* HAAS-WILSON, MANAGED CARE AND MONOPOLY POWER at 105–10. In cases involving insurance there have been disputes, like that in *Ball Memorial Hospital* below, whether diverse insurance products such as indemnity plans, HMOs, PPOs, point-of service plans and the like should be separated or combined. *See, e.g.*, U.S. Healthcare v. Healthsource, Inc., 986 F.2d 589 (1st Cir. 1993); Blue Cross & Blue Shield United of Wisconsin v. Marshfield Clinic, 65 F.3d 1406 (7th Cir. 1995); Ball Memorial Hospital v. Mutual

Hospital Ins., 784 F.2d 1325 (7th Cir. 1986) (reprinted below for discussion of barriers of entry). However, in contrast to hospital cases, these disputes are factual in nature and relatively devoid of difficult conceptual issues. *See, e.g.*, City of New York v. Group Health Inc., 649 F.3d 151 (2d Cir. 2011) (in challenge to merger between two insurance plans, plaintiff's definition of market as "low-cost municipal health benefits market" was rejected because plaintiff failed to prove that other insurance plans were unsuitable).

3. *Defining the geographic market through patient flow-data.* Defining the relevant geographic market is analogous to that of the product market because the former analyzes substitution of products from various locales, which is analogous to analyzing substitution of products of somewhat different physical characteristics. In hospital cases, courts have traditionally analyzed patient-flow patterns, as well as used the sort of evidence the court analyzes in *Long Island Jewish Medical Center*. The courts start with the area from which the hospital (or physician practice group) draws a significant number of its patients—its service area—and combine that area with locales to which a significant number of patients travel (or are willing to travel). We shall have much more to say about this too below but for now merely observe that the same sort of presumptions are at work here too. Starting with the geographic location of a defendant's current customers, one can place the thumb against combining other areas, e.g., hospitals (or physicians) further away, because of evidence showing a reluctance to travel. At the margin this method understates the geographic market, overstates the defendant's power and therefore leads to greater intervention. Coming from the other direction, one could rely on evidence that some defined number of patients do travel to other hospitals and therefore include those hospitals in the geographic market unless other evidence suggests otherwise. At the margin this understates power and diminishes intervention. From which presumption did the Antitrust Division of the Department of Justice operate in *Long Island Jewish Medical Center*? The more recent posture of the FTC is discussed in more detail below in reference to *Evanston Northwestern Healthcare Corporation*.

As we will discuss in far more detail below in the note on *Evanston Northwestern Healthcare Corporation*, defining geographic markets for hospital cases has been very contentious. By contrast, doing so for physician services or insurers has been much easier because markets are always or almost always local.

4. *Section 2 versus section 7. Long Island Jewish Medical Center* involved a section 7 challenge to a merger that had yet to be consummated. Doctrinally section 7 requires a lower threshold for a violation than section 2 because it was designed to preclude mergers that merely threaten to create power—power is to be stopped in its incipiency. In such a situation, possibly presumptions that overstate power are warranted, and decision makers might justifiably err on the side of separating products and different geographic areas unless proven otherwise.

Analysis of horizontal mergers has shifted over time, influenced in good part by contemporaneous views of antitrust as a whole. For many years analysis was dominated by the "structural" perspective reflected in the analysis adumbrated by Judge Hand in *Alcoa* reprinted below—define the relevant market and determine the defendant's share of that market. It was taken as a given that concentrated market structure was highly correlated with the ability to raise price and exclude competitors—hence the name, "structure-conduct-performance." At the height of this perspective, mergers resulting in a significant increase in concentration were very strongly presumed to threaten competition and enjoined, *see* United States v. Philadelphia National Bank, 374 U.S. 321, 363 (1963), with the result that market share, revolving around definition of the relevant market, was usually outcome determinative. However, after withering theoretical criticism from Chicago–School economists and substantial empirical work questioning the underlying "structure-conduct-performance" correlation, the structural presumption was relaxed such that the inquiry became much more flexible, particularly in the consideration of entry and efficiencies. *See, e.g.,* United States v. General Dynamics Corp., 415 U.S. 486 (1974).

Over the last three to four decades, the relevance of market structure has waxed and waned. Greatly influenced, if not dominated, by Chicago–School economics during the 1970s and 1980s, antitrust doctrine swung far away from the structure-conduct-performance hypothesis. Indeed, by 1990, in an influential decision authored by future-Justice Clarence Thomas and joined by future-Justice Ruth Bader Ginsburg, the D.C. Circuit declared that "[e]vidence of market concentration simply provides a convenient starting point for a broader inquiry into future competitiveness." United States v. Baker Hughes, Inc., 908 F.2d 981, 984 (D.C. Cir. 1990). Following, starting with promulgation of the 1992 Horizontal Merger Guidelines, available as amended at http://www.justice.gov/atr/public/guidelines/hmg–2010.html, at least in the enforcement agencies analysis has gradually shifted away from market structure to the so-called "competitive effects" of a merger, whether obtained by coordination among firms ("coordinated effects") or the unilateral conduct of firms ("unilateral effects"), including the firm to be created by the merger (or that was created by the merger). For a discussion of unilateral and coordinated effects, see generally IV Phillip E. Areeda et al., ANTITRUST LAW: AN ANALYSIS OF ANTITRUST PRINCIPLES AND THEIR APPLICATION ¶¶ 914–16 (2d ed., 2006); United States Dep't of Justice & Federal Trade Commission, Commentary on the Horizontal Merger Guidelines 17–36 (2006) (http://www.ftc.gov/os/2006/03/CommentaryontheHorizontalMergerGuidelinesMarch2006.pdf). As discussed below with regard to *Northwestern Evanston*, there is movement in the direction of abandoning the traditional structural approach altogether with regard to highly differentiated products like hospital services.

This history has been canvassed, with varying perspectives, in numerous places. For some examples, see Jonathan B. Baker & Carl Shapiro, Reinvigorating Horizontal Merger Enforcement (2007) (http://papers.ssrn.com/sol3/papers.cfm?abstract_id=1089198); Jonathan B. Baker, *Why Did the Antitrust Agencies Embrace Unilateral Effects?*, 12 GEO. MASON L. REV.

31 (2003); Michael S. Jacobs, *An Essay on the Normative Foundations of Antitrust Economics*, 74 N.C. L. REV. 219 (1995); Malcolm B. Coate, *Economics, the Guidelines and the Evolution of Merger Policy*, 37 ANTITRUST BULLETIN 997 (1992); Leonard W. Weiss, *The Structure–Conduct–Performance Paradigm and Antitrust*, 127 U. PA. L. REV. 1104 (1979). *See generally* HERBERT HOVENKAMP, FEDERAL ANTITRUST POLICY: THE LAW OF COMPETITION AND ITS PRACTICE ¶ 1.7 (3d ed. 2005) ("The Troubled Life of the Structure–Conduct–Performance Paradigm"). For a description of some of the theoretical problems and an assessment of the structure-conduct-performance empirical literature regarding the effects of hospital mergers, see Martin Gaynor & William B. Vogt, *Antitrust and Competition in Health Care Markets, in* 1 HEALTHBOOK OF HEALTH ECONOMICS 1445–51 (A.J. Culyer & J.P. Newhouse eds., 2000) [hereinafter Gaynor & Vogt, *Antitrust and Competition in Health Care Markets*].

5. *Prospective versus retrospective.* In a section 7 prospective challenge to a merger a decision maker must make a prediction about the merger and future conduct's future effect on market structure and price. By contrast, other cases involve challenges to extant structure or conduct. In such instances decision makers must make decisions about present or past structure or price. The former requires evidence that is prospective, the latter necessitates the use of retrospective evidence.

There is, however, less to this distinction than first appears. Although there are methods used to predict prospective structure and conduct, such as merger simulations, *see generally* Gregory J. Werden & Luke M. Froeb, *Unilateral Competitive Effects of Horizontal Mergers, in* HANDBOOK OF ANTITRUST ECONOMICS 43, 64–85 (Paolo Buccirossi ed., 2008) (http://papers.ssrn.com/sol3/papers.cfm?abstract_id=927913), without prophetic vision one must still extrapolate from the past and present into the future. *See generally* 2B Phillip E. Areeda et al., ANTITRUST LAW: AN ANALYSIS OF ANTITRUST PRINCIPLES AND THEIR APPLICATION ¶ 538 (3d ed., 2007). As a prominent example, in defining a market one cannot rely on current substitution patterns but must ask what consumers (or producers) would do in the future in response to an attempt to raise price above a competitive level. "Customers or alternative suppliers who had not previously shifted when ... prices were competitive might readily shift if those prices became supracompetitive." *Id.* ¶ 560, at 359. Going in the other temporal direction, "prior shifts may have occurred only because prices were already monopolistic and thus inadequately constrained by shifts." *Id.* (footnote omitted).

Therefore, the use of current or past structure or conduct to define a market raises a particular problem of circular reasoning known as the "*Cellophane* fallacy," named for the section 2 monopolization case brought against du Pont, the manufacturer of cellophane. *See* United States v. E.I. du Pont (Cellophane), 351 U.S. 377 (1956). Defendant had shown a high degree of substitution between cellophane and other flexible packaging products like waxed paper and tin foil. Based on this evidence, the Supreme Court defined the product market broadly to include all flexible packaging material instead of separating cellophane into its own product market because of its distinctive characteristics—transparency, flexibility, strength, heat resistance, etc. The Court failed to perceive that the high degree of substitution existed *because* the defendant had raised price above the competitive level, thereby causing customers to switch to alternative products. In other words, the Court inferred from the fact of relatively high substitution that defendant lacked power when the high degree of substitution was *caused* by the fact that the defendant had raised price. Paradoxically, then, the defendant, which possessed and was exercising market power, looked less powerful than a firm without power. The latter cannot raise price, with the result that the lower price suppresses the amount of substitution, which in turn makes other products or geographic areas appear not to be good substitutes. If a decision maker relies on this lack of substitution alone, it erroneously increases the market share of the firm without power and infers from this higher share that power exists. The *Cellophane* fallacy threatens to stand antitrust upside down. *See generally* 2B Phillip E. Areeda et al., Antitrust Law: An Analysis of Antitrust Principles and Their Application ¶ 539 (3d ed., 2007); Jonathan B. Baker, *Market Definition: An Analytical Overview*, 74 Antitrust L. J. 129, 159–66, 169–73 (2007) [hereinafter Baker, *Market Definition*].

How to avoid the fallacy is a difficult question because reliance on existing patterns of substitution necessarily involves this problem of circularity. Relatively greater substitution may exist because defendant has raised price and has thereby increased substitution. Equally, relatively greater substitution might reflect an inability to raise price. One cannot infer whether market power exists or doesn't exist from patterns of substitution alone. Instead, courts must rely on evidence concerning the extent to which buyers see different products to be similar or distinctive, evidence concerning differences and similarity in cost and production, and evidence, such as travel time to a hospital or doctor, which is independent of prevailing market conditions. *See, e.g.,* International Boxing Club v. United States, 358 U.S. 242 (1959) (championship professional boxing contests are distinctive from other boxing bouts by virtue of substantial differences in average revenue from all sources, prices for television rights, Nielson ratings, motion picture rights, and ticket prices); United States v. Grinnell Corp., 384 U.S. 563 (1966) (accredited central station protection services are distinctive from other forms of property protection in view of discounts given by insurers and differences in the manner of production); *see also* Baker, *Market Definition* at 162–65, 170–73.

6. *Relevant evidence.* What types of evidence were used in *Long Island Jewish Medical Center* to make predictions concerning the possible effects of the merger? One prominent scholar groups relevant evidence "into five categories: past buyer responses; buyer surveys; product characteristics; seller conduct; and views of industry experts." Baker, *Market Definition* at 139. Various kinds of quantitative and qualitative evidence may be used when available. Data regarding prior attempts to increase price may exist. Various kinds of documents, such as market analyses, may be used. Testimony from market participants is often invaluable, although

of course, in light of self-interest and degrees of knowledge (sometimes puffery too), credibility must be judged. The point is to gain an understanding of prior patterns of buyer substitution and competitors' responses and to make systematic extrapolations into the future. *See, e.g., id.* at 139–42; *see generally* Jonathan B. Baker & Timothy F. Bresnahan, *Economic Evidence in Antitrust: Defining Markets and Measuring Market Power, in* HANDBOOK OF ANTITRUST ECONOMICS 1 (Paolo Buccirossi ed., 2008) (http://papers.ssrn.com/sol3/papers.cfm?abstract_id=931225).

7. *Static versus dynamic analysis.* A market share is merely a snapshot in time, the product of so-called "static analysis." As such, it can be very misleading. Suppose, for example, that a severe freeze in the South wiped out the entire cotton crop except for that of a single producer. Image that this same freeze destroyed all the orange trees in Florida, with the exception of one producer's. Assuming away substitutes, we could say that each surviving producer has a 100% market share. Their power looks the same. Suppose, however, that new cotton crops can be grown and harvested the following year, while it takes ten years for newly planted orange trees to bear fruit. Does power look the same now? Once we take time into account and engage in so-called "dynamic analysis," we see that the question of power requires consideration of how long power can persist. It is for that reason that the question of power must be answered, not just by analyzing market share at one point at time, but also by considering the speed at which new product or substitutes can enter the market in response to supra-competitive prices. Factors that impede such entry are called "barriers to entry" and are discussed immediately below.

8. *Meaning of "concentration."* Market share alone can be misleading in another respect. A firm with a high market share might be able to reduce output, raise price, and perhaps erect barriers to entry. This conduct is known as "unilateral effects" because it occurs through a single firm's unilateral action. However, with regard to some market structures one has to worry about "coordinated effects," which consists of multilateral conduct among a number of firms.

Compare two market structures. In both a firm has a 50% market share. However, in one the remaining 50% is shared by five other firms possessing 10% of the market each, while in the other structure there are 25 firms possessing 2% of the market each. The different structures of these markets raise very different problems. Collaboration among firms in a market is obviously usually easier if there are fewer firms to coordinate. Reaching agreement among them, particularly tacitly by behavior aimed at signaling each other with regard to price and output, is simply easier, as is the task of ensuring, or policing, that all are abiding by the agreement's terms. In the first example market structure there are six competitors who must agree, while in the second there are 26. They are very different.

Accordingly, when coordinated effects are relevant it is useful to have a means to account for these differences or, in other words, a measure of how "concentrated" a market is. Such a tool is the "Herfindahl–Hirschman

Index," which takes into account both market shares and the number of actors across whom those shares are spread.

Coordinated effects are usually not of great concern with regard to hospitals because they produce so many heterogeneous products and the tasks of coordination, particularly implicit, are probably insurmountable. Where firms produce homogeneous products the task of coordination is simpler and therefore the possibility of coordinated effects is greater.

9. *Further reading.* A number of legal scholars have devoted sustained attention to hospital mergers. Professor Tim Greaney has argued that courts should eschew analysis based on simplifying assumptions like those of the Chicago School, which generally minimize the significance of market failure. Like many others, he has been critical of the courts' drawing of broad geographic markets based on patient-flow data and their failure carefully to analyze market conditions and behavior. He claims that in cases like *Long Island Jewish Medical Center* the courts have failed to see that factors like product differentiation allow merged hospitals to assert market power against some types of patients, a subject we address below. He points the finger of blame for courts' careless analysis, which has favored merging hospitals and allowed market power to exist, at the persistence of Chicago–School simplifying assumptions like homogeneous products. *See, e.g.,* Greaney, *Chicago's Procrustean Bed.* Nonetheless, he also argues that courts should still recognize that the nonprofit form might mitigate the effects of market power and, in light of market failure, achieve better results than disaggregated market structure, but that such defenses should displace traditional antitrust structural assumptions regarding market power only after very careful, detailed factual inquiry into behavior and market conditions. He urges caution because defenses based on such factors can be used to disguise anticompetitive conduct. In addition to his work cited elsewhere, see Thomas L. Greaney, *Antitrust and Hospital Mergers: Does the Nonprofit Form Affect Competitive Substance* 31 J. HEALTH POL. POL'Y & L. 511 (2006); Thomas L. Greaney, *Night Landings on an Aircraft Carrier: Hospital Mergers and Antitrust Law,* AM. J.L. & MED. 191 (1997). *See generally* Thomas L. Greaney, *Quality of Care and Market Failure Defenses in Antitrust Health Care Litigation,* 21 CONN. L. REV. 605 (1989).

Writing separately and together Professors Peter Hammer and William Sage have argued that antitrust law in health care should be more broadly conceived as "competition policy" as in Western Europe. As a result, a number of points follow. Antitrust law must focus on more than price competition but also take into account various forms of non-price competition. *See, e.g.,* William M. Sage & Peter J. Hammer, *Competing on Quality of Care: The Need to Develop a Competition Policy for Health Care Markets,* 32 U. MICH. J.L. REFORM 1069 (1999) [hereinafter Sage & Hammer, *Competing on Quality of Care*]; William M. Sage & Peter J. Hammer, *A Copernican View of Health Care Antitrust,* 65 LAW & CONTEMP. PROBS. 241 (2002). Decision makers should apply a general welfare model to hospital mergers in which they pay careful attention to the question whether non-price competition enhances or diminishes welfare. *See, e.g.,* Peter J. Hammer,

Questioning Traditional Antitrust Presumptions: Price and Non-price Competition in Hospital Markets, 32 MICH. J. L. REFORM 727 (1999); Peter J. Hammer, *Antitrust Beyond Competition: Market Failures, Total Welfare, and the Challenge of Intramarket Second–Best Tradeoffs*, 98 MICH. L. REV. 849 (2000). Finally, for our purposes at least, ensuring social benefit from hospital competition rests more in the jurisdiction of regulators and legislators than antitrust courts because of the heavy influence of government as payer through programs like Medicare, Medicaid, and the fact that non-economic values are at stake. *See, e.g.*, Peter J. Hammer & William M. Sage, *Critical Issues in Hospital Antitrust Law*, 22(6) HEALTH AFFAIRS 88 (2003); Peter J. Hammer & William M. Sage, *Antitrust, Health Care Quality, and the Courts*, 102 COLUM. L. REV. 545 (2002) [hereinafter Hammer & Sage, *Antitrust, Health Care Quality, and the Courts*].

Professors Clark C. Havighurst and Barak D. Richman have provided perhaps the best arguments for aggressive merger enforcement. They rely on traditional doctrine and generally reject the relevance of market failure. They claim that providers are generally able to garner surplus to themselves, which most often is retained for expansion of services because of the predominant nonprofit form. The result is an ever-expanding system which is regressively financed. They claim that the power of this system can still be broken were the antitrust laws applied more aggressively. *See* Barak D. Richman, *Antitrust and Nonprofit Hospital Mergers: A Return to Basics*, 156 U. PA. L. REV. 121 (2007); Barak D. Richman, *The Corrosive Combination of Nonprofit Monopolies and U.S.–Style Health Insurance: Implications for Antitrust and Merger Policy*, 68 LAW & CONTEMP. PROBS. 139 (2006); *see also* Clark C. Havighurst and Barak D. Richman, *Who Pays? Who Benefits? Unfairness in American Health Care*, 25 NOTRE DAME J.L. ETHICS & PUB. POL'Y 493 (2011) [hereinafter Havighurst & Richman, *Who Pays? Who Benefits?*]; Clark C. Havighurst and Barak D. Richman, *Distributive Injustice(s) in American Health Care*, 68 LAW & CONTEMP. PROBS. 7 (2006) [hereinafter Havighurst & Richman, *Distributive Injustice(s) in American Health Care*].

Note: Evanston Northwestern Healthcare Corporation

After considerable success challenging hospital mergers during the 1980s and early 1990s, the Federal Trade Commission, the Department of Justice and state enforcers lost all seven cases they litigated in federal courts from 1994 through 2001, largely because courts ruled that the relevant geographic market was broader than they alleged.* In 2002 the

---

* See FTC v. Hospital Board of Lee County, 38 F.3d 1184 (11th Cir. 1994); FTC v. Freeman Hosp., 911 F. Supp. 1213 (W.D. Mo.), *aff'd*, 69 F.3d 260 (8th Cir. 1995); United States v. Mercy Health Servs., 902 F. Supp. 968 (N.D. Iowa 1995), *vacated as moot*, 107 F.3d 632 (8th Cir. 1997); FTC v. Butterworth Health Corp., 946 F.Supp. 1285 (W.D. Mich. 1996), *aff'd*, 1997–2 Trade Cases (CCH) ¶ 71,863 (6th Cir. 1997); United States v. Long Island Jewish Med. Ctr., 983 F. Supp. 121 (E.D.N.Y. 1997); FTC v. Tenet Health Care Corp., 186 F.3d 1045 (8th Cir. 1999); State of California v. Sutter Health Sys., 84 F. Supp.2d 1057 (N.D. Cal. 2000), amended by 130 F. Supp.2d 1109 (N.D. Cal. 2001).

Commission announced the formation of a new task force to "reinvigorate[e] the Commission's hospital merger program, which includes a review of, and potential challenge to, consummated transactions that may have resulted in anticompetitive price increases." Federal Trade Commission Announces Formation of Merger Litigation Task Force (http://www.ftc.gov/opa/2002/08/mergerlitigation.shtm). In a subsequent speech then-Chairman Timothy J. Muris observed that "[o]bviously, the template for trying hospital merger cases that was used with such great success in the 1980s and early 1990s no longer works," and that the "task force will screen targets, select the best cases, and develop new strategies for trying them. The merger task force will also take a hard look at which strategies worked and which did not in the prior hospital merger cases." Timothy J. Muris, "Everything is New Again: Health Care and Competition in the 21st Century," Remarks before the Seventh Annual Competition in Health Care Forum (Nov. 7, 2002), at 19 (http://www.ftc.gov/speeches/muris/murishealth carespeech0211.pdf). A subsequent report, issued by the FTC and DOJ based on hearings, testimony and internal and external research, contained a chapter, "Competition Law: Hospitals," which canvassed existing and alternative methods for defining geographic markets and essentially announced a new path. See IMPROVING HEALTH CARE: A DOSE OF COMPETITION, A REPORT BY THE FEDERAL TRADE COMMISSION AND THE DEPARTMENT OF JUSTICE ch. 4 (July 2004) [hereinafter A DOSE OF COMPETITION].

Perhaps this exercise was simply "an undisguised effort to lighten the agencies' burden," Tom Campbell, *Defending Hospital Mergers after the FTC's Unorthodox Challenge to the Evanston Northwestern—Highland Park Transaction*, 16 ANN. OF HEALTH L. 213, 223 (2007), and it may be questioned whether the casting off of years of traditional analysis in favor of relatively novel methods represents an illegitimate assertion of power or a proper exercise of agency discretion. *See, e.g.*, Neil Horner, *Unilateral Effects and the EC Merger Regulation—How the Commission Had Its Cake and Ate It Too*, 2 HANSE L. REV. 23 (2006). However, there is much more to the story than that.

Over roughly the past two decades, a number of economists, working within and without the FTC and DOJ, have strenuously criticized the courts' use of patient-flow data to define a geographic market. They have complained that this error has led to overly large geographic markets, is responsible for the consecutive losses suffered by antitrust authorities, and has allowed mergers to proceed although they have resulted in market power. *See, e.g.*, Cory S. Capps et al., *Antitrust Policy and Hospital Mergers: Recommendations for a New Approach*, 47 ANTITRUST BULL. 677 (2002) [hereinafter Capps et al., *Antitrust Policy and Hospital Mergers*]; Steven Tenn, *The Price Effects of Hospital Mergers: A Case Study of the Sutter–Summit Transactions*, FEDERAL TRADE COMMISSION BUREAU OF ECONOMICS WORKING PAPER No. 293 (Nov. 2008) (http://www.ftc.gov/be/workpapers/wp 293.pdf); *see also* John Simpson, *Geographic Markets in Hospital Mergers: A Case Study*, 10 INT'L. J. OF ECON. OF BUSINESS 291 (2003). The literature criticizing the courts' use of patient-flow data—and market share altogether—is extremely large, technical and contested. Here we wish only to expose you to the pertinent debates, to raise questions and to link those questions to core questions concerning the application of antitrust to health care. Therefore, we can (overly) simplify the literature into two major complaints.

The first line of attack is scholarship which attempts to show that the courts have relied on a method of analysis that was designed for other types of products and markets and therefore, when applied to hospitals, leads to incorrect results. The courts have used an analysis known as the Elzinga–Hogarty test, named for its two originators. *See* Kenneth Elzinga & Thomas Hogarty, *The Problem of Geographic Market Delineation in Antitrust Suits*, 18 ANTITRUST BULL. 45 (1973); Kenneth Elzinga & Thomas Hogarty, *The Problem of Geographic Market Delineation Revisited: The Case of Coal*, 23 ANTITRUST BULL. 1 (1978). The gist of the test is that for a commodity like beer or coal, courts can define a geographic market by studying the flow of the product into and out of an area. Put generally, a geographic market is an area in which there is relatively little import or export of the product into or out of the locale; if there is such movement into or out of an area, the area must be expanded to encompass the inflow or outflow. When applied to hospitals the test stipulates that if there is sufficient patient flow into or out of geographic areas, the locales are appropriately combined into one market because the patient flows evidence that patients can or do respond to price increases in the area by substituting among the hospitals. *See generally* H.E. Frech III et al., *Elzinga–Hogarty Tests and Alternative Approaches for Market Share Calculations in Hospital Markets*, 71 ANTITRUST L.J. 921 (2004) [hereinafter Frech et al., *Elzinga–Hogarty Tests and Alternative Approaches*].

Critics of the use of the Elzinga–Hogarty test to define hospital markets point out that it was developed for undifferentiated products such that consumers readily substitute production from one area for another subject only to such factors as transportation costs. By contrast, hospitals produce highly differentiated products and patients have heterogeneous tastes.* Regarding the former, patients may bypass a local hospital because the more distant one offers services not available closer to home. Placing the two hospitals in the same market because of this migration would be wrong. More generally, the fact that patients may be willing to travel for one service, say heart surgery, cannot necessarily tell us whether patients needing other services, like ob/gyn, will substitute some more distant facility for the whole host of other services that the more local hospital provides. Therefore, patient-flow data does not necessarily indicate whether that distant hospital can constrain an attempt by the local hospital to increase price.

Regarding patients' heterogeneous tastes, patients decide whether to travel to hospitals for a whole host of reasons: perceived and actual

---

* Many economists hold that product differentiation is a response to heterogeneous consumer tastes, *see, e.g.*, Gaynor & Vogt, *Antitrust and Competition in Health Care Markets* at 1411 n.14, but here we can ignore this chicken-and-egg question whether consumer demand is supplier-induced.

variations in quality, more sophisticated technology, travel costs, insurance coverage, family connections, religious preferences, and so on. Therefore, the fact that some patients travel to another hospital for a service does not necessarily tell us whether other patients likewise would travel for that service. Again, patient-flow data is insufficient to allow antitrust decision makers to decide the geographic area over which patients will readily substitute one hospital for another. Moreover, the use of patient-flow data, the criticism goes, typically defines geographic markets too broadly because the "silent majority" of patients will not travel (hence the term "silent majority fallacy").* *See, e.g.,* Gregory J. Werden, *The Use and Misuse of Shipment Data in Defining Geographic Markets*, 26 ANTITRUST BULLETIN 719 (1981); Gregory J. Werden, *The Limited Relevance of Patient Migration Data in Market Delineation for Hospital Merger Cases*, 8 J. HEALTH ECON. 363 (1989); Cory S. Capps et al., *The Silent Majority Fallacy of the Elzinga–Hogarty Criteria: A Critique and New Approach to Analyzing Hospital Mergers*, NBER WORKING PAPER NO. 8216 (April 2001) (http://www.nber.org/papers/w8216).

The second major line of criticism emphasizes, with much justification, that with regard to most admissions, patients play a relatively minor role in deciding among hospitals and are generally insensitive to price. As a result, modeling of substitution patterns in response to attempted exercise of market power—price elasticity of demand—must account for the fact that physicians and managed care organizations either influence or direct those choices.

One implication is that the relevance or significance of patient-flow data varies depending on one's model of choice. For example, if physicians direct the choice of hospital and if they are insensitive to price, something well supported in the literature, then one cannot infer anything about price-elasticity of demand from actual or potential patient-flow data. Indeed, the whole locus of competition is wrong because, according to this model, hospitals don't compete for patients but compete for physicians in order to obtain strong referral patterns. In this competition, new technology, quality and amenities for physicians are the currency of the realm. In this situation, if location matters at all, it would be the location of physicians, not patients, because what matters is how far physicians—not patients—are willing to travel. *See, e.g.,* Harold S. Luft et al., *The Role of Specialized Clinical Services in Competition Among Hospitals*, 23 INQUIRY 83 (1986); Harold S. Luft et al., *Rejoinder to Dranove and Shanley*, 8 J. HEALTH ECON. 479 (1989); *see also* Jack Zwanziger, *Antitrust Considerations and Hospital Markets*, 8 J. HEALTH ECON. 457, 461 (1989).

Another implication is that market definitions might have to account for multiple "stages" of competition. Probably the leading model here is that of "two-stage" competition proposed by Gregory Vistnes, *Hospitals, Mergers, and Two–Stage Competition*, 67 ANTITRUST L.J. 671 (2000) [herein-

---

* For a fairly recent defense of cautiously using significantly modified forms of the Elzinga–Hogarty test as one factor among others in defining geographic markets, see Frech et al., *Elzinga–Hogarty Tests and Alternative Approaches.*

after Vistnes, *Hospitals, Mergers, and Two–Stage Competition*]; *see also, e.g.*, Robert Town & Gregory Vistnes, *Hospital Competition in HMO Networks*, 20 J. HEALTH ECON. 733 (2001) [hereinafter Town & Vistnes, *Hospital Competition in HMO Networks*]; Cory Capps et al., *Competition and Market Power in Option Demand Markets*, 34 RAND J. ECON. 737 (2003) [hereinafter Capps et al., *Competition and Market Power in Option Demand Markets*]. Under this model, in the world of managed care hospitals first compete to be included in managed care networks; then in a second stage, they compete for patients. Using the facts in *Long Island Jewish Medical Center* as an example, the merged defendant hospitals may have been able to exercise market power against MCOs. In this first stage of competition, as "anchor hospitals," the defendants were a "must" for the MCOs to include in their networks because the MCOs could not market their networks to plan sponsors if the hospitals' primary and secondary care were not included. The market in this stage, therefore, would be local and in this stage, defendants had power. By contrast, the second stage market could have been much larger because, with regard to tertiary care, patients would be willing to travel greater distances to the hospitals in Manhattan. In this geographic market the defendants did not have power. According to Vistnes, "a reduction in competition at *either* stage of competition can harm consumers," Vistnes, *Hospitals, Mergers, and Two–Stage Competition* at 685 (footnote omitted). This result "is no different in principle than any other merger of multiproduct firms in which the merger only reduces competition in one product market," *id.*, an important point to which we return below. The conclusion—that by focusing on patient-flow data, the courts have gotten it wrong—follows:

> Patient flow data say little about key market definition questions: how would a plan induce patients to switch hospitals; and how would diverting patients between hospitals affect the plan's marketability? For example, patient flow data provide no direct information about whether a plan that dropped a hospital from its network would be at a significant marketing disadvantage, nor do they speak to whether the benefits of implementing a within-network steering strategy would exceed the costs. Thus, the true market with respect to first-stage competition might well be one in which there are high levels of patient inflow and outflow.

Id. at 690 (footnotes omitted).*

---

* One would think that if plan sponsors were perfect agents for their plan enrollees, the two stages would be the same. Given overlapping factors in Vistnes' specification of the two stages, it is not clear how distinct they are or whether the degree of difference can support his conclusions. In fact two recent leading applications of this model derive plans' ability to substitute among hospitals from their members' valuation of the inclusion of hospitals in their networks. *See* Town & Vistnes, *Hospital Competition in HMO Networks*; Capps et al., *Competition and Market Power in Option Demand Markets*; *see also* Barry C. Harris & David A. Argue, *FTC v. Northwestern: A Change from Traditional Hospital Merger Analysis?*, 20 ANTITRUST 34 (2006). Town and Vistnes' analysis specifies a utility function based on factors like distance, quality and various characteristics of patients and hospitals, while Capps and colleagues utilize an "option demand" model. Given consumers' uncertainty at the time of

These lines of criticism of the approach used by the courts occurred concurrent with and against the background of increasing consolidation in the hospital sector. According to one analysis, "[i]n 1990, the typical person living in a metropolitan statistical area (MSA) faced a concentrated hospital market with an HHI of 1,576. By 2003, however, the typical MSA resident faced a hospital market with an HHI of 2,323. This change is equivalent to a reduction from six to four competing local hospital systems. By 1990, almost 90 percent of people in populous MSAs sought care in highly concentrated markets." William B. Vogt & Robert Town, *How Has Hospital Consolidation Affected the Price and Quality of Hospital Care?* Research Synthesis Report No. 9, ROBERT WOOD JOHNSON FOUNDATION 3 (2006) (http://www.rwjf.org/publications/synthesis/reports_and_briefs/pdf/no9_research report.pdf). Moreover, a growing literature generally correlated the increased concentration with increased prices. *See generally id.* at 6–10. Fairly clearly, the result, although perhaps not the cause, *see generally id.* at 4–5, was greatly increased consolidation on the provider side, matching greatly increased consolidation on the insurance side. *See, e.g.,* James C. Robinson, *Consolidation and the Transformation of Competition in Health Insurance,* 23(6) HEALTH AFFAIRS 11 (2004).

It was against this background that in 2004 the FTC challenged the merger, already consummated in 2000, between Highland Park Hospital and Evanston Northwestern Healthcare Corporation ("ENHC"), which owned Evanston and Glenbrook Hospitals. *See* In the Matter of Evanston Northwestern Healthcare Corporation, 2007 WL 2286195 (2007). Part of the FTC's overall retrospective review mentioned above, *Evanston Northwestern* presented a good vehicle for the Commission to test its new tools. No one disagreed that ENHC had raised its prices shortly after the merger. The only question was whether the increase reflected market power created by the merger or stemmed from some other cause, such as increased costs, enhanced quality or underpricing by ENHC prior to the merger. Moreover, the fact that the merger had already been consummated meant that retrospective analysis was possible. The data-rich environment enabled the

---

their choosing health plans and the high costs of switching plans, consumers keep their "options" open by valuing hospitals offering a wide array of specialized (i.e., differentiated) products. *See* Capps et al., *Competition and Market Power in Option Demand Markets; see also* David Dranove & Andrew Sfekas, *The Revolution in Health Care Antitrust: New Methods and Provocative Implications,* 87 MILBANK Q. 607 (2009) [hereinafter Dranove & Sfekas, *The Revolution in Health Care Antitrust*]; David Dranove & William D. White, *Specialization, Option Demand, and the Pricing of Medical Specialists,* 5 J. ECON. & MGMT. STRATEGY 277 (1996); Capps et al., *Antitrust Policy and Hospital Mergers.* For an extension of the options-demand bargaining model to account for possible bargaining power conferred from affiliation with physician groups or multi-hospital systems outside the local market, see Matthew S. Lewis & Kevin E. Pflum, *Diagnosing Hospital System Bargaining Power in Managed Care Networks* (http://econweb.tamu.edu/common/files/workshops/PERC% 20Applied% 20Microeconomics/ 2011_11_21_Matthew_Lewis.pdf). For a somewhat different approach in which the authors employ a fully specified model of equilibrium price and quantity in a differentiated product oligopoly model, see Martin Gaynor & William B. Vogt, *Competition Among Hospitals,* 34 RAND J. ECON. 764 (2003); Martin Gaynor et al., *A Structural Approach to Market Definition: An Application to the Hospital Industry,* NBER WORKING PAPER No. 16656 (2011) (http://www.nber. org/papers/w16656).

Commission to deploy econometric methods to analyze the reasons for the price increase and thereby establish the "direct effects" of the merger—increased price caused by market power—obviating the need to infer market power from market share. Since the latter need not be derived if direct effects can be measured—the reasoning goes—power can be established without delineating the geographic market, the shoal upon which enforcement agencies had crashed in most of the last seven cases litigated in court. The stage was set for a break with the past.

The Commission's opinion on liability, therefore, is somewhat of a puzzle. Count one of the complaint had alleged, in traditional fashion, that the merger violated section 7 of the Clayton Act in specified relevant product and geographic markets. Count two, by contrast, alleged that the merger enabled ENHC to raise price above the prices that the hospitals would have charged absent the merger, i.e., the direct effects claim. In a sense the Commission punted. As discussed below, it bootstrapped liability under the first count by inferring the contours of the geographic market from the fact of the price increase. It then found a decision under count two unnecessary.

The most important evidence for the Commission was the econometric evidence purportedly showing that the only statistically valid explanation for the increase in price was market power created by the merger.* Using various control groups, the Commission's expert found that after the merger the Evanston–Northwestern system hospitals had raised prices, that the price increases were greater than those at the control hospitals and that the differential could not be explained by differences between the system hospitals and the control group hospitals regarding relevant factors like cost, case mix, payer mix, and teaching intensity. *See* Debra Haas-Wilson & Christopher Garmon, *Two Hospital Merger's on Chicago's North Shore: A Retrospective Study*, FTC WORKING PAPER No. 294 (2009) (www.ftc.gov/be/workpapers/wp294.pdf). The Commission therefore found that this evidence of the merger's "direct effects" showed that the merger had created market power. Purporting to use the traditional structural analysis of defining a market, the FTC concluded that this evidence of a price increase, explained only by the existence of market power, sufficed to delineate the relevant geographic market, with the result that the section 7 violation under count one had been proved. The Commission then found count two, the one based on direct effects, to be moot.

If you just got confused, it is because this reasoning is indefensible. If it was the direct effects evidence which allowed the delineation of a geographic market, then the definition of a geographic market was not an independent step in the analysis and the violation was established only under count two. As the defendants pointed out, the Commission's reasoning under count one is inexorably circular because it inferred the scope of a geograph-

* There is much more to the decision and evidence than we present here. We are interested only in the manner in which the Commission "defined" the geographic market and the use of econometric evidence to show direct effects and to obviate the need for such a definition.

ic market from the existence of a price increase, taken to be an exercise of market power, while in the traditional, structural analysis the existence of market power itself requires that a geographic market be drawn. Put differently, the reasoning is: the geographic market is the area over which defendants can raise price; defendants raised price; therefore, the geographic market is the area where the defendants raised price. Huh? As one knowledgeable observer has stated, "if the answer to the ultimate question (whether price will rise) is the basis for market definition, market definition and market concentration are conclusory, not an autonomous method of analysis." Jonathan Baker, *Stepping Out in an Old* Brown Shoe: *In Qualified Praise of Submarkets*, 68 ANTITRUST L.J. 203, 215 (2000).*

Even if we take the Commission's decision as one decided under count two sub silentio, numerous questions remain. To begin with, the necessity of defining a market does not disappear because of the econometric evidence. After all, we are still determining whether *market* power exists and must define *market* in the phrase *market* power. When regression analysis is used to make this determination, all the work is shifted to definition of the control group. If the hospitals in the group are not good substitutes for the defendant, whether because of product characteristics or because of geography, then the price differences are potentially explained by the fact that the wrong hospitals were chosen as peers; and what the Commission reasoned is that the proof that these were the right peers was proven by the fact that the hospital raised price against the right peers, i.e., proof that these were the right peers because these were the right peers. *Cf., e.g.,* Jonathan Baker, *Unilateral Competitive Effects Theories in Merger Analysis*, 11 ANTITRUST 21, 25 (1997) (close substitutes must be identified in predicting a merged firm's unilateral incentives to raise price even if market share is not probative).

The Commission attempted to refute the circularity by pointing to the theoretical validity of the direct effects test but this is of no aid. The direct effects test says that one can infer market power from the fact that the merger *caused* a price increase. "Cause" is the key word. To prove cause, the price increases of the merged hospital were compared with a control group. Determining the relevant control group requires defining substitute hospitals, i.e., defining the relevant market. Therefore, proving cause requires defining the relevant market. The tautology is inescapable.

Additionally, actual geography remains crucial, although by using a control group only loosely connected to actual space—the Chicago metropolitan area—the Commission tried to banish it. The usual wisdom, which

---

* "[O]ne could salvage the . . . . [traditional] market delineation paradigm tautologically by declaring that when a sufficient number of customers are 'trapped' between the two merging firms, such that the firms could exercise significant 'unilateral effects' post-merger, then those products (or, if the unilateral effects are based on price discrimination, those products sold to those customers) constitute a relevant market." Lawrence J. White, *Horizontal Merger Antitrust Enforcement: Some Historical Perspectives, Some Current Observations*, at 3 n.6 (2006) (Prepared for the Antitrust Modernization Commission's "Economist's Roundtable on Merger Enforcement" (http://govinfo.library.unt.edu/amc/commission_hearings/pdf/White_Statement_final.pdf)).

the FTC accepts, is that, at least with regard to primary and secondary inpatient services, hospital markets are local. *See, e.g.*, HAAS–WILSON, MANAGED CARE AND MONOPOLY POWER at 118–19. Suppose there is one community hospital within two miles; three community hospitals within three miles; five within ten miles, as well as a teaching hospital; eight community hospitals within twenty miles, as well as the teaching hospital and an academic medical center. Some segment of actual space in this topography constitutes a geographic market because the ultimate question is how far away is too far away for hospitals to be competitors; and it is within this segment of actual space that the defendant hospital has to price. If the control group of hospitals does not conform to the characteristics of the hospitals within this space, then the analysis compares apples and oranges. *See* Werden & Froeb, *Unilateral Competitive Effects of Horizontal Mergers* at 78 ("Antitrust law may overly emphasize market delineation, but variation across local markets can inform merger policy only if observations of prices and market structure are made within geographic areas that constitute relevant markets."); *cf.* Craig M. Newmark, *The Positive Correlation of Price and Concentration in Staples: Market Power or Indivisibility?*, INDEPENDENT INSTITUTE WORKING PAPER No. 31 (http://www.independent. org/publications/working_papers/article.asp?id=742)   (price   differences across local markets may be explained by unobserved variations in product attributes); Craig M. Newmark, *Price–Concentration Studies: There You Go Again* (http://papers.ssrn.com/sol3/papers.cfm?abstract_id=503522) (price differences across local markets may be explained by non-price competition for which there exist no adequate statistical controls); Orley Ashenfelter et al., *Econometric Methods in Staples*, PRINCETON LAW AND PUBLIC AFFAIRS WORKING PAPER No. 04–007, at 16–17 (http://ssrn.com/abstract=529144) (noting that a "more complete analysis of competition" across markets requires measures of non-price competition). *See generally* Gaynor & Vogt, *Antitrust and Competition in Health Care Markets* at 1434–35, 1447. For criticism of the methodology and data used in the empirical study on which the Commission relied, as well as the criticism of the inferences drawn from the empirical findings, see Gregory Adams & Monica Noether, *Comment on "Hospital Mergers and Competitive Effects: Two Retrospective Analyses,"* 18 J. ECON. OF BUS. 33 (2011). For a response to Adams and Noether, see Christopher Garmon & Deborah Haas–Wilson, *The Use of Multiple Control Groups and Data Sources as Validation in Retrospective Studies of Hospital Mergers*, 18 J. ECON. OF BUS. 41 (2011). Similar debates concerning the validity of retrospective studies of other mergers likewise raise questions about the methodology, data and unobserved factors like quality. *See, e.g.*, Gregory K. Leonard & G. Steven Oiley, *What Can Be Learned about the Competitive Effects of Mergers from "Natural Experiments"?*, 18 J. ECON. OF BUS. 103 (2011); Robert Town, *The Effects of US Hospital Consolidations on Hospital Quality: A Comment*, 18 J. ECON. OF BUS. 127 (2011).

What is needed, of course, is the sort of independent evidence of proper selection of control-group peers such as we saw in *Long Island Jewish Medical Center*. The Commission needed evidence regarding which hospitals could serve as substitutes to check an attempted exercise of market power. It could have used patient-flow data, which it rejected because of the "silent majority fallacy" described above, a conclusion with which Dr. Elzinga agrees, at least in the context of a consummated merger such that retrospective data are available. *See* Kenneth G. Elzinga & Anthony W. Swisher, *Limits of the Elzinga–Hogarty Test in Hospital Mergers: The Evanston Case*, 18 J. ECON. OF BUS. 133 (2011). Alternatively, it could have used patient travel time, *see, e.g.*, DaVita, Inc. and Gambro Healthcare, Inc., 70 Fed. Reg. 59,069 (Oct. 11, 2005) (http://www.ftc.gov/opa/2005/10/davita.htm), or even physician travel time. It could have used evidence from market participants regarding patterns of bargaining and substitution, as in *Long Island Jewish Medical Center*. Regardless, it had to use something other than the fact of a price increase across a control group abstracted from actual space; it needed an actual market.

The Commission was clearly disturbed by the simple fact that after the merger the hospitals were able to raise price. Compared with the idealized competitive market discussed above, in which no firm has power over price, this fact alone indicates that the merged hospitals had market power. But recourse to this idealization simply posits the conclusion: In a competitive market sellers cannot raise price. A seller raises price. Therefore, there must be some market that is not competitive (although the only way we know it exists is due to the fact that the seller raised price). Q.E.D. *See* 2007 FTC LEXIS at 155–170. As the Commission wrote:

> [a] market is the smallest possible group of competing products (or geographic area) over which a hypothetical monopolist that sells those products (or competes in that area) could profitably impose a SSNIP [small but significant non-transitory increase in price]. Merger Guidelines §§ 1.11, 1.21. Thus, if a merger enables the combined firm unilaterally to raise prices by a SSNIP for a non-transitory period due to the loss of competition between the merging parties, the merger plainly is anticompetitive, and the merging firms comprise a relevant antitrust market because the merged entity is considered to be a "monopolist" under the Guidelines.

Id. at 161; *see, e.g.*, Jonathan Baker, *Product Differentiation Through Space and Time: Some Antitrust Policy Issues*, 42 ANTITRUST BULLETIN 177, 185 (1997).

However, apart from this idealization—i.e., in actual markets—to varying degrees firms have some power over price depending on the extent of product differentiation,* particularly in bilateral bargaining markets,**

---

* *See, e.g.*, Carl Shapiro, Mergers with Differentiated Products, 10 Antitrust 23, 24 (1996); Christopher A. Vellturo, *Creating an Effective Diversion: Evaluating Mergers with Differentiated Products*, 11 ANTITRUST 16, 19 (1997). *See generally* IIB Phillip E. Areeda et al., ANTITRUST LAW: AN ANALYSIS OF ANTITRUST PRINCIPLES AND THEIR APPLICATION ¶ 517c4 (3d ed., 2007).

** In such a market a seller can distinguish between so-called "captive" or "inframarginal" buyers and "marginal" ones—buyers which can more readily substitute another product in response to a price increase. In such a case, the seller can increase price to the

or in the presence of countervailing market power. Given that in such actual markets power usually exists, the question is the degree of power that is socially tolerable, as reflected in law. To even begin to answer that question, one needs some yardstick, which in antitrust doctrine is provided by determining a firm's position in a well-defined market. That question cannot be wished away by pointing to the increased prices alone.

With regard to hospitals the question of what degree of power is socially tolerable is one of distributional justice among groups of patients (or among whoever pays for diverse services). A hospital is a multi-product firm, selling products that are highly differentiated. The services that it provides in urology, for example, are highly different than those in cardiology, as are those in orthopedics and so forth. Some of the hospital's costs can directly be attributed to a particular type of service or procedure. For example, the cost of the equipment to perform heart tests can be directly attributed to cardiology services. However, many costs, such as maintaining a billing department, are costs that are generated across the hospital's differentiated products, and allocation of those common costs is somewhat arbitrary. Prices of different services, therefore, reflect these arbitrary allocations, a point we have discussed in the payment chapter, in Part Two, and in the tax chapter in this Part.

Suppose that one hospital is preferred for cardiology, another for orthopedics, yet another for gastroenterology, and so on. Let's suppose that each of those hospitals is comparable for the rest of the services it offers. Each hospital, therefore, may have some degree of market power with regard to the services for which it is preferred but have none for the other services. This was the court's insight in dividing the geographic and product markets into primary and secondary, and tertiary services in *Long Island Jewish Medical Center*.

In this situation the effect on a hospital's pricing strategy is the following. For its preferred service it will charge a higher price, allocating joint and common costs there, and earning profit above directly attributable cost. The rest of the services will be priced closer to the costs directly attributable to them and the other components of cost will be recovered where the hospital has more power. *See, e.g.*, Ranjani Krishnan, *Market*

---

infra-marginal buyers only, thereby retaining the marginal ones. By contrast, where a seller cannot distinguish between the two, an increase in price will result in the loss of sales to the latter and therefore is less likely to be profitable. *See, e.g.*, James D. Reitzes & David T. Levy, *Price Discrimination and Mergers*, 28 CANADIAN J. ECON. 427 (1995). The FTC merely asserted that the direct effects analysis applied in such a bargaining market, 2007 FTC LEXIS at 166–68, but did not discuss why some MCOs, in the first stage of two-stage competition, are more captive than others. *See* Capps et al., *Antitrust Policy and Hospital Mergers* at 702 ("There is no a priori expectation for how margin changes should vary by payer. . . ."). For a discussion of some factors that would affect a plan's willingness to substitute, see Vistnes, *Hospitals, Mergers, and Two–Stage Competition* at 685–88. At least for primary and secondary services, in the second stage of competition some buyers may be infra-marginal ones based on their location. For a recent model that hospitals invest in differentiation to cause patients to choose plans that include them and thereby "effectively price discriminate, concentrating high-valuation consumers in the high-priced plans[,]" see Katherine Ho, *Insurer–Provider Networks in the Medical Care Market*, 99 AM. ECON. REV. 393, 408 (2009).

Restructuring and Pricing in the Hospital Industry, 20 J. HEALTH ECON. 213 (2001).

A number of points follow. First, the use of a broad market like "inpatient acute-care services" hides these allocations for it just averages across them. *Evanston Northwestern* provides an example of this in that before the merger Highland Hospital did not provide tertiary services, with the result that if the merger eliminated competition, such effect had to be limited to primary and secondary services only.

Second and following, the method used in *Evanston Northwestern* hides much in that the merged hospitals may well have faced stiff competition from hospitals in some locations with regard to some services but not with regard to others. *See, e.g.,* Seth Sacher & Louis Silvia, *Antitrust Issues in Defining the Product Market for Hospital Services*, 5 INT'L J. ECON. OF BUS. 181 (1998); Krishnan, *Market Restructuring and Pricing in the Hospital Industry* at 217. Evanston Hospital in particular may have faced stiff competition for tertiary services over a much broader geographic area that would have included numerous academic medical centers and teaching hospitals. Put differently, even if it the econometric evidence showed that the hospitals had some degree of power on average, that power might have been borne by some groups of consumers (or their payers) but not others.* *See, e.g.,* Capps et al., *Antitrust Policy and Hospital Mergers* at 699–704; *cf., e.g.,* William D. White & Michael A. Morrisey, *Are Patients Traveling Further?*, 5 INT'L J. ECON. OF BUSINESS 203 (1998) (finding higher travel distances correlated with whether service is discretionary—e.g., for a heart attack, one goes to the nearest hospital immediately—and degree of complexity—e.g., for a kidney transplant, one travels far to a center of excellence). *See generally* 2B Phillip E. Areeda et al., ANTITRUST LAW: AN ANALYSIS OF ANTITRUST PRINCIPLES AND THEIR APPLICATION ¶¶ 533, 562–63 (3d ed., 2007).

Third, if one abandons the fiction that market power is shown by any degree of power over price, it is necessarily the case that some groups of patients (or their payers) will be favored over others; and it is necessarily the case that the goal of eliminating "subsidization" of some by others in the health system is chimerical. Perhaps all this is washed out by the use of insurance but that conclusion is far from certain.

Indeed, to any student of hospitals, the idea of hospitals' competing every service down to cost would be striking. Hospitals have always used "revenue centers"—areas which are profitable—to "cross-subsidize" "cost centers"—areas that lose money. Lucrative services like orthopedics, for example, enable hospitals to continue to offer money-losing services like

---

* Our point pertains only to the distributional issues raised by averaging across groups of patients, not to the fact that the averaging showed that the merged hospitals in *Evanston Northwestern* possessed some degree of market power. Averaging that shows no power can hide the fact that merged hospitals may have power over particular services, an underestimation problem. *See, e.g.,* Krishnan, *Market Restructuring and Pricing in the Hospital Industry* at 217. However, when the average shows power, there exists at least power with regard to some services. If anything, by not breaking out particular services, the averaging may underestimate that documented power.

neonatology. Additionally, the loss of subsidization can cause the contraction of services that no one needs very often but everyone needs to be there when needed, such as trauma centers or burn units (so-called "stand-by capacity"). One can maintain that these services should be supported by explicit and direct governmental funding, but the fact is that such funding often has not been forthcoming and many areas of the country are now without such services because cross-subsidies have been squeezed.

Policy choice concerning degree of power that should trigger enforcement, including normative choices regarding wealth distribution, involves numerous considerations. The degree of wealth transfer itself from the exercise of market power, as well as the magnitude of welfare loss, depend on, among other things, predictions concerning what level of enforcement is necessary for deterrence, whether and how fast entry can occur, and the rate of technological change. The use of resources for enforcement and the risk of error are also relevant. In the end, the decision rests on a mixture of pragmatic considerations and a normative choice regarding what wealth and welfare effects are tolerable. *See generally* 2B Phillip E. Areeda et al., ANTITRUST LAW: AN ANALYSIS OF ANTITRUST PRINCIPLES AND THEIR APPLICATION ¶¶ 530, 537 (3d ed., 2007); *see also id.* ¶ ¶ 532–33. We must stress a point to be developed more fully below in our more general assessment of the application of antitrust to health care: Economics has nothing to say about distributive justice.

The point here is not that *Evanston Northwestern* was wrongly decided but that it raises numerous considerations, some recognized by the Commission and some not, and that these issues were not adequately addressed. One might have thought that perhaps the decision's precedential effect would be limited. As stressed by Commissioner Rosch in his concurring opinion, this particular case involved a consummated merger and direct effects evidence was therefore available. *See* Concurring Opinion of Commissioner J. Thomas Rosch, In the Matter of Evanston Northwestern Healthcare Corp., Docket No. 9315 (http://www.ftc.gov/os/adjpro/d9315/070806rosch.pdf). Perhaps the Commission's abandonment of structural analysis should have been limited to such cases and not applied to prospective Section 7 merger cases. However, as Commissioner Rosch predicted, *see id.* at 9, the Commission's decision has had far reaching consequences because as experts develop tools that are taken to predict future price increases from contemporaneous evidence, the reasoning in this retrospective case can be applied, through simulations and the like, to prospective ones.

This prediction has come true. Clearly emboldened by its new tools, the FTC has become very active again, attacking numerous hospital mergers in recent years, both retrospectively and prospectively. For example, the Commission prospectively challenged a merger in the northern Virginia suburbs of Washington, D.C., which was then abandoned. *See* In re Inova Health System Foundation, Order Dismissing Complaint (June 17, 2008) (http://www.ftc.gov/os/adjpro/d9326/080617orderdismisscmpt.pdf). The challenge was based in part on an analysis by an FTC economist that the suburbs were a distinct market already dominated by the Inova Health System. The analysis used the options-demand model discussed above to predict that the merger would cause an increase in price. *See, e.g.*, Dranove & Sfekas, *The Revolution in Health Care Antitrust* at 614–15. As another example, in a retrospective challenge to a merger in Lucas County, Ohio, FTC complaint counsel has relied on both traditional structural analysis and the new tools, *see* In re ProMedica Health System, Inc., Complaint Counsel's Post–Trial Reply Brief (Sept. 30, 2011), (http://www.ftc.gov/os/adjpro/d9346/110930ccposttrialreplybrief.pdf), as did the Administrative Law Judge in his ruling in favor of Complaint Counsel. *See* 2011 FTC LEXIS 294 (Dec. 12, 2011).*

Additionally, numerous cases brought in courts do involve retrospective evidence, and possibly the Commission's reasoning in *Evanston Northwestern* could be picked up by the courts, as in FTC v. Staples, 970 F. Supp. 1066 (D.D.C. 1997); *see also* FTC v. Whole Foods Market, Inc., 548 F.3d 1028 (D.C. Cir. 2008). *But see* United States v. Oracle Corp., 331 F. Supp.2d 1098, 1168–69 (N.D. Cal. 2004). Given the questions raised above in this note, and others not discussed, one might conclude that caution is in order before the traditional structural analysis, with all its warts, is abandoned. Use of patient-flow data alone may often lead to suspicious conclusions but, as we have seen in *Long Island Jewish Medical Center*, the courts do not simply rely on patient-flow data but also consider evidence from market participants themselves and in particular what they say about the parameters of bargaining and nature of substitution. Moreover, perhaps, at least in all but isolated geographic areas, erring on the side of drawing broader markets might be prudent. *Cf., e.g.*, Derek Ridyard, *The Commission's New Horizontal Merger Guidelines: An Economic Commentary* 6, THE GLOBAL COMPETITION LAW CENTRE WORKING PAPER SERIES No. 02/05 (http://www.coleurope.eu/content/gclc/documents/GCLC% 20WP% 2002–05.pdf) ("Although the traditional dominance test can be artificial and unwieldy in some instances, it did signal a higher burden of proof on the regulator that affirms the need to identify a serious breakdown in competition before a decision to prohibit a merger can be justified."). We are certainly more cautious than those who are willing to declare that a revolution is at hand. See Dranove & Sfekas, *The Revolution in Health Care Antitrust*.

At bottom, here's the problem. There is something intuitively appealing to the notion that if one robber-baron railroad company controls all the freight and passenger transportation east of the Mississippi, it makes more money than if there were many railroads operating there. However, how comfortable is one applying that intuition to something as massively complex as the subject presented here? Given (1) the extreme complexity of

---

* Including the challenge in Lucas County, Ohio, the FTC has brought actions against three mergers over the last two years (as of February, 2012). The other two challenges have been to a merger in Albany, Georgia, that would combine the only two hospitals in that area, *see* FTC v. Phoebe Putney Health System Inc., 663 F.3d 1369 (11th Cir. 2011) (dismissed on state action grounds (discussed below)); and to a merger in Rockford, Illinois, that would combine two of the three hospitals in the area. *See* In re OSF Healthcare System, Administrative Complaint (Nov. 18, 2011) (http://www.ftc.gov/os/adjpro/d9349/111118rockfordcmpt.pdf).

hospital services and of allocating costs across those services; (2) the enormous heterogeneity in both production and consumption; and (3) that in case like *Evanston Northwestern* there are numerous fine hospitals in the pertinent geographic area, how confident is one that the intuitively simple situation is equally applicable? Isn't there an equally appealing intuition, to-wit: given that there are numerous hospitals of all shapes and sizes in these metropolitan areas, as well as some of the world's finest, most sophisticated institutions, how sure can we be that there exists a significant competitive problem? Isn't caution particularly in order when we know that hospitals use lucrative services to fund money-losing ones that remain socially valuable even though not supported by markets?

b.   Barriers to Entry

Ball Memorial Hospital v. Mutual Hospital Insurance, Inc.

784 F.2d 1325 (7th Cir. 1986)

■ EASTERBROOK, CIRCUIT JUDGE:

The provision of health care financing services has become increasingly competitive. Hospitals and physicians (the providers of service) have begun to offer financing packages, much as automobile manufacturers sometimes finance their own products. In health care, where the need for service often depends on events beyond anyone's control, financing often is combined with insurance to spread the risks.

One package is the preferred provider organization (PPO). In exchange for a stated monthly payment, the hospital promises to pay the costs of patients who use particular providers. Patients who use providers other than the "preferred" ones must pay part or all of the fees themselves. A PPO plan specifies in advance the fee it will pay a provider for any given medical service.

The plaintiffs in this case are 80 acute-care hospitals (the Hospitals). All 80 provide care on a fee for service basis. Some of the 80 also offer PPO plans; others are preparing to do so.

The Blues have been losing market share in Indiana for some years. Just how "large" the Blues are turns out not to matter, so we do not pursue the question.

All agree that however large the Blues may be, they are losing business. Concerned about this, the Blues decided to offer a PPO of their own, in addition to their traditional service benefit plans. The Blues asked for bids from all acute-care hospitals in Indiana and invited each to bid a percentage discount from its regular fees. The hospitals that offer PPO plans saw the Blues' decision as a threat to their success. All hospitals saw a PPO plan as a threat to revenues—those who participated in the plan might collect less per service rendered, and those outside the plan might lose volume.

Ninety-one of Indiana's 115 acute-care hospitals submitted bids, and the Blues signed up 61 of the 91. All [hospitals] remain eligible to participate in the regular service benefit plan offered by the Blues, which is the Blues' most popular product. All hospitals in Indiana also may provide services to patients covered by the Blues' PPO, but the Blues will reimburse only 75% of the hospitals' fees; the patients must pay the rest. The Blues will reimburse 100% of the agreed charges when insureds use hospitals within the PPO.

The Hospitals began this suit on November 14, 1984, seeking injunctive relief against the Blues' proposed PPO under sections 1 and 2 of the Sherman Act, 15 U.S.C. §§ 1 and 2.

The district court made extensive findings of fact. The most important of these concern the Hospitals' claim that the Blues have (and abused) "market power," the ability to raise price significantly higher than the competitive level by restricting output. The court found that the Blues do not have the power to restrict output in the market or to raise price because they furnish a fungible product that other people can and do supply easily.

The court treated the product as "health care financing." The Blues, other insurance companies, hospitals offering PPOs, HMOs, and self-insuring employers all offer methods of financing health care. Employers and individual prospective patients easily may switch from one financing package to another; nothing binds an employer or patient to one plan. The court concluded: "Consumers are extremely price sensitive and will readily switch on the basis of price from one company or form of financing to another. Consequently, no competitor . . . has the power to control prices. . . ."

The market in health care financing is competitive, the court concluded, not only because customers can switch readily but also because new suppliers can enter quickly and existing ones can expand their sales quickly. More than 1000 firms are licensed to sell health insurance in Indiana, and more than 500 sell this insurance currently. According to the district court, all can expand on a moment's notice. "Entry barriers into the market for health care financing are extremely low. All that is needed to compete in Indiana, for example, is sufficient capital to underwrite the policies and a license from the Indiana Insurance Commissioner." Of the 500 firms now selling insurance, many operate nationwide and have (or can attract) plenty of capital against which to write policies—if the price is right. The court also observed that firms may elect self-insurance, and HMOs may expand, in response to an increase in the price of insurance.

Buyers' willingness to switch and sellers' ability to enter and expand rapidly, the district court concluded, means that "a firm's share of premium revenues reflects no more than its ability to compete successfully in meeting consumer demands." The Blues cannot exclude competitors, cannot raise prices without losing business quickly; the Blues' size therefore indicates only their success in offering the package of price and service that customers prefer, not any market power.

The district court also found that PPO plans "contain cost by promoting price competition among hospitals" and that many of the large national insurers, as well as the larger hospitals in Indiana, are offering or planning to offer PPO plans. "By thus offering financing arrangements to consumers to pay for hospital services, these hospitals [offering PPOs] are vertically integrating into the health care financing market."

II

The analysis of the adoption of the PPO plan must begin with an assessment of market power. Market power is a necessary ingredient in every case under the Rule of Reason. Unless the defendants possess market power, it is unnecessary to ask whether their conduct may be beneficial to consumers. Firms without power bear no burden of justification. The Hospitals say that the Blues have a large share of the market for medical insurance in Indiana, and that this establishes market power.

In many cases a firm's share of current sales does indicate power. Sales may reflect the ownership of the productive assets in the business. Market power comes from the ability to cut back the market's total output and so raise price; consumers bid more in competing against one another to obtain the smaller quantity available. When a firm (or group of firms) controls a significant percentage of the productive assets in the market, the remaining firms may not have the capacity to increase their sales quickly to make up for any reduction by the dominant firm or group of firms.

In other cases, however, a firm's share of current sales does not reflect an ability to reduce the total output in the market, and therefore it does not convey power over price. Other firms may be able, for example, to divert production into the market from outside. They may be able to convert other productive capacity to the product in question or import the product from out of the area. If firms are able to enter, expand, or import sufficiently quickly, that may counteract a reduction in output by existing firms. And if current sales are not based on the ownership of productive assets—so that entrants do not need to build new plants or otherwise take a long time to supply consumers' wants—the existing firms may have no power at all to cut back the market's output. To put these points a little differently, the lower the barriers to entry, and the shorter the lags of new entry, the less power existing firms have. When the supply is highly elastic, existing market share does not signify power.

The district court found that each of the factors suggesting that market share does not imply market power is present in the market for medical insurance. New firms may enter easily. Existing firms may expand their sales quickly; the district court pointed out that insurers need only a license and capital, and that firms such as Aetna and Prudential have both. There are no barriers to entry—other firms may duplicate the Blues' product at the same cost the Blues incur in furnishing their coverage. See George J. Stigler, *The Organization of Industry* 67–70 (1968) (defining barriers to entry as differentials in the long-term costs of production); cf.

Harold Demsetz, *Barriers to Entry,* 72 Am. Econ. Rev. 47 (1982) (showing that not all barriers, as so defined, injure effective competition).

The Blues do not own any assets that block or delay entry. The insurance industry is not like the steel industry, in which a firm must take years to build a costly plant before having anything to sell. The "productive asset" of the insurance business is money, which may be supplied on a moment's notice, plus the ability to spread risk, which many firms possess and which has no geographic boundary. The district court emphasized that every firm can expand its sales quickly if the price is right, that no firm has captive customers, and that many firms want to serve this market. The conclusion that the Blues face vigorous and effective competition is not clearly erroneous.

Still, the Hospitals say, the conclusion is legally irrelevant. Ease of entry and the absence of barriers do not matter if the defendant has a large market share. The Hospitals are wrong. Market share is just a way of estimating market power, which is the ultimate consideration. When there are better ways to estimate market power, the court should use them. Market share reflects current sales, but today's sales do not always indicate power over sales and price tomorrow. *United States v. General Dynamics Corp.,* 415 U.S. 486 (1974), illustrates the point. The sellers of a large share of all current sales of coal in the midwest merged. The Court held, however, that share did not demonstrate power, because current deliveries of coal were largely committed under long term contracts. The pertinent competitive criterion was the ability to make future commitments of coal, and existing deliveries actually restricted the ability to make such commitments. The real "owners" of the coal currently being delivered were the recipients under the contracts, not the sellers. One of the firms in the merger had committed all of its economically-recoverable coal, and so its disappearance by merger did not remove from the market any competitive force that could be preserved by enjoining the merger. The Court concluded that because market shares did not reflect tomorrow's ability to compete, they did not supply a reason to forbid the merger.

The inquiry in each case is the ability to control output and prices, an ability that depends largely on the ability of other firms to increase their own output in response to a contraction by the defendants. Indeed it is usually best to derive market share *from* ability to exclude other sources of supply. This is the method the Department of Justice adopted in its Merger Guidelines. Cf. Landes & Posner, *supra;* George J. Stigler & Robert A. Sherwin, *The Extent of the Market,* 28 J.L. & Econ. 555 (1985). If the definition of the market builds in a conclusion that there are no significant additional sources of supply and no substitutes from the consumers' perspective, then the market share indicates power over price. But a calculation of the Blues' share of current coverage in Indiana does not capture the possibility of new entry and expanded sales by rivals, and this is why the district court properly held that the geographic market "is regional, if not national." This larger market may not seem useful from the perspective of consumers in Indiana, who must obtain their insurance from firms offering it there. It is highly pertinent, however, from the perspective of the Blues' rivals and potential rivals, and therefore from the perspective of constraints on the Blues' ability to raise price. The Blues' rivals, whose mobility is not restricted, protect consumers, whose mobility is restricted.

Notes

1. *Definition of a barrier to entry*. There has been a long dispute about what constitutes a barrier to entry. Economists who generally are most concerned with efficiency believe in the self-correcting features of markets, are disdainful of antitrust intervention, and define barriers to entry as entry costs not incurred by incumbent firms. *See, e.g.*, GEORGE STIGLER, THE ORGANIZATION OF INDUSTRY 67 (1968). Others concerned more about the possibility of long-lasting market power define an entry barrier as a factor that allows an incumbent firm to raise price for a significant period of time above the competitive level without attracting entry. *See* JOE S. BAIN, BARRIERS TO NEW COMPETITION: THEIR CHARACTER AND CONSEQUENCES IN MANU-FACTURING INDUSTRIES (1962). *See generally* IV Phillip E. Areeda et al., ANTITRUST LAW: AN ANALYSIS OF ANTITRUST PRINCIPLES AND THEIR APPLICATION ¶ 420 (2d ed., 2006). For our purposes, we can divide barriers to entry into two general categories. The first is comprised of the so-called "natural" barriers of entry, commonly listed as exclusive access to a necessary input such as a raw material; economies of scale; product heterogeneity or customer loyalty; nonrecoverable investments; and a legal barrier such as a patent or certificate of need. *See, e.g.*, FREDERIC M. SCHERER & DAVID ROSS, INDUSTRIAL MARKET STRUCTURE AND ECONOMIC PERFORMANCE 56 (3d ed., 1990). The second category consists of costs imposed on an entrant by an incumbent firm. These "barriers" have been more controversial and receive more detailed attention in the next subsection.

2. *Relevance of imperfect competition*. In *Ball Memorial* Judge Easterbrook concluded that market share alone was not a good indicator of market power because there existed few barriers to entry. This conclusion was in part a matter of evidence, because the record showed that employers were switching to PPOs from traditional direct service benefits contracts. The conclusion, however, was also in part based on an ideal for a market and a general failure to account for the manner in which actual markets deviate from that ideal.

In the ideal market, information is irrelevant because all producers and buyers possess perfect knowledge and foresight. Market participants are thus able to predict and plan long-term relationships. One could, in fact, plan from the beginning to the end of time. Furthermore, resources are perfectly mobile and can be switched immediately to highest valued uses in response to a change in those values.

In actual markets, however—what economists term "imperfect competition"—there are often difficulties in obtaining information and in switching, as the Supreme Court recognized in Eastman Kodak Co. v. Image Technical Services, Inc., 504 U.S. 451 (1992). Lacking perfect knowledge and foresight, buyers—or at least unsophisticated ones—possess "imperfect information." Accordingly, when these buyers purchase "durable goods" they are unable to determine their needs in advance but must instead plan incrementally. However, they may get locked in by a decision that causes unforeseen consequences. Unable to switch in the middle, these buyers are then subject to the exercise of market power by a firm that might not have had such power in the initial purchase.

Health care poses such problems. It is very difficult for employers—much less their employees—to anticipate in advance the services that they will need. Hence, in essence what they purchase is not a menu of services but the services of an agent that will exercise discretion in shaping that menu for them after the time of contracting. Even if the purchasers—again, employers and perhaps employees choosing from an offering of insurers—later gain information sufficient to police the action of their chosen agent, itself a dubious proposition, they will still experience switching costs. Employers purchasing a package of services from an insurer will be reluctant to change the agent in the middle of the game so to speak, because the effect will be to force employees to move from one network to another. Even more significant is the fact that employees are often forced to stick with their insurance choice for some contractually determined time, and they suffer even greater consequences from disrupting established relationships with providers. Indeed, the very ideal market—to iterate, one in which resources are perfectly mobile—is at odds with the ideal patient-provider relationship, in which the provider has gained intimate and long-term knowledge of the patient and her social circumstances. For these reasons, Judge Easterbrook's conclusion that no switching costs exist was quite superficial.

As Professor Mark Pauly points out, entry barriers for the risk-spreading function are low, *see* Mark V. Pauly, *Competition in Health Insurance Markets*, 51 LAW & CONTEMP. PROBS. 237, 247–50, and so in this regard Judge Easterbrook was right in his observation that "[t]he 'productive asset' of the insurance business is money, which may be supplied on a moment's notice." However, as discussed above, Judge Easterbrook ignored the other aspects of insurance, for which there are barriers. See *id*. For scathing criticism of Judge Easterbrook's very simplistic analysis, see Frances H. Miller, *Vertical Restraints and Powerful Health Insurers: Exclusionary Conduct Masquerading as Managed Care?*, 51 LAW & CONTEMP. PROBS. 195, 226–30 (1988). Also, for a discussion of the market failure caused by the significant heterogeneity of different insurance products and the resultant "search frictions," see Randall D. Cebul et al., *Unhealthy Insurance Markets: Search Frictions and the Cost and Quality of Health Insurance*, 101 AM. ECON. REV. 1842 (2011).

Finally, one other point regarding information should be noted. Insurance companies themselves need substantial information in order to compete effectively. Not only are there problems of scale, there are also problems of experience in managing networks effectively, particularly in the creation of adequate information systems, and nonrecoverable costs of forming a network. In the early days of managed care many HMOs went belly up, in part because of insufficient scale for risk bearing, but also due to their inexperience in managing and forming networks.

Regardless of whether Judge Easterbrook's factual premises were correct in 1986, the sophistication of his economic analysis regarding the nature of health care financing markets should be compared with that used by the United States Department of Justice (DOJ) in its challenge to the merger of two major national players offering health insurance products, Aetna and Prudential (more precisely, Aetna's acquisition of Prudential's health insurance business). In 1999 the DOJ filed a complaint under sections 7 and 15 of the Clayton Act, 15 U.S.C. §§ 18 and 25, which, as described above, give the DOJ authority to prevent the consummation of mergers, acquisitions, or joint ventures that may substantially lessen competition or tend to create a monopoly. The DOJ's complaint alleged that in Houston and Dallas, Texas, the acquisition would give Aetna sufficient market power that it would be able to increase prices or reduce quality in the sale of HMOs and HMOs with point-of-service (HMO–POS) options, and be able to depress the reimbursements paid to physicians in those networks. *See* United States of America, and the State of Texas v. Aetna Inc. and The Prudential Insurance Company of America Proposed Final Judgment and Competitive Impact Statement, 64 Fed. Reg. 44,946 (1999).*

The analysis of market power is noteworthy in at least two respects. First, in contrast to *Ball Memorial*, the DOJ (and implicitly the court approving the settlement) found that the relevant product market consisted only of managed care products, which are distinguishable from indemnity insurance or PPOs. 64 Fed. Reg. at 44,954–55. On the demand side, the purchasers of HMO and HMO–POS products, i.e., employers and employees, do not view PPOs or indemnity plans to be substitutes for managed care. On the supply side, as we described in Part Two, the products have different characteristics in terms of benefit design, cost, and other factors. Second, in contrast to Judge Easterbrook's opinion, the DOJ accounted for the significant barriers to entry in the two managed care markets at issue, Houston and Dallas. *See id.* at 44,955–56. After the acquisition, Aetna would have a dominant position in those relevant markets because its market shares would climb from 44% to 63% in Houston and 26% to 42% in Dallas. As a "dominant firm," it would have the power to increase the premiums paid by consumers for its managed care products and depress the reimbursements paid to physicians in its networks. Moreover, significant barriers to the entry of new managed care products would enhance Aetna's power both in terms of the magnitude by which Aetna could increase premiums and depress reimbursements and the length of time over which it could exercise that power. Put differently, if entry were to occur at all, it

* The district court before which the DOJ brings an antitrust enforcement action must approve any settlement, and the DOJ is required to file a Competitive Impact Statement, which describes, among other things, the nature of the case and why the proposed settlement is in the public interest. *See* Section 2(b) of the Antitrust Procedures and Penalties Act, 15 U.S.C. § 16(b)–(h).

would be costly and slow. For one thing, it would be costly and time-consuming for new entrants to build the necessary managed care networks. Purchasers, therefore, would be subject to higher premiums for some time. For another, although physicians could execute contracts with new entrants, they have only limited ability to encourage their patients to switch to those new plans. As a result, those physicians' incomes would still largely depend on Aetna's levels of reimbursement for a significant period of time. In sum, health care finance markets evidence the "stickiness" described in this note because on both the demand and supply sides there are substantial costs to "switching."

3. *Barriers to market entry for hospitals and physicians.* It is generally agreed that hospitals' need to obtain regulatory approvals to enter constitutes a significant barrier to entry. *See, e.g.,* A DOSE OF COMPETITION, ch. 4 at 25. By contrast, entry of physicians is usually relatively easy, as witnessed by the fact that hospitals recruit physicians and physician groups all the time. *See, e.g.,* HTI Health Services, Inc. v. Quorum Health Group, Inc., 960 F. Supp. 1104, 1133 (S.D. Miss. 1997). *See generally* HAAS-WILSON, MANAGED CARE AND MONOPOLY POWER at 131–32.*

2.   EXCLUSIONARY CONDUCT OR LAWFULNESS

United States v. Alcoa

148 F.2d 416 (1945)

■ L. HAND, CIRCUIT JUDGE:

[The United States brought an action against Alcoa under section 2 of the Sherman Act. Alcoa was the sole producer of new aluminum ingot in the United States but claimed that it was subject to competition from aluminum ingot producers in foreign countries and from fabricated aluminum products. Alcoa also claimed that its monopoly power, if any, had been gained by lawful means. In an opinion that carries the weight of a Supreme Court decision because of a lack of quorum, Judge Hand set forth the classic structure of analysis which has henceforth governed section 2 cases:]

We shall first consider the amount and character of this competition [from other sources]; next, how far it established a monopoly; and finally, if it did, whether that monopoly was unlawful under § 2 of the Act.

[In other words, in a section 2 case, we first define the relevant market; second, determine whether the defendant has power within that market; and third, decide whether that power is lawful.]

Kartell v. Blue Shield of Massachusetts, Inc.

749 F.2d 922 (1st Cir. 1984), *cert. den.,* 471 U.S. 1029 (1985)

■ BREYER, CIRCUIT JUDGE:

Blue Shield pays doctors for treating patients who are Blue Shield health insurance subscribers, but only if each doctor promises not to make

---

* Combinations among physicians and hospitals or physicians and insurers can raise barriers to entry, an issue we discuss with reference to the *Dentsply* and *Rome* cases below.

any additional charge to the subscriber. The basic issue in this case is whether this Blue Shield practice—called a "ban on balance billing"—violates either Sherman Act § 1 forbidding agreements "in restraint of trade," 15 U.S.C. § 1, or Sherman Act § 2 forbidding "monopolization" and "attempts to monopolize," *id.* § 2. The district court, 582 F. Supp. 734 (D. Mass. 1984) held that the practice constituted an unreasonable restraint of trade in violation of section 1. We conclude that the practice does not violate either section of the Sherman Act; and we reverse the district court.

The consumers of Blue Shield insurance can see any "participating doctor." Under the standard agreement, a participating doctor promises to accept as payment in full an amount determined by Blue Shield's "usual and customary charge" method of compensation.

The district court also found that Blue Shield provides some form of health insurance to about 56 percent of the Massachusetts population. (About 45 percent has coverage carrying a "balance billing" ban.) If one subtracts from the total population universe those Massachusetts residents who rely on government sponsored health care (*e.g.*, Medicare or Medicaid), then Blue Shield (and Blue Cross) provide insurance coverage for about 74 percent of the rest, namely those Massachusetts residents who *privately* insure against health costs. Virtually all practicing doctors agree to take Blue Shield subscribers as patients and to participate in its fee plan. Blue Shield payments made under that plan account for about 13 to 14 percent of all "physician practice revenue."

The district court found that, because of the large number of subscribers, doctors are under "heavy economic pressure" to take them as patients and to agree to Blue Shield's system for charging the cost of their care. The court believed that the effect of this payment system, when combined with Blue Shield's size and buying power, was to produce an unreasonably rigid and unjustifiably low set of prices. In the court's view, the fact that doctors cannot charge Blue Shield subscribers more than the Blue Shield payment-schedule amounts interferes with the doctors' freedom to set higher prices for more expensive services and discourages them from developing and offering patients more expensive (and perhaps qualitatively better) services. For these and related reasons, the district court held that Blue Shield's ban on "balance billing" unreasonably restrains trade, and thereby violates Sherman Act § 1. Blue Shield appeals from this holding. The plaintiff doctors cross-appeal from other rulings of the district court in Blue Shield's favor.

I

A

We disagree with the district court's finding of "restraint." To find an unlawful restraint, one would have to look at Blue Shield as if it were a "third force," intervening in the marketplace in a manner that prevents willing buyers and sellers from independently coming together to strike price/quality bargains. Antitrust law typically frowns upon behavior that impedes the striking of such independent bargains. The persuasive power of the district court's analysis disappears, however, once one looks at Blue Shield, not as an inhibitory "third force," but as itself the purchaser of the doctors' services. *See Group Life & Health Insurance Co. v. Royal Drug Co.,* 440 U.S. 205, 214 (1979) (direct reimbursement to participating pharmacies for subscribers' drugs "merely [an] arrangement [ ] for the purchase of goods and services by Blue Shield"). Antitrust law rarely stops the buyer of a service from trying to determine the price or characteristics of the product that will be sold.

Several circuits have held in antitrust cases that insurer activity closely analogous to that present here amounts to purchasing, albeit for the account of others. And, they have held that an insurer may lawfully engage in such buying of goods and services needed to make the insured whole.

At the same time, the facts before us are unlike those in cases where courts have forbidden an "organization" to buy a good or service—cases in which the buyer was typically a "sham" organization seeking only to combine otherwise independent buyers in order to suppress their otherwise competitive instinct to bid up price. *Mandeville Island Farms, Inc. v. American Crystal Sugar Co.,* 334 U.S. 219, 235 (1948) (horizontal price-fixing by purchasers held *per se* illegal); *United States v. Socony–Vacuum Oil Co.,* 310 U.S. 150 (1940) (same); *National Macaroni Manufacturers Association v. Federal Trade Commission,* 345 F.2d 421 (7th Cir.1965) (competitors in trade association fixing quantity of scarce component to be used in macaroni held *per se* illegal). No one here claims that Blue Shield is such a "sham" organization or anything other than a legitimate, independent medical cost insurer. *But cf. Virginia Academy of Clinical Psychologists v. Blue Shield of Virginia,* 624 F.2d 476 (4th Cir.1980) (Blue Shield found to be a combination, not of policyholders, but of *physicians*), *cert. denied,* 450 U.S. 916 (1981).

[C]onsider some highly simplified examples. Suppose a father buys toys for his son—toys the son picks out. Or suppose a landlord hires a painter to paint his tenant's apartment, to the tenant's specifications. Is it not obviously lawful for the father (the landlord) to make clear to the seller that the father (the landlord) is in charge and will pay the bill? Why can he not then forbid the seller to charge the child (the tenant) anything over and above what the father (the landlord) pays—at least if the seller wants the buyer's business? To bring the example closer to home, suppose that a large manufacturing company hires doctors to treat its employees. Can it not insist that its doctors not charge those employees an additional sum over and above what the company agrees to pay them to do the job? In each of these instances, to refuse to allow the condition would disable the buyer from holding the seller to the price of the contract. Yet, if it is lawful for the buyer to buy for the third party in the first place, how can it be unlawful to bargain for a price term that will stick?

Given this argument, it is not surprising the courts have unanimously upheld contracts analogous in various degrees to the one at issue here—contracts in which those who directly provide goods or services to insureds have agreed to cap or forego completely additional charges to those insureds in return for direct payment by the insurer. Scholarly commentators believe that these cases were correctly decided.

Two arguments might be made in an effort to distinguish these cases. First, the doctors may claim that Blue Shield is not, in essence, a buyer. Traditionally, doctors have opposed financial arrangements that involved the "selling" of their services to anyone but the patient. And medical associations in the past sometimes have argued that selling services to third parties or related "corporate practice" might interfere with the absolute ethical obligation that a doctor owes to the patient. Medical associations have not, however, opposed reimbursement by third party insurers, such as Blue Shield, a fact that arguably suggests an important distinction between "insurance reimbursement" and "purchasing."

In our view, however, any such distinction is irrelevant for antitrust purposes. The relevant antitrust facts are that Blue Shield pays the bill and seeks to set the amount of the charge. Those facts led other courts in similar circumstances to treat insurers as if they were "buyers." The same facts convince us that Blue Shield's activities here are *like* those of a buyer. Whether for ethical, medical, or related professional purposes Blue Shield is, or is not, considered a buyer is beside the point. We here consider only one specific argued application of the antitrust laws and we do not suggest how Blue Shield ought to be characterized in any other context.

Second, the doctors seek to distinguish these precedents by pointing to an important district court finding either not present or not discussed in depth in these other cases. The district court here found that Blue Shield is a buyer with significant "market power"—*i.e.,* the power to force prices below the level that a freely competitive market would otherwise set. They argue that Blue Shield's "market power" makes a significant difference. We do not agree.

To resolve this argument about the existence of market power—an issue hotly debated by the expert economists who testified at trial—would force us to evaluate a record that the district court described as "two competing mountains of mostly meaningless papers." Rather than do so, we shall assume that Blue Shield possesses significant market power. We shall also assume, but purely for the sake of argument, that Blue Shield uses that power to obtain "lower than competitive" prices.

We next ask whether Blue Shield's assumed market power makes a significant legal difference. As a matter of pure logic, to distinguish the examples previously mentioned one must accept at least one of the following three propositions: One must believe either (1) that the law forbids a buyer with market power to bargain for "uncompetitive" or "unreasonable" prices, or (2) that such a buyer cannot buy for the account of others, or (3) that there is some relevant difference between obtaining such price for oneself and obtaining that price for others for whom one can lawfully buy. In our view, each of these propositions is false, as a matter either of law or of logic.

First, the antitrust laws interfere with a firm's freedom to set even uncompetitive prices only in special circumstances, where, for example, a price is below incremental cost. Such a "predatory" price harms competitors, cannot be maintained, and is unlikely to provide consumer benefits. Ordinarily, however, even a monopolist is free to exploit whatever market power it may possess when that exploitation takes the form of charging uncompetitive prices. As Professor Areeda puts it, "Mere monopoly pricing is not a violation of the Sherman Act." P. Areeda, *Antitrust Law* § 710 (Supp. 1982).

The reasons underlying this principle include a judicial reluctance to deprive the lawful monopolist (say a patent monopolist) of its lawful rewards, and a judicial recognition of the practical difficulties of determining what is a "reasonable," or "competitive," price. *See* 2 P. Areeda & D. Turner, *Antitrust Law* §§ 512–14 (1978); 3 *id.* ¶ 710; R. Bork, *The Antitrust Paradox*, 125–29 (1978).

The district court did not suggest here that the prices subject to the "balance billing" ban were "predatory." Nor do the parties point to evidence of any price below anyone's "incremental cost."

Second, as we previously mentioned, there is no law forbidding a legitimate insurance company from itself buying the goods or services needed to make its customer whole. The cases that we have cited are unanimous in allowing such arrangements. The rising costs of medical care, the possibility that patients cannot readily evaluate (as competitive buyers) competing offers of medical service, the desirability of lowering insurance costs and premiums, the availability of state regulation to prevent abuse—all convince us that we ought not create new potentially far-reaching law on the subject. And, the parties have not seriously argued to the contrary.

Third, to reject the first two propositions is, as a matter of logic, to reject the third. If it is lawful for a monopoly buyer to buy for the account of another, how can it be unlawful for him to insist that no additional charge be made to that other? To hold to the contrary is, in practice, to deny the buyer the right to buy for others, for the seller would then be free to obtain a different price from those others by threatening to withhold the service. This reasoning seems sound whether or not the buyer has "market power."

B

We now consider more closely the specific arguments raised by the district court and the parties to show that Blue Shield's "balance billing ban" is anticompetitive in practice. To argue that Blue Shield's pricing system is insufficiently sensitive to service differences, or that it encourages high costs, or does not give the patients what they really need, or to claim that the buyer is making a bad decision is like arguing that the buyer of a fleet of taxicabs ought to buy several different models, or allow the seller to vary color or horsepower or gearshift because doing so either will better satisfy those passengers who use the fleet's services, or will in the long run encourage quality and innovation in automobile manufacture. The short— and conclusive—answer to these arguments is that normally the choice of what to seek to buy and what to offer to pay is the buyer's. And, even if the buyer has monopoly power, an antitrust court (which might, in appropriate circumstances, restructure the market) will not interfere with a buyer's (nonpredatory) determination of price.

The claim that Blue Shield's price scheme is "too rigid" because it ignores qualitative differences among physicians is properly addressed to Blue Shield or to a regulator, not to a court.

Finally, the district court rested its decision in large part upon the Supreme Court's recent case, *Arizona v. Maricopa County Medical Society,* 457 U.S. 332 (1982). *Maricopa,* however, involved a *horizontal* agreement among competing doctors about what to charge. A horizontal agreement among competitors is typically unlawful because the competitors prevent themselves from making *independent* decisions about the terms as to which they will bargain.

The district court saw a similarity between the horizontal agreement cases and this one in the fact that Blue Shield can extract an "uncompetitive price" from doctors while the *Maricopa* court feared that "price-fixing" by competitors might bring about uncompetitive prices. But, the antitrust problems at issue when a single firm sets a price—whether, when, and how courts can identify and control an individual exercise of alleged market power—are very different from those associated with agreements by competitors to limit independent decision-making. A decision about the latter is not strong precedent for a case involving only the former. *Maricopa* is simply not on point. Nor, for similar reasons, is *National Collegiate Athletic Association v. Board of Regents,* 468 U.S. 85 (1984), another "horizontal agreement" case cited by the doctors.

Notes

1. *It's not the size, stupid!* Notice that size, or the possession of monopoly power, does not violate Section 2. Rather, power must be gained or maintained by unlawful means. Exactly what "unlawful" means has filled volumes of federal reporters.

2. *It's the characterization as single-firm, vertical conduct, smart!* Then–Judge Breyer viewed the activity in *Kartell* to consist of vertical conduct. Recall what we wrote in the chapter's introduction. Production processes often involve multiple stages of production. For example, the sale of gasoline to your car starts with the exploration and pumping of crude oil from the ground, its shipment to refining facilities, often through pipelines, its refining at those facilities, followed by distribution of the finished products like gasoline to the station near you. When, as in *Kartell,* a firm at one stage of production enters into an arrangement with a firm or firms at another stage, that conduct is said to be "vertical." By contrast, concert of

action among firms acting at the same stage of production is termed "horizontal." As we shall see, collaboration among competing horizontal providers, as in *Maricopa* discussed below, is treated very differently from vertical conduct; and, as Judge Breyer noted, antitrust courts must be vigilant to the fact that horizontal collaborators will sometimes create "sham" single firms in an attempt to hide the fact that horizontal conduct is involved. Below we discuss the sometimes difficult issues that arise in characterizing conduct as horizontal or vertical and single- or multi-firm.

Stressing language in *Kartell* that Blue Shield bought "for the account of others," Professors Hammer and Sage argue that an "agency theme pervades the opinion," Peter J. Hammer & William M. Sage, *Monopsony as an Agency and Regulatory Problem in Health Care*, 79 ANTITRUST L.J. 949, 956 (2004) [hereinafter Hammer & Sage, *Monopsony as an Agency and Regulatory Problem in Health Care*], and they criticize Judge Breyer and subsequent courts for ignoring the complex agency relationships involved. Their criticism is well taken. Judge Breyer's analogy of the situation to the purchase of automobiles is telling: "To argue that Blue Shield's pricing system is insufficiently sensitive to service differences, or that it encourages high costs, or does not give the patients what they really need, or to claim that the buyer is making a bad decision is like arguing that the buyer of a fleet of taxicabs ought to buy several different models, or allow the seller to vary color or horsepower or gearshift because doing so either will better satisfy those passengers who use the fleet's services, or will in the long run encourage quality and innovation in automobile manufacture." *Kartell*, 749 F.2d at 929. A producer of taxi services buys automobiles as an input necessary for its offering of taxi service. As such it buys "for the account of others," to wit, its passengers. This framing is not one of agency but that of a producer purchasing inputs for a good to be sold to end users. Judge Breyer saw no complicated agency relationship, just the purchase of inputs: A producers of health insurance like Blue Shield buys provider services as an input necessary for its offering of health insurance. As such, it buys "for the account of others," to wit, insureds (or plan sponsors). For purposes of antitrust, as *Kartell* frames the issue, the buyers of taxi-cabs and physician services are no different. Whether this comparison is valid is a different question, to which we turn below when we assess the entire enterprise of applying antitrust to health care and the simplicity of which Hammer and Sage rightfully take to task *Kartell* and later courts that apply it in zombie-like fashion. The long and short of it is that opinions like Judge Breyer's in *Kartell* helped create the "reality" they "perceive" in that antitrust law has gone a long way toward extinguishing the normative possibility that insurers could be agents for insureds. As such, antitrust was a tremendous force in the "struggle for the soul of health insurance." Deborah A. Stone, *The Struggle for the Soul of Health Insurance*, 18 J. HEALTH POL. POL'Y & LAW 287 (1993).

Regardless, because *Kartell* involves single-firm conduct, it provides an example of what is known as the "*Colgate* right," stemming from a case of that name, United States v. Colgate & Co., 250 U.S. 300 (1919), in which the Court held that a trader can decide with whom and under what terms it will deal, market freedom par excellence. As *Kartell* indicates, given the strength of this liberty interest, absent predation or the erection of barriers to entry, discussed in the next subsection, even a monopolist can drive as hard a bargain as it can so long as its power is lawful. Not only can it drive down the price it pays to purchase inputs like physician services, as in *Kartell*, but it can charge as high a price as it can in its sales to customers, *see, e.g.*, Pacific Bell Telephone Co. v. Linkline Communications, Inc., 555 U.S. 438 (2009), and it has no generalized duty to sell to or cooperate with rivals. *See, e.g., id.*; Verizon Communications Inc. v. Law Offices of Curtis V. Trinko, 540 U.S. 398 (2004).

It is important to observe that potentially there are two levels at which Massachusetts Blue Shield possessed market power. As the dominant insurer in the state, Blue Shield could exercise market power against purchasers of its insurance products. Also, again as the dominant insurer in the state, Blue Shield could exercise market power in its purchase of providers' services as inputs into its insurance products. The former is monopoly power, while the latter is termed monopsony power. Crucially, *Kartell* only considered the latter—allegedly driving down the price of its purchase of physician services; and therefore the case stands for one proposition: the fact that a provider gets the short end of a contractual stick in its dealing with an insurer with monopsony power raises no antitrust concern, absent predation. Potentially that contract also affects outsiders, e.g., competing insurers, by raising a barrier to entry. Then antitrust is concerned, as developed in the following subsection. Raising a barrier to entry involves an attempt to maintain monopoly power as the seller of insurance. Hammer and Sage are clearly right in criticizing courts for ignoring the latter antitrust interest, *see* Hammer & Sage, *Monopsony as an Agency and Regulatory Problem in Health Care* at 961–62, which, according to Judge Breyer, was not at issue in *Kartell*. In this respect Judge Breyer got it wrong because he failed to notice that Blue Shield's ability to obtain a discount from physicians—possible only because it was the dominant insurer in the state—actually could raise a barrier to entry against competing insurers, who could obtain no such discount, because it would enable Blue Shield to undercut competing insurers' premiums. This conduct meets even the narrower definition of barrier to entry because it imposes on competitors a cost not borne by the incumbent firm with market power. *See, e.g.*, Pauly, *Competition in Health Insurance Markets* at 255–56. *See generally* Jonathan B. Baker, *Vertical Restraints Among Hospitals, Physicians and Health Insurers That Raise Rivals' Costs*, 14 AM. J.L. & MED. 147 (1988). We leave this issue also to the next subsection.

Given its sole focus on Blue Shield's status as a single-firm monopsonistic purchaser of provider services, *Kartell* has been read to give insurers almost carte blanche under the antitrust laws in their contracting with providers, i.e., subjecting providers to lawfully attained bargaining power raises no antitrust concerns absent predation or the creation of barriers to entry. This principle has been extended to the setting of contractual terms, contractual termination and exclusion from networks. *See, e.g.*, Ambroze v. Aetna Health Plans of New York, Inc., 1996 WL 282069 (S.D.N.Y. 1996), vacated and remanded to permit repleading, 1997 WL 49018 (2d Cir. 1997); Continental Orthopedic Appliances, Inc. v. Health Plan of Greater New York, 956 F. Supp. 367 (E.D.N.Y. 1997).

3. *The Ambiguous effects of monopsony power in health care markets.* There is a substantial literature concerning the welfare effects of the exercise of buyer market power against providers. Aside from the article by Professors Hammer and Sage, for examples see Mark V. Pauly, *Monopsony Power in Health Insurance: Thinking Straight While Standing on Your Head*, 6 J. HEALTH ECON. 73 (1987); Mark V. Pauly, *Market Power, Monopsony, and Health Insurance Markets*, 7 J. HEALTH ECON. 111 (1988); Pauly, *Competition in Health Insurance Markets* at 257; Martin Gaynor et al., *Are Invisible Hands Good Hands? Moral Hazard, Competition, and the Second Best in Health Care Markets*, 108 J. POL. ECON. 992 (2000); Jill Boylston Herndon, *Health Insurer Monopsony Power: The All-or-None Model*, 21 J. HEALTH ECON. 197 (2002). Some of this literature is discussed in the last subsection concerning the application of antitrust to health care more generally.

To disperse monopsony power that might be possessed by health plans, the Patient Protection and Affordable Care Act ("PPACA") has competition among health plans as a principal aim in its establishment of state health insurance Exchanges. *See* 42 U.S.C. 13031 (added by PPACA § 1311). Beyond offering sources of affordable health insurance for individuals with low and moderate incomes who lack minimum essential health coverage (see Part Two), exchanges are supposed to foster a market in which health insurers, selling "qualified health plans," compete on quality and value. Qualified health plan products are, by federal law, designed to be relatively standard, offering "essential health benefits" (see Part Two) according to standardized coverage terms and cost sharing. With basic coverage design off the table as the basis for competitive pricing inside the Exchange, premium pricing, quality and value (e.g., a bigger network, higher quality ratings) are envisioned as the basis of briskly competitive insurance markets. In order to make sure that markets dominated by single insurance companies obtain the benefits of this competition, the Act also requires the federal Office of Management and Budget ("OMB") to assure that all Exchange health plan customers will be able to choose among at least competing multi-state plans. *See* 42 U.S.C. § 18054 (added by PPACA § 1334). The legislation also allows states to develop multi-state certified plans and "CO–OP" plans, nonprofit health plans that are member-owned and, in the spirit of the CO–OP statute, more likely to emphasize quality and value over profits. *See* 42 U.S.C. §§ 18042 and 18052 (added by PPACA §§ 1322 and 1222)

How many states will develop CO–OP or multi-state plans is totally unknown at this point, and as of December 2011, the parameters of the OMB multi-state plan approach have not yet been laid out. Whether the Exchanges will actually create (quality) competition among plans, drive down the price of health care, while improving value and quality, presents an important question for empirical research. One of the biggest concerns about the new Exchange coverage arrangements is that there simply is so large a shortage of raw materials (in this instance, physicians, who are able and willing to treat millions of newly insured persons), from which to build these new insurance products, that it is unclear how much leverage plans will have over provider pricing. Then there is the additional complicating factor, a consumer market that disproportionately is expected to be older and in poorer health to begin with, further driving costs. In other words, even if there will be a bunch of new health plans instead of one or two, the biggest drivers of health care costs—health care status, the cost of health care itself, the use of care—may remain impervious to idealistic notions of competition.

4. *Don't forget the importance of the horizontal–vertical characterization!* To reiterate, the relationships in *Kartell* were interpreted as raising issues of single-firm, vertical conduct rather than issues of horizontal collaboration, which are treated somewhat differently. However, before turning to the special problems raised by horizontal collaboration, we continue to focus on the ''lawfulness'' of single-firm conduct, here the dominant firm's raising a barrier to entry through its own conduct:

United States v. Dentsply International, Inc.

399 F.3d 181 (3d Cir. 2005)

OPINION

■ Weis, Circuit Judge:

In this antitrust case we conclude that an exclusivity policy imposed by a manufacturer on its dealers violates Section 2 of the Sherman Act. We come to that position because of the nature of the relevant market and the established effectiveness of the restraint despite the lack of long term contracts between the manufacturer and its dealers. Accordingly, we will reverse the judgment of the District Court in favor of the defendant and remand with directions to grant the Government's request for injunctive relief.

The Government alleged that Defendant, Dentsply International, Inc., acted unlawfully to maintain a monopoly in violation of Section 2 of the Sherman Act, 15 U.S.C. § 2; entered into illegal restrictive dealing agreements prohibited by Section 3 of the Clayton Act, 15 U.S.C. § 14; and used unlawful agreements in restraint of interstate trade in violation of Section 1 of the Sherman Act, 15 U.S.C. § 1. After a bench trial, the District Court denied the injunctive relief sought by the Government and entered judgment for defendant.

In its comprehensive opinion, the District Court found the following facts. Dentsply International, Inc. manufactures artificial teeth for use in dentures and other restorative appliances and sells them to dental products dealers. The dealers, in turn, supply the teeth and various other materials to dental laboratories, which fabricate dentures for sale to dentists.

The relevant market is the sale of prefabricated artificial teeth in the United States.

Because of advances in dental medicine, artificial tooth manufacturing is marked by a low or no-growth potential. Dentsply has long dominated the industry consisting of 12–13 manufacturers and enjoys a 75%–80% market share on a revenue basis, 67% on a unit basis, and is about 15 times larger than its next closest competitor. The other significant manufacturers and their market shares are:

Ivoclar Vivadent, Inc.	5%
Vita Zahnfabrik	3%
*Myerson LLC	3%
*American Tooth Industries	2%
*Universal Dental Company	1%–2%
Heraeus Kulzer GmbH	1%
Davis, Schottlander & Davis, Ltd.	<1%

* These companies sell directly to dental laboratories as well as to dealers.

Dealers sell to dental laboratories a full range of metals, porcelains, acrylics, waxes, and other materials required to fabricate fixed or removal restorations. Dealers maintain large inventories of artificial teeth and carry thousands of products, other than teeth, made by hundreds of different manufacturers. Dentsply supplies $400 million of products other than teeth to its network of 23 dealers.

There are hundreds of dealers who compete on the basis of price and service among themselves, as well as with manufacturers who sell directly to laboratories. The dealer field has experienced significant consolidation with several large national and regional firms emerging.

For more than fifteen years, Dentsply has operated under a policy that discouraged its dealers from adding competitors' teeth to their lines of products. In 1993, Dentsply adopted "Dealer Criterion 6." It provides that in order to effectively promote Dentsply–York products, authorized dealers "may not add further tooth lines to their product offering." Dentsply operates on a purchase order basis with its distributors and, therefore, the relationship is essentially terminable at will. Dealer Criterion 6 was enforced against dealers with the exception of those who had carried competing products before 1993 and were "grandfathered" for sales of those products. Dentsply rebuffed attempts by those particular distributors to expand their lines of competing products beyond the grandfathered ones.

Dentsply's five top dealers sell competing grandfathered brands of teeth. In 2001, their share of Dentsply's overall sales were

Zahn	39%
Patterson	28%
Darby	8%
Benco	4%
DLDS	<4%
TOTAL	83%

16,000 dental laboratories fabricate restorations and a subset of 7,000 provide dentures. The laboratories compete with each other on the basis of price and service. Patients and dentists value fast service, particularly in the case of lost or damaged dentures. When laboratories' inventories cannot supply the necessary teeth, dealers may fill orders for walk-ins or use overnight express mail as does Dentsply, which dropped-shipped some 60% of orders from dealers.

Dealers have been dissatisfied with Dealer Criterion 6, but, at least in the recent past, none of them have given up the popular Dentsply teeth to take on a competitive line. Dentsply at one time considered selling directly to the laboratories, but abandoned the concept because of fear that dealers would retaliate by refusing to buy its other dental products.

In the 1990's Dentsply implemented aggressive sales campaigns, including efforts to promote its teeth in dental schools, providing rebates for laboratories' increased usage, and deploying a sales force dedicated to teeth, rather than the entire product mix. Its chief competitors did not as actively promote their products. Foreign manufacturers were slow to alter their designs to cope with American preferences, and, in at least one instance, pursued sales of porcelain products rather than plastic teeth.

Dentsply has had a reputation for aggressive price increases in the market and has created a high price umbrella. Its artificial tooth business is characterized as a "cash cow" whose profits are diverted to other operations of the company. A report in 1996 stated its profits from teeth since 1990 had increased 32% from $16.8 million to $22.2 million.

The District Court found that Dentsply's business justification for Dealer Criterion 6 was pretextual and designed expressly to exclude its rivals from access to dealers. The Court however concluded that other dealers were available and direct sales to laboratories was a viable method of doing business. Moreover, it concluded that Dentsply had not created a market with supra competitive pricing, dealers were free to leave the network at any time, and the Government failed to prove that Dentsply's actions "have been or could be successful in preventing 'new or potential competitors from gaining a foothold in the market.' " Accordingly, the Court concluded that the Government had failed to establish violations of Section 3 of the Clayton Act and Sections 1 or 2 of the Sherman Act.

The Government appealed, contending that a monopolist that prevents rivals from distributing through established dealers has maintained its monopoly by acting with predatory intent and violates Section 2. Additionally, the Government asserts that the maintenance of a 75%–80% market share, establishment of a price umbrella, repeated aggressive price increases and exclusion of competitors from a major source of distribution, show that Dentsply possesses monopoly power, despite the fact that rivals are not entirely excluded from the market and some of their prices are higher. The Government did not appeal the rulings under Section 1 of the Sherman Act or Section 3 of the Clayton Act.

Dentsply argues that rivals had obtained a share of the relevant market, that there are no artificially high prices and that competitors have access to all laboratories through existing or readily convertible systems. In addition, Dentsply asserts that its success is due to its leadership in promotion and marketing and not the imposition of Dealer Criterion 6.

II. APPLICABLE LEGAL PRINCIPLES

A violation of Section 2 consists of two elements: (1) possession of monopoly power and (2) "... maintenance of that power as distinguished from growth or development as a consequence of a superior product, business acumen, or historic accident." *Eastman Kodak Co. v. Image Technical Servs., Inc.,* 504 U.S. 451, 480 (1992) (citing *United States v. Grinnell Corp.,* 384 U.S. 563, 571 (1966)). "Monopoly power under § 2 requires ... something greater than market power under § 1." *Eastman Kodak Co.,* 504 U.S. at 481.

To run afoul of Section 2, a defendant must be guilty of illegal conduct "to foreclose competition, gain a competitive advantage, or to destroy a competitor." *Id.* at 482–83 (quoting *United States v. Griffith,* 334 U.S. 100, 107 (1948)). Behavior that otherwise might comply with antitrust law may be impermissibly exclusionary when practiced by a monopolist. As we said in *LePage's, Inc. v. 3M,* 324 F.3d 141, 151–52 (3d Cir. 2003), "a monopolist is not free to take certain actions that a company in a competitive (or even oligopolistic) market may take, because there is no market constraint on a monopolist's behavior." 3 Areeda & Turner, *Antitrust Law* ¶ 813, at 300–02 (1978).

Although not illegal in themselves, exclusive dealing arrangements can be an improper means of maintaining a monopoly. A prerequisite for such a violation is a finding that monopoly power exists. In addition, the exclusionary conduct must have an anti-competitive effect. If those elements are established, the monopolist still retains a defense of business justification.

Unlawful maintenance of a monopoly is demonstrated by proof that a defendant has engaged in anti-competitive conduct that reasonably appears to be a significant contribution to maintaining monopoly power. *United States v. Microsoft,* 253 F.3d 34, 79 (D.C. Cir. 2001); 3 Phillip E. Areeda & Herbert Hovenkamp, *Antitrust Law,* ¶ 651c at 78 (1996). Predatory or exclusionary practices in themselves are not sufficient. There must be proof that competition, not merely competitors, has been harmed.

III. MONOPOLY POWER

A. The Relevant Market

Defining the relevant market is an important part of the analysis. The District Court found the market to be "the sale of prefabricated artificial teeth in the United States." Further, the Court found that "[t]he manufacturers participating in the United States artificial tooth market historically have distributed their teeth into the market in one of three ways: (1) directly to dental labs; (2) through dental dealers; or (3) through a hybrid system combining manufacturer direct sales and dental dealers." The

Court also found that the "labs are the relevant consumers for prefabricated artificial teeth."

There is no dispute that the laboratories are the ultimate consumers because they buy the teeth at the point in the process where they are incorporated into another product. Dentsply points out that its representatives concentrate their efforts at the laboratories as well as at dental schools and dentists.

During oral argument, Dentsply's counsel said, "the dealers are not the market ... [t]he market is the dental labs that consume the product." Emphasizing the importance of end users, Dentsply argues that the District Court understood the relevant market to be the sales of artificial teeth to dental laboratories in the United States. Although the Court used the word "market" in a number of differing contexts, the findings demonstrate that the relevant market is not as narrow as Dentsply would have it. [T]he Court said that Dentsply "has had a persistently high market share between 75% and 80% on a revenue basis, in the artificial tooth market." Dentsply sells only to dealers and the narrow definition of market that it urges upon us would be completely inconsistent with that finding of the District Court.

The Court went on to find that Ivoclar "has the second-highest share of the market, at approximately 5%." Ivoclar sells directly to the laboratories. Therefore, these two findings establish that the relevant market in this case includes sales to dealers and direct sales to the laboratories. Other findings on Dentsply's "market share" are consistent with this understanding.

These findings are persuasive that the District Court understood, as do we, the relevant market to be the total sales of artificial teeth to the laboratories and the dealers combined.

Dentsply's apparent belief that a relevant market cannot include sales both to the final consumer and a middleman is refuted in the closely analogous case of *Allen–Myland, Inc. v. IBM Corp.*, 33 F.3d 194 (3d Cir. 1994). In that case, IBM sold mainframe computers directly to the ultimate consumers and also sold to companies that leased computers to ultimate users. We concluded that the relevant market encompassed the sales directly to consumers as well as those to leasing companies. "... to the extent that leasing companies deal in used, non-IBM mainframes that have not already been counted in the sales market, these machines belong in the relevant market for large-scale mainframe computers."

To resolve any doubt, therefore, we hold that the relevant market here is the sale of artificial teeth in the United States both to laboratories and to the dental dealers.

B. Power to Exclude

Dentsply's share of the market is more than adequate to establish a prima facie case of power. In addition, Dentsply has held its dominant share for more than ten years and has fought aggressively to maintain that imbalance. One court has commented that, "[i]n evaluating monopoly power, it is not market share that counts, but the ability to *maintain* market share."

The District Court found that it could infer monopoly power because of the predominant market share, but despite that factor, concluded that Dentsply's tactics did not preclude competition from marketing their products directly to the dental laboratories. "Dentsply does not have the power to exclude competitors from the ultimate consumer." *United States v. Dentsply Int'l, Inc.*, 277 F. Supp.2d 387, 452.

Moreover, the Court determined that failure of Dentsply's two main rivals, Vident and Ivoclar, to obtain significant market shares resulted from their own business decisions to concentrate on other product lines, rather than implement active sales efforts for teeth.

The District Court's evaluation of Ivoclar and Vident business practices as a cause of their failure to secure more of the market is not persuasive. The reality is that over a period of years, because of Dentsply's domination of dealers, direct sales have not been a practical alternative for most manufacturers. It has not been so much the competitors' less than enthusiastic efforts at competition that produced paltry results, as it is the blocking of access to the key dealers. This is the part of the real market that is denied to the rivals.

The apparent lack of aggressiveness by competitors is not a matter of apathy, but a reflection of the effectiveness of Dentsply's exclusionary policy. Although its rivals could theoretically convince a dealer to buy their products and drop Dentsply's line, that has not occurred. In *United States v. Visa U.S.A.*, 344 F.3d at 229, 240 (2d Cir. 2003), the Court of Appeals held that similar evidence indicated that defendants had excluded their rivals from the marketplace and thus demonstrated monopoly power.

The Supreme Court on more than one occasion has emphasized that economic realities rather than a formalistic approach must govern review of antitrust activity. "Legal presumptions that rest on formalistic distinctions rather than actual market realities are generally disfavored in antitrust law ... in determining the existence of market power ... this Court has examined closely the economic reality of the market at issue." *Eastman Kodak Co. v. Image Technical Servs., Inc.*, 504 U.S. 451, 466–67 (1992).

The realities of the artificial tooth market were candidly expressed by two former managerial employees of Dentsply when they explained their rules of engagement. One testified that Dealer Criterion 6 was designed to "block competitive distribution points." He continued, "Do not allow competition to achieve toeholds in dealers; tie up dealers; do not 'free up' key players."

Another former manager said:

> You don't want your competition with your distributors, you don't want to give the distributors an opportunity to sell a competitive product. And you don't want to give your end user, the customer, meaning a laboratory and/or a dentist, a choice. He has to buy Dentsply teeth. That's the only thing that's available. The only

place you can get it is through the distributor and the only one that the distributor is selling is Dentsply teeth. That's your objective.

These are clear expressions of a plan to maintain monopolistic power.

The District Court detailed some ten separate incidents in which Dentsply required agreement by new as well as long-standing dealers not to handle competitors' teeth. For example, when the DLDS firm considered adding two other tooth lines because of customers' demand, Dentsply threatened to sever access not only to its teeth, but to other dental products as well. DLDS yielded to that pressure. The termination of Trinity Dental, which had previously sold Dentsply products other than teeth, was a similar instance. When Trinity wanted to add teeth to its line for the first time and chose a competitor, Dentsply refused to supply other dental products.

Dentsply also pressured Atlanta Dental, Marcus Dental, Thompson Dental, Patterson Dental and Pearson Dental Supply when they carried or considered adding competitive lines. In another incident, Dentsply recognized DTS as a dealer so as to "fully eliminate the competitive threat that [DTS locations] pose by representing Vita and Ivoclar in three of four regions."

The evidence demonstrated conclusively that Dentsply had supremacy over the dealer network and it was at that crucial point in the distribution chain that monopoly power over the market for artificial teeth was established. The reality in this case is that the firm that ties up the key dealers rules the market.

In concluding that Dentsply lacked the power to exclude competitors from the laboratories, "the ultimate consumers," the District Court overlooked the point that the relevant market was the "sale" of artificial teeth to both dealers and laboratories. Although some sales were made by manufacturers to the laboratories, overwhelming numbers were made to dealers. Thus, the Court's scrutiny should have been applied not to the "ultimate consumers" who used the teeth, but to the "customers" who purchased the teeth, the relevant category which included dealers as well as laboratories. This mis-focus led the District Court into clear error.

The factual pattern here is quite similar to that in *LePage's, Inc. v. 3M,* 324 F.3d 141 (3d Cir. 2003). There, a manufacturer of transparent tape locked up high volume distribution channels by means of substantial discounts on a range of its other products. *LePage's,* 324 F.3d at 144, 160–62. We concluded that the use of exclusive dealing and bundled rebates to the detriment of the rival manufacturer violated Section 2. *See LePage's,* 324 F.3d at 159. Similarly, in *Microsoft,* the Court of Appeals for the D.C. Circuit concluded that, through the use of exclusive contracts with key dealers, a manufacturer foreclosed competitors from a substantial percentage of the available opportunities for product distribution. *See Microsoft,* 253 F.3d at 70–71.

The evidence in this case demonstrates that for a considerable time, through the use of Dealer Criterion 6 Dentsply has been able to exclude competitors from the dealers' network, a narrow, but heavily traveled channel to the dental laboratories.

C.   Pricing

An increase in pricing is another factor used in evaluating existence of market power. Although in this case the evidence of exclusion is stronger than that of Dentsply's control of prices, testimony about suspect pricing is also found in this record.

The District Court found that Dentsply had a reputation for aggressive price increases in the market. It is noteworthy that experts for both parties testified that were Dealer Criterion 6 abolished, prices would fall. A former sales manager for Dentsply agreed that the company's share of the market would diminish should Dealer Criterion 6 no longer be in effect. In 1993, Dentsply's regional sales manager complained, "[w]e need to moderate our increases—twice a year for the last few years was not good." Large scale distributors observed that Dentsply's policy created a high price umbrella.

Although Dentsply's prices fall between those of Ivoclar and Vita's premium tooth lines, Dentsply did not reduce its prices when competitors elected not to follow its increases. Dentsply's profit margins have been growing over the years. The picture is one of a manufacturer that sets prices with little concern for its competitors, "something a firm without a monopoly would have been unable to do." *Microsoft*, 253 F.3d at 58. The results have been favorable to Dentsply, but of no benefit to consumers.

Moreover, even "if monopoly power has been acquired or maintained through improper means, the fact that the power has not been used to extract [a monopoly price] provides no succor to the monopolist." *Microsoft*, 253 F.3d at 57 (quoting *Berkey Photo, Inc. v. Eastman Kodak, Co.*, 603 F.2d 263, 274 (2d Cir. 1979)). The record of long duration of the exclusionary tactics and anecdotal evidence of their efficacy make it clear that power existed and was used effectively. The District Court erred in concluding that Dentsply lacked market power.

IV.   ANTI–COMPETITIVE EFFECTS

Having demonstrated that Dentsply possessed market power, the Government must also establish the second element of a Section 2 claim, that the power was used "to foreclose competition." *United States v. Griffith*, 334 U.S. 100, 107 (1948). Assessing anti-competitive effect is important in evaluating a challenge to a violation of Section 2. Under that Section of the Sherman Act, it is not necessary that all competition be removed from the market. The test is not total foreclosure, but whether the challenged practices bar a substantial number of rivals or severely restrict the market's ambit.

A leading treatise explains,

A set of strategically planned exclusive dealing contracts may slow the rival's expansion by requiring it to develop alternative outlets for its products or rely at least temporarily on inferior or more expensive outlets. Consumer injury results from the delay that the dominant firm imposes on the smaller rival's growth. Herbert Hovenkamp, *Antitrust Law* ¶ 1802c, at 64 (2d ed. 2002).

By ensuring that the key dealers offer Dentsply teeth either as the only or dominant choice, Dealer Criterion 6 has a significant effect in preserving Dentsply's monopoly. It helps keep sales of competing teeth below the critical level necessary for any rival to pose a real threat to Dentsply's market share. As such, Dealer Criterion 6 is a solid pillar of harm to competition. *See LePage's,* 324 F.3d 141, 159 (3d Cir. 2003) ("When a monopolist's actions are designed to prevent one or more new or potential competitors from gaining a foothold in the market by exclusionary, i.e. predatory, conduct, its success in that goal is not only injurious to the potential competitor but also to competition in general.").

A.   Benefits of Dealers

Dentsply has always sold its teeth through dealers. Vita sells through Vident, its exclusive distributor and domestic affiliate, but has a mere 3% of the market. Ivoclar had some relationship with dealers in the past, but its direct relationship with laboratories yields only a 5% share.

A number of factors are at work here. For a great number of dental laboratories, the dealer is the preferred source for artificial teeth. Although the District Court observed that "labs prefer to buy direct because of potential cost savings attributable to the elimination of the dealer middleman, in fact, laboratories are driven by the realities of the marketplace to buy far more heavily from dealers than manufacturers. This may be largely attributed to the beneficial services, credit function, economies of scale and convenience that dealers provide to laboratories, benefits which are otherwise unavailable to them when they buy direct.

The record is replete with evidence of benefits provided by dealers. For example, they provide laboratories the benefit of "one stop-shopping" and extensive credit services. Because dealers typically carry the products of multiple manufacturers, a laboratory can order, with a single phone call to a dealer, products from multiple sources. Without dealers, in most instances laboratories would have to place individual calls to each manufacturer, expend the time, and pay multiple shipping charges to fill the same orders.

The dealer-provided reduction in transaction costs and time represents a substantial benefit, one that the District Court minimized when it characterized "one stop shopping" as merely the ability to order from a single manufacturer all the materials necessary for crown, bridge and denture construction. Although a laboratory can call a manufacturer directly and purchase any product made by it, the laboratory is unable to procure from that source products made by its competitors. Thus, purchasing through dealers, which as a class traditionally carries the products of multiple vendors, surmounts this shortcoming, as well as offers other advantages.

Buying through dealers also enables laboratories to take advantage of obtaining discounts. Because they engage in price competition to gain laboratories' business, dealers often discount manufacturers' suggested laboratory price for artificial teeth. There is no finding on this record that manufacturers offer similar discounts.

Another service dealers perform is taking back tooth returns. Artificial teeth and denture returns are quite common in dentistry. Approximately 30% of all laboratory tooth purchases are returned for exchange or credit. The District Court disregarded this benefit on the ground that all manufacturers except Vita accept tooth returns. However, in equating dealer and manufacturer returns, the District Court overlooked the fact that using dealers, rather than manufacturers, enables laboratories to consolidate their returns. In a single shipment to a dealer, a laboratory can return the products of a number of manufacturers, and so economize on shipping, time, and transaction costs.

Conversely, when returning products directly to manufacturers, a laboratory must ship each vendor's product separately and must track each exchange individually. Consolidating returns yields savings of time, effort, and costs.

Dealers also provide benefits to manufacturers, perhaps the most obvious of which is efficiency of scale. Using select high-volume dealers, as opposed to directly selling to hundreds if not thousands of laboratories, greatly reduces the manufacturer's distribution costs and credit risks. Dentsply, for example, currently sells to twenty three dealers. If it were instead to sell directly to individual laboratories, Dentsply would incur significantly higher transaction costs, extension of credit burdens, and credit risks.

Although a laboratory that buys directly from a manufacturer may be able to avoid the marginal costs associated with "middleman" dealers, any savings must be weighed against the benefits, savings, and convenience offered by dealers.

In addition, dealers provide manufacturers more marketplace exposure and sales representative coverage than manufacturers are able to generate on their own. Increased exposure and sales coverage traditionally lead to greater sales.

B.   "Viability" of Direct Sales

The benefits that dealers provide manufacturers help make dealers the preferred distribution channels—in effect, the "gateways"—to the artificial teeth market. Nonetheless, the District Court found that selling direct is a "viable" method of distributing artificial teeth. But we are convinced that it is "viable" only in the sense that it is "possible," not that it is practical or feasible in the market as it exists and functions. The District Court's conclusion of "viability" runs counter to the facts and is clearly erroneous. On the entire evidence, we are "left with the definite and firm conviction that a mistake has been committed."

It is true that Dentsply's competitors can sell directly to the dental laboratories and an insignificant number do. The undeniable reality, however, is that dealers have a controlling degree of access to the laboratories. The long-entrenched Dentsply dealer network with its ties to the laboratories makes it impracticable for a manufacturer to rely on direct distribution to the laboratories in any significant amount.

That some manufacturers resort to direct sales and are even able to stay in business by selling directly is insufficient proof that direct selling is an effective means of competition. The proper inquiry is not whether direct sales enable a competitor to "survive" but rather whether direct selling "poses a real threat" to defendant's monopoly. The minuscule 5% and 3% market shares eked out by direct-selling manufacturers Ivoclar and Vita, Dentsply's "primary competitors," reveal that direct selling poses little threat to Dentsply.

C. *Efficacy of Dealer Criterion 6*

Although the parties to the sales transactions consider the exclusionary arrangements to be agreements, they are technically only a series of independent sales. Dentsply sells teeth to the dealers on an individual transaction basis and essentially the arrangement is "at-will." Nevertheless, the economic elements involved—the large share of the market held by Dentsply and its conduct excluding competing manufacturers—realistically make the arrangements here as effective as those in written contracts. *See Monsanto Co. v. Spray–Rite Serv. Corp.*, 465 U.S. 752, 764 n. 9 (1984).

Given the circumstances present in this case, there is no ground to doubt the effectiveness of the exclusive dealing arrangement. In *LePage's*, 324 F.3d at 162, we concluded that 3M's aggressive rebate program damaged LePage's ability to compete and thereby harmed competition itself. LePage's simply could not match the discounts that 3M provided. Similarly, in this case, in spite of the legal ease with which the relationship can be terminated, the dealers have a strong economic incentive to continue carrying Dentsply's teeth. Dealer Criterion 6 is not edentulous.[2]

D. *Limitation of Choice*

An additional anti-competitive effect is seen in the exclusionary practice here that limits the choices of products open to dental laboratories, the ultimate users. A dealer locked into the Dentsply line is unable to heed a request for a different manufacturers' product and, from the standpoint of

---

2. In some cases which we find distinguishable, courts have indicated that exclusive dealing contracts of short duration are not violations of the antitrust laws. *See, e.g., CDC Techs., Inc. v. IDEXX Labs., Inc.*, 186 F.3d 74, 81 (2d Cir. 1999) ("distributors" only provided sales leads and sales increased after competitor imposed exclusive dealing arrangements); *Omega Envtl., Inc. v. Gilbarco, Inc.*, 127 F.3d 1157, 1163 (9th Cir. 1997) (manufacturer with 55% market share sold both to consumers and distributors, market showed decreasing prices and fluctuating shares); *Ryko Mfg. Co. v. Eden Servs.*, 823 F.2d 1215 (8th Cir. 1987) (manufacturer sold its products through both direct sales and distributors); *Roland Mach. Co. v. Dresser Indus., Inc.*, 749 F.2d 380 (7th Cir. 1984) (contract between dealer and manufacturer did not contain exclusive dealing provision).

convenience, that inability to some extent impairs the laboratory's choice in the marketplace.

As an example, current and potential customers requested Atlanta Dental to carry Vita teeth. Although these customers could have ordered the Vita teeth from Vident in California, Atlanta Dental's tooth department manager believed that they were interested in a local source. Atlanta Dental chose not to add the Vita line after being advised that doing so would cut off access to Dentsply teeth, which constituted over 90% of its tooth sales revenue.

Similarly, DLDS added Universal and Vita teeth to meet customers' requests, but dropped them after Dentsply threatened to stop supplying its product. Marcus Dental began selling another brand of teeth at one point because of customer demand in response to supply problems with Dentsply. After Dentsply threatened to enforce Dealer Criterion 6, Marcus dropped the other line.

E. Barriers to Entry

Entrants into the marketplace must confront Dentsply's power over the dealers. The District Court's theory that any new or existing manufacturer may "steal" a Dentsply dealer by offering a superior product at a lower price simply has not proved to be realistic. To the contrary, purloining efforts have been thwarted by Dentsply's longtime, vigorous and successful enforcement actions. The paltry penetration in the market by competitors over the years has been a refutation of theory by tangible and measurable results in the real world.

The levels of sales that competitors could project in wooing dealers were minuscule compared to Dentsply's, whose long-standing relationships with these dealers included sales of other dental products. For example, Dentsply threatened Zahn with termination if it started selling Ivoclar teeth. At the time, Ivoclar's projected $1.2 million in sales were 85% lower than Zahn's $8 million in Dentsply's sales.

When approached by Leach & Dillon and Heraeus Kulzer, Zahn's sales of Dentsply teeth had increased to $22–$23 million per year. In comparison, the president of Zahn expected that Leach & Dillon would add up to $200,000 (or less than 1% of its Dentsply's sales) and Heraeus Kulzer would contribute "maybe hundreds of thousands." Similarly, Vident's $1 million in projected sales amounted to 5.5% of its $18 million in annual Dentsply's sales.

The dominant position of Dentsply dealers as a gateway to the laboratories was confirmed by potential entrants to the market. The president of Ivoclar testified that his company was unsuccessful in its approach to the two large national dealers and other regional dealers. He pointed out that it is more efficient to sell through dealers and, in addition, they offered an entre to future customers by promotions in the dental schools.

Further evidence was provided by a Vident executive, who testified about failed attempts to distribute teeth through ten identified dealers. He attributed the lack of success to their fear of losing the right to sell Dentsply teeth.

Another witness, the president of Dillon Company, advised Davis, Schottlander & Davis, a tooth manufacturer, "to go through the dealer network because anything else is futile ... [D]ealers control the tooth industry. If you don't have distribution with the dealer network, you don't have distribution." Some idea of the comparative size of the dealer network was illustrated by the Dillon testimony: "Zahn does $2 billion, I do a million-seven. Patterson does over a billion dollars, I do a million-seven. I have ten employees, they have 6,000."

Dealer Criterion 6 created a strong economic incentive for dealers to reject competing lines in favor of Dentsply's teeth. As in *LePage's,* the rivals simply could not provide dealers with a comparable economic incentive to switch. Moreover, the record demonstrates that Dentsply added Darby as a dealer "to block Vita from a key competitive distribution point." According to a Dentsply executive, the "key issue" was "Vita's potential distribution system." He explained that Vita was "having a tough time getting teeth out to customers. One of their key weaknesses is their distribution system."

Teeth are an important part of a denture, but they are but one component. The dealers are dependent on serving all of the laboratories' needs and must carry as many components as practicable. The artificial teeth business cannot realistically be evaluated in isolation from the rest of the dental fabrication industry.

A leading treatise provides a helpful analogy to this situation:

> [S]uppose that men's bow ties cannot efficiently be sold in stores that deal exclusively in bow ties or even ties generally; rather, they must be sold in department stores where clerks can spread their efforts over numerous products and the ties can be sold in conjunction with shirts and suits. Suppose further that a dominant bow tie manufacturer should impose exclusive dealing on a town's only three department stores. In this case the rival bow tie maker cannot easily enter. Setting up another department store is an unneeded and a very large investment in proportion to its own production, which we assume is only bow ties, but any store that offers less will be an inefficient and costly seller of bow ties. As a result, such exclusive dealing could either exclude the nondominant bow tie maker or else raise its costs in comparison to the costs of the dominant firm. While the department stores might prefer to sell the ties of multiple manufacturers, if faced with an "all-or-nothing" choice they may accede to the dominant firm's wish for exclusive dealing. Herbert Hovenkamp, *Antitrust Law* ¶ 1802e3, at 78–79 (2d ed. 2002).

Criterion 6 imposes an "all-or-nothing" choice on the dealers. The fact that dealers have chosen not to drop Dentsply teeth in favor of a rival's brand demonstrates that they have acceded to heavy economic pressure.

This case does not involve a dynamic, volatile market like that in *Microsoft*, 253 F.3d at 70, or a proven alternative distribution channel. The mere existence of other avenues of distribution is insufficient without an assessment of their overall significance to the market. The economic impact of an exclusive dealing arrangement is amplified in the stagnant, no growth context of the artificial tooth field.

Dentsply's authorized dealers are analogous to the high volume retailers at issue in *LePage's*. Although the dealers are distributors and the stores in *LePage's,* such as K–Mart and Staples, are retailers, this is a distinction in name without a substantive difference. *LePage's,* 324 F.3d at 144. Selling to a few prominent retailers provided "substantially reduced distribution costs" and "cheap, high volume supply lines." *Id.* at 160 n. 14. The manufacturer sold to a few high volume businesses and benefitted from the widespread locations and strong customer goodwill that prominent retailers provided as opposed to selling directly to end-user consumers or to a multitude of smaller retailers. There are other ways across the "river" to consumers, but high volume retailers provided the most effective bridge.

The same is true here. The dealers provide the same advantages to Dentsply, widespread locations and long-standing relationships with dental labs, that the high volume retailers provided to 3M. Even orders that are drop-shipped directly from Dentsply to a dental lab originate through the dealers. This underscores that Dentsply's dealers provide a critical link to end-users.

Although the District Court attributed some of the lack of competition to Ivoclar's and Vident's bad business decisions, that weakness was not ascribed to other manufacturers. Logically, Dealer Criterion 6 cannot be both a cause of the competitors' lower promotional expenditures which hurt their market positions, and at the same time, be unrelated to their exclusion from the marketplace. Moreover, in *Microsoft,* in spite of the competitors' self-imposed problems, the Court of Appeals held that Microsoft possessed monopoly power because it benefitted from a significant barrier to entry. *Microsoft,* 253 F.3d at 55.

Dentsply's grip on its 23 authorized dealers effectively choked off the market for artificial teeth, leaving only a small sliver for competitors. The District Court erred when it minimized that situation and focused on a theoretical feasibility of success through direct access to the dental labs. While we may assume that Dentsply won its preeminent position by fair competition, that fact does not permit maintenance of its monopoly by unfair practices. We conclude that on this record, the Government established that Dentsply's exclusionary policies and particularly Dealer Criterion 6 violated Section 2.

V. BUSINESS JUSTIFICATION

As noted earlier, even if a company exerts monopoly power, it may defend its practices by establishing a business justification. The Government, having demonstrated harm to competition, the burden shifts to

Dentsply to show that Dealer Criterion 6 promotes a sufficiently pro-competitive objective. Significantly, Dentsply has not done so. The District Court found that "Dentsply's asserted justifications for its exclusionary policies are inconsistent with its announced reason for the exclusionary policies, its conduct enforcing the policy, its rival suppliers' actions, and dealers' behavior in the marketplace."

Some of the dealers opposed Dentsply's policy as exerting too much control over the products they may sell, but the grandfathered dealers were no less efficient than the exclusive ones, nor was there any difference in promotional support. Nor was there any evidence of existence of any substantial variation in the level of service provided by exclusive and grandfathered dealers to the laboratories.

The record amply supports the District Court's conclusion that Dentsply's alleged justification was pretextual and did not excuse its exclusionary practices.

Notes

1. *Raising barriers to entry.* High prices invite entry. Therefore, a firm that exercises market power can expect that over time its market power will erode as firms enter the market. In the absence of barriers to entry, the profit-maximizing strategy is to exercise power, take the money and run. However, if a firm with market power can raise barriers to entry, it can have its cake and eat it too. The firm can exercise its power by raising price yet eliminate or deter entry and maintain long-run power by preventing its erosion. That is the sort of conduct at issue in *Dentsply*.

Why does it work? Put yourself in the position of a firm that wishes to enter against the dental manufacturer. Given Dealer Criterion 6, how are you going to get your product to the laboratories? You could sell to them directly, as did Dentsply's fringe competitors, but the fact that the dominant pattern of distribution consisted of sales to the laboratories through dealers strongly indicates that that pattern was more efficient than direct sales; and the record more than amply supported that inference. By foreclosing through the exclusive contracts the possibility that competitors could sell to dealers in the industry, Dentspy forced them to use a more costly method of distribution, direct dealing with laboratories, strongly disfavored by the laboratories, their customers. The imposition of costs on rivals fits any definition of barrier to entry or, as expressed by the term of art, predatory behavior.

Of course, an entrant could try to pick off dealers, but as *Dentsply* indicates, in an industry that is not dynamic, that strategy can fail miserably. To understand the degree of foreclosure, put yourself in the position of a dealer. What incentive would you have to break free of the extant, well-entrenched pattern of distribution? On the one hand, the high side would be attractive. If laboratories truly wished to buy alternative manufacturers' products, numerous sales could be had. On the other hand, the down side was steep. If the gamble did not work, there would be little business for the maverick dealer without Dentsply's. Therefore, why go it alone? The record suggests that collectively the dealers would have been better off had the distribution system been broken, but why should any one of them embark down the gangplank first?

The only alternative mode of entry, therefore, would have been for a firm to enter the marketplace with its own dealers in tow, or, in other words, by vertically integrating two stages of production. However, that strategy would have been problematic in a number of ways. First, entry at more than one stage of production increases the scale of entry. This strategy increases the capital at risk and often creates delay, which in turn may create additional risk because time is money and like in war, one often succeeds through a quick, surprise attack. Second, and probably more important, being forced to enter at more than one stage of production probably produces diseconomies. If the vertical integration of manufacturing and dealing were efficient, one would have expected to see that pattern of distribution already dominant in the marketplace. The fact that it wasn't is evidence that such vertical integration is less efficient than the separation of the two functions.

Here too the record amply supported this inference. Among other things, the court correctly analogized Dentsply's competitor's situation to that of the bow-tie manufacturer that has been foreclosed by exclusive contracts between a dominant competitor and an area's department stores, at which bow ties must be sold. If the bow-tie manufacturer vertically integrated forward and entered with its own department store, it would be at a substantial cost disadvantage unless that store could efficiently sell the numerous other products sold in a department store. Analogously, a competitor of Dentsply could enter with its own dealers but could compete effectively only if those dealers successfully sold the other products offered by dealers with whom Dentsply had exclusive contracts. Therefore, in this regard as well, Dentspy's use of Dealer Criterion 6 imposed costs on its actual or potential rivals, thereby deterring entry and maintaining long-run market share.

2. *Means of entry*. Entry occurs in a number of different ways. The term itself can, but need not, imply that new firms come into a market. Instead, it applies simply to any expansion in capacity. In response to prices above cost, firms already in the market can expand their production. Similarly, firms producing similar goods or services can alter their production processes slightly to compete against the firm or firms that have increased price above cost. A bottler of one kind of soft-drink, let us suppose, might be able to switch from bottling that kind to another because the production processes are similar. This so-called "substitution in production" is the mirror image of consumers' switching their purchases in response to higher prices, so-called "substitution in consumption." In both cases the speed and ease by which such changes can occur are important determinants of the degree to which market power can be exercised.

3. *Chicago–School and beyond*. Cases and commentary regarding a firm's alleged erection of a barrier to entry to maintain or enhance market

power, or exclusionary conduct to attain it, must be read against beliefs regarding the nature and efficiency of markets. As indicated in our discussion of market definition, Chicago–School economics holds that market power is rarely long-lasting because the self-correcting feature of markets will break it down. Given the risk of error and the potential capture of political institutions by market participants seeking protection from the gales of competition, Chicago–School theorists argue that it is better not to intervene into markets, and that courts should be reluctant to find "honestly industrial" conduct to be exclusionary and violate the antitrust laws. At the height of the Chicago–School's influence, in sweeping language the Supreme Court ruled that courts should rarely infer that firms would rationally forego short-term revenues or profits to attain, maintain or enhance long-run market share because such a strategy can rarely succeed. "Given" that such conduct can rarely succeed, and because firms act rationally, absent unambiguous evidence excluding a competitive effect, courts should grant defendants summary judgment because they must infer that challenged conduct cannot have the purpose and effect of attaining, maintaining or enhancing long-run market share. Instead, the conduct "must" provide consumer benefit, i.e., be efficient. *See* Matsushita Electric Industrial Co. v. Zenith Radio Corp., 475 U.S. 574 (1986) ("if the factual context renders respondents' claim implausible—if the claim is one that simply makes no economic sense—respondents must come forward with more persuasive evidence to support their claim than would otherwise be necessary"). Plaintiffs must prove that defendant's conduct makes "no economic sense" except to achieve, maintain or enhance market power. *Id.* at 587.

However, now that we're all "post-Chicago," the tides have changed. Numerous scholars have written to refute the claim that firms rarely or never have an incentive or capability to engage in conduct to attain, maintain or enhance long-run market share. *See, e.g.,* Thomas G. Krattenmaker & Steven C. Salop, *Anticompetitive Exclusion: Raising Rivals' Costs to Achieve Power Over Price*, 96 YALE L.J. 209 (1986); Thomas G. Krattenmaker et al., *Monopoly Power and Market Power in Antitrust Law*, 76 GEO. L.J. 241 (1987); Steven C. Salop & David T. Scheffman, *Cost–Raising Strategies*, 36 J. INDUS. ECON. 19 (1987). These scholars have shown, for example, that vertical foreclosure can work under certain conditions when rivals cannot substitute among inputs without incurring additional costs and barriers to entry exist in the input market. *See, e.g.,* Janusz A. Ordover et al., *Equilibrium Vertical Foreclosure*, 80 AM. ECON. REV. 127 (1990); Oliver Hart & Jean Tirole, *Vertical Mergers and Market Foreclosure*, BROOKINGS PAPERS ON ECONOMIC ACTIVITY: MICROECONOMICS 205–76 (1990); Michael H. Riordan & Steven C. Salop, *Evaluating Vertical Mergers: A Post–Chicago Approach*, 63 ANTITRUST L.J. 513 (1995). Following in the path of this scholarship, courts have been more willing to reject Chicago–School assumptions concerning the nature and efficiency of markets.

In this regard, *Kodak* seemed to have been a watershed case. As discussed previously, in *Kodak* the Supreme Court accepted the economics of imperfect markets in finding plausible plaintiff's claim that the presence of information problems and switching costs—coupled with the ability to price discriminate between sophisticated and unsophisticated buyers—could allow defendant to preclude entry in an aftermarket—the servicing and supply of parts for its copying and micrographic equipment—even if that meant fewer equipment sales. Kodak had asserted "that there is no need to examine the facts when the issue is market power in the aftermarkets. A legal presumption against a finding of market power is warranted in this situation, according to Kodak, because the existence of market power in the service and parts markets absent power in the equipment market 'simply makes no economic sense,' and the absence of a legal presumption would deter procompetitive behavior. *Matsushita*, 475 U.S. at 587; *id.*, at 594–595." *Eastman Kodak Co.*, 504 U.S. at 467. Rejecting that assertion, the Court stated:

> The Court's requirement in *Matsushita* that the plaintiffs' claims make economic sense did not introduce a special burden on plaintiffs facing summary judgment in antitrust cases. The Court did not hold that if the moving party [—the defendant—] enunciates *any* economic theory supporting its behavior, regardless of its accuracy in reflecting the actual market, it is entitled to summary judgment. *Matsushita* demands only that the nonmoving party's inferences be reasonable in order to reach the jury, a requirement that was not invented, but merely articulated, in that decision. If the plaintiff's theory is economically senseless, no reasonable jury could find in its favor, and summary judgment should be granted.

Id. at 468–69.

The point is not that in *Kodak* the Supreme Court necessarily jettisoned *Matsushita's* "no economic sense" criterion for the question whether conduct is exclusionary. The Court may have retained the "no economic sense" criterion, *see* Verizon Communications Inc. v. Law Offices of Curtis V. Trinko, LLP, 540 U.S. 398, 408–09 (2004); *see also* Gregory J. Werden, *The "No Economic Sense" Test for Exclusionary Conduct*, 31 J. CORP. L. 293 (2006), but that the "economics" in the "no economic sense" changed to incorporate a "post-Chicago" version. It now makes "sense" to hold that markets are not inexorably self-correcting, as the Chicago–School would have us believe, and that firms might rationally forego short-run revenues or profits to maintain long-run market share by preventing erosion of market power through conduct that forecloses competition.*

Perhaps. A few terms ago, in Pacific Bell Telephone Co. v. Linkline Communications, Inc., 555 U.S. 438 (2009), the Supreme Court rejected a "price squeeze" claim asserted against defendant AT&T, a vertically inte-

---

* For a discussion of the importance of *Kodak*, see Thomas L. Greaney, *Chicago's Procrustean Bed* at 867–68; *see also, e.g.*, Steven C. Salop, *The First Principles Approach to Antitrust, Kodak, and Antitrust at the Millennium*, 68 ANTITRUST L.J. 187 (2000); Robert H. Lande, *Chicago Takes It on the Chin: Imperfect Information Could Play a Crucial Role in the Post–Kodak World*, 62 ANTITRUST L.J. 193 (1993). For a very critical view of *Kodak*, see Herbert Hovenkamp, *Post–Chicago Antitrust: A Review and Critique*, 2001 COLUM. BUS. L. REV. 257, 283–99.

grated firm that sold digital subscriber line service (DSL) at wholesale to internet service providers (ISPs), which competed against AT&T in offering retail DSL-based internet service. Plaintiffs claimed that AT&T charged such a high price at wholesale for DSL service, and such a low price on its own retail DSL-based service, that retail competitors like plaintiff were "squeezed" and could not compete. The Court rejected the claim because, based on a prior decision, *Verizon Communications Inc.*, 540 U.S. 398, AT&T had no antitrust duty to deal with plaintiff at wholesale, and plaintiff had not established predatory pricing at retail. The Court rejected the claim that the price squeeze might raise a barrier to entry because plaintiff had not identified such an effect, and the Court found irrelevant an assertion that even AT&T could not profit under the pricing scheme it imposed on plaintiff.

The Court's dissection of the alleged price-squeeze scheme into two parts, one at wholesale and one at retail, and its refusal to consider the entire package as a whole might evidence increased skepticism of claims that firms can profit over the long term from strategic pricing at different vertical levels of production—or it might indicate the current Court's (post-post-Chicago?) preference not to do anything about it. Pointing in that direction also is both language in *Trinko* heaping broad praise on monopolists who succeed by virtue of innovation, and concerns expressed in both *Trinko* and *Linkline* about the dangers of "false positives" in finding antitrust violations. *See, e.g.*, Andrew I. Gavil, *Exclusionary Distribution Strategies by Dominant Firms: Striking a Better Balance*, 72 ANTITRUST L.J. 3, 44–51 (2004) (showing how in upholding a motion to dismiss, the Court in *Trinko*, without a factual record, fictively valorized Verizon as the creator of state-of-the-art infrastructure deserving of protection against an interloping parasite like plaintiff that tried to free ride on Verizon's hard-won effort); Eleanor M. Fox, *Is There Life in* Aspen *After* Trinko? *The Silent Revolution of Section 2 of the Sherman Act*, 73 ANTITRUST L.J. 153 (2005) (showing how *Trinko* reversed the presumptions established by prior law, including *Kodak*, and thereby restored the premise that markets are self-correcting and that risks of judicial intervention outweigh risks of judicial forbearance).

The Supreme Court also recently refused to infer that a single-firm's overbuying was predatory because it adopted the view that a single-firm's long-run recoupment of short-run loses through such predation is generally implausible. *See* Weyerhaeuser Co. v. Ross–Simmons Hardwood Lumber Co., 549 U.S. 312 (2007). In doing so, it extended the view expressed in Brooke Group Ltd. v. Brown & Williamson Tobacco Corp., 509 U.S. 209 (1993), that in an oligopoly market predatory pricing was unlikely to explain price discounting because a firm could rarely use predatory pricing as a means to enforce oligopoly pricing and recoup short-run loses from a return to the higher oligopoly prices. In extending this prior ruling, the Court in *Ross–Simmons* completely ignored the fact that recoupment from oligopoly pricing is much harder than from single-firm, monopoly pricing.

In short, these more recent cases might indicate that the Court is stepping away from using post-Chicago models that purport to show how long-run maintenance of market power is possible. Narrower interpretations of these recent rulings are possible, *see, e.g.*, Steven C. Salop, *Refusals to Deal and Price Squeezes by an Unregulated, Vertically Integrated Monopolist*, 76 ANTITRUST L.J. 709 (2010), but it is unclear how broadly these pronouncements were meant to sweep. Stay tuned.

4. *Modes of foreclosing competition.* As Dentsply indicates, the question whether a firm's conduct forecloses competition to attain, maintain or enhance market power is a fact-sensitive inquiry into the specifics of industry practices. The defendant will almost always raise *Kartell* in its defense, arguing that it has the right to deal on any terms of its choosing. When vertical relationships are involved, it will also claim, as described for example in Baker, *Vertical Restraints*, that vertical arrangements in the health care sector are efficient because they reduce transactions costs, take advantage of economies of scope, eliminate externalities, or counter providers' monopoly power (usually described as local power discussed in the section on market definition above). *See generally* HAAS-WILSON, MANAGED CARE AND MONOPOLY POWER, ch. 7. However, once market power and a significant degree of foreclosure and an effect on competition are shown, as *Dentsply* illustrates, the defendant must prove a business justification for its conduct. In the interest of space, we cannot canvass all the means by which a firm can foreclose competition, but can provide examples which illustrate relevant principles.

In reading the examples, be careful to distinguish vertical from horizontal conduct and remember that, as Dentsply indicates, the antitrust problems raised by vertical conduct are the horizontal effects at whatever levels of production are relevant. The exclusivity provisions Dentsply imposed on dealers violated section 2, not because they reduced competition among dealers, but because they foreclosed competing denture manufacturers from using dealers to distribute their products. Most-favored-nations provisions, discussed below, are more complicated because they might reduce competition at two levels of production. We will complicate this discussion even more below in our notes following the *Rome* case because we will see other ways that vertical conduct can sometimes affect competition at multiple stages of production. By contrast, other types of predatory conduct, like the abuse of governmental process described below, are directly aimed at horizontal competitors and do not involve, and their potential effects do not depend on, any vertical relationships.

Before proceeding into different types of conduct, we note that it has been asserted that the different doctrinal categories we discuss, often accorded disparate treatment, engender much confusion, something we address to some degree below here and much more fully in the context of the *Rome* case. It is then claimed that all the doctrinal categories can or should be unified under a single test. Many such unifying tests defining monopolization have been proposed, as conduct that: (1) raises rivals' costs, *see, e.g.*, Krattenmaker & Salop, *Anticompetitive Exclusion: Raising Rivals'*

Costs to Achieve Power Over Price; Baker, *Vertical Restraints* at 162–63; (2) makes "no economic sense," as we just discussed above, *see, e.g.*, Einer Elhauge, *Defining Better Monopolization Standards*, 56 STAN. L. REV. 253 (2003); Werden, *The "No Economic Sense" Test for Exclusionary Conduct*; A. Douglas Melamed, *Exclusive Dealing Agreements and Other Exclusionary Conduct—Are There Unifying Principles?*, 73 ANTITRUST L.J. 375 (2006); (3) sacrifices short-term profit, *see, e.g.*, the discussion in Gregory J. Werden, *Identifying Exclusionary Conduct Under Section 2: The "No Economic Sense" Test*, 73 ANTITRUST L.J. 413, 422–23 (2006); (4) enhances short-run welfare, *see, e.g.*, Steven C. Salop, *Exclusionary Conduct, Effect on Consumers, and the Flawed Profit–Sacrifice Standard*, 73 ANTITRUST L.J. 311, 329–33 (2006), or (5) enhances long-run welfare, *see, e.g.*, Steven C. Salop & R. Craig Romaine, *Preserving Monopoly Economic Analysis, Legal Standards, and* Microsoft, 7 GEO. MASON L. REV. 617, 650–53, 659–65 (1999); Herbert Hovenkamp, *Exclusion and the Sherman Act*, 72 U. CHI. L. REV. 147 (2005). *But see* Mark S. Popofsky, *Defining Exclusionary Conduct: Section 2, The Rule of Reason, and the Unifying Principle Underlying Antitrust Rules*, 73 ANTITRUST L.J. 435 (2006); Mark S. Popofsky, *Section 2, Safe Harbors, and the Rule of Reason*, 15 GEO. MASON L. REV. 1265 (2008) (arguing for conduct-specific tests developed under the principle of the rule of reason).

This subject is remarkably complicated involving questions concerning the workability of different doctrinal categories; decision makers' ability to conduct, and the cost of conducting, relevant inquiries; predictability for purposes of business planning and deterrence; the risk of error; and presumptions regarding which type of error can cause greater harm. We cannot do justice to these questions here. Therefore, for our purposes we will be agnostic whether one unifying test can be applied, and we proceed under the assumption that one size does not fit all, that any one test can be both under and overinclusive—e.g., predatory pricing does not raise rivals' costs but certainly involves sacrificing short-term profits. *See generally* 3 Phillip E. Areeda et al., ANTITRUST LAW: AN ANALYSIS OF ANTITRUST PRINCIPLES AND THEIR APPLICATION & 651b2–b6 (3d ed., 2008). We will consider relevant whether conduct imposes costs on rivals, whether a claim makes economic sense, and whether a firm sacrifices short-run revenues or profits to gain long-term market share; and, at least until we discuss *Rome* below, we'll take the doctrinal categories as they come.

It should also be noted that we present the traditional analysis of inquiring into market power first and then analyzing foreclosure and competitive effect, i.e., the analytical structure we present requires that plaintiff first show some degree of power and effect to force defendant to justify, a burden-shifting approach, *see, e.g.*, 3 Phillip E. Areeda et al., ANTITRUST LAW: AN ANALYSIS OF ANTITRUST PRINCIPLES AND THEIR APPLICATION ¶¶ 651e3, 651j-k (3d ed., 2008). As just stated, we remain agnostic whether courts should undertake to assess welfare effects if defendant shows that its conduct makes economic sense or if plaintiff shows that defendant has sacrificed short-term revenue or profit. Reasonable arguments have been made that other tests, like the "no-economic-sense" or sacrifice tests, *see*, *e.g.*, Melamed, *Exclusive Dealing Agreements and Other Exclusionary Conduct—Are There Unifying Principles?*, at 406–10, or reliance on showings of anticompetitive effects, *see, e.g.*, Steven C. Salop, *The First Principles Approach to Antitrust, Kodak, and Antitrust at the Millennium*, 68 ANTITRUST L.J. 187 (2000); Krattenmaker et al., *Monopoly Power and Market Power in Antitrust Law* at 254–60, can be used to render unnecessary the (burdensome) necessity of litigating market power. We note that like the per-se/rule of reason inquiry, applied to horizontal conduct and discussed with reference to *Maricopa* and *Rome* below, the analysis of foreclosure need not be cabined into discrete, fixed stages with dichotomous answers—first step: there "is" or "isn't" market power; second step, there "is" or "isn't" justification; third step, there "is" or "isn't" a less restrictive alternative; etc.—but can have fluidity. With regard to some types of conduct, showings of greater or lesser degrees of power can call forth different allocations, and greater or lesser burdens of, coming forward or proof of justification. *See, e.g.*, 3 Phillip E. Areeda et al., ANTITRUST LAW: AN ANALYSIS OF ANTITRUST PRINCIPLES AND THEIR APPLICATION ¶¶ 651e3, at 122 (3d ed., 2008) ("The rule of reason applied to cases involving unilateral conduct need not differ significantly from that applied to multilateral conduct."). The questions concerning the order and allocations of burdens of coming forward and burdens of proof in turn relate to the complicated issues of institutional competence, predictability, risk of error and presumptions we cannot fully address here.

a. *Exclusive dealing*. As in *Dentsply*, when a single firm with market power (or one trying to attain market power) imposes exclusivity on firms operating at a different stage of production, this behavior can significantly foreclose competition. Again, those words, "single firm," are crucial. Here we address the situation like that in *Dentsply*, in which for its own benefit a firm with power at one vertical level, like Dentsply, imposes an exclusivity provision on a firm or firms at another level, like Dentsply's distributors—even if the manufacturer shares that benefit with the distributors in some way. In the notes following *Rome* below we discuss how vertical conduct can facilitate, and even hide, horizontal anticompetitive activity, e.g., exclusivity provisions are included at the behest of the distributors for their benefit to protect their market power by foreclosing their competitors. Which situation exists is a matter of proof.

The degree of foreclosure and competitive effects are fact-sensitive issues. If the time period of exclusive dealing is short, entrants are not for long denied access to the firms operating at a different stage of production with which they must deal, and the foreclosure is less significant. What makes *Dentsply* interesting is, among other things, the fact that formally the exclusive dealing provisions' terms were only thirty days but as a practical matter, they were forever renewing. The extent to which contracts are on different cycles, and whether switching costs exist, are likewise important to the temporal dimension of foreclosure. Analogously, if the industry is dynamic, then innovation in alternative modes of distribution should suffice to defeat even long-term exclusivity provisions. Additionally, as the proportion of the industry involved on either side of the exclusive dealing arrangement diminishes—i.e., as the degree of power, on the one side, or the degree of foreclosure, on the other, goes down—so does the exclusionary effect. If Dentsply's market share had been lower, the risk to a dealer of carrying an alternative manufacturer's product would have likewise been diminished. In such a circumstance, fewer dealers would likely have executed such contracts, and they would have been available to deal with other manufacturers.

This effect would have been magnified if entry into the dealership level of the industry had been easy. The exclusionary effect stems from the degree to which one stage of production is locked up in tandem with another. Further, as the input foreclosed to competitors diminishes or increases in importance in the relevant production process, the foreclosure wreaks lesser or greater effect on rivals' costs. It is one thing for an input to constitute 10% of costs, and quite another for it to be 90%. Finally, the competitive effects diminish as efficiencies of scale become less important. If an extant competitor or an entrant can match the cost of the incumbent even if it operates at a lower output than it would absent the preclusion—if it can achieve what is called "minimum viable scale"—then it can still be price and quality competitive at that lower output. The effect is a question of degree.

When analyzing exclusion, one must be careful to define the market by reference to the competitive problem at issue. Contrast the facts in *Dentsply* with those in Jefferson Parish Hospital District No. 2 v. Hyde, 466 U.S. 2 (1984), which we consider more fully below. In that case the defendant had executed an exclusive contract with an anesthesiology group. If the competitive concern is the exclusion of competing anesthesiologists from that hospital due to the exclusive contract—one view of the case, as we shall see—then the market for sale of those services is quite broad, perhaps even national. By contrast, if the concern in the case is that the exclusivity provision denies patients a choice among anesthesiologists—another view of the case—then the market for those purchases is, as we have seen above, fairly local. Necessarily, when addressing the competitive effects of vertical conduct, one must examine market structure, power and barriers at the relevant levels of production involved. *See, e.g.*, 11 HERBERT HOVENKAMP, ANTITRUST LAW: AN ANALYSIS OF ANTITRUST PRINCIPLES AND THEIR APPLICATION ¶ 1821b-c (2d ed., 2005); *see generally id.* ¶ 1802d.

In light of these factors, *Dentsply* was an easy case. Given the factual proof of the degree of power and competitive effects, the defendant's conduct in arranging its mode of distribution clearly imposed very substantial costs on rivals, and there was no showing that exclusivity attained any efficiencies. Further, although Dentsply's imposition of the exclusivity arrangements did not involve its sacrifice of any revenues, it is hard to imagine any reason for its conduct other than imposition of costs on rivals to attain long-run maintenance of market share. The court of appeals was clearly right in holding that the district court engaged in unwarranted speculation in its theory that entry was still possible.

Other cases may be harder if the exclusive dealing arrangements arguably attain efficiencies, i.e., enhance the value of defendant's product. For example, suppose that Dentsply or its dealers engaged in some activity that added value to the product and that such value could not captured by the sale of Dentsply's product alone. Suppose, for example, that Dentsply promoted the use of dentures generally over substitutes like tooth implants and crowns—activity that would expand the sale of all dentures, whether made by Dentsply or not. This externality problem could be solved by exclusivity provisions because those provisions would enable Dentsply to capture the full benefit of the promotion. *See, e.g.,* Beltone Electronics Corp., 100 F.T.C. 68 (1982) (hearing aid manufacturer invested in training dealers and identifying potential customers, expenses that could inure to competing manufacturers absent exclusivity). More recent health-law cases accepting efficiency justifications for exclusivity provisions include: Imaging Center, Inc. v. Western Maryland Health Systems, Inc., 158 Fed. Appx. 413 (4th Cir. 2005) (assured supply, quality and cost control and transactions costs); Digene Corp. v. Third Wave Techs., Inc., 536 F. Supp.2d 996 (W.D. Wis. 2008) (quality control), *aff'd,* 323 Fed.Appx. 902 (Fed. Cir. 2009).

In such a case, the exclusivity provisions would make "economic sense" but could likewise impose costs on Dentsply's competitors by foreclosing dealers from them, and the exclusivity would not involve Dentsply's sacrifice of revenue or profit because the provisions would in fact expand its output. Here the choice among the tests delineated above would matter. A court or enforcer could find that the conduct does not violate Section 2 either because the exclusivity makes "economic sense" or does not involve the sacrifice of revenues or profit. The rationale for such a finding would be that consumers benefit from the creation of such efficiencies; that this conduct is the type that we would want to encourage; and that long-term harm from foreclosure is difficult to measure, perhaps even speculative, and the risk of error is therefore great. The market's dynamism is therefore a better means than governmental intervention to break down such exclusion.

Alternatively, if the facts warrant, a court or enforcer could apply a welfare test and find that the conduct did not enhance either or both short-run and long-run welfare. The rationale for such a finding would be that the antitrust laws are supposed to protect against consumer harm; policing only against conduct that makes no economic sense or involves the sacrifice of revenue or profit fails to accomplish that goal; and that achievement of that welfare requires that decision makers assess the overall effect on consumers. As indicated above, sorting out these arguments is very complicated and turns on issues of institutional competence, predictability, risk of error and presumptions. *See, e.g.,* Melamed, *Exclusive Dealing Agreements and Other Exclusionary Conduct—Are There Unifying Principles?. See generally* Herbert Hovenkamp, *Post–Chicago Antitrust: A Review and Critique,* 2001 COLUM. BUS. L. REV. 257.

b. *Most-favored-nations provisions (MFNs).* An MFN is a contractual term by which one side of the contract promises that it will not offer a better deal to a competitor of the other party without offering it likewise to that party, who is the "most favored nation." In the health care sector, insurance contracts with providers have sometimes stipulated that the providers cannot offer a steeper discount to other insurers, and these clauses have spawned a number of cases. MFNs, which are vertical arrangements, clearly can increase rivals' costs because they ensure that a rival or entrant cannot obtain an input cost lower than that obtained by the contracting insurer. They can thereby raise a barrier to entry: what incentive would a provider have to contract with, and offer a steeper discount to, another insurer when it would have to offer that same discount to the insurer with which it has contracted? On the benefit side of the ledger, perhaps the clauses can aid relatively small, unsophisticated buyers to free ride on larger competitors' search costs, and they might be mechanisms in long-term contracts to deal with unforeseeable market fluctuations. However, neither efficiency justification has been proved in the health care sector. *See generally* Jonathan B. Baker, *Vertical Restraints with Horizontal Consequences: Competitive Effects of "Most–Favored–Customer" Clauses*, 64 ANTITRUST L.J. 517 (1996).*

Nonetheless, the case law has been mixed. In Ocean State Physicians Health Plan, Inc. v. Blue Cross & Blue Shield of Rhode Island, 883 F.2d 1101 (1st Cir. 1989), *cert. den.*, 494 U.S. 1027 (1990), the court "agree[d] with the district court that such a policy of insisting on a supplier's lowest price—assuming that the price is not 'predatory' or below the supplier's incremental cost—tends to further competition on the merits and, as a matter of law, is not exclusionary." *Id.* at 1110. The court also found that such a conclusion is "compelled by this court's holding in *Kartell v. Blue Shield of Massachusetts* that a health insurer's unilateral decisions about the prices it will pay providers do not violate the Sherman Act—unless the prices are 'predatory' or below incremental cost—even if the insurer is assumed to have monopoly power in the relevant market." *Id.* at 1110–11; *see also, e.g.*, Blue Cross & Blue Shield United of Wisconsin v. Marshfield Clinic, 65 F.3d 1406, 1415 (7th Cir. 1995) (Posner, C.J.), *cert. den.*, 516 U.S. 1184 (1996) (assuming without analysis that MFNs would cause lower prices to benefit of consumers).

Commentators have been uniformly critical of the courts' failures in such cases to analyze potential foreclosure carefully, *see, e.g.*, Hammer & Sage, *Monopsony as an Agency and Regulatory Problem in Health Care* at 960–62; HAAS-WILSON, MANAGED CARE AND MONOPOLY POWER at 180–83; Baker, *Vertical Restraints with Horizontal Consequences*, something done in other cases like United States v. Delta Dental of Rhode Island, 943 F. Supp. 172 (D.R.I. 1996). There, the defendant had included MFNs in all its contracts

---

* MFNs can also facilitate horizontal price fixing by reducing the incentive of a cartel member to cheat by offering a discount to a buyer, because the cheater cannot limit that discount to that buyer. Correspondingly, when the clauses are widespread a buyer has less incentive to bargain hard because it cannot gain an advantage over other buyers. We defer our discussion of price fixing and other horizontal collaboration until *Maricopa* in the next section; and we discuss how vertical conduct can facilitate horizontal collaboration in the notes following *Rome*.

with dentists in its network. The court, in approving a magistrate's rejection of defendant's motion to dismiss, ruled that neither *Kartell* nor *Ocean State* established a per se rule of legality—in this regard, the court's reading of those cases was spurious—and held that courts must assess the MFNs' effects, alleged to be: "(1) exclusion of potential competitors from the dental insurance market; (2) prevention of existing competitors from expanding their insurance programs; and (3) substantial increase in the costs of dental insurance and services to all Rhode Island consumers." *Id.* at 179. The *Delta Dental* court surely got it right because when market power and degree of foreclosure are high, the clauses create barriers to entry, and defendant should be forced to justify.

The preclusive effects of MFNs are amply illustration by the facts alleged in a recent filing by the Department of Justice and the State of Michigan in United States v. Blue Cross Blue Shield of Michigan, 2011 WL 3566486 (E.D. Mich. 2011). Defendant Blue Cross Blue Shield of Michigan (BCBS) is the dominant insurer in Michigan, writing policies that cover more than 60% of the commercially insured population. In 70 of its 131 contracts with hospitals it utilizes two types of MFNs. The first type, known as an "MFN-plus" clause, executed with major hospitals and health systems covering 45% of Michigan's tertiary care beds, requires that hospitals charge more than they charge BCBS, sometimes as much as 40% more. The second type, known as "Equal-to MFNs," executed with more than 40 small community hospitals, requires the hospitals to deal with other insurers on terms equal to BCBS, which pays a higher rate to these hospitals. Denying a motion to dismiss, the district court held that these allegations state a cause of action under section 1 because the clauses have substantial exclusionary effects.

What sort of justification could exist for clauses that impose such high costs on rivals? Isn't it one thing for a firm to obtain equal treatment but another to impose much higher costs on rivals for the same input? At some point, aren't these clauses effectively just exclusive dealing arrangements? If so, how could they be justified? However, what do you make of the fact that BCBS is the insurer of last resort in Michigan, meaning that the state obligates it to ensure worse risks than its competitors? The court rejected claims that BCBS is a quasi-public entity or is acting under the state action exemption we discuss immediately below.

For the flip-side of BCBS of Michigan, see United States v. Regional Health Care System ("RHCS"), in which a hospital with a 90% market share of inpatient surgery and a 65% share of outpatient surgery in Wichita Falls, Texas, entered into a consent decree with the United States over its contracts with insurers requiring them to pay 13 to 27% more for inpatient services obtained from RHCS if they contracted with other hospitals. The complaint alleged that these agreements excluded competing insurers from the market and thereby reduced price and quality competition among insurers. *See* United States v. United Regional Health Care System, 2011 WL 846762 (N.D. Tex. 2011) (www.justice.gov/atr/cases/unitedregional.html).

c. *Tying.* Again we can reference the facts in *Jefferson Parish Hospital District No. 2*, 466 U.S. 2, even though we postpone full consideration of the case until later. Suppose that a hospital has market power over inpatient hospital services in a well-defined market (in the actual case, at least according to the Court, defendant did not have such power). Suppose that the hospital executes an exclusive contract with an anesthesiology group. Above we have analyzed such a situation under section 2 as an exclusive dealing arrangement, and we have examined whether the hospital has maintained or enhanced its market power over inpatient services by foreclosing competing hospitals from obtaining a necessary input, anesthesiological services, or by forcing them to obtain it at higher cost. However, this vertical arrangement can also be characterized as a tying arrangement in which the hospital has required that the "tied" product—anesthesiological services—be purchased along with the "tying" product over which the seller has power—inpatient hospital services. Because this situation involves multilateral conduct—it takes two to contract—the exclusive dealing arrangement can also be challenged under as a tying agreement under section 1. Although we argue below that this characterization elevates form over substance, current law does not adopt this position and tying arrangements can still be challenged either under sections 1 or 2. Given this characterization issue, we delay our discussion of tying until after the *Rome* case below.

d. *Invoking governmental processes.* An incumbent firm or firms can try to prevent entry by enlisting the help of government. The most prominent example in health care antitrust is that by filing frivolous objections, submitting false information or engaging in delaying tactics, market incumbents can violate section 2 by trying to take advantage of certificate-of-need regulation to preclude entry. *See, e.g.*, St. Joseph's Hospital, Inc. v. Hospital Corporation of America, 795 F.2d 948 (11th Cir. 1986); Potters Medical Center v. City Hospital Association, 800 F.2d 568 (6th Cir. 1986). A more recent case involves the denial of defendant Glaxo's motion for summary judgment on claims that it tried to delay the entry of generic competition by filing baseless petitions before the FDA. *See* In re Flonase Antitrust Litigation, 795 F. Supp.2d 300 (2011). Other classic instances of potential section 2 violations in other contexts include bad faith enforcement of invalid patents, *see, e.g.*, Handgards, Inc. v. Ethicon, Inc., 601 F.2d 986 (9th Cir. 1979), *cert. den.*, 444 U.S. 1025 (1980); sham litigation, *see, e.g.*, Professional Real Estate Investors, Inc. v. Columbia Pictures Industries, Inc., 508 U.S. 49 (1993); and assertion of patents obtained by fraud against the patent office. *See, e.g.*, Walker Process Equipment, Inc. v. Food Machinery & Chemical Corp., 382 U.S. 172 (1965). On the other hand, the right to petition government is carefully protected and a whole area of antitrust law—the so-called "Noerr–Pennington doctrine"—exists to balance the danger of misuse of government processes to maintain market power against the legitimate right under the First Amendment, and the need, to utilize legal processes. *See* Eastern Railroad Presidents Conference v. Noerr Motor Freight, Inc., 365 U.S. 127 (1961); United Mine Workers of America v. Pennington, 381 U.S. 657 (1965). The basic test is whether the defendant has engaged in "sham petitioning" by asserting "objectively baseless" claims. *See, e.g.,* California Motor Transport Co. v. Trucking Unlimited, 404 U.S. 508 (1972); *Professional Real Estate Investors, Inc.,* 508 U.S. 49.

e.   State action. Some defendants in antitrust actions try to cloak themselves in state authority in order to fall within the state action exemption first established by the Supreme Court in Parker v. Brown, 317 U.S. 341 (1943), a holding that Congress did not intend the federal antitrust laws to cover the acts of sovereign states. This exemption clearly applies to state legislatures but municipalities and private parties sometimes claim that their anticompetitive acts stem from a delegation from the state of authority to displace competition. Municipalities can successfully mount this defense so long as they can show that their actions are consonant with a clearly articulated and affirmatively expressed state policy, *see* Town of Hallie v. City of Eau Claire, 471 U.S. 34, 40 (1985), but private parties, who necessarily possess a conflict of interest, must also show that their actions are actively supervised by the state itself. *See* California Retail Liquor Dealers Ass'n v. Midcal Aluminum, Inc., 445 U.S. 97, 105 (1980).

An FTC enforcement action against the North Carolina State Board of Dental Examiners amply shows why this heightened requirement is necessary. This administrative action, still pending in December 2011, arose from the Dental Board's classification of teeth whitening as the practice of dentistry. Given this interpretation, the Board, authorized by the state to regulate the practice of dentistry, issued cease and desist orders to non-dentist teeth whiteners. Membership of the Board consists of six licensed dentists, one licensed dental hygienist, and one consumer member. The licensed dentists who are members of the Board are elected by the licensed dentists in the state. The dentist-members are entitled to continue to provide for-profit dental services, including teeth whitening.

The FTC complaint charged that the Board, reacting to the competitive threat by non-dentist providers, sought to exclude and did exclude non-dentists from the market for teeth whitening services in North Carolina. The Board sought to dismiss the proceeding on the ground that their conduct constituted state action. The FTC denied this motion. It ruled, first, that the Board is subject to the active supervision requirement, given that it is controlled by elected representatives of the state's dentists and is not politically accountable. This ruling followed from the fact that the active supervision requirement is designed to ensure that private actors pursue state goals, not private ones. The FTC ruled that the active supervision requirement must be applied because the Board effectively represents the collective economic interest of the state's dentists, who are horizontal competitors of non-dentists who perform teeth whitening. The Commission ruled, second, that no active supervision exists in this instance because the state exercises no ultimate control over the challenged anticompetitive conduct. *See* Patrick v. Burget, 486 U.S. 94, 101 (1988). None of the elements evidencing actual control exist: (1) development of an adequate factual record; (2) a written decision on the merits; and (3) a specific assessment—both quantitative and qualitative—of how private action comports with the substantive standards established by the legislature. *See* In re North Carolina State Board of Dental Examiners, 151 F.T.C. 607, 2011 WL 3568990 (2011).

---

3. SPECIAL PROBLEMS RAISED BY HORIZONTAL COLLABORATION

Arizona v. Maricopa County Medical Society

457 U.S. 332 (1982)

■ JUSTICE STEVENS delivered the opinion of the Court.

The question presented is whether Section 1 of the Sherman Act has been violated by agreements among competing physicians setting, by majority vote, the maximum fees that they may claim in full payment for health services provided to policyholders of specified insurance plans. The United States Court of Appeals for the Ninth Circuit held that the question could not be answered without evaluating the actual purpose and effect of the agreements at a full trial. Because the undisputed facts disclose a violation of the statute we granted certiorari and now reverse.

I

In October 1978 the State of Arizona filed a civil complaint against two county medical societies and two "foundations for medical care" that the medical societies had organized. The complaint alleged that the defendants were engaged in illegal price-fixing conspiracies. [T]he State moved for partial summary judgment on the issue of liability. The District Court denied the motion, but entered an order certifying for interlocutory appeal the question "whether the FMC membership agreements, which contain the promise to abide by maximum fee schedules, are illegal per se under section 1 of the Sherman Act."

The Court of Appeals, by a divided vote, affirmed the District Court's order refusing to enter partial summary judgment, but each of the three judges on the panel had a different view of the case. Judge Sneed was persuaded that "the challenged practice is not a per se violation."[4] Judge

---

4. Judge Sneed explained [that] [t]he record did not indicate the actual purpose of the maximum-fee arrangements or their effect on competition in the health care industry. It was not clear whether the assumptions made about typical price restraints could be carried over to that industry. Only recently had this Court applied the antitrust laws to the professions. Moreover, there already were such significant obstacles to pure competition in the industry that a court must compare the prices that obtain under the maximum-fee arrangements with those that would otherwise prevail rather than with those that would prevail under ideal competitive conditions. Furthermore, the Ninth Circuit had not applied [either the Keifer–Stewart or Albrecht decisions] to horizontal agreements that establish maximum prices; some of the economic assumptions underlying the rule against maximum price fixing were not sound.

Kennedy, although concurring, cautioned that he had not found "these reimbursement schedules to be per se proper, [or] that an examination of these practices under the rule of reason at trial will not reveal the proscribed adverse effect on competition, or that this court is foreclosed at some later date, when it has more evidence, from concluding that such schedules do constitute per se violations."[5] Judge Larson dissented, expressing the view that a per se rule should apply and, alternatively, that a rule-of-reason analysis should condemn the arrangement even if a per se approach was not warranted. Id., at 563–569.[6]

Because the ultimate question presented by the certiorari petition is whether a partial summary judgment should have been entered by the District Court, we must assume that the respondents' version of any disputed issue of fact is correct. We therefore first review the relevant undisputed facts and then identify the factual basis for the respondents' contention that their agreements on fee schedules are not unlawful.

II

The Maricopa Foundation for Medical Care is a nonprofit Arizona corporation composed of licensed doctors of medicine, osteopathy, and podiatry engaged in private practice. Approximately 1,750 doctors, representing about 70% of the practitioners in Maricopa County, are members.

The Maricopa Foundation was organized in 1969 for the purpose of promoting fee-for-service medicine and to provide the community with a competitive alternative to existing health insurance plans.[7] The foundation performs three primary activities. It establishes the schedule of maximum fees that participating doctors agree to accept as payment in full for services performed for patients insured under plans approved by the foundation. It reviews the medical necessity and appropriateness of treatment provided by its members to such insured persons. It is authorized to draw checks on insurance company accounts to pay doctors for services

---

5. Judge Kennedy concluded [that] "[t]here does not now appear to be a controlling or definitive analysis of the market impact caused by the arrangements under scrutiny in this case, but trial may reveal that the arrangements are, at least in their essentials, not peculiar to the medical industry and that they should be condemned."

6. Judge Larson stated, in part: "Defendants formulated and dispersed relative value guides and conversion factor lists which together were used to set an upper limit on fees received from third-party payors. It is clear that these activities constituted maximum price-fixing by competitors. Disregarding any 'special industry' facts, this conduct is per se illegal. I find nothing in the nature of either the medical profession or the health care industry that would warrant their exemption from per se rules for price-fixing."

7. Most health insurance plans are of the fee-for-service type. Under the typical insurance plan, the insurer agrees with the insured to reimburse the insured for "usual, customary, and reasonable" medical charges. The third-party insurer, and the insured to the extent of any excess charges, bears the economic risk that the insured will require medical treatment. An alternative to the fee-for-service type of insurance plan is illustrated by health maintenance organizations. Under this form of prepaid health plan, the consumer pays a fixed periodic fee to a functionally integrated group of doctors in exchange for the group's agreement to provide any medical treatment that the subscriber might need. The economic risk is thus borne by the doctors.

performed for covered patients. In performing these functions, the foundation is considered an "insurance administrator" by the Director of the Arizona Department of Insurance. Its participating doctors, however, have no financial interest in the operation of the foundation.

The Pima Foundation for Medical Care, which includes about 400 member doctors,[8] performs similar functions.

At the time this lawsuit was filed, each foundation made use of "relative values" and "conversion factors" in compiling its fee schedule. The fee schedule has been revised periodically. The foundation board of trustees would solicit advice from various medical societies about the need for change in either relative values or conversion factors in their respective specialties. The board would then formulate the new fee schedule and submit it to the vote of the entire membership.[10]

The fee schedules limit the amount that the member doctors may recover for services performed for patients insured under plans approved by the foundations. To obtain this approval the insurers—including self-insured employers as well as insurance companies[11]—agree to pay the doctors' charges up to the scheduled amounts, and in exchange the doctors agree to accept those amounts as payment in full for their services. The doctors are free to charge higher fees to uninsured patients, and they also may charge any patient less than the scheduled maxima. A patient who is insured by a foundation-endorsed plan is guaranteed complete coverage for the full amount of his medical bills only if he is treated by a foundation member. He is free to go to a nonmember physician and is still covered for charges that do not exceed the maximum-fee schedule, but he must pay any excess that the nonmember physician may charge.

The impact of the foundation fee schedules on medical fees and on insurance premiums is a matter of dispute. The State of Arizona contends that the periodic upward revisions of the maximum-fee schedules have the effect of stabilizing and enhancing the level of actual charges by physicians, and that the increasing level of their fees in turn increases insurance premiums. The foundations, on the other hand, argue that the schedules impose a meaningful limit on physicians' charges, and that the advance agreement by the doctors to accept the maxima enables the insurance carriers to limit and to calculate more efficiently the risks they underwrite

---

8.   The record contains divergent figures on the percentage of Pima County doctors that belong to the foundation. A 1975 publication of the foundation reported 80%; a 1978 affidavit by the executive director of the foundation reported 30%.

10.   The parties disagree over whether the increases in the fee schedules are the cause or the result of the increases in the prevailing rate for medical services in the relevant markets. [H]owever 85–95% of physicians bill at or above the maximum reimbursement levels set by the Foundation.

11.   Seven different insurance companies underwrite health insurance plans that have been approved by the Maricopa Foundation, and three companies underwrite the plans approved by the Pima Foundation. The record contains no firm data on the portion of the health care market that is covered by these plans. The State relies upon a 1974 analysis indicating that insurance plans endorsed by the Maricopa Foundation had about 63% of the prepaid health care market, but the respondents contest the accuracy of this analysis.

and therefore serves as an effective cost-containment mechanism that has saved patients and insurers millions of dollars. [W]e must assume that the respondents' view of the genuine issues of fact is correct.

This assumption presents, but does not answer, the question whether the Sherman Act prohibits the competing doctors from adopting, revising, and agreeing to use a maximum-fee schedule in implementation of the insurance plans.

III

The respondents recognize that our decisions establish that price-fixing agreements are unlawful on their face. But they argue that the per se rule does not govern this case because the agreements at issue are horizontal and fix maximum prices, are among members of a profession, are in an industry with which the judiciary has little antitrust experience, and are alleged to have procompetitive justifications. Before we examine each of these arguments, we pause to consider the history and the meaning of the per se rule against price-fixing agreements.

A

Section 1 of the Sherman Act of 1890 literally prohibits every agreement "in restraint of trade."[12] In United States v. Joint Traffic Assn., 171 U.S. 50, we recognized that Congress could not have intended a literal interpretation of the word "every"; since Standard Oil Co. of New Jersey v. United States, 221 U.S. 1, we have analyzed most restraints under the so-called "rule of reason." As its name suggests, the rule of reason requires the factfinder to decide whether under all the circumstances of the case the restrictive practice imposes an unreasonable restraint on competition.[13]

The elaborate inquiry into the reasonableness of a challenged business practice entails significant costs. Litigation of the effect or purpose of a practice often is extensive and complex. Judges often lack the expert understanding of industrial market structures and behavior to determine with any confidence a practice's effect on competition. And the result of the process in any given case may provide little certainty or guidance about the legality of a practice in another context.

---

12. "Every contract, combination in the form of trust or otherwise, or conspiracy, in restraint of trade or commerce among the several States, or with foreign nations, is declared to be illegal...." 15 U.S.C. section 1.

13. Justice Brandeis provided the classic statement of the rule of reason in Chicago Bd. of Trade v. United States, 246 U.S. 231, 238 (1918): "The true test of legality is whether the restraint imposed is such as merely regulates and perhaps thereby promotes competition or whether it is such as may suppress or even destroy competition. To determine that question the court must ordinarily consider the facts peculiar to the business to which the restraint is applied; its condition before and after the restraint was imposed; the nature of the restraint and its effect, actual or probable. The history of the restraint, the evil believed to exist, the reason for adopting the particular remedy, the purpose or end sought to be attained, are all relevant facts. This is not because a good intention will save an otherwise objectionable regulation or the reverse; but because knowledge of intent may help the court to interpret facts and to predict consequences."

The costs of judging business practices under the rule of reason, however, have been reduced by the recognition of per se rules. Once experience with a particular kind of restraint enables the Court to predict with confidence that the rule of reason will condemn it, it has applied a conclusive presumption that the restraint is unreasonable.[15] As in every rule of general application, the match between the presumed and the actual is imperfect. For the sake of business certainty and litigation efficiency, we have tolerated the invalidation of some agreements that a fullblown inquiry might have proved to be reasonable.[16]

Thus "it has often been decided and always assumed that uniform price-fixing by those controlling in any substantial manner a trade or business in interstate commerce is prohibited by the Sherman Law." United States v. Trenton Potteries Co., 273 U.S. 392, 398. "The aim and result of every price-fixing agreement, if effective, is the elimination of one form of competition. The power to fix prices, whether reasonably exercised or not, involves power to control the market and to fix arbitrary and unreasonable prices. Agreements which create such potential power may well be held to be in themselves unreasonable or unlawful restraints, without the necessity of minute inquiry whether a particular price is reasonable or unreasonable as fixed and without placing on the government in enforcing the Sherman Law the burden of ascertaining from day to day whether it has become unreasonable through the mere variation of economic conditions." Id., at 397–398.

Thirteen years later, the Court could report that "for over forty years this Court has consistently and without deviation adhered to the principle that price-fixing agreements are unlawful per se under the Sherman Act and that no showing of so-called competitive abuses or evils which those agreements were designed to eliminate or alleviate may be interposed as a defense." United States v. Socony–Vacuum Oil Co., 310 U.S. 150, 210 (1940). In that case a glut in the spot market for gasoline had prompted the major oil refiners to engage in a concerted effort to purchase and store surplus gasoline in order to maintain stable prices. Absent the agreement, the companies argued, competition was cutthroat and self-defeating. The argument did not carry the day: "Any combination which tampers with price structures is engaged in an unlawful activity. Even though the members of the price-fixing group were in no position to control the

---

15. "Among the practices which the courts have heretofore deemed to be unlawful in and of themselves are price fixing, division of markets, group boycotts, and tying arrangements."

16. Thus, in applying the per se rule to invalidate the restrictive practice in United States v. Topco Associates, Inc., 405 U.S. 5, we stated that "[w]hether or not we would decide this case the same way under the rule of reason used by the District Court is irrelevant to the issue before us." The Court made the same point in Continental T.V., Inc. v. GTE Sylvania Inc., 433 U.S., at 50, n. 16: "Per se rules thus require the Court to make broad generalizations about the social utility of particular commercial practices. The probability that anticompetitive consequences will result from a practice and the severity of those consequences must be balanced against its procompetitive consequences. Cases that do not fit the generalization may arise, but a per se rule reflects the judgment that such cases are not sufficiently common or important to justify the time and expense necessary to identify them."

market, to the extent that they raised, lowered, or stabilized prices they would be directly interfering with the free play of market forces. The Act places all such schemes beyond the pale and protects that vital part of our economy against any degree of interference. Congress has not left with us the determination of whether or not particular price-fixing schemes are wise or unwise, healthy or destructive. It has not permitted the age-old cry of ruinous competition and competitive evils to be a defense to price-fixing conspiracies. It has no more allowed genuine or fancied competitive abuses as a legal justification for such schemes than it has the good intentions of the members of the combination. If such a shift is to be made, it must be done by the Congress. Whatever may be its peculiar problems and characteristics, the Sherman Act, so far as price-fixing agreements are concerned, establishes one uniform rule applicable to all industries alike." Id., at 221–222.

The application of the per se rule to maximum-price-fixing agreements in [Kiefer–Stewart] followed ineluctably from Socony–Vacuum: "For such agreements, no less than those to fix minimum prices, cripple the freedom of traders and thereby restrain their ability to sell in accordance with their own judgment. Over the objection that maximum-price-fixing agreements were not the "economic equivalent" of minimum-price-fixing agreements Kiefer–Stewart was reaffirmed in Albrecht v. Herald Co., 390 U.S. 145 (1968):

"Maximum and minimum price fixing may have different consequences in many situations. But schemes to fix maximum prices, by substituting the perhaps erroneous judgment of a seller for the forces of the competitive market, may severely intrude upon the ability of buyers to compete and survive in that market. Competition, even in a single product, is not cast in a single mold. Maximum prices may be fixed too low for the dealer to furnish services essential to the value which goods have for the consumer or to furnish services and conveniences which consumers desire and for which they are willing to pay. Maximum price fixing may channel distribution through a few large or specifically advantaged dealers who otherwise would be subject to significant nonprice competition. Moreover, if the actual price charged under a maximum price scheme is nearly always the fixed maximum price, which is increasingly likely as the maximum price approaches the actual cost of the dealer, the scheme tends to acquire all the attributes of an arrangement fixing minimum prices." Id., at 152–153.*

B

Our decisions foreclose the argument that the agreements at issue escape per se condemnation because they are horizontal and fix maximum prices. Kiefer–Stewart and Albrecht place horizontal agreements to fix maximum prices on the same legal—even if not economic—footing as

---

* In State Oil Co. v. Khan, 522 U.S. 3 (1997), the Supreme Court expressly overruled *Albrecht* and held that vertical maximum price fixing is no longer a per se violation but is instead subject to the rule of reason.

agreements to fix minimum or uniform prices.[18] In this case the rule is violated by a price restraint that tends to provide the same economic rewards to all practitioners regardless of their skill, their experience, their training, or their willingness to employ innovative and difficult procedures in individual cases. Such a restraint also may discourage entry into the market and may deter experimentation and new developments by individual entrepreneurs. It may be a masquerade for an agreement to fix uniform prices, or it may in the future take on that character.

Nor does the fact that doctors—rather than nonprofessionals—are the parties to the price-fixing agreements support the respondents' position. In Goldfarb v. Virginia State Bar, 421 U.S. 773, 788 (1975), we stated that the "public service aspect, and other features of the professions, may require that a particular practice, which could properly be viewed as a violation of the Sherman Act in another context, be treated differently." The price-fixing agreements in this case, however, are not premised on public service or ethical norms. The respondents do not argue that the quality of the professional service that their members provide is enhanced by the price restraint. The respondents' claim for relief from the per se rule is simply that the doctors' agreement not to charge certain insureds more than a fixed price facilitates the successful marketing of an attractive insurance plan. But the claim that the price restraint will make it easier for customers to pay does not distinguish the medical profession from any other provider of goods or services.

We are equally unpersuaded by the argument that we should not apply the per se rule in this case because the judiciary has little antitrust experience in the health care industry.[19] The argument quite obviously is inconsistent with Socony–Vacuum. In unequivocal terms, we stated that, "[w]hatever may be its peculiar problems and characteristics, the Sherman Act, so far as price-fixing agreements are concerned, establishes one uniform rule applicable to all industries alike." 310 U.S., at 222. We also stated that "[t]he elimination of so-called competitive evils [in an industry] is no legal justification" for price-fixing agreements, id., at 220, yet the Court of Appeals refused to apply the per se rule in this case in part because the health care industry was so far removed from the competitive model. [T]he result of this reasoning was the adoption by the Court of Appeals of a legal standard based on the reasonableness of the fixed prices,[21] an inquiry we have so often condemned.[22] Finally, the argument

---

18. It is true that in Kiefer–Stewart, as in Albrecht, the agreement involved a vertical arrangement in which maximum resale prices were fixed. But the case also involved an agreement among competitors to impose the resale price restraint. In any event, horizontal restraints are generally less defensible than vertical restraints.

19. The argument should not be confused with the established position that a new per se rule is not justified until the judiciary obtains considerable rule-of-reason experience with the particular type of restraint challenged.

21. "[C]onfronted with an industry widely deviant from a reasonably free competitive model, such as agriculture, the proper inquiry is whether the practice enhances the prices charged for the services." [643 F.2d, at 556].

22. In the first price-fixing case arising under the Sherman Act, the Court was required to pass on the sufficiency of the defendants' plea that they had established rates that were

that the per se rule must be rejustified for every industry that has not been subject to significant antitrust litigation ignores the rationale for per se rules.

The respondents' principal argument is that the per se rule is inapplicable because their agreements are alleged to have procompetitive justifications. The argument indicates a misunderstanding of the per se concept. The anticompetitive potential inherent in all price-fixing agreements justifies their facial invalidation even if procompetitive justifications are offered for some. Those claims of enhanced competition are so unlikely to prove significant in any particular case that we adhere to the rule of law that is justified in its general application.

The respondents contend that their fee schedules are procompetitive because they make it possible to provide consumers of health care with a uniquely desirable form of insurance coverage that could not otherwise exist. The features of the foundation-endorsed insurance plans that they stress are a choice of doctors, complete insurance coverage, and lower premiums. The first two characteristics, however, are hardly unique to these plans. Since only about 70% of the doctors in the relevant market are members of either foundation, the guarantee of complete coverage only applies when an insured chooses a physician in that 70%. If he elects to go to a nonfoundation doctor, he may be required to pay a portion of the doctor's fee. It is fair to presume, however, that at least 70% of the doctors in other markets charge no more than the "usual, customary, and reasonable" fee that typical insurers are willing to reimburse in full. Thus, in Maricopa and Pima Counties as well as in most parts of the country, if an insured asks his doctor if the insurance coverage is complete, presumably in about 70% of the cases the doctor will say "Yes" and in about 30% of the cases he will say "No."

It is true that a binding assurance of complete insurance coverage—as well as most of the respondents' potential for lower insurance premiums[25] —can be obtained only if the insurer and the doctor agree in advance on the maximum fee that the doctor will accept as full payment for a particular service. Even if a fee schedule is therefore desirable, it is not necessary that the doctors do the price fixing.[26] The record indicates that

---

actually beneficial to consumers. Assuming the factual validity of the plea, the Court rejected the defense as a matter of law.

25. We do not perceive the respondents' claim of procompetitive justification for their fee schedules to rest on the premise that the fee schedules actually reduce medical fees and accordingly reduce insurance premiums, thereby enhancing competition in the health insurance industry. Such an argument would merely restate the long-rejected position that fixed prices are reasonable if they are lower than free competition would yield. It is arguable, however, that the existence of a fee schedule, whether fixed by the doctors or by the insurers, makes it easier—and to that extent less expensive—for insurers to calculate the risks that they underwrite and to arrive at the appropriate reimbursement on insured claims.

26. According to a Federal Trade Commission staff report: "Until the mid–1960's, most Blue Shield plans determined in advance how much to pay for particular procedures and prepared fee schedules reflecting their determinations. Fee schedules are still used in approximately 25 percent of Blue Shield contracts." Bureau of Competition, Federal Trade Commis-

the Arizona Comprehensive Medical/Dental Program for Foster Children is administered by the Maricopa Foundation pursuant to a contract under which the maximum-fee schedule is prescribed by a state agency rather than by the doctors. This program and the Blue Shield plan challenged in Group Life & Health Insurance Co. v. Royal Drug Co., 440 U.S. 205 (1979), indicate that insurers are capable not only of fixing maximum reimbursable prices but also of obtaining binding agreements with providers guaranteeing the insured full reimbursement of a participating provider's fee. In light of these examples, it is not surprising that nothing in the record even arguably supports the conclusion that this type of insurance program could not function if the fee schedules were set in a different way.

The most that can be said for having doctors fix the maximum prices is that doctors may be able to do it more efficiently than insurers. The validity of that assumption is far from obvious,[28] but in any event there is no reason to believe that any savings that might accrue from this arrangement would be sufficiently great to affect the competitiveness of these kinds of insurance plans. It is entirely possible that the potential or actual power of the foundations to dictate the terms of such insurance plans may more than offset the theoretical efficiencies upon which the respondents' defense ultimately rests.[29]

C

Our adherence to the per se rule is grounded not only on economic prediction, judicial convenience, and business certainty, but also on a recognition of the respective roles of the Judiciary and the Congress in regulating the economy. Congress may consider the exception that we are not free to read into the statute.[30]

---

sion, Medical Participation in Control of Blue Shield and Certain Other Open–Panel Medical Prepayment Plans 128 (1979). We do not suggest that Blue Shield plans are not actually controlled by doctors. Nor does this case present the question whether an insurer may, consistent with the Sherman Act, fix the fee schedule and enter into bilateral contracts with individual doctors. In an amicus curiae brief, the United States expressed its opinion that such an arrangement would be legal unless the plaintiffs could establish that a conspiracy among providers was at work. Our point is simply that the record provides no factual basis for the respondents' claim that the doctors must fix the fee schedule.

28. In order to create an insurance plan under which the doctor would agree to accept as full payment a fee prescribed in a fixed schedule, someone must canvass the doctors to determine what maximum prices would be high enough to attract sufficient numbers of individual doctors to sign up but low enough to make the insurance plan competitive. In this case that canvassing function is performed by the foundation. It would seem that an insurer could simply bypass the foundation by performing the canvassing function and dealing with the doctors itself.

29. In this case it appears that the fees are set by a group with substantial power in the market for medical services, and that there is competition among insurance companies in the sale of medical insurance. Under these circumstances the insurance companies are not likely to have significantly greater bargaining power against a monopoly of doctors than would individual consumers of medical services.

30. "[Congress] can of course make per se rules inapplicable in some or all cases and leave courts free to ramble through the wilds of economic theory in order to maintain a flexible approach." United States v. Topco Associates 405 U.S. at 610, n.10.

IV

Having declined the respondents' invitation to cut back on the per se rule against price fixing, we are left with the respondents' argument that their fee schedules involve price fixing in only a literal sense. For this argument, the respondents rely upon Broadcast Music, Inc. v. Columbia Broadcasting System, Inc., 441 U.S. 1 (1979).

In Broadcast Music we were confronted with an antitrust challenge to the marketing of the right to use copyrighted compositions derived from the entire membership of the American Society of Composers, Authors and Publishers (ASCAP). The so-called "blanket license" was entirely different from the product that any one composer was able to sell by himself.[31] Although there was little competition among individual composers for their separate compositions, the blanket-license arrangement did not place any restraint on the right of any individual copyright owner to sell his own compositions separately to any buyer at any price.[32] But a "necessary consequence" of the creation of the blanket license was that its price had to be established. Id., at 21. We held that the delegation by the composers to ASCAP of the power to fix the price for the blanket license was not a species of the price-fixing agreements categorically forbidden by the Sherman Act. The record disclosed price fixing only in a "literal sense." Id., at 8.

This case is fundamentally different. Each of the foundations is composed of individual practitioners who compete with one another for patients. Neither the foundations nor the doctors sell insurance, and they derive no profits from the sale of health insurance policies. The members of the foundations sell medical services. Their combination in the form of the foundation does not permit them to sell any different product.[33] Their combination has merely permitted them to sell their services to certain customers at fixed prices and arguably to affect the prevailing market price of medical care.

---

31. "Thus, to the extent the blanket license is a different product, ASCAP is not really a joint sales agency offering the individual goods of many sellers, but is a separate seller offering its blanket license, of which the individual compositions are raw material." 441 U.S., at 22.

32. "Here, the blanket-license fee is not set by competition among individual copyright owners, and it is a fee for the use of any of the compositions covered by the license. But the blanket license cannot be wholly equated with a simple horizontal arrangement among competitors. ASCAP does set the price for its blanket license, but that license is quite different from anything any individual owner could issue. The individual composers and authors have neither agreed not to sell individually in any other market nor use the blanket license to mask price fixing in such other markets." Id., at 23–24.

33. It may be true that by becoming a member of the foundation the individual practitioner obtains a competitive advantage in the market for medical services that he could not unilaterally obtain. That competitive advantage is the ability to attract as customers people who value both the guarantee of full health coverage and a choice of doctors. But, as we have indicated, the setting of the price by doctors is not a "necessary consequence" of an arrangement with an insurer in which the doctor agrees not to charge certain insured customers more than a fixed price.

The foundations are not analogous to partnerships or other joint arrangements in which persons who would otherwise be competitors pool their capital and share the risks of loss as well as the opportunities for profit. In such joint ventures, the partnership is regarded as a single firm competing with other sellers in the market. The agreement under attack is an agreement among hundreds of competing doctors concerning the price at which each will offer his own services to a substantial number of consumers. It is true that some are surgeons, some anesthesiologists, and some psychiatrists, but the doctors do not sell a package of three kinds of services. If a clinic offered complete medical coverage for a flat fee, the cooperating doctors would have the type of partnership arrangement in which a price-fixing agreement among the doctors would be perfectly proper. But the fee agreements disclosed by the record in this case are among independent competing entrepreneurs. They fit squarely into the horizontal price-fixing mold.

Notes

1. *The meaning and mysticism of the per se/rule of reason distinction.* As you can see from *Maricopa* the courts distinguish between conduct that is termed a "per se" violation of the Sherman Act and that which is subject to the "rule of reason." Unfortunately, so much lore and rhetoric surround this distinction that it is very difficult for novices in antitrust to have a clue as to its meaning.

Justice Brandeis has passed down to us the classic statement of the rule of reason. Quoted in part in *Maricopa*, it bears iteration:

> The case was rested upon the bald proposition, that a rule or agreement by which men occupying positions of strength in any branch of trade, fixed prices at which they would buy or sell during an important part of the business day, is an illegal restraint of trade under the Anti–Trust Law. But the legality of an agreement or regulation cannot be determined by so simple a test, as whether it restrains competition. Every agreement concerning trade, every regulation of trade, restrains. To bind, to restrain, is of their very essence. The true test of legality is whether the restraint imposed is such as merely regulates and perhaps thereby promotes competition or whether it is such as may suppress or even destroy competition. To determine that question the court must ordinarily consider the facts peculiar to the business to which the restraint is applied; its condition before and after the restraint was imposed; the nature of the restraint and its effect, actual or probable. The history of the restraint, the evil believed to exist, the reason for adopting the particular remedy, the purpose or end sought to be attained, are all relevant facts.

Board of Trade of City of Chicago v. United States, 246 U.S. 231, 238 (1918).

As this quotation readily indicates, analysis of every alleged restraint of trade under the "full-blown" rule of reason would consume substantial resources, introduce great uncertainty and would, with regard to some practices, be completely unnecessary. The per se/rule of reason distinction is a means to rationalize this process.

At one time "per se" did mean that a certain category of conduct was deemed to be always or almost always pernicious such that courts would not, at the risks of creating uncertainty and erroneous decisions, invest the resources necessary to determine if the conduct was actually harmful in any particular case. As such, the category of conduct was indeed deemed always—"per se"—illegal. This meaning developed in early cases dealing with price-fixing by cartels, and there was no reason to litigate whether such conduct consisted of anything other than an attempt to raise price by the exercise of collective market power. In such cases it made perfect sense to rule that such a category of conduct is always illegal.

However, as time went on two related things happened. First, as the antitrust laws were applied, attempts to cartelize an industry were driven underground and hence became more complicated. As its name indicates, the Sherman Antitrust Act was aimed at what were literally trusts: cartels created by formal documents. Early decisions under the Act were targeted at these trusts—the railroad, petroleum, sugar and tobacco trusts, as examples—and once such conduct was deemed per se illegal any attempt to cartelize industries had to be conducted in secret and by increasingly sophisticated means, such as the use of base-point pricing or other facilitative mechanisms in which members of a cartel would agree to use a complicated formula to set a fixed price. *See, e.g.,* FTC v. Cement Institute, 333 U.S. 683 (1948). Over time enforcement of the antitrust laws extended to concerted activity to such an extent that any conduct which in any way "tampers with price structures" was deemed to be "per se." United States v. Socony–Vacuum Oil Co., 310 U.S. 150, 221 (1940).

Second, the extension of the per se rule to relatively complicated behavior came to create the potential that the per se rule would be applied to conduct that was not necessarily, usually or even sometimes injurious to competition. Perhaps the best example of this extension has been Broadcast Music, Inc. v. Columbia Broadcasting System, Inc., 441 U.S. 1 (1979) [*BMI*]. That case involved a challenge to a blanket-pricing system—in other words, a flat-fee license—by which composers licensed media outlets to use their copyrighted songs. Through two associations, BMI and the American Society of Composers, Authors and Publishers (ACAP), composers of songs set a uniform price for the sale of the repertoire of their songs—literally collective price setting. After an eight-week trial on the issue of liability the district court dismissed the case, rejecting the claim that the blanket license was horizontal price fixing and a per se violation of section 1, and holding under the rule of reason that there was no undue restraint. This judgment was reversed by a divided court of appeals, which held that the blanket license did constitute per se price fixing. To be sure, if any conduct "tampers with price structures," this was surely it, but the Supreme Court reversed, holding that the case was rule of reason.

The very fact that *BMI* and other recent important ones like National Collegiate Athletic Association v. Board of Regents of University of Oklahoma, 468 U.S. 85 (1984) (NCAA's rule limiting the number of college football games that may appear on television during a season held to be rule of reason) [*NCAA*], were characterized as per se or rule of reason only after a full trial on the merits in itself tells you that the courts have departed from the rhetoric we see in *Maricopa* that price fixing is per se illegal, with no inquiry into market power, history and characteristics of the particular industry and the particular restraint, or justification. In *BMI* the record showed that thousands of media outlets like radio and television stations needed "unplanned, rapid and indemnified access," 441 U.S. at 19, to any of the millions of songs in the repertoire of songs subject to the blanket license, and that the licensing scheme reduced songwriters' costs of enforcing their copyrights. Accordingly, the Court found that the blanket license could not "automatically be declared illegal in all of its many manifestations," 441 U.S. at 24, but should be examined under the rule of reason.

This result might strike you as odd. Quite literally, through BMI and ASCAP, otherwise competing composers were integrating with regard to price—setting the price for their songs. Unquestionably, BMI and ASCAP possessed market power. Undoubtedly, the restraint directly affected price. Why wasn't this a per se violation?

The contrast with *Maricopa* could hardly be starker. To see this, remind yourself that in *Maricopa* the state of Arizona, the plaintiff, had moved for summary judgment. Given that procedural posture, who was entitled to all inferences from the record? Given who got the benefit of any factual disputes, ask yourself what the summary judgment record showed regarding market power. In Pima County somewhere between 30 and 80% of physicians had executed contracts with the foundation, while in Maricopa County the figure was 70%. Even though the latter figure seems high, what is the significance of the fact that the contracts were not exclusive, meaning that doctors were free to execute participation agreements with non-foundation plans (and vice versa)? Given that, to what degree were actual or potential competing insurance plans excluded from the market, i.e., to what extent did the participation agreements with the foundations foreclose entry by other insurers? Additionally, what did the summary judgment record show regarding the connection between the prices physicians actually charged and those stipulated by the maximum fee schedule? What is the significance of the fact that the record showed substantial deviation from the fee schedules? Given your answers to these questions, to what extent had it been proven that the potential evils of maximum price fixing obtained? Had maximum prices turned into minimum prices? Had the maximum fee schedule deterred innovation? Could the fee schedule deter entry by competing plans, i.e., did the fee schedule represent limit pricing, potentially a barrier to entry?

Finally, what did the record show regarding justification? Justice Stephens found that a maximum fee schedule had to be fixed for this product to exist—someone had to create a network of pooled providers and subject it to a maximum fee constraint such that insurers could have the necessary information to predict risk and establish premiums for complete insurance coverage. Analogously, in *BMI* the Court found that the blanket license fee had to exist in order for the product created by BMI and ASCAP to exist—a repertoire of songs to which users had unplanned, rapid and indemnified access. In *Maricopa* of what significance was the Court's finding that it was not necessary for the doctors to set the price schedule themselves? Given your answers, what could the per se/rule of reason distinction mean and how could it be that this case was treated as per se and Arizona was entitled to summary judgment? How could it be, by contrast, that *BMI* was characterized as a rule of reason case?

2. *Burdens of coming forward and proof.* Exactly what the per se/rule of reason distinction has come to mean is complicated and can be fully explicated only by parsing numerous cases, most saliently by studying its historical development through a line of cases such as is done in an antitrust course. Additionally, as we will see in the notes following *Rome* below, the distinction even has a different meaning for different doctrinal categories. For present purposes, we can only provide a brief summary.

As has become clear particularly through a line of cases starting with *BMI* and running through *Maricopa* and *NCAA*, the per se/rule of reason distinction has come to express a fairly complicated means of ordering complex antitrust litigation such that at different stages of factual development burdens of coming forward and burdens of proof are assigned to plaintiffs or defendants, and further litigation cut off when the burdens are not satisfied. In some situations per se retains its old bite: the category of conduct is always or almost always pernicious such that courts need not examine the particulars before it at all or to any significant degree. For example, bid rigging occurs when members of a market rig a bidding process such that through concerted action a job put out for bid is assigned to a member of the cartel. That member submits the lowest, albeit still inflated bid, while other members pad their fictitious bids even more, so as to lose the bidding contest. A form of price fixing, bid rigging is harmful to consumers under any conceivable circumstances, and always violates section 1. *See, e.g.*, United States v. Addyston Pipe & Steel Co., 85 F. 271 (1898), *aff'd*, 175 U.S. 211 (1899).

By contrast, other conduct in which horizontal competitors "tamper[] with price structures" less unambiguously always harms consumers, and some degree of judicial scrutiny is necessary to sort the wheat from the chaff. Sometimes that examination can be cut off very early and a case called per se, i.e., plaintiff wins; sometimes that examination proceeds all the way to a full trial on the merits and a defendant shows that the category of conduct in its particular situation actually benefits consumers—perhaps even that the challenged conduct is the only way to attain such benefit—and then the case is rule of reason and defendant wins. *Maricopa* was characterized as "per se" based on the record before the Court and that characterization meant that plaintiff prevailed on that record; *BMI* was categorized as "rule of reason" based on its record and that categorization meant that defendant prevailed; *NCAA* was characterized as "rule of reason" based on the record before the Court and that characterization meant that plaintiff prevailed. The categorization of a case as "per se" or "rule of reason" is now a description of a process and an outcome of reasoning. "The point is that we constantly create and revise presumptions of varying strengths to arrive at sensible decisions in the face of the many uncertainties of business reality." 7 Phillip E. Areeda et al., ANTITRUST LAW: AN ANALYSIS OF ANTITRUST PRINCIPLES AND THEIR APPLICATION ¶ 1508c, at 395 (2d ed., 2003).

One can generalize as follows. Once a plaintiff has proven that the usually pernicious conduct exists, e.g., horizontal competitors have set price or divided markets, the plaintiff wins unless the defendants overcome some burden. That burden may consist of some variation of defendants' showing that they have engaged in some beneficial form of horizontal integration other than price setting or market division, defendants' disproving market power, their coming forward with a colorable justification, their proving that justification, or even defendants' showing that the consumer benefit which justifies their conduct can be obtained only by that conduct and by no other means. In *Maricopa* the defendants had proven that a maximum fee schedule was needed for actuarial predictions to exist, but they had not proved that only they could set that fee schedule. Given how inherently dangerous price setting is—and given, perhaps, a past history of such anticompetitive activity by medical associations—defendants had not proven enough to stave off summary judgment by plaintiff even though plaintiff had not shown market power.* By contrast, in some cases once the defendant has produced a plausible justification plaintiff must go so far as show that there exists a less restrictive alternative to obtain the benefit achieved by the challenged conduct. *See, e.g.,* United States v. Brown University, 5 F.3d 658 (3d Cir. 1993). The placement and degree of various burdens vary from situation to situation but this burden-shifting mechanism is now the gist of the per se/rule of reason distinction. *See* California Dental Assn. v. Federal Trade Commission, 526 U.S. 756 (1999) [*California Dental*]; *see generally* 7 Phillip E. Areeda et al., ANTITRUST LAW: AN ANALYSIS OF ANTITRUST PRINCIPLES AND THEIR APPLICATION ¶ ¶ 1500–11 (2d ed., 2003). As the FTC has recently usefully summarized:

> A plaintiff may avoid full rule of reason analysis, including the pleading and proof of market power, if it demonstrates that the conduct at issue is inherently suspect owing to its likely tendency to suppress competition. Such conduct ordinarily encompasses behavior that past judicial experience and current economic learning have shown to warrant summary condemnation. If the plaintiff

---

* *BMI* was distinguishable in part because the price-setting songwriters in *BMI* were enforcing their copyrights, see 441 U.S. at 18–19, and because ASCAP and BMI's licensing practices had already been subjected to considerable judicial scrutiny, enjoyed the continued support of the Department of Justice, and Congress had approved similar practices in somewhat analogous circumstances. See *id.* at 10–16.

makes such an initial showing, and the defendant makes no effort to advance any competitive justification for its practices, then the case is at an end and the practices are condemned.

If the challenged restrictions are of a sort that generally pose significant competitive hazards and thus can be called inherently suspect, then the defendant can avoid summary condemnation only by advancing a legitimate justification for those practices. Such justifications may consist of plausible reasons why practices that are competitively suspect as a general matter may not be expected to have adverse consequences in the context of the particular market in question; or they may consist of reasons why the practices are likely to have beneficial effects for consumers.

At this early stage of the analysis, the defendant need only articulate a legitimate justification.

To be legitimate, a justification must plausibly create or improve competition. A justification is plausible if it cannot be rejected without extensive factual inquiry. The defendant, however, must do more than merely assert that its purported justification benefits consumers. Although the defendant need not produce detailed evidence at this stage, it must articulate the specific link between the challenged restraint and the purported justification to merit a more searching inquiry into whether the restraint may advance procompetitive goals, even though it facially appears of the type likely to suppress competition.

When the defendant advances such cognizable and plausible justifications, the plaintiff must make a more detailed showing that the restraints at issue are indeed likely, in the particular context, to harm competition. Such a showing still need not prove actual anticompetitive effects or entail "the fullest market analysis." [*California Dental*], 526 U.S. at 779. Depending upon the circumstances of the cases and the degree to which antitrust tribunals have experience with restraints in particular markets, such a showing may or may not require evidence about the particular market at issue, but at a minimum must entail the identification of the theoretical basis for the alleged anticompetitive effects and a showing that the effects are indeed likely to be anticompetitive. Such a showing may, for example, be based on a more detailed analysis of economic learning about the likely competitive effects of a particular restraint, in markets with characteristics comparable to the one at issue. The plaintiff may also show that the proffered procompetitive effects could be achieved through means less restrictive of competition. The defendant, of course, can introduce evidence to refute the plaintiff's arguments or to show that detailed evidence supports its proffered justification.

The plaintiff has the burden of persuasion overall, but not necessarily the burden with respect to each step of this analysis. If the plaintiff satisfies its initial burden of showing that the practices in question are inherently suspect, then the defendant must come forward with a substantial reason why there are offsetting procompetitive benefits. If the defendant articulates a legitimate (i.e., cognizable and plausible) justification, then the plaintiff must address the justification, and provide the tribunal with sufficient evidence to show that anticompetitive effects are in fact likely, before the evidentiary burden shifts to the defendant. At this stage, the defendant's burden to respond will likely depend in individual cases upon the quality and amount of evidence that the plaintiff has produced to illuminate the competitive dangers of the defendant's conduct.

Polygram Holding, Inc., 136 F.T.C. 310, 344–50, 2003 WL 25797195, *aff'd*, 416 F.3d 29 (D.C. Cir. 2005).

With this background in mind, now review the answers to the questions posed above about exactly what the summary judgment record in *Maricopa* showed, particularly viewed in light of the fact that the defendants were to get the benefit of any inference as the nonmoving parties. Arizona proved the fact that the foundations performed only a few functions like setting the maximum fee schedules, paying claims and conducting peer review. The record showed that the foundations integrated neither financial risk nor clinical functions. Of what significance were these facts? *See, e.g.*, Texaco Inc. v. Dagher, 547 U.S. 1 (2006) (setting price of product made by lawful, economically integrated joint venture cannot constitute per se price fixing even though the members of the joint venture are otherwise horizontal competitors). Given that the State had proven the existence of horizontal price setting, what burdens were then shifted to the defendants? Which ones did they meet and which ones did they not such that the case was characterized as per se and summary judgment granted to the plaintiff?

   3. *Physician-established fee schedules.* What about defendants' claim that only physicians can set a fee schedule? Do you believe that there is any truth to the notion that only physicians can establish accurate fees? Do the readings in Part Two on the Medicare RBRVS system support or deny the physicians' claim? On the other hand, does providing actuarially valid predictions depend only on the amounts set for given services or more? Do the fee schedules themselves account for the volume of services? Who has control over that? Are providers likely to accommodate to cost control when their income is dictated to them? In most of the industrialized world physician groups are involved in setting fee schedules and in efforts to control volume.

   4. *Physician network joint ventures.* In 1996 the DOJ Antitrust Division and the FTC established a safe harbor for physician network joint ventures. To fall within the safety zone, if the network is exclusive the physician participants must "share substantial financial risk" and constitute at most 20% of the physicians in the relevant market. If the network is non-exclusive the market share for the safe harbor is capped a 30%. Risk-sharing networks outside the safe harbor are analyzed under the rule of

reason. Additionally, two forms of non-financial integration might also satisfy the rule of reason.

a. Clinical Integration. The first involves so-called "clinical integration":

> Physician network joint ventures that do not involve the sharing of substantial financial risk may also involve sufficient integration to demonstrate that the venture is likely to produce significant efficiencies. Such integration can be evidenced by the network implementing an active and ongoing program to evaluate and modify practice patterns by the network's physician participants and create a high degree of interdependence and cooperation among the physicians to control costs and ensure quality. This program may include: (1) establishing mechanisms to monitor and control utilization of health care services that are designed to control costs and assure quality of care; (2) selectively choosing network physicians who are likely to further these efficiency objectives; and (3) the significant investment of capital, both monetary and human, in the necessary infrastructure and capability to realize the claimed efficiencies.

United States Department of Justice & Federal Trade Commission, Statements of Antitrust Enforcement Policy in Health Care 72 (1996) (http://www.ftc.gov/bc/healthcare/industryguide/policy/index.htm).

The FTC staff has considered a number of these arrangements in recent advisory opinions. Illustrative is TriState Health Partners, Inc. (Apr. 13, 2009) (http://www.ftc.gov/os/closings/staff/090413tristateaoletter.pdf), which concerned a physician-hospital organization ("PHO") formed to coordinate care. Among other things, the network would achieve coordination by:

> (a) establishing a largely closed panel of providers committed to practicing consistently with evidence-based medicine standards and clinical guidelines developed or tailored by the program's participants; (b) maintaining continuity and coordination of care through a within-network referral policy; (c) requiring use of health information technology, including electronic health records, to coordinate care, effectively communicate among network providers, eliminate unnecessary duplication of tests, and collect performance data; (d) establishing mechanisms to collect and evaluate treatment and performance data, including data on appropriate use of health care resources; (e) requiring broad participation of the program's physicians in various aspects of the program's development, implementation, and ongoing operation; and (f) establishing procedures and mechanisms, including various committees that include participating physicians, to provide feedback on both individual and group performance, address performance deficiencies and, if necessary, impose sanctions for physicians whose performance is chronically deficient regarding program requirements and standards.

Id. at 19–20.

However, given that the network included approximately two-thirds of the medical staff of the only hospital in a rural county, quite possibly the PHO would be able to exercise market power because it would also engage in (non-exclusive) joint contracting for network members. Nonetheless, analyzing the arrangement under the rule of reason, the FTC staff concluded that the joint contracting was ancillary to the efficiencies attained by the beneficial, partial integration:

> TriState's primary argument of the reasonable necessity of joint contracting on behalf of all of its physicians, in essence, is two sides of the same coin: that not having all member physicians participating under all contracts would seriously undermine the ability of the program to function efficiently and achieve its hoped-for benefits; and that the various aspects of the proposed program, which require physicians to cooperate and interact in both their development and implementation, will be far more effective if all physicians are maximally involved because, through joint contracting, they are participating in all payer contracts under the program.

> Without joint contracting, which will assure, and reinforce, TriState's membership requirement, that all physicians participate under all contracts, TriState potentially could have different provider panels representing a subset of its membership for each payer contract. This, in turn, could make it difficult to effectively maintain the in-network referral requirement, since referring physicians might have to use different physicians for referrals under each contract. Likewise, with varying provider panels for each contract, the ability of TriState to coordinate the care provided to patients, and its ability to obtain information on both patients and providers would be more difficult and the results less robust. Reduced information on provider behavior could interfere with the program's evaluation of, and feedback regarding, physicians' practices in treating patients, again undermining a key component of the program's effort to improve efficiency. Thus, while it might be theoretically possible to have a program without joint contracting on behalf of all physicians in the program, such an approach appears likely to be far more difficult, and potentially could compromise TriState's ability to effectively integrate its physician members' provision of care, and to achieve the program's potential efficiencies.

> On the positive side, uniform participation will facilitate the program's in-network referral requirement, which is central to the program's success in rationalizing and effectively providing evidence-based care to the program's enrollees. With a stable, defined network of participating providers, physicians will easily be able to make referrals to other network physicians, knowing that they also will be participating in the provision of coordinated care under

the program's strictures. Likewise, maintaining a pre-set network makes it easier to assure that data and information on patient treatment and provider activity and use of resources—necessary for monitoring patient status and physician behavior, as well as the program's achievement of its efficiency goals—is available to the greatest extent possible. As noted above, achieving these operational necessities would be far more difficult if different physicians were participating in different payer contracts, referral patterns had to be adjusted accordingly to keep patients within the applicable network, and information on patient treatments and provider behavior were less uniformly available.

Having complete provider participation as a result of joint contracting on their behalf also will maximize the number of patients each physician has that are subject to the program's various efficiency-enhancing mechanisms, thereby increasing the physicians' familiarity with, acceptance of, and efficient participation in those program aspects and requirements. In essence, the more physicians participate in the program, the faster they are likely to climb the learning curve in effectively treating patients under the clinical integration system and its required components.

Guaranteed uniform participation by all physicians under all contracts, through joint contracting, also is likely to contribute to the physicians' commitment to the success of the program. The greater the number of patients that a physician has who are under the proposed program, the more he or she is likely to care about its operation and success, and the greater is likely to be the physician's willingness to invest the necessary time and effort in the various aspects of its operation. Joint contracting on behalf of all TriState physicians will maximize each physician's opportunities to treat patients who are covered by the program which, in turn, should make them more committed to the program's success.

Having a stable provider network for all contracts also appears capable of enhancing TriState's effective business operations by helping to "brand" its product, and identify the program as a single entity with a stable provider panel and a reputation regarding its product, much like the way more highly integrated clinics are identified in the public's mind.

Joint contracting also can reduce administrative costs for the program, and reduce transaction costs for both its members and payers with which it contracts. Administrative and transaction costs efficiencies, by themselves, are unlikely to be of sufficient magnitude to offset the loss of competition from joint negotiation of prices by physicians in a provider network. Nevertheless, these types of efficiencies may be real, and are cognizable under the antitrust laws in the context of an integrated joint venture.

We agree that having a predetermined, identified provider network for all services provided pursuant to contracts with payers for the proposed program appears likely to promote the program's intended integration of its physician members' provision of care, and the efficient operation of the various aspects of the proposed program. It also may help in the effective branding and marketing of the program. Increased physician participation and interaction, in turn, should further TriState's ability to achieve the program's anticipated efficiency benefits. Moreover, without such joint contracting on behalf of all member physicians, effective operation of TriState's proposed program is likely to be far more difficult and its effectiveness could well be compromised. Overall, such joint contracting appears to be subordinate to TriState's legitimate effort to improve efficiency and quality in the delivery of healthcare services through integration by its participants. We therefore conclude that, on balance, joint contracting with payers by TriState on behalf of its entire participating physician membership is an ancillary restraint—one that is subordinate to, and reasonably necessary to further or make more effective the potentially efficiency-enhancing and procompetitive integration that the proposed program represents.

Id. at 26–28.

How do these benefits differ from those obtained in forms of health care financing, extant in the rest of the industrialized world but rarely in the United States, in which stable pools of patients are linked over the long-run to stable pools of providers? For purposes of the antitrust laws should it matter that providers create and run these networks? Is it appropriate for an antitrust enforcement agency to engage in such detailed review of the structure and operations of such networks? If the benefits of this arrangement can be obtained only if both covered lives are treated solely or mostly in-network and network physicians do most or all of their work in-network, then why should it matter, for purposes of the rule of reason, if the contracting is non-exclusive, something stressed by the FTC staff? For a favorable review of the clinical integration provisions, see Lawrence P. Casalino, *The Federal Trade Commission, Clinical Integration, and the Organization of Physician Practice*, 31 J. HEALTH POL. POL'Y & L. 569 (2006).

   b. Messenger models. The second permissible form of integration is the so-called "messenger model arrangement" through which providers use an agent to convey information to and from individual providers concerning prices and price-related terms they are willing to accept. The agent must facilitate individual contracting rather than collective price fixing:

   The Agencies will examine whether the agent facilitates collective decision-making by network providers, rather than independent, unilateral, decisions. In particular, the Agencies will examine whether the agent coordinates the providers' responses to a particular proposal, disseminates to network providers the views or intentions of other network providers as to the proposal, expresses an opinion on the terms offered, collectively negotiates for the providers, or decides whether or not to convey an offer based on the agent's judgment about the attractiveness of the prices or price-related terms. If the agent engages in such activities, the arrangement may amount to a per se illegal price-fixing agreement.

United States Department of Justice & Federal Trade Commission, Statements of Antitrust Enforcement Policy in Health Care 126–27 (1996) (http://www.ftc.gov/bc/healthcare/industryguide/policy/index.htm).

North Texas Specialty Physicians v. Federal Trade Commission, 528 F.3d 346 (5th Cir. 2008), *cert. den.*, 555 U.S. 1170 (2009), provides an example of how to structure a messenger model arrangement so that it operates, illegally, as a joint sales agency that engages in collective bargaining. Each year defendant polled its members regarding the minimum fees they would accept. It then reported to them the responses from their fellow members—i.e., from horizontal competitors—regarding the mean, medium and mode of fees they would accept. When polling, defendant would "remind" its members of the prior year's results. From the responses defendant would then constitute an "offer" to payers. Members were aware of this negotiating process. Members' participation agreements obligated them to refrain from negotiating with payers individually until the joint negotiation was concluded. All offers to individuals from payers before that time were to be funneled to defendant. Payers were told that defendant set a minimum fee schedule for its members and that no offers below the minimum would be transmitted to them. Only if 50% of members approved a payer's offer would it be "messengered" back to them for opting in or out. Finally, at least with regard to one negotiation, defendant transmitted to the payer powers of attorney it had received from many of its members.

This conduct is price fixing, pure and simple. Unfortunately, there have been dozens of such occurrences. *See, e.g.,* Jeff Miles, *Ticking Antitrust Time Bombs: A Message for Messed–Up Messenger Models*, AHLA HEALTH LAWYER NEWS, Nov. 2002, at 5; David Marx, Jr., *Messenger Models: What Can the Agencies Do To Prevent Provider Networks from Violating the Antitrust Laws?*, AHLA HEALTH LAWYER NEWS, Apr. 2004, at 24. For an argument that the messenger model is inherently ambiguous and permissive, see Jeffrey L. Harrison, *The Messenger Model: Don't Ask, Don't Tell?*, 71 ANTITRUST L.J. 1017 (2004). For a discussion why physicians have so blatantly violated the rule against price fixing and why enforcers have been so lenient in response, see Thomas L. Greaney, *Thirty Years of Solicitude: Antitrust Law and Physician Cartels*, 7 HOUS. J. HEALTH L. & POL'Y 189 (2007).

5. *Market division.* Division of markets, like price fixing, remains conduct that is inherently suspect and a per se violation—as close as one gets to the old, rigid meaning of per se. Indeed, many argue that division of markets is if anything a more airtight means of cartelization than price setting. Members of the cartel are assigned a particular type of output, customers or territories—the three ways by which to divide a market. To the extent that sales outside of assigned products, customers or territories

are readily detected, policing cartel discipline is more easily obtained. Moreover, when markets are so divided, each member of the cartel is the sole producer in its assigned market. Therefore, members of the cartel have less incentive to dissipate supra-competitive profits by engaging in forms of non-price competition, e.g., offering longer warranties, something that often occurs to break the ranks of price-fixing cartels.

In some contexts market division arrangements can eliminate free-riding. For example, Blue Cross & Blue Shield United of Wisconsin v. Marshfield Clinic, 65 F.3d 1406 (7th Cir. 1995), cert. den., 516 U.S. 1184 (1996), involved a referral arrangement between Marshfield Clinic and another HMO, North Central Health Protection Plan ("NCHPP"). Although Chief Judge Posner found sufficient evidence of territorial division to affirm a jury verdict, he noted that the arrangement might have been designed to eliminate an externality problem:

> The plan of the physician who rendered the service would bill the other plan for its cost. This was no doubt a valuable service, expanding the range of physicians to whom people enrolled in these two HMOs could turn. But the Clinic has failed to explain why, to provide this service, it was necessary for the two plans to agree not to open offices in each other's territories. We can imagine an argument that would run as follows: if NCHPP, say, opened an office in Marshfield, the doctors staffing that office would constantly be referring patients to the Clinic because it has such a plethora of doctors in Marshfield (remember that it employs all the doctors working in that town). The office would be running a referral business, "free riding" on the reputation and quality of Marshfield's doctors, and perhaps it would be difficult to devise a reimbursement plan under which these doctors would be compensated for these services. It is not a bad argument, but it is not made by the Clinic and it has no support in the record.

Id. at 1416. This type of justification, to be more than a theoretical possibility, would have to rest on the existence of substantial integration to which the market division would be ancillary. *See generally* 12 HERBERT HOVENKAMP, ANTITRUST LAW: AN ANALYSIS OF ANTITRUST PRINCIPLES AND THEIR APPLICATION ¶¶ 2030–33 (2d ed., 2005).

6. *Price v. non-price restraints.* California Dental Association v. Federal Trade Commission, 526 U.S. 756 (1999), is a recent case that well illustrates the fact that horizontal non-price restraints are treated less harshly than price restraints. Other recent cases are discussed in the note on group boycotts following *Rome* below.

In *California Dental* the defendant was a voluntary nonprofit association of local dental societies to which about three-quarters of California dentists belonged. The CDA's ethical code prohibited false and misleading advertising and had been implemented through advisory opinions and guidelines. The FTC claimed that the CDA unreasonably restricted two types of truthful, nondeceptive advertising: price advertising, particularly the offering of discounted fees, and advertising relating to the quality of services. As summarized by the Court, the advisory opinions contained the following propositions:

> Any communication or advertisement which refers to the cost of dental services shall be exact, without omissions, and shall make each service clearly identifiable, without the use of such phrases as "as low as," "and up," "lowest prices," or words or phrases of similar import.

> Any advertisement which refers to the cost of dental services and uses words of comparison or relativity—for example, "low fees,"— must be based on verifiable data substantiating the comparison or statement of relativity. The burden shall be on the dentist who advertises in such terms to establish the accuracy of the comparison or statement of relativity.

> Advertising claims as to the quality of services are not susceptible to measurement or verification; accordingly, such claims are likely to be false or misleading in any material respects.

527 U.S. at 761 n.2.

The FTC had found that these restrictions violated Section 5 of the FTC Act as either per se illegal restraints or as restrictions that are illegal under an "an abbreviated, or 'quick look' rule of reason analysis designed for restraints that are not per se unlawful but are sufficiently anticompetitive on their face that they do not require a full-blown rule of reason inquiry." 128 F.3d at 727. Upon review, the Court of Appeals for the Ninth Circuit rejected the FTC's judgment that per se analysis was appropriate but affirmed the agency's decision under a truncated application of the rule of reason. The court agreed with the FTC that the restrictions on discount advertising "amounted in practice to a fairly 'naked' restraint on price competition itself," *id.*, and found that the CDA's procompetitive justification, that the restrictions encouraged disclosure and prevented false and misleading advertising, carried little weight because "it is simply infeasible to disclose all of the information that is required," *id.* at 728, and because "the record provides no evidence that the rule has in fact led to increased disclosure and transparency of dental pricing." *Id.* Put differently, in a case in which both the FTC and the court of appeals agreed that there was sufficient proof that the CDA possessed market power to show anticompetitive effect, CDA bore the burden of proving that its regulation of price advertising on balance benefitted consumers. The court of appeals also found that the restrictions on advertising relating to quality decreased output, and given this anticompetitive effect, CDA too bore the burden of showing consumer benefit. *See id.*

Read carefully here. The relevant dental markets are local and the FTC did not formally prove power market by market. Instead, it used the CDA's overall statewide membership numbers to show that the advertising restrictions had sufficient anticompetitive effect to shift the burden to defendant to show procompetitive benefit. CDA argued before the Commission, the appellate court and the Supreme Court that the Commission could not prevail without formal proof of market power—the "Full Monty." That claim was never accepted. *See* Stephen Caulkins, California Dental Association: *Not a Quick Look But Not the Full Monty*, 67 ANTITRUST L.J. 495 (2000) [hereinafter Caulkins, *California Dental Association*].

In a 5–4 opinion the Supreme Court vacated the court of appeals' decision, holding that the Ninth Circuit "erred when it held as a matter of law that quick-look analysis was appropriate." *California Dental*, 526 U.S. at 769. The Court observed that in prior cases using a "quick look" standard under the rule of reason, "an observer with even a rudimentary understanding of economics could conclude that the arrangements in question would have an anticompetitive effect on customers and markets." *Id.* at 770. The Court distinguished those prior cases, finding that the CDA's regulation of price and quality advertising differed from a professional association's ban on price competition in the submission of engineering bids, *see* National Society of Professional Engineers v. United States, 435 U.S. 679 (1978), from a prohibition of the submission of dental x-rays to insurers for purposes of reviewing medical necessity, *see* FTC v. Indiana Federation of Dentists, 476 U.S. 447 (1986) (discussed in more detail below in the note on group boycotts after *Rome*), and from the NCAA's rule limiting the number of college football games that may appear on television during a season. *See National Collegiate Athletic Association*, 468 U.S. 85.

The Court found that unlike those restraints, the "CDA's advertising restrictions might plausibly be thought to have a net procompetitive effect, or possibly no effect at all on competition," *California Dental*, 526 U.S. at 771, a question that is "susceptible to empirical but not *a priori* analysis." *Id.* at 774.* The Court thus held it was error to infer net anticompetitive harm, or, in other words, to rule against the CDA because the CDA had failed to establish net procompetitive benefit. Instead, the FTC bore the burden of affirmatively proving net harm. The Court remanded the case to the Ninth Circuit to consider whether the FTC had carried this burden. On remand the court of appeals held that it had not, and the court ordered the case dismissed. *See California Dental*, 224 F.3d 942 (2000).

Notice that the Supreme Court's decision has two facets. First, the CDA's restrictions appear to restrain price and quality competition less directly and comprehensively than a total ban on discussion of prices (*National Society of Professional Engineers*), a ban on the provision of

---

* The lack of empirical support in the record stemmed from the different posture taken by the CDA before the FTC, the Ninth Circuit and the Supreme Court. Until the latter stage, the CDA claimed that its rules proscribed only false and misleading advertising and its principal posture was that it could not be forced to justify its restrictions because the FTC had failed to prove market power. For the first time before the Supreme Court it claimed that a ban on price advertising that is incomplete could benefit consumers by generating more exact, detailed price information; and for the first time it claimed that a complete ban on quality advertising was warranted because of consumers' inability to judge such claims. As a result, many questions regarding the exact implementation of the rules, their effects on the amount and type of advertising, and their effects on the price and quality of dental services, including issues pertaining to professional advertising generally, were never joined below. *See* Caulkins, *California Dental Association*.

dental services in which x-rays are the primary vehicle for medical necessity determinations (*Indiana Federation of Dentists*), and a ban reducing the number of telecast games involving big-time football programs (*NCAA*). Second, and on the other side of the ledger, the restrictions plausibly benefit consumers by preventing advertising that is incomplete or unverifiable. In discussing this point, the Court carefully explicated scholarship showing how markets for professional services differ from other markets in that it is much harder for consumers in a timely fashion to get and assess information regarding the quality of services. *California Dental*, 526 U.S. at 771–76. This is consistent with the Court's discussion of market imperfections in *Eastman Kodak Co.*, 504 U.S. 451, to which we have made reference a number of times already and do so again below.*

Notice how the type of restraint affects the allocation of burdens of producing evidence and burdens of proof and how through this process courts consider the relative anticompetitive harm and procompetitive benefit that a type of conduct typically presents. The plaintiff in *Maricopa*, the State of Arizona, won summary judgment in a case in which horizontal competitors established maximum prices for their services even though the record, construed against the State as the moving party, failed to establish that collectively defendants had market power. Maximum price fixing presented significant danger that the defendant associations might be able to engage in minimum price fixing, deter the development of new means of delivering medical goods and services, and deter the entry of new forms of financing those services. Hence defendants bore the burden of justifying the price fixing either by disproving market power or by showing that only they could establish relative value schedules and thereby create the information necessary for insurers to predict risk and establish premiums.

In opposing the State's motion for summary judgment, defendants had not shown enough in either regard to carry this burden. By contrast, in *California Dental Association*, the regulation of the content of price and quality advertising, while potentially harmful to price and quality competition, was not so obviously harmful as to require defendants to justify. Therefore, even though the FTC, in its reliance on statewide membership figures, had to some degree made a showing of market power and anticompetitive effect, the agency still could not prevail without its proving that on

---

* The Supreme Court found the alleged anticompetitive effect of regulating advertising relating to quality to be an empirical question. *See California Dental*, 526 U.S. at 776–77 & n.13. Others more confidently assert that restriction of advertising increases search costs, which in turn reduces output. *See* Timothy J. Muris, California Dental Assn. v. Federal Trade Commission: *The Revenge of Footnote 17*, 8 S. Ct. Econ. Rev. 265, 291–92 (2000). However, if consumers cannot assess the accuracy of advertising because they cannot judge the price-quality mix of health care services, then advertising may in fact increase search costs. Moreover, in such circumstances increased output from advertising can lead to unnecessary and poor quality care. If application of antitrust to health care is supposed to improve consumer welfare, the Court was right that these are difficult empirical questions that cannot be presumed away by quick looks (based on simplistic economics). Professor Muris is clearly right that advertising with regard to some simple services—like tooth cleaning—may enhance welfare, *see id.* at 290, but decision making must be carefully tailored. Posing questions about the effects of "professional advertising," *see id.* at 288–304, is simply way too broad.

balance the CDA's regulations harmed consumers more than they benefitted them, i.e., the FTC bore the burden of proving net anticompetitive harm. The FTC lost because it failed to carry this burden. If the CDA's conduct had more directly restrained price competition by, for example, banning all forms of advertising, the defendant professional association would have borne the burden of proving benefit. *See, e.g., National Society of Professional Engineers* (rule prohibiting submission of price with technical bid).

7. *The importance of being vertical (or not horizontal) again, e.g., hospital privilege litigation.* An issue that aptly illustrates the importance of characterizing conduct as vertical or horizontal—the subject of the next subpart—is the massive amount of litigation over hospital privileges. Doctors who have been denied privileges or who have lost their privileges have almost routinely attempted to mount section 1 or section 2 claims, or both. For the most part, these claims have failed. Below we question whether it is appropriate to try cases under *both* section 1 and section 2, but for now, we'll ignore that question. Section 2 claims have failed because in most cases, hospitals have not had market power or when they have had power, they've been able to show justification, e.g., the plaintiff lost privileges because of poor quality of care.

In many cases plaintiffs have lost section 1 cases because in 1986, Congress reacted to the mounting tide of litigation by immunizing from antitrust challenge peer review taken in the reasonable belief that patients are at risk and meeting procedural requirements like notice and opportunity to be heard. *See* Health Care Quality Improvement Act of 1986, 42 U.S.C. §§ 11101–11115 (discussed earlier in Part Three). Many other section 1 claims were dismissed, however, because the conduct was deemed to be vertical. Under this reasoning and based on particular facts, the hospital acted as an integrated, single-entity decision maker and determined that it did not wish to contract with the plaintiff. Since a firm cannot conspire with its constitutive parts, within the meaning of section 1, the hospital's action could not form the basis for a section 1 claim despite the involvement of the hospital's organized medical staff and peer-review committees. *See* Copperweld Corp. v. Independence Tube Corp., 467 U.S. 752 (1984) (parent and subsidiary pursuing common economic interest could not engage in section 1 concerted action).

However, every once in a while a court relied on the fact that decisions were made with the involvement of the medical staff, and particular facts supported the suspicion that the action was taken to eliminate horizontal competition among physicians. Under those circumstances, the conduct was undertaken, not by a single, unified entity, but instead by actors such that among separate actors pursuing individual economic interest. Review they might have had reasons to target a horizontal competitor. Review under section 1 was therefore appropriate. *See, e.g.*, Manatee 1993); *see also* Hospitals & Health Systems, Inc., 993 F.2d 1514 (11th Ct. 2201 (2010) American Needle, Inc. v. National Football Leagueams for collective (Section 1 applied to joint venture formed by licensing of team logos because, regardless of revenue pooling from collective licensing, each team is separately owned, independently managed and pursued individual, not collective, economic interests with regard to property rights in team logo). We stress again that the characterization of conduct as horizontal or vertical can be outcome determinative.

4.   CHARACTERIZATION ISSUES

Rome Ambulatory Surgical Center v. Rome Memorial Hospital

349 F. Supp.2d 389 (N.D.Y. 2004)

■ HURD, DISTRICT JUE:

I.   *INTRODUCTN*

Plaintiff RomAmbulatory Surgery Center, LLC ("plaintiff" or "RASC") brought against Rome Memorial Hospital, Inc. ("defendant", "Rome Hospital" the "Hospital") and its corporate parent Greater Affiliates, Inc. ("G' or "defendants").

Plaintiff was eestanding ambulatory surgical facility located in the City of Rome, Newrk within Oneida County. Prior to the events which led to this action, Rome medical community was politically divided. A significant numbearea physicians were affiliated with the Hospital, and another group of pendent physicians had formed their own organization. The plaintiff ity was established by the non-hospital, independent physicians, and theged illegal conduct consists of Hospital efforts aimed at harming the coming facility.

Defendnts' ad conduct falls into two eneral categories. First, plaintiff allges tl defendants engaged in various acts to limit the number of atient errals to RASC. This included ducing and conspiring with affiliatohysicians such that those physicins would not refer patients to RASC forurgery, and intimidation of the physicians who used the facily. The secoi category of alleged illegal conduct invves entering into unlvful exclusive contracts with commercial third party payers. Under the contracts, the patients covered by those health insurance plans were effevely removed from the market in which RASC competed.

RASC ims that this referral restriction and exclusive contracting, not only inj d plaintiff, but forced it to leave the market taking with it the consumer plaintiff, but forced it to leave the market taking with it service, and lotefits it provided; greater customer choice, higher quality rices.

Plaintiff's amended complaint asserts [ten federal] causes of action. There are amended complaint asserts [ten federal] causes of action under Sherman Act 15 U.S.C. § 1:

First Cause of Acti uses of action under Sherman Act 15 U.S.C. § 1:

Second Cause of Acting Contract in Restraint of Trade;

Third Cause of Actionr se Illegal Tying Contract;

l Exclusive Contracts;

Fourth Cause of Action—Market Allocation;

Fifth Cause of Action—Conspiracy to Unreasonably Restrain Trade in Out–Patient Surgery, and;

Sixth Cause of Action—Per se Illegal Boycott.

There are four causes of action under Sherman Act 15 U.S.C. § 2:

Seventh Cause of Action—Monopoly leveraging;

Eighth Cause of Action—Attempted Monopolization;

Ninth Cause of Action—Monopolization of the Outpatient Surgery Market, and;

Tenth Cause of Action—Conspiracy to Monopolize the Outpatient Surgery Market.

Pursuant to Fed. R. Civ. P. 56, defendants moved for summary judgment on the entire complaint, based on lack of standing—causation and failure to demonstrate an antitrust injury—and various insufficiencies of the separate causes of action. Plaintiff cross-moved for summary judgment on the *Fifth* and *Tenth* conspiracy causes of action.

II. *BACKGROUND*

Rome Hospital is a not-for-profit community hospital that provides a full range of patient services including general inpatient acute care and outpatient surgery. It is affiliated with other non-profit and for-profit corporations which provide support to the Hospital and various medical services in the Rome area. While it is the only hospital within the City of Rome, there are four others within a twenty mile radius; Oneida Healthcare, St. Elizabeth Medical Center, Faxton Hospital, and St. Luke's Healthcare. The last two are owned by Mohawk Valley Network which also owns several outpatient facilities in Rome.

There were three significant changes in the Rome healthcare environment in the years immediately preceding the events which led to this action. The first was in 1995 wherein the Hospital transformed from a heavily-indebted publicly-managed hospital to a non-profit private hospital. Following the change in status, the Hospital began another reconfiguration into a managed care system/network. The financial plan of the Hospital presumes that profits from ambulatory surgeries will be used to subsidize other, less profitable, medical services.

The next year brought a change in the regulatory environment, The Healthcare Reform Act of 1996, effective January 1997, replaced Department of Health regulation of hospital rates for most third party payers with a competitive system. Prior to the Reform Act the state set hospital reimbursement rates under a formula which guaranteed higher rates each year. Rome Hospital now had to negotiate for rate changes, both upward and downward. The two largest health insurers in Oneida County throughout the 1990s, measured in terms of patients insured, were Blue Cross/Blue Shield ("BCBS") which covered about 21% of the people who used Rome Hospital, and MVP Health Plan ("MVP"), which covered approximately 8 to 9% of the Hospital's patients. The third party payers used the area's market competitors against each other in negotiating rate reductions, and to pressure area hospitals to deal with market actors the payers could not otherwise reach, i.e. the area's anesthesiologists.

Also during this time, the national boom in free-standing ambulatory surgical centers reached upstate New York. Ambulatory or out-patient surgery is surgery for which the recovery period is less than twenty-four hours and the required post-operative care is not intensive.

RASC claims that the Hospital's change in corporate form contributed to a devise in the local medical community. The change allowed for meetings to be conducted in private, as opposed to previous practice, and for new contractual arrangements with physicians, which weren't entered into evenly across the staff. Regardless of the stimulus, two distinct, and apparently rival, physician groups were formed in Rome, Central New York Medical Alliance PLLC ("CNYMA") and Rome Area Physicians Group ("RAPO"). One example of the alleged conflict between the groups consisted of some CNYMA physicians refusing to work hospital call-schedules with non-CNYMA members.

In 1996, Rome Hospital and certain physicians initiated two physician hospital organizations ("PHOs"). The first was CNYMA, which included Rome Medical Group ("RMG"), the largest primary care practice in the Rome area, and other primary care and specialty physicians. CNYMA negotiated manage care contracts for the physicians. The second PHO was Physician Support Services IPA, Inc. which provided billing and record keeping services to its members.

Because RASC alleges a conspiracy between Rome Hospital and area "cooperating physicians," facts concerning the relationship between them must be related. Among other things, CNYMA was a referral group. Where RMG made an average of 163 referrals per physician to CNYMA physicians, it made an average of 24 referrals to non-CNYMA/non-RMG physicians. The Hospital and CNYMA were financially involved, in large part, because the Hospital relied on CNYMA doctors to refer patients to the hospital. The physicians benefitted from the alliance through arrangements like the Hospital's purchase of RMG's in-office laboratory business. After the purchase, the Hospital continued to pay RMG rent for the laboratory space because it is located on the medical group's premises. Another benefit included income supplements provided by the Hospital for use in recruiting RMG physicians.

Dr. Jeffery Amidon, a RMG partner who spent most of his time at the Hospital, kept the medical group informed about RMG's interaction with the Hospital, specifically its doctors' referral patterns, in order to maintain a strong, tight service network. RMG documents in the record reveal that it kept track of the referrals and that someone at RMG would discuss referral decisions with those doctors who deviated from recommended practice. Prior to RASC's opening, the Hospital tracked physician affiliation with CNYMA and RAPO and use of its surgical facilities.

The same month RASC opened, St. Elizabeth Hospital issued a Letter of Intent to buy RMG. The Hospital subsequently purchased an option to consider its own purchase of the medical group, conducted due diligence and decided to buy the practice. While the Hospital would lose money on the purchase, it was determined that it would lose more by letting the practice, and thus the referrals, go to St. Elizabeth's. The sale was completed six months after RASC's closure.

The other area physician group, RAPO, was also formed in 1996. The group consisted of Rome area primary care physicians and doctors in every specialty. RASC was developed by the non-hospital affiliated physicians, though they maintained Hospital privileges and worked as Hospital staff. Many, but not all, of the doctors who own stock in RASC were RAPO doctors. The physicians felt they could recapture ambulatory service patients who left the area for service, at least in part due to dissatisfaction with Rome Hospital. RAPO members also tend to refer within their physician group. Indeed, RASC's business plan relied heavily on RAPO physician use of the facility.

In December of 1996, RASC filed a Certificate of Need ("CoN") application with New York State Department of Health seeking approval for its proposed ambulatory surgical facility. The Hospital predicted an estimated 2.4 Million Dollar loss to Hospital if RASC opened and met its projected numbers. The Hospital, and others (St. Elizabeth's, Faxton Memorial Hospital, St. Luke's Healthcare, and Auburn Memorial), opposed the application through the regulatory process.

The Hospital's Director of Managed Care, Mr. Paul Tasillo, was the Hospital employee responsible for dealing with the CNYMA physicians. He coordinated a letter writing campaign in opposition to RASC's CoN. He sent the CNYMA physicians a sample opposition letter, collected their responses, and reported the results to the Hospital. He later requested letters in support of the Hospital's own CoN to refurbish its ambulatory surgery facilities.

However, there was support for RASC's application to open its facility from the third party payers or the commercial insurance companies. Both MVP and BCBS stated that they intended to contract with RASC.

RASC's pending entry into the market effected [sic] contract negotiations between Hospital and the commercial payers. MVP and BCBS admitted that they needed Hospital business to do business in Rome. Yet, for the first time they had a direct competitor to use to effect a more favorable deal in ambulatory surgery. In January of 1999, the Hospital and BCBS engaged in negotiations over potential discounted outpatient surgery rates in exchange for an exclusivity designation. Late in the month however, BCBS abruptly stopped the negotiations citing political considerations. Initially, and at the time of these negotiations, BCBS policy in dealing with ambulatory surgery centers was to automatically contract with new facilities. Accordingly, BCBS entered into a contract with RASC. This contract was to expire on December 31, 2000.

The Hospital was, however, able to obtain an exclusivity provision in its contract with MVP. The history of negotiations between those parties was a little different. In the summer of 1997, MVP signed an exclusive contract with another provider, Centrex, for laboratory services. All MVP-covered patients had to have their lab work done at Centrex. Various efforts by RMG doctors and Hospital effected an exception to the agreement which allowed for some lab work to be done through the Hospital.

Considering MVP's exclusive agreement with Centrex, Hospital claims it feared another MVP exclusive, this time with RASC, and so sought one itself beginning in January 1999. MVP agreed to an exclusive designation for ambulatory surgery with Hospital for three years, January 1, 1999 through December 31, 2001, and received reduced rates for ambulatory surgery from the Hospital. The agreement included a ninety-day termination clause. This agreement effected RASC usage because third party payers effectively exercise patient choice since patients must often pay out-of-pocket for uncovered procedures.

In January 1998, the Hospital also had a CoN application with the state seeking permission to improve and expand its own ambulatory surgery facility. New York State Department of Health granted both facilities' CoNs. The Hospital subsequently withdrew its application in July of 1998 because of costs, and declined to improve its ambulatory facilities to provide more direct competition to RASC.

In June 1999, RASC opened in leased space on the former Griffiss Air Force Base in Rome and operated for eighteen months until January 2001.

Submitted testimonials relate RASC patients' satisfaction with the new facility. By RASC's account it was more convenient, patient friendly, and cost effective than the Hospital. However, plaintiff never met its costs. While the reasons are disputed, it is clear that RASC costs were higher than projected, and its income was lower. For one, RASC did a higher percentage of government paid surgery than expected, and this, in turn, meant a lower average pay rate than expected.

RASC's allegations focus on its lower than expected income due to low patient use of RASC as a result of defendants' conduct. Plaintiff alleges that low referral rates were due to Hospital's intimidation of its users, and conspiring with cooperating physicians to choke off referrals. Referral practices affected RASC usage because patients generally follow doctor recommendations.

RASC solicited 144 physicians from Rome, Oneida, Utica, and New Hartford. Forty-four applied, but only twenty-four actually used the facility, and half of those were RASC owners. This was in part because RASC investor physicians gave patients a choice of facilities. This was also in part due to the need to access emergency care if necessary, which meant using the Hospital's services. Scheduling and practicality also determined RASC use. Generally, referrals continued to flow according to the political divisions between CNYMA and RAPO. Overall, even physicians that used RASC used the Hospital more often than they used RASC.

As noted, non-hospital affiliated RASC physicians maintained Hospital privileges and worked as Hospital staff. This meant that RASC investor physicians were in a position to refer Hospital patients to their own facility. It would be possible for them to refer those patients who required profitable procedures to RASC, and leave the costly ones for the Hospital. Whether or not this occurred is disputed by the parties and their experts.

The Hospital experienced a 14.7% decline in out-patient cases in the first six months of RASC operation, and an estimated loss of 18 to 20% of its cases over the full eighteen months. Due to One Million Dollars in cost reductions in the year 2000, overall Hospital profits increased during RASC's tenure, but the Hospital lost money on ambulatory surgery while RASC operated.

The month RASC opened, the Hospital's Board of Trustees amended its bylaws to allow the Board to consider whether a physician competes with the hospital in evaluating medial staff appointments. The bylaw was never used and was removed in 2002 (after RASC closed).

Plaintiff further alleges that the Hospital and/or its co-conspirators harassed the physicians that supported RASC; one doctor received an unfavorable review, one suffered public accusations of disloyalty to the Hospital and was reported to the Department of Health, two lost contracts with the Hospital, two suffered extra competition from doctors that the Hospital recruited to the area, and one happened to be reported for an immigration violation.

Meanwhile the negotiations between BCBS and the Hospital concerning ambulatory surgery intensified. Having declined to enter into an exclusive contract in with the Hospital in 1998, BCBS proceeded to use the Hospital's interest in ambulatory surgery to its advantage. In 1999, BCBS had a specific negotiation plan wherein it threatened to remove Rome Hospital as a provider unless it lowered its ambulatory rates and pressured its independent anesthesiologists to become participating providers with BCBS. BCBS used the same steerage threat against the Utica hospitals. The threat was to steer patients to another facility if each hospital didn't bring the local anesthesiologists into the BCBS network. The Hospital continued to try to bargain for exclusivity, or at least a no steerage provision.

The sequence of events during the 2000 negotiations is disputed, but at some point RASC asked BCBS for a 25% rate increase in the next contract, and BCBS received what it considered to be an unfavorable report concerning RASC's financial status and plans. BCBS noted that one of RASC's problems was that it simply was not getting the expected patient flow. In November 2000, BCBS entered into a two-year contract (2001 and 2002) with the Hospital which gave the Hospital an exclusive in ambulatory surgery. Therefore, the contract between RASC and BCBS which expired on December 31, 2000, was not extended or renewed. BCBS constituted an estimated 25 to 30% of RASC business. Plaintiff claims that the Hospital's exclusive contract with BCBS was the final straw that put it out of business.

Less than a month later, in January 2001, RASC closed.

III. *DISCUSSION*

C. *Sherman Act Claims*

Defendants' alleged illegal conduct falls into two general categories; efforts to restrict referrals to RASC, and exclusive contracting with commercial payers. The different categories and their combinations form the basis of different claims and it is important to be clear exactly what plaintiff has alleged when considering each claim. Section 1 of the Sherman Act forbids every contract, combination in the form of trust or otherwise, or conspiracy, in restraint of trade or commerce among the several states. 15 U.S.C.S. § 1. Plaintiff has characterized the exclusive contracts under four theories of unlawful agreements; tying, illegal exclusive contracting, market allocation, and a group boycott. Plaintiff characterizes the referral restricting conduct as a conspiracy, and brings conspiracy claims under both §§ 1 and 2 of the Sherman Act. Finally, the § 2 Sherman Act monopolization claim combines the conduct categories in an attempt to demonstrate anticompetitive or predatory conduct.

1. *§ I Sherman Act Claims (First through Sixth Causes of Action)*

The restraints at issue here are between the Hospital and its customers, referring physicians, and commercial payers. These are vertical market relationships. Absent price-fixing between a supplier and distributor, vertical restraints are generally subject to "rule of reason" analysis.

a. *Tying Claims (First and Second Causes of Action)*

A tying arrangement is the conditioning of the sale or lease of one item (the "tying" product) on the purchase of another item (the "tied" product). The essence of the claim is that the seller exploits his market power in the tying product to restrain competition in the market for the tied product. Plaintiff alleges that defendants required the third party payers, BCBS and MVP, to contract for outpatient surgery services on an exclusive basis as a condition for contracting for general inpatient acute care hospital services on a discounted basis.

To state prima facie tying arrangement claim under the Sherman Act, plaintiff must allege: (1) two separate and distinct products, (2) actual coercion by seller that forces buyer to take tied product, (3) seller's market power in tying product or ability to force buyer to take tied product, (4) anticompetitive effects in tied product market, and (5) more than insubstantial amount of interstate commerce affected by tying arrangement in tied product market. *See, e.g., Jefferson Parish Hosp. Dist. No. 2 v. Hyde,* 466 U.S. 2, 12–18 (1984).

Plaintiff brings both per se and rule of reason tying claims. Leaving aside all the other elements of either type of tying claim, plaintiff cannot demonstrate that defendants actually coerced the third party payers into entering into exclusive contracts for ambulatory services. Nor has plaintiff set forth sufficient facts to support a reasonable inference of such coercion. On the contrary, the record effectively demonstrates that the exclusive contracts, unreasonably restrictive or not, were the product of negotiation.

Timothy Bozer of BCBS testified as to BCBS's posture at the time BCBS decided to grant the Hospital the exclusive contract in 2000.

Q: The reality was Blue Cross, or Excellus at the time, was not giving up much by agreeing to the exclusivity in light of the past history and in light of what you saw of [RASC's] financial status?

A: Until we saw [the] numbers and reports [RASC] showed us we just weren't going to sever ties on an integrity level. They're doing things. They weren't really monitored. We don't have a staff to monitor every account. That put it right in our face. That was a big turning point in my mind that changed everything. This clarified it for us.

Q: You're giving up something that [the Hospital] wanted but in reality, you weren't giving up much?

A: The doctors weren't going to be upset, because generally they weren't using the surgery center. The patients wouldn't notice ... because they weren't using it very much either ... The groups were fine with us before then, they would be fine with us after. We didn't see by the volume there would be much ripple effect. We didn't want to sever a business relationship we established, and then someone gives you all the information you need to make a quick business decision and it's very compelling.

Plaintiff's attempt to overcome this demonstration consists of pointing to BCBS testimony where it admits that a medical service provider selling in Rome needed the Hospital to do business. This begs the question. Plaintiff must connect that fact to BCBS's agreement to the exclusive contract, and plaintiff has not met its burden.

As for the other exclusive contract with MVP, the record describes complex negotiations between the Hospital and MVP in several service areas. There are simply no viable facts to support an inference of anything but negotiation. The complaint itself lists the long-wanted benefits MVP received as a result of agreeing to the exclusive contract; discounts in outpatient surgery, a fixed three year term, and a new reimbursement structure.

Furthermore, as defendants point out, the third party payers received discounts in outpatient rates in exchange for the exclusive contract. Plaintiff is unable to point to any discounts in the alleged tied product, inpatient rates, as plaintiff alleged in its second amended complaint.

Defendants have met their initial burden of pointing to material facts tending to show there is no genuine issue for trial. RASC has done no more than "show that there is some metaphysical doubt as to the material facts." *Matsushita Elec. Indus. Co.*, 475 U.S. at 586–87. Defendants' motion for summary judgment must be granted as to both tying claims.

b. *Illegal Exclusive Contract (Third Cause of Action)*

Plaintiff claims that the Hospital's contracts for ambulatory surgery services with the commercial health plans are illegal exclusive contracts which foreclose a significant degree of the Rome area third party payer submarket. The Hospital acted to obtain an exclusive contact with MVP and BCBS at its first opportunity. It took longer to obtain an exclusive arrangement with BCBS than MVP, but it was the focus of negotiations as soon as the Hospital discovered RASC's pending market entry.

The claim is subject to the rule of reason analysis because the contracts at issue are not of the pernicious type conclusively presumed to be unreasonable. Indeed, courts have approved vertical arrangements between hospitals and providers and recognized the competitive benefits. *See Jefferson Parish,* 466 U.S. at 29.

Under the rule of reason analysis plaintiff must demonstrate (1) anticompetitive market effects; (2) that the alleged conduct foreclosed a significant degree of trade; and (3) that the defendants' procompetitive justification for the conduct is not valid. The analysis below proceeds accordingly, mindful of the fact that to survive summary judgment plaintiff only needs to raise a question of material fact as to each issue.

(1) *Anticompetitive Effect*

RASC must demonstrate that the challenged activity "has had an actual adverse effect on competition as a whole in the relevant market." As explained above plaintiff has two options for demonstrating anti-competitive effects; competition-reducing effect through evidence of actual effects or by a showing of market power.

Plaintiff may demonstrate actual adverse effects on the market by a showing reduced output, increased prices, decreased quality, or the imposition of entry barriers. Plaintiff alleges that defendants harmed competition in eliminating the benefits RASC provided to consumers while it operated: lower prices, greater customer choice, and higher quality service. Defendants respond that RASC has not demonstrated actual consumer benefits, but illusory ones.

Beginning with price benefits, commercial payers paid approximately 35 percent lower rates during RASC's tenure. Furthermore, it was RASC's presence in the market as a competing contractor that made it possible for the payers to negotiate those rates. RASC presented an opportunity to pressure the Hospital. It would be a reasonable inference that RASC's market presence decreased the market price of ambulatory surgical services and that the exclusive contract preventing RASC's from further competition in contracting caused RASC's failure (and/or inability to compete effectively due to an antitrust injury) and deprived consumers of that benefit.

As to the other market effects, patient choice and quality are challenging to quantify, but they are especially relevant here considered in combination with a demonstrated market price reduction. Certainly, RASC's closure resulted in a loss of choice for Rome area patients. While antitrust policy is not aimed to protect competitors at the sake of market efficiency, the loss of choice is a significant injury to competition.

Demonstrating any given market participant's effect on the quality of a product or service in the market at a particular time is a complex task. Plaintiff's attempt consists of citing survey responses of Hospital patients, statements regarding the Hospital's own CoN application describing the unfavorable conditions of Hospital facilities, and by providing RASC patient testimonials. The weight of such offerings will be left to a fact finder.

While defendants make some persuasive arguments to refute the above averments on price, choice, and quality, the issue of anticompetitive effects remains disputable. Plaintiff has met its burden in this regard.

(2) *Unreasonable Restraint*

Plaintiff must demonstrate that the exclusive contracts unreasonably restricted trade by foreclosing a significant part of the relevant market. While "significance" varies, it is clear that the "plaintiff must both define the relevant market and prove the degree of foreclosure."

For the purpose of this claim, plaintiff has narrowly defined the market as the "submarket for commercial health plans in the greater Rome area," the largest of which are BCBS and MVP. Defendants do not dispute that this is a relevant market in which the Hospital could have restrained trade but only plaintiff's method of defining it and the allocation of market share within it.

Case law supports the proposition that a 40% foreclosure is likely an unreasonable restraint. Plaintiff allocated the proportionate shares of market payers in accordance with what the Hospital received from commercial payers in relation to what the hospital received from the government, self pay and workman's compensation payers. Plaintiff concludes that in 2000 commercial payers made up 49% of Hospital's revenue. BCBS represented roughly 40% of that revenue. The Hospital's payer mix for 1999 was similar, with commercial payers representing 54% of revenue and BCBS constituting almost 39% of that revenue.

A fact finder might reasonably infer that the Hospital was a large enough player in a relatively small market, as plaintiff narrowly defined it, that its payer mix ratio was a reasonable basis for determining market share of its customers. The instant case is not like the example defendants offer in their memorandum, a small medical practice that derives 90% of its income from an exclusive contract with a payer. Defendants' burden here is to provide a conclusive or undisputable alternative allocation formula such that plaintiff could not have foreclosed a legally unreasonable portion. Defendants have not attempted this and as such questions of fact remain.

(3) *Procompetitive Justification*

Under the rule of reason analysis, defendants may defeat plaintiff's illegal exclusive contracting claim by demonstrating that the alleged conduct, however restraining, had procompetitive effects. Defendants' proffered justification is two-fold; first that the conduct was justified in competitive "self-defense" in response to RASC physician investor's ability and motive to steer patients towards their own facility, and second, that there is an efficiency gain in high volume contracts.

This claim addresses defendants' exclusive contracts with the commercial payers. It is difficult to see how exclusive contracting would be considered an appropriate response to the particular behavior defendants claim to be defending against, "cherry picking" or "cream skimming," and possible "free riding" by the RASC investor physicians. Defendants argue that they would have been permitted to exclude those physicians from hospital privileges altogether. Perhaps, and that may have been a more appropriate response, but it is not a defense to the issue of the exclusive contracts. The logical disconnect in defendants' argument is sufficient to raise a question of fact as to its justification.

Defendants also offer that exclusive contracts are not only common, but often considered procompetitive. The MVP and BCBS contracts allegedly benefit competition because they allow for efficiency gains. The greater number of surgeries would provide sufficient volume to allow for some economy of scale which allows for reduced prices or increased input. While the rationale is sound, questions remain as to whether this was actually applied here.

Defendants state that the discounted price to payers proves that the rationale worked here. Interestingly, defendants' own expert, William Lynk, provides the counter argument. Short-term loss for the sake of long-term gain is a legitimate business decision. The lower rates, could simply have been used to secure the contact. While Hospital's maintaining volume certainly could contribute to beneficial pricing as defendants and their expert state, it is not clear that that is what was intended or what occurred here. Maintaining patient volume is certainly good for the Hospital, but defendants have not conclusively demonstrated that it in any way benefitted competition.

Plaintiff has raised questions of fact as to the anticompetitive effect, market foreclosure, and defendants' procompetitive justification of defendants' exclusive contracts with MVP and BCBS. Defendants' motion for summary judgment as to illegal exclusive contracting will be denied.

c. *Market Allocation (Fourth Cause of Action)*

Plaintiff alleges that defendants and cooperating physicians agreed not to compete with each other in certain markets, thereby allocating those markets to each other. This conduct is alleged to be both per se illegal in and of itself, and intended to effectuate a conspiracy to eliminate RASC as a competitor. Defendants oppose by objecting to a per se classification of the claim. Plaintiff failed to respond to defendants' motion in opposition papers or any of the numerous accompanying submissions. Plaintiff has effectively abandoned the claim.

d. *Conspiracy to Restrain Trade (Fifth Cause of Action)*

Plaintiff alleges that the Hospital and Rome area cooperating physicians, including RMG, conspired to restrain trade in the outpatient surgery market. To establish a conspiracy in restraint of trade violation, a plaintiff must produce evidence sufficient to show: (1) a combination or some form of concerted action between at least two legally distinct economic entities; and (2) the combination or conduct constituted an unreasonable restraint of trade either per se or under the rule of reason.

A rule of reason analysis will be applied here because though plaintiff is not specific as to exactly who defendants conspired with, the candidates, RMG and/or other CNYMA cooperating physicians, and the Hospital are in vertical market relationships. Vertical refusals to deal are agreements among persons or organizations at different levels of the market structure not to deal with other market participants. *See United States v. Topco Associates, Inc.,* 405 U.S. 596, 608. Defendants are suppliers of surgical services and the alleged co-conspirators are the customers who bring patients, the actual buyers. There are only two rationales that would allow for per se treatment of this vertical arrangement. The first is price fixing. The alleged agreements, between the Hospital and the cooperating physicians, are non-price agreements.

In support of applying the other per se rationale, plaintiff cites *Klor's, Inc. v. Broadway–Hale Stores, Inc.,* 359 U.S. 207, 79 (1959), where the court did apply per se treatment to a vertical agreement. But *Klor's* is distinguishable. The case involved a vertical agreement between supplier and a customer in combination with a horizontal agreement among the competing customers. The court found a "combination of manufacturers, distributors and a retailer." Plaintiff simply has not set forth sufficient facts from which to infer any horizontal agreement between the Hospital's customers, CNYMA physicians and/or RMG. Business relations and opportunity to conspire are not sufficient in and of themselves for inferring agreement. Accordingly, a rule of reason analysis is required.

Assuming *arguendo,* that plaintiff could demonstrate concerted activity sufficient to constitute a conspiracy, plaintiff's claim fails due to its failure to raise a question of fact as to anticompetitive effects or the unreasonableness of any restraint that may have occurred. Under a rule of reason analysis plaintiff bears the initial burden of demonstrating that the defendants' conduct or policy has had a substantially harmful effect on competition. As explained above, plaintiff has two options for demonstrating anticompetitive effects, direct evidence of actual effects on competition or a demonstration of market power coupled with a showing that the "arrangement has the potential for genuine adverse effects on competition," for example, substantial market foreclosure.

Plaintiff attempts the former method and may satisfy this burden of proving the actual anticompetitive effects by showing a reduction of output, increase in price, or deterioration in quality of goods and services. Plaintiff states in conclusory fashion that there are clear restraints on price, choice, and output as a result of the alleged conspiracy. Plaintiff's demonstration of such effects not only is insufficient to support its motion for summary judgment, it fails to satisfy RASC's burden of raising a triable issue to survive defendants' like motion.

The effect of an alleged restraint is evaluated in the context of the particular facts of a case. What plaintiff has effectively demonstrated is the strength of the referral networks along the CNYMA and RAPO lines prior to RASC's tenure. It seems that to show any effect of an alleged conspiracy plaintiff must argue that the market would have been different, less restrained, in its absence. Furthermore, plaintiff must attempt to quantify that effect in some way to demonstrate that the effect is a significant restraint. Market foreclosure is of course one option, but having declined that method, plaintiff neglects to offer another.

Plaintiff does claim that consumer choice was reduced. Assuming plaintiff means patient choice, RASC fails to explain how the alleged conspiracy did that more than the established referral network did. As defendants' expert, Thomas Dennison, points out, without some added incentive to change, physicians would be unlikely to alter their well established referral patterns just because RASC entered the market.

There is an overwhelming overlap between the alleged conspiracy and the already established referral networks. The network itself has not been opposed, is not at issue and is thus presumed a legitimate business network. This overlap makes it more difficult to demonstrate an effect of the conspiracy as opposed to the effect of the network. The difficulty, however, does not relieve plaintiff of the burden and the attempt made through a few conclusory statements is insufficient in the context of the instant case. Defendants' motion for summary judgment will be granted in regard to this cause of action because plaintiff has failed to demonstrate anticompetitive effects or an unreasonable restraint due to the alleged conspiracy between the Hospital and the cooperating physicians as required under a rule of reason analysis.

e. *Per se Illegal Boycott (Sixth Cause of Action)*

Plaintiff alleges that the Hospital's inducement of BCBS and MVP into exclusive contracts, and the tacit conspiracy among defendants and the two payers to eliminate RASC from the market constitutes a per se illegal boycott.

A per se illegal boycott is an agreement among competitors within the same market tier not to deal with other competitors or market participants. *See Topco Assocs.,* 405 U.S. at 608. Such concerted action is usually termed a horizontal restraint, in contradistinction to combinations of persons at different levels of the market structure, e.g., manufacturers and distributors, which are termed vertical restraints. *Topco Assoc.,* 405 U.S. at 608. Horizontal group boycotts are per se illegal.

The market relationships between the Hospital and the commercial payers are analogous to the relationship between the Hospital and the referring physicians. Defendants are suppliers of surgical services and the alleged co-conspirators are the customers who bring patients, the actual buyers. As explained above, per se treatment does not apply to vertical arrangements absent alleged price fixing and *Klor's* will not be applied to otherwise trigger a per se analysis in absence of evidence of a horizontal agreement. Thus, in order to receive per se treatment, and thus any treatment at all as the claim is pleaded, plaintiff must show a horizontal agreement between MVP and BCBS. No such finding would be reasonable here.

Plaintiff has failed to raise a question of fact as to a possible agreement or understanding between MVP and BCBS concerning RASC. Plaintiff fails to point to specific facts to support any such inference. The MVP contract was entered into prior to the time that Hospital first suggested an exclusive contract to BCBS. There is no reason to draw an inference that MVP, at the time it was negotiating with the Hospital, was considering BCBS or RASC in any way, let alone that it would have agreed with BCBS to boycott RASC.

BCBS knew of MVP's exclusive contract with the Hospital during its contract negotiation with the Hospital, but deposition testimony reveals simply that they used the information to negotiate better deals with both the Hospital and RASC. Defendants' motion for summary judgment will be granted as no reasonable fact finder could infer any agreement or tacit conspiracy between the third party payers based on the instant record. Per se treatment is not applicable, and thus this cause of action fails.

2. § 2 Sherman Act Claims (Seventh through Tenth Causes of Action)

a. Monopoly Leveraging and Monopolization of the Outpatient Surgery Market (Seventh and Ninth Causes of Action)

Plaintiff's second amended complaint alleges that defendants used their monopoly power in the general inpatient acute care hospital services market to harm plaintiff in the secondary, outpatient ambulatory services market. It is "unreasonable, per se, to foreclose competitors from any substantial market." *International Salt Co. v. United States,* 332 U.S. 392 (1947). The anti-trust laws are as much violated by the prevention of competition as by its destruction. *United States v. Aluminum Co. of America,* 148 F.2d 416, 428 (2d Cir. 1945). Thus the use of monopoly power, "however lawfully acquired, to foreclose competition, to gain a competitive advantage, or to destroy a competitor, is unlawful." *United States v. Griffith,* 334 U.S. 100 (1948).

The plaintiff's monopoly leveraging and monopolization causes of action differ only in the alleged effect in the second market, an unfair competitive advantage and acquisition of monopoly power. Monopoly leveraging claims address the use of monopoly power in one market to gain an unfair competitive advantage in a second market. To prove a monopoly leveraging claim in the Second Circuit, the plaintiff must establish that the defendant: "(1) possessed monopoly power in one market; (2) used that power to gain a competitive advantage ... in another distinct market; (3)

caused injury by such anticompetitive conduct; and (4) demonstrate that there is dangerous probability of success in monopolizing a second market." *N.Y. Mercantile Exch., Inc. v. Intercontinental Exchange, Inc.*, 323 F. Supp.2d 559, 572 (S.D.N.Y.2004) (citations omitted).

Both causes of action require plaintiff to demonstrate monopoly power in the general inpatient acute care market. RASC may allege monopoly power by pleading: (1) power to control prices or exclude competition; or (2) possession of a predominant share of the relevant market.

Plaintiff has not satisfied either option. As far as direct evidence of the power to control prices or exclude competition, the record only addresses defendant conduct in the outpatient market. For example, plaintiff claims that success of the alleged conspiracy in restricting referrals to RASC and its ability to foreclose part of the market through exclusive contracting demonstrate defendants' power to exclude competition. While raising questions of fact as to defendants' power in the second market, that evidence will not be accepted as evidence on which to infer power back into the inpatient market, certainly not to the point of monopoly power.

The usual method of demonstrating monopoly power is the second option, showing that the defendant possesses a predominant share of the relevant market. It is "a basic principle in the law of monopolization that the first step in a court's analysis must be a definition of the relevant markets."

Plaintiffs have the burden of defining the relevant product market. This requires the plaintiff to define the market in which such power is held. In neither the voluminous record nor motion memorandum does plaintiff attempt to define the inpatient market or defendants' share of it. The only plaintiff evidence towards this requirement is found in a financial report prepared for the defendants in 1998 that includes a projected market share for defendants during the time of RASC's tenure. This is insufficient; it is only a prediction and the methodology is not adequately explained. Indeed, documents submitted by defendants reveal that this failure to define the inpatient market was not an oversight, but a strategic litigation decision.

The leveraging claim (*Seventh* Cause of Action) fails because it is based on the exercise of monopoly power in the inpatient services market, and plaintiff failed to define that market in order to show market share or, alternatively, to offer direct evidence of defendant's power to "control prices or exclude competition" within it. Plaintiff's monopolization (*Ninth* Cause of Action) claim fails for the same reason because plaintiff framed the cause of action in the same manner as the leveraging claim, in reliance on the use of monopoly power in the inpatient services market which it subsequently declined to define. Defendants' motion for summary judgment on both claims must be granted.

b. *Attempted Monopolization of the Outpatient Surgery Market (Eighth Cause of Action)*

Plaintiff alleges that the Hospital's alleged conduct was part of an attempt to monopolize the outpatient surgery market. Attempted monopolization is proven when a plaintiff can show "(1) that the defendant has engaged in predatory or anti-competitive conduct with (2) a specific intent to monopolize and (3) has a dangerous probability of achieving monopoly power." Plaintiff has raised a question of fact as to all three requirements. These will be addressed in turn.

(1) *Predatory or Anticompetitive Conduct*

Plaintiff relies on the conduct alleged under its § 1 Sherman Act claims to demonstrate anticompetitive conduct for purposes of its § 2 Sherman Act claim. In review, that conduct includes a conspiracy and physician intimidation to restrict referrals to RASC, and illegal exclusive contracts. The alleged conduct would be sufficient to sustain a claim under § 2. The question becomes whether defendants have a sufficient business justification for that conduct.

The Second Circuit has not articulated precise rules for what constitutes anticompetitive conduct for this claim, and thus there is no simple rule for determining when behavior is anticompetitive and when it is efficient and pro-competitive. As the Supreme Court has acknowledged, "it is sometimes difficult to distinguish robust competition from conduct with long-term anticompetitive effects." *Spectrum Sports,* 506 U.S. at 459. The question to be answered is the fact-specific question whether the challenged conduct is "exclusionary" or "predatory." *Aspen Skiing Co. v. Aspen Highlands Skiing Corp.,* 472 U.S. 585, 602 (1985).

Defendants offer two justifications, one for each category of alleged conduct. As for passing the bylaw and any efforts that may be found to limit referrals to RASC, defendants argue that they were justified in light of the potential for "cream skimming" by the RASC physicians. Defendants offer an efficiency rationale for entering into the exclusive contracts. They claim that they were able to offer lower prices if they could be assured of increased volume in patients. Defendants argue that the exclusive contracts were just run of the mill volume discount agreements. As discussed above, under the illegal exclusive contract claim, questions of fact remain as to defendants' justifications.

(2) *Intent to Monopolize*

Specific intent to destroy competition or build monopoly is essential to be guilty of attempt. Proof of the first element of an attempted monopolization claim, anticompetitive or exclusionary conduct, may be used to infer the second element. This is true where the conduct that is alleged to be predatory forms the basis for the substantive claim in restraint. Here the conduct at issue also supports a viable claim for illegal exclusive contracting and, as explained below, a viable claim for conspiracy to monopolize. A reasonable inference of intent is possible based on that combination of conduct.

(3) *Dangerous Probability of Achieving Market Power*

To allege a dangerous probability of achieving monopoly power, plaintiff must plead that defendants possess a sufficient share of the relevant market. Plaintiff asserts that the Hospital held a 70% market share before and after RASC's tenure. This 70% share is generally accepted as an indication of monopoly power, and if proven would be sufficient to support its claim.

The parties do not dispute that ambulatory surgery is the relevant product. The appropriate geographic market definition however is thoroughly disputed by both side's experts.

Plaintiff has come forward with sufficient evidence to create a genuine issue of material fact regarding the scope of the market. Whether or not defendants have a predominant market share depends on how the "greater Rome area" market is defined. As just noted, market definition, by any approach, must consider both the geographic market in which the defendant competes, and then the available substitutes for product within that market. Plaintiff has drawn the boundaries of the outpatient surgery market such that, absent RASC, defendants are the only suppliers in it. Such narrowing is suspect and naturally defendants complain and offer their own market definition by way of their own expert.

The market definition dispute centers on the use of the Eliza–Hogarty [sic] method of market definition.[11] The parties claim that the other's expert failed in application of this method to the instant market. It seems both parties strayed from a pure application, but that need not be resolved at summary judgment. The results of an Eliza–Hogarty [sic] analysis are not dispositive in defining the relevant market. To survive this summary judgment motion the plaintiff need only demonstrate that its market definition would be proper as a matter of law, and provide sufficient data to justify a reasonable inference. The plaintiff has managed this burden, which is of course not to express an opinion on plaintiff's ability to do so at trial.

Plaintiff has raised material issues of fact as to the relevant geographic market. First, plaintiff's E–H test application defines a market at the lower-but-reasonable-in-some circumstances 75% E–H market share threshold. Plaintiff has raised the question of whether defendants' preferred 90% E–H threshold requirement may be inappropriate in the health care market.

---

11. In short, this method amounts to designating the smallest geographic area from which a certain percentage of defendants' patients originate. This is the competitor's "service area." The requisite percentage is in dispute, but the range is between 75 and 90%. The second step is to determine the substitutes available within that market to those original patients. The third step consists of considering the additional patients that those competitors serve. The thinking is that if part of the competitor's market can or would use the alternatives available then they all might use them in response to a price increase or quality decrease. The geographic market is then redrawn to include a threshold percentage of the substitute suppliers' originating patients. The number of patients in the total market is found according to that second drawing. The number of the patients the competitor serves is placed (in the numerator) over the number of patients served by both the competitor and the substitutes combined (the denominator) to arrive at the competitor's market share.

Second [p]laintiff has demonstrated that significant market actors did not view the substitute suppliers that defendants point to within Rome's geographic market as actual substitutes. BCBS for example testified that they considered RASC an opportunity to pressure the Hospital for lower rates being unable to use the other area hospitals as effective substitutes for that purpose.

Assuming plaintiff can prove a predominant market share, its burden is not met. "Courts only infer monopoly power based on predominant market share after considering other relevant factors, such as competitive levels within the relevant market, entry barriers to the relevant market, the nature of the anticompetitive conduct at issue and the elasticity of consumer demand." *Moccio*, 208 F. Supp.2d at 376.

Plaintiff argues that these other factors are present. New York State's CoN process constitutes a significant entry barrier. Plaintiff's expert has explained that surgery patients may be inelastic in demand as they chose where they have surgery based on other factors than just price, but also location and perceptions of quality due to a Hospital's reputation. The weight of such factors is left to the fact finder, here it is enough that plaintiff has raised them and supported them in the record.

Defendants' motion for summary judgment on the attempted monopolization claim must be denied as plaintiff has raised triable issues as to anticompetitive effects, defendants' intent and the probability of success of an alleged conspiracy.

c. *Conspiracy to Monopolize the Outpatient Surgery Market (Tenth Cause of Action)*

Plaintiff alleges that the Hospital has conspired with Rome area cooperating physicians to monopolize the outpatient surgery market. This is alleged as a separate and distinguishable conspiracy from the alleged effort to not use RASC for ambulatory surgery in restraint of trade.

To sustain its claim, plaintiff must demonstrate concerted action, overt acts in furtherance of conspiracy, and specific intent to monopolize. Sherman Act, § 2, as amended, 15 U.S.C.A. § 2. Unlike the elements required to establish an attempt to monopolize, proof of a conspiracy to monopolize does not require a dangerous probability of success. Also, a conspiracy to monopolize violates § 2 even though monopoly power was never acquired.

Both parties have moved for summary judgment claiming the other cannot raise an issue of material fact. Neither party has so conclusively demonstrated their view of the facts to preclude the need for a fact finder.

Plaintiff alleges that RMG only referred ambulatory surgery patients to specialists who used the Hospital. In return, RMG allegedly received direct and indirect financial benefits. Plaintiff provides the following facts from which to infer such an agreement. Plaintiff's expert offers statistics to suggest that referral rates demonstrate the existence of a conspiracy. In 2000, CNYMA physicians performed ambulatory procedures at the Hospital and only two at RASC. The record contains evidence of significant financial dealings between the Hospital and RMG. It was the Hospital Director that negotiated managed care contracts on behalf of CNYMA/RMG physicians. The record contains evidence of RMG efforts to maintain its referral network which used the Hospital. There is testimony that the doctors who did get referrals from RMG physicians knew they should perform the procedures at the Hospital and not RASC. Plaintiff adds that the Hospital's solicitation of letters opposing its CoN and RMG physician responses demonstrate a shared motive between the co-conspirators. It would be a reasonable inference that the Hospital conspired to restrict referrals to RASC.

However, defendants have submitted physician testimony that their referral decisions were not influenced by anything but patient welfare. Defendants argue that Hospital's purchase of RMG followed RASC's closure and shouldn't contribute to an inference of motive for an agreement. Defendants point out that RMG's consideration of sale to St. Elizabeth's in the same month RASC opened, detracts from an inference that RMG and the Hospital were co-conspirators. They claim that it would be a reasonable inference that Hospital and RMG did not conspire to restrict referrals to RASC.

The submitted evidence and the reasonable inferences to be drawn from it require both credibility assessments of the various witnesses and a weighing of the various political and economic factors that would motivate the alleged conspirators conduct. Such is the role of a fact finder.

The allegations refer to numerous overt acts in furthering the conspiracy, the parties thus turn to the requirement of proving specific intent to monopolize. If "one party's intent to monopolize is not shared by another party, there can be no conspiracy to monopolize." Plaintiffs allege the Hospital and RMG shared the intent to monopolize the outpatient market because while RASC's failure benefitted the Hospital, it also benefitted RMG. As noted above, determining intent on the instant record is not possible, credibility and the weighing competing pressures is required.

Since questions of fact remain as to whether or not a conspiracy existed and what the alleged co-conspirators intended if they did so conspire, both parties motions for summary judgment will be denied.

IV. *CONCLUSION*

Defendants' conduct could be found to be a substantial factor in causing a material injury to RASC. Furthermore, that injury is properly considered an antitrust injury. Plaintiff has met the standing requirement.

Under a rule of reason analysis, questions of fact remain as to whether Rome Hospital's exclusive contracts for ambulatory surgery with the third party payers, MVP and BCBS, had anticompetitive effects, unreasonably restrained trade, or were justified by procompetitive effects. Plaintiff has also raised triable issues as to all three requirements of the attempted monopolization claim; anticompetitive conduct, defendants' procompetitive justification and whether defendants had a dangerous probability of success. Finally, questions of fact remain as to whether the Hospital engaged in a conspiracy with RMG, or other cooperating physicians, to monopolize the outpatient surgery market.

Plaintiff failed to provide sufficient allegations of coercion to support its tying claims. Plaintiff abandoned its market allocation claim in failing to respond. Under a rule of reason analysis, plaintiff failed to raise a material issue as to anticompetitive effects of the alleged conspiracy to restrain trade. There are insufficient facts to infer that competition was actually restrained, and if so, to what extent that might have occurred to support a finding that it was unreasonable. Plaintiff's per se boycott claim fails because it was not properly supported by evidence of a horizontal agreement to trigger per se treatment. Finally, the monopoly leveraging and monopolization claims fail because plaintiff did not demonstrate monopoly power in the inpatient surgery market.

Accordingly, it is

ORDERED that

1. Defendants' motion for summary judgment is GRANTED in part, and DENIED in part, as follows:

a. The *First, Second, Fourth, Fifth, Sixth, Seventh, Ninth, Eleventh* and *Twelfth* causes of action are DISMISSED;

b. The *Third, Eighth,* and *Tenth* causes of action are NOT DISMISSED.

2. Plaintiff's motion for summary judgment as to the *Fifth* and *Tenth* causes of action is DENIED.

IT IS SO ORDERED.

Notes

1. *There ought to be a law (or at least a doctrinal category).* For the moment forget any antitrust doctrine and just consider what happened here, according to plaintiff's allegations. Plaintiff was a new ambulatory surgery center that entered into competition against Rome Hospital, the market incumbent. According to the ASC, the hospital reacted in two ways. First, it conspired with, enticed, coerced—for the moment, just pick your verb—the faithful portion of its medical staff to stop sending patients to the ASC. Put differently, by relying on the extant referral network the hospital sought to deprive the ASC of patients. Second, the hospital conspired with, enticed, coerced—again for now just pick your verb—the two largest insurers in the area to enter into exclusive contracts with it for the provision of outpatient surgery. Put differently again, the hospital attempted to deprive the ASC of patients. If proven, these allegations amount to a showing that the ASC went out of business, not because it offered an inferior product to the hospital's in terms of a price-quality mix, but because its competitor was able to cut off its supply of customers, i.e., raise a barrier to entry. There ought to be a law (or at least a doctrinal category)! There certainly have been a number of similar cases, as a result of war breaking about between hospitals and ASCs or specialty hospitals. For

some recent examples, see Little Rock Cardiology Clinic v. Baptist Health, 591 F.3d 591 (8th Cir. 2009), *cert. den.*, 130 S. Ct. 3506 (2010) (allegations similar to that in *Rome* dismissed due to failure to show that hospital possessed market power); Peoria Day Surgery Center v. OSF Healthcare System, 2009 WL 5217344 (C.D. Ill. 2009) (summary judgment denied because plaintiff showed sufficient evidence of hospital's market power and increased prices from alleged tying of inpatient to outpatient services).

2. *An embarrassment of riches.* But do there have to be so many? The use of the insurers to deprive the ASC of patients was at the core of counts one and two (tying of outpatient to inpatient care); three (exclusive contracts for both inpatient and outpatient care); six (conspiracy among insurers to boycott outpatient care at ASC); seven (leveraging market power over inpatient to outpatient care); eight (attempted monopolization of outpatient care); and nine (monopolization of outpatient care). The use of the hospital-physician referral network to deprive the ASC of patients was at the heart of counts four (market allocation of outpatient care to the hospital); five (conspiracy unreasonably to restrain trade in outpatient care); and ten (conspiracy to monopolize outpatient care). Counts one, two, seven and nine were dismissed for lack of evidence that the hospital possessed market power over inpatient care. Count four was abandoned. Count five was dismissed because plaintiff failed to show that the involvement of the physicians loyal to the hospital had any effect more than the extant referral network. Count six was dismissed for lack of evidence of a conspiracy among the insurers.

Left standing were counts three (exclusive contracts with insurers), eight (exclusive contracts with insurers and the use of the referral network), and ten (the use of the referral network). Do you feel it was necessary for the court (and you) to slog your way through no fewer than ten antitrust counts? The fact that identical conduct can be poured through so many doctrinal pigeonholes might indicate to you that there is much doctrinal confusion. You would be right. *See, e.g.*, Melamed, *Exclusive Dealing Agreements and Other Exclusionary Conduct—Are There Unifying Principles?* at 384–86. *But see* Popofsky, *Defining Exclusionary Conduct: Section 2, The Rule of Reason, and the Unifying Principle Underlying Antitrust Rules.*

a. *How can the same conduct give rise to counts under both sections 1 and 2?* Think back to the beginning of this chapter. We wrote that section 2 pertains to single-firm conduct and section 1 to multi-firm behavior. It would seem, therefore, that a case should be analyzed under one or the other of the two. That would be correct, but it is also the case, as *Rome* amply illustrates, that the great majority of economic activity occurs through agreements, explicit or implicit, with the result that creative lawyers can allege concert of action to mount a section 1 claim in additional to one under section 2. Hence, while we focused on section 2 above in considering the conduct in *Dentsply* and the notes after that case, the fact that the conduct occurs in contracts means that the conduct has traditionally given rise to section 1 counts as well as those discussed under section

2. Exclusive *contracts*, after all, involve concert of action, multi-firm conduct. None of this would matter if sections 1 and 2 were applied consistently to a given set of facts but that is not always the case.

There is a converse irrationality. *Dentsply* was brought under both sections 1 and 2, and the fact that we read it only as a section 2 case was solely the result of the fact that the government decided not to appeal the adverse judgment below on the section 1 claims. Once again, the section 1 claims were possible because the exclusivity provisions were expressly included as Criterion 6 in contracts. Suppose that Dentsply had simply refused to fill any orders from dealers which did business with competing denture manufacturers. Most likely, under these facts there would be no concert of action and no basis for a section 1 case.* Yet in substance, with or without contracts, the two situations are the same, indicating again a serious lack of clarity. Moreover, many courts have held that such "unilateral refusals to deal" constitute exercises of the defendant's *Colgate* right and regardless of market power and competitive effects, defendant need not justify.** *See generally* 11 HERBERT HOVENKAMP, ANTITRUST LAW: AN ANALYSIS OF ANTITRUST PRINCIPLES AND THEIR APPLICATION ¶¶ 1800c5, 1821a (2d ed., 2005). By contrast, as we have seen, when concert of action exists, the conduct is analyzed under the rubric of "exclusive dealing"—and possibly other categories as indicated in *Rome* and discussed below. As a result, plaintiff's proof of market power and foreclosure forces defendant to justify, and the different characterizations can be downright outcome determinative. These examples can be multiplied. *See, e.g.,* Melamed, *Exclusive Dealing Agreements and Other Exclusionary Conduct—Are There Unifying Principles?* at 384–86. *But see* Popofsky, *Defining Exclusionary Conduct: Section 2, The Rule of Reason, and the Unifying Principle Underlying Antitrust Rules.*

b. *Is the conduct horizontal or vertical?* The problem is compounded by the fact that many cases like *Rome* (and *Dentsply, Ball Memorial Hospital,* etc.) have mixed horizontal and vertical aspects. By now courts virtually invoke a mantra to make judgments regarding the two forms— "horizontal" is usually bad; "vertical" is usually good—but then they often trip over themselves in characterizing conduct as horizontal or vertical, and the result is often a mess.

To see this, return again to the commonsense view of *Rome,* as alleged by plaintiff: Rome Hospital tried to stamp out an entrant which threatened to take away its outpatient surgery business. It simply used the means at hand, which were the referral network it shared with physicians and its

---

* The reason for our caveat, "most likely," is that even the issue of when concert of action exists in such instances is a morass. *See generally* 11 HERBERT HOVENKAMP, ANTITRUST LAW: AN ANALYSIS OF ANTITRUST PRINCIPLES AND THEIR APPLICATION ¶ 1821a (2d ed., 2005). We spare you these details.

** The law regarding unilateral refusals to deal by firms with market power is likewise complex, see generally 3B Phillip E. Areeda et al., ANTITRUST LAW: AN ANALYSIS OF ANTITRUST PRINCIPLES AND THEIR APPLICATION ¶¶ 770–74 (3d ed., 2008), and space limitations preclude coverage here.

relationship with the two largest insurers. If we focus on the conduct—exclusive agreements and refusals to deal—it involves concert of action among parties which stand in vertical relations. The mantra spits out: "There are two to this tango, and so this is a section 1 case, but vertical is usually good, and so this is rule of reason under section 1." Hence the court began its analysis of the section 1 counts with the statement that "[t]he restraints at issue here are between the Hospital and its customers, referring physicians, and commercial payers. These are vertical market relationships. Absent price-fixing between a supplier and distributor, vertical restraints are generally subject to 'rule of reason' analysis." 349 F. Supp.2d at 406. As we will see, this statement canvasses so many fact patterns as to be worthless. The court then focuses, not on the fact that the conduct involves concert of action among vertical actors, but that for the most part the target of the conduct, again as alleged, was the ASC, which stood in a horizontal relationship with the hospital.* It then analyzes under section 2 the same conduct it took through section 1 without a hint of awareness that there might be any difficulty in invoking both sections with regard to one set of conduct. This mishmash gives rise to redundant count after redundant count.

   c. It's the effects, baby. This confusion can be avoided by going functional—by simply focusing on possible competitive effects at whatever stages of production or markets are relevant, *see, e.g.,* Salop, *The First Principles Approach to Antitrust, Kodak, and Antitrust at the Millennium;* Krattenmaker et al., *Monopoly Power and Market Power in Antitrust Law* at 254–60, which we have done consistently by examining market structure, market share, degree of foreclosure, other evidence of competitive effects, and barriers to entry. A case like *Rome* is complicated because of the mixture of horizontal and vertical aspects: (1) the hospital and the surgery center are horizontal competitors with regard to some services but not others, as are the two feuding camps of physicians; (2) the hospital and the ASC both stand in a vertical relationship with the insurers as sellers and buyers, respectively, while the hospital and ASC both stand in a vertical relationship with the physicians as buyers and sellers, respectively. With regard to these sorts of situations you can help yourselves immensely by creating figures like the following:

---

* Count five seems to be the sole exception in that possibly it alleges that the physicians loyal to the hospital targeted their horizontal competitors, physicians allied with the ASC. We discuss this immediately below.

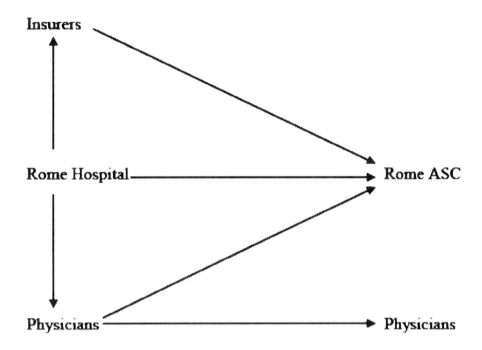

Once you've drawn the figure you can think about the potential existence and location of market power and what the target of that power might be, e.g., if the hospital has or could gain market power over outpatient surgery, it could target the surgery center, a horizontal competitor, to drive it from the market or reduce its output; it could target the insurers, purchasers of outpatient surgery, to increase the price of those services; or it could target the physicians, sellers to it of their services, to drive down the price of those services. You can also then think about the incentives, e.g., do the physicians in the Rome Hospital referral network have an incentive to target the ASC?; do the insurers have an incentive to target the ASC? Not only does such a figure give you a sense of possible incentives, it gives you a pictorial means to display what is happening in a given set of facts.

(1) *What's in it for the insurers, MVP and BCBS?* Were the insurers pleased that Rome ASC entered the market? Payers supported the ASC's application for a CON; BCBS was able to obtain lower prices for outpatient surgery; and had MVP not executed the exclusive contract with the hospital, it too would have enjoyed that benefit. Over the eighteen months the ASC operated, the hospital lost 18–20% of its outpatient cases. As happy campers, would the insurers have been willing to engage in conduct designed to stamp out the surgery center?

All other things being equal, the answer is a resounding "no." In the world of managed care insurers are in the business of connecting pools of covered lives with a network of providers. In this world, hospitals, physicians and all other providers are inputs into the product sold by the insurer to plan sponsors, to wit, a network of providers. Absent special circumstances, a purchaser of an input has no incentive to reduce competition among the suppliers of that input because to do so poses the possibility of a higher price or lower quality for the input and concomitant reduced sales for the purchaser.

But of what relevance is it that the insurers executed contracts, i.e., "agreed"? In some fact patterns, like that in *Dentsply*, the "agreement" is clearly coerced. The dealers in *Dentsply* either complied with the dictates of the defendant and refused to carry competing lines of dentures or defendant cut them off, which meant they would then have little or no business because Dentsply was by far the dominant firm. By contrast, in *Rome*, given that the hospital lacked market power over inpatient care, perhaps the insurers had to be "enticed" somehow to cut off the ASC, but should any of this matter? In our view, the answer is "no" because functionally, at least as we've analyzed it so far, the case remains one in which the hospital, by coercing or enticing the insurers, targeted a horizontal competitor to gain, maintain or enhance market power. This is conduct at the heart of Section 2.

(2) *What's in it for the physicians?* Now we must analyze the role of the physicians who were in a referral pattern that included Rome Hospital. Plaintiff alleged that the physicians conspired with the hospital to remove the ASC from the market. Does that make sense? All other thing being equal, the physicians would prefer two places to do surgery rather than one. As suppliers of an input for the provision of outpatient surgery, the physicians have no incentive to help a buyer of their services eliminate another buyer of their services. The incentives are a mirror image of those pertaining to the insurers. The latter, as we have seen, buy hospital services as an input and have no incentive to reduce competition for the provision of that input because reduction in that competition would increase the input's price. Likewise, as sellers of an input to the hospitals, the physicians have no incentive to reduce competition among the buyers of their services for to do so would reduce the price at which they can sell those services.

However, here things might not have been so equal. Given the sharp division in the physician community, it was clear that the physicians allied with the hospital were not going to operate at the ASC. At the very least, they would have been indifferent to the hospital's alleged effort to eliminate it; or they may have even been willing to help out because of a motive like spite. Additionally, the physicians loyal to the hospital might have had an incentive to eliminate the competition of the other physician camp, their horizontal competitors. If this last point is indicated in the facts, then the concern is a conspiracy among the physicians to eliminate their horizontal competitor, which indeed is a section 1 problem.

Yet, at least on the facts in the record, the latter view of the conduct, which is perhaps embodied in count five, seems implausible. The physicians allied with the ASC still had privileges at the hospital, and even physicians who used the ASC utilized the hospital more often than they did the surgery center. True the hospital had amended its bylaws to provide that a physician doing business with the ASC could lose his or her hospital privileges—and suspiciously this bylaw provision disappeared when the ASC likewise disappeared—but the provision was never invoked. Although the threat was plain and no doubt helped ensure that the ASC got fewer referrals, the fact remained that physicians who used the ASC were not denied a place to perform outpatient surgery when the ASC went out of business. What occurred is only that the hospital successfully moved all of that surgery into its outpatient department by putting the ASC out of business. Hence there appears not to have been any purpose or effect of altering competition among physicians but instead a battle over the site of care, i.e., does the hospital or the ASC get the facility fee? Although the court's analysis of count five could have been, let us say, crisper, perhaps it got the right result in its conclusion that the conspiracy alleged in count five, if it existed, would have had no more effect than did the extant referral pattern.

The court described the conspiracy in count ten, which survived, as distinct from that alleged in count five. Although it's not clear, it appears that in count ten plaintiffs alleged that RMG conspired with the hospital not to refer patients to the ASC, and in return RMG received "direct and indirect financial benefits" in its numerous financial dealings with the hospital. 349 F. Supp.2d at 420–21. Particularly because RMG was a primary-care group, they do not compete with surgeons, and therefore it still appears unlikely that there was a conspiracy among physicians to foreclose competition from surgeons who operated at the ASC. Immediately below in text we look at some fact patterns which suggest that physicians have used "hospital conduct" to eliminate competition from other physicians.

   d.   In the interest of analytic clarity (if not consistent results!). In sum, if we, the authors, were able to choose between which of sections 1 or 2 would apply to this case, we would pick section 2 on these facts. Quite simply, it was alleged that the hospital was trying to protect its alleged control of outpatient surgery. The hospital, fair and square, is at the center of the case as an alleged monopolist. True there was concert of action but the only purpose or effect of this vertical conduct was at the horizontal level of competition between the hospital and the ASC over outpatient surgery, with the allegation that the hospital attempted to maintain market power there. Therefore, we think that this case should have proceeded only under section 2; at the very least, the doctrinal categories applied under both sections should be the same. In this particular case, the results reached under the surviving counts—three (exclusive contracts); eight (attempt to monopolize); and ten (conspiracy to monopolize)—may turn out to be consistent (actually, the case was settled). However, that is not always the case and, moreover, as you can see the different characterizations of the conduct lead to diverse doctrinal categories and elements. This complexity is both unnecessary and potentially confusing. However, since we don't get to pick, the law will continue to see cases brought under both sections so long as inventive lawyers can find two moving parts to constitute concert of action under section 1.

3. *Stir the plot some more.* Let's play with some variations to consider how the analysis might change with different facts.

a. *Vertical conduct with horizontal effects at different levels.* A hospital and an anesthesiology group execute a contract in which the group will provide all anesthesiological services at the hospital. Consider the possibility that the hospital has market power. How does one define that market? At what level or levels is there possible foreclosure? How does one define that market or those markets to determine competitive effects? At which level are barriers to entry relevant, and if they exist, what are they? Consider the possibility that the anesthesiology group has market power. Ask the same questions. Consider the possibility that both the hospital and the group have market power. Same questions. Suppose that the exclusivity runs in the other direction, i.e., that the anesthesiology group will provide services nowhere else than at this one hospital. Finally, how does the analysis change if the contract is two-way (aka "two-sided"), i.e., exclusive in both directions?

b. *Leveraging into different markets.* Suppose that a hospital engages in a joint venture with the orthopedists on its staff to create an ASC at which outpatient orthopedic surgery will be provided. Inpatient and outpatient services are not substitutes. Consider the possibility that the hospital has market power over inpatient services (or a subset of inpatient services). How does one define that market? In which market or markets is there possible foreclosure? How does one define that market or markets to determine competitive effects? At which level are barriers to entry relevant, and if they exist, what are they? Consider the possibility that the orthopedists have market power over the inpatient services (or a subset of those services) they perform. Same questions. What if they possibly have market power over outpatient surgical procedures (or a subset of those services)? Would it make a difference if the ASC has an open or closed staff?

c. *Vertical conduct facilitating horizontal restraints.* Suppose that in a relevant geographic market there are three hospitals and three anesthesiology groups. Suppose that the groups and the hospitals have all executed exclusive contracts or contracts with MFNs. What inferences can be drawn from the fact that the use of these clauses is in every contract in this market? Is it relevant whether such arrangements are used in other markets? If so, why? Change the facts of *Dentsply* somewhat so that there are three manufacturers of dentures, all of which include exclusivity provisions in their contracts with local dealers. Does the fact that the provisions are used industry-wide alter possible inferences? Are barriers to entry, durations of the terms, and switching costs relevant? What about product homogeneity? As in the actual case, are diseconomies of vertical integration relevant? What if the manufacturers cannot come forward with or prove that the exclusivity provisions attain or are the only mean to attain efficiencies? What if there is evidence that the dealers have requested the inclusion of these provisions? In this regard, would it be relevant whether the dealers engaged in activities like product promotion or the provision of services? *See generally* 11 HERBERT HOVENKAMP, ANTITRUST LAW: AN ANALYSIS OF ANTITRUST PRINCIPLES AND THEIR APPLICATION ¶¶ 1805, 1821e-f (2d ed., 2005). For an interesting case involving allegations of a multi-party, multi-market-level war against a specialty hospital with some similarity to *Rome*, see Heartland Surgical Specialty Hospital, LLC v. Midwest Division, Inc., 527 F. Supp.2d 1257 (D. Kan. 2007).

d. *Horizontal conduct masquerading as vertical conduct.* U.S. Health-care, Inc. v. Healthsource, Inc., 986 F.2d 589 (1st Cir. 1993), involved an exclusive dealing arrangement between Healthsource, the defendant, and its network physicians. Healthsource was founded in 1985 by Dr. Norman Payson and a group of doctors. It was an IPA-model HMO in which primary care doctors served as capitated gatekeepers. To create additional incentives to control costs, Dr. Payson had encouraged its physicians to become stockholders, and at least four hundred had done so. However, in 1989 Dr. Payson decided to take Healthsource public, in part to generate greater liquidity for its doctor shareholders. Aware that other HMOs like U.S. Healthcare were considering entry into the New Hampshire market, Dr. Payson "was also concerned that, when Healthsource went public, many of its doctor-shareholders would sell their stock, decreasing their interest in Healthsource and their incentive to control its costs." *Id.* at 592. The exclusive dealing arrangement was conceived as the solution for this problem, and in return for accepting the exclusivity provision, a physician's capitation rate was increased 14%. Plaintiff, U.S. Healthcare, alleged that this arrangement constituted a barrier to entry into the New Hampshire market, but the court disagreed. Characterizing Healthsource's conduct as vertical and applying the rule of reason, it found insufficient foreclosure to warrant a section 1 or 2 violation. Given the fact that physicians were shareholders in Healthsource, is there any other way to characterize the arrangement? Is the fact that Healthsource went public a relevant consideration? Refer to our discussion of *Maricopa* above.

4. *Horizontal effects in light of increasing concentration and increasing vertical integration.* The number of cases with mixed horizontal and vertical components seems to be rising, probably for two reasons. The first reason is that some markets have become concentrated both on the provider and payer side. This point is well illustrated by the recent case of West Penn Allegheny Health System ("West Penn") Inc. v. UPMC, 627 F.3d 85 (3d Cir. 2010). Plaintiff West Penn Allegheny Health System had a share of less than 23% of the market for hospital services in Allegheny County, Pennsylvania, an area that includes Pittsburgh. By contrast, the market is dominated by the University of Pittsburgh Medical Center ("UPMC") and Highmark, which respectively had market shares of 55% and 60–80% (Highmark's share varied over a number of years since 2000). West Penn alleged that the two dominant players on the two sides of the market declared a "truce" such that, among other things, UPMC insulated Highmark from competition on the insurance side by refusing to execute agreements with insurance companies trying to enter the market against Highmark and by intentionally shrinking, and agreeing to withdraw from

the market, the insurer UPMC had created—vertically integrating backward into insurance—precisely to compete against Highmark because Highmark was trying to decrease payments to UPMC. To return the favor, Highmark agreed to drive West Penn from the market through such means as Highmark's paying low rates to West Penn and supra-competitive rates to UPMC, and Highmark's refusal to refinance a loan it had previously extended to West Penn so that West Penn could acquire failing hospitals, thereby preserving, to Highmark's benefit, competition against UPMC. Given these pled facts, the third circuit reversed a district court's dismissal of the complaint. The court found "plausible" the theory on which the case was based—that both UPMC and Highmark stood to gain from the alleged conspiracy. *See id.* at 101, 104–05.

The second related reason for the apparent increase in cases involving both horizontal and vertical elements is the greater degree of vertical integration in the marketplace in recent years, something that may be accelerated by bundled payment and by lucrative reimbursement paid to ACOs and the like. This aspect is well illustrated by the FTC's recent challenge to the pending hospital merger in Rockford, Illinois. Not only would the merger combine two of the three hospitals in the area, but because most primary care physicians in the area are employed by one of the three hospitals, the merger would also, according to the complaint, reduce competition among primary care physicians. *See* In re OSF Healthcare System, Administrative Complaint (Nov. 18, 2011) (http://www.ftc.gov/os/adjpro/d9349/111118rockfordcmpt.pdf).

One final example of both points. Pennsylvania recently entered into a consent decree with a urology practice group, Urology of Central Pennsylvania Inc. (UCPA), which was formed by the merger of five independent urology practices in the Harrisburg area. The complaint alleges that UCPA used its 84% market share to drive up its payments from payers. Additionally, UCPA formed specialized cancer treatment centers, particularly for the treatment of prostate cancer. According to the complaint it hired its own radiation oncologists and referred patients for in-house treatment, thereby reducing the volume of competing radiation oncology centers. Notably, similar to the FTC's decree in *Evanston Northwestern*, the remedies were only conduct-based. Neither the FTC in *Evanston Northwestern* nor the Pennsylvania Attorney General required divestiture—in Pennsylvania that would have meant breaking up UCPA, the source of the power. Rather, behavioral restrictions were imposed such as bargaining in good faith, use of arbitration in case of impasses with payers, barring the use of exclusivity or MFN clauses, and disclosure of non-UCPA radiation oncologists and CT imaging services to patients with the offer to refer them out. *See* Commonwealth of Pa. v. Urology of Central Pa., Inc., No. 3:02–at–06000 (M.D. Pa. 2011) (complaint and consent decree). Although it is difficult to "unscramble the egg," one must wonder how effective these strictures will be.

Ask yourselves, if consolidation continues to increase and if agreements are executed among consolidated entities at multiple levels of production, what is the effect on actual or potential entry? Further, think about the effects on welfare that are occurring *even without* the sorts of agreements in issue in Rockford, Harrisburg and, as alleged, in the Pittsburgh area (and there are a substantial number of similar examples). Recent studies of private insurers and hospitals have consistently shown increased concentration on both sides of the market. *See, e.g.,* Leemore S. Dafny, *Are Health Insurance Markets Competitive?*, 100 AM. ECON. REV. 1399 (2010); Robinson, *Consolidation and the Transformation of Competition in Health Insurance*; David Dranove et al., *Is Managed Care Leading to Consolidation in Healthcare Markets?*, 37 HEALTH SERV. RES. 573 (2002). In some areas of the country, consolidated hospital and payer sides face one another but recent evidence is that concentrated hospital markets outnumber concentrated payer markets. *See* Glenn A. Melnick et al., *The Increased Concentration of Health Plan Markets Can Benefit Consumers Through Lower Hospital Prices*, 30(9) HEALTH AFFAIRS 1728 (2011); *see also* Asako S. Moriya et al., *Hospital Prices and Market Structure in the Hospital and Insurance Industries*, 5 HEALTH ECON., POL'Y & L. 459 (2010). Nonetheless, higher prices and higher margins are generally correlated with higher concentration, on *both* the hospital and payer side. *See, e.g., id.*; Leemore Dafney et al., *Paying a Premium on Your Premium? Consolidation in the U.S. Health Insurance Industry*, NBER WORKING PAPER No. 15434 (2009) (http://papers.ssrn.com/ sol3/papers.cfm?abstract_id=1498916). If we need the consolidation and integration to rationalize care, which is where the payment system is moving with bundling, global payments, ACOs, and the like, then can antitrust possibly succeed in its mission? As we discussed in the payment chapter and elsewhere in Part Two, the evidence of rising payments (and income) on the provider side strongly suggests that antitrust is failing. Does that mean we just try harder? We will return to these points when in the last subpart of this chapter we assess the entire enterprise of applying antitrust to our health care system.

5.   *The persistence of tying as a category.* One of the arrows in the plaintiff's quiver in *Rome*, tying arrangements, has had a long—and many would say, sorry—doctrinal history. For our purposes, discussion of tying must start with the Supreme Court's decision in Jefferson Parish Hospital District No. 2 v. Hyde, 466 U.S. 2 (1984). In that case an anesthesiologist had been denied privileges at the defendant hospital because the defendant had granted another anesthesiology group, Roux & Associates, the exclusive right to provide anesthesiological services there. The defendant alleged, among other things, that this arrangement violated section 1 of the Sherman Act as an illegal tying arrangement or an invalid exclusive dealing contract. After trial, the district court defined the geographic market broadly as the entire New Orleans metropolitan area, in which defendant hospital, East Jefferson, had no power, with the result that the exclusive arrangement had minimal anticompetitive effects that were in any event easily outweighed by the benefits of improved patient care. By contrast, the court of appeals defined the market locally such that East Jefferson had power, with the result that the per se rule against tying was invoked and

plaintiff was entitled to judgment because defendant could have attained its quality objectives by less restrictive means.

Four members of the Supreme Court, in an opinion by Justice O'Connor, rejected the tying claim, which requires that there be two distinct products: the "tying" product—in this case hospital services—which the seller offers only with the "tied" product—here the anesthesiological services. According to Justice O'Connor, the major danger presented by a tying arrangement is that the defendant would use its power over the tying product to gain market power over the tied product, a theory of leveraging power from one market, the hospital, into the other, anesthesia services. Therefore, "[f]or products to be treated as distinct, the tied product must, at a minimum, be one that some consumers might wish to purchase separately *without also purchasing the tying product.* When the tied product has no use other than in conjunction with the tying product, a seller of the tying product can acquire no *additional* market power by selling the two products together." *Jefferson Parish Hospital District No. 2,* 466 U.S. at 39. Given this requirement, resolution of the tying claim was straightforward: "Patients are interested in purchasing anesthesia only in conjunction with hospital services, so the hospital can acquire no *additional* market power by selling the two services together. Accordingly, the link between the hospital's services and anesthesia administered by Roux will affect neither the amount of anesthesia provided nor the combined price of anesthesia and surgery for those who choose to become the hospital's patients." *Id.* at 43. Resolution of the exclusive dealing claim was likewise easy because there was no threat of foreclosure:

> At issue here is an exclusive-dealing arrangement between a firm of four anesthesiologists and one relatively small hospital. There is no suggestion that East Jefferson Hospital is likely to create a "bottleneck" in the availability of anesthesiologists that might deprive other hospitals of access to needed anesthesiological services, or that the Roux associates have unreasonably narrowed the range of choices available to other anesthesiologists in search of a hospital or patients that will buy their services. A firm of four anesthesiologists represents only a very small fraction of the total number of anesthesiologists whose services are available for hire by other hospitals, and East Jefferson is one among numerous hospitals buying such services. Even without engaging in a detailed analysis of the size of the relevant markets we may readily conclude that there is no likelihood that the exclusive-dealing arrangement challenged here will either unreasonably enhance the hospital's market position relative to other hospitals, or unreasonably permit Roux to acquire power relative to other anesthesiologists. Accordingly, this exclusive-dealing arrangement must be sustained under the rule of reason.

Id. at 45–46.

By contrast, the majority of the Court disagreed that there was no tie. Justice O'Connor characterized the provision of anesthesia as an input in the production of hospital services. As such, and as her analysis of competitive effects indicates, the arrangement between the hospital and Roux was vertical. However, the majority viewed the sale of anesthesia and surgery to be one of complements, or, in other words, the purchase by the patient, the end-user, of two distinct products:

> Unquestionably, the anesthesiological component of the package offered by the hospital could be provided separately and could be selected either by the individual patient or by one of the patient's doctors if the hospital did not insist on including anesthesiological services in the package it offers to its customers. As a matter of actual practice, anesthesiological services are billed separately from the hospital services petitioners provide. There was ample and uncontroverted testimony that patients or surgeons often request specific anesthesiologists to come to a hospital and provide anesthesia, and that the choice of an individual anesthesiologist separate from the choice of a hospital is particularly frequent in respondent's specialty, obstetric anesthesiology.

Id. at 22.

Nonetheless, the Court found no violation of section 1. First, agreeing with the district court that the relevant hospital market was broad, the Court ruled that plaintiff could gain no benefit from a per se rule of liability because it had failed to show that defendant had market power over the tying product, hospital services: "Only if patients are forced to purchase Roux's services as a result of the hospital's market power would the arrangement have anticompetitive consequences. If no forcing is present, patients are free to enter a competing hospital and to use another anesthesiologist instead of Roux." *Id.* at 25. Second, plaintiff could not prevail under the rule of reason because he had failed to prove an adverse effect on competition among anesthesiologists:

> The record sheds little light on how this arrangement affected consumer demand for separate arrangements with a specific anesthesiologist. The evidence indicates that some surgeons and patients preferred respondent's services to those of Roux, but there is no evidence that any patient who was sophisticated enough to know the difference between two anesthesiologists was not also able to go to a hospital that would provide him with the anesthesiologist of his choice."

Id. at 30.

These two opinions raise numerous issues.

a. *History of tying as a separate category; the use and meaning of its per se rule; and its unique doctrinal elements.* To understate, the history of tying is arcane and the complexity of the subject, mind-boggling. A leading treatise currently devotes two full volumes, comprised of nearly nine hundred pages, to the subject. *See* 9 & 10 Phillip E. Areeda et al., ANTITRUST LAW: AN ANALYSIS OF ANTITRUST PRINCIPLES AND THEIR APPLICATION (2d ed., 2004). We provide only a brief discussion of the subject, necessary because, as *Rome* illustrates, conduct that allegedly forecloses competition gives rise to claims that are tied (sorry!) with other doctrinal avenues, particularly exclusive dealing. Like other commentators, we question whether tying should be a separate doctrinal category at all, much less one subject to some version of a per se rule.

Early tying doctrine grew out of patent cases in which the patentee required licensees to buy its other products in conjunction with the use of its patented product—e.g., staples with a machine that stapled buttons to shoes, *see* Heaton–Peninsular Button–Fastener Co. v. Eureka Specialty Co., 77 F. 288 (6th Cir. 1896).—and then, a case which reflected concert of action with perhaps hubris that only Hollywood could muster, a conspiracy of the entire motion picture industry to tie together the use of motion picture cameras and projectors with film and exhibition, such that a single enterprise controlled the shooting, development, printing and exhibition of motion pictures. *See* Motion Picture Patents Co. v. Universal Film Mfg. Co., 243 U.S. 502 (1917). The result of this early litigation was such judicial and legislative hostility to tying arrangements that they were perceived as having no legitimate function and simply as "the means of regimenting and monopolizing an entire industry." 9 Phillip E. Areeda et al., ANTITRUST LAW: AN ANALYSIS OF ANTITRUST PRINCIPLES AND THEIR APPLICATION ¶ 1701c, at 22 (2d ed., 2004). A per se category was born, and then expanded to many, many more contexts because linguistically almost any part or service of a product could be said to be "tied" to the whole—is the zipper or are the buttons of pants "tied" to purchase of the pants? *See generally id.* ¶ 1701.

In this context, *Jefferson Parish* is actually part of a retrenchment in that it attempted to place some limitation on what could be characterized as a tie. As we've seen, both opinions agreed that in order for a part to be characterized as "tied" to the whole, there had to be demand and supply-side substitution for bundling—i.e., proof that patients or their surgeons want to unbundle anesthesia services from the rest of an inpatient stay, and proof that hospitals could or do efficiently unbundle these separate elements. The two opinions just reached different conclusions factually whether this requirement was satisfied.

Moreover, per se treatment adumbrated by the case is "most peculiar," *id.* ¶ 1701c, at 24, in that, as you can tell from the holding, to get any benefit from it, a plaintiff must show market power—compare, e.g., price fixing in *Maricopa* in which plaintiff did not have to show market power to force justification. Further, as indicated by dicta at least, its only real bite is that defendant must prove necessity:

> Petitioners argue and the District Court found that the exclusive contract had what it characterized as procompetitive justifications in that an exclusive contract ensures 24–hour anesthesiology coverage, enables flexible scheduling, and facilitates work routine, professional standards, and maintenance of equipment. The Court of Appeals held these findings to be clearly erroneous since the exclusive contract was not necessary to achieve these ends. Roux was willing to provide 24–hour coverage even without an exclusive

contract and the credentials committee of the hospital could impose standards for staff privileges that would ensure staff would
comply with the demands of scheduling, maintenance, and professional standards. 686 F.2d, at 292. In the past, we have refused to
tolerate manifestly anticompetitive conduct simply because the
health care industry is involved. See *Arizona* v. *Maricopa Medical
Society*, 457 U.S., at 348–351. Petitioners seek no special solicitude. We have also uniformly rejected similar "goodwill" defenses
for tying arrangements, finding that the use of contractual quality
specifications are generally sufficient to protect quality without
the use of a tying arrangement. Since the District Court made no
finding as to why contractual quality specifications would not
protect the hospital, there is no basis for departing from our prior
cases here.

Jefferson Parish Hospital District No. 2, 466 U.S. at 25 n.42. The per se
rule against tying lives on but, even though Justice O'Connor and three
other Justices would have gone further, it is a pale shadow of its former
self.

A substantial reason for the changed doctrine concerning tying ar-
rangements is that the rigid per se rule, based on the view that tying is
almost always pernicious, has been the subject of ferocious scholarly attack.
Although at the extreme some Chicago–School law and economics scholars
advocated a rule of per se *legality, see, e.g.,* ROBERT BORK, THE ANTITRUST
PARADOX 365–81 (1978), other criticism was more moderate, *see, e.g.* Tyler
A. Baker, *The Supreme Court and the Per Se Tying Rule: Cutting the
Gordian Knot,* 66 VA. L. REV. 1235 (1980), and was in any event later
balanced by scholarship which, as in other areas, relaxed the simplistic,
static price models used by the Chicago School and showed that tying
arrangement can sometimes have pernicious effects. *See, e.g.,* Louis Kaplow, *Extension of Monopoly Power Through Leverage,* 85 COLUM. L. REV.
515 (1985). We can divide this potential harm into four categories, the first
three of which we have already discussed with regard to vertical conduct—
not surprisingly because, as can be seen from *Rome* and *Jefferson Parish,*
tying arrangements very often take the form of vertical restraints.

First, tying arrangements can sometimes be used to leverage power
from one market to another. *Rome* is a perfect example in that, as alleged,
one purpose and effect of the tie was to use the hospital's purported power
over inpatient care to leverage control over outpatient surgery, as pled in
counts one and two. The alleged means used were the vertical relationships
between the hospital and physicians, and between the hospital and insurers, with regard to inpatient care. The alleged horizontal effect was to
maintain or enhance control over outpatient care by eliminating the ASC,
which competed with the hospital over outpatient, but not inpatient,
surgery.

The second possible harmful use of tying, likewise potentially at issue
in *Rome* and *Jefferson Parish,* is to entrench power in the market in which
the defendant already operates—in contrast to using a tie to leverage power

into another market. In *Rome*, this was the theory of count three, in which it was alleged that the exclusive contracts executed with insurers denied the ASC patients, thereby allowing the hospital to maintain or enhance power in outpatient services. In *Jefferson Parish*, this problem potentially existed because the exclusive contract with Roux was two-way, precluding the anesthesiology group from servicing hospitals other than East Jefferson Hospital. In both cases the issue would be to foreclose the hospital's actual or potential horizontal competitors' access to either patients (*Rome*) or necessary inputs (*Jefferson Parish*). Competitors would therefore have to find alternative sources of customers—alternative insurers in *Rome*—or alternative inputs—alternative anesthesiologists in *Jefferson Parish*. Given this foreclosure, entry would have required vertical integration at two stages rather than one. *Dentsply* was similar in that the exclusive contracts with dealers would have required competing denture manufacturers to bring in their own dealers, two-level entry.

The third potentially harmful use of tying is to facilitate horizontal restraints like price fixing. For example, suppose that the firm with market power over the tying product obtains a dominant position in the market for the tied product. If the fringe firms in the tied market reduce prices for the tied product, the tying firm need not follow their prices down. The customers of the tying firm are locked in by the tie, and therefore even if the fringe firms could expand capacity to service those customers, due to the tie those firms cannot steal them away. Because of this effect, the fringe has less incentive to reduce prices. The tie, therefore, helps facilitate horizontal price fixing in the tied market.

The fourth possible pernicious use of tying is to enable price discrimination through a so-called "requirements" or "variable-proportions" tie. Suppose a firm has a monopoly over an imaging machine and it leases or sells the machine under the condition that customers also buy imaging media from it. The volume of using the media varies among the customers depending on how often they use the imaging machines. Therefore, the amount of tied product used—the imaging media—effectively meters individual demand for the tying product—the imaging machine—and enables the tying firm to engage in price discrimination in the sale of the machine.

Notice that the scheme works even if only a trivial amount of competition in the tied market is obtained because the object is not to obtain a monopoly over the tied product but to meter demand for use of the tying product. Such price discrimination allows the seller to "price along the demand curve," so to speak, charging higher prices to customers willing to pay them, and lower prices, down to the competitive level, to those who won't pay more. At the extreme, price discrimination is perfect in that the price to each consumer is the maximum it would pay, output is not restricted below that of perfect competition, and the dead-weight loss of monopoly is avoided. For that reason, some argue that no antitrust problem exists, while others disagree, pointing to the wealth transfer from consumers to the seller. This debate need not detain us for our limited purposes here.

Against these potential harmful effects are potential efficiencies that can be attained through tying arrangements. Tying arrangements sometimes improve quality, reduce costs, enable evasion of price-fixing, and aid entry. Quality might be improved if the seller's tying product works better with the tied one, e.g., a firm ties sales and service to keep the product it sells working properly. Costs can be reduced through efficiencies in joint production or distribution. Price-fixing can be evaded because a discount for the tied product lowers the overall price to the customer, effectively allowing the seller to chisel against a cartel and possibly avoid detection. Finally, the tied product can help an entrant obtain guaranteed patronage, thereby reducing the risk of entry. In all or most of these instances, less restrictive alternatives might exist, e.g., providing specifications and manuals for service or certification of service personnel can ensure quality, rendering tying of sales and service unnecessary. Therefore, the extent to which defendants can evade liability through justification depends on the aggressiveness of legal intervention. As indicated by the dicta in *Jefferson Parish*, as the degree of power over the tying product increases, so does defendant's burden of justification, even to the point that the per se rule is invoked such that the defendant bears the burden of proof to show that only the tying can attain efficiencies.

It should be the case that defendant's burden should likewise be greater or lesser as the degree of foreclosure over the tied product increases or decreases because, with the possible exception of a requirements tie, the potential harm occurs only if the foreclosure over the tied product is great. However, as noted in the next paragraph, current per se doctrine focuses on power only with regard to the tying product, while the requisite foreclosure over the tied product must just be "not insubstantial." Such a diminished requirement reflects, again, the peculiar history of tying doctrine because, for example, it differs from the analysis applied to foreclosure caused by conduct characterized as an exclusive dealing arrangement. You can see that potentially this difference in doctrinal elements is outcome determinative.

In our view, the fact that tying can sometimes cause harm and can sometimes cause benefit means that courts and other decision makers should simply focus on competitive effects stemming from market power under section 2, as we suggested above. Indeed, as we indicate below, given that nearly all tying arrangements can also be characterized as exclusive dealing, we see no reason for a separate doctrinal category, much less different doctrinal elements or, moreover, the use of any form of per se rule. While the latest Supreme Court decision in a tying case confirmed the continued use of the now-weakened per se rule, it also provided even more doubt concerning its future viability. In Illinois Tool Works Inc. v. Independent Ink, Inc., 547 U.S. 28 (2006), the Court eliminated the presumption that a patent automatically confers the market power necessary to invoke the per se rule against tying. This ruling resulted in part from Congressional changes to the law of patent misuse, but also because the presumption was just "a vestige of the Court's historical distrust of tying arrangements," *id.* at 38, "strong disapproval [which] has substantially diminished." *Id* at 35. The Court even rejected a suggestion to create a rebuttable presumption for a subclass of tying arrangements, "requirements ties," in which, as discussed above, a purchaser must buy the tied unpatented product over a long period of time, thereby providing a means for price discrimination against large purchasers, conduct which can evidence market power. After noting that price discrimination often occurs even in competitive markets—and thereby undercutting the argument that tying arrangements should usually be condemned because they provide a means for price discrimination—the Court more broadly stated that "[m]any tying arrangements, even those involving patents and requirements ties, are fully consistent with a free, competitive market." *Id.* at 45. It is not clear how long any kind of per se rule will survive.

However, given the history delineated above, until the Supreme Court officially overrules prior precedent, such is not the law and tying remains a separate category with its own particular per se doctrinal elements. In brief, as of this writing these are: (1) two separate and distinct products; (2) the two products are tied together coercively; (3) defendant possesses market power over the tying product; (4) the tie causes an anti-competitive effect in the tied market; and (5) a "not insubstantial" amount of interstate commerce in the tied product market is affected. As we have indicated, potentially application of these elements to conduct that can fall into other doctrinal categories can lead to inconsistent results, but given our limited purposes in discussing tying, and the consequent fairly cursory treatment, we cannot go into any further depth.

b. Inputs or complements? Notice the competing characterizations of the role of the anesthesiologists in *Jefferson Parish*. To the majority of the Court, anesthesia services are a distinct product from the surgery for which they are provided because there is a "separable demand" for them and it is possible for hospitals efficiently to supply them separately. This conclusion followed from evidence in the record that patients or their doctors do choose among anesthesiologists and that some hospitals permit that choice. By contrast, to Justice O'Connor, the anesthesia services are inputs because they are useless apart from surgery. They are no different than the brakes that come with a car.

Notice that to this point we have discussed all physician services as inputs, not distinguishing inputs from complements. The reason is that until now the distinction has had no doctrinal significance. Whether we have characterized physician services as complements or inputs has not changed the analysis of the horizontal effects of vertical conduct. However, with our addition of tying as a doctrinal category, the characterization of services as complements or inputs might matter, given that the doctrinal requirements vary among different categories, particularly in the possibility of a per se rule being applied to conduct characterized as a tying arrangement.

Suppose that a hospital executed an exclusive contract with an infectious disease specialty group. That arrangement probably would more easily be characterized as tying than the exclusive contract at issue in

Jefferson Parish because patients and their physicians are more likely to exercise choice over the infectious disease specialist with whom they consult for inpatient care than they would for anesthesiology services. Suppose instead that the exclusive contract is with a pathology group. More than likely that arrangement would not be characterized as tying because patients and their physicians usually do not choose among pathologists.* *See, e.g.,* Collins v. Associated Pathologists, 844 F.2d 473 (7th Cir.), *cert. den.,* 488 U.S. 852 (1988); Drs. Steuer and Latham v. National Medical Enterprises, Inc., 672 F. Supp. 1489 (D.S.C. 1987), *aff'd,* 846 F.2d 70 (4th Cir. 1988). Indeed, in *Jefferson Parish* the Court recognized that distinctions probably should be drawn among types of hospital-based specialties. *See Jefferson Parish Hospital District No. 2,* 466 U.S. at 22 n.36.

Suppose, however, that hospitals in the United States employ all physicians who are on staff, as is the practice in some other countries, and there is no separate billing of facility and professional fees, which is the predominant situation in most of the industrialized world. Now is there a "separable demand" for any physician? If the answer is yes, would that be true of nurses, respiratory therapists, OT, even laundry? The question is whether the internal organization of the hospital, or any other institution, should have such doctrinal significance. Why should an exclusive contract for anesthesiology services, nursing, medical supplies or any other part of the package of services that constitute inpatient care receive distinctive doctrinal treatment as a tying arrangement, potentially subject to a per se rule, while other components of that package would be classified as exclusive contracts, examined as vertical arrangements under the rule of reason? As one learned antitrust scholar has stated, the "economic distinction between [the exclusive dealing and tying categories] is most often slight or nil," 11 HERBERT HOVENKAMP, ANTITRUST LAW: AN ANALYSIS OF ANTITRUST PRINCIPLES AND THEIR APPLICATION ¶ 1800b, at 7 (2d ed., 2005), and "there is no economic or antitrust policy justification other than that the inertia of a history that was unreasonably hostile toward ties but far more benign toward exclusive dealing." 9 Phillip E. Areeda et al., ANTITRUST LAW: AN ANALYSIS OF ANTITRUST PRINCIPLES AND THEIR APPLICATION ¶ 1709e8, at 93 (2d ed., 2004).

c. Basis for finding lack of "forcing." The majority in *Jefferson Parish* found that the "forcing" requirement for invocation of the per se rule could not be satisfied because East Jefferson Hospital exercised no market power in the greater New Orleans metropolitan area, the geographic market it defined by use of patient flow statistics. It reasoned that if patients wanted a different anesthesiologist, they could be admitted to one of the other hospitals to which 70% of Jefferson Parish residents went for inpatient services. Assuming arguendo that patient-flow data indicate accu-

---

* Actually, specimens are often sent from one hospital to an outside pathology lab because specialization does exist, and some pathology services are provided outside of hospitals. *See* Bryan A. Liang, *An Overview and Analysis of Challenges to Medical Exclusive Contracts,* 18 J. LEGAL MED. 1, 11 n.44, 13 n.55 (1997). For purposes of our example, we'll ignore these occurrences.

rately whether hospitals are good substitutes for one another, do those statistics indicate whether patients will substitute one hospital for another in order to obtain the services of different anesthesiologists? How often do you think patients or their doctors choose a hospital based on the anesthesiologist there? What does this say about the Court's conclusion regarding definition of the relevant geographical market or indeed, whether there exists a separable demand for anesthesia services?

The Court rejected plaintiff's argument that market power was much more local because of market imperfections, namely, the lack of price competition and the inability of consumers to judge quality. It stated that "[w]hile these factors may generate 'market power' in some abstract sense, they do not generate the kind of market power that justifies condemnation of tying." *Jefferson Parish Hospital District No. 2*, 466 U.S. at 27. It continued:

> Tying arrangements need only be condemned if they restrain competition on the merits by forcing purchases that would not otherwise be made. A lack of price or quality competition does not create this type of forcing. If consumers lack price consciousness, that fact will not force them to take an anesthesiologist whose services they do not want—their indifference to price will have no impact on their willingness or ability to go to another hospital where they can utilize the services of the anesthesiologist of their choice. Similarly, if consumers cannot evaluate the quality of anesthesiological services, it follows that they are indifferent between certified anesthesiologists even in the absence of a tying arrangement—such an arrangement cannot be said to have foreclosed a choice that would have otherwise been made "on the merits."

Id. at 27–28. If patients do not choose anesthesiologists based on price or quality, then what does consumer demand consist in? Again, what does this say about the Court's conclusion that there exists separable demand for anesthesiological services? What about surgeries that are unplanned, such as those following admissions through the emergency department or unexpectedly after admission for another reason? With regard to both, isn't the situation analogous to the forced purchases of after-market parts and services in *Kodak* discussed above? Finally, suppose that we follow the models of hospital choice, discussed above, in which physicians choose the site of care. If physicians choose among hospitals based on the convenience for them, overall quality, or the level of technology, of what relevance is the identity of the anesthesiologist? What does all this say regarding the Court's delineation of the market and its conclusion of a separable demand for anesthesiological services?

If you haven't gotten the point yet, the majority's view of the provision of anesthesiological services was close to sheer nonsense. The Court's view was that subject to geographical constraints, the anesthesia services of one hospital are a demand-side substitute for those of another hospital. However, given price-insensitivity, the anesthesia services of one hospital are differentiated, if at all, only with regard to non-price dimensions like quality. Moreover, even with regard to this differentiation, choice among hospitals is rarely if ever driven solely—or perhaps even substantially or partly—by differences among anesthesiologists, and patients who undergo unplanned surgery certainly do not choose among hospitals on that basis. Therefore, at most one could conclude that there is separable demand for different anesthesiologists within a given hospital; and if that is the nature of "demand," then at each hospital there would be a local monopoly problem because there is a lock-in, analogous to that in *Kodak*—once a patient or his provider has chosen a hospital on the basis of factors other than anesthesiology, that hospital's execution of an exclusive contract with an anesthesiology group narrows the range of consumer choice to the anesthesiologists in that group. To use an analogy, it would follow that every local restaurant, differentiated from others by the type and quality of the food prepared by its chef, would be potentially liable under the antitrust laws because diners are precluded from choosing their waiters. However, just as demand for the restaurant is an inseparable function of the chef and the wait staff—patrons will not come, no matter how good the food, if it never gets to the table—demand for the hospital is an inseparable function of all the services that together constitute an inpatient stay for surgery. The Court worked itself into an impossible bind by defining demand in one fashion—separable demand for anesthesiological services— and then the relevant market in another way—demand for hospital services. However, as we saw above, markets are defined by demand and supply characteristics, and the Court cannot have it both ways.

In their treatise, *see* 10 Phillip E. Areeda et al., ANTITRUST LAW: AN ANALYSIS OF ANTITRUST PRINCIPLES AND THEIR APPLICATION ¶ ¶ 1733e2, 1735 (2d ed., 2004), the authors try to resolve this inconsistency by describing the Court as distinguishing among sources of power for purposes of the per se rule against tying, with the Court ruling that power conferred by market imperfections does not count as market power for purposes of triggering per se treatment. As a technical matter that is correct, but it does not mean it's a defensible distinction for drawing legal categories. Aside from administrability questions, it would be better to err in favor of a defendant whose market power stems from demand or supply side advantages it has generated, and against one whose power flows from market failure like information asymmetry. Because the former is more deserving, if anything the Court's relaxation of the per se rule against the latter has things exactly backwards. Justice O'Connor was right that this case should have been treated just as an exclusive dealing arrangement and that the only issue in such a case should be the possible horizontal effects of the vertical conduct.

d.   Static or dynamic effects. Suppose the evidence showed that hospitals always bundle together anesthesiology and the other parts of an inpatient surgical stay. Is that necessarily the end of the inquiry? Isn't it possible that judicial intervention can and should foster innovation? Given the risk of error and the premise of the antitrust laws that markets generally reach efficient results, would you distinguish between diverse situations based on the history and structure of the market involved?

e. Justification. In her analysis of the arrangement in *Jefferson Parish*, Justice O'Connor accorded efficiency defenses considerable treatment:

> The tie-in improves patient care and permits more efficient hospital operation in a number of ways. From the viewpoint of hospital management, the tie-in ensures 24–hour anesthesiology coverage, aids in standardization of procedures and efficient use of equipment, facilitates flexible scheduling of operations, and permits the hospital more effectively to monitor the quality of anesthesiological services. Further, the tying arrangement is advantageous to patients because, as the District Court found, the closed anesthesiology department places upon the hospital, rather than the individual patient, responsibility to select the physician who is to provide anesthesiological services. The hospital also assumes the responsibility that the anesthesiologist will be available, will be acceptable to the surgeon, and will provide suitable care to the patient. In assuming these responsibilities—responsibilities that a seriously ill patient frequently may be unable to discharge—the hospital provides a valuable service to its patients.

Jefferson Parish Hospital District No. 2, 466 U.S. at 43–44. Commentators have agreed, adding that like other vertical arrangements, the exclusive dealing arrangement aligns the incentives of the hospital and the anesthesiologists such that the two contractual parties capture the benefits of investments they make—e.g., anesthesiologists' training of nurse anesthetists. Absent exclusivity the two sides would confer an external benefits on others, and the result would be underinvestment. *See* William J. Lynk & Michael A. Morrisey, *The Economic Basis of* Hyde: *Are Market Power and Hospital Exclusive Contracts Related?*, 30 J. L. & ECON. 399, 404 (1987). As we have seen, the majority in the Court did not disagree that efficiencies exist. Rather, they placed the burden on defendants to negate less restrictive alternatives.

If East Jefferson Hospital had no market power over inpatient services, the tying product, should it have had to justify at all, even under the rule of reason? If it had no power over the tying product, what is the likely degree of foreclosure over the tied product? Even if East Jefferson Hospital had market power over inpatient services, is it necessarily the case that there would be foreclosure over the tied product? What else do you need to know? Under the rule of reason doesn't plaintiff have to prove such anticompetitive effect in order to force defendant to justify? Even if plaintiff satisfies that burden, under the rule of reason who has the burden of proof regarding less restrictive alternative? In thinking about the application of the rule of reason to tying, how do your answers differ from analysis of the conduct as an exclusive dealing arrangement? What does this suggest regarding the necessity of a separate category for tying arrangements?

6. *The demise of the "group boycott," aka "concerted refusal to deal," a particularly vacuous category.* In count six of its complaint in *Rome*, the ASC alleged that the two insurers, BCBS and MVP, had conspired to refuse

to deal with it. This conduct is known as a "group boycott" or a "concerted refusal to deal." A particularly vacuous doctrinal category, it has traditionally been accorded per se treatment. Fortunately, it is dead or dying as a separate one.

   a. Its meaning(lessness). Consider the following situations: (1) Suppose that two retailers, *R1* and *R2*, sell a product made by *M*, a manufacturer. They are price fixing. *M* has promised not to compete with them by selling at retail. *M* breaches this promise, *R1* and *R2* refuse to deal any more with *M*, and they buy from *M2* instead; (2) *R1* and *R2* decide jointly to promote a product which they plan to buy from *M*. They condition this purchase on *M's* promise not to compete with them by selling at retail. Again *M* breaches this promise, *R1* and *R2* refuse to deal any more with *M* and buy from *M2* instead; (3) Again *R1* and *R2* decide jointly to promote a product which they plan to buy from *M* but only if *M* can meet certain specifications. *M* offers to meet other specifications, which they reject. They therefore refuse to deal with *M* and buy from *M2* instead because it will satisfy their condition.

   In each situation there is a "concerted refusal to deal," but aren't there crucial differences among them? In situation #(1), the concerted refusal to deal is a means to enforce price fixing by precluding *M* from entering at retail against the retail cartel. As described immediately below, this conduct is the historical root of "group boycott" as a doctrinal category. However, the other two situations are different. In each of them the two "conspirators" who engaged in the "concerted refusal to deal" have integrated in some way other than simply agreeing to fix price. They have made an investment, and to protect that investment they have insisted on a term of trade. In situation #(2), *R1* and *R2* condition their purchase from *M* on *M's* not competing with them at retail. Arguably, if *M* were to enter at retail it would effectively free-ride on *R1* and *R2's* investment and perhaps take advantage of specialized knowledge, possibly even protected intellectual property, gained from the collaboration. In situation #(3), *R1* and *R2* condition their purchase from *M* on the latter's satisfaction of specifications, possibly a means to protect product quality and thereby again a means to guard their investment. If all three situations are lumped together into the category "concerted refusal to deal" and treated alike, these crucial differences are obscured. It may indeed be the case that any one of the examples presents an unreasonable restraint of trade—as price fixing, situation #(1) clearly violates section 1 absent peculiar facts like those in *BMI* or *NCAA* discussed above—but regardless, each situation merits separate analysis in which a decision maker must examine whether the underlying term of trade, enforced by the "concerted refusal to deal," is unreasonable.

   To state the point now more generally, any time two traders insist on a term of trade, one could say that there exists a "concerted refusal to deal." As a result, in very nearly all cases presenting a concerted refusal to deal, the group boycott is a mechanism to enforce an underlying term of trade. To the extent that such conduct is anticompetitive, that problem arises because of the insistence on the term of trade, and therefore examination for possible anticompetitive effect requires analysis of the underlying term of trade. The existence of the "group boycott" adds nothing to this analysis.

The courts' inability to understand this logic, coupled with their inherent distrust of horizontal collaboration, gave rise to the category "concerted refusal to deal," encompassing a seemingly infinite varieties of terms of trade. Similar to the growth of tying doctrine, in which the doctrine grew in large part out of industry-wide cartelization—in that context, cartelization of motion picture production and exhibition—the early cases giving rise to the group boycott doctrine grew out of cases involving cartels operating at multiple levels of an industry. In that context, the refusal to deal was simply a means to enforce price fixing. *See* W.W. Montague & Co. v. Lowry, 193 U.S. 38 (1904); Eastern States Retail Lumber Dealers' Association v. United States, 234 U.S. 600 (1914); United States v. Trenton Potteries Co., 273 U.S. 392 (1927). Similar to tying, the courts' blanket condemnation seemed warranted, but unfortunately, again like tying, the category of group boycott was then expanded to encompass a vast multitude of diverse kinds of conduct.

b. Its demise as an independent doctrinal category. Fortunately, in three recent cases, by explicating a burden-shifting mechanism that focuses on the underlying term of trade enforced by a concerted refusal to deal, the Supreme Court has deprived the group boycott category of its vitality as an independent doctrinal entity. This process started with Northwest Wholesale Stationers, Inc. v. Pacific Stationery & Printing Co., 472 U.S. 284 (1985), in which plaintiff was expelled from a retail office supply cooperative that acted as a wholesaler for its members and sold to them at a price discounted from that provided to nonmembers. The cooperative's bylaws generally precluded members from operating at both retail and wholesale but also grandfathered members like plaintiff which had done so in the past. Plaintiff was expelled, however, for failing to notify defendant of a change of ownership, allegedly in violation of another bylaw.

Plaintiff alleged that its expulsion constituted a concerted refusal to deal, a per se violation of section 1. Reversing a circuit court ruling that this conduct was per se illegal, the Supreme Court first pointed to the efficiencies potentially attained by the retailers' horizontal integration—the cooperative—and stated that "[w]holesale purchasing cooperatives must establish and enforce reasonable rules in order to function effectively. Disclosure rules, such as the one on which Northwest relies, *may* well provide the cooperative with a needed means for monitoring the creditworthiness of its members." *Id.* at 296 (emphasis added). In other words, given the horizontal integration, the defendant was entitled to an inference that its rules, the underlying non-price terms of trade enforced by the group boycott, are efficient, i.e., reasonably related—ancillary—and necessary to the benefits obtained by the lawful horizontal integration. The Court continued that in such circumstances, plaintiff must prove market power or significant foreclosure:

Unless the cooperative possesses market power or exclusive access to an element essential to effective competition, the conclusion that expulsion is virtually always likely to have an anticompetitive effect is not warranted. Cf. *Jefferson Parish Hospital Dist.* v. *Hyde*, 466 U.S. 2, 12–15 (1984) (absent indication of market power, tying arrangement does not warrant *per se* invalidation). See generally *National Collegiate Athletic Assn.* v. *Board of Regents of University of Oklahoma*, 468 U.S., at 104, n. 26 (*"Per se* rules may require considerable inquiry into market conditions before the evidence justifies a presumption of anticompetitive conduct").

Northwest Wholesale Stationers, Inc., 472 U.S. at 296–97. If the plaintiff is able to mount such a showing, defendant must then come forward with "plausible arguments that [its practices] were intended to enhance overall efficiency and make markets more competitive," *id.* at 294, and then, to prevail, plaintiff must prove actual anticompetitive effect. See *id.* at 296 n.8.

The next case in the Court's explicating this burden-shifting mechanism, focused on the underlying term of trade, was FTC v. Indiana Federation of Dentists, 476 U.S. 447 (1986). Defendant, an association of dentists, had successfully coordinated its members' refusal to furnish dental x-rays to insurers who requested them for evaluating submitted claims. The court of appeals had vacated the FTC's cease-and-desist order, holding that it was not supported by the evidence. The court rejected the FTC's claim that the case was per se, and held that as a result the FTC needed to prove the existence of market power or that the concerted refusal to furnish x-rays had increased the price of dental services.

Reversing, the Supreme Court first agreed that the per se rule against group boycotts did not apply:

Although this Court has in the past stated that group boycotts are unlawful *per se*, we decline to resolve this case by forcing the Federation's policy into the "boycott" pigeonhole and invoking the *per se* rule. As we observed last Term in *Northwest Wholesale Stationers, Inc.* v. *Pacific Stationery & Printing Co.*, 472 U.S. 284 (1985), the category of restraints classed as group boycotts is not to be expanded indiscriminately, and the *per se* approach has generally been limited to cases in which firms with market power boycott suppliers or customers in order to discourage them from doing business with a competitor—a situation obviously not present here.

Indiana Federation of Dentists, 476 U.S. at 458. Moreover, this case involved non-price "rules adopted by professional associations," *id.*, i.e., professional associations are a form of horizontal integration that, like the cooperative in *Northwest Wholesale Stationers*, often create efficiencies. Hence, defendant gets the benefit of an inference that its non-price rules, ancillary to that integration, are beneficial.

However, the Court then upheld the Commission's order under the rule of reason. It first found that defendant's non-price conduct inherently restrains trade by eliminating a form of non-price competition: "A refusal to compete with respect to the package of services offered to customers, no less than a refusal to compete with respect to the price term of an agreement, impairs the ability of the market to advance social welfare by ensuring the provision of desired goods and services to consumers at a price approximating the marginal cost of providing them." *Id.* at 459. Second, the Court found that given the inherent nature of the conduct to restrain trade, defendant must offer justification: "Absent some countervailing procompetitive virtue—such as, for example, the creation of efficiencies in the operation of a market or the provision of goods and services, see *Broadcast Music, Inc.* v. *Columbia Broadcasting System, Inc., supra; Chicago Board of Trade, supra;* cf. *National Collegiate Athletic Assn.* v. *Board of Regents of Univ. of Okla.,* 468 U.S. 85 (1984)—such an agreement limiting consumer choice cannot be sustained under the Rule of Reason." 476 U.S. at 459. Third, responding to defendant's argument that its refusal to supply x-rays protected quality of care and that the FTC could not prevail without proof of market power, the Court found sufficient the agency's finding that defendant's conduct had an actual anticompetitive effect:

> The Commission found that in two localities in the State of Indiana (the Anderson and Lafayette areas), Federation dentists constituted heavy majorities of the practicing dentists and that as a result of the efforts of the Federation, insurers in those areas were, over a period of years, actually unable to obtain compliance with their requests for submission of x rays. Since the purpose of the inquiries into market definition and market power is to determine whether an arrangement has the potential for genuine adverse effects on competition, "proof of actual detrimental effects, such as a reduction of output," can obviate the need for an inquiry into market power, which is but a "surrogate for detrimental effects." 7 P. Areeda, Antitrust Law para. 1511, p. 429 (1986).

Indiana Federation of Dentists, 476 U.S. at 460–61. Fourth, the Court found that the Commission's rejection of the quality-of-care justification on the merits was supported by evidence in the record. See *id.* at 462–64. To sum up, the steps in the Court's reasoning were: (1) the restraint, refusal to compete on a non-price dimension—providing dental services with or without x-rays submitted to insurers—inherently restrains trade; (2) therefore defendant must come forward with justification; (3) the FTC could successfully counter that proffer by proving market power or actual anticompetitive effect; and (4) defendant then must prove its justification (which it did not).

The last of the trilogy was Federal Trade Commission v. Superior Court Trial Lawyers Association, 493 U.S. 411 (1990). In that case, the defendant, an association of lawyers who were court-appointed representatives of indigent criminal defendants in the District of Columbia, coordinated the refusal of its members to accept appointments unless the city raised their compensation. The court of appeals held that the FTC's order could not be upheld because it had not proved market power and because defendant's conduct was protected by the First Amendment. It found the per se rule to be not a statutory command but a rule of administrative convenience, from which deviation was warranted in this case, in fact required, given the First Amendment concerns. Reversing, the Supreme Court stated that "while the *per se* rule against price fixing and boycotts is indeed justified in part by 'administrative convenience,' [t]he *per se* rules also reflect a long-standing judgment that the prohibited practices by their nature have 'a substantial potential for impact on competition.' *Jefferson Parish Hospital District*, 466 U.S. at 16." 493 U.S. at 433. The Court held that this group boycott must be condemned without proof of market power. Importantly, the Court noted that this holding was itself compelled by the fact that the concerted refusal to deal enforced price fixing, a per se violation:

> In response to Justice Brennan's opinion [in dissent], and particularly to its observation that some concerted arrangements that might be characterized as "group boycotts" may not merit *per se* condemnation, we emphasize that this case involves not only a boycott but also a horizontal price-fixing arrangement—a type of conspiracy that has been consistently analyzed as a *per se* violation for many decades. All of the "group boycott" cases cited in Justice Brennan's [opinion] involved nonprice restraints.

Id. at 435 n.19.

Starting with the last opinion, one can stitch these three decisions together as follows. Ignore language in the cases concerning what is per se and what is rule of reason and just follow burdens of coming forward and burdens of proof. In all the cases the Court considered the underlying term of trade and did not just jam the case into the boycott "pigeonhole." In cases in which the concerted refusal to deal enforces price fixing, plaintiff need not prove market power to win—that's *Superior Court Trial Lawyer's Association* and a return to the historical roots of viewing group boycotts as a per se doctrinal category because they are a means to enforce price fixing, a per se violation. By contrast, when there is horizontal integration other than the term of trade underlying the concerted refusal to deal, plaintiff must show market power or anticompetitive effect to force defendant to justify—that's *Northwest Wholesale Stationers*; cf. *Texaco Inc. v. Dagher*, 547 U.S. 1 (2006) (setting price of product made by lawful, economically integrated joint venture cannot constitute per se price fixing even though members of joint venture are horizontal competitors outside of joint venture). Alternatively, plaintiff can show that the underlying term of trade inherently eliminates competition—that's the concerted refusal of the dentists in *Indiana Federation of Dentists* to compete over the manner in which utilization review would be conducted, a collective elimination of a non-price dimension of competition. If plaintiff carries this burden defendant must come forward with plausible justification—again, that's *Indiana Federation of Dentists*, in which the dentists claimed that they were protecting quality of care. Plaintiff must then either prove market power—*Northwest Wholesale Stationers*—or actual anticompetitive effect—*Indiana Federation of Dentists*—in which case defendant must actually prove its justification to prevail. Voila: application of the rule of reason, coupled with shifting burdens of coming forward and proof, to order complex litigation! In sum, although this doctrinal category still quacks per se, unless the group boycott is used to enforce horizontal price fixing or another per se violation, the category now smells rule of reason—truncated, full or otherwise—in which courts consider the degree of integration among the horizontal competitors—a vertical contract alone will not constitute concert of action for this purpose, *see* NYNEX Corp. v. Discon, Inc., 525 U.S. 128 (1998)—the degree of market power, the competitive effects stemming from the term of trade underlying the group boycott, and justification.

As we have seen, *Rome* involved an alleged "concerted refusal to deal" in that, if proven, Rome Hospital acted in concert with two insurance companies such that the latter refused to deal with the ASC, the hospital's horizontal competitor, thereby depriving it of patients. Under the doctrinal category of exclusive dealing, we have analyzed the case in terms of the competitive effects of this foreclosure, as did the *Rome* court. The Supreme Court's latest word on group boycotts is that what matters are these competitive effects. Characterizing the conduct as a concerted refusal to deal adds nothing to the analysis at all. The category itself no longer has independent vitality.

7. *The justification of preventing "cherry–picking" in* Rome. Defendants in *Rome* attempted to justify the exclusive contracts with insurers by stating that plaintiff's cherry picking the most lucrative patients made exclusivity necessary. The court summarily dismissed this effort with the statement: "It is difficult to see how exclusive contracting would be considered an appropriate response to the particular behavior defendants claim to be defending against, 'cherry picking' or 'cream skimming,' and possible 'free riding' by the RASC investor physicians." The cream skimming issue rested on defendant's claim that the surgery center would leave the hospital with less lucrative, even money-losing patients. Was the district court correct that the exclusive contracts would not solve the cream-skimming problem? Isn't the division of the lucrative and less lucrative patients solved by forcing them all into the hospital? Perhaps the antitrust laws do not provide the proper vehicle to solve such a problem, if it is considered to be one, but was the district court right that there was a "logical disconnect" between cherry picking and the challenged conduct?

5.   CONCLUDING THOUGHTS: WHAT'S THE PURPOSE?

Let's conclude by stepping back from the details of this complicated doctrinal framework and return to basics: what is the purpose of applying antitrust to health care? We saw at the beginning of the chapter that prior to *Goldfarb* there was a generalized, well-accepted perception that the medical profession, through collective activity, dominated the health care sector—its financing, the conception of what health care consists of, and its delivery. Our quotation in the beginning of the chapter—"It is as if some being from an alien planet landed on the earth and took over all institutions relating to the delivery of health care"—indicates that the standard story overstates the separation of the medical profession from the rest of society. Regardless, the application of antitrust was supposed to eliminate this collective power and, as we have seen in the doctrine, to a great extent, it has.

However, there is much more to professional power than this simple story. Both at the individual and the social level there is dependence on health care professionals, particularly doctors. Economists reduce this dependence to "information asymmetry," but the dependence on professionals is much more than that because, in a society that valorizes science, the claim that health professionals' expertise is grounded in science—even when the reality may be far more custom (as you saw in Part Three) than scientific method—is a foundation that grants special legitimacy. Moreover, because the subject matter of health care is life, quality of life and death, this combination of scientific legitimacy and the basic human desire to be free of illness and death creates a high degree of power. The medical profession in particular is our most important scientific arbiter of the meaning of death, and that role, which has both been ceded and taken—it is futile to try to separate the two halves of this equation—gives it a particularly important place in the social sphere.

However, the use of antitrust law, as well as other elements of health law we've discussed, particularly payment, indicates that the prior linkage of this social power with financial power became intolerable. To a great degree, antitrust in health care represents an attempt to sever that linkage. Yet severance is not possible because even if we target the sources of economic power, various forms of market failure—to stay within the economic framework for purposes of analysis—inevitably exist in the health care market that our society—abetted by our legal system—has enabled and promoted. Because we've canvassed much of this material already in various parts of this book, particularly in the chapter on tax, we can be brief.

The most important source of financial power is the asymmetry of expertise, which gives rise to the problem of agency. No matter how much the collective financial power of the profession is broken—to the point of its being destroyed—this form of power will still exist. This fact can be papered over with vague references about how consumers can rely on their fiscal intermediaries, *see, e.g.*, Clark C. Havighurst, *How the Health Care Revolution Fell Short*, 65 LAW & CONTEMP. PROBS. 55 (2002) [hereinafter Havighurst, *How the Health Care Revolution Fell Short*], but no matter how one slices it, the agency problem won't go away. As we noted in the chapter on fraud, we might move the agency around so that we rely on insurance companies, on plan sponsors, or even on government, but then we need agents to police our agents, and agents to police our agents who police our agents, and agents to police the agents who police the agents who police the agents, ad infinitum. *See* Frankford, *Privatizing Health Care* at 59–60. Regardless of the location of agency, no market, no single-payer system, no all-payer system—nothing—eradicates the dependence that gives rise to agency. This is also true in other nations, which have created more efficient and equitable approaches to developing, organizing, and financing health care; yet here, in the United States, we have empowered agency to an unusual degree, perhaps because our dependence on markets has in turn created an unusually high desire to counter the market's natural instinct, namely, to profit from illness, something we all fear.

This brings us to the core problem: In a market-based system, our reliance on agents also puts them in a position of profiting from this reliance, taking advantage of their agency and increasing their wealth. Consolidation is occurring on both sides of the market, and on both the sides, higher prices and higher margins are generally correlated with higher concentration. Agency is being misused by everyone, everywhere, and those in whom we repose our trust are getting rich from abusing that trust. *See, e.g.*, Thomas (Tim) Greaney, *Competition Policy and Organizational Fragmentation in Health Care*, 71 U. PITT. L. REV. 217, 231–35 (2009); Thomas L. Greaney, *Regulating to Promote Competition in Designing Health Insurance Exchanges*, 20 KAN. J.L. & PUB. POL'Y 237, 245–48 (2011); Thomas Greaney, *The Affordable Care Act and Competition Policy: Antidote or Placebo?*, 89 OR. L. REV. 811, 813–25 (2011). The problem just can't be wished away with the supposed magic of markets.

For that reason, much more nuanced scholarship, like that of Professor Greaney, tries to craft ways by which antitrust doctrine might try to take agency into account, but Professors Hammer and Sage, in their various empirical and theoretical writings, make a cogent case that antitrust doctrine does not, and perhaps cannot, adequately account for the agency problem. These are incredibly complex issues, but as we have pointed out in this chapter, issues regarding "quality" have appeared in antitrust doctrine only to a very limited extent, something that Hammer and Sage document at great length in their empirical study of antitrust cases. *See* Hammer & Sage, *Antitrust, Health Care Quality, and the Courts*. There is simply a mismatch between the traditional tools of antitrust, with its focus on price competition and market structure, and the multitude of non-price variables over which competition occurs.

Another aspect of health care that makes application of antitrust doctrine difficult, if not impossible, is the extreme degree of product differentiation. All of the efforts at bringing industrial techniques to health care, through standardization of the resources and processes of care, cannot mask this fact. Patients, health care systems, and caregivers are unique in some, irreducible, essential ways. A patient with a heart attack and no other defining characteristics—if that could ever be the case—bears only a modest relationship to a patient with a heart attack who also suffers from lupus, diabetes, and depression—and is poor to boot. The interventions needed to treat the former may be a pale version of those essential in treatment of the latter, yet these differences are lost if we attempt to standardize them under an abstraction, like the category "heart attack."

Earlier in the chapter we briefly alluded to a chicken-and-egg question whether patients qua consumers create this differentiation through "heterogeneous tastes" or whether differentiation occurs through the efforts of actors in the health care sector to acquire or maintain economic power. Undoubtedly, health care professionals and their institutions differentiate themselves as a means to preclude standardization, to reduce substitution and to hinder comparison of price and quality. *See, e.g.*, Havighurst & Richman, *Who Pays? Who Benefits?* at 504–05; Havighurst & Richman, *Distributive (In)justices in American Health Care* at 19–20; *see also* Sage & Hammer, *Competing on Quality of Care* at 1062. However, likewise individuals as patients qua consumers differ not only in the biomedical aspects in which they "present" illness but also in their life circumstances, values and aspirations. As a result, it is simply empirically incorrect to claim that health care can be standardized without losing something valuable in the reduction to a standardized unit. Equally, it is normatively reprehensible to reduce patients to standardized cases, units of consumption, to whatever the chosen abstraction may be. *See, e.g.*, Samuel Gorovitz & Alasdair MacIntyre, *Toward a Theory of Medical Fallibility*, J. MED. & PHILOSOPHY 51 (1976). In the payment chapter in Part Two, we explored how the inability to reduce "severity" to a standardized unit renders the task of payment difficult; in Part Three we examined how the inability to reduce "quality" to quantitative measures makes the task of quality assurance difficult; in this chapter, the irreducibility of individuals to some abstract unit likewise makes the application of antitrust extremely hard or impossible because the economic models just don't fit. Extreme differentiation—which exists in both the "consumers" and the "products," the care, they receive—is simply another way of expressing the fact that health care professionals inexorably wield power, and that's just the way things are in our world.

It follows, as we described in Part Two, that any payment method involves averaging—whether applied by government in a single-payer system, by coordinated payers in an all-payer system, or by a multitude of payers in a competitive system like that of the United States. Because product differentiation is so enormous and because any administratively feasible payment system, to be prospective, must rely on some standardized unit of payment, averaging is another fact of life in health care. As a result, the goal of antitrust to force producers to compete the price of services down to the cost of producing just those services, and thereby to eliminate cross-subsidization among services, is chimerical. In health care, everybody cross-subsidizes someone else—the sick cross-subsidize the well; the young cross-subsidize the old; the expensive but highly lucrative arthroscopic knee surgeries cross-subsidize the equally expensive but totally money-losing, neonatal intensive care units. To use economic language again, necessarily there will be externalities in payment because no one can pay exactly just what one receives and just that alone.

It is for that reason that global payment, coupled with close collaboration among physicians, hospitals, and other health care providers, works better, and it is for that reason that despite the hostility of antitrust to the concentration of economic power, that consolidation is occurring. Of course there are other reasons at work, particularly improved ability to bear risk due to larger scale, greater coordination of care delivery, and of course, enhanced bargaining power. Yet, another simple fact of the provision of insured health care services is that it functions better when, as we observed in the chapter on payment, large pools of potential patients are linked with large pools of potential health care providers over the long term. The traditional doctrine of antitrust, grounded in economic models of atomization on both sides of the market and fluidity of relationships, just doesn't comport well with this reality.

Finally, we come last but not least to the biggest of the so-called "noneconomic values"—distributive justice. Economics has absolutely nothing to say about the subject. All economic models start with some proposition like "given an existing distribution of wealth, then ..." Economics, that dismal science, has much to tell us about the problem of scarcity and the means to deal with it, but it is a science of means, not ends, while distributive justice is all about ends, as law too must be. It is the job of law to tell us how much poverty is tolerable, how much lack of access to health care is just, how wealth is to be distributed. Antitrust doctrine is set up to work within those fixed parameters but it cannot tell us how to set them, and because its application necessarily rearranges the distribution of wealth—the distinction between fixing the distribution of wealth and working within that fixed constraint is artificial—antitrust cannot tell us what to do. *See generally* Uwe E. Reinhardt, *Can Efficiency in Health Care Be Left to the Market?*, 26 J. HEALTH POL. POL'Y & L. 967 (2001).

For all these reasons and more, Professors Hammer and Sage are clearly right that antitrust is too narrowly conceived and that it must, at the very least, be more broadly conceptualized as "competition policy" that accounts for the necessary involvement of government activity in the sector both as payer—participant—and as a regulator—a nonparticipant referee. Yet, you should ask whether even that reform goes far enough.

Our society, armed with the best social scientists and legal experts, could continue to debate whether as a theoretical or empirical matter we can fine-tune our market-based system to produce every ounce of quality demanded from the health care sector and no more—allocative efficiency. Likewise, we can put our best minds to work to figure out how to squeeze every ounce of fat out of the sector so that those allocated ounces of quality are produced with the fewest resources possible—production efficiency. Ask yourselves, however, whether we can afford to wait for this fine-tuning to occur.

Look where we are now. Our expenditures already are by far the highest in the industrialized world. As we've discussed in numerous places in this book, the best evidence shows that the reason for this huge and growing gap between our expenditures and those of other nations is the amount we pay for the health care services we receive, which do not differ to a significant degree in quality or quantity purchased elsewhere. We just pay much, much more for the identical level of service. Indeed, in a relatively recent, extremely well-documented article, Professors Havighurst and Richman—among the strongest proponents of market-based health care and aggressive application of traditional antitrust doctrine as one can find—marshal much of the empirical evidence we have in this book and then, stopping on a dime, observe: "It has not escaped our notice that these observations about the consequences for the United States of combining monopoly and health insurance could be cited to support either a shift to a single-payer health system or extensive administrative regulation of prices, especially for hospital services and prescription drugs." Havighurst & Richman, *Distributive Injustice(s) in American Health Care* at 30–31. What follows next is simply a leap of faith: "But private health insurance does not *inevitably* produce the consequences described here and might be reconfigured to allow consumers to make real economizing choices, thereby restoring price elasticity as a constraint on monopolists' pricing." *Id.* at 31.

In the meantime, while we await this hypothesized reconfiguration— notice the use of the subjunctive voice with the word "might"—our *actual* costs continue to grow; a huge amount of wealth keeps flowing into the sector; the growth of technological capacity continues apace; diffusion of technology likewise proceeds; primary care and cognitive services more generally continue to receive the short end of the stick; specialization, subspecialization, and sub-subspecialization continue apace; fewer and fewer medical school graduates choose primary care; huge disparities continue to exist in the care provided to peoples of different races and income levels; administrative costs continue to soar; and so on, and so on, and so on. Theoretical arguments can be mounted that these problems can be overcome. Factual claims can be verified that we still don't know if competition will work because we've never really tried it. Politics has always gotten in the way, and the revolution always cut short. *See, e.g.,* Havighurst, *How the Health Care Revolution Fell Short.* If only we could eliminate politics. . . .

With the full application of antitrust principles to health care and the use of a market-based system more generally, we are in the midst of an approximately 40–year experiment, in which we are trying methods that have never worked anywhere, anytime in the modern, industrialized world; and things keep getting worse. Meanwhile, there are mechanisms that work internationally and could, with appropriate sensitivity, be adapted to the situation and culture of the United States. Isn't it time to conclude that what we're doing is not working and that it's time to try something else?

INDEX

References are to Pages
_____

ELECTRONIC HEALTH RECORDS (EHR)
Generally, 886
Federal funding of adoption, 502
Patient privacy, technology impacts, 768

ELIGIBILITY STANDARDS
Patient Protection and Affordable Care Act, Medicaid improvements, 205

EMERGENCY CARE
See also Emergency Medical Treatment and Labor Act, this index
Ambulance service payment responsibilities, indigents, 44
Common law duties and responsibilities
Generally, 19
State law responses, 41
Federal reforms, historical background, 50
HIPAA, Patient Protection and Affordable Care Act amendments, 423
Historical background, federal reforms, 50
Indigents, ambulance service payment responsibilities, 44
Liabilities, 797
Out-of-network coverage
Generally, 366
Patient Protection and Affordable Care Act, 304
Patient Protection and Affordable Care Act
HIPAA amendments, 423
Out-of-network emergency care, 304
Prudent layperson standard of coverage, 304
Prudent layperson standard of coverage, Patient Protection and Affordable Care Act, 304
Stabilization
Emergency Medical Treatment and Labor Act, this index
ERISA standards, 305
Women in labor, 33

EMERGENCY DEPARTMENTS
Acute care services, 185
Overcrowding, 53
Overcrowding, safety-net hospitals, 170
Residents, working hours, 869
Safety-net hospitals, 170
Scheduled vs unscheduled hospital admissions, 53
Stand–By Capacity, this index

EMERGENCY MEDICAL CONDITIONS
See also Emergency Medical Treatment and Labor Act, this index
Definition, 86

EMERGENCY MEDICAL SERVICES (EMS)
EMTALA duties, 80

EMERGENCY MEDICAL TREATMENT AND LABOR ACT (EMTALA)
Generally, 54 et seq.
Active labor provisions, 52

EMERGENCY MEDICAL TREATMENT AND LABOR ACT (EMTALA)—Cont'd
Administrative enforcement
Generally, 112
Burden of proof, 89
Centers for Medicare and Medicaid Services responsibilities, 113
Judicial review standards, 88
Medically appropriate transfer duties, 87
Office of Inspector General responsibilities, 113
Penalties, 113
Stabilization duties, 87
Transferee hospital duties, 95
Admitted patients. Inpatient stabilization duties, below
Ambulance request for care trigger of act, 77
Ambulances
Emergency service medical transport duties, 80
Third party- vs hospital-owned, 78
Anencephalic infants, stabilization duties
Civil liabilities, 80
Policy considerations, 87
Appropriate screening duties
Generally, 54, 61 et seq.
Civil liabilities, 61
Cursory examinations, 73
Deliberate indifference, 72
Expert testimony, 65
Failure to treat violations, 74
Good faith aspects, 74
Intent, 72
Internal injuries, 66
Misdiagnosis vs disparate diagnosis, 71
Negligent performance, 67
Negligent vs disparate treatment, 69
Non-perception defense, 71
Objective elements, 72
Obvious failures, 74
Protocol standards, 62
Septic shock diagnosis, 61
Spinal fracture, 71
Stabilization duty relationship, 75
Standard of care, 61, 66
Subjective elements, 72
Summary judgment motions standards, 75
Testing, 71
Uniform standards, 68, 83
Appropriate transfer standards, 55
Bad faith issues, consent to transfer, 94
Best meets the need standard, on-call specialists' duties, 97, 99
Burden of proof
Administrative enforcement, 89
Civil liabilities, 65
Centers for Medicare and Medicaid Services rules
Generally, 104
Enforcement responsibilities, 113
On-call specialists, 98

†